THE NORTON ANTHOLOGY OF DRAMA

VOLUME 2: THE NINETEENTH CENTURY TO THE PRESENT

THE NORTON ANTHOLOGY OF DRAMA

J. ELLEN GAINOR
CORNELL UNIVERSITY

STANTON B. GARNER JR.
UNIVERSITY OF TENNESSEE

MARTIN PUCHNER
COLUMBIA UNIVERSITY

VOLUME 2: THE NINETEENTH CENTURY TO THE PRESENT

W. W. NORTON & COMPANY
NEW YORK · LONDON

W. W. Norton & Company has been independent since its founding in 1923, when William Warder Norton and Mary D. Herter Norton first published lectures delivered at the People's Institute, the adult education division of New York City's Cooper Union. The firm soon expanded its program beyond the Institute, publishing books by celebrated academics from America and abroad. By mid-century, the two major pillars of Norton's publishing program—trade books and college texts—were firmly established. In the 1950s, the Norton family transferred control of the company to its employees, and today—with a staff of four hundred and a comparable number of trade, college, and professional titles published each year—W. W. Norton & Company stands as the largest and oldest publishing house owned wholly by its employees.

Printed in the United States of America
First Edition

Editor: Peter Simon
Manuscript Editor: Alice Falk
Reference Editor: Michael Fleming
Assistant Editor: Conor Sullivan
Marketing Associate: Katie Hannah
Electronic Media Editor: Eileen Connell
Project Editors: Kari Gulbrandsen, Pamela Lawson, Barbara Necol, Paula Noonan
Photo Research: Trish Marx, Julie Tesser
Permissions Management: Nancy J. Rodwan
Book Design: Jo Anne Metsch
Production Manager: Benjamin Reynolds
Managing Editor, College: Marian Johnson

Composition by Binghamton Valley Composition.
Manufacturing by R. R. Donnelley & Sons—Crawfordsville, IN

Library of Congress Cataloging-in-Publication Data

The Norton anthology of drama / J. Ellen Gainor, Stanton B. Garner, Jr., H. Martin Puchner.
— 1st ed.
p. cm.
Includes bibliographical references and index.
ISBN 978-0-393-93281-2 (pbk., v. 1) — ISBN 978-0-393-93282-9 (pbk., v. 2)
1. Drama—Collections. I. Gainor, J. Ellen. II. Garner, Stanton B., 1955– III. Puchner, H. Martin.
PN6112.N67 2009
808.2—dc22 2008054942

W. W. Norton & Company, Inc., 500 Fifth Avenue, New York, N.Y. 10110
wwnorton.com
W. W. Norton & Company Ltd., Castle House, 75/76 Wells Street, London W1T 3QT

2 3 4 5 6 7 8 9 0

Contents

PREFACE / *ix*

ACKNOWLEDGMENTS / *xiii*

INTRODUCTION / *1*
Drama and Theater / *1*
A Short History of Theater / *3*
Greek Theater / *4*
Roman Theater / *12*
Classical Indian Theater / *16*
Classical Chinese Theater / *19*
Classical Japanese Theater / *22*
Medieval European Theater / *25*
Theater in Early Modern Europe, 1500–1700 / *31*
English Theater, 1576–1642 / *38*
Spanish Theater, 1580–1700 / *42*
French Theater, 1630–1700 / *45*
English Theater, 1660–1700 / *48*
Eighteenth-Century Theater / *50*
Romanticism and Melodrama, 1800–1880 / *54*
Modern Theater, 1880–1945 / *60*
Postwar Theater, 1945–1970 / *68*
Contemporary Theater / *75*
Reading Drama, Imagining Theater / *81*

THE PLAYS / *87*

GEORG BÜCHNER / *89*
Woyzeck (1836) / *93*

WILLIAM WELLS BROWN / *111*
The Escape; or, A Leap for Freedom (1858) / *116*

AUGUST STRINDBERG / *153*
Miss Julie (1888) / *157*

HENRIK IBSEN / *195*
Hedda Gabler (1891) / *200*

OSCAR WILDE / *255*
The Importance of Being Earnest (1895) / *260*

ALFRED JARRY / *305*
Ubu the King (1896) / *309*

ANTON CHEKHOV / *341*
The Cherry Orchard (1904) / *346*

JOHN MILLINGTON SYNGE / *387*
Riders to the Sea (1904) / *392*

GEORGE BERNARD SHAW / *403*
Pygmalion (1913) / *408*

SUSAN GLASPELL / *471*
Trifles (1916) / *475*

LUIGI PIRANDELLO / *487*
Six Characters in Search of an Author (1921) / *491*

LANGSTON HUGHES / *531*
Soul Gone Home (1936) / *535*

FEDERICO GARCÍA LORCA / *539*
The House of Bernarda Alba (1936) / *544*

BERTOLT BRECHT / *579*
The Good Person of Szechwan (1938–40) / *584*

JEAN GENET / *653*
The Maids (1947) / *657*

TENNESSEE WILLIAMS / *681*
A Streetcar Named Desire (1947) / *686*

ARTHUR MILLER / *753*
Death of a Salesman (1949) / *759*

TAWFIQ AL-HAKIM / *825*
Song of Death (1950) / *831*

SAMUEL BECKETT / *843*
Waiting for Godot (1953) / *849*

DEREK WALCOTT / *907*
The Sea at Dauphin (1954) / *912*

EUGENE O'NEILL / *927*
Long Day's Journey into Night (1957) / *932*

HAROLD PINTER / *1013*
Old Times (1970) / *1018*

WOLE SOYINKA / *1043*
Death and the King's Horseman (1975) / *1048*

SAM SHEPARD / *1097*
Buried Child (1978) / *1102*

JUDITH THOMPSON / *1151*
The Crackwalker (1980) / *1155*

ATHOL FUGARD / *1195*
"MASTER HAROLD" . . . and the boys (1982) / *1199*

MARIA IRENE FORNES / *1231*
Mud (1983) / *1234*

DAVID MAMET / *1253*
Glengarry Glen Ross (1983) / *1257*

LOUIS NOWRA / *1293*
The Golden Age (1985) / *1297*

AUGUST WILSON / *1353*
Fences (1985) / *1358*

DAVID HENRY HWANG / *1407*
M. Butterfly (1988) / *1412*

TONY KUSHNER / *1459*
Angels in America, Part I: Millennium Approaches (1991) / *1464*

SUZAN-LORI PARKS / *1529*
The America Play (1994) / *1533*

EDWARD ALBEE / *1563*
The Goat (2002) / *1567*

CARYL CHURCHILL / *1605*
A Number (2002) / *1609*

SELECTED BIBLIOGRAPHIES / *1629*

PERMISSIONS ACKNOWLEDGMENTS / *1645*

INDEX / *1648*

Preface

DRAMA, one of the oldest of the arts, is also the most multifaceted. Grounded in the different mediums of writing and physical enactment, it offers pleasures both to the spectators of its theatrical realizations and to the solitary reader. In preparing *The Norton Anthology of Drama,* the editors have been mindful of this dual allegiance, and we have taken as our guiding principle that drama is at once a literary document, speaking to us across a vast expanse of time and space, and a live event, taking place in the here and now. Most of the plays collected here can be experienced in theaters today, or at least be seen in performance on film, videotape, or DVD. But even those that are rarely performed in the contemporary era are presented in *The Norton Anthology of Drama* with considerable attention to their life on the stage.

The presentation of plays in *The Norton Anthology of Drama* reflects a commitment to the richness and internationality of the dramatic tradition and to the dialogues that mark dramatic performance across languages, borders, and periods. Most anthologies organize their plays into historical and geographical units with such headings as "Greek Drama," "Renaissance Drama," and "Contemporary Drama." One of the chief results of this kind of demarcation is the separation of Western traditions from non-Western ones, as if these existed in isolation from one another. We, on the other hand, rely on chronology to organize our plays (using actual or estimated dates of first performance, and substituting publication or composition dates for those plays not originally written for performance or plays whose performance was significantly delayed). This decision reflects our belief that theater is historically and geographically more fluid than unit "boxes" imply. We believe, too, that what we call "Western" and "non-Western" texts are marked by concurrent developments across cultures and by similarities of form, subject, and even performance conditions that traditional theatrical and dramatic histories neglect. Chronological presentation allows surprising juxtapositions: Zeami's noh masterpiece *Atsumori* with *The Second Shepherds' Play,* Racine's *Phaedra* with Sor Juana's *Loa* for *The Divine Narcissus,* and Arthur Miller's *Death of a Salesman* with Tawfiq al-Hakim's *Song of Death.* It also enhances flexibility of course development and organization—*The Norton Anthology of Drama* makes possible many different courses while mandating no specific approach. At the same time, those who desire a presentation of theatrical history that emphasizes historical periods and national traditions will find this structure in the anthology's General Introduction.

In determining the table of contents for this anthology, the editors were guided by the desire to select the most thematically rich, performatively engaging, and pedagogically compelling plays available—plays that respond to the historical, cultural, literary, and theatrical contexts in which they were written in new, often groundbreaking, ways. Among the plays assembled here are three masterpieces of the twentieth-century stage for which *The Norton Anthology of Drama* has secured exclusive anthology publication rights. Two of these—Eugene O'Neill's *Long Day's Journey into Night* and Tennessee Williams's *A Streetcar Named Desire*—are numbered in the greatest plays from the modern American theater, while the third—Samuel Beckett's *Waiting for Godot*—is widely considered the century's most important and influential dramatic work. This last inclusion is particularly significant. Since its publication in 1952, Beckett's greatest play has been available in English only in editions from its American and British publishers. It has never before appeared in a general drama anthology, complete with annotation and critical introduction. Our presentation of twentieth-century drama is immeasurably enriched by its presence.

To ensure that reading classic plays written in languages other than English is a lively experience for students, we have selected vibrant translations that speak in a modern idiom while respecting the spirit and sense of the original. When no existing version satisfied us, we commissioned a new one. Whether commissioned specifically for *The Norton Anthology of Drama* or published previously, the translations in this anthology are all not only engaging and accessible on the page but also eminently *performable*. Indeed, several of our translators are themselves playwrights. For example, we have included the translation of Seneca's *Thyestes* by the British playwright Caryl Churchill, whose own recent play, *A Number,* is the final play in the anthology. Our translation of Molière's *Tartuffe,* by the playwright Constance Congdon, premiered at the Two Rivers Theater in 2006 and is now coming alive on other stages throughout North America.

In balancing the literary with the theatrical, we have designed an anthology that will work in both English and theater classrooms. For the instructor of dramatic literature courses at the introductory and advanced levels, the plays in *The Norton Anthology of Drama* reward textual attention of a literary kind while also encouraging analysis of the play's performance possibilities. For the theater instructor, the anthology provides theatrically vibrant texts in actable editions and translations. Students encountering drama for the first time will discover how powerfully the language of these plays comes alive on the tongue, and experienced and inexperienced students alike will find the versions here to be ideal for in-class performance as well as for line and scene reading. The teaching of drama can be conducted through a range of classroom activities, and *The Norton Anthology of Drama* has been designed to facilitate as many as possible.

Not only does *The Norton Anthology of Drama* offer more plays (sixty-five) than any other available drama anthology, but it also provides instructors with a fuller range of periods, texts, and playwrights from which to choose. Thus, in addition to the periods and movements usually covered by general anthologies, *The Norton Anthology of Drama* contains examples of Roman drama; classical Indian, Chinese, and Japanese drama; plays from the European and American theater between the years 1700 and 1880, including Part One of Goethe's *Faust* and William Wells Brown's abolitionist melodrama *The Escape; or, A Leap for Freedom;* French avant-garde drama, represented here by Alfred Jarry's *Ubu the King;* and—for the first time in any introduction to drama anthology—twentieth-century Arabic drama, represented by Tawfiq al-Hakim's *Song of Death.* Our table of contents also provides a fuller presentation of the early modern period in Europe and the Americas, with five plays by English Renaissance playwrights other than Shakespeare and seven plays from the Spanish Golden Age (including the Spanish-speaking New World), the France of Louis XIV, and Restoration England.

Like the Norton anthologies of British, American, and world literatures; *The Norton Anthology of Theory and Criticism;* and the other anthologies with which Norton has shaped classroom teaching over the years, *The Norton Anthology of Drama* provides students and instructors with a wealth of introductory and editorial support. The substantial General Introduction opens by exploring the relationship between dramatic literature and theatrical performance, and it concludes with a discussion of the challenges and opportunities of reading plays as scripts for performance. This final section—"Reading Drama / Imagining Theater"—is designed to give students approaching drama for the first time the tools they need to understand a uniquely hybrid form. The "Short History of Theater and Drama," which makes up the central part of the introduction, provides a detailed yet brisk overview of the political, social, and theatrical contexts within which drama has been embedded through the ages and across the globe.

We illustrate this history—and the headnotes that accompany each play—with vivid images of theaters, playwrights, actors, and audiences; pictures from acting manuals; and other figures related to theatrical performance. Given the importance of manuscript and print culture to the development and dissemination of drama, we have also included examples of the textual appearance of drama: manuscript pages, woodcuts, early printings. Together with images from the other arts (painting and sculpture, for instance), this anthology's generous illustrations convey a rich experience of the visual, performative, and textual cultures from which drama has emerged. Although we have decided to omit pictures from contemporary performances of classic plays, the website that accompanies *The Norton Anthology of Drama* does offer such images of its plays, thereby giving students a glimpse of the creative work performed by actors and directors as they reframe and reimagine plays onstage.

Supplemented by the substantial yet concise historical survey that opens the anthology, the headnotes that accompany each selection offer detailed, accessible introductions to the plays. These headnotes include summaries of the author's life and career, the specific historical and cultural contexts of the play in question, production information (where pertinent), and consideration of the play's importance in terms of its historical period and the broader history of drama and theater. The headnotes also include a discussion of the plays themselves, though we have taken care not to "explain" the plays to students, instead raising issues that will enable them to interpret the works on their own. For those interested in delving more deeply into the subject matter, we provide a carefully chosen and annotated bibliography of books and articles on each play and author. Throughout the headnote and bibliography, the editors have emphasized usefulness, readability, and student interest.

Similar care has been taken with the dramatic texts and their annotations. We have done everything possible to ensure that the texts in *The Norton Anthology of Drama* are the most authoritative ones available; if competing versions of these texts exist, we have selected the ones that are endorsed by contemporary scholarly consensus. In cases in which there is more than one version of a play—Marlowe's *Doctor Faustus,* Shaw's *Pygmalion,* and Shepard's *Buried Child,* for instance—we have selected the text that reflects the playwright's earliest theatrical vision. Our edition of *Hamlet*—a play with one of the most complicated and contested textual histories in world drama—is accompanied by a brief summary of that textual history, an overview of recent attempts to establish or resist an "authoritative" text, and a rationale for the version of the text included here. At the levels of selection and copyediting, we have devoted an exceptional amount of attention to ensuring that the text as it appears here is the most correct published version available.

Whereas other drama anthologies occasionally present historically and linguistically challenging plays without any annotations at all, *The Norton Anthology of Drama* provides footnotes and marginal glosses whenever an unfamiliar word, phrase, or historical/cultural reference risks interfering with a student's understanding of the text. We have tried to avoid cluttering plays with such material—we assume that students have access to a dictionary—but we have worked to annotate those words and references whose significance is obscured or hidden by historical remoteness. A number of our plays—including *Godot*—are annotated here for the first time, and we hope that even those plays that have been annotated before have been given a fresh presentation through our footnotes and marginal glosses.

Comprehensive anthologies of drama, students and instructors have long agreed, are unwieldy affairs, encompassing as they do twenty-five centuries of drama in phone-book-size volumes. *The Norton Anthology of Drama,* by contrast, has been published in companion volumes that fit comfortably in the hand and on a lap, with the play-texts appearing on easy-to-read, single-column pages. Students can carry one volume at a time to class, and the anthology as a whole is an attractive addition to a bookshelf. There are pedagogical reasons for the two-volume choice as well. The first volume ("Antiquity through the Eighteenth Century") contains the periods that typically make up the first half of a two-semester history of theater or drama course, and the second volume ("The Nineteenth Century to the Present") lends itself to the second semester of such courses. Because of their rich historical coverage of specific periods, the two volumes can also be used—together or separately—for advanced courses in Renaissance drama, modern drama, American drama, contemporary drama, script analysis, dramaturgy, tragedy, comedy, and the like and for courses that include extended units in these and other areas. So that the users of the single volumes can have the fullest possible exposure to theatrical antecedents, crosscurrents, and historical developments, the General Introduction has been included in full in each volume.

Finally, the many resources in *The Norton Anthology of Drama*—the General Introduction, individual headnotes, bibliographies, and textual annotations–are complemented by resources outside the anthology itself. An Instructor's Manual by Zander Brietzke, written in consultation with the editors, provides valuable material for teaching both large survey courses and smaller lectures and seminars. This guide presents the most important topics that might be covered in a lecture on a given play; it also suggests creative classroom exercises for students who want to explore the complexities of a scene by performing it in class. Topics and exercises focus on particular passages and scenes, yet also cover larger themes, as do the handy paper topics provided for each play. Teachers will also find a list of prominent productions in the Instructor's Manual, along with a list of the best film adaptations that might be used in class or for further study. Of additional help is an extensive companion website, wwnorton.com/drama. Among other things, it offers students extensive review materials, a comprehensive glossary of terms, a guide to writing about drama, excerpts from well-known statements of drama theory, and thirty "Plays in Performance" features, which present an illustrated overview of significant performances and their critical reception.

Coming from theater and literature departments, the editors of *The Norton Anthology of Drama* bring the perspectives of these overlapping disciplines to dramatic history and performance and to the project of compiling a comprehensive anthology of dramatic literature. We have been aided in our efforts by a number of contributing editors, who have taken responsibilities for plays and playwrights that require special expertise. Numerous other scholars have lent knowledge and experience to this project—reading drafts of the headnotes and General Introduction; clarifying points of fact and interpretation; providing nuance, when needed, to prevent historical overgeneralization; and helping us track down and identify historical images for the anthology. Their names are mentioned in the Acknowledgments section that follows. *The Norton Anthology of Drama,* in short, has been a deeply collaborative process, in which scholars from a number of areas have pooled their expertise to produce the most complete, informative, and engaging anthology of its kind.

Acknowledgments

A project of this magnitude cannot reach its final form without the help and encouragement of many people beyond those whose names appear on the book's cover. Given our appreciation of and love for the collaborative art of theater, we editors of *The Norton Anthology of Drama* are especially sensitive to the countless ways in which we have been helped and inspired by others.

CONTRIBUTING EDITORS

First, we would like to acknowledge the following scholars, who lent us their expertise by editing and introducing specific plays:

Dina Ahmed Amin (Villanova University), *Song of Death*

Art Borreca (University of Iowa), *Old Times; Angels in America: Millennium Approaches*

Karen Brazell (Cornell University), *Atsumori*

Thomas Cartelli (Muhlenberg College), *The Tragical History of the Life and Death of Doctor Faustus*

Sudipto Chatterjee (Loughborough University), *The Little Clay Cart*

Heather Hirschfeld (University of Tennessee), *The Spanish Tragedy; The Duchess of Malfi*

Ivo Kamps (University of Mississippi), *Hamlet; Twelfth Night*

Henry S. Turner (Rutgers University), *The Shoemaker's Holiday*

Evan Darwin Winet (University of Pittsburgh), *Snow in Midsummer*

Each of these scholars has played a critical role in making the anthology what it is, and we are grateful to have had the opportunity to collaborate with them.

We would also like to acknowledge the following people and institutions who provided us with advice, encouragement, administrative support, research assistance, and constructive critiques: Misty G. Anderson, Stephen Bottoms, Zander Brietzke, Meghan Brodie, Bruce E. Bursten, Debra Castillo, Amanda Claybaugh, Leonard Conolly, Jonah Corne, James E. Diamond, Kat Empson, John Ernest, David St. John and Loie Faulkner, Helene Foley, Mary and Charles Gainor, Alison Maerker Garner, Helen Elizabeth Garner, Stanton and Lydia Garner, Monika Gay, Helen Gilbert, Sandra Gilbert, Amy Gillingham, Esther Liu Godfrey, S. E. Gontarski, David Goslee, Cindy Grey, Laura L. Howes, Alexander C. Y. Huang, Shari Huhndorf, Veronica Kelly,

William Kennedy, Daphne Lei, Mechele Leon, Diana Looser, Calvin MacLean, Charles Maland, Jonathan Marks, Meagan Michelson, Judith Milhous, Fred Muratori and the Reference and Interlibrary Loan Staff of Cornell University Libraries, Natalia Pevukhin, Alison G. Power, Gregary Racz, Samuel C. Ramer, Jeffrey Rusten, Sabine Sörgel, Miriam Thaggert, Judith Thompson, Shawkat Toorawa, Dennis Walder, Judith Welch, Pamela Whaley, Katharina Wilson, Katherine Young, John Zomchick, the Yale Repertory Theatre, and the staff of the University of Tennessee Library Interlibrary Loan and Library Express departments.

We also acknowledge Bert Cardullo, who first proposed the anthology to Norton and who brought the original editorial team together.

The publisher and editors are grateful to all of the educators who responded to Norton surveys, questionnaires, and review requests during the early stages of this project. The anthology's shape has changed considerably over the years, in large part because of the good suggestions offered by the following people, whom we thank one and all: Michael Abbott, Gordon S. Armstrong, Yashdip S. Bains, Beulah Baker, Claudia Barnett, Susan Bennett, Linda Ben-Zvi, Robin Bernstein, Dallas Boggs, Scott Boltwood, Kazimierz Braun, Sybil Brinberg, Sarah Bryant-Bertail, Jackson R. Bryer, Ruth Cantrell, Anne Cattaneo, Dorothy Chansky, Kenneth Cox, Margaret Croskery, Marsha Cummins, Richard Cunningham, Koos Daley, Lynda Del Valle, William Demastes, Carlos Dews, Betty Diamond, Maria-Elena Doyle, Robert Duxbury, Michael Erickson, Chris Fisher, Terezinha Fonseca, Valerie L. Gager, Fanni Green, Elissa Guralnick, Janet Haedicke, Jerry Harris, Kevin J. Harty, David Hay, Woody Hood, David Hopes, Elisabeth Schulz Hostetter, Helen M. Housley, Keith N. Hull, William Hutchings, Bill Jenkins, Walter H. Johnson, P. Pennington Jones, Helen Killoran, Matthew Kinservik, Robert Knopf, Michael Kohler, David Kranes, Damon Kupper, James H. Lake, Penne J. Laubenthal, Bruce Leland, Paul M. Levitt, John L'Heureux, Stanley V. Longman, Wayne Luckman, Thomas Luddy, William Luhr, Kevin M. Lynch, Sue Mach, William MacLennan, Philip Manwell, Deborah Martinson, Cary Mazer, Joseph McCadden, Adrienne McCormick, Kirk Melnikoff, Lorraine Mercer, Naomi Miller, Lamata Mitchell, Kathleen Monahan, Deborah J. Montuori, Jonathan Morse, Joan Navarre, I. Nunnari, Pat Onion, Terry Otten, Howard Pearce, June Pulliam, Marjean D. Purinton, Rebecca Rumbo, William Streitberger, Wilbur Thomas, Randolph Umberger, Mardi Valgemae, Martine Van Elk, Ronald Wainscott, Albert Wertheim, David Wheeler, Lisa Whitney, Kayla Wiggins, Don B. Wilmeth, Janet S. Wolf, Leigh Woods, Joyce Wszalek, Kate Wulle, Trisha Yarbrough, Yvonne Yaw, Rick Yeatman, John T. Young, and Kelly Younger.

THE NORTON ANTHOLOGY OF DRAMA

VOLUME 2: THE NINETEENTH CENTURY TO THE PRESENT

Introduction

DRAMA AND THEATER

Audiences gather in a hillside amphitheater under the eastern Mediterranean sun to watch the impersonated figures of Greek myth play out their heroic, terrifying stories. In Kyoto, Japan, the sweep of robes on a railed wooden bridge announces the entry of a masked noh actor, who moves and gestures in front of his aristocratic audience with stylized precision. In London, a group of traveling players are given advice on acting by a Danish prince while the spectators who crowd the theater—aldermen, midwives, apprentices—enjoy the irony of actors meditating on their craft. In Paris, two tramps sitting by a tree on a country road share conversation and stage routines that barely conceal their anguish; an audience, seated in the dark, bears witness to their starkly contemporary situation.

The history of theater and dramatic performance is, in many ways, the history of moments such as these. The collaborative product of actors, playwrights, designers, directors, and spectators, theater achieves its magic in the live moment, rich with its sounds, sights, and feelings. The immediacy of the audience-stage encounter renders the act of theater-making magical and unique. Like other art forms—such as novels, paintings, and movies—theater constructs imaginative worlds that we can marvel at, be moved by, and learn from. Unlike these other forms, however, theater puts its worlds into live motion, in real time. In a kind of alchemy, theater takes the realm of fiction and brings it to life with living beings whose interactions take place before our eyes. At the same time, it takes the experiences of everyday life and transforms them through the magic of performance into something more powerful, deeply felt, and artful than the daily exchanges we witness and participate in. The actor stands in for us, embodies our hopes and fears, boldly enacts what is forbidden or only dreamed of. And like the theater itself, the actor introduces us to the pleasures inherent in recognition, imitation, and the intensity of a life passionately observed and lived.

Theater is the art of the moment, and its ability to captivate us with its illusion is linked to its magical but always precarious sleight of hand. Theater is the most ephemeral of vehicles—a performance, once finished, is lost to time—and the unrepeatability of its accomplishments is a major source of its power. Unlike film, which fixes action in celluloid or other media, theater takes place in the actual, in the here and now that it shares with its spectators, and its illusions are inseparable from its precariousness. Not surprisingly, the most memorable playgoing experiences are often those when something goes wrong—a stage chair collapses, a piece of stage machinery fails, an understudy is rushed on during the middle of a performance when the main actor falls ill—and the carefully constructed dramatic illusion hangs in the balance.

Central to the act of theater-making is the dramatic text, play-text, or script, which serves as the fictional and narrative foundation of the theatrical event. Whether these texts are loosely sketched, as in the improvisational performances of the Renaissance commedia dell'arte, or highly detailed in plot, setting, characterization, and dialogue, the use of scripted narratives is one of the principal features distinguishing theater from other performance types. With the invention of writing, these texts became artworks in and of themselves, and drama assumed its place as the first "literary" form, no longer exclusively dependent on performance for its realization. Plays were available in manuscript form to the educated elite of ancient Greece and Rome; classical India, China, and Japan; and medieval Europe; and after the invention of the printing press in the fifteenth century, they became available to an expanding popular readership. The plays of WILLIAM SHAKESPEARE and TENNESSEE WILLIAMS share space on twenty-first-century bookstore shelves with the novels of Jane Austen and Cormac McCarthy. But the literary dimension of dramatic works remains inseparable from performance—actual, possible, historical, imagined—with the result that drama has different aims and reference points than do more exclusively literary forms. To read a novel is to project characters, actions, and locations within an imaginative realm that is guided and limited by the words on the page; it is to undertake a mental and emotional activity that resembles dreaming more than it does the actions we engage in daily. To read a play, in contrast, is to encounter a text whose primary purpose, with rare exceptions, is to make something happen in real space and time with actors whose bodies and voices are the drama's principal instruments. In this sense, a play resembles a symphonic score, whose printed notations are directions for the production of musical sound. Even those plays that we refer to as "closet dramas," which were usually not performed when written—whether because of political, technical, or cultural barriers or because their authors preferred them to be read or recited rather than subjected to the stage's inherent limitations—often seem to have been created with some ideal performance in mind.

As the final section of this introduction ("Reading Drama, Imagining Theater") will discuss in more detail, drama invites the reader to put her- or himself in the position of a theater artist, alive to the possibilities and choices that bring a play to life, imagining the different ways that a scene, line, or gesture might look, sound, and feel when performed. Being attentive to the conditions of performance allows one to appreciate the features that characterize drama as a literary and theatrical form: the necessary economy of its action, setting, and characterization, which are denied the leisure of novelistic description; the centrality of spoken language, which provides access to offstage and subjective worlds; and the preoccupation with questions of role-playing, impersonation, and the many ways in which we perform for the benefit of others and ourselves. In the absence of an omniscient narrator or other guiding authorial consciousness, drama emerges through the interplay of its characters, who enact their stories in the theater and on the imagined stage of one's reading. The power of these stories resides in the immediacy of the actors and their interactions with the theater environment, which of course includes the audience.

Humans have always told each other stories. From the earliest times for which we have physical or documentary evidence, we have acted our stories for each other. We donned costumes and masks, wielded props, and later created designated places—theaters—where we use the immediacy of live performance to communicate the powerful experiences that have shaped us. Like other forms of organized social performance—games, festivities, sto-

Spectators watch a performance of Anton Chekhov's *Three Sisters* at the Guthrie Theater in Minneapolis, 1963.

rytelling, athletic displays, civic ceremonies, political events, and rituals—these encounters are deeply embedded in specific historical, social, and cultural contexts. To study the history of theater and drama is to confront a range of historical junctures, social and institutional practices, and cultural forms. It is also to encounter one of the most enduring of human activities: make-believe, the act of making oneself other than oneself for purposes of entertainment, commemoration, communication, or devotion.

Through performance and its rituals, we confirm our shared humanity—we acknowledge the importance of each other's existence and suggest that our lives are of value. Collectively, we generate forms of community while articulating the meanings that lend shape to our lives. The sense of communion and reciprocal awareness engendered by live performance, and the dramatic texts written for it, transcends cultures and history; it is foundational to who we are as living beings. As prehistoric cave paintings indicate, imitation and ritual were part of the earliest human societies. We are performers by nature. Although theater and drama are relative latecomers to human history (having been around for a mere 2,500 years), the activities they draw on are as old as humanity itself.

A SHORT HISTORY OF THEATER

The origins of theater—and hence of drama—have long been a subject of scholarly debate. We possess little material evidence concerning the development of theatrical activity in most cultures, and what generalizations we might draw from it are complicated by the fact that the earliest forms of theater were the product of a variety of social, political, and religious forces. However, those studying different dramatic traditions have found theater to be closely connected to hunting, fertility, and other rituals in those early societies where it emerged. The nature of this connection has been debated by scholars, but the consensus view is that theatrical activity represented an extension of ritual's symbolic forms of representation into nonritual contexts. The rituals of early societies involved the enactment of religious and mythic narratives by privileged participants—shaman, priest, ruler, sacrificial victim—and these performances could become quite elaborate. In Egypt, rituals commemorating the death and resurrection of Osiris, a god associated with fertility, took place at the sacred site of Abydos as early as 2500 B.C.E. Evidence suggests that the dramatic events of Osiris's life may have been performed by priests and that these performances were accompanied by lavish spectacle.

Ritual differs from theater, of course, in that its prescribed actions, passed down from generation to generation, are designed to effect change in the natural or spiritual worlds. The ritual performances of Egypt remained tied to their religious and dynastic functions and never developed in the direction of theater. In those cultures in which theater did emerge, symbolic performance asserted itself as an object of interest in its own right, thereby paving the way for institutions, practitioners, and audiences who conceived of theater as a communal artistic activity. The earliest of these transitions—and one of the most important for the subsequent history of theater and drama—occurred in Greece in the fifth century B.C.E.

Greek Theater

ORIGINS OF GREEK THEATER

The theater of classical Greece looms large in the history of Western theater. Not only did the emergence of theater as an institution in Athens during the fifth century B.C.E. establish the world's first theatrical culture, but the characters who confronted their fate on the Greek stage—Orestes, Oedipus, Antigone, Medea—remain among the most imposing characters in the dramatic repertoire. Yet despite the importance of Greek theater to the history of Western drama, little is known about its origins. Scholars have depended, for the most part, on the scattered remarks of later classical writers who were themselves speculating about events hundred of years in the past. Archaeological findings, the history of words associated with the theater, and vase paintings have since provided additional hints as to how the first Greek theaters came into existence. Most scholars subscribe to the notion that the origins of Greek theater lie in religious rituals. Ancient Greek religious life included many different types of ceremonies and public performances: funeral services, festivals celebrating the seasons or individual gods, processions and competitions. But which of these performances provided the decisive impulse is much harder to pinpoint. The Greek word for tragedy, *tragōidia,* originally meant "goat song" and therefore seems to associate tragedy with ritual practices involving the killing of a goat. Other theories hold that theater emerged from rituals performed at the tombs of heroes.

Though we know little about either the goat song or the ritual performances at tombs, other cultural practices that aided the development of theater are much better documented. Among them are the public performances of storytellers, or *rhapsōidoi,* who recited stories of gods and mythical humans to large audiences. The first theorist of theater, the philosopher Plato (ca. 427–ca. 347 B.C.E.), emphasized the similarities between public recitations of epic poetry and simple dramatic performances. What is still the most convincing theory about the origin of Greek theater was developed by Aristotle (384–322 B.C.E.), who wrote a generation after his teacher Plato. Aristotle claimed that theater emerged from a specific ceremony honoring Dionysus, a god associated with fertility, agriculture, wine, and (by extension) physical and spiritual intoxication. During the Attic ceremony honoring him, a chorus and a chorus leader (*koryphaios*) sang and danced a hymn composed in a particular form known as the *dithyrambos.* According to Aristotle, these ritual performances formed the basis for later dramatic performance. The Greek language reinforces Aristotle's claim, for the choral

This image, a detail from a *kylix* (a wine cup) painted by the so-called Brygos Painter in the early fifth century B.C.E., depicts a devotee (a *bacchante* or *maenad*) of the god Dionysus performing a ritualized dance. In her right hand is a *thrysus*, an ivy-covered staff that was an important part of sacred rituals.

performers of dithyrambs were called *tragōidoi*, pointing once again to the later word for tragedy.

The association of theater with the dithyrambs performed in the honor of Dionysus makes sense for many reasons. The first Greek playwright, Thespis (sixth century B.C.E.), whose plays have all been lost, is credited with adding an individual performer to the dithyrambic chorus and chorus leader, and thus enabling dramatic interaction to emerge. Because Thespis himself is said to have performed this newly individual role, he is considered by many to be the world's first actor, and his name has given us the word *thespian.* From this point on the chorus (or chorus leader) was not limited to reciting a hymn but could impersonate an imaginary figure by engaging in a dialogue with the newly introduced actor. The Greek word for actor, *hypokritēs,* by the way, still exists in the English word *hypocrite,* whose now largely negative meaning underscores that acting involves imitation and pretense. Subsequent playwrights added more actors to increase the possibilities for dialogue between individuals, although the chorus remained an important component of Greek, and subsequently of Roman, theater.

Another reason for associating theater with the Dionysian dithyrambs is that the first known Greek plays were performed at the City Dionysia, one of four Athenian festivals (another was the Rural Dionysia) held during the winter in honor of the god. Over the course of the fifth century, when Greek theater was at its height, other festivals incorporated dramatic performances, but the City Dionysia remained the most important event for theater. The City Dionysia, which attracted many visitors from other city-states and from outside Greece, was a multiday affair, whose focus was various competitions. The first was a competition of dithyrambs, first organized around 600 B.C.E., among the four (later ten) "tribes" (*phylai*)—the administrative and military divisions to which all Athenian citizens belonged. Each tribe sponsored two choruses, one consisting of fifty men, the other of fifty boys. Although these dithyrambic performances centered on the worship of Dionysus, they soon included other gods and myths as well. As early as 534 B.C.E., when Thespis became the first recorded winner of the prize for tragedy, plays were added to the program. By the beginning of the fifth century, a system was in place: each dramatist had to compose three tragedies, which were followed by the performance of a short satirical work (called a *satyr play*). Somewhat later, around 486 B.C.E., another type of drama was added: comedy. The City Dionysia held a competition among the different playwrights for first prize, an honor that helped spark the explosive growth in the number of plays written for the occasion and raising the status of theater more generally.

GREEK TRAGEDY

One development necessary for drama to emerge from these various rituals and performances was the invention of writing and the spread of literacy. Greek rituals did not include written scripts but were instead based on formulaic and orally transmitted incantations, hymns, and performances. Likewise, dithyrambic and epic poems were originally memorized and improvised by the performers, but not composed as literature. The first epics to be preserved in writing were those attributed to Homer (ca. 750–700 B.C.E.), the *Iliad* and the *Odyssey;* and in the late seventh century, Arion (active 628–625 B.C.E.) was apparently the first to write down his own dithyrambs (none of which have survived). Consequently, Homer and Arion are considered by some to be the first tragedians, though they did not actually write plays.

The earliest extant tragedies all date from the fifth century and were written by three playwrights: AESCHYLUS (ca. 525–456 B.C.E.), SOPHOCLES (ca. 496–406 B.C.E.), and EURIPIDES (ca. 480–ca. 406 B.C.E.). These plays are set in a mythical past (with one exception—Aeschylus's *Persians*, which takes place during the Persian Wars), using the stories of gods and heroic humans that had been transmitted orally by the early epic poets and subsequently written down. Because Greek audiences already knew the broad outlines of the stories dramatized on the stage, they were able to notice and appreciate subtle differences in the treatments of given myths.

At the center of tragedy is a conflict that eventually results in the downfall of a larger-than-life character. The protagonists of tragedy are socially and morally elevated beings, and the destruction they undergo results, in part, from what Aristotle called *hamartia;* though the term has sometimes been translated as "tragic flaw," it is more accurately understood as referring to a mistaken action or error of judgment. That tragic protagonists bear responsibility for their fate does not mean that they deserve the destruction inflicted on them, however, for their fate is also determined by forces, circumstances, and dilemmas outside their control. For example, while the decision of Antigone (in Sophocles' play of the same name) to bury her brother Polyneices follows the religious imperative, obeying that imperative brings her into conflict with her uncle Creon, the king of Thebes, who has declared him a traitor and therefore has forbidden his burial. Faced with this set of forces not of her making—one, a social and religious mandate; the other, a legal prohibition—Antigone has no alternative but to choose her tragic fate. Similarly, the protagonist of Sophocles' *OEDIPUS THE KING* (ca. 428 B.C.E.), who unknowingly killed his father and married his mother, must accept punishment for deeds performed not with malicious intent but with an overweening pride and belief in his own invulnerability. Ironically, the man of action and the solver of the Sphinx's riddle proves rash in his actions and blind to fate's riddle in his own life. Virtues and flaws, the notion of *hamartia* may also suggest, are intimately tied up in each other: we can trust our talents and strengths too much and learn, in the outcome of our actions, that they are both the reason for our good fortune and the cause of our demise.

As these tragic conflicts unfold, the protagonists find themselves in another contentious relation, namely with the chorus. Not surprisingly, given its origins in choral dithyrambs, tragedy retained the chorus as an important element. Reflecting the perspective of the community, this body observes and comments on the actions and entanglements of the protagonists, trying to rein in their excesses and restore order to the civic realm. The chorus also reminds the audience of the background story of a given myth and often engages the protagonists in a dialogue that draws out the motives of their actions. In keeping with the evolving nature of Greek tragedy during the fifth century, the role of the chorus underwent changes. As dramatic characters grew in number, complexity, and importance, the role of the chorus lessened.

The complexity of the relations between individual actors and the chorus shaped the typical structure of Greek tragedy. Greek tragedies begin either with a prologue that sets the scene or with the entrance—*parodos*—of the chorus. The main body of the tragedy is then composed of a sequence of episodes—*epeisodia,* scenes in which the main actors talk to one another or to the chorus—and choral songs without dialogue, *stasima*. At the end of the play, the characters and the chorus leave the stage in what is called the *exodos*. Greek tragedy, in other words, was a highly structured and formalized art form in which dialogue between two individual actors, today the main component of drama, was relatively unimportant. Instead, choral lyrics and the dialogue between chorus and protagonist took up most of the play. Playwrights used different styles of language and meter to distinguish between the different sections of tragedy. Choral lyrics were a form of poetry highly elevated in diction and intricately composed, while the exchanges between the chorus and individual characters, though still quite stylized, were more conversational. The dialogues in iambic meter between the individual characters, though they too were artfully wrought, were closer still to everyday speech. Such differentiation can clearly be seen in the works of Euripides, who, writing slightly later than Aeschylus and Sophocles, attempted to bring the language of tragedy nearer to the language actually spoken by the audience.

As noted above, in its mature form the City Dionysia included a competition in which each dramatist presented three tragedies followed by a satyr play. Unfortunately, because only one complete satyr play has survived—Euripides' *Cyclops*—it is difficult to generalize about the genre. They plays seem to have dealt with the same mythical and heroic figures and stories as tragedies but irreverently, as burlesque. Accordingly, their language was apparently more colloquial than that of tragedy. The satyr play remained closely connected to Dionysus, for in Greek mythology satyrs were half-human and half-bestial creatures who formed part of his retinue, and the leader of the chorus in satyr plays was Silenus, a satyr who was a constant companion of the god. The satyr play provided the audience with comic relief at the end of a daylong performance of tragedies.

This detail from the so-called Pronomos Vase, painted in the late fifth century B.C.E., depicts actors preparing for a satyr play.

GREEK COMEDY

The satyr play, despite its comic elements, belonged to a genre distinct from comedy. Although comedies had not originally been part of festival competitions, they were incorporated into the City Dionysia festival around 486 B.C.E. The origins of comedy also lie in ritual, most likely in rites that featured groups of men wearing representations of large *phalloi* (male sexual organs) and animal masks. A second source for Greek comedy was a form of mime—short, improvised sketches treating everyday situations humorously. These foundations are visible in what is called Old Comedy, which developed in the fifth century; its only remaining examples are the plays of ARISTOPHANES (ca. 450–ca. 385 B.C.E.), although the names of other comic playwrights are known to us, including Magnes (active 472 B.C.E.) and Aristophanes' main rival, Eupolis (ca. 445–ca. 411 B.C.E.). The choruses of comedy may well represent animals or inanimate objects—Aristophanes' plays have such titles as *The Frogs, The Wasps,* and *The Clouds*—and they often treat explicitly sexual themes. In contrast to both tragedy and the satyr play, comedies take as their subject matter not the gods and heroes of Greek mythology but rather the everyday life of contemporary Athenians, and the topics they engage range from the long Peloponnesian War with Sparta (which provides the background to *LYSISTRATA* [411 B.C.E.], Aristophanes' best-known play) to public personalities such as the philosopher Socrates. Like tragedy, Old Comedy begins with a prologue, which is followed by the entry of the chorus; it contains passages of dialogue; and it concludes with the exit of all the characters. It also features an added element: a section called the *parabasis* (literally, "digression") in which the chorus addresses the audience directly, discussing political and social problems and sometimes praising the playwright. In the *parabasis* and throughout each play, classical comedy engages with political and social issues much more directly than tragedy, although it does so comically, drawing on fantasy, humor that frequently is ribald, and farce.

THE GREEK STAGE

The main performance venue for Athenian theater was the Dionysus theater, located in the hill just below the Acropolis, an elevated area on which stood the Parthenon and which served as the city's religious and political center. Given the elaborate nature of later Greek and Roman theaters, the Dionysus theater in the fifth century was surprisingly simple. A large *amphitheatron,* holding between 14,000 to 17,000 audience members, was built into the hillside, with seating provided by temporary wooden benches. At the center of the amphitheater was the *orchēstra* (or "dancing place"), a semicircle in whose middle stood the *thymelē,* a raised stone used as an altar or a table. Behind the *orchēstra* stood a wooden structure, the *skēnē,* which served as a place where actors could change masks and costumes and, through one or more doors, appear and disappear from the stage. The area in front of the *skēnē* would later be known as the *paraskēnion,* a term from which the modern word *proscenium* derives. On either side of the *skēnē* were passageways.

This physical arrangement was used by the Greek dramatists in increasingly complex ways. The passageways aided the elaborate entrances and exits of the chorus, while the *orchēstra* was the place where the dances performed by the chorus and the interaction between chorus and individual actors took place. The altar or table could be used by individual actors to hide and suddenly appear. The *skēnē* at the back of the performance area provided even more theatrical possibilities. For example, playwrights placed messengers and other figures on its roof, where they could be on the lookout and describe battles and other scenes they pretended to see on its other side (a stage device called *teichoskopeia,* or "watching from a wall"). The doors in the *skēnē* were used not only to aid entrances and exits but also to suddenly reveal characters. To heighten the effect of the doors, a rolling platform, or *ekkyklēma,* was employed to roll the body of a killed character in front of the audience or to make other dramatic disclosures. Such a device was especially important since almost all physical violence—the blinding of Oedipus, for example, or Medea's murder of her children—occurred offstage, often (the audience was led to believe) within the scene building. A second mechanism became increasingly popular: a crane called a *mēchanē,* which could move characters through the air into the space in front of the scene building. Euripides, in particular, used such cranes to introduce gods, who would resolve the plot and mete out punishment at the end of his tragedies; this device became well-known by its Latin name, *deus ex machina* (god from a machine). Various forms of painted panels were probably employed on the stage as well, though little is known about their appearance and function.

Because theater was an integral part of civic and religious festivals, an elaborate system of rules and practices governed the production of plays. A leading figure of the Athenian government, an *archōn eponymos,* selected from among the wealthy citizens a *chorēgos,* or producer, who would provide the funds for the chorus, while the city government provided the funds for the playwright and the leading actors. The playwrights were responsible for rehearsals and sometimes even performed in their own plays. The number of performers was strictly limited. The chorus probably contained twelve to fifteen members, although as many as fifty may have appeared in some early plays of Aeschylus. The number of individual actors was even more crucial, because it directly affected how many characters were available to the playwright. Aeschylus's early plays used two actors, who could take on different roles over the course of a play—but obviously, no more than two speaking parts could be present simultaneously. Either Aeschylus or, more likely, his younger rival Sophocles took the decisive step of introducing a third actor, thereby expanding the playwright's options considerably.

One reason why actors could change so easily from one role to the next was the relative simplicity of their costumes. A thick, richly colored garment covered their bodies; large, high boots made them appear larger than life; and a mask made from either fabric or wood covered their entire face. Given the size of the theater and the bulkiness of their costumes, the actors had to rely on large gestures rather than on small, intimate reactions, and in masks they lacked any recourse to facial expressions.

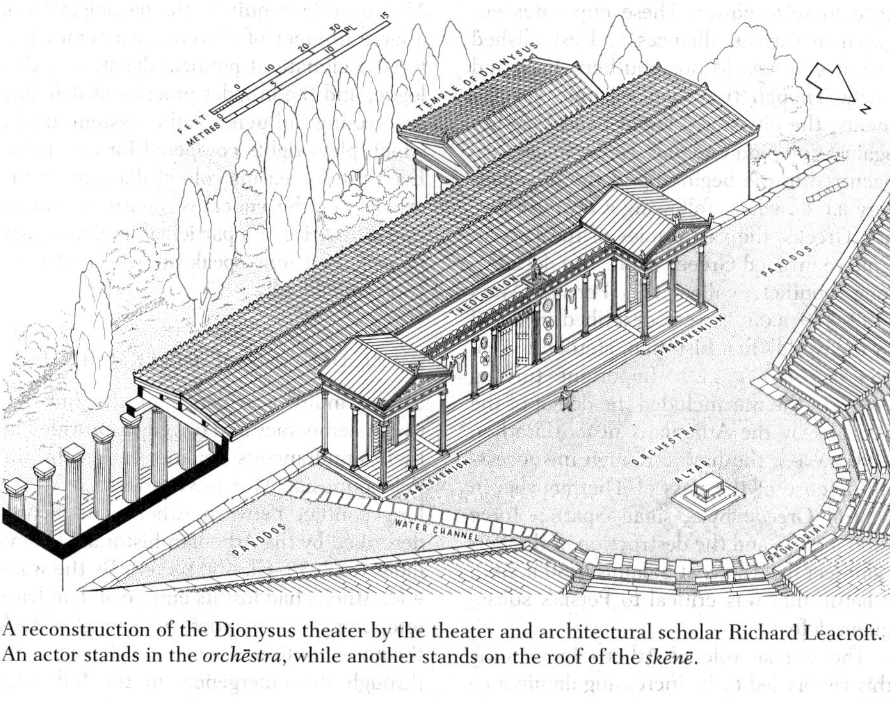

A reconstruction of the Dionysus theater by the theater and architectural scholar Richard Leacroft. An actor stands in the *orchēstra*, while another stands on the roof of the *skēnē*.

Scenes of dialogue alternated with the elaborate dances of the chorus. The performance of Greek plays was accompanied by music, provided mainly by the flute—it was a flute player who led the entrance of the chorus at the beginning of the play—but various other wind and percussion instruments were employed as well. Today's audiences and readers can easily overlook the significance of music, which is generally little used in contemporary revivals of Greek plays, but the scholars and artists who attempted to revive Greek tragedy during the European Renaissance were very conscious of its importance. Indeed, this awareness led to the creation of opera, a form of theater that relies primarily on music and song and only secondarily on spoken dialogue.

THEATER AND ATHENIAN DEMOCRACY

The emergence and rise of Greek theater is intimately tied to the political history of Greece. Greece was not a unified nation but rather a network of city-states—Athens, Sparta, Corinth, and Thebes, among others—ruled by kings or, from the seventh century onward, by nobles who had managed to seize power. These city-states engaged in various alliances and established colonies in Asia Minor, southern Italy, and Sicily. Though they had separate governments, the city-states could band together against common enemies. Such an alliance occurred in the beginning of the fifth century B.C.E., when, following a revolt of Asiatic Greeks, the vast armies of the Persian Empire invaded Greece itself. The decades-long conflict, called the Persian Wars (499–449 B.C.E.), were described in detail by the world's first historian, Herodotus (ca. 484–ca. 425 B.C.E.). Important turning points in the war included the defeat of the Persians by the Athenians near Marathon (490 B.C.E.), the heroic though unsuccessful defense of the pass of Thermopylae in central Greece by a small Spartan force (480 B.C.E.), and the destruction of the Persian fleet by Athens at Salamis (480 B.C.E.), a battle that was critical to Persia's subsequent defeat.

The crucial role of Athens in winning this victory led to its increasing dominance over the rest of Greece, and it built a largely seaborne empire consisting of allies, dependent states, and colonies. It was during this time of military dominance that Athens became a cosmopolitan center for the arts—the birthplace of Greek theater and the center of many other intellectual and cultural pursuits, such as philosophy (although many philosophers living in Athens were foreign-born). Equally important was the development in Athens of an early form of democracy that involved all adult male citizens in the governance of the Athenian empire, serving in the courts, military offices, and other administrative posts. Women, slaves, and foreigners, it is important to note, were not considered citizens. Moreover, though it was a predecessor of modern democracies, Athenian democracy included many features that might strike today's citizens as odd, such as the choosing of important positions by lot (to avoid favoritism). Many scholars consider the rise of Athenian theater and of democracy to be related developments. It is likely that most of the city's inhabitants, including Athenian women and slaves of both sexes, were allowed to attend theater performances, though only adult male citizens could perform in the chorus and as individual actors. Moreover, by requiring the participation of a large number of citizens, democracy fostered a climate of political debate and dialogue, and the broader practice of debating and voting influenced the system under which playwrights competed for first prize. Even the increasing role of dialogue at the expense of the collective chorus seems to mirror the rise of a participatory democracy in which citizens speak out and cast their votes individually.

THE DECLINE OF GREEK THEATER

Strong indirect evidence of the link between democracy and tragedy is provided by their simultaneous decline, caused by the Peloponnesian War (431–404 B.C.E.)—the long conflict between Athens and Sparta described by the Athenian historian Thucydides (ca. 455–ca. 400 B.C.E.). By the war's end, Athens had lost its empire and, at least temporarily, its democracy. Though Greek theater continued to develop—chiefly through the emergence, in the following

The ruins of the theater at Epidaurus, Greece. The theater was built in the middle of the fourth century B.C.E.

century, of New Comedy, whose main practitioner was the playwright Menander (ca. 342–ca. 292 B.C.E.) and whose plays depended much less on fantastic plots and conceits than had their Old Comedy predecessors—by the end of the fifth century the most important era of Greek theater had come to an end.

GREEK THEORIES OF DRAMA

The fourth century's contribution to theater history was the work of two authors who together provided the first written theories of drama: Plato and Aristotle. Though Plato did not take up the subject separately, his philosophy as a whole is deeply engaged with the theater as medium and institution. All of his works were written as dialogues, and although there is no evidence of their performance before large audiences, they may have been recited by students in his Academy, the school that he founded (which took its name from its site, a park sacred to the legendary hero Academus). In these dialogues, Plato—or, more precisely, his main character, Socrates—is often critical of tragedy and comedy as well as of actors, arguing that drama and other works of art offer mere representations of the world and therefore stand in the way of the pursuit of truth, which consists of knowledge of the things themselves. Drawn to the exchange of ideas but suspicious of the seductions of theatrical performance, Plato offered his own philosophical dialogues as an alternative form of drama.

Plato's student Aristotle, by contrast, devoted an entire treatise to the subject of tragedy, describing its classifications, elements, and structure and examining its effect on spectators. In his widely influential *Poetics,* probably composed around 330 B.C.E., Aristotle discusses the origin of tragedy in dithyrambic hymns, the nature of the heroic protagonist, the function of the chorus, and what he considers to be the six crucial elements of theater: plot, character, thought, diction, music, and spectacle (the last is accorded a marginal position in his descriptive hierarchy). He also emphasizes certain plot elements, such as sudden reversals (*peripeteiai*) and the moment of recognition (*anagnōrisis*), and insists that unlike epic poetry, with its meandering plots, tragedy should present a single, unified action. This focus mandates that the action of tragedy be confined to short periods of time, typically one day, and to a single place. Renaissance commentators on the *Poetics* turned these recommendations into the three unities—of time, place, and action—that, according to the strictures of what became known as neoclassical theory, must be maintained by playwrights.

In response to Plato's attack on theatrical representation, Aristotle defended actors by arguing that the drive to imitate, *mimēsis,* was a common human trait and served as a source of pleasure. Perhaps the most influential term introduced in this treatise was *katharsis,* the purging or cleansing of emotions that was the desired effect of tragedy on the audience. Whereas Plato had argued that the extreme emotions depicted in tragedy could have adverse effects on the audience and therefore recommended that playwrights, like other artists, be banished from his ideal republic, Aristotle held that tragedy provided a release, a *katharsis,* of those stirred-up emotions—particularly fear and pity—and that dramatic art thus served a socially therapeutic function. The disagreement between Plato and Aristotle about the value of theater, the reaction of the audience, and the status of actors has persisted to the present—in our debates, for instance, about depictions of violence onstage and on the screen. Much as the playwrights of the fifth century B.C.E. have continued to influence theater history, so the philosophers of the fourth century still shape our thinking about theater.

Roman Theater

The decline of Athens, which at its height had dependent colonies in Italy (where Greeks from several city-states had settled as early as the eighth century B.C.E.), coincided with the rise and expanding influence of Rome. By the middle of the third century B.C.E., the city-state of Rome had managed to unify most of Italy under its leadership, and its victory over its North African rival, Carthage, in the First Punic War (264–241 B.C.E.) enabled Rome to extend its hegemony over Sicily as well as parts of Greece itself. One hundred years later, Rome had absorbed the entire Greek world, on its way to becoming one of the largest empires ever created.

Even though Rome was a rising military power, its art, literature, philosophy, and theater remained heavily influenced by those of Greece. Like Greek theater, Roman theater was performed in the context of civic festivals, here called *ludi,* which by 240 B.C.E. included both tragedies and comedies. The most important of these festivals were the *Ludi Romani,* which honored not Dionysus (or his Roman counterpart, Bacchus) but Jupiter, chief of the gods. This and other festivities differed from their Greek counterparts in significant ways. Influenced by the earlier performance practices of the Etruscans, who belonged to an earlier civilization (centered in present-day Tuscany and part of Umbria) that reached its height in the sixth century B.C.E., the festivities of early Rome included a variety of nondramatic entertainments—chariot races, prize-

Roman masks—one tragic, one comic—as depicted in a wall mosaic from the first century B.C.E.

fighting, dance, farce—that vied with dramatic performance for the spectators' attention. Relatively few early Roman tragedies and comedies survive, although it is clear that most were adaptations of existing Greek plays, which were introduced to Rome in 240 B.C.E. The first known dramatists in Rome, Livius Andronicus (ca. 284–ca. 204 B.C.E.) and Gnaeus Naevius (ca. 270–201 B.C.E.), adapted both Greek tragedies and comedies into Latin, while later playwrights, including the tragedians Quintus Ennius (239–169 B.C.E.) and Lucius Accius (170–ca. 86 B.C.E.), specialized in one or the other genre. Even though Roman tragedies were mostly versions of Greek ones, Roman playwrights introduced considerable alterations, changes, and innovations; far from being a sign of unoriginality, adaptation thus became a special art form. Whereas the Greek playwrights had used known stories and characters in composing their plays, Roman playwrights perfected a more elaborate technique of imitation by working from established dramatic models.

ROMAN COMEDY

Though both tragedies and comedies were performed in Roman theaters, comedy was the genre in which Roman playwrights excelled. Roman comedians could look back at a long tradition of farce, and they drew especially on Atellan farce, a burlesque form based on improvisation and a small set of stock characters that took its name from Atella, a town near Naples in southern Italy. These improvised sketches and stock characters remained popular throughout the history of Rome and beyond, influencing such later theater traditions as Italy's commedia dell'arte. At the same time, a more literary form of comedy, based on Greek Old and New Comedy, was developing. The two most famous Roman playwrights—TITUS MACCIUS PLAUTUS (ca. 254–ca. 184 B.C.E.) and Terence (Publius Terentius Afer, ca. 190–159 B.C.E.)—were authors of such comedies. The most important changes Plautus and Terence made to their Greek models were eliminating the chorus and significantly expanding the use of music, thereby turning their comedies into a kind of musical theater.

EMPIRE AND SPECTACLE

The height of Roman drama, as represented by Plautus and Terence, occurred under the Roman Republic, a political system that allowed a limited number of citizens to participate in government and prevented any single individual from gaining supreme power. It was under the Republic that Rome established its dominance through the Second Punic War with Carthage (218–201 B.C.E.) and finally defeated and destroyed Carthage in 146 at the end of the Third Punic War (149–146 B.C.E.). Rome now dominated not only Italy and Greece

This detail from a Roman mosaic depicts a *venation*—a battle between a leopard and a gladiator.

but also large parts of northern Africa. The resulting flow of wealth and power to Rome increasingly undermined republican institutions, and the Republic gave way to an empire with an absolute ruler. Under the emperors—beginning with Augustus (63 B.C.E.–14 C.E.)—Rome expanded its empire as far as England, Germany, France, Spain, and the Balkans and controlled the entire Mediterranean basin.

The increasing scale of the Roman Empire, and the unheard-of concentration of wealth and power in Rome itself, fueled a tendency toward expensive and lavish spectacles, comparable perhaps to blockbuster Hollywood action films today. These nondramatic varieties of performance, most of them significantly more spectacular than anything seen on the dramatic stage, came to overshadow tragedy and comedy. Among these new public entertainments were chariot races held in sizable arenas, the largest of which, the Circus Maximus in Rome, accommodated more than 60,000 spectators. Other spectacles included elaborately orchestrated, and often lethal, sea battles, which sometimes involved thousands of participants; contests called *venationes,* in which wild animals fought against one another or against humans; and of course the most emblematic and notorious of Roman spectacles—gladiatorial contests, which featured hand-to-hand combat to the death. Although their appetite for staged (but real) violence was voracious, Romans weren't entirely bloodthirsty in their entertainment preferences; pantomime and short comic sketches of mime performances were also very popular.

CLOSET TRAGEDY

The overwhelming popularity of nondramatic entertainments led to a decline of traditional dramatic forms, especially tragedy and comedy. Writers with literary ambitions therefore began to create "closet dramas," plays designed to be recited at small, private gatherings or to be read in private. In fact, the most famous Roman tragic dramatist, LUCIUS ANNAEUS SENECA (4 B.C.E.–65 C.E.), wrote only closet dramas, and his plays were never performed on the great Roman stages of the time. Modeled on Greek tragedy, Seneca's tragedies are composed in an intricate, literary Latin that became a model for many subsequent writers. That these dramas were not written to be performed did not make them less violent. Indeed, unlike Greek tragedy, which had hidden most of its violence offstage, Seneca required that the audience or readers envision it as happening in their "sight." Though few in his own time would have known of his plays, they proved enormously influential on later playwrights, including the Elizabethan playwrights THOMAS KYD and WILLIAM SHAKESPEARE.

THE ROMAN STAGE

Although plays had been written in Latin since the third century B.C.E., the first permanent theater—erected at Pompeii—was not built until 55 B.C.E. Before that time, temporary stages (often quite stable and elaborate) were used for dramatic and other performances. Modeled on their Greek predecessors, Roman theaters included large amphitheaters for the audience; these could be built into hills, like Greek theaters, or erected on level ground. The amphitheater formed a semicircle similar to the Greek *orchēstra,* which was closed on one side by a building, the *scaena,* which was the counterpart of the Greek *skēnē*. In their adaptation from one society to another, however, the function and proportions of these elements changed significantly. For example, the *orchēstra* was used by the chorus, but its Roman equivalent was occupied—as it is in today's theaters—by the most privileged of the audience members. The action of the play took place on a raised stage, or *pulpitum,* located in front of the scene building, which was significantly larger and more elaborate than its Greek predecessor. Supported by several sets of columns and often ornately decorated, the scene building could be many stories high—a change that had profound implications. Unlike the audience of Greek theater, whose view of the stage was framed by landscape and sky, the Roman audience looked entirely at the artificial world created on a stage.

Even as playwrights such as Seneca withdrew from the stage, the Roman taste for spectacle—races, parades, festivals, and staged battles—led to the development of

A digital reconstruction of the interior of the theater of Pompey in Rome. This image—based on a collaborative research project by Richard Beacham, James E. Packer, and John Burge—was generated by the King's Visualization Lab and is copyright © King's College London.

elaborate stage machinery. Roman theater producers not only instituted the stage curtain but also invented sliding panels, cranes, and a type of elevator with which actors or animals could be lifted onto the stage from below. They also introduced more complex, three-dimensional stage decorations, extensive stage props, and even live animals. The actors, called *histriones* in Latin, were not, as had originally been the case in Greece, talented citizen amateurs; instead, they were theater professionals, some of whom were slaves. Their acting style ranged from burlesque and conversational for comedy to more formal and declamatory for tragedy. Costumes and masks were mostly fashioned on Greek models.

THE DECLINE AND INFLUENCE OF ROMAN THEATER

Roman theater declined significantly with the rise of Christianity, which won official toleration in 313 C.E. when the emperor Constantine I issued the Edict of Milan; it soon became the dominant religion in the Roman Empire. Christian clergy were highly critical of theater and in particular its actors, declaring the attendance of theater cause for excommunication and denying actors the holy sacraments (a practice that remained in place in some parts of Europe well into the modern era). Yet despite the theater's waning under Christianity, the influence of classical theater would reverberate through the centuries. The architecture of Roman theater buildings helped shape Renaissance stage design, for example, and Roman comedy and tragedy were important models for English Renaissance playwrights, who often knew of Greek works only through their Roman adaptations and translations. Equally vital for Renaissance theater was Rome's most significant critic, the poet Quintus Horatius Flaccus, known as Horace (65–8 B.C.E.), whose *Ars Poetica* (*The Art of Poetry* [ca. 10 B.C.E.]) discusses the origins, forms, and ends of drama. Recommending such formal practices as the division of plays into five acts, Horace also offered a powerfully moral conception of drama's function. Not only should playwrights cater to their audiences, he asserted, they should also serve as moral instructors: their works, in other words, should prove useful (*utile*) as well as pleasing (*dulce*). In keeping with this conception of theater's social role, he argued against the more fantastic, spectacular, and violent aspects of Roman theater. Like those of Aristotle, his views on drama were taken up by later theorists of drama and theater.

Although Roman theater was in many ways derivative, the influence of its drama, architecture, and practice on subsequent theater history was even greater than that of its Greek predecessor and model. The plays of Plautus, Terence, and Seneca inspired the work of later playwrights, and Roman theater technology—much of it described in *De Architectura* (*On Architecture*), written in the first century B.C.E. by the architect and engineer Vitruvius—made important contributions to theater design during the European Renaissance. One of the most lasting legacies of Roman theater may be the division it opened up between drama as a literary genre and stage as a site of spectacle. In later centuries, in the great ages of world theater, drama and theater have often worked hand in hand; but at times they have become estranged, leading to forms of literary drama disconnected from a theater system mainly interested in extravagant spectacle. To the extent that this division still informs our theater today—when, for example, lavish Broadway spectacles divert attention from serious plays—we are still in the process of working through the inheritance of Roman theater.

Classical Indian Theater

During the millennium after Greece and Rome established the outlines of European theatrical culture, the foundations were being laid for separate traditions in Asia. The earliest, and arguably the most influential, form of Asian theater emerged in India, home to one of the world's oldest civilizations. By 2500 B.C.E. the Indus Valley civilization had introduced city-states and a technologically advanced agricultural society in northwestern and western India. Its decline was caused in part by internal weakness and in part by the incursions of the Aryans, a nomadic people from northern Iran or central Asia. By 1500 B.C.E., the Indian subcontinent had been settled by the Aryans, who developed the Vedic civilization that would subsequently shape Indian history and culture. Central to this culture were the Vedas, or scriptures, that constituted the founding texts of Hinduism (the earliest of these, the *Rig-Veda*, was composed between 1500 and 1000 B.C.E.). Written in Sanskrit, these texts inspired a number of further writings; among them were two epic poems, the *Mahabharata* and the *Ramayana* (both written between 500 and 200 B.C.E.), which exerted a vast influence on later literature and theater in India and Southeast Asia. The Aryans also introduced the system of caste, or social stratification, that divided Indian society into four groups: priests, warriors and rulers, traders and merchants, and workers and peasants. The caste system, which provided the social framework of classical Indian drama and the audience that attended it, remains influential in today's India despite laws mandating equality of treatment for all members of society.

ORIGINS OF INDIAN THEATER

The scarcity of available historical evidence prevents us from knowing much about the origins of Indian, or Sanskrit, theater. In some Vedic rituals priests performed symbolic gestures, and these actions occasionally involved impersonating a represented figure, but it is impossible to tell whether these rites were the seeds of a more purely theatrical tradition. The *Mahabharata* makes references to performers (*nata*), though it is not known if actors were among them. Unlike Greece, India has no surviving theater structures from this period. The earliest plays extant, which date from the first century C.E., display a sophistication that suggests a long period of prior development, but there is no way of determining when a literary theater was first established. What evidence we do have concerning the Sanskrit theater comes from the plays that have survived from later centuries and from the *Natyasastra* (*The Art of Theater*), a compendious treatise on the nature and purpose of dramatic performance ascribed to Bharata Muni and written sometime between 300 B.C.E. and 200 C.E. Longer and more detailed than Aristotle's *Poetics*, the *Natyasastra* includes information concerning acting, theater and stage structures, theater organization, music, dance, playwriting, and aesthetics.

AUDIENCE, PLAYHOUSE, AND ACTORS

Theatrical performances during the classical age of Sanskrit theater (100–900 C.E.) apparently were offered on occasions ranging from sacred festivals to the coronation of kings, marriages, births, or the return of travelers. Although Bharata writes that the ideal spectator for such performances was learned and of high birth, members of all four castes (seated separately) seem to have attended. The *Natyasastra* describes three types of playhouses (square, triangular, and rectangular) and three sizes that these buildings could assume (small, medium-sized, and large), but focuses mainly on a rectangular building measuring 96 by 48 feet. Such a playhouse should resemble a cave, so that the actors' voices would resonate. Its interior was divided into two equal areas, with one half (called the *prekshagriha*) devoted to seating an audience that would have probably have included no more than 500 spectators. The other half

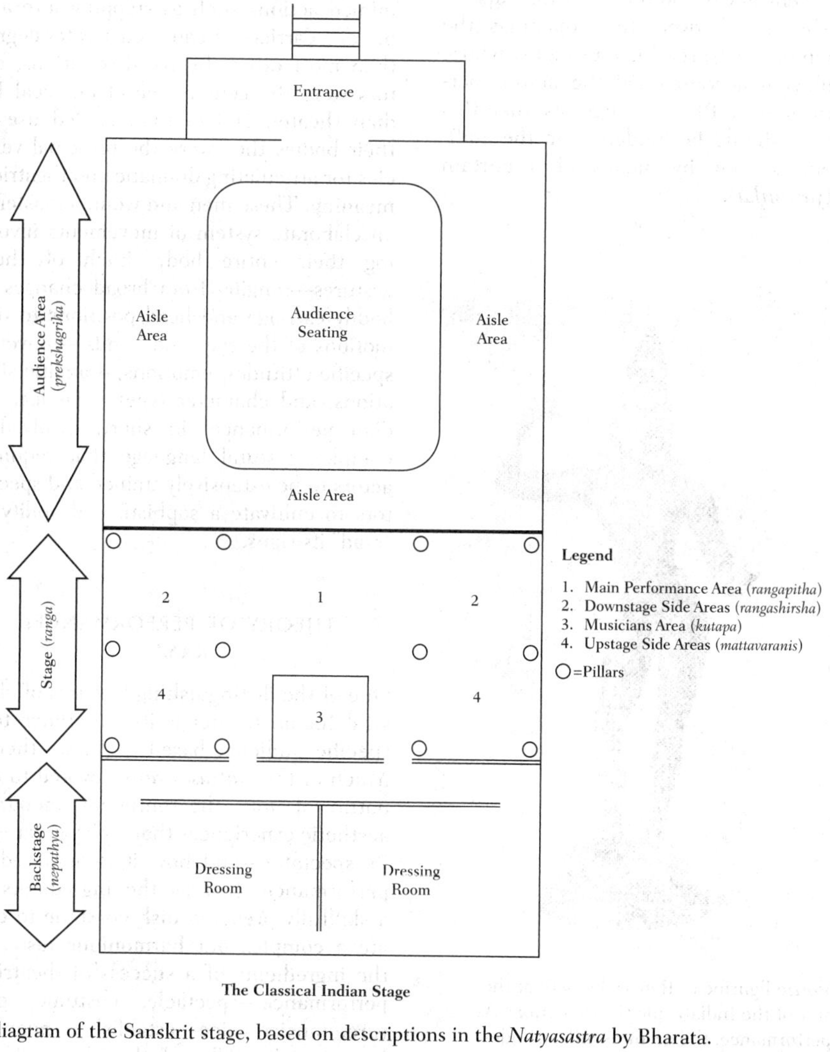

A diagram of the Sanskrit stage, based on descriptions in the *Natyasastra* by Bharata.

was itself divided in two: its back half (the *nepathya*) served as a backstage and dressing room, and its front half (the *ranga*) represented the performance area. The performance area, in turn, contained a number of distinct zones:

1. The main performance space (*rangapitha*) at the center of the stage.
2. The upstage area (*rangashirsha*), which stretched across the width of the performance space, between the back wall and the front performance area. Demarcating the back of this area was an ornamented curtain, possibly held by two attendants, with two openings, one for entrances and the other for exits.
3. The space between these openings (the *kutapa*), an area for musicians, whose playing accompanied the actors' performance. Bharata suggests that this area should be hidden from the audience's view by means of a curtain (*yavanika*).
4. Two downstage side areas (*mattavaranis*) flanking the main performance space.

A bronze figurine of Rama, the hero at the center of the Indian epic the *Ramayana*. As in performance, the gestures and attitudes portrayed in Indian sculpture are highly stylized.

These separate but contiguous acting areas made possible the fluid narrative structure of Sanskrit drama, in which dramatic action shifts between different locations and events and encounters can be staged simultaneously.

Apart from general decorations, which could serve a symbolic function, there were few props and no scenery on the classical Indian stage. Location and specific actions were indicated through a fixed repertoire of highly stylized movements. Actors walked around the stage in a circle to indicate a journey, for example, and mimed actions such as stepping into and out of a carriage. To an even greater degree than most other theatrical traditions, actors were the centerpiece of classical Indian theater, and in their skilled use of their bodies they were the principal vehicles for articulating dramatic and theatrical meaning. These men and women mastered an elaborate system of movements involving their entire body. Each of these gestures—ranging from broad changes in bodily carriage and head positions to tiny motions of the eyes and hands—conveyed specific attitudes, emotions, dramatic situations, and character types. Classical Indian performance, in short, involved a complex gestural language that required actors to be extensively trained and spectators to cultivate a sophisticated ability to "read" its signs.

THEORY OF PERFORMANCE: *RASA*

One of the distinguishing features of classical Indian theater is its adherence to a specific audience-based aesthetic theory. Much of the *Natyasastra* is devoted to the nature of *rasa*—the sentiment, mood, or aesthetic experiences that a play creates in its spectator—and how it is achieved in performance. Just as the ingredients of a skillfully prepared dish combine to create a complex but harmonious taste, so the ingredients of a successful theatrical performance—spectacle, costume, gesture, music, voice—establish a nuanced but overriding "flavor" that the audience can savor. The *Natyasastra* catalogues eight basic *rasas* (a ninth was added by later commentators) and associates these with eight permanent (and thirty-three transitory) human emotions, or *bhavas*. As actors portray these emotions, the spectator experiences the corresponding *rasa*. The effect, akin to that of any good meal, is a sense of aesthetic fullness and satisfaction.

CLASSICAL INDIAN DRAMA

About two dozen Sanskrit plays have survived to the present day, and they demonstrate the formal richness of classical Indian drama. Though Bharata describes ten major categories of play, two types were dominant on the classical Indian stage: *nataka* plays, whose stories are drawn from mythology or history, deal with exploits of kings and heroes; and *prakarana* plays are characterized by invented stories and less exalted characters. All plays combine a central story with numerous subsidiary plots, interweaving the serious and the comic. Indian dramatists employed both verse and prose in their plays and a mixture of Sanskrit and the popular dialects collectively known as Prakrit. The former is reserved for characters of high social standing, whereas the latter is spoken by characters of lesser station.

Most of the finest Sanskrit plays were written during the Gupta dynasty (ca. 320–ca. 550 C.E.), a period that witnessed a golden age of science, mathematics, literature, and philosophy in India. Major playwrights during this period include Bhasa, the author of thirteen surviving plays; Kalidasa, whose epic romance *Shakuntala* is considered by many to be the finest Sanskrit play; and SHUDRAKA, whose lengthy masterpiece ***THE LITTLE CLAY CART*** (ca. 100–300 C.E.) is excerpted in this anthology. Important Sanskrit drama continued to be written through the seventh century. Subsequent Indian history was marked by political instability as the court culture that helped sustain Sanskrit drama was threatened by a series of invasions by Muslim armies from the north from the tenth century onward. Sanskrit theater had largely disappeared as a cultural form by 1000 C.E.

Classical Chinese Theater

ORIGINS OF CHINESE THEATER

China, another of the world's oldest civilizations, has one of its richest performance and theater histories. Ancient Chinese scholars described performances synthesizing dance, music, and poetry as early as the reign of the legendary sage-ruler Yi Shun (2300–2205 B.C.E.), and shamanistic and court rituals involving dance and music were attributed to the Shang dynasty (1600–1045 B.C.E.). There are records dating to the first millennium B.C.E. of court entertainments—performed by jesters and others—that included music, dance, and mime. The integration of various activities in these earliest Chinese performances anticipates the capacious scope of later Chinese theater. The Chinese word that would later be used for "play" (*xi*) also meant "game," and it could be used to describe acrobatics, sports, and other kinds of entertainment. This highly theatrical synthesis of performance forms has flourished in Chinese theater to the present day, as the popularity of Beijing opera—a style of theater combining dance, music, storytelling, acrobatics, and martial arts—demonstrates.

THEATER DURING THE TANG AND SONG DYNASTIES

Theater and other forms of entertainment thrived during the Tang and Song dynasties, whose rulers held power in China between the seventh and thirteenth centuries C.E. During the Tang dynasty (618–907 C.E.), dance stories, skits, shadow and puppet plays, and a popular genre of play satirizing corrupt officials thrived at court and in the marketplace, as did circuslike performances and other forms of staged spectacle. Storytelling flourished as well, in forms that included the oral presentation of religious and secular stories by preachers attempting to disseminate Buddhism to nonliterate audiences. It was during the Tang period that Emperor Minghuang—considered the patron of Chinese theater—established the Pear Orchard Conservatory, the first academy in China devoted to the training of actors and other performers.

During the Song dynasty (960–1279), a period that saw a rise in commerce and the growth and social diversification of Chinese urban centers, amusement centers called "tile districts" (*wazi*) were organized in major cities. These centers, which provided a wide variety of entertainment, included theaters—as many as fifty in the tile districts of the northern capital Bianliang (modern-day Kaifeng)—that could seat up to several thousand spectators. The most accomplished players also performed at the emperor's palace, while itinerant players performed in villages and elsewhere on temporary stages. In addition to viewing such activities as tightrope walking, storytelling, and puppetry, audiences in the tile districts of northern China (a region that was taken over from the Song emperor by invaders from Manchuria in 1127 and ruled thereafter by the Jin dynasty) were entertained by the performance of *zaju:* variety shows that featured dramatic sketches accompanied by musical performance, comic routines, dancing, and acrobatics. In the southern provinces (which remained under Song rule), a separate form of theater known as *nanxi* developed during this period. Longer than their counterparts presented in the north and more intricate in story lines, *nanxi* made use of folk music and a array of familiar character types that influenced subsequent Chinese drama.

YUAN DRAMA: *ZAJU*

Though *nanxi* and the *zaju* have clear dramatic elements, it was not until the Yuan dynasty (1234–1368), when first part and later all of China was under Mongol occupation, that drama flourished as a literary genre. As the Venetian explorer Marco Polo (1254–1324) reported during his travels to the court of Kublai Khan (1215–1294), greatest of the Mongol emperors, China during the Yuan dynasty was a land of prosperity and cultural achievement, enjoying the fruits of increased trade and cultural exchange with western Asia and Europe. Contemporary records mention the titles of some 700 plays written during this period—of which 163 have been preserved, many of them in collections compiled during the late Ming dynasty (1368–1644)—and the names of roughly 550 dramatists, including GUAN HANQING (ca. 1245–ca. 1322), the most prolific and best known of the Yuan playwrights. In its quantity and sophistication, Yuan drama has often been compared to that of Elizabethan and Jacobean England. One of the reasons for its flourishing is that Chinese scholars, who had traditionally served in government posts, found themselves excluded from civil service under Mongol rule; they therefore turned their attention to other careers, such as writing. To appeal to a popular audience, these scholars abandoned the classical Chinese of Confucius (Kong Fuzi, ca. 551–479 B.C.E.)—whose ethical teachings constituted a pillar of traditional Chinese society—and helped develop the vernacular as a dramatic language. The result was a richly poetic drama, literary in conception yet deeply grounded in the performance traditions of Chinese theater.

Most of this drama is referred to as "Yuan *zaju*," to distinguish it from the earlier form of northern theater. These plays treated subjects ranging from the historical, legendary, and supernatural to the contemporary. They told stories of love, war, political intrigue, adventure, religious conversion, domestic drama, crime, and judicial punishment. Their characters—covering a broad spectrum, from gods, emperors, and generals to hermits, outlaws, concubines, and ordinary people—derive from an array of popular types. Yuan *zaju* plays are typically four acts long, though shorter wedge acts (*xiezi*) may be added when additional plot material is required, and they include from ten to twenty songs, all performed by the main character. These songs, often of great poetic beauty, are the lyrical center of *zaju* plays. The remainder of the dramatic action is conveyed through speech and dialogue. In keeping with the Confucian emphasis on right and wrong and on the importance of correct conduct, *zaju* plays end with justice served, even when (as in Guan Hanqing's *SNOW IN MIDSUMMER*) a play's hero or heroine dies.

ACTORS AND STAGE

Yuan acting troupes included men and women performers, and both men and women played male and female roles. From the scattered evidence we possess—

Yuan troupe onstage, from a 1324 temple wall painting in the northern Chinese province of Shanxi.

including a fourteenth-century colored mural from a temple in the northern province of Shanxi that depicts a Yuan acting troupe onstage—we know that actors wore ornate, colorful costumes and highly stylized makeup. Though the physical structure of the stage most likely varied with the venue and performance occasion, the stage depicted in the Shanxi mural—consisting of a bare tile floor with entrances on either side of a decorative wall painting in the rear—was probably typical. There was no formal scenery on the Yuan stage and props were minimal. Musicians performed onstage, and their instruments included the flute, gong, clapper, drum, and a lute-like instrument known as a *pipa*. The audience of these Yuan performers seems to have represented a wide range of Chinese society, from the Mongol emperors and their courts down to merchants, peasants, and poor laborers. Yuan *zaju* was a drama that appealed to educated and uneducated spectators alike.

THE RISE OF *NANXI*

Zaju continued to be popular into the Ming dynasty, which assumed power in 1368 after a rebellion drove the Yuan from power, but in the fourteenth century it was rivaled and eventually eclipsed by the reemergence of *nanxi* drama in the southern provinces and its development into a form markedly different from the theater found in the north. *Nanxi* plays are longer than *zaju* plays, and they contain a variable number of acts (as many as fifty or more, each with its own title). Singing is not restricted to a single character; instead, songs are performed by two or more singers, and sometimes by choruses. Acted to the accompaniment of a bamboo flute, *nanxi* plays drew on folk music, and their overall atmosphere in performance was elegiac. Although *zaju* is considered China's premier classical drama, the development of a "southern style" of drama proved to be more influential. A number of the distinctive character types of *nanxi* drama, in fact, remain popular on today's Chinese stage.

Classical Japanese Theater

When Westerners think of Asian theater, it is the theater of Japan that most often comes to mind. In part, this can be explained by the cultural distinctiveness of Japan's theatrical and dramatic traditions: the meditative dance theater of noh, the stylized acrobatics of kabuki, the sophisticated gestures of bunraku puppet theater. But it also has to do with the preservation of such theatrical traditions through centuries of political and social change. In a country devoted to ritual, ceremony, and other forms of tradition, theatrical practices have been handed down with the formal exactitude of the tea ceremony. As a result, we can come to understand the development of Japanese theater not only by reading histories of theater but by attending live performances.

ORIGINS OF JAPANESE THEATER

Although archaeologists have uncovered clay representations of singers, dancers, and musical instruments from as early as the third century B.C.E., the earliest manifestations of what we would consider theater in Japan were dance-based ritual celebrations collectively known as *kagura*. These performances were connected with Shintoism, a prehistoric religion devoted to the worship of gods and spirits who represented aspects of the natural world. Versions of *kagura* were performed at Shinto shrines by shamanistic priestesses, at the imperial court, and in villages during harvest and other annual festivals. Other theatrical forms emerged in the centuries after Buddhism was introduced to Japan between 538 and 552 C.E., a period during which continental Asian culture was embraced by the imperial court. In the seventh and eighth centuries, two forms of dance theater came from China via Korea: *gigaku*, a Buddhist dance play in which masked figures moved in procession, and *bugaku*, a stately court entertainment that eventually included dances from India, Tibet, and Vietnam in addition to those from China and Korea.

Other popular forms of entertainment also flourished during this time, involving music, dance, masked pantomime, and in some instances acrobatics, juggling, and tightrope walking. Several of these traditions had dramatic components, including *sarugaku* (monkey entertainment), a form of variety theater containing comic dialogues and short skits that came to be performed at Buddhist temples. By the thirteenth century, the dramatic and performance elements of these entertainments had become increasingly sophisticated, and the form was given the name *sarugaku noh*. The term *noh*, which means "skill" or "craft," eventually stood alone as a theatrical category.

THE EMERGENCE OF NOH THEATER: KANAMI AND ZEAMI

The emergence of noh theater reflected the political and social changes that Japan had undergone during the previous two centuries. In 1192 the Japanese emperor relinquished rule of the country to samurai generals, whose rising military and economic power had made them the country's dominant social class. These generals, who gave themselves the title *shogun*, presided over wealthy courts in Kamakura and later Kyoto and established a feudal society with rigidly demarcated social strata. Although many cultural forms that had found favor in the imperial court fell out of fashion, the shoguns patronized the arts, including the theater of *sarugaku noh*. In 1374, Kanami Kiyotsugu (1333–1384), head of one of the country's *sarugaku noh* troupes, performed before the young shogun Ashikaga Yoshimitsu (1358–1408). So impressed was the shogun that he became Kanami's patron and took the performer's son, ZEAMI MOTOKIYO (1363–1443), who was also an accomplished actor, as his companion and lover.

It was through the efforts of Kanami and Zeami that noh became an autonomous form. An innovator by temperament, Kanami combined elements of existing performance traditions into a dramatic form adapted to the tastes of the shogunate and lower warrior classes. Kanami amalgamated popular songs, dance, music, and poetry within an aesthetic of meditative deliberateness and restraint drawn from Zen Buddhism. Limiting his plays to a single protagonist, he advocated a style of acting based on authenticity of physical and vocal characterization. After Kanami's death, Zeami, who would become one of the most important figures in the history of Japanese theater, extended and refined his father's theatrical innovations. In a number of theoretical writings, including the seven-volume *Kadensho* (1400–02), Zeami discussed the intricacies of noh acting, the relationship of noh theater to its audience, and the aesthetic concepts underlying noh performance, such as *yugen,* which denotes suggestive beauty, gracefulness, and an awareness of life's impermanence. In addition to being noh's chief theoretician and one of its greatest actors, Zeami was also its most accomplished playwright, authoring nearly half of the 240 surviving plays that constitute the noh repertoire.

NOH DRAMA

The stories of noh plays are drawn from mythology, legend, and history, particularly (as in Zeami's ***ATSUMORI*** [ca. 1400]) the twelfth-century civil war between rival samurai clans. The main character (or *shite*) is often a ghost, demon, or tormented person who cannot find rest because of his or her past deeds. In the typical two-act structure, the central character appears disguised in the first act and is revealed in the second. He or she speaks an elevated, highly literary verse, and frequently quotes classical Chinese and Japanese poetry. Other established roles include the main character's companion (*tsure*); a third party (*waki*), frequently a priest, who encounters the main character in the first

The *shite*, or primary actor, in a contemporary performance of the noh drama *The Lady Aoi*. Note the mask, costume, folding fan, and stylized gesture of the performer. In the background sit the *hayashikata*, or musicians.

act; and a servant or commoner (*kyogen*), whose language is colloquial and who often provides a narrative summary in the interlude between acts. An onstage chorus sings many of the characters' lines and narrates events within the dramatic action, while three or four onstage musicians accompany the play with drums and flute. The climax of a noh play takes the form of a ritualized dance.

Noh dramas fall into five categories: plays about gods; warrior plays; plays about women, or "wig plays"; miscellaneous plays, including plays about madness and plays about the present time; and demon plays, in which the main character is a good or evil supernatural being. In a traditional noh program, plays from each of these categories were performed, in the order given. Between the plays, farcical sketches known as *kyogen* (wild words) were performed by the same actors who took the colloquial roles in the noh drama. A *nohgaku* program (the term refers to the combination of *noh* and *kyogen* in performance) took seven or eight hours to complete.

ACTORS

The actors of noh drama, who were male—a tradition maintained in all but a few noh companies today—were dressed in elaborate, highly formal silk costumes. These costumes, which included kimonos for male characters, involved variously layered inner and outer garments. Actors were usually wigged. Among the most celebrated features of noh theater are the masks that the main character and his or her companion wore. Treasured for their craftsmanship and elegant yet simple design, these masks offered stylized representations of the established noh character types: male and female, old and young, human and supernatural. Actors in other roles wore masklike makeup. In contrast to the richness of visual presentation that characterized the actors thus attired, the physical setting and props in noh performance were minimal. Movable structures were used to represent a hut, boat, mountain, and other features, while handheld props served to represent emotional states and a range of other objects. A folding fan, for instance, one of the main props in noh theater, could be used to stand for a sword, a flute, or other item. The handling of physical objects formed part of the broader choreography of noh performance, which involved slow, deliberate movement and symbolic, meditative gestures. The acts of walking and dancing, for example, called for painstaking control of body position and motion, and years of training were required for the actor to master such simple gestures as lifting an arm or raising a hand to the eyes, the symbol of weeping.

THE NOH STAGE

Drawn to its formal precision and ceremonial nature, later dramatists and theater artists have sought to appropriate elements of the noh for the modern theater (*Four Plays for Dancers*, published in 1921 by the Irish playwright and poet William Butler Yeats, represents one such attempt). To an extent unrivaled in world theater, however, traditional noh performance is inseparable from the stage for which it was written. The configuration, dimensions, and materials of this stage were standardized during the seventeenth century and have remained unchanged in noh theaters to the present day. The main stage, roughly 18 feet square and raised about 2½ feet above the ground, consists of a polished surface of Japanese cypress with four pillars, roughly 15 feet high, that support a temple-like roof. The audience sits in front of and to the left of this stage. A visible backstage area, at the front of which the musicians sit, features a wooden wall with painted pine trees, while an area to the audience's right of the main acting area is occupied by the chorus, who sit in two rows facing the stage.

One of the most characteristic features of the noh stage is the *hashigakiri,* a railed passageway or bridge that extends from the side of the backstage area on the audience's left to a dressing (or "mirror") room, from which actors make their entrances and to which they exit. A secondary exit to the right of the backstage area is used by the chorus and stage attendants. Reverberating jars are placed under the main stage, backstage, and bridge to provide additional resonance and to amplify the sound of characters walking and stomping their feet. Specific areas of the stage are associated

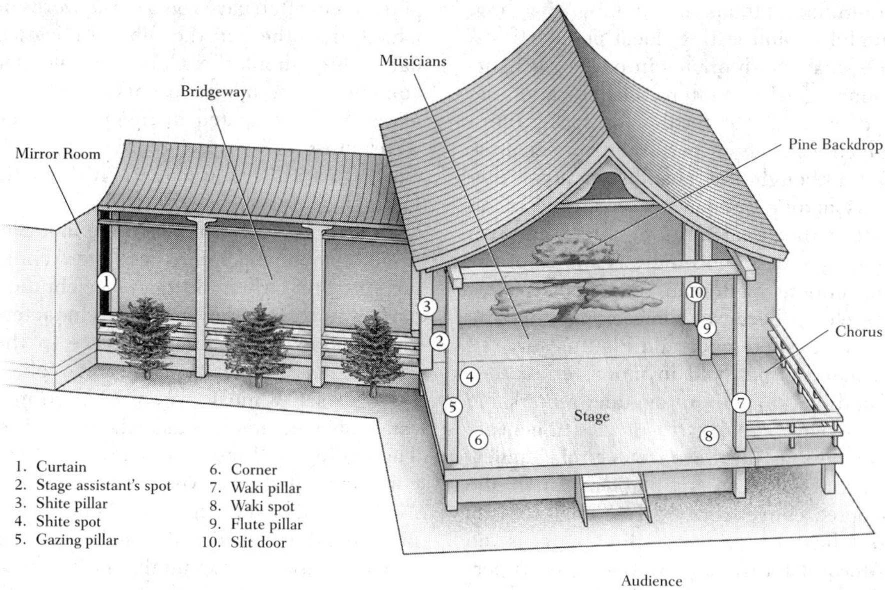

with individual characters and with conventionally assigned functions. The pillar that stands where the bridge meets the stage, for instance, known as the *shite*-pillar, is where the main character stops to announce his name upon entering the stage area.

LATER NOH THEATER

The conventions of modern-day noh theater were standardized during the Tokugawa shogunate (1603–1867), a period when the center of government was moved to Edo (modern-day Tokyo) and the hierarchies of Japanese society were institutionalized to a greater extent. Noh theater companies assumed their modern form as hereditary heads (*iemoto*) were made responsible for preserving the traditions of the major schools of noh. Rooted in the practices and accomplishments of its early masters, noh became an art for connoisseurs; although amateur noh companies found support among the commoners, its principal audience was courtly and upper-class.

KABUKI AND BUNRAKU

By the early seventeenth century, other theatrical forms had emerged to satisfy the tastes of a rising urban middle class. Kabuki—a form of dramatic theater involving music, dance, and acrobatics; ornate costumes and makeup; extensive scenery; and spectacular tricks of stage technology—developed in the early decades of the 1600s from the lively, often erotic, dances that temple maidens performed at religious shrines. The performance of kabuki, which was restricted to adult males in 1653, became a highly conventional and stylized art, and its practitioners—including the popular *onnagata,* or actor of female roles—require decades of training. Bunraku, an elaborate form of puppet (or doll) theater that developed out of earlier puppet and storytelling traditions, also became popular during this period. Like noh, which can be seen in specially built theaters throughout Japan, these centuries-old theater forms remain popular on today's stage.

Medieval European Theater

EUROPE AFTER THE ROMAN EMPIRE

The disintegration of the Roman Empire between the fifth and sixth centuries C.E. marked the end of organized theatrical activity in western and central Europe as it had been practiced in classical Rome. Itinerant groups of performers traveled through southern Europe offering such entertainments as storytelling, juggling, tumbling, and jesting; local popular festivals, many with origins in pagan rites surrounding the winter solstice and the earth's return to fertility in spring, contained a variety of performative elements. But although the abandoned amphitheaters across Europe gave evidence of an earlier theatrical culture, after the sixth century little to nothing was known of the conventions of Roman performance. Nevertheless, because some copies of the comedies of Terence and Plautus survived in manuscripts held in monasteries, they could be drawn on by one remarkable playwright: HROTSVIT, a tenth-century canoness at the Saxon abbey of Gandersheim, who wrote six plays in which she adapted conventions of Terentian comedy to Christian subjects. But there is no record of Hrosvit's plays having been performed during the Middle Ages, and the impact of the Roman playwrights before the Renaissance was limited to scholars and to literary circles; they had no affect on theatrical practice.

EARLY CHURCH DRAMA

A major reason for the absence of organized theater during this era was the opposition of the Christian Church to all such activities. Throughout the Middle Ages (and much of the early modern period), church authorities and moralists denounced theater and other forms of spectacle and impersonation as idolatrous, obscene, and dangerous in their effects on the audience members' passions. Ironically, this same church served as the major site for the reemergence of theater in medieval Europe—but perhaps not surprisingly, since the Catholic liturgy is itself a performed spectacle. During the medieval mass, priests wearing ornate robes officiated before spectators gathered in designated locations within enclosed structures. Processions and other forms of ceremony marked holy days throughout the year, while each day's canonical "offices" or "hours" (such as matins and vespers) were marked by services of their own. Chanting during the liturgy was often antiphonal—with passages sung alternately by two choirs, much like dialogue—and singer-performers often gave voice to the words of Christ and others in the Bible. Individual dates throughout the Christian calendar commemorated biblical events and the figures who participated in them, and thus were inherently associated with a rich trove of narrative and potentially dramatic material.

But ritual and ceremony are not the same as drama, and the latter could emerge only when liturgical celebration gave way to a wider range of characters and actions. This shift took place in the tenth century, when *tropes*—short biblical passages set to music—were inserted into established ceremonies as embellishments. The earliest and most influential of these commemorated the visit by the Three Marys to Christ's sepulcher on Eastern morning, during which they learn from an angel present at the tomb that he has been resurrected. Known as the *Quem quaeritis* trope after its opening line ("Whom are you seeking?"), this chanted dialogue rapidly gained popularity and by the late tenth century had inspired similar tropes

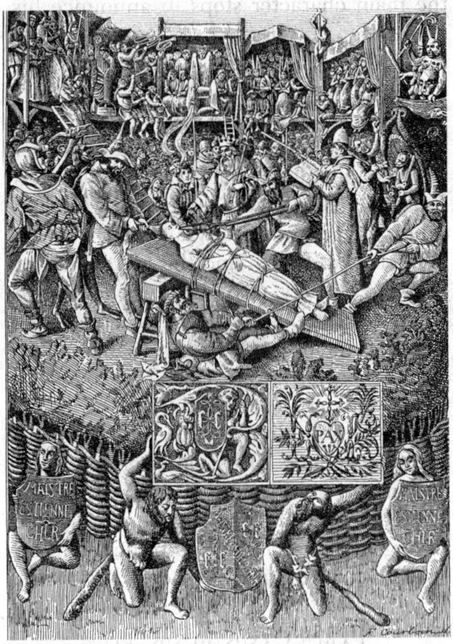

This engraving, a nineteenth-century copy of an original devotional miniature by Jean Fouquet (ca. 1415–1481), depicts the performance of a "miracle play" of the martyrdom of St. Apollonia of Alexandria.

connected with the Christmas liturgy. The connections eventually encompassed other events from the Christmas season, and the *Quem quaeritis* tropes developed into full-length Easter dramas. In their earliest forms liturgical tropes were performed in Benedictine monasteries for fellow monastics; but as cathedrals and other large church buildings were constructed in the eleventh and twelfth centuries, the lay congregations became audiences for these religious performances.

By the twelfth century, church drama had so expanded in scope and complexity that some works—the Christmas and Passion plays from the Benediktbeuern Abbey in Bavarian Germany, for example—were performed outside the context of the liturgy. Eventually, as part of this natural progression, the plays came to be performed outside the context of the church. The range of suitable dramatic subjects grew to include figures and events from the Old and the New Testament: the raising of Lazarus, Daniel in the lion's den, and the conversion of St. Paul, to name a few. Plays commemorating the lives of saints—often called "miracle plays" because they recounted the miracles or martyrdoms that led to the protagonist's conversion—mixed narratives of conflict and romantic adventure with moral exempla. Versions of these saints' plays were written and performed into the late Middle Ages.

CORPUS CHRISTI CYCLES

In a parallel development, religious plays began to be written in the national languages of central and western Europe (rather than the Latin of the church), and during the fourteenth and fifteenth centuries these vernacular forms developed into elaborate dramatic cycles of short plays, or pageants. The most notable of these cycle plays were performed in conjunction with the Feast of Corpus Christi (literally, "The Body of Christ"), a holy day—proposed by Pope Urban IV in 1264 and instituted by the church in 1311—celebrating the redemptive presence of the Holy Eucharist. This feast day, which occurred in late spring or early summer, included an outdoor procession in which the host was displayed; eventually, taking advantage of the generally favorable weather and the longer period of daylight, performers took an entire day and sometimes more to mount plays dramatizing events from biblical history. Though more limited versions of these cycles were performed on the Continent, the best-known achievements in this extended dramatic form were England's Corpus Christi plays, which dramatized the history of the world from the fall of the angels and the creation to the Last Judgment. Local records and the manuscripts of individual plays note performances in London, Coventry, Norwich, Newcastle-on-Tyne, and elsewhere in England, but the great majority of the surviving cycle plays come from just four towns, apparently all in the north: York, Wakefield, Chester, and N Town (where N stands for *nomen*—Latin for "name"—suggesting that this cycle was performed by touring players who would insert whatever name was appropriate as they traveled across the countryside). These cycles are quite extensive, containing between twenty-five pageants (the Chester cycle) to forty-eight (the York cycle). Although English cycle drama was performed as early as 1376, most Corpus Christi plays date from the fifteenth century. This distinctive form of drama continued to be performed—scholars have speculated that as a youth, WILLIAM SHAKESPEARE may have seen a performance of the Coventry cycle; by the late sixteenth century, however, it was effectively suppressed by the newly established Church of England.

The development of theatrical activity on such a scale was made possible by the growth of medieval towns and the formation of guilds: that is, associations governing the practice of individual crafts and trades, which participated in town government and played a major role in both the religious and nonreligious aspects of civic life. In northern England, guilds assumed primary responsibility for the production of the Corpus Christi plays, which therefore are also called "mystery cycles" (the word *mystery*, derived from the Latin *mysterium*, referred to a craft, trade, or profession known only to a few). This arrangement indicates that the cycle plays performed a civic as well as religious function. Given responsibility for individual pageants, guilds provided actors, scenery, costumes, props, and other theatrical elements and materials. In some cases guilds were assigned plays for which they seemed particularly suited: the shipwrights would be given the Noah plays, for instance, while the goldsmiths produced plays about the Three Kings.

STAGING

The manner in which individual Corpus Christi cycles were staged remains a matter of debate. Although practice varied from town to town, there is evidence of two forms of staging: processional and fixed. In certain cities, such as York and Coventry, plays were mounted on pageant wagons that performed, in procession, before spectators gathered at designated viewing sites throughout the town. Scholars disagree on the structure and appearance of these wagons: some speculate that they had two levels (the lower serving as a dressing room), while others argue for a single-platform structure. In addition to the acting area, performers occasionally acted in the street surrounding the pageant wagon; in the Nativity pageant, one of two surviving plays from Coventry, the actor playing Herod "rages in the pagond [pageant wagon] and in the street also." In the alternative staging method, all plays were performed at stationary locations. It is also possible that some combination of processional and fixed staging was practiced: for instance, pageant wagons may have paraded through the town with the actors arranged in tableaux, then gathered in a circle at an open place where they could serve as stages for an audience that stood within the circle's periphery and moved from play to play.

Whether presented on pageant wagons or at fixed locations, the Corpus Christi cycles drew on a staging convention that had characterized medieval drama since its liturgical beginnings. The acting area had two components: one or more structures

This engraved illustration from Thomas Sharp's *Dissertation on the Pageants Anciently Performed at Coventry* (1825) presents an imaginative reconstruction of the performance of a pageant play in Coventry, England.

called *sedes* (mansions) and a nonlocalized playing space adjacent to these that was known as the *platea* (courtyard, or place). The former, usually represented by decorative booths, oriented the dramatic action to specific locations (Heaven, Hell, palace, house, manger), while the latter allowed for extensions of the action into more indeterminate spaces beyond the *sedes*. Financed by prosperous guilds and engineered by skilled craftsmen, Corpus Christi performances could be awe-inspiring affairs, with special effects and elaborate technical devices. Cranes enabled characters to ascend, descend, and fly between locations, while the Hell's Mouth through which sinners were dragged relied on an elaborate contraption of pulleys and smoke-ejecting bellows. Costumes included everyday medieval garments, ecclesiastical vestments, and—in the case of heavenly beings, who wore gilded masks, and devils, who were given the features of grotesque animals—nonnaturalistic adornments.

DRAMATIC TEXTS

Individual plays, or pageants, within specific cycles vary in length, structure, and style. Some are very formal and rely heavily on long-standing conventions, while others combine biblical narratives with scenes and characters from medieval life. Because the authors of these plays often embellished the biblical accounts with more realistic incidents and characterizations, the Corpus Christi cycles established links between sacred history and the world of their audiences. Indeed, the plays reveal as much about the medieval world as they do about the biblical episodes they take as their subjects. Among the greatest of these works blending the sacred and everyday is by an author whom later scholars call the WAKEFIELD MASTER. This unidentified playwright, whose plays display a command of vernacular dialects, complex characterization, and realistic situations, wrote ***THE SECOND SHEPHERDS' PLAY*** (ca. 1475), which parallels and contrasts the scene of the Nativity with a rustic sheep-stealing episode. By counterpointing the mystery of Christ's Incarnation with the earthiness of fallen humanity, this widely known play demonstrates the use of comedy in Corpus Christi drama. Its folk elements remind us of popular forms of entertainment and celebration—folk festivals, songs and stories, mummers' plays (i.e., seasonal folk plays)—and of the drama that emerged from them in the later Middle Ages. In this tradition are the farces of the German poet and dramatist Hans Sachs (1494–1576), written for the festivities of Shrovetide, the three days preceding Lent.

MORALITY PLAYS

At the same time that the mystery cycles were being organized in the late fourteenth century, a different form of religious drama was emerging in England and France: the morality play. Like the Corpus Christi pageants, this drama was concerned with human salvation—but rather than exploring sin and redemption across the vast landscape of human and divine history, as did the cycles, morality plays focused on the moral life of the individual Christian. Written in the mode of allegory, in which abstract ideas and categories of individuals are given concrete form, morality drama featured a representative figure of humanity—Mankind, Everyman, Well-Advised, Ill-Advised—whose identity is universal rather than historical, biblical, or individual. This character interacts with figures personifying virtues and vices, who typically seek to win his soul in a battle between temptation and spiritual obedience. Whereas Corpus Christi plays occasionally employed allegorical characters, morality drama derived neither from these plays nor from the liturgical drama that preceded them. In addition to reflecting the general fondness for allegory in the Middle Ages—Prudentius's poem *Psychomachia* (fourth century C.E.), which introduced the competition of virtues and vices, was widely influential throughout the medieval period—morality drama likely drew on Pater Noster (or Lord's Prayer) plays; these were dramatizations of the seven deadly sins, performed in England during the fourteenth and fifteenth centuries. Since no Pater Noster plays have survived, specific relationships between the two dramatic forms cannot be established.

The oldest extant English morality play is a dramatic fragment titled *The Pride of*

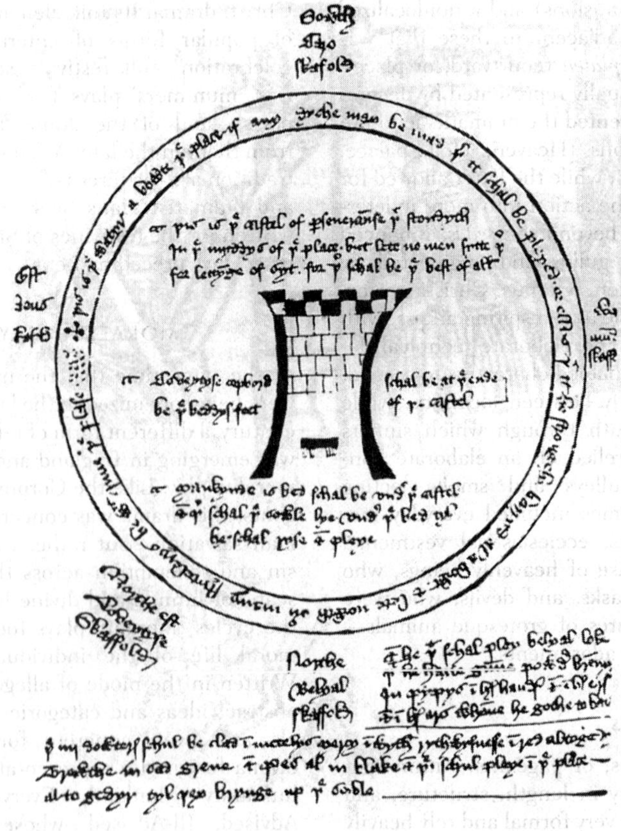

Diagram for staging *The Castle of Perseverance*, from a fifteenth-century manuscript.

Life (ca. 1350). Only a few plays from the following 160 years have survived, but they indicate the drama's variety of forms and staging practices. The longest and most complex of the English moralities, *The Castle of Perseverance* (ca. 1405–25), presents the life of its protagonist Mankind from birth to death, the struggle over his soul by virtues and vices, a debate between Body and Soul, the parliament of heaven, and the final judgment on Mankind's soul. The manuscript for this play, which includes a diagram, offers particular insight into its staging. Located outdoors, the performance area of *The Castle of Perseverance* consisted of a circular playing space with a structure indicating Mankind's castle in the center and five mansions on the periphery. The later *Mankind* (ca. 1465–70), by contrast, was performed before rural audiences by an itinerant group of professional or semiprofessional actors. The staging requirements were necessarily simple—a few props, a small booth for entrances and exits—and the play could be staged both in an open courtyard and indoors. The play itself combines the story of the farmer Mankind's temptation, fall, and repentance with wide-ranging comic business, most having to do with the devil and his attendant mischief-figures. Finally, the best known of the moralities, **EVERYMAN** (ca. 1510, translated from a 1495 Dutch original), eschews the drama of temptation for the more somber story of Everyman's journey to death and final judgment. Although textual evidence suggests that the play was written for a playing area with fixed structures, there are no records of its actual performance.

During the sixteenth century, morality drama became broadly popular with audiences across the social spectrum. A growing number of morality plays were performed in public and private venues throughout England by troupes of professional actors—the direct precursors of the acting companies of Shakespeare's time. As the intellectual and religious climate of England changed in response to Renaissance humanism (a revival in the study of classical literature, science, and philosophy) and to the Reformation (a movement to reform the Catholic Church that led to the founding of Protestant religious denominations), morality drama evolved in its subject matter as well as its ideological function. In the hands of such Tudor humanist writers as Henry Medwall (1462–1501?) and John Skelton (ca. 1460–1529), morality plays engaged with increasingly secular subjects, addressing issues of philosophy, social relations, and politics in addition to moral and religious questions. In this form they frequently resembled Tudor interludes (indoor dramatic entertainments that were usually performed in noble households, guild halls, and schools). During the religious controversies of the English Reformation, morality drama was employed by Catholics and Protestants to dramatize their doctrinal and political divisions. Even more profoundly than the Corpus Christi cycles, which were cumbersome in structure and rooted in a medieval religious consensus that no longer applied in sixteenth-century England, morality plays helped shape subsequent English drama. Because their allegorical conventions were adaptable to a range of issues and ideologies, these plays provided a dramatic structure for such Elizabethan and Jacobean plays as CHRISTOPHER MARLOWE's *DOCTOR FAUSTUS* (ca. 1588). Certainly, the legacy of the Vice characters, with their conniving but theatrically appealing horseplay, can be seen clearly in such later dramatic masterpieces as BEN JONSON's *VOLPONE* (1606).

Theater in Early Modern Europe, 1500–1700

As European theater developed between 1500 and 1700, it was affected by a range of political, economic, social, artistic, and religious changes that were transforming the region and its relationship to the rest of the world. The term *early modern,* which is often used to designate the period in European history between the end of the Middle Ages and the beginning of the Industrial Revolution, focuses attention on those developments that inaugurated the world we know today: the rise of science and accelerating technological innovation, the growth of cities and the emergence of mercantile economies, New World exploration and colonization, and the transformations of church and state through reformation, absolutism, and revolution. But as the competing term *Renaissance*—applied to the fifteenth and sixteenth centuries—suggests, this period is also characterized by a powerful look backward to the classical era of Greece and Rome and to the social, artistic, and intellectual values that scholars, newly given access to many of its rediscovered texts, found there. As they combined the new and the old in fruitful, and also volatile, ways, the years 1500–1700 were a period of unprecedented discovery and rediscovery in the visual, plastic, architectural, and musical arts. But arguably it was theater—where audiences in England, Spain, France, and elsewhere in Europe saw their world represented in action—that witnessed the greatest accomplishments during this extraordinary period.

THE EUROPEAN RENAISSANCE: HUMANISM AND THE CLASSICAL PAST

The European Renaissance played a crucial role in the transformations that Europe underwent in the fifteenth and sixteenth centuries. The term *Renaissance,* which means "rebirth," was first used in 1550 by the artist and critic Giorgio Vasari (1511–1574) to refer to the rediscovery of classical values—which, he claimed, had been eclipsed during the Middle Ages by Christianity and the "barbarian" cultures of northern Europe—in the paintings of Giotto (ca. 1267–1337) and later Florentine artists. This view of medieval civilization as a dark age compared to the civilizations of Greece and Rome is, of course, inaccurate, as is any absolute demarcation between the later Middle Ages and the Renaissance. Europe in the 1500s remained in many ways medieval. But the turn to the classical world represented a driving force behind humanism, the dominant intellectual movement in Renaissance Europe, and it effected a profound shift of cultural direction. Convinced that the civilizations of Greece and Rome represented the highest point of human achievement and that modern Europe should cultivate their ideals and emulate their accomplishments, scholars devoted themselves to the rediscovery, translation, and textual study of classical works, many of which had been preserved in European monasteries and in the libraries of the Byzantine Empire and Islamic Spain. The invention of the printing press in 1450 by Johann Gutenberg (ca. 1400–1468) accelerated the process by which these texts and Renaissance commentaries on them were disseminated.

The deepening understanding of Greek and Roman writers, and of classical civilization as a whole, revolutionized the fields of literature and the arts. The Italian writers Petrarch (Francesco Petrarca, 1304–1374) and Giovanni Boccaccio (1313–1375) urged their peers to study Greek and Roman writers, and the influence of authors, literary forms, historical subjects, and mythological characters from the classical period was widespread in the literature of the next three centuries. Though it is a mistake to see this expanding interest as a departure from the religious concerns of medieval literature—most Renaissance writers explored classical materials in the context of Christian belief—an intensifying concern with human experience and the things of the world makes itself felt throughout the literature of this period, including its finest: the essays of Michel de Montaigne (1533–1592), for example, and the picaresque fiction of Miguel de Cervantes (1547–1616). A similar interest in the world as it is lived and observed is apparent in the work of Leonardo da Vinci (1452–1519), Michelangelo (1475–1564), and other Renaissance artists, who abandoned the flat, often ornamental surfaces of medieval art for more lifelike representations of the human figure and the visible world.

PATRONAGE

The Renaissance as a cultural phenomenon was closely linked to the increasing urbanization and the changing economic and political landscapes of European society. The movement began in the city-states of Italy, where rulers competed with each other to be patrons of scholarship, literature, and the other arts. Here, as elsewhere in Europe, wealth and power were increasingly concentrated in the hands of princes and other monarchs, civic authorities, and an expanding merchant class, and these groups sought to enhance their prestige by funding art, architecture, literature, music, and lavish spectacles. The most prominent of the Italian cultural centers was Florence, which served—under the rule of Lorenzo de' Medici (1449–1492), "the Magnificent"—as a home for humanists, artists, poets, and philosophers. Later centers of patronage included the courts of England's Elizabeth I and James I, Spain's Philip II, and France's Louis XIV. Acting companies, whose members had previously operated on the margins of society, also benefited from the patronage system during the sixteenth and seventeenth centuries. Even as it earned money from the London playgoing public, for instance, the company to which WILLIAM SHAKESPEARE belonged—the Lord Chamberlain's Men, later renamed the King's Men—enjoyed the support, protection, and legitimation conferred by courtly patronage.

SCIENCE AND THE "NEW PHILOSOPHY"

As Renaissance humanism reevaluated medieval learning in light of earlier classical traditions, it profoundly altered established fields of knowledge and inquiry. In the field of political philosophy, for instance, the Italian theorist Niccolò Machiavelli (1469–1527) proposed a view of politics and government in which the maintenance and exercise of power, not moral authority, were the ultimate justification for political action. So controversial were these ideas that his very name became synonymous with cunning and ruthless self-interest. The argument between older and newer conceptions of the world

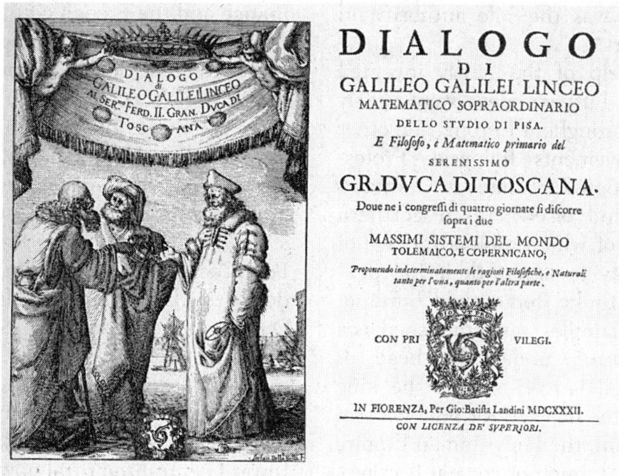

The title page and engraved frontispiece of Galileo's *Dialogue Concerning the Two Chief World Systems*, published in Florence in 1632. In the book, Galileo argued in favor of Copernicus's model of the solar system, in which the planets revolve around the sun, and against the older Ptolemaic system, which placed the earth at the center of the known universe. The engraving shows Aristotle (left), Ptolemy (center), and Copernicus (right).

was a defining feature of the scientific revolution that took place during the sixteenth and seventeenth centuries. In 1543 Nicolaus Copernicus (1473–1543) published his treatise demonstrating that the earth orbited the sun, thereby refuting the geocentric model that had dominated classical and medieval understanding of the heavens.

Further astronomical discoveries were made by Galileo Galilei (1564–1642), who relied on an improved version of the recently invented telescope to make direct celestial observations. The use of empirical observation, experimentation, and inductive reasoning (i.e., drawing general conclusions from data) represented a shift from the more abstract procedures applied by medieval scholars of the natural world. While Aristotle and classical authorities continued to influence Renaissance science and its social practice—the theories of human physiology set forth by the Greek physician Galen (129–ca. 199 C.E.) remained popular during the period, for example—and while most early modern scientists reconciled their scientific methods and discoveries with a literal belief in the Bible, the scientific method worked to undermine traditional notions of authority. As the poet John Donne wrote of recent scientific discoveries in 1611, "[T]he new Philosophy calls all in doubt."

REFORMATION AND COUNTER-REFORMATION

By 1600, the spirits of inquiry and individualism had challenged the authority of the Catholic Church and, in the process, redrawn the political and religious map of Europe. The Protestant Reformation began as a call for reform within the church in 1517, when Martin Luther (1483–1546) wrote a series of theses protesting the sale of indulgences (the remission of temporal punishment for sins) on behalf of the pope. Luther's opposition to the abuses of the Catholic Church quickly expanded to include a broader challenge to its authority. Believing that the church had lost contact with the fundamental truths of Christianity, Luther rejected the doctrine that salvation required the intercession of a religious clergy, arguing instead that salvation was a function of faith alone and that the Bible was the sole authority on spiritual matters.

With the help of the newly invented printing press, Luther's ideas were widely disseminated throughout Europe, and other Protestant movements followed. Protestantism was adopted by states in Germany, Scandinavia, and elsewhere in northern Europe, many of which took advantage of this opportunity to assert their independence from Catholic Rome; the Church of England, for example, was established as a Protestant church under the head of Henry VIII (1491–1547) when the king broke from Rome in 1534 for political reasons. Italy, Spain, the Holy Roman Empire (which included much of central Europe), and eventually France remained within a reviving Catholicism that consolidated its doctrine at the Council of Trent (1545–63) and extended its authority through the Counter-Reformation that followed. Wars, rebellions, and the persecution of religious minorities within states swept across Europe as Catholics, state-sponsored Protestant majorities, and more radical Protestant sects confronted each other over matters of faith, doctrine, and religious and social hierarchy. The conflict between nations that resulted from the Reformation would not begin to be resolved until the Peace of Westphalia, which ended Europe's devastating Thirty Years War (1618–48).

MONARCHY AND GOVERNMENT

Religious controversy and the political turmoil it precipitated contributed to the changing shapes of monarchy and government during the early modern period. In the late sixteenth and early seventeenth centuries, power was increasingly centralized in the hands of monarchs, who justified this movement toward absolutism by invoking the doctrine of the divine right of kings—the right to rule by virtue of birth, a right bestowed by God alone. France offers the most striking example of this development. Following the religious wars that divided the country in the 1500s and the continuation of civil disturbances and political intrigues in the first half of the 1600s, Louis XIV (1638–1715), the "Sun King," assumed the throne in 1643 and began a seventy-two-year reign that saw France and the French court achieve a position of dominance throughout Europe. The statement that is famously attributed to him—"L'état, c'est moi" ("I am the state")—reflects his power over the country's nobility, laws, military, and growing bureaucracy. His model was followed by other European monarchs such as Frederick William I (1688–1740) of Prussia and Peter the Great (1672–1725) of Russia; indeed, the latter built a palace in the recently founded city of St. Petersburg explicitly intended to rival Louis' monumental palace at Versailles.

Absolutism did not triumph everywhere in Europe, however. In England the moves toward centralized royal power undertaken by the Tudor monarchs Henry VII, Henry VIII, and Elizabeth I were checked by Parliament in the 1600s: the Stuart king Charles I (1600–1649) was beheaded in 1649 during the English Civil War, and for the following eleven years—a period divided into the Commonwealth and the Protectorate—England was subject to parliamentary and military rule. The Stuart monarchy was restored in 1660 with the crowning of Charles II (1630–1685), but the next forty years, known as the Restoration, witnessed the overthrow of his brother and successor, the Catholic James II (1633–1701), as a result of conflicts with his Protestant Parliament. Similar clashes awaited European monarchs in the eighteenth century.

NEW WORLD ENCOUNTERS

No overview of early modern Europe would be complete that failed to acknowledge the profound shift in European consciousness brought about by the encounter with the Western Hemisphere. In the Middle Ages Europeans had traveled through Asia by land as far east as Kublai Khan's China, and by 1500 the Portuguese had explored the west coast of Africa. But the "discovery" of an inhabited land across the ocean by the Italian-born Spanish explorer Christopher Columbus (1451–1506), who landed in the Caribbean in 1492 while seeking a western sea route to Asia, had consequences that reached much further. The success of this and subsequent expeditions prompted a race for conquest and settlement of the Americas by Spain and other European powers competing for resources, territorial possessions, and prestige. Over the next hundred years, the Spanish colonized an area stretching from eastern and southern South America to what is today Mexico and much of the United States, while Portugal, the Netherlands, France, and England also established colonies in the New World. The first permanent English settlement was Jamestown (located in the colony of Virginia) in 1607, and by the end of the seventeenth century England's colonial holdings encompassed a good deal of eastern North America.

The history of European colonialism in the Americas is, without doubt, a dark one. The indigenous peoples of South, Central, and North America suffered violence, exploitation, death by disease, and forced conversions, and the relationships between colonizer and colonized were shaped by military power, economic interests, and the religious fervor of missionaries. Europe's colonization of the New World inaugurated a transatlantic system of trade that would eventually bring African slaves to the Americas as part of a highly organized exchange of labor, resources, and commodities. At the same time, even as New World settlers may have sought to Europeanize the indigenous peoples and societies they encountered, their own world was transformed by the contact. Materially, Europe benefited from the introduction of new commodities, such as tobacco, corn, and previously unknown medications. But as Renaissance travel literature reveals, the encounter with the New World also fundamentally changed Europeans' awareness of their recently expanded world. When four delegates (or "kings," as they were called) from the Iroquois Confederacy visited London and Queen Anne's court in 1710, they inspired a fascination whose intensity reveals how deeply their newly discovered hemisphere had penetrated the early modern imagination.

PROFESSIONAL THEATER, 1500–1700

Theater played an important part in the emergence of early modern Europe. As a medium of impersonation and display, theater spoke to a deeply theatricalized society where power was asserted through spectacles, performances, and rituals of display. The spirits of individualism and inquiry found a natural home in an art form in which characters grappled with their destinies on a public stage, and spectators who flocked to attend these performances saw the concerns of their world illuminated and explored. As defenders and critics debated its moral authority, European

An engraving from the mid-1600s showing actors onstage at the Hôtel de Bourgogne.

theater during this period exerted unprecedented social influence.

The years 1500–1700 saw wide-ranging developments in the institution and practices of theater. In addition to those performances that took place in court, private, and university settings, the first professional theaters, public and private, opened in Europe during the second half of the sixteenth century. Paris had the Hôtel de Bourgogne, built in 1548; London the short-lived Red Lion, in 1567; and Madrid the Corral de la Cruz, in 1579; and by 1600 these major cities—and several in Italy—had become thriving theatrical centers. Many of these early theater buildings employed staging arrangements used in courtyard and other outdoor performance venues—the major public theaters of London, such as the Globe, were open-air theaters and contained stages that extended into the audience. But the development of theater architecture and scenic practices during this period was also influenced by the rediscovery of the treatise on architecture by the Roman engineer and architect Vitruvius. Italian architects and theorists drew on it in determining the theater's shape, the relationship between stage and auditorium, and the design of tragic, comic, and pastoral scenes. During the seventeenth and eighteenth centuries, Italian stage design became influential throughout Europe, as such innovations were introduced as the use of perspective, a form of visual representation that creates the impression of three-dimensionality and distance. As it gained popularity, the simultaneous staging that characterized the medieval period and continued into early modern production was replaced by a spatially unified visual field. Italian designers also pioneered the use of the proscenium, an archway or a frame that would become characteristic of European stage design from the late sixteenth to nineteenth centuries.

As the sophistication of theater technology grew, stage design and scenic effects became increasingly elaborate. The spectacular staging for which the theaters of seventeenth-century Italy, France, and Spain became particularly well-known—multiple scenery changes, flying chariots, hidden grottoes, lavish pictorial effects—were manifestations of the baroque style that dominated European arts during this period. The baroque, which stresses exuberance, monumentality, and ornateness, achieved its highest realization in court performances, when royalty spent large sums for the work of Italy's leading designers and those who studied their innovations. This movement toward greater spectacle was accelerated by the development of opera during the 1600s.

COMMEDIA DELL'ARTE

The establishment of theater as a public, private, and courtly institution was paralleled by the professionalization of actors and others involved in theatrical productions. Acting companies operated in England and on the Continent throughout the sixteenth century, and these troupes often performed in other countries in addition to their own. The most widely known were the *commedia dell'arte* (literally, "comedy of art") players who emerged in Italy in the mid-1500s, performed throughout Europe, and occupied an important place in European theatrical history into the eighteenth century. These troupes—which consisted of ten to twelve actors, both male and female—presented comic scenarios centering on love and intrigue. While the narrative outlines of these scenarios were established in advance, their performance depended on improvisation and the use of comic routines or improvisational asides known as *lazzi*. Popular with audiences, *lazzi* were often ingenious bits of comic business that players used to enliven their performances, such as using a wooden arm to slip away from a beating, or engaging in acrobatic contortions in order to catch a flea. Commedia dell'arte actors portrayed a range of stock characters—some masked and some unmasked—that included lovers, masters, and servants (known as *zanni*). Among the best known of the masked characters are Pantalone, a rich miser, and Arlecchino (or Harlequin), an acrobatic servant with a distinctive motley-colored costume.

Commedia dell'arte companies were organized on the sharing plan, an arrangement that enabled performers to share in the risks and profits of their companies. It was just one of the forms of economic or-

A sixteenth-century engraving of two commedia actors dancing.

ganization that acting companies throughout Europe used as actors, managers, playwrights, and others participated in the expanding business of theater. Performing at Europe's courts (often under the patronage of royalty and nobility) while also operating within a newly established network of public and private playhouses, theater companies in the late 1500s and 1600s began to enjoy some measure of economic security. At the same time, the life of theater professionals remained a hard one, with actors and playwrights often living on the edge of poverty and under the threat of debtors' prison. Theater and the profession of acting were regarded with the social ambivalence and antitheatrical prejudice that early modern Europe inherited from the medieval period. In Catholic and Protestant countries alike, the theater was regularly associated with immorality, and such charges came from secular as well as religious sources. Relationships with state and civic authorities were often equally fraught. Dramatic censorship was instituted in Spain and England, and the theater was subject to a range of restrictive laws throughout Europe. Although the licensing of theaters that took place during the 1600s conferred greater legitimacy on the companies that gained state approval, the implementation of such policies had the effect of bringing theatrical activity even more firmly under government control.

THE DRAMA OF EARLY MODERN EUROPE

The profound changes in Europe between 1500 and 1700 and the accompanying theatrical developments helped ensure that the era would become one of the most prominent in the creation of dramatic literature. The rediscovery, translation, and publication of Greek and Roman plays spurred widespread interest in classical drama, and the translation into Italian of Aristotle's *Poetics* in 1549 helped ignite a debate over Aristotelian dramatic theory that lasted into the eighteenth century. Through the efforts of sixteenth-century Italian and French commentators, Aristotle's treatise was interpreted and codified into neoclassical precepts concerning decorum, verisimilitude, dramatic probability, concentrated action, and uniformity of subject and tone. The dramatic unities of time, place, and action, for example, dictated that the playwright not strain a spectator's credulity by having events take place over more than one day and in more than one location and that the play be restricted to a single, focused plotline. Noble characters were appropriate to tragedy, while those of lower social station belonged to the domain of comedy. Neoclassical theory had its greatest impact on the drama of Italy and France; but even in England and Spain, where dramatists generally eschewed its precepts for more episodic, stylistically varied dramatic styles, debates over classical authority took place.

Early in the sixteenth century, comedy, tragedy, tragicomedy, pastoral, and dramatic satire were strongly influenced by classical models. But as the academic performance of plays in Latin gave way to plays written in the vernacular, the drama of early modern Europe began drawing more strongly on native performance traditions inherited from the Middle Ages. The result was a rich tapestry of dramatic styles, ranging from the multiple, episodic plots of Elizabethan and Jacobean English drama to the classical simplicity of the plays of JEAN RACINE (1639–1699). As part of a larger theatrical field that included religious performances, royal pageants, civic commemorations, and such popular forms as mumming, drama during the period 1500–1700 entertained a variety of spectators in numerous venues. Concentrated in Europe's major cities, this drama reflected a lively urban culture and the early stirrings of national self-awareness. And although many of its most enduring technological, performative, and theoretical innovations arose in Italy, the theater of early modern Europe found its highest dramatic achievement in England, Spain, and France.

English Theater, 1576–1642

In 1576, when the actor, manager, and theatrical entrepreneur James Burbage (1531–1597) built the Theatre in Shoreditch (an area to the northeast of the City of London), the commercial theater was in its infancy in England. The performance of plays and other theatrical activity had, of course, enjoyed popularity earlier in the sixteenth century. Dramatists influenced by Renaissance humanism wrote comedies, tragedies, and moral interludes that made use of classical and medieval models alike; they were performed in a variety of places, including at court and in noble households, schools, universities, and London's legal societies, the Inns of Court. Among the best known of these earlier plays are *Ralph Roister Doister* (ca. 1553) and *Gammer Gurton's Needle* (1552–53), two early English comedies, and Thomas Norton and Thomas Sackville's *Gorboduc* (1561), generally considered the first English tragedy. Traveling actors brought mummings, farces, and other forms of popular dramatic entertainment to local communities, and Corpus Christi plays continued to be staged throughout England until the 1570s, when their performance was effectively halted by royal edict. But the expansion of dramatic activity that would make London one of the most vibrant theatrical centers in Europe did not occur until the commercial theater was established during the century's final quarter.

PUBLIC AND PRIVATE THEATERS

In England, as elsewhere in Europe, the construction of theater buildings was essential to the institutionalization of theater. Theater buildings in London were of two kinds: public and private. Burbage's Theatre established the model for subsequent public theaters. Polygonal in shape, it contained three tiers of audience galleries surrounding a roughly circular, unroofed yard. We have sufficient information about this and other public theaters built between 1577 and 1623—notably the Swan, the Rose, the Fortune, and the Globe, which was built in Southwark (on the southern side of the Thames) with timber from the dismantled Theatre in 1599—to know that the stage for these theaters extended into the yard at a height of approximately 5 feet. Partly roofed, this stage featured a structure at the rear known as the *tiring house*, which included two doors for entrances and exits and one or two balcony levels that could be used for audience seating, music, and scenes requiring actors to perform above stage level (the so-called balcony scene in SHAKESPEARE's *Romeo and Juliet* [1595], for example). A trapdoor on the stage floor allowed ghosts and other characters to ascend from a darkened cellar (sometimes referred to as

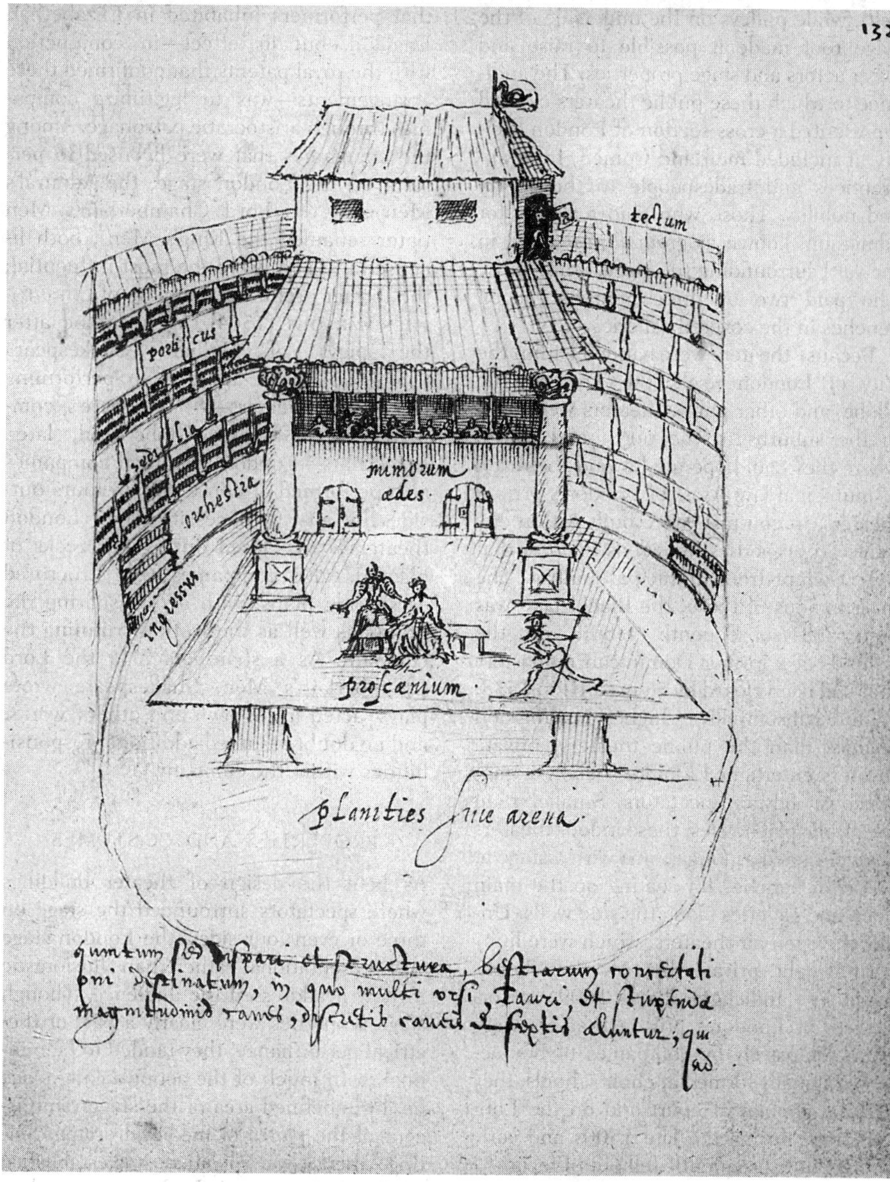

This sketch of the Swan Theater—a copy of an original by a late-sixteenth-century Dutch visitor to London named Johannes de Witt—is the only surviving contemporary likeness of the inside of an Elizabethan theater. Latin words or phrases identify the major parts of the theater: the *proscaenium* (the flat, open stage); the *mimorum aedes* (a dressing room for the actors); the *planities sive* arena (the "yard," in which spectators could stand in front of the stage); the *tectum* (the roof); the *porticus* (covered gallery); the *sedilia* (seats); the *orchestra* (seats for important spectators); and the *ingressus* (the entry into the various galleries).

hell), while pulleys on the underside of the stage roof made it possible to raise and lower actors and stage properties. The audience to which these public theaters catered represented a cross section of London society; it included men and women, from apprentices and tradespeople to the gentry and nobility. Those who paid a penny for admission, known as *groundlings*, stood in the yard surrounding the stage, while those who paid two or three pennies sat on benches in the covered galleries.

Because theaters were banned within the City of London itself, the Theatre, the Globe, and other public theaters were built in the suburbs to the north and south, where they could operate beyond the reach of municipal law. Most of London's private theaters, in contrast, were built within city limits on properties known as *liberties* that were exempt from municipal control. The most famous of these, the Blackfriars, was built and subsequently rebuilt on the grounds of a former Dominican monastery that had been closed by Henry VIII in 1538. With substantially higher admission charges than the public theaters, private theaters entertained a more socially homogeneous body of spectators. Smaller than the public playhouses, these indoor theaters were designed as long rooms with a stage at one end, benches for seating on the main floor, and galleries along the side walls. Unlike the open-air theaters, which were lit by natural light, private theaters were illuminated by candlelight. Until 1609, performances at London's private theaters were given exclusively by companies of boy actors; originally formed at choir schools, they became popular at court and on the London stage during the late 1500s and early 1600s but subsequently fell out of favor.

ACTING COMPANIES

An essential contribution to the rise of professional theater in late sixteenth-century England was a legal shift in the status of actors. In 1572 the government of Elizabeth I passed a law decreeing that itinerant actors and entertainers be arrested and punished as vagabonds if they could not demonstrate that they belonged to the household of a nobleman. The law underscored the socially marginal world that performers inhabited in Elizabethan England, but its effect—in conjunction with the royal patents that confirmed these arrangements—was to legitimize companies through aristocratic patronage. Among the companies that were licensed to perform on the London stage, the Admiral's Men and the Lord Chamberlain's Men (later renamed the King's Men), both licensed in 1594, were the most influential; the former produced the plays of CHRISTOPHER MARLOWE (1564–1593) and the latter the plays of William Shakespeare (1564–1616). In addition to performing in specific theaters—Shakespeare's company played at the Globe and, later, Blackfriars—London theatrical companies also performed at court and on tours outside the city (a necessity when London theaters were closed during outbreaks of plague). Adult companies were structured as sharing plans, with actors sharing the profits as well as the work of running the company. As a shareholder in the Lord Chamberlain's Men, Shakespeare wrote plays, acted in his own and others' works, and no doubt assumed additional responsibilities within the company.

PROPERTIES AND COSTUMES

As befit the design of theater buildings where spectators surrounded the stage on three or even four sides, the London stage was presentational rather than illusionistic in how it addressed the audience. Though stage properties were clearly a part of theatrical performance, they tended to be minimal, with much of the action taking place on an undefined area of the stage reminiscent of the *platea* of medieval drama. Setting, when it was specified, was established more through verbal description than through stage properties. Costumes, on the other hand, were often quite elaborate, with visually luxurious pieces provided by the nobility or purchased by the companies themselves. Whereas actresses were allowed to perform on the Continent, only male actors performed on the London stage before the closing of the theaters in 1642. Women's roles were usually played by boy actors within the companies, a practice that Shakespeare's Cleopatra (played by a boy) alludes to when she imagines her story being performed on a Roman stage: "I shall see / Some squeaking Cleopatra boy my greatness / I'th' posture of a whore." But what may seem like limitations to the modern eye were opportunities for exceptional displays of acting skill by the period's many renowned performers, including the most celebrated actor of his day, Richard Burbage (James Burbage's son, 1568–1619).

PLAYWRIGHTS AND PLAYS

The proliferation of theaters and the rising demand for theatrical entertainment created intense competition for new plays, and a professional class of playwrights emerged to meet this demand. Shakespeare earned enough money from his playwriting and other theatrical efforts to purchase a large house and property in Stratford-upon-Avon, but not all playwrights had equal success, and they often turned their hands to pamphleteering and other activities in London's booming print market. Forced to work under the eye of the Master of the Revels, who in 1581 was granted the power to license plays (and thereby to act as government censor), playwrights were subject to arrest, imprisonment, and even torture if they addressed controversial subjects in their plays. Because plays belonged to the companies that purchased them, playwrights had no rights over their production or publication. Nor were plays accorded the literary standing of poetry and other more strictly literary forms. Company-authorized and pirated versions of plays occasionally appeared in inexpensive quarto editions (on small-sized paper), but it wasn't until 1616, when BEN JONSON (1572–1637) published his plays under the title *The Works of Benjamin Jonson,* that a dramatist presumed to accord his works the status of literary art. Like most of his contemporary dramatists, Shakespeare showed little interest in the publication of his plays, and it was only in 1623, seven years after his death, that two of his colleagues published his plays in a large-format edition, subsequently known as the First Folio.

The drama of Renaissance England was rich and varied, combining the eloquence of dramatic poetry with the vibrant particularity of contemporary life. During the 1580s and 1590s, the London stage offered a wealth of plays in the genres of comedy, tragedy, dramatic pastoral, and history play. With *THE SPANISH TRAGEDY* (1587), THOMAS KYD (1558–1594) inaugurated the genre of revenge tragedy that was to prove popular during the reigns of Elizabeth and James, and before his premature death (in 1593) Marlowe wrote a half-dozen or so tragedies and history plays that remain among the finest of their age. Elizabethan comedy ranged from the pastoral and romantic plays of Robert Greene (1558–1592) to Jonson's early satiric comedies. The exuberance that characterizes much of this drama reflected the optimism of an England that was asserting itself as a European power (the English defeat of the Spanish Armada occurred in 1588). This attitude changed in the years preceding Elizabeth's death in 1603, and the drama of the early seventeenth century was marked by a darkening of tone and subject matter. Shakespeare's greatest tragedies were written during this period, as were the plays of JOHN WEBSTER (1579–1630s?) and other tragic dramatists. In the area of comedy, the closing years of the sixteenth century and the first quarter of the seventeenth saw the sharpening of dramatic satire; a proliferation of city comedies (plays whose characters are drawn from London's urban classes) in the drama of Thomas Middleton (1580–1627), THOMAS DEKKER (ca. 1572–1632), and others; and the popularity of a hybrid genre—tragicomedy—in the plays of Francis Beaumont (ca. 1584–1616) and John Fletcher (1579–1625). The years of Charles I's reign (1625–49) saw the tragedies of John Ford (1586–1639?) and the genteel comedies of James Shirley (1596–1666).

COURT THEATER: MASQUES

The early seventeenth century also witnessed a flowering of theatrical activity in the courts of James I and Charles I. The Stuart court masque was an elaborate form of entertainment that featured lavish spectacle, music, singing, dance, and allegorical or mythological plots celebrating monarchical authority. Jonson was the leading writer of masques during this period, and he worked in collaboration with the architect and stage designer Inigo Jones (1573–

Costume design by Inigo Jones for Ben Jonson's *The Masque of Queens* (1609).

1652), who introduced important aspects of Italian stage design to the English theater. Like the court ballets that were performed in France during the reign of Louis XIV later in the century, the Stuart masques reflect the profound relationship between theatricality and the performance of power in the early modern state.

CIVIL WAR, COMMONWEALTH, AND THE CLOSING OF THE THEATERS

This relationship came to an end during the English Civil War (1642–49), which was followed by the Commonwealth and the Protectorate (1649–60); those eighteen years witnessed the overthrow of the English monarchy by a Puritan-dominated Parliament and the closing of the theaters by parliamentary decree in 1642. The Globe was torn down in 1644 to make room for tenements, and other theaters were subsequently dismantled or allowed to fall into disrepair. Theatrical activity was not entirely eliminated during these years—dramatic performances were given at private houses and other nontheatrical venues, and in the 1650s the musical dramas of William Davenant (1606–1668) marked the beginning of English opera—but the great age of Tudor and Stuart theater had come to a decisive end.

Spanish Theater, 1580–1700

During the sixteenth and seventeenth centuries, a period known as the "Golden Age" of Spanish literature and art, dramatic theater in Spain achieved a level of excellence that rivaled that of SHAKESPEARE's England. The rise of theater and the distinctive shapes it assumed reflected the history of Spain's emergence as a European and global power. During the medieval period much of Spain was under Moslem rule, and the slow reconquest of the Iberian peninsula by Christian armies was not completed until the Battle of Granada in 1492. The kingdoms of Aragon and Castile were joined by the marriage of Ferdinand II (1452–1516) and Isabella I (1451–1504) in 1469, and the resultant unified Spain extended its power through further dynastic alliances and an overseas empire that included vast areas of North, Central, and South America.

While other areas of Europe were feeling the initial shocks of the Protestant Reformation, the Catholic Church consolidated its authority in Spain and, through the office of the Spanish Inquisition, kept religious division beyond its borders. Spain's unique history strongly affected its theatrical development. The centuries of Moslem occupation gave Spanish drama and Spanish literature as a whole their most distinctive theme—that of honor; at the same time, the pervasive Catholicism of Spanish life during the later period ensured that the religious and secular theaters, which were diverging elsewhere in Europe, remained unusually close.

RELIGIOUS DRAMA: THE *AUTO SACRAMENTALE*

The most widely produced form of religious drama in sixteenth- and seventeenth-century Spain was the *auto sacramentale*. Performed, like the earlier mystery cycles throughout Europe, on the Feast of Corpus Christi, *autos sacramentales* celebrated the mystery of the Eucharist in stories mixing the human, the supernatural, and the allegorical. To put on the *autos,* the players used two-story *carros,* or wagons, which were first paraded through Madrid and other cities and towns as part of the Corpus Christi procession and then positioned behind a portable or fixed outdoor stage. Two *carros* were used for each performance until the mid-1600s, when the number was expanded to four (and later to eight). Early *autos* were produced by trade guilds, but by the mid-sixteenth century the responsibility had passed to municipal authorities, who often spent considerable amounts to stage them. Enormously popular events that brought together civic and church authority, *autos sacramentales* were performed by professional acting troupes hired specifically for these occasions, and they commanded the talents of Spain's leading dramatists.

The Corral de Comedias de Almagro, built in 1628 and restored in the 1950s, is the only surviving *corral*. Seats for the audience are positioned in an enclosed courtyard, while the rows of seats known as *gradas* ascend on either side.

PUBLIC THEATER: THE *CORRALES*

Although there was dramatic and theatrical activity—including the performance of secular plays for academic, aristocratic, and popular audiences—in the early and mid-sixteenth century, it was not until the 1570s that a professional public theater was fully established in Spain's major cities. Not surprisingly, the country's theatrical center was Madrid, which in 1561 became the capital under Philip II (1527–1598). The Corral de la Cruz, Madrid's first permanent theater, was built in 1579; it was followed by the Corral del Príncipe in 1583. Like the open-air theaters of Elizabethan England, the design of the *corrales,* or Spanish public theaters, derived from courtyard performances. The *corrales* were constructed within square or rectangular courtyards enclosed on three sides by buildings. A raised stage with permanent backdrop and upper levels was placed on one end of the courtyard, and an open space, or *patio,* for standing spectators was located directly in front of it. In the seventeenth century several rows of benches or stools (called *taburetes*) were installed immediately in front of the stage on a raised platform. On either side of the patio, a section of seats in ascending rows known as the *gradas* extended to the second story. Above the *alojería* (refreshment booth) at the end of the courtyard facing the stage, galleries accommodated additional spectators. The first of these, the *cazuela*, provided seating for women, while higher galleries accommodated officials from the city of Madrid and the Council of Castile and (above them) clergymen and intellectuals. The windows of buildings above the *gradas* served as box seats (*aposentos*), and additional levels of boxed seats or open galleries were available at the third- and fourth-floor levels. The lively, sometimes unruly, audiences who attended performances in the *corrales* represented a cross section of Madrid society.

From its inception the public theater in Madrid was embedded in the city's institutional structures. The *corrales* were originally licensed to confraternities, or charitable organizations, which used theatrical performance as a means of raising money to support hospitals and aid the poor. This arrangement lasted until 1615, when the city of Madrid assumed control of the theaters and the distribution of their revenues for charitable purposes. The theatrical companies it hired—consisting of actor-managers (*autores*), actors, apprentices, and others involved in the productions—were subject to government regulation. After 1603 only licensed companies could operate in Spain, and the number of licenses was limited. Actors who were not hired by these companies joined *compañías de la legua* (companies of the road), which performed throughout the countryside. No company was allowed to perform in any one place for more than two months of the year, and only one could perform there at any one time (more were permitted in Madrid and Seville). As a result, even licensed companies regularly traveled between cities. Women actors were licensed to perform in 1587, but this practice sparked such controversy that a royal decree was issued in 1599 stipulating that only those women married to members of the company perform and that male and female actors not dress in the clothing of the opposite sex. Compromises in response to this final restriction were frequent, however, and actresses who played women disguised as men regularly wore male clothing down to the waist with a skirt below.

THEATER AT COURT

Court performances, which had been infrequent in Spain during the sixteenth century, began to be mounted in the seventeenth century with a splendor that rivaled that displayed in Italy and France. During the reign of Philip III (r. 1598–1621), professional productions and masque-like entertainments involving elaborate settings, costumes, and special effects were given in one of the halls in the Alcázar (the royal palace). When a new palace, the Buen Retiro, was completed on the outskirts of Madrid in 1633, it became the center for court entertainments, which reached their high point during the reign of Philip IV (r. 1621–65). Under the supervision of Italian set designers who were brought to the Spanish court to oversee and engineer these performances, spectacular entertainments were staged both within the palace—a permanent theater, the Coliseo, was constructed there in 1640—and outdoors on the palace grounds. For a 1635 production of *Love Is the Greatest Enchantment* by PEDRO CALDERÓN DE LA BARCA (1600–1681), the Tuscan hydraulics engineer, scenographer, and landscape designer Cosimo (Cosme) Lotti (d. 1643) built a special stage above the waters of a lake, managed to have a silver chariot drawn across the water's surface by two large fish, and transformed a mountain into a palace.

SPANISH GOLDEN AGE DRAMA

The drama of Spain's Golden Age represents one of the period's greatest achievements. Those plays that were performed by early professional troupes in Spain were written by actor-managers for the companies they ran—hence, these versatile men of the theater were given the full title *autores de comedias*. By the 1590s, a class of professional dramatists had emerged to satisfy the increasing demand for original dramatic scripts. The *comedia nueva* (new drama)—or *comedia,* as it became known less formally—proved to be the most popular and enduring dramatic form written during the Spanish Golden Age. Consisting of three-act plays in varying verse forms, *comedia nueva* mixed high and low, tragedy and comedy, in plots that were drawn from history, mythology, legend, Italian *novelle* and other literary sources, the Bible, popular ballads, and the everyday life of country and town. Among its specialized subgenres were the *comedias de capa y espada* (cape and sword plays), which featured stories of romance and intrigue, and *comedias de costumbres* (comedies of manners). Popular character types in the *comedia* included the *cabellero* (gentleman), *galán* (cavalier or gallant), *dama* (lady), and *gracioso* (comic character, or fool, whose actions often parallel the actions of those of superior rank).

Of the many playwrights who contributed to the *comedia nueva,* none played a greater role in its development and success than LOPE DE VEGA (1562–1635), a towering figure in Spanish Golden Age drama and one of the most prolific dramatists ever to write for the stage. He wrote as many as 1,500 plays (of which 470 have survived), and his output included *comedias, autos sacramentales,* and *loas* (prologues) and *entremeses* (interludes), which were performed before and between the acts of plays, respectively. In *The New Art of Writing Plays* (1609), his treatise on dramatic theory, Lope defended his disregard for the classical rules of playwriting in favor of variety and "the likeness of truth." Other dramatists followed in his footsteps—including Tirso de Molina (Gabriel Téllez, ca. 1584–1648), whose play *The Trickster of Seville* is the earliest known version of the Don Juan story—but none achieved a more prominent position in seventeenth-century Spanish theater than Pedro Calderón de la Barca. Calderón—whose plays are marked by meticulous craftsmanship, linguistic complexity, and richness of metaphor—became a leading figure in the *corrales* and in the court of Philip IV, where much of his dramatic activity was concentrated. He also became the leading author of *autos sacramentales;* so exceptional was his mastery of this form that between 1647 and 1681 he wrote all of the *autos* produced in Madrid.

THE LEGACY OF GOLDEN AGE DRAMA

Calderón's death is generally considered to mark the end of Spanish Golden Age drama. Those dramatists who followed in his footsteps conformed to established models rather than pursuing innovation. While spectacular productions continued to be undertaken at court through the end of the century, the heyday of both the court theater and public *corrales* had passed. In their decline they mirrored the condition of Spain itself, which had been weakened and demoralized by a century of wars, declining wealth, and waning influence. Yet during its Golden Age, Spain had achieved one of Europe's most vibrant theatrical cultures, and its dramatic legacy was felt throughout the Continent (particularly in France) and in the world beyond its shores. Colonizing armies and Spanish missionaries brought drama and theatrical performance to the Philippines and the Americas, and the colonial drama that appeared there retained its Spanish heritage (the Philippine vernacular drama known as *komedya,* for instance, derived from European romances brought to the islands by Spanish soldiers). The more developed colonial societies produced dramatists who worked within the forms and conventions of Golden Age drama. The Mexican scholar, poet, and nun SOR JUANA INÉS DE LA CRUZ (1648?–1695), one of the finest writers of the Spanish Golden Age, composed nearly thirty *autos sacramentales,* comedies, and *loas.* The theater of sixteenth- and seventeenth-century Spain, in other words, provided the world with its first truly global drama.

French Theater, 1630–1700

THEATER IN PARIS

During the second half of the seventeenth century, France established one of the most admired and emulated dramatic traditions in Europe. Yet the theatrical institutions needed to underpin this achievement developed significantly later there than they did in Italy, England, and Spain. The delay was largely attributable to external factors, most importantly the Wars of Religion between Catholics and French Protestants (known as Huguenots) that paralyzed the country from 1562 to 1598. The early history of the public theater in Paris certainly did not bode well for establishing an urban theatrical culture. The Hôtel de Bourgogne, Paris's first public theater, was built in 1548 by the Confrérie de la Passion, an association of Paris merchants and tradesmen that had been organized in 1402 to produce religious plays and thereafter held a monopoly on theatrical productions of all kinds in Paris. By the end of the century the Confrérie had ceased to perform plays and was leasing its theater for short periods to theater companies from outside Paris. But traveling companies often avoided Paris, because the cost of renting the Hôtel de Bourgogne was substantial, and because the Confrérie enforced its monopoly by charging a fee to companies who chose to perform elsewhere in the city. The capital lacked a resident theater company until 1629, when a permanent company was allowed to occupy the Hôtel de Bourgogne. In 1634 a second theater—the Théâtre de Marais—opened in a converted tennis court (the sport, popular among the nobility, was played on enclosed courts with a gallery for spectators; these structures often served as theaters in the seventeenth century). It housed a second permanent company, and after a fire in 1644 the theater was rebuilt with many technical improvements. Though Paris had not been without theatrical entertainment during the early decades of the 1600s—commedia dell'arte troupes performed in the city, farce was widely popular, and the foundations of a French dramatic tradition were laid by Alexandre Hardy (ca. 1572–1632), who composed hundreds of tragedies, tragicomedies, and pastoral plays—it was not until the 1630s that the theater became a regular pastime for Paris's middle and upper classes.

STATE PATRONAGE

The growing status of French theater during this time owed much to the support of those in positions of power. Cardinal Richelieu (1585–1642), chief minister to Louis XIII (1601–1643) and one of the figures most responsible for the centralization of power in the French monarchy, was a strong supporter of the arts, and under his patronage the theater acquired a legitimacy it had previously lacked. Richelieu awarded a subsidy to the theater company that occupied the Marais, inaugurating the practice whereby all major French companies received government subsidies. In addition, he had a theater built in his private palace, the Palais Cardinal (renamed the Palais Royal when the palace came under the control of the crown); it was the first in France to include the proscenium arch and side wings characteristic of Italian stage design. The strong link between theater and the French state that Richelieu helped establish was a defining feature of the reigns of Louis XIII and Louis XIV—and this link achieved its clearest institutional expression in 1680, when the latter merged Paris's two leading theater companies to form Europe's first national theater, the Comédie Française.

THEATERS AND AUDIENCE

Like the indoor tennis courts that preceded them and continued to be used as venues for theatrical productions, the public theaters of Paris were rectangular structures, typically long and narrow, with an auditorium for the public and a stage that

An engraving from 1641 showing the stage, complete with proscenium arch and perspectival stage scenery in the background, of the Palais Cardinal.

included room, as the century progressed, for increasingly sophisticated technical machinery. The main floor of the auditorium consisted of a pit (*parterre*) for standing spectators with benches along the wall. The side and rear walls contained three rows of galleries, the first two of which were divided into boxes (*loges*). At the rear of the *parterre* and below the boxes rose the *amphithéâtre,* a section whose rows were raked to provide a better angle for viewing the stage. Both stage and auditorium were illuminated by candlelight. For much of the first half of the seventeenth century, scenic practice followed the conventions of medieval drama, with dramatic locales represented by the separate scenic structures called *mansions.* But as Italian scene design was adopted in the public theaters, the Parisian stage incorporated the spatially unifying principles of perspective staging. Any increase in dramatic illusion that might have resulted from perspective staging, though, was offset by the lively presence of the spectators, whose appearance and behavior in the Paris theater often constituted a performance in their own right. Perhaps more distracting to the actors than the unruly occupants of the *parterre* were those spectators who were allowed to sit onstage during performances. A cross section of Paris society, including the nobility and, on occasion, the king himself, made up the audience.

NEOCLASSICISM AND FRENCH DRAMA

The triumph of Italian scene design, with its concentration on single locations, was aided by the growing influence of neoclassicism on seventeenth-century French drama. During the 1630s and 1640s a number of French authors and intellectuals championed the "rules" that earlier Renaissance commentators had drawn from Aristotle's *Poetics,* and the principles advocated by neoclassical theory (including the dramatic unities) were given official sanction by the newly formed Académie Française. The authority and validity of neoclassicism were fiercely debated, particularly as its strictures might apply to the genre of tragedy. The most passionately argued of these debates concerned *Le Cid* (1636–37), a tragedy written by

An engraving showing the performance of Molière's *The Imaginary Invalid,* in 1664, before Louis XIV and his court.

France's leading playwright at the time, Pierre Corneille (1606–1684). Those who attacked Corneille's play for not observing the principles of verisimilitude, decorum, and purity of genre were supported by the Académie, which entered the debate at the request of Richelieu. Although some writers continued to resist, the principles of neoclassical theory became widely adopted by French playwrights. That these principles could be artistically enabling as well as prescriptive is demonstrated by the formally elegant, psychologically complex plays of JEAN RACINE (1639–1699), France's greatest tragic dramatist.

French comedy also attained a pinnacle of excellence in the later seventeenth century, chiefly through the plays of JEAN-BAPTISTE POQUELIN (1621?–1673), better known by his stage name, MOLIÈRE. Like SHAKESPEARE, Molière was a man of the theater as well as a writer, and his career as a dramatist is intertwined with the professions of actor and company manager. After years touring the French provinces, the theatrical troupe that Molière had helped found in 1643 settled in the French capital. By the 1660s the company had established itself in the Palais Royal, had been awarded an annual subsidy from Louis XIV, and was performing to great acclaim at court and before the Parisian public. Much of this acclaim resulted from Molière's dramatic contributions: farces influenced by the commedia dell'arte, court spectacles, ballets, and, most of all, the comedies of manners in which Molière offered lively and satirical portraits of French society. These plays were not without their controversies—*TARTUFFE* (1664–69), Molière's comic investigation of religious hypocrisy, was attacked on religious grounds and banned from performance for five years—but they quickly became standards of the classical French repertoire.

THE DECLINE OF COURT INFLUENCE

By the end of the seventeenth century, Paris had established itself as the theatrical capital of Europe. The Comédie Française was the leading theatrical company of its time, and under the influence of Jean-Baptiste Lully (1632–1687) French opera had become equally renowned. The brilliance of the theatrical arts in seventeenth-century France owed much to the splendor of the French court, which displayed its power through the culture of spectacle. After Louis XIV moved his court and France's nobility outside Paris to the newly built Palace of Versailles in 1682, however, the role in French theater of the court and its literary tastes declined. As in England at the turn of the eighteenth century, in France public theater was left to thrive on its own terms. That Paris continued to exert a strong influence on European theater in the centuries that followed is powerful testimony to the theater that Corneille, Racine, and Molière helped build.

English Theater, 1660–1700

RESTORATION AND THEATER

When Charles II, eldest son of the executed Charles I, made his triumphant return in 1660 after eighteen years of parliamentary rule, both the monarchy and the public theater were reestablished in England. But the intervening years ensured that both institutions looked very different than they had before the Civil War. Restoration theater (1660–1700) was the product of a largely aristocratic culture, and it catered to a much narrower audience than had the theater of Elizabeth I and James I. Rejecting the Puritanism of the Commonwealth and Protectorate, upper-class Restoration London was an intensely social world, and the licentiousness, materialism, social competition, and love of wit for which the elite society of this period is notorious found ample representation onstage.

The emergence of this theater owes much to broader European theatrical developments. During their exile in France, Charles II and members of his court grew familiar with the theatrical culture that flourished under Louis XIV, and the theater that they helped establish upon their return reflected their taste for Continental stagecraft. Shortly after Charles II was restored to the throne, he issued royal patents to William Davenant (1606–1668) and Thomas Killigrew (1612–1683) to

An early-nineteenth-century engraving of the interior of the Duke's Theatre in Lincoln's Inn Fields during the reign of Charles II.

form theatrical companies and purchase or build theaters. Because the few theaters that survived the Civil War were unable to meet the technical requirements of Italian scenic innovations—sliding upstage shutters and side wings that made possible rapid scene changes, trapdoors, and flying machinery, for instance—new theaters were built to accommodate the new technology. The King's Company (managed by Killigrew and sponsored by Charles II himself) first used an indoor tennis court but soon was performing at the newly built Theatre Royal on Bridges Street; when this burned down in 1672 they performed at a new structure on the same site, the Drury Lane Theatre. The Duke's Company (managed by Davenant and sponsored by the duke of York, the future king James II) used the Lincoln's Inn Fields Theatre (a converted tennis court) and, after 1671, the Dorset Garden Theatre. Given that the patented companies held a monopoly over theatrical production in London—merging in 1682 (after the King's Company fell into dire financial straits) to form the United Company, an arrangement that lasted until 1695—these buildings were the center of London's theatrical life.

PLAYHOUSES, AUDIENCE, AND ACTORS

Restoration playhouses were small structures when compared with the open-air theaters that were built in London in the late sixteenth century. The stage featured a proscenium arch with a curved apron (or open floor) extending into the audience and to the side. The main floor of the auditorium (or pit) contained benches, and these were surrounded on the side and rear by boxed seats and galleries. The play-watching experience in this setting was intimate. Restoration theaters accommodated no more than 600 spectators, and all were seated within 35 feet or so of the stage. Boxes allowed spectators to sit above the sides of the stage (and hence be prominently displayed to the rest of the audience), and by the end of the century spectators were routinely seated onstage. Auditorium and stage were both lit by candelabra, with the result that actors and their spectators were equally illuminated. Restoration actors often played on the forestage (near the audience), and they delivered their lines as much to the spectators as to the play's other characters. It was not uncommon for spectators, who could be quite unruly in the Restoration theater, to interrupt a play by addressing the actors themselves.

As these practices and behaviors begin to suggest, the relationship between Restoration spectators and the performances they attended was marked by mutual interaction and display. Attending the theater was a popular activity for the upper classes of London society and for the king, and the theater became a microcosm of this aristocratic world, its relationships (overt and covert), and its social distinctions. Men and women came to the theater arrayed in the latest fashions, and the theater became an arena for displaying symbols of social distinction. Women—some of them prostitutes—often wore masks (or *vizards*) to disguise their identities, and the rendezvous that were arranged through this and other stratagems mirrored the sexual intrigue being performed onstage. The introduction of women actors for the first time on the English stage contributed to the sexually charged atmosphere of Restoration theaters. Charles II, who had seen actresses perform on the Continent, justified their inclusion in the name of moral reformation, since their presence would eliminate transvestism—boys dressing as women. But the theatrical display of female bodies onstage became an erotic attraction in its own right, particularly when women actors dressed as men, donning tight-fitting, knee-length pants in what were called *breeches roles.* Contemporary moralists viewed actresses as a symbol of the theater's licentiousness; and while their general accusation was unfair, it was certainly true that some actresses did have affairs with theatergoers. Charles II, a well-known libertine, numbered the actress Nell Gwynn (1650–1687) among his many mistresses.

RESTORATION DRAMA

The drama of Restoration England assumed a number of characteristic forms. Even the revivals of English plays written before the Civil War—chiefly, the works of Beaumont and Fletcher, Shakespeare, and JONSON—were often adapted to reflect contemporary tastes and conventions. During this period heroic tragedy flourished; it featured larger-than-life characters, exotic locales, and elevated—occasionally ranting—dramatic verse. Other tragedies written during this time observed the principles of French neoclassicism, such as the concentration of dramatic action according to the dramatic "unities." Adherence to these principles was not as strict in England as it was in France, however, and Restoration tragedy continued to be influenced by Shakespeare and by earlier English dramatic conventions. In his 1668 *An Essay of Dramatic Poesy,* the period's most significant work of dramatic theory, John Dryden (1611–1700)—a leading writer of tragic and other drama—defended "the honour of our *English* writers" against those who overvalued French dramatic models.

But it was in comedy that the Restoration's achievements were most dazzling. Set in contemporary London, the Restoration comedy of manners featured gallants (or rakes), ladies, jealous husbands, cast-off mistresses, unsophisticated country visitors, fops, and clever servants engaged in often predatory games of intrigue and seduction. The wit and wordplay that characterize these plays reflect the importance of language, innuendo, and verbal disguise to Restoration stage interactions. Many of the plays contain a secondary plot involving conventional lovers, but the theatrical energies of the finest Restoration comedies—*THE COUNTRY WIFE* (1675), by WILLIAM WYCHERLEY (1641–1716); *The Man of Mode* (1676), by George Etherege (1636–1692); *THE ROVER* (written in two parts, 1677, 1681), by APHRA BEHN (1640–1689), England's first professional woman playwright; and *The Way of the World* (1700), by William Congreve (1670–1729)—are located in the central, equally matched "wit" couple. The lens provided by these interactions enabled playwrights to investigate fashion, marriage as a social contract, authenticity, masculinity, and social difference. By the end of the century, however, Restoration comedy faced opposition from a growing middle-class audience that rejected its libertinism, amorality, and elitism. When Jeremy Collier (1650–1726), an English clergyman, published *A Short View of the Immorality and Profaneness of the English Stage* in 1698, his attack hastened the end of a comic form that had outlived the courtly world of Charles II.

Eighteenth-Century Theater

The eighteenth century in Europe was characterized by stability and change; it was a period when the new rubbed uncomfortably against the old, and the outlines of the modern world began to emerge with unprecedented clarity. Throughout the century many of the artistic forms that had traditionally been preferred by the social elite continued to thrive. However, the social and economic transformations that would lead, by century's end, to the beginning of the Industrial Revolution hastened the growth of a middle class with its own interests, moral expectations, and tastes. Neoclassicism retained considerable authority on the Continent throughout the century, and the influence of classical ideals was evident in movements in literature, art, architecture, and music late in the century, but these were countered by the growing middle-class demand for nonelite literary and cultural forms such as the novel, which—with the help of an expanding popular press—by 1800 had become a literary form in its own right.

THE ENLIGHTENMENT

The eighteenth century was also the period of the Enlightenment, a philosophical movement centered in France that stressed the authority of reason and universally valid principles in human affairs. While some of the age's thinkers approved of the authoritarian rule of such "enlightened despots" as Frederick the Great (1712–1786) of Prussia and Catherine the Great (1729–1796) of Russia, the Enlightenment's main proponents challenged arbitrary authority and advocated limits to state power. The writings of such theorists as Jean-Jacques Rousseau (1712–1778), who argued that a social contract between individuals constitutes the only legitimate form of political order, established the foundations of modern democracy and were an important influence on the American Revolution (1775–83), the French Revolution (1789–99), and the Latin American revolutions of the early nineteenth century.

THEATERS AND ACTORS

The public theaters of eighteenth-century Europe offered a variety of entertainments—pantomime, comic opera, burlesque, and other popular performance forms in addition to serious and comic drama—to an audience whose numbers grew throughout the century. To accommodate this increase in spectators and keep up with the latest trends in stage design and technology, the major theaters of the period were expanded, renovated, and sometimes replaced by newer, larger buildings. Established theaters and theatrical companies continued to dominate theatrical life in Europe's capitals, usually as a result of government licensing,

A painting by William Hogarth of a scene from John Gay's popular ballad opera *The Beggar's Opera*. Note the audience members onstage in boxes.

though theatrical activity beyond these theaters enjoyed periods of popularity. In London (the capital of what was now known as Great Britain, following the union of England and Scotland in 1707), a number of unlicensed theaters operating in the 1720s and 1730s contributed to a lively theatrical scene that produced the long-running ballad opera *The Beggar's Opera* (1728), by John Gay (1685–1732), and satirical burlesques directed at the government of Sir Robert Walpole (1676–1745), who was in effect Britain's prime minister (a title not yet in official usage). In part as a reaction to this satirical activity, the Theatrical Licensing Act, which confirmed the Drury Lane and Covent Garden as London's only licensed theaters and empowered the Lord Chamberlain to approve plays for performance, was passed in 1737. In Paris, the monopoly of the Comédie Française and the Opéra was challenged by nonlicensed troupes that performed as part of the city's seasonal fairs. These troupes, which presented comic operas, pantomimes, and (by the end of the century) comic and noncomic drama, eventually established themselves as year-round companies housed on the fashionable Boulevard du Temple.

Although theater as an institution changed less in the eighteenth century than in earlier centuries, scenic practice underwent a number of modifications designed to intensify the stage's visual realism. The symmetries of classical perspective were relinquished in favor of angled perspectives, which allowed the scene to be viewed from varying points of view, and mid- and late-century designers introduced picturesque landscapes, historical and exotic locales, and increasingly sophisticated atmospheric settings made possible, in part, by advances in lighting and sound effects. Another development that reinforced the increasing illusionism of the eighteenth-century stage in London and Paris was the removal from it of spectators, a change that was complete by the middle of the century.

Although by modern standards eighteenth-century acting remained stylized in gesture and vocal delivery, in this area, too, practitioners shifted toward realism—and away from rhetorical modes of delivery. David Garrick (1717–1779), the century's greatest English actor, was praised for his natural style of acting, and similar advances in realistic performance took place on the Continent. To be sure, these efforts to bring the stage closer to life were limited in their aspirations and accomplishments. But though realism would not become a fully formed theatrical aesthetic until the nineteenth century, the first steps toward it were taken in the eighteenth.

EIGHTEENTH-CENTURY DRAMA

In the eighteenth century, the genres of tragedy and comedy underwent a number of important modifications that reflected the tastes of a growing middle-class audience and its largely conservative moral outlook. Tragedy, which had traditionally been concerned with actions of the ruling classes, set in historical and mythological locales, was expanded to include the events and scenes of ordinary life. The pioneering play in the subgenre of domestic tragedy was ***THE LONDON MERCHANT*** (1731), by the English playwright **GEORGE LILLO** (1693–1739), which centered on the downfall and moral reclamation of a London apprentice. Comedy was similarly modified as the values of wit, ingenuity, and sexual titillation gave way to noble feeling, moral elevation, and what Sir Richard Steele (1672–1729), one of the new subgenre's earliest champions, called "a joy too exquisite for laughter." Sentimental comedy (known in France as *comédie larmoyante*, or "tearful comedy") became popular throughout Europe during the eighteenth century.

Traditional tragedy and comedy had their supporters and practitioners, as well. For example, the French philosopher and writer Voltaire (François-Marie Arouet, 1694–1778) wrote intricate tragedies in the elevated style, and the Irish-born London playwrights Oliver Goldsmith (ca. 1730–1774) and **RICHARD BRINSLEY SHERIDAN** (1751–1816) championed "laughing comedy" against the drama of sentimentality. In Italy **CARLO GOLDONI** (1707–1793) reformed Italian comedy by transforming the improvisational drama of the commedia dell'arte into a literary genre. While eliminating the bawdiness and nonrealistic devices of the commedia, he nonetheless succeeded in preserving the tradition's comic spirit. Overall, though, sentimental drama and the century's other dramatic innovations crossed and, because of their popularity, undermined the boundaries between the traditional genres. In the 1750s Denis Diderot (1713–1784), one of the leading figures of the French Enlightenment, advocated a genre midway between tragedy and comedy: the *drame bourgeois,* which would take the social and familial problems of the middle class as its subject. Though it produced few plays of note during the late eighteenth century, the *drame bourgeois* was an important precursor to the social problem plays of HENRIK IBSEN (1828–1906) and later modern dramatists.

GERMAN THEATER AND DRAMA

One of the most important theatrical developments in the eighteenth century was the rise of established theater beyond its traditional centers in Italy, Spain, England, and France. This expansion was most striking in the German states of northern and central Europe. Although Vienna was one of the leading centers of opera in the late seventeenth century and troupes of professional actors performed at courts and in public settings throughout German-speaking Europe, an organized German theater did not develop until the eighteenth century. The Thirty Years War, which was fought largely on German soil, had devastated the region in the seventeenth century, and the territories that in the late nineteenth century would become modern Germany consisted of numerous small states within a declining Holy Roman Empire. With the region's resources scattered over a large area rather than concentrated in a capital or in other urban centers, it fell to the individual states to establish and support public theaters. The Hamburg National Theater, established in 1767, was a short-lived venture that paved the way for state-subsidized theaters elsewhere in German-speaking Europe. The Gotha Court Theater was founded in 1775, the Imperial and National Theater of Vienna in 1776, and the Court and National Theater of Mannheim in 1779. Of the numerous state theaters that followed these, the most significant were the Royal National Theater, established in Berlin in 1786, and the Weimar Court Theater (1791), which produced plays by two of the century's greatest dramatists, JOHANN WOLFGANG VON GOETHE (1749–1832) and Friedrich von Schiller (1759–1805). Though these theaters operated independently of each other, their founding reflected a broad cultural concern with the expression of German national identity.

Despite being a relative newcomer to the European dramatic tradition, German drama of the mid- and late eighteenth century was significant in its experimentation and the range of its literary achievement. Gotthold Ephraim Lessing (1729–1781), an early advocate of sentimental drama, wrote plays that dealt with national, social, and philosophical themes and was instrumental in freeing German drama from the influence of French neoclassicism. His *Hamburg Dramaturgy,* a series of essays published in 1767 and 1768, was one of the century's most important works of dramatic theory. A more radical break with neoclassicism was achieved by the playwrights of the *Sturm und Drang* (storm and stress) movement, a revolt against Enlightenment rationalism that flourished between the late 1760s and early 1780s. The drama written as part of this movement—including early plays by Goethe and Schiller—explored intense emotion, nature, rebellion against society, and violent action in irregular, often episodic plots.

Goethe and Schiller eventually rejected *Sturm und Drang* for the "Weimar classicism" of their work created between the former's visit to Italy in 1786–88 and the latter's death in 1805. Ranging over modern European history, classical mythology, and philosophy, the plays of this period pursued the values of harmony, wholeness, and aesthetic distance. This desire to provide Germany with a classical tradition reflected a revived interest in the classical world in late eighteenth-century Europe—the ruins of Herculaneum and Pompeii, which offered Europeans a mesmerizing portrait of Roman life preserved in the ashes of Mount Vesuvius's eruption of 79 C.E., were discovered in Italy in 1709 and 1748. The resultant drama embodied the aesthetic values of beauty, harmony, and form rather than the prescriptive neoclassicism of

An illustration of a scene from one of Schiller's *Sturm und Drang* dramas, *Kabale und Liebe* (1784).

earlier centuries. At the same time, this drama drew its subjects from a Europe facing a period of political and aesthetic changes. Indeed, Goethe's masterpiece, the poetic drama ***FAUST*** (written in two parts, 1808, 1831), owes as much to the Romanticism that flourished in the next century as it does to the classical past.

Romanticism and Melodrama, 1800–1880

THE AGE OF REVOLUTION

At the end of the eighteenth century, two events fundamentally changed the political and cultural landscape of the Western world: the American Revolution and the French Revolution. The American Revolution severed England from its most prosperous colony and launched a radical experiment in democracy in the New World. A few years later, the French Revolution showed that even in Europe the old order was not impervious to change. Begun as a relatively modest revolt against the excesses of a king seeking absolute power, the French Revolution became radical when the lower orders and their revolutionary leaders turned against the aristocracy with increasing violence. The twin revolutions had far-reaching consequences, as neighboring countries watched them and their aftermaths with astonishment, enthusiasm, and fear. Soon, they would be directly affected as well, when Napoleon Bonaparte (1769–1821) rose from the French revolutionary forces to conquer much of Europe, propelled by a powerful army and the promise of freedom from local tyranny. Even after Napoleon had been defeated and the political map of Europe reordered in 1815 at the Congress of Vienna, what historians now term the Age of Revolution would continue well into the second half of the nineteenth century.

ROMANTICISM AND THE THEATER

The two revolutions changed more than the political order of two countries: they also altered how Western societies thought about themselves, with marked effects on cultural institutions and the arts. The French and the American revolutions had been inspired by Enlightenment philosophers such as Voltaire (François-Marie Arouet, 1694–1778), Immanuel Kant (1724–1804), and Thomas Jefferson (1743–1826), who had advocated new social organizations based not on religious beliefs but on rational planning and thought. But as the social upheavals of these revolutions grew more and more violent and unsettling, the Enlightenment insistence on pure reason lost some of its currency. Reflecting these changing historical and intellectual currents, the generation of writers, artists, and thinkers following the revolutions articulated the movement known as Romanticism. The Romantics did not reject the Enlightenment and its social experiments entirely, but they considered its more extreme claims with skepticism. They consequently placed greater emphasis on subjective experience and even on irrational desires and beliefs, which had been rejected by the Enlightenment. By the same token, they turned against the restrained, rational movement in the arts known as classicism.

Whereas artists adhering to classicism respected the boundaries between styles and poetic forms, the Romantics created unusual mixtures and sometimes left their works deliberately in fragments. Ruins of medieval architecture were prized over classical buildings, and folk arts such as fairy tales or rustic idylls over Greek and Roman models.

These developments changed the face of drama and theater as well. Indeed, the battles between the advocates of classicist theater and those of the new Romantic theater were often fierce. The French writer Victor Hugo (1802–1885), whose preface to the play *Cromwell* (1827) served as a manifesto of Romanticism, aroused the ire of traditionalists by rejecting the unities of time and place, advocating the use of historically accurate stage settings, and calling for a theatrical art that included the sublime and the grotesque. So intense were the passions of classicists and romanticists over the future of French theater that the performances of Hugo's play *Hernani* (1830) at the Comédie Française were interrupted by sustained outbursts by supporters and detractors.

An illustration, by Jean Albert Grand-Carteret, of the audience disturbances that followed the final scene of Victor Hugo's *Hernani* at its premiere in 1830.

Like many of their contemporaries, Romantic playwrights developed an ambivalent attitude toward the French Revolution. In the early nineteenth century GEORG BÜCHNER (1813–1837) wanted to bring the legacy of the French Revolution to Germany, where the political system was especially hierarchical and repressive. He even wrote a tragedy about one of the leaders of the French Revolution—*Danton's*

This late-eighteenth-century engraving of King Lear in the storm indicates the passionate intensity with which Shakespeare was often performed on the Romantic stage.

Death (1835), a sympathetic portrait of Georges-Jacques Danton (1759–1794). Other Romantics, such as William Wordsworth (1770–1850) and Samuel Taylor Coleridge (1772–1834), became much more disenchanted with the French Revolution, foregrounding not its social gains but its violence. But though they were divided in their attitudes toward the political and social upheavals of their time, the Romantics could agree on many other things. One was the eminence of WILLIAM SHAKESPEARE, which lead to a revival of the playwright across Europe; French and German Romantics treated the Elizabethan playwright as their most important predecessor. What the Romantics admired in Shakespeare was precisely what classicism had rejected: namely, the mixing of high and low characters and of comedy and tragedy, as well as the fantastic events depicted in Shakespeare's romances.

CLOSET DRAMA

Despite the fascination with theater in general and Shakespeare in particular, Romantic drama was characterized by an increasing distance from the theater audience. Although plays such as Hugo's *Hernani* enjoyed controversy and success on the popular stage, many dramas written by the great Romantic writers either were not performed during their lifetimes or received limited, private performances or readings. Such plays written for reading only, or *closet dramas,* form the most significant genre of dramatic literature during the Romantic era. Among them are *The Borderers* (1796), by Wordsworth; *The Death of Empedocles* (1798; unfinished), by Friedrich Hölderlin (1770–1843); *Remorse* (1813), by Coleridge; *Manfred* (1817), by Lord Byron (1788–1824); *The Cenci* (1819), by Percy Bysshe Shelley (1792–1822); and the plays of Alfred de Musset (1810–1857). The two plays from this era collected in the *Norton Anthology of Drama*—GOETHE's *FAUST* (part 1, 1808) and BÜCHNER's *WOYZECK* (1836)—are closet dramas as well.

THEATERS AND ACTORS

The increasing division between dramatic literature and theatrical performance had to do both with the preferences of writers and with the state of the theater industry. Poets distrusted theater managers and actors, choosing instead to write for the reading public only. At the same time, theaters—which, throughout Europe, continued to expand in size during the nineteenth century—catered to the tastes of the general public by putting on lavish spectacles. (When a similar estrangement between dramatic authors and theater managers had occurred in imperial Rome, SENECA likewise wrote only for readers or small recitations and left the theater to the popular entertainments then dominating the stage.) The demand for such spectacles drove innovation, and thus nineteenth-century theater history is dominated by a series of technical developments—including the use of gaslights (first introduced around 1825) and limelights, an early form of spotlight that greatly enhanced designers' ability to create theatrical illusions and effects. The public also desired equestrian as well as nautical plays, as new traps, elevators, moving panoramas, and, later on, revolving stages expanded the range of theatrical possibilities. Other developments were more in tune with cultural tastes and ideas dominant in the Romantic era. As general interest in the distant past grew, audiences began to pay more attention to historically accurate costumes and sets. At the same time, celebrated actors such as England's Edmund Kean (1787–1833)—famous for his interpretation of Shakespeare—and France's Frédérick Lemaître (1800–1876) developed a Romantic acting style, based on the expression of strong emotions. Such performances may have seemed spontaneous and authentic, but in fact many Romantic actors, who were given little time for rehearsal, followed manuals of gesture and expression.

MELODRAMA

Though most poets refused to write plays for the stage, a second group of writers were only too willing to supply the theaters of Europe with the popular drama they needed. The most popular type of play during this period was melodrama, which suited the public's taste for spectacle, music, and easily digestible characters and plots. The term *melodrama* is taken from the French *melodrame,* which joins the Greek word for music (*melos*) to drama; it was first applied in the late eighteenth century to plays with musical interludes that employ an easily recognizable dramatic formula and unambiguous moral contrasts. Drawing on a set of stock characters—the villain, the hapless maiden in distress, and the hero—melodramatic plots involve extraordinary coincidences and hinge on sudden revelations and encounters. France was the birthplace of melodrama, and its king was René-Charles Guilbert de Pixérécourt (1773–1844). Another prominent author of melodrama was the Irish writer Dion Boucicault (1820?–1890). Boucicault not only wrote popular plays set in Ireland, such as *The Colleen Bawn* (1860), but after spending several years in the United States he set several notable plays there as well, including *The Octoroon; or, Life in Louisiana* (1859).

Sarah Bernhardt in the title role of Victorien Sardou's *Theodora* (1884).

Both in England and in France, many melodramas were produced by adapting novels to the stage. It was a time when the novel experienced an unprecedented rise in status and appeal, and many of the era's most accomplished writers turned their hands to fiction. Prime candidates for adaptation were the immensely popular novels of Charles Dickens (1812–1870). In France, novels by Alexandre Dumas père (1802–1870) and his son, Alexandre Dumas fils (1824–1895), were adapted by the two authors themselves, among them the former's *The Three Musketeers* (1844) and *The Count of Monte Christo* (1845) and the latter's *La Dame aux camélias* (in English known as *Camille;* 1848), which also became the libretto for Giuseppe Verdi's opera *La Traviata* (1853). Because of Paris's dominant cultural position, nineteenth-century French melodramas were imported into many European countries and more distant lands.

THE WELL-MADE PLAY

Alongside melodrama, French playwrights perfected another, related form of drama, the so-called *well-made play* (a name borrowed from the French *pièce bien-fait*). The well-made play was based not on spectacle and music but on complicated, intricately constructed plots. Playwrights relied on well-known techniques such as overheard conversations, mistaken identities, sudden appearances and disappearances, and other forms of confusion that culminated in the main scene of the play—the confrontation of the main antagonists—followed by the final resolution. Because everything in a well-made play led up to such a scene, it was called *scène à faire,* the obligatory scene that "had to be done." Masters of the well-made play included Augustin-Eugène Scribe (1791–1861), who wrote more than 300 plays, and the even more popular Victorien Sardou (1831–1908), who composed several plays specifically for the greatest star of the French nineteenth-century stage, Sarah Bernhardt (1844–1923). Sardou so dominated the second half of the nineteenth century that GEORGE BERNARD SHAW (1856–1950), a radical reformer of the well-made play, referred to his drama as "sardoodledom." Like melodrama, the well-made play was an extremely popular export, imitated everywhere.

EUROPE AT MIDCENTURY

The ever-more sophisticated spectacles, melodramas, and well-made plays were created in the context of Europe's larger economic and political developments. The Age of Revolution had come to a second climax with the Europe-wide revolution of 1848, during which the countries of Continental Europe suffered through protests, strikes, and overturned governments. The revolution of 1848 gave expression to the social consequences of rapid, though uneven, industrialization in various regions of Europe, including the large-scale movements of people to urban centers, the emergence of an industrial proletariat, and the triumph of a bourgeois class. What followed was a period of political reaction and a new focus on economic gains. It was a time when England and France in particular secured and expanded their empires, and from those holdings outside Europe they drew enormous resources. The financial speculation that attended such enterprises as the building of the railroads led a fortunate few to amass unheard-of fortunes, especially in the 1870s and 1880s. This new accumulation of wealth contributed to the development of extravagant and lavish spectacles, the expansion of theaters, and an emphasis on technical developments.

NATIONALISM AND THE THEATER

The nineteenth century was also the century of nationalism, as growing numbers of countries attempted to establish and affirm their own native traditions and values. Nationalists called for national theaters to showcase the new (or old) national self-consciousness, on the model of the Comédie Française, the foremost theater of France. Theatrically the most remarkable of those efforts was undertaken by Richard Wagner (1813–1883) in Germany. Wagner sought to integrate dramatic literature, music, and acting, as well as all the other components of theater such as set design and lighting, into a new and complete synthesis—what he labeled the *Gesamtkunstwerk* (total work of art). Single-handedly, he wrote the libretti, composed the music, and influenced the staging of his operas, which he called music-dramas, at the opera house in Bayreuth newly built under his supervision, the Festspielhaus (Festival Theater). Because Wagner wanted to immerse his spectators in the power of theatrical illusion, he inaugurated what are today common theatrical methods such as dimming the light in the auditorium and hiding the orchestra to encourage the audience to focus exclusively on the stage. Though Wagner himself relied on Romantic plots and folktales, many later theater practitioners, such as the Swiss designer Adolphe Appia (1862–1928), took their inspiration from him as they attempted to create a new and modern theater.

THEATER IN THE UNITED STATES, 1800–1900

The quest for national identity was no less urgent in the United States, but it took a very different form. Theatrical activity in colonial America was recorded in the 1600s, and the first theater was built in Williamsburg, Virginia, in 1716. Even after the American Revolution was over and independence from England had been won, many economic and cultural ties between the newly formed United States of America and its former mother country remained in place. One particularly strong connection was their theaters. In the United States in the late eighteenth century, theatrical activity was largely restricted to the cities of Philadelphia, New York, Boston, and Charleston, South Carolina, and the small but growing number of resident professional companies was dominated by English-born actors and actors who had been trained in England. While the United States produced its own playwrights—including Mercy Otis Warren (1728–1814) and Royall Tyler (1757–1826)—English plays constituted most of the dramatic repertoire well into the nineteenth century.

During the nineteenth century, a new and genuinely American theater culture appeared, owing in no small part to the country's first native-born acting star. Edwin Forrest (1806–1872) established an American school of acting based on a heroic style that relied on grand, physical gestures

The Astor Place Riot, New York City, 1849.

and speech that appealed to popular audiences. While Forrest stayed in America, Charlotte Cushman (1816–1876), the first famous American actress, moved to England once she had become well known, proving that England still had greater cachet and rewards for an ambitious actor. In 1849 the relation between the United States and England, and more specifically the difference between the English and the more physical American acting schools, led to violence. In New York City, both Forrest and the visiting English actor William Charles Macready (1793–1873) were playing Macbeth. The two men were longtime rivals, and when thousands of followers of Forrest invaded the Astor Place Opera House to stop Macready's performance, with thousands more outside, the mayor called out the National Guard. Guardsmen fired into the crowd, and at least twenty-two died in what has become known as the Astor Place Riot.

STAGING RACE

While Americans were fighting for cultural independence, there emerged in the United States another type of theater not found in England or any other part of Europe: the minstrel show. Initially its players were white performers in blackface, their skins darkened with burnt cork or shoe polish, but African American minstrel troupes soon appeared as well. Musicians and singers would form a semicircle, and they would alternate between songs, dances, and short bits of dialogue, mostly between two characters—Tambo (a player of the tambourine) and Bones (a player of the bones, a clacking folk instrument made of bones or wood)—seated at either end of the semicircle, or between them and an interlocutor who sat in the middle. The minstrel show relied on racial stereotypes, for whether whites represented African Americans, as was most often the case, or African Americans made up the troupe, they had to conform to the stereotyped routines that were initially established by white performers and demanded by the predominantly white audiences. In this way, the minstrel show, America's most popular form of theatrical entertainment in the nineteenth century, was part of the fabric of American racism even as it established an American, and especially an African American, performance tradition.

America's most popular play of the nineteenth century also dealt with race relations. Harriet Beecher Stowe's (1811–1896) immensely influential novel *Uncle Tom's Cabin* (1851–52), which some have credited with having helped to start the U.S. Civil War (1861–65) through its moving depiction of the plight of slaves, inspired numerous dramatic adaptations; the most famous was an 1852 version by George L. Aiken (1830–1876), which had the longest run—more than 300 performances—of any single production in nineteenth-century America. Aiken's dramatization was largely faithful to Stowe's antislavery stance, but many other adaptations simply reverted to racial stereotypes. These adaptations, known as Tom shows, helped establish "Uncle Tom" as a derogatory label for African Americans who appeared to make their peace with slavery and suppression rather than rebelling against them. While minstrel shows and the dramatizations of *Uncle Tom's Cabin* played a central role in nineteenth-century American theater, other representations of black life or slavery rarely appeared onstage. As so often in the history of drama, dramatists at odds with popular taste had to write for a smaller reading public instead, as the African American writer and former slave WILLIAM WELLS BROWN (1814–1884) did with his play ***THE ESCAPE; OR, A LEAP FOR FREEDOM*** (1858).

Modern Theater, 1880–1945

THEATER AND THE MODERN WORLD

In the era of Romanticism, theatrical performance and dramatic literature had increasingly drifted apart. During the last two decades of the nineteenth century, however, serious writers were finally drawn to the theater once more. This did not mean that they sought to please the tastes of popular audiences. Indeed, modern drama was often characterized by a tension, even antagonism, between dramatists and audiences, an antagonism sometimes provoked by the playwrights themselves. Riling up audiences had been part of theater history for some time, as demonstrated by various nineteenth-century clashes in theaters, but now an adversarial relationship between producers and consumers became expected. The history of modern drama frequently involved confrontations between supporters of innovation and hostile audiences unprepared for new subjects, dramatic structures, and theatrical techniques. Whether by design or not, being controversial became the very condition for being modern.

Many modern dramatists earned their notoriety by engaging and often confronting audiences with challenging subjects and unusual forms. They wanted to restore theater's serious, moral function and to challenge, rather than please, their audience. To that end, they depicted the most vexing moral problems and dilemmas of their time. During the late nineteenth and early twentieth centuries, Europe and North America underwent a number of profound changes: new technologies, scientific advancement, urbanism, the proliferation of nationalist movements, changing class relationships, an accelerating economic transition from agriculture to industry, and new theories of human nature (including Marxism, Darwinism, and Freudianism).

Challenging the conventions and complacency of late nineteenth and early twentieth century society, modern playwrights addressed the impact of these and other changes. The Norwegian dramatist HENRIK IBSEN (1828–1906) depicted public hypocrisy, restrictive social conventions, and such taboo subjects as hereditary syphilis. His play *A Doll House* (1879), which exposes the hypocrisies and inequalities of Victorian marriage, was denounced in newspapers, sermons, and books. GEORGE BERNARD SHAW (1856–1950), who championed his Norwegian contemporary in *The Quintessence of Ibsenism* (1891), wrote about prostitution and woman's emancipation in *Mrs. Warren's Profession* (1893) and expressed his idiosyncratic form of socialism in such plays as *Man and Superman* (1903). The German writer Gerhart Hauptmann (1862–1946) used his play *The Weavers* (1892) to call attention to the degrading conditions of weavers, while the Swedish playwright AUGUST STRINDBERG (1849–1912) depicted the ruthless battle between the sexes in ***MISS JULIE*** (1888). Even OSCAR WILDE (1854–1900), who delighted audiences with ***THE IMPORTANCE OF BEING EARNEST***

Eleonora Duse as Rebecca in the 1906 production of Ibsen's *Rosmersholm* at the National Theater of Christiana. Rebecca rejects not only the Christian religion but also the entire structure of Christian ethics.

(1895) and other social comedies, violated conventional expectations with *Salomé* (1894), a play based on a sexually charged episode in the New Testament that describes the decapitation of St. John the Baptist. What united these playwrights was that all struggled with official censors; many of their plays could be presented only to small, private audiences because they were banned.

Though provocative themes and characters drew the most immediate hostile reaction, dramatists also deviated radically from the established rules governing dramatic forms. Many modernists criticized and ridiculed the most popular nineteenth-century dramas, such as melodramas and well-made plays. Ibsen and Shaw borrowed the conventions of the well-made play but interrupted its smooth, technically structured plots with lengthy dialogues, set speeches, and other devices that shifted dramatic attention from incidents to social and psychological issues. In such later plays as *The Dream Play* (1902) and *The Ghost Sonata* (1907), Strindberg abandoned dramatic rules for the logic of dreams. Seeking to capture the nuances of everyday life, ANTON CHEKHOV (1860–1904) rejected the stock characters and heightened dramatic incidents of the contemporary Russian theater for a drama of understatement, indirection, and psychological nuance. Traditional forms, when they were used, were adapted to new purposes, and new forms were developed to respond to a changing modern world.

THE INDEPENDENT THEATER MOVEMENT: NATURALISM

These modern playwrights could present their work to the public because of the opening of small, independent theaters intended to provide an alternative to the larger commercial theaters. Particularly important in this respect was André Antoine's (1858–1943) Théâtre Libre in Paris, which introduced the plays of Ibsen, among others. In London the Independent Theatre, founded by J. T. Grein (1862–1935), was devoted to the same task, and later Shaw and Harley Granville-Barker (1877–1946) would find a home at the Court Theatre. In Berlin it was the Freie Bühne of Otto Brahm (1856–1912) and in Moscow the Moscow Art Theater of Konstanin Stanislavsky (1863–1938) that made available performance venues for modern drama. All the theaters named above were associated with naturalism, a movement that originated in France in the 1860s and advocated that literature and art must faithfully present reality, with the writer and artist assuming the position of an objective scientist.

In its concern with the accurate portrayal of human beings and the external world, naturalism represented an extension of the realist movement that came to dominate European and North American art and literature during the middle of the nineteenth century and remains a powerful aesthetic current in today's theater. A reaction against the idealizing tendencies of Romanticism, realism seeks to depict contemporary life and society directly, unmediated by art's distorting conventions. The plays of Ibsen and Chekhov and the early plays of Shaw, which address social realities in recognizably contemporary settings, fall under this rubric. Naturalism differs from realism in that it relies on a more scientifically grounded understanding of the relation between individuals and their environment. Inspired by Charles Darwin (1809–1882) and his theory of natural selection, naturalists believed that humans are not free agents choosing their own destiny but rather are creatures determined by their environment, their physiology, and the social conditions under which they live. In the arts, the chief proponent of naturalism was Émile Zola (1840–1902), who influenced Antoine, Grein, Brahm, and other directors associated with naturalism in the theater. Dramatists who were strongly affected by naturalism include Strindberg and Hauptmann.

MODERN ACTING

Naturalism changed not only the nature of plays but also the modes of staging them. The movement led to an increased emphasis on realistic stage props and décor and a rejection of the histrionic acting practiced in the nineteenth-century commercial theater. The Russian actor and director Konstantin Stanislavsky, for example, pioneered a new acting system based on the actor's psychology and emotions. For performances of Ibsen, he even imported Norwegian furniture to help the actors merge with their roles. What Stanislavsky did for individual roles, George II, the duke of Saxe-Meiningen (1826–1914), did for groups, introducing new systems of ensemble acting and bringing vivid crowds to the stage. Modern plays, with their new and daring female roles, also made it possible for a new generation of female stars to emerge and contribute to a truly modern acting style. Among them were Eleonora Duse (1958–1924) in Italy, Elizabeth Robins (1862–1952) in England, and Eva Le Gallienne (1899–1991) in the United States. In developing their signature roles, many of these actresses chose characters from Ibsen's plays.

AESTHETICISM AND SYMBOLISM

Naturalism was not the only movement that sought to break with the conventions of nineteenth-century theater. Indeed, the rapidity with which such movements followed one another, and their strenuous and public efforts to present a distinctive rationale for artistic innovation, became a distinctive feature of modernism. Aestheticism, which advocated the primacy of beauty over values such as social or political utility, was particularly associated with Oscar Wilde (although Wilde himself was well aware of the importance of societal forces; he expressed a commitment to socialism and suffered prosecution as a homosexual). Symbolism focused on rarified meanings, subjectivity, and suggestion rather than common idioms or everyday speech. Symbolist playwrights included Maurice Maeterlinck (Belgium, 1862–1949), Madame Rachilde (France, 1860–

A set-design sketch by Adolphe Appia, ca. 1910. Note the abstract pattern of lines and angles.

1953), William Butler Yeats (Ireland, 1865–1939), and Aleksandr Blok (Russia, 1880–1921). Symbolism also entailed a return to exalted and poetic speeches and a preference for simple, symbolic designs over the cluttered stage sets of naturalism. Symbolist design was championed especially in Paris, in Aurélien Lugné-Poe's (1869–1940) Théâtre de l'Œuvre. In England, the abstract sets of Edward Gordon Craig (1872–1966) had many affinities with symbolism, as did the monumental and abstract designs of Adolphe Appia (1862–1928).

THEATER AND THE AVANT-GARDE

The battles between different movements became more pronounced and complicated in the first decades of the twentieth century. A host of "isms," often announced through manifestos and declarations, emerged virtually overnight, and many disappeared as quickly. Among those that made a mark was futurism, mostly based in Italy and Russia, which was initiated by F. T. Marinetti (1876–1944). Inspired by an enthusiasm for technology and machines—the products of a belated but rapid industrialization in northern Italy—Marinetti sought to banish the human actor from the theater, relying instead on puppets, machines, and other inanimate objects. He also rejected well-structured plays in favor of short episodes of discontinuous actions and effects. Futurism was followed by Dadaism, which pushed the anarchic provocations of the futurists to an extreme. In the Cabaret Voltaire, which flourished in Zurich during World War I (1914–18), Tristan Tzara (1896–1963) and other Dadaists presented nonsense poems, manifestos, musical pieces, and masked performances of various kinds, often simultaneously. Like futurism, Dadaism quickly became an international movement with followers in the major European cities and beyond. When Dadaism declined in Paris in the early twenties, many of its adherents joined the movement of surrealism, which was led by André Breton (1896–1966). Influenced by the psychoanalytic theory of Sigmund Freud (1865–1939), surrealism focused on

A photograph of the original 1935 production of Antonin Artaud's *Les Cenci*. Based on an Italian story of incest, torture, and patricide, the play embodies the Theater of Cruelty that Artaud espoused in *The Theater and Its Double*. Artaud, in the role of Count Cenci, stands in front.

spontaneous associations, drifting thoughts, and dream images. The surrealists were also interested in earlier writers who shared their concerns, including the provocateur ALFRED JARRY (1873–1907), who had written crude and funny plays violating almost all strictures of decency and proper form. His scatological, grotesque, and irreverent play ***UBU THE KING*** (1896) became an icon of the surrealist movement. The most influential theater maker associated with surrealism (even though he left the movement after a quarrel with Breton) was Antonin Artaud (1896–1948), who, under the name Theater of Cruelty, advocated a primal, physical theater inspired not just by ancient rituals but also by the slapstick comedy of the Marx Brothers. Artaud's writings on theater, which were published on 1938 under the title *The Theater and Its Double,* drew on images such as the plague, primitive myths, and the "animated hieroglyphics" of Balinese theater to establish theater as an antidote to the decadence of modern life.

The increasingly strident movements of the early twentieth century are often grouped together under the classification *avant-garde*. Originally a military term used to designate the advance corps of an army, in the early nineteenth century *avant-garde* became a political label applied to radical and advanced groups seeking social change. It was only in the second half of the nineteenth century that the notion of the avant-garde infiltrated the arts, allowing artists of various movements to present themselves as ahead of everyone else. Yet because the avant-garde groups maintained ties to their political roots, their formation must be understood in the context of the political history of the early twentieth century, and they often strongly promoted socialism, anarchism, or, as in the case of the Italian futurists, fascism. Indeed, the Futurists were extreme Italian nationalists, advocating war as an end in itself as well as a form of self-aggrandizement. The Dadaists, by contrast, formed in opposition to World War I and came to embrace an international socialism as a way to destroy the old class-based societies. They shared that aim with surrealists, many of whom joined various communist parties. Even more closely linked to socialism were the Russian futurists, who participated in the Russian October Revolution of 1917 and strove through artistic means to help it succeed.

POLITICAL THEATER: BRECHT

Socialism had an immense effect on many artists and thinkers of the first half of the twentieth century and later, including those not associated with the more extreme avant-garde movements. The most influential political playwright was BERTOLT BRECHT (1898–1956), who developed a new form of drama and performance called Epic Theater, which relied on a number of techniques meant to interrupt the flow of plot and acting. Brecht believed that such interruptions would ensure that audiences actively ponder, rather than passively consume, the theatrical spectacle. He had also learned from the director Erwin Piscator (1893–1966) the value of bringing many art forms, including film (still relatively new at the time), into the theater, and he collaborated with composers such as Kurt Weill (1900–1950) on new, presentational forms of opera and other forms of musical theater. Brecht, Piscator, and Weill, together with many other European writers and theater makers, fled to the United States during the Nazi era and exerted considerable influence on theater and music there. Besides these émigrés, the best-known political writer in the United States was Clifford Odets (1906–1963), whose plays depicted the plight of working-class families and often included rousing calls for a socialist society.

CULTURAL RENEWAL: IRELAND AND THE UNITED STATES

Not all theaters in the early twentieth century were dominated by avant-garde and socialist plays. The Abbey Theatre (1904) in Dublin, for example, was devoted to gaining the cultural independence of Ireland, which for centuries had been under England's control; it thus followed the nineteenth-century movement for national theaters in European countries other than those—England, France, Spain, and Italy—that had traditionally dominated theater. One of its founding members, Lady Augusta Gregory (1852–1932), advocated a return to the Irish language, which had long been marginalized by English colonizers and settlers. The playwrights associated with the theater took varied approaches to drama. While Ireland's leading poet William Butler Years composed dense, difficult plays filled with highly

A scene from the original 1928 production of *The Threepenny Opera*, a collaboration between the composer Kurt Weill and Bertolt Brecht.

A photograph of the Provincetown Players original production of Eugene O'Neill's *All God's Chill'un Got Wings* (1924). Paul Robeson, seated, played the lead role.

poetic language and mostly set in a mythical past, JOHN MILLINGTON SYNGE (1871–1909) wrote in a more colloquial, highly lyrical idiom. His plays, which undercut romanticized views of the Irish peasantry, proved controversial with the theatergoing Dublin public; so jarring was his presentation of rural Ireland in *The Playboy of the Western World* (1907) that it sparked theatrical riots and a long dispute that threatened the existence of the Abbey Theatre and the Irish Theatre Movement of which it was part.

Cultural independence was also the purpose of the Provincetown Players in the United States, a small theater troupe devoted to presenting new and challenging plays by American playwrights such as SUSAN GLASPELL (1876–1948) and EUGENE O'NEILL (1888–1953). Founded in Cape Cod and then moved to New York City, the company was part of the so-called Little Theatre Movement of the 1910s and 1920s in the United States. This movement, which was inspired by Europe's alternative theater movement of the late nineteenth century, provided the space for staging new and experimental plays without the financial constraints of the commercial theater, which by the late nineteenth century was dominated by New York's Broadway theaters and by touring productions of successful shows that took star performers to theaters in an extensive network across the United States. Some modern playwrights, such as O'Neill, both participated in the Little Theatre Movement and managed to have their plays performed on Broadway, where the largest and most elegant commercial theaters were located. Broadway still retains its unique status, as demonstrated by the distinction drawn today between Broadway, off-Broadway, and even off-off-Broadway theaters.

TRAGEDY, METATRAGEDY, METATHEATER

While the era of modern drama saw an unprecedented explosion of new forms of drama and theater, a number of playwrights also sought to return to one of the oldest dramatic forms: tragedy. In the eyes of Ibsen, the bourgeois family and its struggle against the overwhelming power of the past created the conditions for modern tragedy to take place. A similar view led Eugene O'Neill to adapt Greek tragedies to contemporary America, as in *Mourning Becomes Electra* (1931), and to write new tragedies based on his own family, as in ***LONG DAY'S JOURNEY INTO NIGHT*** (written 1941; produced 1956). Other playwrights in the United States followed his lead: such dramatists as TENNESSEE WILLIAMS (1911–1983), ARTHUR MILLER (1915–2005), SAM SHEPARD (b. 1943), DAVID MAMET (b. 1947), and EDWARD ALBEE (b. 1928) have all explored the intersection of the tragic and the everyday in American life, as characters grapple with the economic, social, and personal challenges of their modern world. Another set of playwrights turned to remote, rural settings in search for appropriate material for modern tragedies. The Spaniard FEDERICO GARCÍA LORCA (1898–1936), for example, set such tragedies as ***THE HOUSE OF BERNARDA ALBA*** (1936) in Andalusia, and Synge turned to the remote western coast of Ireland for ***RIDERS TO THE SEA*** (1904), a play that was later adapted by the Caribbean writer DEREK WALCOTT (b. 1930) in ***THE SEA AT DAUPHIN*** (1957).

A second group of modern playwrights were also drawn to tragedy but did not believe that it was suitable for the modern world. Instead, they wrote plays *about* tragedy—what they called metatragedy or *metatheater*—that focused on the nature of role-playing and the relationship between reality and theatrical illusion. The best-known writer of metatragedies was the Italian LUIGI PIRANDELLO (1867–1936), whose plays—such as the influential ***SIX CHARACTERS IN SEARCH OF AN AUTHOR*** (1921)—are mirrored cabinets in which characters adopt roles, pretend to be mad, or philosophize, in self-referential ways, about the nature of theater itself. Another prominent writer of metatragedies was the French JEAN GENET (1910–1986). Originally a novelist, Genet turned to the theater because of his fascination with costumes and role-playing, and his plays create intricate layers of pretense that are never entirely peeled back. The turn to metatheater proved influential throughout modern and contemporary drama—nontragic as well as tragic—and a self-conscious awareness of theatrical reality is an important part of the twentieth- and early twenty-first-century stage.

WAR, REVOLUTION, AND DEPRESSION: 1900–1945

The explosion of forms, the emergence of politically driven avant-gardes, the return to tragedy, and the rise of metatheater were all responses to the unprecedented turmoil of the first half of the twentieth century in Europe and elsewhere. Nineteenth-century industrialization had effected profound changes in how people lived and worked, leading scores of men and women who formerly had labored in agriculture or trades to join the urban proletariat. The revolutions and wars of the first half of the twentieth century were fueled by these changes. Social unrest was everywhere, even in the relatively stable United States, and the Russian Revolution of 1917 was only one of its most striking manifestations. The unforeseen horrors of World War I, in which the European nations brought on themselves incalculable loss of life, showed once and for all the destructive potential of advances in technology and industrialization. European self-confidence, as well as the belief in progress and the upward course of civilization more generally, was dashed. Peace brought only short-lived relief, as the worldwide stock market crash of 1929 and

Figures silhouetted by the U.S. Constitution in a production of *Triple-A Plowed Under* sponsored by the Federal Theater Project during the 1930s. This play, one of the earliest and best-known of the "living newspapers," addressed the plight of American farmers during the Depression.

the depression that followed it threw the global economy into a crisis—one that, unlike the war, affected the United States as much as it did Europe. Faced with the Great Depression, President Franklin Delano Roosevelt (1882–1945) undertook, as part of his New Deal, an ambitious public works program, which included unprecedented sponsorship of the theater. During its brief existence (1935–39), the Federal Theatre Project rejuvenated theatrical activity across the country and pioneered such innovative forms as the "living newspaper," which addressed social and political issues in innovative, multimedia productions. Other changes affected the theater arts as well. Economic turmoil and racism in the South encouraged the great migration of African Americans to northern cities, which helped make New York's Harlem a cultural center for the arts in the 1910s and 1920s. African American musicians and jazz flourished, and so did such writers, intellectuals, and playwrights of the Harlem Renaissance as Zora Neale Hurston (1891–1960) and LANGSTON HUGHES (1902–1967).

In Europe of the twenties and thirties, fascism and Nazism were on the rise, and soon England and the Continent, the United States, and the world as a whole would be plunged into another and even bloodier war. The cataclysm of World War II (1939–45) brought to a close the era of modern drama that began with Ibsen and other groundbreaking figures of the later nineteenth century, and it cleared the way for new movements and playwrights who would explore the emerging outlines of the contemporary world. The period 1880–1945—which opened with Thomas Edison's first public demonstration of the incandescent lightbulb on December 31, 1879, and ended with the atomic bombing of Hiroshima and Nagasaki in August 1945—was a time of profound and unsettling changes that inevitably affected playwrights. They participated in the political, ideological, and social movements and changes around them, contributing with their plays and performances to urgent debates, problems, and opportunities. They responded to these unsettling times in their stark and jagged plays, in which all the old forms, structures, and certainties seemed to have fallen apart. In the process, they gave rise to the most innovative and influential era of theater-making since the Renaissance. The varied forms of dramatic art that they introduced would influence the shape of theater for generations.

Postwar Theater, 1945–1970

THE POSTWAR WORLD

In political, social, and cultural terms, the latter half of the twentieth century was shaped by the second of two global wars and by the geopolitical changes that followed in its wake. World War II, which was fought between the Axis powers (Germany, Italy, Japan) and the Allies (Britain, France, the Soviet Union, the United States, and China), claimed 60 million military and civilian lives, including 11 million who died in German-controlled concentration camps (6 million of them Jews killed in the Holocaust) and as many as 200,000 who died as a result of the atomic bombs that the United States dropped on the Japanese cities of Hiroshima and Nagasaki. With much of Europe and parts of Asia devastated by warfare, the United States emerged from World War II as the world's dominant military, industrial, and economic power, though its unilateral supremacy proved to be short-lived. The Soviet Union, which successfully tested its own atomic bomb in 1949, established its influence over the countries of Eastern Europe, while the revolution led by Mao Zedong (1893–1976) ended with a communist government ruling mainland China. By 1950 the international landscape had been redrawn between two competing economic and ideological blocs—a capitalist "West" and a communist "East"—and the cold war that would dominate the world for the next forty years was well under way. Although the United States and the Soviet Union avoided direct military confrontation during this period, their struggle for ideological supremacy played itself out in a series of regional wars—notably in Korea, Vietnam, and Afghanistan—and in the internal politics of countries throughout Asia, Africa, and Latin America. They competed as well in the fields of science, technology, culture, and sports. No symbol was more resonant of this bipolar world than the city of Berlin, which was divided into western and eastern sectors by the Berlin Wall, a literal version of the "Iron Curtain" that divided not just Germany but Europe as a whole.

The 1950s inaugurated a period of prosperity for North America, Western Europe, and Japan, and the middle class established itself more firmly as the arbiter of social values. After years of wartime austerity, many in the West began to enjoy the benefits of a thriving consumer-oriented economy that catered to domestic households and an emergent youth subculture. On the surface, the 1950s was a decade of materialism and conformity, a period during which social stability was reinforced—particularly in the United States, where a new "Red Scare," like the one that had followed the Russian Revolution, inflamed anticommunist sentiment in the late 1940s and early 1950s—by the fears of enemy infiltration and nuclear war. Yet many of the social problems that would erupt in the following decade were already visible. The civil rights movement on behalf of African Americans took definitive shape in the United States in the mid-1950s, and London was the site of clashes between white youths and West Indian immigrants in the Notting Hill race riots of 1958. In 1954 France became involved in a war in Algeria that ended eight years later with the independence of its oldest major colony. Decolonization was under way around the globe, as the former holdings of European empires became newly independent countries in what was soon being called the Third World. Even in those nations under Soviet control—the Warsaw Pact countries of Eastern Europe—there were disturbances, as citizens in client states sought more autonomy. In 1956 the Soviet Union brutally suppressed the Hungarian Revolution, as it would Czechoslovakia's "Prague Spring" in 1968.

Driven by these and other impulses for change, an increasing number of challenges arose in the 1960s to the social consensus that had largely prevailed in the United States and Western Europe since the end of World War II. A growing number of intellectuals and activists condemned the inequalities of Western capitalism from the points of view of Marxism/socialism and anarchism, and to their social critique were added the voices of radical trade unionists, an emerging youth subculture, Black Power advocates in the United States, and members of such issue-specific movements as the Campaign for Nuclear Disarmament in Britain and the international protests against the United States' war in Vietnam (1961–73). These movements came to a head in Paris in May 1968, when an escalating series of strikes by students and workers brought France to a standstill and nearly toppled the government of Charles de Gaulle (1890–1970). Similar uprisings took place elsewhere, and it seemed—for the moment, at least—as if capitalism itself was under siege.

POSTWAR THEATER: EXPANSION, CONTINUITY, AND INNOVATION

During the years 1945–70 theater and drama underwent their own changes, many of which intensified trends that had emerged earlier in the century—while others signaled important new directions for the late twentieth-century stage. Even as London, Paris, Berlin, Moscow, New York, Toronto, and other major cities continued to serve and grow as important theatrical centers, more theaters were built and more residential theater companies formed outside these cities. Regional and provincial theaters were established, a number of annual theatrical festivals—such as those in Avignon, France; Edinburgh, Scotland; and Stratford, Ontario—were founded and expanded, and smaller theaters were opened in cities to provide opportunities for productions that the larger commercial theaters were unwilling or unable to undertake. The period also saw the founding of a number of state-sponsored theaters and theater companies, such as London's National Theatre, which was established in 1963. Like other new theaters and companies, these venues opened the way for new kinds of techniques, performance aesthetics outside the mainstream, and unconventional dramatic texts.

Though new theatrical theorists emerged, much of the innovation of these years reflected the influence of two earlier writers: BERTOLT BRECHT and Antonin Artaud.

Brecht's Epic Theater—specifically, its presentational devices and acting style, as well as its view of theater as a medium for social analysis and intervention—maintained a powerful hold on European political theater, while Artaud's conception of a total theater that would surround its audience and address it on a visceral level had a profound impact on the environmental theater movements of the 1960s and the pioneering work of the Polish director Jerzy Grotowski (1933–1999). Both of these traditions helped the theater of the mid-twentieth century to meet one of its greatest challenges: rediscovering its performative uniqueness during an age when competition from film, radio, and television was increasing.

POSTWAR FRENCH THEATER: ABSURDISM

The psychological and social impact of World War II on midcentury drama was felt most immediately in France, where the absurdists established themselves as one of the most important groups of postwar dramatists. The term *absurdism* was not coined until 1961, when the critic and scholar Martin Esslin (1918–2002) published his influential study *The Theater of the Absurd*, and the dramatists who were included under this label are as notable for their differences as for their similarities. But the word does underscore a shared rejection of conventional dramatic structures and a skepticism toward rationality, language, and the coherent subject of traditional philosophy and drama. As they confronted a universe apparently bereft of meaning, divine or otherwise, they echoed the assumptions of Jean-Paul Sartre (1905–1980), Albert Camus (1913–1960), and other proponents of philosophical existentialism, while the dramatic features that defined their plays—nonlinearity, antirealism, lack of traditional coherence, nonsensical language, metadramatic awareness, and the mixture of tragedy, comedy, and farce in a modern form of tragicomedy—owed much to the experiments of Dada, surrealism, and other avant-garde movements earlier in the century. Eugène Ionesco (1909–1994) and JEAN GENET (1910–1986) are among the most prominent of the playwrights whose works show the influence of absurdism, though no figure in this tradition had a greater impact on the drama that followed than the Irish-born playwright SAMUEL BECKETT (1906–1989),

In Eugène Ionesco's *The Bald Soprano*, a classic example of Theater of the Absurd, characters engage in nonsensical banter that calls into question the nature of communication in modern society. Pictured here is the 1950 production at the Théâtre Noctambules in Paris, directed by Nicolas Bataille.

whose play *WAITING FOR GODOT* (1952)—first performed in Paris in 1953—changed the landscape of postwar theater. Although it originated in France, absurdism exerted a pronounced influence on international drama during the 1950s and 1960s. Its challenge to arbitrary forms of order lent itself to social and political critique in the hands of Eastern European dissidents such as the Czech playwright Václav Havel (b. 1936) and dramatists living under repressive regimes throughout the Third World.

POSTWAR GERMAN THEATER: THE BRECHTIAN LEGACY

Postwar drama followed a different trajectory in Germany and the other German-speaking countries of central Europe. Most of Germany's theaters had been destroyed during the war, and the governments of both West Germany and East Germany embarked on major efforts to rebuild their countries' cultural infrastructure. The drama that was written for these theaters in the 1950s dealt mainly with social and political issues, and the subjects of guilt and responsibility loomed particularly large for a people confronting their collective role in World War II. Aiding the development of political theater were Bertolt Brecht's return to East Germany after his self-imposed exile during the Nazi period and the founding of the Berliner Ensemble in 1949 by Brecht and his wife, the actress Helene Weigel (1900–1971). The Berliner Ensemble put Brecht's theories of rehearsal and production into practice and in performing to audiences at home and abroad established Brecht's plays and the "Brechtian style" as major forces in the contemporary theater. In the German-speaking theater Brecht's influence was manifest in the drama of a new generation of playwrights, many of whom adopted the Brechtian focus on social and political issues and employed Brechtian techniques, though usually without the doctrinaire and, at times, utopian Marxism that often shaped Brecht's plays. The Swiss playwright Friedrich Dürrenmatt (1921–1990) made Brechtian and absurdist techniques part of his pessimistic dramatic vision of humanity in the postwar world, while the German playwright Peter Weiss (1916–1982) brought elements of Artaud's Theater of Cruelty to a Brechtian concern with history. Weiss's dramas of the mid- and late 1960s—such as *The Investigation* (1965), which examines the Holocaust through the theatrical re-creation of war crimes testimony—were written in the style of documentary theater, a genre that other dramatists embraced during the decade.

POSTWAR BRITISH THEATER: THE WELFARE STATE AND ITS DISCONTENTS

In the ten years immediately following the war, the theater in Britain gave little evidence of the important role it would play in the history of contemporary drama. The country itself was undergoing historic changes: in 1945 Clement Attlee's (1883–1967) Labour Party achieved a landslide victory over the incumbent prime minister and wartime hero Winston Churchill (1874–1965), and the following six years saw the establishment of the British welfare state. One sign of the increasing role of government in society was the creation of the Arts Council of Great Britain, an independent, government-funded body that—for the first time in Britain—provided state subsidies for the arts. But these changes in society left little mark on the London theater, which for the most part was sustaining itself on an uninspiring diet of West End productions. Two events caused a seismic shift. In 1955 Beckett's *Waiting for Godot* was given its London premiere, and in the following year *Look Back in Anger*, by the playwright John Osborne (1929–1994), electrified the theater world; it was produced by the London Stage Company, a noncommercial company specifically formed to support new playwrights. Osborne's play expressed the restlessness and anger of a generation at odds with the materialism and oppressive class structure of Britain in the mid-1950s, and it reflected the disillusionment permeating an imperial power in the twilight of its ascendancy. Along with the work of the Theatre Workshop—a company in a working-class area in East London that, under the leadership of Joan Littlewood (1914–2002), produced plays

Jimmy Porter (played by Kenneth Haigh) plays his trumpet to distract himself from his cramped quarters and the complacency of postwar Britain in the original 1956 Royal Court production of John Osborne's *Look Back in Anger*.

by such working-class playwrights as Shelagh Delaney (b. 1939)—*Look Back in Anger* opened the door for a new generation of dramatists grappling with social class and other issues central to British national identity.

The subsequent development of social and political theater in Britain was influenced by Brecht's theories and practices; indeed, over the next two decades Brechtian dramaturgy and stagecraft found their widest application outside Germany in British theater. The Berliner Ensemble visited London in 1956 (the year of Brecht's death) and 1965, and its epic style influenced a number of left-wing directors, designers, and playwrights. John Arden (b. 1930) and Edward Bond (b. 1934) belong to the first generation of British dramatists who employed the strategies and techniques of Brechtian theater to strikingly original ends. The Brechtian turn in British drama received greater impetus in the aftermath of 1968, when a new generation of socialist playwrights—inspired by the revolutionary events in Paris and elsewhere and aided by the abolition of government censorship, which had been in effect since the Theatrical Licensing Act of 1737—made Brechtian devices a cornerstone of their more radical political drama. John McGrath (1935–2002), Howard Brenton (b. 1942), and David Hare (b. 1947) are only a few of the many dramatists who drew on Brecht in the 1970s and early 1980s. Among the women playwrights who sought to adapt Brecht within the politics of an emerging feminist movement, CARYL CHURCHILL (b. 1938)—whose plays range with deliberate abandon through space and time in treating their historical and contemporary subjects—is the most accomplished and widely known. This intensification of political playwriting after the events of 1968 was matched by a proliferation of radical (or "fringe") theater groups throughout Britain and Northern Ireland.

PINTER, STOPPARD, ORTON

Other playwrights and dramatic currents helped define postwar British theater. The influence of Samuel Beckett was apparent in the drama of HAROLD PINTER (b. 1930) and Tom Stoppard (b. 1937), two of the country's leading contemporary playwrights. Pinter combined the indeterminacy and linguistic evasions of Beckettian drama with the often gritty realism of interactions within the lower, middle, and upper strata of Britain's class-based society. Stoppard, who was born in Czechoslovakia, drew on Beckett in a technically virtuoso, philosophically sophisticated drama that also has more than a passing kinship to GEORGE BERNARD SHAW's "drama of ideas." Joining Stoppard in reworking the English comic tradition was Joe Orton (1933–1967), whose plays of the mid-1960s exploited the farcical, the macabre, and the surface gentility of English drawing-room comedy within an anarchic drama of sexual desire pursued across boundaries of gender, sexual identity, and class.

POSTWAR AMERICAN THEATER: EXPRESSIVE REALISM, METHOD ACTING

Theater in the United States achieved one of its greatest flowerings in the years immediately following World War II. While Europe found it necessary to revive—and in many cases, rebuild—its theatrical institutions, the Broadway theaters that represented the center of theatrical life in the United States had been left relatively untouched by the war. But with few exceptions—the plays of Thornton Wilder (1897–1975), for instance—this theater had produced little of substance since the mid-1930s. The rebirth of American theater that followed the end of the war resulted from the collaboration between a group of visionary theatrical practitioners and two emerging dramatists—TENNESSEE WILLIAMS (1911–1983) and ARTHUR MILLER (1915–2005)—whose innovative dramaturgy was put to work in plays that captured the aspirations and anxieties of postwar America. The designer Jo Mielziner (1901–1976) pioneered an expressive or "subjective" stage realism that presented the theatrical categories of present and past, here and there, exterior and interior with poetic fluidity. Using the stage designs of Mielziner and under the direction of Elia Kazan (1909–2003), such plays as Williams's ***A STREETCAR NAMED DESIRE*** (1947) and Miller's ***DEATH OF A SALESMAN*** (1949) explored the shifting landscapes of memory and desire on a stage where the external world was at once materially real and evanescent. Such plays created a need for performers to convey greater psychological complexity, and it was met by contemporary developments in American acting. Continuing the interest in Konstantin Stanislavsky's psychological approach to acting that had marked the work of the Group Theater in the 1930s, the Actors Studio (founded in 1947 by members of the earlier company) promoted method acting, a performance style that emphasized psychological motivation, intention, and the importance of subtext in the presentation of dramatic characters. This approach, perhaps most famously realized in the theatrical and film performances of Marlon Brando (1924–2004), dominated American acting through the 1950s.

Director Elia Kazan and playwright Arthur Miller sitting on Jo Mielziner's set for the 1949 Broadway production of *Death of a Salesman*.

OFF-BROADWAY AND OFF-OFF-BROADWAY THEATER

Even as Broadway played a central role in presenting a revitalized American drama, its historically dominant role in American theater was challenged during the postwar years. In an attempt to diversify and expand theatrical activity outside the city of New York, a number of regional theaters were formed with resident companies presenting an annual season of plays. Among the most prominent of these are the Alley Theatre (Houston, 1947), the Arena Stage (Washington, 1950), and the Guthrie Theater (Minneapolis, 1963). Within New York, the increasing conservatism of Broadway theaters in the face of rising production costs led to the opening of off-Broadway theaters. Like the Little Theater Movement of the 1910s, off-Broadway theater involved smaller buildings that often were some distance from the main commercial theater district, and because these spaces served smaller audiences—between 100 and 499 spectators—they could be used to produce plays that the larger Broadway houses found too risky. European writers such as Beckett and Ionesco saw the first New York productions of their plays in off-Broadway theaters, as did a number of new American playwrights, including EDWARD ALBEE (b. 1928). Off-Broadway also played a significant role in the careers of more established American playwrights. The 1956 production of *The Iceman Cometh* by Circle in the Square, one of the decade's most important off-Broadway theaters, revived interest in the plays of EUGENE O'NEILL (1888–1953) and thus helped lead to the Broadway premiere of *LONG DAY'S JOURNEY INTO NIGHT* that same year.

But by the end of the 1950s, off-Broadway theaters were themselves dealing with rising costs; they therefore became more reluctant to gamble on experimental plays or on unproven writers and increasingly reliant on productions whose commercial success seemed guaranteed. In response, off-off-Broadway theaters were founded throughout New York. These low-budget theaters—which were located in coffeehouses, church buildings, various basements, and wherever else space was available—provided opportunities for a generation of younger dramatists with strong antiestablishment leanings and experimental creative interests. During the 1960s—in Caffe Cino (1958), La MaMa Experimental Theatre Club (1961), Judson Poets' Theater (1961), and elsewhere—they launched the careers of such prominent contemporary playwrights as MARIA IRENE FORNES (b. 1930) and SAM SHEPARD (b. 1943). The often radical plays produced in these venues took part in the experimentation more broadly under way in 1960s American theater. For example, under the leadership of Joseph Chaikin (1935–2003), the Open Theater rejected the psychological realism of method acting for a form of acting rooted in improvisation, role-playing, and transformation. Communal theater groups, such as the Living Theater (which had been

Playwright Luis Valdez, right, founder of El Teatro Campesino, with the United Farm Workers president, Cesar Chavez, in front of New York's Winter Garden Theater in 1979. *Zoot Suit*, by Valdez, was the first Chicano play to be performed on Broadway.

founded as an off-Broadway company in 1947), explored a radically participatory theater in which the division between performer and audience became almost imperceptible. Other theater groups—the Free Southern Theater, the Bread and Puppet Theater, and El Teatro Campesino, to name a few—used agitprop techniques, puppetry, and populist theater traditions to engage with social issues such as civil rights, the conditions of migrant farmworkers, and the Vietnam War.

AFRICAN AMERICAN THEATER

The years 1945–70 also saw the rise of contemporary African American drama. Drama and theater, of course, had played a central role in the Harlem Renaissance during the 1920s and 1930s, most notably in the plays of LANGSTON HUGHES (1902–1967), and the government-funded Federal Theatre Project of the 1930s had provided work for African American theater professionals through the "Negro units" that were established in New York and other cities. But it was not until Lorraine Hansberry's (1930–1965) play *A Raisin in the Sun,* which had an acclaimed run on Broadway in 1959, that serious African American drama claimed the attention of mainstream audiences. A product of the 1950s civil rights movement, the play also anticipated the more radical political and cultural movements of the decade that followed. African American theater of the 1960s reflected a deepening militancy; the plays of Amiri Baraka (b. 1934), for instance, reveal the author's growing separatism and revolutionary convictions, while the Black Arts Repertory Theatre (1965) that Baraka helped establish in Harlem was at the forefront of the militant Black Arts Movement. These and other dramatists of the 1950s and 1960s laid the groundwork for such later African American playwrights as Ntozake Shange (b. 1948), AUGUST WILSON (1945–2005), and SUZAN-LORI PARKS (b. 1964).

Contemporary Theater

THE CONTEMPORARY WORLD

The term *contemporary,* always imprecise, is particularly elusive when applied to today's historical moment. In a world of accelerated change—where international events, technological developments, and cultural trends follow each other with dizzying speed—the past of even a few years ago can seem like another age. Much has transpired during the period from the end of the 1960s through the first decade of the twenty-first century, and these years could be subdivided into smaller segments, each with its defining issues and preoccupations. Over the time since 1970, a world has emerged markedly different than that of the postwar years, and the overall trends and transformations of those decades have led to a present whose outlines we are still coming to understand.

In the past forty years a number of pivotal events have remapped the international geopolitical landscape, and two have been particularly important in their immediate and long-range consequences. As the result of intensifying pressure from the outside and the weaknesses of their own economic and social systems, which were unable to adapt to a changing global economy, the Soviet Union and its satellite states rejected communism in favor of Western-style capitalist economies in the years 1989–91, thereby bringing an end to the cold war that had defined international relations since the end of World War II. The fall of the Berlin Wall in November 1989 was the most visual symbol of this rapid change that took the form of peaceful and violent revolutions throughout the former Eastern Bloc, the unification of Germany, the dissolution of the Soviet Union in 1991, and the wars among the newly independent states of the former Yugoslavia. The second major shift was the rise of Islamist militancy as a social and political force. Islamic fundamentalists in Iran overthrew the monarchy of the shahs in 1979, replacing it with a revolutionary Islamic republic; in the 1980s, foreign volunteers joined an Afghan national resistance movement in what they viewed as a fight for Islam and drove the Soviet Union out of Afghanistan (1979–89). Such successes helped foster the growth of organized terrorist organizations, leading to the attacks on the World Trade Center and the Pentagon on September 11, 2001, and the subsequent wars in Afghanistan and Iraq.

THEATER AND GLOBALIZATION

Even more important in shaping the contemporary world than these geopolitical and ideological changes have been developments in the transnational spheres of capital and finance, corporate organization, information, communications, and culture. The world's economy has become literally global: the flow of goods, services, money, and information is increasingly unfettered, as traders move currencies and corporations reconfigure labor forces, production networks, management operations, and marketing strategies without respect to national borders. This process of globalization has been supported by innovations in information and communications technology—most notably, personal and network computing, cellular and electronic communications, and the rapid expansion of the Internet, which has made possible unprecedented access to information. Culture and the arts also show the effects of the global economy, as the products of high, popular, and mass (or commercial) culture reflect an ever-richer dialogue between the local and global. American teenagers read graphic novels that borrow from the latest in Japanese anime, while fans in Asia, Europe, and South America follow the steadily internationalizing game of American basketball. Music and other cultural products circulate between societies, and these encounters generate hybrid forms that draw on and transform both national and more localized styles and traditions.

Not surprisingly, the field of theater has adapted itself to—and been shaped by—this globalizing, technological world. Though one can still speak of national theaters, the activities of theater and drama have become increasingly internationalized over the twentieth and early twenty-first centuries. The 1913 Nobel Prize in Literature was won by the Indian poet and playwright Rabindranath Tagore (1861–1941), whose play *The Post Office* had been performed by Dublin's Abbey Theatre earlier that year; the 2000 prize was awarded to the Chinese playwright and novelist Gao Xingjian (b. 1940). Playwrights, theatrical companies, and productions cross borders with ease, and the encounter of cultural traditions has become both a subject and a collaborative aesthetic of theatrical production. The 1985 theatrical adaptation of the Hindu epic the *Mahabharata* by the British director Peter Brook (b. 1925) was produced at the Avignon Festival in France with actors from sixteen countries; over the next four years it toured internationally. More recently, the French Canadian director, writer, and performer Robert Lepage (b. 1957) has produced a number of the-

The 1987 production at the Theatre des Bouffes du Nord of *Mahabharata*, directed by Peter Brook.

atrical pieces that combine international performance styles in narratives about history, migration, and cultural identity that span the globe. These, too, have been performed around the world. Other prominent contemporary directors—such as Ariane Mnouchkine (b. 1939) and Robert Wilson (b. 1941)—similarly are international theater figures.

THEATER AND MEDIA

One reason for the internationalism of contemporary theater is the shifting relationship of the performing arts to the expanding field of media technologies. For much of the twentieth century, theater was forced to compete with a series of emerging media: film, radio, tape recording, and television. In a number of cases, it responded by incorporating these technologies into its repertoire of staging practices: onstage projections in Brechtian theater, for example, and the disembodied voices of BECKETT's late plays. In the century's final decades, the line separating theater from film and other media continued to blur. The American playwright SAM SHEPARD's (b. 1943) reputation owes as much to his work as a film actor as it does to his theater work, while DAVID MAMET (b. 1947) writes as frequently for cinema as he does for the stage. Plays are regularly adapted for film and television—vastly more people saw TONY KUSHNER's (b. 1956) *ANGELS IN AMERICA* (1991–92) on HBO in 2003 (and subsequently on videotape) than saw it in the theater—and noteworthy productions of such plays as CHEKHOV's *Uncle Vanya* are available for video libraries. As it becomes less reliant on specific performance sites, in other words, theater is more transportable than it has ever been.

The shifting boundary between theater and other media—and the resultant blurring of the distinction between elite and mass culture—is also reflected in the influence of postmodernism on contemporary theater and drama. *Postmodernism,* a term most frequently applied to developments in architecture, the visual arts, and literature in the second half of the twentieth century, denotes a style (or set of styles) that challenges the Enlightenment and modernist belief in metanarratives (i.e., overarching frameworks of meaning) and abandons historical analysis in favor of juxtaposing historical and contemporary elements in the mode of quotation or pastiche.

The theater has also responded to competing media technologies by asserting its uniqueness in the actuality of the theatrical moment and the proximity of live actor to spectator. This impulse, which marked the activities of theater groups influenced by Artaud and the performances of the Living Theater and other communal theater groups of the 1960s, manifested itself in the work of performance artists who began presenting their work in the United States during the 1970s. These artists, often working solo, appeared at a range of locations inside and outside the theater; their performances, which could be scripted or unscripted, often involved the performer's body in situations or encounters that addressed various issues pertaining to social representation, politics, and other matters. By the 1980s, though, even these artists were engaging with contemporary media culture in their performances.

INTERNATIONAL THEATER

In keeping with the overall trend of globalization, in the twentieth and early twenty-first centuries the importance of theater outside Europe and the United States has increased. The rise of national theaters outside Italy, Britain, France, Spain, and Germany is connected to the political and cultural nationalisms that gathered force in Europe and other areas of the world in the late nineteenth and twentieth centuries. From Mexico to Ireland to Egypt, plays were produced that embraced newly emerging cultural identities, often within theaters that were built and designated as national sites. The dramatists who helped drive these movements frequently were influenced by traditional and modern European dramatic forms, and in this sense their dramatic writing represented an attempt to bring Western modernity to local theatrical cultures. This pattern can be observed in Japan, China, and India, where Western-influenced plays entered ancient theatrical traditions. Many of the most influential figures in international theater during the past century brought Western traditions into dialogue with indigenous theatrical, dramatic, and narrative forms. The Egyptian playwright TAWFIQ AL-HAKIM (1898–1987), for instance—who lived in Paris for several years during the 1920s—helped establish an Arabic literary dramatic tradition by applying Western dramatic forms and techniques to traditional Arabic story material (such as *The Thousand and One Nights*). Al-Hakim's plays after 1950, like those of playwrights who followed in his footsteps, addressed the political and social issues of the contemporary Arab world.

POSTCOLONIAL THEATER

The internationalization of drama after the end of World War II received a strong impetus from the decolonization movements that led to the dismantling of Europe's global empires. India achieved its independence from Great Britain in 1947, and by 1970 all but a few of the British, French, and other European colonies in Africa, Asia, and the Caribbean had followed suit. In most cases independence followed intense campaigns by nationalist groups, such as the Viet Minh (the full form of its name means "League for the Independence of Vietnam") of Ho Chi Minh (1890–1969) in French Indochina and the Mouvement National Congolais of Patrice Lumumba (1925–1961) in the Belgian Congo. The newly independent countries faced their own formidable challenges: poverty and underdevelopment; corrupt, often repressive governments; outside political interference; economic exploitation; and tribal, ethnic, and sectarian divisions, in addition to the pervasive political, social, and economic legacies of colonial rule. The unbalanced power relations between indigenous peoples and long-established populations of white settlers caused wide economic disparities, which had political consequences. For example, in South Africa, which became independent of Great Britain in 1910, a system known as *apartheid* (an Afrikaans word that means "separate") restricted political power to citizens of British and Dutch ancestry and legally classified all persons within the country into one of four racial groups. Until it was abolished in 1994, black citizens were forced to live and work in so-called homelands (only those with a work permit could live in a city), were forced into a separate education system, and were compelled to carry government-issued passes for identification. Other former colonies, as well as those nation-states that achieved independence when the Soviet Union dissolved in 1991, have had to deal with their own legacies of colonial suppression.

The term *postcolonial* is frequently used in discussions of national identity in a world still coming to terms with the effects of colonialism—or, according to some, now living under a neocolonial system of new economic and cultural dependencies. The term is often applied to literature and other cultural forms—such as theater—within those nations previously subjected to colonial rule. *Postcolonial,* in this sense, refers less to the historical period after colonialism than it does to the inheritance of a system whose tensions and contradictions—social, psychological, and cultural—remain very much alive. Postcolonial writers and other artists address the metropolitan centers that historically dominated their nations and societies (most prominently, London and Paris), but they do so as subjects who have been partly formed by those centers and their language, educational system, social structures, and culture. Literature, theater, and other postcolonial art forms establish relationships between native and colonial traditions; explore the influence of imperial ideologies, power structures, and discourses on contemporary perceptions and relations; and look for ways in which those who live in postcolonial societies can achieve new forms of identity and cultural resistance.

Postcolonial dramatists, whose work represents one of the most vibrant and important currents in contemporary theater, have been at the forefront of those seeking to rewrite the received traditions of Western culture from a postcolonial point of view. The Nigerian playwright WOLE SOYINKA (b. 1934), who studied in England and worked with the Royal Court Theatre in London before returning to his native country in the late 1950s, draws on the rituals and festivals of Nigeria's Yoruba culture as well as on European dramatic models in plays that address the impact of colonialism and the tyranny of oppressive

Actor-playwrights Percy Mtwa and Mbongeni Ngema in *Woza Albert!*, a play about apartheid performed in 1983 at the Market Theater in Johannesburg.

regimes that followed in its wake. The West Indian playwright DEREK WALCOTT (b. 1930) has also sought fusions of Western and indigenous performance forms, drawing on Caribbean folklore, dance, storytelling, and linguistic patois while celebrating the hybridization of the region's multiple cultures. Because language was central to the dynamics of colonial subjugation—local languages were usually subordinated to an "official" tongue and, in some countries, were even outlawed—the politics of language is an important subject of postcolonial drama. Many of these plays include non-European languages—Gaelic, Zulu, Bengali—within a broadened field of linguistic interaction.

The term *postcolonial* is also used to refer to playwrights who live in the former "settlement colonies," predominantly English-speaking countries where white settlers adopted their own version of British culture and whose relations with London, for most of the colonial period, were largely autonomous. In Canada, which became a dominion in 1867 and achieved legislative independence in 1931, drama challenging the dominant Anglo-Canadian culture has been produced by the country's French-speaking minority—including the leading Quebecois playwright, Michel Tremblay (b. 1942)—and such Native American playwrights as Tomson Highway (Cree, b. 1951). In Australia, which was settled as a British penal colony in the late eighteenth century, a national history that includes the displacement of the indigenous population has been explored by such writers as the Aboriginal playwright Jack Davis (1917–2000) and the white Australian LOUIS NOWRA (b. 1950). And no postcolonial drama is more socially urgent than that which was produced within apartheid South Africa by writers such as ATHOL FUGARD (b. 1932), Zakes Mda (b. 1948), and Maishe Maponya (b. 1951), many of them associated with the pioneering multiracial Market Theatre in Johannesburg (established 1976).

THEATER AND DIVERSITY

The social, cultural, and psychological changes associated with postcolonialism, it is important to note, extend beyond the nations that had been imperial holdings. Many former colonial subjects were among the immigrants who streamed into Europe to work in the decades after World War II, and this growing population of naturalized citizens—South Asians, West Indians, and Africans in Britain; North Africans in France; Turks in West Germany—has redrawn the racial profile of societies that once were homogeneous. Throughout western Europe, cities have become more cosmopolitan—a cosmopolitanism deepened at the end of the twentieth century and the beginning of the twenty-first by the economic integration of nations within the European Union and the liberalization of economies in eastern Europe. The effects on the contemporary theater of Britain, Ireland, and the Continent have been profound. Second- and third-generation writers from immigrant populations—Hanif Kureishi (b. 1954) and Ayub Khan-Din (b. 1961) in Britain, for instance—who find themselves between two cultures and belonging completely to neither, have created plays that explore their often conflicted position, while playwrights from culturally dominant racial groups have produced a drama increasingly concerned with the changing face of nationhood.

A different version of this cultural evolution is evident in the United States, where immigration has been central to national self-definition since the metaphor of the "melting pot" was first used in 1782. Though it has traditionally been assumed that immigrants and their descendents would surrender their particular racial and ethnic differences for a dominant, shared "Americanness," this stance has been replaced in recent decades by an embrace of cultural uniqueness and ethnic/racial identity. Following the development of a contemporary African American drama in the 1950s and 1960s, the American theater has seen the emergence of Asian American drama in the work of DAVID HENRY HWANG (b. 1957) and others, Chicano/a drama, and—since the 1990s—Arab American drama. The growing political and cultural assertiveness of the continent's original inhabitants has also produced an impressive body of Native American drama. This drama is sometimes the product of theater groups, such as the U.S.-based Spiderwoman Theater, that draw on Native American storytelling and performance traditions.

More broadly, the theater has begun to include a wider range of voices and experiences that traditionally have been marginalized within, or excluded from, the stage. The roots of this expansion lie in the "identity" or "liberation" movements that have gathered strength in recent decades in Europe, North America, and other areas of the world. The contemporary women's movement, for example, which burgeoned in the 1970s, has produced a rich body of drama concerned with women's experience, the meaning of "woman" in traditional representations, and the changing manifestations of gender in the late twentieth and early twenty-first centuries. This drama has often formed part of an explicit feminist project to challenge male-directed theatrical practices, institutions, and notions of authorship, and it has sometimes been produced by companies employing newer, more collaborative forms of theatrical practice.

Gay and lesbian drama has also gained a prominent voice in the contemporary theater. Though homosexual rights groups existed in Europe and the United States earlier in the century, agitation for the rights and recognition of gay, lesbian, bisexual, and transgendered individuals did not come to the attention of the general public until the late 1960s. The Sexual Offenses Act of 1967 decriminalized most sexual acts between adults in Britain, and the 1969 Stonewall riots in New York galvanized the gay liberation movement in the United States. Perhaps because of its interest in role-playing and its tolerance for unconventional identities, the modern theater has attracted an impressive number of homosexual and bisexual playwrights, including OSCAR WILDE (1854–1900), Gertrude Stein (1874–1946), FEDERICO GARCÍA LORCA (1898–1936), TENNESSEE WILLIAMS (1911–1983), JEAN GENET (1910–1986), Lorraine Hansberry (1930–1965), EDWARD ALBEE (b. 1928), and Joe Orton (1933–1967). Yet only in the 1970s did an openly gay and lesbian drama emerge in its own right. Among the leading writers of this drama is the American playwright Tony Kushner, whose two-part dramatic fantasia *Angels in America* was one of a number of plays during the 1980s and 1990s that addressed the AIDS epidemic. Important authors of lesbian drama include the contemporary American playwright and performance artist Holly Hughes (b. 1955).

THEATER IN THE TWENTY-FIRST CENTURY

As the works of these and other contemporary playwrights indicate, theater remains deeply responsive to social movements, cultural developments, and historical shifts and transformations. As the twenty-first century unfolds, theater—a medium at once traditional and new—offers a unique perspective on the issues and preoccupations of a changing world. One of the oldest of the arts, theater brings nearly 2,500 years of performance forms and dramatic texts to the current historical moment. At the same time, theater is one of the most immediate of the representational arts, grounded in the physical presence of the actor's body and the irreproducible occasion of live performance. Old plays are performed in new contexts, and the resulting dialogue frames both present and past in mutually illuminating ways. *HAMLET* (1600–01) has been performed thousands of times, but every time the Danish prince picks up Yorick's skull—a stage prop—he does it for different audiences in a performance interaction that changes from moment to moment. Its sensitivity to audience and occasion makes theater exceptionally responsive to the complex web of issues, relationships, and interactions that make up the present moment. For this reason, many of the contemporary theater's most important activities have taken place not in traditional theater buildings but in the squares, community centers, and other sites where people gather and work. Health and theater workers have used theater as a vehicle for vaccination campaigns in South America, AIDS education in Africa, and trauma therapy for those victimized by violence around the world. In these and other forms, theater remains deeply important in regions that may not have access to other media, in cultures that rely for education less on print than on oral modes of transmitting information, and with marginalized social groups in other societies.

Theater is more international than it has ever been, and in its emerging and time-honored forms it constitutes an important part of the global cultural landscape. As the expansion and proliferation of media continue in this digitalizing age of multiple entertainment sources, theater and drama carry on traditions that have been handed down for centuries, reworking these conventions in often striking ways and making them responsive to a new century's changing realities.

READING DRAMA, IMAGINING THEATER

For those of us who are used to reading novels and short stories, opening the text of a play can come as something of a surprise. Characters are identified before the story ever begins, in a listing (often labeled *dramatis personae*) that seems more like the entries in an address book than the stuff of literature. Instead of the designations "he said" or "she said" that embed what these characters say within a novel's or short story's unfolding narrative, dialogue is presented directly, with the speakers' names indicated on the left-hand margin. Stage directions indicate when characters enter or exit the dramatic scene, how they move around in relation to each other, and how they handle the objects of their material world. The very world they inhabit feels constrained—even claustrophobic—next to the expansive, shifting settings of *Don Quixote* or *War and Peace*.

Features such as these point to the essential difference between drama and more strictly literary forms such as fiction and poetry. While the term *playwright* means "maker of plays," the written text that we pick up to read provides only a part of the larger phenomenon we call *performance*. Its meanings, in other words, are not limited to the private worlds created by readers as they encounter words on a page. Rather, the printed play is a blueprint for something that happens in real time and space before an audience. The dramatic text in performance thus depends not on a single literary author but on the collective artistry of actors, designers, directors, and others involved in theatrical production. Even those plays—known as "closet dramas"—that were written with the expectation that they would never (or could never) be performed in an actual theater generate imaginative scenarios that have more in common with an audience's experience of watching a play than with a solitary reader's enjoyment. The fact that plays are written with some form of theater in mind—that they exist as dramatic scripts as well as literary works—ensures that the pleasures associated with dramatic art are rich and complex.

As a consequence, to read drama well requires a theatrical imagination attuned to the possible realizations of the dramatic script onstage. The first time we encounter an unfamiliar play, we seek and respond to its narrative—the story it is telling us. But we cannot fully appreciate the impact of such a play unless we consider *how* that story is told and what kind of performance it suggests. Reading plays is an active process—a creative collaboration with the dramatist that takes place in the mind of the reader. As a way of conceiving the dramatic world of a play, it may be helpful to start by envisioning its physical environment, or setting. Where and when is the play set? What and where are the key markers in that location (a door, for example, or a throne)? Some playwrights—particularly those who write under the influence of theatrical realism—include a great deal of information about the play's physical environment, making the stage materialize by supplying a wealth of particular detail. Other dramatic texts provide minimal, or no, setting specifications; for example, SAMUEL BECKETT'S *WAITING FOR GODOT* (1952) includes the famously minimalist direction "A country road. A tree. Evening." Plays written before the nineteenth century often lack place descriptions and depend on the dramatic action and dialogue to establish what is onstage. The settings of Sanskrit drama, for instance, are suggested through dialogue and mimed actions, as when the courtesan Vasantasena mimes stepping into a carriage in SHUDRAKA'S *THE LITTLE CLAY CART* (ca. 100–300 C.E.), while the plays of SHAKESPEARE and his contemporaries establish location through economical, highly evocative verbal description. Knowing something about the production conventions in use during specific periods can help you re-create how a play might have looked to its original audience, but it should not limit your imagination. As the history of theatrical performance indicates, plays are adaptable to other kinds of theaters, stage resources, and production practices.

When visualizing this physical environment, you may wish to make a rough sketch of the scenic environment (or environments) indicated within the dramatic text, so that you can visualize how the characters and locale interact in each scene. Some theatrical terminology is useful here. In many theatrical traditions, locations and movement on stage are designated by a gridlike pattern. The section farthest away from the audience is considered *upstage,* while the area closest to them is *downstage.* Unless otherwise indicated, the sides of the stage are noted from the actor's perspective; hence, *stage right* will be to the actor's right, and *stage left* will be to the actor's left. The midpoint of the stage is called its *center.* Thus, for example, an actor might be told to enter through a door up right and to move (or "cross") to sit on a chair down left. When imagining the layout of a particular scene, it is important to be aware of who is onstage and where, at all times, even when these characters participate only silently in what is going on. Though the presence of such characters may be easy to forget, they may prove pivotal to the action of individual scenes.

Try to envision each character's appearance, as well as how much flexibility there may be in matching the bodily reality of a given actor to the physical description of the character. At some times and in some places, the correspondence between bodily appearance and role has been fairly conventionalized, with recognizable "types" recurring in similar dramatic performances. But even such roles can be taken by actors who vary in appearance, bearing, age, and manner, or even play against type. Throughout theater history, for example, what we now call cross-gender casting and cross-racial casting have been important elements of performance. As part of your effort to visualize the play in performance, you might cast known actors in your imaginary staging to make it more vivid, then substitute others to see how different personalities and styles of acting might shape a role differently. Here, too, the text can be your guide. Is the performance required by the text naturalistic or stylized, comic or serious? In some cases—the stylized theater of Japanese noh, for example—the answer is clear, and by imposing antithetical acting styles you may violate the play's aesthetic underpinnings. In most cases, however, access to a range of acting styles can liberate possibilities within the dramatic text, offering new perspectives and opening it up to new theatrical energies.

In addition, it is useful to pay close attention to what characters say and how they say it. Language is the playwright's principal means for revealing characters and their dramatic world, and the play relies mainly on the spoken word to communicate with its audience. Dramatic speech often reveals important information about the characters, including their class position, geographic origin (especially through dialect), and personality. In the absence of a narrator who might make known to us a character's inner thoughts and feelings, speech is the conduit through which the play's figures disclose their hopes, fears, and intentions. Such characterization rests not simply on what a specific character says but also on what is said about him or her. Indeed, the richness of a dramatic portrait is often the product of multiple—and differing—accounts, observations, and perspectives offered by a play's characters.

Language, of course, is more than information, and nowhere is this truer than in the theater, where language exists not to be read but to be spoken. The words on the page of a dramatic text are designed for the mouth, and as chosen by the best dramatists their sounds fill and guide the mouth, position the body in specific attitudes, and occupy the stage with their acoustic power. When the playwright JOHN MILLINGTON SYNGE wrote that "in a good play every speech should be as fully flavored as a nut or apple," he was referring not just to his own use of Irish dialect but to the linguistic and syntactical richness that makes all great dialogue a kind of vocal music. When bringing a play to theatrical life in your mind, read its lines aloud, feel the emotions they stir in your body, and enjoy the music that they create within your room. By yourself or with a friend, read some of the dialogue, noticing the contrapuntal rhythms that characters establish when they speak together. Even when reading translations—such as the ones included in this anthology, which were selected with vocal and other forms of performability in mind—you can feel such cadences and musicality. Along with the other sounds that a play may require—the ritualized foot stamping of the noh actor, the swish of regal costumes, Feste's lute in Shakespeare's *TWELFTH NIGHT* (1600–01)—the spoken word makes up the soundscape of dramatic performance. Reading with an awareness of this aural power can enhance your understanding and appreciation of drama.

While noting that the spoken language is a primary determinant of dramatic and theatrical meaning, we must not ignore the other elements that reinforce or complicate the acts of expression, communication, and signification. Three texts, in fact, work together in performance: the spoken text, the action text, and the subtext. Whereas the *spoken text*, or dialogue, is what the characters say to each other (or to the audience) during the play, the *action text*—whether scripted by the playwright or created by the director, the actors, or both—is the physical language of the play: the gestures and movements that significantly shape our understanding of the story. In highly conventionalized theater cultures, such as those of classical India and Japan, the actors' movements and gestures become intricate languages in their own right, signifying to an audience that understands their meaning specific relationships, emotions, and attitudes. But directors and actors of all eras have used the action text as a way of communicating meaning, even when the effect of such gestures and movements may be to undermine the sentiments expressed in the spoken text (as when the villain of nineteenth-century melodrama winks at the audience while professing his sincerity to an onstage character). *Subtext* consists of the unspoken thoughts, feelings, and intentions of the characters that underlie and prompt the action and spoken texts. The relationship between the subtext and its manifestation in word and action is as variable in the theater as it is in life. Sometimes language and gesture express the inner life directly and fully. "Language most shows the man; speak that I may see thee," wrote BEN JONSON in a prose collection published shortly after his death. But as ***VOLPONE*** (1606) and other plays by Jonson demonstrate, drama concerns itself more frequently with the discrepancy between private intention and public expression. Characters hide their meanings from others (and occasionally from themselves), feign indifference when they feel love, say only part of what they mean, pursue their designs under the unsuspecting eyes of those they interact with. Even silence—the choice not to speak—plays an important role in conveying contextual meaning.

The dynamic interplay of these three texts—and their interaction with set design, lighting, and the other elements of production—creates the depth and complexity of live theater. When we speak of an actor's interpretation of a role, or a director's concept for a production, we are thinking about the myriad choices that artists make, using these intersecting texts, to develop fully realized characters and to communicate with the audience through the play and its performance. The key word here is "interpretation," for the dramatic text as it exists on its own is fundamentally incomplete, suspended between possible realizations. Because plays are designed for performance, they depend on the activities of actors, directors, designers, stage managers, musicians, and the other theatrical practitioners who have served in different periods to usher them into life. And every choice that is made by these practitioners helps to realize, or interpret, the play in light of its possible range of meanings. Because the combinations of such choices are infinite, no two productions of a play are ever the same, and a great work of dramatic art has an endless capacity to surprise us with new experiences and insights whenever it is performed.

Because reading drama can and should resemble the process of actual production, you should approach the dramatic text as if you were a theater professional. Instead of reading a play to discern preexisting meanings, look for the places where a role, a scene, or a verbal exchange may be performed in different ways, and make choices as to how such components might be interpreted in the theater of your mind. What happens if an actor dwells on certain words in a speech as opposed to others? Where might he or she pause when delivering the lines, and what would be the effect of such vocal punctuation? What subtextual meanings do you see behind words and actions, and how might your actors bring them out? Consider the other elements of production as well. How would you light a production of your play, and what would be the effect of your decisions? How do the meaning and dynamics of a scene change if you focus your light on certain characters rather than others? What costumes do you imagine for your actors, and what would these tell us about the characters they play? Where would you position actors on the stage, and how would they move in relation to each other? Is the stage busy or relatively still during individual scenes? In those plays that lack detailed set descriptions, what theatrical environment do you envision for the action that takes place? Conversely, with plays that have extensive directions, what specific fixtures and objects might you choose to realize the desired effect? Although some dramatists have indicated that they expect their directions be followed exactly in production, would you want to modify the given directions in any way, either to accommodate different kinds of stages or to offer a more radical vision of the play and its dramatic possibilities? As you imagine your play in the theater, you can also consider how much—if any—of the direction provided by the playwright to employ, and what possible impact on an audience such changes in direction might have. Finally, what stage might you choose for a production of your play: a traditional stage, with the audience seated directly in front of the action (the proscenium stage, for instance), or a different stage arrangement, such as one in which the audience is seated on three sides (i.e., "in the round")? How do the meanings and implications of your play change when the spectators are so close to the actors and can see each other as they look at the stage?

Though reading a play in this way does not require extensive familiarity with the theater, your ability to appreciate the theatrical possibilities of a given play will be greatly enriched by the experience of seeing plays performed onstage. Go to the theater when you can; immerse yourself in the moment when the audience grows quiet, the actors enter, and the stage is taken over by a spectacle that is illusory but feels, in its most powerful moments, more real than life itself. And while attending the theater will enhance your reading of dramatic texts, the reverse is also true. Readers who imagine the theater as part of their reading become more informed and responsive audience members, actively aware of the choices the artists have made in interpreting dramatic texts and better able to evaluate their effectiveness. One of the many pleasures of reading drama is measuring your interpretation against actual performances of the play, and comparing those individual performances with each other. Like the aficionados of other arts, you may develop, over a lifetime, your own repertoire of remembered performances and texts. And as you deepen your awareness of the relationship between what is written and what takes place onstage, you may fall under the spell of drama, which—whether enacted in the theater or in your own mind—is timeless yet always new.

THE PLAYS

GEORG BÜCHNER

1813–1837

WHEN Georg Büchner died of typhus at the age of twenty-three, he was known as a political activist and as a lecturer in anatomy, but not as a playwright. Only one major play, *Danton's Death* (1835), had been published during his lifetime, along with his translations of two plays by Victor Hugo. Indeed, Büchner was doomed to obscurity for the greater part of the nineteenth century, as few knew his other dramatic works, which had never been staged. All this changed in the late nineteenth century, when the writer and editor Karl Emil Franzos rediscovered Büchner and made his works available, many for the first time. In the following decades these works, especially the unfinished *WOYZECK*, were greeted with enthusiasm and astonishment by many playwrights, who hailed Büchner as a fellow modernist ahead of his time. Unknown or overlooked for half a century, Büchner's plays eventually came to be seen as the hidden starting point of modern drama. Because *Woyzeck* seems oddly disconnected from its original context, it must be understood within the evolution of Büchner as an author who produced an astonishingly heterogeneous body of work ranging from medical tracts to political pamphlets. *Woyzeck* remains a singular play, but it is also the logical culmination of Büchner's unusual career as a thinker, researcher, political activist, and writer.

Büchner was born into a family of doctors, and after completing high school in Darmstadt he set out to follow in the footsteps of his father. He enrolled in the medical faculty at Strasbourg and quickly excelled in his studies, even as he pursued many other interests. He continued to work as a researcher in Strasbourg and Giessen, and completed a dissertation on the nervous system of a fish. Finally, he was invited to Zurich, where in 1836 he obtained a teaching post in anatomy. His medical work on the nerves of the human skull not only made a significant contribution to anatomical studies but also displayed considerable philosophical ambition, especially in its detailed discussion of philosophers such as Descartes and Spinoza. For Büchner, as for many of his contemporaries, the fields of philosophy and science were intimately related. Consequently, he did not hesitate to use his findings in science to critique philosophy. Büchner strongly believed in materialism—the notion that the world is composed only of matter and can be explained only through observation, experiment, and empirical evidence—and he shunned speculative philosophies of all kinds. His materialism, his work on the nervous system, and his skill in anatomy are central for understanding the power and peculiar force of his literary work.

More than his academic career impelled Büchner's move to Switzerland: he was a fugitive from the German police. During his student days, Büchner had become a political activist. He had been associated with several secret student organizations, inspired by the French Revolution, that demanded the unification of the scattered German small states, the overthrow of the monarchy, and the foundation of a republic. The brutality of the French government against striking workers in Lyon in the early 1830s radicalized him, and he came to believe that to create a just society would require completely overturning the existing laws and social structures. In 1834 he founded the Society for Human Rights and began to agitate on behalf of peasants and workers, whom he saw as exploited by a small leisure class of aristocrats. It was during this time that Büchner wrote the text that first gained the attention of his contemporaries and that caused him to flee from the police: *The Hessian Courier* (1834). In this pamphlet mixing cold analysis and impassioned prose, Büchner described how the tax and political system of his day—and even the rule of law—systematically exploited the many in favor of the few. The text was coauthored with the pastor Dr. Friedrich Ludwig Weidig, who tried to tone down those passages that seemed to call for an all-out class war. A precursor of Marx and Engels's *Communist Manifesto* (1848), *The Hessian Courier* also provides an essential context for understanding Büchner's later focus on class differences, exploitation, and oppression—especially in his last play, *Woyzeck*.

Weidig's changes were not enough. Betrayed by a police spy, the group around Weidig and Büchner was discovered, several members were arrested, and Büchner fled back to Darmstadt. Weidig died in prison two years later, probably as a result of torture. During this unsettled time, Büchner began to work on his first play, clearly inspired by *The Hessian Courier: Danton's Death*. Now a revolutionary writer himself, Büchner turned to the French Revolution for inspiration, but he did so with a critical edge. *Danton's Death* evokes the immense promise of the French Revolution but also its growing violence, indeed its violent self-destruction. The figure responsible for this self-destruction—representing the increasingly violent and radical wing of the revolution—is Robespierre, who finally wins out over the more moderate Danton. In Büchner's play, this battle over the course of the revolution is fought primarily through long political speeches, delivered both to small groups of revolutionaries and to the more public assembly. A number of these speeches are transcribed more or less directly from the historical record. In a letter, Büchner defined the role of the literary writer as an extension of that of the historian.

Büchner would publish no other play in his lifetime, although we have polished drafts of his final dramatic work and masterpiece, *Woyzeck*. Like *Danton's Death*, *Woyzeck* relies on historical sources. It is based on the criminal case of Johann Christian Woyzeck, a schizophrenic soldier who had killed his lover in a fit of jealousy. The main question in the case, and in Büchner's play, is what drove the lowly soldier to commit this crime. Woyzeck's public trial brought to the forefront the relation between law, oppression, and medical psychiatry, which had always been of special interest to Büchner. He was fascinated by the psychiatric diagnoses, the medical language used to describe the soldier's breakdown, but he was also intrigued by the moral and philosophical consequences of that breakdown. The play Büchner forged from the public record is a medical, literary, and philosophical inquiry into madness, devoted to analyzing the different phases of its protagonist's path toward a final, culminating crisis.

The play offers very little continuous action and instead sketches a character portrait of Woyzeck and his estranged relation to Marie, to his fellow soldiers, and to the world at large. Woyzeck is a low character, the quintessential victim who is driven to commit a crime. Büchner preserved the main motivation of the historical case, jealousy: spurred as Marie gradually falls for the better-positioned Drum Major, it ultimately drives Woyzeck to murder. But Büchner also added dramatic material to the case, paying special attention to the re-

A "rotary machine" designed in the early nineteenth century by the physician Sir Alexander Morison for the treatment of mental maladies.

lation between Woyzeck and his superior, the Captain. The Captain demands many kinds of services from his subaltern, even as he repeatedly scolds Woyzeck for having fathered an illegitimate child. The Captain couches his domination over Woyzeck in moral and religious terms. Such morality is too costly for the likes of Woyzeck, however; the soldier's poverty is a constant underlying theme of his existence. Like Büchner's other plays, *Woyzeck* details the psychology of exploitation: it depicts the reactions of the common soldier who suffers small affronts, constant degradation, and finally the humiliation of seeing the mother of his son fall for a rival.

There is a second mode of exploitation at work in this play as well. In order to earn extra cash, Woyzeck lets a local doctor experiment on him. As he follows a strict and cruel diet consisting of nothing but peas, medicine becomes another mode of oppression and of analysis. In the hands of the doctor, Woyzeck becomes nothing but a disposable guinea pig. Throughout the play, Woyzeck is being observed, measured, and observed. More humiliating still, the doctor exhibits the increasingly feeble Woyzeck to medical students, as if he were one of the performing animals that he and Marie had earlier seen at the carnival. Theatrical display, in *Woyzeck*, becomes one more instrument of degradation.

Woyzeck thrives on the collisions between characters and their styles of speaking. Each character employs a different idiom, ranging from Woyzeck's own heavy local dialect to the somewhat more standard speech of his army superiors to the Latinate vocabulary of the doctor. Büchner's language oscillates between abstract nouns such as "nature," "morality," and "necessity" and minute descriptions of corporeal symptoms charted by the doctor, including sexual drive, the consumption of food, and pissing. To this mix is added a metaphorical language of violence: at one point, Woyzeck compares the moon to a "bloody blade," anticipating the murder he will eventually commit with an old knife purchased for the purpose.

In attempting to dramatize the case of Woyzeck, Büchner drew on a number of his previous works. From *Danton's Death,* Büchner took an interest in theater and theatrical modes of display. Much as *Danton's Death* portrays the French Revolution as a kind of theater, complete with public beheadings, *Woyzeck* features the daily humiliation and display of its protagonist. From his minor early play *Leonce and Lena* (written 1836), Büchner drew a tendency toward social satire. A play loosely based on SHAKESPEARE's *As You Like It* (1599), *Leonce and Lena* is full of spoiled and irresponsible characters, whose main motivation is boredom; at the same time, we see the people, hungry and desolate, forced to line up to cheer their hollow and often idiotic leaders. In *Woyzeck,* Büchner made profitable use of these overdrawn satirical characters, now transposed from satire into the dark key of tragedy. Finally, to capture mental illness Büchner drew on his novella, *Lenz* (written 1835). Similarly unfinished and unpublished in Büchner's lifetime, *Lenz* tells the case of a minor eighteenth-century poet, Jakob Michael Reinhold Lenz, who moves to a remote mountain village and suffers a breakdown caused by schizophrenia. The breakdown is described in ruthless detail, mixing medical language with poetic expression—as does *Woyzeck.* The novella tries to capture schizophrenia subjectively, focusing on the distorted perceptions and manic thoughts racing through the protagonist's head. In *Woyzeck,* Büchner tackles the same problem in a dramatic and therefore less subjective form: we, along with Woyzeck's superiors, observe the protagonist from the outside.

Even as it draws on Büchner's previous literary experiments, *Woyzeck* is a startlingly original play, for Büchner did nothing less than invent a new dramatic form, one suited to representing the tragedy of exploitation, humiliation, and mental instability. Its organization into short and stark scenes, loosely connected, is one of the most remarkable features of *Woyzeck,* and it anticipates early twentieth-century episodic drama. That Büchner never finished readying this play for publication has added to the confusion about the precise sequence and nature of these scenes. While they form a marked trajectory—a downward spiral leading to Woyzeck's final breakdown—they are also disjointed and fragmentary, a series of brief episodes without transitions. This peculiar structure offers a formal analogue of Woyzeck's confusion, his inability to draw logical conclusions and to act rationally. As his mind focuses on single encounters, objects, and figures, so the play as a whole presents isolated moments rather than tightly interconnected scenes. In effect, Büchner applied a subjective narrative technique, such as that used in *Lenz,* to drama. Theorists of modern drama sometimes speak of the intrusion of epic or narratives modes into the theater, and *Woyzeck* is a fine case in point. In this sense, too, *Woyzeck* can be considered ahead of its time, blazing the way for twentieth-century epic and expressionist theaters that would showcase similar forms.

Woyzeck has had enormous influence on modern and contemporary drama. It inspired many writers and artists in the late nineteenth and the twentieth centuries, including the naturalist playwright Gerhart Hauptmann, who was fascinated by Büchner's revolutionary method of portraying mental collapse; the expressionist Frank Wedekind, who echoed Büchner's sexualized language of violence in his own work; and BERTOLT BRECHT, who took from *Woyzeck* its episodic structure and the technique of sketching characters with sharp contours. Many acclaimed directors, both in Europe and in America, have staged *Woyzeck;* notable productions include that of the Bread and Puppet Theater, a company that uses large puppets to stunning aesthetic and political effect. Heightening the influence of this play in the twentieth century was its borrowing by Alban Berg, one of the pioneers of modernist music, who used *Woyzeck* as the libretto for his best-known opera, *Wozzeck* (1925). This operatic tradition extends to the early twenty-first century, when the American director Robert Wilson and the musician Tom Waits created a new musical version of *Woyzeck* (2002) to critical acclaim. Equally important has been a film version of the play (1979), directed by Werner Herzog, with Klaus Kinski in the title role. These adaptations testify to the power that this fragmentary play still holds over contemporary theater.

Woyzeck remains one of the most unusual cases in theater history. Written by a twenty-two-year-old lecturer in anatomy, it lay dormant for many decades; once it came to light, it belatedly became a touchstone of modern drama. With its fragmentary, episodic structure, interest in mental instability, and detached, medical precision, it is now seen as the harbinger of modern drama, composed many decades before the plays of HENRIK IBSEN or AUGUST STRIND-

BERG. Indeed, because *Woyzeck* is more daring and radical than almost all examples of late-nineteenth-century modernism, it thwarts all attempts to tell a linear history of modern drama. Somehow, Büchner anticipated what would become routine only much later. *Woyzeck,* like the few extant Greek tragedies, has survived to be read and performed because of lucky accidents—accidents on which theater history, both ancient and modern, often depends.

M.P.

Woyzeck[1]

CHARACTERS

FRANZ WOYZECK
MARIE
CAPTAIN
DOCTOR
DRUM MAJOR
SERGEANT
ANDRES
MARGRET
BARKER
ANNOUNCER
OLD MAN
CHILD
JEW
INNKEEPER
FIRST APPRENTICE
SECOND APPRENTICE
KARL, an idiot
KATEY
GRANDMOTHER
FIRST CHILD
SECOND CHILD
FIRST PERSON
SECOND PERSON
COURT CLERK
JUDGE
Soldiers, Students, Young Men, Girls, Children

4,1

[SCENE: *Open field. The town in the distance.*]

[WOYZECK *and* ANDRES *are cutting branches in the bushes.*]

WOYZECK Yes, Andres—that stripe there across the grass, that's where heads roll at night; once somebody picked one up, he thought it was a hedgehog. Three days and three nights, and he was lying in a coffin. [*Softly*] Andres, it was the Freemasons,[2] that's it, the Freemasons—shh!

ANDRES [*sings*]

I saw two big rabbits
Chewing up the green, green grass . . .

WOYZECK Shh! Something's moving!

1. Translated by Henry J. Schmidt. Büchner left no definitive version of the play, and even the ordering of its scenes is disputed. All versions of the text are therefore reconstructions; the following is based on the reconstruction by Walter Hinderer and Henry J. Schmidt. The numbers at the beginning of each scene indicate which of Büchner's four drafts supplied the text and, after the comma, the scene in that draft.

2. Members of a secret association, founded in its modern form in England in the early 18th century to promote Enlightenment ideals such as brotherly love and charity. Its secret hierarchies and rituals have long made Freemasonry a target for conspiracy theories.

ANDRES

Chewing up the green, green grass
Till it was all gone.

WOYZECK Something's moving behind me, under me. [*Stamps on the ground.*] Hollow—you hear that? It's all hollow down there. The Freemasons!

ANDRES I'm scared.

WOYZECK It's so strangely quiet. You feel like holding your breath. Andres!

ANDRES What?

WOYZECK Say something! [*Stares off into the distance.*] Andres! Look how bright it is! There's fire raging around the sky, and a noise is coming down like trumpets. It's coming closer! Let's go! Don't look back! [*Drags him into the bushes.*]

ANDRES [*after a pause*] Woyzeck! Do you still hear it?

WOYZECK Quiet, it's all quiet, like the world was dead.

ANDRES Listen! They're drumming. We've got to get back.

4,2

[SCENE: *The town.*]

[MARIE *with her* CHILD *at the window.* MARGRET. *A military patrol goes by, the* DRUM MAJOR *leading.*]

MARIE [*rocking the* CHILD *in her arms*] Hey, boy! Ta-ra-ra-ra! You hear it? They're coming.

MARGRET What a man, like a tree!

MARIE He stands on his feet like a lion.

[*The* DRUM MAJOR *greets them.*]

MARGRET Say, what a friendly look you gave him, neighbor—we're not used to that from you.

MARIE [*sings*]

A soldier is a handsome fellow . . .

MARGRET Your eyes are still shining.

MARIE So what? Why don't you take *your* eyes to the Jew[3] and have them polished—maybe they'll shine enough to sell as two buttons.

MARGRET What? Why, Mrs. Virgin, I'm a decent woman, but you—you can stare through seven pairs of leather pants!

MARIE Bitch! [*Slams the window shut.*] Come, my boy. What do they want from us, anyway? You're only the poor child of a whore, and you make your mother happy with your bastard face. Ta-ta!

[*Sings.*]

Maiden, now what's to be done?
You've got no ring, you've a son.
Oh, why worry my head,
I'll sing here at your bed:
Rockabye baby, my baby are you,
Nobody cares what I do.

3. That is, the pawnbroker (historically, moneylending and pawnbroking were among the few professions open to Jews).

Johnny, hitch up your six horses fleet,
Go bring them something to eat.
From oats they will turn,
From water they'll turn,
Only cool wine will be fine, hooray!
Only cool wine will be fine.

[*A knock at the window.*]

MARIE Who's that? Is that you, Franz? Come on in!

WOYZECK I can't. Have to go to roll call.

MARIE What's the matter with you, Franz?

WOYZECK [*mysteriously*] Marie, there was something out there again—a lot. Isn't it written: "And lo, the smoke of the country went up as the smoke of a furnace"?[4]

MARIE Man alive!

WOYZECK It followed me until I reached town. What's going to happen?

MARIE Franz!

WOYZECK I've got to go.

[*He leaves.*]

MARIE That man! He's so upset. He didn't look at his own child. He'll go crazy with those thoughts of his. Why are you so quiet, son? Are you scared? It's getting so dark, you'd think you were blind. Usually there's a light shining in. I can't stand it. I'm frightened.

[*Goes off.*]

4,3

[SCENE: *Carnival booths. Lights. People.*]

OLD MAN; DANCING CHILD

How long we live, just time will tell,
We all have got to die,
We know that very well!

[WOYZECK] Hey! Whee! Poor man, old man! Poor child! Young child! Hey, Marie, shall I carry you? . . . Beautiful world!

CARNIVAL BARKER [*in front of a booth*] Gentlemen! Gentlemen! [*Points to a monkey.*] Look at this creature, as God made it: he's nothing, nothing at all. Now see the effect of art: he walks upright, wears coat and pants, carries a sword! Ho! Take a bow! Good boy. Give me a kiss! [*Monkey trumpets.*] The little dummy is musical!

Ladies and gentlemen, here is to be seen the astronomical horse and the little cannery-birds[5]—they're favorites of all potentates of Europe and members of all learned societies. They'll tell you everything: how old you are, how many children you have, what kind of illnesses. [*Points to the monkey.*] He shoots a pistol, stands on one leg. It's all a matter of upbringing; he has merely a beastly reason, or rather a very reasonable beastliness—he's no brutish individual like a lot of people, present company excepted. Enter!

4. Genesis 19.28 (describing the destruction of the cities of Sodom and Gomorrah).
5. Canaries, perhaps; the German word used here, *Kanaillevögele*, literally means "riffraff birds."

The presentation will begin. The commencement of the beginning will start immediately.

Observe the progress of civilization. Everything progresses—a horse, a monkey, a cannery-bird. The monkey is already a soldier—that's not much, it's the lowest level of the human race!

[WOYZECK] Want to?

MARIE All right. It ought to be good. Look at his tassels, and the woman's got pants on!

[SERGEANT. DRUM MAJOR. MARIE. WOYZECK.]

SERGEANT Hold it! Over there. Look at her! What a piece!

DRUM MAJOR Damn! Good enough for the propagation of cavalry regiments and the breeding of drum majors.

SERGEANT Look how she holds her head—you'd think that black hair would pull her down like a weight. And those eyes, black . . .

DRUM MAJOR It's like looking down a well or a chimney. Come on, after her!

MARIE Those lights!

WOYZECK Yeah, like a big black cat with fiery eyes. Hey, what a night!

[*Inside the booth.*]

CARNIVAL ANNOUNCER [*presenting a horse*] Show your talent! Show your beastly wisdom! Put human society to shame! Gentlemen, this animal that you see here, with a tail on his body, with his four hooves, is a member of all learned societies, is a professor at our university, with whom the students learn to ride and fight duels. That was simple comprehension! Now think with double *raison.*[6] What do you do when you think with double *raison?* Is there in the learned *société*[7] an ass? [*The horse shakes its head.*] Now you understand double *raison!* That is beastiognomy. Yes, that's no brutish individual, that's a person! A human being, a beastly human being, but still an animal, a *bête.*[8] [*The horse behaves improperly.*] That's right, put *société* to shame! You see, the beast is still nature, unspoiled nature! Take a lesson from him. Go ask the doctor, it's very unhealthy! It is written: man, be natural; you were created from dust, sand, dirt.[9] Do you want to be more than dust, sand, dirt? Observe his power of reason! He can add, but he can't count on his fingers—why is that? He simply can't express himself, explain himself—he's a transformed person! Tell the gentlemen what time it is. Who among the ladies and gentlemen has a watch—a watch?

DRUM MAJOR A watch! [*Slowly and grandly he pulls a watch out of his pocket.*] There you are, sir.

MARIE This I've got to see.

[*She climbs into the first row. The* DRUM MAJOR *helps her.*]

4,4

[SCENE: *Room.*]

[MARIE *sits with her* CHILD *on her lap, a piece of mirror in her hand.*]

MARIE [*looks at herself in the mirror*] These stones really sparkle! What kind are they? What did he say?—Go to sleep, son! Shut your eyes tight. [*The*

6. Reason (French).
7. Society (French).
8. Beast, animal (French).
9. For the creation of man from dust, see Genesis 2.7.

CHILD *covers his eyes with his hands.*] Tighter—stay quiet or he'll come get you.

[*Sings.*]

Close up your shop, fair maid,
A gypsy boy's in the glade.
He'll lead you by the hand
Off into gypsyland.

[*Looks in the mirror again.*] It must be gold. The likes of us only have a little corner in the world and a little piece of mirror, but I have just as red a mouth as the great ladies with their mirrors from top to toe and their handsome lords who kiss their hands. I'm just a poor woman. [*The* CHILD *sits up.*] Shh, son, eyes shut—look, the sandman! He's running along the wall. [*She flashes with the mirror.*] Eyes shut, or he'll look into them, and you'll go blind.

[WOYZECK *enters behind her. She jumps up with her hands over her ears.*]

WOYZECK What's that you got there?

MARIE Nothing.

WOYZECK Something's shining under your fingers.

MARIE An earring—I found it.

WOYZECK I've never found anything like that. Two at once.

MARIE What am I—a whore?

WOYZECK It's all right, Marie.—Look, the boy's asleep. Lift him up under his arms, the chair's hurting him. There are shiny drops on his forehead; everything under the sun is work—sweat, even in our sleep. Us poor people! Here's some more money, Marie, my pay and some from my captain.

MARIE Bless you, Franz.

WOYZECK I have to go. See you tonight, Marie. Bye.

MARIE [*alone, after a pause*] What a bitch I am. I could stab myself.—Oh, what a world! Everything goes to hell anyhow, man and woman alike.

4,5

[*The* CAPTAIN. WOYZECK.]

[*The* CAPTAIN *in a chair,* WOYZECK *shaves him.*]

CAPTAIN Take it easy, Woyzeck, take it easy. One thing at a time; you're making me quite dizzy. You're going to finish early today—what am I supposed to do with the extra ten minutes? Woyzeck, just think, you've still got a good thirty years to live, thirty years! That's 360 months, and days, hours, minutes! What are you going to do with that ungodly amount of time? Get organized, Woyzeck.

WOYZECK Yes, Cap'n.

CAPTAIN I fear for the world when I think about eternity. Activity, Woyzeck, activity! Eternal, that's eternal, that's eternal—you realize that, of course. But then again it's not eternal, it's only a moment, yes, a moment.—Woyzeck, it frightens me to think that the earth rotates in one day—what a waste of time, what will come of that? Woyzeck, I can't look at a mill wheel anymore or I get melancholy.

WOYZECK Yes, Cap'n.

CAPTAIN Woyzeck, you always look so upset. A good man doesn't act like that, a good man with a good conscience. Say something, Woyzeck. What's the weather like today?

WOYZECK It's bad, Cap'n, bad—wind.

CAPTAIN I can feel it, there's something rapid out there. A wind like that reminds me of a mouse. [*Cunningly*] I believe it's coming from the south-north.

WOYZECK Yes, Cap'n.

CAPTAIN Ha! Ha! Ha! South-north! Ha! Ha! Ha! Oh, are you stupid, terribly stupid. [*Sentimentally*] Woyzeck, you're a good man, a good man—[*with dignity*] but Woyzeck, you've got no morality. Morality—that's when you are moral, you understand. It's a good word. You have a child without the blessing of the church, as our Reverend Chaplain says, without the blessing of the church—*I* didn't say it.

WOYZECK Cap'n, the good Lord isn't going to look at a poor little kid only because amen was said over it before it was created. The Lord said: "Suffer little children to come unto me."[1]

CAPTAIN What's that you're saying? What kind of a crazy answer is that? You're getting me all confused with your answer. When I say *you*, I mean you—you!

WOYZECK Us poor people. You see, Cap'n—money, money. If you don't have money. Just try to raise your own kind on morality in this world. After all, we're flesh and blood. The likes of us are wretched in this world and in the next; I guess if we ever got to Heaven, we'd have to help with the thunder.

CAPTAIN Woyzeck, you have no virtue, you're not a virtuous person. Flesh and blood? When I'm lying at the window after it has rained, and I watch the white stockings as they go tripping down the street—damn it, Woyzeck, then love comes all over me. I've got flesh and blood, too. But Woyzeck, virtue, virtue! How else could I make time go by? I always say to myself: you're a virtuous man, [*Sentimentally*] a good man, a good man.

WOYZECK Yes, Cap'n, virtue! I haven't figured it out yet. You see, us common people, we don't have virtue, we act like nature tells us—but if I was a gentleman, and had a hat and a watch and an overcoat and could talk refined, then I'd be virtuous, too. Virtue must be nice, Cap'n. But I'm just a poor guy.

CAPTAIN That's fine, Woyzeck. You're a good man, a good man. But you think too much, that's unhealthy—you always look so upset. This discussion has really worn me out. You can go now—and don't run like that! Slow, nice and slow down the street.

4,6

[MARIE. DRUM MAJOR.]

DRUM MAJOR Marie!

MARIE [*looking at him expressively*] Go march up and down for me.—A chest like a bull and a beard like a lion. Nobody else is like that.—No woman is prouder than me.

1. That is, allow infants to be brought to receive Jesus' blessing (Luke 18.16; see also Matthew 19.14; Mark 10.14).

DRUM MAJOR Sundays when I have my plumed helmet and my white gloves—goddamn, Marie! The prince always says: man, you're quite a guy!

MARIE [*mockingly*] Aw, go on! [*Goes up to him.*] What a man!

DRUM MAJOR What a woman! Hell, let's breed a race of drum majors, hey? [*He embraces her.*]

MARIE [*moody*] Leave me alone!

DRUM MAJOR You wildcat!

MARIE [*violently*] Just try to touch me!

DRUM MAJOR Is the devil in your eyes?

MARIE For all I care. What does it matter?

4,7

[MARIE. WOYZECK.]

WOYZECK [*stares at her, shakes his head*] Hm! I don't see anything, I don't see anything. Oh, I should be able to see it; I should be able to grab it with my fists.

MARIE [*intimidated*] What's the matter, Franz? You're out of your mind, Franz.

WOYZECK A sin so fat and so wide—it stinks enough to smoke the angels out of Heaven. You've got a red mouth, Marie. No blister on it? Good-bye, Marie, you're as beautiful as sin.—Can mortal sin be so beautiful?

MARIE Franz, you're delirious.

WOYZECK Damn it!—Was he standing here like this, like this?

MARIE As the day is long and the world is old, lots of people can stand on one spot, one after another.

WOYZECK I saw him.

MARIE You can see all sorts of things if you've got two eyes and aren't blind, and the sun is shining.

WOYZECK [With my own eyes!]

MARIE [*fresh*] So what!

4,8

[WOYZECK. *The* DOCTOR.]

DOCTOR What's this I saw, Woyzeck? A man of his word!

WOYZECK What is it, Doctor?

DOCTOR I saw it, Woyzeck—you pissed on the street, you pissed on the wall like a dog. And even though you get two cents a day. Woyzeck, that's bad. The world's getting bad, very bad.

WOYZECK But Doctor, the call of nature . . .

DOCTOR The call of nature, the call of nature! Nature! Haven't I proved that the *musculus constrictor vesicae*[2] is subject to the will? Nature! Woyzeck, man is free; in man alone is individuality exalted to freedom. Couldn't hold it in! [*Shakes his head, puts his hands behind his back, and paces back and forth.*] Did you eat your peas already, Woyzeck?—I'm revolutionizing science, I'll blow it sky-high. Urea ten per cent, ammonium chloride, hyperoxidic.[3] Woyzeck, don't you have to piss again? Go in there and try.

2. The muscle that controls the urethral sphincter (Latin).

3. Apparently an analysis (though a somewhat nonsensical one) of Woyzeck's urine.

WOYZECK I can't, Doctor.

DOCTOR [*with emotion*] But pissing on the wall! I have it in writing, here's the contract. I saw it all, saw it with my own eyes—I was just holding my nose out the window, letting the sun's rays hit it, so as to examine the process of sneezing. [*Starts kicking him.*] No, Woyzeck, I'm not getting angry; anger is unhealthy, unscientific. I am calm, perfectly calm—my pulse is beating at its usual sixty, and I'm telling you this in all cold-bloodedness! Who on earth would get excited about a human being, a human being! Now if it were a Proteus lizard[4] that were dying! But you shouldn't have pissed on the wall . . .

WOYZECK You see, Doctor, sometimes you've got a certain character, a certain structure.—But with nature, that's something else, you see, with nature—[*He cracks his knuckles.*] that's like—how should I put it—for example . . .

DOCTOR Woyzeck, you're philosophizing again.

WOYZECK [*confidingly*] Doctor, have you ever seen anything of double nature? When the sun's standing high at noon and the world seems to be going up in flames, I've heard a terrible voice talking to me!

DOCTOR Woyzeck, you've got an *aberratio!*[5]

WOYZECK [*puts his finger to his nose*] The toadstools, Doctor. There—that's where it is. Have you seen how they grow in patterns? If only someone could read that.

DOCTOR Woyzeck, you've got a marvelous *aberratio mentalis partialis,* second species,[6] beautifully developed. Woyzeck, you're getting a raise. Second species: obsession with a generally rational condition. You're doing everything as usual—shaving your captain?

WOYZECK Yes, sir.

DOCTOR Eating your peas?

WOYZECK Same as ever, Doctor. My wife gets the money for the household.

DOCTOR Going on duty?

WOYZECK Yes, sir.

DOCTOR You're an interesting case. Subject Woyzeck, you're getting a raise. Now behave yourself. Show me your pulse! Yes.

4,9

[CAPTAIN. DOCTOR.]

CAPTAIN Doctor, I'm afraid for the horses when I think that the poor beasts have to go everywhere on foot. Don't run like that! Don't wave your cane around in the air like that! You'll run yourself to death that way. A good man with a good conscience doesn't go so fast. A good man. [*He catches the* DOCTOR *by the coat.*] Doctor, allow me to save a human life. You're racing . . .

Doctor, I'm so melancholy, I get so emotional, I always start crying when I see my coat hanging on the wall—there it is.

DOCTOR Hm! Bloated, fat, thick neck, apoplectic constitution. Yes, Captain, you might be stricken by an *apoplexia cerebralis.*[7] But you might get it just on one side and be half paralyzed, or—best of all—you might become mentally affected and just vegetate from then on: those are approximately your

4. A kind of large, rare salamander, found in Austria (also called an olm).
5. Aberration (Latin).
6. Distinct class. *Aberration mentalis partialis:* partial mental aberration (Latin).
7. Cerebral apoplexy (Latin); that is, cerebral hemorrhage, stroke.

prospects for the next four weeks. Moreover, I can assure you that you will be a most interesting case, and if, God willing, your tongue is partially paralyzed, we'll make immortal experiments.

CAPTAIN Doctor, don't frighten me! People have been known to die of fright, of pure, sheer fright.—I can see them now, with their hats in their hands—but they'll say, he was a good man, a good man.—You damn coffin nail!

DOCTOR [*holds out his hat*] What's this, Captain? That's brainless!

CAPTAIN [*makes a crease*] What's this, Doctor? That's in-crease!

DOCTOR I take my leave, most honorable Mr. Drillprick.

CAPTAIN Likewise, dearest Mr. Coffin Nail.

4,10

[SCENE: *The guardroom.*]

[WOYZECK. ANDRES.]

ANDRES [*sings*]

Our hostess has a pretty maid,
She's in her garden night and day,
She sits inside her garden . . .

WOYZECK Andres!

ANDRES Huh?

WOYZECK Nice weather.

ANDRES Sunday weather. There's music outside town. All the broads are out there already, everybody's sweating—it's really moving along.

WOYZECK [*restlessly*] A dance, Andres, they're dancing.

ANDRES Yeah, at the Horse and at the Star.

WOYZECK Dancing, dancing.

ANDRES Big deal.

[*Sings.*]

She sits inside her garden,
Until the bells have all struck twelve,
And stares at all the soo-ooldiers.

WOYZECK Andres, I can't keep still.

ANDRES Fool!

WOYZECK I've got to get out of here. Everything's spinning before my eyes. How hot their hands are. Damn it, Andres!

ANDRES What do you want?

WOYZECK I've got to go.

ANDRES With that whore.

WOYZECK I've got to get out. It's so hot in here.

4,11

[SCENE: *Inn.*]

[*The windows are open, a dance. Benches in front of the house.* APPRENTICES.]

FIRST APPRENTICE

This shirt I've got, I don't know whose,
My soul it stinks like booze . . .

SECOND APPRENTICE Brother, shall I in friendship bore a hole in your nature? Dammit, I want to bore a hole in your nature. I'm quite a guy, too, you know—I'm going to kill all the fleas on his body.

FIRST APPRENTICE My soul, my soul it stinks like booze.—Even money eventually decays. Forget-me-not! Oh, how beautiful this world is. Brother, I could cry a rain barrel full of tears. I wish our noses were two bottles and we could pour them down each other's throats.

OTHERS [*in chorus*]

A hunter from the west
Once went riding through the woods.
Hip-hip, hooray! A hunter has a merry life,
O'er meadow and o'er stream,
Oh, hunting is my dream!

[WOYZECK *stands at the window.* MARIE *and the* DRUM MAJOR *dance past without seeing him.*]

MARIE [*dancing by*] On! and on, on and on!

WOYZECK [*chokes*] On and on—on and on! [*Jumps up violently and sinks back on the bench.*] On and on, on and on. [*Beats his hands together.*] Spin around, roll around. Why doesn't God blow out the sun so that everything can roll around in lust, man and woman, man and beast. Do it in broad daylight, do it on our hands, like flies.—Woman!—That woman is hot, hot! On and on, on and on. [*Jumps up.*] The bastard! Look how he's grabbing her, grabbing her body! He—he's got her now, [like I used to have her.]

FIRST APPRENTICE [*preaches on the table*] Yet when a wanderer stands leaning against the stream of time or gives answer for the wisdom of God, asking himself: Why does man exist? Why does man exist?—But verily I say unto you: how could the farmer, the cooper, the shoemaker, the doctor exist if God hadn't created man? How could the tailor exist if God hadn't given man a feeling of shame? How could the soldier exist, if men didn't feel the necessity of killing one another? Therefore, do not ye despair, yes, yes, it is good and pleasant, yet all that is earthly is passing, even money eventually decays.—In conclusion, my dear friends, let us piss crosswise so that a Jew will die.

4,12

[SCENE: *Open field.*]

WOYZECK On and on! On and on! Shh—music. [*Stretches out on the ground.*] Ha—what, what are you saying? Louder, louder—stab, stab the bitch to death? Stab, stab the bitch to death. Should I? Must I? Do I hear it over there too, is the wind saying it too? Do I hear it on and on—stab her to death, to death.

4,13

[SCENE: *Night.*]

[ANDRES *and* WOYZECK *in a bed.*]

WOYZECK [*shakes* ANDRES] Andres! Andres! I can't sleep—when I close my eyes, everything starts spinning, and I hear the fiddles, on and on, on and on. And then there's a voice from the wall—don't you hear anything?

ANDRES Oh, yeah—let them dance! God bless us, amen. [*Falls asleep again.*]
WOYZECK And it floats between my eyes like a knife.
ANDRES Drink some brandy with a painkiller in it. That'll bring your fever down.

4,14

[SCENE: *Inn.*]

[DRUM MAJOR. WOYZECK. *People.*]

DRUM MAJOR I'm a man! [*Pounds his chest.*] A man, I say. Who wants to start something? If you're not drunk as a lord, stay away from me. I'll shove your nose up your ass. I'll . . . [*To* WOYZECK] Man, have a drink. A man gotta drink. I wish the world was booze, booze.
WOYZECK [*whistles*]
DRUM MAJOR You bastard, you want me to pull your tongue out of your throat and wrap it around you? [*They wrestle,* WOYZECK *loses.*] Shall I leave you as much breath as an old woman's fart? Shall I?

[WOYZECK *sits on the bench, exhausted and trembling.*]

DRUM MAJOR He can whistle till he's blue in the face. Ha!

Oh, brandy, that's my life,
Oh, brandy gives me courage!

A PERSON He sure got what was coming to him.
ANOTHER He's bleeding.
WOYZECK One thing after another.

4,15

[WOYZECK. THE JEW.]

WOYZECK The pistol costs too much.
JEW Well, do you want it or don't you?
WOYZECK How much is the knife?
JEW It's good and straight. You want to cut your throat with it? Well, how about it? I'll give it to you as cheap as anybody else; your death'll be cheap, but not for nothing. How about it? You'll have an economical death.
WOYZECK That can cut more than just bread.
JEW Two cents.
WOYZECK There!

[*Goes off.*]

JEW There! Like it was nothing. But it's money! The dog.

4,16

[MARIE. KARL, *the idiot.* CHILD.]

MARIE [*leafs through the Bible*] "And no guile is found in his mouth"[8] . . . My God, my God! Don't look at me. [*Pages further.*] "And the scribes and Pharisees brought unto him a woman taken in adultery, and set her in the midst . . . And Jesus said unto her, 'Neither do I condemn thee: go, and sin no more.'"[9] [*Clasps her hands together.*] My God! My God! I can't. God,

8. A close echo of 1 Peter 2.22, where Jesus is described as a model of patient suffering.

9. John 8.3, 11.

just give me enough strength to pray. [*The* CHILD *snuggles up to her.*] The boy is like a knife in my heart. [Karl! He's sunning himself!]

KARL [*lies on the ground and tells himself fairy tales on his fingers*] This one has a golden crown—he's a king. Tomorrow I'll go get the queen's child. Blood sausage says, come, liver sausage! [*He takes the* CHILD *and is quiet.*]

[MARIE] Franz hasn't come, not yesterday, not today. It's getting hot in here. [*She opens the window.*] "And stood at his feet weeping, and began to wash his feet with tears, and did wipe them with the hairs of her head, and kissed his feet, and anointed them with ointment."[1] [*Beats her breast.*] It's all dead! Savior, Savior, I wish I could anoint your feet.

4,17

[SCENE: *The barracks.*]

[ANDRES. WOYZECK *rummages through his things.*]

WOYZECK This jacket isn't part of the uniform, Andres; you can use it, Andres. The crucifix is my sister's, and the little ring. I've got an icon, too—two hearts and nice gold. It was in my mother's Bible, and it says:

May pain be my reward,
Through pain I love my Lord.
Lord, like Thy body, red and sore,
So be my heart forevermore.

My mother can only feel the sun shining on her hands now. That doesn't matter.

ANDRES [*blankly, answers to everything*] Yeah.

WOYZECK [*pulls out a piece of paper*] Friedrich Johann Franz Woyzeck, enlisted infantryman in the second regiment, second battalion, fourth company, born . . . Today I'm thirty years, seven months, and twelve days old.

ANDRES Franz, you better go to the infirmary. You poor guy—drink brandy with a painkiller in it. That'll kill the fever.

WOYZECK You know, Andres, when the carpenter nails those boards together, nobody knows who'll be laying his head on them.

[*End of Büchner's revision.*]

[*Scenes from the First Draft:*]

1,14

[SCENE: *Street.*]

[MARIE *with girls in front of the house door.* GRANDMOTHER. *Then* WOYZECK.]

GIRLS

How bright the sun on Candlemas Day,[1]
On fields of golden grain.
As two by two they marched along
Down the country lane.

1. Luke 7.38; the "she" is a woman described in the preceding verse as "a sinner."

1. The Roman Catholic celebration (February 2) of the day on which Jesus first came to the temple and was blessed (see Luke 2.22).

The pipers up in front,
The fiddlers in a chain.
Their red socks . . .

FIRST CHILD That's not nice.
SECOND CHILD What do you want, anyway?
[**OTHERS**] Why'd you start it?

Yeah, why?

I can't.

Because!

Who's going to sing?

Why because?

Marie, you sing to us.
MARIE Come, you little shrimps.

[*Children's games: "Ring-around-a-rosy" and "King Herod."*]

Grandmother, tell a story.
GRANDMOTHER Once upon a time there was a poor child with no father and no mother, everything was dead, and no one was left in the whole world. Everything was dead, and it went and searched day and night. And since nobody was left on the earth, it wanted to go up to the heavens, and the moon was looking at it so friendly, and when it finally got to the moon, the moon was a piece of rotten wood and then it went to the sun and when it got there, the sun was a wilted sunflower and when it got to the stars, they were little golden flies stuck up there like the shrike sticks 'em on the blackthorn and when it wanted to go back down to the earth, the earth was an overturned pot and was all alone and it sat down and cried and there it sits to this day, all alone.
WOYZECK Marie!
MARIE [*startled*] What is it?
WOYZECK Marie, we have to go. It's time.
MARIE Where to?
WOYZECK How do I know?

1,15

[**MARIE** *and* **WOYZECK**.]

MARIE So the town is over there—it's dark.
WOYZECK Stay here. Come on, sit down.
MARIE But I have to get back.
WOYZECK You won't get sore feet.
MARIE What's gotten into you!
WOYZECK Do you know how long it's been, Marie?
MARIE Two years since Pentecost.[2]
WOYZECK And do you know how long it's going to be?
MARIE I've got to go, the evening dew is falling.
WOYZECK Are you freezing, Marie? But you're warm. How hot your lips are!—Hot, the hot breath of a whore—and yet I'd give heaven and earth to

2. A Christian festival celebrated seven weeks after Easter, commemorating the descent of the Holy Spirit upon the apostles.

kiss them once more. And when you're cold, you don't freeze anymore. The morning dew won't make you freeze.

MARIE What are you talking about?

WOYZECK Nothing. [*Silence.*]

MARIE Look how red the moon is.

WOYZECK Like a bloody blade.

MARIE What are you up to? Franz, you're so pale. [*He pulls out the knife.*] Franz—wait! For God's sake—help!

WOYZECK Take that and that! Can't you die? There! There! Ah—she's still twitching—not yet? Not yet? Still alive? [*Stabs once again.*] Are you dead? Dead! Dead!

[*People approach, he runs off.*]

1,16

[*Two people.*]

FIRST PERSON Wait!

SECOND PERSON You hear it? Shh! Over there.

FIRST PERSON Ooh! There! What a sound.

SECOND PERSON That's the water, it's calling. Nobody has drowned for a long time. Let's go—it's bad to hear things like that.

FIRST PERSON Ooh! There it is again. Like someone dying.

SECOND PERSON It's weird. It's so fragrant—some gray fog, and the beetles humming like broken bells. Let's get out of here!

FIRST PERSON No—it's too clear, too loud. Up this way. Come on.

1,17

[SCENE. *The inn.*]

[WOYZECK. KATEY. KARL. INNKEEPER. *People.*]

WOYZECK Dance, all of you, on and on, sweat and stink—he'll get you all in the end.

[*Sings.*]

Our hostess has a pretty maid,
She's in her garden night and day,
She sits inside her garden,
Until the bells have all struck twelve,
And stares at all the soldiers.

[*He dances.*] Come on, Katey! Sit down! I'm hot! Hot. [*He takes off his jacket.*] That's the way it is: the devil takes one and lets the other go. Katey, you're hot! Why? Katey, you'll be cold someday, too. Be reasonable. Can't you sing something?

[KATEY]

For Swabian[3] hills I do not yearn,
And flowing gowns I always spurn,
For flowing gowns and pointed shoes
A servant girl should never choose.

3. Of Swabia, a mountainous region of southwestern Germany.

[WOYZECK] No, no shoes—you can go to hell without shoes, too.
[KATEY]

For shame, my love, I'm not your own,
Just keep your money and sleep alone.

[WOYZECK] Yes, that's right, I don't want to make myself bloody.
KATEY But what's that on your hand?
WOYZECK Who? Me?
KATEY Red! Blood!

[*People gather around.*]

WOYZECK Blood? Blood?
INNKEEPER Ooh, blood.
WOYZECK I guess I must have cut myself, there on my right hand.
INNKEEPER But how'd it get on your elbow?
WOYZECK I wiped it off.
INNKEEPER What, with your right hand on your right elbow? You're talented.
KARL And then the giant said: I smell, I smell, I smell human flesh. Phew! That stinks already.
WOYZECK Damn it, what do you want? What's it got to do with you? Get away, or the first one who—damn it! You think I killed someone? Am I a murderer? What are you staring at? Look at yourselves! Out of my way!

[*He runs out.*]

1,18

[*Children.*]

FIRST CHILD Come on! Marie!
SECOND CHILD What is it?
FIRST CHILD Don't you know? Everybody's gone out there already. Someone's lying there!
SECOND CHILD Where?
FIRST CHILD To the left through the trench, near the red cross.
SECOND CHILD Let's go, so we can still see something. Otherwise they'll carry her away.

1,19

[WOYZECK *alone.*]

WOYZECK The knife? Where's the knife? Here's where I left it. It'll give me away! Closer, still closer! What kind of a place is this? What's that I hear? Something's moving. Shh! Over there. Marie? Ah—Marie! Quiet. Everything's quiet! Why are you so pale, Marie? Why is that red thread around your neck? Who helped you earn that necklace, with your sins? They made you black, black! Now I've made you white. Why does your black hair hang so wild? Didn't you do your braids today? Something's lying over there! Cold, wet, still. Got to get away from here. The knife, the knife—is that it? There! People—over there.

[*He runs off.*]

1,20

[WOYZECK *at a pond.*]

WOYZECK Down it goes! [*He throws the knife in.*] It sinks into the dark water like a stone! The moon is like a bloody blade! Is the whole world going to give me away? No, it's too far in front—when people go swimming—[*He goes into the pond and throws it far out.*] All right, now—but in the summer, when they go diving for shells—bah, it'll rust. Who'll recognize it? I wish I'd smashed it! Am I still bloody? I've got to wash myself. There's a spot[4]—and there's another.

1,21

[COURT CLERK. BARBER. DOCTOR. JUDGE.]

[CLERK] A good murder, a real murder, a beautiful murder—as good a murder as you'd ever want to see. We haven't had one like this for a long time.

3,1[5]

[SCENE: *The* PROFESSOR*'s courtyard.*]

[*Students below, the* PROFESSOR *at the attic window.*]

[PROFESSOR] Gentlemen, I am on the roof like David when he saw Bathsheba,[6] but all I see is underwear on a clothesline in the garden of the girls' boarding house. Gentlemen, we are dealing with the important question of the relationship of subject to object. If we take only one of the things in which the organic self-affirmation of the Divine manifests itself to a high degree, and examine its relationship to space, to the earth, to the planetary system—gentlemen, if I throw this cat out of the window, how will this organism relate to the *centrum gravitationis*[7] and to its own instinct? Hey, Woyzeck. [*Shouts.*] Woyzeck!

WOYZECK Professor, it bites!

PROFESSOR The fellow holds the beast so tenderly, like it was his grandmother!

WOYZECK Doctor [*sic*], I've got the shivers.

DOCTOR [*elated*] Say, that's wonderful, Woyzeck! [*Rubs his hands. He takes the cat.*] What's this I see, gentlemen—a new species of rabbit louse, a beautiful species, quite different, deep in the fur. [*He pulls out a magnifying glass.*] Ricinus,[8] gentlemen! [*The cat runs off.*] Gentlemen, that animal has no scientific instinct. Ricinus—the best examples—bring your fur collars. Gentlemen, instead of that you can see something else: take note of this man—for a quarter of a year he hasn't eaten anything but peas. Notice the result—feel how uneven his pulse is. There—and the eyes.

WOYZECK Doctor, everything's getting black.

[*He sits down.*]

4. A phrase that recalls the attempts of Shakespeare's sleepwalking Lady Macbeth to cleanse her hands after committing murder (*Macbeth* [1606] 5.1).

5. The first of two optional scenes.

6. David, king of Israel (ca. 1010–970 B.C.E.), was said to have seen the beautiful Bathsheba bathing herself (2 Samuel 11.2).

7. Center of gravity (Latin).

8. Tick (Latin); that is, the louse.

DOCTOR Courage, Woyzeck—just a few more days, and then it'll be all over. Feel him, gentlemen, feel him.

[*Students feel his temples, pulse, and chest.*]

Apropos, Woyzeck, wiggle your ears for the gentlemen; I meant to show it to you before. He uses two muscles. Come on, hop to it!

WOYZECK Oh, Doctor!

DOCTOR You dog, shall I wiggle them for you, are you going to act like the cat? So, gentlemen, this represents a transition to the donkey, frequently resulting from being brought up by women and from the use of the mother tongue. How much hair has your mother pulled out for a tender memory? It's gotten very thin in the last few days. Yes, the peas, gentlemen.

3,2[9]

[KARL, *the idiot. The* CHILD. WOYZECK.]

KARL [*holds the* CHILD *on his lap*] He fell in the water, he fell in the water, he fell in the water.

WOYZECK Son—Christian![1]

KARL [*stares at him*] He fell in the water.

WOYZECK [*wants to caress the* CHILD, *who turns away and screams*] My God!

KARL He fell in the water.

WOYZECK Christian, you'll get a hobbyhorse. Da-da! [*The* CHILD *resists. To* KARL] Here, go buy the boy a hobbyhorse.

KARL [*stares at him*]

WOYZECK Hop! Hop! Horsey!

KARL [*cheers*] Hop! Hop! Horsey! Horsey!

[*Runs off with the* CHILD.]

9. The second of two optional scenes.

1. That is, baptized by the water.

WILLIAM WELLS BROWN

1814–1884

William Wells Brown is a remarkable figure in the history of nineteenth-century American literature. An escaped slave who became a successful orator on the northern abolitionist circuit, he earned a place as the first African American man of letters, breaking important ground in a number of literary genres. In addition to producing a widely read narrative of his experiences as a slave, the first African American travel narrative, and a number of other books, Brown wrote the first novel by an African American (*Clotel; or, The President's Daughter: A Narrative of Slave Life in the United States* [1853]), and the first African American play to be published: ***THE ESCAPE; OR, A LEAP FOR FREEDOM*** (1858). Until recently, Brown's activities as a dramatist occupied little more than a footnote to his work in other genres. Now, however, as part of the scholarly effort over the past several decades to revalue forgotten or neglected works in American and dramatic literature, *The Escape* is coming to be seen not only as an important work in mid-nineteenth-century antislavery literature but also as a play of considerable force and interest. Appropriating the dramatic conventions of melodrama, minstrelsy, and other nineteenth-century dramatic forms, *The Escape* offers a fascinating examination of race, representation, and identity in antebellum America.

Brown was born on a plantation near Lexington, Kentucky, in 1814. His mother was a slave named Elizabeth, and his father, a white man, was a relative of the plantation owner, Dr. John Young, who took his slaves and other movable property to Missouri (near St. Louis) in 1816. Young William worked as a coachman, field hand, and physician's assistant, and he was hired out for work in a tavern, hotel, printing office, and steamboat. When he was sixteen he worked for a slave trader named James Walker, and during the three trips he made to the New Orleans slave market over the course of that year he experienced the horrors associated with this commercial aspect of slavery. After a failed attempt to escape with his mother in 1833 he was sold twice, the second time to a St. Louis merchant and steamboat owner named Enoch Price. On a steamboat trip with the Price family in 1834 William escaped for good when the boat docked in Cincinnati. Encountering difficulty on the route to Cleveland, he found help with a Quaker couple; in gratitude for their care and assistance, he adopted the man's name—Wells Brown—as his middle name and surname.

Over the next eight years Brown worked as a steamboatman in Cleveland, then in Buffalo, New York, and as a conductor on the Underground Railroad, a network of sympathetic northern whites and free blacks who ferried fugitive slaves to the northern states or to Canada, where slavery was illegal. In 1843 Brown began lecturing on the antislavery circuit, and four years later he published his autobiography, *Narrative of William W. Brown, A Fugitive Slave,* which went through eight British and American editions by 1851. In 1849 Brown traveled to England, and after passage of the Fugitive Slave Law (1850), which forced escaped slaves in the northern states to be returned to the South, he decided to stay there, delivering hundreds of antislavery lectures until his freedom was purchased from his former master and he returned to Boston in 1854. By this time he had published his travel narrative, *Three Years in Europe; or, Places I Have Seen and People I Have Met* (1852), and the novel *Clotel,* which was based on the long-standing rumor that Thomas Jefferson had fathered a child with Sally Hemings, his slave.

Now legally free, Brown continued to write and lecture extensively in Boston and throughout the northern states. In 1856 he added a performance element to his antislavery appearances with readings of his first play, *Experience; or, How to Give a Northern Man a Backbone.* This play, which we know only through secondhand accounts, was a satire on the Reverend Dr. Nehemiah Adams's rosy portrayal of slavery in *A South-Side View of Slavery; or, Three Months in the South* (1854). Through a clever inversion, Brown exposes the naiveté of Adams's first-person account. Jeremiah Adderson, the northern doctor of divinity in Brown's play, finds himself sold into slavery while on a tour of the South. Exposed in this way to the realities of slavery, he is forced to change his view on the institution and returns to the North to join the Underground Railroad. Brown's readings of the play, which ended with an escaped slave's impassioned appeal against slavery, were immensely popular; in the words of one reviewer, "There are many vivid, graphic, and thrilling passages in the course of the reading, and they are brought out by Mr. B. with telling power."

The following year Brown added a second play, *The Escape,* to his abolitionist lecture repertoire, and this, too, was highly acclaimed by those who heard it. "No description we could give," one reviewer wrote in an upstate New York newspaper, "would convey an adequate idea of the

"A Negro hunt in the southern states," from William Wells Brown's *Clotel; or, The President's Daughter: A Narrative of Slave Life in the United States* (1853).

beauties of this Drama. It must be heard to be appreciated." Though Brown claimed in his author's preface that he had written the play "for my own amusement, and not with the remotest thought that it would ever be seen by the public eye," *The Escape* was published in Boston in 1858.

Brown's second play was based heavily on his own experience as a slave. Like the play's author, for instance, the fictional Cato serves as assistant to his physician-master and at one point extracts the wrong tooth from the mouth of another slave. And true to the author's own "leap for freedom," *The Escape* features a Quaker couple who help the escaped slaves once they reach Ohio. Brown goes to considerable pains in his preface to stress the authenticity of the play's main characters and incidents, stating (for instance) that Glen and Melinda were based on a fugitive slave couple currently living in Canada. But *The Escape* is also faithful to the genres of abolitionist narrative and drama that flourished in the 1840s and 1850s. The most influential single work in this genre was, of course, Harriet Beecher Stowe's *Uncle Tom's Cabin,* which was published in 1852 after appearing in serial form over the previous year and became the greatest-selling book of its time. Stage adaptations of *Uncle Tom's Cabin,* such as George L. Aiken's 1852 version, were similarly popular, and Stowe's Little Eva, Uncle Tom, Simon Legree, and Topsy remained mainstays of the American popular theater throughout the nineteenth century. Combining melodrama, sentimentalism, Christian moralizing, and vernacular comedy with antislavery polemics, Stowe's novel centered on the conditions of slavery and, through the characters George and Eliza Harris, on the thrilling drama of escape.

Brown's *The Escape* draws on the characters and situations familiar from *Uncle Tom's Cabin* and antislavery literature as a whole: the virtuous slave couple faced with separation, unprincipled slave traders, the dramatic crossing of a river to freedom. More broadly, it shares the reformist impulse that made the mid-nineteenth-century American stage an instrument of moral reform for temperance activists and others, including abolitionists. That *The Escape* was read in public as part of abolitionist lectures (it was not performed theatrically) would have intensified its polemical orientation. Like *Experience,* which closes with an oratorical performance, *The Escape* includes speeches on the evils of slavery; in the passion of delivery the voices of the play's characters would have been indistinguishable from the voice of Brown himself.

Brown's performance of his play as reader would have had another, even more radical, effect. While African American characters were frequently represented on the nineteenth-century American stage—notably in the minstrel shows offering stereotyped portraits of plantation and urban blacks, which became phenomenally popular during the 1840s—they were allowed little actual presence on this stage. A well-known victim of this exclusion was the great African American actor Ira Aldridge (1807–1867), who earned critical and popular acclaim for his performances of SHAKESPEARE but had to spend most of his career acting in Britain (where Brown saw him perform). The black characters of antislavery plays and minstrel shows alike were portrayed by white actors in blackface. Against such theatrical disenfranchisement, through which the representation of African American experience was co-opted by a white theatrical institution, Brown's act of reading his drama on the abolitionist platform enabled him to speak the play's many voices and to assert authorship of its dramatic representations.

Like other nineteenth-century reformist plays, *The Escape* draws heavily on the world of melodrama. Melodrama, which emerged at the beginning of the century in France and quickly became the dominant dramatic genre in Europe and the United States, dealt with stock, broadly defined characters who undergo trials within a moral landscape sharply divided between virtue and vice. Its plots, which frequently revolved around threatened virtue (specifically chastity, in the case of women), were geared toward heightened emotion and sensationalistic stage scenes. In *The Escape,* as in other abolitionist drama, the moral polarities of melodrama are adapted to the institution of slavery. The evils of this institution are underscored, with Brown's talent for irony, through those characters who profit from it. Dr. Gaines, who prays for an outbreak of yellow fever in the play's opening scene so that he can have more business, profits from his slaves in more ways than one: he has fathered at least one child already by a female slave and threatens to use Melinda similarly. His wife—like him, a portrait of hypocrisy, social pretension, and cruelty—trumpets her spirituality while whipping her servants at the least provocation. The callousness of their disregard for their slaves' humanity is echoed in the attitudes of those they call their friends and associates: fellow plantation owners, overseers, the clergy, slave speculators.

At the other end of the play's moral spectrum are Glen and Melinda, the virtuous couple whose honest love for each other must contend with their inability to own and control their own lives. They are married by a fellow slave at moonlight; but in the system of chattel slavery instituted in the American South, such a marriage had no legal standing, and slave couples could be broken up and sold separately at the whims of their owners. Unlike the other slaves on Dr. Gaines's plantation, their diction is elevated, and their rhetorically florid speech identifies them simultaneously as protagonists in the melodramatic tradition and as mouthpieces for abolitionist sentiment. Indeed, Glen's speeches on the evils of slavery ("Oh, pity the poor outraged slave!") are indistinguishable from the antislavery tracts that became increasingly fiery in the years leading up to the Civil War.

The slave woman Melinda is a familiar figure from nineteenth-century American drama and literature: the person of mixed race, or mulatto, whose features betray the sexual contacts between whites (usually slave owners) and blacks (usually female slaves) that marked American slavery from its start. In *Clotelle: A Tale of the Southern States,* an 1864 revision of his earlier novel, Brown writes:

> With the growing population in the Southern States, the increase of mulattoes has been very great. Society does not frown upon the man who sits with his half-white child upon his knee whilst the mother stands, a slave, behind his chair. In nearly all the cities and towns of the Slave States, the real negro, or clear black, does not amount to more than one in four of the slave population.

In an effort to police its racial categories against the effects of this miscegenation, Southern law and convention adopted the "one-drop rule." In this system, the presence of any nonwhite blood defined a person as black, and individuals were classified by a set of labels according to their percentage of nonwhite ancestry: mulatto (one black parent), quadroon (one black grandparent), octoroon (one black great-grandparent). Plays such as Dion Boucicault's popular *The Octoroon; or, Life in Louisiana* (1859) explored these microboundaries and popularized the figure of the "tragic mulatto," caught between the racial identities of black and white, excluded from white society by that fatal drop of African blood.

Himself the offspring of an interracial union, Brown shows a keen sense in *The Escape* of the differences and color nuances that made race a complex, ambiguous phenomenon despite legal efforts to codify it. Characters such as the slave boy Sampey are identified as "white" in Brown's script to indicate their lighter-skinned complexion, while (in one telling scene) a white neighbor mistakes a slave child of Dr. Gaines's as a product of his legal marriage. As recent scholars have argued, Brown further complicates the notion of racial identity by subverting conventional cultural representations of black and white. According to John Ernest, "The characters in *The Escape* are rarely who they claim to be. Almost all are involved in a deceptive performance of selfhood, the playing out of a culturally assigned role to veil private motivations." The slave Cato exemplifies how deceptive Brown's characterizations can be. A comic figure whose dialectal speech is laced with malapropisms, Cato evokes Tambo, Bones, and other stock plantation characters from minstrelsy. But Cato does not succumb to this racial typecasting. He takes roles on and off as if they were the doctor's coat he dons in act 1, and he questions the identities that result from such performative transformations: "Cato, is dis you?" When he contemplates making his own leap for freedom toward the play's end, he speaks a language unavailable to his minstrel show prototypes. The image of Cato contemplating himself in the mirror in act 1 underscores that racial identity is a "matter of masquerade" (in Paul Gilmore's phrase) and that its cultural portrayals are self-limiting constructions. Employing the representational conventions of minstrelsy in order to challenge them, Brown invited his audience to examine the cultural imagery by which it constructs identity within racial categories. True to the play's concern with questions of representation, the 1858 edition of *The Escape* includes an epigraph from Shakespeare's *HAMLET* (1600–01) on its title page: "Look on this picture, and on this."

The play's abolitionist underpinnings are also evident in its songs. Among his other literary accomplishments, William Wells Brown published a collection of abolitionist melodies titled *The Anti-Slavery Harp: A Collection of Songs for Anti-Slavery Meetings* (1848). Such songs, which were performed at abolitionist functions, were often based on existing lyrics and popular melodies. In those cases in which the originals were racist in nature, the abolitionist versions served as parodic reappropriations. One of the songs that Brown includes in *The Escape,* Cato's "hyme" to Canada, was based on the minstrel song "Dandy Jim from Caroline," which exploited the stereotype of the flashily dressed black dandy. The excerpt below from one version of this original, which is included in Robert B. Winans's "Early Minstrel Show Music, 1843–1852" (1984), makes clear the ideological transformation accomplished by its abolitionist counterpart:

I've often heard it said ob late,
Dat Souf Carolina was de state,
What a handsome nigga's bound to
shine,
Like Dandy Jim from Caroline.

Chorus: *For my ole massa tole me so,*
I was de best looking nigga in de country,
O,
I look in de glass an found 'twas so,
Just what massa tole me, O.

In keeping with its abolitionist sentiments, *The Escape* includes a stirring tribute to the Underground Railroad and those northerners who helped slaves escape at personal risk. At the same time, abolitionism as a movement was not immune to Brown's critique of racial attitudes. Through the aptly named Mr. White—"a citizen" from Massachusetts, the seat of the abolitionist movement—Brown dramatizes the self-congratulatory stance of those white northerners who took on antislavery rhetoric without coming to terms with its practical and ethical implications. When White arrives in the South he delivers an oration on the slave's "living soul" that could have come from the pages of William Lloyd Garrison's abolitionist paper *The Liberator.* His appearance in the spotlight is brief, however, and he must suffer the indignity of hiding in a basement to escape the wrath of his listeners. In the play's closing scene he appears at the Niagara River, but this border—so important in the ferrying of fugitive slaves to freedom in Canada—becomes, for White, a site for aesthetic rather than ethical contemplation: he berates two impoverished peddlers who approach him for spoiling the "beautiful scene" he is trying to sketch. Although White does join the fight that allows Glen, Melinda, and Cato to cross the river, the largely rhetorical nature of his abolitionist passions elsewhere in the play remains a challenge to those northerners whose antislavery attitudes and commitments are largely untried.

Written by a former slave who experienced much of what he dramatizes, *The Escape* is uncompromising in its attack on slavery and its call to action. Despite being less well-known than *Uncle Tom's Cabin,* Brown's play provides a useful contrast to the earlier work and the numerous dramatic adaptations it inspired. Stowe's novel offers positive portrayals of benevolent slaveholding: the cruelty of Simon Legree is counterbalanced by the good-heartedness of the plantation owner St. Clare and the saintly child Eva. In addition, the Christian moralizing of *Uncle Tom's Cabin* complicates its abolitionist fervor with the suggestion that the ultimate solace for life's evils lies beyond the world and its institutions. Brown's play, to the contrary, refuses otherworldly consolation; its redress for the injustices of slavery consists of action—even violent action—in the present. When Glen declares, "Oh! there is a volcano pent up in the hearts of the slaves of these southern states that will burst forth ere long," he speaks for his author, who championed Toussaint L'Ouverture and the successful Haitian slave revolution of 1801 and who proposed a resolution at the 1857 New England Anti-Slavery Convention asserting the rights of American slaves to free themselves through similar means.

To be sure, *The Escape* is not without its flaws as a play. Like much other popular nineteenth-century drama, its plot is contrived in places, and its dialogue frequently feels artificial, better suited to polemic than to the demands of characterization (a weakness particularly noticeable in the speeches of Glen and Melinda). Yet the play's stylistic and structural roughness are more than matched by the power of its antislavery critique and its subversive manipulation of the conventions of racial representation. One of the most powerful dramas to emerge from the abolitionist movement, *The Escape* dramatized the tensions that would contribute, five years after its publication, to the bloodiest war in United States history. As the first play by an African American writer to be published, it also inaugurated a tradition of dramatic writing by black Americans that would prove vital to the American theater. Brown's play is a worthy progenitor to the drama that followed. Though African American playwrights of the twentieth and twenty-first centuries would address the racial fault lines in post–Civil War American society, none would do so with more passion than this orator, writer, and former slave. S.G.

The Escape or, *A Leap for Freedom*[1]

Author's Preface

This play was written for my own amusement, and not with the remotest thought that it would ever be seen by the public eye. I read it privately, however, to a circle of my friends, and through them was invited to read it before a Literary Society. Since then, the Drama has been given in various parts of the country. By the earnest solicitation of some in whose judgment I have the greatest confidence, I now present it in a printed form to the public. As I never aspired to be a dramatist, I ask no favor for it, and have little or no solicitude for its fate. If it is not readable, no word of mine can make it so; if it is, to ask favor for it would be needless.

The main features in the Drama are true. GLEN and MELINDA are actual characters, and still reside in Canada. Many of the incidents were drawn from my own experience of eighteen years at the South. The marriage ceremony, as performed in the second act, is still adhered to in many of the Southern States, especially in the farming districts.

The ignorance of the slave, as seen in the case of "BIG SALLY," is common wherever chattel slavery exists. The difficulties created in the domestic circle by the presence of beautiful slave women, as found in DR. GAINES's family, is well understood by all who have ever visited the valley of the Mississippi.

The play, no doubt, abounds in defects, but as I was born in slavery, and never had a day's schooling in my life, I owe the public no apology for errors. W. W. B.

CHARACTERS

DR. GAINES, proprietor of the farm at Muddy Creek
REV. JOHN PINCHEN, a clergyman
DICK WALKER, a slave speculator
MR. WILDMARSH, neighbor to Dr. Gaines
MAJOR MOORE, a friend of Dr. Gaines
MR. WHITE, a citizen of Massachusetts
BILL JENNINGS, a slave speculator

1. The present text is based on the 1858 first edition, published by R. F. Wallcut. Spelling and punctuation have been modernized.

JACOB SCRAGG, overseer to Dr. Gaines
MRS. GAINES, wife of Dr. Gaines
MR. and MRS. NEAL, and DAUGHTER, Quakers, in Ohio
THOMAS, Mr. Neal's hired man
GLEN, slave of Mr. Hamilton, brother-in-law of Dr. Gaines
CATO, SAM, SAMPEY, MELINDA, DOLLY, SUSAN, and BIG SALLY, slaves of Dr. Gaines
PETE, NED, BILL, and TAPIOCA, slaves
OFFICERS, LOUNGERS, BARKEEPER, &c.

1.1

[SCENE: *A sitting room.*]

[MRS. GAINES, *looking at some drawings*—SAMPEY, *a white slave,*[2] *stands behind the lady's chair.*]

[*Enter* DR. GAINES, *right.*]

DR. GAINES Well, my dear, my practice is steadily increasing. I forgot to tell you that neighbor Wyman engaged me yesterday as his family physician; and I hope that the fever and ague, which is now taking hold of the people, will give me more patients. I see by the New Orleans papers that the yellow fever is raging there to a fearful extent. Men of my profession are reaping a harvest in that section this year. I would that we could have a touch of the yellow fever here, for I think I could invent a medicine that would cure it. But the yellow fever is a luxury that we medical men in this climate can't expect to enjoy; yet we may hope for the cholera.

MRS. GAINES Yes, I would be glad to see it more sickly here, so that your business might prosper. But we are always unfortunate. Everybody here seems to be in good health, and I am afraid that they'll keep so. However, we must hope for the best. We must trust in the Lord. Providence may possibly send some disease amongst us for our benefit.

[*Enter* CATO, *right.*]

CATO Mr. Campbell is at de door, massa.

DR. GAINES Ask him in, Cato.

[*Enter* MR. CAMPBELL, *right.*]

DR. GAINES Good morning, Mr. Campbell. Be seated.

MR. CAMPBELL Good morning, doctor. The same to you, Mrs. Gaines. Fine morning, this.

MRS. GAINES Yes, sir; beautiful day.

MR. CAMPBELL Well, doctor, I've come to engage you for my family physician. I am tired of Dr. Jones. I've lost another very valuable nigger under his treatment; and, as my old mother used to say, "change of pastures makes fat calves."

DR. GAINES I shall be most happy to become your doctor. Of course, you want me to attend to your niggers, as well as to your family?

MR. CAMPBELL Certainly, sir. I have twenty-three servants. What will you charge me by the year?

DR. GAINES Of course, you'll do as my other patients do, send your servants to me when they are sick, if able to walk?

2. That is, a light-skinned mulatto slave.

MR. CAMPBELL Oh, yes; I always do that.

DR. GAINES Then I suppose I'll have to lump it, and say $500[3] per annum.

MR. CAMPBELL Well, then, we'll consider that matter settled; and as two of the boys are sick, I'll send them over. So I'll bid you good day, doctor. I would be glad if you would come over some time, and bring Mrs. Gaines with you.

DR. GAINES Yes, I will; and shall be glad if you will pay us a visit, and bring with you Mrs. Campbell. Come over and spend the day.

MR. CAMPBELL I will. Good morning, doctor. [*Exit* MR. CAMPBELL, *right.*]

DR. GAINES There, my dear, what do you think of that? Five hundred dollars more added to our income. That's patronage worth having! And I am glad to get all the negroes I can to doctor, for Cato is becoming very useful to me in the shop. He can bleed,[4] pull teeth, and do almost anything that the blacks require. He can put up medicine as well as any one. A valuable boy, Cato!

MRS. GAINES But why did you ask Mr. Campbell to visit you, and to bring his wife? I am sure I could never consent to associate with her, for I understand that she was the daughter of a tanner. You must remember, my dear, that I was born with a silver spoon in my mouth. The blood of the Wyleys runs in my veins. I am surprised that you should ask him to visit you at all; you should have known better.

DR. GAINES Oh, I did not mean for him to visit me. I only invited him for the sake of compliments, and I think he so understood it; for I should be far from wishing you to associate with Mrs. Campbell. I don't forget, my dear, the family you were raised in, nor do I overlook my own family. My father, you know, fought by the side of Washington, and I hope someday to have a handle[5] to my own name. I am certain Providence intended me for something higher than a medical man. Ah! by the by, I had forgotten that I have a couple of patients to visit this morning. I must go at once.

[*Exit* DR. GAINES, *right.*]

[*Enter* HANNAH, *left.*]

MRS. GAINES Go, Hannah, and tell Dolly to kill a couple of fat pullets, and to put the biscuit to rise. I expect brother Pinchen here this afternoon, and I want everything in order. Hannah, Hannah, tell Melinda to come here.

[*Exit* HANNAH, *left.*]

We mistresses do have a hard time in this world; I don't see why the Lord should have imposed such heavy duties on us poor mortals. Well, it can't last always. I long to leave this wicked world, and go home to glory.

[*Enter* MELINDA.]

I am to have company this afternoon, Melinda. I expect brother Pinchen here, and I want everything in order. Go and get one of my new caps, with the lace border, and get out my scalloped-bottomed dimity[6] petticoat, and when you go out, tell Hannah to clean the white-handled knives, and see that not a speck is on them; for I want everything as it should be while brother Pinchen is here.

[*Exit* MRS. GAINES, *left;* HANNAH, *right.*]

3. The equivalent of more than $10,000 today.
4. The centuries-old practice of therapeutic bloodletting was common for a wide variety of ailments.
5. An honorific title, such as "Colonel" (see 2.3, below).
6. A sheer cotton fabric woven in stripes or checks.

1.2

[SCENE: DR. GAINES's *shop*—CATO *making pills.*]

[*Enter* DR. GAINES, *left.*]

DR. GAINES Well, Cato, have you made the batch of ointment that I ordered?

CATO Yes, massa; I dun made de intment, an' now I is making the bread pills.[7] De tater pills is up on the top shelf.

DR. GAINES I am going out to see some patients. If any gentlemen call, tell them I shall be in this afternoon. If any servants come, you attend to them. I expect two of Mr. Campbell's boys over. You see to them. Feel their pulse, look at their tongues, bleed them, and give them each a dose of calomel.[8] Tell them to drink no cold water, and to take nothing but water gruel.

CATO Yes, massa; I'll tend to 'em.

[*Exit* DR. GAINES, *left.*]

CATO I allers knowed I was a doctor, an' now de ole boss has put me at it, I muss change my coat. Ef any niggers comes in, I wants to look suspectable. Dis jacket don't suit a doctor; I'll change it. [*Exit* CATO—*immediately returning in a long coat.*] Ah! now I looks like a doctor. Now I can bleed, pull teef, or cut off a leg. Oh! well, well, ef I aint put de pill stuff an' de intment stuff togedder. By golly, dat ole cuss will be mad when he finds it out, won't he? Nebber mind, I'll make it up in pills, and when de flour is on dem, he won't know what's in 'em; an' I'll make some new intment. Ah! yonder comes Mr. Campbell's Pete an' Ned; dems de ones massa sed was comin'. I'll see ef I looks right. [*Goes to the looking glass and views himself.*] I em some punkins,[9] ain't I? [*Knock at the door.*] Come in.

[*Enter* PETE *and* NED, *right.*]

PETE Whar is de doctor?

CATO Here I is; don't you see me?

PETE But whar is de ole boss?

CATO Dat's none you business. I dun tole you dat I is de doctor, an dat's enuff.

NED Oh! do tell us whar de doctor is. I is almost dead. Oh me! oh dear me! I is so sick. [*Horrible faces.*]

PETE Yes, do tell us; we don't want to stan here foolin'.

CATO I tells you again dat I is de doctor. I larn de trade under massa.

NED Oh! well, den, give me somethin' to stop dis pain. Oh dear me! I shall die. [*He tries to vomit, but can't—ugly faces.*]

CATO Let me feel your pulse. Now put out your tongue. You is berry sick. Ef you don't mine, you'll die. Come out in de shed, an' I'll bleed you.

[*Exit all—re-enter.*]

CATO Dar, now take dese pills, two in de mornin' and two at night, and ef you don't feel better, double de dose. Now, Mr. Pete, what's de matter wid you?

PETE I is got de cole chills, an' has a fever in de night.

CATO Come out, an' I'll bleed you.

[*Exit all—re enter.*]

Now take dese pills, two in de mornin and two at night, an' ef dey don't help you, double de dose. Ah! I like to forget to feel your pulse and look at

7. Such pills (like "tater pills") were placebos.

8. A fungicide used medicinally as a purgative in the 19th century.

9. That is, pretty special.

your tongue. Put out your tongue. [*Feels his pulse.*] Yes, I tells by de feel ob your pulse dat I is gib you de right pills.

[*Enter Mr. Parker's* BILL, *left.*]

CATO What you come in dat door widout knockin' for?

BILL My toof ache so, I didn't tink to knock. Oh, my toof! my toof! Whar is de doctor?

CATO Here I is; don't you see me?

BILL What! you de doctor, you brack cuss! You looks like a doctor! Oh, my toof! my toof! Whar is de doctor?

CATO I tells you I is de doctor. Ef you don't believe me, ax dese men. I can pull your toof in a minnit.

BILL Well, den, pull it out. Oh, my toof! how it aches! Oh, my toof!

[CATO *gets the rusty turnkeys.*[1]]

CATO Now lay down on your back.

BILL What for?

CATO Dat's de way massa does.

BILL Oh, my toof! Well, den, come on. [*Lies down,* CATO *gets astraddle of* BILL's *breast, puts the turnkeys on the wrong tooth, and pulls*—BILL *kicks, and cries out.*]—Oh, do stop! Oh! oh! oh!

[CATO *pulls the wrong tooth*—BILL *jumps up.*]

CATO Dar, now, I tole you I could pull your toof for you.

BILL Oh, dear me! Oh, it aches yet! Oh me! Oh, Lor-e-massy! You dun pull de wrong toof. Drat your skin! ef I don't pay you for this, you brack cuss!

[*They fight, and turn over table, chairs and bench*—PETE *and* NED *look on.*]

[*Enter* DR. GAINES, *right.*]

DR. GAINES Why, dear me, what's the matter? What's all this about? I'll teach you a lesson, that I will.

[*The* DOCTOR *goes at them with his cane.*]

CATO Oh, massa! he's to blame, sir. He's to blame. He struck me fuss.

BILL No, sir; he's to blame; he pull de wrong toof. Oh, my toof! oh, my toof!

DR. GAINES Let me see your tooth. Open your mouth. As I live, you've taken out the wrong tooth. I am amazed. I'll whip you for this; I'll whip you well. You're a pretty doctor. Now lie down, Bill, and let him take out the right tooth; and if he makes a mistake this time, I'll cowhide him well. Lie down, Bill.

[BILL *lies down, and* CATO *pulls the tooth.*]

There now, why didn't you do that in the first place?

CATO He wouldn't hole still, sir.

BILL He lies, sir. I did hole still.

DR. GAINES Now go home, boys; go home.

[*Exit* PETE, NED *and* BILL, *left.*]

DR. GAINES You've made a pretty muss of it, in my absence. Look at the table! Never mind, Cato; I'll whip you well for this conduct of yours today. Go to work now, and clear up the office. [*Exit* DR. GAINES, *right.*]

CATO Confound dat nigger! I wish he was in Ginny.[2] He bite my finger and scratch my face. But didn't I give it to him? Well, den, I reckon I did. [*He*

1. That is, toothkeys: instruments used for extracting teeth.

2. Virginia.

goes to the mirror, and discovers that his coat is torn—weeps.] Oh, dear me! Oh, my coat—my coat is tore! Dat nigger has tore my coat. [*He gets angry, and rushes about the room frantic.*] Cuss dat nigger! Ef I could lay my hands on him, I'd tare him all to pieces,—dat I would. An'de ole boss hit me wid his cane after dat nigger tore my coat. By golly, I wants to fight somebody, Ef ole massa should come in now, I'd fight him. [*Rolls up his sleeves.*] Let 'em come now, ef dey dare—ole massa, or anybody else; I'm ready for 'em.

[*Enter* DR. GAINES, *right.*]

DR. GAINES What's all this noise here?

CATO Nuffin', sir; only jess I is puttin' things to rights, as you tole me. I didn't hear any noise except de rats.

DR. GAINES Make haste, and come in; I want you to go to town.

[*Exit* DR. GAINES, *right.*]

CATO By golly, de ole boss like to cotch me dat time, didn't he? But wasn't I mad? When I is mad, nobody can do nuffin' wid me. But here's my coat, tore to pieces. Cuss dat nigger! [*Weeps.*] Oh, my coat! oh, my coat! I rudder he had broke my head den to tore my coat. Drat dat nigger! Ef he ever comes here agin, I'll pull out every toof he's got in his head—dat I will.

[*Exit, right.*]

1.3

[SCENE: *A room in the quarters.*]

[*Enter* GLEN, *left.*]

GLEN How slowly the time passes away. I've been waiting here two hours, and Melinda has not yet come. What keeps her, I cannot tell. I waited long and late for her last night, and when she approached, I sprang to my feet, caught her in my arms, pressed her to my heart, and kissed away the tears from her moistened cheeks. She placed her trembling hand in mine, and said, "Glen, I am yours; I will never be the wife of another." I clasped her to my bosom, and called God to witness that I would ever regard her as my wife. Old Uncle Joseph joined us in holy wedlock by moonlight; that was the only marriage ceremony. I look upon the vow as ever binding on me, for I am sure that a just God will sanction our union in heaven. Still, this man, who claims Melinda as his property, is unwilling for me to marry the woman of my choice, because he wants her himself. But he shall not have her. What he will say when he finds that we are married, I cannot tell; but I am determined to protect my wife or die. Ah! here comes Melinda.

[*Enter* MELINDA, *right.*]

I am glad to see you, Melinda. I've been waiting long, and feared you would not come. Ah! in tears again?

MELINDA Glen, you are always thinking I am in tears. But what did master say today?

GLEN He again forbade our union.

MELINDA Indeed! Can he be so cruel?

GLEN Yes, he can be just so cruel.

MELINDA Alas! alas! how unfeeling and heartless! But did you appeal to his generosity?

GLEN Yes, I did; I used all the persuasive powers that I was master of, but to no purpose; he was inflexible. He even offered me a new suit of clothes, if I would give you up; and when I told him that I could not, he said he would flog me to death if I ever spoke to you again.

MELINDA And what did you say to him?

GLEN I answered, that, while I loved life better than death, even life itself could not tempt me to consent to a separation that would make life an unchanging curse. Oh, I would kill myself, Melinda, if I thought that, for the sake of life, I could consent to your degradation. No, Melinda, I can die, but shall never live to see you the mistress of another man. But, my dear girl, I have a secret to tell you, and no one must know it but you. I will go out and see that no person is within hearing. I will be back soon. [*Exit* GLEN, *left.*]

MELINDA It is often said that the darkest hour of the night precedes the dawn. It is ever thus with the vicissitudes of human suffering. After the soul has reached the lowest depths of despair, and can no deeper plunge amid its rolling, fetid shades, then the reactionary forces of man's nature begin to operate, resolution takes the place of despondency, energy succeeds instead of apathy, and an upward tendency is felt and exhibited. Men then hope against power, and smile in defiance of despair. I shall never forget when first I saw Glen. It is now more than a year since he came here with his master, Mr. Hamilton. It was a glorious moonlight night in autumn. The wide and fruitful face of nature was silent and buried in repose. The tall trees on the borders of Muddy Creek waved their leafy branches in the breeze, which was wafted from afar, refreshing over hill and vale, over the rippling water, and the waving corn and wheat fields. The starry sky was studded over with a few light, flitting clouds, while the moon, as if rejoicing to witness the meeting of two hearts that should be cemented by the purest love, sailed triumphantly along among the shifting vapors.

Oh, how happy I have been in my acquaintance with Glen! That he loves me, I do well believe it; that I love him, it is most true. Oh, how I would that those who think the slave incapable of the finer feelings, could only see our hearts, and learn our thoughts—thoughts that we dare not utter in the presence of our masters! But I fear that Glen will be separated from me, for there is nothing too base and mean for master to do, for the purpose of getting me entirely in his power. But, thanks to Heaven, he does not own Glen, and therefore cannot sell him. Yet he might purchase him from his brother-in-law, so as to send him out of the way. But here comes my husband.

[*Enter* GLEN, *left.*]

GLEN I've been as far as the overseer's house, and all is quiet. Now, Melinda, as you are my wife, I will confide to you a secret. I've long been thinking of making my escape to Canada, and taking you with me. It is true that I don't belong to your master, but he might buy me from Hamilton, and then sell me out of the neighborhood.

MELINDA But we could never succeed in the attempt to escape.

GLEN We will make the trial, and show that we at least deserve success. There is a slave trader expected here next week, and Dr. Gaines would sell you at once if he knew that we were married. We must get ready and start, and if we can pass the Ohio River, we'll be safe on the road to Canada.[3] [*Exit, right.*]

1.4

[SCENE: *Dining room.*]

[*Rev.* MR. PINCHEN *giving* MRS. GAINES *an account of his experience as a minister*—HANNAH *clearing away the breakfast table*—SAMPEY *standing behind* MRS. GAINES*'s chair.*]

MRS. GAINES Now, do give me more of your experience, brother Pinchen. It always does my soul good to hear religious experience. It draws me nearer and nearer to the Lord's side. I do love to hear good news from God's people.

MR. PINCHEN Well, sister Gaines, I've had great opportunities in my time to study the heart of man. I've attended a great many camp meetings,[4] revival meetings, protracted meetings, and deathbed scenes, and I am satisfied, sister Gaines, that the heart of man is full of sin, and desperately wicked. This is a wicked world, sister Gaines, a wicked world.

MRS. GAINES Were you ever in Arkansas, brother Pinchen? I've been told that the people out there are very ungodly.

MR. PINCHEN Oh, yes, sister Gaines. I once spent a year at Little Rock, and preached in all the towns round about there; and I found some hard cases out there, I can tell you. I was once spending a week in a district where there were a great many horse thieves, and one night, somebody stole my pony. Well, I knowed it was no use to make a fuss, so I told brother Tarbox to say nothing about it, and I'd get my horse by preaching God's everlasting gospel; for I had faith in the truth, and knowed that my Savior would not let me lose my pony. So the next Sunday I preached on horse-stealing, and told the brethren to come up in the evenin' with their hearts filled with the grace of God. So that night the house was crammed brim full with anxious souls, panting for the bread of life. Brother Bingham opened with prayer, and brother Tarbox followed, and I saw right off that we were gwine to have a blessed time. After I got 'em pretty well warmed up, I jumped on to one of the seats, stretched out my hands, and said, "I know who stole my pony; I've found out; and you are in here tryin' to make people believe that you've got religion; but you ain't got it. And if you don't take my horse back to brother Tarbox's pasture this very night, I'll tell your name right out in meetin' tomorrow night. Take my pony back, you vile and wretched sinner, and come up here and give your heart to God." So the next mornin', I went out to brother Tarbox's pasture, and sure enough, there was my bobtail pony. Yes, sister Gaines, there he was, safe and sound. Ha, ha, ha.

MRS. GAINES Oh, how interesting, and how fortunate for you to get your pony! And what power there is in the gospel! God's children are very lucky. Oh, it is so sweet to sit here and listen to such good news from God's

3. Canada was a frequent destination for escaped American slaves even before slavery was formally abolished in Canada and the rest of the British Empire in 1833, and especially after passage of the Fugitive Slave Law in 1850 made them vulnerable to recapture in free states. *The Ohio River*: the border between Kentucky, a slave state, and the "free" northern states of Illinois, Indiana, and Ohio.

4. Religious meetings held in tents or in the open air; they often lasted for several days.

people! You Hannah, what are you standing there listening for, and neglecting your work? [*Aside*] Never mind, my lady, I'll whip you well when I am done here. Go at your work this moment, you lazy hussy! Never mind, I'll whip you well.—Come, do go on, brother Pinchen, with your godly conversation. It is so sweet! It draws me nearer and nearer to the Lord's side.

MR. PINCHEN Well, sister Gaines, I've had some mighty queer dreams in my time, that I have. You see, one night I dreamed that I was dead and in heaven, and such a place I never saw before. As soon as I entered the gates of the celestial empire, I saw many old and familiar faces that I had seen before. The first person that I saw was good old Elder Pike, the preacher that first called my attention to religion. The next person I saw was Deacon Billings, my first wife's father, and then I saw a host of godly faces. Why, sister Gaines, you knowed Elder Goosbee, didn't you?

MRS. GAINES Why, yes; did you see him there? He married me to my first husband.

MR. PINCHEN Oh, yes, sister Gaines, I saw the old Elder, and he looked for all the world as if he had just come out of a revival meetin'.

MRS. GAINES Did you see my first husband there, brother Pinchen?

MR. PINCHEN No, sister Gaines, I didn't see brother Pepper there; but I've no doubt but that brother Pepper was there.

MRS. GAINES Well, I don't know; I have my doubts. He was not the happiest man in the world. He was always borrowing trouble about something or another. Still, I saw some happy moments with Mr. Pepper. I was happy when I made his acquaintance, happy during our courtship, happy awhile after our marriage, and happy when he died. [*Weeps.*]

HANNAH Massa Pinchen, did you see my ole man Ben up dar in hebben?

MR. PINCHEN No, Hannah; I didn't go amongst the niggers.

MRS. GAINES No, of course brother Pinchen didn't go among the blacks. What are you asking questions for? [*Aside*] Never mind, my lady, I'll whip you well when I'm done here. I'll skin you from head to foot.—Do go on with your heavenly conversation, brother Pinchen; it does my very soul good. This is indeed a precious moment for me. I do love to hear of Christ and Him crucified.

MR. PINCHEN Well, sister Gaines, I promised sister Daniels that I'd come over and see her this morning, and have a little season of prayer with her, and I suppose I must go. I'll tell you more of my religious experience when I return.

MRS. GAINES If you must go, then I'll have to let you; but before you do, I wish to get your advice upon a little matter that concerns Hannah. Last week, Hannah stole a goose, killed it, cooked it, and she and her man Sam had a fine time eating the goose; and her master and I would never have known a word about it, if it had not been for Cato, a faithful servant, who told his master. And then, you see, Hannah had to be severely whipped before she'd confess that she stole the goose. Next Sabbath is sacrament day, and I want to know if you think that Hannah is fit to go to the Lord's supper after stealing the goose.

MR. PINCHEN Well, sister Gaines, that depends on circumstances. If Hannah has confessed that she stole the goose, and has been sufficiently whipped, and has begged her master's pardon, and begged your pardon, and thinks she'll never do the like again, why then I suppose she can go to the Lord's supper; for

"While the lamp holds out to burn,
The vilest sinner may return."[5]

But she must be sure that she has repented, and won't steal anymore.

MRS. GAINES Now, Hannah, do you hear that? For my own part, I don't think she's fit to go to the Lord's supper, for she had no occasion to steal the goose. We give our niggers plenty of good wholesome food. They have a full run to the meal tub, meat once a fortnight, and all the sour milk about the place, and I'm sure that's enough for anyone. I do think that our niggers are the most ungrateful creatures in the world, that I do. They aggravate my life out of me.

HANNAH I know, missis, dat I steal de goose, and massa whip me for it, and I confess it, and I is sorry for it. But, missis, I is gwine to de Lord's supper, next Sunday, kase I ain't agwine to turn my back on my bressed Lord an' Massa for no old tough goose, dat I ain't. [*Weeps.*]

MR. PINCHEN Well, sister Gaines, I suppose I must go over and see sister Daniels; she'll be waiting for me. [*Exit* MR. PINCHEN, *center.*]

MRS. GAINES Now, Hannah, brother Pinchen is gone, do you get the cowhide and follow me to the cellar, and I'll whip you well for aggravating me as you have today. It seems as if I can never sit down to take a little comfort with the Lord, without you crossing me. The devil always puts it into your head to disturb me, just when I am trying to serve the Lord. I've no doubt but that I'll miss going to heaven on your account. But I'll whip you well before I leave this world, that I will. Get the cowhide and follow me to the cellar.

[*Exit* MRS. GAINES *and* HANNAH, *right.*]

2.1

[SCENE: *Parlor.*]

[DR. GAINES *at a table, letters and papers before him.*]

[*Enter* SAMPEY, *left.*]

SAMPEY Dar's a gemman at de doe, massa, dat wants to see you, seer.

DR. GAINES Ask him to walk in, Sampey.

[*Exit* SAMPEY, *left.*]

[*Enter* WALKER.]

WALKER Why, how do you do, Dr. Gaines? I em glad to see you, I'll swear.

DR. GAINES How do you do, Mr. Walker? I did not expect to see you up here so soon. What has hurried you?

WALKER Well, you see, doctor, I comes when I em not expected. The price of niggers is up, and I em gwine to take advantage of the times. Now, doctor, ef you've got any niggers that you wants to sell, I em your man. I am paying the highest price of anybody in the market. I pay cash down, and no grumblin'.

DR. GAINES I don't know that I want to sell any of my people now. Still, I've got to make up a little money next month, to pay in bank; and another thing, the doctors say that we are likely to have a touch of the cholera this summer, and if that's the case, I suppose I had better turn as many of my slaves into cash as I can.

5. From Isaac Watts, book 1, hymn 88, *Hymns and Spiritual Songs* (1707).

WALKER Yes, doctor, that is very true. The cholera is death on slaves, and a thousand dollars[6] in your pocket is a great deal better than a nigger in the field, with cholera at his heels. Why, who is that coming up the lane? It's Mr. Wildmarsh, as I live! Jest the very man I wants to see.

[*Enter* MR. WILDMARSH.]

Why, how do you do, Squire? I was jest a thinkin' about you.

WILDMARSH How are you, Mr. Walker? and how are you, doctor? I am glad to see you both looking so well. You seem in remarkably good health, doctor?

DR. GAINES Yes, Squire, I was never in the enjoyment of better health. I hope you left all well at Licking?

WILDMARSH Yes, I thank you. And now, Mr. Walker, how goes times with you?

WALKER Well, you see, Squire, I em in good spirits. The price of niggers is up in the market, and I am lookin' out for bargains; and I was jest intendin' to come over to Lickin' to see you, to see if you had any niggers to sell. But it seems as ef the Lord knowed that I wanted to see you, and directed your steps over here. Now, Squire, ef you've got any niggers you wants to sell, I em your man. I am payin' the highest cash price of anybody in the market. Now's your time, Squire.

WILDMARSH No, I don't think I want to sell any of my slaves now. I sold a very valuable gal to Mr. Haskins last week. I tell you, she was a smart one. I got eighteen hundred dollars for her.

WALKER Why, Squire, how you do talk! Eighteen hundred dollars for one gal? She must have been a screamer[7] to bring that price. What sort of a lookin' critter was she? I should like to have bought her.

WILDMARSH She was a little of the smartest gal I've ever raised; that she was.

WALKER Then she was your own raising, was she?

WILDMARSH Oh, yes; she was raised on my place, and if I could have kept her three or four years longer, and taken her to the market myself, I am sure I could have sold her for three thousand dollars. But you see, Mr. Walker, my wife got a little jealous, and you know jealousy sets the women's heads a teetering, and so I had to sell the gal. She's got straight hair, blue eyes, prominent features, and is almost white. Haskins will make a spec,[8] and no mistake.

WALKER Why, Squire, was she that pretty little gal that I saw on your knee the day that your wife was gone, when I was at your place three years ago?

WILDMARSH Yes, the same.

WALKER Well, now, Squire, I thought that was your daughter; she looked mightily like you. She was your daughter, wasn't she? You need not be ashamed to own it to me, for I am mum upon such matters.

WILDMARSH You know, Mr. Walker, that people will talk, and when they talk, they say a great deal; and people did talk, and many said the gal was my daughter; and you know we can't help people's talking. But here comes the Rev. Mr. Pinchen; I didn't knew that he was in the neighborhood.

WALKER It is Mr. Pinchen, as I live; jest the very man I wants to see.

[*Enter* MR. PINCHEN, *right*.]

Why, how do you do, Mr. Pinchen? What in the name of Jehu[9] brings you down here to Muddy Creek? Any camp meetins, revival meetins, deathbed

6. Equivalent to roughly $25,000 today.
7. An exceptionally attractive woman.
8. That is, will profit (succeed in a speculative commercial venture).
9. A king of Israel (see 2 Kings).

scenes, or anything else in your line going on down here? How is religion prosperin' now, Mr. Pinchen? I always like to hear about religion.

MR. PINCHEN Well, Mr. Walker, the Lord's work is in good condition everywhere now. I tell you, Mr. Walker, I've been in the gospel ministry these thirteen years, and I am satisfied that the heart of man is full of sin and desperately wicked. This is a wicked world, Mr. Walker, a wicked world, and we ought all of us to have religion. Religion is a good thing to live by, and we all want it when we die. Yes, sir, when the great trumpet blows,[1] we ought to be ready. And a man in your business of buying and selling slaves needs religion more than anybody else, for it makes you treat your people as you should. Now, there is Mr. Haskins—he is a slave trader, like yourself. Well, I converted him. Before he got religion, he was one of the worst men to his niggers I ever saw; his heart was as hard as stone. But religion has made his heart as soft as a piece of cotton. Before I converted him, he would sell husbands from their wives, and seem to take delight in it; but now he won't sell a man from his wife, if he can get anyone to buy both of them together. I tell you, sir, religion has done a wonderful work for him.

WALKER I know, Mr. Pinchen, that I ought to have religion, and I feel that I am a great sinner; and whenever I get with good pious people like you and the doctor, and Mr. Wildmarsh, it always makes me feel that I am a desperate sinner. I feel it the more, because I've got a religious turn of mind. I know that I would be happier with religion, and the first spare time I get, I am going to try to get it. I'll go to a protracted meeting, and I won't stop till I get religion. Yes, I'll scuffle with the Lord till I gets forgiven. But it always makes me feel bad to talk about religion, so I'll change the subject. Now, doctor, what about them thar niggers you thought you could sell me?

DR. GAINES I'll see my wife, Mr. Walker, and if she is willing to part with Hannah, I'll sell you Sam and his wife, Hannah. Ah! here comes my wife; I'll mention it.

[*Enter* MRS. GAINES, *left.*]

Ah! my dear, I am glad you've come. I was just telling Mr. Walker, that if you were willing to part with Hannah, I'd sell him Sam and Hannah.

MRS. GAINES Now, Dr. Gaines, I am astonished and surprised that you should think of such a thing. You know what trouble I've had in training up Hannah for a house servant, and now that I've got her so that she knows my ways, you want to sell her. Haven't you niggers enough on the plantation to sell, without selling the servants from under my very nose?

DR. GAINES Oh, yes, my dear; but I can spare Sam, and I don't like to separate him from his wife; and I thought if you could let Hannah go, I'd sell them both. I don't like to separate husbands from their wives.

MRS. GAINES Now, gentlemen, that's just the way with my husband. He thinks more about the welfare and comfort of his slaves, than he does of himself or his family. I am sure you need not feel so bad at the thought of separating Sam from Hannah. They've only been married eight months, and their attachment can't be very strong in that short time. Indeed, I shall be glad if you do sell Sam, for then I'll make Hannah *jump the broomstick*[2]

1. That is, on the Day of Judgment.
2. A quasi-marriage ceremony of unknown origin. Because slaves were considered property, marriages between them had no legal status, and few slaves were married in churches.

with Cato, and I'll have them both here under my eye. I never will again let one of my house servants marry a field hand—never! For when night comes on, the servants are off to the quarters, and I have to holler and holler enough to split my throat before I can make them hear. And another thing: I want you to sell Melinda. I don't intend to keep that mulatto wench about the house any longer.

DR. GAINES My dear, I'll sell any servant from the place to suit you, except Melinda. I can't think of selling her—I can't think of it.

MRS. GAINES I tell you that Melinda shall leave this house, or I'll go. There, now you have it. I've had my life tormented out of me by the presence of that yellow wench, and I'll stand it no longer. I know you love her more than you do me, and I'll—I'll—I'll write—write to my father. [*Weeps.*]

[*Exit* MRS. GAINES, *left.*]

WALKER Why, doctor, your wife's a screamer, ain't she? Ha, ha, ha. Why, doctor, she's got a tongue of her own, ain't she? Why, doctor, it was only last week that I thought of getting a wife myself; but your wife has skeered the idea out of my head. Now, doctor, if you wants to sell the gal, I'll buy her. Husband and wife ought to be on good terms, and your wife won't feel well till the gal is gone. Now, I'll pay you all she's worth, if you wants to sell.

DR. GAINES No, Mr. Walker; the girl my wife spoke of is not for sale. My wife does not mean what she says; she's only a little jealous. I'll get brother Pinchen to talk to her, and get her mind turned upon religious matters, and then she'll forget it. She's only a little jealous.

WALKER I tell you what, doctor, ef you call that a little jealous, I'd like to know what's a heap. I tell you, it will take something more than religion to set your wife right. You had better sell me the gal; I'll pay you cash down, and no grumblin'.

DR. GAINES The girl is not for sale, Mr. Walker; but if you want two good, able-bodied servants, I'll sell you Sam and Big Sally. Sam is trustworthy, and Sally is worth her weight in gold for rough usage.

WALKER Well, doctor, I'll go out and take a look at 'em, for I never buys slaves without examining them well, because they are sometimes injured by overwork or underfeedin'. I don't say that is the case with yours, for I don't believe it is; but as I sell on honor, I must buy on honor.

DR. GAINES Walk out, sir, and you can examine them to your heart's content. Walk right out, sir.

2.2

[SCENE: *View in front of the Great House.*]

[*Examination of* SAM *and* BIG SALLY.—DR. GAINES, WILDMARSH, MR. PINCHEN, *and* WALKER *present.*]

WALKER Well, my boy, what's your name?

SAM Sam, sir, is my name.

WALKER How old are you, Sam?

SAM Ef I live to see next corn plantin' time, I'll be 27, or 30, or 35, or 40—I don't know which, sir.

WALKER Ha, ha, ha. Well, doctor, this is rather a green[3] boy. Well, mer feller, are you sound?

3. Most simple or gullible.

SAM Yes, sir, I spec I is.

WALKER Open your mouth and let me see your teeth. I allers judge a nigger's age by his teeth, same as I dose a hoss. Ah! pretty good set of grinders. Have you got a good appetite?

SAM Yes, sir.

WALKER Can you eat your allowance?

SAM Yes, sir, when I can get it.

WALKER Get out on the floor and dance; I want to see if you are supple.

SAM I don't like to dance; I is got religion.

WALKER Oh, ho! you've got religion, have you? That's so much the better. I likes to deal in the gospel. I think he'll suit me. Now, mer gal, what's your name?

SALLY It is Big Sally, sir.

WALKER How old are you, Sally?

SALLY I don't know, sir; but I heard once dat I was born at sweet pertater diggin' time.

WALKER Ha, ha, ha. Don't know how old you are! Do you know who made you?

SALLY I hev heard who it was in de Bible dat made me, but I dun forget de gentman's name.

WALKER Ha, ha, ha. Well, doctor, this is the greenest lot of niggers I've seen for some time. Well, what do you ask for them?

DR. GAINES You may have Sam for $1000, and Sally for $900. They are worth all I ask for them. You know I never banter,[4] Mr. Walker. There they are; you can take them at that price, or let them alone, just as you please.

WALKER Well, doctor, I reckon I'll take 'em; but it's all they are worth. I'll put the handcuffs on 'em, and then I'll pay you. I likes to go accordin' to Scripter. Scripter says ef eatin' meat will offend your brother, you must quit it; and I say, ef leavin' your slaves without the handcuffs will make 'em run away, you must put the handcuffs on 'em. Now, Sam, don't you and Sally cry. I am of a tender heart, and it allers makes me feel bad to see people cryin'. Don't cry, and the first place I get to, I'll buy each of you a great big *ginger cake*—that I will. Now, Mr. Pinchen, I wish you were going down the river. I'd like to have your company; for I allers likes the company of preachers.

MR. PINCHEN Well, Mr. Walker, I would be much pleased to go down the river with you, but it's too early for me. I expect to go to Natchez[5] in four or five weeks, to attend a camp meetin', and if you were going down then, I'd like it. What kind of niggers sells best in the Orleans[6] market, Mr. Walker?

WALKER Why, field hands. Did you think of goin' in the trade?

MR. PINCHEN Oh, no; only it's a long ways down to Natchez, and I thought I'd just buy five or six niggers, and take 'em down and sell 'em to pay my travelin' expenses. I only want to clear my way.

4. Cheat; in other words, inflate their worth.
5. Mississippi city, a commercial hub on the Mississippi River.
6. New Orleans, which by the 1850s was the center of the U.S. slave trade.

2.3

[SCENE: *Sitting room—Table and rocking chair.*]

[*Enter* MRS. GAINES, *right, followed by* SAMPEY.]

MRS. GAINES I do wish your master would come; I want supper. Run to the gate, Sampey, and see if he is coming.

[*Exit* SAMPEY, *left.*]

That man is enough to break my heart. The patience of an angel could not stand it.

[*Enter* SAMPEY, *left.*]

SAMPEY Yes, missis, master is coming.

[*Enter* DR. GAINES, *left.*]

[*The* DOCTOR *walks about with his hands under his coat, seeming very much elated.*]

MRS. GAINES Why, doctor, what is the matter?

DR. GAINES My dear, don't call me *doctor.*

MRS. GAINES What should I call you?

DR. GAINES Call me Colonel, my dear—Colonel. I have been elected Colonel of the Militia, and I want you to call me by my right name. I always felt that Providence had designed me for something great, and He has just begun to shower His blessings upon me.

MRS. GAINES Dear me, I could never get to calling you Colonel; I've called you Doctor for the last twenty years.

DR. GAINES Now, Sarah, if you will call me Colonel, other people will, and I want you to set the example. Come, my darling, call me Colonel, and I'll give you anything you wish for.

MRS. GAINES Well, as I want a new gold watch and bracelets, I'll commence now. Come, Colonel, we'll go to supper. [*Aside*] Ah! now for my new shawl.—Mrs. Lemme was here today, Colonel, and she had on, Colonel, one of the prettiest shawls, Colonel, I think, Colonel, that I ever saw, Colonel, in my life, Colonel. And there is only one, Colonel, in Mr. Watson's store, Colonel; and that, Colonel, will do, Colonel, for a Colonel's wife.

DR. GAINES Ah! my dear, you never looked so much the lady since I've known you. Go, my darling, get the watch, bracelets and shawl, and tell them to charge them to Colonel Gaines; and when you say "Colonel," always emphasize the word.

MRS. GAINES Come, Colonel, let's go to supper.

DR. GAINES My dear, you're a jewel—you are! [*Exit, right.*]

[*Enter* CATO, *left.*]

CATO Why, whar is massa and missis? I tought dey was here. Ah! by golly, yonder comes a mulatter gal. Yes, it's Mrs. Jones's Tapioca. I'll set up to dat gal, dat I will.

[*Enter* TAPIOCA, *right.*]

Good ebenin', Miss Tappy. How is your folks?

TAPIOCA Pretty well, I tank you.

CATO Miss Tappy, dis wanderin' heart of mine is yours. Come, take a seat! Please to squze my manners; love discommodes me. Take a seat. Now,

Miss Tappy, I loves you; an ef you will jess marry me, I'll make you a happy husband, dat I will. Come, take me as I is.

TAPIOCA But what will Big Jim say?

CATO Big Jim! Why, let dat nigger go to Ginny. I want to know, now, if you is tinkin' about dat common nigger? Why, Miss Tappy, I is surstonished dat you should tink 'bout frowin' yousef away wid a common, ugly lookin' cuss like Big Jim, when you can get a fine lookin', suspectable man like me. Come, Miss Tappy, choose dis day who you have. Afore I go any furder, give me one kiss. Come, give me one kiss. Come, let me kiss you.

TAPIOCA No you shan't—dare now! You shan't kiss me widout you is stronger den I is; and I know you is dat. [*He kisses her.*]

[*Enter* DR. GAINES, *right, and hides.*]

CATO Did you know, Miss Tappy, dat I is de head doctor 'bout dis house? I beats de ole boss all to pieces.

TAPIOCA I hev hearn dat you bleeds and pulls teef.

CATO Yes, Miss Tappy; massa could not get along widout me, for massa was made a doctor by books; but I is a natral doctor. I was born a doctor, jess as Lorenzo Dow[7] was born a preacher. So you see I can't be nuffin' but a doctor, while massa is a bunglin' ole cuss at de bissness.

DR. GAINES [*in a low voice*] Never mind; I'll teach you a lesson, that I will.

CATO You see, Miss Tappy, I was gwine to say—Ah! but afore I forget, jess give me anudder kiss, jess to keep company wid de one dat you give me jess now,—dat's all. [*Kisses her.*] Now, Miss Tappy, duse you know de fuss time dat I seed you?

TAPIOCA No, Mr. Cato, I don't.

CATO Well, it was at de camp meetin'. Oh, Miss Tappy, dat pretty red calliker dress you had on dat time did de work for me. It made my heart flutter—

DR. GAINES [*low voice*] Yes, and I'll make your black hide flutter.

CATO Didn't I hear some noise? By golly, dar is teves in dis house, and I'll drive 'em out.

[*Takes a chair and runs at the* DOCTOR, *and knocks him down. The* DOCTOR *chases* CATO *round the table.*]

CATO Oh, massa, I didn't know 'twas you!

DR. GAINES You scoundrel! I'll whip you well. Stop! I tell you.

3.1

[SCENE: *Sitting room.*]

[MRS. GAINES, *seated in an armchair, reading a letter.*]

[*Enter* HANNAH, *left.*]

MRS. GAINES You need not tell me, Hannah, that you don't want another husband, I know better. Your master has sold Sam, and he's gone down the river, and you'll never see him again. So, go and put on your calico dress, and meet me in the kitchen. I intend for you to *jump the broomstick* with Cato. You need not tell me that you don't want another man. I know

7. Evangelical preacher and abolitionist (1777–1834), famous for his wild and eccentric speaking style.

that there's no woman living that can be happy and satisfied without a husband.

HANNAH Oh, missis, I don't want to jump de broomstick wid Cato. I don't love Cato; I can't love him.

MRS. GAINES Shut up, this moment! What do you know about love? I didn't love your master when I married him, and people don't marry for love now. So go and put on your calico dress, and meet me in the kitchen.

[*Exit* HANNAH, *left.*]

I am glad that the Colonel has sold Sam; now I'll make Hannah marry Cato, and I have them both here under my eye. And I am also glad that the Colonel has parted with Melinda. Still, I'm afraid that he is trying to deceive me. He took the hussy away yesterday, and says he sold her to a trader; but I don't believe it. At any rate, if she's in the neighborhood, I'll find her, that I will. No man ever fools me. [*Exit* MRS. GAINES, *left.*]

3.2

[SCENE: *The kitchen—Slaves at work.*]

[*Enter* HANNAH, *right.*]

HANNAH Oh, Cato, do go and tell missis dat you don't want to jump de broomstick wid me—dat's a good man! Do, Cato; kase I nebber can love you. It was only las week dat massa sold my Sammy, and I don't want any udder man. Do go tell missis dat you don't want me.

CATO No, Hannah, I ain't a gwine to tell missis no such thing, kase I dose want you, and I ain't a-gwine to tell a lie for you ner nobody else. Dar, now yous got it! I don't see why you need to make so much fuss. I is better lookin' den Sam; an' I is a house servant, an' Sam was only a fiel' hand; so you ought to feel proud of a change. So go and do as missis tells you.

[*Exit* HANNAH, *left.*]

Hannah needn't try to get me to tell a lie; I ain't a-gwine to do it, kase I dose want her, an' I is bin wantin' her dis long time, an' soon as massa sold Sam, I knowed I would get her. By golly, I is gwine to be a married man. Won't I be happy! Now, ef I could only jess run away from ole massa, an' get to Canada wid Hannah, den I'd show 'em who I was. Ah! dat reminds me of my song 'bout ole massa and Canada, an' I'll sing it fer yer. Dis is my moriginal hyme. It comed into my head one night when I was fass asleep under an apple tree, looking up at de moon. Now for my song:

AIR—"Dandy Jim."[8]

Come all ye bondmen far and near,
Let's put a song in massa's ear,
It is a song for our poor race,
Who're whipped and trampled with disgrace.

CHORUS

My old massa tells me, Oh,
This is a land of freedom, Oh;

8. That is, sung to the tune of "Dandy Jim from Caroline" (ca. 1844), a popular song by Dan Emmett, who wrote and performed many works for blackface minstrel shows.

Let's look about and see if it's so,
Just as massa tells me, Oh.

He tells us of that glorious one,
I think his name was Washington,
How he did fight for liberty,
To save a threepence tax on tea. [*Chorus.*]

But now we look about and see
That we poor blacks are not so free;
We're whipped and thrashed about like fools,
And have no chance at common schools. [*Chorus.*]

They take our wives, insult and mock,
And sell our children on the block,
They choke us if we say a word,
And say that "niggers" shan't be heard. [*Chorus.*]

Our preachers, too, with whip and cord,
Command obedience in the Lord;
They say they learn it from the big book,
But for ourselves, we dare not look. [*Chorus.*]

There is a country far away,
I think they call it Canada,
And if we reach Victoria's shore,[9]
They say that we are slaves no more.
Now haste, all bondmen, let us go,
And leave this *Christian* country, Oh;
Haste to the land of the British Queen,
Where whips for negroes are not seen.

Now, if we go, we must take the night,
And never let them come in sight;
The bloodhounds will be on our track,
And wo to us if they fetch us back.
Now haste all bondmen, let us go,
And leave this *Christian* country, Oh;
God help us to Victoria's shore,
Where we are free and slaves no more!

[*Enter* MRS. GAINES, *left.*]

MRS. GAINES Ah! Cato, you're ready, are you? Where is Hannah?

CATO Yes, missis; I is bin waitin' dis long time. Hannah has bin here tryin' to swade me to tell you dat I don't want her; but I telled her dat you sed I must jump de broomstick wid her, an' I is gwine to mind you.

MRS. GAINES That's right, Cato; servants should always mind their masters and mistresses, without asking a question.

9. As part of the British Empire, Canada was ruled by Queen Victoria (1819–1901; r. 1837–1901).

CATO Yes, missis, I allers dose what you and massa tells me, an' axes nobody.

[*Enter* HANNAH, *right.*]

MRS. GAINES Ah! Hannah; come, we are waiting for you. Nothing can be done till you come.

HANNAH Oh, missis, I don't want to jump de broomstick wid Cato; I can't love him.

MRS. GAINES Shut up, this moment. Dolly, get the broom. Susan, you take hold of the other end. There, now hold it a little lower—there, a little higher. There, now, that'll do. Now Hannah, take hold of Cato's hand. Let Cato take hold of your hand.

HANNAH Oh, missis, do spare me. I don't want to jump de broomstick wid Cato.

MRS. GAINES Get the cowhide, and follow me to the cellar, and I'll whip you well. I'll let you know how to disobey my orders. Get the cowhide, and follow me to the cellar.

[*Exit* MRS. GAINES *and* HANNAH, *right.*]

DOLLY Oh, Cato, do go an' tell missis dat you don't want Hannah. Don't you hear how she's whippin' her in de cellar? Do go an' tell missis dat you don't want Hannah, and den she'll stop whippin' her.

CATO No, Dolly, I ain't a-gwine to do no such a thing, kase ef I tell missis dat I don't want Hannah, den missis will whip me; ah' I ain't a-gwine to be whipped fer you, ner Hannah, ner nobody else. No, I'll jump de broomstick wid every woman on de place, ef missis wants me to, before I'll be whipped.

DOLLY Cato, ef I was in Hannah's place, I'd see you in de bottomless pit before I'd live wid you, you great big walleyed, empty-headed, knock-kneed fool. You're as mean as your devilish old missis.

CATO Ef you don't quit dat busin' me, Dolly, I'll tell missis as soon as she comes in, an' she'll whip you, you know she will.

[*Enter* MRS. GAINES *and* HANNAH, *right.*]

[MRS. GAINES *fans herself with her handkerchief, and appears fatigued.*]

MRS. GAINES You ought to be ashamed of yourself, Hannah, to make me fatigue myself in this way, to make you do your duty. It's very naughty in you, Hannah. Now, Dolly, you and Susan get the broom, and get out in the middle of the room. There, hold it a little lower—a little higher; there, that'll do. Now, remember that this is a solemn occasion; you are going to jump into matrimony. Now, Cato, take hold of Hannah's hand. There, now, why couldn't you let Cato take hold of your hand before? Now get ready, and when I count three, do you jump. Eyes on the *broomstick!* All ready. One, two, three, and over you go. There, now you're husband and wife, and if you don't live happy together, it's your own fault; for I am sure there's nothing to hinder it. Now, Hannah, come up to the house, and I'll give you some whiskey, and you can make some apple toddy, and you and Cato can have a fine time.

[*Exit* MRS. GAINES *and* HANNAH, *left.*]

DOLLY I tell you what, Susan, when I get married, I is gwine to have a preacher to marry me. I ain't a-gwine to jump de broomstick. Dat will do for fiel' hands, but house servants ought to be 'bove dat.

SUSAN Well, chile, you can't speck anyting else from ole missis. She come from down in Carlina, from 'mong de poor white trash. She don't know any better. You can't speck nothin' more dan a jump from a frog. Missis says she is one of de akastocacy; but she ain't no more of an akastocacy dan I is. Missis says she was born wid a silver spoon in her mouf; ef she was, I wish it had a-choked her, dat's what I wish. Missis wanted to make Linda[1] jump de broomstick wid Glen, but massa ain't a-gwine to let Linda jump de broomstick wid anybody. He's gwine to keep Linda fer heself.

DOLLY You know massa took Linda 'way las' night, an' tell missis dat he has sold her and sent her down de river; but I don't b'lieve he has sold her at all. He went ober towards de poplar farm, an' I tink Linda is ober dar now. Ef she is dar, missis'll find it out, fer she tell'd massa las' night, dat ef Linda was in de neighborhood, she'd find her.

[*Exit* DOLLY *and* SUSAN.]

3.3

[SCENE: *Sitting room—chairs and table.*]

[*Enter* HANNAH, *right.*]

HANNAH I don't keer what missis says; I don't like Cato, an' I won't live wid him. I always love my Sammy, an' I loves him now.

[*Knock at the door—goes to the door.*]

[*Enter* MAJOR MOORE, *center.*]

Walk in, sir; take a seat. I'll call missis, sir; massa is gone away.

[*Exit* HANNAH, *right.*]

MAJOR MOORE So I am here at last, and the Colonel is not at home. I hope his wife is a good-looking woman. I rather like fine-looking women, especially when their husbands are from home. Well, I've studied human nature to some purpose. If you wish to get the goodwill of a man, don't praise his wife, and if you wish to gain the favor of a woman, praise her children, and swear that they are the picture of their father, whether they are or not. Ah! here comes the lady.

[*Enter* MRS. GAINES, *right.*]

MRS. GAINES Good morning, sir!

MAJOR MOORE Good morning, madam! I am Major Moore, of Jefferson. The Colonel and I had seats near each other in the last Legislature.

MRS. GAINES Be seated, sir. I think I've heard the Colonel speak of you. He's away, now; but I expect him every moment. You're a stranger here, I presume?

MAJOR MOORE Yes, madam, I am. I rather like the Colonel's situation here.

MRS. GAINES It is thought to be a fine location.

[*Enter* SAMPEY, *right.*]

Hand me my fan, will you, Sampey?

[SAMPEY *gets the fan and passes near the* MAJOR, *who mistakes the boy for the Colonel's son. He reaches out his hand.*]

1. That is, Melinda.

MAJOR MOORE How do you do, bub? Madam, I should have known that this was the Colonel's son, if I had met him in California; for he looks so much like his papa.

MRS. GAINES [*to the boy*] Get out of here this minute. Go to the kitchen.

[*Exit* SAMPEY, *right.*]

That is one of the niggers, sir.

MAJOR MOORE I beg your pardon, madam; I beg your pardon.

MRS. GAINES No offence, sir; mistakes will be made. Ah! here comes the Colonel.

[*Enter* DR. GAINES, *center.*]

DR. GAINES Bless my soul, how are you, Major? I'm exceedingly pleased to see you. Be seated, be seated, Major.

MRS. GAINES Please excuse me, gentlemen; I must go and look after dinner, for I've no doubt that the Major will have an appetite for dinner, by the time it is ready. [*Exit* MRS. GAINES, *right.*]

MAJOR MOORE Colonel, I'm afraid I've played the devil[2] here today.

DR. GAINES Why, what have you done?

MAJOR MOORE You see, Colonel, I always make it a point, wherever I go, to praise the children, if there are any, and so today, seeing one of your little servants come in, and taking him to be your son, I spoke to your wife of the marked resemblance between you and the boy. I am afraid I've insulted madam.

DR. GAINES Oh! don't let that trouble you. Ha, ha, ha. If you did call him my son, you didn't miss it much. Ha, ha, ha. Come, we'll take a walk, and talk over matters about old times.

[*Exit, left.*]

3.4

[SCENE: *Forest scenery.*]

[*Enter* GLEN, *left.*]

GLEN Oh, how I want to see Melinda! My heart pants and my soul is moved whenever I hear her voice. Human tongue cannot tell how my heart yearns toward her. Oh, God! thou who gavest me life, and implanted in my bosom the love of liberty, and gave me a heart to love, Oh, pity the poor outraged slave! Thou, who canst rend the veil of centuries, speak, Oh, speak, and put a stop to this persecution! What is death, compared to slavery? Oh, heavy curse, to have thoughts, reason, taste, judgment, conscience, and passions like another man, and not have equal liberty to use them! Why was I born with a wish to be free, and still be a slave? Why should I call another man master? And my poor Melinda, she is taken away from me, and I dare not ask the tyrant where she is. It is childish to stand here weeping. Why should my eyes be filled with tears, when my brain is on fire? I will find my wife—I will; and woe to him who shall try to keep me from her!

2. Done mischief.

3.5

[SCENE: *Room in a small cottage on the poplar farm, ten miles from Muddy Creek, and owned by* DR. GAINES.]

[*Enter* MELINDA, *right.*]

MELINDA Here I am, watched, and kept a prisoner in this place. Oh, I would that I could escape, and once more get with Glen. Poor Glen! He does not know where I am. Master took the opportunity, when Glen was in the city with his master, to bring me here to this lonely place, and fearing that mistress would know where I was, he brought me here at night. Oh, how I wish I could rush into the arms of sleep!—that sweet sleep, which visits all alike, descending, like the dews of heaven, upon the bond as well as the free. It would drive from my troubled brain the agonies of this terrible night.

[*Enter* DR. GAINES, *left.*]

DR. GAINES Good evening, Melinda! Are you not glad to see me?

MELINDA Sir, how can I be glad to see one who has made life a burden, and turned my sweetest moments into bitterness?

DR. GAINES Come, Melinda, no more reproaches! You know that I love you, and I have told you, and I tell you again, that if you will give up all idea of having Glen for a husband, I will set you free, let you live in this cottage, and be your own mistress, and I'll dress you like a lady. Come, now, be reasonable!

MELINDA Sir, I am your slave; you can do as you please with the avails of my labor, but you shall never tempt me to swerve from the path of virtue.

DR. GAINES Now, Melinda, that black scoundrel Glen has been putting these notions into your head. I'll let you know that you are my property, and I'll do as I please with you. I'll teach you that there is no limit to my power.

MELINDA Sir, let me warn you that if you compass my ruin, a woman's bitterest curse will be laid upon your head, with all the crushing, withering weight that my soul can impart to it; a curse that shall cling to you throughout the remainder of your wretched life; a curse that shall haunt you like a specter in your dreams by night, and attend upon you by day; a curse, too, that shall embody itself in the ghastly form of the woman whose chastity you will have outraged. Command me to bury myself in yonder stream, and I will obey you. Bid me do anything else, but I beseech you not to commit a double crime—outrage a woman, and make her false to her husband.

DR. GAINES You got a husband! Who is your husband, and when were you married?

MELINDA Glen is my husband, and I've been married four weeks. Old Uncle Joseph married us one night by moonlight. I see you are angry; I pray you not to injure my husband.

DR. GAINES Melinda, you shall never see Glen again. I have bought him from Hamilton, and I will return to Muddy Creek, and roast him at the stake. A black villain, to get into my way in that manner! Here I've come ten miles tonight to see you, and this is the way you receive me!

MELINDA Oh, master, I beg you not to injure my husband! Kill me, but spare him! Do! do! he is my husband!

DR. GAINES You shall never see that black imp again, so good night, my lady! When I come again, you'll give me a more cordial reception. Good night!

[*Exit* DR. GAINES, *left.*]

MELINDA I shall go distracted. I cannot remain here and know that Glen is being tortured on my account. I must escape from this place—I must—I must!

[*Enter* CATO, *right.*]

CATO No, you ain't a-gwine to 'scape, nudder. Massa tells me to keep dese eyes on you, an' I is gwine to do it.

MELINDA Oh, Cato, do let me get away! I beg you, do!

CATO No; I tells you massa telled me to keep you safe; an' ef I let you go, massa will whip me. [*Exit* CATO, *left.*]

[*Enter* MRS. GAINES, *right.*]

MRS. GAINES Ah, you trollop! here you are! Your master told me that he had sold you and sent you down the river, but I knew better; I knew it was a lie. And when he left home this evening, he said he was going to the city on business, and I knew that was a lie too, and determined to follow him, and see what he was up to. I rode all the way over here tonight. My sidesaddle was lent out, and I had to ride ten miles bareback, and I can scarcely walk; and your master has just left here. Now deny that, if you dare.

MELINDA Madam, I will deny nothing which is true. Your husband has just gone from here, but God knows that I am innocent of anything wrong with him.

MRS. GAINES It's a lie! I know better. If you are innocent, what are you doing here, cooped up in this cottage by yourself? Tell me that!

MELINDA God knows that I was brought here against my will, and I beg that you will take me away.

MRS. GAINES Yes, Melinda, I will see that you are taken away, but it shall be after a fashion that you won't like. I know that your master loves you, and I intend to put a stop to it. Here, drink the contents of this vial—drink it!

MELINDA Oh, you will not take my life—you will not!

MRS. GAINES Drink the poison this moment!

MELINDA I cannot drink it.

MRS. GAINES I tell you to drink this poison at once. Drink it, or I will thrust this knife to your heart! The poison or the dagger, this instant!

[*She draws a dagger;* MELINDA *retreats to the back of the room, and seizes a broom.*]

MELINDA I will not drink the poison!

[*They fight;* MELINDA *sweeps off* MRS. GAINES*'s cap, combs, and curls. Curtain falls.*]

4.1

[SCENE: *Interior of a dungeon—*GLEN *in chains.*]

GLEN When I think of my unmerited sufferings, it almost drives me mad. I struck the doctor, and for that, I must remain here loaded with chains. But why did he strike me? He takes my wife from me, sends her off, and then comes and beats me over the head with his cane. I did right to strike him back again. I would I had killed him. Oh! there is a volcano pent up in the hearts of the slaves of these southern states that will burst forth ere long.

When that day comes, woe to those whom its unpitying fury may devour! I would be willing to die, if I could smite down with these chains every man who attempts to enslave his fellow man.

[*Enter* SAMPEY, *right.*]

SAMPEY Glen, I jess bin hear massa call de oberseer, and I spec somebody is gwine to be whipped. Anudder ting: I know whar massa took Linda to. He took her to de poplar farm, an' he went away las' night, an' missis she follow after massa, an' she ain't come back yet. I tell you, Glen, de debil will be to pay on dis place, but don't you tell anybody dat I tole you.

[*Exit* SAMPEY, *right.*]

4.2

[SCENE: *Parlor.*]

[DR. GAINES, *alone.*]

DR. GAINES Yes, I will have the black rascal well whipped, and then I'll sell him. It was most fortunate for me that Hamilton was willing to sell him to me.

[*Enter* MR. SCRAGG, *left.*]

I have sent for you, Mr. Scragg. I want you to take Glen out of the dungeon, take him into the tobacco house, fasten him down upon the stretcher, and give him five hundred lashes upon his bare back; and when you have whipped him, feel his pulse, and report to me how it stands, and if he can bear more, I'll have you give him an additional hundred or two, as the case may be.

SCRAGG I tell you, doctor, that suits me to a charm. I've long wanted to whip that nigger. When your brother-in-law came here to board, and brought that boy with him, I felt bad to see a nigger dressed up in such fine clothes, and I wanted to whip him right off. I tell you, doctor, I had rather whip that nigger than go to heaven, any day—that I had!

DR. GAINES Go, Mr. Scragg, and do your duty. Don't spare the whip!

SCRAGG I will, sir; I'll do it in order. [*Exit* SCRAGG, *left.*]

DR. GAINES Everything works well now, and when I get Glen out of the way, I'll pay Melinda another visit, and she'll give me a different reception. But I wonder where my wife is? She left word that she was going to see her brother, but I am afraid that she has got on my track. That woman is the pest of my life. If there's any place in heaven for her, I'd be glad if the Lord would take her home, for I've had her too long already. But what noise is that? What can that be? What is the matter?

[*Enter* SCRAGG, *left, with face bloody.*]

SCRAGG Oh, dear me! oh, my head! That nigger broke away from me, and struck me over the head with a stick. Oh, dear me! Oh!

DR. GAINES Where is he, Mr. Scragg?

SCRAGG Oh! sir, he jumped out of the window; he's gone. Oh! my head; he's cracked my skull. Oh, dear me, I'm kilt! Oh! oh! oh!

[*Enter* SLAVES, *right.*]

DR. GAINES Go, Dolly, and wash Mr. Scragg's head with some whiskey, and bind it up. Go at once. And Bob, you run over to Mr. Hall, and tell him to come with his hounds; we must go after the rascal.

[*Exit all except the* DOCTOR, *right.*]

This will never do. When I catch the scoundrel, I'll make an example of him; I'll whip him to death. Ah! here comes my wife. I wonder what she comes now for? I must put on a sober face, for she looks angry.

[*Enter* MRS. GAINES, *left.*]

Ah! my dear, I am glad you've come, I've been so lonesome without you. Oh! Sarah, I don't know what I should do if the Lord should take you home to heaven. I don't think that I should be able to live without you.

MRS. GAINES Dr. Gaines, you ought to be ashamed to sit there and talk in that way. You know very well that if the Lord should call me home to glory tonight, you'd jump for joy. But you need not think that I am going to leave this world before you. No; with the help of the Lord, I'll stay here to foil you in your meanness. I've been on your track, and a dirty track it is, too. You ought to be ashamed of yourself. See what promises you made me before we were married; and this is the way you keep your word. When I married you, everybody said that it was a pity that a woman of my sweet temper should be linked to such a man as you.

[*She weeps and wrings her hands.*]

DR. GAINES Come, my dear, don't make a fool of yourself. Come, let's go to supper, and a strong cup of tea will help your head.

MRS. GAINES Tea help my head! Tea won't help my head. You're a brute of a man; I always knew I was a fool for marrying you. There was Mr. Comstock, he wanted me, and he loved me, and he said I was an angel, so he did; and he loved me, and he was rich; and mother always said that he loved me more than you, for when he used to kiss me, he always squeezed my hand. You never did such a thing in your life.

[*She weeps and wrings her hands.*]

DR. GAINES Come, my dear, don't act so foolish.

MRS. GAINES Yes; everything I do is foolish. You're a brute of a man; I won't live with you any longer. I'll leave you—that I will. I'll go and see a lawyer, and get a divorce from you—so I will.

DR. GAINES Well, Sarah, if you want a divorce, you had better engage Mr. Barker. He's the best lawyer in town; and if you want some money to facilitate the business, I'll draw a check for you.

MRS. GAINES So you want me to get a divorce, do you? Well, I won't have a divorce; no, I'll never leave you, as long as the Lord spares me.

[*Exit* MRS. GAINES, *right.*]

4.3

[SCENE: *Forest at night—Large tree.*]

[*Enter* MELINDA, *left.*]

MELINDA This is indeed a dark night to be out and alone on this road. But I must find my husband, I must. Poor Glen! if he only knew that I was here, and could get to me, he would. What a curse slavery is! It separates husbands from their wives, and tears mothers from their helpless offspring, and blights all our hopes for this world. I must try to reach Muddy Creek before daylight, and seek out my husband. What's that I hear?—footsteps? I'll get behind this tree.

[*Enter* GLEN, *right.*]

GLEN It is so dark, I'm afraid I've missed the road. Still, this must be the right way to the poplar farm. And if Bob told me the truth, when he said that Melinda was at the poplar farm, I will soon be with her; and if I once get her in my arms, it will be a strong man that shall take her from me. Aye, a dozen strong men shall not be able to wrest her from my arms.

[MELINDA *rushes from behind the tree.*]

MELINDA Oh, Glen! It is my husband—it is!

GLEN Melinda! Melinda! it is, it is. Oh God! I thank Thee for this manifestation of Thy kindness. Come, come, Melinda, we must go at once to Canada. I escaped from the overseer, whom Dr. Gaines sent to flog me. Yes, I struck him over the head with his own club, and I made the wine flow freely; yes, I pounded his old skillet well for him, and then jumped out of the window. It was a leap for freedom. Yes, Melinda, it was a leap for freedom. I've said "master" for the last time. I am free; I'm bound for Canada. Come, let's be off, at once, for the negro dogs will be put upon our track. Let us once get beyond the Ohio River, and all will be right.

[*Exit right.*]

5.1

[SCENE: *Barroom in the American Hotel—Travelers lounging in chairs, and at the bar.*]

[*Enter* BILL JENNINGS, *right.*]

BARKEEPER Why, Jennings, how do you do?

JENNINGS Say Mr. Jennings, if you please.

BARKEEPER Well, Mr. Jennings, if that suits you better. How are times? We've been expecting you, for some days.

JENNINGS Well, before I talk about the times, I want my horses put up, and want you to tell me where my niggers are to stay tonight. Sheds, stables, barns, and everything else here, seems pretty full, if I am a judge.

BARKEEPER Oh! I'll see to your plunder.

FIRST LOUNGER I say, Barkeeper, make me a brandy cocktail, strong. Why, how do you do, Mr. Jennings?

JENNINGS Pretty well, Mr. Peters. Cold evening, this.

FIRST LOUNGER Yes, this is cold. I heard you speak of your niggers. Have you got a pretty large gang?

JENNINGS No, only thirty-three. But they are the best that the country can afford. I shall clear a few dimes, this trip. I hear that the price is up.

[*Enter* MR. WHITE, *right.*]

WHITE Can I be accommodated here tonight, landlord?

BARKEEPER Yes, sir; we've bed for man and beast. [*To the waiter*] Go, Dick, and take the gentleman's coat and hat. [*To* MR. WHITE] You're a stranger in these parts, I rec'on.

WHITE Yes, I am a stranger here.

SECOND LOUNGER Where mout you come from, ef it's a far question?

WHITE I am from Massachusetts.

THIRD LOUNGER I say, cuss Massachusetts!

FIRST LOUNGER I say so too. There is where the fanatics live; cussed traitors. The President ought to hang 'em all.

WHITE I say, landlord, if this is the language that I am to hear, I would like to go into a private room.

BARKEEPER We ain't got no private room empty.

FIRST LOUNGER Maybe you're mad 'bout what I said 'bout your state. Ef you is, I've only to say that this is a free country, and people talks what they please; an' ef you don't like it, you can better yourself.

WHITE Sir, if this is a free country, why do you have slaves here? I saw a gang at the door, as I came in.

SECOND LOUNGER He didn't mean that this was a free country for niggers. He meant that it's free for white people. And another thing, ef you get to talking 'bout freedom for niggers, you'll catch what you won't like, mister. It's right for niggers to be slaves.

WHITE But I saw some white slaves.

FIRST LOUNGER Well, they're white niggers.

WHITE Well, sir, I am from a free state, and I thank God for it; for the worst act that a man can commit upon his fellow man, is to make him a slave. Conceive of a mind, a living soul, with the germs of faculties which infinity cannot exhaust, as it first beams upon you in its glad morning of existence, quivering with life and joy, exulting in the glorious sense of its developing energies, beautiful, and brave, and generous, and joyous, and free—the clear pure spirit bathed in the auroral light of its unconscious immortality—and then follow it in its dark and dreary passage through slavery, until oppression stifles and kills, one by one, every inspiration and aspiration of its being, until it becomes a dead soul entombed in a living frame!

THIRD LOUNGER Stop that; stop that, I say. That's treason to the country; that's downright rebellion.

BARKEEPER Yes, it is. And another thing—this is not a meeting house.

FIRST LOUNGER Yes, if you talk such stuff as that, you'll get a chunk of cold lead in you, that you will.

[*Enter* DR. GAINES *and* SCRAGG, *followed by* CATO, *right.*]

DR. GAINES Gentlemen, I am in pursuit of two valuable slaves, and I will pay five hundred dollars for their arrest.

[*Exit* MR. WHITE, *left.*]

FIRST LOUNGER I'll bet a picayune[3] that your niggers have been stolen by that cussed feller from Massachusetts. Don't you see he's gone?

DR. GAINES Where is the man? If I can lay my hands on him, he'll never steal another nigger. Where is the scoundrel?

FIRST LOUNGER Let's go after the feller. I'll go with you. Come, foller me.

[*Exit all, left, except* CATO *and the waiter.*]

CATO Why don't you bring in massa's saddlebags? What de debil you standin' dar for? You common country niggers don't know nuffin', no how. Go an' get massa's saddlebags, and bring 'em in.

[*Exit servant, right.*]

By golly! ebry body's gone, an' de barkeeper too. I'll tend de bar myself now; an' de fuss gemman I waits on will be dis gemman of color. [*Goes behind the counter, and drinks.*] Ah, dis is de stuff fer me; it makes my head swim; it makes me happy right off. I'll take a little more.

3. A Spanish half-real piece; that is, a coin of small value.

[*Enter* BARKEEPER, *left.*]

BARKEEPER What are you doing behind that bar, you black cuss?

CATO I is lookin' for massa's saddlebags, sir. Is dey here?

BARKEEPER But what were you drinking there?

CATO Me drinkin'! Why, massa, you muss be mistaken. I ain't drink nuffin'.

BARKEEPER You infernal whelp, to stand there and lie in that way!

CATO Oh, yes, seer, I did tase dat coffee in dat bottle; dat's all I did.

[*Enter* MR. WHITE, *left, excited.*]

MR. WHITE I say, sir, is there no place of concealment in your house? They are after me, and my life is in danger. Say, sir, can't you hide me away?

BARKEEPER Well, you ought to hold your tongue when you come into our state.

MR. WHITE But, sir, the Constitution gives me the right to speak my sentiments, at all times and in all places.

BARKEEPER We don't care for Constitutions nor nothin' else. We made the Constitution, and we'll break it. But you had better hide away; they are coming, and they'll lynch you, that they will. Come with me; I'll hide you in the cellar. Foller me.

[*Exit* BARKEEPER *and* WHITE, *left.*]

[*Enter the mob, right.*]

DR. GAINES If I can once lay my hands on that scoundrel, I'll blow a hole through his head.

JENNINGS Yes, I say so too; for no one knows whose niggers are safe, nowadays. I must look after my niggers. Who is that I see in the distance? I believe it's that cussed Massachusetts feller. Come, let's go after him.

[*Exit the mob, right.*]

5.2

[SCENE: *Forest at night.*]

[*Enter* GLEN *and* MELINDA, *right.*]

MELINDA I am so tired and hungry, that I cannot go further. It is so cloudy that we cannot see the North Star, and therefore cannot tell whether we are going to Canada, or further South. Let's sit down here.

GLEN I know that we cannot see the North Star, Melinda, and I fear we've lost our way. But, see! the clouds are passing away, and it'll soon be clear. See! yonder is a star; yonder is another and another. Ah! yonder is the North Star, and we are safe![4]

"Star of the North! though night winds drift
  The fleecy drapery of the sky
Between thy lamp and me, I lift,
  Yea, lift with hope my sleepless eye,
To the blue heights wherein thou dwellest,
And of a land of freedom tellest.

4. In the following lines, Glen recites in its entirety "The Fugitive Slave's Apostrophe to the North Star" (1840), by the New England minister and abolitionist John Pierpont. (An "apostrophe" is an exclamatory address to a specified person or thing.)

"Star of the North! while blazing day
Pours round me its full tide of light,
And hides thy pale but faithful ray,
I, too, lie hid, and long for night:
For night: I dare not walk at noon,
Nor dare I trust the faithless moon—

"Nor faithless man, whose burning lust
For gold hath riveted my chain—
Nor other leader can I trust
But thee, of even the starry train;
For all the host around thee burning,
Like faithless man, keep turning, turning.

"I may not follow where they go—
Star of the North! I look to thee
While on I press; for well I know,
Thy light and truth shall set me free—
Thy light, that no poor slave deceiveth;
Thy truth, that all my soul believeth.

"Thy beam is on the glassy breast
Of the still spring, upon whose brink
I lay my weary limbs to rest,
And bow my parching lips to drink.
Guide of the friendless negro's way,
I bless thee for this quiet ray!

"In the dark top of southern pines
I nestled, when the Driver's horn
Called to the field, in lengthening lines,
My fellows, at the break of morn.
And there I lay till thy sweet face
Looked in upon 'my hiding place.'

"The tangled cane-brake, where I crept
For shelter from the heat of noon,
And where, while others toiled, I slept,
Till wakened by the rising moon,
As its stalks felt the night wind free,
Gave me to catch a glimpse of thee.

"Star of the North! in bright array
The constellations round thee sweep,
Each holding on its nightly way,
Rising, or sinking in the deep,
And, as it hangs in mid heaven flaming,
The homage of some nation claiming.

"*This* nation to the Eagle cowers;
Fit ensign! she's a bird of spoil—

Like worships like! for each devours
The earnings of another's toil.
I've felt her talons and her beak,
And now the gentler Lion[5] seek.

"The Lion, at the Monarch's feet
Crouches, and lays his mighty paw
Into her lap!—an emblem meet
Of England's Queen, and English law:
Queen, that hath made her Islands free!
Law, that holds out its shield to me!

"Star of the North! upon that shield
Thou shinest—Oh, forever shine!
The negro, from the cotton field
Shall, then, beneath its orb recline,
And feed the Lion, couched before it,
Nor heed the Eagle, screaming o'er it!"

With the thoughts of servitude behind us, and the North Star before us, we will go forward with cheerful hearts. Come, Melinda, let's go on.

[*Exit, left.*]

5.3

[SCENE: *A street.*]

[*Enter* MR. WHITE, *right.*]

MR. WHITE I am glad to be once more in a free state. If I am caught again south of Mason and Dixon's line,[6] I'll give them leave to lynch me. I came near losing my life. This is the way our constitutional rights are trampled upon. But what care these men about Constitutions, or anything else that does not suit them? But I must hasten on. [*Exit, left.*]

[*Enter* CATO, *in disguise, right.*]

CATO I wonder ef dis is me? By golly, I is free as a frog. But maybe I is mistaken; maybe dis ain't me. Cato, is dis you? Yes, seer. Well, now it is me, an' I em a free man. But, stop! I muss change my name, kase ole massa might foller me, and somebody might tell him dat dey seed Cato; so I'll change my name, and den he won't know me ef he sees me. Now, what shall I call myself? I'm now in a suspectable part of de country, an' I muss have a suspectable name. Ah! I'll call myself Alexander Washington Napoleon Pompey Caesar.[7] Dar, now, dat's a good long, suspectable name, and everybody

5. An emblem of England (which has three lions in its heraldic arms), and thus of Canada. The Eagle represents the United States, whose Great Seal features a bald eagle.
6. Literally, the line established (1867–79) by the English surveyors Charles Mason and Jeremiah Dixon to fix the boundary between Maryland and Pennsylvania and between Pennsylvania and present-day West Virginia; it became shorthand for the border between slave and free states.
7. A string of names of heroic figures from modern (Washington, Napoleon) and classical (Alexander, Pompey, Caesar) history; all were notable generals.

will suspect me. Let me see; I wonder ef I can't make up a song on my escape? I'll try.

AIR—"Dearest Mae."[8]

Now, freemen, listen to my song, a story I'll relate,
It happened in de valley of de ole Kentucky State:
Dey marched me out into de fiel', at every break of day,
And work me dar till late sunset, widout a cent of pay.

Chorus.—Dey work me all de day,
Widout a bit of pay,
And thought, because dey fed me well,
I would not run away.

Massa gave me his ole coat, an' thought I'd happy be,
But I had my eye on de North Star, an' thought of liberty;
Ole massa lock de door, an' den he went to sleep,
I dress myself in his bess clothes, an' jump into de street.

Chorus.—Dey work me all de day,
Widout a bit of pay,
So I took my flight, in the middle of de night,
When de sun was gone away.

Sed I, dis chile's a freeman now, he'll be a slave no more;
I travel'd faster all dat night, dan I ever did before.
I came up to a farmer's house, jest at de break of day,
And saw a white man standin' dar, sed he, "You are a runaway."

Chorus.—Dey work me all de day, &c.

I tole him I had left de whip, an' bayin' of de hound,
To find a place where man is man, ef sich dar can be found;
Dat I had heard, in Canada, dat all mankind are free,
An' dat I was going dar in search of liberty.

Chorus.—Dey work me all de day, &c.

I've not committed any crime, why should I run away?
Oh! shame upon your laws, dat drive me off to Canada.
You loudly boast of liberty, an' say your state is free,
But ef I tarry in your midst, will you protect me?

Chorus.—Dey work me all de day, &c.

[*Exit, left.*]

5.4

[SCENE: *Dining room.—Table spread.*]

[MRS. NEAL *and* CHARLOTTE.]

MRS. NEAL Thee may put the tea to draw, Charlotte. Thy father will be in soon, and we must have breakfast.[9]

8. Popular minstrel song by Francis Lynch and L. V. H. Crosby (1848).
9. The use of the familiar "thee" and "thy" for "you" and "your" indicates that the Neals are Quakers, many of whom were active in the abolition movement and the Underground Railroad.

[*Enter* MR. NEAL, *left.*]

I think, Simeon, it is time those people were called. Thee knows that they may be pursued, and we ought not to detain them long here.

MR. NEAL Yes, Ruth, thou art right. Go, Charlotte, and knock on their chamber door, and tell them that breakfast is ready.

[*Exit* CHARLOTTE, *right.*]

MRS. NEAL Poor creatures! I hope they'll reach Canada in safety. They seem to be worthy persons.

[*Enter* CHARLOTTE, *right.*]

CHARLOTTE I've called them, mother, and they'll soon be down. I'll put the breakfast on the table.

[*Enter* NEIGHBOR JONES, *left.*]

MR. NEAL Good morning, James. Thee has heard, I presume, that we have two very interesting persons in the house?

JONES Yes, I heard that you had two fugitives by the Underground road,[1] last night; and I've come over to fight for them, if any persons come to take them back.

[*Enter* THOMAS, *right.*]

MR. NEAL Go, Thomas, and harness up the horses and put them to the covered wagon, and be ready to take these people on, as soon as they get their breakfast. Go, Thomas, and hurry thyself.

[*Exit* THOMAS, *right.*]

And so thee wants to fight this morning, James?

JONES Yes; as you belongs to a society that don't believe in fighting, and I does believe in that sort of thing, I thought I'd come and relieve you of that work, if there is any to be done.

[*Enter* GLEN *and* MELINDA, *right.*]

MR. NEAL Good morning, friends. I hope thee rested well, last night.

MRS. NEAL Yes, I hope thee had a good night's rest.

GLEN I thank you, madam, we did.

MR. NEAL I'll introduce thee to our neighbor, James Jones. He's a staunch friend of thy people.

JONES I am glad to see you. I've come over to render assistance, if any is needed.

MRS. NEAL Come, friends, take seats at the table. Thee'll take seats there. [*To* GLEN *and* MELINDA] [*All take seats at the table.*] Does thee take sugar and milk in thy tea?

MELINDA I thank you, we do.

JONES I'll look at your *Tribune,* Uncle Simeon, while you're eating.

MR. NEAL Thee'll find it on the table.

MRS. NEAL I presume thee's anxious to get to thy journey's end?

GLEN Yes, madam, we are. I am told that we are not safe in any of the free states.

MR. NEAL I am sorry to tell thee, that that is too true. Thee will not be safe until thee gets on British soil. I wonder what keeps Thomas; he should have been here with the team.

1. The Underground Railroad, a loose network of freeborn blacks, former slaves, and sympathetic whites who helped escaped slaves make their way north to the free states or to Canada.

[*Enter* THOMAS, *left.*]

THOMAS All's ready; and I've written the prettiest song that was ever sung. I call it "The Underground Railroad."

MR. NEAL Thomas, thee can eat thy breakfast far better than thee can write a song, as thee calls it. Thee must hurry thyself, when I send thee for the horses, Thomas. Here lately, thee takes thy time.

THOMAS Well, you see I've been writing poetry; that's the reason I've been so long. If you wish it, I'll sing it to you.

JONES Do let us hear the song.

MRS. NEAL Yes, if Thomas has written a ditty, do let us hear it.

MR. NEAL Well, Thomas, if thee has a ditty, thee may recite it to us.

THOMAS Well, I'll give it to you. Remember that I call it "The Underground Railroad."

AIR—"Wait for the Wagon."[2]

Oh, where is the invention
  Of this growing age,
Claiming the attention
  Of statesman, priest, or sage,
In the many railways
  Through the nation found,
Equal to the Yankees'
  Railway underground?

Chorus.—No one hears the whistle,
  Or rolling of the cars,
While negroes ride to freedom
  Beyond the stripes and stars.

On the Southern borders
  Are the Railway stations,
Negroes get free orders
  While on the plantations;
For all, of ev'ry color,
  First-class cars are found,
While they ride to freedom
  By Railway under ground.

Chorus.—No one hears the whistle, &c.

Masters in the morning
  Furiously rage,
Cursing the inventions
  Of this knowing age;
Order out the bloodhounds,
  Swear they'll bring them back,
Dogs return exhausted,
  Cannot find the track.

Chorus.—No one hears the whistle, &c.

2. American folk song popularized in the 1850s.

Travel is increasing,
  Build a double track,
Cars and engines wanted,
  They'll come, we have no lack.
Clear the track of loafers,
  See that crowded car!
Thousands passing yearly,
  Stock is more than par.

Chorus.—No one hears the whistle, &c.

JONES Well done! That's a good song. I'd like to have a copy of them verses.

[*Knock at the door.* CHARLOTTE *goes to the door, and returns.*]

[*Enter* CATO, *left, still in disguise.*]

MR. NEAL Who is this we have? Another of the outcasts, I presume?

CATO Yes, seer; I is gwine to Canada, an' I met a man, an' he tole me dat you would give me some wittals an' help me on de way. By golly! ef dar ain't Glen an' Melinda. Dey don't know me in dese fine clothes. [*Goes up to them.*] Ah, chillen! I is one wid you. I golly, I is here too! [*They shake hands.*]

GLEN Why, it is Cato, as I live!

MELINDA Oh, Cato, I am so glad to see you! But how did you get here?

CATO Ah, chile, I come wid ole massa to hunt you; an' you see I get tired huntin' you, an' I am now huntin' for Canada. I leff de ole boss in de bed at de hotel; an' you see I thought, afore I left massa, I'd jess change clothes wid him; so, you see, I is fixed up—ha, ha, ha. Ah, chillen! I is gwine wid you.

MRS. NEAL Come, sit thee down, and have some breakfast.

CATO Tank you, madam, I'll do dat. [*Sits down and eats.*]

MR. NEAL This is pleasant for thee to meet one of thy friends.

GLEN Yes, sir, it is; I would be glad if we could meet more of them. I have a mother and sister still in slavery, and I would give worlds, if I possessed them, if by so doing I could release them from their bondage.

THOMAS We are all ready, sir, and the wagon is waiting.

MRS. NEAL Yes, thee had better start.

CATO Ef anybody tries to take me back to ole massa, I'll pull ebry toof out of dar heads, dat I will! As soon as I get to Canada, I'll set up a doctor shop, an' won't I be poplar? Den I rec'on I will. I'll pull teef fer all de people in Canada. Oh, how I wish I had Hannah wid me! It makes me feel bad when I tink I ain't a-gwine to see my wife no more. But, come, chillen, let's be makin' tracks. Dey say we is most to de British side.

MR. NEAL Yes, a few miles further, and you'll be safe beyond the reach of the Fugitive Slave Law.[3]

CATO Ah, dat's de talk fer dis chile.

[*Exit, center.*]

3. The 1850 law that required citizens of free as well as slave states to assist in catching fugitive slaves, who were denied jury trials or any opportunity to submit testimony.

5.5

[SCENE: *The Niagara River—A ferry.*]

[FERRYMAN, *fastening his small boat.*]

FERRYMAN [*advancing, takes out his watch*] I swan,[4] if it ain't one o'clock. I thought it was dinner time. Now there's no one here, I'll go to dinner, and if anybody comes, they can wait until I return. I'll go at once. [*Exit, left.*]

[*Enter* MR. WHITE, *right, with an umbrella.*]

MR. WHITE I wonder where that ferryman is? I want to cross to Canada. It seems a little showery, or else the mist from the Falls[5] is growing thicker.

[*Takes out his sketchbook and pencils—sketches.*]

[*Enter* CANE PEDLAR, *right.*]

PEDLAR Want a good cane today, sir? Here's one from Goat Island—very good, sir, straight and neat—only one dollar. I've a wife and nine small children—youngest is nursing, and the oldest only three years old. Here's a cane from Table Rock, sir. Please buy one! I've had no breakfast today. My wife's got the rheumatics, and the children's got the measles. Come, sir, do buy a cane! I've a lame shoulder, and can't work.

MR. WHITE Will you stop your confounded talk, and let me alone? Don't you see that I am sketching? You've spoiled a beautiful scene for me, with your nonsense.

[*Enter* SECOND PEDLAR, *right.*]

SECOND PEDLAR Want any bead bags, or money purses? These are all real Ingen bags, made by the Black Hawk Ingens. Here's a pretty bag, sir, only 75 cents. Here's a money purse, 50 cents. Please, sir, buy something! My wife's got the fever and ague, and the house is full of children, and they're all sick. Come, sir, do help a worthy man!

MR. WHITE Will you hold your tongue? You've spoiled some of the finest pictures in the world. Don't you see that I am sketching?

[*Exit* PEDLARS, *right, grumbling.*]

I am glad those fellows have gone; now I'll go a little further up the shore, and see if I can find another boat. I want to get over. [*Exit, left.*]

[*Enter* DR. GAINES, SCRAGG, *and an* OFFICER.]

OFFICER I don't think that your slaves have crossed yet, and my officers will watch the shore below here, while we stroll up the river. If I once get my hands on them, all the Abolitionists in the state shall not take them from me.

DR. GAINES I hope they have not got over, for I would not lose them for two thousand dollars, especially the gal.

[*Enter* FIRST PEDLAR.]

PEDLAR Wish to get a good cane, sir? This stick was cut on the very spot where Sam Patch[6] jumped over the falls. Only 50 cents. I have a sick wife and thirteen children. Please buy a cane; I ain't had no dinner.

OFFICER Get out of the way! Gentlemen, we'll go up the shore.

[*Exit, left.*]

4. Swear.
5. That is, Niagara Falls, divided by Goat Island; the main vantage point for tourists in the mid-1800s was Table Rock.
6. A daredevil known as the "Yankee Leaper"; in October 1829, he became the first person to jump into Niagara Falls and survive. He died one month later after jumping into the Genesee River from the High Falls of Rochester, New York.

[*Enter* CATO, *right.*]

CATO I is loss fum de cumpny, but dis is de ferry, and I spec dey'll soon come. But didn't we have a good time las' night in Buffalo? Dem dar Buffalo gals make my heart flutter, dat dey did. But, tanks be to de Lord, I is got religion. I got it las' night in de meetin'. Before I got religion, I was a great sinner; I got drunk, an' took de name of de Lord in vain. But now I is a conwerted man; I is bound for hebben; I toats de witness in my bosom; I feel dat my name is rote in de book of life. But dem niggers in de Vine Street Church las' night shout an' make sich a fuss, dey give me de headache. But, tank de Lord, I is got religion, an' now I'll be a preacher, and den dey'll call me de Rev. Alexander Washington Napoleon Pompey Caesar. Now I'll preach and pull teef, bofe at de same time. Oh, how I wish I had Hannah wid me! Cuss ole massa, fer ef it warn't for him, I could have my wife wid me. Ef I hadn't religion, I'd say "Damn ole massa!" but as I is a religious man, an' belongs to de church, I won't say no sich a thing. But who is dat I see comin'? Oh, it's a whole heap of people. Good Lord! what is de matter?

[*Enter* GLEN *and* MELINDA, *left, followed by* OFFICERS.]

GLEN Let them come; I am ready for them. He that lays hands on me or my wife shall feel the weight of this club.

MELINDA Oh, Glen, let's die here, rather than again go into slavery.

OFFICER I am the United States Marshal. I have a warrant from the Commissioner to take you, and bring you before him. I command assistance.

[*Enter* DR. GAINES, SCRAGG, *and* OFFICER, *right.*]

DR. GAINES Here they are. Down with the villain! down with him! but don't hurt the gal!

[*Enter* MR. WHITE, *right.*]

MR. WHITE Why, bless me! these are the slaveholding fellows. I'll fight for freedom!

[*Takes hold of his umbrella with both hands.—The fight commences, in which* GLEN, CATO, DR. GAINES, SCRAGG, WHITE, *and the* OFFICERS *take part.—*FERRYMAN *enters, and runs to his boat.—*DR. GAINES, SCRAGG, *and the* OFFICERS *are knocked down;* GLEN, MELINDA, *and* CATO *jump into the boat, and as it leaves the shore and floats away,* GLEN *and* CATO *wave their hats, and shout loudly for freedom.—Curtain falls.*]

AUGUST STRINDBERG

1849–1912

When scholars try to decide who invented modern drama, their arguments focus on two Scandinavian playwrights: the Norwegian HENRIK IBSEN and the Swede Johan August Strindberg. Ibsen is the more classical writer of the two: his plays are tightly constructed, formally controlled, and carefully paced. Strindberg, by contrast, is a modernist rebel: his plays are flights of fancy, manifestations of a wild imagination that created characters engaged in a perpetual struggle of wills and desires. Strindberg refused to have anything to do with inherited forms of drama. Instead, he reinvented drama from scratch. In order to find new models for his plays, he turned to the most unlikely places. He read contemporary philosophy—for example, the German philosopher Friedrich Nietzsche. He explored the logic of dreams. He studied Eastern religions such as Hinduism. At the same time, he made a name for himself as a painter and wrote a voluminous geographical and cultural history of Sweden as well as a large number of essays, pamphlets, and books on a great variety of subjects, including the occult, magic, and science. Strindberg's career was littered with ill-conceived and quixotic projects, such as his attempts to synthesize gold, which nearly cost him his sanity. Even more disturbing, and notorious, were his anti-Semitic pamphlets and his attacks on the women's rights movement. But somehow out of this volatile life and mind emerged a number of modernism's most compelling and revolutionary plays.

Strindberg was born into a lower-middle-class family, but his mother had been a servant. The stigma attached to this parentage, which Strindberg captured and exaggerated in his first autobiographical novel, *The Son of a Servant* (1886), continued to haunt him to the end of his life. So did his lack of economic resources. He was financially dependent on his friends as early as his student days in Upsala, and even after he had established himself as a writer he could barely make ends meet. His precarious finances forced him to give up his university studies and take jobs as a teacher and also, briefly, as an actor. Eventually he landed a somewhat more secure position as a librarian, which allowed him enough free time to start his career as a writer. But the uneventful and quiet periods in Strindberg's life were few, in part because of his difficult relations with women. His first marriage—to Siri von Essen, an independent and freethinking Finnish aristocrat—lasted for seven tumultuous years and became the subject of his autobiographical novel *A Madman's Defense*

(1888). At the same time, his professional life was in almost as much turmoil. Some of his early plays were staged with relative success, but Strindberg felt attacked by critics and ignored by the theater establishment, a sense that persisted throughout his life. This perceived lack of appreciation was also why he left Sweden in 1883, beginning a long self-imposed exile in France, Germany, Switzerland, and Denmark, interrupted only briefly by returns home.

Many of Strindberg's best-known plays, including *The Father* (1887) and *MISS JULIE* (1888), were first produced outside Sweden, where he first achieved fame as a dramatist. Most of the important influences on Strindberg were likewise European. He engaged in a long correspondence with the influential Danish critic and philosopher Georg Brandes and had less extensive exchanges with Friedrich Nietzsche and Émile Zola. While living in Berlin, he met the director Max Reinhardt, who produced several of Strindberg's plays to great acclaim. Strindberg made friends, but he had a greater talent for making enemies, and he often broke with friends and supporters for no good reason. One of the targets of Strindberg's ire was Ibsen, the older and more established of the two Scandinavian playwrights.

Even though Strindberg had been a professed atheist for much of his life, in the 1890s he increasingly turned to religion, occultism, and pseudo-science. This period also coincided with the end of his volatile second marriage, to Frida Uhl, an Austrian writer. In 1895, after separating from her, he found himself in desolate circumstances in Paris and stopped writing literature entirely. Instead, he spent his scant funds purchasing chemical equipment with which he attempted to produce gold. Paranoid delusions, illness, and failed experiments, together with the mystical writings of Emanuel Swedenborg (1688–1772), fueled his mental instability. The autobiographical *Inferno* (ca. 1898) and his *Occult Diary* (written 1896–1908) sadly testify to this physical and mental decline. In 1897, when he was close to fifty years old, he finally returned permanently to Sweden.

Upon his return to Sweden, Strindberg started to write plays again, but in a very different mode. Whereas his earlier plays had concentrated on single events and encounters, these new, symbolist and expressionist plays, including *The Road to Damascus* (1898) and *The Dream Play* (1901), unfold in loosely connected scenes and episodes. Characters are fluid and shifting, mysterious encounters lead to unforeseen consequences, and the dialogue is infused with religious figures and expressions. These later plays—which also include his so-called chamber plays, among them *The Ghost Sonata* (1907) and *The Pelican* (1907)—revolve around suffering, sin, and redemption. Back in Stockholm Strindberg had also gotten married a third time, to Harriet Bosse, an actress much younger than he. But this marriage was brief, and Strindberg spent his last years alone, in a modest apartment in Stockholm known as the Blue Tower. He never became popular, but in the last years of his life he achieved something of a literary reputation. Although he failed to win the Nobel Prize in Literature—one of the five prizes endowed by the final bequest of the Swedish chemist and armaments manufacturer Alfred Nobel, first awarded in 1901—he was finally honored with a state pension and a so-called Anti-Nobel Prize, a large sum raised by national subscription, one year before his death.

Miss Julie belongs to Strindberg's naturalist period, which also includes *The Father* and *Creditors* (1889). Naturalist drama was a rebellion against the bombastic history plays of Romanticism, the simplistic division between good and evil characters in melodrama, and the neatly constructed drawing-room comedies that flourished in the middle of the century. Naturalism, by contrast, privileged contemporary, and particularly lower-class, settings, which had rarely been seen on the stage except for comic effect. Strindberg's naturalist plays are interested in class differences, especially their effect on the relations between men and women. Like his autobiographical novels and short stories, Strindberg's naturalist plays depict the sexes as engaged in an all-out war. Whether vampires or degenerate creatures, women are always seeking the subjection of men. *The Father* pushes such irrational misogyny to an extreme: it portrays a man who, surrounded by his wife, daughter, mother-in-law, and old nurse, is slowly but surely being driven mad by these vengeful women; finally, he collapses dead in the arms of his nurse. The dramatist's autobiographical novels, as well as his letters and essays, suggest that Strindberg experienced his own marriages as similarly assaultive. But in his plays, at least, he was able to treat his own bitter experiences and paranoid obsessions with more detachment, thereby turning them into more compelling artistic forms.

Miss Julie strives for verisimilitude in its form. The play, confined to a single setting and one long act, represents a single, continuous action that lasts precisely as long as the play itself; it thus strictly obeys the neo-Aristotelian unities of time, place, and action. It is set not in some elaborate drawing room but in the kitchen of an estate, the domain of a cook and her apparent fiancé, another servant in the house in which a count lives with his daughter. Though its opening scene depicts the two servants, the play soon turns to its primary interest: the relation between the emancipated and freethinking mistress of the house, Miss Julie, and the ambitious, virile valet, Jean. The play describes a simple dramatic arc. At first Miss Julie has the upper hand. She flirts with her servant and finally persuades him to dance with her. After a sexual encounter, the dynamics change: now the servant is the dominant one. The play shows in detail the shifting power balance as Jean suggests to Miss Julie that they flee together and fantasizes about setting up a hotel in Italy. But nothing comes of the plan: they are trapped in the kitchen and trapped by their deed. Miss Julie finds herself in the hands of a power-hungry but volatile man, and by the end of the play she has lost her social position and her honor, and has nowhere to turn.

As is to be expected from a self-declared opponent of the New Woman such as Strindberg, Miss Julie does not fare well in this play precisely because she is too emancipated. In keeping with naturalist doctrine, her stance is caused by her parents' corrupting influence; one sign of their moral failings is their initial refusal to be lawfully wedded. Her mother's descent into adultery and arson also helps explain the transformation of the seemingly self-confident and articulate mistress into a moral wreck. Nowhere is Strindberg's reactionary view on marriage and emancipation clearer than in the backstory of Miss Julie, which serves to justify her ultimate downfall. Like many other naturalists, Strindberg was deeply influenced by "social Darwinists," who misapplied evolutionary theory to explain and justify social inequities; here, bad parentage necessarily dooms her. Such plots of social rising and falling are common in naturalist novels and plays alike.

Even though the emancipated aristocrat Miss Julie may in some ways be reminiscent of Strindberg's first wife, the play itself is based not on his own marriage but rather on an account Strindberg had heard of a servant who ended up dominating his former mistress both sexually and socially. In Strindberg's moral universe, the degenerate aristocrat must ultimately be brought down, just as the servant Jean, of humble birth but possessing a forceful will, must rise. The relation between Miss Julie and

Siri von Essen, Strindberg's first wife and the first to play the lead role in the 1889 production of *Miss Julie* at the Scandinavian Experimental Theater.

Jean, couched in a language of dominance, servitude, and struggle, is indebted to Nietzsche, especially those aspects of his philosophy that now seem most troubling.

All the characters in *Miss Julie* are measured in terms of their power and their will to dominate others, but the backdrop of their struggle for dominance is a fixed class structure. Even though in the second part of the play Jean presents himself as the strong servant who will triumph over his mistress, he wavers between arrogance and submission, falling into the latter attitude especially toward Miss Julie's absent father. Throughout the play, the count's return is expected and with it the resumption of Jean's duties, epitomized in the task of polishing his master's shoes. Miss Julie, too, fears the return of her father, who has wholly rejected his former liberal attitudes and now rules sternly and justly, conforming to Strindberg's own conservative ideal. The battle between Jean and Miss Julie is waged in the oppressive atmosphere of the servants' quarters, a setting that underscores the constant threat of retribution. Despite Strindberg's belief in social Darwinism and the survival of the stronger, the determining power of social class can never be entirely overcome in *Miss Julie*: the play and its protagonist remain mired in class resentment. Jean may despise Miss Julie and manage to bring her into his power, but part of him remains a servant.

The oscillation between dominance and subservience within an individual is part of the theory of characterization that Strindberg articulates in his famous preface to the play. He rejects the traditional stage characters, who often manifest a single dominant trait—such stock figures as the hapless victim, the scheming villain, and the trusted friend. Clear motivations and distinct types may be useful in the construction of plots, but in Strindberg's view they fail to represent the conflicted and shifting forces that actually drive human action. Like modernist novelists such as James Joyce and Virginia Woolf, Strindberg wanted to replicate the irregular workings of the human mind. While other naturalists placed great emphasis on external detail of costume and dialect, Strindberg was more interested in interiority and psychology. His characters change their minds constantly; and when they express their thoughts, they are allowed to be inconsistent, shifting, and inarticulate. Strindberg also insisted on abolishing many of the artificial aspects of stagecraft, including painted scenes, makeup, unnatural lighting effects such as those caused by footlights, and the practice of playing to the audience. At the same time, he made no attempt to do away with all elements of theatrical artifice. Even in his naturalist plays, he included theatrical set pieces such as dance, music, and ballet. They often take the place of crowd scenes, which Strindberg did not believe could be staged naturalistically in the theater. He thus pragmatically opted for established theatrical techniques when necessary.

Miss Julie has remained a central play in the canon of modern drama. Early productions were mounted in Copenhagen, Berlin, and, most famously, Paris at André Antoine's Théâtre Libre in 1893, a production that confirmed Strindberg's standing as a leading naturalist playwright. In Sweden, the play was not produced until 1906, when it was staged at the Intima Teater. Upon his return to Sweden, Strindberg had founded this theater with the director August Falck, and many of his late chamber plays were written for it. Decorated in green and white draperies, with a bust of Strindberg in the small foyer, the Intima Teater was in fact modeled on Antoine's Théâtre Libre. But even though Strindberg had control over this theater, he was never entirely content with its productions of his plays. The quality of the acting was mixed, and the theater was under constant financial strain. In 1910 it had to be closed for good. Despite his efforts, Strindberg thus never found a company that could adequately translate his theories and plays into theatrical reality. And not until shortly before his death did he receive the enthusiastic support from the press, publishers, and the theatergoing public that had eluded him for decades.

Strindberg's life was a struggle against the world and against himself. His plays, likewise, are full of struggles among characters, even as they fight for a new type of drama. While Strindberg's struggles were mostly destructive in his life, they were immensely productive in his art. His plays never take anything for granted, and in each play he sought to invent drama anew. In the process, he first created an unusual form of naturalism; then, in his later work, he pioneered what would be known as expressionism—plays full of enigmatic characters, religious language, and episodic plots. But neither label can entirely capture the essence of Strindberg's plays, which are among the most personal and singular in the history of modern drama. Even though readers today are, if anything, more shocked than his contemporaries at his racist, misogynist, and strange religious opinions, Strindberg's unusual plays have continued to compel generations of readers, theatergoers, and critics, and his varied and rich work remains one of the pillars of modern drama. M.P.

Miss Julie[1]

Preface

Like the arts in general, the theater has for a long time seemed to me a *Biblia Pauperum*,[2] a picture Bible for those who cannot read, and the playwright merely a lay preacher who hawks the latest ideals in popular form, so popular that the middle classes—the bulk of the audiences—can grasp them without racking their brains too much. That explains why the theater has always been an elementary school for youngsters and the half-educated, and for women, who still retain a primitive capacity for deceiving themselves and for letting themselves be deceived, that is, for succumbing to illusions and responding hypnotically to the suggestions of the author. Consequently, now that the rudimentary and undeveloped mental processes that operate in the realm of fantasy appear to be evolving to the level of reflection, research, and experimentation, I believe that the theater, like religion, is about to be replaced as a dying institution for whose enjoyment we lack the necessary qualifications. Support for my view is provided by the theater crisis through which all of Europe is now passing, and still more by the fact that in those highly cultured lands which have produced the finest minds of our time—England and Germany—the drama is dead, as for the most part are the other fine arts.

Other countries, however, have thought to create a new drama by filling the old forms with new contents. But since there has not been enough time to popularize the new ideas, the public cannot understand them. And in the second place, controversy has so stirred up the public that they can no longer look on with a pure and dispassionate interest, especially when they see their most cherished ideals assailed or hear an applauding or booing majority openly exercise its tyrannical power, as can happen in the theater. And in the third place, since the new forms for the new ideas have not been created, the new wine has burst the old bottles.

In the play that follows I have not tried to accomplish anything new—that is impossible. I have only tried to modernize the form to satisfy what I believe up-to-date people expect and demand of this art. And with that in mind I have seized upon—or let myself be seized by—a theme that may be said to lie outside current party strife, since the question of being on the way up or on the way down the social ladder, of

1. Translated by Evert Sprinchorn.

2. Bible of the Poor (Latin).

being on the top or on the bottom, superior or inferior, man or woman, is, has been, and will be of perennial interest. When I took this theme from real life—I heard about it a few years ago and it made a deep impression on me—I thought it would be a suitable subject for a tragedy, since it still strikes us as tragic to see a happily favored individual go down in defeat, and even more so to see an entire family line die out. But perhaps a time will come when we shall be so highly developed and so enlightened that we can look with indifference upon the brutal, cynical, and heartless spectacle that life offers us, a time when we shall have laid aside those inferior and unreliable mechanical apparatuses called emotions, which will become superfluous and even harmful as our mental organs develop. The fact that my heroine wins sympathy is due entirely to the fact that we are still too weak to overcome the fear that the same fate might overtake us. The extremely sensitive viewer will of course not be satisfied with mere expressions of sympathy, and the man who believes in progress will demand that certain positive actions be taken for getting rid of the evil, a kind of program, in other words. But in the first place absolute evil does not exist. The decline of one family is the making of another, which now gets its chance to rise. This alternate rising and falling provides one of life's greatest pleasures, for happiness is, after all, relative. As for the man who has a program for changing the disagreeable circumstance that the hawk eats the chicken and that lice eat up the hawk, I should like to ask him why it should be changed. Life is not prearranged with such idiotic mathematical precision that only the larger gets to eat the smaller. Just as frequently the bee destroys the lion (in Aesop's[3] fable)—or at least drives him wild.

If my tragedy makes most people feel sad, that is their fault. When we get to be as strong as the first French Revolutionists were, we shall be perfectly content and happy to watch the forests being cleared of rotting, superannuated trees that have stood too long in the way of others with just as much right to grow and flourish for a while—as content as we are when we see an incurably ill man finally die.

Recently my tragedy *The Father*[4] was censured for being too unpleasant—as if one wanted merry tragedies. "The joy of life" is now the slogan of the day. Theater managers send out orders for nothing but farces, as if the joy of living lay in behaving like a clown and in depicting people as if they were afflicted with St. Vitus's dance[5] or congenital idiocy. I find the joy of living in the fierce and ruthless battles of life, and my pleasure comes from learning something, from being taught something. That is why I have chosen for my play an unusual but instructive case, an exception, in other words—but an important exception of the kind that proves the rule—a choice of subject that I know will offend all lovers of the conventional. The next thing that will bother simple minds is that the motivation for the action is not simple and that the point of view is not single. Usually an event in life—and this is a fairly new discovery—is the result of a whole series of more or less deep-rooted causes. The spectator, however, generally chooses the one that puts the least strain on his mind or reflects most credit on his insight. Consider a case of suicide. "Business failure," says the merchant. "Unhappy love," say the women. "Physical illness," says the sick man. "Lost hopes," says the down-and-out. But it may be that the reason lay in all of these or in none of them, and that the suicide hid his real reason behind a completely different one that would reflect greater glory on his memory.

I have motivated the tragic fate of Miss Julie with an abundance of circumstances: her mother's basic instincts, her father's improper bringing-up of the girl, her own inborn nature, and her fiancé's sway over her weak and degenerate mind. Further and

3. Greek storyteller (early 6th c. B.C.E.), known especially for his moralizing animal fables (Strindberg is here apparently thinking of "The Gnat and the Lion").

4. Published one year earlier, in 1887.

5. Chorea, a disease characterized by involuntary spasmodic movements.

more immediately: the festive atmosphere of Midsummer Eve, her father's absence, her period, her preoccupation with animals, the erotic excitement of the dance, the long summer twilight, the highly aphrodisiac influence of flowers, and finally chance itself, which drives two people together in an out-of-the-way room, plus the boldness of the aroused man.

As one can see, I have not been entirely the physiologist, not been obsessively psychological, not traced everything to her mother's heredity, not found the sole cause in her period, not attributed everything to our "immoral times," and not simply preached a moral lesson. Lacking a priest, I have let the cook handle that.

I am proud to say that this complicated way of looking at things is in tune with the times. And if others have anticipated me in this, I am proud that I am not alone in my paradoxes, as all new discoveries are called. And no one can say this time that I am being one-sided.

As far as the drawing of characters is concerned, I have made the people in my play fairly "characterless" for the following reasons. In the course of time the word *character* has acquired many meanings. Originally it probably meant the dominant and fundamental trait in the soul complex and was confused with temperament. Later the middle class used it to mean an automaton. An individual who once and for all had found his own true nature or adapted himself to a certain role in life, who in fact had ceased to grow, was called a man of character, while the man who was constantly developing, who, like a skillful sailor on the currents of life, did not sail with close-tied sheets but who fell off before the wind in order to luff again, was called a man of no character—derogatorily of course, since he was so difficult to keep track of, to pin down and pigeonhole. This middle-class conception of a fixed character was transferred to the stage, where the middle class has always ruled. A character there came to mean someone who was always one and the same, always drunk, always joking, always melancholy, and who needed to be characterized only by some physical defect such as a club foot, a wooden leg, or a red nose, or by the repetition of some such phrase as, "That's capital," or "Barkis is willin'."[6] This uncomplicated way of viewing people is still to be found in the great Molière. Harpagon[7] is nothing but a miser, although Harpagon could have been both a miser and an exceptional financier, a fine father, and a good citizen. Worse still, his "defect" is extremely advantageous to his son-in-law and his daughter, who will be his heirs and who therefore should not find fault with him, even if they do have to wait a while to jump into bed together. So I do not believe in simple stage characters. And the summary judgments that writers pass on people—he is stupid, this one is brutal, that one is jealous, this one is stingy, and so on—should not pass unchallenged by the naturalists who know how complicated the soul is and who realize that vice has a reverse side very much like virtue.

Since the persons in my play are modern characters, living in a transitional era more hectic and hysterical than the previous one at least, I have depicted them as more unstable, as torn and divided, a mixture of the old and the new. Nor does it seem improbable to me that modern ideas might also have seeped down through newspapers and kitchen talk to the level of the servants. Consequently the valet may belch forth from his inherited slave soul certain modern ideas. And if there are those who find it wrong to allow people in a modern drama to talk Darwin and who recommend the practice of Shakepeare to our attention, may I remind them that the gravedigger in *Hamlet* talks the then-fashionable philosophy of Giordano Bruno

6. A phrase repeated by Mr. Barkis, a character in Charles Dickens's *David Copperfield* (1849–50), to indicate his desire to marry Clara Peggotty; that novel, like many other works by Dickens, was successfully adapted to the stage.

7. The protagonist in *The Miser* (1668), a play by the French dramatist Molière (1622–1673).

(Bacon's philosophy),[8] which is even more improbable, seeing that the means of spreading ideas were fewer then than now. And besides, the fact of the matter is that Darwinism has always existed, ever since Moses' history of creation[9] from the lower animals up to man, but it was not until recently that we discovered it and formulized it.

My souls—or characters—are conglomerations from various stages of culture, past and present, walking scrapbooks, shreds of human lives, tatters torn from old rags that were once Sunday best—hodgepodges just like the human soul. I have even supplied a little source history into the bargain by letting the weaker steal and repeat words of the stronger, letting them get ideas (suggestions as they are called) from one another, from the environment (the songbird's blood), and from objects (the razor). I have also arranged for *Gedankenübertragung*[1] through an inanimate medium to take place (the count's boots, the servant's bell). And I have even made use of "waking suggestions" (a variation of hypnotic suggestion), which have by now been so popularized that they cannot arouse ridicule or skepticism as they would have done in Mesmer's[2] time.

I say Miss Julie is a modern character not because the man-hating half-woman has not always existed but because she has now been brought out into the open, has taken the stage, and is making a noise about herself. Victim of a superstition (one that has seized even stronger minds) that woman, that stunted form of human being, standing with man, the lord of creation, the creator of culture, is meant to be the equal of man or could ever possibly be, she involves herself in an absurd struggle with him in which she falls. Absurd because a stunted form, subject to the laws of propagation, will always be born stunted and can never catch up with the one who has the lead. As follows: A (the man) and B (the woman) start from the same point C, A with a speed of let us say 100 and B with a speed of 60. When will B overtake A? Answer: never. Neither with the help of equal education or equal voting rights—nor by universal disarmament and temperance societies—any more than two parallel lines can ever meet. The half-woman is a type that forces itself on others, selling itself for power, medals, recognition, diplomas, as formerly it sold itself for money. It represents degeneration. It is not a strong species for it does not maintain itself, but unfortunately it propagates its misery in the following generation. Degenerate men unconsciously select their mates from among these half-women, so that they breed and spread, producing creatures of indeterminate sex to whom life is a torture, but who fortunately are overcome eventually either by a hostile reality, or by the uncontrolled breaking loose of their repressed instincts, or else by their frustration in not being able to compete with the male sex. It is a tragic type, offering us the spectacle of a desperate fight against nature; a tragic legacy of romanticism, which is now being dissipated by naturalism—a movement that seeks only happiness, and for that strong and healthy species are required.

Miss Julie, however, is also a vestige of the old warrior nobility that is now being superseded by a new nobility of nerve and brain. She is a victim of the disorder produced within a family by a mother's "crime," of the mistakes of a whole generation gone wrong, of circumstances, of her own defective constitution—all of which put together is equivalent to the fate or universal law of the ancients. The naturalists have banished

8. Perhaps a reference to the extreme logical precision of the gravedigger's wordplay in Shakespeare's *Hamlet* (1600–01), 5.1. Francis Bacon (1561–1626), an English philosopher and essayist, promoted the use of the inductive method of modern science; Bruno (1548–1600), an Italian philosopher, challenged dogmatism (he was burned at the stake for heresy). The major idea of the English naturalist Charles Darwin (1809–1882)—the theory of evolution through natural selection, or Darwinism—was gaining wider acceptance at the end of the 19th century.

9. That is, the account given in Genesis, whose authorship was traditionally ascribed to Moses.

1. Telepathy (German).

2. Franz Anton Mesmer (1734–1815), German physician who devised a therapeutic technique, based on "animal magnetism," that was developed into hypnosis.

guilt along with God, but the consequences of an act—punishment, imprisonment, or the fear of it—cannot be banished for the simple reason that they remain whether or not the naturalist dismisses the case from his court. Those sitting on the sidelines can easily afford to be lenient; but what of the injured parties? And even if her father were compelled to forgo taking his revenge, Miss Julie would take vengeance on herself, as she does in the play, because of that inherited or acquired sense of honor that has been transmitted to the upper classes from—well, where does it come from? From the age of barbarism, from the first Aryans,[3] from the chivalry of the Middle Ages. And a very fine code it was, but now inimical to the survival of the race. It is the aristocrat's form of hara-kiri, a law of conscience that bids the Japanese to slice his own stomach when someone else dishonors him. The same sort of thing survives, slightly modified, in that exclusive prerogative of the aristocracy, the duel. (Example: the husband challenges his wife's lover to a duel; the lover shoots the husband and runs off with the wife. Result: the husband has saved his *honor* but lost his wife.) Hence the servant Jean lives on; but not Miss Julie, who cannot live without honor. The advantage that the slave has over his master is that he has not committed himself to this defeatist principle. In all of us Aryans there is enough of the nobleman, or of the Don Quixote,[4] to make us sympathize with the man who takes his own life after having dishonored himself by shameful deeds. And we are all of us aristocrats enough to be distressed at the sight of a great man lying like a dead hulk ready for the scrap pile, even, I suppose, if he were to raise himself up again and redeem himself by honorable deeds.

The servant Jean is the beginning of a new species in which noticeable differentiation has already taken place. He began as a child of a poor worker and is now evolving through self-education into a future gentleman of the upper classes. He is quick to learn, has highly developed senses (smell, taste, sight), and a keen appreciation of beauty. He has already come up in the world, for he is strong enough not to hesitate to make use of other people. He is already a stranger to his old friends, whom he despises as reminders of past stages in his development, and whom he fears and avoids because they know his secrets, guess his intentions, look with envy on his rise and with joyful expectation toward his fall. Hence his character is unformed and divided. He wavers between an admiration of high positions and a hatred of the men who occupy them. He is an aristocrat—he says so himself—familiar with the ins and outs of good society. He is polished on the outside, but coarse underneath. He wears his frock coat with elegance but offers no guarantee that he keeps his body clean.

Although he respects Miss Julie, he is afraid of Christine, because she knows his innermost secrets. Yet he is sufficiently hard-hearted not to let the events of the night upset his plans for the future. Possessing both the coarseness of the slave and the toughmindedness of the born ruler, he can look at blood without fainting, shake off bad luck like water, and take calamity by the horns. Consequently he will escape from the battle unwounded, probably ending up as proprietor of a hotel. And if he himself does not get to be a Rumanian count, his son will doubtless go to college and possibly end up as a government official.

Now his observations about life as the lower classes see it, from below, are well worth listening to—that is, they are whenever he is telling the truth, which is not too often, because he is more likely to say what is advantageous to him than what is true. When Miss Julie supposes that everyone in the lower classes must feel greatly oppressed by the weight of the classes above, Jean naturally agrees with her since he wants to win her sympathy. But he promptly takes it all back when he finds it expedient to separate himself from the mob.

3. Hypothetical ancient speakers of Indo-European, progenitors of European (especially the Germanic) peoples.

4. The eponymous hero of Miguel de Cervantes's novel (1605, 1615), here invoked as a symbol of unflagging devotion to chivalric ideals.

Apart from the fact that Jean is coming up in the world, he is also superior to Miss Julie in that he is a man. In the sexual sphere, he is the aristocrat. He has the strength of the male, more highly developed senses, and the ability to take the initiative. His inferiority is merely the result of his social environment, which is only temporary and which he will probably slough off along with his livery.

His slave nature expresses itself in his awe of the count (the boots) and his religious superstitions. But he is awed by the count mainly because the count occupies the place he wants most in life; and this awe is still there even after he has won the daughter of the house and seen how empty that beautiful shell was.

I do not believe that any love in the "higher" sense can be born from the union of two such different souls; so I have let Miss Julie's love be refashioned in her imagination as a love that protects and purifies, and I have let Jean imagine that even his love might have a chance to grow under other social circumstances. For I suppose love is very much like the hyacinth that must strike roots deep in the dark earth *before* it can produce a vigorous blossom. Here it shoots up, bursts into bloom, and turns to seed all at once. Such plants can only be short-lived.

Christine—finally to get to her—is a female slave, spineless and phlegmatic after years spent at the kitchen stove, bovinely unconscious of her own hypocrisy, and with a full quota of moral and religious notions that serve as scapegoats and cloaks for her sins—which a stronger soul does not require since he is able either to carry the burden of his own sins or to rationalize them out of existence. She attends church regularly where she deftly unloads unto Jesus her household thefts and picks up from him another load of innocence. She is only a secondary character, and I have deliberately done no more than sketch her in—just as I treated the country doctor and parish priest in *The Father* where I only wanted to draw ordinary everyday people such as most country doctors and parsons are. That some have found my minor characters one-dimensional is due to the fact that ordinary people while at work are to a certain extent one-dimensional and do lack an independent existence, showing only one side of themselves in the performance of their duties. And as long as the audience does not feel it needs to see them from different angles, my abstract sketches will pass muster.

Now as far as the dialogue is concerned, I have broken somewhat with tradition in refusing to make my characters into interlocutors who ask stupid questions to elicit witty answers. I have avoided the symmetrical and mathematical design of the artfully constructed French dialogue and have let minds work as irregularly as they do in real life, where no subject is quite exhausted before another mind engages at random some cog in the conversation and governs it for a while. My dialogue wanders here and there, gathers material in the first scenes which is later picked up, repeated, reworked, developed, and expanded like the theme in a piece of music.

The action of the play poses no problem. Since it really involves only two people, I have limited myself to these two, introducing only one minor character, the cook, and keeping the unhappy spirit of the father brooding over the action as a whole. I have chosen this course because I have noticed that what interests people most nowadays is the psychological action. Our inveterately curious souls are no longer content to see a thing happen; we want to see how it happens. We want to see the strings, look at the machinery, examine the double-bottom drawer, put on the magic ring to find the hidden seam, look in the deck for the marked cards.

In treating the subject this way I have had in mind the case-history novels of the Goncourt brothers,[5] which appeal to me more than anything else in modern literature.

As far as play construction is concerned, I have made a stab at getting rid of act divisions. I was afraid that the spectator's declining susceptibility to illusion might not carry him through the intermission, when he would have time to think about what

5. Edmond de Goncourt (1822–1896) and Jules de Goncourt (1830–1870), coauthors of six novels set in 18th-century France.

he has seen and to escape the suggestive influence of the author-hypnotist. I figure my play lasts about ninety minutes. Since one can listen to a lecture, a sermon, or a political debate for that long or even longer, I have convinced myself that a play should not exhaust an audience in that length of time. As early as 1872 in one of my first attempts at the drama, *The Outlaw,* I tried out this concentrated form, although with little success. I had finished the work in five acts when I noticed the disjointed and disturbing effect it produced. I burned it, and from the ashes there arose a single, complete reworked act of fifty pages that would run for less than an hour. Although this play form is not completely new, it seems to be my special property and has a good chance of gaining favor with the public when tastes change. My hope is to educate a public to sit through a full evening's show in one act. But this whole question must first be probed more deeply. In the meantime, in order to establish resting places for the audience and the actors without destroying the illusion, I have made use of three arts that belong to the drama: the monologue, the pantomime, and the ballet, all of which were part of classic tragedy, the monody having become the monologue and the choral dance, the ballet.

The realists have banished the monologue from the stage as implausible. But if I can motivate it, I make it plausible, and I can then use it to my advantage. Now it is certainly plausible for a speaker to pace the floor and read his speech aloud to himself. It is plausible for an actor to practice his part aloud, for a child to talk to her cat, a mother to babble to her baby, an old lady to chatter to her parrot, and a sleeping man to talk in his sleep. And in order to give the actor a chance to work on his own for once and for a moment not be obliged to follow the author's directions, I have not written out the monologues in detail but simply outlined them. Since it makes very little difference what is said while asleep, or to the parrot or the cat, inasmuch as it does not affect the main action, a gifted player who is in the midst of the situation and mood of the play can probably improvise the monologue better than the author, who cannot estimate ahead of time how much may be said and for how long before the illusion is broken.

Some theaters in Italy have, as we know, returned to the art of improvisation[6] and have thereby trained actors who are truly inventive—without, however, violating the intentions of the author. This seems to be a step in the right direction and possibly the beginning of a new, fertile form of art that will be genuinely *creative.*

In places where the monologue cannot be properly motivated, I have resorted to pantomime. Here I have given the actor even more freedom to be creative and win honor on his own. Nevertheless, not to try the audience beyond its limits, I have relied on music—well motivated by the Midsummer Eve dance—to exercise its hypnotic powers during the pantomime scene. I beg the music director to select his tunes with great care, so that associations foreign to the mood of the play will not be produced by reminders of popular operattas or current dance numbers or by folk music of interest only to ethnologists.

The ballet that I have introduced cannot be replaced by a so-called crowd scene. Such scenes are always badly acted, with a pack of babbling fools taking advantage of the occasion to "gag it up," thereby destroying the illusion. Inasmuch as country people do not improvise their taunts but make use of material already to hand by giving it a double meaning, I have not composed an original lampoon but have made use of a little-known round dance that I noted down in the Stockholm district. The words do not fit the situation exactly, which is what I intended, since the slave in his cunning (that is, weakness) never attacks directly. At any rate, let us have no comedians in this serious story and no obscene smirking over an affair that nails the lid on a family coffin.

As far as the scenery is concerned, I have borrowed from impressionistic painting the idea of asymmetrical and open composition, and I believe that I have thereby

6. That is, the commedia dell'arte, which relies on improvisation by stock characters along conventional plotlines.

gained something in the way of greater illusion. Because the audience cannot see the whole room and all the furniture, they will have to surmise what's missing; that is, their imagination will be stimulated to fill in the rest of the picture. I have gained something else by this: I have avoided those tiresome exits through doors. Stage doors are made of canvas and rock at the slightest touch. They cannot even be used to indicate the wrath of an angry father who storms out of the house after a bad dinner, slamming the door behind him "so that the whole house shakes." (In the theater it sways and billows.) Furthermore, I have confined the action to one set, both to give the characters a chance to become part and parcel of their environment and to cut down on scenic extravagance. If there is only one set, one has a right to expect it to be as realistic as possible. Yet nothing is more difficult than to make a room look like a room, however easy it may be for the scene painter to create waterfalls and erupting volcanos. I suppose we shall have to put up with walls made of canvas, but isn't it about time that we stopped painting shelves and pots and pans on the canvas? There are so many other conventions in the theater that we are told to accept in good faith that we should be spared the strain of believing in painted saucepans.

I have placed the backdrop and the table at an angle to force the actors to play face to face or in half profile when they are seated opposite each other at the table. In a production of *Aida*[7] I saw a flat placed at such an angle, which led the eye out in an unfamiliar perspective. Nor did it look as if it had been set that way simply to be different or to avoid those monotonous right angles.

Another desirable innovation would be the removal of the footlights. I understand that the purpose of lighting from below is to make the actors look more full in the face. But may I ask why all actors should have full faces? Doesn't this kind of lighting wipe out many of the finer features in the lower part of the face, especially around the jaws? Doesn't it distort the shape of the nose and throw false shadows above the eyes? If not, it certainly does something else: it hurts the actor's eyes. The footlights hit the retina at an angle from which it is usually shielded (except in sailors who must look at the sunlight reflected in the water), and the result is the loss of any effective play of the eyes. All one ever sees on stage are goggle-eyed glances sideways at the boxes or upward at the balcony, with only the whites of the eyes being visible in the latter case. And this probably also accounts for that tiresome fluttering of the eyelashes that the female performers are particularly guilty of. If an actor nowadays wants to express something with his eyes, he can only do it looking right at the audience, in which case he makes direct contact with someone outside the proscenium arch—a bad habit known, justifiably or not, as "saying hello to friends."

I should think that the use of sufficiently strong side lights (through the use of reflectors or something like them) would provide the actor with a new asset: an increased range of expression made possible by the play of the eyes, the most expressive part of the face.

I have scarcely any illusions about getting actors to play for the audience and not directly at them, although this should be the goal. Nor do I dream of ever seeing an actor play through all of an important scene with his back to the audience. But is it too much to hope that crucial scenes could be played where the author indicated and not in front of the prompter's box as if they were duets demanding applause? I am not calling for a revolution, only for some small changes. I am well aware that transforming the stage into a real room with the fourth wall missing and with some of the furniture placed with backs to the auditorium would only upset the audience, at least for the present.

If I bring up the subject of makeup, it is not because I dare hope to be heeded by the ladies, who would rather be beautiful than truthful. But the male actor might do well to consider if it is an advantage to paint his face with character lines that remain

7. An Italian opera by Giuseppe Verdi (1871), set in ancient Egypt.

there like a mask. Let us imagine an actor who pencils in with soot a few lines between his eyes to indicate great anger, and let us suppose that in that permanently enraged state he finds he has to smile on a certain line. Imagine the horrible grimace! And how can the old character actor wrinkle his brows in anger when his false bald pate is as smooth as a billiard ball?

In a modern psychological drama, in which every tremor of the soul should be reflected more by facial expressions than by gestures and grunts, it would probably be most sensible to experiment with strong side lighting on a small stage, using actors without any makeup or a minimum of it.

And then, if we could get rid of the visible orchestra with its disturbing lights and the faces turned toward the public; if the auditorium floor could be raised so that the spectator's eyes are not level with the actor's knees; if we could get rid of the proscenium boxes and their occupants, arriving giggling and drunk from their dinners; and if we could have it dark in the auditorium during the performance; and if, above everything else, we could have a *small* stage and an *intimate* auditorium—then possibly a new drama might arise and at least one theater become a refuge for cultured audiences. While we are waiting for such a theater, we shall have to write for the dramatic stockpile and prepare the repertory that one day shall come.

Here is my attempt. If I have failed, there is still time to try again!

CHARACTERS

MISS JULIE, twenty-five years old
JEAN, valet, thirty years old
CHRISTINE, cook, thirty-five years old
THE CHORUS, a party of country folk

The scene is a country estate in Sweden.

The time: A Midsummer Night in the 1880s. The hours after midnight, June 24, St. John the Baptist's Day.

The Set

The scene is the kitchen of the estate belonging to the count, MISS JULIE's *father. It is a large kitchen, situated along with the servants' quarters in the basement of the manor house. The side walls and the ceiling of the kitchen are masked by the tormentors*[8] *and borders of the set. The rear wall runs obliquely upstage from the left. On this wall to the left are two shelves with pots and pans of copper, iron, and pewter. The shelves are decorated with goffered*[9] *paper. A little to the right can be seen three-fourths of a deep arched entry with two glass doors, and through them can be seen a fountain with a statue of a cupid,*[1] *lilac bushes in bloom, and the tops of some Lombardy poplars.*

From the left of the stage the corner of a large, Dutch-tile kitchen stove protrudes with part of the hood showing.

Projecting from the right side of the stage is one end of the servants' dining table of white pine, with a few chairs around it.

The stove is decorated with branches of birch leaves; the floor is strewn with juniper twigs.

On the end of the table is a large Japanese spice jar filled with lilacs.

8. Curtains or doors on the sides of a stage set that hide the wings from the view of the audience.

9. Embossed to produce patterns of raised figures.

1. A representation of the Roman god of love.

An icebox, a sink, a washbasin.

Over the door a big old-fashioned bell; and to the left of the door the gaping mouth of a speaking tube.[2]

[CHRISTINE *is standing at the stove, frying something in a pan. She is wearing a light-colored cotton dress and an apron.*]

[JEAN *enters, dressed in livery and carrying a pair of high-top boots with spurs. He sets them where they are clearly visible.*]

JEAN What a night! She's wild again! Miss Julie's absolutely wild!

CHRISTINE You sure took your time getting back!

JEAN I took the count down to the station, and on my way back, I passed the barn and went in for a dance. And there was Miss Julie leading the dance with the game warden. Then she noticed me. And she ran right into my arms and chose me for the ladies' waltz. And she's been dancing ever since like—like I don't know what. Wild, I tell you, absolutely wild!

CHRISTINE That's nothing new. But she's been worse than ever during the last two weeks, ever since her engagement was broken off.

JEAN Yes. I never did hear all there was to that. He was a good man, too, even if he wasn't rich. Well, they've got such crazy ideas. [*He sits down at the end of the table.*] Tell me, isn't it strange that a young girl like her—all right, young woman—prefers to stay home here with the servants rather than go with her father to visit her relatives?

CHRISTINE I suppose she's ashamed to face them after that fiasco with her young man.

JEAN No doubt. He wouldn't take any nonsense from her. Do you know what happened, Christine? I saw the whole thing. Of course, I didn't let on.

CHRISTINE You were there? I don't believe it.

JEAN Well, I was. They were in the stable yard one evening—and she was training him, that's what she called it. Do you know what? She was making him jump over her riding whip—training him like a dog. He jumped over twice, and she whipped him both times. But the third time, he grabbed the whip from her, [scratched her face with it—long scratch on her left cheek;][3] then broke it in a thousand pieces—and walked off.

CHRISTINE I don't believe it! What do you know!

JEAN Yes, that put an end to that affair. —What have you got for me that's really good, Christine?

CHRISTINE [*serving him from the frying pan*] Just a little bit of kidney. Cut it from the veal roast.

JEAN [*smelling it*] Wonderful! One of my special *délices!*[4] [*Feeling the plate*] Hey, you didn't warm the plate!

CHRISTINE You're more fussy than the count himself when you set your mind to it. [*She rumples his hair affectionately.*]

JEAN [*irritated*] Cut it out! Don't muss up my hair. You know how particular I am!

2. A hollow pipe connecting two cones, used in businesses and upper-class homes in the 19th century for communicating over distances.

3. The passage in brackets was deleted in Strindberg's manuscript, probably by Strindberg himself [translator's note].

4. Pleasures, delights (French).

CHRISTINE Oh, don't get mad. Can I help it if I like you?

[JEAN *eats.* CHRISTINE *gets out a bottle of beer.*]

JEAN Beer on Midsummer Eve! No thank you! I've got something much better than that. [*He opens a drawer in the table and takes out a bottle of red wine with a gold seal.*] Do you see that? Gold Seal. Now give me a glass.

[*She hands him a tumbler.*]

—No, a wineglass of course. This has to be drunk properly. No water.

CHRISTINE [*goes back to the stove and puts on a small saucepan*] Lord help the woman who gets you for a husband. You're an old fussbudget!

JEAN Talk, talk! You'd consider yourself lucky if you got yourself a man as good as me. It hasn't done you any harm to have people think I'm your fiancé. [*He tastes the wine.*] Very good. Excellent. But warmed just a little too little. [*Warming the glass in his hands*] We bought this in Dijon. Four francs a liter, unbottled—and the tax on top of that. . . . What on earth are you cooking? It stinks like hell!

CHRISTINE Some damn mess that Miss Julie wants for her Diana, that damn dog of hers.

JEAN You should watch your language, Christine. . . . Why do you have to stand in front of the stove on a holiday, cooking for that mutt? Is it sick?

CHRISTINE Oh, she's sick, all right! She sneaked out to the gatekeeper's pug and—got herself in a fix. And you know Miss Julie, she can't stand anything like that.

JEAN She's too stuck-up in some ways and not proud enough in others. Just like her mother. The countess felt right at home in the kitchen or down in the barn with the cows, but when she went driving, one horse wasn't enough for her, she had to have a pair. Her sleeves were always dirty, but her buttons had the royal crown on them. As for Miss Julie, she doesn't give a hoot in hell how she looks and acts. I mean, she's not really refined, not really. Just now, down at the barn, she grabbed the game warden right from under Anna's eyes and asked him to dance. You wouldn't see anybody in our class behaving like that. But that's what happens when the gentry try to act like the common people—they become common! . . . However, I'll say one thing for her: she *is* beautiful! Statuesque! Ah, those shoulders—those—and so forth, and so forth!

CHRISTINE Oh, don't exaggerate. Clara tells me all about her, and Clara dresses her.

JEAN Clara, pooh! You women are always jealous of each other. I've been out riding with her. . . . And how she can dance . . . !

CHRISTINE Listen, Jean, you *are* going to dance with me, aren't you, when I'm finished here?

JEAN Certainly! Of course I am.

CHRISTINE Promise?

JEAN Promise! Listen—if I say I'm going to do a thing, I do it. . . . Christine, I thank you for a delicious meal. Superb! [*He shoves the cork back into the bottle.*]

[MISS JULIE *appears in the entry, talking to someone outside.*]

MISS JULIE I'll be right back. Don't wait for me.

[JEAN *slips the bottle into the table drawer quickly and rises respectfully.* MISS JULIE *comes in and crosses over to* CHRISTINE, *who is at the stove.*]

MISS JULIE Did you get it ready?

[CHRISTINE *signals that* JEAN *is present.*]

JEAN [*polite and charming*] Are you ladies sharing secrets?

MISS JULIE [*flipping her handkerchief in his face*] Don't be nosy!

JEAN Oh, that smells good! Violets.

MISS JULIE [*flirting with him*] Don't be impudent! And don't tell me you're an expert on perfumes, too. I love the way you dance!—No, mustn't look! Go away!

JEAN [*cocky but pleasant*] What are the ladies cooking up? A witches' brew for Midsummer Eve? So they can tell the future?[5] Read what's in the cards for them, and see who they'll marry?

MISS JULIE [*curtly*] You'd have to have good eyes to see that. [*To* CHRISTINE] Pour it into a small bottle, and seal it tight. . . . Jean, come and dance a schottische[6] with me.

JEAN [*hesitating*] I hope you don't think I'm being rude, but I've already promised this dance to Christine.

MISS JULIE She can always find someone. Isn't that so, Christine? You don't mind if I borrow Jean for a minute, do you?

CHRISTINE It ain't up to me. If Miss Julie is gracious enough to invite you, it ain't right for you to say no, Jean. You go on, and thank her for the honor.

JEAN Frankly, Miss Julie, I don't want to hurt your feelings, but I wonder if it's wise—I mean for you to dance twice in a row with the same partner. Especially since the people around here love to talk.

MISS JULIE [*bridling*] What do you mean? What kind of talk? What are you trying to say?

JEAN [*retreating*] I wish you wouldn't misunderstand me, Miss Julie. It just doesn't look right for you to prefer one of your servants to the others who are hoping for the same unusual honor.

MISS JULIE Prefer! What an idea! I'm really surprised. I, the mistress of the house, am good enough to come to their dance, and when I feel like dancing, I want to dance with someone who knows how to lead. After all I don't want to look ridiculous.

JEAN As you wish, Miss Julie. I am at your orders.

MISS JULIE [*gently*] Don't take it as an order. Tonight we're all just having a good time. There's no question of rank. Now give me your arm. —Don't worry, Christine. I won't run off with your boyfriend.

[JEAN *gives her his arm and leads her out.*]

Pantomime Scene

This should be played as if the actress were actually alone. She turns her back on the audience when she feels like it; she does not look out into the auditorium; she does not rush through the scene as if afraid the audience will grow impatient.

CHRISTINE *alone. In the distance the sound of the violins playing the schottische.* CHRISTINE, *humming in time with the music, cleans up after* JEAN, *washes the dishes, dries them, and puts them away in a cupboard. Then she takes off her apron, takes a little mir-*

5. In Swedish folklore, Midsummer Eve is a time of fortune-telling.

6. Literally, "Scottish" (German), a country dance similar to the polka.

ror from one of the table drawers, and leans it against the jar of lilacs on the table. She lights a tallow candle, heats a curling iron, and curls the bangs on her forehead. Then she goes to the doorway and stands listening to the music. She comes back to the table and finds the handkerchief that MISS JULIE *left behind. She smells it, spreads it out, and then, as if lost in thought, stretches it, smooths it out, and folds it in four.*

[JEAN *enters alone.*]

JEAN Wild! I told you she was wild! You should have seen the way she was dancing. Everyone was peeking at her from behind the doors and laughing at her. What's the matter with her, Christine?

CHRISTINE You might know it's her monthlies, Jean. She always acts peculiar then. . . . Well, are you going to dance with me?

JEAN You're not mad at me because I broke my promise?

CHRISTINE Of course not. Not for a little thing like that, you know that. I know my place.

JEAN [*grabs her around the waist*] You're a sensible girl, Christine. You're going to make somebody a good wife—

[MISS JULIE, *coming in, sees them together. She is unpleasantly surprised.*]

MISS JULIE [*with forced gaiety*] Well, aren't you the gallant beau—running away from your partner!

JEAN On the contrary, Miss Julie. As you can see, I've hurried back to the partner I deserted.

MISS JULIE [*changing tack*] You know, you're the best dancer I've met. —Why are you wearing livery on a holiday? Take it off at once.

JEAN I'd have to ask you to leave for a minute. My black coat is hanging right here—[*He moves to the right and points.*]

MISS JULIE You're not embarrassed because I'm here, are you? Just to change your coat? Go in your room and come right back again. Or else stay here and I'll turn my back.

JEAN If you'll excuse me, Miss Julie.

[*He goes off to the right. His arm can be seen as he changes his coat.*]

MISS JULIE [*to* CHRISTINE] Tell me something, Christine. Is Jean your fiancé? He acts so familiar with you.

CHRISTINE Fiancé? I suppose so. At least we say we are.

MISS JULIE What do you mean?

CHRISTINE Well, Miss Julie, you have had fiancés yourself, and you know—

MISS JULIE But we were properly engaged—!

CHRISTINE I know, but did anything come of it?

[JEAN *comes back, wearing a black cutaway coat and derby.*]

MISS JULIE *Très gentil, monsieur Jean! Très gentil!*

JEAN *Vous voulez plaisanter, madame.*

MISS JULIE *Et vous voulez parler français!*[7] Where did you learn to speak French?

JEAN In Switzerland. I was *sommelier*[8] in one of the biggest hotels in Lucerne.

MISS JULIE My! but you look quite the gentleman in that coat! *Charmant!*[9]

[*She sits down at the table.*]

7. "Very nice, Mister Jean! Very nice!" "You are trying to flatter me, madam." "And you are trying to speak French!" (French).

8. Wine steward.

9. Charming (French).

JEAN Flatterer!

MISS JULIE [*stiffening*] Who said I was flattering you?

JEAN My natural modesty would not allow me to presume that you were paying sincere compliments to someone like me, and therefore I could only assume that you were exaggerating, which, in this case, means flattering me.

MISS JULIE You certainly have a way with words. Where did you learn to talk like that? Seeing plays?

JEAN And other places. You don't think I stayed in the house for six years when I was a valet in Stockholm, do you?

MISS JULIE I thought you were born in this district. Weren't you?

JEAN My father worked as a farmhand on the district attorney's estate, next door to yours. I used to see you when you were little. Of course you didn't notice me.

MISS JULIE Did you really?

JEAN Yes. I remember one time in particular—. But I can't tell you about that!

MISS JULIE Of course you can. . . . Oh, come on. Just this once—for me.

JEAN No. No, I really couldn't. Not now. Some other time maybe.

MISS JULIE Some other time? That means never. What's the harm in telling me now?

JEAN There's no harm. I just don't feel like it. —Look at her.

[*He nods at* CHRISTINE, *who has fallen asleep in a chair by the stove.*]

MISS JULIE Won't she make somebody a pretty wife! I'll bet she snores, too.

JEAN No, she doesn't. But she talks in her sleep.

MISS JULIE [*archly*] Now how could you know she talks in her sleep?

JEAN [*coolly*] I've heard her . . .

[*Pause. They look at each other.*]

MISS JULIE Why don't you sit down?

JEAN I wouldn't take the liberty in your presence.

MISS JULIE Not even if I ordered you?

JEAN Of course I'd obey.

MISS JULIE Well then: sit down. —Wait a minute. Could you get me something to drink?

JEAN I don't know what there is in the icebox. Only beer, I suppose.

MISS JULIE Only beer?! I have simple tastes. I prefer beer to wine.

[JEAN *takes a bottle of beer from the icebox and opens it. He looks in the cupboard for a glass and a plate, and serves her.*]

JEAN At your service, *mademoiselle*.[1]

MISS JULIE Thank you. What about you?

JEAN I'm not much of a beer-drinker, thank you, but if it's your wish—

MISS JULIE My wish! I should think a gentleman would want to keep his lady company.

JEAN A point well taken! [*He opens another bottle and takes a glass.*]

MISS JULIE Now drink a toast to me!

[JEAN *hesitates.*]

You're not shy, are you? A big, strong man like you?

[*Playfully,* JEAN *kneels and raises his glass in mock gallantry.*]

1. Miss (French).

JEAN To my lady's health!

MISS JULIE Bravo! Now you have to kiss my shoe, too. Then you will have hit it off perfectly.

[JEAN *hesitates, then boldly grasps her foot and touches it lightly with his lips.*]

Superb! You should have been an actor.

JEAN [*rising*] This has got to stop, Miss Julie! Someone might come in and see us.

MISS JULIE So what?

JEAN People would talk, that's what! If you knew how their tongues were wagging out there just a few minutes ago!

MISS JULIE What did they say? Tell me. Sit down and tell me.

JEAN I don't want to hurt your feelings. . . . They used expressions that—that hinted at certain—you know what I mean. You're not a child. And when they see a woman drinking, alone with a man—and a servant at that—in the middle of the night—well . . .

MISS JULIE Well what?! Besides, we're not alone. Christine is here.

JEAN Sleeping!

MISS JULIE I'll wake her up. [*She goes over to* CHRISTINE.] Christine! Are you asleep? [CHRISTINE *babbles in her sleep.*] Christine! —My, how sound she sleeps!

CHRISTINE [*talking in her sleep*] Count's boots are brushed . . . put on the coffee . . . right away, right away, right . . . mm—mm . . . poofff . . .

[MISS JULIE *shakes* CHRISTINE.]

MISS JULIE Wake up, will you!

JEAN [*sternly*] Let her alone! Let her sleep!

MISS JULIE [*sharply*] What?

JEAN She's been standing over the stove all day. She's worn out when night comes. Anyone asleep is entitled to some consideration.

MISS JULIE [*changing her tone*] That's a very kind thought. It does you credit, Jean. You're right, of course. [*She offers* JEAN *her hand.*] Now come on out and pick some lilacs for me.

[*During the following,* CHRISTINE *wakes up and, drunk with sleep, shuffles off to the right to go to bed. A polka can be heard in the distance.*]

JEAN With you, Miss Julie?

MISS JULIE Yes, with me.

JEAN That's no good. Absolutely not.

MISS JULIE I don't know what you're thinking. Aren't you letting your imagination run away with you?

JEAN No. Other people are.

MISS JULIE How? Imagining that I'm—*verliebt*[2] with a servant?

JEAN I'm not conceited, but it's been known to happen. And to these people nothing's sacred.

MISS JULIE "These people!" Why, I do believe you're an aristocrat!

JEAN Yes, I am.

MISS JULIE I'm climbing down—

JEAN Don't climb down, Miss Julie! Take my advice. No one will believe that you climbed down deliberately. They'll say you fell.

2. In love (German).

MISS JULIE I have a higher opinion of these people than you do. Let's see who's right! Come on! [*She gives him a long, steady look.*]

JEAN You know, you're very strange.

MISS JULIE Perhaps. But then so are you. . . . Besides, everything is strange. Life, people, everything. It's all scum, drifting and drifting on the water until it sinks—drowns. There's a dream I have every now and then. It's coming back to me now. I'm sitting on top of a pillar. I've climbed up it somehow and I don't know how to get back down. When I look down I get dizzy. I have to get down but I don't have the courage to jump. I can't hold on much longer and I want to fall; but I don't fall. I know I won't have any peace until I get down; no rest until I get down, down on the ground. And if I ever got down on the ground, I'd want to go farther down, right down into the earth. . . . Have you ever felt anything like that?

JEAN Never! I used to dream that I'm lying under a tall tree in a dark woods. I want to get up, up to the very top, to look out over the bright landscape with the sun shining on it, to rob the bird's nest up there with the golden eggs in it. And I climb and I climb, but the trunk is so thick, and so smooth, and it's such a long way to that first branch. But I know that if I could just reach that first branch, I'd go right to the top as if on a ladder. I've never reached it yet, but someday I will—even if only in my dreams.

MISS JULIE Here I am talking about dreams with you. Come out with me. Only into the park a way. [*She offers him her arm, and they start to go.*]

JEAN Let's sleep on nine midsummer flowers, Miss Julie, and then our dreams will come true![3]

[MISS JULIE *and* JEAN *suddenly turn around in the doorway.* JEAN *is holding his hand over one eye.*]

MISS JULIE You've caught something in your eye. Let me see.

JEAN It's nothing. Just a bit of dust. It'll go away.

MISS JULIE The sleeve of my dress must have grazed your eye. Sit down and I'll help you. [*She takes him by the arm and sits him down. She takes his head and leans it back. With the corner of her handkerchief she tries to get out the bit of dust.*] Now sit still, absolutely still. [*She slaps his hand.*] Do as you're told. Why, I believe you're trembling—a big, strong man like you. [*She feels his biceps.*] With such big arms!

JEAN [*warningly*] Miss Julie!

MISS JULIE Yes, *Monsieur Jean?*

JEAN *Attention! Je ne suis qu'un homme!*[4]

MISS JULIE Sit still, I tell you! . . . There now! It's out. Kiss my hand and thank me!

JEAN [*rising to his feet.*] Listen to me, Miss Julie—Christine has gone to bed! —Listen to me, I tell you!

MISS JULIE Kiss my hand first!

JEAN Listen to me!

MISS JULIE Kiss my hand first!

JEAN All right. But you'll have no one to blame but yourself.

3. A girl would pick in silence on Midsummer Eve nine different sorts of flowers, make a bouquet of them, and place them under her pillow. The man who appeared in her dreams would be the man she would marry [translator's note].

4. Be careful! I am just a man! (French).

MISS JULIE For what?

JEAN For what! Are you twenty-five years old and still a child? Don't you know it's dangerous to play with fire?

MISS JULIE Not for me, I'm insured!

JEAN [*boldly*] Oh, no, you're not! And even if you are, there's inflammable stuff next door.

MISS JULIE Meaning you?

JEAN Yes. Not just because it's me, but because I'm young and—

MISS JULIE And irresistibly handsome? What incredible conceit! A Don Juan, maybe! Or a Joseph![5] Yes, bless my soul, that's it: you're a Joseph!

JEAN You think so?!

MISS JULIE I'm almost afraid so!

[JEAN *boldly steps up to her, grabs her around the waist, tries to kiss her. She slaps his face.*]

None of that!

JEAN More games? Or are you serious?

MISS JULIE I'm serious.

JEAN Then you must have been serious a moment ago, too! You take your games too seriously; that's dangerous. Well, I'm tired of your games, and if you'll excuse me, I'll return to my work. [*Takes up the boots and starts to brush them.*] The count will be wanting his boots on time, and it's long past midnight.

MISS JULIE Put those boots down.

JEAN No! This is my job. It's what I'm here for. I never undertook to be your playmate. That's something I could never be. I consider myself too good for that.

MISS JULIE You are proud.

JEAN In some ways. Not in others.

MISS JULIE Have you ever been in love?

JEAN We don't use that word around here. But I've hankered after some girls, if that's what you mean. . . . I even got sick once because I couldn't have the one I wanted—really sick, like the princes in the Arabian Nights[6]—who couldn't eat or drink for love.

MISS JULIE Who was she?

[JEAN *does not reply.*]

Who was the girl?

JEAN You can't get that out of me.

MISS JULIE Even if I ask you as an equal—ask you—as a friend? . . . Who was she?

JEAN You.

MISS JULIE [*sitting down*] How—amusing . . .

JEAN Yes, maybe so. Ridiculous. . . . That's why I didn't want to tell you about it before. Want to hear the whole story? . . . Have you any idea what

5. In the Bible, a son of Jacob: after Joseph was sold into slavery by his brothers, his good looks led his master's wife to make sexual advances toward him; when he refused her, she falsely accused him of rape (Genesis 39.6–18). *Don Juan:* the legendary Spanish seducer of women, whose story is told in a number of European dramas and in Mozart's opera *Don Giovanni* (1787).

6. *The Thousand and One Nights,* a collection of ancient tales in Arabic, arranged in its present form in the 15th century.

you and your people look like from down below? Of course not. Like hawks or eagles, that's what: you hardly ever see their backs because they're always soaring so high up. I lived with seven brothers and sisters—and a pig—out on the wasteland where there wasn't even a tree growing. But from my window I could see the wall of the count's garden with the apple trees sticking up over it. That was the Garden of Eden for me, and there were many angry angels with flaming swords standing guard over it.[7] But in spite of them, I and the other boys found a way to the Tree of Life. . . . How contemptible, that's what you're thinking.

MISS JULIE For stealing apples? All boys do that.

JEAN That's what you say now. All the same, you think me contemptible. Never mind. One day I went with my mother into this paradise to weed the onion beds. Next to the vegetable garden stood a Turkish pavilion, shaded by jasmine and hung all over with honeysuckle. I couldn't imagine what it was used for; I only knew I had never seen such a beautiful building. People went in, and came out again. And then one day the door was left open. I sneaked in. The walls were covered with portraits of kings and emperors, and the windows had red curtains with tassels on them. —Recognize it? Yes, the count's private privy. . . . I— [*He breaks off a lilac and holds it under* MISS JULIE*'s nose.*] I had never been inside a castle, never seen anything besides the church. This was more beautiful. And no matter what I tried to think about, my thoughts always came back—to that little pavilion. And little by little there arose in me a desire to experience just for once the whole pleasure of—. *Enfin,*[8] I sneaked in, looked about, and marveled. And just then I heard someone coming! There was only one way out—for the upper-class people. But for me there was one more—a lower one.[9] And I had no other choice but to take it. [MISS JULIE, *who has taken the lilac from* JEAN, *lets it fall to the table.*] Then I began to run like mad, plunging through the raspberry bushes, plowing through the strawberry patches, and came up on the rose terrace. And there I caught sight of a pink dress and a pair of white stockings. You! I crawled under—well, you can imagine what it was like—under thistles that pricked me and wet dirt that stank to high heaven. And all the while I could see you walking among the roses. I said to myself, "If it's true that a thief can enter heaven and be with the angels,[1] isn't it strange that a poor man's child here on God's green earth can't enter the count's park and play with the count's daughter."

MISS JULIE [*sentimentally*] Do you think all poor children have felt that way?

JEAN [*hesitatingly at first, then with mounting conviction*] If all poor ch—? Yes—yes, naturally. Of course!

MISS JULIE It must be terrible to be poor.

JEAN [*with exaggerated intensity*] Oh, Miss Julie! You don't know! A dog can lie on the sofa with its mistress; a horse can have its nose stroked by the hand of a countess; but a servant—! [*Changing his tone*] Of course, now and then you meet somebody with guts enough to work his way up in the world, but how often? —Anyway, you know what I did afterward? I threw myself into the millstream with all my clothes on. Got fished out and spanked. But the following Sunday, when Pa and everybody else in the house went to visit

7. See Genesis 3.24.
8. Finally (French).
9. That is, through the pit or trench under the outhouse.
1. According to 1 Corinthians 6.9–10, the thief cannot enter heaven.

Grandma, I arranged things so I'd be left behind. Then I washed myself all over with soap and warm water, put on my best clothes, and went off to church—just to see you there once more. I saw you, and then I went home determined to die. But I wanted to die beautifully and comfortably, without pain. I remembered some stories I had heard about how fatal it was to sleep under an elderberry bush. And we had a big one that had just blossomed out. I stripped it of every leaf and blossom it had and made a bed of them in a bin of oats. Have you ever noticed how smooth oats are? As smooth to the touch as human skin. . . . So I pulled the lid of the bin shut and closed my eyes. Fell asleep. And when they woke me I was really very sick. However, I didn't die, as you can see. —What was I trying to prove? I don't know. There was no hope of winning you. It was just that you were a symbol of the absolute hopelessness of my ever getting out of the class I was born in.

MISS JULIE You know, you have a real gift for telling stories. Did you go to school?

JEAN A little. But I've read a lot of novels and gone to the theater. And I've also listened to educated people talk. That way I learned the most.

MISS JULIE You mean to tell me you stand around listening to what we're saying!

JEAN Certainly! And I've heard an awful lot, I can tell you—sitting on the coachman's seat or rowing the boat. One time I heard you and a girlfriend talking—

MISS JULIE Really? . . . And just what did you hear?

JEAN Well, now, I don't know if I can repeat it. I can tell you I was a little amazed. I couldn't imagine where you had learned such words. Maybe at bottom there isn't such a big difference as you might think, between people and people.

MISS JULIE How vulgar! At least people in my class don't behave like you when we're engaged.

JEAN [*looking her in the eye*] Are you sure? —Come on now, it's no use playing the innocent with me.

MISS JULIE He was a beast. The man I offered my love was a beast.

JEAN That's what you all say—afterward.

MISS JULIE All?

JEAN I'd say so. I've heard the same expression used several times before in similar circumstances.

MISS JULIE What kind of circumstances?

JEAN The kind we're talking about. I remember the last time I—

MISS JULIE [*rising*] That's enough! I don't want to hear any more.

JEAN How strange! Neither did she! . . . Well, now if you'll excuse me, I'll go to bed.

MISS JULIE [*softly*] Go to bed on Midsummer Eve?

JEAN That's right. Dancing with that crowd up there really doesn't amuse me.

MISS JULIE Jean, get the key to the boathouse and row me out on the lake. I want to see the sun come up.

JEAN Do you think that's wise?

MISS JULIE You sound as if you were worried about your reputation.

JEAN Why not? I don't particularly care to be made ridiculous, or to be kicked out without a recommendation just when I'm trying to establish myself. Besides, I have a certain obligation to Christine.

MISS JULIE Oh, I see. It's Christine now.

JEAN Yes, but I'm thinking of you, too. Take my advice, Miss Julie. Go up to your room.

MISS JULIE When did you start giving me orders?

JEAN Just this once. For your own sake! Please! It's very late. You're so tired, you're drunk; you don't know what you're doing. Go to bed, Miss Julie. —Besides, if my ears aren't deceiving me, they're coming this way, looking for me. If they find us here together, you're done for!

THE CHORUS [*is heard coming nearer, singing*]

Said Jill to Jack, "Soil needs a tilling."
Tri-di-ri-di-ralla, tri-di-ri-di-ra.
Said Jack to Jill, "Time's a-spilling."
Tri-di-ri-di-ralla-la.
Said Jill to Jack, "Gold's a-hoarding."
Tri-di-ri-di-ralla, tri-di-ri-di-ra.
Said Jack to Jill, "Tell not my lording."
Tri-di-ri-di-ralla-la.
Said Jill to Jack, "Hair is for plaiting."
Tri-di-ri-di-ralla, tri-di-ri-di-ra.
"But Jill for Jack is not waiting."
Tri-di-ri-di-ralla-la![2]

MISS JULIE I know these people. I love them just as they love me. Let them come. You'll see.

JEAN Oh, no, Miss Julie, they don't love you! They take the food you give them, but they spit on it as soon as your back is turned. Believe me! Just listen to them. Listen to what they're singing. —No, you'd better not listen.

MISS JULIE [*listening*] What are they singing?

JEAN A nasty song—about you and me!

MISS JULIE How disgusting! Oh, what cowardly, sneaking—

JEAN That's what the mob always is—cowards! You can't fight them; you can only run away.

MISS JULIE Run away? Where? There's no way out of here. And we can't go in to Christine.

JEAN What about my room? What do you say? Rules don't count in a situation like this. You can trust me. —You said, let's be friends. Remember? Well, I'm your friend—your true, devoted, respectful friend.

MISS JULIE But suppose—suppose they looked for you there?

JEAN I'll bolt the door. If they try to break it down, I'll shoot. Come, Miss Julie! [*On his knees*] Please, Miss Julie!

MISS JULIE [*meaningfully*] You promise me that you won't—

JEAN I swear to you!

[MISS JULIE *goes out quickly to the right. Jean follows her impetuously.*]

The Ballet

The country people enter in festive costumes, with flowers in their hats. The fiddler is in the lead. A keg of small beer and a little keg of liquor, decorated with greenery, are set up on the table. Glasses are brought out. They all drink. Then they form a circle and sing

2. A peasants' folk song.

"Said Jill to Jack," dancing the round dance as they sing. At the end of the dance, they all leave singing.

MISS JULIE *comes in alone; looks at the devastated kitchen; clasps her hands together; then takes out a powder puff and powders her face.* JEAN *enters. He is in high spirits.*

JEAN You see! You heard them, didn't you? You've got to admit it's impossible to stay here.

MISS JULIE No, I don't. But even if I did, what could we do?

JEAN Go away, travel, get away from here!

MISS JULIE Travel? Yes—but where?

JEAN Switzerland, the Italian lakes. You've never been there?

MISS JULIE No. Is it beautiful?

JEAN Eternal summer, oranges, laurel trees, ah . . . !

MISS JULIE What do we do when we get there?

JEAN I'll set up a hotel—a first-class hotel with a first-class clientele.

MISS JULIE Hotel?

JEAN I tell you that's the life! Always new faces, new languages. Not a minute to think about yourself or worry about your nerves. No looking for something to do. The work keeps you busy. Day and night the bells ring, the trains whistle, the buses come and go. And all the while the money comes rolling in. I tell you it's the life!

MISS JULIE Yes, that's the life. But what about me?

JEAN The mistress of the whole place, the star of the establishment! With your looks—and your personality—it can't fail. It's perfect! You'll sit in the office like a queen, setting your slaves in motion by pressing an electric button. The guests will file before your throne and timidly lay their treasures on your table. You can't imagine how people tremble when you shove a bill in their face! I'll salt the bills and you'll sugar them with your prettiest smile. Come on, let's get away from here—[*He takes a timetable from his pocket.*]—right away—the next train! We'll be in Malmö at six-thirty, Hamburg eight-forty in the morning; Frankfurt to Basel in one day, and to Como[3] by way of the Gotthard tunnel in—let me see—three days! Three days!

MISS JULIE You make it sound so wonderful. But, Jean, you have to give me strength. Tell me you love me. Come and put your arms around me.

JEAN [*hesitates*] I want to . . . but I don't dare. Not anymore, not in this house. I do love you—without a shadow of a doubt. How can you doubt that, Miss Julie?

MISS JULIE [*shyly, very becomingly*] You don't have to be formal with me, Jean. You can call me Julie. There aren't any barriers between us now. Call me Julie.

JEAN [*agonized*] I can't! There are still barriers between us, Miss Julie, as long as we stay in this house! There's the past, there's the count. I've never met anyone I feel so much respect for. I've only got to see his gloves lying on a table and I shrivel up. I only have to hear that bell ring and I shy like a frightened horse. I only have to look at his boots standing there so stiff and proud and I feel my spine bending. [*He kicks the boots.*] Superstitions, prejudices that they've drilled into us since we were children! But they can be forgotten just as easily! Just get us to another country where they have a republic!

3. A city on the southwest end of Lake Como, in northern Italy; Jean outlines the journey there from Sweden through Germany and Switzerland.

They'll crawl on their hands and knees when they see my uniform. On their hands and knees, I tell you! But not me! Oh, no. I'm not made for crawling. I've got guts, backbone. And once I grab that first branch, you just watch me climb. I may be a valet now, but next year I'll be owning property; in ten years, I'll be living off my investments. Then I'll go to Rumania, get myself some decorations, and maybe—notice I only say maybe—end up as a count!

MISS JULIE How wonderful, wonderful.

JEAN Listen, in Rumania you can buy titles. You'll be a countess after all. My countess.

MISS JULIE But I'm not interested in that. I'm leaving all that behind. Tell me you love me, Jean, or else—or else what difference does it make what I am?

JEAN I'll tell you a thousand times—but later! Not now. And not here. Above all, let's keep our feelings out of this or we'll make a mess of everything. We have to look at this thing calmly and coolly, like sensible people. [*He takes out a cigar, clips the end, and lights it.*] Now you sit there and I'll sit here, and we'll talk as if nothing had happened.

MISS JULIE [*in anguish*] My God, what are you? Don't you have any feelings?

JEAN Feelings? Nobody's got more feelings than I have. But I've learned to control them.

MISS JULIE A few minutes ago you were kissing my shoe—and now—!

JEAN [*harshly*] That was a few minutes ago. We've got other things to think about now!

MISS JULIE Don't speak to me like that, Jean!

JEAN I'm just trying to be sensible. We've been stupid once; let's not be stupid again. Your father might be back at any moment, and we've got to decide our future before then. —Now what do you think about my plans? Do you approve or don't you?

MISS JULIE I don't see anything wrong with them. Except one thing. For a big undertaking like that, you'd need a lot of capital. Have you got it?

JEAN [*chewing on his cigar*] Have I got it? Of course I have. I've got my knowledge of the business, my vast experience, my familiarity with languages. That's capital that counts for something, let me tell you.

MISS JULIE You can't even buy the railway tickets with it.

JEAN That's true. That's why I need a backer—someone to put up the money.

MISS JULIE Where can you find him on a moment's notice?

JEAN You'll find him—if you want to be my partner.

MISS JULIE I can't. And I don't have a penny to my name.

[*Pause.*]

JEAN Then you can forget the whole thing.

MISS JULIE Forget—?

JEAN And things will stay just the way they are.

MISS JULIE Do you think I'm going to live under the same roof with you as your mistress? Do you think I'm going to have people sneering at me behind my back? How do you think I'll ever be able to look my father in the face after this? No, no! Take me away from here, Jean—the shame, the humiliation. . . . What have I done? Oh, my God, my God! What have I done! [*She bursts into tears.*]

JEAN Now don't start singing that tune. It won't work. What have you done that's so awful? You're not the first.

MISS JULIE [*crying hysterically*] Now you think me contemptible—I'm falling, falling!

JEAN Fall down to me, and I'll lift you up again!

MISS JULIE What awful hold did you have over me? What drove me to you? The weak to the strong? The falling to the rising! Or maybe it was love? Love? This? You don't know what love is!

JEAN Want to bet? Did you think I was a virgin?

MISS JULIE You're coarse—vulgar! The things you say, the things you think!

JEAN That's the way I was brought up. It's the way I am! Now don't get hysterical. And don't play the fine lady with me. We're eating off the same platter now. . . . That's better. Come over here and be a good girl and I'll treat you to something special. [*He opens the table drawer and takes out the wine bottle. He pours the wine into two used glasses.*]

MISS JULIE Where did you get that wine?

JEAN From the wine cellar.

MISS JULIE My father's burgundy!

JEAN Should be good enough for his son-in-law.

MISS JULIE I was drinking beer and you—!

JEAN Shows I have better taste than you.

MISS JULIE Thief!

JEAN You going to squeal on me?

MISS JULIE Oh, God! Partner in crime with a petty house thief! I must have been drunk; I must have been walking in my sleep. Midsummer Night! Night of innocent games—

JEAN Yes, very innocent!

MISS JULIE [*pacing up and down*] Is there anyone here on earth as miserable as I am?

JEAN Why be miserable? Look at the conquest you've made! Think of poor Christine in there. Don't you think she's got any feelings?

MISS JULIE I thought so a while ago; I don't now. A servant's a servant—

JEAN And a whore's a whore!

MISS JULIE [*falls to her knees and clasps her hands together*] Oh, God in heaven, put an end to my worthless life! Lift me out of this awful filth I'm sinking in! Save me! Save me!

JEAN I feel sorry for you, I have to admit it. When I was lying in the onion beds, looking up at you on the rose terrace, I—I'm telling you the truth now—I had the same dirty thoughts that all boys have.

MISS JULIE And you said you wanted to die for me!

JEAN In the oat bin? That was only a story.

MISS JULIE A lie, you mean.

JEAN [*getting sleepy*] Practically. I think I read it in a paper about a chimney sweep who curled up in a wood-bin with some lilacs because they were going to arrest him for nonsupport of his child.

MISS JULIE Now I see you as you really are.

JEAN What did you expect me to do? It's always the fancy talk that gets the women.

MISS JULIE You dog!

JEAN You bitch!

MISS JULIE Well, now you've seen the eagle's back—

JEAN Wasn't exactly its back—!

MISS JULIE I was going to be the window dressing for your hotel—!

JEAN And I the hotel—!

MISS JULIE Sitting at the desk, attracting your customers, padding your bills—!

JEAN I could manage that myself—!

MISS JULIE How can a human soul be so dirty and filthy?

JEAN Then why don't you clean it up?

MISS JULIE You lackey! You shoeshine boy! Stand up when I talk to you!

JEAN You lackey lover! You bootblack's tramp! Shut your mouth and get out of here! Who do you think you are telling me I'm coarse? I've never seen anybody in my class behave as crudely as you did tonight. Have you ever seen any of the girls around here grab at a man like you did? Do you think any of the girls of my class would throw themselves at a man like that? I've never seen the like of it except in animals and prostitutes!

MISS JULIE [*crushed*] That's right! Hit me! Walk all over me! It's all I deserve. I'm rotten. But help me! Help me to get out of this—if there is any way out for me!

JEAN [*less harsh*] I'd be doing myself an injustice if I didn't admit that part of the credit for this seduction belongs to me. But do you think a person in my position would have dared to look twice at you if you hadn't asked for it? I'm still amazed—

MISS JULIE And still proud.

JEAN Why not? But I've got to confess the victory was a little too easy to give me any real thrill.

MISS JULIE Go on, hit me again!

JEAN [*standing up*] No. . . . I'm sorry I said that. I never hit a person who's down, especially a woman. I can't deny that, in one way, it was good to find out that what I saw glittering up above was only fool's gold, to see that the eagle's back was as gray as its belly, that the smooth cheek was just powder, and that there could be dirt under the manicured nails, that the handkerchief was soiled even though it smelled of perfume. But, in another way, it hurts to find that everything I was striving for wasn't very high above me after all, wasn't even real. It hurts me to see you sink far lower than your own cook. Hurts, like seeing the last flowers cut to pieces by the autumn rains and turned to muck.

MISS JULIE You talk as if you already stood high above me.

JEAN Well, don't I? Don't forget I could make you a countess but you can never make me a count.

MISS JULIE I have a father for a count. You can never have that!

JEAN True. But I might father my own counts—that is, if—

MISS JULIE You're a thief! I'm not!

JEAN There are worse things than being a thief. A lot worse. And besides, when I take a position in a house, I consider myself a member of the family—in a way, like a child in the house. It's no crime for a child to steal a few ripe cherries when they're falling off the trees, is it? [*He begins to feel passionate again.*] Miss Julie, you're a beautiful woman, much too good for the likes of me. You got carried away by your emotions and now you want to cover up your mistake by telling yourself that you love me. You don't love me. Maybe you were attracted by my looks—in which case your kind of love is no better than mine. But I could never be satisfied to be just an animal for you, and I could never make you love me.

MISS JULIE How do you know that for sure?

JEAN You mean there's a chance? I could love you, there's no doubt about that. You're beautiful, you're refined—[*He goes up to her and takes her hand.*]—educated, lovable when you want to be, and once you set a man's heart on fire, I'll bet it burns forever. [*He puts his arm around her waist.*] You're like hot wine with strong spices. One of your kisses is enough to—

[*He attempts to lead her out, but she rather reluctantly breaks away from him.*]

MISS JULIE Let me go. You don't get me that way.

JEAN Then how? Not by petting you and not with pretty words, not by planning for the future, not by saving you from humiliation! Then how, tell me how?

MISS JULIE How? How? I don't know how! I don't know at all! —I hate you like I hate rats, but I can't get away from you.

JEAN Then come away with me!

MISS JULIE [*pulling herself together*] Away? Yes, we'll go away! —But I'm so tired. Pour me a glass of wine, will you?

[JEAN *pours the wine,* MISS JULIE *looks at her watch.*]

Let's talk first. We still have a little time. [*She empties the glass of wine and holds it out for more.*]

JEAN Don't overdo it. You'll get drunk.

MISS JULIE What difference does it make?

JEAN What difference? It looks cheap. —What did you want to say to me?

MISS JULIE We're going to run away together, right? But we'll talk first—that is, I'll talk. So far you've done all the talking. You've told me your life, now I'll tell you mine. That way we'll know each other through and through before we become . . . traveling companions.

JEAN Wait a minute. Are you sure you won't regret this afterward—surrendering your secrets to me?

MISS JULIE I thought you were my friend.

JEAN I am—sometimes. Just don't count on it.

MISS JULIE You don't mean that. Anyway, everybody knows my secrets. —My mother's parents were very ordinary people, just commoners. She was brought up, according to the theories of her time, to believe in equality, the independence of women, and all that. And she had a strong aversion to marriage. When my father proposed to her, she swore she would never become his wife but that she might possibly consent to become his mistress. So he told her he didn't want to see the woman he loved enjoy less respect than he did. But she said she didn't care what the world thought—and he, believing that he couldn't live without her, accepted her conditions. That did it. From then on he was cut off from his old circle of friends and left without anything to do in the house, which couldn't have kept him occupied anyway. Then I came into the world—against my mother's wishes, as far as I can make out. My mother decided to bring me up as a nature child. And on top of that I had to learn everything a boy learns, so I could be living proof that women were just as good as men. I had to wear boy's clothes, learn to handle horses—but not to milk the cows! Girls did that! I was made to groom the horses and harness them, and learn farming and go hunting—I even had to learn how to slaughter the animals. It was disgusting. Awful! And on the estate all the men were set to doing women's chores, and the women to doing men's work—with the result that the whole place fell to pieces, and we became the local laughing-stock. Finally, my father must have come out of his trance. He rebelled, and everything was changed according to his wishes. They got married—very quietly. Then my mother got sick. I don't know what kind of sickness it was, but she often had convulsions, and she would hide herself in the attic or in the garden, and sometimes she would stay out all night. Then there occurred that big fire you've heard about. The house, the stables, the cowsheds, all burned down—and under very peculiar circumstances that led one to suspect arson. You see, the accident occurred the day after the insurance expired, and the premiums on the new policy, which my father had sent in, were delayed through the messenger's carelessness, and didn't arrive in time. [*She refills her glass and drinks.*]

JEAN You've had enough.

MISS JULIE Who cares! —We were left without a penny to our name. We had to sleep in the carriages. My father didn't know where to turn for money to rebuild the house. Then Mother suggested to him that he might try to borrow money from an old friend of hers, who owned a brick factory not far from here. Father took out a loan, but there wasn't any interest charged, which surprised him. So the place was rebuilt. [*She drinks some more.*] Do you know who set fire to the place?

JEAN Your honorable mother!

MISS JULIE Do you know who the brick manufacturer was?

JEAN Your mother's lover?

MISS JULIE Do you know whose money it was?

JEAN Let me think a minute. . . . No, I give up.

MISS JULIE It was my mother's!

JEAN The count's, you mean. Or was there a marriage settlement?[4]

MISS JULIE There wasn't a settlement. My mother had a little money of her own which she didn't want under my father's control, so she invested it with her—friend.

JEAN Who pinched it!

MISS JULIE Right! He kept it for himself. Well, my father found out what happened. But he couldn't go to court, couldn't pay his wife's lover, couldn't prove that it was his wife's money. That was how my mother got her revenge because he had taken control of the house. He was on the verge of shooting himself. There was even a rumor that he tried and failed. But somehow he took a new lease on life and he forced my mother to pay for her mistakes. Can you imagine what those five years were like for me? I loved my father, but I took my mother's side because I didn't know the whole story. She had taught me to hate all men—I'm sure you've heard how she hated men—and I swore to her that I'd never be slave to any man.

JEAN You got engaged to the attorney, didn't you?

MISS JULIE Only to make him my slave.

JEAN I guess he didn't go for that, did he?

MISS JULIE Oh, he wanted to well enough. I didn't give him the chance. I got bored with him.

JEAN Yes, so I noticed—in the stable yard.

4. An agreement, made before a marriage, to transfer some property to the wife.

MISS JULIE What did you notice?

JEAN I saw how he—. [Still see it on your cheek.

MISS JULIE What!

JEAN The stripe on your cheek.][5] He broke it off.

MISS JULIE It's a lie! I broke it off! Did he tell you that? He's beneath contempt!

JEAN Come on now, as bad as that? So you hate men, hm?

MISS JULIE Yes, I do. . . . Most of the time. But sometimes, when I can't help myself—oh . . . [*She shudders in disgust.*]

JEAN Then you hate me, too?

MISS JULIE You have no idea how much! I'd like to see you killed like an animal—

JEAN Like when you're caught having sex with an animal: you get two years at hard labor and the animal is killed. Right?

MISS JULIE Right.

JEAN But there's no one to catch us—and *no animal!*—So what are we going to do?

MISS JULIE Go away from here.

JEAN To torture ourselves to death?

MISS JULIE No. To enjoy ourselves for a day or two, or a week, for as long as we can—and then—to die—

JEAN Die? That's stupid! I've got a better idea: start a hotel!

MISS JULIE [*continuing without hearing* JEAN] —on the shores of Lake Como, where the sun is always shining, where the laurels bloom at Christmas, and the golden oranges glow on the trees.

JEAN Lake Como is a stinking wet hole, and the only oranges I saw there were on the fruit stands. But it's a good tourist spot with a lot of villas and cottages that are rented out to lovers. Now there's a profitable business. You know why? They rent the villa for the whole season, but they leave after three weeks.

MISS JULIE [*naively*] Why after only three weeks?

JEAN Because that's about as long as they can stand each other. Why else? But they still have to pay the rent. You see? Then you rent it out again to another couple, and so on. There's no shortage of love—even if it doesn't last very long.

MISS JULIE Then you don't want to die with me?

JEAN I don't want to die at all! I enjoy life too much. And moreover, I consider taking your own life a sin against the Providence that gave us life.

MISS JULIE You believe in God? You?

JEAN Yes, certainly I do! I go to church every other Sunday—. Honestly, I've had enough of this talk. I'm going to bed.

MISS JULIE Really? You think you're going to get off that easy? Don't you know that a man owes something to the woman he's dishonored?

JEAN [*takes out his purse and throws a silver coin on the table*] There you are. I don't want to owe anybody anything.

MISS JULIE [*pretending not to notice*] Do you know what the law says—?

JEAN Lucky for you the law says nothing about women who seduce men!

MISS JULIE [*as before*] What else can we do but go away from here, get married, and get divorced?

5. The passage in brackets was deleted in Strindberg's manuscript, probably by Strindberg himself [translator's note].

JEAN Suppose I refuse to enter into this *mésalliance?*[6]

MISS JULIE *Mésalliance?*

JEAN For me! I've got better ancestors than you. I don't have a female arsonist in my family.

MISS JULIE You can't prove that.

JEAN You can't prove the opposite—because we don't have any family records—except in the police files. But I've read the whole history of your family in that peerage book in the drawing room. Do you know who the founder of your family line was? A miller—who let his wife sleep with the king one night during the Danish war.[7] I don't have any ancestors like that. I don't have any ancestors at all! But I can become an ancestor myself.

MISS JULIE This is what I get for baring my heart and soul to someone too low to understand, for sacrificing the honor of my family—

JEAN Dishonor! —I warned you, remember? Drinking makes one talk, and talking's bad.

MISS JULIE Oh, how sorry I am! . . . If only it had never happened! . . . If only you at least loved me!

JEAN For the last time—what do you want me to do? Cry? Jump over your whip? Kiss you? Lure you to Lake Como for three weeks and then—? What am I supposed to do? What do you want? I've had more than I can take. This is what I get for involving myself with women. . . . Miss Julie, I can see that you're unhappy; I know that you're suffering; but I simply cannot understand you. My people don't behave like this. We don't hate each other. We make love for the fun of it, when we can get any time off from our work. But we don't have time for it all day and all night like you do. If you ask me, you're sick, Miss Julie. Your mother's mind was affected, you know. There are whole counties affected with pietism. That was your mother's trouble—pietism. It's spreading like the plague.

MISS JULIE You can be understanding, Jean. You're talking to me like a human being now.

JEAN Well, be human yourself. You spit on me, but you don't let me wipe it off—on you.

MISS JULIE Help me, Jean. Help me. Tell me what I should do, that's all—which way to go.

JEAN For Christ's sake, if only I knew myself!

MISS JULIE I've been crazy—I've been out of my mind—but does that mean there's no way out for me?

JEAN Stay here as if nothing had happened. Nobody knows anything.

MISS JULIE Impossible! Everybody who works here knows. Christine knows.

JEAN They don't know a thing. Anyhow they'd never believe it.

MISS JULIE [*slowly, significantly*] But . . . it might happen again.

JEAN That's true!

MISS JULIE And one time there might be . . . consequences.

JEAN [*stunned*] Consequences!! What on earth have I been thinking of! You're right. There's only one thing to do: get away from here! Immediately!

6. Literally, "misalliance" (French), an ill-advised marriage.
7. That is, the war begun by Denmark in 1657 that ended with the Treaty of Copenhagen (1660), which restored to Sweden its southern provinces.

I can't go with you—that would give the whole game away. You'll have to go by yourself. Somewhere—I don't care where!

MISS JULIE By myself? Where? —Oh, no, Jean, I can't. I can't!

JEAN You've got to! Before the count comes back. You know as well as I do what will happen if you stay here. After one mistake, you figure you might as well go on—the damage is already done. Then you get more and more careless until—finally you're exposed. I tell you, you've got to get out of the country. Afterward you can write to the count and tell him everything—leaving me out, of course. He'd never figure it was me. He wouldn't even let himself think it was me.

MISS JULIE I'll go—if you'll come with me!

JEAN Lady, are you out of your mind? "Miss Julie elopes with her footman." The day after tomorrow it would be in all the papers. The count would never live it down.

MISS JULIE I can't go away. I can't stay. Help me. I'm so tired, so awfully tired. . . . Tell me what to do. Order me. Start me going. I can't think anymore, can't move anymore . . .

JEAN Now do you realize how weak you all are? What gives you the right to go strutting around with your noses in the air as if you owned the world? All right, I'll give you your orders. Go up and get dressed. Get some traveling money. And come back down here.

MISS JULIE [*almost in a whisper*] Come up with me!

JEAN To your room? . . . You're going crazy again! [*He hesitates a moment.*] No! No! Go! Right now! [*He takes her hand and leads her out.*]

MISS JULIE [*as she is leaving*] Don't be so harsh, Jean.

JEAN Orders always sound harsh. You've never had to take them.

[JEAN, *left alone, heaves a sigh of relief and sits down at the table. He takes out a notebook and a pencil and begins to calculate, counting aloud now and then. The pantomime continues until* CHRISTINE *enters, dressed for church, and carrying* JEAN*'s white tie and shirtfront in her hand.*]

CHRISTINE Lord in Heaven, what a mess! What on earth have you been doing?

JEAN It was Miss Julie. She dragged the whole crowd in here. You must have been sleeping awfully sound if you didn't hear anything.

CHRISTINE I slept like a log.

JEAN You already dressed for church?

CHRISTINE Yes, indeed. Don't you remember you promised to go to communion with me today?

JEAN Oh, yes. Of course, I remember. I see you've brought my things. All right. Come on, put it on me. [*He sits down, and* CHRISTINE *starts to put the white tie and shirtfront on him. Pause.*]

JEAN [*yawning*] What's the lesson for today?

CHRISTINE The beheading of John the Baptist, what else? It's Midsummer. It's his feast day.

JEAN My God, that will go on forever. —Hey, you're choking me! . . . Oh, I'm so sleepy, so sleepy.

CHRISTINE What were you doing up all night? You look green in the face.

JEAN I've been sitting here talking with Miss Julie.

CHRISTINE That girl! She doesn't know how to behave herself!

[*Pause.*]

JEAN Tell me something, Christine . . .

CHRISTINE Well, what?

JEAN Isn't it strange when you think about it? Her, I mean.

CHRISTINE What's so strange?

JEAN Everything!

[*Pause.* CHRISTINE *looks at the half-empty glasses on the table.*]

CHRISTINE Have you been drinking with her?

JEAN Yes!

CHRISTINE Shame on you! —Look me in the eyes! You haven't . . . ?

JEAN Yes!

CHRISTINE Is it possible? Is it really possible?

JEAN [*thinking about it*] Yes. It is.

CHRISTINE Oh, how disgusting! I could never have believed anything like this would happen! No. No. This is too much!

JEAN Don't tell me you're jealous of her?

CHRISTINE No, not of her. If it had been Clara—or Sophie—I would have scratched your eyes out! But her—? That's different. I don't know why. . . . But it's still disgusting!

JEAN You're not mad at her?

CHRISTINE No. Mad at you. You were mean and cruel to do a thing like that, very mean. The poor girl! . . . Let me tell you, I'm not going to stay in this house a moment longer, not when I can't have any respect for my employers.

JEAN Why do you want to respect them?

CHRISTINE Don't try to be smart. You don't want to work for people who behave like pigs, do you? Well, do you? If you ask me, you'd be lowering yourself by doing that.

JEAN Oh, I don't know. I think it's rather comforting to find out that they're not one damn bit better than we are.

CHRISTINE Well, I don't. If they're not any better, there's no point in us trying to be like them. —And think of the count. Think of all the sorrows he's been through in his time. My God! I won't stay in this house any longer. . . . Imagine! You, of all people! If it had been the attorney fellow; if it had been somebody respectable—

JEAN Now just a minute—!

CHRISTINE Oh, you're all right in your own way. But there's a big difference between one class and another. You can't deny that. —No, this is something I can never get over. She was so proud, and so sarcastic about men, you'd never believe she'd go and throw herself at one. And at someone like you! And she was going to have Diana shot because the poor thing ran after the gatekeeper's mongrel! —Well, I tell you, I've had enough! I'm not going to stay here any longer. When my term's up, I'm leaving.

JEAN Then what'll you do?

CHRISTINE Well, since you brought it up, it's about time that you got yourself a decent place, if we're going to get married.

JEAN Why should I go looking for another place? I could never get a job like this if I'm married.

CHRISTINE Well, I know that! But you could get a job as a porter, or maybe try to get a government job as a caretaker somewhere. A square deal and a square meal, that's what you get from the government—and a pension for the wife and children.

JEAN [*wryly*] Fine, fine! But I'm not the kind of guy who thinks about dying for his wife and children this early in the game. Let me tell you, I've got slightly bigger plans than that.

CHRISTINE Plans! Ha! What about your obligations? You'd better start giving them a little thought!

JEAN Don't start nagging me about obligations! I know what I have to do without you telling me. [*He hears a sound upstairs.*] Anyhow, we'll have plenty of chance to talk about this later. You just go and get yourself ready, and we'll be off to church.

CHRISTINE Who is that walking around up there?

JEAN I don't know. Clara, I suppose. Who else?

CHRISTINE [*starting to leave*] It can't be the count, can it? Could he have come back without anybody hearing him?

JEAN [*frightened*] The count? No, it can't be. He would have rung.

CHRISTINE [*leaving*] God help us! I've never heard the like of this.

[*The sun has now risen and strikes the tops of the trees in the park. As the scene progresses, the light shifts gradually until it is shining very obliquely through the windows.* JEAN *goes to the door and signals.* MISS JULIE *enters, dressed for travel, and carrying a small birdcage, covered with a towel. She sets the cage down on a chair.*]

MISS JULIE I'm ready now.

JEAN Shh! Christine's awake.

MISS JULIE [*extremely tense and nervous during the following*] Did she suspect anything?

JEAN She doesn't know a thing. —My God, what happened to you?

MISS JULIE What do you mean? Do I look so strange?

JEAN You're white as a ghost, and you've—excuse me—you've got dirt on your face.

MISS JULIE Let me wash it off. [*She goes over to the washbasin and washes her face and hands.*] There! Do you have a towel? . . . Oh, look, the sun's coming up!

JEAN That breaks the magic spell!

MISS JULIE Yes, we were spellbound last night, weren't we? Midsummer madness . . . Jean, listen to me! Come with me. I've got the money!

JEAN [*suspiciously*] Enough?

MISS JULIE Enough for a start. Come with me, Jean. I can't travel alone today. Midsummer Day on a stifling hot train, packed in with crowds of people, all staring at me—stopping at every station when I want to be flying. I can't, Jean, I can't! . . . And everything will remind me of the past. Midsummer Day when I was a child and the church was decorated with leaves—birch leaves and lilacs . . . the table spread for dinner with friends and relatives . . . and after dinner, dancing in the park, with flowers and games. Oh, no matter how far you travel, the memories tag right along in the baggage car . . . and the regrets and the remorse.

JEAN All right, I'll go with you! But it's got to be now—before it's too late! This very instant!

MISS JULIE Hurry and get dressed! [*She picks up the birdcage.*]

JEAN No baggage! It would give us away.

MISS JULIE Nothing. Only what we can take to our seats.

JEAN [*as he gets his hat*] What in the devil have you got there? What is that?

MISS JULIE It's only my canary. I can't leave it behind.

JEAN A canary! My God, do you expect us to carry a birdcage around with us? You're crazy. Put that cage down!

MISS JULIE It's the only thing I'm taking with me from my home—the only living thing who loves me since Diana was unfaithful to me! Don't be cruel, Jean. Let me take it with me.

JEAN I told you to put that cage down! —And don't talk so loud. Christine can hear us.

MISS JULIE No, I won't leave it with a stranger. I won't. I'd rather have you kill it.

JEAN Give it here, the little pest. I'll wring its neck.

MISS JULIE Oh, don't hurt it. Don't—. No, I can't do it!

JEAN Don't worry, I can. Give it here.

[MISS JULIE *takes the bird out of the cage and kisses it.*]

MISS JULIE Oh, my little Serena, must you die and leave your mistress?

JEAN You don't have to make a scene of it. It's a question of your whole life and future. You're wasting time!

[JEAN *grabs the canary from her, carries it to the chopping block, and picks up a meat cleaver.* MISS JULIE *turns away.*]

You should have learned how to kill chickens instead of shooting revolvers—[*He brings the cleaver down.*]—then a drop of blood wouldn't make you faint.

MISS JULIE [*screaming*] Kill me too! Kill me! You can kill an innocent creature without turning a hair—then kill me. Oh, how I hate you! I loathe you! There's blood between us. I curse the moment I first laid eyes on you! I curse the moment I was conceived in my mother's womb.

JEAN What good does your cursing do? Let's get out of here!

MISS JULIE [*approaches the chopping block, drawn to it against her will*]. No, I don't want to go yet. I can't. —I have to see. —Shh! [*She listens but keeps her eyes fastened on the chopping block and cleaver.*] You don't think I can stand the sight of blood, do you? You think I'm so weak, don't you? Oh, how I'd love to see your blood, your brains on that chopping block. I'd love to see the whole of your sex swimming in a sea of blood just like that. I could drink blood out of your skull. Use your chest as a foot bath, dip my toes in your guts! I could eat your heart roasted whole! —You think I'm weak! You think I loved you because my womb hungered for your semen. You think I want to carry your brood under my heart and feed it with my blood? Bear your child and take your name? —Come to think of it, what is your name? I've never even heard your last name. I'll bet you don't have one. I'd be Mrs. Doorman or Madame Garbageman. You dog with *my* name on your collar—you lackey with *my* initials on your buttons! Do you think I'm going to share you with my cook and fight over you with my maid?! Ohh! —You think I'm a coward who's going to run away! No, I'm going to stay—come hell or high water. My father will come home—find his desk broken into—his money gone. He'll ring—on that bell—two rings for the valet. And then he'll send for the sheriff—and I'll tell him everything. Everything! Oh, what a relief it'll be to have it all over . . . over and done with . . . if only it will be over. . . . He'll have a stroke and die . . . and there'll be an end to all of us. There'll be peace . . . and quiet . . . forever. . . . The coat of arms will be broken on his coffin; the count's line will be extinct—while the valet's breed will continue in an orphanage, win triumphs in the gutter, and end in jail!

[CHRISTINE *enters, dressed for church and with a hymnbook in her hand.* MISS JULIE *rushes over to her and throws herself into her arms as if seeking protection.*]

MISS JULIE Help me, Christine! Protect me against this man!

CHRISTINE [*cold and unmoved*] This is a fine way to behave on a holy day! [*She sees the chopping block.*] Just look at the mess you've made there! How do you explain that? And what's all this shouting and screaming about?

MISS JULIE Christine, you're a woman, you're my friend! I warn you, watch out for this—this monster!

JEAN [*feeling awkward*] If you ladies are going to talk, you won't want me around. I think I'll go and shave. [*He slips out to the right.*]

MISS JULIE You've got to understand, Christine! You've got to listen to me!

CHRISTINE No, I don't. I don't understand this kind of shenanigans at all. Where do you think you're going dressed like that? And Jean with his hat on? —Well? —Well?

MISS JULIE Listen to me, Christine! If you'll just listen to me, I'll tell you everything.

CHRISTINE I don't want to know anything.

MISS JULIE You've got to listen to me—!

CHRISTINE What about? About your stupid behavior with Jean? I tell you that doesn't bother me at all, because it's none of my business. But if you have any silly idea about talking him into skipping out with you, I'll soon put a stop to that.

MISS JULIE [*extremely tense*] Christine, please don't get upset. Listen to me. I can't stay here, and Jean can't stay here. So you see, we have to go away.

CHRISTINE Hm, hm, hm.

MISS JULIE [*suddenly brightening up*] Wait! I've got an idea! Why couldn't all three of us go away together?—out of the country—to Switzerland—and start a hotel? I've got the money, you see. Jean and I would be responsible for the whole affair—and Christine, you could run the kitchen, I thought. Doesn't that sound wonderful! Say you'll come, Christine, then everything will be settled. Say you will! Please! [*She throws her arms around* CHRISTINE *and pats her.*]

CHRISTINE [*remaining aloof and unmoved*] Hm. Hm.

MISS JULIE [*presto tempo*[8]] You've never been traveling, Christine. You have to get out and see the world. You can't imagine how wonderful it is to travel by train—constantly new faces, new countries. We'll go to Hamburg, and stop over to look at the zoo—it's famous, has everything—you'll love that. And we'll go to the theater and the opera. And then when we get to Munich, we'll go to the museums, Christine. They have Rubenses and Raphaels there—those great painters, you know. Of course you've heard about Munich where King Ludwig[9] lived—you know, the king who went mad. And then we can go and see his castles—they're just like the ones you read about in fairy tales. And from there it's just a short trip to Switzerland—with the

8. Quick time (Italian), a musical direction.
9. King Ludwig II of Bavaria (1845–1886; r. 1864–86), known as "the Fairy-Tale King," built several extravagant palaces—most famously Neuschwanstein, the so-called Cinderella castle; he was declared insane in 1886. Peter Paul Rubens (1577–1640) was a Flemish baroque painter; Raphael (Raffaello Sanzio, 1483–1520), a master of the Italian Renaissance.

Alps. Think of the Alps, Christine, covered with snow in the middle of summer. And oranges grow there, and laurel trees that are green the whole year round—

[JEAN *can be seen in the wings at the right, sharpening his straight razor on a strop held between his teeth and his left hand. He listens to* MISS JULIE *with a satisfied expression on his face, now and then nodding approvingly.* MISS JULIE *continues tempo prestissimo.*[1]]

—and that's where we'll get a hotel. I'll sit at the desk while Jean stands at the door and receives the guests, goes out shopping, writes the letters. What a life that will be! The train whistle blowing, then the bus arriving, then a bell ringing upstairs, then the bell in the restaurant rings—and I'll be making out the bills—and I know just how much to salt them—you can't imagine how timid tourists are when you shove a bill in their face! —And you, Christine, you'll run the whole kitchen—there'll be no standing at the stove for you—of course not. If you're going to talk to the people, you'll have to dress. And with your looks—I'm not trying to flatter you, Christine—you'll run off with some man one fine day—a rich Englishman, that's who it'll be, they're so easy to—[*Slowing down*]—to catch. —Then we'll all be rich. —We'll build a villa on Lake Como. —Maybe it does rain there sometimes, but—[*More and more lifelessly*]—the sun has to shine sometimes, too—even if it looks cloudy. —And—then . . . or else we can always travel some more—and come back . . . [*Pause*]—here . . . or somewhere else . . .

CHRISTINE Do you really believe a word of that yourself, Miss Julie?

MISS JULIE [*completely beaten*] Do I believe a word of it myself?

CHRISTINE Do you?

MISS JULIE [*exhausted*] I don't know. I don't believe anything anymore. [*She sinks down on the bench and lays her head between her arms on the table.*] Nothing. Nothing at all.

CHRISTINE [*turns to the right and faces* JEAN] So! You were planning to run away, were you?

JEAN [*taken aback, lays his razor down on the table*] We weren't exactly going to run away! Don't exaggerate. You heard Miss Julie's plans. Even if she's tired now after being up all night, her plans are perfectly practical.

CHRISTINE Well, just listen to you! Did you really think you could get me to cook for that little—!

JEAN [*sharply*] You keep a respectful tongue in your mouth when you talk to your mistress! Understand?

CHRISTINE Mistress!

JEAN Yes, mistress!

CHRISTINE Well of all the—! I don't have to listen—

JEAN Yes, you do! You need to listen more and blabber less. Miss Julie is your mistress. Don't you forget that! And if you're going to despise her for what she did, you ought to despise yourself for the same reason.

CHRISTINE I've always held myself high enough to—

JEAN High enough to make you look down on others!

CHRISTINE —enough to keep from lowering myself beneath my station. Don't you dare say that the count's cook has ever had anything to do with the stable groom or the swineherd. Don't you dare!

1. At a very rapid tempo (Italian).

JEAN Yes, you got yourself a decent man. Lucky you!

CHRISTINE What kind of a decent man is it who sells the oats from the count's stables?

JEAN Listen to who's talking! You get the gravy on the groceries and take bribes from the butcher!

CHRISTINE How dare you say a thing like that!

JEAN And you say you can't respect your employers. You of all people! You!

CHRISTINE Are you going to church or aren't you? You need a good sermon after your great exploits.

JEAN No, I'm not going to church! Go yourself. Go tell God how bad you are.

CHRISTINE Yes, I'll do just that. And I'll come back with enough forgiveness for your sins, too. Our Redeemer suffered and died on the cross for all our sins, and if we come to Him in faith and with a penitent heart, He will take all our sins upon Himself.

JEAN Rake-offs[2] included?

MISS JULIE Do you really believe that, Christine?

CHRISTINE With all my heart, as sure as I'm standing here. It was the faith I was born into, and I've held on to it since I was a little girl, Miss Julie. Where sin aboundeth, there grace aboundeth also.[3]

MISS JULIE If I had your faith, Christine, if only—

CHRISTINE But you see, that's something you can't have without God's special grace. And it is not granted to everyone to receive it.

MISS JULIE Then who receives it?

CHRISTINE That's the secret of the workings of grace, Miss Julie, and God is no respecter of persons. With Him the last shall be first[4]—

MISS JULIE In that case, he does have respect for the last, doesn't he?

CHRISTINE [*continuing*] —and it is easier for a camel to go through the eye of a needle than for a rich man to enter the kingdom of God.[5] That's how things are, Miss Julie. I'm going to leave now—alone. And on my way out I'm going to tell the stable boy not to let any horses out, in case anyone has any ideas about leaving before the count comes home. Goodbye.

[*She leaves.*]

JEAN She's a devil in skirts! —All because of a canary!

MISS JULIE [*listlessly*] Never mind the canary. . . . Do you see any way out of this, any end to it?

JEAN [*after thinking for a moment*] No.

MISS JULIE What would you do if you were in my place?

JEAN In your place? Let me think. . . . An aristocrat, a woman, and—fallen. . . . I don't know. —Or maybe I do.

MISS JULIE [*picks up the razor and makes a gesture with it*] Like this?

JEAN Yes. But I wouldn't do it, you understand. That's the difference between us.

MISS JULIE Because you're a man and I'm a woman? What difference does that make?

JEAN Just the difference that there is—between a man and a woman.

2. Cuts; money or goods skimmed off the top.
3. Romans 5.20.
4. Matthew 19.30, 20.16; Luke 13.30; Mark 10.31.
5. Matthew 19.24.

MISS JULIE [*holding the razor in her hand*] I want to! But I can't do it. My father couldn't do it either, that time when he should have.

JEAN No, he was right not to. He had to get his revenge first.

MISS JULIE And now my mother is getting her revenge again through me.

JEAN Didn't you ever love your father, Miss Julie?

MISS JULIE Yes, enormously. But I must have hated him too. I must have hated him without knowing it. It was he who brought me up to despise my own sex, to be half woman and half man. Who's to blame for what has happened? My father, my mother, myself? Myself? I don't have a self that's my own. I don't have a single thought I didn't get from my father, not an emotion I didn't get from my mother. And that last idea—about all people being equal—I got that from him, my fiancé. That's why I say he's beneath contempt. How can it be my own fault? Put the blame on Jesus, like Christine does? I'm too proud to do that—and too intelligent, thanks to what my father taught me. . . . A rich man can't get into heaven? That's a lie. But at least Christine, who's got money in the savings bank, won't get in. . . . Who's to blame? What difference does it make who's to blame? I'm still the one who has to bear the guilt, suffer the consequences—

JEAN Yes, but—

[*The bell rings sharply twice.* MISS JULIE *jumps up.* JEAN *changes his coat.*]

JEAN The count's back! What if Christine—[*He goes to the speaking tube, taps on it, and listens.*]

MISS JULIE Has he looked in his desk yet?

JEAN This is Jean, sir! [*Listens. The audience cannot hear what the count says.*] Yes, sir! [*Listens.*] Yes, sir! Yes, as soon as I can. [*Listens.*] Yes, at once, sir! [*Listens.*] Very good, sir! In half an hour.

MISS JULIE [*trembling with anxiety*] What did he say? For God's sake, what did he say?

JEAN He ordered his boots and his coffee in half an hour.

MISS JULIE Half an hour then! . . . Oh, I'm so tired. I can't bring myself to do anything. Can't repent, can't run away, can't stay, can't live . . . can't die. Help me, Jean. Command me, and I'll obey like a dog. Do me this last favor. Save my honor, save his name. You know what I ought to do but can't force myself to do. Let me use your willpower. You command me and I'll obey.

JEAN I don't know—. I can't either, not now. I don't know why. It's as if this coat made me—I can't give you orders in this. And now, after the count has spoken to me, I—I can't really explain it—but—I've got the backbone of a damned lackey! If the count came down here now and ordered me to cut my throat, I'd do it on the spot.

MISS JULIE Then pretend you're him. Pretend I'm you. You were such a good actor just a while ago, when you were kneeling before me. You were the aristocrat then. Or else—have you been to the theater and seen a hypnotist?

[JEAN *nods.*]

He says to his subject, "Take this broom!" and he takes it. He says, "Now sweep!" and he sweeps.

JEAN The person has to be asleep!

MISS JULIE [*ecstatic, transported*] I'm already asleep. The whole room has turned to smoke. You seem like an iron stove, a stove that looks like a man in black with a high hat. Your eyes are glowing like fading coals in a dying fire. Your face is a white smudge, like ashes.

[*The sun is now shining in on the floor and falls on* JEAN.]

It's so good and warm—[*She rubs her hands together as if warming them at a fire.*]—and so bright—and so peaceful.

JEAN [*takes the razor and puts it in her hand*] There's the broom. Go now, when the sun is up—out into the barn—and—[*He whispers in her ear.*]

MISS JULIE [*waking up*] Thanks! I'm going to get my rest. But tell me one thing. Tell me that the first can also receive the gift of grace. Tell me that, even if you don't believe it.

JEAN The first? I can't tell you that. —Wait a moment, Miss Julie. I know what I can tell you. You're no longer one of the first. You're one of—the last.

MISS JULIE That's true! I'm one of the last. I am the very last! —Oh! —Now I can't go! Tell me just once more, tell me to go!

JEAN Now I can't either. I can't!

MISS JULIE And the first shall be the last . . .

JEAN Don't think—don't think! You're taking all my strength from me. You're making me a coward. . . . What?! I thought I saw the bell move. No. . . . Let me stuff some paper in it. —Afraid of a bell! But it isn't just a bell. There's somebody behind it. A hand that makes it move. And there's something that makes the hand move. —Stop your ears, that's it, stop your ears! But it only rings louder. Rings louder and louder until you answer it. And then it's too late. Then the sheriff comes—and then—[*There are two sharp rings on the bell.* JEAN *gives a start, then straightens himself up.*] It's horrible! But there's no other way for it to end. —Go!

[MISS JULIE *walks resolutely out through the door.*]

in black with a high hat. Your eyes are glowing like fading coals in a dying fire. Your face is a white smudge, like ashes.

[*The sun is now shining in on the floor and falls on* JEAN.]

It's so good and warm—[*She rubs her hands together as if warming them at a fire.*]—and so bright—and so peaceful.

JEAN [*takes the razor and puts it in her hand*]. There's the broom. Go now, when the sun is up—out into the barn—and—[*He whispers in her ear.*]

MISS JULIE [*waking up*]. Thanks! I'm going to get my rest. But tell me one thing. Tell me that the first can also receive the gift of grace. Tell me that, even if you don't believe it.

JEAN. The first? I can't tell you that.—Wait a moment, Miss Julie. I know what I can tell you. You're no longer one of the first. You're one of—the last.

MISS JULIE. That's true! I'm one of the last. I am the very last.—Oh!—Now I can't go! Tell me just once more, tell me to go!

JEAN. Now I can't either. I can't!

MISS JULIE. And the first shall be the last . . .

JEAN. Don't think—don't think! You're taking all my strength from me. You're making me a coward. . . . What? I thought I saw the bell move. No. . . . Let me stuff some paper in it.—Afraid of a bell! But it isn't just a bell. There's somebody behind it. A hand that makes it move. And there's something that makes the hand move.—Stop your ears, that's it, stop your ears! But it only rings louder. Rings louder and louder until you answer it. And then it's too late. Then the sheriff comes—and then—[*There are two sharp rings on the bell.* JEAN *gives a start, then straightens himself up.*] It's horrible! But there's no other way for it to end.—Go!

[MISS JULIE *walks resolutely out through the door.*]

HENRIK IBSEN

1828–1906

WRITING in an era when the theater had become a second-rate occupation, with most gifted writers turning instead to novels or poetry, Henrik Johan Ibsen restored to drama its prestige and relevance. During the nineteenth century, the invention of new theatrical machinery and techniques had turned theater into spectacle. Producers spent their time and money on special effects, dazzling audiences with lighting, horses, or even sea battles to add to—and sometimes replace—the appeal of popular actors. Nineteenth-century theater was in some ways comparable to present-day Hollywood and its focus on blockbuster action movies filled with special effects and big-name stars. Ibsen showed Europe that drama could be more than just spectacle: it could be an art form addressing the most serious moral and social questions of the time. The theatergoing public was first shocked, and later thrilled, to have controversial figures and themes presented on the stage, in plays that relied not on special effects but on carefully drawn characters and well-constructed dramatic situations. Honing his dramatic technique over half a century, Ibsen almost single-handedly brought a new seriousness to drama, and in doing so he won enduring acclaim as the originator of modern drama.

Ibsen achieved his unparalleled success against all odds. He was born in Skien, a small town in Norway, far removed from the cultural centers of Europe both physically and linguistically. When Ibsen left his provincial home at the age of fifteen, he was apprenticed to a pharmacist for more than six years; during that time he began to write occasional pieces, including his first play, *Catiline* (written 1848–49). Only at the age of twenty-two was he able to free himself from his apprenticeship—as well as from a liaison with a maid that had resulted in an illegitimate child—and move to the capital, Christiania (now Oslo), to study for the university entrance exam, which he failed. His efforts as a dramatist were better received, as one of his plays—the one-act *The Burial Mound* (1850)—was performed. The true beginning of his career occurred several years later, however, when he moved to Bergen to take his first job in the theater. After a few years spent learning the craft, he assumed positions of greater responsibility—as artistic director and dramatist—at a theater back in Christiania, where in 1857 he also married and had another child. By the time Ibsen was thirty-five, the foundation for his subsequent success as a dramatist had been laid.

While working at the theaters in Bergen and Christiania, Ibsen got to know the standard dramatic form of the time, the so-called well-made play (a literal translation of the French *pièce bien-fait*). Popularized by the French playwrights Victorien Sardou (1831–1908) and Augustin-Eugène Scribe (1791–1861), well-made plays were formulaic dramas focused less on well-developed characters than on complicated plots and well-timed confrontations. They offered fast-moving action, intrigues, alliances, and sudden revelations. Immensely popular at the time, the genre was also attacked by proponents of modern drama for favoring cheap suspense and empty entertainment over social relevance and meaningful art.

Ibsen's own drama can be viewed as an evolving series of reactions to the well-made play, beginning with *Brand* (1866) and *Peer Gynt* (1867)—the two plays that established him throughout Europe as a writer of significance. They mark Ibsen's rejection not only of the well-made play but of the theater as such, for they were "dramatic poems"—plays written exclusively to be read, not performed. All the rules that governed stage action, the rules of the well-made play, could thus be ignored entirely. Both plays were built around a single character on a singular and willful mission. *Brand* is the more tragic of the two; it presents a fanatical preacher who seeks to impose an uncompromising religion on his small parish high up in the Norwegian mountains, demanding increasingly large sacrifices of his congregants and of himself until he finally dies in utter isolation. In *Peer Gynt*, the protagonist's quest is cast in a more satirical form. The adventures of the title character, a notorious liar, take him from the fairy-tale realm of the Norwegian mountain trolls to the Moroccan desert and then back to Norway, where he dies not as a hero but as a mediocrity, even in his sinning. Drawing on literary models such as GOETHE's *Faust* (1808, 1832) and Byron's *Don Juan* (1819–24), *Peer Gynt* freely mixes fantasy and reality, conjuring mountain trolls, mad German philosophers, and the devil himself.

By the time he wrote *Brand* and *Peer Gynt*, Ibsen had left Norway. He would spend twenty-seven years on the Continent, mostly in Italy and Germany, before returning to his homeland in 1891, at the age of sixty-three. Exile became the condition in which he thrived and from which he suffered. After *Brand* and *Peer Gynt* had secured his reputation, Ibsen started writing for the stage once more, but in an entirely different style. Whereas his earliest dramas had dealt with Norway's history, he now chose to write, once and for all, about the contemporary world he knew best—namely, the contemporary Norwegian middle class—in prose, not verse. His single purpose was to lay bare the ugly reality behind the facade of middle-class respectability, to expose the lies of bourgeois characters and indeed of bourgeois society as a whole. The five plays of this period—*The Pillars of Society* (1877), *A Doll House* (1879), *Ghosts* (1881), *An Enemy of the People* (1882), and *The Wild Duck* (1884)—made Ibsen notorious throughout Europe and established him as an author of shock, confrontation, and revolt: in short, as a modern. With these plays, Ibsen struck a nerve and secured his place in the pantheon of world drama.

The main cause of audiences' consternation also explains why these plays are now seen as the beginning of modern drama: they introduced realism, long established in the novel, to the theater. Using idiomatic language, Ibsen created a drama devoted to unveiling hidden motives and past misdeeds so that the truth would shine forth on the stage. In this way, Ibsen campaigned not only against a theater of special effects but also against a theater of convention. Realism, for Ibsen, required a theater of emotional and moral truth, a theater centered on understanding the subjective experience and objective conditions of modern life.

After winning fame and some infamy with his realist plays, Ibsen changed course once more as he attempted to write modern versions of Greek tragedy. In this last phase of his career, he managed to give definite shape to the tragedy of modern middle-class life. *HEDDA GABLER* (1890) is the most compelling and famous of the plays from this period, but it shares many features with the others—*Rosmersholm* (1886), *Lady from the Sea* (1888), *The Master Builder* (1892), *Little Eyolf* (1894), *John Gabriel Borkman* (1896), and

When We Dead Awaken (1899). All are set in the same bourgeois milieu as his realist plays, but they are less concerned with social deceptions and pretense. Instead, they are interested in the bourgeois characters themselves, presented as complex figures with hidden yearnings and fantasies that take them outside of the constricted worlds in which they live.

The title character of *Hedda Gabler* is the daughter of a general; she has married an aspiring scholar (Tesman) waiting for his university post. As the play begins, upon the couple's return from their honeymoon, we see almost immediately that the marriage is an unequal, and unsettled, one. Tesman is eager to start his new life and he is clearly proud of his beautiful wife. Hedda, by contrast, is dismissive of both his affectionate tone and his values. She snubs him, is impatient, abruptly changes the topic of conversation, and sulks. The class difference between the upper-middle-class Hedda and lower-middle-class Tesman is starkly drawn, as the collision between Hedda's and Tesman's respective classes, expectations, and attitudes occurs in and in fact centers on the bourgeois home. Like many of Ibsen's late plays, the home in *Hedda Gabler* bears and reveals the contradictions of bourgeois life. While Tesman thinks he has provided an ideal house, his wife from the bottom of her heart despises it and the life it offers. Gradually we learn that Hedda married Tesman and encouraged his purchase of the house only out of boredom and because she felt that her time and options were running out. But now she finds herself trapped in her marriage, and in the house.

Inger Munch, Sister of the Artist, by Edvard Munch (1892).

For that reason, Ibsen has Hedda focus her scorn on the house and its furnishings, as the play revolves around what they represent: class and taste. Hedda Gabler demands a new piano, because her old one does not "fit in" with the "other things" in this house and expects to have horses so that she can keep up the lifestyle to which she is accustomed. At the same time, she despises those objects associated with Tesman and his class—the déclassé hat of one of his aunts and his old and worn slippers, which his other aunt has hand embroidered. She admires the remnants of her former life, preserved in the towering portrait of the general and his set of pistols. Tesman's scholarly area is the handicrafts of the Middle Ages. What he does not see is that around him a battle is occurring over a different set of objects, which become the game pieces in a struggle of two classes and two wills.

Hedda Gabler, bored and without a function except to bear children—a thought she rejects with horror—manipulates everyone around her in order to exert control. Her coaxing Tesman to get a house he cannot afford is just the beginning. Hedda is equally calculating in her dealings with the other characters, from Tesman's aunt to Løvborg and his companion, Mrs. Elvsted, whom she knew as a schoolgirl. She gets them to do her bidding through force, lies, flattery, and utter ruthlessness. As the play progresses, we find her destroying careers and lives without blinking an eye; she lacks any moral compass beyond her own will. Although her actions at times seem to have some motive, they more often have no apparent goal. Hedda seems to value power as an end in itself.

The main victim of Hedda's plotting is Tesman's rival, Løvborg, who not only has published a well-received history of civilization but has just completed a book about the future. At an earlier moment in his career, Ibsen might have shown interest in the content of Løvborg's ideas, as he had done in examining the idealist drive for truth in *The Wild Duck,* for example, or in discussing marriage in *A Doll House*; here, the ideas are reduced to their container, Løvberg's manuscript, which becomes a central plot device—lost, found, and finally burned. Ibsen had learned from the well-made play how to weave objects and characters into suspenseful plots. But these props also convey something important about those who possess them: they are multifaceted devices that take on a life of their own.

Hedda may be a manipulator, but she is a manipulator with a vision. She is driven by her hunger for a more fulfilling, ideal, and beautiful life. She fantasizes about acts of heroism and beauty, which she tries to bring about by assigning roles to the people around her as if she were the director of a play. Hedda shares her desire for a better life with many tragic characters of Ibsen's later plays, characters who cannot rid themselves of the chains that bind them to their houses, their objects, their habits, their class, and their past. The architect Solness falls from the tower of his final house in the play *The Master Builder* and the sculptor Rubek, in *When We Dead Awaken,* climbs higher and higher into the dangerous mountains with his former love only to be killed by an avalanche. Ibsen's attitude toward his characters' desire for beauty is ambivalent. On the one hand, he sympathizes with them—even the cold-hearted Hedda Gabler. On the other hand, his plays show that the single-minded desire to achieve an ideal life wreaks destruction. Hedda Gabler's vision is an escape fantasy, the stuff of historical and idealist plays of the kind Ibsen had written in his youth. Ibsen perceived and understood both the desire for ideals and their destructive effects.

Ibsen is a dramatist of singular importance in part because he has consistently inspired the most important actors and directors. In England, Ibsen initially owed his influence to GEORGE BERNARD SHAW and William Archer, writers who led what some have called the Ibsen campaign. Shaw's defense of Ibsen against the scornful reception given his drama in the popular press and Archer's translations and productions of Ibsen's plays turned the Norwegian into the most important figure in British modern drama. Directors and playwrights elsewhere soon championed Ibsen as well. André Antoine, whose Théâtre Libre had pioneered a naturalist style of acting and design, played Oswald in *Ghosts* in 1890,

Elizabeth Robins as Hedda. Robins was the first actress to play Hedda in English, at the Vaudeville Theatre in London in 1891.

and the influential Russian director Konstantin Stanislavski, whose Moscow Art Theater promoted an acting style based on authentic emotional responses, played Doctor Stockman in *An Enemy of the People* in 1900. Ibsen's later plays, including *Hedda Gabler,* attracted a different set of directors, more interested in symbolism and poetry than in naturalism and truth. Aurélien Lugné-Poe, who had attacked realist drama and instead pioneered a symbolist theater full of ominous allusions and hieratic moods, staged *Rosmersholm* (1893) and *The Master Builder* (1894) in Paris, and directors interested in surrealism and suggestive stagecraft, such as Ingmar Bergman, have continued to be attracted first and foremost to Ibsen's late plays.

Ibsen is acknowledged as a founder of modern drama, but his place in theater history is full of enigmas and contradictions. He started his career with historical dramas that were typical nineteenth-century fare, yet became the herald of modern drama. Rather than simply rejecting the dramatic techniques of his time, he transformed them into a drama that seemed new, shocking, and modern to his audience. He received the most attention for his realist plays, but later turned realism in a more poetic and symbolist direction. In the end, Ibsen created a dramatic oeuvre of unparalleled variety and complexity. His plays could be many things to many people, viewed as stirring manifestos against social injustice or modern tragedies of striking poetic and dramatic force. This versatility, more than anything else, is responsible for Ibsen's having remained one of the most popular dramatists of all time. Today, he ranks second only after SHAKESPEARE as the world's most-performed playwright, a position that testifies to Ibsen's dramatic art: shocking and novel when it was first presented to audiences, it has stood the test of time.

M.P.

Hedda Gabler[1]

CHARACTERS

GEORGE TESMAN, research fellow in cultural history
HEDDA TESMAN, his wife
MISS JULIANA TESMAN, his aunt
MRS. ELVSTED
JUDGE BRACK
EILERT LØVBORG
BERTA, the TESMANS' maid

The action takes place in TESMAN's *residence in the fashionable part of town.*

Act 1

[*A large, attractively furnished drawing room, decorated in dark colors. In the rear wall, a wide doorway with curtains drawn back. The doorway opens into a smaller room in the same style as the drawing room. In the right wall of the front room, a folding door that leads to the hall. In the left wall opposite, a glass door, with curtains similarly drawn back. Through the panes one can see part of an overhanging veranda and trees in autumn colors. In the foreground is an oval table with tablecloth and chairs around it. By the right wall, a wide, dark porcelain stove, a high-backed armchair, a cushioned footstool, and two taborets. In the right-hand corner, a settee with a small round table in front. Nearer, on the left and slightly out from the wall, a piano. On either side of the doorway in back, étagères with terra-cotta and majolica ornaments. Against the back wall of the inner room, a sofa, a table, and a couple of chairs can be seen. Above this sofa hangs a portrait of a handsome, elderly man in a general's uniform. Over the table, a hanging lamp with an opalescent glass shade. A number of bouquets of flowers are placed about the drawing room in vases and glasses. Others lie on the tables. The floors in both rooms are covered with thick carpets. Morning light. The sun shines in through the glass door.*

MISS JULIANA TESMAN, *wearing a hat and carrying a parasol, comes in from the hall, followed by* BERTA, *who holds a bouquet wrapped in paper.* MISS TESMAN *is a lady around sixty-five with a kind and good-natured look, nicely but simply dressed in a gray tailored suit.* BERTA *is a maid somewhat past middle age, with a plain and rather provincial appearance.*]

MISS TESMAN [*stops close by the door, listens, and says softly*] Goodness, I don't think they're even up yet!

BERTA [*also softly*] That's just what I said, Miss Juliana. Remember how late the steamer got in last night. Yes, and afterward! My gracious, how much the young bride had to unpack before she could get to bed.

MISS TESMAN Well, then—let them enjoy a good rest. But they must have some of this fresh morning air when they do come down. [*She goes to the glass door and opens it wide.*]

1. Translated by Rolf Fjelde.

BERTA [*by the table, perplexed, with the bouquet in her hand*] I swear there isn't a bit of space left. I think I'll have to put it here, miss. [*Places the bouquet on the piano.*]

MISS TESMAN So now you have a new mistress, Berta dear. Lord knows it was misery for me to give you up.

BERTA [*on the verge of tears*] And for me, miss! What can I say? All those many blessed years I've been in your service, you and Miss Rina.

MISS TESMAN We must take it calmly, Berta. There's really nothing else to do. George needs you here in this house, you know that. You've looked after him since he was a little boy.

BERTA Yes, but miss, I'm all the time thinking of her, lying at home. Poor thing—completely helpless. And with that new maid! She'll never take proper care of an invalid, that one.

MISS TESMAN Oh, I'll manage to teach her. And most of it, you know, I'll do myself. So you mustn't be worrying over my poor sister.

BERTA Well, but there's something else too, miss. I'm really so afraid I won't please the young mistress.

MISS TESMAN Oh, well—there might be something or other at first—

BERTA Because she's so very particular.

MISS TESMAN Well, of course. General Gabler's daughter. What a life she had in the general's day! Remember seeing her out with her father—how she'd go galloping past in that long black riding outfit, with a feather in her hat?

BERTA Oh yes—I remember! But I never would have dreamed then that she and George Tesman would make a match of it.

MISS TESMAN Nor I either. But now, Berta—before I forget: from now on, you mustn't say George Tesman. You must call him Doctor Tesman.

BERTA Yes, the young mistress said the same thing—last night, right after they came in the door. Is that true then, miss?

MISS TESMAN Yes, absolutely. Think of it, Berta—they gave him his doctor's degree. Abroad, that is—on this trip, you know. I hadn't heard one word about it, till he told me down on the pier.

BERTA Well, he's clever enough to be anything. But I never thought he'd go in for curing people.

MISS TESMAN No, he wasn't made that kind of doctor. [*Nods significantly.*] But as a matter of fact, you may soon now have something still greater to call him.

BERTA Oh, really! What's that, miss?

MISS TESMAN [*smiling*] Hm, wouldn't you like to know! [*Moved*] Ah, dear God—if only my poor brother could look up from his grave and see what his little boy has become! [*Glancing about*] But what's this, Berta? Why, you've taken all the slipcovers off the furniture—?

BERTA Madam told me to. She doesn't like covers on chairs, she said.

MISS TESMAN Are they going to make this their regular living room, then?

BERTA It seems so—with her. For his part—the doctor—he said nothing.

[GEORGE TESMAN *enters the inner room from the right, singing to himself and carrying an empty, unstrapped suitcase. He is a youngish-looking man of thirty-three, medium sized, with an open, round, cheerful face, blond hair and beard. He wears glasses and is somewhat carelessly dressed in comfortable lounging clothes.*]

MISS TESMAN Good morning, good morning, George!

TESMAN [*in the doorway*] Aunt Julie! Dear Aunt Julie! [*Goes over and warmly shakes her hand.*] Way out here—so early in the day—uh?

MISS TESMAN Yes, you know I simply had to look in on you a moment.

TESMAN And that without a decent night's sleep.

MISS TESMAN Oh, that's nothing at all to me.

TESMAN Well, then you did get home all right from the pier? Uh?

MISS TESMAN Why, of course I did—thank goodness. Judge Brack was good enough to see me right to my door.

TESMAN We were sorry we couldn't drive you up. But you saw for yourself—Hedda had all those boxes to bring along.

MISS TESMAN Yes, that was quite something, the number of boxes she had.

BERTA [*to* TESMAN] Should I go in and ask Mrs. Tesman if there's anything I can help her with?

TESMAN No, thanks, Berta—don't bother. She said she'd ring if she needed anything.

BERTA [*going off toward the right*] All right.

TESMAN But wait now—you can take this suitcase with you.

BERTA [*taking it*] I'll put it away in the attic. [*She goes out by the hall door.*]

TESMAN Just think, Aunt Julie—I had that whole suitcase stuffed full of notes. You just can't imagine all I've managed to find, rummaging through archives. Marvelous old documents that nobody knew existed—

MISS TESMAN Yes, you've really not wasted any time on your wedding trip, George.

TESMAN I certainly haven't. But do take your hat off, Auntie. Here—let me help you—uh?

MISS TESMAN [*as he does so*] Goodness—this is exactly as if you were still back at home with us.

TESMAN [*turning the hat in his hand and studying it from all sides*] My—what elegant hats you go in for!

MISS TESMAN I bought that for Hedda's sake.

TESMAN For Hedda's sake? Uh?

MISS TESMAN Yes, so Hedda wouldn't feel ashamed of me if we walked down the street together.

TESMAN [*patting her cheek*] You think of everything, Aunt Julie! [*Laying the hat on a chair by the table*] Sh—look, suppose we sit down on the sofa and have a little chat till Hedda comes. [*They settle themselves. She puts her parasol on the corner of the sofa.*]

MISS TESMAN [*takes both of his hands and gazes at him*] How wonderful it is having you here, right before my eyes again, George! You—dear Jochum's own boy!

TESMAN And for me too, to see you again, Aunt Julie! You, who've been father and mother to me both.

MISS TESMAN Yes, I'm sure you'll always keep a place in your heart for your old aunts.

TESMAN But Auntie Rina—hm? Isn't she any better?

MISS TESMAN Oh no—we can hardly expect that she'll ever be better, poor thing. She lies there, just as she has all these years. May God let me keep her a little while longer! Because otherwise, George, I don't know what I'd do with my life. The more so now, when I don't have you to look after.

TESMAN [*patting her on the back*] There, there, there—

MISS TESMAN [*suddenly changing her tone*] No, but to think of it, that now you're a married man! And that it was *you* who carried off Hedda Gabler. The beautiful Hedda Gabler! Imagine! She, who always had so many admirers!

TESMAN [*hums a little and smiles complacently*] Yes, I rather suspect I have several friends who'd like to trade places with me.

MISS TESMAN And then to have such a wedding trip! Five—almost six months—

TESMAN Well, remember, I used it for research, too. All those libraries I had to check—and so many books to read!

MISS TESMAN Yes, no doubt. [*More confidentially; lowering her voice*] But now listen, George—isn't there something—something special you have to tell me?

TESMAN From the trip?

MISS TESMAN Yes.

TESMAN No, I can't think of anything beyond what I wrote in my letters. I got my doctor's degree down there—but I told you that yesterday.

MISS TESMAN Yes, of course. But I mean—whether you have any kind of—expectations—?

TESMAN Expectations?

MISS TESMAN My goodness, George—I'm your old aunt!

TESMAN Why, naturally I have expectations.

MISS TESMAN Ah!

TESMAN I have every expectation in the world of becoming a professor shortly.

MISS TESMAN Oh, a professor, yes—

TESMAN Or I might as well say, I'm sure of it. But, Aunt Julie—you know that perfectly well yourself.

MISS TESMAN [*with a little laugh*] That's right, so I do. [*Changing the subject*] But we were talking about your trip. It must have cost a terrible amount of money.

TESMAN Well, that big fellowship, you know—it took us a good part of the way.

MISS TESMAN But I don't see how you could stretch it enough for two.

TESMAN No, that's not so easy to see—uh?

MISS TESMAN And especially traveling with a lady. For I hear tell that's much more expensive.

TESMAN Yes, of course—it's a bit more expensive. But Hedda just had to have that trip. She *had* to. There was nothing else to be done.

MISS TESMAN No, no, I guess not. A honeymoon abroad seems to be the thing nowadays. But tell me—have you had a good look around your house?

TESMAN You can bet I have! I've been up since daybreak.

MISS TESMAN And how does it strike you, all in all?

TESMAN First-rate! Absolutely first-rate! Only, I don't know what we'll do with the two empty rooms between the back parlor and Hedda's bedroom.

MISS TESMAN [*laughing again*] Oh, my dear George, I think you can use them—as time goes on.

TESMAN Yes, you're quite right about that, Aunt Julie! In time, as I build up my library—uh?

MISS TESMAN Of course, my dear boy. It was your library I meant.

TESMAN I'm happiest now for Hedda's sake. Before we were engaged, she used to say so many times there was no place she'd rather live than here, in Secretary Falk's town house.

MISS TESMAN Yes, and then to have it come on the market just after you'd sailed.

TESMAN We really have had luck, haven't we?

MISS TESMAN But expensive, George dear! You'll find it expensive, all this here.

TESMAN [*looks at her, somewhat crestfallen*] Yes, I suppose I will.

MISS TESMAN Oh, Lord, yes!

TESMAN How much do you think? Approximately? Hm?

MISS TESMAN It's impossible to say till the bills are all in.

TESMAN Well, fortunately Judge Brack has gotten me quite easy terms. That's what he wrote Hedda.

MISS TESMAN Don't worry yourself about that, dear. I've also put up security to cover the carpets and furniture.

TESMAN Security? Aunt Julie, dear—you? What kind of security could *you* give?

MISS TESMAN I took out a mortgage on our pension.

TESMAN [*jumping up*] What! On your—and Auntie Rina's pension!

MISS TESMAN I saw nothing else to do.

TESMAN [*standing in front of her*] But you're out of your mind, Aunt Julie! That pension—it's all Aunt Rina and you have to live on.

MISS TESMAN Now, now—don't make so much of it. It's only a formality; Judge Brack said so. He was good enough to arrange the whole thing for me. Just a formality, he said.

TESMAN That's all well enough. But still—

MISS TESMAN You'll be drawing your own salary now. And, good gracious, if we have to lay out a bit, just now at the start—why, it's no more than a pleasure for us.

TESMAN Oh, Aunt Julie—you never get tired of making sacrifices for me!

MISS TESMAN [*rises and places her hands on his shoulders*] What other joy do I have in this world than smoothing the path for you, my dear boy? You, without father or mother to turn to. And now we've come to the goal, George! Things may have looked black at times; but now, thank heaven, you've made it.

TESMAN Yes, it's remarkable, really, how everything's turned out for the best.

MISS TESMAN Yes—and those who stood against you—who wanted to bar your way—they've gone down. They've fallen, George. The one most dangerous to you—he fell farthest. And he's lying there now, in the bed he made—poor, misguided creature.

TESMAN Have you heard any news of Eilert? I mean, since I went away.

MISS TESMAN Only that he's supposed to have brought out a new book.

TESMAN What's that? Eilert Løvborg? Just recently, uh?

MISS TESMAN So they say. But considering everything, it can hardly amount to much. Ah, but when *your* new book comes out—it'll be a different story, George! What will it be about?

TESMAN It's going to treat the domestic handicrafts of Brabant[2] in the Middle Ages.

MISS TESMAN Just imagine—that you can write about things like that!

TESMAN Actually, the book may take quite a while yet. I have this tremendous collection of material to put in order, you know.

MISS TESMAN Yes, collecting and ordering—you do that so well. You're not my brother's son for nothing.

TESMAN I look forward so much to getting started. Especially now, with a comfortable home of my own to work in.

MISS TESMAN And most of all, dear, now that you've won her, the wife of your heart.

TESMAN [*embracing her*] Yes, yes, Aunt Julie! Hedda—that's the most beautiful part of it all! [*Glancing toward the doorway*] But I think she's coming—uh?

[HEDDA *enters from the left through the inner room. She is a woman of twenty-nine. Her face and figure show breeding and distinction; her complexion is pallid and opaque. Her steel gray eyes express a cool, unruffled calm. Her hair is an attractive medium brown, but not particularly abundant. She wears a tasteful, rather loose-fitting gown.*]

MISS TESMAN [*going to meet* HEDDA] Good morning, Hedda dear—how good to see you!

HEDDA [*holding out her hand*] Good morning, my dear Miss Tesman! Calling so early? This *is* kind of you.

MISS TESMAN [*slightly embarrassed*] Well—did the bride sleep well in her new home?

HEDDA Oh yes, thanks. Quite adequately.

TESMAN Adequately! Oh, I like that, Hedda! You were sleeping like a stone when I got up.

HEDDA Fortunately. But of course one has to grow accustomed to anything new, Miss Tesman—little by little. [*Looking toward the left*] Oh! That maid has left the door open—and the sunlight's just flooding in.

MISS TESMAN [*going toward the door*] Well, we can close it.

HEDDA No, no—don't! [*To* TESMAN] There, dear, draw the curtains. It gives a softer light.

TESMAN [*by the glass door*] All right—all right. Look, Hedda—now you have shade and fresh air both.

HEDDA Yes, we really need some fresh air here, with all these piles of flowers— But—won't you sit down, Miss Tesman?

MISS TESMAN Oh no, thank you. Now that I know that everything's fine—thank goodness—I will have to run along home. My sister's lying there waiting, poor thing.

TESMAN Give her my very, very best, won't you? And say I'll be looking in on her later today.

MISS TESMAN Oh, you can be sure I will. But what do you know, George—[*Searching in her bag*]—I nearly forgot. I have something here for you.

TESMAN What's that, Aunt Julie? Hm?

MISS TESMAN [*brings out a flat package wrapped in newspaper and hands it to him*] There, dear. Look.

2. A province of central Belgium.

TESMAN [*opening it*] Oh, my—you kept them for me, Aunt Julie! Hedda! That's really touching! Uh!

HEDDA [*by the étagère on the right*] Yes, dear, what is it?

TESMAN My old bedroom slippers! My slippers!

HEDDA Oh yes. I remember how often you spoke of them during the trip.

TESMAN Yes, I missed them terribly. [*Going over to her*] Now you can see them, Hedda!

HEDDA [*moves toward the stove*] Thanks, but I really don't care to.

TESMAN [*following her*] Imagine—Auntie Rina lay and embroidered them, sick as she was. Oh, you couldn't believe how many memories are bound up in them.

HEDDA [*at the table*] But not for me.

MISS TESMAN I think Hedda is right, George.

TESMAN Yes, but I only thought, now that she's part of the family—

HEDDA [*interrupting*] We're never going to manage with this maid, Tesman.

MISS TESMAN Not manage with Berta?

TESMAN But dear—why do you say that? Uh?

HEDDA [*pointing*] See there! She's left her old hat lying out on a chair.

TESMAN [*shocked; dropping the slippers*] But Hedda—!

HEDDA Suppose someone came in and saw it.

TESMAN Hedda—that's Aunt Julie's hat!

HEDDA Really?

MISS TESMAN [*picking it up*] That's right, it's mine. And what's more, it certainly is not old—Mrs. Tesman.

HEDDA I really hadn't looked closely at it, Miss Tesman.

MISS TESMAN [*putting on the hat*] It's actually the first time I've had it on. The very first time.

TESMAN And it's lovely, too. Most attractive!

MISS TESMAN Oh, it's hardly all that, George. [*Looks about.*] My parasol—? Ah, here. [*Takes it.*] For that's mine too. [*Murmurs.*] Not Berta's.

TESMAN New hat and new parasol! Just imagine, Hedda!

HEDDA Quite charming, really.

TESMAN Yes, aren't they, uh? But Auntie, take a good look at Hedda before you leave. See how charming *she* is!

MISS TESMAN But George dear, there's nothing new in that. Hedda's been lovely all her life. [*She nods and starts out, right.*]

TESMAN [*following her*] But have you noticed how plump and buxom she's grown? How much she's filled out on the trip?

HEDDA [*crossing the room*] Oh, do be quiet—!

MISS TESMAN [*who has stopped and turned*] Filled out?

TESMAN Of course, you can't see it so well when she has that dressing gown on. But I, who have the opportunity to—

HEDDA [*by the glass door, impatiently*] Oh, you have no opportunity for anything!

TESMAN It must have been the mountain air, down in the Tyrol[3]—

HEDDA [*brusquely interrupting*] I'm exactly as I was when I left.

TESMAN Yes, that's your claim. But you certainly are not. Auntie, don't you agree?

3. A region of the eastern Alps, mainly in western Austria but partly in northern Italy.

MISS TESMAN [*gazing at her with folded hands*] Hedda is lovely—lovely—lovely. [*Goes up to her, takes her head in both hands, bends it down and kisses her hair.*] God bless and keep Hedda Tesman—for George's sake.

HEDDA [*gently freeing herself*] Oh—! Let me go.

MISS TESMAN [*with quiet feeling*] I won't let a day go by without looking in on you two.

TESMAN Yes, please do that, Aunt Julie! Uh?

MISS TESMAN Good-bye—good-bye!

[*She goes out by the hall door.* TESMAN *accompanies her, leaving the door half open. He can be heard reiterating his greetings to Aunt Rina and his thanks for the slippers. At the same time,* HEDDA *moves about the room, raising her arms and clenching her fists as if in a frenzy. Then she flings back the curtains from the glass door and stands there, looking out. A moment later* TESMAN *comes back, closing the door after him.*]

TESMAN [*retrieving the slippers from the floor*] What are you standing and looking at, Hedda?

HEDDA [*again calm and controlled*] I'm just looking at the leaves—they're so yellow—and so withered.

TESMAN [*wraps up the slippers and puts them on the table*] Yes, well, we're into September now.

HEDDA [*once more restless*] Yes, to think—that already we're in—in September.

TESMAN Didn't Aunt Julie seem a bit strange? A little—almost formal? What do you suppose was bothering her? Hm?

HEDDA I hardly know her at all. Isn't that how she usually is?

TESMAN No, not like this, today.

HEDDA [*leaving the glass door*] Do you think this thing with the hat upset her?

TESMAN Oh, not very much. A little, just at the moment, perhaps—

HEDDA But really, what kind of manners has she—to go throwing her hat about in a drawing room! It's just not proper.

TESMAN Well, you can be sure Aunt Julie won't do it again.

HEDDA Anyhow, I'll manage to smooth it over with her.

TESMAN Yes, Hedda dear, I wish you would!

HEDDA When you go in to see them later on, you might ask her out for the evening.

TESMAN Yes, I'll do that. And there's something else you could do that would make her terribly happy.

HEDDA Oh?

TESMAN If only you could bring yourself to speak to her warmly, by her first name. For my sake, Hedda? Uh?

HEDDA No, no—don't ask me to do that. I told you this once before. I'll try to call her "Aunt."[4] That should be enough.

TESMAN Oh, all right. I was only thinking, now that you belong to the family—

HEDDA Hm—I really don't know— [*She crosses the room to the doorway.*]

4. In the original Norwegian text, Tesman has just asked his wife to address his aunt with the familiar *du* (thou), used only by intimate friends and family, rather than with the formal *De* (you). Hedda refuses, but suggests the compromise of calling her "Aunt."

TESMAN [*after a pause*] Is something the matter, Hedda? Uh?

HEDDA I'm just looking at my old piano. It doesn't really fit in with all these other things.

TESMAN With the first salary I draw, we can see about trading it in on a new one.

HEDDA No, not traded in. I don't want to part with it. We can put it there, in the inner room, and get another here in its place. When there's a chance, I mean.

TESMAN [*slightly cast down*] Yes, we could do that, of course.

HEDDA [*picks up the bouquet from the piano*] These flowers weren't here when we got in last night.

TESMAN Aunt Julie must have brought them for you.

HEDDA [*examining the bouquet*] A visiting card. [*Takes it out and reads it.*] "Will stop back later today." Can you guess who this is from?

TESMAN No. Who? Hm?

HEDDA It says "Mrs. Elvsted."

TESMAN No, really? Sheriff Elvsted's wife. Miss Rysing, she used to be.

HEDDA Exactly. The one with the irritating hair that she was always showing off. An old flame of yours, I've heard.

TESMAN [*laughing*] Oh, that wasn't for long. And it was before I knew you, Hedda. But imagine—that she's here in town.

HEDDA It's odd that she calls on us. I've hardly seen her since we were in school.

TESMAN Yes, I haven't seen her either—since God knows when. I wonder how she can stand living in such an out-of-the-way place. Hm?

HEDDA [*thinks a moment, then bursts out*] But wait—isn't it somewhere up in those parts that he—that Eilert Løvborg lives?

TESMAN Yes, it's someplace right around there.

[BERTA *enters by the hall door.*]

BERTA She's back again, ma'am—that lady who stopped by and left the flowers an hour ago. [*Pointing*] The ones you have in your hand, ma'am.

HEDDA Oh, is she? Good. Would you ask her to come in.

[BERTA *opens the door for* MRS. ELVSTED *and goes out.* MRS. ELVSTED *is a slender woman with soft, pretty features. Her eyes are light blue, large, round, and somewhat prominent, with a startled, questioning look. Her hair is remarkably light, almost a white-gold, and unusually abundant and wavy. She is a couple of years younger than* HEDDA. *She wears a dark visiting dress, tasteful, but not quite in the latest fashion.*]

HEDDA [*going to greet her warmly*] Good morning, my dear Mrs. Elvsted. How delightful to see you again!

MRS. ELVSTED [*nervously; struggling to control herself*] Yes, it's a very long time since we last met.

TESMAN [*gives her his hand*] Or since *we* met, uh?

HEDDA Thank you for your beautiful flowers—

MRS. ELVSTED Oh, that's nothing—I would have come straight out here yesterday afternoon, but then I heard you weren't at home—

TESMAN Have you just now come to town? Uh?

MRS. ELVSTED I got in yesterday toward noon. Oh, I was in desperation when I heard that you weren't at home.

HEDDA Desperation! Why?

TESMAN But my dear Mrs. Rysing—Mrs. Elvsted, I mean—

HEDDA You're not in some kind of trouble?

MRS. ELVSTED Yes, I am. And I don't know another living soul down here I can turn to.

HEDDA [*putting the bouquet down on the table*] Come, then—let's sit here on the sofa—

MRS. ELVSTED Oh, I can't sit down. I'm really too much on edge!

HEDDA Why, of course you can. Come here.

[*She draws* MRS. ELVSTED *down on the sofa and sits beside her.*]

TESMAN Well? What is it, Mrs. Elvsted?

HEDDA Has anything particular happened at home?

MRS. ELVSTED Yes, that's both it—and not it. Oh, I do want so much that you don't misunderstand me—

HEDDA But then the best thing, Mrs. Elvsted, is simply to speak your mind.

TESMAN Because I suppose that's why you've come. Hm?

MRS. ELVSTED Oh yes, that's why. Well, then, I have to tell you—if you don't already know—that Eilert Løvborg's also in town.

HEDDA Løvborg—!

TESMAN What! Is Eilert Løvborg back! Just think, Hedda!

HEDDA Good Lord, I can hear.

MRS. ELVSTED He's been back all of a week's time now. A whole week—in this dangerous town! Alone! With all the bad company that's around.

HEDDA But my dear Mrs. Elvsted, what does *he* have to do with you?

MRS. ELVSTED [*glances anxiously at her and says quickly*] He was the children's tutor.

HEDDA Your children's?

MRS. ELVSTED My husband's. I have none.

HEDDA Your stepchildren's, then.

MRS. ELVSTED Yes.

TESMAN [*somewhat hesitantly*] But was he—I don't know quite how to put it—was he sufficiently—responsible in his habits for such a job? Uh?

MRS. ELVSTED In these last two years, there wasn't a word to be said against him.

TESMAN Not a word? Just think of that, Hedda!

HEDDA I heard it.

MRS. ELVSTED Not even a murmur, I can assure you! Nothing. But anyway—now that I know he's here—in this big city—and with so much money in his hands—then I'm just frightened to death for him.

TESMAN But why didn't he stay up there where he was? With you and your husband? Uh?

MRS. ELVSTED After the book came out, he just couldn't rest content with us.

TESMAN Yes, that's right—Aunt Julie was saying he'd published a new book.

MRS. ELVSTED Yes, a great new book, on the course of civilization—in all its stages. It's been out two weeks. And now it's been bought and read so much—and it's made a tremendous stir—

TESMAN Has it really? It must be something he's had lying around from his better days.

MRS. ELVSTED Years back, you mean?

TESMAN I suppose.

MRS. ELVSTED No, he's written it all up there with us. Now—in this last year.

TESMAN That's marvelous to hear. Hedda! Just imagine!

MRS ELVSTED Yes, if only it can go on like this!

HEDDA Have you seen him here in town?

MRS. ELVSTED No, not yet. I had such trouble finding out his address. But this morning I got it at last.

HEDDA [*looks searchingly at her*] I must say it seems rather odd of your husband—

MRS. ELVSTED [*with a nervous start*] Of my husband—! What?

HEDDA To send you to town on this sort of errand. Not to come and look after his friend himself.

MRS. ELVSTED No, no, my husband hasn't the time for that. And then I had—some shopping to do.

HEDDA [*with a slight smile*] Oh, that's different.

MRS. ELVSTED [*getting up quickly and uneasily*] I beg you, please, Mr. Tesman—be good to Eilert Løvborg if he comes to you. And he will, I'm sure. You know—you were such good friends in the old days. And you're both doing the same kind of work. The same type of research—from what I can gather.

TESMAN We were once, at any rate.

MRS. ELVSTED Yes, and that's why I'm asking you, please—you too—to keep an eye on him. Oh, you will do that, Mr. Tesman—promise me that?

TESMAN I'll be only too glad to, Mrs. Rysing—

HEDDA Elvsted.

TESMAN I'll certainly do everything in my power for Eilert. You can depend on that.

MRS. ELVSTED Oh, how terribly kind of you! [*Pressing his hands*] Many, many thanks! [*Frightened*] He means so much to my husband, you know.

HEDDA [*rising*] You ought to write him, dear. He might not come by on his own.

TESMAN Yes, that probably would be the best, Hedda? Hm?

HEDDA And the sooner the better. Right now, I'd say.

MRS. ELVSTED [*imploringly*] Oh yes, if you could!

TESMAN I'll write him this very moment. Have you got his address, Mrs.—Mrs. Elvsted?

MRS. ELVSTED Yes. [*Takes a slip of paper from her pocket and hands it to him.*] Here it is.

TESMAN Good, good. Then I'll go in— [*Looking about*] But wait—my slippers? Ah! Here. [*Takes the package and starts to leave.*]

HEDDA Write him a really warm, friendly letter. Nice and long, too.

TESMAN Don't worry, I will.

MRS. ELVSTED But please, not a word that I asked you to!

TESMAN No, that goes without saying. Uh? [*Leaves by the inner room, to the right.*]

HEDDA [*goes over to* MRS. ELVSTED, *smiles, and speaks softly*] How's that! Now we've killed two birds with one stone.

MRS. ELVSTED What do you mean?

HEDDA Didn't you see that I wanted him out of the room?

MRS. ELVSTED Yes, to write the letter—

HEDDA But also to talk with you alone.

MRS. ELVSTED [*confused*] About this same thing?

HEDDA Precisely.

MRS. ELVSTED [*upset*] But Mrs. Tesman, there's nothing more to say! Nothing!

HEDDA Oh yes, but there is. There's a great deal more—I can see that. Come, sit here—and let's speak openly now, the two of us. [*She forces* MRS. ELVSTED *down into the armchair by the stove and sits on one of the taborets.*]

MRS. ELVSTED [*anxiously glancing at her watch*] But Mrs. Tesman, dear—I was just planning to leave.

HEDDA Oh, you can't be in such a rush— Now! Tell me a little about how things are going at home.

MRS. ELVSTED Oh, that's the last thing I'd ever want to discuss.

HEDDA But with me, dear—? After all, we were in school together.

MRS. ELVSTED Yes, but you were a class ahead of me. Oh, I was terribly afraid of you then!

HEDDA Afraid of me?

MRS. ELVSTED Yes, terribly. Because whenever we met on the stairs, you'd always pull my hair.

HEDDA Did I really?

MRS. ELVSTED Yes, and once you said you would burn it off.

HEDDA Oh, that was just foolish talk, you know.

MRS. ELVSTED Yes, but I was so stupid then. And, anyway, since then—we've drifted so far—far apart from each other. We've moved in such different circles.

HEDDA Well, let's try now to come closer again. Listen, at school we were quite good friends, and we called each other by our first names[5]—

MRS. ELVSTED No, I'm sure you're mistaken.

HEDDA Oh, I couldn't be! I remember it clearly. And that's why we have to be perfectly open, just as we were. [*Moves the stool nearer* MRS. ELVSTED.] There now! [*Kissing her cheek*] You have to call me Hedda.

MRS. ELVSTED [*pressing and patting her hands*] Oh, you're so good and kind—! It's not at all what I'm used to.

HEDDA There, there! And I'm going to call you my own dear Thora.

MRS. ELVSTED My name is Thea.

HEDDA Oh yes, of course. I meant Thea. [*Looks at her compassionately.*] So you're not much used to goodness or kindness, Thea? In your own home?

MRS. ELVSTED If only I had a home! But I don't. I never have.

HEDDA [*glances quickly at her*] I thought it had to be something like that.

MRS. ELVSTED [*gazing helplessly into space*] Yes—yes—yes.

HEDDA I can't quite remember now—but wasn't it as a housekeeper that you first came up to the Elvsteds?

MRS. ELVSTED Actually as a governess. But his wife—his first wife—she was an invalid and mostly kept to her bed. So I had to take care of the house too.

HEDDA But finally you became mistress of the house yourself.

MRS. ELVSTED [*heavily*] Yes, I did.

HEDDA Let me see—about how long ago was that?

MRS. ELVSTED That I was married?

5. In the original Norwegian text, Hedda claims that they used to address each other with the familiar *du*. Not used to this level of intimacy, Mrs. Elvsted will slip back into the formal *De* before adopting *du*.

HEDDA Yes.

MRS. ELVSTED It's five years now.

HEDDA That's right. It must be.

MRS. ELVSTED Oh, these five years—! Or the last two or three, anyway. Oh, if you only knew, Mrs. Tesman—

HEDDA [*gives her hand a little slap*] Mrs. Tesman! Now, Thea!

MRS. ELVSTED I'm sorry; I'll try— Yes, if you could only understand— Hedda—

HEDDA [*casually*] Eilert Løvborg has lived up there about three years too, hasn't he?

MRS. ELVSTED [*looks at her doubtfully*] Eilert Løvborg? Yes—he has.

HEDDA Had you already known him here in town?

MRS. ELVSTED Hardly at all. Well, I mean—by name, of course.

HEDDA But up there—I suppose he'd visit you both?

MRS. ELVSTED Yes, he came to see us every day. He was tutoring the children, you know. Because, in the long run, I couldn't do it all myself.

HEDDA No, that's obvious. And your husband—? I suppose he often has to be away?

MRS. ELVSTED Yes, you can imagine, as sheriff, how much traveling he does around in the district.

HEDDA [*leaning against the chair arm*] Thea—my poor, sweet Thea—now you must tell me everything—just as it is.

MRS. ELVSTED Well, then you have to ask the questions.

HEDDA What sort of man is your husband, Thea? I mean—you know—to be with. Is he good to you?

MRS. ELVSTED [*evasively*] He believes he does everything for the best.

HEDDA I only think he must be much too old for you. More than twenty years older, isn't he?

MRS. ELVSTED [*irritated*] That's true. Along with everything else. I just can't stand him! We haven't a single thought in common. Nothing at all—he and I.

HEDDA But doesn't he care for you all the same—in his own way?

MRS. ELVSTED Oh, I don't know what he feels. I'm no more than useful to him. And then it doesn't cost much to keep me. I'm inexpensive.

HEDDA That's stupid of you.

MRS. ELVSTED [*shaking her head*] It can't be otherwise. Not with him. He really doesn't care for anyone but himself—and maybe a little for the children.

HEDDA And for Eilert Løvborg, Thea.

MRS. ELVSTED [*looking at her*] Eilert Løvborg! Why do you think so?

HEDDA But my dear—it seems to me, when he sends you all the way into town to look after him— [*Smiles almost imperceptibly.*] Besides, it's what you told my husband.

MRS. ELVSTED [*with a little nervous shudder*] Really? Yes, I suppose I did. [*In a quiet outburst*] No—I might as well tell you here and now! It's bound to come out in time.

HEDDA But my dear Thea—?

MRS. ELVSTED All right, then! My husband never knew I was coming here.

HEDDA What! Your husband never knew—

MRS. ELVSTED Of course not. Anyway, he wasn't at home. Off traveling somewhere. Oh, I couldn't bear it any longer, Hedda. It was impossible! I would have been so alone up there now.

HEDDA Well? What then?

MRS. ELVSTED So I packed a few of my things together—the barest necessities—without saying a word. And I slipped away from the house.

HEDDA Right then and there?

MRS. ELVSTED Yes, and took the train straight into town.

HEDDA But my dearest girl—that you could dare to do such a thing!

MRS. ELVSTED [*rising and walking about the room*] What else could I possibly do!

HEDDA But what do you think your husband will say when you go back home?

MRS. ELVSTED [*by the table, looking at her*] Back to *him?*

HEDDA Yes, of course.

MRS. ELVSTED I'll never go back to him.

HEDDA [*rising and approaching her*] You mean you've left, in dead earnest, for good?

MRS. ELVSTED Yes. There didn't seem anything else to do.

HEDDA But—to go away so openly.

MRS. ELVSTED Oh, you can't keep a thing like that secret.

HEDDA But what do you think people will say about you, Thea?

MRS. ELVSTED God knows they'll say what they please. [*Sitting wearily and sadly on the sofa*] I only did what I had to do.

HEDDA [*after a short silence*] What do you plan on now? What kind of work?

MRS. ELVSTED I don't know yet. I only know I have to live here, where Eilert Løvborg is—if I'm going to live at all.

HEDDA [*moves a chair over from the table, sits beside her, and strokes her hands*] Thea dear—how did this—this friendship—between you and Eilert Løvborg come about?

MRS. ELVSTED Oh, it happened little by little. I got some kind of power, almost, over him.

HEDDA Really?

MRS. ELVSTED He gave up his old habits. Not because I'd asked him to. I never dared do that. But he could tell they upset me, and so he dropped them.

HEDDA [*hiding an involuntary, scornful smile*] My dear little Thea—just as they say—you rehabilitated him.

MRS. ELVSTED Well, he says so, at any rate. And he—on his part—he's made a real human being out of me. Taught me to think—and understand so many things.

HEDDA You mean he tutored you also?

MRS. ELVSTED No, not exactly. But he'd talk to me—talk endlessly on about one thing after another. And then came the wonderful, happy time when I could share in his work! When I could help him!

HEDDA Could you really?

MRS. ELVSTED Yes! Whenever he wrote anything, we'd always work on it together.

HEDDA Like two true companions.

MRS. ELVSTED [*eagerly*] Companions! You know, Hedda—that's what he said too! Oh, I ought to feel so happy—but I can't. I just don't know if it's going to last.

HEDDA You're no more sure of him than that?

MRS. ELVSTED [*despondently*] There's a woman's shadow between Eilert Løvborg and me.

HEDDA [*looks at her intently*] Who could that be?

MRS. ELVSTED I don't know. Someone out of his—his past. Someone he's really never forgotten.

HEDDA What has he said—about this!

MRS. ELVSTED It's only once—and just vaguely—that he touched on it.

HEDDA Well! And what did he say!

MRS. ELVSTED He said that when they broke off she was going to shoot him with a pistol.

HEDDA [*with cold constraint*] That's nonsense! Nobody behaves that way around here.

MRS. ELVSTED No. And that's why I think it must have been that redheaded singer that at one time he—

HEDDA Yes, quite likely.

MRS. ELVSTED I remember they used to say about her that she carried loaded weapons.

HEDDA Ah—then of course it must have been her.

MRS. ELVSTED [*wringing her hands*] But you know what, Hedda—I've heard that this singer—that she's in town again! Oh, it has me out of my mind—

HEDDA [*glancing toward the inner room*] Shh! Tesman's coming. [*Gets up and whispers.*] Thea—keep all this just between us.

MRS. ELVSTED [*jumping up*] Oh yes! In heaven's name—!

[GEORGE TESMAN, *with a letter in his hand, enters from the right through the inner room.*]

TESMAN There, now—the letter's signed and sealed.

HEDDA That's fine. I think Mrs. Elvsted was just leaving. Wait a minute. I'll go with you to the garden gate.

TESMAN Hedda, dear—could Berta maybe look after this?

HEDDA [*taking the letter*] I'll tell her to.

[BERTA *enters from the hall.*]

BERTA Judge Brack is here and says he'd like to greet you and the Doctor, ma'am.

HEDDA Yes, ask Judge Brack to come in. And, here—put this letter in the mail.

BERTA [*takes the letter*] Yes, ma'am.

[*She opens the door for* JUDGE BRACK *and goes out.* BRACK *is a man of forty-five, thickset, yet well-built, with supple movements. His face is roundish, with a distinguished profile. His hair is short, still mostly black, and carefully groomed. His eyes are bright and lively. Thick eyebrows; a mustache to match, with neatly clipped ends. He wears a trimly tailored walking suit, a bit too youthful for his age. Uses a monocle, which he now and then lets fall.*]

JUDGE BRACK [*hat in hand, bowing*] May one dare to call so early?

HEDDA Of course one may.

TESMAN [*shakes his hand*] You're always welcome here. [*Introducing him*] Judge Brack—Miss Rysing—

HEDDA Ah—!

BRACK [*bowing*] I'm delighted.

HEDDA [*looks at him and laughs*] It's really a treat to see you by daylight, Judge!

BRACK You find me—changed?

HEDDA Yes. A bit younger, I think.

BRACK Thank you, most kindly.

TESMAN But what do you say for Hedda, uh? Doesn't she look flourishing? She's actually—

HEDDA Oh, leave me out of it! You might thank Judge Brack for all the trouble he's gone to—

BRACK Nonsense—it was a pleasure—

HEDDA Yes, you're a true friend. But here's Thea, standing here, aching to get away. Excuse me, Judge; I'll be right back.

[*Mutual good-byes.* MRS. ELVSTED *and* HEDDA *go out by the hall door.*]

BRACK So—is your wife fairly well satisfied, then—?

TESMAN Yes, we can't thank you enough. Of course—I gather there's some rearrangement called for here and there. And one or two things are lacking. We still have to buy a few minor items.

BRACK Really?

TESMAN But that's nothing for you to worry about. Hedda said she'd pick up those things herself. Why don't we sit down, hm?

BRACK Thanks. Just for a moment. [*Sits by the table.*] There's something I'd like to discuss with you, Tesman.

TESMAN What? Oh, I understand! [*Sitting*] It's the serious part of the banquet we're coming to, uh?

BRACK Oh, as far as money matters go, there's no great rush—though I must say I wish we'd managed things a bit more economically.

TESMAN But that was completely impossible! Think about Hedda, Judge! You, who know her so well—I simply couldn't have her live like a grocer's wife.

BRACK No, no—that's the trouble, exactly.

TESMAN And then—fortunately—it can't be long before I get my appointment.

BRACK Well, you know—these things can often hang fire.

TESMAN Have you heard something further? Hm?

BRACK Nothing really definite— [*Changing the subject*] But incidentally—I do have one piece of news for you.

TESMAN Well?

BRACK Your old friend Eilert Løvborg is back in town.

TESMAN I already know.

BRACK Oh? How did you hear?

TESMAN She told me. The lady that left with Hedda.

BRACK I see. What was her name again? I didn't quite catch it—

TESMAN Mrs. Elvsted.

BRACK Aha—Sheriff Elvsted's wife. Yes—it's up near them he's been staying.

TESMAN And, just think—what a pleasure to hear that he's completely stable again!

BRACK Yes, that's what they claim.

TESMAN And that he's published a new book, uh?

BRACK Oh yes!

TESMAN And it's created quite a sensation.

BRACK An extraordinary sensation.

TESMAN Just imagine—isn't that marvelous? He, with his remarkable talents—I was so very afraid that he'd really gone down for good.

BRACK That's what everyone thought.

TESMAN But I've no idea what he'll find to do now. How on earth can he ever make a living? Hm?

[*During the last words,* HEDDA *comes in by the hall door.*]

HEDDA [*to* BRACK, *laughing, with a touch of scorn*] Tesman always goes around worrying about how people are going to make a living.

TESMAN My Lord—it's poor Eilert Løvborg we're talking of, dear.

HEDDA [*glancing quickly at him*] Oh, really? [*Sits in the armchair by the stove and asks casually.*] What's the matter with him?

TESMAN Well—he must have run through his inheritance long ago. And he can't write a new book every year. Uh? So I was asking, really, what's going to become of him.

BRACK Perhaps I can shed some light on that.

TESMAN Oh?

BRACK You must remember that he does have relatives with a great deal of influence.

TESMAN Yes, but they've washed their hands of him altogether.

BRACK They used to call him the family's white hope.

TESMAN They used to, yes! But he spoiled all that himself.

HEDDA Who knows? [*With a slight smile*] He's been rehabilitated up at the Elvsteds—

BRACK And then this book that he's published—

TESMAN Oh, well, let's hope they really help him some way or other. I just now wrote to him. Hedda dear, I asked him out here this evening.

BRACK But my dear fellow, you're coming to my stag party this evening. You promised down on the pier last night.

HEDDA Had you forgotten, Tesman?

TESMAN Yes, I absolutely had.

BRACK For that matter, you can rest assured that he'd never come.

TESMAN What makes you say that, hm?

BRACK [*hesitating, rising and leaning on the back of the chair*] My dear Tesman—and you too, Mrs. Tesman—I can't, in all conscience, let you go on without knowing something that—that—

TESMAN Something involving Eilert—?

BRACK Both you and him.

TESMAN But my dear Judge, then tell us!

BRACK You must be prepared that your appointment may not come through as quickly as you've wished or expected.

TESMAN [*jumping up nervously*] Has something gone wrong? Uh?

BRACK It may turn out that there'll have to be a competition for the post—

TESMAN A competition! Imagine, Hedda!

HEDDA [*leaning farther back in the chair*] Ah, there—you see!

TESMAN But with whom! You can't mean—?

BRACK Yes, exactly. With Eilert Løvborg.

TESMAN [*striking his hands together*] No, no—that's completely unthinkable! It's impossible! Uh?

BRACK Hm—but it may come about, all the same.

TESMAN No, but, Judge Brack—that would just be incredibly inconsiderate toward me! [*Waving his arms*] Yes, because—you know—I'm a married man! We married on my prospects, Hedda and I. We went into debt. And even borrowed money from Aunt Julie. Because that job—my Lord, it was as good as promised to me, uh?

BRACK Easy now—I'm sure you'll get the appointment. But you will have to compete for it.

HEDDA [*motionless in the armchair*] Just think, Tesman—it will be like a kind of championship match.

TESMAN But Hedda dearest, how can you take it so calmly!

HEDDA [*as before*] I'm not the least bit calm. I can't wait to see how it turns out.

BRACK In any case, Mrs. Tesman, it's well that you know now how things stand. I mean—with respect to those little purchases I hear you've been threatening to make.

HEDDA This business can't change anything.

BRACK I see! Well, that's another matter. Good-bye. [*To* TESMAN] When I take my afternoon walk, I'll stop by and fetch you.

TESMAN Oh yes, please do—I don't know where I'm at.

HEDDA [*leaning back and reaching out her hand*] Good-bye, Judge. And come again soon.

BRACK Many thanks. Good-bye now.

TESMAN [*accompanying him to the door*] Good-bye, Judge! You really must excuse me—

[BRACK *goes out by the hall door.*]

TESMAN [*pacing about the room*] Oh, Hedda—one should never go off and lose oneself in dreams, uh?

HEDDA [*looks at him and smiles*] Do *you* do *that?*

TESMAN No use denying it. It was living in dreams to go and get married and set up house on nothing but expectations.

HEDDA Perhaps you're right about that.

TESMAN Well, at least we have our comfortable home, Hedda! The home that we always wanted. That we both fell in love with, I could almost say. Hm?

HEDDA [*rising slowly and wearily*] It was part of our bargain that we'd live in society—that we'd keep a great house—

TESMAN Yes of course—how I'd looked forward to that! Imagine—seeing you as a hostess—in our own select circle of friends! Yes, yes—well, for a while, we two will just have to get on by ourselves, Hedda. Perhaps have Aunt Julie here now and then. Oh, you—for you I wanted to have things so—so utterly different—!

HEDDA Naturally this means I can't have a butler now.

TESMAN Oh no—I'm sorry, a butler—we can't even talk about that, you know.

HEDDA And the riding horse I was going to have—

TESMAN [*appalled*] Riding horse!

HEDDA I suppose I can't think of that anymore.

TESMAN Good Lord, no—that's obvious!

HEDDA [*crossing the room*] Well, at least I have one thing left to amuse myself with.

TESMAN [*beaming*] Ah, thank heaven for that! What is it, Hedda? Uh?

HEDDA [*in the center doorway, looking at him with veiled scorn*] My pistols, George.

TESMAN [*in fright*] Your pistols!

HEDDA [*her eyes cold*] General Gabler's pistols.

[*She goes through the inner room and out to the left.*]

TESMAN [*runs to the center doorway and calls after her*] No, for heaven's sake, Hedda darling—don't touch those dangerous things! For my sake, Hedda! Uh?

Act 2

[*The rooms at the* TESMANS', *same as in the first act, except that the piano has been moved out, and an elegant little writing table with a bookcase put in its place. A smaller table stands by the sofa to the left. Most of the flowers have been removed.* MRS. ELVSTED'*s bouquet stands on the large table in the foreground. It is afternoon.*

HEDDA, *dressed to receive callers, is alone in the room. She stands by the open glass door, loading a revolver. The match to it lies in an open pistol case on the writing table.*]

HEDDA [*looking down into the garden and calling*] Good to see you again, Judge!

BRACK [*heard from below, at a distance*] Likewise, Mrs. Tesman!

HEDDA [*raises the pistol and aims*] And now, Judge, I'm going to shoot you!

BRACK [*shouting from below*] No-no-no! Don't point that thing at me!

HEDDA That's what comes of sneaking in the back way. [*She fires.*]

BRACK [*nearer*] Are you out of your mind—!

HEDDA Oh, dear—I didn't hit you, did I?

BRACK [*still outside*] Just stop this nonsense!

HEDDA All right, you can come in, Judge.

[JUDGE BRACK, *dressed for a stag party, enters through the glass door. He carries a light overcoat on his arm.*]

BRACK Good God! Are you still playing such games? What are you shooting at?

HEDDA Oh, I was just shooting into the sky.

BRACK [*gently taking the pistol out of her hand*] Permit me. [*Looks at it.*] Ah, this one—I know it well. [*Glancing around*] Where's the case? Ah, here. [*Puts the pistol away and shuts the case.*] We'll have no more of that kind of fun today.

HEDDA Well, what in heaven's name do you want me to do with myself?

BRACK You haven't had any visitors?

HEDDA [*closing the glass door*] Not a single one. All of our set are still in the country, I guess.

BRACK And Tesman isn't home either?

HEDDA [*at the writing table, putting the pistol case away in a drawer*] No. Right after lunch he ran over to his aunts. He didn't expect you so soon.

BRACK Hm— I should have realized. That was stupid of me.

HEDDA [*turning her head and looking at him*] Why stupid?

BRACK Because in that case I would have stopped by a little bit—earlier.

HEDDA [*crossing the room*] Well, you'd have found no one here then at all. I've been up in my room dressing since lunch.

BRACK And there's not the least little crack in the door we could have conferred through.

HEDDA You forgot to arrange it.

BRACK Also stupid of me.

HEDDA Well, we'll just have to settle down here—and wait. Tesman won't be back for a while.

BRACK Don't worry, I can be patient.

[HEDDA *sits in the corner of the sofa.* BRACK *lays his coat over the back of the nearest chair and sits down, keeping his hat in his hand. A short pause. They look at each other.*]

HEDDA Well?

BRACK [*in the same tone*] Well?

HEDDA I spoke first.

BRACK [*leaning slightly forward*] Then let's have a nice little cozy chat, Mrs. Hedda.[6]

HEDDA [*leaning farther back on the sofa*] Doesn't it seem like a whole eternity since the last time we talked together? Oh, a few words last night and this morning—but they don't count.

BRACK You mean, like this—between ourselves? Just the two of us?

HEDDA Well, more or less.

BRACK There wasn't a day that I didn't wish you were home again.

HEDDA And I was wishing exactly the same.

BRACK You? Really, Mrs. Hedda? And I thought you were having such a marvelous time on this trip.

HEDDA Oh, you can imagine!

BRACK But that's what Tesman always wrote.

HEDDA Oh, him! There's nothing he likes better than grubbing around in libraries and copying out old parchments, or whatever you call them.

BRACK [*with a touch of malice*] But after all, it's his calling in life. In good part, anyway.

HEDDA Yes, that's true. So there's nothing wrong with it— But what about *me!* Oh, Judge, you don't know—I've been so dreadfully bored.

BRACK [*sympathetically*] You really mean that? In all seriousness?

HEDDA Well, you can understand—! To go for a whole six months without meeting a soul who knew the least bit about our circle. No one that one could talk to about our kind of things.

BRACK Ah, yes—I think that would bother me too.

HEDDA But then the most unbearable thing of all—

BRACK What?

HEDDA To be everlastingly together with—with one and the same person—

BRACK [*nodding in agreement*] Morning, noon, and night—yes. At every conceivable hour.

HEDDA I said "everlastingly."

BRACK All right. But with our good friend Tesman, I really should have thought—

HEDDA My dear Judge, Tesman is—a specialist.

BRACK Undeniably.

HEDDA And specialists aren't at all amusing to travel with. Not in the long run, anyway.

6. Although Brack uses the playful "Mrs. Hedda" when they are alone, in Ibsen's original Norwegian text he addresses her with the formal *De* throughout the play.

BRACK Not even—the specialist that one *loves?*

HEDDA Ugh—don't use that syrupy word!

BRACK [*startled*] What's that, Mrs. Hedda!

HEDDA [*half laughing, half annoyed*] Well, just try it yourself! Try listening to the history of civilization morning, noon, and—

BRACK Everlastingly.

HEDDA Yes! Yes! And then all this business about domestic crafts in the Middle Ages—! That really is just too revolting!

BRACK [*looks searchingly at her*] But tell me—I can't see how it ever came about that—? Hm—

HEDDA That George Tesman and I could make a match?

BRACK All right, let's put it that way.

HEDDA Good Lord, does it seem so remarkable?

BRACK Well, yes—and no, Mrs. Hedda.

HEDDA I really had danced myself out, Judge. My time was up. [*With a slight shudder*] Ugh! No, I don't want to say that. Or think it, either.

BRACK You certainly have no reason to.

HEDDA Oh—reasons— [*Watching him carefully*] And George Tesman—he is, after all, a thoroughly acceptable choice.

BRACK Acceptable and dependable, beyond a doubt.

HEDDA And I don't find anything especially ridiculous about him. Do you?

BRACK Ridiculous? No-o-o, I wouldn't say that.

HEDDA Hm. Anyway, he works incredibly hard on his research! There's every chance that, in time, he could still make a name for himself.

BRACK [*looking at her with some uncertainty*] I thought you believed, like everyone else, that he was going to be quite famous some day.

HEDDA [*wearily*] Yes, so I did. And then when he kept pressing and pleading to be allowed to take care of me—I didn't see why I ought to resist.

BRACK No. From that point of view, of course not—

HEDDA It was certainly more than my other admirers were willing to do for me, Judge.

BRACK [*laughing*] Well, I can't exactly answer for all the others. But as far as I'm concerned, you know that I've always cherished a—a certain respect for the marriage bond. Generally speaking, that is.

HEDDA [*bantering*] Oh, I never really held out any hopes for *you.*

BRACK All I want is to have a warm circle of intimate friends, where I can be of use one way or another, with the freedom to come and go as—as a trusted friend—

HEDDA Of the man of the house, you mean?

BRACK [*with a bow*] Frankly—I prefer the lady. But the man, too, of course, in his place. That kind of—let's say, triangular arrangement—you can't imagine how satisfying it can be all around.

HEDDA Yes, I must say I longed for some third person so many times on that trip. Oh—those endless tête-à-têtes in railway compartments—!

BRACK Fortunately the wedding trip's over now.

HEDDA [*shaking her head*] The trip will go on—and on. I've only come to one stop on the line.

BRACK Well, then what you do is jump out—and stretch yourself a little, Mrs. Hedda.

HEDDA I'll never jump out.

BRACK Never?

HEDDA No. Because there's always someone on the platform who—

BRACK [*with a laugh*] Who looks at your legs, is that it?

HEDDA Precisely.

BRACK Yes, but after all—

HEDDA [*with a disdainful gesture*] I'm not interested. I'd rather keep my seat—right here, where I am. Tête-à-tête.

BRACK Well, but suppose a third person came on board and joined the couple.

HEDDA Ah! That's entirely different.

BRACK A trusted friend, who understands—

HEDDA And can talk about all kinds of lively things—

BRACK Who's not in the least a specialist.

HEDDA [*with an audible sigh*] Yes, that would be a relief.

BRACK [*hearing the front door open and glancing toward it*] The triangle is complete.

HEDDA [*lowering her voice*] And the train goes on.

[GEORGE TESMAN, *in a gray walking suit and a soft felt hat, enters from the hall. He has a good number of unbound books under his arm and in his pockets.*]

TESMAN [*going up to the table by the corner settee*] Phew! Let me tell you, that's hot work—carrying all these. [*Setting the books down*] I'm actually sweating, Hedda. And what's this—you're already here, Judge? Hm? Berta didn't tell me.

BRACK [*rising*] I came in through the garden.

HEDDA What are all these books you've gotten?

TESMAN [*stands leafing through them*] They're new publications in my special field. I absolutely need them.

HEDDA Your special field?

BRACK Of course. Books in his special field, Mrs. Tesman.

[BRACK *and* HEDDA *exchange a knowing smile.*]

HEDDA You need still more books in your special field?

TESMAN Hedda, my dear, it's impossible ever to have too many. You have to keep up with what's written and published.

HEDDA Oh, I suppose so.

TESMAN [*searching among the books*] And look—I picked up Eilert Løvborg's new book too. [*Offering it to her*] Maybe you'd like to have a look at it? Uh?

HEDDA No, thank you. Or—well, perhaps later.

TESMAN I skimmed through some of it on the way home.

BRACK Well, what do you think of it—as a specialist?

TESMAN I think it's amazing how well it holds up. He's never written like this before. [*Gathers up the books.*] But I'll take these into the study now. I can't wait to cut the pages—![7] And then I better dress up a bit. [*To* BRACK] We don't have to rush right off, do we? Hm?

BRACK No, not at all. There's ample time.

7. When books are published, four or eight pages are usually printed on one sheet, which is subsequently folded to properly order the leaves; formerly, books were often sold with the outer edges of the folded pages left uncut.

TESMAN Ah, then I'll be at my leisure. [*Starts out with the books, but pauses and turns in the doorway.*] Oh, incidentally, Hedda—Aunt Julie won't be by to see you this evening.

HEDDA She won't? I suppose it's that business with the hat?

TESMAN Not at all. How can you think that of Aunt Julie? Imagine—! No, it's Auntie Rina—she's very ill.

HEDDA She always is.

TESMAN Yes, but today she really took a turn for the worse.

HEDDA Well, then it's only sensible for her sister to stay with her. I'll have to bear with it.

TESMAN But you can't imagine how delighted Aunt Julie was all the same—because you'd filled out so nicely on the trip!

HEDDA [*under her breath; rising*] Oh, these eternal aunts!

TESMAN What?

HEDDA [*going over to the glass door*] Nothing.

TESMAN All right, then. [*He goes through the inner room and out, right.*]

BRACK What were you saying about a hat?

HEDDA Oh, it's something that happened with Miss Tesman this morning. She'd put her hat down over there on the chair. [*Looks at him and smiles.*] And I pretended I thought it was the maid's.

BRACK [*shaking his head*] But my dear Mrs. Hedda, how could you do that! Hurt that nice old lady!

HEDDA [*nervously, pacing the room*] Well, it's—these things come over me, just like that, suddenly. And I can't hold back. [*Throws herself down in the armchair by the stove.*] Oh, I don't know myself how to explain it.

BRACK [*behind the armchair*] You're not really happy—that's the heart of it.

HEDDA [*gazing straight ahead*] And I don't know why I ought to be—happy. Or maybe you can tell me why?

BRACK Yes—among other things, because you've gotten just the home you've always wanted.

HEDDA [*looks up at him and laughs*] You believe that story too?

BRACK You mean there's nothing to it?

HEDDA Oh yes—there's something to it.

BRACK Well?

HEDDA There's this much to it, that I used Tesman as my escort home from parties last summer—

BRACK Unfortunately—I was headed quite a different way.

HEDDA How true. Yes, you went several different ways last summer.

BRACK [*laughing*] For shame, Mrs. Hedda! Well—so you and Tesman—?

HEDDA Yes, so one evening we walked by this place. And Tesman, poor thing, was writhing in torment, because he couldn't find anything to say. And I felt sorry for a man of such learning—

BRACK [*smiling skeptically*] Did you? Hm—

HEDDA No, I honestly did. And so—just to help him off the hook—I came out with some rash remark about this lovely house being where I'd always wanted to live.

BRACK No more than that?

HEDDA No more that evening.

BRACK But afterward?

HEDDA Yes, my rashness had its consequences, Judge.

BRACK I'm afraid our rashness all too often does, Mrs. Hedda.

HEDDA Thanks! But don't you see, it was this passion for the old Falk mansion that drew George Tesman and me together! It was nothing more than that, that brought on our engagement and the marriage and the wedding trip and everything else. Oh yes, Judge—I was going to say, you make your bed and then you lie in it.

BRACK But that's priceless! So actually you couldn't care less about all this?

HEDDA God knows, not in the least.

BRACK But even now? Now that we've got it furnished a bit cosier for you here?

HEDDA Ugh—all the rooms seem to smell of lavender and dried roses. But maybe that scent was brought in by Aunt Julie.

BRACK [*laughing*] No, I think it's a bequest from the late Mrs. Falk.

HEDDA Yes, there's something in it of the odor of death. It's like a corsage—the day after the dance. [*Folds her hands behind her neck, leans back in her chair, and looks at him.*] Oh, my dear Judge—you can't imagine how horribly I'm going to bore myself here.

BRACK But couldn't you find some goal in life to work toward? Others do, Mrs. Hedda.

HEDDA A goal—that would really absorb me?

BRACK Yes, preferably.

HEDDA God only knows what that could be. I often wonder if— [*Breaks off.*] But that's impossible too.

BRACK Who knows? Tell me.

HEDDA I was thinking—if I could get Tesman to go into politics.

BRACK [*laughing*] Tesman! No, I can promise you—politics is absolutely out of his line.

HEDDA No, I can believe you. But even so, I wonder if I could get him into it?

BRACK Well, what satisfaction would you have in that, if he can't succeed? Why push him in that direction?

HEDDA Because, I've told you, I'm bored! [*After a pause*] Then you think it's really out of the question that he could ever be a cabinet minister?

BRACK Hm—you see, Mrs. Hedda—to be anything like that, he'd have to be fairly wealthy to start with.

HEDDA [*rising impatiently*] Yes, there it is! It's this tight little world I've stumbled into— [*Crossing the room*] That's what makes life so miserable! So utterly ludicrous! Because that's what it *is*.

BRACK I'd say the fault lies elsewhere.

HEDDA Where?

BRACK You've never experienced anything that's really stirred you.

HEDDA Anything serious, you mean.

BRACK Well, you can call it that, if you like. But now perhaps it's on the way.

HEDDA [*tossing her head*] Oh, you mean all the fuss over that wretched professorship! But that's Tesman's problem. I'm not going to give it a single thought.

BRACK No, that isn't—ah, never mind. But suppose you were to be confronted now by what—in rather elegant language—is called your most solemn responsibility. [*Smiling*] A new responsibility, Mrs. Hedda.

HEDDA [*angrily*] Be quiet! You'll never see me like that!

BRACK [*delicately*] We'll discuss it again in a year's time—at the latest.

HEDDA [*curtly*] I have no talent for such things, Judge. I won't have responsibilities!

BRACK Don't you think you've a talent for what almost every woman finds the most meaningful—

HEDDA [*over by the glass door*] Oh, I told you, be quiet! I often think I have talent for only one thing in life.

BRACK [*moving closer*] And what, may I ask, is that?

HEDDA [*stands looking out*] Boring myself to death. And that's the truth. [*Turns, looks toward the inner room, and laughs.*] See what I mean! Here comes the professor.

BRACK [*in a low tone of warning*] Ah-ah-ah, Mrs. Hedda!

[GEORGE TESMAN, *dressed for the party, with hat and gloves in hand, enters from the right through the inner room.*]

TESMAN Hedda—there's been no word from Eilert Løvborg, has there? Hm?

HEDDA No.

TESMAN Well, he's bound to be here soon then. You'll see.

BRACK You really believe he'll come?

TESMAN Yes, I'm almost positive of it. Because I'm sure they're nothing but rumors, what you told us this morning.

BRACK Oh?

TESMAN Yes. At least Aunt Julie said she couldn't for the world believe that he'd stand in my way again. Can you imagine that!

BRACK So, then everything's well and good.

TESMAN [*putting his hat with the gloves inside on a chair to the right*] Yes, but I really would like to wait for him as long as possible.

BRACK We have plenty of time for that. There's no one due at my place till seven or half past.

TESMAN Why, then we can keep Hedda company for a while. And see what turns up. Uh?

HEDDA [*taking* BRACK's *hat and coat over to the settee*] And if worst comes to worst, Mr. Løvborg can sit and talk with me.

BRACK [*trying to take his things himself*] Ah, please, Mrs. Tesman—! What do you mean by "worst," in this case?

HEDDA If he won't go with you and Tesman.

TESMAN [*looks doubtfully at her*] But Hedda dear—is it quite right that he stays with you here? Uh? Remember that Aunt Julie isn't coming.

HEDDA No, but Mrs. Elvsted is. The three of us can have tea together.

TESMAN Oh, well, that's all right.

BRACK [*smiling*] And that might be the soundest plan for him too.

HEDDA Why?

BRACK Well, really, Mrs. Tesman, you've made enough pointed remarks about my little bachelor parties. You've always said they're only fit for men of the strictest principles.

HEDDA But Mr. Løvborg is surely a man of principle now. After all, a reformed sinner—

[BERTA *appears at the hall door.*]

BERTA Ma'am, there's a gentleman here who'd like to see you—

HEDDA Yes, show him in.

TESMAN [*softly*] I'm sure it's him! Just think!

[EILERT LØVBORG *enters from the hall. He is lean and gaunt, the same age as* TESMAN, *but looks older and somewhat run-down. His hair and beard are dark brown, his face long and pale, but with reddish patches over the cheekbones. He is dressed in a trim black suit, quite new, and holds dark gloves and a top hat in his hand. He hesitates by the door and bows abruptly. He seems somewhat embarrassed.*]

TESMAN [*crosses over and shakes his hand*] Ah, my dear Eilert—so at last we meet again!

EILERT LØVBORG [*speaking in a hushed voice*] Thanks for your letter, George! [*Approaching* HEDDA] May I shake hands with you too, Mrs. Tesman?

HEDDA [*taking his hand*] So glad to see you, Mr. Løvborg. [*Gesturing with her hand*] I don't know if you two gentlemen—?

LØVBORG [*bowing slightly*] Judge Brack, I believe.

BRACK [*reciprocating*] Of course. It's been some years—

TESMAN [*to* LØVBORG, *with his hands on his shoulders*] And now, Eilert, make yourself at home, completely! Right, Hedda? I hear you'll be settling down here in town again? Uh?

LØVBORG I plan to.

TESMAN Well, that makes sense. Listen—I just got hold of your new book. But I really haven't had time to read it yet.

LØVBORG You can save yourself the bother.

TESMAN Why? What do you mean?

LØVBORG There's very little to it.

TESMAN Imagine—you can say that!

BRACK But it's won such high praise, I hear.

LØVBORG That's exactly what I wanted. So I wrote a book that everyone could agree with.

BRACK Very sound.

TESMAN Yes, but my dear Eilert—!

LØVBORG Because now I want to build up my position again—and try to make a fresh start.

TESMAN [*somewhat distressed*] Yes, that is what you want, I suppose. Uh?

LØVBORG [*smiling, puts down his hat and takes a packet wrapped in brown paper out of his coat pocket*] But when this comes out—George Tesman—you'll have to read it. Because this is the real book—the one that speaks for my true self.

TESMAN Oh, really? What sort of book is that?

LØVBORG It's the sequel.

TESMAN Sequel? To what?

LØVBORG To the book.

TESMAN The one just out?

LØVBORG Of course.

TESMAN Yes, but my dear Eilert—that comes right down to our own time!

LØVBORG Yes, it does. And this one deals with the future.

TESMAN The future! But good Lord, there's nothing we know about that!

LØVBORG True. But there are one or two things worth saying about it all the same. [*Opens the packet.*] Here, take a look—

TESMAN But that's not your handwriting.

LØVBORG I dictated it. [*Paging through the manuscript*] It's divided into two sections. The first is about the forces shaping the civilization of the future.

And the second part, here—[*Paging further on*] suggests what lines of development it's likely to take.

TESMAN How extraordinary! It never would have occurred to me to write about anything like that.

HEDDA [*at the glass door, drumming on the pane*] Hm—no, of course not.

LØVBORG [*puts the manuscript back in its wrapping and lays it on the table*] I brought it along because I thought I might read you a bit of it this evening.

TESMAN Ah, that's very good of you, Eilert; but this evening— [*Glancing at* BRACK] I'm really not sure that it's possible—

LØVBORG Well, some other time, then. There's no hurry.

BRACK I should explain, Mr. Løvborg—there's a little party at my place tonight. Mostly for Tesman, you understand.

LØVBORG [*looking for his hat*] Ah—then I won't stay—

BRACK No, listen—won't you give me the pleasure of having you join us?

LØVBORG [*sharply and decisively*] No, I can't. Thanks very much.

BRACK Oh, nonsense! Do that. We'll be a small, select group. And you can bet we'll have it "lively," as Mrs. Hed—Mrs. Tesman says.

LØVBORG I don't doubt it. But nevertheless—

BRACK You could bring your manuscript with you and read it to Tesman there, at my place. I have plenty of rooms.

TESMAN Why, of course, Eilert—you could do that, couldn't you? Uh?

HEDDA [*intervening*] But dear, if Mr. Løvborg simply doesn't want to! I'm sure Mr. Løvborg would much prefer to settle down here and have supper with me.

LØVBORG [*looking at her*] With you, Mrs. Tesman!

HEDDA And with Mrs. Elvsted.

LØVBORG Ah. [*Casually*] I saw her a moment this afternoon.

HEDDA Oh, did you? Well, she'll be here soon. So it's almost essential for you to stay, Mr. Løvborg. Otherwise, she'll have no one to see her home.

LØVBORG That's true. Yes, thank you, Mrs. Tesman—I'll be staying, then.

HEDDA Then let me just tell the maid—

[*She goes to the hall door and rings.* BERTA *enters.* HEDDA *talks to her quietly and points toward the inner room.* BERTA *nods and goes out again.*]

TESMAN [*at the same time, to* LØVBORG] Tell me, Eilert—is it this new material—about the future—that you're going to be lecturing on?

LØVBORG Yes.

TESMAN Because I heard at the bookstore that you'll be giving a lecture series here this autumn.

LØVBORG I intend to. I hope you won't be offended, Tesman.

TESMAN Why, of course not! But—?

LØVBORG I can easily understand that it makes things rather difficult for you.

TESMAN [*dispiritedly*] Oh, I could hardly expect that for my sake you'd—

LØVBORG But I'm going to wait till you have your appointment.

TESMAN You'll wait! Yes, but—but—you're not competing for it, then? Uh?

LØVBORG No. I only want to win in the eyes of the world.

TESMAN But, my Lord—then Aunt Julie was right after all! Oh yes—I knew it all along! Hedda! Can you imagine—Eilert Løvborg won't stand in our way!

HEDDA [*brusquely*] Our way? Leave me out of it.

[*She goes up toward the inner room where* BERTA *is putting a tray with decanters and glasses on the table.* HEDDA *nods her approval and comes back again.* BERTA *goes out.*]

TESMAN [*at the same time*] But you, Judge—what do you say to all this? Uh?

BRACK Well, I'd say that victory and honor—hm—after all, they're very sweet—

TESMAN Yes, of course. But still—

HEDDA [*regarding* TESMAN *with a cold smile*] You look as if you'd been struck by lightning.

TESMAN Yes—something like it—I guess—

BRACK That's because a thunderstorm just passed over us, Mrs. Tesman.

HEDDA [*pointing toward the inner room*] Won't you gentlemen please help yourselves to a glass of cold punch?

BRACK [*looking at his watch*] A parting cup? That's not such a bad idea.

TESMAN Marvelous, Hedda! Simply marvelous! The way I feel now, with this weight off my mind—

HEDDA Please, Mr. Løvborg, you too,

LØVBORG [*with a gesture of refusal*] No, thank you. Not for me.

BRACK Good Lord, cold punch—it isn't poison, you know.

LØVBORG Perhaps not for everyone.

HEDDA I'll keep Mr. Løvborg company a while.

TESMAN All right, Hedda dear, you do that.

[*He and* BRACK *go into the inner room, sit down, drink punch, smoke cigarettes, and talk animatedly during the following.* LØVBORG *remains standing by the stove.* HEDDA *goes to the writing table.*]

HEDDA [*slightly raising her voice*] I can show you some photographs, if you like. Tesman and I traveled through the Tyrol on our way home.

[*She brings over an album and lays it on the table by the sofa, seating herself in the farthest corner.* EILERT LØVBORG *comes closer, stops, and looks at her. Then he takes a chair and sits down on her left, his back toward the inner room.*]

HEDDA [*opening the album*] You see this view of the mountains, Mr. Løvborg. That's the Ortler group. Tesman's labeled them underneath. Here it is: "The Ortler group, near Meran."[8]

LØVBORG [*whose eyes have never left her, speaking in a low, soft voice*] Hedda—Gabler!

HEDDA [*with a quick glance at him*] Ah! Shh!

LØVBORG [*repeating softly*] Hedda Gabler!

HEDDA [*looks at the album*] Yes, I used to be called that. In those days—when we two knew each other.

LØVBORG And from now on—for the rest of my life—I have to teach myself not to say Hedda Gabler.

HEDDA [*turning the pages*] Yes, you have to. And I think you ought to start practicing it. The sooner the better, I'd say.

LØVBORG [*resentment in his voice*] Hedda Gabler married? And to George Tesman!

8. Merano, a district in northeastern Italy on the southern slope of the Alps.

HEDDA Yes—that's how it goes.

LØVBORG Oh, Hedda, Hedda—how could you throw yourself away like that![9]

HEDDA [*looks at him sharply*] All right—no more of that!

LØVBORG What do you mean?

[TESMAN *comes in and over to the sofa.*]

HEDDA [*hears him coming and says casually*] And this one, Mr. Løvborg, was taken from the Val d'Ampezzo.[1] Just look at the peaks of those mountains. [*Looks warmly up at* TESMAN.] Now what were those marvelous mountains called, dear?

TESMAN Let me see. Oh, those are the Dolomites.

HEDDA Why, of course! Those are the Dolomites, Mr. Løvborg.

TESMAN Hedda dear—I only wanted to ask if we shouldn't bring in some punch anyway. At least for you, hm?

HEDDA Yes, thank you. And a couple of *petits fours*, please.

TESMAN No cigarettes?

HEDDA No.

TESMAN Right.

[*He goes through the inner room and out to the right.* BRACK *remains sitting inside, keeping his eye from time to time on* HEDDA *and* LØVBORG.]

LØVBORG [*softly, as before*] Answer me, Hedda—how could you go and do such a thing?

HEDDA [*apparently immersed in the album*] If you keep on saying Hedda like that to me, I won't talk to you.

LØVBORG Can't I say Hedda even when we're alone?

HEDDA No. You can think it, but you mustn't say it like that.

LØVBORG Ah, I understand. It offends your—love for George Tesman.

HEDDA [*glances at him and smiles*] Love? You *are* absurd!

LØVBORG Then you don't love him!

HEDDA I don't expect to be unfaithful, either. I'm not having any of that!

LØVBORG Hedda, just answer me one thing—

HEDDA Shh!

[TESMAN, *carrying a tray, enters from the inner room.*]

TESMAN Look out! Here come the goodies. [*He sets the tray on the table.*]

HEDDA Why do you do the serving?

TESMAN [*filling the glasses*] Because I think it's such fun to wait on you, Hedda.

HEDDA But now you've poured out two glasses. And you know Mr. Løvborg doesn't want—

TESMAN Well, but Mrs. Elvsted will be along soon.

HEDDA Yes, that's right—Mrs. Elvsted—

TESMAN Had you forgotten her? Uh?

HEDDA We've been so caught up in these. [*Showing him a picture*] Do you remember this little village?

9. When addressing Hedda, Løvborg uses the familiar *du* in the first part of this scene; here, he reverts to the formal *De*. However, he calls her by her first name throughout. Hedda, by contrast, addresses him as "Mr. Løvborg" and uses only the formal *De*.

1. A valley in northern Italy in the Dolomites, a section of the Tyrolean Alps.

TESMAN Oh, that's the one just below the Brenner Pass![2] It was there that we stayed overnight—

HEDDA And met all those lively summer people.

TESMAN Yes, that's the place. Just think—if we could have had *you* with us, Eilert! My! [*He goes back and sits beside* BRACK.]

LØVBORG Answer me just one thing, Hedda—

HEDDA Yes?

LØVBORG Was there no love with respect to me, either? Not a spark—not one glimmer of love at all?

HEDDA I wonder, really, was there? To me it was as if we were two true companions—two very close friends. [*Smiling*] You, especially, were so open with me.

LØVBORG You wanted it that way.

HEDDA When I look back on it now, there was really something beautiful and fascinating—and daring, it seems to me, about—about our secret closeness—our companionship that no one, not a soul, suspected.

LØVBORG Yes, Hedda, that's true! Wasn't there? When I'd come over to your father's in the afternoon—and the general sat by the window reading his papers—with his back to us—

HEDDA And we'd sit on the corner sofa—

LØVBORG Always with the same illustrated magazine in front of us—

HEDDA Yes, for the lack of an album.

LØVBORG Yes, Hedda—and the confessions I used to make—telling you things about myself that no one else knew of then. About the way I'd go out, the drinking, the madness that went on day and night, for days at a time. Ah, what power was it in you, Hedda, that made me tell you such things?

HEDDA You think it was some kind of power in me?

LØVBORG How else can I explain it? And all those—those devious questions you asked me—

HEDDA That you understood so remarkably well—

LØVBORG To think you could sit there and ask such questions! So boldly.

HEDDA Deviously, please.

LØVBORG Yes, but boldly, all the same. Interrogating me about—all that kind of thing!

HEDDA And to think you could answer, Mr. Løvborg.

LØVBORG Yes, that's exactly what I don't understand—now, looking back. But tell me, Hedda—the root of that bond between us, wasn't it love? Didn't you feel, on your part, as if you wanted to cleanse and absolve me—when I brought those confessions to you? Wasn't that it?

HEDDA No, not quite.

LØVBORG What made you do it, then?

HEDDA Do you find it so very surprising that a young girl—if there's no chance of anyone knowing—

LØVBORG Yes?

HEDDA That she'd like some glimpse of a world that—

LØVBORG That—?

HEDDA That she's forbidden to know anything about.

2. One of the main passes in the Alps, between Austria and Italy.

LØVBORG So that was it?

HEDDA Partly. Partly that, I guess.

LØVBORG Companionship in a thirst for life. But why, then, couldn't it have gone on?

HEDDA But that was your fault.

LØVBORG You broke it off.

HEDDA Yes, when that closeness of ours threatened to grow more serious. Shame on you, Eilert Løvborg! How could you violate my trust when I'd been so—so bold with my friendship?

LØVBORG [*clenching his fists*] Oh, why didn't you do what you said! Why didn't you shoot me down!

HEDDA I'm—much too afraid of scandal.

LØVBORG Yes, Hedda, you're a coward at heart.

HEDDA A terrible coward. [*Changing her tone*] But that was lucky for you. And now you're so nicely consoled at the Elvsteds'.

LØVBORG I know what Thea's been telling you.

HEDDA And perhaps you've been telling her all about us?

LØVBORG Not a word. She's too stupid for that sort of thing.

HEDDA Stupid?

LØVBORG When it comes to those things, she's stupid.

HEDDA And I'm a coward. [*Leans closer, without looking him in the eyes, and speaks softly.*] But there *is* something now that I can tell you.

LØVBORG [*intently*] What?

HEDDA When I didn't dare shoot you—

LØVBORG Yes?

HEDDA That wasn't my worst cowardice—that night.

LØVBORG [*looks at her a moment, understands, and whispers passionately*] Oh, Hedda! Hedda Gabler! Now I begin to see it, the hidden reason why we've been so close! You and I—![3] It was the hunger for *life* in you—

HEDDA [*quietly, with a sharp glance*] Careful! That's no way to think!

[*It has begun to grow dark. The hall door is opened from without by* BERTA.]

HEDDA [*clapping the album shut and calling out with a smile*] Well, at last! Thea dear—please come in!

[MRS. ELVSTED *enters from the hall. She is in evening dress. The door is closed behind her.*]

HEDDA [*on the sofa, stretching her arms out toward her*] Thea, my sweet—I thought you were never coming!

[*In passing,* MRS. ELVSTED *exchanges light greetings with the gentlemen in the inner room, then comes over to the table and extends her hand to* HEDDA. LØVBORG *has gotten up. He and* MRS. ELVSTED *greet each other with a silent nod.*]

MRS. ELVSTED Perhaps I ought to go in and talk a bit with your husband?

HEDDA Oh, nonsense. Let them be. They're leaving soon.

MRS. ELVSTED They're leaving?

HEDDA Yes, for a drinking party.

MRS. ELVSTED [*quickly, to* LØVBORG] But you're not?

3. Here Løvborg reverts to the familiar *du* while Hedda continues to address him with the formal *De*.

LØVBORG No.

HEDDA Mr. Løvborg—is staying with us.

MRS. ELVSTED [*taking a chair, about to sit down beside him*] Oh, it's so good to be here!

HEDDA No, no, Thea dear! Not there! You have to come over here by me. I want to be in the middle.

MRS. ELVSTED Any way you please.

[*She goes around the table and sits on the sofa to* HEDDA'S *right.* LØVBORG *resumes his seat.*]

LØVBORG [*after a brief pause, to* HEDDA] Isn't she lovely to look at?

HEDDA [*lightly stroking her hair*] Only to look at?

LØVBORG Yes. Because we two—she and I—we really *are* true companions. We trust each other completely. We can talk things out together without any reservations—

HEDDA Never anything devious, Mr. Løvborg?

LØVBORG Well—

MRS. ELVSTED [*quietly, leaning close to* HEDDA] Oh, Hedda, you don't know how happy I am! Just think—he says that I've inspired him.

HEDDA [*regarding her with a smile*] Really, dear; did he say that?

LØVBORG And then the courage she has, Mrs. Tesman, when it's put to the test.

MRS. ELVSTED Good heavens, me! Courage!

LØVBORG Enormous courage—where I'm concerned.

HEDDA Yes, courage—yes! If one only had that.

LØVBORG Then what?

HEDDA Then life might still be bearable. [*Suddenly changing her tone*] But now, Thea dearest—you really must have a nice glass of cold punch.

MRS. ELVSTED No, thank you. I never drink that sort of thing.

HEDDA Well, then you, Mr. Løvborg.

LØVBORG Thanks, not for me either.

MRS. ELVSTED No, not for him either!

HEDDA [*looking intently at him*] But if I insist?

LØVBORG Makes no difference.

HEDDA [*with a laugh*] Poor me, then I have no power over you at all?

LØVBORG Not in that area.

HEDDA But seriously, I think you ought to, all the same. For your own sake.

MRS. ELVSTED But Hedda—!

LØVBORG Why do you think so?

HEDDA Or, to be more exact, for others' sakes.

LØVBORG Oh?

HEDDA Otherwise, people might get the idea that you're not very bold at heart. That you're not really sure of yourself at all.

MRS. ELVSTED [*softly*] Oh, Hedda, don't—!

LØVBORG People can think whatever they like, for all I care.

MRS. ELVSTED [*happily*] Yes, that's right!

HEDDA I saw it so clearly in Judge Brack a moment ago.

LØVBORG What did you see?

HEDDA The contempt in his smile when you didn't dare join them for a drink.

LØVBORG Didn't dare! Obviously I'd rather stay here and talk with you.

MRS. ELVSTED That's only reasonable, Hedda.

HEDDA But how could the judge know that? And besides, I noticed him smile and glance at Tesman when you couldn't bring yourself to go to their wretched little party.

LØVBORG Couldn't! Are you saying I couldn't?

HEDDA I'm not. But that's the way Judge Brack sees it.

LØVBORG All right, let him.

HEDDA Then you won't go along?

LØVBORG I'm staying here with you and Thea.

MRS. ELVSTED Yes, Hedda—you can be sure he is!

HEDDA [*smiles and nods approvingly at* LØVBORG] I see. Firm as a rock. True to principle, to the end of time. There, that's what a man ought to be! [*Turning to* MRS. ELVSTED *and patting her*] Well, now, didn't I tell you that, when you came here so distraught this morning—

LØVBORG [*surprised*] Distraught?

MRS. ELVSTED [*terrified*] Hedda—! But Hedda—!

HEDDA Can't you see for yourself? There's no need at all for your going around so deathly afraid that— [*Changing her tone*] There! Now we can all enjoy ourselves!

LØVBORG [*shaken*] What is all this, Mrs. Tesman?

MRS. ELVSTED Oh, God, oh, God, Hedda! What are you saying! What are you doing!

HEDDA Not so loud. That disgusting judge is watching you.

LØVBORG So deathly afraid? For my sake?

MRS. ELVSTED [*in a low moan*] Oh, Hedda, you've made me so miserable!

LØVBORG [*looks intently at her a moment, his face drawn*] So that's how completely you trusted me.

MRS. ELVSTED [*imploringly*] Oh, my dearest—if you'll only listen—!

LØVBORG [*takes one of the glasses of punch, raises it, and says in a low, hoarse voice*] Your health, Thea! [*He empties the glass, puts it down, and takes the other.*]

MRS. ELVSTED [*softly*] Oh, Hedda, Hedda—how could you want such a thing!

HEDDA Want it? I? Are you crazy?

LØVBORG And your health too, Mrs. Tesman. Thanks for the truth. Long live truth! [*Drains the glass and starts to refill it.*]

HEDDA [*laying her hand on his arm*] All right—no more for now. Remember, you're going to a party.

MRS. ELVSTED No, no, no!

HEDDA Shh! They're watching you.

LØVBORG [*putting down his glass*] Now, Thea—tell me honestly—

MRS. ELVSTED Yes!

LØVBORG Did your husband know that you followed me?

MRS. ELVSTED [*wringing her hands*] Oh, Hedda—listen to him!

LØVBORG Did you have it arranged, you and he, that you should come down into town and spy on me? Or maybe he got you to do it himself? Ah, yes—I'm sure he needed me back in the office! Or maybe he missed my hand at cards?

MRS. ELVSTED [*softly, in anguish*] Oh, Eilert, Eilert—!

LØVBORG [*seizing his glass to fill it*] Skoal to the old sheriff, too!

HEDDA [*stopping him*] That's enough. Don't forget, you're giving a reading for Tesman.

LØVBORG [*calmly, setting down his glass*] That was stupid of me, Thea. I mean, taking it like this. Don't be angry at me, my dearest. You'll see—you and all the others—that if I stumbled and fell—I'm back on my feet again now! With your help, Thea.

MRS. ELVSTED [*radiant with joy*] Oh, thank God—!

[BRACK, *in the meantime, has looked at his watch. He and* TESMAN *stand up and enter the drawing room.*]

BRACK [*takes his hat and overcoat*] Well, Mrs. Tesman, our time is up.

HEDDA I suppose it is.

LØVBORG [*rising*] Mine too, Judge.

MRS. ELVSTED [*softly pleading*] Oh, Eilert—don't!

HEDDA [*pinching her arm*] They can hear you!

MRS. ELVSTED [*with a small cry*] Ow!

LØVBORG [*to* BRACK] You were kind enough to ask me along.

BRACK Oh, then you *are* coming, after all?

LØVBORG Yes, thank you.

BRACK I'm delighted—

LØVBORG [*putting the packet back in his pocket, to* TESMAN] I'd like to show you one or two things before I turn this in.

TESMAN Just think—how exciting! But Hedda dear, how will Mrs. Elvsted get home? Uh?

HEDDA Oh, we'll hit on something.

LØVBORG [*glancing toward the ladies*] Mrs. Elvsted? Don't worry, I'll stop back and fetch her. [*Coming nearer*] Say about ten o'clock, Mrs. Tesman? Will that do?

HEDDA Yes. That will do very nicely.

TESMAN Well, then everything's all set. But you mustn't expect *me* that early, Hedda.

HEDDA Dear, you stay as long—just as long as you like.

MRS. ELVSTED [*with suppressed anxiety*] Mr. Løvborg—I'll be waiting here till you come.

LØVBORG [*his hat in his hand*] Yes, I understand.

BRACK So, gentlemen—the excursion train is leaving! I hope it's going to be lively, as a certain fair lady puts it.

HEDDA Ah, if only that fair lady could be there, invisible—

BRACK Why invisible?

HEDDA To hear a little of your unadulterated liveliness, Judge.

BRACK [*laughs*] I wouldn't advise the fair lady to try.

TESMAN [*also laughing*] Oh, Hedda, that's a good one! Just imagine!

BRACK Well, good night. Good night, ladies.

LØVBORG [*bowing*] About ten o'clock, then.

[BRACK, LØVBORG, *and* TESMAN *go out the hall door. At the same time,* BERTA *enters from the inner room with a lighted lamp, which she sets on the drawing room table, then goes out the same way.*]

MRS. ELVSTED [*having risen, moving restlessly about the room*] Hedda—Hedda—what's going to come of all this?

HEDDA At ten o'clock—he'll be here. I can see him now—with vine leaves in his hair[4]—fiery and bold—

MRS. ELVSTED Oh, how good that would be!

4. That is, adorned like Dionysus, the Greek god of wine, whose worship is associated with mad frenzy (his rites were called orgies) and with the origins of Greek tragedy.

HEDDA And then, you'll see—he'll be back in control of himself. He'll be a free man, then, for the rest of his days.

MRS. ELVSTED Oh, God—if only he comes as you see him now!

HEDDA He'll come back like that, and no other way! [*Gets up and goes closer.*] Go on and doubt him as much as you like. *I* believe in him. And now we'll find out—

MRS. ELVSTED There's something behind what you're doing, Hedda.

HEDDA Yes, there is. For once in my life, I want to have power over a human being.

MRS. ELVSTED But don't you have that?

HEDDA I don't have it. I've never had it.

MRS. ELVSTED Not with your husband?

HEDDA Yes, what a bargain *that* was! Oh, if you only could understand how poor I am. And you're allowed to be so rich! [*Passionately throws her arms about her.*] I think I'll burn your hair off, after all!

MRS. ELVSTED Let go! Let me go! I'm afraid of you, Hedda!

BERTA [*in the doorway to the inner room*] Supper's waiting in the dining room, ma'am.

HEDDA All right, we're coming.

MRS. ELVSTED No, no, no! I'd rather go home alone! Right away—now!

HEDDA Nonsense! First you're going to have tea, you little fool. And then—ten o'clock—Eilert Løvborg comes—with vine leaves in his hair.

[*She drags* MRS. ELVSTED, *almost by force, toward the doorway.*]

Act 3

[*The same rooms at the* TESMANS'. *The curtains are drawn across the doorway to the inner room, and also across the glass door. The lamp, shaded and turned down low, is burning on the table. The door to the stove stands open; the fire has nearly gone out.*

MRS. ELVSTED, *wrapped in a large shawl, with her feet up on a foot-stool, lies back in the armchair close by the stove.* HEDDA, *fully dressed, is asleep on the sofa, with a blanket over her. After a pause,* MRS. ELVSTED *suddenly sits straight up in the chair, listening tensely. Then she sinks wearily back again.*]

MRS. ELVSTED [*in a low moan*] Not yet—oh, God—oh, God—not yet!

[BERTA *slips in cautiously by the hall door. She holds a letter in her hand.*]

MRS. ELVSTED [*turns and whispers anxiously*] Yes? Has anyone come?

BERTA [*softly*] Yes, a girl just now stopped by with this letter.

MRS. ELVSTED [*quickly, reaching out her hand*] A letter! Give it to me!

BERTA No, it's for the Doctor, ma'am.

MRS. ELVSTED Oh.

BERTA It was Miss Tesman's maid that brought it. I'll leave it here on the table.

MRS. ELVSTED Yes, do.

BERTA [*putting the letter down*] I think I'd best put out the lamp. It's smoking.

MRS. ELVSTED Yes, put it out. It'll be daylight soon.

BERTA [*does so*] It's broad daylight already, ma'am.

MRS. ELVSTED It's daylight! And still no one's come—!

BERTA Oh, mercy—I knew it would go like this.

MRS. ELVSTED You knew?

BERTA Yes, when I saw that a certain gentleman was back here in town—and that he went off with them. We've heard plenty about that gentleman over the years.

MRS. ELVSTED Don't talk so loud. You'll wake Mrs. Tesman.

BERTA [*looks toward the sofa and sighs*] Goodness me—yes, let her sleep, poor thing. Should I put a bit more on the fire?

MRS. ELVSTED Thanks, not for me.

BERTA All right. [*She goes quietly out the hall door.*]

HEDDA [*wakes as the door shuts and looks up*] What's that?

MRS. ELVSTED It was just the maid—

HEDDA [*glancing about*] In here—? Oh yes, I remember now. [*Sits up on the sofa, stretches, and rubs her eyes.*] What time is it, Thea?

MRS. ELVSTED [*looking at her watch*] It's after seven.

HEDDA When did Tesman get in?

MRS. ELVSTED He isn't back.

HEDDA Not back yet?

MRS. ELVSTED [*getting up*] No one's come in.

HEDDA And we sat here and waited up for them till four o'clock—

MRS. ELVSTED [*wringing her hands*] And *how* I've waited for him!

HEDDA [*yawns, and speaks with her hand in front of her mouth*] Oh, dear—we could have saved ourselves the trouble.

MRS. ELVSTED Did you get any sleep?

HEDDA Oh yes. I slept quite well, I think. Didn't you?

MRS. ELVSTED No, not at all. I couldn't, Hedda! It was just impossible.

HEDDA [*rising and going toward her*] There, there, now! There's nothing to worry about. It's not hard to guess what happened.

MRS. ELVSTED Oh, what? Tell me!

HEDDA Well, it's clear that the party must have gone on till all hours—

MRS. ELVSTED Oh, Lord, yes—it must have. But even so—

HEDDA And then, of course, Tesman didn't want to come home and make a commotion in the middle of the night. [*Laughs.*] Probably didn't care to show himself, either—so full of his party spirits.

MRS. ELVSTED But where else could he have gone?

HEDDA He must have gone up to his aunts' to sleep. They keep his old room ready.

MRS. ELVSTED No, he can't be with them. Because he just now got a letter from Miss Tesman. It's over there.

HEDDA Oh? [*Looking at the address*] Yes, that's Aunt Julie's handwriting, all right. Well, then he must have stayed over at Judge Brack's. And Eilert Løvborg—he's sitting with vine leaves in his hair, reading away.

MRS. ELVSTED Oh, Hedda, you say these things, and you really don't believe them at all.

HEDDA You're such a little fool, Thea.

MRS. ELVSTED That's true; I guess I am.

HEDDA And you really look dead tired.

MRS. ELVSTED Yes, I feel dead tired.

HEDDA Well, you just do as I say, then. Go in my room and stretch out on the bed for a while.

MRS. ELVSTED No, no—I still wouldn't get any sleep.

HEDDA Why, of course you would.

MRS. ELVSTED Well, but your husband's sure to be home now soon. And I've got to know right away—

HEDDA I'll call you the moment he comes.

MRS. ELVSTED Yes? Promise me, Hedda?

HEDDA You can count on it. Just go and get some sleep.

MRS. ELVSTED Thanks. I'll try. [*She goes out through the inner room.*]

[HEDDA *goes over to the glass door and draws the curtains back. Bright daylight streams into the room. She goes over to the writing table, takes out a small hand mirror, regards herself and arranges her hair. She then goes to the hall door and presses the bell. After a moment,* BERTA *enters.*]

BERTA Did you want something, ma'am?

HEDDA Yes, you can build up the fire. I'm freezing in here.

BERTA Why, my goodness—we'll have it warm in no time. [*She rakes the embers together and puts some wood on, then stops and listens.*] There's the front doorbell, ma'am.

HEDDA Go see who it is. I'll take care of the stove.

BERTA It'll be burning soon. [*She goes out the hall door.*]

[HEDDA *kneels on the footstool and lays more wood on the fire. After a moment,* GEORGE TESMAN *comes in from the hall. He looks tired and rather serious. He tiptoes toward the doorway to the inner room and is about to slip through the curtains.*]

HEDDA [*at the stove, without looking up*] Good morning.

TESMAN [*turns*] Hedda! [*Approaching her*] But what on earth—! You're up so early? Uh?

HEDDA Yes, I'm up quite early today.

TESMAN And I was so sure you were still in bed sleeping. Isn't that something, Hedda!

HEDDA Not so loud. Mrs. Elvsted's resting in my room.

TESMAN Was Mrs. Elvsted here all night?

HEDDA Well, no one returned to take her home.

TESMAN No, I guess that's right.

HEDDA [*shuts the door to the stove and gets up*] So—did you enjoy your party?

TESMAN Were you worried about me? Hm?

HEDDA No, that never occurred to me. I just asked if you'd had a good time.

TESMAN Oh yes, I really did, for once. But more at the beginning, I'd say—when Eilert read to me out of his book. We got there more than an hour too soon—imagine! And Brack had so much to get ready. But then Eilert read to me.

HEDDA [*sitting at the right-hand side of the table*] Well? Tell me about it—

TESMAN [*sitting on a footstool by the stove*] Really, Hedda—you can't imagine what a book that's going to be! I do believe it's one of the most remarkable things ever written. Just think!

HEDDA Yes, yes, I don't care about that—

TESMAN But I have to make a confession, Hedda. When he'd finished reading—I had such a nasty feeling—

HEDDA Nasty?

TESMAN I found myself envying Eilert, that he was able to write such a book. Can you imagine, Hedda!

HEDDA Oh yes, I can imagine!

TESMAN And then how sad to see—that with all his gifts—he's still quite irreclaimable.

HEDDA Don't you mean that he has more courage to live than the others?

TESMAN Good Lord, no—I mean, he simply can't take his pleasures in moderation.

HEDDA Well, what happened then—at the end?

TESMAN I suppose I'd have to say it turned into an orgy, Hedda.

HEDDA Were there vine leaves in his hair?

TESMAN Vine leaves? Not that I noticed. But he gave a long, muddled speech in honor of the woman who'd inspired his work. Yes, that was his phrase for it.

HEDDA Did he give her name?

TESMAN No, he didn't. But it seems to me it has to be Mrs. Elvsted. Wait and see!

HEDDA Oh? Where did you leave him?

TESMAN On the way here. We broke up—the last of us—all together. And Brack came along with us too, to get a little fresh air. And then we did want to make sure that Eilert got home safe. Because he really had a load on, you know.

HEDDA He must have.

TESMAN But here's the curious part of it, Hedda. Or perhaps I should say, the distressing part. Oh, I'm almost ashamed to speak of it—for Eilert's sake—

HEDDA Yes, go on—

TESMAN Well, as we were walking toward town, you see, I happened to drop back a little behind the others. Only for a minute or two—you follow me?

HEDDA Yes, yes, so—?

TESMAN And then when I was catching up with the rest of them, what do you think I found on the sidewalk? Uh?

HEDDA Oh, how should I know!

TESMAN You mustn't breathe a word to anyone, Hedda—you hear me? Promise me that, for Eilert's sake. [*Takes a manila envelope out of his coat pocket.*] Just think—I found this.

HEDDA Isn't that what he had with him yesterday?

TESMAN That's right. It's the whole of his precious, irreplaceable manuscript. And he went and lost it—without even noticing. Can you imagine, Hedda! How distressing—

HEDDA But why didn't you give it right back to him?

TESMAN No, I didn't dare do that—in the state he was in—

HEDDA And you didn't tell any of the others you'd found it?

TESMAN Of course not. I'd never do that, you know—for Eilert's sake.

HEDDA Then there's no one who knows you have Eilert Løvborg's manuscript?

TESMAN No. And no one must ever know, either.

HEDDA What did you say to him afterwards?

TESMAN I had no chance at all to speak with him. As soon as we reached the edge of town, he and a couple of others got away from us and disappeared. Imagine!

HEDDA Oh? I expect they saw him home.

TESMAN Yes, they probably did, I suppose. And also Brack went home.

HEDDA And where've you been carrying on since then?

TESMAM Well, I and some of the others—we were invited up by one of the fellows and had morning coffee at his place. Or a post-midnight snack, maybe—uh? But as soon as I've had a little rest—and given poor Eilert time to sleep it off, then I've got to take this back to him.

HEDDA [*reaching out for the envelope*] No—don't give it back! Not yet, I mean. Let me read it first.

TESMAN Hedda dearest, no. My Lord, I can't do that.

HEDDA You can't?

TESMAN No. Why, you can just imagine the anguish he'll feel when he wakes up and misses the manuscript. He hasn't any copy of it, you know. He told me that himself.

HEDDA [*looks searchingly at him*] Can't such a work be rewritten? I mean, over again?

TESMAN Oh, I don't see how it could. Because the inspiration, you know—

HEDDA Yes, yes—that's the thing, I suppose. [*Casually*] Oh, by the way—there's a letter for you.

TESMAN No, really—?

HEDDA [*handing it to him*] It came early this morning.

TESMAN Dear, from Aunt Julie! What could that be? [*Sets the envelope on the other taboret, opens the letter, skims through it, and springs to his feet.*] Oh, Hedda—she says poor Auntie Rina's dying!

HEDDA It's no more than we've been expecting.

TESMAN And if I want to see her one last time, I've got to hurry. I'll have to hop right over.

HEDDA [*suppressing a smile*] Hop?

TESMAN Oh, Hedda dearest, if you could only bring yourself to come with me! Think of it!

HEDDA [*rises and dismisses the thought wearily*] No, no, don't ask me to do such things. I don't want to look on sickness and death. I want to be free of everything ugly.

TESMAN Yes, all right, then— [*Dashing about*] My hat—? My overcoat—? Oh, in the hall—I do hope I'm not there too late, Hedda! Hm?

HEDDA Oh, if you just hop to it—

[BERTA *appears at the hall door.*]

BERTA Judge Brack's outside, asking if he might stop in.

TESMAN At a time like this! No, I can't possibly see him now.

HEDDA But I can. [*To* BERTA] Ask the judge to come in.

[BERTA *goes out.*]

HEDDA [*quickly, in a whisper*] Tesman, the manuscript! [*She snatches it from the taboret.*]

TESMAN Yes, give it here!

HEDDA No, no, I'll keep it till you're back.

[*She moves over to the writing table and slips it in the bookcase.* TESMAN *stands flustered, unable to get his gloves on.* BRACK *enters from the hall.*]

HEDDA Well, aren't you the early bird.

BRACK Yes, wouldn't you say so? [*To* TESMAN] Are you off and away too?

TESMAN Yes, I absolutely have to get over to my aunts'. Just think—the invalid one, she's dying.

BRACK Good Lord, she is? But then you mustn't let me detain you. Not at a moment like this—

TESMAN Yes, I really must run— Good-bye! Good-bye!

[*He goes hurriedly out the hall door.*]

HEDDA It would seem you had quite a time of it last night, Judge.

BRACK I've not been out of my clothes yet, Mrs. Hedda.

HEDDA Not you, either?

BRACK No, as you can see. But what's Tesman been telling you about our night's adventures?

HEDDA Oh, some tedious tale. Something about stopping up somewhere for coffee.

BRACK Yes, I know all about the coffee party. Eilert Løvborg wasn't with them, I expect?

HEDDA No, they'd already taken him home.

BRACK Tesman, as well.

HEDDA No, but he said some others had.

BRACK [*smiles*] George Tesman is really a simple soul, Mrs. Hedda.

HEDDA God knows he's that. But was there something else that went on?

BRACK Oh, you might say so.

HEDDA Well, now! Let's sit down, Judge; you'll talk more easily then.

[*She sits at the left-hand side of the table, with* BRACK *at the long side, near her.*]

HEDDA So?

BRACK I had particular reasons for keeping track of my guests—or, I should say, certain of my guests, last night.

HEDDA And among them Eilert Løvborg, perhaps?

BRACK To be frank—yes.

HEDDA Now you really have me curious—

BRACK You know where he and a couple of the others spent the rest of the night, Mrs. Hedda?

HEDDA Tell me—if it's fit to be told.

BRACK Oh, it's very much fit to be told. Well, it seems they showed up at a quite animated soirée.

HEDDA Of the lively sort.

BRACK Of the liveliest.

HEDDA Do go on, Judge—

BRACK Løvborg, and the others also, had advance invitations. I knew all about it. But Løvborg had begged off, because now, of course, he was supposed to have become a new man, as you know.

HEDDA Up at the Elvsteds', yes. But he went anyway?

BRACK Well, you see, Mrs. Hedda—unfortunately the spirit moved him up at my place last evening—

HEDDA Yes, I hear that he *was* inspired there.

BRACK To a very powerful degree, I'd say. Well, so his mind turned to other things, that's clear. We males, sad to say—we're not always so true to principle as we ought to be.

HEDDA Oh, I'm sure you're an exception, Judge. But what about Løvborg—?

BRACK Well, to cut it short—the result was that he wound up in Mademoiselle Diana's parlors.

HEDDA Mademoiselle Diana's?

BRACK It was Mademoiselle Diana who was holding the soirée. For a select circle of lady friends and admirers.

HEDDA Is she a redhaired woman?

BRACK Precisely.

HEDDA Sort of a—singer?

BRACK Oh yes—she's that too. And also a mighty huntress—of men,[5] Mrs. Hedda. You've undoubtedly heard about her. Løvborg was one of her ruling favorites—back there in his palmy days.

HEDDA And how did all this end?

BRACK Less amicably, it seems. She gave him a most tender welcoming, with open arms, but before long she'd taken to fists.

HEDDA Against Løvborg?

BRACK That's right. He accused her or her friends of having robbed him. He claimed that his wallet was missing—along with some other things. In short, he must have made a frightful scene.

HEDDA And what did it come to?

BRACK It came to a regular free-for-all, the men and the women both. Luckily the police finally got there.

HEDDA The police too?

BRACK Yes. But it's likely to prove an expensive little romp for Eilert Løvborg. That crazy fool.

HEDDA So?

BRACK He apparently made violent resistance. Struck one of the officers on the side of the head and ripped his coat. So they took him along to the station house.

HEDDA Where did you hear all this?

BRACK From the police themselves.

HEDDA [*gazing straight ahead*] So that's how it went. Then he had no vine leaves in his hair.

BRACK Vine leaves, Mrs. Hedda?

HEDDA [*changing her tone*] But tell me, Judge—just why do you go around like this, spying on Eilert Løvborg?

BRACK In the first place, it's hardly a matter of no concern to me, if it's brought out during the investigation that he'd come direct from my house.

HEDDA There'll be an investigation—?

BRACK Naturally. Anyway, that takes care of itself. But I felt that as a friend of the family I owed you and Tesman a full account of his nocturnal exploits.

HEDDA Why, exactly?

BRACK Well, because I have a strong suspicion that he'll try to use you as a kind of screen.

HEDDA Oh, how could you ever think such a thing!

BRACK Good Lord—we're really not blind, Mrs. Hedda. You'll see! This Mrs. Elvsted, she won't be going home now so quickly.

HEDDA Well, even supposing there were something between them, there are plenty of other places where they could meet.

BRACK Not one single home. From now on, every decent house will be closed to Eilert Løvborg.

5. Diana was the Roman virgin goddess of the hunt.

HEDDA So mine ought to be too, is that what you mean?

BRACK Yes. I'll admit I'd find it more than annoying if that gentleman were to have free access here. If he came like an intruder, an irrelevancy, forcing his way into—

HEDDA Into the triangle?

BRACK Precisely. It would almost be like turning me out of my home.

HEDDA [*looks at him with a smile*] I see. The one cock of the walk—that's what you want to be.

BRACK [*nodding slowly and lowering his voice*] Yes, that's what I want to be. And that's what I'll fight for—with every means at my disposal.

HEDDA [*her smile vanishing*] You can be a dangerous person, can't you—in a tight corner.

BRACK Do you think so?

HEDDA Yes, now I'm beginning to think so. And I'm thoroughly grateful—that you have no kind of hold over me.

BRACK [*with an ambiguous laugh*] Ah, yes, Mrs. Hedda—perhaps you're right about that. If I had, then who knows just what I might do?

HEDDA Now you listen here, Judge! That sounds too much like a threat.

BRACK [*rising*] Oh, nothing of the kind! A triangle, after all—is best fortified and defended by volunteers.

HEDDA There we're agreed.

BRACK Well, now that I've said all I have to say, I'd better get back to town. Good-bye, Mrs. Hedda. [*He goes toward the glass door.*]

HEDDA [*rising*] Are you going through the garden?

BRACK Yes, I find it's shorter.

HEDDA Yes, and then it's the back way, too.

BRACK How true. I have nothing against back ways. At certain times they can be rather piquant.

HEDDA You mean, when somebody's sharpshooting?

BRACK [*in the doorway, laughing*] Oh, people don't shoot their tame roosters!

HEDDA [*also laughing*] I guess not. Not when there's only one—

[*Still laughing, they nod good-bye to each other. He goes. She shuts the door after him, then stands for a moment, quite serious, looking out. She then goes over and glances through the curtains to the inner room. Moves to the writing table, takes* LØVBORG'*s envelope from the bookcase, and is about to page through it, when* BERTA'*s voice is heard loudly in the hall.* HEDDA *turns and listens. She hurriedly locks the envelope in the drawer and lays the key on the desk.* EILERT LØVBORG, *with his overcoat on and his hat in his hand, throws open the hall door. He looks confused and excited.*]

LØVBORG [*turned toward the hall*] And I'm telling you, I have to go in! I will, you hear me! [*He shuts the door, turns, sees* HEDDA, *immediately gains control of himself and bows.*]

HEDDA [*at the writing table*] Well, Mr. Løvborg, it's late to call for Thea.

LØVBORG Or rather early to call on you. You must forgive me.

HEDDA How did you know she was still with me?

LØVBORG. They said at her lodgings that she'd been out all night.

HEDDA [*goes to the center table*] Did you notice anything in their faces when they said that?

LØVBORG [*looking at her inquiringly*] Notice anything?

HEDDA I mean, did it look like they had their own thoughts on the matter?

LØVBORG [*suddenly understanding*] Oh yes, that's true! I'm dragging her down with me! Actually, I didn't notice anything. Tesman—I don't suppose he's up yet?

HEDDA No, I don't think so.

LØVBORG When did he get in?

HEDDA Very late.

LØVBORG Did he tell you anything?

HEDDA Well, I heard you'd had a high time of it out at Judge Brack's.

LØVBORG Anything else?

HEDDA No, I don't think so. As a matter of fact, I was terrible sleepy—

[MRS. ELVSTED *comes in through the curtains to the inner room.*]

MRS. ELVSTED [*running toward him*] Oh, Eilert! At last—!

LØVBORG Yes, at last. And too late.

MRS. ELVSTED [*looking anxiously at him*] What's too late?

LØVBORG Everything's too late now. It's over with me.

MRS. ELVSTED Oh no, no—don't say that!

LØVBORG You'll say the same thing when you've heard—

MRS. ELVSTED I won't hear anything!

HEDDA Maybe you'd prefer to talk with her alone. I can leave.

LØVBORG No, stay—you too. Please.

MRS. ELVSTED But I tell you, I don't want to hear anything!

LØVBORG It's nothing about last night.

MRS. ELVSTED What is it, then—?

LØVBORG It's simply this, that from now on, we separate.

MRS. ELVSTED Separate!

HEDDA [*involuntarily*] I knew it!

LØVBORG Because I have no more use for you, Thea.

MRS. ELVSTED And you can stand there and say that! No more use for me! Then I'm not going to help you now, as I have? We're not going to go on working together?

LØVBORG I have no plans for any more work.

MRS. ELVSTED [*in desperation*] Then what will I do with my life?

LØVBORG You must try to go on living as if you'd never known me.

MRS. ELVSTED But I can't do that!

LØVBORG You must try to, Thea. You'll have to go home again—

MRS. ELVSTED [*in a fury of protest*] Never! No! Where you are, that's where I want to be! I won't be driven away like this! I'm going to stay right here—and be together with you when the book comes out.

HEDDA [*in a tense whisper*] Ah, yes—the book!

LØVBORG [*looks at her*] My book and Thea's—for that's what it is.

MRS. ELVSTED Yes, that's what I feel it is. And that's why I have the right, as well, to be with you when it comes out. I want to see you covered with honor and respect again. And the joy—I want to share the joy of it with you too.

LØVBORG Thea—our book's never coming out.

HEDDA Ah!

MRS. ELVSTED Never coming out!

LØVBORG *Can* never come out.

MRS. ELVSTED [*with anguished foreboding*] Eilert—what have you done with the manuscript?

HEDDA [*watching him intently*] Yes, the manuscript—?

MRS. ELVSTED Where is it!

LØVBORG Oh, Thea—don't ask me that.

MRS. ELVSTED Yes, yes, I have to know. I've got a right to know, this minute!

LØVBORG The manuscript—well, you see—I tore the manuscript into a thousand pieces.

MRS. ELVSTED [*screams*] Oh no, no—!

HEDDA [*involuntarily*] But that just isn't—!

LØVBORG [*looks at her*] Isn't so, you think?

HEDDA [*composing herself*] All right. Of course; if you say it yourself. But it sounds so incredible—

LØVBORG It's true, all the same.

MRS. ELVSTED [*wringing her hands*] Oh, God—oh, God, Hedda—to tear his own work to bits!

LØVBORG I've torn my own life to bits. So why not tear up my life's work as well—

MRS. ELVSTED And you did this thing last night!

LØVBORG Yes, you heard me. In a thousand pieces. And scattered them into the fjord. Far out. At least there, there's clean salt water. Let them drift out to sea—drift with the tide and the wind. And after a while, they'll sink. Deeper and deeper. As I will, Thea.

MRS. ELVSTED Do you know, Eilert, this thing you've done with the book—for the rest of my life it will seem to me as if you'd killed a little child.

LØVBORG You're right. It was like murdering a child.

MRS. ELVSTED But how could you do it—! It was my child too.

HEDDA [*almost inaudible*] Ah, the child—

MRS. ELVSTED [*breathes heavily*] Then it *is* all over. Yes, yes, I'm going now, Hedda.

HEDDA But you're not leaving town, are you?

MRS. ELVSTED Oh, I don't know myself what I'll do. Everything's dark for me now. [*She goes out the hall door.*]

HEDDA [*stands waiting a moment*] You're not going to take her home, then, Mr. Løvborg?

LØVBORG I? Through the streets? So people could see that she'd been with me?

HEDDA I don't know what else may have happened last night. But is it so completely irredeemable?

LØVBORG It won't just end with last night—I know that well enough. But the thing is, I've lost all desire for that kind of life. I don't want to start it again, not now. It's the courage and daring for life—that's what she's broken in me.

HEDDA [*staring straight ahead*] To think that pretty little fool could have a man's fate in her hands. [*Looks at him.*] But still, how could you treat her so heartlessly?

LØVBORG Oh, don't say it was heartless!

HEDDA To go ahead and destroy what's filled her whole being for months and years! That's not heartless?

LØVBORG To you, Hedda—I can tell the truth.

HEDDA The truth?

LØVBORG Promise me first—give me your word that what I tell you now, you'll never let Thea know.

HEDDA You have my word.

LØVBORG Good. I can tell you, then, that what I said here just now isn't true.

HEDDA About the manuscript?

LØVBORG Yes. I didn't tear it up—or throw it in the fjord.

HEDDA No, but—where is it, then?

LØVBORG I've destroyed it all the same, Hedda. Utterly destroyed it.

HEDDA I don't understand.

LØVBORG Thea said that what I've done, for her was like killing a child.

HEDDA Yes—that's what she said.

LØVBORG But killing his child—that's not the worst thing a father can do.

HEDDA *That's* not the worst?

LØVBORG No. I wanted to spare Thea the worst.

HEDDA And what's that—the worst?

LØVBORG Suppose now, Hedda, that a man—in the early morning hours, say—after a wild, drunken night, comes home to his child's mother and says: "Listen—I've been out to this place and that—here and there. And I had our child with me. In this place and that. And I lost the child. Just lost it. God only knows what hands it's come into. Or who's got hold of it."

HEDDA Well—but when all's said and done—it was only a book—

LØVBORG Thea's pure soul was in that book.

HEDDA Yes, I understand.

LØVBORG Well, then you can understand that for her and me there's no future possible any more.

HEDDA What do you intend to do?

LØVBORG Nothing. Just put an end to it all. The sooner the better.

HEDDA [*coming a step closer*] Eilert Løvborg—listen to me. Couldn't you arrange that—that it's done beautifully?

LØVBORG Beautifully? [*Smiles.*] With vine leaves in my hair, as you used to dream in the old days—

HEDDA No. I don't believe in vine leaves any more. But beautifully, all the same. For this once—! Good-bye! You must go now—and never come here again.

LØVBORG Good-bye, then. And give my best to George Tesman. [*He turns to leave.*]

HEDDA No. wait. I want you to have a souvenir from me.

[*She goes to the writing desk and opens the drawer and the pistol case, then comes back to* LØVBORG *with one of the pistols.*]

LØVBORG [*looks at her*] That? Is that the souvenir?

HEDDA [*nods slowly*] Do you recognize it? It was aimed at you once.

LØVBORG You should have used it then.

HEDDA Here! Use it now.

LØVBORG [*puts the pistol in his breast pocket*] Thanks.

HEDDA And beautifully, Eilert Løvborg. Promise me that!

LØVBORG Good-bye, Hedda Gabler.

[*He goes out the hall door.* HEDDA *listens a moment at the door. Then she goes over to the writing table, takes out the envelope with the manuscript, glances inside, pulls some of the sheets half out and looks at them. She then goes over to the armchair by the stove and sits, with the envelope in her lap. After a moment, she opens the stove door, then brings out the manuscript.*]

HEDDA [*throwing some of the sheets into the fire and whispering to herself*] Now I'm burning your child, Thea! You, with your curly hair! [*Throwing another sheaf in the stove*] Your child and Eilert Løvborg's. [*Throwing in the rest*] Now I'm burning—I'm burning the child.

Act 4

[*The same rooms at the* TESMANS'. *It is evening. The drawing room is in darkness. The inner room is lit by the hanging lamp over the table. The curtains are drawn across the glass door.* HEDDA, *dressed in black, is pacing back and forth in the dark room. She then enters the inner room, moving out of sight toward the left. Several chords are heard on the piano. She comes in view again, returning into the drawing room.* BERTA *enters from the right through the inner room with a lighted lamp, which she puts on the table in front of the settee in the drawing room. Her eyes are red from crying, and she has black ribbons on her cap.*[6] *She goes quietly and discreetly out to the right.* HEDDA *moves to the glass door, lifts the curtains aside slightly, and gazes out into the darkness.*

Shortly after, MISS TESMAN, *in mourning, with a hat and veil, comes in from the hall.* HEDDA *goes toward her, extending her hand.*]

MISS TESMAN Well, Hedda, here I am, all dressed in mourning. My poor sister's ordeal is finally over.

HEDDA As you see, I've already heard. Tesman sent me a note.

MISS TESMAN Yes, he promised he would. But all the same I thought that, to Hedda—here in the house of life—I ought to bear the news of death myself.

HEDDA That was very kind of you.

MISS TESMAN Ah, Rina ought not to have passed on just now. This is no time for grief in Hedda's house.

HEDDA [*changing the subject*] She had a peaceful death, then, Miss Tesman?

MISS TESMAN Oh, she went so calmly, so beautifully. And so inexpressibly happy that she could see George once again. And say good-bye to him properly. Is it possible that he's still not home?

HEDDA No, he wrote that I shouldn't expect him too early. But won't you sit down?

MISS TESMAN No, thank you, my dear—blessed Hedda. I'd love to, but I have so little time. I want to see her dressed and made ready as best as I can. She should go to her grave looking her finest.

HEDDA Can't I help you with something?

MISS TESMAN Oh, you mustn't think of it. This is nothing for Hedda Tesman to put her hands to. Or let her thoughts dwell on, either. Not at a time like this, no.

HEDDA Ah, thoughts—they're not so easy to control—

MISS TESMAN [*continuing*] Well, there's life for you. At my house now we'll be sewing a shroud for Rina. And here, too, there'll be sewing soon, I imagine. But a far different kind, praise God!

[GEORGE TESMAN *enters from the hall.*]

6. Worn to signify mourning.

HEDDA Well, at last! It's about time.

TESMAN Are you here, Aunt Julie? With Hedda? Think of that!

MISS TESMAN I was just this minute leaving, dear boy. Well, did you get done all you promised you would?

TESMAN No, I'm really afraid I've forgotten half. I'll have to run over and see you tomorrow. My brain's completely in a whirl today. I can't keep my thoughts together.

MISS TESMAN But George dear, you mustn't take it that way.

TESMAN Oh? Well, how should I, then?

MISS TESMAN You should rejoice in your grief. Rejoice in everything that's happened, as I do.

TESMAN Oh yes, of course. You're thinking of Auntie Rina.

HEDDA It's going to be lonely for you, Miss Tesman.

MISS TESMAN For the first few days, yes. But it won't be for long, I hope. I won't let dear Rina's little room stand empty.

TESMAN No? Who would you want to have in it? Hm?

MISS TESMAN Oh, there's always some poor invalid in need of care and attention.

HEDDA Would you really take another burden like that on yourself?

MISS TESMAN Burden! Mercy on you, child—it's been no burden for me.

HEDDA But now, with a stranger—

MISS TESMAN Oh, you soon make friends with an invalid. And I do so much need someone to live for—I, too. Well, thank God, in this house as well, there soon ought to be work that an old aunt can turn her hand to.

HEDDA Oh, forget about us—

TESMAN Yes, think how pleasant it could be for the three of us if—

HEDDA If—?

TESMAN [*uneasily*] Oh, nothing. It'll all take care of itself. Let's hope so. Uh?

MISS TESMAN Ah, yes. Well, I expect you two have things to talk about. [*Smiles.*] And perhaps Hedda has something to tell you, George. Good-bye. I'll have to get home now to Rina. [*Turning at the door*] Goodness me, how strange! Now Rina's both with me and with poor dear Jochum as well.

TESMAN Yes, imagine that, Aunt Julie! Hm?

[MISS TESMAN *goes out the hall door.*]

HEDDA [*follows* TESMAN *with a cold, probing look*] I almost think you feel this death more than she.

TESMAN Oh, it's not just Auntie Rina's death. It's Eilert who has me worried.

HEDDA [*quickly*] Any news about him?

TESMAN I stopped up at his place this afternoon, thinking to tell him that the manuscript was safe.

HEDDA Well? Didn't you see him then?

TESMAN No, he wasn't home. But afterward I met Mrs. Elvsted, and she said he'd been here early this morning.

HEDDA Yes, right after you left.

TESMAN And apparently he said he'd torn his manuscript up. Uh?

HEDDA Yes, he claimed that he had.

TESMAN But good Lord, then he must have been completely demented! Well, then I guess you didn't dare give it back to him, Hedda, did you?

HEDDA No, he didn't get it.

TESMAN But you did tell him we had it, I suppose?

HEDDA No. [*Quickly*] Did you tell Mrs. Elvsted anything?

TESMAN No, I thought I'd better not. But you should have said something to him. Just think, if he goes off in desperation and does himself some harm! Give me the manuscript, Hedda! I'm taking it back to him right away. Where do you have it?

HEDDA [*cold and impassive, leaning against the armchair*] I don't have it anymore.

TESMAN You don't have it! What on earth do you mean by that?

HEDDA I burned it—the whole thing.

TESMAN [*with a start of terror*] Burned it! Burned Eilert Løvborg's manuscript!

HEDDA Stop shouting. The maid could hear you.

TESMAN Burned it! But my God in heaven—! No, no, no—that's impossible!

HEDDA Yes, but it's true, all the same.

TESMAN But do you realize what you've done, Hedda! It's illegal disposition of lost property. Just think! Yes, you can ask Judge Brack; he'll tell you.

HEDDA It would be wiser not mentioning this—either to the judge or to anyone else.

TESMAN But how could you go and do such an incredible thing! Whatever put it into your head? What got into you, anyway? Answer me! Well?

HEDDA [*suppressing an almost imperceptible smile*] I did it for your sake, George.

TESMAN For my sake!

HEDDA When you came home this morning and told about how he'd read to you—

TESMAN Yes, yes, then what?

HEDDA Then you confessed that you envied him this book.

TESMAN Good Lord, I didn't mean it literally.

HEDDA Never mind. I still couldn't bear the thought that anyone should eclipse you.

TESMAN [*in an outburst of mingled doubt and joy*] Hedda—is this true, what you say? Yes, but—but—I never dreamed you could show your love like this. Imagine!

HEDDA Well, then it's best you know that—that I'm going to— [*Impatiently, breaking off*] No, no—you ask your Aunt Julie. She's the one who can tell you.

TESMAN Oh, I'm beginning to understand you, Hedda! [*Claps his hands together.*] Good heavens, no! Is it actually *that?* Can it be? Uh?

HEDDA Don't shout so. The maid can hear you.

TESMAN The maid! Oh, Hedda, you're priceless, really! The maid—but that's Berta! Why, I'll go out and tell her myself.

HEDDA [*clenching her fists in despair*] Oh, I'll die—I'll die of all this!

TESMAN Of what, Hedda? Uh?

HEDDA Of all these—absurdities—George.

TESMAN Absurdities? What's absurd about my being so happy? Well, all right—I guess there's no point in my saying anything to Berta.

HEDDA Oh, go ahead—why not that, too?

TESMAN No, no, not yet. But Aunt Julie will have to hear. And then, that you've started to call me George, too! Imagine! Oh, Aunt Julie will be so glad—so glad!

HEDDA When she hears that I burned Eilert Løvborg's book—for your sake?

TESMAN Well, as far as that goes—this thing with the book—of course, no one's to know about that. But that you have a love that burns for me, Hedda—Aunt Julie can certainly share in that! You know, I wonder, really, if things such as this are common among young wives? Hm?

HEDDA I think you should ask Aunt Julie about that, too.

TESMAN Yes, I'll do it definitely, when I have the chance. [*Again looks distressed and preoccupied.*] No, but—but the manuscript! My Lord, it's just terrible to think about poor Eilert.

[MRS. ELVSTED, *dressed as on her first visit, with hat and coat, comes in the hall door.*]

MRS. ELVSTED [*greets them hurriedly and speaks in agitation*] Oh, Hedda dear, don't be annoyed that I'm back again.

HEDDA Has something happened, Thea?

TESMAN Something with Eilert Løvborg? Uh?

MRS. ELVSTED Yes, I'm so terribly afraid he's met with an accident.

HEDDA [*seizing her arm*] Ah—you think so!

TESMAN But, Mrs. Elvsted, where did you get that idea?

MRS. ELVSTED Well, because I heard them speaking of him at the boardinghouse, just as I came in. Oh, there are the most incredible rumors about him in town today.

TESMAN Yes, you know, I heard them too! And yet I could swear that he went right home to bed last night. Imagine!

HEDDA Well—what did they say at the boardinghouse?

MRS. ELVSTED Oh, I couldn't get anything clearly. They either didn't know much themselves, or else—They stopped talking when they saw me. And I didn't dare to ask.

TESMAN [*restlessly moving about*] Let's hope—let's hope you misunderstood them, Mrs. Elvsted!

MRS. ELVSTED No, no, I'm sure they were talking of him. And then I heard them say something or other about the hospital, or—

TESMAN The hospital!

HEDDA No—but that's impossible!

MRS. ELVSTED Oh, I'm so deathly afraid for him now. And later I went up to his lodging to ask about him.

HEDDA But was that very wise to do, Thea?

MRS. ELVSTED What else could I do? I couldn't bear the uncertainty any longer.

TESMAN But didn't you find him there either? Hm?

MRS. ELVSTED No. And no one had any word of him. He hadn't been in since yesterday afternoon, they said.

TESMAN Yesterday! Imagine them saying that!

MRS. ELVSTED I think there can only be one reason—something terrible must have happened to him!

TESMAN Hedda dear—suppose I went over and made a few inquiries—?

HEDDA No, no—don't you get mixed up in this business.

[JUDGE BRACK, *with hat in hand, enters from the hall,* BERTA *letting him in and shutting the door after him. He looks grave and bows silently.*]

TESMAN Oh, is that you, Judge? Uh?

BRACK Yes, it's imperative that I see you this evening.

TESMAN I can see that you've heard the news from Aunt Julie.

BRACK Among other things, yes.

TESMAN It's sad, isn't it? Uh?

BRACK Well, my dear Tesman, that depends on how you look at it.

TESMAN [*eyes him doubtfully*] Has anything else happened?

BRACK Yes, as a matter of fact.

HEDDA [*intently*] Something distressing, Judge?

BRACK Again, that depends on how you look at it, Mrs. Tesman.

MRS. ELVSTED [*in an uncontrollable outburst*] Oh, it's something about Eilert Løvborg!

BRACK [*glancing at her*] Now how did you hit upon that, Mrs. Elvsted? Have you, perhaps, heard something already—?

MRS. ELVSTED [*in confusion*] No, no, nothing like that—but—

TESMAN Oh, for heaven's sake, tell us!

BRACK [*with a shrug*] Well—I'm sorry, but—Eilert Løvborg's been taken to the hospital. He's dying.

MRS. ELVSTED [*crying out*] Oh, God, oh, God—!

TESMAN To the hospital! And dying!

HEDDA [*involuntarily*] All so soon—!

MRS. ELVSTED [*wailing*] And we parted in anger, Hedda!

HEDDA [*in a whisper*] Thea—be careful, Thea!

MRS. ELVSTED [*ignoring her*] I have to see him! I have to see him alive!

BRACK No use, Mrs. Elvsted. No one's allowed in to see him.

MRS. ELVSTED Oh, but tell me, at least, what happened to him! What is it?

TESMAN Don't tell me he tried to—! Uh?

HEDDA Yes, he did, I'm sure of it.

TESMAN Hedda—how can you say—!

BRACK [*his eyes steadily on her*] Unhappily, you've guessed exactly right, Mrs. Tesman.

MRS. ELVSTED Oh, how horrible!

TESMAN Did it himself! Imagine!

HEDDA Shot himself!

BRACK Again, exactly right, Mrs. Tesman.

MRS. ELVSTED [*trying to control herself*] When did it happen, Mr. Brack?

BRACK This afternoon. Between three and four.

TESMAN But good Lord—where did he do it, then? Hm?

BRACK [*hesitating slightly*] Where? Why—in his room, I suppose.

MRS. ELVSTED No, that can't be right. I was there between six and seven.

BRACK Well, somewhere else, then. I don't know exactly. I only know he was found like that. Shot—in the chest.

MRS. ELVSTED What a horrible thought! That he should end that way!

HEDDA [*to* BRACK] In the chest, you say.

BRACK Yes—I told you.

HEDDA Not the temple?

BRACK In the chest, Mrs. Tesman.

HEDDA Well—well, the chest is just as good.

BRACK Why, Mrs. Tesman?

HEDDA [*evasively*] Oh, nothing—never mind.

TESMAN And the wound is critical, you say? Uh?

BRACK The wound is absolutely fatal. Most likely, it's over already.

MRS. ELVSTED Yes, yes, I can feel that it is! It's over! All over! Oh, Hedda—!

TESMAN But tell me now—how did you learn about this?

BRACK [*brusquely*] One of the police. Someone I had to talk to.

HEDDA [*in a clear, bold voice*] At last, something truly done!

TESMAN [*shocked*] My God, what are you saying, Hedda!

HEDDA I'm saying there's beauty in all this.

BRACK Hm, Mrs. Tesman—

TESMAN Beauty! What an idea!

MRS. ELVSTED Oh, Hedda, how can you talk about beauty in such a thing?

HEDDA Eilert Løvborg's settled accounts with himself. He's had the courage to do what—what had to be done.

MRS. ELVSTED Don't you believe it! It never happened like that. When he did this, he was in a delirium!

TESMAN In despair, you mean.

HEDDA No, he wasn't. I'm certain of that.

MRS. ELVSTED But he was! In delirium! The way he was when he tore up our book.

BRACK [*startled*] The book? His manuscript, you mean? He tore it up?

MRS. ELVSTED Yes. Last night.

TESMAN [*in a low whisper*] Oh, Hedda, we'll never come clear of all this.

BRACK Hm, that's very strange.

TESMAN [*walking about the room*] To think Eilert could be gone like that! And then not to have left behind the one thing that could have made his name live on.

MRS. ELVSTED Oh, if it could only be put together again!

TESMAN Yes, imagine if that were possible! I don't know what I wouldn't give—

MRS. ELVSTED Perhaps it can, Mr. Tesman.

TESMAN What do you mean?

MRS. ELVSTED [*searching in the pockets of her dress*] Look here. I've kept all these notes that he used to dictate from.

HEDDA [*coming a step closer*] Ah—!

TESMAN You've kept them, Mrs. Elvsted! Uh?

MRS. ELVSTED Yes, here they are. I took them along when I left home. And they've stayed right here in my pocket—

TESMAN Oh, let me look!

MRS. ELVSTED [*hands him a sheaf of small papers*] But they're in such a mess. All mixed up.

TESMAN But just think, if we could decipher them, even so! Maybe the two of us could help each other—

MRS. ELVSTED Oh yes! At least, we could try—

TESMAN We can do it! We *must!* I'll give my whole life to this!

HEDDA You, George? Your life?

TESMAN Yes. Or, let's say, all the time I can spare. My own research will have to wait. You can understand, Hedda. Hm! It's something I owe to Eilert's memory.

HEDDA Perhaps.

TESMAN And so, my dear Mrs. Elvsted, let's pull ourselves together. Good Lord, there's no use brooding over what's gone by. Uh? We must try to compose our thoughts as much as we can, in order that—

MRS. ELVSTED Yes, yes, Mr. Tesman, I'll do the best I can.

TESMAN Come on, then. Let's look over these notes right away. Where shall we sit? Here? No, in there, in the back room. Excuse us, Judge. You come with me, Mrs. Elvsted.

MRS. ELVSTED Dear God—if only we can do this!

[TESMAN *and* MRS. ELVSTED *go into the inner room. She takes off her hat and coat. They both sit at the table under the hanging lamp and become totally immersed in examining the papers.* HEDDA *goes toward the stove and sits in the armchair. After a moment,* BRACK *goes over by her.*]

HEDDA [*her voice lowered*] Ah, Judge—what a liberation it is, this act of Eilert Løvborg's.

BRACK Liberation, Mrs. Hedda? Well, yes, for him; you could certainly say he's been liberated—

HEDDA I mean for me. It's liberating to know that there can still actually be a free and courageous action in this world. Something that shimmers with spontaneous beauty.

BRACK [*smiling*] Hm—my dear Mrs. Hedda—

HEDDA Oh, I already know what you're going to say. Because you're a kind of specialist too, you know, just like— Oh, well!

BRACK [*looking fixedly at her*] Eilert Løvborg meant more to you than you're willing to admit, perhaps even to yourself. Or am I wrong about that?

HEDDA I won't answer that sort of question. I simply know that Eilert Løvborg's had the courage to live life after his own mind. And now—this last great act, filled with beauty! That he had the strength and the will to break away from the banquet of life—so young.

BRACK It grieves me, Mrs. Hedda—but I'm afraid I have to disburden you of this beautiful illusion.

HEDDA Illusion?

BRACK One that, in any case, you'd soon be deprived of.

HEDDA And what's that?

BRACK He didn't shoot himself—of his own free will.

HEDDA He didn't—!

BRACK No. This whole affair didn't go off quite the way I described it.

HEDDA [*in suspense*] You've hidden something? What is it?

BRACK For poor Mrs. Elvsted's sake, I did a little editing here and there.

HEDDA Where?

BRACK First, the fact that he's already dead.

HEDDA In the hospital?

BRACK Yes. Without regaining consciousness.

HEDDA What else did you hide?

BRACK That the incident didn't occur in his room.

HEDDA Well, that's rather unimportant.

BRACK Not entirely. Suppose I were to tell you that Eilert Løvborg was found shot in—in Mademoiselle Diana's boudoir.

HEDDA [*half rises, then sinks back again*] That's impossible, Judge! He wouldn't have gone there again today!

BRACK He was there this afternoon. He went there, demanding something he said they'd stolen from him. Kept raving about a lost child—

HEDDA Ah—so that was it—

BRACK I thought perhaps that might be his manuscript. But, I hear now, he destroyed that himself. So it must have been his wallet.

HEDDA I suppose so. Then, there—that's where they found him.

BRACK Yes, there. With a discharged pistol in his breast pocket. The bullet had wounded him fatally.

HEDDA In the chest—yes.

BRACK No—in the stomach—more or less.

HEDDA [*stares up at him with a look of revulsion*] That too! What is it, this—this curse—that everything I touch turns ridiculous and vile?

BRACK There's something else, Mrs. Hedda. Another ugly aspect to the case.

HEDDA What's that?

BRACK The pistol he was carrying—

HEDDA [*breathlessly*] Well! What about it!

BRACK He must have stolen it.

HEDDA [*springs up*] Stolen! That's not true! He didn't!

BRACK It seems impossible otherwise. He must have stolen it—shh!

[TESMAN *and* MRS. ELVSTED *have gotten up from the table in the inner room and come into the drawing room.*]

TESMAN [*with both hands full of papers*] Hedda dear—it's nearly impossible to see in there under that overhead lamp. You know?

HEDDA Yes, I know.

TESMAN Do you think it would be all right if we used your table for a while? Hm?

HEDDA Yes, I don't mind. [*Quickly*] Wait! No, let me clear it off first.

TESMAN Oh, don't bother, Hedda. There's plenty of room.

HEDDA No, no, let me just clear it off, can't you? I'll put all this in by the piano. There!

[*She has pulled out an object covered with sheet music from under the bookcase, adds more music to it, and carries the whole thing into the inner room and off left.* TESMAN *puts the scraps of paper on the writing table and moves the lamp over from the corner table. He and* MRS. ELVSTED *sit down and go on with their work.* HEDDA *comes back.*]

HEDDA [*behind* MRS. ELVSTED*'s chair, gently ruffling her hair*] Well, my sweet little Thea—how is it going with Eilert Løvborg's monument?

MRS. ELVSTED [*looking despondently up at her*] Oh, dear—it's going to be terribly hard to set these in order.

TESMAN It's got to be done. There's just no alternative. Besides, setting other people's papers in order—it's exactly what I can do best.

[HEDDA *goes over by the stove and sits on one of the taborets.* BRACK *stands over her, leaning on the armchair.*]

HEDDA [*whispering*] What did you say about the pistol?

BRACK [*softly*] That he must have stolen it.

HEDDA Why, necessarily, that?

BRACK Because every other explanation would seem impossible, Mrs. Hedda.

HEDDA I see.

BRACK [*glancing at her*] Of course, Eilert Løvborg was here this morning. Wasn't he?

HEDDA Yes.

BRACK Were you alone with him?

HEDDA Yes, briefly.

BRACK Did you leave the room while he was here?

HEDDA No.

BRACK Consider. You didn't leave, even for a moment.

HEDDA Well, yes, perhaps, just for a moment—into the hall.

BRACK And where did you have your pistol case?

HEDDA I had it put away in—

BRACK Yes, Mrs. Hedda?

HEDDA It was lying over there, on the writing table.

BRACK Have you looked since to see if both pistols are there?

HEDDA No.

BRACK No need to. I saw the pistol. Løvborg had it on him. I knew it immediately, from yesterday. And other days too.

HEDDA Do you have it, maybe?

BRACK No, the police have it.

HEDDA What will they do with it?

BRACK Try to trace it to the owner.

HEDDA Do you think they'll succeed?

BRACK [*bending over her and whispering*] No, Hedda Gabler—as long as I keep quiet.

HEDDA [*looking at him anxiously*] And if you don't keep quiet—then what?

BRACK [*with a shrug*] Counsel could always claim that the pistol was stolen.

HEDDA [*decisively*] I'd rather die!

BRACK [*smiling*] People *say* such things. But they don't *do* them.

HEDDA [*without answering*] And what, then, if the pistol wasn't stolen. And they found the owner. What would happen?

BRACK Well, Hedda—there'd be a scandal.

HEDDA A scandal!

BRACK A scandal, yes—the kind you're so deathly afraid of. Naturally, you'd appear in court—you and Mademoiselle Diana. She'd have to explain how the whole thing occurred. Whether it was an accident or homicide. Was he trying to pull the pistol out of his pocket to threaten her? Is that why it went off? Or had she torn the pistol out of his hand, shot him, and slipped it back in his pocket again? It's rather like her to do that, you know. She's a solid piece of work, this Mademoiselle Diana.

HEDDA But all that sordid business is no concern of mine.

BRACK No. But you'll have to answer the question: why did you give Eilert Løvborg the pistol? And what conclusions will people draw from the fact that you did give it to him?

HEDDA [*her head sinking*] That's true. I hadn't thought of that.

BRACK Well, luckily there's no danger, as long as I keep quiet.

HEDDA So I'm in your power, Judge. You have your hold over me from now on.

BRACK [*whispers more softly*] My dearest Hedda—believe me—I won't abuse my position.

HEDDA All the same, I'm in your power. Tied to your will and desire. Not free. Not free, then! [*Rises angrily.*] No—I can't bear the thought of it. Never!

BRACK [*looks at her half mockingly*] One usually manages to adjust to the inevitable.

HEDDA [*returning his look*] Yes, perhaps so. [*She goes over to the writing table. Suppressing an involuntary smile, she imitates* TESMAN's *intonation.*] Well? Getting on with it, George? Uh?

TESMAN Goodness knows, dear. It's going to mean months and months of work, in any case.

HEDDA [*as before*] Imagine that! [*Runs her hand lightly through* MRS. ELVSTED's *hair.*] Don't you find it strange, Thea? Here you are, sitting now beside Tesman—just as you used to sit with Eilert Løvborg.

MRS. ELVSTED Oh, if I could only inspire your husband in the same way.

HEDDA Oh, that will surely come—in time.

TESMAN Yes, you know what, Hedda—I really think I'm beginning to feel something of the kind. But you go back and sit with Judge Brack.

HEDDA Is there nothing the two of you can use me for here?

TESMAN No, nothing in the world. [*Turning his head*] From now on, Judge, you'll have to be good enough to keep Hedda company.

BRACK [*with a glance at* HEDDA] I'll take the greatest pleasure in that.

HEDDA Thanks. But I'm tired this evening. I want to rest a while in there on the sofa.

TESMAN Yes, do that, dear. Uh?

[HEDDA *goes into the inner room, pulling the curtains closed after her. Short pause. Suddenly she is heard playing a wild dance melody on the piano.*]

MRS. ELVSTED [*starting up from her chair*] Oh—what's that?

TESMAN [*running to the center doorway*] But Hedda dearest—don't go playing dance music tonight! Think of Auntie Rina! And Eilert, too!

HEDDA [*putting her head out between the curtains*] And Auntie Julie. And all the rest of them. From now on I'll be quiet. [*She closes the curtains again.*]

TESMAN [*at the writing table*] She can't feel very happy seeing us do this melancholy work. You know what, Mrs. Elvsted—you must move in with Aunt Julie. Then I can come over evenings. And then we can sit and work *there*. Uh?

MRS. ELVSTED Yes, perhaps that would be best—

HEDDA [*from the inner room*] I can hear everything you say, Tesman. But what will I do evenings over here?

TESMAN [*leafing through the notes*] Oh, I'm sure Judge Brack will be good enough to stop by and see you.

BRACK [*in the armchair, calling out gaily*] Gladly, every blessed evening, Mrs. Tesman! We'll have great times here together, the two of us!

HEDDA [*in a clear, ringing voice*] Yes, don't you hope so, Judge? You, the one cock of the walk—

[*A shot is heard within.* TESMAN, MRS. ELVSTED, *and* BRACK *start from their chairs.*]

TESMAN Oh, now she's fooling with those pistols again.

[*He throws the curtains back and runs in.* MRS. ELVSTED *follows.* HEDDA *lies, lifeless, stretched out on the sofa. Confusion and cries.* BERTA *comes in, bewildered, from the right.*]

TESMAN [*shrieking to* BRACK] Shot herself! Shot herself in the temple! Can you imagine!

BRACK [*in the armchair, prostrated*] But good God! People don't *do* such things!

OSCAR WILDE

1854–1900

OSCAR Wilde cut a remarkable figure within the literary, cultural, and theatrical worlds of late nineteenth-century Britain. Dandy, man of letters, public speaker, proponent of aestheticism (the movement championing "Art for Art's Sake"), and prolific author of poetry, fiction, essays, children's stories, criticism, and drama, he entertained London high society with his epigrammatic wit even as he flouted some of the most deeply held values of late-Victorian society. His 1890 novel, *The Picture of Dorian Gray,* scandalized many of its readers with its decadence and perceived amorality, and his society comedies of the early 1890s both entertained and satirized their West End audience. Something of an outsider by virtue of his Irishness and homosexuality, he fashioned a distinctly modern form of celebrity that challenged the norms of Victorian respectability. But Wilde's position in the society of his day was, it turned out, a precarious one. In 1895, even as two of his dramas played on the West End, he was convicted and imprisoned on the charge of "gross indecency" after three sensational trials that represent, to this day, a landmark in the public perception of homosexuality. "I'll be a poet, a writer, a dramatist," he wrote to a friend before leaving Oxford University in 1878. "Somehow or other, I'll be famous, and if not famous, notorious." One of the most accomplished writers for the theater in fin de siècle London, Oscar Wilde became, in the end, his own greatest drama.

Oscar Fingal O'Flahertie Wills Wilde was born in Dublin on October 16, 1854, to William Wilde, an eye and ear surgeon, and the former Jane Francesca Elgee, who wrote Irish Nationalist poetry under the pseudonym "Speranza." After graduating from Portora Royal School in Enniskillen, he attended Trinity College, Dublin, where he distinguished himself as a student of the classics; he won a number of awards, including the prestigious Berkeley Prize for Greek. In 1874 he was awarded a scholarship to Magdalen College, Oxford, which he attended for the next four years. Wilde later referred to two great turning points in his life: "the first when my father sent me to Oxford, the second when Society sent me to prison." At Oxford Wilde studied with John Ruskin and Walter Pater, two leading scholars of aesthetics. Pater exerted the most lasting influence on the young Irishman. In his recently published *Studies in the History of the Renaissance* (1873), Pater celebrated "poetic passion, the desire for beauty, and the love of art for art's sake." Wilde, who had been attracted to aestheticism even before he arrived in Oxford, adopted the movement's beliefs, manners, and poses. He wore his hair long, dressed flamboyantly, and decorated his room in the aesthetic mode, with such accessories as lilies (associated with the Pre-Raphaelite painters) and studiously artistic furnishings. "I find it harder and harder every day to live up to my blue china," he famously stated, and the mannered self-consciousness of such sentiments would make him one of England's most visible aesthetes. During this time Wilde also wrote many of the poems that would appear in an 1881 collection of verse.

When Wilde moved from Oxford to London in 1878, he quickly established himself in high society through his brilliant conversation and wit. Within two years the newspaper *Punch* was regularly caricaturing him as a figurehead of the aesthetic movement, and in 1881 W. S. Gilbert and Sir Arthur Sullivan's comic opera *Patience* satirized aestheticism through the "perfectly precious" Wilde-like character Bunthorne. When the producer of *Patience* took the opera on tour in the United States and Canada the following year, Wilde accompanied the production as a lecturer and representative aesthete. Wilde traveled from coast to coast; met Ulysses S. Grant, Walt Whitman, and other prominent Americans; and registered his impressions of the New World in such epigrams as this: "When good Americans die they go to Paris; when bad Americans die they stay in America." Back in England, Wilde toured the British Isles as lecturer, worked as a journalist and book reviewer, and assumed the editorship of *Woman's World*, a popular late-Victorian periodical. In 1884 Wilde married Constance Mary Lloyd, with whom he had two sons over the next two years. But while Wilde continued to entertain the fashionable society of London with his witty conversation, and while his marriage established a degree of social respectability, he was known for little beyond being a celebrity. That began to change in 1888 with the publication of *The Happy Prince and Other Tales*, the first of two collections of original fairy tales. Over the next seven years, Wilde published a collection of critical essays (which included "The Artist as Critic" [1890]); two additional collections of stories; *The Picture of Dorian Gray*, his novel about a hedonistic aristocrat that shocked the Victorian public; and his five major plays.

An avid theatergoer since his college days and a friend of such theater luminaries as the actresses Lillie Langtry and Sarah Bernhardt, Wilde first tried his hand at drama with *Vera; or, The Nihilists* and *The Duchess of Padua*, which were written in the early 1880s and given short runs in New York. In 1891 Wilde agreed to write a social comedy for George Alexander, manager of the St. James's Theatre, and it was this play that would catapult him to the forefront of the London theater scene. *Lady Windermere's Fan*, produced in 1892, uses the narrative frame of the "problem play"—a nineteenth-century dramatic genre that dealt with controversial social issues—but deploys provocative social commentary and witty epigram to undermine the comfortable moral conclusions that plays in this genre frequently adopted. The play was widely popular, and the attention it received was intensified by Wilde himself, who strolled onstage, cigarette in hand, to greet the opening night applause and congratulated the audience for thinking as highly of his play as he did. *Lady Windermere's Fan* was followed by three more extremely successful social comedies: *A Woman of No Importance* (1893), *An Ideal Husband* (1895), and—Wilde's greatest play—***THE IMPORTANCE OF BEING EARNEST*** (1895). *Salomé*, which Wilde wrote in 1891, dramatized the love of Salomé, Herodias's daughter, for John the Baptist (or Iokanaan) and her incantatory dance with his severed head. Deeply influenced by the symbolist drama of Stéphane Mallarmé (1842–1898) and Maurice Maeterlinck (1862–1949), *Salomé* was refused production by the Lord Chamberlain, who invoked a centuries-old law that prohibited the theatrical depiction of biblical figures. Wilde's poetic tragedy would not be seen on the English stage until after the playwright's death.

But even as Wilde was establishing himself as London's leading literary figure, the elements of his precipitous change in fortune were being set in place. In 1891 he met Lord Alfred Douglas, third son of the ninth marquess of Queensberry, and the two became inseparable. It is not clear when Wilde first became involved in homosexual relationships, but by the 1890s he was leading an active hidden life in London and

Wilde and his lover, Lord Alfred Douglas, in 1893.

abroad. The antagonism of Douglas's father toward what he understood to be a scandalous connection came to a head in February 1895 when Queensberry delivered a card to the London club of which Wilde was a member with the inscription "To Oscar Wilde, posing Somdomite [*sic*]." Wilde took out a warrant charging Queensberry with criminal libel, and in April the case went to trial. When Queensberry presented a list of male prostitutes who would testify concerning Wilde's illegal activities, however, Wilde withdrew the prosecution and the marquess was acquitted. Wilde, who was quickly arrested, now found himself the defendant, and after two trials (the first ended with a hung jury), he was sentenced to two years' hard labor for homosexual conduct. Over the next twenty-four months he suffered the misery and deprivations of the Victorian prison system. Initially allowed only a Bible, hymnbook, and prayerbook, he was eventually able to obtain other books and writing materials. Under these somewhat more lenient conditions he wrote *De Profundis* (published in part in 1905; unexpurgated, in 1962), a book-length letter to Douglas that included a meditation on his own life and fate. When Wilde was released from prison in May 1897, he left for France and never again set foot in England. In 1898 Wilde published *The Ballad of Reading Gaol*—inspired by his experience in prison—but his career as a writer was effectively over. He died in Paris on November 30, 1900, at the age of forty-six.

In *De Profundis,* which became his own eulogy, Wilde summed up what he felt to be the nature of his contribution to the cultural and philosophical life of his times:

> I made art a philosophy, and philosophy an art: I altered the minds of men and the colors of things: there was nothing I said or did that did not make people wonder: I took the drama, the most objective form known to art, and made it as personal a mode of expression as the lyric or the sonnet, at the same time that I widened its range and enriched its characterization. . . . I treated Art as the supreme reality, and life as a mere mode of fiction: I awoke the imagination of my century so that it created myth and legend around me: I summed up all systems in a phrase, and all existence in an epigram.

Wilde's conception of art resists both the moral seriousness of much nineteenth-century literature and what he considered to be the Philistine tendencies of the Victorian middle and upper classes. Writing that "all art is quite useless," he sought to dissociate artistic creation from traditional notions of social usefulness and moral edification. The result of this creative principle was a sophisticated manipulation of literary and social form. Indeed, Wilde became one of his age's most visible celebrities by also serving as its most clever critic. Even as his writing detailed the rituals and conventions of Victorian high society, Wilde subverted the hierarchy of values that structured this world.

Nowhere is this transgressive impulse more evident than in the famous Wildean epigrams, which invert traditional platitudes through clever turns of phrase. Take one example: "Ignorance is like a delicate exotic fruit; touch it and the bloom is gone." The immediate effect of such a remark is studied frivolity: as Algernon says of another epigram, similarly found in *The Importance of Being Earnest,* "It is perfectly phrased! and quite as true as any observation in civilized life should be." At the same time, the line offers a pointed commentary on those segments of the British upper class who value privilege over education. Wilde's plays draw on the manners tradition of social comedy, but in their boundary-assaulting wit they bear more than passing kinship to the more explicitly political drama of his fellow Irishman GEORGE BERNARD SHAW.

The Importance of Being Earnest, which opened to widespread acclaim at the St. James's Theatre on February 14, 1895, is the epitome of Wilde's subversive mode of playwriting. Its philosophy, as Wilde defined it, is straightforward: "That we should treat all the trivial things of life seriously, and all the serious things of life with sincere and studied triviality." Unlike Wilde's earlier comedies, which borrowed the situations and plot devices of contemporary popular drama and were occasionally marred by the uneasy blend of melodrama and wit, *The Importance of Being Earnest* embraces the logic of a thoroughly stylized world in which action borders on farce, epigram rules the day, and even the butler speaks with exceptional propriety. Its world is ruthlessly superficial—"In matters of grave importance," Gwendolen insists, "style, not sincerity is the vital thing"—and its irreverent wit satirizes the institutions and ideals of Victorian society: marriage, religion, gender roles, family, the class system, colonialism, English country living, science, education, romantic idealism, and (of course) earnestness, the habit of taking oneself and one's cherished beliefs quite seriously.

Algernon and Jack, the play's central male characters, pursue a life of leisure and pleasure untroubled by the codes of respectability and responsibility that govern the society around them. Wilde's audience would have recognized them as "dandies" within a nineteenth-century tradition of mannered individualism that included the

Allan Aynesworth as Algernon and George Alexander as Jack in the original 1895 production of *The Importance of Being Earnest.*

fashionable man-about-town Beau Brummell (1778–1840). The dandy, as Alan Sinfield observes, rejected the middle-class values of work and purity through a display of "conspicuous idleness, moral skepticism, and effeminacy." As much an attitude toward life as a manner and style of dress, dandyism called attention to its originality even as it embraced the outward forms of aristocratic society. Unlike Wilde's earlier comedies, which introduce dandy characters in conventional social settings, *The Importance of Being Earnest* presents a world in which wit, pleasure, and studied superficiality are the moral norm. It is a world of erased distinctions and inverted expectations, where smoking is as good an occupation for a man as any other and the most important thing to do in a moment of crisis is eat a muffin in the proper manner. Even Lady Bracknell, that most formidable representative of British social propriety, carries the observance of appearance and form to a dandiacal level of irreverence: "To lose one parent may be regarded as a misfortune—to lose *both* seems like carelessness."

In "The Critic as Artist" Wilde wrote: "Man is least himself when he talks in his own person. Give him a mask, and he will tell you the truth." Few characters in The Importance of Being Earnest are what they appear. Jack Worthing takes on his alter ego, Ernest, when he slips away to the city to see his nonexistent brother, and Algernon assumes the same name when he visits Cecily on the pretense of visiting his imaginary friend Bunbury. Gwendolen hides the secret of her romance with Jack from her mother, Cecily creates an imaginary engagement, and Lady Bracknell's authoritarian manner hides the fact that she married into her social position from decidedly nonaristocratic origins. Even Lane, the butler, and Miss Prism, the governess, have their secrets. In a play that pivots on the question of who one is, "Bunburying" becomes a metaphor for more fundamental shifts of identity. As Neil Sammells points out, *The Importance of Being Earnest* is obsessed with public and private documents—letters, diaries, birth certificates, Army Lists, novels—and with "their fallibility as a means of establishing 'authenticity,' whether of person or incident." But in "an age of surfaces" (the phrase belongs to Lady Bracknell), such categories as truth and identity remain elusive, caught in the play of social conventions and outward forms. The play on the word "Earnest" in the comedy's title reflects a society where who one is may hinge on a name, and where Sincerity is the stepchild of Accident. "It is a terrible thing," Jack laments, "for a man to find out suddenly that all his life he has been speaking nothing but the truth."

In the end, Victorian earnestness had its revenge, and for those who know the playwright's biography it is hard not to view Wilde's final comedy in light of the events that followed shortly upon its premiere. When Wilde was arrested after the first trial, his name was taken off the billboards for *The Ideal Husband* and *The Importance of Being Earnest*, and in view of the author's sudden notoriety the two productions were soon canceled. The Bunburying in which Wilde's protagonists engage must have felt, to many in his audience, uncomfortably close to the secret life of which he was accused and for which he was convicted. In fact, the connections are more than coincidental. As recent scholars have demonstrated, Wilde wove a series of homosexual allusions within the play: in addition to its other meanings, for instance, *earnest* was a Victorian code word for homosexual. But though *The Importance of Being Earnest* engages and is framed by the trenchant realities of late-nineteenth-century society, its strategy of taking seriousness lightly and lightness seriously ensures that its world maintains the studied refinement for which Wilde strove. Dandyism, Wilde wrote, "is the assertion of the absolute modernity of beauty." What dominates this greatest of nineteenth-century comedies—"written by a butterfly for butterflies" (as Wilde wrote a friend)—is the power of wit, satire, and unscrupulous elegance.

S.G.

The Importance of Being Earnest
A Trivial Comedy for Serious People

CHARACTERS

JOHN WORTHING, J.P.[1]	LADY BRACKNELL
ALGERNON MONCRIEFF	HON. GWENDOLEN FAIRFAX
REV. CANON CHASUBLE, D.D.[2]	CECILY CARDEW
MERRIMAN, butler	MISS PRISM, governess
LANE, manservant	

Time
The Present.

First Act

[SCENE: *Morning-room in Algernon's flat in Half Moon Street.*[3] *The room is luxuriously and artistically furnished. The sound of a piano is heard in the adjoining room.*]

[LANE *is arranging afternoon tea on the table, and after the music has ceased,* ALGERNON *enters.*]

ALGERNON Did you hear what I was playing, Lane?

LANE I didn't think it polite to listen, sir.

ALGERNON I'm sorry for that, for your sake. I don't play accurately—anyone can play accurately—but I play with wonderful expression. As far as the piano is concerned, sentiment is my forte. I keep science for Life.

LANE Yes, sir.

ALGERNON And, speaking of the science of Life, have you got the cucumber sandwiches cut for Lady Bracknell?

LANE Yes, sir. [*Hands them on a salver.*]

ALGERNON [*inspects them, takes two, and sits down on the sofa*] Oh! . . . by the way, Lane, I see from your book that on Thursday night, when Lord Shoreham and Mr Worthing were dining with me, eight bottles of champagne are entered as having been consumed.

LANE Yes, sir; eight bottles and a pint.

ALGERNON Why is it that at a bachelor's establishment the servants invariably drink the champagne? I ask merely for information.

LANE I attribute it to the superior quality of the wine, sir. I have often observed that in married households the champagne is rarely of a first-rate brand.

ALGERNON Good Heavens! Is marriage so demoralizing as that?

LANE I believe it *is* a very pleasant state, sir. I have had very little experience of it myself up to the present. I have only been married once. That was in consequence of a misunderstanding between myself and a young person.

1. Justice of the Peace.
2. Doctor of Divinity.
3. Located off Piccadilly Street in Mayfair, a fashionable district of London's West End.

Morning-room: an informal room for receiving morning visitors. Later visitors would be received in the more formal drawing room.

ALGERNON [*languidly*] I don't know that I am much interested in your family life, Lane.

LANE No, sir; it is not a very interesting subject. I never think of it myself.

ALGERNON Very natural, I am sure. That will do, Lane, thank you.

LANE Thank you, sir. [LANE *goes out.*]

ALGERNON Lane's views on marriage seem somewhat lax. Really, if the lower orders don't set us a good example, what on earth is the use of them? They seem, as a class, to have absolutely no sense of moral responsibility.

[*Enter* LANE.]

LANE Mr Ernest Worthing.

[*Enter* JACK.] [LANE *goes out.*]

ALGERNON How are you, my dear Ernest? What brings you up to town?

JACK Oh, pleasure, pleasure! What else should bring one anywhere? Eating as usual, I see, Algy!

ALGERNON [*stiffly*] I believe it is customary in good society to take some slight refreshment at five o'clock. Where have you been since last Thursday?

JACK [*sitting down on the sofa*] In the country.

ALGERNON What on earth do you do there?

JACK [*pulling off his gloves*] When one is in town one amuses oneself. When one is in the country one amuses other people. It is excessively boring.

ALGERNON And who are the people you amuse?

JACK [*airily*] Oh, neighbours, neighbours.

ALGERNON Got nice neighbours in your part of Shropshire?[4]

JACK Perfectly horrid! Never speak to one of them.

ALGERNON How immensely you must amuse them! [*Goes over and takes sandwich.*] By the way, Shropshire is your county, is it not?

JACK Eh? Shropshire? Yes, of course. Hallo! Why all these cups? Why cucumber sandwiches? Why such reckless extravagance in one so young? Who is coming to tea?

ALGERNON Oh! merely Aunt Augusta and Gwendolen.

JACK How perfectly delightful!

ALGERNON Yes, that is all very well; but I am afraid Aunt Augusta won't quite approve of your being here.

JACK May I ask why?

ALGERNON My dear fellow, the way you flirt with Gwendolen is perfectly disgraceful. It is almost as bad as the way Gwendolen flirts with you.

JACK I am in love with Gwendolen. I have come up to town expressly to propose to her.

ALGERNON I thought you had come up for pleasure? . . . I call that business.

JACK How utterly unromantic you are!

ALGERNON I really don't see anything romantic in proposing. It is very romantic to be in love. But there is nothing romantic about a definite proposal. Why, one may be accepted. One usually is, I believe. Then the excitement is all over. The very essence of romance is uncertainty. If ever I get married, I'll certainly try to forget the fact.

4. A county of England in the west Midlands, adjoining the Welsh border (about 150 miles northwest of London).

JACK I have no doubt about that, dear Algy. The Divorce Court was specially invented for people whose memories are so curiously constituted.

ALGERNON Oh! there is no use speculating on that subject. Divorces are made in Heaven——[JACK *puts out his hand to take a sandwich.* ALGERNON *at once interferes.*] Please don't touch the cucumber sandwiches. They are ordered specially for Aunt Augusta. [*Takes one and eats it.*]

JACK Well, you have been eating them all the time.

ALGERNON That is quite a different matter. She is my aunt. [*Takes plate from below.*] Have some bread and butter. The bread and butter is for Gwendolen. Gwendolen is devoted to bread and butter.

JACK [*advancing to table and helping himself*] And very good bread and butter it is too.

ALGERNON Well, my dear fellow, you need not eat as if you were going to eat it all. You behave as if you were married to her already. You are not married to her already, and I don't think you ever will be.

JACK Why on earth do you say that?

ALGERNON Well, in the first place girls never marry the men they flirt with. Girls don't think it right.

JACK Oh, that is nonsense!

ALGERNON It isn't. It is a great truth. It accounts for the extraordinary number of bachelors that one sees all over the place. In the second place, I don't give my consent.

JACK Your consent!

ALGERNON My dear fellow, Gwendolen is my first cousin. And before I allow you to marry her, you will have to clear up the whole question of Cecily. [*Rings bell.*]

JACK Cecily! What on earth do you mean? What do you mean, Algy, by Cecily? I don't know anyone of the name of Cecily.

[*Enter* LANE.]

ALGERNON Bring me that cigarette case Mr Worthing left in the smoking-room the last time he dined here.

LANE Yes, sir. [LANE *goes out.*]

JACK Do you mean to say you have had my cigarette case all this time? I wish to goodness you had let me know. I have been writing frantic letters to Scotland Yard[5] about it. I was very nearly offering a large reward.

ALGERNON Well, I wish you would offer one. I happen to be more than usually hard up.

JACK There is no good offering a large reward now that the thing is found.

[*Enter* LANE *with the cigarette case on a salver.* ALGERNON *takes it at once.* LANE *goes out.*]

ALGERNON I think that is rather mean of you, Ernest, I must say. [*Opens case and examines it.*] However, it makes no matter, for, now that I look at the inscription inside, I find that the thing isn't yours after all.

JACK Of course it's mine. [*Moving to him*] You have seen me with it a hundred times, and you have no right whatsoever to read what is written inside. It is a very ungentlemanly thing to read a private cigarette case.

5. The headquarters of the London Metropolitan Police Force.

ALGERNON Oh! it is absurd to have a hard-and-fast rule about what one should read and what one shouldn't. More than half of modern culture depends on what one shouldn't read.

JACK I am quite aware of the fact, and I don't propose to discuss modern culture. It isn't the sort of thing one should talk of in private. I simply want my cigarette case back.

ALGERNON Yes; but this isn't your cigarette case. This cigarette case is a present from someone of the name of Cecily, and you said you didn't know anyone of that name.

JACK Well, if you want to know, Cecily happens to be my aunt.

ALGERNON Your aunt!

JACK Yes. Charming old lady she is, too. Lives at Tunbridge Wells.[6] Just give it back to me, Algy.

ALGERNON [*retreating to back of sofa*] But why does she call herself little Cecily if she is your aunt and lives at Tunbridge Wells. [*Reading*] 'From little Cecily with her fondest love.'

JACK [*moving to sofa and kneeling upon it*] My dear fellow, what on earth is there in that? Some aunts are tall, some aunts are not tall. That is a matter that surely an aunt may be allowed to decide for herself. You seem to think that every aunt should be exactly like your aunt! That is absurd! For Heaven's sake give me back my cigarette case. [*Follows* ALGERNON *round the room.*]

ALGERNON Yes. But why does your aunt call you her uncle? 'From little Cecily, with her fondest love to her dear Uncle Jack.' There is no objection, I admit, to an aunt being a small aunt, but why an aunt, no matter what her size may be, should call her own nephew her uncle, I can't quite make out. Besides, your name isn't Jack at all; it is Ernest.

JACK It isn't Ernest; it's Jack.

ALGERNON You have always told me it was Ernest. I have introduced you to everyone as Ernest. You answer to the name of Ernest. You look as if your name was Ernest. You are the most earnest looking person I ever saw in my life. It is perfectly absurd your saying that your name isn't Ernest. It's on your cards. Here is one of them. [*Taking it from case*] 'Mr Ernest Worthing, B. 4, The Albany.'[7] I'll keep this as a proof that your name is Ernest if ever you attempt to deny it to me, or to Gwendolen, or to anyone else. [*Puts the card in his pocket.*]

JACK Well, my name is Ernest in town and Jack in the country, and the cigarette case was given to me in the country.

ALGERNON Yes, but that does not account for the fact that your small Aunt Cecily, who lives at Tunbridge Wells, calls you her dear uncle. Come, old boy, you had much better have the thing out at once.

JACK My dear Algy, you talk exactly as if you were a dentist. It is very vulgar to talk like a dentist when one isn't a dentist. It produces a false impression.

ALGERNON Well, that is exactly what dentists always do. Now, go on! Tell me the whole thing. I may mention that I have always suspected you of being a confirmed and secret Bunburyist, and I am quite sure of it now.

JACK Bunburyist? What on earth do you mean by a Bunburyist?

ALGERNON I'll reveal to you the meaning of that incomparable expression as soon as you are kind enough to inform me why you are Ernest in town and Jack in the country.

6. A fashionable spa town in Kent, about 30 miles southeast of London.

7. Popular bachelors' quarters near Piccadilly Street, in central London.

JACK Well, produce my cigarette case first.

ALGERNON Here it is. [*Hands cigarette case.*] Now produce your explanation, and pray make it improbable. [*Sits on sofa.*]

JACK My dear fellow, there is nothing improbable about my explanation at all. In fact it's perfectly ordinary. Old Mr Thomas Cardew, who adopted me when I was a little boy, made me in his will guardian to his grand-daughter, Miss Cecily Cardew. Cecily who addresses me as her uncle from motives of respect that you could not possibly appreciate, lives at my place in the country under the charge of her admirable governess, Miss Prism.

ALGERNON Where is that place in the country, by the way?

JACK That is nothing to you, dear boy. You are not going to be invited. . . . I may tell you candidly that the place is not in Shropshire.

ALGERNON I suspected that, my dear fellow! I have Bunburyed all over Shropshire on two separate occasions. Now, go on. Why are you Ernest in town and Jack in the country?

JACK My dear Algy, I don't know whether you will be able to understand my real motives. You are hardly serious enough. When one is placed in the position of guardian, one has to adopt a very high moral tone on all subjects. It's one's duty to do so. And as a high moral tone can hardly be said to conduce very much to either one's health or one's happiness, in order to get up to town I have always pretended to have a younger brother of the name of Ernest, who lives in the Albany, and gets into the most dreadful scrapes. That, my dear Algy, is the whole truth pure and simple.

ALGERNON The truth is rarely pure and never simple. Modern life would be very tedious if it were either, and modern literature a complete impossibility!

JACK That wouldn't be at all a bad thing.

ALGERNON Literary criticism is not your forte, my dear fellow. Don't try it. You should leave that to people who haven't been at a University. They do it so well in the daily papers. What you really are is a Bunburyist. I was quite right in saying you were a Bunburyist. You are one of the most advanced Bunburyists I know.

JACK What on earth do you mean?

ALGERNON You have invented a very useful younger brother called Ernest, in order that you may be able to come up to town as often as you like. I have invented an invaluable permanent invalid called Bunbury, in order that I may be able to go down into the country whenever I choose. Bunbury is perfectly invaluable. If it wasn't for Bunbury's extraordinary bad health, for instance, I wouldn't be able to dine with you at Willis's[8] tonight, for I have been really engaged to Aunt Augusta for more than a week.

JACK I haven't asked you to dine with me anywhere tonight.

ALGERNON I know. You are absurdly careless about sending out invitations. It is very foolish of you. Nothing annoys people so much as not receiving invitations.

JACK You had much better dine with your Aunt Augusta.

ALGERNON I haven't the smallest intention of doing anything of the kind. To begin with, I dined there on Monday, and once a week is quite enough to dine with one's own relations. In the second place, whenever I do dine

8. A fashionable restaurant on King Street, near Piccadilly, frequented by Wilde and his companion Alfred Lord Douglas.

there I am always treated as a member of the family, and sent down[9] with either no woman at all, or two. In the third place, I know perfectly well whom she will place me next to, tonight. She will place me next Mary Farquhar, who always flirts with her own husband across the dinner-table. That is not very pleasant. Indeed, it is not even decent . . . and that sort of thing is enormously on the increase. The amount of women in London who flirt with their own husbands is perfectly scandalous. It looks so bad. It is simply washing one's clean linen in public. Besides, now that I know you to be a confirmed Bunburyist I naturally want to talk to you about Bunburying. I want to tell you the rules.

JACK I'm not a Bunburyist at all. If Gwendolen accepts me, I am going to kill my brother, indeed I think I'll kill him in any case. Cecily is a little too much interested in him. It is rather a bore. So I am going to get rid of Ernest. And I strongly advise you to do the same with Mr . . . with your invalid friend who has the absurd name.

ALGERNON Nothing will induce me to part with Bunbury, and if you ever get married, which seems to me extremely problematic, you will be very glad to know Bunbury. A man who marries without knowing Bunbury has a very tedious time of it.

JACK That is nonsense. If I marry a charming girl like Gwendolen, and she is the only girl I ever saw in my life that I would marry, I certainly won't want to know Bunbury.

ALGERNON Then your wife will. You don't seem to realize, that in married life three is company and two is none.

JACK [*sententiously*] That, my dear young friend, is the theory that the corrupt French Drama[1] has been propounding for the last fifty years.

ALGERNON Yes; and that the happy English home has proved in half the time.

JACK For heaven's sake, don't try to be cynical. It's perfectly easy to be cynical.

ALGERNON My dear fellow, it isn't easy to be anything nowadays. There's such a lot of beastly competition about. [*The sound of an electric bell is heard.*] Ah! that must be Aunt Augusta. Only relatives, or creditors, ever ring in that Wagnerian[2] manner. Now, if I get her out of the way for ten minutes, so that you can have an opportunity for proposing to Gwendolen, may I dine with you tonight at Willis's?

JACK I suppose so, if you want to.

ALGERNON Yes, but you must be serious about it. I hate people who are not serious about meals. It is so shallow of them.

[*Enter* LANE.]

LANE Lady Bracknell and Miss Fairfax.

[ALGERNON *goes forward to meet them. Enter* LADY BRACKNELL *and* GWENDOLEN.]

LADY BRACKNELL Good afternoon, dear Algernon, I hope you are behaving very well.

ALGERNON I'm feeling very well, Aunt Augusta.

9. Directed to accompany someone to dinner. Victorian dinner guests would gather upstairs in the drawing room, and then gentlemen would escort ladies to the dining room in arranged couples.

1. Because its plots frequently involved adultery and infidelity, French drama was often viewed by the English as immoral.

2. Loud and imposing, like the operas of the German composer Richard Wagner (1813–1883).

LADY BRACKNELL That's not quite the same thing. In fact the two things rarely go together. [*Sees* JACK *and bows to him with icy coldness.*]

ALGERNON [*to* GWENDOLEN] Dear me, you are smart![3]

GWENDOLEN I am always smart! Aren't I, Mr Worthing?

JACK You're quite perfect, Miss Fairfax.

GWENDOLEN Oh! I hope I am not that. It would leave no room for developments, and I intend to develop in many directions. [GWENDOLEN *and* JACK *sit down together in the corner.*]

LADY BRACKNELL I'm sorry if we are a little late, Algernon, but I was obliged to call on dear Lady Harbury. I hadn't been there since her poor husband's death. I never saw a woman so altered; she looks quite twenty years younger. And now I'll have a cup of tea, and one of those nice cucumber sandwiches you promised me.

ALGERNON Certainly, Aunt Augusta. [*Goes over to tea-table.*]

LADY BRACKNELL Won't you come and sit here, Gwendolen?

GWENDOLEN Thanks, mamma, I'm quite comfortable where I am.

ALGERNON [*picking up empty plate in horror*] Good heavens! Lane! Why are there no cucumber sandwiches? I ordered them specially.

LANE [*gravely*] There were no cucumbers in the market this morning, sir. I went down twice.

ALGERNON No cucumbers!

LANE No, sir. Not even for ready money.[4]

ALGERNON That will do, Lane, thank you.

LANE Thank you, sir. [*Goes out.*]

ALGERNON I am greatly distressed, Aunt Augusta, about there being no cucumbers, not even for ready money.

LADY BRACKNELL It really makes no matter, Algernon. I had some crumpets with Lady Harbury, who seems to me to be living entirely for pleasure now.

ALGERNON I hear her hair has turned quite gold from grief.

LADY BRACKNELL It certainly has changed its colour. From what cause I, of course, cannot say. [ALGERNON *crosses and hands tea.*] Thank you. I've quite a treat for you tonight, Algernon. I am going to send you down with Mary Farquhar. She is such a nice woman, and so attentive to her husband. It's delightful to watch them.

ALGERNON I am afraid, Aunt Augusta, I shall have to give up the pleasure of dining with you tonight after all.

LADY BRACKNELL [*frowning*] I hope not, Algernon. It would put my table completely out.[5] Your uncle would have to dine upstairs. Fortunately he is accustomed to that.

ALGERNON It is a great bore, and, I need hardly say, a terrible disappointment to me, but the fact is I have just had a telegram to say that my poor friend Bunbury is very ill again. [*Exchanges glances with* JACK.] They seem to think I should be with him.

LADY BRACKNELL It is very strange. This Mr Bunbury seems to suffer from curiously bad health.

ALGERNON Yes; poor Bunbury is a dreadful invalid.

3. Neatly stylish in appearance.
4. Immediate cash payment (the well-off often bought goods on credit).
5. That is, ruin the seating arrangement, which was always carefully planned to balance male and female guests.

LADY BRACKNELL Well, I must say, Algernon, that I think it is high time that Mr Bunbury made up his mind whether he was going to live or to die. This shilly-shallying with the question is absurd. Nor do I in any way approve of the modern sympathy with invalids. I consider it morbid. Illness of any kind is hardly a thing to be encouraged in others. Health is the primary duty of life. I am always telling that to your poor uncle, but he never seems to take much notice . . . as far as any improvement in his ailments goes. I should be much obliged if you would ask Mr Bunbury, from me, to be kind enough not to have a relapse on Saturday, for I rely on you to arrange my music for me. It is my last reception, and one wants something that will encourage conversation, particularly at the end of the season[6] when everyone has practically said whatever they had to say, which, in most cases, was probably not much.

ALGERNON I'll speak to Bunbury, Aunt Augusta, if he is still conscious, and I think I can promise you he'll be all right by Saturday. Of course the music is a great difficulty. You see, if one plays good music, people don't listen, and if one plays bad music people don't talk. But I'll run over the programme I've drawn out, if you will kindly come into the next room for a moment.

LADY BRACKNELL Thank you, Algernon. It is very thoughtful of you. [*Rising, and following* ALGERNON] I'm sure the programme will be delightful, after a few expurgations. French songs I cannot possibly allow. People always seem to think that they are improper, and either look shocked, which is vulgar, or laugh, which is worse. But German sounds a thoroughly respectable language, and indeed, I believe is so. Gwendolen, you will accompany me.

GWENDOLEN Certainly, mamma.

[LADY BRACKNELL *and* ALGERNON *go into the music-room,* GWENDOLEN *remains behind.*]

JACK Charming day it has been, Miss Fairfax.

GWENDOLEN Pray don't talk to me about the weather, Mr Worthing. Whenever people talk to me about the weather, I always feel quite certain that they mean something else. And that makes me so nervous.

JACK I do mean something else.

GWENDOLEN I thought so. In fact, I am never wrong.

JACK And I would like to be allowed to take advantage of Lady Bracknell's temporary absence . . .

GWENDOLEN I would certainly advise you to do so. Mamma has a way of coming back suddenly into a room that I have often had to speak to her about.

JACK [*nervously*] Miss Fairfax, ever since I met you I have admired you more than any girl . . . I have ever met since . . . I met you.

GWENDOLEN Yes, I am quite aware of the fact. And I often wish that in public, at any rate, you had been more demonstrative. For me you have always had an irresistible fascination. Even before I met you I was far from indifferent to you. [JACK *looks at her in amazement.*] We live, as I hope you know, Mr Worthing, in an age of ideals. The fact is constantly mentioned in the more expensive monthly magazines, and has reached the provincial pulpits I am told: and my ideal has always been to love some one of the name of Ernest. There is something in that name that inspires absolute

6. That is, the social season in London, which began in May and lasted through July; during this time fashionable society attended balls, dinners, and other entertainments.

confidence. The moment Algernon first mentioned to me that he had a friend called Ernest, I knew I was destined to love you.

JACK You really love me, Gwendolen?

GWENDOLEN Passionately!

JACK Darling! You don't know how happy you've made me.

GWENDOLEN My own Ernest!

JACK But you don't really mean to say that you couldn't love me if my name wasn't Ernest?

GWENDOLEN But your name is Ernest.

JACK Yes, I know it is. But supposing it was something else? Do you mean to say you couldn't love me then?

GWENDOLEN [*glibly*] Ah! that is clearly a metaphysical speculation, and like most metaphysical speculations has very little reference at all to the actual facts of real life, as we know them.

JACK Personally, darling, to speak quite candidly, I don't much care about the name of Ernest . . . I don't think the name suits me at all.

GWENDOLEN It suits you perfectly. It is a divine name. It has a music of its own. It produces vibrations.

JACK Well, really, Gwendolen, I must say that I think there are lots of other much nicer names. I think Jack, for instance, a charming name.

GWENDOLEN Jack? . . . No, there is very little music in the name Jack, if any at all, indeed. It does not thrill. It produces absolutely no vibrations. . . . I have known several Jacks, and they all, without exception, were more than usually plain. Besides, Jack is a notorious domesticity[7] for John! And I pity any woman who is married to a man called John. She would probably never be allowed to know the entrancing pleasure of a single moment's solitude. The only really safe name is Ernest.

JACK Gwendolen, I must get christened at once—I mean we must get married at once. There is no time to be lost.

GWENDOLEN Married, Mr Worthing?

JACK [*astounded*] Well . . . surely. You know that I love you, and you led me to believe, Miss Fairfax, that you were not absolutely indifferent to me.

GWENDOLEN I adore you. But you haven't proposed to me yet. Nothing has been said at all about marriage. The subject has not even been touched on.

JACK Well . . . may I propose to you now?

GWENDOLEN I think it would be an admirable opportunity. And to spare you any possible disappointment, Mr Worthing, I think it only fair to tell you quite frankly beforehand that I am fully determined to accept you.

JACK Gwendolen!

GWENDOLEN Yes, Mr Worthing, what have you got to say to me?

JACK You know what I have got to say to you.

GWENDOLEN Yes, but you don't say it.

JACK Gwendolen, will you marry me? [*Goes on his knees.*]

GWENDOLEN Of course I will, darling. How long you have been about it! I am afraid you have had very little experience in how to propose.

JACK My own one, I have never loved anyone in the world but you.

GWENDOLEN Yes, but men often propose for practice. I know my brother Gerald does. All my girl-friends tell me so. What wonderfully blue eyes you

7. A domestic or familiar expression.

have, Ernest! They are quite, quite, blue. I hope you will always look at me just like that, especially when there are other people present.

[*Enter* LADY BRACKNELL.]

LADY BRACKNELL Mr Worthing! Rise, sir, from this semi-recumbent posture. It is most indecorous.

GWENDOLEN Mamma! [*He tries to rise; she restrains him.*] I must beg you to retire. This is no place for you. Besides, Mr Worthing has not quite finished yet.

LADY BRACKNELL Finished what, may I ask?

GWENDOLEN I am engaged to Mr Worthing, mamma. [*They rise together.*]

LADY BRACKNELL Pardon me, you are not engaged to anyone. When you do become engaged to some one, I, or your father, should his health permit him, will inform you of the fact. An engagement should come on a young girl as a surprise, pleasant or unpleasant, as the case may be. It is hardly a matter that she could be allowed to arrange for herself. . . . And now I have a few questions to put to you, Mr Worthing. While I am making these inquiries, you, Gwendolen, will wait for me below in the carriage.

GWENDOLEN [*reproachfully*] Mamma!

GWENDOLEN In the carriage, Gwendolen! [GWENDOLEN *goes to the door. She and* JACK *blow kisses to each other behind* LADY BRACKNELL*'s back.* LADY BRACKNELL *looks vaguely about as if she could not understand what the noise was. Finally turns round.*] Gwendolen, the carriage!

GWENDOLEN Yes, mamma. [*Goes out, looking back at* JACK.]

LADY BRACKNELL [*sitting down*] You can take a seat, Mr Worthing.

[*Looks in her pocket for note-book and pencil.*]

JACK Thank you, Lady Bracknell, I prefer standing.

LADY BRACKNELL [*pencil and note-book in hand*] I feel bound to tell you that you are not down on my list of eligible young men, although I have the same list as the dear Duchess of Bolton has. We work together, in fact. However, I am quite ready to enter your name, should your answers be what a really affectionate mother requires. Do you smoke?

JACK Well, yes, I must admit I smoke.

LADY BRACKNELL I am glad to hear it. A man should always have an occupation of some kind. There are far too many idle men in London as it is. How old are you?

JACK Twenty-nine.

LADY BRACKNELL A very good age to be married at. I have always been of opinion that a man who desires to get married should know either everything or nothing. Which do you know?

JACK [*after some hesitation*] I know nothing, Lady Bracknell.

LADY BRACKNELL I am pleased to hear it. I do not approve of anything that tampers with natural ignorance. Ignorance is like a delicate exotic fruit; touch it and the bloom is gone. The whole theory of modern education is radically unsound. Fortunately in England, at any rate, education produces no effect whatsoever. If it did, it would prove a serious danger to the upper classes, and probably lead to acts of violence in Grosvenor Square.[8] What is your income?

8. A Mayfair neighborhood east of Speakers' Corner in Hyde Park.

JACK Between seven and eight thousand[9] a year.

LADY BRACKNELL [*makes a note in her book*] In land, or in investments?

JACK In investments, chiefly.

LADY BRACKNELL That is satisfactory. What between the duties expected of one during one's lifetime, and the duties exacted from one after one's death,[1] land has ceased to be either a profit or a pleasure. It gives one position, and prevents one from keeping it up. That's all that can be said about land.

JACK I have a country house with some land, of course, attached to it, about fifteen hundred acres, I believe; but I don't depend on that for my real income. In fact, as far as I can make out, the poachers are the only people who make anything out of it.

LADY BRACKNELL A country house! How many bedrooms? Well, that point can be cleared up afterwards. You have a town house, I hope? A girl with a simple, unspoiled nature, like Gwendolen, could hardly be expected to reside in the country.

JACK Well, I own a house in Belgrave Square,[2] but it is let by the year to Lady Bloxham. Of course, I can get it back whenever I like, at six months' notice.

LADY BRACKNELL Lady Bloxham? I don't know her.

JACK Oh, she goes about very little. She is a lady considerably advanced in years.

LADY BRACKNELL Ah, nowadays that is no guarantee of respectability of character. What number in Belgrave Square?

JACK 149.

LADY BRACKNELL [*shaking her head*] The unfashionable side. I thought there was something. However, that could easily be altered.

JACK Do you mean the fashion, or the side?

LADY BRACKNELL [*sternly*] Both, if necessary, I presume. What are your politics?

JACK Well, I am afraid I really have none. I am a Liberal Unionist.[3]

LADY BRACKNELL Oh, they count as Tories. They dine with us. Or come in the evening, at any rate. Now to minor matters. Are your parents living?

JACK I have lost both my parents.

LADY BRACKNELL Both? To lose one parent may be regarded as a misfortune—to lose *both* seems like carelessness. Who was your father? He was evidently a man of some wealth. Was he born in what the Radical papers call the purple of commerce, or did he rise from the ranks of the aristocracy?

JACK I am afraid I really don't know. The fact is, Lady Bracknell, I said I had lost my parents. It would be nearer the truth to say that my parents seem to have lost me . . . I don't actually know who I am by birth. I was . . . well, I was found.

LADY BRACKNELL Found!

JACK The late Mr Thomas Cardew, an old gentleman of a very charitable and kindly disposition, found me, and gave me the name of Worthing, because

9. That is £7,000 to £8,000, roughly equivalent to $1 million today.
1. That is, inheritance taxes, a play on the secondary meaning of "duties."
2. The center of Belgravia, a fashionable neighborhood just west of Buckingham Palace.
3. The Liberal Unionists were a splinter group of the Liberal Party that joined with the Conservatives (known as the Tories) to defeat William Gladstone's Home Rule Bill of 1886, which would have granted political autonomy to Ireland.

he happened to have a first-class ticket for Worthing in his pocket at the time. Worthing is a place in Sussex.[4] It is a seaside resort.

LADY BRACKNELL Where did the charitable gentleman who had a first-class ticket for this seaside resort find you?

JACK [*gravely*] In a hand-bag.

LADY BRACKNELL A hand-bag?

JACK [*very seriously*] Yes, Lady Bracknell. I was in a hand-bag—a somewhat large, black leather hand-bag, with handles to it—an ordinary hand-bag in fact.

LADY BRACKNELL In what locality did this Mr James, or Thomas, Cardew come across this ordinary hand-bag?

JACK In the cloak-room at Victoria Station.[5] It was given to him in mistake for his own.

LADY BRACKNELL The cloak-room at Victoria Station?

JACK Yes. The Brighton line.[6]

LADY BRACKNELL The line is immaterial. Mr Worthing, I confess I feel somewhat bewildered by what you have just told me. To be born, or at any rate bred, in a hand-bag, whether it had handles or not, seems to me to display a contempt for the ordinary decencies of family life that reminds one of the worst excesses of the French Revolution. And I presume you know what that unfortunate movement led to? As for the particular locality in which the hand-bag was found, a cloak-room at a railway station might serve to conceal a social indiscretion—has probably, indeed, been used for that purpose before now—but it could hardly be regarded as an assured basis for a recognized position in good society.

JACK May I ask you then what you would advise me to do? I need hardly say I would do anything in the world to ensure Gwendolen's happiness.

LADY BRACKNELL I would strongly advise you, Mr Worthing, to try and acquire some relations as soon as possible, and to make a definite effort to produce at any rate one parent, of either sex, before the season is quite over.

JACK Well, I don't see how I could possibly manage to do that. I can produce the hand-bag at any moment. It is in my dressing-room at home. I really think that should satisfy you, Lady Bracknell.

LADY BRACKNELL Me, sir! What has it to do with me? You can hardly imagine that I and Lord Bracknell would dream of allowing our only daughter—a girl brought up with the utmost care—to marry into a cloak-room, and form an alliance with a parcel? Good morning, Mr Worthing!

[LADY BRACKNELL *sweeps out in majestic indignation.*]

JACK Good morning! [ALGERNON, *from the other room, strikes up the Wedding March.*[7] JACK *looks perfectly furious, and goes to the door.*] For goodness' sake don't play that ghastly tune, Algy! How idiotic you are!

[*The music stops, and* ALGERNON *enters cheerily.*]

4. Wilde, who frequently named characters after places, wrote *The Importance of Being Earnest* while vacationing with his family in the coastal town of Worthing. Sussex is a county south of London.

5. One of London's main rail stations, located in Belgravia.

6. The rail line to Brighton, a popular seaside resort in Sussex on England's south coast.

7. The recessional often played at weddings, from Felix Mendelssohn's *A Midsummer Night's Dream* (1842).

ALGERNON Didn't it go off all right, old boy? You don't mean to say Gwendolen refused you? I know it is a way she has. She is always refusing people. I think it is most ill-natured of her.

JACK Oh, Gwendolen is as right as a trivet.[8] As far as she is concerned, we are engaged. Her mother is perfectly unbearable. Never met such a Gorgon[9] . . . I don't really know what a Gorgon is like, but I am quite sure that Lady Bracknell is one. In any case, she is a monster, without being a myth, which is rather unfair . . . I beg your pardon, Algy, I suppose I shouldn't talk about your own aunt in that way before you.

ALGERNON My dear boy, I love hearing my relations abused. It is the only thing that makes me put up with them at all. Relations are simply a tedious pack of people, who haven't got the remotest knowledge of how to live, nor the smallest instinct about when to die.

JACK Oh, that is nonsense!

ALGERNON It isn't!

JACK Well, I won't argue about the matter. You always want to argue about things.

ALGERNON That is exactly what things were originally made for.

JACK Upon my word, if I thought that, I'd shoot myself . . . [*A pause*] You don't think there is any chance of Gwendolen becoming like her mother in about a hundred and fifty years, do you Algy?

ALGERNON All women become like their mothers. That is their tragedy. No man does. That's his.

JACK Is that clever?

ALGERNON It is perfectly phrased! and quite as true as any observation in civilized life should be.

JACK I am sick to death of cleverness. Everybody is clever nowadays. You can't go anywhere without meeting clever people. The thing has become an absolute public nuisance. I wish to goodness we had a few fools left.

ALGERNON We have.

JACK I should extremely like to meet them. What do they talk about?

ALGERNON The fools? Oh! about the clever people, of course.

JACK What fools!

ALGERNON By the way, did you tell Gwendolen the truth about your being Ernest in town, and Jack in the country?

JACK [*in a very patronizing manner*] My dear fellow, the truth isn't quite the sort of thing one tells to a nice sweet refined girl. What extraordinary ideas you have about the way to behave to a woman!

ALGERNON The only way to behave to a woman is to make love to her,[1] if she is pretty, and to someone else if she is plain.

JACK Oh, that is nonsense.

ALGERNON What about your brother? What about the profligate Ernest?

JACK Oh, before the end of the week I shall have got rid of him. I'll say he died in Paris of apoplexy. Lots of people die of apoplexy, quite suddenly, don't they?

ALGERNON Yes, but it's hereditary, my dear fellow. It's a sort of thing that runs in families. You had much better say a severe chill.

8. Proverbial expression for steadiness; a trivet is a three-footed stand used to support cooking vessels over a fire.

9. In Greek mythology, one of three snake-haired sisters, the sight of whom turned all who looked at them to stone.

1. That is, flirt with her, court her.

JACK You are sure a severe chill isn't hereditary, or anything of that kind?

ALGERNON Of course it isn't!

JACK Very well, then. My poor brother Ernest is carried off suddenly in Paris, by a severe chill. That gets rid of him.

ALGERNON But I thought you said that . . . Miss Cardew was a little too much interested in your poor brother Ernest? Won't she feel his loss a good deal?

JACK Oh, that is all right. Cecily is not a silly romantic girl, I am glad to say. She has got a capital appetite, goes on long walks, and pays no attention at all to her lessons.

ALGERNON I would rather like to see Cecily.

JACK I will take very good care you never do. She is excessively pretty, and she is only just eighteen.

ALGERNON Have you told Gwendolen yet that you have an excessively pretty ward who is only just eighteen?

JACK Oh! one doesn't blurt these things out to people. Cecily and Gwendolen are perfectly certain to be extremely great friends. I'll bet you anything you like that half an hour after they have met, they will be calling each other sister.

ALGERNON Women only do that when they have called each other a lot of other things first. Now, my dear boy, if we want to get a good table at Willis's, we really must go and dress. Do you know it is nearly seven?

JACK [*irritably*] Oh! it always is nearly seven.

ALGERNON Well, I'm hungry.

JACK I never knew you when you weren't. . . .

ALGERNON What shall we do after dinner? Go to a theatre?

JACK Oh no! I loathe listening.

ALGERNON Well, let us go to the Club?[2]

JACK Oh, no! I hate talking.

ALGERNON Well, we might trot round to the Empire[3] at ten?

JACK Oh no! I can't bear looking at things. It is so silly.

ALGERNON Well, what shall we do?

JACK Nothing!

ALGERNON It is awfully hard work doing nothing. However, I don't mind hard work where there is no definite object of any kind.

[*Enter* LANE.]

LANE Miss Fairfax.

[*Enter* GWENDOLEN. LANE *goes out.*]

ALGERNON Gwendolen, upon my word!

GWENDOLEN Algy, kindly turn your back. I have something very particular to say to Mr Worthing.

ALGERNON Really, Gwendolen, I don't think I can allow this at all.

GWENDOLEN Algy, you always adopt a strictly immoral attitude towards life. You are not quite old enough to do that.

[ALGERNON *retires to the fireplace.*]

2. Any one of a number of exclusive, members-only clubs for men.

3. The Empire Theatre of Varieties, a well-known music hall in Leicester Square, a center of entertainments in London's West End.

JACK My own darling!

GWENDOLEN Ernest, we may never be married. From the expression on mamma's face I fear we never shall. Few parents nowadays pay any regard to what their children say to them. The old-fashioned respect for the young is fast dying out. Whatever influence I ever had over mamma, I lost at the age of three. But although she may prevent us from becoming man and wife, and I may marry someone else, and marry often, nothing that she can possibly do can alter my eternal devotion to you.

JACK Dear Gwendolen!

GWENDOLEN The story of your romantic origin, as related to me by mamma, with unpleasing comments, has naturally stirred the deeper fibres of my nature. Your Christian name has an irresistible fascination. The simplicity of your character makes you exquisitely incomprehensible to me. Your town address at the Albany I have. What is your address in the country?

JACK The Manor House, Woolton, Hertfordshire.[4]

[ALGERNON, *who has been carefully listening, smiles to himself, and writes the address on his shirt-cuff. Then picks up the Railway Guide.*]

GWENDOLEN There is a good postal service, I suppose? It may be necessary to do something desperate. That of course will require serious consideration. I will communicate with you daily.

JACK My own one!

GWENDOLEN How long do you remain in town?

JACK Till Monday.

GWENDOLEN Good! Algy, you may turn round now.

ALGERNON Thanks, I've turned round already.

GWENDOLEN You may also ring the bell.

JACK You will let me see you to your carriage, my own darling?

GWENDOLEN Certainly.

JACK [*to* LANE, *who now enters*] I will see Miss Fairfax out.

LANE Yes, sir.

[JACK *and* GWENDOLEN *go off.*]

[LANE *presents several letters on a salver to Algernon. It is to be surmised that they are bills, as* ALGERNON, *after looking at the envelopes, tears them up.*]

ALGERNON A glass of sherry, Lane.

LANE Yes, sir.

ALGERNON Tomorrow, Lane, I'm going Bunburying.

LANE Yes, sir.

ALGERNON I shall probably not be back till Monday. You can put up my dress clothes, my smoking jacket,[5] and all the Bunbury suits . . .

LANE Yes, sir. [*Handing sherry*]

ALGERNON I hope tomorrow will be a fine day, Lane.

LANE It never is, sir.

ALGERNON Lane, you're a perfect pessimist.

LANE I do my best to give satisfaction, sir.

[*Enter* JACK. LANE *goes off.*]

4. A rural county just northeast of London.

5. A loose-fitting casual jacket worn at home, usually in the evening. *Put up:* pack.

JACK There's a sensible, intellectual girl! the only girl I ever cared for in my life. [ALGERNON *is laughing immoderately.*] What on earth are you so amused at?

ALGERNON Oh, I'm a little anxious about poor Bunbury, that is all.

JACK If you don't take care, your friend Bunbury will get you into a serious scrape some day.

ALGERNON I love scrapes. They are the only things that are never serious.

JACK Oh, that's nonsense, Algy. You never talk anything but nonsense.

ALGERNON Nobody ever does.

[JACK *looks indignantly at him, and leaves the room.* ALGERNON *lights a cigarette, reads his shirt-cuff, and smiles.*]

Act Drop.[6]

Second Act

[SCENE: *Garden at the Manor House. A flight of gray stone steps leads up to the house. The garden, an old-fashioned one, full of roses. Time of year, July. Basket chairs, and a table covered with books, are set under a large yew tree.*]

[MISS PRISM *discovered seated at the table.* CECILY *is at the back watering flowers.*]

MISS PRISM [*calling*] Cecily, Cecily! Surely such a utilitarian occupation as the watering of flowers is rather Moulton's duty[7] than yours? Especially at a moment when intellectual pleasures await you. Your German grammar is on the table. Pray open it at page fifteen. We will repeat yesterday's lesson.

CECILY [*coming over very slowly*] But I don't like German. It isn't at all a becoming language. I know perfectly well that I look quite plain after my German lesson.

MISS PRISM Child, you know how anxious your guardian is that you should improve yourself in every way. He laid particular stress on your German, as he was leaving for town yesterday. Indeed, he always lays stress on your German when he is leaving for town.

CECILY Dear Uncle Jack is so very serious! Sometimes he is so serious that I think he cannot be quite well.

MISS PRISM [*drawing herself up*] Your guardian enjoys the best of health, and his gravity of demeanour is especially to be commended in one so comparatively young as he is. I know no one who has a higher sense of duty and responsibility.

CECILY I suppose that is why he often looks a little bored when we three are together.

MISS PRISM Cecily! I am surprised at you. Mr Worthing has many troubles in his life. Idle merriment and triviality would be out of place in his conversation. You must remember his constant anxiety about that unfortunate young man his brother.

CECILY I wish Uncle Jack would allow that unfortunate young man, his brother, to come down here sometimes. We might have a good influence over him, Miss Prism. I am sure you certainly would. You know German,

6. The painted curtain lowered to indicate divisions between acts or scenes.

7. The gardener Moulton appears in Wilde's earlier, four-act version of the play.

and geology, and things of that kind influence a man very much. [CECILY *begins to write in her diary.*]

MISS PRISM [*shaking her head*] I do not think that even I could produce any effect on a character that according to his own brother's admission is irretrievably weak and vacillating. Indeed I am not sure that I would desire to reclaim him. I am not in favour of this modern mania for turning bad people into good people at a moment's notice. As a man sows so let him reap.[8] You must put away your diary, Cecily. I really don't see why you should keep a diary at all.

CECILY I keep a diary in order to enter the wonderful secrets of my life. If I didn't write them down I should probably forget all about them.

MISS PRISM Memory, my dear Cecily, is the diary that we all carry about with us.

CECILY Yes, but it usually chronicles the things that have never happened, and couldn't possibly have happened. I believe that Memory is responsible for nearly all the three-volume novels that Mudie[9] sends us.

MISS PRISM Do not speak slightingly of the three-volume novel, Cecily. I wrote one myself in earlier days.

CECILY Did you really, Miss Prism? How wonderfully clever you are! I hope it did not end happily? I don't like novels that end happily. They depress me so much.

MISS PRISM The good ended happily, and the bad unhappily. That is what Fiction means.

CECILY I suppose so. But it seems very unfair. And was your novel ever published?

MISS PRISM Alas! no. The manuscript unfortunately was abandoned. I use the word in the sense of lost or mislaid.[1] To your work, child, these speculations are profitless.

CECILY [*smiling*] But I see dear Dr Chasuble coming up through the garden.

MISS PRISM [*rising and advancing*] Dr Chasuble! This is indeed a pleasure.

[*Enter* CANON CHASUBLE.]

CHASUBLE And how are we this morning? Miss Prism, you are, I trust, well?

CECILY Miss Prism has just been complaining of a slight headache. I think it would do her so much good to have a short stroll with you in the Park, Dr Chasuble.

MISS PRISM Cecily, I have not mentioned anything about a headache.

CECILY No, dear Miss Prism, I know that, but I felt instinctively that you had a headache. Indeed I was thinking about that, and not about my German lesson, when the Rector came in.

CHASUBLE I hope Cecily, you are not inattentive.

CECILY Oh, I am afraid I am.

CHASUBLE That is strange. Were I fortunate enough to be Miss Prism's pupil, I would hang upon her lips. [MISS PRISM *glares.*] I spoke metaphorically.—My

8. A New Testament proverb: "Be not deceived; God is not mocked: for whatsoever a man soweth, that shall he also reap" (Galatians 6.7).
9. Charles Edward Mudie (1818–1890), an English publisher who in 1842 founded a lending library that charged subscribers to borrow books; most Victorian fiction was published in three volumes (a practice that benefited for-fee libraries).
1. That is, not in the sense of "licentious" or "unrestrained."

metaphor was drawn from bees.[2] Ahem! Mr Worthing I suppose, has not returned from town yet?

MISS PRISM We do not expect him till Monday afternoon.

CHASUBLE Ah yes, he usually likes to spend his Sunday in London. He is not one of those whose sole aim is enjoyment, as, by all accounts, that unfortunate young man his brother seems to be. But I must not disturb Egeria and her pupil any longer.

MISS PRISM Egeria? My name is Lætitia,[3] Doctor.

CHASUBLE [*bowing*] A classical allusion merely, drawn from the Pagan authors. I shall see you both no doubt at Evensong?[4]

MISS PRISM I think, dear Doctor, I will have a stroll with you. I find I have a headache after all, and a walk might do it good.

CHASUBLE With pleasure, Miss Prism, with pleasure. We might go as far as the schools and back.

MISS PRISM That would be delightful. Cecily, you will read your Political Economy in my absence. The chapter on the Fall of the Rupee[5] you may omit. It is somewhat too sensational. Even these metallic problems have their melodramatic side. [*Goes down the garden with* DR CHASUBLE.]

CECILY [*picks up books and throws them back on table*] Horrid Political Economy! Horrid Geography! Horrid, horrid German!

[*Enter* MERRIMAN *with a card on a salver.*]

MERRIMAN Mr Ernest Worthing has just driven over from the station. He has brought his luggage with him.

CECILY [*takes the card and reads it*] 'Mr Ernest Worthing, B.4 The Albany, W.' Uncle Jack's brother! Did you tell him Mr Worthing was in town?

MERRIMAN Yes, Miss. He seemed very much disappointed. I mentioned that you and Miss Prism were in the garden. He said he was anxious to speak to you privately for a moment.

CECILY Ask Mr Ernest Worthing to come here. I suppose you had better talk to the housekeeper about a room for him.

MERRIMAN Yes, Miss. [MERRIMAN *goes off.*]

CECILY I have never met any really wicked person before. I feel rather frightened. I am so afraid he will look just like everyone else.

[*Enter* ALGERNON, *very gay and debonnair.*]

He does!

ALGERNON [*raising his hat*] You are my little cousin Cecily, I'm sure.

CECILY You are under some strange mistake. I am not little. In fact, I believe I am more than usually tall for my age. [ALGERNON *is rather taken aback.*] But I am your cousin Cecily. You, I see from your card, are Uncle Jack's brother, my cousin Ernest, my wicked cousin Ernest.

ALGERNON Oh! I am not really wicked at all, cousin Cecily. You mustn't think that I am wicked.

2. A reference to the honey of Miss Prism's instruction.

3. A Latin name (literally, "beauty, grace, joy"). *Egeria:* in Roman mythology, one of the Camenae (prophetic nymphs), said to have counseled Numa Pompilius, the legendary second king of Rome; thus, any female adviser or patron.

4. Evening church services.

5. India's currency had been declining in value for a number of years. *Political Economy:* that is, an economics textbook.

CECILY If you are not, then you have certainly been deceiving us all in a very inexcusable manner. I hope you have not been leading a double life, pretending to be wicked and being really good all the time. That would be hypocrisy.

ALGERNON [*looks at her in amazement*] Oh! Of course I have been rather reckless.

CECILY I am glad to hear it.

ALGERNON In fact, now you mention the subject, I have been very bad in my own small way.

CECILY I don't think you should be so proud of that, although I am sure it must have been very pleasant.

ALGERNON It is much pleasanter being here with you.

CECILY I can't understand how you are here at all. Uncle Jack won't be back till Monday afternoon.

ALGERNON That is a great disappointment. I am obliged to go up by the first train on Monday morning. I have a business appointment that I am anxious . . . to miss.

CECILY Couldn't you miss it anywhere but in London?

ALGERNON No: the appointment is in London.

CECILY Well, I know, of course, how important it is not to keep a business engagement, if one wants to retain any sense of the beauty of life, but still I think you had better wait till Uncle Jack arrives. I know he wants to speak to you about your emigrating.

ALGERNON About my what?

CECILY Your emigrating. He has gone up to buy your outfit.

ALGERNON I certainly wouldn't let Jack buy my outfit. He has no taste in neckties at all.

CECILY I don't think you will require neckties. Uncle Jack is sending you to Australia.[6]

ALGERNON Australia! I'd sooner die.

CECILY Well, he said at dinner on Wednesday night, that you would have to choose between this world, the next world, and Australia.

ALGERNON Oh, well! The accounts I have received of Australia and the next world, are not particularly encouraging. This world is good enough for me, cousin Cecily.

CECILY Yes, but are you good enough for it?

ALGERNON I'm afraid I'm not that. That is why I want you to reform me. You might make that your mission, if you don't mind, cousin Cecily.

CECILY I'm afraid I've no time, this afternoon.

ALGERNON Well, would you mind my reforming myself this afternoon?

CECILY It is rather Quixotic[7] of you. But I think you should try.

ALGERNON I will. I feel better already.

CECILY You are looking a little worse.

ALGERNON That is because I am hungry.

CECILY How thoughtless of me. I should have remembered that when one is going to lead an entirely new life, one requires regular and wholesome meals. Won't you come in?

6. While Australia was no longer a penal colony in Wilde's day, it was still widely seen as a place where disreputable family members might be sent.

7. Impulsively idealistic, like the hero of Miguel de Cervantes's *Don Quixote* (1605, 1615).

ALGERNON Thank you. Might I have a buttonhole[8] first? I never have any appetite unless I have a buttonhole first.

CECILY A Maréchal Niel?[9] [*Picks up scissors.*]

ALGERNON No, I'd sooner have a pink rose.

CECILY Why? [*Cuts a flower.*]

ALGERNON Because you are like a pink rose, Cousin Cecily.

CECILY I don't think it can be right for you to talk to me like that. Miss Prism never says such things to me.

ALGERNON Then Miss Prism is a short-sighted old lady. [CECILY *puts the rose in his buttonhole.*] You are the prettiest girl I ever saw.

CECILY Miss Prism says that all good looks are a snare.

ALGERNON They are a snare that every sensible man would like to be caught in.

CECILY Oh! I don't think I would care to catch a sensible man. I shouldn't know what to talk to him about.

[*They pass into the house.* MISS PRISM *and* DR CHASUBLE *return.*]

MISS PRISM You are too much alone, dear Dr Chasuble. You should get married. A misanthrope I can understand—a womanthrope, never!

CHASUBLE [*with a scholar's shudder*] Believe me, I do not deserve so neologistic a phrase.[1] The precept as well as the practice of the Primitive Church was distinctly against matrimony.[2]

MISS PRISM [*sententiously*] That is obviously the reason why the Primitive Church has not lasted up to the present day. And you do not seem to realize, dear Doctor, that by persistently remaining single, a man converts himself into a permanent public temptation. Men should be more careful; this very celibacy leads weaker vessels astray.

CHASUBLE But is a man not equally attractive when married?

MISS PRISM No married man is ever attractive except to his wife.

CHASUBLE And often, I've been told, not even to her.

MISS PRISM That depends on the intellectual sympathies of the woman. Maturity can always be depended on. Ripeness can be trusted. Young women are green.[3] [DR CHASUBLE *starts.*] I spoke horticulturally. My metaphor was drawn from fruits. But where is Cecily?

CHASUBLE Perhaps she followed us to the schools.

[*Enter* JACK *slowly from the back of the garden. He is dressed in the deepest mourning, with crape hat-band*[4] *and black gloves.*]

MISS PRISM Mr Worthing!

CHASUBLE Mr Worthing?

MISS PRISM This is indeed a surprise. We did not look for you till Monday afternoon.

8. A flower worn in the lapel of a man's jacket.

9. A fragrant yellow rose, developed in France and first grown in England in 1864; it was named after Adolphe Niel, marshal of France under Napoleon III.

1. Chasuble is pained by the illogical coinage "womanthrope," which mixes Old English and Greek roots.

2. That is, the marriage of clergy (permitted in the Church of England). *The Primitive Church*: the Early Christian church. As his comment on celibacy indicates, the High Church Anglicanism practiced by Chasuble—whose name evokes a vestment worn during services—saw itself as maintaining that tradition.

3. Unripe, and thus inexperienced, easily deceived; understood by Chasuble as suffering from greensickness, an anemic condition found especially in adolescent girls and long believed to be caused by celibacy.

4. A band of crepe material, worn to signify mourning.

JACK [*shakes* MISS PRISM*'s hand in a tragic manner*] I have returned sooner than I expected. Dr Chasuble, I hope you are well?

CHASUBLE Dear Mr Worthing, I trust this garb of woe does not betoken some terrible calamity?

JACK My brother.

MISS PRISM More shameful debts and extravagance?

CHASUBLE Still leading his life of pleasure?

JACK [*shaking his head*] Dead!

CHASUBLE Your brother Ernest dead?

JACK Quite dead.

MISS PRISM What a lesson for him! I trust he will profit by it.

CHASUBLE Mr Worthing, I offer you my sincere condolence. You have at least the consolation of knowing that you were always the most generous and forgiving of brothers.

JACK Poor Ernest! He had many faults, but it is a sad, sad blow.

CHASUBLE Very sad indeed. Were you with him at the end?

JACK No. He died abroad; in Paris, in fact. I had a telegram last night from the manager of the Grand Hotel.[5]

CHASUBLE Was the cause of death mentioned?

JACK A severe chill, it seems.

MISS PRISM As a man sows, so shall he reap.

CHASUBLE [*raising his hand*] Charity, dear Miss Prism, charity! None of us are perfect. I myself am peculiarly susceptible to draughts. Will the interment take place here?

JACK No. He seemed to have expressed a desire to be buried in Paris.

CHASUBLE In Paris! [*Shakes his head.*] I fear that hardly points to any very serious state of mind at the last. You would no doubt wish me to make some slight allusion to this tragic domestic affliction next Sunday. [JACK *presses his hand convulsively.*] My sermon on the meaning of the manna in the wilderness[6] can be adapted to almost any occasion, joyful, or, as in the present case, distressing. [*All sigh.*] I have preached it at harvest celebrations, christenings, confirmations, on days of humiliation and festal days. The last time I delivered it was in the Cathedral, as a charity sermon on behalf of the Society for the Prevention of Discontent among the Upper Orders. The Bishop, who was present, was much struck by some of the analogies I drew.

JACK Ah! that reminds me, you mentioned christenings I think, Dr Chasuble? I suppose you know how to christen all right? [DR CHASUBLE *looks astounded.*] I mean, of course, you are continually christening, aren't you?

MISS PRISM It is, I regret to say, one of the Rector's most constant duties in this parish. I have often spoken to the poorer classes on the subject. But they don't seem to know what thrift is.

CHASUBLE But is there any particular infant in whom you are interested, Mr Worthing? Your brother was, I believe, unmarried, was he not?

JACK Oh, yes.

MISS PRISM [*bitterly*] People who live entirely for pleasure usually are.

5. A luxurious Paris hotel.

6 The food said to have miraculously fallen from heaven for the hungry Israelites when they wandered in the wilderness (Exodus 16).

JACK But it is not for any child, dear Doctor. I am very fond of children. No! the fact is, I would like to be christened myself, this afternoon, if you have nothing better to do.

CHASUBLE But surely, Mr Worthing, you have been christened already?

JACK I don't remember anything about it.

CHASUBLE But have you any grave doubts on the subject?

JACK I certainly intend to have. Of course I don't know if the thing would bother you in any way, or if you think I am a little too old now.

CHASUBLE Not at all. The sprinkling, and, indeed, the immersion of adults is a perfectly canonical practice.

JACK Immersion!

CHASUBLE You need have no apprehensions. Sprinkling is all that is necessary, or indeed I think advisable. Our weather is so changeable. At what hour would you wish the ceremony performed?

JACK Oh, I might trot round about five if that would suit you.

CHASUBLE Perfectly, perfectly! In fact I have two similar ceremonies to perform at that time. A case of twins that occurred recently in one of the outlying cottages on your own estate. Poor Jenkins the carter, a most hard-working man.

JACK Oh! I don't see much fun in being christened along with other babies. It would be childish. Would half-past five do?

CHASUBLE Admirably! Admirably! [*Takes out watch.*] And now, dear Mr Worthing, I will not intrude any longer into a house of sorrow. I would merely beg you not to be too much bowed down by grief. What seem to us bitter trials are often blessings in disguise.

MISS PRISM This seems to me a blessing of an extremely obvious kind.

[*Enter* CECILY *from the house.*]

CECILY Uncle Jack! Oh, I am pleased to see you back. But what horrid clothes you have got on! Do go and change them.

MISS PRISM Cecily!

CHASUBLE My child! my child!

[CECILY *goes towards* JACK; *he kisses her brow in a melancholy manner.*]

CECILY What is the matter, Uncle Jack? Do look happy! You look as if you had toothache, and I have got such a surprise for you. Who do you think is in the dining-room? Your brother!

JACK Who?

CECILY Your brother Ernest. He arrived about half an hour ago.

JACK What nonsense! I haven't got a brother.

CECILY Oh, don't say that. However badly he may have behaved to you in the past he is still your brother. You couldn't be so heartless as to disown him. I'll tell him to come out. And you will shake hands with him, won't you, Uncle Jack? [*Runs back into the house.*]

CHASUBLE These are very joyful tidings.

MISS PRISM After we had all been resigned to his loss, his sudden return seems to me peculiarly distressing.

JACK My brother is in the dining-room? I don't know what it all means. I think it is perfectly absurd.

[*Enter* ALGERNON *and* CECILY *hand in hand. They come slowly up to* JACK.]

JACK Good heavens! [*Motions* ALGERNON *away.*]

ALGERNON Brother John, I have come down from town to tell you that I am very sorry for all the trouble I have given you, and that I intend to lead a better life in the future.

[JACK *glares at him and does not take his hand.*]

CECILY Uncle Jack, you are not going to refuse your own brother's hand?

JACK Nothing will induce me to take his hand. I think his coming down here disgraceful. He knows perfectly well why.

CECILY Uncle Jack, do be nice. There is some good in everyone. Ernest has just been telling me about his poor invalid friend Mr Bunbury whom he goes to visit so often. And surely there must be much good in one who is kind to an invalid, and leaves the pleasures of London to sit by a bed of pain.

JACK Oh! he has been talking about Bunbury has he?

CECILY Yes, he has told me all about poor Mr Bunbury, and his terrible state of health.

JACK Bunbury! Well, I won't have him talk to you about Bunbury or about anything else. It is enough to drive one perfectly frantic.

ALGERNON Of course I admit that the faults were all on my side. But I must say that I think that Brother John's coldness to me is peculiarly painful. I expected a more enthusiastic welcome, especially considering it is the first time I have come here.

CECILY Uncle Jack, if you don't shake hands with Ernest I will never forgive you.

JACK Never forgive me?

CECILY Never, never, never!

JACK Well, this is the last time I shall ever do it. [*Shakes hands with* ALGERNON *and glares.*]

CHASUBLE It's pleasant, is it not, to see so perfect a reconciliation? I think we might leave the two brothers together.

MISS PRISM Cecily, you will come with us.

CECILY Certainly, Miss Prism. My little task of reconciliation is over.

CHASUBLE You have done a beautiful action today, dear child.

MISS PRISM We must not be premature in our judgments.

CECILY I feel very happy.

[*They all go off.*]

JACK You young scoundrel, Algy, you must get out of this place as soon as possible. I don't allow any Bunburying here.

[*Enter* MERRIMAN.]

MERRIMAN I have put Mr Ernest's things in the room next to yours, sir. I suppose that is all right?

JACK What?

MERRIMAN Mr Ernest's luggage, sir. I have unpacked it and put it in the room next to your own.

JACK His luggage?

MERRIMAN Yes, sir. Three portmanteaus, a dressing-case,[7] two hat-boxes, and a large luncheon-basket.

ALGERNON I am afraid I can't stay more than a week this time.

7. A case for toiletries.

JACK Merriman, order the dog-cart[8] at once. Mr Ernest has been suddenly called back to town.

MERRIMAN Yes, sir. [*Goes back into the house.*]

ALGERNON What a fearful liar you are, Jack. I have not been called back to town at all.

JACK Yes, you have.

ALGERNON I haven't heard anyone call me.

JACK Your duty as a gentleman calls you back.

ALGERNON My duty as a gentleman has never interfered with my pleasures in the smallest degree.

JACK I can quite understand that.

ALGERNON Well, Cecily is a darling.

JACK You are not to talk of Miss Cardew like that. I don't like it.

ALGERNON Well, I don't like your clothes. You look perfectly ridiculous in them. Why on earth don't you go up and change? It is perfectly childish to be in deep mourning for a man who is actually staying for a whole week with you in your house as a guest. I call it grotesque.

JACK You are certainly not staying with me for a whole week as a guest or anything else. You have got to leave . . . by the four-five train.

ALGERNON I certainly won't leave you so long as you are in mourning. It would be most unfriendly. If I were in mourning you would stay with me, I suppose. I should think it very unkind if you didn't.

JACK Well, will you go if I change my clothes?

ALGERNON Yes, if you are not too long. I never saw anybody take so long to dress, and with such little result.

JACK Well, at any rate, that is better than being always over-dressed as you are.

ALGERNON If I am occasionally a little over-dressed, I make up for it by being always immensely over-educated.

JACK Your vanity is ridiculous, your conduct an outrage, and your presence in my garden utterly absurd. However, you have got to catch the four-five, and I hope you will have a pleasant journey back to town. This Bunburying, as you call it, has not been a great success for you. [*Goes into the house.*]

ALGERNON I think it has been a great success. I'm in love with Cecily, and that is everything.

[*Enter* CECILY *at the back of the garden. She picks up the can and begins to water the flowers.*]

But I must see her before I go, and make arrangements for another Bunbury. Ah, there she is.

CECILY Oh, I merely came back to water the roses. I thought you were with Uncle Jack.

ALGERNON He's gone to order the dog-cart for me.

CECILY Oh, is he going to take you for a nice drive?

ALGERNON He's going to send me away.

CECILY Then have we got to part?

ALGERNON I am afraid so. It's a painful parting.

CECILY It is always painful to part from people whom one has known for a very brief space of time. The absence of old friends one can endure with

8. A light, two-wheeled open carriage, originally designed with a small rear compartment to hold sportsmen's dogs.

equanimity. But even a momentary separation from anyone to whom one has just been introduced is almost unbearable.

ALGERNON Thank you.

[*Enter* MERRIMAN.]

MERRIMAN The dog-cart is at the door, sir.

[ALGERNON *looks appealingly at* CECILY.]

CECILY It can wait, Merriman . . . for . . . five minutes.

MERRIMAN Yes, Miss. [*Exit* MERRIMAN.]

ALGERNON I hope, Cecily, I shall not offend you if I state quite frankly and openly that you seem to me to be in every way the visible personification of absolute perfection.

CECILY I think your frankness does you great credit, Ernest. If you will allow me I will copy your remarks into my diary. [*Goes over to table and begins writing in diary.*]

ALGERNON Do you really keep a diary? I'd give anything to look at it. May I?

CECILY Oh no. [*Puts her hand over it.*] You see, it is simply a very young girl's record of her own thoughts and impressions, and consequently meant for publication. When it appears in volume form I hope you will order a copy. But pray, Ernest, don't stop. I delight in taking down from dictation. I have reached 'absolute perfection'. You can go on. I am quite ready for more.

ALGERNON [*somewhat taken aback*] Ahem! Ahem!

CECILY Oh, don't cough, Ernest. When one is dictating one should speak fluently and not cough. Besides, I don't know how to spell a cough. [*Writes as* ALGERNON *speaks.*]

ALGERNON [*speaking very rapidly*] Cecily, ever since I first looked upon your wonderful and incomparable beauty, I have dared to love you wildly, passionately, devotedly, hopelessly.

CECILY I don't think that you should tell me that you love me wildly, passionately, devotedly, hopelessly. Hopelessly doesn't seem to make much sense, does it?

ALGERNON Cecily!

[*Enter* MERRIMAN.]

MERRIMAN The dog-cart is waiting, sir.

ALGERNON Tell it to come round next week, at the same hour.

MERRIMAN [*looks at* CECILY, *who makes no sign*] Yes, sir. [MERRIMAN *retires.*]

CECILY Uncle Jack would be very much annoyed if he knew you were staying on till next week, at the same hour.

ALGERNON Oh, I don't care about Jack. I don't care for anybody in the whole world but you. I love you, Cecily. You will marry me, won't you?

CECILY You silly boy! Of course. Why, we have been engaged for the last three months.

ALGERNON For the last three months?

CECILY Yes, it will be exactly three months on Thursday.

ALGERNON But how did we become engaged?

CECILY Well, ever since dear Uncle Jack first confessed to us that he had a younger brother who was very wicked and bad, you of course have formed the chief topic of conversation between myself and Miss Prism. And of course a man who is much talked about is always very attractive. One feels there must be something in him after all. I daresay it was foolish of me, but I fell in love with you, Ernest.

ALGERNON Darling! And when was the engagement actually settled?

CECILY On the 14th of February last.[9] Worn out by your entire ignorance of my existence, I determined to end the matter one way or the other, and after a long struggle with myself I accepted you under this dear old tree here. The next day I bought this little ring in your name, and this is the little bangle with the true lovers' knot I promised you always to wear.

ALGERNON Did I give you this? It's very pretty, isn't it?

CECILY Yes, you've wonderfully good taste, Ernest. It's the excuse I've always given for your leading such a bad life. And this is the box in which I keep all your dear letters. [*Kneels at table, opens box, and produces letters tied up with blue ribbon.*]

ALGERNON My letters! But my own sweet Cecily, I have never written you any letters.

CECILY You need hardly remind me of that, Ernest. I remember only too well that I was forced to write your letters for you. I wrote always three times a week, and sometimes oftener.

ALGERNON Oh, do let me read them, Cecily?

CECILY Oh, I couldn't possibly. They would make you far too conceited. [*Replaces box.*] The three you wrote me after I had broken off the engagement are so beautiful, and so badly spelled, that even now I can hardly read them without crying a little.

ALGERNON But was our engagement ever broken off?

CECILY Of course it was. On the 22nd of last March. You can see the entry if you like. [*Shows diary.*] 'Today I broke off my engagement with Ernest. I feel it is better to do so. The weather still continues charming.'

ALGERNON But why on earth did you break it off? What had I done? I had done nothing at all. Cecily, I am very much hurt indeed to hear you broke it off. Particularly when the weather was so charming.

CECILY It would hardly have been a really serious engagement if it hadn't been broken off at least once. But I forgave you before the week was out.

ALGERNON [*crossing to her, and kneeling*] What a perfect angel you are, Cecily.

CECILY You dear romantic boy. [*He kisses her, she puts her fingers through his hair.*] I hope your hair curls naturally, does it?

ALGERNON Yes, darling, with a little help from others.

CECILY I am so glad.

ALGERNON You'll never break off our engagement again, Cecily?

CECILY I don't think I could break it off now that I have actually met you. Besides, of course, there is the question of your name.

ALGERNON Yes, of course. [*Nervously*]

CECILY You must not laugh at me, darling, but it had always been a girlish dream of mine to love some one whose name was Ernest. [ALGERNON *rises,* CECILY *also.*] There is something in that name that seems to inspire absolute confidence. I pity any poor married woman whose husband is not called Ernest.

ALGERNON But, my dear child, do you mean to say you could not love me if I had some other name?

CECILY But what name?

9. Valentine's Day, also the date when *The Importance of Being Earnest* premiered at St. James's Theatre in 1895.

ALGERNON Oh, any name you like—Algernon—for instance . . .

CECILY But I don't like the name of Algernon.

ALGERNON Well, my own dear, sweet, loving little darling, I really can't see why you should object to the name of Algernon. It is not at all a bad name. In fact, it is rather an aristocratic name. Half of the chaps who get into the Bankruptcy Court are called Algernon. But seriously, Cecily . . . [*Moving to her*] . . . if my name was Algy, couldn't you love me?

CECILY [*rising*] I might respect you, Ernest, I might admire your character, but I fear that I should not be able to give you my undivided attention.

ALGERNON Ahem! Cecily! [*Picking up hat*] Your Rector here is, I suppose, thoroughly experienced in the practice of all the rites and ceremonials of the Church?

CECILY Oh yes. Dr Chasuble is a most learned man. He has never written a single book, so you can imagine how much he knows.

ALGERNON I must see him at once on a most important christening—I mean on most important business.

CECILY Oh!

ALGERNON I shan't be away more than half an hour.

CECILY Considering that we have been engaged since February the 14th, and that I only met you today for the first time, I think it is rather hard that you should leave me for so long a period as half an hour. Couldn't you make it twenty minutes?

ALGERNON I'll be back in no time. [*Kisses her and rushes down the garden.*]

CECILY What an impetuous boy he is! I like his hair so much. I must enter his proposal in my diary.

[*Enter* MERRIMAN.]

MERRIMAN A Miss Fairfax has just called to see Mr Worthing. On very important business Miss Fairfax states.

CECILY Isn't Mr Worthing in his library?

MERRIMAN Mr Worthing went over in the direction of the Rectory some time ago.

CECILY Pray ask the lady to come out here; Mr Worthing is sure to be back soon. And you can bring tea.

MERRIMAN Yes, Miss. [*Goes out.*]

CECILY Miss Fairfax! I suppose one of the many good elderly women who are associated with Uncle Jack in some of his philanthropic work in London. I don't quite like women who are interested in philanthropic work. I think it is so forward of them.

[*Enter* MERRIMAN.]

MERRIMAN Miss Fairfax.

[*Enter* GWENDOLEN.] [*Exit* MERRIMAN.]

CECILY [*advancing to meet her*] Pray let me introduce myself to you. My name is Cecily Cardew.

GWENDOLEN Cecily Cardew? [*Moving to her and shaking hands*] What a very sweet name! Something tells me that we are going to be great friends. I like you already more than I can say. My first impressions of people are never wrong.

CECILY How nice of you to like me so much after we have known each other such a comparatively short time. Pray sit down.

GWENDOLEN [*still standing up*] I may call you Cecily, may I not?

CECILY With pleasure!

GWENDOLEN And you will always call me Gwendolen, won't you.

CECILY If you wish.

GWENDOLEN Then that is all quite settled, is it not?

CECILY I hope so.

[*A pause. They both sit down together.*]

GWENDOLEN Perhaps this might be a favourable opportunity for my mentioning who I am. My father is Lord Bracknell. You have never heard of papa, I suppose?

CECILY I don't think so.

GWENDOLEN Outside the family circle, papa, I am glad to say, is entirely unknown. I think that is quite as it should be. The home seems to me to be the proper sphere for the man.[1] And certainly once a man begins to neglect his domestic duties he becomes painfully effeminate, does he not? And I don't like that. It makes men so very attractive. Cecily, mamma, whose views on education are remarkably strict, has brought me up to be extremely short-sighted; it is part of her system; so do you mind my looking at you through my glasses?

CECILY Oh! not at all, Gwendolen. I am very fond of being looked at.

GWENDOLEN [*after examining* CECILY *carefully through a lorgnette*] You are here on a short visit I suppose.

CECILY Oh no! I live here.

GWENDOLEN [*severely*] Really? Your mother, no doubt, or some female relative of advanced years, resides here also?

CECILY Oh no! I have no mother, nor, in fact, any relations.

GWENDOLEN Indeed?

CECILY My dear guardian, with the assistance of Miss Prism, has the arduous task of looking after me.

GWENDOLEN Your guardian?

CECILY Yes, I am Mr Worthing's ward.

GWENDOLEN Oh! It is strange he never mentioned to me that he had a ward. How secretive of him! He grows more interesting hourly. I am not sure, however, that the news inspires me with feelings of unmixed delight. [*Rising and going to her*] I am very fond of you, Cecily; I have liked you ever since I met you! But I am bound to state that now that I know that you are Mr Worthing's ward, I cannot help expressing a wish you were—well just a little older than you seem to be—and not quite so very alluring in appearance. In fact, if I may speak candidly——

CECILY Pray do! I think that whenever one has anything unpleasant to say, one should always be quite candid.

GWENDOLEN Well, to speak with perfect candour, Cecily, I wish that you were fully forty-two, and more than usually plain for your age. Ernest has a strong upright nature. He is the very soul of truth and honour. Disloyalty would be as impossible to him as deception. But even men of the noblest possible moral character are extremely susceptible to the influence of the physical charms of others. Modern, no less than Ancient History, supplies

1. The 19th-century doctrine of separate spheres divided life into two domains: public (male) and private (female).

us with many most painful examples of what I refer to. If it were not so, indeed, History would be quite unreadable.

CECILY I beg your pardon, Gwendolen, did you say Ernest?

GWENDOLEN Yes.

CECILY Oh, but it is not Mr Ernest Worthing who is my guardian. It is his brother—his elder brother.

GWENDOLEN [*sitting down again*] Ernest never mentioned to me that he had a brother.

CECILY I am sorry to say they have not been on good terms for a long time.

GWENDOLEN Ah! that accounts for it. And now that I think of it I have never heard any man mention his brother. The subject seems distasteful to most men. Cecily, you have lifted a load from my mind. I was growing almost anxious. It would have been terrible if any cloud had come across a friendship like ours, would it not? Of course you are quite, quite sure that it is not Mr Ernest Worthing who is your guardian?

CECILY Quite sure. [*A pause*] In fact, I am going to be his.

GWENDOLEN [*enquiringly*] I beg your pardon?

CECILY [*rather shy and confidingly*] Dearest Gwendolen, there is no reason why I should make a secret of it to you. Our little county newspaper is sure to chronicle the fact next week. Mr Ernest Worthing and I are engaged to be married.

GWENDOLEN [*quite politely, rising*] My darling Cecily, I think there must be some slight error. Mr Ernest Worthing is engaged to me. The announcement will appear in the 'Morning Post'[2] on Saturday at the latest.

CECILY [*very politely, rising*] I am afraid you must be under some misconception. Ernest proposed to me exactly ten minutes ago. [*Shows diary.*]

GWENDOLEN [*examines diary through her lorgnette carefully*] It is certainly very curious, for he asked me to be his wife yesterday afternoon at 5.30. If you would care to verify the incident, pray do so. [*Produces diary of her own.*] I never travel without my diary. One should always have something sensational to read in the train. I am so sorry, dear Cecily, if it is any disappointment to you, but I am afraid *I* have the prior claim.

CECILY It would distress me more than I can tell you, dear Gwendolen, if it caused you any mental or physical anguish, but I feel bound to point out that since Ernest proposed to you he clearly has changed his mind.

GWENDOLEN [*meditatively*] If the poor fellow has been entrapped into any foolish promise I shall consider it my duty to rescue him at once, and with a firm hand.

CECILY [*thoughtfully and sadly*] Whatever unfortunate entanglement my dear boy may have got into, I will never reproach him with it after we are married.

GWENDOLEN Do you allude to me, Miss Cardew, as an entanglement? You are presumptuous. On an occasion of this kind it becomes more than a moral duty to speak one's mind. It becomes a pleasure.

CECILY Do you suggest, Miss Fairfax, that I entrapped Ernest into an engagement? How dare you? This is no time for wearing the shallow mask of manners. When I see a spade I call it a spade.

GWENDOLEN [*satirically*] I am glad to say that I have never seen a spade. It is obvious that our social spheres have been widely different.

2. The London *Morning Post*, a conservative daily newspaper.

[*Enter* MERRIMAN, *followed by the footman. He carries a salver, table cloth, and plate stand.* CECILY *is about to retort. The presence of the servants exercises a restraining influence, under which both girls chafe.*]

MERRIMAN Shall I lay tea here as usual, Miss?

CECILY [*sternly, in a calm voice*] Yes, as usual.

[MERRIMAN *begins to clear table and lay cloth. A long pause.* CECILY *and* GWENDOLEN *glare at each other.*]

GWENDOLEN Are there many interesting walks in the vicinity, Miss Cardew?

CECILY Oh! yes! a great many. From the top of one of the hills quite close one can see five counties.

GWENDOLEN Five counties! I don't think I should like that. I hate crowds.

CECILY [*sweetly*] I suppose that is why you live in town?

[GWENDOLEN *bites her lip, and beats her foot nervously with her parasol.*]

GWENDOLEN [*looking round*] Quite a well-kept garden this is, Miss Cardew.

CECILY So glad you like it, Miss Fairfax.

GWENDOLEN I had no idea there were any flowers in the country.

CECILY Oh, flowers are as common here, Miss Fairfax, as people are in London.

GWENDOLEN Personally, I cannot understand how anybody manages to exist in the country, if anybody who is anybody does. The country always bores me to death.

CECILY Ah! This is what the newspapers call agricultural depression,[3] is it not? I believe the aristocracy are suffering very much from it just at present. It is almost an epidemic amongst them, I have been told. May I offer you some tea, Miss Fairfax?

GWENDOLEN [*with elaborate politeness*] Thank you. [*Aside*] Detestable girl! But I require tea!

CECILY [*sweetly*] Sugar?

GWENDOLEN [*superciliously*] No, thank you. Sugar is not fashionable any more.

[CECILY *looks angrily at her, takes up the tongs and puts four lumps of sugar into the cup.*]

CECILY [*severely*] Cake or bread and butter?

GWENDOLEN [*in a bored manner*] Bread and butter, please. Cake is rarely seen at the best houses nowadays.

CECILY [*cuts a very large slice of cake, and puts it on the tray*] Hand that to Miss Fairfax.

[MERRIMAN *does so, and goes out with footman.* GWENDOLEN *drinks the tea and makes a grimace. Puts down cup at once, reaches out her hand to the bread and butter, looks at it, and finds it is cake. Rises in indignation.*]

GWENDOLEN You have filled my tea with lumps of sugar, and though I asked most distinctly for bread and butter, you have given me cake. I am known for the gentleness of my disposition, and the extraordinary sweetness of my nature, but I warn you, Miss Cardew, you may go too far.

CECILY [*rising*] To save my poor, innocent, trusting boy from the machinations of any other girl there are no lengths to which I would not go.

3. British agriculture had been in an economic slump since the 1870s.

GWENDOLEN From the moment I saw you I distrusted you. I felt that you were false and deceitful. I am never deceived in such matters. My first impressions of people are invariably right.

CECILY It seems to me, Miss Fairfax, that I am trespassing on your valuable time. No doubt you have many other calls of a similar character to make in the neighbourhood.

[*Enter* JACK.]

GWENDOLEN [*catching sight of him*] Ernest! My own Ernest!

JACK Gwendolen! Darling! [*Offers*[4] *to kiss her.*]

GWENDOLEN [*drawing back*] A moment! May I ask if you are engaged to be married to this young lady? [*Points to* CECILY.]

JACK [*laughing*] To dear little Cecily! Of course not! What could have put such an idea into your pretty little head?

GWENDOLEN Thank you. You may! [*Offers her cheek.*]

CECILY [*very sweetly*] I knew there must be some misunderstanding, Miss Fairfax. The gentleman whose arm is at present round your waist is my dear guardian, Mr John Worthing.

GWENDOLEN I beg your pardon?

CECILY This is Uncle Jack.

GWENDOLEN [*receding*] Jack! Oh!

[*Enter* ALGERNON.]

CECILY Here is Ernest.

ALGERNON [*goes straight over to* CECILY *without noticing anyone else*] My own love! [*Offers to kiss her.*]

CECILY [*drawing back*] A moment, Ernest! May I ask you—are you engaged to be married to this young lady?

ALGERNON [*looking round*] To what young lady? Good heavens! Gwendolen!

CECILY Yes, to good heavens, Gwendolen, I mean to Gwendolen.

ALGERNON [*laughing*] Of course not! What could have put such an idea into your pretty little head?

CECILY Thank you. [*Presenting her cheek to be kissed*] You may.

[ALGERNON *kisses her.*]

GWENDOLEN I felt there was some slight error, Miss Cardew. The gentleman who is now embracing you is my cousin, Mr Algernon Moncrieff.

CECILY [*breaking away from* ALGERNON] Algernon Moncrieff! Oh!

[*The two girls move towards each other and put their arms round each other's waists as if for protection.*]

CECILY Are you called Algernon?

ALGERNON I cannot deny it.

CECILY Oh!

GWENDOLEN Is your name really John?

JACK [*standing rather proudly*] I could deny it if I liked. I could deny anything if I liked. But my name certainly is John. It has been John for years.

CECILY [*to* GWENDOLEN] A gross deception has been practised on both of us.

GWENDOLEN My poor wounded Cecily!

CECILY My sweet wronged Gwendolen!

GWENDOLEN [*slowly and seriously*] You will call me sister, will you not?

4. Attempts.

[*They embrace.* JACK *and* ALGERNON *groan and walk up and down.*]

CECILY [*rather brightly*] There is just one question I would like to be allowed to ask my guardian.

GWENDOLEN An admirable idea! Mr Worthing, there is just one question I would like to be permitted to put to you. Where is your brother Ernest? We are both engaged to be married to your brother Ernest, so it is a matter of some importance to us to know where your brother Ernest is at present.

JACK [*slowly and hesitatingly*] Gwendolen—Cecily—it is very painful for me to be forced to speak the truth. It is the first time in my life that I have ever been reduced to such a painful position, and I am really quite inexperienced in doing anything of the kind. However I will tell you quite frankly that I have no brother Ernest. I have no brother at all. I never had a brother in my life, and I certainly have not the smallest intention of ever having one in the future.

CECILY [*surprised*] No brother at all?

JACK [*cheerily*] None!

GWENDOLEN [*severely*] Had you never a brother of any kind?

JACK [*pleasantly*] Never. Not even of any kind.

GWENDOLEN I am afraid it is quite clear, Cecily, that neither of us is engaged to be married to anyone.

CECILY It is not a very pleasant position for a young girl suddenly to find herself in. Is it?

GWENDOLEN Let us go into the house. They will hardly venture to come after us there.

CECILY No, men are so cowardly, aren't they?

[*They retire into the house with scornful looks.*]

JACK This ghastly state of things is what you call Bunburying, I suppose?

ALGERNON Yes, and a perfectly wonderful Bunbury it is. The most wonderful Bunbury I have ever had in my life.

JACK Well, you've no right whatsoever to Bunbury here.

ALGERNON That is absurd. One has a right to Bunbury anywhere one chooses. Every serious Bunburyist knows that.

JACK Serious Bunburyist! Good heavens!

ALGERNON Well, one must be serious about something, if one wants to have any amusement in life. I happen to be serious about Bunburying. What on earth you are serious about I haven't got the remotest idea. About everything, I should fancy. You have such an absolutely trivial nature.

JACK Well, the only small satisfaction I have in the whole of this wretched business is that your friend Bunbury is quite exploded. You won't be able to run down to the country quite so often as you used to do, dear Algy. And a very good thing too.

ALGERNON Your brother is a little off colour,[5] isn't he, dear Jack? You won't be able to disappear to London quite so frequently as your wicked custom was. And not a bad thing either.

JACK As for your conduct towards Miss Cardew, I must say that your taking in a sweet, simple, innocent girl like that is quite inexcusable. To say nothing of the fact that she is my ward.

5. That is, in poor health.

ALGERNON I can see no possible defence at all for your deceiving a brilliant, clever, thoroughly experienced young lady like Miss Fairfax. To say nothing of the fact that she is my cousin.

JACK I wanted to be engaged to Gwendolen, that is all. I love her.

ALGERNON Well, I simply wanted to be engaged to Cecily. I adore her.

JACK There is certainly no chance of your marrying Miss Cardew.

ALGERNON I don't think there is much likelihood, Jack, of you and Miss Fairfax being united.

JACK Well, that is no business of yours.

ALGERNON If it was my business, I wouldn't talk about it. [*Begins to eat muffins.*] It is very vulgar to talk about one's business. Only people like stock-brokers do that, and then merely at dinner parties.

JACK How you can sit there, calmly eating muffins when we are in this horrible trouble, I can't make out. You seem to me to be perfectly heartless.

ALGERNON Well, I can't eat muffins in an agitated manner. The butter would probably get on my cuffs. One should always eat muffins quite calmly. It is the only way to eat them.

JACK I say it's perfectly heartless your eating muffins at all, under the circumstances.

ALGERNON When I am in trouble, eating is the only thing that consoles me. Indeed, when I am in really great trouble, as anyone who knows me intimately will tell you, I refuse everything except food and drink. At the present moment I am eating muffins because I am unhappy. Besides, I am particularly fond of muffins. [*Rising*]

JACK [*rising*] Well, that is no reason why you should eat them all in that greedy way. [*Takes muffins from* ALGERNON.]

ALGERNON [*offering tea-cake*] I wish you would have tea-cake instead. I don't like tea-cake.

JACK Good heavens! I suppose a man may eat his own muffins in his own garden.

ALGERNON But you have just said it was perfectly heartless to eat muffins.

JACK I said it was perfectly heartless of you, under the circumstances. That is a very different thing.

ALGERNON That may be. But the muffins are the same. [*He seizes the muffin-dish from* JACK.]

JACK Algy, I wish to goodness you would go.

ALGERNON You can't possibly ask me to go without having some dinner. It's absurd. I never go without my dinner. No one ever does, except vegetarians and people like that. Besides I have just made arrangements with Dr Chasuble to be christened at a quarter to six under the name of Ernest.

JACK My dear fellow, the sooner you give up that nonsense the better. I made arrangements this morning with Dr Chasuble to be christened myself at 5.30, and I naturally will take the name of Ernest. Gwendolen would wish it. We can't both be christened Ernest. It's absurd. Besides, I have a perfect right to be christened if I like. There is no evidence at all that I ever have been christened by anybody. I should think it extremely probable I never was, and so does Dr Chasuble. It is entirely different in your case. You have been christened already.

ALGERNON Yes, but I have not been christened for years.

JACK Yes, but you have been christened. That is the important thing.

ALGERNON Quite so. So I know my constitution can stand it. If you are not quite sure about your ever having been christened, I must say I think it rather dangerous your venturing on it now. It might make you very unwell. You can hardly have forgotten that someone very closely connected with you was very nearly carried off this week in Paris by a severe chill.

JACK Yes, but you said yourself that a severe chill was not hereditary.

ALGERNON It usen't to be, I know—but I daresay it is now. Science is always making wonderful improvements in things.

JACK [*picking up the muffin-dish*] Oh, that is nonsense; you are always talking nonsense.

ALGERNON Jack, you are at the muffins again! I wish you wouldn't. There are only two left. [*Takes them.*] I told you I was particularly fond of muffins.

JACK But I hate tea-cake.

ALGERNON Why on earth then do you allow tea-cake to be served up for your guests? What ideas you have of hospitality!

JACK Algernon! I have already told you to go. I don't want you here. Why don't you go!

ALGERNON I haven't quite finished my tea yet! and there is still one muffin left.

[JACK *groans, and sinks into a chair.* ALGERNON *still continues eating.*]

Act Drop.

Third Act

[SCENE: *Morning-room at the Manor House.*]

[GWENDOLEN *and* CECILY *are at the window, looking out into the garden.*]

GWENDOLEN The fact that they did not follow us at once into the house, as anyone else would have done, seems to me to show that they have some sense of shame left.

CECILY They have been eating muffins. That looks like repentance.

GWENDOLEN [*after a pause*] They don't seem to notice us at all. Couldn't you cough?

CECILY But I haven't got a cough.

GWENDOLEN They're looking at us. What effrontery!

CECILY They're approaching. That's very forward of them.

GWENDOLEN Let us preserve a dignified silence.

CECILY Certainly. It's the only thing to do now.

[*Enter* JACK *followed by* ALGERNON. *They whistle some dreadful popular air from a British Opera.*[6]]

GWENDOLEN This dignified silence seems to produce an unpleasant effect.

CECILY A most distasteful one.

GWENDOLEN But we will not be the first to speak.

CECILY Certainly not.

GWENDOLEN Mr Worthing, I have something very particular to ask you. Much depends on your reply.

6. Possibly a reference to the comic operas of W. S. Gilbert (1836–1911) and Sir Arthur Sullivan (1842–1900), whose 1881 *Patience* satirized Wilde and the aesthetic movement.

CECILY Gwendolen, your common sense is invaluable. Mr Moncrieff, kindly answer me the following question. Why did you pretend to be my guardian's brother?

ALGERNON In order that I might have an opportunity of meeting you.

CECILY [*to* GWENDOLEN] That certainly seems a satisfactory explanation, does it not?

GWENDOLEN Yes, dear, if you can believe him.

CECILY I don't. But that does not affect the wonderful beauty of his answer.

GWENDOLEN True. In matters of grave importance, style, not sincerity is the vital thing. Mr Worthing, what explanation can you offer to me for pretending to have a brother? Was it in order that you might have an opportunity of coming up to town to see me as often as possible?

JACK Can you doubt it, Miss Fairfax?

GWENDOLEN I have the gravest doubts upon the subject. But I intend to crush them. This is not the moment for German scepticism.[7] [*Moving to* CECILY] Their explanations appear to be quite satisfactory, especially Mr Worthing's. That seems to me to have the stamp of truth upon it.

CECILY I am more than content with what Mr Moncrieff said. His voice alone inspires one with absolute credulity.

GWENDOLEN Then you think we should forgive them?

CECILY Yes. I mean no.

GWENDOLEN True! I had forgotten. There are principles at stake that one cannot surrender. Which of us should tell them? The task is not a pleasant one.

CECILY Could we not both speak at the same time?

GWENDOLEN An excellent idea! I nearly always speak at the same time as other people. Will you take the time from me?

CECILY Certainly.

[GWENDOLEN *beats time with uplifted finger.*]

GWENDOLEN and CECILY [*speaking together*] Your Christian names are still an insuperable barrier. That is all!

JACK and ALGERNON [*speaking together*] Our Christian names! Is that all? But we are going to be christened this afternoon.

GWENDOLEN [*to* JACK] For my sake you are prepared to do this terrible thing?

JACK I am.

CECILY [*to* ALGERNON] To please me you are ready to face this fearful ordeal?

ALGERNON I am!

GWENDOLEN How absurd to talk of the equality of the sexes! Where questions of self-sacrifice are concerned, men are infinitely beyond us.

JACK We are. [*Clasps hands with* ALGERNON.]

CECILY They have moments of physical courage of which we women know absolutely nothing.

GWENDOLEN [*to* JACK] Darling!

ALGERNON [*to* CECILY] Darling! [*They fall into each other's arms.*]

[*Enter* MERRIMAN. *When he enters he coughs loudly, seeing the situation.*]

7. German biblical scholars of the 19th century were notorious among the British for their skepticism toward scriptural authority and claims of divine revelation.

MERRIMAN Ahem! Ahem! Lady Bracknell!

JACK Good heavens!

[*Enter* LADY BRACKNELL. *The couples separate in alarm.*]

[*Exit* MERRIMAN.]

LADY BRACKNELL Gwendolen! What does this mean?

GWENDOLEN Merely that I am engaged to be married to Mr Worthing, mamma.

LADY BRACKNELL Come here. Sit down. Sit down immediately. Hesitation of any kind is a sign of mental decay in the young, of physical weakness in the old. [*Turns to* JACK.] Apprised, sir, of my daughter's sudden flight by her trusty maid, whose confidence I purchased by means of a small coin, I followed her at once by a luggage train.[8] Her unhappy father is, I am glad to say, under the impression that she is attending a more than usually lengthy lecture by the University Extension Scheme[9] on the Influence of a permanent income on Thought. I do not propose to undeceive him. Indeed I have never undeceived him on any question. I would consider it wrong. But of course, you will clearly understand that all communication between yourself and my daughter must cease immediately from this moment. On this point, as indeed on all points, I am firm.

JACK I am engaged to be married to Gwendolen, Lady Bracknell!

LADY BRACKNELL You are nothing of the kind, sir. And now, as regards Algernon! . . . Algernon!

ALGERNON Yes, Aunt Augusta.

LADY BRACKNELL May I ask if it is in this house that your invalid friend Mr Bunbury resides?

ALGERNON [*stammering*] Oh! No! Bunbury doesn't live here. Bunbury is somewhere else at present. In fact, Bunbury is dead.

LADY BRACKNELL Dead! When did Mr Bunbury die? His death must have been extremely sudden.

ALGERNON [*airily*] Oh! I killed Bunbury this afternoon. I mean poor Bunbury died this afternoon.

LADY BRACKNELL What did he die of?

ALGERNON Bunbury? Oh, he was quite exploded.

LADY BRACKNELL Exploded! Was he the victim of a revolutionary outrage? I was not aware that Mr Bunbury was interested in social legislation. If so, he is well punished for his morbidity.

ALGERNON My dear Aunt Augusta, I mean he was found out! The doctors found out that Bunbury could not live, that is what I mean—so Bunbury died.

LADY BRACKNELL He seems to have had great confidence in the opinion of his physicians. I am glad, however, that he made up his mind at the last to some definite course of action, and acted under proper medical advice. And now that we have finally got rid of this Mr Bunbury, may I ask, Mr Worthing, who is that young person whose hand my nephew Algernon is now holding in what seems to me a peculiarly unnecessary manner?

JACK That lady is Miss Cecily Cardew, my ward.

[LADY BRACKNELL *bows coldly to* CECILY.]

8. Freight train.

9. An extramural education program in which university instructors delivered lectures to students not pursuing regular degrees.

ALGERNON I am engaged to be married to Cecily, Aunt Augusta.

LADY BRACKNELL I beg your pardon?

CECILY Mr Moncrieff and I are engaged to be married, Lady Bracknell.

LADY BRACKNELL [*with a shiver, crossing to the sofa and sitting down*] I do not know whether there is anything peculiarly exciting in the air of this particular part of Hertfordshire, but the number of engagements that go on seems to me considerably above the proper average that statistics have laid down for our guidance. I think some preliminary enquiry on my part would not be out of place. Mr Worthing, is Miss Cardew at all connected with any of the larger railway stations in London? I merely desire information. Until yesterday I had no idea that there were any families or persons whose origin was a Terminus.[1]

[JACK *looks perfectly furious, but restrains himself.*]

JACK [*in a clear, cold voice*] Miss Cardew is the granddaughter of the late Mr Thomas Cardew of 149, Belgrave Square, S.W.; Gervase Park, Dorking, Surrey; and the Sporran, Fifeshire, N.B.[2]

LADY BRACKNELL That sounds not unsatisfactory. Three addresses always inspire confidence, even in tradesmen. But what proof have I of their authenticity?

JACK I have carefully preserved the Court Guides[3] of the period. They are open to your inspection, Lady Bracknell.

LADY BRACKNELL [*grimly*] I have known strange errors in that publication.

JACK Miss Cardew's family solicitors are Messrs[4] Markby, Markby, and Markby.

LADY BRACKNELL Markby, Markby, and Markby? A firm of the very highest position in their profession. Indeed I am told that one of the Mr Markbys is occasionally to be seen at dinner parties. So far I am satisfied.

JACK [*very irritably*] How extremely kind of you, Lady Bracknell! I have also in my possession, you will be pleased to hear, certificates of Miss Cardew's birth, baptism, whooping cough, registration, vaccination, confirmation, and the measles; both the German and the English variety.[5]

LADY BRACKNELL Ah! A life crowded with incident, I see; though perhaps somewhat too exciting for a young girl. I am not myself in favour of premature experiences. [*Rises, looks at her watch.*] Gwendolen! the time approaches for our departure. We have not a moment to lose. As a matter of form, Mr Worthing, I had better ask you if Miss Cardew has any little fortune?

JACK Oh! about a hundred and thirty thousand pounds in the Funds.[6] That is all. Goodbye, Lady Bracknell. So pleased to have seen you.

LADY BRACKNELL [*sitting down again*] A moment, Mr Worthing. A hundred and thirty thousand pounds! And in the Funds! Miss Cardew seems to me

1. The station at the end of a railway line.
2. That is, with residences in Belgravia, in a county south of London, and in Scotland ("North Britain").
3. Annual publications listing the names and addresses of those presented at court—that is, the British nobility, gentry, and anyone else of social importance.
4. The plural of "Mister." *Solicitors:* British lawyers who advise and represent clients, but do not argue cases in court.
5. That is, both rubeola and rubella.
6. Interest-bearing government bonds—and a considerable fortune (roughly equivalent to $20 million today).

a most attractive young lady, now that I look at her. Few girls of the present day have any really solid qualities, any of the qualities that last, and improve with time. We live, I regret to say, in an age of surfaces. [*To* CECILY] Come over here, dear. [CECILY *goes across.*] Pretty child! your dress is sadly simple, and your hair seems almost as Nature might have left it. But we can soon alter all that. A thoroughly experienced French maid produces a really marvellous result in a very brief space of time. I remember recommending one to young Lady Lancing, and after three months her own husband did not know her.

JACK [*aside*] And after six months nobody knew her.[7]

LADY BRACKNELL [*glares at* JACK *for a few moments. Then bends, with a practised smile, to* CECILY] Kindly turn round, sweet child. [CECILY *turns completely round.*] No, the side view is what I want. [CECILY *presents her profile.*] Yes, quite as I expected. There are distinct social possibilities in your profile. The two weak points in our age are its want of principle and its want of profile. The chin a little higher, dear. Style largely depends on the way the chin is worn. They are worn very high, just at present. Algernon!

ALGERNON Yes, Aunt Augusta!

LADY BRACKNELL There are distinct social possibilities in Miss Cardew's profile.

ALGERNON Cecily is the sweetest, dearest, prettiest girl in the whole world. And I don't care twopence about social possibilities.

LADY BRACKNELL Never speak disrespectfully of Society, Algernon. Only people who can't get into it do that. [*To* CECILY] Dear child, of course you know that Algernon has nothing but his debts to depend upon. But I do not approve of mercenary marriages. When I married Lord Bracknell I had no fortune of any kind. But I never dreamed for a moment of allowing that to stand in my way. Well, I suppose I must give my consent.

ALGERNON Thank you, Aunt Augusta.

LADY BRACKNELL Cecily, you may kiss me!

CECILY [*kisses her*] Thank you, Lady Bracknell.

LADY BRACKNELL You may also address me as Aunt Augusta for the future.

CECILY Thank you, Aunt Augusta.

LADY BRACKNELL The marriage, I think, had better take place quite soon.

ALGERNON Thank you, Aunt Augusta.

CECILY Thank you, Aunt Augusta.

LADY BRACKNELL To speak frankly, I am not in favour of long engagements. They give people the opportunity of finding out each other's character before marriage, which I think is never advisable.

JACK I beg your pardon for interrupting you, Lady Bracknell, but this engagement is quite out of the question. I am Miss Cardew's guardian, and she cannot marry without my consent until she comes of age. That consent I absolutely decline to give.

LADY BRACKNELL Upon what grounds may I ask? Algernon is an extremely, I may almost say an ostentatiously, eligible young man. He has nothing, but he looks everything. What more can one desire?

JACK It pains me very much to have to speak frankly to you, Lady Bracknell, about your nephew, but the fact is that I do not approve at all of his moral character. I suspect him of being untruthful.

7. Acknowledged her socially (i.e., her behavior had become scandalous).

[ALGERNON *and* CECILY *look at him in indignant amazement.*]

LADY BRACKNELL Untruthful! My nephew Algernon? Impossible! He is an Oxonian.[8]

JACK I fear there can be no possible doubt about the matter. This afternoon, during my temporary absence in London on an important question of romance, he obtained admission to my house by means of the false pretence of being my brother. Under an assumed name he drank, I've just been informed by my butler, an entire pint bottle of my Perrier-Jouet, Brut, '89;[9] a wine I was specially reserving for myself. Continuing his disgraceful deception, he succeeded in the course of the afternoon in alienating the affections of my only ward. He subsequently stayed to tea, and devoured every single muffin. And what makes his conduct all the more heartless is, that he was perfectly well aware from the first that I have no brother, that I never had a brother, and that I don't intend to have a brother, not even of any kind. I distinctly told him so myself yesterday afternoon.

LADY BRACKNELL Ahem! Mr Worthing, after careful consideration I have decided entirely to overlook my nephew's conduct to you.

JACK That is very generous of you, Lady Bracknell. My own decision, however, is unalterable. I decline to give my consent.

LADY BRACKNELL [*to* CECILY] Come here, sweet child. [CECILY *goes over.*] How old are you, dear?

CECILY Well, I am really only eighteen, but I always admit to twenty when I go to evening parties.

LADY BRACKNELL You are perfectly right in making some slight alteration. Indeed, no woman should ever be quite accurate about her age. It looks so calculating. . . . [*In a meditative manner*] Eighteen, but admitting to twenty at evening parties. Well, it will not be very long before you are of age and free from the restraints of tutelage. So I don't think your guardian's consent is, after all, a matter of any importance.

JACK Pray excuse me, Lady Bracknell, for interrupting you again, but it is only fair to tell you that according to the terms of her grandfather's will Miss Cardew does not come legally of age till she is thirty-five.

LADY BRACKNELL That does not seem to me to be a grave objection. Thirty-five is a very attractive age. London society is full of women of the very highest birth who have, of their own free choice, remained thirty-five for years. Lady Dumbleton is an instance in point. To my own knowledge she has been thirty-five ever since she arrived at the age of forty, which was many years ago now. I see no reason why our dear Cecily should not be even still more attractive at the age you mention than she is at present. There will be a large accumulation of property.

CECILY Algy, could you wait for me till I was thirty-five?

ALGERNON Of course I could, Cecily. You know I could.

CECILY Yes, I felt it instinctively, but I couldn't wait all that time. I hate waiting even five minutes for anybody. It always makes me rather cross. I am not punctual myself, I know, but I do like punctuality in others, and waiting, even to be married, is quite out of the question.

ALGERNON Then what is to be done, Cecily?

CECILY I don't know, Mr Moncrieff.

8. A student at or graduate of Oxford University.

9. A particularly fine vintage of dry champagne.

LADY BRACKNELL My dear Mr Worthing, as Miss Cardew states positively that she cannot wait till she is thirty-five—a remark which I am bound to say seems to me to show a somewhat impatient nature—I would beg of you to reconsider your decision.

JACK But my dear Lady Bracknell, the matter is entirely in your own hands. The moment you consent to my marriage with Gwendolen, I will most gladly allow your nephew to form an alliance with my ward.

LADY BRACKNELL [*rising and drawing herself up*] You must be quite aware that what you propose is out of the question.

JACK Then a passionate celibacy is all that any of us can look forward to.

LADY BRACKNELL That is not the destiny I propose for Gwendolen. Algernon, of course, can choose for himself. [*Pulls out her watch.*] Come, dear; [GWENDOLEN *rises.*] we have already missed five, if not six, trains. To miss any more might expose us to comment on the platform.

[*Enter* DR CHASUBLE.]

CHASUBLE Everything is quite ready for the christenings.

LADY BRACKNELL The christenings, sir! Is not that somewhat premature?

CHASUBLE [*looking rather puzzled, and pointing to* JACK *and* ALGERNON] Both these gentlemen have expressed a desire for immediate baptism.

LADY BRACKNELL At their age? The idea is grotesque and irreligious! Algernon, I forbid you to be baptized. I will not hear of such excesses. Lord Bracknell would be highly displeased if he learned that that was the way in which you wasted your time and money.

CHASUBLE Am I to understand then that there are to be no christenings at all this afternoon?

JACK I don't think that, as things are now, it would be of much practical value to either of us, Dr Chasuble.

CHASUBLE I am grieved to hear such sentiments from you, Mr Worthing. They savour of the heretical views of the Anabaptists,[1] views that I have completely refuted in four of my unpublished sermons. However, as your present mood seems to be one peculiarly secular, I will return to the church at once. Indeed, I have just been informed by the pew-opener[2] that for the last hour and a half Miss Prism has been waiting for me in the vestry.

LADY BRACKNELL [*starting*] Miss Prism! Did I hear you mention a Miss Prism?

CHASUBLE Yes, Lady Bracknell. I am on my way to join her.

LADY BRACKNELL Pray allow me to detain you for a moment. This matter may prove to be one of vital importance to Lord Bracknell and myself. Is this Miss Prism a female of repellent aspect, remotely connected with education?

CHASUBLE [*somewhat indignantly*] She is the most cultivated of ladies, and the very picture of respectability.

LADY BRACKNELL It is obviously the same person. May I ask what position she holds in your household?

1. Members of a radical Protestant sect, established in Germany in the 16th century, that advocated the baptism only of adult believers (*Anabaptist* literally means "one who baptizes over again"); the label was sometimes applied pejoratively to Baptists or to others who rejected Anglican doctrine.

2. An usher who unlocked the private pews provided by many churches.

CHASUBLE [*severely*] I am a celibate, madam.

JACK [*interposing*] Miss Prism, Lady Bracknell, has been for the last three years Miss Cardew's esteemed governess and valued companion.

LADY BRACKNELL In spite of what I hear of her, I must see her at once. Let her be sent for.

CHASUBLE [*looking off*] She approaches; she is nigh.

[*Enter* MISS PRISM *hurriedly.*]

MISS PRISM I was told you expected me in the vestry, dear Canon. I have been waiting for you there for an hour and three quarters. [*Catches sight of* LADY BRACKNELL *who has fixed her with a stony glare.* MISS PRISM *grows pale and quails. She looks anxiously round as if desirous to escape.*]

LADY BRACKNELL [*in a severe, judicial voice*] Prism! [MISS PRISM *bows her head in shame.*] Come here, Prism! [MISS PRISM *approaches in a humble manner.*] Prism! Where is that baby? [*General consternation. The* CANON *starts back in horror.* ALGERNON *and* JACK *pretend to be anxious to shield* CECILY *and* GWENDOLEN *from hearing the details of a terrible public scandal.*] Twenty-eight years ago, Prism, you left Lord Bracknell's house, Number 104, Upper Grosvenor Street, in charge of a perambulator[3] that contained a baby, of the male sex. You never returned. A few weeks later, through the elaborate investigations of the Metropolitan police, the perambulator was discovered at midnight, standing by itself in a remote corner of Bayswater.[4] It contained the manuscript of a three-volume novel of more than usually revolting sentimentality. [MISS PRISM *starts in involuntary indignation.*] But the baby was not there! [*Everyone looks at* MISS PRISM.] Prism! Where is that baby? [*A pause.*]

MISS PRISM Lady Bracknell, I admit with shame that I do not know. I only wish I did. The plain facts of the case are these. On the morning of the day you mention, a day that is for ever branded on my memory, I prepared as usual to take the baby out in its perambulator. I had also with me a somewhat old, but capacious hand-bag in which I had intended to place the manuscript of a work of fiction that I had written during my few unoccupied hours. In a moment of mental abstraction, for which I never can forgive myself, I deposited the manuscript in the bassinette, and placed the baby in the hand-bag.

JACK [*who has been listening attentively*] But where did you deposit the hand-bag?

MISS PRISM Do not ask me, Mr Worthing.

JACK Miss Prism, this is a matter of no small importance to me. I insist on knowing where you deposited the hand-bag that contained that infant.

MISS PRISM I left it in the cloak-room of one of the larger railway stations in London.

JACK What railway station?

MISS PRISM [*quite crushed*] Victoria. The Brighton line. [*Sinks into a chair.*]

JACK I must retire to my room for a moment. Gwendolen, wait here for me.

GWENDOLEN If you are not too long, I will wait here for you all my life.

[*Exit* JACK *in great excitement.*]

3. Baby carriage (pram).

4. A fashionable residential area of west London, north of Kensington Gardens.

CHASUBLE What do you think this means, Lady Bracknell?

LADY BRACKNELL I dare not even suspect, Dr Chasuble. I need hardly tell you that in families of high position strange coincidences are not supposed to occur. They are hardly considered the thing.

[*Noises heard overhead as if someone was throwing trunks about. Everyone looks up.*]

CECILY Uncle Jack seems strangely agitated.

CHASUBLE Your guardian has a very emotional nature.

LADY BRACKNELL This noise is extremely unpleasant. It sounds as if he was having an argument. I dislike arguments of any kind. They are always vulgar, and often convincing.

CHASUBLE [*looking up*] It has stopped now. [*The noise is redoubled.*]

LADY BRACKNELL I wish he would arrive at some conclusion.

GWENDOLEN This suspense is terrible. I hope it will last.

[*Enter* JACK *with a hand-bag of black leather in his hand.*]

JACK [*rushing over to* MISS PRISM] Is this the hand-bag, Miss Prism? Examine it carefully before you speak. The happiness of more than one life depends on your answer.

MISS PRISM [*calmly*] It seems to be mine. Yes, here is the injury it received through the upsetting of a Gower Street omnibus[5] in younger and happier days. Here is the stain on the lining caused by the explosion of a temperance beverage, an incident that occurred at Leamington.[6] And here, on the lock, are my initials. I had forgotten that in an extravagant mood I had had them placed there. The bag is undoubtedly mine. I am delighted to have it so unexpectedly restored to me. It has been a great inconvenience being without it all these years.

JACK [*in a pathetic voice*] Miss Prism, more is restored to you than this hand-bag. I was the baby you placed in it.

MISS PRISM [*amazed*] You?

JACK [*embracing her*] Yes . . . mother!

MISS PRISM [*recoiling in indignant astonishment*] Mr Worthing! I am unmarried!

JACK Unmarried! I do not deny that is a serious blow. But after all, who has the right to cast a stone[7] against one who has suffered? Cannot repentance wipe out an act of folly? Why should there be one law for men, and another for women. Mother, I forgive you. [*Tries to embrace her again.*]

MISS PRISM [*still more indignant*] Mr Worthing, there is some error. [*Pointing to* LADY BRACKNELL] There is the lady who can tell you who you really are.

JACK [*after a pause*] Lady Bracknell, I hate to seem inquisitive, but would you kindly inform me who I am?

LADY BRACKNELL I am afraid that the news I have to give you will not altogether please you. You are the son of my poor sister, Mrs Moncrieff, and consequently Algernon's elder brother.

5. Public carriage (bus). *Gower Street*: a street in the Bloomsbury section of central London (where the University of London and the British Museum are located).

6. Royal Leamington Spa, in Warwickshire, about 100 miles northwest of London. *Temperance beverage:* in the 1890s, carbonated soda drinks were marketed as wholesome alternatives to alcohol.

7. That is, condemn a sinner—in the phrase's original context, a woman caught committing adultery (see John 8.7).

JACK Algy's elder brother! Then I have a brother after all. I knew I had a brother! I always said I had a brother! Cecily—how could you have ever doubted that I had a brother. [*Seizes hold of* ALGERNON.] Dr Chasuble, my unfortunate brother. Miss Prism, my unfortunate brother. Gwendolen, my unfortunate brother. Algy, you young scoundrel, you will have to treat me with more respect in the future. You have never behaved to me like a brother in all your life.

ALGERNON Well, not till today, old boy, I admit. I did my best, however, though I was out of practice. [*Shakes hands.*]

GWENDOLEN [*to* JACK] My own! But what own are you? What is your Christian name, now that you have become someone else?

JACK Good heavens! . . . I had quite forgotten that point. Your decision on the subject of my name is irrevocable, I suppose?

GWENDOLEN I never change, except in my affections.

CECILY What a noble nature you have, Gwendolen!

JACK Then the question had better be cleared up at once. Aunt Augusta, a moment. At the time when Miss Prism left me in the hand-bag, had I been christened already?

LADY BRACKNELL Every luxury that money could buy, including christening, had been lavished on you by your fond and doting parents.

JACK Then I was christened! That is settled. Now, what name was I given? Let me know the worst.

LADY BRACKNELL Being the eldest son you were naturally christened after your father.

JACK [*irritably*] Yes, but what was my father's Christian name?

LADY BRACKNELL [*meditatively*] I cannot at the present moment recall what the General's Christian name was. But I have no doubt he had one. He was eccentric, I admit. But only in later years. And that was the result of the Indian climate, and marriage, and indigestion, and other things of that kind.

JACK Algy! Can't you recollect what our father's Christian name was?

ALGERNON My dear boy, we were never even on speaking terms. He died before I was a year old.

JACK His name would appear in the Army Lists[8] of the period, I suppose, Aunt Augusta?

LADY BRACKNELL The General was essentially a man of peace, except in his domestic life. But I have no doubt his name would appear in any military directory.

JACK The Army Lists of the last forty years are here. These delightful records should have been my constant study. [*Rushes to bookcase and tears the books out.*] M. Generals . . . Mallam, Maxbohm, Magley, what ghastly names they have—Markby, Migsby, Mobbs, Moncrieff! Lieutenant 1840, Captain, Lieutenant-Colonel, Colonel, General 1869, Christian names, Ernest John. [*Puts book very quietly down and speaks quite calmly.*] I always told you, Gwendolen, my name was Ernest, didn't I? Well, it is Ernest after all. I mean it naturally is Ernest.

LADY BRACKNELL Yes, I remember now that the General was called Ernest. I knew I had some particular reason for disliking the name.

8. The official lists of all the commissioned officers in the army.

GWENDOLEN Ernest! My own Ernest! I felt from the first that you could have no other name!

JACK Gwendolen, it is a terrible thing for a man to find out suddenly that all his life he has been speaking nothing but the truth. Can you forgive me?

GWENDOLEN I can. For I feel that you are sure to change.

JACK My own one!

CHASUBLE [*to* MISS PRISM] Lætitia! [*Embraces her.*]

MISS PRISM [*enthusiastically*] Frederick! At last!

ALGERNON Cecily! [*Embraces her.*] At last!

JACK Gwendolen! [*Embraces her.*] At last!

LADY BRACKNELL My nephew, you seem to be displaying signs of triviality.

JACK On the contrary, Aunt Augusta, I've now realized for the first time in my life the vital Importance of Being Earnest.

Tableau.[9]

Curtain.

9. That is, a tableau vivant: having characters freeze in a final pose as the curtain fell was a vogue in 19th-century theater.

ALFRED JARRY

1873–1907

THOUGH Alfred Jarry composed a large variety of works during his short life, his name is linked almost exclusively with that of the title character of his best-known play: *UBU THE KING* (1896). Even before the play was first performed, it had become notorious. At the dress rehearsal, Jarry had given a rousing curtain speech that, together with the play that followed, managed to enrage the audience. By the time the play opened officially, word had gotten around that a young and hitherto unknown playwright was intent on violating all rules of decency. *Ubu the King* begins with the word "merdre"—an almost imperceptible distortion of *merde,* the French word for "shit." Fecal expressions dominate the play, in which toilet brushes are thrown onto dinner tables and dishes such as "cauliflower à la shitsky" are served with glee. At the opening, conservative detractors and a small number of supporters started to riot as soon as the offensive word was uttered. A quarter hour of pandemonium ensued, with the two factions outdoing one another in booing, cheering, whistling, and shouting. Somehow, the performance continued, but with frequent interruptions and disturbances. Although the Ubu riot, as it came to be known, led to the immediate closing of the play, it also ensured *Ubu the King*'s place in the mythology of modernism. The riot shored up Jarry's credentials as a daring rebel willing to affront his audience. Offending the audience became the hallmark of modernist playwrights, and no one pursued the practice more avidly than Jarry.

Jarry was born in the provincial town of Laval, in northwest France, but before he was six his mother took him and his older sister to Saint-Brieuc, where they lived with her father. In 1888 they moved to the larger town of Rennes. There Alfred attended high school—an experience that proved crucial for his later career, for it provided the foundation of the figure of Ubu, first conceived as a satirical portrait of his physics teacher, Félix Hébert. Jarry subsequently transformed this character, but all his later Ubu plays retain an element of the sophomoric humor of the initial caricature.

To prepare for the demanding nationwide entrance exam for France's elite university, the École Normale Supérieur, Jarry enrolled in the famous École Henry IV in Paris. Distracted by life in the capital, he failed the exam three years in a row and eventually abandoned the effort. Instead, he devoted himself to café society and artistic circles. During the early 1890s, he wrote poetry and short prose in the symbolist style that dominated the literary and theatrical arts in Paris at the time; he managed to place his pieces in the main symbolist journals such as the *Mercure de France,* whose editor, Alfred Vallette, and his wife, Rachilde, took a liking to Jarry and supported his career whenever they could. Representative of this period is Jarry's *Caesar-Antichrist* (1895), a play populated by biblical figures including Saint Peter and Christ, fantasy creatures such as unicorns and five-winged animals, and the play's title character, the Antichrist. Jarry adds to the standard repertoire of symbolism—rarified poetic expressions and religious, metaphysical topics—some peculiar and unusual elements, including the rude character from his school days, Ubu. The result is an odd mixture, a symbolist play with a crude interlude dominated by Jarry's unseemly protagonist.

Symbolism, the aesthetic doctrine favoring refined poetry over base realism, continued to be important for Jarry throughout his life. In his narrative satire *Exploits and Opinions of Dr. Faustroll, Pataphysician* (published posthumously in 1911), he dedicated each section to a symbolist poet or artist, including Stéphane Mallarmé (1842–1898), Aubrey Beardsley (1872–1898), and Rachilde (1860–1953). Whether imitating their style or otherwise reacting to their work, these sections can be seen as Jarry's most programmatic engagement with symbolism, a retrospective account of the movement that had taught him how to become a writer.

Even more important than symbolist poetry for Jarry's artistic formation was symbolist theater, especially its unrivaled center: Aurélien Lugné-Poe's Théâtre de l'Œuvre. Not much older than Jarry, Lugné-Poe had produced such symbolist playwrights as Maurice Maeterlinck (1862–1949) as well as a wide range of other international playwrights—among them HENRIK IBSEN, AUGUST STRINDBERG, and OSCAR WILDE, whose play *Salomé,* which was banned in England, he had staged to critical acclaim in 1896. Jarry did not just admire this theater from afar, but began to seek a more active role in it. In 1896 he became a sort of manager with some artistic responsibilities. At the same time, he began to lobby Lugné-Poe to produce his play *Ubu the King.* After some hesitation and delays, Lugné-Poe gave in and scheduled the opening for later that year. It proved to be a decision with consequences. The ensuing Ubu riot almost ruined the Théâtre de l'Œuvre, though the uproar ultimately contributed to its place in theater history.

Ubu the King is a strange mixture of styles. The plot and language seem borrowed from a historical play in the manner of SHAKESPEARE, and there are direct Shakespearean echoes as well. The play begins when Ubu's wife, Mama Ubu, apparently imitating Lady Macbeth, incites her husband to kill the King of Poland and usurp his rule. Once the king is killed and Ubu is installed on the throne, he turns more violent, killing nobles, raising taxes, and amassing great wealth. He personally goes out to extract heavy taxes from the impoverished and starving peasants. When he is finally faced with a popular uprising, led by the surviving son of the former king and an army raised in Russia, he flees and is eventually vanquished in battle.

This rough description may capture the play insofar as it resembles a historical drama, but history was the last thing Jarry cared about. He conducted no historical research and did not seek to re-create life in Poland at some remote time. In fact, the opening stage direction gives the place of the action as "*Poland—in other words, nowhere.*" The setting and the characters' bombastic phrases serve only as a foil for the deliberate crudity and vulgarity of the play. Ubu's main feature is extreme childishness, manifest in part in a complete lack of moral introspection. He is motivated to act by hunger and greed, and only fear deters him from following his instincts. In battle, the smallest opposition has him fleeing like Falstaff, the drinker and coward who is Prince Hal's companion in Shakespeare's *Henry IV.* Whether driven by greed or by fear, Ubu acts entirely without forethought or reflection. His impulsive and repulsive behavior has no redeeming features, not even dramatic ones. He is no evil genius whose plots, however objectionable, we can admire. He simply acts randomly from moment to moment, without plan, without a conscience, without a moment of hesitation or doubt. The only thing in which he reliably shows interest is consuming food. He is persuaded to kill the king when his wife points out that once

Poster art by Jarry for a performance of *Ubu the King*.

on the throne, he could "eat stuffed sausages all the time." It was Ubu's fixation on food and excretion that put the play most directly at odds with symbolism and with his audience's expectations. Jarry deliberately violated the most elevated and refined ideals of symbolism, which had sought to ignore everything having to do with the corporeal. In *Ubu the King,* Jarry confronted symbolist audiences with the most unseemly aspects of life.

As if its vulgarity were not upsetting enough, the play exhibits another feature designed to provoke the ire of audiences used to the conventions of symbolism. Its gratuitous violence, so at odds with the refined symbolist plays that Jarry helped produce at the Théâtre de l'Œuvre, reflects a very different theatrical tradition: the puppet theater of Punch and Judy. Jarry had experimented with marionettes and puppets as a teenager, and in fact the early versions of Ubu plays that he created with his classmates had been written for such theaters. One distinctive trait of the Punch and Judy show is that violence never leads to real-life consequences—characters can be hit on the head with a hammer and suffer no injury. In *Ubu the King,* too, characters are run through with sabers, and Ubu himself is perforated by bullets, only to walk away without much difficulty. By the same token, this cartoonish violence in *Ubu* is never cause for tragedy. When Ubu kills the entire nobility to increase his revenue, the murders are accomplished with a simple mechanical device: each noble in turn is pushed through a trapdoor and then "disembrained." At moments in the play, violence seems lamentable—but the mode of inconsequential and exaggerated carnage quickly returns.

The puppet theater was also an important inspiration for Jarry's stage design. His characters were written to be one-dimensional and simple, an effect that Jarry enhanced with the actors' costumes and style of acting and speaking. He created full-body costumes and masks that significantly reduced the mobility of those wearing them. Ubu's entire body was covered by an egg-shaped, stiff costume, eliminating the actor's ability to convey subtle points with facial expressions, gestures, or poses. To make the performance even more stylized, Jarry also instructed his actors to speak unnaturally. For this purpose, he created what he called an acoustic

Jarry's woodcut engraving of Ubu (1896).

mask, demanding that Ubu deliver his lines in a staccato fashion, giving each syllable equal emphasis. The appearance, movements, and speech of Ubu were thus reduced to a set of mechanical expressions. Ubu was no longer a character taken from life; he was a plainly artificial and crude creation.

For all of its particular use of vulgarity and violence—or because of them—*Ubu the King* is best understood as farce: that is, as a form that turns vulgarity and violence into laughter. The theorist of laughter most useful for explaining Jarry's combination of vulgarity, verbal tics, violence, and puppetlike characters is the turn-of-the-century philosopher Henri Bergson (1859–1941). Indeed, Bergson's influence on Jarry was direct, since the playwright was one of his students at the École Henry IV, where Bergson taught parts of what would become his famous essay on comedy, *Laughter* (1900). In its most basic form, Bergson's theory holds that laughter is provoked by the imposition of something mechanical (i.e., nonliving) onto a living organism. The strength of this theory lies in its ability to work on many levels. In the realm of language, Bergson identifies moments of the mechanical in the form of linguistic tics. *Ubu the King* is full of recurring nonsense phrases such as "by my green candlestick." At the same time, Jarry demanded mechanical repetitions of single characteristic gestures, such as tapping oneself on the head. Bergson's theory also describes the type of violence at work in *Ubu the King*. As king, Ubu treats other characters as if they were mere machines: everywhere, human bodies are penetrated and taken apart, only to be reassembled with ease. From this perspective, *Ubu the King* is a compilation of techniques meant to create laughter.

The daring mixture of pseudo-historical language and vulgarity, violence and laughter, made Jarry famous overnight. Through countless interviews, features, articles, and commentaries following the Ubu riot, Jarry became a notorious figure in the Parisian cultural world. Exploiting this position to the full, he published different versions of the text of *Ubu the King* and wrote new plays based on the Ubu figure. The title character in *Ubu Cocu* (*Ubu Cuckolded*, published posthumously in 1944) is by and large the same; he relies on gratuitous acts of violence to take possession of the house of a scholar of geometrical shapes. From time to time, a character called Conscience appears, only to be dismissed. Another Ubu play, called *Ubu in Chains* (1899), is set after Ubu flees Poland at the end of *Ubu the King*, seeking exile in France. Whereas in *Ubu the King,* Ubu had been hungry for power and ready to use all means available to obtain it, in *Ubu in Chains* he insists on becoming a slave. However, the main features associated with this character—wanton violence, abrupt changes, and motiveless decisions—remain the same. Several years later, Jarry wrote a final Ubu play, *Ubu sur la Butte* (*Ubu on the Mound*, 1901), which includes a prologue about theater and, like *Ubu Cuckolded,* many songs and musical interludes, an element absent from the original *Ubu the King*. In addition, Jarry published different kinds of Ubu paraphernalia, including an Ubu *Almanach* (1901). None of these texts and publications repeated the success of *Ubu the King,* in part because none managed to replicate its juxtaposition of high and low, symbolism and farce, or repeat the imaginative implementation of Bergson's theory of laughter that had turned *Ubu the King* into a succès de scandale.

What the various Ubu publications did

accomplish was to keep the figure of Ubu alive. Making this achievement all the more important was that Jarry had begun to imitate Ubu's character in his own life. Jarry spoke like Ubu, sometimes acted like Ubu, and more generally turned his own life into a kind of Ubu performance piece. He lived in extremely strange quarters—a room with a half-height ceiling, which allowed him but few of his guests to stand without stooping—and cultivated other peculiar habits. He also began to drink excessively, especially absinthe. He became a self-stylized figure of the Parisian bohemia, well-known enough that André Gide, France's most famous novelist of the early twentieth century, modeled a character on Jarry in his novel *The Counterfeiters* (1926). Ubu, Jarry's earliest creation, thus also became a kind of curse. None of Jarry's other artistic endeavors ever came close to having the impact of *Ubu the King,* although *Exploits and Opinions of Dr. Faustroll, Pataphysician* has received scholarly attention and is in some ways a more rewarding artistic achievement. But notoriety prevented Jarry from moving beyond *Ubu the King* and the scandals it had caused.

In fact, it was the reaction to the play more than the play itself that turned *Ubu the King* into the harbinger of a new phase of modern drama, which became an aggressive, shocking type of avant-garde art. After the Ubu scandal, radical artists in France and elsewhere tried to elicit a similar response to their own work. Provocation, shock, deliberate attacks on the audience—these became the ingredients of a new brand of shrill theater. The audience was turned into the natural enemy of the artist: to establish one's credentials as an avant-garde artist, it was necessary to provoke a riot. Many twentieth-century artists followed suit, among them Antonin Artaud (1896–1948), who named his own short-lived theater Théâtre Alfred Jarry. After Jarry, modern drama had become an art of scandal.

M.P.

Ubu the King[1]

CHARACTERS

PAPA UBU
MAMA UBU
CAPTAIN BARBAGE
KING WENCESLAS, QUEEN ROSEMONDE, and their sons: BOLESLAS, LADISLAS, BUGGERLAS

COUNCILLORS
GENERAL LASKY
STANISLAS LECZINSKY
JOHANNES SOBIESKY
NICHOLAS RENSKY
CZAR ALEXIS
TAILS
HEADS
The Disembraining Machine

COTISE
Conspirators and Soldiers
Scribes
Crowds
MICHAEL FEDOROVITCH
NOBLES
JUDGES

FINANCIERS
Lackeys of Phynance
Peasants

The Whole Russian Army
The Whole Polish Army
Mama Ubu's Guards
A CAPTAIN

1. Translated by David Ball.

A Bear
The Phynancial Horse
Knighties
The Crew
The Ship's CAPTAIN

The play takes place in Poland—in other words, nowhere.[2]

1.1

[PAPA UBU, MAMA UBU.]

PAPA UBU Shitsky![3]

MAMA UBU Oh! such language! Papa Ubu, thou art a big bad boy.

PAPA UBU What stoppeth me from slaying thee, Mama Ubu?

MAMA UBU It is not I, Papa Ubu, it is someone else who should be assassinated.

PAPA UBU By my green candlestick, I understand not.

MAMA UBU What, Papa Ubu, are you happy with your lot?

PAPA UBU By my green candlestick, shitsky! my dear, verily, verily, I am happy. A man could be happy with less: captain of the Dragoons, an officer with the confidence of King Wenceslas, decorated with the Order of the Red Eagle of Poland, and former King of Aragon,[4] what more could you want?

MAMA UBU What! You, who were once King of Aragon, now you think it's good enough to march in a parade at the head of forty attendants armed with cabbage-cutters when after the crown of Aragon you could place the crown of Poland on your noggin?

PAPA UBU Ah! Mama Ubu, I can't understand a word you say.

MAMA UBU You're so dumb!

PAPA UBU By my green candlestick, King Wenceslas is still very much alive; and even assuming he dies, does he not have swarms of children?

MAMA UBU What's stopping you from massacrating the whole family and taking their place?

PAPA UBU Ah! Mama Ubu, you are insulting me and you will soon get dumped in the lobster pot.

MAMA UBU Ah! miserable wretch, if I got dumped in the lobster pot, who then would mend the seat of your pants?

PAPA UBU Hey, come on! don't I have an ass like everybody else?

MAMA UBU If I were you, it's that very ass I'd want to put on a throne. You could get infinitely rich, eat stuffed sausage all the time, and drive through the streets in a horse and carriage.

PAPA UBU If I were king, I'd have me a big cape made like the one I had in Aragon, the one those rascally Spaniards impudently stole from me.

MAMA UBU You could also get an umbrella and a big pea jacket that goes all the way down to your heels.

PAPA UBU Oh! I'll give in to the temptation. For shitsky's sakesky, for sakesky's shitsky, if I ever meet him somewhere in the woods, he'll have a hard time of it.

2. Even though most places mentioned in this play actually exist, Jarry uses place-names irreverently and inconsistently, with no regard for geographic specificity.

3. In Jarry's original French text, the play's first word is *Merdre*, a distortion of *merde* (shit).

4. A kingdom in northeast Spain (united with Castile in 1479).

MAMA UBU Oh good! Papa Ubu, now you have become a real man.

PAPA UBU Oh no! a Captain of the Dragoons massacrating the King of Poland! Never! I'd die first!

MAMA UBU [*aside*] Oh, shitsky! [*To* UBU] So, you will remain poor as a church rat, Papa Ubu.

PAPA UBU Oddsbellyzooks! by my green candlestick, I'd rather be poor as a good thin rat than rich as a wicked fat cat.

MAMA UBU What about the cape? And the umbrella? And the great big pea jacket?

PAPA UBU Well! what about them, Mama Ubu? Who needs them?

[*He exits, slamming the door.*]

MAMA UBU Crapsky, shitsky, he was an old meanie, but crapsky, shitsky, I do think I have shaken him. Thank God! and myself. In a week I may be Queen of Poland.

1.2

[SCENE: *The stage represents a room in* PAPA UBU's *house where a splendid table is laid.*]

[PAPA UBU, MAMA UBU.]

MAMA UBU Oh, our guests are really late.

PAPA UBU Yes, by my green candlestick. I'm dying of hunger. Mama Ubu, you are quite ugly today. Could it be because we're having guests for dinner?

MAMA UBU [*shrugging*] Shitsky.

PAPA UBU [*grabbing a roast chicken*] Hey, I'm hungry. I am going to bite into this bird. It is a chicken, I believe. . . . Hey! this isn't bad!

MAMA UBU What are you doing, you wretch? What will our guests eat?

PAPA UBU There will be quite enough for them. I won't touch another thing. Mama Ubu, go to the window and see if our guests are coming.

MAMA UBU [*going there*] I don't see anything. [*Meanwhile* PAPA UBU *filches a slice of veal.*]

MAMA UBU Ah! here are Captain Barbage and his followers. What are you eating, Papa Ubu?

PAPA UBU Nothing—a little veal.

MAMA UBU Oh, the veal! the veal! veal! He ate the veal! Help!

PAPA UBU By my green candlestick, I'm going to scratch thine eyes out!

[*The door opens.*]

1.3

[PAPA UBU, MAMA UBU, CAPTAIN BARBAGE, *and his followers.*]

MAMA UBU Good evening, gentlemen. We have been waiting for you most eagerly. Do be seated.

CAPTAIN BARBAGE Good evening, Madam. But where is Papa Ubu?

PAPA UBU Here I am, here I am! Gadzookspot, by my green candlestick, I'm fat enough to be visible.

CAPTAIN BARBAGE Good day, Papa Ubu. Be seated, men. [*They all sit down.*]

PAPA UBU Whew! I almost went right through my chair.

CAPTAIN BARBAGE Hey, Ubu! what've you got that's good today?

MAMA UBU Here's the menu.

PAPA UBU Ah! this is interesting.

MAMA UBU Polish soup, ratsky cutlets, veal, chicken, dog paté, turkey rumps, charlotte russe.

PAPA UBU Hey! that's quite enough, it seems to me. Is there more?

MAMA UBU [*continuing*] Ice pudding,[5] salad, fruit, dessert, oatmeal, Jerusalem artichokes, cauliflower à la shitsky.

PAPA UBU Hey! what do you think I am to spend that much, the Emperor of the Orient?

MAMA UBU Don't listen to him, he's a half-wit.

PAPA UBU Oh! I'm going to sharpen my teeth against your calves.

MAMA UBU Have dinner instead, Papa Ubu. Here's some of the Polish.

PAPA UBU Buggersky! it's terrible!

CAPTAIN BARBAGE Indeed, it is not good.

MAMA UBU You barbarians, what more do you want?

PAPA UBU [*striking his forehead*] Ah! I have an idea. I'll be back in a minute.

[*He leaves.*]

MAMA UBU Gentlemen, we are going to sample the veal.

CAPTAIN BARBAGE It's very good, I'm done.

MAMA UBU Not the rumps.

CAPTAIN BARBAGE Exquisite, exquisite! Long live Mama Ubu!

ALL Long live Mama Ubu.

PAPA UBU [*coming back onstage*] And soon you'll shout, "Long live Papa Ubu." [*He is holding an incredibly disgusting toilet brush that he throws into the midst of the banquet.*]

MAMA UBU Wretch, what have you done?

PAPA UBU Just taste that! [*Several guests taste it and fall, poisoned.*] Mama Ubu, pass me the ratsky cutlets so that I can serve them.

MAMA UBU Here they are.

PAPA UBU Everybody, out! . . . Captain Barbage, I'd like to have a few words with you.

THE OTHERS Hey, we haven't had dinner.

PAPA UBU What do you mean, you haven't had dinner! Everybody out! Stay, Barbage. [*Nobody moves.*]

PAPA UBU You still haven't left? By my green candlestick, I'm going to knock you out with ratsky cutlets. [*He starts throwing some at them.*]

ALL Oh! help! Defend us! Alas, I am dead!

PAPA UBU Shitsky, shitsky, shitsky. Out! . . . I'm really making a hit.

ALL Every man for himself! Wretched Papa Ubu! The traitor, the beggarly ruffian!

PAPA UBU Ah! they're gone. I can breathe again, but I have dined most execrably. Come, Barbage.

[*They exit with* MAMA UBU.]

1.4

[PAPA UBU, MAMA UBU, CAPTAIN BARBAGE.]

PAPA UBU Well! Captain, have you dined well?

CAPTAIN BARBAGE Quite well, sir, except for the shitsky.

5. That is, a frozen pudding.

PAPA UBU Hey! the shitsky wasn't bad.

MAMA UBU To each his own.

PAPA UBU Captain Barbage, I have decided to make you Duke of Lithuania.

CAPTAIN BARBAGE What? I thought you were poor as a beggar, Papa Ubu.

PAPA UBU In a few days, if you wish, I shall reign over Poland.

CAPTAIN BARBAGE You're going to kill Wenceslas?

PAPA UBU He's no dumbbell, the little bugger, he guessed it.

CAPTAIN BARBAGE If it's a matter of killing Wenceslas, count me in. I am his mortal enemy, and I'll answer for my men.

PAPA UBU [*throwing himself on him to embrace him*] Oh! oh! I love you dearly, Barbage!

CAPTAIN BARBAGE Hey, you stink, Papa Ubu. Don't you ever wash?

PAPA UBU Rarely.

MAMA UBU Never!

PAPA UBU I'm going to stamp on thy toes!

MAMA UBU You big shitsky!

PAPA UBU All right, Barbage, I have finished talking to you. But by my green candlestick, I swear on Mama Ubu here I'll make you Duke of Lithuania.

MAMA UBU But . . .

PAPA UBU Be still, my child.

[*They exit.*]

1.5

[PAPA UBU, MAMA UBU, *a* MESSENGER.]

PAPA UBU Sirrah,[6] what would you? Beat it, scram! you're getting on my nerves.

MESSENGER Sir, you are summoned by the King. [*He exits.*]

PAPA UBU Oh! shitsky, oddsbellyzooksy, by my green candlestick, I am discovered, I am going to be beheaded! Alas, alas!

MAMA UBU What a milksop! And time presses.

PAPA UBU Oh! I have an idea! I'll say it was Mama Ubu and Barbage.

MAMA UBU Ah, Big Ubu, if you do that . . .

PAPA UBU Hey! I'm going there right away. [*He exits.*]

MAMA UBU Oh, Papa Ubu, Papa Ubu, *I'll* give you stuffed sausage . . .

[*She exits.*]

PAPA UBU [*from the wings*] Oh! shitsky! you're a fine stuffed sausage yourself!

1.6

[SCENE: *The* KING*'s palace.*]

[KING WENCESLAS, *surrounded by his officers;* BARBAGE; *the* KING*'s sons:* BOLESLAS, LADISLAS, *and* BUGGERLAS. *Then,* PAPA UBU.]

PAPA UBU [*entering*] Oh! you know, I didn't do it, it was Mama Ubu and Barbage.

THE KING What's the matter, Papa Ubu?

6. An archaic form of address to male social inferiors.

BARBAGE He has had too much to drink.

THE KING So did I, this morning.

PAPA UBU Yes, I'm drunk; that's because I drank too much French wine.

THE KING Papa Ubu, I wish to reward you for your many services as Captain of the Dragoons, and I hereby name you Count of Sandomir.[7]

PAPA UBU Oh! Mr. Wenceslas, I hardly know how to thank you.

THE KING Do not thank me, Papa Ubu; but do appear in our grand review tomorrow morning.

PAPA UBU I'll be there, but do accept, I beg of you, this little party noisemaker. [*He presents a coiled-up noisemaker to the* KING.]

THE KING At my age, what do you expect me to do with a noisemaker? I'll give it to Buggerlas.

YOUNG BUGGERLAS Man! is that Papa Ubu dumb!

PAPA UBU And now, I'm gonna split. [*As he turns around, he falls down.*] Oh! ow! help! By my green candlestick, I broke my intestine and split my bagpipe!

THE KING [*helping him up*] Papa Ubu, art thou hurt?

PAPA UBU Yea, verily, and I'm sure I'm going to drop dead. Oh! what will become of Mama Ubu?

THE KING We shall provide for her.

PAPA UBU You are kind indeed. [*He exits.*]

Yes, but, King Wenceslas, you shall be massacrated all the same.

1.7

[SCENE: PAPA UBU*'s house.*]

[TAILS, HEADS, COTISE, PAPA UBU, MAMA UBU, *Conspirators and Soldiers,* CAPTAIN BARBAGE.]

PAPA UBU Hey! my dear friends, it is high time we drew up the plan for our conspiracy. Let each man give his opinion. First I'll give mine, if you will.

CAPTAIN BARBAGE Speak, Papa Ubu.

PAPA UBU Well, friends, my opinion is we just poison the King by stuffing some arsenic into his lunch. When he begins to graze on it he'll drop dead and so I'll be king.

EVERYBODY Fie on you, you big ape! Fie, fie!

PAPA UBU So, you don't like that? Then let Barbage give his opinion.

CAPTAIN BARBAGE My opinion is, to take a big sword and slit him from his guggle to his zatch.

EVERYBODY Yes! that is noble and valiant.

PAPA UBU And what if he kicks you? Now I seem to remember that for his reviews, he puts on iron shoes that really hurt. If I thought that's what you were going to do, I'd get out of this dirty business, run to him and turn you in. And I think he'd also give me back some change.

MAMA UBU Oh! the traitor, the coward, the villainous downright miser.

EVERYBODY Booo, Papa Ubu!

PAPA UBU Now, gentlemen, be still, if you don't want to pay a visit to my pockets. All right, I agree to put myself in danger for you. So, Barbage, you'll take care of slitting the King from one end to the other.

7. A city in southeast central Poland (Sandomierz).

CAPTAIN BARBAGE And wouldn't it be better if we all jumped on him at the same time, yelling and screaming? That way we have a chance of getting his troops to go along with us.

PAPA UBU OK, here goes. I'll try to step on his toes, he'll jump, then I'll say to him: SHITSKY! That's the signal for all of you to jump him.

MAMA UBU Yes, and as soon as he's dead you'll take his scepter and his crown.

CAPTAIN BARBAGE And I'll go after the royal family with my men.

PAPA UBU Yes, and I especially recommend young Buggerlas to your attention.

[*They exit.*]

PAPA UBU [*running after them and making them come back*] Gentlemen, we have forgotten an indispensable ceremony; we must vow to fight valiantly.

CAPTAIN BARBAGE How can we do that? We don't have a priest.

PAPA UBU Mama Ubu will fill in.

EVERYBODY So be it.

PAPA UBU So, you swear to really kill the king?

EVERYBODY Yes we do. Long live Papa Ubu!

End of the First Act.

2.1

[SCENE: *The* KING*'s palace.*]

THE KING Mr. Buggerlas, this morning you were quite rude to Mr. Ubu, Knight of my Orders and Count of Sandomir. That is why I am forbidding you to appear in my review.

THE QUEEN But Wenceslas, even your whole family might not be enough to defend you.

THE KING Madam, I never go back on my word. I'm tired of your nonsense.

YOUNG BUGGERLAS I submit, Sire.

THE QUEEN Sire, are you still set on going to that review?

THE KING Why not, Madam?

THE QUEEN Must I tell you again, did I not see him in a dream striking you with his mace and throwing you into the Vistula,[8] and an eagle like the one in the royal arms of Poland putting a crown on his head?

THE KING On whose head?

THE QUEEN On Papa Ubu's head.

THE KING What folly. Monsieur de Ubu is a fine gentleman, who would let himself be drawn and quartered to serve me.

THE QUEEN and BUGGERLAS What a mistake.

THE KING Be quiet, you young ape. And you, Madam, to show you how little I fear Monsieur Ubu, I shall go to the review just as I am, without a weapon, without a sword.

THE QUEEN O fatal imprudence! I shall never see you alive again.

THE KING Come, Ladislas, come, Boleslas.

[*They exit. The* QUEEN *and* BUGGERLAS *go to the window.*]

8. The principal river of Poland.

THE QUEEN and BUGGERLAS May God and Saint Nicholas preserve you!

THE QUEEN Buggerlas, come to the chapel with me to pray for your father and your brothers.

2.2

[SCENE: *The reviewing grounds.*]

[*The Polish Army, the* KING, BOLESLAS, LADISLAS, PAPA UBU, CAPTAIN BARBAGE *and his men,* TAILS, HEADS, COTISE.]

THE KING Noble Papa Ubu, come next to me with your suite to inspect the troops.

PAPA UBU [*to his followers*] Careful, men. [*To the* KING] We're coming, Sire, we're coming. [PAPA UBU'*s men surround the* KING.]

THE KING Ah! here is the regiment of the Danzig Horse Guards. My word, they are gallant-looking lads indeed.

PAPA UBU You think so? They don't look so hot to me. Look at this one. [*To the soldier*] How long has it been since you've washed, you beastly rogue?

THE KING But this soldier is quite clean. What can be the matter with you, Papa Ubu?

PAPA UBU There, take that! [*He stamps on his foot.*]

THE KING Miserable wretch!

PAPA UBU SHITSKY!! follow me, men!

BARBAGE Hurrah! Forward! [*They all strike the* KING*; a Knightie explodes.*]

THE KING Oh! Help! Help! By the Blessed Virgin, I am dead.

BOLESLAS [*to* LADISLAS] What's this? Let us draw!

PAPA UBU Ah! I've got the crown! On to the others, now!

CAPTAIN BARBAGE Death to the traitors!!

[*The* KING'*s sons flee; they all run after them.*]

2.3

[*The* QUEEN *and* BUGGERLAS.]

THE QUEEN At last my misgivings are beginning to fade.

BUGGERLAS You have no reason to fear.

[*A frightful clamor is heard outside.*]

BUGGERLAS Ah! what do I see? My two brothers pursued by Papa Ubu and his men.

THE QUEEN Oh my God! Blessed Virgin, they're losing, they're losing ground!

BUGGERLAS The whole army is following Papa Ubu. The King is no longer there. Horrors! Help!

THE QUEEN Now Boleslas is dead! He has been shot.

BUGGERLAS Hey! [LADISLAS *turns around.*] Defend yourself! Hurrah for Ladislas!

THE QUEEN Oh! he is surrounded.

BUGGERLAS It's all over for him. Barbage has just sliced him in half like a sausage.

THE QUEEN Ah! Alas! those madmen are entering the palace, they are coming up the stairs.

[*The clamor increases.*]

THE QUEEN and BUGGERLAS [*kneeling*] Oh Lord, help us.

BUGGERLAS Oh, that Papa Ubu! The villain, the wretch, if I had him . . .

2.4

[*The* QUEEN, BUGGERLAS. *The door is smashed in;* PAPA UBU *and his frenzied followers enter.*]

PAPA UBU Hey, Buggerlas! what would you do with me?

BUGGERLAS Good God! I shall defend my mother to the death! The first one who moves is a dead man.

PAPA UBU Oh, Barbage! I'm afraid! Get me out of here.

A SOLDIER [*advancing*] Surrender, Buggerlas!

BUGGERLAS Here, you thug, take that! [*He smashes in his skull.*]

THE QUEEN Hold fast, Buggerlas, hold fast!

SEVERAL [*coming forward*] Buggerlas, we promise to spare your life.

BUGGERLAS Rapscallions, wine bags, mercenary monkeys!

[*Twirling his sword around his head, he mows them down with it.*]

PAPA UBU Oh, I'll get the best of you anyhow!

BUGGERLAS Flee, Mother, escape through the secret stairway!

THE QUEEN And you, my son, what about you?

BUGGERLAS I shall follow.

PAPA UBU Try to catch the Queen. Ah! she's gone. As for you, you wretch! . . . [*He advances on* BUGGERLAS.]

BUGGERLAS Ah! sweet God, here is my vengeance! [*With a terrible blow of his sword,* BUGGERLAS *slits his begizzard.*] Mother, I follow!

[*He disappears through the secret stairs.*]

2.5

[SCENE: *A cavern in the mountains.*]

[*Young* BUGGERLAS *followed by* QUEEN ROSEMONDE]

BUGGERLAS We'll be safe here.

THE QUEEN Yes, I think so! Buggerlas, sustain me! [*She falls on the snow.*]

BUGGERLAS Ah! what ails thee, Mother?

THE QUEEN I am very ill, believe me, Buggerlas. I have but two hours left to live.

BUGGERLAS What! have you been struck by the cold?

THE QUEEN How can I possibly bear up under so many blows? The King massacrated, our family struck down, and you, a representative of the noblest race ever to carry a sword, forced to flee into the mountains like a smuggler.

BUGGERLAS And forced by whom, great God! by whom? By a vulgar Papa Ubu, an adventurer sprung from the Lord knows where, a vile scoundrel, a shameful vagabond! And to think that my father decorated him and made him a count, and the very next day that villain blushed not to raise his hand against him.

THE QUEEN O Buggerlas! When I recall how happy we were before the coming of that Papa Ubu! But now, alas! everything has changed!

BUGGERLAS What can we do? Let us wait in hope and never give up our rights.

THE QUEEN I wish it so for you, my dear child, but as for me, I shall never see that happy day.

BUGGERLAS Ah! what ails thee? She pales, she falls, o help! But I am in the wilderness! O my God! her heart is no longer beating. She is dead! Can such things be? Another victim of Papa Ubu! [*He hides his face in his hands and cries.*] O my God! how sad it is to be alone at the age of fourteen with a terrible vengeance to pursue! [*He falls prey to the most violent despair.*]

[*Meanwhile the souls of* WENCESLAS, BOLESLAS, LADISLAS, *and* ROSEMONDE *have entered the grotto; their ancestors accompany them and fill up the cave. The oldest goes over to* BUGGERLAS *and gently wakes him.*]

BUGGERLAS Eh! what do I see? My whole family, my ancestors . . . Through what miracle?

THE SHADE Learn, Buggerlas, that during my life I was Lord Mathias of Königsberg,[9] the first king and founder of your house. I entrust you with the task of avenging us. [*He gives him a large sword.*] And may the sword I am giving you know no rest till it has struck the usurper dead.

2.6

[SCENE: *The* KING*'s palace.*]

[PAPA UBU, MAMA UBU, CAPTAIN BARBAGE.]

PAPA UBU No, I won't! I won't! Do you want to ruin me with all this foodsky?

CAPTAIN BARBAGE But, Papa Ubu, can't you see that the people expect the gift of the happy accession?

MAMA UBU If you don't distribute meat and gold, you'll be overthrown within two hours.

PAPA UBU Meat, OK! gold, never! Slaughter three old horses. That's quite good enough for apes like these.

MAMA UBU Ape yourself! Who ever built me an animal like that?

PAPA UBU I tell you again, I want to get rich, I'm not gonna give up a red cent.

MAMA UBU When he has all the treasures of Poland in his hands!

CAPTAIN BARBAGE Yes, I know there's a huge treasure in the chapel. We'll distribute it to the people.

PAPA UBU You wretch, if you do that . . . !

CAPTAIN BARBAGE But, Papa Ubu, if you don't distribute some things, the people won't want to pay their taxes.

PAPA UBU Is that really true?

MAMA UBU Yes, yes!

PAPA UBU Oh, in that case I agree to everything. Get a hold of three million, cook a hundred and fifty oxen and sheep—especially since I'll have some too!

[*They exit.*]

9. The former capital of East Prussia, a port on the Baltic Sea (north of Poland). Part of the German Empire during Jarry's lifetime, it was annexed by the Soviet Union in 1945 and renamed Kaliningrad in 1946.

2.7

[SCENE: *The courtyard of the palace, full of people.*]

[PAPA UBU, *crowned,* MAMA UBU, CAPTAIN BARBAGE, *lackeys laden with meat.*]

PEOPLE There's the King! Long live the King! Hurray!

PAPA UBU [*throwing food to the people*] Here, there's something for everyone. I had no desire to give you any money, but you know, Mama Ubu wanted me to. At least promise me to pay your taxes.

EVERYBODY Yes, yes!

CAPTAIN BARBAGE Look, Mama Ubu, look how they're fighting for the gold! What a battle!

MAMA UBU It really is horrible. Feh! there's a man with his skull split open.

PAPA UBU What a fine sight! Bring in more chests full of gold.

CAPTAIN BARBAGE Let's have a race.

PAPA UBU Yes, good idea. [*To the people*] My friends, you see this chest full of gold; it contains three hundred thousand pink nobles in gold, in good Polish money. Let those who wish to run go to the end of the courtyard. You will start when I wave my handkerchief and the first one there will get the chest. Those who do not win will have a consolation prize: this other chest, which will be distributed among them.

EVERYBODY Yes! Long live Papa Ubu! What a good king! There was nothing like this in the days of Wenceslas.

PAPA UBU [*to* MAMA UBU, *happily*] Just listen to them!

[*All the people go line up at the end of the courtyard.*]

PAPA UBU One, two, three! Are you ready?

EVERYBODY Yes, yes!

PAPA UBU Go!

[*They begin to run, tripping all over each other. Shouts, tumult.*]

CAPTAIN BARBAGE They're coming closer, they're coming closer!

PAPA UBU Hey! the leader is losing ground.

MAMA UBU No, he's winning again now.

CAPTAIN BARBAGE Oh! he's losing, he's losing! It's over! The other one won! [*The man who was second comes in first.*]

EVERYBODY Long live Michael Fedorovitch! Long live Michael Fedorovitch!

MICHAEL FEDOROVITCH Sire, I really don't know how to thank your Majesty . . .

PAPA UBU Oh! my dear friend, it's really nothing. Take the chest home with you, Michael, and you others, share this other chest between you, take a coin each until there is no more.

EVERYBODY Long live Michael Fedorovitch! Long live Papa Ubu!

PAPA UBU And you, my friends, come dine with me! Today the doors of my palace are open to you: pray come honor my table!

PEOPLE In we go! Long live Papa Ubu! the noblest of monarchs!

[*They go into the palace. We hear the noise of an orgy, which will continue till the next day. The curtain falls.*]

End of the Second Act.

3.1

[SCENE: *The palace.*]

[PAPA UBU, MAMA UBU.]

PAPA UBU By my green candlestick, now I am king in this country. I already got indigestion and now they're gonna bring me my big cape.

MAMA UBU What is it made of, Papa Ubu? For we may be kings, but still we must be economical.

PAPA UBU Madam my Female, it is made of sheepskin, with stitching and reins of dogskin.

MAMA UBU That is fine, but it is finer still to be kings.

PAPA UBU Yes, you are right, Mama Ubu.

MAMA UBU We are extremely grateful to the Duke of Lithuania.

PAPA UBU Who's that?

MAMA UBU Hey, Captain Barbage.

PAPA UBU I pray thee, Mama Ubu, speak to me not of that buggersky. Now that I no longer need him, he can go jump in the lake, he won't have his dukedom.

MAMA UBU You are making a great mistake, Papa Ubu, he will turn against you.

PAPA UBU Oh! I'm really sorry for that little man. I'm worried about him about as much as I am about Buggerlas.

MAMA UBU And you think you have heard the last of Buggerlas, eh?

PAPA UBU By my Financial Saber, of course I do! What do you think he can do to me, that little ape of fourteen?

MAMA UBU Papa Ubu, heed what I say. Believe me, try to win over Buggerlas with your generosity.

PAPA UBU Give away more money? Hey, no way! you've already made me waste twenty-two million.

MAMA UBU Just do whatever you want, Papa Ubu, and your goose will be cooked.

PAPA UBU Well, you'll be in the pot with me.

MAMA UBU Listen, I'll tell you once again: I'm sure that young Buggerlas will triumph, for he has right on his side.

PAPA UBU Ah, you filthy wretch! Isn't the wrong side as good as the right? Ah! you are insulting me, Mama Ubu, and I'm going to rip you to bits.

[MAMA UBU *runs out, followed by* PAPA UBU.]

3.2

[SCENE: *The great hall of the palace.*]

[PAPA UBU, MAMA UBU, *Officers and Soldiers,* TAILS, HEADS, COTISE, NOBLES *in chains,* FINANCIERS, JUDGES, *Scribes.*]

PAPA UBU Bring in the Noble Chest and the Noble Hook and the Noble Knife and the Noble Book! Then bring forth the Nobles.

[*The* NOBLES *are brutally pushed forward.*]

MAMA UBU I pray thee, take it easy, Papa Ubu.

PAPA UBU I am pleased to inform you that in order to enrich the kingdom, I am going to execute all the Nobles and take their property.

NOBLES Horrors! soldiers and people, follow us!

PAPA UBU Bring up the first Noble and pass me the Noble Hook. Those who receive the death penalty will be pushed through the trapdoor; they'll fall into the cellars of Pig-Pincher and Penny-Chamber, where they'll be disembrained. [*To the* NOBLE] Who are you, you buggersky?

THE NOBLE Count of Vitebsk.[1]

PAPA UBU What is your income?

THE NOBLE Three million rixdalers.[2]

PAPA UBU Guilty! [*He spikes him with the hook and pushes him into the hole.*]

MAMA UBU What base ferocity!

PAPA UBU Second Noble, who are you? [*The* NOBLE *does not reply.*] Will you answer, you buggersky?

THE NOBLE The Grand Duke of Posen.[3]

PAPA UBU Fine! fine! That's all I need to know. Into the trapdoor with him. Third Noble, who are you? You have an ugly face.

THE NOBLE Duke of Curland, of the cities of Riga, Revel, and Mitau.[4]

PAPA UBU Good! good! You don't have anything else?

THE NOBLE Nothing.

PAPA UBU OK, down the trapdoor. Fourth Noble, who are you?

THE NOBLE The Prince of Poxdolia.[5]

PAPA UBU What is your revenue?

THE NOBLE Alas, I am ruined!

PAPA UBU For that bad word, you go through the trapdoor. Fifth Noble, who are you?

THE NOBLE Margrave of Thorn,[6] Palatine of Polack.

PAPA UBU That's not much. You don't have anything else?

THE NOBLE That was enough for me.

PAPA UBU Well, better little than nothing. Into the trapdoor. What're you crying about, Mama Ubu?

MAMA UBU You are too fierce, Papa Ubu.

PAPA UBU Hey! I'm getting rich. I'm going to read out MY List of MY Property. Clerk, read us MY List of MY Property.

CLERK County of Sandomir.

PAPA UBU Begin by the Principalities, you dumb bugger!

CLERK Principality of Poxdolia, Grand Duchy of Posen, Duchy of Curland, County of Sandomir, County of Vitebsk, Palatinate of Polack, Margraviate of Thorn.

PAPA UBU And then what?

CLERK That's it.

PAPA UBU Whaddya mean, that's it? In that case, Nobles, forward, march! And since I'm going to get rich endlessly I'm going to have all the Nobles executed so I'll get all their vacant property. Come on, throw the Nobles

1. A city in northeastern Belarus (east of Poland).
2. That is, rix-dollars: silver coins. This was a denomination used in keeping accounts in a number of European countries (from the older Dutch *rijcksdaler*, "kingdom's dollar").
3. Poznań, a city in west central Poland.
4. Curland is a region that corresponds to western Latvia. Riga is now the capital of Latvia; Revel is the former name of Tallinn, now the capital of Estonia (more than 100 miles from Curland); Mitau is the former name of Jelgava, in Latvia.
5. Podalia is a historical region in western Ukraine.
6. A province in northern Poland (Toruń).

into the trapdoor. [*The* NOBLES *are piled into the trapdoor.*] Hurry up, faster, I want to make some laws now.

SEVERAL We'll see about that.

PAPA UBU First I'm going to reform the legal system, then we'll proceed to state finance.

SEVERAL JUDGES We are opposed to any changes.

PAPA UBU Shitsky. First of all judges will no longer be paid.

JUDGES And what will we live on? We are poor.

PAPA UBU You'll have the fines you give out and the property of the people who get the death penalty.

A JUDGE Horrors!

SECOND Infamous.

THIRD Scandalous.

FOURTH An indignity.

ALL We refuse to judge under such conditions.

PAPA UBU Down the trapdoor with the judges! [*They struggle in vain.*]

MAMA UBU Oh! what are you doing, Papa Ubu? Who will deliver judgments now?

PAPA UBU Hey! I will! You'll see, it'll go great.

MAMA UBU Sure, it will be a real joy.

PAPA UBU Come on, be quiet, you buggeress. Now, gentlemen, we shall proceed to the finances of the state.

FINANCIERS There is nothing to change.

PAPA UBU Whaddya mean? I want to change everything. First of all I want to keep half the taxes for myself.

FINANCIERS Makes himself right at home.

PAPA UBU Gentlemen, we shall establish a tax of ten percent on property, another on commerce and industry, a third on weddings, and a fourth one on deaths, fifteen francs each.

FIRST FINANCIER But that's idiotic, Papa Ubu.

SECOND FINANCIER It's absurd.

THIRD FINANCIER That is absolutely senseless.

PAPA UBU What are you, kidding?! Down the trapdoor with the financiers! [*The* FINANCIERS *are shoveled in.*]

MAMA UBU Now come on, Papa Ubu, what kind of king are you? You're massacrating everybody.

PAPA UBU Oh, shitsky!

MAMA UBU No more judges, no more financiers.

PAPA UBU Fear nothing, my child, I shall go from village to village myself and collect the taxes.

3.3

[SCENE: *A farmhouse near Warsaw. Several* PEASANTS *are gathered there.*]

A PEASANT [*entering*] Did you hear the news? The King is dead, so are the Dukes, and young Buggerlas ran away into the mountains with his mother. What's more, Papa Ubu has taken over the throne.

ANOTHER PEASANT I know a lot more. I come from Cracow,[7] where I saw the bodies of more than three hundred nobles and five hundred judges carried

7. The city in southern Poland where the kings of Poland lived (14th–16th centuries) and were crowned (until the 18th century).

away—they'd been killed. And it seems they're going to double the taxes and Papa Ubu's going to come get them himself.

ALL Great God! what will become of us? Papa Ubu is a horrible baboon and it is said that his family is absolutely abominable.

A PEASANT But listen, wouldn't you say someone is knocking at the door?

A VOICE [*outside*] Oddsbellikins! open, by my shitsky, by Saint John, Saint Peter, and Saint Nicholas! Open, by my Financial Saber, my Financial Horn, I've come to get the taxes! [*The door is smashed in and* PAPA UBU *enters, followed by a legion of lackeys.*]

3.4

PAPA UBU Who's the oldest one here? [*A peasant steps forward.*] What is your name?

THE PEASANT Stanislas Leczinsky.

PAPA UBU Well, oddsbellikins, listen carefully, or else these gentlemen will cut your earies off. Look, are you going to listen to me? Will you listen?!

STANISLAS But your Excellency hasn't said anything yet.

PAPA UBU Whaddya mean, I've been talkin' for an hour. Think you that I have come here to preach in the desert?

STANISLAS Far be it from me to have such a thought.

PAPA UBU So. I have come to tell you, order you, and announce to you that you must promptly produce and exhibit your Finance, or else you will be massacrated. Come, my Lords Sonsabiddies of Finance, wagon the Phynance[8] Wagonette over here. [*The wagonette is brought in.*]

STANISLAS Sire, we are only registered for one hundred and fifty two rixdalers that we have already paid, about two weeks ago on Saint Matthew's Day.[9]

PAPA UBU That is quite possible, but I've changed the government and I had the newspapers announce that taxes will be paid twice—and three times for the ones that can be levied later by decree. With this system I'll get rich quick, then I'll kill everybody and get the hell out.

PEASANTS Papa Ubu, we beg of you, have pity on us. We are poor citizens.

PAPA UBU I don't give a damn. Pay up.

PEASANTS I cannot, we have paid.

PAPA UBU Pay up! Or I'll put you in my pocket with torture and chopping off of neck and head! Oddshornikins, I'm the King, aren't I?

ALL Ah! so that's the way it is! To arms! Long live Buggerlas, by God's grace King of Poland and Lithuania!

PAPA UBU Forward, Gentlemen of Finance, do your duty.

[*There is a struggle, the house is destroyed, and old* STANISLAS *flees alone across the plain.* PAPA UBU *remains to pick up the Finance.*]

3.5

[SCENE: *A bunker in the fortifications of Thorn.*]

[CAPTAIN BARBAGE *in chains,* PAPA UBU.]

PAPA UBU So! citizen, you see how it is, you wanted me to pay you what I owed you, I didn't want to, you conspired, and now here you are in the

8. Jarry coined the words "phynance" and "phynancial," playing on "finance" and "financial"; all are used to characterize some of his possessions and other objects.

9. September 21.

slammer. Oddsfinancesky, that's what you get, and it's such a good trick that you should appreciate it yourself.

CAPTAIN BARBAGE Take care, Papa Ubu. In the five days you have been king, you have committed more murders than it would take to damn all the saints in heaven. The blood of the King and his nobles cries for vengeance and their cries will be heard.

PAPA UBU Well! my fine-feathered friend, you speak very freely indeed. I have no doubt that there might well be complications if you escaped, but I don't think the bunkers of Thorn have ever released a single one of the honest lads who were turned over to them. That's why, good night, and I suggest you sleep tight, though the rats do dance a fine saraband in these cellies.

[*He exits. The lackeys come in and lock up all the doors.*]

3.6

[SCENE: *The Moscow palace.*]

[CZAR ALEXIS *and his Court,* BARBAGE.]

CZAR ALEXIS Was it you, you infamous adventurer, who cooperated in the death of our cousin Wenceslas?

BARBAGE Sire, forgive me, I was carried away by Papa Ubu despite myself.

ALEXIS Oh! what a frightful liar. Well, what do you want?

BARBAGE Papa Ubu had me thrown in jail on the pretext of conspiracy. I succeeded in escaping and I galloped for five days and five nights across the steppes to come and beg Your gracious mercy.

ALEXIS What do you bring me as a token of your surrender?

BARBAGE My adventurer's sword and a detailed map of the city of Thorn.

ALEXIS I accept the sword, but by Saint George, burn this map; I do not wish to owe my victory to an act of treachery.

BARBAGE One of the sons of Wenceslas is still alive—young Buggerlas. I will do anything to restore him to his throne.

ALEXIS What was your rank in the Polish army?

BARBAGE I commanded the Fifth Regiment of Vilna Dragoons and a Company of Freebooters in the service of Papa Ubu.

ALEXIS All right, I name you Second Lieutenant in the Tenth Regiment of Cossacks, and woe betide you if you betray me. If you fight well, you will be rewarded.

BARBAGE Courage is not a thing I lack, Sire.

ALEXIS All right, vanish from my presence.

[BARBAGE *exits.*]

3.7

[SCENE: UBU's *Council Room.*]

[PAPA UBU, MAMA UBU, *Finance* COUNCILLORS.]

PAPA UBU Gentlemen, the session is opened. Listen up and try to be quiet. First we are going to tackle the finance question, next we will talk about a little system I've dreamed up to bring good weather and prevent rain.

A COUNCILLOR Very good, Mr. Ubu.

MAMA UBU What a blockhead.

PAPA UBU Madame of my shitsky, watch out! for I won't stand for your nonsense. . . . As I was saying, gentlemen, our finances are doing reasonably well. A large number of woolstocking dogs go out into the streets every morning, and the Sonsabiddies are doing wonders. On every side, all you can see is burned-down houses and people crushed under the weight of our phynances.

THE COUNCILLOR How about the new taxes, Mr. Ubu, are they doing well?

MAMA UBU Absolutely not. The tax on weddings has only yielded eleven cents, even though Papa Ubu goes running after people everywhere to force them to get married.

PAPA UBU By my Financial Saber, gads of my oddzooks, Madame Financier, I have earies for talking and you have a mouth to hear me with. [*Bursts of laughter.*] Oh, no! you're making me make a mistake and you're the reason why I'm being stupid! But, by Ubu's oddsbelly . . .

[*A messenger enters.*]

OK, OK, what's wrong with *him?* Get out of here, you baboon, or I'll pocket you, with decapitation and twisting of the legs.

MAMA UBU OK, he's gone, but there's a letter.

PAPA UBU Read it. I think I'm losing my mind, or I don't know how to read. Hurry up, you buffoodsky, it must be from Barbage.

MAMA UBU Exactly. He says the czar gave him a warm welcome, he's going to invade your states to bring back Buggerlas, and you'll be killed.

PAPA UBU Oh! oh! I'm scared! I'm scared! Ah! I think I'm dying. Oh, what a poor man I am. Good God, what will become of me? That wicked man will kill me. Saint Anthony[1] and all the saints, protect me, I will give you phynance and I'll burn candles for you. Lord, what will become of me? [*He weeps and sobs.*]

MAMA UBU There is only one course to take, Papa Ubu.

PAPA UBU Which, my love?

MAMA UBU War!!!

ALL God be praised! How noble!

PAPA UBU Yeah, and I'll get beat up again.

FIRST COUNCILLOR Quick, let us hasten to organize the army.

SECOND And stock up on food.

THIRD And prepare the artillery and the fortresses.

FOURTH And get the money for the troops.

PAPA UBU Hell no! I'll *kill* you, I don't want to give away any money. Money! now there's good one! I was paid to make war and now I have to do it at my own expense. No, by my green candlestick, we'll make war, since you're so enraged, but we will not spend a red cent.

ALL Three cheers for war!

3.8

[SCENE: *The camp near Warsaw.*]

SOLDIERS and KNIGHTIES Three cheers for Poland! Three cheers for Papa Ubu!

PAPA UBU Ah! Mama Ubu, give me my armor and my little piece of wood. Soon I'll be so heavily loaded down I won't be able to walk if I am pursued.

1. St. Anthony of Padua (1195–1231), a great miracle worker.

MAMA UBU Fie, what a coward.

PAPA UBU Ah! the Shitsky Saber is getting away and the Financial Hook's coming loose!!! I'll never get out of this, and the Russians are advancing and they'll kill me.

A SOLDIER My Lord Ubu, the Earie Scissors are falling.

PAPA UBU I keel you weez ze Shitsky Hook and ze Face Knife.

MAMA UBU How handsome he is with his helmet and his armor; he looks like an armed pumpkin.

PAPA UBU Ah! now I shall mount my steed. Gentlemen, bring in the Phynancial Horse.

MAMA UBU Papa Ubu, your horse can no longer carry you; he hasn't had anything to eat for five days and he's almost dead.

PAPA UBU Now there's a good one! They charge me twelve cents a day for this nag and he can't carry me any more. Are you kidding me, by Ubu's horn, or . . . what if you're robbing me? [MAMA UBU *blushes and lowers her eyes.*] Well then, bring me in another horse, I'm not going to walk, oddshornikins!

[*An enormous horse is brought in.*]

PAPA UBU I'm going to mount. Oh! down, horsie, down! for I am going to fall. [*The horse takes off.*] Ah! stop this beast. Good God, I'm going to fall down and be dead!!!

MAMA UBU He's a real imbecile. Ah! now he's gotten up again. But he fell down.

PAPA UBU Physical horn, I'm half dead! But that's all right, I'm going off to war and I'll kill everybody. Whoever doesn't walk the straight and narrow, look out! I poot heem in my pock*ett* with twisting of nose and teeth and extraction of tongue.

MAMA UBU Good luck, Mr. Ubu.

PAPA UBU I forgot to tell you—I'm giving you the regency. But I'm keeping my book of finances on me, and it'll be too bad for you if you cheat me. I leave you Knightie Lap to aid and assist you. Farewell, Mama Ubu.

MAMA UBU Farewell, Papa Ubu. Have a good czar-killing.

PAPA UBU For sure. Twisting of the nose and teeth, extraction of the tongue and driving of the little piece of wood into his earies.

[*The army goes off, to the sound of fanfares.*]

MAMA UBU [*alone*] Now that that fat puppet has departed, let us attend to our own business, kill Buggerlas and seize the treasure.

End of the Third Act.

4.1

[SCENE: *The crypt of the ancient kings of Poland in the Warsaw cathedral.*[2]

MAMA UBU Where the devil is that treasure? Not one stone slab has sounded hollow. Yet I did count thirteen stones after the tomb of Ladislav the Great following the wall, and nothing's there. They must have fooled me. But here: the stone sounds hollow. Let's get to work, Mama Ubu. Courage, let us unseal this stone. It's holding firm. We'll take this end of

2. The ancient kings of Poland are actually buried in Kraków.

the Financial Hook; it will perform its office once again. There! here's the gold, in the midst of the bones of kings. Into our bag now, all of it! Hey! what is that sound? Could there still be living souls in these old vaults? No, it's nothing, let us hurry. We'll take everything. This money will be better in the light of day than in the midst of the tombs of ancient princes. Let us replace the stone. My presence in this place inspires me with a strange fear. I'll take the rest of this gold another time; I'll come back tomorrow.

A VOICE [*coming from the tomb of John Sigismund*[3]] Never, Mama Ubu!

[MAMA UBU *runs away, terrified, carrying off the stolen gold through a secret door.*]

4.2

[SCENE: *The Warsaw palace.*]

[BUGGERLAS *and his followers, People and Soldiers, then* GUARDS, MAMA UBU, KNIGHTIE LAP.]

BUGGERLAS Forward, my friends! Long live Wenceslas and Poland! That old rascal Papa Ubu is gone, all that's left is that witch Mama Ubu with her Knightie. I offer to march at your head and reestablish the race of my fathers.

EVERYONE Long live Buggerlas!

BUGGERLAS And we will do away with all the taxes raised by that frightful Papa Ubu.

EVERYONE Hurray! forward! Let us run to the palace and massacrate that breed.

BUGGERLAS Hey! there's Mama Ubu coming out with her guards on the palace steps!

MAMA UBU What do you want, gentlemen? Ah! it's Buggerlas.

[*The crowd throws stones.*]

FIRST GUARD All our windows are broken.

SECOND GUARD By Saint George, I am knocked out.

THIRD GUARD Oddshornikins, I am dying.

BUGGERLAS Throw stones, my friends.

KNIGHTIE LAP So! that's the way it is! [*He unsheathes his sword and rushes forward, causing frightful carnage.*]

BUGGERLAS I'll take you on! Defend yourself, you cowardly little pistol.

[*They fight.*]

KNIGHTIE LAP I am dead!

BUGGERLAS Victory, my friends! On to Mama Ubu, let her have it!

[*Trumpets are heard.*]

BUGGERLAS Ah! the Nobles are coming. Run, let's get that evil harpy!

EVERYONE And then we'll strangle the old bandit!

[MAMA UBU *runs off, followed by all the Poles. Rifle shots, hail of stones.*]

3. Prince-elector of the Margraviate of Brandenburg and a duke of Prussia (1572–1619).

4.3

[*The Polish army marching through Ukraine.*]

PAPA UBU Oddshornikins, godsleggikins, by the cow's head! we shall perish, for we are dying of thirst and are tired. Sire Soldier, be good enough to wear our Financial Helmet, and you, Sire Lancer, take up the Shitsky Scissors and the Physical Stick to ease our person, for, I repeat, we are tired.

[*The soldiers obey.*]

HEADS Eh! Meesterr! it is astonishing that ye Russians appear not.

PAPA UBU It is regrettable that the state of our finances does not allow us to have a coach of our size; for, out of fear of demolishing our steed, we have walked all the way, leading our horse by the bridle. But with our knowledge of physics and the help of the wisdom of our councillors, when we are back in Poland, we will dream up a wind-driven coach to transport the whole army.

COTISE Here's Nicholas Rensky running up to us.

PAPA UBU What's the matter with that boy?

RENSKY All is lost, Sire, the Poles have revolted, Lap is killed, Mama Ubu has taken flight in the mountains.

PAPA UBU You wretched beast, you night bird, you owl with spats! Where'd you get that garbage? There's a good one! And who did it? Buggerlas, I'll bet. Where are you coming from?

RENSKY From Warsaw, my noble lord.

PAPA UBU Boy of my shitsky, if I believed you I'd have the whole army do an about-face. But, my lord boy, you have more plumes than brains on your shoulders and you have dreamed up a lot of nonsense. Go to the outposts, my boy, the Russians are not far and soon we will have to thrust with our weapons, both shitskied and phynancials—and physicals.

GENERAL LASKY Papa Ubu, do you not see the Russians in the plain?

PAPA UBU It's true, the Russians! Now I'm really in for it. At least if there were some way of getting out of here, but no, we're on a height and we'll be perfect targets.

THE ARMY The Russians! The enemy!

PAPA UBU Come, gentlemen, let us draw up our plans for the battle. We shall remain on the hill and will not commit the blunder of descending below. I shall stay in the middle like a living fortress and you people will gravitate around me. I must enjoin you to insert into your rifles as many bullets as they can hold, for eight bullets can kill eight Russians and that makes so many more off my back. We'll station the infantrymen at the bottom of the hill to receive the Russians and kill them a bit, the horsemen behind to throw themselves into the confusion, and the artillery around ye windmill here to fire into the crowd. As for us, we shall remain in the windmill and shall shoot through the window with the Phynancial Pistol, across the door we shall place the Physical Stick, and if anyone tries to get in, watch out for the Shitsky Hook!!!

OFFICERS Sire Ubu, your orders will be carried out.

PAPA UBU Ha! that's good, we shall be victorious. What time is it?

GENERAL LASKY Eleven A.M.

PAPA UBU Well then, let us have lunch, for the Russians will not attack before noon. Lord General, tell the soldiers to relieve themselves and to strike up the Finance Song.

[LASKY *leaves.*]

SOLDIERS and KNIGHTIES Long live Papa Ubu, our great Financier! Ting, ting, ting; ting, ting, ting; ting, ting, ta-ting!

PAPA UBU O what fine soldiers, I love them. [*A Russian cannonball comes in and breaks the sail of the windmill.*] Oh! I am afraid, Sire God, I am dead! And yet no, I'm quite all right.

4.4

[*The same, a* CAPTAIN, *then the Russian Army.*]

A CAPTAIN [*entering*] Sire Ubu, the Russians are attacking.

PAPA UBU So what do you want me to do about it? *I* didn't tell them to do it! Still, Gentlemen of Finance, let us prepare for combat.

GENERAL LASKY A second cannonball.

PAPA UBU Ah! I can stand no more. It is raining lead and fire and we might damage our precious person. Let us go down the hill.

[*They all race down. The battle has just begun. They disappear in torrents of smoke at the foot of the hill.*]

A RUSSIAN [*striking*] For God and the Czar!

RENSKY Ah! I am dead.

PAPA UBU Forward! Ah! you, Sir, let me get a hold of you, for you hurt me, do you hear! you wine bag! with your piece that can't fire.

THE RUSSIAN Ah! watch this. [*He fires a revolver shot at him.*]

PAPA UBU Ah! Oh! I am wounded, I am punctured, I am perforated, I am administrated, I am cremated. Ah, still and all, ah! I've got him. [*He rips him apart.*] There! Will you start up again now?

GENERAL LASKY Forward, push ahead vigorously, over the ditch, victory is ours.

PAPA UBU Think so? Up to here I feel more bumps than laurels[4] on my brow.

RUSSIAN HORSEMEN Hurrah! Make way for the Czar!

[*The* CZAR *enters, accompanied by* BARBAGE *in disguise.*]

A POLE Ah! Lord! Every man for himself, here comes the Czar!

ANOTHER Oh! my God! he has crossed the ditch.

ANOTHER Bing! Bang! there go four soldiers, struck down by that big bugger of a lieutenant.

BARBAGE Ah! it's not over yet for you! Here, Johannes Sobiesky, now you're going to get yours. [*He strikes him down.*] Now for the others! [*He makes a massacre of the Poles.*]

PAPA UBU Forward, my friends! Get that good-for-nothing! Make applesauce out of those Muscovites! Victory is ours. Long live the Red Eagle!

EVERYONE Forward! Hurrah! Godsleg! Get the big bugger.

BARBAGE By Saint George, I have fallen.

PAPA UBU [*recognizing him*] Ah! it's you, Barbage! Aha! my friend. We are quite happy to meet you once again. So is the whole Company. I am going

4. Symbolic of victory in battle.

to cook you over a slow fire. Gentlemen of Finance, light the fire. Oh! Ah! Oh! I am dead. I've been hit by a cannon shot at the very least. Ah! God, forgive me my sins. Yes, it is a cannon shot.

BARBAGE It's a shot from a pistol loaded with powder.

PAPA UBU Ah! you're kidding me! Again! Into my poke-et!

[*He charges at him and rips him apart.*]

GENERAL LASKY Papa Ubu, we are advancing on all fronts.

PAPA UBU I can see that very well, I can't take any more, I've been kicked all over, I would like to sit down upon the ground . . . Oh! my bottle.

GENERAL LASKY Go take the Czar's, Papa Ubu.

PAPA UBU Hey! I'm going for it right away. Let's go! Shitsky Saber, do your duty, and you, Financial Hook, do not remain behind. Let the Physical Stick work with generous emulation and share with the little wedge of wood the honor of massacrating, gouging out, and exploiting the Muscovite Czar. Forward, Sir Horse of Finance!

[*He charges at the* CZAR.]

A RUSSIAN OFFICER On guard, Your Majesty!

PAPA UBU Here's for you! Oh! Ouch! Come *on!* Ah! excuse me, sir, do leave me alone. Oh! really, I didn't do it on purpose!

[*He runs away. The* CZAR *follows him.*]

PAPA UBU Blessed Virgin, that madman is following me! Great God, what have I done! Ah! OK, we've still got the ditch to cross over again. Ah! I can feel him behind me, and the ditch ahead! Courage, let us close our eyes.

[*He jumps the ditch. The* CZAR *falls into it.*]

THE CZAR Well, I'm in it.

POLES Hurrah! the Czar is down!

PAPA UBU I hardly dare turn around! He's in it. Ah! and a good thing too, and they're beating on him. Come on Poles, give it to him good, he has a broad back, that wretch! *I* don't dare look at him! And yet our prediction has come completely true, the Physical Stick has wrought marvels, and there is no doubt that I would have killed him completely if terror had not inexplicably come in to combat and nullify in us the effects of our courage. But we were obliged suddenly to turn turncoat, and we were obliged to owe our salvation solely to our skill as a horseman as well as to the legs of our Financial Horse—whose rapidity is only equaled by his stability and whose lightness is justly celebrated—as well as to the depth of the ditch that quite luckily happened to be under the feet of the enemy of Us, the present-and-accounted-for Master of Phynances. Now this is all very well, but no one is listening to me. . . . Uh oh! here we go again!

[*The Russian Dragoons make a charge and deliver the* CZAR.]

GENERAL LASKY This time, we're in a general rout.

PAPA UBU Ah! here's a chance to bust outta here. And now, good Polish Lords, forward! Or rather, backward!

POLE Every man for himself!

PAPA UBU Come on, let's get going! What a lot of people, what a stampede, what a multitude, how can I get out of this mess? [*He is roughly jostled.*] Hey, you! watch out, or you will feel the burning valor of the Master of

Finances. Ah! he has gone, let us get out of here, and fast, while Lasky can't see us.

[*He exits. Then the* CZAR *goes by, and the Russian Army pursuing the Poles.*]

4.5

[SCENE: *A cavern in Lithuania (it is snowing).*]

[PAPA UBU, HEADS, COTISE.]

PAPA UBU Ah! what filthy weather, it's cold enough to split rocks, and the person of the Master of Finances has been quite damaged by it.

HEADS Oh! Milaird Ubu, have you recovered from your terror and your flight?

PAPA UBU Yes! I'm not scared any more, but I've still got the flights.

COTISE [*aside*] What a pig.

PAPA UBU Hey! Sire Cotise, how is the health of your earie?

COTISE Milaird, it's as good as it can be seeing as it's bad. Quinsecontly, the lead makes it lean toward the earth and I have not been able to extract the bullet.

PAPA UBU Well! you asked for it! You're one of those guys who always wanted to beat up on other people. As for me, I displayed the greatest valor, and without exposing myself at all I massacrated four enemies with my own hand, not counting all the ones who were already dead that we finished off.

COTISE Heads, do you know what happened to little Rensky?

HEADS He was shot in the head.

PAPA UBU AS the wild poppy and the dandelion in their prime are scythed down by the pitiless scythe of the pitiless scyther who pitilessly scythes their pitiful noggins, EVEN SO has little Rensky played poppy; he did fight well however, but also there were too many Russians.

HEADS and COTISE Ooh, Milaird!

AN ECHO Ooooh!

HEADS What have we here? Let us arm ourselves with our bladies.

PAPA UBU Not on your life! I'll bet it's the Russians again, for Godsakes. I'm sick and tired of this! Well, the hell with it, if they get me I sticka dem inna de pocket.

4.6[5]

[SCENE: *The same.*]

[*Enter a bear.*]

COTISE Yoo-hoo, Milaird of Finances!

PAPA UBU Oh, hey! look at the little doggie. My word, but he's cute.

HEADS Watch out! Ah! what a huge bear: my cartridges!

PAPA UBU A bear! Ah! what a horrible beast. Oh! poor man, I am eaten alive. God protect me. And he's coming right at me. No, he's got Cotise. Ah! I can breathe again.

[*The bear jumps on* COTISE. HEADS *attacks it with his knife.* UBU *takes shelter on a rock.*]

5. This scene, adapted from an intermezzo in one of Molière's minor plays, was cut when *Ubu* was first performed in Paris [translator's note].

COTISE To me, Heads! Help, Milaird Ubu!

PAPA UBU Nothing doing! You can shift for yourself, my friend; for the moment, we are reciting an Our Father.[6] Everybody has to take his turn at being eaten.

HEADS I've got him, I've got him.

COTISE Hold firm, friend, he's beginning to let go.

PAPA UBU Hallowèd be thy name.

COTISE Let go, you bugger!

HEADS Ah! he's biting me! Oh good Lord, save us, I am dead.

PAPA UBU Thy will be done.

COTISE Ah! I've succeeded in wounding him.

HEADS Hurray! he's losing blood.

[*In the midst of the shouting Knighties, the bear bellows with pain and* UBU *continues to mutter.*]

COTISE Hold on to him, so I can let loose an explosive punch.

UBU Give us this day our daily bread.

HEADS Do you have him, for godsakes, I can't take any more.

PAPA UBU Forgive us our debts, as we forgive our debtors.

COTISE Ah! I've got him.

[*An explosion rings out and the bear falls, dead.*]

HEADS and COTISE Victory!

PAPA UBU But deliver us from evil. Well, is he good and dead? Can I come down from my rock?

HEADS [*scornfully*] As much as you like.

PAPA UBU [*climbing down*] You may rest assured that if you are still alive and still treading the snow of Lithuania, you owe it to the magnanimous virtue of the Master of Finances, who wore his throat, his back, and his self to a frazzle reciting Our Fathers for your safety and salvation, and who was as brave in wielding the spiritual sword of prayer as you were skillful with the temporal one of the present-and-accounted-for-Knightie Heads's explosive punch. We even went still further in our devotion, for we did not hesitate to climb an extremely high rock so that our prayers would have less distance to travel up to heaven.

HEADS You disgusting jackass.

PAPA UBU Now here's a fat beast. Thanks to me, you have something for supper. What a belly, gentlemen! The Greeks would have had more room in it than inside the wooden horse,[7] and, my dear friends, we very nearly went and verified its inner capacity with our own eyes.

HEADS I'm dying of hunger. What can we eat?

COTISE The bear!

PAPA UBU Hey! you poor fools, are you going to eat it raw? We have nothing to make fire with.

HEADS Have we not the flints from our muskets?

6. That is, the Lord's Prayer, which begins "Our Father which art in heaven" (Matthew 6.9–13). Ubu continues to quote from this prayer through "But deliver us from evil."

7. That is, the Trojan Horse. According to legend, the Trojan War was finally brought to an end when the Trojans were tricked into pulling this hollow construction—filled with the best Greek warriors—within the city walls.

PAPA UBU Huh! that's true. And then it seems to me that not far from here there is a little wood where there should be some dry branches. Go get some, Sire Cotise.

[COTISE *goes off through the snow.*]

HEADS And now, Sire Ubu, go cut up the bear.

PAPA UBU Oh no! he might not be dead. Whereas you, who are already half eaten and bitten all over, it's just your kind of job. I'll light a fire while we wait for him to bring wood.

[HEADS *begins to cut up the bear.*]

PAPA UBU Oh! watch out! he moved.

HEADS But Sire Ubu, he is already quite cold.

PAPA UBU What a shame, it would have been better to eat him hot. This will cause indigestion in the Master of Finances.

HEADS [*aside*] This is revolting. [*Aloud*] Give us a hand, Mr. Ubu, I can't do the whole job.

PAPA UBU No, I don't wanna do a thing! I'm tired, of course!

COTISE [*entering*] What snow, my friends, one would think we were in Spain or at the North Pole. Night is beginning to fall. In an hour it will be dark. Let us hurry so that we can still see clearly.

PAPA UBU Yes, do you hear, Heads? Hurry. Both of you, hurry up! Spit the beast, cook the beast, I'm hungry!

HEADS Ah! this is really too much! You'll have to work or you won't get a thing, do you hear, you glutton!

PAPA UBU Oh! I don't care, I'd just as soon eat it raw, you're the ones who'll be sorry. And anyway, I'm sleepy!

COTISE What can we do, Heads? Let's make dinner all by ourselves. He won't get any, that's all. Or else we can give him the bones.

HEADS Fine. Ah! there's the fire flaming up.

PAPA UBU Oh! that's nice, it's warm now. But I see Russians everywhere. What a rout, good God! Ah! [*He falls asleep.*]

COTISE I wonder if what Rensky said is true, if Mama Ubu has really lost her throne. It does not sound impossible.

HEADS Let's finish making supper.

COTISE No, we have more important things to talk about. I think it would be good to inquire as to the veracity of that bit of news.

HEADS That's true; should we abandon Papa Ubu or stay with him?

COTISE The night brings counsel. Let us sleep, tomorrow we shall see what we must do.

HEADS No, it's better to take advantage of the night to get out of here.

COTISE In that case, let us go.

[*They go.*]

4.7

[PAPA UBU *talking in his sleep.*]

PAPA UBU Ah! Sire Russian Dragoon, be careful, don't shoot this way, there are people here. Ah! here's Barbage, how bad-natured he is, you'd think he was a bear. And Buggerlas coming right at me! The bear, the bear! Ah! he's down! good God, he's tough! I don't want to do anything! Get out of here, Buggerlas! Do you hear, you idiot? Now here's Rensky and the Czar! Oh!

they're going to beat me. And Mabubu. Where did you get all that gold? You took my gold, you wretch, you went and rummaged around in my tomb which is in the Warsaw Cathedral, near the moon. I've really been dead for a long time, Buggerlas is the one who killed me, and I'm buried in Warsaw near Vladislas the Great, and also in Cracow near John Sigismund and also in Thorn in the bunker with Barbage! Here he comes again. Would you get out of here, you beastly bear. You look like Barbage. Do you hear, you damned beast? No, he can't hear, the Sonsabiddies have cut his earies off. De-brain 'em, kill 'em, cut all their earies off, rip out the finance and drink to the death, that's the life for Sonsabiddies, and for the Master of Finances, that's what makes his day.

[*He stops talking and sleeps.*]

End of the Fourth Act.

5.1

[*Night.* PAPA UBU *is asleep. Enter* MAMA UBU, *who does not see him. Total darkness.*]

MAMA UBU Shelter at last. I am alone here, and none too soon, but what a mad race: crossing all of Poland in four days! Every misfortune assailed me at once. As soon as that fat jackass had left, I went to the crypt to get rich. Right after that I almost got stoned to death by Buggerlas and his madmen. I lost my Knightie—Lap, who was so in love with my charms that he swooned with pleasure when he saw me, and even (so I have been assured) when he didn't see me, which is the height of love. He would have cut himself in two for me, poor boy. The proof of that is, he was cut in four by Buggerlas. Slish slash slish! . . . Ah! I thought I would die. So then I ran away, pursued by the angry crowd. I left the palace, I reached the Vistula, all the bridges were guarded. I swam across the river, hoping to wear out my persecutors. On all sides the nobility assembled and pursued me. A thousand times I almost perished, smothered in a circle of Poles determined to end my days. At last I got the better of their rage, and after four days of racing through the snow of what was once my kingdom I managed to find shelter here. I have neither eaten nor drunk these four days, Buggerlas was on my heels . . . . Well! at last I am safe. Ah! I am dying of weariness and cold. But I *would* like to know what happened to my fat puppet, I mean my dear husband. Boy, did I take finance from him! Did I ever steal rixdalers from him! Did I ever ever get his carrots! And his Financial Horse that was dying of hunger: he didn't see oats very often, the poor devil. Ah! what a story. But alas! I have lost my treasure! It is in Warsaw, and he who wants may seek it.

PAPA UBU [*beginning to wake up*] Get Mama Ubu, cut her earies off!

MAMA UBU Oh, God! where am I? I'm losing my mind. Oh, no, Lord!

> Put out the light, and then put out the light.
> Without quenching thee, thou flaming minister,
> I see again my former Ubu sleep . . .

. . . Let's act nice. Well, has Mama's big boy had a good sleep?

PAPA UBU A very bad one! That bear was tough as hell! A battle of the ravenous against the cavernous, but the ravenous have completely eaten up and devoured the cavernous, as you will see when daylight comes—do you hear, noble Knighties!

MAMA UBU What's he jabbering about? He's even dumber than when he left. Who's he mad at?

PAPA UBU Cotise, Heads, answer me, you shitsky-bags! Where are you? Ah! I'm scared. But someone spoke. Who spoke? It can't be the bear. Shitsky! Where are my matches? Ah! I lost them in the battle.

MAMA UBU [*aside*] Let us take advantage of the situation and the night, let us simulate a supernatural apparition and make him promise to forgive us our theft.

PAPA UBU Oh! by Saint Anthony! someone's talking. Godslegs! well, blow me down!

MAMA UBU [*amplifying her voice*] Yes, Mr. Ubu, someone is talking indeed, and the trumpet of the archangel who will pull the dead from the ashes and the final dust would speak no other way! Listen to that severe voice. It is the voice of Saint Gabriel[8] who can only give you good advice.

PAPA UBU Oh sure! *that* he can give!

MAMA UBU Don't interrupt me or I'll be quiet and that'll be the end of your bogsbelliskin!

PAPA UBU Ah! my godsbellysky! I'll be quiet, I say no more. Continue, Madam Apparition!

MAMA UBU We were saying, Mr. Ubu, that you were a big, big boy.

PAPA UBU Very big, indeed, this is true.

MAMA UBU Shut up, for God's sake!

PAPA UBU Oh! angels don't swear!

MAMA UBU [*aside*] Shitsky! [*Continuing*] You are married, Mr. Ubu.

PAPA UBU Absolutely, to the worst shrew in the world!

MAMA UBU You mean she's a charming woman.

PAPA UBU She's horrible. She has claws everywhere, there's no way of handling her.

MAMA UBU Handle her with gentleness, Sire Ubu, and if you handle her like that you will see that she is at least the equal of the Venus of Milo.[9]

PAPA UBU Who's that you say should be in a silo?

MAMA UBU You are not listening, Mr. Ubu; lend us a more attentive ear. [*Aside*] But let us hasten, for day is going to break—Mr. Ubu, your wife is adorable and delightful, she does not have one single fault.

PAPA UBU You're wrong, there's not one fault she doesn't have.

MAMA UBU Silence, I say! your wife is not unfaithful to you!

PAPA UBU I'd really like to know who could possibly fall in love with her. She's a harpy!

MAMA UBU She doesn't drink!

PAPA UBU Ever since I took the key to the wine cellar. Before that, she was drunk at seven in the morning and the perfume she used was pure booze. Now the perfume she uses is heliotrope and she smells a lot better. I don't care. But now I'm the only one who's drunk!

MAMA UBU Silly fool!—Your wife doesn't take your gold.

PAPA UBU No she doesn't—*that's* funny!

MAMA UBU She doesn't swindle you out of a cent!

8. According to legend, the archangel Gabriel is the seventh angel who, in the book of Revelation (11.15), sounds the final trumpet that announces Judgment Day.

9. An ancient Greek statue of Aphrodite, the goddess of love; its arms have been lost.

PAPA UBU Witness our noble and unfortunate Phynancial Horse, who, since he had not been fed for three months, was obliged to go through the whole campaign led across Ukraine by the bridle. And so he died in harness, poor beast!

MAMA UBU That's all a pack of lies, your wife is a model wife and as for you, you're a monster!

PAPA UBU That's all true, my wife is a rascal, and as for you, you're a nattering ninny!

MAMA UBU Beware, Papa Ubu, beware!

PAPA UBU Ah, that's true, I forgot who I was talking to. OK, no, I didn't say that!

MAMA UBU You killed Wenceslas.

PAPA UBU That's not *my* fault, of course. Mama Ubu's the one who wanted to do that.

MAMA UBU You put Boleslas and Ladislas to death.

PAPA UBU Too bad for them! They wanted to borrow from me!

MAMA UBU You did not keep your promise to Barbage and later you killed him.

PAPA UBU I'd rather it be me than he who reigns in Lithuania. For the moment it's neither one of us. So you can see it's not me.

MAMA UBU There is only one way for you to be forgiven for all your evil deeds.

PAPA UBU What way? I am quite ready to become a holy man; I want to be a bishop and see my name in the calendar.

MAMA UBU You must forgive Mama Ubu for having embezzled a little money.

PAPA UBU Well, there you are! I'll forgive her when she has given enough back to me and when she has been soundly beaten. And when she has brought my Financial Horse back to life.

MAMA UBU God, he's crazy about his horse! . . . Ah! I am lost, day is breaking.

PAPA UBU At any rate, I am glad to have learned with certainty that my dear wife was stealing from me. Now I have it from a good source. *Omnis a Deo scientia*, which means: *Omnis*—all; *a Deo*—knowledge; *scientia*—comes from God.[1] There's the explanation of the phenomenon. But Madame the Apparition isn't saying anything any more. Would that I could offer her something to comfort her. What she was saying was very amusing. Hey, it's broad daylight! Oh, good God, by my Financial Horse . . . it's Mama Ubu!

MAMA UBU [*brazenly*] That's not true, I'll excommunicate you.

PAPA UBU Ah! you animal!

MAMA UBU What impiety.

PAPA UBU Oh! this is too much. I can see it's you, you stupid shrew! What the devil are you doing here?

MAMA UBU Lap is dead and the Poles threw me out.

PAPA UBU On my side, it's the Russians who threw me out. Great minds meet.

MAMA UBU Let's say a great mind has met a jackass!

1. Ubu's translation is accurate, but his explanation reverses the meanings of *a Deo* (from God) and *scientia* (knowledge).

PAPA UBU Oh! well, now it's going to meet a palmiped![2] [*He throws the bear at her.*]

MAMA UBU [*falling crushed under the weight of the bear*] Ah! good God! how horrible! Ah! I am dying! I am smothering! He's biting me! He's swallowing me! He's digesting me!

PAPA UBU He's dead! you grotesque woman, you. . . . Uh oh! or maybe not! Lord! he's not dead, let's get out of here. [*Climbing back on his rock*] Our Father who art . . .

MAMA UBU [*extricating herself*] Hey! where is he?

PAPA UBU Oh, Lord! here she is again! The stupid beast, there's no way of getting rid of her. Is the bear dead?

MAMA UBU Of course he is, you stupid donkey, he's already stone cold. How did he get here?

PAPA UBU [*embarrassed*] I don't know. Oh yes, I do! He wanted to eat Heads and Cotise and I killed him with one stroke of my Lord's Prayer.

MAMA UBU Heads, Cotise, Lord's Prayer. What *is* all this? He's crazy, that Finance of mine!

PAPA UBU It's true, it's true, what I'm tellin' you! And you're an idiot, Bogsbelliskin of mine!

MAMA UBU Tell me about your campaign, Papa Ubu.

PAPA UBU Oh! for heaven's sake, no! It's too long. All I know is that despite my incontrovertible valiance everybody beat me.

MAMA UBU What! even the Poles?

PAPA UBU They shouted: Long live Wenceslas and Buggerlas. I thought they wanted me drawn and quartered. Oh! the madmen! And then they went and killed Rensky.

MAMA UBU I don't care! You know, Buggerlas killed Knightie Lap!

PAPA UBU I don't care! And then they went and killed poor Lasky!

MAMA UBU I don't care!

PAPA UBU Oh! not *that!* Get over here, you animal! Fall on your knees before your master [*He grabs her and throws her to her knees.*], you are going to pay the ultimate penalty.

MAMA UBU Oh, oh, Mr. Ubu!

PAPA UBU Oh! oh! oh! so, have you finished? Now *I'll* start: twisting of the nose, pulling out of the hair, penetration of the little piece of wood into the earies, extraction of the brain by the heels, laceration of the posterior, partial or even total suppression of the spine marrow (if only that would get rid of her spiny character!), not to forget opening of the swimming bladder and finally renewal of the great decapitation of Saint John the Baptist,[3] all adapted from the very holy Scriptures, both from the Old and New Testament, arranged, corrected, and perfected by the present-and-accounted-for Master of Finances!

[*He tears her apart.*]

MAMA UBU Mercy, Mr. Ubu!

[*Loud noise at the entrance of the cavern.*]

2. A web-footed bird.
3. See Matthew 14.1–12 (a similar account appears in the other three Gospels).

5.2

[*The same, with* BUGGERLAS, *charging into the cavern with his Soldiers.*]

BUGGERLAS Forward, my friends! Long live Poland!

PAPA UBU Oh! oh! just you wait, Mr. Polesky. Just wait till I've finished with Madame my Better Half!

BUGGERLAS [*striking him*] There, you coward, you blackguard, you beggar, you infidel, you moslem!

PAPA UBU [*riposting*] There! You Polesky, drunksky, bastardsky, troopsky, Turksky, kibumsky, snoopsky, doopsky, Commie!

MAMA UBU [*also beating him*] There, you chicken, piggen, felon, bacon, villain, slattern, Polen!

[*The Soldiers charge at the* UBUS, *who defend themselves as best they can.*]

PAPA UBU Ye gods! what reenfortments!

MAMA UBU We've got feet, Sir Poles.

PAPA UBU By my green candlestick, will it never end, finally? Another one! Ah! if only I had my Phynancial Horse here!

BUGGERLAS Hit, and keep hitting.

VOICE OUTSIDE Long live Papa Ubu, our great financier!

PAPA UBU Ah! there they are. Hurrah! there are the Papa Ubus. Forward, come on, we need you, gentlemen of the Finance.

[*Enter the Knighties, who throw themselves into the fray.*]

COTISE Out with the Poles!

TAILS Ooh! we are together again, Ghentlemen of the Finance. Forward, thrust vigorously, gain the door; once outside all we'll have to do is run away.

PAPA UBU Oh! there, that's my strongest. O how he can hit.

BUGGERLAS God! I am wounded.

STANISLAS LECZINSKY It is nothing, Sire.

JOHANNES SOBIESKY Hit, keep hitting, they are gaining the door, the beggars.

COTISE We're drawing near, follow the people. In consequence of whyche, I can see ye sky.

HEADS Courage, Sire Ubu.

PAPA UBU Ah! I'm doing number one in my pants. Forward, oddsbellikins! kiddiddle 'em, blideedle 'em, skin 'em, massmur-murder 'em, by Ubu's horn! Ah! there are less of 'em now!

COTISE There are only two left guarding the door.

PAPA UBU [*knocking them down with blows of the bear*] One down, two to go! Whew! I'm out! Let's get out of here! The rest of you, follow me, and fast!

5.3

[SCENE: *The stage represents the Province of Livonia covered with snow.*]

[*The* UBUS *and their suite in flight.*]

PAPA UBU Ah! I think they've given up trying to catch us.

MAMA UBU Yes, Buggerlas has gone to be crowned.

PAPA UBU He can keep it; I don't envy him his crown.

MAMA UBU You are absolutely right, Papa Ubu.

[*They disappear in the distance.*]

5.4

[SCENE: *The deck of a ship sailing close to the wind on the Baltic.*]

[*On the deck* PAPA UBU *and his whole band.*]

THE CAPTAIN Ah! what a fine breeze.

PAPA UBU It is a fact that we are sailing with a speed that borders on the prodigious. We must be going a million knots an hour, and the good thing about those knots is that once they're done, they don't come undone. It is true we have the wind behind us.

TAILS What a sorry imbecile.

[*A squall blows up, the ship tilts sharply and whitens the sea.*]

PAPA UBU Oh! ah! God! we've capsized! Why, your boat's all crooked, it's going to fall.

THE CAPTAIN All hands to the leeward, haul in the foresail!

PAPA UBU Oh! no, for heaven's sake! Don't all stand on the same side! That's really reckless. And just suppose the wind should change sides: everybody would go straight to the bottom and fish will eat us.

THE CAPTAIN Don't bear down, furl sails, close and hard!

PAPA UBU No, no, bear down, unfurl those sails, I'm in a hurry! We'll never get there, you brute of a Captain, and it's all your fault! We should be there already. OK, if that's the way it is, I'll take the command! Get ready to veer about! Farewell. Drop anchor, veer wind ahead, veer wind behind. Raise sails, furl sails, tiller up, tiller down, tiller sideways. See, we're going along just fine. Go broadside to the wave and then it'll be perfect.

[*Everyone twists and turns, the breeze freshens.*]

THE CAPTAIN Take in the main jib, reef in the sails!

PAPA UBU That's not bad, in fact it's good! Listen up, Mr. Crew! "Take a plain rib, beef with ales!"

[*A few collapse with laughter. A wave comes in.*]

PAPA UBU Oh! what a flood! This is an effect of the maneuvers he ordered.

MAMA UBU and TAILS Navigation is a delightful thing.

[*Second wave pours in.*]

TAILS [*drenched*] Beware of Satan and all his works.

PAPA UBU Sire waiter, bring us something to drink.

[*They all sit down to drink.*]

MAMA UBU Ah! what a pleasure to see fair France again soon, our old friends, and our castle of Mondragon!

PAPA UBU Hey! we'll be there soon. In a minute we'll be coming in under the castle of Elsinore.[4]

TAILS My spirits revive at the thought of seeing my beloved Spain again.

COTISE Yes, and we'll dazzle our friends with tales of our wonderful adventures.

4. On the east coast of Denmark (Hilsingør), the setting of Shakespeare's *Hamlet* (1600–01).

PAPA UBU Oh, you bet! And I'll get myself appointed Master of Finances in Paris.

MAMA UBU That's right! . . . Ah! what a jolt!

COTISE It's nothing, we've just passed the Point of Elsinore.

TAILS And now our noble ship skims rapidly over the darkening waves of the North Sea.

PAPA UBU A wild and inhospitable sea that washes the shores of a land called Germania, so named because the comments of its inhabitants are all germane.

MAMA UBU Now there's scholarship for you. They say that country is quite beautiful.

PAPA UBU Ah, gentlemen! Beautiful as it may be, it cannot compare to Poland. If there were no Poland, there would be no Poles!

End.[5]

5. The original edition ends here. Jarry added a "Disembraining Song" when he put on an earlier version of the play [translator's note].

ANTON CHEKHOV

1860–1904

ANTON Chekhov, who died four years after the dawn of the new century, casts a long shadow over the history of modern theater. The greatest dramatist the Russian stage has ever seen, he stands as a central figure in the emergence of twentieth-century drama. At first glance, Chekhov may seem an unlikely candidate for this historical role. Inheriting a tradition of Russian fiction that included such literary monuments as Fyodor Dostoevsky's novel *Crime and Punishment* (1866) and Leo Tolstoy's *War and Peace* (1865–89), Chekhov achieved his initial literary reputation through the writing of novellas and short stories rather than drama. Of the dozen and a half plays that he wrote, the majority are comic one acts, and those on which his reputation chiefly rests—*The Seagull*, *Uncle Vanya*, *The Three Sisters*, and *THE CHERRY ORCHARD*—are only four in number and were written relatively late in his career. In Chekhov's case, though, numbers are misleading, for the dramatic terrain that these plays opened up proved so innovative that their influence can be felt more than a century after his death. Rewriting the aesthetic of theatrical realism through a drama of understatement, indirection, and psychological nuance, Chekhov's major plays offer a new vision of the relationship between theater and everyday life.

Chekhov was born on January 17, 1860, in Taganrog, a small seaport on the Sea of Azov (a northern arm of the Black Sea) in southern Russia. His father was a merchant and his paternal grandfather a serf who had purchased his freedom and that of his family in 1841. Only one generation removed from serfdom, Chekhov remained acutely aware of his background: in an autobiographical letter to his friend and publisher Alexei Suvorin in 1889, he described an imaginary character who, after squeezing the slave blood out of himself "drop by drop," awakes one day to find that "the blood coursing through his veins is no longer that of a slave but that of a real human being." After attending local schools, he graduated in 1879 with a scholarship for university study. Chekhov's father had moved the rest of his family to Moscow three years earlier in order to escape debtor's prison, and when Anton joined them he enrolled at the Moscow University School of Medicine, from which he earned a degree at the age of twenty-four. Although Chekhov soon gave up private practice to focus on writing, his medical training remained an essential part of his personal and professional identity. "Medicine is my lawful wife and literature is my mistress," he later commented. "When I get tired of one I go to the other." He continued to treat patients, often for free, and he demonstrated a lifelong interest in matters of public health. During the famine and cholera epidemic of 1892–93, he served as head of a district sanitary committee and treated many of the epidemic's poorest victims.

Chekhov began writing in his teens. He edited a school newspaper and, encouraged by his older brothers, wrote humorous anecdotes and sketches. By the time he graduated from medical school, he was publishing comic sketches, parodies, dialogues, and short stories in small-press periodicals. As the popularity of his fiction grew, Chekhov's stories began appearing in more established periodicals and newspapers, and in 1884 he published his first collection of short stories, *Fairy Tales of Melpomene*. Dmitri Grigorovich, a leading short-story writer and a prominent figure in Russia's literary establishment, praised Chekhov as the most talented writer of his generation; the young writer's accomplishment was given official recognition when his second collection of stories, *In the Twilight*, was awarded the Pushkin Prize by the Imperial Academy of Science in 1888. Although Chekhov attempted unsuccessfully to write a novel, he was attracted—and his artistic temperament was suited—to more condensed fictional forms. Focusing on the particularities of character, social class, and setting while maintaining the authorial objectivity for which he became renowned, he developed the short story into a vehicle of unprecedented psychological complexity and acute social observation. His finest stories—such as "Ward No. 6" (1892), "My Life" (1896), and "Peasants" (1897)—are considered masterpieces of the genre.

Chekhov's interest in the theater also developed at an early age. As a schoolboy, he participated in amateur theatrical skits with his siblings (he had four brothers and one sister), and he and his friends saw professional plays at the Taganrog theater. In his late teens he composed two plays that have not survived, a one-act farce and a full-length drama titled "Fatherlessness," and during his first two years of medical school he produced a cumbersome four-act drama that may have been a reworked version of the latter play. Though he subsequently destroyed this play, a copy was discovered after his death and has been published under the title *Platonov*. Chekhov's first theatrical production did not occur until 1887, when *Ivanov*, a play about a bored and disillusioned landowner, premiered in Moscow to critical and popular acclaim. It was followed in 1889 by *The Wood Demon*, a full-length comedy, and by a series of one-act comedies that Chekhov wrote between 1887 and 1901. Conceived in the tradition of vaudeville farce, these "airy trifles" (as Chekhov called them) were little more than curtain-raisers, though *The Bear* (1888) proved popular throughout Russia and *The Proposal* (1889) entertained a St. Petersburg audience that included Czar Alexander III.

A gap of five years separates this early drama from the earliest of the four mature plays that figure so prominently in the history of modern drama. In 1895, Chekhov wrote *The Seagull*, a play about art, disappointed love, and the psychology of survival. Set, like his other major plays, on a provincial Russian estate, it explores the shifting relationships in a quartet of central characters: Arkádina, an aging actress; her son Tréplev, an avant-garde writer; Trigórin, an established novelist; and Nína, a young actress whose aspirations, hardships, and disappointments identify her with a seagull that Tréplev has shot. At the play's premiere in St. Petersburg on October 17, 1896, the audience responded so negatively that Chekhov fled the auditorium during the second act and vowed never to write another play. However, when Konstantin Stanislavsky and Vladimir Nemirovich-Danchenko, founders of the newly formed Moscow Art Theatre, revived *The Seagull* two years later, the play proved so popular that the theater company adopted its title bird as their emblem. With Stanislavsky as director, the MAT staged the Moscow premieres of Chekhov's remaining plays: *Uncle Vanya*, a reworked version of *The Wood Demon*, in 1899; *The Three Sisters* in 1901; and *The Cherry Orchard* in 1904. Six months after *The Cherry Orchard* opened, Chekhov died of tuberculosis at the age of forty-four.

The innovations of dramaturgy and stagecraft in these plays are both subtle and wide-ranging. Late nineteenth-century Russian theater was dominated by farce and melodrama, genres that relied on stock characters and heightened dramatic incident. Reacting against these theatrical conventions, Chekhov insisted that drama imitate the textures, issues, and actions of everyday life and that its characters reflect the complexity of human experience. In a statement of his artistic principles, Chekhov wrote:

> The demand is made that the hero and heroine should be dramatically effective. But in life people do not shoot themselves, or hang themselves, or fall in love, or deliver themselves of clever sayings every minute. They spend most of their time eating, drinking, running after women or men, talking nonsense. It is therefore necessary that this should be shown on the stage. A play ought to be written in which the people should come and go, dine, talk of the weather, or play cards, not because the author wants it but because that is what happens in real life. Life on the stage should be as it really is, and the people, too, should be as they are and not on stilts.

In order to accomplish this objective, Chekhov reduced the importance of traditional dramatic climaxes by minimizing their impact or eliminating them altogether. His characters resist dramatic stereotype, and the stage they occupy generates multiple points of attention rather than central protagonists and antagonists. These characters talk, do ordinary things, and are defined more by the actions they don't take than those they do. In keeping with Chekhov's belief that a dramatist's job is not to judge the characters created but to present them in the light of dispassionate observation, his plays give little evidence of their author's point of view. The result is a drama of understatement, indirection, and nuance, where action and emotion lie beneath the words. Chekhov famously observed: "People are having a meal, just having a meal, but at the same time their happiness is being created, or their lives are being destroyed."

The Cherry Orchard is one of the finest examples of Chekhov's "drama of the undramatic" (in the critic Richard Gilman's phrase). Its plot hinges on the fate of the Ranyévskaya estate, famed for its beautiful cherry orchard but no longer able to support its occupants or their privileged lifestyle. Its threatened sale is the stuff of French "mortgage melodramas," which often hinged on the possible or actual loss of property at the hands of a villainous manipulator; but the climactic event of Chekhov's play—the auction at which the estate is sold—occurs offstage, and its outcome is recounted after the fact. In a similar undermining of expectations, the participants in this crisis do not fit the moral categories of conventional melodrama. Liubóv (Madame Ranyévskaya) and her brother Gáyev, who cling to their childhood memories of the orchard, lose the estate through a mixture of paralysis and fecklessness, not victimization; indeed, their inaction in the face of the imminent loss of their property is the play's most sustained narrative thread. For his part, Lopákhin—the former serf who eventually buys the estate—is a far cry from the stock villain of melodrama. He urges Liubóv and Gáyev to sell the orchard as a way of saving the estate, and in the giddiness of having bought the property he speaks movingly (if somewhat thoughtlessly) about his social transformation. In terms of dramatic technique, the moment in act 3 when he delivers this speech is a rare example in Chekhov's play of a character's dominating the stage and claiming attention. The rest of the time characters engage in conversation with each other, sometimes listening, sometimes not. In keeping with its muted sphere of action, *The Cherry Orchard* opens with the arrival of characters and ends with their departure.

Chekhov wrote *The Cherry Orchard* while living as a semi-invalid in Yalta, and its composition was long and difficult. Yet the play is the most comic of his mature dramas. In September 1903 he wrote to his wife, Olga Knipper, who would play the role of Madame Ranyévskaya, "My play . . . hasn't turned out as a drama, but as a comedy, at times almost a farce." Subtitling his play "A Comedy in Four Acts," Chekhov insisted on this view of the play throughout its rehearsals and found himself in frequent disagreement with his director, Stanislavsky, who considered the play a tragedy and accentuated the atmosphere

The Moscow Art Theater's original 1904 production of *The Cherry Orchard*, directed by Constantin Stanislavsky. Stanislavsky, who performed the role of Gayev in this production, is on the far left, gesturing toward the bookcase.

of pathos and loss. In Chekhov's hands, comedy is central to the play's mixture of tones. In addition to the obvious moments of slapstick—Liubóv's adopted daughter Várya swings a stick at the accountant Yepikhódov in anger but hits Lopákhin instead, while "the eternal student" Trofímov falls noisily down the stairs after an argument with Liubóv—Chekhov employs comedy as a vehicle of irony and distance. His use of comedy is particularly evident in those moments when the physical world intrudes on private emotion and in those tics and mannerisms that signal a character's self-absorption. When the governess Carlotta laments that she doesn't own a birth certificate at the start of the play's second act—"Where I'm from . . . who I am . . . no idea"—the painful undertones of her meditation are deflected when she reaches into her pocket and absent-mindedly takes a bite out of a cucumber pickle. And when Gáyev plays his imaginary billiards game or delivers an oration to the family bookcase, these humorous moments measure the extent to which he, like all the play's characters, inhabits a world of his own.

The problem in Stanislavsky's "tearful" direction of *The Cherry Orchard,* in other words, was that he sought to reveal the play's emotions through overt gesture rather than through the ironic counterpoint of surface activity and emotional undercurrents. In Chekhovian drama the weight of emotion lies in what is not said, as when the forced gaiety of the ball in act 3 is undercut by the audience's awareness that the auction is taking place offstage. And few scenes in all of Chekhov's plays hold the emotional power of Várya's exchange with Lopákhin near the play's end, when the two exchange small talk while failing to address the life-deciding issue that hangs over them.

As elsewhere in Chekhov's writing, individual psychology in *The Cherry Orchard* is deeply embedded within the social, economic, and political landscape of turn-of-the-century Russia. In the sale of the Ranyévskaya estate, Chekhov dramatizes the historical eclipse of the landowning class that had formed the historical pillar of feudal Russia. Semyónov-Píshchik, a neighboring landowner, must borrow money from Liubóv to meet his financial needs, and he pays her back only after selling the rights to extract the white clay that has been discovered on his property. In Lopákhin's plan to cut down the cherry orchard and build vacation homes we feel the emerging class of others, like him, who have grown prosperous through acquired wealth. Social mobility defines *The Cherry Orchard,* and as the contrasting destinies of Chekhov's central characters demonstrate, this mobility extends in both directions. Beyond the circle of property and money, of course, is the vast number of Russia's poor and uneducated. Firs, the family's aging house servant, recalls the emancipation of the serfs in 1861, and Chekhov's play provides ample evidence of

Chekhov's home in Melikhovo, Russia, where he and his family lived from 1892 to 1899.

the poverty and social dislocation that this class has had to endure. Indigent peasants have been staying in the old servants' quarters, and a homeless man intrudes upon the pastoral quiet of act 2. The student Trofímov addresses this poverty and its history in a speech to Liubóv's daughter Ánya: "Your grandfather, and his father, and his father's fathers, they *owned* the people who slaved away for them all over this estate, and now the voices and faces of human beings hide behind every cherry in the orchard, every leaf, every tree trunk." Envisioning a future of happiness and social justice, he calls on Ánya to devote her life to working in the cause of human progress. "This whole country is our orchard," he proclaims, widening the scope of the play's issues to include czarist Russia as a whole.

In view of subsequent Russian history—in 1917 the Communist-led Russian Revolution overthrew Czar Nicholas II and proclaimed an era of social equality—Trofímov's speeches in act 2 have sometimes been taken as Chekhov's own call for transformative social change. Not surprisingly, Soviet productions of *The Cherry Orchard* made Trofímov the herald of a new revolutionary order. To be sure, Chekhov's Trofímov articulates the revolutionary sentiment that had gained increasing force in Russia by the turn of the century. Universities were major sites of antigovernment agitation, and (as Chekhov indicated in a letter to his wife) Trofímov's extended career as a graduate student reflects the fact that he has been expelled more than once for political reasons. At the same time, though Trofímov's rhetoric is stirring, his vision of a future that will redeem the present resembles the beautiful dreams that other Chekhov characters use to escape the drabness and disappointment of their lives. Trofímov does little to translate language into action, and this character who likes the sound of his own voice cuts a somewhat ridiculous figure at times. The optimism of his predictions exist in ironic counterpoint with the present, just as the historical evolution represented by change in *The Cherry Orchard* coexists with the painfulness of individual loss. To push the tone of *The Cherry Orchard* in one direction at the expense of another—to stress its resignation or its desire for something better, its comedy or its tears—is to deny the multiple perspectives that Chekhov so masterfully calls into play.

S.G.

The Cherry Orchard
A Comedy in Four Acts[1]

CHARACTERS

LIUBÓV RANYÉVSKAYA [Lyúba, Liúba Andréyevna], who owns the estate
ÁNYA, her daughter, seventeen years old
VÁRYA, her adopted daughter, twenty-four years old
LEONÍD GÁYEV [Lonya, Lyónya Andréyich], Liubóv's brother
YERMOLÁI LOPÁKHIN [Yermolái Alexéyich], a businessman
PÉTYA TROFÍMOV, a graduate student
BORÍS SEMYÓNOV-PÍSHCHIK, who owns land in the neighborhood
CARLOTTA, the governess
SEMYÓN YEPIKHÓDOV, an accountant
DUNYÁSHA [Avdótya Fyódorovna, Dunyáhsa Kozoyédov], the maid
FIRS, the butler, eighty-seven years old
YÁSHA, the valet
A HOMELESS MAN
The STATIONMASTER
The POSTMASTER
Guests, servants

The action takes place on Ranyévskaya's estate.

Act 1

[*A room they still call the nursery. A side door leads to* ÁNYA'S *room. Almost dawn; the sun is about to rise. It's May; the cherry orchard is already in bloom, but there's a chill in the air. The windows are shut. Enter* DUNYÁSHA *with a lamp, and* LOPÁKHIN *with a book in his hand.*]

LOPÁKHIN The train's finally in, thank God. What time is it?

DUNYÁSHA Almost two. [*She blows out the lamp.*] It's getting light.

LOPÁKHIN How late is the train this time? Must be at least two hours. [*He yawns and stretches.*] That was dumb. I came over on purpose just to meet them at the station, and then I fell asleep. Sat right here and fell asleep. Too bad. You should have woke me up.

DUNYÁSHA I thought you already left. [*She listens.*] Listen, that must be them.

LOPÁKHIN [*he listens*] No, they still have the luggage to get, and all that. [*Pause*] She's been away five years now; no telling how she's changed. She was always a good person. Very gentle, never caused a fuss. I remember one time when I was a kid, fifteen or so, they had my old man working in the store down by the village, and he hit me, hard, right in the face; my nose started to bleed. And we had to come up here to make a delivery or something; he was still drunk. And Liubóv Andréyevna—she wasn't much older than I was, kind of thin—she brought me inside the house, right into the nursery here, and washed the blood off my face for me. "Don't cry," she told me. "Don't cry, poor boy; you'll live long enough to get married." [*Pause*] Poor boy . . . Well, my father was poor, but take a look at me now,

1. Translated by Paul Schmidt.

all dressed up, brand-new suit and tan shoes. Silk purse out of a sow's ear, I guess . . . I'm rich now, got lots of money, but when you think about it, I guess I'm still a poor boy from the country. [*He flips the pages of the book.*] I tried reading this book, couldn't figure out a word it said. Put me to sleep.

[*Pause.*]

DUNYÁSHA The dogs were barking all night long; they know their mistress is coming home.

LOPÁKHIN Don't be silly.

DUNYÁSHA I'm so excited I'm shaking. I may faint.

LOPÁKHIN You're getting too full of yourself, Dunyásha. Look at you, all dressed up like that, and that hairdo. You watch out for that. You got to remember who you are.

[*Enter* YEPIKHÓDOV *with a bunch of flowers; he wears a jacket and tie and brightly polished boots, which squeak loudly. As he comes in, he drops the flowers.*]

YEPIKHÓDOV [*picking up the flowers*] Here. The gardener sent these over; he said put them on the dining room table. [*He gives the flowers to* DUNYÁSHA.]

LOPÁKHIN And bring me a beer.

DUNYÁSHA Right away.

[*She goes out.*]

YEPIKHÓDOV It's freezing this morning—it must be in the thirties—and the cherry blossoms are out already. I cannot abide the climate here. [*He sighs.*] I never have abided it, ever. [*Beat*][2] Yermolái Alexéyich, would you examinate something for me, please? Day before yesterday I bought myself a new pair of boots, and listen to them squeak, will you? I just cannot endear it. Do you know anything I can put on them?

LOPÁKHIN Will you shut up? You drive me crazy.

YEPIKHÓDOV Every day something awful happens to me. It's like a habit. But I don't complain. I just try to keep smiling.

[*Enter* DUNYÁSHA; *she brings* LOPÁKHIN *a beer.*]

YEPIKHÓDOV I'm going. [*He bumps into a chair, which falls over.*] You see? [*He seems proud of it.*] You see what I was referring about? Excuse my expressivity, but what a concurrence. It's almost uncanny, isn't it?

[*He leaves.*]

DUNYÁSHA You know what? That Yepikhódov proposed to me!

LOPÁKHIN Oh?

DUNYÁSHA I just don't know what to think. He's kind of nice. . . . He's a real quiet boy, but then he opens his mouth, and you can't ever understand what he's talking about. I mean, it sounds nice, but it just doesn't make any sense. I do like him, though. Kind of. And he's crazy about me. It's funny, you know, every day something awful happens to him. People around here call him Double Trouble.

LOPÁKHIN [*he listens*] That must be them.

DUNYÁSHA It's them! Oh, I don't know what's the matter with me! I feel so funny; I'm cold all over.

LOPÁKHIN It really is them this time. Let's go; we should be there at the door. You think she'll recognize me? It's been five years.

2. Pause.

DUNYÁSHA [*excited*] Oh, my God! I'm going to faint! I think I'm going to faint!

[*The sound of two carriages outside the house.* LOPÁKHIN *and* DUNYÁSHA *hurry out. The stage is empty. The sound outside gets louder.* FIRS, *leaning heavily on his cane, crosses the room, heading for the door; he wears an old-fashioned butler's livery and a top hat; he says something to himself, but you can't make out the words. The offstage noise and bustle increases. A voice: "Here we are . . . this way." Enter* LIUBÓV ANDRÉYEVNA, ÁNYA, *and* CARLOTTA, *dressed in traveling clothes.* VÁRYA *wears an overcoat, and a kerchief on her head.* GÁYEV, SEMYÓNOV-PÍSHCHIK, LOPÁKHIN, DUNYÁSHA *with a bundle and an umbrella, Servants with the luggage—all pass across the stage.*]

ÁNYA Here we are. Oh, Mama, do you remember this room?

LIUBÓV ANDRÉYEVNA The nursery!

VÁRYA It's freezing; my hands are like ice. We kept your room exactly as you left it, Mama. The white and lavender one.

LIUBÓV ANDRÉYEVNA The nursery! Oh, this house, this beautiful house! I slept in this room when I was a child. . . . [*She weeps.*] And I feel like a child again! [*She hugs* GÁYEV, VÁRYA, *then* GÁYEV *again.*] And Várya hasn't changed at all—still looks like a nun! And Dunyásha dear! Of course I remember you! [*She hugs* DUNYÁSHA.]

GÁYEV The train was two hours late. What kind of efficiency is that? Eh?

CARLOTTA And my dog loves nuts.

SEMYÓNOV-PÍSHCHIK Really! I don't believe it!

[*Everyone leaves, except* ÁNYA *and* DUNYÁSHA.]

DUNYÁSHA We've been up all night, waiting. . . . [*She takes* ÁNYA'*s coat and hat.*]

ÁNYA I've been up for four nights now. . . . I didn't sleep the whole trip. And now I'm freezing.

DUNYÁSHA When you went away it was still winter, it was snowing, and now look! Oh, sweetie, you're back! [*She laughs and hugs Ánya.*] I've been up all night, waiting to see you. Sweetheart, I just can't wait—I've got to tell you what happened. I can't wait another minute!

ÁNYA [*wearily*] Now what?

DUNYÁSHA Yepikhódov proposed the day after Easter! He wants to marry me!

ÁNYA That's all you ever think about. . . . [*She fixes her hair.*] I lost all my hairpins. . . .

DUNYÁSHA I just don't know what to do about him. He really, really loves me!

ÁNYA [*looking through the door to her room*] My own room, just as if I'd never left. I'm back home! Tomorrow I'll get up and go for a walk in the orchard. I just wish I could get some sleep. I didn't sleep the whole trip, I was so worried.

DUNYÁSHA Pétya's here. He got here day before yesterday.

ÁNYA [*joyfully*] Pétya!

DUNYÁSHA He's staying out in the barn. Said he didn't want to bother anybody. [*She looks at her watch.*] He told me to get him up, but Várya said not to. You let him sleep, she said.

[*Enter* VÁRYA. *She has a big bunch of keys attached to her belt.*]

VÁRYA Dunyásha, go get the coffee. Mama wants her coffee.

DUNYÁSHA Oh, I forgot!

[*She goes out.*]

VÁRYA You're back. Thank God! You're home again! [*She embraces Ánya.*] My angel is home again! My beautiful darling!

ÁNYA You won't believe what I've been through!

VÁRYA I can imagine.

ÁNYA I left just before Easter; it was cold. Carlotta never shut up the whole trip; she kept doing those silly tricks of hers. I don't know why you had to stick me with her.

VÁRYA Darling, you couldn't go all that way by yourself! You're only seventeen!

ÁNYA We got to Paris, it was cold and snowy, and my French is just awful! Mama was living in this fifth-floor apartment, we had to walk up, we get there and there's all these French people, some old priest reading some book, and it was crowded, and everybody was smoking these awful cigarettes—and I felt so sorry for Mama, I just threw my arms around her and couldn't let go. And she was so glad to see me, she cried—

VÁRYA [*almost crying*] I know, I know . . .

ÁNYA And she sold the villa in Mentón,[3] and the money was already gone, all of it! And I spent everything you gave me for the trip; I haven't got a thing left. And Mama still doesn't understand! We have dinner at the train station, and she orders the most expensive things on the menu, and then she tips the waiters a ruble[4] each! And Carlotta does the same! And Yásha expects the same treatment—he's just awful. You know, Yásha, that flunky of Mama's—he came back with us.

VÁRYA I saw him, the lazy good-for-nothing.

ÁNYA So what happened? Did you get the interest paid?

VÁRYA With what?

ÁNYA Oh, my God, my God . . .

VÁRYA The place goes up for sale in August.

ÁNYA Oh, my God.

[LOPÁKHIN *sticks his head in the doorway and makes a mooing sound, then goes away.*]

VÁRYA Oh, that man! I'd like to—[*She shakes her fist.*]

ÁNYA [*she hugs her*] Várya, did he propose yet? [VÁRYA *shakes her head no.*] But you know he loves you! Why don't the two of you just sit down and be honest with each other? What are you waiting for?

VÁRYA I don't think anything will ever come of it. He's always so busy, he never has time for me. He just isn't interested! It's hard for me when I see him, but I don't care anymore. Everybody talks about us getting married, people even congratulate me, but there's nothing. . . . I mean, it's all just a dream. [*A change of tone*] Oh, you've got a new pin, a little bee. . . .

ÁNYA [*with a sigh*] I know. Mama bought it for me. [*She goes into her room and starts to giggle, like a little girl.*] You know what? In Paris I went for a ride in a balloon!

VÁRYA Oh, darling, you're back! My angel is home again!

3. A resort town on the French Mediterranean coast.

4. Roughly equivalent to $20 today.

[DUNYÁSHA *comes in, carrying a tray with coffee things, and begins setting them out on the table.* VÁRYA *stands at the doorway and talks to* ÁNYA *in the other room.*]

You know, dear, I spend the livelong day trying to keep this house going, and all I do is dream. I want to see you married off to somebody rich, then I can rest easy. And I think then I'll go away by myself, maybe live in a convent, or just go traveling: Kiev, Moscow . . . spend all my time making visits to churches. I'd start walking and just go and go and go. That would be heaven!

ÁNYA Listen to the birds in the orchard! What time is it?

VÁRYA It must be almost three. You should get some sleep, darling. [*She goes into* ÁNYA*'s room.*] Yes, that would be heaven!

[*Enter* YÁSHA *with a suitcase and a lap robe. He walks with an affected manner.*]

YÁSHA I beg pardon! May I intrude?

DUNYÁSHA I didn't even recognize you, Yásha. You got so different there in France.

YÁSHA *I'm* sorry—who are you exactly?

DUNYÁSHA When you left, I wasn't any higher than this. [*She holds her hand a distance from the floor.*] I'm Dunyásha. You know, Dunyásha Kozoyédov. Don't you remember me?

YÁSHA Well! You sure turned out cute, didn't you? [*He looks around carefully, then grabs and kisses her; she screams and drops a saucer;* YÁSHA *leaves in a hurry.*]

VÁRYA [*at the door, annoyed*] Now what happened?

DUNYÁSHA [*almost in tears*] I broke a saucer.

VÁRYA [*ironically*] Well, isn't that lucky!

ÁNYA [*entering*] Somebody should let Mama know Pétya's here.

VÁRYA I told them to let him sleep.

ÁNYA [*lost in thought*] Father died six years ago, and a month later our little brother, Grísha, drowned. Sweet boy, he was only seven. And Mama couldn't face it, that's why she went away, just went away and never looked back. [*Shivers.*] And I understand exactly how she felt. I wish she knew that.

[*Pause.*]

And Pétya Trofímov was Grísha's tutor. He might remind her . . .

[*Enter* FIRS *in his old-fashioned butler's livery. He crosses to the table and begins looking over the coffee things.*]

FIRS The missus will have her breakfast here. [*He puts on a pair of white gloves.*] Is the coffee ready? [*To* DUNYÁSHA, *crossly*] Where's the cream? Go get the cream!

DUNYÁSHA Oh, my God, I'm sorry. . . .

[*Hurries off.*]

FIRS [*he starts fussing with the coffee things*] Young flibbertigibbet . . . [*He mumbles to himself.*] They're all back from Paris. . . . In the old days they went to Paris too . . . had to go the whole way in a horse and buggy. [*He laughs.*]

VÁRYA Firs, what are you talking about?

FIRS Beg pardon? [*Joyfully*] The missus is home! Going to see her at last! Now I can die happy. . . . [*He starts to cry with joy.*]

[*Enter* LIUBÓV, GÁYEV, LOPÁKHIN, *and* SEMYÓNOV-PÍSHCHIK, *who wears a crumpled linen suit. As* GÁYEV *enters, he gestures as if he were making a billiard shot.*]

LIUBÓV ANDRÉYEVNA How did it go? I'm trying to remember. . . . Yellow ball in the side pocket! Bank shot off the corner!

GÁYEV And right down the middle! Oh, sister, sister, just think . . . when you and I were little we used to sleep in this room, and now I'm almost fifty-one! Strange, isn't it?

LOPÁKHIN Time sure passes. . . .

GÁYEV [*beat*] Say again?

LOPÁKHIN I said, time sure passes.

GÁYEV [*looking at* LOPÁKHIN] Who's wearing that cheap cologne?

ÁNYA I'm going to bed. Good night, Mama. [*She kisses her mother.*]

LIUBÓV ANDRÉYEVNA Oh, my darling little girl, my baby! Are you glad you're home? I still can't quite believe I'm here.

ÁNYA Good night, Uncle.

GÁYEV [*he kisses her*] God bless you, dear. You're getting to look so much like your mother! Liúba, she looks just like you when you were her age. She really does.

[ÁNYA *says good night to* LOPÁKHIN *and* PÍSHCHIK, *goes into her room, and closes the door behind her.*]

LIUBÓV ANDRÉYEVNA She's tired to death.

PÍSHCHIK Well, that's such a long trip!

VÁRYA Gentlemen, please. It's almost three; time you were going.

LIUBÓV ANDRÉYEVNA [*laughs*] You're the same as ever, Várya. [*Hugs and kisses her.*] Just let me have my coffee, then we'll all be going.

[FIRS *puts a pillow beneath her feet.*]

Thank you, dear. I've really gotten addicted to coffee; I drink it day and night. You old darling, you! Thank you.

VÁRYA I'll just go make sure they've got everything unloaded.

[*Goes out.*]

LIUBÓV ANDRÉYEVNA I can't believe I'm really here! [*Laughs.*] I feel like jumping up and waving my arms in the air! [*Covers her face with her hands.*] It's still like a dream. I love this country, really I do, I adore it. I started to cry every time I looked out the train windows. [*Almost in tears*] But I do need my coffee! Thank you, Firs, thank you, darling. I'm so glad you're still alive.

FIRS Day before yesterday.

GÁYEV He doesn't hear too well anymore.

LOPÁKHIN Time for me to go. I have to leave for Hárkov[5] at five. I'm really disappointed; I was looking forward to seeing you, have a chance to talk. . . . You look wonderful, just the way you always did.

PÍSHCHIK [*breathes hard*] Better than she always did. That Paris outfit. . . . She makes me feel young again!

LOPÁKHIN Your brother here thinks I'm crude, calls me a money grubber. That doesn't bother me; he can call me whatever he wants. I just hope you'll trust me the way you used to, look at me the way you used to. . . . My

5. That is, Kharkov, the second-largest city in Ukraine (then part of the Russian Empire).

God, my father slaved for your father and grandfather, my whole family worked for yours; but you, you treated me different. You did so much for me I forgot about all that. Fact is, I . . . I love you like you were family . . . more, even.

LIUBÓV ANDRÉYEVNA I can't sit still; I'm just not in the mood! [*Gets up excitedly, moves about the room.*] I'm so happy I could die! I know I sound stupid—go ahead, laugh. . . . Dear old bookcase. . . . [*Kisses the bookcase.*] My little desk . . .

GÁYEV Did I tell you Nanny died while you were away?

LIUBÓV ANDRÉYEVNA [*sits back down and drinks her coffee*] Yes, you wrote me. God rest her.

GÁYEV Stásy died too. And Petrúsha Kosói quit and moved into town; he works at the police station. [*Takes out a little box of hard candies and puts one in his mouth.*]

PÍSHCHIK Dáshenka—you remember Dáshenka? My daughter? Anyway, she sends her regards. . . .

LOPÁKHIN Well, I'd like to give you some very good news. [*Looks at his watch.*] Afraid there's no time to talk now, though; I've got to go. Well, just to make it short, you know you haven't kept up the mortgage payments on your place here. So now they foreclosed and your estate is up for sale. At auction. They set a date already, August twenty-second, but don't you worry, you can rest easy. We can take care of this—I've got a great idea. Now listen, here's how it works: your place here is fifteen miles from town, and it's only a short drive from the train station. All you've got to do is clear out the old cherry orchard, plus that land down by the river, and subdivide! You lease the plots, build vacation homes, and I swear that'll bring you in twenty-five thousand[6] a year, maybe more.

GÁYEV What an outrageous thing to say!

LIUBÓV ANDRÉYEVNA Excuse me . . . Excuse me, I don't think I quite understand. . . .

LOPÁKHIN You'll get at least twenty-five hundred an acre! And if you start advertising right away, I swear to God come this fall you won't have a single plot left. You see what I'm saying? Your troubles are over! Congratulations! The location is terrific; the river's a real selling point. Only thing is, you've got to start clearing right away. Get rid of all the old buildings. This house, for instance, will have to go. You can't get people to live in a barn like this anymore. And you'll have to cut down that old cherry orchard.

LIUBÓV ANDRÉYEVNA Cut down the cherry orchard? My dear man, you don't understand! Our cherry orchard is a landmark! It's famous for miles around!

LOPÁKHIN The only thing famous about it is how big it is. You only get cherries every two years, and even then you can't get rid of them. Nobody buys them. It's just not a commercial crop.

GÁYEV Our cherry orchard is mentioned in the encyclopedia![7]

LOPÁKHIN [*looks at his watch*] We have to think of something to do and then do it. Otherwise the cherry orchard will be sold at auction on August twenty-second, this house and all the land with it. Make up your minds!

6. Roughly equivalent to $500,000 today (all references to money are in rubles).

7. Probably a reference to the *Great Russian Encyclopedic Dictionary* (1890–1906), an authoritative 86-volume reference work published by F. A. Brockhaus and I. A. Efron.

Believe me, I've thought this through; there isn't any other way to do it. There just isn't.

FIRS Back in the old days, forty, fifty years ago, they used to make dried cherries, pickled cherries, preserved cherries, cherry jam, and sometimes—

GÁYEV Oh, Firs, just shut up.

FIRS —sometimes they sent them off to Moscow by the wagonload. People paid a lot for them! Back then the dried cherries were soft and juicy and sweet, and they smelled just lovely; back then they knew how to fix them. . . .

LIUBÓV ANDRÉYEVNA Does anybody know how to fix them nowadays?

FIRS Nope. They all forgot.

PÍSHCHIK Tell us about Paris. What was it like? Did you eat frogs?

LIUBÓV ANDRÉYEVNA I ate crocodiles.

PÍSHCHIK Crocodiles? Really! I don't believe it!

LOPÁKHIN You see, it used to be out here in the country there were only landlords and poor farmers, but now all of a sudden there are summer people moving in; they want vacation homes. Every town you can name is surrounded by them—it's the coming thing. In twenty years they'll expand and multiply! Right now maybe they're only places to relax on the weekend, but I bet you eventually people will put down roots out here, they'll create neighborhoods, and then your cherry orchard will blossom and bear fruit once again—and even bring in a profit!

GÁYEV [*indignantly*] That's outrageous!

[*Enter* VÁRYA *and* YÁSHA.]

VÁRYA Mama, a couple of telegrams came for you. [*Takes a key and opens the old bookcase; the lock creaks.*] Here they are.

LIUBÓV ANDRÉYEVNA They're from Paris. [*She tears them up without opening then.*] I'm through with Paris.

GÁYEV Liúba, have you any idea how old this bookcase is? Last week I pulled out the bottom drawer, and there was the date on the back, burned right into the wood. A hundred years! This bookcase is exactly a hundred years old! What do you say to that, eh? We should have a birthday celebration. Of course, it's an inanimate object, any way you look at it, but still, it's a . . . well, it's a . . . a bookcase.

PÍSHCHIK A hundred years old! Really! I don't believe it!

GÁYEV Yes, yes, it is. [*He caresses the bookcase.*] Dear old bookcase! Wonderful old bookcase! I rejoice in your existence. For a hundred years now you have borne the shining ideals of goodness and justice, a hundred years have not dimmed your silent summons to useful labor. To generations of our family [*Almost in tears*] you have offered courage, a belief in a better future, you have instructed us in ideals of goodness and social awareness. . . .

[*Pause.*]

LOPÁKHIN Right. Well . . .

LIUBÓV ANDRÉYEVNA Oh, Lonya, you're still the same as ever!

GÁYEV [*somewhat embarrassed*] Yellow ball in the side pocket! Bank shot off the center!

LOPÁKHIN Well, I've got to be off.

YÁSHA [*gives* LIUBÓV *a pillbox*] Isn't it perhaps time for your pills?

PÍSHCHIK No, no, no, dear lady! Never take medicine! Won't do any good! Won't do any harm either, though. Watch! [*Takes the pillbox, dumps the *contents into his hand, puts them in his mouth, and swallows them with a swig of beer.*] There! All gone!

LIUBÓV ANDRÉYEVNA [*alarmed*] Are you out of your mind?

PÍSHCHIK I have just taken all your pills for you.

LOPÁKHIN What a glutton.

[*Everybody laughs.*]

FIRS He was here over the holidays, ate half a crock of pickles. . . . [*Mumbles.*]

LIUBÓV ANDRÉYEVNA What's he mumbling about?

VÁRYA He's been going on like that for the last three years. We're used to it by now.

YÁSHA He's getting senile.

[*Enter* CARLOTTA, *in a white dress with a lorgnette on a chain. She starts to cross the room.*]

LOPÁKHIN Oh, excuse me, Carlotta, I didn't get a chance to say hello yet. [*Tries to kiss her hand.*]

CARLOTTA [*takes her hand away*] I let you kiss my hand, first thing I know, you'll want to kiss my elbow, then my shoulder . . .

LOPÁKHIN This isn't my lucky day.

[*Everybody laughs.*]

Carlotta, show us a trick!

LIUBÓV ANDRÉYEVNA Yes, do, Carlotta—show us a trick!

CARLOTTA Not now. I'm off to bed.

[*Leaves.*]

LOPÁKHIN Well, I'll see you in three weeks. [*Kisses* LIUBÓV*'s hand.*] Goodbye now. I've got to be off. [*To* GÁYEV] Goodbye. [*Hugs* PÍSHCHIK.] So long. [*Shakes hands with* VÁRYA, *then with* FIRS *and* YÁSHA.] I sort of hate to leave. [*To* LIUBÓV] Think over what I said about subdividing the place. You decide to do it, let me know, and I'll take care of everything. I'll get you a loan of fifty thousand. Think it over now, seriously.

VÁRYA [*angry*] Will you please just go?

LOPÁKHIN I'm going, I'm going.

[*Leaves.*]

GÁYEV What a bore. Oh, excuse me, *pardon*,[8] I forgot—that's Várya's boyfriend. He's going to marry our Várya.

VÁRYA Uncle, will you please not talk nonsense?

LIUBÓV ANDRÉYEVNA Oh, but Várya, that's wonderful! He's a fine man!

PÍSHCHIK One of the finest, in fact . . . the very, very finest . . . My Dáshenka always says . . . she says . . . she says a lot of things. [*Snores, but immediately wakes up.*] Dear lady, yes, always respected you, hmm. . . . You think you could lend me, say, two hundred and forty rubles? Mortgage payment, you know, due tomorrow . . .

VÁRYA [*terrified*] We can't; we don't have any!

LIUBÓV ANDRÉYEVNA I'm afraid that's the truth. We haven't any money.

PÍSHCHIK I'll get it somewhere. [*Laughs.*] I never give up hope. There was that time I thought I was finished, it was all over, and all of a sudden—boom!

8. Gáyev's interjection of the French word *pardon* (excuse me) is typical of the upper classes, who in pre-Soviet Russia spoke French as a second language.

The railroad cut across some of my land and paid me for it. You'll see, something will turn up tomorrow or the next day. Dáshenka will win two hundred thousand in the lottery; she just bought a ticket.

LIUBÓV ANDRÉYEVNA Well, the coffee's gone. We might as well go to bed.

FIRS [*takes out a clothes brush and brushes* GÁYEV's *clothes; scolds him*] You've got on the wrong trousers again. What am I supposed to do with you?

VÁRYA [*softly*] Ánya's asleep. [*Quietly opens the window.*] The sun's coming up; it's not as cold as it was. Look, Mama, what wonderful trees! Smell the perfume! Oh, Lord! And the orioles are singing!

GÁYEV [*opens another window*] The whole orchard is white. You remember, Liúba? That long path, stretched out like a ribbon, on and on, the way it used to shine in the moonlight? You remember? You haven't forgotten?

LIUBÓV ANDRÉYEVNA Oh, my childhood! My innocence! I slept in this room, I could look out over the orchard, when I woke up in the morning I was happy, and it all looked exactly the same as this! Nothing has changed! [*Laughs delightedly.*] White, white, all white! My whole orchard is white! Autumn was dark and drizzly, and winter was cold, but now you're young again, flowering with happiness—the angels of heaven have never abandoned you. If only I could shake off this weight I've been carrying so long. If only I could forget my past!

GÁYEV Yes, and now they're selling the orchard to pay our debts. Strange, isn't it?

LIUBÓV ANDRÉYEVNA Look! There . . . in the orchard . . . it's Mother! In her white dress! [*Laughs delightedly.*] It's Mother!

GÁYEV Where?

VÁRYA Oh, Mama, for God's sake . . .

LIUBÓV ANDRÉYEVNA It's all right; I was just imagining things. There to the right, by the path to the summerhouse, that little white tree all bent over . . . it looked just like a woman.

[*Enter* TROFÍMOV. *He is dressed like a student and wears wire-rimmed glasses.*]

What a glorious orchard! All those white blossoms, and the blue sky—

TROFÍMOV Liubóv Andréyevna!

[*She turns to look at him.*]

I don't mean to disturb you; I just wanted to say hello. [*Shakes her hand warmly.*] They told me to wait until later, but I couldn't. . . .

[LIUBÓV *stares at him, bewildered.*]

VÁRYA It's Pétya Trofímov. . . .

TROFÍMOV Pétya Trofímov—I was your little boy Grísha's tutor. . . . Have I really changed all that much?

[LIUBÓV *embraces him and begins to weep softly.*]

GÁYEV [*embarrassed*] Liúba, that'll do, that'll do. . . .

VÁRYA [*weeps*] Oh, Pétya, I told you to wait till tomorrow.

LIUBÓV ANDRÉYEVNA Grísha . . . my little boy. Grísha . . . my son . . .

VÁRYA Oh, Mama, don't; it was God's will.

TROFÍMOV [*gently, almost in tears*] There, there . . .

LIUBÓV ANDRÉYEVNA [*weeps softly*] My little boy drowned, lost forever . . . Why? What for? My dear boy, why? [*Quiets down.*] Ánya's asleep, and here I am carrying on like this. . . . Pétya, what's happened to you? You used to be such a nice-looking boy. What happened? You look dreadful. You've gotten so old!

TROFÍMOV Some lady on the train called me a high-class tramp.

LIUBÓV ANDRÉYEVNA You were only a boy then, just out of high school, you were adorable, and now you've got glasses and you're losing your hair. And haven't you graduated yet? [*Goes to the door.*]

TROFÍMOV I suppose I'm what you'd call a permanent graduate student.

LIUBÓV ANDRÉYEVNA [*kisses* GÁYEV, *then* VÁRYA] Time for bed. You've gotten old too, Leoníd.

PÍSHCHIK [*follows* LIUBÓV] Time for bed, time to go . . . Ooh, my gout! I'd better stay the night. Now, dear, look, look . . . Liubóv Andréyevna, tomorrow morning I need . . . two hundred and forty rubles. . . .

GÁYEV He never gives up, does he?

PÍSHCHIK Two hundred and forty rubles; my mortgage payment due. . . .

LIUBÓV ANDRÉYEVNA Darling, I simply have no money.

PÍSHCHIK But, dear, I'll give it right back. . . . It's such a *trivial* amount. . . .

LIUBÓV ANDRÉYEVNA Oh, all right. Leoníd will get it for you. Leoníd, you give him the money.

GÁYEV I should give him money? That'll be the day.

LIUBÓV ANDRÉYEVNA We have to give it to him; he needs it. He'll give it back.

[*Exit* LIUBÓV, TROFÍMOV, PÍSHCHIK, *and* FIRS. GÁYEV, VÁRYA, *and* YÁSHA *remain.*]

GÁYEV She still thinks money grows on trees. [*To* YÁSHA] My good man, will you leave us, please? Go back to the barn, where you belong.

YÁSHA [*smiles*] Leoníd Andréyich, you're the same as you always were.

GÁYEV What say? [*To* VÁRYA] What did he just say?

VÁRYA [*to* YÁSHA] Your mother came in from the country to see you. She's been sitting in the kitchen for two days now, waiting.

YÁSHA Oh, for God's sake, can't she leave me alone?

VÁRYA You are really disgraceful!

YÁSHA That's all I need right now. Why couldn't she wait till tomorrow?

[*Goes out.*]

VÁRYA Mama hasn't changed; she's the same as she always was. If it were up to her, she'd give away everything.

GÁYEV Yes. . . . [*Pause*] Someone gets sick, you know, and the doctor tries one thing after another, that means there's no cure. I've been thinking and thinking, racking my brains, I come up with one thing, then another, but the truth is, none of them will work. It would be wonderful if somebody left us a lot of money, it would be wonderful if we could marry off Ánya to somebody with a lot of money, it would be wonderful if we could go see Ánya's godmother in Yároslavl,[9] try to borrow the money from her. She's very, very rich.

VÁRYA [*weeps*] If only God would help us!

GÁYEV Oh, stop crying. She's very, very rich, but she doesn't like us. Because in the first place, my sister married a mere lawyer instead of a man with a title. . . .

[ÁNYA *appears in the doorway.*]

9. A city on the Volga River, about 160 miles northeast of Moscow.

She married a lawyer, and then her behavior has not been—how shall I put it?—particularly exemplary. She's a lovely woman, goodhearted, charming, and of course she's my sister and I love her very much, and there are extenuating circumstances and such, but the fact is, she's what you'd have to call a . . . a loose woman. And she doesn't care who knows it; you can feel it in every move she makes.

VÁRYA [*whispers*] Ánya's here.

GÁYEV What say? [*Pause*] Funny, I must have gotten something in my eye: I can't see too well. . . . Did I tell you what happened Thursday, when I was at the county courthouse?

[ÁNYA *comes into the room.*]

VÁRYA Why aren't you asleep?

ÁNYA I tried. I couldn't sleep.

GÁYEV Kitten . . . [*Kisses* ÁNYA'*s cheek, then her hands.*] My dear child . . . [*Almost in tears*] You're more than just my niece, you're my angel, you know that? You're my whole world, believe me, believe me. . . .

ÁNYA I believe you, Uncle. And I love you; we all love you. . . . But, Uncle dear, you should learn not to talk so much. The things you were saying just now about Mama, about your own sister . . . What were you saying all that for?

GÁYEV I know, I know. . . . [*Covers his face with her hand.*] It's awful, I know. My God, a few minutes ago I made a speech to a piece of furniture. . . . It was so stupid! The thing is, I never realize how stupid I sound until I'm done.

VÁRYA She's right, Uncle. You just have to learn to keep still, that's all.

ÁNYA If you do, you'll feel much better about yourself, you know you will. . . .

GÁYEV I will, I will, I promise. [*Kisses* ÁNYA'*s and* VÁRYA'*s hands.*] I'll keep still. Only right now I have to talk a little more. Business! On Thursday I was at the county courthouse; there was a group of us talking—just this and that—and it turns out I might be able to arrange a promissory note for enough money to pay off the mortgage.

VÁRYA If only God would help us!

GÁYEV I'm going in on Tuesday, I'll talk to them again. [*To* VÁRYA] Don't whine! [*To* ÁNYA] Your mother will talk to Lopákhin; he can't refuse to help her. And you, as soon as you're rested, you go to Yároslavl, go talk to your godmother. There. We'll be operating on three fronts at once; we're sure to succeed. We *will* pay off this mortgage, I know we will. . . . [*He pops a hard candy into his mouth.*] I swear by my honor, I swear by anything you want, the estate will not be sold! [*Excitedly*] I swear by my own happiness! Here, you have my hand on it. You may call me . . . dishonorable, call me anything you will, if I ever let this estate go on the auction block! I swear by my entire existence!

ÁNYA [*her calm mood has returned; she is happy*] You're so smart, Uncle! You're such a wonderful man! [*Hugs* GÁYEV.] Now I feel better! So much better! I'm happy again!

[*Enter* FIRS.]

FIRS [*reproachfully*] Leoníd Andréyich, why aren't you in bed, like decent God-fearing people?

GÁYEV I'm coming, I'm coming. You go to bed, Firs. I can get undressed by myself. All right, children, nighty-night. We can talk about the details tomorrow, now it's time for bed. [*Kisses* ÁNYA *and* VÁRYA.] I am a man of the eighties, you know. People don't think much of that era now, but I can tell you frankly that I have had the courage of my convictions and often had to pay the price.[1] But these local peasants all love me. You have to get to know them, that's all. You have to get to know them, and—

ÁNYA Uncle. You're at it again.

VÁRYA Just be quiet, Uncle.

FIRS [*angrily*] Leoníd Andréyich!

GÁYEV I'm coming, I'm coming. . . . Go to bed now. Yellow ball in the side pocket! Clean shot!

[*Goes out;* FIRS *follows him, limping.*]

ÁNYA I feel much better. I don't much want to go to Yároslavl, I don't like my godmother, but I feel better now. Thanks to Uncle [*Sits down.*]

VÁRYA We've got to get some sleep. I'm going to bed. Oh, there's something came up since you left. You know we've got all those old retired servants living out back—Paulina, old Karp, and the rest of them. And what happened, they started inviting people in to spend the night. Well, it's annoying, but I never said a thing. Then what happened was, they started telling everybody all they were getting to eat was beans. Because I was so cheap, you see. It was that old Karp was doing it. So I said to myself, All right, that's the way you want it, all right, just wait, and I sent for him [*Yawns*], and in he comes, so I say, Karp, you're such an idiot—[*Looks at* ÁNYA.] Ánya!

[*Pause.*]

She's asleep. [*Lifts* ÁNYA *by the arms.*] Come on, time for bed. . . . Come on, let's go. . . . [*Leads her off.*] My angel fell asleep! Come on. . . . [*They start out.*]

[*In the distance, beyond the orchard, a shepherd plays a pipe.* TROFÍMOV *enters, sees* ÁNYA *and* VÁRYA, *stops.*]

VÁRYA Shh! She's asleep. . . . Come on, darling, let's go. . . .

ÁNYA [*softly, half asleep*] I was so tired. . . . All those bells . . . Uncle dear . . . and Mama. Uncle and Mama.

VÁRYA Come on, darling, come on. . . .

[*They go off into* ÁNYA'*s room.*]

TROFÍMOV [*deeply moved*] My sunshine! My springtime!

Curtain.

Act 2

[*An open space. The overgrown ruin of an abandoned chapel. There is a well beside it and some large stones that must once have been grave markers. An old bench. Beyond, the road to the Gáyev estate. On one side a shadowy row of poplar trees; they mark the limits of the cherry orchard. A row of telegraph poles, and on the far distant horizon, on a clear day, you can just make out the city. It's late afternoon, almost sunset.* CARLOTTA, YÁSHA, *and* DUNYÁSHA *are sitting on the bench;* YEPIKHÓDOV *stands nearby, strumming his guitar; each seems lost in his own thoughts.* CARLOTTA *wears an old military cap and is adjusting the strap on a hunting rifle.*]

1. When Alexander III (1845–1894) became czar in 1881, he initiated a series of repressive measures designed to combat liberal and revolutionary elements in Russian society.

CARLOTTA [*meditatively*] I haven't got a birth certificate, so I don't know how old I really am. I just think of myself as young. When I was a little girl, Mama and my father used to travel around to fairs and put on shows, good ones. I did back flips, things like that. And after they died this German woman brought me up, taught me a few things. And that was it. Then I grew up and had to go to work. As a governess. Where I'm from . . . who I am . . . no idea. Who my parents were—maybe they weren't even married—no idea. [*Takes a large cucumber pickle out of her pocket and takes a bite.*] No idea at all.

[*Pause.*]

And I feel like talking all the time, but there's no one to talk to. No one.

YEPIKHÓDOV [*plays the guitar and sings*]

"What do I care for the rest of the world,
or care what it cares for me . . ."[2]

Very agreeable, playing a mandolin.

DUNYÁSHA That's not a mandolin, it's a guitar. [*Takes out a compact with a mirror and powders herself.*]

YEPIKHÓDOV When a man is madly in love, a guitar is a mandolin. [*Sings.*]

"As long as my heart is on fire with love,
and the one I love loves me."

[YÁSHA *sings harmony.*]

CARLOTTA Oof! You people sound like hyenas.

DUNYÁSHA But it must have been just lovely, being in Europe.

YÁSHA Oh, it was. Quite, quite lovely. I have to agree with you there. [*Yawns, then lights a cigar.*]

YEPIKHÓDOV That's understandable. In Europe, things have already come to a complex.

YÁSHA [*beat*] I suppose you could say that.

YEPIKHÓDOV I'm a true product of the educational system; I read all the time. All the right books too, but I have no chosen directive in life. For me, strictly speaking, it's live or shoot myself. That's why I always carry a loaded pistol. See? [*Takes out a revolver.*]

CARLOTTA All done. Time to go. [*Slings the rifle over her shoulder.*] You're a very smart man, Yepikhódov, and a very scary one. Ooh! The women must adore you. [*Starts off.*] They're all so dumb, these smart boys. Never anyone to talk to . . . Always alone, all by myself, no one to talk to . . . and I still don't know who I am. Or why. No idea.

[*Walks slowly off.*]

YEPIKHÓDOV I should explain, by the way, for the sake of expressivity, that fate has been, ah, *rigorous* to me. I am, strictly speaking, tempest-tossed. Always have been. Now, you may say to me, Oh, you're imagining things, but then why, when I wake up this morning—here's an example—and I look down, why is there this spider on my stomach? Detrimentally large too. [*Makes a circle with his two hands.*] Big as that. Or take a beer, let's say.

2. Words from a popular turn-of-the-century ballad.

I go to drink it, what do I see floating around in it? Something highly unappreciative, like a cockroach.

[*Pause.*]

Have you ever read Henry Thomas Buckle?[3]

[*Pause.*]

May I design to disturb you, Avdótya Fyódorovna, with something I have to say?

DUNYÁSHA So say it.

YEPIKHÓDOV Preferentially alone. [*Sighs.*]

DUNYÁSHA [*embarrassed*] All right. . . . Only first get me my wrap; it's by the kitchen door. It's getting kind of damp.

YEPIKHÓDOV Ah, I see. Yes, get the wrap, of course. Now I know what to do with my gun.

[*Takes his guitar and goes off, strumming.*]

YÁSHA Double Trouble. He's an idiot, if you ask me. [*Yawns.*]

DUNYÁSHA I hope to God he doesn't shoot himself.

[*Pause.*]

I get upset over every little thing anymore. Ever since I started working for them here, I've gotten used to their *lifestyle.* Just look at my hands. Look at how white they are, just like I was rich. I'm different now from like I was. I'm more delicate, I'm more sensitive; everything upsets me. . . . It's just awful how things upset me. So if you cheat on me, Yásha, I may just have a nervous breakdown.

YÁSHA [*kisses her*] Oh, you little cutie! Just remember, though: a girl has to watch her step. What I'm after is a *nice* girl.

DUNYÁSHA I really love you, Yásha, I really do. You're so smart, you know so many things. . . .

[*Pause.*]

YÁSHA [*yawns*] Yeah. . . . But my theory is, a girl says she loves you, she's not a nice girl.

[*Pause.*]

Nothing like smoking a cigar out here in the fresh air. . . . [*Listens.*] Somebody's coming. . . . It's them. . . .

[DUNYÁSHA *hugs him impulsively.*]

YÁSHA Go on back to the house. Go back the other way, make believe you've been swimming down by the river, so they don't think we've been . . . we've been getting together out here like this. I don't want them to think that.

DUNYÁSHA [*a little cough*] That cigar smoke is giving me a headache. . . .

[*Goes out.*]

[YÁSHA *sits beside the chapel wall. Enter* LIUBÓV, GÁYEV, *and* LOPÁKHIN.]

LOPÁKHIN You have to make up your mind one way or the other; time's running out. There's no argument left. You want to subdivide or don't you? Just give me an answer, one word, yes or no.

3. English historian (1821–1862), author of *History of Civilization in England* (1857–61), an unfinished attempt to present history as an exact science.

LIUBÓV ANDRÉYEVNA Who's been smoking those cheap cigars? [*Sits down.*]

GÁYEV Everything's so convenient, now that there's the railroad. We went into town just to have lunch. Yellow ball in the side pocket! What do you say—why don't we go back to the house, eh? Have ourselves a little game . . .

LIUBÓV ANDRÉYEVNA Let's wait till later.

LOPÁKHIN Just one word! [*Imploringly*] Why don't you give me an answer?

GÁYEV [*yawns*] To what?

LIUBÓV ANDRÉYEVNA [*rummages in her purse*] Yesterday I had a lot of money, today it's all gone. My poor Várya feeds us all on soup to economize, the poor old people get nothing but beans, and I just spend and spend. . . . [*Drops her purse; gold coins spill out.*] Oh, I've spilled everything. . . .

YÁSHA Here, allow me. [*Picks up the money.*]

LIUBÓV ANDRÉYEVNA Oh, please do, Yásha; thank you. And why I had to go into that town for lunch—that stupid restaurant of yours, those stupid musicians, those stupid tablecloths; they smelled of soap. . . . Why do we drink so much, Lyónya? And eat so much? Why do we talk so much? The whole time we were in the restaurant, you kept talking, and none of it made any sense. Talking about the seventies, about Symbolism.[4] And to who? The waiters! Talking about Symbolism to waiters!

LOPÁKHIN Yes.

GÁYEV [*makes a deprecating gesture*] I'm incorrigible, I suppose. . . . [*To* YÁSHA, *irritably*] What are *you* doing here? Why are you always underfoot every time I turn around?

YÁSHA [*laughs*] Because every time I hear your voice it makes me laugh.

GÁYEV Either he goes or I do!

LIUBÓV ANDRÉYEVNA Yásha, please . . . just go 'way, will you?

YÁSHA [*gives* LIUBÓV *her purse*] I'm going. Right now. [*Barely containing his laughter*] Right this very minute . . .

[*Goes out.*]

LOPÁKHIN You know who Derigánov is? You know how much money he has? You know he's planning to buy your property? They say he's coming to the auction himself.

LIUBÓV ANDRÉYEVNA Who told you that?

LOPÁKHIN Everybody in town knows about it.

GÁYEV The old lady in Yároslavl promised to send money. . . . But when, and how much, she didn't say.

LOPÁKHIN How much will she send? A hundred thousand? Two hundred?

LIUBÓV ANDRÉYEVNA Ten or fifteen thousand. And we're lucky to get that much.

LOPÁKHIN Excuse me, but you people . . . I have never met anyone so unbusinesslike, so impractical, so . . . so *crazy* as the pair of you! Somebody tells you flat out your land is about to be sold, you don't even seem to understand!

LIUBÓV ANDRÉYEVNA But what should we do? Just tell us what we should do!

4. A movement in literature and art that began in France in the last third of the 19th century; it emphasized the evocation of subjective emotion, via symbol and metaphor, rather than objective description, and it had its greatest influence in Russia in the 1880s. *The seventies:* a time of widespread populist agitation among Russia's peasant population.

LOPÁKHIN I tell you every day what you should do! Every day I come out here and say the same thing. The cherry orchard and the rest of the land has to be subdivided and developed for leisure homes, and it has to be done right away. The auction date is getting closer! Can't you understand? All you have to do is make up your mind to subdivide, you'll have more money than even you can spend! Your troubles will be over!

LIUBÓV ANDRÉYEVNA Subdivide, leisure homes . . . excuse me, but it's all so hopelessly vulgar.

GÁYEV I couldn't agree more.

LOPÁKHIN You people drive me crazy! Another minute, I'll be shouting my head off! Oh, I give up, I give up! Why do I even bother? [*To* GÁYEV] You're worse than an old lady!

GÁYEV What say?

LOPÁKHIN I said you're an old lady! [*Starts to leave.*]

LIUBÓV ANDRÉYEVNA [*fearfully*] No, no, no, please, my dear, don't go. Please. I'm sure we'll think of something.

LOPÁKHIN What's there to think of?

LIUBÓV ANDRÉYEVNA Please. Don't go. Things are easier when you're around. . . .

[*Pause.*]

I keep waiting for something to happen. It's as if the house were about to fall down around our ears or something. . . .

GÁYEV [*meditatively*] Yellow ball in the side pocket . . . Clean shot down the middle . . .

LIUBÓV ANDRÉYEVNA We're guilty of so many sins, I know—

LOPÁKHIN Sins? What are you talking about?

GÁYEV [*pops a hard candy into his mouth*] People say I've eaten up my entire inheritance in candy. [*Laughs.*]

LIUBÓV ANDRÉYEVNA All my sins . . . I've always wasted money, just thrown it away like a madwoman, and I married a man who never paid a bill in his life. He was an alcoholic; he drank himself to death—on champagne. And I was so unhappy I fell in love with another man, *unfortunately,* and had an affair with him, and that was when—that was the first thing, my first punishment, right down there, in the river, my little boy drowned, and I left, I went to France, I left and never wanted to come back, I never wanted to see that river again, I just closed my eyes and *ran,* forgot about everything, and that man followed me. He just wouldn't let up. And he was so mean to me, so cruel! I bought a villa in Mentón because he got sick while we were there, and for the next three years I never had a moment's peace, day or night. He tormented me from his sickbed. I could feel my soul dry up. And last year I couldn't afford the villa anymore, so I sold it and we moved to Paris, and once we were in Paris he took everything I had left and ran off with another woman, and I tried to kill myself. It was so stupid, and so shameful! Finally all I wanted was to come back home, to where I was born, to my daughter. [*Wipes away her tears.*] Oh, dear God, dear God, forgive me! Forgive me my sins! Don't punish me again! [*Takes a telegram from her purse.*] This came today, from Paris. . . . He says he's sorry, he wants me back. . . . [*Tears up the telegram.*] Where's [*Listens.*] . . . where's that music coming from?

GÁYEV That's our famous local orchestra. Those Jewish musicians, you remember? Four fiddles, a clarinet, and a double bass.

LIUBÓV ANDRÉYEVNA Are they still around? We should have them over some evening and throw a party.

LOPÁKHIN [*listens*] I don't hear anything. [*Sings to himself.*]

"Ooh-la-la . . .
Just a little bit of money
makes a lady very French . . ."

[*Laughs.*] I went to the theater last night, saw this musical. Very funny.

LIUBÓV ANDRÉYEVNA I doubt there was anything funny about it. You ought to stop going to see playacting and take a good look at your own reality. What a boring life you lead! And what uninteresting things you talk about.

LOPÁKHIN Well . . . yeah, there's some truth to that. It is a pretty dumb life we lead. . . .

[*Pause.*]

My father was a . . . he was a dirt farmer, an idiot, never understood me, never taught me anything, just got drunk and beat me up. With a stick. Fact is, I'm not much better myself. Never did well in school, my writing's terrible, I'm ashamed if anybody sees it. I write like a pig.

LIUBÓV ANDRÉYEVNA My dear man, you should get married.

LOPÁKHIN Yes. . . . Yes, I should.

LIUBÓV ANDRÉYEVNA And you should marry our Várya. She's a wonderful girl.

LOPÁKHIN She is.

LIUBÓV ANDRÉYEVNA Her people were quite ordinary, but she works like a dog, and the main thing is, she loves you. And you like her, I know you do. You always have.

LOPÁKHIN Look, I've got nothing against it. I . . . She's a wonderful girl.

[*Pause.*]

GÁYEV They offered me a position at the bank. Six thousand a year. Did I tell you?

LIUBÓV ANDRÉYEVNA Don't be silly! You stay right here where you belong.

[*Enter* FIRS, *carrying an overcoat.*]

FIRS Sir, sir, please put this on. It's getting damp.

GÁYEV [*puts it on*] Firs, you're getting to be a bore.

FIRS That so? Went out this morning, didn't even tell me. [*Tries to adjust* GÁYEV*'s clothes.*]

LIUBÓV ANDRÉYEVNA Poor Firs! You've gotten so old!

FIRS Beg pardon?

LOPÁKHIN She said you got very old!

FIRS I've lived a long time. They were trying to marry me off way back before your daddy was born. [*Laughs.*] By the time we got our freedom back,[5] I was already head butler. I had all the freedom I needed, so I stayed right here with the masters.

[*Pause.*]

I remember everybody got all excited about it, but they never even knew what they were getting excited about.

5. That is, 1861, when the serfs—feudal agricultural workers bound to their lord's land, who made up one-third of Russia's total population—were freed by Alexander II's Edict of Emancipation.

LOPÁKHIN Oh, sure, things were wonderful back in the good old days! They had the right to beat you if they wanted, remember?

FIRS [*doesn't hear*] That's right. Masters stood by the servants, servants stood by the masters. Nowadays it's all mixed up; you can't tell who's who.

GÁYEV Shut up, Firs. . . . I have to go into town tomorrow. A friend promised to introduce me to someone who might be able to arrange a loan. Some general.

LOPÁKHIN That's never going to work. Trust me, you won't get enough even for the interest payments.

LIUBÓV ANDRÉYEVNA He's imagining things. There's no general.

[*Enter* ÁNYA, VÁRYA, *and* TROFÍMOV.]

GÁYEV Here come our young people.

ÁNYA Mama's resting.

LIUBÓV ANDRÉYEVNA [*tenderly*] Here we are, dears, over here. [*Kisses* ÁNYA *and Várya.*] If you only knew how much I love you both. Come sit here by me . . . that's right.

[*They all sit down.*]

LOPÁKHIN Our permanent graduate student seems to spend all his time studying the ladies.

TROFÍMOV Mind your own business.

LOPÁKHIN Almost in his fifties, he's still in school.

TROFÍMOV Just stop the silly jokes, will you?

LOPÁKHIN Oh, the *scholar* is losing his temper!

TROFÍMOV Will you please just leave me alone?

LOPÁKHIN [*laughs*] Let me ask you a question: You look at me, what do you see?

TROFÍMOV When I look at you, Yermolái Alexéyich, what I see is a rich man. One who will soon be a millionaire. You are as necessary a part of the evolution of the species as the wild animal that eats up anything in its path.

[*Everybody laughs.*]

VÁRYA Forget biology, Pétya. You should stick to counting stars.

LIUBÓV ANDRÉYEVNA I want to hear more about what we were talking about last night.

TROFÍMOV What were we talking about?

GÁYEV About human dignity.

TROFÍMOV We talked about a lot last night, but we never got anywhere. You people talk about human dignity as if it were something mystical. I suppose it is, in a way, for you anyway, but when you really get down to it, what have humans got to be proud of? Biologically we're pretty minor specimens—besides which, the great majority of human beings are vulgar and unhappy and totally *un*dignified. We should stop patting ourselves on the back and get to work.

GÁYEV You still have to die.

TROFÍMOV Who says? Anyway, what does that mean, to die? Maybe we have a hundred senses, and all we lose when we die are the five we're familiar with, and the other ninety-five go on living.

LIUBÓV ANDRÉYEVNA Oh, Pétya, you're so smart!

LOPÁKHIN [*with irony*] Oh, yes, very.

TROFÍMOV Remember, human beings are constantly progressing, and their power keeps growing. Things that seem impossible to us nowadays, the day will come when they're not a problem at all, only we have to work toward that day. We have to seek out the truth. We don't do that, you know. Most of the people in this country aren't working toward anything. People I come in contact with—at the university, for instance—they're supposed to be educated, but they're not interested in the truth. They're not interested in much of anything, actually. They certainly don't *do* much. They call themselves intellectuals and think that gives them the right to look down on the rest of the world. They never read anything worthwhile, they're completely ignorant where science is concerned, they talk about art and they don't even know what it is they're talking about. They take themselves so seriously, they're full of theories and ideas, but just go look at the cities they live in. Miles and miles of slums, where people go hungry and where they live packed into unheated tenements full of cockroaches and garbage, and their lives are full of violence and immorality. So what are all the theories for? To keep people like us from seeing all that. Where are the day-care centers they talk so much about, and the literacy programs? It's all just talk. You go out to the parts of town where the poor people live, you can't find them. All you find is dirt and ignorance and crime. That's why I don't like all this talk, all these theories. Bothers me, makes me afraid. If that's all our talk is good for, we'd better just shut up.

LOPÁKHIN I get up at five and work from morning to night, and you know, my business involves a lot of money, my own and other people's, so I see lots of people, see what they're like. And you just try to get anything accomplished: you'll see how few decent, honest people there really are. Sometimes at night I can't sleep, and I think: Dear God, you gave us this beautiful earth to live on, these great forests, these wide fields, the broad horizons . . . by rights we should be giants.

LIUBÓV ANDRÉYEVNA What do you want giants for? The only good giants are in fairy tales. Real ones would scare you to death.

[*Upstage,* YEPIKHÓDOV *strolls by, playing his guitar.*]

[*Dreamily*] There goes Yepikhódov. . . .

ÁNYA [*dreamily*] There goes Yepikhódov. . . .

GÁYEV The sun, ladies and gentlemen, has just set.

TROFÍMOV Yes.

GÁYEV [*as if reciting a poem, but not too loud*] O wondrous nature, cast upon us your eternal rays, forever beautiful, forever indifferent. . . . Mother, we call you; life and death reside within you; you bring forth and lay waste—

VÁRYA [*pleading*] Uncle, please!

ÁNYA Uncle, you're doing it again.

TROFÍMOV We'd rather have the yellow ball in the side pocket.

GÁYEV Sorry, sorry. I'll keep still.

[*They all sit in silence. The only sound we hear is old* FIRS *mumbling. Suddenly a distant sound seems to fall from the sky, a sad sound, like a harp string breaking. It dies away.*]

LIUBÓV ANDRÉYEVNA What was that?

LOPÁKHIN Can't tell. Sounds like it could be an echo from a mine shaft. But it must be far away.

GÁYEV Or some kind of bird . . . like a heron.

TROFÍMOV Or an owl.

LIUBÓV ANDRÉYEVNA [*shivers*] Makes me nervous.

[*Pause.*]

FIRS It's like just before the trouble started. They heard an owl screech, and the kettle wouldn't stop whistling. . . .

GÁYEV Before what trouble?

FIRS The day we got our freedom back.

[*Pause.*]

LIUBÓV ANDRÉYEVNA My dears, it's getting dark; we should be going in. [*To* ÁNYA] You've got tears in your eyes, darling. What's the matter? [*Hugs* ÁNYA.]

ÁNYA Nothing, Mama. It's all right.

TROFÍMOV Someone's coming.

[*Enter a* HOMELESS MAN *in a white cap and an overcoat; he's slightly drunk.*]

HOMELESS MAN Can anyone please tell me, can I get to the train station this way?

GÁYEV Of course you can. Just follow this road.

HOMELESS MAN Much obliged. [*Bows.*] Wonderful weather we're having . . . [*Recites.*] "Behold one of the poor in spirit, just trying to inherit a little of the earth. . . ."[6] [*To* VÁRYA] Listen, you think you could spare some money for a hungry man?

[VÁRYA *is terrified; she screams.*]

LOPÁKHIN [*angrily*] Now hold on just a minute!

LIUBÓV ANDRÉYEVNA [*panicked*] Here . . . here . . . take this. [*Fumbles in her purse.*] Oh, I don't seem to have anything smaller. Here, take this. [*Gives him a gold piece.*]

HOMELESS MAN Very much obliged!

[*Goes out.*]

[*Everybody laughs.*]

VÁRYA Get me out of here! Oh, please get me out! Mama, how could you! We can't even feed the servants, and you go and give him a gold piece!

LIUBÓV ANDRÉYEVNA I know, darling, I'm just stupid about money. When we get home I'll give you whatever I've got left; you can take care of it. Yermolái Alexéyich, can you lend me some money?

LOPÁKHIN Of course.

LIUBÓV ANDRÉYEVNA My darlings, it really is time to go in. Várya dear, we've just gotten you engaged. Congratulations.

VÁRYA [*almost in tears*] Mama, that's nothing to joke about!

LOPÁKHIN Amelia, get thee to a nunnery![7]

GÁYEV Look how my hands shake. I don't know if I could play billiards anymore. . . .

6. An allusion to two of the beatitudes from Jesus' Sermon on the Mount: "Blessed are the poor in spirit, for theirs is the kingdom of heaven. . . . Blessed are the meek, for they shall inherit the earth" (Matthew 5.3, 5).

7. Hamlet's charge to Ophelia in Shakespeare's *Hamlet* (1600–01; 3.1.122). Lopákhin's next line also quotes Hamlet though he substitutes "horizons" for "orisons" 3.1.91–92).

LOPÁKHIN Nymph, in thy horizons be all my sins remembered!

LIUBÓV ANDRÉYEVNA Please, let's go. It's almost suppertime.

VÁRYA He scared me half to death. I can feel my heart pounding.

LOPÁKHIN But keep in mind, the cherry orchard is going to be sold. On August twenty-second! You hear what I'm saying? You've got to think about this! You've got to!

[*They all go off except* ÁNYA *and* TROFÍMOV.]

ÁNYA [*laughs*] I'm so glad that tramp scared Várya off. Now we can be alone.

TROFÍMOV Várya's afraid we're going to fall in love; that's why she never leaves us alone. She's so narrow-minded; she simply can't understand that we are above love. Our goal is to get rid of the silly illusions that keep us from being free and happy. We are moving forward, toward the future! Toward one bright star that burns ahead of us! Forward, friends! Come join us in our journey!

ÁNYA [*claps her hands*] Oh, you talk so beautifully!

[*Pause.*]

It's just heavenly out here today!

TROFÍMOV Yes, the weather's been really good lately.

ÁNYA I don't know what it is you've done to me, Pétya, but I don't love the cherry orchard anymore, not the way I used to. I used to think there was no place on earth like our orchard.

TROFÍMOV This whole country is our orchard. It's a big country and a beautiful one; it has lots of wonderful places in it.

[*Pause.*]

Just think, Ánya: your grandfather, and his father, and his father's fathers, they *owned* the people who slaved away for them all over this estate, and now the voices and faces of human beings hide behind every cherry in the orchard, every leaf, every tree trunk. Can't you see them? And hear them? And owning human beings has left its mark on all of you. Look at your mother and your uncle! They live off the labor of others, they always have, and they've never even noticed! They owe their entire lives to those other people, people they wouldn't even let walk through the front gate of their beloved cherry orchard! This whole country has fallen behind; it'll take us at least two hundred years to catch up. The thing is, we don't have any real sense of our own history; all we do is sit around and talk, talk, talk, then we feel depressed, so we go out and get drunk. If there's one thing that's clear to me, it's this: if we want to have any real life in the present, we have to do something to make up for our past, we have to get over it, and the only way to do that is to make sacrifices, get down to work, and work harder than we've ever worked before. Do you understand what I mean, Ánya?

ÁNYA The house we live in isn't our house anymore. It hasn't ever been, really. And I'll leave it all behind, I promise you I will.

TROFÍMOV Yes, you will! Throw away your house keys and go as far away as you can! You'll be free as the wind.

ÁNYA [*radiant*] I love the way you say things!

TROFÍMOV You have to understand me, Ánya. I'm not thirty yet, I'm still young; I may still be in school, but I've learned a lot. Winter comes, sometimes I get cold and hungry, or sick and upset, I don't have a cent to my name; things work out or they don't. . . . But no matter what, my heart and soul are always full of feelings, all kinds . . . I can't even explain them. And I feel happiness coming, Ánya, I can feel it, I can almost see it—

ÁNYA [*dreamily*] Look, the moon's rising.

[*The sound of* YEPIKHÓDOV*'s guitar, still playing the same mournful song. The moon rises. Somewhere beyond the poplar trees,* VÁRYA *can be heard calling.*]

VÁRYA [*off*] Anya! Ánya, where are you?

TROFÍMOV Yes, the moon is rising.

[*Pause.*]

It's happiness, that's what it is: it's rising, it's coming closer and closer, I can hear it. And even if we miss it, if we never find it, that's all right! Someone will!

VÁRYA [*off*] Ánya! Ánya, where are you?

TROFÍMOV [*angrily*] That Várya! Why won't she let us alone!

ÁNYA Don't let her bother you. Let's take a walk by the river. It's so nice there.

TROFÍMOV All right, let's go.

[*They leave. The stage is empty.*]

VÁRYA [*off*] Ánya! Ánya!

Curtain.

Act 3

[*A sitting room, separated from the ballroom in back by an archway. The chandeliers are lit. From the entrance hall comes the sounds of an orchestra, the Jewish musicians* GÁYEV *mentioned in Act 2. Evening. In the ballroom, everyone is dancing a grande ronde.* SEMYÓNOV-PÍSHCHIK*'s voice is heard calling the figures of the dance: "Promenade à une paire!"*[8] *The dancers dance through the sitting room in pairs in the following order:* PÍSHCHIK *and* CARLOTTA, TROFÍMOV *and* LIUBÓV ANDREYÉVNA, ÁNYA *and the* POSTMASTER, VÁRYA *and the* STATIONMASTER, *etc.* VÁRYA *is in tears, which she tries to wipe away as she dances. The final pair includes* DUNYÁSHA. *As the dancers return to the ballroom,* PÍSHCHIK *calls out: "Grande ronde, balancez!" and "Les cavaliers à genoux et remercier vos dames."*[9] FIRS *in his butler's uniform crosses the stage, carrying a seltzer bottle on a tray.* PÍSHCHIK *and* TROFÍMOV *come into the sitting room.*]

PÍSHCHIK I'm prone to strokes, already had two of 'em, I really shouldn't be dancing, but you know what they say: When in Rome. Besides, I'm really strong as a horse. Speaking of Romans, my father—what a joker he was—he used to claim our family was descended from the emperor Caligula's horse—you know, the one he made a senator?[1] [*Sits down.*] The only problem is we have no money. [*His head nods, he snores, then immediately wakes up.*] So the only thing I ever think about is money.

8. "Promenade with your partner!" (French).
9. "Large circle, swing with your arms!"; "Gentlemen, kneel down and thank your ladies" (French).
1. According to the Roman historian Suetonius, the emperor Caligula (r. 37–41 C.E.) considered making his favorite racehorse a consul; the version in popular lore is that he appointed the animal a senator.

TROFÍMOV Your father was right. You do look a little like a horse.

PÍSHCHIK Nothing wrong with horses. Wonderful animals. If I had one, I could sell it. . . .

[*From the adjacent billiard room come the sounds of a game.* VÁRYA *appears in the archway.*]

TROFÍMOV [*teases her*] Mrs. Lopákhin! Mrs. Lopákhin!

VÁRYA [*angrily*] High-class tramp!

TROFÍMOV Yes, I'm a high-class tramp, and I'm proud of it!

VÁRYA [*bitterly*] We've hired an orchestra! And what are we supposed to pay them with?

[*Goes out.*]

TROFÍMOV [*to* PÍSHCHIK] All the energy you've used trying to find money to pay your mortgage, if you'd spent that energy on something else, you could have moved the world.

PÍSHCHIK Nietzsche,[2] you know, the philosopher—a great thinker, Nietzsche, a man of genius, one of the great minds of the century—now Nietzsche, you know, says, in his memoirs, that counterfeit money's just as good as real. . . .

TROFÍMOV I didn't know you'd read Nietzsche.

PÍSHCHIK Well . . . actually, Dáshenka told me. And I'm desperate enough. I'm ready to start counterfeiting. I need three hundred and ten rubles, day after tomorrow. All I've got so far is a hundred and thirty. . . . [*He feels in his pockets anxiously.*] It's gone! My money's gone! [*Almost in tears*] I've lost my money! [*Joyfully*] Oh, here it is! It slipped down into the lining of my coat! God, I'm all in a sweat!

[*Enter* LIUBÓV *and* CARLOTTA.]

LIUBÓV ANDREYÉVNA [*she hums a dance tune*] Why is it taking so long? What's Leoníd doing all this time in town? He should be back by now. [*Calls to* DUNYÁSHA *in the ballroom.*] Dunyásha, tell the musicians they can take a break.

TROFÍMOV They probably postponed the auction.

LIUBÓV ANDREYÉVNA I suppose it was a mistake to hire an orchestra. Or to have a party in the first place. Oh, well . . . what difference does it make? [*Sits down and hums quietly.*]

CARLOTTA [*hands* PÍSHCHIK *a deck of cards*] Here's the deck. Pick a card, any card. . . . No, no, just think of one.

PÍSHCHIK All right, I'm thinking of one.

CARLOTTA Good. Now shuffle the deck. Very good. Now give it to me. Observe, my dear Píshchik! *Eins, zwei, drei!*[3] Now look in your jacket pocket, and you will find your card.

PÍSHCHIK [*takes a card from his jacket pocket*] That's it, the eight of spades! [*Amazed*] Really! I don't believe it!

CARLOTTA [*holds out the deck to* TROFÍMOV] Quick, what's the top card?

TROFÍMOV The top card? Oh . . . uh . . . the queen of spades.

CARLOTTA Correct! [*To* PÍSHCHIK] Now which card's on top?

PÍSHCHIK Ace of hearts!

2. Friedrich Nietzsche (1844–1900), German philosopher who was among the most influential of modern thinkers.

3. One, two, three! (German).

CARLOTTA Correct! [*Claps her hands, and the deck disappears.*] Well, isn't this a lovely day we're having?

[*A mysterious woman's voice answers; it seems to come from the floorboards: "A lovely day indeed. I couldn't agree more."*]

Whoever you are, I adore you!

[*The voice: "I adore you too!"*]

STATIONMASTER [*applauds*] Bravo! A lady ventriloquist!

PÍSHCHIK [*amazed*] Really! I don't believe it! Carlotta, you are amazing! I'm completely in love with you!

CARLOTTA In love? [*Shrugs her shoulders.*] What do you know about love? *Guter Mensch aber schlechter Musikant.*[4]

TROFÍMOV [*slaps* PÍSHCHIK *on the shoulder*] You're just an old horse!

CARLOTTA All right, everybody, watch closely! One more trick! [*Takes a lap robe from a chair.*] See, what a lovely blanket! I'm thinking of selling it. [*Shakes out the lap robe and holds it up.*] Who wants to buy?

PÍSHCHIK [*amazed*] Really! I don't believe it!

CARLOTTA *Eins, zwei, drei!* [*Quickly raises the lap robe.*]

[ÁNYA *appears behind the lap robe; she curtsies, runs to her mother and kisses her, then runs back into the ballroom. General applause and cries of delight.*]

LIUBÓV ANDREYÉVNA [*applauding*] Bravo! Bravo!

CARLOTTA Now one more! *Eins, zwei, drei!*

[*She raises the lap robe;* VÁRYA *appears; she takes a bow.*]

PÍSHCHIK Really! I don't believe it!

CARLOTTA That's all. The show is over.

[*Throws the lap robe to* PÍSHCHIK, *takes a bow, goes through the ballroom and out.*]

PÍSHCHIK [*goes after her*] Enchanting! What a woman! What a woman!

[*Goes out.*]

LIUBÓV ANDREYÉVNA Leoníd still isn't back from town yet. I don't understand what could be taking him so long! It's got to be all over by now: either the estate has been sold or they've postponed the auction. Why does he have to keep us in suspense like this?

VÁRYA [*tries to comfort her*] Uncle bought the estate, I'm sure he has.

TROFÍMOV [*ironically*] Oh, I'm sure.

VÁRYA Ánya's godmother sent him a power of attorney to buy the estate in her name; she agreed to take over the mortgage. She did it for Ánya. So God *has* helped us. Uncle has saved the estate.

LIUBÓV ANDREYÉVNA The old lady in Yároslavl sent us fifteen thousand to buy the place in her name—she doesn't trust us—but that's not even enough to pay the interest. [*Covers her face with her hands.*] My fate . . . my entire life . . . It's all being decided today.

TROFÍMOV [*teases* VÁRYA] Mrs. Lopákhin! Mrs. Lopákhin!

VÁRYA [*angrily*] And you're a permanent graduate student! Who's been suspended twice!

LIUBÓV ANDRÉYEVNA Don't get so angry, Várya; he's only teasing you. What's wrong with that? And what's wrong with Lopákhin? If you want to marry

4. A good man but a bad musician (German); that is, an incompetent.

him, do; he's a nice man. Interesting, even. If you don't want to marry him, don't; nobody's forcing you.

VÁRYA It's not a joking matter, Mama, believe me. I'm serious about him. He is a nice man, and I like him.

LIUBÓV ANDRÉYEVNA Then go ahead and marry him! I don't understand what you're waiting for!

VÁRYA Mama, I can't propose to him myself! For two years now everybody's been telling me to marry him, everybody, but he never mentions it. Or he jokes about it! Look, I understand, he's busy getting rich, he doesn't have time for me. Oh, if I had just a little money—I don't care how much, even a couple of hundred—I'd get out of here and go someplace far away. I'd go join a convent.

TROFÍMOV Now, there's an exalted idea!

VÁRYA [*to* TROFÍMOV] I thought students were supposed to be smart! [*Her tone softens; almost crying.*] Oh, Pétya, you used to be so nice-looking, and now you're getting old! [*To* LIUBÓV, *in a normal tone*] It's just that I need something to do all the time, Mama; it's the way I am. I can't sit around and do nothing.

[*Enter* YÁSHA.]

YÁSHA [*barely controlling his laughter*] Yepikhódov broke a billiard cue!

[*Goes out.*]

VÁRYA What is Yepikhódov doing here? Who asked him to come? And what's he doing playing billiards? I just don't understand these people. . . .

[*Goes out.*]

LIUBÓV ANDRÉYEVNA Pétya, don't tease her like that; you can see she's upset already.

TROFÍMOV Oh, she's such a busybody, always poking her nose into other people's business. She hasn't left Ánya and me alone the whole summer; she's afraid we're having a . . . an *affair.* What business is it of hers? Besides, it's not true. I'd never do anything so sordid. We're above love!

LIUBÓV ANDRÉYEVNA And I, I suppose, am beneath love. [*Upset*] Why isn't Leoníd back yet? I just want to know: has the estate been sold or not? The whole disaster seems so impossible to me, I don't know what to think, or do. . . . Oh, God, I'm losing my mind! I want to scream, or do something completely stupid . . . Help me, Pétya! Save me! Say something, say something!

TROFÍMOV Whether they sell it or not, does it make any difference really? You can't go back to the past. Everything here came to an end a long time ago. Try to calm down. You can't go on deceiving yourself; at least once in your life you have to look the truth straight in the eye.

LIUBÓV ANDRÉYEVNA What truth? You seem so sure what's truth and what isn't, but I'm not. I've lost any sense of it, I've lost sight of the truth. You're so sure of yourself, aren't you, so sure you have all the answers to everything, but darling, have you ever really had to live with one of your answers? You're too young. Of course *you* look into the future and see a brave new world, you don't expect any difficulties, but that's because you know nothing about life! Yes, you have more courage than my generation has, and better morals, and you're better educated, but for God's sake have a little sense of what it's like for me, and be easier on me. Pétya, I was born here! My parents lived here all their lives; so did my grandfather. I love this house! Without the cherry orchard my life makes no sense, and if you have to sell it, you might as well sell me with it. [*She embraces* TROFÍMOV *and kisses his forehead.*] And it was here my son drowned, you know that. . . . [*Weeps.*] Have some feeling for me, Pétya, you're such a good, sweet boy.

TROFÍMOV I pity you. [*Beat*] I do, from the bottom of my heart.

LIUBÓV ANDRÉYEVNA You should have said that differently, just a little differently. . . . [*Takes out her handkerchief; a telegram falls to the floor.*] You can't imagine how miserable I am today. All this noise, and every new sound makes me shake. I can't get away from it, but then when I'm alone in my room I can't stand the silence. Don't judge me, Pétya! I love you like one of my own family; I'd be very happy to see you and Ánya married, you know I would, only, darling, you must finish school first! You have *got* to graduate! You don't do anything except drift around from place to place—what kind of life is that? It's true, isn't it? Isn't that the truth? And we have to do something about that beard of yours; it's so scraggly. . . . [*Laughs.*] You've gotten so funny-looking!

TROFÍMOV [*picks up the telegram*] I have no desire to be good-looking.

LIUBÓV ANDRÉYEVNA The telegram's from Paris. I get a new one every day. One yesterday, now again today. That madman is sick again and in trouble. . . . He wants me to forgive him, he wants me back . . . and I suppose I should go back to Paris to be with him. Now see, Pétya, you're giving me that superior look, but darling, what am I supposed to do? He's sick, he's alone, he's unhappy, and who has he got to look after him? To give him his medicine and keep him out of trouble? And I love him—why do I have to pretend I don't, or not talk about it? I love him. That's just the way it is: I love him. I love him! He's a millstone around my neck, and he'll drown me with him, but he's *my* millstone! I love him and I can't live without him! [*Grabs* TROFÍMOV*'s hand.*] Don't judge me, Pétya, don't think badly of me, just don't say anything, please just don't say anything. . . .

TROFÍMOV [*almost in tears*] But for God's sake, you have to face the facts! He robbed you blind!

LIUBÓV ANDRÉYEVNA No, no, please, you mustn't say that, you mustn't—

TROFÍMOV He doesn't care a thing for you—you're the only person who doesn't seem to understand that! He's rotten!

LIUBÓV ANDRÉYEVNA [*gets angry but tries to control it*] And you, you're what? Twenty-six, twenty-seven? Listen to you: you sound like you'd never even graduated to long pants!

TROFÍMOV That's fine with me!

LIUBÓV ANDRÉYEVNA You're supposed to be a man; at your age you ought to know something about love. You ought to be in love yourself! [*Angrily*] Really! You think you're so smart, you're just a kid who doesn't know the first thing about it, you're probably a virgin, you're ridiculous, you're grotesque—

TROFÍMOV [*horrified*] What are you saying!

LIUBÓV ANDREYÉVNA "I'm above love!" You're not above love; you've just never gotten down to it! You're all wet, like Firs says. At your age, you ought to be sleeping with someone!

TROFÍMOV [*horrified*] What a terrible thing to say! That's terrible! [*He runs toward the ballroom, covering his ears.*] That's just horrible. . . . I can't listen to that; I'm leaving. [*Goes out, but reappears immediately.*] All is over between us!

[*Goes out into the entrance hall.*]

LIUBÓV ANDRÉYEVNA [*calls after him*] Pétya, wait a minute! Come back! I was just joking, Pétya, don't be so silly! Pétya!

[*A great clatter from the entrance hall; someone has fallen downstairs.* ÁNYA *and* VÁRYA *scream.*]

What happened?

[ÁNYA *and* VÁRYA *suddenly howl with laughter.*]

ÁNYA [*runs in, laughing*] Pétya just fell headfirst down the stairs!

[*Runs out.*]

LIUBÓV ANDRÉYEVNA Oh, what a silly boy!

[*The* STATIONMASTER *in the ballroom gets on a chair and begins declaiming the opening lines of "The Magdalen" by Alexei Tolstoy.*[5]]

STATIONMASTER "The splendid ballroom gleams with gold and candles,
a crowd of dancers whirls around the room;
and there apart, an empty glass beside her,
behold the fallen beauty, the lost, the doomed.

Her lavish gown and jewels make all eyes wonder,
her shameless glance bespeaks a life of sin;
young men and old cast longing glances at her—
see, how her fatal beauty draws them in!"

[*Everyone gathers to listen, but soon the orchestra returns and the strains of a waltz are heard from the entrance hall. The reading breaks off, and everybody begins to dance.* TROFÍMOV, ÁNYA, *and* VÁRYA *come in from the entrance hall.*]

LIUBÓV ANDRÉYEVNA Pétya . . . oh, darling, I'm *so* sorry. . . . You sweet thing, please forgive me. . . . Come on, let's dance. [*Dances with* TROFÍMOV.]

[ÁNYA *and* VÁRYA *dance together.* FIRS *enters, leans his walking stick against the side door.* YÁSHA *appears and stands watching the dancers.*]

YÁSHA What's the matter, pops?

FIRS I don't feel so good. The old days, we had a dance, we had generals and barons and admirals; nowadays we have to send out for the postmaster and the stationmaster. And they're none too eager to come, either. Oh, I'm getting old and feeble. The old master, their grandfather, anybody got sick, he used to dose 'em all with sealing wax. Didn't matter what they had, they all got sealing wax. I've been taking sealing wax myself now for nigh onto twenty years. Take some every day. That's probably why I'm still alive.

YÁSHA You're getting boring, pops. [*Yawns.*] Time for you to crawl off and die.

FIRS Oh, you . . . you young flibbertigibbet. [*Mumbles.*]

[TROFÍMOV *and* LIUBÓV *dance through the ballroom, into the sitting room.*]

5. Russian novelist, poet, and playwright (1817–1875), a distant relative of the more famous novelist Leo Tolstoy. "The Magdalen" is sometimes translated "The Sinful Woman" (a *magdalen* is a reformed prostitute).

LIUBÓV ANDRÉYEVNA *Merci.*[6] I need to sit down and rest a bit. . . . [*Sits.*] I'm so tired.

[*Enter* ÁNYA.]

ÁNYA [*upset*] There was a man in the kitchen just now, he said the cherry orchard's already been sold!

LIUBÓV ANDRÉYEVNA Who bought it?

ÁNYA He didn't say. And he's gone now. [*Dances with* TROFÍMOV; *they dance off across the ballroom.*]

YÁSHA That was just some old guy talking crazy. It wasn't anybody from around here.

FIRS And Leoníd Andréyich still isn't back. All he had on was his topcoat; you watch, he'll catch cold. He's all wet, that one.

LIUBÓV ANDRÉYEVNA I'll never live through this. Yásha, go out and see if anybody knows who bought it.

YÁSHA It was just some old guy. He left long ago. [*Laughs.*]

LIUBÓV ANDRÉYEVNA [*somewhat annoyed*] What are you laughing at? What's so funny?

YÁSHA That Yepikhódov. What a dope. Old Double Trouble.

LIUBÓV ANDRÉYEVNA Firs, suppose the estate is sold—where are you going to go?

FIRS I'll go wherever you tell me to.

LIUBÓV ANDRÉYEVNA What's the matter? Your face looks so funny. . . . Are you sick? You should go to bed.

FIRS Yes . . . [*Smirks.*] Yes, sure, go to bed, and then who'll take care of things? I'm the only one you've got.

YÁSHA Liubóv Andréyevna, there's a favor I have *got* to ask you; it's very important. If you go back to Paris, please take me with you. Please! You've got to! I positively cannot stay around here. [*Looks around, lowers his voice.*] You can see for yourself this place is hopeless. The whole country's a mess, nobody has any culture, it's boring, the food is lousy, and there's that old Firs drooling all over the place and talking like an idiot. Please, take me with you—you've just got to!

[*Enter* PÍSHCHIK.]

PÍSHCHIK Beautiful lady, what about a waltz? Just one little waltz! [LIUBÓV *crosses to him.*] You dazzler, you! And what about a loan, just one little loan, just a hundred and eighty, that's all I need. [*They begin to dance.*] Just a hundred and eighty . . .

[*They dance off into the ballroom.*]

YÁSHA [*sings to himself*] "Can't you see my heart is breaking . . ."

[*In the ballroom, a figure appears dressed in checkered trousers and a gray top hat, jumping and waving its arms. We hear shouts of "Bravo, Carlotta!"*]

DUNYÁSHA [*stops to powder her nose*] The missus told me to dance—there's too many gentlemen and not enough ladies—so I did, I've been dancing all night and my heart won't stop beating, and you know what, Firs? Just now, the postmaster, you know? He said something almost made me faint.

[*The orchestra stops playing.*]

6. Thank you (French).

FIRS What did he say?

DUNYÁSHA That I was like a flower. That's what he said.

YÁSHA [*yawns*] What does he know about it?

[*Goes out.*]

DUNYÁSHA Just like a flower. I'm a very romantic girl, really. I just adore that kind of talk.

FIRS You're out of your mind.

[*Enter* YEPIKHÓDOV.]

YEPIKHÓDOV [*to* DUNYÁSHA] Why are you deliberating not to notice me? You act as if I wasn't here, like I was a bug or something [*Sighs.*] Ah, life!

DUNYÁSHA Excuse me?

YEPIKHÓDOV Of course, you may be right. [*Sighs.*] But if you look at it, let's say, from a . . . a point of view, then you're the faulty one—excuse my expressivity—because you led me on. Into this predictament. Look at me! Every day something awful happens to me. It's like a habit. But I can look disaster in the face and keep smiling. You gave me your word, you know, and you even—

DUNYÁSHA Do you mind? Let's talk about it later. Right now I'd rather be left alone. With my dreams. [*Plays with a fan.*]

YEPIKHÓDOV Every day. Something awful. But all I do—excuse my expressivity—is try to keep smiling. Sometimes I even laugh.

[*Enter* VÁRYA *from the ballroom.*]

VÁRYA [*to* YEPIKHÓDOV] Are you still here? I thought I told you to go home. Really, you have no consideration. [*To* DUNYÁSHA] Dunyásha, go back to the kitchen! [*To* YEPIKHÓDOV] You come in here and start playing billiards, you break one of our cues, now you hang around in here as if we'd invited you.

YEPIKHÓDOV Excuse my expressivity, but you have no right to penalize me.

VÁRYA I'm not penalizing you, I'm telling you! All you do here is wander around and bump into the furniture. You're supposed to be working for us, and you don't do a thing. I don't know why we hired you in the first place.

YEPIKHÓDOV [*offended*] Whether I work or not or wander around or not or play billiards or not is none of your business! You do not have the know-it-all to make my estimation!

VÁRYA How dare you talk to me like that! [*In a rage*] How dare you! What do you mean, I don't have the know-it-all? You get yourself out of here right this minute! Right this minute!

YEPIKHÓDOV [*apprehensively*] I wish you wouldn't use language like that—

VÁRYA [*beside herself*] Get out of here right this minute! Out! [*He goes to the door; she follows him.*] Double Trouble! I don't want to see hide or hair of you, I don't want to lay eyes on you ever again! [YEPIKHÓDOV *goes out; from behind the door we hear him screech: "I'll call the police on you!"*] Oh, you coming back for more? [*Grabs the stick that* FIRS *has left by the door.*] Come on . . . Come on . . . Come on, I'll show you! All right, all right, you asked for it—[*Swings the stick; the door opens, and she hits* LOPÁKHIN *over the head as he enters.*]

LOPÁKHIN Thanks a lot.

VÁRYA [*still angry, sarcastic*] Oh, I'm so sorry!

LOPÁKHIN S'all right. Always appreciate a warm welcome.

VÁRYA I don't need appreciation. [*Walks off, then turns and asks gently.*] I didn't hurt you, did I?

LOPÁKHIN No, I'm fine. Just a whopping big lump, that's all.

[*Voices from the ballroom: "Lopákhin! Lopákhin's here! He's back! Lopákhin's back!" People crowd into the sitting room.*]

PÍSHCHIK The great man in person! [*Hugs* LOPÁKHIN.] Is that cognac I smell? It is! You've been celebrating! Well, so have we. Join the party!

LIUBÓV ANDRÉYEVNA It's you, Yermolái Alexéyich. Where have you been all this time? Where's Leoníd?

LOPÁKHIN He's coming; we took the same train.

LIUBÓV ANDRÉYEVNA What happened? Did they have the auction? Tell me!

LOPÁKHIN [*embarrassed, afraid to show his joy*] The auction was all over by four this afternoon, but we missed the train. We had to wait for the nine-thirty. [*Exhales heavily.*] Oof! My head is really spinning. . . .

[*Enter* GÁYEV; *he holds a wrapped package in one hand, wipes his eyes with the other.*]

LIUBÓV ANDRÉYEVNA Lyónya, what's the matter? Lyónya! [*Impatiently, beginning to cry*] For God's sake, what happened!

GÁYEV [*weeps and can't answer her; makes a despairing gesture with his free hand and turns to* FIRS] Here, take these . . . some anchovies . . . imported. I haven't eaten a thing all day. You have no idea what I've been through! [*The door to the billiard room is open; we hear the click of billiard balls and* YÁSHA'*s voice: "Seven ball in the left pocket!"* GÁYEV'*s expression changes; he stops crying.*] I'm all worn out. Firs, come help me get ready for bed.

[*Goes through the ballroom and out;* FIRS *follows him.*]

PÍSHCHIK What about the auction? Tell us what happened!

LIUBÓV ANDRÉYEVNA Is the cherry orchard sold?

LOPÁKHIN It's sold.

LIUBÓV ANDRÉYEVNA Who bought it?

LOPÁKHIN I did.

[*Pause.* LIUBÓV *is overcome; she would fall, if she weren't standing beside a table and the armchair.* VÁRYA *takes the keys from her belt, throws them on the floor, crosses the room, and goes out.*]

I did! I bought it! No, wait, don't go, please. I'm still a little mixed up about it, I can't talk yet. . . . [*Laughs.*] We get to the auction, and there's Derigánov, all ready and waiting. Leoníd Andréyich only had fifteen thousand, so right away Derigánov raises the bid to thirty, that's on top of the balance on the mortgage. So I see what he's up to, and I bid against him. Raise it to forty. He bids forty-five. I bid fifty-five. See, he was raising by five, and I double him, I raise him ten each time. Anyway, finally it's all over, and I got it! Ninety thousand plus the balance on the mortgage.[7] And now the cherry orchard is mine! Mine! [*A loud laugh*] My God, the cherry orchard belongs to me! Tell me I'm drunk, tell me it's all a dream, I'm making this up—[*Stomps on the floor.*] And don't anybody laugh! My God, if my father and my grandfather could be here now and see this, see *me*, their Yermolái, the boy they beat, who went barefoot in winter and never

7. The winning bid for the estate was equivalent to nearly $2 million today—about twice what Lopákhin had offered to lend Liubóv and her family to save the estate (act 1).

went to school, see how that poor boy just bought the most beautiful estate in the whole world! I bought the estate where my father and my grandfather slaved away their lives, where they wouldn't even let them in the kitchen! My God, I must be dreaming—I can't believe all this is happening! [*Picks up* VÁRYA'*s keys; smiles gently.*] See, she threw away her keys; she knows she isn't running the place anymore. . . . [*Jingles the keys.*] Well, that's all right.

[*The orchestra starts tuning up again.*]

That's it, let's have some music—come on, I want to hear it! Everybody come watch! Come on and watch what I do! I'm going to chop down every tree in that cherry orchard, every goddamn one of them, and then I'm going to develop that land! Watch me! I'm going to do something our children and grandchildren can be proud of! Come on, you musicians, play!

[*The orchestra begins to play.* LIUBÓV *curls up in the armchair and weeps bitterly.*]

LOPÁKHIN [*reproachfully*] Oh, why didn't you listen to me? You dear woman, you dear good woman, you can't ever go back to the past. [*With tears in his eyes*] Oh, if only we could change things, if only life were different, this unhappy, messy life . . .

PÍSHCHIK [*takes his arm; quietly*] She's crying. Come on, we'll go in the other room, leave her alone for a while. Come on. . . . [*Leads him into the ballroom.*]

LOPÁKHIN What's the matter? Tell the band to keep playing! Louder! [*Ironic*] It's my house now! The cherry orchard belongs to me! I can do what I want to! [*Bumps into a small table, almost knocking over a candlestick.*] Don't worry about that: I can pay for it! I can pay for everything!

[*Goes out with* PÍSHCHIK.]

[*The sitting room is empty except for* LIUBÓV, *who sits tightly clenched and weeping bitterly. The orchestra plays softly. Suddenly* ÁNYA *and* TROFÍMOV *enter.* ÁNYA *goes and kneels before her mother.* TROFÍMOV *remains by the archway.*]

ÁNYA Mama! Mama, you're crying. Mama dear, I love you, I'll take care of you. The cherry orchard is sold, it's gone now, that's the truth, Mama, that's the truth, but don't cry. You still have your life to lead, you're still a good person. . . . Come with me, Mama, we'll go away, someplace far away from here. We'll plant a new orchard, even better than this one, you'll see, Mama, you'll understand, and you'll feel a new kind of joy, like a light in your soul. . . . Let's go, Mama. Let's go!

Curtain.

Act 4

[*The same room as Act 1. The curtains have been taken down, the pictures are gone from the walls, and there are only a few pieces of furniture shoved into a corner, as if for sale. The place feels empty. By the doorway, a pile of trunks, suitcases, etc. The door on the right is open; we hear* ÁNYA *and* VÁRYA *talking in the room beyond.* LOPÁKHIN *stands waiting. Beside him,* YÁSHA *holds a tray of glasses filled with champagne. Through the door we see* YEPIKHÓDOV *in the front hall, fastening the straps on a trunk. The sound of murmured voices offstage; some of the local people have come to say goodbye.* GÁYEV'S *voice: "Thank you all, good people, thanks, thanks very much for coming."*]

YÁSHA It's some of these poor yokels, come to say goodbye. I'm of the opinion, you know, these people around here . . . ? They're okay, but they're . . . they're just a bunch of know-nothings.

[*The murmur of voices dies away.* LIUBÓV *and* GÁYEV *come in from the entrance hall; she has stopped crying, but she is shaking slightly, and her face is pale. She cannot speak.*]

GÁYEV You gave them all the money you had, Liúba. You can't do that! You can't do that anymore!

LIUBÓV ANDREYÉVNA I couldn't help it! I just couldn't help it!

[*They both go out.* LOPÁKHIN *follows them to the door.*]

LOPÁKHIN Wait, please. How about a little glass of champagne, just to celebrate? I forgot to bring some from town, but I got this one bottle at the station. It was all they had.

[*Pause.*]

No? What's the matter, don't you want any? [*Comes back from the door.*] If I'd known that, I wouldn't have bought it. I don't feel like any myself.

[YÁSHA *carefully puts the tray down on a chair.*]

Go on, Yásha, you might as well have one.

YÁSHA *Bon voyage!* And here's to the girls we leave behind! [*Drinks.*] This is not your real French champagne, I can tell.

LOPÁKHIN Cost me enough.

[*Pause.*]

It's cold as hell in here.

YÁSHA They figured they were going away today anyway—they decided not to heat the place. [*Laughs.*]

LOPÁKHIN What's with you?

YÁSHA I'm laughing because everything worked out just the way I wanted.

LOPÁKHIN It's October already, but the sun's out; it feels like summer. Good weather for home builders. [*Looks at his watch, then at the door.*] Listen, everybody, you got forty-six minutes till train time! And it's twenty minutes from here to the station, so you better get a move on.

[*Enter* TROFÍMOV *from outside; he's wearing an overcoat.*]

TROFÍMOV It must be time to go. The carts are here. Where the hell are my galoshes? I've lost them somewhere. [*At the door*] Ánya, where are my galoshes? I can't find them anyplace!

LOPÁKHIN I'm off to Hárkov. I'll be taking the same train as you. Off to Hárkov, spend the winter there. I've been hanging around here too long, doing nothing; I can't stand that. I got to keep working, otherwise I don't know what to do with my hands; if they're not doing something, they feel like they don't belong to me.

TROFÍMOV So. We're leaving, and you're going back to your useful labors in the real world.

LOPÁKHIN Have a glass of champagne.

TROFÍMOV No, thanks.

LOPÁKHIN So you're off to Moscow?

TROFÍMOV Yes. I'll go into town with them today, and then leave tomorrow for Moscow.

LOPÁKHIN Sure. I'll bet all those professors are waiting for you to show up, wouldn't want to start their lectures without you!

TROFÍMOV Mind your own business.

LOPÁKHIN How long you say you've been at that university?

TROFÍMOV Come on! Think up something new, will you? You're getting boring. [*Pokes around, looking for his galoshes.*] You know, we probably won't ever see each other again, so you mind my giving you a little advice? As a farewell present? Don't wave your arms around so much. Bad habit. And this development you're putting in out here—you think that's going to improve the world? You think your leisure home buyers are going to turn into yeoman farmers? That's a lot of arm waving too. Well, what the hell. I like you anyway. You've got nice hands. Gentle and sensitive. You could have been an artist. And you're like that inside too—gentle and sensitive.

LOPÁKHIN [*hugs him*] Goodbye, boy. Thanks for everything. Here, let me give you a little money. You may need it for the trip.

TROFÍMOV What for? I don't need money!

LOPÁKHIN What *for*? You don't have any!

TROFÍMOV I do too. Thanks all the same. I got paid for a translation I did. I have money right here in my pocket. [*Worried*] I just wish I could find my galoshes!

VÁRYA [*from the next room*] Here they are! The smelly things . . . [*Throws a pair of galoshes into the room.*]

TROFÍMOV What are you always getting mad for? Hmm . . . These aren't my galoshes.

LOPÁKHIN This past spring I planted a big crop of poppies. Three hundred acres. Sold the poppy seed, made forty thousand clear. And when those poppies were all in flower, what a picture that was! So look, I just made forty thousand, I can afford to loan you some money. Why turn up your nose at it? Because you think I'm just a dirt farmer?

TROFÍMOV So your father was a dirt farmer. Mine worked in a drugstore. What does that prove?

[LOPÁKHIN *takes out his wallet.*]

Forget it, forget it. Look, you could give me a couple of hundred thousand, I still wouldn't take it. I'm a free man. And you people, everything you think is so valuable, it doesn't mean a thing to me. I don't care whether you're rich or poor; you've got no power over me. I can do without you, I can go right on past you, because I am proud and I am strong. Humanity is moving onward, toward a higher truth and a higher happiness, higher than anyone can imagine. And I'm ahead of the rest!

LOPÁKHIN You think you'll ever get there?

TROFÍMOV I'll get there.

[*Pause.*]

I'll get there. Or I'll make sure the rest of them get there.

[*From the orchard comes the sound of axes; they've started chopping down the cherry trees.*]

LOPÁKHIN Well, boy, goodbye. Time to go. You and I don't see eye to eye, but life goes on anyway. Whenever I work real hard, round the clock practically, that clears my mind somehow, and for a minute I think maybe I know what we're all here for. But God, boy, think of the thousands of people in this country who don't know what they're doing or why they're doing it.

But . . . I guess that doesn't have much to do with the price of eggs. They told me Leoníd Andréyich got a job at the bank, six thousand a year. He won't last; he's too lazy.

ÁNYA [*at the door*] Mama asks you to please wait until she's gone before you start cutting down the orchard.

TROFÍMOV I agree. That isn't very tactful, you know.

[*Goes out into the front hall.*]

LOPÁKHIN All right, all right, I'll take care of it. God, these people . . .

[*Goes out after him.*]

ÁNYA Have they taken Firs to the nursing home?

YÁSHA I told them about it this morning. So I imagine they have.

ÁNYA [*to* YEPIKHÓDOV, *who crosses the room*] Yepikhódov, could you please go and make sure they've taken Firs to the nursing home?

YÁSHA [*offended*] I already told them this morning! Why keep asking?

YEPIKHÓDOV The aged Firs, in my ultimate opinion, is beyond nursing. They ought to take him to the cemetery. And I can only envy him. [*Sets a suitcase down on a cardboard hatbox and crushes it.*] There. Finally. Wouldn't you know.

[*Goes out.*]

YÁSHA [*snickers*] Old Double Trouble.

VÁRYA [*from the next room*] Have they taken Firs to the nursing home?

ÁNYA They took him this morning.

VÁRYA Then why didn't they take the letter for the doctor?

ÁNYA They must have forgotten. We'll have to send someone after them with it.

VÁRYA Where's Yásha? Tell him his mother is here; she wants to say goodbye.

YÁSHA [*with a dismissive gesture*] What a bore! Why can't she just leave me alone?

[DUNYÁSHA *has been drifting in and out, fussing with the baggage; now that she sees* YÁSHA *alone, she goes to him.*]

DUNYÁSHA Oh . . . oh, Yásha, why won't you even look at me? You're going away . . . you're leaving me behind. . . . [*Starts to cry and throws her arms around his neck.*]

YÁSHA What are you crying about? [*Drinks some champagne.*] Six days from now, I'll be back in Paris. Tomorrow we get on the express train, and we're off! And that's the last you'll ever see of me! I can't hardly believe it myself. *Vive la France!*[8] I can't live around here anymore; it's just not my kind of place. They're all so ignorant, and I can't stand that. [*Drinks more champagne.*] What are you crying about? If you'd been a nice girl, you wouldn't have anything to cry about.

DUNYÁSHA [*powders her nose in a mirror*] Don't forget to send me a letter from Paris. Because I loved you, Yásha, I really did. I'm a very sensitive person, Yásha, I really am—

YÁSHA Watch it, someone's coming. [*He starts fussing with the luggage, whistling quietly.*]

[*Enter* LIUBÓV, GÁYEV, ÁNYA, *and* CARLOTTA.]

8. Long live France! (French).

GÁYEV We should be going. We're already a little late. [*Looks at* YÁSHA.] Who smells like herring?

LIUBÓV ANDRÉYEVNA We've only got ten minutes; then we absolutely must start out. [*Glances around the room.*] Goodbye, house! Wonderful old house! Winter's almost here, and come spring you'll be gone. They'll tear you down. Think of everything these walls have seen! [*Kisses* ÁNYA *with great feeling.*] My treasure, look at you! You're radiant today! Your eyes are shining like diamonds! Are you happy? Really happy?

ÁNYA Oh, yes, Mama, really! We're starting a new life!

GÁYEV She's right—everything worked out extremely well. Before the cherry orchard was sold we were at our wit's end—remember how painful it was?—and now everything's finally settled, once and for all, no turning back, and see? We've all calmed down. We're even rather happy. I'm going to work at the bank, I'm about to become a financier! Yellow ball in the side pocket . . . And you look better than you have in a long time, Lyúba; you do, you know.

LIUBÓV ANDRÉYEVNA I know. My nerves have quieted down. You're quite right.

[*Someone holds out her hat and coat.*]

And I sleep much better now. Take my things, Yásha, will you? It's time to go. [*To* ÁNYA] Darling, we'll see each other soon enough. I'm off to Paris—I kept the money your godmother in Yároslavl sent to buy the estate. [*A hard laugh*] Thank God for the old lady! That ought to get me through the winter at least. . . .

ÁNYA And you'll come back soon, won't you? You promise? I'll study hard and get my diploma, and then I'll get a job and help you out. We can read together the way we used to, can't we? [*Kisses her mother's hands.*] We'll spend long autumn evenings together; we'll read lots of books and learn all about the wonderful new world of the future. . . . [*Dreamily*] Don't forget, Mama, you promised. . . .

LIUBÓV ANDRÉYEVNA I will, my angel, I promise. [*Embraces her.*]

[*Enter* LOPÁKHIN. CARLOTTA *hums a tune under her breath.*]

GÁYEV Carlotta must be happy; she's singing!

CARLOTTA [*picks up a bundle that looks like a baby in swaddling clothes*] Here's my little baby. Bye, bye, baby . . .

[*We hear a baby's voice: "Wah! Wah!"*]

Shh, baby, shh, shh . . . good little children don't cry. . . .

[*Again: "Wah! Wah!"*]

I feel so sorry for the poor thing. [*Hurls the bundle to the floor.*] You will find me a job, won't you? I can't go on like this anymore.

LOPÁKHIN Don't worry, Carlotta; we'll take care of you.

GÁYEV Everybody's just thrown us away. Várya's leaving. . . . All of a sudden we're useless.

CARLOTTA How can I live in that town of yours? There must be someplace I can go. . . . [*Hums.*] What difference does it make . . . ?

[*Enter* PÍSHCHIK.]

LOPÁKHIN Here comes the wonder boy.

PÍSHCHIK [*panting*] Ooh, give me a minute . . . I'm all worn out. Good morning, good morning, good morning. Could I get a drink of water?

GÁYEV [*sarcastic*] You're sure it isn't money you want? You'll all have to excuse me if I remove myself from the approaching negotiations.

[*Goes out.*]

PÍSHCHIK I'm so glad to see you all. . . . Dear lady . . . I've been a stranger, I know. [*To* LOPÁKHIN] And you're here too. Delighted, delighted, a man I admire, always have. . . . Here. Here. This is for you. [*Gives* LOPÁKHIN *money.*] Four hundred. And I still owe you eight hundred and forty.

LOPÁKHIN [*a bewildered shrug*] I must be dreaming. Where did you get money?

PÍSHCHIK Wait a minute; let me cool off. Well, it was an absolutely extraordinary thing. These Englishmen showed up, they poked around on my land, found some kind of white clay. . . . [*To* LIUBÓV] Here . . . Here's the four hundred. You've been so kind . . . so sweet . . . [*Gives her money.*] And you'll have the rest before you know it. [*Takes a drink of water.*] You know, there was a young man on the train just now, he was saying . . . there was this philosopher, he said, who wanted us all to jump off the roof. "Jump!" he said. "Jump!" That was his whole philosophy. [*Amazed*] Really! I don't believe it! Give me some more water. . . .

LOPÁKHIN What Englishmen are you talking about?

PÍSHCHIK I gave them a lease on the land, the place where the clay is, a twenty-four-year lease. And now excuse me, but I'm off. Lots of people to see, pay back what I owe. I owe money all over the place. [*Takes a drink of water.*] Well, I just wanted to say hello. I'll come by again on Thursday.

LIUBÓV ANDRÉYEVNA But we're leaving for town today. And tomorrow I'm going back to Paris.

PÍSHCHIK What? [*Astonished*] Leaving for town? Oh, my . . . Oh, of course; the furniture's gone. And all these trunks. I didn't realize. [*Almost in tears*] I didn't realize. Great thinkers, these English . . . God bless you all. And be happy. I didn't realize. Well, all things must come to an end. [*Kisses* LIUBÓV*'s hand.*] I'll come to an end myself one of these days. And when I do, I want you all to say: "Semyónov-Píshchik . . . he was a good old horse. God bless him." Wonderful weather we're having. Yes. . . . [*Starts out, overcome with emotion, stops in the doorway and turns.*] Oh, by the way, Dáshenka says hello.

[*Goes out.*]

LIUBÓV ANDRÉYEVNA Now we can go. There are just two things still on my mind. The first is old Firs. [*Looks at her watch.*] We've still got five minutes. . . .

ÁNYA Mama, they took Firs to the nursing home this morning. Yásha took care of it.

LIUBÓV ANDRÉYEVNA . . . And then there's our Várya. She's used to getting up early and working around here all day long, and now she's . . . out of a job. Like a fish out of water. Poor thing—she's so nervous, she cries, she's losing weight . . .

[*Pause.*]

You know, Yermolái Alexéyich—well, of course you know—I'd always dreamed . . . always dreamed she'd marry you; you know we all think it's a wonderful idea. . . . [*Whispers to* ÁNYA, *who nods to* CARLOTTA; *they both leave.*] She loves you, you like her. . . . I don't know why, I just don't know why the two of you keep avoiding the issue. Really!

LOPÁKHIN I don't know why either. It's all a little funny. Well, I don't mind. If there's still time, I'll do it. . . . All right, *basta,*[9] let's just get it over with. But I don't know, I don't think I can propose without you—

LIUBÓV ANDRÉYEVNA Of course you can. All it takes is a minute. I'll send her right in. . . .

LOPÁKHIN We've even got some champagne all ready. [*Looks at the tray of empty glasses.*] Or at least we did. Somebody must have drunk it all up.

[YÁSHA *coughs.*]

Guzzled it down, I should say.

LIUBÓV ANDRÉYEVNA Wonderful! We'll leave you alone. Yásha, *allez!*[1] I'll go call her. [*At the door*] Várya, leave that alone; come here a minute, will you? Come on, dear!

[*Goes out with* YÁSHA.]

LOPÁKHIN [*looks at his watch*] Well . . .

[*Pause. A few stifled laughs and whispers behind the door. Finally* VÁRYA *enters.*]

VÁRYA [*examines the luggage; takes her time*] That's funny, I can't find them. . . .

LOPÁKHIN What are you looking for?

VÁRYA I packed them myself, and now I don't remember where.

[*Pause.*]

LOPÁKHIN What . . . ah . . . where are you off to, Várya?

VÁRYA Me? I'm going to work for the Ragúlins. I talked to them about it already; they need a housekeeper. And look after things, you know. . . .

LOPÁKHIN All the way over there? That's fifty miles away.

[*Pause.*]

Well, looks like this is the end of things around here. . . .

VÁRYA [*still examining the luggage*] Where are they . . . ? Or maybe I put them in the trunk. You're right: this is the end of things here. The end of one life—

LOPÁKHIN I'm going too. To Hárkov. Taking the same train, actually. I've got a million things waiting for me. I'm leaving Yepikhódov, though. Hired him to take charge here.

VÁRYA You hired *who?*

LOPÁKHIN Last year this time it was snowing already, remember? Today it's still sunny. Nice day. A little chilly, though . . . It was freezing this morning; must have been in the thirties.

VÁRYA I didn't notice.

[*Pause.*]

Anyway, the thermometer's broken.

[*Pause. A voice from outside calls: "Lopákhin!"*]

LOPÁKHIN [*as if he'd been waiting for the call*] I'm coming!

[*Goes out.*]

[VÁRYA *sits down on the floor, leans her head on a bundle of dresses, and cries. The door opens;* LIUBÓV *enters carefully.*]

LIUBÓV ANDRÉYEVNA Well?

[*Pause.*]

9. Enough (Italian).

1. Go on! (French).

We have to go.

VÁRYA [*already stopped crying, wipes her eyes*] Right, Mama, we have to go. I can get to the Ragúlins' today, if I don't miss the train.

LIUBÓV ANDRÉYEVNA Ánya, get your coat on.

[*Enter* ÁNYA, GÁYEV, CARLOTTA. GÁYEV *wears a winter overcoat. Servants and drivers come in to pick up the luggage.* YEPIKHÓDOV *directs the operation.*]

Well, we're ready to start.

ÁNYA [*joyfully*] Ready to start!

GÁYEV My dear friends, my very dear friends! On this occasion, this farewell to our beloved house, I cannot keep still. I feel I must say a few words to express the emotion that overwhelms me, overwhelms us all—

ÁNYA [*pleads*] Uncle, please!

VÁRYA That's enough, Uncle.

GÁYEV [*crushed*] All right . . . Yellow ball in the side pocket . . . I'll keep still.

[*Enter* TROFÍMOV, *then* LOPÁKHIN.]

TROFÍMOV Ladies and gentlemen, time to go! You'll be late!

LOPÁKHIN Yepikhódov, get my coat.

LIUBÓV ANDRÉYEVNA Let me stay a little minute longer. I never really noticed these walls before, or the ceilings. I want a last look, one last long look. . . .

GÁYEV I remember when I was six, I was watching out that window, right over there. It was a holy day, Trinity Sunday,[2] I think, and I saw Father on his way to church. . . .

LIUBÓV ANDRÉYEVNA Have we got everything?

LOPÁKHIN I guess so. [*To* YEPIKHÓDOV, *who helps him on with his coat*] You keep an eye on things, Yepikhódov.

YEPIKHÓDOV [*loud, businesslike tone*] You can count on me, Yermolái Alexéyich!

LOPÁKHIN Why are you talking like that all of a sudden?

YEPIKHÓDOV I just had a drink—water. . . . It went down the wrong way.

YÁSHA [*with contempt*] Dumb hick!

LIUBÓV ANDRÉYEVNA We're all going away. There won't be a soul left on the place. . . .

LOPÁKHIN But wait till you see what happens here come spring!

[VÁRYA *grabs an umbrella from the luggage, as if she were going to hit him.* LOPÁKHIN *pretends to be terrified.*]

VÁRYA Don't get excited. It was just a joke.

TROFÍMOV You've all got to get moving! It's time to go! You'll miss your train!

VÁRYA Here's your galoshes, Pétya, behind this suitcase. [*With tears in her eyes*] Smelly old things . . .

TROFÍMOV [*puts them on*] It's time to go!

GÁYEV [*deeply moved, afraid he'll start crying*] Yes, the train . . . mustn't miss the train . . . Yellow ball in the side pocket, white in the corner . . .

LIUBÓV ANDRÉYEVNA Let's go!

LOPÁKHIN Everybody here? Nobody left? [*Closes and locks the door, left.*] Got to lock up; I've got a few things stored here. All right, let's go!

2. A celebration of the Christian doctrine of the Trinity (the belief that the Father, Son, and Holy Spirit exist together in God); in Eastern Christianity it falls on Pentecost (seven weeks after Easter).

ÁNYA Goodbye, house! Goodbye, old life!

TROFÍMOV No, hello, new life!

[Goes out with Ánya.]

*[*VÁRYA *looks around the room again; she's not eager to go.* YÁSHA *goes out with* CARLOTTA *and her little dog.]*

LOPÁKHIN So. Until next spring. Come on, let's go, everybody. Goodbye!

*[*LIUBÓV *and* GÁYEV *are left alone. It's as if they'd been waiting for this moment. They throw their arms around each other and burst out crying, but try to keep the others outside from hearing.]*

GÁYEV *[in despair]* Oh, sister, sister . . .

LIUBÓV ANDRÉYEVNA Oh, my orchard, my beautiful orchard! My life, my youth, my happiness, goodbye! Goodbye! Goodbye!

*[*ÁNYA*'s voice, joyful: "Mama!"* TROFÍMOV*'s voice, joyful, excited: "Yoo-hoo!"]*

These walls, these windows, for the last time . . . And Mama loved this room . . .

GÁYEV Oh, sister, sister . . .

*[*ÁNYA*: "Mama!"* TROFÍMOV*: "Yoo-hoo!"]*

LIUBÓV ANDRÉYEVNA We're coming!

[They leave.]

[The stage is empty. We hear the sound of the door being locked, then the carriages as they drive away. It grows very quiet. In the silence, we hear the occasional sound of an ax chopping down the cherry trees, a mournful, lonely sound. Then we hear steps. Enter FIRS *from the door, right. He wears his usual butler's livery, but with bedroom slippers. He's very ill.]*

FIRS *[goes to the door, tries the handle]* Locked. They're gone. *[Sits on the sofa.]* They forgot about me. That's all right; I'll just sit here for a bit. . . . And Leoníd Andréyich probably forgot his winter coat. *[A worried sigh]* I should have looked. . . . He's still all wet, that one. . . . *[Mumbles something we can't make out.]* Well, it's all over now, and I never even had a life to live. . . . *[Lies back.]* I'll just lie here for a bit. . . . No strength left, nothing left, not a thing . . . Oh, you. You young flibbertigibbet. *[Lies there, no longer moving.]*

[In the distance we hear a sound that seems to come from the sky, a sad sound, like a string snapping. It dies away. Everything grows quiet. We can hear the occasional sound of an ax on a tree.]

Curtain.

JOHN MILLINGTON SYNGE

1871–1909

IRELAND, which has spent much of the past five hundred years under the political and cultural domination of its larger neighbor, has played an important role in the modern English theater. William Congreve (1670–1729), RICHARD BRINSLEY SHERIDAN (1751–1816), Oliver Goldsmith (1730–1774), OSCAR WILDE (1854–1900), and GEORGE BERNARD SHAW (1856–1950) were all raised in Ireland before making their fortunes on the London stage. But although Dublin had long been an important theatrical center, Ireland did not achieve a truly national drama until the Irish Renaissance of the late nineteenth century. This movement, which brought to culture and the arts the same drive for self-determination that marked Irish nationalism in the political arena, was distinguished by a reaction against the English literary tradition, an interest in Irish folklore and the Gaelic language, and a focus on Irish themes and topics. Though the Irish Renaissance saw remarkable achievements in poetry and the other arts, some of its most enduring contributions were in drama and theater. In 1899, the Irish poet William Butler Yeats, Lady Augusta Gregory, and Edward Martyn formed the Irish Literary Theatre "to bring upon the stage the deeper thoughts and emotions of Ireland." Their vision of a native Irish theater was soon realized. The Abbey Theatre, which opened in Dublin in 1904, became one of the leading theaters of the twentieth century, and its actors were quickly recognized as forming one of the premier English-speaking companies of their time. In conjunction with these theatrical developments, the Irish Renaissance witnessed a flourishing of dramatic writing as authors availed themselves of a medium newly dedicated to Irish subjects. In one of these writers—John Millington Synge—Ireland produced one of the greatest playwrights of the modern stage. Embracing the poetic as well as the ironic, Synge challenged the theatrical assumptions of his contemporaries with a drama of exceptional vitality, lyricism, and satiric power.

Synge's reputation rests on six plays written between 1902 and 1909. With the exception of *Deirdre of the Sorrows* (1909), which dramatizes a tragic story from Celtic mythology, these plays are set in the hills and hearths of contemporary rural Ireland. In Wicklow, Galway, Kerry, Mayo, and the Aran Islands—regions of the country that he visited throughout his life—Synge found a natural world characterized by beauty and elemental power and a people steeped in folklore and tradition. The Irish peasants also spoke poetic, syntactically rich dialects of English that set them apart from the metropolitan inhabitants of Dublin and cities elsewhere in the British Isles. In his preface to *The Playboy of the Western World* (1907), Synge contrasted the natural poetry of rural speech with the language of cities and towns, and he set himself against HENRIK IBSEN (1828–1906), Émile Zola (1840–1902), and other proponents of dramatic naturalism who dealt with the reality of life "in joyless and pallid words." Arguing that every speech in a good play should be "as fully flavored as a nut or apple," Synge justified his dramatic use of this dialect: "In Ireland, for a few years more, we have a popular imagination that is fiery and magnificent, and tender; so that those of us who wish to write start with a chance that is not given to writers in places where the springtime of the local life has been forgotten, and the harvest is a memory only, and the straw has been turned into bricks."

The beliefs and concerns expressed in Synge's preface were not new, of course. European Romantic writers had celebrated nature and its rural inhabitants since the early nineteenth century, and the study of folklore and popular legends and mythology had been central to Romantic nationalism since Johann Gottfried von Herder first advocated preserving indigenous folk material in the eighteenth century. In Ireland, amateur and professional ethnographers began conducting fieldwork in the western counties in the 1890s, and the Gaelic League was founded in Dublin in 1893 "for the purpose of keeping the Irish language spoken in Ireland." But though Synge's interest in rural Ireland may have been inspired by these broader intellectual and cultural currents, his plays refuse to idealize or sentimentalize the primitive life he found there. While Synge's drama captures the traditions and lyricism of the Irish peasantry, it also portrays the harsher side of its behaviors and beliefs. In his essay "J. M. Synge and the Ireland of His Time," published two years after the playwright's death, Yeats wrote: "He loves all that has edge, all that is salt in the mouth, all that is rough to the hand, all that heightens the emotions by contrast, all that stings into life the sense of tragedy." Deeply ironic, even satiric at times, plays such as *In the Shadow of the Glen* (1903) and *The Playboy of the Western World* juxtapose poetic celebration with bitter comedy and a tragic sense of loss. Given how deeply his Dublin audience was invested in heroic or nostalgic images of the Irish peasantry during a time of intense nationalism, it should come as no surprise that this greatest of Irish playwrights was harshly criticized by many of his contemporaries.

Edmund John Millington Synge (the name is pronounced "sing") was born on April 16, 1871, in Rathfarnham, a suburb south of Dublin, to landowning Anglo-Irish parents of Protestant descent. A sickly child whose early years were solitary, he eventually was tutored at home in lieu of attending school. Having discovered a love for taking long walks in the Irish countryside, he developed an early interest in natural history; he later would join the Dublin Naturalists' Field Club. When, at the age of fourteen, he read *The Descent of Man* (1871) by Charles Darwin, Synge underwent a crisis of faith that led him, three years later, to renounce Christianity. Turning his attention from science to the arts, he began studying the violin at the age of sixteen. While enrolled at Trinity College in Dublin, where he studied Gaelic and Hebrew, he also attended the Royal Irish Academy of Music; upon receiving a B.A. from Trinity he continued his musical studies in Germany. Synge lacked the temperament to be a professional musician, however, and in 1894 he moved to Paris to study language and literature at the Sorbonne and support himself teaching English. He had been composing poems for several years and was determined to launch a career as a writer and critic.

During the years in which he distanced himself from his Protestant family upbringing, Synge had grown increasingly engaged with Irish culture. "Everything Irish became sacred," he later wrote, "and had a charm that was neither quite human nor divine." At the Sorbonne, he attended lectures on Celtic civilization; and in 1896 he met Yeats and Maud Gonne, who were at the center of a circle of revolutionary nationalists living in Paris. It was Yeats who advised him to abandon the self-consciously modern poetry he had been writing and to embrace the life of one of Ireland's most primitive regions: "Give up Paris, you will never create anything by reading Racine and Arthur Symons will al-

Fishermen with nets on the coast of Inishmore, ca. 1955.

ways be a better critic of French literature. Go to the Aran Islands. Live there as if you were one of the people themselves; express a life that has never found expression." The Aran Islands (Inishmore, Inishmaan, and Inisheer) are located 30 miles off the west coast of Ireland in Galway Bay; bearing the brunt of the North Atlantic, they are characterized by harsh conditions and a rugged, treeless beauty. Following Yeats's advice, Synge spent two weeks on the islands in 1898, the first of five such visits he would make over the next four and a half years. He stayed with the Aran Islanders, who spoke Gaelic (and only occasionally English); observed their lives, customs, and speech; and listened to their stories and other lore. In Aran, he wrote, he felt in touch with a "world of inarticulate power." While Synge gathered his notes into a book titled *The Aran Islands* (published in 1907), his observations and experiences in Aran (and elsewhere in Ireland) would find their fullest artistic form in the drama they inspired.

Synge's earliest attempt at playwriting was *When the Moon Has Set* (written 1901), a melodramatic, loosely autobiographical drama that Yeats and Lady Gregory rejected for production by the Irish Literary Theater on artistic grounds. It was not until 1902 that Synge abandoned autobiography and wrote two one-act plays set in the communities of rural Ireland. *In the Shadow of the Glen,* produced in October 1903 by the newly formed Irish National Theatre Society at Molesworth Hall, also established his turbulent relationship with the Dublin theatergoing public. The story of a Wicklow man who feigns death in order to catch his wife in an act of infidelity, *In the Shadow of the Glen* was condemned by many of its reviewers as an attack on Irish womanhood and the institution of marriage. ***RIDERS TO THE SEA,*** which opened on February 25, 1904, at Molesworth, received scattered criticism, though its tragic beauty was also recognized, and it quickly became Synge's most acclaimed play. Other plays soon followed, including *The Well of the Saints,* produced at the recently opened Abbey Theatre in February 1905. This play, about a blind couple who have their sight miraculously restored but eventually choose to return to blindness, was attacked by many as un-Irish. *The Tinker's Wedding,* which Synge wrote between 1902 and 1906, is the story of an indigent couple who try to trick a priest into marrying them; broadly comic, it was considered so inflammatory that it was not staged in Ireland until after Synge's death.

Nothing in the critical responses to these earlier plays, contentious though they often were, could have prepared Synge and his colleagues at the Irish National Theatre Society for the uproar that greeted his three-act play *The Playboy of the Western World* in January 1907 (in 1905 Synge had become the company's co-director; it had replaced the Irish Literary Theatre). Based on a tale that Synge heard in the Aran Islands, *Playboy* is the story of villagers on the coast of Mayo who take in a fugitive claiming to have murdered his father. The young man, named Christy, captivates his protectors with his tale of heroic transgression, and he woos the tavern keeper's daughter, Pegeen Mike, with his poetic speech. After his father unexpectedly shows up, though, wounded but not dead, the villagers turn on Christy—and when he tries in earnest to kill his father they set about to lynch him in a scene of jarring cruelty. With the lines between comedy and the noncomic blurred beyond recognition, Christy and his father depart, cursing the villagers for their villainy.

"The Playboy Riots," as the play's initial performances have come to be known, were among the most violent in the history of the modern theater. The play's opening-night audience sat through the first two acts in relative, if ominous, calm; but when one of the play's characters used the word "shift" (i.e., a woman's undergarment) in the third act, an uproar ensued. At performances over the following week, police were repeatedly called in as audience members grew increasingly violent in their attempts to shout down the actors. Yeats stood up and lectured the audience on their obligation to let the play be heard. Those in the audience who rioted were clearly outraged at Synge's portrayal of rural Ireland, a representation at odds with the idealized images championed by Irish nationalism. One reviewer called *The Playboy of the Western World* "an unmitigated, protracted libel upon Irish peasant men and, worse still, upon Irish peasant girlhood." That Synge himself had come from the Anglo-Irish ruling class only fanned the resentment of his audience. Though the play drew favorable attention when it was performed in London one year later, its Dublin reception guaranteed its notoriety in Ireland for decades.

Riders to the Sea, considered by many to be the finest one-act play ever written, is an exception among Synge's mature plays. Lacking the satiric realism of the later comedies, it resembles the drama of AESCHYLUS and SOPHOCLES in its simplicity of action and its atmosphere of tragic inevitability. Its world is harsh, elemental, and marked by hardship and loss but also given to moments of intense lyricism. *Riders* opens in the Aran cottage of Maurya, who has lost her husband and four of six sons to the sea. The setting is stark: nets, oilskins, a spinning wheel, and a pot-oven for cooking bread on the fire are among the few props. Several new boards stand by the wall, purchased (it turns out) to furnish a coffin for her son Michael, who is presumed to be lost at sea. Cathleen and Nora, Maurya's daughters, have been given articles of clothing found on a drowned man in Donegal, and they hide these from their mother until they have the chance to positively identify them as Michael's. Before they can do so, Maurya's youngest son, Bartley, announces that he will travel by sea in order to sell horses at the Galway fair. She pleads with him not to go, but he dismisses her concerns and leaves before she gives him her blessing. When Maurya follows Bartley to provide that blessing and some bread for his journey, she has a vision that foretells his death: as Bartley rides by the spring well on his red mare, she sees Michael riding in fine clothes on the gray pony that follows him. This fatal omen is shortly fulfilled, and the remainder of Synge's play deals with the aftermath of such irrevocable loss.

Synge drew extensively on his experiences in the Aran Islands when writing *Riders to the Sea:* riding in a curragh on a turbulent sea, attending the burial and funeral of a young man who had drowned, listening to stories like one about a woman who had a vision of her dead son riding a horse. For the original Irish National Theatre Society production, Synge insisted the play's realistic elements be recognized: the actors were shod in authentic pampooties (a form of footwear used on the slippery rocks of the Aran Islands), and they were taught how to deliver the funeral keen by a woman from Galway. But realism in

Brigit O'Dempsey, Sara Algood, and Maire O'Neill in the 1906 production of *Riders to the Sea*.

Riders to the Sea continually drifts into the mythic and the supernatural. Maurya and her two daughters recall Clotho, Lachesis, and Atropos, the three Fates of Greek mythology, who determine human life and death. Maurya's name echoes *moira* (the Greek word for fate or destiny), and the prominent spinning wheel suggests the wheel on which Clotho spins the thread of life. The death of Bartley recalls that of Hippolytus, dragged along the seacoast by his horses, as told in EURIPIDES' *Hippolytus* (428 B.C.E.) and RACINE's *Phaedra* (1677). There is Christian imagery, as well: the bread that Maurya forgets to give to her son resembles the Eucharist, and the gray horse with its ghostly rider recalls the book of Revelation: "And I saw, and behold, a pale horse, and its rider's name was Death." Finally, the action of *Riders to the Sea* is also shaped by Irish folk beliefs and traditions. The gray horse bears traces of the *púca,* a malevolent fairy spirit of Irish myth that takes the form of a horse and lures people to their death.

In part because of these mythic elements, the play's characters and actions acquire a quality of timelessness: present and past give way to a vision of universal loss that transcends time and place. In *The Aran Islands* Synge describes sitting with a group of fishermen on the shore: "I could not help feeling that I was talking with men who were under a judgment of death." The sense of fatality that permeates *Riders to the Sea* derives from a tragic loss enacted over and over again. This inevitability is conveyed in the play's language, which moves in cadences and participial phrases that interrupt linear sequence and bring the past into the present: "I'm after seeing him this day, and he riding and galloping." Individual words and phrases, such as Cathleen's description of string tied around a bundle of clothes as "perished with the salt water," have a fatalistic resonance. When Maurya delivers her powerful laments at the end of the play, surrounded by the women who represent the island community, she speaks not only of individual loss but of a condition. Religion—represented by the young priest who assures Nora that God would not leave her mother destitute "with no son living"—offers little solace in this case. The afterlife of Christian faith is decidedly absent from Synge's play. As in the tragedies of Sophocles or the elegies of Anglo-Saxon England, the mood is much darker. Writing of the play, Yeats observed, "The old woman in *Riders to the Sea,* in mourning for her six fine sons, mourns for the passing of all beauty and strength."

The years after Synge's early plays were themselves shadowed by mortality. In 1906 Synge became engaged to Molly Allgood, an actress of the Abbey company who would play the role of Pegeen Mike in *The Playboy of the Western World.* Because of Synge's deteriorating health, though, they never married. Swelling in his neck, which had first troubled him in 1897, confirmed that he had Hodgkin's disease, and a tumor discovered in his side in 1908 proved inoperable. Synge died in a Dublin nursing home on March 24, 1909. *Deirdre of the Sorrows,* which Synge left incomplete at his death, was arranged into an acting version by Yeats, Lady Gregory, and Allgood and performed at the Abbey Theatre the following year. A story of tragic love, the play is set in the world of Irish mythology with its kings, bards, warriors, and maidens. In dramatizing this world *Deirdre of the Sorrows* recalls the work of others in the Irish Renaissance, such as Yeats, who wrote about the heroic age of Irish myth and legend. But as one contemporary reviewer noted, Synge's concern in working with this mythological material was less to celebrate this age, ethereal and remote, than "to wrest the legend from its exalted plane and breathe the commonplaces of everyday life into it." In that effort, Synge's unfinished drama achieves what *Riders to the Sea* and his other plays do so notably: it brings the ordinary and the poetic together in new, deeply theatrical ways.

S.G.

Riders to the Sea

CHARACTERS

MAURYA, an old woman
BARTLEY, her son
CATHLEEN, her daughter
NORA, a younger daughter
MEN and WOMEN

SCENE: *An island off the West of Ireland.*[1]

[Cottage kitchen, with nets, oilskins, spinning-wheel, some new boards standing by the wall, etc. CATHLEEN, *a girl of about twenty, finishes kneading cake, and puts it down in the pot-oven*[2] *by the fire; then wipes*

1. Synge's play is set on Inishmore, the largest of the three Aran Islands, located about 15 miles off the west coast of Ireland.
2. A heated iron plate, made into an oven by being covered by a pot on which embers are heaped; it was used to bake "cake," a small, flattened form of bread.

her hands, and begins to spin at the wheel. NORA, *a young girl, puts her head in at the door.*]

NORA [*in a low voice*] Where is she?

CATHLEEN She's lying down, God help her, and maybe sleeping, if she's able.

[NORA *comes in softly, and takes a bundle from under her shawl.*]

[*Spinning the wheel rapidly*] What is it you have?

NORA The young priest is after bringing them. It's a shirt and a plain stocking were got off a drowned man in Donegal.[3]

[CATHLEEN *stops her wheel with a sudden movement, and leans out to listen.*]

We're to find out if it's Michael's they are, some time herself will be down looking by the sea.

CATHLEEN How would they be Michael's, Nora? How would he go the length of that way to the far north?

NORA The young priest says he's known the like of it. 'If it's Michael's they are,' says he, 'you can tell herself he's got a clean burial, by the grace of God; and if they're not his, let no one say a word about them, for she'll be getting her death,' says he, 'with crying and lamenting.'

[*The door which* NORA *half closed is blown open by a gust of wind.*]

CATHLEEN [*looking out anxiously*] Did you ask him would he stop Bartley going this day with the horses to the Galway[4] fair?

NORA 'I won't stop him,' says he; 'but let you not be afraid. Herself does be saying prayers half through the night, and the Almighty God won't leave her destitute,' says he, 'with no son living.'

CATHLEEN Is the sea bad by the white rocks, Nora?

NORA Middling bad, God help us. There's a great roaring in the west, and it's worse it'll be getting when the tide's turned to° the wind. [*She goes over to the table with the bundle.*] Shall I open it now? *against*

CATHLEEN Maybe she'd wake up on us, and come in before we'd done. [*Coming to the table*] It's a long time we'll be, and the two of us crying.

NORA [*goes to the inner door and listens*] She's moving about on the bed. She'll be coming in a minute.

CATHLEEN Give me the ladder, and I'll put them up in the turf loft,[5] the way° she won't know of them at all, and maybe when the tide turns she'll be going down to see would he be floating from the east. *so that*

3. A county on the northwest coast of Ireland, more than 100 miles north of the Aran Islands. *After:* to have just (done something).

4. A county and town on the west coast of Ireland, northeast of the Aran Islands.

5. Loft for storing turf (peat), which was used as fuel for fires.

[*They put the ladder against the gable of the chimney;* CATHLEEN *goes up a few steps and hides the bundle in the turf loft.* MAURYA *comes from the inner room.*]

MAURYA [*looking up at* CATHLEEN *and speaking querulously*] Isn't it turf enough you have for this day and evening?

CATHLEEN There's a cake baking at the fire for a short space [*throwing down the turf*], and Bartley will want it when the tide turns if he goes to Connemara.[6]

[NORA *picks up the turf and puts it round the pot-oven.*]

MAURYA [*sitting down on a stool at the fire*] He won't go this day with the wind rising from the south and west. He won't go this day, for the young priest will stop him surely.

NORA He'll not stop him, mother; and I heard Eamon Simon and Stephen Pheety and Colum Shawn saying he would go.

MAURYA Where is he itself?° *(i.e, himself)*

NORA He went down to see would there be another boat sailing in the week, and I'm thinking it won't be long till he's here now, for the tide's turning at the green head, and the hooker's[7] tacking from the east.

CATHLEEN I hear someone passing the big stones.

NORA [*looking out*] He's coming now, and he in a hurry.

BARTLEY [*comes in and looks round the room. Speaking sadly and quietly*] Where is the bit of new rope, Cathleen, was bought in Connemara?

CATHLEEN [*coming down*] Give it to him, Nora; it's on a nail by the white boards. I hung it up this morning, for the pig with the black feet was eating it.

NORA [*giving him a rope*] Is that it, Bartley?

MAURYA You'd do right to leave that rope, Bartley, hanging by the boards. [BARTLEY *takes the rope.*] It will be wanting in this place, I'm telling you, if Michael is washed up tomorrow morning, or the next morning, or any morning in the week; for it's a deep grave we'll make him, by the grace of God.

BARTLEY [*beginning to work with the rope*] I've no halter the way I can ride down on the mare, and I must go now quickly. This is the one boat going for two weeks or beyond it, and the fair will be a good fair for horses, I heard them saying below.

MAURYA It's a hard thing they'll be saying below if the body is washed up and there's no man in it to make the coffin, and I after giving a big price for the finest white boards you'd find in Connemara. [*She looks round at the boards.*]

BARTLEY How would it be washed up, and we after looking each day for nine days, and a strong wind blowing a while back from the west and south?

6. A mountainous peninsula on the Galway coast, north of the Aran Islands.

7. A light single-masted fishing vessel. *Green head:* grassy headland or promontory.

MAURYA If it isn't found itself, that wind is raising the sea, and there was a star up against the moon, and it rising in the night. If it was a hundred horses, or a thousand horses you had itself, what is the price of a thousand horses against a son where there is one son only?

BARTLEY [*working at the halter, to* CATHLEEN] Let you go down each day, and see the sheep aren't jumping in on the rye, and if the jobber° comes you can sell the pig with the black feet if there is a good price going. *livestock dealer*

MAURYA How would the like of her get a good price for a pig?

BARTLEY [*to* CATHLEEN] If the west winds holds with the last bit of the moon let you and Nora get up weed enough for another cock for the kelp.[8] It's hard set we'll be from this day with no one in it but one man to work.

MAURYA It's hard set we'll be surely the day you're drowned with the rest. What way will I live and the girls with me, and I an old woman looking for the grave?

[BARTLEY *lays down the halter, takes off his old coat, and puts on a newer one of the same flannel.*]

BARTLEY [*to* NORA] Is she coming to the pier?

NORA [*looking out*] She's passing the green head and letting fall her sails.

BARTLEY [*getting his purse° and tobacco*] I'll have half an hour to go down, and you'll see me coming again in two days, or in three days, or maybe in four days if the wind is bad. *money bag*

MAURYA [*turning round to the fire, and putting her shawl over her head*] Isn't it a hard and cruel man won't hear a word from an old woman, and she holding him from the sea?

CATHLEEN It's the life of a young man to be going to the sea, and who would listen to an old woman with one thing and she saying it over?

BARTLEY [*taking the halter*] I must go now quickly. I'll ride down on the red mare, and the grey pony 'ill run behind me. . . . The blessing of God on you. [*He goes out.*]

MAURYA [*crying out as he is in the door*] He's gone now, God spare us, and we'll not see him again. He's gone now, and when the black night is falling I'll have no son left me in the world.

CATHLEEN Why wouldn't you give him your blessing and he looking round in the door? Isn't it sorrow enough is on every one in this house without your sending him out with an unlucky word behind him, and a hard word in his ear?

[MAURYA *takes up the tongs and begins raking the fire aimlessly without looking round.*]

8. That is, gather enough kelp (used as fertilizer) to form another cone-shaped mound.

NORA [*turning towards her*] You're taking away the turf from the cake.[9]

CATHLEEN [*crying out*] The Son of God forgive us, Nora, we're after forgetting his bit of bread. [*She comes over to the fire.*]

NORA And it's destroyed° he'll be going till dark night, and he after eating nothing since the sun went up. *exhausted*

CATHLEEN [*turning the cake out of the oven*] It's destroyed he'll be surely. There's no sense left on any person in a house where an old woman will be talking for ever.

[MAURYA *sways herself on her stool.*]

[*Cutting off some of the bread and rolling it in a cloth; to* MAURYA.]

Let you go down now to the spring well and give him this and he passing. You'll see him then and the dark word will be broken, and you can say 'God speed you,' the way he'll be easy in his mind.

MAURYA [*taking the bread*] Will I be in it° as soon as himself? *there*

CATHLEEN If you go now quickly.

MAURYA [*standing up unsteadily*] It's hard set I am to walk.

CATHLEEN [*looking at her anxiously*] Give her the stick, Nora, or maybe she'll slip on the big stones.

NORA What stick?

CATHLEEN The stick Michael brought from Connemara.

MAURYA [*taking a stick* NORA *gives her*] In the big world the old people do be leaving things after them for their sons and children, but in this place it is the young men do be leaving things behind for them that do be old.

[*She goes out slowly.* NORA *goes over to the ladder.*]

CATHLEEN Wait, Nora, maybe she'd turn back quickly. She's that sorry,° God help her, you wouldn't know the thing she'd do. *wretched*

NORA Is she gone round by the bush?

CATHLEEN [*looking out*] She's gone now. Throw it down quickly, for the Lord knows when she'll be out of it again.

NORA [*getting the bundle from the loft*] The young priest said he'd be passing tomorrow, and we might go down and speak to him below if it's Michael's they are surely.

CATHLEEN [*taking the bundle*] Did he say what way they were found?

NORA [*coming down*] 'There were two men,' said he, 'and they rowing round with poteen[1] before the cocks crowed, and the oar of one of them caught the body, and they passing the black cliffs of the north.'

9. That is, preventing the bread from baking.

1. Literally, "small pot" (Irish; pronounced *puh-cheen*); illegal whiskey, often made from potatoes.

CATHLEEN [*trying to open the bundle*] Give me a knife, Nora; the string's perished with° the salt water, and there's a black knot on it you wouldn't loosen in a week. *destroyed by*

NORA [*giving her a knife*] I've heard tell it was a long way to Donegal.

CATHLEEN [*cutting the string*] It is surely. There was a man in here a while ago—the man sold us that knife—and he said if you set off walking from the rocks beyond, it would be in seven days you'd be in Donegal.

NORA And what time would a man take, and he floating?

[CATHLEEN *opens the bundle and takes out a bit of a shirt and a stocking. They look at them eagerly.*]

CATHLEEN [*in a low voice*] The Lord spare us, Nora! isn't it a queer hard thing to say if it's his they are surely?

NORA I'll get his shirt off the hook the way we can put the one flannel on the other. [*She looks through some clothes hanging in the corner.*] It's not with them, Cathleen, and where will be it?

CATHLEEN I'm thinking Bartley put it on him in the morning, for his own shirt was heavy with the salt in it. [*Pointing to the corner*] There's a bit of a sleeve was of the same stuff. Give me that and it will do.

[NORA *brings it to her and they compare the flannel.*]

It's the same stuff, Nora; but if it is itself, aren't there great rolls of it in the shops of Galway, and isn't it many another man may have a shirt of it as well as Michael himself?

NORA [*who has taken up the stocking and counted the stitches, crying out*] It's Michael, Cathleen, it's Michael; God spare his soul, and what will herself say when she hears this story, and Bartley on the sea?

CATHLEEN [*taking the stocking*] It's a plain stocking.

NORA It's the second one of the third pair I knitted, and I put up three-score stitches, and I dropped four of them.

CATHLEEN [*counts the stitches*] It's that number is in it. [*Crying out*] Ah, Nora, isn't it a bitter thing to think of him floating that way to the far north, and no one to keen him but the black hags[2] that do be flying on the sea?

NORA [*swinging herself half round, and throwing out her arms on the clothes*] And isn't it a pitiful thing when there is nothing left of a man who was a great rower and fisher but a bit of an old shirt and a plain stocking?

CATHLEEN [*after an instant*] Tell me is herself coming, Nora? I hear a little sound on the path.

NORA [*looking out*] She is, Cathleen. She's coming up to the door.

CATHLEEN Put these things away before she'll come in. Maybe it's easier she'll be after giving her blessing to

2. That is, cormorants, black diving birds with hooked beaks. *Keen:* lament bitterly; specifically, utter the traditional Irish wail of lamentation for the dead.

Bartley, and we won't let on we've heard anything the time he's on the sea.

NORA [*helping* CATHLEEN *to close the bundle*] We'll put them here in the corner.

[*They put them into a hole in the chimney corner.* CATHLEEN *goes back to the spinning-wheel.*]

Will she see it was crying I was?

CATHLEEN Keep your back to the door the way the light'll not be on you.

[NORA *sits down at the chimney corner, with her back to the door.* MAURYA *comes in very slowly, without looking at the girls, and goes over to her stool at the other side of the fire. The cloth with the bread is still in her hand. The girls look at each other, and* NORA *points to the bundle of bread.*]

[*After spinning for a moment*] You didn't give him his bit of bread?

[MAURYA *begins to keen softly, without turning round.*]

Did you see him riding down?

[MAURYA *goes on keening.*]

[*A little impatiently*] God forgive you; isn't it a better thing to raise your voice and tell what you seen, than to be making lamentation for a thing that's done? Did you see Bartley, I'm saying to you?

MAURYA [*with a weak voice*] My heart's broken from this day.

CATHLEEN [*as before*] Did you see Bartley?

MAURYA I seen the fearfullest thing.

CATHLEEN [*leaves her wheel and looks out*] God forgive you; he's riding the mare now over the green head, and the grey pony behind him.

MAURYA [*starts so that her shawl falls back from her head and shows her white tossed hair. With a frightened voice*] The grey pony behind him. . . .

CATHLEEN [*coming to the fire*] What is it ails you at all?

MAURYA [*speaking very slowly*] I've seen the fearfullest thing any person has seen since the day Bride Dara seen the dead man with the child in his arms.

CATHLEEN *and* NORA Uah.[3]

[*They crouch down in front of the old woman at the fire.*]

NORA Tell us what it is you seen.

MAURYA I went down to the spring well, and I stood there saying a prayer to myself. Then Bartley came along, and he riding on the red mare with the grey pony behind him. [*She puts up her hands, as if to hide something from her eyes.*] The Son of God spare us, Nora!

3. They are keening.

CATHLEEN What is it you seen?

MAURYA I seen Michael himself.

CATHLEEN [*speaking softly*] You did not, mother. It wasn't Michael you seen, for his body is after being found in the far north, and he's got a clean burial, by the grace of God.

MAURYA [*a little defiantly*] I'm after seeing him this day, and he riding and galloping. Bartley came first on the red mare, and I tried to say 'God speed you,' but something choked the words in my throat. He went by quickly; and 'The blessing of God on you,' says he, and I could say nothing. I looked up then, and I crying, at the grey pony, and there was Michael upon it—with fine clothes on him, and new shoes on his feet.

CATHLEEN [*begins to keen*] It's destroyed we are from this day. It's destroyed, surely.

NORA Didn't the young priest say the Almighty God won't leave her destitute with no son living?

MAURYA [*in a low voice, but clearly*] It's little the like of him knows of the sea. . . . Bartley will be lost now, and let you call in Eamon and make me a good coffin out of the white boards, for I won't live after them. I've had a husband, and a husband's father, and six sons in this house—six fine men, though it was a hard birth I had with every one of them and they coming into the world—and some of them were found and some of them were not found, but they're gone now the lot of them. . . . There were Stephen and Shawn were lost in the great wind, and found after in the Bay of Gregory[4] of the Golden Mouth, and carried up the two of them on one plank, and in by that door.

[*She pauses for a moment; the girls start as if they heard something through the door that is half open behind them.*]

NORA [*in a whisper*] Did you hear that, Cathleen? Did you hear a noise in the north-east?

CATHLEEN [*in a whisper*] There's someone after crying out by the seashore.

MAURYA [*continues without hearing anything*] There was Sheamus and his father, and his own father again, were lost in a dark night, and not a stick or sign was seen of them when the sun went up. There was Patch after was drowned out of a curragh[5] that turned over. I was sitting here with Bartley, and he a baby lying on my two knees, and I seen two women, and three women, and four women coming in, and they crossing themselves and not

4. Gregory Sound, which separates the islands of Inishmore and Inishmaan (the name is perhaps derived from the legend that Saint Gregory I, credited with inventing Gregorian chant, was buried on the Aran Islands after his coffin miraculously floated there from Rome).

5. Literally, "little ship" (Irish; pronounced *kur-uh*); a light-weight boat, made of hide or tarred canvas stretched over a wood or wicker work frame, common on the west coast of Ireland.

saying a word. I looked out then, and there were men coming after them, and they holding a thing in the half of a red sail, and water dripping out of it—it was a dry day, Nora—and leaving a track to the door.

[*She pauses with her hand stretched out towards the door. It opens softly and old women begin to come in, crossing themselves on the threshold, and kneeling down in front of the stage with red petticoats over their heads.*]

[*Half in a dream, to* CATHLEEN] Is it Patch, or Michael, or what is it at all?

CATHLEEN Michael is after being found in the far north, and when he is found there how could he be here in this place?

MAURYA There does be a power of young men floating round in the sea, and what way would they know if it was Michael they had, or another man like him, for when a man is nine days in the sea, and the wind blowing, it's hard set his own mother would be to say what man was in it.

CATHLEEN It's Michael, God spare him, for they're after sending us a bit of his clothes from the far north.

[*She reaches out and hands* MAURYA *the clothes that belonged to* MICHAEL. MAURYA *stands up slowly, and takes them in her hands.* NORA *looks out.*]

NORA They're carrying a thing among them, and there's water dripping out of it and leaving a track by the big stones.

CATHLEEN [*in a whisper to the women who have come in*] Is it Bartley it is?

ONE OF THE WOMEN It is, surely, God rest his soul.

[*Two younger women come in and pull out the table. Then men carry in the body of* BARTLEY, *laid on a plank, with a bit of a sail over it, and lay it on the table.*]

CATHLEEN [*to the women as they are doing so*] What way was he drowned?

ONE OF THE WOMEN The grey pony knocked him over into the sea, and he was washed out where there is a great surf on the white rocks.

[MAURYA *has gone over and knelt down at the head of the table. The women are keening softly and swaying themselves with a slow movement.* CATHLEEN *and* NORA *kneel at the other end of the table. The men kneel near the door.*]

MAURYA [*raising her head and speaking as if she did not see the people around her*] They're all gone now, and there isn't anything more the sea can do to me. . . . I'll have no call now to be up crying and praying when the wind breaks from the south, and you can hear the surf is in the east, and the surf is in the west, making a great stir with the two noises, and they hitting one on the other. I'll have no call now to be going down and getting Holy Water in the dark nights after Samhain,[6] and I won't care what way the sea is when the other women will be keening. [*To* NORA] Give me the Holy Water, Nora; there's a small sup° still on the dresser. *sip, mouthful*

[NORA *gives it to her.*]

[*Drops* MICHAEL*'s clothes across* BARTLEY*'s feet, and sprinkles the Holy Water over him.*] It isn't that I haven't prayed for you, Bartley, to the Almighty God. It isn't that I haven't said prayers in the dark night till you wouldn't know what I'd be saying; but it's a great rest I'll have now, and it's time, surely. It's a great rest I'll have now, and great sleeping in the long nights after Samhain, if it's only a bit of wet flour we do have to eat, and maybe a fish that would be stinking.

[*She kneels down again, crossing herself, and saying prayers under her breath.*]

CATHLEEN [*to an old man*] Maybe yourself and Eamon would make a coffin when the sun rises. We have fine white boards herself bought, God help her, thinking Michael would be found, and I have a new cake you can eat while you'll be working.

THE OLD MAN [*looking at the boards*] Are there nails with them?

CATHLEEN There are not, Colum; we didn't think of the nails.

ANOTHER MAN It's a great wonder she wouldn't think of the nails, and all the coffins she's seen made already.

CATHLEEN It's getting old she is, and broken.

[MAURYA *stands up again very slowly and spreads out the pieces of* MICHAEL*'s clothes beside the body, sprinkling them with the last of the Holy Water.*]

NORA [*in a whisper to* CATHLEEN] She's quiet now and easy; but the day Michael was drowned you could hear her crying out from this to the spring well. It's fonder she was of Michael, and would any one have thought that?

CATHLEEN [*slowly and clearly*] An old woman will be soon tired with anything she will do, and isn't it nine days herself is after crying and keening, and making great sorrow in the house?

MAURYA [*puts the empty cup mouth downwards on the table, and lays her hands together on* BARTLEY*'s feet*] They're all together this time, and the end is come. May the Almighty God have mercy on Bartley's soul, and on Michael's soul, and on the souls of Sheamus and Patch, and Stephen and Shawn [*bending her head*]; and may He

6. Literally, probably "Summer's End" (Irish; pronounced *sah-win*); November 1, in the Christian calendar All Saints' Day, originally celebrated as the end of the harvest and the beginning of winter.

have mercy on my soul, Nora, and on the soul of every one is left living in the world.

[*She pauses, and the keen rises a little more loudly from the women, then sinks away.*]

[*Continuing*] Michael has a clean burial in the far north, by the grace of the Almighty God. Bartley will have a fine coffin out of the white boards, and a deep grave surely. What more can we want than that? No man at all can be living for ever, and we must be satisfied.

[*She kneels down again and the curtain falls slowly.*]

GEORGE BERNARD SHAW

1856–1950

In the history of English drama, George Bernard Shaw stands second only to SHAKESPEARE as the playwright with the most profound influence on his own era and beyond. Winner of the Nobel Prize for Literature in 1925, Shaw was not only the most famous author of his time but also a highly regarded social critic, routinely sought after for his responses to world events and political issues. Although in the latter part of his career he was best known globally as a public intellectual, his theatrical writing was responsible for his place, long after his death in 1950, as one of the leading cultural forces of the twentieth century. Shaw's plays are still regularly revived and continue to strike audiences as relevant and compelling. This "timeliness" in his work in part reflects how little has changed at the very core of modern civilization over the past century; Shaw's tireless dissection of social ills as well as his insightful grasp of human motivations and foibles also enables his plays to speak to each generation anew. Yet the truthfulness and acuity of his vision would not matter much to audiences if the plays themselves were not such exemplars of theatrical craftsmanship. Shaw's ability to interweave captivating narratives and memorable characters with social critique and, above all, humor sets him apart in the pantheon of modern drama. ***PYGMALION*** (1913) is one of the most popular, and arguably among the very finest, of Shaw's comedies. Gently poking fun at the pretensions of the lower class, and the idiosyncrasies of the upper class, *Pygmalion* entrances us with fairy-tale transformations and the possibility of romance; at the same time, it exposes the very real economic and gender inequities that continue to plague our modern world.

Shaw was born in 1856 to an Irish Protestant family that had more aspirations to social position than their father's income—reduced by his alcoholism—could sustain. George Carr Shaw cut short his son's formal education at age fifteen and sent him to work to help support his mother and two older sisters. Shaw spent five years as a clerk in a land agency, experience he would later use in his first play, *Widowers' Houses* (1892), which considers the hypocrisies of slum landlords. Shaw's mother, Lucinda Elizabeth Gurly Shaw, a talented singer, focused much of her time and energy on her music and, apparently, on her voice teacher, George J. Vandeleur Lee, with whom she may have been romantically involved. In 1873, Shaw's mother followed Lee to London, taking her two daughters with her. Shaw joined them in 1876. His first employment there was as a ghostwriter of music reviews for Lee, and he parlayed what he learned into lifelong journalistic work as a music, art, theater, and social critic. But Shaw desired a literary career, and he drafted a novel, *Immaturity* (written 1879), that he hoped would establish him both professionally and financially. Over the next four years, he composed four additional novels, only one of which, *Cashel Byron's Profession* (1886; rev. ed., 1901), saw any real success.

In 1884, Shaw discovered the newly organized Fabian Society, a socialist organization named after the Roman general Fabius Cunctator (the Delayer); its guiding principle was the idea that the best way to accomplish political and social reform was through the calculated, gradual infiltration of established channels of power. In the late nineteenth century and into the first decades of the twentieth, the Fabian Society came to have increasing influence on English politics, attracting into its ranks some of the foremost figures of the era—including its leaders, Sidney and Beatrice Webb, and the novelist H. G. Wells. Through the Fabians Shaw also met Charlotte Payne Townshend, whom he married in 1898. Shaw's writing skills and lecturing acumen soon made him the most visible member of this elite group dedicated to the pursuit of what Shaw deemed its "Socialist and Democratic objects."

In 1890, Shaw began to draw together his passionate commitment to the arts and to socialism by delivering a series of lectures for the Society on HENRIK IBSEN, whose dramas had recently been translated into English by Shaw's friend William Archer. As these plays began to be produced on the London stage, they galvanized broader public debate, especially about marriage and the role of women in modern society. Shaw published his talks the following year as *The Quintessence of Ibsenism,* and his analysis of these pioneering works of the modern theater helped him discover his own vocation as a dramatist.

The timing of these events could not have been more auspicious. Shaw emerged as a playwright just as theatrical modernism was beginning to coalesce as a movement across Europe. Shaw championed the arrival of the "New Drama" in England, leading a theatrical revolution that sought to replace formulaic native melodrama and Continental well-made plays with works closely engaged with the pressing issues of the day. Shaw also quickly learned that humor was a highly effective vehicle for social critique, and he exploited its didactic potential throughout his career. A remarkably prolific author, Shaw generated new plays and essays annually through the early 1920s, and was still writing steadily through World War II.

Pygmalion brings together many of Shaw's lifelong concerns: class and economic structures, shifting gender roles, and England's global influence and power, among others. The play's opening scene, set in London's Covent Garden, provides an opportunity for Shaw to introduce a cross section of character types and ranks in English society. As members of the upper class search for taxis to take them home from an evening at the theater, a "poor girl," Eliza Doolittle, tries to earn her meager income selling bunches of flowers to the passersby. Henry Higgins, a professor of phonetics who frequents the area to study its range of English idioms, hears Eliza, whose Cockney speech interests him. Quite by accident, he also encounters an amateur linguist, Colonel Pickering, an expert in Indian dialects who has come to London to meet him, and Higgins invites Pickering to his home. Eliza overhears Higgins giving out his address, and she shows up the next day to ask Higgins to teach her "genteel" speech, so that she will be qualified to work in a flower shop instead of on the streets. Higgins bets Pickering that he can teach Eliza convincingly to speak as a member of the upper class and comport herself as a duchess. But what will it mean for Eliza to appear to be what she is not? What happens when one is removed from one's "natural" place in the social order? While in its plot *Pygmalion* echoes such tales as "The Ugly Duckling," Shaw's transformation narrative also reflects the real and pressing concerns faced by working-class women with severely limited financial options to improve their lives.

Shaw took his title from a classical myth, best known today in the version that appears in book 10 of Ovid's *Metamorphoses*. Pygmalion, "revolted by the many faults which nature has implanted in the female sex," carves a statue "lovelier than any woman born." He promptly falls in love with his creation, and prays to the goddess of love for a wife like his "ivory maid" (translation by Mary M. Innes). Venus brings the statue to life, and Pygmalion immediately marries and impregnates Galatea. Such stories of male construction of idealized womanhood pervade Western literature, and Shaw could have drawn on many versions of this myth, including W. S. Gilbert's theatrical extravaganza *Pygmalion and Galatea* (1871). Higgins's claim "I said I'd make a woman of you; and I have," coupled with his assertion (also in act 5) that he has "created this thing out of the squashed cabbage leaves of Covent Garden," indisputably connects him to this tradition. Shaw's rendition may also have been influenced by even darker variants of such tales, such as Mary Shelley's gothic novel *Frankenstein* (1818), which depicts the uncontrollability of creations once they are brought to life. Echoing Shelley's label for Frankenstein's monster, Higgins refers to Eliza as "the creature," ultimately damning his "own folly in having lavished hard-earned knowledge and the treasure of [his] regard" on her.

Shaw weaves together this creation myth with another equally powerful narrative, a tale of a girl magically transformed, as was Cinderella, from rags to riches. By asserting that he can make a "duchess" from a "draggle-tailed guttersnipe," Higgins presents himself as the modern-day fairy godfather who will provide Eliza with clothes fit for an ambassador's party and with rides in a taxi, almost as magical to her as a pumpkin coach. But here, too, Shaw introduces a darker tone by also depicting Higgins as the evil stepfather/witch out of a story like "Snow White," tempting Eliza with sweets and munching on an apple taken from the same dessert stand.

For audiences *Pygmalion*'s enduring appeal clearly lies in part in the teasingly undefined and unresolved relationship of Higgins and Eliza. Shaw builds the comedy, which he subtitled a "A Romance in Five Acts," around Higgins's disavowals of romantic interest in Eliza as well as Eliza's need for "a little kindness" and her "right to be loved." Eliza maintains that "the sort of feeling" she wants from Higgins is not the same as that experienced by men such as the poor but aristocratic Freddy Eynsford Hill, who writes "sheets and sheets" of love letters to her. Shaw always insisted that his subtitle should suggest an older sense of the term *romance*—the sense in which it is

Left to right: Edmund Gurney as Alfred Doolittle, Stella Campbell as his daughter, Eliza Doolittle, and Herbert Beerbohm Tree as Professor Henry Higgins in the original 1914 production of *Pygmalion*.

applied to the late plays of Shakespeare, which similarly depict mythic transformations and adventures beyond the everyday. Nevertheless, the agonistic dynamic between Higgins and Eliza has struck many audiences and critics as the verbal equivalent of sexual foreplay, in the tradition of Beatrice and Benedick in Shakespeare's *Much Ado about Nothing* (ca. 1598), or Mirabel and Millimant in William Congreve's *The Way of the World* (1700). From the first production of *Pygmalion* forward, Shaw had to fight both actors' inclinations and audiences' expectations that the comedy end conventionally, in marriage. In that legendary first staging, Herbert Beerbohm Tree (Higgins) got around Shaw by tossing flowers to Stella Campbell (Eliza) right before the final curtain to signal the pair's ultimate union. Well aware of theatergoers' delight at this gesture, Tree told the irate Shaw, "My ending makes money; you ought to be grateful." Shaw responded, "Your ending is damnable: you ought to be shot."

The critical and theatrical controversy that erupted over the play's lack of narrative closure has perennially overshadowed explorations of other social and political issues raised in the play. It is certainly possible that Shaw perceived the amatory dynamic at work in *Pygmalion,* but actively sought to expose the darker realities behind such romantic fantasies. Shortly before Shaw conceived the play, the London periodical *Pall Mall Gazette* featured an exposé of white slavery that prompted a public debate over sexual predation and may have contributed to the drama's aura of barely disguised sexual threat. The journal's revelations of the sexual availability and vulnerability of young working-class women, and their exploitation by men in more economically privileged positions, would certainly have been familiar to Shaw's audiences. That Stella Campbell, for whom Shaw created the role of Eliza, was already known to audiences through her prior star turns in highly sexualized "fallen woman" roles, such as in Arthur Pinero's *The Second Mrs. Tanqueray* (1893), only complicated their perception of her and the reception of *Pygmalion*.

Shaw uses details of language—what he calls "phonetics"—to explore class boundaries and their potential malleability. He overtly links economics with dialect and grammar by suggesting that class position is culturally bound to speech. Through Higgins (whom Shaw partly modeled on Henry Sweet, a noted philologist he had met in 1880), Shaw states that the lower class's acquisition of "new speech"—by which he means what came to be known as Standard British English—can "fil[l] up the deepest gulf that separates class from class and soul from soul." He sets up this major arc of the play in act 1, when Higgins remarks: "You see this creature with her kerbstone English: the English that will keep her in the gutter to the end of her days. . . . [I]n three months I could pass that girl off as a duchess. . . . I could even get her a place as lady's maid or shop assistant, which requires better English." In Higgins's idealized vision, once the marker of lower-class status is removed from speech, individuals

Stella Campbell, for whom Shaw created the role of Eliza.

not only will be able to move upward through social ranks, they will also be able to realize their full potential economically, intellectually, and spiritually.

The juxtaposition of two branches of linguistic inquiry undertaken by Higgins and Pickering—one rooted in the British class system, the other emerging from its imperial endeavors—cannot be accidental. Shaw had already anonymously written the manifesto *Fabianism and the Empire* (1900) for the Fabian Society and had dramatized the familiar parallel of the British and Roman empires in *Caesar and Cleopatra* (written 1898). In *Pygmalion* Shaw demonstrates how language can be used either to perpetuate or to level social distinctions both at home and, by extension, in the colonies. He combines the established idea that British English should be the vehicle for the education and enculturation of colonized natives with social reformers' notions that Britain's underclass had much in common with its colonial "Others."

Shaw uses a streamlined version of the Elizabethan dramatic structure of main plot and comic subplot to develop his themes of language and class. Eliza's willing transfiguration through speech has its comic counterpart in her father's resistance to his removal from the legions of "the undeserving poor" and forced embrace of "middle-class morality" when he unexpectedly receives a sizable legacy. The character of Alfred Doolittle owes much to earlier Victorian literature, especially the novels of Charles Dickens (1812–1870) and the dramas of T. W. Robertson (1829–1871), with their depictions of colorful laggards and other lowlifes. These Victorian characterological influences emerged in Shaw's earliest plays—including *Widowers' Houses,* which featured the rent collector Lickcheese; in *Pygmalion* Shaw more fully and pointedly uses Doolittle to expose the hypocrisy and pretensions of elevated class position through the resolutely unreformed dustman's lectures on "Moral Reform"—lectures that, under the terms of the will that irrevocably changes his social position, he must deliver.

Some critics have contrasted the "human" comedy of Eliza to the "social" comedy of her father, claiming that only the latter is about class. But Shaw's grounding in socialism was too thorough to allow him to separate an understanding of modern humanity from individuals' placement in a class system. Rather, through the triangulated relations of Eliza, Pickering, and Higgins, we come to realize that class position has both external markers and intrinsic qualities. Eliza learns that "apart from the things anyone can pick up (the dressing and the proper way of speaking, and so on), the difference between a lady and a flower girl is not how she behaves, but how shes treated." Henry's mother sees Eliza's transformation from still another perspective: the tension between the appearance of elevated class position and the economic realities of women's lives. Mrs. Higgins questions her son's having taught Eliza "the manners and habits that disqualify a fine lady from earning her own living without giving her a fine lady's income." Eliza pointedly comes to understand the price of class standing for women without independent means—the necessity of finding a husband in a society that still saw marriage as the only "profession" appropriate to real ladies: "I sold flowers. I didnt sell myself. Now youve made a lady of me I'm not fit to sell anything else."

Though Shaw's postscript spells out Eliza's later career in some detail, his play's intentionally ambiguous ending leaves unclear whether she will marry the impecunious Freddy Eynsford Hill, "as soon as hes able to support me," or teach phonetics. It could well be that the financial and emotional independence she craves if she "cant have kindness" proved too threatening to dramatize fully at that time. Tree's conventionally romantic gesture at the final curtain reassured his audiences—members of a society that could not yet accept women's suffrage and other struggles for human equality—that the social problems Shaw placed within the spotlight could be easily resolved. Yet the continued theatrical appeal of *Pygmalion* suggests that the issues Shaw depicts are with us still. Not only can we appreciate the value of complexity and indeterminacy, but such ambiguity may well affirm, better than any pat ending, the realities of our lives.

J.E.G.

Pygmalion
A Romance in Five Acts

CHARACTERS

CLARA EYNSFORD HILL
MRS. EYNSFORD HILL
FREDDY EYNSFORD HILL
ELIZA DOOLITTLE
COLONEL PICKERING
HENRY HIGGINS
MRS. PEARCE
ALFRED DOOLITTLE
MRS. HIGGINS
A PARLOR-MAID
BYSTANDERS

Act 1

[*Covent Garden*[1] *at* 11.15 *p.m. Torrents of heavy summer rain. Cab whistles blowing frantically in all directions. Pedestrians running for shelter into the market and under the portico of St. Paul's Church, where there are already several people, among them a lady and her daughter in evening dress. They are all peering out gloomily at the rain, except one man with his back turned to the rest, who seems wholly preoccupied with a notebook in which he is writing busily.*

The church clock strikes the first quarter.]

THE DAUGHTER [*in the space between the central pillars, close to the one on her left*] I'm getting chilled to the bone. What can Freddy be doing all this time? Hes[2] been gone twenty minutes.

THE MOTHER [*on her daughter's right*] Not so long. But he ought to have got us a cab by this.

A BYSTANDER [*on the lady's right*] He wont get no cab not until half-past eleven, missus, when they come back after dropping their theatre fares.

THE MOTHER But we must have a cab. We cant stand here until half-past eleven. It's too bad.

THE BYSTANDER Well, it aint my fault, missus.

THE DAUGHTER If Freddy had a bit of gumption, he would have got one at the theatre door.

THE MOTHER What could he have done, poor boy?

THE DAUGHTER Other people got cabs. Why couldnt he?

[FREDDY *rushes in out of the rain from the Southampton Street side, and comes between them closing a dripping umbrella. He is a young man of twenty, in evening dress, very wet around the ankles.*]

THE DAUGHTER Well, havnt you got a cab?

FREDDY Theres not one to be had for love or money.

1. The site of London's main produce and flower market from the 1600s until 1974, in Westminster; also the site of major entertainment venues, including the Royal Opera House and the Drury Lane Theatre.

2. An example of one of the spelling reforms advocated by Shaw, who argued that the apostrophe was unnecessary in most contractions (he also insisted on dropping the final *e* from Shakespeare).

THE MOTHER Oh, Freddy, there must be one. You cant have tried.

THE DAUGHTER It's too tiresome. Do you expect us to go and get one ourselves?

FREDDY I tell you theyre all engaged. The rain was so sudden: nobody was prepared; and everybody had to take a cab. Ive been to Charing Cross one way and nearly to Ludgate Circus the other;[3] and they were all engaged.

THE MOTHER Did you try Trafalgar Square?[4]

FREDDY There wasnt one at Trafalgar Square.

THE DAUGHTER Did you try?

FREDDY I tried as far as Charing Cross Station. Did you expect me to walk to Hammersmith?[5]

THE DAUGHTER You havnt tried at all.

THE MOTHER You really are very helpless, Freddy. Go again; and dont come back until you have found a cab.

FREDDY I shall simply get soaked for nothing.

THE DAUGHTER And what about us? Are we to stay here all night in this draught, with next to nothing on. You selfish pig—

FREDDY Oh, very well: I'll go, I'll go.

[*He opens his umbrella and dashes off Strandwards,*[6] *but comes into collision with a flower girl, who is hurrying in for shelter, knocking her basket out of her hands. A blinding flash of lightning, followed instantly by a rattling peal of thunder, orchestrates the incident.*]

THE FLOWER GIRL Nah then, Freddy: look wh' y' gowin, deah.

FREDDY Sorry.

[*He rushes off.*]

THE FLOWER GIRL [*picking up her scattered flowers and replacing them in the basket*] Theres menners f' yer! Te-oo banches o voylets trod into the mad.

[*She sits down on the plinth of the column, sorting her flowers, on the lady's right. She is not at all an attractive person. She is perhaps eighteen, perhaps twenty, hardly older. She wears a little sailor hat of black straw that has long been exposed to the dust and soot of London and has seldom if ever been brushed. Her hair needs washing rather badly: its mousy color can hardly be natural. She wears a shoddy black coat that reaches nearly to her knees and is shaped to her waist. She has a brown skirt with a coarse apron. Her boots are much the worse for wear. She is no doubt as clean as she can afford to be; but compared to the ladies she is very dirty. Her features are no worse than theirs; but their condition leaves something to be desired; and she needs the services of a dentist.*]

THE MOTHER How do you know that my son's name is Freddy, pray?

THE FLOWER GIRL Ow, eez ye-ooa san, is e? Wal, fewd dan y' de-ooty bawmz a mather should, eed now bettern to spawl a pore gel's flahrzn than ran awy athaht[7] pyin. Will ye-oo py me f'them? [*Here, with apologies, this desperate*

3. Freddy has walked more than a half mile in different directions: first southwest to Charing Cross, the busy intersection of a number of major Westminster thoroughfares, and then east to Ludgate Circus, near the entrance to the old City of London.
4. A large plaza near Charing Cross.
5. The westernmost of the inner London boroughs, several miles beyond Charing Cross.
6. That is, toward the Strand, a street in Westminster south of Covent Garden where many theaters were located.
7. Without. *Fewd dan y' de-ooty bawmz:* if you'd done your duty by him.

attempt to represent her dialect without a phonetic alphabet must be abandoned as unintelligible outside London.][8]

THE DAUGHTER Do nothing of the sort, mother. The idea!

THE MOTHER Please allow me, Clara. Have you any pennies?

THE DAUGHTER No. I've nothing smaller than sixpence.[9]

THE FLOWER GIRL [*hopefully*] I can give you change for a tanner,[1] kind lady.

THE MOTHER [*to* CLARA] Give it to me. [CLARA *parts reluctantly.*] Now [*To the* GIRL] This is for your flowers.

THE FLOWER GIRL Thank you kindly, lady.

THE DAUGHTER Make her give you the change. These things are only a penny a bunch.

THE MOTHER Do hold your tongue, Clara. [*To the* GIRL] You can keep the change.

THE FLOWER GIRL Oh, thank you, lady.

THE MOTHER Now tell me how you know that young gentleman's name.

THE FLOWER GIRL I didnt.

THE MOTHER I heard you call him by it. Dont try to deceive me.

THE FLOWER GIRL [*protesting*] Whos trying to deceive you? I called him Freddy or Charlie same as you might yourself if you was talking to a stranger and wished to be pleasant. [*She sits down beside her basket.*]

THE DAUGHTER Sixpence thrown away! Really, mamma, you might have spared Freddy that. [*She retreats in disgust behind the pillar.*]

[*An elderly gentleman of the amiable military type rushes into shelter, and closes a dripping umbrella. He is in the same plight as* FREDDY, *very wet about the ankles. He is in evening dress, with a light overcoat. He takes the place left vacant by the daughter's retirement.*]

THE GENTLEMAN Phew!

THE MOTHER [*to the* GENTLEMAN] Oh, sir, is there any sign of its stopping?

THE GENTLEMAN I'm afraid not. It started worse than ever about two minutes ago. [*He goes to the plinth beside the flower girl; puts up his foot on it; and stoops to turn down his trouser ends.*]

THE MOTHER Oh, dear! [*She retires sadly and joins her daughter.*]

THE FLOWER GIRL [*taking advantage of the military gentleman's proximity to establish friendly relations with him*] If it's worse it's a sign it's nearly over. So cheer up, Captain; and buy a flower off a poor girl.

THE GENTLEMAN I'm sorry, I havnt any change.

THE FLOWER GIRL I can give you change, Captain.

THE GENTLEMAN For a sovereign?[2] Ive nothing less.

THE FLOWER GIRL Garn! Oh do buy a flower off me, Captain. I can change half-a-crown.[3] Take this for tuppence.[4]

8. Shaw's note.
9. That is, six pennies, roughly equivalent in value to $2 today. Before the decimalization of U.K. currency in 1971, the pound was worth twenty shillings, and each shilling was worth twelve pence.
1. Nickname for a sixpence coin.
2. A coin worth one pound, roughly equivalent to $80 today.
3. Go on!
4. Two pence (a single coin). *Half-a-crown:* a coin worth two and a half shillings, roughly equivalent to $10 today.

THE GENTLEMAN Now dont be troublesome: theres a good girl. [*Trying his pockets*] I really havnt any change—Stop: heres three hapence,[5] if thats any use to you. [*He retreats to the other pillar.*]

THE FLOWER GIRL [*disappointed, but thinking three halfpence better than nothing*] Thank you, sir.

THE BYSTANDER [*to the girl*] You be careful: give him a flower for it. Theres a bloke[6] here behind taking down every blessed word youre saying. [*All turn to the man who is taking notes.*]

THE FLOWER GIRL [*springing up terrified*] I aint done nothing wrong by speaking to the gentleman. Ive a right to sell flowers if I keep off the kerb.[7] [*Hysterically*] I'm a respectable girl: so help me, I never spoke to him except to ask him to buy a flower off me. [*General hubbub, mostly sympathetic to the* FLOWER GIRL, *but deprecating her excessive sensibility. Cries of* Dont start hollerin. Whos hurting you? Nobody's going to touch you. Whats the good of fussing? Steady on. Easy, easy, etc., *come from the elderly staid spectators, who pat her comfortingly. Less patient ones bid her shut her head,*[8] *or ask her roughly what is wrong with her. A remoter group, not knowing what the matter is, crowd in and increase the noise with question and answer:* Whats the row? What she do? Where is he? A tec[9] taking her down. What! him? Yes: him over there: Took money off the gentleman, etc. *The* FLOWER GIRL, *distraught and mobbed, breaks through them to the gentleman, crying wildly.*] Oh, sir, dont let him charge me. You dunno what it means to me. Theyll take away my character[1] and drive me on the streets for speaking to gentlemen. They—

THE NOTE TAKER [*coming forward on her right, the rest crowding after him*] There, there, there, there! whos hurting you, you silly girl? What do you take me for?

THE BYSTANDER It's all right: hes a gentleman: look at his boots. [*Explaining to the* NOTE TAKER] She thought you was a copper's nark, sir.

THE NOTE TAKER [*with quick interest*] Whats a copper's nark?

THE BYSTANDER [*inapt at definition*] It's a—well, it's a copper's nark, as you might say. What else would you call it? A sort of informer.

THE FLOWER GIRL [*still hysterical*] I take my Bible oath I never said a word—

THE NOTE TAKER [*overbearing but good-humored*] Oh, shut up, shut up. Do I look like a policeman?

THE FLOWER GIRL [*far from reassured*] Then what did you take down my words for? How do I know whether you took me down right? You just shew[2] me what youve wrote about me. [*The* NOTE TAKER *opens his book and holds it steadily under her nose, though the pressure of the mob trying to read it over his shoulders would upset a weaker man.*] Whats that? That aint proper writing. I cant read that.

THE NOTE TAKER I can. [*Reads, reproducing her pronunciation exactly.*] "Cheer ap, Keptin; n' baw ya flahr orf a pore gel."

5. Half-penny coins.
6. Man.
7. Curb.
8. That is, shut up.
9. Detective (slang).
1. Testimony about an employee's qualities, provided by the employer; more generally, reputation. A woman who lost her reputation, and who therefore was unable to find legal work, was in danger of being driven into prostitution ("on the streets").
2. Show.

THE FLOWER GIRL [*much distressed*] It's because I called him Captain. I meant no harm. [*To the* GENTLEMAN] Oh, sir, dont let him lay a charge agen[3] me for a word like that. You—

THE GENTLEMAN Charge! I make no charge. [*To the* NOTE TAKER] Really, sir, if you are a detective, you need not begin protecting me against molestation by young women until I ask you. Anybody could see that the girl meant no harm.

THE BYSTANDERS GENERALLY [*demonstrating against police espionage*] Course they could. What business is it of yours? You mind your own affairs. He wants promotion, he does. Taking down people's words! Girl never said a word to him. What harm if she did? Nice thing a girl cant shelter from the rain without being insulted, etc., etc., etc. [*She is conducted by the more sympathetic demonstrators back to her plinth, where she resumes her seat and struggles with her emotion.*]

THE BYSTANDER He aint a tec. Hes a blooming busybody: thats what he is. I tell you, look at his boots.

THE NOTE TAKER [*turning on him genially*] And how are all your people down at Selsey?[4]

THE BYSTANDER [*suspiciously*] Who told you my people come from Selsey?

THE NOTE TAKER Never you mind. They did. [*To the* GIRL] How do you come to be up so far east? You were born in Lisson Grove.[5]

THE FLOWER GIRL [*appalled*] Oh, what harm is there in my leaving Lisson Grove? It wasnt fit for a pig to live in; and I had to pay four-and-six[6] a week. [*In tears*] Oh, boo—hoo—oo—

THE NOTE TAKER Live where you like; but stop that noise.

THE GENTLEMAN [*to the* GIRL] Come, come! he cant touch you: you have a right to live where you please.

A SARCASTIC BYSTANDER [*thrusting himself between the* NOTE TAKER *and the* GENTLEMAN] Park Lane, for instance. Id like to go into the Housing Question[7] with you, I would.

THE FLOWER GIRL [*subsiding into a brooding melancholy over her basket, and talking very low-spiritedly to herself*] I'm a good girl, I am.

THE SARCASTIC BYSTANDER [*not attending to her*] Do you know where *I* come from?

THE NOTE TAKER [*promptly*] Hoxton.[8]

[*Titterings. Popular interest in the* NOTE TAKER*'s performance increases.*]

THE SARCASTIC ONE [*amazed*] Well, who said I didnt? Bly me![9] You know everything, you do.

THE FLOWER GIRL [*still nursing her sense of injury*] Aint no call to meddle with me, he aint.

3. Against.
4. A town on the coast of England, directly south of London.
5. A district of northwest London notorious in Shaw's day for slums, crime, and prostitution.
6. That is, four shillings and sixpence (the standard form of expressing amounts of these currencies).
7. The early twentieth-century debate over the need to provide adequate, affordable housing for the working classes. *Park Lane:* one of the most fashionable streets in London, about a mile west of Covent Garden.
8. A district of central London known for its theaters and music halls, as well as its overcrowding and slums.
9. That is, blimey, a shortened form of "gorblimey" (God blind me!), an exclamation of surprise.

THE BYSTANDER [*to her*] Of course he aint. Dont you stand it from him. [*To the* NOTE TAKER] See here: what call have you to know about people what never offered to meddle with you? Wheres your warrant?

SEVERAL BYSTANDERS [*encouraged by this seeming point of law*] Yes: wheres your warrant?

THE FLOWER GIRL Let him say what he likes. I dont want to have no truck with him.

THE BYSTANDER You take us for dirt under your feet, dont you? Catch you taking liberties with a gentleman!

THE SARCASTIC BYSTANDER Yes: tell him where he come from if you want to go fortune-telling.

THE NOTE TAKER Cheltenham, Harrow, Cambridge, and India.[1]

THE GENTLEMAN Quite right. [*Great laughter. Reaction in the* NOTE TAKER*'s favor. Exclamations of* He knows all about it. Told him proper. Hear him tell the toff[2] where he come from? etc.] May I ask, sir, do you do this for your living at a music hall?

THE NOTE TAKER Ive thought of that. Perhaps I shall some day.

[*The rain has stopped; and the persons on the outside of the crowd begin to drop off.*]

THE FLOWER GIRL [*resenting the reaction*] Hes no gentleman, he aint, to interfere with a poor girl.

THE DAUGHTER [*out of patience, pushing her way rudely to the front and displacing the* GENTLEMAN, *who politely retires to the other side of the pillar*] What on earth is Freddy doing? I shall get pneumonia if I stay in this draught any longer.

THE NOTE TAKER [*to himself, hastily making a note of her pronunciation of "monia"*] Earlscourt.[3]

THE DAUGHTER [*violently*] Will you please keep your impertinent remarks to yourself?

THE NOTE TAKER Did I say that out loud? I didnt mean to. I beg your pardon. Your mother's Epsom,[4] unmistakeably.

THE MOTHER [*advancing between her* DAUGHTER *and the* NOTE TAKER] How very curious! I was brought up in Largelady Park, near Epsom.

THE NOTE TAKER [*uproariously amused*] Ha! ha! What a devil of a name! Excuse me. [*To the* DAUGHTER] You want a cab, do you?

THE DAUGHTER Dont dare speak to me.

THE MOTHER Oh, please, please Clara. [*Her* DAUGHTER *repudiates her with an angry shrug and retires haughtily.*] We should be so grateful to you, sir, if you found us a cab. [*The* NOTE TAKER *produces a whistle.*] Oh, thank you. [*She joins her* DAUGHTER.]

[*The* NOTE TAKER *blows a piercing blast.*]

THE SARCASTIC BYSTANDER There! I knowed he was a plain-clothes copper.

1. In effect, a summary of the gentleman's life: born in Cheltenham, a town in Gloucestershire, west of London; educated first at Harrow, a prestigious private school for boys in a borough of London, and then at Cambridge University, in Cambridge; and finally embarked on a career in India, which, as a large part of the British Empire, required the services of many British army officers and administrators.

2. Slightly derogatory slang term for a well-dressed gentleman.

3. That is, Earls Court, a well-to-do section of west London.

4. A suburb on the western periphery of greater London, known for horseracing.

THE BYSTANDER That aint a police whistle: thats a sporting whistle.

THE FLOWER GIRL [*still preoccupied with her wounded feelings*] Hes no right to take away my character. My character is the same to me as any lady's.

THE NOTE TAKER I dont know whether youve noticed it; but the rain stopped about two minutes ago.

THE BYSTANDER So it has. Why didnt you say so before? and us losing our time listening to your silliness. [*He walks off towards the Strand.*]

THE SARCASTIC BYSTANDER I can tell where you come from. You come from Anwell. Go back there.

THE NOTE TAKER [*helpfully*] Hanwell.[5]

THE SARCASTIC BYSTANDER [*affecting great distinction of speech*] Thenk you, teacher. Haw haw! So long.

[*He touches his hat with mock respect and strolls off.*]

THE FLOWER GIRL Frightening people like that! How would he like it himself.

THE MOTHER It's quite fine now, Clara. We can walk to a motor bus. Come.

[*She gathers her skirts above her ankles and hurries off towards the Strand.*]

THE DAUGHTER But the cab—[*Her mother is out of hearing.*] Oh, how tiresome!

[*She follows angrily.*]

[*All the rest have gone except the* NOTE TAKER, *the* GENTLEMAN, *and the* FLOWER GIRL, *who sits arranging her basket, and still pitying herself in murmurs.*]

THE FLOWER GIRL Poor girl! Hard enough for her to live without being worrited and chivied.[6]

THE GENTLEMAN [*returning to his former place on the* NOTE TAKER*'s left*] How do you do it, if I may ask?

THE NOTE TAKER Simply phonetics. The science of speech. Thats my profession: also my hobby. Happy is the man who can make a living by his hobby! You can spot an Irishman or a Yorkshireman by his brogue. *I* can place any man within six miles. I can place him within two miles in London. Sometimes within two streets.

THE FLOWER GIRL Ought to be ashamed of himself, unmanly coward!

THE GENTLEMAN But is there a living in that?

THE NOTE TAKER Oh yes. Quite a fat one. This is an age of upstarts. Men begin in Kentish Town with £80 a year, and end in Park Lane with a hundred thousand.[7] They want to drop Kentish Town; but they give themselves away every time they open their mouths. Now I can teach them—

THE FLOWER GIRL Let him mind his own business and leave a poor girl—

THE NOTE TAKER [*explosively*] Woman: cease this detestable boohooing instantly; or else seek the shelter of some other place of worship.

THE FLOWER GIRL [*with feeble defiance*] Ive a right to be here if I like, same as you.

5. Dropped *h*s are typical of Cockney pronunciation. Hanwell, a working-class precinct of western London, contained a lunatic asylum founded in 1831.

6. That is, worried and hounded.

7. That is, men rise from grim working-class beginnings (Kentish Town is in northwest London) to become millionaires.

THE NOTE TAKER A woman who utters such depressing and disgusting sounds has no right to be anywhere—no right to live. Remember that you are a human being with a soul and the divine gift of articulate speech: that your native language is the language of Shakespear and Milton and The Bible;[8] and dont sit there crooning like a bilious pigeon.

THE FLOWER GIRL [*quite overwhelmed, and looking up at him in mingled wonder and deprecation without daring to raise her head*] Ah-ah-ah-ow-ow-ow-oo!

THE NOTE TAKER [*whipping out his book*] Heavens! what a sound! [*He writes; then holds out the book and reads, reproducing her vowels exactly.*] Ah-ah-ah-ow-ow-ow-oo!

THE FLOWER GIRL [*tickled by the performance, and laughing in spite of herself*] Garn!

THE NOTE TAKER You see this creature with her kerbstone English: the English that will keep her in the gutter to the end of her days. Well, sir, in three months I could pass that girl off as a duchess at an ambassador's garden party. I could even get her a place as lady's maid or shop assistant, which requires better English. Thats the sort of thing I do for commercial millionaires. And on the profits of it I do genuine scientific work in phonetics, and a little as a poet on Miltonic lines.

THE GENTLEMAN I am myself a student of Indian dialects; and—

THE NOTE TAKER [*eagerly*] Are you? Do you know Colonel Pickering, the author of Spoken Sanscrit?

THE GENTLEMAN I am Colonel Pickering. Who are you?

THE NOTE TAKER Henry Higgins, author of Higgins's Universal Alphabet.

PICKERING [*with enthusiasm*] I came from India to meet you.

HIGGINS I was going to India to meet you.

PICKERING Where do you live?

HIGGINS 27A Wimpole Street.[9] Come and see me tomorrow.

PICKERING I'm at the Carlton.[1] Come with me now and lets have a jaw over some supper.

HIGGINS Right you are.

THE FLOWER GIRL [*to* PICKERING, *as he passes her*] Buy a flower, kind gentleman. I'm short for my lodging.

PICKERING I really havnt any change. I'm sorry.

[*He goes away.*]

HIGGINS [*shocked at girl's mendacity*] Liar. You said you could change half-a-crown.

THE FLOWER GIRL [*rising in desperation*] You ought to be stuffed with nails, you ought. [*Flinging the basket at his feet*] Take the whole blooming basket for sixpence.

[*The church clock strikes the second quarter.*]

8. Three of the greatest literary influences on the English language: the playwright William Shakespeare (1564–1616), the poet John Milton (1608–1674), and the translation of the Bible commissioned by King James (1611).

9. A street in Westminster; its most famous resident was Elizabeth Barrett, who eloped with Robert Browning from her family's home at 50 Wimpole St. in 1846.

1. An elegant London hotel on Haymarket, near Piccadilly Circus.

HIGGINS [*hearing in it the voice of God, rebuking him for his Pharisaic*[2] *want of charity to the poor girl*] A reminder.

[*He raises his hat solemnly; then throws a handful of money into the basket and follows Pickering.*]

THE FLOWER GIRL [*picking up a half-crown*] Ah-ow-ooh! [*Picking up a couple of florins*] Aaah-ow-ooh! [*Picking up several coins*] Aaaaaah-ow-ooh! [*Picking up a half-sovereign*][3] Aaaaaaaaaaaah-ow-ooh!!!

FREDDY [*springing out of a taxicab*] Got one at last. Hallo! [*To the* GIRL] Where are the two ladies that were here?

THE FLOWER GIRL They walked to the bus when the rain stopped.

FREDDY And left me with a cab on my hands. Damnation!

THE FLOWER GIRL [*with grandeur*] Never you mind, young man. I'm going home in a taxi. [*She sails off to the cab. The driver puts his hand behind him and holds the door firmly shut against her. Quite understanding his mistrust, she shews him her handful of money.*] Eightpence aint no object to me, Charlie. [*He grins and opens the door.*] Angel Court, Drury Lane,[4] round the corner of Micklejohn's oil shop. Lets see how fast you can make her hop it.[5] [*She gets in and pulls the door to with a slam as the taxicab starts.*]

FREDDY Well, I'm dashed![6]

Act 2

[*Next day at 11 a.m. Higgins's laboratory in Wimpole Street. It is a room on the first floor, looking on the street, and was meant for the drawing-room. The double doors are in the middle of the back wall; and persons entering find in the corner to their right two tall file cabinets at right angles to one another against the walls. In this corner stands a flat writing-table, on which are a phonograph, a laryngoscope,*[7] *a row of tiny organ pipes with a bellows, a set of lamp chimneys for singeing flames with burners attached to a gas plug in the wall by an indiarubber tube, several tuning-forks of different sizes, a life-size image of half a human head, showing in section the vocal organs, and a box containing a supply of wax cylinders for the phonograph.*

Further down the room, on the same side, is a fireplace, with a comfortable leather-covered easy-chair at the side of the hearth nearest the door, and a coal-scuttle. There is a clock on the mantelpiece. Between the fireplace and the phonograph table is a stand for newspapers.

On the other side of the central door, to the left of the visitor, is a cabinet of shallow drawers. On it is a telephone and the telephone directory. The corner beyond, and most of the side wall, is occupied by a grand piano, with the keyboard at the end furthest from the door, and a bench for the player extending the full length of the keyboard. On the piano is a dessert dish heaped with fruit and sweets, mostly chocolates.

The middle of the room is clear. Besides the easy-chair, the piano bench, and two chairs at the phonograph table, there is one stray chair. It stands near the fireplace. On the walls, engravings; mostly Piranesis[8] *and mezzotint portraits. No paintings.*

2. That is, self-righteous and hypocritical, like the Pharisees as depicted in The New Testament.
3. A half-pound coin. *Florins:* two-shilling coins.
4. A street close to Covent Garden; once fashionable, by the nineteenth century it became one of London's worst slums.
5. Go away quickly.
6. That is, "I'll be damned!"
7. An instrument for examining the larynx, invented in the mid-19th century.
8. Reproductions of works by Giovanni Battista Piranesi (1720–1778), an Italian printmaker known for his depictions of classical and contemporary Roman sites.

PICKERING *is seated at the table, putting down some cards and a tuning-fork which he has been using.* HIGGINS *is standing up near him, closing two or three file drawers which are hanging out. He appears in the morning light as a robust, vital, appetizing sort of man of forty or thereabouts, dressed in a professional-looking black frock-coat with a white linen collar and black silk tie. He is of the energetic, scientific type, heartily, even violently interested in everything that can be studied as a scientific subject, and careless about himself and other people, including their feelings. He is, in fact, but for his years and size, rather like a very impetuous baby "taking notice"*[9] *eagerly and loudly, and requiring almost as much watching to keep him out of unintended mischief. His manner varies from genial bullying when he is in a good humor to stormy petulance when anything goes wrong; but he is so entirely frank and void of malice that he remains likeable even in his least reasonable moments.*]

HIGGINS [*as he shuts the last drawer*] Well, I think thats the whole show.

PICKERING It's really amazing. I havnt taken half of it in, you know.

HIGGINS Would you like to go over any of it again?

PICKERING [*rising and coming to the fireplace, where he plants himself with his back to the fire*] No, thank you; not now. I'm quite done up for this morning.

HIGGINS [*following him, and standing beside him on his left*] Tired of listening to sounds?

PICKERING Yes. It's a fearful strain. I rather fancied myself because I can pronounce twenty-four distinct vowel sounds; but your hundred and thirty beat me. I cant hear a bit of difference between most of them.

HIGGINS [*chuckling, and going over to the piano to eat sweets*] Oh, that comes with practice. You hear no difference at first; but you keep on listening, and presently you find theyre all as different as A from B. [MRS. PEARCE *looks in: she is* HIGGINS*'s housekeeper.*] Whats the matter?

MRS. PEARCE [*hesitating, evidently perplexed*] A young woman wants to see you, sir.

HIGGINS A young woman! What does she want?

MRS. PEARCE Well, sir, she says youll be glad to see her when you know what shes come about. Shes quite a common girl, sir. Very common indeed. I should have sent her away, only I thought perhaps you wanted her to talk into your machines. I hope Ive not done wrong; but really you see such queer people sometimes—youll excuse me, I'm sure, sir—

HIGGINS Oh, thats all right, Mrs. Pearce. Has she an interesting accent?

MRS. PEARCE Oh, something dreadful, sir, really. I dont know how you can take an interest in it.

HIGGINS [*to* PICKERING] Lets have her up. Shew her up, Mrs. Pearce. [*He rushes across to his working table and picks out a cylinder to use on the phonograph.*]

MRS. PEARCE [*only half resigned to it*] Very well, sir. It's for you to say.

[*She goes downstairs.*]

HIGGINS This is rather a bit of luck. I'll shew you how I make records. We'll set her talking; and I'll take it down first in Bell's Visible Speech, then in

9. Showing signs of intelligent observation (a phrase used specifically of babies).

broad Romic,[1] and then we'll get her on the phonograph so that you can turn her on as often as you like with the written transcript before you.

MRS. PEARCE [*returning*] This is the young woman, sir.

[*The* FLOWER GIRL *enters in state. She has a hat with three ostrich feathers, orange, sky-blue, and red. She has a nearly clean apron, and the shoddy coat has been tidied a little. The pathos of this deplorable figure, with its innocent vanity and consequential air, touches* PICKERING, *who has already straightened himself in the presence of* MRS. PEARCE. *But as to* HIGGINS, *the only distinction he makes between men and women is that when he is neither bullying nor exclaiming to the heavens against some featherweight cross, he coaxes women as a child coaxes its nurse when it wants to get anything out of her.*]

HIGGINS [*brusquely, recognizing her with unconcealed disappointment, and at once, babylike, making an intolerable grievance of it*] Why, this is the girl I jotted down last night. Shes no use: Ive got all the records I want of the Lisson Grove lingo; and I'm not going to waste another cylinder on it. [*To the* GIRL] Be off with you: I dont want you.

THE FLOWER GIRL Dont you be so saucy. You aint heard what I come for yet. [*To* MRS. PEARCE, *who is waiting at the door for further instruction*] Did you tell him I come in a taxi?

MRS. PEARCE Nonsense, girl! what do you think a gentleman like Mr. Higgins cares what you came in?

THE FLOWER GIRL Oh, we are proud! He aint above giving lessons, not him: I heard him say so. Well, I aint come here to ask for any compliment; and if my money's not good enough I can go elsewhere.

HIGGINS Good enough for what?

THE FLOWER GIRL Good enough for ye-oo. Now you know, dont you? I'm come to have lessons, I am. And to pay for em too: make no mistake.

HIGGINS [*stupent*][2] Well ! ! ! [*Recovering his breath with a gasp*] What do you expect me to say to you?

THE FLOWER GIRL Well, if you was a gentleman, you might ask me to sit down, I think. Dont I tell you I'm bringing you business?

HIGGINS Pickering: shall we ask this baggage to sit down or shall we throw her out of the window?

THE FLOWER GIRL [*running away in terror to the piano, where she turns at bay*] Ah-ah-ah-ow-ow-ow-oo! [*Wounded and whimpering*] I wont be called a baggage when Ive offered to pay like any lady.

[*Motionless, the two men stare at her from the other side of the room, amazed.*]

PICKERING [*gently*] What is it you want, my girl?

1. The system of phonetic notation—a precursor of the International Phonetic Alphabet (IPA) used today—devised by Henry Sweet (1845–1912), a linguist on whose career Shaw drew in creating Higgins and who defined a "broad" transcription as less detailed (and less scientific) than a narrow one. *Bell's Visible Speech:* a system of notation created a decade earlier than Sweet's by the educator Alexander Melville Bell (1819–1905), the father of the inventor Alexander Graham Bell; it attempts to represent the position of the vocal organs as individual sounds are produced.

2. In a state of stupefied amazement.

THE FLOWER GIRL I want to be a lady in a flower shop stead of selling at the corner of Tottenham Court Road.[3] But they wont take me unless I can talk more genteel. He said he could teach me. Well, here I am ready to pay him—not asking any favor—and he treats me as if I was dirt.

MRS. PEARCE How can you be such a foolish ignorant girl as to think you could afford to pay Mr. Higgins?

THE FLOWER GIRL Why shouldnt I? I know what lessons cost as well as you do; and I'm ready to pay.

HIGGINS How much?

THE FLOWER GIRL [*coming back to him, triumphant*] Now youre talking! I thought youd come off it when you saw a chance of getting back a bit of what you chucked at me last night. [*Confidentially*] Youd had a drop in,[4] hadnt you?

HIGGINS [*peremptorily*] Sit down.

THE FLOWER GIRL Oh, if youre going to make a compliment of it—

HIGGINS [*thundering at her*] Sit down.

MRS. PEARCE [*severely*] Sit down, girl. Do as youre told. [*She places the stray chair near the hearthrug between* HIGGINS *and* PICKERING, *and stands behind it waiting for the girl to sit down.*]

THE FLOWER GIRL Ah-ah-ah-ow-ow-oo! [*She stands, half rebellious, half bewildered.*]

PICKERING [*very courteous*] Wont you sit down?

THE FLOWER GIRL [*coyly*] Dont mind if I do. [*She sits down.* PICKERING *returns to the hearthrug.*]

HIGGINS Whats your name?

THE FLOWER GIRL Liza Doolittle.

HIGGINS [*declaiming gravely*]
Eliza, Elizabeth, Betsy and Bess,
They went to the woods to get a birds nes':

PICKERING They found a nest with four eggs in it:

HIGGINS They took one apiece, and left three in it.

They laugh heartily at their own wit.

LIZA Oh, dont be silly.

MRS. PEARCE You mustnt speak to the gentleman like that.

LIZA Well, why wont he speak sensible to me?

HIGGINS Come back to business. How much do you propose to pay me for the lessons?

LIZA Oh, I know whats right. A lady friend of mine gets French lessons for eighteenpence an hour from a real French gentleman. Well, you wouldnt have the face to ask me the same for teaching me my own language as you would for French; so I wont give more than a shilling. Take it or leave it.

HIGGINS [*walking up and down the room, rattling his keys and his cash in his pockets*] You know, Pickering, if you consider a shilling, not as a simple shilling, but as a percentage of this girl's income, it works out as fully equivalent to sixty or seventy guineas[5] from a millionaire.

3. A busy central London shopping street, within a half mile of Covent Garden.
4. That is, you'd had something to drink.
5. Roughly equivalent to $6,000 today; a guinea is a gold coin worth twenty-one shillings.

PICKERING How so?

HIGGINS Figure it out. A millionaire has about £150 a day. She earns about half-a-crown.

LIZA [*haughtily*] Who told you I only—

HIGGINS [*continuing*] She offers me two-fifths of her day's income for a lesson. Two-fifths of a millionaire's income for a day would be somewhere about £60. It's handsome. By George, it's enormous! it's the biggest offer I ever had.

LIZA [*rising, terrified*] Sixty pounds! What are you talking about? I never offered you sixty pounds. Where would I get—

HIGGINS Hold your tongue.

LIZA [*weeping*] But I aint got sixty pounds. Oh—

MRS. PEARCE Dont cry, you silly girl. Sit down. Nobody is going to touch your money.

HIGGINS Somebody is going to touch you, with a broomstick, if you dont stop snivelling. Sit down.

LIZA [*obeying slowly*] Ah-ah-ah-ow-oo-o! One would think you was my father.

HIGGINS If I decide to teach you, I'll be worse than two fathers to you. Here! [*He offers her his silk handkerchief.*]

LIZA Whats this for?

HIGGINS To wipe your eyes. To wipe any part of your face that feels moist. Remember: thats your handkerchief; and thats your sleeve. Dont mistake the one for the other if you wish to become a lady in a shop.

[LIZA, *utterly bewildered, stares helplessly at him.*]

MRS. PEARCE It's no use talking to her like that, Mr. Higgins: she doesnt understand you. Besides, youre quite wrong: she doesnt do it that way at all. [*She takes the handkerchief.*]

LIZA [*snatching it*] Here! You give me that handkerchief. He give it to me, not to you.

PICKERING [*laughing*] He did. I think it must be regarded as her property, Mrs. Pearce.

MRS. PEARCE [*resigning herself*] Serve you right, Mr. Higgins.

PICKERING Higgins: I'm interested. What about the ambassador's garden party? I'll say youre the greatest teacher alive if you make that good. I'll bet you all the expenses of the experiment you cant do it. And I'll pay for the lessons.

LIZA Oh, you are real good. Thank you, Captain.

HIGGINS [*tempted, looking at her*] It's almost irresistible. Shes so deliciously low—so horribly dirty—

LIZA [*protesting extremely*] Ah-ah-ah-ah-ow-ow-oo-oo!!! I aint dirty: I washed my face and hands afore I come, I did.

PICKERING Youre certainly not going to turn her head with flattery, Higgins.

MRS. PEARCE [*uneasy*] Oh, dont say that, sir: theres more ways than one of turning a girl's head; and nobody can do it better than Mr. Higgins, though he may not always mean it. I do hope, sir, you wont encourage him to do anything foolish.

HIGGINS [*becoming excited as the idea grows on him*] What is life but a series of inspired follies? The difficulty is to find them to do. Never lose a chance: it doesnt come every day. I shall make a duchess of this draggle-tailed guttersnipe.

LIZA [*strongly deprecating this view of her*] Ah-ah-ah-ow-ow-oo!

HIGGINS [*carried away*] Yes: in six months—in three if she has a good ear and a quick tongue—I'll take her anywhere and pass her off as anything. We'll start today: now! this moment! Take her away and clean her, Mrs. Pearce. Monkey Brand,[6] if it wont come off any other way. Is there a good fire in the kitchen?

MRS. PEARCE [*protesting*] Yes; but—

HIGGINS [*storming on*] Take all her clothes off and burn them. Ring up Whiteley[7] or somebody for new ones. Wrap her up in brown paper til they come.

LIZA Youre no gentleman, youre not, to talk of such things. I'm a good girl, I am; and I know what the like of you are, I do.

HIGGINS We want none of your Lisson Grove prudery here, young woman. Youve got to learn to behave like a duchess. Take her away, Mrs. Pearce. If she gives you any trouble wallop her.

LIZA [*springing up and running between* PICKERING *and* MRS. PEARCE *for protection*] No! I'll call the police, I will.

MRS. PEARCE But Ive no place to put her.

HIGGINS Put her in the dustbin.

LIZA Ah-ah-ah-ow-ow-oo!

PICKERING Oh come, Higgins! be reasonable.

MRS. PEARCE [*resolutely*] You must be reasonable, Mr. Higgins: really you must. You cant walk over everybody like this.

[HIGGINS, *thus scolded, subsides. The hurricane is succeeded by a zephyr of amiable surprise.*]

HIGGINS [*with professional exquisiteness of modulation*] I walk over everybody! My dear Mrs. Pearce, my dear Pickering, I never had the slightest intention of walking over anyone. All I propose is that we should be kind to this poor girl. We must help her to prepare and fit herself for her new station in life. If I did not express myself clearly it was because I did not wish to hurt her delicacy, or yours.

[LIZA, *reassured, steals back to her chair.*]

MRS. PEARCE [*to* PICKERING] Well, did you ever hear anything like that, sir?

PICKERING [*laughing heartily*] Never, Mrs. Pearce: never.

HIGGINS [*patiently*] Whats the matter?

MRS. PEARCE Well, the matter is, sir, that you cant take a girl up like that as if you were picking up a pebble on the beach.

HIGGINS Why not?

MRS. PEARCE Why not! But you dont know anything about her. What about her parents? She may be married.

LIZA Garn!

HIGGINS There! As the girl very properly says, Garn! Married indeed! Dont you know that a woman of that class looks a worn out drudge of fifty a year after shes married.

LIZA Whood marry me?

HIGGINS [*suddenly resorting to the most thrillingly beautiful low tones in his best elocutionary style*] By George, Eliza, the streets will be strewn with

6. A popular brand of scouring soap.

7. A large department store in London.

the bodies of men shooting themselves for your sake before Ive done with you.

MRS. PEARCE Nonsense, sir. You mustnt talk like that to her.

LIZA [*rising and squaring herself determinedly*] I'm going away. He's off his chump, he is. I dont want no balmies[8] teaching me.

HIGGINS [*wounded in his tenderest point by her insensibility to his elocution*] Oh, indeed! I'm mad, am I? Very well, Mrs. Pearce: you neednt order the new clothes for her. Throw her out.

LIZA [*whimpering*] Nah-ow. You got no right to touch me.

MRS. PEARCE You see now what comes of being saucy. [*Indicating the door*] This way, please.

LIZA [*almost in tears*] I didnt want no clothes. I wouldnt have taken them. [*She throws away the handkerchief.*] I can buy my own clothes.

HIGGINS [*deftly retrieving the handkerchief and intercepting her on her reluctant way to the door*] Youre an ungrateful wicked girl. This is my return for offering to take you out of the gutter and dress you beautifully and make a lady of you.

MRS. PEARCE Stop, Mr. Higgins. I wont allow it. It's you that are wicked. Go home to your parents, girl; and tell them to take better care of you.

LIZA I aint got no parents. They told me I was big enough to earn my own living and turned me out.

MRS. PEARCE Wheres your mother?

LIZA I aint got no mother. Her that turned me out was my sixth stepmother. But I done without them. And I'm a good girl, I am.

HIGGINS Very well, then, what on earth is all this fuss about? The girl doesnt belong to anybody—is no use to anybody but me. [*He goes to* MRS. PEARCE *and begins coaxing.*] You can adopt her, Mrs. Pearce: I'm sure a daughter would be a great amusement to you. Now dont make any more fuss. Take her downstairs; and—

MRS. PEARCE But whats to become of her? Is she to be paid anything? Do be sensible, sir.

HIGGINS Oh, pay her whatever is necessary: put it down in the housekeeping book. [*Impatiently*] What on earth will she want with money? She'll have her food and her clothes. She'll only drink if you give her money.

LIZA [*turning on him*] Oh you are a brute. It's a lie: nobody ever saw the sign of liquor on me. [*She goes back to her chair and plants herself there defiantly.*]

PICKERING [*in good-humored remonstrance*] Does it occur to you, Higgins, that the girl has some feelings?

HIGGINS [*looking critically at her*] Oh no, I dont think so. Not any feelings that we need bother about. [*Cheerily*] Have you, Eliza?

LIZA I got my feelings same as anyone else.

HIGGINS [*to* PICKERING, *reflectively*] You see the difficulty?

PICKERING Eh? What difficulty?

HIGGINS To get her to talk grammar. The mere pronunciation is easy enough.

LIZA I dont want to talk grammar. I want to talk like a lady.

8. Crazies, madmen (slang). *Off his chump*: out of his senses (*chump* is slang for "head").

MRS. PEARCE Will you please keep to the point, Mr. Higgins. I want to know on what terms the girl is to be here. Is she to have any wages? And what is to become of her when youve finished your teaching? You must look ahead a little.

HIGGINS [*impatiently*] Whats to become of her if I leave her in the gutter? Tell me that, Mrs. Pearce.

MRS. PEARCE Thats her own business, not yours, Mr. Higgins.

HIGGINS Well, when Ive done with her, we can throw her back into the gutter; and then it will be her own business again; so thats all right.

LIZA Oh, youve no feeling heart in you: you dont care for nothing but yourself. [*She rises and takes the floor resolutely.*] Here! Ive had enough of this. I'm going. [*Making for the door*] You ought to be ashamed of yourself, you ought.

HIGGINS [*snatching a chocolate cream from the piano, his eyes suddenly beginning to twinkle with mischief*] Have some chocolates, Eliza.

LIZA [*halting, tempted*] How do I know what might be in them? Ive heard of girls being drugged by the like of you.

[HIGGINS *whips out his penknife; cuts a chocolate in two; puts one half into his mouth and bolts it; and offers her the other half.*]

HIGGINS Pledge of good faith, Eliza. I eat one half: you eat the other. [LIZA *opens her mouth to retort: he pops the half chocolate into it.*] You shall have boxes of them, barrels of them, every day. You shall live on them. Eh?

LIZA [*who has disposed of the chocolate after being nearly choked by it*] I wouldnt have ate it, only I'm too ladylike to take it out of my mouth.

HIGGINS Listen, Eliza. I think you said you came in a taxi.

LIZA Well, what if I did? Ive as good a right to take a taxi as anyone else.

HIGGINS You have, Eliza; and in future you shall have as many taxis as you want. You shall go up and down and round the town in a taxi every day. Think of that, Eliza.

MRS. PEARCE Mr. Higgins: youre tempting the girl. It's not right. She should think of the future.

HIGGINS At her age! Nonsense! Time enough to think of the future when you havnt any future to think of. No, Eliza: do as this lady does: think of other people's futures; but never think of your own. Think of chocolates, and taxis, and gold, and diamonds.

LIZA No: I dont want no gold and no diamonds. I'm a good girl, I am. [*She sits down again, with an attempt at dignity.*]

HIGGINS You shall remain so, Eliza, under the care of Mrs. Pearce. And you shall marry an officer in the Guards, with a beautiful moustache: the son of a marquis, who will disinherit him for marrying you, but will relent when he sees your beauty and goodness—

PICKERING Excuse me, Higgins; but I really must interfere. Mrs. Pearce is quite right. If this girl is to put herself in your hands for six months for an experiment in teaching, she must understand thoroughly what shes doing.

HIGGINS How can she? Shes incapable of understanding anything. Besides, do any of us understand what we are doing? If we did, would we ever do it?

PICKERING Very clever, Higgins; but not sound sense. [*To* ELIZA] Miss Doolittle—

LIZA [*overwhelmed*] Ah-ah-ow-oo!

HIGGINS There! Thats all you get out of Eliza. Ah-ah-ow-oo! No use explaining. As a military man you ought to know that. Give her her orders: thats what she wants. Eliza: you are to live here for the next six months, learning how to speak beautifully, like a lady in a florist's shop. If youre good and do whatever youre told, you shall sleep in a proper bedroom, and have lots to eat, and money to buy chocolates and take rides in taxis. If youre naughty and idle you will sleep in the back kitchen among the black beetles, and be walloped by Mrs. Pearce with a broomstick. At the end of six months you shall go to Buckingham Palace in a carriage, beautifully dressed. If the King finds out youre not a lady, you will be taken by the police to the Tower of London, where your head will be cut off as a warning to other presumptuous flower girls. If you are not found out, you shall have a present of seven-and-sixpence to start life with as a lady in a shop. If you refuse this offer you will be a most ungrateful and wicked girl; and the angels will weep for you. [*To* PICKERING] Now are you satisfied, Pickering? [*To* MRS. PEARCE] Can I put it more plainly and fairly, Mrs. Pearce?

MRS. PEARCE [*patiently*] I think youd better let me speak to the girl properly in private. I dont know that I can take charge of her or consent to the arrangement at all. Of course I know you dont mean her any harm; but when you get what you call interested in people's accents, you never think or care what may happen to them or you. Come with me, Eliza.

HIGGINS Thats all right. Thank you, Mrs. Pearce. Bundle her off to the bathroom.

LIZA [*rising reluctantly and suspiciously*] Youre a great bully, you are. I wont stay here if I dont like. I wont let nobody wallop me. I never asked to go to Bucknam Palace, I didnt. I was never in trouble with the police, not me. I'm a good girl—

MRS. PEARCE Dont answer back, girl. You dont understand the gentleman. Come with me. [*She leads the way to the door, and holds it open for* ELIZA.]

LIZA [*as she goes out*] Well, what I say is right. I wont go near the king, not if I'm going to have my head cut off. If I'd known what I was letting myself in for, I wouldnt have come here. I always been a good girl; and I never offered to say a word to him; and I dont owe him nothing; and I dont care; and I wont be put upon; and I have my feelings the same as anyone else—

[MRS. PEARCE *shuts the door; and* ELIZA'*s plaints are no longer audible.* PICKERING *comes from the hearth to the chair and sits astride it with his arms on the back.*]

PICKERING Excuse the straight question, Higgins. Are you a man of good character where women are concerned?

HIGGINS [*moodily*] Have you ever met a man of good character where women are concerned?

PICKERING Yes: very frequently.

HIGGINS [*dogmatically, lifting himself on his hands to the level of the piano, and sitting on it with a bounce*] Well, I havnt. I find that the moment I let a woman make friends with me, she becomes jealous, exacting, suspicious, and a damned nuisance. I find that the moment I let myself make friends with a woman, I become selfish and tyrannical. Women upset everything. When you let them into your life, you find that the woman is driving at one thing and youre driving at another.

PICKERING At what, for example?

HIGGINS [*coming off the piano restlessly*] Oh, Lord knows! I suppose the woman wants to live her own life; and the man wants to live his; and each tries to drag the other on to the wrong track. One wants to go north and the other south; and the result is that both have to go east, though they both hate the east wind. [*He sits down on the bench at the keyboard.*] So here I am, a confirmed old bachelor, and likely to remain so.

PICKERING [*rising and standing over him gravely*] Come, Higgins! You know what I mean. If I'm to be in this business I shall feel responsible for that girl. I hope it's understood that no advantage is to be taken of her position.

HIGGINS What! That thing! Sacred, I assure you. [*Rising to explain*] You see, she'll be a pupil; and teaching would be impossible unless pupils were sacred. Ive taught scores of American millionairesses how to speak English: the best looking women in the world. I'm seasoned. They might as well be blocks of wood. I might as well be a block of wood. It's—

[MRS. PEARCE *opens the door. She has* ELIZA'S *hat in her hand.* PICKERING *retires to the easy-chair at the hearth and sits down.*]

HIGGINS [*eagerly*] Well, Mrs. Pearce: is it all right?

MRS. PEARCE [*at the door*] I just wish to trouble you with a word, if I may, Mr. Higgins.

HIGGINS Yes, certainly. Come in. [*She comes forward.*] Dont burn that, Mrs. Pearce. I'll keep it as a curiosity. [*He takes the hat.*]

MRS. PEARCE Handle it carefully, sir, please. I had to promise her not to burn it; but I had better put it in the oven for a while.

HIGGINS [*putting it down hastily on the piano*] Oh! thank you. Well, what have you to say to me?

PICKERING Am I in the way?

MRS. PEARCE Not at all, sir. Mr. Higgins: will you please be very particular what you say before the girl?

HIGGINS [*sternly*] Of course. I'm always particular about what I say. Why do you say this to me?

MRS. PEARCE [*unmoved*] No, sir: youre not at all particular when youve mislaid anything or when you get a little impatient. Now it doesnt matter before me: I'm used to it. But you really must not swear before the girl.

HIGGINS [*indignantly*] I swear! [*Most emphatically*] I never swear. I detest the habit. What the devil do you mean?

MRS. PEARCE [*stolidly*] Thats what I mean, sir. You swear a great deal too much. I dont mind your damning and blasting, and what the devil and where the devil and who the devil—

HIGGINS Mrs. Pearce: this language from your lips! Really!

MRS. PEARCE [*not to be put off*] —but there is a certain word I must ask you not to use. The girl has just used it herself because the bath was too hot. It begins with the same letter as bath.[9] She knows no better: she learnt it at her mother's knee. But she must not hear it from your lips.

HIGGINS [*loftily*] I cannot charge myself with having ever uttered it, Mrs. Pearce. [*She looks at him steadfastly. He adds, hiding an uneasy conscience with a judicial air.*] Except perhaps in a moment of extreme and justifiable excitement.

MRS. PEARCE Only this morning, sir, you applied it to your boots, to the butter, and to the brown bread.

HIGGINS Oh, that! Mere alliteration, Mrs. Pearce, natural to a poet.

9. That is, "bloody," a colloquial intensifier that came to be considered highly offensive and profane (folk etymology linked it to the oath "God's blood!").

MRS. PEARCE Well, sir, whatever you choose to call it, I beg you not to let the girl hear you repeat it.

HIGGINS Oh, very well, very well. Is that all?

MRS. PEARCE No, sir. We shall have to be very particular with this girl as to personal cleanliness.

HIGGINS Certainly. Quite right. Most important.

MRS. PEARCE I mean not to be slovenly about her dress or untidy in leaving things about.

HIGGINS [*going to her solemnly*] Just so. I intended to call your attention to that. [*He passes on to* PICKERING, *who is enjoying the conversation immensely.*] It is these little things that matter, Pickering. Take care of the pence and the pounds will take care of themselves is as true of personal habits as of money. [*He comes to anchor on the hearthrug, with the air of a man in an unassailable position.*]

MRS. PEARCE Yes, sir. Then might I ask you not to come down to breakfast in your dressing-gown, or at any rate not to use it as a napkin to the extent you do, sir. And if you would be so good as not to eat everything off the same plate, and to remember not to put the porridge saucepan out of your hand on the clean tablecloth, it would be a better example to the girl. You know you nearly choked yourself with a fishbone in the jam only last week.

HIGGINS [*rounded from the hearthrug and drifting back to the piano*] I may do these things sometimes in absence of mind; but surely I dont do them habitually. [*Angrily*] By the way: my dressing-gown smells most damnably of benzine.[1]

MRS. PEARCE No doubt it does, Mr. Higgins. But if you will wipe your fingers—

HIGGINS [*yelling*] Oh very well, very well: I'll wipe them in my hair in future.

MRS. PEARCE I hope youre not offended, Mr. Higgins.

HIGGINS [*shocked at finding himself thought capable of an unamiable sentiment*] Not at all, not at all. Youre quite right, Mrs. Pearce: I shall be particularly careful before the girl. Is that all?

MRS. PEARCE No, sir. Might she use some of those Japanese dresses you brought from abroad? I really cant put her back into her old things.

HIGGINS Certainly. Anything you like. Is that all?

MRS. PEARCE Thank you, sir. Thats all. [*She goes out.*]

HIGGINS You know, Pickering, that woman has the most extraordinary ideas about me. Here I am, a shy, diffident sort of man. Ive never been able to feel really grown-up and tremendous, like other chaps. And yet shes firmly persuaded that I'm an arbitrary overbearing bossing kind of person. I cant account for it.

[MRS. PEARCE *returns.*]

MRS. PEARCE If you please, sir, the trouble's beginning already. Theres a dustman[2] downstairs, Alfred Doolittle, wants to see you. He says you have his daughter here.

PICKERING [*rising*] Phew! I say! [*He retreats to the hearthrug.*]

HIGGINS [*promptly*] Send the blackguard up.

MRS. PEARCE Oh, very well, sir. [*She goes out.*]

PICKERING He may not be a blackguard, Higgins.

HIGGINS Nonsense. Of course hes a blackguard.

1. A solvent used to remove grease spots. 2. Garbage collector.

PICKERING Whether he is or not, I'm afraid we shall have some trouble with him.

HIGGINS [*confidently*] Oh no: I think not. If theres any trouble he shall have it with me, not I with him. And we are sure to get something interesting out of him.

PICKERING About the girl?

HIGGINS No. I mean his dialect.

PICKERING Oh!

MRS. PEARCE [*at the door*] Doolittle, sir. [*She admits* DOOLITTLE *and retires.*]

[ALFRED DOOLITTLE *is an elderly but vigorous dustman, clad in the costume of his profession, including a hat with a back brim covering his neck and shoulders. He has well marked and rather interesting features, and seems equally free from fear and conscience. He has a remarkably expressive voice, the result of a habit of giving vent to his feelings without reserve. His present pose is that of wounded honor and stern resolution.*]

DOOLITTLE [*at the door, uncertain which of the two gentlemen is his man*] Professor Higgins?

HIGGINS Here. Good morning. Sit down.

DOOLITTLE Morning, Governor. [*He sits down magisterially.*] I come about a very serious matter, Governor.

HIGGINS [*to* PICKERING] Brought up in Hounslow.[3] Mother Welsh, I should think. [DOOLITTLE *opens his mouth, amazed.* HIGGINS *continues.*] What do you want, Doolittle?

DOOLITTLE [*menacingly*] I want my daughter: thats what I want. See?

HIGGINS Of course you do. Youre her father, arnt you? You dont suppose anyone else wants her, do you? I'm glad to see you have some spark of family feeling left. Shes upstairs. Take her away at once.

DOOLITTLE [*rising, fearfully taken aback*] What!

HIGGINS Take her away. Do you suppose I'm going to keep your daughter for you?

DOOLITTLE [*remonstrating*] Now, now, look here, Governor. Is this reasonable? Is it fairity[4] to take advantage of a man like this? The girl belongs to me. You got her. Where do I come in? [*He sits down again.*]

HIGGINS Your daughter had the audacity to come to my house and ask me to teach her how to speak properly so that she could get a place in a flowershop. This gentleman and my housekeeper have been here all the time. [*Bullying him*] How dare you come here and attempt to blackmail me? You sent her here on purpose.

DOOLITTLE [*protesting*] No, Governor.

HIGGINS You must have. How else could you possibly know that she is here?

DOOLITTLE Dont take a man up like that, Governor.

HIGGINS The police shall take you up. This is a plant—a plot to extort money by threats. I shall telephone for the police. [*He goes resolutely to the telephone and opens the directory.*]

DOOLITTLE Have I asked you for a brass farthing?[5] I leave it to the gentleman here: have I said a word about money?

3. A working-class suburb west of central London.
4. Fair (Doolittle's fanciful coinage).
5. An expression equivalent to "one red cent"; a farthing is one-quarter of a penny, and "brass" here is emphatic.

HIGGINS [*throwing the book aside and marching down on* DOOLITTLE *with a poser*] What else did you come for?

DOOLITTLE [*sweetly*] Well, what would a man come for? Be human, Governor.

HIGGINS [*disarmed*] Alfred: did you put her up to it?

DOOLITTLE So help me, Governor, I never did. I take my Bible oath I aint seen the girl these two months past.

HIGGINS Then how did you know she was here?

DOOLITTLE [*"most musical, most melancholy"*[6]] I'll tell you, Governor, if youll only let me get a word in. I'm willing to tell you. I'm wanting to tell you. I'm waiting to tell you.

HIGGINS Pickering: this chap has a certain natural gift of rhetoric. Observe the rhythm of his native wood-notes wild.[7] "I'm willing to tell you: I'm wanting to tell you: I'm waiting to tell you." Sentimental rhetoric! thats the Welsh strain in him. It also accounts for his mendacity and dishonesty.

PICKERING Oh, please, Higgins: I'm west country[8] myself. [*To* DOOLITTLE] How did you know the girl was here if you didnt send her?

DOOLITTLE It was like this, Governor. The girl took a boy in the taxi to give him a jaunt. Son of her landlady, he is. He hung about on the chance of her giving him another ride home. Well, she sent him back for her luggage when she heard you was willing for her to stop here. I met the boy at the corner of Long Acre and Endell Street.

HIGGINS Public house.[9] Yes?

DOOLITTLE The poor man's club, Governor: why shouldnt I?

PICKERING Do let him tell his story, Higgins.

DOOLITTLE He told me what was up. And I ask you, what was my feelings and my duty as a father? I says to the boy, "You bring me the luggage," I says—

PICKERING Why didnt you go for it yourself?

DOOLITTLE Landlady wouldnt have trusted me with it, Governor. Shes that kind of woman: you know. I had to give the boy a penny afore he trusted me with it, the little swine. I brought it to her just to oblige you like, and make myself agreeable. Thats all.

HIGGINS How much luggage?

DOOLITTLE Musical instrument, Governor. A few pictures, a trifle of jewelry, and a bird-cage. She said she didnt want no clothes. What was I to think from that, Governor? I ask you as a parent what was I to think?

HIGGINGS So you came to rescue her from worse than death, eh?

DOOLITTLE [*appreciatively. relieved at being so well understood*] Just so, Governor. Thats right.

PICKERING But why did you bring her luggage if you intended to take her away?

DOOLITTLE Have I said a word about taking her away? Have I now?

HIGGINS [*determinedly*] Youre going to take her away, double quick. [*He crosses to the hearth and rings the bell.*]

6. From John Milton's poem "Il Penseroso" (ca. 1631), line 62.

7. A quotation from Milton's "L'Allegro" (ca. 1631), line 134; in the poem (a companion piece to "Il Penseroso"), the phrase refers to Shakespeare.

8. The southwestern counties of England—Somerset, Dorset, Devon, and Cornwall. The inhabitants of Cornwall and Wales are connected by their related languages, and the English long regarded (and often denigrated) them as separate cultural groups.

9. That is, a pub.

DOOLITTLE [*rising*] No, Governor. Dont say that. I'm not the man to stand in my girl's light. Heres a career opening for her, as you might say; and—

[MRS. PEARCE *opens the door and awaits orders.*]

HIGGINS Mrs. Pearce: this is Eliza's father. He has come to take her away. Give her to him. [*He goes back to the piano, with an air of washing his hands of the whole affair.*]

DOOLITTLE No. This is a misunderstanding. Listen here—

MRS. PEARCE He cant take her away, Mr. Higgins: how can he? You told me to burn her clothes.

DOOLITTLE Thats right. I cant carry the girl through the streets like a blooming monkey, can I? I put it to you.

HIGGINS You have put it to me that you want your daughter. Take your daughter. If she has no clothes go out and buy her some.

DOOLITTLE [*desperate*] Wheres the clothes she come in? Did I burn them or did your missus here?

MRS. PEARCE I am the housekeeper, if you please. I have sent for some clothes for your girl. When they come you can take her away. You can wait in the kitchen. This way, please.

[DOOLITTLE, *much troubled, accompanies her to the door; then hesitates; finally turns confidentially to* HIGGINS.]

DOOLITTLE Listen here, Governor. You and me is men of the world, aint we?

HIGGINS Oh! Men of the world, are we? Youd better go, Mrs. Pearce.

MRS. PEARCE I think so, indeed, sir.

[*She goes, with dignity.*]

PICKERING The floor is yours, Mr. Doolittle.

DOOLITTLE [*to* PICKERING] I thank you, Governor. [*To* HIGGINS, *who takes refuge on the piano bench, a little overwhelmed by the proximity of his visitor; for* DOOLITTLE *has a professional flavor of dust about him*] Well, the truth is, Ive taken a sort of fancy to you, Governor; and if you want the girl, I'm not so set on having her back home again but what I might be open to an arrangement. Regarded in the light of a young woman, shes a fine handsome girl. As a daughter shes not worth her keep; and so I tell you straight. All I ask is my rights as a father; and youre the last man alive to expect me to let her go for nothing; for I can see youre one of the straight sort, Governor. Well, whats a five pound note to you? And whats Eliza to me? [*He returns to his chair and sits down judicially.*]

PICKERING I think you ought to know, Doolittle, that Mr. Higgins's intentions are entirely honorable.

DOOLITTLE Course they are, Governor. If I thought they wasnt, Id ask fifty.

HIGGINS [*revolted*] Do you mean to say, you callous rascal, that you would sell your daughter for £50?

DOOLITTLE Not in a general way I wouldnt; but to oblige a gentleman like you I'd do a good deal, I do assure you.

PICKERING Have you no morals, man?

DOOLITTLE [*unabashed*] Cant afford them, Governor. Neither could you if you was as poor as me. Not that I mean any harm, you know. But if Liza is going to have a bit out of this, why not me too?

HIGGINS [*troubled*] I dont know what to do, Pickering. There can be no question that as a matter of morals it's a positive crime to give this chap a farthing. And yet I feel a sort of rough justice in his claim.

DOOLITTLE Thats it, Governor. Thats all I say. A father's heart, as it were.

PICKERING Well, I know the feeling; but really it seems hardly right—

DOOLITTLE Dont say that, Governor. Dont look at it that way. What am I, Governors both? I ask you, what am I? I'm one of the undeserving poor: thats what I am. Think of what that means to a man. It means that hes up agen[1] middle class morality all the time. If theres anything going, and I put in for a bit of it, it's always the same story: "Youre undeserving; so you cant have it." But my needs is as great as the most deserving widow's that ever got money out of six different charities in one week for the death of the same husband. I dont need less than a deserving man: I need more. I dont eat less hearty than him; and I drink a lot more. I want a bit of amusement, cause I'm a thinking man. I want cheerfulness and a song and a band when I feel low. Well, they charge me just the same for everything as they charge the deserving. What is middle class morality? Just an excuse for never giving me anything. Therefore, I ask you, as two gentlemen, not to play that game on me. I'm playing straight with you. I aint pretending to be deserving. I'm undeserving; and I mean to go on being undeserving. I like it; and thats the truth. Will you take advantage of a man's nature to do him out of the price of his own daughter what hes brought up and fed and clothed by the sweat of his brow until shes growed big enough to be interesting to you two gentlemen? Is five pounds unreasonable? I put it to you; and I leave it to you.

HIGGINS [*rising, and going over to* PICKERING] Pickering: if we were to take this man in hand for three months, he could choose between a seat in the Cabinet and a popular pulpit in Wales.

PICKERING What do you say to that, Doolittle?

DOOLITTLE Not me, Governor, thank you kindly. Ive heard all the preachers and all the prime ministers—for I'm a thinking man and game for politics or religion or social reform same as all the other amusements—and I tell you it's a dog's life anyway you look at it. Undeserving poverty is my line. Taking one station in society with another, it's—it's—well, it's the only one that has any ginger in it, to my taste.

HIGGINS I suppose we must give him a fiver.

PICKERING He'll make a bad use of it, I'm afraid.

DOOLITTLE Not me, Governor, so help me I wont. Dont you be afraid that I'll save it and spare it and live idle on it. There wont be a penny of it left by Monday: I'll have to go to work same as if I'd never had it. It wont pauperize me, you bet. Just one good spree for myself and the missus, giving pleasure to ourselves and employment to others, and satisfaction to you to think it's not been throwed away. You couldnt spend it better.

HIGGINS [*taking out his pocket book and coming between* DOOLITTLE *and the piano*] This is irresistible. Lets give him ten. [*He offers two notes to the dustman.*]

DOOLITTLE No, Governor. She wouldnt have the heart to spend ten; and perhaps I shouldnt neither. Ten pounds is a lot of money: it makes a man feel prudent like: and then good-bye to happiness. You give me what I ask you, Governor: not a penny more, and not a penny less.

PICKERING Why dont you marry that missus of yours? I rather draw the line at encouraging that sort of immorality.

1. Against.

DOOLITTLE Tell her so, Governor: tell her so. *I'm* willing. It's me that suffers by it. Ive no hold on her. I got to be agreeable to her. I got to give her presents. I got to buy her clothes something sinful. I'm a slave to that woman, Governor, just because I'm not her lawful husband. And she knows it too. Catch her marrying me! Take my advice, Governor: marry Eliza while shes young and dont know no better. If you dont youll be sorry for it after. If you do, she'll be sorry for it after; but better you than her, because youre a man, and shes only a woman and dont know how to be happy anyhow.

HIGGINS Pickering: if we listen to this man another minute, we shall have no convictions left. [*To* DOOLITTLE] Five pounds I think you said.

DOOLITTLE Thank you kindly, Governor.

HIGGINS Youre sure you wont take ten?

DOOLITTLE Not now. Another time, Governor.

HIGGINS [*handing him a five-pound note*] Here you are.

DOOLITTLE Thank you, Governor. Good morning.

[*He hurries to the door, anxious to get away with his booty. When he opens it he is confronted with a dainty and exquisitely clean young Japanese lady in a simple blue cotton kimono printed cunningly with small white jasmine blossoms.* MRS. PEARCE *is with her. He gets out of her way deferentially and apologizes.*]

Beg pardon, miss.

THE JAPANESE LADY Garn! Dont you know your own daughter?

DOOLITTLE } *exclaiming simultaneously* { Bly me! it's Eliza!
HIGGINS } { Whats that! This!
PICKERING } { By Jove!

LIZA Dont I look silly?

HIGGINS Silly?

MRS. PEARCE [*at the door*] Now, Mr. Higgins, please dont say anything to make the girl conceited about herself.

HIGGINS [*conscientiously*] Oh! Quite right, Mrs. Pearce. [*To* ELIZA] Yes: damned silly.

MRS. PEARCE Please, sir.

HIGGINS [*correcting himself*] I mean extremely silly.

LIZA I should look all right with my hat on. [*She takes up her hat; puts it on; and walks across the room to the fireplace with a fashionable air.*]

HIGGINS A new fashion, by George! And it ought to look horrible!

DOOLITTLE [*with fatherly pride*] Well, I never thought she'd clean up as good looking as that, Governor. Shes a credit to me, aint she?

LIZA I tell you, it's easy to clean up here. Hot and cold water on tap, just as much as you like, there is. Woolly towels, there is; and a towel horse[2] so hot, it burns your fingers. Soft brushes to scrub yourself, and a wooden bowl of soap smelling like primroses. Now I know why ladies is so clean. Washing's a treat for them. Wish they saw what it is for the like of me!

HIGGINS I'm glad the bath-room met with your approval.

LIZA It didnt: not all of it; and I dont care who hears me say it. Mrs. Pearce knows.

HIGGINS What was wrong, Mrs. Pearce?

MRS. PEARCE [*blandly*] Oh, nothing, sir. It doesnt matter.

2. A towel rack, in this case apparently a metal pipe filled with hot water (usually such racks were made of wood).

LIZA I had a good mind to break it. I didnt know which way to look. But I hung a towel over it, I did.

HIGGINS Over what?

MRS. PEARCE Over the looking-glass, sir.

HIGGINS Doolittle: you have brought your daughter up too strictly.

DOOLITTLE Me! I never brought her up at all, except to give her a lick of a strap now and again. Dont put it on me, Governor. She aint accustomed to it, you see: thats all. But she'll soon pick up your free-and-easy ways.

LIZA I'm a good girl, I am; and I wont pick up no free and easy ways.

HIGGINS Eliza: if you say again that youre a good girl, your father shall take you home.

LIZA Not him. You dont know my father. All he come here for was to touch you for some money to get drunk on.

DOOLITTLE Well, what else would I want money for? To put into the plate in church, I suppose. [*She puts out her tongue at him. He is so incensed by this that* PICKERING *presently finds it necessary to step between them.*] Dont you give me none of your lip; and dont let me hear you giving this gentleman any of it neither, or youll hear from me about it. See?

HIGGINS Have you any further advice to give her before you go, Doolittle? Your blessing, for instance.

DOOLITTLE No, Governor: I aint such a mug[3] as to put up my children to all I know myself. Hard enough to hold them in without that. If you want Eliza's mind improved, Governor, you do it yourself with a strap. So long, gentlemen. [*He turns to go.*]

HIGGINS [*impressively*] Stop. Youll come regularly to see your daughter. It's your duty, you know. My brother is a clergyman; and he could help you in your talks with her.

DOOLITTLE [*evasively*] Certainly. I'll come, Governor. Not just this week, because I have a job at a distance. But later on you may depend on me. Afternoon, gentlemen. Afternoon, maam.

[*He takes off his hat to* MRS. PEARCE, *who disdains the salutation and goes out. He winks at* HIGGINS, *thinking him probably a fellow-sufferer from* MRS. PEARCE*'s difficult disposition, and follows her.*]

LIZA Dont you believe the old liar. He'd as soon you set a bull-dog on him as a clergyman. You wont see him again in a hurry.

HIGGINS I dont want to, Eliza. Do you?

LIZA Not me. I dont want never to see him again, I dont. Hes a disgrace to me, he is, collecting dust, instead of working at his trade.

PICKERING What is his trade, Eliza?

LIZA Talking money out of other people's pockets into his own. His proper trade's a navvy;[4] and he works at it sometimes too—for exercise—and earns good money at it. Aint you going to call me Miss Doolittle any more?

PICKERING I beg your pardon, Miss Doolittle. It was a slip of the tongue.

LIZA Oh, I dont mind; only it sounded so genteel. I should just like to take a taxi to the corner of Tottenham Court Road and get out there and tell it to wait for me, just to put the girls in their place a bit. I wouldnt speak to them, you know.

PICKERING Better wait til we get you something really fashionable.

3. Fool.

4. An unskilled laborer who digs earth.

HIGGINS Besides, you shouldnt cut[5] your old friends now that you have risen in the world. Thats what we call snobbery.

LIZA You dont call the like of them my friends now, I should hope. Theyve took it out of me often enough with their ridicule when they had the chance; and now I mean to get a bit of my own back. But if I'm to have fashionable clothes, I'll wait. I should like to have some. Mrs. Pearce says youre going to give me some to wear in bed at night different to what I wear in the daytime; but it do seem a waste of money when you could get something to shew. Besides, I never could fancy changing into cold things on a winter night.

MRS. PEARCE [*coming back*] Now, Eliza. The new things have come for you to try on.

LIZA Ah-ow-oo-ooh!

[*She rushes out.*]

MRS. PEARCE [*following her*] Oh, dont rush about like that, girl.

[*She shuts the door behind her.*]

HIGGINS Pickering: we have taken on a stiff job.

PICKERING [*with conviction*] Higgins: we have.

Act 3

[*It is* MRS. HIGGINS*'s at-home day.*[6] *Nobody has yet arrived. Her drawing-room, in a flat on Chelsea Embankment,*[7] *has three windows looking on the river; and the ceiling is not so lofty as it would be in an older house of the same pretension. The windows are open, giving access to a balcony with flowers in pots. If you stand with your face to the windows, you have the fireplace on your left and the door in the right-hand wall close to the corner nearest the windows.*

MRS. HIGGINS *was brought up on Morris and Burne Jones,*[8] *and her room, which is very unlike her son's room in Wimpole Street, is not crowded with furniture and little tables and nicknacks. In the middle of the room there is a big ottoman; and this, with the carpet, the Morris wall-papers, and the Morris chintz windows curtains and brocade covers of the ottoman and its cushions, supply all the ornament, and are much too handsome to be hidden by odds and ends of useless things. A few good oil-paintings from the exhibitions in the Grosvenor Gallery thirty years ago (the Burne Jones, not the Whistler side of them)*[9] *are on the walls. The only landscape is a Cecil Lawson on the scale of a Rubens.*[1] *There is a portrait of* MRS. HIGGINS *as she was when she defied fashion in her youth in one of the beautiful Rossettian*[2] *costumes which, when caricatured by people*

5. Break off acquaintance with; pretend not to know.
6. In middle- and upper-class society, a set time each week for receiving visitors.
7. A roadway along the north bank of the Thames in central London, developed in the late 19th century with residences for the well-to-do.
8. Two highly influential Victorian artists and designers, who were friends and colleagues. William Morris (1834–1896), associated with the Pre-Raphaelites, was one of the founders of the Arts and Crafts movement and is especially well-known for his wallpaper and fabric designs; Edward Burne-Jones (1833–1898), known for his medieval-style paintings, came under the influence of the Pre-Raphaelites at about the same time as Morris.
9. An allusion to an 1877 exhibition; the painting by the American artist James McNeill Whistler (1834–1903) was so severely attacked in a review by John Ruskin (who praised Burne-Jones's work) that Whistler sued for libel.
1. Peter Paul Rubens (1577–1640), a Flemish artist identified with the baroque style and known for very large paintings. Lawson (1851–1882), an English landscape painter whose early works included a number of studies of Chelsea.
2. In the style of Dante Gabriel Rossetti (1828–1882), an English poet and painter who was a founding member of the Pre-Raphaelite Brotherhood; many of his works depict idealized, sensuous women in flowing garments.

who did not understand, let to the absurdities of popular estheticism in the eighteen-seventies.

In the corner diagonally opposite the door MRS. HIGGINS, *now over sixty and long past taking the trouble to dress out of the fashion, sits writing at an elegantly simple writing-table with a bell button within reach of her hand. There is a Chippendale*[3] *chair further back in the room between her and the window nearest her side. At the other side of the room, further forward, is an Elizabethan chair roughly carved in the taste of Inigo Jones.*[4] *On the same side a piano in a decorated case. The corner between the fireplace and the window is occupied by a divan cushioned in Morris chintz.*

It is between four and five in the afternoon.

The door is opened violently; and Higgins enters with his hat on.]

MRS. HIGGINS [*dismayed*] Henry! [*Scolding him*] What are you doing here to-day? It is my at-home day: you promised not to come. [*As he bends to kiss her, she takes his hat off, and presents it to him.*]

HIGGINS Oh bother! [*He throws the hat down on the table.*]

MRS. HIGGINS Go home at once.

HIGGINS [*kissing her*] I know, mother. I came on purpose.

MRS. HIGGINS But you mustnt. I'm serious, Henry. You offend all my friends: they stop coming whenever they meet you.

HIGGINS Nonsense! I know I have no small talk; but people dont mind. [*He sits on the settee.*]

MRS. HIGGINS Oh! dont they? Small talk indeed! What about your large talk? Really, dear, you mustnt stay.

HIGGINS I must. Ive a job for you. A phonetic job.

MRS. HIGGINS No use, dear. I'm sorry; but I cant get round your vowels; and though I like to get pretty postcards in your patent shorthand, I always have to read the copies in ordinary writing you so thoughtfully send me.

HIGGINS Well, this isnt a phonetic job.

MRS. HIGGINS You said it was.

HIGGINS Not your part of it. Ive picked up a girl.

MRS. HIGGINS Does that mean that some girl has picked you up?

HIGGINS Not at all. I dont mean a love affair.

MRS. HIGGINS What a pity!

HIGGINS Why?

MRS. HIGGINS Well, you never fall in love with anyone under forty-five. When will you discover that there are some rather nice-looking young women about?

HIGGINS Oh, I cant be bothered with young women. My idea of a loveable woman is something as like you as possible. I shall never get into the way of seriously liking young women: some habits lie too deep to be changed. [*Rising abruptly and walking about, jingling his money and his keys in his trouser pockets*] Besides, theyre all idiots.

MRS. HIGGINS Do you know what you would do if you really loved me, Henry?

HIGGINS Oh bother! What? Marry, I suppose?

MRS. HIGGINS No. Stop fidgeting and take your hands out of your pockets. [*With a gesture of despair, he obeys and sits down again.*] Thats a good boy. Now tell me about the girl.

3. A popular 18th-century furniture style, graceful and often ornate; it was named for the English cabinetmaker Thomas Chippendale (1718–1779).

4. The founder of English classical architecture (1573–1652); he designed stage sets as well as buildings.

HIGGINS Shes coming to see you.

MRS. HIGGINS I dont remember asking her.

HIGGINS You didnt. *I* asked her. If youd known her you wouldnt have asked her.

MRS. HIGGINS Indeed! Why?

HIGGINS Well, it's like this. Shes a common flower girl. I picked her off the kerbstone.

MRS. HIGGINS And invited her to my at-home!

HIGGINS [*rising and coming to her to coax her*] Oh, thatll be all right. Ive taught her to speak properly; and she has strict orders as to her behavior. Shes to keep to two subjects: the weather and everybody's health—Fine day and How do you do, you know—and not to let herself go on things in general. That will be safe.

MRS. HIGGINS Safe! To talk about our health! about our insides! perhaps about our outsides! How could you be so silly, Henry?

HIGGINS [*impatiently*] Well, she must talk about something. [*He controls himself and sits down again.*] Oh, she'll be all right: dont you fuss. Pickering is in it with me. Ive a sort of bet on that I'll pass her off as a duchess in six months. I started on her some months ago; and shes getting on like a house on fire. I shall win my bet. She has a quick ear; and shes been easier to teach than my middle-class pupils because shes had to learn a complete new language. She talks English almost as you talk French.

MRS. HIGGINS Thats satisfactory, at all events.

HIGGINS Well, it is and it isnt.

MRS. HIGGINS What does that mean?

HIGGINS You see, Ive got her pronunciation all right; but you have to consider not only how a girl pronounces, but what she pronounces; and thats where—

[*They are interrupted by the* PARLOR-MAID, *announcing guests.*]

THE PARLOR-MAID Mrs. and Miss Eynsford Hill.

[*She withdraws.*]

HIGGINS Oh Lord! [*He rises; snatches his hat from the table; and makes for the door; but before he reaches it his mother introduces him.*]

[MRS. *and* MISS EYNSFORD HILL *are the mother and daughter who sheltered from the rain in Covent Garden. The mother is well bred, quiet, and has the habitual anxiety of straitened means. The daughter has acquired a gay air of being very much at home in society: the bravado of genteel poverty.*]

MRS. EYNSFORD HILL [*to* MRS. HIGGINS] How do you do? [*They shake hands.*]

MISS EYNSFORD HILL How d'you do? [*She shakes.*]

MRS. HIGGINS [*introducing*] My son Henry.

MRS. EYNSFORD HILL Your celebrated son! I have so longed to meet you, Professor Higgins.

HIGGINS [*glumly, making no movement in her direction*] Delighted. [*He backs against the piano and bows brusquely.*]

MISS EYNSFORD HILL [*going to him with confident familiarity*] How do you do?

HIGGINS [*staring at her*] Ive seen you before somewhere. I havnt the ghost of a notion where; but Ive heard your voice. [*Drearily*] It doesnt matter. Youd better sit down.

MRS. HIGGINS I'm sorry to say that my celebrated son has no manners. You mustnt mind him.

MISS EYNSFORD HILL [*gaily*] I dont. [*She sits in the Elizabethan chair.*]

MRS. EYNSFORD HILL [*a little bewildered*] Not at all. [*She sits on the ottoman between her daughter and* MRS. HIGGINS, *who has turned her chair away from the writing-table.*]

HIGGINS Oh, have I been rude? I didnt mean to be.

[*He goes to the central window, through which, with his back to the company, he contemplates the river and the flowers in Battersea Park on the opposite bank as if they were a frozen desert.*]

[*The* PARLOR-MAID *returns, ushering in* PICKERING.]

THE PARLOR-MAID Colonel Pickering.

[*She withdraws.*]

PICKERING How do you do, Mrs. Higgins?

MRS. HIGGINS So glad youve come. Do you know Mrs. Eynsford Hill—Miss Eynsford Hill? [*Exchange of bows. The* COLONEL *brings the Chippendale chair a little forward between* MRS. HILL *and* MRS. HIGGINS, *and sits down.*]

PICKERING Has Henry told you what weve come for?

HIGGINS [*over his shoulder*] We were interrupted: damn it!

MRS. HIGGINS Oh Henry, Henry, really!

MRS. EYNSFORD HILL [*half rising*] Are we in the way?

MRS. HIGGINS [*rising and making her sit down again*] No, no. You couldnt have come more fortunately: we want you to meet a friend of ours.

HIGGINS [*turning hopefully*] Yes, by George! We want two or three people. Youll do as well as anybody else.

[*The* PARLOR-MAID *returns, ushering* FREDDY.]

THE PARLOR-MAID Mr. Eynsford Hill.

HIGGINS [*almost audibly, past endurance*] God of Heaven! another of them.

FREDDY [*shaking hands with* MRS. HIGGINS] Ahdedo?[5]

MRS. HIGGINS Very good of you to come. [*Introducing*] Colonel Pickering.

FREDDY [*bowing*] Ahdedo?

MRS. HIGGINS I dont think you know my son, Professor Higgins.

FREDDY [*going to Higgins*] Ahdedo?

HIGGINS [*looking at him much as if he were a pickpocket*] I'll take my oath Ive met you before somewhere. Where was it?

FREDDY I dont think so.

HIGGINS [*resignedly*] It dont matter, anyhow. Sit down.

[*He shakes* FREDDY*'s hand, and almost slings him on the ottoman with his face to the windows; then comes round to the other side of it.*]

HIGGINS Well, here we are, anyhow! [*He sits down on the ottoman next* MRS. EYNSFORD HILL, *on her left.*] And now, what the devil are we going to talk about until Eliza comes?

MRS. HIGGINS Henry: you are the life and soul of the Royal Society's[6] soirées; but really youre rather trying on more commonplace occasions.

HIGGINS Am I? Very sorry. [*Beaming suddenly*] I suppose I am, you know. [*Uproariously*] Ha, ha!

5. That is, "How do you do?"
6. An independent academy of science in the United Kingdom (formally named in its 1663 charter "The Royal Society of London for Improving Natural Knowledge").

MISS EYNSFORD HILL [*who considers* HIGGINS *quite eligible matrimonially*] I sympathize. *I* havnt any small talk. If people would only be frank and say what they really think!

HIGGINS [*relapsing into gloom*] Lord forbid!

MRS. EYNSFORD HILL [*taking up her daughter's cue*] But why?

HIGGINS What they think they ought to think is bad enough, Lord knows; but what they really think would break up the whole show. Do you suppose it would be really agreeable if I were to come out now with what *I* really think?

MISS EYNSFORD HILL [*gaily*] Is it so very cynical?

HIGGINS Cynical! Who the dickens said it was cynical? I mean it wouldnt be decent.

MRS. EYNSFORD HILL [*seriously*] Oh! I'm sure you dont mean that, Mr. Higgins.

HIGGINS You see, we're all savages, more or less. We're supposed to be civilized and cultured—to know all about poetry and philosophy and art and science, and so on; but how many of us know even the meanings of these names? [*To* MISS HILL] What do you know of poetry? [*To* MRS. HILL] What do you know of science? [*Indicating* FREDDY] What does he know of art or science or anything else? What the devil do you imagine I know of philosophy?

MRS. HIGGINS [*warningly*] Or of manners, Henry?

THE PARLOR-MAID [*opening the door*] Miss Doolittle. [*She withdraws.*]

HIGGINS [*rising hastily and running to* MRS. HIGGINS] Here she is, mother. [*He stands on tiptoe and makes signs over his mother's head to* ELIZA *to indicate to her which lady is her hostess.*]

[ELIZA, *who is exquisitely dressed, produces an impression of such remarkable distinction and beauty as she enters that they all rise, quite fluttered. Guided by* HIGGINS*'s signals, she comes to* MRS. HIGGINS *with studied grace.*]

LIZA [*speaking with pedantic correctness of pronunciation and great beauty of tone*] How do you do, Mrs. Higgins? [*She gasps slightly in making sure of the H in Higgins, but is quite successful.*] Mr. Higgins told me I might come.

MRS. HIGGINS [*cordially*] Quite right: I'm very glad indeed to see you.

PICKERING How do you do, Miss Doolittle?

LIZA [*shaking hands with him*] Colonel Pickering, is it not?

MRS. EYNSFORD HILL I feel sure we have met before, Miss Doolittle. I remember your eyes.

LIZA How do you do? [*She sits down on the ottoman gracefully in the place just left vacant by* HIGGINS.]

MRS. EYNSFORD HILL [*introducing*] My daughter Clara.

LIZA How do you do?

CLARA [*impulsively*] How do you do? [*She sits down on the ottoman beside* ELIZA, *devouring her with her eyes.*]

FREDDY [*coming to their side of the ottoman*] Ive certainly had the pleasure.

MRS. EYNSFORD HILL [*introducing*] My son Freddy.

LIZA How do you do?

[FREDDY *bows and sits down in the Elizabethan chair, infatuated.*]

HIGGINS [*suddenly*] By George, yes: it all comes back to me! [*They stare at him.*] Covent Garden! [*Lamentably*] What a damned thing!

MRS. HIGGINS Henry, please! [*He is about to sit on the edge of the table.*] Dont sit on my writing-table: youll break it.

HIGGINS [*sulkily*] Sorry.

[*He goes to the divan, stumbling into the fender*[7] *and over the fire-irons on his way; extricating himself with muttered imprecations; and finishing his disastrous journey by throwing himself so impatiently on the divan that he almost breaks it. Mrs. Higgins looks at him, but controls herself and says nothing.*]

[*A long and painful pause ensues.*]

MRS. HIGGINS [*at last, conversationally*] Will it rain, do you think?

LIZA The shallow depression in the west of these islands is likely to move slowly in an easterly direction. There are no indications of any great change in the barometrical situation.

FREDDY Ha! ha! how awfully funny!

LIZA What is wrong with that, young man? I bet I got it right.

FREDDY Killing!

MRS. EYNSFORD HILL I'm sure I hope it wont turn cold. Theres so much influenza about. It runs right through our whole family regularly every spring.

LIZA [*darkly*] My aunt died of influenza: so they said.

MRS. EYNSFORD HILL [*clicks her tongue sympathetically*] !!!

LIZA [*in the same tragic tone*] But it's my belief they done the old woman in.

MRS. HIGGINS [*puzzled*] Done her in?

LIZA Y-e-e-e-es, Lord love you! Why should she die of influenza? She come through diphtheria right enough the year before. I saw her with my own eyes. Fairly blue with it, she was. They all thought she was dead; but my father he kept ladling gin down her throat til she came to so sudden that she bit the bowl off the spoon.

MRS. EYNSFORD HILL [*startled*] Dear me!

LIZA [*piling up the indictment*] What call would a woman with that strength in her have to die of influenza? What become of her new straw hat that should have come to me? Somebody pinched it; and what I say is, them as pinched it done her in.

MRS. EYNSFORD HILL What does doing her in mean?

HIGGINS [*hastily*] Oh, thats the new small talk. To do a person in means to kill them.

MRS. EYNSFORD HILL [*to* ELIZA, *horrified*] You surely dont believe that your aunt was killed?

LIZA Do I not! Them she lived with would have killed her for a hat-pin, let alone a hat.

MRS. EYNSFORD HILL But it cant have been right for your father to pour spirits down her throat like that. It might have killed her.

LIZA Not her. Gin was mother's milk to her. Besides, he'd poured so much down his own throat that he knew the good of it.

MRS. EYNSFORD HILL Do you mean that he drank?

LIZA Drank! My word! Something chronic.

MRS. EYNSFORD HILL How dreadful for you!

LIZA Not a bit. It never did him no harm what I could see. But then he did not keep it up regular. [*Cheerfully*] On the burst,[8] as you might say, from time to time. And always more agreeable when he had a drop in. When he was out of work, my mother used to give him fourpence and tell him to go

7. A low metal fire screen.

8. A bout of drunkenness; a binge.

out and not come back until he'd drunk himself cheerful and loving-like. Theres lots of women has to make their husbands drunk to make them fit to live with. [*Now quite at her ease*] You see, it's like this. If a man has a bit of a conscience, it always takes him when he's sober; and then it makes him low-spirited. A drop of booze just takes that off and makes him happy. [*To* FREDDY, *who is in convulsions of suppressed laughter*] Here! what are you sniggering at?

FREDDY The new small talk. You do it so awfully well.

LIZA If I was doing it proper, what was you laughing at? [*To* HIGGINS] Have I said anything I oughtnt?

MRS. HIGGINS [*interposing*] Not at all, Miss Doolittle.

LIZA Well, thats a mercy, anyhow. [*Expansively*] What I always say is—

HIGGINS [*rising and looking at his watch*] Ahem!

LIZA [*looking round at him; taking the hint; and rising*] Well: I must go. [*They all rise.* FREDDY *goes to the door.*] So pleased to have met you. Good-bye. [*She shakes hands with* MRS. HIGGINS.]

MRS. HIGGINS. Good-bye.

LIZA Good-bye, Colonel Pickering.

PICKERING Good-bye, Miss Doolittle. [*They shake hands.*]

LIZA [*nodding to the others*] Good-bye, all.

FREDDY [*opening the door for her*] Are you walking across the Park, Miss Doolittle? If so—

LIZA Walk! Not bloody likely. [*Sensation*] I am going in a taxi. [*She goes out.*]

[PICKERING *gasps and sits down.* FREDDY *goes out on the balcony to catch another glimpse of* ELIZA.]

MRS. EYNSFORD HILL [*suffering from shock*] Well, I really cant get used to the new ways.

CLARA [*throwing herself discontentedly into the Elizabethan chair*] Oh, it's all right, mamma, quite right. People will think we never go anywhere or see anybody if you are so old-fashioned.

MRS. EYNSFORD HILL I daresay I am very old-fashioned; but I do hope you wont begin using that expression, Clara. I have got accustomed to hear you talking about men as rotters, and calling everything filthy and beastly; though I do think it horrible and unladylike. But this last is really too much. Dont you think so, Colonel Pickering?

PICKERING Dont ask me. Ive been away in India for several years; and manners have changed so much that I sometimes dont know whether I'm at a respectable dinner-table or in a ship's forecastle.

CLARA It's all a matter of habit. Theres no right or wrong in it. Nobody means anything by it. And it's so quaint, and gives such a smart emphasis to things that are not in themselves very witty. I find the new small talk delightful and quite innocent.

MRS. EYNSFORD HILL [*rising*] Well, after that, I think it's time for us to go.

[PICKERING *and* HIGGINS *rise.*]

CLARA [*rising*] Oh yes: we have three at-homes to go to still. Good-bye, Mrs. Higgins. Good-bye, Colonel Pickering. Good-bye, Professor Higgins.

HIGGINS [*coming grimly at her from the divan, and accompanying her to the door*] Good-bye. Be sure you try on that small talk at the three at-homes. Dont be nervous about it. Pitch it in strong.

CLARA [*all smiles*] I will. Good-bye. Such nonsense, all this early Victorian prudery!

HIGGINS [*tempting her*] Such damned nonsense!

CLARA Such bloody nonsense!

MRS. EYNSFORD HILL [*convulsively*] Clara!

CLARA. Ha! ha!

[*She goes out radiant, conscious of being thoroughly up to date, and is heard descending the stairs in a stream of silvery laughter.*]

FREDDY [*to the heavens at large*] Well, I ask you—[*He gives it up, and comes to* MRS. HIGGINS]. Good-bye.

MRS. HIGGINS [*shaking hands*] Good-bye. Would you like to meet Miss Doolittle again?

FREDDY [*eagerly*] Yes, I should, most awfully.

MRS. HIGGINS Well, you know my days.

FREDDY Yes. Thanks awfully. Good-bye. [*He goes out.*]

MRS. EYNSFORD HILL Good-bye, Mr. Higgins.

HIGGINS Good-bye. Good-bye.

MRS. EYNSFORD HILL [*to* PICKERING] It's no use. I shall never be able to bring myself to use that word.

PICKERING Dont. It's not compulsory, you know. Youll get on quite well without it.

MRS. EYNSFORD HILL Only, Clara is so down on me if I am not positively reeking with the latest slang. Good-bye.

PICKERING Good-bye. [*They shake hands.*]

MRS. EYNSFORD HILL [*to* MRS. HIGGINS] You mustnt mind Clara. [PICKERING, *catching from her lowered tone that this is not meant for him to hear, discreetly joins* HIGGINS *at the window.*] We're so poor! and she gets so few parties, poor child! She doesnt quite know. [MRS. HIGGINS, *seeing that her eyes are moist, takes her hand sympathetically and goes with her to the door.*] But the boy is nice. Dont you think so?

MRS. HIGGINS Oh, quite nice. I shall always be delighted to see him.

MRS. EYNSFORD HILL Thank you, dear. Good-bye.

[*She goes out.*]

HIGGINS [*eagerly*] Well? Is Eliza presentable? [*He swoops on his mother and drags her to the ottoman, where she sits down in* ELIZA's *place with her son on her left.*]

[PICKERING *returns to his chair on her right.*]

MRS. HIGGINS You silly boy, of course shes not presentable. Shes a triumph of your art and of her dressmaker's; but if you suppose for a moment that she doesnt give herself away in every sentence she utters, you must be perfectly cracked about[9] her.

PICKERING But dont you think something might be done? I mean something to eliminate the sanguinary element[1] from her conversation.

MRS. HIGGINS Not as long as she is in Henry's hands.

HIGGINS [*aggrieved*] Do you mean that my language is improper?

MRS. HIGGINS No, dearest: it would be quite proper—say on a canal barge; but it would not be proper for her at a garden party.

HIGGINS [*deeply injured*] Well I must say—

9. Infatuated with.

1. That is, the word "bloody."

PICKERING [*interrupting him*] Come, Higgins: you must learn to know yourself. I havnt heard such language as yours since we used to review the volunteers[2] in Hyde Park twenty years ago.

HIGGINS [*sulkily*] Oh, well, if you say so, I suppose I dont always talk like a bishop.

MRS. HIGGINS [*quieting* HENRY *with a touch*] Colonel Pickering: will you tell me what is the exact state of things in Wimpole Street?

PICKERING [*cheerfully: as if this completely changed the subject*] Well, I have come to live there with Henry. We work together at my Indian Dialects; and we think it more convenient—

MRS. HIGGINS Quite so. I know all about that: it's an excellent arrangement. But where does this girl live?

HIGGINS With us, of course. Where would she live?

MRS. HIGGINS But on what terms? Is she a servant? If not, what is she?

PICKERING [*slowly*] I think I know what you mean, Mrs. Higgins.

HIGGINS Well, dash me if *I* do! Ive had to work at the girl every day for months to get her to her present pitch. Besides, shes useful. She knows where my things are, and remembers my appointments and so forth.

MRS. HIGGINS How does your housekeeper get on with her?

HIGGINS Mrs. Pearce? Oh, shes jolly glad to get so much taken off her hands; for before Eliza came, she used to have to find things and remind me of my appointments. But shes got some silly bee in her bonnet about Eliza. She keeps saying "You dont think, sir": doesnt she, Pick?

PICKERING Yes: thats the formula. "You dont think, sir." Thats the end of every conversation about Eliza.

HIGGINS As if I ever stop thinking about the girl and her confounded vowels and consonants. I'm worn out, thinking about her, and watching her lips and her teeth and her tongue, not to mention her soul, which is the quaintest of the lot.

MRS. HIGGINS You certainly are a pretty pair of babies, playing with your live doll.

HIGGINS Playing! The hardest job I ever tackled: make no mistake about that, mother. But you have no idea how frightfully interesting it is to take a human being and change her into a quite different human being by creating a new speech for her. It's filling up the deepest gulf that separates class from class and soul from soul.

PICKERING [*drawing his chair closer to* MRS. HIGGINS *and bending over to her eagerly*] Yes: it's enormously interesting. I assure you, Mrs. Higgins, we take Eliza very seriously. Every week—every day almost—there is some new change. [*Closer again*] We keep records of every stage—dozens of gramophone disks and photographs—

HIGGINS [*assailing her at the other ear*] Yes, by George: it's the most absorbing experiment I ever tackled. She regularly fills our lives up; doesnt she, Pick?

PICKERING We're always talking Eliza.

HIGGINS Teaching Eliza.

PICKERING Dressing Eliza.

MRS. HIGGINS What!

HIGGINS Inventing new Elizas.

2. Inspect the troops. Hyde Park, a large park in central London northwest of Buckingham Palace, was frequently used for large-scale military reviews in the 19th century.

HIGGINS [*speaking together*] You know, she has the most extraordinary quickness of ear:
PICKERING I assure you, my dear Mrs. Higgins, that girl
HIGGINS just like a parrot. Ive tried her with every
PICKERING is a genius. She can play the piano quite beautifully.
HIGGINS possible sort of sound that a human being can make—
PICKERING We have taken her to classical concerts and to music
HIGGINS Continental dialects, African dialects, Hottentot
PICKERING halls; and it's all the same to her: she plays everything
HIGGINS clicks,[3] things it took me years to get hold of; and
PICKERING she hears right off when she comes home, whether it's
HIGGINS she picks them up like a shot, right away, as if she had
PICKERING Beethoven and Brahms or Lehar and Lionel Monckton;[4]
HIGGINS been at it all her life.
PICKERING though six months ago, she'd never as much as touched a piano—

MRS. HIGGINS [*putting her fingers in her ears, as they are by this time shouting one another down with an intolerable noise*] Sh-sh-sh—sh! [*They stop.*]

PICKERING I beg your pardon. [*He draws his chair back apologetically.*]

HIGGINS Sorry. When Pickering starts shouting nobody can get a word in edgeways.

MRS. HIGGINS Be quiet, Henry. Colonel Pickering: dont you realize that when Eliza walked into Wimpole Street, something walked in with her?

PICKERING Her father did. But Henry soon got rid of him.

MRS. HIGGINS It would have been more to the point if her mother had. But as her mother didnt something else did.

PICKERING But what?

MRS. HIGGINS [*unconsciously dating herself by the word*] A problem.

PICKERING Oh, I see. The problem of how to pass her off as a lady.

HIGGINS I'll solve that problem. Ive half solved it already.

MRS. HIGGINS No, you two infinitely stupid male creatures: the problem of what is to be done with her afterwards.

HIGGINS I dont see anything in that. She can go her own way, with all the advantages I have given her.

MRS. HIGGINS The advantages of that poor woman who was here just now! The manners and habits that disqualify a fine lady from earning her own living without giving her a fine lady's income! Is that what you mean?

3. *Hottentot clicks:* implosive consonant sounds used in a number of languages of southern Africa.

4. Examples of composers featured in classical concerts—the Germans Ludwig van Beethoven (1770–1827) and Johannes Brahms (1833–1897)—and those celebrated for more popular fare, the Hungarian Franz Lehár (1870–1948), known for his operettas, and the English Lionel Monckton (1861–1924), who wrote many hit songs for musical theater.

PICKERING [*indulgently, being rather bored*] Oh, that will be all right, Mrs. Higgins. [*He rises to go.*]

HIGGINS [*rising also*] We'll find her some light employment.

PICKERING Shes happy enough. Dont you worry about her. Good-bye. [*He shakes hands as if he were consoling a frightened child, and makes for the door.*]

HIGGINS Anyhow, theres no good bothering now. The things done. Good-bye, mother. [*He kisses her, and follows* PICKERING.]

PICKERING [*turning for a final consolation*] There are plenty of openings. We'll do whats right. Good-bye.

HIGGINS [*to* PICKERING *as they go out together*] Let's take her to the Shakespear exhibition at Earls Court.

PICKERING Yes: lets. Her remarks will be delicious.

HIGGINS She'll mimic all the people for us when we get home.

PICKERING Ripping.

[*Both are heard laughing as they go downstairs.*]

MRS. HIGGINS [*rises with an impatient bounce, and returns to her work at the writing-table. She sweeps a litter of disarranged papers out of her way; snatches a sheet of paper from her stationery case; and tries resolutely to write. At the third line she gives it up; flings down her pen; grips the table angrily and exclaims.*] Oh, men! men!! men!!!

Act 4

[*The Wimpole Street laboratory. Midnight. Nobody in the room. The clock on the mantelpiece strikes twelve. The fire is not alight: it is a summer night.*

Presently HIGGINS *and* PICKERING *are heard on the stairs.*]

HIGGINS [*calling down to* PICKERING] I say, Pick: lock up, will you. I shant be going out again.

PICKERING Right. Can Mrs. Pearce go to bed? We dont want anything more, do we?

HIGGINS Lord, no!

[ELIZA *opens the door and is seen on the lighted landing in opera cloak, brilliant evening dress, and diamonds, with fan, flowers, and all accessories. She comes to the hearth, and switches on the electric lights there. She is tired: her pallor contrasts strongly with her dark eyes and hair; and her expression is almost tragic. She takes off her cloak; puts her fan and flowers on the piano; and sits down on the bench, brooding and silent.* HIGGINS, *in evening dress, with overcoat and hat, comes in, carrying a smoking jacket*[5] *which he has picked up downstairs. He takes off the hat and overcoat; throws them carelessly on the newspaper stand; disposes of his coat in the same way; puts on the smoking jacket; and throws himself wearily into the easy-chair at the hearth.* PICKERING *similarly attired, comes in. He also takes off his hat and overcoat, and is about to throw them on* HIGGINS*'s when he hesitates.*]

PICKERING I say: Mrs. Pearce will row[6] if we leave these things lying about in the drawing-room.

5. A casual jacket worn at home, usually in the evening.

6. That is, start a quarrel.

HIGGINS Oh, chuck them over the bannisters into the hall. She'll find them there in the morning and put them away all right. She'll think we were drunk.

PICKERING We are, slightly. Are there any letters?

HIGGINS I didnt look. [PICKERING *takes the overcoats and hats and goes downstairs. Higgins begins half singing half yawning an air from La Fanciulla del Golden West.*[7] *Suddenly he stops and exclaims*] I wonder where the devil my slippers are!

[ELIZA *looks at him darkly; then rises suddenly and leaves the room.*]

[HIGGINS *yawns again, and resumes his song.*]

[PICKERING *returns, with the contents of the letter-box in his hand.*]

PICKERING Only circulars, and this coroneted billet-doux[8] for you. [*He throws the circulars into the fender, and posts himself on the hearthrug, with his back to the grate.*]

HIGGINS [*glancing at the billet-doux*] Money-lender. [*He throws the letter after the circulars.*]

[ELIZA *returns with a pair of large down-at-heel slippers. She places them on the carpet before* HIGGINS, *and sits as before without a word.*]

HIGGINS [*yawning again*] Oh Lord! What an evening! What a crew! What a silly tomfoollery! [*He raises his shoe to unlace it, and catches sight of the slippers. He stops unlacing and looks at them as if they had appeared there of their own accord.*] Oh! theyre there, are they?

PICKERING [*stretching himself*] Well, I feel a bit tired. It's been a long day. The garden party, a dinner party, and the opera! Rather too much of a good thing. But youve won your bet, Higgins. Eliza did the trick, and something to spare, eh?

HIGGINS [*fervently*] Thank God it's over!

[ELIZA *flinches violently; but they take no notice of her; and she recovers herself and sits stonily as before.*]

PICKERING Were you nervous at the garden party? *I* was. Eliza didnt seem a bit nervous.

HIGGINS Oh, she wasnt nervous. I knew she'd be all right. No: it's the strain of putting the job through all these months that has told on me. It was interesting enough at first, while we were at the phonetics; but after that I got deadly sick of it. If I hadnt backed myself to do it I should have chucked the whole thing up two months ago. It was a silly notion: the whole thing has been a bore.

PICKERING Oh come! the garden party was frightfully exciting. My heart began beating like anything.

HIGGINS Yes, for the first three minutes. But when I saw we were going to win hands down, I felt like a bear in a cage, hanging about doing nothing. The dinner was worse: sitting gorging there for over an hour, with nobody but a damned fool of a fashionable woman to talk to! I tell you, Pickering, never again for me. No more artificial duchesses. The whole thing has been simple purgatory.

PICKERING Youve never been broken in properly to the social routine. [*Strolling over to the piano*] I rather enjoy dipping into it occasionally

7. That is, *La Fanciulla del West* (*The Girl of the Golden West,* 1910), an opera by Giacomo Puccini.

8. A love letter on fine stationery (coronets signify nobility).

myself: it makes me feel young again. Anyhow, it was a great success: an immense success. I was quite frightened once or twice because Eliza was doing it so well. You see, lots of the real people cant do it at all: theyre such fools that they think style comes by nature to people in their position; and so they never learn. Theres always something professional about doing a thing superlatively well.

HIGGINS Yes: thats what drives me mad: the silly people dont know their own silly business. [*Rising*] However, it's over and done with; and now I can go to bed at last without dreading tomorrow.

[ELIZA's *beauty becomes murderous.*]

PICKERING I think I shall turn in too. Still, it's been a great occasion: a triumph for you. Good-night.

[*He goes.*]

HIGGINS [*following him*] Good-night. [*Over his shoulder, at the door*] Put out the lights, Eliza; and tell Mrs. Pearce not to make coffee for me in the morning: I'll take tea.

[*He goes out.*]

[ELIZA *tries to control herself and feel indifferent as she rises and walks across to the hearth to switch off the lights. By the time she gets there she is on the point of screaming. She sits down in* HIGGINS*'s chair and holds on hard to the arms. Finally she gives way and flings herself furiously on the floor raging.*]

HIGGINS [*in despairing wrath outside*] What the devil have I done with my slippers? [*He appears at the door.*]

LIZA [*snatching up the slippers, and hurling them at him one after the other with all her force*] There are your slippers. And there. Take your slippers; and may you never have a day's luck with them!

HIGGINS [*astounded*] What on earth—! [*He comes to her.*] Whats the matter? Get up. [*He pulls her up.*] Anything wrong?

LIZA [*breathless*] Nothing wrong—with you. Ive won your bet for you, havnt I? That enough for you. *I* dont matter, I suppose.

HIGGINS You won my bet! You! Presumptuous insect! *I* won it. What did you throw those slippers at me for?

LIZA Because I wanted to smash your face. I'd like to kill you, you selfish brute. Why didnt you leave me where you picked me out of—in the gutter? You thank God it's all over, and that now you can throw me back again there, do you? [*She crisps*[9] *her fingers frantically.*]

HIGGINS [*looking at her in cool wonder*] The creature is nervous, after all.

LIZA [*gives a suffocated scream of fury, and instinctively darts her nails at his face*] !!

HIGGINS [*catching her wrists*] Ah! would you? Claws in, you cat. How dare you shew your temper to me? Sit down and be quiet. [*He throws her roughly into the easy-chair.*]

LIZA [*crushed by superior strength and weight*] Whats to become of me? Whats to become of me?

HIGGINS How the devil do I know whats to become of you? What does it matter what becomes of you?

9. Curls.

LIZA You dont care. I know you dont care. You wouldnt care if I was dead. I'm nothing to you—not so much as them slippers.

HIGGINS [*thundering*] Those slippers.

LIZA [*with bitter submission*] Those slippers. I didnt think it made any difference now.

[*A pause.* ELIZA *hopeless and crushed.* HIGGINS *a little uneasy.*]

HIGGINS [*in his loftiest manner*] Why have you begun going on like this? May I ask whether you complain of your treatment here?

LIZA No.

HIGGINS Has anybody behaved badly to you? Colonel Pickering? Mrs. Pearce? Any of the servants?

LIZA No.

HIGGINS I presume you dont pretend that *I* have treated you badly.

LIZA No.

HIGGINS I am glad to hear it. [*He moderates his tone.*] Perhaps youre tired after the strain of the day. Will you have a glass of champagne? [*He moves towards the door.*]

LIZA No. [*Recollecting her manners*] Thank you.

HIGGINS [*good-humored again*] This has been coming on you for some days. I suppose it was natural for you to be anxious about the garden party. But thats all over now. [*He pats her kindly on the shoulder. She writhes.*] Theres nothing more to worry about.

LIZA No. Nothing more for you to worry about. [*She suddenly rises and gets away from him by going to the piano bench, where she sits and hides her face.*] Oh God! I wish I was dead.

HIGGINS [*staring after her in sincere surprise*] Why? in heaven's name, why? [*Reasonably, going to her*] Listen to me, Eliza. All this irritation is purely subjective.

LIZA I dont understand. I'm too ignorant.

HIGGINS It's only imagination. Low spirits and nothing else. Nobody's hurting you. Nothing's wrong. You go to bed like a good girl and sleep it off. Have a little cry and say your prayers: that will make you comfortable.

LIZA I heard your prayers. "Thank God it's all over!"

HIGGINS [*impatiently*] Well, dont you thank God it's all over? Now you are free and can do what you like.

LIZA [*pulling herself together in desperation*] What am I fit for? What have you left me fit for? Where am I to go? What am I to do? Whats to become of me?

HIGGINS [*enlightened, but not at all impressed*] Oh, thats whats worrying you, is it? [*He thrusts his hands into his pockets, and walks about in his usual manner, rattling the contents of his pockets, as if condescending to a trivial subject out of pure kindness.*] I shouldnt bother about it if I were you. I should imagine you wont have much difficulty in settling yourself somewhere or other, though I hadnt quite realized that you were going away. [*She looks quickly at him: he does not look at her, but examines the dessert stand on the piano and decides that he will eat an apple.*] You might marry, you know. [*He bites a large piece out of the apple, and munches it noisily.*] You see, Eliza, all men are not confirmed old bachelors like me and the Colonel. Most men are the marrying sort (poor devils!); and youre not bad-looking; it's quite a pleasure to look at you sometimes—not now, of course, because youre crying and looking as ugly as the very devil; but when youre all right and quite yourself, youre what I should call attractive. That is, to the people in the marrying line, you understand. You go to bed and have a good nice rest; and then get up and look at yourself in the glass; and you wont feel so cheap.

[ELIZA *again looks at him, speechless, and does not stir.*]

[*The look is quite lost on him: he eats his apple with a dreamy expression of happiness, as it is quite a good one.*]

HIGGINS [*a genial afterthought occurring to him*] I daresay my mother could find some chap or other who would do very well.

LIZA We were above that at the corner of Tottenham Court Road.

HIGGINS [*waking up*] What do you mean?

LIZA I sold flowers. I didnt sell myself. Now youve made a lady of me I'm not fit to sell anything else. I wish youd left me where you found me.

HIGGINS [*slinging the core of the apple decisively into the grate*] Tosh, Eliza. Dont you insult human relations by dragging all this cant about buying and selling into it. You neednt marry the fellow if you dont like him.

LIZA What else am I to do?

HIGGINS Oh, lots of things. What about your old idea of a florist's shop? Pickering could set you up in one: hes lots of money. [*Chuckling*] He'll have to pay for all those togs you have been wearing today; and that, with the hire of the jewellery, will make a big hole in two hundred pounds. Why, six months ago you would have thought it the millennium to have a flower shop of your own. Come! youll be all right. I must clear off to bed: I'm devilish sleepy. By the way, I came down for something: I forget what it was.

LIZA Your slippers.

HIGGINS Oh yes, of course. You shied them at me. [*He picks them up, and is going out when she rises and speaks to him.*]

LIZA Before you go, sir—

HIGGINS [*dropping the slippers in his surprise at her calling him Sir*] Eh?

LIZA Do my clothes belong to me or to Colonel Pickering?

HIGGINS [*coming back into the room as if her question were the very climax of unreason*] What the devil use would they be to Pickering?

LIZA He might want them for the next girl you pick up to experiment on.

HIGGINS [*shocked and hurt*] Is that the way you feel towards us?

LIZA I dont want to hear anything more about that. All I want to know is whether anything belongs to me. My own clothes were burnt.

HIGGINS But what does it matter? Why need you start bothering about that in the middle of the night?

LIZA I want to know what I may take away with me. I dont want to be accused of stealing.

HIGGINS [*now deeply wounded*] Stealing! You shouldnt have said that, Eliza. That shews a want of feeling.

LIZA I'm sorry. I'm only a common ignorant girl; and in my station I have to be careful. There cant be any feelings between the like of you and the like of me. Please will you tell me what belongs to me and what doesn't?

HIGGINS [*very sulky*] You may take the whole damned houseful if you like. Except the jewels. Theyre hired. Will that satisfy you? [*He turns on his heel and is about to go in extreme dudgeon.*]

LIZA [*drinking in his emotion like nectar, and nagging him to provoke a further supply*] Stop, please. [*She takes off her jewels.*] Will you take these to your room and keep them safe? I dont want to run the risk of their being missing.

HIGGINS [*furious*] Hand them over. [*She puts them into his hands.*] If these belonged to me instead of to the jeweler, I'd ram them down your ungrateful throat. [*He perfunctorily thrusts them into his pockets, unconsciously decorating himself with the protruding ends of the chains.*]

LIZA [*taking a ring off*] This ring isnt the jeweler's: it's the one you bought me in Brighton.[1] I dont want it now. [*Higgins dashes the ring violently into the fireplace, and turns on her so threateningly that she crouches over the piano with her hands over her face, and exclaims.*] Don't you hit me.

HIGGINS Hit you! You infamous creature, how dare you accuse me of such a thing? It is you who have hit me. You have wounded me to the heart.

LIZA [*thrilling with hidden joy*] I'm glad. Ive got a little of my own back, anyhow.

HIGGINS [*with dignity, in his finest professional style*] You have caused me to lose my temper: a thing that has hardly ever happend to me before. I prefer to say nothing more tonight. I am going to bed.

LIZA [*pertly*] Youd better leave a note for Mrs. Pearce about the coffee; for she wont be told by me.

HIGGINS [*formally*] Damn Mrs. Pearce; and damn the coffee; and damn you; and damn my own folly in having lavished hard-earned knowledge and the treasure of my regard and intimacy on a heartless guttersnipe.

[*He goes out with impressive decorum, and spoils it by slamming the door savagely.*]

[ELIZA *smiles for the first time; expresses her feelings by a wild pantomime in which an imitation of* HIGGINS*'s exit is confused with her own triumph; and finally goes down on her knees on the hearthrug to look for the ring.*]

Act 5

[*Mrs.* HIGGINS*'s drawing-room. She is at her writing-table as before. The* PARLOR-MAID *comes in.*]

THE PARLOR-MAID [*at the door*] Mr. Henry, mam, is downstairs with Colonel Pickering.

MRS. HIGGINS Well, shew them up.

THE PARLOR-MAID Theyre using the telephone, mam. Telephoning to the police, I think.

MRS. HIGGINS What!

THE PARLOR-MAID [*coming further in and lowering her voice*] Mr. Henry's in a state, mam. I thought I'd better tell you.

MRS. HIGGINS If you had told me that Mr. Henry was not in a state it would have been more surprising. Tell them to come up when theyve finished with the police. I suppose hes lost something.

THE PARLOR-MAID Yes, mam. [*Going*]

MRS. HIGGINS Go upstairs and tell Miss Doolittle that Mr. Henry and the Colonel are here. Ask her not to come down till I send for her.

THE PARLOR-MAID Yes, mam.

[HIGGINS *bursts in. He is, as the* PARLOR-MAID *has said, in a state.*]

1. A seaside resort on the English Channel, about 50 miles south of London.

HIGGINS Look here, mother: heres a confounded thing!

MRS. HIGGINS Yes, dear. Good-morning. [*He checks his impatience and kisses her, whilst the* PARLOR-MAID *goes out.*] What is it?

HIGGINS Eliza's bolted.

MRS. HIGGINS [*calmly continuing her writing*] You must have frightened her.

HIGGINS Frightened her! nonsense! She was left last night, as usual, to turn out the lights and all that; and instead of going to bed she changed her clothes and went right off: her bed wasnt slept in. She came in a cab for her things before seven this morning; and that fool Mrs. Pearce let her have them without telling me a word about it. What am I to do?

MRS. HIGGINS Do without, I'm afraid, Henry. The girl has a perfect right to leave if she chooses.

HIGGINS [*wandering distractedly across the room*] But I cant find anything. I dont know what appointments Ive got. I'm— [PICKERING *comes in.* MRS. HIGGINS *puts down her pen and turns away from the writing-table.*]

PICKERING [*shaking hands*] Good-morning, Mrs. Higgins. Has Henry told you? [*He sits down on the ottoman.*]

HIGGINS What does that ass of an inspector say? Have you offered a reward?

MRS. HIGGINS [*rising in indignant amazement*] You dont mean to say you have set the police after Eliza?

HIGGINS Of course. What are the police for? What else could we do? [*He sits in the Elizabethan chair.*]

PICKERING The inspector made a lot of difficulties. I really think he suspected us of some improper purpose.

MRS. HIGGINS Well, of course he did. What right have you to go to the police and give the girl's name as if she were a thief, or a lost umbrella, or something? Really! [*She sits down again, deeply vexed.*]

HIGGINS But we want to find her.

PICKERING We cant let her go like this, you know, Mrs. Higgins. What were we to do?

MRS. HIGGINS You have no more sense, either of you, than two children. Why—

[*The* PARLOR-MAID *comes in and breaks off the conversation.*]

THE PARLOR-MAID Mr. Henry: a gentleman wants to see you very particular. Hes been sent on from Wimpole Street.

HIGGINS Oh, bother! I cant see anyone now. Who is it?

THE PARLOR-MAID A Mr. Doolittle, sir.

PICKERING Doolittle! Do you mean the dustman?

THE PARLOR-MAID Dustman! Oh no, sir: a gentleman.

HIGGINS [*springing up excitedly*] By George, Pick, it's some relative of hers that shes gone to. Somebody we know nothing about. [*To the* PARLOR-MAID] Send him up, quick.

THE PARLOR-MAID Yes, sir.

[*She goes.*]

HIGGINS [*eagerly, going to his mother*] Genteel relatives! now we shall hear something. [*He sits down in the Chippendale chair.*]

MRS. HIGGINS Do you know any of her people?

PICKERING Only her father: the fellow we told you about.

THE PARLOR-MAID [*announcing*] Mr. Doolittle.

[*She withdraws.*]

[DOOLITTLE *enters. He is brilliantly dressed in a new fashionable frock-coat, with white waistcoat and grey trousers. A flower in his buttonhole, a dazzling silk hat, and patent leather shoes complete the effect. He is too concerned with the business he has come on to notice* MRS. HIGGINS. *He walks straight to* HIGGINS, *and accosts him with vehement reproach.*]

DOOLITTLE [*indicating his own person*] See here! Do you see this? You done this.

HIGGINS Done what, man?

DOOLITTLE This, I tell you. Look at it. Look at this hat. Look at this coat.

PICKERING Has Eliza been buying you clothes?

DOOLITTLE Eliza! not she. Not half. Why would she buy me clothes?

MRS. HIGGINS Good-morning, Mr. Doolittle. Wont you sit down?

DOOLITTLE [*taken aback as he becomes conscious that he has forgotten his hostess*] Asking your pardon, maam. [*He approaches her and shakes her proffered hand.*] Thank you. [*He sits down on the ottoman, on Pickering's right.*] I am that full of what has happened to me that I cant think of anything else.

HIGGINS What the dickens has happened to you?

DOOLITTLE I shouldnt mind if it had only happened to me: anything might happen to anybody and nobody to blame but Providence, as you might say. But this is something that you done to me: yes, you, Henry Higgins.

HIGGINS Have you found Eliza? Thats the point.

DOOLITTLE Have you lost her?

HIGGINS Yes.

DOOLITTLE You have all the luck, you have. I aint found her; but she'll find me quick enough now after what you done to me.

MRS. HIGGINS But what has my son done to you, Mr. Doolittle?

DOOLITTLE Done to me! Ruined me. Destroyed my happiness. Tied me up and delivered me into the hands of middle class morality.

HIGGINS [*rising intolerantly and standing over Doolittle*] Youre raving. Youre drunk. Youre mad. I gave you five pounds. After that I had two conversations with you, at half-a-crown an hour. Ive never seen you since.

DOOLITTLE Oh! Drunk! am I? Mad! am I? Tell me this. Did you or did you not write a letter to an old blighter in America that was giving five millions to found Moral Reform Societies all over the world, and that wanted you to invent a universal language for him?

HIGGINS What! Ezra D. Wannafeller![2] Hes dead. [*He sits down again carelessly.*]

DOOLITTLE Yes: hes dead; and I'm done for. Now did you or did you not write a letter to him to say that the most original moralist at present in England, to the best of your knowledge, was Alfred Doolittle, a common dustman.

HIGGINS Oh, after your last visit I remember making some silly joke of the kind.

DOOLITTLE Ah! you may well call it a silly joke. It put the lid on me right enough. Just give him the chance he wanted to shew that Americans is not like us: that they recognize and respect merit in every class of life, however humble. Them words is in his blooming will, in which, Henry Higgins, thanks to your silly joking, he leaves me a share in his Pre-digested Cheese

2. Shaw conflates the names of two actual American millionaires, the merchant John Wanamaker (1838–1922) and the industrialist John D. Rockefeller (1839–1937).

Trust worth three thousand a year[3] on condition that I lecture for his Wannafeller Moral Reform World League as often as they ask me up to six times a year.

HIGGINS The devil he does! Whew! [*Brightening suddenly*] What a lark!

PICKERING A safe thing for you, Doolittle. They wont ask you twice.

DOOLITTLE It aint the lecturing I mind. I'll lecture them blue in the face, I will, and not turn a hair. It's making a gentleman of me that I object to. Who asked him to make a gentleman of me? I was happy. I was free. I touched pretty nigh everybody for money when I wanted it, same as I touched you, Henry Higgins. Now I am worrited; tied neck and heels; and everybody touches me for money. It's a fine thing for you, says my solicitor. Is it? says I. You mean it's a good thing for you, I says. When I was a poor man and had a solicitor once when they found a pram in the dust cart, he got me off, and got shut of[4] me and got me shut of him as quick as he could. Same with the doctors: used to shove me out of the hospital before I could hardly stand on my legs, and nothing to pay. Now they finds out that I'm not a healthy man and cant live unless they looks after me twice a day. In the house I'm not let do a hand's turn for myself: somebody else must do it and touch me for it. A year ago I hadnt a relative in the world except two or three that wouldnt speak to me. Now Ive fifty, and not a decent week's wages among the lot of them. I have to live for others and not for myself: thats middle class morality. You talk of losing Eliza. Dont you be anxious: I bet shes on my doorstep by this: she that could support herself easy by selling flowers if I wasnt respectable. And the next one to touch me will be you, Henry Higgins. I'll have to learn to speak middle class language from you, instead of speaking proper English. Thats where youll come in; and I daresay thats what you done it for.

MRS. HIGGINS But, my dear Mr. Doolittle, you need not suffer all this if you are really in earnest. Nobody can force you to accept this bequest. You can repudiate it. Isnt that so, Colonel Pickering?

PICKERING I believe so.

DOOLITTLE [*softening his manner in deference to her sex*] Thats the tragedy of it, maam. It's easy to say chuck it; but I havent the nerve. Which of us has? We're all intimidated. Intimidated, maam: thats what we are. What is there for me if I chuck it but the workhouse in my old age? I have to dye my hair[5] already to keep my job as a dustman. If I was one of the deserving poor, and had put by a bit, I could chuck it; but then why should I, acause[6] the deserving poor might as well be millionaires for all the happiness they ever has. They dont know what happiness is. But I, as one of the undeserving poor, have nothing between me and the pauper's uniform but this here blasted three thousand a year that shoves me into the middle class. (Excuse the expression, maam: youd use it yourself if you had my provocation.) Theyve got you every way you turn: it's a choice between the Skilly of the workhouse and the Char Bydis of the middle class;[7] and I havnt the nerve

3. Roughly equivalent to $250,000 today.
4. Rid of.
5. That is, to keep from being fired because of his advancing age (no laws prevented such firing).
6. Because.
7. That is, between two equal dangers. In Greek mythology, Scylla and Charybdis are two monsters (who become a rock and whirlpool, respectively) that endanger sailors between Sicily and Italy.

for the workhouse. Intimidated: thats what I am. Broke. Bought up. Happier men than me will call for my dust, and touch me for their tip; and I'll look on helpless, and envy them. And thats what your son has brought me to. [*He is overcome by emotion.*]

MRS. HIGGINS Well, I'm very glad youre not going to do anything foolish, Mr. Doolittle. For this solves the problem of Eliza's future. You can provide for her now.

DOOLITTLE [*with melancholy resignation*] Yes, maam: I'm expected to provide for everyone now, out of three thousand a year.

HIGGINS [*jumping up*] Nonsense! he cant provide for her. He shant provide for her. She doesnt belong to him. I paid him five pounds for her. Doolittle: either youre an honest man or a rogue.

DOOLITTLE [*tolerantly*] A little of both, Henry, like the rest of us: a little of both.

HIGGINS Well, you took that money for the girl; and you have no right to take her as well.

MRS. HIGGINS Henry: dont be absurd. If you really want to know where Eliza is, she is upstairs.

HIGGINS [*amazed*] Upstairs!!! Then I shall jolly soon fetch her downstairs. [*He makes resolutely for the door.*]

MRS. HIGGINS [*rising and following him*] Be quiet, Henry. Sit down.

HIGGINS I—

MRS. HIGGINS Sit down, dear; and listen to me.

HIGGINS Oh very well, very well, very well. [*He throws himself ungraciously on the ottoman, with his face towards the windows.*] But I think you might have told me this half an hour ago.

MRS. HIGGINS Eliza came to me this morning. She passed the night partly walking about in a rage, partly trying to throw herself into the river and being afraid to, and partly in the Carlton Hotel. She told me of the brutal way you two treated her.

HIGGINS [*bounding up again*] What!

PICKERING [*rising also*] My dear Mrs. Higgins, shes been telling you stories. We didnt treat her brutally. We hardly said a word to her; and we parted on particularly good terms. [*Turning on* HIGGINS] Higgins: did you bully her after I went to bed?

HIGGINS Just the other way about. She threw my slippers in my face. She behaved in the most outrageous way. I never gave her the slightest provocation. The slippers came bang into my face the moment I entered the room—before I had uttered a word. And used perfectly awful language.

PICKERING [*astonished*] But why? What did we do to her?

MRS. HIGGINS I think I know pretty well what you did. The girl is naturally rather affectionate, I think. Isnt she, Mr. Doolittle?

DOOLITTLE Very tender-hearted, maam. Takes after me.

MRS. HIGGINS Just so. She had become attached to you both. She worked very hard for you, Henry! I dont think you quite realize what anything in the nature of brain work means to a girl like that. Well, it seems that when the great day of trial came, and she did this wonderful thing for you without making a single mistake, you two sat there and never said a word to her, but talked together of how glad you were that it was all over and how you had been bored with the whole thing. And then you were surprised because she threw your slippers at you! *I* should have thrown the fire-irons at you.

HIGGINS We said nothing except that we were tired and wanted to go to bed. Did we, Pick?

PICKERING [*shrugging his shoulders*] That was all.

MRS. HIGGINS [*ironically*] Quite sure?

PICKERING Absolutely. Really, that was all.

MRS. HIGGINS You didn't thank her, or pet her, or admire her, or tell her how splendid she'd been.

HIGGINS [*impatiently*] But she knew all about that. We didnt make speeches to her, if thats what you mean.

PICKERING [*conscience stricken*] Perhaps we were a little inconsiderate. Is she very angry?

MRS. HIGGINS [*returning to her place at the writing-table*] Well, I'm afraid she wont go back to Wimpole Street, especially now that Mr. Doolittle is able to keep up the position you have thrust on her; but she says she is quite willing to meet you on friendly terms and to let bygones be bygones.

HIGGINS [*furious*] Is she, by George? Ho!

MRS. HIGGINS If you promise to behave yourself, Henry, I'll ask her to come down. If not, go home; for you have taken up quite enough of my time.

HIGGINS Oh, all right. Very well. Pick: you behave yourself. Let us put on our best Sunday manners for this creature that we picked out of the mud. [*He flings himself sulkily into the Elizabethan chair.*]

DOOLITTLE [*remonstrating*] Now, now, Henry Higgins! have some consideration for my feelings as a middle class man.

MRS. HIGGINS Remember your promise, Henry. [*She presses the bell-button on the writing-table.*] Mr. Doolittle: will you be so good as to step out on the balcony for a moment. I dont want Eliza to have the shock of your news until she has made it up with these two gentlemen. Would you mind?

DOOLITTLE As you wish, lady. Anything to help Henry to keep her off my hands.

[*He disappears through the window.*]

[*The* PARLOR-MAID *answers the bell.* PICKERING *sits down in Doolittle's place.*]

MRS. HIGGINS Ask Miss Doolittle to come down, please.

THE PARLOR-MAID Yes, mam. [*She goes out.*]

MRS. HIGGINS Now, Henry: be good.

HIGGINS I am behaving myself perfectly.

PICKERING He is doing his best, Mrs. Higgins.

[*A pause.* HIGGINS *throws back his head; stretches out his legs; and begins to whistle.*]

MRS. HIGGINS Henry, dearest, you dont look at all nice in that attitude.

HIGGINS [*pulling himself together*] I was not trying to look nice, mother.

MRS. HIGGINS It doesnt matter, dear. I only wanted to make you speak.

HIGGINS Why?

MRS. HIGGINS Because you cant speak and whistle at the same time.

[HIGGINS *groans. Another very trying pause.*]

HIGGINS [*springing up, out of patience*] Where the devil is that girl? Are we to wait here all day?

[ELIZA *enters, sunny, self-possessed, and giving a staggeringly convincing exhibition of ease of manner. She carries a little work-basket, and is very much at home.* PICKERING *is too much taken aback to rise.*]

LIZA How do you do, Professor Higgins? Are you quite well?

HIGGINS [*choking*] Am I— [*He can say no more*].

LIZA But of course you are: you are never ill. So glad to see you again, Colonel Pickering. [*He rises hastily; and they shake hands.*] Quite chilly this morning, isnt it? [*She sits down on his left. He sits beside her.*]

HIGGINS Dont you dare try this game on me. I taught it to you; and it doesnt take me in. Get up and come home; and dont be a fool.

[ELIZA *takes a piece of needlework from her basket, and begins to stitch at it, without taking the least notice of this outburst.*]

MRS. HIGGINS Very nicely put, indeed, Henry. No woman could resist such an invitation.

HIGGINS You let her alone, mother. Let her speak for herself. You will jolly soon see whether she has an idea that I havnt put into her head or a word that I havnt put into her mouth. I tell you I have created this thing out of the squashed cabbage leaves of Covent Garden; and now she pretends to play the fine lady with me.

MRS. HIGGINS [*placidly*] Yes, dear; but youll sit down, wont you?

[HIGGINS *sits down again, savagely.*]

LIZA [*to* PICKERING, *taking no apparent notice of* HIGGINS, *and working away deftly*] Will you drop me altogether now that the experiment is over, Colonel Pickering?

PICKERING Oh dont. You mustnt think of it as an experiment. It shocks me, somehow.

LIZA Oh, I'm only a squashed cabbage leaf—

PICKERING [*impulsively*] No.

LIZA [*continuing quietly*] —but I owe so much to you that I should be very unhappy if you forgot me.

PICKERING It's very kind of you to say so, Miss Doolittle.

LIZA It's not because you paid for my dresses. I know you are generous to everybody with money. But it was from you that I learnt really nice manners; and that is what makes one a lady, isnt it? You see it was so very difficult for me with the example of Professor Higgins always before me. I was brought up to be just like him, unable to control myself, and using bad language on the slightest provocation. And I should never have known that ladies and gentlemen didnt behave like that if you hadnt been there.

HIGGINS Well!!

PICKERING Oh, thats only his way, you know. He doesnt mean it.

LIZA Oh, *I* didnt mean it either, when I was a flower girl. It was only my way. But you see I did it; and thats what makes the difference after all.

PICKERING No doubt. Still, he taught you to speak; and I couldnt have done that, you know.

LIZA [*trivially*] Of course: that is his profession.

HIGGINS Damnation!

LIZA [*continuing*] It was just like learning to dance in the fashionable way: there was nothing more than that in it. But do you know what began my real education?

PICKERING What?

LIZA [*stopping her work for a moment*] Your calling me Miss Doolittle that day when I first came to Wimpole Street. That was the beginning of self-respect for me. [*She resumes her stitching.*] And there were a hundred little things you never noticed, because they came naturally to you. Things about standing up and taking off your hat and opening door—

PICKERING Oh, that was nothing.

LIZA Yes: things that shewed you thought and felt about me as if I were something better than a scullery-maid; though of course I know you would have been just the same to a scullery-maid if she had been let in the drawing-room. You never took off your boots in the dining room when I was there.

PICKERING You mustnt mind that. Higgins takes off his boots all over the place.

LIZA I know. I am not blaming him. It is his way, isnt it? But it made such a difference to me that you didnt do it. You see, really and truly, apart from the things anyone can pick up (the dressing and the proper way of speaking, and so on), the difference between a lady and a flower girl is not how she behaves, but how shes treated. I shall always be a flower girl to Professor Higgins, because he always treats me as a flower girl, and always will; but I know I can be a lady to you, because you always treat me as a lady, and always will.

MRS. HIGGINS Please dont grind your teeth, Henry.

PICKERING Well, this is really very nice of you, Miss Doolittle.

LIZA I should like you to call me Eliza, now, if you would.

PICKERING Thank you. Eliza, of course.

LIZA And I should like Professor Higgins to call me Miss Doolittle.

HIGGINS I'll see you damned first.

MRS. HIGGINS Henry! Henry!

PICKERING [*laughing*] Why dont you slang back[8] at him? Dont stand it. It would do him a lot of good.

LIZA I cant. I could have done it once; but now I cant go back to it. Last night, when I was wandering about, a girl spoke to me; and I tried to get back into the old way with her; but it was no use. You told me, you know, that when a child is brought to a foreign country, it picks up the language in a few weeks, and forgets its own. Well, I am a child in your country. I have forgotten my own language, and can speak nothing but yours. Thats the real break-off with the corner of Tottenham Court Road. Leaving Wimpole Street finishes it.

PICKERING [*much alarmed*] Oh! but youre coming back to Wimpole Street, arnt you? Youll forgive Higgins?

HIGGINS [*rising*] Forgive! Will she, by George! Let her go. Let her find out how she can get on without us. She will relapse into the gutter in three weeks without me at her elbow.

[DOOLITTLE *appears at the centre window. With a look of dignified reproach at* HIGGINS, *he comes slowly and silently to his daughter, who, with her back to the window, is unconscious of his approach.*]

PICKERING Hes incorrigible, Eliza. You wont relapse, will you?

8. That is, respond with equal abuse.

LIZA No: Not now. Never again. I have learnt my lesson. I dont believe I could utter one of the old sounds if I tried. [DOOLITTLE *touches her on her left shoulder. She drops her work, losing her self-possession utterly at the spectacle of her father's splendor.*] A-a-a-a-ah-ow-ooh!

HIGGINS [*with a crow of triumph*] Aha! Just so. A-a-a-a-ahowooh! A-a-a-a-ahowooh! A-a-a-a-ahowooh! Victory! Victory! [*He throws himself on the divan, folding his arms, and spraddling arrogantly.*]

DOOLITTLE Can you blame the girl? Dont look at me like that, Eliza. It aint my fault. Ive come into some money.

LIZA You must have touched a millionaire this time, dad.

DOOLITTLE I have. But I'm dressed something special today. I'm going to St. George's,[9] Hanover Square. Your stepmother is going to marry me.

LIZA [*angrily*] Youre going to let yourself down to marry that low common woman!

PICKERING [*quietly*] He ought to, Eliza. [*To* DOOLITTLE] Why has she changed her mind?

DOOLITTLE [*sadly*] Intimidated, Governor. Intimidated. Middle class morality claims its victim. Wont you put on your hat, Liza, and come and see me turned off?

LIZA If the Colonel says I must, I—I'll [*Almost sobbing*] I'll demean myself. And get insulted for my pains, like enough.

DOOLITTLE Dont be afraid: she never comes to words with anyone now, poor woman! respectability has broke all the spirit out of her.

PICKERING [*squeezing* ELIZA'*s elbow gently*] Be kind to them, Eliza. Make the best of it.

LIZA [*forcing a little smile for him through her vexation*] Oh well, just to shew theres no ill feeling. I'll be back in a moment. [*She goes out.*]

DOOLITTLE [*sitting down beside* PICKERING] I feel uncommon nervous about the ceremony, Colonel. I wish youd come and see me through it.

PICKERING But youve been through it before, man. You were married to Eliza's mother.

DOOLITTLE Who told you that, Colonel?

PICKERING Well, nobody told me. But I concluded—naturally—

DOOLITTLE No: that aint the natural way, Colonel: it's only the middle class way. My way was always the undeserving way. But dont say nothing to Eliza. She dont know: I always had a delicacy about telling her.

PICKERING Quite right. We'll leave it so, if you dont mind.

DOOLITTLE And youll come to the church, Colonel, and put me through straight?

PICKERING With pleasure. As far as a bachelor can.

MRS. HIGGINS May I come, Mr. Doolittle? I should be very sorry to miss your wedding.

DOOLITTLE I should indeed be honored by your condescension,[1] maam; and my poor old woman would take it as a tremenjous compliment. Shes been very low, thinking of the happy days that are no more.

MRS. HIGGINS [*rising*] I'll order the carriage and get ready. [*The men rise, except* HIGGINS.] I shant be more than fifteen minutes. [*As she goes to the*

9. A church in Mayfair, a fashionable area of Westminster.

1. Here, courteous disregard of differences in rank (without the negative connotation common in today's usage).

door ELIZA *comes in, hatted and buttoning her gloves.*] I'm going to the church to see your father married, Eliza. You had better come in the brougham[2] with me. Colonel Pickering can go on with the bridegroom.

[MRS. HIGGINS *goes out.* ELIZA *comes to the middle of the room between the centre window and the ottoman.* PICKERING *joins her.*]

DOOLITTLE Bridegroom! What a word! It makes a man realize his position, somehow. [*He takes up his hat and goes towards the door.*]

PICKERING Before I go, Eliza, do forgive him and come back to us.

LIZA I dont think papa would allow me. Would you, dad?

DOOLITTLE [*sad but magnanimous*] They played you off very cunning, Eliza, them two sportsmen. If it had been only one of them, you could have nailed him. But you see, there was two; and one of them chaperoned the other, as you might say. [*To* PICKERING] It was artful of you, Colonel; but I bear no malice: I should have done the same myself. I been the victim of one woman after another all my life; and I dont grudge you two getting the better of Eliza. I shant interfere. It's time for us to go, Colonel. So long, Henry. See you in St. George's, Eliza.

[*He goes out.*]

PICKERING [*coaxing*] Do stay with us, Eliza.

[*He follows* DOOLITTLE.]

[ELIZA *goes out on the balcony to avoid being alone with* HIGGINS. *He rises and joins her there. She immediately comes back into the room and makes for the door; but he goes along the balcony quickly and gets his back to the door before she reaches it.*]

HIGGINS Well, Eliza, youve had a bit of your own back, as you call it. Have you had enough? and are you going to be reasonable? Or do you want any more?

LIZA You want me back only to pick up your slippers and put up with your tempers and fetch and carry for you.

HIGGINS I havnt said I wanted you back at all.

LIZA Oh, indeed. Then what are we talking about?

HIGGINS About you, not about me. If you come back I shall treat you just as I have always treated you. I cant change my nature; and I dont intend to change my manners. My manners are exactly the same as Colonel Pickering's.

LIZA Thats not true. He treats a flower girl as if she was a duchess.

HIGGINS And I treat a duchess as if she was a flower girl.

LIZA I see. [*She turns away composedly, and sits on the ottoman, facing the window.*] The same to everybody.

HIGGINS Just so.

LIZA Like father.

HIGGINS [*grinning, a little taken down*[3]] Without accepting the comparison at all points, Eliza, it's quite true that your father is not a snob, and that he will be quite at home in any station of life to which his eccentric destiny may call him. [*Seriously*] The great secret, Eliza, is not having bad manners or good manners or any other particular sort of manners, but having the

2. A one-horse closed carriage, which holds two or four.

3. Humbled.

same manner for all human souls: in short, behaving as if you were in Heaven, where there are no third-class carriages, and one soul is as good as another.

LIZA Amen. You are a born preacher.

HIGGINS [*irritated*] The question is not whether I treat you rudely, but whether you ever heard me treat anyone else better.

LIZA [*with sudden sincerity*] I dont care how you treat me. I dont mind your swearing at me. I dont mind a black eye: Ive had one before this. But [*Standing up and facing him*] I wont be passed over.[4]

HIGGINS Then get out of my way; for I wont stop for you. You talk about me as if I were a motor bus.

LIZA So you are a motor bus: all bounce and go, and no consideration for anyone. But I can do without you: dont think I cant.

HIGGINS I know you can. I told you you could.

LIZA [*wounded, getting away from him to the other side of the ottoman with her face to the hearth*] I know you did, you brute. You wanted to get rid of me.

HIGGINS Liar.

LIZA Thank you. [*She sits down with dignity.*]

HIGGINS You never asked yourself, I suppose, whether *I* could do without you.

LIZA [*earnestly*] Dont you try to get round me.[5] Youll have to do without me.

HIGGINS [*arrogant*] I can do without anybody. I have my own soul: my own spark of divine fire. But [*With sudden humility*] I shall miss you, Eliza. [*He sits down near her on the ottoman.*] I have learnt something from your idiotic notions: I confess that humbly and gratefully. And I have grown accustomed to your voice and appearance. I like them, rather.

LIZA Well, you have both of them on your gramophone and in your book of photographs. When you feel lonely without me, you can turn the machine on. It's got no feelings to hurt.

HIGGINS I cant turn your soul on. Leave me those feelings; and you can take away the voice and the face. They are not you.

LIZA Oh, you are a devil. You can twist the heart in a girl as easy as some could twist her arms to hurt her. Mrs. Pearce warned me. Time and again she has wanted to leave you; and you always got round her at the last minute. And you dont care a bit for her. And you dont care a bit for me.

HIGGINS I care for life, for humanity; and you are a part of it that has come my way and been built into my house. What more can you or anyone ask?

LIZA I wont care for anybody that doesnt care for me.

HIGGINS Commercial principles, Eliza. Like [*Reproducing her Covent Garden pronunciation with professional exactness*] s'yollin voylets [selling violets], isnt it?

LIZA Dont sneer at me. It's mean to sneer at me.

HIGGINS I have never sneered in my life. Sneering doesnt become either the human face or the human soul. I am expressing my righteous contempt for Commercialism. I dont and wont trade in affection. You call me a brute because you couldnt buy a claim on me by fetching my slippers and finding my spectacles. You were a fool: I think a woman fetching a man's slippers is a disgusting sight: did I ever fetch your slippers? I think a good deal more

4. Ignored.

5. That is, don't try to deceive or outsmart me.

of you for throwing them in my face. No use slaving for me and then saying you want to be cared for: who cares for a slave? If you come back, come back for the sake of good fellowship; for youll get nothing else. Youve had a thousand times as much out of me as I have out of you; and if you dare to set up your little dog's tricks of fetching and carrying slippers against my creation of a Duchess Eliza, I'll slam the door in your silly face.

LIZA What did you do it for if you didnt care for me?

HIGGINS [*heartily*] Why, because it was my job.

LIZA You never thought of the trouble it would make for me.

HIGGINS Would the world ever have been made if its maker had been afraid of making trouble? Making life means making trouble. Theres only one way of escaping trouble; and thats killing things. Cowards, you notice, are always shrieking to have troublesome people killed.

LIZA I'm no preacher: I dont notice things like that. I notice that you dont notice me.

HIGGINS [*jumping up and walking about intolerantly*] Eliza: youre an idiot. I waste the treasures of my Miltonic mind by spreading them before you. Once for all, understand that I go my way and do my work without caring twopence what happens to either of us. I am not intimidated, like your father and your stepmother. So you can come back or go to the devil: which you please.

LIZA What am I to come back for?

HIGGINS [*bouncing up on his knees on the ottoman and leaning over it to her*] For the fun of it. Thats why I took you on.

LIZA [*with averted face*] And you may throw me out tomorrow if I dont do everything you want me to?

HIGGINS Yes; and you may walk out tomorrow if I dont do everything you want me to.

LIZA And live with my stepmother?

HIGGINS Yes, or sell flowers.

LIZA Oh! if I only could go back to my flower basket! I should be independent of both you and father and all the world! Why did you take my independence from me? Why did I give it up? I'm a slave now, for all my fine clothes.

HIGGINS Not a bit. I'll adopt you as my daughter and settle money on you if you like. Or would you rather marry Pickering?

LIZA [*looking fiercely round at him*] I wouldnt marry you if you asked me; and youre nearer my age than what he is.

HIGGINS [*gently*] Than he is: not "than what he is."

LIZA [*losing her temper and rising*] I'll talk as I like. Youre not my teacher now.

HIGGINS [*reflectively*] I dont suppose Pickering would, though. Hes as confirmed an old bachelor as I am.

LIZA Thats not what I want; and dont you think it. Ive always had chaps enough wanting me that way. Freddy Hill writes to me twice and three times a day,[6] sheets and sheets.

6. At the time, most places in England had two or three mail deliveries daily, and London had even more.

HIGGINS [*disagreeably surprised*] Damn his impudence! [*He recoils and finds himself sitting on his heels.*]

LIZA He has a right to if he likes, poor lad. And he does love me.

HIGGINS [*getting off the ottoman*] You have no right to encourage him.

LIZA Every girl has a right to be loved.

HIGGINS What! By fools like that?

LIZA Freddy's not a fool. And if hes weak and poor and wants me, may be hed make me happier than my betters that bully me and dont want me.

HIGGINS Can he make anything of you? Thats the point.

LIZA Perhaps I could make something of him. But I never thought of us making anything of one another; and you never think of anything else. I only want to be natural.

HIGGINS In short, you want me to be as infatuated about you as Freddy? Is that it?

LIZA No I dont. Thats not the sort of feeling I want from you. And dont you be too sure of yourself or of me. I could have been a bad girl if I'd liked. Ive seen more of some things than you, for all your learning. Girls like me can drag gentlemen down to make love to[7] them easy enough. And they wish each other dead the next minute.

HIGGINS Of course they do. Then what in thunder are we quarrelling about?

LIZA [*much troubled*] I want a little kindness. I know I'm a common ignorant girl, and you a book-learned gentleman; but I'm not dirt under your feet. What I done [*Correcting herself*] what I did was not for the dresses and the taxis: I did it because we were pleasant together and I come—came—to care for you; not to want you to make love to me, and not forgetting the difference between us, but more friendly like.

HIGGINS Well, of course. Thats just how I feel. And how Pickering feels. Eliza: youre a fool.

LIZA Thats not a proper answer to give me. [*She sinks on the chair at the writing-table in tears.*]

HIGGINS It's all youll get until you stop being a common idiot. If youre going to be a lady, youll have to give up feeling neglected if the men you know dont spend half their time snivelling over you and the other half giving you black eyes. If you cant stand the coldness of my sort of life, and the strain of it, go back to the gutter. Work til you are more a brute than a human being; and then cuddle and squabble and drink til you fall asleep. Oh, it's a fine life, the life of the gutter. It's real: it's warm: it's violent: you can feel it through the thickest skin: you can taste it and smell it without any training or any work. Not like Science and Literature and Classical Music and Philosophy and Art. You find me cold, unfeeling, selfish, dont you? Very well: be off with you to the sort of people you like. Marry some sentimental hog or other with lots of money, and a thick pair of lips to kiss you with and a thick pair of boots to kick you with. If you cant appreciate what youve got, youd better get what you can appreciate.

LIZA [*desperate*] Oh, you are a cruel tyrant. I cant talk to you: you turn everything against me: I'm always in the wrong. But you know very well all the time that youre nothing but a bully. You know I cant go back to the gutter, as you call it, and that I have no real friends in the world but you and

7. To pay amorous attention to, to court.

the Colonel. You know well I couldnt bear to live with a low common man after you two; and it's wicked and cruel of you to insult me by pretending I could. You think I must go back to Wimpole Street because I have nowhere else to go but father's. But dont you be too sure that you have me under your feet to be trampled on and talked down. I'll marry Freddy, I will, as soon as hes able to support me.

HIGGINS [*sitting down beside her*] Rubbish! you shall marry an ambassador. You shall marry the Governor-General of India or the Lord-Lieutenant of Ireland, or somebody who wants a deputy-queen. I'm not going to have my masterpiece thrown away on Freddy.

LIZA You think I like you to say that. But I havnt forgot what you said a minute ago; and I wont be coaxed round as if I was a baby or a puppy. If I cant have kindness, I'll have independence.

HIGGINS Independence? Thats middle class blasphemy. We are all dependent on one another, every soul of us on earth.

LIZA [*rising determinedly*] I'll let you see whether I'm dependent on you. If you can preach, I can teach. I'll go and be a teacher.

HIGGINS Whatll you teach, in heaven's name?

LIZA What you taught me. I'll teach phonetics.

HIGGINS Ha! Ha! Ha!

LIZA I'll offer myself as an assistant to Professor Nepean.

HIGGINS [*rising in a fury*] What! That impostor! that humbug! that toadying ignoramus! Teach him my methods! my discoveries! You take one step in his direction and I'll wring your neck. [*He lays hands on her.*] Do you hear?

LIZA [*defiantly non-resistant*] Wring away. What do I care? I knew youd strike me some day. [*He lets her go, stamping with rage at having forgotten himself, and recoils so hastily that he stumbles back into his seat on the ottoman.*] Aha! Now I know how to deal with you. What a fool I was not to think of it before! You cant take away the knowledge you gave me. You said I had a finer ear than you. And I can be civil and kind to people, which is more than you can. Aha! Thats done[8] you, Henry Higgins, it has. Now I dont care that [*Snapping her fingers*] for your bullying and your big talk. I'll advertize it in the papers that your duchess is only a flower girl that you taught, and that she'll teach anybody to be a duchess just the same in six months for a thousand guineas. Oh, when I think of myself crawling under your feet and being trampled on and called names, when all the time I had only to lift up my finger to be as good as you, I could just kick myself.

HIGGINS [*wondering at her*] You damned impudent slut, you! But it's better than snivelling; better than fetching slippers and finding spectacles, isnt it? [*Rising*] By George, Eliza, I said I'd make a woman of you; and I have. I like you like this.

LIZA Yes: you turn round and make up to me now that I'm not afraid of you, and can do without you.

HIGGINS Of course I do, you little fool. Five minutes ago you were like a millstone round my neck. Now youre a tower of strength: a consort[9] battleship. You and I and Pickering will be three old bachelors together instead of only two men and a silly girl.

8. Defeated.

9. A ship sailing in company with another.

[MRS. HIGGINS *returns, dressed for the wedding.* ELIZA *instantly becomes cool and elegant.*]

MRS. HIGGINS The carriage is waiting, Eliza. Are you ready?

LIZA Quite. Is the Professor coming?

MRS. HIGGINS Certainly not. He cant behave himself in church. He makes remarks out loud all the time on the clergyman's pronunciation.

LIZA Then I shall not see you again, Professor. Good-bye. [*She goes to the door.*]

MRS. HIGGINS [*coming to* HIGGINS] Good-bye, dear.

HIGGINS Good-bye, mother. [*He is about to kiss her, when he recollects something.*] Oh, by the way, Eliza, order a ham and a Stilton cheese, will you? And buy me a pair of reindeer gloves, number eights, and a tie to match that new suit of mine, at Eale & Binman's. You can choose the color. [*His cheerful, careless, vigorous voice shows that he is incorrigible.*]

LIZA [*disdainfully*] Buy them yourself.

[*She sweeps out.*]

MRS. HIGGINS I'm afraid youve spoiled that girl, Henry. But never mind, dear: I'll buy you the tie and gloves.

HIGGINS [*sunnily*] Oh, dont bother. She'll buy em all right enough. Good-bye.

[*They kiss.* MRS. HIGGINS *runs out.* HIGGINS, *left alone, rattles his cash in his pocket; chuckles; and disports himself in a highly self-satisfied manner.*]

* * * * *

The rest of the story need not be shown in action, and indeed, would hardly need telling if our imaginations were not so enfeebled by their lazy dependence on the ready-mades and reach-me-downs of the ragshop[1] in which Romance keeps its stock of "happy endings" to misfit all stories. Now, the history of Eliza Doolittle, though called a romance because of the transfiguration it records seems exceedingly improbable, is common enough. Such transfigurations have been achieved by hundreds of resolutely ambitious young women since Nell Gwynne[2] set them the example by playing queens and fascinating kings in the theatre in which she began by selling oranges. Nevertheless, people in all directions have assumed, for no other reason than that she became the heroine of a romance, that she must have married the hero of it. This is unbearable, not only because her little drama, if acted on such a thoughtless assumption, must be spoiled, but because the true sequel is patent to anyone with a sense of human nature in general, and of feminine instinct in particular.

Eliza, in telling Higgins she would not marry him if he asked her, was not coquetting: she was announcing a well-considered decision. When a bachelor interests, and dominates, and teaches, and becomes important to a spinster, as Higgins with Eliza, she always, if she has character enough to be capable of it, considers very seriously indeed whether she will play for becoming that bachelor's wife, especially if he is so little interested in marriage that a determined and devoted woman might capture him if she set herself resolutely to do it.

1. That is, a shop selling cheap mass-produced and secondhand clothing ("ready-mades and reach-me-downs").

2. Eleanor Gwynn (1650–1687), one of the first prominent English actresses and a mistress of King Charles II.

Her decision will depend a good deal on whether she is really free to choose; and that, again, will depend on her age and income. If she is at the end of her youth, and has no security for her livelihood, she will marry him because she must marry anybody who will provide for her. But at Eliza's age a good-looking girl does not feel that pressure: she feels free to pick and choose. She is therefore guided by her instinct in the matter. Eliza's instinct tells her not to marry Higgins. It does not tell her to give him up. It is not in the slightest doubt as to his remaining one of the strongest personal interests in her life. It would be very sorely strained if there was another woman likely to supplant her with him. But as she feels sure of him on that last point, she has no doubt at all as to her course, and would not have any, even if the difference of twenty years in age, which seems so great to youth, did not exist between them.

As our own instincts are not appealed to by her conclusion, let us see whether we cannot discover some reason in it. When Higgins excused his indifference to young women on the ground that they had an irresistible rival in his mother, he gave the clue to his inveterate old-bachelordom. The case is uncommon only to the extent that remarkable mothers are uncommon. If an imaginative boy has a sufficiently rich mother who has intelligence, personal grace, dignity of character without harshness, and a cultivated sense of the best art of her time to enable her to make her house beautiful, she sets a standard for him against which very few women can struggle, besides effecting for him a disengagement of his affections, his sense of beauty, and his idealism from his specifically sexual impulses. This makes him a standing puzzle to the huge number of uncultivated people who have been brought up in tasteless homes by commonplace or disagreeable parents, and to whom, consequently, literature, painting, sculpture, music, and affectionate personal relations come as modes of sex if they come at all. The word passion means nothing else to them; and that Higgins could have a passion for phonetics and idealize his mother instead of Eliza, would seem to them absurd and unnatural. Nevertheless, when we look round and see that hardly anyone is too ugly or disagreeable to find a wife or a husband if he or she wants one, whilst many old maids and bachelors are above the average in quality and culture, we cannot help suspecting that the disentanglement of sex from the associations with which it is so commonly confused, a disentanglement which persons of genius achieve by sheer intellectual analysis, is sometimes produced or aided by parental fascination.

Now, though Eliza was incapable of thus explaining to herself Higgins's formidable powers of resistance to the charm that prostrated Freddy at the first glance, she was instinctively aware that she could never obtain a complete grip of him, or come between him and his mother (the first necessity of the married woman). To put it shortly, she knew that for some mysterious reason he had not the makings of a married man in him, according to her conception of a husband as one to whom she would be his nearest and fondest and warmest interest. Even had there been no mother-rival, she would still have refused to accept an interest in herself that was secondary to philosophic interests. Had Mrs. Higgins died, there would still have been Milton and the Universal Alphabet. Landor's[3] remark that to those who have the greatest power of loving, love is a secondary affair, would not have recommended Landor to

3. The English poet Walter Savage Landor (1775–1864); in "Roger Ascham and the Lady Jane Grey," in *Imaginary Conversations of Literary Men and Statesmen* (1824), he wrote, "Love is a secondary passion in those who love most, a primary in those who love least."

Eliza. Put that along with her resentment of Higgins's domineering superiority, and her mistrust of his coaxing cleverness in getting round her and evading her wrath when he had gone too far with his impetuous bullying, and you will see that Eliza's instinct had good grounds for warning her not to marry her Pygmalion.

And now, whom did Eliza marry? For if Higgins was a predestinate old bachelor, she was most certainly not a predestinate old maid. Well, that can be told very shortly to those who have not guessed it from the indications she has herself given them.

Almost immediately after Eliza is stung into proclaiming her considered determination not to marry Higgins, she mentions the fact that young Mr. Frederick Eynsford Hill is pouring out his love for her daily through the post. Now Freddy is young, practically twenty years younger than Higgins: he is a gentleman (or, as Eliza would qualify him, a toff), and speaks like one; he is nicely dressed, is treated by the Colonel as an equal, loves her unaffectedly, and is not her master, nor ever likely to dominate her in spite of his advantage of social standing. Eliza has no use for the foolish romantic tradition that all women love to be mastered, if not actually bullied and beaten. "When you go to women," says Nietzsche, "take your whip with you."[4] Sensible despots have never confined that precaution to women: they have taken their whips with them when they have dealt with men, and been slavishly idealized by the men over whom they have flourished the whip much more than by women. No doubt there are slavish women as well as slavish men; and women, like men, admire those that are stronger than themselves. But to admire a strong person and to live under that strong person's thumb are two different things. The weak may not be admired and hero-worshipped; but they are by no means disliked or shunned; and they never seem to have the least difficulty in marrying people who are too good for them. They may fail in emergencies; but life is not one long emergency: it is mostly a string of situations for which no exceptional strength is needed, and with which even rather weak people can cope if they have a stronger partner to help them out. Accordingly, it is a truth everywhere in evidence that strong people, masculine or feminine, not only do not marry stronger people, but do not shew any preference for them in selecting their friends. When a lion meets another with a louder roar "the first lion thinks the last a bore."[5] The man or woman who feels strong enough for two, seeks for every other quality in a partner than strength.

The converse is also true. Weak people want to marry strong people who do not frighten them too much; and this often leads them to make the mistake we describe metaphorically as "biting off more than they can chew." They want too much for too little; and when the bargain is unreasonable beyond all bearing, the union becomes impossible: it ends in the weaker party being either discarded or borne as a cross, which is worse. People who are not only weak, but silly or obtuse as well, are often in these difficulties.

This being the state of human affairs, what is Eliza fairly sure to do when she is placed between Freddy and Higgins? Will she look forward to a lifetime

4. Spoken by a fictional old woman in *Thus Spoke Zarathustra* (1883), by the German philosopher Friedrich Nietzsche (1844–1900).

5. Shaw slightly misquotes the popular comic opera *Bombastes Furioso* (1810), by English dramatist William Barnes Rhodes: "So have I heard on Afric's burning shore / Another lion give a grievous roar; / And the first lion thought the last a bore."

of fetching Higgins's slippers or to a lifetime of Freddy fetching hers? There can be no doubt about the answer. Unless Freddy is biologically repulsive to her, and Higgins biologically attractive to a degree that overwhelms all her other instincts, she will, if she marries either of them, marry Freddy.

And that is just what Eliza did.

Complications ensued; but they were economic, not romantic. Freddy had no money and no occupation. His mother's jointure, a last relic of the opulence of Largelady Park, had enabled her to struggle along in Earlscourt with an air of gentility, but not to procure any serious secondary education for her children, much less give the boy a profession. A clerkship at thirty shillings a week was beneath Freddy's dignity, and extremely distasteful to him besides. His prospects consisted of a hope that if he kept up appearances somebody would do something for him. The something appeared vaguely to his imagination as a private secretaryship or a sinecure of some sort. To his mother it perhaps appeared as a marriage to some lady of means who could not resist her boy's niceness. Fancy her feelings when he married a flower girl who had become déclassée under extraordinary circumstances which were now notorious!

It is true that Eliza's situation did not seem wholly ineligible. Her father, though formerly a dustman, and now fantastically disclassed, had become extremely popular in the smartest society by a social talent which triumphed over every prejudice and every disadvantage. Rejected by the middle class, which he loathed, he had shot up at once into the highest circles by his wit, his dustmanship (which he carried like a banner), and his Nietzschean transcendence of good and evil.[6] At intimate ducal dinners he sat on the right hand of the Duchess; and in country houses he smoked in the pantry and was made much of by the butler when he was not feeding in the dining-room and being consulted by cabinet ministers. But he found it almost as hard to do all this on four thousand a year as Mrs. Eynsford Hill to live in Earlscourt on an income so pitiably smaller that I have not the heart to disclose its exact figure. He absolutely refused to add the last straw to his burden by contributing to Eliza's support.

Thus Freddy and Eliza, now Mr. and Mrs. Eynsford Hill, would have spent a penniless honeymoon but for a wedding present of £500[7] from the Colonel to Eliza. It lasted a long time because Freddy did not know how to spend money, never having had any to spend, and Eliza, socially trained by a pair of old bachelors, wore her clothes as long as they held together and looked pretty, without the least regard to their being many months out of fashion. Still, £500 will not last two young people for ever; and they both knew, and Eliza felt as well, that they must shift for themselves in the end. She could quarter herself on Wimpole Street because it had come to be her home; but she was quite aware that she ought not to quarter Freddy there, and that it would not be good for his character if she did.

Not that the Wimpole Street bachelors objected. When she consulted them, Higgins declined to be bothered about her housing problem when that solution was so simple. Eliza's desire to have Freddy in the house with her seemed of no more importance than if she had wanted an extra piece of bedroom furniture. Pleas as to Freddy's character, and the moral obligation on

6. A well-known work by Nietzsche is titled *Beyond Good and Evil* (1886).

7. Roughly equivalent to $40,000 today.

him to earn his own living, were lost on Higgins. He denied that Freddy had any character, and declared that if he tried to do any useful work some competent person would have the trouble of undoing it: a procedure involving a net loss to the community; and great unhappiness to Freddy himself, who was obviously intended by Nature for such light work as amusing Eliza, which, Higgins declared, was a much more useful and honorable occupation than working in the city.[8] When Eliza referred again to her project of teaching phonetics, Higgins abated not a jot of his violent opposition to it. He said she was not within ten years of being qualified to meddle with his pet subject; and as it was evident that the Colonel agreed with him, she felt she could not go against them in this grave matter, and that she had no right, without Higgins's consent, to exploit the knowledge he had given her; for his knowledge seemed to her as much his private property as his watch: Eliza was no communist. Besides, she was superstitiously devoted to them both, more entirely and frankly after her marriage than before it.

It was the Colonel who finally solved the problem, which had cost him much perplexed cogitation. He one day asked Eliza, rather shyly, whether she had quite given up her notion of keeping a flower shop. She replied that she had thought of it, but had put it out of her head, because the Colonel had said, that day at Mrs. Higgins's, that it would never do. The Colonel confessed that when he said that, he had not quite recovered from the dazzling impression of the day before. They broke the matter to Higgins that evening. The sole comment vouchsafed by him very nearly led to a serious quarrel with Eliza. It was to the effect that she would have in Freddy an ideal errand boy.

Freddy himself was next sounded on the subject. He said he had been thinking of a shop himself; though it had presented itself to his pennilessness as a small place in which Eliza should sell tobacco at one counter whilst he sold newspapers at the opposite one. But he agreed that it would be extraordinarily jolly to go early every morning with Eliza to Covent Garden and buy flowers on the scene of their first meeting: a sentiment which earned him many kisses from his wife. He added that he had always been afraid to propose anything of the sort, because Clara would make an awful row about a step that must damage her matrimonial chances, and his mother could not be expected to like it after clinging for so many years to that step of the social ladder on which retail trade is impossible.

This difficulty was removed by an event highly unexpected by Freddy's mother. Clara, in the course of her incursions into those artistic circles which were the highest within her reach, discovered that her conversational qualifications were expected to include a grounding in the novels of Mr. H. G. Wells.[9] She borrowed them in various directions so energetically that she swallowed them all within two months. The result was a conversion of a kind quite common today. A modern Acts of the Apostles would fill fifty whole Bibles if anyone were capable of writing it.

Poor Clara, who appeared to Higgins and his mother as a disagreeable and ridiculous person, and to her own mother as in some inexplicable way a social failure, had never seen herself in either light; for, though to some extent

8. That is, working in London's finance district.

9. The English writer Herbert George Wells (1866–1946), a prominent member of the socialist Fabian Society and the author not only of science-fiction novels such as *The War of the Worlds* (1898) but also novels of social criticism such as *Tono-Bungay* (1908).

ridiculed and mimicked in West Kensington[1] like everybody else there, she was accepted as a rational and normal—or shall we say inevitable?—sort of human being. At worst they called her The Pusher;[2] but to them no more than to herself had it ever occurred that she was pushing the air, and pushing it in a wrong direction. Still, she was not happy. She was growing desperate. Her one asset, the fact that her mother was what the Epsom greengrocer called a carriage lady had no exchange value, apparently. It had prevented her from getting educated, because the only education she could have afforded was education with the Earlscourt greengrocer's daughter. It had led her to seek the society of her mother's class; and that class simply would not have her, because she was much poorer than the greengrocer, and, far from being able to afford a maid,[3] could not afford even a housemaid, and had to scrape along at home with an illiberally treated general servant. Under such circumstances nothing could give her an air of being a genuine product of Largelady Park. And yet its tradition made her regard a marriage with anyone within her reach as an unbearable humiliation. Commercial people and professional people in a small way were odious to her. She ran after painters and novelists; but she did not charm them; and her bold attempts to pick up and practise artistic and literary talk irritated them. She was, in short, an utter failure, an ignorant, incompetent, pretentious, unwelcome, penniless, useless little snob; and though she did not admit these disqualifications (for nobody ever faces unpleasant truths of this kind until the possibility of a way out dawns on them) she felt their effects too keenly to be satisfied with her position.

Clara had a startling eyeopener when, on being suddenly wakened to enthusiasm by a girl of her own age who dazzled her and produced in her a gushing desire to take her for a model, and gain her friendship, she discovered that this exquisite apparition had graduated from the gutter in a few months' time. It shook her so violently, that when Mr. H. G. Wells lifted her on the point of his puissant pen, and placed her at the angle of view from which the life she was leading and the society to which she clung appeared in its true relation to real human needs and worthy social structure, he effected a conversion and a conviction of sin comparable to the most sensational feats of General Booth or Gypsy Smith.[4] Clara's snobbery went bang. Life suddenly began to move with her. Without knowing how or why, she began to make friends and enemies. Some of the acquaintances to whom she had been a tedious or indifferent or ridiculous affliction, dropped her: others became cordial. To her amazement she found that some "quite nice" people were saturated with Wells, and that this accessibility to ideas was the secret of their niceness. People she had thought deeply religious, and had tried to conciliate on that tack with disastrous results, suddenly took an interest in her, and revealed a hostility to conventional religion which she had never conceived possible except among the most desperate characters. They made her read Galsworthy;[5] and Galsworthy exposed the vanity of Largelady Park and finished her. It exasperated her to think that the dungeon in which she had languished for so

1. An area of London at the western edge of the inner suburbs.
2. That is, The Social Climber.
3. A personal attendant, as distinct from a general servant who does housework.
4. That is, feats of religious conversion. William Booth (1829–1912), a Methodist revivalist, founded the Salvation Army; Rodney Smith (1860–1947), briefly a captain in the Salvation Army, became an internationally renowned evangelist.
5. John Galsworthy (1867–1933), an English playwright and novelist whose writings cast a realistic and critical light on the upper middle class.

many unhappy years had been unlocked all the time, and that the impulses she had so carefully struggled with and stifled for the sake of keeping well with society, were precisely those by which alone she could have come into any sort of sincere human contact. In the radiance of these discoveries, and the tumult of their reaction, she made a fool of herself as freely and conspicuously as when she so rashly adopted Eliza's expletive in Mrs. Higgins's drawing-room; for the new-born Wellsian had to find her bearings almost as ridiculously as a baby; but nobody hates a baby for its ineptitudes, or thinks the worse of it for trying to eat the matches; and Clara lost no friends by her follies. They laughed at her to her face this time; and she had to defend herself and fight it out as best she could.

When Freddy paid a visit to Earlscourt (which he never did when he could possibly help it) to make the desolating announcement that he and his Eliza were thinking of blackening the Largelady scutcheon[6] by opening a shop, he found the little household already convulsed by a prior announcement from Clara that she also was going to work in an old furniture shop in Dover Street, which had been started by a fellow Wellsian. This appointment Clara owed, after all, to her old social accomplishment of Push. She had made up her mind that, cost what it might, she would see Mr. Wells in the flesh; and she had achieved her end at a garden party. She had better luck than so rash an enterprise deserved. Mr. Wells came up to her expectations. Age had not withered him, nor could custom stale his infinite variety in half an hour.[7] His pleasant neatness and compactness, his small hands and feet, his teeming ready brain, his unaffected accessibility, and a certain fine apprehensiveness which stamped him as susceptible from his topmost hair to his tipmost toe, proved irresistible. Clara talked of nothing else for weeks and weeks afterwards. And as she happened to talk to the lady of the furniture shop, and that lady also desired above all things to know Mr. Wells and sell pretty things to him, she offered Clara a job on the chance of achieving that end through her.

And so it came about that Eliza's luck held, and the expected opposition to the flower shop melted away. The shop is in the arcade of a railway station not very far from the Victoria and Albert Museum; and if you live in that neighborhood you may go there any day and buy a buttonhole[8] from Eliza.

Now here is a last opportunity for romance. Would you not like to be assured that the shop was an immense success, thanks to Eliza's charms and her early business experience in Covent Garden? Alas! the truth is the truth: the shop did not pay for a long time, simply because Eliza and her Freddy did not know how to keep it. True, Eliza had not to begin at the very beginning: she knew the names and prices of the cheaper flowers; and her elation was unbounded when she found that Freddy, like all youths educated at cheap, pretentious, and thoroughly inefficient schools, knew a little Latin. It was very little, but enough to make him appear to her a Porson or Bentley,[9] and to put him at his ease with botanical nomenclature. Unfortunately he knew nothing else; and Eliza, though she could count money up to eighteen shillings or so, and had acquired a certain familiarity with the language of

6. Reputation (literally, a heraldic shield).
7. An allusion to the description of Cleopatra in Shakespeare's *Antony and Cleopatra* (1606–07): "Age cannot wither her, nor custom stale / Her infinite variety" (2.2.240–41).
8. A flower worn in the buttonhole of a lapel.
9. A great classicist, such as the English scholars Richard Porson (1759–1808) and Richard Bentley (1662–1742).

Milton from her struggles to qualify herself for winning Higgins's bet, could not write out a bill without utterly disgracing the establishment. Freddy's power of stating in Latin that Balbus built a wall and that Gaul was divided into three parts[1] did not carry with it the slightest knowledge of accounts or business: Colonel Pickering had to explain to him what a cheque book and a bank account meant. And the pair were by no means easily teachable. Freddy backed up Eliza in her obstinate refusal to believe that they could save money by engaging a bookkeeper with some knowledge of the business. How, they argued, could you possibly save money by going to extra expense when you already could not make both ends meet? But the Colonel, after making the ends meet over and over again, at last gently insisted; and Eliza, humbled to the dust by having to beg from him so often, and stung by the uproarious derision of Higgins, to whom the notion of Freddy succeeding at anything was a joke that never palled, grasped the fact that business, like phonetics, has to be learned.

On the piteous spectacle of the pair spending their evenings in shorthand schools and polytechnic classes, learning bookkeeping and typewriting with incipient junior clerks, male and female, from the elementary schools, let me not dwell. There were even classes at the London School of Economics, and a humble personal appeal to the director of that institution to recommend a course bearing on the flower business. He, being a humorist, explained to them the method of the celebrated Dickensian essay on Chinese Metaphysics by the gentleman who read an article on China and an article on Metaphysics and combined the information.[2] He suggested that they should combine the London School with Kew Gardens. Eliza, to whom the procedure of the Dickensian gentleman seemed perfectly correct (as in fact it was) and not in the least funny (which was only her ignorance) took his advice with entire gravity. But the effort that cost her the deepest humiliation was a request to Higgins, whose pet artistic fancy, next to Milton's verse, was caligraphy, and who himself wrote a most beautiful Italian hand, that he would teach her to write. He declared that she was congenitally incapable of forming a single letter worthy of the least of Milton's words; but she persisted; and again he suddenly threw himself into the task of teaching her with a combination of stormy intensity, concentrated patience, and occasional bursts of interesting disquisition on the beauty and nobility, the august mission and destiny, of human handwriting. Eliza ended by acquiring an extremely uncommercial script which was a positive extension of her personal beauty, and spending three times as much on stationery as anyone else because certain qualities and shapes of paper became indispensable to her. She could not even address an envelope in the usual way because it made the margins all wrong.

Their commercial school days were a period of disgrace and despair for the young couple. They seemed to be learning nothing about flower shops. At last they gave it up as hopeless, and shook the dust of the shorthand schools, and the polytechnics, and the London School of Economics from their feet for ever. Besides, the business was in some mysterious way beginning to take care of itself. They had somehow forgotten their objections to employing other people. They came to the conclusion that their own way was the best,

1. Phrases from standard Latin exercise books (the second is the opening of Caesar's *Gallic War* [ca. 50 B.C.E.]).

2. An allusion to *The Pickwick Papers* (1836–37), a novel by Charles Dickens.

and that they had really a remarkable talent for business. The Colonel, who had been compelled for some years to keep a sufficient sum on current account at his bankers to make up their deficits, found that the provision was unnecessary: the young people were prospering. It is true that there was not quite fair play between them and their competitors in trade. Their week-ends in the country cost them nothing, and saved them the price of their Sunday dinners; for the motor car was the Colonel's; and he and Higgins paid the hotel bills. Mr. F. Hill, florist and greengrocer (they soon discovered that there was money in asparagus; and asparagus led to other vegetables), had an air which stamped the business as classy; and in private life he was still Frederick Eynsford Hill, Esquire. Not that there was any swank about him: nobody but Eliza knew that he had been christened Frederick Challoner. Eliza herself swanked like anything.

That is all. That is how it has turned out. It is astonishing how much Eliza still manages to meddle in the housekeeping at Wimpole Street in spite of the shop and her own family. And it is notable that though she never nags her husband, and frankly loves the Colonel as if she were his favorite daughter, she has never got out of the habit of nagging Higgins that was established on the fatal night when she won his bet for him. She snaps his head off on the faintest provocation, or on none. He no longer dares to tease her by assuming an abysmal inferiority of Freddy's mind to his own. He storms and bullies and derides; but she stands up to him so ruthlessly that the Colonel has to ask her from time to time to be kinder to Higgins; and it is the only request of his that brings a mulish expression into her face. Nothing but some emergency or calamity great enough to break down all likes and dislikes, and throw them both back on their common humanity—and may they be spared any such trial!—will ever alter this. She knows that Higgins does not need her, just as her father did not need her. The very scrupulousness with which he told her that day that he had become used to having her there, and dependent on her for all sorts of little services, and that he should miss her if she went away (it would never have occurred to Freddy or the Colonel to say anything of the sort) deepens her inner certainty that she is "no more to him than them slippers," yet she has a sense, too, that his indifference is deeper than the infatuation of commoner souls. She is immensely interested in him. She has even secret mischievous moments in which she wishes she could get him alone, on a desert island, away from all ties and with nobody else in the world to consider, and just drag him off his pedestal and see him making love like any common man. We all have private imaginations of that sort. But when it comes to business, to the life that she really leads as distinguished from the life of dreams and fancies, she likes Freddy and she likes the Colonel; and she does not like Higgins and Mr. Doolittle. Galatea never does quite like Pygmalion: his relation to her is too godlike to be altogether agreeable.[3]

3. In classical mythology, Pygmalion was a legendary king of Cyprus who fell in love with an ivory statue of a woman that he had carved. In answer to his prayers, Aphrodite (called Venus by the Romans), the goddess of love, gave it life and they married; the most familiar version of the story is found in Ovid, *Metamorphoses* (ca. 10 C.E.), 10.243–97.

SUSAN GLASPELL

1876–1948

THE rediscovery of Susan Glaspell's writing by feminist critics and theater artists has, over the past few decades, exposed new generations of readers and audiences to this groundbreaking American playwright, novelist, and short story author, who received the Pulitzer Prize for drama in 1931. Glaspell came of age in the late nineteenth century, during the heyday of the "local color" movement in American literature. Works in this tradition—such as those of Glaspell's fellow Davenport, Iowa, resident Alice French (writing as Octave Thanet, 1850–1934)—celebrated regional American life and exposed its idiosyncrasies. By the early twentieth century, however, writers were increasingly focusing on the cultural, economic, and political differences growing between the country's burgeoning urban centers and its established rural locales. Glaspell and her contemporaries felt compelled to share with the nation their large and probing questions about American beliefs, values, and goals. In their creative endeavors, they framed these questions through the lenses of the Progressive era and their modern age, most notably the recent discoveries about human psychology. Glaspell's writing—especially her plays—reflects her keen engagement with the pressing issues of her day: how to foster a democratic and equitable society, what to think about the evolving roles of men and women, and how to honor the nation's founding principles while embracing the spirit of modernism. Artists like Glaspell were also engaged in formal experimentation, and their works reveal a sense of creative excitement as they sought new ways, structurally and aesthetically, to represent these cogent contemporary themes. Glaspell's 1916 play *Trifles* has emerged as a canonical text precisely because it exemplifies these intertwining artistic and social goals within American modernism.

Like many American modernists, Glaspell grew up in the nation's heartland. Her father, Elmer Glaspell, was a feed dealer; her mother, born Alice Keating, had been a schoolteacher before her marriage. Glaspell began her career as a journalist, writing a society column for her local paper before leaving home to attend Drake University. After graduation, she secured a post with the *Des Moines Daily News* as a statehouse and legislative reporter, but after two years, she decided to devote herself to fiction. She quickly had success writing short stories, which she placed in such national magazines as *McClure's* and *Harper's.* Following in the local-color tradition, Glaspell based many of her narratives on her experiences growing up in and around Davenport. But she interlaced these intimate portraits of midwestern life with the sharper edge of social critique that epitomizes her evolution as a Progressive and modernist artist. She published her first novel in 1909 and her second in 1911, as she continued to write short fiction. Following her marriage to George Cram "Jig" Cook in 1913, she and her new husband moved to Greenwich Village, as did many other young writers and artists of their generation. They were drawn to New York's bohemian lifestyle and creative freedom, which they felt were unattainable in the Midwest.

During this early twentieth-century moment, a growing number of American modernists recognized the potential of the stage to convey vivid images of life in the contemporary United States and, even more importantly, to engage audiences directly with larger social concerns. Eschewing the commercial theater and its devotion to profit-making entertainment, they sought to create a new kind of theater that would foster the development of a distinctly American culture. As a co-founder of the influential Provincetown Players—the company originally based in Provincetown, Massachusetts, that first produced the work of EUGENE O'NEILL during summer vacations—Glaspell played a central role in this movement. With Cook and other friends and colleagues such as John Reed, Djuna Barnes, Edna St. Vincent Millay, Theodore Dreiser, and Wallace Stevens, Glaspell participated in establishing a national theater dedicated to artistically innovative and political drama reflecting the explosive arrival of modernism in the United States.

For financial, practical, and philosophical reasons, most of the works produced by the Provincetown Players in their early years were one acts. Having been influenced by a U.S. tour of what was still called the Irish Players—the group founded in 1899 by the poet William Butler Yeats, Lady Gregory, and others that in 1904 became the Abbey Theatre—Cook believed that their repertoire of one-act plays had great impact as both artistic and nationalist creations, and he encouraged the Provincetown dramatists to use this form. Glaspell wrote eleven plays, seven of which were one acts (two written with Cook), for the Provincetown group between 1915 and 1922. Glaspell and Cook then departed from New York for Greece, leaving the Provincetown Players to reconfigure themselves under others' leadership. After Cook died unexpectedly in 1924, Glaspell chose to return to their home on Cape Cod rather than renew her life in the bohemian Greenwich Village milieu. She also chose to return to her first creative form, fiction, producing six new novels and a children's tale. Glaspell did not abandon the theater however. With her new companion Norman Matson, with whom she lived until 1932, Glaspell wrote *The Comic Artist* (1927); soon thereafter she composed *Alison's House* (1930), based on the life and family of Emily Dickinson, for which she won the Pulitzer Prize. From 1936 to 1938 she lived in Chicago, serving as the director of the Midwest Play Bureau of the Federal Theater Project. Glaspell wrote one additional play, *Springs Eternal* (written 1944), which was neither published nor produced. She died in Provincetown in 1948.

Glaspell's first play, *Trifles,* was quickly identified by critics as an exemplar of one-act dramaturgy, and it was soon both widely produced and anthologized. Although Glaspell had initially conceived the piece as another short story, her husband persuaded her to write it first as a play; its short story version, "A Jury of Her Peers," was equally praised on its publication the following year. *Trifles* established Glaspell as a dramatist of real power; like all her short dramatic pieces, it displays her skill at constructing tight plots and using distinctive images in the service of theme. Like her American modernist contemporaries, Glaspell experimented freely with the various "isms" that defined the period, including realism, symbolism, and expressionism, often combining these approaches to achieve a specific thematic or stylistic effect. She demonstrated the effectiveness of both comedy and tragedy as vehicles for social critique. And she capitalized on the power of live theater to examine issues of particular concern to women, placing female characters and their struggles at the center of her dramaturgy. *The Outside* (1917), set in a lifesaving station on Cape Cod, epitomizes her method of integrating the symbolism of her setting with the play's action, as she portrays characters literally and figuratively in need of salvation. Such one acts as *Woman's Honor* (1918) showcase Glaspell's gifts as a comic playwright, particularly her ability to depict the foibles of all her characters equally, as she introduces a group of allegorical women responding to what they take to be a demonstration of chivalry. This even-handedness in her dramaturgical technique gives her plays a sense of balance, which is especially important when her theme is politically charged. Her ability to represent differing ideological perspectives is clearly displayed in *Inheritors* (1921), a full-length play that explores the Espionage Act (1917) and the Sedition Act (1918), which were intended to silence opposition to U.S. involvement in World War I. Other longer dramas, such as her highly regarded *The Verge* (1921), feature Glaspell's engagement with questions of gender identity and feminist consciousness, as well as stylistic experimentation with realism and expressionism. Though some earlier critics faulted Glaspell for what they perceived as inconsistencies in style or thematic focus, more recently this variety and breadth have been championed as integral to the modernist movement in America and its willingness to engage with many facets of contemporary life.

Between December 1900 and April 1901, while working as a journalist, Glaspell had written a series of articles on the murder case that became the genesis for *Trifles:* the story of an Iowa farmer named Hossack whose wife was accused of killing him with an axe, and her subsequent trial and conviction. Glaspell transformed the details disclosed in the trial into a dramatic work of remarkable power, economy, and artistry. *Trifles* is set in the kitchen of "the now abandoned farmhouse" of John and Minnie Wright. We soon learn that shortly after the murder, a neighbor, Lewis Hale, discovered John strangled in his bed upstairs and Minnie dazedly rocking in her kitchen. With the body removed and the accused wife in jail, the play opens with the arrival of Hale; the sheriff, Henry Peters; and the county prosecutor, George Henderson, to inspect the crime scene. The wives of the sheriff and the neighbor, Mrs. Peters and Mrs. Hale, remain in the kitchen area to collect a few things Minnie has requested from prison. Glaspell's choice to identify them only by their married names underscores the traditional assumption that women have significance only through their relation to their husbands. Once the men leave the room, however, the women begin to explore the domestic space on their own. As they interact with the stage environment, the two women discover clues to the couple's personalities, as well as potential evidence in the case. Despite their absence from the scene, Minnie and John Wright become

The Hossack family in front of their farmhouse, ca. 1892.

The 1916 production of *Trifles* by the Washington Square Players at the Comedy Theater. Pictured, from left to right, are Marjorie Vonnegut (Mrs. Peters), Elinor M. Cox (Mrs. Hale), John King (Lewis Hale), Arthur E. Hohl (Henry Peters), and T. W. Gibson (George Henderson).

vivid figures for us via the dialogue and actions of Mrs. Hale and Mrs. Peters. Glaspell's technique of building a plot around these absent centers is a hallmark of her dramaturgy, recurring in *Bernice* (1919) and *Alison's House,* among other plays. This device enables her to show that identity is as much constructed as innate. Moreover, it creates a distance between the audience and these characters that thwarts identification, thus making it possible for theatergoers to see them and their reported actions from multiple points of view. The irony that Glaspell emphasizes throughout the play (and in its very title) is the inconsequentiality—to the men who are empowered to solve the crime—of the domestic details these women embrace. The "trifles" of women's lives and work that the men dismiss hold great significance for the women who understand how to read their import empathically. Although the women do not really know each other at the beginning of the play, they come to find they have much in common, just as they do with the absent Minnie. Recognizing a sense of responsibility for and community with this other woman, Mrs. Hale exclaims: "I might have known she needed help! I know how things can be—for women. . . . We all go through the same things—it's all just a different kind of the same thing."

By reversing the narrative conventions that place men at the center of a plot as figures of power and knowledge, Glaspell guides her audience toward the recognition that different perspectives and values are essential to appreciate women's lives. The short story's title, "A Jury of Her Peers," adds another layer of irony by highlighting the impossibility of a woman facing such a jury at a time when women were systematically denied the right to be jurors. In effect, Mrs. Peters and Mrs. Hale (played by Glaspell in the first production) try Minnie Wright in an alternative venue, using a process that reveals details of her experience and possible motives—aspects of the case that the men's investigation will never discover. While Minnie's ultimate fate is left unresolved at the play's end, we sense that these women have come to their own verdict, one that exonerates Minnie and makes the audience wonder who in the couple was the victim.

Part of the ongoing appeal of *Trifles* surely stems from its reliance on the conventions of the murder mystery. Glaspell capitalized on the growing interest in this form of narrative, a genre that was popularized first in the United States by Edgar Allan Poe (1809–1849) and that gained an even wider readership with the Sherlock Holmes stories of England's Arthur Conan Doyle (1859–1930). Like many writers of mysteries, Glaspell uses amateur detectives—the two women—who turn out to be more perceptive than the male experts investigating the case. Glaspell involves her audience in the process of discovery and deduction intrinsic to the form. Her employment of the mystery genre thus advances her feminist agenda: all members of the audience, regardless of sex, come to understand each piece of the puzzle through the perspectives of the women sleuths as they grapple with the evidence. As feminist critics point out, Glaspell's play teaches its viewers to see as women, to resist the conventions that have dominated the Western theater since its inception.

Glaspell's deft layering of imagery, her poignant representation of her midwestern locale, and the specificity of her characterizations and dialect in such a brief work all point to her mastery of the one-act form and her significance as an American dramatist. During her period of greatest productivity, she was considered by many to be one of the country's two most important dramatists—O'Neill being the other. The prominent cultural critic Ludwig Lewisohn wrote in 1932, "Susan Glaspell was followed by Eugene O'Neill. The rest was silence; the rest is silence still." Though recent critical attention has focused on Glaspell primarily as a feminist writer, her dramatic work reflects a number of compelling aesthetic and political concerns. She made important contributions to the development of American modernism, and her writing reflects a forceful commitment to the country's foundational principles of democracy and personal liberty. For those wishing to grasp essential nuances of our cultural and political heritage, Susan Glaspell provides eloquent renditions of our nation a century ago.

J.E.G.

Trifles

A Play in One Act

CHARACTERS

GEORGE HENDERSON, county attorney
HENRY PETERS, sheriff
LEWIS HALE, a neighboring farmer
MRS. PETERS
MRS. HALE

SCENE: *The kitchen in the now abandoned farmhouse of* JOHN WRIGHT, *a gloomy kitchen, and left without having been put in order—unwashed pans under the sink, a loaf of bread outside the breadbox, a dish towel on the table—other signs of incompleted work.*

[*At the rear the outer door opens and the* SHERIFF *comes in followed by the* COUNTY ATTORNEY *and* HALE. *The* SHERIFF *and* HALE *are men in middle life, the* COUNTY ATTORNEY *is a young man; all are much bundled up and go at once to the stove. They are followed by the two women—the* SHERIFF*'s wife first; she is a slight wiry woman, a thin nervous face.* MRS. HALE *is larger and would ordinarily be called more comfortable*[1] *looking, but she is disturbed now and looks fearfully about as she enters. The women have come in slowly, and stand close together near the door.*]

COUNTY ATTORNEY [*rubbing his hands*] This feels good. Come up to the fire, ladies.

MRS. PETERS [*after taking a step forward*] I'm not—cold.

SHERIFF [*unbuttoning his overcoat and stepping away from the stove as if to mark the beginning of official business*] Now, Mr. Hale, before we move things about, you explain to Mr. Henderson just what you saw when you came here yesterday morning.

COUNTY ATTORNEY By the way, has anything been moved? Are things just as you left them yesterday?

SHERIFF [*looking about*] It's just the same. When it dropped below zero last night I thought I'd better send Frank out this morning to make a fire for us—no use getting pneumonia with a big case on, but I told him not to touch anything except the stove—and you know Frank.

COUNTY ATTORNEY Somebody should have been left here yesterday.

SHERIFF Oh—yesterday. When I had to send Frank to Morris Center for that man who went crazy—I want you to know I had my hands full yesterday. I knew you could get back from Omaha by today and as long as I went over everything here myself—

COUNTY ATTORNEY Well, Mr. Hale, tell just what happened when you came here yesterday morning.

HALE Harry and I had started to town with a load of potatoes. We came along the road from my place and as I got here I said, "I'm going to see if I can't get John Wright to go in with me on a party telephone."[2] I spoke to Wright about it once before and he put me off, saying folks talked too much anyway, and all he asked was peace and quiet—I guess you know about how much he talked himself; but I thought maybe if I went to the house and talked about it before his wife, though I said to Harry that I didn't know as what his wife wanted made much difference to John—

COUNTY ATTORNEY Let's talk about that later, Mr. Hale. I do want to talk about that, but tell now just what happened when you got to the house.

HALE I didn't hear or see anything; I knocked at the door, and still it was all quiet inside. I knew they must be up, it was past eight o'clock. So I knocked again, and I thought I heard somebody say, "Come in." I wasn't sure, I'm not sure yet, but I opened the door—this door [*indicating the door by which the two women are still standing*] and there in that rocker—[*pointing to it*] sat Mrs. Wright.

[*They all look at the rocker.*]

COUNTY ATTORNEY What—was she doing?

HALE She was rockin' back and forth. She had her apron in her hand and was kind of—pleating it.

COUNTY ATTORNEY And how did she—look?

1. That is, appearing more relaxed.
2. That is, a single telephone line shared by two or four households.

HALE Well, she looked queer.

COUNTY ATTORNEY How do you mean—queer?

HALE Well, as if she didn't know what she was going to do next. And kind of done up.[3]

COUNTY ATTORNEY How did she seem to feel about your coming?

HALE Why, I don't think she minded—one way or other. She didn't pay much attention. I said, "How do, Mrs. Wright, it's cold, ain't it?" And she said, "Is it?"—and went on kind of pleating at her apron. Well, I was surprised; she didn't ask me to come up to the stove, or to set down, but just sat there, not even looking at me, so I said, "I want to see John." And then she—laughed. I guess you would call it a laugh. I thought of Harry and the team outside, so I said a little sharp: "Can't I see John?" "No," she says, kind o' dull like. "Ain't he home?" says I. "Yes," says she, "he's home." "Then why can't I see him?" I asked her, out of patience. "'Cause he's dead," says she. *"Dead?"* says I. She just nodded her head, not getting a bit excited, but rockin' back and forth. "Why—where is he?" says I, not knowing what to say. She just pointed upstairs—like that [*himself pointing to the room above*]. I got up, with the idea of going up there. I walked from there to here—then I says, "Why, what did he die of?" "He died of a rope round his neck," says she, and just went on pleatin' at her apron. Well, I went out and called Harry. I thought I might—need help. We went upstairs and there he was lyin'—

COUNTY ATTORNEY I think I'd rather have you go into that upstairs, where you can point it all out. Just go on now with the rest of the story.

HALE Well, my first thought was to get that rope off. It looked . . . [*Stops, his face twitches.*] . . . but Harry, he went up to him, and he said, "No, he's dead all right, and we'd better not touch anything." So we went back down stairs. She was still sitting that same way. "Has anybody been notified?" I asked. "No," says she, unconcerned. "Who did this, Mrs. Wright?" said Harry. He said it business-like—and she stopped pleatin' of her apron. "I don't know," she says. "You don't *know?*" says Harry. "No," says she. "Weren't you sleepin' in the bed with him?" says Harry. "Yes," says she, "but I was on the inside." "Somebody slipped a rope round his neck and strangled him and you didn't wake up?" says Harry. "I didn't wake up," she said after him. We must 'a looked as if we didn't see how that could be, for after a minute she said, "I sleep sound." Harry was going to ask her more questions but I said maybe we ought to let her tell her story first to the coroner, or the sheriff, so Harry went fast as he could to Rivers' place, where there's a telephone.

COUNTY ATTORNEY And what did Mrs. Wright do when she knew that you had gone for the coroner?

HALE She moved from that chair to this one over here [*pointing to a small chair in the corner*] and just sat there with her hands held together and looking down. I got a feeling that I ought to make come conversation, so I said I had come in to see if John wanted to put in a telephone, and at that she started to laugh, and then she stopped and looked at me—scared. [*The* COUNTY ATTORNEY, *who has had his notebook out, makes a note.*] I dunno, maybe it wasn't scared. I wouldn't like to say it was. Soon Harry got back,

3. Worn out.

and then Dr. Lloyd came, and you, Mr. Peters, and so I guess that's all I know that you don't.

COUNTY ATTORNEY [*looking around*] I guess we'll go upstairs first—and then out to the barn and around there. [*To the* SHERIFF] You're convinced that there was nothing important here—nothing that would point to any motive.

SHERIFF Nothing here but kitchen things.

[*The* COUNTY ATTORNEY, *after again looking around the kitchen, opens the door of a cupboard closet. He gets up on a chair and looks on a shelf. Pulls his hand away, sticky.*]

COUNTY ATTORNEY Here's a nice mess.

[*The women draw nearer.*]

MRS. PETERS [*to the other woman*] Oh, her fruit; it did freeze. [*To the* LAWYER] She worried about that when it turned so cold. She said the fire'd go out and her jars would break.

SHERIFF Well, can you beat the women! Held for murder and worryin' about her preserves.

COUNTY ATTORNEY I guess before we're through she may have something more serious than preserves to worry about.

HALE Well, women are used to worrying over trifles.

[*The two women move a little closer together.*]

COUNTY ATTORNEY [*with the gallantry of a young politician*] And yet, for all their worries, what would we do without the ladies? [*The women do not unbend. He goes to the sink, takes a dipperful of water from the pail and pouring it into a basin, washes his hands. Starts to wipe them on the roller towel, turns it for a cleaner place.*] Dirty towels! [*Kicks his foot against the pans under the sink.*] Not much of a housekeeper, would you say, ladies?

MRS. HALE [*stiffly*] There's a great deal of work to be done on a farm.

COUNTY ATTORNEY To be sure. And yet [*with a little bow to her*] I know there are some Dickson county farmhouses which do not have such roller towels.

[*He gives it a pull to expose its full length again.*]

MRS. HALE Those towels get dirty awful quick. Men's hands aren't always as clean as they might be.

COUNTY ATTORNEY Ah, loyal to your sex, I see. But you and Mrs. Wright were neighbors. I suppose you were friends, too.

MRS. HALE [*shaking her head*] I've not seen much of her of late years. I've not been in this house—it's more than a year.

COUNTY ATTORNEY And why was that? You didn't like her?

MRS. HALE I liked her all well enough. Farmers' wives have their hands full, Mr. Henderson. And then—

COUNTY ATTORNEY Yes—?

MRS. HALE [*looking about*] It never seemed a very cheerful place.

COUNTY ATTORNEY No—it's not cheerful. I shouldn't say she had the homemaking instinct.

MRS. HALE Well, I don't know as Wright had, either.

COUNTY ATTORNEY You mean that they didn't get on very well?

MRS. HALE No, I don't mean anything. But I don't think a place'd be any cheerfuller for John Wright's being in it.

COUNTY ATTORNEY I'd like to talk more of that a little later. I want to get the lay of things upstairs now.

[*He goes to the left, where three steps lead to a stair door.*]

SHERIFF I suppose anything Mrs. Peters does'll be all right. She was to take in some clothes for her, you know, and a few little things. We left in such a hurry yesterday.

COUNTY ATTORNEY Yes, but I would like to see what you take, Mrs. Peters, and keep an eye out for anything that might be of use to us.

MRS. PETERS Yes, Mr. Henderson.

[*The women listen to the men's steps on the stairs, then look about the kitchen.*]

MRS. HALE I'd hate to have men coming into my kitchen, snooping around and criticising.

[*She arranges the pans under sink which the* LAWYER *had shoved out of place.*]

MRS. PETERS Of course it's no more than their duty.

MRS. HALE Duty's all right, but I guess that deputy sheriff that came out to make the fire might have got a little of this on. [*Gives the roller towel a pull.*] Wish I'd thought of that sooner. Seems mean to talk about her for not having things slicked up when she had to come away in such a hurry.

MRS. PETERS [*who has gone to a small table in the left rear corner of the room, and lifted one end of a towel that covers a pan*] She had bread set.

[*Stands still.*]

MRS. HALE [*Eyes fixed on a loaf of bread beside the bread box, which is on a low shelf at the other side of the room. Moves slowly toward it.*] She was going to put this in there. [*Picks up loaf, then abruptly drops it. In a manner of returning to familiar things.*] It's a shame about her fruit. I wonder if it's all gone. [*Gets up on the chair and looks.*] I think there's some here that's all right, Mrs. Peters. Yes—here; [*holding it toward the window*] this is cherries, too. [*Looking again*] I declare I believe that's the only one. [*Gets down, bottle in her hand. Goes to the sink and wipes it off on the outside.*] She'll feel awful bad after all her hard work in the hot weather. I remember the afternoon I put up my cherries last summer.

[*She puts the bottle on the big kitchen table, center of the room. With a sigh, is about to sit down in the rocking chair. Before she is seated realizes what chair it is; with a slow look at it, steps back. The chair which she has touched rocks back and forth.*]

MRS. PETERS Well, I must get those things from the front room closet. [*She goes to the door at the right, but after looking into the other room, steps back.*] You coming with me, Mrs. Hale? You could help me carry them.

[*They go in the other room; reappear,* MRS. PETERS *carrying a dress and skirt,* MRS. HALE *following with a pair of shoes.*]

MRS. PETERS My, it's cold in there.

[*She puts the clothes on the big table, and hurries to the stove.*]

MRS. HALE [*examining the skirt*] Wright was close.[4] I think maybe that's why she kept so much to herself. She didn't even belong to the Ladies Aid. I suppose she felt she couldn't do her part, and then you don't enjoy things when you feel shabby. She used to wear pretty clothes and be lively, when

4. Stingy.

she was Minnie Foster, one of the town girls singing in the choir. But that—oh, that was thirty years ago. This all you was to take in?

MRS. PETERS She said she wanted an apron. Funny thing to want, for there isn't much to get you dirty in jail, goodness knows. But I suppose just to make her feel more natural. She said they was in the top drawer in this cupboard. Yes, here. And then her little shawl that always hung behind the door. [*Opens stair door and looks.*] Yes, here it is.

[*Quickly shuts door leading upstairs.*]

MRS. HALE [*abruptly moving toward her*] Mrs. Peters?

MRS. PETERS Yes, Mrs. Hale?

MRS. HALE Do you think she did it?

MRS. PETERS [*in a frightened voice*] Oh, I don't know.

MRS. HALE Well, I don't think she did. Asking for an apron and her little shawl. Worrying about her fruit.

MRS. PETERS [*starts to speak, glances up, where footsteps are heard in the room above. In a low voice*] Mr. Peters says it looks bad for her. Mr. Henderson is awful sarcastic in a speech and he'll make fun of her sayin' she didn't wake up.

MRS. HALE Well, I guess John Wright didn't wake when they was slipping that rope under his neck.

MRS. PETERS No, it's strange. It must have been done awful crafty and still. They say it was such a—funny way to kill a man, rigging it all up like that.

MRS. HALE That's just what Mr. Hale said. There was a gun in the house. He says that's what he can't understand.

MRS. PETERS Mr. Henderson said coming out that what was needed for the case was a motive; something to show anger, or—sudden feeling.

MRS. HALE [*who is standing by the table*] Well, I don't see any signs of anger around here. [*She puts her hand on the dish towel which lies on the table, stands looking down at table, one half of which is clean, the other half messy.*] It's wiped to here. [*Makes a move as if to finish work, then turns and looks at loaf of bread outside the breadbox. Drops towel. In that voice of coming back to familiar things*] Wonder how they are finding things upstairs. I hope she had it a little more red-up[5] up there. You know, it seems kind of *sneaking*. Locking her up in town and then coming out here and trying to get her own house to turn against her!

MRS. PETERS But Mrs. Hale, the law is the law.

MRS. HALE I s'pose 'tis. [*Unbuttoning her coat*] Better loosen up your things, Mrs. Peters. You won't feel them when you go out.

[MRS. PETERS *takes off her fur tippet, goes to hang it on hook at back of room, stands looking at the under part of the small corner table.*]

MRS. PETERS She was piecing a quilt.

[*She brings the large sewing basket and they look at the bright pieces.*]

MRS. HALE It's log cabin pattern. Pretty, isn't it? I wonder if she was goin' to quilt it or just knot it?

[*Footsteps have been heard coming down the stairs. The* SHERIFF *enters followed by* HALE *and the* COUNTY ATTORNEY.]

SHERIFF They wonder if she was going to quilt it or just knot it!

5. Tidied up.

[*The men laugh, the women look abashed.*]

COUNTY ATTORNEY [*rubbing his hands over the stove*] Frank's fire didn't do much up there, did it? Well, let's go out to the barn and get that cleared up.

[*The men go outside.*]

MRS. HALE [*resentfully*] I don't know as there's anything so strange, our takin' up our time with little things while we're waiting for them to get the evidence. [*She sits down at the big table smoothing out a block with decision.*] I don't see as it's anything to laugh about.

MRS. PETERS [*apologetically*] Of course they've got awful important things on their minds.

[*Pulls up a chair and joins* MRS. HALE *at the table.*]

MRS. HALE [*examining another block*] Mrs. Peters, look at this one. Here, this is the one she was working on, and look at the sewing! All the rest of it has been so nice and even. And look at this! It's all over the place! Why, it looks as if she didn't know what she was about!

[*After she has said this they look at each other, then start to glance back at the door. After an instant* MRS. HALE *has pulled at a knot and ripped the sewing.*

MRS. PETERS Oh, what are you doing, Mrs. Hale?

MRS. HALE [*mildly*] Just pulling out a stitch or two that's not sewed very good. [*Threading a needle*] Bad sewing always made me fidgety.

MRS. PETERS [*nervously*] I don't think we ought to touch things.

MRS. HALE I'll just finish up this end. [*Suddenly stopping and leaning forward*] Mrs. Peters?

MRS. PETERS Yes, Mrs. Hale?

MRS. HALE What do you suppose she was so nervous about?

MRS. PETERS Oh—I don't know. I don't know as she was nervous. I sometimes sew awful queer when I'm just tired. [MRS. HALE *starts to say something, looks at* MRS. PETERS, *then goes on sewing.*] Well I must get these things wrapped up. They may be through sooner than we think. [*Putting apron and other things together*] I wonder where I can find a piece of paper, and string.

MRS. HALE In that cupboard, maybe.

MRS. PETERS [*looking in cupboard*] Why, here's a bird-cage. [*Holds it up.*] Did she have a bird, Mrs. Hale?

MRS. HALE Why, I don't know whether she did or not—I've not been here for so long. There was a man around last year selling canaries cheap, but I don't know as she took one; maybe she did. She used to sing real pretty herself.

MRS. PETERS [*glancing around*] Seems funny to think of a bird here. But she must have had one, or why would she have a cage? I wonder what happened to it.

MRS. HALE I s'pose maybe the cat got it.

MRS. PETERS No, she didn't have a cat. She's got that feeling some people have about cats—being afraid of them. My cat got in her room and she was real upset and asked me to take it out.

MRS. HALE My sister Bessie was like that. Queer, ain't it?

MRS. PETERS [*examining the cage*] Why, look at this door. It's broke. One hinge is pulled apart.

MRS. HALE [*looking too*] Looks as if someone must have been rough with it.

MRS. PETERS Why, yes.

[*She brings the cage forward and puts it on the table.*]

MRS. HALE I wish if they're going to find any evidence they'd be about it. I don't like this place.

MRS. PETERS But I'm awful glad you came with me, Mrs. Hale. It would be lonesome for me sitting here alone.

MRS. HALE It would, wouldn't it? [*Dropping her sewing*] But I tell you what I do wish, Mrs. Peters. I wish I had come over sometimes when *she* was here. I—[*looking around the room*]—wish I had.

MRS. PETERS But of course you were awful busy, Mrs. Hale—your house and your children.

MRS. HALE I could've come. I stayed away because it weren't cheerful—and that's why I ought to have come. I—I've never liked this place. Maybe because it's down in a hollow and you don't see the road. I dunno what it is, but it's a lonesome place and always was. I wish I had come over to see Minnie Foster sometimes. I can see now—[*Shakes her head.*]

MRS. PETERS Well, you mustn't reproach yourself, Mrs. Hale. Somehow we just don't see how it is with other folks until—something comes up.

MRS. HALE Not having children makes less work—but it makes a quiet house, and Wright out to work all day, and no company when he did come in. Did you know John Wright, Mrs. Peters?

MRS. PETERS Not to know him; I've seen him in town. They say he was a good man.

MRS. HALE Yes—good; he didn't drink, and kept his word as well as most, I guess, and paid his debts. But he was a hard man, Mrs. Peters. Just to pass the time of day with him— [*Shivers.*] Like a raw wind that gets to the bone. [*Pauses, her eye falling on the cage.*] I should think she would 'a wanted a bird. But what do you suppose went with it?

MRS. PETERS I don't know, unless it got sick and died.

[*She reaches over and swings the broken door, swings it again, both women watch it.*]

MRS. HALE You weren't raised round here, were you? [MRS. PETERS *shakes her head.*] You didn't know—her?

MRS. PETERS Not till they brought her yesterday.

MRS. HALE She—come to think of it, she was kind of like a bird herself—real sweet and pretty, but kind of timid and—fluttery. How—she—did—change. [*Silence; then as if struck by a happy thought and relieved to get back to everyday things.*] Tell you what, Mrs. Peters, why don't you take the quilt in with you? It might take up her mind.

MRS. PETERS Why, I think that's a real nice idea, Mrs. Hale. There couldn't possibly be any objection to it, could there? Now, just what would I take? I wonder if her patches are in here—and her things.

[*They look in the sewing basket.*]

MRS. HALE Here's some red. I expect this has got sewing things in it. [*Brings out a fancy box.*] What a pretty box. Looks like something somebody would give you. Maybe her scissors are in here. [*Opens box. Suddenly puts her hand to her nose.*] Why — [MRS. PETERS *bends nearer, then turns her face away.*] There's something wrapped up in this piece of silk.

MRS. PETERS Why, this isn't her scissors.

MRS. HALE [*lifting the silk*] Oh, Mrs. Peters—it's—

[MRS. PETERS *bends closer.*]

MRS. PETERS It's the bird.

MRS. HALE [*jumping up*] But, Mrs. Peters—look at it! It's neck! Look at its neck! It's all—other side *to*.[6]

MRS. PETERS Somebody—wrung—its—neck.

[*Their eyes meet. A look of growing comprehension, of horror, Steps are heard outside.* MRS. HALE *slips box under quilt pieces, and sinks into her chair. Enter* SHERIFF *and* COUNTY ATTORNEY. MRS. PETERS *rises.*]

COUNTY ATTORNEY [*as one turning from serious things to little pleasantries*] Well, ladies, have you decided whether she was going to quilt it or knot it?

MRS. PETERS We think she was going to—knot it.

COUNTY ATTORNEY Well, that's interesting, I'm sure. [*Seeing the birdcage*] Has the bird flown?

MRS. HALE [*putting more quilt pieces over the box*] We think the—cat got it.

COUNTY ATTORNEY [*preoccupied*] Is there a cat?

[MRS. HALE *glances in a quick covert way at* MRS. PETERS.]

MRS. PETERS Well, not *now*. They're superstitious, you know. They leave.

COUNTY ATTORNEY [*to* SHERIFF PETERS, *continuing an interrupted conversation*] No sign at all of anyone having come from the outside. Their own rope. Now let's go up again and go over it piece by piece. [*They start upstairs.*] It would have to have been someone who knew just the—

[MRS. PETERS *sits down. The two women sit there not looking at one another, but as if peering into something and at the same time holding back. When they talk now it is in the manner of feeling their way over strange ground, as if afraid of what they are saying, but as if they cannot help saying it.*]

MRS. HALE She liked the bird. She was going to bury it in that pretty box.

MRS. PETERS [*in a whisper*] When I was a girl—my kitten—there was a boy took a hatchet, and before my eyes—and before I could get there—[*covers her face an instant*] If they hadn't held me back I would have—[*catches herself, looks upstairs where steps are heard, falters weakly.*]—hurt him.

MRS. HALE [*with a slow look around her*] I wonder how it would seem never to have had any children around. [*Pause*] No, Wright wouldn't like the bird — a thing that sang. She used to sing. He killed that, too.

MRS. PETERS [*moving uneasily*] We don't know who killed the bird.

MRS. HALE I knew John Wright.

MRS. PETERS It was an awful thing was done in this house that night, Mrs. Hale. Killing a man while he slept, slipping a rope around his neck that choked the life out of him.

MRS. HALE His neck. Choked the life out of him.

[*Her hand goes out and rests on the birdcage.*]

MRS. PETERS [*with rising voice*] We don't know who killed him. We don't *know*.

MRS. HALE [*her own feeling not interrupted*] If there'd been years and years of nothing, then a bird to sing to you, it would be awful—still, after the bird was still.

MRS. PETERS [*something within her speaking*] I know what stillness is. When we homesteaded in Dakota, and my first baby died—after he was two years old, and me with no other then—

6. Twisted around.

MRS. HALE [*moving*] How soon do you suppose they'll be through, looking for the evidence?

MRS. PETERS I know what stillness is. [*Pulling herself back*] The law has got to punish crime, Mrs. Hale.

MRS. HALE [*not as if answering that*] I wish you'd seen Minnie Foster when she wore a white dress with blue ribbons and stood up there in the choir and sang. [*A look around the room*] Oh, I *wish* I'd come over here once in a while! That was a crime! That was a crime! Who's going to punish that?

MRS. PETERS [*looking upstairs*] We mustn't—take on.

MRS. HALE I might have known she needed help! I know how things can be—for women. I tell you, it's queer, Mrs. Peters. We live close together and we live far apart. We all go through the same things—it's all just a different kind of the same thing. [*Brushes her eyes, noticing the bottle of fruit, reaches out for it.*] If I was you I wouldn't tell her her fruit was gone. Tell her it *ain't*. Tell her it's all right. Take this in to prove it to her. She—she may never know whether it was broke or not.

MRS. PETERS [*Takes the bottle, looks about for something to wrap it in; takes petticoat from the clothes brought from the other room, very nervously begins winding this around the bottle. In a false voice.*] My, it's a good thing the men couldn't hear us. Wouldn't they just laugh! Getting all stirred up over a little thing like a—dead canary. As if that could have anything to do with—with—wouldn't they *laugh!*

[*The men are heard coming down stairs.*]

MRS. HALE [*under her breath*] Maybe they would—maybe they wouldn't.

COUNTY ATTORNEY No, Peters, it's all perfectly clear except a reason for doing it. But you know juries when it comes to women. If there was some definite thing. Something to show—something to make a story about—a thing that would connect up with this strange way of doing it—

[*The women's eyes meet for an instant. Enter* HALE *from outer door.*]

HALE Well, I've got the team around. Pretty cold out there.

COUNTY ATTORNEY I'm going to stay here a while by myself. [*To the* SHERIFF] You can send Frank out for me, can't you? I want to go over everything. I'm not satisfied that we can't do better.

SHERIFF Do you want to see what Mrs. Peters is going to take in?

[*The* LAWYER *goes to the table, picks up the apron, laughs.*]

COUNTY ATTORNEY Oh, I guess they're not very dangerous things the ladies have picked out. [*Moves a few things about, disturbing the quilt pieces which cover the box. Steps back.*] No, Mrs. Peters doesn't need supervising. For that matter, a sheriff's wife is married to the law. Ever think of it that way, Mrs. Peters?

MRS. PETERS Not—just that way.

SHERIFF [*chuckling*] Married to the law. [*Moves toward the other room.*] I just want you to come in here a minute, George. We ought to take a look at these windows.

COUNTY ATTORNEY [*scoffingly*] Oh, windows!

SHERIFF We'll be right out, Mr. Hale.

[HALE *goes outside. The* SHERIFF *follows the* COUNTY ATTORNEY *into the other room. Then* MRS. HALE *rises, hands tight together, looking intensely at* MRS. PETERS, *whose eyes make a slow turn, finally meeting* MRS.

HALE'S. *A moment* MRS. HALE *holds her, then her own eyes point the way to where the box is concealed. Suddenly* MRS. PETERS *throws back quilt pieces and tries to put the box in the bag she is wearing. It is too big. She opens box, starts to take bird out, cannot touch it, goes to pieces, stands there helpless. Sound of a knob turning in the other room.* MRS. HALE *snatches the box and puts it in the pocket of her big coat. Enter* COUNTY ATTORNEY *and* SHERIFF.]

COUNTY ATTORNEY [*facetiously*] Well, Henry, at least we found out that she was not going to quilt it. She was going to—what is it you call it, ladies?

MRS. HALE [*her hand against her pocket*] We call it—knot it, Mr. Henderson.

Curtain.

LUIGI PIRANDELLO

1867–1937

When Pirandello received the Nobel Prize in Literature in 1934, at the age of sixty-seven, he was widely known as the author of intricate philosophical comedies. One in particular, *SIX CHARACTERS IN SEARCH OF AN AUTHOR* (1921), had catapulted him onto the international scene in the early 1920s, leading to acclaimed performances all over Europe and the Americas. Like his contemporaries GEORGE BERNARD SHAW for the English-speaking world and Maurice Maeterlinck for the French-speaking world, Pirandello became the Italian representative of the New Drama. Pirandello's worldwide success occurred relatively late in his life, at the end of a busy writing career that included hundreds of short stories, dozens of early plays, and a handful of novels as well as essays, a dissertation in linguistics, and several film scripts. Outside Italy, however, Pirandello's name remained tied to the invention of a new, intellectual drama thriving on arguments, paradoxes, and inversions. These plays, of which *Six Characters* is the best known, apply their wit to the theater itself, turning actors, directors, and dramatic authors into the material from which to fashion outrageous plots and far-fetched conceits. Somehow, Pirandello managed to transform himself from an author of local and rather traditional novellas and plays into the most fashionable and advanced European dramatist of his age.

Luigi Pirandello was born into a nineteenth-century Sicily where a small landowning class lorded over impoverished peasants. It was a society with many lingering feudal structures and a deeply traditional literature and culture to go with it. Pirandello himself was rather fortunate, since his father was quite wealthy and was therefore capable of financing Pirandello's studies in Rome, his doctorate at the University of Bonn, and his early career as a writer. Despite his cosmopolitan education, however, Pirandello did not reject the social values of Sicily and agreed to an arranged marriage to Antonietta Portulano, the daughter of one of his father's business partners, whom he barely knew. His marriage of 1894, business interests, the sulphur mine—these were the pillars of Pirandello's life. But they did not last. His father's fortune and his wife's dowry were heavily invested in a mine that was flooded in 1903, and everything was lost. In the meantime, Pirandello had began teaching at a women's college in Rome, an occupation he continued until his international breakthrough in the early twenties. Just as the economic foundations of his life crumbled, so did the personal ones. His wife was subject to increasingly pathological fits of jealousy and other delusional behavior, and Pirandello retired more and more from social life, maintaining his three children and suffering from an untenable domestic arrangement until Antonietta was eventually committed to a mental institution in 1914.

In the early twentieth century, Pirandello withdrew from life, but he also became a prolific writer of short stories, with which he supplemented his teacher's income. Over the years, he perfected his command of the genre and reissued selected short stories in a collection, *Novellas for a Year* (15 vols., 1922–37), that still enjoys great popularity in Italy. Pirandello's later mastery of drama can be traced back to these works. Like drama, the short story is a genre that requires economy and constraint and is often built around very few scenes and exchanges. Pirandello would frequently recycle his short stories in his dramas, including *Six Characters*.

The world in which Pirandello had grown up had fallen to pieces, but it continued to make itself felt in his literary work. His short stories, novels, and plays often revolve around closed family structures made insufferable by arranged marriages, jealousy, and betrayal. They are set in deeply patriarchal worlds in which women are seen as mothers, virgins, or whores. Even when Pirandello shows the extent to which these roles lead to pathologies, he held onto them to the end. His acclaimed comedies, such as *Six Characters* and *Henry IV* (1922), with their plays-within-the-play, philosophizing characters, and modern structures, contain under their surface the traditional plots of marriage and fertility, jealousy and adultery that are premised on the most traditional of family roles. Pirandello could never quite let go of Sicily—even during his time in Germany, when he studied philology and philosophy at Bonn, he chose as his dissertation subject the Sicilian dialects of his home region.

A similar fascination with Sicily also prompted Pirandello to turn from the short story to drama. After having become acquainted with a Sicilian dialect theater group headed by the charismatic Angelo Musco, Pirandello started writing dialect plays of high passion and melodrama. It was a traditionalist and provincial beginning for the future modern dramatist, but it gave him a first taste of the pleasures of the theater, which would come to full fruition in his most successful plays. Musco's group acted in a style reminiscent of the commedia dell'arte, the tradition of improvised theater based on fixed types that are often accentuated with masks. Pirandello continued to use this technique later in his career: for example, in *Six Characters*, where a number of actors wear such masks. Indeed, it was CARLO GOLDONI (1707–1793), the playwright most closely associated with commedia dell'arte, rather than HENRIK IBSEN, Shaw, or any of the other modern dramatists, who was Pirandello's favorite playwright. Pirandello's best and bestknown dialect play, *Liolà* (1916), whose plot is taken entirely from the first chapters of his novel *The Late Mattia Pascal* (1904), is representative of this phase of his work in that it revolves around fertility, adultery, and the necessity of producing an heir. Yet all these subjects are presented in a particular form of comedy. In a long essay written to qualify for his teaching position, Pirandello had defined humor as the collision of ideals and harsh reality, as a sentiment of contradiction, as a moment when one position merges with its opposite, and as an art of quick reversals and inversions. This theory of humor underlies much of Pirandello's later drama.

Despite some considerable success in the theater, however, Pirandello still viewed it as a secondary art form. He put actors in the same category as illustrators of novels or translators—merely necessary but lamentable vehicles for bringing works of literature to the public. But over time, he became more interested in theatrical representation as well as in modernist forms of literature and drama. The first of his modernist plays, *It Is So! (If You Think So)* (1917), introduced the philosophizing *raisonneur*—a character that comments on the main action of the play, expressing skepticism about the truth of appearances. More important than the validity of this skepticism as a philosophical position is its close relation to Pirandello's theory of humor, which is premised on sudden reversals and quick changes from one appearance to the next. Many of his later plays, including *Six Characters, Henry IV*, and *Each in His Own Way* (1923), exploit philosophical relativism as a vehicle for a comedy, and they often rely on the figure of the *raisonneur*. Because of the prominence of this figure in many of his plays, Pirandello's works are sometimes considered too theoretical or intellectual, too dependent on words and conceits. But in his most successful plays, Pirandello manages to draw these explanatory figures into the action, exposing their own blindness, missteps, and mistakes. After decades of writing more or less realistic literature set in Sicily and Rome, Pirandello found that the theater formed the perfect setting and subject matter for his art.

The best-known and most cunning of these plays about theater is *Six Characters*. Here Pirandello highlights the difference between the fixed dramatic text and its ever-changing performances by staging a conflict between two groups: a set of characters and the actors who want to impersonate these characters according to the traditions and rules of theatrical representation. Even though the characters are putatively searching for an author who will write down their story, that story already exists within them. The real conflict breaks out not over how to transform these characters into a play but over how to bring the story that they represent onto the stage. The title, in this sense, is a misnomer, one that can be explained by the history of the play's composition; like many of Pirandello's dramas, it originated as a short story. In fact, it originated as three short stories, all of which featured "characters" appearing before an author and demanding to be turned into literature: "Character" (1906), "A Character's Tragedy" (1911), and "Interview of Characters" (1915). But once this conceit is transported to the theater, characters and actors engage in a struggle over the question of what it means to stage a play. While the characters demand absolute fidelity to their story, the director and the actors recast that story into one suitable for the theater. They simplify the plot, reduce the number of scenes, and do everything necessary for an audience to be able to follow the play.

Having characters appear on stage as characters and not as full-fledged persons creates a number of interesting problems and conundrums, which Pirandello exploits to the full. Since the story is enclosed inside these characters, they have to tell their story to the director and the actors so that it can be brought to the stage. Most of the narration is done by the father, another version of Pirandello's *raisonneur* figure; he also explains the predicament of the actors, who are caught in their roles and hope to find release through an author. Far from being detached observers, however, these characters, including the father, are fully immersed in their story and therefore lack the capacity to tell it coherently and succinctly. Every time they begin to narrate what happened and how it happened, they "fall into character," as the common theatrical idiom has it—that is, they stop narrating and start feeling and enacting their plight. Indeed, they are entirely trapped inside their story and are forced to live it over and over again. It is only at the very end of the play, after many conflicts between characters and actors, that the audience can surmise that story's contours.

But living the story is one thing, playing it is another. While the characters *feel* their passions, the actors need to *represent* them. The director and the actors in this play argue directly against the common critique of acting as falsifying the author's intentions (a position Pirandello himself had maintained early in his career)—or, more precisely, they prove the necessity of such falsifications in the interest of art. *Six Characters* is thus essentially a play about acting, about theater, about the rules and integrity of theatrical representation. As eccentric and unusual as this piece of metatheater may be, the actual story inside the characters is strikingly traditional. It is precisely the kind of story that had populated Pirandello's earlier works, featuring an adulterous affair, a separation between husband and wife, the threat of incest, and rivalries between stepsiblings, as well as hatred and shame. *Six Characters* is metatheater, but metatheater with a traditional, melodramatic core.

The difference between the unchanging eternal play to which the characters are tied and its variations every time they relive it on the stage was something Pirandello had absorbed from the Italian critic Adriano Tilgher. Tilgher supplied Pirandello with an aesthetic philosophy, borrowed from such theorists as Henri Bergson (1859–1941) and Friedrich Nietzsche (1844–1900), according to which life is a perpetual chaos onto which the human mind seeks to impose order and form. Art, in Tilgher's view, is the highest imposition of form onto life, connecting the ever-changing with eternal and ideal forms. Pirandello realized that this difference between eternal works of art and ever-changing life corresponded directly to

Benito Mussolini in *The Yellow Caesar* (1941), an Italian fascist propaganda film.

the relation between a fixed literary text and its ever-new performances through live actors. This insight was put into practice most brilliantly in Pirandello's plays about the theater. Some of these metatheatrical pieces—*Six Characters, Each in His Own Way*, and *Tonight We Improvise* (1930)—actually take place in the theater, but many others that draw on the same aesthetic theory do not.

Six Characters, and Pirandello's metatheater more generally, has a more sinister, political side, which is often ignored: it supplied the language in which Pirandello formulated his strong and unwavering allegiance to Benito Mussolini and Italian fascism. Pirandello favored a powerful leader who could stand above the chaos of democratic multiplicity and lead the country with a strong and fatherly hand. In Mussolini he got precisely the leader he was looking for. He met Mussolini in 1923 and immediately began to heap praise on him in the right-wing press, in the precise terms of his aesthetic doctrine—namely, as a strong leader capable of imposing onto the chaos of the nation a single and eternal form. Pirandello thus envisioned Mussolini as the artist of the Italian nation. The playwright who often declared that his art had nothing to do with his politics here treated politics as if it were nothing but an extension of art.

Pirandello's antidemocratic and profascist sympathies were not isolated moments of enthusiasm but were deeply felt. Indeed, he made his strongest gesture of support for fascism at a time of the movement's greatest weakness, after fascist supporters had brutally murdered a socialist member of parliament, Giacomo Matteotti. Rather than being outraged at this level of brutality, as many otherwise sympathetic to fascism were, Pirandello publicly declared his allegiance to the National Fascist Party and finally applied for membership. This political dimension may also account for a somewhat puzzling aspect of Pirandello's work: its violence. Even and especially his most philosophical and metatheatrical plays end with acts of extreme violence; *Six Characters*, for instance, culminates in two sudden deaths, one a suicide. This unexpectedly violent turn in an otherwise talkative and intellectual play corresponds structurally to the fascist doctrine of action: talking is what democracy practices in parliament and it must be ended by pure and bloody acts. It is as if Pirandello felt that his verbose and witty plays likewise needed to be concluded with bloodshed, so that mere talking could stop and real action could start.

In addition to Pirandello's genuine attraction to fascism, there was also a mercenary element to his relationship with Mussolini—he hoped that the fascist leader would establish a national theater and place him in charge of it. After his success with *Six Characters,* which received multiple stagings by Europe's most innovative directors, Pirandello founded a theater of his own, the Teatro d'Arte. Although Mussolini never gave sufficient funds to satisfy Pirandello's ambitious plans for a national theater, he supplied enough to enable Pirandello's theater company to tour Europe and the Americas with *Six Characters* and other plays, thereby functioning, as Pirandello never tired of telling Mussolini, as cultural ambassadors for fascist Italy. These tours also exposed Pirandello to Europe's most innovative directors, such as the Russian Nikolai Evreinov and the Austrian Max Reinhardt, who had perfected new forms of spectacular theater. Indeed, one of Pirandello's last pieces of metatheater set in a theater, *Tonight We Improvise,* contains a parody of Max Reinhardt as a director disrespectful of the playwright and interested only in creating spectacles.

It was during his own work as director and producer that Pirandello in 1925 met the young actress Marta Abba, whom he fell in love with and continued to adore for the rest of his life. It was for her that he wrote his final plays, all of which feature strong female protagonists, such as the utopian *The New Colony* (1928) or his last play, *The Mountain Giants* (1937), a metatheatrical work that features a group of actors and magicians living in a remote mountain region. After a tumultuous life of personal tragedy, political entanglement, and artistic fame, Pirandello ended with a eulogy to the art that he had first rejected but that turned out to be his calling: the theater.

M.P.

Six Characters in Search of an Author[1]

CHARACTERS OF THE PLAY-IN-THE-MAKING

The FATHER
The MOTHER
The SON, aged 22
The STEPDAUGHTER, 18
The BOY, 14
The LITTLE GIRL, 4
(these two last do not speak)
Then, called into being:
MADAM PACE

ACTORS IN THE COMPANY

The DIRECTOR (DIRETTORE-CAPOCOMICO)[2]
LEADING LADY
LEADING MAN
SECOND ACTRESS
INGENUE
JUVENILE LEAD
Other actors and actresses
STAGE MANAGER
PROMPTER
PROPERTY MAN
TECHNICIAN
Director's SECRETARY
STAGE DOOR MAN
STAGE CREW

1. Translated by Eric Bentley.
2. Pirandello here combines the modern 20th-century role of director (*direttore* in Italian) with the older position of actor-manager (or "chief actor," *capocomico* in Italian), who fulfilled the function of supervising a theatrical production.

THE PLACE: *The stage of a playhouse.*[3]

When the audience arrives in the theater, the curtain is raised; and the stage, as normally in the daytime, is without wings or scenery and almost completely dark and empty. From the beginning we are to receive the impression of an unrehearsed performance.

Two stairways, left and right respectively, connect the stage with the auditorium.

Onstage the dome of the prompter's box[4] *has been placed on one side of the box itself. On the other side, at the front of the stage, a small table and an armchair with its back to the audience, for the* DIRETTORE-CAPOCOMICO [DIRECTOR].

Two other small tables of different sizes with several chairs around them have also been placed at the front of the stage, ready as needed for the rehearsal. Other chairs here and there, left and right, for the actors, and at the back, a piano, on one side and almost hidden.

As soon as the houselights dim, the TECHNICIAN *is seen entering at the door onstage. He is wearing a blue shirt, and a tool bag hangs from his belt. From a corner at the back he takes several stage braces,*[5] *then arranges them on the floor downstage, and kneels down to hammer some nails in. At the sound of the hammering, the* STAGE MANAGER *comes running from the door that leads to the dressing rooms.*

STAGE MANAGER Oh! What are you doing?

TECHNICIAN What am I doing? Hammering.

STAGE MANAGER At this hour? [*He looks at the clock.*] It's ten-thirty already. The Director will be here any moment. For the rehearsal.

TECHNICIAN I gotta have time to work, too, see.

STAGE MANAGER You will have. But not now.

TECHNICIAN When?

STAGE MANAGER Not during rehearsal hours. Now move along, take all this stuff away, and let me set the stage for the second act of, um, *The Game of Role Playing.*[6]

[*Muttering, grumbling, the* TECHNICIAN *picks up the stage braces and goes away. Meanwhile, from the door onstage, the* ACTORS OF THE COMPANY *start coming in, both men and women, one at a time at first, then in twos, at random, nine or ten of them, the number one would expect as the cast in rehearsals of Pirandello's play "The Game of Role Playing," which is the order of the day. They enter, greet the* STAGE MANAGER *and each other, all saying good-morning to all. Several go to their dressing rooms. Others, among them the* PROMPTER, *who has a copy of the script rolled up under his arm, stay onstage, waiting for the* DIRECTOR *to begin the rehearsal. Meanwhile, either seated in conversational groups, or*

3. The play has neither acts nor scenes. The performance should be interrupted twice; first—without any lowering of the curtain—when the Director and the chief among the Characters retire to put the scenario together and the Actors leave the stage; second when the Technician lets the curtain down by mistake [Pirandello's note].

4. A box in the apron or on the side of a stage, opening toward the actors, that houses someone with a script (sitting below the stage) who is ready to prompt the actors when they forget their lines.

5. Braces used to support a stage set from behind.

6. *Il Gioco delle Parti* (1918), a stage adaptation of Pirandello's own novella.

standing, they exchange a few words among themselves. One lights a cigarette, one complains about the part he has been assigned, one reads aloud to his companions items of news from a theater journal. It would be well if both the Actresses and the Actors wore rather gay and brightly colored clothes and if this first improvised scene [scena a soggetto] *combined vivacity with naturalness. At a certain point, one of the actors can sit down at the piano and strike up a dance tune. The younger actors and actresses start dancing.*]

STAGE MANAGER [*clapping his hands to call them to order*] All right, that's enough of that. The Director's here.

[*The noise and the dancing stop at once. The Actors turn and look toward the auditorium from the door of which the* DIRECTOR *is now seen coming. A bowler hat on his head, a walking stick under his arm, and a big cigar in his mouth, he walks down the aisle and, greeted by the Actors, goes onstage by one of the two stairways. The* SECRETARY *hands him his mail: several newspapers and a script in a wrapper.*]

DIRECTOR Letters?

SECRETARY None. That's all the mail there is.

DIRECTOR [*handing him the script*] Take this to my room. [*Then, looking around and addressing himself to the* STAGE MANAGER] We can't see each other in here. Want to give us a little light?

STAGE MANAGER OK.

[*He goes to give the order, and shortly afterward, the whole left side of the stage where the Actors are is lit by a vivid white light. Meanwhile, the* PROMPTER *has taken up his position in his box. He uses a small lamp and has the script open in front of him.*]

DIRECTOR [*clapping his hands*] Very well, let's start. [*To the* STAGE MANAGER] Someone missing?

STAGE MANAGER The Leading Lady.

DIRECTOR As usual! [*He looks at the clock.*] We're ten minutes late already. Fine her for that, would you, please? Then she'll learn to be on time.

[*He has not completed his rebuke when the voice of the* LEADING LADY *is heard from the back of the auditorium.*]

LEADING LADY No, no, for heaven's sake! I'm here! I'm here! [*She is dressed all in white with a big, impudent hat on her head and a cute little dog in her arms. She runs down the aisle and climbs one of the sets of stairs in great haste.*]

DIRECTOR You've sworn an oath always to keep people waiting.

LEADING LADY You must excuse me. Just couldn't find a taxi. But you haven't even begun, I see. And I'm not on right away. [*Then, calling the* STAGE MANAGER *by name, and handing the little dog over to him*] Would you please shut him in my dressing room?

DIRECTOR [*grumbling*] And the little dog to boot! As if there weren't enough dogs around here. [*He claps his hands again and turns to the* PROMPTER.] Now then, the second act of *The Game of Role Playing*. [*As he sits down in his armchair*] Quiet, gentlemen. Who's onstage?

[*The Actresses and Actors clear the front of the stage and go and sit on one side, except for the three who will start the rehearsal and the* LEADING LADY *who, disregarding the* DIRECTOR'*s request, sits herself down at one of the two small tables.*]

DIRECTOR [*to the* LEADING LADY] You're in this scene, are you?

LEADING LADY Me? No, no.

DIRECTOR [*irritated*] Then how about getting up, for Heaven's sake?

[*The* LEADING LADY *rises and goes and sits beside the other Actors who have already gone to one side.*]

DIRECTOR [*to the* PROMPTER] Start, start.

PROMPTER [*reading from the script*] "In the house of Leone Gala. A strange room, combined study and dining room."

DIRECTOR [*turning to the* STAGE MANAGER] We'll use the red room.

STAGE MANAGER [*making a note on a piece of paper*] Red room. Very good.

PROMPTER [*continuing to read from the script*] "The table is set and the desk has books and papers on it. Shelves with books on them, and cupboards with lavish tableware. Door in the rear through which one goes to Leone's bedroom. Side door on the left through which one goes to the kitchen. The main entrance is on the right."

DIRECTOR [*rising and pointing*] All right, now listen carefully. That's the main door. This is the way to the kitchen. [*Addressing himself to the Actor playing the part of Socrates*] You will come on and go out on this side. [*To the* STAGE MANAGER] The compass at the back. And curtains. [*He sits down again.*]

STAGE MANAGER [*making a note*] Very good.

PROMPTER [*reading as before*] "Scene One. Leone Gala, Guido Venanzi, Filippo called Socrates." [*To the* DIRECTOR] Am I supposed to read the stage directions, too?

DIRECTOR Yes, yes, yes! I've told you that a hundred times!

PROMPTER [*reading as before*] "At the rise of the curtain, Leone Gala, wearing a chef's hat and apron, is intent on beating an egg in a saucepan with a wooden spoon. Filippo, also dressed as a cook, is beating another egg. Guido Venanzi, seated, is listening."

LEADING ACTOR [*to the* DIRECTOR] Excuse me, but do I really have to wear a chef's hat?

DIRECTOR [*annoyed by this observation*] I should say so! It's in the script. [*And he points at it.*]

LEADING ACTOR But it's ridiculous, if I may say so.

DIRECTOR [*leaping to his feet, furious*] "Ridiculous, ridiculous!" What do you want me to do? We never get a good play from France any more, so we're reduced to producing plays by Pirandello, a fine man and all that, but neither the actors, the critics, nor the audience are ever happy with his plays, and if you ask me, he does it all on purpose. [*The Actors laugh. And now he rises and coming over to the* LEADING ACTOR *shouts.*] A cook's hat, yes, my dear man! And you beat eggs. And you think you have nothing more on your hands than the beating of eggs? Guess again. You symbolize the shell of those eggs. [*The Actors resume their laughing, and start making ironical comments among themselves.*] Silence! And pay attention while I explain. [*Again addressing himself to the* LEADING ACTOR] Yes, the shell: that is to say, the empty *form* of reason without the *content* of instinct, which is blind. You are reason, and your wife is instinct in the game of role playing. You play the part assigned you, and you're your own puppet—of your own free will. Understand?

LEADING ACTOR [*extending his arms, palms upward*] Me? No.

DIRECTOR [*returning to his place*] Nor do I. Let's go on. Wait and see what I do with the ending. [*In a confidential tone*] I suggest you face three-quarters front. Otherwise, what with the abstruseness of the dialogue, and an audience that can't hear you, good-bye play! [*Again clapping*] Now, again, order! Let's go.

PROMPTER Excuse me, sir, may I put the top back on the prompter's box? There's rather a draft.

DIRECTOR Yes, yes, do that.

[*The* STAGE DOOR MAN *has entered the auditorium in the meanwhile, his braided cap on his head. Proceeding down the aisle, he goes up onstage to announce to the* DIRECTOR *the arrival of the Six Characters, who have also entered the auditorium, and have started following him at a certain distance, a little lost and perplexed, looking around them.*

Whoever is going to try and translate this play into scenic terms must take all possible measures not *to let these Six Characters get confused with the Actors of the Company. Placing both groups correctly, in accordance with the stage directions, once the Six are onstage, will certainly help, as will lighting the two groups in contrasting colors. But the most suitable and effective means to be suggested here is the use of special masks for the Characters: masks specially made of material which doesn't go limp when sweaty and yet masks which are not too heavy for the Actors wearing them, cut out and worked over so they leave eyes, nostrils, and mouth free. This will also bring out the inner significance of the play. The Characters in fact should not be presented as ghosts but as created realities, unchanging constructs of the imagination, and therefore more solidly real than the Actors with their fluid naturalness. The masks will help to give the impression of figures constructed by art, each one unchangeably fixed in the expression of its own fundamental sentiment, thus:*

remorse *in the case of the* FATHER; revenge *in the case of the* STEPDAUGHTER; disdain *in the case of the* SON; grief *in the case of the* MOTHER, *who should have wax tears fixed in the rings under her eyes and on her cheeks, as with the sculpted and painted images of the* mater dolorosa[7] *in church. Their clothes should be of special material and design, without extravagance, with rigid, full folds like a statue, in short not suggesting a material you might buy at any store in town, cut out and tailored at any dressmaker's.*

The FATHER *is a man of about fifty, hair thin at the temples, but not bald, thick mustache coiled round a still youthful mouth that is often open in an uncertain, pointless smile. Pale, most notably on his broad forehead: blue eyes, oval, very clear and piercing; dark jacket and light trousers: at times gentle and smooth, at times he has hard, harsh outbursts.*

The MOTHER *seems scared and crushed by an intolerable weight of shame and self-abasement. Wearing a thick black crepe widow's veil, she is modestly dressed in black, and when she lifts the veil, the face does not show signs of suffering, and yet seems made of wax. Her eyes are always on the ground.*

The STEPDAUGHTER, *eighteen, is impudent, almost insolent. Very beautiful, and also in mourning, but mourning of a showy elegance. She shows contempt for the timid, afflicted, almost humiliated manner of her little brother, rather a mess of a* BOY, *fourteen, also dressed in black, but a lively tenderness for her little sister, a* LITTLE GIRL *of around four, dressed in white with a black silk sash round her waist.*

7. Grieving mother (Latin); specifically, Mary, mother of Jesus, grieving over the body of her dead son.

The SON, *twenty-two, tall, almost rigid with contained disdain for the* FATHER *and supercilious indifference toward the* MOTHER, *wears a mauve topcoat and a long green scarf wound round his neck.*]

STAGE DOOR MAN [*beret in hand*] Excuse me, your honor.

DIRECTOR [*rudely jumping on him*] What is it now?

STAGE DOOR MAN [*timidly*] There are some people here asking for you.

[*The* DIRECTOR *and the Actors turn in astonishment to look down into the auditorium.*]

DIRECTOR [*furious again*] But I'm rehearsing here! And you know perfectly well no one can come in during rehearsal! [*Turning again toward the house*] Who are these people? What do they want?

THE FATHER [*stepping forward, followed by the others, to one of the two little stairways to the stage*] We're here in search of an author.

DIRECTOR [*half angry, half astounded*] An author? What author?

FATHER Any author, sir.

DIRECTOR There's no author here at all. It's not a new play we're rehearsing.

STEPDAUGHTER [*very vivaciously as she rushes up the stairs*] Then so much the better, sir! *We* can be your new play!

ONE OF THE ACTORS [*among the racy comments and laughs of the others*] Did you hear that?

FATHER [*following the* STEPDAUGHTER *onstage*] Certainly, but if the author's not here . . . [*To the* DIRECTOR] Unless *you'd* like to be the author?

[*The* MOTHER, *holding the* LITTLE GIRL *by the hand, and the* BOY *climb the first steps of the stairway and remain there waiting. The* SON *stays morosely below.*]

DIRECTOR Is this your idea of a joke?

FATHER Heavens, no! Oh, sir, on the contrary: we bring you a painful drama.

STEPDAUGHTER We can make your fortune for you.

DIRECTOR Do me a favor, and leave. We have no time to waste on madmen.

FATHER [*wounded, smoothly*] Oh, sir, you surely know that life is full of infinite absurdities which, brazenly enough, do not need to appear probable, because they're true.

DIRECTOR What in God's name are you saying?

FATHER I'm saying it can actually be considered madness, sir, to force oneself to do the opposite: that is, to give probability to things so they will seem true. But permit me to observe that, if this is madness, it is also the *raison d'être* of your profession.

[*The Actors become agitated and indignant.*]

DIRECTOR [*rising and looking him over*] It is, is it? It seems to you an affair for madmen, our profession?

FATHER Well, to make something seem true which is not true . . . without any need, sir: just for fun . . . Isn't it your job to give life onstage to creatures of fantasy?

DIRECTOR [*immediately, making himself spokesman for the growing indignation of his Actors*] Let me tell you something, my good sir. The actor's profession is a very noble one. If, as things go nowadays, our new playwrights give us nothing but stupid plays, with puppets in them instead of men, it is our boast, I'd have you know, to have given life—on these very boards—to immortal works of art.

[*Satisfied, the Actors approve and applaud their* DIRECTOR.]

FATHER [*interrupting and bearing down hard*] Exactly! That's just it. You have created living beings—*more* alive than those that breathe and wear clothes! Less real, perhaps; but more true! We agree completely!

[*The Actors look at each other, astounded.*]

DIRECTOR What? You were saying just now . . .

FATHER No, no, don't misunderstand me. You shouted that you hadn't time to waste on madmen. So I wanted to tell you that no one knows better than you that Nature employs the human imagination to carry her work of creation on to a higher plane!

DIRECTOR All right, all right. But what are you getting at, exactly?

FATHER Nothing, sir. I only wanted to show that one may be born to this life in many modes, in many forms: as tree, as rock, water or butterfly . . . or woman. And that . . . characters are born too.

DIRECTOR [*his amazement ironically feigned*] And you—with these companions of yours—were born a character?

FATHER Right, sir. And alive, as you see.

[*The* DIRECTOR *and the Actors burst out laughing as at a joke.*]

FATHER [*wounded*] I'm sorry to hear you laugh, because, I repeat, we carry a painful drama within us, as you all might deduce from the sight of that lady there, veiled in black.

[*As he says this, he gives his hand to the* MOTHER *to help her up the last steps and, still holding her by the hand, he leads her with a certain tragic solemnity to the other side of the stage, which is suddenly bathed in fantastic light. The* LITTLE GIRL *and the* BOY *follow the* MOTHER; *then the* SON, *who stands on one side at the back; then the* STEPDAUGHTER *who also detaches herself from the others—downstage and leaning against the proscenium arch. At first astonished at this development, then overcome with admiration, the Actors now burst into applause as at a show performed for their benefit.*]

DIRECTOR [*bowled over at first, then indignant*] Oh, stop this! Silence please! [*Then, turning to the Characters*] And you, leave! Get out of here! [*To the* STAGE MANAGER] For God's sake, get them out!

STAGE MANAGER [*stepping forward but then stopping, as if held back by a strange dismay*] Go! Go!

FATHER [*to the* DIRECTOR] No, look, we, um—

DIRECTOR [*shouting*] I tell you we've got to work!

LEADING MAN It's not right to fool around like this . . .

FATHER [*resolute, stepping forward*] I'm amazed at your incredulity! You're accustomed to seeing the created characters of an author spring to life, aren't you, right here on this stage, the one confronting the other? Perhaps the trouble is there's no script *there* [*Pointing to the* PROMPTER'*s box*] with us in it?

STEPDAUGHTER [*going right up to the* DIRECTOR, *smiling, coquettish*] Believe me, we really are six characters, sir. Very interesting ones at that. But lost. Adrift.

FATHER [*brushing her aside*] Very well: lost, adrift. [*Going right on*] In the sense, that is, that the author who created us, made us live, did not wish, or simply and materially was not able, to place us in the world of art. And that was a real crime, sir, because whoever has the luck to be born a living character can also laugh at death. He will never die! The man will die, the writer, the instrument of creation; the creature will never die! And to have eternal life it doesn't even take extraordinary gifts, nor the performance of miracles. Who was Sancho Panza? Who was Don Abbondio?[8] But they live forever because, as live germs, they have the luck to find a fertile matrix, an imagination which knew how to raise and nourish them, make them live through all eternity!

DIRECTOR That's all well and good. But what do you people want here?

FATHER We want to live, sir.

DIRECTOR [*ironically*] Through all eternity?

FATHER No, sir. But for a moment at least. In you.

AN ACTOR Well, well, well!

LEADING LADY They want to live in us.

JUVENILE LEAD [*pointing to the* STEPDAUGHTER] Well, I've no objection, so long as I get that one.

FATHER Now look, look. The play is still in the making. [*To the* DIRECTOR] But if you wish, and your actors wish, we can make it right away. Acting in concert.

LEADING MAN [*annoyed*] Concert? We don't put on concerts! We do plays, dramas, comedies!

FATHER Very good. That's why we came.

DIRECTOR Well, where's the script?

FATHER Inside us, sir. [*The Actors laugh.*] The drama is inside us. It *is* us. And we're impatient to perform it. According to the dictates of the passion within us.

STEPDAUGHTER [*scornful, with treacherous grace, deliberate impudence*] My passion—if you only knew, sir! My passion—for him! [*She points to the* FATHER *and makes as if to embrace him but then breaks into a strident laugh.*]

FATHER [*an angry interjection*] You keep out of this now. And please don't laugh that way!

STEPDAUGHTER No? Then, ladies and gentlemen, permit me. A two months' orphan, I shall dance and sing for you all. Watch how! [*She mischievously starts to sing "Beware of Chu Chin Chow" by Dave Stamper, reduced to fox-trot or slow one-step by Francis Salabert:*[9] *the first verse, accompanied by a step or two of dancing. While she sings and dances, the Actors, especially the young ones, as if drawn by some strange fascination, move toward her and half raise their hands as if to take hold of her. She runs away and when the Actors burst into applause she just stands there, remote, abstracted, while the* DIRECTOR *protests.*]

ACTORS and ACTRESSES [*laughing and clapping*] Brava![1] Fine! Splendid!

DIRECTOR [*annoyed*] Silence! What do you think this is, a night spot? [*Taking the* FATHER *a step or two to one side, with a certain amount of consternation*] Tell me something. Is she crazy?

8. A rural priest in Alessandro Manzoni's novel *I Promessi sposi* (*The Betrothed,* 1825–27). *Sancho Panza:* the servant and companion of the title character in Miguel de Cervantes' novel *Don Quixote* (1605, 1615).

9. A French music publisher (1884–1946); his company released numerous recordings of dance music in the 1920s and 1930s. "Beware of Chu Chin Chow" (1917), with music by Dave Stamper (1883–1963) and words by Gene Buck and Charles Wilmott, was a popular novelty song.

1. An Italian exclamation of approval, used when applauding a woman (as *bravo* is used of a man).

FATHER Crazy? Of course not. It's much worse than that.

STEPDAUGHTER [*running over at once to the* DIRECTOR] Worse! Worse! Not crazy but worse! Just listen: I'll play it for you right now, this drama, and at a certain point you'll see me—when this dear little thing—[*She takes the* LITTLE GIRL *who is beside the* MOTHER *by the hand and leads her to the* DIRECTOR.]—isn't she darling? [*Takes her in her arms and kisses her.*] Sweetie! Sweetie! [*Puts her down again and adds with almost involuntary emotion.*] Well, when God suddenly takes this little sweetheart away from her poor mother, and that idiot there—[*Thrusting the* BOY *forward, rudely seizing him by a sleeve*] does the stupidest of things, like the nitwit that he is, [*With a shove she drives him back toward the* MOTHER] then you will see me take to my heels. Yes, ladies and gentlemen, take to my heels! I can hardly wait for that moment. For after what happened between him and me—[*She points to the* FATHER *with a horrible wink.*] something very intimate, you understand—I can't stay in such company any longer, witnessing the anguish of our mother on account of that fool there—[*She points to the* SON.] Just look at him, look at him!—how indifferent, how frozen, because he is the legitimate son, that's what he is, full of contempt for me, for him [*the* BOY], and for that little creature [*the* LITTLE GIRL], because we three are bastards, d'you see? Bastards. [*Goes to the* MOTHER *and embraces her.*] And this poor mother, the common mother of us all, he—well, he doesn't want to acknowledge her as *his* mother too, and he looks down on her, that's what he does, looks on her as only the mother of us three bastards, the wretch! [*She says this rapidly in a state of extreme excitement. Her voice swells to the word: "bastards!" and descends again to the final "wretch," almost spitting it out.*]

MOTHER [*to the* DIRECTOR, *with infinite anguish*] In the name of these two small children, sir, I implore you . . . [*She grows faint and sways.*] Oh, heavens . . .

FATHER [*rushing over to support her with almost all the Actors, who are astonished and scared*] Please! Please, a chair, a chair for this poor widow!

ACTORS [*rushing over*] —Is it true then?—She's *really* fainting?

DIRECTOR A chair!

[*One of the Actors proffers a chair. The others stand around, ready to help. The* MOTHER, *seated, tries to stop the* FATHER *from lifting the veil that hides her face.*]

FATHER [*to the* DIRECTOR] Look at her, look at her . . .

MOTHER Heavens, no, stop it!

FATHER Let them see you. [*He lifts her veil.*]

MOTHER [*rising and covering her face with her hands, desperate*] Oh, sir, please stop this man from carrying out his plan. It's horrible for me!

DIRECTOR [*surprised, stunned*] I don't know where we're at! What's this all about? [*To the* FATHER] Is this your wife?

FATHER [*at once*] Yes, sir, my wife.

DIRECTOR Then how is she a widow, if you're alive?

[*The Actors relieve their astonishment in a loud burst of laughter.*]

FATHER [*wounded, with bitter resentment*] Don't laugh! Don't laugh like that! Please! Just that is her drama, sir. She had another man. Another man who should be here!

MOTHER [*with a shout*] No! No!

STEPDAUGHTER He had the good luck to die. Two months ago, as I told you. We're still in mourning as you see.

FATHER But he's absent, you see, not just because he's dead. He's absent—take a look at her, sir, and you will understand at once!—Her drama wasn't in the love of two men for whom she was incapable of feeling anything—except maybe a little gratitude [not to me, but to him]—She is not a woman, she is a mother!—And her drama—a powerful one, very powerful—is in fact all in those four children which she bore to her two men.

MOTHER *My* men? Have you the gall to say I wanted two men? It was him, sir. He forced the other man on me. Compelled—yes, compelled—me to go off with him!

STEPDAUGHTER [*cutting in, roused*] It's not true!

MOTHER [*astounded*] How d'you mean, not true?

STEPDAUGHTER It's not true! It's not true!

MOTHER And what can you know about it?

STEPDAUGHTER It's not true. [*To the* DIRECTOR] Don't believe it. Know why she says it? For his sake. [*Pointing to the* SON] His indifference tortures her, destroys her. She wants him to believe that, if she abandoned him when he was two, it was because he [*the* FATHER] compelled her to.

MOTHER [*with violence*] He did compel me, he did compel me, as God is my witness! [*To the* DIRECTOR] Ask him if that isn't true. [*Her husband*] Make him tell him. [*The* SON] She couldn't know anything about it.

STEPDAUGHTER With my father, while he lived, I know you were always happy and content. Deny it if you can.

MOTHER I don't deny it, I don't . . .

STEPDAUGHTER He loved you, he cared for you! [*To the* BOY, *with rage*] Isn't that so? Say it! Why don't you speak, you dope?

MOTHER Leave the poor boy alone. Why d'you want to make me out ungrateful, daughter? I have no wish to offend your father! I told him [*the* FATHER] I didn't abandon my son and my home for my own pleasure. It wasn't my fault.

FATHER That's true, sir. It was mine.

[*Pause.*]

LEADING MAN [*to his companions*] What a show!

LEADING LADY And *they* put it on—for us.

JUVENILE LEAD Quite a change!

DIRECTOR [*who is now beginning to get very interested*] Let's listen to this, let's listen! [*And saying this, he goes down one of the stairways into the auditorium, and stands in front of the stage, as if to receive a spectator's impression of the show.*]

SON [*without moving from his position, cold, quiet, ironic*] Oh yes, you can now listen to the philosophy lecture. He will tell you about the Demon of Experiment.

FATHER You are a cynical idiot, as I've told you a hundred times. [*To the* DIRECTOR, *now in the auditorium*] He mocks me, sir, on account of that phrase I found to excuse myself with.

SON [*contemptuously*] Phrases!

FATHER Phrases! Phrases! As if they were not a comfort to everyone: in the face of some unexplained fact, in the face of an evil that eats into us, to find a word that says nothing but at least quiets us down!

STEPDAUGHTER Quiets our guilt feelings too. That above all.

FATHER Our guilt feelings? Not so. I have never quieted my guilt feelings with words alone.

STEPDAUGHTER It took a little money as well, didn't it, it took a little dough! The hundred lire[2] he was going to pay me, ladies and gentlemen!

[*Movement of horror among the Actors.*]

SON [*with contempt toward the* STEPDAUGHTER] That's filthy.

STEPDAUGHTER Filthy? The dough was there. In a small pale blue envelope on the mahogany table in the room behind the shop. Madam Pace's [*she pronounces it "Pah-chay"*] shop. One of those Madams who lure us poor girls from good families into their *ateliers* under the pretext of selling *Robes et Manteaux*.[3]

SON And with those hundred lire he was going to pay she has bought the right to tyrannize over us all. Only it so happens—I'd have you know—that he never actually incurred the debt.

STEPDAUGHTER Oh, oh, but we were really going to it, I assure you! [*She bursts out laughing.*]

MOTHER [*rising in protest*] Shame, daughter! Shame!

STEPDAUGHTER [*quickly*] Shame? It's my revenge! I am frantic, sir, frantic to live it, live that scene! The room . . . here's the shop window with the coats in it; there's the bed-sofa; the mirror; a screen; and in front of the window the little mahogany table with the hundred lire in the pale blue envelope. I can see it. I could take it. But you men should turn away now: I'm almost naked. I don't blush anymore. It's he that blushes now. [*Points to the* FATHER.] But I assure you he was very pale, very pale, at that moment. [*To the* DIRECTOR] You must believe me, sir.

DIRECTOR You lost me some time ago.

FATHER Of course! Getting it thrown at you like that! Restore a little order, sir, and let *me* speak. And never mind this ferocious girl. She's trying to heap opprobrium on me by withholding the relevant explanations!

STEPDAUGHTER This is no place for long-winded narratives!

FATHER I said—explanations.

STEPDAUGHTER Oh, certainly. Those that suit your turn.

[*At this point, the* DIRECTOR *returns to the stage to restore order.*]

FATHER But that's the whole root of the evil. Words. Each of us has, inside him, a world of things—to everyone, his world of things. And how can we understand each other, sir, if, in the words I speak, I put the sense and value of things as they are inside me, whereas the man who hears them inevitably receives them in the sense and with the value they have for him, the sense and value of the world inside him? We think we understand each other but we never do. Consider: the compassion, all the compassion I feel for this woman [*the* MOTHER] has been received by her as the most ferocious of cruelties!

MOTHER You ran me out of the house.

FATHER Hear that? Ran her out. It *seemed to her* that I ran her out.

MOTHER You can talk; I can't . . . But, look, sir, after he married me . . . and who knows why he did? I was poor, of humble birth . . .

2. Equivalent to about $50 today.

3. Dressing gowns and coats (French). *Ateliers:* workshops (French).

FATHER And that's why I married you for your . . . humility. I loved you for it, believing . . . [*He breaks off, seeing her gestured denials; seeing the impossibility of making himself understood by her, he opens his arms wide in a gesture of despair, and turns to the* DIRECTOR.] See that? She says No. It's scarifying, isn't it, sir, scarifying, this deafness of hers, this mental deafness! She has a heart, oh yes, where her children are concerned! But she's deaf, deaf in the brain, deaf, sir, to the point of desperation!

STEPDAUGHTER [*to the* DIRECTOR] All right, but now make him tell you what his intelligence has ever done for us.

FATHER If we could only foresee all the evil that can result from the good we believe we're doing!

[*At this point, the* LEADING LADY, *who has been on hot coals seeing the* LEADING MAN *flirt with the* STEPDAUGHTER, *steps forward and asks of the* DIRECTOR:]

LEADING LADY Excuse me, is the rehearsal continuing?

DIRECTOR Yes, of course! But let me listen a moment.

JUVENILE LEAD This is something quite new.

INGENUE Very interesting!

LEADING LADY If that sort of thing interests you. [*And she darts a look at the* LEADING MAN.]

DIRECTOR [*to the* FATHER] But you must give us *clear* explanations. [*He goes and sits down.*]

FATHER Right. Yes. Listen. There was a man working for me. A poor man. As my secretary. Very devoted to me. Understood *her* [*the* MOTHER] very well. There was mutual understanding between them. Nothing wrong in it. They thought no harm at all. Nothing off-color about it. No, no, he knew his place, as she did. They didn't do anything wrong. Didn't even think it.

STEPDAUGHTER So he thought it *for* them. And did it.

FATHER It's not true! I wanted to do them some good. And myself too, oh yes, I admit. I'd got to this point, sir: I couldn't say a word to either of them but they would exchange a significant look. The one would consult the eyes of the other, asking how what I had said should be taken, if they didn't want to put me in a rage. That sufficed, you will understand, to keep me continually in a rage, in a state of unbearable exasperation.

DIRECTOR Excuse me, why didn't you fire him, this secretary?

FATHER Good question! That's what I did do, sir. But then I had to see that poor woman remain in my house, a lost soul. Like an animal without a master that one takes pity on and carries home.

MOTHER No, no, it's—

FATHER [*at once, turning to her to get it in first*] Your son? Right?

MOTHER He'd already snatched my son from me.

FATHER But not from cruelty. Just so he'd grow up strong and healthy. In touch with the soil.

STEPDAUGHTER [*pointing at the latter, ironic*] And just look at him!

FATHER [*at once*] Uh? Is it also my fault if he then grew up this way? I sent him to a wet nurse, sir, in the country, a peasant woman. I didn't find her [*the* MOTHER] strong enough, despite her humble origin. I'd married her for similar reasons, as I said. All nonsense maybe, but there we are. I always had these confounded aspirations toward a certain solidity, toward what is morally sound. [*Here the* STEPDAUGHTER *bursts out laughing.*] Make her stop that! It's unbearable!

DIRECTOR Stop it. I can't hear, for Heaven's sake!

[*Suddenly, again, as the* DIRECTOR *rebukes her, she is withdrawn and remote, her laughter cut off in the middle. The* DIRECTOR *goes down again from the stage to get an impression of the scene.*]

FATHER I couldn't bear to be with that woman anymore. [*Points to the* MOTHER] Not so much, believe me, because she irritated me, and even made me feel physically ill, as because of the pain—a veritable anguish—that I felt on her account.

MOTHER And he sent me away!

FATHER. Well provided for. And to that man. Yes, sir. So she could be free of me.

MOTHER And so *he* could be free.

FATHER That, too. I admit it. And much evil resulted. But I intended good. And more for her than for me, I swear it! [*He folds his arms across his chest. Then, suddenly, turning to the* MOTHER] I never lost sight of you, never lost sight of you till, from one day to the next, unbeknown to me, he carried you off to another town. He noticed I was interested in her, you see, but that was silly, because my interest was absolutely pure, absolutely without ulterior motive. The interest I took in her new family, as it grew up, had an unbelievable tenderness to it. Even she should bear witness to that! [*He points to the* STEPDAUGHTER.]

STEPDAUGHTER Oh, very much so! I was a little sweetie. Pigtails over my shoulders. Panties coming down a little bit below my skirt. A little sweetie. He would see me coming out of school, at the gate. He would come and see me as I grew up . . .

FATHER This is outrageous. You're betraying me!

STEPDAUGHTER I'm not! What do you mean?

FATHER Outrageous. Outrageous. [*Immediately, still excited, he continues in a tone of explanation, to the* DIRECTOR.] My house, sir, when she had left it, at once seemed empty. [*Points to the* MOTHER.] She was an incubus. But she filled my house for me. Left alone, I wandered through these rooms like a fly without a head. This fellow here [*the* SON] was raised away from home. Somehow, when he got back, he didn't seem mine anymore. Without a mother between me and him, he grew up on his own, apart, without any relationship to me, emotional or intellectual. And then—strange, sir, but true—first I grew curious, then I was gradually attracted toward *her* family, which I had brought into being. The thought of *this* family began to fill the void around me. I had to—really had to—believe she was at peace, absorbed in the simplest cares of life, lucky to be away and far removed from the complicated torments of my spirit. And to have proof of this, I would go and see that little girl at the school gate.

STEPDAUGHTER Correct! He followed me home, smiled at me and, when I was home, waved to me, like this! I would open my eyes wide and look at him suspiciously. I didn't know who it was. I told mother. And she guessed right away it was him. [*The* MOTHER *nods.*] At first she didn't want to send me back to school for several days. When I did go, I saw him again at the gate—the clown!—with a brown paper bag in his hand. He came up to me, caressed me, and took from the bag a lovely big Florentine straw hat with a ring of little May roses round it—for me!

DIRECTOR You're making too long a story of this.

SON [*contemptuously*] Story is right! Fiction! Literature!

FATHER Literature? This is life, sir. Passion!

DIRECTOR Maybe! But not actable!

FATHER I agree. This is all preliminary. I wouldn't *want* you to act it. As you see, in fact, she [*the* STEPDAUGHTER] is no longer that little girl with pigtails—

STEPDAUGHTER —and the panties showing below her skirt!

FATHER The drama comes now, sir. Novel, complex—

STEPDAUGHTER [*gloomy, fierce, steps forward*] —What my father's death meant for us was—

FATHER [*not giving her time to continue*] —poverty, sir. They returned, unbeknownst to me. She's so thickheaded. [*Pointing to the* MOTHER] It's true she can hardly write herself, but she could have had her daughter write, or her son, telling me they were in need!

MOTHER But, sir, how could I have guessed he felt the way he did?

FATHER Which is just where you always went wrong. You could never guess how I felt about anything!

MOTHER After so many years of separation, with all that had happened . . . .

FATHER And is it my fault if that fellow carried you off as he did? [*Turning to the* DIRECTOR] From one day to the next, as I say. He'd found some job someplace. I couldn't even trace them. Necessarily, then, my interest dwindled, with the years. The drama breaks out, sir, unforeseen and violent, at their return. When I, alas, was impelled by the misery of my still-living flesh . . . Oh, and what misery that is for a man who is alone, who has not wanted to form debasing relationships, not yet old enough to do without a woman, and no longer young enough to go and look for one without shame! Misery? It's horror, horror, because no woman can give him love anymore.—Knowing this, one should go without! Well, sir, on the outside, when other people are watching, each man is clothed in dignity: but, on the inside, he knows what unconfessable things are going on within him. One gives way, gives way to temptation, to rise again, right afterward, of course, in a great hurry to put our dignity together again, complete, solid, a stone on a grave that hides and buries from our eyes every sign of our shame and even the very memory of it! It's like that with everybody. Only the courage to say it is lacking—to say certain things.

STEPDAUGHTER The courage to do them, though—everybody's got that.

FATHER Everybody. But in secret. That's why it takes more courage to say them. A man only has to say them and it's all over: he's labeled a cynic. But, sir, he isn't! He's just like everybody else. Better! He's better because he's not afraid to reveal, by the light of intelligence, the red stain of shame, there, in the human beast, which closes its eyes to it. Woman—yes, woman—what is she like, actually? She looks at us, inviting, tantalizing. You take hold of her. She's no sooner in your arms than she shuts her eyes. It is the sign of her submission. The sign with which she tells the man: Blind yourself for I am blind.

STEPDAUGHTER How about when she no longer keeps them shut? When she no longer feels the need to hide the red stain of shame from herself by closing her eyes, and instead, her eyes now dry and impassive, sees the shame of the man, who has blinded himself even without love? They make me vomit, all those intellectual elaborations, this philosophy that begins by revealing the beast and then goes on to excuse it and save its soul . . . I can't bear to hear about it! Because when a man feels obliged to *reduce* life this way, reduce it all to "the beast," throwing overboard every vestige of the truly human, every aspiration after chastity, all feelings of purity, of the ideal, of duties, of modesty, of shame, then nothing is more contemptible, more nauseating than his wretched guilt feelings! Crocodile tears!

DIRECTOR Let's get to the facts, to the facts! This is just discussion.

FATHER Very well. But a fact is like a sack. When it's empty, it won't stand up. To make it stand up you must first pour into it the reasons and feelings by which it exists. I couldn't know that—when that man died and they returned here in poverty—she went out to work as a dressmaker to support the children, nor that the person she went to work for was that . . . that Madam Pace!

STEPDAUGHTER A high-class dressmaker, if you'd all like to know! To all appearances, she serves fine ladies, but then she arranges things so that the fine ladies serve *her* . . . without prejudice to ladies not so fine!

MOTHER Believe me, sir, I never had the slightest suspicion that that old witch hired me because she had her eye on my daughter . . .

STEPDAUGHTER Poor mama! Do you know, sir, what the woman did when I brought her my mother's work? She would point out to me the material she'd ruined by giving it to my mother to sew. And she deducted for that, she deducted. And so, you understand, *I* paid, while that poor creature thought she was making sacrifices for me and those two by sewing, even at night, Madam Pace's material!

[*Indignant movements and exclamations from the Actors.*]

DIRECTOR [*without pause*] And there, one day, you met—

STEPDAUGHTER [*pointing to the* FATHER] —him, him, yes sir! An old client! Now there's a scene for you to put on! Superb!

FATHER Interrupted by her—the mother—

STEPDAUGHTER [*without pause, treacherously*] —almost in time!—

FATHER [*shouting*] No, no, *in* time! Because, luckily, I recognized the girl in time. And I took them all back, sir, into my home. Now try to visualize my situation and hers, the one confronting the other—she as you see her now, myself unable to look her in the face anymore.

STEPDAUGHTER It's too absurd! But—afterward—was it possible for me to be a modest little miss, virtuous and well-bred, in accordance with those confounded aspirations toward a certain solidity, toward what is morally sound?

FATHER And therein lies the drama, sir, as far as I'm concerned: in my awareness that each of us thinks of himself as *one* but that, well, it's not true, each of us is many, oh so many, sir, according to the possibilities of being that are in us. We are one thing for this person, another for that! Already *two* utterly different things! And with it all, the illusion of being always one thing for all men, and always this one thing in every single action. It's not true! Not true! We realize as much when, by some unfortunate chance, in one or another of our acts, we find ourselves suspended, hooked. We see, I mean, that we are not wholly in that act, and that therefore it would be abominably unjust to judge us by that act alone, to hold us suspended, hooked, in the pillory, our whole life long, as if our life were summed up in that act! Now do you understand this girl's treachery? She surprised me in a place, in an act, in which she should never have had to know me—I couldn't be that way for her. And she wants to give me a reality such as I could never had expected I would have to assume for her, the reality of a fleeting moment, a shameful one, in my life! This, sir, this is what I feel most strongly. And you will see that the drama will derive tremendous value from this. But now add the situation of the others! His . . . [*He points to the* SON.]

SON [*shrugging contemptuously*] Leave me out of this! It's none of my business.

FATHER What? None of your business?

SON None. And I *want* to be left out. I wasn't made to be one of you, and you know it.

STEPDAUGHTER We're common, aren't we?—And he's so refined.—But from time to time I give him a hard, contemptuous look, and he looks down at the ground. You may have noticed that, sir. He looks down at the ground. For he knows the wrong he's done me.

SON [*hardly looking at her*] Me?

STEPDAUGHTER You! You! I'm on the streets because of you! [*A movement of horror from the Actors*] Did you or did you not, by your attitude, deny us—I won't say the intimacy of home but even the hospitality which puts guests at their ease? We were the intruders, coming to invade the kingdom of your legitimacy! I'd like to have you see, sir, certain little scenes between just him and me! He says I tyrannized over them all. But it was entirely because of his attitude that I started to exploit the situation he calls filthy, a situation which had brought me into his home with my mother, who is also *his* mother, *as its mistress!*

SON [*coming slowly forward*] They can't lose, sir, three against one, an easy game. But figure to yourself a son, sitting quietly at home, who one fine day sees a young woman arrive, an impudent type with her nose in the air, asking for his father, with whom she has heaven knows what business; and then he sees her return, in the same style, accompanied by that little girl over there; and finally he sees her treat his father—who can say why?—in a very ambiguous and cool manner, demanding money, in a tone that takes for granted that he *has* to give it, has to, is obligated—

FATHER —but I *am* obligated: it's for your mother!

SON How would I know? When, sir, [*To the* DIRECTOR] have I ever seen her? When have I ever heard her spoken of? One day I see her arrive with her [*the* STEPDAUGHTER], with that boy, with that little girl. They say to me: "It's your mother too, know that?" I manage to figure out from her carryings-on [*Pointing at the* STEPDAUGHTER] why they arrived in our home from one day to the next . . . What I'm feeling and experiencing I can't put into words, and wouldn't want to. I wouldn't want to confess it, even to myself. It cannot therefore result in any action on my part. You can see that. Believe me, sir, I'm a character that, dramatically speaking, remains unrealized. I'm out of place in their company. So please leave me out of it all!

FATHER What? But it's just because you're so—

SON [*in violent exasperation*] —I'm so what? How would *you* know? When did you ever care about me?

FATHER *Touché! Touché!* But isn't even that a dramatic situation? This withdrawnness of yours, so cruel to me, and to your mother who, on her return home is seeing you almost for the first time, a grown man she doesn't recognize, though she knows you're her son . . . [*Pointing out the* MOTHER *to the* DIRECTOR] Just look at her, she's crying.

STEPDAUGHTER [*angrily, stamping her foot*] Like the fool she is!

FATHER [*pointing her out to the* DIRECTOR] And she can't abide him, you know. [*Again referring to the* SON]—He says it's none of his business. The truth is he's almost the pivot of the action. Look at that little boy, clinging to his mother all the time, scared, humiliated . . . It's all because of *him* [*the* SON]. Perhaps the most painful situation of all is that little boy's: he feels alien, more than all the others, and the poor little thing is so mortified, so anguished at being taken into our home—out of charity, as it were . . . [*Confidentially*] He's just like his father: humble, doesn't say anything . . .

DIRECTOR He won't fit anyway. You've no idea what a nuisance children are onstage.

FATHER But he wouldn't be a nuisance for long. Nor would the little girl, no, she's the first to go . . .

DIRECTOR Very good, yes! The whole thing interests me very much indeed. I have a hunch, a definite hunch, that there's material here for a fine play!

STEPDAUGHTER [*trying to inject herself*] With a character like me in it!

FATHER [*pushing her to one side in his anxiety to know what the* DIRECTOR *will decide*] You be quiet!

DIRECTOR [*going right on, ignoring the interruption*] Yes, it's new stuff . . .

FATHER Very new!

DIRECTOR You had some gall, though, to come and throw it at me this way . . .

FATHER Well, you see, sir, born as we are to the stage . . .

DIRECTOR You're amateurs, are you?

FATHER No. I say: "born to the stage" because . . .

DIRECTOR Oh, come on, you must have done some acting!

FATHER No, no, sir, only as every man acts the part assigned to him—by himself or others—in this life. In me you see passion itself, which—in almost all people, as it rises—invariably becomes a bit theatrical . . .

DIRECTOR Well, never mind! Never mind about that!—You see, my dear sir, without the author . . . I could direct you to an author . . .

FATHER No, no, look: you be the author!

DIRECTOR Me? What are you talking about?

FATHER Yes, you. You. Why not?

DIRECTOR Because I've never been an author, that's why not!

FATHER Couldn't you be one now, hm? There's nothing to it. Everyone's doing it. And your job is made all the easier by the fact that you have us—here—alive—right in front of your nose!

DIRECTOR It wouldn't be enough.

FATHER Not enough? Seeing us live our own drama . . .

DIRECTOR I know, but you always need someone to write it!

FATHER No. Just someone to take it down, maybe, since you have us here—in action—scene by scene. It'll be enough if we piece together a rough sketch for you, then you can rehearse it.

DIRECTOR [*tempted, goes up onstage again*] Well, I'm almost, almost tempted . . . Just for kicks . . . We could actually rehearse . . .

FATHER Of course you could! What scenes you'll see emerge! I can list them for you right away.

DIRECTOR I'm tempted . . . I'm tempted . . . Let's give it a try . . . Come to my office. [*Turns to the Actors.*] Take a break, will you? But don't go away. We'll be back in fifteen or twenty minutes. [*To the* FATHER] Let's see what we can do . . . Maybe we can get something very extraordinary out of all this . . .

FATHER We certainly can. Wouldn't it be better to take *them* along? [*He points to the Characters.*]

DIRECTOR Yes, let them all come. [*Starts going off, then comes back to address the Actors.*] Now don't forget. Everyone on time. Fifteen minutes.

[DIRECTOR *and Six Characters cross the stage and disappear. The Actors stay there and look at one another in amazement.*]

LEADING MAN Is he serious? What's he going to do?

JUVENILE This is outright insanity.

A THIRD ACTOR We have to improvise a drama right off the bat?

JUVENILE LEAD That's right. Like Commedia dell'Arte.[4]

LEADING LADY Well, if he thinks *I'm* going to lend myself to that sort of thing . . .

INGENUE Count me out.

A FOURTH ACTOR [*alluding to the Characters*] I'd like to know who those people are.

THE THIRD ACTOR Who would they be? Madmen or crooks!

JUVENILE LEAD And he's going to pay attention to them?

INGENUE Carried away by vanity! Wants to be an author now . . .

LEADING MAN It's out of this world. If this is what the theater is coming to, my friends . . .

A FIFTH ACTOR I think it's rather fun.

THE THIRD ACTOR Well! We shall see. We shall see. [*And chatting thus among themselves, the Actors leave the stage, some using the little door at the back, others returning to their dressing rooms.*]

The curtain remains raised. The performance is interrupted by a twenty-minute intermission.

Bells ring. The performance is resumed.

[*From dressing rooms, from the door, and also from the house, the Actors, the* STAGE MANAGER, *the* TECHNICIAN, *the* PROMPTER, *the* PROPERTY MAN *return to the stage; at the same time the* DIRECTOR *and the Six Characters emerge from the office.*

As soon as the house lights are out, the stage lighting is as before.]

DIRECTOR Let's go, everybody! Is everyone here? Quiet! We're beginning. [*Calls the* TECHNICIAN *by name.*]

4. A traditional form of Italian comedy featuring stock characters, some in masks, who improvise dialogue.

TECHNICIAN Here!

DIRECTOR Set the stage for the parlor scene. Two wings and a backdrop with a door in it will do, quickly please!

[*The* TECHNICIAN *at once runs to do the job, and does it while the* DIRECTOR *works things out with the* STAGE MANAGER, *the* PROPERTY MAN, *the* PROMPTER, *and the Actors. This indication of a set consists of two wings, a drop with a door in it, all in pink and gold stripes.*]

DIRECTOR [*to the* PROPERTY MAN] See if we have some sort of bed-sofa in the prop room.

PROPERTY MAN Yes, sir, there's the green one.

STEPDAUGHTER No, no, not green! It was yellow, flowered, plush, and very big. Extremely comfortable.

PROPERTY MAN Well, we have nothing like that.

DIRECTOR But it doesn't matter. Bring the one you have.

STEPDAUGHTER Doesn't matter? Madam Pace's famous chaise longue!

DIRECTOR This is just for rehearsal. Please don't meddle! [*To the* STAGE MANAGER] See if we have a display case—long and rather narrow.

STEPDAUGHTER The table, the little mahogany table for the pale blue envelope!

STAGE MANAGER [*to the* DIRECTOR] There's the small one. Gilded.

DIRECTOR All right. Get that one.

FATHER A large mirror.

STEPDAUGHTER And the screen. A screen, please, or what'll I do?

STAGE MANAGER Yes, ma'am, we have lots of screens, don't worry.

DIRECTOR [*to the* STEPDAUGHTER] A few coat hangers?

STEPDAUGHTER A great many, yes.

DIRECTOR [*to the* STAGE MANAGER] See how many we've got, and have them brought on.

STAGE MANAGER Right, sir, I'll see to it.

[*The* STAGE MANAGER *also hurries to do his job and while the* DIRECTOR *goes on talking with the* PROMPTER *and then with the Characters and the Actors, has the furniture carried on by stagehands and arranges it as he thinks fit.*]

DIRECTOR [*to the* PROMPTER] Meanwhile you can get into position. Look: this is the outline of the scenes, act by act. [*He gives him several sheets of paper.*] You'll have to be a bit of a virtuoso today.

PROMPTER Shorthand?

DIRECTOR [*pleasantly surprised*] Oh, good! You know shorthand?

PROMPTER I may not know prompting, but shorthand . . . [*Turning to a stagehand*] Get me some paper from my room—quite a lot—all you can find!

[*The stagehand runs off and returns a little later with a wad of paper which he gives to the* PROMPTER.]

DIRECTOR [*going right on, to the* PROMPTER] Follow the scenes line by line as we play them, and try to pin down the speeches, at least the most important ones. [*Then, turning to the Actors*] Clear the stage please, everyone! Yes, come over to this side and pay close attention. [*He indicates the left.*]

LEADING LADY Excuse me but—

DIRECTOR [*forestalling*] There'll be no improvising, don't fret.

LEADING MAN Then what are we to do?

DIRECTOR Nothing. For now, just stop, look, and listen. Afterward you'll be given written parts. Right now we'll rehearse. As best we can. With them doing the rehearsing for us. [*He points to the Characters.*]

FATHER [*amid all the confusion onstage, as if he'd fallen from the clouds*] *We're* rehearsing? How d'you mean?

DIRECTOR Yes, for them. You rehearse for them. [*Indicates the Actors.*]

FATHER But if we are the characters . . .

DIRECTOR All right, you're characters, but, my dear sir, characters don't perform here, actors perform here. The characters are there, in the script [*He points to the* PROMPTER*'s box.*]—when there *is* a script!

FATHER Exactly! Since there isn't, and you gentlemen have the luck to have them right here, alive in front of you, those characters . . .

DIRECTOR Oh, great! Want to do it all yourselves? Appear before the public, do the acting yourselves?

FATHER Of course. Just as we are.

DIRECTOR [*ironically*] I'll bet you'd put on a splendid show!

LEADING MAN Then what's the use of staying?

DIRECTOR [*without irony, to the Characters*] Don't run away with the idea that you can act! That's laughable . . . [*And in fact the Actors laugh.*] Hear that? They're laughing. [*Coming back to the point*] I was forgetting. I must cast the show. It's quite easy. It casts itself. [*To the* SECOND ACTRESS] You, ma'am, will play the Mother. [*To the* FATHER] You'll have to find her a name.

FATHER Amalia, sir.

DIRECTOR But that's this lady's real name. We wouldn't want to call her by her real name!

FATHER Why not? If that is her name . . . But of course, if it's to be this lady . . . [*He indicates the* SECOND ACTRESS *with a vague gesture.*] To me *she* [*the* MOTHER] is Amalia. But suit yourself . . . [*He is getting more and more confused.*] I don't know what to tell you . . . I'm beginning to . . . oh, I don't know . . . to find my own words ringing false, they sound different somehow.

DIRECTOR Don't bother about that, just don't bother about it. We can always find the right sound. As for the name, if you say Amalia, Amalia it shall be; or we'll find another. For now, we'll designate the characters thus: [*To the* JUVENILE LEAD] You're the Son. [*To the* LEADING LADY] You, ma'am, are of course the Stepdaughter.

STEPDAUGHTER [*excitedly*] What, what? That one there is me? [*She bursts out laughing.*]

DIRECTOR [*mad*] What is there to laugh at?

LEADING LADY [*aroused*] No one has ever dared laugh at me! I insist on respect—or I quit!

STEPDAUGHTER But, excuse me, I'm not laughing at you.

DIRECTOR [*to the* STEPDAUGHTER] You should consider yourself honored to be played by . . .

LEADING LADY [*without pause, contemptuously*] —"That one there!"

STEPDAUGHTER But I wasn't speaking of you, believe me. I was speaking of me. I don't see me in you, that's all. I don't know why . . . I guess you're just not like me!

FATHER That's it, exactly, my dear sir! What is *expressed* in us . . .

DIRECTOR Expression, expression! You think that's your business? Not at all!

FATHER Well, but what *we* express . . .

DIRECTOR But you don't. You don't express. You provide us with raw material. The actors give it body and face, voice and gesture. They've given expression to much loftier material, let me tell you. Yours is on such a small scale that, if it stands up onstage at all, the credit, believe me, should all go to my actors.

FATHER I don't dare contradict you, sir, but it's terribly painful for us who are as you see us—with these bodies, these faces—

DIRECTOR [*cutting in, out of patience*] —that's where makeup comes in, my dear sir, for whatever concerns the face, the remedy is makeup!

FATHER Yes. But the voice, gesture—

DIRECTOR Oh, for Heaven's sake! You can't exist here! Here the actor acts you, and that's that!

FATHER I understand, sir. But now perhaps I begin to guess also why our author who saw us, alive as we are, did not want to put us onstage. I don't want to offend your actors. God forbid! But I feel that seeing myself acted . . . I don't know by whom . . .

LEADING MAN [*rising with dignity and coming over, followed by the gay young Actresses who laugh*] By me, if you've no objection.

FATHER [*humble, smooth*] I'm very honored, sir. [*He bows.*] But however much art and willpower the gentleman puts into absorbing me into himself . . . [*He is bewildered now.*]

LEADING MAN Finish. Finish.

[*The Actresses laugh.*]

FATHER Well, the performance he will give, even forcing himself with makeup to resemble me, well, with that figure [*All the Actors laugh.*] he can hardly play me as I am. I shall rather be—even apart from the face—what he interprets me to be, as he feels I am—if he feels I am anything—and not as I feel myself inside myself. And it seems to me that whoever is called upon to judge us should take this into account.

DIRECTOR So now you're thinking of what the critics will say? And I was still listening! Let the critics say what they want. We will concentrate on putting on your play! [*He walks away a little, and looks around.*] Come on, come on. Is the set ready? [*To the Actors and the Characters*] Don't clutter up the stage, I want to be able to see! [*He goes down from the stage.*] Let's not lose any more time! [*To the* STEPDAUGHTER] Does the set seem pretty good to you?

STEPDAUGHTER Oh! But I can't recognize it!

DIRECTOR Oh my God, don't tell me we should reconstruct Madam Pace's back room for you! [*To the* FATHER] Didn't you say a parlor with flowered wallpaper?

FATHER Yes, sir. White.

DIRECTOR It's not white. Stripes. But it doesn't matter. As for furniture we're in pretty good shape. That little table—bring it forward a bit! [*Stagehands do this. To the* PROPERTY MAN] Meanwhile you get an envelope, possibly a light blue one, and give it to the gentleman. [*Indicating the* FATHER]

PROPERTY MAN A letter envelope?

DIRECTOR and FATHER Yes, a letter envelope.

PROPERTY MAN I'll be right back.

[*He exits.*]

DIRECTOR Come on, come on. It's the young lady's scene first. [*The* LEADING LADY *comes forward.*] No, no, wait. I said the young lady. [*Indicating the* STEPDAUGHTER] You will just watch—

STEPDAUGHTER [*adding, without pause*] —watch me live it!

LEADING LADY [*resenting this*] I'll know how to live it too, don't worry, once I put myself in the role!

DIRECTOR [*raising his hands to his head*] Please! No more chatter! Now, scene one. The Young Lady with Madam Pace. Oh, and how about this Madam Pace? [*Bewildered, looking around him, he climbs back onstage.*]

FATHER She isn't with us, sir.

DIRECTOR Then what do we do?

FATHER But she's alive. She's alive too.

DIRECTOR Fine. But where?

FATHER I'll tell you. [*Turning to the Actresses*] If you ladies will do me the favor of giving me your hats for a moment.

THE ACTRESSES [*surprised a little, laughing a little, in chorus*] —What?—Our hats?—What does he say?—Why?—Oh, dear!

DIRECTOR What are you going to do with the ladies' hats?

[*The Actors laugh.*]

FATHER Oh, nothing. Just put them on these coathooks for a minute. And would some of you be so kind as to take your coats off too?

ACTORS [*as before*] Their coats too?—And then?—He's nuts!

AN ACTRESS OR TWO [*as above*] —But why?—Just the coats?

FATHER Just so they can be hung there for a moment. Do me this favor. Will you?

ACTRESSES [*taking their hats off, and one or two of them their coats, too, continuing to laugh, and going to hang the hats here and there on the coathooks*] —Well, why not?—There!—This is getting to be really funny!—Are we to put them on display?

FATHER Exactly! That's just right, ma'am: on display!

DIRECTOR May one inquire *why* you are doing this?

FATHER Yes, sir. If we set the stage better, who knows but she may come to us, drawn by the objects of her trade . . . [*Inviting them to look toward the entrance at the back*] Look! Look!

[*The entrance at the back opens, and* MADAM PACE *walks a few paces downstage, a hag of enormous fatness with a pompous wig of carrot-colored wool and a fiery red rose on one side of it,* à l'espagnole,[5] *heavily made up, dressed with gauche elegance in garish red silk, a feathered fan in one hand and the other hand raised to hold a lighted cigarette between two fingers. At the sight of this apparition, the* DIRECTOR *and the Actors at once dash off the stage with a yell of terror, rushing down the stairs and making as if to flee up the aisle. The* STEPDAUGHTER, *on the other hand runs to* MADAM PACE—*deferentially, as to her boss.*]

STEPDAUGHTER [*running to her*] Here she is, here she is!

FATHER [*beaming*] It's she! What did I tell you? Here she is!

DIRECTOR [*overcoming his first astonishment, and incensed now*] What tricks are these?

[*The next four speeches are more or less simultaneous.*]

LEADING MAN What goes on around here?

JUVENILE LEAD Where on earth did she come from?

INGENUE They must have been holding her in reserve.

5. Spanish-style (French).

LEADING LADY Hocus pocus! Hocus pocus!

FATHER [*dominating these protests*] Excuse me, though! Why, actually, would you want to destroy this prodigy in the name of vulgar truth, this miracle of a reality that is born of the stage itself—called into being by the stage, drawn here by the stage, and shaped by the stage—and which has more right to live on the stage than you have because it is much truer? Which of you actresses will later re-create Madam Pace? This lady *is* Madam Pace. You must admit that the actress who re-creates her will be less true than this lady—who is Madam Pace. Look: my daughter recognized her, and went right over to her. Stand and watch the scene!

[*Hesitantly, the* DIRECTOR *and the Actors climb back onstage. But the scene between the* STEPDAUGHTER *and* MADAM PACE *has begun during the protest of the Actors and the* FATHER*'s answer: sotto voce,*[6] *very quietly, in short naturally—as would never be possible on a stage. When, called to order by the* FATHER, *the Actors turn again to watch, they hear* MADAM PACE, *who has just placed her hand under the* STEPDAUGHTER*'s chin in order to raise her head, talk unintelligibly. After trying to hear for a moment, they just give up.*]

DIRECTOR Well?

LEADING MAN What's she saying?

LEADING LADY One can't hear a thing.

JUVENILE LEAD Louder!

STEPDAUGHTER [*leaving* MADAM PACE, *who smiles a priceless smile, and walking down toward the Actors*] Louder, huh? How d'you mean: louder? These aren't things that can be said louder. *I* was able to say them loudly—to shame him [*Indicating the* FATHER]—that was my revenge. For Madam, it's different, my friends: it would mean—jail.

DIRECTOR Oh my God! It's like that, is it? But, my dear young lady, in the theater one must be heard. And even we couldn't hear you, right here on the stage. How about an audience out front? There's a scene to be done. And anyway you *can* speak loudly—it's just between yourselves, we won't be standing here listening like now. Pretend you're alone. In a room. The back room of the shop. No one can hear you. [*The* STEPDAUGHTER *charmingly and with a mischievous smile tells him No with a repeated movement of the finger.*] Why not?

STEPDAUGHTER [*sotto voce, mysteriously*] There's someone who'll hear if she [MADAM PACE] speaks loudly.

DIRECTOR [*in consternation*] Is someone else going to pop up now?

[*The Actors make as if to quit the stage again.*]

FATHER No, no, sir. She means me. I'm to be there—behind the door—waiting. And Madam knows. So if you'll excuse me. I must be ready for my entrance. [*He starts to move.*]

DIRECTOR [*stopping him*] No, wait. We must respect the exigencies of the theater. Before you get ready—

STEPDAUGHTER [*interrupting him*] Let's get on with it! I tell you I'm dying with desire to live it, to live that scene! If he's ready, I'm more than ready!

DIRECTOR [*shouting*] But first we have to get that scene out of you and her! [*Indicating* MADAM PACE] Do you follow me?

6. Under the voice (Italian); that is, spoken very softly, under the breath.

STEPDAUGHTER Oh dear, oh dear, she was telling me things you already know—that my mother's work had been badly done once again, the material is ruined, and I'm going to have to bear with her if I want her to go on helping us in our misery.

MADAM PACE [*coming forward with a great air of importance*] Sí, sí, señor, porque yo[7] no want profit. No advantage, no.

DIRECTOR [*almost scared*] What, what? She talks like *that?!*

[*All the Actors loudly burst out laughing.*]

STEPDAUGHTER [*also laughing*] Yes, sir, she talks like that—halfway between Spanish and English—very funny, isn't it?

MADAM PACE Now that is not good manners, no, that you laugh at me! Yo hablo[8] the English as good I can, señor!

DIRECTOR And it *is* good! Yes! Do talk that way, ma'am! It's a surefire effect! There couldn't be anything better to, um, soften the crudity of the situation! Do talk that way! It's fine!

STEPDAUGHTER Fine! Of course! To have certain propositions put to you in a lingo like that. Surefire, isn't it? Because, sir, it seems almost a joke. When I hear there's "an old señor" who wants to "have good time conmigo,"[9] I start to laugh—don't I, Madam Pace?

MADAM PACE Old, viejo, no. Viejito—leetle beet old, sí, darling? Better like that: if he no give you fun, he bring you prudencia.[1]

MOTHER [*jumping up, to the stupefaction and consternation of all the Actors, who had been taking no notice of her, and who now respond to her shouts with a start and, smiling, try to restrain her, because she has grabbed* MADAM PACE*'s wig and thrown it on the floor*] Witch! Witch! Murderess! My daughter!

STEPDAUGHTER [*running over to restrain her* MOTHER] No, no, mama, no, please!

FATHER [*running over too at the same time*] Calm down, calm down! Sit here.

MOTHER Then send that woman away!

STEPDAUGHTER [*to the* DIRECTOR, *who also has run over*] It's not possible, not possible that my mother should be here!

FATHER [*also to the* DIRECTOR] They can't be together. That's why, you see, the woman wasn't with us when we came. Their being together would spoil it, you understand.

DIRECTOR It doesn't matter, doesn't matter at all. This is just a preliminary sketch. Everything helps. However confusing the elements, I'll piece them together somehow. [*Turning to the* MOTHER *and sitting her down again in her place*] Come along, come along, ma'am, calm down: sit down again.

STEPDAUGHTER [*who meanwhile has moved center stage again. Turning to* MADAM PACE] All right, let's go!

MADAM PACE Ah, no! No thank you! Yo aquí no do nada[2] with your mother present.

STEPDAUGHTER Oh, come on! Bring in that old señor who wants to have

7. Yes, yes, yes, Mister, because I . . . (Spanish). In Pirandello's original Italian text, Madam Pace mixes Spanish and Italian.
8. I speak (Spanish).
9. With me (Spanish).
1. Care, caution (Spanish).
2. I do nothing here (Spanish and English).

good time conmigo! [*Turning imperiously to all the others*] Yes, we've got to have it, this scene!—Come on, let's go! [*To* MADAM PACE] You may leave.

MADAM PACE Ah sí, I go, I go, go seguramente[3] . . . [*She makes her exit furiously, putting her wig back on, and looking haughtily at the Actors who applaud mockingly.*]

STEPDAUGHTER [*to the* FATHER] And you can make your entrance. No need to go out and come in again. Come here. Pretend, you're already in. Right. Now I'm here with bowed head, modest, huh? Let's go! Speak up! With a different voice, the voice of someone just in off the street: "Hello, miss."

DIRECTOR [*by this time out front again*] Now look: are you directing this, or am I? [*To the* FATHER *who looks undecided and perplexed.*] Do it, yes. Go to the back. Don't leave the stage, though. And then come forward.

[*The* FATHER *does it, almost dismayed. Very pale; but already clothed in the reality of his created life, he smiles as he approaches from the back, as if still alien to the drama which will break upon him. The Actors now pay attention to the scene which is beginning.*]

DIRECTOR [*softly, in haste, to the* PROMPTER *in the box*] And you, be ready now, ready to write!

THE SCENE

FATHER [*coming forward, with a different voice*] Hello, miss.

STEPDAUGHTER [*with bowed head and contained disgust*] Hello.

FATHER [*scrutinizing her under her hat which almost hides her face and noting that she is very young, exclaims, almost to himself, a little out of complaisance and a little out of fear of compromising himself in a risky adventure*] Oh . . . —Well, I was thinking, it wouldn't be the first time, hm? The first time you came here.

STEPDAUGHTER [*as above*] No, sir.

FATHER You've been here other times? [*And when the* STEPDAUGHTER *nods*] More than once? [*He waits a moment for her to answer, then again scrutinizes her under her hat; smiles; then says*] Well then, hm . . . it shouldn't any longer be so . . . May I take this hat off for you?

STEPDAUGHTER [*without pause, to forestall him, not now containing her disgust*] No, sir, *I* will take it off! [*And she does so in haste, convulsed.*]

[*The* MOTHER, *watching the scene with the* SON *and with the two others, smaller and more her own, who are close to her all the time, forming a group at the opposite side of the stage from the Actors, is on tenterhooks as she follows the words and actions of* FATHER *and* STEPDAUGHTER *with varied expression: grief, disdain, anxiety, horror, now hiding her face, now emitting a moan.*]

MOTHER Oh God! My God!

FATHER [*is momentarily turned to stone by the moaning; then he reassumes the previous tone*] Now give it to me: I'll hang it up for you. [*He takes the hat from her hands.*] But I could wish for a little hat worthier of such a dear, lovely little head! Would you like to help me choose one? From the many Madam has?—You wouldn't?

INGENUE [*interrupting*] Oh now, come on, those are *our* hats!

3. Certainly (Spanish).

DIRECTOR [*without pause, very angry*] Silence, for Heaven's sake, don't try to be funny!—This is the stage. [*Turning back to the* STEPDAUGHTER] Would you begin again, please?

STEPDAUGHTER [*beginning again*] No, thank you, sir.

FATHER Oh, come on now, don't say no. Accept one from me. To please me . . . There are some lovely ones you know. And we would make Madam happy. Why else does she put them on display?

STEPDAUGHTER No, no, sir, look: I wouldn't even be able to wear it.

FATHER You mean because of what the family would think when they saw you come home with a new hat on? Think nothing of it. Know how to handle that? What to tell them at home?

STEPDAUGHTER [*breaking out, at the end of her rope*] But that's not why, sir. I couldn't wear it because I'm . . . as you see me. You might surely have noticed! [*Points to her black attire.*]

FATHER In mourning, yes. Excuse me. It's true: I do see it. I beg your pardon. I'm absolutely mortified, believe me.

STEPDAUGHTER [*forcing herself and plucking up courage to conquer her contempt and nausea*] Enough! Enough! It's for me to thank you, it is not for you to be mortified or afflicted. Please pay no more attention to what I said. Even for me, you understand . . . [*She forces herself to smile and adds*] I need to forget I am dressed like this.

DIRECTOR [*interrupting, addressing himself to the* PROMPTER *in his box, and going up onstage again*] Wait! Wait! Don't write. Leave that last sentence out, leave it out! [*Turning to the* FATHER *and* STEPDAUGHTER] It's going very well indeed. [*Then to the* FATHER *alone*] This is where you go into the part we prepared. [*To the Actors*] Enchanting, that little hat scene, don't you agree?

STEPDAUGHTER Oh, but the best is just coming. Why aren't we continuing?

DIRECTOR Patience one moment. [*Again addressing himself to the Actors*] Needs rather delicate handling, of course . . .

LEADING MAN —With a certain *ease*—

LEADING LADY Obviously. But there's nothing to it. [*To the* LEADING MAN] We can rehearse it at once, can't we?

LEADING MAN As far as I'm . . . Very well, I'll go out and make my entrance. [*And he does go out by the back door, ready to reenter.*]

DIRECTOR [*to the* LEADING LADY] And so, look, your scene with that Madam Pace is over. I'll write it up later. You are standing . . . Hey, where are you going?

LEADING LADY Wait. I'm putting my hat back on . . . [*She does so, taking the hat from the hook.*]

DIRECTOR Oh yes, good.—Now, you're standing here with your head bowed.

STEPDAUGHTER [*amused*] But she's not wearing black!

LEADING LADY *I shall* wear black! And I'll carry it better than you!

DIRECTOR [*to the* STEPDAUGHTER] Keep quiet, please! Just watch. You can learn something. [*Claps his hands.*] Get going, get going! The entrance! [*And he goes back out front to get an impression of the stage.*]

[*The door at the back opens, and the* LEADING MAN *comes forward, with the relaxed, waggish manner of an elderly Don Juan.*[4] *From the first*

4. That is, a great lover or seducer of women (from the legendary Spaniard of that name).

speeches, the performance of the scene by the Actors is quite a different thing, without, however, having any element of parody in it—rather, it seems corrected, set to rights. Naturally, the STEPDAUGHTER *and the* FATHER, *being quite unable to recognize themselves in this* LEADING LADY *and* LEADING MAN *but hearing them speak their own words express in various ways, now with gestures, now with smiles, now with open protests, their surprise, their wonderment, their suffering, etc., as will be seen forthwith.*

The PROMPTER*'s voice is clearly heard from the box.*]

LEADING MAN Hello, miss.

FATHER [*without pause, unable to contain himself*] No, no!

[*The* STEPDAUGHTER, *seeing how the* LEADING MAN *makes his entrance, has burst out laughing.*]

DIRECTOR [*coming from the proscenium, furious*] Silence here! And stop that laughing at once! We can't go ahead till it stops.

STEPDAUGHTER [*coming from the proscenium*] How can I help it? This lady [*the* LEADING LADY] just stands there. If she's supposed to be me, let me tell you that if anyone said hello to me in that manner and that tone of voice, I'd burst out laughing just as I actually did!

FATHER [*coming forward a little too*] That's right . . . the manner, the tone . . .

DIRECTOR Manner! Tone! Stand to one side now, and let me see the rehearsal.

LEADING MAN [*coming forward*] If I'm to play an old man entering a house of ill—

DIRECTOR Oh, pay no attention, please. Just begin again. It was going fine. [*Waiting for the Actor to resume*] Now then . . .

LEADING MAN Hello, miss.

LEADING LADY Hello.

LEADING MAN [*re-creating the* FATHER*'s gesture of scrutinizing her under her hat, but then expressing very distinctly first the complaisance and then the fear*] Oh . . . Well . . . I was thinking it wouldn't be the first time, I hope . . .

FATHER [*unable to help correcting him*] Not "I hope." "Would it?" "Would it?"

DIRECTOR He says: "would it?" A question.

LEADING MAN [*pointing to the* PROMPTER] I heard: "I hope."

DIRECTOR Same thing! "Would it." Or: "I hope." Continue, continue.—Now, maybe a bit less affected . . . Look, I'll do it for you. Watch me . . . [*Returns to the stage, then repeats the bit since the entrance*]—Hello, miss.

LEADING LADY Hello.

DIRECTOR Oh, well . . . I was thinking . . . [*Turning to the* LEADING MAN *to have him note how he has looked at the* LEADING LADY *under her hat*] Surprise . . . fear and complaisance. [*Then, going on, and turning to the* LEADING LADY] It wouldn't be the first time, would it? The first time you came here. [*Again turning to the* LEADING MAN *with an inquiring look*] Clear? [*To the* LEADING LADY] Then you say: No, sir. [*Back to the* LEADING MAN] How shall I put it? Plasticity! [*Goes back out front.*]

LEADING LADY No, sir.

LEADING MAN You came here other times? More than once?

DIRECTOR No, no, wait. [*Indicating the* LEADING LADY] First let her nod. "You came here other times?"

[*The* LEADING LADY *raises her head a little, closes her eyes painfully as if in disgust, then nods twice at the word "Down" from the* DIRECTOR.]

STEPDAUGHTER [*involuntarily*] Oh, my God! [*And she at once puts her hand on her mouth to keep the laughter in.*]

DIRECTOR [*turning round*] What is it?

STEPDAUGHTER [*without pause*] Nothing, nothing.

DIRECTOR [*to the* LEADING MAN That's your cue. Go straight on.

LEADING MAN More than once? Well then, hm . . . it shouldn't any longer be so . . . May I take this little hat off for you?

[*The* LEADING MAN *says this last speech in such a tone and accompanies it with such a gesture that the* STEPDAUGHTER, *her hands on her mouth, much as she wants to hold herself in, cannot contain her laughter, which comes bursting out through her fingers irresistibly and very loud.*]

LEADING LADY [*returning to her place, enraged*] Now look, I'm not going to be made a clown of by that person!

LEADING MAN Nor am I. Let's stop.

DIRECTOR [*to the* STEPDAUGHTER, *roaring*] Stop it! Stop it!

STEPDAUGHTER Yes, yes. Forgive me, forgive me . . .

DIRECTOR You have no manners! You're presumptuous! So there!

FATHER [*seeking to intervene*] That's true, yes, that's true, sir, but forgive . . .

DIRECTOR [*onstage again*] Forgive nothing! It's disgusting!

FATHER Yes, sir. But believe me, it has such a strange effect—

DIRECTOR Strange? Strange? What's strange about it?

FATHER I admire your actors, sir, I really admire them, this gentleman [LEADING MAN] and that lady [LEADING LADY] but assuredly . . . well, they're not us . . .

DIRECTOR So what? How *could* they be you, if they're the actors?

FATHER Exactly, the actors! And they play our parts well, both of them. But of course, to us, they seem something else—that tries to be the same but simply isn't!

DIRECTOR How d'you mean: isn't? What is it then?

FATHER Something that . . . becomes theirs. And stops being ours.

DIRECTOR Necessarily! I explained that to you!

FATHER Yes. I understand, I do under—

DIRECTOR Then that will be enough! [*Turning to the Actors*] We'll be rehearsing by ourselves as we usually do. Rehearsing with authors present has always been hell, in my experience. There's no satisfying them. [*Turning to the* FATHER and the STEPDAUGHTER] Come along then. Let's resume. And let's hope you find it possible not to laugh this time.

STEPDAUGHTER Oh, no, I won't be laughing this time around. My big moment comes up now. Don't worry!

DIRECTOR Very well, when she says: "Please pay no more attention to what I said . . . Even for me—you understand . . ." [*Turning to the* FATHER] You'll have to cut right in with: "I understand, oh yes, I understand . . ." and ask her right away—

STEPDAUGHTER [*interrupting*] Oh? Ask me what?

DIRECTOR —why she is in mourning.

STEPDAUGHTER No, no, look: when I told him I needed to forget I was dressed like this, do you know what his answer was? "Oh, good! Then let's take that little dress right off, shall we?"

DIRECTOR Great! Terrific! It'll knock 'em right out of their seats!

STEPDAUGHTER But it's the truth.

DIRECTOR Truth, is it? Well, well, well. This is the theater! Our motto is: truth up to a certain point!

STEPDAUGHTER Then what would you propose?

DIRECTOR You'll see. You'll see it. Just leave me alone.

STEPDAUGHTER Certainly not. From my nausea—from all the reasons one more cruel than another why I am what I am, why I am "that one there"—you'd like to cook up some romantic, sentimental concoction, wouldn't you? He asks me why I'm in mourning, and I tell him, through my tears, that Papa died two months ago! No, my dear sir! He has to say what he did say: "Then let's take that little dress right off, shall we?" And I, with my two-months mourning in my heart, went back there—you see? behind that screen—and—my fingers quivering with shame, with loathing—I took off my dress, took off my corset . . .

DIRECTOR [*running his hands through his hair*] Good God, what are you saying?

STEPDAUGHTER [*shouting frantically*] The truth, sir, the truth!

DIRECTOR Well, yes, of course, that must be the truth . . . and I quite understand your horror, young lady. Would you try to understand that all that is impossible *on the stage*?

STEPDAUGHTER Impossible? Then, thanks very much, I'm leaving.

DIRECTOR No, no, look . . .

STEPDAUGHTER I'm leaving, I'm leaving! You went in that room, you two, didn't you, and figured out "what is possible on the stage"? Thanks very much. I see it all. He wants to skip to the point where he can act out his [*Exaggerating*] spiritual travail! But I want to play *my* drama. Mine!

DIRECTOR [*annoyed, and shrugging haughtily*] Oh well, *your* drama. This is not just your drama, if I may say so. How about the drama of the others? His drama [*the* FATHER], hers [*the* MOTHER]? We can't let one character hog the limelight, just taking the whole stage over, and overshadowing all the others! Everything must be placed within the frame of one harmonious picture! We must perform only what is performable! I know as well as you do that each of us has a whole life of his own inside him and would like to bring it all out. But the difficult thing is this: to bring out only as much as is needed—in relation to the others—and in this to *imply* all the rest, *suggest* what remains inside! Oh, it would be nice if every character could come down to the footlights and tell the audience just what is brewing inside him—in a fine monologue or, if you will, a lecture! [*Good-natured, conciliatory*] Miss, you will have to *contain yourself*. And it will be in your interest. It could make a bad impression—let me warn you—this tearing fury, this desperate disgust—since, if I may say so, you confessed having been with others at Madam Pace's—before him—more than once!

STEPDAUGHTER [*lowering her head, pausing to recollect, a deeper note in her voice*] It's true. But to me the others are also *him*, all of them equally!

DIRECTOR [*not getting it*] The others? How d'you mean?

STEPDAUGHTER People "go wrong." And wrong follows on the heels of wrong. Who is responsible, if not whoever it was who first brought them down? Isn't that always the case? And for me that is him. Even before I was born. Look at him, and see if it isn't so.

DIRECTOR Very good. And if he has so much to feel guilty about, can't you appreciate how it must weigh him down? So let's at least permit him to act it out.

STEPDAUGHTER And how, may I ask, how could he act out all that "noble" guilt, all those so "moral" torments, if you propose to spare him the horror of one day finding in his arms—after having bade her take off the black clothes that marked her recent loss—a woman now, and already gone wrong—that little girl, sir, that little girl whom he used to go watch coming out of school?

[*She says these last words in a voice trembling with emotion. The* MOTHER, *hearing her say this, overcome with uncontrollable anguish, which comes out first in suffocated moans and subsequently bursts out in bitter weeping. The emotion takes hold of everyone. Long pause.*]

STEPDAUGHTER [*as soon as the* MOTHER *gives signs of calming down, somber, determined*] We're just among ourselves now. Still unknown to the public. Tomorrow you will make of us the show you have in mind. You will put it together in your way. But would you like to really see—our drama? Have it explode—the real thing?

DIRECTOR Of course. Nothing I'd like better. And I'll use as much of it as I possibly can!

STEPDAUGHTER Very well. Have this Mother here go out.

MOTHER [*ceasing to weep, with a loud cry*] No, no! Don't allow this, don't allow it!

DIRECTOR I only want to take a look, ma'am.

MOTHER I can't, I just can't!

DIRECTOR But if it's already happened? Excuse me but I just don't get it.

MOTHER No, no, it's happening now. It's always happening. My torment is not a pretense! I am alive and present—always, in every moment of my torment—it keeps renewing itself, it too is alive and always present. But those two little ones over there—have you heard them speak? They cannot speak, sir, not anymore! They still keep clinging to me—to keep my torment alive and present. For themselves they don't exist, don't exist any longer. And she [*the* STEPDAUGHTER], she just fled, ran away from me, she's lost, lost . . . If I see her before me now, it's for the same reason: to renew the torment, keep it always alive and present forever—the torment I've suffered on her account too—forever!

FATHER [*solemn*] The eternal moment, sir, as I told you. She [*the* STEPDAUGHTER] is here to catch me, fix me, hold me there in the pillory, hanging there forever, hooked, in that single fleeting shameful moment of my life! She cannot give it up. And, actually, sir, *you* cannot spare me.

DIRECTOR But I didn't say I wouldn't use that. On the contrary, it will be the nucleus of the whole first act. To the point where she [*the* MOTHER] surprises you.

FATHER Yes, exactly. Because that is the sentence passed upon me: all our passion which has to culminate in her [*the* MOTHER's] final cry!

STEPDAUGHTER It still rings in my ears. It's driven me out of my mind, that cry!—You can present me as you wish, sir, it doesn't matter. Even dressed. As long as at least my arms—just my arms—are bare. Because it was like this. [*She goes to the* FATHER *and rests her head on his chest.*] I was standing like this with my head on his chest and my arms round his neck like this. Then I saw something throbbing right here on my arm. A vein. Then, as if it was just this living vein that disgusted me, I jammed my eyes shut, like this, d'you see? and buried my head on his chest. [*Turning to the* MOTHER] Scream, scream, mama! [*Buries her head on the* FATHER*'s chest and with her shoulders raised as if to avoid hearing the scream she adds in a voice stifled with torment.*] Scream as you screamed then!

MOTHER [*rushing forward to part them*] No! My daughter! My daughter! [*Having pulled her from him*] Brute! Brute! It's my daughter, don't you see—my daughter!

DIRECTOR [*the outburst having sent him reeling to the footlights, while the Actors show dismay*] Fine! Splendid! And now: curtain, curtain!

FATHER [*running to him, convulsed*] Right! Yes! Because that, sir, is how it actually was!

DIRECTOR [*in admiration and conviction*] Yes, yes, of course! Curtain! Curtain!

[*Hearing this repeated cry of the* DIRECTOR, *the* TECHNICIAN *lets down the curtain, trapping the* DIRECTOR *and the* FATHER *between curtain and footlights.*]

DIRECTOR [*looking up, with raised arms*] What an idiot! I say Curtain, meaning that's how the act should end, and they let down the actual curtain! [*He lifts a corner of the curtain so he can get back onstage. To the* FATHER] Yes, yes, fine, splendid! Absolutely surefire! Has to end that way. I can vouch for the first act. [*Goes behind the curtain with the* FATHER.]

[*When the curtain rises we see that the stagehands have struck that first "indication of a set," and have put onstage in its stead a small garden fountain. On one side of the stage, the Actors are sitting in a row, and on the other are the Characters. The* DIRECTOR *is standing in the middle of the stage, in the act of meditating with one hand, fist clenched, on his mouth.*]

DIRECTOR [*shrugging after a short pause*] Yes, well then, let's get to the second act. Just leave it to me as we agreed beforehand and everything will be all right.

STEPDAUGHTER Our entrance into his house [*the* FATHER] in spite of him [*the* SON].

DIRECTOR [*losing patience*] Very well. But leave it all to me, I say.

STEPDAUGHTER In spite of him. Just let that be clear.

MOTHER [*shaking her head from her corner*] For all the good that's come out of it . . .

STEPDAUGHTER [*turning quickly on her*] It doesn't matter. The more damage to us, the more guilt feelings for him.

DIRECTOR [*still out of patience*] I understand, I understand. All this will be taken into account, especially at the beginning. Rest assured.

MOTHER [*supplicatingly*] Do make them understand, I beg you, sir, for my conscience' sake, for I tried in every possible way—

STEPDAUGHTER [*continuing her* MOTHER*'s speech, contemptuously*] To placate me, to advise me not to give him trouble. [*To the* DIRECTOR] Do what she wants, do it because it's true. I enjoy the whole thing very much because, look: the more she plays the suppliant and tries to gain entrance into his heart, the more he holds himself aloof: he's an absentee! How I relish this!

DIRECTOR We want to get going—on the second act, don't we?

STEPDAUGHTER I won't say another word. But to play it all in the garden, as you want to, won't be possible.

DIRECTOR Why won't it be possible?

STEPDAUGHTER Because he [*the* SON] stays shut up in his room, on his own. Then again we need the house for the part about this poor bewildered little boy, as I told you.

DIRECTOR Quite right. But on the other hand, we can't change the scenery in view of the audience three or four times in one act, nor can we stick up signs—

LEADING MAN They used to at one time . . .

DIRECTOR Yes, when the audiences were about as mature as that little girl.

LEADING LADY They got the illusion more easily.

FATHER [*suddenly, rising*] The illusion, please don't say illusion! Don't use that word! It's especially cruel to us.

DIRECTOR [*astonished*] And why, if I may ask?

FATHER Oh yes, cruel, cruel! You should understand that.

DIRECTOR What word would you have us use anyway? The illusion of creating here for our spectators—

LEADING MAN —By our performance—

DIRECTOR —the illusion of a reality.

FATHER I understand, sir, but perhaps you do not understand us. Because, you see, for you and for your actors all this—quite rightly—is a game—

LEADING LADY [*indignantly interrupting*] Game! We are not children, sir. We act in earnest.

FATHER I don't deny it. I just mean the game of your art which, as this gentleman rightly says, must provide a perfect illusion of reality.

DIRECTOR Yes, exactly.

FATHER But consider this. We [*He quickly indicates himself and the other five Characters.*], we have no reality outside this illusion.

DIRECTOR [*astonished, looking at his Actors who remain bewildered and lost*] And that means?

FATHER [*after observing them briefly, with a pale smile*] Just that, ladies and gentlemen. How should we have any other reality? What for you is an illusion, to be created, is for us our unique reality. [*Short pause. He takes several short steps toward the* DIRECTOR, *and adds*] But not for us alone, of course. Think a moment. [*He looks into his eyes.*] Can you tell me who you are? [*And he stands there pointing his first finger at him.*]

DIRECTOR [*upset, with a half-smile*] How do you mean, who I am? I am I.

FATHER And if I told you that wasn't true because you are me?

DIRECTOR I would reply that you are out of your mind. [*The Actors laugh.*]

FATHER You are right to laugh: because this is a game. [*To the* DIRECTOR] And you can object that it's only in a game that that gentleman there [LEADING MAN], who is himself, must be me, who am *myself*. I've caught you in a trap, do you see that?

[*Actors start laughing again.*]

DIRECTOR [*annoyed*] You said all this before. Why repeat it?

FATHER I won't—I didn't intend to say that. I'm inviting you to emerge from this game. [*He looks at the* LEADING LADY *as if to forestall what she might say.*] This game of art which you are accustomed to play here with your actors. Let me again ask quite seriously: Who are you?

DIRECTOR [*turning to the Actors, amazed and at the same time irritated*] The gall of this fellow! Calls himself a character and comes here to ask me who I am!

FATHER [*dignified, but not haughty*] A character, sir, can always ask a man who he is. Because a character really has his own life, marked with his own characteristics, by virtue of which he is always someone. Whereas, a man—I'm not speaking of you now—*a man* can be no one.

DIRECTOR Oh sure. But you are asking me! And I am the manager, understand?

FATHER [*quite softly with mellifluous modesty*] Only in order to know, sir, if you as you now are see yourself . . . for example, at a distance in time. Do you see the man you once were, with all the illusions you had then, with everything, inside you and outside, as it seemed then—as it was then for you?—Well sir, thinking back to those illusions which you don't have anymore, to all those things which no longer seem to be what at one time they were for you, don't you feel, not just the boards of this stage, but the very earth beneath slipping away from you? For will not all that you feel yourself to be now, your whole reality of today, as it is now, inevitably seem an illusion tomorrow?

DIRECTOR [*who has not followed exactly, but has been staggered by the plausibilities of the argument*] Well, well, what do you want to prove?

FATHER Oh nothing, sir. I just wanted to make you see that if *we* [*pointing again at himself and the other Characters*] have no reality outside of illusion, it would be well if you should distrust your reality because, though you breathe it and touch it today, it is destined like that of yesterday to stand revealed to you tomorrow as illusion.

DIRECTOR [*deciding to mock him*] Oh splendid! And you'll be telling me next that you and this play that you have come to perform for me are truer and more real than I am.

FATHER [*quite seriously*] There can be no doubt of that, sir.

DIRECTOR Really?

FATHER I thought you had understood that from the start.

DIRECTOR More real than me?

FATHER If your reality can change overnight . . .

DIRECTOR Of course it can, it changes all the time, like everyone else's.

FATHER [*with a cry*] But ours does not, sir. You see, that is the difference. It does not change, it cannot ever change or be otherwise because it is already fixed, it is what is, just that, forever—a terrible thing, sir!—an immutable reality. You should shudder to come near us.

DIRECTOR [*suddenly struck by a new idea, he steps in front of the* FATHER] I should like to know, however, when anyone ever saw a character get out of his part and set about expounding and explicating it, delivering lectures on it. Can you tell me? I have never seen anything like that.

FATHER You have never seen it, sir, because authors generally hide the travail of their creations. When characters are alive and turn up, living, before their author, all that author does is follow the words and gestures which they propose to him. He has to want them to be as they themselves want to be. Woe betide him if he doesn't! When a character is born, he at once acquires such an independence, even of his own author, that the whole world can imagine him in innumerable situations other than those the author thought to place him in. At times he acquires a meaning that the author never dreamt of giving him.

DIRECTOR Certainly, I know that.

FATHER Then why all this astonishment at us? Imagine what a misfortune it is for a character such as I described to you—given life in the imagination of an author who then wished to deny him life—and tell me frankly: isn't such a character, given life and left without life, isn't he right to set about doing just what we are doing now as we stand here before you, after having done just the same—for a very long time, believe me—before *him*, trying to persuade him, trying to push him . . . I would appear before him sometimes, sometimes she [*looks at* STEPDAUGHTER] would go to him, sometimes that poor mother . . .

STEPDAUGHTER [*coming forward as if in a trance*] It's true. I too went there, sir, to tempt him, many times, in the melancholy of that study of his, at the twilight hour, when he would sit stretched out in his armchair, unable to make up his mind to switch the light on, and letting the evening shadows invade the room, knowing that these shadows were alive with us and that we were coming to tempt him . . . [*As if she saw herself still in that study and felt only annoyance at the presence of all of these Actors*] Oh, if only you would all go away! Leave us alone! My mother there with her son—I with this little girl—the boy there always alone—then I with him [*the* FATHER]—then I by myself, I by myself . . . in those shadows. [*Suddenly she jumps up as if she wished to take hold of herself in the vision she has of herself lighting up the shadows and alive.*] Ah, my life! What scenes, what scenes we went there to propose to him: I, I tempted him more than the others.

FATHER Right, but perhaps that was the trouble: you insisted too much. You thought you could seduce him.

STEPDAUGHTER Nonsense. He wanted me that way. [*She comes up to the* DIRECTOR *to tell him as in confidence.*] If you ask me, sir, it was because he was so depressed, or because he despised the theater the public knows and wants . . .

DIRECTOR Let's continue. Let's continue, for heaven's sake. Enough theories, I'd like some facts. Give me some facts.

STEPDAUGHTER It seems to me that we have already given you more facts than you can handle—with our entry into his [*the* FATHER'*s*] house! You said you couldn't change the scene every five minutes or start hanging signs.

DIRECTOR Nor can we, of course not, we have to combine the scenes and group them in one simultaneous close-knit action. Not your idea at all. You'd like to see your brother come home from school and wander through the house like a ghost, hiding behind the doors, and brooding on a plan which—how did you put it—?

STEPDAUGHTER —shrivels him up, sir, completely shrivels him up, sir.

DIRECTOR "Shrivels!" What a word! All right then: his growth was stunted except for his eyes. Is that what you said?

STEPDAUGHTER Yes, sir. Just look at him. [*She points him out next to the* MOTHER.]

DIRECTOR Good girl. And then at the same time you want this little girl to be playing in the garden, dead to the world. Now, the boy in the house, the girl in the garden, is that possible?

STEPDAUGHTER Happy in the sunshine! Yes, that is my only reward, her pleasure, her joy in that garden! After the misery, the squalor of a horrible room where we slept, all four of us, she with me: just think, of the horror of my contaminated body next to hers! She held me tight, oh so tight with her loving innocent little arms! In the garden she would run and take my hand as soon as she saw me. She did not see the big flowers, she ran around looking for the teeny ones and wanted to show them to me, oh the joy of it!

[*Saying this and tortured by the memory she breaks into prolonged desperate sobbing, dropping her head onto her arms which are spread out on the work table. Everyone is overcome by her emotion. The* DIRECTOR *goes to her almost paternally and says to comfort her*]

DIRECTOR We'll do the garden. We'll do the garden, don't worry, and you'll be very happy about it. We'll bring all the scenes together in the garden. [*Calling a* STAGEHAND *by name*] Hey, drop me a couple of trees, will you, two small cypress trees, here in front of the fountain.

[*Two small cypress trees are seen descending from the flies.*[5] *A* STAGEHAND *runs on to secure them with nails and a couple of braces.*]

DIRECTOR [*to the* STEPDAUGHTER] Something to go on with anyway. Gives us an idea. [*Again calling the* STAGEHAND *by name*] Hey, give me a bit of sky.

STAGEHAND [*from above*] What?

DIRECTOR Bit of sky, a backcloth, to go behind that fountain. [*A white backdrop is seen descending from the flies.*] Not white, I said sky. It doesn't matter, leave it, I'll take care of it. [*Shouting*] Hey, Electrician, put these lights out. Let's have a bit of atmosphere, lunar atmosphere, blue background, and give me a blue spot on that backcloth. That's right. That's enough. [*At his command a mysterious lunar scene is created which induces the Actors to talk and move as they would on an evening in the garden beneath the moon.*] [*To* STEPDAUGHTER] You see? And now instead of hiding behind doors in the house the boy could move around here in the garden and hide behind trees. But it will be difficult, you know, to find a little girl to play the scene where she shows you the flowers. [*Turning to the* BOY] Come down this way a bit. Let's see how this can be worked out. [*And when the* BOY *doesn't move*] Come on, come on. [*Then dragging him forward he tries to make him hold his head up but it falls down again every time.*] Oh dear, another problem, this boy . . . What *is* it? . . . My God, he'll have to say something . . . [*He goes up to him, puts a hand on his shoulder and leads him behind one of the tree drops.*] Come on. Come on. Let me see. You can hide a bit here . . . Like this . . . You can stick your head out a bit to look . . . [*He goes to one side to see the effect. The* BOY *has scarcely run through the actions when the Actors are deeply affected; and they remain quite overwhelmed.*] Ah! Fine! Splendid! [*He turns again to the* STEPDAUGHTER.] If the little girl surprises him looking out and runs over to him, don't you think she might drag a few words out of him too?

STEPDAUGHTER [*jumping to her feet*] Don't expect him to speak while *he's* here. [*She points to the* SON.] You have to send *him* away first.

5. The space over the stage from which scenery and equipment can be lowered.

SON [*going resolutely toward one of the two stairways*] Suits me. Glad to go. Nothing I want more.

DIRECTOR [*immediately calling him*] No. Where are you going? Wait.

[*The* MOTHER *rises, deeply moved, in anguish at the thought that he is really going. She instinctively raises her arms as if to halt him, yet without moving away from her position.*]

SON [*arriving at the footlights, where the* DIRECTOR *stops him*] I have absolutely nothing to do here. So let me go please. Just let me go.

DIRECTOR How do you mean, you have nothing to do?

STEPDAUGHTER [*placidly, with irony*] Don't hold him! He won't go.

FATHER He has to play the terrible scene in the garden with his mother.

SON [*unhesitating, resolute, proud*] I play nothing. I said so from the start. [*To the* DIRECTOR] Let me go.

STEPDAUGHTER [*running to the* DIRECTOR *to get him to lower his arms so that he is no longer holding the* SON *back*] Let him go. [*Then turning to the* SON *as soon as the* DIRECTOR *has let him go*] Very well, go. [*The* SON *is all set to move toward the stairs but, as if held by some occult power, he cannot go down the steps. While the Actors are both astounded and deeply troubled, he moves slowly across the footlights straight to the other stairway. But having arrived there he remains poised for the descent but unable to descend. The* STEPDAUGHTER, *who has followed him with her eyes in an attitude of defiance, bursts out laughing.*] He can't, you see. He can't. He has to stay here, has to. Bound by a chain, indissolubly. But if I who do take flight, sir, when that happens which has to happen, and precisely because of the hatred I feel for him, precisely so as not to see him again—very well, if *I* am still here and can bear the sight of him and his company—you can imagine whether *he* can go away. He who really must, must remain here with that fine father of his and that mother there who no longer has any other children. [*Turning again to the* MOTHER] Come on, Mother, come on. [*Turning again to the* DIRECTOR *and pointing to the* MOTHER] Look, she got up to hold him back. [*To the* MOTHER, *as if exerting a magical power over her*] Come. Come . . . [*Then to the* DIRECTOR] You can imagine how little she wants to display her love in front of your actors. But so great is her desire to get at him that—look, you see—she is even prepared to live her scene.

[*In fact the* MOTHER *has approached and no sooner has the* STEPDAUGHTER *spoken her last words than she spreads her arms to signify consent.*]

SON [*without pause*] But *I* am not, *I* am not. If I cannot go I will stay here, but I repeat: I will play nothing.

FATHER [*to the* DIRECTOR, *enraged*] You can force him, sir.

SON No one can force me.

FATHER I will force you.

STEPDAUGHTER Wait, wait. First the little girl must be at the fountain. [*She runs to take the* LITTLE GIRL, *drops on her knees in front of her, takes her little face in her hands.*] My poor little darling, you look bewildered with those lovely big eyes of yours. Who knows where you think you are? We are on a stage my dear. What is a stage? It is a place where you play at being serious, a place for playacting, where we will now playact. But seriously! For real! You too . . . [*She embraces her, presses her to her bosom, and rocks her a little.*] Oh, little darling, little darling, what an ugly play you will enact! What a horrible thing has been planned for you, the garden, the fountain . . . All pretense, of course, that's the trouble, my sweet, everything is make-believe here, but perhaps for you, my child, a make-believe fountain is nicer than a real one for playing in, hmm? It will be a game for the others, but not for you, alas, because you are real, my darling, and are actually playing in a fountain that is real, beautiful, big, green with many bamboo plants reflected in it and giving it shade. Many, many ducklings can swim in it, breaking the shade to bits. You want to take hold of one of these ducklings . . . [*With a shout that fills everyone with dismay*] No! No, my Rosetta! Your mother is not looking after you because of that beast of a son. A thousand devils are loose in my head . . . and *he* . . . [*She leaves the* LITTLE GIRL *and turns with her usual hostility to the* BOY.] And what are you doing here, always looking like a beggar child? It will be your fault too if this little girl drowns—with all your standing around like that. As if I hadn't paid for everybody when I got you all into this house. [*Grabbing one of his arms to force him to take a hand out of his pocket*] What have you got there? What are you hiding? Let's see this hand. [*Tears his hand out of his pocket, and to the horror of everyone discovers that it holds a small revolver. She looks at it for a moment as if satisfied and then says*] Ah! Where did you get that and how? [*And as the* BOY *in his confusion, with his eyes staring and vacant all the time, does not answer her*] Idiot, if I were you I wouldn't have killed myself, I would have killed one of those two—or both of them—the father and the son! [*She hides him behind the small cypress tree from which he had been looking out, and she takes the* LITTLE GIRL *and hides her in the fountain, having her lie down in it in such a way as to be quite hidden. Finally, the* STEPDAUGHTER *goes down on her knees with her face in her hands, which are resting on the rim of the fountain.*]

DIRECTOR Splendid! [*Turning to the* SON] And at the same time . . .

SON [*with contempt*] And at the same time, nothing. It is not true, sir. There was never any scene between me and her. [*He points to the* MOTHER.] Let her tell you herself how it was.

[*Meanwhile the* SECOND ACTRESS *and the* JUVENILE LEAD *have detached themselves from the group of Actors. The former has started to observe the* MOTHER, *who is opposite her, very closely. And the other has started to observe the* SON. *Both are planning how they will re-create the roles.*]

MOTHER Yes, it is true, sir. I had gone to his room.

SON My room, did you hear that? Not the garden.

DIRECTOR That is of no importance. We have to rearrange the action, I told you that.

SON [*noticing that the* JUVENILE LEAD *is observing him*] What do *you* want?

JUVENILE LEAD Nothing. I am observing you.

SON [*turning to the other side where the* SECOND ACTRESS *is*] Ah, and here we have you to re-create the role, eh? [*He points to the* MOTHER.]

DIRECTOR Exactly, exactly. You should be grateful, it seems to me, for the attention they are giving you.

SON Oh yes, thank you. But you still haven't understood that you cannot do this drama. We are not inside you, not in the least, and your actors are looking at us from the outside. Do you think it's possible for us to live before a mirror which, not content to freeze us in the fixed image it provides of our expression, also throws back at us an unrecognizable grimace purporting to be ourselves?

FATHER That is true. That is true. You must see that.

DIRECTOR [*to the* JUVENILE LEAD *and the* SECOND ACTRESS] Very well, get away from here.

SON No good. I won't cooperate.

DIRECTOR Just be quiet a minute and let me hear your mother. [*To the* MOTHER] Well? You went into his room?

MOTHER Yes sir, into his room. I was at the end of my tether. I wanted to pour out all of the anguish which was oppressing me. But as soon as he saw me come in—

SON —There was no scene. I went away. I went away so there would be no scene. Because I have never made scenes, never, understand?

MOTHER That's true. That's how it was. Yes.

DIRECTOR But now there's got to be a scene between you and him. It is indispensable.

MOTHER As for me, sir, I am ready. If only you could find some way to have me speak to him for one moment, to have me say what is in my heart.

FATHER [*going right up to the* SON, *very violent*] You will do it! For your mother! For your mother!

SON [*more decisively than ever*] I will do nothing!

FATHER [*grabbing him by the chest and shaking him*] By God, you will obey! Can't you hear how she is talking to you? Aren't you her son?

SON [*grabbing his* FATHER] No! No! Once and for all let's have done with it!

[*General agitation. The* MOTHER, *terrified, tries to get between them to separate them.*]

MOTHER [*as before*] Please, please!

FATHER [*without letting go of the* SON] You must obey, you must obey!

SON [*wrestling with his* FATHER *and in the end throwing him to the ground beside the little stairway, to the horror of everyone*] What's this frenzy that's taken hold of you? To show your shame and ours to everyone? Have you no restraint? I won't cooperate, I won't cooperate! And that is how I interpret the wishes of the man who did not choose to put us onstage.

DIRECTOR But you came here.

SON [*pointing to his* FATHER] He came here—not me!

DIRECTOR But aren't you here too?

SON It was he who wanted to come, dragging the rest of us with him, and then getting together with you to plot not only what really happened, but also—as if that did not suffice—*what did not happen*.

DIRECTOR Then tell me. Tell me what did happen. Just tell me. You came out of your room without saying a thing?

SON [*after a moment of hesitation*] Without saying a thing. In order not to make a scene.

DIRECTOR [*driving him on*] Very well, and then, what did you do then?

SON [*while everyone looks on in anguished attention, he moves a few steps on the front part of the stage*] Nothing . . . crossing the garden . . . [*He stops, gloomy, withdrawn.*]

DIRECTOR [*always driving him on to speak, impressed by his reticence*] Very well, crossing the garden?

SON [*desperate, hiding his face with one arm*] Why do you want to make me say it, sir? It is horrible.

[*The* MOTHER *trembles all over, and stifles groans, looking toward the fountain.*]

DIRECTOR [*softly, noticing this look of hers, turning to the* SON, *with growing apprehension*] The little girl?

SON [*looking out into the auditorium*] Over there—in the fountain . . .

FATHER [*on the ground, pointing compassionately toward the* MOTHER] And she followed him, sir.

DIRECTOR [*to the* SON, *anxiously*] And then you . . .

SON [*slowly, looking straight ahead all the time*] I ran out. I started to fish her out . . . but all of a sudden I stopped. Behind those trees I saw something that froze me: the boy, the boy was standing there, quite still. There was madness in the eyes. He was looking at his drowned sister in the fountain. [*The* STEPDAUGHTER, *who has been bent over the fountain, hiding the* LITTLE GIRL, *is sobbing desperately, like an echo from the bottom. Pause.*] I started to approach and then . . .

[*From behind the trees where the* BOY *has been hiding, a revolver shot rings out.*]

MOTHER [*running up with a tormented shout, accompanied by the* SON *and all the Actors in a general tumult*] Son! My son! [*And then amid the hubbub and the disconnected shouts of the others*] Help! Help!

DIRECTOR [*amid the shouting, trying to clear a space while the* BOY *is lifted by his head and feet and carried away behind the backcloth*] Is he wounded, is he wounded, really?

[*Everyone except the* DIRECTOR *and the* FATHER, *who has remained on the ground beside the steps, has disappeared behind the backcloth which has served for a sky, where they can still be heard for a while whispering anxiously. Then from one side and the other of this curtain, the Actors come back onstage.*]

LEADING LADY [*reentering from the right, very much upset*] He's dead! Poor boy! He's dead! What a terrible thing!

LEADING MAN [*reentering from the left, laughing*] How do you mean, dead? Fiction, fiction, one doesn't believe such things.

OTHER ACTORS [*on the right*] Fiction? Reality! Reality! He is dead!

OTHER ACTORS [*on the left*] No! Fiction! Fiction!

FATHER [*rising, and crying out to them*] Fiction indeed! Reality, reality, gentlemen, reality! [*Desperate, he too disappears at the back.*]

DIRECTOR [*at the end of his rope*] Fiction! Reality! To hell with all of you! Lights, lights, lights! [*At a single stroke the whole stage and auditorium is flooded with very bright light. The* DIRECTOR *breathes again, as if freed from an incubus, and they all look each other in the eyes, bewildered and lost.*] Things like this don't happen to me, they've made me lose a whole day. [*He looks at his watch.*] Go, you can all go. What could we do now anyway? It is too late to pick up the rehearsal where we left off. See you this evening. [*As soon as the Actors have gone he talks to the* ELECTRICIAN *by name.*] Hey, Electrician, lights out. [*He has hardly said the words when the theater is plunged for a moment into complete darkness.*] Hey, for God's sake, leave me at least one light! I like to see where I am going!

[*Immediately, from behind the backcloth, as if the wrong switch had been pulled, a green light comes on which projects the silhouettes, clear-cut and large, of the Characters, minus the* BOY *and the* LITTLE GIRL. *Seeing the silhouettes, the* DIRECTOR, *terrified, rushes from the stage. At the same time the light behind the backcloth goes out and the stage is again lit in nocturnal blue as before.*

Slowly, from the right side of the curtain, the SON *comes forward first, followed by the* MOTHER *with her arms stretched out toward him; then from the left side, the* FATHER. *They stop in the middle of the stage and stay there as if in a trance. Last of all from the right, the* STEPDAUGHTER *comes out and runs toward the two stairways. She stops on the first step, to look for a moment at the other three, and then breaks into a harsh laugh before throwing herself down the steps; she runs down the aisle between the rows of seats; she stops one more time and again laughs, looking at the three who are still onstage; she disappears from the auditorium, and from the lobby her laughter is still heard. Shortly thereafter the curtain falls.*]

LANGSTON HUGHES

1902–1967

LANGSTON Hughes, who made his name as a writer during the Harlem Renaissance of the 1920s, is widely considered one of the leading African American literary figures of the twentieth century. The author of novels, short stories, autobiographies, nonfiction, screenplays, and translations, he is best known for his poetry, which expressed the aspirations and painful realities of African American life in a language that drew on the rhythms of jazz, the blues, and African American vernacular. Perhaps because of his fame as a poet, Hughes's importance as a dramatist has, until recently, been overlooked. But between 1920 and his death in 1967, Hughes wrote nearly seventy plays for theater, radio, and television; pageants; musicals; and operas. The Broadway version of his play *Mulatto* (1935) ran for more performances than any previous play by an African American playwright. Arguably, no African American dramatist worked more deliberately—and across a wider range of theatrical forms and genres—to explore the social, psychological, and cultural experience of twentieth-century African Americans.

Like the Harlem Renaissance itself, Langston Hughes's early life was shaped by a variety of forces: the Jim Crow legal and social practices of a United States that still practiced racial segregation, a demographic shift that brought tens of thousands of black Americans to northern cities in the early and mid-twentieth century, and the international sensibility that characterized modernism as a cultural movement. Hughes was born on February 1, 1902, in Joplin, Missouri. His childhood was marked by frequent moves and family instability. His father, James, who could not take the Oklahoma bar exam because he was black, abandoned the family when Hughes was five and moved to Mexico, where his race did not prevent him from practicing law. Hughes lived for much of his childhood with his maternal grandmother in Lawrence, Kansas; after she died in 1915, he joined his mother, who had remarried, and they eventually settled in Cleveland. At an integrated high school there he was named editor of the yearbook and class poet during his senior year.

Upon graduating from high school, Hughes spent a year with his father in Mexico, and during that time he made plans to attend Columbia University. In September 1921, he arrived in New York. That year, his poems appeared in two periodicals of the National Association for the Advancement of Colored People (NAACP)—*The Brownie's Book*, a magazine for children, and *The Crisis*, the organization's chief publication. One of these poems, "The Negro Speaks of Rivers," was to become one of the most anthologized of all twentieth-century American poems. Hughes enrolled as a freshman at Columbia but dropped out after a year in order to support himself and to take greater advantage of the life and culture that surrounded him in Harlem. After working at a variety of jobs, he determined to see the world by sea. Long fascinated by the idea of Africa as an ancestral home, in 1923 he embarked on a freighter headed to the West Coast of Africa. He visited a number of ports from Senegal to Angola, and then spent ten months living and working in Paris. Back in the United States and with his reputation growing as one of the leading young African American writers, he published his first collection of poems (*The Weary Blues* [1926]); earned a bachelor's degree from Lincoln University, a historically black college in Pennsylvania; and grew close to such leading figures of the Harlem Renaissance as Countee Cullen, Wallace Thurman, and Zora Neale Hurston. But while Harlem would remain his spiritual and physical home until his death, he never abandoned the wandering life that he had known since childhood. Beginning in the early 1930s he traveled to Cuba, Haiti, the Soviet Union (where he lived for a year), China, Japan, and Mexico.

The Harlem that Hughes embraced in the 1920s was the center of a growing social, economic, political, and cultural self-consciousness on the part of black America. As its population rose from 50,000 to 300,000 in the years 1914–30, Harlem became the symbol of the "New Negro Renaissance," as it was often called. Books were written by and about African Americans, the politics of black nationalism were debated in an emerging black press, and a vogue for things "Negro" was evident in the popularity of jazz, such dances as the Charleston, *Shuffle Along* (1921) and other musicals, and the careers of such entertainers as Josephine Baker and Paul Robeson. Later scholars have debated the nature and scope of the Harlem Renaissance; as some have pointed out, a number of its participants lived outside New York; the emergence of a black self-consciousness was evident before the end of World War I and continued well after the Depression; and the prominence of its activities and personalities did not alter the fact that (in Hughes's own words) "[t]he ordinary Negroes hadn't heard of the Negro Renaissance. And if they had, it hadn't raised their wages any." That said, in the years 1910–40 black writers, thinkers, and artists enjoyed unprecedented opportunities and a cultural visibility that African Americans have only recently surpassed.

Drama and the theater played an important part in the Harlem Renaissance. Faced with the popularity of "black" plays by white playwrights (most importantly, Ridgely Torrence's *Three Plays for a Negro Theater* [1917] and EUGENE O'NEILL's *The Emperor Jones* [1920]) and the enormous success of *Shuffle Along* (written by African Americans but with a cartoonist plot that relied on racial stereotypes), black cultural figures called for a drama grounded in the experiences of African Americans themselves. In 1916, W. E. B. Du Bois predicted "the slow growth of a new folk drama built around the actual experience of Negro American life." And in 1924 he wrote: "No greater mine of dramatic material ever lay ready for the great artist's hands than the situation of men of Negro blood in modern America." During the 1920s, the NAACP instituted a commission on drama, the periodicals *Crisis* and *Opportunity* (published by the Urban League) offered awards for playwriting, and the first anthologies of plays by African American writers appeared in the 1920s and 1930s, collecting the works of such dramatists as Angelina Weld Grimké, Willis Richardson, Theophilus Lewis, and Georgia Douglas Johnson. In keeping with Du Bois's dictum that a "real Negro theater" should be "in a Negro neighborhood near the mass of ordinary Negro people," a number of black theater groups—with Du Bois's own Krigwa Players prominent among them—were established between 1920 and 1930.

Hughes's first attempt at playwriting was a short children's play titled *The Gold Piece,* which was published in 1921. His next attempt—*Mulatto: A Tragedy of the Deep South,* written in the summer of 1930—would establish his reputation in the theater. An exploration of the theme of the tragic mulatto, or person of mixed-race ancestry, *Mulatto* takes place on a Georgia plantation whose white owner has had several children with his black housekeeper, who has been his mistress for thirty years. In defiance of the arrangements that his parents have made in order to live as a family while maintaining the South's racial hierarchies, Robert, the youngest of these children, asserts his right to public recognition as his father's son. In the end, Robert kills his father during a violent struggle, takes his life to avoid a mob seeking his death, and leaves his mother to question the racial contradictions that have defined her life. A production of *Mulatto* opened in 1935 on Broadway, where it ran for more than a year before touring the country for two additional seasons, but the play was altered by its producer, who made its plot even more sensationalistic by adding an attempted rape scene and introducing other changes.

In this and other plays Hughes explored a variety of dramatic styles and genres. A great deal of politically and socially engaged drama was produced in the 1930s, and Hughes wrote explicitly political plays about such issues as a farmworkers' strike in California and the notorious case of the "Scottsboro Boys," the 1931 trial in Alabama of nine black youths falsely accused of rape. But despite his interests in agitprop theater, his talents as a playwright led him more frequently toward a tradition of folk realism. In 1930 Hughes collaborated with Zora Neale Hurston on *Mule Bone: A Comedy of Negro Life*, which employed folk material that Hurston had collected (because the two quarreled over authorship, *Mule Bone* was not produced until 1991). Hughes's first urban comedy, *Little Ham* (1936), features Hamlet Jones, a diminutive shoe shiner and lady's man in late 1920s Harlem, and a cast of other vividly drawn characters. *Simply Heavenly* (1957), which is also set in Harlem, showcases Jesse B. Semple ("Simple"), a humorous character first introduced by Hughes in a popular series of sketches that began appearing in the *Chicago Defender* in 1943. Other plays revealed Hughes's interest in the role of music in black society and culture. *Tambourines to Glory* (1963), for instance—a "folk ballad in stage form"—incorporates the rhythms of gospel hymns and spirituals in its tale of duplicity and goodness within a storefront church.

None of Hughes's plays is richer in its mix of genres and tones than ***SOUL GONE HOME***, a one-act "tragi-comedy" that Hughes wrote in January 1936 for the Gilpin Players of Cleveland. This dramatized confrontation between a mother and her dead son was not performed then, however, perhaps (as Hughes's biographer Faith Berry speculates) because Hughes's own mother was ill with cancer and would recognize the play's unresolved mother-son conflict. *Soul Gone Home* was published in the July 1937 issue of *One Act Play* magazine, has been performed a number of times since then, and was produced as an opera by Ulysses Kay in 1954. Scholars and critics have been alternately bewildered and intrigued by this brief play, which mixes naturalism and surrealism, comedy and the tragic, in the sardonic darkness of Hughes's urban fantasy.

The title *Soul Gone Home* evokes the lyrical emotionalism of a gospel hymn, but the play itself refuses such sentimentality. The play opens in a "bare, ugly, dirty" tenement room in an unnamed northern city, where a Mother kneels weeping beside

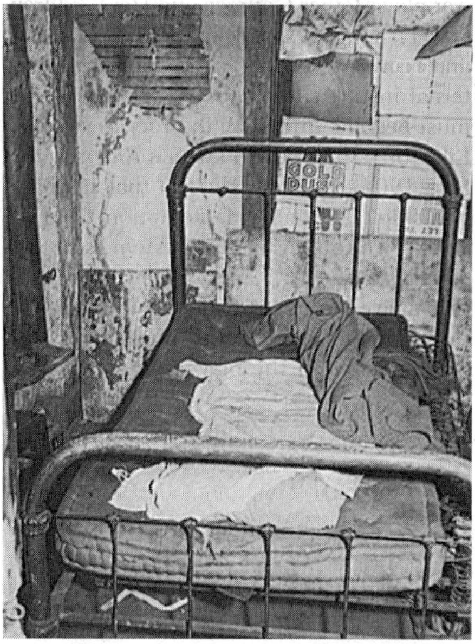

"Room in rooming house for negroes. Chicago, Illinois" (1941). Photo by Russell Lee.

the body of her Son lying on a cot. The Mother's grief is simulated, Hughes's directions indicate, and the action that follows deepens this discrepancy between the ideal of the sorrowing mother and the realities of family relationships in this harsh urban setting. When Ronnie, her son, rises from the dead, he charges her with neglect: "You been a hell of a mama!" Having seen his life for what it was during his brief stay in the spirit world, Ronnie accuses his mother, who earns her living as a prostitute, of letting him grow up in the streets, putting him to work selling newspapers as soon as he could walk, and contributing to the tuberculosis that killed him by failing to feed him properly. For her part, his mother accuses him of ingratitude, of causing her pain at birth, and of failing to earn his keep. Like his, her speech is distinguished by its darkly comic streetwise vernacular: "Well, damn your hide, you ain't even decent dead." But while *Soul Gone Home* portrays an intimate landscape of incrimination and failure, its condemnation is directed toward a racially unjust society that forces the black urban poor to pit love against survival. Even Ronnie must acknowledge that his mother's claim not to have enough money to buy him milk and eggs was valid. Like BERTOLT BRECHT's antiwar play *Mother Courage and Her Children* (1941), Hughes's play dramatizes a social and economic system in which normal maternal instincts are a luxury for those who must become unfeeling in order to survive. Like JOHN MILLINGTON SYNGE's *Riders to the Sea* (1904), it shows the toll that material hardship takes on human emotion.

The white face of this system is represented by the two ambulance attendants who arrive in the play's closing moments to take Ronnie's body to the undertaker. For the first time in the play, mother and son act in unison. When the men enter the room, they are met by the spectacle of a grieving mother weeping "hysterically." As it was in the play's opening moments, the scene of grief is a performance, this time for a white America that is denied access to the lives of those it marginalizes. Like the country beyond it, the tenement room is a theater with forestages and backstages, and its inhabitants are actors to their outside audience. The final image of *Soul Gone Home* is of the Mother, now alone, powdering (or whitening) her face in a mirror in order to attract that evening's customers. In a play so deeply engaged with questions of simulation and role-playing, race may be the most pervasive performance of all.

Hughes stressed on several occasions that *Soul Gone Home* should be performed with attention to its comedy. In reference to the operatic version of the play he wrote: "[I]t is NOT a heavy tragic sentimental play. . . . There should be as many laughs as possible in the way the SON's part is written and played—otherwise the tragi-comedy will not come through, and it will be merely an over sentimental and unpleasantly grim piece." He added: "[B]oth of [the characters] are hard-boiled marginal people, slum-shocked products of the rip tides of life." By playing sentimentality against itself and bringing humor to such painful subjects, Hughes allows the play's ironies and outrages to be experienced in jarring, unsettling ways. And by crossing the boundaries separating realism from nonrealistic dramatic modes, he incorporates in social commentary the surreal, the self-consciously theatrical, and the macabre. It is a short distance from *Soul Gone Home* to the more recent plays of Amiri Baraka, AUGUST WILSON, and SUZAN-LORI PARKS. S.G.

Soul Gone Home

CHARACTERS

THE MOTHER
THE SON
TWO MEN

Night.

[*A tenement room, bare, ugly, dirty. An unshaded electric-light bulb. In the middle of the room a cot on which the body of a* NEGRO YOUTH *is lying. His hands are folded across his chest. There are pennies on his eyes.*[1] *He is a soul gone home.*

As the curtain rises, his MOTHER, *a large, middle-aged woman in a red sweater, kneels weeping beside the cot, loudly simulating grief.*]

MOTHER Oh, Gawd! Oh, Lawd! Why did you take my son from me? Oh, Gawd, why did you do it? He was all I had! Oh, Lawd, what am I gonna do? [*Looking at the dead boy and stroking his head*] Oh, son! Oh, Ronnie! Oh, my boy, speak to me! Ronnie, say something to me! Son, why don't you talk to your mother? Can't you see she's bowed down in sorrow? Son, speak to me, just a word! Come back from the spirit-world and speak to me! Ronnie, come back from the dead and speak to your mother!

SON [*lying there dead as a doornail. Speaking loudly*] I wish I wasn't dead, so I *could* speak to you. You been a hell of a mama!

MOTHER [*falling back from the cot in astonishment, but still on her knees*] Ronnie! Ronnie! What's that you say? What you sayin' to your mother? [*Wild-eyed*] Is you done opened your mouth and spoke to me?

SON I said you a hell of a mama!

MOTHER [*rising suddenly and backing away, screaming loudly*] Awo-ooo-o! Ronnie, that ain't you talkin'!

SON Yes, it is me talkin', too! I say you been a no-good mama.

MOTHER What for you talkin' to me like that, Ronnie? You ain't never said nothin' like that to me before.

SON I know it, but I'm dead now—and I can say what I want to say. [*Stirring*] You done called on me to talk, ain't you? Lemme take these pennies off my eyes so I can see. [*He takes the coins off his eyes, throws them across the room, and sits up in bed. He is a very dark boy in a torn white shirt. He looks hard at his mother.*] Mama, you know you ain't done me right.

MOTHER What you mean, I ain't done you right? [*She is rooted in horror.*] What you mean, huh?

SON You know what I mean.

1. In the 18th and 19th centuries, African Americans often put coins on the eyes of the dead to keep them closed and, in accordance with West African folk tradition, provide the deceased with money to pay for the journey to the spirit world.

MOTHER No, I don't neither. [*Trembling violently*] What you mean comin' back to haunt your poor old mother? Ronnie, what does you mean?

SON [*leaning forward*] I'll tell you just what I mean! You been a bad mother to me.

MOTHER Shame! Shame! Shame, talkin' to your mama that away. Damn it! Shame! I'll slap your face. [*She starts toward him, but he rolls his big white eyes at her, and she backs away.*] Me, what borned you! Me, what suffered the pains o' death to bring you into this world! Me, what raised you up, what washed your dirty didies.[2] [*Sorrowfully*] And now I'm left here mighty nigh prostrate 'cause you gone from me! Ronnie, what you mean talkin' to *me* like that—what brought you into this world?

SON You never did feed me good, that's what I mean! Who wants to come into the world hongry, and go out the same way?

MOTHER What you mean hongry? When I had money, ain't I fed you?

SON [*Sullenly*] Most of the time you ain't had no money.

MOTHER 'Twarn't my fault then.

SON 'Twarnt *my* fault then.

MOTHER [*defensively*] You always was so weak and sickly, you couldn't earn nothin' sellin' papers.

SON I know it.

MOTHER You never was no use to me.

SON So you just lemme grow up in the street, and I ain't had no manners nor morals, neither.

MOTHER Manners and morals? Ronnie, where'd you learn all them big words?

SON I learnt 'em just now in the spirit-world.

MOTHER [*coming nearer*] But you ain't been dead no more'n an hour.

SON That's long enough to learn a lot.

MOTHER Well, what else did you find out?

SON I found out you was a hell of a mama puttin' me out in the cold to sell papers soon as I could even walk.

MOTHER What? You little liar!

SON If I'm lyin', I'm dyin'! And lettin' me grow up all bowlegged and stunted from undernourishment.

MOTHER Under-nurse-mint?

SON Undernourishment. You heard what the doctor said last week?

MOTHER Naw, what'd he say?

SON He said I was dyin' o' undernourishment, that's what he said. He said I had TB 'cause I didn't have enough to eat never when I were a child. And he said I couldn't get well, nohow eating nothin' but beans ever since I been sick. Said I needed milk and eggs. And you said you ain't got no money for milk and eggs, which I know you ain't. [*Gently*] We never had no money, mama, not even since you took up hustlin' on the streets.

MOTHER Son, money ain't everything.

SON Naw, but when you got TB you have to have milk and eggs.

MOTHER [*advancing sentimentally*] Anyhow, I love you, Ronnie!

SON [*rudely*] Sure you love me—but here I am dead.

MOTHER [*angrily*] Well, damn your hide, you ain't even decent dead. If you was, you wouldn't be sittin' there jawin' at your mother when she's sheddin' every tear she's got for you tonight.

2. Diapers.

SON First time you ever did cry for me, far as I know.

MOTHER Tain't! You's a liar! I cried when I borned you—you was such a big child—ten pounds.

SON Then *I* did the cryin' after that, I reckon.

MOTHER [*proudly*] Sure, I could of let you die, but I didn't. Naw, I kept you with me—off and on. And I lost the chance to marry many a good man, too—if it weren't for you. No man wants to take care o' nobody else's child. [*Self-pityingly*] You been a burden to me, Randolph.

SON [*angrily*] What did you have me for then, in the first place?

MOTHER How could I help havin' you, you little bastard? Your father ruint me—and you's the result. And I been worried with you for sixteen years. [*Disgustedly*] Now, just when you get big enough to work and do me some good, you have to go and die.

SON I sure am dead!

MOTHER But you ain't decent dead! Here you come back to haunt your poor old mama, and spoil her cryin' spell, and spoil the mournin'. [*There is the noise of an ambulance gong outside. The* MOTHER *goes to the window and looks down into the street. Turns to* SON.] Ronnie, lay down quick! Here comes the city's ambulance to take you to the undertaker's. Don't let them white men see you dead, sitting up here quarrelin' with your mother. Lay down and fold your hands back like I had 'em.

SON [*passing his hand across his head*] All right, but gimme that comb yonder and my stocking cap. I don't want to go out of here with my hair standin' straight up in front, even if I is dead. [*The* MOTHER *hands him a comb and his stocking cap. The* SON *combs his hair and puts the cap on. Noise of men coming up the stairs.*]

MOTHER Hurry up, Ronnie, they'll be here in no time.

SON Aw, they got another flight to come yet. Don't rush me, ma!

MOTHER Yes, but I got to put these pennies back on your eyes, boy! [*She searches in a corner for the coins as her* SON *lies down and folds his hands, stiff in death. She finds the coins and puts them nervously on his eyes, watching the door meanwhile. A knock.*] Come in.

[*Enter two* MEN *in the white coats of city health employees.*]

MAN Somebody sent for us to get the body of Ronnie Bailey? Third floor, apartment five.

MOTHER Yes, sir, here he is! [*Weeping loudly*] He's my boy! Oh, Lawd, he's done left me! Oh, Lawdy, he's done gone home! His soul's gone home! Oh, what am I gonna do? Mister! Mister! Mister, the Lawd's done took him home! [*As the* MEN *unfold the stretchers, she continues to weep hysterically. They place the boy's thin body on the stretchers and cover it with a rubber cloth. Each man takes his end of the stretchers. Silently, they walk out the door as the* MOTHER *wails.*] Oh, my son! Oh, my boy! Come back, come back, come back! Ronnie, come back! [*One loud scream as the door closes*] Awo-ooo-o!

[*As the footsteps of the men die down on the stairs, the* MOTHER *becomes suddenly quiet. She goes to a broken mirror and begins to rouge and powder her face. In the street the ambulance gong sounds fainter and fainter in the distance. The* MOTHER *takes down an old fur coat from a nail and puts it on. Before she leaves, she smooths back the quilts on the cot from which the dead boy has been removed. She looks into the mirror again, and once more whitens her face with powder. She dons a red hat. From a handbag she takes a cigarette, lights it, and walks slowly out the door. At the door she switches off the light. The hallway is dimly illuminated. She turns before closing the door, looks back into the room, and speaks.*]

MOTHER Tomorrow, Ronnie, I'll buy you some flowers—if I can pick up a dollar tonight. You was a hell of a no-good son, I swear!

Curtain.

FEDERICO GARCÍA LORCA

1898–1936

When Federico García Lorca was arrested and executed by fascist militia at the beginning of the Spanish Civil War, he was already the best-known Spanish poet and dramatist of his generation. During the long years of Generalissimo Franco's rule, which lasted until 1975, the memory and work of García Lorca were systematically suppressed in Spain even as he achieved worldwide fame for his poetry and his three greatest tragedies, *The Blood Wedding* (1933), *Yerma* (1934), and *THE HOUSE OF BERNARDA ALBA* (written 1936; produced 1945). Like other modern dramatists, such as the Irish JOHN MILLINGTON SYNGE, the Italian LUIGI PIRANDELLO, and the West Indian DEREK WALCOTT, García Lorca used remote, rural settings for his particular brand of modern tragedy. Like them, he transformed colloquial dialects into an intensely poetic language, creating plays of unusual resonance and beauty. But García Lorca did not excel only at tragedy. Inspired by an early interest in puppet theater, he composed several plays and curtain-raisers in the crude form of the Punch-and-Judy show, as well as farces and other pieces of popular entertainment. He worked, throughout his short life, on a visionary piece of metatheater, which was not performed until the 1980s. And he became well-known as the author of several collections of poetry, some traditional and others daring and modernist. Despite this wide-ranging oeuvre, García Lorca will be remembered as an author of modern tragedies whose own life made him a martyr in the fight against fascism.

García Lorca was born into a small village in a relatively remote region of Andalusia, in southern Spain; his father, a farmer and landowner, had managed to amass a small fortune, enabling him to support García Lorca during his studies and early career as a writer. After undertaking his first poetic and dramatic experiments as a student in Granada, García Lorca moved to Madrid to study law. There he encountered the leading Spanish artists of his generation, including the surrealist filmmaker Luis Buñuel, the composer Manuel de Falla, and the painter Salvador Dalí. His friendship with the latter two led to artistic collaborations and exchanges. With Falla, he organized an arts festival, during which Falla performed the 1927 Spanish premiere of Igor Stravinsky's *The Soldier's Tale* (1918), and Dalí created the sets for García Lorca's historical play *Mariana Pineda* (1927). The collaborative experimental films made by Dalí and Buñuel in the late 1920s (the most famous of which is *Un Chien Andalou* [1928]) also left a lasting impact on García Lorca; he later wrote several short film scripts, including *Trip to the Moon* (written ca.

1930), as well as an homage to the American silent film star Buster Keaton in the form of a short dialogue. García Lorca was deeply involved with various experimental avant-garde movements, especially surrealism—he was a contributor to the Spanish surrealist journal *Gallo*—and he was on his way to becoming a leading experimental artist himself.

At the same time, however, García Lorca had a serious interest in an entirely different type of art: folklore. An accomplished pianist, he became familiar with the flamenco tradition by taking some guitar lessons from an aunt. His most successful book of poetry was his collection *Gypsy Ballads* (1928), and he drew on a gypsy form popular in his home region, *conte jondo* (deep song), in his *Poem of the Deep Song* (1931). Most importantly, he sought to revive the puppet theater. García Lorca was intrigued by the unapologetically colloquial and rough language, the sharply drawn characters, and the economy of action characteristic of this popular art form. In this fascination, he was not alone. Many modern dramatists, from Maurice Maeterlinck and William Butler Yeats to E. G. Craig and ALFRED JARRY, turned to the puppet theater for inspiration; in García Lorca's own circle, Falla had composed several operas involving puppet theater, in particular his acclaimed *Master Peter's Puppet Show* (1923). García Lorca's main work for the puppet theater, often revised and adapted to different occasions, was the *Tragicomedy of Don Cristóbal and Donna Rosita* (1921–22), which, like Jarry's *Ubu the King* (1896), became an important example of the avant-garde mixture of crude puppet theater and modern drama. But García Lorca also wrote more traditional, short pieces of puppet theater—for example, *The Girl Who Waters the Basil and the Very Inquisitive Prince Cristobical* (1923), a play aimed mainly at children. Although not written explicitly for the puppet theater, several of García Lorca's comical farces—*The Shoemaker's Prodigious Wife* (1930) and *The Love of Don Perlimpín and Belisa in Her Garden* (1933) among them—are clearly influenced by the tradition of the Punch-and-Judy show.

Before completing *The Shoemaker's Prodigious Wife,* García Lorca took a lengthy trip to the United States, which included a semester studying at Columbia University. The most important product of his time in New York was his collection *A Poet in New York* (written 1930; published 1940), a widely read and translated homage to the city. At the same time, García Lorca started to work on his most private work, ironically titled *The Public* (written in 1930), a play depicting the homosexuality that he had to hide throughout his life. Like many writers with a secret, García Lorca had a public side and a private side, and many of his works, especially his tragedies, revolve around the differences between the two spheres.

Upon his return to Spain, García Lorca also returned to working actively in the theater. In 1931 he started the Barraca, a traveling student theater troupe that performed both the classics and several of García Lorca's own plays. With this group, García Lorca went to smaller towns and villages, trying to introduce a new theatrical culture to remote places. This enterprise was part of the spirit of progress and reform that took hold in Spain after the election of the country's first democratic-republican government in 1931. But Spanish traditionalists and defenders of established interests—monarchists, the church, landowners, and a large portion of the military—fought against the reforms, and were joined by a new fascist party, the Falange. As the struggle between the republican Loyalists and the conservative Nationalists grew, García Lorca was among the many Spaniards who became more politically engaged. His political awakening and his support for the republican cause would soon have tragic consequences, forcing García Lorca into hiding and leading to his execution by a Nationalist death squad.

During the last years of his life García Lorca wrote the three tragedies for which he is mainly known today: *The Blood Wedding, Yerma,* and *The House of Bernarda Alba.* All are set in the rural parts of Spain that García Lorca knew from his own childhood—a world of poverty, restrictive Catholic morality, and submerged passions. The first, *The Blood Wedding,* a drama partly in prose and partly in verse, is most fully attuned to the poetic possibilities of the dialect of Andalusia. Like García Lorca's other tragedies, *The Blood Wedding* revolves around the strict moral codes and customs governing life in this world: a bride lets herself be abducted by a former admirer whom she had been forced to reject because of his poverty—with tragic consequences. The second tragedy, *Yerma,* approaches the enforced marriage of convenience from another angle. Yerma, whose name echoes the Spanish word for infertility, is interested in nothing but having children, a desire not shared by her husband. The tension between them is followed by the playwright until its climax, when in desperation she strangles her husband. The strictures of the honor code, blood revenge, and marriage expectations trap these characters into lives from which they can escape only through violence and death.

The abduction of *The Blood Wedding* and the tragedy of infertility in *Yerma* are brought to a perfect union in García Lorca's last play and masterpiece: *The House of Bernarda Alba.* Here, adherence to the strictest morality, in particular the moral codes governing women and female sexuality, is ensured not by men but by a mother, Bernarda Alba, who controls her five marriageable daughters (as well as her own mother) as best she can. The oldest, the thirty-nine-year-old Angustias, is from Bernarda's first marriage and has inherited a small fortune from her deceased father. All Bernarda wants is to match Angustias with a suitable husband, and she seems to have found a halfway acceptable candidate in the much younger Pepe. But all too quickly she loses control when Pepe falls in love with her youngest daughter, Adela. When the two are discovered, the orderly world of the House of Bernarda Alba comes crashing down on its inhabitants with sudden force.

A drawing by García Lorca to illustrate one of his poems.

Bernarda's desire for control, which dominates the entire play, is partially motivated by misguided class arrogance: since the Albas are the richest family in the village, appearances have to be kept up—and consequently no one is good enough to marry the daughters. When it is suggested to Bernarda that she could have moved to a larger village, where she would no longer have the burden of maintaining the finest establishment, Bernarda dismisses this thought, thus showing that her aims of upholding her class position and controlling her daughters are inextricably intertwined. Bernarda has so fully internalized the rules she imposes on her house—the laws of propriety, position, and social expectations—that she can no longer see their damaging effects. This damage is particularly severe for the younger daughters, but in the end all suffer: marriage and having children are the only purposes for women in this world, without which they shrivel and waste away. Like García Lorca's other plays, *The House of Bernarda Alba* takes a tragic turn precisely at the moment when these ends of matrimony and motherhood cannot be achieved. This repeated pattern suggests a critical attitude on the part of the author, who as a bohemian and homosexual certainly did not subscribe to the view of life presented by Bernarda and the other characters in his plays. García Lorca's own experience of having to hide his sexuality from a hostile world made him all too familiar with the repressive force of society that is brought to bear on these characters. At the same time, his play does not explicitly denounce the traditional moral system that informs it. Rather, *The House of Bernarda Alba* shows how the obsessive pursuit of this conservative morality invariably has tragic consequences.

Bernarda seeks to control not just whom her daughters marry but everything about their existence, down to their smallest movements and gestures. She insists, for example, on a complete separation between men and women, a separation much stricter than is customary in her community. The play opens with a funeral scene; because the men are kept outdoors, we see only the women on the stage. Indeed, the play's cast is composed exclusively of women. All their thoughts revolve around men, focusing on how much they would like to be married and how to achieve that goal. Thus, through their absence, the men dominate the play. Moreover, the play is confined entirely to the inside of the house. One is reminded here of other modern plays that emphasize even more strongly the entrapment of their protagonists in enclosed spaces: for example, Jean-Paul Sartre's *No Exit* (1944) and SAMUEL BECKETT's *Endgame* (1957). In these plays, the interior space of the house and the interior space of the theater fuse, and that identity gives them their unique claustrophobic power. Such confinement also imposes on these plays a great economy of means—a simplicity that is the hallmark of much modernist theater, which García Lorca here anticipates.

Enclosure and the absence of men also determine the structure of the play, as the women inside the house are obsessed with trying to break through to the outside or, alternatively, to lure someone from the outside in. The one character who moves freely between the outside and inside is the old maid, La Poncia. Bernarda sends her out to inquire about daily events and, more importantly, about the honor and standing of the Alba family. Even though Poncia is only a maid, her mobility gives her a position of power, but she does not use that power to resist Bernarda's strict regime: she is as interested as her mistress in upholding the honor of the house. The other somewhat anomalous figure in the household, and another victim of Bernarda's regime, is her mother. At the beginning of the play, María Josefa is locked into a closet, and her unending efforts to escape her daughter's control set the scene for the rebellion of Bernarda's own daughters. They constantly spy through cracks in the door or various windows in order to have some relation with the outside world;

García Lorca's sketch for a stage backdrop.

they exhibit themselves in the windows, to attract the attention of passersby; they jealously watch one another for signs of successful communication. All this we surmise only indirectly, as the daughters fight among themselves and with their mother and their maid. We are as enclosed and in the dark as Bernarda herself, who tries to understand what is going on at each moment and who desperately holds on to the vestiges of her power.

Based apparently on childhood neighbors of García Lorca, *The House of Bernarda Alba* is "intended as a photographic document." Its language is markedly different from that of his other tragedies and indeed all his previous plays. With *The House of Barnarda Alba*, García Lorca inaugurates a new style—more economical, more functional, and much less prone to lyrical interludes, songs, flights of fancy, metaphors, and rhetorical embellishments. Nor does the play seek to render the dialect of peasants. Its language, like the lives of the characters, is tightly controlled, in this regard making good its claim of photographic realism. At the same time, however, the play is subtitled "A Drama about Women in the Villages of Spain," underscoring that it has much larger scope and significance than a single photo-realist snapshot of one particular family. It is a play that aspires to tell a more general truth about an entire world.

We can only speculate about the contribution to modern drama that García Lorca could have made in this new mode had his life not been cut short, at the age of thirty-eight, by fascist violence. But even the works he was able to write are remarkable documents of a modernism that is rooted in local culture and tradition. Somehow, García Lorca was able to combine an unusual number of influences and styles. From the folk music of Andalusia and its popular puppet theater to his collaborations with avant-garde artists such as Falla and Dalí, García Lorca forged a modernist drama that sought not to overthrow tradition but instead to continue it. Given this sensibility, it is perhaps not surprising that he met with his greatest success in the most traditional art form of them all: tragedy. While other writers of modern tragedy felt that they had to battle against the long history of that form since Greek antiquity, García Lorca welcomed this legacy, which he enriched by embedding it in the rural traditions he knew best. The result was an art of tragedy that is rooted in a specific place but that also speaks eloquently to audiences around the world.

M.P.

The House of Bernarda Alba
A Drama about Women in the Villages of Spain[1]

CHARACTERS

BERNARDA (age: 60)
MARÍA JOSEFA, Bernarda's mother (age: 80)
ANGUSTIAS, Bernarda's daughter (age: 39)
MAGDALENA, Bernarda's daughter (age: 30)
AMELIA, Bernarda's daughter (age: 27)
MARTIRIO, Bernarda's daughter (age: 24)
ADELA, Bernarda's daughter (age: 20)
A SERVANT (age: 50)
LA PONCIA, a maid (age: 60)
PRUDENCIA (age: 50)
A BEGGAR WOMAN
Women in mourning

The writer states that these Three Acts are intended as a photographic document.

Act 1

[SCENE: *A very white room in* BERNARDA ALBA'S *house. The walls are white. There are arched doorways white jute curtains tied back with tassels and ruffles. Wicker chairs. On the walls, pictures of unlikely landscapes full of nymphs or legendary kings.*

It is summer. A great brooding silence fills the stage. It is empty when the curtain rises. Bells can be heard tolling outside.]

FIRST SERVANT [*entering*] The tolling of those bells hits me right between the eyes.

PONCIA [*she enters, eating bread and sausage*] More than two hours of mumbo jumbo. Priests are here from all the towns. The church looks beautiful. At the first responsory for the dead,[2] Magdalena fainted.

FIRST SERVANT She's the one who's left most alone.

PONCIA She's the only one who loved her father. Ay! Thank God we're alone for a little. I came over to eat.

FIRST SERVANT If Bernarda sees you . . . !

PONCIA She's not eating today so she'd just as soon we'd all die of hunger! Domineering old tyrant! But she'll be fooled! I opened the sausage crock.

FIRST SERVANT [*with an anxious sadness*] Couldn't you give me some for my little girl, Poncia?

PONCIA Go ahead! And take a fistful of peas too. She won't know the difference today.

VOICE [*within*] Bernarda!

PONCIA There's the grandmother! Isn't she locked up tight?

FIRST SERVANT Two turns of the key.

PONCIA You'd better put the cross-bar up too. She's got the fingers of a lockpicker!

1. Translated by James Graham-Luján and Richard L. O'Connell.

2. A section of the Roman Catholic memorial service.

VOICE [*within*] Bernarda!

PONCIA [*shouting*] She's coming! [*To the* SERVANT] Clean everything up good. If Bernarda doesn't find things shining, she'll pull out the few hairs I have left.

SERVANT What a woman!

PONCIA Tyrant over everyone around her. She's perfectly capable of sitting on your heart and watching you die for a whole year without turning off that cold little smile she wears on her wicked face. Scrub, scrub those dishes!

SERVANT I've got blood on my hands from so much polishing of everything.

PONCIA She's the cleanest, she's the decentest, she's the highest everything! A good rest her poor husband's earned!

[*The bells stop.*]

SERVANT Did all the relatives come?

PONCIA Just hers. His people hate her. They came to see him dead and make the sign of the cross over him; that's all.

SERVANT Are there enough chairs?

PONCIA More than enough. Let them sit on the floor. When Bernarda's father died people stopped coming under this roof. She doesn't want them to see her in her "domain." Curse her!

SERVANT She's been good to you.

PONCIA Thirty years washing her sheets. Thirty years eating her leftovers. Nights of watching when she had a cough. Whole days peeking through a crack in the shutters to spy on the neighbors and carry her the tale. Life without secrets one from the other. But in spite of that—curse her! May the "pain of the piercing nail"[3] strike her in the eyes.

SERVANT Poncia!

PONCIA But I'm a good watchdog! I bark when I'm told and bite beggars' heels when she sics me on 'em. My sons work in her fields—both of them already married, but one of these days I'll have enough.

SERVANT And then . . . ?

PONCIA Then I'll lock myself up in a room with her and spit in her face—a whole year. "Bernarda, here's for this, that and the other!" Till I leave her—just like a lizard the boys have squashed. For that's what she is—she and her whole family! Not that I envy her her life. Five girls are left her, five ugly daughters—not counting Angustias the eldest, by her first husband, who has money—the rest of them, plenty of eyelets to embroider, plenty of linen petticoats, but bread and grapes when it comes to inheritance.

SERVANT Well, *I'd* like to have what they've got!

PONCIA All we have is our hands and a hole in God's earth.

SERVANT And that's the only earth they'll ever leave to us—to us who have nothing!

PONCIA [*at the cupboard*] This glass has some specks.

SERVANT Neither soap nor rag will take them off.

[*The bells toll.*]

PONCIA The last prayer! I'm going over and listen. I certainly like the way

3. That is, one of the nails holding Jesus to the cross.

our priest sings. In the Pater Noster[4] his voice went up, and up—like a pitcher filling with water little by little. Of course, at the end his voice cracked, but it's glorious to hear it. No, there never was anybody like the old Sacristan[5]—Tronchapinos. At my mother's Mass, may she rest in peace, he sang. The walls shook—and when he said "Amen," it was as if a wolf had come into the church. [*Imitating him*] A-a-a-a-men! [*She starts coughing.*]

SERVANT Watch out—you'll strain your windpipe!

PONCIA I'd rather strain something else!

[*Goes out laughing.*]

[*The* SERVANT *scrubs. The bells toll.*]

SERVANT [*imitating the bells*] Dong, dong, dong. Dong, dong, dong. May God forgive him!

BEGGAR WOMAN [*at the door, with a little girl*] Blessèd be God!

SERVANT Dong, dong, dong. I hope he waits many years for us! Dong, dong, dong.

BEGGAR [*loudly, a little annoyed*] Blessèd be God!

SERVANT [*annoyed*] Forever and ever![6]

BEGGAR I came for the scraps.

[*The bells stop tolling.*]

SERVANT You can go right out the way you came in. Today's scraps are for me.

BEGGAR But you have somebody to take care of you—and my little girl and I are all alone!

SERVANT Dogs are alone too, and they live.

BEGGAR They always give them to me.

SERVANT Get out of here! Who let you in anyway? You've already tracked up the place.

[*The* BEGGAR WOMAN *and little girl leave. The* SERVANT *goes on scrubbing.*]

Floors finished with oil, cupboards, pedestals, iron beds—but us servants, we can suffer in silence—and live in mud huts with a plate and a spoon. I hope someday not a one will be left to tell it.

[*The bells sound again.*]

Yes, yes—ring away. Let them put you in a coffin with gold inlay and brocade to carry it on—you're no less dead than I'll be, so take what's coming to you, Antonio María Benavides—stiff in your broadcloth suit and your high boots—take what's coming to you! You'll never again lift my skirts behind the corral door!

[*From the rear door, two by two, women in mourning with large shawls and black skirts and fans, begin to enter. They come in slowly until the stage is full.*]

4. Our Father (Latin); that is, the Lord's Prayer, which begins "Our Father which art in heaven" (Matthew 6.9–13).

5. The church officer in charge of the sacristy, the room where vestments, sacred vessels, and valuable items are kept.

6. The formulaic responses given here and later echo the Roman Catholic ritual of burial.

SERVANT [*breaking into a wail*] Oh, Antonio María Benavides, now you'll never see these walls, nor break bread in this house again! I'm the one who loved you most of all your servants. [*Pulling her hair*] *Must* I live on after you've gone? Must I go on living?

[*The two hundred women finish coming in, and* BERNARDA *and her five daughters enter.* BERNARDA *leans on a cane.*]

BERNARDA [*to the* SERVANT] Silence!

SERVANT [*weeping*] Bernarda!

BERNARDA Less shrieking and more work. You should have had all this cleaner for the wake. Get out. This isn't your place.

[*The* SERVANT *goes off crying.*]

The poor are like animals—they seem to be made of different stuff.

FIRST WOMAN The poor feel their sorrows too.

BERNARDA But they forget them in front of a plateful of peas.

FIRST GIRL [*timidly*] Eating is necessary for living.

BERNARDA At your age one doesn't talk in front of older people.

WOMAN Be quiet, child.

BERNARDA I've never taken lessons from anyone. Sit down.

[*They sit down. Pause. Loudly.*]

Magdalena, don't cry. If you want to cry, get under your bed. Do you hear me?

SECOND WOMAN [*to* BERNARDA] Have you started to work the fields?

BERNARDA Yesterday.

THIRD WOMAN The sun comes down like lead.

FIRST WOMAN I haven't known heat like this for years.

[*Pause. They all fan themselves.*]

BERNARDA Is the lemonade ready?

PONCIA Yes, Bernarda.

[*She brings in a large tray full of little white jars which she distributes.*]

BERNARDA Give the men some.

PONCIA They're already drinking in the patio.

BERNARDA Let them get out the way they came in. I don't want them walking through here.

A GIRL [*to* ANGUSTIAS] Pepe el Romano was with the men during the service.

ANGUSTIAS There he was.

BERNARDA His mother was there. She saw his mother. Neither she nor I saw Pepe . . .

GIRL I thought . . .

BERNARDA The one who *was* there was Darajalí, the widower. Very close to your aunt. We all of us saw him.

SECOND WOMAN [*aside, in a low voice*] Wicked, worse than wicked woman!

THIRD WOMAN A tongue like a knife!

BERNARDA Women in church shouldn't look at any man but the priest—and him only because he wears skirts. To turn your head is to be looking for the warmth of corduroy.

FIRST WOMAN Sanctimonious old snake!

PONCIA [*between her teeth*] Itching for a man's warmth.

BERNARDA [*beating with her cane on the floor*] Blessèd be God!

ALL [*crossing themselves*] Forever blessèd and praised.

BERNARDA Rest in peace with holy company at your head.

ALL Rest in peace!

BERNARDA With the Angel Saint Michael, and his sword of justice.

ALL Rest in peace!

BERNARDA With the key that opens, and the hand that locks.

ALL Rest in peace!

BERNARDA With the most blessèd, and the little lights of the field.

ALL Rest in peace!

BERNARDA With our holy charity, and all souls on land and sea.

ALL Rest in peace!

BERNARDA Grant rest to your servant, Antonio María Benavides, and give him the crown of your blessèd glory.

ALL Amen.

BERNARDA [*she rises and chants*] Requiem aeternam dona eis domine.[7]

ALL [*standing and chanting in the Gregorian fashion*][8] Et lux perpetua luce ab eis.

[*They cross themselves.*]

FIRST WOMAN May you have health to pray for his soul.

[*They start filing out.*]

THIRD WOMAN You won't lack loaves of hot bread.

SECOND WOMAN Nor a roof for your daughters.

[*They are all filing in front of* BERNARDA *and going out.*]

[ANGUSTIAS *leaves by the door to the patio.*]

FOURTH WOMAN May you go on enjoying your wedding wheat.

PONCIA [*she enters, carrying a money bag*] From the men—this bag of money for Masses.[9]

BERNARDA Thank them—and let them have a glass of brandy.

GIRL [*to* MAGDALENA] Magdalena . . .

BERNARDA [*to* MAGDALENA, *who is starting to cry*] Sh-h-h-h!

[*She beats with her cane on the floor.*]

[*All the women have gone out.*]

BERNARDA [*to the women who have just left*] Go back to your houses and criticize everything you've seen! I hope it'll be many years before you pass under the archway of my door again.

PONCIA You've nothing to complain about. The whole town came.

BERNARDA Yes, to fill my house with the sweat from their wraps and the poison of their tongues.

AMELIA Mother, don't talk like that.

BERNARDA What other way is there to talk about this cursèd village with no river—this village full of wells where you drink water always fearful it's been poisoned?

7. Grant them eternal rest, Lord (Latin); the first words of the Requiem Mass. She is answered with the next line, "And let eternal light shine on them."

8. That is, like the antiphonal plain chant whose invention is credited to Saint Gregory I (ca. 540–604).

9. The money will be given to the church so that the priest will mention the dead man's name at Mass.

PONCIA Look what they've done to the floor!

BERNARDA As though a herd of goats had passed through.

[PONCIA *cleans the floor.*]

Adela, give me a fan.

ADELA Take this one.

[*She gives her a round fan with green and red flowers.*]

BERNARDA [*throwing the fan on the floor*] Is that the fan to give to a widow? Give me a black one and learn to respect your father's memory.

MARTIRIO Take mine.

BERNARDA And you?

MARTIRIO I'm not hot.

BERNARDA Well, look for another, because you'll need it. For the eight years of mourning, not a breath of air will get in this house from the street. We'll act as if we'd sealed up doors and windows with bricks. That's what happened in my father's house—and in my grandfather's house. Meantime, you can all start embroidering your hope-chest linens. I have twenty bolts of linen in the chest from which to cut sheets and coverlets. Magdalena can embroider them.

MAGDALENA It's all the same to me.

ADELA [*sourly*] If you don't want to embroider them—they can go without. That way yours will look better.

MAGDALENA Neither mine nor yours. I know I'm not going to marry. I'd rather carry sacks to the mill. Anything except sit here day after day in this dark room.

BERNARDA That's what a woman is for.

MAGDALENA Cursèd be all women.

BERNARDA In this house you'll do what I order. You can't run with the story to your father anymore. Needle and thread for women. Whiplash and mules for men. That's the way it has to be for people who have certain obligations.

[ADELA *goes out.*]

VOICE Bernarda! Let me out!

BERNARDA [*calling*] Let her out now!

[*The* FIRST SERVANT *enters.*]

FIRST SERVANT I had a hard time holding her. In spite of her eighty years, your mother's strong as an oak.

BERNARDA It runs in the family. My grandfather was the same way.

SERVANT Several times during the wake I had to cover her mouth with an empty sack because she wanted to shout out to you to give her dishwater to drink at least, and some dog meat, which is what she says you feed her.

MARTIRIO She's mean!

BERNARDA [*to* SERVANT] Let her get some fresh air in the patio.

SERVANT She took her rings and the amethyst earrings out of the box, put them on, and told me she wants to get married.

[*The daughters laugh.*]

BERNARDA Go with her and be careful she doesn't get near the well.

SERVANT You don't need to be afraid she'll jump in.

BERNARDA It's not that—but the neighbors can see her there from their windows.

[*The* SERVANT *leaves.*]

MARTIRIO We'll go change our clothes.

BERNARDA Yes, but don't take the kerchiefs from your heads.

[ADELA *enters.*]

And Angustias?

ADELA [*meaningfully*] I saw her looking out through the cracks of the back door. The men had just gone.

BERNARDA And you, what were *you* doing at the door?

ADELA I went there to see if the hens had laid.

BERNARDA But the men had already gone!

ADELA [*meaningfully*] A group of them were still standing outside.

BERNARDA [*furiously*] Angustias! Angustias!

ANGUSTIAS [*entering*] Did you want something?

BERNARDA For what—and at whom—were you looking?

ANGUSTIAS Nobody.

BERNARDA Is it decent for a woman of your class to be running after a man the day of her father's funeral? Answer me! Whom were you looking at? [*Pause*]

ANGUSTIAS I . . .

BERNARDA Yes, you!

ANGUSTIAS Nobody.

BERNARDA Soft! Honeytongue!

[*She strikes her.*]

PONCIA [*running to her*] Bernarda, calm down!

[*She holds her.* ANGUSTIAS *weeps.*]

BERNARDA Get out of here, all of you!

[*They all go out.*]

PONCIA She did it not realizing what she was doing—although it's bad, of course. It really disgusted me to see her sneak along to the patio. Then she stood at the window listening to the men's talk which, as usual, was not the sort one should listen to.

BERNARDA That's what they come to funerals for. [*With curiosity*] What were they talking about?

PONCIA They were talking about Paca la Roseta. Last night they tied her husband up in a stall, stuck her on a horse behind the saddle, and carried her away to the depths of the olive grove.

BERNARDA And what did she do?

PONCIA She? She was just as happy—they say her breasts were exposed and Maximiliano held on to her as if he were playing a guitar. Terrible!

BERNARDA And what happened?

PONCIA What had to happen. They came back almost at daybreak. Paca la Roseta with her hair loose and a wreath of flowers on her head.

BERNARDA She's the only bad woman we have in the village.

PONCIA Because she's not from here. She's from far away. And those who went with her are the sons of outsiders too. The men from here aren't up to a thing like that.

BERNARDA No, but they like to see it, and talk about it, and suck their fingers over it.

PONCIA They were saying a lot more things.

BERNARDA [*looking from side to side with a certain fear*] What things?

PONCIA I'm ashamed to talk about them.

BERNARDA And my daughter heard them?

PONCIA Of course!

BERNARDA That one takes after her aunts: white and mealymouthed and casting sheep's eyes at any little barber's compliment. Oh, what one has to go through and put up with so people will be decent and not too wild!

PONCIA It's just that your daughters are of an age when they ought to have husbands. Mighty little trouble they give you. Angustias must be much more than thirty now.

BERNARDA Exactly thirty-nine.

PONCIA Imagine. And she's never had a beau . . .

BERNARDA [*furiously*] None of them has ever had a beau and they've never needed one! They get along very well.

PONCIA I didn't mean to offend you.

BERNARDA For a hundred miles around there's no one good enough to come near them. The men in this town are not of their class. Do you want me to turn them over to the first shepherd?

PONCIA You should have moved to another town.

BERNARDA That's it. To sell them!

PONCIA No, Bernarda, to change . . . Of course, anyplace else, they'd be the poor ones.

BERNARDA Hold your tormenting tongue!

PONCIA One can't even talk to you. Do we, or do we not share secrets?

BERNARDA We do not. You're a servant and I pay you. Nothing more.

PONCIA But . . .

FIRST SERVANT [*entering*] Don Arturo's here. He's come to see about dividing the inheritance.

BERNARDA Let's go. [*To the* SERVANT] You start whitewashing the patio. [*To* LA PONCIA] And you start putting all the dead man's clothes away in the chest.

PONCIA We could give away some of the things.

BERNARDA Nothing—not a button even! Not even the cloth we covered his face with.

[*She goes out slowly, leaning on her cane. At the door she turns to look at the two servants. They go out. She leaves.*]

[AMELIA *and* MARTIRIO *enter.*]

AMELIA Did you take the medicine?

MARTIRIO For all the good it'll do me.

AMELIA But you took it?

MARTIRIO I do things without any faith, but like clockwork.

AMELIA Since the new doctor came you look livelier.

MARTIRIO I feel the same.

AMELIA Did you notice? Adelaida wasn't at the funeral.

MARTIRIO I know. Her sweetheart doesn't let her go out even to the front doorstep. Before, she was gay. Now, not even powder on her face.

AMELIA These days a girl doesn't know whether to have a beau or not.

MARTIRIO It's all the same.

AMELIA The whole trouble is all these wagging tongues that won't let us live. Adelaida has probably had a bad time.

MARTIRIO She's afraid of our mother. Mother is the only one who knows the story of Adelaida's father and where he got his lands. Every time she comes here, Mother twists the knife in the wound. Her father killed his first wife's husband in Cuba so he could marry her himself. Then he left her here and went off with another woman who already had one daughter, and then he took up with this other girl, Adelaida's mother, and married her after his second wife died insane.

AMELIA But why isn't a man like that put in jail?

MARTIRIO Because men help each other cover up things like that and no one's able to tell on them.

AMELIA But Adelaida's not to blame for any of that.

MARTIRIO No. But history repeats itself. I can see that everything is a terrible repetition. And she'll have the same fate as her mother and grandmother—both of them wife to the man who fathered her.

AMELIA What an awful thing!

MARTIRIO It's better never to look at a man. I've been afraid of them since I was a little girl. I'd see them in the yard, yoking the oxen and lifting grain sacks, shouting and stamping, and I was always afraid to grow up for fear one of them would suddenly take me in his arms. God has made me weak and ugly and has definitely put such things away from me.

AMELIA Don't say that! Enrique Humanas was after you and he liked you.

MARTIRIO That was just people's ideas! One time I stood in my nightgown at the window until daybreak because he let me know through his shepherd's little girl that he was going to come, and he didn't. It was all just talk. Then he married someone else who had more money than I.

AMELIA And ugly as the devil.

MARTIRIO What do men care about ugliness? All they care about is lands, yokes of oxen, and a submissive bitch who'll feed them.

AMELIA Ay!

[MAGDALENA *enters.*]

MAGDALENA What are you doing?

MARTIRIO Just here.

AMELIA And you?

MAGDALENA I've been going through all the rooms. Just to walk a little, and look at Grandmother's needlepoint pictures—the little woolen dog, and the black man wrestling with the lion—which we liked so much when we were children. Those were happier times. A wedding lasted ten days and evil tongues weren't in style. Today people are more refined. Brides wear white veils, just as in the cities, and we drink bottled wine, but we rot inside because of what people might say.

MARTIRIO Lord knows what went on then!

AMELIA [*to* MAGDALENA] One of your shoelaces has come untied.

MAGDALENA What of it?

AMELIA You'll step on it and fall.

MAGDALENA One less!

MARTIRIO And Adela?

MAGDALENA Ah! She put on the green dress she made to wear for her birthday, went out to the yard, and began shouting: "Chickens! Chickens, look at me!" I had to laugh.

AMELIA If Mother had only seen her!

MAGDALENA Poor little thing! She's the youngest one of us and still has her illusions. I'd give something to see her happy.

[*Pause.* ANGUSTIAS *crosses the stage, carrying some towels.*]

ANGUSTIAS What time is it?

MAGDALENA It must be twelve.

ANGUSTIAS So late?

AMELIA It's about to strike.

[ANGUSTIAS *goes out.*]

MAGDALENA [*meaningfully*] Do you know what? [*Pointing after* ANGUSTIAS]

AMELIA No.

MAGDALENA Come on!

MARTIRIO I don't know what you're talking about!

MAGDALENA Both of you know it better than I do, always with your heads together, like two little sheep, but not letting anybody else in on it. I mean about Pepe el Romano!

MARTIRIO Ah!

MAGDALENA [*mocking her*] Ah! The whole town's talking about it. Pepe el Romano is coming to marry Angustias. Last night he was walking around the house and I think he's going to send a declaration soon.

MARTIRIO I'm glad. He's a good man.

AMELIA Me too. Angustias is well off.

MAGDALENA Neither one of you is glad.

MARTIRIO Magdalena! What do you mean?

MAGDALENA If he were coming because of Angustias's looks, for Angustias as a woman, I'd be glad too, but he's coming for her money. Even though Angustias is our sister, we're her family here and we know she's old and sickly, and always has been the least attractive one of us! Because if she looked like a dressed-up stick at twenty, what can she look like now, now that she's forty?

MARTIRIO Don't talk like that. Luck comes to the one who least expects it.

AMELIA But Magdalena's right after all! Angustias has all her father's money; she's the only rich one in the house and that's why, now that Father's dead and the money will be divided, they're coming for her.

MAGDALENA Pepe el Romano is twenty-five years old and the best-looking man around here. The natural thing would be for him to be after you, Amelia, or our Adela, who's twenty—not looking for the least likely one in this house, a woman who, like her father, talks through her nose.

MARTIRIO Maybe he likes that!

MAGDALENA I've never been able to bear your hypocrisy.

MARTIRIO Heavens!

[ADELA *enters.*]

MAGDALENA Did the chickens see you?

ADELA What did you want me to do?

AMELIA If Mother sees you, she'll drag you by your hair!

ADELA I had a lot of illusions about this dress. I'd planned to put it on the day we were going to eat watermelons at the well. There wouldn't have been another like it.

MARTIRIO It's a lovely dress.

ADELA And one that looks very good on me. It's the best thing Magdalena's ever cut.

MAGDALENA And the chickens, what did they say to you?

ADELA They presented me with a few fleas that riddled my legs.

[*They laugh.*]

MARTIRIO What you can do is dye it black.

MAGDALENA The best thing you can do is give it to Angustias for her wedding with Pepe el Romano.

ADELA [*with hidden emotion*] But Pepe el Romano . . .

AMELIA Haven't you heard about it?

ADELA No.

MAGDALENA Well, now you know!

ADELA But it can't be!

MAGDALENA Money can do anything.

ADELA Is that why she went out after the funeral and stood looking through the door? [*Pause*] And that man would . . .

MAGDALENA Would do anything. [*Pause*]

MARTIRIO What are you thinking, Adela?

ADELA I'm thinking that this mourning has caught me at the worst moment of my life for me to bear it.

MAGDALENA You'll get used to it.

ADELA [*bursting out, crying with rage*] I will not get used to it! I can't be locked up. I don't want my skin to look like yours. I don't want my skin's whiteness lost in these rooms. Tomorrow I'm going to put on my green dress and go walking in the streets. I want to go out!

[*The* FIRST SERVANT *enters.*]

MAGDALENA [*in a tone of authority*] Adela!

SERVANT The poor thing! How she misses her father. . . .

[*She goes out.*]

MARTIRIO Hush!

AMELIA What happens to one will happen to all of us.

[ADELA *grows calm.*]

MAGDALENA The servant almost heard you.

SERVANT [*entering*] Pepe el Romano is coming along at the end of the street.

[AMELIA, MARTIRIO, *and* MAGDALENA *run hurriedly.*]

MAGDALENA Let's go see him!

[*They leave rapidly.*]

SERVANT [*to* ADELA] Aren't you going?

ADELA It's nothing to me.

SERVANT Since he has to turn the corner, you'll see him better from the window of your room.

[*The* SERVANT *goes out.* ADELA *is left on the stage, standing doubtfully; after a moment, she also leaves rapidly, going toward her room.* BERNARDA *and* LA PONCIA *come in.*]

BERNARDA Damned portions and shares!

PONCIA What a lot of money is left to Angustias!

BERNARDA Yes.

PONCIA And for the others, considerably less.

BERNARDA You've told me that three times now, when you know I don't want it mentioned! Considerably less; a lot less! Don't remind me anymore.

[ANGUSTIAS *comes in, her face heavily made up.*]

ANGUSTIAS Mother.

BERNARDA Have you dared to powder your face? Have you dared to wash your face on the day of your father's death?

ANGUSTIAS He wasn't my father. Mine died a long time ago. Have you forgotten that already?

BERNARDA You owe more to this man, father of your sisters, than to your own. Thanks to him, your fortune is intact.

ANGUSTIAS We'll have to see about that first!

BERNARDA Even out of decency! Out of respect!

ANGUSTIAS Let me go out, mother!

BERNARDA Let you go out? After I've taken that powder off your face, I will. Spineless! Painted hussy! Just like your aunts!

[*She removes the powder violently with her handkerchief.*]

Now get out!

PONCIA Bernarda, don't be so hateful!

BERNARDA Even though my mother is crazy, I still have my five senses and I know what I'm doing.

[*They all enter.*]

MAGDALENA What's going on here?

BERNARDA Nothing's "going on here"!

MAGDALENA [*to* ANGUSTIAS] If you're fighting over the inheritance, you're the richest one and can hang on to it all.

ANGUSTIAS Keep your tongue in your pocketbook!

BERNARDA [*beating on the floor*] Don't fool yourselves into thinking you'll sway me. Until I go out of this house feet first I'll give the orders for myself and for you!

[*Voices are heard and* MARÍA JOSEFA, BERNARDA*'s mother, enters. She is very old and has decked out her head and breast with flowers.*]

MARÍA JOSEFA Bernarda, where is my mantilla? Nothing, nothing of what I own will be for any of you. Not my rings nor my black moiré dress.[1] Because not a one of you is going to marry—not a one. Bernarda, give me my necklace of pearls.

BERNARDA [*to the* SERVANT] Why did you let her get in here?

SERVANT [*trembling*] She got away from me!

MARÍA JOSEFA I ran away because I want to marry—I want to get married to a beautiful manly man from the shore of the sea. Because here the men run from women.

BERNARDA Hush, hush, Mother!

MARÍA JOSEFA No, no—I won't hush. I don't want to see these single women, longing for marriage, turning their hearts to dust; and I want to go to my hometown. Bernarda, I want a man to get married to and be happy with!

BERNARDA Lock her up!

MARÍA JOSEFA Let me go out, Bernarda!

[*The* SERVANT *seizes* MARÍA JOSEFA.]

BERNARDA Help her, all of you!

[*They all grab the old woman.*]

1. A dress made of watered silk, or a fabric with a similar shimmering appearance.

MARÍA JOSEFA I want to get away from here! Bernarda! To get married by the shore of the sea—by the shore of the sea!

Quick Curtain.

Act 2

[SCENE: *A white room in Bernarda's house. The doors on the left lead to the bedrooms.*]

[BERNARDA'*s daughters are seated on low chairs, sewing.* MAGDALENA *is embroidering.* LA PONCIA *is with them.*]

ANGUSTIAS I've cut the third sheet.

MARTIRIO That one goes to Amelia.

MAGDALENA Angustias, shall I put Pepe's initials here too?

ANGUSTIAS [*dryly*] No.

MAGDALENA [*calling, from offstage to* ADELA] Adela, aren't you coming?

AMELIA She's probably stretched out on the bed.

PONCIA Something's wrong with that one. I find her restless, trembling, frightened—as if a lizard were between her breasts.

MARTIRIO There's nothing, more or less, wrong with her than there is with all of us.

MAGDALENA All of us except Angustias.

ANGUSTIAS I feel fine, and anybody who doesn't like it can pop.

MAGDALENA We all have to admit the nicest things about you are your figure and your tact.

ANGUSTIAS Fortunately, I'll soon be out of this hell.

MAGDALENA Maybe you won't get out!

MARTIRIO Stop this talk!

ANGUSTIAS Besides, a good dowry is better than dark eyes in one's face!

MAGDALENA All you say just goes in one ear and out the other.

AMELIA [*to* LA PONCIA] Open the patio door[2] and see if we can get a bit of a breeze.

[LA PONCIA *opens the door.*]

MARTIRIO Last night I couldn't sleep because of the heat.

AMELIA Neither could I.

MAGDALENA I got up for a bit of air. There was a black storm cloud and a few drops even fell.

PONCIA It was one in the morning and the earth seemed to give off fire. I got up too. Angustias was still at the window with Pepe.

MAGDALENA [*with irony*] That late? What time did he leave?

ANGUSTIAS Why do you ask, if you saw him?

AMELIA He must have left about one-thirty.

ANGUSTIAS Yes. How did you know?

AMELIA I heard him cough and heard his mare's hoofbeats.

PONCIA But I heard him leave around four.

ANGUSTIAS It must have been someone else!

PONCIA No, I'm sure of it!

AMELIA That's what it seemed to me, too.

2. That is, the door to an inner courtyard (a common feature in Spanish residences).

MAGDALENA That's very strange! [*Pause*]

PONCIA Listen, Angustias, what did he say to you the first time he came by your window?

ANGUSTIAS Nothing. What should he say? Just talked.

MARTIRIO It's certainly strange that two people who never knew each other should suddenly meet at a window and be engaged.

ANGUSTIAS Well, I didn't mind.

AMELIA I'd have felt very strange about it.

ANGUSTIAS No, because when a man comes to a window he knows, from all the busybodies who come and go and fetch and carry, that he's going to be told "yes."

MARTIRIO All right, but he'd have to ask you.

ANGUSTIAS Of course!

AMELIA [*inquisitively*] And how did he ask you?

ANGUSTIAS Why, no way:—"You know I'm after you. I need a good, well-brought-up woman, and that's you—if it's agreeable."

AMELIA These things embarrass me!

ANGUSTIAS They embarrass me too, but one has to go through it!

PONCIA And did he say anything more?

ANGUSTIAS Yes, he did all the talking.

MARTIRIO And you?

ANGUSTIAS I couldn't have said a word. My heart was almost coming out of my mouth. It was the first time I'd ever been alone at night with a man.

MAGDALENA And such a handsome man.

ANGUSTIAS He's not bad looking!

PONCIA Those things happen among people who have an idea how to do things, who talk and say and move their hand. The first time my husband, Evaristo the Short-tailed, came to my window . . . Ha! Ha! Ha!

AMELIA What happened?

PONCIA It was very dark. I saw him coming along and as he went by he said, "Good evening." "Good evening," I said. Then we were both silent for more than half an hour. The sweat poured down my body. Then Evaristo got nearer and nearer as if he wanted to squeeze in through the bars and said in a very low voice—"Come here and let me feel you!"

[*They all laugh.* AMELIA *gets up, runs, and looks through the door.*]

AMELIA Ay, I thought mother was coming!

MAGDALENA What she'd have done to us!

[*They go on laughing.*]

AMELIA Sh-h-h! She'll hear us.

PONCIA Then he acted very decently. Instead of getting some other idea, he went to raising birds, until he died. You aren't married but it's good for you to know, anyway, that two weeks after the wedding a man gives up the bed for the table, then the table for the tavern, and the woman who doesn't like it can just rot, weeping in a corner.

AMELIA You liked it.

PONCIA I learned how to handle him!

MARTIRIO Is it true that you sometimes hit him?

PONCIA Yes, and once I almost poked out one of his eyes!

MAGDALENA All women ought to be like that!

PONCIA I'm one of your mother's school. One time I don't know what he said to me, and then I killed all his birds—with the pestle!

[*They laugh.*]

MAGDALENA Adela, child! Don't miss this.

AMELIA Adela! [*Pause*]

MAGDALENA I'll go see!

[*She goes out.*]

PONCIA That child is sick!

MARTIRIO Of course. She hardly sleeps!

PONCIA What *does* she do, then?

MARTIRIO How do I know what she does?

PONCIA You probably know better than we do, since you sleep with just a wall between you.

ANGUSTIAS Envy gnaws on people.

AMELIA Don't exaggerate.

ANGUSTIAS I can tell it in her eyes. She's getting the look of a crazy woman.

MARTIRIO Don't talk about crazy women. This is one place you're not allowed to say that word.

[MAGDALENA *and* ADELA *enter.*]

MAGDALENA Didn't you say she was asleep?

ADELA My body aches.

MARTIRIO [*with a hidden meaning*] Didn't you sleep well last night?

ADELA Yes.

MARTIRIO Then?

ADELA [*loudly*] Leave me alone. Awake or asleep, it's no affair of yours. I'll do whatever I want to with my body.

MARTIRIO I was just concerned about you!

ADELA Concerned? Curious! Weren't you sewing? Well, continue! I wish I were invisible so I could pass through a room without being asked where I was going!

SERVANT [*entering*] Bernarda is calling you. The man with the laces is here.

[*All but* ADELA *and* LA PONCIA *go out, and as* MARTIRIO *leaves, she looks fixedly at* ADELA.]

ADELA Don't look at me like that! If you want, I'll give you my eyes, for they're younger, and my back to improve that hump you have, but look the other way when I go by.

PONCIA Adela, she's your sister, and the one who most loves you besides!

ADELA She follows me everywhere. Sometimes she looks in my room to see if I'm sleeping. She won't let me breathe, and always, "Too bad about that face!" "Too bad about that body! It's going to waste!" But I won't let that happen. My body will be for whomever I choose.

PONCIA [*insinuatingly, in a low voice*] For Pepe el Romano, no?

ADELA [*frightened*] What do you mean?

PONCIA What I said, Adela!

ADELA Shut up!

PONCIA [*loudly*] Don't you think I've noticed?

ADELA Lower your voice!

PONCIA Then forget what you're thinking about!

ADELA What do you know?

PONCIA We old ones can see through walls. Where do you go when you get up at night?

ADELA I wish you were blind!

PONCIA But my head and hands are full of eyes, where something like this is concerned. I couldn't possibly guess your intentions. Why did you sit almost naked at your window, and with the light on and the window open, when Pepe passed by the second night he came to talk with your sister?

ADELA That's not true!

PONCIA Don't be a child! Leave your sister alone. And if you like Pepe el Romano, keep it to yourself.

[ADELA *weeps.*]

Besides, who says you can't marry him? Your sister Angustias is sickly. She'll die with her first child. Narrow waisted, old—and out of my experience I can tell you she'll die. Then Pepe will do what all widowers do in these parts: he'll marry the youngest and most beautiful, and that's you. Live on that hope, forget him, anything; but don't go against God's law.

ADELA Hush!

PONCIA I won't hush!

ADELA Mind your own business. Snooper, traitor!

PONCIA I'm going to stick to you like a shadow!

ADELA Instead of cleaning the house and then going to bed and praying for the dead, you root around like an old sow about goings-on between men and women—so you can drool over them.

PONCIA I keep watch; so people won't spit when they pass our door.

ADELA What a tremendous affection you've suddenly conceived for my sister.

PONCIA I don't have any affection for any of you. I want to live in a decent house. I don't want to be dirtied in my old age!

ADELA Save your advice. It's already too late. For I'd leap not over you, just a servant, but over my mother to put out this fire I feel in my legs and my mouth. What can you possibly say about me? That I lock myself in my room and will not open the door? That I don't sleep? I'm smarter than you! See if you can catch the hare with your hands.

PONCIA Don't defy me, Adela, don't defy me! Because I can shout, light lamps, and make bells ring.

ADELA Bring four thousand yellow flares and set them about the walls of the yard. No one can stop what has to happen.

PONCIA You like him that much?

ADELA That much! Looking in his eyes I seem to drink his blood in slowly.

PONCIA I won't listen to you.

ADELA Well, you'll have to! I've been afraid of you. But now I'm stronger than you!

[ANGUSTIAS *enters.*]

ANGUSTIAS Always arguing!

PONCIA Certainly. She insists that in all this heat I have to go bring her I don't know what from the store.

ANGUSTIAS Did you buy me the bottle of perfume?

PONCIA The most expensive one. And the face powder. I put them on the table in your room.

[ANGUSTIAS *goes out.*]

ADELA And be quiet!

PONCIA We'll see!

[MARTIRIO *and* AMELIA *enter.*]

MARTIRIO [*to* ADELA] Did you see the laces?

AMELIA Angustias's, for her wedding sheets, are beautiful.

ADELA [*to* MARTIRIO, *who is carrying some lace*] And these?

MARTIRIO They're for me. For a nightgown.

ADELA [*with sarcasm*] One needs a sense of humor around here!

MARTIRIO [*meaningfully*] But only for me to look at. I don't have to exhibit myself before anybody.

PONCIA No one ever sees us in our nightgowns.

MARTIRIO [*meaningfully, looking at* ADELA] Sometimes they don't! But I love nice underwear. If I were rich, I'd have it made of Holland cloth.[3] It's one of the few tastes I've left.

PONCIA These laces are beautiful for babies' caps and christening gowns. I could never afford them for my own. Now let's see if Angustias will use them for hers. Once she starts having children, they'll keep her running night and day.

MAGDALENA I don't intend to sew a stitch on them.

AMELIA And much less bring up some stranger's children. Look how our neighbors across the road are—making sacrifices for four brats.

PONCIA They're better off than you. There at least they laugh and you can hear them fight.

MARTIRIO Well, you go work for them, then.

PONCIA No, fate has sent me to this nunnery!

[*Tiny bells are heard distantly as though through several thicknesses of wall.*]

MAGDALENA It's the men going back to work.

PONCIA It was three o'clock a minute ago.

MARTIRIO With this sun!

ADELA [*sitting down*] Ay! If only we could go out in the fields too!

MAGDALENA [*sitting down*] Each class does what it has to!

MARTIRIO [*sitting down*] That's it!

AMELIA [*sitting down*] Ay!

PONCIA There's no happiness like that in the fields right at this time of year. Yesterday morning the reapers arrived. Forty or fifty handsome young men.

MAGDALENA Where are they from this year?

PONCIA From far, far away. They came from the mountains! Happy! Like weathered trees! Shouting and throwing stones! Last night a woman who dresses in sequins and dances, with an accordion, arrived, and fifteen of them made a deal with her to take her to the olive grove. I saw them from far away. The one who talked with her was a boy with green eyes—tight-knit as a sheaf of wheat.

AMELIA Really?

ADELA Are you sure?

PONCIA Years ago another one of those women came here, and I myself gave my eldest son some money so he could go. Men need things like that.

3. An expensive linen fabric from Holland.

ADELA Everything's forgiven *them.*

AMELIA To be born a woman's the worst possible punishment.

MAGDALENA Even our eyes aren't our own.

[*A distant song is heard, coming nearer.*]

PONCIA There they are. They have a beautiful song.

AMELIA They're going out to reap now.

CHORUS

The reapers have set out
Looking for ripe wheat;
They'll carry off the hearts
Of any girls they meet.

[*Tambourines and carrañacas*[4] *are heard. Pause. They all listen in the silence cut by the sun.*]

AMELIA And they don't mind the sun!

MARTIRIO They reap through flames.

ADELA How I'd like to be a reaper so I could come and go as I pleased. Then we could forget what's eating at us all.

MARTIRIO What do you have to forget?

ADELA Each one of us has something.

MARTIRIO [*intensely*] Each one!

PONCIA Quiet! Quiet!

CHORUS [*very distantly*]

Throw wide your doors and windows,
You girls who live in the town
The reaper asks you for roses
With which to deck his crown.

PONCIA What a song!

MARTIRIO [*with nostalgia*]

Throw wide your doors and windows,
You girls who live in the town.

ADELA [*passionately*]

The reaper asks you for roses
With which to deck his crown.

[*The song grows more distant.*]

PONCIA Now they're turning the corner.

ADELA Let's watch them from the window of my room.

PONCIA Be careful not to open the shutters too much because they're likely to give them a push to see who's looking.

[*The three leave.* MARTIRIO *is left sitting on the low chair with her head between her hands.*]

AMELIA [*drawing near her*] What's wrong with you?

MARTIRIO The heat makes me feel ill.

AMELIA And it's no more than that?

MARTIRIO I was wishing it were November, the rainy days, the frost—anything except this unending summertime.

AMELIA It'll pass and come again.

4. Rattles (Spanish).

MARTIRIO Naturally. [*Pause*] What time did you go to sleep last night?

AMELIA I don't know. I sleep like a log. Why?

MARTIRIO Nothing. Only I thought I heard someone in the yard.

AMELIA Yes?

MARTIRIO Very late.

AMELIA And weren't you afraid?

MARTIRIO No. I've heard it other nights.

AMELIA We'd better watch out! Couldn't it have been the shepherds?

MARTIRIO The shepherds come at six.

AMELIA Maybe a young, unbroken mule?

MARTIRIO [*to herself, with double meaning*] That's it! That's it. An unbroken little mule.

AMELIA We'll have to set a watch.

MARTIRIO No. No. Don't say anything. It may be I've just imagined it.

AMELIA Maybe.

[*Pause.* AMELIA *starts to go.*]

MARTIRIO Amelia!

AMELIA [*at the door*] What? [*Pause*]

MARTIRIO Nothing. [*Pause*]

AMELIA Why did you call me? [*Pause*]

MARTIRIO It just came out. I didn't mean to. [*Pause*]

AMELIA Lie down for a little.

ANGUSTIAS [*she bursts in furiously, in a manner that makes a great contrast with previous silence*] Where's that picture of Pepe I had under my pillow? Which one of you has it?

MARTIRIO No one.

AMELIA You'd think he was a silver St. Bartholomew.[5]

ANGUSTIAS Where's the picture?

[PONCIA, MAGDALENA, *and* ADELA *enter.*]

ADELA What picture?

ANGUSTIAS One of you has hidden it from me.

MAGDALENA Do you have the effrontery to say that?

ANGUSTIAS I had it in my room, and now it isn't there.

MARTIRIO But couldn't it have jumped out into the yard at midnight? Pepe likes to walk around in the moonlight.

ANGUSTIAS Don't joke with me! When he comes I'll tell him.

PONCIA Don't do that! Because it'll turn up. [*Looking at* ADELA]

ANGUSTIAS I'd like to know which one of you has it.

ADELA [*looking at* MARTIRIO] Somebody has it! But not me!

MARTIRIO [*with meaning*] Of course not you!

BERNARDA [*entering, with her cane*] What scandal is this in my house in the heat's heavy silence? The neighbors must have their ears glued to the walls.

ANGUSTIAS They've stolen my sweetheart's picture!

BERNARDA [*fiercely*] Who? Who?

ANGUSTIAS They have!

5. That is, a silver medal depicting Bartholomew, one of the Twelve Apostles.

BERNARDA Which one of you? [*Silence*] Answer me! [*Silence*] [*To* LA PONCIA] Search their rooms! Look in their beds. This comes of not tying you up with shorter leashes. But I'll teach you now! [*To* ANGUSTIAS] Are you sure?

ANGUSTIAS Yes.

BERNARDA Did you look everywhere?

ANGUSTIAS Yes, Mother.

[*They all stand in an embarrassed silence.*]

BERNARDA At the end of my life—to make me drink the bitterest poison a mother knows. [*To* PONCIA] Did you find it?

PONCIA Here it is.

BERNARDA Where did you find it?

PONCIA It was . . .

BERNARDA Say it! Don't be afraid.

PONCIA [*wonderingly*] Between the sheets in Martirio's bed.

BERNARDA [*to* MARTIRIO] Is that true?

MARTIRIO It's true.

BERNARDA [*advancing on her, beating her with her cane*] You'll come to a bad end yet, you hypocrite! Trouble maker!

MARTIRIO [*fiercely*] Don't hit me, Mother!

BERNARDA All I want to!

MARTIRIO If I let you! You hear me? Get back!

PONCIA Don't be disrespectful to your mother!

ANGUSTIAS [*holding* BERNARDA] Let her go, please!

BERNARDA Not even tears in your eyes.

MARTIRIO I'm not going to cry just to please you.

BERNARDA Why did you take the picture?

MARTIRIO Can't I play a joke on my sister? What else would I want it for?

ADELA [*leaping forward, full of jealousy*] It wasn't a joke! You never liked to play jokes. It was something else bursting in her breast—trying to come out. Admit it openly now.

MARTIRIO Hush, and don't make me speak; for if I should speak the walls would close together one against the other with shame.

ADELA An evil tongue never stops inventing lies.

BERNARDA Adela!

MAGDALENA You're crazy.

AMELIA And you stone us all with your evil suspicions.

MARTIRIO But some others do things more wicked!

ADELA Until all at once they stand forth stark naked and the river carries them along.

BERNARDA Spiteful!

ANGUSTIAS It's not my fault Pepe el Romano chose me!

ADELA For your money.

ANGUSTIAS Mother!

BERNARDA Silence!

MARTIRIO For your fields and your orchards.

MAGDALENA That's only fair.

BERNARDA Silence, I say! I saw the storm coming but I didn't think it'd burst so soon. Oh, what an avalanche of hate you've thrown on my heart! But I'm not old yet—I have five chains for you, and this house my father built, so not even the weeds will know of my desolation. Out of here!

[*They go out.* BERNARDA *sits down desolately.* LA PONCIA *is standing close to the wall.* BERNARDA *recovers herself, and beats on the floor.*]

I'll have to let them feel the weight of my hand! Bernarda, remember your duty!

PONCIA May I speak?

BERNARDA Speak. I'm sorry you heard. A stranger is always out of place in a family.

PONCIA What I've seen, I've seen.

BERNARDA Angustias must get married right away.

PONCIA Certainly. We'll have to get her away from here.

BERNARDA Not her, him!

PONCIA Of course. He's the one to get away from here. You've thought it all out.

BERNARDA I'm not thinking. There are things that shouldn't and can't be thought out. I give orders.

PONCIA And you think he'll be satisfied to go away?

BERNARDA [*rising*] What are you imagining now?

PONCIA He will, of course, marry Angustias.

BERNARDA Speak up! I know you well enough to see that your knife's out for me.

PONCIA I never knew a warning could be called murder.

BERNARDA Have you some "warning" for me?

PONCIA I'm not making any accusations, Bernarda. I'm only telling you to open your eyes and you'll see.

BERNARDA See what?

PONCIA You've always been smart, Bernarda. You've seen other people's sins a hundred miles away. Many times I've thought you could read minds. But, your children are your children, and now you're blind.

BERNARDA Are you talking about Martirio?

PONCIA Well, yes—about Martirio . . . [*With curiosity*] I wonder why she hid the picture?

BERNARDA [*shielding her daughter*] After all, she says it was a joke. What else could it be?

PONCIA [*scornfully*] Do you believe that?

BERNARDA [*sternly*] I don't merely believe it. It's so!

PONCIA Enough of this. We're talking about your family. But if we were talking about your neighbor across the way, what would it be?

BERNARDA Now you're beginning to pull the point of the knife out.

PONCIA [*always cruelly*] No, Bernarda. Something very grave is happening here. I don't want to put the blame on your shoulders, but you've never given your daughters any freedom. Martirio is lovesick, I don't care what you say. Why didn't you let her marry Enrique Humanas? Why, on the very day he was coming to her window did you send him a message not to come?

BERNARDA [*loudly*] I'd do it a thousand times over! My blood won't mingle with the Humanases' while I live! His father was a shepherd.

PONCIA And you see now what's happening to you with these airs!

BERNARDA I have them because I can afford to. And you don't have them because you know where you came from!

PONCIA [*with hate*] Don't remind me! I'm old now. I've always been grateful for your protection.

BERNARDA [*emboldened*] You don't seem so!

PONCIA [*with hate, behind softness*] Martirio will forget this.

BERNARDA And if she doesn't—the worse for her. I don't believe this is that "very grave thing" that's happening here. Nothing's happening here. It's just that you wish it would! And if it should happen one day, you can be sure it won't go beyond these walls.

PONCIA I'm not so sure of that! There are people in town who can also read hidden thoughts, from afar.

BERNARDA How you'd like to see me and my daughters on our way to a whorehouse!

PONCIA No one knows her own destiny!

BERNARDA I know my destiny! And my daughters'! The whorehouse was for a certain woman, already dead. . . .

PONCIA [*fiercely*] Bernarda, respect the memory of my mother!

BERNARDA Then don't plague me with your evil thoughts! [*Pause*]

PONCIA I'd better stay out of everything.

BERNARDA That's what you ought to do. Work and keep your mouth shut. The duty of all who work for a living.

PONCIA But we can't do that. Don't you think it'd be better for Pepe to marry Martirio or . . . yes! . . . Adela?

BERNARDA No, I *don't* think so.

PONCIA [*with meaning*] Adela! She's Romano's real sweetheart!

BERNARDA Things are never the way we want them!

PONCIA But it's hard work to turn them from their destined course. For Pepe to be with Angustias seems wrong to me—and to other people—and even to the wind. Who knows if they'll get what they want?

BERNARDA There you go again! Sneaking up on me—giving me bad dreams. But I won't listen to you, because if all you say should come to pass—I'd scratch your face.

PONCIA Frighten someone else with that.

BERNARDA Fortunately, my daughters respect me and have never gone against my will!

PONCIA That's right! But, as soon as they break loose they'll fly to the rooftops!

BERNARDA And I'll bring them down with stones!

PONCIA Oh, yes! You were always the bravest one!

BERNARDA I've always enjoyed a good fight!

PONCIA But aren't people strange. You should see Angustias's enthusiasm for her lover, at her age! And he seems very smitten too. Yesterday my oldest son told me that when he passed by with the oxen at four-thirty in the morning they were still talking.

BERNARDA At four-thirty?

ANGUSTIAS [*entering*] That's a lie!

PONCIA That's what he told me.

BERNARDA [*to* ANGUSTIAS] Speak up!

ANGUSTIAS For more than a week Pepe has been leaving at one. May God strike me dead if I'm lying.

MARTIRIO [*entering*] I heard him leave at four too.

BERNARDA But did you see him with your eyes?

MARTIRIO I didn't want to look out. Don't you talk now through the side window?

ANGUSTIAS We talk through my bedroom window.

[ADELA *appears at the door.*]

MARTIRIO Then . . .

BERNARDA What's going on here?

PONCIA If you're not careful, you'll find out! At least Pepe was at *one* of your windows—and at four in the morning too!

BERNARDA Are you sure of that?

PONCIA You can't be sure of anything in this life!

ADELA Mother, don't listen to someone who wants us to lose everything we have.

BERNARDA I know how to take care of myself! If the townspeople want to come bearing false witness against me, they'll run into a stone wall! Don't any of you talk about this! Sometimes other people try to stir up a wave of filth to drown us.

MARTIRIO I don't like to lie.

PONCIA So there must be something.

BERNARDA There won't be anything. I was born to have my eyes always open. Now I'll watch without closing them 'til I die.

ANGUSTIAS I have the right to know.

BERNARDA You don't have any right except to obey. No one's going to fetch and carry for me. [*To* LA PONCIA] And don't meddle in our affairs. No one will take a step without my knowing it.

SERVANT [*entering*] There's a big crowd at the top of the street, and all the neighbors are at their doors!

BERNARDA [*to* PONCIA] Run see what's happening!

[*The girls are about to run out.*]

Where are you going? I always knew you for window-watching women and breakers of your mourning. All of you, to the patio!

[*They go out.* BERNARDA *leaves. Distant shouts are heard.* MARTIRIO *and* ADELA *enter and listen, not daring to step farther than the front door.*]

MARTIRIO You can be thankful I didn't happen to open my mouth.

ADELA I would have spoken too.

MARTIRIO And what were you going to say? Wanting isn't doing!

ADELA I do what I can and what happens to suit me. You've wanted to, but haven't been able.

MARTIRIO You won't go on very long.

ADELA I'll have everything!

MARTIRIO I'll tear you out of his arms!

ADELA [*pleadingly*] Martirio, let me be!

MARTIRIO None of us will have him!

ADELA He wants me for his house!

MARTIRIO I saw how he embraced you!

ADELA I didn't want him to. It's as if I were dragged by a rope.

MARTIRIO I'll see you dead first!

[MAGADALENA *and* ANGUSTIAS *look in. The tumult is increasing. A* SERVANT *enters with* BERNARDA. PONCIA *also enters from another door.*]

PONCIA Bernarda!

BERNARDA What's happening?

PONCIA Librada's daughter, the unmarried one, had a child and no one knows whose it is!

ADELA A child?

PONCIA And to hide her shame she killed it and hid it under the rocks, but the dogs, with more heart than most Christians, dug it out and, as though directed by the hand of God, left it at her door. Now they want to kill her. They're dragging her through the streets—and down the paths and across the olive groves the men are coming, shouting so the fields shake.

BERNARDA Yes, let them all come with olive whips and hoe handles—let them all come and kill her!

ADELA No, not to kill her!

MARTIRIO Yes—and let us go out too!

BERNARDA And let whoever loses her decency pay for it!

[*Outside a woman's shriek and a great clamor is heard.*]

ADELA Let her escape! Don't you go out!

MARTIRIO [*looking at* ADELA] Let her pay what she owes!

BERNARDA [*at the archway*] Finish her before the guards come! Hot coals in the place where she sinned!

ADELA [*holding her belly*] No! No!

BERNARDA Kill her! Kill her!

Curtain.

Act 3

[SCENE: *Four white walls, lightly washed in blue, of the interior patio of* BERNARDA ALBA's *house. The doorways, illumined by the lights inside the rooms, give a tenuous glow to the stage.*]

[*At the center there is a table with a shaded oil lamp about which* BERNARDA *and her daughters are eating.* LA PONCIA *serves them.* PRUDENCIA *sits apart. When the curtain rises, there is a great silence interrupted only by the noise of plates and silverware.*]

PRUDENCIA I'm going. I've made you a long visit.

[*She rises.*]

BERNARDA But wait, Prudencia. We never see one another.

PRUDENCIA Have they sounded the last call to rosary?[6]

PONCIA Not yet.

[PRUDENCIA *sits down again.*]

BERNARDA And your husband, how's he getting on?

PRUDENCIA The same.

BERNARDA We never see him either.

PRUDENCIA You know how he is. Since he quarrelled with his brothers over the inheritance, he hasn't used the front door. He takes a ladder and climbs over the back wall.

BERNARDA He's a real man! And your daughter?

PRUDENCIA He's never forgiven her.

BERNARDA He's right.

6. A form of devotion that consists of a set of repeated prayers.

PRUDENCIA I don't know what he told you. I suffer because of it.

BERNARDA A daughter who's disobedient stops being a daughter and becomes an enemy.

PRUDENCIA I let water run. The only consolation I've left is to take refuge in the church, but, since I'm losing my sight, I'll have to stop coming so the children won't make fun of me.

[*A heavy blow is heard against the walls.*]

What's that?

BERNARDA The stallion. He's locked in the stall and he kicks against the wall of the house. [*Shouting*] Tether him and take him out in the yard! [*In a lower voice*] He must be too hot.

PRUDENCIA Are you going to put the new mares to him?

BERNARDA At daybreak.

PRUDENCIA You've known how to increase your stock.

BERNARDA By dint of money and struggling.

PONCIA [*interrupting*] And she has the best herd in these parts. It's a shame that prices are low.

BERNARDA Do you want a little cheese and honey?

PRUDENCIA I have no appetite.

[*The blow is heard again.*]

PONCIA My God!

PRUDENCIA It quivered in my chest!

BERNARDA [*rising, furiously*] Do I have to say things twice? Let him out to roll on the straw. [*Pause. Then, as though speaking to the stableman*] Well then, lock the mares in the corral, but let him run free or he may kick down the walls.

[*She returns to the table and sits again.*]

Ay, what a life!

PRUDENCIA You have to fight like a man.

BERNARDA That's it.

[ADELA *gets up from the table.*]

Where are you going?

ADELA For a drink of water.

BERNARDA [*raising her voice*] Bring a pitcher of cool water. [*To* ADELA] You can sit down.

[ADELA *sits down.*]

PRUDENCIA And Angustias, when will she get married?

BERNARDA They're coming to ask for her within three days.

PRUDENCIA You must be happy.

ANGUSTIAS Naturally!

AMELIA [*to* MAGDALENA] You've spilled the salt!

MAGDALENA You can't possibly have worse luck than you're having.

AMELIA It always brings bad luck.

BERNARDA That's enough!

PRUDENCIA [*to* ANGUSTIAS] Has he given you the ring yet?

ANGUSTIAS Look at it.

[*She holds it out.*]

PRUDENCIA It's beautiful. Three pearls. In my day, pearls signified tears.

ANGUSTIAS But things have changed now.

ADELA I don't think so. Things go on meaning the same. Engagement rings should be diamonds.

PONCIA The most appropriate.

BERNARDA With pearls or without them, things are as one proposes.

MARTIRIO Or as God disposes.

PRUDENCIA I've been told your furniture is beautiful.

BERNARDA It cost sixteen thousand *reales*.[7]

PONCIA [*interrupting*] The best is the wardrobe with the mirror.

PRUDENCIA I never saw a piece like that.

BERNARDA We had chests.

PRUDENCIA The important thing is that everything be for the best.

ADELA And that you never know.

BERNARDA There's no reason why it shouldn't be.

[*Bells are heard very distantly.*]

PRUDENCIA The last call. [*To* ANGUSTIAS] I'll be coming back to have you show me your clothes.

ANGUSTIAS Whenever you like.

PRUDENCIA Good evening—God bless you!

BERNARDA Good-bye, Prudencia.

ALL FIVE DAUGHTERS [*at the same time*] God go with you!

[*Pause.* PRUDENCIA *goes out.*]

BERNARDA Well, we've eaten.

[*They rise.*]

ADELA I'm going to walk as far as the gate to stretch my legs and get a bit of fresh air.

[MAGDALENA *sits down in a low chair and leans against the wall.*]

AMELIA I'll go with you.

MARTIRIO I too.

ADELA [*with contained hate*] I'm not going to get lost!

AMELIA One needs company at night.

[*They go out.* BERNARDA *sits down.* ANGUSTIAS *is clearing the table.*]

BERNARDA I've told you once already! I want you to talk to your sister Martirio. What happened about the picture was a joke and you must forget it.

ANGUSTIAS You know she doesn't like me.

BERNARDA Each one knows what she thinks inside. I don't pry into anyone's heart, but I want to put up a good front and have family harmony. You understand?

ANGUSTIAS Yes.

BERNARDA Then that's settled.

MAGDALENA [*she is almost asleep*] Besides, you'll be gone in no time.

[*She falls asleep.*]

ANGUSTIAS Not soon enough for me.

BERNARDA What time did you stop talking last night?

7. Originally, silver coins (the 8-real coin was the Spanish dollar). The real was the chief unit in Spain's first decimal currency; though from 1868 until 2002 it was replaced in that role by the peseta (worth 4 reales), the term remained in common use.

ANGUSTIAS Twelve-thirty.

BERNARDA What does Pepe talk about?

ANGUSTIAS I find him absent-minded. He always talks to me as though he were thinking of something else. If I ask him what's the matter, he answers—"We men have our worries."

BERNARDA You shouldn't ask him. And when you're married, even less. Speak if he speaks, and look at him when he looks at you. That way you'll get along.

ANGUSTIAS But, Mother, I think he's hiding things from me.

BERNARDA Don't try to find out. Don't ask him, and above all, never let him see you cry.

ANGUSTIAS I should be happy, but I'm not.

BERNARDA It's all the same.

ANGUSTIAS Many nights I watch Pepe very closely through the window bars and he seems to fade away—as though he were hidden in a cloud of dust like those raised by the flocks.

BERNARDA That's just because you're not strong.

ANGUSTIAS I hope so!

BERNARDA Is he coming tonight?

ANGUSTIAS No, he went into town with his mother.

BERNARDA Good, we'll get to bed early. Magdalena!

ANGUSTIAS She's asleep.

[ADELA, MARTIRIO, *and* AMELIA *enter.*]

AMELIA What a dark night!

ADELA You can't see two steps in front of you.

MARTIRIO A good night for robbers, for anyone who needs to hide.

ADELA The stallion was in the middle of the corral. White. Twice as large. Filling all the darkness.

AMELIA It's true. It was frightening. Like a ghost.

ADELA The sky has stars as big as fists.

MARTIRIO This one stared at them till she almost cracked her neck.

ADELA Don't you like them up there?

MARTIRIO What goes on over the roof doesn't mean a thing to me. I have my hands full with what happens under it.

ADELA Well, that's the way it goes with you!

BERNARDA And it goes the same for you as for her.

ANGUSTIAS Good night.

ADELA Are you going to bed now?

ANGUSTIAS Yes, Pepe isn't coming tonight.

[*She goes out.*]

ADELA Mother, why, when a star falls or lightning flashes, does one say:
Holy Barbara,[8] blessed on high
May your name be in the sky
With holy water written high?

BERNARDA The old people know many things we've forgotten.

AMELIA I close my eyes so I won't see them.

8. Saint Barbara, an early Christian martyr traditionally invoked for protection from lightning. Lightning and falling stars were thought to bring bad luck, which this rhyme is meant to avert.

ADELA Not I. I like to see what's quiet and been quiet for years on end, running with fire.

MARTIRIO But all that has nothing to do with us.

BERNARDA And it's better not to think about it.

ADELA What a beautiful night! I'd like to stay up till very late and enjoy the breeze from the fields.

BERNARDA But we have to go to bed. Magdalena!

AMELIA She's just dropped off.

BERNARDA Magdalena!

MAGDALENA [*annoyed*] Leave me alone!

BERNARDA To bed!

MAGDALENA [*rising, in a bad humor*] You don't give anyone a moment's peace!

[*She goes off grumbling.*]

AMELIA Good night!

[*She goes out.*]

BERNARDA You two get along, too.

MARTIRIO How is it Angustias's sweetheart isn't coming tonight?

BERNARDA He went on a trip.

MARTIRIO [*looking at* ADELA] Ah!

ADELA I'll see you in the morning!

[*She goes out.* MARTIRIO *drinks some water and goes out slowly, looking at the door to the yard.* LA PONCIA *enters.*]

PONCIA Are you still here?

BERNARDA Enjoying this quiet and not seeing anywhere the "very grave thing" that's happening here—according to you.

PONCIA Bernarda, let's not go any further with this.

BERNARDA In this house there's no question of a yes or a no. My watchfulness can take care of anything.

PONCIA Nothing's happening outside. That's true, all right. Your daughters act and are as though stuck in a cupboard. But neither you nor anyone else can keep watch inside a person's heart.

BERNARDA My daughters breathe calmly enough.

PONCIA That's your business, since you're their mother. I have enough to do just with serving you.

BERNARDA Yes, you've turned quiet now.

PONCIA I keep my place—that's all.

BERNARDA The trouble is you've nothing to talk about. If there were grass in this house, you'd make it your business to put the neighbors' sheep to pasture here.

PONCIA I hide more than you think.

BERNARDA Do your sons still see Pepe at four in the morning? Are they still repeating this house's evil litany?

PONCIA They say nothing.

BERNARDA Because they can't. Because there's nothing for them to sink their teeth in. And all because my eyes keep constant watch!

PONCIA Bernarda, I don't want to talk about this because I'm afraid of what you'll do. But don't you feel so safe.

BERNARDA Very safe!

PONCIA Who knows, lightning might strike suddenly. Who knows but what all of a sudden, in a rush of blood, your heart might stop.

BERNARDA Nothing will happen here. I'm on guard now against all your suspicions.

PONCIA All the better for you.

BERNARDA Certainly, all the better!

SERVANT [*entering*] I've just finished with the dishes. Is there anything else, Bernarda?

BERNARDA [*rising*] Nothing. I'm going to get some rest.

PONCIA What time do you want me to call you?

BERNARDA No time. Tonight I intend to sleep well.

[*She goes out.*]

PONCIA When you're powerless against the sea, it's easier to turn your back on it and not look at it.

SERVANT She's so proud! She herself pulls the blindfold over her eyes.

PONCIA I can do nothing. I tried to head things off, but now they frighten me too much. You feel this silence?—in each room there's a thunderstorm—and the day it breaks, it'll sweep all of us along with it. But I've said what I had to say.

SERVANT Bernarda thinks nothing can stand against her, yet she doesn't know the strength a man has among women alone.

PONCIA It's not all the fault of Pepe el Romano. It's true last year he was running after Adela; and she was crazy about him—but she ought to keep her place and not lead him on. A man's a man.

SERVANT And some there are who believe he didn't have to talk many times with Adela.

PONCIA That's true. [*In a low voice*] And some other things.

SERVANT I don't know what's going to happen here.

PONCIA How I'd like to sail across the sea and leave this house, this battleground, behind!

SERVANT Bernarda's hurrying the wedding and it's possible nothing will happen.

PONCIA Things have gone much too far already. Adela is set no matter what comes, and the rest of them watch without rest.

SERVANT Martirio too . . . ?

PONCIA That one's the worst. She's a pool of poison. She sees El Romano is not for her, and she'd sink the world if it were in her hand to do so.

SERVANT How bad they all are!

PONCIA They're women without men, that's all. And in such matters even blood is forgotten. Sh-h-h-h!

[*She listens.*]

SERVANT What's the matter?

PONCIA [*she rises*] The dogs are barking.

SERVANT Someone must have passed by the back door.

[ADELA *enters wearing a white petticoat and corselet.*]

PONCIA Aren't you in bed yet?

ADELA I want a drink of water.

[*She drinks from a glass on the table.*]

PONCIA I imagined you were asleep.

ADELA I got thirsty and woke up. Aren't you two going to get some rest?

SERVANT Soon now.

[ADELA *goes out.*]

PONCIA Let's go.

SERVANT We've certainly earned some sleep. Bernarda doesn't let me rest the whole day.

PONCIA Take the light.

SERVANT The dogs are going mad.

PONCIA They're not going to let us sleep.

[*They go out. The stage is left almost dark.* MARÍA JOSEFA *enters with a lamb in her arms.*]

MARÍA JOSEFA [*singing*]

Little lamb, child of mine,
Let's go to the shore of the sea,
The tiny ant will be at his doorway,
I'll nurse you and give you your bread.
Bernarda, old leopard-face,
And Magdalena, hyena-face,
Little lamb . . .
Rock, rock-a-bye,
Let's go to the palms at Bethlehem's gate.

[*She laughs.*]

Neither you nor I would want to sleep
The door will open by itself
And on the beach we'll go and hide
In a little coral cabin.

Bernarda, old leopard-face,
And Magdalena, hyena-face,
Little lamb . . .
Rock, rock-a-bye,
Let's go to the palms at Bethlehem's gate.

[*She goes off singing.*]

[ADELA *enters. She looks about cautiously and disappears out the door leading to the corral.* MARTIRIO *enters by another door and stands in anguished watchfulness near the center of the stage. She also is in petticoats. She covers herself with a small black scarf.* MARÍA JOSEFA *crosses before her.*]

MARTIRIO Grandmother, where are you going?

MARÍA JOSEFA You are going to open the door for me? Who are you?

MARTIRIO How did you get out here?

MARÍA JOSEFA I escaped. You, who are you?

MARTIRIO Go back to bed.

MARÍA JOSEFA You're Martirio. Now I see you. Martirio, face of a martyr. And when are you going to have a baby? I've had this one.

MARTIRIO Where did you get that lamb?

MARÍA JOSEFA I know it's a lamb. But can't a lamb be a baby? It's better to have a lamb than not to have anything. Old Bernarda, leopard-face, and Magdalena, hyena-face!

MARTIRIO Don't shout.

MARÍA JOSEFA It's true. Everything's very dark. Just because I have white hair you think I can't have babies, but I can—babies and babies and babies. This baby will have white hair, and I'd have *this* baby, and another, and this *one* other; and with all of us with snow-white hair we'll be like the waves—one, then another, and another. Then we'll all sit down and all of us will have white heads, and we'll be sea-foam. Why isn't there any sea-foam here? Nothing but mourning shrouds here.

MARTIRIO Hush, hush.

MARÍA JOSEFA When my neighbor had a baby, I'd carry her some chocolate and later she'd bring me some, and so on—always and always and always. You'll have white hair, but your neighbors won't come. Now I have to go away, but I'm afraid the dogs will bite me. Won't you come with me as far as the fields? I don't like fields. I like houses, but open houses, and the neighbor women asleep in their beds with their little tiny tots, and the men outside sitting in their chairs. Pepe el Romano is a giant. All of you love him. But he's going to devour you because you're grains of wheat. No, not grains of wheat. Frogs with no tongues!

MARTIRIO [*angrily*] Come, off to bed with you.

[*She pushes her.*]

MARÍA JOSEFA Yes, but then you'll open the door for me, won't you?

MARTIRIO Of course.

MARÍA JOSEFA [*weeping*]

Little lamb, child of mine,
Let's go to the shore of the sea,
The tiny ant will be at his doorway,
I'll nurse you and give you your bread.

[MARTIRIO *locks the door through which* MARÍA JOSEFA *came out and goes to the yard door. There she hesitates, but goes two steps farther.*]

MARTIRIO [*in a low voice*] Adela!

[*Pause. She advances to the door. Then, calling*]

Adela!

[ADELA *enters. Her hair is disarranged.*]

ADELA And what are you looking for me for?

MARTIRIO Keep away from him.

ADELA Who are you to tell me that?

MARTIRIO That's no place for a decent woman.

ADELA How you wish *you'd* been there!

MARTIRIO [*shouting*] This is the moment for me to speak. This can't go on.

ADELA This is just the beginning. I've had strength enough to push myself forward—the spirit and looks you lack. I've seen death under this roof, and gone out to look for what was mine, what belonged to me.

MARTIRIO That soulless man came for another woman. You pushed yourself in front of him.

ADELA He came for the money, but his eyes were always on me.

MARTIRIO I won't allow you to snatch him away. He'll marry Angustias.

ADELA You know better than I he doesn't love her.

MARTIRIO I know.

ADELA You know because you've seen—he loves me, me!

MARTIRIO [*desperately*] Yes.

ADELA [*close before her*] He loves me, *me!* He loves me, *me!*

MARTIRIO Stick me with a knife if you like, but don't tell me that again.

ADELA That's why you're trying to fix it so I won't go away with him. It makes no difference to you if he puts his arms around a woman he doesn't love. Nor does it to me. He could be a hundred years with Angustias, but for him to have his arms around me seems terrible to you—because you too love him! You love him!

MARTIRIO [*dramatically*] Yes! Let me say it without hiding my head. Yes! My breast's bitter, bursting like a pomegranate! I love him!

ADELA [*impulsively, hugging her*] Martirio, Martirio, I'm not to blame!

MARTIRIO Don't put your arms around me! Don't try to smooth it over. My blood's no longer yours, and even though I try to think of you as a sister, I see you as just another woman.

[*She pushes her away.*]

ADELA There's no way out here. Whoever has to drown—let her drown. Pepe is mine. He'll carry me to the rushes along the river bank. . . .

MARTIRIO He won't!

ADELA I can't stand this horrible house after the taste of his mouth. I'll be what he wants me to be. Everybody in the village against me, burning me with their fiery fingers; pursued by those who claim they're decent, and I'll wear, before them all, the crown of thorns that belongs to the mistress of a married man.

MARTIRIO Hush!

ADELA Yes, yes. [*In a low voice*] Let's go to bed. Let's let him marry Angustias. I don't care anymore, but I'll go off alone to a little house where he'll come to see me whenever he wants, whenever he feels like it.

MARTIRIO That'll never happen! Not while I have a drop of blood left in my body.

ADELA Not just weak you, but a wild horse I could force to his knees with just the strength of my little finger.

MARTIRIO Don't raise that voice of yours to me. It irritates me. I have a heart full of a force so evil that, without my wanting to be, I'm drowned by it.

ADELA You show us the way to love our sisters. God must have meant to leave me alone in the midst of darkness, because I can see you as I've never seen you before.

[*A whistle is heard and* ADELA *runs toward the door, but* MARTIRIO *gets in front of her.*]

MARTIRIO Where are you going?

ADELA Get away from that door!

MARTIRIO Get by me if you can!

ADELA Get away!

[*They struggle.*]

MARTIRIO [*shouts*] Mother! Mother!

ADELA Let me go!

[BERNARDA *enters. She wears petticoats and a black shawl.*]

BERNARDA Quiet! Quiet! How poor I am without even a man to help me!

MARTIRIO [*pointing to* ADELA] She was with him. Look at those skirts covered with straw!

BERNARDA [*going furiously toward* ADELA] That's the bed of a bad woman!

ADELA [*facing her*] There'll be an end to prison voices here!

[ADELA *snatches away her mother's cane and breaks it in two.*]

This is what I do with the tyrant's cane. Not another step. No one but Pepe commands me!

[MAGDALENA *enters.*]

MAGDALENA Adela!

[LA PONCIA *and* ANGUSTIAS *enter.*]

ADELA I'm his. [*To* ANGUSTIAS] Know that—and go out in the yard and tell him. He'll be master in this house.

ANGUSTIAS My God!

BERNARDA The gun! Where's the gun?

[*She rushes out.* LA PONCIA *runs ahead of her.* AMELIA *enters and looks on frightened, leaning her head against the wall. Behind her comes* MARTIRIO.]

ADELA No one can hold me back!

[*She tries to go out.*]

ANGUSTIAS [*holding her*] You're not getting out of here with your body's triumph! Thief! Disgrace of this house!

MAGDALENA Let her go where we'll never see her again!

[*A shot is heard.*]

BERNARDA [*entering*] Just try looking for him now!

MARTIRIO [*entering*] That does away with Pepe el Romano.

ADELA Pepe! My God! Pepe!

[*She runs out.*]

PONCIA Did you kill him?

MARTIRIO No. He raced away on his mare!

BERNARDA It was my fault. A woman can't aim.

MAGDALENA Then, why did you say . . . ?

MARTIRIO For her! I'd like to pour a river of blood over her head!

PONCIA Curse you!

MAGDALENA Devil!

BERNARDA Although it's better this way!

[*A thud is heard.*]

Adela! Adela!

PONCIA [*at her door*] Open this door!

BERNARDA Open! Don't think the walls will hide your shame!

SERVANT [*entering*] All the neighbors are up!

BERNARDA [*in a low voice, but like a roar*] Open! Or I'll knock the door down!

[*Pause. Everything is silent.*]

Adela!

[*She walks away from the door.*]

A hammer!

[LA PONCIA *throws herself against the door. It opens and she goes in. As she enters, she screams and backs out.*]

What is it?

PONCIA [*she puts her hands to her throat*] May we never die like that!

[*The sisters fall back. The* SERVANT *crosses herself.* BERNARDA *screams and goes forward.*]

Don't go in!

BERNARDA No, not I! Pepe, you're running now, alive, in the darkness, under the trees, but another day you'll fall. Cut her down! My daughter died a virgin. Take her to another room and dress her as though she were a virgin. No one will say anything about this! She died a virgin. Tell them, so that at dawn, the bells will ring twice.

MARTIRIO A thousand times happy she, who had him.

BERNARDA And I want no weeping. Death must be looked at face to face. Silence! [*To one daughter*] Be still, I said! [*To another daughter*] Tears when you're alone! We'll drown ourselves in a sea of mourning. She, the youngest daughter of Bernarda Alba, died a virgin. Did you hear me? Silence, silence, I said. Silence!

Curtain.

BERTOLT BRECHT

1898–1956

ARGUABLY the most influential dramatist of the twentieth century, Bertolt Brecht developed and popularized a provocative form of theater that has changed the course of theater history. Through dozens of plays and adaptations, elaborate theories of acting, and a whole new approach to theatrical performance, Brecht touched every aspect of theater making and imposed on it his distinct style and method. Collaborating with leading musicians, writers, actors, and designers, such as the composers Kurt Weill and Hanns Eisler, the writer Elisabeth Hauptmann, the actor Helene Weigel (Brecht's wife), and the designer Caspar Neher, Brecht sought to combine these different arts into a new and jarring theatrical experience. He was also intrigued by radio and film, the newest media at the time, and sought to transform the theater in their light, making sure that it would remain "up to date," as he liked to put it. Brecht wanted to create new theater fit for an age dominated by science and progress. The product also of an intensely felt political and social vision, Brecht's reform sought above all to change the relation between theater and its audience, seeking to instill in the audience a critical and analytical attitude. The lasting impact of his work can be measured by the fact that the adjective *Brechtian* has long ceased to refer to Brecht's particular reforms and practices, and often stands for much modernist theater in general.

Born in the city of Augsburg in southern Germany, Brecht studied philosophy and medicine in Munich; but in 1924, he left Munich in order to work with Max Reinhardt, the acclaimed director of the Deutsches Theater in Berlin. By that time, he had already won some recognition with a number of plays, including *Baal* (1922), *Drums in the Night* (1922), and *In the Jungle of Cities* (1923; 1927). Influenced by the episodic structures and jagged style of German expressionist playwrights such as Ernst Toller (1893–1939) and Georg Kaiser (1878–1945), these plays are set in a world whose social fabric has broken down; even the language spoken by the characters is ruptured, shifting abruptly from colloquial speech to abstract metaphysical and religious terms, never resting in a single, stable idiom.

In the course of the 1920s, Brecht gradually moved away from the topics and the characteristic language of his early expressionist plays, although he retained their episodic structure. Increasingly, his theater became a vehicle for understanding, analyzing, and criticizing the social world. *Man Equals Man* (1926) is a good example of this change, focused as it is on the analysis of a single problem: the transformation of a porter, Galy Gay, into a cold-blooded soldier, or rather into a "human fighting machine," as the play puts it. A similar purpose of critical analysis informs *The Rise and Fall of the City of Mahagonny* (1927; 1930), which identifies different forms of greed and consumption in a capitalist Sodom and Gomorrah. Brecht's greatest success during this period was *The Threepenny Opera* (1928), inspired by John Gay's *Beggar's Opera* (1728). *The Threepenny Opera* depicts a reality as cold as that of *Mahagonny:* the criminal underworld of London, where the king of the beggars, Peachum, and a crook, Macheath, fight for Peachum's daughter. This criminal sphere itself is not the main object of critique, however; instead, it functions as a metaphor for the criminality of capitalism. Though never a member of the Communist Party, Brecht shared with Marxist intellectuals an interest in power relations, and he sought to expose, through his plays, the hidden mechanisms of exploitation. Theater for him had become part of the struggle for a better society.

Even though the subject matter of Brecht's plays had grown more sober during the 1920s, their form and style remained exuberant. *Man Equals Man, Mahagonny*, and *The Threepenny Opera*—as well as many subsequent works, including *THE GOOD PERSON OF SZECHWAN* (1943)—were conceived as musical plays. In some cases, the music has come to overshadow the plays themselves. The popularity of *The Threepenny Opera,* perhaps the most entertaining work of them all, was due mostly to Kurt Weill's catchy songs; the best known is "Mack the Knife," which hit the top of the American charts after being recorded in the 1950s by Louis Armstrong and by Bobby Darin. On stage, however, Brecht did not so much use the conventions of musical theater as transform them. Rather than being smoothly integrated into these plays, the music was deliberately set apart. The same was true of the other elements of performance—dialogue, acting, set design. Brecht called this technique the "separation of the elements"; it was an attempt to use the different components of performance in such a way that they would interrupt one another rather than work in unison. Brecht and his collaborators thought of the resulting productions as antioperas: operas whose components had been pulled apart and put back together in a new and startling manner.

The result was the *Verfremdungseffekt* or the "estrangement effect," the attempt to "make strange" the entire experience of watching theater (an alternate translation sometimes used, "alienation effect," misleadingly implies an alienation from nature rather than the defamiliarization emphasized by Brecht). This was the heart of the theory of drama that made Brecht famous. Instead of enchanting the audience through well-integrated, harmonious spectacles, Brecht and his collaborators meant to disentangle the different sensory experiences associated with music, acting, scene design, language, and suspenseful plots and to set them against one another. Ultimately, they envisioned estrangement as the foundation of a new relation between theatrical performance and the audience, aimed at making the audience pause, examine, reflect, and criticize—that is, to look at the performance as if from a distance. Brecht once compared this attitude to that displayed by spectators at a boxing match or a similar sporting event; such audiences examine the skill of the players, appreciating their strategies and techniques from a critical distance, rather than being drawn unreflectively into a simulated world.

The technique of estrangement also extended to acting. Whereas traditionally the actor was supposed to inhabit the role completely, Brecht wanted his actors to remind the audience that they were only playing, that they were pretending to be another person for the duration of the performance. Put in the language of the theater, this meant that actor and role were to be clearly distinguished. Accomplishing this separation was a difficult task, but Brecht helped the actors by often having them speak about the character they are impersonating in the third person—commenting on the role as if from the outside. To illustrate his ideal of estranged acting, Brecht used the example of a courtroom in which witnesses are asked to demonstrate to the jury how a particular accident occurred. They take on different roles, Brecht explains, and go through the action, but do not seek to become completely absorbed in their performance. They never lose sight of their specific purpose. To encourage playgoers to shift their attention from the "what" (what happened) to the "how" (how did it happen), Brecht often gave away the plot at the beginning of each scene, sometimes writing a brief summary on a half-curtain. The audience (the "jury") was meant to analyze the events depicted on stage, focusing on how they had taken place and how they could be altered, rather than be engrossed by the suspense.

The final dimension of estrangement Brecht employed was geographic. Many of his plays are set in non-European locales: America (*Jungle of Cities; Mahagonny; St. Joan of the Stockyards* [1932]), South Asia (*Man Equals Man*), China (*The Good Person of Szechwan*), Japan (*The Yea Sayer* [1930]). Brecht's goal here was not to represent, as accurately as possible, these different cultures. Instead he used settings that were foreign (to his German audience) to facilitate a distanced, analytical attitude toward the events depicted on stage, rather than one complicated by familiar investments and opinions. At the same time, however, Brecht was genuinely influenced by the tradition of Chinese acting and by the Japanese noh theater; his play *The Yea Sayer,* for example, is based on the noh play *Taniko* (fifteenth century).

The geographic displacement of the plays was mirrored by Brecht's later life. Fearing rise of National Socialism, he fled first to Denmark in 1933 and then to the United States in 1941, where he tried and mostly failed to produce his plays or make a living by writing Hollywood screenplays. In 1947, as the McCarthyite anticommunist witch hunts began, Brecht was called before the House Un-American Activities Committee (HUAC); he left the United States directly after the harrowing experience, going first to Switzerland and then, in 1949, to East Germany, where he built the Berliner Ensemble into one of the premier theaters of the world. It was during the years in exile that he wrote not only some of his best-known plays, including *Mother Courage* (1941), *The Life of Galileo Galilei* (1943), and *The Good Person of Szechwan,* but also his adaptation of AESCHYLUS's *Antigone* (1948; his other famous adaptation, of SHAKESPEARE's *Coriolanus,* was written and left incomplete in 1952). In his last years, Brecht withdrew from the public eye, though he was accompanied, as he had been throughout his life, not only by his wife, Helene Weigel, but also by a number of lovers; indeed, many of his plays were collaborations with lovers (especially Elisabeth Hauptmann). He died in East Berlin in 1956, having become the most important cultural representative of socialist East Germany.

The Good Person of Szechwan, written between 1930 and 1942 but not published until 1953, combines many of Brecht's characteristic techniques. It is set in a remote locale, the Chinese province of Sichuan (spelled "Sezuan" by Brecht and "Szechwan" in the following translation). A prelude, interludes, and the play's scenes are organized episodically and not into a tightly constructed plot; the play is also scattered with songs, written by Paul Dessau, that interrupt the flow of the action. In accordance with Brecht's the-

Brecht and Elizabeth Hauptmann working, Berlin, 1927.

ory of acting, actors address the audience directly, commenting on the action and explaining their problems and thus destroying any illusion of realism. Brecht worked on this play over a long period of time—precisely the period in which he formulated the tenets of his theory of estrangement. It therefore became the chief representative of estranged theater, or what Brecht himself preferred to call "epic theater."

Like many of Brecht's plays, *The Good Person of Szechwan* presents a relatively simple dilemma: the inability of the female protagonist, Shen Teh, to be good in the world as it is. Brecht even uses a didactic genre, the parable, to drive this point home: three gods visit Szechwan in order to find a single good person. The only good person they can find, the only one to offer them shelter, is the prostitute Shen Teh, whom they reward by giving her a considerable sum of money. They then leave her to her own devices, urging her only to remain good. Doing so, however, is not all that easy. Shen Teh uses the money to buy a tobacco store. As a good person, she soon begins taking in all kinds of people in need and distributing food to the poor, until finally the tobacco store itself is in danger of failing. It is at this point that she calls on the services of Shui Ta, her hard-nosed cousin, to keep her business afloat. Immediately, Shui Ta cuts down on Shen Teh's philanthropy, and thus restores her business to a sound economic footing. Therein lies the play's central concern: being a good person and getting by in this world are mutually incompatible goals.

The play presents this point through an intriguing variation on the estrangement technique—Shen Teh and Shui Ta are the same person and are played by the same actor. The device is revealed to the audience relatively early, when the change in costume occurs in front of the spectators' eyes; yet all but one of the other characters on the stage remain in the dark.

The 1957 Berliner Ensemble production of *The Good Person of Szechwan*.

Brecht thereby ensures that the audience has more information at its disposal than the characters and can thus observe their motivations and actions. No attention is wasted on a state of suspense, trying to discover this identity (the "what"); the focus instead is entirely on understanding why Shen Teh depends on Shui Ta. Brecht employs a split character to show not psychological conflict but social conflict.

Another source of dramatic conflict is the demand made by the gods that Shen Teh must be good, which fails to take into account whether she can afford goodness. The state of the world, the fact that the world as it is does not allow a person be good and survive, does not concern them. This discrepancy between the world and the gods is mediated by a man named Wang, a water carrier. No angel himself, Wang knows what this world requires and how it forces those who live in it to behave. At the same time, he honors the gods, striving to please them as best he can, even as he recognizes the impossibility of their demands. He seeks shelter for them and tries to hide most people's indifference toward them. He is a figure of compromise and attempts to mediate the clash between the gods and the harsh realities of the world—with limited success.

Fueling this clash is not just the gods' disinterest in the world but ultimately their ignorance of it. Wang first recognizes them because their very appearance bears no traces of labor; they are creatures of leisure who know nothing of the world's hard realities; their conception of goodness is merely a lofty ideal. In particular, the gods refuse to interfere in the area of economics, assuming instead that morality and economics have nothing to do with one another. They cling to Shen Teh's goodness without recognizing that it depends on the constant interventions of her harder self, of which the gods disapprove. By revealing to the audience that Shui Ta is just the other side of Shen Teh, Brecht constructs a disjunction between the audience and the gods of which only the audience is aware. The gods are thus in a position of ignorance and the audience, of knowledge.

Like Brecht's other didactic plays, *The Good Person of Szechwan* does not offer, or preach, a particular solution to the dilemma it presents, such as a socialist society or a new conception of goodness. What it does do, however, is suggest a problem or a set of contradictions, here between the conception of goodness imposed by the gods and the (economic) requisites of the world. It is clear that such a contradiction offers two lines of attack: to get rid of the gods or to get rid of the economic system that does not allow for goodness.

These two consequences are suggested throughout, but they come to the fore in the final scene, which is a trial. Now the contradictions on which the entire play is built are brought into the open: the audience, both onstage and offstage, has to make up its mind. Indeed, trial scenes can be found frequently in Brecht's works, for they offer an opportunity to expose false morals, false laws, and other abuses. At the same time, trial scenes resonate with Brecht's ideal audience: an audience willing to make its own judgments and to come to its own conclusions.

Brecht's theater shaped many of the most important theater makers of the twentieth century, including the German experimental writers Heiner Müller and Peter Weiss, the British feminist playwright CARYL CHURCHILL, and the Brazilian political dramatist Augusto Boal. That they, despite their enormous differences, all refer to Brecht as their primary influence testifies to the long and varied impact he has had on contemporary theater the world over. This unparalleled influence was due to Brecht's ability to institute a coherent theater reform in every dimension of performance, a reform that other artists could then adopt, alter, or rebel against. But despite all his fame, Brecht did not achieve—or at least he did not fully achieve—his ultimate end: namely, to transform the theater from a vehicle of entertainment into a vehicle of critical thought. His legacy is thus an ambiguous one: he single-handedly changed the course of theater history, and yet this change fell short of his grand goal. M.P.

The Good Person of Szechwan[1]

CHARACTERS

WANG, a water-seller
THREE GODS
SHEN TEH–SHUI TA
YANG SUN, an unemployed airman
MRS YANG, his mother
MRS SHIN, a widow
The family of eight
Lin To, a CARPENTER
MRS MI TZU, a property owner
The POLICEMAN
The CARPET-DEALER and his WIFE
The OLD PROSTITUTE
SHU FU, the barber
The PRIEST
The UNEMPLOYED MAN
The WAITER
Passersby of the Prologue

Prologue

A Street in the Capital of Szechwan[2]

[*It is evening.* WANG, *the water-seller, introduces himself to the audience.*]

WANG I am a water-seller in the capital of Szechwan province. My job is tedious. When water is short I have to go far for it. And when it is plentiful I earn nothing. But utter poverty is the rule in our province. All agree that only the gods can help us. To my inexpressible joy a widely travelled cattle dealer has told me that some of the highest gods are already on their way, and that Szechwan may see them too. They say that the heavens are deeply disturbed by the many complaints that have been going up. For the last three days I have waited at this entrance to the city, especially towards evening, so that I may be the first to greet them. There will hardly be a chance for me later; they will be surrounded by important people and there will be far too many demands on them. But shall I be able to recognise them? They may not arrive in a group. Perhaps they will come singly, so as not to attract attention. It cannot be those men—[*He studies some workmen passing by.*]—they are coming away from work. Their shoulders are bent by the burdens they have to carry. That fellow is no god either, he has inky fingers. At most he may be some kind of clerk in a cement works. I would not take those gentlemen—[*Two gentlemen walk past.*]—for gods even: they have the brutal faces of men who beat people, and the gods find that unnecessary. But look at these three! They seem very different. They are well nourished, show no evidence of any kind of employment, and have dust on their shoes, so they must have travelled far. It is them! Yours to command, Illustrious Ones!

1. Translated by John Willett.
2. Chengdu is the capital of Szechwan (Sichuan), a province in western China. However, the Chinese setting of this play is drawn largely from Brecht's imagination, not from historical or geographical fact.

[*He flings himself to the ground.*]

THE FIRST GOD [*pleased*] Have you been expecting us?

WANG [*gives them a drink*] For a long while. But only I knew that you were coming.

THE FIRST GOD We must find a lodging for tonight. Do you know of one?

WANG One? Lots! The city is at your service, O Illustrious Ones. Where do you wish to stay?

[*The* GODS *exchange significant looks.*]

THE FIRST GOD Try the first house, my son. Take the very first one first.

WANG I only fear that I may attract the enmity of the powerful, if I give one of them the preference.

THE FIRST GOD Then take it as an order: try the first one.

WANG That's Mr Fo opposite. One moment.

[*He runs to a house and hammers on the door. It opens, but one can see him being turned away. He comes hesitantly back.*]

WANG How stupid. Mr Fo happens to be out just now, and his servants dare not take the responsibility, as he is very strict. Won't he be angry when he finds who has been turned away!

THE GODS [*smiling*] Indeed.

WANG Another moment then! The house next door is the widow Su's. She will be beside herself with joy.

[*He runs there, but is apparently turned away once more.*]

I shall have to ask across the road. She says she has only one very small room, and it's in no fit state. I will go straight to Mr Cheng's.

THE SECOND GOD But a small room is all we need. Tell her that we are coming.

WANG Even if it has not been cleaned? Suppose it is crawling with spiders?

THE SECOND GOD No matter. The more spiders, the fewer flies.

THE THIRD GOD [*in an amiable way*] Try Mr Cheng or anybody else you like, my son. I admit I find spiders a little unattractive.

[WANG *knocks at another door and is admitted.*]

A VOICE FROM THE HOUSE Get away with your gods! We've got enough troubles of our own.

WANG [*returning to the gods*] Mr Cheng is extremely sorry, he has his whole house full of relatives and dare not appear before you, Illustrious Ones. Between ourselves, I think there are evil men among them whom he would prefer you not to see. He is much too frightened of your judgment. That must be it.

THE THIRD GOD Are we all that frightening?

WANG Only to evil people, isn't it? We all know that Kwan province has suffered from floods for years.

THE SECOND GOD Oh? And why is that?

WANG Because they are not god-fearing people, I suppose.

THE SECOND GOD Rubbish. Because they didn't look after the dam properly.

THE FIRST GOD Sh! [*To* WANG] Any other prospects, my son?

WANG How can you ask? I have only to go to the next house, and I can have my pick. They are all falling over each other to entertain you. An unlucky combination of circumstances, you understand. Half a minute.

[He walks away hesitantly and stands in the street unable to make up his mind.]

THE SECOND GOD What did I tell you?

THE THIRD GOD It may just be circumstances.

THE SECOND GOD Circumstances in Shun, circumstances in Kwan, and now circumstances in Szechwan. There are no god-fearing people left: that is the naked truth which you will not recognize. Our mission is hopeless, and you had better admit it.

THE FIRST GOD We may still come across good people at any moment. We cannot expect to have things all our own way.

THE THIRD GOD The resolution says: the world can go on as it is if we find enough good people, able to lead a decent human existence. The water-seller himself is such a person, if I am not deceived.

[He goes up to WANG, *who is still standing uncertain.]*

THE SECOND GOD He is always deceived. When the water man let us drink out of his measure I saw something. Look.

[He shows it to the FIRST GOD.]

THE FIRST GOD It has got a false bottom.

THE SECOND GOD A swindler.

THE FIRST GOD Very well, we strike him out. But what does it matter if one man is corrupted? We shall soon find plenty who fulfil the conditions. We must find someone. For two thousand years we have been hearing the same complaint, that the world cannot go on as it is. No one can stay on earth and remain good. We must at last be able to show some people who are in a position to keep our commandments.

THE THIRD GOD [*to* WANG] Is it too difficult for you to find us a place?

WANG Such guests as you? What are you thinking of? It is my fault that you were not taken in immediately; I am a bad guide.

THE THIRD GOD Not that, certainly.

[He turns back to the others.]

WANG They have begun to realise. [*He accosts a* GENTLEMAN.] Honoured sir, forgive me for addressing you, but three of the highest gods, whose impending advent has been the talk of all Szechwan for years, have now really arrived and are looking for a place to spend the night. Don't walk away. Look for yourself. One glance will convince you. For heaven's sake do something about it. It's the chance of a lifetime! Invite the gods to visit your home before someone else snaps them up; they are sure to accept.

[The GENTLEMAN *has walked on.* WANG *turns to another.]*

You, sir, you heard what it's about. Have you any room? It needn't be palatial. The intention is what matters.

THE GENTLEMAN How am I to tell what sort of gods yours are? Heaven knows who I might be letting into my house.

[He goes into a tobacconist's. WANG *runs back to the three.]*

WANG I have found somebody who is sure to take you.

[He sees his measure on the ground, looks embarrassedly at the GODS, *picks it up, and runs back again.]*

THE FIRST GOD That does not sound encouraging.

WANG [*as the man steps out of the shop*] What about the accommodation?

THE GENTLEMAN How do you know I'm not living in rooms myself?

THE FIRST GOD He will find nothing. We had better write Szechwan off too.

WANG It's three of the chief gods. Truly. Their images in the temples are just like them. If you get your invitation in now they might perhaps accept.

THE GENTLEMAN [*laughs*] I suppose they're a lot of prize swindlers you're trying to foist off on someone.

[*Off.*]

WANG [*shouting after him*] You swivel-eyed chiseller! Have you no reverence? You'll all roast in brimstone for your lack of interest. The gods crap on the lot of you. And you'll be sorry for it. You shall pay for it unto the fourth generation. You have disgraced the whole province. [*Pause*] That leaves us with Shen Teh, the prostitute; she can't refuse.

[*He calls 'Shen Teh!'* SHEN TEH *looks out of the window above.*]

They've arrived, and I can't find them a room. Could you possibly have them for one night?

SHEN TEH Not much hope, Wang. I am expecting someone. But how is it that you can't find a room for them?

WANG I can't explain now. Szechwan is nothing but one big muck-heap.

SHEN TEH I should have to hide when he arrives. Then he might go away. He was supposed to be taking me out.

WANG Can we come up in the meantime?

SHEN TEH If you don't talk too loudly. Do I have to be careful what I say?

WANG Very. They mustn't find out how you earn your living. We had better wait downstairs. But you won't be going off with him, will you?

SHEN TEH I've had no luck lately, and if I can't find the rent by tomorrow they'll throw me out.

WANG You shouldn't think of money at a moment like this.

SHEN TEH I don't know: I'm afraid that a rumbling stomach is no respecter of persons. But very well, I will take them in.

[*She is seen to put out her light.*]

THE FIRST GOD It looks hopeless to me.

[*They go up to* WANG.]

WANG [*startled to see them standing behind him*] You are fixed up for the night.

[*He wipes the sweat off his face.*]

THE GODS Really? Then let us go.

WANG There is no great hurry. Take your time. The room is not quite ready.

THE THIRD GOD Very good, we will sit here and wait.

WANG But isn't there too much traffic here? Let's cross the road.

THE SECOND GOD We like looking at people. That is exactly what we came for.

WANG It's a windy spot.

THE THIRD GOD Does this seem all right to you?

[*They sit on a doorstep.* WANG *sits on the ground somewhat to one side.*]

WANG [*with a rush*] You are lodging with a girl who lives on her own. She is the best person in Szechwan.

THE THIRD GOD That is gratifying.

WANG [*to the audience*] When I picked up my mug just then they gave me a peculiar look. Do you think they noticed anything? I daren't look them in the face any longer.

THE THIRD GOD You seem exhausted.

WANG A little. I have been running.

THE FIRST GOD Do people here find life very hard?

WANG Good people do.

THE FIRST GOD [*seriously*] Do you?

WANG I know what you mean. I am not good. But I too find life hard.

[*Meanwhile a gentleman has appeared in front of* SHEN TEH*'s house and whistled a number of times. Each time* WANG *gives a nervous jerk.*]

THE THIRD GOD [*in an undertone to* WANG] It looks as if he has given up.

WANG [*confused*] It does.

[*He jumps up and runs into the open, leaving his carrying-pole behind. But the following has occurred: the man waiting has gone off, and* SHEN TEH, *after opening the door quietly and calling 'Wang!' in a low voice, has gone down the street in search of* WANG. *When* WANG *in turn calls 'Shen Teh!' in a low voice he gets no reply.*]

WANG She has let me down. She has gone off to get the money for the rent, and I have no place for the Illustrious Ones. They are waiting there, exhausted. I cannot go back yet again and tell them: no good, sorry. My own sleeping place under the culvert is out of the question. And I am sure the gods would not care to lodge with a man whose dirty business they have seen through. I would not go back for anything in the world. But my carrying-pole is still there. What shall I do? I dare not fetch it. I shall leave the capital and find somewhere where I can hide from their eyes, for I failed to do anything to help those I honour.

[*He hurries away. As soon as he has gone,* SHEN TEH *returns, searches for him on the opposite side and sees the* GODS.]

SHEN TEH Are you the Illustrious Ones? My name is Shen Teh. I should be happy if you consented to make do with my small room.

THE THIRD GOD But where has the water-seller disappeared to?

SHEN TEH I must have missed him.

THE FIRST GOD He probably thought you were not coming, and then felt too scared to come back to us.

THE THIRD GOD [*picks up the carrying-pole*] We will ask you to look after it. He needs it.

[*They enter the house led by* SHEN TEH. *It grows dusk, then light again. In the half-light of the dawn the* GODS *again leave the door, led by* SHEN TEH *guiding them with a lantern. They take their leave.*]

THE FIRST GOD Dear Shen Teh, we are grateful for your hospitality. We shall not forget that it was you who took us in. Will you give the water-seller his pole back? And tell him that we are grateful to him too for having shown us a good person.

SHEN TEH I am not good. I have an admission to make: when Wang asked me if I could shelter you I had hesitations.

THE FIRST GOD Hesitations do not count if you overcome them. Know that you gave us more than a lodging. There are many, including even certain of us gods, who have begun to doubt whether such a thing as a good person still exists. To check up was the main object of our journey. We are now happy to continue it, for we have succeeded in finding one. Farewell.

SHEN TEH Wait, Illustrious Ones. I am by no means sure that I am good. I should certainly like to be, but how am I to pay the rent? Let me admit: I sell myself in order to live, and even so I cannot manage, for there are so many forced to do this. I would take on anything, but who would not? Of course I should like to obey the commandments: to honour my parents and respect the truth. Not to covet my neighbour's house would be a joy to me, and to love, honour, and cherish a husband would be very pleasant. Nor do I wish to exploit other men or to rob the defenceless. But how can it be done? Even by breaking one or two of the commandments I can barely manage.

THE FIRST GOD All these, Shen Teh, are but the doubts of a good person.

THE THIRD GOD Goodbye, Shen Teh. And give our warmest greetings to the water-seller. He was a good friend to us.

THE SECOND GOD I fear we did but little good to him.

THE THIRD GOD The best of luck.

THE FIRST GOD Above all, be good, Shen Teh. Goodbye.

[*They turn to go. They begin to wave goodbye.*]

SHEN TEH [*nervously*] But I am not certain of myself, Illustrious Ones. How can I be good when everything is so expensive?

THE SECOND GOD Alas, that is beyond our powers. We cannot meddle in the sphere of economics.

THE THIRD GOD Wait! Just a minute. If she were better provided she might stand more chance.

THE SECOND GOD We cannot give her anything. We could not answer for it up there.

THE FIRST GOD Why not?

[*They put their heads together and confer animatedly.*]

THE FIRST GOD [*awkwardly, to* SHEN TEH] We understand that you have no money for the rent. We are not poor people, so it is natural that we should pay for our lodging. Here you are. [*He gives her money.*] But please let nobody know that we paid. It might be misinterpreted.

THE SECOND GOD Only too easily.

THE THIRD GOD No, it is permissible. We can quite well pay for our lodging. There was nothing against it in the resolution. So fare you well.

[*The* GODS *exeunt*[3] *rapidly.*]

Scene 1

A Small Tobacconist's

[*The shop is not yet properly installed, and not yet open.*]

SHEN TEH [*to the audience*] It is now three days since the gods left. They told me they wanted to pay for their lodging. And when I looked at what they had given me I saw that it was more than a thousand silver dollars. I have used the money to buy a tobacconist's business. I moved in here yesterday, and now I hope to be able to do a great deal of good. Look at Mrs Shin, for instance, the old owner of the shop. Yesterday she came to ask for rice for her children. And today I again see her bringing her pot across the square.

[*Enter* MRS SHIN. *The women bow to one another.*]

SHEN TEH Good evening, Mrs Shin.

3. Leave (literally, "they exit"; Latin).

MRS SHIN Good evening, Miss Shen Teh. What do you think of your new home?

SHEN TEH I like it. How did the children spend the night?

MRS SHIN Oh, in someone's house, if you can call that shack a house. The baby's started coughing.

SHEN TEH That's bad.

MRS SHIN You don't know what's bad. You've got it good. But you'll find plenty to learn in a dump like this. The whole district's a slum.

SHEN TEH That is right what you told me, though? That the cement workers call in here at midday?

MRS SHIN But not a customer otherwise, not even the locals.

SHEN TEH You didn't tell me that when you sold me the business.

MRS SHIN That's right: throw it in my face. First you take the roof away over the children's heads, and then it's nothing but dump and slum. It's more than I can bear.

[*She weeps.*]

SHEN TEH [*quickly*] I'll get your rice.

MRS SHIN I was going to ask you if you could lend me some money.

SHEN TEH [*as she pours rice into her bowl*] I can't do that. I haven't sold anything yet.

MRS SHIN But I need it. What am I to live on? You've taken everything I've got. Now you're cutting my throat. I'll leave my children on your door-step, you bloodsucker!

[*She snatches the pot from her hands.*]

SHEN TEH Don't be so bad-tempered. You'll spill your rice.

[*Enter an* ELDERLY COUPLE *and a shabbily dressed* MAN.]

THE WOMAN Ah, Shen Teh, my dear, we heard you were doing so nicely now. Why, you've set up in business! Just fancy, we're without a home. Our tobacconist's shop has folded up. We wondered if we mightn't spend a night with you. You know my nephew? He can't abide being separated from us.

THE NEPHEW [*looking round*] Smashing shop.

MRS SHIN Who's this lot?

SHEN TEH When I arrived here from the country they were my first landlords. [*To the audience*] When my small funds ran out they threw me on the street. They are probably frightened that I will say no. They are poor.

They have no shelter.
They have no friends.
They need someone.
How can they be refused?

[*Addressing the woman in a friendly voice*] Welcome to you, I will gladly give you lodging. But all I have is a tiny room at the back of the shop.

THE MAN That'll do us. Don't you worry. [*While* SHEN TEH *fetches them tea*] We'd better move in behind here, so as not to be in your way. I suppose you picked on a tobacconist's to remind you of your first home? We'll be able to give you one or two tips. That's another reason for coming to you.

MRS SHIN [*sardonically*] Let's hope one or two customers come too.

THE WOMAN Is that meant for us?

THE MAN Sh. Here's a customer already.

[*Enter a tattered* MAN.]

THE UNEMPLOYED MAN Excuse me, miss, I'm out of a job.

[MRS SHIN *laughs.*]

SHEN TEH What can I do for you?

THE UNEMPLOYED MAN They say you're opening up tomorrow. I thought people sometimes find things in bad condition when they unpack them. Can you spare a fag?

THE WOMAN What cheek, begging for tobacco. 'Tisn't as if it had been bread.

THE UNEMPLOYED MAN Bread's expensive. A few puffs at a fag and I'm a new man. I'm so done in.[4]

SHEN TEH [*gives him cigarettes*] That's very important, being a new man. I shall open up with you, you'll bring me luck.

[*The* UNEMPLOYED MAN *hastily lights a cigarette, inhales, and goes off coughing.*]

THE WOMAN Was that wise, my dear?

MRS SHIN If that's how you open up you'll be closing down before three days are out.

THE MAN I bet he had money on him, all right.

SHEN TEH But he said he hadn't anything.

THE NEPHEW How do you know he wasn't having you on?

SHEN TEH [*worked up*] How do I know he was having me on?

THE WOMAN [*shaking her head*] She can't say no. You're too good, Shen Teh. If you want to hang on to your shop you'd better be able to refuse sometimes.

THE MAN Say it isn't yours. Say it belongs to a relation and he insists on strict accounts. Why not try it?

MRS SHIN Anyone would who didn't always want to play Lady Bountiful.[5]

SHEN TEH [*laughs*] Grumble away. The room won't be available and the rice goes back in the sack.

THE WOMAN [*shocked*] Is the rice yours too?

SHEN TEH [*to the audience*]

They are bad.
They are no man's friend.
They grudge even a bowl of rice.
They need it all themselves.
How can they be blamed?

[*Enter a* LITTLE MAN.]

MRS SHIN [*sees him and leaves hurriedly*] I'll look in tomorrow, then. [*Off.*]

THE LITTLE MAN [*starts after her*] Hey, Mrs Shin! Just the person I want.

THE WOMAN Does she come regularly? Has she got some claim on you?

SHEN TEH No claim, but she's hungry: and that's more important.

THE LITTLE MAN She knows why she's running away. Are you the new proprietress? I see you're stocking up your shelves. But they aren't yours, let me tell you. Unless you pay for them. That old ragamuffin who was squatting here didn't pay. [*To the others*] I'm the carpenter, see?

SHEN TEH But I thought that was part of the fittings I paid for.

4. Exhausted.
5. A character in George Farquhar's comedy *The Beaux' Stratagem* (1707), who displays striking generosity to the poor.

THE CARPENTER Crooks. A pack of crooks. You and this Mrs Shin are thick as thieves. I want my 100 silver dollars, or my name's not Lin To.

SHEN TEH How can I pay? I've got no money left.

THE CARPENTER Then I'll have you sold up![6] On the spot. Pay on the spot or you'll be sold up.

THE MAN [*prompts* SHEN TEH] Your cousin . . .

SHEN TEH Can't you make it next month?

THE CARPENTER [*shouting*] No.

SHEN TEH Don't be too hard, Mr Lin To. I can't satisfy all demands at once. [*To the audience*]

A slight connivance, and one's powers are doubled.
Look how the cart-horse stops before a tuft of grass:
Wink one eye for an instant and the horse pulls better.
Show but a little patience in June and the tree
By August is sagging with peaches. How
But for patience could we live together?
A brief postponement
Brings the most distant goal within reach.

[*To the* CARPENTER] Please be patient, just a little, Mr Lin To.

THE CARPENTER And who is going to be patient with me and my family? [*He pulls some of the shelving away from the wall, as if to take it down.*] You pay, else I take the shelves with me.

THE WOMAN My dear Shen Teh, why don't you refer the whole thing to your cousin? [*To the* CARPENTER] Put your claim in writing, and Miss Shen Teh's cousin will pay.

THE CARPENTER We all know those cousins.

THE NEPHEW Don't stand there laughing like an idiot. He's a personal friend of mine.

THE MAN He's sharp as a knife.

THE CARPENTER All right, he'll get my bill.

[*He tips the shelving over, sits down on it, and writes out his bill.*]

THE WOMAN He'll have the clothes off your back for his rotten old planks if you don't stop him. My advice is never admit a claim, right or wrong, or you'll be smothered in claims, right or wrong. Throw a bit of meat in your dustbin, and every mongrel in the place will be at each other's throats in your backyard. What are solicitors for?

SHEN TEH He has done some work and can't go away with nothing. He has a family too. It's dreadful that I can't pay him. What will the gods say?

THE MAN You did your bit when you took us in, that's more than enough.

[*Enter a* LIMPING MAN *and a pregnant* WOMAN.]

THE LIMPING MAN [*to the couple*] So there you are. A credit to the family, I don't think. Going and leaving us waiting at the corner.

THE WOMAN [*embarrassed*] This is my brother Wung and my sister-in-law. [*To the two*] Stop nagging and sit quietly out of the way, and don't bother our old friend Miss Shen Teh. [*To* SHEN TEH] We ought to take them both in, I think, what with my sister-in-law being four months gone.[7] Or are you against it?

6. That is, all her goods will be sold for the benefit of her creditors.

7. That is, pregnant.

SHEN TEH You are welcome.

THE WOMAN Thank her. The cups are over there. [*To* SHEN TEH] They would never have known where to go. Just as well you've got this shop.

SHEN TEH [*laughing to the audience as she brings tea*] Yes, just as well I have got it.

[*Enter* MRS MI TZU, *the proprietress, with a document in her hand.*]

MRS MI TZU Miss Shen Teh, I am Mrs Mi Tzu, the proprietress of this building. I hope we will get on together. Here is the agreement for the lease. [*While* SHEN TEH *studies the agreement*] An auspicious moment, do you not think, gentlemen, when a small business is opened? [*She looks round her.*] A few gaps on the shelves still, but it will do. I suppose you can provide me with one or two references?

SHEN TEH Is that necessary?

MRS MI TZU You see, I have really no idea who you are.

THE MAN Can we vouch for Miss Shen Teh, maybe? We've known her ever since she first came to town, and we'd cut off our right hands for her.

MRS MI TZU And who are you?

THE MAN I am Ma Fu, tobacconist.

MRS MI TZU Where's your shop?

THE MAN I haven't got a shop at the moment. It's like this: I've just sold it.

MRS MI TZU Aha. [*To* SHEN TEH] And is there no one else who can give me any information about you?

THE WOMAN [*prompting*] Cousin . . . your cousin . . .

MRS MI TZU But you must have someone who can tell me what kind of tenant I'm getting in my house. This is a respectable house, my dear. I can't sign any agreement with you otherwise.

SHEN TEH [*slowly, with lowered eyes*] I have got a cousin.

MRS MI TZU Oh, so you've got a cousin? Round here? We could go straight over now. What is he?

SHEN TEH He doesn't live here; he's in another town.

THE WOMAN In Shung, weren't you saying?

SHEN TEH Mr Shui Ta. In Shung.

THE MAN But of course I know him. Tall, skinny.

THE NEPHEW [*to the* CARPENTER] You've had to do with Miss Shen Teh's cousin too, chum. Over the shelving.

THE CARPENTER [*grumpily*] I'm just making out his bill. There you are. [*He hands it over.*] I'll be back first thing in the morning.

[*Exit.*]

THE NEPHEW [*calling after him, for the proprietress's benefit*] Don't you worry. Her cousin will pay.

MRS MI TZU [*with a keen look at* SHEN TEH] Well, I shall also be glad to meet him. Good evening, madam.

[*Exit.*]

THE WOMAN [*after an interval*] It's bound to come out now. You can bet she'll know all about you by the morning.

THE SISTER-IN-LAW [*quietly to the* NEPHEW] This set-up won't last long!

[*Enter an* OLD MAN, *guided by a* BOY.]

THE BOY [*calling back*] Here they are.

THE WOMAN Hello, grandpa. [*To* SHEN TEH] The dear old man. He must have been worrying about us. And the youngster, look how he's grown. He eats like an ostrich. Who else have you got with you?

THE MAN [*looking out*] Only your niece. [*To* SHEN TEH] A young relation up from the country. I hope we aren't too many for you. We weren't such a big family when you used to live with us, were we? Ah yes, we grew and grew. The worse it got, the more of us there seemed to be. And the more of us there were the worse it got. But we'd better lock up or we'll have no peace.

[*She shuts the door and all sit down.*]

THE WOMAN The great thing is, we mustn't get in your way in the shop. It's up to you to keep the home fires burning. We planned it like this: the kids'll be out during the day, and only grandpa and my sister-in-law will stay, and perhaps me. The others will just be looking in once or twice during the daytime, see? Light that lamp, boys, and make yourselves at home.

THE NEPHEW [*facetiously*] I hope that cousin doesn't blow in tonight, tough old Mr Shui Ta! [*The* SISTER-IN-LAW *laughs.*]

THE BROTHER [*reaching for a cigarette*] One more or less won't matter.

THE MAN You bet.

[*They all help themselves to something to smoke. The* BROTHER *hands round a jug of wine.*]

THE NEPHEW Drinks on old cousin!

THE GRANDFATHER [*solemnly to* SHEN TEH] Hullo!

[SHEN TEH *is confused by this delayed greeting, and bows. In one hand she holds the* CARPENTER'*s bill, in the other the agreement for the lease.*]

THE WOMAN Can't you people sing something to entertain our hostess?

THE NEPHEW Grandpa can kick off.

[*They sing.*]

Song of the Smoke

THE GRANDFATHER

Once I believed intelligence would aid me
I was an optimist when I was younger
Now that I'm old I see it hasn't paid me:
How can intelligence compete with hunger?
  And so I said: drop it!
  Like smoke twisting grey
  Into ever colder coldness you'll
  Blow away.

THE MAN

I saw the conscientious man get nowhere
And so I tried the crooked path instead
But crookedness makes our sort travel slower.
There seems to be no way to get ahead.
  Likewise I say: drop it!
  Like smoke twisting grey
  Into ever colder coldness you'll
  Blow away.

THE NIECE

The old, they say, find little fun in hoping.
Time's what they need, and time begins to press.
But for the young, they say, the gates are open.
They open, so they say, on nothingness.
  And I too say: drop it!
  Like smoke twisting grey
  Into ever colder coldness you'll
  Blow away.

THE NEPHEW Where did that wine come from?

THE SISTER-IN-LAW He pawned the sack of tobacco.

THE MAN What? That tobacco was all we had left. We didn't touch it even to get a bed. You dirty bastard!

THE BROTHER Call me a bastard just because my wife's half frozen? And who's been drinking it? Give me that jug.

[*They struggle. The shelves collapse.*]

SHEN TEH [*touches them*] O look out for the shop, don't smash everything! It's a gift of the gods. Take whatever's there if you want, but don't smash it!

THE WOMAN [*sceptically*] It's a smaller shop than I thought. A pity we went and told Aunty and the others. If they turn up too there won't be much room.

THE SISTER-IN-LAW Our hostess is getting a bit frosty too.

[*There are voices outside, and a knocking on the door.*]

CRIES Open up! It's us!

THE WOMAN Is that you, Aunty? How are we going to manage now?

SHEN TEH My beautiful shop! Oh, such hopes! No sooner opened, than it is no more. [*To the audience*]

The dinghy which might save us
Is straightway sucked into the depths:
Too many of the drowning
Snatch greedily at it.

CRIES [*from outside*] Open up!

Interlude

Under a Bridge

[*The water-seller is crouching by the stream.*]

WANG [*looking round*] All quiet. That makes four days I have been hiding. They won't find me, I've got my eyes open. I took the same direction as them on purpose. The second day they crossed the bridge; I heard their footsteps overhead. By now they must be a long way off; I have nothing more to fear.

[*He has leant back and gone to sleep. Music. The slope becomes transparent, and the* GODS *appear.*]

WANG [*holding his arm in front of his face, as though he were about to be struck*] Don't say anything! I know! I failed to find anybody who would take you into his house! Now I have told you! Now go your way!

THE FIRST GOD No, you did find somebody. As you left they came up. They took us in for the night; they watched over our sleep; and they lighted our way next morning when we left them. You had told us that she was a good person, and she was good.

WANG So it was Shen Teh who lodged you?

THE THIRD GOD Of course.

WANG And I ran away, I had so little faith! Just because I thought she couldn't come. Because she had been down on her luck she couldn't come.

THE GODS

O feeble one!
Well-meaning but feeble man!
Where hardship is, he thinks there is no goodness.
Where danger lies, he thinks there is no courage.
O feebleness, that believes no good whatever!
O hasty judgement! O premature despair!

WANG I am deeply ashamed, Illustrious Ones.

THE FIRST GOD And now, O water-seller, be so good as to return quickly to the city and look to dear Shen Teh, so that you can keep us posted about her. She is doing well now. She is said to have acquired the money to set up a small shop, so she can freely follow the impulses of her gentle heart. Show some interest in her goodness, for no one can be good for long if goodness is not demanded of him. We for our part wish to travel further and continue our search, and discover still more people like our good person in Szechwan, so that we can put a stop to the rumour which says that the good have found our earth impossible to live on.

[*They vanish.*]

Scene 2

The Tobacconist's

[*Sleeping bodies everywhere. The lamp is still burning. A knock.*]

THE WOMAN [*raises herself, drunk with sleep*] Shen Teh! Somebody knocking! Where has the girl got to?

THE NEPHEW Getting breakfast, I expect. It's on her cousin.

[*The* WOMAN *laughs and slouches to the door. Enter a* YOUNG GENTLEMAN, *the* CARPENTER *behind him.*]

THE YOUNG GENTLEMAN I am her cousin.

THE WOMAN [*falling from the clouds*[8]] What did you say you were?

THE YOUNG GENTLEMAN My name is Shui Ta.

THE FAMILY [*shaking one another awake*] Her cousin! But it was all a joke, she's got no cousin! But here's someone who says he's her cousin! Don't tell me, and at this hour of the day!

THE NEPHEW If you're our hostess's cousin, mister, get us some breakfast right away, will you?

SHUI TA [*turning out the lamp*] The first customers will be arriving any moment. Please be quick and get dressed so that I can open up my shop.

THE MAN Your shop? I fancy this shop belongs to our friend Shen Teh? [SHUI TA *shakes his head.*] What, do you mean to say it's not her shop at all?

THE SISTER-IN-LAW So she's been having us on. Where's she slunk off to?

8. That is, with surprise.

SHUI TA She has been detained. She wishes me to tell you that now I am here she can no longer do anything for you.

THE WOMAN [*shaken*] And we thought she was such a good person.

THE NEPHEW Don't you believe him! Go and look for her!

THE MAN Right, we will. [*He organises them.*] You and you and you and you, go and comb the place for her. Grandpa and us will stay here and hold the fort. The boy can go and find us something to eat. [*To the* BOY] See that baker's at the corner. Nip over and stuff your shirt full.

THE SISTER-IN-LAW And don't forget some of those little round cakes.

THE MAN But mind the baker doesn't catch you. And keep clear of the policeman!

[*The* BOY *nods and goes off. The others get fully dressed.*]

SHUI TA Won't cake-stealing damage the reputation of the shop which has given you refuge?

THE NEPHEW Don't mind him, we'll soon find her. She'll tell him what's what.

[*Exeunt* NEPHEW, BROTHER, SISTER-IN-LAW, *and* NIECE.]

THE SISTER-IN-LAW [*as she goes*] Leave us a bit of breakfast.

SHUI TA [*calmly*] You won't find her. My cousin naturally regrets being unable to make unbounded concessions to the laws of hospitality. But I fear you are too numerous. This is a tobacconist's, and it is Miss Shen Teh's livelihood.

THE MAN Our Shen Teh could never bring herself to say such things.

SHUI TA You may be right. [*To the* CARPENTER] The unfortunate fact is that the poverty in this city is too much for any individual to correct. Alas, nothing has changed in the eleven centuries since a poet wrote:

> That so many of the poor should suffer from cold what can
> we do to prevent?
> To bring warmth to a single body is not much use.
> I wish I had a big rug ten thousand feet long,
> Which at one time could cover up every inch of the City.[9]

[*He starts clearing up the shop.*]

THE CARPENTER I see you are trying to straighten out your cousin's affairs. There is a small bill to be settled for the shelves; she has admitted it before witnesses. 100 silver dollars.

SHUI TA [*drawing the bill out of his pocket, not unkindly*] Wouldn't you say that 100 silver dollars was rather much?

THE CARPENTER No. I can't do it for less. I've a wife and family to look after.

SHUI TA [*hard*] How many children?

THE CARPENTER Four.

SHUI TA Then my offer is 20 silver dollars.

THE CARPENTER [*laughs*] Are you crazy? These shelves are walnut.

SHUI TA Then take them away.

THE CARPENTER What do you mean?

SHUI TA I can't afford it. I suggest you take your walnut shelves away.

THE WOMAN One up to you.[1] [*She in turn laughs.*]

THE CARPENTER [*uncertainly*] I would like Miss Shen Teh to be fetched. She seems to be a decent person, unlike you.

9. "The Big Rug," by Po Chü-I (772–846), translated by Arthur Waley.

1. That is, one point for you.

SHUI TA Obviously. She is ruined.

THE CARPENTER [*resolutely seizes some shelving and takes it to the door*] You can stack your goods on the floor then. It doesn't matter to me.

SHUI TA [*to the* MAN] Give him a hand.

THE MAN [*takes some more shelving and takes it to the door with a grin*] Here we go. Chuck the lot out!

THE CARPENTER You bastard. Do you want my family to starve?

SHUI TA Let me repeat my offer: you can have 20 silver dollars, to save me stacking my goods on the floor.

THE CARPENTER 100.

[SHUI TA *looks indifferently out of the window. The* MAN *sets about removing the shelves.*]

THE CARPENTER Anyway, don't smash them into the doorpost, you fool! [*In confusion*] But they're made to fit. They won't go anywhere else. The boards had to be cut to size, sir.

SHUI TA Exactly. That's why I can't offer you more than 20 silver dollars. Because the boards were cut to size.

[*The* WOMAN *squeals with delight.*]

THE CARPENTER [*suddenly decides he has had enough*] I can't go on. Keep the shelves and pay me what you like.

SHUI TA 20 silver dollars.

[*He lays two big coins on the table. The* CARPENTER *takes them.*]

THE MAN [*bringing back the shelves*] Good enough for a lot of cut-up boards!

THE CARPENTER About good enough to get drunk on!

[*Exit.*]

THE MAN Good riddance!

THE WOMAN [*wiping away tears of laughter*] 'But they're walnut!'—'Take them away!'—'100 silver dollars, I've got four children!'—'Then I'll pay 20!'—'But they've been cut to fit!'—'Exactly, 20 silver dollars!' That's the way to deal with his sort!

SHUI TA Yes. [*Seriously*] Leave here at once.

THE MAN What, us?

SHUI TA Yes, you. You are thieves and parasites. Leave at once, waste no time in arguing, and you can still save your skins.

THE MAN It is better not to take any notice of him. No arguing on an empty stomach. I wonder where the nipper is?

SHUI TA Yes, where is he? I told you I will not have him here with stolen cakes. [*Suddenly shouting*] For the second time. Get out!

[*They remain seated.*]

SHUI TA [*calm once more*] All right then.

[*He walks to the door and bows deeply to someone outside. A* POLICEMAN *looms up in the doorway.*]

SHUI TA I take it I am addressing the police representative for this district?

THE POLICEMAN You are, Mr . . .

SHUI TA Shui Ta. [*They exchange smiles.*] Pleasant weather today!

THE POLICEMAN A trifle warm, perhaps.

SHUI TA Perhaps a trifle warm.

THE MAN [*softly to his wife*] If he goes on gassing till the kid gets back we'll be done for.

[*He tries to make* SHUI TA *a surreptitious sign.*]

SHUI TA [*without noticing*] It all depends whether one is contemplating the weather from a cool establishment like this or from the dusty street.

THE POLICEMAN It certainly does.

THE WOMAN Don't worry. He'll keep away when he sees the copper standing in the door.

SHUI TA But do come in. It really is cooler here. My cousin and I have opened a shop. Let me tell you that we consider it highly important to be on good terms with the authorities.

THE POLICEMAN [*enters*] That is very kind of you, sir. Why yes, it really is cooler in here.

THE MAN [*softly*] He's asked him in just so the kid won't see him.

SHUI TA Some guests. Distant acquaintances of my cousin's, apparently. They have a journey to make. [*Bows are exchanged.*] We were just saying goodbye.

THE MAN [*hoarsely*] All right then, we'll be going.

SHUI TA I will tell my cousin that you thanked her for her hospitality, but could not wait for her return.

[*Noises from the street and cries of 'Stop thief!'*]

THE POLICEMAN What's that about?

[*The* BOY *appears in the door. Cakes and rolls are tumbling out of his shirt. The* WOMAN *motions him desperately to get out. He turns and tries to go off.*]

THE POLICEMAN You stay here. [*He catches hold of him.*] Where d'you get those cakes from?

THE BOY Over there.

THE POLICEMAN Aha. Stolen, eh?

THE WOMAN We knew nothing about it. It was the boy's own idea. Little wretch.

THE POLICEMAN Mr Shui Ta, can you throw any light on this?

[SHUI TA *remains silent.*]

THE POLICEMAN Right. You all come along to the station with me.

SHUI TA I am exceedingly sorry that anything like this should happen in my shop.

THE WOMAN He watched the boy go off!

SHUI TA I can assure you, officer, that I should hardly have invited you in if I had been wanting to conceal a robbery.

THE POLICEMAN I quite see. You realise I'm only doing my duty, Mr Shui Ta, in taking these persons in custody. [SHUI TA *bows.*] Get moving, you! [*He pushes them out.*]

THE GRANDFATHER [*peacefully from the doorway*] Hullo.

[*Exeunt all except* SHUI TA. *Enter* MRS MI TZU.]

MRS MI TZU So you are the cousin I've heard about? How do the police come to be escorting people away from my building? What does your cousin mean by starting a boarding-house here? That's what comes of taking in people who a moment ago were in cheap digs, begging for crusts from the baker on the corner. I know all about it, you see.

SHUI TA I do see. People have been speaking against my cousin. They have blamed her for being hungry! She has a bad name for living in poverty. Her reputation is the worst possible: she was down and out!

MRS MI TZU She was a common or garden . . .

SHUI TA Pauper; let's say the nasty word aloud.

MRS MI TZU Oh, don't try and play on my feelings. I am speaking of her way of life, not her income. I have no doubt there was an income from somewhere, or she would hardly have started this shop. No doubt one or two elderly gentlemen looked after that. How does one get hold of a shop? This is a respectable house, sir. The tenants here aren't paying to live under the same roof as that sort of person: no, sir. [*Pause*] I am not inhuman, but I have got my obligations.

SHUI TA [*coldly*] Mrs Mi Tzu, I'm a busy man. Just tell me what it will cost to live in this highly respectable house.

MRS MI TZU Well, you are a cold fish, I'll give you that!

SHUI TA [*takes the form of agreement out of the drawer*] It is a very high rent. I take it from this agreement that it is to be paid monthly?

MRS MI TZU [*quickly*] Not for your cousin's sort.

SHUI TA What does that mean?

MRS MI TZU That means that people like your cousin have to pay six months' rent in advance: 200 silver dollars.

SHUI TA 200 silver dollars! That is plain murder! Where am I to find that much? I cannot count on a big turnover here. My one hope is the girls who sew sacks in the cement works, who are supposed to smoke a lot because they find the work so exhausting. But they are badly paid.

MRS MI TZU You should have thought of that sooner.

SHUI TA Mrs Mi Tzu, please have a heart! I realise that my cousin made the unforgiveable mistake of giving shelter to some unfortunates. But she will learn. I shall see that she learns. Against that, where could you find a better tenant than one who knows the gutter because he came from there? He'll work his fingers to the bone to pay his rent punctually, he'll do anything, go without anything, sell anything, stick at nothing, and at the same time be as quiet as a mouse, gentle as a fly, submit to you utterly rather than return there. A tenant like that is worth his weight in gold.

MRS MI TZU 200 silver dollars in advance, or she goes back on the street, where she came from.

[*Enter the* POLICEMAN.]

THE POLICEMAN Don't let me disturb you, Mr Shui Ta!

MRS MI TZU The police really seem remarkably interested in this shop.

THE POLICEMAN Mrs Mi Tzu, I hope you haven't got a wrong impression. Mr Shui Ta did us a service, and I have come in the name of the police to thank him.

MRS MI TZU Well, that's no affair of mine. Mr Shui Ta, I trust my proposition will be agreeable to your cousin. I like to be on good terms with my tenants. Good morning, gentlemen.

[*Exit.*]

SHUI TA Good morning, Mrs Mi Tzu.

THE POLICEMAN Have you been having trouble with Mrs Mi Tzu?

SHUI TA She is demanding the rent in advance, as she doesn't think my cousin is respectable.

THE POLICEMAN And can't you raise the money? [SHUI TA *remains silent.*] But Mr Shui Ta, surely someone like you ought to be able to get credit.

SHUI TA I dare say. But how is someone like Shen Teh to get credit?

THE POLICEMAN Are you not staying here then?

SHUI TA No. And I shall not be able to come again. I could only give her a hand because I was passing through; I just saved her from the worst. Any minute she will be thrown back on her own resources. I am worried as to what will happen.

THE POLICEMAN Mr Shui Ta, I am sorry to hear that you are having trouble over the rent. I must admit that we began by viewing this shop with mixed feelings, but your decisive action just now showed us the sort of man you are. Speaking for the authorities, we soon find out who we can rely on as a friend of law and order.

SHUI TA [*bitterly*] To save this little shop, officer, which my cousin regards as a gift of the gods, I am prepared to go to the utmost limits of the law. But toughness and duplicity will serve only against one's inferiors, for those limits have been cleverly defined. I am in the position of a man who has just got the rats out of his cellar, when along come the floods. [*After a short pause*] Do you smoke?

THE POLICEMAN [*putting two cigars in his pocket*] Our station would be sorry to see you go, Mr Shui Ta. But you've got to understand Mrs Mi Tzu's point of view. Shen Teh, let's face it, lived by selling herself to men. You may ask, what else was she to do? For instance, how was she to pay her rent? But the fact remains: it is not respectable. Why not? A: you can't earn your living by love, or it becomes immoral earnings. B: respectability means, not with the man who can pay, but with the man one loves. C: it mustn't be for a handful of rice but for love. All right, you may say: what's the good of being so clever over spilt milk? What's she to do? When she has to find six months' rent? Mr Shui Ta, I must admit I don't know. [*He thinks hard.*] Mr Shui Ta, I have got it! All you need do is to find a husband for her.

[*Enter a little* OLD WOMAN.]

THE OLD WOMAN I want a good cheap cigar for my husband. Tomorrow is our fortieth wedding anniversary, you see, and we are having a little celebration.

SHUI TA [*politely*] Forty years, and still something to celebrate!

THE OLD WOMAN As far as our means allow! That's our carpet shop over the way. I hope we are going to be good neighbours, it's important in these hard times.

SHUI TA [*spreads various boxes before her*] Two very familiar words, I'm afraid.

THE POLICEMAN Mr Shui Ta, what we need is capital. So I suggest a marriage.

SHUI TA [*excusing himself to the* OLD WOMAN] I have been allowing myself to tell the officer some of my private troubles.

THE POLICEMAN We've got to find six months' rent. Right, we marry a bit of money.

SHUI TA That will not be easy.

THE POLICEMAN Why not? She's a good match. She owns a small and promising business. [*To the* OLD WOMAN] What do you think?

THE OLD WOMAN [*doubtfully*] Well . . .

THE POLICEMAN An advertisement in the personal column.

THE OLD WOMAN [*reluctant*] If the young lady agrees . . .

THE POLICEMAN Why shouldn't she agree? I'll draft it out for you. One good turn deserves another. Don't think the authorities have no sympathy for the small and struggling shopkeeper. You play along with us, and in return we draft your matrimonial advertisements! Hahaha!

[*He hastens to pull out his notebook, licks his pencil stump, and starts writing.*]

SHUI TA [*slowly*] It's not a bad idea.

THE POLICEMAN 'What respectable gentleman . . . small capital . . . widower considered . . . desires marriage . . . into progressive tobacconist's?' And then we'll add: 'With charming attractive brunette.' How's that?

SHUI TA You don't feel that's overstating it?

THE OLD WOMAN [*kindly*] Certainly not. I have seen her.

[*The* POLICEMAN *tears the page out of his notebook and hands it to* SHUI TA.]

SHUI TA With horror I begin to realise how much luck one needs to avoid being crushed! What brilliant ideas! What faithful friends! [*To the* POLICEMAN] Thus for all my decisiveness I was at my wits' end over the rent. And then you came along and helped me with good advice. I really begin to see a way out.

Scene 3

Evening in a Public Park

[*A young man in tattered clothes is watching an aeroplane, which is evidently making a high sweep over the park. He takes a rope from his pocket and looks round him for something. He is making for a big willow tree, when* TWO PROSTITUTES *come up to him. One of them is old, the other is the* NIECE *from the family of eight.*]

THE YOUNG ONE Evening, young fellow. Coming home with me, dear?

SUN It could be done, ladies, if you'll stand me a meal.

THE OLD ONE Are you nuts? [*To the* YOUNG ONE] Come on, love. He's just a waste of time. That's that out-of-work pilot.

THE YOUNG ONE But there won't be a soul in the park now, it's going to rain.

THE OLD ONE There's always a chance.

[*They walk on.* SUN *looks round him, pulls out his rope, and throws it over a branch of a willow tree. But he is interrupted again. The* TWO PROSTITUTES *return rapidly. They do not see him.*]

THE YOUNG ONE It's going to pelt with rain.

[SHEN TEH *is walking up.*]

THE OLD ONE Hullo, here she is, the bitch! She got your lot into trouble, all right!

THE YOUNG ONE Not her. It was her cousin. She took us in, and in the end she offered to pay for the cakes. I haven't any bone to pick with her.

THE OLD ONE I have. [*Loudly*] Why, there's our fancy friend with all the money. She's got a shop, but she still wants to pinch our boys off us.

SHEN TEH Don't jump down my throat! I'm going down to the teahouse by the lake.

THE YOUNG ONE Is it true you're marrying a widower with three children?

SHEN TEH Yes, I'm meeting him there.

SUN [*impatiently*] Do your cackling somewhere else, will you? Isn't there anywhere one can get a bit of peace?

[*Exeunt the* TWO PROSTITUTES.]

SUN [*calls after them*] Scavengers! [*To the audience*] Even in this remote spot they fish tirelessly for victims, even in the thickets, in the rain, they pursue their desperate hunt for custom.

SHEN TEH [*angry*] What call have you got to slang them? [*She sees the rope.*] Oh!

SUN What are you gooping[2] at?

SHEN TEH What's that rope for?

SUN Move on, sister, move on! I've got no money, nothing, not a copper. And if I had I'd buy a drink of water, not you.

[*It starts raining.*]

SHEN TEH What's that rope for? You're not to do it!

SUN Mind your own business! And get out of the way!

SHEN TEH It's raining.

SUN Don't you try sheltering under my tree.

SHEN TEH [*remains motionless in the rain*] No.

SUN Why not give up, sister, it's no use. You can't do business with me. Besides, you're too ugly, Bandy Legs.

SHEN TEH That's not true.

SUN I don't want to see them! All right, come under the bloody tree, since it's raining!

[*She approaches slowly and sits down under the tree.*]

SHEN TEH Why do you want to do that?

SUN Would you like to know? Then I'll tell you, so as to be rid of you. [*Pause*] Do you know what an airman is?

SHEN TEH Yes, I once saw some airmen in a teahouse.

SUN Oh no you didn't. One or two windy idiots in flying helmets, I expect: the sort who's got no ear for his engine and no feeling for his machine. Gets into a kite by bribing the hangar superintendent. Tell a type like that: now stall your crate at 2,000, down through the clouds, then catch her up with the flick of the stick, and he'll say: But that's not in the book. If you can't land your kite gently as lowering your bottom you're not an airman, you're an idiot. Me, I'm an airman. And yet I'm the biggest idiot of the lot, because I read all the manuals in flying school at Pekin.[3] But just one page of one manual I happened to miss, the one where it says Airmen Not Wanted. And so I became an airman without an aircraft, a mail pilot without mail. What that means you wouldn't understand.

SHEN TEH I think I do understand all the same.

SUN No, I'm telling you you can't understand. And that means you can't understand.

SHEN TEH [*half laughing, half crying*] When we were children we had a crane with a broken wing. He was very tame and didn't mind our teasing him, and used to come strutting after us and scream if we went too fast for him. But in the autumn and the spring, when the great flocks of birds flew over our village, he became very restless, and I could understand why.

SUN Stop crying.

SHEN TEH Yes.

2. Gawking.

3. That is, Beijing, the capital of China.

SUN It's bad for the complexion.

SHEN TEH I'm stopping.

[She dries her tears on her sleeve. Leaning against the tree, but without turning towards her, he reaches for her face.]

SUN You don't even know how to wipe your face properly.

[He wipes it for her with a handkerchief.]

SUN If you've got to sit there and stop me from hanging myself you might at least say something.

SHEN TEH I don't know what.

SUN Why do you want to hack me down, sister, as a matter of interest?

SHEN TEH It frightens me. I'm sure you only felt like that because the evening's so dreary. [*To the audience*]

In our country
There should be no dreary evenings
Or tall bridges over rivers
Even the hour between night and morning
And the whole winter season too, that is dangerous.
For in face of misery
Only a little is needed
Before men start throwing
Their unbearable life away.

SUN Tell me about yourself.

SHEN TEH What is there? I've got a small shop.

SUN [*ironically*] Oh, so you haven't got a flat, you've got a shop!

SHEN TEH [*firmly*] I've got a shop, but before that I was on the streets.

SUN And the shop, I take it, was a gift of the gods?

SHEN TEH Yes.

SUN One fine evening they stood before you and said: Here's some money for you.

SHEN TEH [*laughing quietly*] One morning.

SUN You're not exactly entertaining.

SHEN TEH [*after a pause*] I can play the zither a bit, and do imitations. [*In a deep voice she imitates a dignified gentleman.*] 'How idiotic, I must have come without my wallet!' But then I got the shop. The first thing I did was give away my zither. From now on, I told myself, you can be a complete jellyfish and it won't matter.

How rich I am, I told myself.
I walk alone. I sleep alone.
For one whole year, I told myself
I'll have no dealings with a man.

SUN But now you're going to marry one? The one in the teahouse by the lake.

[SHEN TEH *says nothing.*]

SUN As a matter of interest, what do you know of love?

SHEN TEH Everything.

SUN Nothing, sister. Or was it perhaps pleasant?

SHEN TEH No.

[SUN *strokes her face, without turning towards her.*]

SUN Is that pleasant?

SHEN TEH Yes.

SUN Easily satisfied, you are. God, what a town.

SHEN TEH Haven't you got friends?

SUN A whole lot, but none that like hearing that I'm still out of a job. They make a face as if someone were complaining that the sea's wet. Have you got a friend, if it comes to that?

SHEN TEH [*hesitantly*] A cousin.

SUN Then don't you trust him an inch.

SHEN TEH He was only here once. Now he has gone off and is never coming back. But why do you talk as if you'd given up hope? They say: to give up hope is to give up kindness.

SUN Just talk on! At least it's something to hear a human voice.

SHEN TEH [*eagerly*] There are still friendly people, for all our wretchedness. When I was little once I was carrying a bundle of sticks and fell. An old man helped me up and even gave me a penny. I have often thought of it. Those who have least to eat give most gladly. I suppose people just like showing what they are good at; and how can they do it better than by being friendly? Crossness is just a way of being inefficient. Whenever someone is singing a song or building a machine or planting rice it is really friendliness. You are friendly too.

SUN It doesn't seem hard by your definition.

SHEN TEH And that was a raindrop.

SUN Where?

SHEN TEH Between my eyes.

SUN More to the left or more to the right?

SHEN TEH More to the left.

SUN Good. [*After a moment, sleepily*] So you're through with men?

SHEN TEH [*smiling*] But my legs aren't bandy.

SUN Perhaps not.

SHEN TEH Definitely not.

SUN [*wearily leaning back against the tree*] But as I haven't eaten for two days or drunk for one, I couldn't love you, sister, even if I wanted.

SHEN TEH It is good in the rain.

[WANG *the water-seller, appears. He sings.*]

WANG

THE WATER-SELLER'S SONG IN THE RAIN

I sell water. Who will taste it?
—Who would want to in this weather?
All my labour has been wasted
Fetching these few pints together.
I stand shouting Buy my Water!
And nobody thinks it
Worth stopping and buying
Or greedily drinks it.
(Buy water, you devils!)

O to stop the leaky heaven
Hoard what stock I've got remaining:

Recently I dreamt that seven
Years went by without it raining.
How they'd all shout Give me Water!
How they'd fight for my good graces
And I'd make their further treatment
Go by how I liked their faces.
(Stay thirsty, you devils!)

Wretched weeds, you're through with thirsting
Heaven must have heard you praying.
You can drink until you're bursting
Never bother about paying.
I'm left shouting Buy my Water!
And nobody thinks it
Worth stopping and buying
Or greedily drinks it.
(Buy water, you devils!)

[*The rain has stopped.* SHEN TEH *sees* WANG *and runs towards him.*]

SHEN TEH Oh Wang, so you have come back. I have looked after your pole for you.

WANG Thank you for taking care of it! How are you, Shen Teh?

SHEN TEH Well. I have got to know a very brave and clever person. And I should like to buy a cup of your water.

WANG Throw your head back and open your mouth, and you can have as much water as you want. The willow tree is still dripping.

SHEN TEH But I want your water, Wang.

Laboriously carried
Exhausting to its bearer
And hard to sell, because it is raining.
And I need it for the man over yonder.
He is an airman. An airman
Is braver than other humans. With the clouds for companions
Daring enormous tempests
He flies through the heavens and brings
To friends in far countries
The friendly post.

[*She pays and runs over to* SUN *with the cup.*]

SHEN TEH [*calls back to* WANG, *laughing*] He has fallen asleep. Hopelessness and the rain and I have tired him out.

Interlude

Wang's Sleeping Place under a Culvert

[*The water-seller is asleep. Music. The culvert becomes transparent, and the* GODS *appear to him as he dreams.*]

WANG [*beaming*] I have seen her, O Illustrious Ones! She has not changed.

THE FIRST GOD That gives us pleasure.

WANG She is in love! She showed me her friend. Truly things are going well for her.

THE FIRST GOD That is good to hear. Let us hope that she will be strengthened in her pursuit of goodness.

WANG Indeed yes! She is performing all the charitable deeds she can.

THE FIRST GOD Charitable deeds? What sort? Tell us about them, dear Wang.

WANG She has a friendly word for everyone.

THE FIRST GOD [*keenly*] What else?

WANG It is rare that a man is allowed to leave her shop without something to smoke, just for lack of money.

THE FIRST GOD That sounds satisfactory. Any more?

WANG She has taken in a family of eight.

THE FIRST GOD [*triumphantly to the* SECOND] Eight, indeed! [*To* WANG] Have you anything else you can tell us?

WANG Although it was raining she bought a cup of water from me.

THE FIRST GOD Yes, minor charities of that sort. Of course.

WANG But they eat into the money. A small business doesn't make all that much.

THE FIRST GOD True, true! But a prudent gardener can work wonders with his little patch.

WANG That is just what she does! Every morning she distributes rice; believe me, it must cost more than half her earnings!

THE FIRST GOD [*slightly disappointed*] I am not denying it. I am not displeased with her start.

WANG Remember, times are not easy! She had to call in a cousin once, as her shop was getting into difficulties.

Hardly was a shelter erected against the wind
Than the ruffled birds of the whole wintry heaven
Came tumbling flying and
Squabbled for a place and the hungry fox gnawed through
The flimsy wall and the one-legged wolf
Knocked the little rice-bowl over.

In other words the business was too much for her to manage. But everyone agrees that she is a good girl. They have begun to call her 'The Angel of the Slums'. So much good goes out from her shop. Whatever Lin To the carpenter may say!

THE FIRST GOD What's that? Does Lin To the carpenter speak ill of her?

WANG Oh, he only says the shelving in the shop wasn't quite paid for.

THE SECOND GOD What are you telling us? A carpenter not paid? In Shen Teh's shop? How could she permit that?

WANG I suppose she didn't have the money.

THE SECOND GOD No matter: one pays one's debts. One cannot afford even the appearance of irregularity. The letter of the law has first to be fulfilled; then its spirit.

WANG But Illustrious Ones, it was only her cousin, not herself.

THE SECOND GOD Then that cousin must never again enter her door.

WANG [*dejected*] I have understood, Illustrious One! But in Shen Teh's defence let me just say that her cousin is supposed to be a most reputable businessman. Even the police respect him.

THE FIRST GOD This cousin will not be condemned without a hearing either. I know nothing of business, I admit; perhaps we ought to find out what is thought usual in such matters. But business indeed! Is it so very necessary?

Nowadays there is nothing but business. Were the Seven Good Kings in business? Did Kung the Just[4] sell fish? What has business to do with an upright and honourable life?

THE SECOND GOD [*with a bad cold*] In any case it must not be allowed to occur again.

[*He turns to leave. The other two* GODS *likewise turn.*]

THE THIRD GOD [*the last to leave, embarrassedly*] Forgive our rather sharp tone today! We are very tired, and we have slept too little. Oh, those nights! The well-off give us the best possible recommendations to the poor, but the poor have too few rooms.

THE GODS [*grumble as they move off*] Broken reeds, even the best of them! Nothing conclusive! Pitiful, pitiful! All from the heart, of course, but it adds up to nothing! At least she ought to . . .

[*They can no longer be heard.*]

WANG [*calls after them*] Do not be too hard on us, O Illustrious Ones! Do not ask for everything at once!

Scene 4

Square in Front of Shen Teh's Shop

[*A barber's, a carpet shop, and* SHEN TEH*'s tobacconist's shop. It is Monday. Outside* SHEN TEH*'s shop wait two survivors of the family of eight—the* GRANDFATHER *and the* SISTER-IN-LAW. *Also the* UNEMPLOYED MAN *and* MRS SHIN.]

THE SISTER-IN-LAW She never came home last night!

MRS SHIN Astonishing behaviour! We manage to get rid of this maniac of a cousin and there's nothing to stop her having a little rice to spare now and again, when off she goes for the night chasing around God knows where!

[*Loud voices are heard from the barber's.* WANG *staggers out followed by* MR SHU FU, *the stout barber, with a heavy pair of curling tongs in his hand.*]

MR SHU FU I'll teach you to come bothering my customers with your stinking water! Take your mug and get out!

[WANG *reaches for the mug which* MR SHU FU *is holding out to him, and gets a blow on the hand with the curling tongs, so that he screams.*]

MR SHU FU Take that! Let that be a lesson to you.

[*He puffs back to his shop.*]

THE UNEMPLOYED MAN [*picks up the mug and hands it to* WANG] You can have him up[5] for hitting you.

WANG My hand's gone.

THE UNEMPLOYED MAN Any bones broken?

WANG I can't move it.

THE UNEMPLOYED MAN Sit down and bathe it a bit.

MRS SHIN The water won't cost you much, anyway.

4. K'ung Futzu (Master K'ung), the Chinese philosopher better known by his latinized name, Confucius (551–479 B.C.E.). *Seven Good Kings:* rulers of the first historical dynasty of China (traditionally dated ca. 1766–ca. 1122 B.C.E.), whom the Confucian scholar Mencius called "sage worthies."

5. That is, have him brought before a magistrate on civil charges.

THE SISTER-IN-LAW Eight o'clock already, and one can't even lay hands on a bit of rag here. She has to go gallivanting off! A disgrace!

MRS SHIN [*darkly*] She's forgotten us, that's what!

[SHEN TEH *comes down the street carrying a pot of rice.*]

SHEN TEH [*to the audience*] I had never seen the city at dawn. These were the hours when I used to lie with my filthy blanket over my head, terrified to wake up. Today I mixed with the newsboys, with the men who were washing down the streets, with the ox-carts bringing fresh vegetables in from the fields. It was a long walk from Sun's neighbourhood to here, but with every step I grew happier. I had always been told that when one is in love one walks on air, but the wonderful thing is that one walks on earth, on tarmac. I tell you, at dawn the blocks of buildings are like rubbish heaps with little lights glowing in them; the sky is pink but still transparent, clear of dust. I tell you, you miss a great deal if you are not in love and cannot see your city at that hour when she rises from her couch like a sober old craftsman, filling his lungs with fresh air and reaching for his tools, as the poets have it. [*To the group waiting*] Good morning! Here is your rice! [*She shares it out, then notices* WANG.] Good morning, Wang. I am light-headed today. All along the way I looked at my reflection in the shop windows, and now I would like to buy myself a shawl. [*After a short hesitation*] I should so like to look beautiful.

[*She turns quickly into the carpet shop.*]

MR SHU FU [*who is again standing in his doorway, to the audience*] I am smitten today with the beauty of Miss Shen Teh, the owner of the tobacconist's opposite, whom I have never previously noticed. I have watched her for three minutes, and I believe I am already in love. An infinitely charming person! [*To* WANG] Get to hell, you lout!

[*He turns back into the barber's shop.* SHEN TEH *and an extremely old couple, the* CARPET-DEALER *and his* WIFE, *come out of the carpet-shop.* SHEN TEH *is carrying a shawl, the* CARPET-DEALER *a mirror.*]

THE OLD WOMAN It's very pretty and not at all dear; there's a small hole at the bottom.

SHEN TEH [*trying the shawl on the* OLD WOMAN'S *arm*] I like the green one too.

THE OLD WOMAN [*smiling*] But I'm afraid it's in perfect condition.

SHEN TEH Yes, a pity. I cannot undertake too much with my shop. The income is small, and there are many expenses.

THE OLD WOMAN For charity; don't you do so much. When you are starting every bowl of rice counts, eh?

SHEN TEH [*tries on the shawl with the hole in it*] Except that I have to; only at present I'm light-headed. Do you think the colour suits me?

THE OLD WOMAN You had better ask a man that question.

SHEN TEH [*calls to the* OLD MAN] Does it suit me?

THE OLD MAN Why don't you ask . . .

SHEN TEH [*very politely*] No, I am asking you.

THE OLD MAN [*equally politely*] The shawl suits you. But wear it dull side out.

[SHEN TEH *pays.*]

THE OLD WOMAN If you don't like it I will always change it for another. [*Draws her aside.*] Has he any money?

SHEN TEH [*laughing*] O goodness no.

THE OLD WOMAN Will you be able to pay your half-year's rent?

SHEN TEH The rent! It had clean gone out of my mind!

THE OLD WOMAN I thought it had! And Monday will be the first of the month. I have something to suggest. You know: my husband and I were a little doubtful about the marriage advertisement once we had got to know you. We decided we'd help you out if need be. We've put something by, and we can lend you the 200 silver dollars. If you like you can make over your stock to us as security. But of course we don't need anything in writing.

SHEN TEH Would you really lend money to such a scatter-brained person?

THE OLD WOMAN To be honest, we'd think twice about lending it to your cousin, who is definitely not scatter-brained, but we'd gladly lend it to you.

THE OLD MAN [*comes up*] All fixed?

SHEN TEH I wish the gods could have heard your wife just then, Mr Deng. They are looking for good and happy people. And I'm sure you must be happy, to be helping me out of the troubles that love has brought me.

[*The two* OLD PEOPLE *smile at one another.*]

THE OLD MAN Here is the money.

[*He hands her an envelope.* SHEN TEH *accepts it and bows. The* OLD PEOPLE *bow too. They go back to their shop.*]

SHEN TEH [*to* WANG, *holding up the envelope*] This is six months' rent. Isn't that a miracle? And Wang, what do you think of my new shawl?

WANG Did you buy it for the man I saw in the park?

[SHEN TEH *nods.*]

MRS SHIN You might choose to look at his hand instead of retailing your shady adventures!

SHEN TEH [*alarmed*] What's the matter with your hand?

MRS SHIN The barber smashed it with his curling tongs in front of our eyes.

SHEN TEH [*horrified at her heedlessness*] And I didn't notice! You must go to the doctor at once, or your hand will go stiff and you'll never be able to work properly again. It's a frightful disaster. Come on, get up! Hurry!

THE UNEMPLOYED MAN He doesn't want the doctor; he wants the magistrate! The barber's a rich man, and he ought to get compensation.

WANG Do you think there's a chance?

MRS SHIN If you really can't use it. Can you?

WANG I don't think so. It's already very swollen. Would it mean a pension for life?

MRS SHIN You need a witness, of course.

WANG But you all saw! You can all of you bear me out.

[*He looks round.* UNEMPLOYED MAN, GRANDFATHER, SISTER-IN-LAW: *all are sitting against the wall and eating. No one looks up.*]

SHEN TEH [*to* MRS SHIN] You yourself saw it, didn't you?

MRS SHIN I don't want to get mixed up with the police.

SHEN TEH [*to the* SISTER-IN-LAW] What about you then?

THE SISTER-IN-LAW Me? I wasn't looking!

MRS SHIN Of course you were looking. I saw you looking! You're just scared because the barber's got too much pull.

SHEN TEH [*to the* GRANDFATHER] I am sure that you will confirm what happened.

THE SISTER-IN-LAW They wouldn't listen to him. He's gaga.

SHEN TEH [*to the* UNEMPLOYED MAN] It may mean a pension for life.

THE UNEMPLOYED MAN They've taken my name twice for begging. It won't do him much good if I give evidence.

SHEN TEH [*incredulous*] Do you mean to say that not one of you will say what happened? His hand gets broken in full daylight, in front of you all, and not one will open his mouth. [*Angrily*]

O you unfortunates!
Your brother is mishandled before you, and you just shut your eyes.
Injured, he screams aloud, and you keep mum.
The bully swaggers round, picks out his victim
And you say: he'll spare us, for we hide our displeasure.
What sort of a town is that, what sort of humans are you?
When an injustice takes place in a town there must be an uproar
And where there is no uproar it is better the town disappears
In flames before the night falls.

Wang, if nobody who saw it will be your witness, then I will be your witness and say that I saw it.

MRS SHIN It'll be perjury.

WANG I don't know if I can allow that. But perhaps I have to allow it. [*Looking anxiously at his hand*] Do you think it has swollen enough? It looks to me as if it has started to go down?

THE UNEMPLOYED MAN [*calming him*] No, it certainly hasn't gone down.

WANG Are you sure? Ah yes, I do believe it's swelling a bit more. Possibly my wrist is broken! I'd better go straight to the magistrate.

[*Holding his hand carefully and still looking at it, he hurries off.* MRS SHIN *enters the barber's shop.*]

THE UNEMPLOYED MAN She's gone to the barber's to butter him up.

THE SISTER-IN-LAW It's not for us to change the world.

SHEN TEH [*discouraged*] I didn't mean to be rude to you. It's just that I was shocked. No, I did mean to be rude to you. Get out of my sight!

[*The* UNEMPLOYED MAN, *the* SISTER-IN-LAW, *and the* GRANDFATHER *go off eating and grumbling.*]

SHEN TEH [*to the audience*]

They cannot respond. Where they are stationed
They stay put, and when turned away
They quickly yield place!
Nothing now moves them. Only
The smell of cooking will make them look up.

[*An old woman comes hurrying up. It is* SUN'S *mother,* MRS YANG.]

MRS YANG [*out of breath*] Are you Miss Shen Teh? My son has told me everything. I am Sun's mother, Mrs Yang. Think of it, he has got the chance of a job as a pilot! He got a letter from Pekin this morning, just now. From one of the superintendents in the postal service.

SHEN TEH That means he can fly again? Oh, Mrs Yang!

MRS YANG But it will cost a lot: 500 silver dollars.

SHEN TEH That's a great deal, but money must not stand in his way. After all, I've got the shop.

MRS YANG If you could only do something!

SHEN TEH [*embraces her*] If I could help him!

MRS YANG You would be giving a chance to a very gifted individual!

SHEN TEH Why should they stop a man from applying his gifts? [*After a pause*] Except that I shall not get enough for the shop, and the 200 silver dollars which I have got in cash are only a loan. Of course you can have those now. I will sell my stock and pay them back out of that.

[*She gives her the old couple's money.*]

MRS YANG O Miss Shen Teh, a friend in need is a friend indeed. And they were all calling him the dead pilot, because they said he has as much chance of flying again as a corpse.

SHEN TEH We still need 300 silver dollars for the job, though. Mrs Yang, we must think. [*Slowly*] I know someone who might perhaps help. Someone who has advised me before. I didn't really want to have to resort to him again; he is too smart and too tough. This will definitely be the last time. But a pilot has got to fly, that is obvious.

[*Sound of engines in the distance.*]

MRS YANG If your friend could only raise the money! Look, there goes the morning mail service to Pekin!

SHEN TEH [*with determination*] Wave to it, Mrs Yang. I'm sure the pilot can see us! [*She waves her shawl.*] Go on, wave!

MRS YANG [*waving*] Do you know the pilot?

SHEN TEH No. I know a pilot. For the man without hope shall fly, Mrs Yang. One of us at least shall be able to fly above all this wretchedness; one at least shall rise above us all!

[*To the audience*]

Yang Sun, my loved one, with the clouds for companions!
Daring enormous tempests
Flying through the heavens and bringing
To friends in far countries
The friendly post.

Interlude

in front of the curtain

[SHEN TEH *enters, carrying* SHUI TA's *mask and costume, and sings the*]

SONG OF THE DEFENCELESSNESS OF THE
GOOD AND THE GODS

SHEN TEH

In our country
The capable man needs luck. Only
If he has mighty backers
Can he prove his capacity.
The good
Have no means of helping themselves and the gods are powerless.
So why can't the gods launch a great operation
With bombers and battleships, tanks and destroyers
And rescue the good by a ruthless invasion?
Then maybe the wicked would cease to annoy us.

[*She puts on* SHUI TA'*s costume and takes a few steps in his way of walking.*]

The good
Cannot remain good for long in our country
Where cupboards are bare, housewives start to squabble.
Oh, the divine commandments
Are not much use against hunger.
So why can't the gods share out what they've created
Come down and distribute the bounties of nature
And allow us, once hunger and thirst have been sated
To mix with each other in friendship and pleasure?

[*She dons* SHUI TA'*s mask and sings on in his voice.*]

In order to win one's mid-day meal
One needs the toughness which elsewhere builds empires.
Except twelve others be trampled down
The unfortunate cannot be helped.
So why can't the gods make a simple decision
That goodness must conquer in spite of its weakness?—
Then back up the good with an armoured division
Command it to 'fire!' and not tolerate meekness?

Scene 5

The Tobacconist's

[SHUI TA *sits behind the counter and reads the paper. He takes no notice of* MRS SHIN, *who is cleaning the place and talking.*]

MRS SHIN A small business like this soon goes downhill, believe me, once certain rumours get around locally. This shady affair between the young lady and that fellow Yang Sun from the Yellow Alley, it was high time a proper gentleman like you came and cleared it up. Don't forget that Mr Shu Fu, the hairdresser next door, a gentleman who owns twelve houses and has only one wife, and an old one at that, hinted to me yesterday that he took a rather flattering interest in the young lady. He went so far as to ask about her financial standing. I'd say that showed real partiality.

[*Getting no answer, she finally leaves with her bucket.*]

SUN'S VOICE [*from outside*] Is this Miss Shen Teh's shop?

MRS SHIN'S VOICE Yes. But her cousin's there today.

[SHUI TA *runs to a mirror, with* SHEN TEH'*s light steps, and is just beginning to arrange his hair when he realises his mistake. He turns away with a soft laugh. Enter* YANG SUN. *Behind him appears the inquisitive* MRS SHIN. *She goes past him into the back of the shop.*]

SUN I am Yang Sun. [SHUI TA *bows.*] Is Shen Teh in?

SHUI TA No, she is not in.

SUN But I expect you're in the picture about me and her? [*He begins to take stock of the shop.*] A real shop, large as life. I always thought she was putting it on a bit. [*He examines the boxes and china pots with satisfaction.*] Oh boy, I'm going to be flying again. [*He helps himself to a cigar, and* SHUI TA *gives him a light.*] Do you think we can squeeze another 300 dollars out of the business?

SHUI TA May I ask: is it your intention to proceed to an immediate sale?

SUN Why? Have we got the 300 in cash? [SHUI TA *shakes his head.*] It was good of her to produce the 200 at once. But I've got to have the other 300 or I'm stuck.

SHUI TA Perhaps she was a bit hasty in offering you the money. It may cost her her business. They say, haste is the wind that blew the house down.

SUN I need it now or not at all. And the girl's not one to hesitate when it's a question of giving. Between ourselves, she hasn't hesitated much so far.

SHUI TA Really?

SUN All to her credit, of course.

SHUI TA May I ask how the 500 dollars will be used?

SUN Why not? As you seem to be checking up on me. The airport superintendent in Pekin is a friend of mine from flying school, and he can get me the job if I cough up 500 silver dollars.

SHUI TA Isn't that an unusually large sum?

SUN No. He has got to prove negligence against a highly conscientious pilot with a large family. You get me? That's between us, by the way, and there's no need for Shen Teh to know.

SHUI TA Perhaps not. One point though: won't the superintendent be selling you up the river a month later?

SUN Not me. No negligence with me. I've been long enough without a job.

SHUI TA [*nods*] It is the hungry dog who pulls the cart home quickest. [*He studies him for a moment or two.*] That's a very big responsibility. You are asking my cousin, Mr Yang Sun, to give up her small property and all her friends in this town, and to place herself entirely in your hands. I take it your intention is to marry Shen Teh?

SUN I'd be prepared to.

SHUI TA Then wouldn't it be a pity to let the business go for a few silver dollars? You won't get much for a quick sale. The 200 silver dollars that you've already got would guarantee the rent for six months. Do you not feel at all tempted to carry on the tobacconist's business?

SUN What, me? Have people see Yang Sun the pilot serving behind a counter? 'Good morning, sir; do you prefer Turkish or Virginia?' That's no career for Yang Suns, not in the twentieth century!

SHUI TA And is flying a career, may I ask?

SUN [*takes a letter from his pocket*] They're paying me 250 silver dollars a month, sir. Here is the letter; see for yourself. Look at the stamp, postmarked Pekin.

SHUI TA 250 silver dollars? That is a lot.

SUN Do you think I'd fly for nothing?

SHUI TA It sounds like a good job. Mr Yang Sun, my cousin has asked me to help you get this pilot's job which means so much to you. Looking at it from her point of view I see no insuperable objection to her following the bidding of her heart. She is fully entitled to share in the delights of love. I am prepared to realise everything here. Here comes Mrs Mi Tzu, the landlady; I will ask her advice about the sale.

MRS MI TZU [*enters*] Good morning, Mr Shui Ta. I suppose it's about your rent that's due the day after tomorrow?

SHUI TA Mrs Mi Tzu, circumstances have arisen which make it doubtful whether my cousin will carry on with the business. She is contemplating marriage, and her future husband—[*he introduces* YANG SUN]—Mr Yang Sun, is taking her to Pekin where they wish to start a new life. If I can get a good price for my tobacco I shall sell it.

MRS MI TZU How much do you need?

SUN 300 in cash.

SHUI TA [*quickly*] No, no. 500!

MRS MI TZU [*to* SUN] Perhaps I can help you out. How much did your stock cost?

SHUI TA My cousin originally paid 1000 silver dollars, and very little of it has been sold.

MRS MI TZU 1000 silver dollars! She was swindled, of course. I'll make you an offer: you can have 300 silver dollars for the whole business, if you move out the day after tomorrow.

SUN All right. That's it, old boy!

SHUI TA It's too little!

SUN It's enough!

SHUI TA I must have at least 500.

SUN What for?

SHUI TA May I just discuss something with my cousin's fiancé? [*Aside to* SUN] All this stock of tobacco is pledged to two old people against the 200 silver dollars which you got yesterday.

SUN [*slowly*] Is there anything about it in writing?

SHUI TA No.

SUN [*to* MRS MI TZU *after a short pause*] 300 will do us.

MRS MI TZU But I have to be sure that the business has no outstanding debts.

SUN You answer.

SHUI TA The business has no outstanding debts.

SUN How soon can we have the 300?

MRS MI TZU The day after tomorrow, and you had better think it over. Put the sale off for a month and you will get more. I can offer you 300, and that's only because I'm glad to help where it seems to be a case of young love.

[*Exit.*]

SUN [*calling after her*] It's a deal! Lock, stock, and barrel for 300, and our troubles are over. [*To* SHUI TA] I suppose we might get a better offer in the next two days? Then we could even pay back the 200.

SHUI TA Not in the time. We shan't get a single dollar over Mrs Mi Tzu's 300. Have you got the money for both your tickets, and enough to tide you over?

SUN Sure.

SHUI TA How much?

SUN Anyway, I'll raise it even if I have to steal it!

SHUI TA Oh, so that's another sum that has to be raised?

SUN Don't worry, old boy. I'll get to Pekin all right.

SHUI TA It costs quite a bit for two.

SUN Two? I'm leaving the girl here. She'd only be a liability at first.

SHUI TA I see.

SUN Why do you look at me as if I was something the cat had brought in? Beggars can't be choosers.

SHUI TA And what is my cousin to live on?

SUN Can't you do something for her?

SHUI TA I will look into it. [*Pause*] I should like you to hand me back the 200 silver dollars, Mr Yang Sun, and leave them with me until you are in a position to show me two tickets to Pekin.

SUN My dear cousin, I should like you to mind your own business.

SHUI TA Miss Shen Teh . . .

SUN You just leave her to me.

SHUI TA . . . may not wish to proceed with the sale of her business when she hears . . .

SUN O yes she will.

SHUI TA And you are not afraid of what I may have to say against it?

SUN My dear man!

SHUI TA You seem to forget that she is flesh and blood, and has a mind of her own.

SUN [*amused*] It astounds me what people imagine about their female relations and the effect of sensible argument. Haven't they ever told you about the power of love, the twitching of the flesh? You want to appeal to her reason? She hasn't any reason! All she's had is a lifetime of ill-treatment, poor thing! If I put my hand on her shoulder and say 'You're coming with me,' she'll hear bells and not recognise her own mother.

SHUI TA [*laboriously*] Mr Yang Sun!

SUN Mr . . . whatever your name is!

SHUI TA My cousin is indebted to you because . . .

SUN Let's say because I've got my hand inside her blouse? Stuff that in your pipe and smoke it! [*He takes another cigar, then sticks a few in his pocket, and finally puts the box under his arm.*] You're not to go to her empty-handed: we're getting married, and that's settled. And she'll bring the 300 with her or else you will: either her or you.

[*Exit.*]

MRS SHIN [*sticks her head out of the back room*] How very disagreeable! And the whole Yellow Alley knows that he's got the girl exactly where he wants her.

SHUI TA [*crying out*] The business has gone! He's not in love. This means ruin. I am lost! [*He begins to rush round like a captive animal, continually repeating, 'The business has gone!'—until he suddenly stops and addresses* MRS SHIN.] Mrs Shin, you grew up in the gutter and so did I. Are we irresponsible? No. Do we lack the necessary brutality? No. I am ready to take you by the scruff of the neck and shake you until you spit out the farthing you stole from me, and you know it. Times are frightful, the town is hell, but we scrabble up the naked walls. Then one of us is overcome by disaster: he is in love. That is enough, he is lost. A single weakness, and you can be shovelled away. How can one remain free of every weakness, above all of the most deadly, of love? It is intolerable! It costs too much! Tell me, has one got to spend one's whole life on the lookout? What sort of world do we live in?

Love's caresses merge in strangulation.
Love's sighs grow into a scream of fear.
What are the vultures hovering for?
A girl is keeping an appointment.

MRS SHIN I think I had better fetch the barber. You must talk to the barber. He is a man of honour. The barber: that's the right man for your cousin.

[*Getting no answer, she hurries away.* SHUI TA *continues rushing around until* MR SHU FU *enters, followed by* MRS SHIN, *who however is forced to withdraw at a gesture from* MR SHU FU.]

SHUI TA [*turns to him*] My dear sir, rumour has it that you have shown a certain interest in my cousin. You must allow me to set aside the laws of propriety, which call for a measure of reserve, for the young lady is at the moment in great danger.

MR SHU FU Oh!

SHUI TA Proprietress of her own business until a few hours ago, my cousin is now little more than a beggar. Mr Shu Fu, this shop is bankrupt.

MR SHU FU Mr Shui Ta, Miss Shen Teh's attraction lies less in the soundness of her business than in the goodness of her heart. You can tell a lot from the name they give the young lady round here: The Angel of the Slums!

SHUI TA My dear sir, this goodness has cost my cousin 200 silver dollars in a single day! There are limits.

MR SHU FU Allow me to put forward a different opinion: is it not time that all limits to this goodness were removed? It is the young lady's nature to do good. What is the sense of her feeding four people, as she so moves me by doing every morning! Why should she not feed four hundred? I hear for instance that she is desperate to find shelter for a few homeless. My buildings across the cattleyard are unoccupied. They are at her disposal. And so on and so forth. Mr Shui Ta, have I the right to hope that such thoughts as these which I have lately been entertaining may find a willing listener in Miss Shen Teh?

SHUI TA Mr Shu Fu, she will listen with admiration to such lofty thoughts.

[*Enter* WANG *with the* POLICEMAN. MR SHU FU *turns round and examines the shelves.*]

WANG Is Miss Shen Teh here?

SHUI TA No.

WANG I am Wang, the water-seller. I suppose you are Mr Shui Ta?

SHUI TA Quite correct. Good morning, Wang.

WANG I am a friend of Shen Teh's.

SHUI TA I know that you are one of her oldest friends.

WANG [*to the* POLICEMAN] See? [*To* SHUI TA] I have come about my hand.

THE POLICEMAN He can't use it, there's no denying.

SHUI TA [*quickly*] I see you want a sling for your arm. [*He fetches a shawl from the back room and tosses it to* WANG.]

WANG But that's her new shawl.

SHUI TA She won't need it.

WANG But she bought it specially to please a particular person.

SHUI TA As things have turned out that is no longer necessary.

WANG [*makes a sling out of the shawl*] She is my only witness.

THE POLICEMAN Your cousin is supposed to have seen Shu Fu the barber strike the water-carrier with his curling-tongs. Do you know anything about that?

SHUI TA I only know that my cousin was not present when this slight incident took place.

WANG It's a misunderstanding! When Shen Teh comes she will clear it all up. Shen Teh will bear me out. Where is she?

SHUI TA [*seriously*] Mr Wang, you call yourself my cousin's friend. At the moment my cousin has really serious worries. She has been disgracefully exploited on all sides. From now on she cannot permit herself the slightest weakness. I am convinced that you will not ask her to ruin herself utterly by testifying in your case to anything but the truth.

WANG [*puzzled*] But she told me to go to the magistrate.

SHUI TA Was the magistrate supposed to cure your hand?

THE POLICEMAN No. But he was to make the barber pay up.

[MR SHU FU *turns round.*]

SHUI TA Mr Wang, one of my principles is never to interfere in a dispute between my friends.

[SHUI TA *bows to* MR SHU FU, *who bows back.*]

WANG [*sadly, as he takes off the sling and puts it back*] I see.

THE POLICEMAN Which means I can go, eh? You tried your game on the wrong man, on a proper gentleman that is. You be a bit more careful with your complaints next time, fellow. If Mr Shu Fu doesn't choose to waive his legal rights you can still land in the cells for defamation. Get moving!

[*Both exeunt.*]

SHUI TA I beg you to excuse this episode.

MR SHU FU It is excused. [*Urgently*] And this business about a 'particular person?' [*He points to the shawl.*] Is it really over? Finished and done with?

SHUI TA Completely. She has seen through him. Of course, it will take time for it all to heal.

MR SHU FU One will be careful, considerate.

SHUI TA Her wounds are fresh.

MR SHU FU She will go away to the country.

SHUI TA For a few weeks. But she will be glad to talk things over first with someone she can trust.

MR SHU FU Over a little supper, in a small but good restaurant.

SHUI TA Discreetly. I shall hasten to inform my cousin. She will show her good sense. She is greatly upset about her business, which she regards as a gift from the gods. Please be so good as to wait for a few minutes.

[*Exit into the back room.*]

MRS SHIN [*sticks her head in*] Can we congratulate you?

MR SHU FU You can. Mrs Shin, will you tell Shen Teh's dependents from me before tonight that I am giving them shelter in my buildings across the yard?

[*She grins and nods.*]

MR SHU FU [*standing up, to the audience*] What do you think of me, ladies and gentlemen? Could one do more? Could one be more unselfish? More delicate? More farsighted? A little supper. How crude and vulgar that would normally sound. Yet there will be nothing of that kind, not a thing. No contact, not even an apparently accidental touch when passing the salt. All that will happen will be an exchange of ideas. Two souls will discover one another, across the flowers on the table—white chrysanthemums, by the way. [*He notes it down.*] No, this will be no exploiting of an unfortunate situation, no profiting from a disappointment. Understanding and assistance will be offered, but almost unspoken. By a glance alone will they be acknowledged, a glance that can also signify rather more.

MRS SHIN Has it all turned out as you wanted, Mr Shu Fu?

MR SHU FU Oh, quite as I wanted. You can take it that there will be changes in this neighbourhood. A certain character has been sent packing, and one or two hostile movements against this shop are due to be foiled. Certain persons who have no hesitation in trampling on the good name of the most respectable girl in this town will in future have me to deal with. What do you know about this Yang Sun?

MRS SHIN He is the idlest, dirtiest . . .

MR SHU FU He is nothing. He does not exist. He is simply not present, Mrs Shin.

[*Enter* SUN.]

SUN What's this about?

MRS SHIN Would you like me to call Mr Shui Ta, sir? He won't like strangers wandering round the shop.

MR SHU FU Miss Shen Teh is having an important discussion with Mr Shui Ta, and they cannot be interrupted.

SUN She's here, is she? I didn't see her go in! What are they discussing? They can't leave me out!

MR SHU FU [*prevents him from going into the back room*] You will have to be patient, sir. I think I know who you are. Kindly take note that Miss Shen Teh and I are about to announce our engagement.

SUN What?

SHIN That is a surprise for you, isn't it?

[SUN *struggles with the barber in an effort to get into the back room;* SHEN TEH *emerges.*]

MR SHU FU Forgive us, my dear Shen Teh. Perhaps you will explain.

SUN What's up, Shen Teh? Have you gone crazy?

SHEN TEH [*breathlessly*] Sun, Mr Shu Fu and my cousin have agreed that I ought to listen to Mr Shu Fu's ideas of how to help the people round here. [*Pause*] My cousin is against our relationship.

SUN And you have agreed?

SHEN TEH Yes.

[*Pause.*]

SUN Have they told you I'm a bad character?

[SHEN TEH *remains silent.*]

SUN Perhaps I am, Shen Teh. And that is why I need you. I am a debased character. No capital, no manners. But I can put up a fight. They're wrecking your life, Shen Teh. [*He goes up to her, subdued.*] Just look at him! Haven't you got eyes in your head? [*Putting his hand on her shoulder*] Poor creature, what are they trying to shove you into now? Into a sensible marriage! If it weren't for me they would simply have put you out of your misery. Tell me yourself: but for me, wouldn't you have gone off with him?

SHEN TEH Yes.

SUN A man you don't love!

SHEN TEH Yes.

SUN Have you completely forgotten? The rain?

SHEN TEH No.

SUN How you hacked me down from the tree, how you brought me a glass of water, how you promised me the money so I could fly again?

SHEN TEH [*trembling*] What do you want?

SUN Come away with me.

SHEN TEH Mr Shu Fu, forgive me, I want to go away with Sun.

SUN We are in love, you know. [*He escorts her to the door.*] Have you got the key of the shop? [*He takes it from her and gives it to* MRS SHIN.] Put it on the step when you've finished. Come, Shen Teh.

MR SHU FU But this is rape! [*He shouts into the back room.*] Mr Shui Ta!

SUN Tell him not to make so much row here.

SHEN TEH Please don't call my cousin, Mr Shu Fu. We are not of one mind, I know. But he is not in the right, I can sense it.

[*To the audience*]

I would go with the man whom I love.
I would not reckon what it costs me.
I would not consider what is wiser.
I would not know whether he loves me.
I would go with the man whom I love.

SUN Just like that.

[*Both walk off.*]

Interlude

in front of the curtain

[SHEN TEH *in her wedding clothes, on her way to the wedding, turns and addresses the audience.*]

SHEN TEH I have had a fearful experience. As I stepped out of the door, joyous and full of expectation, I found the carpet-dealer's old wife standing in the street, shakily telling me that her husband was so excited and troubled about the money she lent me that he had fallen ill. She thought it best for me in any case to give her back the money. Of course I promised. She was greatly relieved and, weeping, gave me her good wishes, begging me to excuse her for not completely trusting my cousin, nor, alas, Sun. I had to sit down on the steps when she left, I had so scared myself. In the tumult of my feelings I had thrown myself once more into Yang Sun's arms. I could resist neither his voice nor his caresses. The evil that he had spoken to Shui Ta could not teach Shen Teh a lesson. Sinking into his arms, I still thought; the gods wanted me to be kind to myself too.

To let none go to waste, not oneself either
To bring happiness to all, even oneself, that
Is good.

How could I simply have forgotten the two good old people? Like a small hurricane Sun just swept my shop off in the direction of Pekin, and with it all my friends. But he is not evil, and he loves me. As long as I am near him he will do nothing wicked; what a man tells other men means nothing. He wants to seem big and strong then, and particularly hard-boiled. If I tell him that the old people cannot pay their taxes he will understand. He would rather get a job at the cement works than owe his flying to a wrong action. True, flying is a tremendous passion with him. Shall I be strong enough to call out the goodness in him? At the moment, on the way to my wedding, I am hovering between fear and joy.

[*She goes off quickly.*]

Scene 6

Private Room in a Cheap Suburban Restaurant

[*A* WAITER *is pouring out wine for the wedding guests. Round* SHEN TEH *stand the* GRANDFATHER, *the* SISTER-IN-LAW, *the* NIECE, MRS. SHIN, *and the* UNEMPLOYED MAN. *A* PRIEST *stands by himself in a corner.* SUN *is talking to his mother,* MRS YANG, *in front. He is wearing a dinner jacket.*]

SUN Bad news, mother. She just told me, oh so innocently, that she can't sell the shop for me. Some people are dunning her to pay back those 200 silver dollars she gave you. Though her cousin says there's nothing about it in writing.

MRS YANG What did you say to her? You can't marry her, of course.

SUN There's no point in discussing all that with her; she is too pig-headed. I have sent for her cousin.

MRS YANG But he wants to get her married to the barber.

SUN I've dealt with that marriage. The barber has been seen off. Her cousin will soon realise the business has gone if I don't produce the 200, as the creditors will seize it, but that the job's gone too if I don't get the 300 on top.

MRS YANG I'll go and look for him outside. Go and talk to your bride now, Sun!

SHEN TEH [*to the audience as she pours out wine*] I was not mistaken in him. Not a line of his face betrayed disappointment. Despite the heavy blow that it must have been to renounce his flying he is perfectly cheerful. I love him very much. [*She motions* SUN *to come to her.*] Sun, you have not yet drunk with the bride!

SUN What shall we drink to?

SHEN TEH Let it be to the future.

[*They drink.*]

SUN When the bridegroom's dinner jacket is his own!

SHEN TEH But the bride's dress is still sometimes exposed to the rain.

SUN To all we want for ourselves!

SHEN TEH May it come soon!

MRS YANG [*to* MRS SHIN *as she leaves*] I am delighted with my son. I've always tried to make him realise that he can get any girl he wants. Him, a trained pilot and mechanic. And what does he go and tell me now? I am marrying for love, mother, he says. Money isn't everything. It's a love match! [*To the* SISTER-IN-LAW] Sooner or later these things have to happen, don't they? But it's hard on a mother, very hard. [*Calling to the* PRIEST] Don't cut it too short. If you take as long over the ceremony as you did arguing about the fee, that will make it nice and dignified. [*To* SHEN TEH] We shall have to hold things up a bit, my dear. One of our most valued guests has still to arrive. [*To all*] Please excuse us.

[*Exit.*]

THE SISTER-IN-LAW It's a pleasure to be patient as long as there's something to drink.

[*They sit down.*]

THE UNEMPLOYED MAN We're not missing much.

SUN [*loudly and facetiously in front of the guests*] Before the ceremony starts I ought to give you a little test. There's some point when the wedding's at such short notice. [*To the guests*] I have no idea what sort of wife I'm going to get. It's most disturbing. For instance, can you use three tea leaves to make five cups of tea?

SHEN TEH No.

SUN Then I shan't be getting any tea. Can you sleep on a straw mattress the size of that book the priest's reading?

SHEN TEH Double?

SUN Single.

SHEN TEH In that case, no.

SUN Dreadful, what a wife I'm getting.

[*All laugh. Behind* SHEN TEH MRS YANG *appears in the doorway. She shrugs her shoulders to tell* SUN *that the expected guest is not to be seen.*]

MRS YANG [*to the* PRIEST, *who is pointing to his watch*] Don't be in such a hurry. It can't be more than a matter of minutes. There they are, all drinking and smoking, and none of them's in a hurry. [*She sits down with her guests.*]

SHEN TEH But oughtn't we to discuss how it's all going to be settled?

MRS YANG Now, not a word about business today. It so lowers the tone of a party, don't you think?

[*The bell at the door rings. All look towards the door, but nobody comes in.*]

SHEN TEH Who is your mother waiting for, Sun?

SUN It's to be a surprise for you. By the way, where is your cousin, Shui Ta? I get on well with him. A very sensible fellow! Brainy! Why don't you say something?

SHEN TEH I don't know. I don't want to think about him.

SUN Why not?

SHEN TEH Because I wish you didn't get on with him. If you like me, you can't like him.

SUN Then I hope the gremlins got him: the engine gremlin, the petrol gremlin, and the fog gremlin. Drink, you old obstinate!

[*He forces her.*]

THE SISTER-IN-LAW [*to* MRS SHIN] Something fishy here.

MRS SHIN What else did you expect?

THE PRIEST [*comes firmly up to* MRS YANG, *with his watch in his hand*] I must go, Mrs Yang. I've got a second wedding, and a funeral first thing in the morning.

MRS YANG Do you imagine I'm holding things up for pleasure? We hoped that one jug of wine would see us through. Now look how low it's getting. [*Loudly, to* SHEN TEH] I can't understand, my dear Shen Teh, why your cousin should let us wait for him like this!

SHEN TEH My cousin?

MRS YANG But my dear girl, it's him we're waiting for. I am old-fashioned enough to feel that such a close relation of the bride ought to be at the wedding.

SHEN TEH Oh Sun, is it about the 300 dollars?

SUN [*without looking at her*] You've heard what it's about. She is old-fashioned. I've got to consider her. We'll just wait a quarter of an hour, and if he hasn't come by then it'll mean the three gremlins have got him, and we'll start without!

MRS YANG I expect you have all heard that my son is getting a position as a mail pilot. I am delighted about it. It's important to have a well-paid job in these days.

THE SISTER-IN-LAW In Pekin, they say: is that right?

MRS YANG Yes, in Pekin.

SHEN TEH Sun, hadn't you better tell your mother that Pekin is off?

SUN Your cousin can tell her if he feels the same way as you. Between you and me, I don't.

SHEN TEH [*shocked*] Sun!

SUN God, how I loathe Szechwan! What a town! Do you realise what they all look like when I half shut my eyes? Like horses. They look up nervously: what's that thundering over their heads? What, won't people need them anymore? Have they outlived their time? They can bite each other to death in their horse town! All I want is to get out of here!

SHEN TEH But I promised the old couple I'd pay them back.

SUN Yes, that's what you told me. And it's a good thing your cousin's coming as you're so silly. Drink your wine and leave business to us! We'll fix it.

SHEN TEH [*horrified*] But my cousin can't come!

SUN What do you mean?

SHEN TEH He's not there.

SUN And how do you picture our future: will you kindly tell me?

SHEN TEH I thought you still had the 200 silver dollars. We can pay them back tomorrow and keep the tobacco, which is worth much more, and sell it together outside the cement works as we can't pay the rent.

SUN Forget it! Put it right out of your mind, sister! Me stand in the street and hawk tobacco to the cement workers: me, Yang Sun the pilot? I'd sooner blow the whole 200 in a single night. I'd sooner chuck it in the river! And your cousin knows me. I fixed with him he was to bring the 300 to the wedding.

SHEN TEH My cousin cannot come.

SUN And I thought he couldn't possibly stay away.

SHEN TEH It is impossible for him to be where I am.

SUN How very mysterious!

SHEN TEH Sun, you must realise he is no friend of yours. It is I who love you. My cousin Shui Ta loves nobody— He is a friend to me, but not to my friends. He agreed that you should have the old people's money because he was thinking of your pilot's job in Pekin. But he will not bring the 300 silver dollars to the wedding.

SUN And why not?

SHEN TEH [*looking him in the eyes*] He says you only bought one ticket to Pekin.

SUN Yes, but that was yesterday, and look what I've got to show him today! [*He half pulls two tickets out of his breast pocket.*] There's no need for the old woman to see. That's two tickets to Pekin, for me and for you. Do you still think your cousin's against the marriage?

SHEN TEH No. The job is a good one. And my business has gone.

SUN It's for your sake I sold the furniture.

SHEN TEH Don't say any more! Don't show me the tickets! It makes me too afraid that I might simply go off with you. But do you see, Sun, I can't give you the 300 silver dollars, or what is to become of the two old people?

SUN What's to become of me? [*Pause*] You'd better have a drink! Or do you believe in being careful? I can't stick a careful woman. When I drink I start flying again. And you: if you drink there's just the faintest shadow of a possibility you may understand me.

SHEN TEH Don't think I don't understand you. You want to fly, and I can't be any help.

SUN 'Here's your plane, beloved, but I'm afraid it's a wing short.'

SHEN TEH Sun, there's no honourable way for us to get that job in Pekin. That's why I need you to hand back the 200 silver dollars I gave you. Give them to me now, Sun!

SUN 'Give them to me now, Sun!' What do you think you are talking about? Are you my wife or aren't you? Because you're ratting on me, don't you realise? Luckily—and luckily for you too—it doesn't depend on you, because it's all been settled.

MRS YANG [*icily*] Sun, are you certain the bride's cousin will be coming? It almost looks as though he had something against this marriage, as he doesn't appear.

SUN But what are you thinking of, mother! Him and me are like that. I'll open the door wide so that he spots us at once as he comes rushing up to act as best man to his old friend Sun. [*He goes to the door and kicks it open. Then he comes back, swaying slightly because he has already drunk too much, and sits down again by* SHEN TEH.] We'll wait. Your cousin has got more sense than you. Love is an essential part of living, he wisely says. And what's more he knows what it would mean for you: no shop left and no wedding either!

[*They wait.*]

MRS YANG At last!

[*Footsteps are heard, and all look towards the door. But the footsteps move on.*]

MRS SHIN There's going to be a scandal. One can feel it; one can sniff it in the air. The bride is waiting for the ceremony, but the bridegroom is waiting for her honourable cousin.

SUN The honourable cousin is taking his time.

SHEN TEH [*softly*] Oh, Sun!

SUN Sitting here with the tickets in my pocket, and an idiot beside me who can't do arithmetic! And I see the day coming when you'll be putting the police on me to get your 200 silver dollars back.

SHEN TEH [*to the audience*] He is evil and he would like me to be evil too. Here am I who love him, and he stays waiting for a cousin. But round me sit the defenceless: the old woman with her sick husband, the poor who wait at the door every morning for rice, and an unknown man from Pekin who is worried about his job. And they all protect me because they all have faith in me.

SUN [*stares at the glass jug in which the wine is near the bottom*] The wine jug is our clock. We are poor people, and once the guests have drunk the wine the clock has run down forever.

[MRS YANG *signs to him to keep silent, and footsteps can be heard once more.*]

THE WAITER [*enters*] Do you wish to order another jug of wine, Mrs Yang?

MRS YANG No, I think there will be enough. Wine only makes one too hot, don't you think?

MRS SHIN I imagine it costs a lot too.

MRS YANG Drinking always makes me perspire.

THE WAITER Would you mind settling the bill now, madam?

MRS YANG [*ignores him*] Ladies and gentlemen, I hope you can be patient a little longer: our relative must be on his way by now. [*To the* WAITER] Don't interrupt the party.

THE WAITER My orders are not to let you leave until the bill is settled.

MRS YANG But I am well known here!

THE WAITER Exactly!

MRS YANG The service nowadays is really outrageous! Don't you think so, Sun?

THE PRIEST I fear that I must leave.

[*Exit weightily.*]

MRS YANG [*desperate*] Please all of you remain seated! The priest will be back in a few minutes.

SUN Drop it, mother. Ladies and gentlemen, now that the priest has left we cannot detain you any longer.

THE SISTER-IN-LAW Come on, Grandpa!

THE GRANDFATHER [*solemnly empties his glass*] The bride!

THE NIECE [*to* SHEN TEH] Don't mind him. He means it friendly-like. He's fond of you.

MRS SHIN That's what I call a flop!

[*All the guests leave.*]

SHEN TEH Shall I leave too, Sun?

SUN No, you wait. [*He pulls at her wedding finery so that it is askew.*] It's your wedding, isn't it? I'm going to wait on, and the old lady will wait on. She is anxious to see her bird in the air again anyhow. It's my opinion that the moon will be nothing but green cheese before she can step outside and see his plane thundering over the house. [*To the empty chairs as if the guests were still there*] Ladies and gentlemen, can't you make conversation? Don't you like it here? The wedding has only been somewhat postponed, on account of the non-arrival of influential relations, and because the bride doesn't know what love is. To keep you amused I, the bridegroom, will sing you a song. [*He sings.*]

The Song of Green Cheese

A day will come, so the poor were informed
As they sat at their mother's knees
When a child of low birth shall inherit the earth
And the moon shall be made of green cheese.
  When the moon is green cheese
  The poor shall inherit the earth.

Then goodness will be a thing to reward
And evil a mortal offence.
'Where there's merit, there's money' won't sound quite
so funny
There will really be no difference.
When the moon is green cheese
There won't be this difference.

Then the grass will look down on the blue sky below
And the pebbles will roll up the stream
And man is a king. Without doing a thing
He gorges on honey and cream.
When the moon is green cheese
The world flows with honey and cream.

Then I shall become a pilot again
And you'll get a deputy's seat.
You, man on the loose, will find you're some use
And you, Ma, can put up your feet.
When the moon is green cheese
The weary can put up their feet.

And as we have waited quite long enough
This new world has got to be born
Not at the last minute so there's nothing left in it
But at the first glimmer of dawn
When the moon is green cheese
The very first glimmer of dawn.

MRS YANG He won't come now.

[*The three of them sit there and two of them look towards the door.*]

Interlude

Wang's Sleeping Place

[*Once more the* GODS *appear to the water-seller in a dream. He has fallen asleep over a large book. Music.*]

WANG How good that you have come, Illustrious Ones! Permit me a question which disturbs me greatly. In the tumbledown hut belonging to a priest who has left to become an unskilled labourer in the cement works I discovered a book, and in it I found a remarkable passage. I should like to read it to you. It runs: [*With his left hand he thumbs through an imaginary book laid over the book in his lap, and lifts this imaginary book up to read from it, leaving the real one lying where it was.*] 'In Sung there is a place known as Thorn Hedge. There catalpas, cypresses, and mulberries flourish. Now those trees which are nine or ten inches in circumference are chopped down by the people who need stakes for their dog kennels. Those which are three or four feet in circumference are chopped down by rich and respectable families who want planks for their coffins. Those which are seven or eight feet in circumference are chopped down by persons seeking beams for their luxurious villas. And so none reaches its full quota of years, but is brought down prematurely by saw or by axe. That is the price of utility.'

THE THIRD GOD That would mean that the least useful is the best.

WANG No, only the most fortunate. The least good is the most fortunate.

THE FIRST GOD Ah, what things they write!

THE SECOND GOD Why are you so deeply moved by this comparison, O water-seller?

WANG On account of Shen Teh, Illustrious Ones! She has failed in her love because she obeyed the commandment to love her neighbours. Perhaps she really is too good for this world, O Illustrious Ones!

THE FIRST GOD Nonsense. You poor, feeble creature! It seems to me that you are half eaten away by scepticism and lice.

WANG Certainly, O Illustrious One! I only thought you might perhaps intervene.

THE FIRST GOD Out of the question. Our friend here—[*He points to the* THIRD GOD, *who has a black eye.*]—intervened in a quarrel only yesterday; you see the result.

WANG But they had to send for her cousin yet again. He is an unusually capable man, I know from experience, but even he could not set things straight. It looks as if the shop were already lost.

THE THIRD GOD [*disturbed*] Do you think perhaps we ought to help?

THE FIRST GOD My view is that she has got to help herself.

THE SECOND GOD [*strictly*] The worse the difficulties, the better the good man will prove to be. Suffering ennobles!

THE FIRST GOD We are putting all our hopes in her.

THE THIRD GOD Our search is not progressing well. Now and again we come across a good start, admirable intentions, a lot of high principles, but it hardly adds up to a good person. When we do find people who are halfway good, they are not living a decent human existence. [*Confidentially*] The nights are getting worse and worse. You can tell where we have been spending them from the straws sticking to our clothes.

WANG Just one request. Could you not at least . . .

THE GODS Nothing. We are but observers. We firmly believe that our good person will find her own feet on this sombre earth. Her powers will wax with her burden. Only wait a little, O water-seller, and you will find all's well that ends . . .

[*The* GODS' *figures have been growing steadily paler, their voices steadily fainter. Now they disappear, and their voices cease.*]

Scene 7

Yard behind Shen Teh's Shop

[*A few household goods on a cart.* SHEN TEH *and* MRS SHIN *are taking washing down from the line.*]

MRS SHIN I can't think why you don't put up a better fight for your business.

SHEN TEH How? I can't even pay the rent. I have got to pay the old people their 200 silver dollars back today, and because I've given them to someone else I shall have to sell my stock to Mrs Mi Tzu.

MRS SHIN All gone, eh? No man, no stock, no home! That comes of trying to set oneself up as a cut above our lot. How do you propose to live now?

SHEN TEH I don't know. I might earn a bit as a tobacco sorter.

MRS SHIN What are Mr Shui Ta's trousers doing here? He must have gone off in his shirt.

SHEN TEH He's got another pair.

MRS SHIN I thought you said he had gone away for good. What does he want to leave his trousers behind for?

SHEN TEH Perhaps he's finished with them.

MRS SHIN Oughtn't you to make a parcel of them?

SHEN TEH No.

[MR SHU FU *bursts in.*]

MR SHU FU Don't tell me. I know it all. You have sacrificed your young love so that two old people who trusted you should not be ruined. It was not for nothing that this malicious and mistrustful district christened you 'The Angel of the Slums'. The gentleman to whom you were engaged proved unable to raise himself to your moral stature; you threw him over. And now you are closing your shop, that little haven of refuge for so many! I cannot stand by and see it. Day after day I have stood at the door of my shop and seen the knot of down-and-outs before your window, and you yourself doling out rice. Must all that vanish forever? Must goodness be defeated? Ah, if only you will allow me to assist you in your good works! No, don't say a thing! I wish for no assurances. No promises that you will accept my help! But herewith—[*He takes out a cheque-book and writes a cheque, which he lays on the cart.*]—I make you out a blank cheque, which you can fill in for any sum you like; and now I shall go, quietly and modestly, demanding nothing in return, on tiptoe, full of respectful admiration, not a thought for myself.

[*Exit.*]

MRS SHIN [*examines the cheque*] This'll save you! People like you have some luck! You can always find a mug. Now hurry up. Write in 1,000 silver dollars and I'll run to the bank with it before he comes to his senses.

SHEN TEH Put the laundry basket on the cart. I can pay for the washing without that cheque.

MRS SHIN What do you mean? You're not going to take the cheque? That's criminal! Is it just because you feel you would have to marry him? That would be plain crazy. A fellow like that just asks to be led by the nose! That sort really likes it. Are you still wanting to hang on to that pilot of yours, when everyone here and in Yellow Alley knows how badly he's treated you?

SHEN TEH It all comes from poverty. [*To the audience*]

At night I watched him blow out his cheeks in his sleep: they were evil
And at dawn I held his coat up to the light, and saw the wall through it.
When I saw his sly smile I was afraid, but
When I saw the holes in his shoes I loved him dearly.

MRS SHIN So you're still sticking up for him? I never heard anything so idiotic. [*Angry*] I shall be relieved when we have got you out of the district.

SHEN TEH [*staggers as she takes down the washing*] I'm feeling a bit giddy.

MRS SHIN [*takes the washing from her*] Do you often feel giddy when you bend or stretch? Let's only hope it isn't a little one! [*Laughs.*] He has fixed you good and proper! If that's it then the big cheque will turn sour. It wasn't meant for that sort of situation. [*She goes to the rear with a basket.*]

[SHEN TEH *looks after her without moving. Then she examines her body, feels it, and a great joy appears in her face.*]

SHEN TEH [*softly*] Oh joy! A small being is coming to life in my body. There is nothing to see yet. But he is already there. The world awaits him in secret. In the cities they have heard the rumour: someone is coming now with whom we must reckon. [*She presents her small son to the audience.*] An airman!

Salute a new conqueror
Of unknown mountains, inaccessible countries! One
Carrying letters from man to man
Across the wastes where no man yet has trod!

[*She begins to walk up and down, leading her small son by the hand.*] Come my son, inspect your world. Here, that is a tree. Bow politely, greet him. [*She performs a bow.*] There, now you know one another. Listen, that is the water-seller coming. A friend, shake hands with him. Don't be nervous. 'A glass of cool water for my son, please. It's a hot day.' [*She hands him the glass.*] Ah, the policeman! I think we will avoid him. Perhaps we might collect one or two cherries over there, from rich old Mr Feh Pung's orchard. This is a moment not to be seen. Come, poor little bastard! You too like cherries! Soft, soft, my son! [*They walk cautiously, looking around them.*] No, round this way, where the bushes will shield us. No, no going straight to the point in this case. [*He seems to be dragging away; she resists.*] We've got to be sensible. [*Suddenly she gives in.*] Very well, if you can't do it any other way. . . . [*She lifts him up.*] Can you reach the cherries? Shove them in your mouth, that's the best place for them. [*She eats one herself, which he puts into her mouth.*] Tastes fine. O god, the police. This is where we run. [*They flee.*] Here's the road. Now gently, walk slowly so we don't attract attention. As if nothing whatever had happened. . . . [*She sings as she walks along with the child.*]

A plum off my tree
Bit a man on the knee
The man had a thirst
Got his own bite in first.

[WANG *the water-seller has entered, leading a child by the hand. He watches* SHEN TEH *in astonishment.*]

SHEN TEH [*as* WANG *coughs*] Oh, Wang! Good day.

WANG Shen Teh, I have heard you are in difficulties, that you must even sell your business to pay debts. But here's this child without any home. It was playing about in the slaughterhouse. They say it belongs to Lin To the carpenter, who had to give up his workshop a few weeks ago and is now on the drink. His children are wandering around starving. What can be done with them?

SHEN TEH [*takes the child from him*] Come on, little man! [*To the audience*]

Here, you! Someone begging for shelter.
A chip of tomorrow begging you for a today.
His friend, the conqueror, whom you know
Can answer for him.

[*To* WANG] He can quite well live in Mr Shu Fu's sheds, where I may be going too. I myself am expecting a child. But do not repeat that, or Yang Sun may hear of it, and we can only hamper him. See if you can find Lin To in the lower town, and tell him to come here.

WANG Many thanks, Shen Teh. I knew you would find an answer. [*To the child*] See? A good person always knows a way. I'll go off quickly and fetch your father. [*He starts to go.*]

SHEN TEH Oh, Wang, I have just remembered. What happened about your hand? I did want to give evidence for you, but my cousin . . .

WANG Don't bother about my hand. Look, I've already learnt to do without my right hand. I hardly need it at all. [*He shows her how he can manage his carrying pole without his right hand.*] See how I manage?

SHEN TEH But you mustn't let it get stiff! Take that cart, sell the lot, and use the money to go to the doctor. I am ashamed of having let you down like that. And what must you think of me for accepting the barber's offer of the sheds!

WANG The homeless can live there now, and you yourself. After all, that matters more than my hand. I'll go and fetch the carpenter.

[*Exit.*]

SHEN TEH [*calls after him*] Promise me you'll let me take you to the doctor!

[MRS SHIN *has come back and has been making repeated signs.*]

SHEN TEH What is it?

MRS SHIN Are you mad? Giving away the cart with all you've got left? What's his hand to do with you? If the barber gets to know he'll throw you out of the last lodging you're likely to find. You haven't paid me for the washing yet!

SHEN TEH Why are you so unpleasant?

To trample on one's fellows
Is surely exhausting? Veins in your temples
Stick out with the strenuousness of greed.
Loosely held forth
A hand gives and receives with the same suppleness. Yet
Greedily snatching it has got to strain. Oh
How tempting it is to be generous. How welcome
Friendliness can somehow feel. A kindly word
Escapes like a sigh of contentment.

[MRS SHIN *goes off angrily.*]

SHEN TEH [*to the child*] Sit here and wait till your father comes.

[*The child sits on the ground. Enter the elderly couple who visited* SHEN TEH *on the day of the opening of her shop.* MAN *and* WIFE *are dragging big sacks.*]

THE WOMAN Are you by yourself, Shen Teh? [*When* SHEN TEH *nods she calls in her nephew, who is also carrying a sack.*] Where's your cousin?

SHEN TEH He went away.

THE WOMAN Is he coming back?

SHEN TEH No. I'm giving up the shop.

THE WOMAN So we heard. That's why we've come. These are a few sacks of leaf tobacco which somebody owed us, and we'd be ever so grateful if you could move them to your new home with your own things. We've no place to put them yet, and if we have them in the street people are bound to notice. I don't see how you can refuse to do us this little favour after the bad luck we had in your shop.

SHEN TEH I will do it for you gladly.

THE MAN And if anyone happens to ask you whose sacks these are you can say they're yours.

SHEN TEH Who would want to know?

THE WOMAN [*giving her a sharp look*] The police for one. They've got it in for us, and they're out to ruin us. Where do we put the sacks?

SHEN TEH I don't know; just at this moment I'd sooner not do anything that might get me into gaol.

THE WOMAN Isn't that like you? All we've been able to save of our things is a few rotten old sacks of tobacco, and a lot you care if we lose them!

[SHEN TEH *is stubbornly silent.*]

THE MAN Don't you see that this stock of tobacco might allow us to start manufacturing in a small way? Then we could work our way up.

SHEN TEH All right, I'll keep your sacks for you. They can go in the back room for the present.

[*She goes in with them. The child has been watching her. Now it looks round timidly, goes to the dustbin, and starts fishing in it. It begins to eat something that it has found.* SHEN TEH *and the others return.*]

THE WOMAN You realise we're completely in your hands?

SHEN TEH Yes. [*She notices the child and stiffens.*]

THE MAN We'll call on you the day after tomorrow in Mr Shu Fu's buildings.

SHEN TEH Please leave at once; I'm not well. [*She pushes them out. Exeunt the three.*] He's hungry. Fishing in the dustbin.

[*She lifts up the child and expresses her horror at the fate of poor children in a speech, showing the audience his dirty mouth. She proclaims her determination never to treat her own child in such a heartless way.*]

O son, O airman! What sort of a world
Awaits you? Will you too
Be left to fish in the garbage? Observe
The greyness round his mouth! [*She exhibits the child.*] Is that
How you treat your fellow creatures? Have you
Not the least compassion for the fruit
Of your bodies? No pity
For yourselves, you unfortunates? Henceforth I
Shall fight at least for my own, if I have to be
Sharp as a tiger. Yes, from the hour
When I saw this thing I shall cut myself off
From them all, never resting
Till I have at least saved my son, if only him.
What I learnt from my schooling, the gutter
By violence and trickery now
Shall serve you, my son: to you
I would be kind; a tiger, a savage beast
To all others if need be. And
It need be.

[*She goes off to change herself into her cousin.*]

SHEN TEH [*walking off*] Once more it must be done, for the last time I hope.

[*She has taken* SHUI TA'*s trousers with her.* MRS SHIN *returns and stares inquisitively after her. Enter the* SISTER-IN-LAW *and the* GRANDFATHER.]

THE SISTER-IN-LAW Shop shut, all her stuff in the yard! It's the finish!

MRS SHIN That's what comes of selfishness, irresponsibility, and the lusts of the flesh! And where is she heading? Downwards! To Mr Shu Fu's sheds, along with the rest of you!

THE SISTER-IN-LAW She'll be surprised at what she finds there! We've come to complain! A damp rabbit-warren with half-rotten floors! The barber only let us have them because his stock of soap was going bad there. 'I can give you shelter, what do you say to that?' We say, it's a scandal!

[*Enter the* UNEMPLOYED MAN.]

THE UNEMPLOYED MAN Is it true Shen Teh's clearing out?

THE SISTER-IN-LAW Yes. She meant to sneak away so we shouldn't know.

MRS SHIN She's ashamed because she's broke.

THE UNEMPLOYED MAN [*excited*] She must send for her cousin! All of you, advise her to send for her cousin! He's the only one can do anything.

THE SISTER-IN-LAW That's right! He's mean enough, but at least he'll save her business, and then she'll be generous.

THE UNEMPLOYED MAN I wasn't thinking of us, I was thinking of her. But it's a fact: he must be sent for for our sakes too.

[*Enter* WANG *with the* CARPENTER. *He is leading two children by the hand.*]

THE CARPENTER Truly, I can't thank you enough. [*To the others*] We're to get a lodging.

MRS SHIN Where?

THE CARPENTER In Mr Shu Fu's buildings. And it was little Feng who managed it! Ah, there you are! 'Here's someone begging for shelter,' Miss Shen Teh's supposed to have said, and she finds us lodgings there and then. Say thank you to your brother, all of you!

[*The* CARPENTER *and his children make pretence of bowing to the child.*]

THE CARPENTER Our thanks, shelter-beggar!

[SHUI TA *has entered.*]

SHUI TA May I ask what you are all doing here?

THE UNEMPLOYED MAN Mr Shui Ta!

WANG Good day, Mr Shui Ta. I didn't realise you were back. You know Lin To the carpenter. Miss Shen Teh promised to find him a corner in one of Mr Shu Fu's buildings.

SHUI TA Mr Shu Fu's buildings are booked.

THE CARPENTER Does that mean we can't lodge there?

SHUI TA No. These premises are reserved for another purpose.

THE SISTER-IN-LAW Have we got to move out too then?

SHUI TA Unfortunately.

THE SISTER-IN-LAW But where can we all go?

SHUI TA [*shrugging his shoulders*] Miss Shen Teh, who has left town, gave me to understand that she had no intention of neglecting you. In future, however, it must all be rather more sensibly arranged. No more free meals without working for it. Instead every man shall have the opportunity to improve his condition honourably by his labour. Miss Shen Teh has decided to find work for you all. Those of you who now choose to follow me into Mr Shu Fu's buildings will not be led into the blue.

THE SISTER-IN-LAW Do you mean we've all got to start working for Shen Teh?

SHUI TA Yes. You will shred tobacco. There are three full bales in the back room there. Get them!

THE SISTER-IN-LAW Don't forget we used to have a shop of our own. We'd rather work for ourselves. We've got our own tobacco.

SHUI TA [*to the* UNEMPLOYED MAN *and the* CARPENTER] Perhaps you would like to work for Shen Teh, as you have no tobacco of your own?

[*The* CARPENTER *and the* UNEMPLOYED MAN *comply reluctantly, and exeunt. Mrs Mi Tzu enters.*]

MRS MI TZU Now then, Mr Shui Ta, how about the sale of the stock? I have your 300 silver dollars here with me.

SHUI TA Mrs Mi Tzu, I have decided not to sell, but to sign the lease.

MRS MI TZU What? Don't you want the money for the pilot any more?

SHUI TA No.

MRS MI TZU And can you find the rent?

SHUI TA [*takes the barber's cheque off the cart and fills it in*] I have here a cheque for 10,000 silver dollars, signed by Mr Shu Fu, who is taking an interest in my cousin. Look for yourself, Mrs Mi Tzu! You will get your 200 silver dollars for the next half-year's rent before six this evening. And now, Mrs Mi Tzu, you will allow me to go on with my own work. I am extremely busy today and must ask you to excuse me.

MRS MI TZU So Mr Shu Fu is in the pilot's shoes now! 10,000 silver dollars! All the same I am astounded that young girls nowadays should be so frivolous and unstable, Mr Shui Ta.

[*Exit.*]

[*The* CARPENTER *and the* UNEMPLOYED MAN *bring in the sacks.*]

THE CARPENTER I can't think why I should have to cart your sacks for you.

SHUI TA The point is that I can. Your son has a healthy appetite. He wants to eat, Mr Lin To.

THE SISTER-IN-LAW [*sees the sacks*] Has my brother-in-law been here?

MRS SHIN Yes.

THE SISTER-IN-LAW I thought so. I know those sacks. That's our tobacco.

SHUI TA I advise you not to say that so loudly. That is my tobacco, as you can see from the fact that it was in my room. But if you have any doubts about it we can go to the police and clear them up. Do you wish to?

THE SISTER-IN-LAW [*crossly*] No.

SHUI TA Evidently you haven't got your own stock of tobacco after all. Perhaps under those circumstances you will accept the helping hand which Miss Shen Teh is offering you? Be so good now as to show me the way to Mr Shu Fu's buildings.

[*Taking the hand of the* CARPENTER'*s youngest child,* SHUI TA *walks off, followed by the* CARPENTER, *his remaining children, the* SISTER-IN-LAW, *the* GRANDFATHER, *the* UNEMPLOYED MAN. SISTER-IN-LAW, CARPENTER, *and* UNEMPLOYED MAN *drag out the sacks.*]

WANG He is not a wicked man, but Shen Teh is good.

MRS SHIN I'm not sure. There's a pair of trousers missing from the clothes line, and her cousin is wearing them. That must mean something. I'd like to know what.

[*Enter the two old people.*]

THE OLD WOMAN Is Miss Shen Teh not here?

MRS SHIN [*absently*] Left town.

THE OLD WOMAN That's strange. She was going to bring us something.

WANG [*looking painfully at his hand*] And she was going to help me. My hand's going stiff. She's sure to be back soon. Her cousin never stays long.

MRS SHIN He doesn't, does he?

Interlude
Wang's Sleeping Place

[*Music. In a dream the water-seller informs the* GODS *of his fears. The gods are still engaged on their long pilgrimage. They seem tired. Unresponsive at first, they turn and look back at the water-seller.*]

WANG Before you appeared and awoke me, O Illustrious Ones, I was dreaming and saw my dear sister Shen Teh in great distress among the reeds by the river, at the spot where the suicides are found. She was staggering in a strange way and held her head bent as if she were carrying something soft and heavy that was pressing her into the mud. When I called to her she called back that she must carry the whole bundle of precepts across to the other bank, keeping it dry so that the ink should not run. In fact I could see nothing on her shoulder. But I was sharply reminded that you gods had lectured her about the major virtues as a reward for her taking you in when you were stuck for a night's lodging, the more shame to us! I am certain you understand my worries for her.

THE THIRD GOD What do you suggest?

WANG A slight reduction of the precepts, Illustrious Ones. A slight alleviation of the bundle of precepts, O gracious ones, in view of the difficulty of the times.

THE THIRD GOD For instance, Wang, for instance?

WANG For instance, that only good will should be required instead of love, or . . .

THE THIRD GOD But that is far harder, you unhappy man!

WANG Or fairness instead of justice.

THE THIRD GOD But that means more work!

WANG Then plain decency instead of honour!

THE THIRD GOD But that is far more, you man of doubts!

[*They wander wearily on.*]

Scene 8
Shui Ta's Tobacco Factory

[SHUI TA *has set up a small tobacco factory in* MR SHU FU'S *huts. Horribly constricted, a number of families huddle behind bars. Women and children predominate, among them the* SISTER-IN-LAW, *the* GRANDFATHER, *the* CARPENTER, *and his children. In front of them enter* MRS YANG, *followed by her son,* SUN.]

MRS YANG [*to the audience*] I must describe to you how the wisdom and discipline of our universally respected Mr Shui Ta turned my son Sun from a broken wreck into a useful citizen. Near the cattle-yard, as the whole neighbourhood quickly came to hear, Mr Shui Ta started a small but rapidly prospering tobacco factory. Three months ago I found it advisable to call on him there with my son. He received me after a brief wait.

[SHUI TA *comes up to* MRS YANG *from the factory.*]

SHUI TA What can I do for you, Mrs Yang?

MRS YANG Mr Shui Ta, I should like to put in a word for my son. The police came round this morning, and we heard that you were suing in Miss Shen Teh's name for breach of promise and fraudulent conversion of 200 silver dollars.

SHUI TA Quite correct, Mrs Yang.

MRS YANG Mr Shui Ta, in the gods' name can you not temper justice with mercy once more? The money has gone. He ran through it in a couple of days as soon as the idea of the pilot's job fell through. I know he is a bad lot. He had already sold my furniture and was going to set off to Pekin without his poor old mother. [*She weeps.*] There was a time when Miss Shen Teh thought very highly of him.

SHUI TA Have you got anything to say to me, Mr Yang Sun?

SUN [*sombrely*] The money's gone.

SHUI TA Mrs Yang, in view of the weakness which my cousin for some inexplicable reason felt for your broken-down son, I am prepared to give him another chance. She told me she thought honest work might bring an improvement. I can find him a place in my factory. The 200 silver dollars will be deducted in instalments from his wages.

SUN So it's to be factory or clink?

SHUI TA It's your own choice.

SUN And no chance of talking to Shen Teh, I suppose.

SHUI TA No.

SUN Show me where I work.

MRS YANG A thousand thanks, Mr Shui Ta. Your kindness is overwhelming, and the gods will repay you. [*To* SUN] You have strayed from the narrow path. See if honest work will make you fit to look your mother in the face again.

[SUN *follows* SHUI TA *into the factory.* MRS YANG *returns to the front of the stage.*]

MRS YANG The first weeks were difficult for Sun. The work was not what he was used to. He had little chance to show what he could do. It was only in the third week that a small incident brought him luck. He and Lin To who used to be a carpenter were shifting bales of tobacco.

[SUN *and the* FORMER CARPENTER LIN TO *are each shifting two bales of tobacco.*]

THE FORMER CARPENTER [*comes to a halt groaning, and lowers himself on to one of the bales*] I'm about done in. I'm too old for this sort of work.

SUN [*likewise sits down*] Why don't you tell them they can stuff their bales?

THE FORMER CARPENTER How would we live then? To get the barest necessities I must even set the kids to work. A pity Miss Shen Teh can't see it! She was good.

SUN I've known worse. If things had been a bit less miserable we'd have hit it off quite well together. I'd like to know where she is. We had better get on. He usually comes about now.

[*They get up.*]

SUN [*sees* SHUI TA *coming*] Give us one of your sacks, you old cripple! [SUN *adds one of* LIN TO*'s bales to his own load.*]

THE FORMER CARPENTER Thanks a lot! Yes, if she were there you'd certainly go up a peg when she saw how helpful you were to an old man. Ah yes!

[*Enter* SHUI TA.]

MRS YANG And a glance is enough for Mr Shui Ta to spot a good worker who will tackle anything. And he takes a hand.

SHUI TA Hey, you two! What's happening here? Why are you only carrying one sack?

THE FORMER CARPENTER I feel a bit run down today, Mr Shui Ta, and Yang Sun was so kind . . .

SHUI TA You go back and pick up three bales, my friend. If Yang Sun can do it, so can you. Yang Sun puts his heart in it, and you don't.

MRS YANG [*while the* FORMER CARPENTER *fetches two more bales*] Not a word to Sun, of course, but Mr Shui Ta had noticed. And next Saturday, at the pay desk . . .

[*A table is set up and* SHUI TA *comes with a small bag of money. Standing next to the* OVERSEER*—the former unemployed man—he pays out the wages.* SUN *steps up to the table.*

THE OVERSEER Yang Sun—6 silver dollars.

SUN Sorry, but it can't be more than five. Not more than 5 silver dollars. [*He takes the list which the* OVERSEER *is holding.*] Look, here you are, you've got me down for six full days, but I was off one day, as I had to go to court. [*Ingratiatingly*] I wouldn't like to be paid money I hadn't earned, however lousy the pay is.

THE OVERSEER 5 silver dollars, then! [*To* SHUI TA] Very unusual that, Mr Shui Ta!

SHUI TA How do you come to have six days down here when it was only five?

THE OVERSEER Quite correct, Mr Shui Ta, I must have made a mistake. [*To* SUN, *coldly*] It won't occur again.

SHUI TA [*calls* SUN *aside*] I have noticed lately that you have plenty of strength and don't grudge it to the firm. Now I see that you are to be trusted too. Does it often happen that the overseer makes mistakes to the firm's loss?

SUN He's friends with some of the workers, and they count him as one of them.

SHUI TA I see. One good turn deserves another. Would you like a bonus?

SUN No. But perhaps I might point out that I have also got a brain. I have had a fair education, you know. The overseer has the right ideas about the men, but being uneducated he can't see what's good for the firm. Give me a week's trial, Mr Shui Ta, and I think I can prove to you that my brains are worth more to the firm than the mere strength of my muscles.

MRS YANG They were bold words, but that evening I told my Sun: 'You are a flying man. Show that you can get to the top where you are now! Fly, my eagle!' And indeed it is remarkable what brains and education will achieve! How can a man hope to better himself without them? Absolute miracles were performed by my son in the factory directed by Mr Shui Ta!

[SUN *stands behind the workers, his legs apart. They are passing a basket of raw tobacco above their heads.*]

SUN Here you, that's not proper work! The basket has got to be kept moving! [*To a child*] Sit on the ground, can't you? It takes up less room! And you might as well get on with a bit of pressing: yes, it's you I'm talking to! You idle loafers, what do you think you're paid for? Come on with that basket! O hell and damnation! Put grandpa over there and let him shred with the kids! There's been enough dodging here! Now take your time from me! [*He claps time with his hands and the basket moves faster*.]

MRS YANG And no enmities, no slanderous allegations by the uneducated—for he was not spared that—could hold my son back from the fulfilment of his duty.

[*One of the workers begins singing the song of the eighth elepant. The others join in the chorus.*]

WORKERS' CHORUS

SONG OF THE EIGHTH ELEPHANT

1

Seven elephants worked for Major Chung
And an eighth one followed the others.
Seven were wild and the eighth was tame
And the eighth had to spy on his brothers.
    Keep moving!
    Major Chung owns a wood
    See it's cleared before tonight.
    That's orders. Understood?

2

Seven elephants were clearing the wood
The eighth bore the Major in person
Number eight merely checked that the work was correct
And spared himself any exertion.
    Dig harder!
    Major Chung owns a wood
    See it's cleared before tonight.
    That's orders. Understood?

3

Seven elephants got tired of their work
Of shoving and digging and felling.
The Major was annoyed with the seven he employed
But rewarded the eighth one for telling.
    What's up now?
    Major Chung owns a wood
    See it's cleared before tonight.
    That's orders. Understood?

4

Seven elephants, not a tusk in their heads
The eighth's were in excellent order.
So eight used his wits, slashed the seven to bits
And the Major had never laughed harder.

Dig away!
Major Chung owns a wood
See it's cleared before tonight
That's orders. Understood?

[SHUI TA *has lounged forward, smoking a cigar.* YANG SUN *has laughingly joined in the chorus of the third verse and quickened the tempo in the fourth verse by clapping his hands.*]

MRS YANG We really owe everything to Mr Shui Ta. With wisdom and discipline, but with hardly a word of interference, he has brought out all the good that lay in Sun! He made no fantastic promises like his much overrated cousin, but forced him to do good honest work. Today Sun is a different person from what he was three months ago. I think you will admit it! 'The noble soul is like a bell, strike it and it rings, strike it not and it rings not,'[6] as our forebears used to say.

Scene 9

Shen Teh's Shop

[*The shop has been turned into an office, with easy chairs and fine carpets. It is raining.* SHUI TA, *now become fat, is showing out the old couple of carpet-dealers.* MRS SHIN *watches with amusement. It is plain that she is wearing new clothes.*]

SHUI TA I regret that I cannot say when she will be back.

THE OLD WOMAN We had a letter today enclosing the 200 silver dollars we once lent her. It didn't say who from. But it can only be Shen Teh who sent it. We'd like to write to her: what's her address?

SHUI TA I'm afraid I don't know that either.

THE OLD MAN We'd better go.

THE OLD WOMAN Sooner or later she is bound to come back.

[SHUI TA *bows. The two old people go off uncertain and upset.*]

MRS SHIN It was too late when they got their money back. Now they've lost their shop because they couldn't pay their taxes.

SHUI TA Why didn't they come to me?

MRS SHIN People don't like coming to you. I expect they started by waiting for Shen Teh to come back as they'd got nothing in writing. Then the old man got ill at the critical moment, and his wife had to nurse him night and day.

SHUI TA [*has to sit down because he feels sick*] I feel giddy again.

MRS SHIN [*fusses around him*] You're six months gone! You mustn't let yourself get worked up. Lucky for you you've got me. Everyone can do with a helping hand. Yes, when your time comes I shall be at your side. [*She laughs.*]

SHUI TA [*feebly*] Can I count on that, Mrs Shin?

MRS SHIN You bet! It'll cost money of course. Undo your collar, and you'll feel better.

SHUI TA [*pitifully*] It's all for the baby's sake, Mrs Shin.

6. A saying by the Chinese philosopher Mo-tzu (ca. 470–ca. 391 B.C.E.).

MRS SHIN All for the baby's sake.

SHUI TA I'm getting fat so quickly, though. People are bound to notice.

MRS SHIN They think it's because you're doing so well.

SHUI TA And what will happen to him?

MRS SHIN You're always asking that. He will be looked after. The best that money can buy.

SHUI TA Yes. [*Anxiously*] And he must never see Shui Ta.

MRS SHIN Never. Only Shen Teh.

SHUI TA But all the gossip round here! The water-seller and his rumours! They're watching the shop!

MRS SHIN As long as the barber doesn't hear there's no harm done. Come on dear, have a drop of water.

[*Enter* SUN *in a smart suit carrying a businessman's briefcase. He is amazed to see* SHUI TA *in* MRS SHIN*'s arms.*]

SUN Am I disturbing you?

SHUI TA [*gets up with difficulty and goes unsteadily to the door*] Till tomorrow, then, Mrs Shin!

[MRS SHIN *puts on her gloves and goes off smiling.*]

SUN Gloves! How, why, what for? Is she milking you? [*On* SHUI TA *not replying*] Don't tell me even you have your softer moments. Curious. [*He takes a document from his briefcase.*] Anyway, you haven't been on form lately, not on your old form. Moody. Hesitant. Are you ill? It's doing no good to the business. Here's another notice from the police. They want to shut the factory. They say they can't possibly allow more than twice the legal number of people to a room. It's about time you took some action, Mr Shui Ta!

[SHUI TA *looks at him distractedly for a moment. Then he goes into the back room and returns with a box. He takes out a new bowler and throws it on the table.*]

SHUI TA The firm wishes its representatives to dress according to their position.

SUN Did you get that for me?

SHUI TA [*indifferently*] See if it fits.

[SUN *looks astounded, then puts it on.* SHUI TA *tries adjusting it at the right angle.*]

SUN At your service, sir. But don't try and dodge the question. You must see the barber today and talk about the new scheme.

SHUI TA The barber makes impossible conditions.

SUN I wish you'd tell me what conditions.

SHUI TA [*evasively*] The sheds are quite good enough.

SUN Good enough for the riffraff who work there, but not good enough for the tobacco. The damp's getting in it. Before we have another meeting I'll see Mrs Mi Tzu again about her premises. If we can get them we can chuck out this rag, tag, and bobtail.[7] They're not good enough. I'll tickle Mrs Mi Tzu's fat knees over a cup of tea, and we'll get the place for half the money.

SHUI TA [*sharply*] That is out of the question. For the sake of the firm's reputation I wish you always to be coolly businesslike, and to be reserved in personal matters.

7. This whole (disreputable) lot.

SUN What are you so irritable for? Is it the unpleasant local gossip?

SHUI TA I am not concerned with gossip.

SUN Then it must be the weather again. Rain always makes you so touchy and melancholic. I'd like to know why.

WANG'S VOICE [*from without*]

I sell water. Who would taste it?
—Who would want to in this weather?
All my labour has been wasted
Fetching these few pints together.
I stand shouting Buy my Water!
And nobody thinks it
Worth stopping and buying
Or greedily drinks it.

SUN There's that bloody water-seller. Now he'll be nagging us again.

WANG'S VOICE [*from without*] Isn't there a good person left in this town? Not even on the square where the good Shen Teh used to live? Where is the woman who once bought a mug of water from me in the rain, months ago, in the joy of her heart? Where is she now? Has nobody seen her? Has none of you heard from her? This is the house which she entered one evening and never left!

SUN Hadn't I better shut his mouth for good? What's it got to do with him, where she is? Incidentally, I believe the only reason why you don't say is so that I shouldn't know.

WANG [*enters*] Mr Shui Ta, I ask you once more: when is Shen Teh coming back? It's now six months since she went off on her travels. [*On* SHUI TA *remaining silent*] Since then a lot has happened which could never have taken place if she'd been here. [*On* SHUI TA *still remaining silent*] Mr Shui Ta, the rumour round here is that something must have happened to Shen Teh. Her friends are very worried. Would you please be so good as to let us know her address?

SHUI TA I fear I have no time at the moment, Mr Wang. Come again next week.

WANG [*worked up*] People have also begun to notice that the rice she used to give the needy is being put out at the door again.

SHUI TA What do they conclude from that?

WANG That Shen Teh hasn't gone away at all.

SHUI TA But? [*On* WANG*'s remaining silent*] In that case I will give you my answer. It is final. If you consider yourself a friend of Shen Teh's, Mr Wang, then you will refrain from enquiring as to her whereabouts. That is my advice.

WANG Marvellous advice! Mr Shui Ta, Shen Teh told me before she disappeared that she was pregnant!

SUN What?

SHUI TA [*quickly*] A lie!

WANG [*most seriously, to* SHUI TA] Mr Shui Ta, please don't think Shen Teh's friends will ever give up the search for her. A good person is not easily forgotten. There are not many.

[*Exit.*]

[SHUI TA *stares after him. Then he goes quickly into the back room.*]

SUN [*to the audience*] Shen Teh pregnant! That makes me livid! I've been done![8] She must have told her cousin, and of course that swine hurried her off at once. 'Pack your bags and clear out, before the child's father gets wind of it!' It's utterly against nature. Inhuman, in fact. I've got a son. A Yang is about to appear on the scene! And what happens? The girl vanishes, and I'm left here to work like a slave. [*He is losing his temper.*] They buy me off with a hat! [*He tramples on it.*] Crooks! Thieves, kidnappers! And the girl has nobody to look after her! [*Sobbing is heard from the back room. He stops still.*] Wasn't that someone crying? Who's there? It's stopped. What's that crying in the back room? I bet that half-baked swine Shui Ta doesn't cry. So who's crying? And what's the meaning of the rice being put outside the door every morning? Is the girl there after all? Is he simply hiding her? Who else could be crying in there? That would be a fine kettle of fish! I've absolutely got to find her if she's pregnant!

[SHUI TA *returns from the back room. He goes to the door and peers out into the rain.*]

SUN Well, where is she?

SHUI TA [*raises his hand and listens*] Just a moment! Nine o'clock. But one can't hear today. The rain is too heavy.

SUN [*ironically*] What do you hope to hear?

SHUI TA The mail plane.

SUN Don't be funny.

SHUI TA I thought they told me you were interested in flying? Have you dropped that?

SUN I have no complaints about my present job, if that's what you mean. I'd sooner not do night work, you know. The mail service means flying at night. I've begun to get a sort of soft spot for the firm. After all, it is my former fiancée's firm, even if she is away. She did go away, didn't she?

SHUI TA Why do you ask?

SUN Maybe because her affairs don't leave me entirely cold.

SHUI TA My cousin might like to hear that.

SUN Anyway I'm concerned enough to be unable to shut my eyes if I find, for instance, that she is being deprived of her freedom.

SHUI TA By whom?

SUN By you!

[*Pause.*]

SHUI TA What would you do in such an eventuality?

SUN I might start by wanting to reconsider my position in the firm.

SHUI TA Indeed. And supposing the firm—that is to say I—found a suitable position for you, would it be able to count on your giving up all further enquiries about your former fiancée?

SUN Possibly.

SHUI TA And how do you picture your new position in the firm?

SUN Full control. For instance, I picture chucking you out.

SHUI TA And suppose the firm chucked you out instead?

SUN Then I should probably return, but not on my own.

SHUI TA But?

SUN With the police.

8. Cheated.

SHUI TA With the police. Let us suppose the police found no one here.

SUN Then I presume they would look in that room! Mr Shui Ta, my longing for the lady of my heart cannot be suppressed. I feel I shall have to take steps if I am to enfold her in my arms once more. [*Quietly*] She's pregnant, and needs a man beside her. I must talk it over with the water-seller.

[*He leaves.*]

[SHUI TA *looks after him without moving. Then he goes quickly into the back room once more. He fetches all kinds of everyday articles of* SHEN TEH*'s: underwear, dresses, toilet things. He looks lengthily at the shawl which* SHEN TEH *bought from the old carpet-dealers. Then he packs it all into a bundle and hides it under the table, as he hears sounds. Enter* MRS MI TZU *and* MR SHU FU. *They greet* SHUI TA *and dispose of their umbrellas and galoshes.*]

MRS MI TZU Autumn's on the way, Mr Shui Ta.

MR SHU FU A melancholy time of year!

MRS MI TZU And where is that charming manager of yours? A shocking lady-killer! But of course you don't know that side of him. Still, he knows how to reconcile his charm with his business obligations, so you only profit from it.

SHUI TA [*bows*] Will you please sit down?

[*They sit and start smoking.*]

SHUI TA My friends, an unpredictable eventuality, which may have certain consequences, compels me to speed up the negotiations which I have recently initiated as to the future of my business. Mr Shu Fu, my factory is in difficulties.

MR SHU FU It always is.

SHUI TA But now the police are frankly threatening to shut it down if I cannot show that I am negotiating for a new arrangement. Mr Shu Fu, what is at stake is nothing less than the sole remaining property of my cousin, in whom you have always shown such interest.

MR SHU FU Mr Shui Ta, it is deeply repugnant to me to discuss your ever-expanding projects. I suggest a small supper with your cousin, you indicate financial difficulties. I offer your cousin buildings for the homeless, you use them to set up a factory. I hand her a cheque, you cash it. Your cousin vanishes, you ask for 100,000 silver dollars and tell me my buildings are not big enough. Sir, where is your cousin?

SHUI TA Mr Shu Fu, please be calm. I can now inform you that she will very shortly be back.

MR SHU FU 'Shortly.' When? You have been saying 'shortly' for weeks.

SHUI TA I have not asked you to sign anything further. I have simply asked whether you would be more closely associated with my project supposing my cousin came back.

MR SHU FU I have told you a thousand times that I am not prepared to go on discussing with you, but will discuss anything with your cousin. However, you seem to want to put obstacles in the way of such a discussion.

SHUI TA Not now.

MR SHU FU Can we fix a date?

SHUI TA [*uncertainly*] In three months.

MR SHU FU [*irritably*] Then you can have my signature in three months too.

SHUI TA But it must all be prepared.

MR SHU FU You can prepare everything yourself, Shui Ta, if you are sure this time that your cousin really is coming.

SHUI TA Mrs Mi Tzu, are you for your part ready to certify to the police that I can have your workshops?

MRS MI TZU Certainly, if you will let me take over your manager. I told you weeks ago that that was my condition. [*To* MR SHU FU] The young man is so conscientious, and I must have someone to run things.

SHUI TA Please understand that I cannot let Mr Yang Sun go at this moment: there are all these problems, and my health has been so uncertain lately. I was always prepared to let you have him but . . .

MRS MI TZU Ha! But!

[*Pause.*]

SHUI TA Very well, he shall report at your office tomorrow.

MR SHU FU I am glad you could arrive at this decision, Mr Shui Ta. If Miss Shen Teh really comes back it will be most undesirable that this young man should be here. We all know that in his time he has had a most pernicious influence on her.

SHUI TA [*bowing*] No doubt. Forgive my undue hesitation in these questions relating to my cousin Shen Teh and Mr Yang Sun: it was quite unworthy of a businessman. These two were once very close to each other.

MRS MI TZU We forgive you.

SHUI TA [*looking towards the door*] My friends, it is time for us to come to a decision. At this spot, in what used to be the drab little shop where the poor of the district bought the good Shen Teh's tobacco, we, her friends, herewith resolve to establish twelve fine new branches, which from now on shall retail Shen Teh's good tobacco. I am told that people have begun calling me the Tobacco King of Szechwan. But the fact is that I have conducted this enterprise solely and exclusively in my cousin's interest. It will belong to her, and to her children, and to her children's children.

[*From without come sounds of a crowd of people. Enter* WANG, SUN, *and the* POLICEMAN.]

THE POLICEMAN Mr Shui Ta, I am extremely sorry, but in view of the disturbed state of the district I have to follow up certain information received from your own firm, according to which you are alleged to be keeping your cousin Miss Shen Teh under illegal restraint.

SHUI TA That is not true.

THE POLICEMAN Mr Yang Sun here states that he heard crying from the room behind your office, and that it can only have proceeded from a female person.

MRS MI TZU That is absurd. Mr Shu Fu and I, two respected citizens of this town whose word the police can hardly doubt, will witness that there has been no crying here. We have been smoking our cigars perfectly quietly.

THE POLICEMAN I'm afraid I have an order to search the aforementioned room.

[SHUI TA *opens the door. The* POLICEMAN *bows and crosses the threshold. He looks in, then turns round and smiles.*]

THE POLICEMAN Perfectly true, there's no one there.

SUN [*who has accompanied him*] But someone was crying! [*His eye falls on the table under which* SHUI TA *shoved the bundle. He pounces on it.*] That wasn't there before!

[*He opens it and reveals* SHEN TEH*'s clothes, etc.*]

WANG Those are Shen Teh's things! [*He runs to the door and calls out.*] They've found her clothes!

THE POLICEMAN [*taking charge of things*] You state that your cousin is away. A bundle containing her property is found concealed beneath your desk. Where can the young lady be contacted, Mr Shui Ta?

SHUI TA I don't know her address.

THE POLICEMAN That is a great pity.

SHOUTS FROM THE CROWD Shen Teh's things have been found! The Tobacco King did the girl in and got rid of her!

THE POLICEMAN Mr Shui Ta, I must ask you to come to the station with me.

SHUI TA [*bowing to* MRS MI TZU *and to* MR SHU FU] Please forgive this disturbance, my dear colleagues. But we still have magistrates in Szechwan. I am sure it will all be cleared up quickly.

[*He precedes the* POLICEMAN *out.*]

WANG There has been a most frightful crime!

SUN [*overcome*] But I did hear somebody crying!

Interlude

Wang's Sleeping Place

[*Music. For the last time the* GODS *appear to the water-seller in a dream. They are greatly changed. It is impossible to mistake the symptoms of prolonged travel, utter exhaustion, and unhappy experiences of every kind. One of them has had his hat knocked off his head, one has lost a leg in a fox-trap, and all three are going barefoot.*]

WANG At last you have appeared! Fearful things are happening in Shen Teh's shop, Illustrious Ones! Shen Teh has again been away, this time for months! Her cousin has been grabbing everything! Today they arrested him. He is supposed to have murdered her in order to get hold of her shop. But I cannot believe that, for I had a dream in which she appeared to me and said that her cousin was keeping her a prisoner. Oh, Illustrious Ones, you must come back at once and find her.

THE FIRST GOD That is terrible. Our whole search has been in vain. We found few good people, and those we found were not living a decent human existence. We had already decided to settle on Shen Teh.

THE SECOND GOD If only she is still good!

WANG That she surely is, but she has vanished!

THE FIRST GOD Then all is lost!

THE SECOND GOD You forget yourself.

THE FIRST GOD What's wrong with forgetting oneself? We shall have to give up if she cannot be found! What a world we have found here: nothing but poverty, debasement, and dilapidation! Even the landscape crumbles away before our eyes. Beautiful trees are lopped off by cables, and over the mountains we see great clouds of smoke and hear the thunder of guns, and nowhere a good person who survives it!

THE THIRD GOD Alas, water-seller, our commandments seem to be fatal! I fear that all the moral principles that we have evolved will have to be cancelled. People have enough to do to save their bare lives. Good precepts bring them to the edge of the precipice; good deeds drag them over. [*To the other* GODS] The world is unfit to live in, you have got to admit it!

THE FIRST GOD [*emphatically*] No, mankind is worthless!

THE THIRD GOD Because the world is too chilling!

THE SECOND GOD Because men are too feeble!

THE FIRST GOD Remember your dignity, my friends! Brothers, we cannot afford to despair. We did discover one who was good and has not become evil, and she has only disappeared. Let us hasten to find her. One is enough. Did we not say that all could still be redeemed if just one can be found who stands up to this world, just one?

[*They swiftly disappear.*]

Scene 10

Courtroom

[*In groups:* MR SHU FU *and* MRS MI TZU. SUN *and his mother.* WANG, *the* CARPENTER, *the* GRANDFATHER, *the* YOUNG PROSTITUTE, *the* TWO OLD PEOPLE. MRS SHIN. *The* POLICEMAN. *The* SISTER-IN-LAW.]

THE OLD WOMAN He is too powerful.

WANG He means to open twelve new branches.

THE CARPENTER How can the magistrate give a fair verdict when the defendant's friends, Shu Fu the barber and Mrs Mi Tzu the property owner, are his friends too?

THE SISTER-IN-LAW Last night old Shin was seen carrying a fat goose into the judge's kitchen on Mr Shui Ta's orders. The grease was oozing through the basket.

THE OLD WOMAN [*to* WANG] Our poor Shen Teh will never be found again.

WANG Yes, it will take the gods to get at the truth.

THE POLICEMAN Silence! The court is assembling.

[*The* THREE GODS *appear in magistrates' robes. As they pass along the front of the stage to go to their places they can be heard whispering.*]

THE THIRD GOD There will be trouble. The certificates were most incompetently forged.

THE SECOND GOD And people will be curious about the magistrate's sudden indisposition.

THE FIRST GOD It is natural enough after eating half a goose.

MRS SHIN We've got new magistrates!

WANG And very good ones!

[*The* THIRD GOD, *last of the three, hears him, turns, and smiles at him. The* GODS *take their seats. The* FIRST GOD *taps on the table with a hammer. The* POLICEMAN *brangs in* SHUI TA, *who is received with catcalls but maintains an air of arrogance as he enters.*]

THE POLICEMAN This may be a shock to you. Fu Yi Cheng is not on the bench. But the new magistrates look pretty soft too.

[SHUI TA *catches sight of the* GODS *and faints.*]

THE YOUNG PROSTITUTE What's happened? The Tobacco King has fainted.

THE SISTER-IN-LAW As soon as he saw the new magistrates!

WANG He seems to know them! That's beyond me.

THE FIRST GOD Are you Shui Ta, tobacco merchant?

SHUI TA [*very faintly*] Yes.

THE FIRST GOD You are charged with having made away with your cousin Miss Shen Teh, in order to gain control of her business. Do you plead guilty?

SHUI TA No.

THE FIRST GOD [*thumbing through the papers*] The court will begin with the local constable's evidence as to the characters of the accused and his cousin.

THE POLICEMAN [*steps forward*] Miss Shen Teh was a girl who made herself pleasant to everyone—live and let live, as they say. Mr Shui Ta, on the other hand, is a man of principle. The young lady's warmhearted nature sometimes drove him to strict measures. But unlike the girl he was always on the side of the law, your worships. There were some people whom his cousin had trusted and taken in, and he was able to show them up as a gang of thieves, and another time he barely managed to save Shen Teh from straight perjury—Mr Shui Ta is known to me as a respectable citizen who respects the law.

THE FIRST GOD Are there other witnesses in court who wish to testify that the accused is incapable of a crime of the sort attributed to him?

[MR SHU FU *and* MRS MI TZU *step forward.*]

THE POLICEMAN [*whispers to the* GODS] Mr Shu Fu, one of our more prominent citizens!

MR SHU FU The town looks up to Mr Shui Ta as an able businessman. He is vice-chairman of the chamber of commerce and has been proposed as a justice of the peace.

WANG [*interrupting*] By you! You two are hand in glove with him.

THE POLICEMAN [*whispering*] An undesirable character!

MRS MI TZU In my capacity as Chairman of the Charitable Welfare Association I should like to point out to the court that Mr Shui Ta is not only turning over the best possible rooms in his tobacco works—all light and healthy—to a considerable number of the homeless, but also makes regular subscriptions to our Disabled Persons' Institution.

THE POLICEMAN [*whispering*] Mrs Mi Tzu, a close friend of our magistrate Fu Yi Cheng!

THE FIRST GOD Yes, yes, but now we must also hear whether anyone has a less favourable report to make on the accused.

[*There step forward:* WANG, *the* CARPENTER, *the* OLD COUPLE, *the* UNEMPLOYED MAN, *the* SISTER-IN-LAW, *the* YOUNG PROSTITUTE.]

THE POLICEMAN The scum of the district.

THE FIRST GOD Tell us, what do you know of Shui Ta's general conduct?

CRIES [*confusedly*] He ruined us! He bled me white! Led us into bad ways! Exploited the helpless! Lied! Swindled! Murdered!

THE FIRST GOD Accused, what have you to say for yourself?

SHUI TA All I did was to save my cousin's bare means of existence, your worships. I only came when she was in danger of losing her small business. Three times I had to come. I never meant to stay. Circumstances were such that last time I was forced to remain. All the time I have had nothing but trouble. They loved my cousin, and I had to do the dirty work. That is why they hate me.

THE SISTER-IN-LAW You bet we do. Look at our boy, your worships. [*To* SHUI TA] Not to mention the sacks.

SHUI TA Why not? Why not?

THE SISTER-IN-LAW [*to the* GODS] Shen Teh put us up, and he had us arrested.

SHUI TA You were stealing cakes!

THE SISTER-IN-LAW Now he's pretending he cared about the baker and his cakes! He wanted the shop for himself!

SHUI TA The shop wasn't a doss-house,[9] you selfish brutes!

THE SISTER-IN-LAW But we had nowhere to go!

SHUI TA There were too many of you!

WANG And these two! [*He points to the* OLD COUPLE.] Are they also too selfish?

THE OLD WOMAN We put our savings into Shen Teh's business. Why did you do us out of our own?

SHUI TA Because my cousin was helping an airman to get back into the air again. I was supposed to find the money!

WANG She may have wanted that, but you had your eye on that good job in Pekin. The shop wasn't good enough for you.

SHUI TA The rent was too high!

MRS SHIN I can confirm that.

SHUI TA And my cousin had no idea of business.

MRS SHIN That too! Besides, she was in love with the airman.

SHUI TA Hadn't she the right to love?

WANG Of course she had! So why did you try to make her marry a man she didn't love: the barber there?

SHUI TA The man she loved was a crook.

WANG Him?

[*He indicates* SUN.]

SUN [*leaps up*] Was it because he was a crook you took him into your office?

SHUI TA To help you! To help you improve!

THE SISTER-IN-LAW To turn him into a slave-driver!

WANG And when you had finished improving him, didn't you sell him to her? [*He indicates* MRS MI TZU.] She was crowing all over the place about it!

SHUI TA Because she wouldn't let me have her workshops unless he tickled her knees!

MRS MI TZU Lies! Don't ever mention my workshops again! I'll have nothing more to do with you. Murderer!

[*She rushes off in a dudgeon.*]

SUN [*firmly*] Your worships, I must put in a word for him!

THE SISTER-IN-LAW You've got to; he's your boss.

THE UNEMPLOYED MAN He's the worst slave-driver there ever was. They completely broke him.

SUN Your worships, whatever the accused made of me he is not a murderer. A few minutes before his arrest I heard Shen Teh's voice from the room behind the shop!

THE FIRST GOD [*intrigued*] She was alive, was she? Describe exactly what you heard.

SUN [*triumphantly*] Crying, your worships, crying!

THE THIRD GOD You could recognise it?

SUN Absolutely certain. Don't I know her voice?

MR SHU FU Yes, you've made her cry often enough!

9. A flophouse (British).

SUN But I've also made her happy. And then he wanted—[*pointing to* SHUI TA]—to sell her to you.

SHUI TA [*to* SUN] Because you didn't love her!

WANG No—for the money!

SHUI TA But what was the money needed for, your worships? [*To* SUN] You would have liked her to give up all her friends, but the barber offered his buildings and his money so that she could help the poor. I had to promise her to the barber even to allow her to do good.

WANG Why didn't you allow her to do good when the big cheque was filled in? Why did you shove Shen Teh's friends in your stinking sweatshops, your tobacco factory, you tobacco king?

SHUI TA It was for the child's sake!

THE CARPENTER And what about my children? What did you do to them?

[SHUI TA *remains silent.*]

WANG That has made you think! The gods gave Shen Teh her shop to be a little source of goodness. And she always tried to do good, and you always came and brought it to nothing.

SHUI TA [*beside himself*] Because they'd have stifled the source, you fool.

MRS SHIN That's quite true, your worships!

WANG What's the good of a source that can't be drawn on?

SHUI TA Good deeds are the road to ruin!

WANG [*wildly*] And evil deeds are the road to the good life, I suppose? What have you done with the good Shen Teh, you evil man? How many good people are there left, Illustrious Ones? She was certainly good! When that barber broke my hand she wanted to give evidence for me. And now I'm giving evidence for her. She was good, I swear it.

[*He raises his hand to swear.*]

THE THIRD GOD What is wrong with your hand, water-seller? It seems stiff.

WANG [*points to* SHUI TA] He's to blame, no one else! She was going to give me the money for the doctor, then he came along. You were her mortal enemy!

SHUI TA I was her only friend!

ALL Where is she?

SHUI TA Gone away.

WANG Where to?

SHUI TA I shan't tell!

ALL What made her go?

SHUI TA [*screaming*] You were tearing her to bits!

[*There is a sudden silence.*]

SHUI TA [*has collapsed on to his chair*] I can't go on. If the court can be cleared so that only the magistrates are present I will make a confession.

ALL Confession! We've won!

THE FIRST GOD [*taps on the table with his hammer*] Clear the court.

[*The* POLICEMAN *clears the court.*]

MRS SHIN [*as she goes out, laughing*] They've got a surprise coming!

SHUI TA Have they gone? All of them? I cannot hold out any longer. Illustrious Ones, I have recognised you!

THE SECOND GOD What have you done with our good person of Szechwan?

SHUI TA Let me confess the frightful truth. I am your good person!

[*He takes off his mask and rips away his costume.* SHEN TEH *stands there.*]

THE SECOND GOD Shen Teh!

SHEN TEH

Yes, it is me. Shui Ta and Shen Teh, I am both of them.
Your original order
To be good while yet surviving
Split me like lightning into two people. I
Cannot tell what occurred: goodness to others
And to myself could not both be achieved.
To serve both self and others I found too hard.
Oh, your world is arduous! Such need, such desperation!
The hand which is held out to the starving
Is quickly wrenched off! He who gives help to the lost
Is lost for his own part! For who could
Hold himself back from anger when the hungry are dying?
Where could I find so much that was needed, if not
In myself? But that was my downfall! The load of commandments
Forced me into the sludge. Yet if I broke the rules
I strode proudly around, and could eat myself full!
Something is wrong with this world of yours. Why
Is wickedness so rewarded, and why is so much suffering
Reserved for the good? Oh, I felt such
Temptation to treat myself kindly! I felt too
A secret awareness inside me, for my foster mother
Washed me with slops from the gutter! So I acquired
A sharp eye. And yet pity
Brought me such pain that I at once felt wolfish anger
At the sight of misery. Then
I could feel how I gradually altered and
My lips grew tight and hard. Bitter as ashes
The kind word felt in my mouth. And yet
I should gladly have been an Angel to the slums. For giving
Was still my delight. A smiling face
And I walked in the clouds.
Condemn me: each of my crimes
Was committed to help out my neighbour
To love my beloved or
To save my young son from going without.
O gods, for your vast projects
I, poor human, was too small.

THE FIRST GOD [*with every indication of horror*] Speak no further, you unhappy creature! What are we to think, who so rejoice to have found you again?

SHEN TEH But do you not understand that I am the wicked person whose many crimes you have heard described?

THE FIRST GOD The good person, of whom no one speaks anything but good!

SHEN TEH No, the wicked person as well!

THE FIRST GOD A misunderstanding! A few unfortunate incidents. One or two hard-hearted neighbours! A little too much zeal!

THE SECOND GOD But how is she to go on living?

THE FIRST GOD She can manage! She is strong, healthy, and well-built, and can endure much.

THE SECOND GOD But didn't you hear what she said?

THE FIRST GOD [*emphatically*] Muddled, completely muddled! Hard to accept, extremely hard to accept! Are we to admit that our commandments are fatal? Are we to sacrifice them? [*Grimly*] Never! Is the world to be altered? How? By whom? No, everything is as it should be.

[*He taps rapidly on the table with his hammer. And now—at a sign from him—music is heard. A rosy glow is seen.*]

Now we return to heaven. This little world
Still fascinates us. All its joys and hurts
Encouraged us or caused us pain. And still
We'll gladly think, away beyond the planets
Of you, Shen Teh, the good person we sought
Who makes our spirit manifest down here
And through this bitter darkness bears the tiny lamp.
Farewell, good luck!

[*At a sign from him the ceiling opens. A pink cloud descends. On it the three* GODS *mount slowly upwards.*]

SHEN TEH Oh no, Illustrious Ones! Do not go away! Don't leave me! How am I to face the two good old people who lost their shop, or the water-seller with his stiff hand? And how can I protect myself against the barber, whom I don't love, and how against Sun, whom I do? And my body has been blessed; soon my little son will be there and wanting to eat. I cannot remain here!

[*She looks frantically towards the door through which her tormentors will come.*]

THE FIRST GOD You can manage. Only be good, and all will be well!

[*Enter the witnesses. They are amazed to see the magistrates floating on their pink cloud.*]

WANG Show your respect! The gods have appeared among us! Three of the mightiest gods have come to Szechwan in search of a good person. They thought they had found one, but . . .

THE FIRST GOD No but! Here she is!

ALL Shen Teh!

THE FIRST GOD She was not dead, she lay but hidden. She will remain among you, a good person!

SHEN TEH But I must have my cousin!

THE FIRST GOD Not too often!

SHEN TEH Once a week anyway!

THE FIRST GOD Once a month: that will be enough!

SHEN TEH Oh, do not go away, Illustrious Ones! I haven't told you all! I need you terribly!

THE GODS [*sing*]

TRIO OF THE VANISHING GODS ON THEIR CLOUD

All too long on earth we lingered.
Swiftly droops the lovely day:
Shrewdly studied, closely fingered
Precious treasures melt away.
Now the golden flood is dying
While your shadows onward press
Time that we too started flying
Homeward to our nothingness.

SHEN TEH Help!

THE GODS

Now let us go: the search at last is o'er
We have to hurry on!
Then give three cheers, and one cheer more
For the good person of Szechwan!

[*As* SHEN TEH *stretches desperately towards them they disappear upwards, waving and smiling.*]

Epilogue

[*A* PLAYER *appears before the curtain and addresses the audience apologetically in an epilogue.*]

THE PLAYER

Ladies and gentlemen, don't feel let down:
We know this ending makes some people frown.
We had in mind a sort of golden myth
Then found the finish had been tampered with.
Indeed it is a curious way of coping:
To close the play, leaving the issue open.
Especially since we live by your enjoyment.
Frustrated audiences mean unemployment.
Whatever optimists may have pretended
Our play will fail if you can't recommend it.
Was it stage fright made us forget the rest?
Such things occur. But what would you suggest?
What is your answer? Nothing's been arranged.
Should men be better? Should the world be changed?
Or just the gods? Or ought there to be none?
We for our part feel well and truly done.
There's only one solution that we know:
That you should now consider as you go
What sort of measures you would recommend
To help good people to a happy end.
Ladies and gentlemen, in you we trust:
There must be happy endings, must, must, must!

JEAN GENET

1910–1986

A WARD of the state, a vagabond, deserter, prostitute, thief, and convict, Jean Genet is an unlikely candidate for the role of great author. After he had served many short prison sentences for theft, a mandatory sentence of life imprisonment threatened to remove Genet from the world for good. He was hardly the first French author who was also a social outcast; indeed, in the late nineteenth century, Paul Verlaine applied the label "accursed poets" to those who—like Genet's models, Baudelaire and Rimbaud—wrote from the margins of society. It was this tradition that Genet's supporters invoked both to prevent the imposition of a life sentence in 1944 and to win an official pardon from the president of the Republic in 1949. Genet was able to live and write for the rest of his life in freedom, creating an astonishingly oeuvre that included not just novels and plays but also film and ballet scripts, art criticism, and political writings.

Even though Genet was abandoned by his mother, his childhood was not one of extreme deprivation. Placed in a family in a small mountain town, Genet was a good student but began stealing; at the age of fifteen he was put in a psychiatric clinic, from which he promptly ran away. He was soon caught, spent three months in prison, and was sentenced to live in the Mettray Reformatory, an agricultural penitentiary for adolescents. His experiences in this closed world began his lifelong fascination with life in penal institutions; here, too, his homosexuality was openly expressed. In 1929, he gained early release from Mettray by enlisting in the army, which sent him to Syria and Morocco. After deserting in 1936, he began a period of drifting through Europe and its prisons. During this phase of his life, Genet supported himself by panhandling, stealing, prostitution, and smuggling. But when he found himself again in prison in 1941, Genet did not simply sink back into the familiar routine of prison life. Instead, he began work on his first novel, *Our Lady of the Flowers* (1943), which attracted the attention of Jean Cocteau and other literary figures in Paris. The outcast was in the process of transforming himself into a writer.

Between 1942 and 1948, Genet wrote several largely autobiographical novels in quick succession: *Our Lady of the Flowers* was followed by *Miracle of the Rose* (1946), *Funeral Rites* (1947), *Querelle of Brest* (1947), and *The Thief's Journal* (1948). With the exception of *Querelle,* these novels are narrated by a figure based on Jean Genet and set in the different milieus that Genet had come to know intimately, from the reform school at Mettray and Fontevrault State Prison (*Miracle*), the bohemian and homosexual scene of Montmartre (*Our Lady*), and the German occupation of Paris (*Funeral*) to the experience of drifting through Europe (*Thief*). They are frank and often graphic in depicting the world of pimps and criminals, as well as homosexuality. Defying almost all ethical norms, these novels revel in the abject and strategically evoke disgust even as they dwell on aesthetic objects such as flowers. Like Genet's later plays, these novels pay almost fetishistic attention to body parts, individual gestures, flowers, and pieces of clothing, including and especially uniforms. Indeed, his protagonists are alternately attracted to and repulsed by figures of authority, around which many of these works revolve.

The juxtaposition of the abject and the beautiful is part of the most surprising aspect of Genet's work: its fascination with the saintly and the sacred. Raised in the Catholicism of small-town France, Genet continued to invoke such ascetic qualities as submission and self-negation, even when he associated them with such acts as passively submitting to sodomy. Nor was this language of sainthood intended as blasphemy, at least in any simple sense. Rather it works as a mode of thinking, behaving, and writing that undergirds much of Genet's work. The person who first noted this constant underlying theme was Jean-Paul Sartre, whose monumental study of Genet, *Saint Genet: Actor and Martyr* (1952), had a decisive impact on his career. That France's most eminent philosopher would dedicate a 700-page book to a relatively unknown author was remarkable—particularly since he was presented as the embodiment of Sartre's existentialist philosophy of freedom. Genet was flattered and accepted Sartre's analysis, but he also felt exposed—and he knew that he could no longer claim the role of the cultural outsider.

Even before Sartre published his study, Genet had recognized that he had exhausted the autobiographical material on which his novels had relied and decided to transform himself once more: this time into a playwright. His choice did not reflect a long-standing love for the theater; in fact, he had shown very little interest in this art form and often claimed that he did not much like it. He rarely went to rehearsals or performances of his plays, and even after he had made a name as a dramatist, he continued to consider his great models not the playwrights but the "accursed poets" Baudelaire and Rimbaud, as well as the novelist Marcel Proust. His preference for poetry and the novel over drama did not keep him from expressing intense preferences when it came to directors and their productions of his work, however. Genet strongly favored Roger Blin, for example, the director of SAMUEL BECKETT's *Waiting for Godot* (1953), and turned sharply against Peter Brook, whose earlier productions he had admired. Genet's letters to Blin offer a fascinating insight into his conception of the theater, in particular his vision of costumes and stage props.

What drove Genet to write plays was the inner logic of his literary style, built as it was around the artificial and the fake, around masks and poses, mirrors and props. Many commentators, including Sartre, had sensed something decidedly theatrical in Genet's novels from the beginning, and this theatricality now came into its own. His first play, *Deathwatch* (1947), is a transitional piece, which, like several of his novels, is set in a prison. It also anticipates the ceremonial rituals, role-playing, and manipulations that would become hallmarks of Genet's most successful plays. In *The Blacks* (1959), for example, a group of black actors puts on white masks to play the white slaveholders for whose benefit a group of black actors enact a ritualistic punishment, one that has clearly been rehearsed and performed innumerable times before. *The Blacks,* like many of Genet's plays, employs a play-within-the-play and therefore belongs to the tradition of metatheater—theater about theater. *The Balcony* (1956) is also set in a world of artifice, but of a different sort. It takes place in an elaborate brothel whose decorated rooms represent different fantasy worlds for clients who play at being a general, bishop, or judge. Around the brothel, a revolt is under way; and when the real general, bishop, and judge flee, the brothel clients take their places. In the end, it is impossible to determine what is real and what is fantasy; even the real rebellion

Scene from the 1948 staging of *The Maids* at Stockholm's Royal Dramatic Theatre, starring Maj-Britt Nilsson (foreground) and Anita Bjork (background).

happening outside the brothel relies on theatrical techniques to achieve its goal. The form Genet chose for this play enhances the impression of different fake worlds colliding: The fantasy worlds are painted on large screens whose arrangement repeatedly changes. Indeed, screens became Genet's favorite device, finding their most elaborate application in his longest play, *The Screens* (1961), which is set in Algeria during the struggle against French colonialism.

Formal restraint and manipulative games also characterize Genet's most important play, ***THE MAIDS*** (1946), which was his first play to be performed and the first to bring him fame as a dramatist. Like *Deathwatch,* which was not staged until 1949, *The Maids* takes place in a single contained space—one room in a house inhabited by two maids, who are sisters, and their mistress, Madame. The atmosphere is one of complete control: Everything in this household is precisely proscribed, and the maids are trained to obey Madame's every order. But once Madame is out of the house—as is the case for most of the play—things change. The two maids then engage in an elaborate game in which one of them plays Madame and the other plays a maid. They push this role-playing so far that even the one pretending to be a maid usually acts as her sister, not herself; thus both play roles. In fact, role-playing is the main focus of this drama. Only well into the action do we recognize that what appeared to be an exchange between Madame and her maid was just such a game, a play-within-the-play that is interrupted by the ringing of an alarm clock.

At first sight, the maids seem to be engaging in this game merely to pass the time while Madame is away. One of its important components, and the main source of pleasure for those engaged in it, is the handling of clothing and accessories—the simple act of getting dressed and undressed.

The two sisters relish taking out Madame's beautiful dresses, jewelry, and flowers and putting them on. Like so much of Genet's work, *The Maids* seems baroque in its delight in elaborate attire and the energy spent on getting a bow right or a piece of jewelry placed at just the perfect spot. The excessive beauty of Madame's clothes stands in stark contrast to the maids' ordinary garb and their ugly kitchen gloves. Clearly, the maids seek to escape their utilitarian everyday life through this game of dressing up. Genet here transposes his fetishistic attention to clothes and objects onto the stage, creating a theater of objects, of stage props, and of costumes.

The game of dressing up as Madame is more than a benign diversion, however. It becomes increasingly obvious that it is full of violence, a violence that the maid playing Madame directs toward her sister playing "maid." The maids appear to be willfully reenacting their daily suffering, the countless humiliations to which they are subjected. As in many of Genet's novels and plays, the infliction of pain causes a strange kind of pleasure, bringing the game nearer to a sadomasochistic ritual. The maids clearly delight not just in humiliating one another but also in being humiliated, in deliciously and elaborately enacting the power games usually played by Madame with them. Their play focuses on the disturbing connection between power, domination, and pleasure. Here, as elsewhere in Genet's work, it is difficult to find human relations among equals. He always constructs constellations that are infused with authority, even as he subverts that authority.

As the play progresses, it becomes evident that the maids' role-playing is indeed such an act of subversion: The maids are plotting a revolt, for what they are rehearsing is the killing of Madame. At this point, *The Maids* turns into a kind of murder mystery revolving around the question of whether the sisters will be able to carry out their plan. A forged letter that leads to the temporary arrest of Madame's lover and withheld information about a phone call are some of the ingredients of this suspenseful dimension of the play. Indeed, *The Maids* is partly based on the famous murder case of Lea and Christine Papin, who brutally murdered their employer and her daughter in Le Mans, France, in 1933.

Yet ultimately, Genet cares little about the historical case or the murder mystery. Each merely serves as a vehicle that can carry his primary interest in theater and theatricality. Like Genet's other plays, *The Maids* is a particular brand of metatheater: Nothing on the stage can be taken at face value, not even the actors, who may be playing any number of roles. In this sense, Genet's theater is the opposite of naturalism, which emphasizes authentic decoration and acting. To increase the sense of artifice, Genet originally envisioned that the three women be played—and played badly—by adolescent boys. An unauthorized, though widely noted, 1965 production of *The Maids* by the experimental American company the Living Theater took up this suggestion and presented the play with an all-male cast to stunning effect.

The games and role-playing of Genet's play call to mind a number of cultural practices, including the ceremonies and rituals of the Catholic mass as well as children's games. Genet was an avid reader of Friedrich Nietzsche (1844–1900), the philosopher who insisted on the seriousness of children's games and who also envisioned a renewal of Western theater by returning it to its roots in ancient Greek ritual. Among the many theorists of the early twentieth century who took up Nietzsche's vision was Antonin Artaud, whose so-called Theater of Cruelty is often compared to Genet's. In the eyes of many, Genet was the playwright who finally fulfilled these dreams. In a note, Genet even imagined a performance of *The Maids* at Epidaurus, the largest and best-preserved classical Greek theater. Whereas Genet's novels were steeped in the language of saintliness, his plays translate this religious vocabulary into ritual.

After winning early fame with his novels and later succeeding with drama, Genet published no literary works for decades. He stopped writing about revolutions and freedom struggles to become an activist, speaking in support of and even living with such groups as the Palestine Liberation Organization and, in the United States, the Black Panthers. In September 1982, Genet was one of the first Westerners to set foot in Shatila, a UN-sanctioned refugee camp for

Palestinians near Beirut, after the Israeli army allowed the Lebanese Christian militia to enter Sabra and Shatila and to massacre hundreds of their inhabitants—a criminal act that shocked the world. More broadly, Genet incorporated these experiences into his last great work of literature, *Prisoner of Love* (1986), an autobiographical account of his time with the Palestinians and the Panthers. This meditation on the troubling relationship between revolutionary struggles and theatricality made use of many of his earlier styles and forms.

Dramatizing the intimate if contentious links between theater, power, and revolution is Genet's most significant achievement. His plays embody two seemingly contradictory impulses: On the one hand, they are deeply immersed in the theater, in artificiality and role-play; on the other hand, they refuse to turn away from the world in order to celebrate the theater, as many metaplays do. Instead, they manage to turn theatricality into an effective tool for analyzing power—its attractions, its erotic charge, and its violence. Genet, who himself suffered from the tyranny and brutality of prison wardens, army superiors, and police, did not denounce the exploitation of power directly. But his plays are profound indictments of authoritarian behavior of every kind. They also seek to plant in the audience the seeds of rebellion that may bring authoritarianism to an end. M.P.

The Maids[1]

CHARACTERS

SOLANGE, CLAIRE — Two housemaids, sisters, thirty to thirty-five years old. Solange is the elder.
MADAME — Their mistress. She is about twenty-five.

MADAME's *bedroom. Louis-Quinze furniture,*[2] *Lace. Rear, a window opening on the front of the house opposite. Right, a bed. Left, a door and a dressing table. Flowers in profusion. The time is evening.*

[CLAIRE, *wearing a slip, is standing with her back to the dressing table. Her gestures—arm extended—and tone are exaggeratedly tragic.*]

CLAIRE Those gloves! Those eternal gloves! I've told you time and again to leave them in the kitchen. You probably hope to seduce the milkman with them. No, no, don't lie; that won't get you anywhere! Hang them over the sink. When *will* you understand that this room is not to be sullied. Everything, yes, everything that comes out of the kitchen is spit! So stop it! [*During this speech,* SOLANGE *has been playing with a pair of rubber gloves and observing her gloved hands, which are alternately spread fanwise and folded in the form of a bouquet.*] Make yourself quite at home. Preen like a peacock. And above all, don't hurry, we've plenty of time. Go!

1. Translated by Bernard Frechtman.
2. The richly ornamental style of furniture and decoration common during the reign of Louis XV (r. 1715–74). *Quinze*: fifteen (French).

[SOLANGE's *posture changes and she leaves humbly, holding the rubber gloves with her fingertips.* CLAIRE *sits down at the dressing table. She sniffs at the flowers, runs her hand over the toilet articles, brushes her hair, pats her face.*]

Get my dress ready. Quick! Time presses. Are you there? [*She turns round.*] Claire! Claire!

[SOLANGE *enters.*]

SOLANGE I beg Madame's pardon, I was preparing her tea. [*She pronounces it "tay."*]

CLAIRE Lay out my things. The white spangled dress. The fan. The emeralds.

SOLANGE Very well, Madame. All Madame's jewels?

CLAIRE Put them out and I shall choose. And, of course, my patent-leather slippers. The ones you've had your eye on for years. [SOLANGE *takes a few jewel boxes from the closet, opens them, and lays them out on the bed.*] For your wedding, no doubt. Admit he seduced you! Just look at you! How big you are! Admit it! [SOLANGE *squats on the rug, spits on the patent-leather slippers, and polishes them.*] I've told you, Claire, with*out* spit. Let it sleep in you, my child, let it stagnate. Ah! Ah! [*She giggles nervously.*] May the lost wayfarer drown in it. Ah! Ah! You *are* hideous. Lean forward and look at yourself in my shoes. Do you think I find it pleasant to know that my foot is shrouded by the veils of your saliva? By the mists of your swamps?

SOLANGE [*on her knees, and very humble*] I wish Madame to be lovely.

CLAIRE I shall be. [*She primps in front of the mirror.*] You hate me, don't you? You crush me with your attentions and your humbleness; you smother me with gladioli and mimosa. [*She stands up and, lowering her tone*] There are too many flowers. The room is needlessly cluttered. It's *impossible.* [*She looks at herself again in the glass.*] I shall be lovely. Lovelier than you'll ever be. With a face and body like that, you'll never seduce Mario. [*Dropping the tragic tone*] A ridiculous young milkman despises us, and if we're going to have a kid by him—

SOLANGE Oh! I've never—

CLAIRE [*resuming*] Be quiet, you fool. My dress!

SOLANGE [*she looks in the closet, pushing aside a few dresses*] The red dress. Madame will wear the red dress.

CLAIRE I said the white dress, the one with spangles.

SOLANGE [*firmly*] I'm sorry. Madame will wear the scarlet velvet dress this evening.

CLAIRE [*naively*] Ah? Why?

SOLANGE [*coldly*] It's impossible to forget Madame's bosom under the velvet folds. And the jet brooch, when Madame was sighing and telling Monsieur[3] of my devotion! Your widowhood really requires that you be entirely in black.

CLAIRE Eh?

SOLANGE Need I say more? A word to the wise—

3. Mister (French); literally, "my lord" (as *madame* is "my lady"), and thus used alone as a courtesy title.

CLAIRE Ah! So you want to talk. . . . Very well. Threaten me. Insult your mistress, Solange. You want to talk about Monsieur's misfortunes, don't you? Fool. It was hardly the moment to allude to him, but I can turn this matter to fine account! You're smiling? Do you doubt it?

SOLANGE The time is not yet ripe to unearth—

CLAIRE What a word! My infamy? My infamy! To unearth!

SOLANGE Madame!

CLAIRE Am I to be at your mercy for having denounced Monsieur to the police, for having sold him? And yet I'd have done even worse, or better. You think I haven't suffered? Claire, I forced my hand to pen the letter—without mistakes in spelling or syntax, without crossing anything out—the letter that sent my lover to prison. And you, instead of standing by me, you mock me. You force your colors on me! You speak of widowhood! He isn't dead. Claire, Monsieur will be led from prison to prison, perhaps even to Devil's Island,[4] where I, his mistress, mad with grief, shall follow him. I shall be in the convoy. I shall share his glory. You speak of widowhood and deny me the white gown—the mourning of queens. You're unaware of that, Claire—

SOLANGE [*coldly*] Madame will wear the red dress.

CLAIRE [*simply*] Quite. [*Severely*] Hand me the dress. Oh! I'm so alone and friendless. I can see in your eyes that you loathe me. You don't care what happens to me.

SOLANGE I'll follow you everywhere. I love you.

CLAIRE No doubt. As one loves a mistress. You love and respect me. And you're hoping for a legacy, a codicil in your favor—

SOLANGE I'd do all in my power—

CLAIRE [*ironically*] I know. You'd go through fire for me. [SOLANGE *helps* CLAIRE *put on her dress.*] Fasten it. Don't pull so hard. Don't try to bind me. [SOLANGE *kneels at* CLAIRE*'s feet and arranges the folds of the dress.*] Avoid pawing me. You smell like an animal. You've brought those odors from some foul attic, where the lackeys visit us at night. The maid's room! The garret! [*Graciously*] Claire, if I speak of the smell of garrets, it is for memory's sake. And of the twin beds where two sisters fall asleep, dreaming of one another. There, [*She points to a spot in the room.*] there, the two iron beds with the night table between them. There, [*She points to a spot opposite.*] the pinewood dresser with the little altar to the Holy Virgin![5] That's right, isn't it?

SOLANGE We're so unhappy. I could cry! If you go on—

CLAIRE It *is* right, isn't it! Let's skip the business of your prayers and kneeling. I won't even mention the paper flowers. . . . [*She laughs.*] Paper flowers! And the branch of holy boxwood! [*She points to the flowers in the room.*] Just look at these flowers open in my honor! Claire, am I not a lovelier Virgin?

SOLANGE [*as if in adoration*] Be quiet—

CLAIRE And there, [*She points to a very high spot at the window.*] that notorious skylight from which a half-naked milkman jumps to your bed!

SOLANGE Madame is forgetting herself, Madame—

4. The notorious French penal colony; located several miles off the shore of French Guiana, on the northern coast of South America, it operated from 1852 to 1952.

5. That is, the Virgin Mary; the mother of Jesus.

CLAIRE And what about your hands? Don't *you* forget your hands. How often have I [*She hesitates.*] murmured: they befoul the sink.

SOLANGE The fall!

CLAIRE Eh?

SOLANGE [*arranging the dress on* CLAIRE*'s hips*] The fall of your dress. I'm arranging your fall from grace.

CLAIRE Get away, you bungler! [*She kicks* SOLANGE *in the temple with her Louis-Quinze heel.* SOLANGE, *who is kneeling, staggers and draws back.*]

SOLANGE Oh! Me a burglar?

CLAIRE I said bungler; and if you must whimper, do it in your garret. Here, in my bedroom, I will have only noble tears. A time will come when the hem of my gown will be studded with them, but those will be precious tears. Arrange my train, you clod.

SOLANGE [*in ecstasy*] Madame's being carried away!

CLAIRE By the devil! He's carrying me away in his fragrant arms. He's lifting me up, I leave the ground, I'm off. . . . [*She stamps with her heel.*] And I stay behind. Get my necklace! But hurry, we won't have time. If the gown's too long, make a hem with some safety pins. [SOLANGE *gets up and goes to take the necklace from a jewel case, but* CLAIRE *rushes ahead of her and seizes the jewels. Her fingers graze those of* SOLANGE, *and she recoils in horror.*] Keep your hands off mine! I can't stand your touching me. Hurry up!

SOLANGE There's no need to overdo it. Your eyes are ablaze.

CLAIRE [*shocked astonishment*] What's that you said?

SOLANGE Limits, boundaries, Madame. Frontiers are not conventions but laws. Here, my lands; there, your shore—

CLAIRE What language, my dear. Claire, do you mean that I've already crossed the seas? Are you offering me the dreary exile of your imagination? You're taking revenge, aren't you? You feel the time coming when, no longer a maid—

SOLANGE You see straight through me. You divine my thoughts.

CLAIRE [*increasingly carried away*] —the time coming when, no longer a maid, you become vengeance itself, but, Claire, don't forget—Claire, are you listening?—don't forget, it was the maid who hatched schemes of vengeance, and I—Claire, you're not listening.

SOLANGE [*absent-mindedly*] I'm listening.

CLAIRE And I contain within me both vengeance and the maid and give them a chance for life, a chance for salvation. Claire, it's a burden, it's terribly painful to be a mistress, to contain all the springs of hatred, to be the dunghill on which you grow. You want to see me naked every day. I *am* beautiful, am I not? And the desperation of my love makes me even more so, but you have no idea what strength I need!

SOLANGE [*contemptuously*] Your lover!

CLAIRE My unhappy lover heightens my nobility. Yes. Yes, my child. All that you'll ever know is your own baseness.

SOLANGE That'll do! Now hurry! Are you ready?

CLAIRE Are you?

SOLANGE [*she steps back to the wardrobe*] I'm ready.—I'm tired of being an object of disgust. I hate you, too. I despise you. I hate your scented bosom. Your . . . *ivory* bosom! Your . . . *golden* thighs! Your . . . *amber* feet! I hate you! [*She spits on the red dress.*]

CLAIRE [*aghast*] Oh! . . . Oh! . . . But . . .

SOLANGE [*walking up to her*] Yes, my proud beauty. You think you can always do just as you like. You think you can deprive me forever of the beauty of the sky, that you can choose your perfumes and powders, your nail polish and silk and velvet and lace, and deprive *me* of them? That you can steal the milkman from me? Admit it! Admit about the milkman. His youth and vigor excite you, don't they? Admit about the milkman. For Solange says: to hell with you!

CLAIRE [*panic-stricken*] Claire! Claire!

SOLANGE Eh?

CLAIRE [*in a murmur*] Claire, Solange, Claire.

SOLANGE Ah! Yes, Claire, Claire says: to hell with you! Claire is here, more dazzling than ever. Radiant! [*She slaps* CLAIRE.]

CLAIRE Oh! . . . Oh! Claire . . . You . . . Oh!

SOLANGE Madame thought she was protected by her barricade of flowers, saved by some special destiny, by a sacrifice. But she reckoned without a maid's rebellion. Behold her wrath, Madame. She turns your pretty speeches to nought. She'll cut the ground from under your fine adventure. Your Monsieur was just a cheap thief, and you—

CLAIRE I forbid you! Confound your impudence!

SOLANGE Twaddle! She forbids me! It's Madame who's confounded. Her face is all convulsed. Would you like a mirror? Here. [*She hands* CLAIRE *a mirror.*]

CLAIRE [*regarding herself with satisfaction*] I see the marks of a slap, but now I'm more beautiful than ever!

SOLANGE Yes, a slap!

CLAIRE Danger is my halo, Claire; and you, you dwell in darkness. . . .

SOLANGE But the darkness is dangerous.—I know. I've heard all that before. I can tell by your face what I'm supposed to answer. So I'll finish it up. Now, here are the two maids, the faithful servants! They're standing in front of you. Despise them. Look more beautiful.—We no longer fear you. We're merged, enveloped in our fumes, in our revels, in our hatred of you. The mold is setting. We're taking shape, Madame. Don't laugh—ah! above all, don't laugh at my grandiloquence. . . .

CLAIRE Get out!

SOLANGE But only to be of further service to Madame! I'm going back to my kitchen, back to my gloves and the smell of my teeth. To my belching sink. You have your flowers, I my sink. I'm the maid. You, at least, you can't defile me. But! But! . . . [*She advances on* CLAIRE, *threateningly.*] But before I go back, I'm going to finish the job. [*Suddenly an alarm clock goes off.* SOLANGE *stops. The two actresses, in a state of agitation, run together. They huddle and listen.*] Already?

CLAIRE Let's hurry! Madame'll be back. [*She starts to unfasten her dress.*] Help me. It's over already. And you didn't get to the end.

SOLANGE [*helping her. In a sad tone of voice*] The same thing happens every time. And it's all your fault, you're never ready. I can't finish you off.

CLAIRE We waste too much time with the preliminaries. But we've still . . .

SOLANGE [*as she helps* CLAIRE *out of her dress*] Watch at the window.

CLAIRE We've still got a little time left. I set the clock so we'd be able to put the things in order. [*She drops wearily into the armchair.*]

SOLANGE [*gently*] It's so close this evening. It's been close all day.

CLAIRE [*gently*] Yes.

SOLANGE Is that what's killing us, Claire?

CLAIRE Yes.

SOLANGE It's time now.

CLAIRE Yes. [*She gets up wearily.*] I'm going to make the tea.

SOLANGE Watch at the window.

CLAIRE There's time. [*She wipes her face.*]

SOLANGE Still looking at yourself . . . Claire, dear . . .

CLAIRE Let me alone. I'm exhausted.

SOLANGE [*sternly*] Watch at the window. Thanks to you, the whole place is in a mess again. And I've got to clean Madame's gown. [*She stares at her sister.*] Well, what's the matter with you? You can be like me now. Be yourself again. Come on, Claire, be my sister again.

CLAIRE I'm finished. That light's killing me. Do you think the people opposite . . .

SOLANGE Who cares! You don't expect us to . . . [*She hesitates.*] organize things in the dark? Have a rest. Shut your eyes. Shut your eyes, Claire.

CLAIRE [*she puts on her short black dress*] Oh! When I say I'm exhausted, it's just a way of talking. Don't use it to pity me. Stop trying to dominate me.

SOLANGE I've never tried to dominate you. I only want you to rest. You'll help me more by resting.

CLAIRE I understand, don't explain.

SOLANGE Yes, I will explain. It was you who started it. When you mentioned the milkman. You think I couldn't see what you were driving at? If Mario—

CLAIRE Oh!

SOLANGE If the milkman says indecent things to me, he does to you, too. But you loved mingling. . . .

CLAIRE [*shrugging her shoulders*] You'd better see whether everything's in order. Look, the key of the secretary[6] was like this [*She arranges the key.*] and, as Monsieur says—

SOLANGE [*violently*] You loved mingling your insults—

CLAIRE He's always finding the maids' hairs all over the pinks and roses!

SOLANGE And things about our private life with—

CLAIRE With? With? With what? Say it! Go on, name it! The ceremony? Besides, we've no time to start a discussion now. She'll be back, back, back! But, Solange, this time we've got her. I envy you; I wish I could have seen the expression on her face when she heard about her lover's arrest. For once in my life, I did a good job. You've got to admit it. If it weren't for me, if it hadn't been for my anonymous letter, you'd have missed a pretty sight: the lover handcuffed and Madame in tears. It's enough to kill her. This morning she could hardly stand up.

SOLANGE Fine. She can drop dead! And I'll inherit! Not to have to set foot again in that filthy garret, with those two idiots, that cook and that butler.

CLAIRE I really liked our garret.

SOLANGE Just to contradict me. Don't start getting sentimental about it. I loathe it and I see it as it really is, bare and mean. And shabby. But what of it! We're just scum!

6. A writing desk, usually topped by a cabinet.

CLAIRE Ah! No, don't start that again. Better watch at the window. I can't see a thing. It's too dark outside.

SOLANGE Let me talk. Let me get it out of my system. I liked the garret because it was plain and I didn't have to put on a show. No hangings to push aside, no rugs to shake, no furniture to caress—with my eyes or with a rag, no mirrors, no balcony. Nothing forced us to make pretty gestures. Don't worry, you'll be able to go on playing queen, playing at Marie Antoinette,[7] strolling about the apartment at night.

CLAIRE You're mad! I've never strolled about the apartment.

SOLANGE [*ironically*] Oh, no. Mademoiselle has never gone strolling! Wrapped in the curtains or the lace bedcover. Oh no! Looking at herself in the mirrors, strutting on the balcony at two in the morning, and greeting the populace which has turned out to parade beneath her windows. Never, oh no, never.

CLAIRE But, Solange—

SOLANGE It's too dark at night for spying on Madame, and you thought you were invisible on your balcony. What do you take me for? Don't try to tell me you walk in your sleep. At the stage we've reached you can admit it.

CLAIRE But, Solange, you're shouting. Please, please lower your voice. Madame may come in without making a sound. . . . [*She runs to the window and lifts the curtain.*]

SOLANGE All right, I've had my say. Let go of the curtains. Oh, I can't stand the way you lift them. Let go of them. It upsets me; that's how Monsieur did it when he was spying on the police, the morning he was arrested.

CLAIRE So you're scared now? The slightest gesture makes you feel like a murderer trying to slip away by the service stairway.

SOLANGE Go on, be sarcastic, work me up! Go on, be sarcastic! Nobody loves me! Nobody loves us!

CLAIRE *She* does, *she* loves us. She's kind. Madame is kind! Madame adores us.

SOLANGE She loves us the way she loves her armchair. Not even *that* much! Like her bidet, rather. Like her pink enamel toilet seat. And we, can't love one another. Filth . . .

CLAIRE Ah! . . .

SOLANGE . . . doesn't love filth. D'you think I'm going to put up with it, that I'm going to keep playing this game and then at night go back to my folding cot? The game! Will we even be able to go on with it? And if I have to stop spitting on someone who calls me Claire, I'll simply choke! My spurt of saliva is my spray of diamonds!

CLAIRE [*she stands up and cries*] Speak more softly, please, please. Speak—speak of Madame's kindness.

SOLANGE Her kindness, is it? It's easy to be kind, and smiling, and sweet—ah! that sweetness of hers!—when you're beautiful and rich. But what if you're only a maid? The best you can do is to give yourself airs while you're doing the cleaning or washing up. You twirl a feather duster like a fan. You make fancy gestures with the dishcloth. Or like *you*, you treat yourself to historical parades in Madame's apartment.

7. As the wife of Louis XVI, the queen of France (1755–1793), legendary for her extravagance. She and her husband were executed by the revolutionary government in 1793.

CLAIRE Solange! You're starting again! What are you trying to do? We'll never calm down if you talk like that! I could say a thing or two about you.

SOLANGE You? You?

CLAIRE Yes, me. If I wanted to. Because, after all . . .

SOLANGE All? After all? What are you insinuating? It was you who started talking about that man. Claire, I hate you.

CLAIRE Same to you and more! But if I wanted to provoke you, I wouldn't have to use the milkman as an excuse. I've got something better on you and you know it.

SOLANGE Who's going to get the better of who? Eh? Well, say something?

CLAIRE Go on, start it! You hit first. It's you who're backing out, Solange. You don't dare accuse me of the worst: my letters. Pages and pages of them. The garret was littered with them. I invented the most fantastic stories and you used them for your own purposes. You frittered away my frenzy. Yesterday, when you were Madame, I could see how delighted you were at the chance they gave you to stow away on the *Lamartiniere*,[8] to flee France in the company of your lover—

SOLANGE Claire—

CLAIRE Your lover, to Devil's Island, to Guiana. You were delighted that my letters allowed you to be the prostitute kneeling at the feet of the thief. You were happy to sacrifice yourself, to bear the cross of the impenitent thief, to wipe his face, to stand by him, to take his place in the galleys so that he could rest. And you felt yourself growing. Your brow rose higher than mine, it rose above the palm trees.

SOLANGE But what about you, just before, when you were talking about following him. . . .

CLAIRE Right. I don't deny it. I took up where you left off. But with less violence than you. Even in the garret, amidst all the letters, you started swaying back and forth with the pitching of the boat.

SOLANGE You didn't see yourself—

CLAIRE I did. I'm more sensible than you. You're the one who concocted the story. Turn your head. Ha! If only you could see yourself, Solange. Your face is still lit up by the sun setting through the virgin forest! You're planning his escape! [*She laughs nervously.*] You certainly do work yourself up! But don't let it worry you; it would be cruel to disturb your blissful voyage. I hate you for other reasons, and you know what they are.

SOLANGE [*lowering her voice*] I'm not afraid of you. I know you hate me and that you're a sneak, but be careful now. I'm older than you.

CLAIRE So what?—Older! And stronger too? You're trying to put me off by making me talk about that man. Hmph! You think I haven't found you out? You tried to kill her.

SOLANGE Are you accusing me?

CLAIRE Don't deny it. I saw you.

[*A long silence.*]

And I was frightened. Frightened, Solange. Through her, it was me you were aiming at. I'm the one who's in danger. When we finish the ceremony, I'll protect my neck.

[*A long silence.* SOLANGE *shrugs her shoulders.*]

8. A prison ship.

SOLANGE [*with decision*] Is that all? Yes, I did try. I wanted to free you. I couldn't bear it any longer. It made me suffocate to see you suffocating, to see you turning red and green, rotting away in that woman's bittersweetness. Blame me for it, you're right. I loved you too much. Had I killed her, you'd have been the first to denounce me. You'd have turned me over to the police, yes, you.

CLAIRE [*she seizes her by the wrists*] Solange. . . .

SOLANGE [*freeing herself*] What are *you* afraid of? It's *my* concern.

CLAIRE Solange, my little sister, she'll be back soon.

SOLANGE I didn't kill anyone. I was a coward, you realize. I did the best I could, but she turned over in her sleep. [*Rising exaltation*] She was breathing softly. She swelled out the sheets: it was Madame.

CLAIRE Stop it.

SOLANGE Now you want to stop me. You wanted to know, didn't you. Well, wait, I've got some more to tell you. You'll see what your sister's made of. What stuff she's made of. What a servant girl really is. I wanted to strangle her—

CLAIRE Let me alone. Think of what comes after.

SOLANGE Nothing comes after. I'm sick and tired of kneeling in pews. In church I'd have had the red velvet of abbesses or the stone of the penitents, but my bearing at least would have been noble. Look, just look at how she suffers. How she suffers in beauty. Grief transfigures her, doesn't it? Beautifies her? When she learned that her lover was a thief, she stood up to the police. She exulted. Now she is forlorn and splendid, supported under each arm by two devoted servants whose hearts bleed to see her grief. Did you see it? Her grief sparkling with the glint of her jewels, with the satin of her gowns, in the glow of the chandelier! Claire, I wanted to make up for the poverty of my grief by the splendor of my crime. Afterward, I'd have set fire to the lot.

CLAIRE Solange, calm down. The fire might not have caught. You'd have been found out. You know what happens to incendiaries.

SOLANGE I know everything. I kept my eye and ear to the keyhole. No servant ever listened at doors as I did. I know everything. Incendiary! It's a splendid title.

CLAIRE Be quiet. I'm stifling. You're stifling me. [*She wants to open the window.*] Oh! Let's have some air!

SOLANGE Get away from the window. Open the anteroom and the kitchen doors. [CLAIRE *opens both doors.*] Go and see whether the water's boiling.

CLAIRE All alone?

SOLANGE Wait, all right, wait till she comes. She's bringing her stars, her tears, her smiles, her sighs. She'll corrupt us with her sweetness.

[*The telephone rings. The two sisters listen.*]

CLAIRE [*at the telephone*] Monsieur? It's Monsieur! . . . This is Claire, Monsieur. . . . [SOLANGE *wants to hear too, but* CLAIRE *pushes her away.*] Very well. I'll inform Madame. Madame will be overjoyed to hear that Monsieur is free. . . . Yes, Monsieur. . . . Very well. . . . Good-by, Monsieur. [*She wants to hang up, but her hand trembles, and she lays the receiver on the table.*]

SOLANGE Is he out?

CLAIRE The judge let him out on bail.

SOLANGE Well, you've done a fine job. My compliments. Your denunciations, your letters, it's working out beautifully. And if they recognize your handwriting, it'll be perfect.

CLAIRE Please, please, don't overwhelm me. Since you're so clever, you should have managed your business with Madame. But you were afraid. The bed was warm. The air thick with perfume. It was Madame! We've got to carry on with the same kind of life. With the same old game. But, you poor wretch! Even the game is dangerous. I'm sure we've left traces. We leave them every time. I see a host of traces I'll never be able to cover up. And she, she walks about in her tamed menagerie. She unravels the clues. She points to our traces with the tip of her pink toe. She discovers us, one by one. Madame jeers at us. And it's your fault. All's lost because you lacked strength.

SOLANGE I can still find whatever strength I need.

CLAIRE Where? Where? You've been outstripped by *me*. You don't live above the treetops. A milkman passing through your mind gets you all flustered.

SOLANGE It was because I couldn't see her face, Claire. Because I was so close to Madame, so close to her sleep. I lost my strength. In order to get at her throat, I'd have had to lift the sheet from her heaving bosom.

CLAIRE [*ironically*] And the sheets were warm. The night dark. That kind of thing has to be done in broad daylight. You're incapable of it. It's too terrible a deed. But *I* can manage it.

SOLANGE Claire!

CLAIRE Where you botched it, *I'll* succeed.

SOLANGE [*she runs a comb through her hair*] Claire, don't get carried away, don't be rash—

CLAIRE What makes you think I'm being rash? First of all, don't mix your hairpins up with mine! You . . . Oh! All right, mix your muck with mine. Mix it! Mix your rags with my tatters! Mix it all up. It'll stink of the maids. So Monsieur won't have any trouble discovering us. And we'll die in a flood of shame. [*Suddenly calm*] I'm capable of anything, you know.

SOLANGE The sleeping pills.

CLAIRE Yes. Let's talk calmly. I'm strong. You tried to dominate me. . . .

SOLANGE But, Claire—

CLAIRE [*calmly*] I beg your pardon, but I know what I'm saying. I've made up my mind. I'm ready. I'm tired of it all. Tired of being the spider, the umbrella case, the shabby, godless nun, without a family! I'm tired of having a stove for an altar. I'm that disagreeable, sullen, smelly girl. To you, too.

SOLANGE Claire . . . we're both nervous. [*Anxiously*] Where's Madame? I can't stand it anymore either. I can't stand our being so alike, I can't stand my hands, my black stockings, my hair. I'm not reproaching you for anything, my little sister. I understand that your strolls through the apartment helped ease the strain.

CLAIRE [*irritated*] Ah! Stop it!

SOLANGE I want to help you. I want to comfort you, but I know I disgust you. I'm repulsive to you. And I know it because you disgust me. When slaves love one another, it's not love.

CLAIRE And me, I'm sick of seeing my image thrown back at me by a mirror, like a bad smell. You're my bad smell. Well, I'm ready. Ready to bite. I'll have my crown and I shall stroll about the apartment.

SOLANGE That's not reason enough to kill her.

CLAIRE Really? Why, please? For what other reason? Where and when could we find a better excuse? Ah, so it's not enough, not enough to be raped by a milkman who goes blithely through our garrets? Tonight Madame will witness our shame. Bursting with laughter, laughing until the tears roll down her face, with her flabby sighs. No. I shall have my crown. I shall be the poisoner that you failed to be. It's my turn now to dominate you!

SOLANGE But I never . . .

CLAIRE Hand me the towel! Hand me the clothespins! Peel the onions! Scrape the carrots! Scrub the tiles! It's over. Over. Ah! I almost forgot! Turn off the tap! It's over. [*Exalted*] I'll run the world!

SOLANGE My little baby sister!

CLAIRE You'll help me.

SOLANGE You won't know what gestures to make. Things are more serious, Claire, and simpler too.

CLAIRE [*exalted*] We've read the story of Sister Holy Cross of the Blessed Valley who poisoned twenty-seven Arabs. She walked without shoes, with her feet all stiff. She was lifted up, carried off to the crime. We've read the story of Princess Albanarez who caused the death of her lover and her husband. She uncorked the bottle and made a big sign of the cross over the goblet. As she stood before the corpses, she saw only death and, off in the distance, the fleet image of herself being carried by the wind. She made all the gestures of earthly despair. In the book about the Marquise de Venosa, the one who poisoned her children, we're told that, as she approached the bed, her arms were supported by the ghost of her lover.[9]

SOLANGE Baby sister, my angel!

CLAIRE I'll be supported by the sturdy arms of the milkman. I'll lean my left hand on the back of his neck. He won't flinch. You'll help me. And, far away, Solange, if we have to go far away, if I have to leave for Devil's Island, you'll come with me. You'll board the boat. The flight you were planning for him can be used for me. We shall be that eternal couple, Solange, the two of us, the eternal couple of the criminal and the saint. We'll be saved, Solange, saved, I swear to you! [*She falls on* MADAME'*s bed.*]

SOLANGE Be calm. You're going to sleep. I'll carry you upstairs.

CLAIRE Let me alone. Turn out the light. Please turn out the light. [SOLANGE *turns out the light.*]

SOLANGE Rest. Rest, little sister. [*She kneels, removes* CLAIRE'*s shoes, kisses her feet.*] Be calm, my darling. [*She caresses her.*] Put your feet on my shoulders. There. Close your eyes.

CLAIRE [*she sighs*] I'm ashamed, Solange.

SOLANGE [*very gently*] Don't talk. Leave things to me. I'm going to put you to bed and, when you fall asleep, I'll carry you upstairs, to the garret. I'll undress you and put you into your little cot. Sleep. I'll be here.

CLAIRE I'm ashamed, Solange.

9. These stories were apparently invented by Genet.

SOLANGE Sh! Let me tell you a story.

CLAIRE [*simply*] Solange.

SOLANGE My angel?

CLAIRE Solange, listen . . .

SOLANGE Sleep. [*A long silence*]

CLAIRE You have lovely hair. You have such lovely hair. Hers—

SOLANGE Don't talk about her anymore.

CLAIRE Hers is false. [*A long silence*] Do you remember? Under the tree, just the two of us? Our feet in the sun? Solange?

SOLANGE I'm here. Sleep. I'm your big sister.

[*Silence. A moment later* CLAIRE *gets up.*]

CLAIRE No! No weakness! Put the light on! Put it on! Quick! It's too great a moment! [SOLANGE *puts the light on.*] Stand up. And let's eat. What's in the kitchen? Eh? We've got to eat. To be strong. Come along, you'll advise me. The phenobarbital.[1]

SOLANGE I'm too exhausted. Yes, the phenobarbital.

CLAIRE The phenobarbital! Don't make such a face. We must be joyous. And sing. Let's sing! Sing, the way you'll sing when you go begging in the courts and embassies! Laugh! [*They burst out laughing.*] Otherwise, it'll be so tragic that we'll go flying out the window. Shut the window. [SOLANGE, *laughing, shuts the window.*] Murder is a thing that's . . . unspeakable!

SOLANGE Let's sing! We'll carry her off to the woods, and under the fir trees we'll cut her to bits by the light of the moon. And we'll sing. We'll bury her beneath the flowers, in our flower beds, and at night—we'll water her *toes* with a little *hose!* [*The front doorbell rings.*]

CLAIRE It's Madame!

SOLANGE It must be her! Straighten the bed. [*She seizes her sister by the wrists.*] Claire, are you sure you can go through with it?

CLAIRE How many do we need?

SOLANGE About ten. Put ten pills into her tea. Will you do it?

CLAIRE [*she frees herself, goes to tidy the bed, stares at it for a moment*] Yes. I've got the tube in my pocket.

[*Exit* SOLANGE, *left.* CLAIRE *continues tidying the room and leaves right. A few seconds elapse. A burst of nervous laughter backstage.* MADAME, *in a fur coat, enters laughing, with* SOLANGE *behind her.*]

MADAME There's no end to it! Such horrible gladioli, such a sickly pink, and mimosa! They probably hunt through the market before dawn to get them cheaper. [SOLANGE *helps her off with her coat.*]

SOLANGE Madame wasn't too cold?

MADAME Yes, Solange, I was very cold. I've been trailing through corridors all night long. I've been seeing frozen men and stony faces, but I did manage to catch a glimpse of Monsieur. From a distance. I waved to him. I've only just left the wife of a magistrate. Claire!

SOLANGE She's preparing Madame's tea.

MADAME I wish she'd hurry. I'm ashamed to ask for tea when Monsieur is all alone, without a thing, without food, without cigarettes.

SOLANGE But Monsieur won't stay there long. They'll see right away that he's not guilty.

1. A barbiturate, prescribed as an anticonvulsant and, formerly, as a sedative.

MADAME Guilty or not, I shall never desert him, never. You see, Solange, it's at times like this that you realize how much you love someone. I don't think he's guilty either, but if he were, I'd become his accomplice. I'd follow him to Devil's Island, to Siberia.[2]

SOLANGE There's no need to get panicky. I've seen worse cases acquitted. There was a trial in Bordeaux[3]—

MADAME Do you go to trials? You?

SOLANGE I read the crime news. It was about a man who—

MADAME You can't compare Monsieur's case. He's been accused of the most idiotic thefts. I know he'll get out of it. All I mean is that, as a result of this preposterous affair, I've come to realize how deeply attached I am to him. Of course, none of this is serious, but if it were, Solange, it would be a joy for me to bear his cross. I'd follow him from place to place, from prison to prison, on foot if need be, as far as the penal colony.

SOLANGE They wouldn't let you. Only bandits' wives, or their sisters, or their mothers, are allowed to follow them.

MADAME A condemned man is no longer a bandit. And then I'd force my way in, past the guards. [*Suddenly conquettish*] And, Solange, I'd be utterly fearless. I'd use my weapons. What do you take me for?

SOLANGE Madame mustn't get such ideas into her head. You must rest.

MADAME I'm not tired. You treat me like an invalid. You're always ready to coddle me and pamper me as if I were dying. Thank God, I've got my wits about me. I'm ready for the fight. [*She looks at* SOLANGE *and, feeling that she has hurt her, adds, with a smile*] Come, come, don't make such a face. [*With sudden violence*] All right, it's true! There are times when you're so sweet that I simply can't stand it. It crushes me, stifles me! And those flowers which are there for the very opposite of a celebration!

SOLANGE If Madame means that we lack discretion . . .

MADAME But I didn't mean anything of the kind, my dear girl. It's just that I'm so upset. You see what a state I'm in.

SOLANGE Would Madame like to see the day's accounts?

MADAME You certainly picked the right time. You must be mad. Do you think I could look at figures now? Show them to me tomorrow.

SOLANGE [*putting away the fur cape*] The lining's torn. I'll take it to the furrier tomorrow.

MADAME If you like. Though it's hardly worthwhile. I'm giving up my wardrobe. Besides, I'm an old woman.

SOLANGE There go those gloomy ideas again.

MADAME I'm thinking of going into mourning. Don't be surprised if I do. How can I lead a worldly life when Monsieur is in prison? If you find the house too sad . . .

SOLANGE We'll never desert Madame.

MADAME I know you won't, Solange. You've not been too unhappy with me, have you?

SOLANGE Oh!

2. A region used as a place of exile and penal colonies, first by czarist Russia and then, beginning in the 1930s, by the Soviet Union.

3. A major city in the Aquitaine region of southwestern France.

MADAME When you needed anything, I saw that you got it. With my old gowns alone you both could have dressed like princesses. Besides . . . [*She goes to the closet and looks at her dresses.*] of what use will they be to me? I'm through with finery and all that goes with it.

[CLAIRE *enters carrying the tea.*]

CLAIRE The tea is ready.

MADAME Farewell to parties and dances and the theater. You'll inherit all that.

CLAIRE Madame is losing her self-control. She must pull herself together.

SOLANGE The tea is ready.

MADAME Put it down. I'm going to bed. It's all over. [*She runs her hand over the red velvet dress.*] My lovely "Fascination," the loveliest of them all. [*She takes it down and runs her hand over it.*] It was designed for me by Chanel.[4] Specially. Here, you may have it. It's yours. [*She gives it to* CLAIRE *and searches in the closet.*]

CLAIRE For me?

MADAME [*smiling sadly*] Of course. I said so, didn't I?

SOLANGE Madame is very kind. [*To* CLAIRE] You might thank Madame. You've been admiring it so long.

CLAIRE It's so beautiful. I'll never dare wear it.

MADAME You can have it altered. There's enough velvet in the train alone for the sleeves. And for you, Solange, I'm going to give you. . . . What shall I give you? Here, this coat. [*She hands* SOLANGE *the magnificent fur cape.*]

CLAIRE Oh! the fur cape!

SOLANGE [*thrilled*] Oh! Madame . . . never . . . Madame's too kind.

MADAME No, no, don't thank me. It's such a pleasure to make people happy. Now I'm going to get undressed. [*She looks at the telephone.*] Who left the receiver off?

CLAIRE It was Monsieur. . . . [*She stops suddenly.*]

MADAME [*dumbfounded*] Eh? Monsieur? [CLAIRE *is silent.*] What do you mean? Speak up!

SOLANGE [*slowly and as if in spite of herself*] When Monsieur rang up.

MADAME What are you talking about? Monsieur phoned?

SOLANGE We wanted to surprise Madame. Monsieur's out on bail. He's waiting for Madame at the Hong-Kong Bar.

MADAME [*rising to her feet*] And you didn't say anything! Go get a taxi! Solange, quick, quick, get me a taxi. And hurry up. Go on, run. [*She pushes* SOLANGE *out of the room.*] My furs! Quick, quick! You're both mad. You let me go on talking. You really are mad. Or am *I* going mad! [*She puts on her fur coat. To* CLAIRE] When did he phone?

CLAIRE [*in a toneless voice*] Five minutes before Madame came in.

MADAME But you should have told me. And this cold tea! I'll never be able to wait for Solange to get back! Oh! What did he say?

CLAIRE What I've just told you. He was very calm.

MADAME Ah, him, he always is. He'd be utterly unconcerned if he were condemned to death. The man's unique! What else did he say?

CLAIRE Nothing. He said the judge was letting him out.

MADAME How can anyone leave police headquarters at midnight? Do judges work as late as that?

4. Coco Chanel (1883–1971), prominent French fashion designer.

CLAIRE Sometimes, much later.

MADAME Much later? How do *you* know that?

CLAIRE I read *True Detective*.[5] I know those things.

MADAME [*astonished*] Oh you do? You really are an odd little girl, Claire. She *might* hurry. [*She looks at her wristwatch.*] You won't forget to have the lining of my coat sewn?

CLAIRE I'll take it to the furrier tomorrow. [*A long silence*]

MADAME What about the accounts? The day's accounts. Let me see them. I've got time!

CLAIRE Solange attends to that.

MADAME That's right. I'm all in a dither. I'll look at them tomorrow. [*Staring at* CLAIRE] Come a little closer! Come here! Why . . . you've got makeup on! [*Laughing*] Why Claire, you've been putting makeup on!

CLAIRE [*very embarrassed*] Madame . . .

MADAME Ah, don't lie! Besides, you've every right to. Live, my child, live. In whose honor is it? Eh? Got a crush on someone? Own up!

CLAIRE I put a little powder on. . . .

MADAME That's not powder, it's makeup. But there's nothing wrong in that, you're still young. Make yourself attractive. Smarten up. [*She puts a flower in* CLAIRE*'s hair. She looks at her wristwatch.*] What *can* she be doing? It's midnight and she's not back!

CLAIRE There aren't many taxis at this hour. She probably had to run to the cab-stand.

MADAME You think so? I've lost track of time. I'm wild with happiness. Monsieur ringing up at a time like that! And that he's free.

CLAIRE Madame ought to sit down. I'll go and heat up the tea. [*She starts to leave.*]

MADAME Don't bother, I'm not thirsty. It's champagne we'll be drinking tonight. You can be sure we won't be coming home.

CLAIRE Really, just a little tea . . .

MADAME [*laughing*] I'm nervous enough as it is. I don't want you and Solange to wait up for us. Go upstairs and get to bed right away. [*Suddenly she sees the alarm clock.*] But . . . That alarm clock, what's that doing here? Where does it come from?

CLAIRE [*very embarrassed*] The alarm clock? It's the kitchen clock.

MADAME It is? I've never seen it before.

CLAIRE [*she takes the alarm clock*] It belongs on the shelf. It's always been there.

MADAME [*smiling*] It's true I'm something of a stranger in the kitchen. You're at home there. It's your domain. You're its sovereigns. But, I wonder why you brought it in here?

CLAIRE It was Solange, for the cleaning. She'd never dare trust the big clock.

MADAME How odd.

[CLAIRE *goes out carrying the alarm clock.*]

How odd. [*She looks at her wristwatch.*] She's certainly taking her time. You can find taxis at every street corner. [*She sits down at her dressing table. She*

5. The earliest magazine of this title, which claimed to present true stories of crime, was published in the United States (1924–95).

looks at herself in the mirror and talks to herself.] And what about you, you fool, will you be beautiful enough to receive him? No wrinkles, eh? It's been such a long separation, it'll have been like a thousand years! Eh? Let's see, now. Gay? Wistful? Idiot, you idiot, there I go talking to myself. Happiness makes me giddy. And Solange not back yet. All those flowers! Those girls do worship me, but—[*She looks at the top of the dressing table and blows at the powder.*] but they haven't dusted the dressing table. Their housekeeping is the most extraordinary combination of luxury and filth.

[*As she utters the last sentence,* CLAIRE *enters the room on tiptoe. She stands silently behind* MADAME *who suddenly notices her in the mirror.*]

Eh? I'm raving, Claire, my mind's wandering. Forgive me. Today's been too dreadful.

CLAIRE Isn't Madame satisfied with our work?

MADAME [*smiling*] But I am, Claire. Delighted. In seventh heaven.

CLAIRE Madame's making fun of us.

MADAME [*laughing*] Oh, stop nagging me. After what I've been through today, I've got a right to be out of sorts. In the first place, there's that business of the letters to the police. . . . I wonder who could have sent them. I suppose you wouldn't have any idea?

CLAIRE Does Madame mean . . . ?

MADAME I don't mean anything. I'd like to know, that's all. I've been groping around the whole day long as if I were blind. I felt like the police hunting in the bushes for a girl's corpse.

CLAIRE That's all over with. Monsieur is free.

MADAME Thank heavens. Which still doesn't account for those letters. What *can* she be doing? She's been gone an hour. Why didn't you tell me at once that Monsieur had phoned? He'll be furious.

CLAIRE We were terribly afraid of alarming Madame, of giving her a shock.

MADAME That was very bright. You're quietly killing me with flowers and kindness. One fine day I'll be found dead beneath the roses. Claire, what do you think of this coiffure? Do you like it?

CLAIRE If I might venture . . .

MADAME Eh? If you might venture? Well, venture. I've full confidence in your opinion. Well? What do you think of it?

CLAIRE If I might be so bold as to make a suggestion, Madame's hair would look fluffier worn over the forehead.

MADAME Are you sure?

CLAIRE It would soften Madame's face.

MADAME Like that? You're right. You *are* a bright girl, Claire. You know, Claire, I've always thought you had a great deal of taste and that you were meant for better things.

CLAIRE I'm not complaining.

MADAME No, no, I know. But after all, you *are* more sensitive than the others. I realize that it's not much fun living with them. Fortunately you're with your sister. You're a family. But with a bit of luck you—

CLAIRE Oh! If I had wanted to!

MADAME I don't doubt it! [*She listens.*] Listen! [*She stands up.*] Listen! A car. It's her. Ah! [*She looks at herself again in the mirror.*]

CLAIRE Madame should have some tea because of the cold.

MADAME [*laughing*] You're trying to kill me with your tea and your flowers and your suggestions. You're too much for me, Claire. No. I've never felt so alive. Oh! And served in the best tea set, the *very best* set! Such pomp! Such elegance! [*She wants to leave, but* CLAIRE *stands between her and the door.*]

CLAIRE [*imploringly*] Madame *must* drink it. Otherwise . . .

[SOLANGE *dashes in. She pushes her sister aside and turns to* MADAME.]

MADAME Well!

SOLANGE [*surprised*] Ah! Madame's still here. I've looked everywhere. No one wanted to come as late as this!

MADAME Did you get a taxi?

SOLANGE It's here, Madame. It's downstairs, Madame.

MADAME Let's hurry. So it's understood, you're to go upstairs and to bed. And tomorrow morning we'll just sleep and sleep and sleep. Claire, come and close the door behind me. And you're not to latch it.

[*She leaves, followed by* CLAIRE. SOLANGE *is left alone.* CLAIRE *returns. The two sisters look at one another.*]

SOLANGE [*ironically*] You certainly did a fine job. And you sneered at me.

CLAIRE Don't. I tried so hard not to say it, but I just couldn't help myself.

SOLANGE Didn't she drink it? [CLAIRE *shakes her head "no."*] Obviously. It was to be expected.

CLAIRE I'd have liked to see *you* in my place. [*She remains motionless for a moment and then starts walking toward the kitchen.*]

SOLANGE Where are you going?

CLAIRE [*without turning around and in a weary voice*] To sleep!

[*She leaves.*]

SOLANGE Claire! [*Silence*] Claire! [*She goes to the door and calls her.*] Claire, I'm calling you.

CLAIRE [*offstage*] Who cares?

SOLANGE [*facing the door at the right*] Come here. Do you hear me? Come here.

[CLAIRE *comes in untying her apron.*]

CLAIRE [*very wearily*] What do you want? Is it my fault? The "tay"—as she says—was ready. I put in the pills. She wouldn't drink it!

SOLANGE And so you think we're just going to sit here and shake? [*She stares hard at her sister.*] They'll both be back tomorrow, drunk probably and vicious, like conquerors. They'll know where the letters came from. They—I hate her. [CLAIRE *shrugs her shoulders.*] Oh, I hate her! I loathe her. And you, you just stand there! Didn't you see how she sparkled? How disgustingly happy she was? *Her* joy feeds on *our* shame. Her carnation is the red of our shame. Her dress . . . [*She kicks at the red velvet dress.*] It's the red of our shame. Her furs . . . Ah! She took back her furs! And you just stand there! You don't scream. Are you dead?

CLAIRE What do you want me to do? She got away from us. You came back too soon.

SOLANGE She gets away and you just stand there!

CLAIRE What do you want to do? Make a scene? Eh? [*She screams in the face of* SOLANGE, *who remains motionless.*] You want to make a scene? Answer. Answer. Well, answer. We've got time. We've got all night.

SOLANGE [*in a very calm tone*] Let's get on with it.

CLAIRE What's the hurry? No, we'll take our time. Shall we? [*She unties her apron.*]

SOLANGE Keep your apron on. It's your turn.

CLAIRE No, that doesn't matter.

SOLANGE It's my turn to be Madame.

CLAIRE Take the apron.

SOLANGE But Claire . . .

CLAIRE [*simply*] I'm used to it. Here. [*She delicately hands the apron to* SOLANGE.] Do you think I've really got too much rouge on?

SOLANGE Rouge? Yes, there's some rouge left. . . . But you're not rouged. You're all made-up.

CLAIRE That's what she said.

SOLANGE That's all over. [*She grabs the apron.*] Forced to wear that! But I want to be a real maid. [*She ties the strings behind her back.*] Put out the light.

CLAIRE [*timidly*] You . . . You don't want us to . . . to organize things in the dark?

SOLANGE Do as I say. [*She puts out the light. The room is in semi-darkness. The two sisters look at one another and speak, without moving.*]

CLAIRE Oh! Let's wait a little while, Solange. Suppose she comes back? Madame might have forgotten something. At times like that one always forgets . . . one's bag, or money, or . . .

SOLANGE Naive!

CLAIRE [*muttering*] She left in such a hurry. It's a trap. Madame suspects something.

SOLANGE [*shrugging her shoulders*] What? For instance?

CLAIRE She's suspicious. We're being watched. . . .

SOLANGE What of it? We're beyond that!

CLAIRE [*she wants to gain time*] You're not listening to me, Solange. I assure you, I feel something, I feel it. Listen, we're being spied on. I'm sure she'll come back unexpectedly. She'll have forgotten her handkerchief. Or her gloves. [SOLANGE *shrugs her shoulders.*] Or her compact, God knows what. But I feel there's something here, Solange—something in this room—that can record our gestures and play them back. Remember, Madame told us not to latch the front door. . . .

SOLANGE You're raving.

CLAIRE I'm not! No! Please, wait, please, it's so serious. Suppose she came back. . . .

SOLANGE Too bad for her!

CLAIRE You're growing terrible, Solange. You've got an answer for everything. At least . . .

SOLANGE What?

CLAIRE [*timidly*] At least . . . suppose we said a prayer?

SOLANGE Do you dare bring God . . .

CLAIRE But to the Holy . . .

SOLANGE Bring the *Mother* of God into the ceremony? Really, you've got more nerve than I thought. You've no shame.

CLAIRE More softly, Solange, the walls are thin.

SOLANGE [*less loudly*] You're going mad, Claire. It's God who's listening to us. We know that it's for Him that the last act is to be performed, but we mustn't forewarn Him. We'll play it to the hilt.

CLAIRE Not so loud!

SOLANGE The walls are His ears.

CLAIRE Then I'll put on the white dress.

SOLANGE If you like. It makes no difference. But hurry up! Let's drop the preliminaries and get on with it. We've long since stopped needing the twists and turns and the lies. Let's get right into the transformation. Hurry up! Hurry up! I can't stand the shame and humiliation any longer. Who cares if the world listens to us and smiles and shrugs its shoulders and says I'm crazy and envious! I'm quivering, I'm shuddering with pleasure. Claire, I'm going to whinny with joy!

[*During this speech,* CLAIRE *has taken down the white dress and, hidden behind a screen, has put it on over her black dress whose black sleeves show.*]

CLAIRE [*appearing, all in white, with an imperious voice*] Begin!

SOLANGE [*ecstatically*] You're beautiful!

CLAIRE Skip that. You said we're skipping the prelude. Start the insults.

SOLANGE I'll never be able to. You dazzle me.

CLAIRE I said the insults! Let them come, let them unfurl, let them drown me, for, as you well know, I loathe servants. A vile and odious breed, I loathe them. They're not of the human race. Servants ooze. They're a foul effluvium drifting through our rooms and hallways, seeping into us, entering our mouths, corrupting us. I vomit you!

SOLANGE Go on. [*Silence.* CLAIRE *coughs.*] Go on! I'm getting there, I'm getting there!

CLAIRE I know they're necessary, just as gravediggers and scavengers and policemen are necessary. Nevertheless, they're a putrid lot.

SOLANGE Go on, go on!

CLAIRE Your frightened guilty faces, your puckered elbows, your outmoded clothes, your wasted bodies, only fit for our castoffs! You're our distorting mirrors, our loathsome vent, our shame, our dregs!

SOLANGE Go on, go on!

CLAIRE Please hurry. Please! I can't go on. You're . . . you're . . . My God, I can't think of anything. My mind's a blank. I've run out of insults. Claire, you exhaust me.

SOLANGE Stop. I've got there. It's my turn.—Madame had her billing and cooing, her lovers, her milkman. . . .

CLAIRE Solange . . .

SOLANGE Silence! Her morning milkman, her messenger of dawn, her handsome clarion, her pale and charming lover. That's over. [*She takes down a riding whip.*] Take your place for the ball.

CLAIRE What are you doing?

SOLANGE [*solemnly*] I'm checking the flow. Down on your knees!

CLAIRE Solange . . .

SOLANGE Down on your knees! [CLAIRE *hesitates and kneels.*] Ah! Ah! You were so beautiful, the way you wrung your precious arms! Your tears, your petals oozed down your lovely face. Ah! Ah! Down! [CLAIRE *does not move.*] Down! [SOLANGE *strikes her.*] *Get down!* [CLAIRE *lies down.*] Ah! You amuse me, my dear! Crawl! Crawl, I say, like a worm! And you were going to follow in the wake of the boats, to cross the sea to aid and comfort your handsome exile! Look at yourself again! That role is only for the fairest of the fair. The guards would snicker. People would point at you. Your lover would hang his head in shame! And are you strong enough? Strong enough to carry his bag? And spry enough, Madame, spry enough on your feet? Don't worry. I'm not jealous. I don't need that thief where I'm going. No, Madame. I myself am both the thief and his slavish shadow. I move alone toward the brightest shores.

CLAIRE I'm losing him!

SOLANGE Aren't I enough for you?

CLAIRE Solange, please, I'm sinking.

SOLANGE Sink! But rise again to the surface. I know what my final destiny is to be. I've reached shelter. I can be bountiful. [*She takes a breath.*] Stand up! I'll marry you standing up! Ah! Ah! Groveling on the rug at a man's feet. What a sorry, facile gesture. The great thing is to end in beauty. How are you going to get up?

CLAIRE [*getting up slowly and clumsily*] You're killing me.

SOLANGE [*ironically*] Careful now, watch your movements.

CLAIRE [*on her feet*] We're out of our depth. We must go to bed. My throat's—

SOLANGE [*striding up to her*] Madame has a very lovely throat. The throat of a queen. [CLAIRE *moves back to the kitchen door.*] Of a dove. Come, my turtle dove!

CLAIRE [*she withdraws farther back, putting her hands to her neck as if to protect it*] It's late.

SOLANGE Never too late.

CLAIRE Madame . . .

SOLANGE . . . is drinking champagne with Monsieur who has returned from the dead.

CLAIRE She'll be back any moment. Let me go.

SOLANGE Stop worrying. She's waltzing! She's waltzing! She's guzzling fine wine! She's delirious.

CLAIRE Let's get out of here, Solange. I tell you we're in danger.

SOLANGE Go into the vestry.[6] [*She points to the kitchen door.*] Go on in. You've got to finish the linoleum.

CLAIRE [*she screams in a hollow voice*] Help!

SOLANGE Don't yell! It's useless. Death is present, and is stalking you. Don't yell! I, who kept you the way they keep kittens for drowning. I, yes I, who trimmed my belly with pins to stab all the foetuses I threw into the gutter! In order to keep you, to have *you* alive!

CLAIRE [*running about the room*] Solange, Solange, come to yourself!

SOLANGE [*running after her*] To *yourself*!

CLAIRE [*in a dull voice*] Help!

SOLANGE Stop yelling! No one can hear you! We're both beyond the pale.

CLAIRE Solange . . .

SOLANGE Everyone's listening, but no one will hear.

CLAIRE I'm ill. . . .

SOLANGE You'll be taken care of there.

CLAIRE I'm ill . . . I . . . I'm going to be sick. . . . [*She seems to be gagging.*]

6. A room in a church.

SOLANGE [*she approaches her and says sympathetically*] Really? Are you really ill? Claire, are you really feeling ill?

CLAIRE I'm, I'm going to—

SOLANGE Not here, Claire, hold it in. [*She supports her.*] Not here, please, please. Come. Lean on me. There. Walk gently. We'll be better off there, in our flowered domain. I have such sure ways of putting an end to all suffering.

> [*They leave by the kitchen door. The stage remains empty for a few seconds. A gust of wind opens the unlocked window. Enter* SOLANGE, *right, wearing her short black dress. Throughout the scene she will seem to be addressing characters who are imaginary, though present.*]

SOLANGE Madame . . . At last! Madame is dead! . . . laid out on the linoleum . . . strangled by the dish-gloves. What? Oh, Madame may remain seated. . . . Madame may call me Mademoiselle[7] Solange. . . . Exactly. It's because of what I've done. Madame and Monsieur will call me Mademoiselle Solange Lemercier. . . . Madame should have taken off that black dress. It's grotesque. [*She imitates* MADAME'*s voice.*] So I'm reduced to wearing mourning for my maid. As I left the cemetery all the servants of the neighborhood marched past me as if I were a member of the family. I've so often been part of the family. Death will see the joke through to the bitter end. . . . What? Oh! Madame needn't feel sorry for me. I'm Madame's equal and I hold my head high. . . . Oh! And there are things Monsieur doesn't realize. He doesn't know that he used to obey our orders. [*She laughs.*] Ah! Ah! Monsieur was a tiny little boy. Monsieur toed the line when we threatened. No, Inspector, no . . . I won't talk! I won't say a word. I refuse to speak about our complicity in this murder. . . . The dresses? Oh, Madame could have kept them. My sister and I had our own. Those we used to put on at night, in secret. Now, I have my own dress, and I'm your equal. I wear the red garb of criminals. Monsieur's laughing at me? He's smiling at me. Monsieur thinks I'm mad. He's thinking maids should have better taste than to make gestures reserved for Madame! Monsieur really forgives me? Monsieur is the soul of kindness. He'd like to vie with me in grandeur. But I've scaled the fiercest heights. Madame now sees my loneliness—at last! Yes, I am alone. And fearsome. I might say cruel things, but I can be kind. . . . Madame will get over her fright. She'll get over it well enough. What with her flowers and perfumes and gowns and jewels and lovers. As for me, I've my sister. . . . Yes. I dare speak of these things. I do, Madame. There's nothing I won't dare. And who could silence me, who? Who would be so bold as to say to me: "My dear child!" I've been a servant. Well and good. I've made the gestures a servant must make. I've smiled at Madame. I've bent down to make the bed, bent down to scrub the tiles, bent down to peel vegetables, to listen at doors, to glue my eye to keyholes! But now I stand upright. And firm. I'm the strangler. Mademoiselle Solange, the one who strangled her sister! . . . Me be still? Madame is delicate, really. But I pity Madame. I pity Madame's whiteness, her satiny skin, and her little ears, and little wrists. . . . Eh? I'm the black crow. . . . Oh! Oh! I have my judges. I belong to the police. Claire? She was really

7. That is, use the respectful title "Miss" rather than her first name alone (as servants were addressed).

very fond of Madame. . . . YOUR dresses again! And THAT white dress, THAT one, which I forbade her to put on, the one you wore the night of the Opera Ball, the night you poked fun at her, because she was sitting in the kitchen admiring a photo of Gary Cooper[8] . . . Madame will remember. Madame will remember her gentle irony, the maternal grace with which she took the magazine from us, and smiled. Nor will Madame forget that she called her Clarinette.[9] Monsieur laughed until the tears rolled down his cheeks. . . . Eh? Who am I? The monstrous soul of servantdom! . . . No, Inspector, I'll explain nothing in their presence. That's *our* business. It would be a fine thing if masters could pierce the shadows where servants live. . . . That, my child, is our darkness, ours. [*She lights a cigarette and smokes clumsily. The smoke makes her cough.*] Neither you nor anyone else will be told anything. Just tell yourselves that this time Solange has gone through with it. . . . You see her dressed in red. She is going out. [*She goes to the window, opens it, and steps out on the balcony. Facing the night, with her back to the audience, she delivers the following speech. A slight breeze makes the curtains stir.*] Going out. Descending the great stairway. Accompanied by the police. Out on your balconies to see her making her way among the shadowy penitents! It's noon. She's carrying a nine-pound torch. The hangman follows close behind. He's whispering sweet nothings in her ear. Claire! The hangman's by my side! Now take your hand off my waist. He's trying to kiss me! Let go of me! Ah! Ah! [*She laughs.*] The hangman's trifling with me. She will be led in procession by all the maids of the neighborhood, by all the servants who accompanied Claire to her final resting place. They'll all be wearing crowns, flowers, streamers, banners. They'll toll the bell. The funeral will unfold its pomp. It's beautiful, isn't it? First come the butlers, in full livery, but without silk lining. They're wearing their crowns. Then come the footmen, the lackeys in knee breeches and white stockings. They're wearing their crowns. Then come the valets, and then the chambermaids wearing our colors. Then the porters. And then come the delegations from heaven. And I'm leading them. The hangman's lulling me. I'm being acclaimed. I'm pale and I'm about to die. . . . [*She returns to the room.*] And what flowers! They gave her such a lovely funeral, didn't they? Oh! Claire, poor little Claire! [*She bursts into tears and collapses into an armchair*] What? [*She gets up.*] It's no use, Madame, I'm obeying the police. They're the only ones who understand me. They too belong to the world of outcasts, the world you touch only with tongs.

[*Visible only to the audience,* CLAIRE, *during the last few moments, has been leaning with her elbows against the jamb of the kitchen door and listening to her sister.*]

Now we are Mademoiselle Solange Lemercier, that Lemercier woman. The famous criminal. And above all, Monsieur need not be uneasy. I'm not a maid. I have a noble soul. . . . [*She shrugs her shoulders.*] No, no, not another word, my dear fellow. Ah, Madame's not forgetting what I've done for her. . . . No, no she must not forget my devotion. . . .

[*Meanwhile* CLAIRE *enters through the door at the left. She is wearing the white dress.*]

8. An American film star (1901–1961).

9. In French, *-ette* is a feminine diminutive ("little one").

And in spite of my forbidding it, Madame continues to stroll about the apartment. She will please sit down . . . and listen to me. . . . [*To* CLAIRE] Claire . . . we're raving!

CLAIRE [*complainingly,* MADAME*'s voice*] You're talking far too much, my child. Far too much. Shut the window. [SOLANGE *shuts the window.*] Draw the curtains. Very good, Claire!

SOLANGE It's late. Everyone's in bed. . . . We're playing an idiotic game.

CLAIRE [*she signals with her hand for silence*] Claire, pour me a cup of tea.

SOLANGE But . . .

CLAIRE I said a cup of tea.

SOLANGE We're dead tired. We've got to stop. [*She sits down in an armchair.*]

CLAIRE Ah, by no means! Poor servant girl, you think you'll get out of it as easily as that? It would be too simple to conspire with the wind, to make the night one's accomplice. Solange, you will contain me within you. Now pay close attention.

SOLANGE Claire . . .

CLAIRE Do as I tell you. I'm going to help you. I've decided to take the lead. Your role is to keep me from backing out, nothing more.

SOLANGE What more do you want? We're at the end. . . .

CLAIRE We're at the very beginning.

SOLANGE They'll be coming. . . .

CLAIRE Forget about them. We're alone in the world. Nothing exists but the altar where one of the two maids is about to immolate herself—

SOLANGE But—

CLAIRE Be still. It will be your task, yours alone, to keep us both alive. You must be very strong. In prison no one will know that I'm with you, secretly. On the sly.

SOLANGE I'll never be able . . .

CLAIRE Please, stand up straight. Up straight, Solange! Claire! Darling, stand straight now. Up straight. Pull yourself together.

SOLANGE You're overwhelming me.

CLAIRE A staff! A standard! Claire, up straight! I call upon you to represent me—

SOLANGE I've been working too hard. I'm exhausted.

CLAIRE To represent me in the world. [*She tries to lift her sister and keep her on her feet.*] My darling, stand up straight.

SOLANGE Please, I beg of you.

CLAIRE [*domineeringly*] I beg of you, stand up straight. Solemnly, Claire! Pretty does it, pretty does it! Up Claire! Up on your paws! [*She holds her by the wrists and lifts her from her chair.*] Up on your paws! Now then! Up! Up!

SOLANGE You don't realize the danger—

CLAIRE But, Solange, you're immortal! Repeat after me—

SOLANGE Talk. But not so loud.

CLAIRE [*mechanically*] Madame must have her tea.

SOLANGE [*firmly*] No, I won't.

CLAIRE [*holding her by the wrists*] You bitch! Repeat. Madame must have her tea.

SOLANGE I've just been through such a lot. . . .

CLAIRE [*more firmly*] Madame will have her tea. . . .

SOLANGE Madame will have her tea. . . .

CLAIRE Because she must sleep . . .

SOLANGE Because she must sleep . . .

CLAIRE And I must stay awake.

SOLANGE And I must stay awake.

CLAIRE [*she lies down on* MADAME*'s bed*] Don't interrupt again. I repeat. Are you listening? Are you obeying? [SOLANGE *nods "yes."*] I repeat: My tea!

SOLANGE [*hesitating*] But . . .

CLAIRE I say: my tea.

SOLANGE But, Madame.

CLAIRE Good. Continue.

SOLANGE But, Madame, it's cold.

CLAIRE I'll drink it anyway. Let me have it. [SOLANGE *brings the tray.*] And you've poured it into the best, the finest tea set. [*She takes the cup and drinks, while* SOLANGE, *facing the audience, delivers the end of her speech.*]

SOLANGE The orchestra is playing brilliantly. The attendant is raising the red velvet curtain. He bows. Madame is descending the stairs. Her furs brush against the green plants. Madame steps into the car. Monsieur is whispering sweet nothings in her ear. She would like to smile, but she is dead. She rings the bell. The porter yawns. He opens the door. Madame goes up the stairs. She enters her apartment—but, Madame is dead. Her two maids are alive: they've just risen up, free, from Madame's icy form. All the maids were present at her side—not they themselves, but rather the hellish agony of their names. And all that remains of them to float about Madame's airy corpse is the delicate perfume of the holy maidens which they were in secret. We are beautiful, joyous, drunk, and free!

Curtain.

TENNESSEE WILLIAMS

1911–1983

WHEN Tennessee Williams's play *The Glass Menagerie* premiered in 1944, American drama found itself at a crossroads. EUGENE O'NEILL, whose plays helped establish the American theater as a serious artistic medium, had been absent from the stage since 1934, and the drama of social protest that dominated the 1930s was eclipsed by the outbreak of World War II. American society was undergoing a transition, as traditional values and institutions were shaken by the mid-twentieth century's accelerating economic and social transformations. In this theatrical and social climate, the plays of Williams and ARTHUR MILLER restored the centrality of theater to the nation's cultural life. But whereas Miller's *All My Sons* (1947) and *Death of a Salesman* (1949) concentrated on the ethical conflicts of individuals and society, Williams's drama explored the deeper (and often darker) regions of America's psyche: the psychological fault lines between convention and romantic individualism; the dynamics of sexuality, violence, and alienation; and the place of art and the artist's visionary temperament in a society seen as increasingly hostile to the imagination. Drawn to characters who cling to failing illusions—outsiders who have difficulty fitting in the modern world—Williams pioneered a lyrical dramatic style that confronted but also transcended the harsh realities of contemporary life. In plays such as *The Glass Menagerie*, *A STREETCAR NAMED DESIRE* (1947), and *Cat on a Hot Tin Roof* (1955), the clash of cultures, generations, and psyches is marked by a lyricism reminiscent of the works of ANTON CHEKHOV (1860–1904) and FEDERICO GARCÍA LORCA (1898–1936). After Williams's death, the playwright DAVID MAMET called these plays "the greatest dramatic poetry in the American language."

Williams was, before all else, a Southern writer; like his fellow twentieth-century authors William Faulkner, Eudora Welty, and Flannery O'Connor, he explored the region's self-defining myths and codes of behavior, its changing economy, and its multiple—often conflicting—cultures. The playwright was born Thomas Lanier Williams III on March 26, 1911, in Columbus, Mississippi, to Edwina Dakin Williams, the daughter of an Episcopal minister, and Cornelius Coffin Williams, a shoe salesman from east Tennessee. (The playwright would later change his first name to Tennessee in recognition of his paternal ancestors.) Although he suffered a near-fatal bout of diphtheria at the age of five that kept him out of school, his childhood in Mississippi was an idyllic one. But the idyll ended in 1918 when his father moved the family to St. Louis to take a managerial position at the International Shoe Company. Living in what he later recalled as "a perpetually dim little apartment in a wilderness of identical brick and concrete structures with no grass and no trees nearer than the park," mocked by other children for their southern accents, Williams and his sister Rose (with whom he was very close) found themselves isolated and unhappy in this harsh urban setting. The situation at home was hardly better: his parents quarreled frequently, and his relationship with his father was strained.

Williams began writing at the age of twelve and saw his first article published in a popular magazine at the age of sixteen. He attended the University of Missouri from 1929 to 1932 and majored in journalism, but his father withdrew him from college after he failed a mandatory ROTC course. For the next several years, he worked at his father's company while writing stories at night. Williams eventually attended Washington University in St. Louis and the University of Iowa, where he earned a B.A. in English in 1938. During these years Williams turned his attention to playwriting. A year after his first play—a farce about sailors titled *Cairo! Shanghai! Bombay!*—was produced in a backyard theater in 1935, Williams became involved with the Mummers, a semiprofessional St. Louis theater group specializing in plays of social protest. The country was in the throes of the Depression, and the theater had become an outlet for expressing social and political discontent. Clifford Odets's *Waiting for Lefty* took the theater world by storm in 1935, and the Federal Theatre Project (part of the New Deal's Works Progress Administration) was popularizing the multimedia "Living Newspaper" format as a way of commenting on poverty and other social issues. Reflecting this theatrical climate, Williams's drama during these years was socially and politically engaged. In 1937 the Mummers produced *Candles to the Sun,* a play about Alabama coal miners, and *Fugitive Kind,* which explored the hardships of Depression America through a group of characters living in a St. Louis flophouse. Williams also completed *Not About Nightingales,* a play about prison conditions that he had started at the University of Iowa; the Mummers considered this play, but it would not be produced until 1998.

Buoyed by the local success of these plays, Williams submitted three works to a playwriting competition sponsored by the Group Theater, one of the leading American theater companies of the 1930s. He also moved to New Orleans for two months, a city to which he would return throughout his career and to which he would later refer as his "spiritual home." Williams received a special prize from the Group Theater for a collection of one-act plays and subsequently won a Rockefeller Foundation fellowship, which he used to write *The Battle of Angels.* The Theater Guild of New York produced this play in Boston in 1940, but the production was condemned by spectators and critics.

Over the next four years Williams held a variety of jobs, including a two-month scriptwriting stint for MGM in Hollywood, and he worked on a number of other writing projects. One of these, a play titled *The Gentleman Caller,* would earn Williams the fame that had eluded him in Boston. Under the revised title *The Glass Menagerie,* this play opened in Chicago in December 1944. Response was initially lukewarm, but the glowing review by a prominent Chicago theater critic led to sold-out houses. After transferring to Broadway in March 1945, the play ran for 561 performances and won the New York Drama Critics' Circle Award for Best Play. Williams's most deeply autobiographical drama—its narrator, Tom Wingfield, is modeled on Williams himself, and his sister Laura is a portrait of Rose Williams—*The Glass Menagerie* was important to American theater (and to the playwright's subsequent career) as much for its technical and stylistic innovations as for its subject matter. Seeking to express the fluidity of memory in theatrical terms, Williams employs setting, music, and light in ways that blur the lines between realism and expressionism. The playwright's production notes to *The Glass Menagerie* call for "a new, plastic theatre which must take the place of the exhausted theatre of realistic conventions if the theatre is to resume vitality as a part of our culture." Such a theater must not escape reality; rather, the use of expressionistic and poetic devices allows fuller access to the truth. "[T]ruth, life, or reality," Williams wrote, "is an organic thing which the poetic imagination can represent or suggest, in essence, only through transformation, through changing into other forms than those which were merely present in appearance."

The success of *The Glass Menagerie* catapulted Williams to the forefront of public attention and generated a celebrity toward which he remained profoundly ambivalent. His reputation as one of America's leading dramatists was underscored by the success of his next play, *A Streetcar Named Desire*. Williams had conceived the play's outlines in the early 1940s and had written a number of early versions: *Blanche's Chair on the Moon, The Moth, The Primary Colors,* and *The Poker Night* were among the titles he tried. The completed *A Streetcar Named Desire* opened on December 3, 1947, at the Ethel Barrymore Theater in New York in a production directed by Elia Kazan. Starring a little-known actor, Marlon Brando, in the role of Stanley Kowalski, the play ran for 855 performances over the next two years and was awarded a Pulitzer Prize and the New York Drama Critics' Circle Award. The 1951 film version of *Streetcar* (also directed by Kazan) was equally celebrated. In addition to receiving a number of major revivals, *A Streetcar Named Desire* has been translated into nearly twenty-five languages and staged around the world.

During the decade and a half after *A Streetcar Named Desire,* Williams had a string of plays produced on Broadway: *The Rose Tattoo* (1951), *Camino Real* (1953), *Cat on a Hot Tin Roof* (1955, Pulitzer Prize), *Orpheus Descending* (1957), *Suddenly Last Summer* (1958), *Sweet Bird of Youth* (1959), and *The Night of the Iguana* (1961). Although Williams continued to write plays in the 1960s and 1970s—including *In the Bar of a Tokyo Hotel* (1969), *The Two-Character Play/Out Cry* (1967, 1971), *The Red Devil Battery Sign* (1975), and *Clothes for a Summer Hotel* (1980)—his dramatic work after *Night of the Iguana* failed to receive the acclaim of his earlier plays. Convinced for most of his life that he would die young, Tennessee Williams passed away at the age of seventy-one on February 25, 1983.

A Streetcar Named Desire is set in the French Quarter of New Orleans, a city known for its international influences (French, Spanish, Caribbean) as well as its theatricalized ceremonies and celebrations

Final scene from the original 1947 Broadway production of *A Streetcar Named Desire*.

and its bohemian subculture. The play is full of references to the city's sites and institutions; indeed, the streetcar named Desire, which brings Blanche DuBois to her sister's apartment in the play's opening scene, did run through the French Quarter in the 1940s. At the same time, William's New Orleans is as much an atmosphere as an actual location. Like the blues music rising from a nearby bar, the turquoise evening sky that opens the play "invests the scene with a kind of lyricism and gracefully attenuates the atmosphere of decay." Throughout *A Streetcar Named Desire,* the play's setting embodies moods and states of mind, accentuating points of crisis and imbuing realism with expressionism's more subjective reach. The apartment of Stanley and Stella Kowalski reflects this shifting border between inside and outside. Obscured in darkness when the play's action takes place outside, it appears as an interior acting space when the lighting changes. Its back wall consists of a scrim (or see-through fabric), which appears solid when lit from the front but transparent when lit from behind, allowing a view of the alley beyond the apartment.

Reviewers and scholars who have written about *A Streetcar Named Desire* have focused, for the most part, on the characters of Stanley and Blanche. While such an emphasis risks obscuring the important roles of other characters (particularly Stella and Stanley's friend Mitch), the interaction between Stanley and Blanche represents one of the great *agones,* or dramatic conflicts, in Western drama. The two characters are, in many ways, dramatic antitheses. From his initial appearance, Stanley is defined by his rough manners, working-class pride, and sexual confidence. Polish American by birth, he inhabits a neighborhood defined by its relaxed—at times violent—behavior and its ethnic and racial mix. Stanley's is a male-centered world of poker nights, Jax beer, and sexual pleasure; as Williams writes in introducing the character, "Since earliest manhood the center of his being has been pleasure with women, the giving and taking of it, not with weak indulgence, dependently, but with the

Vivien Leigh as Blanche DuBois and Marlon Brando as Stanley Kowalski, in Elia Kazan's 1951 film adaptation of *A Streetcar Named Desire.*

power and pride of a richly feathered male bird among hens." Given to explosive outbursts but also a man of shrewdness and calculation, he defends his territory with a fierceness that masks an awareness of his own limitations. His charismatic yet threatening presence in Williams's play derives from the aggressive masculinity that he wears like a badge. In this mode of interacting with others he contrasts markedly with Mitch, a man of sensitivity and deep emotional attachments who lives with his mother.

Unlike Stanley, Blanche comes from a plantation world of landed wealth, breeding, and sexual decorum, a world (encapsulated in the plantation's name, Belle Reve—French for "beautiful dream") that was, in reality, already yielding in the 1940s to a newly industrializing South. With her white suit, bodice, and gloves, Blanche's mothlike appearance in the opening scene is incongruous with her urban surroundings. Whereas Stanley represents the vitality, dynamism, and swagger of a country emerging from World War II, Blanche represents more traditional ideals of culture, civilization, and manners. Yet even as Blanche articulates these ideals, the audience is aware that they have failed her. Belle Reve has been lost to the sexual appetites and financial improvidence of its inhabitants, and the history of decline and death that Blanche recounts is gothic in tone. Traumatized by the suicide of her homosexual husband years earlier, Blanche has led a life of promiscuity and fleeting encounters. As age begins to threaten her attractiveness, her efforts to maintain the southern belle image that she was raised to project grow more strained. Standing as the centerpiece of Williams's theatrical world, Blanche becomes stage manager in her own right, controlling the lighting by which she is seen and adding music, decorating the Kowalski apartment, and dressing herself and applying makeup in order to play the starring role in her interactions with others. "I don't want realism. I want magic!" she tells Mitch, and these words capture her increasingly desperate faith in the compensatory power of illusion. Her attempts to maintain this illusion and the accompanying struggle to hold together the different parts of her personality break down the lines between her subjective life and the ever more hostile surroundings in which she finds herself. Of all the characters, it is Blanche who is most closely linked to the expressionistic devices of *A Streetcar Named Desire*. In the play's early scenes she hears the Varsouviana polka that was playing the night her husband shot himself; and as the play progresses, the lighting and sound effects of the stage increasingly mirror her mental and emotional turmoil.

In the aftermath of Stanley's violent outburst at the poker night he hosts for his friends in scene 3, Blanche pleads with Stella to choose tenderness and civilization over the bestiality and violence that Stanley embodies: "*Don't—don't hang back with the brutes!*" By framing the choice of values so explicitly, Blanche seeks to triumph over Stanley in the battle for Stella's love and allegiance. But the claims presented by the characters engage the audience's sympathies as well. Though scholars and reviewers have often sided with Stanley or Blanche in their assessments of the play's central confrontation, such judgments violate the complex balances and counterpoints that Williams establishes. In their sympathies, audiences must come to terms with competing social and moral codes, and they must deal with the fact that Williams's character portrayals amplify and change as the play progresses. For his part, while Williams condemned what he called "the ravishment of the tender, the sensitive, the delicate, by the savage and brutal forces of modern society," his sympathies extended in both directions: "[Blanche] was broken on the rock of the world; I find her a sympathetic character, but I also find Stanley sympathetic."

With its exploration of traditional and contemporary gender roles and its juxtaposition of the old South with the new, *A Streetcar Named Desire* offers a powerful portrait of the changing social landscape of postwar America. In keeping with this achievement, its characters, actions, and lines of dialogue became potent cultural symbols in the decades that followed. Brando's Stanley—memorialized by the widely successful film adaptation—became an image of masculinity for a generation that also worshipped such male icons as John Wayne, Elvis Presley, and James Dean. Subsequent actors playing Stanley have had to work to free their role from this mesmerizing performance. But the figure of Blanche DuBois—introduced on stage by Jessica Tandy and popularized on screen by Vivien Leigh—may be more resonant in the latter half of the twentieth century and the early years of the twenty-first. Embodying the strains in female social roles during the supposed return to normalcy following World War II, Blanche serves as an image of the conflicted place of both women and men in a society in which expected ideals and behaviors no longer match the realities of contemporary gender relations. Like Stanley, she deals with the realities of desire—physical and emotional—that fly in the face of death itself. That she cannot control her journey on the streetcar named Desire says as much about the society she inhabits as it does her precarious psyche. Though the contemporary world is no longer that of postwar America, issues of sexuality remain pressing in both traditional and cosmopolitan societies. When the drag queen Prior Walters quotes Blanche in TONY KUSHNER's *Angels in America* (1991–92), he acknowledges the line between Williams's female protagonist—trapped between roles—and a more contemporary field of sexual identities. S.G.

A Streetcar Named Desire

And so it was I entered the broken world
To trace the visionary company of love, its voice
An instant in the wind (I know not whither hurled)
But not for long to hold each desperate choice.
"*The Broken Tower*" by *Hart Crane*[1]

CHARACTERS

BLANCHE	PABLO
STELLA	A NEGRO WOMAN
STANLEY	A DOCTOR
MITCH	A NURSE
EUNICE	A YOUNG COLLECTOR
STEVE	A MEXICAN WOMAN

Scene 1

The exterior of a two-story corner building on a street in New Orleans which is named Elysian Fields and runs between the L & N tracks[2] *and the river. The section is poor but,*

1. American poet (1899–1932); "The Broken Tower" was the last poem Crane wrote before committing suicide at the age of 32.
2. Tracks used by trains of the Louisville and Nashville Railroad—formerly a major freight and passenger company in the southeastern United States. *Elysian Fields:* a street just north of the French Quarter, the oldest neighborhood of New Orleans; also, in classical mythology, the abode of the blessed dead.

unlike corresponding sections in other American cities, it has a raffish charm. The houses are mostly white frame, weathered grey, with rickety outside stairs and galleries and quaintly ornamented gables. This building contains two flats, upstairs and down. Faded white stairs ascend to the entrances of both.

It is first dark of an evening early in May. The sky that shows around the dim white building is a peculiarly tender blue, almost a turquoise, which invests the scene with a kind of lyricism and gracefully attenuates the atmosphere of decay. You can almost feel the warm breath of the brown river beyond the river warehouses with their faint redolences of bananas and coffee. A corresponding air is evoked by the music of Negro entertainers at a barroom around the corner. In this part of New Orleans you are practically always just around the corner, or a few doors down the street, from a tinny piano being played with the infatuated fluency of brown fingers. This "blue piano" expresses the spirit of the life which goes on here.

Two women, one white and one colored, are taking the air on the steps of the building. The white woman is EUNICE, *who occupies the upstairs flat; the colored woman a neighbor, for New Orleans is a cosmopolitan city where there is a relatively warm and easy intermingling of races in the old part of town.*

Above the music of the "blue piano" the voices of people on the street can be heard overlapping.

[*Two men come around the corner,* STANLEY KOWALSKI *and* MITCH. *They are about twenty-eight or thirty years old, roughly dressed in blue denim work clothes.* STANLEY *carries his bowling jacket and a red-stained package from a butcher's. They stop at the foot of the steps.*]

STANLEY [*bellowing*] Hey, there! Stella, baby!

[STELLA *comes out on the first floor landing, a gentle young woman, about twenty-five, and of a background obviously quite different from her husband's.*]

STELLA [*mildly*] Don't holler at me like that. Hi, Mitch.

STANLEY Catch!

STELLA What?

STANLEY Meat!

[*He heaves the package at her. She cries out in protest but manages to catch it: then she laughs breathlessly. Her husband and his companion have already started back around the corner.*]

STELLA [*calling after him*] Stanley! Where are you going?

STANLEY Bowling!

STELLA Can I come watch?

STANLEY Come on.

[*He goes out.*]

STELLA Be over soon. [*To the white woman*] Hello, Eunice. How are you?

EUNICE I'm all right. Tell Steve to get him a poor boy's sandwich[3] 'cause nothing's left here.

[*They all laugh; the* COLORED WOMAN *does not stop.* STELLA *goes out.*]

COLORED WOMAN What was that package he th'ew at 'er? [*She rises from steps, laughing louder.*]

EUNICE You hush, now!

NEGRO WOMAN Catch *what!*

3. A po'boy, the Gulf Coast version of a submarine sandwich, featuring beef, shrimp, or other fillings in a hollowed-out loaf of French bread.

[*She continues to laugh.* BLANCHE *comes around the corner, carrying a valise. She looks at a slip of paper, then at the building, then again at the slip and again at the building. Her expression is one of shocked disbelief. Her appearace is incongruous to this setting. She is daintily dressed in a white suit with a fluffy bodice, necklace and earrings of pearl, white gloves and hat, looking as if she were arriving at a summer tea or cocktail party in the garden district.*[4] *She is about five years older than* STELLA. *Her delicate beauty must avoid a strong light. There is something about her uncertain manner, as well as her white clothes, that suggests a moth.*]

EUNICE [*finally*] What's the matter, honey? Are you lost?

BLANCHE [*with faintly hysterical humor*] They told me to take a streetcar named Desire, and then transfer to one called Cemeteries[5] and ride six blocks and get off at—Elysian Fields!

EUNICE That's where you are now.

BLANCHE At Elysian Fields?

EUNICE This here is Elysian Fields.

BLANCHE They mustn't have—understood—what number I wanted . . .

EUNICE What number you lookin' for?

[BLANCHE *wearily refers to the slip of paper.*]

BLANCHE Six thirty-two.

EUNICE You don't have to look no further.

BLANCHE [*uncomprehendingly*] I'm looking for my sister, Stella DuBois. I mean—Mrs. Stanley Kowalski.

EUNICE That's the party.—You just did miss her, though.

BLANCHE This—can this be—her home?

EUNICE She's got the downstairs here and I got the up.

BLANCHE Oh. She's—out?

EUNICE You noticed that bowling alley around the corner?

BLANCHE I'm—not sure I did.

EUNICE Well, that's where she's at, watchin' her husband bowl. [*There is a pause.*] You want to leave your suitcase here an' go find her?

BLANCHE No.

NEGRO WOMAN I'll go tell her you come.

BLANCHE Thanks.

NEGRO WOMAN You welcome.

[*She goes out.*]

EUNICE She wasn't expecting you?

BLANCHE No. No, not tonight.

EUNICE Well, why don't you just go in and make yourself at home till they get back.

BLANCHE How could I—do that?

EUNICE We own this place so I can let you in.

[*She gets up and opens the downstairs door. A light goes on behind the blind, turning it light blue.* BLANCHE *slowly follows her into the downstairs flat. The surrounding areas dim out as the interior is lighted.*]

4. An elegant New Orleans neighborhood known for its Greek Revival and Italianate architecture.

5. Streetcar routes in New Orleans at the time the play was written; the Desire line, which went through the French Quarter, was replaced by a bus in 1948.

[*Two rooms can be seen, not too clearly defined. The one first entered is primarily a kitchen but contains a folding bed to be used by* BLANCHE. *The room beyond this is a bedroom. Off this room is a narrow door to a bathroom.*]

EUNICE [*defensively, noticing* BLANCHE*'s look*] It's sort of messed up right now but when it's clean it's real sweet.

BLANCHE Is it?

EUNICE Uh-huh, I think so. So you're Stella's sister?

BLANCHE Yes. [*Wanting to get rid of her*] Thanks for letting me in.

EUNICE *Por nada,*[6] as the Mexicans say, *por nada!* Stella spoke of you.

BLANCHE Yes?

EUNICE I think she said you taught school.

BLANCHE Yes.

EUNICE And you're from Mississippi, huh?

BLANCHE Yes.

EUNICE She showed me a picture of your home-place, the plantation.

BLANCHE Belle Reve?[7]

EUNICE A great big place with white columns.

BLANCHE Yes . . .

EUNICE A place like that must be awful hard to keep up.

BLANCHE If you will excuse me, I'm just about to drop.

EUNICE Sure, honey. Why don't you set down?

BLANCHE What I meant was I'd like to be left alone.

EUNICE [*offended*] Aw. I'll make myself scarce, in that case.

BLANCHE I didn't mean to be rude, but—

EUNICE I'll drop by the bowling alley an' hustle her up.

[*She goes out the door.*]

[BLANCHE *sits in a chair very stiffly with her shoulders slightly hunched and her legs pressed close together and her hands tightly clutching her purse as if she were quite cold. After a while the blind look goes out of her eyes and she begins to look slowly around. A cat screeches. She catches her breath with a startled gesture. Suddenly she notices something in a half-opened closet. She springs up and crosses to it, and removes a whiskey bottle. She pours a half tumbler of whiskey and tosses it down. She carefully replaces the bottle and washes out the tumbler at the sink. Then she resumes her seat in front of the table.*]

BLANCHE [*faintly to herself*] I've got to keep hold of myself!

[STELLA *comes quickly around the corner of the building and runs to the door of the downstairs flat.*]

STELLA [*calling out joyfully*] *Blanche!*

[*For a moment they stare at each other. Then* BLANCHE *springs up and runs to her with a wild cry.*]

BLANCHE Stella, oh, Stella, Stella! Stella for Star![8]

[*She begins to speak with feverish vivacity as if she feared for either of them to stop and think. They catch each other in a spasmodic embrace.*]

BLANCHE Now, then, let me look at you. But don't you look at me, Stella, no, no, no, not till later, not till I've bathed and rested! And turn that over-light

6. It's nothing (Spanish).
7. Beautiful Dream (French).
8. *Stella* means "star" in Latin.

off! Turn that off! I won't be looked at in this merciless glare! [STELLA *laughs and complies.*] Come back here now! Oh, my baby! Stella! Stella for Star! [*She embraces her again.*] I thought you would never come back to this horrible place! What am I saying? I didn't mean to say that. I meant to be nice about it and say—Oh, what a convenient location and such—Ha-a-ha! Precious lamb! You haven't said a *word* to me.

STELLA You haven't given me a chance to, honey! [*She laughs, but her glance at* BLANCHE *is a little anxious.*]

BLANCHE Well, now you talk. Open your pretty mouth and talk while I look around for some liquor! I know you must have some liquor on the place! Where could it be, I wonder? Oh, I spy, I spy!

[*She rushes to the closet and removes the bottle; she is shaking all over and panting for breath as she tries to laugh. The bottle nearly slips from her grasp.*]

STELLA [*noticing*] Blanche, you sit down and let me pour the drinks. I don't know what we've got to mix with. Maybe a coke's[9] in the icebox. Look'n see, honey, while I'm—

BLANCHE No coke, honey, not with my nerves tonight! Where—where—where is—?

STELLA Stanley? Bowling! He loves it. They're having a—found some soda!—tournament . . .

BLANCHE Just water, baby, to chase it! Now don't get worried, your sister hasn't turned into a drunkard, she's just all shaken up and hot and tired and dirty! You sit down, now, and explain this place to me! What are you doing in a place like this?

STELLA Now, Blanche—

BLANCHE Oh, I'm not going to be hypocritical, I'm going to be honestly critical about it! Never, never, never in my worst dreams could I picture—Only Poe! Only Mr. Edgar Allan Poe!—could do it justice! Out there I suppose is the ghoul-haunted woodland of Weir![1] [*She laughs.*]

STELLA No, honey, those are the L & N tracks.

BLANCHE No, now seriously, putting joking aside. Why didn't you tell me, why didn't you write me, honey, why didn't you let me know?

STELLA [*carefully, pouring herself a drink*] Tell you what, Blanche?

BLANCHE Why, that you had to live in these conditions!

STELLA Aren't you being a little intense about it? It's not that bad at all! New Orleans isn't like other cities.

BLANCHE This has got nothing to do with New Orleans. You might as well say—forgive me, blessed baby! [*She suddenly stops short.*] The subject is closed!

STELLA [*a little drily*] Thanks.

[*During the pause,* BLANCHE *stares at her. She smiles at* BLANCHE.]

BLANCHE [*looking down at her glass, which shakes in her hand*] You're all I've got in the world, and you're not glad to see me!

STELLA [*sincerely*] Why, Blanche, you know that's not true.

BLANCHE No?—I'd forgotten how quiet you were.

9. In the South, *coke* is often used as a generic term for any soft drink.

1. The setting of the gothic ballad "Ulalume" (1847), by Poe, the American short story writer and poet (1809–1849).

STELLA You never did give me a chance to say much, Blanche. So I just got in the habit of being quiet around you.

BLANCHE [*vaguely*] A good habit to get into . . . [*Then, abruptly*] You haven't asked me how I happened to get away from the school before the spring term ended.

STELLA Well, I thought you'd volunteer that information—if you wanted to tell me.

BLANCHE You thought I'd been fired?

STELLA No, I—thought you might have—resigned . . .

BLANCHE I was so exhausted by all I'd been through my—nerves broke. [*Nervously tamping cigarette*] I was on the verge of—lunacy, almost! So Mr. Graves—Mr. Graves is the high school superintendent—he suggested I take a leave of absence. I couldn't put all of those details into the wire[2] . . . [*She drinks quickly.*] Oh, this buzzes right through me and feels so *good!*

STELLA Won't you have another?

BLANCHE No, one's my limit.

STELLA Sure?

BLANCHE You haven't said a word about my appearance.

STELLA You look just fine.

BLANCHE God love you for a liar! Daylight never exposed so total a ruin! But you—you've put on some weight, yes, you're just as plump as a little partridge! And it's so becoming to you!

STELLA Now, Blanche—

BLANCHE Yes, it is, it is or I wouldn't say it! You just have to watch around the hips a little. Stand up.

STELLA Not now.

BLANCHE You hear me? I said stand up! [STELLA *complies reluctantly.*] You messy child, you, you've spilt something on that pretty white lace collar! About your hair—you ought to have it cut in a feather bob with your dainty features. Stella, you have a maid, don't you?

STELLA No. With only two rooms it's—

BLANCHE What? *Two* rooms, did you say?

STELLA This one and— [*She is embarrassed.*]

BLANCHE The other one? [*She laughs sharply. There is an embarrassed silence.*] I am going to take just one little tiny nip more, sort of to put the stopper on, so to speak. . . . Then put the bottle away so I won't be tempted. [*She rises.*] I want you to look at *my* figure! [*She turns around.*] You know I haven't put on one ounce in ten years, Stella? I weigh what I weighed the summer you left Belle Reve. The summer Dad died and you left us . . .

STELLA [*a little wearily*] It's just incredible, Blanche, how well you're looking.

[*They both laugh uncomfortably.*]

BLANCHE But, Stella, there's only two rooms, I don't see where you're going to put me!

STELLA We're going to put you in here.

2. Telegram.

BLANCHE What kind of bed's this—one of those collapsible things? [*She sits on it.*]

STELLA Does it feel all right?

BLANCHE [*dubiously*] Wonderful, honey. I don't like a bed that gives much. But there's no door between the two rooms, and Stanley—will it be decent?

STELLA Stanley is Polish, you know.

BLANCHE Oh, yes. They're something like Irish, aren't they?

STELLA Well—

BLANCHE Only not so—highbrow? [*They both laugh again in the same way.*] I brought some nice clothes to meet all your lovely friends in.

STELLA I'm afraid you won't think they are lovely.

BLANCHE What are they like?

STELLA They're Stanley's friends.

BLANCHE Polacks?

STELLA They're a mixed lot, Blanche.

BLANCHE Heterogeneous—types?

STELLA Oh, yes. Yes, types is right!

BLANCHE Well—anyhow—I brought nice clothes and I'll wear them. I guess you're hoping I'll say I'll put up at a hotel, but I'm not going to put up at a hotel. I want to be *near* you, got to be *with* somebody, I *can't* be *alone!* Because—as you must have noticed—I'm—*not* very *well* . . . [*Her voice drops and her look is frightened.*]

STELLA You seem a little bit nervous or overwrought or something.

BLANCHE Will Stanley like me, or will I be just a visiting in-law, Stella? I couldn't stand that.

STELLA You'll get along fine together, if you'll just try not to—well—compare him with men that we went out with at home.

BLANCHE Is he so—different?

STELLA Yes. A different species.

BLANCHE In what way; what's he like?

STELLA Oh, you can't describe someone you're in love with! Here's a picture of him! [*She hands a photograph to* BLANCHE.]

BLANCHE An officer?

STELLA A Master Sergeant in the Engineers' Corps.[3] Those are decorations!

BLANCHE He had those on when you met him?

STELLA I assure you I wasn't just blinded by all the brass.

BLANCHE That's not what I—

STELLA But of course there were things to adjust myself to later on.

BLANCHE Such as his civilian background! [STELLA *laughs uncertainly.*] How did he take it when you said I was coming?

STELLA Oh, Stanley doesn't know yet.

BLANCHE [*frightened*] You—haven't told him?

STELLA He's on the road a good deal.

BLANCHE Oh. Travels?

STELLA Yes.

BLANCHE Good. I mean—isn't it?

3. A branch of the U.S. Army that provides construction and engineering services in support of combat soldiers and federal agencies.

STELLA [*half to herself*] I can hardly stand it when he is away for a night . . .

BLANCHE Why, Stella!

STELLA When he's away for a week I nearly go wild!

BLANCHE Gracious!

STELLA And when he comes back I cry on his lap like a baby . . . [*She smiles to herself.*]

BLANCHE I guess that is what is meant by being in love . . . [STELLA *looks up with a radiant smile.*] Stella—

STELLA What?

BLANCHE [*in an uneasy rush*] I haven't asked you the things you probably thought I was going to ask. And so I'll expect you to be understanding about what *I* have to tell *you*.

STELLA What, Blanche? [*Her face turns anxious.*]

BLANCHE Well, Stella—you're going to reproach me, I know that you're bound to reproach me—but before you do—take into consideration—you left! I stayed and struggled! You came to New Orleans and looked out for yourself! *I* stayed at *Belle Reve* and tried to hold it together! I'm not meaning this in any reproachful way, but *all* the burden descended on *my* shoulders.

STELLA The best I could do was make my own living, Blanche.

[*Blanche begins to shake again with intensity.*]

BLANCHE I know, I know. But you are the one that abandoned Belle Reve, not I! I stayed and fought for it, bled for it, almost died for it!

STELLA Stop this hysterical outburst and tell me what's happened? What do you mean fought and bled? What kind of—

BLANCHE I knew you would, Stella. I knew you would take this attitude about it!

STELLA About—what?—please!

BLANCHE [*slowly*] The loss—the loss . . .

STELLA Belle Reve? Lost, is it? No!

BLANCHE Yes, Stella.

[*They stare at each other across the yellow-checked linoleum of the table.* BLANCHE *slowly nods her head and* STELLA *looks slowly down at her hands folded on the table. The music of the "blue piano" grows louder.* BLANCHE *touches her handkerchief to her forehead.*]

STELLA But how did it go? What happened?

BLANCHE [*springing up*] You're a fine one to ask me how it went!

STELLA Blanche!

BLANCHE You're a fine one to sit there *accusing me* of it!

STELLA *Blanche!*

BLANCHE I, I, *I* took the blows in my face and my body! All of those deaths! The long parade to the graveyard! Father, Mother! Margaret, that dreadful way! So big with it, it couldn't be put in a coffin! But had to be burned like rubbish! You just came home in time for the funerals, Stella. And funerals are pretty compared to deaths. Funerals are quiet, but deaths—not always. Sometimes their breathing is hoarse, and sometimes it rattles, and sometimes they even cry out to you, "Don't let me go!" Even the old, sometimes, say, "Don't let me go." As if you were able to stop them! But funerals are quiet, with pretty flowers. And, oh, what gorgeous boxes they pack them away in! Unless you were there at the bed when they cried out, "Hold me!"

you'd never suspect there was the struggle for breath and bleeding. You didn't dream, but I saw! *Saw! Saw!* And now you sit there telling me with your eyes that I let the place go! How in hell do you think all that sickness and dying was paid for? Death is expensive, Miss Stella! And old Cousin Jessie's right after Margaret's, hers! Why, the Grim Reaper had put up his tent on our doorstep! . . . Stella. Belle Reve was his headquarters! Honey—that's how it slipped through my fingers! Which of them left us a fortune? Which of them left a cent of insurance even? Only poor Jessie—one hundred to pay for her coffin. That was all, Stella! And I with my pitiful salary at the school. Yes, accuse me! Sit there and stare at me, thinking I let the place go! *I* let the place go? Where were *you!* In bed with your—Polack!

STELLA [*springing*] Blanche! You be still! That's enough! [*She starts out.*]

BLANCHE Where are you going?

STELLA I'm going into the bathroom to wash my face.

BLANCHE Oh, Stella, Stella, you're crying!

STELLA Does that surprise you?

BLANCHE Forgive me—I didn't mean to—

[*The sound of men's voices is heard.* STELLA *goes into the bathroom, closing the door behind her. When the men appear, and* BLANCHE *realizes it must be* STANLEY *returning, she moves uncertainly from the bathroom door to the dressing table, looking apprehensively toward the front door.* STANLEY *enters, followed by* STEVE *and* MITCH. STANLEY *pauses near his door,* STEVE *by the foot of the spiral stair, and* MITCH *is slightly above and to the right of them, about to go out. As the men enter, we hear some of the following dialogue.*]

STANLEY Is that how he got it?

STEVE Sure that's how he got it. He hit the old weather-bird for 300 bucks on a six-number-ticket.[4]

MITCH Don't tell him those things; he'll believe it.

[MITCH *starts out.*]

STANLEY [*restraining* MITCH] Hey, Mitch—come back here.

[BLANCHE, *at the sound of voices, retires in the bedroom. She picks up* STANLEY'S *photo from dressing table, looks at it, puts it down. When* STANLEY *enters the apartment, she darts and hides behind the screen at the head of bed.*]

STEVE [*to* STANLEY *and* MITCH] Hey, are we playin' poker tomorrow?

STANLEY Sure—at Mitch's.

MITCH [*hearing this, returns quickly to the stair rail*] No—not at my place. My mother's still sick!

STANLEY Okay, at my place . . . [MITCH *starts out again.*] But you bring the beer!

[MITCH *pretends not to hear—calls out "Goodnight, all," and goes out, singing.*]

EUNICE [*heard from above*] Break it up down there! I made the spaghetti dish and ate it myself.

4. That is, he won $300 on a six-number lottery ticket. *Hit the old weather-bird:* got extraordinarily lucky (as one would have to be to shoot at and hit an ornamental weather vane, which traditionally was shaped like a rooster).

STEVE [*going upstairs*] I told you and phoned you we was playing. [*To the men*] Jax beer![5]

EUNICE You never phoned me once.

STEVE I told you at breakfast—and phoned you at lunch . . .

EUNICE Well, never mind about that. You just get yourself home here once in a while.

STEVE You want it in the papers?

[*More laughter and shouts of parting come from the men.* STANLEY *throws the screen door of the kitchen open and comes in. He is of medium height, about five feet eight or nine, and strongly, compactly built. Animal joy in his being is implicit in all his movements and attitudes. Since earliest manhood the center of his life has been pleasure with women, the giving and taking of it, not with weak indulgence, dependently, but with the power and pride of a richly feathered male bird among hens. Branching out from this complete and satisfying center are all the auxiliary channels of his life, such as his heartiness with men, his appreciation of rough humor, his love of good drink and food and games, his car, his radio, everything that is his, that bears his emblem of the gaudy seed-bearer. He sizes women up at a glance, with sexual classifications, crude images flashing into his mind and determining the way he smiles at them.*]

BLANCHE [*drawing involuntarily back from his stare*] You must be Stanley. I'm Blanche.

STANLEY Stella's sister?

BLANCHE Yes.

STANLEY H'lo. Where's the little woman?

BLANCHE In the bathroom.

STANLEY Oh. Didn't know you were coming in town.

BLANCHE I—uh—

STANLEY Where you from, Blanche?

BLANCHE Why, I—live in Laurel.[6]

[*He has crossed to the closet and removed the whiskey bottle.*]

STANLEY In Laurel, huh? Oh, yeah. Yeah, in Laurel, that's right. Not in my territory. Liquor goes fast in hot weather.

[*He holds the bottle to the light to observe its depletion.*]

Have a shot?

BLANCHE No, I—rarely touch it.

STANLEY Some people rarely touch it, but it touches them often.

BLANCHE [*faintly*] Ha-ha.

STANLEY My clothes're stickin' to me. Do you mind if I make myself comfortable? [*He starts to remove his shirt.*]

BLANCHE Please, please do.

STANLEY Be comfortable is my motto.

BLANCHE It's mine, too. It's hard to stay looking fresh. I haven't washed or even powdered my face and—here you are!

5. Made by the Jackson Brewing Company of New Orleans until 1974. The brewery sponsored a bowling team in nearby St. Charles.

6. A town in southeast Mississippi, about 135 miles from New Orleans.

STANLEY You know you can catch cold sitting around in damp things, especially when you been exercising hard like bowling is. You're a teacher, aren't you?

BLANCHE Yes.

STANLEY What do you teach, Blanche?

BLANCHE English.

STANLEY I never was a very good English student. How long you here for, Blanche?

BLANCHE I—don't know yet.

STANLEY You going to shack up here?

BLANCHE I thought I would if it's not inconvenient for you all.

STANLEY Good.

BLANCHE Traveling wears me out.

STANLEY Well, take it easy.

[*A cat screeches near the window.* BLANCHE *spring up.*]

BLANCHE What's that?

STANLEY Cats . . . Hey, Stella!

STELLA [*faintly, from the bathroom*] Yes, Stanley.

STANLEY Haven't fallen in, have you? [*He grins at* BLANCHE. *She tries unsuccessfully to smile back. There is a silence.*] I'm afraid I'll strike you as being the unrefined type. Stella's spoke of you a good deal. You were married once, weren't you?

[*The music of the polka rises up, faint in the distance.*]

BLANCHE Yes. When I was quite young.

STANLEY What happened?

BLANCHE The boy—the boy died. [*She sinks back down.*] I'm afraid I'm—going to be sick!

[*Her head falls on her arms.*]

Scene 2

It is six o'clock the following evening. BLANCHE *is bathing.* STELLA *is completing her toilette.* BLANCHE*'s dress, a flowered print, is laid out on* STELLA*'s bed.*

STANLEY *enters the kitchen from outside, leaving the door open on the perpetual "blue piano" around the corner.*

STANLEY What's all this monkey doings?

STELLA Oh, Stan! [*She jumps up and kisses him, which he accepts with lordly composure.*] I'm taking Blanche to Galatoire's[7] for supper and then to a show, because it's your poker night.

STANLEY How about my supper, huh? I'm not going to no Galatoire's for supper!

STELLA I put you a cold plate on ice.

STANLEY Well, isn't that just dandy!

STELLA I'm going to try to keep Blanche out till the party breaks up because I don't know how she would take it. So we'll go to one of the little places in the Quarter[8] afterward and you'd better give me some money.

STANLEY Where is she?

7. An elegant restaurant on Bourbon Street, specializing in French Creole cuisine.

8. The French Quarter.

STELLA She's soaking in a hot tub to quiet her nerves. She's terribly upset.

STANLEY Over what?

STELLA She's been through such an ordeal.

STANLEY Yeah?

STELLA Stan, we've—lost Belle Reve!

STANLEY The place in the country?

STELLA Yes.

STANLEY How?

STELLA [*vaguely*] Oh, it had to be—sacrificed or something. [*There is a pause while* STANLEY *considers.* STELLA *is changing into her dress.*] When she comes in be sure to say something nice about her appearance. And, oh! Don't mention the baby. I haven't said anything yet, I'm waiting until she gets in a quieter condition.

STANLEY [*ominously*] So?

STELLA And try to understand her and be nice to her, Stan.

BLANCHE [*singing in the bathroom*] "From the land of the sky blue water, They brought a captive maid!"[9]

STELLA She wasn't expecting to find us in such a small place. You see I'd tried to gloss things over a little in my letters.

STANLEY So?

STELLA And admire her dress and tell her she's looking wonderful. That's important with Blanche. Her little weakness!

STANLEY Yeah. I get the idea. Now let's skip back a little to where you said the country place was disposed of.

STELLA Oh!—yes . . .

STANLEY How about that? Let's have a few more details on that subjeck.

STELLA It's best not to talk much about it until she's calmed down.

STANLEY So that's the deal, huh? Sister Blanche cannot be annoyed with business details right now!

STELLA You saw how she was last night.

STANLEY Uh-hum, I saw how she was. Now let's have a gander at the bill of sale.

STELLA I haven't seen any.

STANLEY She didn't show you no papers, no deed of sale or nothing like that, huh?

STELLA It seems like it wasn't sold.

STANLEY Well, what in hell was it then, give away? To charity?

STELLA Shhh! She'll hear you.

STANLEY I don't care if she hears me. Let's see the papers!

STELLA There weren't any papers, she didn't show any papers, I don't care about papers.

STANLEY Have you ever heard of the Napoleonic code?[1]

STELLA No, Stanley, I haven't heard of the Napoleonic code and if I have, I don't see what it—

9. From "From the Land of the Sky-Blue Water" (1908), by Nelle Richmond Eberhart and Charles Wakefield Cadman, a song popularized by the Andrews Sisters in the late 1930s.

1. The civil law code established in France under Napoleon in 1804 and adopted by most other European countries. In 1808, after Louisiana had been purchased from France but before it became a state, it adopted a version of the Napoleonic code; all other U.S. states follow the British common law model.

STANLEY Let me enlighten you on a point or two, baby.

STELLA Yes?

STANLEY In the state of Louisiana we have the Napoleonic code according to which what belongs to the wife belongs to the husband and vice versa. For instance if I had a piece of property, or you had a piece of property—

STELLA My head is swimming!

STANLEY All right. I'll wait till she gets through soaking in a hot tub and then I'll inquire if *she* is acquainted with the Napoleonic code. It looks to me like you have been swindled, baby, and when you're swindled under the Napoleonic code I'm swindled *too.* And I don't like to be *swindled.*

STELLA There's plenty of time to ask her questions later but if you do now she'll go to pieces again. I don't understand what happened to Belle Reve but you don't know how ridiculous you are being when you suggest that my sister or I or anyone of our family could have perpetrated a swindle on anyone else.

STANLEY Then where's the money if the place was sold?

STELLA Not sold—*lost, lost!*

[*He stalks into bedroom, and she follows him.*]

Stanley!

[*He pulls open the wardrobe trunk standing in middle of room and jerks out an armful of dresses.*]

STANLEY Open your eyes to this stuff! You think she got them out of a teacher's pay?

STELLA Hush!

STANLEY Look at these feathers and furs that she come here to preen herself in! What's this here? A solid-gold dress, I believe! And this one! What is these here? Fox-pieces! [*He blows on them.*] Genuine fox fur-pieces, a half a mile long! Where are your fox-pieces, Stella? Bushy snow-white ones, no less! Where are your white fox-pieces?

STELLA Those are inexpensive summer furs that Blanche has had a long time.

STANLEY I got an acquaintance who deals in this sort of merchandise. I'll have him in here to appraise it. I'm willing to bet you there's thousands of dollars invested in this stuff here!

STELLA Don't be such an idiot, Stanley!

[*He hurls the furs to the day bed. Then he jerks open small drawer in the trunk and pulls up a fistful of costume jewelry.*]

STANLEY And what have we here? The treasure chest of a pirate!

STELLA Oh, Stanley!

STANLEY Pearls! Ropes of them! What is this sister of yours, a deep-sea diver? Bracelets of solid gold, too! Where are your pearls and gold bracelets?

STELLA Shhh! Be still, Stanley!

STANLEY And diamonds! A crown for an empress!

STELLA A rhinestone tiara she wore to a costume ball.

STANLEY What's rhinestone?

STELLA Next door to glass.

STANLEY Are you kidding? I have an acquaintance that works in a jewelry store. I'll have him in here to make an appraisal of this. Here's your plantation, or what was left of it, here!

STELLA You have no idea how stupid and horrid you're being! Now close that trunk before she comes out of the bathroom!

[*He kicks the trunk partly closed and sits on the kitchen table.*]

STANLEY The Kowalskis and the DuBoises have different notions.

STELLA [*angrily*] Indeed they have, thank heavens!—*I'm* going outside.

[*She snatches up her white hat and gloves and crosses to the outside door.*]

You come out with me while Blanche is getting dressed.

STANLEY Since when do you give me orders?

STELLA Are you going to stay here and insult her?

STANLEY You're damn tootin' I'm going to stay here.

[STELLA *goes out to the porch.* BLANCHE *comes out of the bathroom in a red satin robe.*]

BLANCHE [*airily*] Hello, Stanley! Here I am, all freshly bathed and scented, and feeling like a brand-new human being!

[*He lights a cigarette.*]

STANLEY That's good.

BLANCHE [*drawing the curtains at the windows*] Excuse me while I slip on my pretty new dress!

STANLEY Go right ahead, Blanche.

[*She closes the drapes between the rooms.*]

BLANCHE I understand there's to be a little card party to which we ladies are cordially *not* invited!

STANLEY [*ominously*] Yeah?

[BLANCHE *throws off her robe and slips into a flowered print dress.*]

BLANCHE Where's Stella?

STANLEY Out on the porch.

BLANCHE I'm going to ask a favor of you in a moment.

STANLEY What could that be, I wonder?

BLANCHE Some buttons in back! You may enter!

[*He crosses through drapes with a smoldering look.*]

How do I look?

STANLEY You look all right.

BLANCHE Many thanks! Now the buttons!

STANLEY I can't do nothing with them.

BLANCHE You men with your big clumsy fingers. May I have a drag on your cig?

STANLEY Have one for yourself.

BLANCHE Why, thanks! . . . It looks like my trunk has exploded.

STANLEY Me an' Stella were helping you unpack.

BLANCHE Well, you certainly did a fast and thorough job of it!

STANLEY It looks like you raided some stylish shops in Paris.

BLANCHE Ha-ha! Yes—clothes are my passion!

STANLEY What does it cost for a string of fur-pieces like that?

BLANCHE Why, those were a tribute from an admirer of mine!

STANLEY He must have had a lot of—admiration!

BLANCHE Oh, in my youth I excited some admiration. But look at me now! [*She smiles at him radiantly.*] Would you think it possible that I was once considered to be—attractive?

STANLEY Your looks are okay.

BLANCHE I was fishing for a compliment, Stanley.

STANLEY I don't go in for that stuff.

BLANCHE What—stuff?

STANLEY Compliments to women about their looks. I never met a woman that didn't know if she was good-looking or not without being told, and some of them give themselves credit for more than they've got. I once went out with a doll who said to me, "I am the glamorous type, I am the glamorous type!" I said, "So what?"

BLANCHE And what did she say then?

STANLEY She didn't say nothing. That shut her up like a clam.

BLANCHE Did it end the romance?

STANLEY It ended the conversation—that was all. Some men are took in by this Hollywood glamor stuff and some men are not.

BLANCHE I'm sure you belong in the second category.

STANLEY That's right.

BLANCHE I cannot imagine any witch of a woman casting a spell over you.

STANLEY That's—right.

BLANCHE You're simple, straightforward and honest, a little bit on the primitive side I should think. To interest you a woman would have to— [*She pauses with an indefinite gesture.*]

STANLEY [*slowly*] Lay . . . her cards on the table.

BLANCHE [*smiling*] Well, I never cared for wishy-washy people. That was why, when you walked in here last night, I said to myself—"My sister has married a man!"—Of course that was all that I could tell about you.

STANLEY [*booming*] Now let's cut the re-bop![2]

BLANCHE [*pressing hands to her ears*] Ouuuuu!

STELLA [*calling from the steps*] Stanley! You come out here and let Blanche finish dressing!

BLANCHE I'm through dressing, honey.

STELLA Well, you come out, then.

STANLEY Your sister and I are having a little talk.

BLANCHE [*lightly*] Honey, do me a favor. Run to the drugstore and get me a lemon Coke with plenty of chipped ice in it!—Will you do that for me, sweetie?

STELLA [*uncertainly*] Yes.

[*She goes around the corner of the building.*]

BLANCHE The poor little thing was out there listening to us, and I have an idea she doesn't understand you as well as I do. . . . All right; now, Mr. Kowalski, let us proceed without any more double-talk. I'm ready to answer all questions. I've nothing to hide. What is it?

STANLEY There is such a thing in this state of Louisiana as the Napoleonic code, according to which whatever belongs to my wife is also mine—and vice versa.

BLANCHE My, but you have an impressive judicial air!

[*She sprays herself with her atomizer; then playfully sprays him with it. He seizes the atomizer and slams it down on the dresser. She throws back her head and laughs.*]

2. Nonsense (a variant of *bebop* or *bop*, the virtuosic jazz of the late 1940s and a term meaning "glib or deceptive talk").

STANLEY If I didn't know that you was my wife's sister I'd get ideas about you!

BLANCHE Such as what!

STANLEY Don't play so dumb. You know what!

BLANCHE [*she puts the atomizer on the table*] All right. Cards on the table. That suits me. [*She turns to* STANLEY.] I know I fib a good deal. After all, a woman's charm is fifty per cent illusion, but when a thing is important I tell the truth, and this is the truth: I haven't cheated my sister or you or anyone else as long as I have lived.

STANLEY Where's the papers? In the trunk?

BLANCHE Everything that I own is in that trunk.

[STANLEY *crosses to the trunk, shoves it roughly open and begins to open compartments.*]

BLANCHE What in the name of heaven are you thinking of! What's in the back of that little boy's mind of yours? That I am absconding with something, attempting some kind of treachery on my sister?—Let me do that! It will be faster and simpler . . . [*She crosses to the trunk and takes out a box.*] I keep my papers mostly in this tin box. [*She opens it.*]

STANLEY What's them underneath? [*He indicates another sheaf of paper.*]

BLANCHE These are love-letters, yellowing with antiquity, all from one boy. [*He snatches them up. She speaks fiercely.*] Give those back to me!

STANLEY I'll have a look at them first!

BLANCHE The touch of your hands insults them!

STANLEY Don't pull that stuff!

[*He rips off the ribbon and starts to examine them.* BLANCHE *snatches them from him, and they cascade to the floor.*]

BLANCHE Now that you've touched them I'll burn them!

STANLEY [*staring, baffled*] What in hell are they?

BLANCHE [*on the floor gathering them up*] Poems a dead boy wrote. I hurt him the way that you would like to hurt me, but you can't! I'm not young and vulnerable any more. But my young husband was and I—never mind about that! Just give them back to me!

STANLEY What do you mean by saying you'll have to burn them?

BLANCHE I'm sorry, I must have lost my head for a moment. Everyone has something he won't let others touch because of their—intimate nature . . .

[*She now seems faint with exhaustion and she sits down with the strong box and puts on a pair of glasses and goes methodically through a large stack of papers.*]

Ambler & Ambler. Hmmmmm. . . . Crabtree. . . . More Ambler & Ambler.

STANLEY What is Ambler & Ambler?

BLANCHE A firm that made loans on the place.

STANLEY Then it *was* lost on a mortgage?

BLANCHE [*touching her forehead*] That must've been what happened.

STANLEY I don't want no ifs, ands or buts! What's all the rest of them papers?

[*She hands him the entire box. He carries it to the table and starts to examine the papers.*]

BLANCHE [*picking up a large envelope containing more papers*] There are thousands of papers, stretching back over hundreds of years, affecting Belle Reve as, piece by piece, our improvident grandfathers and father and uncles and brothers exchanged the land for their epic fornications—to put it plainly! [*She removes her glasses with an exhausted laugh.*] The four-letter word deprived us of our plantation, till finally all that was left—and Stella can verify that!—was the house itself and about twenty acres of ground, including a graveyard, to which now all but Stella and I have retreated. [*She pours the contents of the envelope on the table.*] Here all of them are, all papers! I hereby endow you with them! Take them, peruse them—commit them to memory, even! I think it's wonderfully fitting that Belle Reve should finally be this bunch of old papers in your big, capable hands! . . . I wonder if Stella's come back with my lemon Coke . . . [*She leans back and closes her eyes.*]

STANLEY I have a lawyer acquaintance who will study these out.

BLANCHE Present them to him with a box of aspirin tablets.

STANLEY [*becoming somewhat sheepish*] You see, under the Napoleonic code—a man has to take an interest in his wife's affairs—especially now that she's going to have a baby.

[BLANCHE *opens her eyes. The "blue piano" sounds louder.*]

BLANCHE Stella? Stella going to have a baby? [*Dreamily*] I didn't know she was going to have a baby!

[*She gets up and crosses to the outside door.* STELLA *appears around the corner with a carton from the drugstore.*]

[STANLEY *goes into the bedroom with the envelope and the box.*]

[*The inner rooms fade to darkness and the outside wall of the house is visible.* BLANCHE *meets* STELLA *at the foot of the steps to the sidewalk.*]

BLANCHE Stella, Stella for Star! How lovely to have a baby! It's all right. Everything's all right.

STELLA I'm sorry he did that to you.

BLANCHE Oh, I guess he's just not the type that goes for jasmine perfume, but maybe he's what we need to mix with our blood now that we've lost Belle Reve. We thrashed it out. I feel a bit shaky, but I think I handled it nicely, I laughed and treated it all as a joke. [STEVE *and* PABLO *appear, carrying a case of beer.*] I called him a little boy and laughed and flirted. Yes, I was flirting with your husband! [*As the men approach*] The guests are gathering for the poker party. [*The two men pass between them, and enter the house.*] Which way do we go now, Stella—this way?

STELLA No, this way. [*She leads* BLANCHE *away.*]

BLANCHE [*laughing*] The blind are leading the blind![3]

[*A tamale* VENDOR *is heard calling.*]

VENDOR'S VOICE Red-hot!

Scene 3

The Poker Night[4]

There is a picture of Van Gogh's of a billiard-parlor at night.[5] *The kitchen now suggests that sort of lurid nocturnal brilliance, the raw colors of childhood's spectrum. Over the*

3. See Matthew 15.14: "And if the blind lead the blind, both shall fall into the ditch."
4. "The Poker Night" was Williams's working title for *A Streetcar Named Desire.*
5. *The Night Café* (1888), by the Dutch painter Vincent Van Gogh (1853–1890).

*yellow linoleum of the kitchen table hangs an electric bulb with a vivid green glass shade. The poker players—*STANLEY, STEVE, MITCH, *and* PABLO*—wear colored shirts, solid blue, a purple, a red-and-white check, a light green, and they are men at the peak of their physical manhood, as coarse and direct and powerful as the primary colors. There are vivid slices of watermelon on the table, whiskey bottles and glasses. The bedroom is relatively dim with only the light that spills between the portieres*[6] *and through the wide window on the street. For a moment, there is absorbed silence as a hand is dealt.*

STEVE Anything wild this deal?

PABLO One-eyed jacks are wild.

STEVE Give me two cards.

PABLO You, Mitch?

MITCH I'm out.

PABLO One.

MITCH Anyone want a shot?

STANLEY Yeah. Me.

PABLO Why don't somebody go to the Chinaman's and bring back a load of chop suey?

STANLEY When I'm losing you want to eat! Ante up! Openers? Openers! Get y'r ass off the table, Mitch. Nothing belongs on a poker table but cards, chips, and whiskey.

[*He lurches up and tosses some watermelon rinds to the floor.*]

MITCH Kind of on your high horse, ain't you?

STANLEY How many?

STEVE Give me three.

STANLEY One.

MITCH I'm out again. I oughta go home pretty soon.

STANLEY Shut up.

MITCH I gotta sick mother. She don't go to sleep until I come in at night.

STANLEY Then why don't you stay home with her?

MITCH She says to go out, so I go, but I don't enjoy it. All the while I keep wondering how she is.

STANLEY Aw, for the sake of Jesus, go home, then!

PABLO What've you got?

STEVE Spade flush.

MITCH You all are married. But I'll be alone when she goes.—I'm going to the bathroom.

STANLEY Hurry back and we'll fix you a sugar-tit.[7]

MITCH Aw, go rut. [*He crosses through the bedroom into the bathroom.*]

STEVE [*dealing a hand*] Seven card stud. [*Telling his joke as he deals.*] This ole farmer is out in back of his house sittin' down th'owing corn to the chickens when all at once he hears a loud cackle and this young hen comes lickety split around the side of the house with the rooster right behind her and gaining on her fast.

STANLEY [*impatient with the story*] Deal!

STEVE But when the rooster catches sight of the farmer th'owing the corn he puts on the brakes and lets the hen get away and starts pecking corn. And the old farmer says, "Lord God, I hopes I never gits *that* hongry!"

6. Heavy curtains hung across a doorway.
7. A pacifier dipped in sugar.

[STEVE *and* PABLO *laugh. The sisters appear around the corner of the building.*]

STELLA The game is still going on.

BLANCHE How do I look?

STELLA Lovely, Blanche.

BLANCHE I feel so hot and frazzled. Wait till I powder before you open the door. Do I look done in?

STELLA Why no. You are as fresh as a daisy.

BLANCHE One that's been picked a few days.

[STELLA *opens the door and they enter.*]

STELLA Well, well, well. I see you boys are still at it!

STANLEY Where you been?

STELLA Blanche and I took in a show. Blanche, this is Mr. Gonzales and Mr. Hubbell.

BLANCHE Please don't get up.

STANLEY Nobody's going to get up, so don't be worried.

STELLA How much longer is this game going to continue?

STANLEY Till we get ready to quit.

BLANCHE Poker is so fascinating. Could I kibitz?

STANLEY You could not. Why don't you women go up and sit with Eunice?

STELLA Because it is nearly two-thirty. [BLANCHE *crosses into the bedroom and partially closes the portieres.*] Couldn't you call it quits after one more hand?

[*A chair scrapes.* STANLEY *gives a loud whack of his hand on her thigh.*]

STELLA [*sharply*] That's not fun, Stanley.

[*The men laugh.* STELLA *goes into the bedroom.*]

STELLA It makes me so mad when he does that in front of people.

BLANCHE I think I will bathe.

STELLA Again?

BLANCHE My nerves are in knots. Is the bathroom occupied?

STELLA I don't know.

[BLANCHE *knocks.* MITCH *opens the door and comes out, still wiping his hands on a towel.*]

BLANCHE Oh!—good evening.

MITCH Hello. [*He stares at her.*]

STELLA Blanche, this is Harold Mitchell. My sister, Blanche DuBois.

MITCH [*with awkward courtesy*] How do you do, Miss DuBois.

STELLA How is your mother now, Mitch?

MITCH About the same, thanks. She appreciated your sending over that custard.—Excuse me, please.

[*He crosses slowly back into the kitchen, glancing back at* BLANCHE *and coughing a little shyly. He realizes he still has the towel in his hands and with an embarrassed laugh hands it to* STELLA. BLANCHE *looks after him with a certain interest.*]

BLANCHE That one seems—superior to the others.

STELLA Yes, he is.

BLANCHE I thought he had a sort of sensitive look.

STELLA His mother is sick.

BLANCHE Is he married?

STELLA No.

BLANCHE Is he a wolf?

STELLA Why, Blanche! [BLANCHE *laughs.*] I don't think he would be.

BLANCHE What does—what does he do?

[*She is unbuttoning her blouse.*]

STELLA He's on the precision bench in the spare parts department. At the plant Stanley travels for.

BLANCHE Is that something much?

STELLA No. Stanley's the only one of his crowd that's likely to get anywhere.

BLANCHE What makes you think Stanley will?

STELLA Look at him.

BLANCHE I've looked at him.

STELLA Then you should know.

BLANCHE I'm sorry, but I haven't noticed the stamp of genius even on Stanley's forehead.

[*She takes off the blouse and stands in her pink silk brassiere and white skirt in the light through the portieres. The game has continued in undertones.*]

STELLA It isn't on his forehead and it isn't genius.

BLANCHE Oh. Well, what is it, and where? I would like to know.

STELLA It's a drive that he has. You're standing in the light, Blanche!

BLANCHE Oh, am I!

[*She moves out of the yellow streak of light. Stella has removed her dress and put on a light blue satin kimona.*[8]]

STELLA [*with girlish laughter*] You ought to see their wives.

BLANCHE [*laughingly*] I can imagine. Big, beefy things, I suppose.

STELLA You know that one upstairs? [*More laughter*] One time [*Laughing*] the plaster—[*Laughing*] cracked—

STANLEY You hens cut out that conversation in there!

STELLA You can't hear us.

STANLEY Well, you can hear me and I said to hush up!

STELLA This is my house and I'll talk as much as I want to!

BLANCHE Stella, don't start a row.

STELLA He's half drunk!—I'll be out in a minute.

[*She goes into the bathroom.* BLANCHE *rises and crosses leisurely to a small white radio and turns it on.*]

STANLEY Awright, Mitch, you in?

MITCH What? Oh!—No, I'm out!

[BLANCHE *moves back into the streak of light. She raises her arms and stretches, as she moves indolently back to the chair.*]

[*Rhumba music comes over the radio.* MITCH *rises at the table.*]

STANLEY Who turned that on in there?

BLANCHE I did. Do you mind?

STANLEY Turn it off!

STEVE Aw, let the girls have their music.

PABLO Sure, that's good, leave it on!

STEVE Sounds like Xavier Cugat![9]

8. Kimono.

9. The Cuban American bandleader (1900–1990) whose hits of the 1930s won him the nickname "Rhumba King."

[STANLEY *jumps up and, crossing to the radio, turns it off. He stops short at the sight of* BLANCHE *in the chair. She returns his look without flinching. Then he sits again at the poker table.*]

[*Two of the men have started arguing hotly.*]

STEVE I didn't hear you name it.

PABLO Didn't I name it, Mitch?

MITCH I wasn't listenin'.

PABLO What were you doing, then?

STANLEY He was looking through them drapes. [*He jumps up and jerks roughly at curtains to close them.*] Now deal the hand over again and let's play cards or quit. Some people get ants[1] when they win.

[MITCH *rises as* STANLEY *returns to his seat.*]

STANLEY [*yelling*] Sit down!

MITCH I'm going to the "head."[2] Deal me out.

PABLO Sure he's got ants now. Seven five-dollar bills in his pants pocket folded up tight as spitballs.

STEVE Tomorrow you'll see him at the cashier's window getting them changed into quarters.

STANLEY And when he goes home he'll deposit them one by one in a piggy bank his mother give him for Christmas. [*Dealing*] This game is Spit in the Ocean.

[MITCH *laughs uncomfortably and continues through the portieres. He stops just inside.*]

BLANCHE [*softly*] Hello! The Little Boys' Room is busy right now.

MITCH We've—been drinking beer.

BLANCHE I hate beer.

MITCH It's—a hot weather drink.

BLANCHE Oh, I don't think so; it always makes me warmer. Have you got any cigs? [*She has slipped on the dark red satin wrapper.*]

MITCH Sure.

BLANCHE What kind are they?

MITCH Luckies.

BLANCHE Oh, good. What a pretty case. Silver?

MITCH Yes. Yes; read the inscription.

BLANCHE Oh, is there an inscription? I can't make it out. [*He strikes a match and moves closer.*] Oh! [*Reading with feigned difficulty.*]

"And if God choose,
I shall but love thee better—after—death!"

Why, that's from my favorite sonnet by Mrs. Browning![3]

MITCH You know it?

BLANCHE Certainly I do!

MITCH There's a story connected with that inscription.

BLANCHE It sounds like a romance.

MITCH A pretty sad one.

1. Antsy.
2. Navy slang for a ship's toilet.
3. The English poet Elizabeth Barrett Browning (1806–1861). She is best known for her *Sonnets from the Portuguese* (1850), a sequence of love poems written before her marriage to Robert Browning; Blanche quotes from the most famous of them, Sonnet XLIII ("How do I love thee? Let me count the ways").

BLANCHE Oh?

MITCH The girl's dead now.

BLANCHE [*in a tone of deep sympathy*] *Oh!*

MITCH She knew she was dying when she give me this. A very strange girl, very sweet—very!

BLANCHE She must have been fond of you. Sick people have such deep, sincere attachments.

MITCH That's right, they certainly do.

BLANCHE Sorrow makes for sincerity, I think.

MITCH It sure brings it out in people.

BLANCHE The little there is belongs to people who have experienced some sorrow.

MITCH I believe you are right about that.

BLANCHE I'm positive that I am. Show me a person who hasn't known any sorrow and I'll show you a shuperficial—Listen to me! My tongue is a little—thick! You boys are responsible for it. The show let out at eleven and we couldn't come home on account of the poker game so we had to go somewhere and drink. I'm not accustomed to having more than one drink. Two is the limit—and *three!* [*She laughs.*] Tonight I had three.

STANLEY Mitch!

MITCH Deal me out. I'm talking to Miss—

BLANCHE DuBois.

MITCH Miss DuBois?

BLANCHE It's a French name. It means woods and Blanche means white, so the two together mean white woods. Like an orchard in spring! You can remember it by that.

MITCH You're French?

BLANCHE We are French by extraction. Our first American ancestors were French Huguenots.[4]

MITCH You are Stella's sister, are you not?

BLANCHE Yes, Stella is my precious little sister. I call her little in spite of the fact she's somewhat older than I. Just slightly. Less than a year. Will you do something for me?

MITCH Sure. What?

BLANCHE I bought this adorable little colored paper lantern at a Chinese shop on Bourbon.[5] Put it over the light bulb! Will you, please?

MITCH Be glad to.

BLANCHE I can't stand a naked light bulb, any more than I can a rude remark or a vulgar action.

MITCH [*adjusting the lantern*] I guess we strike you as being a pretty rough bunch.

BLANCHE I'm very adaptable—to circumstances.

MITCH Well, that's a good thing to be. You are visiting Stanley and Stella?

BLANCHE Stella hasn't been so well lately, and I came down to help her for a while. She's very run down.

4. French Protestants, repeatedly persecuted by the Catholic monarchy. Many Huguenots emigrated to the American colonies after Louis XIV's Edict of Fontainebleau declared Protestantism illegal in 1685.

5. Bourbon Street, the center of the French Quarter's nightlife.

MITCH You're not—?

BLANCHE Married? No, no. I'm an old maid schoolteacher!

MITCH You may teach school but you're certainly not an old maid.

BLANCHE Thank you, sir! I appreciate your gallantry!

MITCH So you are in the teaching profession?

BLANCHE Yes. Ah, yes . . .

MITCH Grade school or high school or—

STANLEY [*bellowing*] *Mitch!*

MITCH *Coming!*

BLANCHE Gracious, what lung-power! . . . I teach high school. In Laurel.

MITCH What do you teach? What subject?

BLANCHE Guess!

MITCH I bet you teach art or music? [BLANCHE *laughs delicately.*] Of course I could be wrong. You might teach arithmetic.

BLANCHE Never arithmetic, sir; never arithmetic! [*With a laugh*] I don't even know my multiplication tables! No, I have the misfortune of being an English instructor. I attempt to instill a bunch of bobby-soxers and drugstore Romeos with reverence for Hawthorne and Whitman and Poe![6]

MITCH I guess that some of them are more interested in other things.

BLANCHE How very right you are! Their literary heritage is not what most of them treasure above all else! But they're sweet things! And in the spring, it's touching to notice them making their first discovery of love! As if nobody had ever known it before!

[*The bathroom door opens and* STELLA *comes out.* BLANCHE *continues talking to* MITCH.]

Oh! Have you finished? Wait—I'll turn on the radio.

[*She turns the knobs on the radio and it begins to play "Wien, Wien, nur du allein."*[7] BLANCHE *waltzes to the music with romantic gestures.* MITCH *is delighted and moves in awkward imitation like a dancing bear.*]

[STANLEY *stalks fiercely through the portieres into the bedroom. He crosses to the small white radio and snatches it off the table. With a shouted oath, he tosses the instrument out the window.*]

STELLA *Drunk—drunk—animal thing, you!* [*She rushes through to the poker table.*] All of you—please go home! If any of you have one spark of decency in you—

BLANCHE [*wildly*] Stella, watch out, he's—

[STANLEY *charges after* STELLA.]

MEN [*feebly*] Take it easy, Stanley. Easy, fellow.—Let's all—

STELLA You lay your hands on me and I'll—

[*She backs out of sight. He advances and disappears. There is the sound of a blow.* STELLA *cries out.* BLANCHE *screams and runs into the kitchen.*

6. Classic American authors: Nathaniel Hawthorne (1804–1864), Walt Whitman (1819–1892), and Edgar Allan Poe. *Bobby-soxers and drugstore Romeos:* teenage boys and girls. "Bobby-soxer" was a term first applied to the girls in ankle socks who cried and swooned at Frank Sinatra's concerts in the early 1940s; and boys were "drugstore Romeos" because drugstores usually had soda fountains, where teenagers socialized.

7. "Vienna, Vienna, only you alone" (German); from the popular waltz "Wien, du Stadt meiner Träume" ("Vienna, You City of My Dreams," 1914), by the Austrian composer Rudolf Sieczynski.

The men rush forward and there is grappling and cursing. Something is overturned with a crash.]

BLANCHE [*shrilly*] My sister is going to have a baby!

MITCH This is terrible.

BLANCHE Lunacy, absolute lunacy!

MITCH Get him in here, men.

[STANLEY *is forced, pinioned by the two men, into the bedroom. He nearly throws them off. Then all at once he subsides and is limp in their grasp.*]

[*They speak quietly and lovingly to him and he leans his face on one of their shoulders.*]

STELLA [*in a high, unnatural voice, out of sight*] I want to go away, I want to go away!

MITCH Poker shouldn't be played in a house with women.

[BLANCHE *rushes into the bedroom.*]

BLANCHE I want my sister's clothes! We'll go to that woman's upstairs!

MITCH Where is the clothes?

BLANCHE [*opening the closet*] I've got them! [*She rushes through to* STELLA.] Stella, Stella, precious! Dear, dear little sister, don't be afraid!

[*With her arms around* STELLA, BLANCHE *guides her to the outside door and upstairs.*]

STANLEY [*dully*] What's the matter; what's happened?

MITCH You just blew your top, Stan.

PABLO He's okay, now.

STEVE Sure, my boy's okay!

MITCH Put him on the bed and get a wet towel.

PABLO I think coffee would do him a world of good, now.

STANLEY [*thickly*] I want water.

MITCH Put him under the shower!

[*The men talk quietly as they lead him to the bathroom.*]

STANLEY Let the rut go of me, you sons of bitches!

[*Sounds of blows are heard. The water goes on full tilt.*]

STEVE Let's get quick out of here!

[*They rush to the poker table and sweep up their winings on their way out.*]

MITCH [*sadly but firmly*] Poker should not be played in a house with women.

[*The door closes on them and the place is still. The Negro entertainers in the bar around the corner play "Paper Doll"*[8] *slow and blue. After a moment Stanley comes out of the bathroom dripping water and still in his clinging wet polka-dot drawers.*]

STANLEY Stella! [*There is a pause.*] My baby doll's left me!

[*He breaks into sobs. Then he goes to the phone and dials, still shuddering with sobs.*]

Eunice? I want my baby! [*He waits a moment; then he hangs up and dials again.*] Eunice! I'll keep on ringin' until I talk with my baby!

8. A song written by Johnny S. Black in 1915; the Mills Brothers' 1943 version was a huge hit.

[*An indistinguishable shrill voice is heard. He hurls phone to floor. Dissonant brass and piano sounds as the rooms dim out to darkness and the outer walls appear in the night light. The "blue piano" plays for a brief interval.*]

[*Finally,* STANLEY *stumbles half-dressed out to the porch and down the wooden steps to the pavement before the building. There he throws back his head like a baying hound and bellows his wife's name: "Stella! Stella, sweetheart! Stella!"*]

STANLEY Stell-*lahhhhh!*

EUNICE [*calling down from the door of her upper apartment*] Quit that howling out there an' go back to bed!

STANLEY I want my baby down here. Stella, Stella!

EUNICE She ain't comin' down so you quit! Or you'll git th' law on you!

STANLEY Stella!

EUNICE You can't beat on a woman an' then call 'er back! She won't come! And her goin' t' have a baby! . . . You stinker! You whelp of a Polack, you! I hope they do haul you in and turn the fire hose on you, same as the last time!

STANLEY [*humbly*] Eunice, I want my girl to come down with me!

EUNICE Hah! [*She slams her door.*]

STANLEY [*with heaven-splitting violence*] *STELL-LAHHHHH!*

[*The low-tone clarinet moans. The door upstairs opens again.* STELLA *slips down the rickety stairs in her robe. Her eyes are glistening with tears and her hair loose about her throat and shoulders. They stare at each other. Then they come together with low, animal moans. He falls to his knees on the steps and presses his face to her belly, curving a little with maternity. Her eyes go blind with tenderness as she catches his head and raises him level with her. He snatches the screen door open and lifts her off her feet and bears her into the dark flat.*]

[BLANCHE *comes out on the upper landing in her robe and slips fearfully down the steps.*]

BLANCHE Where is my little sister? Stella? Stella?

[*She stops before the dark entrance of her sister's flat. Then catches her breath as if struck. She rushes down to the walk before the house. She looks right and left as if for a sanctuary.*]

[*The music fades away.* MITCH *appears from around the corner.*]

MITCH Miss DuBois?

BLANCHE Oh!

MITCH All quiet on the Potomac[9] now?

BLANCHE She ran downstairs and went back in there with him.

MITCH Sure she did.

BLANCHE I'm terrified!

MITCH Ho-ho! There's nothing to be scared of. They're crazy about each other.

BLANCHE I'm not used to such—

MITCH Naw, it's a shame this had to happen when you just got here. But don't take it serious.

9. Because of the inaction of the Union general George McClellan in 1861–62, newspaper correspondents frequently reported "All quiet on the Potomac"; it became a bitter catchphrase, featured in ballads and a popular song.

BLANCHE Violence! Is so—

MITCH Set down on the steps and have a cigarette with me.

BLANCHE I'm not properly dressed.

MITCH That don't make no difference in the Quarter.

BLANCHE Such a pretty silver case.

MITCH I showed you the inscription, didn't I?

BLANCHE Yes. [*During the pause, she looks up at the sky.*] There's so much—so much confusion in the world . . . [*He coughs diffidently.*] Thank you for being so kind! I need kindness now.

Scene 4

It is early the following morning. There is a confusion of street cries like a choral chant.

STELLA *is lying down in the bedroom. Her face is serene in the early morning sunlight. One hand rests on her belly, rounding slightly with new maternity. From the other dangles a book of colored comics. Her eyes and lips have that almost narcotized tranquility that is in the faces of Eastern idols.*

The table is sloppy with remains of breakfast and the debris of the preceding night, and STANLEY'S *gaudy pyjamas lie across the threshold of the bathroom. The outside door is slightly ajar on a sky of summer brilliance.*

BLANCHE *appears at this door. She has spent a sleepless night and her appearance entirely contrasts with Stella's. She presses her knuckles nervously to her lips as she looks through the door, before entering.*

BLANCHE Stella?

STELLA [*stirring lazily*] Hmmh?

[BLANCHE *utters a moaning cry and runs into the bedroom, throwing herself down beside* STELLA *in a rush of hysterical tenderness.*]

BLANCHE Baby, my baby sister!

STELLA [*drawing away from her*] Blanche, what is the matter with you?

[BLANCHE *straightens up slowly and stands beside the bed looking down at her sister with knuckles pressed to her lips.*]

BLANCHE He's left?

STELLA Stan? Yes.

BLANCHE Will he be back?

STELLA He's gone to get the car greased. Why?

BLANCHE Why! I've been half crazy, Stella! When I found out you'd been insane enough to come back in here after what happened—I started to rush in after you!

STELLA I'm glad you didn't.

BLANCHE What were you thinking of? [STELLA *makes an indefinite gesture.*] Answer me! What? What?

STELLA Please, Blanche! Sit down and stop yelling.

BLANCHE All right, Stella. I will repeat the question quietly now. How could you come back in this place last night? Why, you must have slept with him!

[STELLA *gets up in a calm and leisurely way.*]

STELLA Blanche, I'd forgotten how excitable you are. You're making much too much fuss about this.

BLANCHE Am I?

STELLA Yes, you are, Blanche. I know how it must have seemed to you and I'm awful sorry it had to happen, but it wasn't anything as serious as you seem to take it. In the first place, when men are drinking and playing poker anything can happen. It's always a powder-keg. He didn't know what he was doing. . . . He was as good as a lamb when I came back and he's really very, very ashamed of himself.

BLANCHE And that—that makes it all right?

STELLA No, it isn't all right for anybody to make such a terrible row, but—people do sometimes. Stanley's always smashed things. Why, on our wedding night—soon as we came in here—he snatched off one of my slippers and rushed about the place smashing light bulbs with it.

BLANCHE He did—*what?*

STELLA He smashed all the light bulbs with the heel of my slipper! [*She laughs.*]

BLANCHE And you—you *let* him? Didn't *run,* didn't *scream?*

STELLA I was—sort of—thrilled by it. [*She waits for a moment.*] Eunice and you had breakfast?

BLANCHE Do you suppose I wanted any breakfast?

STELLA There's some coffee left on the stove.

BLANCHE You're so—matter-of-fact about it, Stella.

STELLA What other can I be? He's taken the radio to get it fixed. It didn't land on the pavement so only one tube[1] was smashed.

BLANCHE And you are standing there smiling!

STELLA What do you want me to do?

BLANCHE Pull yourself together and face the facts.

STELLA What are they, in your opinion?

BLANCHE In my opinion? You're married to a madman!

STELLA No!

BLANCHE Yes, you are, your fix is worse than mine is! Only you're not being sensible about it. I'm going to *do* something. Get hold of myself and make myself a new life!

STELLA Yes?

BLANCHE But you've given in. And that isn't right, you're not old! You can get out.

STELLA [*slowly and emphatically*] I'm not in anything I want to get out of.

BLANCHE [*incredulously*] What—Stella?

STELLA I said I am not in anything that I have a desire to get out of. Look at the mess in this room! And those empty bottles! They went through two cases last night! He promised this morning that he was going to quit having these poker parties, but you know how long such a promise is going to keep. Oh, well, it's his pleasure, like mine is movies and bridge. People have got to tolerate each other's habits, I guess.

BLANCHE I don't understand you. [STELLA *turns toward her.*] I don't understand your indifference. Is this a Chinese philosophy you've—cultivated?

STELLA Is what—what?

BLANCHE This—shuffling about and mumbling—'One tube smashed—beer bottles—mess in the kitchen!'—as if nothing out of the ordinary has happened! [STELLA *laughs uncertainly and picking up the broom, twirls it in her hands.*]

BLANCHE Are you deliberately shaking that thing in my face?

1. Vacuum tube (used in radios before the invention of transistors).

STELLA No.

BLANCHE Stop it. Let go of that broom. I won't have you cleaning up for him!

STELLA Then who's going to do it? Are you?

BLANCHE I? I!

STELLA No, I didn't think so.

BLANCHE Oh, let me think, if only my mind would function! We've got to get hold of some money, that's the way out!

STELLA I guess that money is always nice to get hold of.

BLANCHE Listen to me. I have an idea of some kind. [*Shakily she twists a cigarette into her holder.*] Do you remember Shep Huntleigh? [STELLA *shakes her head.*] Of course you remember Shep Huntleigh. I went out with him at college and wore his pin[2] for a while. Well—

STELLA Well?

BLANCHE I ran into him last winter. You know I went to Miami during the Christmas holidays?

STELLA No.

BLANCHE Well, I did. I took the trip as an investment, thinking I'd meet someone with a million dollars.

STELLA Did you?

BLANCHE Yes. I ran into Shep Huntleigh—I ran into him on Biscayne Boulevard, on Christmas Eve, about dusk . . . getting into his car—Cadillac convertible; must have been a block long!

STELLA I should think it would have been—inconvenient in traffic!

BLANCHE You've heard of oil wells?

STELLA Yes—remotely.

BLANCHE He has them, all over Texas. Texas is literally spouting gold in his pockets.

STELLA My, my.

BLANCHE Y'know how indifferent I am to money. I think of money in terms of what it does for you. But he could do it, he could certainly do it!

STELLA Do what, Blanche?

BLANCHE Why—set us up in a—shop!

STELLA What kind of a shop?

BLANCHE Oh, a—shop of some kind! He could do it with half what his wife throws away at the races.

STELLA He's married?

BLANCHE Honey, would I be here if the man weren't married? [STELLA *laughs a little.* BLANCHE *suddenly springs up and crosses to phone. She speaks shrilly.*] How do I get Western Union?[3]—Operator! Western Union!

STELLA That's a dial phone,[4] honey.

BLANCHE I can't dial, I'm too—

STELLA Just dial O.

BLANCHE O?

2. A fraternity pin, worn as a sign that a couple were "going steady."
3. The dominant American telegraph company for most of the twentieth century.
4. Though dial telephones came into use in the 1930s, in some parts of the country (rural Mississippi presumably among them) operators placed all calls for another decade or more.

STELLA Yes, "O" for Operator! [BLANCHE *considers a moment; then she puts the phone down.*]

BLANCHE Give me a pencil. Where is a slip of paper? I've got to write it down first—the message, I mean . . .

[*She goes to the dressing table, and grabs up a sheet of Kleenex and an eyebrow pencil for writing equipment.*]

Let me see now . . . [*She bites the pencil.*] 'Darling Shep. Sister and I in desperate situation.'

STELLA I beg your pardon!

BLANCHE 'Sister and I in desperate situation. Will explain details later. Would you be interested in—?' [*She bites the pencil again.*] 'Would you be—interested—in . . .' [*She smashes the pencil on the table and springs up.*] You never get anywhere with direct appeals!

STELLA [*with a laugh*] Don't be so ridiculous, darling!

BLANCHE But I'll think of something, I've *got* to think of—*some*thing! Don't, don't laugh at me, Stella! Please, please don't—I—I want you to look at the contents of my purse! Here's what's in it! [*She snatches her purse open.*] Sixty-five measly cents in coin of the realm!

STELLA [*crossing to bureau*] Stanley doesn't give me a regular allowance, he likes to pay bills himself, but—this morning he gave me ten dollars to smooth things over. You take five of it, Blanche, and I'll keep the rest.

BLANCHE Oh, no. No, Stella.

STELLA [*insisting*] I know how it helps your morale just having a little pocket money on you.

BLANCHE No, thank you—I'll take to the streets!

STELLA Talk sense! How did you happen to get so low on funds?

BLANCHE Money just goes—it goes places. [*She rubs her forehead.*] Sometime today I've got to get hold of a Bromo![5]

STELLA I'll fix you one now.

BLANCHE Not yet—I've got to keep thinking!

STELLA I wish you'd just let things go, at least for a—while . . .

BLANCHE Stella, I can't live with him! You can, he's your husband. But how could I stay here with him, after last night, with just those curtains between us?

STELLA Blanche, you saw him at his worst last night.

BLANCHE On the contrary, I saw him at his best! What such a man has to offer is animal force and he gave a wonderful exhibition of that! But the only way to live with such a man is to—go to bed with him! And that's your job—not mine!

STELLA After you've rested a little, you'll see it's going to work out. You don't have to worry about anything while you're here. I mean—expenses . . .

BLANCHE I have to plan for us both, to get us both—out!

STELLA You take it for granted that I am in something that I want to get out of.

BLANCHE I take it for granted that you still have sufficient memory of Belle Reve to find this place and these poker players impossible to live with.

STELLA Well, you're taking entirely too much for granted.

BLANCHE I can't believe you're in earnest.

5. Bromo-Seltzer, a headache remedy and antacid introduced in 1891; its effervescent granules are dissolved in water.

STELLA No?

BLANCHE I understand how it happened—a little. You saw him in uniform, an officer, not here but—

STELLA I'm not sure it would have made any difference where I saw him.

BLANCHE Now don't say it was one of those mysterious electric things between people! If you do I'll laugh in your face.

STELLA I am not going to say anything more at all about it!

BLANCHE All right, then, don't!

STELLA But there are things that happen between a man and a woman in the dark—that sort of make everything else seem—unimportant. [*Pause*]

BLANCHE What you are talking about is brutal desire—just—Desire!—the name of that rattletrap streetcar that bangs through the Quarter, up one old narrow street and down another . . .

STELLA Haven't you ever ridden on that streetcar?

BLANCHE It brought me here.—Where I'm not wanted and where I'm ashamed to be . . .

STELLA Then don't you think your superior attitude is a bit out of place?

BLANCHE I am not being or feeling at all superior, Stella. Believe me I'm not! It's just this. This is how I look at it. A man like that is someone to go out with—once—twice—three times when the devil is in you. But live with? Have a child by?

STELLA I have told you I love him.

BLANCHE Then I *tremble* for you! I just—*tremble* for you. . . .

STELLA I can't help your trembling if you insist on trembling!

[*There is a pause.*]

BLANCHE May I—speak—*plainly?*

STELLA Yes, do. Go ahead. As plainly as you want to.

[*Outside, a train approaches. They are silent till the noise subsides. They are both in the bedroom.*]

[*Under cover of the train's noise* STANLEY *enters from outside. He stands unseen by the women, holding some packages in his arms, and overhears their following conversation. He wears an undershirt and grease-stained seersucker pants.*]

BLANCHE Well—if you'll forgive me—he's *common!*

STELLA Why, yes, I suppose he is.

BLANCHE Suppose! You can't have forgotten that much of our bringing up, Stella, that you just *suppose* that any part of a gentleman's in his nature! *Not one particle, no!* Oh, if he was just—*ordinary!* Just *plain*—but good and wholesome, but—*no*. There's something downright—*bestial*—about him! You're hating me saying this, aren't you?

STELLA [*coldly*] Go on and say it all, Blanche.

BLANCHE He acts like an animal, has an animal's habits! Eats like one, moves like one, talks like one! There's even something—subhuman—something not quite to the stage of humanity yet! Yes, something—apelike about him, like one of those pictures I've seen in—anthropological studies! Thousands and thousands of years have passed him right by, and there he is—Stanley Kowalski—survivor of the Stone Age! Bearing the raw meat home from the kill in the jungle! And you—*you* here—*waiting* for him! Maybe he'll strike you or maybe grunt and kiss you! That is, if kisses have been discovered yet! Night falls and the other apes gather! There in the front of the cave, all grunting like him, and swilling and gnawing and hulking! His poker night!—you call it—this party of apes! Somebody growls—some creature snatches at something—the fight is on! *God!* Maybe we are a long way from being made in God's image, but Stella—my sister—there has been *some* progress since then! Such things as art—as poetry and music—such kinds of new light have come into the world since then! In some kinds of people some tenderer feelings have had some little beginning! That we have got to make *grow!* And *cling* to, and hold as our flag! In this dark march toward whatever it is we're approaching. . . . *Don't—don't hang back with the brutes!*

[*Another train passes outside.* STANLEY *hesitates, licking his lips. Then suddenly he turns stealthily about and withdraws through front door. The women are still unaware of his presence. When the train has passed he calls through the closed front door.*]

STANLEY Hey! Hey, Stella!

STELLA [*who has listened gravely to* BLANCHE] Stanley!

BLANCHE Stell, I—

[*But* STELLA *has gone to the front door.* STANLEY *enters casually with his packages.*]

STANLEY Hiyuh, Stella. Blanche back?

STELLA Yes, she's back.

STANLEY Hiyuh, Blanche. [*He grins at her.*]

STELLA You must've got under the car.

STANLEY Them darn mechanics at Fritz's don't know their ass fr'm—*Hey!*

[STELLA *has embraced him with both arms, fiercely, and full in the view of* BLANCHE. *He laughs and clasps her head to him. Over her head he grins through the curtains at* BLANCHE.]

[*As the lights fade away, with a lingering brightness on their embrace, the music of the "blue piano" and trumpet and drums is heard.*]

Scene 5

BLANCHE *is seated in the bedroom fanning herself with a palm leaf as she reads over a just-completed letter. Suddenly she bursts into a peal of laughter.* STELLA *is dressing in the bedroom.*

STELLA What are you laughing at, honey?

BLANCHE Myself, myself, for being such a liar! I'm writing a letter to Shep. [*She picks up the letter.*] "Darling Shep. I am spending the summer on the wing, making flying visits here and there. And who knows, perhaps I shall take a sudden notion to *swoop* down on *Dallas!* How would you feel about that? Ha-ha! [*She laughs nervously and brightly, touching her throat as if actually talking to Shep.*] Forewarned is forearmed, as they say!"—How does that sound?

STELLA Uh-huh . . .

BLANCHE [*going on nervously*] "Most of my sister's friends go north in the summer but some have homes on the Gulf and there has been a continued round of entertainments, teas, cocktails, and luncheons—"

[*A disturbance is heard upstairs at the Hubbells' apartment.*]

STELLA Eunice seems to be having some trouble with Steve.

[EUNICE's *voice shouts in terrible wrath.*]

EUNICE I heard about you and that blonde!

STEVE That's a damn lie!

EUNICE You ain't pulling the wool over my eyes! I wouldn't mind if you'd stay down at the Four Deuces, but you always going up.

STEVE Who ever seen me up?

EUNICE I seen you chasing her 'round the balcony—I'm gonna call the vice squad!

STEVE Don't you throw that at me!

EUNICE [*shrieking*] You hit me! I'm gonna call the police!

[*A clatter of aluminum striking a wall is heard, followed by a man's angry roar, shouts and overturned furniture. There is a crash; then a relative hush.*]

BLANCHE [*brightly*] Did he *kill* her?

[EUNICE *appears on the steps in daemonic disorder.*]

STELLA No! She's coming downstairs.

EUNICE Call the police, I'm going to call the police! [*She rushes around the corner.*]

[*They laugh lightly.* STANLEY *comes around the corner in his green and scarlet silk bowling shirt. He trots up the steps and bangs into the kitchen.* BLANCHE *registers his entrance with nervous gestures.*]

STANLEY What's a matter with Eun-uss?

STELLA She and Steve had a row. Has she got the police?

STANLEY Naw. She's gettin' a drink.

STELLA That's much more practical!

[STEVE *comes down nursing a bruise on his forehead and looks in the door.*]

STEVE She here?

STANLEY Naw, naw. At the Four Deuces.

STEVE That rutting hunk! [*He looks around the corner a bit timidly, then turns with affected boldness and runs after her.*]

BLANCHE I must jot that down in my notebook. Ha-ha! I'm compiling a notebook of quaint little words and phrases I've picked up here.

STANLEY You won't pick up nothing here you ain't heard before.

BLANCHE Can I count on that?

STANLEY You can count on it up to five hundred.

BLANCHE That's a mighty high number. [*He jerks open the bureau drawer, slams it shut and throws shoes in a corner. At each noise* BLANCHE *winces slightly. Finally she speaks.*] What sign were you born under?

STANLEY [*while he is dressing*] Sign?

BLANCHE Astrological sign. I bet you were born under Aries. Aries people are forceful and dynamic. They dote on noise! They love to bang things around! You must have had lots of banging around in the army and now that you're out, you make up for it by treating inanimate objects with such a fury!

[STELLA *has been going in and out of closet during this scene. Now she pops her head out of the closet.*]

STELLA Stanley was born just five minutes after Christmas.

BLANCHE Capricorn—the Goat!

STANLEY What sign were *you* born under?

BLANCHE Oh, my birthday's next month, the fifteenth of September; that's under Virgo.

STANLEY What's Virgo?

BLANCHE Virgo is the Virgin.

STANLEY [*contemptuously*] *Hah!* [*He advances a little as he knots his tie.*] Say, do you happen to know somebody named Shaw?

[*Her face expresses a faint shock. She reaches for the cologne bottle and dampens her handkerchief as she answers carefully.*]

BLANCHE Why, everybody knows somebody named Shaw!

STANLEY Well, this somebody named Shaw is under the impression he met you in Laurel, but I figure he must have got you mixed up with some other party because this other party is someone he met at a hotel called the Flamingo.

[BLANCHE *laughs breathlessly as she touches the cologne-dampened handkerchief to her temples.*]

BLANCHE I'm afraid he does have me mixed up with this "other party." The Hotel Flamingo is not the sort of establishment I would dare to be seen in!

STANLEY You know of it?

BLANCHE Yes, I've seen it and smelled it.

STANLEY You must've got pretty close if you could smell it.

BLANCHE The odor of cheap perfume is penetrating.

STANLEY That stuff you use is expensive?

BLANCHE Twenty-five dollars an ounce! I'm nearly out. That's just a hint if you want to remember my birthday! [*She speaks lightly but her voice has a note of fear.*]

STANLEY Shaw must've got you mixed up. He goes in and out of Laurel all the time so he can check on it and clear up any mistake.

[*He turns away and crosses to the portieres.* BLANCHE *closes her eyes as if faint. Her hand trembles as she lifts the handkerchief again to her forehead.*]

[STEVE *and* EUNICE *come around corner.* STEVE*'s arm is around* EUNICE*'s shoulder and she is sobbing luxuriously and he is cooing love-words. There is a murmur of thunder as they go slowly upstairs in a tight embrace.*]

STANLEY [*to* STELLA] I'll wait for you at the Four Deuces!

STELLA Hey! Don't I rate one kiss?

STANLEY Not in front of your sister.

[*He goes out.* BLANCHE *rises from her chair. She seems faint; looks about her with an expression of almost panic.*]

BLANCHE Stella! What have you heard about me?

STELLA Huh?

BLANCHE What have people been telling you about me?

STELLA Telling?

BLANCHE You haven't heard any—unkind—gossip about me?

STELLA Why, no, Blanche, of course not!

BLANCHE Honey, there was—a good deal of talk in Laurel.

STELLA About *you,* Blanche?

BLANCHE I wasn't so good the last two years or so, after Belle Reve had started to slip through my fingers.

STELLA All of us do things we—

BLANCHE I never was hard or self-sufficient enough. When people are soft—soft people have got to shimmer and glow—they've got to put on soft colors, the colors of butterfly wings, and put a—paper lantern over the light. . . . It isn't enough to be soft. You've got to be soft *and attractive*. And I—I'm fading now! I don't know how much longer I can turn the trick.

[*The afternoon has faded to dusk.* STELLA *goes into the bedroom and turns on the light under the paper lantern. She holds a bottled soft drink in her hand.*]

BLANCHE Have you been listening to me?

STELLA I don't listen to you when you are being morbid! [*She advances with the bottled Coke.*]

BLANCHE [*with abrupt change to gaiety*] Is that Coke for me?

STELLA Not for anyone else!

BLANCHE Why, you precious thing, you! Is it just Coke?

STELLA [*turning*] You mean you want a shot in it!

BLANCHE Well, honey, a shot never does a Coke any harm! Let me! You mustn't wait on me!

STELLA I like to wait on you, Blanche. It makes it seem more like home. [*She goes into the kitchen, finds a glass and pours a shot of whiskey into it.*]

BLANCHE I have to admit I love to be waited on . . .

[*She rushes into the bedroom.* STELLA *goes to her with the glass.* BLANCHE *suddenly clutches* STELLA*'s free hand with a moaning sound and presses the hand to her lips.* STELLA *is embarrassed by her show of emotion.* BLANCHE *speaks in a choked voice.*]

You're—you're—so *good* to me! And I—

STELLA Blanche.

BLANCHE I know, I won't! You hate me to talk sentimental! But honey, *believe* I feel things more than I *tell* you! I *won't* stay long! I won't, I *promise* I—

STELLA Blanche!

BLANCHE [*hysterically*] I won't, I promise, *I'll* go! Go *soon!* I will *really!* I *won't* hang around until he—throws me out . . .

STELLA Now will you stop talking foolish?

BLANCHE Yes, honey. Watch how you pour—that fizzy stuff foams over!

[BLANCHE *laughs shrilly and grabs the glass, but her hand shakes so it almost slips from her grasp.* STELLA *pours the Coke into the glass. It foams over and spills.* BLANCHE *gives a piercing cry.*]

STELLA [*shocked by the cry*] Heavens!

BLANCHE Right on my pretty white skirt!

STELLA Oh . . . Use my hanky. Blot gently.

BLANCHE [*slowly recovering*] I know—gently—gently . . .

STELLA Did it stain?

BLANCHE Not a bit. Ha-ha! Isn't that lucky? [*She sits down shakily, taking a grateful drink. She holds the glass in both hands and continues to laugh a little.*]

STELLA Why did you scream like that?

BLANCHE I don't know why I screamed! [*Continuing nervously*] Mitch—Mitch is coming at seven. I guess I am just feeling nervous about our relations. [*She begins to talk rapidly and breathlessly.*] He hasn't gotten a thing but a good-night kiss, that's all I have given him, Stella. I want his respect. And men don't want anything they get too easy. But on the other hand men lose interest quickly. Especially when the girl is over—thirty. They think a girl over thirty ought to—the vulgar term is—"put out." . . . And I—I'm not "putting out." Of course he—he doesn't know—I mean I haven't informed him—of my real age!

STELLA Why are you sensitive about your age?

BLANCHE Because of hard knocks my vanity's been given. What I mean is—he thinks I'm sort of—prim and proper, you know! [*She laughs out sharply.*] I want to *deceive* him enough to make him—want me . . .

STELLA Blanche, do you want *him?*

BLANCHE I want to *rest!* I want to breathe quietly again! Yes—I *want* Mitch . . . *very badly!* Just think! If it happens! I can leave here and not be anyone's problem . . .

[STANLEY *comes around the corner with a drink under his belt.*]

STANLEY [*bawling*] Hey, Steve! Hey, Eunice! Hey, Stella!

[*There are joyous calls from above. Trumpet and drums are heard from around the corner.*]

STELLA [*kissing* BLANCHE *impulsively*] It *will* happen!

BLANCHE [*doubtfully*] It will?

STELLA It *will!* [*She goes across into the kitchen, looking back at* BLANCHE.] It will, honey, *it will.* . . . But don't take another drink! [*Her voice catches as she goes out the door to meet her husband.*

[BLANCHE *sinks faintly back in her chair with her drink.* EUNICE *shrieks with laughter and runs down the steps.* STEVE *bounds after her with goat-like screeches and chases her around corner.* STANLEY *and* STELLA *twine arms as they follow, laughing.*]

[*Dusk settles deeper. The music from the Four Deuces is slow and blue.*]

BLANCHE Ah, me, ah, me, ah, me . . .

[*Her eyes fall shut and the palm leaf fan drops from her fingers. She slaps her hand on the chair arm a couple of times. There is a little glimmer of lightning about the building.*]

[*A* YOUNG MAN *comes along the street and rings the bell.*]

BLANCHE Come in.

[*The* YOUNG MAN *appears through the portieres. She regards him with interest.*]

BLANCHE Well, well! What can I do for *you?*

YOUNG MAN I'm collecting for *The Evening Star.*

BLANCHE I didn't know that stars took up collections.

YOUNG MAN It's the paper.

BLANCHE I know, I was joking—feebly! Will you—have a drink?

YOUNG MAN No, ma'am. No, thank you. I can't drink on the job.

BLANCHE Oh, well, now, let's see. . . . No, I don't have a dime! I'm not the lady of the house. I'm her sister from Mississippi. I'm one of those poor relations you've heard about.

YOUNG MAN That's all right. I'll drop by later. [*He starts to go out. She approaches a little.*]

BLANCHE Hey! [*He turns back shyly. She puts a cigarette in a long holder.*] Could you give me a light? [*She crosses toward him. They meet at the door between the two rooms.*]

YOUNG MAN Sure. [*He takes out a lighter.*] This doesn't always work.

BLANCHE It's temperamental? [*It flares.*] Ah!—thank you. [*He starts away again.*] Hey! [*He turns again, still more uncertainly. She goes close to him.*] Uh—what time is it?

YOUNG MAN Fifteen of seven, ma'am.

BLANCHE So late? Don't you just love these long rainy afternoons in New Orleans when an hour isn't just an hour—but a little piece of eternity dropped into your hands—and who knows what to do with it? [*She touches his shoulders.*] You—uh—didn't get wet in the rain?

YOUNG MAN No, ma'am. I stepped inside.

BLANCHE In a drugstore? And had a soda?

YOUNG MAN Uh-huh.

BLANCHE Chocolate?

YOUNG MAN No, ma'am. Cherry.

BLANCHE [*laughing*] Cherry!

YOUNG MAN A cherry soda.

BLANCHE You make my mouth water. [*She touches his cheek lightly, and smiles. Then she goes to the trunk.*]

YOUNG MAN Well, I'd better be going—

BLANCHE [*stopping him*] Young man!

[*He turns. She takes a large, gossamer scarf from the trunk and drapes it about her shoulders.*]

[*In the ensuing pause, the "blue piano" is heard. It continues through the rest of this scene and the opening of the next. The young man clears his throat and looks yearningly at the door.*]

Young man! Young, young, young man! Has anyone ever told you that you look like a young Prince out of the Arabian Nights?[6]

[*The* YOUNG MAN *laughs uncomfortably and stands like a bashful kid.* BLANCHE *speaks softly to him.*]

Well, you do, honey lamb! Come here. I want to kiss you, just once, softly and sweetly on your mouth!

[*Without waiting for him to accept, she crosses quickly to him and presses her lips to his.*]

Now run along, now, quickly! It would be nice to keep you, but I've got to be good—and keep my hands off children.

[*He stares at her a moment. She opens the door for him and blows a kiss at him as he goes down the steps with a dazed look. She stands there a little dreamily after he has disappeared. Then* MITCH *appears around the corner with a bunch of roses.*]

BLANCHE [*gaily*] Look who's coming! My Rosenkavalier! Bow to me first . . . now present them! *Ahhhh—Merciiii!*[7]

[*She looks at him over them, coquettishly pressing them to her lips. He beams at her self-consciously.*]

6. That is, *The Thousand and One Nights*, a collection of ancient tales in Arabic, arranged in its present form in the 15th century.

7. Thank you (French). *Rosenkavalier:* literally, "Knight of the Rose" (German), an allusion to Richard Strauss's romantic opera *Der Rosenkavalier* (1911).

Scene 6

It is about two A.M. *on the same evening. The outer wall of the building is visible.* BLANCHE *and* MITCH *come in. The utter exhaustion which only a neurasthenic personality*[8] *can know is evident in* BLANCHE'S *voice and manner.* MITCH *is stolid but depressed. They have probably been out to the amusement park on Lake Pontchartrain, for* MITCH *is bearing, upside down, a plaster statuette of Mae West,*[9] *the sort of prize won at shooting galleries and carnival games of chance.*

BLANCHE [*stopping lifelessly at the steps*] Well—

[MITCH *laughs uneasily.*]

Well . . .

MITCH I guess it must be pretty late—and you're tired.

BLANCHE Even the hot tamale man has deserted the street, and he hangs on till the end. [MITCH *laughs uneasily again.*] How will you get home?

MITCH I'll walk over to Bourbon and catch an owl-car.[1]

BLANCHE [*laughing grimly*] Is that streetcar named Desire still grinding along the tracks at this hour?

MITCH [*heavily*] I'm afraid you haven't gotten much fun out of this evening, Blanche.

BLANCHE I spoiled it for *you.*

MITCH No, you didn't, but I felt all the time that I wasn't giving you much—entertainment.

BLANCHE I simply couldn't rise to the occasion. That was all. I don't think I've ever tried so hard to be gay and made such a dismal mess of it. I get ten points for trying!—I *did* try.

MITCH Why did you try if you didn't feel like it, Blanche?

BLANCHE I was just obeying the law of nature.

MITCH Which law is that?

BLANCHE The one that says the lady must entertain the gentleman—or no dice! See if you can locate my door key in this purse. When I'm so tired my fingers are all thumbs!

MITCH [*rooting in her purse*] This it?

BLANCHE No, honey, that's the key to my trunk which I must soon be packing.

MITCH You mean you are leaving here soon?

BLANCHE I've outstayed my welcome.

MITCH This it?

[*The music fades away.*]

BLANCHE Eureka! Honey, you open the door while I take a last look at the sky. [*She leans on the porch rail. He opens the door and stands awkwardly behind her.*] I'm looking for the Pleiades, the Seven Sisters,[2] but these girls are not out tonight. Oh, yes they are, there they are! God bless them! All in

8. Someone suffering from neurasthenia, a psychological disorder characterized by nervous exhaustion. A common clinical diagnosis during the late 19th century, the term is no longer in scientific use.

9. An American actress of burlesque shows, stage, and screen (1893–1980), famous for her sexual double entendres. *Lake Ponchartrain:* the large, shallow lake immediately north of New Orleans.

1. A late-night streetcar (i.e., for "night owls").

2. In Greek mythology, the Pleiades are the seven daughters of Atlas who were changed into a cluster of stars in the constellation Taurus.

a bunch going home from their little bridge party. . . . Y' get the door open? Good boy! I guess you—want to go now . . .

[*He shuffles and coughs a little.*]

MITCH Can I—uh—kiss you—good night?

BLANCHE Why do you always ask me if you may?

MITCH I don't know whether you want me to or not.

BLANCHE Why should you be so doubtful?

MITCH That night when we parked by the lake and I kissed you, you—

BLANCHE Honey, it wasn't the kiss I objected to. I liked the kiss very much. It was the other little—familiarity—that I—felt obliged to—discourage. . . . I didn't resent it! Not a bit in the world! In fact, I was somewhat flattered that you—desired me! But, honey, you know as well as I do that a single girl, a girl alone in the world, has got to keep a firm hold on her emotions or she'll be lost!

MITCH [*solemnly*] Lost?

BLANCHE I guess you are used to girls that like to be lost. The kind that get lost immediately, on the first date!

MITCH I like you to be exactly the way that you are, because in all my—experience—I have never known anyone like you.

[BLANCHE *looks at him gravely; then she bursts into laughter and then claps a hand to her mouth.*]

MITCH Are you laughing at me?

BLANCHE No, honey. The lord and lady of the house have not yet returned, so come in. We'll have a nightcap. Let's leave the lights off. Shall we?

MITCH You just—do what you want to.

[BLANCHE *precedes him into the kitchen. The outer wall of the building disappears and the interiors of the two rooms can be dimly seen.*]

BLANCHE [*remaining in the first room*] The other room's more comfortable—go on in. This crashing around in the dark is my search for some liquor.

MITCH You want a drink?

BLANCHE I want *you* to have a drink! You have been so anxious and solemn all evening, and so have I; we have both been anxious and solemn and now for these few last remaining moments of our lives together—I want to create—*joie de vivre!*[3] I'm lighting a candle.

MITCH That's good.

BLANCHE We are going to be very Bohemian. We are going to pretend that we are sitting in a little artists' cafe on the Left Bank[4] in Paris! [*She lights a candle stub and puts it in a bottle.*] *Je suis la Dame aux Camellias! Vous êtes—Armand!*[5] Understand French?

MITCH [*heavily*] Naw. Naw, I—

3. Joy of life (French).
4. A neighborhood on the western ("left") bank of the river Seine, known for cultural and intellectual activities.
5. I am the Lady of the Camellias. You are—Armand! (French). The reference is to Alexandre Dumas's novel *La Dame aux camélias* (1848), the tragic story of Marguerite Gautier, a Parisian courtesan who falls in love with Armand Duval, a respectable member of middle-class society, and dies of consumption. Dumas's 1852 theatrical adaptation of this novel (often titled *Camille* in English) was highly popular with late 19th-century audiences.

BLANCHE *Voulez-vous couchez avec moi ce soir? Vous ne comprenez pas? Ah, quelle dommage!*[6] I mean it's a damned good thing. . . . I've found some liquor! Just enough for two shots without any dividends, honey . . .

MITCH [*heavily*] That's—good.

[*She enters the bedroom with the drinks and the candle.*]

BLANCHE Sit down! Why don't you take off your coat and loosen your collar?

MITCH I better leave it on.

BLANCHE No. I want you to be comfortable.

MITCH I am ashamed of the way I perspire. My shirt is sticking to me.

BLANCHE Perspiration is healthy. If people didn't perspire they would die in five minutes. [*She takes his coat from him.*] This is a nice coat. What kind of material is it?

MITCH They call that stuff alpaca.

BLANCHE Oh. Alpaca.

MITCH It's very light-weight alpaca.

BLANCHE Oh. Light-weight alpaca.

MITCH I don't like to wear a wash-coat[7] even in summer because I sweat through it.

BLANCHE Oh.

MITCH And it don't look neat on me. A man with a heavy build has got to be careful of what he puts on him so he don't look too clumsy.

BLANCHE You are not too heavy.

MITCH You don't think I am?

BLANCHE You are not the delicate type. You have a massive bone-structure and a very imposing physique.

MITCH Thank you. Last Christmas I was given a membership to the New Orleans Athletic Club.

BLANCHE Oh, good.

MITCH It was the finest present I ever was given. I work out there with the weights and I swim and I keep myself fit. When I started there, I was getting soft in the belly but now my belly is hard. It is so hard now that a man can punch me in the belly and it don't hurt me. Punch me! Go on! See? [*She pokes lightly at him.*]

BLANCHE Gracious. [*Her hand touches her chest.*]

MITCH Guess how much I weigh, Blanche?

BLANCHE Oh, I'd say in the vicinity of—one hundred and eighty?

MITCH Guess again.

BLANCHE Not that much?

MITCH No. More.

BLANCHE Well, you're a tall man and you can carry a good deal of weight without looking awkward.

MITCH I weigh two hundred and seven pounds and I'm six feet one and one half inches tall in my bare feet—without shoes on. And that is what I weigh stripped.

BLANCHE Oh, my goodness, me! It's awe-inspiring.

6. Would you like to go to bed with me tonight? You don't understand? Ah, what a shame! (French).

7. A light washable jacket, here made of a silky wool.

MITCH [*embarrassed*] My weight is not a very interesting subject to talk about. [*He hesitates for a moment.*] What's yours?

BLANCHE My weight?

MITCH Yes.

BLANCHE Guess!

MITCH Let me lift you.

BLANCHE Samson![8] Go on, lift me. [*He comes behind her and puts his hands on her waist and raises her lightly off the ground.*] Well?

MITCH You are light as a feather.

BLANCHE Ha-ha! [*He lowers her but keeps his hands on her waist.* BLANCHE *speaks with an affectation of demureness.*] You may release me now.

MITCH Huh?

BLANCHE [*gaily*] I said unhand me, sir. [*He fumblingly embraces her. Her voice sounds gently reproving.*] Now, Mitch. Just because Stanley and Stella aren't at home is no reason why you shouldn't behave like a gentleman.

MITCH Just give me a slap whenever I step out of bounds.

BLANCHE That won't be necessary. You're a natural gentleman, one of the very few that are left in the world. I don't want you to think that I am severe and old maid school-teacherish or anything like that. It's just—well—

MITCH Huh?

BLANCHE I guess it is just that I have—old-fashioned ideals! [*She rolls her eyes, knowing he cannot see her face.* MITCH *goes to the front door. There is a considerable silence between them.* BLANCHE *sighs and* MITCH *coughs self-consciously.*]

MITCH [*finally*] Where's Stanley and Stella tonight?

BLANCHE They have gone out. With Mr. and Mrs. Hubbell upstairs.

MITCH Where did they go?

BLANCHE I think they were planning to go to a midnight prevue at Loew's State.

MITCH We should all go out together some night.

BLANCHE No. That wouldn't be a good plan.

MITCH Why not?

BLANCHE You are an old friend of Stanley's?

MITCH We was together in the Two-forty-first.[9]

BLANCHE I guess he talks to you frankly?

MITCH Sure.

BLANCHE Has he talked to you about me?

MITCH Oh—not very much.

BLANCHE The way you say that, I suspect that he has.

MITCH No, he hasn't said much.

BLANCHE But what he *has* said. What would you say his attitude toward me was?

MITCH Why do you want to ask that?

BLANCHE Well—

MITCH Don't you get along with him?

BLANCHE What do you think?

MITCH I don't think he understands you.

8. An Israelite hero of great strength (see Judges 13–16).

9. The 241st Battalion of the Army Corps of Engineers.

BLANCHE That is putting it mildly. If it weren't for Stella about to have a baby, I wouldn't be able to endure things here.

MITCH He isn't—nice to you?

BLANCHE He is insufferably rude. Goes out of his way to offend me.

MITCH In what way, Blanche?

BLANCHE Why, in every conceivable way.

MITCH I'm surprised to hear that.

BLANCHE Are you?

MITCH Well, I—don't see how anybody could be rude to you.

BLANCHE It's really a pretty frightful situation. You see, there's no privacy here. There's just these portieres between the two rooms at night. He stalks through the rooms in his underwear at night. And I have to ask him to close the bathroom door. That sort of commonness isn't necessary. You probably wonder why I don't move out. Well, I'll tell you frankly. A teacher's salary is barely sufficient for her living expenses. I didn't save a penny last year and so I had to come here for the summer. That's why I have to put up with my sister's husband. And he has to put up with me, apparently so much against his wishes. . . . Surely he must have told you how much he hates me!

MITCH I don't think he hates you.

BLANCHE He hates me. Or why would he insult me? The first time I laid eyes on him I thought to myself, that man is my executioner! That man will destroy me, unless—

MITCH Blanche—

BLANCHE Yes, honey?

MITCH Can I ask you a question?

BLANCHE Yes. What?

MITCH How old are you?

[*She makes a nervous gesture.*]

BLANCHE Why do you want to know?

MITCH I talked to my mother about you and she said, "How old is Blanche?" And I wasn't able to tell her. [*There is another pause.*]

BLANCHE You talked to your mother about me?

MITCH Yes.

BLANCHE Why?

MITCH I told my mother how nice you were, and I liked you.

BLANCHE Were you sincere about that?

MITCH You know I was.

BLANCHE Why did your mother want to know my age?

MITCH Mother is sick.

BLANCHE I'm sorry to hear it. Badly?

MITCH She won't live long. Maybe just a few months.

BLANCHE Oh.

MITCH She worries because I'm not settled.

BLANCHE Oh.

MITCH She wants me to be settled down before she—[*His voice is hoarse and he clears his throat twice, shuffling nervously around with his hands in and out of his pockets.*]

BLANCHE You love her very much, don't you?

MITCH Yes.

BLANCHE I think you have a great capacity for devotion. You will be lonely when she passes on, won't you? [MITCH *clears his throat and nods.*] I understand what that is.

MITCH To be lonely?

BLANCHE I loved someone, too, and the person I loved I lost.

MITCH Dead? [*She crosses to the window and sits on the sill, looking out. She pours herself another drink.*] A man?

BLANCHE He was a boy, just a boy, when I was a very young girl. When I was sixteen, I made the discovery—love. All at once and much, much too completely. It was like you suddenly turned a blinding light on something that had always been half in shadow, that's how it struck the world for me. But I was unlucky. Deluded. There was something different about the boy, a nervousness, a softness and tenderness which wasn't like a man's, although he wasn't the least bit effeminate-looking—still—that thing was there. . . . He came to me for help. I didn't know that. I didn't find out anything till after our marriage when we'd run away and come back and all I knew was I'd failed him in some mysterious way and wasn't able to give the help he needed but couldn't speak of! He was in the quicksands and clutching at me—but I wasn't holding him out, I was slipping in with him! I didn't know that. I didn't know anything except I loved him unendurably but without being able to help him or help myself. Then I found out. In the worst of all possible ways. By coming suddenly into a room that I thought was empty—which wasn't empty, but had two people in it . . . the boy I had married and an older man who had been his friend for years . . .

[*A locomotive is heard approaching outside. She claps her hands to her ears and crouches over. The headlight of the locomotive glares into the room as it thunders past. As the noise recedes she straightens slowly and continues speaking.*]

Afterward we pretended that nothing had been discovered. Yes, the three of us drove out to Moon Lake Casino,[1] very drunk and laughing all the way.

[*Polka music sounds, in a minor key faint with distance.*]

We danced the Varsouviana![2] Suddenly in the middle of the dance the boy I had married broke away from me and ran out of the casino. A few moments later—a shot!

[*The polka stops abruptly.*]

[BLANCHE *rises stiffly. Then, the polka resumes in a major key.*]

I ran out—all did!—all ran and gathered about the terrible thing at the edge of the lake! I couldn't get near for the crowding. Then somebody caught my arm. "Don't go any closer! Come back! You don't want to see!" See? See what! Then I heard voices say—Allan! Allan! The Grey boy! He'd stuck the revolver into his mouth, and fired—so that the back of his head had been—blown away!

[*She sways and covers her face.*]

It was because—on the dance floor—unable to stop myself—I'd suddenly said—"I saw! I know! You disgust me . . ." And then the searchlight which had been turned on the world was turned off again and never for one

1. A popular night spot and casino during the 1940s, located in Dundee, Mississippi.

2. A jaunty polka dance.

moment since has there been any light that's stronger than this—kitchen—candle . . .

[MITCH *gets up awkwardly and moves toward her a little. The polka music increases.* MITCH *stands beside her.*]

MITCH [*drawing her slowly into his arms*] You need somebody. And I need somebody, too. Could it be—you and me, Blanche?

[*She stares at him vacantly for a moment. Then with a soft cry huddles in his embrace. She makes a sobbing effort to speak but the words won't come. He kisses her forehead and her eyes and finally her lips. The polka tune fades out. Her breath is drawn and released in long, grateful sobs.*]

BLANCHE Sometimes—there's God—so quickly!

Scene 7

It is late afternoon in mid-September.

The portieres are open and a table is set for a birthday supper, with cake and flowers. STELLA *is completing the decorations as* STANLEY *comes in.*

STANLEY What's all this stuff for?

STELLA Honey, it's Blanche's birthday.

STANLEY She here?

STELLA In the bathroom.

STANLEY [*mimicking*] "Washing out some things"?

STELLA I reckon so.

STANLEY How long she been in there?

STELLA All afternoon.

STANLEY [*mimicking*] "Soaking in a hot tub"?

STELLA Yes.

STANLEY Temperature 100 on the nose, and she soaks herself in a hot tub.

STELLA She says it cools her off for the evening.

STANLEY And you run out an' get her cokes, I suppose? And serve 'em to Her Majesty in the tub? [STELLA *shrugs.*] Set down here a minute.

STELLA Stanley, I've got things to do.

STANLEY Set down! I've got th' dope on your big sister, Stella.

STELLA Stanley, stop picking on Blanche.

STANLEY That girl calls *me* common!

STELLA Lately you been doing all you can think of to rub her the wrong way, Stanley, and Blanche is sensitive and you've got to realize that Blanche and I grew up under very different circumstances than you did.

STANLEY So I been told. And told and told and told! You know she's been feeding us a pack of lies here?

STELLA No, I don't, and—

STANLEY Well, she has, however. But now the cat's out of the bag! I found out some things!

STELLA What—things?

STANLEY Things I already suspected. But now I got proof from the most reliable sources—which I have checked on!

[BLANCHE *is singing in the bathroom a saccharine popular ballad which is used contrapuntally with Stanley's speech.*]

STELLA [*to* STANLEY] Lower your voice!

STANLEY Some canary bird, huh!

STELLA Now please tell me quietly what you think you've found out about my sister.

STANLEY Lie Number One: All this squeamishness she puts on! You should just know the line she's been feeding to Mitch. He thought she had never been more than kissed by a fellow! But Sister Blanche is no lily! Ha-ha! Some lily she is!

STELLA What have you heard and who from?

STANLEY Our supply-man down at the plant has been going through Laurel for years and he knows all about her and everybody else in the town of Laurel knows all about her. She is as famous in Laurel as if she was the President of the United States, only she is not respected by any party! This supply-man stops at a hotel called the Flamingo.

BLANCHE [*singing blithely*]

> "Say, it's only a paper moon, Sailing over a cardboard sea—But it wouldn't be make-believe If you believed in me!"[3]

STELLA What about the—Flamingo?

STANLEY She stayed there, too.

STELLA My sister lived at Belle Reve.

STANLEY This is after the home-place had slipped through her lily-white fingers! She moved to the Flamingo! A second-class hotel which has the advantage of not interfering in the private social life of the personalities there! The Flamingo is used to all kinds of goings-on. But even the management of the Flamingo was impressed by Dame Blanche! In fact they was so impressed by Dame Blanche that they requested her to turn in her room key—for permanently! This happened a couple of weeks before she showed here.

BLANCHE [*singing*]

> "It's a Barnum and Bailey world,[4] Just as phony as it can be—
> But it wouldn't be make-believe If you believed in me!"

STELLA What—contemptible—lies!

STANLEY Sure, I can see how you would be upset by this. She pulled the wool over your eyes as much as Mitch's!

STELLA It's pure invention! There's not a word of truth in it and if I were a man and this creature had dared to invent such things in my presence—

BLANCHE [*singing*]

> "Without your love,
> It's a honky-tonk parade!
> Without your love,
> It's a melody played In a penny arcade . . ."

STANLEY Honey, I told you I thoroughly checked on these stories! Now wait till I finished. The trouble with Dame Blanche was that she couldn't put on her act any more in Laurel! They got wised up after two or three dates with her and then they quit, and she goes on to another, the same old line, same old act, same old hooey! But the town was too small for this to go on forever!

3. From "It's Only a Paper Moon" (lyrics by Yip Harburg and Billy Rose, music by Harold Arlen), used in the film *Take a Chance* (1933).

4. That is, a circus performance. P. T. Barnum (1810–1891) and James A. Bailey (1847–1906) merged their circuses in 1881.

And as time went by she became a town character. Regarded as not just different but downright loco—nuts.

[STELLA *draws back.*]

And for the last year or two she has been washed up like poison. That's why she's here this summer, visiting royalty, putting on all this act—because she's practically told by the mayor to get out of town! Yes, did you know there was an army camp near Laurel and your sister's was one of the places called "Out-of-Bounds"?

BLANCHE

"It's only a paper moon, Just as phony as it can be—
But it wouldn't be make-believe If you believed in me!"

STANLEY Well, so much for her being such a refined and particular type of girl. Which brings us to Lie Number Two.

STELLA I don't want to hear any more!

STANLEY She's not going back to teach school! In fact I am willing to bet you that she never had no idea of returning to Laurel! She didn't resign temporarily from the high school because of her nerves! No, siree, Bob! She didn't. They kicked her out of that high school before the spring term ended—and I hate to tell you the reason that step was taken! A seventeen-year-old boy—she'd gotten mixed up with!

BLANCHE

"It's a Barnum and Bailey world, Just as phony as it can be—"

[*In the bathroom the water goes on loud; little breathless cries and peals of laughter are heard as if a child were frolicking in the tub.*]

STELLA This is making me—sick!

STANLEY The boy's dad learned about it and got in touch with the high school superintendent. Boy, oh, boy, I'd like to have been in that office when Dame Blanche was called on the carpet! I'd like to have seen her trying to squirm out of that one! But they had her on the hook good and proper that time and she knew that the jig was all up! They told her she better move on to some fresh territory. Yep, it was practickly a town ordinance passed against her!

[*The bathroom door is opened and* BLANCHE *thrusts her head out, holding a towel about her hair.*]

BLANCHE Stella!

STELLA [*faintly*] Yes, Blanche?

BLANCHE Give me another bath-towel to dry my hair with. I've just washed it.

STELLA Yes, Blanche. [*She crosses in a dazed way from the kitchen to the bathroom door with a towel.*]

BLANCHE What's the matter, honey?

STELLA Matter? Why?

BLANCHE You have such a strange expression on your face!

STELLA Oh—[*She tries to laugh.*] I guess I'm a little tired!

BLANCHE Why don't you bathe, too, soon as I get out?

STANLEY [*calling from the kitchen*] How soon is that going to be?

BLANCHE Not so terribly long! Possess your soul in patience![5]

5. "In your patience possess ye your souls" (Luke 21:19).

STANLEY It's not my soul, it's my kidneys I'm worried about!

[BLANCHE *slams the door.* STANLEY *laughs harshly.* STELLA *comes slowly back into the kitchen.*]

STANLEY Well, what do you think of it?

STELLA I don't believe all of those stories and I think your supply-man was mean and rotten to tell them. It's possible that some of the things he said are partly true. There are things about my sister I don't approve of—things that caused sorrow at home. She was always—flighty!

STANLEY Flighty!

STELLA But when she was young, very young, she married a boy who wrote poetry. . . . He was extremely good-looking. I think Blanche didn't just love him but worshipped the ground he walked on! Adored him and thought him almost too fine to be human! But then she found out—

STANLEY What?

STELLA This beautiful and talented young man was a degenerate. Didn't your supply-man give you that information?

STANLEY All we discussed was recent history. That must have been a pretty long time ago.

STELLA Yes, it was—a pretty long time ago . . .

[STANLEY *comes up and takes her by the shoulders rather gently. She gently withdraws from him. Automatically she starts sticking little pink candles in the birthday cake.*]

STANLEY How many candles you putting in that cake?

STELLA I'll stop at twenty-five.

STANLEY Is company expected?

STELLA We asked Mitch to come over for cake and ice-cream.

[STANLEY *looks a little uncomfortable. He lights a cigarette from the one he has just finished.*]

STANLEY I wouldn't be expecting Mitch over tonight.

[STELLA *pauses in her occupation with candles and looks slowly around at* STANLEY.]

STELLA *Why?*

STANLEY Mitch is a buddy of mine. We were in the same outfit together—Two-forty-first Engineers. We work in the same plant and now on the same bowling team. You think I could face him if—

STELLA Stanley Kowalski, did you—did you repeat what that—?

STANLEY You're goddam right I told him! I'd have that on my conscience the rest of my life if I knew all that stuff and let my best friend get caught!

STELLA Is Mitch through with her?

STANLEY Wouldn't you be if—?

STELLA I said, *Is Mitch through with her?*

[BLANCHE*'s voice is lifted again, serenely as a bell. She sings "But it wouldn't be make-believe If you believed in me."*]

STANLEY No, I don't think he's necessarily through with her—just wised up!

STELLA Stanley, she thought Mitch was—going to—going to marry her. I was hoping so, too.

STANLEY Well, he's not going to marry her. Maybe he *was*, but he's not going to jump in a tank with a school of sharks—now! [*He rises.*] Blanche! Oh, Blanche! Can I please get in my bathroom? [*There is a pause.*]

BLANCHE Yes, indeed, sir! Can you wait one second while I dry?

STANLEY Having waited one hour I guess one second ought to pass in a hurry.

STELLA And she hasn't got her job? Well, what will she do!

STANLEY She's not stayin' here after Tuesday. You know that, don't you? Just to make sure I bought her ticket myself. A bus ticket?

STELLA In the first place, Blanche wouldn't go on a bus.

STANLEY She'll go on a bus and like it.

STELLA No, she won't, no, she won't, Stanley!

STANLEY *She'll go!* Period. P.S. She'll go *Tuesday!*

STELLA [*slowly*] What'll—she—do? What on earth will she—*do!*

STANLEY Her future is mapped out for her.

STELLA What do you mean?

[BLANCHE *sings.*]

STANLEY Hey, canary bird! Toots! Get *OUT* of the *BATHROOM!*

[*The bathroom door flies open and* BLANCHE *emerges with a gay peal of laughter, but as* STANLEY *crosses past her, a frightened look appears in her face, almost a look of panic. He doesn't look at her but slams the bathroom door shut as he goes in.*]

BLANCHE [*snatching up a hairbrush*] Oh, I feel so good after my long, hot bath, I feel so good and cool and—rested!

STELLA [*sadly and doubtfully from the kitchen*] Do you, Blanche?

BLANCHE [*brushing her hair vigorously*] Yes, I do, so refreshed! [*She tinkles her highball glass.*] A hot bath and a long, cold drink always give me a brand new outlook on life! [*She looks through the portieres at* STELLA, *standing between them, and slowly stops brushing.*] Something has happened!—What is it?

STELLA [*turning away quickly*] Why, nothing has happened, Blanche.

BLANCHE You're lying! Something has!

[*She stares fearfully at* STELLA, *who pretends to be busy at the table. The distant piano goes into a hectic breakdown.*]

Scene 8

Three-quarters of an hour later.

The view through the big windows is fading gradually into a still-golden dusk. A torch of sunlight blazes on the side of a big water-tank or oil-drum across the empty lot toward the business district which is now pierced by pinpoints of lighted windows or windows reflecting the sunset.

The three people are completing a dismal birthday supper. STANLEY *looks sullen.* STELLA *is embarrassed and sad.* BLANCHE *has a tight, artificial smile on her drawn face. There is a fourth place at the table which is left vacant.*

BLANCHE [*suddenly*] Stanley, tell us a joke, tell us a funny story to make us all laugh. I don't know what's the matter, we're all so solemn. Is it because I've been stood up by my beau?

[STELLA *laughs feebly.*]

It's the first time in my entire experience with men, and I've had a good deal of all sorts, that I've actually been stood up by anybody! Ha-ha! I don't know how to take it. . . . Tell us a funny little story, Stanley! Something to help us out.

STANLEY I didn't think you liked my stories, Blanche.

BLANCHE I like them when they're amusing but not indecent.

STANLEY I don't know any refined enough for your taste.

BLANCHE Then let me tell one.

STELLA Yes, you tell one, Blanche. You used to know lots of good stories.

[The music fades.]

BLANCHE Let me see, now. . . . I must run through my repertoire! Oh, yes—I love parrot stories! Do you all like parrot stories? Well, this one's about the old maid and the parrot. This old maid, she had a parrot that cursed a blue streak and knew more vulgar expressions than Mr. Kowalski!

STANLEY Huh.

BLANCHE And the only way to hush the parrot up was to put the cover back on its cage so it would think it was night and go back to sleep. Well, one morning the old maid had just uncovered the parrot for the day—when who should she see coming up the front walk but the preacher! Well, she rushed back to the parrot and slipped the cover back on the cage and then she let in the preacher. And the parrot was perfectly still, just as quiet as a mouse, but just as she was asking the preacher how much sugar he wanted in his coffee—the parrot broke the silence with a loud—[*She whistles.*]—and said—"God *damn,* but that was a short day!"

[*She throws back her head and laughs.* STELLA *also makes an ineffectual effort to seem amused.* STANLEY *pays no attention to the story but reaches way over the table to spear his fork into the remaining chop which he eats with his fingers.*]

BLANCHE Apparently Mr. Kowalski was not amused.

STELLA Mr. Kowalski is too busy making a pig of himself to think of anything else!

STANLEY That's right, baby.

STELLA Your face and your fingers are disgustingly greasy. Go and wash up and then help me clear the table.

[*He hurls a plate to the floor.*]

STANLEY That's how I'll clear the table! [*He seizes her arm.*] Don't ever talk that way to me! "Pig—Polack—disgusting—vulgar—greasy!"—them kind of words have been on your tongue and your sister's too much around here! What do you two think you are? A pair of queens? Remember what Huey Long said—"Every Man is a King!"[6] And I am the king around here, so don't forget it! [*He hurls a cup and saucer to the floor.*] My place is cleared! You want me to clear your places?

[STELLA *begins to cry weakly.* STANLEY *stalks out on the porch and lights a cigarette.*]

[*The Negro entertainers around the corner are heard.*]

BLANCHE What happened while I was bathing? What did he tell you, Stella?

STELLA Nothing, nothing, nothing!

BLANCHE I think he told you something about Mitch and me! You know why Mitch didn't come but you won't tell me! [STELLA *shakes her head helplessly.*] I'm going to call him!

STELLA I wouldn't call him, Blanche.

BLANCHE I am, I'm going to call him on the phone.

6. The slogan used by the populist Democrat Long (1893–1935) in his successful campaigns for governor of and then senator from Louisiana.

STELLA [*miserably*] I wish you wouldn't.

BLANCHE I intend to be given some explanation from someone!

[*She rushes to the phone in the bedroom.* STELLA *goes out on the porch and stares reproachfully at her husband. He grunts and turns away from her.*]

STELLA I hope you're pleased with your doings. I never had so much trouble swallowing food in my life, looking at that girl's face and the empty chair! [*She cries quietly.*]

BLANCHE [*at the phone*] Hello. Mr. Mitchell, please. . . . Oh. . . . I would like to leave a number if I may. Magnolia 9047. And say it's important to call. . . . Yes, very important. . . . Thank you. [*She remains by the phone with a lost, frightened look.*]

[STANLEY *turns slowly back toward his wife and takes her clumsily in his arms.*]

STANLEY Stell, it's gonna be all right after she goes and after you've had the baby. It's gonna be all right again between you and me the way that it was. You remember that way that it was? Them nights we had together? God, honey, it's gonna be sweet when we can make noise in the night the way that we used to and get the colored lights going with nobody's sister behind the curtains to hear us!

[*Their upstairs neighbors are heard in bellowing laughter at something.* STANLEY *chuckles.*]

Steve an' Eunice . . .

STELLA Come on back in. [*She returns to the kitchen and starts lighting the candles on the white cake.*] Blanche?

BLANCHE Yes. [*She returns from the bedroom to the table in the kitchen.*] Oh, those pretty, pretty little candles! Oh, don't burn them, Stella.

STELLA I certainly will.

[STANLEY *comes back in.*]

BLANCHE You ought to save them for baby's birthdays. Oh, I hope candles are going to glow in his life and I hope that his eyes are going to be like candles, like two blue candles lighted in a white cake!

STANLEY [*sitting down*] What poetry!

BLANCHE [*she pauses reflectively for a moment*] I shouldn't have called him.

STELLA There's lots of things could have happened.

BLANCHE There's no excuse for it, Stella. I don't have to put up with insults. I won't be taken for granted.

STANLEY Goddamn, it's hot in here with the steam from the bathroom.

BLANCHE I've said I was sorry three times. [*The piano fades out.*] I take hot baths for my nerves. Hydrotherapy, they call it. You healthy Polack, without a nerve in your body, of course you don't know what anxiety feels like!

STANLEY I am not a Polack. People from Poland are Poles, not Polacks. But what I am is a one-hundred-per-cent American, born and raised in the greatest country on earth and proud as hell of it, so don't ever call me a Polack.

[*The phone rings.* BLANCHE *rises expectantly.*]

BLANCHE Oh, that's for me, I'm sure.

STANLEY *I'm* not sure. Keep your seat. [*He crosses leisurely to phone.*] H'lo. Aw, yeh, hello, Mac.

[*He leans against wall, staring insultingly in at* BLANCHE. *She sinks back in her chair with a frightened look.* STELLA *leans over and touches her shoulder.*]

BLANCHE Oh, keep your hands off me, Stella. What is the matter with you? Why do you look at me with that pitying look?

STANLEY [*bawling*] QUIET IN THERE!—We've got a noisy woman on the place.—Go on, Mac. At Riley's? No, I don't wanta bowl at Riley's. I had a little trouble with Riley last week. I'm the team captain, ain't I? All right, then, we're not gonna bowl at Riley's, we're gonna bowl at the West Side or the Gala! All right, Mac. See you!

[*He hangs up and returns to the table.* BLANCHE *fiercely controls herself, drinking quickly from her tumbler of water. He doesn't look at her but reaches in a pocket. Then he speaks slowly and with false amiability.*]

Sister Blanche, I've got a little birthday remembrance for you.

BLANCHE Oh, have you, Stanley? I wasn't expecting any, I—I don't know why Stella wants to observe my birthday! I'd much rather forget it—when you—reach twenty-seven! Well—age is a subject that you'd prefer to—ignore!

STANLEY Twenty-seven?

BLANCHE [*quickly*] What is it? Is it for *me?*

[*He is holding a little envelope toward her.*]

STANLEY Yes, I hope you like it!

BLANCHE Why, why—Why, it's a—

STANLEY Ticket! Back to Laurel! On the Greyhound![7] Tuesday!

[*The Varsouviana music steals in softly and continues playing.* STELLA *rises abruptly and turns her back.* BLANCHE *tries to smile. Then she tries to laugh. Then she gives both up and springs from the table and runs into the next room. She clutches her throat and then runs into the bathroom. Coughing, gagging sounds are heard.*]

Well!

STELLA You didn't need to do that.

STANLEY Don't forget all that I took off her.

STELLA You needn't have been so cruel to someone alone as she is.

STANLEY Delicate piece she is.

STELLA She is. She was. You didn't know Blanche as a girl. Nobody, nobody, was tender and trusting as she was. But people like you abused her, and forced her to change.

[*He crosses into the bedroom, ripping off his shirt, and changes into a brilliant silk bowling shirt. She follows him.*]

Do you think you're going bowling now?

STANLEY Sure.

STELLA You're not going bowling. [*She catches hold of his shirt.*] Why did you do this to her?

STANLEY I done nothing to no one. Let go of my shirt. You've torn it.

STELLA I want to know why. Tell me why.

STANLEY When we first met, me and you, you thought I was common. How right you was, baby. I was common as dirt. You showed me the snapshot of

7. That is, the long-distance bus.

the place with the columns. I pulled you down off them columns and how you loved it, having them colored lights going! And wasn't we happy together, wasn't it all okay till she showed here?

[STELLA *makes a slight movement. Her look goes suddenly inward as if some interior voice had called her name. She begins a slow, shuffling progress from the bedroom to the kitchen, leaning and resting on the back of the chair and then on the edge of a table with a blind look and listening expression. Stanley, finishing with his shirt, is unaware of her reaction.*]

And wasn't we happy together? Wasn't it all okay? Till she showed here. Hoity-toity, describing me as an ape. [*He suddenly notices the change in* STELLA.] Hey, what is it, Stell? [*He crosses to her.*]

STELLA [*quietly*] Take me to the hospital.

[*He is with her now, supporting her with his arm, murmuring indistinguishably as they go outside.*]

Scene 9

A while later that evening. BLANCHE *is seated in a tense hunched position in a bedroom chair that she has recovered with diagonal green and white stripes. She has on her scarlet satin robe. On the table beside chair is a bottle of liquor and a glass. The rapid, feverish polka tune, the "Varsouviana," is heard. The music is in her mind; she is drinking to escape it and the sense of disaster closing in on her, and she seems to whisper the words of the song. An electric fan is turning back and forth across her.*

MITCH *comes around the corner in work clothes: blue denim shirt and pants. He is unshaven. He climbs the steps to the door and rings.* BLANCHE *is startled.*

BLANCHE Who is it, please?

MITCH [*hoarsely*] Me. Mitch.

[*The polka tune stops.*]

BLANCHE Mitch!—Just a minute.

[*She rushes about frantically, hiding the bottle in a closet, crouching at the mirror and dabbing her face with cologne and powder. She is so excited that her breath is audible as she dashes about. At last she rushes to the door in the kitchen and lets him in.*]

Mitch!—Y'know, I really shouldn't let you in after the treatment I have received from you this evening! So utterly uncavalier! But hello, beautiful!

[*She offers him her lips. He ignores it and pushes past her into the flat. She looks fearfully after him as he stalks into the bedroom.*]

My, my, what a cold shoulder! And such uncouth apparel! Why, you haven't even shaved! The unforgivable insult to a lady! But I forgive you. I forgive you because it's such a relief to see you. You've stopped that polka tune that I had caught in my head. Have you ever had anything caught in your head? No, of course you haven't, you dumb angel-puss, you'd never get anything awful caught in your head!

[*He stares at her while she follows him while she talks. It is obvious that he has had a few drinks on the way over.*]

MITCH Do we have to have that fan on?

BLANCHE No!

MITCH I don't like fans.

BLANCHE Then let's turn it off, honey. I'm not partial to them!

[*She presses the switch and the fan nods slowly off. She clears her throat uneasily as* MITCH *plumps himself down on the bed in the bedroom and lights a cigarette.*]

I don't know what there is to drink. I—haven't investigated.

MITCH I don't want Stan's liquor.

BLANCHE It isn't Stan's. Everything here isn't Stan's. Some things on the premises are actually mine! How is your mother? Isn't your mother well?

MITCH Why?

BLANCHE Something's the matter tonight, but never mind. I won't cross-examine the witness. I'll just—[*She touches her forehead vaguely. The polka tune starts up again.*]—pretend I don't notice anything different about you! That—music again . . .

MITCH What music?

BLANCHE The "Varsouviana"! The polka tune they were playing when Allan—Wait!

[*A distant revolver shot is heard.* BLANCHE *seems relieved.*]

There now, the shot! It always stops after that.

[*The polka music dies out again.*]

Yes, now it's stopped.

MITCH Are you boxed out of your mind?

BLANCHE I'll go and see what I can find in the way of—[*She crosses into the closet, pretending to search for the bottle.*] Oh, by the way, excuse me for not being dressed. But I'd practically given you up! Had you forgotten your invitation to supper?

MITCH I wasn't going to see you anymore.

BLANCHE Wait a minute. I can't hear what you're saying and you talk so little that when you do say something, I don't want to miss a single syllable of it. . . . What am I looking around here for? Oh, yes—liquor! We've had so much excitement around here this evening that I *am* boxed out of my mind! [*She pretends suddenly to find the bottle. He draws his foot up on the bed and stares at her contemptuously.*] Here's something. Southern Comfort![8] What is that, I wonder?

MITCH If you don't know, it must belong to Stan.

BLANCHE Take your foot off the bed. It has a light cover on it. Of course you boys don't notice things like that. I've done so much with this place since I've been here.

MITCH I bet you have.

BLANCHE You saw it before I came. Well, look at it now! This room is almost—dainty! I want to keep it that way. I wonder if this stuff ought to be mixed with something? Ummm, it's sweet, so sweet! It's terribly, terribly sweet! Why, it's a *liqueur,* I believe! Yes, that's what it *is,* a liqueur! [MITCH *grunts.*] I'm afraid you won't like it, but try it, and maybe you will.

MITCH I told you already I don't want none of his liquor and I mean it. You ought to lay off his liquor. He says you been lapping it up all summer like a wild cat!

BLANCHE What a fantastic statement! Fantastic of him to say it, fantastic of you to repeat it! I won't descend to the level of such cheap accusations to answer them, even!

8. A flavored whiskey liqueur.

MITCH Huh.

BLANCHE What's in your mind? I see something in your eyes!

MITCH [*getting up*] It's dark in here.

BLANCHE I like it dark. The dark is comforting to me.

MITCH I don't think I ever seen you in the light. [BLANCHE *laughs breathlessly.*] That's a fact!

BLANCHE Is it?

MITCH I've never seen you in the afternoon.

BLANCHE Whose fault is that?

MITCH You never want to go out in the afternoon.

BLANCHE Why, Mitch, you're at the plant in the afternoon!

MITCH Not Sunday afternoon. I've asked you to go out with me sometimes on Sundays but you always make an excuse. You never want to go out till after six and then it's always some place that's not lighted much.

BLANCHE There is some obscure meaning in this but I fail to catch it.

MITCH What it means is I've never had a real good look at you, Blanche. Let's turn the light on here.

BLANCHE [*fearfully*] Light? Which light? What for?

MITCH This one with the paper thing on it. [*He tears the paper lantern off the light bulb. She utters a frightened gasp.*]

BLANCHE What did you do that for?

MITCH So I can take a look at you good and plain!

BLANCHE Of course you don't really mean to be insulting!

MITCH No, just realistic.

BLANCHE I don't want realism. I want magic! [MITCH *laughs.*] Yes, yes, magic! I try to give that to people. I misrepresent things to them. I don't tell truth, I tell what *ought* to be truth. And if that is sinful, then let me be damned for it!—*Don't turn the light on!*

[MITCH *crosses to the switch. He turns the light on and stares at her. She cries out and covers her face. He turns the light off again.*]

MITCH [*slowly and bitterly*] I don't mind you being older than what I thought. But all the rest of it—Christ! That pitch about your ideals being so old-fashioned and all the malarkey that you've dished out all summer. Oh, I knew you weren't sixteen anymore. But I was a fool enough to believe you was straight.

BLANCHE Who told you I wasn't—"straight"? My loving brother-in-law. And you believed him.

MITCH I called him a liar at first. And then I checked on the story. First I asked our supply-man who travels through Laurel. And then I talked directly over long-distance to this merchant.

BLANCHE Who is this merchant?

MITCH Kiefaber.

BLANCHE The merchant Kiefaber of Laurel! I know the man. He whistled at me. I put him in his place. So now for revenge he makes up stories about me.

MITCH Three people, Kiefaber, Stanley, and Shaw, swore to them!

BLANCHE Rub-a-dub-dub, three men in a tub![9] And such a filthy tub!

9. A reference to the nursery rhyme.

MITCH Didn't you stay at a hotel called The Flamingo?

BLANCHE Flamingo? No! Tarantula was the name of it! I stayed at a hotel called The Tarantula Arms!

MITCH [*stupidly*] Tarantula?

BLANCHE Yes, a big spider! That's where I brought my victims. [*She pours herself another drink.*] Yes, I had many intimacies with strangers. After the death of Allan—intimacies with strangers was all I seemed able to fill my empty heart with. . . . I think it was panic, just panic, that drove me from one to another, hunting for some protection—here and there, in the most—unlikely places—even, at last, in a seventeen-year-old boy but—somebody wrote the superintendent about it—"This woman is morally unfit for her position!"

[*She throws back her head with convulsive, sobbing laughter. Then she repeats the statement, gasps, and drinks.*]

True? Yes, I suppose—unfit somehow—anyway. . . . So I came here. There was nowhere else I could go. I was played out. You know what played out is? My youth was suddenly gone up the water-spout, and—I met you. You said you needed somebody. Well, I needed somebody, too. I thanked God for you, because you seemed to be gentle—a cleft in the rock of the world that I could hide in! But I guess I was asking, hoping—too much! Kiefaber, Stanley, and Shaw have tied an old tin can to the tail of the kite.

[*There is a pause.* MITCH *stares at her dumbly.*]

MITCH You lied to me, Blanche.

BLANCHE Don't say I lied to you.

MITCH Lies, lies, inside and out, all lies.

BLANCHE Never inside, I didn't lie in my heart . . .

[*A vendor comes around the corner. She is a blind* MEXICAN WOMAN *in a dark shawl, carrying bunches of those gaudy tin flowers that lower-class Mexicans display at funerals and other festive occasions. She is calling barely audibly. Her figure is only faintly visible outside the building.*]

MEXICAN WOMAN Flores. Flores. Flores para los muertos.[1] Flores. Flores.

BLANCHE What? Oh! Somebody outside . . . [*She goes to the door, opens it and stares at the* MEXICAN WOMAN.]

MEXICAN WOMAN [*she is at the door and offers* BLANCHE *some of her flowers*] Flores? Flores para los muertos?

BLANCHE [*frightened*] No, no! Not now! Not now!

[*She darts back into the apartment, slamming the door.*]

MEXICAN WOMAN [*she turns away and starts to move down the street*] Flores para los muertos.

[*The polka tune fades in.*]

BLANCHE [*as if to herself*] Crumble and fade and—regrets—recriminations . . . "If you'd done this, it wouldn't've cost me that!"

MEXICAN WOMAN Corones[2] para los muertos. Corones . . .

BLANCHE Legacies! Huh. . . . And other things such as bloodstained pillow-slips—"Her linen needs changing"—"Yes, Mother. But couldn't we get a colored girl to do it?" No, we couldn't of course. Everything gone but the—

1. Flowers for the dead (Spanish).
2. Crowns (Spanish); wreaths of flowers.

MEXICAN WOMAN Flores.

BLANCHE Death—I used to sit here and she used to sit over there and death was as close as you are. . . . We didn't dare even admit we had ever heard of it!

MEXICAN WOMAN Flores para los muertos, flores—flores . . .

BLANCHE The opposite is desire. So do you wonder? How could you possibly wonder! Not far from Belle Reve, before we had lost Belle Reve, was a camp where they trained young soldiers. On Saturday nights they would go in town to get drunk—

MEXICAN WOMAN [*softly*] Corones . . .

BLANCHE —and on the way back they would stagger onto my lawn and call—"Blanche! Blanche!"—the deaf old lady remaining suspected nothing. But sometimes I slipped outside to answer their calls. . . . Later the paddy-wagon would gather them up like daisies . . . the long way home . . .

[*The* MEXICAN WOMAN *turns slowly and drifts back off with her soft mournful cries.* BLANCHE *goes to the dresser and leans forward on it. After a moment,* MITCH *rises and follows her purposefully. The polka music fades away. He places his hands on her waist and tries to turn her about.*]

BLANCHE What do you want?

MITCH [*fumbling to embrace her*] What I been missing all summer.

BLANCHE Then marry me, Mitch!

MITCH I don't think I want to marry you anymore.

BLANCHE No?

MITCH [*dropping his hands from her waist*] You're not clean enough to bring in the house with my mother.

BLANCHE Go away, then. [*He stares at her.*] Get out of here quick before I start screaming fire! [*Her throat is tightening with hysteria.*] Get out of here quick before I start screaming fire.

[*He still remains staring. She suddenly rushes to the big window with its pale blue square of the soft summer light and cries wildly.*]

Fire! Fire! Fire!

[*With a startled gasp,* MITCH *turns and goes out the outer door, clatters awkwardly down the steps and around the corner of the building.* BLANCHE *staggers back from the window and falls to her knees. The distant piano is slow and blue.*]

Scene 10

It is a few hours later that night.

BLANCHE *has been drinking fairly steadily since* MITCH *left. She has dragged her wardrobe trunk into the center of the bedroom. It hangs open with flowery dresses thrown across it. As the drinking and packing went on, a mood of hysterical exhilaration came into her and she has decked herself out in a somewhat soiled and crumpled white satin evening gown and a pair of scuffed silver slippers with brilliants*[3] *set in their heels.*

Now she is placing the rhinestone tiara on her head before the mirror of the dressing-table and murmuring excitedly as if to a group of spectral admirers.

BLANCHE How about taking a swim, a moonlight swim at the old rock quarry? If anyone's sober enough to drive a car! Ha-ha! Best way in the

3. Sparkling gems.

world to stop your head buzzing! Only you've got to be careful to dive where the deep pool is—if you hit a rock you don't come up till tomorrow. . . .

[Tremblingly she lifts the hand mirror for a closer inspection. She catches her breath and slams the mirror face down with such violence that the glass cracks. She moans a little and attempts to rise.]

*[*STANLEY *appears around the corner of the building. He still has on the vivid green silk bowling shirt. As he rounds the corner the honky-tonk music is heard. It continues softly throughout the scene.]*

[He enters the kitchen, slamming the door. As he peers in at BLANCHE, *he gives a low whistle. He has had a few drinks on the way and has brought some quart beer bottles home with him.]*

BLANCHE How is my sister?

STANLEY She is doing okay.

BLANCHE And how is the baby?

STANLEY *[grinning amiably]* The baby won't come before morning so they told me to go home and get a little shut-eye.

BLANCHE Does that mean we are to be alone in here?

STANLEY Yep. Just me and you, Blanche. Unless you got somebody hid under the bed. What've you got on those fine feathers for?

BLANCHE Oh, that's right. You left before my wire came.

STANLEY You got a wire?

BLANCHE I received a telegram from an old admirer of mine.

STANLEY Anything good?

BLANCHE I think so. An invitation.

STANLEY What to? A fireman's ball?

BLANCHE *[throwing back her head]* A cruise of the Caribbean on a yacht!

STANLEY Well, well. What do you know?

BLANCHE I have never been so surprised in my life.

STANLEY I guess not.

BLANCHE It came like a bolt from the blue!

STANLEY Who did you say it was from?

BLANCHE An old beau of mine.

STANLEY The one that give you the white fox-pieces?

BLANCHE Mr. Shep Huntleigh. I wore his ATO[4] pin my last year at college. I hadn't seen him again until last Christmas. I ran in to him on Biscayne Boulevard. Then—just now—this wire—inviting me on a cruise of the Caribbean! The problem is clothes. I tore into my trunk to see what I have that's suitable for the tropics!

STANLEY And come up with that—gorgeous—diamond—tiara?

BLANCHE This old relic? Ha-ha! It's only rhinestones.

STANLEY Gosh. I thought it was Tiffany diamonds.[5] *[He unbuttons his shirt.]*

BLANCHE Well, anyhow, I shall be entertained in style.

STANLEY Uh-huh. It goes to show, you never know what is coming.

BLANCHE Just when I thought my luck had begun to fail me—

STANLEY Into the picture pops this Miami millionaire.

BLANCHE This man is not from Miami. This man is from Dallas.

STANLEY This man is from Dallas?

4. The fraternity Alpha Tau Omega.
5. That is, diamonds from the famous jewelry store in New York.

BLANCHE Yes, this man is from Dallas where gold spouts out of the ground!

STANLEY Well, just so he's from somewhere! [*He starts removing his shirt.*]

BLANCHE Close the curtains before you undress any further.

STANLEY [*amiably*] This is all I'm going to undress right now. [*He rips the sack off a quart beer bottle.*] Seen a bottle-opener?

[*She moves slowly toward the dresser, where she stands with her hands knotted together.*]

I used to have a cousin who could open a beer bottle with his teeth. [*Pounding the bottle cap on the corner of table.*] That was his only accomplishment, all he could do—he was just a human bottle-opener. And then one time, at a wedding party, he broke his front teeth off! After that he was so ashamed of himself he used t' sneak out of the house when company came . . .

[*The bottle cap pops off and a geyser of foam shoots up.* STANLEY *laughs happily, holding up the bottle over his head.*]

Ha-ha! Rain from heaven! [*He extends the bottle toward her.*] Shall we bury the hatchet and make it a loving-cup? Huh?

BLANCHE No, thank you.

STANLEY Well, it's a red-letter night for us both. You having an oil millionaire and me having a baby.

[*He goes to the bureau in the bedroom and crouches to remove something from the bottom drawer.*]

BLANCHE [*drawing back*] What are you doing in here?

STANLEY Here's something I always break out on special occasions like this. The silk pyjamas I wore on my wedding night!

BLANCHE Oh.

STANLEY When the telephone rings and they say, "You've got a son!" I'll tear this off and wave it like a flag! [*He shakes out a brilliant pyjama coat.*] I guess we are both entitled to put on the dog.[6] [*He goes back to the kitchen with the coat over his arm.*]

BLANCHE When I think of how divine it is going to be to have such a thing as privacy once more—I could weep with joy!

STANLEY This millionaire from Dallas is not going to interfere with your privacy any?

BLANCHE It won't be the sort of thing you have in mind. This man is a gentleman and he respects me. [*Improvising feverishly.*] What he wants is my companionship. Having great wealth sometimes makes people lonely! A cultivated woman, a woman of intelligence and breeding, can enrich a man's life—immeasurably! I have those things to offer, and this doesn't take them away. Physical beauty is passing. A transitory possession. But beauty of the mind and richness of the spirit and tenderness of the heart—and I have all of those things—aren't taken away, but grow! Increase with the years! How strange that I should be called a destitute woman! When I have all of these treasures locked in my heart. [*A choked sob comes from her.*] I think of myself as a very, very rich woman! But I have been foolish—casting my pearls before swine![7]

STANLEY Swine, huh?

6. That is, put on uncharacteristic stylishness, show off.

7. An allusion to Jesus' Sermon on the Mount (Matthew 7.6).

BLANCHE Yes, swine! Swine! And I'm thinking not only of you but of your friend, Mr. Mitchell. He came to see me tonight. He dared to come here in his work clothes! And to repeat slander to me, vicious stories that he had gotten from you! I gave him his walking papers. . . .

STANLEY You did, huh?

BLANCHE But then he came back. He returned with a box of roses to beg my forgiveness! He implored my forgiveness. But some things are not forgivable. Deliberate cruelty is not forgivable. It is the one unforgivable thing in my opinion and it is the one thing of which I have never, never been guilty. And so I told him, I said to him, "Thank you," but it was foolish of me to think that we could ever adapt ourselves to each other. Our ways of life are too different. Our attitudes and our backgrounds are incompatible. We have to be realistic about such things. So farewell, my friend! And let there be no hard feelings . . .

STANLEY Was this before or after the telegram came from the Texas oil millionaire?

BLANCHE What telegram? No! No, after! As a matter of fact, the wire came just as—

STANLEY As a matter of fact there wasn't no wire at all!

BLANCHE Oh, oh!

STANLEY There isn't no millionaire! And Mitch didn't come back with roses 'cause I know where he is—

BLANCHE Oh!

STANLEY There isn't a goddam thing but imagination!

BLANCHE Oh!

STANLEY And lies and conceit and tricks!

BLANCHE Oh!

STANLEY And look at yourself! Take a look at yourself in that worn-out Mardi Gras[8] outfit, rented for fifty cents from some rag-picker! And with the crazy crown on! What queen do you think you are?

BLANCHE Oh—God . . .

STANLEY I've been on to you from the start! Not once did you pull any wool over this boy's eyes! You come in here and sprinkle the place with powder and spray perfume and cover the lightbulb with a paper lantern, and lo and behold the place has turned into Egypt and you are the Queen of the Nile! Sitting on your throne and swilling down my liquor! I say—*Ha!—Ha!* Do you hear me? *Ha—ha—ha!* [*He walks into the bedroom.*]

BLANCHE Don't come in here!

[*Lurid reflections appear on the walls around* BLANCHE. *The shadows are of a grotesque and menacing form. She catches her breath, crosses to the phone and jiggles the hook.* STANLEY *goes into the bathroom and closes the door.*]

Operator, operator! Give me long-distance, please. . . . I want to get in touch with Mr. Shep Huntleigh of Dallas. He's so well known he doesn't require any address. Just ask anybody who—Wait!!—No, I couldn't find it

8. Fat Tuesday (French), or Shrove Tuesday, the final day before Lent, traditionally a time of penitence and prayer for Christians, begins. In many places it is celebrated with merrymaking and parades; the festivities are particularly famous and extensive in New Orleans.

right now. . . . Please understand, I—No! No, wait! . . . One moment! Someone is—Nothing! Hold on, please!

[*She sets the phone down and crosses warily into the kitchen. The night is filled with inhuman voices like cries in a jungle.*]

[*The shadows and lurid reflections move sinuously as flames along the wall spaces.*]

[*Through the back wall of the rooms, which have become transparent, can be seen the sidewalk. A prostitute has rolled*[9] *a drunkard. He pursues her along the walk, overtakes her and there is a struggle. A policeman's whistle breaks it up. The figures disappear.*]

[*Some moments later the* NEGRO WOMAN *appears around the corner with a sequined bag which the prostitute had dropped on the walk. She is rooting excitedly through it.*]

[BLANCHE *presses her knuckles to her lips and returns slowly to the phone. She speaks in a hoarse whisper.*]

BLANCHE Operator! Operator! Never mind long-distance. Get Western Union. There isn't time to be—Western—Western Union!

[*She waits anxiously.*]

Western Union? Yes! I—want to—Take down this message! "In desperate, desperate circumstances! Help me! Caught in a trap. Caught in—" *Oh!*

[*The bathroom door is thrown open and* STANLEY *comes out in the brilliant silk pyjamas. He grins at her as he knots the tasseled sash about his waist. She gasps and backs away from the phone. He stares at her for a count of ten. Then a clicking becomes audible from the telephone, steady and rasping.*]

STANLEY You left th' phone off th' hook.

[*He crosses to it deliberately and sets it back on the hook. After he has replaced it, he stares at her again, his mouth slowly curving into a grin, as he weaves between* BLANCHE *and the outer door.*]

[*The barely audible "blue piano" begins to drum up louder. The sound of it turns into the roar of an approaching locomotive.* BLANCHE *crouches, pressing her fists to her ears until it has gone by.*]

BLANCHE [*finally straightening*] Let me—let me get by you!

STANLEY Get by me? Sure. Go ahead. [*He moves back a pace in the doorway.*]

BLANCHE You—you stand over there! [*She indicates a further position.*]

STANLEY [*grinning*] You got plenty of room to walk by me now.

BLANCHE Not with you there! But I've got to get out somehow!

STANLEY You think I'll interfere with you? Ha-ha!

[*The "blue piano" goes softly. She turns confusedly and makes a faint gesture. The inhuman jungle voices rise up. He takes a step toward her, biting his tongue which protrudes between his lips.*]

STANLEY [*softly*] Come to think of it—maybe you wouldn't be bad to—interfere with . . .

[BLANCHE *moves backward through the door into the bedroom.*]

BLANCHE Stay back! Don't you come toward me another step or I'll—

STANLEY What?

9. Robbed (by going through the pockets of someone drunk, unconscious, or asleep).

BLANCHE Some awful thing will happen! It will!

STANLEY What are you putting on now?

[They are now both inside the bedroom.]

BLANCHE I warn you, don't, I'm in danger!

[He takes another step. She smashes a bottle on the table and faces him, clutching the broken top.]

STANLEY What did you do that for?

BLANCHE So I could twist the broken end in your face!

STANLEY I bet you would do that!

BLANCHE I would! I will if you—

STANLEY Oh! So you want some roughhouse! All right, let's have some roughhouse!

[He springs toward her, overturning the table. She cries out and strikes at him with the bottle top but he catches her wrist.]

Tiger—tiger! Drop the bottle-top! Drop it! We've had this date with each other from the beginning!

[She moans. The bottle-top falls. She sinks to her knees. He picks up her inert figure and carries her to the bed. The hot trumpet and drums from the Four Deuces sound loudly.]

Scene 11

It is some weeks later. STELLA *is packing* BLANCHE's *things. Sound of water can be heard running in the bathroom.*

*The portieres are partly open on the poker players—*STANLEY, STEVE, MITCH, *and* PABLO*—who sit around the table in the kitchen. The atmosphere of the kitchen is now the same raw, lurid one of the disastrous poker night.*

The building is framed by the sky of turquoise. STELLA *has been crying as she arranges the flowery dresses in the open trunk.*

EUNICE *comes down the steps from her flat above and enters the kitchen. There is an outburst from the poker table.*

STANLEY Drew to an inside straight and made it, by God.

PABLO *Maldita sea tu suerto!*

STANLEY Put it in English, greaseball.

PABLO I am cursing your rutting luck.

STANLEY *[prodigiously elated]* You know what luck is? Luck is believing you're lucky. Take at Salerno.[1] I believed I was lucky. I figured that 4 out of 5 would not come through but I would . . . and I did. I put that down as a rule. To hold front position in this rat race you've got to believe you are lucky.

MITCH You . . . you . . . you. . . . Brag . . . brag . . . bull . . . bull.

*[*STELLA *goes into the bedroom and starts folding a dress.]*

STANLEY What's the matter with him?

EUNICE *[walking past the table]* I always did say that men are callous things with no feelings, but this does beat anything. Making pigs of yourselves. *[She comes through the portieres into the bedroom.]*

STANLEY What's the matter with her?

1. A city in southern Italy on the Gulf of Salerno, an important beachhead in the Allied invasion of Italy during World War II.

STELLA How is my baby?

EUNICE Sleeping like a little angel. Brought you some grapes. [*She puts them on a stool and lowers her voice.*] Blanche?

STELLA Bathing.

EUNICE How is she?

STELLA She wouldn't eat anything but asked for a drink.

EUNICE What did you tell her?

STELLA I—just told her that—we'd made arrangements for her to rest in the country. She's got it mixed in her mind with Shep Huntleigh.

[BLANCHE *opens the bathroom door slightly.*]

BLANCHE Stella.

STELLA Yes, Blanche?

BLANCHE If anyone calls while I'm bathing take the number and tell them I'll call right back.

STELLA Yes.

BLANCHE That cool yellow silk—the bouclé.[2] See if it's crushed. If it's not too crushed I'll wear it and on the lapel that silver and turquoise pin in the shape of a seahorse. You will find them in the heart-shaped box I keep my accessories in. And Stella . . . Try and locate a bunch of artificial violets in that box, too, to pin with the seahorse on the lapel of the jacket.

[*She closes the door.* STELLA *turns to* EUNICE.]

STELLA I don't know if I did the right thing.

EUNICE What else could you do?

STELLA I couldn't believe her story and go on living with Stanley.

EUNICE Don't ever believe it. Life has got to go on. No matter what happens, you've got to keep on going.

[*The bathroom door opens a little.*]

BLANCHE [*looking out*] Is the coast clear?

STELLA Yes, Blanche. [*To* EUNICE] Tell her how well she's looking.

BLANCHE Please close the curtains before I come out.

STELLA They're closed.

STANLEY —How many for you?

PABLO —Two.

STEVE —Three.

[BLANCHE *appears in the amber light of the door. She has a tragic radiance in her red satin robe following the sculptural lines of her body. The "Varsouviana" rises audibly as* BLANCHE *enters the bedroom.*]

BLANCHE [*with faintly hysterical vivacity*] I have just washed my hair.

STELLA Did you?

BLANCHE I'm not sure I got the soap out.

EUNICE Such fine hair!

BLANCHE [*accepting the compliment*] It's a problem. Didn't I get a call?

STELLA Who from, Blanche?

BLANCHE Shep Huntleigh . . .

STELLA Why, not yet, honey!

BLANCHE How strange! I—

2. A rough-textured fabric made of looped yarn.

[*At the sound of* BLANCHE'*s voice* MITCH'*s arm supporting his cards has sagged and his gaze is dissolved into space.* STANLEY *slaps him on the shoulder.*]

STANLEY Hey, Mitch, come to!

[*The sound of this new voice shocks* BLANCHE. *She makes a shocked gesture, forming his name with her lips.* STELLA *nods and looks quickly away.* BLANCHE *stands quite still for some moments—the silver-backed mirror in her hand and a look of sorrowful perplexity as though all human experience shows on her face.* BLANCHE *finally speaks but with sudden hysteria.*]

BLANCHE What's going on here?

[*She turns from* STELLA *to* EUNICE *and back to* STELLA. *Her rising voice penetrates the concentration of the game.* MITCH *ducks his head lower but* STANLEY *shoves back his chair as if about to rise.* STEVE *places a restraining hand on his arm.*]

BLANCHE [*continuing*] What's happened here? I want an explanation of what's happened here.

STELLA [*agonizingly*] Hush! Hush!

EUNICE Hush! Hush! Honey.

STELLA Please, Blanche.

BLANCHE Why are you looking at me like that? Is something wrong with me?

EUNICE You look wonderful, Blanche. Don't she look wonderful?

STELLA Yes.

EUNICE I understand you are going on a trip.

STELLA Yes, Blanche *is*. She's going on a vacation.

EUNICE I'm green with envy.

BLANCHE Help me, help me get dressed!

STELLA [*handing her dress*] Is this what you—

BLANCHE Yes, it will do! I'm anxious to get out of here—this place is a trap!

EUNICE What a pretty blue jacket.

STELLA It's lilac colored.

BLANCHE You're both mistaken. It's Della Robbia blue.[3] The blue of the robe in the old Madonna pictures. Are these grapes washed?

[*She fingers the bunch of grapes which* EUNICE *had brought in.*]

EUNICE Huh?

BLANCHE Washed, I said. Are they washed?

EUNICE They're from the French Market.[4]

BLANCHE That doesn't mean they've been washed. [*The cathedral bells chime.*] Those cathedral bells—they're the only clean thing in the Quarter. Well, I'm going now. I'm ready to go.

EUNICE [*whispering*] She's going to walk out before they get here.

STELLA Wait, Blanche.

BLANCHE I don't want to pass in front of those men.

EUNICE Then wait'll the game breaks up.

STELLA Sit down and . . .

3. The distinctive blue backgrounds of the reliefs made first by the Florentine sculptor Luca della Robbia (ca. 1400–1482), and then by his descendants. The color blue is symbolic of heaven and is associated with fidelity, chastity, and modesty.

4. A city market—partly open-air, partly enclosed—in the French Quarter, on the bank of the Mississippi, since 1791.

[BLANCHE *turns weakly, hesitantly about. She lets them push her into a chair.*]

BLANCHE I can smell the sea air. The rest of my time I'm going to spend on the sea. And when I die, I'm going to die on the sea. You know what I shall die of? [*She plucks a grape.*] I shall die of eating an unwashed grape one day out on the ocean. I will die—with my hand in the hand of some nice-looking ship's doctor, a very young one with a small blond mustache and a big silver watch. "Poor lady," they'll say, "the quinine[5] did her no good. That unwashed grape has transported her soul to heaven." [*The cathedral chimes are heard.*] And I'll be buried at sea sewn up in a clean white sack and dropped overboard—at noon—in the blaze of summer—and into an ocean as blue as [*Chimes again*] my first lover's eyes!

[*A* DOCTOR *and a* MATRON *have appeared around the corner of the building and climbed the steps to the porch. The gravity of their profession is exaggerated—the unmistakable aura of the state institution with its cynical detachment. The* DOCTOR *rings the doorbell. The murmur of the game is interrupted.*]

EUNICE [*whispering to* STELLA] That must be them.

[STELLA *presses her fists to her lips.*]

BLANCHE [*rising slowly*] What is it?

EUNICE [*affectedly casual*] Excuse me while I see who's at the door.

STELLA Yes.

[EUNICE *goes into the kitchen.*]

BLANCHE [*tensely*] I wonder if it's for me.

[*A whispered colloquy takes place at the door.*]

EUNICE [*returning, brightly*] Someone is calling for Blanche.

BLANCHE It *is* for me, then! [*She looks fearfully from one to the other and then to the portieres. The "Varsouviana" faintly plays.*] Is it the gentleman I was expecting from Dallas?

EUNICE I think it is, Blanche.

BLANCHE I'm not quite ready.

STELLA Ask him to wait outside.

BLANCHE I . . .

[EUNICE *goes back to the portieres. Drums sound very softly.*]

STELLA Everything packed?

BLANCHE My silver toilet articles are still out.

STELLA Ah!

EUNICE [*returning*] They're waiting in front of the house.

BLANCHE They! Who's "they"?

EUNICE There's a lady with him.

BLANCHE I cannot imagine who this "lady" could be! How is she dressed?

EUNICE Just—just a sort of a—plain-tailored outfit.

BLANCHE Possibly she's— [*Her voice dies out nervously.*]

STELLA Shall we go, Blanche?

BLANCHE Must we go through that room?

STELLA I will go with you.

BLANCHE How do I look?

5. A salt used to treat malaria and reduce fever.

STELLA Lovely.

EUNICE [*echoing*] Lovely.

[BLANCHE *moves fearfully to the portieres.* EUNICE *draws them open for her.* BLANCHE *goes into the kitchen.*]

BLANCHE [*to the men*] Please don't get up. I'm only passing through.

[*She crosses quickly to outside door.* STELLA *and* EUNICE *follow. The poker players stand awkwardly at the table—all except* MITCH, *who remains seated, looking down at the table.* BLANCHE *steps out on a small porch at the side of the door. She stops short and catches her breath.*]

DOCTOR How do you do?

BLANCHE You are not the gentleman I was expecting. [*She suddenly gasps and starts back up the steps. She stops by* STELLA, *who stands just outside the door, and speaks in a frightening whisper.*] That man isn't Shep Huntleigh.

[*The "Varsouviana" is playing distantly.*]

[STELLA *stares back at* BLANCHE. EUNICE *is holding* STELLA'*s arm. There is a moment of silence—no sound but that of* STANLEY *steadily shuffling the cards.*]

[BLANCHE *catches her breath again and slips back into the flat. She enters the flat with a peculiar smile, her eyes wide and brilliant. As soon as her sister goes past her,* STELLA *closes her eyes and clenches her hands.* EUNICE *throws her arms comfortingly about her. Then she starts up to her flat.* BLANCHE *stops just inside the door.* MITCH *keeps staring down at his hands on the table, but the other men look at her curiously. At last she starts around the table toward the bedroom. As she does,* STANLEY *suddenly pushes back his chair and rises as if to block her way. The* MATRON *follows her into the flat.*]

STANLEY Did you forget something?

BLANCHE [*shrilly*] Yes! Yes, I forgot something!

[*She rushes past him into the bedroom. Lurid reflections appear on the walls in odd, sinuous shapes. The "Varsouviana" is filtered into a weird distortion, accompanied by the cries and noises of the jungle.* BLANCHE *seizes the back of a chair as if to defend herself.*]

STANLEY [*sotto voce*[6]] Doc, you better go in.

DOCTOR [*sotto voce, motioning to the* MATRON] Nurse, bring her out.

[*The* MATRON *advances on one side,* STANLEY *on the other. Divested of all the softer properties of womanhood, the* MATRON *is a peculiarly sinister figure in her severe dress. Her voice is bold and toneless as a fire-bell.*]

MATRON Hello, Blanche.

[*The greeting is echoed and re-echoed by other mysterious voices behind the walls, as if reverberated through a canyon of rock.*]

STANLEY She says that she forgot something.

[*The echo sounds in threatening whispers.*]

MATRON That's all right.

STANLEY What did you forget, Blanche?

BLANCHE I—I—

MATRON It don't matter. We can pick it up later.

STANLEY Sure. We can send it along with the trunk.

6. Under his breath, in an undertone (Italian).

BLANCHE [*retreating in panic*] I don't know you—I don't know you. I want to be—left alone—please!

MATRON Now, Blanche!

ECHOES [*rising and falling*] Now, Blanche—now, Blanche—now, Blanche!

STANLEY You left nothing here but spilt talcum and old empty perfume bottles—unless it's the paper lantern you want to take with you. You want the lantern?

[*He crosses to dressing table and seizes the paper lantern, tearing it off the light bulb, and extends it toward her. She cries out as if the lantern was herself. The* MATRON *steps boldly toward her. She screams and tries to break past the* MATRON. *All the men spring to their feet.* STELLA *runs out to the porch, with* EUNICE *following to comfort her, simultaneously with the confused voices of the men in the kitchen.* STELLA *rushes into* EUNICE*'s embrace on the porch.*]

STELLA Oh, my God, Eunice help me! Don't let them do that to her, don't let them hurt her! Oh, God, oh, please God, don't hurt her! What are they doing to her? What are they doing? [*She tries to break from* EUNICE*'s arms.*]

EUNICE No, honey, no, no, honey. Stay here. Don't go back in there. Stay with me and don't look.

STELLA What have I done to my sister? Oh, God, what have I done to my sister?

EUNICE You done the right thing, the only thing you could do. She couldn't stay here; there wasn't no other place for her to go.

[*While* STELLA *and* EUNICE *are speaking on the porch the voices of the men in the kitchen overlap them.* MITCH *has started toward the bedroom.* STANLEY *crosses to block him.* STANLEY *pushes him aside.* MITCH *lunges and strikes at* STANLEY. STANLEY *pushes* MITCH *back. Mitch collapses at the table, sobbing.*]

[*During the preceding scenes, the* MATRON *catches hold of* BLANCHE*'s arm and prevents her flight.* BLANCHE *turns wildly and scratches at the* MATRON. *The heavy woman pinions her arms.* BLANCHE *cries out hoarsely and slips to her knees.*]

MATRON These fingernails have to be trimmed. [*The* DOCTOR *comes into the room and she looks at him.*] Jacket,[7] Doctor?

DOCTOR Not unless necessary.

[*He takes off his hat and now he becomes personalized. The unhuman quality goes. His voice is gentle and reassuring as he crosses to* BLANCHE *and crouches in front of her. As he speaks her name, her terror subsides a little. The lurid reflections fade from the walls, the inhuman cries and noises die out and her own hoarse crying is calmed.*]

DOCTOR Miss DuBois.

[*She turns her face to him and stares at him with desperate pleading. He smiles; then he speaks to the* MATRON.]

It won't be necessary.

BLANCHE [*faintly*] Ask her to let go of me.

DOCTOR [*to the* MATRON] Let go.

[*The* MATRON *releases her.* BLANCHE *extends her hands toward the* DOCTOR. *He draws her up gently and supports her with his arm and leads her through the portieres.*]

7. Straitjacket.

BLANCHE [*holding tight to his arm*] Whoever you are—I have always depended on the kindness of strangers.

[*The poker players stand back as* BLANCHE *and the* DOCTOR *cross the kitchen to the front door. She allows him to lead her as if she were blind. As they go out on the porch,* STELLA *cries out her sister's name from where she is crouched a few steps up on the stairs.*]

STELLA Blanche! Blanche, Blanche!

[BLANCHE *walks on without turning, followed by the* DOCTOR *and the* MATRON. *They go around the corner of the building.*]

[EUNICE *descends to* STELLA *and places the child in her arms. It is wrapped in a pale blue blanket. Stella accepts the child, sobbingly.* EUNICE *continues downstairs and enters the kitchen where the men, except for* STANLEY, *are returning silently to their places about the table.* STANLEY *has gone out on the porch and stands at the foot of the steps looking at* STELLA.]

STANLEY [*a bit uncertainly*] Stella?

[*She sobs with inhuman abandon. There is something luxurious in her complete surrender to crying now that her sister is gone.*]

STANLEY [*voluptuously, soothingly*] Now, honey. Now, love. Now, now, love. [*He kneels beside her and his fingers find the opening of her blouse.*] Now, now, love. Now, love. . . .

[*The luxurious sobbing, the sensual murmur fade away under the swelling music of the "blue piano" and the muted trumpet.*]

STEVE This game is seven-card stud.

Curtain.

ARTHUR MILLER

1915–2005

In a career that lasted sixty-one years and garnered national and international acclaim, Arthur Miller established himself as one of the American theater's most visible and publicly engaged playwrights. He was born two years before the United States' entry into World War I, and his political and artistic convictions were forged in the crucible of national crisis: the Great Depression, World War II, McCarthyism. While Miller felt the impact of these turbulent years in very personal ways—like EUGENE O'NEILL and TENNESSEE WILLIAMS, he is a deeply autobiographical playwright—his plays situate the personal within social realms where the individual is defined as an ethical and moral agent. The son of an Eastern European Jewish immigrant, Miller grew up in a country struggling to come to terms with its national identity, with the social contracts that underlie this identity, and with the increasing tension between its various animating myths and ideologies. Following what the playwright called "the age-old tradition of theatre as a civic art," Miller's plays trace the fault lines running through social psyche of twentieth-century America.

In plays such as *DEATH OF A SALESMAN* (1949), Miller determined many of the directions that postwar American drama would follow. But the roots of his drama and the central experiences to which it gives form lie in the century's earlier decades. Miller was born in Manhattan on October 17, 1915, to Isadore Miller, a clothing manufacturer, and his wife, Augusta Barnett Miller. The family lived in an apartment on the edge of Harlem overlooking Central Park and enjoyed an affluent life during Miller's childhood. When his father's business failed in 1928, however, they were forced to move to a small house in Brooklyn. The stock market crash in 1929 and the Depression years that followed deepened the future playwright's awareness of the narrow line separating success and failure and the discrepancy between myth and reality in the American capitalist system. Attending high school in Brooklyn, Miller played on the football team but was an average student; for two years after he graduated he held a series of jobs, including deliveryman for his father and sales clerk in an auto parts warehouse in Manhattan. Having saved enough money to attend college, Miller applied and was accepted to the University of Michigan in 1934.

In Ann Arbor, Miller wrote for the school newspaper, majored in English, and began writing drama. He studied playwriting with the English professor Kenneth Rowe and became aware of Clifford Odets, the author of *Waiting for Lefty* (1935), and other dramatists who made the theater an instrument of social protest during the 1930s. His first two plays won the university's prestigious Avery Hopwood Award in drama in successive years, and he won the Theatre Guild Bureau of New Plays award in 1937. After graduating in June of that year, Miller went to New York to work with the Federal Theatre Project, which was established in 1935 to offer employment to promising young playwrights as part of the New Deal's Works Progress Administration. When the program was abolished by Congress in 1939, he worked in a series of jobs, sold a number of radio scripts, and published *Situation Normal* (1944), a work of military reportage, and *Focus* (1945), a novel dealing with anti-Semitism. At that time, he was living in Brooklyn Heights with his first wife, Mary Grace Slattery, and their two children.

Miller's emergence onto the New York theater scene came in November 1944, when his play *The Man Who Had All the Luck* was produced on Broadway. Although this production received some favorable notice, most reviews were negative and it closed after only four performances. Three more years would elapse before Miller found Broadway success with *All My Sons* (1947). This play—which is about Joe Keller, a manufacturer of airplane engines, and the disclosure that he had sold defective airplane parts that led to the death of twenty-one pilots and, indirectly, his eldest son—won the New York Drama Critics' Circle Award and was made into a movie in 1948. Its critical and financial success would pale, of course, next to the acclaim that greeted Miller's next play. After a brief preview run in Philadelphia, *Death of a Salesman* opened on February 10, 1949, at Broadway's Morosco Theater in a production directed by Elia Kazan (who had also directed *All My Sons*) and starring Lee J. Cobb as the aging salesman Willy Loman. Hailed by many reviewers as one of the finest plays to emerge in the American theater, *Salesman* won the Critics' Circle Award and the inaugural Pulitzer Prize for Drama. The play ran for 742 productions on Broadway, and by early 1950, eleven foreign productions had opened in Europe, South America, and Israel.

The success of *Salesman* catapulted Miller into the ranks of America's leading writers. But the country itself, growing increasingly obsessed with what it perceived as the Communist threat to its way of life, was undergoing a different kind of transformation. In response to the heightened paranoia of the postwar Red Scare, Miller wrote a play about the 1692 witch persecutions in Salem, Massachusetts. *The Crucible* (1953) is the story of John Proctor, a Salem individualist who struggles with questions of guilt, responsibility, and moral conduct as the witch hunt develops and he is accused. Miller himself was subpoenaed to appear before the House Un-American Activities Committee in June 1956; and while he was forthright in answering questions concerning his own brief involvement with so-called subversive organizations during the war, he, like Proctor, refused to provide the names of others who attended meetings of Communist writers. As a result, he was found guilty of contempt of Congress in May 1957, a conviction that was reversed the following year by the U.S. Court of Appeals.

In the decade after *The Crucible,* Miller wrote several important plays for the theater, including *A View from The Bridge* (1955), *After the Fall* (1964), and *Incident at Vichy* (1964). *After the Fall,* Miller's most autobiographical play, drew on the playwright's often troubled marriage (1956–61) with his second wife, the film star Marilyn Monroe. He married Inge Morath, an Austrian-born photographer, in 1962 (they had two children, and they remained together until Inge's death in 2002). After a four-year break from playwriting—during which he was appointed president of PEN, an international organization that fights censorship and other political pressures on writers—Miller returned to the theater in 1968 with *The Price,* which ran on Broadway for more than a year. But the American theater was changing, and in ways that proved less hospitable to Miller's drama of the individual, society, and the ethical life. Miller wrote a number of plays after *The Price*—including *The Creation of the World and Other Business* (1972), *The Archbishop's Ceiling* (1977), *The American Clock* (1980), *The Last Yankee* (1991; 1993), *The Ride Down Mt. Morgan* (1991), *Broken Glass* (1994),

The set, designed by Jo Mielziner, for the original 1949 Broadway production of *Death of a Salesman* at the Morosco Theater in New York.

Mr. Peters' Connections (1998), and *Resurrection Blues* (2002)—but these later works received a mixed reception from American reviewers.

Death of a Salesman is one of the most widely known and influential plays of the twentieth-century theater, and in its narrative techniques and stagecraft, it represents an important development in Miller's career. His preceding play, *All My Sons,* which hinges on the gradual revelation of past events, follows the cause-and-effect structure of discovery and consequence that he admired in the plays of HENRIK IBSEN. In *Salesman*, in contrast, the playwright sought to capture the lived experience of time, with its fluid boundaries between past and present, inner world and outer world. He wanted a play, he later wrote, that would "cut through time like a knife through a layer cake or a road through a mountain revealing its geologic layers, and instead of one incident in one time-frame succeeding another, display past and present concurrently, with neither one ever coming to a stop." Miller's initial image of the set was of a face as tall as the proscenium arch that would open up to reveal the inside of a man's head, a conception captured in his early working title: *The Inside of His Head*. But as the play developed—and as he incorporated the theatrical contributions of Kazan and the stage designer, Jo Mielziner—Miller abandoned such an expressionistic approach for the mode of subjective realism that Mielziner had pioneered in productions of Tennessee Williams's *A Glass Menagerie* (1945) and *A Streetcar Named Desire* (1947).

By drawing on realist stagecraft while simultaneously transcending it, subjective realism renders porous the boundaries between internal and external reality. *Death of a Salesman* takes place in the house and backyard of the Loman family in midcentury Brooklyn. Surrounding this area, marked by a harsh orange glow, loom the towering shapes of city buildings. The house itself, which creates an impression of fragility, is indicated only in outline, with imaginary walls, a one-dimensional roofline, and minimal furnishings. An apron that curves into the audience provides the setting for other city scenes and for Willy Loman's memories and imaginings. When the play's action takes place in the present, characters observe the conventions of realistic time and space, entering the house only through its doors. When the scene shifts to the past, however, characters walk through the imaginary walls as if they didn't exist. In keeping with Willy's memories of a more pastoral Brooklyn when the neighborhood was covered with elms, the surrounding buildings recede and the stage is lit with a pattern of leaves during those scenes when Willy relives his past.

Even before Miller wrote *Death of a Salesman* in the spring of 1948, the figure of the salesman occupied an important place in his life and imagination. His father had worked as a salesman for Miller's grandfather's company, traveling around the country selling coats, and two of his uncles—both of whom lived with their families in Brooklyn, where Miller visited them before his own family moved to the borough—were career salesmen. The traveling salesmen whom Miller knew embodied the entrepreneurial dreams and haunting failures that marked American capitalism. "[T]hese men lived like artists," Miller declared, "like actors whose product is first of all themselves, forever imagining triumphs in a world that either ignores them or denies their presence altogether." While working for his father in the early 1930s, Miller wrote a short story, "In Memoriam," that was based on a salesman in his father's business who had committed suicide by throwing himself in front of a New York elevated train.

In the twenty-four hours during which the play takes place, Willy Loman searches for some way of reconciling the aspirations that have shaped his life with what he fears is the failure of that life. More than sixty years old, he can no longer earn his keep as a traveling salesman, his sons have not fulfilled the dreams he held for them, and the contradictions that have defined his personality are becoming increasingly apparent. Faced with a desperate present, he seeks refuge in a past that is the product more of nostalgia than of accurate recall. The "remembered" scenes with his family a quarter century earlier, in which he basks in his sons' adoration, are clearly idealized, polished and buffed like his old car. The glow of this past is the glow of an America with a limitless panorama of opportunity and promise, a place where the sky's the limit and all things are possible for a man with personal magnetism. This America has roots in the nineteenth-century frontier: specifically, the American West, where Willy's father sold flutes with his family in a covered wagon, and the territories—Alaska and Africa—where his brother Ben earned a fortune. "[T]hat's the wonder, the wonder of this country," Willy rhapsodizes, "that a man can end with diamonds here on the basis of being liked!" These myths of individualism and success are epitomized in Dave Singleman, a salesman of the previous generation who, after a successful career spent crisscrossing the country, winning customers and making friends, dies "the death of a salesman"—in green velvet slippers in the smoking car of a train—and is fondly remembered by hundreds of salesmen and buyers at his funeral.

Willy holds fiercely to this entrepreneurial dream and all it entails—competition, consumerism, status, the marketing of oneself as a commodity—as if his faith in the American dream guaranteed him a place within it. His slogans about success and popularity are repeated like mantras. But the discrepancies between myth and reality, as well as the contradictions between different facets of the myth itself, create powerful ironies. Willy buys the refrigerator that has the "biggest ads" but finds it in constant need of repairs. He boasts of his popularity on the road—"I can park my car in any street in New England, and the cops protect it like their own"—but minutes later confides to his wife that prospective customers laugh at him behind his back. Willy champions his sons Biff and Happy over their neighbor Bernard, but it is the latter who achieves economic and social success. Once a promising high school football star, Biff drifts from job to job, compulsively stealing things in a self-destructive flight from himself. And the ironically named Happy, who works as an assistant manager, womanizes as a way of bolstering his self-image. Willy has tried to imbue his sons with the secrets of success, but what they inherit from him are the pathological undersides of the ethic he advocates.

To the director and drama critic Harold Clurman, *Death of a Salesman* represents a challenge to the American dream, or at least the capitalist version of it: "[S]ince the Civil War, and particularly since 1900, the American dream has become distorted by the dream of business success." From a Marxist perspective, Willy's tragedy reflects the logic of commodification, whereby the value of something is what it can sell for. Alienated from the work of his hands and the genuineness of relationships, this salesman is worth, in the end, only the dollar amount of the insurance policy on his life. Reacting to this component of Miller's critique, one right-wing publication called *Death of a Salesman* "a time bomb expertly placed under the edifice of Americanism." But Miller's attitude toward the capitalist culture that produced Willy Loman was ambivalent. As he himself pointed out, the most decent person in the play is Charley, a successful businessman, and the dreams that he and his son hold come to pass, as far as we can see. And while Biff Loman finds himself by rejecting his father's aspirations—"He had the wrong dreams"—Charley offers an alternative perspective: "A salesman is got to dream, boy. It comes with the territory."

The last words in *Salesman* belong to Linda Loman, and her presence underscores the centrality of family to Miller's tragedy. *Death of a Salesman* was written and produced in the years immediately after World War II, and its dramatic concerns reflect pressures on the institution of the family that mounted in the postwar United States: urbanization, the emergence (and increasing isolation) of the nuclear family, and a hardening of gender roles that would continue into the 1950s. Miller registers the impact of these forces on the relation-

Willy Loman (played by Lee Cobb, center) in a "memory" scene with his boys Happy (left; played by Cameron Mitchell) and Biff (right; played by Arthur Kennedy), from the 1949 Broadway production of *Death of a Salesman.*

ships within the Loman family, particularly those between fathers and sons. The sense of need that drives Willy—he confesses to feeling "kind of temporary about [him]self"—is linked to his having been abandoned by his father at an early age, and he turns to his brother Ben as a surrogate for that missing paternal presence. Looking to the generation ahead, he seeks to consolidate through his two sons what identity he does possess. Despite the heightened images of male accomplishment throughout the play—high school football hero, wilderness explorer, business tycoon, ladies' man—masculinity, for Miller, is a source of anxiety, and the struggles, exaggerations, and rule breaking in which Willy engages are compensations for his failure to live up to these images. Emphasizing this dynamic, feminist and other analysts have drawn attention to Linda's role within the play. Some critics view her as a source of Willy's problems, arguing that she fails to understand him, encourages him in self-deception or illusion, or interjects materialistic values of her own. Others see her as a source of strength, acting forcefully at a number of moments while trying to balance the claims of reality with her husband's need for self-esteem. In the eyes of one of the play's early reviewers, the single-mindedness of Linda's love holds the play together; more recently, a number of feminist critics have contended that her characterization is circumscribed by the roles available to her in the masculine value system that dominates Miller's play.

In a 1999 essay commemorating the play's fiftieth anniversary, Miller described what he considered to be the power of *Death of a Salesman*: "Being human—a father, mother, son—is something most of us fail at most of the time, and a little mercy is eminently in order given the societies we live in, which purport to be stable and sound as mountains when in fact they are all trembling in a fast wind blowing mindlessly around the earth." In countries as remote from postwar America as Communist China (where *Salesman* was produced to great acclaim in 1983), the play has spoken to the dreams and anxieties of the late twentieth- and early twenty-first-century world. Indeed, as national economies become part of an ever-expanding global capitalism—and developed nations deal with outsourced labor, international finance markets, and the loss of blue-collar jobs—its insistence on the dignity of the individual is as urgent as ever. S.G.

Death of a Salesman

CHARACTERS

WILLY LOMAN
LINDA
BIFF
HAPPY
BERNARD
THE WOMAN
CHARLEY
UNCLE BEN
HOWARD WAGNER
JENNY
STANLEY
MISS FORSYTHE
LETTA

The action takes place in Willy Loman's house and yard and in various places he visits in the New York and Boston of today.

Act 1

A melody is heard, played upon a flute. It is small and fine, telling of grass and trees and the horizon. The curtain rises.

Before us is the Salesman's house. We are aware of towering, angular shapes behind it, surrounding it on all sides. Only the blue light of the sky falls upon the house and forestage; the surrounding area shows an angry glow of orange. As more light appears, we see a solid vault of apartment houses around the small, fragile-seeming home. An air of the dream clings to the place, a dream rising out of reality. The kitchen at center seems actual enough, for there is a kitchen table with three chairs, and a refrigerator. But no other fixtures are seen. At the back of the kitchen there is a draped entrance, which leads to the living room. To the right of the kitchen, on a level raised two feet, is a bedroom furnished only with a brass bedstead and a straight chair. On a shelf over the bed a silver athletic trophy stands. A window opens onto the apartment house at the side.

Behind the kitchen, on a level raised six and a half feet, is the boys' bedroom, at present barely visible. Two beds are dimly seen, and at the back of the room a dormer window. (This bedroom is above the unseen living room.) At the left a stairway curves up to it from the kitchen.

The entire setting is wholly, or, in some places, partially transparent. The roofline of the house is one-dimensional; under and over it we see the apartment buildings. Before the house lies an apron,[1] curving beyond the forestage into the orchestra. This forward area serves as the backyard as well as the locale of all WILLY'S *imaginings and of his city scenes. Whenever the action is in the present the actors observe the imaginary wall-lines, entering the house only through its door at the left. But in the scenes of the past these boundaries are broken, and characters enter or leave a room by stepping "through" a wall onto the forestage.*

From the right, WILLY LOMAN, *the Salesman, enters, carrying two large sample cases. The flute plays on. He hears but is not aware of it. He is past sixty years of age, dressed quietly. Even as he crosses the stage to the doorway of the house, his exhaustion is apparent.*

1. The foremost part of the stage, in front of the proscenium arch.

He unlocks the door, comes into the kitchen, and thankfully lets his burden down, feeling the soreness of his palms. A word-sigh escapes his lips—it might be "Oh, boy, oh, boy." He closes the door, then carries his cases out into the living room, through the draped kitchen doorway.

LINDA, *his wife, has stirred in her bed at the right. She gets out and puts on a robe, listening. Most often jovial, she has developed an iron repression of her exceptions to Willy's behavior—she more than loves him, she admires him, as though his mercurial nature, his temper, his massive dreams and little cruelties, served her only as sharp reminders of the turbulent longings within him, longings which she shares but lacks the temperament to utter and follow to their end.*

LINDA [*hearing* WILLY *outside the bedroom, calls with some trepidation*] Willy!

WILLY It's all right. I came back.

LINDA Why? What happened? [*Slight pause*] Did something happen, Willy?

WILLY No, nothing happened.

LINDA You didn't smash the car, did you?

WILLY [*with casual irritation*] I said nothing happened. Didn't you hear me?

LINDA Don't you feel well?

WILLY I'm tired to the death. [*The flute has faded away. He sits on the bed beside her, a little numb.*] I couldn't make it. I just couldn't make it, Linda.

LINDA [*very carefully, delicately*] Where were you all day? You look terrible.

WILLY I got as far as a little above Yonkers. I stopped for a cup of coffee. Maybe it was the coffee.

LINDA What?

WILLY [*after a pause*] I suddenly couldn't drive anymore. The car kept going off onto the shoulder, y'know?

LINDA [*helpfully*] Oh. Maybe it was the steering again. I don't think Angelo knows the Studebaker.

WILLY No, it's me, it's me. Suddenly I realize I'm goin' sixty miles an hour and I don't remember the last five minutes. I'm—I can't seem to—keep my mind to it.

LINDA Maybe it's your glasses. You never went for your new glasses.

WILLY No, I see everything. I came back ten miles an hour. It took me nearly four hours from Yonkers.

LINDA [*resigned*] Well, you'll just have to take a rest, Willy, you can't continue this way.

WILLY I just got back from Florida.

LINDA But you didn't rest your mind. Your mind is overactive, and the mind is what counts, dear.

WILLY I'll start out in the morning. Maybe I'll feel better in the morning. [*She is taking off his shoes.*] These goddam arch supports are killing me.

LINDA Take an aspirin. Should I get you an aspirin? It'll soothe you.

WILLY [*with wonder*] I was driving along, you understand? And I was fine. I was even observing the scenery. You can imagine, me looking at scenery, on the road every week of my life. But it's so beautiful up there, Linda, the trees are so thick, and the sun is warm. I opened the windshield and just let the warm air bathe over me. And then all of a sudden I'm goin' off the road! I'm tellin' ya, I absolutely forgot I was driving. If I'd've gone the other way over the white line I might've killed somebody. So I went on again—and five minutes later I'm dreamin' again, and I nearly—[*He presses two fingers against his eyes.*] I have such thoughts, I have such strange thoughts.

LINDA Willy, dear. Talk to them again. There's no reason why you can't work in New York.

WILLY They don't need me in New York. I'm the New England man. I'm vital in New England.

LINDA But you're sixty years old. They can't expect you to keep traveling every week.

WILLY I'll have to send a wire to Portland. I'm supposed to see Brown and Morrison tomorrow morning at ten o'clock to show the line. Goddammit, I could sell them! [*He starts putting on his jacket.*]

LINDA [*taking the jacket from him*] Why don't you go down to the place tomorrow and tell Howard you've simply got to work in New York? You're too accommodating, dear.

WILLY If old man Wagner was alive I'd a been in charge of New York now! That man was a prince, he was a masterful man. But that boy of his, that Howard, he don't appreciate. When I went north the first time, the Wagner Company didn't know where New England was!

LINDA Why don't you tell those things to Howard, dear?

WILLY [*encouraged*] I will, I definitely will. Is there any cheese?

LINDA I'll make you a sandwich.

WILLY No, go to sleep. I'll take some milk. I'll be up right away. The boys in?

LINDA They're sleeping. Happy took Biff on a date tonight.

WILLY [*interested*] That so?

LINDA It was so nice to see them shaving together, one behind the other, in the bathroom. And going out together. You notice? The whole house smells of shaving lotion.

WILLY Figure it out. Work a lifetime to pay off a house. You finally own it, and there's nobody to live in it.

LINDA Well, dear, life is a casting off. It's always that way.

WILLY No, no, some people—some people accomplish something. Did Biff say anything after I went this morning?

LINDA You shouldn't have criticized him, Willy, especially after he just got off the train. You mustn't lose your temper with him.

WILLY When the hell did I lose my temper? I simply asked him if he was making any money. Is that a criticism?

LINDA But, dear, how could he make any money?

WILLY [*worried and angered*] There's such an undercurrent in him. He became a moody man. Did he apologize when I left this morning?

LINDA He was crestfallen, Willy. You know how he admires you. I think if he finds himself, then you'll both be happier and not fight any more.

WILLY How can he find himself on a farm? Is that a life? A farmhand? In the beginning, when he was young, I thought, well, a young man, it's good for him to tramp around, take a lot of different jobs. But it's more than ten years now and he has yet to make thirty-five dollars[2] a week!

LINDA He's finding himself, Willy.

WILLY Not finding yourself at the age of thirty-four is a disgrace!

LINDA Shh!

WILLY The trouble is he's lazy, goddammit!

2. The equivalent of about $325 in 2008.

LINDA Willy, please!

WILLY Biff is a lazy bum!

LINDA They're sleeping. Get something to eat. Go on down.

WILLY Why did he come home? I would like to know what brought him home.

LINDA I don't know. I think he's still lost, Willy. I think he's very lost.

WILLY Biff Loman is lost. In the greatest country in the world a young man with such—personal attractiveness, gets lost. And such a hard worker. There's one thing about Biff—he's not lazy.

LINDA Never.

WILLY [*with pity and resolve*] I'll see him in the morning; I'll have a nice talk with him. I'll get him a job selling. He could be big in no time. My God! Remember how they used to follow him around in high school? When he smiled at one of them their faces lit up. When he walked down the street . . . [*He loses himself in reminiscences.*]

LINDA [*trying to bring him out of it*] Willy, dear, I got a new kind of American-type cheese today. It's whipped.

WILLY Why do you get American when I like Swiss?

LINDA I just thought you'd like a change—

WILLY I don't want a change! I want Swiss cheese. Why am I always being contradicted?

LINDA [*with a covering laugh*] I thought it would be a surprise.

WILLY Why don't you open a window in here, for God's sake?

LINDA [*with infinite patience*] They're all open, dear.

WILLY The way they boxed us in here. Bricks and windows, windows and bricks.

LINDA We should've bought the land next door.

WILLY The street is lined with cars. There's not a breath of fresh air in the neighborhood. The grass don't grow anymore, you can't raise a carrot in the backyard. They should've had a law against apartment houses. Remember those two beautiful elm trees out there? When I and Biff hung the swing between them?

LINDA Yeah, like being a million miles from the city.

WILLY They should've arrested the builder for cutting those down. They massacred the neighborhood. [*Lost*] More and more I think of those days, Linda. This time of year it was lilac and wisteria. And then the peonies would come out, and the daffodils. What fragrance in this room!

LINDA Well, after all, people had to move somewhere.

WILLY No, there's more people now.

LINDA I don't think there's more people. I think—

WILLY There's more people! That's what's ruining this country! Population is getting out of control. The competition is maddening! Smell the stink from that apartment house! And another one on the other side . . . How can they whip cheese?

[*On* WILLY*'s last line,* BIFF *and* HAPPY *raise themselves up in their beds, listening.*]

LINDA Go down, try it. And be quiet.

WILLY [*turning to* LINDA, *guiltily*] You're not worried about me, are you, sweetheart?

BIFF What's the matter?

HAPPY Listen!

LINDA You've got too much on the ball to worry about.

WILLY You're my foundation and my support, Linda.

LINDA Just try to relax, dear. You make mountains out of molehills.

WILLY I won't fight with him anymore. If he wants to go back to Texas, let him go.

LINDA He'll find his way.

WILLY Sure. Certain men just don't get started till later in life. Like Thomas Edison, I think. Or B. F. Goodrich.[3] One of them was deaf. [*He starts for the bedroom doorway.*] I'll put my money on Biff.

LINDA And Willy—if it's warm Sunday we'll drive in the country. And we'll open the windshield, and take lunch.

WILLY No, the windshields don't open on the new cars.

LINDA But you opened it today.

WILLY Me? I didn't. [*He stops.*] Now isn't that peculiar! Isn't that a remarkable—[*He breaks off in amazement and fright as the flute is heard distantly.*]

LINDA What, darling?

WILLY That is the most remarkable thing.

LINDA What, dear?

WILLY I was thinking of the Chevvy. [*Slight pause*] Nineteen twenty-eight . . . when I had that red Chevvy—[*Breaks off.*] That funny? I coulda sworn I was driving that Chevvy today.

LINDA Well, that's nothing. Something must've reminded you.

WILLY Remarkable. Ts. Remember those days? The way Biff used to simonize[4] that car? The dealer refused to believe there was eighty thousand miles on it. [*He shakes his head.*] Heh! [*To* LINDA] Close your eyes, I'll be right up. [*He walks out of the bedroom.*]

HAPPY [*to* BIFF] Jesus, maybe he smashed up the car again!

LINDA [*calling after* WILLY] Be careful on the stairs, dear! The cheese is on the middle shelf! [*She turns, goes over to the bed, takes his jacket, and goes out of the bedroom.*]

[*Light has risen on the boys' room. Unseen,* WILLY *is heard talking to himself, "Eighty thousand miles," and a little laugh.* BIFF *gets out of bed, comes downstage a bit, and stands attentively.* BIFF *is two years older than his brother* HAPPY, *well built, but in these days bears a worn air and seems less self-assured. He has succeeded less, and his dreams are stronger and less acceptable than* HAPPY'S. HAPPY *is tall, powerfully made. Sexuality is like a visible color on him, or a scent that many women have discovered. He, like his brother, is lost, but in a different way, for he has never allowed himself to turn his face toward defeat and is thus more confused and hard-skinned, although seemingly more content.*]

HAPPY [*getting out of bed*] He's going to get his license taken away if he keeps that up. I'm getting nervous about him, y'know, Biff?

3. An American industrialist (1851–1888); his first investment venture into rubber manufacturing failed, but in 1870 he helped form the company that soon bore only his name. The legendary American inventor Edison (1847–1931) is most famous for creating the phonograph and the first commercially viable incandescent lightbulb; his rapid rise to success and early hearing loss are well-known chapters in his life story.

4. To polish (the Simoniz brand of car wax was first sold in 1935).

BIFF His eyes are going.

HAPPY No, I've driven with him. He sees all right. He just doesn't keep his mind on it. I drove into the city with him last week. He stops at a green light and then it turns red and he goes. [*He laughs.*]

BIFF Maybe he's color-blind.

HAPPY Pop? Why he's got the finest eye for color in the business. You know that.

BIFF [*sitting down on his bed*] I'm going to sleep.

HAPPY You're not still sour on Dad, are you, Biff?

BIFF He's all right, I guess.

WILLY [*underneath them, in the living room*] Yes, sir, eighty thousand miles—eighty-two thousand!

BIFF You smoking?

HAPPY [*holding out a pack of cigarettes*] Want one?

BIFF [*taking a cigarette*] I can never sleep when I smell it.

WILLY What a simonizing job, heh!

HAPPY [*with deep sentiment*] Funny, Biff, y'know? Us sleeping in here again? The old beds. [*He pats his bed affectionately.*] All the talk that went across those two beds, huh? Our whole lives.

BIFF Yeah. Lotta dreams and plans.

HAPPY [*with a deep and masculine laugh*] About five hundred women would like to know what was said in this room.

[*They share a soft laugh.*]

BIFF Remember that big Betsy something—what the hell was her name—over on Bushwick Avenue?[5]

HAPPY [*combing his hair*] With the collie dog!

BIFF That's the one. I got you in there, remember?

HAPPY Yeah, that was my first time—I think. Boy, there was a pig! [*They laugh, almost crudely.*] You taught me everything I know about women. Don't forget that.

BIFF I bet you forgot how bashful you used to be. Especially with girls.

HAPPY Oh, I still am, Biff.

BIFF Oh, go on.

HAPPY I just control it, that's all. I think I got less bashful and you got more so. What happened, Biff? Where's the old humor, the old confidence? [*He shakes* BIFF*'s knee.* BIFF *gets up and moves restlessly about the room.*] What's the matter?

BIFF Why does Dad mock me all the time?

HAPPY He's not mocking you, he—

BIFF Everything I say there's a twist of mockery on his face. I can't get near him.

HAPPY He just wants you to make good, that's all. I wanted to talk to you about Dad for a long time, Biff. Something's—happening to him. He—talks to himself.

BIFF I noticed that this morning. But he always mumbled.

HAPPY But not so noticeable. It got so embarrassing I sent him to Florida. And you know something? Most of the time he's talking to you.

BIFF What's he say about me?

5. A major thoroughfare in Brooklyn, New York.

HAPPY I can't make it out.

BIFF What's he say about me?

HAPPY I think the fact that you're not settled, that you're still kind of up in the air . . .

BIFF There's one or two other things depressing him, Happy.

HAPPY What do you mean?

BIFF Never mind. Just don't lay it all to me.

HAPPY But I think if you just got started—I mean—is there any future for you out there?

BIFF I tell ya, Hap, I don't know what the future is. I don't know—what I'm supposed to want.

HAPPY What do you mean?

BIFF Well, I spent six or seven years after high school trying to work myself up. Shipping clerk, salesman, business of one kind or another. And it's a measly manner of existence. To get on that subway on the hot mornings in summer. To devote your whole life to keeping stock, or making phone calls, or selling or buying. To suffer fifty weeks of the year for the sake of a two-week vacation, when all you really desire is to be outdoors, with your shirt off. And always to have to get ahead of the next fella. And still—that's how you build a future.

HAPPY Well, you really enjoy it on a farm? Are you content out there?

BIFF [*with rising agitation*] Hap, I've had twenty or thirty different kinds of jobs since I left home before the war, and it always turns out the same. I just realized it lately. In Nebraska when I herded cattle, and the Dakotas, and Arizona, and now in Texas. It's why I came home now, I guess, because I realized it. This farm I work on, it's spring there now, see? And they've got about fifteen new colts. There's nothing more inspiring or—beautiful than the sight of a mare and a new colt. And it's cool there now, see? Texas is cool now, and it's spring. And whenever spring comes to where I am, I suddenly get the feeling, my God, I'm not gettin' anywhere! What the hell am I doing, playing around with horses, twenty-eight dollars a week! I'm thirty-four years old, I oughta be makin' my future. That's when I come running home. And now, I get here, and I don't know what to do with myself. [*After a pause*] I've always made a point of not wasting my life, and every time I come back here I know that all I've done is to waste my life.

HAPPY You're a poet, you know that, Biff? You're a—you're an idealist!

BIFF No, I'm mixed up very bad. Maybe I oughta get married. Maybe I oughta get stuck into something. Maybe that's my trouble. I'm like a boy. I'm not married, I'm not in business, I just—I'm like a boy. Are you content, Hap? You're a success, aren't you? Are you content?

HAPPY Hell, no!

BIFF Why? You're making money, aren't you?

HAPPY [*moving about with energy, expressiveness*] All I can do now is wait for the merchandise manager to die. And suppose I get to be merchandise manager? He's a good friend of mine, and he just built a terrific estate on Long Island. And he lived there about two months and sold it, and now he's building another one. He can't enjoy it once it's finished. And I know that's just what I would do. I don't know what the hell I'm workin' for. Sometimes I sit in my apartment—all alone. And I think of the rent I'm paying. And it's crazy. But then, it's what I always wanted. My own apartment, a car, and plenty of women. And still, goddammit, I'm lonely.

BIFF [*with enthusiasm*] Listen, why don't you come out West with me?

HAPPY You and I, heh?

BIFF Sure, maybe we could buy a ranch. Raise cattle, use our muscles. Men built like we are should be working out in the open.

HAPPY [*avidly*] The Loman Brothers, heh?

BIFF [*with vast affection*] Sure, we'd be known all over the counties!

HAPPY [*enthralled*] That's what I dream about, Biff. Sometimes I want to just rip my clothes off in the middle of the store and outbox that goddam merchandise manager. I mean I can outbox, outrun, and outlift anybody in that store, and I have to take orders from those common, petty sons-of-bitches till I can't stand it anymore.

BIFF I'm tellin' you, kid, if you were with me I'd be happy out there.

HAPPY [*enthused*] See, Biff, everybody around me is so false that I'm constantly lowering my ideals . . .

BIFF Baby, together we'd stand up for one another, we'd have someone to trust.

HAPPY If I were around you—

BIFF Hap, the trouble is we weren't brought up to grub for money. I don't know how to do it.

HAPPY Neither can I!

BIFF Then let's go!

HAPPY The only thing is—what can you make out there?

BIFF But look at your friend. Builds an estate and then hasn't the peace of mind to live in it.

HAPPY Yeah, but when he walks into the store the waves part in front of him. That's fifty-two thousand dollars a year coming through the revolving door, and I got more in my pinky finger than he's got in his head.

BIFF Yeah, but you just said—

HAPPY I gotta show some of those pompous, self-important executives over there that Hap Loman can make the grade. I want to walk into the store the way he walks in. Then I'll go with you, Biff. We'll be together yet, I swear. But take those two we had tonight. Now weren't they gorgeous creatures?

BIFF Yeah, yeah, most gorgeous I've had in years.

HAPPY I get that anytime I want, Biff. Whenever I feel disgusted. The only trouble is, it gets like bowling or something. I just keep knockin' them over and it doesn't mean anything. You still run around a lot?

BIFF Naa. I'd like to find a girl—steady, somebody with substance.

HAPPY That's what I long for.

BIFF Go on! You'd never come home.

HAPPY I would! Somebody with character, with resistance! Like Mom, y'know? You're gonna call me a bastard when I tell you this. That girl Charlotte I was with tonight is engaged to be married in five weeks. [*He tries on his new hat.*]

BIFF No kiddin'!

HAPPY Sure, the guy's in line for the vice-presidency of the store. I don't know what gets into me, maybe I just have an overdeveloped sense of competition or something, but I went and ruined her, and furthermore I can't get rid of her. And he's the third executive I've done that to. Isn't that a crummy characteristic? And to top it all, I go to their weddings! [*Indignantly, but laughing*] Like I'm not supposed to take bribes. Manufacturers offer me a hundred-dollar bill now and then to throw an order their way. You know how honest I am, but it's like this girl, see. I hate myself for it. Because I don't want the girl, and, still, I take it and—I love it!

BIFF Let's go to sleep.

HAPPY I guess we didn't settle anything, heh?

BIFF I just got one idea that I think I'm going to try.

HAPPY What's that?

BIFF Remember Bill Oliver?

HAPPY Sure, Oliver is very big now. You want to work for him again?

BIFF No, but when I quit he said something to me. He put his arm on my shoulder, and he said, "Biff, if you ever need anything, come to me."

HAPPY I remember that. That sounds good.

BIFF I think I'll go to see him. If I could get ten thousand or even seven or eight thousand dollars I could buy a beautiful ranch.

HAPPY I bet he'd back you. 'Cause he thought highly of you, Biff. I mean, they all do. You're well liked, Biff. That's why I say to come back here, and we both have the apartment. And I'm tellin' you, Biff, any babe you want . . .

BIFF No, with a ranch I could do the work I like and still be something. I just wonder though. I wonder if Oliver still thinks I stole that carton of basketballs.

HAPPY Oh, he probably forgot that long ago. It's almost ten years. You're too sensitive. Anyway, he didn't really fire you.

BIFF Well, I think he was going to. I think that's why I quit. I was never sure whether he knew or not. I know he thought the world of me, though. I was the only one he'd let lock up the place.

WILLY [*below*] You gonna wash the engine, Biff?

HAPPY Shh!

[BIFF *looks at* HAPPY, *who is gazing down, listening.* WILLY *is mumbling in the parlor.*]

HAPPY You hear that?

[*They listen.* WILLY *laughs warmly.*]

BIFF [*growing angry*] Doesn't he know Mom can hear that?

WILLY Don't get your sweater dirty, Biff!

[*A look of pain crosses* BIFF*'s face.*]

HAPPY Isn't that terrible? Don't leave again, will you? You'll find a job here. You gotta stick around. I don't know what to do about him, it's getting embarrassing.

WILLY What a simonizing job!

BIFF Mom's hearing that!

WILLY No kiddin', Biff, you got a date? Wonderful!

HAPPY Go on to sleep. But talk to him in the morning, will you?

BIFF [*reluctantly getting into bed*] With her in the house. Brother!

HAPPY [*getting into bed*] I wish you'd have a good talk with him.

[*The light on their room begins to fade.*]

BIFF [*to himself in bed*] That selfish, stupid . . .

HAPPY Sh . . . Sleep, Biff.

[*Their light is out. Well before they have finished speaking,* WILLY'S *form is dimly seen below in the darkened kitchen. He opens the refrigerator, searches in there, and takes out a bottle of milk. The apartment houses are fading out, and the entire house and surroundings become covered with leaves. Music insinuates itself as the leaves appear.*]

WILLY Just wanna be careful with those girls, Biff, that's all. Don't make any promises. No promises of any kind. Because a girl, y'know, they always believe what you tell 'em, and you're very young, Biff, you're too young to be talking seriously to girls.

[*Light rises on the kitchen.* WILLY, *talking, shuts the refrigerator door and comes downstage to the kitchen table. He pours milk into a glass. He is totally immersed in himself, smiling faintly.*]

WILLY Too young entirely, Biff. You want to watch your schooling first. Then when you're all set, there'll be plenty of girls for a boy like you. [*He smiles broadly at a kitchen chair.*] That so? The girls pay for you? [*He laughs.*] Boy, you must really be makin' a hit.

[WILLY *is gradually addressing—physically—a point offstage, speaking through the wall of the kitchen, and his voice has been rising in volume to that of a normal conversation.*]

WILLY I been wondering why you polish the car so careful. Ha! Don't leave the hubcaps, boys. Get the chamois to the hubcaps. Happy, use newspaper on the windows, it's the easiest thing. Show him how to do it, Biff! You see, Happy? Pad it up, use it like a pad. That's it, that's it, good work. You're doin' all right, Hap. [*He pauses, then nods in approbation for a few seconds, then looks upward.*] Biff, first thing we gotta do when we get time is clip that big branch over the house. Afraid it's gonna fall in a storm and hit the roof. Tell you what. We get a rope and sling her around, and then we climb up there with a couple of saws and take her down. Soon as you finish the car, boys, I wanna see ya. I got a surprise for you, boys.

BIFF [*offstage*] Whatta ya got, Dad?

WILLY No, you finish first. Never leave a job till you're finished—remember that. [*Looking toward the "big trees"*] Biff, up in Albany I saw a beautiful hammock. I think I'll buy it next trip, and we'll hang it right between those two elms. Wouldn't that be something? Just swingin' there under those branches. Boy, that would be . . .

[YOUNG BIFF *and* YOUNG HAPPY *appear from the direction* WILLY *was addressing.* HAPPY *carries rags and a pail of water.* BIFF, *wearing a sweater with a block "S," carries a football.*]

BIFF [*pointing in the direction of the car offstage*] How's that, Pop, professional?

WILLY Terrific. Terrific job, boys. Good work, Biff.

HAPPY Where's the surprise, Pop?

WILLY In the back seat of the car.

HAPPY Boy! [*He runs off.*]

BIFF What is it, Dad? Tell me, what'd you buy?

WILLY [*laughing, cuffs him*] Never mind, something I want you to have.

BIFF [*turns and starts off*] What is it, Hap?

HAPPY [*offstage*] It's a punching bag!

BIFF Oh, Pop!

WILLY It's got Gene Tunney's[6] signature on it!

[HAPPY *runs onstage with a punching bag.*]

BIFF Gee, how'd you know we wanted a punching bag?

WILLY Well, it's the finest thing for the timing.

HAPPY [*lies down on his back and pedals with his feet*] I'm losing weight, you notice, Pop?

WILLY [*to* HAPPY] Jumping rope is good too.

BIFF Did you see the new football I got?

WILLY [*examining the ball*] Where'd you get a new ball?

BIFF The coach told me to practice my passing.

WILLY That so? And he gave you the ball, heh?

BIFF Well, I borrowed it from the locker room. [*He laughs confidentially.*]

WILLY [*laughing with him at the theft*] I want you to return that.

HAPPY I told you he wouldn't like it!

BIFF [*angrily*] Well, I'm bringing it back!

WILLY [*stopping the incipient argument, to* HAPPY] Sure, he's gotta practice with a regulation ball, doesn't he? [*To* BIFF] Coach'll probably congratulate you on your initiative!

BIFF Oh, he keeps congratulating my initiative all the time, Pop.

WILLY That's because he likes you. If somebody else took that ball there'd be an uproar. So what's the report, boys, what's the report?

BIFF Where'd you go this time, Dad? Gee, we were lonesome for you.

WILLY [*pleased, puts an arm around each boy and they come down to the apron*] Lonesome, heh?

BIFF Missed you every minute.

WILLY Don't say? Tell you a secret, boys. Don't breathe it to a soul. Someday I'll have my own business, and I'll never have to leave home anymore.

HAPPY Like Uncle Charley, heh?

WILLY Bigger than Uncle Charley! Because Charley is not—liked. He's liked, but he's not—well liked.

BIFF Where'd you go this time, Dad?

WILLY Well, I got on the road, and I went north to Providence. Met the Mayor.

BIFF The Mayor of Providence!

WILLY He was sitting in the hotel lobby.

BIFF What'd he say?

WILLY He said, "Morning!" And I said, "You got a fine city here, Mayor." And then he had coffee with me. And then I went to Waterbury. Waterbury is a fine city. Big clock city, the famous Waterbury clock. Sold a nice bill[7] there. And then Boston—Boston is the cradle of the Revolution. A fine city. And a couple of other towns in Mass., and on to Portland and Bangor and straight home!

BIFF Gee, I'd love to go with you sometime, Dad.

WILLY Soon as summer comes.

HAPPY Promise?

6. James Joseph Tunney (1897–1978), an American boxer who was undefeated world heavyweight champion, 1926–28.

7. That is, a bill of goods; a consignment of merchandise.

WILLY You and Hap and I, and I'll show you all the towns. America is full of beautiful towns and fine, upstanding people. And they know me, boys, they know me up and down New England. The finest people. And when I bring you fellas up, there'll be open sesame for all of us, 'cause one thing, boys: I have friends. I can park my car in any street in New England, and the cops protect it like their own. This summer, heh?

BIFF and HAPPY [*together*] Yeah! You bet!

WILLY We'll take our bathing suits.

HAPPY We'll carry your bags, Pop!

WILLY Oh, won't that be something! Me comin' into the Boston stores with you boys carryin' my bags. What a sensation!

[BIFF *is prancing around, practicing passing the ball.*]

WILLY You nervous, Biff, about the game?

BIFF Not if you're gonna be there.

WILLY What do they say about you in school, now that they made you captain?

HAPPY There's a crowd of girls behind him every time the classes change.

BIFF [*taking* WILLY*'s hand*] This Saturday, Pop, this Saturday—just for you, I'm going to break through for a touchdown.

HAPPY You're supposed to pass.

BIFF I'm takin' one play for Pop. You watch me, Pop, and when I take off my helmet, that means I'm breakin' out. Then you watch me crash through that line!

WILLY [*kisses* BIFF] Oh, wait'll I tell this in Boston!

[BERNARD *enters in knickers. He is younger than* BIFF, *earnest and loyal, a worried boy.*]

BERNARD Biff, where are you? You're supposed to study with me today.

WILLY Hey, looka Bernard. What're you lookin' so anemic about, Bernard?

BERNARD He's gotta study, Uncle Willy. He's got Regents[8] next week.

HAPPY [*tauntingly, spinning* BERNARD *around*] Let's box, Bernard!

BERNARD Biff! [*He gets away from* HAPPY.] Listen, Biff, I heard Mr. Birnbaum say that if you don't start studyin' math he's gonna flunk you, and you won't graduate. I heard him!

WILLY You better study with him, Biff. Go ahead now.

BERNARD I heard him!

BIFF Oh, Pop, you didn't see my sneakers! [*He holds up a foot for* WILLY *to look at.*]

WILLY Hey, that's a beautiful job of printing!

BERNARD [*wiping his glasses*] Just because he printed University of Virginia on his sneakers doesn't mean they've got to graduate him, Uncle Willy!

WILLY [*angrily*] What're you talking about? With scholarships to three universities they're gonna flunk him?

BERNARD But I heard Mr. Birnbaum say—

WILLY Don't be a pest, Bernard! [*To his boys*] What an anemic!

BERNARD Okay, I'm waiting for you in my house, Biff.

[BERNARD *goes off. The Lomans laugh.*]

8. That is, Regents examinations: tests in specific subject areas administered by the state of New York to all students in public high schools.

WILLY Bernard is not well liked, is he?

BIFF He's liked, but he's not well liked.

HAPPY That's right, Pop.

WILLY That's just what I mean. Bernard can get the best marks in school, y'understand, but when he gets out in the business world, y'understand, you are going to be five times ahead of him. That's why I thank Almighty God you're both built like Adonises.[9] Because the man who makes an appearance in the business world, the man who creates personal interest, is the man who gets ahead. Be liked and you will never want. You take me, for instance. I never have to wait in line to see a buyer. "Willy Loman is here!" That's all they have to know, and I go right through.

BIFF Did you knock them dead, Pop?

WILLY Knocked 'em cold in Providence, slaughtered 'em in Boston.

HAPPY [*on his back, pedaling again*] I'm losing weight, you notice, Pop?

[LINDA *enters, as of old, a ribbon in her hair, carrying a basket of washing.*]

LINDA [*with youthful energy*] Hello, dear!

WILLY Sweetheart!

LINDA How'd the Chevvy run?

WILLY Chevrolet, Linda, is the greatest car ever built. [*To the boys*] Since when do you let your mother carry wash up the stairs?

BIFF Grab hold there, boy!

HAPPY Where to, Mom?

LINDA Hang them up on the line. And you better go down to your friends, Biff. The cellar is full of boys. They don't know what to do with themselves.

BIFF Ah, when Pop comes home they can wait!

WILLY [*laughs appreciatively*] You better go down and tell them what to do, Biff.

BIFF I think I'll have them sweep out the furnace room.

WILLY Good work, Biff.

BIFF [*goes through wall-line of kitchen to doorway at back and calls down*] Fellas! Everybody sweep out the furnace room! I'll be right down!

VOICES All right! Okay, Biff.

BIFF George and Sam and Frank, come out back! We're hangin' up the wash! Come on, Hap, on the double! [*He and* HAPPY *carry out the basket.*]

LINDA The way they obey him!

WILLY Well, that's training, the training. I'm tellin' you, I was sellin' thousands and thousands, but I had to come home.

LINDA Oh, the whole block'll be at that game. Did you sell anything?

WILLY I did five hundred gross in Providence and seven hundred gross in Boston.

LINDA No! Wait a minute, I've got a pencil. [*She pulls pencil and paper out of her apron pocket.*] That makes your commission . . . Two hundred—my God! Two hundred and twelve dollars!

WILLY Well, I didn't figure it yet, but . . .

LINDA How much did you do?

WILLY Well, I—I did—about a hundred and eighty gross in Providence. Well, no—it came to—roughly two hundred gross on the whole trip.

9. In Greek mythology, Adonis was a beautiful youth.

LINDA [*without hesitation*] Two hundred gross. That's . . . [*She figures.*]

WILLY The trouble was that three of the stores were half closed for inventory in Boston. Otherwise I woulda broke records.

LINDA Well, it makes seventy dollars and some pennies. That's very good.

WILLY What do we owe?

LINDA Well, on the first there's sixteen dollars on the refrigerator—

WILLY Why sixteen?

LINDA Well, the fan belt broke, so it was a dollar eighty.

WILLY But it's brand new.

LINDA Well, the man said that's the way it is. Till they work themselves in, y'know.

[*They move through the wall-line into the kitchen.*]

WILLY I hope we didn't get stuck on that machine.

LINDA They got the biggest ads of any of them!

WILLY I know, it's a fine machine. What else?

LINDA Well, there's nine-sixty for the washing machine. And for the vacuum cleaner there's three and a half due on the fifteenth. Then the roof, you got twenty-one dollars remaining.

WILLY It don't leak, does it?

LINDA No, they did a wonderful job. Then you owe Frank for the carburetor.

WILLY I'm not going to pay that man! That goddam Chevrolet, they ought to prohibit the manufacture of that car!

LINDA Well, you owe him three and a half. And odds and ends, comes to around a hundred and twenty dollars by the fifteenth.

WILLY A hundred and twenty dollars! My God, if business don't pick up I don't know what I'm gonna do!

LINDA Well, next week you'll do better.

WILLY Oh, I'll knock 'em dead next week. I'll go to Hartford. I'm very well liked in Hartford. You know, the trouble is, Linda, people don't seem to take to me.

[*They move onto the forestage.*]

LINDA Oh, don't be foolish.

WILLY I know it when I walk in. They seem to laugh at me.

LINDA Why? Why would they laugh at you? Don't talk that way, Willy.

[WILLY *moves to the edge of the stage.* LINDA *goes into the kitchen and starts to darn stockings.*]

WILLY I don't know the reason for it, but they just pass me by. I'm not noticed.

LINDA But you're doing wonderful, dear. You're making seventy to a hundred dollars a week.

WILLY But I gotta be at it ten, twelve hours a day. Other men—I don't know—they do it easier. I don't know why—I can't stop myself—I talk too much. A man oughta come in with a few words. One thing about Charley. He's a man of few words, and they respect him.

LINDA You don't talk too much, you're just lively.

WILLY [*smiling*] Well, I figure, what the hell, life is short, a couple of jokes. [*To himself*] I joke too much! [*The smile goes.*]

LINDA Why? You're—

WILLY I'm fat. I'm very—foolish to look at, Linda. I didn't tell you, but Christmastime I happened to be calling on F. H. Stewart's, and a salesman

I know, as I was going in to see the buyer I heard him say something about—walrus. And I—I cracked him right across the face. I won't take that. I simply will not take that. But they do laugh at me. I know that.

LINDA Darling . . .

WILLY I gotta overcome it. I know I gotta overcome it. I'm not dressing to advantage, maybe.

LINDA Willy, darling, you're the handsomest man in the world—

WILLY Oh, no, Linda.

LINDA To me you are. [*Slight pause*] The handsomest.

[*From the darkness is heard the laughter of a woman.* WILLY *doesn't turn to it, but it continues through* LINDA'*s lines.*]

LINDA And the boys, Willy. Few men are idolized by their children the way you are.

[*Music is heard as behind a scrim, to the left of the house,* THE WOMAN, *dimly seen, is dressing.*]

WILLY [*with great feeling*] You're the best there is, Linda, you're a pal, you know that? On the road—on the road I want to grab you sometimes and just kiss the life outa you.

[*The laughter is loud now, and he moves into a brightening area at the left, where* THE WOMAN *has come from behind the scrim and is standing, putting on her hat, looking into a "mirror" and laughing.*]

WILLY 'Cause I get so lonely—especially when business is bad and there's nobody to talk to. I get the feeling that I'll never sell anything again, that I won't make a living for you, or a business, a business for the boys. [*He talks through* THE WOMAN'*s subsiding laughter;* THE WOMAN *primps at the "mirror."*] There's so much I want to make for—

THE WOMAN Me? You didn't make me, Willy. I picked you.

WILLY [*pleased*] You picked me?

THE WOMAN [*who is quite proper-looking,* WILLY'*s age*] I did. I've been sitting at that desk watching all the salesmen go by, day in, day out. But you've got such a sense of humor, and we do have such a good time together, don't we?

WILLY Sure, sure. [*He takes her in his arms.*] Why do you have to go now?

THE WOMAN It's two o'clock . . .

WILLY No, come on in! [*He pulls her.*]

THE WOMAN . . . my sisters'll be scandalized. When'll you be back?

WILLY Oh, two weeks about. Will you come up again?

THE WOMAN Sure thing. You do make me laugh. It's good for me. [*She squeezes his arm, kisses him.*] And I think you're a wonderful man.

WILLY You picked me, heh?

THE WOMAN Sure. Because you're so sweet. And such a kidder.

WILLY Well, I'll see you next time I'm in Boston.

THE WOMAN I'll put you right through to the buyers.

WILLY [*slapping her bottom*] Right. Well, bottoms up!

THE WOMAN [*slaps him gently and laughs*] You just kill me, Willy. [*He suddenly grabs her and kisses her roughly.*] You kill me. And thanks for the stockings. I love a lot of stockings. Well, good night.

WILLY Good night. And keep your pores open!

THE WOMAN Oh, Willy!

[THE WOMAN *bursts out laughing, and* LINDA*'s laughter blends in.* THE WOMAN *disappears into the dark. Now the area at the kitchen table brightens.* LINDA *is sitting where she was at the kitchen table, but now is mending a pair of her silk stockings.*]

LINDA You are, Willy. The handsomest man. You've got no reason to feel that—

WILLY [*coming out of* THE WOMAN*'s dimming area and going over to* LINDA] I'll make it all up to you, Linda, I'll—

LINDA There's nothing to make up, dear. You're doing fine, better than—

WILLY [*noticing her mending*] What's that?

LINDA Just mending my stockings. They're so expensive—

WILLY [*angrily, taking them from her*] I won't have you mending stockings in this house! Now throw them out!

[LINDA *puts the stockings in her pocket.*]

BERNARD [*entering on the run*] Where is he? If he doesn't study!

WILLY [*moving to the forestage, with great agitation*] You'll give him the answers!

BERNARD I do, but I can't on a Regents! That's a state exam! They're liable to arrest me!

WILLY Where is he? I'll whip him, I'll whip him!

LINDA And he'd better give back that football, Willy, it's not nice.

WILLY Biff! Where is he? Why is he taking everything?

LINDA He's too rough with the girls, Willy. All the mothers are afraid of him!

WILLY I'll whip him!

BERNARD He's driving the car without a license!

[THE WOMAN*'s laugh is heard.*]

WILLY Shut up!

LINDA All the mothers—

WILLY Shut up!

BERNARD [*backing quietly away and out*] Mr. Birnbaum says he's stuck up.

WILLY Get outa here!

BERNARD If he doesn't buckle down he'll flunk math! [*He goes off.*]

LINDA He's right, Willy, you've gotta—

WILLY [*exploding at her*] There's nothing the matter with him! You want him to be a worm like Bernard? He's got spirit, personality . . .

[*As he speaks,* LINDA, *almost in tears, exits into the living room.* WILLY *is alone in the kitchen, wilting and staring. The leaves are gone. It is night again, and the apartment houses look down from behind.*]

WILLY Loaded with it. Loaded! What is he stealing? He's giving it back, isn't he? Why is he stealing? What did I tell him? I never in my life told him anything but decent things.

[HAPPY *in pajamas has come down the stairs;* WILLY *suddenly becomes aware of* HAPPY*'s presence.*]

HAPPY Let's go now, come on.

WILLY [*sitting down at the kitchen table*] Huh! Why did she have to wax the floors herself? Everytime she waxes the floors she keels over. She knows that!

HAPPY Shh! Take it easy. What brought you back tonight?

WILLY I got an awful scare. Nearly hit a kid in Yonkers. God! Why didn't I go to Alaska with my brother Ben that time! Ben! That man was a genius, that man was success incarnate! What a mistake! He begged me to go.

HAPPY Well, there's no use in—

WILLY You guys! There was a man started with the clothes on his back and ended up with diamond mines!

HAPPY Boy, someday I'd like to know how he did it.

WILLY What's the mystery? The man knew what he wanted and went out and got it! Walked into a jungle, and comes out, the age of twenty-one, and he's rich! The world is an oyster, but you don't crack it open on a mattress!

HAPPY Pop, I told you I'm gonna retire you for life.

WILLY You'll retire me for life on seventy goddam dollars a week? And your women and your car and your apartment, and you'll retire me for life! Christ's sake, I couldn't get past Yonkers today! Where are you guys, where are you? The woods are burning! I can't drive a car!

[CHARLEY *has appeared in the doorway. He is a large man, slow of speech, laconic, immovable. In all he says, despite what he says, there is pity, and, now, trepidation. He has a robe over pajamas, slippers on his feet. He enters the kitchen.*]

CHARLEY Everything all right?

HAPPY Yeah, Charley, everything's . . .

WILLY What's the matter?

CHARLEY I heard some noise. I thought something happened. Can't we do something about the walls? You sneeze in here, and in my house hats blow off.

HAPPY Let's go to bed, Dad. Come on.

[CHARLEY *signals to* HAPPY *to go.*]

WILLY You go ahead, I'm not tired at the moment.

HAPPY [*to* WILLY] Take it easy, huh? [*He exits.*]

WILLY What're you doin' up?

CHARLEY [*sitting down at the kitchen table opposite* WILLY] Couldn't sleep good. I had a heartburn.

WILLY Well, you don't know how to eat.

CHARLEY I eat with my mouth.

WILLY No, you're ignorant. You gotta know about vitamins and things like that.

CHARLEY Come on, let's shoot. Tire you out a little.

WILLY [*hesitantly*] All right. You got cards?

CHARLEY [*taking a deck from his pocket*] Yeah, I got them. Someplace. What is it with those vitamins?

WILLY [*dealing*] They build up your bones. Chemistry.

CHARLEY Yeah, but there's no bones in a heartburn.

WILLY What are you talkin' about? Do you know the first thing about it?

CHARLEY Don't get insulted.

WILLY Don't talk about something you don't know anything about.

[*They are playing. Pause.*]

CHARLEY What're you doin' home?

WILLY A little trouble with the car.

CHARLEY Oh. [*Pause*] I'd like to take a trip to California.

WILLY Don't say.

CHARLEY You want a job?

WILLY I got a job, I told you that. [*After a slight pause*] What the hell are you offering me a job for?

CHARLEY Don't get insulted.

WILLY Don't insult me.

CHARLEY I don't see no sense in it. You don't have to go on this way.

WILLY I got a good job. [*Slight pause*] What do you keep comin' in here for?

CHARLEY You want me to go?

WILLY [*after a pause, withering*] I can't understand it. He's going back to Texas again. What the hell is that?

CHARLEY Let him go.

WILLY I got nothin' to give him, Charley, I'm clean, I'm clean.

CHARLEY He won't starve. None a them starve. Forget about him.

WILLY Then what have I got to remember?

CHARLEY You take it too hard. To hell with it. When a deposit bottle is broken you don't get your nickel back.

WILLY That's easy enough for you to say.

CHARLEY That ain't easy for me to say.

WILLY Did you see the ceiling I put up in the living room?

CHARLEY Yeah, that's a piece of work. To put up a ceiling is a mystery to me. How do you do it?

WILLY What's the difference?

CHARLEY Well, talk about it.

WILLY You gonna put up a ceiling?

CHARLEY How could I put up a ceiling?

WILLY Then what the hell are you bothering me for?

CHARLEY You're insulted again.

WILLY A man who can't handle tools is not a man. You're disgusting.

CHARLEY Don't call me disgusting. Willy.

[UNCLE BEN, *carrying a valise and an umbrella, enters the forestage from around the right corner of the house. He is a stolid man, in his sixties, with a mustache and an authoritative air. He is utterly certain of his destiny, and there is an aura of far places about him. He enters exactly as* WILLY *speaks.*]

WILLY I'm getting awfully tired, Ben.

[BEN'*s music is heard.* BEN *looks around at everything.*]

CHARLEY Good, keep playing; you'll sleep better. Did you call me Ben?

[BEN *looks at his watch.*]

WILLY That's funny. For a second there you reminded me of my brother Ben.

BEN I only have a few minutes. [*He strolls, inspecting the place.* WILLY *and* CHARLEY *continue playing.*]

CHARLEY You never heard from him again, heh? Since that time?

WILLY Didn't Linda tell you? Couple of weeks ago we got a letter from his wife in Africa. He died.

CHARLEY That so.

BEN [*chuckling*] So this is Brooklyn, eh?

CHARLEY Maybe you're in for some of his money.

WILLY Naa, he had seven sons. There's just one opportunity I had with that man . . .

BEN I must make a train, William. There are several properties I'm looking at in Alaska.

WILLY Sure, sure! If I'd gone with him to Alaska that time, everything would've been totally different.

CHARLEY Go on, you'd froze to death up there.

WILLY What're you talking about?

BEN Opportunity is tremendous in Alaska, William. Surprised you're not up there.

WILLY Sure, tremendous.

CHARLEY Heh?

WILLY There was the only man I ever met who knew the answers.

CHARLEY Who?

BEN How are you all?

WILLY [*taking a pot,*[1] *smiling*] Fine, fine.

CHARLEY Pretty sharp tonight.

BEN Is Mother living with you?

WILLY No, she died a long time ago.

CHARLEY Who?

BEN That's too bad. Fine specimen of a lady, Mother.

WILLY [*to Charley*] Heh?

BEN I'd hoped to see the old girl.

CHARLEY Who died?

BEN Heard anything from Father, have you?

WILLY [*unnerved*] What do you mean, who died?

CHARLEY [*taking a pot*] What're you talkin' about?

BEN [*looking at his watch*] William, it's half-past eight!

WILLY [*as though to dispel his confusion he angrily stops* CHARLEY'*s hand*] That's my build![2]

CHARLEY I put the ace—

WILLY If you don't know how to play the game I'm not gonna throw my money away on you!

CHARLEY [*rising*] It was my ace, for God's sake!

WILLY I'm through, I'm through!

BEN When did Mother die?

WILLY Long ago. Since the beginning you never knew how to play cards.

CHARLEY [*picks up the cards and goes to the door*] All right! Next time I'll bring a deck with five aces.

WILLY I don't play that kind of game!

CHARLEY [*turning to him*] You ought to be ashamed of yourself!

WILLY Yeah?

CHARLEY Yeah! [*He goes out.*]

WILLY [*slamming the door after him*] Ignoramus!

BEN [*as* WILLY *comes toward him through the wall-line of the kitchen*] So you're William.

WILLY [*shaking* BEN'*s hand*] Ben! I've been waiting for you so long! What's the answer? How did you do it?

BEN Oh, there's a story in that.

[LINDA *enters the forestage, as of old, carrying the wash basket.*]

LINDA Is this Ben?

BEN [*gallantly*] How do you do, my dear.

1. The bets at stake in a hand of casino, the card game they are playing.
2. Casino players must take in builds (cards that combine to form a declared total) to win.

LINDA Where've you been all these years? Willy's always wondered why you—

WILLY [*pulling* BEN *away from her impatiently*] Where is Dad? Didn't you follow him? How did you get started?

BEN Well, I don't know how much you remember.

WILLY Well, I was just a baby, of course, only three or four years old—

BEN Three years and eleven months.

WILLY What a memory, Ben!

BEN I have many enterprises, William, and I have never kept books.

WILLY I remember I was sitting under the wagon in—was it Nebraska?

BEN It was South Dakota, and I gave you a bunch of wild flowers.

WILLY I remember you walking away down some open road.

BEN [*laughing*] I was going to find Father in Alaska.

WILLY Where is he?

BEN At that age I had a very faulty view of geography, William. I discovered after a few days that I was heading due south, so instead of Alaska, I ended up in Africa.

LINDA Africa!

WILLY The Gold Coast![3]

BEN Principally diamond mines.

LINDA Diamond mines!

BEN Yes, my dear. But I've only a few minutes—

WILLY No! Boys! Boys! [YOUNG BIFF *and* HAPPY *appear*.] Listen to this. This is your Uncle Ben, a great man! Tell my boys, Ben!

BEN Why, boys, when I was seventeen I walked into the jungle, and when I was twenty-one I walked out. [*He laughs*.] And by God I was rich.

WILLY [*to the boys*] You see what I been talking about? The greatest things can happen!

BEN [*glancing at his watch*] I have an appointment in Ketchikan Tuesday week.[4]

WILLY No, Ben! Please tell about Dad. I want my boys to hear. I want them to know the kind of stock they spring from. All I remember is a man with a big beard, and I was in Mamma's lap, sitting around a fire, and some kind of high music.

BEN His flute. He played the flute.

WILLY Sure, the flute, that's right!

[*New music is heard, a high, rollicking tune*.]

BEN Father was a very great and a very wild-hearted man. We would start in Boston, and he'd toss the whole family into the wagon, and then he'd drive the team right across the country; through Ohio, and Indiana, Michigan, Illinois, and all the Western states. And we'd stop in the towns and sell the flutes that he'd made on the way. Great inventor, Father. With one gadget he made more in a week than a man like you could make in a lifetime.

WILLY That's just the way I'm bringing them up, Ben—rugged, well liked, all-around.

3. The region of West Africa that is now Ghana (still a British colony in 1949); industrial diamonds are one of its major exports.

4. That is, in Ketchikan, Alaska, one week from Tuesday.

BEN Yeah? [*To* BIFF] Hit that, boy—hard as you can. [*He pounds his stomach.*]

BIFF Oh, no, sir!

BEN [*taking boxing stance*] Come on, get to me! [*He laughs.*]

WILLY Go to it, Biff! Go ahead, show him!

BIFF Okay! [*He cocks his fists and starts in.*]

LINDA [*to* WILLY] Why must he fight, dear?

BEN [*sparring with* BIFF] Good boy! Good boy!

WILLY How's that, Ben, heh?

HAPPY Give him the left, Biff!

LINDA Why are you fighting?

BEN Good boy! [*Suddenly comes in, trips* BIFF, *and stands over him, the point of his umbrella poised over* BIFF*'s eye.*]

LINDA Look out, Biff!

BIFF Gee!

BEN [*patting* BIFF*'s knee*] Never fight fair with a stranger, boy. You'll never get out of the jungle that way. [*Taking* LINDA*'s hand and bowing*] It was an honor and a pleasure to meet you, Linda.

LINDA [*withdrawing her hand coldly, frightened*] Have a nice—trip.

BEN [*to* WILLY] And good luck with your—what do you do?

WILLY Selling.

BEN Yes. Well . . . [*He raises his hand in farewell to all.*]

WILLY No, Ben, I don't want you to think . . . [*He takes* BEN*'s arm to show him.*] It's Brooklyn, I know, but we hunt too.

BEN Really, now.

WILLY Oh, sure, there's snakes and rabbits and—that's why I moved out here. Why, Biff can fell any one of these trees in no time! Boys! Go right over to where they're building the apartment house and get some sand. We're gonna rebuild the entire front stoop right now! Watch this, Ben!

BIFF Yes, sir! On the double, Hap!

HAPPY [*as he and* BIFF *run off*] I lost weight, Pop, you notice?

[CHARLEY *enters in knickers, even before the boys are gone.*]

CHARLEY Listen, if they steal any more from that building the watchman'll put the cops on them!

LINDA [*to Willy*] Don't let Biff . . .

[BEN *laughs lustily.*]

WILLY You shoulda seen the lumber they brought home last week. At least a dozen six-by-tens worth all kinds a money.

CHARLEY Listen, if that watchman—

WILLY I gave them hell, understand. But I got a couple of fearless characters there.

CHARLEY Willy, the jails are full of fearless characters.

BEN [*clapping* WILLY *on the back, with a laugh at* CHARLEY] And the stock exchange, friend!

WILLY [*joining in Ben's laughter*] Where are the rest of your pants?

CHARLEY My wife bought them.

WILLY Now all you need is a golf club and you can go upstairs and go to sleep. [*To* BEN] Great athlete! Between him and his son Bernard they can't hammer a nail!

BERNARD [*rushing in*] The watchman's chasing Biff!

WILLY [*angrily*] Shut up! He's not stealing anything!

LINDA [*alarmed, hurrying off left*] Where is he? Biff, dear! [*She exits.*]

WILLY [*moving toward the left, away from* BEN] There's nothing wrong. What's the matter with you?

BEN Nervy boy. Good!

WILLY [*laughing*] Oh, nerves of iron, that Biff!

CHARLEY Don't know what it is. My New England man comes back and he's bleedin', they murdered him up there.

WILLY It's contacts, Charley, I got important contacts!

CHARLEY [*sarcastically*] Glad to hear it, Willy. Come in later, we'll shoot a little casino. I'll take some of your Portland money. [*He laughs at Willy and exits.*]

WILLY [*turning to* BEN] Business is bad, it's murderous. But not for me, of course.

BEN I'll stop by on my way back to Africa.

WILLY [*longingly*] Can't you stay a few days? You're just what I need, Ben, because I—I have a fine position here, but I—well, Dad left when I was such a baby and I never had a chance to talk to him and I still feel—kind of temporary about myself.

BEN I'll be late for my train.

[*They are at opposite ends of the stage.*]

WILLY Ben, my boys—can't we talk? They'd go into the jaws of hell for me, see, but I—

BEN William, you're being first-rate with your boys. Outstanding, manly chaps!

WILLY [*hanging on to his words*] Oh, Ben, that's good to hear! Because sometimes I'm afraid that I'm not teaching them the right kind of—Ben, how should I teach them?

BEN [*giving great weight to each word, and with a certain vicious audacity*] William, when I walked into the jungle, I was seventeen. When I walked out I was twenty-one. And, by God, I was rich! [*He goes off into the darkness around the right corner of the house.*]

WILLY . . . was rich! That's just the spirit I want to imbue them with! To walk into a jungle! I was right! I was right! I was right!

[BEN *is gone, but* WILLY *is still speaking to him as* LINDA, *in nightgown and robe, enters the kitchen, glances around for* WILLY, *then goes to the door of the house, looks out and sees him. Comes down to his left. He looks at her.*]

LINDA Willy, dear? Willy?

WILLY I was right!

LINDA Did you have some cheese? [*He can't answer.*] It's very late, darling. Come to bed, heh?

WILLY [*looking straight up*] Gotta break your neck to see a star in this yard.

LINDA You coming in?

WILLY Whatever happened to that diamond watch fob? Remember? When Ben came from Africa that time? Didn't he give me a watch fob with a diamond in it?

LINDA You pawned it, dear. Twelve, thirteen years ago. For Biff's radio correspondence course.

WILLY Gee, that was a beautiful thing. I'll take a walk.

LINDA But you're in your slippers.

WILLY [*starting to go around the house at the left*] I was right! I was! [*Half to* LINDA, *as he goes, shaking his head*] What a man! There was a man worth talking to. I was right!

LINDA [*calling after* WILLY] But in your slippers, Willy!

[WILLY *is almost gone when* BIFF, *in his pajamas, comes down the stairs and enters the kitchen.*]

BIFF What is he doing out there?

LINDA Sh!

BIFF God Almighty, Mom, how long has he been doing this?

LINDA Don't, he'll hear you.

BIFF What the hell is the matter with him?

LINDA It'll pass by morning.

BIFF Shouldn't we do anything?

LINDA Oh, my dear, you should do a lot of things, but there's nothing to do, so go to sleep.

[HAPPY *comes down the stair and sits on the steps.*]

HAPPY I never heard him so loud, Mom.

LINDA Well, come around more often; you'll hear him. [*She sits down at the table and mends the lining of* WILLY's *jacket.*]

BIFF Why didn't you ever write me about this, Mom?

LINDA How would I write to you? For over three months you had no address.

BIFF I was on the move. But you know I thought of you all the time. You know that, don't you, pal?

LINDA I know, dear, I know. But he likes to have a letter. Just to know that there's still a possibility for better things.

BIFF He's not like this all the time, is he?

LINDA It's when you come home he's always the worst.

BIFF When I come home?

LINDA When you write you're coming, he's all smiles, and talks about the future, and—he's just wonderful. And then the closer you seem to come, the more shaky he gets, and then, by the time you get here, he's arguing, and he seems angry at you. I think it's just that maybe he can't bring himself to—to open up to you. Why are you so hateful to each other? Why is that?

BIFF [*evasively*] I'm not hateful, Mom.

LINDA But you no sooner come in the door than you're fighting!

BIFF I don't know why. I mean to change. I'm tryin', Mom, you understand?

LINDA Are you home to stay now?

BIFF I don't know. I want to look around, see what's doin'.

LINDA Biff, you can't look around all your life, can you?

BIFF I just can't take hold, Mom. I can't take hold of some kind of a life.

LINDA Biff, a man is not a bird, to come and go with the springtime.

BIFF Your hair . . . [*He touches her hair.*] Your hair got so gray.

LINDA Oh, it's been gray since you were in high school. I just stopped dyeing it, that's all.

BIFF Dye it again, will ya? I don't want my pal looking old. [*He smiles.*]

LINDA You're such a boy! You think you can go away for a year and . . . You've got to get it into your head now that one day you'll knock on this door and there'll be strange people here—

BIFF What are you talking about? You're not even sixty, Mom.

LINDA But what about your father?

BIFF [*lamely*] Well, I meant him too.

HAPPY He admires Pop.

LINDA Biff, dear, if you don't have any feeling for him, then you can't have any feeling for me.

BIFF Sure I can, Mom.

LINDA No. You can't just come to see me, because I love him. [*With a threat, but only a threat, of tears*] He's the dearest man in the world to me, and I won't have anyone making him feel unwanted and low and blue. You've got to make up your mind now, darling, there's no leeway any more. Either he's your father and you pay him that respect, or else you're not to come here. I know he's not easy to get along with—nobody knows that better than me—but . . .

WILLY [*from the left, with a laugh*] Hey, hey, Biffo!

BIFF [*starting to go out after* WILLY] What the hell is the matter with him? [HAPPY *stops him.*]

LINDA Don't—don't go near him!

BIFF Stop making excuses for him! He always, always wiped the floor with you. Never had an ounce of respect for you.

HAPPY He's always had respect for—

BIFF What the hell do you know about it?

HAPPY [*surlily*] Just don't call him crazy!

BIFF He's got no character—Charley wouldn't do this. Not in his own house—spewing out that vomit from his mind.

HAPPY Charley never had to cope with what he's got to.

BIFF People are worse off than Willy Loman. Believe me, I've seen them!

LINDA Then make Charley your father, Biff. You can't do that, can you? I don't say he's a great man. Willy Loman never made a lot of money. His name was never in the paper. He's not the finest character that ever lived. But he's a human being, and a terrible thing is happening to him. So attention must be paid. He's not to be allowed to fall into his grave like an old dog. Attention, attention must be finally paid to such a person. You called him crazy—

BIFF I didn't mean—

LINDA No, a lot of people think he's lost his—balance. But you don't have to be very smart to know what his trouble is. The man is exhausted.

HAPPY Sure!

LINDA A small man can be just as exhausted as a great man. He works for a company thirty-six years this March, opens up unheard-of territories to their trademark, and now in his old age they take his salary away.

HAPPY [*indignantly*] I didn't know that, Mom.

LINDA You never asked, my dear! Now that you get your spending money someplace else you don't trouble your mind with him.

HAPPY But I gave you money last—

LINDA Christmastime, fifty dollars! To fix the hot water it cost ninety-seven fifty! For five weeks he's been on straight commission, like a beginner, an unknown!

BIFF Those ungrateful bastards!

LINDA Are they any worse than his sons? When he brought them business, when he was young, they were glad to see him. But now his old friends, the old buyers that loved him so and always found some order to hand him in a pinch—they're all dead, retired. He used to be able to make six, seven calls a day in Boston. Now he takes his valises out of the car and puts them back and takes them out again and he's exhausted. Instead of walking he talks now. He drives seven hundred miles, and when he gets there no one knows him anymore, no one welcomes him. And what goes through a man's mind, driving seven hundred miles home without having earned a cent? Why shouldn't he talk to himself? Why? When he has to go to Charley and borrow fifty dollars a week and pretend to me that it's his pay? How long can that go on? How long? You see what I'm sitting here and waiting for? And you tell me he has no character? The man who never worked a day but for your benefit? When does he get the medal for that? Is this his reward—to turn around at the age of sixty-three and find his sons, who he loved better than his life, one a philandering bum—

HAPPY Mom!

LINDA That's all you are, my baby! [*To* BIFF] And you! What happened to the love you had for him? You were such pals! How you used to talk to him on the phone every night! How lonely he was till he could come home to you!

BIFF All right, Mom. I'll live here in my room, and I'll get a job. I'll keep away from him, that's all.

LINDA No, Biff. You can't stay here and fight all the time.

BIFF He threw me out of this house, remember that.

LINDA Why did he do that? I never knew why.

BIFF Because I know he's a fake and he doesn't like anybody around who knows!

LINDA Why a fake? In what way? What do you mean?

BIFF Just don't lay it all at my feet. It's between me and him—that's all I have to say. I'll chip in from now on. He'll settle for half my paycheck. He'll be all right. I'm going to bed. [*He starts for the stairs.*]

LINDA He won't be all right.

BIFF [*turning on the stairs, furiously*] I hate this city and I'll stay here. Now what do you want?

LINDA He's dying, Biff.

[HAPPY *turns quickly to her, shocked.*]

BIFF [*after a pause*] Why is he dying?

LINDA He's been trying to kill himself.

BIFF [*with great horror*] How?

LINDA I live from day to day.

BIFF What're you talking about?

LINDA Remember I wrote you that he smashed up the car again? In February?

BIFF Well?

LINDA The insurance inspector came. He said that they have evidence. That all these accidents in the last year—weren't—weren't—accidents.

HAPPY How can they tell that? That's a lie.

LINDA It seems there's a woman . . . [*She takes a breath as*]

BIFF [*sharply but contained*] What woman?

LINDA [*simultaneously*] . . . and this woman . . .

LINDA What?

BIFF Nothing. Go ahead.

LINDA What did you say?

BIFF Nothing. I just said what woman?

HAPPY What about her?

LINDA Well, it seems she was walking down the road and saw his car. She says that he wasn't driving fast at all, and that he didn't skid. She says he came to that little bridge, and then deliberately smashed into the railing, and it was only the shallowness of the water that saved him.

BIFF Oh, no, he probably just fell asleep again.

LINDA I don't think he fell asleep.

BIFF Why not?

LINDA Last month . . . [*With great difficulty*] Oh, boys, it's so hard to say a thing like this! He's just a big stupid man to you, but I tell you there's more good in him than in many other people. [*She chokes, wipes her eyes.*] I was looking for a fuse. The lights blew out, and I went down the cellar. And behind the fuse box—it happened to fall out—was a length of rubber pipe—just short.

HAPPY No kidding?

LINDA There's a little attachment on the end of it. I knew right away. And sure enough, on the bottom of the water heater there's a new little nipple on the gas pipe.

HAPPY [*angrily*] That—jerk.

BIFF Did you have it taken off?

LINDA I'm—I'm ashamed to. How can I mention it to him? Every day I go down and take away that little rubber pipe. But, when he comes home, I put it back where it was. How can I insult him that way? I don't know what to do. I live from day to day, boys. I tell you, I know every thought in his mind. It sounds so old-fashioned and silly, but I tell you he put his whole life into you and you've turned your backs on him. [*She is bent over in the chair, weeping, her face in her hands.*] Biff, I swear to God! Biff, his life is in your hands!

HAPPY [*to* BIFF] How do you like that damned fool!

BIFF [*kissing her*] All right, pal, all right. It's all settled now. I've been remiss. I know that, Mom. But now I'll stay, and I swear to you, I'll apply myself. [*Kneeling in front of her, in a fever of self-reproach*] It's just—you see, Mom, I don't fit in business. Not that I won't try. I'll try, and I'll make good.

HAPPY Sure you will. The trouble with you in business was you never tried to please people.

BIFF I know, I—

HAPPY Like when you worked for Harrison's. Bob Harrison said you were tops, and then you go and do some damn fool thing like whistling whole songs in the elevator like a comedian.

BIFF [*against* HAPPY] So what? I like to whistle sometimes.

HAPPY You don't raise a guy to a responsible job who whistles in the elevator!

LINDA Well, don't argue about it now.

HAPPY Like when you'd go off and swim in the middle of the day instead of taking the line around.

BIFF [*his resentment rising*] Well, don't you run off? You take off sometimes, don't you? On a nice summer day?

HAPPY Yeah, but I cover myself!

LINDA Boys!

HAPPY If I'm going to take a fade[5] the boss can call any number where I'm supposed to be and they'll swear to him that I just left. I'll tell you something that I hate to say, Biff, but in the business world some of them think you're crazy.

BIFF [*angered*] Screw the business world!

HAPPY All right, screw it! Great, but cover yourself!

LINDA Hap, Hap!

BIFF I don't care what they think! They've laughed at Dad for years, and you know why? Because we don't belong in this nuthouse of a city! We should be mixing cement on some open plain, or—or carpenters. A carpenter is allowed to whistle!

[WILLY *walks in from the entrance of the house, at left.*]

WILLY Even your grandfather was better than a carpenter. [*Pause. They watch him.*] You never grew up. Bernard does not whistle in the elevator, I assure you.

BIFF [*as though to laugh* WILLY *out of it*] Yeah, but you do, Pop.

WILLY I never in my life whistled in an elevator! And who in the business world thinks I'm crazy?

BIFF I didn't mean it like that, Pop. Now don't make a whole thing out of it, will ya?

WILLY Go back to the West! Be a carpenter, a cowboy, enjoy yourself!

LINDA Willy, he was just saying—

WILLY I heard what he said!

HAPPY [*trying to quiet* WILLY] Hey, Pop, come on now . . .

WILLY [*continuing over* HAPPY'*s line*] They laugh at me, heh? Go to Filene's, go to the Hub,[6] go to Slattery's, Boston. Call out the name Willy Loman and see what happens! Big shot!

BIFF All right, Pop.

WILLY Big!

BIFF All right!

WILLY Why do you always insult me?

BIFF I didn't say a word. [*To* LINDA] Did I say a word?

LINDA He didn't say anything, Willy.

WILLY [*going to the doorway of the living room*] All right, good night, good night.

LINDA Willy, dear, he just decided . . .

WILLY [*to* BIFF] If you get tired hanging around tomorrow, paint the ceiling I put up in the living room.

BIFF I'm leaving early tomorrow.

HAPPY He's going to see Bill Oliver, Pop.

WILLY [*interestedly*] Oliver? For what?

BIFF [*with reserve, but trying, trying*] He always said he'd stake me. I'd like to go into business, so maybe I can take him up on it.

LINDA Isn't that wonderful?

WILLY Don't interrupt. What's wonderful about it? There's fifty men in the City of New York who'd stake him. [*To* BIFF] Sporting goods?

5. Disappear.
6. Boston (label given the Massachusetts State House in 1858 by Oliver Wendell Holmes).

BIFF I guess so. I know something about it and—

WILLY He knows something about it! You know sporting goods better than Spalding,[7] for God's sake! How much is he giving you?

BIFF I don't know, I didn't even see him yet, but—

WILLY Then what're you talkin' about?

BIFF [*getting angry*] Well, all I said was I'm gonna see him, that's all!

WILLY [*turning away*] Ah, you're counting your chickens again.

BIFF [*starting left for the stairs*] Oh, Jesus, I'm going to sleep!

WILLY [*calling after him*] Don't curse in this house!

BIFF [*turning*] Since when did you get so clean?

HAPPY [*trying to stop them*] Wait a . . .

WILLY Don't use that language to me! I won't have it!

HAPPY [*grabbing* BIFF, *shouts*] Wait a minute! I got an idea. I got a feasible idea. Come here, Biff, let's talk this over now, let's talk some sense here. When I was down in Florida last time, I thought of a great idea to sell sporting goods. It just came back to me. You and I, Biff—we have a line, the Loman Line. We train a couple of weeks, and put on a couple of exhibitions, see?

WILLY That's an idea!

HAPPY Wait! We form two basketball teams, see? Two water-polo teams. We play each other. It's a million dollars' worth of publicity. Two brothers, see? The Loman Brothers. Displays in the Royal Palms—all the hotels. And banners over the ring and the basketball court: "Loman Brothers." Baby, we could sell sporting goods!

WILLY That is a one-million-dollar idea!

LINDA Marvelous!

BIFF I'm in great shape as far as that's concerned.

HAPPY And the beauty of it is, Biff, it wouldn't be like a business. We'd be out playin' ball again . . .

BIFF [*enthused*] Yeah, that's . . .

WILLY Million-dollar . . .

HAPPY And you wouldn't get fed up with it, Biff. It'd be the family again. There'd be the old honor, and comradeship, and if you wanted to go off for a swim or somethin'—well, you'd do it! Without some smart cooky gettin' up ahead of you!

WILLY Lick the world! You guys together could absolutely lick the civilized world.

BIFF I'll see Oliver tomorrow. Hap, if we could work that out . . .

LINDA Maybe things are beginning to—

WILLY [*wildly enthused, to* LINDA] Stop interrupting! [*To* BIFF] But don't wear sport jacket and slacks when you see Oliver.

BIFF No, I'll—

WILLY A business suit, and talk as little as possible, and don't crack any jokes.

BIFF He did like me. Always liked me.

LINDA He loved you!

7. The sporting goods company named after the American baseball star A. G. Spalding (1850–1915), who founded it.

WILLY [*to* LINDA] Will you stop! [*To* BIFF] Walk in very serious. You are not applying for a boy's job. Money is to pass. Be quiet, fine, and serious. Everybody likes a kidder, but nobody lends him money.

HAPPY I'll try to get some myself, Biff. I'm sure I can.

WILLY I see great things for you kids, I think your troubles are over. But remember, start big and you'll end big. Ask for fifteen. How much you gonna ask for?

BIFF Gee, I don't know—

WILLY And don't say "Gee." "Gee" is a boy's word. A man walking in for fifteen thousand dollars does not say "Gee!"

BIFF Ten, I think, would be top though.

WILLY Don't be so modest. You always started too low. Walk in with a big laugh. Don't look worried. Start off with a couple of your good stories to lighten things up. It's not what you say, it's how you say it—because personality always wins the day.

LINDA Oliver always thought the highest of him—

WILLY Will you let me talk?

BIFF Don't yell at her, Pop, will ya?

WILLY [*angrily*] I was talking, wasn't I?

BIFF I don't like you yelling at her all the time, and I'm tellin' you, that's all.

WILLY What're you, takin' over this house?

LINDA Willy—

WILLY [*turning on her*] Don't take his side all the time, goddammit!

BIFF [*furiously*] Stop yelling at her!

WILLY [*suddenly pulling on his cheek, beaten down, guilt ridden*] Give my best to Bill Oliver—he may remember me. [*He exits through the living room doorway.*]

LINDA [*her voice subdued*] What'd you have to start that for? [BIFF *turns away.*] You see how sweet he was as soon as you talked hopefully? [*She goes over to* BIFF.] Come up and say good night to him. Don't let him go to bed that way.

HAPPY Come on, Biff, let's buck him up.

LINDA Please, dear. Just say good night. It takes so little to make him happy. Come. [*She goes through the living room doorway, calling upstairs from within the living room.*] Your pajamas are hanging in the bathroom, Willy!

HAPPY [*looking toward where* LINDA *went out*] What a woman! They broke the mold when they made her. You know that, Biff?

BIFF He's off salary. My God, working on commission!

HAPPY Well, let's face it: he's no hot-shot selling man. Except that sometimes, you have to admit, he's a sweet personality.

BIFF [*deciding*] Lend me ten bucks, will ya? I want to buy some new ties.

HAPPY I'll take you to a place I know. Beautiful stuff. Wear one of my striped shirts tomorrow.

BIFF She got gray. Mom got awful old. Gee, I'm gonna go in to Oliver tomorrow and knock him for a—

HAPPY Come on up. Tell that to Dad. Let's give him a whirl. Come on.

BIFF [*steamed up*] You know, with ten thousand bucks, boy!

HAPPY [*as they go into the living room*] That's the talk, Biff, that's the first time I've heard the old confidence out of you! [*From within the living room, fading off*] You're gonna live with me, kid, and any babe you want just say the word . . . [*The last lines are hardly heard. They are mounting the stairs to their parents' bedroom.*]

LINDA [*entering her bedroom and addressing* WILLY, *who is in the bathroom. She is straightening the bed for him.*] Can you do anything about the shower? It drips.

WILLY [*from the bathroom*] All of a sudden everything falls to pieces! Goddam plumbing, oughta be sued, those people. I hardly finished putting it in and the thing . . . [*His words rumble off.*]

LINDA I'm just wondering if Oliver will remember him. You think he might?

WILLY [*coming out of the bathroom in his pajamas*] Remember him? What's the matter with you, you crazy? If he'd've stayed with Oliver he'd be on top by now! Wait'll Oliver gets a look at him. You don't know the average caliber any more. The average young man today—[*He is getting into bed.*]—is got a caliber of zero. Greatest thing in the world for him was to bum around.

[BIFF *and* HAPPY *enter the bedroom. Slight pause.*]

WILLY [*stops short, looking at* BIFF] Glad to hear it, boy.

HAPPY He wanted to say good night to you, sport.

WILLY [*to* BIFF] Yeah. Knock him dead, boy. What'd you want to tell me?

BIFF Just take it easy, Pop. Good night. [*He turns to go.*]

WILLY [*unable to resist*] And if anything falls off the desk while you're talking to him—like a package or something—don't you pick it up. They have office boys for that.

LINDA I'll make a big breakfast—

WILLY Will you let me finish? [*To* BIFF] Tell him you were in the business in the West. Not farm work.

BIFF All right, Dad.

LINDA I think everything—

WILLY [*going right through her speech*] And don't undersell yourself. No less than fifteen thousand dollars.

BIFF [*unable to bear him*] Okay. Good night, Mom. [*He starts moving.*]

WILLY Because you got a greatness in you, Biff, remember that. You got all kinds a greatness . . . [*He lies back, exhausted.* BIFF *walks out.*]

LINDA [*calling after Biff*] Sleep well, darling!

HAPPY I'm gonna get married, Mom. I wanted to tell you.

LINDA Go to sleep, dear.

HAPPY [*going*] I just wanted to tell you.

WILLY Keep up the good work. [HAPPY *exits.*] God . . . remember that Ebbets Field[8] game? The championship of the city?

LINDA Just rest. Should I sing to you?

WILLY Yeah. Sing to me. [LINDA *hums a soft lullaby.*] When that team came out—he was the tallest, remember?

LINDA Oh, yes. And in gold.

[BIFF *enters the darkened kitchen, takes a cigarette, and leaves the house. He comes downstage into a golden pool of light. He smokes, staring at the night.*]

8. Brooklyn's baseball stadium, home of the Dodgers before the team's move to Los Angeles in 1957. Football was also played there.

WILLY Like a young god. Hercules[9]—something like that. And the sun, the sun all around him. Remember how he waved to me? Right up from the field, with the representatives of three colleges standing by? And the buyers I brought, and the cheers when he came out—Loman, Loman, Loman! God Almighty, he'll be great yet. A star like that, magnificent, can never really fade away!

[*The light on* WILLY *is fading. The gas heater begins to glow through the kitchen wall, near the stairs, a blue flame beneath red coils.*]

LINDA [*timidly*] Willy dear, what has he got against you?

WILLY I'm so tired. Don't talk anymore.

[BIFF *slowly returns to the kitchen. He stops, stares toward the heater.*]

LINDA Will you ask Howard to let you work in New York?

WILLY First thing in the morning. Everything'll be all right.

[BIFF *reaches behind the heater and draws out a length of rubber tubing. He is horrified and turns his head toward* WILLY*'s room, still dimly lit, from which the strains of* LINDA*'s desperate but monotonous humming rise.*]

WILLY [*staring through the window into the moonlight*] Gee, look at the moon moving between the buildings!

[BIFF *wraps the tubing around his hand and quickly goes up the stairs.*]

Curtain.

Act 2

Music is heard, gay and bright. The curtain rises as the music fades away. WILLY, *in shirt sleeves, is sitting at the kitchen table, sipping coffee, his hat in his lap.* LINDA *is filling his cup when she can.*

WILLY Wonderful coffee. Meal in itself.

LINDA Can I make you some eggs?

WILLY No. Take a breath.

LINDA You look so rested, dear.

WILLY I slept like a dead one. First time in months. Imagine, sleeping till ten on a Tuesday morning. Boys left nice and early, heh?

LINDA They were out of here by eight o'clock.

WILLY Good work!

LINDA It was so thrilling to see them leaving together. I can't get over the shaving lotion in this house!

WILLY [*smiling*] Mmm—

LINDA Biff was very changed this morning. His whole attitude seemed to be hopeful. He couldn't wait to get downtown to see Oliver.

WILLY He's heading for a change. There's no question, there simply are certain men that take longer to get—solidified. How did he dress?

LINDA His blue suit. He's so handsome in that suit. He could be a—anything in that suit!

[WILLY *gets up from the table.* LINDA *holds his jacket for him.*]

WILLY There's no question, no question at all. Gee, on the way home tonight I'd like to buy some seeds.

9. In classical mythology, the greatest of all heroes (a son of Zeus, king of the gods, and the mortal Alcmene).

LINDA [*laughing*] That'd be wonderful. But not enough sun gets back there. Nothing'll grow anymore.

WILLY You wait, kid, before it's all over we're gonna get a little place out in the country, and I'll raise some vegetables, a couple of chickens . . .

LINDA You'll do it yet, dear.

[WILLY *walks out of his jacket.* LINDA *follows him.*]

WILLY And they'll get married, and come for a weekend. I'd build a little guest house. 'Cause I got so many fine tools, all I'd need would be a little lumber and some peace of mind.

LINDA [*joyfully*] I sewed the lining . . .

WILLY I could build two guest houses, so they'd both come. Did he decide how much he's going to ask Oliver for?

LINDA [*getting him into the jacket*] He didn't mention it, but I imagine ten or fifteen thousand. You going to talk to Howard today?

WILLY Yeah. I'll put it to him straight and simple. He'll just have to take me off the road.

LINDA And Willy, don't forget to ask for a little advance, because we've got the insurance premium. It's the grace period now.

WILLY That's a hundred . . . ?

LINDA A hundred and eight, sixty-eight. Because we're a little short again.

WILLY Why are we short?

LINDA Well, you had the motor job on the car . . .

WILLY That goddam Studebaker!

LINDA And you got one more payment on the refrigerator . . .

WILLY But it just broke again!

LINDA Well, it's old, dear.

WILLY I told you we should've bought a well-advertised machine. Charley bought a General Electric and it's twenty years old and it's still good, that son-of-a-bitch.

LINDA But, Willy—

WILLY Whoever heard of a Hastings refrigerator? Once in my life I would like to own something outright before it's broken! I'm always in a race with the junkyard! I just finished paying for the car and it's on its last legs. The refrigerator consumes belts like a goddam maniac. They time those things. They time them so when you finally paid for them, they're used up.

LINDA [*buttoning up his jacket as he unbuttons it*] All told, about two hundred dollars would carry us, dear. But that includes the last payment on the mortgage. After this payment, Willy, the house belongs to us.

WILLY It's twenty-five years!

LINDA Biff was nine years old when we bought it.

WILLY Well, that's a great thing. To weather a twenty-five year mortgage is—

LINDA It's an accomplishment.

WILLY All the cement, the lumber, the reconstruction I put in this house! There ain't a crack to be found in it anymore.

LINDA Well, it served its purpose.

WILLY What purpose? Some stranger'll come along, move in, and that's that. If only Biff would take this house, and raise a family . . . [*He starts to go.*] Good-by, I'm late.

LINDA [*suddenly remembering*] Oh, I forgot! You're supposed to meet them for dinner.

WILLY Me?

LINDA At Frank's Chop House on Forty-eighth near Sixth Avenue.

WILLY Is that so! How about you?

LINDA No, just the three of you. They're gonna blow you to a big meal![1]

WILLY Don't say! Who thought of that?

LINDA Biff came to me this morning, Willy, and he said, "Tell Dad, we want to blow him to a big meal." Be there six o'clock. You and your two boys are going to have dinner.

WILLY Gee whiz! That's really somethin'. I'm gonna knock Howard for a loop, kid. I'll get an advance, and I'll come home with a New York job. Goddammit, now I'm gonna do it!

LINDA Oh, that's the spirit, Willy!

WILLY I will never get behind a wheel the rest of my life!

LINDA It's changing, Willy, I can feel it changing!

WILLY Beyond a question. G'by, I'm late. [*He starts to go again.*]

LINDA [*calling after him as she runs to the kitchen table for a handkerchief*] You got your glasses?

WILLY [*feels for them, then comes back in*] Yeah, yeah, got my glasses.

LINDA [*giving him the handkerchief*] And a handkerchief.

WILLY Yeah, handkerchief.

LINDA And your saccharine?

WILLY Yeah, my saccharine.

LINDA Be careful on the subway stairs.

[*She kisses him, and a silk stocking is seen hanging from her hand.* WILLY *notices it.*]

WILLY Will you stop mending stockings? At least while I'm in the house. It gets me nervous. I can't tell you. Please.

[LINDA *hides the stocking in her hand as she follows* WILLY *across the forestage in front of the house.*]

LINDA Remember, Frank's Chop House.

WILLY [*passing the apron*] Maybe beets would grow out there.

LINDA [*laughing*] But you tried so many times.

WILLY Yeah. Well, don't work hard today. [*He disappears around the right corner of the house.*]

LINDA Be careful!

[*As* WILLY *vanishes, Linda waves to him. Suddenly the phone rings. She runs across the stage and into the kitchen and lifts it.*]

LINDA Hello? Oh, Biff! I'm so glad you called, I just . . . Yes, sure, I just told him. Yes, he'll be there for dinner at six o'clock, I didn't forget. Listen, I was just dying to tell you. You know that little rubber pipe I told you about? That he connected to the gas heater? I finally decided to go down the cellar this morning and take it away and destroy it. But it's gone! Imagine? He took it away himself, it isn't there! [*She listens*]. When? Oh, then you took it. Oh—nothing, it's just that I'd hoped he'd taken it away himself. Oh, I'm not worried, darling, because this morning he left in such high spirits, it was like the old days! I'm not afraid anymore. Did Mr. Oliver see you? . . . Well, you wait there then. And make a nice impression on him, darling.

1. That is, treat him to dinner, spending extravagantly on it.

Just don't perspire too much before you see him. And have a nice time with Dad. He may have big news too! . . . That's right, a New York job. And be sweet to him tonight, dear. Be loving to him. Because he's only a little boat looking for a harbor. [*She is trembling with sorrow and joy.*] Oh, that's wonderful, Biff, you'll save his life. Thanks, darling. Just put your arm around him when he comes into the restaurant. Give him a smile. That's the boy . . . Good-by, dear. . . . You got your comb? . . . That's fine. Good-by, Biff dear.

[*In the middle of her speech,* HOWARD WAGNER, *thirty-six, wheels in a small typewriter table on which is a wire-recording machine*[2] *and proceeds to plug it in. This is on the left forestage. Light slowly fades on* LINDA *as it rises on* HOWARD. HOWARD *is intent on threading the machine and only glances over his shoulder as* WILLY *appears.*]

WILLY Pst! Pst!

HOWARD Hello, Willy, come in.

WILLY Like to have a little talk with you, Howard.

HOWARD Sorry to keep you waiting. I'll be with you in a minute.

WILLY What's that, Howard?

HOWARD Didn't you ever see one of these? Wire recorder.

WILLY Oh. Can we talk a minute?

HOWARD Records things. Just got delivery yesterday. Been driving me crazy, the most terrific machine I ever saw in my life. I was up all night with it.

WILLY What do you do with it?

HOWARD I bought it for dictation, but you can do anything with it. Listen to this. I had it home last night. Listen to what I picked up. The first one is my daughter. Get this. [*He flicks the switch and "Roll out the Barrel"*[3] *is heard being whistled.*] Listen to that kid whistle.

WILLY That is lifelike, isn't it?

HOWARD Seven years old. Get that tone.

WILLY Ts, ts. Like to ask a little favor if you . . .

[*The whistling breaks off, and the voice of* HOWARD*'s daughter is heard.*]

HIS DAUGHTER "Now you, Daddy."

HOWARD She's crazy for me! [*Again the same song is whistled.*] That's me! Ha! [*He winks.*]

WILLY You're very good!

[*The whistling breaks off again. The machine runs silent for a moment.*]

HOWARD Sh! Get this now, this is my son.

HIS SON "The capital of Alabama is Montgomery; the capital of Arizona is Phoenix; the capital of Arkansas is Little Rock; the capital of California is Sacramento . . ." [*And on, and on.*]

HOWARD [*holding up five fingers*] Five years old, Willy!

WILLY He'll make an announcer some day!

HIS SON [*continuing*] "The capital . . ."

HOWARD Get that—alphabetical order! [*The machine breaks off suddenly.*] Wait a minute. The maid kicked the plug out.

2. The earliest practical magnetic sound recording machine, first commercially available after World War II (soon made obsolete by the tape recorder).

3. "The Beer Barrel Polka" (music written 1927; English lyrics written 1939), a song that became very popular during World War II.

WILLY It certainly is a—

HOWARD Sh, for God's sake!

HIS SON "It's nine o'clock, Bulova watch time.[4] So I have to go to sleep."

WILLY That really is—

HOWARD Wait a minute! The next is my wife.

[*They wait.*]

HOWARD'S VOICE "Go on, say something." [*Pause*] "Well, you gonna talk?"

HIS WIFE "I can't think of anything."

HOWARD'S VOICE "Well, talk—it's turning."

HIS WIFE [*shyly, beaten*] "Hello." [*Silence*] "Oh, Howard, I can't talk into this . . ."

HOWARD [*snapping the machine off*] That was my wife.

WILLY That is a wonderful machine. Can we—

HOWARD I tell you, Willy, I'm gonna take my camera, and my bandsaw, and all my hobbies, and out they go. This is the most fascinating relaxation I ever found.

WILLY I think I'll get one myself.

HOWARD Sure, they're only a hundred and a half. You can't do without it. Supposing you wanna hear Jack Benny,[5] see? But you can't be at home at that hour. So you tell the maid to turn the radio on when Jack Benny comes on, and this automatically goes on with the radio . . .

WILLY And when you come home you . . .

HOWARD You can come home twelve o'clock, one o'clock, anytime you like, and you get yourself a Coke and sit yourself down, throw the switch, and there's Jack Benny's program in the middle of the night!

WILLY I'm definitely going to get one. Because lots of time I'm on the road, and I think to myself, what I must be missing on the radio!

HOWARD Don't you have a radio in the car?

WILLY Well, yeah, but who ever thinks of turning it on?

HOWARD Say, aren't you supposed to be in Boston?

WILLY That's what I want to talk to you about, Howard. You got a minute? [*He draws a chair in from the wing.*]

HOWARD What happened? What're you doing here?

WILLY Well . . .

HOWARD You didn't crack up again, did you?

WILLY Oh, no. No . . .

HOWARD Geez, you had me worried there for a minute. What's the trouble?

WILLY Well, tell you the truth, Howard. I've come to the decision that I'd rather not travel any more.

HOWARD Not travel! Well, what'll you do?

WILLY Remember, Christmastime, when you had the party here? You said you'd try to think of some spot for me here in town.

HOWARD With us?

WILLY Well, sure.

HOWARD Oh, yeah, yeah. I remember. Well, I couldn't think of anything for you, Willy.

4. A phrase used for years in Bulova's radio advertisements, beginning in 1926.

5. American comedian and actor (Benjamin Kubelsky, 1894–1974), host of a popular comedy show on radio (1932–55) and television (1950–65).

WILLY I tell ya, Howard. The kids are all grown up, y'know. I don't need much anymore. If I could take home—well, sixty-five dollars a week, I could swing it.

HOWARD Yeah, but Willy, see I—

WILLY I tell ya why, Howard. Speaking frankly and between the two of us, y'know—I'm just a little tired.

HOWARD Oh, I could understand that, Willy. But you're a road man, Willy, and we do a road business. We've only got a half-dozen salesmen on the floor here.

WILLY God knows, Howard, I never asked a favor of any man. But I was with the firm when your father used to carry you in here in his arms.

HOWARD I know that, Willy, but—

WILLY Your father came to me the day you were born and asked me what I thought of the name of Howard, may he rest in peace.

HOWARD I appreciate that, Willy, but there just is no spot here for you. If I had a spot I'd slam you right in, but I just don't have a single solitary spot.

[*He looks for his lighter.* WILLY *has picked it up and gives it to him. Pause.*]

WILLY [*with increasing anger*] Howard, all I need to set my table is fifty dollars a week.

HOWARD But where am I going to put you, kid?

WILLY Look, it isn't a question of whether I can sell merchandise, is it?

HOWARD No, but it's a business, kid, and everybody's gotta pull his own weight.

WILLY [*desperately*] Just let me tell you a story, Howard—

HOWARD 'Cause you gotta admit, business is business.

WILLY [*angrily*] Business is definitely business, but just listen for a minute. You don't understand this. When I was a boy—eighteen, nineteen—I was already on the road. And there was a question in my mind as to whether selling had a future for me. Because in those days I had a yearning to go to Alaska. See, there were three gold strikes in one month in Alaska, and I felt like going out. Just for the ride, you might say.

HOWARD [*barely interested*] Don't say.

WILLY Oh, yeah, my father lived many years in Alaska. He was an adventurous man. We've got quite a little streak of self-reliance in our family. I thought I'd go out with my older brother and try to locate him, and maybe settle in the North with the old man. And I was almost decided to go, when I met a salesman in the Parker House.[6] His name was Dave Singleman. And he was eighty-four years old, and he'd drummed merchandise in thirty-one states. And old Dave, he'd go up to his room, y'understand, put on his green velvet slippers—I'll never forget—and pick up his phone and call the buyers, and without ever leaving his room, at the age of eighty-four, he made his living. And when I saw that, I realized that selling was the greatest career a man could want. 'Cause what could be more satisfying than to be able to go, at the age of eighty-four, into twenty or thirty different cities, and pick up a phone, and be remembered and loved and helped by so many different people? Do you know? when he died—and by the way

6. A venerable Boston luxury hotel.

he died the death of a salesman, in his green velvet slippers in the smoker[7] of the New York, New Haven and Hartford, going into Boston—when he died, hundreds of salesmen and buyers were at his funeral. Things were sad on a lotta trains for months after that. [*He stands up.* HOWARD *has not looked at him.*] In those days there was personality in it, Howard. There was respect, and comradeship, and gratitude in it. Today, it's all cut and dried, and there's no chance for bringing friendship to bear—or personality. You see what I mean? They don't know me anymore.

HOWARD [*moving away, to the right*] That's just the thing, Willy.

WILLY If I had forty dollars a week—that's all I'd need. Forty dollars, Howard.

HOWARD Kid, I can't take blood from a stone, I—

WILLY [*desperation is on him now*] Howard, the year Al Smith was nominated,[8] your father came to me and—

HOWARD [*starting to go off*] I've got to see some people, kid.

WILLY [*stopping him*] I'm talking about your father! There were promises made across this desk! You mustn't tell me you've got people to see—I put thirty-four years into this firm, Howard, and now I can't pay my insurance! You can't eat the orange and throw the peel away—a man is not a piece of fruit! [*After a pause*] Now pay attention. Your father—in 1928 I had a big year. I averaged a hundred and seventy dollars a week in commissions.

HOWARD [*impatiently*] Now, Willy, you never averaged—

WILLY [*banging his hand on the desk*] I averaged a hundred and seventy dollars a week in the year of 1928! And your father came to me—or rather, I was in the office here—it was right over this desk—and he put his hand on my shoulder—

HOWARD [*getting up*] You'll have to excuse me, Willy, I gotta see some people. Pull yourself together. [*Going out*] I'll be back in a little while.

[*On* HOWARD*'s exit, the light on his chair grows very bright and strange.*]

WILLY Pull myself together! What the hell did I say to him? My God, I was yelling at him! How could I! [WILLY *breaks off, staring at the light, which occupies the chair, animating it. He approaches this chair, standing across the desk from it.*] Frank, Frank, don't you remember what you told me that time? How you put your hand on my shoulder, and Frank . . . [*He leans on the desk and as he speaks the dead man's name he accidentally switches on the recorder, and instantly.*]

HOWARD'S SON ". . . of New York is Albany. The capital of Ohio is Cincinnati, the capital of Rhode Island is . . ." [*The recitation continues.*]

WILLY [*leaping away with fright, shouting*] Ha! Howard! Howard! Howard!

HOWARD [*rushing in*] What happened?

WILLY [*pointing at the machine, which continues nasally, childishly, with the capital cities*] Shut it off! Shut it off!

HOWARD [*pulling the plug out*] Look, Willy . . .

WILLY [*pressing his hands to his eyes*] I gotta get myself some coffee. I'll get some coffee . . .

[WILLY *starts to walk out.* HOWARD *stops him.*]

7. The smoking car on a train (Willy names the specific railroad).

8. That is, in 1928; Smith (1873–1944) was the Democratic Party's presidential nominee.

HOWARD [*rolling up the cord*] Willy, look . . .

WILLY I'll go to Boston.

HOWARD Willy, you can't go to Boston for us.

WILLY Why can't I go?

HOWARD I don't want you to represent us. I've been meaning to tell you for a long time now.

WILLY Howard, are you firing me?

HOWARD I think you need a good long rest, Willy.

WILLY Howard—

HOWARD And when you feel better, come back, and we'll see if we can work something out.

WILLY But I gotta earn money, Howard. I'm in no position to—

HOWARD Where are your sons? Why don't your sons give you a hand?

WILLY They're working on a very big deal.

HOWARD This is no time for false pride, Willy. You go to your sons and you tell them that you're tired. You've got two great boys, haven't you?

WILLY Oh, no question, no question, but in the meantime . . .

HOWARD Then that's that, heh?

WILLY All right, I'll go to Boston tomorrow.

HOWARD No, no.

WILLY I can't throw myself on my sons. I'm not a cripple!

HOWARD Look, kid, I'm busy this morning.

WILLY [*grasping* HOWARD'*s arm*] Howard, you've got to let me go to Boston!

HOWARD [*hard, keeping himself under control*] I've got a line of people to see this morning. Sit down, take five minutes, and pull yourself together, and then go home, will ya? I need the office, Willy. [*He starts to go, turns, remembering the recorder, starts to push off the table holding the recorder.*] Oh, yeah. Whenever you can this week, stop by and drop off the samples. You'll feel better, Willy, and then come back and we'll talk. Pull yourself together, kid, there's people outside.

[HOWARD *exits, pushing the table off left.* WILLY *stares into space, exhausted. Now the music is heard—*BEN'*s music—first distantly, then closer, closer. As* WILLY *speaks,* BEN *enters from the right. He carries valise and umbrella.*]

WILLY Oh, Ben, how did you do it? What is the answer? Did you wind up the Alaska deal already?

BEN Doesn't take much time if you know what you're doing. Just a short business trip. Boarding ship in an hour. Wanted to say good-by.

WILLY Ben, I've got to talk to you.

BEN [*glancing at his watch*] Haven't the time, William.

WILLY [*crossing the apron to Ben*] Ben, nothing's working out. I don't know what to do.

BEN Now, look here, William. I've bought timberland in Alaska and I need a man to look after things for me.

WILLY God, timberland! Me and my boys in those grand outdoors!

BEN You've a new continent at your doorstep, William. Get out of these cities, they're full of talk and time payments and courts of law. Screw on your fists and you can fight for a fortune up there.

WILLY Yes, yes! Linda, Linda!

[LINDA *enters as of old, with the wash.*]

LINDA Oh, you're back?

BEN I haven't much time.

WILLY No, wait! Linda, he's got a proposition for me in Alaska.

LINDA But you've got—[*To* BEN] He's got a beautiful job here.

WILLY But in Alaska, kid, I could—

LINDA You're doing well enough, Willy!

BEN [*to* LINDA] Enough for what, my dear?

LINDA [*frightened of* BEN *and angry at him*] Don't say those things to him! Enough to be happy right here, right now. [*To* WILLY, *while* BEN *laughs*] Why must everybody conquer the world? You're well liked, and the boys love you, and someday—[*To* BEN]—why, old man Wagner told him just the other day that if he keeps it up he'll be a member of the firm, didn't he, Willy?

WILLY Sure, sure. I am building something with this firm, Ben, and if a man is building something he must be on the right track, mustn't he?

BEN What are you building? Lay your hand on it. Where is it?

WILLY [*hesitantly*] That's true, Linda, there's nothing.

LINDA Why? [*To* BEN] There's a man eighty-four years old—

WILLY That's right, Ben, that's right. When I look at that man I say, what is there to worry about?

BEN Bah!

WILLY It's true, Ben. All he has to do is go into any city, pick up the phone, and he's making his living and you know why?

BEN [*picking up his valise*] I've got to go.

WILLY [*holding* BEN *back*] Look at this boy!

[BIFF, *in his high school sweater, enters carrying suitcase.* HAPPY *carries* BIFF*'s shoulder guards, gold helmet, and football pants.*]

WILLY Without a penny to his name, three great universities are begging for him, and from there the sky's the limit, because it's not what you do, Ben. It's who you know and the smile on your face! It's contacts, Ben, contacts! The whole wealth of Alaska passes over the lunch table at the Commodore Hotel, and that's the wonder, the wonder of this country, that a man can end with diamonds here on the basis of being liked! [*He turns to* BIFF.] And that's why when you get out on that field today it's important. Because thousands of people will be rooting for you and loving you. [*To* BEN, *who has again begun to leave*] And Ben! when he walks into a business office his name will sound out like a bell and all the doors will open to him! I've seen it, Ben, I've seen it a thousand times! You can't feel it with your hand like timber, but it's there!

BEN Good-by, William.

WILLY Ben, am I right? Don't you think I'm right? I value your advice.

BEN There's a new continent at your doorstep, William. You could walk out rich. Rich! [*He is gone.*]

WILLY We'll do it here, Ben! You hear me? We're gonna do it here!

[YOUNG BERNARD *rushes in. The gay music of the Boys is heard.*]

BERNARD Oh, gee, I was afraid you left already!

WILLY Why? What time is it?

BERNARD It's half-past one!

WILLY Well, come on, everybody! Ebbets Field next stop! Where's the pennants? [*He rushes through the wall-line of the kitchen and out into the living room.*]

LINDA [*to* BIFF] Did you pack fresh underwear?

BIFF [*who has been limbering up*] I want to go!

BERNARD Biff, I'm carrying your helmet, ain't I?

HAPPY No, I'm carrying the helmet.

BERNARD Oh, Biff, you promised me.

HAPPY I'm carrying the helmet.

BERNARD How am I going to get in the locker room?

LINDA Let him carry the shoulder guards. [*She puts her coat and hat on in the kitchen.*]

BERNARD Can I, Biff? 'Cause I told everybody I'm going to be in the locker room.

HAPPY In Ebbets Field it's the clubhouse.

BERNARD I meant the clubhouse. Biff!

HAPPY Biff!

BIFF [*grandly, after a slight pause*] Let him carry the shoulder guards.

HAPPY [*as he gives* BERNARD *the shoulder guards*] Stay close to us now.

[WILLY *rushes in with the pennants.*]

WILLY [*handing them out*] Everybody wave when Biff comes out on the field. [HAPPY *and* BERNARD *run off.*] You set now, boy?

[*The music has died away.*]

BIFF Ready to go, Pop. Every muscle is ready.

WILLY [*at the edge of the apron*] You realize what this means?

BIFF That's right, Pop.

WILLY [*feeling* BIFF*'s muscle*] You're comin' home this afternoon captain of the All-Scholastic Championship Team of the City of New York.

BIFF I got it, Pop. And remember, pal, when I take off my helmet, that touchdown is for you.

WILLY Let's go! [*He is starting out, with his arm around Biff, when* CHARLEY *enters, as of old, in knickers.*] I got no room for you, Charley.

CHARLEY Room? For what?

WILLY In the car.

CHARLEY You goin' for a ride? I wanted to shoot some casino.

WILLY [*furiously*] Casino! [*Incredulously*] Don't you realize what today is?

LINDA Oh, he knows, Willy. He's just kidding you.

WILLY That's nothing to kid about!

CHARLEY No. Linda, what's goin' on?

LINDA He's playing in Ebbets Field.

CHARLEY Baseball in this weather?

WILLY Don't talk to him. Come on, come on! [*He is pushing them out.*]

CHARLEY Wait a minute, didn't you hear the news?

WILLY What?

CHARLEY Don't you listen to the radio? Ebbets Field just blew up.

WILLY You go to hell! [CHARLEY *laughs. Pushing them out*] Come on, come on! We're late.

CHARLEY [*as they go*] Knock a homer, Biff, knock a homer!

WILLY [*the last to leave, turning to* CHARLEY] I don't think that was funny, Charley. This is the greatest day of his life.

CHARLEY Willy, when are you going to grow up?

WILLY Yeah, heh? When this game is over, Charley, you'll be laughing out of the other side of your face. They'll be calling him another Red Grange.[9] Twenty-five thousand a year.

CHARLEY [*kidding*] Is that so?

WILLY Yeah, that's so.

CHARLEY Well, then, I'm sorry, Willy. But tell me something.

WILLY What?

CHARLEY Who is Red Grange?

WILLY Put up your hands. Goddam you, put up your hands!

[CHARLEY, *chuckling, shakes his head and walks away, around the left corner of the stage.* WILLY *follows him. The music rises to a mocking frenzy.*]

WILLY Who the hell do you think you are, better than everybody else? You don't know everything, you big, ignorant, stupid . . . Put up your hands!

[*Light rises, on the right side of the forestage, on a small table in the reception room of* CHARLEY'S *office. Traffic sounds are heard.* BERNARD, *now mature, sits whistling to himself. A pair of tennis rackets and an overnight bag are on the floor beside him.*]

WILLY [*offstage*] What are you walking away for? Don't walk away! If you're going to say something say it to my face! I know you laugh at me behind my back. You'll laugh out of the other side of your goddam face after this game. Touchdown! Touchdown! Eighty thousand people! Touchdown! Right between the goal posts.

[BERNARD *is a quiet, earnest, but self-assured young man.* WILLY'S *voice is coming from right upstage now.* BERNARD *lowers his feet off the table and listens.* JENNY, *his father's secretary, enters.*]

JENNY [*distressed*] Say, Bernard, will you go out in the hall?

BERNARD What is that noise? Who is it?

JENNY Mr. Loman. He just got off the elevator.

BERNARD [*getting up*] Who's he arguing with?

JENNY Nobody. There's nobody with him. I can't deal with him any more, and your father gets all upset everytime he comes. I've got a lot of typing to do, and your father's waiting to sign it. Will you see him?

WILLY [*entering*] Touchdown! Touch—[*He sees* JENNY.] Jenny, Jenny, good to see you. How're ya? Workin'? Or still honest?

JENNY Fine. How've you been feeling?

WILLY Not much anymore, Jenny. Ha, ha! [*He is surprised to see the rackets.*]

BERNARD Hello, Uncle Willy.

WILLY [*almost shocked*] Bernard! Well, look who's here! [*He comes quickly, guiltily, to* BERNARD *and warmly shakes his hand.*]

BERNARD How are you? Good to see you.

WILLY What are you doing here?

BERNARD Oh, just stopped by to see Pop. Get off my feet till my train leaves. I'm going to Washington in a few minutes.

WILLY Is he in?

9. Harold Edward Grange (1903–1991), a football player who was a three-time All-American halfback at the University of Illinois (1923–25); after starting for the Chicago Bears, he became a sportscaster.

BERNARD Yes, he's in his office with the accountant. Sit down.

WILLY [*sitting down*] What're you going to do in Washington?

BERNARD Oh, just a case I've got there, Willy.

WILLY That so? [*Indicating the rackets*] You going to play tennis there?

BERNARD I'm staying with a friend who's got a court.

WILLY Don't say. His own tennis court. Must be fine people, I bet.

BERNARD They are, very nice. Dad tells me Biff's in town.

WILLY [*with a big smile*] Yeah, Biff's in. Working on a very big deal, Bernard.

BERNARD What's Biff doing?

WILLY Well, he's been doing very big things in the West. But he decided to establish himself here. Very big. We're having dinner. Did I hear your wife had a boy?

BERNARD That's right. Our second.

WILLY Two boys! What do you know!

BERNARD What kind of a deal has Biff got?

WILLY Well, Bill Oliver—very big sporting-goods man—he wants Biff very badly. Called him in from the West. Long distance, carte blanche, special deliveries. Your friends have their own private tennis court?

BERNARD You still with the old firm, Willy?

WILLY [*after a pause*] I'm—I'm overjoyed to see how you made the grade, Bernard, overjoyed. It's an encouraging thing to see a young man really—really—Looks very good for Biff—very—[*He breaks off, then*] Bernard—[*He is so full of emotion, he breaks off again.*]

BERNARD What is it, Willy?

WILLY [*small and alone*] What—what's the secret?

BERNARD What secret?

WILLY How—how did you? Why didn't he ever catch on?

BERNARD I wouldn't know that, Willy.

WILLY [*confidentially, desperately*] You were his friend, his boyhood friend. There's something I don't understand about it. His life ended after that Ebbets Field game. From the age of seventeen nothing good ever happened to him.

BERNARD He never trained himself for anything.

WILLY But he did, he did. After high school he took so many correspondence courses. Radio mechanics; television; God knows what, and never made the slightest mark.

BERNARD [*taking off his glasses*] Willy, do you want to talk candidly?

WILLY [*rising, faces* BERNARD] I regard you as a very brilliant man, Bernard. I value your advice.

BERNARD Oh, the hell with the advice, Willy. I couldn't advise you. There's just one thing I've always wanted to ask you. When he was supposed to graduate, and the math teacher flunked him—

WILLY Oh, that son-of-a-bitch ruined his life.

BERNARD Yeah, but, Willy, all he had to do was go to summer school and make up that subject.

WILLY That's right, that's right.

BERNARD Did you tell him not to go to summer school?

WILLY Me? I begged him to go. I ordered him to go!

BERNARD Then why wouldn't he go?

WILLY Why? Why! Bernard, that question has been trailing me like a ghost for the last fifteen years. He flunked the subject, and laid down and died like a hammer hit him!

BERNARD Take it easy, kid.

WILLY Let me talk to you—I got nobody to talk to. Bernard, Bernard, was it my fault? Y'see? It keeps going around in my mind, maybe I did something to him. I got nothing to give him.

BERNARD Don't take it so hard.

WILLY Why did he lay down? What is the story there? You were his friend!

BERNARD Willy, I remember, it was June, and our grades came out. And he'd flunked math.

WILLY That son-of-a-bitch!

BERNARD No, it wasn't right then. Biff just got very angry, I remember, and he was ready to enroll in summer school.

WILLY [*surprised*] He was?

BERNARD He wasn't beaten by it at all. But then, Willy, he disappeared from the block for almost a month. And I got the idea that he'd gone up to New England to see you. Did he have a talk with you then?

[WILLY *stares in silence.*]

BERNARD Willy?

WILLY [*with a strong edge of resentment in his voice*] Yeah, he came to Boston. What about it?

BERNARD Well, just that when he came back—I'll never forget this, it always mystifies me. Because I'd thought so well of Biff, even though he'd always taken advantage of me. I loved him, Willy, y'know? And he came back after that month and took his sneakers—remember those sneakers with "University of Virginia" printed on them? He was so proud of those, wore them every day. And he took them down in the cellar, and burned them up in the furnace. We had a fist fight. It lasted at least half an hour. Just the two of us, punching each other down the cellar, and crying right through it. I've often thought of how strange it was that I knew he'd given up his life. What happened in Boston, Willy?

[WILLY *looks at him as at an intruder.*]

BERNARD I just bring it up because you asked me.

WILLY [*angrily*] Nothing. What do you mean, "What happened?" What's that got to do with anything?

BERNARD Well, don't get sore.

WILLY What are you trying to do, blame it on me? If a boy lays down is that my fault?

BERNARD Now, Willy, don't get—

WILLY Well, don't—don't talk to me that way! What does that mean, "What happened?"

[CHARLEY *enters. He is in his vest, and he carries a bottle of bourbon.*]

CHARLEY Hey, you're going to miss that train. [*He waves the bottle.*]

BERNARD Yeah, I'm going. [*He takes the bottle.*] Thanks, Pop. [*He picks up his rackets and bag.*] Good-by, Willy, and don't worry about it. You know, "If at first you don't succeed . . ."

WILLY Yes, I believe in that.

BERNARD But sometimes, Willy, it's better for a man just to walk away.

WILLY Walk away?

BERNARD That's right.

WILLY But if you can't walk away?

BERNARD [*after a slight pause*] I guess that's when it's tough. [*Extending his hand*] Good-by, Willy.

WILLY [*shaking* BERNARD'*s hand*] Good-by, boy.

CHARLEY [*an arm on* BERNARD'*s shoulder*] How do you like this kid? Gonna argue a case in front of the Supreme Court.

BERNARD [*protesting*] Pop!

WILLY [*genuinely shocked, pained, and happy*] No! The Supreme Court!

BERNARD I gotta run. 'By, Dad!

CHARLEY Knock 'em dead, Bernard!

[BERNARD *goes off.*]

WILLY [*as* CHARLEY *takes out his wallet*] The Supreme Court! And he didn't even mention it!

CHARLEY [*counting out money on the desk*] He don't have to—he's gonna do it.

WILLY And you never told him what to do, did you? You never took any interest in him.

CHARLEY My salvation is that I never took any interest in anything. There's some money—fifty dollars. I got an accountant inside.

WILLY Charley, look . . . [*With difficulty*] I got my insurance to pay. If you can manage it—I need a hundred and ten dollars.

[CHARLEY *doesn't reply for a moment; merely stops moving.*]

WILLY I'd draw it from my bank but Linda would know, and I . . .

CHARLEY Sit down, Willy.

WILLY [*moving toward the chair*] I'm keeping an account of everything, remember. I'll pay every penny back. [*He sits.*]

CHARLEY Now listen to me, Willy.

WILLY I want you to know I appreciate . . .

CHARLEY [*sitting down on the table*] Willy, what're you doin'? What the hell is goin' on in your head?

WILLY Why? I'm simply . . .

CHARLEY I offered you a job. You can make fifty dollars a week. And I won't send you on the road.

WILLY I've got a job.

CHARLEY Without pay? What kind of a job is a job without pay? [*He rises.*] Now, look, kid, enough is enough. I'm no genius but I know when I'm being insulted.

WILLY Insulted!

CHARLEY Why don't you want to work for me?

WILLY What's the matter with you? I've got a job.

CHARLEY Then what're you walkin' in here every week for?

WILLY [*getting up*] Well, if you don't want me to walk in here—

CHARLEY I am offering you a job.

WILLY I don't want your goddam job!

CHARLEY When the hell are you going to grow up?

WILLY [*furiously*] You big ignoramus, if you say that to me again I'll rap you one! I don't care how big you are! [*He's ready to fight.*]

[*Pause.*]

CHARLEY [*kindly, going to him*] How much do you need, Willy?

WILLY Charley, I'm strapped, I'm strapped. I don't know what to do. I was just fired.

CHARLEY Howard fired you?

WILLY That snotnose. Imagine that? I named him. I named him Howard.

CHARLEY Willy, when're you gonna realize that them things don't mean anything? You named him Howard, but you can't sell that. The only thing you got in this world is what you can sell. And the funny thing is that you're a salesman, and you don't know that.

WILLY I've always tried to think otherwise, I guess. I always felt that if a man was impressive, and well liked, that nothing—

CHARLEY Why must everybody like you? Who liked J. P. Morgan?[1] Was he impressive? In a Turkish bath he'd look like a butcher. But with his pockets on he was very well liked. Now listen, Willy, I know you don't like me, and nobody can say I'm in love with you, but I'll give you a job because—just for the hell of it, put it that way. Now what do you say?

WILLY I—I just can't work for you, Charley.

CHARLEY What're you, jealous of me?

WILLY I can't work for you, that's all, don't ask me why.

CHARLEY [*angered, takes out more bills*] You been jealous of me all your life, you damned fool! Here, pay your insurance. [*He puts the money in* WILLY'S *hand.*]

WILLY I'm keeping strict accounts.

CHARLEY I've got some work to do. Take care of yourself. And pay your insurance.

WILLY [*moving to the right*] Funny, y'know? After all the highways, and the trains, and the appointments, and the years, you end up worth more dead than alive.

CHARLEY Willy, nobody's worth nothin' dead. [*After a slight pause*] Did you hear what I said?

[WILLY *stands still, dreaming.*]

CHARLEY Willy!

WILLY Apologize to Bernard for me when you see him. I didn't mean to argue with him. He's a fine boy. They're all fine boys, and they'll end up big—all of them. Someday they'll all play tennis together. Wish me luck, Charley. He saw Bill Oliver today.

CHARLEY Good luck.

WILLY [*on the verge of tears*] Charley, you're the only friend I got. Isn't that a remarkable thing? [*He goes out.*]

CHARLEY Jesus!

[CHARLEY *stares after him a moment and follows. All light blacks out. Suddenly raucous music is heard, and a red glow rises behind the screen at right.* STANLEY, *a young waiter, appears, carrying a table, followed by* HAPPY, *who is carrying two chairs.*]

STANLEY [*putting the table down*] That's all right, Mr. Loman, I can handle it myself. [*He turns and takes the chairs from* HAPPY *and places them at the table.*]

1. American financier, industrialist, and philanthropist (1837–1913); he amassed an enormous fortune.

HAPPY [*glancing around*] Oh, this is better.

STANLEY Sure, in the front there you're in the middle of all kinds a noise. Whenever you got a party, Mr. Loman, you just tell me and I'll put you back here. Y'know, there's a lotta people they don't like it private, because when they go out they like to see a lotta action around them because they're sick and tired to stay in the house by theirself. But I know you, you ain't from Hackensack.[2] You know what I mean?

HAPPY [*sitting down*] So how's it coming, Stanley?

STANLEY Ah, it's a dog's life. I only wish during the war they'd a took me in the Army. I coulda been dead by now.

HAPPY My brother's back, Stanley.

STANLEY Oh, he come back, heh? From the Far West.

HAPPY Yeah, big cattle man, my brother, so treat him right. And my father's coming too.

STANLEY Oh, your father too!

HAPPY You got a couple of nice lobsters?

STANLEY Hundred per cent, big.

HAPPY I want them with the claws.

STANLEY Don't worry, I don't give you no mice. [HAPPY *laughs.*] How about some wine? It'll put a head on the meal.

HAPPY No. You remember, Stanley, that recipe I brought you from overseas? With the champagne in it?

STANLEY Oh, yeah, sure. I still got it tacked up yet in the kitchen. But that'll have to cost a buck apiece anyways.

HAPPY That's all right.

STANLEY What'd you, hit a number[3] or somethin'?

HAPPY No, it's a little celebration. My brother is—I think he pulled off a big deal today. I think we're going into business together.

STANLEY Great! That's the best for you. Because a family business, you know what I mean?—that's the best.

HAPPY That's what I think.

STANLEY 'Cause what's the difference? Somebody steals? It's in the family. Know what I mean? [*Sotto voce*[4]] Like this bartender here. The boss is goin' crazy what kinda leak he's got in the cash register. You put it in but it don't come out.

HAPPY [*raising his head*] Sh!

STANLEY What?

HAPPY You notice I wasn't lookin' right or left, was I?

STANLEY No.

HAPPY And my eyes are closed.

STANLEY So what's the—?

HAPPY Strudel's comin'.

STANLEY [*catching on, looks around*] Ah, no, there's no—

[*He breaks off as a furred, lavishly dressed girl enters and sits at the next table. Both follow her with their eyes.*]

STANLEY Geez, how'd ya know?

2. A mainly working-class town in northern New Jersey, several miles from Manhattan.
3. That is, win in an illegal lottery.
4. Under the voice (Italian); that is, spoken very softly, under the breath.

HAPPY I got radar or something. [*Staring directly at her profile*] Ooooooo . . . Stanley.

STANLEY I think that's for you, Mr. Loman.

HAPPY Look at that mouth. Oh, God. And the binoculars.

STANLEY Geez, you got a life, Mr. Loman.

HAPPY Wait on her.

STANLEY [*going to the girl's table*] Would you like a menu, ma'am?

GIRL I'm expecting someone, but I'd like a—

HAPPY Why don't you bring her—excuse me, miss, do you mind? I sell champagne, and I'd like you to try my brand. Bring her a champagne, Stanley.

GIRL That's awfully nice of you.

HAPPY Don't mention it. It's all company money. [*He laughs.*]

GIRL That's a charming product to be selling, isn't it?

HAPPY Oh, gets to be like everything else. Selling is selling, y'know.

GIRL I suppose.

HAPPY You don't happen to sell, do you?

GIRL No, I don't sell.

HAPPY Would you object to a compliment from a stranger? You ought to be on a magazine cover.

GIRL [*looking at him a little archly*] I have been.

[STANLEY *comes in with a glass of champagne.*]

HAPPY What'd I say before, Stanley? You see? She's a cover girl.

STANLEY Oh, I could see, I could see.

HAPPY [*to the* GIRL] What magazine?

GIRL Oh, a lot of them. [*She takes the drink.*] Thank you.

HAPPY You know what they say in France, don't you? "Champagne is the drink of the complexion"—Hya, Biff!

[BIFF *has entered and sits with* HAPPY.]

BIFF Hello, kid. Sorry I'm late.

HAPPY I just got here. Uh, Miss—?

GIRL Forsythe.

HAPPY Miss Forsythe, this is my brother.

BIFF Is Dad here?

HAPPY His name is Biff. You might've heard of him. Great football player.

GIRL Really? What team?

HAPPY Are you familiar with football?

GIRL No, I'm afraid I'm not.

HAPPY Biff is quarterback with the New York Giants.

GIRL Well, that is nice, isn't it? [*She drinks.*]

HAPPY Good health.

GIRL I'm happy to meet you.

HAPPY That's my name. Hap. It's really Harold, but at West Point they called me Happy.

GIRL [*now really impressed*] Oh, I see. How do you do? [*She turns her profile.*]

BIFF Isn't Dad coming?

HAPPY You want her?

BIFF Oh, I could never make that.

HAPPY I remember the time that idea would never come into your head. Where's the old confidence, Biff?

BIFF I just saw Oliver—

HAPPY Wait a minute. I've got to see that old confidence again. Do you want her? She's on call.[5]

BIFF Oh, no. [*He turns to look at the* GIRL.]

HAPPY I'm telling you. Watch this. [*Turning to the* GIRL] Honey? [*She turns to him.*] Are you busy?

GIRL Well, I am . . . but I could make a phone call.

HAPPY Do that, will you, honey? And see if you can get a friend. We'll be here for a while. Biff is one of the greatest football players in the country.

GIRL [*standing up*] Well, I'm certainly happy to meet you.

HAPPY Come back soon.

GIRL I'll try.

HAPPY Don't try, honey, try hard.

[*The* GIRL *exits.* STANLEY *follows, shaking his head in bewildered admiration.*]

HAPPY Isn't that a shame now? A beautiful girl like that? That's why I can't get married. There's not a good woman in a thousand. New York is loaded with them, kid!

BIFF Hap, look—

HAPPY I told you she was on call!

BIFF [*strangely unnerved*] Cut it out, will ya? I want to say something to you.

HAPPY Did you see Oliver?

BIFF I saw him all right. Now look, I want to tell Dad a couple of things and I want you to help me.

HAPPY What? Is he going to back you?

BIFF Are you crazy? You're out of your goddam head, you know that?

HAPPY Why? What happened?

BIFF [*breathlessly*] I did a terrible thing today, Hap. It's been the strangest day I ever went through. I'm all numb, I swear.

HAPPY You mean he wouldn't see you?

BIFF Well, I waited six hours for him, see? All day. Kept sending my name in. Even tried to date his secretary so she'd get me to him, but no soap.

HAPPY Because you're not showin' the old confidence, Biff. He remembered you, didn't he?

BIFF [*stopping* HAPPY *with a gesture*] Finally, about five o'clock, he comes out. Didn't remember who I was or anything. I felt like such an idiot, Hap.

HAPPY Did you tell him my Florida idea?

BIFF He walked away. I saw him for one minute. I got so mad I could've torn the walls down! How the hell did I ever get the idea I was a salesman there? I even believed myself that I'd been a salesman for him! And then he gave me one look and—I realized what a ridiculous lie my whole life has been! We've been talking in a dream for fifteen years. I was a shipping clerk.

HAPPY What'd you do?

BIFF [*with great tension and wonder*] Well, he left, see. And the secretary went out. I was all alone in the waiting-room. I don't know what came over

5. That is, a call girl, a prostitute.

me, Hap. The next thing I know I'm in his office—paneled walls, everything. I can't explain it. I—Hap, I took his fountain pen.

HAPPY Geez, did he catch you?

BIFF I ran out. I ran down all eleven flights. I ran and ran and ran.

HAPPY That was an awful dumb—what'd you do that for?

BIFF [*agonized*] I don't know, I just—wanted to take something, I don't know. You gotta help me, Hap, I'm gonna tell Pop.

HAPPY You crazy? What for?

BIFF Hap, he's got to understand that I'm not the man somebody lends that kind of money to. He thinks I've been spiting him all these years and it's eating him up.

HAPPY That's just it. You tell him something nice.

BIFF I can't.

HAPPY Say you got a lunch date with Oliver tomorrow.

BIFF So what do I do tomorrow?

HAPPY You leave the house tomorrow and come back at night and say Oliver is thinking it over. And he thinks it over for a couple of weeks, and gradually it fades away and nobody's the worse.

BIFF But it'll go on forever!

HAPPY Dad is never so happy as when he's looking forward to something!

[WILLY *enters.*]

HAPPY Hello, scout!

WILLY Gee, I haven't been here in years!

[STANLEY *has followed* WILLY *in and sets a chair for him.* STANLEY *starts off but* HAPPY *stops him.*]

HAPPY Stanley!

[STANLEY *stands by, waiting for an order.*]

BIFF [*going to* WILLY *with guilt, as to an invalid*] Sit down, Pop. You want a drink?

WILLY Sure, I don't mind.

BIFF Let's get a load on.

WILLY You look worried.

BIFF N-no. [*To* STANLEY] Scotch all around. Make it doubles.

STANLEY Doubles, right. [*He goes.*]

WILLY You had a couple already, didn't you?

BIFF Just a couple, yeah.

WILLY Well, what happened, boy? [*Nodding affirmatively, with a smile*] Everything go all right?

BIFF [*takes a breath, then reaches out and grasps* WILLY'S *hand*] Pal . . . [*He is smiling bravely, and* WILLY *is smiling too.*] I had an experience today.

HAPPY Terrific, Pop.

WILLY That so? What happened?

BIFF [*high, slightly alcoholic, above the earth*] I'm going to tell you everything from first to last. It's been a strange day. [*Silence. He looks around, composes himself as best he can, but his breath keeps breaking the rhythm of his voice.*] I had to wait quite a while for him, and—

WILLY Oliver?

BIFF Yeah, Oliver. All day, as a matter of cold fact. And a lot of—instances—facts, Pop, facts about my life came back to me. Who was it, Pop? Who ever said I was a salesman with Oliver?

WILLY Well, you were.

BIFF No, Dad, I was a shipping clerk.

WILLY But you were practically—

BIFF [*with determination*] Dad, I don't know who said it first, but I was never a salesman for Bill Oliver.

WILLY What're you talking about?

BIFF Let's hold on to the facts tonight, Pop. We're not going to get anywhere bullin' around. I was a shipping clerk.

WILLY [*angrily*] All right, now listen to me—

BIFF Why don't you let me finish?

WILLY I'm not interested in stories about the past or any crap of that kind because the woods are burning, boys, you understand? There's a big blaze going on all around. I was fired today.

BIFF [*shocked*] How could you be?

WILLY I was fired, and I'm looking for a little good news to tell your mother, because the woman has waited and the woman has suffered. The gist of it is that I haven't got a story left in my head, Biff. So don't give me a lecture about facts and aspects. I am not interested. Now what've you got to say to me?

[STANLEY *enters with three drinks. They wait until he leaves.*]

WILLY Did you see Oliver?

BIFF Jesus, Dad!

WILLY You mean you didn't go up there?

HAPPY Sure he went up there.

BIFF I did. I—saw him. How could they fire you?

WILLY [*on the edge of his chair*] What kind of a welcome did he give you?

BIFF He won't even let you work on commission?

WILLY I'm out! [*Driving*] So tell me, he gave you a warm welcome?

HAPPY Sure, Pop, sure!

BIFF [*driven*] Well, it was kind of—

WILLY I was wondering if he'd remember you. [*To* HAPPY] Imagine, man doesn't see him for ten, twelve years and gives him that kind of a welcome!

HAPPY Damn right!

BIFF [*trying to return to the offensive*] Pop, look—

WILLY You know why he remembered you, don't you? Because you impressed him in those days.

BIFF Let's talk quietly and get this down to the facts, huh?

WILLY [*as though* BIFF *had been interrupting*] Well, what happened? It's great news, Biff. Did he take you into his office or'd you talk in the waiting room?

BIFF Well, he came in, see, and—

WILLY [*with a big smile*] What'd he say? Betcha he threw his arm around you.

BIFF Well, he kinda—

WILLY He's a fine man. [*To* HAPPY] Very hard man to see, y'know.

HAPPY [*agreeing*] Oh, I know.

WILLY [*to Biff*] Is that where you had the drinks?

BIFF Yeah, he gave me a couple of—no, no!

HAPPY [*cutting in*] He told him my Florida idea.

WILLY Don't interrupt. [*To* BIFF] How'd he react to the Florida idea?

BIFF Dad, will you give me a minute to explain?

WILLY I've been waiting for you to explain since I sat down here! What happened? He took you into his office and what?

BIFF Well—I talked. And—and he listened, see.

WILLY Famous for the way he listens, y'know. What was his answer?

BIFF His answer was—[*He breaks off, suddenly angry.*] Dad, you're not letting me tell you what I want to tell you!

WILLY [*accusing, angered*] You didn't see him, did you?

BIFF I did see him!

WILLY What'd you insult him or something? You insulted him, didn't you?

BIFF Listen, will you let me out of it, will you just let me out of it!

HAPPY What the hell!

WILLY Tell me what happened!

BIFF [*to* HAPPY] I can't talk to him!

[*A single trumpet note jars the ear. The light of green leaves stains the house, which holds the air of night and a dream.* YOUNG BERNARD *enters and knocks on the door of the house.*]

YOUNG BERNARD [*frantically*] Mrs. Loman, Mrs. Loman!

HAPPY Tell him what happened!

BIFF [*to* HAPPY] Shut up and leave me alone!

WILLY No, no! You had to go and flunk math!

BIFF What math? What're you talking about?

YOUNG BERNARD Mrs. Loman, Mrs. Loman!

[LINDA *appears in the house, as of old.*]

WILLY [*wildly*] Math, math, math!

BIFF Take it easy, Pop!

YOUNG BERNARD Mrs. Loman!

WILLY [*furiously*] If you hadn't flunked you'd've been set by now!

BIFF Now, look, I'm gonna tell you what happened, and you're going to listen to me.

YOUNG BERNARD Mrs. Loman!

BIFF I waited six hours—

HAPPY What the hell are you saying?

BIFF I kept sending in my name but he wouldn't see me. So finally he . . . [*He continues unheard as light fades low on the restaurant.*]

YOUNG BERNARD Biff flunked math!

LINDA No!

YOUNG BERNARD Birnbaum flunked him! They won't graduate him!

LINDA But they have to. He's gotta go to the university. Where is he? Biff! Biff!

YOUNG BERNARD No, he left. He went to Grand Central.[6]

LINDA Grand—You mean he went to Boston!

YOUNG BERNARD Is Uncle Willy in Boston?

LINDA Oh, maybe Willy can talk to the teacher. Oh, the poor, poor boy!

[*Light on house area snaps out.*]

BIFF [*at the table, now audible, holding up a gold fountain pen*] . . . so I'm washed up with Oliver, you understand? Are you listening to me?

6. Grand Central Terminal, one of New York City's two main railroad stations.

WILLY [*at a loss*] Yeah, sure. If you hadn't flunked—

BIFF Flunked what? What're you talking about?

WILLY Don't blame everything on me! I didn't flunk math—you did! What pen?

HAPPY That was awful dumb, Biff, a pen like that is worth—

WILLY [*seeing the pen for the first time*] You took Oliver's pen?

BIFF [*weakening*] Dad, I just explained it to you.

WILLY You stole Bill Oliver's fountain pen!

BIFF I didn't exactly steal it! That's just what I've been explaining to you!

HAPPY He had it in his hand and just then Oliver walked in, so he got nervous and stuck it in his pocket!

WILLY My God, Biff!

BIFF I never intended to do it, Dad!

OPERATOR'S VOICE Standish Arms, good evening!

WILLY [*shouting*] I'm not in my room!

BIFF [*frightened*] Dad, what's the matter? [*He and* HAPPY *stand up.*]

OPERATOR Ringing Mr. Loman for you!

WILLY I'm not there, stop it!

BIFF [*horrified, gets down on one knee before* WILLY] Dad, I'll make good, I'll make good. [WILLY *tries to get to his feet.* BIFF *holds him down.*] Sit down now.

WILLY No, you're no good, you're no good for anything.

BIFF I am, Dad, I'll find something else, you understand? Now don't worry about anything. [*He holds up* WILLY's *face.*] Talk to me, Dad.

OPERATOR Mr. Loman does not answer. Shall I page him?

WILLY [*attempting to stand, as though to rush and silence the* OPERATOR] No, no, no!

HAPPY He'll strike something, Pop.

WILLY No, no . . .

BIFF [*desperately, standing over* WILLY] Pop, listen! Listen to me! I'm telling you something good. Oliver talked to his partner about the Florida idea. You listening? He—he talked to his partner, and he came to me . . . I'm going to be all right, you hear? Dad, listen to me, he said it was just a question of the amount!

WILLY Then you . . . got it?

HAPPY He's gonna be terrific, Pop!

WILLY [*trying to stand*] Then you got it, haven't you? You got it! You got it!

BIFF [*agonized, holds* WILLY *down*] No, no. Look, Pop. I'm supposed to have lunch with them tomorrow. I'm just telling you this so you'll know that I can still make an impression, Pop. And I'll make good somewhere, but I can't go tomorrow, see?

WILLY Why not? You simply—

BIFF But the pen, Pop!

WILLY You give it to him and tell him it was an oversight!

HAPPY Sure, have lunch tomorrow!

BIFF I can't say that—

WILLY You were doing a crosswood puzzle and accidentally used his pen!

BIFF Listen, kid, I took those balls years ago, now I walk in with his fountain pen? That clinches it, don't you see? I can't face him like that! I'll try elsewhere.

PAGE'S VOICE Paging Mr. Loman!

WILLY Don't you want to be anything?

BIFF Pop, how can I go back?

WILLY You don't want to be anything, is that what's behind it?

BIFF [*now angry at* WILLY *for not crediting his sympathy*] Don't take it that way! You think it was easy walking into that office after what I'd done to him? A team of horses couldn't have dragged me back to Bill Oliver!

WILLY Then why'd you go?

BIFF Why did I go? Why did I go! Look at you! Look at what's become of you!

[*Off left,* THE WOMAN *laughs.*]

WILLY Biff, you're going to go to that lunch tomorrow, or—

BIFF I can't go. I've got no appointment!

HAPPY Biff, for . . . !

WILLY Are you spiting me?

BIFF Don't take it that way! Goddammit!

WILLY [*strikes* BIFF *and falters away from the table*] You rotten little louse! Are you spiting me?

THE WOMAN Someone's at the door, Willy!

BIFF I'm no good, can't you see what I am?

HAPPY [*separating them*] Hey, you're in a restaurant! Now cut it out, both of you! [*The girls enter.*] Hello, girls, sit down.

[THE WOMAN *laughs, off left.*]

MISS FORSYTHE I guess we might as well. This is Letta.

THE WOMAN Willy, are you going to wake up?

BIFF [*ignoring* WILLY] How're ya, miss, sit down. What do you drink?

MISS FORSYTHE Letta might not be able to stay long.

LETTA I gotta get up very early tomorrow. I got jury duty. I'm so excited! Were you fellows ever on a jury?

BIFF No, but I been in front of them! [*The girls laugh.*] This is my father.

LETTA Isn't he cute? Sit down with us, Pop.

HAPPY Sit him down, Biff!

BIFF [*going to him*] Come on, slugger, drink us under the table. To hell with it! Come on, sit down, pal.

[*On* BIFF*'s last insistence,* WILLY *is about to sit.*]

THE WOMAN [*now urgently*] Willy, are you going to answer the door!

[THE WOMAN*'s call pulls* WILLY *back. He starts right, befuddled.*]

BIFF Hey, where are you going?

WILLY Open the door.

BIFF The door?

WILLY The washroom . . . the door . . . where's the door?

BIFF [*leading* WILLY *to the left*] Just go straight down.

[WILLY *moves left.*]

THE WOMAN Willy, Willy, are you going to get up, get up, get up, get up?

[WILLY *exits left.*]

LETTA I think it's sweet you bring your daddy along.

MISS FORSYTHE Oh, he isn't really your father!

BIFF [*at left, turning to her resentfully*] Miss Forsythe, you've just seen a prince walk by. A fine, troubled prince. A hard-working, unappreciated prince. A pal, you understand? A good companion. Always for his boys.

LETTA That's so sweet.

HAPPY Well, girls, what's the program? We're wasting time. Come on, Biff. Gather round. Where would you like to go?

BIFF Why don't you do something for him?

HAPPY Me!

BIFF Don't you give a damn for him, Hap?

HAPPY What're you talking about? I'm the one who—

BIFF I sense it, you don't give a good goddam about him. [*He takes the rolled-up hose from his pocket and puts it on the table in front of* HAPPY.] Look what I found in the cellar, for Christ's sake. How can you bear to let it go on?

HAPPY Me? Who goes away? Who runs off and—

BIFF Yeah, but he doesn't mean anything to you. You could help him—I can't! Don't you understand what I'm talking about? He's going to kill himself, don't you know that?

HAPPY Don't I know it! Me!

BIFF Hap, help him! Jesus . . . help him . . . Help me, help me, I can't bear to look at his face! [*Ready to weep, he hurries out, up right.*]

HAPPY [*starting after him*] Where are you going?

MISS FORSYTHE What's he so mad about?

HAPPY Come on, girls, we'll catch up with him.

MISS FORSYTHE [*as Happy pushes her out*] Say, I don't like that temper of his!

HAPPY He's just a little overstrung, he'll be all right!

WILLY [*off left, as* THE WOMAN *laughs*] Don't answer! Don't answer!

LETTA Don't you want to tell your father—

HAPPY No, that's not my father. He's just a guy. Come on, we'll catch Biff, and, honey, we're going to paint this town! Stanley, where's the check! Hey, Stanley!

[*They exit.* STANLEY *looks toward left.*]

STANLEY [*calling to* HAPPY *indignantly*] Mr. Loman! Mr. Loman!

[STANLEY *picks up a chair and follows them off. Knocking is heard off left.* THE WOMAN *enters, laughing.* WILLY *follows her. She is in a black slip; he is buttoning his shirt. Raw, sensuous music accompanies their speech.*]

WILLY Will you stop laughing? Will you stop?

THE WOMAN Aren't you going to answer the door? He'll wake the whole hotel.

WILLY I'm not expecting anybody.

THE WOMAN Whyn't you have another drink, honey, and stop being so damn self-centered?

WILLY I'm so lonely.

THE WOMAN You know you ruined me, Willy? From now on, whenever you come to the office, I'll see that you go right through to the buyers. No waiting at my desk anymore, Willy. You ruined me.

WILLY That's nice of you to say that.

THE WOMAN Gee, you are self-centered! Why so sad? You are the saddest, self-centeredest soul I ever did see-saw. [*She laughs. He kisses her.*] Come on inside, drummer[7] boy. It's silly to be dressing in the middle of the night. [*As knocking is heard*] Aren't you going to answer the door?

7. A commercial traveler, a salesman.

WILLY They're knocking on the wrong door.

THE WOMAN But I felt the knocking. And he heard us talking in here. Maybe the hotel's on fire!

WILLY [*his terror rising*] It's a mistake.

THE WOMAN Then tell him to go away!

WILLY There's nobody there.

THE WOMAN It's getting on my nerves, Willy. There's somebody standing out there and it's getting on my nerves!

WILLY [*pushing her away from him*] All right, stay in the bathroom here, and don't come out. I think there's a law in Massachusetts about it,[8] so don't come out. It may be that new room clerk. He looked very mean. So don't come out. It's a mistake, there's no fire.

[*The knocking is heard again. He takes a few steps away from her, and she vanishes into the wing. The light follows him, and now he is facing* YOUNG BIFF, *who carries a suitcase. Biff steps toward him. The music is gone.*]

BIFF Why didn't you answer?

WILLY Biff! What are you doing in Boston?

BIFF Why didn't you answer? I've been knocking for five minutes, I called you on the phone—

WILLY I just heard you. I was in the bathroom and had the door shut. Did anything happen home?

BIFF Dad—I let you down.

WILLY What do you mean?

BIFF Dad . . .

WILLY Biffo, what's this about? [*Putting his arm around* BIFF] Come on, let's go downstairs and get you a malted.

BIFF Dad, I flunked math.

WILLY Not for the term?

BIFF The term. I haven't got enough credits to graduate.

WILLY You mean to say Bernard wouldn't give you the answers?

BIFF He did, he tried, but I only got a sixty-one.

WILLY And they wouldn't give you four points?

BIFF Birnbaum refused absolutely. I begged him, Pop, but he won't give me those points. You gotta talk to him before they close the school. Because if he saw the kind of man you are, and you just talked to him in your way, I'm sure he'd come through for me. The class came right before practice, see, and I didn't go enough. Would you talk to him? He'd like you, Pop. You know the way you could talk.

WILLY You're on. We'll drive right back.

BIFF Oh, Dad, good work! I'm sure he'll change it for you!

WILLY Go downstairs and tell the clerk I'm checkin' out. Go right down.

BIFF Yes, sir! See, the reason he hates me, Pop—one day he was late for class so I got up at the blackboard and imitated him. I crossed my eyes and talked with a lithp.

WILLY [*laughing*] You did? The kids like it?

BIFF They nearly died laughing!

8. That is, adultery, which is a felony in Massachusetts, though this law was rarely enforced even in the 1940s.

WILLY Yeah? What'd you do?

BIFF The thquare root of thixthy twee is . . . [WILLY *bursts out laughing;* BIFF *joins him.*] And in the middle of it he walked in!

[WILLY *laughs and* THE WOMAN *joins in offstage.*]

WILLY [*without hesitation*] Hurry downstairs and—

BIFF Somebody in there?

WILLY No, that was next door.

[THE WOMAN *laughs offstage.*]

BIFF Somebody got in your bathroom!

WILLY No, it's the next room, there's a party—

THE WOMAN [*enters, laughing. She lisps this*] Can I come in? There's something in the bathtub, Willy, and it's moving!

[WILLY *looks at* BIFF, *who is staring open-mouthed and horrified at* THE WOMAN.]

WILLY Ah—you better go back to your room. They must be finished painting by now. They're painting her room so I let her take a shower here. Go back, go back . . . [*He pushes her.*]

THE WOMAN [*resisting*] But I've got to get dressed, Willy, I can't—

WILLY Get out of here! Go back, go back . . . [*Suddenly striving for the ordinary*] This is Miss Francis, Biff, she's a buyer. They're painting her room. Go back, Miss Francis, go back . . .

THE WOMAN But my clothes, I can't go out naked in the hall!

WILLY [*pushing her offstage*] Get outa here! Go back, go back!

[BIFF *slowly sits down on his suitcase as the argument continues offstage.*]

THE WOMAN Where's my stockings? You promised me stockings, Willy!

WILLY I have no stockings here!

THE WOMAN You had two boxes of size nine sheers for me, and I want them!

WILLY Here, for God's sake, will you get outa here!

THE WOMAN [*enters holding a box of stockings*] I just hope there's nobody in the hall. That's all I hope. [*To* BIFF] Are you football or baseball?

BIFF Football.

THE WOMAN [*angry, humiliated*] That's me too. G'night. [*She snatches her clothes from* WILLY, *and walks out.*]

WILLY [*after a pause*] Well, better get going. I want to get to the school first thing in the morning. Get my suits out of the closet. I'll get my valise. [BIFF *doesn't move.*] What's the matter? [BIFF *remains motionless, tears falling.*] She's a buyer. Buys for J. H. Simmons. She lives down the hall—they're painting. You don't imagine—[*He breaks off. After a pause*] Now listen, pal, she's just a buyer. She sees merchandise in her room and they have to keep it looking just so . . . [*Pause. Assuming command*] All right, get my suits. [BIFF *doesn't move.*] Now stop crying and do as I say. I gave you an order. Biff, I gave you an order! Is that what you do when I give you an order? How dare you cry! [*Putting his arm around Biff*] Now look, Biff, when you grow up you'll understand about these things. You mustn't—you mustn't overemphasize a thing like this. I'll see Birnbaum first thing in the morning.

BIFF Never mind.

WILLY [*getting down beside* BIFF] Never mind! He's going to give you those points. I'll see to it.

BIFF He wouldn't listen to you.

WILLY He certainly will listen to me. You need those points for the U. of Virginia.

BIFF I'm not going there.

WILLY Heh? If I can't get him to change that mark you'll make it up in summer school. You've got all summer to—

BIFF [*his weeping breaking from him*] Dad . . .

WILLY [*infected by it*] Oh, my boy . . .

BIFF Dad . . .

WILLY She's nothing to me, Biff. I was lonely, I was terribly lonely.

BIFF You—you gave her Mama's stockings! [*His tears break through and he rises to go.*]

WILLY [*grabbing for* BIFF] I gave you an order!

BIFF Don't touch me, you—liar!

WILLY Apologize for that!

BIFF You fake! You phony little fake! You fake! [*Overcome, he turns quickly and weeping fully goes out with his suitcase.* WILLY *is left on the floor on his knees.*]

WILLY I gave you an order! Biff, come back here or I'll beat you! Come back here! I'll whip you!

[STANLEY *comes quickly in from the right and stands in front of* WILLY.]

WILLY [*shouts at Stanley*] I gave you an order . . .

STANLEY Hey, let's pick it up, pick it up, Mr. Loman. [*He helps* WILLY *to his feet.*] Your boys left with the chippies.[9] They said they'll see you home.

[*A second waiter watches some distance away.*]

WILLY But we were supposed to have dinner together.

[*Music is heard,* WILLY's *theme.*]

STANLEY Can you make it?

WILLY I'll—sure, I can make it. [*Suddenly concerned about his clothes*] Do I—I look all right?

STANLEY Sure, you look all right. [*He flicks a speck off* WILLY's *lapel.*]

WILLY Here—here's a dollar.

STANLEY Oh, your son paid me. It's all right.

WILLY [*putting it in* STANLEY's *hand*] No, take it. You're a good boy.

STANLEY Oh, no, you don't have to . . .

WILLY Here—here's some more, I don't need it anymore. [*After a slight pause*] Tell me—is there a seed store in the neighborhood?

STANLEY Seeds? You mean like to plant?

[*As* WILLY *turns,* STANLEY *slips the money back into his jacket pocket.*]

WILLY Yes. Carrots, peas . . .

STANLEY Well, there's hardware stores on Sixth Avenue, but it may be too late now.

WILLY [*anxiously*] Oh, I'd better hurry, I've got to get some seeds. [*He starts off to the right.*] I've got to get some seeds, right away. Nothing's planted. I don't have a thing in the ground.

[WILLY *hurries out as the light goes down.* STANLEY *moves over to the right after him, watches him off. The other waiter has been staring at* WILLY.]

9. Tramps, prostitutes.

STANLEY [*to the waiter*] Well, whatta you looking at?

[*The waiter picks up the chairs and moves off right.* STANLEY *takes the table and follows him. The light fades on this area. There is a long pause, the sound of the flute coming over. The light gradually rises on the kitchen, which is empty.* HAPPY *appears at the door of the house, followed by* BIFF. HAPPY *is carrying a large bunch of long-stemmed roses. He enters the kitchen, looks around for* LINDA. *Not seeing her, he turns to* BIFF, *who is just outside the house door, and makes a gesture with his hands, indicating "Not here, I guess." He looks into the living room and freezes. Inside, Linda, unseen, is seated,* WILLY'S *coat on her lap. She rises ominously and quietly and moves toward* HAPPY, *who backs up into the kitchen, afraid.*]

HAPPY Hey, what're you doing up? [LINDA *says nothing but moves toward him implacably.*] Where's Pop? [*He keeps backing to the right, and now* LINDA *is in full view in the doorway to the living room.*] Is he sleeping?

LINDA Where were you?

HAPPY [*trying to laugh it off*] We met two girls, Mom, very fine types. Here, we brought you some flowers. [*Offering them to her*] Put them in your room, Ma.

[*She knocks them to the floor at* BIFF'S *feet. He has now come inside and closed the door behind him. She stares at* BIFF, *silent.*]

HAPPY Now what'd you do that for? Mom, I want you to have some flowers—

LINDA [*cutting* HAPPY *off, violently to* BIFF] Don't you care whether he lives or dies?

HAPPY [*going to the stairs*] Come upstairs, Biff.

BIFF [*with a flare of disgust, to* HAPPY] Go away from me! [*To* LINDA] What do you mean, lives or dies? Nobody's dying around here, pal.

LINDA Get out of my sight! Get out of here!

BIFF I wanna see the boss.

LINDA You're not going near him!

BIFF Where is he? [*He moves into the living room and* LINDA *follows.*]

LINDA [*shouting after* BIFF] You invite him for dinner. He looks forward to it all day—[BIFF *appears in his parents' bedroom, looks around, and exits.*]—and then you desert him there. There's no stranger you'd do that to!

HAPPY Why? He had a swell time with us. Listen, when I—[LINDA *comes back into the kitchen.*]—desert him I hope I don't outlive the day!

LINDA Get out of here!

HAPPY Now look, Mom . . .

LINDA Did you have to go to women tonight? You and your lousy rotten whores!

[BIFF *reenters the kitchen.*]

HAPPY Mom, all we did was follow Biff around trying to cheer him up! [*To* BIFF] Boy, what a night you gave me!

LINDA Get out of here, both of you, and don't come back! I don't want you tormenting him anymore. Go on now, get your things together! [*To* BIFF] You can sleep in his apartment. [*She starts to pick up the flowers and stops herself.*] Pick up this stuff, I'm not your maid anymore. Pick it up, you bum, you!

[HAPPY *turns his back to her in refusal.* BIFF *slowly moves over and gets down on his knees, picking up the flowers.*]

LINDA You're a pair of animals! Not one, not another living soul would have had the cruelty to walk out on that man in a restaurant!

BIFF [*not looking at her*] Is that what he said?

LINDA He didn't have to say anything. He was so humiliated he nearly limped when he came in.

HAPPY But, Mom, he had a great time with us—

BIFF [*cutting him off violently*] Shut up!

[*Without another word,* HAPPY *goes upstairs.*]

LINDA You! You didn't even go in to see if he was all right!

BIFF [*still on the floor in front of* LINDA, *the flowers in his hand; with self-loathing*] No. Didn't. Didn't do a damned thing. How do you like that, heh? Left him babbling in a toilet.

LINDA You louse. You . . .

BIFF Now you hit it on the nose! [*He gets up, throws the flowers in the wastebasket.*] The scum of the earth, and you're looking at him!

LINDA Get out of here!

BIFF I gotta talk to the boss, Mom. Where is he?

LINDA You're not going near him. Get out of this house!

BIFF [*with absolute assurance, determination*] No. We're gonna have an abrupt conversation, him and me.

LINDA You're not talking to him!

[*Hammering is heard from outside the house, off right.* BIFF *turns toward the noise.*]

LINDA [*suddenly pleading*] Will you please leave him alone?

BIFF What's he doing out there?

LINDA He's planting the garden!

BIFF [*quietly*] Now? Oh, my God!

[BIFF *moves outside,* LINDA *following. The light dies down on them and comes up on the center of the apron as* WILLY *walks into it. He is carrying a flashlight, a hoe, and a handful of seed packets. He raps the top of the hoe sharply to fix it firmly, and then moves to the left, measuring off the distance with his foot. He holds the flashlight to look at the seed packets, reading off the instructions. He is in the blue of night.*]

WILLY Carrots . . . quarter-inch apart. Rows . . . one-foot rows. [*He measures it off.*] One foot. [*He puts down a package and measures off.*] Beets. [*He puts down another package and measures again.*] Lettuce. [*He reads the package, puts it down.*] One foot—[*He breaks off as* BEN *appears at the right and moves slowly down to him.*] What a proposition, ts, ts. Terrific, terrific. 'Cause she's suffered, Ben, the woman has suffered. You understand me? A man can't go out the way he came in, Ben, a man has got to add up to something. You can't, you can't—[BEN *moves toward him as though to interrupt.*] You gotta consider, now. Don't answer so quick. Remember, it's a guaranteed twenty-thousand-dollar proposition. Now look, Ben, I want you to go through the ins and outs of this thing with me. I've got nobody to talk to, Ben, and the woman has suffered, you hear me?

BEN [*standing still, considering*] What's the proposition?

WILLY It's twenty thousand dollars on the barrelhead. Guaranteed, gilt-edged, you understand?

BEN You don't want to make a fool of yourself. They might not honor the policy.

WILLY How can they dare refuse? Didn't I work like a coolie to meet every premium on the nose? And now they don't pay off? Impossible!

BEN It's called a cowardly thing, William.

WILLY Why? Does it take more guts to stand here the rest of my life ringing up a zero?

BEN [*yielding*] That's a point, William. [*He moves, thinking, turns.*] And twenty thousand—that *is* something one can feel with the hand, it is there.

WILLY [*now assured, with rising power*] Oh, Ben, that's the whole beauty of it! I see it like a diamond, shining in the dark, hard and rough, that I can pick up and touch in my hand. Not like—like an appointment! This would not be another damned-fool appointment, Ben, and it changes all the aspects. Because he thinks I'm nothing, see and so he spites me. But the funeral—[*Straightening up*] Ben, that funeral will be massive! They'll come from Maine, Massachusetts, Vermont, New Hampshire! All the old-timers with the strange license plates—that boy will be thunder-struck, Ben, because he never realized—I am known! Rhode Island, New York, New Jersey—I am known, Ben, and he'll see it with his eyes once and for all. He'll see what I am, Ben! He's in for a shock, that boy!

BEN [*coming down to the edge of the garden*] He'll call you a coward.

WILLY [*suddenly fearful*] No, that would be terrible.

BEN Yes. And a damned fool.

WILLY No, no, he mustn't, I won't have that! [*He is broken and desperate.*]

BEN He'll hate you, William.

[*The gay music of the Boys is heard.*]

WILLY Oh, Ben, how do we get back to all the great times? Used to be so full of light, and comradeship, the sleigh-riding in winter, and the ruddiness on his cheeks. And always some kind of good news coming up, always something nice coming up ahead. And never even let me carry the valises in the house, and simonizing, simonizing that little red car! Why, why can't I give him something and not have him hate me?

BEN Let me think about it. [*He glances at his watch.*] I still have a little time. Remarkable proposition, but you've got to be sure you're not making a fool of yourself.

[BEN *drifts off upstage and goes out of sight.* BIFF *comes down from the left.*]

WILLY [*suddenly conscious of* BIFF, *turns and looks up at him, then begins picking up the packages of seeds in confusion*] Where the hell is that seed? [*Indignantly*] You can't see nothing out here! They boxed in the whole goddam neighborhood!

BIFF There are people all around here. Don't you realize that?

WILLY I'm busy. Don't bother me.

BIFF [*taking the hoe from* WILLY] I'm saying good-by to you, Pop. [WILLY *looks at him, silent, unable to move.*] I'm not coming back anymore.

WILLY You're not going to see Oliver tomorrow?

BIFF I've got no appointment, Dad.

WILLY He put his arm around you, and you've got no appointment?

BIFF Pop, get this now, will you? Everytime I've left it's been a fight that sent me out of here. Today I realized something about myself and I tried to explain it to you and I—I think I'm just not smart enough to make any sense out of it for you. To hell with whose fault it is or anything like that. [*He takes* WILLY*'s arm.*] Let's just wrap it up, heh? Come on in, we'll tell Mom. [*He gently tries to pull* WILLY *to left.*]

WILLY [*frozen, immobile, with guilt in his voice*] No, I don't want to see her.

BIFF Come on! [*He pulls again, and* WILLY *tries to pull away.*]

WILLY [*highly nervous*] No, no, I don't want to see her.

BIFF [*tries to look into* WILLY*'s face, as if to find the answer there*] Why don't you want to see her?

WILLY [*more harshly now*] Don't bother me, will you?

BIFF What do you mean, you don't want to see her? You don't want them calling you yellow, do you? This isn't your fault; it's me, I'm a bum. Now come inside! [WILLY *strains to get away.*] Did you hear what I said to you?

[WILLY *pulls away and quickly goes by himself into the house.* BIFF *follows.*]

LINDA [*to* WILLY] Did you plant, dear?

BIFF [*at the door, to* LINDA] All right, we had it out. I'm going and I'm not writing anymore.

LINDA [*going to* WILLY *in the kitchen*] I think that's the best way, dear. 'Cause there's no use drawing it out, you'll just never get along.

[WILLY *doesn't respond.*]

BIFF People ask where I am and what I'm doing, you don't know, and you don't care. That way it'll be off your mind and you can start brightening up again. All right? That clears it, doesn't it? [WILLY *is silent, and* BIFF *goes to him.*] You gonna wish me luck, scout? [*He extends his hand.*] What do you say?

LINDA Shake his hand, Willy.

WILLY [*turning to her, seething with hurt*] There's no necessity to mention the pen at all, y'know.

BIFF [*gently*] I've got no appointment, Dad.

WILLY [*erupting fiercely*] He put his arm around . . . ?

BIFF Dad, you're never going to see what I am, so what's the use of arguing? If I strike oil I'll send you a check. Meantime forget I'm alive.

WILLY [*to* LINDA] Spite, see?

BIFF Shake hands, Dad.

WILLY Not my hand.

BIFF I was hoping not to go this way.

WILLY Well, this is the way you're going. Good-by.

[BIFF *looks at him a moment, then turns sharply and goes to the stairs.*]

WILLY [*stops him with*] May you rot in hell if you leave this house!

BIFF [*turning*] Exactly what is it that you want from me?

WILLY I want you to know, on the train, in the mountains, in the valleys, wherever you go, that you cut down your life for spite!

BIFF No, no.

WILLY Spite, spite, is the word of your undoing! And when you're down and out, remember what did it. When you're rotting somewhere beside the railroad tracks, remember, and don't you dare blame it on me!

BIFF I'm not blaming it on you!

WILLY I won't take the rap for this, you hear?

[HAPPY *comes down the stairs and stands on the bottom step, watching.*]

BIFF That's just what I'm telling you!

WILLY [*sinking into a chair at the table, with full accusation*] You're trying to put a knife in me—don't think I don't know what you're doing!

BIFF All right, phony! Then let's lay it on the line. [*He whips the rubber tube out of his pocket and puts it on the table.*]

HAPPY You crazy—

LINDA Biff! [*She moves to grab the hose, but* BIFF *holds it down with his hand.*]

BIFF Leave it there! Don't move it!

WILLY [*not looking at it*] What is that?

BIFF You know goddam well what that is.

WILLY [*caged, wanting to escape*] I never saw that.

BIFF You saw it. The mice didn't bring it into the cellar! What is this supposed to do, make a hero out of you? This supposed to make me sorry for you?

WILLY Never heard of it.

BIFF There'll be no pity for you, you hear it? No pity!

WILLY [*to* LINDA] You hear the spite!

BIFF No, you're going to hear the truth—what you are and what I am!

LINDA Stop it!

WILLY Spite!

HAPPY [*coming down toward* BIFF] You cut it now!

BIFF [*to* HAPPY] The man don't know who we are! The man is gonna know! [*To* WILLY] We never told the truth for ten minutes in this house!

HAPPY We always told the truth!

BIFF [*turning on him*] You big blow, are you the assistant buyer? You're one of the two assistants to the assistant, aren't you?

HAPPY Well, I'm practically—

BIFF You're practically full of it! We all are! And I'm through with it. [*To* WILLY] Now hear this, Willy, this is me.

WILLY I know you!

BIFF You know why I had no address for three months? I stole a suit in Kansas City and I was in jail. [*To* LINDA, *who is sobbing*] Stop crying. I'm through with it.

[LINDA *turns away from them, her hands covering her face.*]

WILLY I suppose that's my fault!

BIFF I stole myself out of every good job since high school!

WILLY And whose fault is that?

BIFF And I never got anywhere because you blew me so full of hot air I could never stand taking orders from anybody! That's whose fault it is!

WILLY I hear that!

LINDA Don't, Biff!

BIFF It's goddam time you heard that! I had to be boss big shot in two weeks, and I'm through with it!

WILLY Then hang yourself! For spite, hang yourself!

BIFF No! Nobody's hanging himself, Willy! I ran down eleven flights with a pen in my hand today. And suddenly I stopped, you hear me? And in the middle of that office building, do you hear this? I stopped in the middle of that building and I saw—the sky. I saw the things that I love in this world. The work and the food and time to sit and smoke. And I looked at the pen and said to myself, what the hell am I grabbing this for? Why am I trying to become what I don't want to be? What am I doing in an office, making a contemptuous, begging fool of myself, when all I want is out there, waiting for me the minute I say I know who I am! Why can't I say that, Willy? [*He tries to make* WILLY *face him, but* WILLY *pulls away and moves to the left.*]

WILLY [*with hatred, threateningly*] The door of your life is wide open!

BIFF Pop! I'm a dime a dozen, and so are you!

WILLY [*turning on him now in an uncontrolled outburst*] I am not a dime a dozen! I am Willy Loman, and you are Biff Loman!

[BIFF *starts for* WILLY, *but is blocked by* HAPPY. *In his fury,* BIFF *seems on the verge of attacking his father.*]

BIFF I am not a leader of men, Willy, and neither are you. You were never anything but a hard-working drummer who landed in the ash can like all the rest of them! I'm one dollar an hour, Willy! I tried seven states and couldn't raise it. A buck an hour! Do you gather my meaning? I'm not bringing home any prizes anymore, and you're going to stop waiting for me to bring them home!

WILLY [*directly to* BIFF] You vengeful, spiteful mut!

[BIFF *breaks from* HAPPY. WILLY, *in fright, starts up the stairs.* BIFF *grabs him.*]

BIFF [*at the peak of his fury*] Pop, I'm nothing! I'm nothing, Pop. Can't you understand that? There's no spite in it anymore. I'm just what I am, that's all.

[BIFF'*s fury has spent itself, and he breaks down, sobbing, holding on to* WILLY, *who dumbly fumbles for* BIFF'*s face.*]

WILLY [*astonished*] What're you doing? What're you doing? [*To* LINDA] Why is he crying?

BIFF [*crying, broken*] Will you let me go, for Christ's sake? Will you take that phony dream and burn it before something happens? [*Struggling to contain himself, he pulls away and moves to the stairs.*] I'll go in the morning. Put him—put him to bed. [*Exhausted,* BIFF *moves up the stairs to his room.*]

WILLY [*after a long pause, astonished, elevated*] Isn't that—isn't that remarkable? Biff—he likes me!

LINDA He loves you, Willy!

HAPPY [*deeply moved*] Always did, Pop.

WILLY Oh, Biff! [*Staring wildly*] He cried! Cried to me. [*He is choking with his love, and now cries out his promise*] That boy—that boy is going to be magnificent!

[BEN *appears in the light just outside the kitchen.*]

BEN Yes, outstanding, with twenty thousand behind him.

LINDA [*sensing the racing of his mind, fearfully, carefully*] Now come to bed, Willy. It's all settled now.

WILLY [*finding it difficult not to rush out of the house*] Yes, we'll sleep. Come on. Go to sleep, Hap.

BEN And it does take a great kind of a man to crack the jungle.

[*In accents of dread,* BEN'*s idyllic music starts up.*]

HAPPY [*his arm around* LINDA] I'm getting married, Pop, don't forget it. I'm changing everything. I'm gonna run that department before the year is up. You'll see, Mom. [*He kisses her.*]

BEN The jungle is dark but full of diamonds, Willy.

[WILLY *turns, moves, listening to* BEN.]

LINDA Be good. You're both good boys, just act that way, that's all.

HAPPY Night, Pop. [*He goes upstairs.*]

LINDA [*to* WILLY] Come, dear.

BEN [*with greater force*] One must go in to fetch a diamond out.

WILLY [*to* LINDA, *as he moves slowly along the edge of the kitchen, toward the door*] I just want to get settled down, Linda. Let me sit alone for a little.

LINDA [*almost uttering her fear*] I want you upstairs.

WILLY [*taking her in his arms*] In a few minutes, Linda. I couldn't sleep right now. Go on, you look awful tired. [*He kisses her.*]

BEN Not like an appointment at all. A diamond is rough and hard to the touch.

WILLY Go on now. I'll be right up.

LINDA I think this is the only way, Willy.

WILLY Sure, it's the best thing.

BEN Best thing!

WILLY The only way. Everything is gonna be—go on, kid, get to bed. You look so tired.

LINDA Come right up.

WILLY Two minutes.

[LINDA *goes into the living room, then reappears in her bedroom.* WILLY *moves just outside the kitchen door.*]

WILLY Loves me. [*Wonderingly*] Always loved me. Isn't that a remarkable thing? Ben, he'll worship me for it!

BEN [*with promise*] It's dark there, but full of diamonds.

WILLY Can you imagine that magnificence with twenty thousand dollars in his pocket?

LINDA [*calling from her room*] Willy! Come up!

WILLY [*calling into the kitchen*] Yes! Yes. Coming! It's very smart, you realize that, don't you, sweetheart? Even Ben sees it. I gotta go, baby. 'By! 'By! [*Going over to Ben, almost dancing*] Imagine? When the mail comes he'll be ahead of Bernard again!

BEN A perfect proposition all around.

WILLY Did you see how he cried to me? Oh, if I could kiss him, Ben!

BEN Time, William, time!

WILLY Oh, Ben, I always knew one way or another we were gonna make it, Biff and I!

BEN [*looking at his watch*] The boat. We'll be late. [*He moves slowly off into the darkness.*]

WILLY [*elegiacally, turning to the house*] Now when you kick off, boy, I want a seventy-yard boot, and get right down the field under the ball, and when you hit, hit low and hit hard, because it's important, boy. [*He swings around and faces the audience.*] There's all kinds of important people in the stands, and the first thing you know . . . [*Suddenly realizing he is alone*] Ben! Ben, where do I . . . ? [*He makes a sudden movement of search.*] Ben, how do I . . . ?

LINDA [*calling*] Willy, you coming up?

WILLY [*uttering a gasp of fear, whirling about as if to quiet her*] Sh! [*He turns around as if to find his way; sounds, faces, voices, seem to be swarming in upon him and he flicks at them, crying*] Sh! Sh! [*Suddenly music, faint and high, stops him. It rises in intensity, almost to an unbearable scream. He goes up and down on his toes, and rushes off around the house.*] Shhh!

LINDA Willy?

[*There is no answer.* LINDA *waits.* BIFF *gets up off his bed. He is still in his clothes.* HAPPY *sits up.* BIFF *stands listening.*]

LINDA [*with real fear*] Willy, answer me! Willy!

[*There is the sound of a car starting and moving away at full speed.*]

LINDA No!

BIFF [*rushing down the stairs*] Pop!

[*As the car speeds off, the music crashes down in a frenzy of sound, which becomes the soft pulsation of a single cello string.* BIFF *slowly returns to his bedroom. He and* HAPPY *gravely don their jackets.* LINDA *slowly walks out of her room. The music has developed into a dead march. The leaves of day are appearing over everything.* CHARLEY *and* BERNARD, *somberly dressed, appear and knock on the kitchen door.* BIFF *and* HAPPY *slowly descend the stairs to the kitchen as* CHARLEY *and* BERNARD *enter. All stop a moment when* LINDA, *in clothes of mourning, bearing a little bunch of roses, comes through the draped doorway into the kitchen. She goes to* CHARLEY *and takes his arm. Now all move toward the audience, through the wall-line of the kitchen. At the limit of the apron,* LINDA *lays down the flowers, kneels, and sits back on her heels. All stare down at the grave.*]

Requiem[1]

CHARLEY It's getting dark, Linda.

[LINDA *doesn't react. She stares at the grave.*]

BIFF How about it, Mom? Better get some rest, heh? They'll be closing the gate soon.

[LINDA *makes no move. Pause.*]

HAPPY [*deeply angered*] He had no right to do that. There was no necessity for it. We would've helped him.

CHARLEY [*grunting*] Hmmm.

BIFF Come along, Mom.

LINDA Why didn't anybody come?

CHARLEY It was a very nice funeral.

LINDA But where are all the people he knew? Maybe they blame him.

CHARLEY Naa. It's a rough world, Linda. They wouldn't blame him.

LINDA I can't understand it. At this time especially. First time in thirty-five years we were just about free and clear. He only needed a little salary. He was even finished with the dentist.

CHARLEY No man only needs a little salary.

LINDA I can't understand it.

BIFF There were a lot of nice days. When he'd come home from a trip; or on Sundays, making the stoop; finishing the cellar; putting on the new porch; when he built the extra bathroom; and put up the garage. You know something, Charley, there's more of him in that front stoop than in all the sales he ever made.

CHARLEY Yeah. He was a happy man with a batch of cement.

1. In Roman Catholicism, a special mass for the repose of departed souls; also, a musical setting for such a mass, and by extension any solemn dirge or chant for the dead.

LINDA He was so wonderful with his hands.

BIFF He had the wrong dreams. All, all, wrong.

HAPPY [*almost ready to fight* BIFF] Don't say that!

BIFF He never knew who he was.

CHARLEY [*stopping* HAPPY*'s movement and reply. To* BIFF] Nobody dast blame this man. You don't understand: Willy was a salesman. And for a salesman, there is no rock bottom to the life. He don't put a bolt to a nut, he don't tell you the law or give you medicine. He's a man way out there in the blue, riding on a smile and a shoeshine. And when they start not smiling back—that's an earthquake. And then you get yourself a couple of spots on your hat, and you're finished. Nobody dast blame this man. A salesman is got to dream, boy. It comes with the territory.

BIFF Charley, the man didn't know who he was.

HAPPY [*infuriated*] Don't say that!

BIFF Why don't you come with me, Happy?

HAPPY I'm not licked that easily. I'm staying right in this city, and I'm gonna beat this racket! [*He looks at* BIFF, *his chin set.*] The Loman Brothers!

BIFF I know who I am, kid.

HAPPY All right, boy. I'm gonna show you and everybody else that Willy Loman did not die in vain. He had a good dream. It's the only dream you can have—to come out number-one man. He fought it out here, and this is where I'm gonna win it for him.

BIFF [*with a hopeless glance at* HAPPY, *bends toward his mother*] Let's go, Mom.

LINDA I'll be with you in a minute. Go on, Charley. [*He hesitates.*] I want to, just for a minute. I never had a chance to say good-by.

[CHARLEY *moves away, followed by* HAPPY. BIFF *remains a slight distance up and left of* LINDA. *She sits there, summoning herself. The flute begins, not far away, playing behind her speech.*]

LINDA Forgive me, dear. I can't cry. I don't know what it is, but I can't cry. I don't understand it. Why did you ever do that? Help me, Willy, I can't cry. It seems to me that you're just on another trip. I keep expecting you. Willy, dear, I can't cry. Why did you do it? I search and search and I search, and I can't understand it, Willy. I made the last payment on the house today. Today, dear. And there'll be nobody home. [*A sob rises in her throat.*] We're free and clear. [*Sobbing more fully, released*] We're free. [BIFF *comes slowly toward her.*] We're free . . . We're free . . .

[BIFF *lifts her to her feet and moves out up right with her in his arms.* LINDA *sobs quietly.* BERNARD *and* CHARLEY *come together and follow them, followed by* HAPPY. *Only the music of the flute is left on the darkening stage as over the house the hard towers of the apartment buildings rise into sharp focus, and*]

The curtain falls.

TAWFIQ AL-HAKIM

1898–1987

COMMONLY regarded as the founder of modern Egyptian drama, Tawfiq al-Hakim is a towering literary figure in Egypt and the Arab world. His diverse literary output includes plays, short stories, poems, autobiographies, essays, and novels, but his reputation rests mostly on his dramatic work. Driven by what he called a "creative panic" to explore new artistic terrain and new modes of expression, al-Hakim continuously examined fresh perspectives and challenged the social and artistic status quo. Throughout his long life, al-Hakim was also involved in the intellectual and political ferment of his country, and by the 1980s, he was widely revered as a sage and elder statesman as well as one of the most prominent Arab writers. Produced domestically and internationally, such plays as *SONG OF DEATH* (1950), address the shifting cultural and political landscapes of twentieth-century Egypt and the broader Arab world.

Born to a rural upper-middle-class family, al-Hakim was pushed by his parents to become a lawyer. In 1920, he was sent to live with his uncles in Cairo to finish his undergraduate studies in law, but al-Hakim spent this unsupervised time attending plays and getting to know Cairo's theatrical community. Before long, he started writing musicals and farces—the most popular theatrical forms at that time—for the well-known 'Ukasha Brothers Troupe. Between 1920 and 1925, he wrote four plays: three of them were adaptations of French plays and the fourth, *al-Mar'ah al-Jadida* (*The Modern Woman*, 1923), was an original play inspired by the nascent feminist movement in Egypt. Though al-Hakim had assumed a pseudonym, hoping to avoid his parents' disapproval, they discovered his increasingly active participation in Cairo's theater world. After al-Hakim finished his *Licence en droit* (Bachelor's in Law) in 1925 at Cairo University, his father attempted to break his son's attachment to the theater by sending him to France to obtain a doctorate in law. But the move only encouraged the young playwright, for in Paris al-Hakim had the opportunity to attend the plays of such modern European dramatists as HENRIK IBSEN, Maurice Maeterlinck, GEORGE BERNARD SHAW, Jean Cocteau, and LUIGI PIRANDELLO. He found himself drawn to the intellectual content in these plays and to the craftsmanship of the European stage. Al-Hakim also read widely during this time in philosophy, poetry, and fiction. Among the writers who affected him deeply were LOPE DE VEGA, JOHANN WOLFGANG VON GOETHE, Edgar Allan Poe, Arthur Rimbaud, Friedrich Nietzsche, and Andre Gide. Al-Hakim's time in Paris profoundly expanded his aesthetic and creative consciousness,

The Opera House at Ezbekiah Garden, ca. 1930. This theater, built in the mid-nineteeth century at the height of European influence in Cairo, was one of the major venues for Egypt's cultural and economic elite prior to the socialist revolution of Gamal Abdel Nasser in 1952.

transforming him into a full-fledged writer and intellectual.

Realizing after a few years that his son was not going to earn his doctorate, al-Hakim's father summoned him back to Cairo and encouraged him to become a public prosecutor in the Egyptian provinces. Upon his return to Cairo in 1928, al-Hakim embarked on an important new stage in his playwriting career, as he ceased to collaborate with popular theater troupes. Determined that Arab theater not remain an ephemeral art form, al-Hakim set out to write serious plays that would help establish an Arab dramatic literary heritage. In choosing this path, he was consciously working against the long-held belief in Egypt and the Arab world more generally that theater was a popular form, not high literature, and that plays therefore need not be preserved for future generations or even published at all. Most of Egypt's theater producers were convinced that to achieve commercial success, they must stage popular drama, in colloquial language. At the same time, Egypt's cultural elite scorned any texts not written in classical Arabic, a language in which few were proficient; they viewed colloquial texts as beneath the dignity of the Arabic literary canon. Consequently, though theater was a vital part of popular culture, Egypt had no written dramatic literary tradition to speak of.

In choosing to write plays in a literary mode, al-Hakim thus filled a glaring gap in modern Arabic literature. His plays of the 1930s were inspired by history, Greek and Arab mythology, folklore, and religion and were written in the classical Arabic known as *Fusha:* they belonged to what he called the "theater of ideas" (or "theater of the mind"). Al-Hakim considered these plays—among them, *Ahl al-Kahf* (*People of the Cave,* 1933), *Shahrazad* (1934), *Praxagora* (1939; enlarged, 1954), *Pygmalion* (1942), *Sulayman al-Hakim* (*Solomon the Wise,* 1943), and *Al-Malik Udib* (*King Oedipus,* 1949)—works to be read, not staged; he insisted that they should be categorized as dramatic literature, not theatrical pieces.

The earliest of these plays, *People of the Cave,* was both a turning point in al-Hakim's career and a milestone in Egyptian and Arab drama. Based on a Christian tale retold in the Qur'an, *People of the Cave* tells the story of three Christian converts who seek refuge in a cave in order to escape the wrath of a brutal king who is persecuting converts. The three characters and a dog sleep there for three hundred years. When they rise from their long slumber, they realize that the world around them has changed. Overwhelmed by these changes and aware that they have become representatives of the past, the characters decide to retreat to the cave. Addressed to Egyptians unsure of how to respond to a rapidly changing modern world, al-Hakim's play suggests that if nations do not modernize, they perish. The intellectual content of this play (as well as others that al-Hakim wrote during the early 1930s) and the classical Arabic language in which it was written gained the approval of Egypt's literary and intellectual elite, who praised al-Hakim for winning drama a place in the canon of Arabic literature. In recognition of its importance, *People of the Cave* was the first play staged at Egypt's National Theater when it opened in 1935. Though the play's use of classical Arabic—and its division into four very long acts—guaranteed that *People of the Cave* would not appeal to a broad audience, it remains a touchstone in Egyptian cultural memory.

Al-Hakim continued to compose philosophy-steeped plays through the 1940s, but in the 1950s, he started to write in a more populist vein. This shift in al-Hakim's career was tied in part to political changes in the country. In 1952, a peaceful coup d'état led by Gamal Abdel Nasser transformed Egypt from a 150-year-old monarchy into a socialist republic. Nasser and his allies instituted educational and cultural reforms designed to publicize and promote the socialist principles of the new republic. Many Egyptian authors, including the novelist Naguib Mahfouz (who would win the Nobel Prize in Literature in 1988), supported Nasser's reforms and embraced a "social realist" style that reflected his ideology.

Under the leadership of the Ministry of Culture, those engaged in the performance arts turned away from the adaptations of Western plays, musicals, and farces that had dominated the pre-Nasser period and directed their efforts toward establishing a national literacy dramatic canon. While the National Theater continued to provide a venue for classic Arab plays and world classics in translation, additional theaters were built that featured other kinds of performance: the Puppet Theater for children's drama, the Pocket Theater for experimental drama, the Balloon Theater for ballet and folkloric dance, and the Modern Theater for contemporary texts. A number of new initiatives were also undertaken to support artists, such as artist-in-residence programs, and prizes were granted to honor excellence in the arts. Al-Hakim himself received two important playwriting awards in the 1950s.

During this decade of social and political reform, both Nasser's government and the creative community were mainly concerned with giving artistic expression to the lives of the masses. The young playwrights who emerged in the postrevolutionary period with the state's encouragement and financial support generally advocated commitment to social change. The dramas (and films) that they produced during this period focused on social issues, the family, and the place of the new postcolonial Egyptian in the world, and did so in a realist and naturalistic vein. Playwrights and intellectuals during the 1950s paid equal attention to the remaking of Egyptian theater arts and of Arab theater more generally. For most Egyptian intellectuals, this work of creating a uniquely Arab theater depended on their establishing a connection to the Arab past—a period of intellectual and cultural flowering that, they believed, was cut off by European colonialism. As part of this cultural effort, many playwrights, including al-Hakim, incorporated Arab history and folklore into their plays.

The issue of language played a central role in this nationalist project. Wanting both to reach a wide audience and to help shape the identity of Egyptian and Arab theater, al-Hakim realized that the longstanding dispute over the use of classical versus colloquial language in drama had to be resolved if Arab theater was to continue developing at all. His solution was a new stage language, which he called "the third language." He proposed that writers compose plays in a style that could both entertain and serve literature, accessible to the layperson as well as the intellectual; such a style could accommodate realist topics and express a variety of themes, including tragic ones. The language of these plays was similar to classical Arabic, or *Fusha,* but with some concessions to everyday speech. By writing in this modified version of *Fusha* rather than the local Egyptian dialect, al-Hakim also ensured that his plays could be understood in each of the twenty-two Standard Arabic–speaking countries that constitute the Arab world. Al-Hakim's approach could easily be adapted to Arabic's many local dialects, and by the 1960s, the period many consider the heyday of Arab drama, a number of other playwrights had taken it up.

In his introduction to *Masrah al-Mujtama* (*Theater of Social Themes,* 1950), a collection of short plays from this period that contains some of his most widely read and produced works, al-Hakim emphasizes that every play in the volume—even ones whose plots seem to be far-fetched—authentically reflects Egyptian social realities in the 1940s and 1950s. One central reality is the place of women in traditional Arab society. Three plays in the collection underscore women's power and represent female characters in nonstereotypical ways: *Urid Hadha'l-Rajul* (*I Want This Man*), *al-Na'iba al-Muhtarama* (*The Honorable Lady Member of Parliament*), and *Ughiniyyat al-Mawt* (*Song of Death*), which is included here. In keeping with the dictates of social realism, al-Hakim wished to depict the opportunities for education and work that became increasingly available to women during the 1940s and 1950s. Although feminist and other critics have taken issue with aspects of his representation of women—arguing, for instance, that these characters are given to irrationality and often pursue domestic bliss more avidly than independence—the works in this collection explore the social, familial, and psychological demands with which Arab women contend and the conflicting roles they have traditionally assumed.

No play of al-Hakim's more powerfully captures the pressures of tradition on women—and on Egyptian society as a whole—than *Song of Death*, whose well-crafted structure and poignant, tragic tone have won it praise as one of the finest modern Arabic plays. An unsparing critique of brutal village customs and the tyranny of traditional gender roles, *Song of Death* takes as its subject the long-standing peasant tradition of blood revenge. For centuries, cycles of blood revenge were the undisputed law of the land for country folk in Egypt, and since the beginning of the twentieth century, governments have combated the deeply ingrained belief that the murder of a family member should be punished privately, not by the state's justice

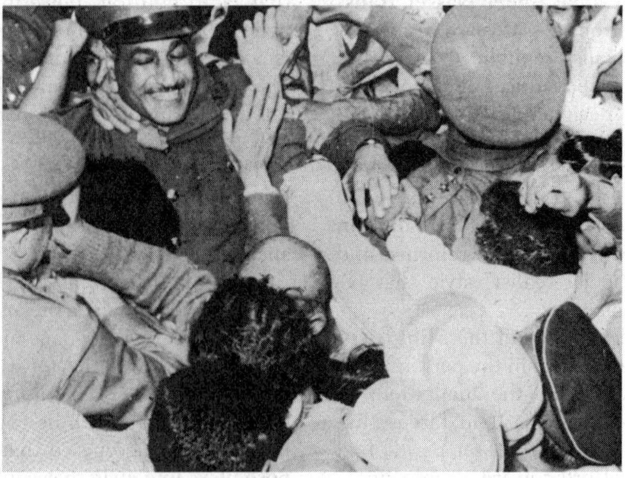

Egyptian president Gamal Abdel Nasser, mobbed by enthusiastic supporters in the early 1960s.

system. As a public prosecutor who had confronted this provincial mind-set directly, al-Hakim strongly believed that private vengeance was a barbaric and regressive custom—a tradition that had to end if society was to move forward. *Song of Death* was his attempt in dramatic form to address his professional and humanistic concerns about this destructive tradition.

Al-Hakim's play takes place in a peasant house in Upper Egypt, the region of the Nile Valley that stretches south of Cairo. Asakir, a widow, has spent seventeen years yearning for retribution for the death of her husband, murdered by a member of a rival family as part of a generations-long blood feud. As the play opens, she is awaiting the arrival of her son, Ilwan, who was sent away as a child and raised as a student at one of Cairo's oldest theology schools (housed in an ancient mosque), with the expectation that he will take the weapon with which his father was killed and exact vengeance. When Ilwan arrives and challenges the cycle of violence, maintaining that the law is more important, his refusal to meet traditional expectations precipitates an equally devastating tragedy, and Asakir must face the consequences of her commitment to retribution and family honor. *Song of Death* embeds its story of vengeance and loss in the images and remembered sounds of rural Egyptian life: a reference to walls painted in mud, the joyful trilling of women, ritual gestures.

Hard and single-minded, the figure of Asakir dominates the play. With "a memory that can never forget and a heart that cannot relent," she has put her implacable fantasy of revenge before maternal and other feelings. The events of the past have shaped her view of the world, but the hardness to which she has given herself also reflects the social role that she, as woman and mother, has been asked to assume. The deliberately masculine name Asakir (which means "soldiers" in Arabic) indicates that although she is a woman, she is expected to act as a man. In peasant societies, such as the one depicted in the play, masculinity has historically signified strength and status; thus, sons have been valued more than daughters. This power imbalance forces women to act in conformity with masculine ways—to teach their sons to be "men" and to inspire their daughters to become more like men (by giving them ruthless-sounding names, for instance). Women in such communities are responsible for upholding the laws of their village and passing them down to their children. As *Song of Death* illustrates, women also play central roles in preserving and defending family honor.

But such hardening comes with a price. What makes Asakir such a richly dramatic figure is the conflict between her consuming desire for vengeance and the emotional bond that connects her, despite her struggles to escape it, to her son, Ilwan. Asakir is portrayed as both nurturing and controlling, but her excessive determination to take revenge for her husband's murder turns her into a tragic figure: her single-minded focus on killing drives all tenderness from her motherly love, leaving her with nothing but hatred on her mind and in her heart. By upholding the code that requires sons to avenge their fathers, she places the imperatives of the past over life in the present. In the play's climactic scene, as her desires pull her in opposite directions, Asakir confronts the grim logic of her vengeance in a growing spectacle of loss.

Song of Death delves deeply into the particularities of Egyptian rural life and exposes universal human flaws, such as excessive hatred, adherence to illogical traditions, and the blindness caused by anger and pride. Its themes are as relevant to our contemporary world as to al-Hakim's Egypt in 1950. Because of its poignant message—its insistence on the need to put an end to violence between nations and to the cycles of grievance that perpetuate this violence—it continues to be staged by Arab directors. The local and universal layers of *Song of Death* suggest why al-Hakim's name remains synonymous with modern Arab theater, and why his concerns, vision, and tireless experimentation are still points of reference for emerging dramatic voices in the Arab world. DINA AHMED AMIN

Song of Death[1]

CHARACTERS[2]

ASAKIR, a widowed peasant woman
MABRUKA, her sister-in-law
SIMEIDA, son of Mabruka
ILWAN, son of Asakir

[*A peasant hut in an Upper Egyptian village.*[3] ASAKIR *and* MABRUKA, *both dressed in black, are sitting near the entrance, with heads bowed in silence. Close by them a calf and a kid are seen eating herbage and dried clover. The whistle of a train is heard.*]

MABRUKA [*raising her head*] There's the train.

ASAKIR [*without moving*] Do you think he has come on it?

MABRUKA Didn't he say he would, in his letter? Sheikh[4] Isnawi, the schoolteacher, read it out for us yesterday.

ASAKIR Are you sure you've told no one at all that he's my son?

MABRUKA Do you think I've gone mad? Your son Ilwan died when he was a mere child of two. He was drowned in the sluice of the waterwheel.[5] The whole village knows that.

ASAKIR But *they* no longer believe it.

MABRUKA Who are "they"? The Tahawis?

ASAKIR Didn't your son Simeida tell you what he heard in the market the other day?

MABRUKA No. What did he hear?

ASAKIR He heard someone say to a group of people, "Either the Azizes have no more men left among them or else they're concealing a man in order to take revenge, a man closer to the victim then his nephew Simeida." And who but a man's own son can be any closer than his nephew?

MABRUKA Oh yes: Simeida told me about that. If it hadn't been for this rumor he would never have been able to hold up his head in the village.

ASAKIR Well, let them know now that the dead man's son is still alive. We've no fear for him now that he's a grown man. I'm not the one who is afraid now. It's them that fear keeps awake of a night. Hurry up, train, and bring him soon. I've waited a long time—seventeen years, I've counted them

---

1. Translated by Mustafa Badawi; revised by Andrew Parkin and Mahmoud Manzalaoui.
2. The characters' names in this play, like most Arabic names, have specific meanings: *Asakir*, "army of soldiers"; *Mabruka*, "blessed"; *Simeida*, "stiff" or "stonelike"; *Ilwan*, "transcendent" or "sublime."
3. That is, a village in the less populous southern region of Egypt, up the Nile River from Cairo.
4. An honorary title given to teachers in provincial religious schools (and to graduates of al-Azhar University). The local schoolteacher reads the letter to Asakir and Mabruka because they are illiterate.
5. An irrigation device.

hour by hour. Seventeen whole years and I've milked them out of Time's udders, drop after drop, with all the hard tugging you'd need if you were milking a cow that's far gone in her age.

MABRUKA [*listening to a far-off sound*] There's the train arrived in the station. He'll find my son Simeida waiting to meet him.

ASAKIR [*as if talking to herself*] That's right.

MABRUKA [*turning to her*] What's the matter with you, Asakir? You're trembling.

ASAKIR [*as if to herself*] Simeida's song will tell me.

MABRUKA Tell you?

ASAKIR That he's come.

MABRUKA Did you tell my son to sing as a sign that Ilwan was here?

ASAKIR Yes, as soon as they set foot across the village bounds.

MABRUKA Patience, Asakir. Be patient. The worst is over now.

ASAKIR It's not fear nor weakness that I'm feeling now.

MABRUKA The fearsome days have now gone. Gone forever, they are. I shan't ever forget the day when you hid your son Ilwan—and he a mere child of two then—hid him in the flour basket and carried him under cover of darkness out of the village. Took him all the way to Cairo, and gave him into the care of that kinsman of yours, the flour merchant who kept shop in the spice dealer's row near the mosque of our blessed Hussein.[6]

ASAKIR Bring him up as a butcher, I said to him. Let him learn to use the knife like a master.

MABRUKA But he never did as you asked him.

ASAKIR He did that! Soon as he was seven years old he placed him in a butcher's shop. But run away, he did, some time later.

MABRUKA And went into the Holy al-Azhar[7] as a student.

ASAKIR That's it. When I visited him last year I saw him in his gown and turban[8] looking most dignified. I said to him, "If only your father could have seen you looking like that, he'd have been mighty proud." But they didn't spare him to enjoy watching his son grow up.

MABRUKA Wouldn't it have been better if he'd stayed on in the butcher's shop?

ASAKIR What makes you say that, Mabruka?

MABRUKA I don't know. It's only a thought that came into my head.

ASKIR I reckon I know your thought.

MABRUKA What is it, then, Asakir?

ASAKIR It grieves you to see my son in gown and turban while yours goes on wearing his woolly skull cap and his smock.[9]

MABRUKA By the memory of the dear departed, I give you my oath, nothing of the kind was in my mind.

ASAKIR Why then don't you like Ilwan to be at the Holy al-Azhar?

MABRUKA I give you my oath, it isn't that I don't like it, it's just that I'm afraid . . .

6. That is, the ancient mosque and shrine of Hussein (also spelled al-Husayn, ca. 629–680), the grandson of the Prophet Muhammad, in the heart of old Cairo.

7. That is, Cairo's al-Azhar University; established in 975, it is one of the oldest universities in the world and a leading center for the study of Islam and the Arabic language.

8. Attire worn by students and graduates of al-Azhar, highly respected as clerics and scholars.

9. That is, wearing attire typical of peasants.

ASAKIR Afraid?

MABRUKA That he might not be such a master at wielding his knife.

ASAKIR Set your mind at rest, Mabruka. When you see Ilwan now, a full-grown man, you'll realize that he has the lean, strong-thewed arm of the Aziz family.

MABRUKA [*listening to the train whistle*] The train's moving out of the station now.

ASAKIR Let it go where it will, so long as it's brought us Ilwan to force the murderer's soul out of his body, and to leave him for the farm dogs in scattered gobbets of flesh.

MABRUKA What if he hasn't come?

ASAKIR Why do you say that, Mabruka?

MABRUKA I don't know. Just a feeling I've got.

ASAKIR What would stop him coming?

MABRUKA What would drive him to leave Cairo and the city life and the Holy al-Azhar and come to this—?

ASAKIR This is where he was born, where blood is calling out to him.

MABRUKA Our village is a long, long way away from Cairo! Can blood make itself heard as far as the cities?

ASAKIR Do you really think he hasn't come?

MABRUKA I know no more about it than you do.

ASAKIR And what about the letter that the schoolmaster read out to us?

MABRUKA Don't you recall his words: "I hope to come if my circumstances allow it." Who knows whether or not his circumstances have allowed it?

ASAKIR Don't dampen my spirits, Mabruka. Don't dash my hope. I've just heard the train whistle turning into trills[1] of joy in my heart, announcing that the end of this long mourning is near. Ilwan not come? What would become of me if that were true? And how much longer would I have to wait then?

MABRUKA The station isn't so far from here, nor the main road. If he'd arrived, Simeida would be singing now.

ASAKIR Perhaps they're taking their time, chatting. After all, they haven't seen each other for more than three years . . . since your son was in Cairo last during the Fair of the Blessed Hussein.[2]

MABRUKA If he'd come my son's heart would have brimmed over with joy and he'd have started his singing even before he'd reached the main road.

ASAKIR Perhaps he's forgotten to sing.

MABRUKA It's impossible: he can't forget.

ASAKIR [*listening*] I can hear no one singing.

MABRUKA [*listening*] Nor I neither.

ASAKIR [*continuing to listen*] There's no one singing, not even a shepherd lad. There's not a single creature singing, not even the owl over in the ruins. You're right, Mabruka. He hasn't come.

MABRUKA [*as if to herself*] My heart tells me things.

ASAKIR No, not yours—mine. Mine, that's as secret as the grave, as hard as rock, is now beginning to tell me things.

MABRUKA What things?

1. High-pitched sounds traditionally made by women to express joy on such happy occasions as weddings, pregnancy announcements, and the births of children.
2. In the Islamic world, fairs are popular festivals in honor of venerated religious figures.

ASAKIR Things that will happen.

MABRUKA Do tell me.

ASAKIR [*listening intently*] Hush! Listen, listen. Can you not hear, Mabruka? Can you not hear?

MABRUKA Simeida singing.

ASAKIR The heavens be thanked for that!

[*They listen for a while to* SIMEIDA*'s song, which grows increasingly clear.*]

SIMEIDA [*sings*]

O my dear one,
Your bitter voice accuses:
Repentance and excuses
Were all I ever gave!
You reproached me then the more,
And out of grief
My clothes
To shreds I tore.
When they told me of your father,
It was my silent shame
Which set unmanly cheeks aflame,
Where eyes ran dry
And made a desert of my face.

ASAKIR He's come, Ilwan is here! And now it's off with the shirt of my shame and on with my garment of honor.

MABRUKA And now we can hold the true rites[3] over the body of the dear one—and may he rest in peace.

ASAKIR And sacrifice to his spirit the kid and the calf.

MABRUKA O joy! O happiness! [*Makes as though to give out a loud trill.*]

ASAKIR [*restrains her*] Not now. Otherwise we'll be known to the world too early.

MABRUKA Your hours are numbered, Suweilam Tahawi![4]

[*A knock on the door.* ASAKIR *rushes to open it:* SIMEIDA *appears carrying a bag.*]

SIMEIDA I have brought you Sheikh Ilwan. [*Puts the bag on the floor and is soon followed in by* ILWAN.]

ASAKIR [*with open arms*] Ilwan, my son.

ILWAN [*kisses her head*] Mother.

ASAKIR [*to her son*] Say your greetings to your Aunt Mabruka.

ILWAN [*turns to* MABRUKA] Are you well, Aunt Mabruka?

MABRUKA You can see for yourself, Ilwan. You are our only hope now.

SIMEIDA Let us go home now, Mother.

MABRUKA Come. It's close now, Asakir—the hour of relief.

[MABRUKA *and* SIMEIDA *go out.*]

ASAKIR You must be hungry, Ilwan. I've a bowl of sour milk.

ILWAN Thank you, Mother. No, I'm not hungry. I had some hard-boiled eggs and some barley cake on the train.

3. By village custom, a person killed in a blood feud is not officially mourned until his family has avenged his death.

4. Either the man or the son of the man who killed Asakir's husband.

ASAKIR You'll be thirsty then?

ILWAN No, not thirsty either.

ASAKIR Of course you haven't come here for food or drink. You've come to eat of his flesh and drink of his blood.

ILWAN [*as if in a trance*] I have come here to do something truly great, Mother.

ASAKIR I know, I know, my son. Wait till I bring you something: something you've never set your eyes on before. [*Rushes to an inner room where she disappears for a while.*]

ILWAN [*casting a look around the room*] My eyes can still see animals and their droppings in your houses. The dirty water jar, firewood, and dried stalks of maize forming a shaky roof.

ASAKIR [*emerges from the inner room holding a saddlebag which she lays before her son*] Here. For seventeen years I have kept these things for you.

ILWAN [*looks at the saddlebag without moving*] What is this?

ASAKIR The saddlebag that your father's body was sent to me in, carried on his donkey. In this pouch I found his severed head, and in the other one the rest of his body, hacked to pieces. With his own knife they stabbed him to death—the knife he was carrying, then they put knife and body in the saddlebag. See, here is the knife. I left the blood on it until it's turned to rust as you can see. As for the donkey that brought me the body of your murdered father, tracing its steps back to this house by force of habit, with its head bowed down, as if it was grieving over its master—I couldn't keep it alive for you. It couldn't endure for all these years: it's died.

ILWAN Who did this?

ASAKIR Suweilam Tahawi.

ILWAN How do you know?

ASAKIR The whole village knows.

ILWAN I know you've told me that. You've told that name to me over and over again, whenever you came to visit me in Cairo. I was too young to think then or to argue. But now my reason needs to be satisfied. What's the evidence? Did the police ever look into the crime?

ASAKIR Look into the crime?

ILWAN Yes. What did you say to the Public Prosecutor?

ASAKIR Public Prosecutor? The shame of it! We say anything to the Public Prosecutor? We the Azizes do that? Did even the Tahawis ever do that?

ILWAN Didn't the Public Prosecutor ask you any questions?

ASAKIR Of course. But we said we knew nothing about the business, that we'd seen no corpse. Meantime we had buried your father in secret under cover of darkness.

ILWAN [*as if addressing himself*] So that we may exact requital with our own hands.

ASAKIR With the selfsame knife that stabbed your father.

ILWAN And the murderer?

ASAKIR Alive and hearty. There's not a saint or a holy man in the neighborhood but whose shrine I visited. I held on to the railings of their sanctuary, uncovered my head and heaped dust from their ground over my hair,[5] and

5. A traditional gesture of abasement and supplication.

I prayed to them to beseech our God for me that He might prolong the slayer's days until you, my son, should take his life—with your own hands.

ILWAN Are you sure, Mother, that he was the murderer?

ASAKIR We've no enemies beside the Tahawis.

ILWAN But how do you know it was Suweilam himself who did it?

ASAKIR Because he believed it was your father who'd murdered his father.

ILWAN And is that true? Did my father kill his father?

ASAKIR God alone knows.

ILWAN But what started this family feud in the first place?

ASAKIR I don't know. Nobody knows. It's something far gone in the past. All that we know is that there's always been blood spilt between us.

ILWAN The cause may well be that one of our calves happened to drink from a water-channel in a field that belonged to their ancestors!

ASAKIR God alone knows. As for us mortals, all that we know is that between the Azizes and Tahawis rivers of blood have flowed.

ILWAN Rivers that water neither crop nor fruit.

ASAKIR Rivers that stopped flowing only with the death of your father. And that because of your tender age. Years then went past dry as the thirsty season, and people whispered lies and false rumors, while I was writhing in the flames of my hidden anger, waiting for this hour. And now the hour has come, so get up, son, and put out my fire and slake my thirst for the blood of Suweilam Tahawi.

ILWAN Has this Suweilam Tahawi got a son?

ASAKIR Yes. Fourteen years old.

ILWAN So I have no more than another four or five years to live.

ASAKIR What is it you are saying?

ILWAN . . . Only until he grows strong enough to do to me what I am supposed to do to his father.

ASAKIR Do you fear for your life, Ilwan?

ILWAN And what about you, Mother? Do you fear for my life?

ASAKIR The Lord be my witness, how I fear for every hair on your head.

ILWAN You really care about my life, Mother?

ASAKIR Has my life any worth without yours? Or for that matter, the lives of all the Azizes? It's your life alone has made it possible for every one of us to live through the past seventeen years.

ILWAN [*bows his head*] I see.

ASAKIR How often we suffered shame and humiliation. But as soon as your image crossed our minds our energy would revive, our resolution would strengthen and we were united in the hope that we placed upon you.

ILWAN [*his head still bowed and as if talking to himself*] You certainly need my life.

ASAKIR Even your father's funeral waits for you, Ilwan. These sacrifices here are ready for the slaughter. My lamentation which I've been choking down in my throat all these years is waiting for you to set it free. My frock, which I've kept myself from tearing open all that time, is waiting for you,[6] too. Everything in our existence is dead. Stagnant. Looking to you to breathe life into it.

6. In Egyptian villages, the tearing of one's outer garments is a ritualized expression of extreme grief.

ILWAN Is this how life is breathed into you?

ASAKIR Yes, Ilwan. Bring the appointed hour closer. Be quick, for we've been waiting for it for so long.

ILWAN [*in wonder*] The appointed hour?

ASAKIR I've forgotten nothing. Even the stone to whet the rusty knife I've brought for you and hidden in this room.

ILWAN But how am I to know this Suweilam? I've never set eyes on him in the whole of my life.

ASAKIR Simeida will show you where to find him. He'll point him out to you.

ILWAN [*looks at his clothes*] Am I to commit this deed while I'm dressed in this way?

ASAKIR Take off those clothes. I've a cloak that belonged to your father. I've kept it for you. [*She turns to go into the inner room.*]

ILWAN [*stops her*] Just a minute, Mother. Why the hurry?

ASAKIR Every breath Suweilam draws while you are here is a gift which you are granting to him.

ILWAN And what harm is there in that?

ASAKIR It's taken from our breaths; it's drawn out of our well-being. Against our wishes we were forced to extend his life by as much as nearly brought us to the grave. Look at your mother, Ilwan. I was a young woman when your father died. But look what all those years have done to me. It is as if they were forty years, not seventeen. The sap of my youth has dried up and my bones have grown weak. All I have left is a memory that can never forget and a heart that cannot relent.

ILWAN [*as if to himself*] What a price it costs to avenge one's blood.

ASAKIR [*uncomprehending*] What did you say, Ilwan?

ILWAN I said that God the Mighty Avenger is merciful to us: He offers to relive us of this burden without any cost to us.

ASAKIR [*in a suspicious tone*] What do you mean?

ILWAN Nothing, Mother, nothing.

ASAKIR [*decisively*] Take off those clothes. I'll bring you the cloak and sharpen the knife for you myself.

ILWAN Isn't there a mosque nearby?

ASAKIR We've only a little chapel next to Sheikh Isnawi's schoolhouse.

ILWAN [*moving*] I'll go there and say my evening prayers.

ASAKIR At this hour?

ILWAN I think the sun is about to set.[7]

ASAKIR Do you want to be seen in the mosque by everyone in the village?

ILWAN That would be the best opportunity for my purpose.

ASAKIR [*stares him in the face*] Have you gone mad, Ilwan?

ILWAN It's most important for me to meet the villagers. Haven't I just told you that I have come to do something truly great?

ASAKIR [*as if mocking him*] I shouldn't imagine you'll want to reveal to the village the reason for your coming here?

ILWAN It's essential to let them all hear what I have to tell.

7. Every healthy adult Muslim is required to pray five times daily—at dawn, at midday, in late afternoon, at sunset, and at night before retiring—and it is better to pray in a mosque than alone.

ASAKIR Ilwan, my son! What is it that I hear you say? Are you serious? Are you in your right mind? What is it that you want to tell them?

ILWAN [*as if in a dream*] I'll tell them what I have come here to say. I have often thought about my village and its people, in spite of the long time I've been away from it. There, at al-Azhar, when the classes were over, we—the students, that is—we'd gather together and read the newspapers. And we'd think of the places we'd come from. We were very homesick. And we often worried about when our people in the countryside would be able to live like human beings, in clean houses where they wouldn't share their meals with animals. When the roofs of their houses would be something better than dry stalks of cotton and maize, and the walls painted with something better than mud and the droppings of their beasts. When the water pot would disappear and there would be clean piped water in the house. When electric lights would replace the oil lamp. Was that too much to ask for our people? Don't they have the same rights as others?

ASAKIR [*as if uncomprehending*] What is all this you're saying, Ilwan?

ILWAN This is what the people of the village ought to know. And those of us who were educated in Cairo—it's our duty to make them see and realize their human rights. It shouldn't be difficult for them to achieve this aim: if only they would unite, join hands, and co-operate. They ought to set up a council. Elect a council, that's it, from amongst themselves. And they could tax those who had money enough to pay. They'd form a team of able-bodied men to spend those long hours when there's nothing doing in making dykes and bridges and other constructive things. Not wasting time in squabbles and feuds. Why, if they worked together like that, if they would only make the effort, we'd make this a model village. And it would soon be an example for all the other villages in the country to follow.

ASAKIR You're talking the language of books. You can keep that for later. For when you have your evening talk with Sheikh Muhammad Isnawi. He can understand it—I can't. As for the present, there's something more important that we've to do, Ilwan.

ILWAN [*shocked*] What is it that's more important?

ASAKIR No. Don't go to the mosque to pray tonight. Else our plan might fail. Pray here tonight, if you wish to. Go and take off those clothes. I'll fetch water from the water pot for you to prepare for your prayers.[8] Put on the cloak and help me sharpen the knife.

ILWAN [*his head bowed, whispers*] Your mercy, O God, Your favor and forgiveness!

ASAKIR What are you saying, Ilwan?

ILWAN [*raises his head*] I am saying that I have come here only to make you see and realize what life is, to bring you life.

ASAKIR And that's exactly what we've been waiting for patiently for all these long nights. For seventeen years all the Azizes have been dead, waiting for your return to bring life back to them.

ILWAN [*whispers with his head bowed down*] God! What am I to do with these people?

ASAKIR What is wrong with you, Ilwan? You keep bowing your head. Come on. Get up. Don't waste any more time.

8. In Islam, ritual washing before prayer is obligatory.

ILWAN [*raises his head and takes courage*] Mother, I will not kill.

ASAKIR [*tries to conceal her distress*] What do I hear?

ILWAN I will not kill.

ASAKIR [*in a rough voice*] The blood of your father!

ILWAN It's you yourselves who left it spilt and wasted by hiding the crime from the government. It's up to the authorities to punish.

ASAKIR [*beside herself*] The blood of your father!

ILWAN My hand wasn't made to destroy a human being.

ASAKIR [*as if in a trance*] The blood of your father!

ILWAN [*alarmed at her condition*] Mother, Mother: what is the matter with you?

ASAKIR [*as if she can see nobody in front of her*] The blood of your father! Seventeen years. The blood of your father. Seventeen years . . . !

ILWAN Mother, calm yourself. Of course it's a shock to you. But you must realize that I could never be an assassin and use my knife on a man.

ASAKIR [*whispers as if out of her mind*] Seventeen years . . . Vengeance for your father's murder . . . Seventeen years . . .

ILWAN [*as if to himself*] Mother, I know that you've stood it patiently for so long. If only this patience and endurance of yours were given up to a useful cause you would perform miracles! But you must understand that I—

ASAKIR [*with a quaver in her throat*] The blood of your father!

ILWAN [*rushes towards her, alarmed*] Mother! Mother! Mother!

ASAKIR [*recovers awareness of her surroundings*] Who are you?

ILWAN Your son, Ilwan. Your son.

ASAKIR [*screams*] Son? *My* son? No, no! Never, never, never!

ILWAN [*astonished*] Mother!

ASAKIR I'm not your mother. I don't know you. No son has ever been born out of my womb. No son have I ever given birth to.

ILWAN [*pleading*] Please, Mother! Try to understand that I—

ASAKIR Out of my house . . . God's curse be upon you to the Day of Judgment. Out of my house.

ILWAN Mother!

ASAKIR [*screams*] Out of my house . . . or else I'll ask the help of our men to throw you out. We still have men. There are still men among the Azizes. But you—you're not one of them. Out of my house with you.

ILWAN [*picks up his bag*] I'll go to the station and go back to where I came from. And I'll pray to God that your disturbed soul may find peace, and that I may see you in Cairo soon to explain my way of looking at things, in quiet, far away from here. Goodbye, Mother.

[*He leaves. His mother remains motionless in her place. After a while,* SIMEIDA *enters, first putting his head round the door, then gently pushing it open.*]

SIMEIDA Was it you screaming, Aunt Asakir?

ASAKIR [*with determination: she is fully recovered now*] Come here, Simeida.

SIMEIDA [*looks round*] Where's Ilwan? Where's your son?

ASAKIR I have no son. I never bore a son.

SIMEIDA What are you saying, Aunt Asakir?

ASAKIR If I had a son he'd now be avenging his father's murder.

SIMEIDA Where has he gone?

ASAKIR To the station. On his way back to Cairo.

SIMEIDA My mother was right. As soon as she saw him just now, she said, as we were leaving, "That turbaned preacher will never kill Suweilam Tahawi."

ASAKIR I wish my womb had been torn to shreds before it brought such a son into the world!

SIMEIDA Don't upset yourself, Aunt. There are still men among the Azizes.

ASAKIR Our hope is now in you, Simeida.

SIMEIDA A nephew can stand in for a son.

ASAKIR But in this case the son's alive. It's his duty before anybody else, to avenge the shedding of his father's blood. He's alive. Alive. He's about amongst the living.

SIMEIDA Just try to tell yourself that he's dead.

ASAKIR I wish he had really died, drowned in the sluice of the waterwheel when he was a child. We would then never have had to wait all those years, writhing and roasting on the live coals of our pent-up anger, waiting to no purpose. I wish he had truly died. We would have been able to live honorably then, and not be wearing our garment of shame. But he is alive, and it has been broadcast in the market places and in the whole neighborhood that he is alive. Oh, the shame. The ignominy. The disgrace!

SIMEIDA Aunt, don't be so upset.

ASAKIR It's impossible not to be upset by a disgrace like this. Carrying such a shame, life will be impossible. How can I go on living in this village now that people know that I have a son like this. How many a mouth'll spit whenever his name is mentioned. From all directions the cry will be heard: "Cursed be the womb that brought him forth!" Yes, this womb [*striking her belly hard and wildly*]. A curse on this womb. All the women of the village will mock it: even the ugly, the dim-witted, the barren. This womb . . . this womb . . . this womb.

SIMEIDA [*tries to stop her*] Aunt Asakir, don't punish yourself so!

ASAKIR Fetch the knife, Simeida, fetch the knife, and rip it open.

SIMEIDA Have you gone mad?

ASAKIR [*screams*] Simeida: are you a man?

SIMEIDA [*looks at her intently*] What is it you want?

ASAKIR Stop your cousin's disgrace.

SIMEIDA Ilwan's?

ASAKIR And his mother's, your Aunt Asakir's. Prevent her shame.

SIMEIDA How?

ASAKIR [*takes the knife from the saddle bag*] Kill him with this knife.

SIMEIDA Kill who?

ASAKIR Ilwan. Dig this knife into his heart.

SIMEIDA I kill Ilwan? Your son?

ASAKIR Yes. Kill him. Send him to join the dead.

SIMEIDA Pull yourself together, Aunt.

ASAKIR Do this, Simeida . . . for my sake and for his!

SIMEIDA For his sake!

ASAKIR Yes. Better for him and better for me that it should be said he was killed, than for folk to say that he fled from his duty of avenging his father's murder.

SIMEIDA My own cousin!

ASAKIR If you're a man, Simeida, you must never let him bring shame upon the Azizes. Never again will you be able to carry yourself like a man. Men will whisper and laugh behind their hands at you and point at you in the marketplace, and say: "There goes no more than a woman and one who's given shelter to another mere woman, at that."

SIMEIDA [*to himself*] A woman!

ASAKIR If the Tahawis had such a son they'd never have let him live for an hour.

SIMEIDA [*to himself*] A woman—giving shelter to another woman!

ASAKIR Yes, that's so; that'll be you if you allow him to behave as he means to.

SIMEIDA [*stretches out his hand resolutely*] Give me the knife.

ASAKIR [*hands him the knife*] Here it is. But wait till I wash the dried blood and the rust off its blade.

SIMEIDA [*impatiently*] Give it to me, before he slips away by the evening train.

ASAKIR [*gives him the knife eagerly and forcefully*] Take it. Let his blood wash away the blood of his father that's dried upon the blade.

SIMEIDA [*goes off with the knife*] If I manage to kill him, you'll at hear my voice raised in song at the outskirts of the village, Aunt.

[*Exit quickly.* ASAKIR *remains alone, fixed to the spot like a statue, gazing motionless and absently. After a while,* MABRUKA *appears, carrying a water pitcher on her head.*]

MABRUKA [*puts down the pitcher*] I've brought some dried fish for Sheikh Ilwan.

ASAKIR [*turns to her slowly*] May your life be longer than his,[9] Mabruka.

MABRUKA Who are you talking about?

ASAKIR Ilwan.

MABRUKA Your son?

ASAKIR He's no longer mine; he belongs to the dust.

MABRUKA What are you saying, Asakir? I left him with you only a moment ago. Where is he?

ASAKIR Gone to the station on his way back to where he came from. Giving his back to the duty of avenging his father's murder.

MABRUKA [*her head bowed down*] Just as my heart has been telling me.

ASAKIR Your prophecy has come true, Mabruka.

MABRUKA If only he had never come.

ASAKIR Seventeen years we've been waiting.

MABRUKA Every year you used to say, "He's growing." You measured him by the handspan as if he were a shoot of maize. But then, when he grew tall and his cob was ripe, you stripped him, only to find that there was no grain on the cob.

ASAKIR It wouldn't have been such a disaster if he were no more than a bare cob. We never expected any material gain through him. We expected him to give us back our dignity—that was all. How proud I was of him, Mabruka, how often I boasted about him to you. I thought I'd brought forth the son who'd cleanse the stain off the honor of the family. And how

9. According to funeral etiquette throughout the Arab world, the blessing "May you live long after the departed one" is directed to the deceased family; the customary response is "May your life be longer than his."

has he turned out now? The very son I've given birth to, the son I took great care to hide like a treasure in a crock of clay—he's no more than a stain on our tree, like a blight overtaking a cotton plant. God's mercy be on your soul, my husband: they spilt your blood and it has not been avenged. I've given you a son who brings comfort to your enemies and makes them gloat.

MABRUKA Oh shame, shame on the Azizes!

ASAKIR If he stays alive. But before long he'll be buried in the earth.

MABRUKA [*turns round suddenly*] Where's Simeida?

[*The whistling of a train is heard.*]

ASAKIR [*listening intently*] Hush! There's the evening train entering the station.

MABRUKA Asakir, where's Simeida?

ASAKIR [*still listening intently*] Be quiet. Now, at this instant, at this very instant.

MABRUKA [*astonished*] What happens at this instant?

ASAKIR [*as if to herself*] Do you think the train has carried him off? Or has he been carried off by—

MABRUKA If he's gone to the station, as you say, he must have got on the train. All these curses you are heaping on his head will do no good.

ASAKIR Do you really think he has got on the train?

MABRUKA What could have stopped him?

ASAKIR [*slipping out the answer*] Simeida!

MABRUKA Simeida? Did he go after him to stop him leaving?

ASAKIR Yes.

MABRUKA When did he go?

ASAKIR A short while before you came.

MABRUKA I shouldn't think he could have overtaken him.

ASAKIR [*sighs in relief*] Do you really think so?

MABRUKA Unless he ran very fast.

[*The train whistle is heard again.*]

ASAKIR [*listens intently*] There, the train is leaving the station.

MABRUKA [*stares at her*] What's wrong with you, Asakir? Why have you gone so pale?

ASAKIR What does your heart tell you, Mabruka?

MABRUKA It tells me that he has gone.

ASAKIR Gone. Gone—where?

MABRUKA Where he came from.

ASAKIR What do you mean?

MABRUKA [*watches her*] Why is your breast heaving like that?

ASAKIR [*in a whisper, her eyes wandering*] Gone where he came from!

MABRUKA Do you still hope for some good from him?

ASAKIR No.

MABRUKA You must think of him as if he'd never been.

ASAKIR [*as if to herself*] Yes. His death is less shameful than his life.

MABRUKA And thank God that he's far away.

ASAKIR [*to herself*] Is he on the train now?

MABRUKA Who knows? Perhaps Simeida was able to catch him up and persuade him not to go: perhaps he'll bring him back now.

ASAKIR [*as if dreaming*] Bring him back now?

MABRUKA Why not? If Simeida ran really fast he wouldn't have missed the train.

ASAKIR [*whispers*] . . . Was able to catch him up . . .

MABRUKA And it may not be long before we see them coming back again together.

ASAKIR [*to herself*] No. This time Simeida will be coming alone.

MABRUKA [*watches her anxiously*] Your face, Asakir: it fills me with terror.

ASAKIR [*listens intently*] Hush! Listen! Listen! Can't you hear anything?

MABRUKA No. What do you want me to hear?

ASAKIR Singing.

MABRUKA No, I cannot hear any singing.

ASAKIR [*with relief*] Nor can I.

MABRUKA Did Simeida tell you he was going to sing?

ASAKIR [*to herself, anxiously*] Perhaps he hasn't reached the edge of the village yet.

MABRUKA I should imagine he has, by now.

ASAKIR [*breathing more freely*] And he is not singing!

MABRUKA Now the blood has come back to your cheeks.

ASAKIR [*whispers*] He hasn't caught him up.

MABRUKA You'd rather he didn't come back, Asakir, wouldn't you? You'd rather the train carried him away from this village. So would I. I'd much rather he returned to his Cairo, to his preachers and the other students. He doesn't belong to us, nor we to him. He's done well to leave us so soon, before the people of the village could meet him and get to know what we know about him. [ASAKIR *listens to a distant sound.*] You're not listening to me, Asakir. Don't you think I'm right?

ASAKIR [*in a rough, alarmed voice*] No, no, I can't hear anything!

MABRUKA [*listens*] It is Simeida singing. [*Turns, alarmed, to* ASAKIR, *whose eyes have glazed over.*] Asakir! Asakir! What's wrong? You scare me!

SIMEIDA [*outside, sings*]

O my dear one,
Your bitter voice accuses:
Repentance and excuses
Were all I ever gave!
You reproached me then the more,
And out of grief
My clothes
To shreds I tore.
When they told me of your father,
It was my silent shame
Which set unmanly cheeks aflame,
Where eyes ran dry
And made a desert of my face.

ASAKIR [*pulls herself together, to stop herself from collapsing, but lets slip a faint choking cry like a death rattle*] My son!

Curtain.

SAMUEL BECKETT

1906–1989

THE career of Samuel Beckett, one of the modern period's most influential dramatists, bridges the most important artistic currents of the early and late twentieth century. A member of the novelist James Joyce's literary circle in Paris during the late 1920s and early 1930s, Beckett was one of the last of the high modernists, and his drama and fiction mark the twilight of a movement that produced such works as Joyce's *Ulysses* and T. S. Eliot's *The Waste Land* (both published in 1922). A writer who lived in France most of his life (and who often composed in French), he also continued a tradition of modern Irish playwriting that flourished in the plays of William Butler Yeats and JOHN MILLINGTON SYNGE. Even as they are rooted in the past, however, Beckett's works opened paths for later twentieth-century writers. His trailblazing is particularly evident in the theater, whose boundaries Beckett's plays extended in radically individual ways. *WAITING FOR GODOT*, which premiered in Paris in 1953 and became a symbol of the crisis of meaning in post–World War II Europe, stands as the landmark play of contemporary drama. With its drama of non-action announcing the exhaustion of traditional dramatic structures, *Waiting for Godot*—like Beckett's other plays—inaugurated new theatrical possibilities for dramatists as diverse as HAROLD PINTER, SAM SHEPARD, ATHOL FUGARD, and CARYL CHURCHILL.

Samuel Barclay Beckett was born in 1906 to an affluent Protestant family who lived in the Dublin suburb of Foxrock. His date of birth is listed on his birth certificate as May 13, though he was actually born on April 13 (Beckett relished the fact that this date coincided not only with Friday the thirteenth but also with Good Friday). Beckett was educated in Portora Royal School in County Fermanagh, the alma mater of his fellow Irish writer OSCAR WILDE, and Trinity College, Dublin, where he excelled as a student while studying Dante as well as English and French literature. Upon graduation, Beckett taught French in Belfast for two terms; he then was chosen to represent Trinity as *lecteur* in English at the Ecole Normale Supérieure in Paris, and he began this two-year position in 1928. It was in Paris that Beckett met Joyce, who was at work on his final novel, *Finnegans Wake* (1939), and who became a powerful influence on the younger Irishman. Beckett's own career as a writer was launched with an essay on Joyce's work (published in 1929 as the lead essay in a collection of essays on *Finnegans Wake,* then known as *Work in Progress*) and a poetic parody of the seventeenth-century French philosopher Descartes titled *Whoroscope,* which was published in 1930. In

1930, Beckett also wrote a study of Marcel Proust, the French author whose novel *Remembrance of Things Past* (1913–27) explores questions of time, memory, and human consciousness that would prove central to Beckett's later writing.

After completing his term as *lecteur,* Beckett spent seven years living in Dublin, Paris, and London before returning to France for good in 1937. In addition to *Proust,* which appeared in 1931, these years saw the publication of a collection of short stories, *More Kicks Than Pricks* (1934), and the novel *Murphy* (1938). Twenty years after the end of World War I, war was on the horizon again; and when Germany invaded France in 1940 Beckett joined the French Resistance, typing and translating information concerning German troop movements. As a result of his activities he was forced to flee Paris in 1942; he spent the rest of the war in hiding in Roussillon, in the Vichy-controlled south of France, where he wrote the novel *Watt* (published in 1953).

The period immediately after World War II was, for Beckett, a time of enormous creativity. In fiction, Beckett wrote a trilogy that helped revolutionize the novel form: *Molloy* (1951), *Malone Dies* (1951), and *The Unnamable* (1953). Composed originally in French, then translated (primarily by Beckett) into English, these novels establish deeply self-referential narrative worlds; they explore the limits of fiction, as consciousness engages in an increasingly urgent struggle with the language in which it seeks to articulate itself. It was in part to escape the constrictions of language in these novels that Beckett turned to the stage. In 1948–49, between completing the second and third novels in his trilogy, Beckett wrote *En attendant Godot*—soon to be translated by the author himself as *Waiting for Godot*—"as a relaxation, to get away from the awful prose I was writing at the time." It was not his first play. *Eleuthéria,* a drawing room play that was written in January 1947 but never pub-

The cast and set of the original 1953 production of *Waiting for Godot* at the Théâtre de Babylone. From left to right, Jean Martin as Lucky, Lucien Raimbourg as Vladimir, Pierre Latour as Estragon, and Roger Blin (the director of the production) as Pozzo.

lished or produced during Beckett's lifetime, gave little indication of what he would achieve less than two years later. When *Godot* opened at the 230-seat Théâtre de Babylone in Paris on January 5, 1953, audiences were confronted by a radically new conception of drama. Over the course of two acts that mix vaudeville routines with metaphysical speculation, two tramps wait on a country road for a figure—referred to as Godot—who never arrives. *Waiting for Godot,* which ran for more than 100 performances, became an immediate cause célèbre, and critics struggled to come to terms with its reduced but undeniably powerful dramatic vision. Beckett's "tragicomedy" was soon produced in Berlin (1953), London (1955), and Miami (the United States premiere, 1956); in the decades since, it has received theatrical productions all over the world.

In the plays that followed *Godot,* Beckett continued his theatrical innovations as he explored the human predicament. The action of *Endgame* (1957), one of Beckett's most bleakly comic plays, is restricted to a room set against a postapocalyptic landscape; its characters, positioned like pieces in the terminal stage of a chess match, play out their diminished existence within a world that is winding down. *Krapp's Last Tape* (1958) explores the existence of the individual in time as its lone protagonist plays the recorded voices of his earlier selves. In *Happy Days* (1961), a woman buried in a mound up to her waist—then neck—plays with the objects and words that are all that is left of her world. *Play* (1963) offers one of Beckett's most arresting stage images: three characters, entombed up to their necks in urns, recount the details of a love triangle in alternating confessional fragments. In the late 1950s and early 1960s, he also wrote several plays for radio—including *All That Fall,* which was broadcast by the British Broadcasting Company in 1957—that allowed him to experiment with the staging of disembodied voices.

Following the principle that less is more, Beckett's drama from *Godot* to *Play* is increasingly minimalistic, with its characters progressively immobilized and its dialogue transformed into interiorized monologues. Through that process, this drama laid the foundation for his remarkable plays of the 1970s and 1980s, where character and setting are more radically reduced and even the human body is subject to fragmentation. The protagonist of *Not I* (1972) is a mouth: illuminated at a height of 8 feet above the stage floor, it narrates the disconnected pieces of a life that it refuses to acknowledge as its own. A companion play, *That Time* (1976), features a suspended head listening to the voices of intersecting memories. Inhabiting an increasingly spectral space, the figures who people these and other late Beckett plays—*Footfalls* (1976), *Rockaby* (1981), *Ohio Impromptu* (1981), and *What Where* (1983), to name some of the most prominent—encounter the voices of their own ghosted lives within a field of emptiness and silence. This deepening minimalism also characterizes Beckett's late plays for television, a medium whose dramatic possibilities first interested him in the 1960s. His television plays of the 1970s and 1980s—including *Ghost Trio* (1977), *. . . but the clouds . . .* (1977), and *Nacht und Träume* (1983)—exploit the medium's technical possibilities in order to achieve unearthly, and deeply lyrical, visual landscapes. By the 1970s, Beckett's dramatic writing—and his continuing work in fiction—had garnered an international reputation; he received the Nobel Prize in Literature in 1969, and he was revered as one of the greatest living writers until his death in 1989. Since then, his plays have continued to be produced around the world.

Waiting for Godot, the play that launched Beckett's career in the theater, reflects the intellectual and artistic climate of a Europe still recovering from the devastation of World War II. In the aftermath of the war's unprecedented horrors, a number of Continental dramatists rejected dramatic coherence and logic and the centuries-old tradition of rationality on which they stood. In 1961, the critic Martin Esslin coined the influential phrase "Theater of the Absurd" to describe the drama of Beckett, Eugène Ionesco, JEAN GENET, and others. Philosophically akin to the writings of Albert Camus, Jean-Paul Sartre, and other existential philosophers who were writing about human existence in a world without meaning, the Theater of the Absurd, according to Esslin, sought to convey this human condition in nontraditional dramatic forms. In *The Myth of Sisyphus* (1942), Albert Camus wrote:

> A world that can be explained by reasoning, however faulty, is a familiar world. But in a universe that is suddenly deprived of illusions and of light, man feels a stranger. His is an irremediable exile, because he is deprived of memories of a lost homeland as much as he lacks the hope of a promised land to come. This divorce between man and his life, the actor and his setting, truly constitutes the feeling of Absurdity.

Playing out the implications of Camus' theatrical metaphor, Beckett dismantles the elements, or meaning structures, that have sustained and defined dramatic literature. In place of a plot that might organize onstage incidents in relation to each other and that generates movement toward a conclusion, *Waiting for Godot* is organized around activities—pacing, speaking, remembering, falling down—that refuse to cohere into a beginning, middle, and end. Instead of presenting dramatic action, Beckett dramatizes the condition of waiting, a quintessential non-action that depends on forces and events beyond the acting subject. Time, for its part, loses what claim it has to linearity and becomes disconnected and unknowable. The amount of time that elapses between acts 1 and 2 of *Godot* remains mysterious: the latter act seems to take place the next day, but the lone onstage tree has sprouted leaves—a change that suggests a longer temporal span—and neither Vladimir (Didi) nor Estragon (Gogo), the play's protagonists, can determine how much time has passed. The play's minimalist setting—"A country road. A tree."—is equally indeterminate. Unlike the coherent settings of such modern dramatists as HENRIK IBSEN or GEORGE BERNARD SHAW, Beckett's setting is a kind of nonplace. Uncongenial, not humanized in any way, it is obviously a stage, and an empty one at that. The world beyond the stage is even more frightening and unknown. The characters make references

The second act of *Waiting for Godot* in the 1961 Paris Odeon production. The tree was designed by Beckett's friend, the Italian sculptor Alberto Giacometti.

to more idyllic times and places—climbing the Eiffel Tower in the 1890s, grape harvesting near the Rhône—but it is barely conceivable that these realms could be continuous with the inert, radically reduced world the text describes.

Like all of Beckett's characters, Vladimir and Estragon try to understand this world and to come to terms with their own being (or nonbeing) as its inhabitants. Waiting for a figure whose arrival might give meaning to their lives, the two ponder their condition while devising strategies to pass the time. It is worth noting, in this regard, that the play's original French title—*En attendant Godot*—translates into English more accurately as "While waiting for Godot," a participial phrase that shifts attention from the act of waiting to what one does to kill time during that time of waiting. Didi and Gogo develop routines—putting on boots, engaging in crosstalk "canters," even (they fantasize) hanging themselves—that provide distractions from the tedium of waiting. Much of the crosstalk and many of the routines that these tramps devise recall vaudeville and music hall entertainment, clown performances, and the silent films of Charlie Chaplin; indeed, the many visual gags (pants falling down, pratfalls, exchanges of hats) of *Waiting for Godot* help explain why this play has attracted many of the theater's finest comic actors. But there is no mistaking either the urgency of the characters' attempts to distract themselves through such activities or the high stakes for these figures whose very reality and purpose elude their grasp. As Estragon says to Vladimir, "We always find something, eh Didi, to give us the impression we exist?" The absurdity of their predicament and the meaninglessness of their existence repeatedly interrupt their attempts at play, particularly at those times when language gives way to silence. In such moments, as Beckett wrote in his study of Proust, "the boredom of living is replaced by the suffering of being." After one particularly long silence, Vladimir's anguish is undisguisable: "Say something! . . . Say anything at all!"

The two tramps' greatest distraction in each of the two acts is the arrival and departure of Pozzo and Lucky, whose master-slave relationship is reflected in the rope that connects them. Pozzo, a former landowner, seeks to dominate the stage and those around him with oratorical declamations and physical assertions of power. The ironically named Lucky, his servant, carries his bags like a packhorse and submits to Pozzo's abuse. Lucky remains silent until commanded to "think" near the end of the first act, at which point he delivers a disjointed monologue consisting of quasi-philosophical and quasi-theological discourse, arcane and invented references, and sexual/scatological wordplay. This monologue, which teases the audience with fragmentary structures and half-meanings amid its barrage of apparent nonsense, offers a mock-academic portrayal of an intellectual tradition whose religious and rational frameworks have imploded. The very notion of an originative thinking subject is undermined by Lucky's performance. His torrent of words issues forth—involuntarily, it seems—like water from a faucet, and it is turned off just as mechanically when Vladimir wrestles away his hat.

Pozzo and Lucky cross the stage in each act, moving on a linear course between unknown points. In this regard, they differ from Vladimir and Estragon, who return to the same point each evening, who mark the boundaries of their familiar space by marking the edges of the stage, and whose existence is one of familiarities and recurrences. Pozzo and Lucky undergo catastrophic changes between acts—Pozzo becomes blind, and Lucky loses the ability to speak—while the two tramps seem largely unchanged. Like the German drinking song that Vladimir sings to open it—in which a dog's death is recounted in an endlessly repeating narrative—the play's second act recapitulates many of the situations, actions, and changes of the first act. At the same time, it is not an exact repetition. The scholar Vivian Mercier may have characterized Godot, famously, as "a play in which nothing happens, twice," but the shape and feel of nothing assume different forms in the two acts. The second act is noticeably darker than the first, the comic efforts of its central figures more strained. Time for Didi and Gogo is a process of diminishment, in which "lessness" (to borrow a title from one of Beckett's late prose pieces) makes itself felt with increasing force. The carrot of act 1 is gone in act 2. Even memory seems to weaken between acts. The two characters labor to remember what happened in act 1, and the uncertainty that they confront renders their lives even more out of their control.

And what about Godot, the object of their waiting? Scholars have speculated on the origins of this name—Godeau is the name of an absent character in a Balzac novel, and *godillot* and *godasse* are French slang terms for "boot"—but whatever echoes the name may carry, the identity of this figure remains, in the end, unknowable. A frequent assumption by spectators, readers, and critics is that Godot represents the Christian God and that his absence marks the twentieth-century historical moment when the Age of Faith had passed and the idea of God no longer served, in the minds of leading artists and intellectuals, as the foundation of moral order. The play is filled, to be sure, with Christian references and allusions: Didi and Gogo speak of the two thieves who were crucified on either side of Jesus, and references to crucifixion, salvation, and other Christian motifs occur throughout. But the name "Godot" is not linguistically identical with "God"; and as Beckett himself noted, this resemblance is wholly absent from the text in French, the play's original language. Beckett also said that if he knew who Godot was, he would have said so in the play. In the absence of such direct identification, we can conclude little more than the following: Godot is that for which Didi and Gogo wait, the absent promise on which they pin their desires for meaningfulness and purpose. Does he really exist? Though his repeated failure to arrive may suggest that he doesn't, the entrance of a boy who brings a message from him at the end of each act undermines even this potential certainty. Beckett once stated, not surprisingly, that his favorite word was "perhaps."

Against their uncertainty and disappointment, the dignity of these two tramps lies in their insistence on keeping their appointment and their refusal to succumb to despair, close though they may come to it. They also have the presence of each other and their shared familiarity, which keeps them together even though they ask themselves, in moments of weariness, whether they should part. Finally, they have the consolation of language, which finds poetry in the most painful of recognitions: "Astride of a grave and a difficult birth. Down in the hole, lingeringly, the grave-digger puts on the forceps. We have time to grow old. The air is full of our cries." In its gritty lyricism and daringly innovative use of the stage, this most original of plays offers a theatrically rich portrayal of boredom, anguish, hope, and resiliency. In urging his London audience to see *Waiting for Godot,* Harold Hobson, one of the play's first English reviewers, captured its haunting power for a generation that had experienced nothing like it: "At the worst you will discover a curiosity, a four-leaved clover, a black tulip; at the best, something that will securely lodge in a corner of your mind for as long as you live."

S.G.

Waiting for Godot

A Tragicomedy in Two Acts[1]

CHARACTERS

ESTRAGON — POZZO
VLADIMIR — A BOY
LUCKY

Act 1

A country road. A tree.
Evening.

[ESTRAGON, *sitting on a low mound, is trying to take off his boot. He pulls at it with both hands, panting. He gives up, exhausted, rests, tries again. As before.*]

[*Enter* VLADIMIR.]

ESTRAGON [*giving up again*] Nothing to be done.

VLADIMIR [*advancing with short, stiff strides, legs wide apart*] I'm beginning to come round to that opinion. All my life I've tried to put it from me, saying, Vladimir, be reasonable, you haven't yet tried everything. And I resumed the struggle. [*He broods, musing on the struggle. Turning to* ESTRAGON.] So there you are again.

ESTRAGON Am I?

VLADIMIR I'm glad to see you back. I thought you were gone for ever.

ESTRAGON Me too.

VLADIMIR Together again at last! We'll have to celebrate this. But how? [*He reflects.*] Get up till I embrace you.

ESTRAGON [*irritably*] Not now, not now.

VLADIMIR [*hurt, coldly*] May one enquire where His Highness spent the night?

ESTRAGON In a ditch.

VLADIMIR [*admiringly*] A ditch! Where?

ESTRAGON [*without gesture*] Over there.

VLADIMIR And they didn't beat you?

ESTRAGON Beat me? Certainly they beat me.

VLADIMIR The same lot as usual?

ESTRAGON The same? I don't know.

VLADIMIR When I think of it . . . all these years . . . but for me . . . where would you be . . . [*Decisively*] You'd be nothing more than a little heap of bones at the present minute, no doubt about it.

ESTRAGON And what of it?

1. Translated from the original French text by the author.

VLADIMIR [*gloomily*] It's too much for one man. [*Pause. Cheerfully.*] On the other hand what's the good of losing heart now, that's what I say. We should have thought of it a million years ago, in the nineties.[2]

ESTRAGON Ah stop blathering and help me off with this bloody thing.

VLADIMIR Hand in hand from the top of the Eiffel Tower, among the first. We were respectable in those days. Now it's too late. They wouldn't even let us up. [ESTRAGON *tears at his boot.*] What are you doing?

ESTRAGON Taking off my boot. Did that never happen to you?

VLADIMIR Boots must be taken off every day, I'm tired telling you that. Why don't you listen to me?

ESTRAGON [*feebly*] Help me!

VLADIMIR It hurts?

ESTRAGON [*angrily*] Hurts! He wants to know if it hurts!

VLADIMIR [*angrily*] No one ever suffers but you. I don't count. I'd like to hear what you'd say if you had what I have.

ESTRAGON It hurts?

VLADIMIR [*angrily*] Hurts! He wants to know if it hurts!

ESTRAGON [*pointing*] You might button it all the same.

VLADIMIR [*stooping*] True. [*He buttons his fly.*] Never neglect the little things of life.

ESTRAGON What do you expect, you always wait till the last moment.

VLADIMIR [*musingly*] The last moment . . . [*He meditates.*] Hope deferred maketh the something sick, who said that?[3]

ESTRAGON Why don't you help me?

VLADIMIR Sometimes I feel it coming all the same. Then I go all queer. [*He takes off his hat, peers inside it, feels about inside it, shakes it, puts it on again.*] How shall I say? Relieved and at the same time . . . [*He searches for the word.*] . . . appalled. [*With emphasis*] AP-PALLED. [*He takes off his hat again, peers inside it.*] Funny. [*He knocks on the crown as though to dislodge a foreign body, peers into it again, puts it on again.*] Nothing to be done. [ESTRAGON *with a supreme effort succeeds in pulling off his boot. He peers inside it, feels about inside it, turns it upside down, shakes it, looks on the ground to see if anything has fallen out, finds nothing, feels inside it again, staring sightlessly before him.*] Well?

ESTRAGON Nothing.

VLADIMIR Show.

ESTRAGON There's nothing to show.

VLADIMIR Try and put it on again.

ESTRAGON [*examining his foot*] I'll air it for a bit.

VLADIMIR There's man all over for you, blaming on his boots the faults of his feet. [*He takes off his hat again, peers inside it, feels about inside it, knocks on the crown, blows into it, puts it on again.*] This is getting alarming. [*Silence. Vladimir deep in thought, Estragon pulling at his toes.*] One of the thieves was saved.[4] [*Pause*] It's a reasonable percentage. [*Pause*] Gogo.

2. That is, the 1890s.

3. "Hope deferred maketh the heart sick: but when the desire cometh, it is a tree of life" (Proverbs 13.12).

4. That is, one of the two thieves crucified at the same time as Jesus. One of the Gospels describes one thief railing at him and the other asking to be remembered in heaven. To the second thief Jesus replied, "Verify I say unto thee, Today shalt thou be with me in paradise" (Luke 23.43).

ESTRAGON What?

VLADIMIR Suppose we repented.

ESTRAGON Repented what?

VLADIMIR Oh . . . [*He reflects.*] We wouldn't have to go into the details.

ESTRAGON Our being born?

[VLADIMIR *breaks into a hearty laugh which he immediately stifles, his hand pressed to his pubis, his face contorted.*]

VLADIMIR One daren't even laugh any more.

ESTRAGON Dreadful privation.

VLADIMIR Merely smile. [*He smiles suddenly from ear to ear, keeps smiling, ceases as suddenly.*] It's not the same thing. Nothing to be done. [*Pause*] Gogo.

ESTRAGON [*irritably*] What is it?

VLADIMIR Did you ever read the Bible?

ESTRAGON The Bible . . . [*He reflects.*] I must have taken a look at it.

VLADIMIR Do you remember the Gospels?

ESTRAGON I remember the maps of the Holy Land. Coloured they were. Very pretty. The Dead Sea[5] was pale blue. The very look of it made me thirsty. That's where we'll go, I used to say, that's where we'll go for our honeymoon. We'll swim. We'll be happy.

VLADIMIR You should have been a poet.

ESTRAGON I was. [*Gesture towards his rags*] Isn't that obvious?

[*Silence.*]

VLADIMIR Where was I . . . How's your foot?

ESTRAGON Swelling visibly.

VLADIMIR Ah yes, the two thieves. Do you remember the story?

ESTRAGON No.

VLADIMIR Shall I tell it to you?

ESTRAGON No.

VLADIMIR It'll pass the time. [*Pause*] Two thieves, crucified at the same time as our Saviour. One—

ESTRAGON Our what?

VLADIMIR Our Saviour. Two thieves. One is supposed to have been saved and the other . . . [*He searches for the contrary of saved.*] . . . damned.

ESTRAGON Saved from what?

VLADIMIR Hell.

ESTRAGON I'm going.

[*He does not move.*]

VLADIMIR And yet . . . [*Pause*] . . . how is it—this is not boring you I hope—how is it that of the four Evangelists only one speaks of a thief being saved. The four of them were there—or thereabouts—and only one speaks of a thief being saved. [*Pause*] Come on, Gogo, return the ball, can't you, once in a way?

ESTRAGON [*with exaggerated enthusiasm*] I find this really most extraordinarily interesting.

5. A salt lake, about 45 miles long and up to 10 miles wide, on the boundary between Israel and Jordan.

VLADIMIR One out of four. Of the other three two don't mention any thieves at all and the third says that both of them abused him.[6]

ESTRAGON Who?

VLADIMIR What?

ESTRAGON What's all this about? Abused who?

VLADIMIR The Saviour.

ESTRAGON Why?

VLADIMIR Because he wouldn't save them.

ESTRAGON From hell?

VLADIMIR Imbecile! From death.

ESTRAGON I thought you said hell.

VLADIMIR From death, from death.

ESTRAGON Well what of it?

VLADIMIR Then the two of them must have been damned.

ESTRAGON And why not?

VLADIMIR But one of the four says that one of the two was saved.

ESTRAGON Well? They don't agree and that's all there is to it.

VLADIMIR But all four were there. And only one speaks of a thief being saved. Why believe him rather than the others?

ESTRAGON Who believes him?

VLADIMIR Everybody. It's the only version they know.

ESTRAGON People are bloody ignorant apes.

[*He rises painfully, goes limping to extreme left, halts, gazes into distance off with his hand screening his eyes, turns, goes to extreme right, gazes into distance.* VLADIMIR *watches him, then goes and picks up the boot, peers into it, drops it hastily.*]

VLADIMIR Pah!

[*He spits.* ESTRAGON *moves to center, halts with his back to auditorium.*]

ESTRAGON Charming spot. [*He turns, advances to front, halts facing auditorium.*] Inspiring prospects. [*He turns to* VLADIMIR.] Let's go.

VLADIMIR We can't.

ESTRAGON Why not?

VLADIMIR We're waiting for Godot.

ESTRAGON [*despairingly*] Ah! [*Pause*] You're sure it was here?

VLADIMIR What?

ESTRAGON That we were to wait.

VLADIMIR He said by the tree. [*They look at the tree.*] Do you see any others?

ESTRAGON What is it?

VLADIMIR I don't know. A willow.[7]

ESTRAGON Where are the leaves?

VLADIMIR It must be dead.

ESTRAGON No more weeping.

VLADIMIR Or perhaps it's not the season.

ESTRAGON Looks to me more like a bush.

VLADIMIR A shrub.

ESTRAGON A bush.

6. See Matthew 27.44. Both Mark (15.27) and John (who calls them simply "two others"; 19.18) mention the thieves.

7. A tree associated with mourning.

VLADIMIR A—. What are you insinuating? That we've come to the wrong place?

ESTRAGON He should be here.

VLADIMIR He didn't say for sure he'd come.

ESTRAGON And if he doesn't come?

VLADIMIR We'll come back tomorrow.

ESTRAGON And then the day after tomorrow.

VLADIMIR Possibly.

ESTRAGON And so on.

VLADIMIR The point is—

ESTRAGON Until he comes.

VLADIMIR You're merciless.

ESTRAGON We came here yesterday.

VLADIMIR Ah no, there you're mistaken.

ESTRAGON What did we do yesterday?

VLADIMIR What did we do yesterday?

ESTRAGON Yes.

VLADIMIR Why . . . [*Angrily*] Nothing is certain when you're about.

ESTRAGON In my opinion we were here.

VLADIMIR [*looking round*] You recognize the place?

ESTRAGON I didn't say that.

VLADIMIR Well?

ESTRAGON That makes no difference.

VLADIMIR All the same . . . that tree . . . [*Turning towards auditorium*] that bog . . .

ESTRAGON You're sure it was this evening?

VLADIMIR What?

ESTRAGON That we were to wait.

VLADIMIR He said Saturday. [*Pause*] I think.

ESTRAGON You think.

VLADIMIR I must have made a note of it. [*He fumbles in his pockets, bursting with miscellaneous rubbish.*]

ESTRAGON [*very insidious*] But what Saturday? And is it Saturday? Is it not rather Sunday? [*Pause*] Or Monday? [*Pause*] Or Friday?

VLADIMIR [*looking wildly about him, as though the date was inscribed in the landscape*] It's not possible!

ESTRAGON Or Thursday?

VLADIMIR What'll we do?

ESTRAGON If he came yesterday and we weren't here you may be sure he won't come again today.

VLADIMIR But you say we were here yesterday.

ESTRAGON I may be mistaken. [*Pause*] Let's stop talking for a minute, do you mind?

VLADIMIR [*feebly*] All right. [ESTRAGON *sits down on the mound.* VLADIMIR *paces agitatedly to and fro, halting from time to time to gaze into distance off.* ESTRAGON *falls asleep.* VLADIMIR *halts finally before* ESTRAGON.] Gogo! . . . Gogo! . . . GOGO!

[ESTRAGON *wakes with a start.*]

ESTRAGON [*restored to the horror of his situation*] I was asleep! [*Despairingly*] Why will you never let me sleep?

VLADIMIR I felt lonely.

ESTRAGON I had a dream.

VLADIMIR Don't tell me!

ESTRAGON I dreamt that—

VLADIMIR DON'T TELL ME!

ESTRAGON [*gesture towards the universe*] This one is enough for you? [*Silence*] It's not nice of you, Didi. Who am I to tell my private nightmares to if I can't tell them to you?

VLADIMIR Let them remain private. You know I can't bear that.

ESTRAGON [*coldly*] There are times when I wonder if it wouldn't be better for us to part.

VLADIMIR You wouldn't go far.

ESTRAGON That would be too bad, really too bad. [*Pause*] Wouldn't it, Didi, be really too bad? [*Pause*] When you think of the beauty of the way. [*Pause*] And the goodness of the wayfarers. [*Pause. Wheedling.*] Wouldn't it, Didi?

VLADIMIR Calm yourself.

ESTRAGON [*voluptuously*] Calm . . . calm . . . The English say cawm. [*Pause*] You know the story of the Englishman in the brothel?

VLADIMIR Yes.

ESTRAGON Tell it to me.

VLADIMIR Ah stop it!

ESTRAGON An Englishman having drunk a little more than usual proceeds to a brothel. The bawd asks him if he wants a fair one, a dark one or a red-haired one. Go on.

VLADIMIR STOP IT!

[*Exit* VLADIMIR *hurriedly.* ESTRAGON *gets up and follows him as far as the limit of the stage. Gestures of* ESTRAGON *like those of a spectator encouraging a pugilist. Enter* VLADIMIR. *He brushes past* ESTRAGON, *crosses the stage with bowed head.* ESTRAGON *takes a step towards him, halts.*]

ESTRAGON [*gently*] You wanted to speak to me? [*Silence.* ESTRAGON *takes a step forward.*] You had something to say to me? [*Silence. Another step forward.*] Didi . . .

VLADIMIR [*without turning*] I've nothing to say to you.

ESTRAGON [*step forward*] You're angry? [*Silence. Step forward.*] Forgive me. [*Silence. Step forward.* ESTRAGON *lays his hand on* VLADIMIR's *shoulder.*] Come, Didi. [*Silence*] Give me your hand. [VLADIMIR *half turns.*] Embrace me! [VLADIMIR *stiffens.*] Don't be stubborn! [VLADIMIR *softens. They embrace.* ESTRAGON *recoils.*] You stink of garlic!

VLADIMIR It's for the kidneys. [*Silence.* ESTRAGON *looks attentively at the tree.*] What do we do now?

ESTRAGON Wait.

VLADIMIR Yes, but while waiting.

ESTRAGON What about hanging ourselves?

VLADIMIR Hmm. It'd give us an erection.

ESTRAGON [*highly excited*] An erection!

VLADIMIR With all that follows. Where it[8] falls mandrakes grow. That's why they shriek when you pull them up. Did you not know that?

8. That is, semen. The mandrake, whose root sometimes splits in a way that resembles a man's body, was long believed to be inhabited by a demon (its shriek at being uprooted was said to be fatal). The idea that mandrakes grow from the semen of hanged men was widespread in Europe in the Middle Ages.

ESTRAGON Let's hang ourselves immediately!

VLADIMIR From a bough? [*They go towards the tree.*] I wouldn't trust it.

ESTRAGON We can always try.

VLADIMIR Go ahead.

ESTRAGON After you.

VLADIMIR No no, you first.

ESTRAGON Why me?

VLADIMIR You're lighter than I am.

ESTRAGON Just so!

VLADIMIR I don't understand.

ESTRAGON Use your intelligence, can't you?

[**VLADIMIR** *uses his intelligence.*]

VLADIMIR [*finally*] I remain in the dark.

ESTRAGON This is how it is. [*He reflects.*] The bough . . . the bough . . . [*Angrily*] Use your head, can't you?

VLADIMIR You're my only hope.

ESTRAGON [*with effort*] Gogo light—bough not break—Gogo dead. Didi heavy—bough break—Didi alone. Whereas—

VLADIMIR I hadn't thought of that.

ESTRAGON If it hangs you it'll hang anything.

VLADIMIR But am I heavier than you?

ESTRAGON So you tell me. I don't know. There's an even chance. Or nearly.

VLADIMIR Well? What do we do?

ESTRAGON Don't let's do anything. It's safer.

VLADIMIR Let's wait and see what he says.

ESTRAGON Who?

VLADIMIR Godot.

ESTRAGON Good idea.

VLADIMIR Let's wait till we know exactly how we stand.

ESTRAGON On the other hand it might be better to strike the iron before it freezes.[9]

VLADIMIR I'm curious to hear what he has to offer. Then we'll take it or leave it.

ESTRAGON What exactly did we ask him for?

VLADIMIR Were you not there?

ESTRAGON I can't have been listening.

VLADIMIR Oh . . . Nothing very definite.

ESTRAGON A kind of prayer.

VLADIMIR Precisely.

ESTRAGON A vague supplication.

VLADIMIR Exactly.

ESTRAGON And what did he reply?

VLADIMIR That he'd see.

ESTRAGON That he couldn't promise anything.

VLADIMIR That he'd have to think it over.

ESTRAGON In the quiet of his home.

VLADIMIR Consult his family.

9. A version of the proverb "Strike while the iron is hot," whose earliest attribution is to Publilius Syrus (1st c. B.C.E.).

ESTRAGON His friends.
VLADIMIR His agents.
ESTRAGON His correspondents.
VLADIMIR His books.
ESTRAGON His bank account.
VLADIMIR Before taking a decision.[1]
ESTRAGON It's the normal thing.
VLADIMIR Is it not?
ESTRAGON I think it is.
VLADIMIR I think so too.
[*Silence.*]
ESTRAGON [*anxious*] And we?
VLADIMIR I beg your pardon?
ESTRAGON I said, And we?
VLADIMIR I don't understand.
ESTRAGON Where do we come in?
VLADIMIR Come in?
ESTRAGON Take your time.
VLADIMIR Come in? On our hands and knees.
ESTRAGON As bad as that?
VLADIMIR Your Worship wishes to assert his prerogatives?
ESTRAGON We've no rights any more?
[*Laugh of* VLADIMIR, *stifled as before, less the smile.*]
VLADIMIR You'd make me laugh if it wasn't prohibited.
ESTRAGON We've lost our rights?
VLADIMIR [*distinctly*] We got rid of them.
[*Silence. They remain motionless, arms dangling, heads sunk, sagging at the knees.*]
ESTRAGON [*feebly*] We're not tied? [*Pause*] We're not—
VLADIMIR Listen!
[*They listen, grotesquely rigid.*]
ESTRAGON I hear nothing.
VLADIMIR Hsst! [*They listen.* ESTRAGON *loses his balance, almost falls. He clutches the arm of* VLADIMIR *who totters. They listen, huddled together.*] Nor I.
[*Sighs of relief. They relax and separate.*]
ESTRAGON You gave me a fright.
VLADIMIR I thought it was he.
ESTRAGON Who?
VLADIMIR Godot.
ESTRAGON Pah! The wind in the reeds.
VLADIMIR I could have sworn I heard shouts.
ESTRAGON And why would he shout?
VLADIMIR At his horse.
[*Silence.*]
ESTRAGON [*violently*] I'm hungry!
VLADIMIR Do you want a carrot?

1. That is, making a decision (a British idiom).

ESTRAGON Is that all there is?

VLADIMIR I might have some turnips.

ESTRAGON Give me a carrot. [VLADIMIR *rummages in his pockets, takes out a turnip and gives it to* ESTRAGON *who takes a bite out of it. Angrily.*] It's a turnip!

VLADIMIR Oh pardon! I could have sworn it was a carrot. [*He rummages again in his pockets, finds nothing but turnips.*] All that's turnips. [*He rummages.*] You must have eaten the last. [*He rummages.*] Wait, I have it. [*He brings out a carrot and gives it to* ESTRAGON.] There, dear fellow. [ESTRAGON *wipes the carrot on his sleeve and begins to eat it.*] Make it last, that's the end of them.

ESTRAGON [*chewing*] I asked you a question.

VLADIMIR Ah.

ESTRAGON Did you reply?

VLADIMIR How's the carrot?

ESTRAGON It's a carrot.

VLADIMIR So much the better, so much the better. [*Pause.*] What was it you wanted to know?

ESTRAGON I've forgotten. [*Chews.*] That's what annoys me. [*He looks at the carrot appreciatively, dangles it between finger and thumb.*] I'll never forget this carrot. [*He sucks the end of it meditatively.*] Ah yes, now I remember.

VLADIMIR Well?

ESTRAGON [*his mouth full, vacuously*] We're not tied?

VLADIMIR I don't hear a word you're saying.

ESTRAGON [*chews, swallows*] I'm asking you if we're tied.

VLADIMIR Tied?

ESTRAGON Ti-ed.

VLADIMIR How do you mean tied?

ESTRAGON Down.

VLADIMIR But to whom? By whom?

ESTRAGON To your man.

VLADIMIR To Godot? Tied to Godot! What an idea! No question of it. [*Pause*] For the moment.

ESTRAGON His name is Godot?

VLADIMIR I think so.

ESTRAGON Fancy that. [*He raises what remains of the carrot by the stub of leaf, twirls it before his eyes.*] Funny, the more you eat the worse it gets.

VLADIMIR With me it's just the opposite.

ESTRAGON In other words?

VLADIMIR I get used to the muck as I go along.

ESTRAGON [*after prolonged reflection*] Is that the opposite?

VLADIMIR Question of temperament.

ESTRAGON Of character.

VLADIMIR Nothing you can do about it.

ESTRAGON No use struggling.

VLADIMIR One is what one is.

ESTRAGON No use wriggling.

VLADIMIR The essential doesn't change.

ESTRAGON Nothing to be done. [*He proffers the remains of the carrot to* VLADIMIR.] Like to finish it?

[*A terrible cry, close at hand.* ESTRAGON *drops the carrot. They remain motionless, then together make a sudden rush towards the wings.* ESTRAGON *stops halfway, runs back, picks up the carrot, stuffs it in his pocket, runs to rejoin* VLADIMIR *who is waiting for him, stops again, runs back, picks up his boot, runs to rejoin* VLADIMIR. *Huddled together, shoulders hunched, cringing away from the menace, they wait.*]

[*Enter* POZZO *and* LUCKY. POZZO *drives* LUCKY *by means of a rope passed round his neck, so that* LUCKY *is the first to enter, followed by the rope which is long enough to let him reach the middle of the stage before* POZZO *appears.* LUCKY *carries a heavy bag, a folding stool, a picnic basket and a greatcoat,* POZZO *a whip.*]

POZZO [*off*] On! [*Crack of whip.* POZZO *appears. They cross the stage.* LUCKY *passes before* VLADIMIR *and* ESTRAGON *and exit.* POZZO *at the sight of* VLADIMIR *and* ESTRAGON *stops short. The rope tautens.* POZZO *jerks at it violently.*] Back!

[*Noise of* LUCKY *falling with all his baggage.* VLADIMIR *and* ESTRAGON *turn towards him, half wishing half fearing to go to his assistance.* VLADIMIR *takes a step towards Lucky,* ESTRAGON *holds him back by the sleeve.*]

VLADIMIR Let me go!

ESTRAGON Stay where you are!

POZZO Be careful! He's wicked. [VLADIMIR *and* ESTRAGON *turn towards* POZZO.] With strangers.

ESTRAGON [*undertone*] Is that him?

VLADIMIR Who?

ESTRAGON [*trying to remember the name*] Er . . .

VLADIMIR Godot?

ESTRAGON Yes.

POZZO I present myself: Pozzo.

VLADIMIR [*to* ESTRAGON] Not at all!

ESTRAGON He said Godot.

VLADIMIR Not at all!

ESTRAGON [*timidly, to* POZZO] You're not Mr. Godot, Sir?

POZZO [*terrifying voice*] I am Pozzo! [*Silence*] Pozzo! [*Silence*] Does that name mean nothing to you? [*Silence*] I say does that name mean nothing to you?

[VLADIMIR *and* ESTRAGON *look at each other questioningly.*]

ESTRAGON [*pretending to search*] Bozzo . . . Bozzo . . .

VLADIMIR [*ditto*] Pozzo . . . Pozzo . . .

POZZO PPPOZZZO!

ESTRAGON Ah! Pozzo . . . let me see . . . Pozzo . . .

VLADIMIR Is it Pozzo or Bozzo?

ESTRAGON Pozzo . . . no . . . I'm afraid I . . . no . . . I don't seem to . . .

[POZZO *advances threateningly.*]

VLADIMIR [*conciliating*] I once knew a family called Cozzo. The mother had the clap.[2]

ESTRAGON [*hastily*] We're not from these parts, Sir.

POZZO [*halting*] You are human beings none the less. [*He puts on his glasses.*] As far as one can see. [*He takes off his glasses.*] Of the same species as my-

2. Gonorrhea (slang).

self. [*He bursts into an enormous laugh.*] Of the same species as Pozzo! Made in God's image!

VLADIMIR Well you see—

POZZO [*peremptory*] Who is Godot?

ESTRAGON Godot?

POZZO You took me for Godot.

VLADIMIR Oh no, Sir, not for an instant, Sir.

POZZO Who is he?

VLADIMIR Oh he's a . . . he's a kind of acquaintance.

ESTRAGON Nothing of the kind, we hardly know him.

VLADIMIR True . . . we don't know him very well . . . but all the same . . .

ESTRAGON Personally I wouldn't even know him if I saw him.

POZZO You took me for him.

ESTRAGON [*recoiling before* POZZO] That's to say . . . you understand . . . the dusk . . . the strain . . . waiting . . . I confess . . . I imagined . . . for a second . . .

POZZO Waiting? So you were waiting for him?

VLADIMIR Well you see—

POZZO Here? On my land?

VLADIMIR We didn't intend any harm.

ESTRAGON We meant well.

POZZO The road is free to all.

VLADIMIR That's how we looked at it.

POZZO It's a disgrace. But there you are.

ESTRAGON Nothing we can do about it.

POZZO [*with magnanimous gesture*] Let's say no more about it. [*He jerks the rope.*] Up pig! [*Pause*] Every time he drops he falls asleep. [*Jerks the rope.*] Up hog! [*Noise of* LUCKY *getting up and picking up his baggage.* POZZO *jerks the rope.*] Back! [*Enter* LUCKY *backwards.*] Stop! [LUCKY *stops.*] Turn! [LUCKY *turns. To* VLADIMIR *and* ESTRAGON, *affably.*] Gentlemen, I am happy to have met you. [*Before their incredulous expression*] Yes yes, sincerely happy. [*He jerks the rope.*] Closer! [LUCKY *advances.*] Stop! [LUCKY *stops.*] Yes, the road seems long when one journeys all alone for . . . [*He consults his watch.*] . . . yes . . . [*He calculates.*] . . . yes, six hours, that's right, six hours on end, and never a soul in sight. [*To* LUCKY] Coat! [LUCKY *puts down the bag, advances, gives the coat, goes back to his place, takes up the bag.*] Hold that! [POZZO *holds out the whip.* LUCKY *advances and, both his hands being occupied, takes the whip in his mouth, then goes back to his place.* POZZO *begins to put on his coat, stops.*] Coat! [LUCKY *puts down bag, basket and stool, advances, helps* POZZO *on with his coat, goes back to his place and takes up bag, basket and stool.*] Touch of autumn in the air this evening. [POZZO *finishes buttoning his coat, stoops, inspects himself, straightens up.*] Whip! [LUCKY *advances, stoops,* POZZO *snatches the whip from his mouth,* LUCKY *goes back to his place.*] Yes, gentlemen, I cannot go for long without the society of my likes [*He puts on his glasses and looks at the two likes.*] even when the likeness is an imperfect one. [*He takes off his glasses.*] Stool! [LUCKY *puts down bag and basket, advances, opens stool, puts it down, goes back to his place, takes up bag and basket.*] Closer! [LUCKY *puts down bag and basket, advances, moves stool, goes back to his place, takes up bag and basket.* POZZO *sits down, places the butt of his whip against* LUCKY*'s chest and pushes.*]

Back! [LUCKY *takes a step back.*] Further! [LUCKY *takes another step back.*] Stop! [LUCKY *stops. To* VLADIMIR *and* ESTRAGON.] That is why, with your permission, I propose to dally with you a moment, before I venture any further. Basket! [LUCKY *advances, gives the basket, goes back to his place.*] The fresh air stimulates the jaded appetite. [*He opens the basket, takes out a piece of chicken and a bottle of wine.*] Basket! [LUCKY *advances, picks up the basket and goes back to his place.*] Further! [LUCKY *takes a step back.*] He stinks. Happy days!

[*He drinks from the bottle, puts it down and begins to eat. Silence.* VLADIMIR *and* ESTRAGON, *cautiously at first, then more boldly, begin to circle about* LUCKY, *inspecting him up and down.* POZZO *eats his chicken voraciously, throwing away the bones after having sucked them.* LUCKY *sags slowly, until bag and basket touch the ground, then straightens up with a start and begins to sag again. Rhythm of one sleeping on his feet.*]

ESTRAGON What ails him?
VLADIMIR He looks tired.
ESTRAGON Why doesn't he put down his bags?
VLADIMIR How do I know? [*They close in on him.*] Careful!
ESTRAGON Say something to him.
VLADIMIR Look!
ESTRAGON What?
VLADIMIR [*pointing*] His neck!
ESTRAGON [*looking at the neck*] I see nothing.
VLADIMIR Here.

[ESTRAGON *goes over beside* VLADIMIR.]

ESTRAGON Oh I say!
VLADIMIR A running sore!
ESTRAGON It's the rope.
VLADIMIR It's the rubbing.
ESTRAGON It's inevitable.
VLADIMIR It's the knot.
ESTRAGON It's the chafing.

[*They resume their inspection, dwell on the face.*]

VLADIMIR [*grudgingly*] He's not bad looking.
ESTRAGON [*shrugging his shoulders, wry face*] Would you say so?
VLADIMIR A trifle effeminate.
ESTRAGON Look at the slobber.
VLADIMIR It's inevitable.
ESTRAGON Look at the slaver.[3]
VLADIMIR Perhaps he's a halfwit.
ESTRAGON A cretin.
VLADIMIR [*looking closer*] Looks like a goiter.
ESTRAGON [*ditto*] It's not certain.
VLADIMIR He's panting.
ESTRAGON It's inevitable.
VLADIMIR And his eyes!
ESTRAGON What about them?
VLADIMIR Goggling out of his head.

3. Saliva falling from the mouth.

ESTRAGON Looks at his last gasp to me.

VLADIMIR It's not certain. [*Pause*] Ask him a question.

ESTRAGON Would that be a good thing?

VLADIMIR What do we risk?

ESTRAGON [*timidly*] Mister . . .

VLADIMIR Louder.

ESTRAGON [*louder*] Mister . . .

POZZO Leave him in peace! [*They turn towards* POZZO *who, having finished eating, wipes his mouth with the back of his hand.*] Can't you see he wants to rest? Basket! [*He strikes a match and begins to light his pipe.* ESTRAGON *sees the chicken bones on the ground and stares at them greedily. As* LUCKY *does not move* POZZO *throws the match angrily away and jerks the rope.*] Basket! [LUCKY *starts, almost falls, recovers his senses, advances, puts the bottle in the basket and goes back to his place.* ESTRAGON *stares at the bones.* POZZO *strikes another match and lights his pipe.*] What can you expect, it's not his job. [*He pulls at his pipe, stretches out his legs.*] Ah! That's better.

ESTRAGON [*timidly*] Please Sir . . .

POZZO What is it, my good man?

ESTRAGON Er . . . you've finished with the . . . er . . . you don't need the . . . er . . . bones, Sir?

VLADIMIR [*scandalized*] You couldn't have waited?

POZZO No no, he does well to ask. Do I need the bones? [*He turns them over with the end of his whip.*] No, personally I do not need them any more. [ESTRAGON *takes a step towards the bones.*] But . . . [ESTRAGON *stops short.*] . . . but in theory the bones go to the carrier. He is therefore the one to ask. [ESTRAGON *turns towards* LUCKY, *hesitates.*] Go on, go on, don't be afraid, ask him, he'll tell you.

[ESTRAGON *goes towards* LUCKY, *stops before him.*]

ESTRAGON Mister . . . excuse me, Mister . . .

POZZO You're being spoken to, pig! Reply! [*To* ESTRAGON] Try him again.

ESTRAGON Excuse me, Mister, the bones, you won't be wanting the bones?

[LUCKY *looks long at* ESTRAGON.]

POZZO [*in raptures*] Mister! [LUCKY *bows his head.*] Reply! Do you want them or don't you? [*Silence of* LUCKY. *To* ESTRAGON.] They're yours. [ESTRAGON *makes a dart at the bones, picks them up and begins to gnaw them.*] I don't like it. I've never known him refuse a bone before. [*He looks anxiously at* LUCKY.] Nice business it'd be if he fell sick on me! [*He puffs at his pipe.*]

VLADIMIR [*exploding*] It's a scandal!

[*Silence. Flabbergasted,* ESTRAGON *stops gnawing, looks at* POZZO *and* VLADIMIR *in turn.* POZZO *outwardly calm.* VLADIMIR *embarrassed.*]

POZZO [*to* VLADIMIR] Are you alluding to anything in particular?

VLADIMIR [*stutteringly resolute*] To treat a man . . . [*Gesture towards* LUCKY] . . . like that . . . I think that . . . no . . . a human being . . . no . . . it's a scandal!

ESTRAGON [*not to be outdone*] A disgrace! [*He resumes his gnawing.*]

POZZO You are severe. [*To* VLADIMIR] What age are you, if it's not a rude question? [*Silence*] Sixty? Seventy? [*To* ESTRAGON] What age would you say he was?

ESTRAGON Eleven.

POZZO I am impertinent. [*He knocks out his pipe against the whip, gets up.*] I must be getting on. Thank you for your society. [*He reflects.*] Unless I smoke another pipe before I go. What do you say? [*They say nothing.*] Oh I'm only a small smoker, a very small smoker, I'm not in the habit of smoking two pipes one on top of the other, it makes [*Hand to heart, sighing*] my heart go pit-a-pat. [*Silence*] It's the nicotine, one absorbs it in spite of one's precautions. [*Sighs*] You know how it is. [*Silence*] But perhaps you don't smoke? Yes? No? It's of no importance. [*Silence*] But how am I to sit down now, without affectation, now that I have risen? Without appearing to—how shall I say—without appearing to falter. [*To* VLADIMIR] I beg your pardon? [*Silence*] Perhaps you didn't speak? [*Silence*] It's of no importance. Let me see . . . [*He reflects.*]

ESTRAGON Ah! That's better. [*He puts the bones in his pocket.*]

VLADIMIR Let's go.

ESTRAGON So soon?

POZZO One moment! [*He jerks the rope.*] Stool! [*He points with his whip.* LUCKY *moves the stool.*] More! There! [*He sits down.* LUCKY *goes back to his place.*] Done it! [*He fills his pipe.*]

VLADIMIR [*vehemently*] Let's go!

POZZO I hope I'm not driving you away. Wait a little longer, you'll never regret it.

ESTRAGON [*sensing charity*] We're in no hurry.

POZZO [*having lit his pipe*] The second is never so sweet . . . [*He takes the pipe out of his mouth, contemplates it.*] . . . as the first I mean. [*He puts the pipe back in his mouth.*] But it's sweet just the same.

VLADIMIR I'm going.

POZZO He can no longer endure my presence. I am perhaps not particularly human, but who cares? [*To* VLADIMIR] Think twice before you do anything rash. Suppose you go now while it is still day, for there is no denying it is still day. [*They all look up at the sky.*] Good. [*They stop looking at the sky.*] What happens in that case—[*He takes the pipe out of his mouth, examines it.*]—I'm out—[*He relights his pipe.*]—in that case—[*Puff*]—in that case—[*Puff*]—what happens in that case to your appointment with this . . . Godet . . . Godot . . . Godin . . . anyhow you see who I mean, who has your future in his hands . . . [*Pause*] . . . at least your immediate future?

VLADIMIR Who told you?

POZZO He speaks to me again! If this goes on much longer we'll soon be old friends.

ESTRAGON Why doesn't he put down his bags?

POZZO I too would be happy to meet him. The more people I meet the happier I become. From the meanest creature one departs wiser, richer, more conscious of one's blessings. Even you . . . [*He looks at them ostentatiously in turn to make it clear they are both meant.*] . . . even you, who knows, will have added to my store.

ESTRAGON Why doesn't he put down his bags?

POZZO But that would surprise me.

VLADIMIR You're being asked a question.

POZZO [*delighted*] A question! Who? What? A moment ago you were calling me Sir, in fear and trembling. Now you're asking me questions. No good will come of this!

VLADIMIR [*to* ESTRAGON] I think he's listening.

ESTRAGON [*circling about* LUCKY] What?

VLADIMIR You can ask him now. He's on the alert.

ESTRAGON Ask him what?

VLADIMIR Why he doesn't put down his bags.

ESTRAGON I wonder.

VLADIMIR Ask him, can't you?

POZZO [*who has followed these exchanges with anxious attention, fearing lest the question get lost*] You want to know why he doesn't put down his bags, as you call them.

VLADIMIR That's it.

POZZO [*to* ESTRAGON] You are sure you agree with that?

ESTRAGON He's puffing like a grampus.[4]

POZZO The answer is this. [*To* ESTRAGON] But stay still, I beg of you, you're making me nervous!

VLADIMIR Here.

ESTRAGON What is it?

VLADIMIR He's about to speak.

[ESTRAGON *goes over beside* VLADIMIR. *Motionless, side by side, they wait.*]

POZZO Good. Is everybody ready? Is everybody looking at me? [*He looks at* LUCKY, *jerks the rope.* LUCKY *raises his head.*] Will you look at me, pig! [LUCKY *looks at him.*] Good. [*He puts the pipe in his pocket, takes out a little vaporizer and sprays his throat, puts back the vaporizer in his pocket, clears his throat, spits, takes out the vaporizer again, sprays his throat again, puts back the vaporizer in his pocket.*] I am ready. Is everybody listening? Is everybody ready? [*He looks at them all in turn, jerks the rope.*] Hog! [LUCKY *raises his head.*] I don't like talking in a vacuum. Good. Let me see. [*He reflects.*]

ESTRAGON I'm going.

POZZO What was it exactly you wanted to know?

VLADIMIR Why he—

POZZO [*angrily*] Don't interrupt me! [*Pause. Calmer.*] If we all speak at once we'll never get anywhere. [*Pause.*] What was I saying? [*Pause. Louder.*] What was I saying?

[VLADIMIR *mimics one carrying a heavy burden.* POZZO *looks at him, puzzled.*]

ESTRAGON [*forcibly*] Bags. [*He points at* LUCKY.] Why? Always hold. [*He sags, panting.*] Never put down. [*He opens his hands, straightens up with relief.*] Why?

POZZO Ah! Why couldn't you say so before? Why he doesn't make himself comfortable? Let's try and get this clear. Has he not the right to? Certainly he has. It follows that he doesn't want to. There's reasoning for you. And why doesn't he want to? [*Pause*] Gentlemen, the reason is this.

VLADIMIR [*to* ESTRAGON] Make a note of this.

POZZO He wants to impress me, so that I'll keep him.

ESTRAGON What?

POZZO Perhaps I haven't got it quite right. He wants to mollify me, so that I'll give up the idea of parting with him. No, that's not exactly it either.

4. A variety of dolphin.

VLADIMIR You want to get rid of him?

POZZO He wants to cod[5] me, but he won't.

VLADIMIR You want to get rid of him?

POZZO He imagines that when I see how well he carries I'll be tempted to keep him on in that capacity.

ESTRAGON You've had enough of him?

POZZO In reality he carries like a pig. It's not his job.

VLADIMIR You want to get rid of him?

POZZO He imagines that when I see him indefatigable I'll regret my decision. Such is his miserable scheme. As though I were short of slaves! [*All three look at* LUCKY.] Atlas, son of Jupiter![6] [*Silence*] Well, that's that I think. Anything else?

[*Vaporizer.*]

VLADIMIR You want to get rid of him?

POZZO Remark that I might just as well have been in his shoes and he in mine. If chance had not willed otherwise. To each one his due.

VLADIMIR You waagerrim?

POZZO I beg your pardon?

VLADIMIR You want to get rid of him?

POZZO I do. But instead of driving him away as I might have done, I mean instead of simply kicking him out on his arse, in the goodness of my heart I am bringing him to the fair, where I hope to get a good price for him. The truth is you can't drive such creatures away. The best thing would be to kill them.

[LUCKY *weeps.*]

ESTRAGON He's crying!

POZZO Old dogs have more dignity. [*He proffers his handkerchief to* ESTRAGON.] Comfort him, since you pity him. [ESTRAGON *hesitates.*] Come on. [ESTRAGON *takes the handkerchief.*] Wipe away his tears, he'll feel less forsaken.

[ESTRAGON *hesitates.*]

VLADIMIR Here, give it to me, I'll do it.

[ESTRAGON *refuses to give the handkerchief. Childish gestures.*]

POZZO Make haste, before he stops. [ESTRAGON *approaches* LUCKY *and makes to wipe his eyes.* LUCKY *kicks him violently in the shins.* ESTRAGON *drops the handkerchief, recoils, staggers about the stage howling with pain.*] Hanky!

[LUCKY *puts down bag and basket, picks up handkerchief and gives it to* POZZO, *goes back to his place, picks up bag and basket.*]

ESTRAGON Oh the swine! [*He pulls up the leg of his trousers.*] He's crippled me!

POZZO I told you he didn't like strangers.

VLADIMIR [*to* ESTRAGON] Show. [ESTRAGON *shows his leg. To* POZZO, *angrily*] He's bleeding!

POZZO It's a good sign.

5. Play a joke on, tease; or, perhaps, a shortened version of *coddle.*

6. In classical mythology, Atlas's father was the Titan Iapetus, not Jupiter; as punishment for leading the Titans in their war against the Olympian gods, Atlas was condemned to hold the heavens on his shoulders.

ESTRAGON [*on one leg*] I'll never walk again!

VLADIMIR [*tenderly*] I'll carry you. [*Pause*] If necessary.

POZZO He's stopped crying. [*To* ESTRAGON] You have replaced him as it were. [*Lyrically*] The tears of the world are a constant quantity. For each one who begins to weep somewhere else another stops. The same is true of the laugh. [*He laughs.*] Let us not then speak ill of our generation, it is not any unhappier than its predecessors. [*Pause*] Let us not speak well of it either. [*Pause*] Let us not speak of it at all. [*Pause. Judiciously.*] It is true the population has increased.

VLADIMIR Try and walk.

[ESTRAGON *takes a few limping steps, stops before* LUCKY *and spits on him, then goes and sits down on the mound.*]

POZZO Guess who taught me all these beautiful things. [*Pause. Pointing to* LUCKY] My Lucky!

VLADIMIR [*looking at the sky*] Will night never come?

POZZO But for him all my thoughts, all my feelings, would have been of common things. [*Pause. With extraordinary vehemence.*] Professional worries! [*Calmer*] Beauty, grace, truth of the first water,[7] I knew they were all beyond me. So I took a knook.[8]

VLADIMIR [*startled from his inspection of the sky*] A knook?

POZZO That was nearly sixty years ago . . . [*He consults his watch.*] . . . yes, nearly sixty. [*Drawing himself up proudly*] You wouldn't think it to look at me, would you? Compared to him I look like a young man, no? [*Pause*] Hat! [LUCKY *puts down the basket and takes off his hat. His long white hair falls about his face. He puts his hat under his arm and picks up the basket.*] Now look. [POZZO *takes off his hat.*[9] *He is completely bald. He puts on his hat again.*] Did you see?

VLADIMIR And now you turn him away? Such an old and faithful servant!

ESTRAGON Swine!

[POZZO *more and more agitated.*]

VLADIMIR After having sucked all the good out of him you chuck him away like a . . . like a banana skin. Really . . .

POZZO [*groaning, clutching his head*] I can't bear it . . . any longer . . . the way he goes on . . . you've no idea . . . it's terrible . . . he must go . . . [*He waves his arms.*] . . . I'm going mad . . . [*He collapses, his head in his hands.*] . . . I can't bear it . . . any longer . . .

[*Silence. All look at* POZZO.]

VLADIMIR He can't bear it.

ESTRAGON Any longer.

VLADIMIR He's going mad.

ESTRAGON It's terrible.

VLADIMIR [*to* LUCKY] How dare you! It's abominable! Such a good master! Crucify him like that! After so many years! Really!

7. Of the highest quality (formerly, a technical term used of diamonds).

8. A coinage of Beckett's, possibly echoing *knut* (the Russian word for "whip"). In a passage from the original French version that Beckett did not include in his English translation, Pozzo expounds on the word to Vladimir as follows: "You are not from these parts. Are you so out of touch with the times? Years ago people used to have jesters. Now they have knouks. Those who are able to afford them."

9. All four wear bowlers [Beckett's note].

POZZO [*sobbing*] He used to be so kind . . . so helpful . . . and entertaining . . . my good angel . . . and now . . . he's killing me.

ESTRAGON [*to* VLADIMIR] Does he want to replace him?

VLADIMIR What?

ESTRAGON Does he want someone to take his place or not?

VLADIMIR I don't think so.

ESTRAGON What?

VLADIMIR I don't know.

ESTRAGON Ask him.

POZZO [*calmer*] Gentlemen, I don't know what came over me. Forgive me. Forget all I said. [*More and more his old self*] I don't remember exactly what it was, but you may be sure there wasn't a word of truth in it. [*Drawing himself up, striking his chest*] Do I look like a man that can be made to suffer? Frankly? [*He rummages in his pockets.*] What have I done with my pipe?

VLADIMIR Charming evening we're having.

ESTRAGON Unforgettable.

VLADIMIR And it's not over.

ESTRAGON Apparently not.

VLADIMIR It's only beginning.

ESTRAGON It's awful.

VLADIMIR Worse than the pantomime.

ESTRAGON The circus.

VLADIMIR The music-hall.

ESTRAGON The circus.

POZZO What can I have done with that briar?[1]

ESTRAGON He's a scream. He's lost his dudeen.[2] [*Laughs noisily.*]

VLADIMIR I'll be back. [*He hastens towards the wings.*]

ESTRAGON End of the corridor, on the left.

VLADIMIR Keep my seat. [*Exit* VLADIMIR.]

POZZO [*on the point of tears*] I've lost my Kapp and Peterson![3]

ESTRAGON [*convulsed with merriment*] He'll be the death of me!

POZZO You didn't see by any chance—. [*He misses* VLADIMIR.] Oh! He's gone! Without saying goodbye! How could he! He might have waited!

ESTRAGON He would have burst.

POZZO Oh! [*Pause*] Oh well then of course in that case . . .

ESTRAGON Come here.

POZZO What for?

ESTRAGON You'll see.

POZZO You want me to get up?

ESTRAGON Quick! [POZZO *gets up and goes over beside* ESTRAGON. ESTRAGON *points off.*] Look!

POZZO [*having put on his glasses*] Oh I say!

ESTRAGON It's all over.

1. That is, his pipe made from briar wood.
2. A short-stemmed clay tobacco pipe (Irish Gaelic).
3. A brand of pipe. Kapp and Peterson were Dublin's most renowned manufacturers and purveyors of smoking pipes and other tobacco products.

[*Enter* VLADIMIR, *somber. He shoulders* LUCKY *out of his way, kicks over the stool, comes and goes agitatedly.*]

POZZO He's not pleased.

ESTRAGON [*to* VLADIMIR] You missed a treat. Pity.

[VLADIMIR *halts, straightens the stool, comes and goes, calmer.*]

POZZO He subsides. [*Looking round*] Indeed all subsides. A great calm descends. [*Raising his hand*] Listen! Pan sleeps.[4]

VLADIMIR Will night never come?

[*All three look at the sky.*]

POZZO You don't feel like going until it does?

ESTRAGON Well you see—

POZZO Why it's very natural, very natural. I myself in your situation, if I had an appointment with a Godin . . . Godet . . . Godot . . . anyhow you see who I mean, I'd wait till it was black night before I gave up. [*He looks at the stool.*] I'd very much like to sit down, but I don't quite know how to go about it.

ESTRAGON Could I be of any help?

POZZO If you asked me perhaps.

ESTRAGON What?

POZZO If you asked me to sit down.

ESTRAGON Would that be a help?

POZZO I fancy so.

ESTRAGON Here we go. Be seated, Sir, I beg of you.

POZZO No no, I wouldn't think of it! [*Pause. Aside.*] Ask me again.

ESTRAGON Come come, take a seat I beseech you, you'll get pneumonia.

POZZO You really think so?

ESTRAGON Why it's absolutely certain.

POZZO No doubt you are right. [*He sits down.*] Done it again! [*Pause*] Thank you, dear fellow. [*He consults his watch.*] But I must really be getting along, if I am to observe my schedule.

VLADIMIR Time has stopped.

POZZO [*cuddling his watch to his ear*] Don't you believe it, Sir, don't you believe it. [*He puts his watch back in his pocket.*] Whatever you like, but not that.

ESTRAGON [*to* POZZO] Everything seems black to him today.

POZZO Except the firmament. [*He laughs, pleased with this witticism.*] But I see what it is, you are not from these parts, you don't know what our twilights can do. Shall I tell you? [*Silence.* ESTRAGON *is fiddling with his boot again,* VLADIMIR *with his hat.*] I can't refuse you. [*Vaporizer*] A little attention, if you please. [VLADIMIR *and* ESTRAGON *continue their fiddling,* LUCKY *is half asleep.* POZZO *cracks his whip feebly.*] What's the matter with this whip? [*He gets up and cracks it more vigorously, finally with success.* LUCKY *jumps.* VLADIMIR*'s hat,* ESTRAGON*'s boot,* LUCKY*'s hat, fall to the ground.* POZZO *throws down the whip.*] Worn out, this whip. [*He looks at* VLADIMIR *and* ESTRAGON.] What was I saying?

VLADIMIR Let's go.

4. Pan, the Greek god of pastures, flocks, and wild places, was said to sleep at noon; to accommodate him, all of nature fell quiet.

ESTRAGON But take the weight off your feet, I implore you, you'll catch your death.

POZZO True. [*He sits down. To* ESTRAGON.] What is your name?

ESTRAGON Adam.

POZZO [*who hasn't listened*] Ah yes! The night. [*He raises his head.*] But be a little more attentive, for pity's sake, otherwise we'll never get anywhere. [*He looks at the sky.*] Look! [*All look at the sky except* LUCKY *who is dozing off again.* POZZO *jerks the rope.*] Will you look at the sky, pig! [LUCKY *looks at the sky.*] Good, that's enough. [*They stop looking at the sky.*] What is there so extraordinary about it? Qua[5] sky. It is pale and luminous like any sky at this hour of the day. [*Pause*] In these latitudes. [*Pause*] When the weather is fine. [*Lyrical*] An hour ago [*He looks at his watch, prosaic.*] roughly [*Lyrical*] after having poured forth even since [*He hesitates, prosaic.*] say ten o'clock in the morning [*Lyrical*] tirelessly torrents of red and white light it begins to lose its effulgence, to grow pale [*Gesture of the two hands lapsing by stages*] pale, ever a little paler, a little paler until [*Dramatic pause, ample gesture of the two hands flung wide apart*] pppfff! finished! it comes to rest. But—[*Hand raised in admonition*]—but behind this veil of gentleness and peace night is charging [*Vibrantly*] and will burst upon us [*Snaps his fingers.*] pop! like that! [*His inspiration leaves him.*] just when we least expect it. [*Silence. Gloomily.*] That's how it is on this bitch of an earth.

[*Long silence.*]

ESTRAGON So long as one knows.

VLADIMIR One can bide one's time.

ESTRAGON One knows what to expect.

VLADIMIR No further need to worry.

ESTRAGON Simply wait.

VLADIMIR We're used to it. [*He picks up his hat, peers inside it, shakes it, puts it on.*]

POZZO How did you find me? [VLADIMIR *and* ESTRAGON *look at him blankly.*] Good? Fair? Middling? Poor? Positively bad?

VLADIMIR [*first to understand*] Oh very good, very very good.

POZZO [*to* ESTRAGON] And you, Sir?

ESTRAGON Oh tray bong, tray tray tray bong.[6]

POZZO [*fervently*] Bless you, gentlemen, bless you! [*Pause*] I have such need of encouragement! [*Pause*] I weakened a little towards the end, you didn't notice?

VLADIMIR Oh perhaps just a teeny weeny little bit.

ESTRAGON I thought it was intentional.

POZZO You see my memory is defective.

[*Silence.*]

ESTRAGON In the meantime nothing happens.

POZZO You find it tedious?

ESTRAGON Somewhat.

POZZO [*to* VLADIMIR] And you, Sir?

5. As (a term common in philosophical discourse).
6. "Oui! Tray bong!" (which plays on the French phrase *oui très bon*—"yes, very good") was the title of a late 19th-century song made popular in English music halls by Charles Chaplin Sr., father of the famous film actor.

VLADIMIR I've been better entertained.

[*Silence.* POZZO *struggles inwardly.*]

POZZO Gentlemen, you have been . . . civil to me.

ESTRAGON Not at all!

VLADIMIR What an idea!

POZZO Yes yes, you have been correct. So that I ask myself is there anything I can do in my turn for these honest fellows who are having such a dull, dull time.

ESTRAGON Even ten francs would be a help.

VLADIMIR We are not beggars!

POZZO Is there anything I can do, that's what I ask myself, to cheer them up? I have given them bones, I have talked to them about this and that, I have explained the twilight, admittedly. But is it enough, that's what tortures me, is it enough?

ESTRAGON Even five.

VLADIMIR [*to* ESTRAGON, *indignantly*] That's enough!

ESTRAGON I couldn't accept less.

POZZO Is it enough? No doubt. But I am liberal. It's my nature. This evening. So much the worse for me. [*He jerks the rope.* LUCKY *looks at him.*] For I shall suffer, no doubt about that. [*He picks up the whip.*] What do you prefer? Shall we have him dance, or sing, or recite, or think, or—

ESTRAGON Who?

POZZO Who! You know how to think, you two?

VLADIMIR He thinks?

POZZO Certainly. Aloud. He even used to think very prettily once, I could listen to him for hours. Now . . . [*He shudders.*] So much the worse for me. Well, would you like him to think something for us?

ESTRAGON I'd rather he'd dance, it'd be more fun.

POZZO Not necessarily.

ESTRAGON Wouldn't it, Didi, be more fun?

VLADIMIR I'd like well to hear him think.

ESTRAGON Perhaps he could dance first and think afterwards, if it isn't too much to ask him.

VLADIMIR [*to* POZZO] Would that be possible?

POZZO By all means, nothing simpler. It's the natural order. [*He laughs briefly.*]

VLADIMIR Then let him dance.

[*Silence.*]

POZZO Do you hear, hog?

ESTRAGON He never refuses?

POZZO He refused once. [*Silence*] Dance, misery!

[LUCKY *puts down bag and basket, advances towards front, turns to* POZZO. LUCKY *dances. He stops.*]

ESTRAGON Is that all?

POZZO Encore!

[LUCKY *executes the same movements, stops.*]

ESTRAGON Pooh! I'd do as well myself. [*He imitates* LUCKY, *almost falls.*] With a little practice.

POZZO He used to dance the farandole, the fling, the brawl, the jig, the fandango and even the hornpipe.[7] He capered. For joy. Now that's the best he can do. Do you know what he calls it?

ESTRAGON The Scapegoat's Agony.

VLADIMIR The Hard Stool.

POZZO The Net. He thinks he's entangled in a net.

VLADIMIR [*squirming like an aesthete*] There's something about it . . .

[LUCKY *makes to return to his burdens.*]

POZZO Woaa!

[LUCKY *stiffens.*]

ESTRAGON Tell us about the time he refused.

POZZO With pleasure, with pleasure. [*He fumbles in his pockets.*] Wait. [*He fumbles.*] What have I done with my spray? [*He fumbles.*] Well now isn't that . . . [*He looks up, consternation on his features. Faintly.*] I can't find my pulverizer![8]

ESTRAGON [*faintly*] My left lung is very weak! [*He coughs feebly. In ringing tones.*] But my right lung is as sound as a bell!

POZZO [*normal voice*] No matter! What was I saying. [*He ponders.*] Wait. [*Ponders.*] Well now isn't that . . . [*He raises his head.*] Help me!

ESTRAGON Wait!

VLADIMIR Wait!

POZZO Wait!

[*All three take off their hats simultaneously, press their hands to their foreheads, concentrate.*]

ESTRAGON [*triumphantly*] Ah!

VLADIMIR He has it.

POZZO [*impatient*] Well?

ESTRAGON Why doesn't he put down his bags?

VLADIMIR Rubbish!

POZZO Are you sure?

VLADIMIR Damn it haven't you already told us?

POZZO I've already told you?

ESTRAGON He's already told us?

VLADIMIR Anyway he has put them down.

ESTRAGON [*glance at Lucky*] So he has. And what of it?

VLADIMIR Since he has put down his bags it is impossible we should have asked why he does not do so.

POZZO Stoutly reasoned!

ESTRAGON And why has he put them down?

POZZO Answer us that.

VLADIMIR In order to dance.

ESTRAGON True!

POZZO True!

[*Silence. They put on their hats.*]

ESTRAGON Nothing happens, nobody comes, nobody goes, it's awful!

VLADIMIR [*to* POZZO] Tell him to think.

7. All energetic dances, associated (respectively) with Provence, the Scottish highlands, France, Ireland, Spain, and England.

8. That is, his vaporizer, mentioned earlier.

POZZO Give him his hat.

VLADIMIR His hat?

POZZO He can't think without his hat.

VLADIMIR [*to* ESTRAGON] Give him his hat.

ESTRAGON Me! After what he did to me! Never!

VLADIMIR I'll give it to him. [*He does not move.*]

ESTRAGON [*to* POZZO] Tell him to go and fetch it.

POZZO It's better to give it to him.

VLADIMIR I'll give it to him.

[*He picks up the hat and tenders it at arm's length to* LUCKY, *who does not move.*]

POZZO You must put it on his head.

ESTRAGON [*to* POZZO] Tell him to take it.

POZZO It's better to put it on his head.

VLADIMIR I'll put it on his head.

[*He goes round behind* LUCKY, *approaches him cautiously, puts the hat on his head and recoils smartly.* LUCKY *does not move. Silence.*]

ESTRAGON What's he waiting for?

POZZO Stand back! [VLADIMIR *and* ESTRAGON *move away from* LUCKY. POZZO *jerks the rope.* LUCKY *looks at* POZZO.] Think, pig! [*Pause.* LUCKY *begins to dance.*] Stop! [LUCKY *stops.*] Forward! [LUCKY *advances.*] Stop! [LUCKY *stops.*] Think!

[*Silence.*]

LUCKY On the other hand with regard to—

POZZO Stop! [LUCKY *stops.*] Back! [LUCKY *moves back.*] Stop! [LUCKY *stops.*] Turn! [LUCKY *turns towards auditorium.*] Think!

LUCKY Given the existence as uttered forth in the public works of Puncher and Wattmann[9] of a personal God quaquaquaqua with white beard quaquaquaqua outside time without extension who from the heights of divine apathia divine athambia divine aphasia[1] loves us dearly with some exceptions for reasons unknown but time will tell and suffers like the divine Miranda[2] with those who for reasons unknown but time will tell are plunged in torment plunged in fire whose fire flames if that continues and who can doubt it will fire the firmament that is to say blast hell to heaven so blue still and calm so calm with a calm which even though intermittent is better than nothing but not so fast and considering what is more that as a result of the labors left unfinished crowned by the Acacacacademy of Anthropopopometry of Essy-in-Possy[3] of

[VLADIMIR *and* ESTRAGON *all attention,* POZZO *dejected and*

9. Fictitious academics, as are "Testew and Cunard," "Fartov and Belcher," "Steinweg and Peterman," and so on, below. Mixing quasi-philosophical discourse, arcane language, and sexual/scatological wordplay, this speech uses invented and altered proper names, technical terms, and allusions to create half-meanings amid apparent nonsense.

1. Of the three Greek words employed here—*apatheia* (freedom from emotion), *athambia* (freedom from fear or surprise), and *aphasia* (lack or loss of speech)—only the last is actually used in English.

2. The character in William Shakespeare's *The Tempest* (1611) who agonizes over a shipwreck she has witnessed: "O, I have sufferèd / With those that I saw suffer!" (1.2.5–6).

3. An echo of the Latin verbs *esse* (to be) and *posse* (to be able to). *Acacacacademy:* in several Romance languages, including French, *caca* is a child's word for excrement. *Anthropopopometry:* that is, anthropometry (the study of measurement of the human body).

disgusted.]

Testew and Cunard it is established beyond all doubt all other doubt than that which clings to the labors of men that as a

[VLADIMIR *and* ESTRAGON *begin to protest,* POZZO*'s sufferings increase.*]

result of the labors unfinished of Testew and Cunard it is established as hereinafter but not so fast for reasons unknown that as a result of the public works of Puncher and Wattmann it is established beyond all doubt that in view of the labors of Fartov and Belcher left unfinished for reasons unknown of Testew and Cunard left unfinished it is established what many deny that man in Possy of Testew and Cunard that man in Essy that man in short that man in brief in spite of the strides of alimentation and defecation wastes and pines wastes and pines

[VLADIMIR *and* ESTRAGON *attentive again,* POZZO *more and more agitated and groaning.*]

and concurrently simultaneously what is more for reasons unknown in spite of the strides of physical culture the practice of sports such as tennis football running cycling swimming flying floating riding gliding conating camogie[4] skating tennis of all kinds dying flying sports of all sorts autumn summer winter winter tennis of all kinds hockey of all sorts penicillin and succedanea[5] in a word I resume flying gliding golf over nine and eighteen holes tennis of all sorts in a word for reasons unknown in Feckham Peckham Fulham Clapham[6] namely concurrently simultaneously what is more for reasons unknown but time will tell fades away I resume Fulham Clapham in a word the dead loss per head since the death of Bishop Berkeley[7] being to the tune of one inch four ounce per head approximately by and large more or less to the nearest decimal

[VLADIMIR *and* ESTRAGON *protest violently.* POZZO *jumps up, pulls on the rope. General outcry.* LUCKY *pulls on the rope, staggers, shouts his text. All three throw themselves*

good measure round figures stark naked in the stockinged feet in Connemara[8] in a word for reasons unknown no matter what matter the facts are there and considering what is more much more grave that in the light of the labors lost of Steinweg and Peterman it appears what is more much more grave that in the light the light the light of the labors lost of Steinweg and Peterman that in the plains in the mountains by the seas by the rivers running water running fire the air is the same and then the earth namely the air and then the earth in the great cold the great dark the air and the earth abode of stones in the great cold alas alas in the year of their Lord six hundred and something the air the earth the sea the earth abode of stones in the great deeps the great cold on sea on land and in the air I resume for reasons unknown in spite of the tennis the facts are there but time will tell I resume alas alas on on in short in fine on on abode of stones who can doubt it I resume but not so fast I resume the skull fading fading fading and concurrently simultaneously what is more for reasons

4. A Celtic team sport played with sticks and a ball (the women's version of hurling). *Conating:* desiring, attempting (Beckett's back-formation from *conation*).
5. Substitutes.
6. Three areas of south London, preceded by an obscene pun on them.
7. George Berkeley (1685–1753), Irish idealist philosopher and bishop in the Church of Ireland. Berkeley's theory, which held that the world exists only insofar as it is perceived by the senses, is summed up in his Latin dictum *Esse est percipi* (To be is to be perceived).
8. A region of Galway in western Ireland.

on LUCKY *who struggles and shouts his text.*]

unknown in spite of the tennis on on the beard the flames the tears the stones so blue so calm alas alas on on the skull the skull the skull the skull in Connemara in spite of the tennis the labors abandoned left unfinished graver still abode of stones in a word I resume alas alas abandoned unfinished the skull the skull in Connemara in spite of the tennis the skull alas the stones Cunard [*Mêlée, final vociferations*] tennis . . . the stones . . . so calm . . . Cunard . . . unfinished . . .

POZZO His hat!

[VLADIMIR *seizes* LUCKY*'s hat. Silence of* LUCKY. *He falls. Silence. Panting of the victors.*]

ESTRAGON Avenged!

[VLADIMIR *examines the hat, peers inside it.*]

POZZO Give me that! [*He snatches the hat from* VLADIMIR, *throws it on the ground, tramples on it.*] There's an end to his thinking!

VLADIMIR But will he be able to walk?

POZZO Walk or crawl! [*He kicks* LUCKY.] Up pig!

ESTRAGON Perhaps he's dead.

VLADIMIR You'll kill him.

POZZO Up scum! [*He jerks the rope.*] Help me!

VLADIMIR How?

POZZO Raise him up!

[VLADIMIR *and* ESTRAGON *hoist* LUCKY *to his feet, support him an instant, then let him go. He falls.*]

ESTRAGON He's doing it on purpose!

POZZO You must hold him. [*Pause*] Come on, come on, raise him up.

ESTRAGON To hell with him!

VLADIMIR Come on, once more.

ESTRAGON What does he take us for?

[*They raise* LUCKY, *hold him up.*]

POZZO Don't let him go! [VLADIMIR *and* ESTRAGON *totter.*] Don't move! [POZZO *fetches bag and basket and brings them towards* LUCKY.] Hold him tight! [*He puts the bag in* LUCKY*'s hand.* LUCKY *drops it immediately.*] Don't let him go! [*He puts back the bag in* LUCKY*'s hand. Gradually, at the feel of the bag,* LUCKY *recovers his senses and his fingers finally close round the handle.*] Hold him tight! [*As before with basket*] Now! You can let him go. [VLADIMIR *and* ESTRAGON *move away from* LUCKY *who totters, reels, sags, but succeeds in remaining on his feet, bag and basket in his hands.* POZZO *steps back, cracks his whip.*] Forward! [LUCKY *totters forward.*] Back! [LUCKY *totters back.*] Turn! [LUCKY *turns.*] Done it! He can walk. [*Turning to* VLADIMIR *and* ESTRAGON] Thank you, gentlemen, and let me . . . [*He fumbles in his pockets*] . . . let me wish you . . . [*Fumbles.*] . . . wish you . . . [*Fumbles.*] . . . what have I done with my watch? [*Fumbles.*] A genuine half-hunter, gentlemen, with deadbeat escapement![9] [*Sobbing.*] Twas my granpa gave it to me! [*He searches on the ground,* VLADIMIR *and* ESTRAGON *likewise.* POZZO *turns over with his foot the remains of* LUCKY*'s hat.*] Well now isn't that just—

9. The mechanism in watches that regulates the movement of the hands, here "deadbeat" because it does not recoil. *Half-hunter:* a kind of pocket watch featuring a metal case with a small glass window through which the hands are visible.

VLADIMIR Perhaps it's in your fob.[1]

POZZO Wait! [*He doubles up in an attempt to apply his ear to his stomach, listens. Silence.*] I hear nothing. [*He beckons them to approach.* VLADIMIR *and* ESTRAGON *go over to him, bend over his stomach.*] Surely one should hear the tick-tick.

VLADIMIR Silence!

[*All listen, bent double.*]

ESTRAGON I hear something.

POZZO Where?

VLADIMIR It's the heart.

POZZO [*disappointed*] Damnation!

VLADIMIR Silence!

ESTRAGON Perhaps it has stopped.

[*They straighten up.*]

POZZO Which of you smells so bad?

ESTRAGON He has stinking breath and I have stinking feet.

POZZO I must go.

ESTRAGON And your half-hunter?

POZZO I must have left it at the manor.

[*Silence.*]

ESTRAGON Then adieu.

POZZO Adieu.

VLADIMIR Adieu.

POZZO Adieu.

[*Silence. No one moves.*]

VLADIMIR Adieu.

POZZO Adieu.

ESTRAGON Adieu.

[*Silence.*]

POZZO And thank you.

VLADIMIR Thank *you.*

POZZO Not at all.

ESTRAGON Yes yes.

POZZO No no.

VLADIMIR Yes yes.

ESTRAGON No no.

[*Silence.*]

POZZO I don't seem to be able . . . [*Long hesitation*] . . . to depart.

ESTRAGON Such is life.

[POZZO *turns, moves away from* LUCKY *towards the wings, paying out the rope as he goes.*]

VLADIMIR You're going the wrong way.

POZZO I need a running start. [*Having come to the end of the rope, i.e. off stage, he stops, turns and cries.*] Stand back! [VLADIMIR *and* ESTRAGON *stand back, look towards* POZZO. *Crack of whip.*] On! On!

1. A small pocket, originally in the waistband (also known as a "watch pocket").

ESTRAGON On!

VLADIMIR On!

[LUCKY *moves off.*]

POZZO Faster! [*He appears, crosses the stage preceded by* LUCKY. VLADIMIR *and* ESTRAGON *wave their hats. Exit* LUCKY.] On! On! [*On the point of disappearing in his turn he stops and turns. The rope tautens. Noise of* LUCKY *falling off.*] Stool! [VLADIMIR *fetches stool and gives it to* POZZO *who throws it to* LUCKY.] Adieu!

VLADIMIR }
ESTRAGON } [*waving*] Adieu! Adieu!

POZZO Up! Pig! [*Noise of* LUCKY *getting up.*] On! [*Exit* POZZO.] Faster! On! Adieu! Pig! Yip! Adieu!

[*Long silence.*]

VLADIMIR That passed the time.

ESTRAGON It would have passed in any case.

VLADIMIR Yes, but not so rapidly.

[*Pause.*]

ESTRAGON What do we do now?

VLADIMIR I don't know.

ESTRAGON Let's go.

VLADIMIR We can't.

ESTRAGON Why not?

VLADIMIR We're waiting for Godot.

ESTRAGON [*despairingly*] Ah!

[*Pause.*]

VLADIMIR How they've changed!

ESTRAGON Who?

VLADIMIR Those two.

ESTRAGON That's the idea, let's make a little conversation.

VLADIMIR Haven't they?

ESTRAGON What?

VLADIMIR Changed.

ESTRAGON Very likely. They all change. Only we can't.

VLADIMIR Likely! It's certain. Didn't you see them?

ESTRAGON I suppose I did. But I don't know them.

VLADIMIR Yes you do know them.

ESTRAGON No I don't know them.

VLADIMIR We know them, I tell you. You forget everything. [*Pause. To himself.*] Unless they're not the same . . .

ESTRAGON Why didn't they recognize us then?

VLADIMIR That means nothing. I too pretended not to recognize them. And then nobody ever recognizes us.

ESTRAGON Forget it. What we need—ow! [VLADIMIR *does not react.*] Ow!

VLADIMIR [*to himself*] Unless they're not the same . . .

ESTRAGON Didi! It's the other foot! [*He goes hobbling towards the mound.*]

VLADIMIR Unless they're not the same . . .

BOY [*off*] Mister!

[ESTRAGON *halts. Both look towards the voice.*]

ESTRAGON Off we go again.

VLADIMIR Approach, my child.

[*Enter* BOY, *timidly. He halts.*]

BOY Mister Albert . . . ?

VLADIMIR Yes.

ESTRAGON What do you want?

VLADIMIR Approach!

[*The* BOY *does not move.*]

ESTRAGON [*forcibly*] Approach when you're told, can't you?

[*The* BOY *advances timidly, halts.*]

VLADIMIR What is it?

BOY Mr. Godot . . .

VLADIMIR Obviously . . . [*Pause*] Approach.

ESTRAGON [*violently*] Will you approach! [*The* BOY *advances timidly.*] What kept you so late?

VLADIMIR You have a message from Mr. Godot?

BOY Yes Sir.

VLADIMIR Well, what is it?

ESTRAGON What kept you so late?

[*The* BOY *looks at them in turn, not knowing to which he should reply.*]

VLADIMIR [*to* ESTRAGON] Let him alone.

ESTRAGON [*violently*] You let me alone. [*Advancing, to the* BOY] Do you know what time it is?

BOY [*recoiling*] It's not my fault, Sir.

ESTRAGON And whose is it? Mine?

BOY I was afraid, Sir.

ESTRAGON Afraid of what? Of us? [*Pause*] Answer me!

VLADIMIR I know what it is, he was afraid of the others.

ESTRAGON How long have you been here?

BOY A good while, Sir.

VLADIMIR You were afraid of the whip?

BOY Yes Sir.

VLADIMIR The roars?

BOY Yes Sir.

VLADIMIR The two big men.

BOY Yes Sir.

VLADIMIR Do you know them?

BOY No Sir.

VLADIMIR Are you a native of these parts? [*Silence*] Do you belong to these parts?

BOY Yes Sir.

ESTRAGON That's all a pack of lies. [*Shaking the* BOY *by the arm*] Tell us the truth!

BOY [*trembling*] But it is the truth, Sir!

VLADIMIR Will you let him alone! What's the matter with you? [ESTRAGON *releases the* BOY, *moves away, covering his face with his hands.* VLADIMIR *and the* BOY *observe him.* ESTRAGON *drops his hands. His face is convulsed.*] What's the matter with you?

ESTRAGON I'm unhappy.

VLADIMIR Not really! Since when?

ESTRAGON I'd forgotten.

VLADIMIR Extraordinary the tricks that memory plays!

[ESTRAGON *tries to speak, renounces, limps to his place, sits down and begins to take off his boots. To* BOY]

Well?

BOY Mr. Godot—

VLADIMIR I've seen you before, haven't I?

BOY I don't know, Sir.

VLADIMIR You don't know me?

BOY No Sir.

VLADIMIR It wasn't you came yesterday?

BOY No Sir.

VLADIMIR This is your first time?

BOY Yes Sir.

[*Silence.*]

VLADIMIR Words words. [*Pause*] Speak.

BOY [*in a rush*] Mr. Godot told me to tell you he won't come this evening but surely tomorrow.

[*Silence.*]

VLADIMIR Is that all?

BOY Yes Sir.

[*Silence.*]

VLADIMIR You work for Mr. Godot?

BOY Yes Sir.

VLADIMIR What do you do?

BOY I mind the goats, Sir.

VLADIMIR Is he good to you?

BOY Yes Sir.

VLADIMIR He doesn't beat you?

BOY No Sir, not me.

VLADIMIR Whom does he beat?

BOY He beats my brother, Sir.

VLADIMIR Ah, you have a brother?

BOY Yes Sir.

VLADIMIR What does he do?

BOY He minds the sheep, Sir.

VLADIMIR And why doesn't he beat you?

BOY I don't know, Sir.

VLADIMIR He must be fond of you.

BOY I don't know, Sir.

[*Silence.*]

VLADIMIR Does he give you enough to eat? [*The* BOY *hesitates.*] Does he feed you well?

BOY Fairly well, Sir.

VLADIMIR You're not unhappy? [*The* BOY *hesitates.*] Do you hear me?

BOY Yes Sir.

VLADIMIR Well?

BOY I don't know, Sir.

VLADIMIR You don't know if you're unhappy or not?

BOY No Sir.

VLADIMIR You're as bad as myself. [*Silence*] Where do you sleep?

BOY In the loft, Sir.

VLADIMIR With your brother?

BOY Yes Sir.

VLADIMIR In the hay?

BOY Yes Sir.

[*Silence.*]

VLADIMIR All right, you may go.

BOY What am I to tell Mr. Godot, Sir?

VLADIMIR Tell him . . . [*He hesitates.*] . . . tell him you saw us. [*Pause*] You did see us, didn't you?

BOY Yes Sir.

[*He steps back, hesitates, turns and exits running. The light suddenly fails. In a moment it is night. The moon rises at back, mounts in the sky, stands still, shedding a pale light on the scene.*]

VLADIMIR At last! [ESTRAGON *gets up and goes towards* VLADIMIR, *a boot in each hand. He puts them down at edge of stage, straightens and contemplates the moon.*] What are you doing?

ESTRAGON Pale for weariness.

VLADIMIR Eh?

ESTRAGON Of climbing heaven and gazing on the likes of us.

VLADIMIR Your boots, what are you doing with your boots?

ESTRAGON [*turning to look at the boots*] I'm leaving them there. [*Pause*] Another will come, just as . . . as . . . as me, but with smaller feet, and they'll make him happy.

VLADIMIR But you can't go barefoot!

ESTRAGON Christ did.

VLADIMIR Christ! What has Christ got to do with it? You're not going to compare yourself to Christ!

ESTRAGON All my life I've compared myself to him.

VLADIMIR But where he lived it was warm, it was dry!

ESTRAGON Yes. And they crucified quick.

[*Silence.*]

VLADIMIR We've nothing more to do here.

ESTRAGON Nor anywhere else.

VLADIMIR Ah Gogo, don't go on like that. Tomorrow everything will be better.

ESTRAGON How do you make that out?

VLADIMIR Did you not hear what the child said?

ESTRAGON No.

VLADIMIR He said that Godot was sure to come tomorrow. [*Pause*] What do you say to that?

ESTRAGON Then all we have to do is to wait on here.

VLADIMIR Are you mad? We must take cover. [*He takes* ESTRAGON *by the arm.*] Come on.

[*He draws* ESTRAGON *after him.* ESTRAGON *yields, then resists. They halt.*]

ESTRAGON [*looking at the tree*] Pity we haven't got a bit of rope.

VLADIMIR Come on. It's cold.

[*He draws* ESTRAGON *after him. As before.*]

ESTRAGON Remind me to bring a bit of rope tomorrow.

VLADIMIR Yes. Come on.

[*He draws him after him. As before.*]

ESTRAGON How long have we been together all the time now?

VLADIMIR I don't know. Fifty years maybe.

ESTRAGON Do you remember the day I threw myself into the Rhône?[2]

VLADIMIR We were grape harvesting.

ESTRAGON You fished me out.

VLADIMIR That's all dead and buried.

ESTRAGON My clothes dried in the sun.

VLADIMIR There's no good harking back on that. Come on.

[*He draws him after him. As before.*]

ESTRAGON Wait!

VLADIMIR I'm cold!

ESTRAGON Wait! [*He moves away from* VLADIMIR.] I sometimes wonder if we wouldn't have been better off alone, each one for himself. [*He crosses the stage and sits down on the mound.*] We weren't made for the same road.

VLADIMIR [*without anger*] It's not certain.

ESTRAGON No, nothing is certain.

[VLADIMIR *slowly crosses the stage and sits down beside* ESTRAGON.]

VLADIMIR We can still part, if you think it would be better.

ESTRAGON It's not worthwhile now.

[*Silence.*]

VLADIMIR No, it's not worthwhile now.

[*Silence.*]

ESTRAGON Well, shall we go?

VLADIMIR Yes, let's go.

[*They do not move.*]

Curtain.

Act 2

Next day. Same time.
Same place.

[ESTRAGON'*s boots front center, heels together, toes splayed.* LUCKY'*s hat at same place.*]

[*The tree has four or five leaves.*]

[*Enter* VLADIMIR *agitatedly. He halts and looks long at the tree, then suddenly begins to move feverishly about the stage. He halts before the boots, picks one up, examines it, sniffs it, manifests disgust, puts it back carefully. Comes and goes. Halts extreme right and gazes into distance off, shading his eyes with his hand. Comes and goes. Halts extreme left, as before. Comes and goes. Halts suddenly and begins to sing loudly.*]

VLADIMIR A dog came in—

2. A major river in southeastern France.

[*Having begun too high he stops, clears his throat, resumes.*]

A dog came in the kitchen
And stole a crust of bread.
Then cook up with a ladle
And beat him till he was dead.

Then all the dogs came running
And dug the dog a tomb—

[*He stops, broods, resumes.*]

Then all the dogs came running
And dug the dog a tomb
And wrote upon the tombstone
For the eyes of dogs to come:

A dog came in the kitchen
And stole a crust of bread.
Then cook up with a ladle
And beat him till he was dead.

Then all the dogs came running
And dug the dog a tomb—

[*He stops, broods, resumes.*]

Then all the dogs came running
And dug the dog a tomb—

[*He stops, broods. Softly.*]

And dug the dog a tomb . . .

[*He remains a moment silent and motionless, then begins to move feverishly about the stage. He halts before the tree, comes and goes, before the boots, comes and goes, halts extreme right, gazes into distance, extreme left, gazes into distance. Enter* ESTRAGON *right, barefoot, head bowed. He slowly crosses the stage.* VLADIMIR *turns and sees him.*]

VLADIMIR You again! [ESTRAGON *halts but does not raise his head.* VLADIMIR *goes towards him.*] Come here till I embrace you.

ESTRAGON Don't touch me!

[VLADIMIR *holds back, pained.*]

VLADIMIR Do you want me to go away? [*Pause*] Gogo! [*Pause.* VLADIMIR *observes him attentively.*] Did they beat you? [*Pause*] Gogo! [ESTRAGON *remains silent, head bowed.*] Where did you spend the night?

ESTRAGON Don't touch me! Don't question me! Don't speak to me! Stay with me!

VLADIMIR Did I ever leave you?

ESTRAGON You let me go.

VLADIMIR Look at me. [ESTRAGON *does not raise his head. Violently.*] Will you look at me!

[ESTRAGON *raises his head. They look long at each other, then suddenly embrace, clapping each other on the back. End of the embrace.* ESTRAGON, *no longer supported, almost falls.*]

ESTRAGON What a day!

VLADIMIR Who beat you? Tell me.

ESTRAGON Another day done with.

VLADIMIR Not yet.

ESTRAGON For me it's over and done with, no matter what happens. [*Silence*] I heard you singing.

VLADIMIR That's right, I remember.

ESTRAGON That finished me. I said to myself, He's all alone, he thinks I'm gone for ever, and he sings.

VLADIMIR One is not master of one's moods. All day I've felt in great form. [*Pause*] I didn't get up in the night, not once!

ESTRAGON [*sadly*] You see, you piss better when I'm not there.

VLADIMIR I missed you . . . and at the same time I was happy. Isn't that a queer thing?

ESTRAGON [*shocked*] Happy?

VLADIMIR Perhaps it's not quite the right word.

ESTRAGON And now?

VLADIMIR Now? . . . [*Joyous*] There you are again . . . [*Indifferent*] There we are again . . . [*Gloomy*] There I am again.

ESTRAGON You see, you feel worse when I'm with you. I feel better alone too.

VLADIMIR [*vexed*] Then why do you always come crawling back?

ESTRAGON I don't know.

VLADIMIR No, but I do. It's because you don't know how to defend yourself. I wouldn't have let them beat you.

ESTRAGON You couldn't have stopped them.

VLADIMIR Why not?

ESTRAGON There was ten of them.

VLADIMIR No, I mean before they beat you. I would have stopped you from doing whatever it was you were doing.

ESTRAGON I wasn't doing anything.

VLADIMIR Then why did they beat you?

ESTRAGON I don't know.

VLADIMIR Ah no, Gogo, the truth is there are things escape you that don't escape me, you must feel it yourself.

ESTRAGON I tell you I wasn't doing anything.

VLADIMIR Perhaps you weren't. But it's the way of doing it that counts, the way of doing it, if you want to go on living.

ESTRAGON I wasn't doing anything.

VLADIMIR You must be happy too, deep down, if you only knew it.

ESTRAGON Happy about what?

VLADIMIR To be back with me again.

ESTRAGON Would you say so?

VLADIMIR Say you are, even if it's not true.

ESTRAGON What am I to say?

VLADIMIR Say, I am happy.

ESTRAGON I am happy.

VLADIMIR So am I.

ESTRAGON So am I.

VLADIMIR We are happy.

ESTRAGON We are happy. [*Silence*] What do we do now, now that we are happy?

VLADIMIR Wait for Godot. [ESTRAGON *groans. Silence.*] Things have changed here since yesterday.

ESTRAGON And if he doesn't come.

VLADIMIR [*after a moment of bewilderment*] We'll see when the time comes. [*Pause*] I was saying that things have changed here since yesterday.

ESTRAGON Everything oozes.

VLADIMIR Look at the tree.

ESTRAGON It's never the same pus from one second to the next.

VLADIMIR The tree, look at the tree.

[ESTRAGON *looks at the tree.*]

ESTRAGON Was it not there yesterday?

VLADIMIR Yes of course it was there. Do you not remember? We nearly hanged ourselves from it. But you wouldn't. Do you not remember?

ESTRAGON You dreamt it.

VLADIMIR Is it possible you've forgotten already?

ESTRAGON That's the way I am. Either I forget immediately or I never forget.

VLADIMIR And Pozzo and Lucky, have you forgotten them too?

ESTRAGON Pozzo and Lucky?

VLADIMIR He's forgotten everything!

ESTRAGON I remember a lunatic who kicked the shins off me. Then he played the fool.

VLADIMIR That was Lucky.

ESTRAGON I remember that. But when was it?

VLADIMIR And his keeper, do you not remember him?

ESTRAGON He gave me a bone.

VLADIMIR That was Pozzo.

ESTRAGON And all that was yesterday, you say?

VLADIMIR Yes of course it was yesterday.

ESTRAGON And here where we are now?

VLADIMIR Where else do you think? Do you not recognize the place?

ESTRAGON [*suddenly furious*] Recognize! What is there to recognize? All my lousy life I've crawled about in the mud! And you talk to me about scenery! [*Looking wildly about him*] Look at this muckheap! I've never stirred from it!

VLADIMIR Calm yourself, calm yourself.

ESTRAGON You and your landscapes! Tell me about the worms!

VLADIMIR All the same, you can't tell me that this [*Gesture*] bears any resemblance to . . . [*He hesitates.*] . . . to the Mâcon country[3] for example. You can't deny there's a big difference.

ESTRAGON The Mâcon country! Who's talking to you about the Mâcon country?

VLADIMIR But you were there yourself, in the Mâcon country.

ESTRAGON No I was never in the Mâcon country! I've puked my puke of a life away here, I tell you! Here! In the Cackon country!

VLADIMIR But we were there together, I could swear to it! Picking grapes for a man called . . . [*He snaps his fingers.*] . . . can't think of the name of the

3. A wine-producing district in the Bourgogne region of east-central France.

man, at a place called . . . [*Snaps his fingers.*] . . . can't think of the name of the place, do you not remember?

ESTRAGON [*a little calmer*] It's possible. I didn't notice anything.

VLADIMIR But down there everything is red!

ESTRAGON [*exasperated*] I didn't notice anything, I tell you!

[*Silence.* VLADIMIR *sighs deeply.*]

VLADIMIR You're a hard man to get on with, Gogo.

ESTRAGON It'd be better if we parted.

VLADIMIR You always say that and you always come crawling back.

ESTRAGON The best thing would be to kill me, like the other.

VLADIMIR What other? [*Pause*] What other?

ESTRAGON Like billions of others.

VLADIMIR [*sententious*] To every man his little cross. [*He sighs.*] Till he dies. [*Afterthought*] And is forgotten.

ESTRAGON In the meantime let us try and converse calmly, since we are incapable of keeping silent.

VLADIMIR You're right, we're inexhaustible.

ESTRAGON It's so we won't think.

VLADIMIR We have that excuse.

ESTRAGON It's so we won't hear.

VLADIMIR We have our reasons.

ESTRAGON All the dead voices.

VLADIMIR They make a noise like wings.

ESTRAGON Like leaves.

VLADIMIR Like sand.

ESTRAGON Like leaves.

[*Silence.*]

VLADIMIR They all speak at once.

ESTRAGON Each one to itself.

[*Silence.*]

VLADIMIR Rather they whisper.

ESTRAGON They rustle.

VLADIMIR They murmur.

ESTRAGON They rustle.

[*Silence.*]

VLADIMIR What do they say?

ESTRAGON They talk about their lives.

VLADIMIR To have lived is not enough for them.

ESTRAGON They have to talk about it.

VLADIMIR To be dead is not enough for them.

ESTRAGON It is not sufficient.

[*Silence.*]

VLADIMIR They make a noise like feathers.

ESTRAGON Like leaves.

VLADIMIR Like ashes.

ESTRAGON Like leaves.

[*Long silence.*]

VLADIMIR Say something!

ESTRAGON I'm trying.

[*Long silence.*]

VLADIMIR [*in anguish*] Say anything at all!

ESTRAGON What do we do now?

VLADIMIR Wait for Godot.

ESTRAGON Ah!

[*Silence.*]

VLADIMIR This is awful!

ESTRAGON Sing something.

VLADIMIR No no! [*He reflects.*] We could start all over again perhaps.

ESTRAGON That should be easy.

VLADIMIR It's the start that's difficult.

ESTRAGON You can start from anything.

VLADIMIR Yes, but you have to decide.

ESTRAGON True.

[*Silence.*]

VLADIMIR Help me!

ESTRAGON I'm trying.

[*Silence.*]

VLADIMIR When you seek you hear.

ESTRAGON You do.

VLADIMIR That prevents you from finding.

ESTRAGON It does.

VLADIMIR That prevents you from thinking.

ESTRAGON You think all the same.

VLADIMIR No no, impossible.

ESTRAGON That's the idea, let's contradict each other.

VLADIMIR Impossible.

ESTRAGON You think so?

VLADIMIR We're in no danger of ever thinking any more.

ESTRAGON Then what are we complaining about?

VLADIMIR Thinking is not the worst.

ESTRAGON Perhaps not. But at least there's that.

VLADIMIR That what?

ESTRAGON That's the idea, let's ask each other questions.

VLADIMIR What do you mean, at least there's that?

ESTRAGON That much less misery.

VLADIMIR True.

ESTRAGON Well? If we gave thanks for our mercies?

VLADIMIR What is terrible is to *have* thought.

ESTRAGON But did that ever happen to us?

VLADIMIR Where are all these corpses from?

ESTRAGON These skeletons.

VLADIMIR Tell me that.

ESTRAGON True.

VLADIMIR We must have thought a little.

ESTRAGON At the very beginning.

VLADIMIR A charnel-house! A charnel-house![4]

4. A building or vault in which the bodies or bones of the dead are placed.

ESTRAGON You don't have to look.

VLADIMIR You can't help looking.

ESTRAGON True.

VLADIMIR Try as one may.

ESTRAGON I beg your pardon?

VLADIMIR Try as one may.

ESTRAGON We should turn resolutely towards Nature.

VLADIMIR We've tried that.

ESTRAGON True.

VLADIMIR Oh it's not the worst, I know.

ESTRAGON What?

VLADIMIR To have thought.

ESTRAGON Obviously.

VLADIMIR But we could have done without it.

ESTRAGON Que voulez-vous?[5]

VLADIMIR I beg your pardon?

ESTRAGON Que voulez-vous.

VLADIMIR Ah! que voulez-vous. Exactly.

[*Silence.*]

ESTRAGON That wasn't such a bad little canter.

VLADIMIR Yes, but now we'll have to find something else.

ESTRAGON Let me see. [*He takes off his hat, concentrates.*]

VLADIMIR Let me see. [*He takes off his hat, concentrates. Long silence.*] Ah! [*They put on their hats, relax.*]

ESTRAGON Well?

VLADIMIR What was I saying, we could go on from there.

ESTRAGON What were you saying when?

VLADIMIR At the very beginning.

ESTRAGON The very beginning of WHAT?

VLADIMIR This evening . . . I was saying . . . I was saying . . .

ESTRAGON I'm not a historian.

VLADIMIR Wait . . . we embraced . . . we were happy . . . happy . . . what do we do now that we're happy . . . go on waiting . . . waiting . . . let me think . . . it's coming . . . go on waiting . . . now that we're happy . . . let me see . . . ah! The tree!

ESTRAGON The tree?

VLADIMIR Do you not remember?

ESTRAGON I'm tired.

VLADIMIR Look at it.

[*They look at the tree.*]

ESTRAGON I see nothing.

VLADIMIR But yesterday evening it was all black and bare. And now it's covered with leaves.

ESTRAGON Leaves?

VLADIMIR In a single night.

ESTRAGON It must be the Spring.

VLADIMIR But in a single night!

5. What do you want? (French).

ESTRAGON I tell you we weren't here yesterday. Another of your nightmares.

VLADIMIR And where were we yesterday evening according to you?

ESTRAGON How would I know? In another compartment. There's no lack of void.

VLADIMIR [*sure of himself*] Good. We weren't here yesterday evening. Now what did we do yesterday evening?

ESTRAGON Do?

VLADIMIR Try and remember.

ESTRAGON Do . . . I suppose we blathered.

VLADIMIR [*controlling himself*] About what?

ESTRAGON Oh . . . this and that I suppose, nothing in particular. [*With assurance*] Yes, now I remember, yesterday evening we spent blathering about nothing in particular. That's been going on now for half a century.

VLADIMIR You don't remember any fact, any circumstance?

ESTRAGON [*weary*] Don't torment me, Didi.

VLADIMIR The sun. The moon. Do you not remember?

ESTRAGON They must have been there, as usual.

VLADIMIR You didn't notice anything out of the ordinary?

ESTRAGON Alas!

VLADIMIR And Pozzo? And Lucky?

ESTRAGON Pozzo?

VLADIMIR The bones.

ESTRAGON They were like fishbones.

VLADIMIR It was Pozzo gave them to you.

ESTRAGON I don't know.

VLADIMIR And the kick.

ESTRAGON That's right, someone gave me a kick.

VLADIMIR It was Lucky gave it to you.

ESTRAGON And all that was yesterday?

VLADIMIR Show your leg.

ESTRAGON Which?

VLADIMIR Both. Pull up your trousers. [ESTRAGON *gives a leg to* VLADIMIR, *staggers.* VLADIMIR *takes the leg. They stagger.*] Pull up your trousers.

ESTRAGON I can't.

[VLADIMIR *pulls up the trousers, looks at the leg, lets it go.* ESTRAGON *almost falls.*]

VLADIMIR The other. [ESTRAGON *gives the same leg.*] The other, pig! [ESTRAGON *gives the other leg. Triumphantly.*] There's the wound! Beginning to fester!

ESTRAGON And what about it?

VLADIMIR [*letting go the leg*] Where are your boots?

ESTRAGON I must have thrown them away.

VLADIMIR When?

ESTRAGON I don't know.

VLADIMIR Why?

ESTRAGON [*exasperated*] I don't know why I don't know!

VLADIMIR No, I mean why did you throw them away?

ESTRAGON [*exasperated*] Because they were hurting me!

VLADIMIR [*triumphantly, pointing to the boots*] There they are! [ESTRAGON *looks at the boots.*] At the very spot where you left them yesterday!

[ESTRAGON *goes towards the boots, inspects them closely.*]

ESTRAGON They're not mine.

VLADIMIR [*stupefied*] Not yours!

ESTRAGON Mine were black. These are brown.

VLADIMIR You're sure yours were black?

ESTRAGON Well they were a kind of grey.

VLADIMIR And these are brown. Show.

ESTRAGON [*picking up a boot*] Well they're a kind of green.

VLADIMIR Show. [ESTRAGON *hands him the boot.* VLADIMIR *inspects it, throws it down angrily.*] Well of all the—

ESTRAGON You see, all that's a lot of bloody—

VLADIMIR Ah! I see what it is. Yes, I see what's happened.

ESTRAGON All that's a lot of bloody—

VLADIMIR It's elementary. Someone came and took yours and left you his.

ESTRAGON Why?

VLADIMIR His were too tight for him, so he took yours.

ESTRAGON But mine were too tight.

VLADIMIR For you. Not for him.

ESTRAGON [*having tried in vain to work it out*] I'm tired! [*Pause*] Let's go.

VLADIMIR We can't.

ESTRAGON Why not?

VLADIMIR We're waiting for Godot.

ESTRAGON Ah! [*Pause. Despairing*] What'll we do, what'll we do!

VLADIMIR There's nothing we can do.

ESTRAGON But I can't go on like this!

VLADIMIR Would you like a radish?

ESTRAGON Is that all there is?

VLADIMIR There are radishes and turnips.

ESTRAGON Are there no carrots?

VLADIMIR No. Anyway you overdo it with your carrots.

ESTRAGON Then give me a radish. [VLADIMIR *fumbles in his pockets, finds nothing but turnips, finally brings out a radish and hands it to* ESTRAGON *who examines it, sniffs it.*] It's black!

VLADIMIR It's a radish.

ESTRAGON I only like the pink ones, you know that!

VLADIMIR Then you don't want it?

ESTRAGON I only like the pink ones!

VLADIMIR Then give it back to me. [ESTRAGON *gives it back.*]

ESTRAGON I'll go and get a carrot. [*He does not move.*]

VLADIMIR This is becoming really insignificant.

ESTRAGON Not enough.

[*Silence.*]

VLADIMIR What about trying them.

ESTRAGON I've tried everything.

VLADIMIR No, I mean the boots.

ESTRAGON Would that be a good thing?

VLADIMIR It'd pass the time. [ESTRAGON *hesitates.*] I assure you, it'd be an occupation.

ESTRAGON A relaxation.

VLADIMIR A recreation.

ESTRAGON A relaxation.

VLADIMIR Try.

ESTRAGON You'll help me?

VLADIMIR I will of course.

ESTRAGON We don't manage too badly, eh Didi, between the two of us?

VLADIMIR Yes yes. Come on, we'll try the left first.

ESTRAGON We always find something, eh Didi, to give us the impression we exist?

VLADIMIR [*impatiently*] Yes yes, we're magicians. But let us persevere in what we have resolved, before we forget. [*He picks up a boot.*] Come on, give me your foot. [ESTRAGON *raises his foot.*] The other, hog! [ESTRAGON *raises the other foot.*] Higher! [*Wreathed together they stagger about the stage.* VLADIMIR *succeeds finally in getting on the boot.*] Try and walk. [ESTRAGON *walks.*] Well?

ESTRAGON It fits.

VLADIMIR [*taking string from his pocket*] We'll try and lace it.

ESTRAGON [*vehemently*] No no, no laces, no laces!

VLADIMIR You'll be sorry. Let's try the other. [*As before*] Well?

ESTRAGON [*grudgingly*] It fits too.

VLADIMIR They don't hurt you?

ESTRAGON Not yet.

VLADIMIR Then you can keep them.

ESTRAGON They're too big.

VLADIMIR Perhaps you'll have socks some day.

ESTRAGON True.

VLADIMIR Then you'll keep them?

ESTRAGON That's enough about these boots.

VLADIMIR Yes, but—

ESTRAGON [*violently*] Enough! [*Silence*] I suppose I might as well sit down. [*He looks for a place to sit down, then goes and sits down on the mound.*]

VLADIMIR That's where you were sitting yesterday evening.

ESTRAGON If I could only sleep.

VLADIMIR Yesterday you slept.

ESTRAGON I'll try. [*He resumes his foetal posture, his head between his knees.*]

VLADIMIR Wait. [*He goes over and sits down beside* ESTRAGON *and begins to sing in a loud voice.*]

Bye bye bye bye
Bye bye—

ESTRAGON [*looking up angrily*] Not so loud!

VLADIMIR [*softly*]

Bye bye bye bye
Bye bye bye bye
Bye bye bye bye
Bye bye . . .

[ESTRAGON *sleeps.* VLADIMIR *gets up softly, takes off his coat and lays it across* ESTRAGON*'s shoulders, then starts walking up and down, swinging* *his arms to keep himself warm.* ESTRAGON *wakes with a start, jumps up, casts about wildly.* VLADIMIR *returns to him, puts his arms round him.*]

There . . . there . . . Didi is there . . . don't be afraid . . .

ESTRAGON Ah!

VLADIMIR There . . . there . . . it's all over.

ESTRAGON I was falling—

VLADIMIR It's all over, it's all over.

ESTRAGON I was on top of a—

VLADIMIR Don't tell me! Come, we'll walk it off.

[*He takes* ESTRAGON *by the arm and walks him up and down until* ESTRAGON *refuses to go any further.*]

ESTRAGON That's enough. I'm tired.

VLADIMIR You'd rather be stuck there doing nothing?

ESTRAGON Yes.

VLADIMIR Please yourself.

[*He releases* ESTRAGON, *picks up his coat and puts it on.*]

ESTRAGON Let's go.

VLADIMIR We can't.

ESTRAGON Why not?

VLADIMIR We're waiting for Godot.

ESTRAGON Ah! [VLADIMIR *walks up and down.*] Can you not stay still?

VLADIMIR I'm cold.

ESTRAGON We came too soon.

VLADIMIR It's always at nightfall.

ESTRAGON But night doesn't fall.

VLADIMIR It'll fall all of a sudden, like yesterday.

ESTRAGON Then it'll be night.

VLADIMIR And we can go.

ESTRAGON Then it'll be day again. [*Pause. Despairing.*] What'll we do, what'll we do!

VLADIMIR [*halting, violently*] Will you stop whining! I've had about my bellyful of your lamentations!

ESTRAGON I'm going.

VLADIMIR [*seeing* LUCKY's *hat*] Well!

ESTRAGON Farewell.

VLADIMIR Lucky's hat. [*He goes towards it.*] I've been here an hour and never saw it. [*Very pleased*] Fine!

ESTRAGON You'll never see me again.

VLADIMIR I knew it was the right place. Now our troubles are over. [*He picks up the hat, contemplates it, straightens it.*] Must have been a very fine hat. [*He puts it on in place of his own which he hands to* ESTRAGON.] Here.

ESTRAGON What?

VLADIMIR Hold that.

[ESTRAGON *takes* VLADIMIR's *hat.* VLADIMIR *adjusts* LUCKY's *hat on his head.* ESTRAGON *puts on* VLADIMIR's *hat in place of his own which he hands to* VLADIMIR. VLADIMIR *takes* ESTRAGON's *hat.* ESTRAGON *adjusts* VLADIMIR's *hat on his head.* VLADIMIR *puts on* ESTRAGON's *hat in place of* LUCKY's *which he hands to* ESTRAGON. ESTRAGON *takes* LUCKY's *hat.* VLADIMIR *adjusts* ESTRAGON's *hat on his head.* ESTRAGON *puts on* LUCKY's *hat in place of* VLADIMIR*'s which he hands to* VLADIMIR. VLADIMIR *takes his hat.* ESTRAGON *adjusts* LUCKY*'s hat on his head.* VLADIMIR *puts on his hat in place of* ESTRAGON*'s which he hands to* ESTRAGON. ESTRAGON *takes his hat.* VLADIMIR *adjusts his hat on his head.* ESTRAGON *puts on his hat in place of* LUCKY*'s which he hands to* VLADIMIR. VLADIMIR *takes* LUCKY*'s hat.* ESTRAGON *adjusts his hat on his head.* VLADIMIR *puts on* LUCKY*'s hat in place of his own which he hands to* ESTRAGON. ESTRAGON *takes* VLADIMIR*'s hat.* VLADIMIR *adjusts* LUCKY*'s hat on his head.* ESTRAGON *hands* VLADIMIR*'s hat back to* VLADIMIR *who takes it and hands it back to* ESTRAGON *who takes it and hands it back to* VLADIMIR *who takes it and throws it down.*]

How does it fit me?

ESTRAGON How would I know?

VLADIMIR No, but how do I look in it? [*He turns his head coquettishly to and fro, minces like a mannequin.*]

ESTRAGON Hideous.

VLADIMIR Yes, but not more so than usual?

ESTRAGON Neither more nor less.

VLADIMIR Then I can keep it. Mine irked me. [*Pause*] How shall I say? [*Pause*] It itched me. [*He takes off* LUCKY*'s hat, peers into it, shakes it, knocks on the crown, puts it on again.*]

ESTRAGON I'm going.

[*Silence.*]

VLADIMIR Will you not play?

ESTRAGON Play at what?

VLADIMIR We could play at Pozzo and Lucky.

ESTRAGON Never heard of it.

VLADIMIR I'll do Lucky, you do Pozzo. [*He imitates* LUCKY *sagging under the weight of his baggage.* ESTRAGON *looks at him with stupefaction.*] Go on.

ESTRAGON What am I to do?

VLADIMIR Curse me!

ESTRAGON [*after reflection*] Naughty!

VLADIMIR Stronger!

ESTRAGON Gonococcus! Spirochete![6]

[VLADIMIR *sways back and forth, doubled in two.*]

VLADIMIR Tell me to think.

ESTRAGON What?

VLADIMIR Say, Think, pig!

ESTRAGON Think, pig!

[*Silence.*]

VLADIMIR I can't!

ESTRAGON That's enough of that.

VLADIMIR Tell me to dance.

ESTRAGON I'm going.

VLADIMIR Dance, hog! [*He writhes. Exit* ESTRAGON *left, precipitately.*] I can't! [*He looks up, misses* ESTRAGON.] Gogo! [*He moves wildly about the stage. Enter* ESTRAGON *left, panting. He hastens towards* VLADIMIR, *falls into his arms.*] There you are again at last!

6. Bacteria that cause venereal diseases. The gonococcus bacterium is associated with gonorrhea; the spirochete, with syphilis as well as other diseases.

ESTRAGON I'm accursed!

VLADIMIR Where were you? I thought you were gone for ever.

ESTRAGON They're coming!

VLADIMIR Who?

ESTRAGON I don't know.

VLADIMIR How many?

ESTRAGON I don't know.

VLADIMIR [*triumphantly*] It's Godot! At last! Gogo! It's Godot! We're saved! Let's go and meet him! [*He drags* ESTRAGON *towards the wings.* ESTRAGON *resists, pulls himself free, exit right.*] Gogo! Come back! [VLADIMIR *runs to extreme left, scans the horizon. Enter* ESTRAGON *right, he hastens towards* VLADIMIR, *falls into his arms.*] There you are again again!

ESTRAGON I'm in hell!

VLADIMIR Where were you?

ESTRAGON They're coming there too!

VLADIMIR We're surrounded! [ESTRAGON *makes a rush towards back.*] Imbecile! There's no way out there. [*He takes* ESTRAGON *by the arm and drags him towards front. Gesture towards front.*] There! Not a soul in sight! Off you go! Quick! [*He pushes* ESTRAGON *towards auditorium.* ESTRAGON *recoils in horror.*] You won't? [*He contemplates auditorium.*] Well I can understand that. Wait till I see. [*He reflects.*] Your only hope left is to disappear.

ESTRAGON Where?

VLADIMIR Behind the tree. [ESTRAGON *hesitates.*] Quick! Behind the tree. [ESTRAGON *goes and crouches behind the tree, realizes he is not hidden, comes out from behind the tree.*] Decidedly this tree will not have been the slightest use to us.

ESTRAGON [*calmer*] I lost my head. Forgive me. It won't happen again. Tell me what to do.

VLADIMIR There's nothing to do.

ESTRAGON You go and stand there. [*He draws* VLADIMIR *to extreme right and places him with his back to the stage.*] There, don't move, and watch out. [VLADIMIR *scans horizon, screening his eyes with his hand.* ESTRAGON *runs and takes up same position extreme left. They turn their heads and look at each other.*] Back to back like in the good old days. [*They continue to look at each other for a moment, then resume their watch. Long silence.*] Do you see anything coming?

VLADIMIR [*turning his head.*] What?

ESTRAGON [*louder*] Do you see anything coming?

VLADIMIR No.

ESTRAGON Nor I.

[*They resume their watch. Silence.*]

VLADIMIR You must have had a vision.

ESTRAGON [*turning his head*] What?

VLADIMIR [*louder*] You must have had a vision.

ESTRAGON No need to shout!

[*They resume their watch. Silence.*]

VLADIMIR } ESTRAGON } [*turning simultaneously*] Do you—

VLADIMIR Oh pardon!

ESTRAGON Carry on.

VLADIMIR No no, after you.
ESTRAGON No no, you first.
VLADIMIR I interrupted you.
ESTRAGON On the contrary.
[*They glare at each other angrily.*]
VLADIMIR Ceremonious ape!
ESTRAGON Punctilious pig!
VLADIMIR Finish your phrase, I tell you!
ESTRAGON Finish your own!
[*Silence. They draw closer, halt.*]
VLADIMIR Moron!
ESTRAGON That's the idea, let's abuse each other.
[*They turn, move apart, turn again and face each other.*]
VLADIMIR Moron!
ESTRAGON Vermin!
VLADIMIR Abortion!
ESTRAGON Morpion![7]
VLADIMIR Sewer-rat!
ESTRAGON Curate!
VLADIMIR Cretin!
ESTRAGON [*with finality*] Crritic!
VLADIMIR Oh! [*He wilts, vanquished, and turns away.*]
ESTRAGON Now let's make it up.
VLADIMIR Gogo!
ESTRAGON Didi!
VLADIMIR Your hand!
ESTRAGON Take it!
VLADIMIR Come to my arms!
ESTRAGON Your arms?
VLADIMIR My breast!
ESTRAGON Off we go!
[*They embrace. They separate. Silence.*]
VLADIMIR How time flies when one has fun!
[*Silence.*]
ESTRAGON What do we do now?
VLADIMIR While waiting.
ESTRAGON While waiting.
[*Silence.*]
VLADIMIR We could do our exercises.
ESTRAGON Our movements.
VLADIMIR Our elevations.
ESTRAGON Our relaxations.
VLADIMIR Our elongations.
ESTRAGON Our relaxations.
VLADIMIR To warm us up.
ESTRAGON To calm us down.

7. Crab louse (a French word, obsolete in English).

VLADIMIR Off we go.

[VLADIMIR *hops from one foot to the other.* ESTRAGON *imitates him.*]

ESTRAGON [*stopping*] That's enough. I'm tired.

VLADIMIR [*stopping*] We're not in form. What about a little deep breathing?

ESTRAGON I'm tired breathing.

VLADIMIR You're right. [*Pause*] Let's just do the tree, for the balance.

ESTRAGON The tree?

[VLADIMIR *does the tree, staggering about on one leg.*]

VLADIMIR [*stopping*] Your turn.

[ESTRAGON *does the tree, staggers.*]

ESTRAGON Do you think God sees me?

VLADIMIR You must close your eyes.

[ESTRAGON *closes his eyes, staggers worse.*]

ESTRAGON [*stopping, brandishing his fists, at the top of his voice*] God have pity on me!

VLADIMIR [*vexed*] And me?

ESTRAGON On me! On me! Pity! On me!

[*Enter* POZZO *and* LUCKY. POZZO *is blind.* LUCKY *burdened as before. Rope as before, but much shorter, so that* POZZO *may follow more easily.* LUCKY *wearing a different hat. At the sight of* VLADIMIR *and* ESTRAGON *he stops short.* POZZO, *continuing on his way, bumps into him.*]

VLADIMIR Gogo!

POZZO [*clutching on to* LUCKY *who staggers*] What is it? Who is it?

[LUCKY *falls, drops everything and brings down* POZZO *with him. They lie helpless among the scattered baggage.*]

ESTRAGON Is it Godot?

VLADIMIR At last! [*He goes towards the heap.*] Reinforcements at last!

POZZO Help!

ESTRAGON Is it Godot?

VLADIMIR We were beginning to weaken. Now we're sure to see the evening out.

POZZO Help!

ESTRAGON Do you hear him?

VLADIMIR We are no longer alone, waiting for the night, waiting for Godot, waiting for . . . waiting. All evening we have struggled, unassisted. Now it's over. It's already tomorrow.

POZZO Help!

VLADIMIR Time flows again already. The sun will set, the moon rise, and we away . . . from here.

POZZO Pity!

VLADIMIR Poor Pozzo!

ESTRAGON I knew it was him.

VLADIMIR Who?

ESTRAGON Godot.

VLADIMIR But it's not Godot.

ESTRAGON It's not Godot?

VLADIMIR It's not Godot.

ESTRAGON Then who is it?

VLADIMIR It's Pozzo.

POZZO Here! Here! Help me up!

VLADIMIR He can't get up.

ESTRAGON Let's go.

VLADIMIR We can't.

ESTRAGON Why not?

VLADIMIR We're waiting for Godot.

ESTRAGON Ah!

VLADIMIR Perhaps he has another bone for you.

ESTRAGON Bone?

VLADIMIR Chicken. Do you not remember?

ESTRAGON It was him?

VLADIMIR Yes.

ESTRAGON Ask him.

VLADIMIR Perhaps we should help him first.

ESTRAGON To do what?

VLADIMIR To get up.

ESTRAGON He can't get up?

VLADIMIR He wants to get up.

ESTRAGON Then let him get up.

VLADIMIR He can't.

ESTRAGON Why not?

VLADIMIR I don't know.

[POZZO *writhes, groans, beats the ground with his fists.*]

ESTRAGON We should ask him for the bone first. Then if he refuses we'll leave him there.

VLADIMIR You mean we have him at our mercy?

ESTRAGON Yes.

VLADIMIR And that we should subordinate our good offices to certain conditions?

ESTRAGON What?

VLADIMIR That seems intelligent all right. But there's one thing I'm afraid of.

POZZO Help!

ESTRAGON What?

VLADIMIR That Lucky might get going all of a sudden. Then we'd be ballocksed.[8]

ESTRAGON Lucky?

VLADIMIR The one that went for you yesterday.

ESTRAGON I tell you there was ten of them.

VLADIMIR No, before that, the one that kicked you.

ESTRAGON Is he there?

VLADIMIR As large as life. [*Gesture towards* LUCKY.] For the moment he is inert. But he might run amuck any minute.

POZZO Help!

ESTRAGON And suppose we gave him a good beating the two of us?

VLADIMIR You mean if we fell on him in his sleep?

ESTRAGON Yes.

8. Ruined, screwed (slang).

VLADIMIR That seems a good idea all right. But could we do it? Is he really asleep? [*Pause*] No, the best would be to take advantage of Pozzo's calling for help—

POZZO Help!

VLADIMIR To help him—

ESTRAGON *We* help *him*?

VLADIMIR In anticipation of some tangible return.

ESTRAGON And suppose he—

VLADIMIR Let us not waste our time in idle discourse! [*Pause. Vehemently.*] Let us do something, while we have the chance! It is not every day that we are needed. Not indeed that we personally are needed. Others would meet the case equally well, if not better. To all mankind they were addressed, those cries for help still ringing in our ears! But at this place, at this moment of time, all mankind is us, whether we like it or not. Let us make the most of it, before it is too late! Let us represent worthily for once the foul brood to which a cruel fate consigned us! What do you say? [**ESTRAGON** *says nothing.*] It is true that when with folded arms we weigh the pros and cons we are no less a credit to our species. The tiger bounds to the help of his congeners[9] without the least reflexion, or else he slinks away into the depths of the thickets. But that is not the question. What are we doing here, *that* is the question. And we are blessed in this, that we happen to know the answer. Yes, in this immense confusion one thing alone is clear. We are waiting for Godot to come—

ESTRAGON Ah!

POZZO Help!

VLADIMIR Or for night to fall. [*Pause*] We have kept our appointment and that's an end to that. We are not saints, but we have kept our appointment. How many people can boast as much?

ESTRAGON Billions.

VLADIMIR You think so?

ESTRAGON I don't know.

VLADIMIR You may be right.

POZZO Help!

VLADIMIR All I know is that the hours are long, under these conditions, and constrain us to beguile them with proceedings which—how shall I say—which may at first sight seem reasonable, until they become a habit. You may say it is to prevent our reason from foundering. No doubt. But has it not long been straying in the night without end of the abyssal depths? That's what I sometimes wonder. You follow my reasoning?

ESTRAGON [*aphoristic for once*] We are all born mad. Some remain so.

POZZO Help! I'll pay you!

ESTRAGON How much?

POZZO One hundred francs!

ESTRAGON It's not enough.

VLADIMIR I wouldn't go so far as that.

ESTRAGON You think it's enough?

VLADIMIR No, I mean so far as to assert that I was weak in the head when I came into the world. But that is not the question.

9. Members of his class or kind.

POZZO Two hundred!

VLADIMIR We wait. We are bored. [*He throws up his hand.*] No, don't protest, we are bored to death, there's no denying it. Good. A diversion comes along and what do we do? We let it go to waste. Come, let's get to work! [*He advances towards the heap, stops in his stride.*] In an instant all will vanish and we'll be alone once more, in the midst of nothingness! [*He broods.*]

POZZO Two hundred!

VLADIMIR We're coming!

[*He tries to pull* POZZO *to his feet, fails, tries again, stumbles, falls, tries to get up, fails.*]

ESTRAGON What's the matter with you all?

VLADIMIR Help!

ESTRAGON I'm going.

VLADIMIR Don't leave me! They'll kill me!

POZZO Where am I?

VLADIMIR Gogo!

POZZO Help!

VLADIMIR Help!

ESTRAGON I'm going.

VLADIMIR Help me up first, then we'll go together.

ESTRAGON You promise?

VLADIMIR I swear it!

ESTRAGON And we'll never come back?

VLADIMIR Never!

ESTRAGON We'll go to the Pyrenees.[1]

VLADIMIR Wherever you like.

ESTRAGON I've always wanted to wander in the Pyrenees.

VLADIMIR You'll wander in them.

ESTRAGON [*recoiling*] Who farted?

VLADIMIR Pozzo.

POZZO Here! Here! Pity!

ESTRAGON It's revolting!

VLADIMIR Quick! Give me your hand!

ESTRAGON I'm going. [*Pause. Louder.*] I'm going.

VLADIMIR Well I suppose in the end I'll get up by myself. [*He tries, fails.*] In the fullness of time.

ESTRAGON What's the matter with you?

VLADIMIR Go to hell.

ESTRAGON Are you staying there?

VLADIMIR For the time being.

ESTRAGON Come on, get up, you'll catch a chill.

VLADIMIR Don't worry about me.

ESTRAGON Come on, Didi, don't be pig-headed!

[*He stretches out his hand which* VLADIMIR *makes haste to seize.*]

VLADIMIR Pull!

[ESTRAGON *pulls, stumbles, falls. Long silence.*]

1. The mountain range on the border between Spain and France, extending from the Atlantic Ocean to the Mediterranean Sea.

POZZO Help!

VLADIMIR We've arrived.

POZZO Who are you?

VLADIMIR We are men.

[*Silence.*]

ESTRAGON Sweet mother earth!

VLADIMIR Can you get up?

ESTRAGON I don't know.

VLADIMIR Try.

ESTRAGON Not now, not now.

[*Silence.*]

POZZO What happened?

VLADIMIR [*violently*] Will you stop it, you! Pest! He can think of nothing but himself!

ESTRAGON What about a little snooze?

VLADIMIR Did you hear him? He wants to know what happened!

ESTRAGON Don't mind him. Sleep.

[*Silence.*]

POZZO Pity! Pity!

ESTRAGON [*with a start*] What is it?

VLADIMIR Were you asleep?

ESTRAGON I must have been.

VLADIMIR It's this bastard Pozzo at it again.

ESTRAGON Make him stop it. Kick him in the crotch.

VLADIMIR [*striking Pozzo*] Will you stop it! Crablouse! [POZZO *extricates himself with cries of pain and crawls away. He stops, saws the air blindly, calling for help.* VLADIMIR, *propped on his elbow, observes his retreat.*] He's off! [POZZO *collapses.*] He's down!

ESTRAGON What do we do now?

VLADIMIR Perhaps I could crawl to him.

ESTRAGON Don't leave me!

VLADIMIR Or I could call to him.

ESTRAGON Yes, call to him.

VLADIMIR Pozzo! [*Silence*] Pozzo! [*Silence*] No reply.

ESTRAGON Together.

VLADIMIR }
ESTRAGON } Pozzo! Pozzo!

VLADIMIR He moved.

ESTRAGON Are you sure his name is Pozzo?

VLADIMIR [*alarmed*] Mr. Pozzo! Come back! We won't hurt you!

[*Silence.*]

ESTRAGON We might try him with other names.

VLADIMIR I'm afraid he's dying.

ESTRAGON It'd be amusing.

VLADIMIR What'd be amusing?

ESTRAGON To try him with other names, one after the other. It'd pass the time. And we'd be bound to hit on the right one sooner or later.

VLADIMIR I tell you his name is Pozzo.

ESTRAGON We'll soon see. [*He reflects.*] Abel! Abel!

POZZO Help!

ESTRAGON Got it in one!

VLADIMIR I begin to weary of this motif.

ESTRAGON Perhaps the other is called Cain.[2] Cain! Cain!

POZZO Help!

ESTRAGON He's all humanity. [*Silence*] Look at the little cloud.

VLADIMIR [*raising his eyes*] Where?

ESTRAGON There. In the zenith.[3]

VLADIMIR Well? [*Pause*] What is there so wonderful about it?

[*Silence.*]

ESTRAGON Let's pass on now to something else, do you mind?

VLADIMIR I was just going to suggest it.

ESTRAGON But to what?

VLADIMIR Ah!

[*Silence.*]

ESTRAGON Suppose we got up to begin with?

VLADIMIR No harm trying.

[*They get up.*]

ESTRAGON Child's play.

VLADIMIR Simple question of will-power.

ESTRAGON And now?

POZZO Help!

ESTRAGON Let's go.

VLADIMIR We can't.

ESTRAGON Why not?

VLADIMIR We're waiting for Godot.

ESTRAGON Ah! [*Despairing*] What'll we do, what'll we do!

POZZO Help!

VLADIMIR What about helping him?

ESTRAGON What does he want?

VLADIMIR He wants to get up.

ESTRAGON Then why doesn't he?

VLADIMIR He wants us to help him to get up.

ESTRAGON Then why don't we? What are we waiting for?

[*They help* POZZO *to his feet, let him go. He falls.*]

VLADIMIR We must hold him. [*They get him up again.* POZZO *says between them, his arms round their necks.*] Feeling better?

POZZO Who are you?

VLADIMIR Do you not recognize us?

POZZO I am blind.

[*Silence.*]

ESTRAGON Perhaps he can see into the future.

VLADIMIR Since when?

POZZO I used to have wonderful sight—but are you friends?

ESTRAGON [*laughing noisily*] He wants to know if we are friends!

2. In the Bible, the first murderer (a son of Adam and Eve); after Cain killed his brother Abel, God made him "a fugitive and a vagabond" (Genesis 4.12).

3. Literally, the point of the sky directly overhead.

VLADIMIR No, he means friends of his.

ESTRAGON Well?

VLADIMIR We've proved we are, by helping him.

ESTRAGON Exactly. Would we have helped him if we weren't his friends?

VLADIMIR Possibly.

ESTRAGON True.

VLADIMIR Don't let's quibble about that now.

POZZO You are not highwaymen?

ESTRAGON Highwaymen! Do we look like highwaymen?

VLADIMIR Damn it can't you see the man is blind!

ESTRAGON Damn it so he is. [*Pause*] So he says.

POZZO Don't leave me!

VLADIMIR No question of it.

ESTRAGON For the moment.

POZZO What time is it?

VLADIMIR [*inspecting the sky*] Seven o'clock . . . eight o'clock . . .

ESTRAGON That depends what time of year it is.

POZZO Is it evening?

[*Silence.* VLADIMIR *and* ESTRAGON *scrutinize the sunset.*]

ESTRAGON It's rising.

VLADIMIR Impossible.

ESTRAGON Perhaps it's the dawn.

VLADIMIR Don't be a fool. It's the west over there.

ESTRAGON How do you know?

POZZO [*anguished*] Is it evening?

VLADIMIR Anyway it hasn't moved.

ESTRAGON I tell you it's rising.

POZZO Why don't you answer me?

ESTRAGON Give us a chance.

VLADIMIR [*reassuring*] It's evening, Sir, it's evening, night is drawing nigh. My friend here would have me doubt it and I must confess he shook me for a moment. But it is not for nothing I have lived through this long day and I can assure you it is very near the end of its repertory. [*Pause*] How do you feel now?

ESTRAGON How much longer are we to cart him around. [*They half release him, catch him again as he falls.*] We are not caryatids![4]

VLADIMIR You were saying your sight used to be good, if I heard you right.

POZZO Wonderful! Wonderful, wonderful sight!

[*Silence.*]

ESTRAGON [*irritably*] Expand! Expand!

VLADIMIR Let him alone. Can't you see he's thinking of the days when he was happy. [*Pause*] *Memoria praeteritorum bonorum*[5]—that must be unpleasant.

ESTRAGON We wouldn't know.

VLADIMIR And it came on you all of a sudden?

POZZO Quite wonderful!

4. In architecture, draped female figures that act as supporting columns.

5. Memory of past goods (Latin); a phrase quoted from St. Thomas Aquinas, *Summa Theologica* (1269–73), 2.2.36.1.

VLADIMIR I'm asking you if it came on you all of a sudden.

POZZO I woke up one fine day as blind as Fortune.[6] [*Pause*] Sometimes I wonder if I'm not still asleep.

VLADIMIR And when was that?

POZZO I don't know.

VLADIMIR But no later than yesterday—

POZZO [*violently*] Don't question me! The blind have no notion of time. The things of time are hidden from them too.

VLADIMIR Well just fancy that! I could have sworn it was just the opposite.

ESTRAGON I'm going.

POZZO Where are we?

VLADIMIR I couldn't tell you.

POZZO It isn't by any chance the place known as the Board?[7]

VLADIMIR Never heard of it.

POZZO What is it like?

VLADIMIR [*looking round*] It's indescribable. It's like nothing. There's nothing. There's a tree.

POZZO Then it's not the Board.

ESTRAGON [*sagging*] Some diversion!

POZZO Where is my menial?

VLADIMIR He's about somewhere,

POZZO Why doesn't he answer when I call?

VLADIMIR I don't know. He seems to be sleeping. Perhaps he's dead.

POZZO What happened exactly?

ESTRAGON Exactly!

VLADIMIR The two of you slipped. [*Pause*] And fell.

POZZO Go and see is he hurt.

VLADIMIR We can't leave you.

POZZO You needn't both go.

VLADIMIR [*to* ESTRAGON] You go.

ESTRAGON After what he did to me? Never!

POZZO Yes yes, let your friend go, he stinks so. [*Silence.*] What is he waiting for?

VLADIMIR What you waiting for?

ESTRAGON I'm waiting for Godot.

[*Silence.*]

VLADIMIR What exactly should he do?

POZZO Well to begin with he should pull on the rope, as hard as he likes so long as he doesn't strangle him. He usually responds to that. If not he should give him a taste of his boot, in the face and the privates as far as possible.

VLADIMIR [*to* ESTRAGON] You see, you've nothing to be afraid of. It's even an opportunity to revenge yourself.

ESTRAGON And if he defends himself?

POZZO No no, he never defends himself.

VLADIMIR I'll come flying to the rescue.

6. The Roman goddess Fortuna, the personification of fortune, was sometimes depicted wearing a blindfold.

7. The stage itself is often referred to as "the boards."

ESTRAGON Don't take your eyes off me. [*He goes towards* LUCKY.]

VLADIMIR Make sure he's alive before you start. No point in exerting yourself if he's dead.

ESTRAGON [*bending over* LUCKY] He's breathing.

VLADIMIR Then let him have it.

[*With sudden fury* ESTRAGON *starts kicking* LUCKY, *hurling abuse at him as he does so. But he hurts his foot and moves away, limping and groaning.* LUCKY *stirs.*]

ESTRAGON Oh the brute!

[*He sits down on the mound and tries to take off his boot. But he soon desists and disposes himself for sleep, his arms on his knees and his head on his arms.*]

POZZO What's gone wrong now?

VLADIMIR My friend has hurt himself

POZZO And Lucky?

VLADIMIR So it is he?

POZZO What?

VLADIMIR It is Lucky?

POZZO I don't understand.

VLADIMIR And you are Pozzo?

POZZO Certainly I am Pozzo.

VLADIMIR The same as yesterday?

POZZO Yesterday?

VLADIMIR We met yesterday. [*Silence*] Do you not remember?

POZZO I don't remember having met anyone yesterday. But tomorrow I won't remember having met anyone today. So don't count on me to enlighten you.

VLADIMIR But—

POZZO Enough! Up pig!

VLADIMIR You were bringing him to the fair to sell him. You spoke to us. He danced. He thought. You had your sight.

POZZO As you please. Let me go! [VLADIMIR *moves away.*] Up! [LUCKY *gets up, gathers up his burdens.*]

VLADIMIR Where do you go from here.

POZZO On. [LUCKY, *laden down, takes his place before* POZZO.] Whip! [LUCKY *puts everything down, looks for whip, finds it, puts it into* POZZO*'s hand, takes up everything again.*] Rope!

[LUCKY *puts everything down, puts end of rope into* POZZO*'s hand, takes up everything again.*]

VLADIMIR What is there in the bag?

POZZO Sand. [*He jerks the rope.*] On!

VLADIMIR Don't go yet.

POZZO I'm going.

VLADIMIR What do you do when you fall far from help?

POZZO We wait till we can get up. Then we go on. On!

VLADIMIR Before you go tell him to sing.

POZZO Who?

VLADIMIR Lucky.

POZZO To sing?

VLADIMIR Yes. Or to think. Or to recite.

POZZO But he is dumb.
VLADIMIR Dumb!
POZZO Dumb. He can't even groan.
VLADIMIR Dumb! Since when?
POZZO [*suddenly furious*] Have you not done tormenting me with your accursed time! It's abominable! When! When! One day, is that not enough for you, one day he went dumb, one day I went blind, one day we'll go deaf, one day we were born, one day we shall die, the same day, the same second, is that not enough for you? [*Calmer*] They give birth astride of a grave, the light gleams an instant, then it's night once more. [*He jerks the rope.*] On!

[*Exeunt*[8] *Pozzo and Lucky. Vladimir follows them to the edge of the stage, looks after them. The noise of falling, reinforced by mimic of Vladimir, announces that they are down again. Silence. Vladimir goes towards Estragon, contemplates him a moment, then shakes him awake.*]

ESTRAGON [*wild gestures, incoherent words. Finally*] Why will you never let me sleep?
VLADIMIR I felt lonely.
ESTRAGON I was dreaming I was happy.
VLADIMIR That passed the time.
ESTRAGON I was dreaming that—
VLADIMIR [*violently*] Don't tell me! [*Silence*] I wonder is he really blind.
ESTRAGON Blind? Who?
VLADIMIR Pozzo.
ESTRAGON Blind?
VLADIMIR He told us he was blind.
ESTRAGON Well what about it?
VLADIMIR It seemed to me he saw us.
ESTRAGON You dreamt it. [*Pause*] Let's go. We can't. Ah! [*Pause*] Are you sure it wasn't him?
VLADIMIR Who?
ESTRAGON Godot.
VLADIMIR But who?
ESTRAGON Pozzo.
VLADIMIR Not at all! [*Less sure*] Not at all! [*Still less sure*] Not at all!
ESTRAGON I suppose I might as well get up. [*He gets up painfully.*] Ow! Didi!
VLADIMIR I don't know what to think any more.
ESTRAGON My feet! [*He sits down again and tries to take off his boots.*] Help me!
VLADIMIR Was I sleeping, while the others suffered? Am I sleeping now? Tomorrow, when I wake, or think I do, what shall I say of today? That with Estragon my friend, at this place, until the fall of night, I waited for Godot? That Pozzo passed, with his carrier, and that he spoke to us? Probably. But in all that what truth will there be? [ESTRAGON, *having struggled with his boots in vain, is dozing off again.* VLADIMIR *looks at him.*] He'll know nothing. He'll tell me about the blows he received and I'll give him a carrot. [*Pause*] Astride of a grave and a difficult birth. Down in the hole, lingeringly,

8. [They] exit (Latin).

the grave-digger puts on the forceps.[9] We have time to grow old. The air is full of our cries. [*He listens.*] But habit is a great deadener. [*He looks again at* ESTRAGON.] At me too someone is looking, of me too someone is saying, He is sleeping, he knows nothing, let him sleep on. [*Pause*] I can't go on! [*Pause*] What have I said?

[*He goes feverishly to and fro, halts finally at extreme left, broods. Enter* BOY *right. He halts. Silence.*]

BOY Mister . . . [VLADIMIR *turns.*] Mister Albert . . .

VLADIMIR Off we go again. [*Pause*] Do you not recognize me?

BOY No Sir.

VLADIMIR It wasn't you came yesterday.

BOY No Sir.

VLADIMIR This is your first time.

BOY Yes Sir.

[*Silence.*]

VLADIMIR You have a message from Mr. Godot.

BOY Yes Sir.

VLADIMIR He won't come this evening.

BOY No Sir.

VLADIMIR But he'll come tomorrow.

BOY Yes Sir.

VLADIMIR Without fail.

BOY Yes Sir.

[*Silence.*]

VLADIMIR Did you meet anyone?

BOY No Sir.

VLADIMIR Two other . . . [*He hesitates.*] . . . men?

BOY I didn't see anyone, Sir.

[*Silence.*]

VLADIMIR What does he do, Mr. Godot? [*Silence*] Do you hear me?

BOY Yes Sir.

VLADIMIR Well?

BOY He does nothing, Sir.

[*Silence*]

VLADIMIR How is your brother?

BOY He's sick, Sir.

VLADIMIR Perhaps it was he came yesterday.

BOY I don't know, Sir.

[*Silence*]

VLADIMIR [*softly*] Has he a beard, Mr. Godot?

BOY Yes Sir.

VLADIMIR Fair or . . . [*He hesitates.*] . . . or black?

BOY I think it's white, Sir.

[*Silence.*]

VLADIMIR Christ have mercy on us!

[*Silence.*]

9. An instrument for grasping (obstetrical forceps help pull a baby from the birth canal).

BOY What am I to tell Mr. Godot, Sir?

VLADIMIR Tell him . . . [*He hesitates.*] . . . tell him you saw me and that . . . [*He hesitates.*] . . . that you saw me. [*Pause.* VLADIMIR *advances, the* BOY *recoils.* VLADIMIR *halts, the* BOY *halts. With sudden violence.*] You're sure you saw me, you won't come and tell me tomorrow that you never saw me!

[*Silence.* VLADIMIR *makes a sudden spring forward, the* BOY *avoids him and exit running. Silence. The sun sets, the moon rises. As in Act 1.* VLADIMIR *stands motionless and bowed.* ESTRAGON *wakes, takes off his boots, gets up with one in each hand and goes and puts them down center front, then goes towards* VLADIMIR.]

ESTRAGON What's wrong with you?

VLADIMIR Nothing.

ESTRAGON I'm going.

VLADIMIR So am I.

ESTRAGON Was I long asleep?

VLADIMIR I don't know.

[*Silence.*]

ESTRAGON Where shall we go?

VLADIMIR Not far.

ESTRAGON Oh yes, let's go far away from here.

VLADIMIR We can't.

ESTRAGON Why not?

VLADIMIR We have to come back tomorrow.

ESTRAGON What for?

VLADIMIR To wait for Godot.

ESTRAGON Ah! [*Silence.*] He didn't come?

VLADIMIR No.

ESTRAGON And now it's too late.

VLADIMIR Yes, now it's night.

ESTRAGON And if we dropped him? [*Pause*] If we dropped him?

VLADIMIR He'd punish us. [*Silence. He looks at the tree.*] Everything's dead but the tree.

ESTRAGON [*looking at the tree*] What is it?

VLADIMIR It's the tree.

ESTRAGON Yes, but what kind?

VLADIMIR I don't know. A willow.

[ESTRAGON *draws* VLADIMIR *towards the tree. They stand motionless before it. Silence.*]

ESTRAGON Why don't we hang ourselves?

VLADIMIR With what?

ESTRAGON You haven't got a bit of rope?

VLADIMIR No.

ESTRAGON Then we can't.

[*Silence.*]

VLADIMIR Let's go.

ESTRAGON Wait, there's my belt.

VLADIMIR It's too short.

ESTRAGON You could hang on to my legs.

VLADIMIR And who'd hang on to mine?

ESTRAGON True.

VLADIMIR Show all the same. [**ESTRAGON** *loosens the cord that holds up his trousers which, much too big for him, fall about his ankles. They look at the cord.*] It might do at a pinch. But is it strong enough?

ESTRAGON We'll soon see. Here.

[*They each take an end of the cord and pull. It breaks. They almost fall.*]

VLADIMIR Not worth a curse.

[*Silence.*]

ESTRAGON You say we have to come back tomorrow?

VLADIMIR Yes.

ESTRAGON Then we can bring a good bit of rope.

VLADIMIR Yes.

[*Silence.*]

ESTRAGON Didi.

VLADIMIR Yes.

ESTRAGON I can't go on like this.

VLADIMIR That's what you think.

ESTRAGON If we parted? That might be better for us.

VLADIMIR We'll hang ourselves tomorrow. [*Pause*] Unless Godot comes.

ESTRAGON And if he comes?

VLADIMIR We'll be saved.

[**VLADIMIR** *takes off his hat (***LUCKY***'s), peers inside it, feels about inside it, shakes it, knocks on the crown, puts it on again.*]

ESTRAGON Well? Shall we go?

VLADIMIR Pull on your trousers.

ESTRAGON What?

VLADIMIR Pull on your trousers.

ESTRAGON You want me to pull off my trousers?

VLADIMIR Pull ON your trousers.

ESTRAGON [*realizing his trousers are down*] True. [*He pulls up his trousers.*]

VLADIMIR Well? Shall we go?

ESTRAGON Yes, let's go.

[*They do not move.*]

Curtain.

DEREK WALCOTT

b. 1930

In his long epic poems, collections of lyric poetry, and plays, Derek Walcott has captured the dynamic cultural mix of African, Amerindian, and European influences that is unique to the Caribbean. An advocate and producer of the arts as well as a writer, Walcott co-founded and was the first president of the St. Lucia Arts Guild at age twenty; he created what would become the flagship professional theater company of the Caribbean, the acclaimed Trinidad Theatre Workshop, nine years later. Seen as less overtly political than some other Caribbean artists and intellectuals, such as Aimé Césaire or Franz Fanon, or than the Nigerian dramatist WOLE SOYINKA, a contemporary with whom he is often compared, Walcott has created poetry and drama that nonetheless powerfully indict colonialism and its effect on culture and language. Concerned primarily with defining the Caribbean as a culture distinct from yet in dialogue with Western traditions, Walcott gives voice to what he called in his 1992 speech accepting the Nobel Prize in Literature "an ancestral, an ecstatic rhythm in the blood that cannot be subdued by slavery or indenture." From the history of slavery and colonialism, Walcott forged a literature at once realistic and lyrical, insistent both on showing oppression and on giving the suppressed a literary voice of their own through an unusual mixture of folklore, dance, and storytelling.

Derek Walcott was born on the small island of St. Lucia, one of the Windward Islands of the West Indies, to mixed-race parents—both his grandfathers were white, his grandmothers black. His father, a civil servant, died before he was two, and he was raised by his mother, a teacher, who encouraged Walcott's forays into literature; Walcott dedicates one of his earliest poetic achievements to her. While still a schoolboy, he started to write poetry and plays; he avidly engaged in student theater, exploring the art forms that would continue to dominate his life. In his twenties, he received a Rockefeller Fellowship to New York, where he trained with José Quintero at the Circle in the Square, a leading off-Broadway theater. Walcott received further support from the Rockefeller Foundation as he attempted to establish a professional theater company in Port of Spain, Trinidad, where he made his home. The funding enabled Walcott's company, the Trinidad Theatre Workshop, to establish ties with New York theater and even to initiate some artistic exchanges—for example, with the playwright, actor, and director André Gregory. But unlike many Caribbean writers of his generation, such as V. S. Naipaul, Walcott did not leave the islands to live in London or New York.

Instead, he spent more than twenty years trying to foster a national culture of modernist theater in Port of Spain.

But in the mid-1970s, relations both in his marriage and at the Trinidad Theatre Workshop were under strain. He resigned from the workshop in 1976, his marriage ended, and he started to spend more time abroad to teach, first at the College of the Virgin Islands and then in visiting posts at Yale, Columbia, New York University, and Boston University, which in 1986 made him a professor of English—a position he still holds.

Because the schools in St. Lucia, like those of most colonies, followed the same curriculum as schools in the mother country, Walcott grew up not just with English literature but also with the classical literature of Rome and Greece. This background is visible everywhere in his poetry and plays, which frequently bear epigraphs from Greek tragedies or allude to them in other ways. Walcott even composed a dramatic adaptation of the *Odyssey*, commissioned by the Royal Shakespeare Company and produced in 1992. Walcott has also turned to North American themes and topics, in *The Ghost Dance* (1989), a play about the religious movement that swept through Native Americans in the late nineteenth century, and *Walker* (1993; 2001), a play set in Cambridge, Massachusetts, which revolves around an abolitionist who is shot by a Southern slave holder.

At the same time, Walcott knew that to find a distinct literary voice and language—one representative of the unique cultural amalgam of the Caribbean—he would have to adapt, transform, and reimagine the various Western traditions with which he was deeply familiar. In that endeavor, he turned to the Caribbean's African heritage, which had been largely suppressed for centuries and had to be revived in the drive toward independence. But despite his emphasis on African traditions, Walcott never subscribed to the more radical forms of black nationalism, which hoped to find in Africa the cultural roots of an authentic Caribbean identity free from the taint of the European colonizers. Many of his plays center on the violence and the shattered illusions that, through the islands' history, accompanied revolts and revolutions—especially the Haitian Revolution (1791–1804), which features in three of his plays (later collected under the name *The Haitian Trilogy*): *Henri Christophe* (1950), *Drums and Colours* (1958), and *The Haitian Earth* (1984). *Henri Christophe* deals with the struggle between the title character, who successfully plotted against Toussaint L'Ouverture (leader of the uprising against French rule) and another guerrilla leader. *Drums and Colours*, commissioned to mark the launch of the newly formed West Indian Federation, a short-lived attempt to combine ten British colonies into a single political unit, is perhaps Walcott's most overtly political play. A history pageant, it spans the colonial and postcolonial history of the Caribbean: its four main episodes feature Christopher Columbus; the quest for the legendary El Dorado, a land rich in gold and gems, by Sir Walter Raleigh; the betrayal of Toussaint; and George William Gordon, a mixed-race Jamaican businessman and critic of colonial rule who was executed in 1865 after a local uprising. *The Haitian Earth*, set after the Haitian Revolution, was produced by the government of St. Lucia to commemorate the 150th anniversary of passage of the British Emancipation Act, which abolished slavery throughout most of the British Empire (Haiti itself had been independent since 1804). These plays demonstrate how important political questions of emancipation and statehood were for Walcott's project of finding a literary voice for the Caribbean.

A number of other works address the political history of the Caribbean from a more literary perspective. *Pantomime* (1978), for example, reworks Daniel Defoe's *Robinson Crusoe* (1719), a central text in the European imagination of colonialism; indeed, Walcott also dedicated a series of poems and essays to Defoe. Walcott's best-known meditation on colonialism is probably his acclaimed book-length poem *Omeros* (1990), which sets Helen, Hector, and Achille in a fishing village on St. Lucia, and which is regarded by many as the paradigmatic postcolonial epic. At once autobiographical and historical, *Omeros* transposes the Homeric themes of anger and betrayal into a world populated by British colonial landowners and dispossessed castaways.

Though Walcott and other Caribbean authors could not look back on a long local tradition of written literature, they could build on a rich heritage of theater and dance as well as the unique forms of Caribbean carnival as they created new kinds of theater and performance. Some cultural figures, such as the playwright, actor, and theater scholar Errol Hill, even espoused the carnival as the source for a specifically Caribbean theater. The position of Walcott, who dedicated some of his plays to Hill, was more ambivalent, as he feared that by celebrating the carnival the young Caribbean nations would promote a kind of folklore that is closer to tourism than to art. Despite these misgivings, however, many of Walcott's plays use the carnival as a backdrop, both to distinguish themselves from it and to signal that it remains a foundation of any Caribbean theater. Indeed, those of his plays that are immersed in the carnival, including *Dream on Monkey Mountain* (1967) and *Last Carnival* (1982), are among Walcott's strongest.

Walcott believed that rather than subsidizing folklore, the government should support the kind of modernist art to which he himself aspired. His most important essayistic statement on drama, "What the Twilight Says" (1970), emphasizes modernism, not the carnival, and quotes SAMUEL BECKETT, JEAN GENET, W. B. Yeats, Antonin Artaud, Naipaul, and Ernest Hemingway. Walcott's dedication to modernist art is also reflected in his fascination—shared by the modernists—with East Asian theatrical traditions, in particular with Japanese noh and kabuki theater. Walcott draws on many other theatrical styles as well, including Greek tragedy, the history pageant, and social drama. *Pantomime* is partly modeled on the British music hall tradition; *Ti-Jean and His Brothers* (1957; 1970), on a simple folktale. Walcott even collaborated with the composer of the musical *Hair* (1967), Galt MacDermot, on a musical called *Marie Laveau* (1979), based on the life of a mysterious New Orleans voodoo queen. At the same time, he wrote lyrical plays that, like those of many poets before him, are rarely performed.

THE SEA AT DAUPHIN (1954), a short play in one act, is one of Walcott's most compelling and best-known dramas. It takes place on a wind-lashed island, where poor fishermen venture forth on the dangerous sea in small boats to seize their meager sustenance. The action of the play is as spare as the characters' lives. Hounakin, an old man, wants to join two younger fishermen, Afa and Augustin, on a fishing excursion, even though the sea is unusually threatening. After much pleading, Afa consents; once in the boat, though, Hounakin freezes with terror, which leads to his leaving the boat. But he is not the only one who stays behind. Another fisherman, Gacia, is driven back by the rough waters, choosing to wait for better weather. Only Afa seems to embrace the challenge and the necessity of battling the waves, no matter the risk. The daily struggle has hardened his heart and become his entire existence: he will never prefer the safe land to the dangerous sea.

In *The Sea at Dauphin*, we clearly see the myriad influences that have shaped Walcott's oeuvre. The play was inspired by a modernist Irish play, JOHN MILLINGTON SYNGE's *Riders to the Sea* (1904). Both plays are set in an extremely remote outpost: a fishing village far from centers of power and civilization. The inhabitants live in poverty as they struggle against the sea, which at once sustains fishermen and destroys them. In both plays, the victims of the sea are evoked time and again, casting long shadows over the living. And both plays seek to forge a new literary language that incorporates nonstandard dialects. Synge had shocked audiences with his literary version of the speech of Irish fishermen; Walcott similarly uses St. Lucia's distinctive patois, a mixture of French and English that reflects the island's colonial history. For Walcott, Synge was not simply a European modernist whose themes he could borrow and rework from a postcolonial perspective: he identified with Synge and other writers of the Irish drama movement, such as Yeats, as fellow victims of the

Jamaican fishermen. From *The West Indies, Illustrated* (1909).

British Empire. They too had suffered from a long history of English colonial occupation; they too lived on a rural island; and they too had created a unique form of English.

Though *Riders to the Sea* is important to *The Sea at Dauphin*, Walcott made significant changes to Synge's framework. Whereas *Riders to the Sea* unfolds from the perspective of a mother, who has already lost several sons to the sea and who must watch another head to the waves, *The Sea at Dauphin* has an almost entirely male cast. The habits and values they portray—loyalty, respect for the old, attitudes toward work, regular drinking of rum, among others—set these characters on a collision course. It is a hard male world, and Afa, who has renounced women to focus entirely on his daily battle against the sea, is the hardest of them all. Compared to him, everyone else seems undedicated, distracted, and weak—even the priest, whom he scolds as a parasite.

Yet in this world, the influence and voices of women are not entirely absent. The play is divided into two sections, separated by a chorus of women that marks the passing of time. While Afa views the earlier deaths by sea as a threat to the living, the women remember the dead in a lyrical lamentation, mourning yet accepting the dangers that fishermen confront. Still, no women appear as individual characters—an absence that is especially striking in light of the focus on women in Synge's play. Walcott thus changes not only the location of the action but also the sexes of the main actors.

The necessity of going out and fighting against the sea determines the lives of these characters, leaving them little room for change and variation. The epigraph from EURIPIDES that begins the play, "The sea doth wash away all human ills," signals that the sea is more than a mere backdrop. It imposes a cyclical rhythm onto the play—the rhythm of the tides flowing out and coming in, of quiet and storm. The sea is the main adversary of the struggling characters; it can even be seen as the play's protagonist, the main actor in this drama that pits men against nature.

One event shifts the focus of the play

away from the relentless sea: the suicide around which this play revolves, which takes place on land. Unlike Synge's play, which focuses almost exclusively on the sea, *The Sea at Dauphin* also clearly conveys the harshness of the fight for survival on land. The island is rocky and hard to farm, and cutting sugarcane is backbreaking labor. Indeed, Afa claims that unlike the land, with its stony heart, "The sea / It have compassion in the end": it is a place where bravery can be tested and manhood proven. Old Hounakin seems to agree, as despair over his wife's death leads him to seek the heroic death of a fisherman, though he has never fished from a boat before. The fisherman's life is a curse, but it is also a sign of vitality. Insofar as the play is structured by divisions—young and old, men and women, sea and land—Afa allies himself with the first one. He is still young enough to battle the sea, he has renounced women, and he rejects life on land. He thus is made to represent an extreme position, setting the terms by which all others are understood and against which they are measured.

In *The Sea at Dauphin,* Walcott has brilliantly given the ancient genre of tragedy a modern form. Whereas the Greeks had pitted their drama's protagonists against an inexorable fate, Walcott presents humans who are dwarfed by a forbidding nature against which they must relentlessly struggle. While in some respects Walcott's play hews close to classical tragedy—for example, in the chorus of women between its two parts—in others it offers a radical and modern reinvention of the form. In Greek tragedy, the protagonist had to be a socially elevated personage, who almost invariably was taken from myth; Walcott, like other writers of modern tragedy, endows characters from everyday life with the dignity formerly denied those viewed as lowly. This expansion of tragedy's social range is accompanied by a shift in its language: instead of writing in an especially elevated register, as did the Greeks, Walcott, like Synge before him, uses a nonstandard dialect in creating a contemporary language of tragedy. The result of this combination of the traditional and new is a compelling modern tragedy, one that breaks with strictures of the classical form yet stays true to its spirit. Later in his career, Walcott would turn to social drama as well as to comedy, farce, musical theater, and many other theatrical genres with great success, but in its dramatic simplicity and poetic inventiveness, *The Sea at Dauphin* remains an important contribution to a project that has occupied Walcott throughout his life: drawing on the island culture of the Caribbean for new settings, languages, and forms that nevertheless resonate richly with both Western and non-Western theater. M.P.

The Sea at Dauphin

The sea doth wash away all human ills.[1]
Euripides

CHARACTERS

AFA, a fisherman
GACIA, a fisherman
AUGUSTIN, Afa's mate
HOUNAKIN, an old East Indian
A PRIEST [P. Lavoisier]
JULES, a boy
WOMEN OF DAUPHIN

A Windward Island in the West Indies, on its nerve-wracked Atlantic coast, two hours from sunrise. Age-grey morning before the fishermen file, gum-eyed, hitching their trousers, to the latrine on the beach's spit in the bay. Nothing on the beach now so early, except a sail, patched square from used flour sacks, washing its slack cheeks with the wind. In the sleep-tightened village a dog is coughing among the lanes, then by the grey false light of daybreak a fisherman comes down the littered beach, barefooted, wrapped in a moth-riddled sweater against the October cold, carrying a dented tin, coils of marlin twine,[2] *and a bamboo pole. He wears a cap with the braid shredded, and pants quilted with patches. In the bow of a canoe that protrudes from a clump of stunted grapes he rests the pail down, then the rod, picks dead leaves floating in the bilge of the boat, then squints unwillingly at the bad weather; fiddles in his cap for a butt, lights it against the wind, then rubs it out. He sits on a stone near the canoe. Its bow is lettered with the words* Our Daily Bread.[3] *This man is* AFA, *over forty, and gritty-tempered as he unpacks the twine, mumbling, and thins it out between finger and thumb. Soon another fisherman,* GACIA, *stale drunk, twice as tattered, in his old constable's cloak comes dead-footed down the beach.*

GACIA *Bon matin, boug.*[4]

AFA *Matin*, Gacia, *bon matin.* Wind hard, eh? [*Looking at the sky*] Wind still savage.

GACIA Ay, *oui,*[5] the cold will drop, but this just half the wind. The next half in the sea back-pocket, by Sablisse. Where Augustin?

1. From *Iphigenia in Tauris*, line 1193 (ca. 413 B.C.E.), by the Greek tragedian Euripides (480–ca. 406 B.C.E.).
2. A two-strand line, usually tarred, used for repairing nets.
3. A reference to Matthew 6.11 ("Give us this day our daily bread"), a verse of the Lord's Prayer.
4. Good morning, man (Antillean Creole, the French patois spoken throughout this play).
5. Yes.

AFA You know Augustin. Augustin is his woman blanket. Where Debel?

GACIA Debel? Debel sick. [*Imitates a man vomiting*] *Rhum.*

AFA You see, cousin? Rum is a bad wife.

GACIA But you must sleep with it. Debel finish. Between him and his woman not much leave. He should die, since to beg is worse. [*Shivering*] I don't even take my little coffee yet. [*Looks at sky.*] Two weeks now, this sea whiter than spit, two weeks is rain.

AFA It white like the time when Bolo drown. [*Points off-shore.*] There so!

GACIA *Garçcon,*[6] to see a next day so like when Bolo drown . . . [*Shakes his head.*] I remember . . .

AFA But the sea forget.

GACIA The sea do what it have to do, like wind, like birds. Like me. Cigawette? [*Offers* AFA *a cigarette.*] American.

AFA [*wiping his hands*] *Merci*[7] . . . [*Looks at it.*] Ay, ay, *boug. 'Ous riche,*[8] a whole one? [*They laugh.*] Is only natural for wind to blow so hard, but to turn, and turn. You going out, you one? The others, they making one with their woman, only both of us two so stupid.

GACIA It staying so for a next month, *compère,* and in all my life I never see it more *vex* and it have many season, fishing *nasse,*[9] I see it bad; but never in a life, like this. But is work or starve. They have many garden wash down in Fond River. We curse, *compère.* God forget us . . . *Bonne chance*[1] . . . the sail have a hole . . . [*Goes off, singing.*]

AFA Eh-heh, I know, I know . . .

[GACIA *exits.* AFA *stands to watch him go, impatiently stamping his foot. He is fixing the twine angrily when a yell from the hill stops him. AFAaaaaaah ooooh, AFAoooooy, and suddenly a lithe, agitated young man breaks through the bushes, stuffing his merino*[2] *into his pants, and chattering in the cold. The young man is* AUGUSTIN, AFA'S *mate. He throws his things in the canoe and hugs himself.*]

AUGUSTIN *Bon matin, bon matin,* Admiral. *Bon Dieu, Jesi Marie La Vierge en ciel, mwen fwette,*[3] it making cold, woy!

AFA Is time for this old man to come, morning break and you can't smell this wind? Gacia pass now so going for his canoe.

AUGUSTIN You mean Gacia one? Make me aid you with the twine. Gacia one? Where Debel?

AFA Is sick. Is time for this old man, *oui.*

AUGUSTIN Debel sick? Rum and sea water not a good drink. Ay, where *you going?*

AFA Look! Just now sun will rise, and wind working already. And fish waiting for nobody is working late. Mind you foot by the hook there!

AUGUSTIN You have a cigawette? It making cold.

AFA Not now, not now, when you want one for true. [*Exasperated*] Look, Monsieur Augustin, this fish you know it have now fifteen years, does wait for people line to hook them up? I tired use me tongue and tell you, don't

6. Boy.
7. Thanks.
8. You [are] rich.
9. Fishing net. *Compère:* friend. *Vex:* that is, vexed—angry, turbulent.
1. Good luck.
2. An undershirt made of merino wool.
3. Good morning, Admiral. Good God, Jesus Virgin Mary up in heaven, I'm cold.

care how you drinking in Samuel café, or talking how you brave in front of them Dauphin women, work is work, and sea and I don't sleep. I tell you when you pass, pass for the old man. Where he is now? Where this old man?

AUGUSTIN Last night in Samuel café, when white rum scald you tongue, is not you tell this old man he can come? Not you what have water in you eyes from Samuel onions, and cry on the old man shoulder?

AFA Well, today I feel to say *non.*[4] *Non!* Last night did drunk. Everybody drunk, you ask me when I did drunk. This morning I have sense, and so is *non, non!*

AUGUSTIN The old man is my godfather!

AFA What a man, to drown he godfather!

AUGUSTIN Is my godfather, and I want to drown him is my business! Piece of the canoe is mine you know.

AFA *Bien!*[5] So is for that you doing you don't know what season sea have now, as if is not September pass that Bolo drown, there self, so close you can hear scissor bird cutting the wind, you can hear gaulin[6] feather fall on rock. Forty years, *quarante,*[7] I work this water, and this is one bitch wind on Dauphin side today!

AUGUSTIN [*sitting down*] *Eh bien,*[8] we bound to go, Admiral?

AFA Eh-heh, we bound to go, because nobody going; when is nice even woman going.

AUGUSTIN Fish know wind too, Afa, come bet today fish hiding?

AFA *Eh bien,* stay home and make garden with you woman!

AUGUSTIN Make garden! *Cooyon!*[9] Is only you one who know current? Is only you who have need to work like nigger? Only you who brave? They have bigger than you on the sand under the sea, they have brave we don't hear yet is food for fish. *Cooyon!*

AFA Look, give me my respect you hear! I know you since you wetting this same pants you have; piece of the canoe is yours but gi' me my respect or we mashing up now self![1]

AUGUSTIN *Tiens!*[2] We always mashing up, just like you and you woman.

AFA I have no woman.

AUGUSTIN Don't have no woman only? You don't have no love, no time, no child, you have a hole where man heart should be, you have no God, no dog, no friend, that is why Dauphin fraid you, because you always enrage, and nobody will give you help of the hand, so you make it, live with it . . . Woman will leave you till you dead.

AFA Look, eh!

AUGUSTIN And when you dead, who will cry? Only blind Batal is peeling onions for Samuel on a bench behind the café, and a few grains of rain. Not me, not Gacia. And at your wake, if they so stupid to have wake for fool like you, women saying only "They had this man Afa, who greedy make fisherman, a man that beat his woman, that have no love, no mercy, no

4. No.
5. Fine!
6. A kind of egret, a bird that bears long plumes during the breeding season.
7. Forty.
8. Okay.
9. Fool.
1. That is, or we're having a quarrel right now.
2. What!

compassion!" I pass the old man *ajoupa*[3] before daybreak, the house eyes close, and the cannot sleep, he crying in the making dark, making ehhhh like dog, and the dog self watching him, waiting to die. I run here fast to tell you wait.—But why I talking to you? . . . [AFA *has turned away. Silence.*] You fix the hole was in the bottom of the canoe?

AFA Ah, God, you hear?

AUGUSTIN You fix the hole, pal? *Doux, doux,*[4] ay, papa, give Agos a little kiss . . . you vex? Pal, pal, . . . you fix the hole was in the bottom of . . .

AFA I bring *the calebasse*[5] to bail. The old man have to bail.

AUGUSTIN He have a old hurt in his back, you know that?

AFA So when we pass Point Jesu, and where water making white after Sablisse, I must take my two eyes from the wind, and my hand from the boat to rub his back?

AUGUSTIN *Bon Dieu,*[6] Afa, Sablisse? Why we going so far, and you can hear sea grinding his teeth in the making dark? . . . *'Ous malice,*[7] Afa, *malice, malice* . . .

AFA Malice! Compassion! What it have in this morning before sun even wipe his eye, that I must take this dirty tongue from you, eh? When I did working your age with Bolo, you think I could show my teeth in disrespect? And this new thing, compassion? Where is compassion? Is I does make poor people poor, or this sea vex? Is I that put rocks where should dirt by Dauphin side, man cannot make garden grow? Is I that swell little children belly with bad worm,[8] and woman to wear clothes white people use to wipe their foot? In my head is stone, and my heart is another, and without stone, my eyes would burst for that, would look for compassion on woman belly. I born and deading in this coast that have no compassion to grow food for children, no fish enough to buy new sail, no twine. Every day sweat, sun, and salt, and night is salt and sleep, and all the dead days pack away and stink, is Dauphin life. Not I who make it! So I must work the sea, that is my pasture, *garce.*[9] If is compassion you want talk to the sea, ask it where Bolo bones, and Rafael, and friends I did have before you even born . . .

AUGUSTIN So you not taking the old man?

AFA What right a man is blind, two holes where had his eyes,
To work this sea? He think is land,
But you cannot plant it, the sea food does move,
And we must follow it. Today he will learn.

AUGUSTIN *Est*-you[1] taking him?

AFA And Gacia pass Point Jesu long! *Gadez!*[2] [*Smashes a calabash down in anger.*] I have no time to wipe old man pants is frighten. He your godfather, and promise is to break. He coming, look at him coming, like piece of break-up stick. Not me in this thing!

AUGUSTIN He can hear you.

3. House.
4. Soft; easy.
5. Calabash, gourd.
6. Good God.
7. You are mean.
8. *Strongyloides stercolis*, an intestinal parasite; it is often fatal to infants.
9. Boy (short for *garçon*).
1. Are you.
2. Be careful!

AFA Make him hear then!

AUGUSTIN Do what you want! [*He sucks his teeth and starts to break up a twig.*]

AFA [*loudly*] I say I not carrying nobody dead in my boat.

AUGUSTIN Half the boat is mine.

AFA I not carrying nobody dead in my half the boat, no old man on my shoulder. I know old man, dribbling in bed. Since Rama, his old woman dead, he think everybody must go round their face long like bamboo, the world work must stop because one old woman dead.

[*Now the old man for whom they have been waiting,* HOUNAKIN, *comes through the bushes. He is an old East Indian, wrapped in almost rags, a green gourd in his hand, carrying a cutlass. He wears a large straw hat, is barefooted, and walks painfully, squinting through narrow gummed eyes set in a face worn and cracked with heat. He has overheard* AFA*'s words. Now he waits with the weary smile of the aged and near-deaf. He is suffering from cataract and a cramp has stiffened one hand.* AFA *looks at him, then turns his back on the old man.* AUGUSTIN *gestures in despair.*]

HOUNAKIN [*coming forward wearily*] *Bon matin, mes messieurs.*[3] I late . . .

AUGUSTIN *Bo' jou',*[4] *papa.*

HOUNAKIN *Ey, M'sieu Afa, bon matin . . .*

AFA *Vieux corps!*[5] Sea is waiting for nobody, old not old. You know how many *canot*[6] gone? Sunrise is sun lying down when fisherman late. You know early you go early you come back, and fish must sell quick quick or fish rotten fast, faster than old woman dead.

AUGUSTIN [*rushes at him*] Afa, *Sacré salop!*[7]

AFA [*facing him*] *Vini, vini, 'ti cooyon!*[8] Come!

[*They stand facing each other,* AUGUSTIN *with a stone.*]

AUGUSTIN You don't have no heart, [*Beating his breast*] you don't have no compassion, all you want is money, money, money, you same like a damn dog, a dog is what you are [*Getting nearer and nearer*] and your mother and your mother mother . . .

HOUNAKIN *Mes enfants, mes enfants!*[9] [*He stands between them.*]

AFA You want to fish is seventy years you have! Fisherman at seventy! But if you want it you doing like a boy is five years. And when Afa say four in the morning is four. All right, put down the cutlass in the boat, Houna, take off the stones in the *canot*. Augustin, take guard of the sail!

[AUGUSTIN *waits to pull down the sail.*]

HOUNAKIN God will bless you.

AFA He taking long, old man. Ay! Augustin, I have a tin[1] belonging Ratal in the bow, see if it there. [AFA *is helping* HOUNAKIN *unballast the canoe.*] You ever sail yet, pap? [HOUNAKIN *shakes his head.*] Fish line? [HOUNAKIN *shakes his head.*] Fish net? Nothing?

AUGUSTIN No tin[2] not there!

AFA You never fishing?

3. Good morning, gentlemen.
4. Good day.
5. Old man (literally, "old body").
6. Canoe.
7. Holy shit!
8. Come here, come here, little fool!
9. My children.
1. A thing.
2. Nothing.

HOUNAKIN On jetty alone.

AFA Is not the same thing.

HOUNAKIN I know, captain.

AFA You know why we taking out stone? Is more rough than you will see this sea again for many weeks, but we must go or belly full of wind, the *canot* must be fast and light to ride high white water, and if the pots have enough it will be heavy coming back. [*Turns and notices* AUGUSTIN *struggling with some twine.*] The cord stick, you fool! He is the most ignorant nigger they have in the world. All he know is white rum and black woman. [*Now he helps* AUGUSTIN *furl the sail into the boat.*] Repose your body under the wood-trees, old man, and watch sun breaking and guard us make *canot* ready for sea. The sea is very funny, papa. But it not making me laugh. Some say this sea is dead fisherman laughing. Some say is noise of all the fisherman woman crying. Sea in Dauphin never quiet. Always noise, noise. [*Pauses. Spits in the water. He leaves* AUGUSTIN *to fix the canoe and stands up over the old man.*] It will not make you laugh, old man, every night it getting whiter, and the birds running hungry on the rocks by Maingot side.

AUGUSTIN [*pauses, looks up*] Old man don't frighten. You playing with you death today, M'sieu Afa.

AFA Since Bolo drown. Everybody say Boileau would never drown. And Habal, Habal drowning there last year. And in September is not Annelles, Gacia brother they find two mile behind Dennery, one afternoon a boy catching crab, walking, see him on sand, when all the *maître*[3] boat looking for him by Trou Pamphile, his body swell, and the boy turn this thing with his foot and when he finish it was Annelles, drown like what, like Raphael, and Boileau. Ay, Augustin behind! *Derrière, derrière!*[4] [*He changes the position of the sail to the front of the canoe so that it now projects from the bow.*]

AUGUSTIN [*suddenly straightening up*] Afa!

AFA What?

AUGUSTIN Look Gacia coming back!

AFA You lie . . .

> [*The fisherman,* GACIA, *who has passed earlier, now returns, dejected and soaked, trailing his pole, and beating his hat against his thighs. He stops when he sees the three men.*]

GACIA

They have some men who don't believe in nothing.
Unless is accident, who don't believe in love, unless
They breed their woman. Their head like Dauphin land,
All rock, and in the rock, worm, and in the worm head
Is only death. Afa, you are this man. Greedy
Will kill you. Old man, you choose a hard companion.
Go home and sleep, die in your hut.
This sea not make for men. God self can't sail it.

AFA You going back?

GACIA What you think? By Pointe it is like mad dog fighting. *Augustin ni un cigawette?*[5] All mine wet. [AFA *gives him his cigarette.*] *Merci.*

AUGUSTIN Is so bad truly?

3. Authorities (police or coast guard).
4. Behind.
5. You don't have a cigarette?

GACIA Go and see. You can take my fish too. [*Exit.*]

AUGUSTIN You hear what Gacia say? You hear old man? Afa?

AFA We going still.

HOUNAKIN *À nous, à nous.*[6] I not afraid to die.

AUGUSTIN You want to die! You old! I different. It have a lot I don't do yet to die. Sun coming up, Afa, what to do?

HOUNAKIN To die is once. *À nous.*

AUGUSTIN [*restraining him*] You mad? Wait, wait!

AFA What happen now? Gacia is God?

AUGUSTIN No. You is God.

AFA We waiting for sun. This sea is Gacia woman no man must touch it?

AUGUSTIN The sea is the sea. [*He sits down and removes some bread from a pocket, eating angrily.*] I know you, Afa. All your life is to be better than Bolo. You can't dead better than what is dead. You want Dauphin and the whole coast to say Afa was brave! Is when you drown you brave? You have no respect for man, animal, sea, or God.

AFA

This brave I have it come from many years,
Many years of sea, many years *dolour.*[7]
That crack my face, and make my heart so hard.
If none going, then I will go alone.
If I don't have no love I don't have hate,
If I don't have woman, there is sea and sky.
God is a white man. The sky is his blue eye,
His spit on Dauphin people is the sea.
Don't ask me why a man must work so hard
To eat for worm to get more fat. Maybe I bewitch.
You never curse God, I curse him, and cannot die,
Until His time. This basin men call sea
Never get red for men blood it have. My turn is next.
I cannot sleep on land, like Gacia.
The land is hard, this Dauphin land have stone
Where it should have some heart. The sea
It have compassion in the end.

AUGUSTIN [*clapping in mockery*]

What it have across the sea?
You leave something in *Africa*?
Between there and Dauphin, ten thousand miles?
Is there you going?
And furthermore I can't swim.

AFA [*to* HOUNAKIN] You can swim, papa?

HOUNAKIN *Non.*

AFA [*sitting down suddenly, interested now that the canoe is equipped for work*] Tell me again, old man, why for you want to work the sea? And you so old? You never stay in your house and hear wind breaking wood-trees? You never go down on your two knees and thank the Virgin you never work this sea by Maingot side? Where is Habal, Raphael, Annelles, Boileau? Sun breaking,

6. Together.

7. Pain.

papa, talk fast. Where Boileau used to pull *canot* with his one hand? [HOUNAKIN, *frightened, cannot talk.*] The onliest fisherman better than Boileau was Saint Pierre,[8] both of them dead.

AUGUSTIN You will not talk, old man? He want to die.

AFA [*rises*] Today is a good day. [*Businesslike*] *Alors!* All right. *Nous parti.*[9] [*Giving orders expertly*] Augustin, we going; old man, we ready. [AUGUSTIN *pauses, looks seaward, then crosses himself.* AFA *and* AUGUSTIN *get ready to push the canoe, when the old man rises, dazed, and sits in it.*] All right, Augustin, watch for the big wave. [*To the old man*] Get out the *canot,* old man, not time to sit. [*Turns away, his back to the old man*] When I say *poussez, poussez!*[1] Ready?

AUGUSTIN Come, papa. Not yet to sit down in the *canot.* Come, come . . . [HOUNAKIN *is petrified;* AFA *turns round. His anger is mounting.*] *Sorti, sorti, vieux corps.*[2] [*Touches* HOUNAKIN *on the shoulder.*] He is trembling.

AFA What happen now?

AUGUSTIN He is crying.

AFA [*striding over to the old man*] *Sorti, sorti,* papa, get up, get up. [AUGUSTIN *lifts* HOUNAKIN's *chin with his hand.* AFA *shakes him roughly.*] Get up, get up, papa, sun break long.

HOUNAKIN *Non, non,* is cold, is cold . . .

AFA [*shaking him harder*] I say get up! Is making cold in this hot sun! Is late!

AUGUSTIN [*pleading*] Papa, *sou 'plait, levez!*[3] [HOUNAKIN *is mumbling to himself.*] He is like a man is dead, he is so cold . . . papa.

AFA [*completely enraged*] *Ça c'est bettise,*[4] man! Pull him out! Haul the old man skin out the boat. Is not me kill his woman. You want me to pull him out? Smell him! Stink of white rum! He drunk! [*Begins to pull the old man.*] Get out the backside boat, man time going!

AUGUSTIN [*raising his cutlass and weeping with rage*] Son of Man, Afa! Touch this old man once, once! *Avec un fois encore*[5] and I cut you belly open and put a heart in it! *Touchez-lui! Touchez-lui!*[6]

AFA So is tongue and cutlass now? [*He looks at him steadily;* AUGUSTIN *throws down the cutlass and turns away.*] Old man, your wife is dead, and sorry[7] make you mad. Go on the morne[8] and count the birds like Ragamin, and play bamboo under the wood-trees for you' goat. Is land you know, old man, you don't know sea, you know the fifteen kind of grass this island have, land hard under a old man foot and hard on old woman body, but this sea is no cemetery for old men; go on the morne behind the presbytery, watch goat, talk with priest, and drink your white rum after the night come. When we come back we will talk of this sea.

AUGUSTIN Afa and Augustin will bring Hounakin fish, and bread, and vegetable from Gacia garden, and when Noel come will drink red rum and talk. Because you woman dead you want to drown?

HOUNAKIN [*touching* AFA's *hand*] Cousin, it cold, it always making cold.

8. Saint Peter (d. ca. 64 C.E.), a Galilean fisherman who became one of Jesus' Twelve Apostles.
9. We leave; let's go. *Alors!*: well then.
1. Push.
2. Get out, old man.
3. Please, get up, get up!
4. This is stupid.
5. One more time.
6. Touch him!
7. Sorrow.
8. Small hill.

AUGUSTIN [*kneeling near the canoe*] So what you have, old man, you cannot sleep? Sixty years you work in cane[9] field, rice swamp, Barnard land, your two eyes come so small you cannot see. Old man, the sun come up, and sea have work. Let Afa and Augustin go to work for you . . . [HOUNAKIN *puts* AFA*'s hand away. It is now broad daylight.* HOUNAKIN *gets up from the narrow canoe, takes his things and is leaving, the two fishermen watching him, when, thinking again, he turns to them.*]

HOUNAKIN [*resting his pail*] Cousin, I must give my heart tongue, or it will break. You know the stories Rama did tell you Augustin . . . ?

AFA And me, when I was small . . . *messieurs, crik-crack*[1] . . .

AUGUSTIN I never forget, papa . . . that is long time . . .

HOUNAKIN [*walks painfully nearer*] Like you say, Afa, and my son Augustin, God bless.

[*He sits.*]

Since she dead it have two days I only counting birds,
And even bird have woman, fisherman know;
I know where they fly making nest for wind by Pointe,
But they still screaming: "Rama dead, old man, old man, Rama dead."
To dead; what is to dead? not dead I fraid . . .
For old man that is nothing, wind.
But when one woman you loving fifty years,
That time they dead, it don't like they should have bird,
And bread to eat, a house, and dog to feed.
It is to take a net in you hand to catch the wind,
To beat head on a stone, to take sand in you' hand,
And that is it, *compère*, that is it true,
When Rama dead I cry after the dog tired.

AFA All Dauphin know that old man . . . Sit down . . . You want some bread?

HOUNAKIN *Non, non, merci*, I only keep you back . . . The sun break long . . .

AUGUSTIN Today Afa can wait . . .

HOUNAKIN Don't worry, you will not see this old man so again, only, a man must talk, old man talk to the wind or man go mad . . . [AFA *offers him bread.*] I have no heart to eat. I old, old, more old than Dauphin self. Rama and I see when didn't have no Dauphin, only cane, and a green river by the canes. We come here first.

AFA Sit down, papa. [*He gives him some bread, the old man smiles, then puts it in his shirt.* AUGUSTIN *gives him a cigarette, which he holds absently, unlit, while talking. He has sat down.*]

HOUNAKIN

When Rama dying she did want more medicine,
You know we could not beg, but then I beg
For one whole year, then she catch sick again.
And Rama say no medicine we must not beg.
I did not want to beg and Rama die.
The first time I did beg you was last night.

9. That is, sugarcane.

1. In the Caribbean, Creole storytellers traditionally begin a tale with "Krik-krak," the equivalent of "Once upon a time . . ."

To work. I cannot beg or bend down to make garden.
I know have friend, but friend and pride is different . . .
Is just a work to feed a old man and the dog . . .

AFA Sea will go down, *vieux corps*, come with your cousin.

HOUNAKIN *Non*. You must go. The sea rough for two weeks. If Afa not go, will have no more fish again. *Non* . . . God is good . . .

AUGUSTIN
A *canot* not no coffin for a old man.
Tonight we will drunk and joke in Samuel café,
Bringing back good fish, and for Rama grave
A white shell is at the bottom of the sea . . .
And when sea calm, and God not so vex . . .

HOUNAKIN
Paix, paix, garçon[2] . . . An old man must have strength. Nobody
know God height, and nobody know the deep the green sea is,
Wind does not pull bird where wind want, look there!
It looking like somebody shaking this basin of the world,
And making waves where man and boats is drowning. Is God.
All that; but me self, Hounakin, what I do wrong?
I poor is not my fault. I sin, I make sorry, did have pride,
But that gone now. Me one alone, who don't know night from day,
My two eyes come so small. I kneel on my two knees,
I say, when Rama coughing all this time,
God you is old man like me, you put me here, I pray, I work,
I never steal when my belly full of wind . . .
I sin, I make confession, is the same.
I work, make absolution is the same.
I love, I have no child, and is the same,
Is seventy years they giving man to live,[3] even old coolie,
But I spit in the face of nothing.
You break your back for seventy cane reap times[4]
And then is ashes. A man cannot fight nothing, after all.
But wind is coming high, Houna must go.

AUGUSTIN Papa . . . do not do nothing to yourself . . .

HOUNAKIN Houna will not kill himself. This sea have many navels, many waves, and I did feel to die in Dauphin sea, so I could born. *Au'voir*[5] cousin . . . [*Goes off.*]

AUGUSTIN Another day, old man, when sea is calm and wind is soft . . .

AFA He cannot hear . . .

AUGUSTIN And a white shell for Rama is in the ground . . .

AFA [*starting to push canoe*] *À nous, à nous, compère*, sea going down, and the sun hot . . . [*They start to haul the canoe.*] *Plus fort. Poussez! Poussez!*[6] [*The old man can be seen a little above them, watching them at work.*] Mind the sail, Agos, mind the sail! [*The old man remains watching them dazedly, and waves a worn, tired hand, then goes off as the lights fade into*

2. Peace, boy.
3. See Psalms 90.10: "The days of our years are threescore years and ten."
4. That is, annual harvests of sugarcane.
5. Good-bye.
6. Harder. Push! Push!

evening and the almost blinding twilight. The sunset is reddening as the villagers of Dauphin can be heard singing; they are mostly women and a boy, dressed poorly, with bare feet and baskets for the catch, and they come from different parts of the beach, with the young French PRIEST, *Father Lavoisier.*]

CHORUS OF DAUPHIN WOMEN [*singing*]

La mer pwend Bolo qui 'tait si bwave, oy!
Si la mer pwend mwen 'ous pas kai save, oy!
Ba-bye doux-doux, ba-bye, mwen ka aller,
Si mwen mort jourd'hui, pas pleurez!

(The sea took Bolo who was so brave, oh!
When the sea takes me you will not know, oh!
Farewell, darling, farewell, I must go,
If I should die today, don't cry, don't cry.)

'Ous ni un 'tit mouton blanc tout moune save, woy!
Pas quittez-li pleurer pis 'ous pas brave, woy!
Mwen pas ni l'argent pous ba'ous m'a ni l'or
Pwend vieux canot mwen l'heure mwen mort.

(You have a little white sheep everyone knows, oh!
Don't let it bleat because you aren't brave, oh!
I have no money to give you, I have no gold,
When I die, take this canoe that is too old.)

Ba-bye doux-doux, ba-bye, priez-Dieu pour mwen,
Prie-Dieu pour toute nomme qui ni vent en la main.
Ba-bye doux-doux, ba-bye, l'heure pêcheur mort
Pas ni malheur, pas ni la mer encore.

(Farewell, my love, farewell, pray for me,
Pray for all men with only the wind in their hands
Farewell, my love, farewell, when fishermen die
There is no more bad luck and no more sea.)

A WOMAN The *canot* is there, where Afa and Augustin?

ANOTHER I tell you I see them go up by Houna house. Looking for the old man—

FIRST WOMAN [*pointing left*] Look. They coming.

[AFA *and* AUGUSTIN *come in.* AUGUSTIN *is worried and carries a white shell in his hand.* AFA *carries a pail of fish, cord, etc. They see the small group, and wait.*]

AFA Is true, then, priest?

AUGUSTIN We come back long, before the sun lying down, his house is close. Is true this thing we hear? We stand up by his house and hear this singing. If is fish you want, don't have no fish.

AFA When it happen, *père*?[7]

P. LAVOISIER [*urges the boy forward gently*] Jules, go and talk to your uncle, Augustin.

7. Father (this "P. Lavoisier" is "Father Lavoisier").

AFA *Oui!* Is better than any priest saying *bettise*[8] about God for me to fling salt water in his face!

AUGUSTIN Afa, you mad?

JULES What to say, *père*?

AUGUSTIN Jules, my nephew, tell us what you see?

AFA Tell us what you see, *garçon*, and you put God in it, I cut your throat!

JULES I find him by . . . I was looking for whelks with Baptiste, M'sieu Afa, I find him by the rocks by Pointe . . . Baptiste was frighten and take run . . . I run and call the *père* . . .

AUGUSTIN [*breaks down*] I cannot take no more, I cannot take no more . . .

[*A woman goes over to him.*]

P. LAVOISIER Augustin, my son, let the wind come, sea come, let the hurricane blow. It will blow the sand from the heart of many a man and change this world . . .

AUGUSTIN [*to the woman*] He was mad, he had nothing, he beg us this morning to take him, but we go . . . Afa have fish for him, half a bonito, and I have this shell . . .

JULES Is fall he fall down from the high rocks by Point Side. His face mash up; I wasn't fraid, he fall and the sea take him . . .

WOMAN True. When you old you don't have nothing.

AUGUSTIN He didn't have nobody or nothing.

P. LAVOISIER He had God . . .

AFA God! [*He turns and empties the fish pail on the sand.*] That is God! A big fish eating small ones. And the sea, that thing there, not a priest white, pale like a shark belly we must feed until we dead, not no young Frenchman lock up in a church don't know coolie man dying because he will not beg! [*The women break up and retreat before him.*] *Sacrés cooyons! Sacrés jamettes saintes!*[9] All you can do is what, sing way! way! Hounakin dead and Bolo dead, is all mouth! mouth! [*He turns and tears a scapular*[1] *from his neck and hurls it to the ground.*] *Mi! Mi!* Pick it up, *père*, is not ours. This scapular not Dauphin own! Dauphin people build the church and pray and feed you, not their own people, and look at Dauphin! *Gadez lui!*[2] Look at it! You see? Poverty, dirty woman, dirty children, where all the prayers? Where all the money a man should have and friends when his skin old? Dirt and prayers is Dauphin life, in Dauphin, in Canaries, Micoud.[3] Where they have priest is poverty. [*The people leave.*] Go home! *Allez-la-caille 'ous! . . . Allez!* Idiots, *garces!*[4] . . . [*The* PRIEST, AUGUSTIN, *and* JULES *remain.*]

AUGUSTIN Don't mind him, Father. He must curse or he will cry.

P. LAVOISIER We are all trying, Afa. I am young here. We must help one another. [*The* PRIEST *picks up the scapular.*] You must take it back . . .

AFA Why for?

P. LAVOISIER Afa, leave what you cannot understand to me . . .

AFA Move in front of me.

AUGUSTIN Give it to me, *père*. He will take it tomorrow.

8. Stupid [things].

9. Holy fools! Holy gutter saints!

1. That is, a scapular medal, originally intended to replace the cloth scapular (part of the monastic habit) but later worn more generally as a religious medallion.

2. Look at it!

3. Canaries and Micoud are the names of actual towns on St. Lucia, the island in the West Indies where Walcott was born.

4. Boys (short for *garçons*). *Allez-la-caille 'ous* go home, all of you.

AFA Like dog!

P. LAVOISIER You fishermen are a hard race. You think we cannot help you? You are wrong. It is a sacred profession, Afa, the first saints followed your profession, Saint Pierre, Saint Jean.[5] They were hard-headed men too . . .

AFA Eh, heh . . . priest, I have nothing against you, leave me alone. You curse me, I curse you, all right?

P. LAVOISIER I will pray for you . . .

AFA Pray for the dead.

P. LAVOISIER Augustin has your scapular. [*Exit*]

[AUGUSTIN *and the boy* JULES *wait, watching* AFA *fix some twine, pause, then fix it again.* JULES *tugs at* AUGUSTIN*'s shoulder and whispers.* AUGUSTIN *walks over to* AFA, *who is staring, mumbling, out to sea.*]

AUGUSTIN Tomorrow again?

AFA Unless you going to church. Because one old man dead, the sea will stop?

AUGUSTIN *Quant-même*[6] we don't have to wait for no old man . . . We start too late this morning . . .

AFA *À quatre heures juste*[7] . . . Four o'clock.

[JULES *tugs at* AUGUSTIN*'s shoulder.*]

AUGUSTIN Afa [*Whose back is still turned to them*], you always saying in Samuel café we want another man is not too heavy to bail, and haul up the *nasse*, this one here want to go with us tomorrow. His father was Habal, you used to work sea first in Habal boat, when you did half the old he is . . .

AFA Half the boat is yours.

AUGUSTIN *Captaine*, he have to sit in your half too when fishpots in.

AFA [*turning*] Tell him if he know what it have in this trade, in this season any day is to die. And tell the boy it make you sour and old and good for nothing standing on two feet when forty years you have. Ask him why he not going to Castries[8] to learn mechanic or work in canes. Ask him if he remember Habal, and then Bolo. If he say yes, tell him he must brave like Hounakin, from young he is. Brave like Habal to fight sea at Dauphin. This piece of coast is make for men like that. Tell him Afa do it for his father sake. Although Augustin say he have no gratitude . . . Four o'clock . . .

[JULES *runs over and hugs* AFA. AFA *gives* AUGUSTIN *the fish, and the boy and* AUGUSTIN *go out.* AFA *sits on the stage, exactly as he did before, wrapping some twine and smoking. The sound of the* WOMEN *singing faintly throughout.* GACIA *the fisherman comes in, his straw hat flapping, quite drunk. He sees* AFA, *then rests his hat down on the ground. He has a pint bottle of white rum, which he rests carefully against the canoe.*]

GACIA [*spelling lettering of the canoe*] Our Daily Bread . . . Our Daily Bread. [*Holds up the bottle.*] You want one?

AFA [*takes a drink*] *Merci, boug.* [*Rests his hand on* GACIA*'s shoulder.*] *Merci.* [*Offers a cigarette.*] Cigarette?

GACIA [*shakes his head, mouth full*] Woy! Whole day! . . . Tonight they have his wake. You going?

[*A* WOMAN*'s* VOICE *calling "Gacia, Gacia, oy!"*]

5. Saint John the Evangelist (1st c. C.E.), another of the Twelve Apostles and another former fisherman.

6. However.

7. At four o'clock sharp.

8. The capital city of St. Lucia.

AFA Your woman calling you.

GACIA [*shaking his shoulders in disgust*] *Quittez-lui crier!*[9] Is woman work to cry. When you woman Anna coming back?

AFA I have no woman. I cannot love woman. [*Takes another drink.*] My head is full of madness. I make my heart hard long. From the first time it break. Nothing breaking it again. [*Passes back the bottle.*]

GACIA A man cannot live so. Man not a rock.

AFA I don't know, *boug*. They had a time was like Augustin could cry in front of woman. No more, *jamais encore, garçon.* [*Looks to the sea.*] *Belle jour demain.*[1]

GACIA *Peut-être.*[2] I finish with the sea . . .

AFA You always finish with the sea. But you and I, *compère*, we cannot finish.

GACIA If you leave women I can leave the sea . . . Why you must curse the priest?

AFA I was vex . . . It mean nothing.

GACIA *Alors,*[3] the old man die. He kill himself they say. Sorry can make old man mad. You catch anything?

AFA One bonito. And a shell.

GACIA Eh-heh . . .

AFA In the evening when sun go down behind Maria Island we come back and don't see the old man. We walk up all the beach where we leave him, and go up to his *ajoupa* . . . It have white sea all day around Maingot, but no good fish . . .

GACIA Ay, *boug!*

AFA And Augustin have half a bonito for the old man, and so we go up the *ajoupa* on the hill by Dauphin side. And he not there, is only his woman grave. And the garden dead, the old corn dying standing up and the yellow dog is hungry. And Augustin wrap the fish, half a bonito, and put it on top the house and a banana leaf to mark it. And coming down the hill just now we hear the woman singing, and I look at Agos and he look at me afraid. And we meet Debel drunk looking for us and Debel say this morning he see him sitting on the sand and counting bird. [*Takes a drink.*] And this afternoon Debel come back, was to catch crab, and he is not there, only the wood-trees and the sand blowing . . . And Debel say he look for him and meet a old man was driving goat from dry grass, and say he see him climbing on the high rocks by where they have the statue of Sainte Vierge[4] . . . And this afternoon they had a boy was fishing for whelks under La Vierge by Maingot side, and see this thing, and the boy turn it over on the sand with his foot, and when they look is him. And the fish on top his house is rotten, faster than old man is dead . . .

WOMAN'S VOICE Gacia! Gacia!

GACIA *Alors?*

AFA [*looking to sea*] Last year Annelles, and Bolo, and this year Hounakin . . . And one day, tomorrow, you Gacia, and me . . . And Augustin . . . And we have only this shell for his old woman is in the

9. Stop crying!
1. Never again, boy. . . . Nice day tomorrow.
2. Could be.
3. So.
4. The Blessed Virgin (Mary, mother of Jesus).

cimetière[5] behind the church, where Fond River coming down by the canes and making one with the sea at Dauphin . . .

GACIA Sun going down . . .

AFA The sea too . . .

GACIA Tomorrow again. *Un autre demain*[6] . . .

[WOMAN'S VOICE *calling "Gacia, Gacia."*]

AFA [*rising*] Your woman crying for you . . . Help me with this sail. *Aidez, aidez-moi avec voile-là.*[7]

[*They furl the sail.*]

Night.

5. Cemetery.
6. Another tomorrow.
7. Help me with this sail.

EUGENE O'NEILL

1888–1953

EVER since his breakthrough in the 1920s, Eugene O'Neill has been regarded as the first truly modern playwright of the United States—a status confirmed in 1936, when he became the first American dramatist to receive the Nobel Prize in Literature. O'Neill made full use of the cultural and artistic achievements of modernism. We find in his oeuvre the vernacular voices of working-class characters, typical of naturalism; the exaggerated, shrill voices of expressionism; the eruptions of repressed feelings associated with Freudian psychology; the chorus and masks of ancient tragedy that were being revived in the early twentieth century; and the multiple voices and open structures of modern ensemble pieces that have no main protagonist. In bringing the new experimental dramas of modernism to America, O'Neill drew on a panoply of styles, thereby providing in effect a condensed history of the various stages of modern drama. At the same time, however, O'Neill did more than merely channel artistic and intellectual trends invented elsewhere. He managed to create out of them original plays that capture the forces of the modern world through unusual dramatic structures as well as through deeply felt and often tragic characters. For many, O'Neill remains not only the founder of modern drama in America but also its most distinguished representative.

O'Neill was born into an Irish American family, with a dominating father who was a successful actor and a doting mother from a wealthy family. While his father's career in the theater would prove an important inspiration for the dramatist, it was also a cautionary tale. James O'Neill, born in Ireland and raised in poverty in America, had once been a rising star. Then he was offered the title role in a melodrama that would dominate the rest of his life: *The Count of Monte Cristo* (1846). He bought the rights to the work and played its wrongly accused hero more than 5,000 times, only to find that the role and its endless performances had blunted his talent, bringing him fame and financial rewards but thwarting his true artistic achievement. For much of his youth, Eugene seemed to be rebelling against parental expectations—failing to complete his freshman year at Princeton, working odd jobs, and marrying a respectable young woman, Kathleen Jenkins, against his father's wishes. Leaving behind his wife and infant son, he then went to sea as a crewman on a cargo ship; he spent considerable time on a number of freighters and passenger liners. When he returned to New York, he and his wife divorced, and he began working for the New London *Telegraph*, writing both news stories and occasional verse. Soon thereafter he was diagnosed with a life-threatening case of tuberculosis. During the months he spent at a sanatorium, 1912–13, O'Neill found a new focus: He decided to become a playwright.

His first significant teacher and champion was George Pierce Baker of Harvard University, a pioneer in offering workshop-like courses in modern dramatic literature; O'Neill attended his seminar in 1914–15. Another early supporter was the influential New York theater critic George Jean Nathan, who became O'Neill's close friend. Equally if not more important for his success was a group that formed as an experimental summer theater in Provincetown on Cape Cod and later relocated to New York City. The Provincetown Players, founded in 1915, were devoted to fostering a new American theater; under the leadership of George Cram (Jig) Cook and SUSAN GLASPELL, the group—which had its first New York City season in 1916—helped establish off-Broadway theaters as essential venues for serious drama. One of the plays featured in that first season was O'Neill's *Bound East for Cardiff* (1916); and over the next ten years, the Provincetown Players staged many of his plays, some of which later moved to Broadway.

Even during this relatively stable and highly productive period of his life, O'Neill was restless. He had married Agnes Boulton in 1918, and they moved between Provincetown and New York before taking up residence in a series of houses purchased on Cape Cod, in Connecticut, and finally in Bermuda. But in 1927, he left Agnes and their two children for Carlotta Monterey, whom he married in Paris in 1929. After living in France for two years, they returned to the United States, living first in Georgia and then in California. His final decades were marred by declining health as well as by disappointment in and estrangement from his children; his eldest child, Eugene Jr., an alcoholic who failed to live up to his early promise, committed suicide in 1950; his other son, Shane, became a heroin addict; and he disowned his eighteen-year-old daughter, Oona, in 1943, after she married Charlie Chaplin, who was three times her age and was widely reputed to be a womanizer. As early as the mid-1930s, O'Neill was showing signs of physical weakness, no doubt exacerbated by his lifelong struggles with depression and alcohol; he was too ill to attend his own Nobel Prize ceremony. By 1940, hand tremors were making it difficult for him to hold a pencil—the Parkinson-like shaking was caused by the degenerative neurological disease that ultimately led to his death at the age of sixty-five. He had stopped writing ten years earlier, in 1943. Yet in his last years of work, he produced his finest plays, *The Iceman Cometh* (written 1939; produced 1946) and *LONG DAY'S JOURNEY INTO NIGHT* (written 1941; produced 1956).

O'Neill's early plays drew extensively on his life at sea. The one-act plays *Bound East for Cardiff* and *The Moon of the Caribbees* (1918), as well as the full-length drama *Anna Christie* (1921), are set on ships, and many of his mature later works also pay homage to the sea. These plays brought O'Neill recognition, and soon he began writing the plays with which he staked his claim to be the first modernist playwright in the United States. In *The Hairy Ape* (1922), he channeled the themes of his early one acts into an expressionistic play about a stoker who identifies himself with the powerful engine of a steamship. A second expressionist play, *The Emperor Jones* (1920), is set on an island in the West Indies; it revolves around a megalomaniac ruler, with a plot inspired by Joseph Conrad's modernist story "Heart of Darkness" (1902). Indeed, O'Neill frequently drew on the techniques of novels, as is clear from his long and descriptive stage directions and characterizations. More specifically, in having characters express their secret thoughts through long asides, as he did in *Strange Interlude* (1928), he sought to introduce the new stream-of-consciousness technique of James Joyce and Virginia Woolf to drama. In some plays—such as *The Great God Brown* (1926), whose title character is an architect who ultimately assumes the persona of his rival—O'Neill relied on masks to help reveal characters' innermost thoughts and express hidden conflicts.

Though O'Neill worked with an astonishing range of theatrical styles, he concentrated on modern tragedy, a thrust that culminated in his great late plays. O'Neill owed his tragic worldview in part to his enthusiasm for the writings of Friedrich Nietzsche, who in *The Birth of Tragedy* (1872) advocated a revival of Greek tragedy, a project to which O'Neill remained dedicated throughout his career as a dramatist. Several of his most significant plays are rewritings of specific Greek tragedies; for example, *Desire under the Elms* (1924) transfers the story of the love felt for Hippolytus by his young stepmother, Phaedra, to a New England farm, and O'Neill's magisterial trilogy, *Mourning Becomes Electra* (1931), is a modern version of AESCHYLUS's plays about the house of Atreus.

The high point of O'Neill's oeuvre is *Long Day's Journey into Night,* perhaps the finest tragedy written in the twentieth century, which draws on his lifelong work in this form. At the same time, it differs from most of his important plays in that it is unabashedly autobiographical. In fact, it is so closely interwoven with his own family history that O'Neill kept it secret throughout his life and demanded it not be published or performed until twenty-five years after his death. When Carlotta nevertheless allowed its premiere in Stockholm in 1956, it cast a new light on his entire career. Audiences and critics sought out autobiographical elements and figures in O'Neill's other plays as well, and soon biographers began using the play as a unique window onto his formative years. Like O'Neill's father, James Tyrone has made his name and fortune playing the title role in a commercially successful but artistically mediocre play. Like O'Neill's mother, Mary Tyrone is unhappy in the itinerant life forced on her by her husband's tours across the United States and she, too, becomes addicted to morphine while recovering from childbirth. Like O'Neill's older brother, Jamie Tyrone leads a life devoted to the bar and the whorehouse, remaining financially dependent on his wealthy but stingy father. And like O'Neill himself, Edmund Tyrone is an aspiring poet, immersed in Nietzsche and Baudelaire, who is about to be sent to a cheap state sanatorium to treat his tuberculosis. Finally, the whole play is set in a summer residence in Connecticut of the kind the O'Neills possessed and which his mother could never bring herself to regard as a proper home.

The close connection between the play and the O'Neill family is remarkable, but it does not explain the play's unique power. Indeed, those of O'Neill's early works, such as *Bread and Butter* (written 1914), that are based on particular family members

Scene from the world premiere, in February 1956, of *Long Day's Journey into Night* at the Royal Dramatic Theatre, Stockholm.

and that contain a poet figure with whom the author clearly identifies are among O'Neill's weakest plays. *Long Day's Journey into Night* is a masterpiece of twentieth-century tragedy not because of but despite its autobiographical elements. O'Neill may have used some events and family structures he knew from his childhood and adolescence, but he significantly compressed and altered them, imposing on them a carefully balanced dramatic form.

The play conforms to the neoclassical unities of time, space, and action: The time is confined to one evening, and the entire play takes place in the living room of the Tyrone household. The quality of its dramatic action is more difficult to grasp, for unlike most tragedies, *Long Day's Journey into Night* presents the audience with little action, onstage or (as in Greek tragedy) offstage. Nothing seems to happen except the talking of characters who slowly but surely descend into drunken or drugged reverie. The rhythms of speech vary, as periods of introspection and silence are followed by heated exchanges, accusations, and monologues, and as characters enter and exit. But the net effect is their inexorable movement into the night evoked in the play's title.

The dearth of action on the stage does not mean that *Long Day's Journey into Night* lacks development, turning points, or suspense. On the contrary, the play contains plenty of action, but it has all happened in the past. What occurs on the stage is the gradual discovery of that past, as words lay bare hidden events, emotions, and relations. O'Neill borrowed this technique from the most important but also most unusual of Greek tragedies, SOPHOCLES' *Oedipus the King* (ca. 428 B.C.E.). Rather than presenting confrontations and dilemmas as they arise in the present, *Oedipus* reveals the true meaning of what has already happened. O'Neill is among a number of modern writers and thinkers, from HENRIK IBSEN to Sigmund Freud, who saw *Oedipus* as the most modern of Greek tragedies.

Out of his studies in tragedy and selected elements of his own life, O'Neill creates a network of relations among characters hopelessly tangled in a web of guilt and dependence, love and hate—all the human passions. There is not a single in-

A caricature by Al Hirschfeld drawn to accompany the *New York Times* review of the Broadway premiere of *Long Day's Journey into Night* in November 1956.

nocent figure in this play, which constantly shifts blame from one to the next. James Tyrone speculates in real estate, but he is too tightfisted to provide a real home of the kind his wife dreams of. In addition, his stinginess is at least partially responsible for his wife's morphine addiction, which began when he sought medical advice on the cheap. Yet Tyrone himself, no less than his family, is a victim of his desire for financial security—a desire he has pursued at the expense of his larger artistic ambitions. And on another level, Mary's addiction was caused not by his cheapness but by the pain of Edmund's difficult birth, which the morphine originally was treating. Though Edmund clearly bears no direct responsibility, there is unquestionably a link between his existence and his mother's condition. Nor can Mary herself be viewed simply as a victim. By insisting on the Tyrones' social superiority to others in town, she has isolated herself; and by idolizing her father, she has intensified her dissatisfaction with her husband. It seems that in her eyes no home could ever equal the one in which she grew up. O'Neill cruelly knots his characters together so that the more they attack one another, the more tightly the bonds tie them.

The power of *Long Day's Journey into Night* lies in O'Neill's subtle unveiling of a terrible history. The past, which determines the inner quality of these figures and their relationships, must be made visible in the present. In part, this revelation is accomplished through long confessional speeches, embellished with quotes from SHAKESPEARE, made by increasingly drunk characters. Yet these declarations are not always trustworthy, skewed as they are by a toxic mixture of guilt, self-justification, and self-deception. This blend of confession and dissimulation becomes manifest on stage though characters' habits, poses, and tics, as well as stage props. The living room is barely lit, because James Tyrone tries to save every penny. And when one of his sons insists on turning on a few lights upon reentering the house, an argument ensues. O'Neill here uses a significant element of the theater—lighting—to capture a character trait and to trigger one of the conflicts whose progression will reveal another piece of the past, another knot of causation and guilt.

More significant than stage props are the physiognomy and gestures of these characters, whose present actions are driven entirely by past events, becoming in effect symptoms through which their histories can be read. The most legible, and the most closely scrutinized, are Mary's. The audience and the other characters on the stage constantly examine her appearance and gestures to determine whether she has gone back to using drugs. We learn that Mary once aspired to become a pianist and prided herself on her fine hands. Now, however, they are crippled with rheumatism and shake nervously, a result of the detoxification she has just undergone; her husband desperately tries to still them. They are quieted only by the several doses of morphine she takes over the course of the play. Similarly, James's mode of speech and acting are mere extensions of his roles on the stage, but he cannot escape them: Grand gestures and grandiose speech have become his second nature. Nor can Jamie stop his cynical invectives, the product of a long and bitter fight against his own failure. When the play begins, it appears to be firmly rooted in a single day in 1912 as it reaches back in time; by its end, the present has almost disappeared, overwhelmed by the past that holds these characters in its grip.

Long Day's Journey into Night is O'Neill's most compelling play because it uniquely balances such externals as the shabbiness of the house, the significance of each stage prop, and the symptomatic quality of each gesture, habit, and tic as the characters interact. It displays impressive elegance of form, whose elements function like interwoven signs and signals that reveal the past. Through such simple and economical means, *Long Day's Journey into Night* develops characters that are complex and internally divided, drifting through violence and silence into the abysmal darkness of the play's close.

M.P.

Long Day's Journey into Night

For Carlotta, on our 12th Wedding Anniversary

Dearest: I give you the original script of this play of old sorrow, written in tears and blood. A sadly inappropriate gift, it would seem, for a day celebrating happiness. But you will understand. I mean it as a tribute to your love and tenderness which gave me the faith in love that enabled me to face my dead at last and write this play—write it with deep pity and understanding and forgiveness for all the four haunted Tyrones.

These twelve years, Beloved One, have been a Journey into Light—into love. You know my gratitude. And my love! GENE

Tao House
July 22, 1941.

CHARACTERS

JAMES TYRONE
MARY CAVAN TYRONE, his wife
JAMES TYRONE, JR., their elder son
EDMUND TYRONE, their younger son
CATHLEEN, second girl

SCENES

ACT 1 *Living room of the Tyrones' summer home 8:30 A.M. of a day in August, 1912*

ACT 2 SCENE 1 *The same, around 12:45*
SCENE 2 *The same, about a half hour later*

ACT 3 *The same, around 6:30 that evening*

ACT 4 *The same, around midnight*

Act 1

SCENE: *Living room of James Tyrone's summer home on a morning in August, 1912.*

At rear are two double doorways with portieres.[1] *The one at right leads into a front parlor with the formally arranged, set appearance of a room rarely occupied. The other opens on a dark, windowless back parlor, never used except as a passage from living room to dining room. Against the wall between the doorways is a small*

1. Heavy curtains hung over the doorway.

bookcase, with a picture of Shakespeare above it, containing novels by Balzac, Zola, Stendhal, philosophical and sociological works by Schopenhauer, Nietzsche, Marx, Engels, Kropotkin, Max Stirner, plays by Ibsen, Shaw, Strindberg, poetry by Swinburne, Rossetti, Wilde, Ernest Dawson, Kipling, etc.

In the right wall, rear, is a screen door leading out on the porch which extends halfway around the house. Farther forward, a series of three windows looks over the front lawn to the harbor and the avenue that runs along the waterfront. A small wicker table and an ordinary oak desk are against the wall, flanking the windows.

In the left wall, a similar series of windows looks out on the grounds in back of the house. Beneath them is a wicker couch with cushions, its head toward rear. Farther back is a large, glassed-in bookcase with sets of Dumas, Victor Hugo, Charles Lever, three sets of Shakespeare, The World's Best Literature *in fifty large volumes, Hume's* History of England, *Thiers'* History of the Consulate and Empire, *Smollett's* History of England, *Gibbon's* Roman Empire, *and miscellaneous volumes of old plays, poetry, and several histories of Ireland. The astonishing thing about these sets is that all the volumes have the look of having been read and reread.*

The hardwood floor is nearly covered by a rug, inoffensive in design and color. At center is a round table with a green-shaded reading lamp, the cord plugged in one of the four sockets in the chandelier above. Around the table within reading-light range are four chairs, three of them wicker armchairs, the fourth (at right front of table) a varnished oak rocker with leather bottom.

It is around 8:30. Sunshine comes through the windows at right.

As the curtain rises, the family have just finished breakfast. MARY TYRONE *and her husband enter together from the back parlor, coming from the dining room.*

MARY *is fifty-four, about medium height. She still has a young, graceful figure, a trifle plump, but showing little evidence of middle-aged waist and hips, although she is not tightly corseted. Her face is distinctly Irish in type. It must once have been extremely pretty, and is still striking. It does not match her healthy figure but is thin and pale with the bone structure prominent. Her nose is long and straight, her mouth wide with full, sensitive lips. She uses no rouge or any sort of makeup. Her high forehead is framed by thick pure white hair. Accentuated by her pallor and white hair, her dark brown eyes appear black. They are unusually large and beautiful, with black brows and long curling lashes.*

What strikes one immediately is her extreme nervousness. Her hands are never still. They were once beautiful hands, with long, tapering fingers, but rheumatism has knotted the joints and warped the fingers, so that now they have an ugly crippled look. One avoids looking at them, the more so because one is conscious she is sensitive about their appearance and humiliated by her inability to control the nervousness which draws attention to them.

She is dressed simply but with a sure sense of what becomes her. Her hair is arranged with fastidious care. Her voice is soft and attractive. When she is merry, there is a touch of Irish lilt in it.

Her most appealing quality is the simple, unaffected charm of a shy convent-girl youthfulness she has never lost—an innate unworldly innocence.

JAMES TYRONE *is sixty-five but looks ten years younger. About five feet eight, broad-shouldered and deep-chested, he seems taller and slenderer because of his bearing, which has a soldierly quality of head up, chest out, stomach in, shoulders squared. His face has begun to break down but he is still remarkably good-looking—a big, finely shaped head, a handsome profile, deep-set light-brown eyes. His grey hair is thin with a bald spot like a monk's tonsure.*

The stamp of his profession is unmistakably on him. Not that he indulges in any of the deliberate temperamental posturings of the stage star. He is by nature and preference a simple, unpretentious man, whose inclinations are still close to his humble beginnings and his Irish farmer forebears. But the actor shows in all his unconscious habits of speech, movement, and gesture. These have the quality of belonging to a studied technique. His voice is remarkably fine, resonant and flexible, and he takes great pride in it.

His clothes, assuredly, do not costume any romantic part. He wears a threadbare, ready-made, grey sack suit[2] *and shineless black shoes, a collarless shirt with a thick white handkerchief knotted loosely around his throat. There is nothing picturesquely careless about this get-up. It is commonplace shabby. He believes in wearing his clothes to the limit of usefulness, is dressed now for gardening, and doesn't give a damn how he looks.*

He has never been really sick a day in his life. He has no nerves. There is a lot of stolid, earthy peasant in him, mixed with streaks of sentimental melancholy and rare flashes of intuitive sensibility.

TYRONE*'s arm is around his wife's waist as they appear from the back parlor. Entering the living room he gives her a playful hug.*

TYRONE You're a fine armful now, Mary, with those twenty pounds you've gained.

MARY [*smiles affectionately*] I've gotten too fat, you mean, dear. I really ought to reduce.

TYRONE None of that, my lady! You're just right. We'll have no talk of reducing. Is that why you ate so little breakfast?

MARY So little? I thought I ate a lot.

TYRONE You didn't. Not as much as I'd like to see, anyway.

MARY [*teasingly*] Oh you! expect everyone to eat the enormous breakfast you do. No one else in the world could without dying of indigestion.

[*She comes forward to stand by the right of table.*]

TYRONE [*following her*] I hope I'm not as big a glutton as that sounds. [*With hearty satisfaction*] But thank God, I've kept my appetite and I've the digestion of a young man of twenty, if I am sixty-five.

MARY You surely have, James. No one could deny that.

[*She laughs and sits in the wicker armchair at right rear of table. He comes around in back of her and selects a cigar from a box on the table and cuts off the end with a little clipper. From the dining room* JAMIE*'s and* EDMUND*'s voices are heard.* MARY *turns her head that way.*]

Why did the boys stay in the dining room, I wonder? Cathleen must be waiting to clear the table.

TYRONE [*jokingly but with an undercurrent of resentment*] It's a secret confab they don't want me to hear, I suppose. I'll bet they're cooking up some new scheme to touch the Old Man.[3]

[*She is silent on this, keeping her head turned toward their voices. Her hands appear on the table top, moving restlessly. He lights his cigar and sits down in the rocker at right of table, which is his chair, and puffs contentedly.*]

2. A suit with a straight, loose-fitting jacket.

3. That is, to get money from their father.

There's nothing like the first after-breakfast cigar, if it's a good one, and this new lot have the right mellow flavor. They're a great bargain, too. I got them dead cheap. It was McGuire put me on to them.

MARY [*a trifle acidly*] I hope he didn't put you on to any new piece of property at the same time. His real estate bargains don't work out so well.

TYRONE [*defensively*] I wouldn't say that, Mary. After all, he was the one who advised me to buy that place on Chestnut Street and I made a quick turnover on it for a fine profit.

MARY [*smiles now with teasing affection*] I know. The famous one stroke of good luck. I'm sure McGuire never dreamed— [*Then she pats his hand.*] Never mind, James. I know it's a waste of breath trying to convince you you're not a cunning real estate speculator.

TYRONE [*huffily*] I've no such idea. But land is land, and it's safer than the stocks and bonds of Wall Street swindlers. [*Then placatingly*] But let's not argue about business this early in the morning.

[*A pause. The boys' voices are again heard and one of them has a fit of coughing.* MARY *listens worriedly. Her fingers play nervously on the table top.*]

MARY James, it's Edmund you ought to scold for not eating enough. He hardly touched anything except coffee. He needs to eat to keep up his strength. I keep telling him that but he says he simply has no appetite. Of course, there's nothing takes away your appetite like a bad summer cold.

TYRONE Yes, it's only natural. So don't let yourself get worried—

MARY [*quickly*] Oh, I'm not. I know he'll be all right in a few days if he takes care of himself. [*As if she wanted to dismiss the subject but can't.*] But it does seem a shame he should have to be sick right now.

TYRONE Yes, it is bad luck. [*He gives her a quick, worried look.*] But you mustn't let it upset you, Mary. Remember, you've got to take care of yourself, too.

MARY [*quickly*] I'm not upset. There's nothing to be upset about. What makes you think I'm upset?

TYRONE Why, nothing, except you've seemed a bit high-strung the past few days.

MARY [*forcing a smile*] I have? Nonsense, dear. It's your imagination. [*With sudden tenseness*] You really must not watch me all the time, James. I mean, it makes me self-conscious.

TYRONE [*putting a hand over one of her nervously playing ones*] Now, now, Mary. That's your imagination. If I've watched you it was to admire how fat and beautiful you looked. [*His voice is suddenly moved by deep feeling.*] I can't tell you the deep happiness it gives me, darling, to see you as you've been since you came back to us, your dear old self again.

[*He leans over and kisses her cheek impulsively—then turning back adds with a constrained air.*]

So keep up the good work, Mary.

MARY [*has turned her head away*] I will, dear.

[*She gets up restlessly and goes to the windows at right.*]

Thank heavens, the fog is gone. [*She turns back.*] I do feel out of sorts this morning. I wasn't able to get much sleep with that awful foghorn going all night long.

TYRONE Yes, it's like having a sick whale in the backyard. It kept me awake, too.

MARY [*affectionately amused*] Did it? You had a strange way of showing your restlessness. You were snoring so hard I couldn't tell which was the foghorn!

[*She comes to him, laughing, and pats his cheek playfully.*]

Ten foghorns couldn't disturb you. You haven't a nerve in you. You've never had.

TYRONE [*his vanity piqued—testily*] Nonsense. You always exaggerate about my snoring.

MARY I couldn't. If you could only hear yourself once—

[*A burst of laughter comes from the dining room. She turns her head, smiling.*]

What's the joke, I wonder?

TYRONE [*grumpily*] It's on me. I'll bet that much. It's always on the Old Man.

MARY [*teasingly*] Yes, it's terrible the way we all pick on you, isn't it? You're so abused!

[*She laughs—then with a pleased, relieved air.*]

Well, no matter what the joke is about, it's a relief to hear Edmund laugh. He's been so down in the mouth lately.

TYRONE [*ignoring this—resentfully*] Some joke of Jamie's, I'll wager. He's forever making sneering fun of somebody, that one.

MARY Now don't start in on poor Jamie, dear. [*Without conviction*] He'll turn out all right in the end, you wait and see.

TYRONE He'd better start soon, then. He's nearly thirty-four.

MARY [*ignoring this*] Good heavens, are they going to stay in the dining room all day?

[*She goes to the back parlor doorway and calls.*]

Jamie! Edmund! Come in the living room and give Cathleen a chance to clear the table.

[EDMUND *calls back*, "We're coming, Mama." *She goes back to the table.*]

TYRONE [*grumbling*] You'd find excuses for him no matter what he did.

MARY [*sitting down beside him, pats his hand*] Shush.

[*Their sons* JAMES, JR., *and* EDMUND *enter together from the back parlor. They are both grinning, still chuckling over what had caused their laughter, and as they come forward they glance at their father and their grins grow broader.*

JAMIE, *the elder, is thirty-three. He has his father's broad-shouldered, deep-chested physique, is an inch taller and weighs less, but appears shorter and stouter because he lacks* TYRONE'*s bearing and graceful carriage. He also lacks his father's vitality. The signs of premature disintegration are on him. His face is still good-looking, despite marks of dissipation, but it has never been handsome like* TYRONE'*s, although* JAMIE *resembles him rather than his mother. He has fine brown eyes, their color midway between his father's lighter and his mother's darker ones. His hair is thinning and already there is indication of a bald spot like* TYRONE'*s. His nose is unlike that of any other member of the family, pronouncedly aquiline. Combined with his habitual expression of cynicism it gives his countenance a Mephistophelian cast.*[4] *But on the rare*

4. A devilish aspect; that is, resembling Mephistopheles, the devil in the Faust legend.

occasions when he smiles without sneering, his personality possesses the remnant of a humorous, romantic, irresponsible Irish charm—that of the beguiling ne'er-do-well, with a strain of the sentimentally poetic, attractive to women and popular with men.

He is dressed in an old sack suit, not as shabby as TYRONE*'s, and wears a collar and tie. His fair skin is sunburned a reddish, freckled tan.*

EDMUND *is ten years younger than his brother, a couple of inches taller, thin and wiry. Where* JAMIE *takes after his father, with little resemblance to his mother,* EDMUND *looks like both his parents, but is more like his mother. Her big, dark eyes are the dominant feature in his long, narrow Irish face. His mouth has the same quality of hypersensitiveness hers possesses. His high forehead is hers accentuated, with dark brown hair, sunbleached to red at the ends, brushed straight back from it. But his nose is his father's and his face in profile recalls* TYRONE*'s.* EDMUND*'s hands are noticeably like his mother's, with the same exceptionally long fingers. They even have to a minor degree the same nervousness. It is in the quality of extreme nervous sensibility that the likeness of* EDMUND *to his mother is most marked.*

He is plainly in bad health. Much thinner than he should be, his eyes appear feverish and his cheeks are sunken. His skin, in spite of being sunburned a deep brown, has a parched sallowness. He wears a shirt, collar and tie, no coat, old flannel trousers, brown sneakers.]

MARY [*turns smilingly to them, in a merry tone that is a bit forced*] I've been teasing your father about his snoring. [*To* TYRONE] I'll leave it to the boys, James. They must have heard you. No, not you, Jamie. I could hear you down the hall almost as bad as your father. You're like him. As soon as your head touches the pillow you're off and ten foghorns couldn't wake you.

[*She stops abruptly, catching* JAMIE*'s eyes regarding her with an uneasy, probing look. Her smile vanishes and her manner becomes self-conscious.*]

Why are you staring, Jamie? [*Her hands flutter up to her hair.*] Is my hair coming down? It's hard for me to do it up properly now. My eyes are getting so bad and I never can find my glasses.

JAMIE [*looks away guiltily*] Your hair's all right, Mama. I was only thinking how well you look.

TYRONE [*heartily*] Just what I've been telling her, Jamie. She's so fat and sassy, there'll soon be no holding her.

EDMUND Yes, you certainly look grand, Mama.

[*She is reassured and smiles at him lovingly. He winks with a kidding grin.*]

I'll back you up about Papa's snoring. Gosh, what a racket!

JAMIE I heard him, too. [*He quotes, putting on a ham-actor manner.*] "The Moor, I know his trumpet."[5]

[*His mother and brother laugh.*]

TYRONE [*scathingly*] If it takes my snoring to make you remember Shakespeare instead of the dope sheet[6] on the ponies, I hope I'll keep on with it.

MARY Now, James! You mustn't be so touchy.

5. Quoting Iago, from William Shakespeare's *Othello* (1604), 2.1.177.

6. A piece of paper containing information about racehorses.

[JAMIE *shrugs his shoulders and sits down in the chair on her right.*]

EDMUND [*irritably*] Yes, for Pete's sake, Papa! The first thing after breakfast! Give it a rest, can't you?

[*He slumps down in the chair at left of table next to his brother. His father ignore him.*]

MARY [*reprovingly*] Your father wasn't finding fault with you. You don't have to always take Jamie's part. You'd think you were the one ten years older.

JAMIE [*boredly*] What's all the fuss about? Let's forget it.

TYRONE [*contemptuously*] Yes, forget! Forget everything and face nothing! It's a convenient philosophy if you've no ambition in life except to—

MARY James, do be quiet.

[*She puts an arm around his shoulder—coaxingly.*]

You must have gotten out of the wrong side of the bed this morning. [*To the boys, changing the subject*] What were you two grinning about like Cheshire cats[7] when you came in? What was the joke?

TYRONE [*with a painful effort to be a good sport*] Yes, let us in on it, lads. I told your mother I knew damned well it would be one on me, but never mind that, I'm used to it.

JAMIE [*dryly*] Don't look at me. This is the Kid's story.

EDMUND [*grins*] I meant to tell you last night, Papa, and forgot it. Yesterday when I went for a walk I dropped in at the Inn—

MARY [*worriedly*] You shouldn't drink now, Edmund.

EDMUND [*ignoring this*] And who do you think I met there, with a beautiful bun on,[8] but Shaughnessy, the tenant on that farm of yours.

MARY [*smiling*] That dreadful man! But he is funny.

TYRONE [*scowling*] He's not so funny when you're his landlord. He's a wily Shanty Mick,[9] that one. He could hide behind a corkscrew. What's he complaining about now, Edmund—for I'm damned sure he's complaining. I suppose he wants his rent lowered. I let him have the place for almost nothing, just to keep someone on it, and he never pays that till I threaten to evict him.

EDMUND No, he didn't beef about anything. He was so pleased with life he even bought a drink, and that's practically unheard of. He was delighted because he'd had a fight with your friend, Harker, the Standard Oil[1] millionaire, and won a glorious victory.

MARY [*with amused dismay*] Oh, Lord! James, you'll really have to do something—

TYRONE Bad luck to Shaughnessy, anyway!

JAMIE [*maliciously*] I'll bet the next time you see Harker at the Club and give him the old respectful bow, he won't see you.

EDMUND Yes. Harker will think you're no gentleman for harboring a tenant who isn't humble in the presence of a king of America.

TYRONE Never mind the Socialist gabble. I don't care to listen—

MARY [*tactfully*] Go on with your story, Edmund.

7. That is, like the broadly grinning cat (as drawn by John Tenniel) in *Alice's Adventures in Wonderland* (1865), by Lewis Carroll.
8. That is, highly intoxicated.
9. Derogatory term for a lower-class Irish immigrant.
1. The oil company founded by John D. Rockefeller and forced to break up in 1911 because it was a monopoly. (Its successor companies, some of which originally had "Standard Oil" in their names, continue to dominate the U.S. oil industry.)

EDMUND [*grins at his father provocatively*] Well, you remember, Pap, the ice pond on Harker's estate is right next to the farm, and you remember Shaughnessy keeps pigs. Well, it seems there's a break in the fence and the pigs have been bathing in the millionaire's ice pond, and Harker's foreman told him he was sure Shaughnessy had broken the fence on purpose to give his pigs a free wallow.

MARY [*shocked and amused*] Good heavens!

TYRONE [*sourly, but with a trace of admiration*] I'm sure he did, too, the dirty scallywag. It's like him.

EDMUND So Harker came in person to rebuke Shaughnessy. [*He chuckles.*] A very bonehead play! If I needed any further proof that our ruling plutocrats, especially the ones who inherited their boodle, are not mental giants, that would clinch it.

TYRONE [*with appreciation, before he thinks*] Yes, he'd be no match for Shaughnessy. [*Then he growls.*] Keep your damned anarchist remarks to yourself. I won't have them in my house. [*But he is full of eager anticipation.*] What happened?

EDMUND Harker had as much chance as I would with Jack Johnson.[2] Shaughnessy got a few drinks under his belt and was waiting at the gate to welcome him. He told me he never gave Harker a chance to open his mouth. He began by shouting that he was no slave Standard Oil could trample on. He was a King of Ireland, if he had his rights, and scum was scum to him, no matter how much money it had stolen from the poor.

MARY Oh, Lord! [*But she can't help laughing.*]

EDMUND Then he accused Harker of making his foreman break down the fence to entice the pigs into the ice pond in order to destroy them. The poor pigs, Shaughnessy yelled, had caught their death of cold. Many of them were dying of pneumonia, and several others had been taken down with cholera from drinking the poisoned water. He told Harker he was hiring a lawyer to sue him for damages. And he wound up by saying that he had to put up with poison ivy, ticks, potato bugs, snakes and skunks on his farm, but he was an honest man who drew the line somewhere, and he'd be damned if he'd stand for a Standard Oil thief trespassing. So would Harker kindly remove his dirty feet from the premises before he sicked the dog on him. And Harker did!

[*He and* JAMIE *laugh.*]

MARY [*shocked but giggling*] Heavens, what a terrible tongue that man has!

TYRONE [*admiringly before he thinks*] The damned old scoundrel! By God, you can't beat him!

[*He laughs—then stops abruptly and scowls.*]

The dirty blackguard! He'll get me in serious trouble yet. I hope you told him I'd be mad as hell—

EDMUND I told him you'd be tickled to death over the great Irish victory, and so you are. Stop faking, Papa.

TYRONE Well, I'm not tickled to death.

MARY [*teasingly*] You are, too, James. You're simply delighted!

TYRONE No, Mary, a joke is a joke, but—

2. African American boxer (1878–1946); in 1908, he became the first black world heavyweight champion.

EDMUND I told Shaughnessy he should have reminded Harker that a Standard Oil millionaire ought to welcome the flavor of hog in his ice water as an appropriate touch.

TYRONE The devil you did! [*Frowning*] Keep your damned Socialist anarchist sentiments out of my affairs!

EDMUND Shaughnessy almost wept because he hadn't thought of that one, but he said he'd include it in a letter he's writing to Harker, along with a few other insults he'd overlooked.

[*He and* JAMIE *laugh.*]

TYRONE What are you laughing at? There's nothing funny— A fine son you are to help that blackguard get me into a lawsuit!

MARY Now, James, don't lose your temper.

TYRONE [*turns on* JAMIE] And you're worse than he is, encouraging him. I suppose you're regretting you weren't there to prompt Shaughnessy with a few nastier insults. You've a fine talent for that, if for nothing else.

MARY James! There's no reason to scold Jamie.

[JAMIE *is about to make some sneering remark to his father, but he shrugs his shoulders.*]

EDMUND [*with sudden nervous exasperation*] Oh, for God's sake, Papa! If you're starting that stuff again, I'll beat it. [*He jumps up.*] I left my book upstairs, anyway. [*He goes to the front parlor, saying disgustedly*] God, Papa, I should think you'd get sick of hearing yourself—

[*He disappears.* TYRONE *looks after him angrily.*]

MARY You mustn't mind Edmund, James. Remember he isn't well.

[EDMUND *can be heard coughing as he goes upstairs. She adds nervously.*]

A summer cold makes anyone irritable.

JAMIE [*genuinely concerned*] It's not just a cold he's got. The Kid is damned sick.

[*His father gives him a sharp warning look but he doesn't see it.*]

MARY [*turns on him resentfully*] Why do you say that? It *is* just a cold! Anyone can tell that! You always imagine things!

TYRONE [*with another warning glance at* JAMIE*—easily*] All Jamie meant was Edmund might have a touch of something else, too, which makes his cold worse.

JAMIE Sure, Mama. That's all I meant.

TYRONE Doctor Hardy thinks it might be a bit of malarial fever he caught when he was in the tropics. If it is, quinine will soon cure it.

MARY [*a look of contemptuous hostility flashes across her face*] Doctor Hardy! I wouldn't believe a thing he said, if he swore on a stack of Bibles! I know what doctors are. They're all alike. Anything, they don't care what, to keep you coming to them.

[*She stops short, overcome by a fit of acute self-consciousness as she catches their eyes fixed on her. Her hands jerk nervously to her hair. She forces a smile.*]

What is it? What are you looking at? Is my hair—?

TYRONE [*puts his arm around her—with guilty heartiness, giving her a playful hug*] There's nothing wrong with your hair. The healthier and fatter you get, the vainer you become. You'll soon spend half the day primping before the mirror.

MARY [*half reassured*] I really should have new glasses. My eyes are so bad now.

TYRONE [*with Irish blarney*] Your eyes are beautiful, and well you know it.

[*He gives her a kiss. Her face lights up with a charming, shy embarrassment. Suddenly and startlingly one sees in her face the girl she had once been, not a ghost of the dead, but still a living part of her.*]

MARY You mustn't be so silly, James. Right in front of Jamie!

TYRONE Oh, he's on to you, too. He knows this fuss about eyes and hair is only fishing for compliments. Eh, Jamie?

JAMIE [*his face has cleared, too, and there is an old boyish charm in his loving smile at his mother*] Yes. You can't kid us, Mama.

MARY [*laughs and an Irish lilt comes into her voice*] Go along with both of you! [*Then she speaks with a girlish gravity.*] But I did truly have beautiful hair once, didn't I, James?

TYRONE The most beautiful in the world!

MARY It was a rare shade of reddish brown and so long it came down below my knees. You ought to remember it, too, Jamie. It wasn't until after Edmund was born that I had a single grey hair. Then it began to turn white.

[*The girlishness fades from her face.*]

TYRONE [*quickly*] And that made it prettier than ever.

MARY [*again embarrassed and pleased*] Will you listen to your father, Jamie—after thirty-five years of marriage! He isn't a great actor for nothing, is he? What's come over you, James? Are you pouring coals of fire on my head for teasing you about snoring? Well then, I take it all back. It must have been only the foghorn I heard. [*She laughs, and they laugh with her. Then she changes to a brisk businesslike air.*] But I can't stay with you any longer, even to hear compliments. I must see the cook about dinner and the day's marketing. [*She gets up and sighs with humorous exaggeration.*] Bridget is so lazy. And so sly. She begins telling me about her relatives so I can't get a word in edgeways and scold her. Well, I might as well get it over.

[*She goes to the back-parlor doorway, then turns, her face worried again.*]

You mustn't make Edmund work on the grounds with you, James, remember. [*Again with the strange obstinate set to her face*] Not that he isn't strong enough, but he'd perspire and he might catch more cold.

[*She disappears through the back parlor.* TYRONE *turns on* JAMIE *condemningly.*]

TYRONE You're a fine lunkhead! Haven't you any sense? The one thing to avoid is saying anything that would get her more upset over Edmund.

JAMIE [*shrugging his shoulders*] All right. Have it your way. I think it's the wrong idea to let Mama go on kidding herself. It will only make the shock worse when she has to face it. Anyway, you can see she's deliberately fooling herself with that summer cold talk. She knows better.

TYRONE Knows? Nobody knows yet.

JAMIE Well, I do. I was with Edmund when he went to Doc Hardy on Monday. I heard him pull that touch of malaria stuff. He was stalling. That isn't what he thinks anymore. You know it as well as I do. You talked to him when you went uptown yesterday, didn't you?

TYRONE He couldn't say anything for sure yet. He's to phone me today before Edmund goes to him.

JAMIE [*slowly*] He thinks it's consumption,[3] doesn't he, Papa?

TYRONE [*reluctantly*] He said it might be.

JAMIE [*moved, his love for his brother coming out*] Poor kid! God damn it!

[*He turns on his father accusingly.*]

It might never have happened if you'd sent him to a real doctor when he first got sick.

TYRONE What's the matter with Hardy? He's always been our doctor up here.

JAMIE Everything's the matter with him! Even in this hick burg he's rated third class! He's a cheap old quack!

TYRONE That's right! Run him down! Run down everybody! Everyone is a fake to you!

JAMIE [*contemptuously*] Hardy only charges a dollar. That's what makes you think he's a fine doctor!

TYRONE [*stung*] That's enough! You're not drunk now! There's no excuse—

[*He controls himself—a bit defensively.*]

If you mean I can't afford one of the fine society doctors who prey on the rich summer people—

JAMIE Can't afford? You're one of the biggest property owners around here.

TYRONE That doesn't mean I'm rich. It's all mortgaged—

JAMIE Because you always buy more instead of paying off mortgages. If Edmund was a lousy acre of land you wanted, the sky would be the limit!

TYRONE That's a lie! And your sneers against Doctor Hardy are lies! He doesn't put on frills, or have an office in a fashionable location, or drive around in an expensive automobile. That's what you pay for with those other five-dollars-to-look-at-your-tongue fellows, not their skill.

JAMIE [*with a scornful shrug of his shoulders*] Oh, all right. I'm a fool to argue. You can't change the leopard's spots.

TYRONE [*with rising anger*] No, you can't. You've taught me that lesson only too well. I've lost all hope you will ever change yours. You dare tell me what I can afford? You've never known the value of a dollar and never will! You've never saved a dollar in your life! At the end of each season you're penniless! You've thrown your salary away every week on whores and whiskey!

JAMIE My salary! Christ!

TYRONE It's more than you're worth, and you couldn't get that if it wasn't for me. If you weren't my son, there isn't a manager in the business who would give you a part, your reputation stinks so. As it is, I have to humble my pride and beg for you, saying you've turned over a new leaf, although I know it's a lie!

JAMIE I never wanted to be an actor. You forced me on the stage.

TYRONE That's a lie! You made no effort to find anything else to do. You left it to me to get you a job and I have no influence except in the theater. Forced you! You never wanted to do anything except loaf in barrooms! You'd have been content to sit back like a lazy lunk and sponge on me for the rest of your life! After all the money I'd wasted on your education, and all you did was get fired in disgrace from every college you went to!

3. A wasting disease, especially pulmonary tuberculosis.

JAMIE Oh, for God's sake, don't drag up that ancient history!

TYRONE It's not ancient history that you have to come home every summer to live on me.

JAMIE I earn my board and lodging working on the grounds. It saves you hiring a man.

TYRONE Bah! You have to be driven to do even that much! [*His anger ebbs into a weary complaint.*] I wouldn't give a damn if you ever displayed the slightest sign of gratitude. The only thanks is to have you sneer at me for a dirty miser, sneer at my profession, sneer at every damned thing in the world—except yourself.

JAMIE [*wryly*] That's not true, Papa. You can't hear me talking to myself, that's all.

TYRONE [*stares at him puzzledly, then quotes mechanically*] "Ingratitude, the vilest weed that grows"![4]

JAMIE I could see that line coming! God, how many thousand times—! [*He stops, bored with their quarrel, and shrugs his shoulders.*] All right, Papa. I'm a bum. Anything you like, so long as it stops the argument.

TYRONE [*with indignant appeal now*] If you'd get ambition in your head instead of folly! You're young yet. You could still make your mark. You had the talent to become a fine actor! You have it still. You're my son—!

JAMIE [*boredly*] Let's forget me. I'm not interested in the subject. Neither are you.

[TYRONE *gives up.* JAMIE *goes on casually.*]

What started us on this? Oh, Doc Hardy. When is he going to call you up about Edmund?

TYRONE Around lunch time [*He pauses—then defensively.*] I couldn't have sent Edmund to a better doctor. Hardy's treated him whenever he was sick up here, since he was knee high. He knows his constitution as no other doctor could. It's not a question of my being miserly, as you'd like to make out. [*Bitterly*] And what could the finest specialist in America do for Edmund, after he's deliberately ruined his health by the mad life he's led ever since he was fired from college? Even before that when he was in prep school, he began dissipating and playing the Broadway sport to imitate you, when he's never had your constitution to stand it. You're a healthy hulk like me—or you were at his age—but he's always been a bundle of nerves like his mother. I've warned him for years his body couldn't stand it, but he wouldn't heed me, and now it's too late.

JAMIE [*sharply*] What do you mean, too late? You talk as if you thought—

TYRONE [*guiltily explosive*] Don't be a damned fool! I meant nothing but what's plain to anyone! His health has broken down and he may be an invalid for a long time.

JAMIE [*stares at his father, ignoring his explanation*] I know it's an Irish peasant idea consumption is fatal. It probably is when you live in a hovel on a bog, but over here, with modern treatment—

TYRONE Don't I know that! What are you gabbing about, anyway? And keep your dirty tongue off Ireland, with your sneers about peasants and bogs

4. Perhaps Tyrone's own adaptation of a line from *King Edward III* (1596), a play sometimes attributed to Shakespeare: "Ingratitude, the basest weed that grows" (2.1.165).

and hovels! [*Accusingly*] The less you say about Edmund's sickness, the better for your conscience! You're more responsible than anyone!

JAMIE [*stung*] That's a lie! I won't stand for that, Papa!

TYRONE It's the truth! You've been the worst influence for him. He grew up admiring you as a hero! A fine example you set him! If you ever gave him advice except in the ways of rottenness, I've never heard of it! You made him old before his time, pumping him full of what you consider worldly wisdom, when he was too young to see that your mind was so poisoned by your own failure in life, you wanted to believe every man was a knave with his soul for sale, and every woman who wasn't a whore was a fool!

JAMIE [*with a defensive air of weary indifference again*] All right. I did put Edmund wise to things, but not until I saw he'd started to raise hell, and knew he'd laugh at me if I tried the good advice, older brother stuff. All I did was make a pal of him and be absolutely frank so he'd learn from my mistakes that— [*He shrugs his shoulders—cynically.*] Well, that if you can't be good you can at least be careful.

[*His father snorts contemptuously. Suddenly* JAMIE *becomes really moved.*]

That's a rotten accusation, Papa. You know how much the Kid means to me, and how close we've always been—not like the usual brothers! I'd do anything for him.

TYRONE [*impressed—mollifyingly*] I know you may have thought it was for the best, Jamie. I didn't say you did it deliberately to harm him.

JAMIE Besides it's damned rot! I'd like to see anyone influence Edmund more than he wants to be. His quietness fools people into thinking they can do what they like with him. But he's stubborn as hell inside and what he does is what he wants to do, and to hell with anyone else! What had I to do with all the crazy stunts he's pulled in the last few years—working his way all over the map as a sailor and all that stuff. I thought that was a damned fool idea, and I told him so. You can't imagine me getting fun out of being on the beach in South America, or living in filthy dives, drinking rotgut, can you? No, thanks! I'll stick to Broadway, and a room with a bath, and bars that serve bonded Bourbon.[5]

TYRONE You and Broadway! It's made you what you are! [*With a touch of pride*] Whatever Edmund's done, he's had the guts to go off on his own, where he couldn't come whining to me the minute he was broke.

JAMIE [*stung into sneering jealousy*] He's always come home broke finally, hasn't he? And what did his going away get him? Look at him now! [*He is suddenly shamefaced.*] Christ! That's a lousy thing to say. I don't mean that.

TYRONE [*decides to ignore this*] He's been doing well on the paper. I was hoping he'd found the work he wants to do at last.

JAMIE [*sneering jealously again*] A hick town rag! Whatever bull they hand you, they tell me he's a pretty bum reporter. If he weren't your son— [*Ashamed again*] No, that's not true! They're glad to have him, but it's the special stuff that gets him by. Some of the poems and parodies he's written are damned good. [*Grudgingly again*] Not that they'd ever get him any-

5. That is, good bourbon. Bonded whiskey is aged, bottled, and stored under government supervision, in accordance with the Bottled in Bond Act of 1897; it must be at least four years old and bottled at 100 proof.

where on the big time. [*Hastily*] But he's certainly made a damned good start.

TYRONE Yes. He's made a start. You used to talk about wanting to become a newspaperman but you were never willing to start at the bottom. You expected—

JAMIE Oh, for Christ's sake, Papa! Can't you lay off me!

TYRONE [*stares at him—then looks away—after a pause*] It's damnable luck Edmund should be sick right now. It couldn't have come at a worse time for him. [*He adds, unable to conceal an almost furtive uneasiness.*] Or for your mother. It's damnable she should have this to upset her, just when she needs peace and freedom from worry. She's been so well in the two months since she came home. [*His voice grows husky and trembles a little.*] It's been heaven to me. This home has been a home again. But I needn't tell you, Jamie.

[*His son looks at him, for the first time with an understanding sympathy. It is as if suddenly a deep bond of common feeling existed between them in which their antagonisms could be forgotten.*]

JAMIE [*almost gently*] I've felt the same way, Papa.

TYRONE Yes, this time you can see how strong and sure of herself she is. She's a different woman entirely from the other times. She has control of her nerves—or she had until Edmund got sick. Now you can feel her growing tense and frightened underneath. I wish to God we could keep the truth from her, but we can't if he has to be sent to a sanatorium. What makes it worse is her father died of consumption. She worshiped him and she's never forgotten. Yes, it will be hard for her. But she can do it! She has the willpower now! We must help her, Jamie, in every way we can!

JAMIE [*moved*] Of course, Papa. [*Hesitantly*] Outside of nerves, she seems perfectly all right this morning.

TYRONE [*with hearty confidence now*] Never better. She's full of fun and mischief. [*Suddenly he frowns at Jamie suspiciously.*] Why do you say, seems? Why shouldn't she be all right? What the hell do you mean?

JAMIE Don't start jumping down my throat! God, Papa, this ought to be one thing we can talk over frankly without a battle.

TYRONE I'm sorry, Jamie. [*Tensely*] But go on and tell me—

JAMIE There's nothing to tell. I was all wrong. It's just that last night— Well, you know how it is, I can't forget the past. I can't help being suspicious. Any more than you can. [*Bitterly*] That's the hell of it. And it makes it hell for Mama! She watches us watching her—

TYRONE [*sadly*] I know. [*Tensely*] Well, what was it? Can't you speak out?

JAMIE Nothing, I tell you. Just my damned foolishness. Around three o'clock this morning, I woke up and heard her moving around in the spare room. Then she went to the bathroom. I pretended to be asleep. She stopped in the hall to listen, as if she wanted to make sure I was.

TYRONE [*with forced scorn*] For God's sake, is that all? She told me herself the foghorn kept her awake all night, and every night since Edmund's been sick she's been up and down, going to his room to see how he was.

JAMIE [*eagerly*] Yes, that's right, she did stop to listen outside his room. [*Hesitantly again*] It was her being in the spare room that scared me. I couldn't help remembering that when she starts sleeping alone in there, it has always been a sign—

TYRONE It isn't this time! It's easily explained. Where else could she go last night to get away from my snoring? [*He gives way to a burst of resentful anger.*] By God, how you can live with a mind that sees nothing but the worst motives behind everything is beyond me!

JAMIE [*stung*] Don't pull that! I've just said I was all wrong. Don't you suppose I'm as glad of that as you are!

TYRONE [*mollifyingly*] I'm sure you are, Jamie.

[*A pause. His expression becomes somber. He speaks slowly with a superstitious dread.*]

It would be like a curse she can't escape if worry over Edmund—It was in her long sickness after bringing him into the world that she first—

JAMIE She didn't have anything to do with it!

TYRONE I'm not blaming her.

JAMIE [*bitingly*] Then who are you blaming? Edmund, for being born?

TYRONE You damned fool! No one was to blame.

JAMIE The bastard of a doctor was! From what Mama's said, he was another cheap quack like Hardy! You wouldn't pay for a first-rate—

TYRONE That's a lie! [*Furiously*] So I'm to blame! That's what you're driving at, is it? You evil-minded loafer!

JAMIE [*warningly as he hears his mother in the dining room*] Ssh!

[TYRONE *gets hastily to his feet and goes to look out the windows at right.* JAMIE *speaks with a complete change of tone.*]

Well, if we're going to cut the front hedge today, we'd better go to work.

[MARY *comes in from the back parlor. She gives a quick, suspicious glance from one to the other, her manner nervously self-conscious.*]

TYRONE [*turns from the window—with an actor's heartiness*] Yes, it's too fine a morning to waste indoors arguing. Take a look out the window, Mary. There's no fog in the harbor. I'm sure the spell of it we've had is over now.

MARY [*going to him*] I hope so, dear. [*To* JAMIE, *forcing a smile*] Did I actually hear you suggesting work on the front hedge, Jamie? Wonders will never cease! You must want pocket money badly.

JAMIE [*kiddingly*] When don't I? [*He winks at her, with a derisive glance at his father.*] I expect a salary of at least one large iron man[6] at the end of the week—to carouse on!

MARY [*does not respond to his humor—her hands fluttering over the front of her dress*] What were you two arguing about?

JAMIE [*shrugs his shoulders*] The same old stuff.

MARY I heard you say something about a doctor, and your father accusing you of being evil-minded.

JAMIE [*quickly*] Oh, that. I was saying again Doc Hardy isn't my idea of the world's greatest physician.

MARY [*knows he is lying—vaguely*] Oh. No, I wouldn't say he was, either. [*Changing the subject—forcing a smile*] That Bridget! I thought I'd never get away. She told me all about her second cousin on the police force in St. Louis. [*Then with nervous irritation*] Well, if you're going to work on the hedge why don't you go? [*Hastily*] I mean, take advantage of the sunshine

6. A dollar (slang).

before the fog comes back. [*Strangely, as if talking aloud to herself*] Because I know it will. [*Suddenly she is self-consciously aware that they are both staring fixedly at her—flurriedly, raising her hands.*] Or I should say, the rheumatism in my hands knows. It's a better weather prophet than you are, James. [*She stares at her hands with fascinated repulsion.*] Ugh! How ugly they are! Who'd ever believe they were once beautiful?

[*They stare at her with a growing dread.*]

TYRONE [*takes her hands and gently pushes them down*] Now, now, Mary. None of that foolishness. They're the sweetest hands in the world.

[*She smiles, her face lighting up, and kisses him gratefully. He turns to his son.*]

Come on Jamie. Your mother's right to scold us. The way to start work is to start work. The hot sun will sweat some of that booze fat off your middle.

[*He opens the screen door and goes out on the porch and disappears down a flight of steps leading to the ground.* JAMIE *rises from his chair and, taking off his coat, goes to the door. At the door he turns back but avoids looking at her, and she does not look at him.*]

JAMIE [*with an awkward, uneasy tenderness*] We're all so proud of you, Mama, so darned happy.

[*She stiffens and stares at him with a frightened defiance. He flounders on.*]

But you've still got to be careful. You mustn't worry so much about Edmund. He'll be all right.

MARY [*with a stubborn, bitterly resentful look*] Of course, he'll be all right. And I don't know what you mean, warning me to be careful.

JAMIE [*rebuffed and hurt, shrugs his shoulders*] All right, Mama. I'm sorry I spoke.

[*He goes out on the porch. She waits rigidly until he disappears down the steps. Then she sinks down in the chair he had occupied, her face betraying a frightened, furtive desperation, her hands roving over the tabletop, aimlessly moving objects around. She hears* EDMUND *descending the stairs in the front hall. As he nears the bottom he has a fit of coughing. She springs to her feet, as if she wanted to run away from the sound, and goes quickly to the windows at right. She is looking out, apparently calm, as he enters from the front parlor, a book in one hand. She turns to him, her lips set in a welcoming, motherly smile.*]

MARY Here you are. I was just going upstairs to look for you.

EDMUND I waited until they went out. I don't want to mix up in any arguments. I feel too rotten.

MARY [*almost resentfully*] Oh, I'm sure you don't feel half as badly as you make out. You're such a baby. You like to get us worried so we'll make a fuss over you. [*Hastily*] I'm only teasing, dear. I know how miserably uncomfortable you must be. But you feel better today, don't you? [*Worriedly, taking his arm*] All the same, you've grown much too thin. You need to rest all you can. Sit down and I'll make you comfortable.

[*He sits down in the rocking chair and she puts a pillow behind his back.*]

There. How's that?

EDMUND Grand. Thanks, Mama.

MARY [*kisses him—tenderly*] All you need is your mother to nurse you. Big as you are, you're still the baby of the family to me, you know.

EDMUND [*takes her hand—with deep seriousness*] Never mind me. You take care of yourself. That's all that counts.

MARY [*evading his eyes*] But I am, dear. [*Forcing a laugh.*] Heavens, don't you see how fat I've grown! I'll have to have all my dresses let out.

[*She turns away and goes to the windows at right. She attempts a light, amused tone.*]

They've started clipping the hedge. Poor Jamie! How he hates working in front where everyone passing can see him. There go the Chatfields in their new Mercedes. It's a beautiful car, isn't it? Not like our secondhand Packard.[7] Poor Jamie! He bent almost under the hedge so they wouldn't notice him. They bowed to your father and he bowed back as if he were taking a curtain call. In that filthy old suit I've tried to make him throw away. [*Her voice has grown bitter.*] Really, he ought to have more pride than to make such a show of himself.

EDMUND He's right not to give a damn what anyone thinks. Jamie's a fool to care about the Chatfields. For Pete's sake, who ever heard of them outside this hick burg?

MARY [*with satisfaction*] No one. You're quite right, Edmund. Big frogs in a small puddle. It is stupid of Jamie. [*She pauses, looking out the window—then with an undercurrent of lonely yearning.*] Still, the Chatfields and people like them stand for something. I mean they have decent, presentable homes they don't have to be ashamed of. They have friends who entertain them and whom they entertain. They're not cut off from everyone. [*She turns back from the window.*] Not that I want anything to do with them. I've always hated this town and everyone in it. You know that. I never wanted to live here in the first place, but your father liked it and insisted on building this house, and I've had to come here every summer.

EDMUND Well, it's better than spending the summer in a New York hotel, isn't it? And this town's not so bad. I like it well enough. I suppose because it's the only home we've had.

MARY I've never felt it was my home. It was wrong from the start. Everything was done in the cheapest way. Your father would never spend the money to make it right. It's just as well we haven't any friends here. I'd be ashamed to have them step in the door. But he's never wanted family friends. He hates calling on people, or receiving them. All he likes is to hobnob with men at the Club or in a barroom. Jamie and you are the same way, but you're not to blame. You've never had a chance to meet decent people here. I know you both would have been so different if you'd been able to associate with nice girls instead of— You'd never have disgraced yourselves as you have, so that now no respectable parents will let their daughters be seen with you.

EDMUND [*irritably*] Oh, Mama, forget it! Who cares? Jamie and I would be bored stiff. And about the Old Man, what's the use of talking? You can't change him.

MARY [*mechanically rebuking*] Don't call your father the Old Man. You should have more respect. [*Then dully*] I know it's useless to talk. But sometimes I feel so lonely. [*Her lips quiver and she keeps her head turned away.*]

7. A brand of American luxury automobile (manufactured from 1899 to 1958).

EDMUND Anyway, you've got to be fair, Mama. It may have been all his fault in the beginning, but you know that later on, even if he'd wanted to, we couldn't have had people here— [*He flounders guiltily.*] I mean, you wouldn't have wanted them.

MARY [*wincing—her lips quivering pitifully*] Don't. I can't bear having you remind me.

EDMUND Don't take it that way! Please, Mama! I'm trying to help. Because it's bad for you to forget. The right way is to remember. So you'll always be on your guard. You know what's happened before. [*Miserably*] God, Mama, you know I hate to remind you. I'm doing it because it's been so wonderful having you home the way you've been, and it would be terrible—

MARY [*strickenly*] Please, dear. I know you mean it for the best, but— [*A defensive uneasiness comes into her voice again.*] I don't understand why you should suddenly say such things. What put it in your mind this morning?

EDMUND [*evasively*] Nothing. Just because I feel rotten and blue, I suppose.

MARY Tell me the truth. Why are you so suspicious all of a sudden?

EDMUND I'm not!

MARY Oh, yes you are. I can feel it. Your father and Jamie, too—particularly Jamie.

EDMUND Now don't start imagining things, Mama.

MARY [*her hands fluttering*] It makes it so much harder, living in this atmosphere of constant suspicion, knowing everyone is spying on me, and none of you believe in me, or trust me.

EDMUND That's crazy, Mama. We do trust you.

MARY If there was only some place I could go to get away for a day, or even an afternoon, some woman friend I could talk to—not about anything serious, simply laugh and gossip and forget for a while—someone besides the servants—that stupid Cathleen!

EDMUND [*gets up worriedly and puts his arm around her*] Stop it, Mama. You're getting yourself worked up over nothing.

MARY Your father goes out. He meets his friends in barrooms or at the Club. You and Jamie have the boys you know. You go out. But I am alone. I've always been alone.

EDMUND [*soothingly*] Come now! You know that's a fib. One of us always stays around to keep you company, or goes with you in the automobile when you take a drive.

MARY [*bitterly*] Because you're afraid to trust me alone! [*She turns on him—sharply.*] I insist you tell me why you act so differently this morning—why you felt you had to remind me—

EDMUND [*hesitates—then blurts out guiltily*] It's stupid. It's just that I wasn't asleep when you came in my room last night. You didn't go back to your and Papa's room. You went in the spare room for the rest of the night.

MARY Because your father's snoring was driving me crazy! For heaven's sake, haven't I often used the spare room as my bedroom? [*Bitterly*] But I see what you thought. That was when—

EDMUND [*too vehemently*] I didn't think anything!

MARY So you pretended to be asleep in order to spy on me!

EDMUND No! I did it because I knew if you found out I was feverish and couldn't sleep, it would upset you.

MARY Jamie was pretending to be asleep, too, I'm sure, and I suppose your father—

EDMUND Stop it, Mama!

MARY Oh, I can't bear it, Edmund, when even you—!

[*Her hands flutter up to pat her hair in their aimless, distracted way. Suddenly a strange undercurrent of revengefulness comes into her voice.*]

It would serve all of you right if it was true!

EDMUND Mama! Don't say that! That's the way you talk when—

MARY Stop suspecting me! Please, dear! You hurt me! I couldn't sleep because I was thinking about you. That's the real reason! I've been so worried ever since you've been sick.

[*She puts her arms around him and hugs him with a frightened, protective tenderness.*]

EDMUND [*soothingly*] That's foolishness. You know it's only a bad cold.

MARY Yes, of course, I know that!

EDMUND But listen, Mama. I want you to promise me that even if it should turn out to be something worse, you'll know I'll soon be all right again, anyway, and you won't worry yourself sick, and you'll keep on taking care of yourself—

MARY [*frightenedly*] I won't listen when you're so silly! There's absolutely no reason to talk as if you expected something dreadful! Of course, I promise you. I give you my sacred word of honor! [*Then with a sad bitterness*] But I suppose you're remembering I've promised before on my word of honor.

EDMUND No!

MARY [*her bitterness receding into a resigned helplessness*] I'm not blaming you, dear. How can you help it? How can any one of us forget? [*Strangely*] That's what makes it so hard—for all of us. We can't forget.

EDMUND [*grabs her shoulder*] Mama! Stop it!

MARY [*forcing a smile*] All right, dear. I didn't mean to be so gloomy. Don't mind me. Here. Let me feel your head. Why, it's nice and cool. You certainly haven't any fever now.

EDMUND Forget! It's you—

MARY But I'm quite all right, dear. [*With a quick, strange, calculating, almost sly glance at him*] Except I naturally feel tired and nervous this morning, after such a bad night. I really ought to go upstairs and lie down until lunch time and take a nap.

[*He gives her an instinctive look of suspicion—then, ashamed of himself, looks quickly away. She hurries on nervously.*]

What are you going to do? Read here? It would be much better for you to go out in the fresh air and sunshine. But don't get overheated, remember. Be sure and wear a hat.

[*She stops, looking straight at him now. He avoids her eyes. There is a tense pause. Then she speaks jeeringly.*]

Or are you afraid to trust me alone?

EDMUND [*tormentedly*] No! Can't you stop talking like that! I think you ought to take a nap. [*He goes to the screen door—forcing a joking tone.*] I'll go down and help Jamie bear up. I love to lie in the shade and watch him work.

[*He forces a laugh in which she makes herself join. Then he goes out on the porch and disappears down the steps. Her first reaction is one of re-*

lief. She appears to relax. She sinks down in one of the wicker armchairs at rear of table and leans her head back, closing her eyes. But suddenly she grows terribly tense again. Her eyes open and she strains forward, seized by a fit of nervous panic. She begins a desperate battle with herself. Her long fingers, warped and knotted by rheumatism, drum on the arms of the chair, driven by an insistent life of their own, without her consent.]

Curtain.

Act 2, Scene 1

SCENE: *The same. It is around quarter to one. No sunlight comes into the room now through the windows at right. Outside the day is still fine but increasingly sultry, with a faint haziness in the air which softens the glare of the sun.*

EDMUND *sits in the armchair at left of table, reading a book. Or rather he is trying to concentrate on it but cannot. He seems to be listening for some sound from upstairs. His manner is nervously apprehensive and he looks more sickly than in the previous act.*

The second girl, CATHLEEN, *enters from the back parlor. She carries a tray on which is a bottle of bonded Bourbon, several whiskey glasses, and a pitcher of ice water. She is a buxom Irish peasant, in her early twenties, with a red-cheeked comely face, black hair and blue eyes—amiable, ignorant, clumsy, and possessed by a dense, well-meaning stupidity. She puts the tray on the table.* EDMUND *pretends to be so absorbed in his book he does not notice her, but she ignores this.*

CATHLEEN [*with garrulous familiarity*] Here's the whiskey. It'll be lunchtime soon. Will I call your father and Mister Jamie, or will you?

EDMUND [*without looking up from his book*] You do it.

CATHLEEN It's a wonder your father wouldn't look at his watch once in a while. He's a divil for making the meals late, and then Bridget curses me as if I was to blame. But he's a grand handsome man, if he is old. You'll never see the day you're as good-looking—nor Mister Jamie, either. [*She chuckles.*] I'll wager Mister Jamie wouldn't miss the time to stop work and have his drop of whiskey if he had a watch to his name!

EDMUND [*gives up trying to ignore her and grins*] You win that one.

CATHLEEN And here's another I'd win, that you're making me call them so you can sneak a drink before they come.

EDMUND Well, I hadn't thought of that—

CATHLEEN Oh no, not you! Butter wouldn't melt in your mouth, I suppose.

EDMUND But now you suggest it—

CATHLEEN [*suddenly primly virtuous*] I'd never suggest a man or a woman touch drink, Mister Edmund. Sure, didn't it kill an uncle of mine in the old country. [*Relenting*] Still, a drop now and then is no harm when you're in low spirits, or have a bad cold.

EDMUND Thanks for handing me a good excuse. [*Then with forced casualness*] You'd better call my mother, too.

CATHLEEN What for? She's always on time without any calling. God bless her, she has some consideration for the help.

EDMUND She's been taking a nap.

CATHLEEN She wasn't asleep when I finished my work upstairs a while back. She was lying down in the spare room with her eyes wide open. She'd a terrible headache, she said.

EDMUND [*his casualness more forced*] Oh well then, just call my father.

CATHLEEN [*goes to the screen door, grumbling good-naturedly*] No wonder my feet kill me each night. I won't walk out in this heat and get sunstroke. I'll call from the porch.

[*She goes out on the side porch, letting the screen door slam behind her, and disappears on her way to the front porch. A moment later she is heard shouting.*]

Mister Tyrone! Mister Jamie! It's time!

[EDMUND, *who has been staring frightenedly before him, forgetting his book, springs to his feet nervously.*]

EDMUND God, what a wench!

[*He grabs the bottle and pours a drink, adds ice water and drinks. As he does so, he hears someone coming in the front door. He puts the glass hastily on the tray and sits down again, opening his book. Jamie comes in from the front parlor, his coat over his arm. He has taken off collar*[8] *and tie and carries them in his hand. He is wiping sweat from his forehead with a handkerchief. Edmund looks up as if his reading was interrupted. Jamie takes one look at the bottle and glasses and smiles cynically.*]

JAMIE Sneaking one, eh? Cut out the bluff, Kid. You're a rottener actor than I am.

EDMUND [*grins*] Yes, I grabbed one while the going was good.

JAMIE [*puts a hand affectionately on his shoulder*] That's better. Why kid me? We're pals, aren't we?

EDMUND I wasn't sure it was you coming.

JAMIE I made the Old Man look at his watch. I was halfway up the walk when Cathleen burst into song. Our wild Irish lark! She ought to be a train announcer.

EDMUND That's what drove me to drink. Why don't you sneak one while you've got a chance?

JAMIE I was thinking of that little thing.

[*He goes quickly to the window at right.*]

The Old Man was talking to old Captain Turner. Yes, he's still at it.

[*He comes back and takes a drink.*]

And now to cover up from his eagle eye. He memorizes the level in the bottle after every drink.

[*He measures two drinks of water and pours them in the whiskey bottle and shakes it up.*]

There. That fixes it.

[*He pours water in the glass and sets it on the table by* EDMUND.]

And here's the water you've been drinking.

EDMUND Fine! You don't think it will fool him, do you?

JAMIE Maybe not, but he can't prove it. [*Putting on his collar and tie*] I hope he doesn't forget lunch listening to himself talk. I'm hungry. [*He sits across the table from Edmund—irritably.*] That's what I hate about working down in front. He puts on an act for every damned fool that comes along.

EDMUND [*gloomily*] You're in luck to be hungry. The way I feel I don't care if I ever eat again.

8. Detachable collars—of starched linen or paper and celluloid—were common from the mid-19th century until after World War I.

JAMIE [*gives him a glance of concern*] Listen, Kid. You know me. I've never lectured you, but Doctor Hardy was right when he told you to cut out the red-eye.[9]

EDMUND Oh, I'm going to after he hands me the bad news this afternoon. A few before then won't make any difference.

JAMIE [*hesitates—then slowly*] I'm glad you've got your mind prepared for bad news. It won't be such a jolt. [*He catches* EDMUND *staring at him.*] I mean, it's a cinch you're really sick, and it would be wrong dope to kid yourself.

EDMUND [*disturbed*] I'm not. I know how rotten I feel, and the fever and chills I get at night are no joke. I think Doctor Hardy's last guess was right. It must be the damned malaria come back on me.

JAMIE Maybe, but don't be too sure.

EDMUND Why? What do you think it is?

JAMIE Hell, how would I know? I'm no doc. [*Abruptly*] Where's Mama?

EDMUND Upstairs.

JAMIE [*looks at him sharply*] When did she go up?

EDMUND Oh, about the time I came down to the hedge, I guess. She said she was going to take a nap.

JAMIE You didn't tell me—

EDMUND [*defensively*] Why should I? What about it? She was tired out. She didn't get much sleep last night.

JAMIE I know she didn't.

[*A pause. The brothers avoid looking at each other.*]

EDMUND That damned foghorn kept me awake, too.

[*Another pause.*]

JAMIE She's been upstairs alone all morning, eh? You haven't seen her?

EDMUND No. I've been reading here. I wanted to give her a chance to sleep.

JAMIE Is she coming down to lunch?

EDMUND Of course.

JAMIE [*dryly*] No of course about it. She might not want any lunch. Or she might start having most of her meals alone upstairs. That's happened, hasn't it?

EDMUND [*with frightened resentment*] Cut it out, Jamie! Can't you think anything but—? [*Persuasively*] You're all wrong to suspect anything. Cathleen saw her not long ago. Mama didn't tell her she wouldn't be down to lunch.

JAMIE Then she wasn't taking a nap?

EDMUND Not right then, but she was lying down, Cathleen said.

JAMIE In the spare room?

EDMUND Yes. For Pete's sake, what of it?

JAMIE [*bursts out*] You damned fool! Why did you leave her alone so long? Why didn't you stick around?

EDMUND Because she accused me—and you and Papa—of spying on her all the time and not trusting her. She made me feel ashamed. I know how rotten it must be for her. And she promised on her sacred word of honor—

JAMIE [*with a bitter weariness*] You ought to know that doesn't mean anything.

EDMUND It does this time!

9. Cheap whiskey.

JAMIE That's what we thought the other times. [*He leans over the table to give his brother's arm an affectionate grasp.*] Listen, Kid, I know you think I'm a cynical bastard, but remember I've seen a lot more of this game than you have. You never knew what was really wrong until you were in prep school. Papa and I kept it from you. But I was wise ten years or more before we had to tell you. I know the game backwards and I've been thinking all morning of the way she acted last night when she thought we were asleep. I haven't been able to think of anything else. And now you tell me she got you to leave her alone upstairs all morning.

EDMUND She didn't! You're crazy!

JAMIE [*placatingly*] All right, Kid. Don't start a battle with me. I hope as much as you do I'm crazy. I've been as happy as hell because I'd really begun to believe that this time— [*He stops—looking through the front parlor toward the hall—lowering his voice, hurriedly.*] She's coming downstairs. You win on that. I guess I'm a damned suspicious louse.

[*They grow tense with a hopeful, fearful expectancy. Jamie mutters.*]

Damn! I wish I'd grabbed another drink.

EDMUND Me, too.

[*He coughs nervously and this brings on a real fit of coughing.* JAMIE *glances at him with worried pity.* MARY *enters from the front parlor. At first one notices no change except that she appears to be less nervous, to be more as she was when we first saw her after breakfast, but then one becomes aware that her eyes are brighter, and there is a peculiar detachment in her voice and manner, as if she were a little withdrawn from her words and actions.*]

MARY [*goes worriedly to* EDMUND *and puts her arm around him*] You mustn't cough like that. It's bad for your throat. You don't want to get a sore throat on top of your cold.

[*She kisses him. He stops coughing and gives her a quick apprehensive glance, but if his suspicious are aroused her tenderness makes him renounce them and he believes what he wants to believe for the moment. On the other hand,* JAMIE *knows after one probing look at her that his suspicions are justified. His eyes fall to stare at the floor, his face sets in an expression of embittered, defensive cynicism.* MARY *goes on, half sitting on the arm of* EDMUND'S *chair, her arm around him, so her face is above and behind his and he cannot look into her eyes.*]

But I seem to be always picking on you, telling you don't do this and don't do that. Forgive me, dear. It's just that I want to take care of you.

EDMUND I know, Mama. How about you? Do you feel rested?

MARY Yes, ever so much better. I've been lying down ever since you went out. It's what I needed after such a restless night. I don't feel nervous now.

EDMUND That's fine.

[*He pats her hand on his shoulder.* JAMIE *gives him a strange, almost contemptuous glance, wondering if his brother can really mean this.* EDMUND *does not notice but his mother does.*]

MARY [*in a forced teasing tone*] Good heavens, how down in the mouth you look, Jamie. What's the matter now?

JAMIE [*without looking at her*] Nothing.

MARY Oh, I'd forgotten you've been working on the front hedge. That accounts for your sinking into the dumps, doesn't it?

JAMIE If you want to think so, Mama.

MARY [*keeping her tone*] Well, that's the effect it always has, isn't it? What a big baby you are! Isn't he, Edmund?

EDMUND He's certainly a fool to care what anyone thinks.

MARY [*strangely*] Yes, the only way is to make yourself not care.

[*She catches* JAMIE *giving her a bitter glance and changes the subject.*]

Where is your father? I heard Cathleen call him.

EDMUND Gabbing with old Captain Turner, Jamie says. He'll be late, as usual.

[JAMIE *gets up and goes to the windows at right, glad of an excuse to turn his back.*]

MARY I've told Cathleen time and again she must go wherever he is and tell him. The idea of screaming as if this were a cheap boardinghouse!

JAMIE [*looking out the window*] She's down there now. [*Sneeringly*] Interrupting the famous Beautiful Voice! She should have more respect.

MARY [*sharply—letting her resentment toward him come out*] It's you who should have more respect! Stop sneering at your father! I won't have it! You ought to be proud you're his son! He may have his faults. Who hasn't? But he's worked hard all his life. He made his way up from ignorance and poverty to the top of his profession! Everyone else admires him and you should be the last one to sneer—you, who, thanks to him, have never had to work hard in your life!

[*Stung,* JAMIE *has turned to stare at her with accusing antagonism. Her eyes waver guiltily and she adds in a tone which begins to placate.*]

Remember your father is getting old, Jamie. You really ought to show more consideration.

JAMIE *I* ought to?

EDMUND [*uneasily*] Oh, dry up, Jamie!

[JAMIE *looks out the window again.*]

And, for Pete's sake, Mama, why jump on Jamie all of a sudden?

MARY [*bitterly*] Because he's always sneering at someone else, always looking for the worst weakness in everyone. [*Then with a strange, abrupt change to a detached, impersonal tone*] But I suppose life has made him like that, and he can't help it. None of us can help the things life has done to us. They're done before you realize it, and once they're done they make you do other things until at last everything comes between you and what you'd like to be, and you've lost your true self forever.

[EDMUND *is made apprehensive by her strangeness. He tries to look up in her eyes but she keeps them averted.* JAMIE *turns to her—then looks quickly out of the window again.*]

JAMIE [*dully*] I'm hungry. I wish the Old Man would get a move on. It's a rotten trick the way he keeps meals waiting, and then beefs because they're spoiled.

MARY [*with a resentment that has a quality of being automatic and on the surface while inwardly she is indifferent*] Yes, it's very trying, Jamie. You don't know how trying. You don't have to keep house with summer servants who don't care because they know it isn't a permanent position. The really good servants are all with people who have homes and not merely summer places. And your father won't even pay the wages the best summer help ask. So every year I have stupid, lazy greenhorns to deal with. But you've heard me say this a thousand times. So has he, but it goes in one ear and out the other. He thinks money spent on a home is money wasted. He's lived too much in hotels. Never the best hotels, of course. Second-rate hotels. He doesn't understand a home. He doesn't feel at home in it. And yet, he wants a home. He's even proud of having this shabby place. He loves it here. [*She laughs—a hopeless and yet amused laugh.*] It's really funny, when you come to think of it. He's a peculiar man.

EDMUND [*again attempting uneasily to look up in her eyes*] What makes you ramble on like that, Mama?

MARY [*quickly casual—patting his cheek*] Why, nothing in particular, dear. It *is* foolish.

[*As she speaks,* CATHLEEN *enters from the back parlor.*]

CATHLEEN [*volubly*] Lunch is ready, Ma'am, I went down to Mister Tyrone, like you ordered, and he said he'd come right away, but he kept on talking to that man, telling him of the time when—

MARY [*indifferently*] All right, Cathleen. Tell Bridget I'm sorry but she'll have to wait a few minutes until Mister Tyrone is here.

[CATHLEEN *mutters,* "Yes, Ma'am," *and goes off through the back parlor, grumbling to herself.*]

JAMIE Damn it! Why don't you go ahead without him? He's told us to.

MARY [*with a remote, amused smile*] He doesn't mean it. Don't you know your father yet? He'd be so terribly hurt.

EDMUND [*jumps up—as if he was glad of an excuse to leave*] I'll make him get a move on.

[*He goes out on the side porch. A moment later he is heard calling from the porch exasperatedly.*]

Hey! Papa! Come on! We can't wait all day!

[MARY *has risen from the arm of the chair. Her hands play restlessly over the tabletop. She does not look at* JAMIE *but she feels the cynically appraising glance he gives her face and hands.*]

MARY [*tensely*] Why do you stare like that?

JAMIE You know.

[*He turns back to the window.*]

MARY I don't know.

JAMIE Oh, for God's sake, do you think you can fool me, Mama? I'm not blind.

MARY [*looks directly at him now, her face set again in an expression of blank, stubborn denial*] I don't know what you're talking about.

JAMIE No? Take a look at your eyes in the mirror!

EDMUND [*coming in from the porch*] I got Papa moving. He'll be here in a minute. [*With a glance from one to the other, which his mother avoids—uneasily*] What's happened? What's the matter, Mama?

MARY [*disturbed by his coming, gives way to a flurry of guilty, nervous excitement*] Your brother ought to be ashamed of himself. He's been insinuating I don't know what.

EDMUND [*turns on* JAMIE] God damn you!

[*He takes a threatening step toward him.* JAMIE *turns his back with a shrug and looks out the window.*]

MARY [*more upset, grabs* EDMUND*'s arm—excitedly*] Stop this at once, do you hear me? How dare you use such language before me! [*Abruptly her tone and manner change to the strange detachment she has shown before.*] It's wrong to blame your brother. He can't help being what the past has made him. Any more than your father can. Or you. Or I.

EDMUND [*frightenedly—with a desperate hoping against hope*] He's a liar! It's a lie, isn't it, Mama?

MARY [*keeping her eyes averted*] What is a lie? Now you're talking in riddles like Jamie.

[*Then her eyes meet his stricken, accusing look. She stammers.*]

Edmund! Don't! [*She looks away and her manner instantly regains the quality of strange detachment—calmly.*] There's your father coming up the steps now. I must tell Bridget.

[*She goes through the back parlor.* EDMUND *moves slowly to his chair. He looks sick and hopeless.*]

JAMIE [*from the window, without looking around*] Well?

EDMUND [*refusing to admit anything to his brother yet—weakly defiant*] Well, what? You're a liar.

[JAMIE *again shrugs his shoulders. The screen door on the front porch is heard closing.* EDMUND *says dully*]

Here's Papa. I hope he loosens up with the old bottle.

[TYRONE *comes in through the front parlor. He is putting on his coat.*]

TYRONE Sorry I'm late. Captain Turner stopped to talk and once he starts gabbing you can't get away from him.

JAMIE [*without turning—dryly*] You mean once he starts listening.

[*His father regards him with dislike. He comes to the table with a quick measuring look at the bottle of whiskey. Without turning,* JAMIE *senses this.*]

It's all right. The level in the bottle hasn't changed.

TYRONE I wasn't noticing that. [*He adds caustically.*] As if it proved anything with you around. I'm on to your tricks.

EDMUND [*dully*] Did I hear you say, let's all have a drink?

TYRONE [*frowns at him*] Jamie is welcome after his hard morning's work, but I won't invite you. Doctor Hardy—

EDMUND To hell with Doctor Hardy! One isn't going to kill me. I feel—all in,[1] Papa.

TYRONE [*with a worried look at him—putting on a fake heartiness*] Come along, then. It's before a meal and I've always found that good whiskey, taken in moderation as an appetizer, is the best of tonics.

[EDMUND *gets up as his father passes the bottle to him. He pours a big drink.* TYRONE *frowns admonishingly.*]

I said, in moderation.

[*He pours his own drink and passes the bottle to* JAMIE*, grumbling.*]

It'd be a waste of breath mentioning moderation to you.

[*Ignoring the hint,* JAMIE *pours a big drink. His father scowls—then, giving it up, resumes his hearty air, raising his glass.*]

1. Exhausted.

Well, here's health and happiness!

[EDMUND *gives a bitter laugh.*]

EDMUND That's a joke!

TYRONE What is?

EDMUND Nothing. Here's how.

[*They drink.*]

TYRONE [*becoming aware of the atmosphere*] What's the matter here? There's gloom in the air you could cut with a knife. [*Turns on* JAMIE *resentfully.*] You got the drink you were after, didn't you? Why are you wearing that gloomy look on your mug?

JAMIE [*shrugging his shoulders*] You won't be singing a song yourself soon.

EDMUND Shut up, Jamie.

TYRONE [*uneasy now—changing the subject*] I thought lunch was ready. I'm hungry as a hunter. Where is your mother?

MARY [*returning through the back parlor, calls*] Here I am.

[*She comes in. She is excited and self-conscious. As she talks, she glances everywhere except at any of their faces.*]

I've had to calm down Bridget. She's in a tantrum over your being late again, and I don't blame her. If your lunch is dried up from waiting in the oven, she said it served you right, you could like it or leave it for all she cared. [*With increasing excitement*] Oh, I'm so sick and tired of pretending this is a home! You won't help me! You won't put yourself out the least bit! You don't know how to act in a home! You don't really want one! You never have wanted one—never since the day we were married! You should have remained a bachelor and lived in second-rate hotels and entertained your friends in barrooms! [*She adds strangely, as if she were now talking aloud to herself rather than to* TYRONE] Then nothing would ever have happened.

[*They stare at her.* TYRONE *knows now. He suddenly looks a tired, bitterly sad old man.* EDMUND *glances at his father and sees that he knows, but he still cannot help trying to warn his mother.*]

EDMUND Mama! Stop talking. Why don't we go in to lunch.

MARY [*starts and at once the quality of unnatural detachment settles on her face again. She even smiles with an ironical amusement to herself.*] Yes, it is inconsiderate of me to dig up the past, when I know your father and Jamie must be hungry. [*Putting her arm around Edmund's shoulder—with a fond solicitude which is at the same time remote*] I do hope you have an appetite, dear. You really must eat more. [*Her eyes become fixed on the whiskey glass on the table beside him—sharply.*] Why is that glass there? Did you take a drink? Oh, how can you be such a fool? Don't you know it's the worst thing?

[*She turns on* TYRONE.] You're to blame, James. How could you let him? Do you want to kill him? Don't you remember my father? He wouldn't stop after he was stricken. He said doctors were fools! He thought, like you, that whiskey is a good tonic! [*A look of terror comes into her eyes and she stammers.*] But, of course, there's no comparison at all. I don't know why I— Forgive me for scolding you, James. One small drink won't hurt Edmund. It might be good for him, if it gives him an appetite.

[*She pats* EDMUND*'s cheek playfully, the strange detachment again in her manner. He jerks his head away. She seems not to notice, but she moves instinctively away.*]

JAMIE [*roughly, to hide his tense nerves*] For God's sake, let's eat. I've been working in the damned dirt under the hedge all morning. I've earned my grub.

[*He comes around in back of his father, not looking at his mother, and grabs* EDMUND*'s shoulder.*]

Come on, Kid. Let's put on the feed bag.

[EDMUND *gets up, keeping his eyes averted from his mother. They pass her, heading for the back parlor.*]

TYRONE [*dully*] Yes, you go in with your mother, lads. I'll join you in a second.

[*But they keep on without waiting for her. She looks at their backs with a helpless hurt and, as they enter the back parlor, starts to follow them.* TYRONE*'s eyes are on her, sad and condemning. She feels them and turns sharply without meeting his stare.*]

MARY Why do you look at me like that? [*Her hands flutter up to pat her hair.*] Is it my hair coming down? I was so worn out from last night. I thought I'd better lie down this morning. I drowsed off and had a nice refreshing nap. But I'm sure I fixed my hair again when I woke up. [*Forcing a laugh*] Although, as usual, I couldn't find my glasses. [*Sharply*] Please stop staring! One would think you were accusing me— [*Then pleadingly*] James! You don't understand!

TYRONE [*with dull anger*] I understand that I've been a God-damned fool to believe in you!

[*He walks away from her to pour himself a big drink.*]

MARY [*her face again sets in stubborn defiance*] I don't know what you mean by "believing in me." All I've felt was distrust and spying and suspicion. [*Then accusingly*] Why are you having another drink? You never have more than one before lunch. [*Bitterly*] I know what to expect. You will be drunk tonight. Well, it won't be the first time, will it—or the thousandth? [*Again she bursts out pleadingly.*] Oh, James, please! You don't understand! I'm so worried about Edmund! I'm so afraid he—

TYRONE I don't want to listen to your excuses, Mary.

MARY [*strickenly*] Excuses? You mean—? Oh, you can't believe that of me! You mustn't believe that, James! [*Then slipping away into her strange detachment—quite casually*] Shall we not go into lunch, dear? I don't want anything but I know you're hungry.

[*He walks slowly to where she stands in the doorway. He walks like an old man. As he reaches her she bursts out piteously.*]

James! I tried so hard! I tried so hard! Please believe—!

TYRONE [*moved in spite of himself—helplessly*] I suppose you did, Mary. [*Then grief-strickenly*] For the love of God, why couldn't you have the strength to keep on?

MARY [*her face setting into that stubborn denial again*] I don't know what you're talking about. Have the strength to keep on what?

TYRONE [*hopelessly*] Never mind. It's no use now.

[*He moves on and she keeps beside him as they disappear in the back parlor.*]

Curtain.

Act 2, Scene 2

SCENE: *The same, about a half hour later. The tray with the bottle of whiskey has been removed from the table. The family are returning from lunch as the curtain rises.* MARY *is the first to enter from the back parlor. Her husband follows. He is not with her as he was in the similar entrance after breakfast at the opening of Act 1. He avoids touching her or looking at her. There is condemnation in his face, mingled now with the beginning of an old weary, helpless resignation.* JAMIE *and* EDMUND *follow their father.* JAMIE*'s face is hard with defensive cynicism.* EDMUND *tries to copy this defense but without success. He plainly shows he is heartsick as well as physically ill.*

MARY *is terribly nervous again, as if the strain of sitting through lunch with them had been too much for her. Yet at the same time, in contrast to this, her expression shows more of that strange aloofness which seems to stand apart from her nerves and the anxieties which harry them.*

She is talking as she enters—a stream of words that issues casually, in a routine of family conversation, from her mouth. She appears indifferent to the fact that their thoughts are not on what she is saying any more than her own are. As she talks, she comes to the left of the table and stands, facing front, one hand fumbling with the bosom of her dress, the other playing over the tabletop. TYRONE *lights a cigar and goes to the screen door, staring out.* JAMIE *fills a pipe from a jar on top of the bookcase at rear. He lights it as he goes to look out the window at right.* EDMUND *sits in a chair by the table, turned half away from his mother so he does not have to watch her.*

MARY It's no use finding fault with Bridget. She doesn't listen. I can't threaten her, or she'd threaten she'd leave. And she does do her best at times. It's too bad they seem to be just the times you're sure to be late, James. Well, there's this consolation: it's difficult to tell from her cooking whether she's doing her best or her worst. [*She gives a little laugh of detached amusement—indifferently.*] Never mind. The summer will soon be over, thank goodness. Your season will open again and we can go back to second-rate hotels and trains. I hate them, too, but at least I don't expect them to be like a home, and there's no housekeeping to worry about. It's unreasonable to expect Bridget or Cathleen to act as if this was a home. They know it isn't as well as we know it. It never has been and it never will be.

TYRONE [*bitterly without turning around*] No, it never can be now. But it was once, before you—

MARY [*her face instantly set in blank denial*] Before I what?

[*There is a dead silence. She goes on with a return of her detached air.*]

No, no. Whatever you mean, it isn't true, dear. It was never a home. You've always preferred the Club or a barroom. And for me it's always been as lonely as a dirty room in a one-night-stand hotel. In a real home one is never lonely. You forget I know from experience what a home is like. I gave up one to marry you—my father's home.

[*At once, through an association of ideas she turns to* EDMUND. *Her manner becomes tenderly solicitous, but there is the strange quality of detachment in it.*]

I'm worried about you, Edmund. You hardly touched a thing at lunch. That's no way to take care of yourself. It's all right for me not to have an appetite. I've been growing too fat. But you must eat. [*Coaxingly maternal*] Promise me you will, dear, for my sake.

EDMUND [*dully*] Yes, Mama.

MARY [*pats his cheek as he tries not to shrink away*] That's a good boy.

[*There is another pause of dead silence. Then the telephone in the front hall rings and all of them stiffen startledly.*]

TYRONE [*hastily*] I'll answer. McGuire said he'd call me.

[*He goes out through the front parlor.*]

MARY [*indifferently*] McGuire. He must have another piece of property on his list that no one would think of buying except your father. It doesn't matter any more, but it's always seemed to me your father could afford to keep on buying property but never to give me a home. [*She stops to listen as* TYRONE*'s voice is heard from the hall.*]

TYRONE Hello. [*With forced heartiness*] Oh, how are you, Doctor?

[JAMIE *turns from the window.* MARY*'s fingers play more rapidly on the tabletop.* TYRONE*'s voice, trying to conceal, reveals that he is hearing bad news.*]

I see— [*Hurriedly*] Well, you'll explain all about it when you see him this afternoon. Yes, he'll be in without fail. Four o'clock. I'll drop in myself and have a talk with you before that. I have to go uptown on business, anyway. Goodbye, Doctor.

EDMUND [*dully*] That didn't sound like glad tidings.

[JAMIE *gives him a pitying glance—then looks out the window again.* MARY*'s face is terrified and her hands flutter distractedly.* TYRONE *comes in. The strain is obvious in his casualness as he addresses* EDMUND.]

TYRONE It was Doctor Hardy. He wants you to be sure and see him at four.

EDMUND [*dully*] What did he say? Not that I give a damn now.

MARY [*bursts out excitedly*] I wouldn't believe him if he swore on a stack of Bibles. You mustn't pay attention to a word he says, Edmund.

TYRONE [*sharply*] Mary!

MARY [*more excitedly*] Oh, we all realize why you like him, James! Because he's cheap! But please don't try to tell me! I know all about Doctor Hardy. Heaven knows I ought to after all these years. He's an ignorant fool! There should be a law to keep men like him from practicing. He hasn't the slightest idea— When you're in agony and half insane, he sits and holds your hand and delivers sermons on willpower!

[*Her face is drawn in an expression of intense suffering by the memory. For the moment, she loses all caution. With bitter hatred.*]

He deliberately humiliates you! He makes you beg and plead! He treats you like a criminal! He understands nothing! And yet it was exactly the same type of cheap quack who first gave you the medicine—and you never knew what it was until too late! [*Passionately*] I hate doctors! They'll do anything—anything to keep you coming to them. They'll sell their souls! What's worse, they'll sell yours, and you never know it till one day you find yourself in hell!

EDMUND Mama! For God's sake, stop talking.

TYRONE [*shakenly*] Yes, Mary, it's no time—

MARY [*suddenly is overcome by guilty confusion—stammers*] I— Forgive me, dear. You're right. It's useless to be angry now.

[*There is again a pause of dead silence. When she speaks again, her face has cleared and is calm, and the quality of uncanny detachment is in her voice and manner.*]

I'm going upstairs for a moment, if you'll excuse me. I have to fix my hair. [*She adds smilingly.*] That is if I can find my glasses. I'll be right down.

TYRONE [*as she starts through the doorway—pleading and rebuking*] Mary!

MARY [*turns to stare at him calmly*] Yes, dear? What is it?

TYRONE [*helplessly*] Nothing.

MARY [*with a strange derisive smile*] You're welcome to come up and watch me if you're so suspicious.

TYRONE As if that could do any good! You'd only postpone it. And I'm not your jailor. This isn't a prison.

MARY No. I know you can't help thinking it's a home. [*She adds quickly with a detached contrition.*] I'm sorry, dear. I don't mean to be bitter. It's not your fault.

[*She turns and disappears through the back parlor. The three in the room remain silent. It is as if they were waiting until she got upstairs before speaking.*]

JAMIE [*cynically brutal*] Another shot in the arm!

EDMUND [*angrily*] Cut out that kind of talk!

TYRONE Yes! Hold your foul tongue and your rotten Broadway loafer's lingo! Have you no pity or decency? [*Losing his temper*] You ought to be kicked out in the gutter! But if I did it, you know damned well who'd weep and plead for you, and excuse you and complain till I let you come back.

JAMIE [*a spasm of pain crosses his face*] Christ, don't I know that? No pity? I have all the pity in the world for her. I understand what a hard game to beat she's up against—which is more than you ever have! My lingo didn't mean I had no feeling. I was merely putting bluntly what we all know, and have to live with now, again. [*Bitterly*] The cures are no damned good except for a while. The truth is there is no cure and we've been saps to hope— [*Cynically*] They never come back!

EDMUND [*scornfully parodying his brother's cynicism*] They never come back! Everything is in the bag! It's all a frame-up! We're all fall guys and suckers and we can't beat the game! [*Disdainfully*] Christ, if I felt the way you do—!

JAMIE [*stung for a moment—then shrugging his shoulders, dryly*] I thought you did. Your poetry isn't very cheery. Nor the stuff you read and claim you admire. [*He indicates the small bookcase at rear.*] Your pet with the unpronounceable name, for example.

EDMUND Nietzsche.[2] You don't know what you're talking about. You haven't read him.

JAMIE Enough to know it's a lot of bunk!

TYRONE Shut up, both of you! There's little choice between the philosophy you learned from Broadway loafers, and the one Edmund got from his books. They're both rotten to the core. You've both flouted the faith you were born and brought up in—the one true faith of the Catholic Church—and your denial has brought nothing but self-destruction!

[*His two sons stare at him contemptuously. They forget their quarrel and are as one against him on this issue.*]

2. Friedrich Nietzsche (1844–1900), the German philosopher who, in such works as *Thus Spake Zarathustra* (1883–85), challenged religion and conventional philosophy. He also influenced modern dramatists such as August Strindberg and O'Neill with his theory of tragedy, as put forth in *The Birth of Tragedy* (1872).

EDMUND That's the bunk, Papa!

JAMIE We don't pretend, at any rate. [*Caustically*] I don't notice you've worn any holes in the knees of your pants going to Mass.

TYRONE It's true I'm a bad Catholic in the observance, God forgive me. But I believe! [*Angrily*] And you're a liar! I may not go to church but every night and morning of my life I get on my knees and pray!

EDMUND [*bitingly*] Did you pray for Mama?

TYRONE I did. I've prayed to God these many years for her.

EDMUND Then Nietzsche must be right. [*He quotes from* Thus Spake Zarathustra.] "God is dead: of His pity for man hath God died."

TYRONE [*ignores this*] If your mother had prayed, too— She hasn't denied her faith, but she's forgotten it, until now there's no strength of the spirit left in her to fight against her curse. [*Then dully resigned*] But what's the good of talk? We've lived with this before and now we must again. There's no help for it. [*Bitterly*] Only I wish she hadn't led me to hope this time. By God, I never will again!

EDMUND That's a rotten thing to say, Papa! [*Defiantly*] Well, I'll hope! She's just started. It can't have got a hold on her yet. She can still stop. I'm going to talk to her.

JAMIE [*shrugs his shoulders*] You can't talk to her now. She'll listen but she won't listen. She'll be here but she won't be here. You know the way she gets.

TYRONE Yes, that's the way the poison acts on her always. Every day from now on, there'll be the same drifting away from us until by the end of each night—

EDMUND [*miserably*] Cut it out, Papa! [*He jumps up from his chair.*] I'm going to get dressed. [*Bitterly, as he goes*] I'll make so much noise she can't suspect I've come to spy on her.

[*He disappears through the front parlor and can be heard stamping noisily upstairs.*]

JAMIE [*after a pause*] What did Doc Hardy say about the Kid?

TYRONE [*dully*] It's what you thought. He's got consumption.

JAMIE God damn it!

TYRONE There is no possible doubt, he said.

JAMIE He'll have to go to a sanatorium.

TYRONE Yes, and the sooner the better, Hardy said, for him and everyone around him. He claims that in six months to a year Edmund will be cured, if he obeys orders. [*He sighs—gloomily and resentfully.*] I never thought a child of mine— It doesn't come from my side of the family. There wasn't one of us that didn't have lungs as strong as an ox.

JAMIE Who gives a damn about that part of it! Where does Hardy want to send him?

TYRONE That's what I'm to see him about.

JAMIE Well, for God's sake, pick out a good place and not some cheap dump!

TYRONE [*stung*] I'll send him wherever Hardy thinks best!

JAMIE Well, don't give Hardy your old over-the-hills-to-the-poorhouse song about taxes and mortgages.

TYRONE I'm no millionaire who can throw money away! Why shouldn't I tell Hardy the truth?

JAMIE Because he'll think you want him to pick a cheap dump, and because he'll know it isn't the truth—especially if he hears afterwards you've seen McGuire and let that flannel-mouth, gold-brick merchant sting you with another piece of bum property!

TYRONE [*furiously*] Keep your nose out of my business!

JAMIE This is Edmund's business. What I'm afraid of is, with your Irish bog-trotter[3] idea that consumption is fatal, you'll figure it would be a waste of money to spend any more than you can help.

TYRONE You liar!

JAMIE All right. Prove I'm a liar. That's what I want. That's why I brought it up.

TYRONE [*his rage still smouldering*] I have every hope Edmund will be cured. And keep your dirty tongue off Ireland! You're a fine one to sneer, with the map of it on your face!

JAMIE Not after I wash my face. [*Then before his father can react to this insult to the Old Sod, he adds dryly, shrugging his shoulders.*] Well, I've said all I have to say. It's up to you. [*Abruptly*] What do you want me to do this afternoon, now you're going uptown? I've done all I can do on the hedge until you cut more of it. You don't want me to go ahead with your clipping, I know that.

TYRONE No. You'd get it crooked, as you get everything else.

JAMIE Then I'd better go uptown with Edmund. The bad news coming on top of what's happened to Mama may hit him hard.

TYRONE [*forgetting his quarrel*] Yes, go with him, Jamie. Keep up his spirits, if you can. [*He adds caustically.*] If you can without making it an excuse to get drunk!

JAMIE What would I use for money? The last I heard they were still selling booze, not giving it away. [*He starts for the front-parlor doorway.*] I'll get dressed.

[*He stops in the doorway as he sees his mother approaching from the hall, and moves aside to let her come in. Her eyes look brighter, and her manner is more detached. This change becomes more marked as the scene goes on.*]

MARY [*vaguely*] You haven't seen my glasses anywhere, have you, Jamie?

[*She doesn't look at him. He glances away, ignoring her question but she doesn't seem to expect an answer. She comes forward, addressing her husband without looking at him.*]

You haven't seen them, have you, James?

[*Behind her* JAMIE *disappears through the front parlor.*]

TYRONE [*turns to look out the screen door*] No, Mary.

MARY What's the matter with Jamie? Have you been nagging at him again? You shouldn't treat him with such contempt all the time. He's not to blame. If he'd been brought up in a real home, I'm sure he would have been different. [*She comes to the windows at right—lightly.*] You're not much of a weather prophet, dear. See how hazy it's getting. I can hardly see the other shore.

TYRONE [*trying to speak naturally*] Yes, I spoke too soon. We're in for another night of fog, I'm afraid.

3. A derogatory nickname for the Irish.

MARY Oh, well, I won't mind it tonight.

TYRONE No, I don't imagine you will, Mary.

MARY [*flashes a glance at him—after a pause*] I don't see Jamie going down to the hedge. Where did he go?

TYRONE He's going with Edmund to the doctor's. He went up to change his clothes. [*Then, glad of an excuse to leave her*] I'd better do the same or I'll be late for my appointment at the Club.

[*He makes a move toward the front-parlor doorway, but with a swift impulsive movement she reaches out and clasps his arm.*]

MARY [*a note of pleading in her voice*] Don't go yet, dear. I don't want to be alone. [*Hastily*] I mean, you have plenty of time. You know you boast you can dress in one-tenth the time it takes the boys. [*Vaguely*] There is something I wanted to say. What is it? I've forgotten. I'm glad Jamie is going uptown. You didn't give him any money, I hope.

TYRONE I did not.

MARY He'd only spend it on drink and you know what a vile, poisonous tongue he has when he's drunk. Not that I would mind anything he said tonight, but he always manages to drive you into a rage, especially if you're drunk, too, as you will be.

TYRONE [*resentfully*] I won't. I never get drunk.

MARY [*teasing indifferently*] Oh, I'm sure you'll hold it well. You always have. It's hard for a stranger to tell, but after thirty-five years of marriage—

TYRONE I've never missed a performance in my life. That's the proof! [*Then bitterly*] If I did get drunk it is not you who should blame me. No man has ever had a better reason.

MARY Reason? What reason? You always drink too much when you go to the Club, don't you? Particularly when you meet McGuire. He sees to that. Don't think I'm finding fault, dear. You must do as you please. I won't mind.

TYRONE I know you won't [*He turns toward the front parlor, anxious to escape.*] I've got to get dressed.

MARY [*again she reaches out and grasps his arm—pleadingly*] No, please wait a little while, dear. At least, until one of the boys comes down. You will all be leaving me so soon.

TYRONE [*with bitter sadness*] It's you who are leaving us, Mary.

MARY I? That's a silly thing to say, James. How could I leave? There is nowhere I could go. Who would I go to see? I have no friends.

TYRONE It's your own fault— [*He stops and sighs helplessly—persuasively.*] There's surely one thing you can do this afternoon that will be good for you, Mary. Take a drive in the automobile. Get away from the house. Get a little sun and fresh air. [*Injuredly*] I bought the automobile for you. You know I don't like the damned things. I'd rather walk any day, or take a trolley. [*With growing resentment*] I had it here waiting for you when you came back from the sanatorium. I hoped it would give you pleasure and distract your mind. You used to ride in it every day, but you've hardly used it at all lately. I paid a lot of money I couldn't afford, and there's the chauffeur I have to board and lodge and pay high wages whether he drives you or not. [*Bitterly*] Waste! The same old waste that will land me in the poorhouse in my old age! What good did it do you? I might as well have thrown the money out the window.

MARY [*with detached calm*] Yes, it was a waste of money, James. You shouldn't have bought a secondhand automobile. You were swindled again as you always are, because you insist on secondhand bargains in everything.

TYRONE It's one of the best makes! Everyone says it's better than any of the new ones!

MARY [*ignoring this*] It was another waste to hire Smythe, who was only a helper in a garage and had never been a chauffeur. Oh, I realize his wages are less than a real chauffeur's, but he more than makes up for that, I'm sure, by the graft he gets from the garage on repair bills. Something is always wrong. Smythe sees to that, I'm afraid.

TYRONE I don't believe it! He may not be a fancy millionaire's flunky but he's honest! You're as bad as Jamie, suspecting everyone!

MARY You mustn't be offended, dear. I wasn't offended when you gave me the automobile. I knew you didn't mean to humiliate me. I knew that was the way you had to do everything. I was grateful and touched. I knew buying the car was a hard thing for you to do, and it proved how much you loved me, in your way, especially when you couldn't really believe it would do me any good.

TYRONE Mary! [*He suddenly hugs her to him—brokenly.*] Dear Mary! For the love of God, for my sake and the boys' sake and your own, won't you stop now?

MARY [*stammers in guilty confusion for a second*] I— James! Please! [*Her strange, stubborn defense comes back instantly.*] Stop what? What are you talking about?

[*He lets his arm fall to his side brokenly. She impulsively puts her arm around him.*]

James! We've loved each other! We always will! Let's remember only that, and not try to understand what we cannot understand, or help things that cannot be helped—the things life has done to us we cannot excuse or explain.

TYRONE [*as if he hadn't heard—bitterly*] You won't even try?

MARY [*her arms drop hopelessly and she turns away—with detachment*] Try to go for a drive this afternoon, you mean? Why, yes, if you wish me to, although it makes me feel lonelier than if I stayed here. There is no one I can invite to drive with me, and I never know where to tell Smythe to go. If there was a friend's house where I could drop in and laugh and gossip awhile. But, of course, there isn't. There never has been. [*Her manner becoming more and more remote*] At the Convent I had so many friends. Girls whose families lived in lovely homes. I used to visit them and they'd visit me in my father's home. But, naturally, after I married an actor—you know how actors were considered in those days—a lot of them gave me the cold shoulder. And then, right after we were married, there was the scandal of that woman who had been your mistress, suing you. From then on, all my old friends either pitied me or cut me dead.[4] I hated the ones who cut me much less than the pitiers.

TYRONE [*with guilty resentment*] For God's sake, don't dig up what's long forgotten. If you're that far gone in the past already, when it's only the beginning of the afternoon, what will you be tonight?

4. Pretended not to know her; broke off their acquaintance.

MARY [*stares at him defiantly now*] Come to think of it, I do have to drive uptown. There's something I must get at the drugstore.

TYRONE [*bitterly scornful*] Leave it to you to have some of the stuff hidden, and prescriptions for more! I hope you'll lay in a good stock ahead so we'll never have another night like the one when you screamed for it, and ran out of the house in your nightdress half crazy, to try and throw yourself off the dock!

MARY [*tries to ignore this*] I have to get tooth powder and toilet soap and cold cream— [*She breaks down pitiably.*] James! You mustn't remember! You mustn't humiliate me so!

TYRONE [*ashamed*] I'm sorry. Forgive me, Mary!

MARY [*defensively detached again*] It doesn't matter. Nothing like that ever happened. You must have dreamed it.

[*He stares at her hopelessly. Her voice seems to drift farther and farther away.*]

I was so healthy before Edmund was born. You remember, James. There wasn't a nerve in my body. Even traveling with you season after season, with week after week of one-night stands, in trains without Pullmans,[5] in dirty rooms of filthy hotels, eating bad food, bearing children in hotel rooms, I still kept healthy. But bearing Edmund was the last straw. I was so sick afterwards, and that ignorant quack of a cheap hotel doctor— All he knew was I was in pain. It was easy for him to stop the pain.

TYRONE Mary! For God's sake, forget the past!

MARY [*with strange objective calm*] Why? How can I? The past is the present, isn't it? It's the future, too. We all try to lie out of that but life won't let us. [*Going on*] I blame only myself. I swore after Eugene died I would never have another baby. I was to blame for his death. If I hadn't left him with my mother to join you on the road, because you wrote telling me you missed me and were so lonely, Jamie would never have been allowed, when he still had measles, to go in the baby's room. [*Her face hardening*] I've always believed Jamie did it on purpose. He was jealous of the baby. He hated him. [*As Tyrone starts to protest.*] Oh, I know Jamie was only seven, but he was never stupid. He'd been warned it might kill the baby. He knew. I've never been able to forgive him for that.

TYRONE [*with bitter sadness*] Are you back with Eugene now? Can't you let our dead baby rest in peace?

MARY [*as if she hadn't heard him*] It was my fault. I should have insisted on staying with Eugene and not have let you persuade me to join you, just because I loved you. Above all, I shouldn't have let you insist I have another baby to take Eugene's place, because you thought that would make me forget his death. I knew from experience by then that children should have homes to be born in, if they are to be good children, and women need homes, if they are to be good mothers. I was afraid all the time I carried Edmund. I knew something terrible would happen. I knew I'd proved by the way I'd left Eugene that I wasn't worthy to have another baby, and that God would punish me if I did. I never should have borne Edmund.

TYRONE [*with an uneasy glance through the front parlor*] Mary! Be careful

5. Sleeping cars.

with your talk. If he heard you he might think you never wanted him. He's feeling bad enough already without—

MARY [*violently*] It's a lie! I did want him! More than anything in the world! You don't understand! I meant, for his sake. He has never been happy. He never will be. Nor healthy. He was born nervous and too sensitive, and that's my fault. And now, ever since he's been so sick I've kept remembering Eugene and my father and I've been so frightened and guilty— [*Then, catching herself, with an instant change to stubborn denial*] Oh, I know it's foolish to imagine dreadful things when there's no reason for it. After all, everyone has colds and gets over them.

[TYRONE *stares at her and sighs helplessly. He turns away toward the front parlor and sees* EDMUND *coming down the stairs in the hall.*]

TYRONE [*sharply, in a low voice*] Here's Edmund. For God's sake try and be yourself—at least until he goes! You can do that much for him!

[*He waits, forcing his face into a pleasantly paternal expression. She waits frightenedly, seized again by a nervous panic, her hands fluttering over the bosom of her dress, up to her throat and hair, with a distracted aimlessness. Then, as* EDMUND *approaches the doorway, she cannot face him. She goes swiftly away to the windows at left and stares out with her back to the front parlor.* EDMUND *enters. He has changed to a ready-made blue serge suit, high stiff collar and tie, black shoes.*]

[*With an actor's heartiness*] Well! You look spic and span. I'm on my way up to change, too.

[*He starts to pass him.*]

EDMUND [*dryly*] Wait a minute, Papa. I hate to bring up disagreeable topics, but there's the matter of carfare. I'm broke.

TYRONE [*starts automatically on a customary lecture*] You'll always be broke until you learn the value— [*Checks himself guiltily, looking at his son's sick face with worried pity.*] But you've been learning, lad. You worked hard before you took ill. You've done splendidly. I'm proud of you.

[*He pulls out a small roll of bills from his pants pocket and carefully selects one.* EDMUND *takes it. He glances at it and his face expresses astonishment. His father again reacts customarily—sarcastically.*]

Thank you. [*He quotes.*] "How sharper than a serpent's tooth it is—"

EDMUND "To have a thankless child."[6] I know. Give me a chance, Papa. I'm knocked speechless. This isn't a dollar. It's a ten spot.

TYRONE [*embarrassed by his generosity*] Put it in your pocket. You'll probably meet some of your friends uptown and you can't hold your end up and be sociable with nothing in your jeans.

EDMUND You meant it? Gosh, thank you, Papa. [*He is genuinely pleased and grateful for a moment—then he stares at his father's face with uneasy suspicion.*] But why all of a sudden—? [*Cynically*] Did Doc Hardy tell you I was going to die? [*Then he sees his father is bitterly hurt.*] No! That's a rotten crack. I was only kidding, Papa.

[*He puts an arm around his father impulsively and gives him an affectionate hug.*]

I'm very grateful. Honest, Papa.

TYRONE [*touched, returns his hug*] You're welcome, lad.

6. Quoting Lear, from Shakespeare's *King Lear* (1605), 1.4.251–52.

MARY [*suddenly turns to them in a confused panic of frightened anger*] I won't have it! [*She stamps her foot.*] Do you hear, Edmund! Such morbid nonsense! Saying you're going to die! It's the books you read! Nothing but sadness and death! Your father shouldn't allow you to have them. And some of the poems you've written yourself are even worse! You'd think you didn't want to live! A boy of your age with everything before him! It's just a pose you get out of books! You're not really sick at all!

TYRONE Mary! Hold your tongue!

MARY [*instantly changing to a detached tone*] But, James, it's absurd of Edmund to be so gloomy and make such a great to-do about nothing. [*Turning to* EDMUND *but avoiding his eyes—teasingly affectionate*] Never mind, dear. I'm on to you. [*She comes to him.*] You want to be petted and spoiled and made a fuss over, isn't that it? You're still such a baby.

[*She puts her arm around him and hugs him. He remains rigid and unyielding. Her voice begins to tremble.*]

But please don't carry it too far, dear. Don't say horrible things. I know it's foolish to take them seriously but I can't help it. You've got me—so frightened.

[*She breaks and hides her face on his shoulder, sobbing.* EDMUND *is moved in spite of himself. He pats her shoulder with an awkward tenderness.*]

EDMUND Don't, mother. [*His eyes meet his father's.*]

TYRONE [*huskily—clutching at hopeless hope*] Maybe if you asked your mother now what you said you were going to— [*He fumbles with his watch.*] By God, look at the time! I'll have to shake a leg.

[*He hurries away through the front parlor.* MARY *lifts her head. Her manner is again one of detached motherly solicitude. She seems to have forgotten the tears which are still in her eyes.*]

MARY How do you feel, dear? [*She feels his forehead.*] Your head is a little hot, but that's just from going out in the sun. You look ever so much better than you did this morning. [*Taking his hand*] Come and sit down. You mustn't stand on your feet so much. You must learn to husband your strength.

[*She gets him to sit and she sits sideways on the arm of his chair, an arm around his shoulder, so he cannot meet her eyes.*]

EDMUND [*starts to blurt out the appeal he now feels is quite hopeless*] Listen, Mama—

MARY [*interrupting quickly*] Now, now! Don't talk. Lean back and rest. [*Persuasively*] You know, I think it would be much better for you if you stayed home this afternoon and let me take care of you. It's such a tiring trip uptown in the dirty old trolley on a hot day like this. I'm sure you'd be much better off here with me.

EDMUND [*dully*] You forget I have an appointment with Hardy. [*Trying again to get his appeal started*] Listen, Mama—

MARY [*quickly*] You can telephone and say you don't feel well enough. [*Excitedly*] It's simply a waste of time and money seeing him. He'll only tell you some lie. He'll pretend he's found something serious the matter because that's his bread and butter. [*She gives a hard sneering little laugh.*] The old idiot! All he knows about medicine is to look solemn and preach willpower!

EDMUND [*trying to catch her eyes*] Mama! Please listen! I want to ask you something! You— You're only just started. You can still stop. You've got the willpower! We'll all help you. I'll do anything! Won't you, Mama?

MARY [*stammers pleadingly*] Please don't—talk about things you don't understand!

EDMUND [*dully*] All right, I give up. I knew it was no use.

MARY [*in blank denial now*] Anyway, I don't know what you're referring to. But I do know you should be the last one— Right after I returned from the sanatorium, you began to be ill. The doctor there had warned me I must have peace at home with nothing to upset me, and all I've done is worry about you. [*Then distractedly*] But that's no excuse! I'm only trying to explain. It's not an excuse! [*She hugs him to her—pleadingly.*] Promise me, dear, you won't believe I made you an excuse.

EDMUND [*bitterly*] What else can I believe?

MARY [*slowly takes her arm away—her manner remote and objective again*] Yes, I suppose you can't help suspecting that.

EDMUND [*ashamed but still bitter*] What do you expect?

MARY Nothing, I don't blame you. How could you believe me—when I can't believe myself? I've become such a liar. I never lied about anything once upon a time. Now I have to lie, especially to myself. But how can you understand, when I don't myself. I've never understood anything about it, except that one day long ago I found I could no longer call my soul my own. [*She pauses—then lowering her voice to a strange tone of whispered confidence.*] But someday, dear, I will find it again—someday when you're all well, and I see you healthy and happy and successful, and I don't have to feel guilty anymore—someday when the Blessed Virgin Mary forgives me and gives me back the faith in Her love and pity I used to have in my convent days, and I can pray to Her again—when She sees no one in the world can believe in me even for a moment anymore, then She will believe in me, and with Her help it will be so easy. I will hear myself scream with agony, and at the same time I will laugh because I will be so sure of myself. [*Then as Edmund remains hopelessly silent, she adds sadly.*] Of course, you can't believe that, either.

[*She rises from the arm of his chair and goes to stare out the windows at right with her back to him—casually.*]

Now I think of it, you might as well go uptown. I forgot I'm taking a drive. I have to go to the drugstore. You would hardly want to go there with me. You'd be so ashamed.

EDMUND [*brokenly*] Mama! Don't!

MARY I suppose you'll divide that ten dollars your father gave you with Jamie. You always divide with each other, don't you? Like good sports. Well, I know what he'll do with his share. Get drunk someplace where he can be with the only kind of woman he understands or likes. [*She turns to him, pleading frightenedly.*] Edmund! Promise me you won't drink! It's so dangerous! You know Doctor Hardy told you—

EDMUND [*bitterly*] I thought he was an old idiot. Anyway, by tonight, what will you care?

MARY [*pitifully*] Edmund!

[JAMIE's *voice is heard from the front hall,* "Come on, Kid, let's beat it."]

[MARY's *manner at once becomes detached again.*]

Go on, Edmund. Jamie's waiting.

[*She goes to the front-parlor doorway.*]

There comes your father downstairs, too.

[TYRONE*'s voice calls,* "Come on, Edmund."]

EDMUND [*jumping up from his chair*] I'm coming.

[*He stops beside her—without looking at her.*]

Goodbye, Mama.

MARY [*kisses him with detached affection*] Goodbye, dear. If you're coming home for dinner, try not to be late. And tell your father. You know what Bridget is.

[*He turns and hurries away.* TYRONE *calls from the hall,* "Goodbye, Mary," *and then* JAMIE, "Goodbye, Mama."]

[*She calls back.*] Goodbye.

[*The front screen door is heard closing after them. She comes and stands by the table, one hand drumming on it, the other fluttering up to pat her hair. She stares about the room with frightened, forsaken eyes and whispers to herself.*]

It's so lonely here. [*Then her face hardens into bitter self-contempt.*] You're lying to yourself again. You wanted to get rid of them. Their contempt and disgust aren't pleasant company. You're glad they're gone. [*She gives a little despairing laugh.*] Then Mother of God, why do I feel so lonely?

Curtain.

Act 3

SCENE: *The same. It is around half past six in the evening. Dusk is gathering in the living room, an early dusk due to the fog which has rolled in from the Sound*[7] *and is like a white curtain drawn down outside the windows. From a lighthouse beyond the harbor's mouth, a foghorn is heard at regular intervals, moaning like a mournful whale in labor, and from the harbor itself, intermittently, comes the warning ringing of bells on yachts at anchor.*

The tray with the bottle of whiskey, glasses, and pitcher of ice water is on the table, as it was in the pre-luncheon scene of the previous act.

MARY *and the second girl,* CATHLEEN, *are discovered. The latter is standing at left of table. She holds an empty whiskey glass in her hand as if she'd forgotten she had it. She shows the effects of drink. Her stupid, good-humored face wears a pleased and flattered simper.*

MARY *is paler than before and her eyes shine with unnatural brilliance. The strange detachment in her manner has intensified. She has hidden deeper within herself and found refuge and release in a dream where present reality is but an appearance to be accepted and dismissed unfeelingly—even with a hard cynicism—or entirely ignored. There is at times an uncanny gay, free youthfulness in her manner, as if in spirit she were released to become again, simply and without self-consciousness, the naive, happy, chattering schoolgirl of her convent days. She wears the dress into which she had changed for her drive to town, a simple, fairly expensive affair, which would be extremely becoming if it were not for the careless, almost slovenly way she wears it. Her hair is no longer fastidiously*

7. Long Island Sound.

in place. It has a slightly disheveled, lopsided look. She talks to CATHLEEN *with a confiding familiarity, as if the second girl were an old, intimate friend. As the curtain rises, she is standing by the screen door looking out. A moan of the foghorn is heard.*

MARY [*amused—girlishly*] That foghorn! Isn't it awful, Cathleen?

CATHLEEN [*talks more familiarly than usual but never with intentional impertinence because she sincerely likes her mistress*] It is indeed, Ma'am. It's like a banshee.[8]

MARY [*goes on as if she hadn't heard. In nearly all the following dialogue there is the feeling that she has* CATHLEEN *with her merely as an excuse to keep talking.*] I don't mind it tonight. Last night it drove me crazy. I lay awake worrying until I couldn't stand it anymore.

CATHLEEN Bad cess[9] to it. I was scared out of my wits riding back from town. I thought that ugly monkey, Smythe, would drive us in a ditch or against a tree. You couldn't see your hand in front of you. I'm glad you had me sit in back with you, Ma'am. If I'd been in front with that monkey— He can't keep his dirty hands to himself. Give him half a chance and he's pinching me on the leg or you-know-where—asking your pardon, Ma'am, but it's true.

MARY [*dreamily*] It wasn't the fog I minded, Cathleen. I really love fog.

CATHLEEN They say it's good for the complexion.

MARY It hides you from the world and the world from you. You feel that everything has changed, and nothing is what it seemed to be. No one can find or touch you anymore.

CATHLEEN I wouldn't care so much if Smythe was a fine, handsome man like some chauffeurs I've seen—I mean, if it was all in fun, for I'm a decent girl. But for a shriveled runt like Smythe—! I've told him, you must think I'm hard up that I'd notice a monkey like you. I've warned him, one day I'll give a clout that'll knock him into next week. And so I will!

MARY It's the foghorn I hate. It won't let you alone. It keeps reminding you, and warning you, and calling you back. [*She smiles strangely.*] But it can't tonight. It's just an ugly sound. It doesn't remind me of anything. [*She gives a teasing, girlish laugh.*] Except, perhaps, Mr. Tyrone's snores. I've always had such fun teasing him about it. He has snored ever since I can remember, especially when he's had too much to drink, and yet he's like a child, he hates to admit it. [*She laughs, coming to the table.*] Well, I suppose I snore at times, too, and I don't like to admit it. So I have no right to make fun of him, have I?

[*She sits in the rocker at right of table.*]

CATHLEEN Ah, sure, everybody healthy snores. It's a sign of sanity, they say. [*Then, worriedly*] What time is it, Ma'am? I ought to go back in the kitchen. The damp is in Bridget's rheumatism and she's like a raging divil. She'll bite my head off.

[*She puts her glass on the table and makes a movement toward the back parlor.*]

MARY [*with a flash of apprehension*] No, don't go, Cathleen. I don't want to be alone, yet.

8. In Irish folklore, a female spirit whose wailing cry warns of an impending death.

9. That is, bad luck (a chiefly Irish curse).

CATHLEEN You won't be for long. The Master and the boys will be home soon.

MARY I doubt if they'll come back for dinner. They have too good an excuse to remain in the barrooms where they feel at home.

[CATHLEEN *stares at her, stupidly puzzled.* MARY *goes on smilingly.*]

Don't worry about Bridget. I'll tell her I kept you with me, and you can take a big drink of whiskey to her when you go. She won't mind then.

CATHLEEN [*grins—at her ease again*] No, Ma'am. That's the one thing can make her cheerful. She loves her drop.

MARY Have another drink yourself, if you wish, Cathleen.

CATHLEEN I don't know if I'd better, Ma'am. I can feel what I've had already. [*Reaching for the bottle*] Well, maybe one more won't harm. [*She pours a drink.*] Here's your good health, Ma'am.

[*She drinks without bothering about a chaser.*]

MARY [*dreamily*] I really did have good health once, Cathleen. But that was long ago.

CATHLEEN [*worried again*] The Master's sure to notice what's gone from the bottle. He has the eye of a hawk for that.

MARY [*amusedly*] Oh, we'll play Jamie's trick on him. Just measure a few drinks of water and pour them in.

CATHLEEN [*does this—with a silly giggle*] God save me, it'll be half water. He'll know by the taste.

MARY [*indifferently*] No, by the time he comes home he'll be too drunk to tell the difference. He has such a good excuse, he believes, to drown his sorrows.

CATHLEEN [*philosophically*] Well, it's a good man's failing. I wouldn't give a trauneen[1] for a teetotaler. They've no high spirits. [*Then, stupidly puzzled*] Good excuse? You mean Master Edmund, Ma'am? I can tell the Master is worried about him.

MARY [*stiffens defensively—but in a strange way the reaction has a mechanical quality, as if it did not penetrate to real emotion*] Don't be silly, Cathleen. Why should he be? A touch of grippe[2] is nothing. And Mr. Tyrone never is worried about anything, except money and property and the fear he'll end his days in poverty. I mean, deeply worried. Because he cannot really understand anything else. [*She gives a little laugh of detached, affectionate amusement.*] My husband is a very peculiar man, Cathleen.

CATHLEEN [*vaguely resentful*] Well, he's a fine, handsome, kind gentleman just the same, Ma'am. Never mind his weakness.

MARY Oh, I don't mind. I've loved him dearly for thirty-six years. That proves I know he's lovable at heart and can't help being what he is, doesn't it?

CATHLEEN [*hazily reassured*] That's right, Ma'am. Love him dearly, for any fool can see he worships the ground you walk on. [*Fighting the effect of her last drink and trying to be soberly conversational*] Speaking of acting, Ma'am, how is it you never went on the stage?

MARY [*resentfully*] I? What put that absurd notion in your head? I was brought up in a respectable home and educated in the best convent in the Middle West. Before I met Mr. Tyrone I hardly knew there was such a

1. Long, thin blade of grass (Irish Gaelic). 2. Influenza.

thing as a theater. I was a very pious girl. I even dreamed of becoming a nun. I've never had the slightest desire to be an actress.

CATHLEEN [*bluntly*] Well, I can't imagine you a holy nun, Ma'am. Sure, you never darken the door of a church, God forgive you.

MARY [*ignores this*] I've never felt at home in the theater. Even though Mr. Tyrone has made me go with him on all his tours, I've had little to do with the people in his company, or with anyone on the stage. Not that I have anything against them. They have always been kind to me, and I to them. But I've never felt at home with them. Their life is not my life. It has always stood between me and— [*She gets up—abruptly.*] But let's not talk of old things that couldn't be helped.

[*She goes to the porch door and stares out.*]

How thick the fog is. I can't see the road. All the people in the world could pass by and I would never know. I wish it was always that way. It's getting dark already. It will soon be night, thank goodness. [*She turns back—vaguely.*] It was kind of you to keep me company this afternoon, Cathleen. I would have been lonely driving uptown alone.

CATHLEEN Sure, wouldn't I rather ride in a fine automobile than stay here and listen to Bridget's lies about her relations? It was like a vacation, Ma'am. [*She pauses—then stupidly.*] There was only one thing I didn't like.

MARY [*vaguely*] What was that, Cathleen?

CATHLEEN The way the man in the drugstore acted when I took in the prescription for you. [*Indignantly*] The impidence of him!

MARY [*with stubborn blankness*] What are you talking about? What drugstore? What prescription? [*Then hastily, as Cathleen stares in stupid amazement*] Oh, of course, I'd forgotten. The medicine for the rheumatism in my hands. What did the man say? [*Then with indifference*] Not that it matters, as long as he filled the prescription.

CATHLEEN It mattered to me, then! I'm not used to being treated like a thief. He gave me a long look and says insultingly, "Where did you get hold of this?" and I says, "It's none of your damned business, but if you must know, it's for the lady I work for, Mrs. Tyrone, who's sitting out in the automobile." That shut him up quick. He gave a look out at you and said, "Oh," and went to get the medicine.

MARY [*vaguely*] Yes, he knows me.

[*She sits in the armchair at right rear of table. She adds in a calm, detached voice.*]

It's a special kind of medicine. I have to take it because there is no other that can stop the pain—*all* the pain—I mean, in my hands.

[*She raises her hands and regards them with melancholy sympathy. There is no tremor in them now.*]

Poor hands! You'd never believe it, but they were once one of my good points, along with my hair and eyes, and I had a fine figure, too. [*Her tone has become more and more far-off and dreamy.*] They were a musician's hands. I used to love the piano. I worked so hard at my music in the Convent—if you can call it work when you do something you love. Mother Elizabeth and my music teacher both said I had more talent than any student they remembered. My father paid for special lessons. He spoiled me. He would do anything I asked. He would have sent me to Europe to study after I graduated from the Convent. I might have gone—if I hadn't fallen in love with Mr. Tyrone. Or I might have become a nun. I had two dreams. To be a nun, that was the more beautiful one. To become a concert pianist, that was the other.

[*She pauses, regarding her hands fixedly. Cathleen blinks her eyes to fight off drowsiness and a tipsy feeling.*]

I haven't touched a piano in so many years. I couldn't play with such crippled fingers, even if I wanted to. For a time after my marriage I tried to keep up my music. But it was hopeless. One-night stands, cheap hotels, dirty trains, leaving children, never having a home— [*She stares at her hands with fascinated disgust.*] See, Cathleen, how ugly they are! So maimed and crippled! You would think they'd been through some horrible accident! [*She gives a strange little laugh.*] So they have, come to think of it. [*She suddenly thrusts her hands behind her back.*] I won't look at them. They're worse than the foghorn for reminding me— [*Then with defiant self-assurance*] But even they can't touch me now. [*She brings her hands from behind her back and deliberately stares at them—calmly.*] They're far away. I see them, but the pain has gone.

CATHLEEN [*stupidly puzzled*] You've taken some of the medicine? It made you act funny, Ma'am. If I didn't know better, I'd think you'd a drop taken.

MARY [*dreamily*] It kills the pain. You go back until at last you are beyond its reach. Only the past when you were happy is real.

[*She pauses—then as if her words had been an evocation which called back happiness she changes in her whole manner and facial expression. She looks younger. There is a quality of an innocent convent girl about her, and she smiles shyly.*]

If you think Mr. Tyrone is handsome now, Cathleen, you should have seen him when I first met him. He had the reputation of being one of the best-looking men in the country. The girls in the Convent who had seen him act, or seen his photographs, used to rave about him. He was a great matinee idol then, you know. Women used to wait at the stage door just to see him come out. You can imagine how excited I was when my father wrote me he and James Tyrone had become friends, and that I was to meet him when I came home for Easter vacation. I showed the letter to all the girls, and how envious they were! My father took me to see him act first. It was a play about the French Revolution and the leading part was a nobleman.[3] I couldn't take my eyes off him. I wept when he was thrown in prison—and then was so mad at myself because I was afraid my eyes and nose would be red. My father had said we'd go backstage to his dressing room right after the play, and so we did. [*She gives a little excited, shy laugh.*] I was so bashful all I could do was stammer and blush like a little fool. But he didn't seem to think I was a fool. I know he liked me the first moment we were introduced. [*Coquettishly*] I guess my eyes and nose couldn't have been red, after all. I was really very pretty then, Cathleen. And he was handsomer than my wildest dream, in his makeup and his nobleman's costume that was so becoming to him. He was different from all ordinary men, like

3. O'Neill's Irish-born father, James O'Neill, spent years touring the United States playing the lead in *The Count of Monte Cristo* (1846), a melodrama adapted from Alexandre Dumas' novel (1844–45).

someone from another world. At the same time he was simple, and kind, and unassuming, not a bit stuck-up or vain. I fell in love right then. So did he, he told me afterwards. I forgot all about becoming a nun or a concert pianist. All I wanted was to be his wife. [*She pauses, staring before her with unnaturally bright, dreamy eyes, and a rapt, tender, girlish smile.*] Thirty-six years ago, but I can see it as clearly as if it were tonight! We've loved each other ever since. And in all those thirty-six years, there has never been a breath of scandal about him. I mean, with any other woman. Never since he met me. That has made me very happy, Cathleen. It has made me forgive so many other things.

CATHLEEN [*fighting tipsy drowsiness—sentimentally*] He's a fine gentleman and you're a lucky woman. [*Then, fidgeting*] Can I take the drink to Bridget, Ma'am? It must be near dinnertime and I ought to be in the kitchen helping her. If she don't get something to quiet her temper, she'll be after me with the cleaver.

MARY [*with a vague exasperation at being brought back from her dream*] Yes, yes, go. I don't need you now.

CATHLEEN [*with relief*] Thank you, Ma'am.

[*She pours out a big drink and starts for the back parlor with it.*]

You won't be alone long. The Master and the boys—

MARY [*impatiently*] No, no, they won't come. Tell Bridget I won't wait. You can serve dinner promptly at half past six. I'm not hungry but I'll sit at the table and we'll get it over with.

CATHLEEN You ought to eat something, Ma'am. It's a queer medicine if it takes away your appetite.

MARY [*has begun to drift into dreams again—reacts mechanically*] What medicine? I don't know what you mean. [*In dismissal*] You better take the drink to Bridget.

CATHLEEN Yes, Ma'am.

[*She disappears through the back parlor.* MARY *waits until she hears the pantry door close behind her. Then she settles back in relaxed dreaminess, staring fixedly at nothing. Her arms rest limply along the arms of the chair, her hands with long, warped, swollen-knuckled, sensitive fingers drooping in complete calm. It is growing dark in the room. There is a pause of dead quiet. Then from the world outside comes the melancholy moan of the foghorn, followed by a chorus of bells, muffled by the fog, from the anchored craft in the harbor.* MARY'S *face gives no sign she has heard, but her hands jerk and the fingers automatically play for a moment on the air. She frowns and shakes her head mechanically as if a fly had walked across her mind. She suddenly loses all the girlish quality and is an aging, cynically sad, embittered woman.*]

MARY [*bitterly*] You're a sentimental fool. What is so wonderful about that first meeting between a silly romantic schoolgirl and a matinee idol? You were much happier before you knew he existed, in the Convent when you used to pray to the Blessed Virgin. [*Longingly*] If I could only find the faith I lost, so I could pray again! [*She pauses—then begins to recite the Hail Mary in a flat, empty tone.*] "Hail, Mary, full of grace! The Lord is with Thee; blessed art Thou among women." [*Sneeringly*] You expect the Blessed Virgin to be fooled by a lying dope fiend reciting words! You can't hide from her!

[*She springs to her feet. Her hands fly up to pat her hair distractedly.*]

I must go upstairs. I haven't taken enough. When you start again you never know exactly how much you need.

[*She goes toward the front parlor—then stops in the doorway as she hears the sound of voices from the front path. She starts guiltily.*]

That must be them—

[*She hurries back to sit down. Her face sets in stubborn defensiveness—resentfully.*]

Why are they coming back? They don't want to. And I'd much rather be alone.

[*Suddenly her whole manner changes. She becomes pathetically relieved and eager.*]

Oh, I'm so glad they've come! I've been so horribly lonely!

[*The front door is heard closing and Tyrone calls uneasily from the hall.*]

TYRONE Are you there, Mary?

[*The light in the hall is turned on and shines through the front parlor to fall on* MARY.]

MARY [*rises from her chair, her face lighting up lovingly—with excited eagerness*] I'm here, dear. In the living room. I've been waiting for you.

[TYRONE *comes in through the front parlor.* EDMUND *is behind him.* TYRONE *has had a lot to drink but beyond a slightly glazed look in his eyes and a trace of blur in his speech, he does not show it.* EDMUND *has also had more than a few drinks without much apparent effect, except that his sunken cheeks are flushed and his eyes look bright and feverish. They stop in the doorway to stare appraisingly at her. What they see fulfills their worst expectations. But for the moment* MARY *is unconscious of their condemning eyes. She kisses her husband and then* EDMUND. *Her manner is unnaturally effusive. They submit shrinkingly. She talks excitedly.*]

I'm so happy you've come. I had given up hope. I was afraid you wouldn't come home. It's such a dismal, foggy evening. It must be much more cheerful in the barrooms uptown, where there are people you can talk and joke with. No, don't deny it. I know how you feel. I don't blame you a bit. I'm all the more grateful to you for coming home. I was sitting here so lonely and blue. Come and sit down.

[*She sits at left rear of table,* EDMUND *at left of table, and* TYRONE *in the rocker at right of it.*]

Dinner won't be ready for a minute. You're actually a little early. Will wonders never cease. Here's the whiskey, dear. Shall I pour a drink for you? [*Without waiting for a reply she does so.*] And you, Edmund? I don't want to encourage you, but one before dinner, as an appetizer, can't do any harm.

[*She pours a drink for him. They make no move to take the drinks. She talks on as if unaware of their silence.*]

Where's Jamie? But, of course, he'll never come home so long as he has the price of a drink left. [*She reaches out and clasps her husband's hand—sadly.*] I'm afraid Jamie has been lost to us for a long time, dear. [*Her face hardens.*] But we mustn't allow him to drag Edmund down with him, as he'd like to do. He's jealous because Edmund has always been the baby—just as he used to be of Eugene. He'll never be content until he makes Edmund as hopeless a failure as he is.

EDMUND [*miserably*] Stop talking, Mama.

TYRONE [*dully*] Yes, Mary, the less you say now— [*Then to Edmund, a bit tipsily*] All the same there's truth in your mother's warning. Beware of that brother of yours, or he'll poison life for you with his damned sneering serpent's tongue!

EDMUND [*as before*] Oh, cut it out, Papa.

MARY [*goes on as if nothing had been said*] It's hard to believe, seeing Jamie as he is now, that he was ever my baby. Do you remember what a healthy, happy baby he was, James? The one-night stands and filthy trains and cheap hotels and bad food never made him cross or sick. He was always smiling or laughing. He hardly ever cried. Eugene was the same, too, happy and healthy, during the two years he lived before I let him die through my neglect.

TYRONE Oh, for the love of God! I'm a fool for coming home!

EDMUND Papa! Shut up!

MARY [*smiles with detached tenderness at* EDMUND] It was Edmund who was the crosspatch when he was little, always getting upset and frightened about nothing at all. [*She pats his hand—teasingly.*] Everyone used to say, dear, you'd cry at the drop of a hat.

EDMUND [*cannot control his bitterness*] Maybe I guessed there was a good reason not to laugh.

TYRONE [*reproving and pitying*] Now, now, lad. You know better than to pay attention—

MARY [*as if she hadn't heard—sadly again*] Who would have thought Jamie would grow up to disgrace us. You remember, James, for years after he went to boarding school, we received such glowing reports. Everyone liked him. All his teachers told us what a fine brain he had, and how easily he learned his lessons. Even after he began to drink and they had to expel him, they wrote us how sorry they were, because he was so likable and such a brilliant student. They predicted a wonderful future for him if he would only learn to take life seriously. [*She pauses—then adds with a strange, sad detachment.*] It's such a pity. Poor Jamie! It's hard to understand—

[*Abruptly a change comes over her. Her face hardens and she stares at her husband with accusing hostility.*]

No, it isn't at all. You brought him up to be a boozer. Since he first opened his eyes, he's seen you drinking. Always a bottle on the bureau in the cheap hotel rooms! And if he had a nightmare when he was little, or a stomachache, your remedy was to give him a teaspoonful of whiskey to quiet him.

TYRONE [*stung*] So I'm to blame because that lazy hulk has made a drunken loafer of himself? Is that what I came home to listen to? I might have known! When you have the poison in you, you want to blame everyone but yourself!

EDMUND Papa! You told me not to pay attention. [*Then, resentfully*] Anyway it's true. You did the same thing with me. I can remember that teaspoonful of booze every time I woke up with a nightmare.

MARY [*in a detached reminiscent tone*] Yes, you were continually having nightmares as a child. You were born afraid. Because I was so afraid to bring you into the world. [*She pauses—then goes on with the same detachment.*] Please don't think I blame your father, Edmund. He didn't know any better. He never went to school after he was ten. His people were the most ignorant kind of poverty-stricken Irish. I'm sure they honestly believed whiskey is the healthiest medicine for a child who is sick or frightened.

[TYRONE *is about to burst out in angry defense of his family but* EDMUND *intervenes.*]

EDMUND [*sharply*] Papa! [*Changing the subject*] Are we going to have this drink, or aren't we?

TYRONE [*controlling himself—dully*] You're right. I'm a fool to take notice. [*He picks up his glass listlessly.*] Drink hearty, lad.

[EDMUND *drinks but* TYRONE *remains staring at the glass in his hand.* EDMUND *at once realizes how much the whiskey has been watered. He frowns, glancing from the bottle to his mother—starts to say something but stops.*]

MARY [*in a changed tone—repentently*] I'm sorry if I sounded bitter, James. I'm not. It's all so far away. But I did feel a little hurt when you wished you hadn't come home. I was so relieved and happy when you came, and grateful to you. It's very dreary and sad to be here alone in the fog with night falling.

TYRONE [*moved*] I'm glad I came, Mary, when you act like your real self.

MARY I was so lonesome I kept Cathleen with me just to have someone to talk to. [*Her manner and quality drift back to the shy convent girl again.*] Do you know what I was telling her, dear? About the night my father took me to your dressing room and I first fell in love with you. Do you remember?

TYRONE [*deeply moved—his voice husky*] Can you think I'd ever forget, Mary?

[EDMUND *looks away from them, sad and embarrassed.*]

MARY [*tenderly*] No. I know you still love me, James, in spite of everything.

TYRONE [*his face works and he blinks back tears—with quiet intensity*] Yes! As God is my judge! Always and forever, Mary!

MARY And I love you, dear, in spite of everything.

[*There is a pause in which* EDMUND *moves embarrassedly. The strange detachment comes over her manner again as if she were speaking impersonally of people seen from a distance.*]

But I must confess, James, although I couldn't help loving you, I would never have married you if I'd known you drank so much. I remember the first night your barroom friends had to help you up to the door of our hotel room, and knocked and then ran away before I came to the door. We were still on our honeymoon, do you remember?

TYRONE [*with guilty vehemence*] I don't remember! It wasn't on our honeymoon! And I never in my life had to be helped to bed, or missed a performance!

MARY [*as though he hadn't spoken*] I had waited in that ugly hotel room hour after hour. I kept making excuses for you. I told myself it must be some business connected with the theater. I knew so little about the theater. Then I became terrified. I imagined all sorts of horrible accidents. I got on my knees and prayed that nothing had happened to you—and then they brought you up and left you outside the door. [*She gives a little, sad sigh.*] I didn't know how often that was to happen in the years to come, how many times I was to wait in ugly hotel rooms. I became quite used to it.

EDMUND [*bursts out with a look of accusing hate at his father*] Christ! No wonder—! [*He controls himself—gruffly.*] When is dinner, Mama? It must be time.

TYRONE [*overwhelmed by shame which he tries to hide, fumbles with his watch*] Yes. It must be. Let's see.

[*He stares at his watch without seeing it. Pleadingly.*]

Mary! Can't you forget—?

MARY [*with detached pity*] No, dear. But I forgive. I always forgive you. So don't look so guilty. I'm sorry I remembered out loud. I don't want to be sad, or to make you sad. I want to remember only the happy part of the past. [*Her manner drifts back to the shy, gay convent girl.*] Do you remember our wedding, dear? I'm sure you've completely forgotten what my wedding gown looked like. Men don't notice such things. They don't think they're important. But it was important to me, I can tell you! How I fussed and worried! I was so excited and happy! My father told me to buy anything I wanted and never mind what it cost. The best is none too good, he said. I'm afraid he spoiled me dreadfully. My mother didn't. She was very pious and strict. I think she was a little jealous. She didn't approve of my marrying—especially an actor. I think she hoped I would become a nun. She used to scold my father. She'd grumble, "You never tell me, never mind what it costs, when I buy anything! You've spoiled that girl so, I pity her husband if she ever marries. She'll expect him to give her the moon. She'll never make a good wife." [*She laughs affectionately.*] Poor mother! [*She smiles at* TYRONE *with a strange, incongruous coquetry.*] But she was mistaken, wasn't she, James? I haven't been such a bad wife, have I?

TYRONE [*huskily, trying to force a smile*] I'm not complaining, Mary.

MARY [*a shadow of vague guilt crosses her face*] At least, I've loved you dearly, and done the best I could—under the circumstances. [*The shadow vanishes and her shy, girlish expression returns.*] That wedding gown was nearly the death of me and the dressmaker, too! [*She laughs.*] I was so particular. It was never quite good enough. At last she said she refused to touch it anymore or she might spoil it, and I made her leave so I could be alone to examine myself in the mirror. I was so pleased and vain. I thought to myself, "Even if your nose and mouth and ears are a trifle too large, your eyes and hair and figure, and your hands, make up for it. You're just as pretty as any actress he's ever met, and you don't have to use paint." [*She pauses, wrinkling her brow in an effort of memory.*] Where is my wedding gown now, I wonder? I kept it wrapped up in tissue paper in my trunk. I used to hope I would have a daughter and when it came time for her to marry— She couldn't have bought a lovelier gown, and I knew, James, you'd never tell her, never mind the cost. You'd want her to pick up something at a bargain. It was made of soft, shimmering satin, trimmed with wonderful old duchesse lace, in tiny ruffles around the neck and sleeves, and worked in with the folds that were draped round in a bustle effect at the back. The basque was boned[4] and very tight. I remember I held my breath when it was fitted, so my waist would be as small as

4. That is, the bodice was stiffened with whalebone.

possible. My father even let me have duchesse lace on my white satin slippers, and lace with the orange blossoms in my veil. Oh, how I loved that gown! It was so beautiful! Where is it now, I wonder? I used to take it out from time to time when I was lonely, but it always made me cry, so finally a long while ago— [*She wrinkles her forehead again.*] I wonder where I hid it? Probably in one of the old trunks in the attic. Someday I'll have to look.

[*She stops, staring before her.* TYRONE *sighs, shaking his head hopelessly, and attempts to catch his son's eye, looking for sympathy, but* EDMUND *is staring at the floor.*]

TYRONE [*forces a casual tone*] Isn't it dinner time, dear? [*With a feeble attempt at teasing*] You're forever scolding me for being late, but now I'm on time for once, it's dinner that's late.

[*She doesn't appear to hear him. He adds, still pleasantly.*]

Well, if I can't eat yet, I can drink. I'd forgotten I had this.

[*He drinks his drink.* EDMUND *watches him.* TYRONE *scowls and looks at his wife with sharp suspicion—roughly.*]

Who's been tampering with my whiskey? The damned stuff is half water! Jamie's been away and he wouldn't overdo his trick like this, anyway. Any fool could tell—Mary, answer me! [*With angry disgust*] I hope to God you haven't taken to drink on top of—

EDMUND Shut up, Papa! [*To his mother, without looking at her*] You treated Cathleen and Bridget, isn't that it, Mama?

MARY [*with indifferent casualness*] Yes, of course. They work hard for poor wages. And I'm the housekeeper, I have to keep them from leaving. Besides, I wanted to treat Cathleen because I had her drive uptown with me, and sent her to get my prescription filled.

EDMUND For God's sake, Mama! You can't trust her! Do you want everyone on earth to know?

MARY [*her face hardening stubbornly*] Know what? That I suffer from rheumatism in my hands and have to take medicine to kill the pain? Why should I be ashamed of that? [*Turns on* EDMUND *with a hard, accusing antagonism—almost a revengeful enmity.*] I never knew what rheumatism was before you were born! Ask your father!

[EDMUND *looks away, shrinking into himself.*]

TYRONE Don't mind her, lad. It doesn't mean anything. When she gets to the stage where she gives the old crazy excuse about her hands she's gone far away from us.

MARY [*turns on him—with a strangely triumphant, taunting smile*] I'm glad you realize that, James! Now perhaps you'll give up trying to remind me, you and Edmund! [*Abruptly, in a detached, matter-of-fact tone*] Why don't you light the light, James? It's getting dark. I know you hate to, but Edmund has proved to you that one bulb burning doesn't cost much. There's no sense letting your fear of the poorhouse make you too stingy.

TYRONE [*reacts mechanically*] I never claimed one bulb cost much! It's having them on, one here and one there, that makes the Electric Light Company rich.

[*He gets up and turns on the reading lamp—roughtly.*]

But I'm a fool to talk reason to you. [*To* EDMUND] I'll get a fresh bottle of whiskey, lad, and we'll have a real drink.

[*He goes through the back parlor.*]

MARY [*with detached amusement*] He'll sneak around to the outside cellar door so the servants won't see him. He's really ashamed of keeping his whiskey padlocked in the cellar. Your father is a strange man, Edmund. It took many years before I understood him. You must try to understand and forgive him, too, and not feel contempt because he's close-fisted. His father deserted his mother and their six children a year or so after they came to America. He told them he had a premonition he would die soon, and he was homesick for Ireland, and wanted to go back there to die. So he went and he did die. He must have been a peculiar man, too. Your father had to go to work in a machine shop when he was only ten years old.

EDMUND [*protests dully*] Oh, for Pete's sake, Mama. I've heard Papa tell that machine shop story ten thousand times.

MARY Yes, dear, you've had to listen, but I don't think you've ever tried to understand.

EDMUND [*ignoring this—miserably*] Listen, Mama! You're not so far gone yet you've forgotten everything. You haven't asked me what I found out this afternoon. Don't you care a damn?

MARY [*shakenly*] Don't say that! You hurt me, dear!

EDMUND What I've got is serious, Mama. Doc Hardy knows for sure now.

MARY [*stiffens into scornful, defensive stubbornness*] That lying old quack! I warned you he'd invent—!

EDMUND [*miserably dogged*] He called in a specialist to examine me, so he'd be absolutely sure.

MARY [*ignoring this*] Don't tell me about Hardy! If you heard what the doctor at the sanatorium, who really knows something, said about how he'd treated me! He said he ought to be locked up! He said it was a wonder I hadn't gone mad! I told him I had once, that time I ran down in my nightdress to throw myself off the dock. You remember that, don't you? And yet you want me to pay attention to what Doctor Hardy says. Oh, no!

EDMUND [*bitterly*] I remember, all right. It was right after that Papa and Jamie decided they couldn't hide it from me anymore. Jamie told me. I called him a liar! I tried to punch him in the nose. But I knew he wasn't lying. [*His voice trembles, his eyes begin to fill with tears.*] God, it made everything in life seem rotten!

MARY [*pitiably*] Oh, don't. My baby! You hurt me so dreadfully!

EDMUND [*dully*] I'm sorry, Mama. It was you who brought it up. [*Then with a bitter, stubborn persistence*] Listen, Mama. I'm going to tell you whether you want to hear or not. I've got to go to a sanatorium.

MARY [*dazedly, as if this was something that had never occurred to her*] Go away? [*Violently*] No! I won't have it! How dare Doctor Hardy advise such a thing without consulting me! How dare your father allow him! What right has he? You are my baby! Let him attend to Jamie! [*More and more excited and bitter*] I know why he wants you sent to a sanatorium. To take you from me! He's always tried to do that. He's been jealous of every one of my babies! He kept finding ways to make me leave them. That's what caused Eugene's death. He's been jealous of you most of all. He knew I loved you most because—

EDMUND [*miserably*] Oh, stop talking crazy, can't you, Mama! Stop trying to blame him. And why are you so against my going away now? I've been away a lot, and I've never noticed it broke your heart!

MARY [*bitterly*] I'm afraid you're not very sensitive, after all. [*Sadly*] You might have guessed, dear, that after I knew you knew—about me—I had to be glad whenever you were where you couldn't see me.

EDMUND [*brokenly*] Mama! Don't!

[*He reaches out blindly and takes her hand—but he drops it immediately, overcome by bitterness again.*]

All this talk about loving me—and you won't even listen when I try to tell you how sick—

MARY [*with an abrupt transformation into a detached bullying motherliness*] Now, now. That's enough! I don't care to hear because I know it's nothing but Hardy's ignorant lies.

[*He shrinks back into himself. She keeps on in a forced, teasing tone but with an increasing undercurrent of resentment.*]

You're so like your father, dear. You love to make a scene out of nothing so you can be dramatic and tragic. [*With a belittling laugh*] If I gave you the slightest encouragement, you'd tell me next you were going to die—

EDMUND People do die of it. Your own father—

MARY [*sharply*] Why do you mention him? There's no comparison at all with you. He had consumption. [*Angrily*] I hate you when you become gloomy and morbid! I forbid you to remind me of my father's death, do you hear me?

EDMUND [*his face hard—grimly*] Yes, I hear you, Mama. I wish to God I didn't!

[*He gets up from his chair and stands staring condemningly at her—bitterly.*]

It's pretty hard to take at times, having a dope fiend for a mother!

[*She winces—all life seeming to drain from her face, leaving it with the appearance of a plaster cast. Instantly* EDMUND *wishes he could take back what he has said. He stammers miserably.*]

Forgive me, Mama. I was angry. You hurt me.

[*There is a pause in which the foghorn and the ships' bells are heard.*]

MARY [*goes slowly to the windows at right like an automaton—looking out, a blank, far-off quality in her voice*] Just listen to that awful foghorn. And the bells. Why is it fog makes everything sound so sad and lost, I wonder?

EDMUND [*brokenly*] I—I can't stay here. I don't want any dinner.

[*He hurries away through the front parlor. She keeps staring out the window until she hears the front door close behind him. Then she comes back and sits in her chair, the same blank look on her face.*]

MARY [*vaguely*] I must go upstairs. I haven't taken enough. [*She pauses—then longingly*] I hope, sometime, without meaning it, I will take an overdose. I never could do it deliberately. The Blessed Virgin would never forgive me, then.

[*She hears* TYRONE *returning and turns as he comes in, through the back parlor, with a bottle of whiskey he has just uncorked. He is fuming.*]

TYRONE [*wrathfully*] The padlock is all scratched. That drunken loafer has tried to pick the lock with a piece of wire, the way he's done before. [*With satisfaction, as if this was a perpetual battle of wits with his elder son*] But

I've fooled him this time. It's a special padlock a professional burglar couldn't pick. [*He puts the bottle on the tray and suddenly is aware of* EDMUND's *absence.*] Where's Edmund?

MARY [*with a vague far-away air*] He went out. Perhaps he's going uptown again to find Jamie. He still has some money left, I suppose, and it's burning a hole in his pocket. He said he didn't want any dinner. He doesn't seem to have any appetite these days. [*Then stubbornly*] But it's just a summer cold.

[TYRONE *stares at her and shakes his head helplessly and pours himself a big drink and drinks it. Suddenly it is too much for her and she breaks out and sobs.*]

Oh, James, I'm so frightened!

[*She gets up and throws her arms around him and hides her face on his shoulder—sobbingly.*]

I know he's going to die!

TYRONE Don't say that! It's not true! They promised me in six months he'd be cured.

MARY You don't believe that! I can tell when you're acting! And it will be my fault. I should never have borne him. It would have been better for his sake. I could never hurt him then. He wouldn't have had to know his mother was a dope fiend—and hate her!

TYRONE [*his voice quivering*] Hush, Mary, for the love of God! He loves you. He knows it was a curse put on you without your knowing or willing it. He's proud you're his mother! [*Abruptly as he hears the pantry door opening*] Hush, now! Here comes Cathleen. You don't want her to see you crying.

[*She turns quickly away from him to the windows at right, hastily wiping her eyes. A moment later* CATHLEEN *appears in the back-parlor doorway. She is uncertain in her walk and grinning woozily.*]

CATHLEEN [*starts guiltily when she sees Tyrone—with dignity*] Dinner is served, Sir. [*Raising her voice unnecessarily*] Dinner is served, Ma'am. [*She forgets her dignity and addresses* TYRONE *with good-natured familiarity.*] So you're here, are you? Well, well. Won't Bridget be in a rage! I told her the Madame said you wouldn't be home. [*Then reading accusation in his eye*] Don't be looking at me that way. If I've a drop taken, I didn't steal it. I was invited.

[*She turns with huffy dignity and disappears through the back parlor.*]

TYRONE [*sighs—then summoning his actor's heartiness*] Come along, dear. Let's have our dinner. I'm hungry as a hunter.

MARY [*comes to him—her face is composed in plaster again and her tone is remote*] I'm afraid you'll have to excuse me, James. I couldn't possibly eat anything. My hands pain me dreadfully. I think the best thing for me is to go to bed and rest. Good night, dear.

[*She kisses him mechanically and turns toward the front parlor.*]

TYRONE [*harshly*] Up to take more of that God-damned poison, is that it? You'll be like a mad ghost before the night's over!

MARY [*starts to walk away—blankly*] I don't know what you're talking about, James. You say such mean, bitter things when you've drunk too much. You're as bad as Jamie or Edmund.

[*She moves off through the front parlor. He stands a second as if not knowing what to do. He is a sad, bewildered, broken old man. He walks wearily off through the back parlor toward the dining room.*]

Curtain.

Act 4

SCENE: *The same. It is around midnight. The lamp in the front hall has been turned out, so that now no light shines through the front parlor. In the living room only the reading lamp on the table is lighted. Outside the windows the wall of fog appears denser than ever. As the curtain rises, the foghorn is heard, followed by the ships' bells from the harbor.*

TYRONE *is seated at the table. He wears his pince-nez, and is playing solitaire. He has taken off his coat and has on an old brown dressing gown. The whiskey bottle on the tray is three-quarters empty. There is a fresh full bottle on the table, which he has brought from the cellar so there will be an ample reserve at hand. He is drunk and shows it by the owlish, deliberate manner in which he peers at each card to make certain of its identity, and then plays it as if he wasn't certain of his aim. His eyes have a misted, oily look and his mouth is slack. But despite all the whiskey in him, he has not escaped, and he looks as he appeared at the close of the preceding act, a sad, defeated old man, possessed by hopeless resignation.*

As the curtain rises, he finishes a game and sweeps the cards together. He shuffles them clumsily, dropping a couple on the floor. He retrieves them with difficulty, and starts to shuffle again, when he hears someone entering the front door. He peers over his pince-nez through the front parlor.

TYRONE [*his voice thick*] Who's that? Is it you, Edmund?

[EDMUND'*s voice answers curtly,* "Yes." *Then he evidently collides with something in the dark hall and can be heard cursing. A moment later the hall lamp is turned on.* TYRONE *frowns and calls.*]

Turn that light out before you come in.

[*But* EDMUND *doesn't. He comes in through the front parlor. He is drunk now, too, but like his father he carries it well, and gives little physical sign of it except in his eyes and a chip-on-the-shoulder aggressiveness in his manner.* TYRONE *speaks, at first with a warm, relieved welcome.*]

I'm glad you've come, lad. I've been damned lonely. [*Then resentfully*] You're a fine one to run away and leave me to sit alone here all night when you know— [*with sharp irritation*] I told you to turn out that light! We're not giving a ball. There's no reason to have the house ablaze with electricity at this time of night, burning up money!

EDMUND [*angrily*] Ablaze with electricity! One bulb! Hell, everyone keeps a light on in the front hall until they go to bed. [*He rubs his knee.*] I damned near busted my knee on the hat stand.

TYRONE The light from here shows in the hall. You could see your way well enough if you were sober.

EDMUND If *I* was sober? I like that!

TYRONE I don't give a damn what other people do. If they want to be wasteful fools, for the sake of show, let them be!

EDMUND One bulb! Christ, don't be such a cheapskate! I've proved by figures if you left the lightbulb on all night it wouldn't be as much as one drink!

TYRONE To hell with your figures! The proof is in the bills I have to pay!

EDMUND [*sits down opposite his father—contemptuously*] Yes, facts don't mean a thing, do they? What you want to believe, that's the only truth! [*Derisively*] Shakespeare was an Irish Catholic,[5] for example.

TYRONE [*stubbornly*] So he was. The proof is in his plays.

EDMUND Well he wasn't, and there's no proof of it in his plays, except to you! [*Jeeringly*] The Duke of Wellington,[6] there was another good Irish Catholic!

TYRONE I never said he was a good one. He was a renegade but a Catholic just the same.

EDMUND Well, he wasn't. You just want to believe no one but an Irish Catholic general could beat Napoleon.[7]

TYRONE I'm not going to argue with you. I asked you to turn out that light in the hall.

EDMUND I heard you, and as far as I'm concerned it stays on.

TYRONE None of your damned insolence! Are you going to obey me or not?

EDMUND Not! If you want to be a crazy miser put it out yourself!

TYRONE [*with threatening anger*] Listen to me! I've put up with a lot from you because from the mad things you've done at times I've thought you weren't quite right in your head. I've excused you and never lifted my hand to you. But there's a straw that breaks the camel's back. You'll obey me and put out that light or, big as you are, I'll give you a thrashing that'll teach you—! [*Suddenly he remembers* EDMUND*'s illness and instantly becomes guilty and shamefaced.*] Forgive me, lad. I forgot— You shouldn't goad me into losing my temper.

EDMUND [*ashamed himself now*] Forget it, Papa. I apologize, too. I had no right being nasty about nothing. I am a bit soused, I guess. I'll put out the damned light.

[*He starts to get up.*]

TYRONE No, stay where you are. Let it burn.

[*He stands up abruptly—and a bit drunkenly—and begins turning on the three bulbs in the chandelier, with a childish, bitterly dramatic self-pity.*]

We'll have them all on! Let them burn! To hell with them! The poorhouse is the end of the road, and it might as well be sooner as later! [*He finishes turning on the lights.*]

EDMUND [*has watched this proceeding with an awakened sense of humor—now he grins, teasing affectionately*] That's a grand curtain. [*He laughs.*] You're a wonder, Papa.

TYRONE [*sits down sheepishly—grumbles pathetically*] That's right, laugh at the old fool! The poor old ham! But the final curtain will be in the poor-

5. Few biographical facts are known about Shakespeare; according to one theory, which scholars have generally dismissed, he was secretly a practicing Catholic (secrecy would have been necessary, because Roman Catholics were persecuted during the reign of Elizabeth I). Tyrone may be alone in believing the playwright to have been Irish.

6. Arthur Wellesley, first duke of Wellington (1769–1852), a statesman and military hero. Although born in Ireland, he was a member of the Anglo-Irish aristocracy and thus Protestant, not Roman Catholic.

7. Napoléon Bonaparte (1769–1821), the French military leader who became emperor of France; one of the greatest military strategists of history, he was overcome by the European countries allied against him and suffered his final defeat at the hands of British forces under Wellington's command at Waterloo (in Belgium) in 1815.

house just the same, and that's not comedy! [*Then as Edmund is still grinning, he changes the subject.*] Well, well, let's not argue. You've got brains in that head of yours, though you do your best to deny them. You'll live to learn the value of a dollar. You're not like your damned tramp of a brother. I've given up hope he'll ever get sense. Where is he, by the way?

EDMUND How would I know?

TYRONE I thought you'd gone back uptown to meet him.

EDMUND No. I walked out to the beach. I haven't seen him since this afternoon.

TYRONE Well, if you split the money I gave you with him, like a fool—

EDMUND Sure I did. He's always staked me when he had anything.

TYRONE Then it doesn't take a soothsayer to tell he's probably in the whorehouse.

EDMUND What of it if he is? Why not?

TYRONE [*contemptuously*] Why not, indeed. It's the fit place for him. If he's ever had a loftier dream than whores and whiskey, he's never shown it.

EDMUND Oh, for Pete's sake, Papa! If you're going to start that stuff, I'll beat it.

[*He starts to get up.*]

TYRONE [*placatingly*] All right, all right, I'll stop. God knows, I don't like the subject either. Will you join me in a drink?

EDMUND Ah! Now you're talking!

TYRONE [*passes the bottle to him—mechanically*] I'm wrong to treat you. You've had enough already.

EDMUND [*pouring a big drink—a bit drunkenly*] Enough is *not* as good as a feast.

[*He hands back the bottle.*]

TYRONE It's too much in your condition.

EDMUND Forget my condition! [*He raises his glass.*] Here's how.

TYRONE Drink hearty. [*They drink.*] If you walked all the way to the beach you must be damp and chilled.

EDMUND Oh, I dropped in at the Inn on the way out and back.

TYRONE It's not a night I'd pick for a long walk.

EDMUND I loved the fog. It was what I needed. [*He sounds more tipsy and looks it.*]

TYRONE You should have more sense than to risk—

EDMUND To hell with sense! We're all crazy. What do we want with sense? [*He quotes from Dowson sardonically.*]

"They are not long, the weeping and the laughter,
Love and desire and hate:
I think they have no portion in us after
We pass the gate.

They are not long, the days of wine and roses:
Out of a misty dream
Our path emerges for a while, then closes
Within a dream."[8]

8. "They Are Not Long" (1896), by the English poet Ernest Dowson (1867–1900).

[*Staring before him*] The fog was where I wanted to be. Halfway down the path you can't see this house. You'd never know it was here. Or any of the other places down the avenue. I couldn't see but a few feet ahead. I didn't meet a soul. Everything looked and sounded unreal. Nothing was what it is. That's what I wanted—to be alone with myself in another world where truth is untrue and life can hide from itself. Out beyond the harbor, where the road runs along the beach, I even lost the feeling of being on land. The fog and the sea seemed part of each other. It was like walking on the bottom of the sea. As if I had drowned long ago. As if I was a ghost belonging to the fog, and the fog was the ghost of the sea. It felt damned peaceful to be nothing more than a ghost within a ghost.

[*He sees his father staring at him with mingled worry and irritated disapproval. He grins mockingly.*]

Don't look at me as if I'd gone nutty. I'm talking sense. Who wants to see life as it is, if they can help it? It's the three Gorgons[9] in one. You look in their faces and turn to stone. Or it's Pan.[1] You see him and you die—that is, inside you—and have to go on living as a ghost.

TYRONE [*impressed and at the same time revolted*] You have a poet in you but it's a damned morbid one! [*Forcing a smile*] Devil take your pessimism. I feel low-spirited enough. [*He sighs.*] Why can't you remember your Shakespeare and forget the third-raters. You'll find what you're trying to say in him—as you'll find everything else worth saying. [*He quotes, using his fine voice.*] "We are such stuff as dreams are made on, and our little life is rounded with a sleep."[2]

EDMUND [*ironically*] Fine! That's beautiful. But I wasn't trying to say that. We are such stuff as manure is made on, so let's drink up and forget it. That's more my idea.

TYRONE [*disgustedly*] Ach! Keep such sentiments to yourself. I shouldn't have given you that drink.

EDMUND It did pack a wallop, all right. On you, too. [*He grins with affectionate teasing.*] Even if you've never missed a performance! [*Aggressively*] Well, what's wrong with being drunk? It's what we're after, isn't it? Let's not kid each other, Papa. Not tonight. We know what we're trying to forget. [*Hurriedly*] But let's not talk about it. It's no use now.

TYRONE [*dully*] No. All we can do is try to be resigned—again.

EDMUND Or be so drunk you can forget.

[*He recites, and recites well, with bitter, ironical passion, the Symons' translation of Baudelaire's prose poem.*]

"Be always drunken. Nothing else matters: that is the only question. If you would not feel the horrible burden of Time weighing on your shoulders and crushing you to the earth, be drunken continually.

"Drunken with what? With wine, with poetry, or with virtue, as you will. But be drunken.

"And if sometimes, on the stairs of a palace, or on the green side of a ditch, or in the dreary solitude of your own room, you should awaken and the

9. In Greek mythology, three snake-haired sisters, the sight of whom turned all who looked at them to stone.

1. The Greek god of pastures, flocks, and wild places, who had horns and goat's feet; he was also believed responsible for irrational terrors that seize animals and humans (i.e., panic).

2. Quoting Prospero, from Shakespeare's *The Tempest* (1611), 4.1.156–58.

drunkenness be half or wholly slipped away from you, ask of the wind, or of the wave, or of the star, or of the bird, or of the clock, of whatever flies, or sighs, or rocks, or sings, or speaks, ask what hour it is; and the wind, wave, star, bird, clock, will answer you: 'It is the hour to be drunken! Be drunken, if you would not be martyred slaves of Time; be drunken continually! With wine, with poetry, or with virtue, as you will.' "[3]

[*He grins at his father provocatively.*]

TYRONE [*thickly humorous*] I wouldn't worry about the virtue part of it, if I were you. [*Then disgustedly*] Pah! It's morbid nonsense! What little truth is in it you'll find nobly said in Shakespeare. [*Then appreciatively*] But you recited it well, lad. Who wrote it?

EDMUND Baudelaire.

TYRONE Never heard of him.

EDMUND [*grins provocatively*] He also wrote a poem about Jamie and the Great White Way.

TYRONE That loafer! I hope to God he misses the last car and has to stay uptown!

EDMUND [*goes on, ignoring this*] Although he was French and never saw Broadway and died before Jamie was born. He knew him and Little Old New York just the same.

[*He recites the Symons' translation of Baudelaire's "Epilogue."*[4]]

"With heart at rest I climbed the citadel's
Steep height, and saw the city as from a tower,
Hospital, brothel, prison, and such hells,

"Where evil comes up softly like a flower.
Thou knowest, O Satan, patron of my pain,
Not for vain tears I went up at that hour;

"But like an old sad faithful lecher, fain[5]
To drink delight of that enormous trull
Whose hellish beauty makes me young again.

"Whether thou sleep, with heavy vapours full,
Sodden with day, or, new apparelled, stand
In gold-laced veils of evening beautiful,

"I love thee, infamous city! Harlots and
Hunted have pleasures of their own to give,
The vulgar herd can never understand."

TYRONE [*with irritable disgust*] Morbid filth! Where the hell do you get your taste in literature? Filth and despair and pessimism! Another atheist, I suppose. When you deny God, you deny hope. That's the trouble with you. If you'd get down on your knees—

3. Quoted from the prose poem "Get Drunk" (1862), by the French poet Charles Baudelaire (1821–1867). The poet Arthur Symons (1865–1945) translated and introduced to England Baudelaire and many other French poets associated with symbolism and decadence.

4. The final poem in *Petits poèmes en prose* (1862), the volume in which "Get Drunk" appeared.

5. Eager.

EDMUND [*as if he hadn't heard—sardonically*] It's a good likeness of Jamie, don't you think, hunted by himself and whiskey, hiding in a Broadway hotel room with some fat tart—he likes them fat—reciting Dowson's Cynara to her.

[*He recites derisively, but with deep feeling.*]

"All night upon mine heart I felt her warm heart beat,
Night-long within mine arms in love and sleep she lay;
Surely the kisses of her bought red mouth were sweet;
But I was desolate and sick of an old passion,
When I awoke and found the dawn was gray:
I have been faithful to thee, Cynara! in my fashion."[6]

[*Jeeringly*] And the poor fat burlesque queen doesn't get a word of it, but suspects she's being insulted! And Jamie never loved any Cynara, and was never faithful to a woman in his life, even in his fashion! But he lies there, kidding himself he is superior and enjoys pleasures "the vulgar herd can never understand"! [*He laughs.*] It's nuts—completely nuts!

TYRONE [*vaguely—his voice thick*] It's madness, yes. If you'd get on your knees and pray. When you deny God, you deny sanity.

EDMUND [*ignoring this*] But who am I to feel superior? I've done the same damned thing. And it's no more crazy than Dowson himself, inspired by an absinthe[7] hangover, writing it to a dumb barmaid, who thought he was a poor crazy souse, and gave him the gate[8] to marry a waiter! [*He laughs—then soberly, with genuine sympathy.*] Poor Dowson. Booze and consumption got him.

[*He starts and for a second looks miserable and frightened. Then with defensive irony.*]

Perhaps it would be tactful of me to change the subject.

TYRONE [*thickly*] Where you get your taste in authors— That damned library of yours! [*He indicates the small bookcase at rear.*] Voltaire, Rousseau, Schopenhauer, Nietzsche, Ibsen![9] Atheists, fools, and madmen! And your poets! This Dowson, and this Baudelaire, and Swinburne and Oscar Wilde, and Whitman and Poe![1] Whoremongers and degenerates! Pah! When I've three good sets of Shakespeare there [*he nods at the large bookcase*] you could read.

EDMUND [*provocatively*] They say he was a souse, too.

TYRONE They lie! I don't doubt he liked his glass—it's a good man's failing—but he knew how to drink so it didn't poison his brain with morbidness and filth. Don't compare him with the pack you've got in there. [*He indicates the small bookcase again.*] Your dirty Zola! And your Dante Gabriel Rossetti[2] who was a dope fiend! [*He starts and looks guilty.*]

6. The third stanza of "Cynara" (1891).
7. A green liqueur distilled from herbs (including wormwood), highly popular in late 19th-century Paris; it was alleged to be an addictive hallucinogen.
8. That is, rejected or dismissed him.
9. All philosophers, except for the Norwegian dramatist Henrik Ibsen (1828–1906).
1. The writers Algernon Charles Swinburne (1837–1909), Oscar Wilde (1854–1900), Walt Whitman (1819–1892), and Edgar Allan Poe (1809–1849) were all attacked for sexual deviancy, on various grounds.
2. The English poet (1828–1882) became increasingly morbid toward the end of his life, when he was addicted to the sedative chloral. The French novelist Émile Zola (1840–1902) was a leading proponent of naturalism; his scientific observations of working-class French life struck many readers as sordid.

EDMUND [*with defensive dryness*] Perhaps it would be wise to change the subject.

[*A pause.*]

You can't accuse me of not knowing Shakespeare. Didn't I win five dollars from you once when you bet me I couldn't learn a leading part of his in a week, as you used to do in stock in the old days. I learned Macbeth and recited it letter perfect, with you giving me the cues.

TYRONE [*approvingly*] That's true. So you did. [*He smiles teasingly and sighs.*] It was a terrible ordeal, I remember, hearing you murder the lines. I kept wishing I'd paid over the bet without making you prove it.

[*He chuckles and* EDMUND *grins. Then he starts as he hears a sound from upstairs—with dread.*]

Did you hear? She's moving around. I was hoping she'd gone to sleep.

EDMUND Forget it! How about another drink?

[*He reaches out and gets the bottle, pours a drink and hands it back. Then with a strained casualness, as his father pours a drink.*]

When did Mama go to bed?

TYRONE Right after you left. She wouldn't eat any dinner. What made you run away?

EDMUND Nothing. [*Abruptly raising his glass*] Well, here's how.

TYRONE [*mechanically*] Drink hearty, lad.

[*They drink.* TYRONE *again listens to sounds upstairs—with dread.*]

She's moving around a lot. I hope to God she doesn't come down.

EDMUND [*dully*] Yes. She'll be nothing but a ghost haunting the past by this time. [*He pauses—then miserably.*] Back before I was born—

TYRONE Doesn't she do the same with me? Back before she ever knew me. You'd think the only happy days she's ever known were in her father's home, or at the Convent, praying and playing the piano. [*Jealous resentment in his bitterness*] As I've told you before, you must take her memories with a grain of salt. Her wonderful home was ordinary enough. Her father wasn't the great, generous, noble Irish gentleman she makes out. He was a nice enough man, good company and a good talker. I liked him and he liked me. He was prosperous enough, too, in his wholesale grocery business, an able man. But he had his weakness. She condemns my drinking but she forgets his. It's true he never touched a drop till he was forty, but after that he made up for lost time. He became a steady champagne drinker, the worst kind. That was his grand pose, to drink only champagne. Well, it finished him quick—that and the consumption—

[*He stops with a guilty glance at his son.*]

EDMUND [*sardonically*] We don't seem able to avoid unpleasant topics, do we?

TYRONE [*sighs sadly*] No. [*Then with a pathetic attempt at heartiness*] What do you say to a game or two of Casino,[3] lad?

3. A card game in which players capture cards exposed on the table by matching them with cards from their own hands.

EDMUND All right.

TYRONE [*shuffling the cards clumsily*] We can't lock up and go to bed till Jamie comes on the last trolley—which I hope he won't—and I don't want to go upstairs, anyway, till she's asleep.

EDMUND Neither do I.

TYRONE [*keeps shuffling the cards fumblingly, forgetting to deal them*] As I was saying, you must take her tales of the past with a grain of salt. The piano playing and her dream of becoming a concert pianist. That was put in her head by the nuns flattering her. She was their pet. They loved her for being so devout. They're innocent women, anyway, when it comes to the world. They don't know that not one in a million who shows promise ever rises to concert playing. Not that your mother didn't play well for a schoolgirl, but that's no reason to take it for granted she could have—

EDMUND [*sharply*] Why don't you deal, if we're going to play.

TYRONE Eh? I am. [*Dealing with very uncertain judgment of distance*] And the idea she might have become a nun. That's the worst. Your mother was one of the most beautiful girls you could ever see. She knew it, too. She was a bit of a rogue and a coquette, God bless her, behind all her shyness and blushes. She was never made to renounce the world. She was bursting with health and high spirits and the love of loving.

EDMUND For God's sake, Papa! Why don't you pick up your hand?

TYRONE [*picks it up—dully*] Yes, let's see what I have here.

[*They both stare at their cards unseeingly. Then they both start.* TYRONE *whispers.*]

Listen!

EDMUND She's coming downstairs.

TYRONE [*hurriedly*] We'll play our game. Pretend not to notice and she'll soon go up again.

EDMUND [*staring through the front parlor—with relief*] I don't see her. She must have started down and then turned back.

TYRONE Thank God.

EDMUND Yes. It's pretty horrible to see her the way she must be now. [*With bitter misery*] The hardest thing to take is the blank wall she builds around her. Or it's more like a bank of fog in which she hides and loses herself. Deliberately, that's the hell of it! You know something in her does it deliberately—to get beyond our reach, to be rid of us, to forget we're alive! It's as if, in spite of loving us, she hated us!

TYRONE [*remonstrates gently*] Now, now, lad. It's not her. It's the damned poison.

EDMUND [*bitterly*] She takes it to get that effect. At least, I know she did this time! [*Abruptly*] My play, isn't it? Here. [*He plays a card.*]

TYRONE [*plays mechanically—gently reproachful*] She's been terribly frightened about your illness, for all her pretending. Don't be too hard on her, lad. Remember she's not responsible. Once that cursed poison gets a hold on anyone—

EDMUND [*his face grows hard and he stares at his father with bitter accusation*] It never should have gotten a hold on her! I know damned well she's not to blame! And I know who is! You are! Your damned stinginess! If you'd spent money for a decent doctor when she was so sick after I was born, she'd never have known morphine existed! Instead you put her in the hands of a hotel quack who wouldn't admit his ignorance and took the easiest way out, not giving a damn what happened to her afterwards! All because his fee was cheap! Another one of your bargains!

TYRONE [*stung—angrily*] Be quiet! How dare you talk of something you know nothing about! [*Trying to control his temper.*] You must try to see my side of it, too, lad. How was I to know he was that kind of a doctor? He had a good reputation—

EDMUND Among the souses in the hotel bar, I suppose!

TYRONE That's a lie! I asked the hotel proprietor to recommend the best—

EDMUND Yes! At the same time crying poorhouse and making it plain you wanted a cheap one! I know your system! By God, I ought to after this afternoon!

TYRONE [*guiltily defensive*] What about this afternoon?

EDMUND Never mind now. We're talking about Mama! I'm saying no matter how you excuse yourself you know damned well your stinginess is to blame—

TYRONE And I say you're a liar! Shut your mouth right now, or—

EDMUND [*ignoring this*] After you found out she'd been made a morphine addict, why didn't you send her to a cure then, at the start, while she still had a chance? No, that would have meant spending some money! I'll bet you told her all she had to do was use a little willpower! That's what you still believe in your heart, in spite of what doctors, who really know something about it, have told you!

TYRONE You lie again! I know better than that now! But how was I to know then? What did I know of morphine? It was years before I discovered what was wrong. I thought she'd never got over her sickness, that's all. Why didn't I send her to a cure, you say? [*Bitterly*] Haven't I? I've spent thousands upon thousands in cures! A waste. What good have they done her? She always started again.

EDMUND Because you've never given her anything that would help her want to stay off it! No home except this summer dump in a place she hates and you've refused even to spend money to make this look decent, while you keep buying more property, and playing sucker for every con man with a gold mine, or a silver mine, or any kind of get-rich-quick swindle! You've dragged her around on the road, season after season, on one-night stands, with no one she could talk to, waiting night after night in dirty hotel rooms for you to come back with a bun on after the bars closed! Christ, is it any wonder she didn't want to be cured. Jesus, when I think of it I hate your guts!

TYRONE [*strickenly*] Edmund! [*Then in a rage*] How dare you talk to your father like that, you insolent young cub! After all I've done for you.

EDMUND We'll come to that, what you're doing for me!

TYRONE [*looking guilty again—ignores this*] Will you stop repeating your mother's crazy accusations, which she never makes unless it's the poison talking? I never dragged her on the road against her will. Naturally, I wanted her with me. I loved her. And she came because she loved me and wanted to be with me. That's the truth, no matter what she says when she's not herself. And she needn't have been lonely. There was always the members of my company to talk to, if she'd wanted. She had her children, too, and I insisted, in spite of the expense, on having a nurse to travel with her.

EDMUND [*bitterly*] Yes, your one generosity, and that because you were jealous of her paying too much attention to us, and wanted us out of your way! It was another mistake, too! If she'd had to take care of me all by herself, and had that to occupy her mind, maybe she'd have been able—

TYRONE [*goaded into vindictiveness*] Or for that matter, if you insist on judging things by what she says when she's not in her right mind, if you hadn't been born she'd never— [*He stops ashamed.*]

EDMUND [*suddenly spent and miserable*] Sure. I know that's what she feels, Papa.

TYRONE [*protests penitently*] She doesn't! She loves you as dearly as ever mother loved a son! I only said that because you put me in such a God-damned rage, raking up the past, and saying you hate me—

EDMUND [*dully*] I didn't mean it, Papa. [*He suddenly smiles—kidding a bit drunkenly.*] I'm like Mama, I can't help liking you, in spite of everything.

TYRONE [*grins a bit drunkenly in return*] I might say the same of you. You're no great shakes as a son. It's a case of "A poor thing but mine own."[4]

[*They both chuckle with real, if alcoholic, affection.* TYRONE *changes the subject.*]

What's happened to our game? Whose play is it?

EDMUND Yours, I guess.

[TYRONE *plays a card which* EDMUND *takes and the game gets forgotten again.*]

TYRONE You mustn't let yourself be too downhearted, lad, by the bad news you had today. Both the doctors promised me, if you obey orders at this place you're going, you'll be cured in six months, or a year at most.

EDMUND [*his face hard again*] Don't kid me. You don't believe that.

TYRONE [*too vehemently*] Of course I believe it! Why shouldn't I believe it when both Hardy and the specialist—?

EDMUND You think I'm going to die.

TYRONE That's a lie! You're crazy!

EDMUND [*more bitterly*] So why waste money? That's why you're sending me to a state farm—

TYRONE [*in guilty confusion*] What state farm? It's the Hilltown Sanatorium, that's all I know, and both doctors said it was the best place for you.

EDMUND [*scathingly*] For the money! That is, for nothing, or practically nothing. Don't lie, Papa! You know damned well Hilltown Sanatorium is a state institution! Jamie suspected you'd cry poorhouse to Hardy and he wormed the truth out of him.

TYRONE [*furiously*] That drunken loafer! I'll kick him out in the gutter! He's poisoned your mind against me ever since you were old enough to listen!

EDMUND You can't deny it's the truth about the state farm, can you?

TYRONE It's not true the way you look at it! What if it is run by the state? That's nothing against it. The state has the money to make a better place than any private sanatorium. And why shouldn't I take advantage of it? It's my right—and yours. We're residents. I'm a property owner. I help to support it. I'm taxed to death—

EDMUND [*with bitter irony*] Yes, on property valued at a quarter of a million.

4. A shortened version of what Touchstone says in Shakespeare's *As You Like It* (1599): "A poor virgin, sir, an ill-favoured thing, sir, but mine own" (5.4.55–56).

TYRONE Lies! It's all mortgaged!

EDMUND Hardy and the specialist know what you're worth. I wonder what they thought of you when they heard you moaning poorhouse and showing you wanted to wish me on charity!

TYRONE It's a lie! All I told them was I couldn't afford any millionaire's sanatorium because I was land-poor.[5] That's the truth!

EDMUND And then you went to the Club to meet McGuire and let him stick you with another bum piece of property! [*As* TYRONE *starts to deny*] Don't lie about it! We met McGuire in the hotel bar after he left you. Jamie kidded him about hooking you, and he winked and laughed!

TYRONE [*lying feebly*] He's a liar if he said—

EDMUND Don't lie about it! [*With gathering intensity*] God, Papa, ever since I went to sea and was on my own, and found out what hard work for little pay was, and what it felt like to be broke, and starve, and camp on park benches because I had no place to sleep, I've tried to be fair to you because I knew what you'd been up against as a kid. I've tried to make allowances. Christ, you have to make allowances in this damned family or go nuts! I have tried to make allowances for myself when I remember all the rotten stuff I've pulled! I've tried to feel like Mama that you can't help being what you are where money is concerned. But God Almighty, this last stunt of yours is too much! It makes me want to puke! Not because of the rotten way you're treating me. To hell with that! I've treated you rottenly, in my way, more than once. But to think when it's a question of your son having consumption, you can show yourself up before the whole town as such a stinking old tightwad! Don't you know Hardy will talk and the whole damned town will know! Jesus, Papa, haven't you any pride or shame? [*Bursting with rage*] And don't think I'll let you get away with it! I won't go to any damned state farm just to save you a few lousy dollars to buy more bum property with! You stinking old miser—!

[*He chokes huskily, his voice trembling with rage, and then is shaken by a fit of coughing.*]

TYRONE [*has shrunk back in his chair under this attack, his guilty contrition greater than his anger. He stammers*] Be quiet! Don't say that to me! You're drunk! I won't mind you. Stop coughing, lad. You've got yourself worked up over nothing. Who said you had to go to this Hilltown place? You can go anywhere you like. I don't give a damn what it costs. All I care about is to have you get well. Don't call me a stinking miser, just because I don't want doctors to think I'm a millionaire they can swindle.

[EDMUND *has stopped coughing. He looks sick and weak. His father stares at him frightenedly.*]

You look weak, lad. You'd better take a bracer.

EDMUND [*grabs the bottle and pours his glass brimfull—weakly*] Thanks. [*He gulps down the whiskey.*]

TYRONE [*pours himself a big drink, which empties the bottle, and drinks it. His head bows and he stares dully at the cards on the table—vaguely.*] Whose play is it? [*He goes on dully, without resentment.*] A stinking old miser. Well, maybe you're right. Maybe I can't help being, although all my life since I

5. That is, short on cash because his wealth is tied up in the ownership of unprofitable land.

had anything I've thrown money over the bar to buy drinks for everyone in the house, or loaned money to sponges I knew would never pay it back— [*With a loose-mouthed sneer of self-contempt*] But, of course, that was in barrooms, when I was full of whiskey. I can't feel that way about it when I'm sober in my home. It was at home I first learned the value of a dollar and the fear of the poorhouse. I've never been able to believe in my luck since. I've always feared it would change and everything I had would be taken away. But still, the more property you own, the safer you think you are. That may not be logical, but it's the way I have to feel. Banks fail, and your money's gone, but you think you can keep land beneath your feet. [*Abruptly his tone becomes scornfully superior*] You said you realized what I'd been up against as a boy. The hell you do! How could you? You've had everything—nurses, schools, college, though you didn't stay there. You've had food, clothing. Oh, I know you had a fling of hard work with your back and hands, a bit of being homeless and penniless in a foreign land, and I respect you for it. But it was a game of romance and adventure to you. It was play.

EDMUND [*dully sarcastic*] Yes, particularly the time I tried to commit suicide at Jimmie the Priest's, and almost did.

TYRONE You weren't in your right mind. No son of mine would ever— You were drunk.

EDMUND I was stone cold sober. That was the trouble. I'd stopped to think too long.

TYRONE [*with drunken peevishness*] Don't start your damned atheist morbidness again! I don't care to listen. I was trying to make plain to you— [*Scornfully*] What do you know of the value of a dollar? When I was ten my father deserted my mother and went back to Ireland to die. Which he did soon enough, and deserved to, and I hope he's roasting in hell. He mistook rat poison for flour, or sugar, or something. There was gossip it wasn't by mistake but that's a lie. No one in my family ever—

EDMUND My bet is, it wasn't by mistake.

TYRONE More morbidness! Your brother put that in your head. The worst he can suspect is the only truth for him. But never mind. My mother was left, a stranger in a strange land,[6] with four small children, me and a sister a little older and two younger than me. My two older brothers had moved to other parts. They couldn't help. They were hard put to it to keep themselves alive. There was no damned romance in our poverty. Twice we were evicted from the miserable hovel we called home, with my mother's few sticks of furniture thrown out in the street, and my mother and sisters crying. I cried, too, though I tried hard not to, because I was the man of the family. At ten years old! There was no more school for me. I worked twelve hours a day in a machine shop, learning to make files. A dirty barn of a place where rain dripped through the roof, where you roasted in summer, and there was no stove in winter, and your hands got numb with cold, where the only light came through two small filthy windows, so on grey days I'd have to sit bent over with my eyes almost touching the files in order to see! You talk of work! And what do you think I got

6. A phrase from Exodus 2.22.

for it? Fifty cents a week! It's the truth! Fifty cents a week! And my poor mother washed and scrubbed for the Yanks by the day, and my older sister sewed, and my two younger stayed at home to keep the house. We never had clothes enough to wear, nor enough food to eat. Well I remember one Thanksgiving, or maybe it was Christmas, when some Yank in whose house mother had been scrubbing gave her a dollar extra for a present, and on the way home she spent it all on food. I can remember her hugging and kissing us and saying with tears of joy running down her tired face: "Glory be to God, for once in our lives we'll have enough for each of us!" [*He wipes tears from his eyes.*] A fine, brave, sweet woman. There never was a braver or finer.

EDMUND [*moved*] Yes, she must have been.

TYRONE Her one fear was she'd get old and sick and have to die in the poorhouse. [*He pauses—then adds with grim humor.*] It was in those days I learned to be a miser. A dollar was worth so much then. And once you've learned a lesson, it's hard to unlearn it. You have to look for bargains. If I took this state farm sanatorium for a good bargain, you'll have to forgive me. The doctors did tell me it's a good place. You must believe that, Edmund. And I swear I never meant you to go there if you didn't want to. [*Vehemently*] You can choose any place you like! Never mind what it costs! Any place I can afford. Any place you like—within reason.

[*At this qualification, a grin twitches* EDMUND*'s lips. His resentment has gone. His father goes on with an elaborately offhand, casual air.*]

There was another sanatorium the specialist recommended. He said it had a record as good as any place in the country. It's endowed by a group of millionaire factory owners, for the benefit of their workers principally, but you're eligible to go there because you're a resident. There's such a pile of money behind it, they don't have to charge much. It's only seven dollars a week but you get ten times that value. [*Hastily*] I don't want to persuade you to anything, understand. I'm simply repeating what I was told.

EDMUND [*concealing his smile—casually*] Oh, I know that. It sounds like a good bargain to me. I'd like to go there. So that settles that. [*Abruptly he is miserably desperate again—dully.*] It doesn't matter a damn now, anyway. Let's forget it! [*Changing the subject*] How about our game? Whose play is it?

TYRONE [*mechanically*] I don't know. Mine, I guess. No, it's yours.

[EDMUND *plays a card. His father takes it. Then about to play from his hand, he again forgets the game.*]

Yes, maybe life overdid the lesson for me, and made a dollar worth too much, and the time came when that mistake ruined my career as a fine actor. [*Sadly*] I've never admitted this to anyone before, lad, but tonight I'm so heartsick I feel at the end of everything, and what's the use of fake pride and pretense. That God-damned play I bought for a song and made such a great success in—a great money success—it ruined me with its promise of an easy fortune. I didn't want to do anything else, and by the time I woke up to the fact I'd become a slave to the damned thing and did try other plays, it was too late. They had identified me with that one part, and didn't want me in anything else. They were right, too. I'd lost the great talent I once had through years of easy repetition, never learning a new part, never really working hard. Thirty-five to forty thousand dollars net profit a season like snapping your fingers! It was too great a temptation. Yet before I bought the damned thing I was considered one of the three or four young actors with the greatest artistic promise in America. I'd worked like hell. I'd left a good job as a machinist to take supers' parts[7] because I loved the theater. I was wild with ambition. I read all the plays ever written. I studied Shakespeare as you'd study the Bible. I educated myself. I got rid of an Irish brogue you could cut with a knife. I loved Shakespeare. I would have acted in any of his plays for nothing, for the joy of being alive in his great poetry. And I acted well in him. I felt inspired by him. I could have been a great Shakespearean actor, if I'd kept on. I know that! In 1874 when Edwin Booth[8] came to the theater in Chicago where I was leading man, I played Cassius to his Brutus one night, Brutus to his Cassius the next, Othello to his Iago, and so on.[9] The first night I played Othello, he said to our manager, "That young man is playing Othello better than I ever did!" [*Proudly*] That from Booth, the greatest actor of his day or any other! And it was true! And I was only twenty-seven years old! As I look back on it now, that night was the high spot in my career. I had life where I wanted it! And for a time after that I kept on upward with ambition high. Married your mother. Ask her what I was like in those days. Her love was an added incentive to ambition. But a few years later my good bad luck made me find the big moneymaker. It wasn't that in my eyes at first. It was a great romantic part I knew I could play better than anyone. But it was a great box office success from the start—and then life had me where it wanted me—at from thirty-five to forty thousand net profit a season! A fortune in those days—or even in these. [*Bitterly*] What the hell was it I wanted to buy, I wonder, that was worth— Well, no matter. It's a late day for regrets. [*He glances vaguely at his cards.*] My play, isn't it?

EDMUND [*moved, stares at his father with understanding—slowly*] I'm glad you've told me this, Papa. I know you a lot better now.

TYRONE [*with a loose, twisted smile*] Maybe I shouldn't have told you. Maybe you'll only feel more contempt for me. And it's a poor way to convince you of the value of a dollar.

[*Then as if this phrase automatically aroused an habitual association in his mind, he glances up at the chandelier disapprovingly.*]

The glare from those extra lights hurts my eyes. You don't mind if I turn them out, do you? We don't need them, and there's no use making the Electric Company rich.

EDMUND [*controlling a wild impulse to laugh—agreeably*] No, sure not. Turn them out.

TYRONE [*gets heavily and a bit waveringly to his feet and gropes uncertainly for the lights—his mind going back to its line of thought*] No, I don't know what the hell it was I wanted to buy. [*He clicks out one bulb.*] On my solemn oath, Edmund, I'd gladly face not having an acre of land to call my own, nor a penny in the bank— [*He clicks out another bulb.*] I'd be willing

7. That is, to be an extra; supernumerary roles are nonspeaking parts.
8. The foremost American actor of the 19th century (1833–1893), and the first to gain international fame (especially for his interpretations of Shakespeare).
9. Cassius and Brutus are principal roles in Shakespeare's *Julius Caesar* (1599); Othello and Iago are principal roles in *Othello*.

to have no home but the poorhouse in my old age if I could look back now on having been the fine artist I might have been.

[*He turns out the third bulb, so only the reading lamp is on, and sits down again heavily.* EDMUND *suddenly cannot hold back a burst of strained, ironical laughter.* TYRONE *is hurt.*]

What the devil are you laughing at?

EDMUND Not at you, Papa. At life. It's so damned crazy.

TYRONE [*growls*] More of your morbidness! There's nothing wrong with life. It's we who— [*He quotes.*] "The fault, dear Brutus, is not in our stars, but in ourselves that we are underlings."[1] [*He pauses—then sadly.*] The praise Edwin Booth gave my Othello. I made the manager put down his exact words in writing. I kept it in my wallet for years. I used to read it every once in a while until finally it made me feel so bad I didn't want to face it any more. Where is it now, I wonder? Somewhere in this house. I remember I put it away carefully—

EDMUND [*with a wry ironical sadness*] It might be in an old trunk in the attic, along with Mama's wedding dress. [*Then as his father stares at him, he adds quickly.*] For Pete's sake, if we're going to play cards, let's play.

[*He takes the card his father had played and leads. For a moment, they play the game, like mechanical chess players. Then* TYRONE *stops, listening to a sound upstairs.*]

TYRONE She's still moving around. God knows when she'll go to sleep.

EDMUND [*pleads tensely*] For Christ's sake, Papa, forget it!

[*He reaches out and pours a drink.* TYRONE *starts to protest, then gives it up.* EDMUND *drinks. He puts down the glass. His expression changes. When he speaks it is as if he were deliberately giving way to drunkenness and seeking to hide behind a maudlin manner.*]

Yes, she moves above and beyond us, a ghost haunting the past, and here we sit pretending to forget, but straining our ears listening for the slightest sound, hearing the fog drip from the eaves like the uneven tick of a rundown, crazy clock—or like the dreary tears of a trollop spattering in a puddle of stale beer on a honky-tonk tabletop! [*He laughs with maudlin appreciation.*] Not so bad, that last, eh? Original, not Baudelaire. Give me credit! [*Then with alcoholic talkativeness*] You've just told me some high spots in your memories. Want to hear mine? They're all connected with the sea. Here's one. When I was on the Squarehead square-rigger,[2] bound for Buenos Aires. Full moon in the Trades. The old hooker[3] driving fourteen knots. I lay on the bowsprit, facing astern, with the water foaming into spume under me, the masts with every sail white in the moonlight, towering high above me. I became drunk with the beauty and singing rhythm of it, and for a moment I lost myself—actually lost my life. I was set free! I dissolved in the sea, became white sails and flying spray, became beauty and rhythm, became moonlight and the ship and the high dim-starred sky! I belonged, without past or future, within peace and unity and a wild joy, within something greater than my own life, or the life of Man, to Life itself! To God, if you want to put it that way. Then another time, on the American

1. Quoting Cassius, from Shakespeare's *Julius Caesar*, 1.2.141–42.
2. A large sailing vessel with square sails on two or more masts.
3. An affectionate term for an older ship.

Line,[4] when I was lookout on the crow's nest in the dawn watch. A calm sea, that time. Only a lazy ground swell and a slow drowsy roll of the ship. The passengers asleep and none of the crew in sight. No sound of man. Black smoke pouring from the funnels behind and beneath me. Dreaming, not keeping lookout, feeling alone, and above, and apart, watching the dawn creep like a painted dream over the sky and sea which slept together. Then the moment of ecstatic freedom came. The peace, the end of the quest, the last harbor, the joy of belonging to a fulfillment beyond men's lousy, pitiful, greedy fears and hopes and dreams! And several other times in my life, when I was swimming far out, or lying alone on a beach, I have had the same experience. Became the sun, the hot sand, green seaweed anchored to a rock, swaying in the tide. Like a saint's vision of beatitude. Like the veil of things as they seem drawn back by an unseen hand. For a second you see—and seeing the secret, are the secret. For a second there is meaning! Then the hand lets the veil fall and you are alone, lost in the fog again, and you stumble on toward nowhere, for no good reason! [*He grins wryly.*] It was a great mistake, my being born a man, I would have been much more successful as a seagull or a fish. As it is, I will always be a stranger who never feels at home, who does not really want and is not really wanted, who can never belong, who must always be a little in love with death!

TYRONE [*stares at him—impressed*] Yes, there's the makings of a poet in you all right. [*Then protesting uneasily*] But that's morbid craziness about not being wanted and loving death.

EDMUND [*sardonically*] The *makings* of a poet. No, I'm afraid I'm like the guy who is always panhandling for a smoke. He hasn't even got the makings. He's got only the habit. I couldn't touch what I tried to tell you just now. I just stammered. That's the best I'll ever do, I mean, if I live. Well, it will be faithful realism, at least. Stammering is the native eloquence of us fog people.

[*A pause. Then they both jump startledly as there is a noise from outside the house, as if someone had stumbled and fallen on the front steps.* EDMUND *grins.*]

Well, that sounds like the absent brother. He must have a peach of a bun on.

TYRONE [*scowling*] That loafer! He caught the last car, bad luck to it. [*He gets to his feet.*] Get him to bed, Edmund. I'll go out on the porch. He has a tongue like an adder when he's drunk. I'd only lose my temper.

[*He goes out the door to the side porch as the front door in the hall bangs shut behind* JAMIE. EDMUND *watches with amusement* JAMIE'*s wavering progress through the front parlor.* JAMIE *comes in. He is very drunk and woozy on his legs. His eyes are glassy, his face bloated, his speech blurred, his mouth slack like his father's, a leer on his lips.*]

JAMIE [*swaying and blinking in the doorway—in a loud voice*] What ho! What ho!

EDMUND [*sharply*] Nix on the loud noise!

JAMIE [*blinks at him*] Oh, hello, Kid. [*With great seriousness*] I'm as drunk as a fiddler's bitch.

4. The American Steamship Line, which provided transatlantic passenger service in the late 19th century.

EDMUND [*dryly*] Thanks for telling me your great secret.

JAMIE [*grins foolishly*] Yes. Unneshesary information Number One, eh? [*He bends and slaps at the knees of his trousers.*] Had serious accident. The front steps tried to trample on me. Took advantage of fog to waylay me. Ought to be a lighthouse out there. Dark in here, too. [*Scowling*] What the hell is this, the morgue? Lesh have some light on subject.

[*He sways forward to the table, reciting Kipling.*]

"Ford, ford, ford o' Kabul river,
Ford o' Kabul river in the dark!
Keep the crossing-stakes beside you, an' they will surely guide you
'Cross the ford o' Kabul river in the dark."[5]

[*He fumbles at the chandelier and manages to turn on the three bulbs.*]

Thash more like it. To hell with old Gaspard.[6] Where is the old tightwad?

EDMUND Out on the porch.

JAMIE Can't expect us to live in the Black Hole of Calcutta.[7] [*His eyes fix on the full bottle of whiskey.*] Say! Have I got the d.t.'s? [*He reaches out fumblingly and grabs it.*] By God, it's real. What's matter with the Old Man tonight? Must be ossified to forget he left this out. Grab opportunity by the forelock. Key to my success.

[*He slops a big drink into a glass.*]

EDMUND You're stinking now. That will knock you stiff.

JAMIE Wisdom from the mouth of babes. Can the wise stuff, Kid. You're still wet behind the ears.

[*He lowers himself into a chair, holding the drink carefully aloft.*]

EDMUND All right. Pass out if you want to.

JAMIE Can't, that's trouble. Had enough to sink a ship, but can't sink. Well, here's hoping. [*He drinks.*]

EDMUND Shove over the bottle. I'll have one, too.

JAMIE [*with sudden, big-brotherly solicitude, grabbing the bottle*] No, you don't. Not while I'm around. Remember doctor's orders. Maybe no one else gives a damn if you die, but I do. My kid brother. I love your guts, Kid. Everything else is gone. You're all I've got left. [*Pulling bottle closer to him.*] So no booze for you, if I can help it. [*Beneath his drunken sentimentality there is a genuine sincerity.*]

EDMUND [*irritably*] Oh, lay off it.

JAMIE [*is hurt and his face hardens*] You don't believe I care, eh? Just drunken bull. [*He shoves the bottle over.*] All right. Go ahead and kill yourself.

EDMUND [*seeing he is hurt—affectionately*] Sure I know you care, Jamie, and I'm going on the wagon. But tonight doesn't count. Too many damned things have happened today. [*He pours a drink.*] Here's how. [*He drinks.*]

JAMIE [*sobers up momentarily and with a pitying look*] I know, Kid. It's been

5. From "Ford o' Kabul River" (1892), by the English poet and novelist Rudyard Kipling (1865–1936).

6. A miserly character who cheats two heirs out of their inheritance in the 1877 operetta *Les cloches de Corneville* (*The Bells of Corneville*), by Louis Clairville and Charles Gabet.

7. The small, stifling room into which, in 1756, captured British soldiers were packed so tightly that most did not survive the night.

a lousy day for you. [*Then with sneering cynicism*] I'll bet old Gaspard hasn't tried to keep you off booze. Probably give you a case to take with you to the state farm for pauper patients. The sooner you kick the bucket, the less expense. [*With contemptuous hatred*] What a bastard to have for a father! Christ, if you put him in a book, no one would believe it!

EDMUND [*defensively*] Oh, Papa's all right, if you try to understand him—and keep your sense of humor.

JAMIE [*cynically*] He's been putting on the old sob act for you, eh? He can always kid you. But not me. Never again. [*Then slowly*] Although, in a way, I do feel sorry for him about one thing. But he has even that coming to him. He's to blame. [*Hurriedly*] But to hell with that. [*He grabs the bottle and pours another drink, appearing very drunk again.*] That lash drink's getting me. This one ought to put the lights out. Did you tell Gaspard I got it out of Doc Hardy this sanatorium is a charity dump?

EDMUND [*reluctantly*] Yes. I told him I wouldn't go there. It's all settled now. He said I can go anywhere I want. [*He adds, smiling without resentment.*] Within reason, of course.

JAMIE [*drunkenly imitating his father*] Of course, lad. Anything within reason. [*Sneering*] That means another cheap dump. Old Gaspard, the miser in "The Bells," that's a part he can play without makeup.

EDMUND [*irritably*] Oh, shut up, will you. I've heard that Gaspard stuff a million times.

JAMIE [*shrugs his shoulders—thickly*] Aw right, if you're shatisfied—let him get away with it. It's your funeral—I mean, I hope it won't be.

EDMUND [*changing the subject*] What did you do uptown tonight? Go to Mamie Burns?

JAMIE [*very drunk, his head nodding*] Sure thing. Where else could I find suitable feminine companionship? And love. Don't forget love. What is a man without a good woman's love? A God-damned hollow shell.

EDMUND [*chuckles tipsily, letting himself go now and be drunk*] You're a nut.

JAMIE [*quotes with gusto from Oscar Wilde's "The Harlot's House"*]

"Then, turning to my love, I said,
'The dead are dancing with the dead,
The dust is whirling with the dust.'

But she—she heard the violin,
And left my side and entered in:
Love passed into the house of lust.

Then suddenly the tune went false,
The dancers wearied of the waltz . . ."[8]

[*He breaks off, thickly.*] Not strictly accurate. If my love was with me, I didn't notice it. She must have been a ghost. [*He pauses.*] Guess which one of Mamie's charmers I picked to bless me with her woman's love. It'll hand you a laugh, Kid. I picked Fat Violet.

EDMUND [*laughs drunkenly*] No, honest? Some pick! God, she weighs a ton. What the hell for, a joke?

JAMIE No joke. Very serious. By the time I hit Mamie's dump I felt very sad

8. This 1881 poem is said to have been inspired by a night Wilde spent with a French prostitute.

about myself and all the other poor bums in the world. Ready for a weep on any old womanly bosom. You know how you get when John Barleycorn[9] turns on the soft music inside you. Then, soon as I got in the door, Mamie began telling me all her troubles. Beefed how rotten business was, and she was going to give Fat Violet the gate. Customers didn't fall for Vi. Only reason she'd kept her was she could play the piano. Lately Vi's gone on drunks and been too boiled to play, and was eating her out of house and home, and although Vi was a goodhearted dumbbell, and she felt sorry for her because she didn't know how the hell she'd make a living, still business was business, and she couldn't afford to run a home for fat tarts. Well, that made me feel sorry for Fat Violet, so I squandered two bucks of your dough to escort her upstairs. With no dishonorable intentions whatever. I like them fat, but not that fat. All I wanted was a little heart-to-heart talk concerning the infinite sorrow of life.

EDMUND [*chuckles drunkenly*] Poor Vi! I'll bet you recited Kipling and Swinburne and Dowson and gave her "I have been faithful to thee, Cynara, in my fashion."

JAMIE [*grins loosely*] Sure—with the Old Master, John Barleycorn, playing soft music. She stood it for a while. Then she got good and sore. Got the idea I took her upstairs for a joke. Gave me a grand bawling out. Said she was better than a drunken bum who recited poetry. Then she began to cry. So I had to say I loved her because she was fat, and she wanted to believe that, and I stayed with her to prove it, and that cheered her up, and she kissed me when I left, and said she'd fallen hard for me, and we both cried a little more in the hallway, and everything was fine, except Mamie Burns thought I'd gone bughouse.

EDMUND [*quotes derisively*] "Harlots and
Hunted have pleasures of their own to give,
The vulgar herd can never understand."[1]

JAMIE [*nods his head drunkenly*] Egzactly! Hell of a good time, at that. You should have stuck around with me, Kid. Mamie Burns inquired after you. Sorry to hear you were sick. She meant it, too. [*He pauses—then with maudlin humor, in a ham-actor tone.*] This night has opened my eyes to a great career in store for me, my boy! I shall give the art of acting back to the performing seals, which are its most perfect expression. By applying my natural God-given talents in their proper sphere, I shall attain the pinnacle of success! I'll be the lover of the fat woman in Barnum and Bailey's circus![2]

[EDMUND *laughs.* JAMIE'*s mood changes to arrogant disdain.*]

Pah! Imagine me sunk to the fat girl in a hick town hooker shop! Me! Who have made some of the best-lookers on Broadway sit up and beg!

[*He quotes from Kipling's "Sestina of the Tramp-Royal."*]

9. That is, alcohol. In an English folksong John Barleycorn is the personification of barley and the alcoholic beverages made from it, beer and whiskey.

1. From Baudelaire's "Epilogue" (see above.)

2. The circuses owned by P. T. Barnum (1810–1891) and James Bailey (1847–1906) merged in 1881, becoming America's most celebrated circus.

"Speakin' in general, I 'ave tried 'em all,
The 'appy roads that take you o'er the world."[3]

[*With sodden melancholy*] Not so apt. Happy roads is bunk. Weary roads is right. Get you nowhere fast. That's where I've got—nowhere. Where everyone lands in the end, even if most of the suckers won't admit it.

EDMUND [*derisively*] Can it! You'll be crying in a minute.

JAMIE [*starts and stares at his brother for a second with bitter hostility—thickly*] Don't get—too damned fresh. [*Then abruptly*] But you're right. To hell with repining! Fat Violet's a good kid. Glad I stayed with her. Christian act. Cured her blues. Hell of a good time. You should have stuck with me, Kid. Taken your mind off your troubles. What's the use coming home to get the blues over what can't be helped. All over—finished now—not a hope!

[*He stops, his head nodding drunkenly, his eyes closing—then suddenly he looks up, his face hard, and quotes jeeringly.*]

"If I were hanged on the highest hill,
Mother o' mine, O mother o' mine!
I know whose love would follow me still . . ."[4]

EDMUND [*violently*] Shut up!

JAMIE [*in a cruel, sneering tone with hatred in it*] Where's the hophead? Gone to sleep?

[EDMUND *jerks as if he'd been struck. There is a tense silence.* EDMUND'S *face looks stricken and sick. Then in a burst of rage he springs from his chair.*]

EDMUND You dirty bastard!

[*He punches his brother in the face, a blow that glances off the cheekbone. For a second* JAMIE *reacts pugnaciously and half rises from his chair to do battle, but suddenly he seems to sober up to a shocked realization of what he has said and he sinks back limply.*]

JAMIE [*miserably*] Thanks, Kid. I certainly had that coming. Don't know what made me—booze talking—You know me, Kid.

EDMUND [*his anger ebbing*] I know you'd never say that unless— But God, Jamie, no matter how drunk you are, it's no excuse! [*He pauses—miserably.*] I'm sorry I hit you. You and I never scrap—that bad.

[*He sinks back on his chair.*]

JAMIE [*huskily*] It's all right. Glad you did. My dirty tongue. Like to cut it out. [*He hides his face in his hands—dully.*] I suppose it's because I feel so damned sunk. Because this time Mama had me fooled. I really believed she had it licked. She thinks I always believe the worst, but this time I believed the best. [*His voice flutters.*] I suppose I can't forgive her—yet. It meant so much. I'd begun to hope, if she'd beaten the game, I could, too.

[*He begins to sob, and the horrible part of his weeping is that it appears sober, not the maudlin tears of drunkenness.*]

3. Kipling's 1896 poem, written in Cockney dialect, celebrates the life of the itinerant seaman.

4. Lines from the dedication poem to Kipling's novel *The Light That Failed* (1890).

EDMUND [*blinking back tears himself*] God, don't I know how you feel! Stop it, Jamie!

JAMIE [*trying to control his sobs*] I've known about Mama so much longer than you. Never forget the first time I got wise. Caught her in the act with a hypo. Christ, I'd never dreamed before that any women but whores took dope! [*He pauses.*] And then this stuff of you getting consumption. It's got me licked. We've been more than brothers. You're the only pal I've ever had. I love your guts. I'd do anything for you.

EDMUND [*reaches out and pats his arm*] I know that, Jamie.

JAMIE [*his crying over—drops his hands from his face—with a strange bitterness*] Yet I'll bet you've heard Mama and old Gaspard spill so much bunk about my hoping for the worst, you suspect right now I'm thinking to myself that Papa is old and can't last much longer, and if you were to die, Mama and I would get all he's got, and so I'm probably hoping—

EDMUND [*indignantly*] Shut up, you damned fool! What the hell put that in your nut? [*He stares at his brother accusingly.*] Yes, that's what I'd like to know. What put that in your mind?

JAMIE [*confusedly—appearing drunk again*] Don't be a dumbbell! What I said! Always suspected of hoping for the worst. I've got so I can't help — [*Then drunkenly resentful*] What are you trying to do, accuse me? Don't play the wise guy with me! I've learned more of life than you'll ever know! Just because you've read a lot of highbrow junk, don't think you can fool me! You're only an overgrown kid! Mama's baby and Papa's pet! The family White Hope![5] You've been getting a swelled head lately. About nothing! About a few poems in a hick town newspaper! Hell, I used to write better stuff for the Lit magazine in college! You better wake up! You're setting no rivers on fire! You let hick town boobs flatter you with bunk about your future—

[*Abruptly his tone changes to disgusted contrition.* EDMUND *has looked away from him, trying to ignore this tirade.*]

Hell, Kid, forget it. That goes for Sweeny.[6] You know I don't mean it. No one hopes more than I do you'll knock 'em all dead. No one is prouder you've started to make good. [*Drunkenly assertive*] Why shouldn't I be proud? Hell, it's purely selfish. You reflect credit on me. I've had more to do with bringing you up than anyone. I wised you up about women, so you'd never be a fall guy, or make any mistakes you didn't want to make! And who steered you on to reading poetry first? Swinburne, for example? I did! And because I once wanted to write, I planted it in your mind that someday you'd write! Hell, you're more than my brother. I made you! You're my Frankenstein![7]

[*He has risen to a note of drunken arrogance.* EDMUND *is grinning with amusement now.*]

EDMUND All right, I'm your Frankenstein. So let's have a drink. [*He laughs.*] You crazy nut!

JAMIE [*thickly*] I'll have a drink. Not you. Got to take care of you.

5. That is, the person on whom hopes are centered (first used of the unknown white boxer who might defeat Jack Johnson).

6. An early 20th-century catchphrase meaning "forget it" or "pay no attention."

7. That is, his creation, like the unnamed monster brought to life by Victor Frankenstein in Mary Shelley's novel *Frankenstein: or, The Modern Prometheus* (1818).

[*He reaches out with a foolish grin of doting affection and grabs his brother's hand.*]

Don't be scared of this sanatorium business. Hell, you can beat that standing on your head. Six months and you'll be in the pink. Probably haven't got consumption at all. Doctors lot of fakers. Told me years ago to cut out booze or I'd soon be dead—and here I am. They're all con men. Anything to grab your dough. I'll bet this state farm stuff is political graft game. Doctors get a cut for every patient they send.

EDMUND [*disgustedly amused*] You're the limit! At the Last Judgment, you'll be around telling everyone it's in the bag.

JAMIE And I'll be right. Slip a piece of change to the Judge and be saved, but if you're broke you can go to hell!

[*He grins at this blasphemy and* EDMUND *has to laugh.* JAMIE *goes on.*]

"Therefore put money in thy purse."[8] That's the only dope. [*Mockingly*] The secret of my success! Look what it's got me!

[*He lets* EDMUND*'s hand go to pour a big drink, and gulps it down. He stares at his brother with bleary affection—takes his hand again and begins to talk thickly but with a strange, convincing sincerity.*]

Listen, Kid, you'll be going away. May not get another chance to talk. Or might not be drunk enough to tell you truth. So got to tell you now. Something I ought to have told you long ago—for your own good.

[*He pauses—struggling with himself.* EDMUND *stares, impressed and uneasy.* JAMIE *blurts out.*]

Not drunken bull, but "in vino veritas"[9] stuff. You better take it seriously. Want to warn you—against me. Mama and Papa are right. I've been rotten bad influence. And worst of it is, I did it on purpose.

EDMUND [*uneasily*] Shut up! I don't want to hear—

JAMIE Nix, Kid! You listen! Did it on purpose to make a bum of you. Or part of me did. A big part. That part that's been dead so long. That hates life. My putting you wise so you'd learn from my mistakes. Believed that myself at times, but it's a fake. Made my mistakes look good. Made getting drunk romantic. Made whores fascinating vampires instead of poor, stupid, diseased slobs they really are. Made fun of work as sucker's game. Never wanted you succeed and make me look even worse by comparison. Wanted you to fail. Always jealous of you. Mama's baby, Papa's pet! [*He stares at* EDMUND *with increasing enmity.*] And it was your being born that started Mama on dope. I know that's not your fault, but all the same, God damn you, I can't help hating your guts— !

EDMUND [*almost frightenedly*] Jamie! Cut it out! You're crazy!

JAMIE But don't get wrong idea, Kid. I love you more than I hate you. My saying what I'm telling you now proves it. I run the risk you'll hate me—and you're all I've got left. But I didn't mean to tell you that last stuff—go that far back. Don't know what made me. What I wanted to say is, I'd like to see you become the greatest success in the world. But you'd better be on your guard. Because I'll do my damnedest to make you fail. Can't help it. I

8. Quoting Iago from Shakespeare's *Othello*, 1.3.343–44. The phrase means "you can believe me" (cf. "you can bank on it").

9. "In wine [lies] truth" (Latin proverb).

hate myself. Got to take revenge. On everyone else. Especially you. Oscar Wilde's "Reading Gaol"[1] has the dope twisted. The man was dead and so he had to kill the thing he loved. That's what it ought to be. The dead part of me hopes you won't get well. Maybe he's even glad the game has got Mama again! He wants company, he doesn't want to be the only corpse around the house! [*He gives a hard, tortured laugh.*]

EDMUND Jesus, Jamie! You really have gone crazy!

JAMIE Think it over and you'll see I'm right. Think it over when you're away from me in the sanatorium. Make up your mind you've got to tie a can to me—get me out of your life—think of me as dead—tell people, "I had a brother, but he's dead." And when you come back, look out for me. I'll be waiting to welcome you with that "my old pal" stuff, and give you the glad hand, and at the first good chance I get stab you in the back.

EDMUND Shut up! I'll be God-damned if I'll listen to you anymore—

JAMIE [*as if he hadn't heard*] Only don't forget me. Remember I warned you—for your sake. Give me credit. Greater love hath no man than this, that he saveth his brother from himself.[2] [*Very drunkenly, his head bobbing*] That's all. Feel better now. Gone to confession. Know you absolve me, don't you, Kid? You understand. You're a damned fine kid. Ought to be. I made you. So go and get well. Don't die on me. You're all I've got left. God bless you, Kid. [*His eyes close. He mumbles.*] That last drink—the old K.O.[3]

[*He falls into a drunken doze, not completely asleep.* EDMUND *buries his face in his hands miserably.* TYRONE *comes in quietly through the screen door from the porch, his dressing gown wet with fog, the collar turned up around his throat. His face is stern and disgusted but at the same time pitying.* EDMUND *does not notice his entrance.*]

TYRONE [*In a low voice*] Thank God he's asleep.

[EDMUND *looks up with a start.*]

I thought he'd never stop talking. [*He turns down the collar of his dressing gown.*] We'd better let him stay where he is and sleep it off.

[EDMUND *remains silent.* TYRONE *regards him—then goes on.*]

I heard the last part of his talk. It's what I've warned you. I hope you'll heed the warning, now it comes from his own mouth.

[EDMUND *gives no sign of having heard.* TYRONE *adds pityingly*]

But don't take it too much to heart, lad. He loves to exaggerate the worst of himself when he's drunk. He's devoted to you. It's the one good thing left in him. [*He looks down on* JAMIE *with a bitter sadness.*] A sweet spectacle for me! My first-born, who I hoped would bear my name in honor and dignity, who showed such brilliant promise!

EDMUND [*miserably*] Keep quiet, can't you, Papa?

TYRONE [*pours a drink*] A waste! A wreck, a drunken hulk, done with and finished!

1. "The Ballad of Reading Gaol," which Wilde wrote upon his 1897 release from prison ("gaol") in Reading, England; the poem's most famous line is "Yet each man kills the thing he loves."

2. See John 15.13: "Greater love hath no man than this, that a man lay down his life for his friends."

3. Knockout.

[*He drinks.* JAMIE *has become restless, sensing his father's presence, struggling up from his stupor. Now he gets his eyes open to blink up at* TYRONE. *The latter moves back a step defensively, his face growing hard.*]

JAMIE [*suddenly points a finger at him and recites with dramatic emphasis*]

"Clarence is come, false, fleeting, perjured Clarence,
That stabbed me in the field by Tewksbury.
Seize on him, Furies, take him into torment."[4]

[*Then resentfully*] What the hell are you staring at?

[*He recites sardonically from Rossetti.*]

"Look in my face. My name is Might-Have-Been;
I am also called No More, Too Late, Farewell."[5]

TYRONE I'm well aware of that, and God knows I don't want to look at it.

EDMUND Papa! Quit it!

JAMIE [*derisively*] Got a great idea for you, Papa. Put on revival of "The Bells" this season. Great part in it you can play without makeup. Old Gaspard, the miser!

[TYRONE *turns away, trying to control his temper.*]

EDMUND Shut up, Jamie!

JAMIE [*jeeringly*] I claim Edwin Booth never saw the day when he could give as good a performance as a trained seal. Seals are intelligent and honest. They don't put up any bluffs about the Art of Acting. They admit they're just hams earning their daily fish.

TYRONE [*stung, turns on him in a rage*] You loafer!

EDMUND Papa! Do you want to start a row that will bring Mama down? Jamie, go back to sleep! You've shot off your mouth too much already.

[TYRONE *turns away.*]

JAMIE [*thickly*] All right, Kid. Not looking for argument. Too damned sleepy.

[*He closes his eyes, his head nodding.* TYRONE *comes to the table and sits down, turning his chair so he won't look at* JAMIE. *At once he becomes sleepy, too.*]

TYRONE [*heavily*] I wish to God she'd go to bed so that I could, too. [*Drowsily*] I'm dog tired. I can't stay up all night like I used to. Getting old—old and finished. [*With a bone-cracking yawn*] Can't keep my eyes open. I think I'll catch a few winks. Why don't you do the same, Edmund? It'll pass the time until she—

[*His voice trails off. His eyes close, his chin sags, and he begins to breathe heavily through his mouth.* EDMUND *sits tensely. He hears something and jerks nervously forward in his chair, staring through the front parlor into the hall. He jumps up with a hunted, distracted expression. It seems for a second he is going to hide in the back parlor. Then he sits down again and waits, his eyes averted, his hands gripping the arms of his chair. Suddenly all five bulbs of the chandelier in the front parlor are turned on from a wall switch, and a moment later someone starts playing the piano in there—the opening of one of Chopin's simpler waltzes, done with a forgetful, stiff-fingered groping, as if an awkward schoolgirl were practic-*

4. Quoting Clarence from Shakespeare's *Richard III* (1592–93), 1.4.55–57.

5. The opening lines of sonnet 97, "A Superscription," from *The House of Life* (1870).

ing it for the first time. TYRONE *starts to wide-awakeness and sober dread, and* JAMIE*'s head jerks back and his eyes open. For a moment they listen frozenly. The playing stops as abruptly as it began, and* MARY *appears in the doorway. She wears a sky-blue dressing gown over her nightdress, dainty slippers with pompons on her bare feet. Her face is paler than ever. Her eyes look enormous. They glisten like polished black jewels. The uncanny thing is that her face now appears so youthful. Experience seems ironed out of it. It is a marble mask of girlish innocence, the mouth caught in a shy smile. Her white hair is braided in two pigtails which hang over her breast. Over one arm, carried neglectfully, trailing on the floor, as if she had forgotten she held it, is an old-fashioned white satin wedding gown, trimmed with duchesse lace. She hesitates in the doorway, glancing round the room, her forehead puckered puzzledly, like someone who has come to a room to get something but has become absent-minded on the way and forgotten what it was. They stare at her. She seems aware of them merely as she is aware of other objects in the room, the furniture, the windows, familiar things she accepts automatically as naturally belonging there but which she is too preoccupied to notice.*]

JAMIE [*breaks the cracking silence—bitterly, self-defensively sardonic*] The Mad Scene. Enter Ophelia![6]

[*His father and brother both turn on him fiercely.* EDMUND *is quicker. He slaps* JAMIE *across the mouth with the back of his hand.*]

TYRONE [*his voice trembling with suppressed fury*] Good boy, Edmund. The dirty blackguard! His own mother!

JAMIE [*mumbles guiltily, without resentment*] All right, Kid. Had it coming. But I told you how much I'd hoped—

[*He puts his hands over his face and begins to sob.*]

TYRONE I'll kick you out in the gutter tomorrow, so help me God.

[*But* JAMIE*'s sobbing breaks his anger, and he turns and shakes his shoulder, pleading.*]

Jamie, for the love of God, stop it!

[*Then* MARY *speaks, and they freeze into silence again, staring at her. She has paid no attention whatever to the incident. It is simply a part of the familiar atmosphere of the room, a background which does not touch her preoccupation; and she speaks aloud to herself, not to them.*]

MARY I play so badly now. I'm all out of practice. Sister Theresa will give me a dreadful scolding. She'll tell me it isn't fair to my father when he spends so much money for extra lessons. She's quite right, it isn't fair, when he's so good and generous, and so proud of me. I'll practice every day from now on. But something horrible has happened to my hands. The fingers have gotten so stiff— [*She lifts her hands to examine them with a frightened puzzlement.*] The knuckles are all swollen. They're so ugly. I'll have to go to the Infirmary and show Sister Martha. [*With a sweet smile of affectionate trust.*] She's old and a little cranky, but I love her just the same, and she has things in her medicine chest that'll cure anything. She'll give me something to rub on my hands, and tell me to pray to the Blessed Virgin, and they'll be well again in no time.

6. In Shakespeare's *Hamlet* (ca. 1600), 4.5, Ophelia enters—apparently mad, but conveying a good deal of matter in her distracted words.

[*She forgets her hands and comes into the room, the wedding gown trailing on the floor. She glances around vaguely, her forehead puckered again.*]

Let me see. What did I come here to find? It's terrible, how absent-minded I've become. I'm always dreaming and forgetting.

TYRONE [*in a stifled voice*] What's that she's carrying, Edmund?

EDMUND [*dully*] Her wedding gown, I suppose.

TYRONE Christ!

[*He gets to his feet and stands directly in her path—in anguish.*]

Mary! Isn't it bad enough—? [*Controlling himself—gently persuasive*] Here, let me take it, dear. You'll only step on it and tear it and get it dirty dragging it on the floor. Then you'd be sorry afterwards.

[*She lets him take it, regarding him from somewhere far away within herself, without recognition, without either affection or animosity.*]

MARY [*with the shy politeness of a well-bred young girl toward an elderly gentleman who relieves her of a bundle*] Thank you. You are very kind. [*She regards the wedding gown with a puzzled interest.*] It's a wedding gown. It's very lovely, isn't it? [*A shadow crosses her face and she looks vaguely uneasy.*] I remember now. I found it in the attic hidden in a trunk. But I don't know what I wanted it for. I'm going to be a nun—that is, if I can only find— [*She looks around the room, her forehead puckered again.*] What is it I'm looking for? I know it's something I lost.

[*She moves back from* TYRONE, *aware of him now only as some obstacle in her path.*]

TYRONE [*in hopeless appeal*] Mary!

[*But it cannot penetrate her preoccupation. She doesn't seem to hear him. He gives up helplessly, shrinking into himself, even his defensive drunkenness taken from him, leaving him sick and sober. He sinks back on his chair, holding the wedding gown in his arms with an unconscious clumsy, protective gentleness.*]

JAMIE [*drops his hand from his face, his eyes on the tabletop. He has suddenly sobered up, too—dully.*] It's no good, Papa.

[*He recites from Swinburne's "A Leave-taking" and does it well, simply but with a bitter sadness.*]

"Let us rise up and part; she will not know.
Let us go seaward as the great winds go,
Full of blown sand and foam; what help is here?
There is no help, for all these things are so,
And all the world is bitter as a tear.
And how these things are, though ye strove to show,
She would not know."[7]

MARY [*looking around her*] Something I miss terribly. It can't be altogether lost.

[*She starts to move around in back of* JAMIE'S *chair.*]

JAMIE [*turns to look up into her face—and cannot help appealing pleadingly in his turn*] Mama!

7. The second stanza of the 1866 poem (he then quotes the first stanza, followed by the sixth, and final stanza).

[*She does not seem to hear. He looks away hopelessly.*]

Hell! What's the use? It's no good.

[*He recites from "A Leave-taking" again with increased bitterness.*]

"Let us go hence, my songs; she will not hear.
Let us go hence together without fear;
Keep silence now, for singing-time is over,
And over all old things and all things dear.
She loves not you nor me as all we love her.
Yea, though we sang as angels in her ear,
She would not hear."

MARY [*looking around her*] Something I need terribly. I remember when I had it I was never lonely nor afraid. I can't have lost it forever, I would die if I thought that. Because then there would be no hope.

[*She moves like a sleepwalker, around the back of* JAMIE's *chair, then forward toward left front, passing behind* EDMUND.]

EDMUND [*turns impulsively and grabs her arm. As he pleads he has the quality of a bewilderedly hurt little boy.*] Mama! It isn't a summer cold! I've got consumption!

MARY [*for a second he seems to have broken through to her. She trembles and her expression becomes terrified. She calls distractedly, as if giving a command to herself.*] No!

[*And instantly she is far away again. She murmurs gently but impersonally.*]

You must not try to touch me. You must not try to hold me. It isn't right, when I am hoping to be a nun.

[*He lets his hand drop from her arm. She moves left to the front end of the sofa beneath the windows and sits down, facing front, her hands folded in her lap, in a demure schoolgirlish pose.*]

JAMIE [*gives* EDMUND *a strange look of mingled pity and jealous gloating*] You damned fool. It's no good.

[*He recites again from the Swinburne poem.*]

"Let us go hence, go hence; she will not see.
Sing all once more together; surely she,
She too, remembering days and words that were,
Will turn a little toward us, sighing; but we,
We are hence, we are gone, as though we had not been there.
Nay, and though all men seeing had pity on me,
She would not see."

TYRONE [*trying to shake off his hopeless stupor*] Oh, we're fools to pay any attention. It's the damned poison. But I've never known her to drown herself in it as deep as this. [*Gruffly*] Pass me that bottle, Jamie. And stop reciting that damned morbid poetry. I won't have it in my house!

[JAMIE *pushes the bottle toward him. He pours a drink without disarranging the wedding gown he holds carefully over his other arm and on his lap, and shoves the bottle back.* JAMIE *pours his and passes the bottle to* EDMUND, *who, in turn, pours one.* TYRONE *lifts his glass and his sons follow suit mechanically, but before they can drink* MARY *speaks and they slowly lower their drinks to the table, forgetting them.*]

MARY [*staring dreamily before her. Her face looks extraordinarily youthful and innocent. The shyly eager, trusting smile is on her lips as she talks aloud to herself.*] I had a talk with Mother Elizabeth. She is so sweet and good. A saint on earth. I love her dearly. It may be sinful of me but I love her better than my own mother. Because she always understands, even before you say a word. Her kind blue eyes look right into your heart. You can't keep any secrets from her. You couldn't deceive her, even if you were mean enough to want to. [*She gives a little rebellious toss of her head—with girlish pique.*] All the same, I don't think she was so understanding this time. I told her I wanted to be a nun. I explained how sure I was of my vocation, that I had prayed to the Blessed Virgin to make me sure, and to find me worthy. I told Mother I had had a true vision when I was praying in the shrine of Our Lady of Lourdes,[8] on the little island in the lake. I said I knew, as surely as I knew I was kneeling there, that the Blessed Virgin had smiled and blessed me with her consent. But Mother Elizabeth told me I must be more sure than that, even, that I must prove it wasn't simply my imagination. She said, if I was so sure, then I wouldn't mind putting myself to a test by going home after I graduated, and living as other girls lived, going out to parties and dances and enjoying myself; and then if after a year or two I still felt sure, I could come back to see her and we would talk it over again. [*She tosses her head—indignantly.*] I never dreamed Holy Mother would give me such advice! I was really shocked. I said, of course, I would do anything she suggested, but I knew it was simply a waste of time. After I left her, I felt all mixed up, so I went to the shrine and prayed to the Blessed Virgin and found peace again because I knew she heard my prayer and would always love me and see no harm ever came to me so long as I never lost my faith in her.

[*She pauses and a look of growing uneasiness comes over her face. She passes a hand over her forehead as if brushing cobwebs from her brain—vaguely.*]

That was in the winter of senior year. Then in the spring something happened to me. Yes, I remember. I fell in love with James Tyrone and was so happy for a time.

[*She stares before her in a sad dream.* TYRONE *stirs in his chair.* EDMUND *and* JAMIE *remain motionless.*]

Curtain.

Tao House
September 20, 1940

8. The town of Lourdes, in southwestern France, has been a major destination for Christian pilgrims since 1858, when Bernadette Soubirous reported seeing apparitions of the Virgin Mary.

HAROLD PINTER

1930–2008

HAROLD Pinter, who won the Nobel Prize in Literature in 2005, is, in the opinion of many, the most important British dramatist since GEORGE BERNARD SHAW. Despite the obvious differences between the playwrights, they shared a similar relationship to the theater and society of their times. An Irishman and outsider to the English stage at the turn of the twentieth century, Shaw turned one of its dominant genres, the well-made play, into a mode of ironic social drama recalling the socially conscious realist plays of HENRIK IBSEN that he had championed. Likewise Pinter, a Jewish, working-class outsider from London's East End, remade the dominant conventions of the London stage after World War II—those of psychological realism and the drawing-room play—into vehicles of modern tragicomedy. Although both the playwright and his work lacked Shaw's didacticism, Pinter became a leading figure in the movement for a new British drama in the late 1950s and 1960s. More than those of any other playwright associated with that movement, Pinter's plays moved the British theater nearer to the Absurdist vision of SAMUEL BECKETT and the Continental avant-garde.

Beginning with his first play, *The Room* (1957), and continuing with *The Birthday Party* (1958), *The Caretaker* (1960), and *The Homecoming* (1965), Pinter developed a dramaturgy so distinctive it has earned the label "Pinteresque." Employing a mix of familiar and indecipherable dramatic events, the Pinteresque is associated with the following elements: a sparsely furnished room; an ongoing and precarious balance of power—physical, verbal, and psychological—between the inhabitants of the room; and the entrance of an outsider who disturbs the balance, provoking power struggles that issue in a violent or near-violent denouement. The term "Pinteresque" also refers to Pinter's characteristic use of dramatic language. In Pinter's plays, every line (and every silence) serves to maintain, disturb, or renegotiate the balance of power between characters. Speech often reflects a need for dominance and displaces a physical violence that would break out if that need were not contained or redirected. The dialogue is marked by patterns of verbal repetition, crosstalk (characters speaking "past" or "around" each other), outbursts of uneasy garrulity (trivial banter, jokes, anecdotes, philosophical ruminations), and, above all, silence. The patterns emerge from what Pinter called the "desire for verification"—the speaker's desire to have an assertion, and often his or her very sense of identity, affirmed by the other character. Silence is pivotal in this cat-and-mouse game as characters refuse or become unable to say what they think or feel, or to verify what their interlocutor has asserted. Early in his career, Pinter wrote: "The speech we hear . . . is a necessary avoidance, a violent, sly, and anguished or mocking smoke screen which keeps the other in its place. When true silence falls we are still left with the echo but are nearer nakedness. One way of looking at speech is to say that it is a constant stratagem to cover nakedness."

The facts of Pinter's early life provide clues to his obsession with violence and the power of language to embody and repress it. Born in 1930, Pinter grew up in Hackney, a run-down working-class area in London's East End. His father was a women's tailor, and his ancestors were Jews who had escaped pogroms in Poland and Ukraine. At the start of World War II, the ten-year-old Pinter was sent to the countryside to escape the German bombing of London, though he returned home a year later and experienced the Blitz firsthand. While Pinter was a teenager, a fascist movement led by Sir Oswald Mosley was active in the East End. Pinter and his friends, many of whom were Jewish, regularly encountered gangs of young toughs who were roaming the streets with broken milk bottles and threatening to attack Jews and Communists. They escaped assault by engaging gang members in verbal banter, using language to defer violence in a manner that would become typical in Pinter's plays.

During 1944–47 Pinter attended Hackney Downs, the local all-boys grammar school, where he was an accomplished runner, cricketer, and soccer player. He also wrote poetry, acted in productions of Shakespeare, and developed a close circle of friends who shared his interests in art and literature. After graduation, Pinter trained as an actor at the Royal Academy of Dramatic Art (RADA) and the Central School of Speech and Drama, both in London. In the 1950s, he acted in provincial repertory theaters, most notably Andrew McMaster's Shakespearean touring company; there he met his first wife, Vivien Merchant, who became a leading interpreter of his female characters in the 1960s and early 1970s. (They divorced in 1980, and Pinter married the novelist and historian Lady Antonia Fraser.) During this time, Pinter wrote steadily: poems, short stories, and a semi-autobiographical novel, *The Dwarfs* (published 1990). He turned to playwriting in 1957 after being invited to write a play for the Bristol University Drama Department. The resulting one act, *The Room*, was performed in the Sunday Times Student Drama Festival and received an enthusiastic review from the influential *Times* critic Harold Hobson. The review brought Pinter to the attention of the West End producer Michael Codron, who staged Pinter's first full-length play, *The Birthday Party*, in 1958. The daily reviewers (with the exception of Hobson) attacked the play, but it caught the interest of critics and directors in the United States and Germany as well as in Britain. In 1959–60 Pinter premiered two additional works: a one act, *The Dumb Waiter* (1959), and a second full-length play, *The Caretaker*. More naturalistic than his previous plays, *The Caretaker* was Pinter's first critical success, winning prestigious prizes in London and New York and solidifying his reputation as a major if controversial dramatist.

In the late 1950s and early 1960s, several other young authors—most notably John Osborne, Arnold Wesker, and John Arden—received widespread critical attention for plays that decried the rise of social affluence and complacency in Britain after the war. Dubbed the "Angry Young Men" by the press, these playwrights offered both innovative naturalistic depictions of British working-class life and epic historical dramas that used the past to mirror present-day political concerns. Unlike the Angry Young Men, Pinter never sought to lead a theatrical movement or advocate a new kind of drama. Pinter's early plays reflect the realities of working-class life in their settings, characters, and language; yet social class is not so much a dramatic focus of the plays as simply an aspect of the sense of identity over which Pinter's characters struggle. It was not until the 1980s that Pinter's plays expressed explicit political commitment. Even then, such plays as *One for the Road* (1984), *Mountain Language* (1988), and *Party Time* (1991) dramatize political torture and repression as metaphors for the essential dynamics of power at all levels of human relationship—physical, emotional, and psychological as well as political.

Both *The Room* and *The Birthday Party* present mundane situations that disintegrate into scenes of ominous danger. The latter opens with a breakfast at a seaside boarding house, as the landlady fusses over her husband and a young boarder. The domestic scene is disturbed when two men visit the boarder and interrogate him with unanswerable questions; in the end, they take him away. These plays turn a seemingly familiar situation into something mystifying and inexplicable: characters and their pasts are not revealed but instead are shown to be perplexing, beyond explanation. In *The Caretaker,* and to even greater effect in *The Homecoming* (1965), the tensions between the familiar and the inexplicable remain constant while the dramatic action grows more complex. In *The Caretaker,* a young man takes in an elderly homeless man to serve as "caretaker" of the apartment that the young man shares with his brother; the three men become entwined in a territorial struggle that ends when one of them is evicted and humiliated. In *The Homecoming,* a philosophy professor returns from an American university to his working-class home in London, where he introduces his father, brothers, and uncle to his English-born wife. The struggles that ensue among the men are heightened by sexual tension between the men and the wife, by the couple's deployment of the higher social position to which they have risen, and by the tough "male" occupations (boxer, pimp) of the brothers. In both plays, the territorial struggle for dominance within the room is wedded to intricate psychological encounters that occur over issues of class, education, age, sex, and gender.

This deepening of Pinter's psychological exploration in *The Caretaker* and *The Homecoming* anticipated the tone and focus of Pinter's major plays of the 1970s: *OLD TIMES* (1971), *No Man's Land* (1975), and *Betrayal* (1978). Abandoning the physically menacing environments of the earlier works, these plays dwell more deeply on the remembered past and the importance of memory to self-identity. Though they are grounded in realistic portrayals of the English middle class, the plays unfold in a fragmented, dreamlike manner. *Betrayal,* for example, traces the relationship between two old university friends and a woman who is the wife of one and the lover of the other. The play presents the development of these relationships over many years but does so in reverse chronological order; it thereby highlights the duplicities, both small and large, on which friendship, marriage, and infidelity are founded. Here as in *Old Times* and *No Man's Land,* the exploration of memory, time, and subjectivity affects the tone and style of Pinter's writing: minimalist dialogue is refined into lyricism, and subtextual indications of repressed violence are redirected into an acute sense of human loss and aloneness. In their dramatic structure, the plays use the outward conventions of realism—"real" behavior and settings—to dramatize a recognizable reality that ultimately turns mystifying. Here, though, the mystification derives less from contradictory statements and actions about the past that are difficult to verify or reconcile than from the past's wounding impact on the present.

Old Times displays the features of Pinter's memory plays in their purest form. The play has an apparently realistic setting—a converted farmhouse with minimal furniture and French windows upstage. It is the home of a middle-aged, middle-class husband and wife, Deeley and Kate, who have been married for an unspecified time. When the lights first come up, the couple sits downstage, anticipating a visit from Kate's oldest friend, Anna, whom Kate has not seen in many years. The scene of reminiscence is perplexing in several ways, however. First, Kate's replies to Deeley's questions about Anna are terse, strangely lacking in specific detail about her "best and oldest" friend. The only detail Kate recalls is that Anna "was a thief. She used to steal things," including Kate's underwear. The image stands out from her otherwise laconic replies, both striking and puzzling.

Intertwined with these replies are pauses and silences, which seem to intimate something forgotten, or something denied by or cut off from memory. Also unsettling is the upstage presence of a figure looking out the window in dim light with her back to Kate and Deeley. When Kate and Deeley's opening dialogue ends, the figure reveals itself as Anna, the friend who has come to visit. She turns quickly downstage, speaking a richly detailed monologue recollecting Kate's and her life together as young roommates in London. The monologue, it becomes apparent, is part of the characters' after-dinner conversation during Anna's visit. Its vividness contrasts sharply with Kate's memory of the past; her silence and Anna's upstage presence in that scene emerge as metaphors for a past whose effects are deeply felt in the present, yet whose origins remain out of memory's reach.

The opening moments of *Old Times*—the contrast between spare and abundant recollection, the recurring silences, and the presence of a past forcefully but differently recalled by the characters—encapsulate the action of the play as a whole. As the evening unfolds, Anna and Deeley vividly describe their times with Kate, who continues to say little or nothing. The dialogue is charged with unspoken sexual competition over Kate, as well as with yearning for a past that cannot be regained. Dialogue gives way to intense monologues of recollection, whose details suggest that the characters have experienced some of the same events but are either unable or unwilling to acknowledge that fact or that their perspectives on them conflict. As memories collide, an image of the past as collage takes shape: no single version of what took place is absolutely accurate. Indeed, it is hard to know if some events even "happened" at all. As Anna ob-

Scene from the original 1971 production of *Old Times* by the Royal Shakespeare Company at the Aldwych Theatre, London. From left to right: Colin Blakely as Deeley, Dorothy Tutin as Kate, and Vivien Merchant as Anna.

serves, "There are some things one remembers even though they may never have happened. There are things I remember which may never have happened but as I recall them so they take place." Its indeterminate outlines make the past an arena in which characters struggle to control the account of what happened. In their game of "Odd Man Out" (a title taken from a 1947 film that Deeley recalls watching when he first saw Kate), characters can exclude or marginalize each other by "remembering" the past in certain ways.

Presented within a context that appears realistic on the surface, though lacking the explanatory background of traditional psychological realism, *Old Times* might seem to be a puzzle that could be solved if only one could get the right perspective on the events dramatized and described. Yet what distinguishes the play is its fragmentation, at once dreamlike and well-grounded as it dramatizes the elusive and inexorable force of the past in the present. Here Pinter acknowledges Samuel Beckett's influence on his work. Beckett's connection to the Theatre of the Absurd is reflected in his characters' drive to establish a sense of self, of coherent memory and meaningful existence, in the face of a universe that lacks ultimate meaning. In *Old Times,* Pinter explores an essential part of that drive—the use of memory to make meaning of one's life—from the perspective of upper-middle-class characters who are endeavoring to find professional, domestic, and sexual fulfillment.

Together with *No Man's Land* and *Betrayal, Old Times* has often been described as "cinematic"—making theatrical use of time-jumping and time-eliding strategies more common to film, and thus exhibiting some of the impact of Pinter's work as a screenwriter on his playwriting. That career included screen adaptations of his plays and of novels by other authors (notably, John Fowles's *The French Lieutenant's Woman* [1969; film, 1981] and Margaret Atwood's *The Handmaid's Tale* [1985; film, 1990]). In bringing works of fiction to the screen, the playwright exploited the structural flexibility of film to find a cinematic equivalent of the novel's complex point of view and use of time. Pinter's foremost achievement in this regard is his adaptation of *Remembrance of Things Past* (1913–27), Marcel Proust's fictional reminiscence of childhood, love, and sexual awakening, on which Pinter worked in the years between *Old Times* and *No Man's Land*; it was never filmed. And while those plays were informed by Pinter's experience with film, so too, conversely, his interest in Proust's novel was partly driven by the same concerns that found voice in his own memory plays.

Pinter's stage plays of the 1990s—including *Moonlight* (1993), *Ashes to Ashes* (1996), and *Celebration* (1999)—revisit the subject of memory while sometimes conveying the political overtones that marked his work in the 1980s. As these plays demonstrate, the "Pinteresque" is a resilient and adaptable dramatic mode, and Pinter's dramaturgy of minimal words and maximal silence continues, like that of Beckett, to speak to the anxieties of contemporary life.

ART BORRECCA

Old Times

CHARACTERS

DEELEY, KATE, ANNA — All in their early forties

A converted farmhouse.

Act 1

A long window up center. Bedroom door up left.
Front door up right.
Spare modern furniture.
Two sofas. An armchair.
Autumn. Night.

[*Light dim. Three figures discerned.*]
[DEELEY *slumped in armchair, still.*
KATE *curled on a sofa, still.*
ANNA *standing at the window, looking out.*]
[*Silence.*]
[*Lights up on* DEELEY *and* KATE, *smoking cigarettes.*]
[ANNA'*s figure remains still in dim light at the window.*]

KATE [*reflectively*] Dark.

[*Pause.*]

DEELEY Fat or thin?

KATE Fuller than me. I think.

[*Pause.*]

DEELEY She was then?

KATE I think so.

DEELEY She may not be now.

[*Pause.*]

Was she your best friend?

KATE Oh, what does that mean?

DEELEY What?

KATE The word friend . . . when you look back . . . all that time.

DEELEY Can't you remember what you felt?

[*Pause.*]

KATE It is a very long time.

DEELEY But you remember her. She remembers you. Or why would she be coming here tonight?

KATE I suppose because she remembers me.

[*Pause.*]

DEELEY Did you *think* of her as your best friend?

KATE She was my only friend.

DEELEY Your best and only.

KATE My one and only.

[*Pause.*]

If you have only one of something you can't say it's the best of anything.

DEELEY Because you have nothing to compare it with?

KATE Mmnn.

[*Pause.*]

DEELEY [*smiling*] She was incomparable.

KATE Oh, I'm sure she wasn't.

[*Pause.*]

DEELEY I didn't know you had so few friends.

KATE I had none. None at all. Except her.

DEELEY Why her?

KATE I don't know.

[*Pause.*]

She was a thief. She used to steal things.

DEELEY Who from?

KATE Me.

DEELEY What things?

KATE Bits and pieces. Underwear.

[DEELEY *chuckles.*]

DEELEY Will you remind her?

KATE Oh . . . I don't think so.

[*Pause.*]

DEELEY Is that what attracted you to her?

KATE What?

DEELEY The fact that she was a thief.

KATE No.

[*Pause.*]

DEELEY Are you looking forward to seeing her?

KATE No.

DEELEY I am. I shall be very interested.

KATE In what?

DEELEY In you. I'll be watching you.

KATE Me? Why?

DEELEY To see if she's the same person.

KATE You think you'll find that out through me?

DEELEY Definitely.

[*Pause.*]

KATE I hardly remember her. I've almost totally forgotten her.

[*Pause.*]

DEELEY Any idea what she drinks?

KATE None.

DEELEY She may be a vegetarian.

KATE Ask her.

DEELEY It's too late. You've cooked your casserole.

[*Pause.*]

Why isn't she married? I mean, why isn't she bringing her husband?

KATE Ask her.

DEELEY Do I have to ask her everything?

KATE Do you want me to ask your questions for you?

DEELEY No. Not at all.

[*Pause.*]

KATE Of course she's married.

DEELEY How do you know?

KATE Everyone's married.

DEELEY Then why isn't she bringing her husband?

KATE Isn't she?

[*Pause.*]

DEELEY Did she mention a husband in her letter?

KATE No.

DEELEY What do you think he'd be like? I mean, what sort of man would she have married? After all, she was your best — your only — friend. You must have some idea. What kind of man would he be?

KATE I have no idea.

DEELEY Haven't you any curiosity?

KATE You forget. I know her.

DEELEY You haven't seen her for twenty years.

KATE You've never seen her. There's a difference.

[*Pause.*]

DEELEY At least the casserole is big enough for four.

KATE You said she was a vegetarian.

[*Pause.*]

DEELEY Did *she* have many friends?

KATE Oh . . . the normal amount, I suppose.

DEELEY Normal? What's normal? You had none.

KATE One.

DEELEY Is that normal?

[*Pause.*]

She . . . had quite a lot of friends, did she?

KATE Hundreds.

DEELEY You met them?

KATE Not all, I think. But after all, we were living together. There were visitors, from time to time. I met them.

DEELEY Her visitors?

KATE What?

DEELEY Her visitors. Her friends. You had no friends.

KATE Her friends, yes.

DEELEY You met them.

[*Pause.*]

[*Abruptly*] You lived together?

KATE Of course.

DEELEY I didn't know that.

KATE Didn't you?

DEELEY You never told me that. I thought you just knew each other.

KATE We did.

DEELEY But in fact you lived with each other.

KATE Of course we did. How else would she steal my underwear from me? In the street?

[*Pause.*]

DEELEY I knew you had shared with someone at one time . . .

[*Pause.*]

But I didn't know it was her.

KATE Of course it was.

[*Pause.*]

DEELEY Anyway, none of this matters.

[ANNA *turns from the window, speaking, and moves down to them, eventually sitting on the second sofa.*]

ANNA Queuing[1] all night, the rain, do you remember? my goodness, the Albert Hall, Covent Garden,[2] what did we eat? to look back, half the night, to do things we loved, we were young then of course, but what stamina, and to work in the morning, and to a concert, or the opera, or the ballet, that night, you haven't forgotten? and then riding on top of the bus down Kensington High Street,[3] and the bus conductors, and then dashing for the matches for the gasfire and then I suppose scrambled eggs, or did we? who cooked? both giggling and chattering, both huddling to the heat, then bed and sleeping, and all the hustle and bustle in the morning, rushing for the bus again for work, lunchtimes in Green Park,[4] exchanging all our news, with our very own sandwiches, innocent girls, innocent secretaries, and then the night to come, and goodness knows what excitement in store, I mean the sheer expectation of it all, the looking-forwardness of it all, and so poor, but to be poor and young, and a girl, in London then . . . and the cafés we found, almost private ones, weren't they? where artists and writers and sometimes actors collected, and others with dancers, we sat hardly breathing with our coffee, heads bent, so as not to be seen, so as not to disturb, so as not to distract, and listened and listened to all those words, all those cafés and all those people, creative undoubtedly, and does it still exist I wonder? do you know? can you tell me?

[*Slight pause.*]

DEELEY We rarely get to London.

[KATE *stands, goes to a small table and pours coffee from a pot.*]

KATE Yes, I remember.

[*She adds milk and sugar to one cup and takes it to* ANNA. *She takes a black coffee to* DEELEY *and then sits with her own.*]

1. That is, waiting in a queue or line (British).
2. The Royal Opera House, home of the Royal Opera and the Royal Ballet, located in the central London district of Covent Garden (an area filled with entertainment venues and restaurants). *Albert Hall:* the Royal Albert Concert Hall, located in Kensington, a fashionable residential and shopping district in West London.
3. The main thoroughfare in Kensington.
4. A royal park in London, located north of Buckingham Palace.

DEELEY [*to* ANNA] Do you drink brandy?

ANNA I would love some brandy.

[DEELEY *pours brandy for all and hands the glasses. He remains standing with his own.*]

ANNA Listen. What silence. Is it always as silent?

DEELEY It's quite silent here, yes. Normally.

[*Pause.*]

You can hear the sea sometimes if you listen very carefully.

ANNA How wise you were to choose this part of the world, and how sensible and courageous of you both to stay permanently in such a silence.

DEELEY My work takes me away quite often, of course. But Kate stays here.

ANNA No one who lived here would want to go far. I would not want to go far, I would be afraid of going far, lest when I returned the house would be gone.

DEELEY Lest?

ANNA What?

DEELEY The word lest. Haven't heard it for a long time.

[*Pause.*]

KATE Sometimes I walk to the sea. There aren't many people. It's a long beach.

[*Pause.*]

ANNA But I would miss London, nevertheless. But of course I was a girl in London. We were girls together.

DEELEY I wish I had known you both then.

ANNA Do you?

DEELEY Yes.

[DEELEY *pours more brandy for himself.*]

ANNA You have a wonderful casserole.

DEELEY What?

ANNA I mean wife. So sorry. A wonderful wife.

DEELEY Ah.

ANNA I was referring to the casserole. I was referring to your wife's cooking.

DEELEY You're not a vegetarian, then?

ANNA No. Oh no.

DEELEY Yes, you need good food in the country, substantial food, to keep you going, all the air . . . you know.

[*Pause.*]

KATE Yes, I quite like those kind of things, doing it.

ANNA What kind of things?

KATE Oh, you know, that sort of thing.

[*Pause.*]

DEELEY Do you mean cooking?

KATE All that thing.

ANNA We weren't terribly elaborate in cooking, didn't have the time, but every so often dished up an incredibly enormous stew, guzzled the lot, and then more often than not sat up half the night reading Yeats.[5]

[*Pause.*]

5. William Butler Yeats (1865–1939), Irish poet, dramatist, and Nobel laureate.

[*To herself*] Yes. Every so often. More often than not.

[ANNA *stands, walks to the window.*]

And the sky is so still.

[*Pause.*]

Can you see that tiny ribbon of light? Is that the sea? Is that the horizon?

DEELEY You live on a very different coast.

ANNA Oh, very different. I live on a volcanic island.

DEELEY I know it.

ANNA Oh, do you?

DEELEY I've been there.

[*Pause.*]

ANNA I'm so delighted to be here.

DEELEY It's nice I know for Katey to see you. She hasn't many friends.

ANNA She has you.

DEELEY She hasn't made many friends, although there's been every opportunity for her to do so.

ANNA Perhaps she has all she wants.

DEELEY She lacks curiosity.

ANNA Perhaps she's happy.

[*Pause.*]

KATE Are you talking about me?

DEELEY Yes.

ANNA She was always a dreamer.

DEELEY She likes taking long walks. All that. You know. Raincoat on. Off down the lane, hands deep in pockets. All that kind of thing.

[ANNA *turns to look at* KATE.]

ANNA Yes.

DEELEY Sometimes I take her face in my hands and look at it.

ANNA Really?

DEELEY Yes, I look at it, holding it in my hands. Then I kind of let it go, take my hands away, leave it floating.

KATE My head is quite fixed. I have it on.

DEELEY [*to* ANNA] It just floats away.

ANNA She was always a dreamer.

[ANNA *sits.*]

Sometimes, walking, in the park, I'd say to her, you're dreaming, you're dreaming, wake up, what are you dreaming? and she'd look round at me, flicking her hair, and look at me as if I were part of her dream.

[*Pause.*]

One day she said to me, I've slept through Friday. No you haven't, I said, what do you mean? I've slept right through Friday, she said. But today is Friday, I said, it's been Friday all day, it's now Friday night, you haven't slept through Friday. Yes I have, she said, I've slept right through it, today is Saturday.

DEELEY You mean she literally didn't know what day it was?

ANNA No.

KATE Yes I did. It was Saturday.

[*Pause.*]

DEELEY What month are we in?

KATE September.

[*Pause.*]

DEELEY We're forcing her to think. We must see you more often. You're a healthy influence.

ANNA But she was always a charming companion.

DEELEY Fun to live with?

ANNA Delightful.

DEELEY Lovely to look at, delightful to know.[6]

ANNA Ah, those songs. We used to play them, all of them, all the time, late at night, lying on the floor, lovely old things. Sometimes I'd look at her face, but she was quite unaware of my gaze.

DEELEY Gaze?

ANNA What?

DEELEY The word gaze. Don't hear it very often.

ANNA Yes, quite unaware of it. She was totally absorbed.

DEELEY In Lovely to look at, delightful to know?

KATE [*to* ANNA] I don't know that song. Did we have it?

DEELEY [*singing, to* KATE] You're lovely to look at, delightful to know . . .

ANNA Oh we did. Yes, of course. We had them all.

DEELEY [*singing*] Blue moon, I see you standing alone . . . [7]

ANNA [*singing*] The way you comb your hair . . . [8]

DEELEY [*singing*] Oh no they can't take that away from me . . .

ANNA [*singing*] Oh but you're lovely, with your smile so warm . . . [9]

DEELEY [*singing*] I've got a woman crazy for me. She's funny that way.[1]

[*Slight pause.*]

ANNA [*singing*] You are the promised kiss of springtime . . . [2]

DEELEY [*singing*]

And someday I'll know that moment divine,
When all the things you are, are mine!

[*Slight pause.*]

ANNA [*singing*]

I get no kick from champagne,[3]
Mere alcohol doesn't thrill me at all,
So tell me why should it be true—

6. From "Lovely to Look At" (music by Jerome Kern, lyrics by Dorothy Fields and Jimmy McHugh), a song from the movie musical *Roberta* (1935).

7. From "Blue Moon" (music by Richard Rogers, lyrics by Lorenz Hart), an American popular ballad published in 1934; the line actually reads "Blue moon, / You saw me standing alone."

8. This and the following line are from "They Can't Take That Away from Me" (music by George Gershwin, lyrics by Ira Gershwin), a song from the movie musical *Shall We Dance?* (1937).

9. From "The Way You Look Tonight" (music by Jerome Kern, lyrics by Dorothy Fields), a song from the movie musical *Swing Time* (1936); the song won that year's Academy Award for Best Original Song.

1. From "She's Funny That Way" (1928; music by Neil Moret, lyrics by Richard A. Whiting). The song became Frank Sinatra's radio theme song.

2. This and following two lines are from "All the Things You Are" (music by Jerome Kern, lyrics by Oscar Hammerstein II), a song from the Broadway musical *Very Warm for May* (1939).

3. This and the following three lines are from "I Get a Kick Out of You" (music and lyrics by Cole Porter), a song from the movie musical *Anything Goes* (1934).

DEELEY [*singing*]
That I get a kick out of you?
[*Pause.*]

ANNA [*singing*]
They asked me how I knew[4]
My true love was true,
I of course replied,
Something here inside
Cannot be denied.

DEELEY [*singing*]
When a lovely flame dies . . .

ANNA [*singing*]
Smoke gets in your eyes.
[*Pause.*]

DEELEY [*singing*]
The sigh of midnight trains in empty stations . . . [5]
[*Pause.*]

ANNA [*singing*]
The park at evening when the bell has sounded . . .
[*Pause.*]

DEELEY [*singing*] The smile of Garbo[6] and the scent of roses . . .

ANNA [*singing*] The waiters whistling as the last bar closes . . .

DEELEY [*singing*] Oh, how the ghost of you clings . . .
[*Pause.*]

They don't make them like that anymore.
[*Silence.*]

What happened to me was this. I popped into a fleapit to see Odd Man Out.[7] Some bloody awful summer afternoon, walking in no direction. I remember thinking there was something familiar about the neighbourhood and suddenly recalled that it was in this very neighbourhood that my father bought me my first tricycle, the only tricycle in fact I ever possessed. Anyway, there was the bicycle shop and there was this fleapit showing Odd Man Out and there were two usherettes standing in the foyer and one of them was stroking her breasts and the other one was saying 'dirty bitch' and the one stroking her breasts was saying 'mmnnn' with a very sensual relish and smiling at her fellow usherette, so I marched in on this excruciatingly hot summer afternoon in the middle of nowhere and watched Odd Man

4. This and following six lines are from "Smoke Gets in Your Eyes" (music by Jerome Kern, lyrics by Otto A. Harbach), a song from the operetta *Roberta* (1933), from which the 1935 Hollywood musical was adapted.

5. This and the following four lines are from "These Foolish Things (Remind Me of You)" (music by Jack Strachey and Harry Link, lyrics by Holt Marvell), from the British musical revue *Spread It Around* (1935); the song became a U.S. hit the following year.

6. Greta Garbo (1905–1990), the Swedish-born actor who became one of Hollywood's most famous movie stars.

7. A 1947 film directed by Carol Reed. In addition to the English actor James Mason (1909–1984), who played the lead, *Odd Man Out* features Robert Newton (1905–1956), also English, and F. J. McCormick (1889–1947), an Irish actor better known for his work on stage with the Abbey Theatre than for his few roles in movies.

Out and thought Robert Newton was fantastic. And I still think he was fantastic. And I would commit murder for him, even now. And there was only one other person in the cinema, one other person in the whole of the whole cinema, and there she is. And there she was, very dim, very still, placed more or less I would say at the dead center of the auditorium. I was off-center and have remained so. And I left when the film was over, noticing, even though James Mason was dead, that the first usherette appeared to be utterly exhausted, and I stood for a moment in the sun, thinking I suppose about something and then this girl came out and I think looked about her and I said wasn't Robert Newton fantastic, and she said something or other, Christ knows what, but looked at me, and I thought Jesus this is it, I've made a catch, this is a trueblue pickup, and when we had sat down in the café with tea she looked into her cup and then up at me and told me she thought Robert Newton was remarkable. So it was Robert Newton who brought us together and it is only Robert Newton who can tear us apart.

[*Pause.*]

ANNA F. J. McCormick was good too.

DEELEY I know F. J. McCormick was good too. But he didn't bring us together.

[*Pause.*]

DEELEY You've seen the film then?

ANNA Yes.

DEELEY When?

ANNA Oh . . . long ago.

[*Pause*]

DEELEY [*to* KATE] Remember that film?

KATE Oh yes. Very well.

[*Pause.*]

DEELEY I think I am right in saying the next time we met we held hands. I held her cool hand, as she walked by me, and I said something which made her smile, and she looked at me, didn't you, flicking her hair back, and I thought she was even more fantastic than Robert Newton.

[*Pause.*]

And then at a slightly later stage our naked bodies met, hers cool, warm, highly agreeable, and I wondered what Robert Newton would think of this. What would he think of this I wondered as I touched her profoundly all over. [*To* ANNA] What do you think he'd think?

ANNA I never met Robert Newton but I do know I know what you mean. There are some things one remembers even though they may never have happened. There are things I remember which may never have happened but as I recall them so they take place.

DEELEY *What?*

ANNA This man crying in our room. One night late I returned and found him sobbing, his hand over his face, sitting in the armchair, all crumpled in the armchair and Katey sitting on the bed with a mug of coffee and no one spoke to me, no one spoke, no one looked up. There was nothing I could do. I undressed and switched out the light and got into my bed, the curtains were thin, the light from the street came in, Katey still, on her bed, the man sobbed, the light came in, it flicked the wall, there was a slight breeze, the curtains occasionally shook, there was nothing but sobbing, suddenly it stopped. The man came over to me, quickly, looked down at me, but I would have absolutely nothing to do with him, nothing.

[*Pause.*]

No, no, I'm quite wrong . . . he didn't move quickly . . . that's quite wrong . . . he moved . . . very slowly, the light was bad, and stopped. He stood in the center of the room. He looked at us both, at our beds. Then he turned towards me. He approached my bed. He bent down over me. But I would have nothing to do with him, absolutely nothing.

[*Pause.*]

DEELEY What kind of man was he?

ANNA But after a while I heard him go out. I heard the front door close, and footsteps in the street, then silence, then the footsteps fade away, and then silence.

[*Pause.*]

But then sometime later in the night I woke up and looked across the room to her bed and saw two shapes.

DEELEY He'd come back!

ANNA He was lying across her lap on her bed.

DEELEY A man in the dark across my wife's lap?

[*Pause.*]

ANNA But then in the early morning . . . he had gone.

DEELEY Thank Christ for that.

ANNA It was as if he had never been.

DEELEY Of course he'd been. He went twice and came once.[8]

[*Pause.*]

Well, what an exciting story that was.

[*Pause.*]

What did he look like, this fellow?

ANNA Oh, I never saw his face clearly. I don't know.

DEELEY But was he—?

[KATE *stands. She goes to a small table, takes a cigarette from a box and lights it. She looks down at* ANNA.]

KATE You talk of me as if I were dead.

ANNA No, no, you weren't dead, you were so lively, so animated, you used to laugh—

DEELEY Of course you did. I made you smile myself, didn't I? walking along the street, holding hands. You smiled fit to bust.

ANNA Yes, she could be so . . . animated.

DEELEY Animated is no word for it. When she smiled . . . how can I describe it?

ANNA Her eyes lit up.

DEELEY I couldn't have put it better myself.

[DEELEY *stands, goes to cigarette box, picks it up, smiles at* KATE. KATE *looks at him, watches him light a cigarette, takes the box from him, crosses to* ANNA, *offers her a cigarette.* ANNA *takes one.*]

8. An obvious sexual pun.

ANNA You weren't dead. Ever. In any way.

KATE I said you talk about me as if I *am* dead. Now.

ANNA How can you say that? How can you say that, when I'm looking at you now, seeing you so shyly poised over me, looking down at me—

DEELEY Stop that!

[*Pause.*]

[KATE *sits.*

DEELEY *pours a drink.*]

DEELEY Myself I was a student then, juggling with my future, wondering should I bejasus[9] saddle myself with a slip of a girl not long out of her swaddling clothes whose only claim to virtue was silence but who lacked any sense of fixedness, any sense of decisiveness, but was compliant only to the shifting winds, with which she went, but not *the* winds, and certainly not my winds, such as they are, but I suppose winds that only she understood, and that of course with no understanding whatsoever, at least as I understand the word, at least that's the way I figured it. A classic female figure, I said to myself, or is it a classic female posture, one way or the other long outworn.

[*Pause.*]

That's the position as I saw it then. I mean, that is my categorical pronouncement on the position as I saw it then. Twenty years ago.

[*Silence.*]

ANNA When I heard that Katey was married my heart leapt with joy.

DEELEY How did the news reach you?

ANNA From a friend.

[*Pause.*]

Yes, it leapt with joy. Because you see I knew she never did things loosely or carelessly, recklessly. Some people throw a stone into a river to see if the water's too cold for jumping, others, a few others, will always wait for the ripples before they will jump.

DEELEY Some people do *what?* [*To* KATE] What did she say?

ANNA And I knew that Katey would always wait not just for the first emergence of ripple but for the ripples to pervade and pervade the surface, for of course as you know ripples on the surface indicate a shimmering in depth down through every particle of water down to the river bed, but even when she felt that happen, when she was assured it was happening, she still might not jump. But in this case she did jump and I knew therefore she had fallen in love truly and was glad. And I deduced it must also have happened to you.

DEELEY You mean the ripples?

ANNA If you like.

DEELEY Do men ripple too?

ANNA Some, I would say.

DEELEY I see.

[*Pause.*]

ANNA And later when I found out the kind of man you were I was doubly delighted because I knew Katey had always been interested in the arts.

KATE I was interested once in the arts, but I can't remember now which ones they were.

9. That is, "by Jesus" (said with an Irish brogue).

ANNA Don't tell me you've forgotten our days at the Tate[1] and how we explored London and all the old churches and all the old buildings, I mean those that were left from the bombing, in the City and south of the river in Lambeth and Greenwich.[2] Oh my goodness. Oh yes. And the Sunday papers! I could never get her away from the review pages. She ravished them, and then insisted we visit that gallery, or this theatre, or that chamber concert, but of course there was so much, so much to see and to hear, in lovely London then, that sometimes we missed things, or had no more money, and so missed some things. For example, I remember one Sunday she said to me, looking up from the paper, come quick, quick, come with me quickly, and we seized our handbags and went, on a bus, to some totally obscure, some totally unfamiliar district and, almost alone, saw a wonderful film called Odd Man Out.

[*Silence.*]

DEELEY Yes, I do quite a bit of traveling in my job.

ANNA Do you enjoy it?

DEELEY Enormously. Enormously.

ANNA Do you go far?

DEELEY I travel the globe in my job.

ANNA And poor Katey when you're away? What does she do?

[ANNA *looks at* KATE.]

KATE Oh, I continue.

ANNA Is he away for long periods?

KATE I think, sometimes. Are you?

ANNA You leave your wife for such long periods? How can you?

DEELEY I have to do a lot of traveling in my job.

ANNA [*to* KATE] I think I must come and keep you company when he's away.

DEELEY Won't your husband miss you?

ANNA Of course. But he would understand.

DEELEY Does he understand now?

ANNA Of course.

DEELEY We had a vegetarian dish prepared for him.

ANNA He's not a vegetarian. In fact he's something of a gourmet. We live in a rather fine villa and have done so for many years. It's very high up, on the cliffs.

DEELEY You eat well up there, eh?

ANNA I would say so, yes.

DEELEY Yes, I know Sicily slightly. Just slightly. Taormina.[3] Do you live in Taormina?

ANNA Just outside.

1. The Tate Gallery, a national museum of British and foreign art, located in central London.
2. Two boroughs of southeast London: Lambeth, an inner borough, is the site of Lambeth Palace (the official London residence of the archbishop of Canterbury), which dates in part to the 15th century; Greenwich, to its east, contains many Georgian and Victorian buildings as well as the historic Royal Observatory and the Royal Naval College. Both areas were extensively damaged during Germany's bombing of England early in World War II (the Blitz).
3. A town in eastern Sicily; located high on a ridge, it has been a popular tourist destination since the 19th century.

DEELEY Just outside, yes. Very high up. Yes, I've probably caught a glimpse of your villa.

[*Pause.*]

My work took me to Sicily. My work concerns itself with life all over, you see, in every part of the globe. With people all over the globe. I use the word globe because the word world possesses emotional political sociological and psychological pretensions and resonances which I prefer as a matter of choice to do without, or shall I say to steer clear of, or if you like to reject. How's the yacht?

ANNA Oh, very well.

DEELEY Captain steer a straight course?

ANNA As straight as we wish, when we wish it.

DEELEY Don't you find England damp, returning?

ANNA Rather beguilingly so.

DEELEY Rather beguilingly so? [*To himself*] What the hell does she mean by that?

[*Pause.*]

Well, any time your husband finds himself in this direction my little wife will be only too glad to put the old pot on the old gas stove and dish him up something luscious if not voluptuous. No trouble.

[*Pause.*]

I suppose his business interests kept him from making the trip. What's his name? Gian Carlo or Per Paulo?[4]

KATE [*to* ANNA] Do you have marble floors?

ANNA Yes.

KATE Do you walk in bare feet on them?

ANNA Yes. But I wear sandals on the terrace, because it can be rather severe on the soles.

KATE The sun, you mean? The heat.

ANNA Yes.

DEELEY I had a great crew in Sicily. A marvelous cameraman. Irving Shultz. Best in the business. We took a pretty austere look at the women in black. The little old women in black. I wrote the film and directed it. My name is Orson Welles.[5]

KATE [*to* ANNA] Do you drink orange juice on your terrace in the morning, and bullshots[6] at sunset, and look down at the sea?

ANNA Sometimes, yes.

DEELEY As a matter of fact I am at the top of my profession, as a matter of fact, and I have indeed been associated with substantial numbers of articulate and sensitive people, mainly prostitutes of all kinds.

KATE [*to* ANNA] And do you like the Sicilian people?

4. Common Italian names, though they also bring to mind the actor Giancarlo Giannini (b. 1942) and the writer and director Pier Paolo Pasolini (1922–1975).

5. The American actor, director, and producer (1915–1985); at the end of his film *The Magnificent Ambersons* (1942), he narrates the credits, which include the lines "I wrote the script and directed it. My name is Orson Welles." *Women in black:* in Sicily, a largely rural and conservative region of Italy, it is still common for women, once widowed, to dress in black for the rest of their lives.

6. Drinks made with vodka and bouillon.

DEELEY I've been there. There's nothing more to see, there's nothing more to investigate, nothing. There's nothing more in Sicily to investigate.

KATE [*to* ANNA] Do you like the Sicilian people?

[ANNA *stares at her.*]

[*Silence.*]

ANNA [*quietly*] Don't let's go out tonight, don't let's go anywhere tonight, let's stay in. I'll cook something, you can wash your hair, you can relax, we'll put on some records.

KATE Oh, I don't know. We could go out.

ANNA Why do you want to go out?

KATE We could walk across the park.

ANNA The park is dirty at night, all sorts of horrible people, men hiding behind trees and women with terrible voices, they scream at you as you go past, and people come out suddenly from behind trees and bushes and there are shadows everywhere and there are policemen, and you'll have a horrible walk, and you'll see all the traffic and the noise of the traffic and you'll see all the hotels, and you know you hate looking through all those swing doors, you hate it, to see all that, all those people in the lights in the lobbies all talking and moving . . . and all the chandeliers . . .

[*Pause.*]

You'll only want to come home if you go out. You'll want to run home . . . and into your room. . . .

[*Pause.*]

KATE What shall we do then?

ANNA Stay in. Shall I read to you? Would you like that?

KATE I don't know.

[*Pause.*]

ANNA Are you hungry?

KATE No.

DEELEY Hungry? After that casserole?

[*Pause.*]

KATE What shall I wear tomorrow? I can't make up my mind.

ANNA Wear your green.

KATE I haven't got the right top.

ANNA You have. You have your turquoise blouse.

KATE Do they go?

ANNA Yes, they do go. Of course they go.

KATE I'll try it.

[*Pause.*]

ANNA Would you like me to ask someone over?

KATE Who?

ANNA Charley . . . or Jake?

KATE I don't like Jake.

ANNA Well, Charley . . . or . . .

KATE Who?

ANNA McCabe.

[*Pause.*]

KATE I'll think about it in the bath.

ANNA Shall I run your bath for you?

KATE [*standing*] No. I'll run it myself tonight.

[KATE *slowly walks to the bedroom door, goes out, closes it.*]

[DEELEY *stands looking at* ANNA.

ANNA *turns her head towards him.*]

[*They look at each other.*]

Fade.

Act 2

The bedroom.

A long window up center. Door to bathroom up left. Door to sitting-room up right.

Two divans. An armchair.

The divans and armchair are disposed in precisely the same relation to each other as the furniture in the first act, but in reversed positions.

[*Lights dim.* ANNA *discerned sitting on divan. Faint glow from glass panel in bathroom door.*]

[*Silence.*]

[*Lights up. The other door opens.* DEELEY *comes in with tray.*]

[DEELEY *comes into the room, places the tray on a table.*]

DEELEY Here we are. Good and hot. Good and strong and hot. You prefer it white with sugar, I believe?

ANNA Please.

DEELEY [*pouring*] Good and strong and hot with white and sugar.

[*He hands her the cup.*]

Like the room?

ANNA Yes.

DEELEY We sleep here. These are beds. The great thing about these beds is that they are susceptible to any amount of permutation. They can be separated as they are now. Or placed at right angles, or one can bisect the other, or you can sleep feet to feet, or head to head, or side by side. It's the castors that make all this possible.

[*He sits with coffee.*]

Yes, I remember you quite clearly from The Wayfarers.

ANNA The what?

DEELEY The Wayfarers Tavern, just off the Brompton Road.[7]

ANNA When was that?

DEELEY Years ago.

ANNA I don't think so.

DEELEY Oh yes, it was you, no question. I never forget a face. You sat in the corner, quite often, sometimes alone, sometimes with others. And here you are, sitting in my house in the country. The same woman. Incredible. Fellow called Luke used to go in there. You knew him.

7. A main thoroughfare of Knightsbridge, a fashionable area of West London between Kensington and Chelsea.

ANNA Luke?

DEELEY Big chap. Ginger hair. Ginger beard.

ANNA I don't honestly think so.

DEELEY Yes, a whole crowd of them, poets, stunt men, jockeys, stand-up comedians, that kind of setup. You used to wear a scarf, that's right, a black scarf, and a black sweater, and a skirt.

ANNA Me?

DEELEY And black stockings. Don't tell me you've forgotten The Wayfarers Tavern? You might have forgotten the name but you must remember the pub. You were the darling of the saloon bar.[8]

ANNA I wasn't rich, you know. I didn't have money for alcohol.

DEELEY You had escorts. You didn't have to pay. You were looked after. I bought you a few drinks myself.

ANNA You?

DEELEY Sure.

ANNA Never.

DEELEY It's the truth. I remember clearly.

[*Pause.*]

ANNA You?

DEELEY I've bought you drinks.

[*Pause.*]

Twenty years ago . . . or so.

ANNA You're saying we've met before?

DEELEY Of course we've met before.

[*Pause.*]

We've talked before. In that pub, for example. In the corner. Luke didn't like it much but we ignored him. Later we all went to a party. Someone's flat, somewhere in Westbourne Grove.[9] You sat on a very low sofa, I sat opposite and looked up your skirt. Your black stockings were very black because your thighs were so white. That's something that's all over now, of course, isn't it, nothing like the same palpable profit in it now, it's all over. But it was worthwhile then. It was worthwhile that night. I simply sat sipping my light ale and gazed . . . gazed up your skirt. You didn't object, you found my gaze perfectly acceptable.

ANNA I was aware of your gaze, was I?

DEELEY There was a great argument going on, about China or something, or death, or China *and* death, I can't remember which, but nobody but I had a thigh-kissing view, nobody but you had the thighs which kissed. And here you are. Same woman. Same thighs.

[*Pause.*]

Yes. Then a friend of yours came in, a girl, a girl friend. She sat on the sofa with you, you both chatted and chuckled, sitting together, and I settled lower to gaze at you both, at both your thighs, squealing and hissing, you aware, she unaware, but then a great multitude of men surrounded me,

8. English pubs are traditionally divided into a public bar and a saloon bar, which offers more services and is sometimes more expensive.

9. A fashionable shopping street in West London. *Flat:* apartment.

and demanded my opinion about death, or about China, or whatever it was, and they would not let me be but bent down over me, so that what with their stinking breath and their broken teeth and the hair in their noses and China and death and their arses on the arms of my chair I was forced to get up and plunge my way through them, followed by them with ferocity, as if I were the cause of their argument, looking back through smoke, rushing to the table with the linoleum cover to look for one more full bottle of light ale, looking back through smoke, glimpsing two girls on the sofa, one of them you, heads close, whispering, no longer able to see anything, no longer able to see stocking or thigh, and then you were gone. I wandered over to the sofa. There was no one on it. I gazed at the indentations of four buttocks. Two of which were yours.

[*Pause.*]

ANNA I've rarely heard a sadder story.

DEELEY I agree.

ANNA I'm terribly sorry.

DEELEY That's all right.

[*Pause.*]

I never saw you again. You disappeared from the area. Perhaps you moved out.

ANNA No. I didn't.

DEELEY I never saw you in The Wayfarers Tavern again. Where were you?

ANNA Oh, at concerts, I should think, or the ballet.

[*Silence.*]

Katey's taking a long time over her bath.

DEELEY Well, you know what she's like when she gets in the bath.

ANNA Yes.

DEELEY Enjoys it. Takes a long time over it.

ANNA She does, yes.

DEELEY A hell of a long time. Luxuriates in it. Gives herself a great soaping all over.

[*Pause.*]

Really soaps herself all over, and then washes the soap off, sud by sud. Meticulously. She's both thorough and, I must say it, sensuous. Gives herself a comprehensive going over, and apart from everything else she does emerge as clean as a new pin. Don't you think?

ANNA Very clean.

DEELEY Truly so. Not a speck. Not a tidemark. Shiny as a balloon.

ANNA Yes, a kind of floating.

DEELEY What?

ANNA She floats from the bath. Like a dream. Unaware of anyone standing, with her towel, waiting for her, waiting to wrap it round her. Quite absorbed.

[*Pause.*]

Until the towel is placed on her shoulders.

[*Pause.*]

DEELEY Of course she's so totally incompetent at drying herself properly, did you find that? She gives herself a really good *scrub*, but can she with the same efficiency give herself an equally good *rub*? I have found, in my experience of her, that this is not in fact the case. You'll always find a few odd unexpected unwanted cheeky[1] globules dripping about.

ANNA Why don't you dry her yourself?

DEELEY Would you recommend that?

ANNA You'd do it properly.

DEELEY In her bath towel?

ANNA How out?

DEELEY How out?

ANNA How could you dry her out? Out of her bath towel?

DEELEY I don't know.

ANNA Well, dry her yourself, in her bath towel.

[*Pause.*]

DEELEY Why don't *you* dry her in her bath towel?

ANNA Me?

DEELEY You'd do it properly.

ANNA No, no.

DEELEY Surely? I mean, you're a woman, you know how and where and in what density moisture collects on women's bodies.

ANNA No two women are the same.

DEELEY Well, that's true enough.

[*Pause.*]

I've got a brilliant idea. Why don't we do it with powder?

ANNA Is that a brilliant idea?

DEELEY Isn't it?

ANNA It's quite common to powder yourself after a bath.

DEELEY It's quite common to powder yourself after a bath but it's quite uncommon to be powdered. Or is it? It's not common where I come from, I can tell you. My mother would have a fit.

[*Pause.*]

Listen. I'll tell you what. I'll do it. I'll do the whole lot. The towel and the powder. After all, I am her husband. But you can supervise the whole thing. And give me some hot tips while you're at it. That'll kill two birds with one stone.

[*Pause.*]

[*To himself*] Christ.

[*He looks at her slowly.*]

You must be about forty, I should think, by now.

[*Pause.*]

If I walked into The Wayfarers Tavern now, and saw you sitting in the corner, I wouldn't recognize you.

[*The bathroom door opens.* KATE *comes into the bedroom. She wears a bathrobe.*]

[*She smiles at* DEELEY *and* ANNA.]

KATE [*with pleasure*] Aaahh.

1. Insolent, impudent.

[*She walks to the window and looks out into the night.* DEELEY *and* ANNA *watch her.*]

[DEELEY *begins to sing softly.*]

DEELEY [*singing*] The way you wear your hat . . . [2]

ANNA [*singing, softly*] The way you sip your tea . . .

DEELEY [*singing*] The memory of all that . . .

ANNA [*singing*] No, no, they can't take that away from me . . .

[KATE *turns from the window to look at them.*]

ANNA [*singing*] The way your smile just beams . . .

DEELEY [*singing*] The way you sing off key . . .

ANNA [*singing*] The way you haunt my dreams . . .

DEELEY [*singing*] No, no, they can't take that away from me . . .

[KATE *walks down towards them and stands, smiling.* ANNA *and* DEELEY *sing again, faster on cue, and more perfunctorily.*]

ANNA [*singing*] The way you hold your knife—

DEELEY [*singing*] The way we danced till three—

ANNA [*singing*] The way you've changed my life—

DEELEY No, no, they can't take that away from me.

[KATE *sits on a divan.*]

ANNA [*to* DEELEY] Doesn't she look beautiful?

DEELEY Doesn't she?

KATE Thank you. I feel fresh. The water's very soft here. Much softer than London. I always find the water very hard in London. That's one reason I like living in the country. Everything's softer. The water, the light, the shapes, the sounds. There aren't such edges here. And living close to the sea too. You can't say where it begins or ends. That appeals to me. I don't care for harsh lines. I deplore that kind of urgency. I'd like to go to the East, or somewhere like that, somewhere very hot, where you can lie under a mosquito net and breathe quite slowly. You know . . . somewhere where you can look through the flap of a tent and see sand, that kind of thing. The only nice thing about a big city is that when it rains it blurs everything, and it blurs the lights from the cars, doesn't it, and blurs your eyes, and you have rain on your lashes. That's the only nice thing about a big city.

ANNA That's not the only nice thing. You can have a nice room and a nice gas fire and a warm dressing gown and a nice hot drink, all waiting for you for when you come in.

[*Pause.*]

KATE Is it raining?

ANNA No.

KATE Well, I've decided I will stay in tonight anyway.

ANNA Oh good. I am glad. Now you can have a good strong cup of coffee after your bath.

[ANNA *stands, goes to coffee, pours.*]

I could do the hem on your black dress. I could finish it and you could try it on.

2. This and the following eleven lines (until Kate sits on a divan) are from the song "They Can't Take That Away from Me."

KATE Mmmnn.

[ANNA *hands her her coffee.*]

ANNA Or I could read to you.

DEELEY Have you dried yourself properly, Kate?

KATE I think so.

DEELEY Are you sure? All over?

KATE I think so. I feel quite dry.

DEELEY Are you quite sure? I don't want you sitting here damply all over the place.

[KATE *smiles.*]

See that smile? That's the same smile she smiled when I was walking down the street with her, after Odd Man Out, well, quite some time after. What did you think of it?

ANNA It is a very beautiful smile.

DEELEY Do it again.

KATE I'm still smiling.

DEELEY You're not. Not like you were a moment ago, not like you did then. [*To* ANNA] You know the smile I'm talking about?

KATE This coffee's cold.

[*Pause.*]

ANNA Oh, I'm sorry. I'll make some fresh.

KATE No, I don't want any, thank you.

[*Pause.*]

Is Charley coming?

ANNA I can ring him if you like.

KATE What about McCabe?

ANNA Do you really want to see anyone?

KATE I don't think I like McCabe.

ANNA Nor do I.

KATE He's strange. He says some very strange things to me.

ANNA What things?

KATE Oh, all sorts of funny things.

ANNA I've never liked him.

KATE Duncan's nice though, isn't he?

ANNA Oh yes.

KATE I like his poetry so much.

[*Pause.*]

But you know who I like best?

ANNA Who?

KATE Christy.

ANNA He's lovely.

KATE He's so gentle, isn't he? And his humor. Hasn't he got a lovely sense of humor? And I think he's . . . so sensitive. Why don't you ask him round?

DEELEY He can't make it. He's out of town.

KATE Oh, what a pity.

[*Silence.*]

DEELEY [*to* ANNA] Are you intending to visit anyone else while you're in England? Relations? Cousins? Brothers?

ANNA No. I know no one. Except Kate.

[*Pause.*]

DEELEY Do you find her changed?

ANNA Oh, just a little, not very much. [*To* KATE] You're still shy, aren't you?

[KATE *stares at her.*]

[*To* DEELEY] But when I knew her first she was *so* shy, as shy as a fawn, she really was. When people leaned to speak to her she would fold away from them, so that though she was still standing within their reach she was no longer accessible to them. She folded herself from them, they were no longer able to speak or go through with their touch. I put it down to her upbringing, a parson's daughter, and indeed there was a good deal of Bronte about her.[3]

DEELEY *Was* she a parson's daughter?

ANNA But if I thought Brontë I did not think she was Brontë in passion but only in secrecy, in being so stubbornly private.

[*Slight pause.*]

I remember her first blush.

DEELEY What? What was it? I mean why was it?

ANNA I had borrowed some of her underwear, to go to a party. Later that night I confessed. It was naughty of me. She stared at me, nonplussed, perhaps, is the word. But I told her that in fact I had been punished for my sin, for a man at the party had spent the whole evening looking up my skirt.

[*Pause.*]

DEELEY She blushed at that?

ANNA Deeply.

DEELEY Looking up *your* skirt in *her* underwear. Mmnn.

ANNA But from that night she insisted, from time to time, that I borrow her underwear—she had more of it than I, and a far greater range—and each time she proposed this she would blush, but propose it she did, nevertheless. And when there was anything to tell her, when I got back, anything of interest to tell her, I told her.

DEELEY Did she blush then?

ANNA I could never see then. I would come in late and find her reading under the lamp, and begin to tell her, but she would say no, turn off the light, and I would tell her in the dark. She preferred to be told in the dark. But of course it was never completely dark, what with the light from the gasfire or the light through the curtains, and what she didn't know was that, knowing her preference, I would choose a position in the room from which I could see her face, although she could not see mine. She could hear my voice only. And so she listened and I watched her listening.

DEELEY Sounds a perfect marriage.

ANNA We were great friends.

[*Pause.*]

DEELEY You say she was Brontë in secrecy but not in passion. What was she in passion?

ANNA I feel that is your province.

DEELEY You feel it's my province? Well, you're damn right. It is my province.

3. The Brontë sisters—Charlotte (1816–1855), Emily (1818–1848), and Anne (1820–1849)—all published novels; they grew up with their brother, Branwell (1817–1848), in their father's rectory on the moors of Yorkshire and together created and wrote about elaborate imaginary worlds.

I'm glad someone's showing a bit of taste at last. Of course it's my bloody province. I'm her husband.

[*Pause.*]

I mean I'd like to ask a question. Am I alone in beginning to find all this distasteful?

ANNA But what can you possibly find distasteful? I've flown from Rome to see my oldest friend, after twenty years, and to meet her husband. What is it that worries you?

DEELEY What worries me is the thought of your husband rumbling about alone in his enormous villa living hand to mouth on a few hardboiled eggs and unable to speak a damn word of English.

ANNA I interpret, when necessary.

DEELEY Yes, but you're here, with us. He's there, alone, lurching up and down the terrace, waiting for a speedboat, waiting for a speedboat to spill out beautiful people, at least. Beautiful Mediterranean people. Waiting for all *that*, a kind of elegance we know nothing about, a slim-bellied Cote d'Azur[4] thing we know absolutely nothing about, a lobster and lobster sauce ideology we know fuck-all about, the longest legs in the world, the most phenomenally soft voices. I can hear them now. I mean let's put it on the table, I have my eye on a number of pulses, pulses all round the globe, deprivations and insults, why should I waste valuable space listening to two—

KATE [*swiftly*] If you don't like it go.

[*Pause.*]

DEELEY Go? Where can I go?

KATE To China. Or Sicily.

DEELEY I haven't got a speedboat. I haven't got a white dinner jacket.

KATE China then.

DEELEY You know what they'd do to me in China if they found me in a white dinner jacket. They'd bloodywell kill me. You know what they're like over there.

[*Slight pause.*]

ANNA You are welcome to come to Sicily at any time, both of you, and be my guests.

[*Silence.*]

[KATE *and* DEELEY *stare at her.*]

ANNA [*to* DEELEY, *quietly*] I would like you to understand that I came here not to disrupt but to celebrate.

[*Pause.*]

To celebrate a very old and treasured friendship, something that was forged between us long before you knew of our existence.

[*Pause.*]

I found her. She grew to know wonderful people, through my introduction. I took her to cafés, almost private ones, where artists and writers and sometimes actors collected, and others with dancers, and we sat hardly breath-

4. The Azure Coast (French); the Mediterranean coast of France, particularly the French Riviera, whose beauty and mild winters have long made it a resort destination for the wealthy.

ing with our coffee, listening to the life around us. All I wanted for her was her happiness. That is all I want for her still.

[*Pause.*]

DEELEY [*to* KATE] We've met before, you know. Anna and I.

[KATE *looks at him.*]

Yes, we met in the Wayfarers Tavern. In the corner. She took a fancy to me. Of course I was slimhipped in those days. Pretty nifty. A bit squinky,[5] quite honestly. Curly hair. The lot. We had a scene together. She freaked out. She didn't have any bread,[6] so I bought her a drink. She looked at me with big eyes, shy, all that bit. She was pretending to be you at the time. Did it pretty well. Wearing your underwear she was too, at the time. Amiably allowed me a gander.[7] Trueblue generosity. Admirable in a woman. We went to a party. Given by philosophers. Not a bad bunch. Edgware Road[8] gang. Nice lot. Haven't seen any of them for years. Old friends. Always thinking. Spoke their thoughts. Those are the people I miss. They're all dead, anyway I've never seen them again. The Maida Vale[9] group. Big Eric and little Tony. They lived somewhere near Paddington library.[1] On the way to the party I took her into a café, bought her a cup of coffee, beards with faces. She thought she was you, said little, so little. Maybe she was you. Maybe it was you, having coffee with me, saying little, so little.

[*Pause.*]

KATE What do you think attracted her to you?

DEELEY I don't know. What?

KATE She found your face very sensitive, vulnerable.

DEELEY Did she?

KATE She wanted to comfort it, in the way only a woman can.

DEELEY Did she?

KATE Oh yes.

DEELEY She wanted to comfort my face, in the way only a woman can?

KATE She was prepared to extend herself to you.

DEELEY I beg your pardon?

KATE She fell in love with you.

DEELEY With me?

KATE You were so unlike the others. We knew men who were brutish, crass.

DEELEY There really are such men, then? Crass men?

KATE Quite crass.

DEELEY But I was crass, wasn't I, looking up her skirt?

KATE That's not crass.

DEELEY If it was her skirt. If it was her.

ANNA [*coldly*] Oh, it was my skirt. It was me. I remember your look . . . very well. I remember you well.

KATE [*to* ANNA] But I remember you. I remember you dead.

[*Pause.*]

I remember you lying dead. You didn't know I was watching you. I leaned

5. Having a sultry, narrow-eyed look.
6. Money (slang).
7. A look.
8. A major thoroughfare running through Marylebone and Paddington, in central London.
9. An affluent residential area of Paddington.
1. That is, the community library in west Paddington.

over you. Your face was dirty. You lay dead, your face scrawled with dirt, all kinds of earnest inscriptions, but unblotted, so that they had run, all over your face, down to your throat. Your sheets were immaculate. I was glad. I would have been unhappy if your corpse had lain in an unwholesome sheet. It would have been graceless. I mean as far as I was concerned. As far as my room was concerned. After all, you were dead in my room. When you woke my eyes were above you, staring down at you. You tried to do my little trick, one of my tricks you had borrowed, my little slow smile, my little slow shy smile, my bend of the head, my half closing of the eyes, that we knew so well, but it didn't work, the grin only split the dirt at the sides of your mouth and stuck. You stuck in your grin. I looked for tears but could see none. Your pupils weren't in your eyes. Your bones were breaking through your face. But all was serene. There was no suffering. It had all happened elsewhere. Last rites I did not feel necessary. Or any celebration. I felt the time and season appropriate and that by dying alone and dirty you had acted with proper decorum. It was time for my bath. I had quite a lengthy bath, got out, walked about the room, glistening, drew up a chair, sat naked beside you and watched you.

[*Pause.*]

When I brought him into the room your body of course had gone. What a relief it was to have a different body in my room, a male body behaving quite differently, doing all those things they do and which they think are good, like sitting with one leg over the arm of an armchair. We had a choice of two beds. Your bed or my bed. To lie in, or on. To grind noses together, in or on. He liked your bed, and thought he was different in it because he was a man. But one night I said let me do something, a little thing, a little trick. He lay there in your bed. He looked up at me with great expectation. He was gratified. He thought I had profited from his teaching. He thought I was going to be sexually forthcoming, that I was about to take a long-promised initiative. I dug about in the windowbox, where you had planted our pretty pansies, scooped, filled the bowl, and plastered his face with dirt. He was bemused, aghast, resisted, resisted with force. He would not let me dirty his face, or smudge it, he wouldn't let me. He suggested a wedding instead, and a change of environment.

[*Slight pause.*]

Neither mattered.

[*Pause.*]

He asked me once, at about that time, who had slept in that bed before him. I told him no one. No one at all.

[*Long silence.*]

[ANNA *stands, walks towards the door, stops, her back to them.*]

[*Silence.*]

[DEELEY *starts to sob, very quietly.*]

[ANNA *stands still.*]

[ANNA *turns, switches off the lamps, sits on her divan, and lies down.*]

[*The sobbing stops.*]

[*Silence.*]

[DEELEY *stands. He walks a few paces, looks at both divans. He goes to* ANNA'*s divan, looks down at her. She is still.*]

[*Silence.*]

[DEELEY *moves towards the door, stops, his back to them.*]

[*Silence.*]

[DEELEY *turns. He goes towards* KATE'*s divan. He sits on her divan, lies across her lap.*]

[*Long silence.*]

[DEELEY *very slowly sits up.*
He gets off the divan.
He walks slowly to the armchair.
He sits, slumped.]

[*Silence.*]

[*Lights up full sharply. Very bright.*]

[DEELEY *in armchair.*
ANNA *lying on divan.*
KATE *sitting on divan.*]

WOLE SOYINKA

b. 1934

An active writer for more than five decades, Wole Soyinka is widely regarded as Africa's foremost dramatist and one of the most compelling contemporary writers in English more generally, a judgment affirmed by his being awarded the Nobel Prize in Literature in 1986. Though he is also an accomplished poet, novelist, and essayist, Soyinka's worldwide acclaim rests mainly on his dramatic oeuvre. His plays make use of the rituals and festivals of Nigeria's Yoruba culture and are marked by Nigeria's volatile history, but they also reflect the influences of other cultures, such as that of classical Greece. Soyinka has been one of the continent's most outspoken critics of abuses of power, in Nigeria and elsewhere, even as he has crafted plays that cannot be tied to a particular political creed. For many, his most significant achievement is the creation of a new form of tragedy that draws on both Western and Yoruba traditions, a form that is perhaps most fully realized in ***DEATH AND THE KING'S HORSEMAN*** (1975).

During Soyinka's formative years, Nigeria was in its last decades of British rule. Consequently, Soyinka received a traditional education in English, first at an elite grammar school and then at Government College, Ibadan, where he excelled in the study of various Western literatures, including French and Greek. He continued his education in England, where he studied drama at the University of Leeds. In Leeds and later in London, Soyinka also intensified his engagement with the theater and wrote his first plays, which helped win him a research grant and begin his swift rise as a dramatist. He returned to Nigeria in 1960, the year of its independence from Britain and the start of a period of intense conflict between different regions of the country. Over the next few years, Soyinka founded theater groups; wrote fiction and verse as well as plays for stage, television, and radio; and taught as a university lecturer in English. At the same time, he attempted to prevent the civil war that ultimately broke out in 1967 when the southeast of Nigeria declared its independence as Biafra; these efforts led to his imprisonment. He spent much of his two years of detention in solitary confinement, an experience he later described in one of his autobiographical prose works, *The Man Died: Prison Notes of Wole Soyinka* (1972). His subsequent career has been marked by a series of exiles and returns. Soyinka has taught at the University of Cambridge and Yale University and has directed shows in Europe and the United States, but his most sustained project has been the fostering of Nigeria's literary culture and democracy.

The clearest indications of Soyinka's changing attitude toward nationalism and cultural autonomy can be found in his essays. Writing in the sixties, Soyinka was often critical of those seeking an "authentic" culture that existed before Europeans colonized Africa, and focused instead on cultural mixture. By the 1970s, however, he had turned more fully to Yoruba culture—to which he was exposed early, despite his mother's fervent Christianity—as a resource for drama. In the 1980s, as Soyinka once more became disenchanted with Nigeria's political realities, he placed less emphasis on Yoruba culture. His critical writings thus chart a path through the cultural struggles of a former colony dealing with an imposed culture that has now fused with local ones; after the terrible experience of colonialism, Western and indigenous cultures had become permanently intertwined. Soyinka's relation to colonialism was further complicated by his decision to write in English, albeit an English shot through with metaphors, idioms, and sayings from Yoruba. At various times in his career, he advocated the use of Swahili throughout the continent as a lingua franca to replace the languages of Africa's former European colonizers, but this proposal won few followers.

Soyinka's oeuvre oscillates between tradition and modernity. His earliest plays, *The Swamp Dwellers* (1958) and *The Lion and the Jewel* (1959), present a critique of traditional Yoruba practices and social structures as they come under increasing pressure from forces of modernization both from within and from without. Each play contains a village priest or ruler who opposes modernization and who cunningly seeks to hold on to vestiges of power predicated on the old ways. Soyinka clearly does not endorse this defensive rejection of modernization, although he recognizes the pain that accompanied the transformation of the Nigerian hinterland. Ultimately, these plays satirize the attempt to preserve the old at all cost. A similar critique is developed in *The Trials of Brother Jero* (1960) and *Jero's Metamorphosis* (1973), two plays that revolve around a pseudo-prophet who attracts followers solely for his own economic gain and who is ready to employ every trick possible to outsmart his rivals. In other works, Soyinka is more fully concerned with the social reality of the outcast. In *The Road* (1965), one of his best plays, a number of lowlifes are assembled around a figure called Professor, who is akin to the sham prophet Jero. As Professor ekes out a living by forging documents, he is also engaged in an unlikely quest for spiritual enlightenment. These plays show that modernity is not something imposed onto Yoruba culture from the outside but a force at work within it.

Some of Soyinka's plays aim squarely at Nigerian politics—for example, *From Zia, with Love* (1992), which harshly indicts the dictatorship—but his best-known plays avoid direct political engagement, seeking instead to weave together different cultures and traditions. In his drama, Soyinka has continually insisted on the affinities between Greek and Yoruba tragedy. Most significantly, he has related the Yoruba god Ogun, the deity to whom he himself feels closest, to the Greek god Dionysus, who is connected with the origins of Greek tragedy. This attempt to forge new forms of tragedy out of Western and African traditions led to a long-standing controversy between Soyinka and a group of Nigerian intellectuals and critics—dubbed by Soyinka the "Leftocracy"—who accused him of seeking universal human meaning while ignoring the specifics of Nigeria's political and social situation after independence.

The tensions between political drama and tragedy as well as the tensions between the use of Western and Yoruba traditions are most visible in Soyinka's adaptations of EURIPIDES' *The Bacchae* (406 B.C.E.) and of BERTOLT BRECHT's *The Threepenny Opera* (1928). *The Bacchae of Euripides* (1973) provided Soyinka with an occasion to gauge the similarities and differences between Greek and Yoruba myths. Soyinka's Dionysus is less vindictive than Euripides', and his play displays a broader social range (its chorus is made up of slaves). Yet he shares with Euripides the attempt to connect drama to its lost origin in ritual. Brecht's *Threepenny Opera* is much more overtly political; *Opera Wonyosi* (1977) replaces the underworld of London, which Brecht himself had borrowed from the eighteenth-century British playwright John

Gay, with a politically corrupt West Africa. In both adaptations, Soyinka demonstrates the power of translation and transposition, encouraging cultural mixture and cross-fertilization in a way that respects the integrity of different traditions and practices.

Soyinka's project of inventing a new tragic form culminates in *Death and the King's Horseman*, a play based on a historical incident. In 1946, a British colonial district officer interrupted the ritual suicide of a village notable, the King's Horseman—a suicide prescribed by the Yoruba religious and social system—without realizing how his interference would affect the village and, most importantly, the King's Horseman's son, who is also his protégé. This historical incident thus ties the officer, the King's Horseman, and his son in an inextricable and fatal knot. The officer himself is presented as a relatively two-dimensional figure, distinguished mainly by his colonial arrogance: Simon Pilkings interferes with local customs without knowing anything about their role in the social order or their religious significance. As a result, some critics have read the play as a defense of Yoruba customs. In his author's note, however, Soyinka takes issue with all readings that reduce the play to a simple "clash of cultures"; indeed, the play spends considerable energy trying—and failing—to bridge the gulf between them.

The two cultures are connected by various mediating figures, who participate in or have knowledge of both worlds. The officer, for example, depends on his Yoruba employees for information about local customs and religion. While Pilkings, who arrogantly dismisses their culture, often finds it difficult to interpret what his informants say, his wife is somewhat more open-minded and thus more aware of the inescapable cultural clash. The most competent intermediary is Olunde, the son of Elesin, the King's Horseman. Sent by Pilkings to England to study medicine against his father's wishes, Olunde has now returned for his father's burial. Although he is Westernized (as evidenced by the suit he wears), he does not dismiss the requirement that his father commit suicide, knowing how deeply the ritual is woven

British colonial administrators meeting tribal representatives in Lagos, Nigeria, ca. 1900.

Death and the King's Horseman

Dedicated
In Affectionate Greeting
to
My Father, Ayodele
who lately danced, and joined the Ancestors.

Author's Note

This play is based on events which took place in Oyo,[1] ancient Yoruba city of Nigeria, in 1946. That year, the lives of Elesin (Olori Elesin), his son, and the Colonial District Officer intertwined with the disastrous results set out in the play. The changes I have made are in matters of detail, sequence, and of course characterisation. The action has also been set back two or three years to while the war was still on,[2] for minor reasons of dramaturgy.

The factual account still exists in the archives of the British Colonial Administration. It has already inspired a fine play in Yoruba (Oba Wàjà[3]) by Duro Ladipo. It has also misbegotten a film by some German television company.

The bane of themes of this genre is that they are no sooner employed creatively than they acquire the facile tag of 'clash of cultures', a prejudicial label which, quite apart from its frequent misapplication, presupposes a potential equality *in every given situation* of the alien culture and the indigenous, on the actual soil of the latter. (In the area of misapplication, the overseas prize for illiteracy and mental conditioning undoubtedly goes to the blurb-writer for the American edition of my novel *Season of Anomy*[4] who unblushingly declares that this work portrays the 'clash between old values and new ways, between western methods and African traditions'!) It is thanks to this kind of perverse mentality that I find it necessary to caution the would-be producer of this play against a sadly familiar reductionist tendency, and to direct his vision instead to the far more difficult and risky task of eliciting the play's threnodic[5] essence.

One of the more obvious alternative structures of the play would be to make the District Officer the victim of a cruel dilemma. This is not to my taste and it is not by chance that I have avoided dialogue or situation which would encourage this. No attempt should be made in production to suggest it. The Colonial Factor is an incident, a catalytic incident merely. The confrontation in the play is largely metaphysical, contained in the human vehicle which is Elesin and the universe of the Yoruba mind—the world of the living, the dead and the unborn, and the numinous passage which links all: transition. *Death and the King's Horseman* can be fully realised only through an evocation of music from the abyss of transition.

W.S.

1. A city in western Nigeria, about 100 miles north of Lagos.
2. That is, World War II.
3. *The King Is Dead* (1964).
4. Published in New York in 1974 (London, 1973).
5. Resembling a threnody, or song of lament for the dead.

CHARACTERS

PRAISE-SINGER
ELESIN, Horseman of the King
IYALOJA, 'Mother' of the market
SIMON PILKINGS, District Officer
JANE PILKINGS, his wife
SERGEANT AMUSA
JOSEPH, houseboy to the Pilkingses
BRIDE
H.R.H. THE PRINCE
THE RESIDENT[6]
AIDE-DE-CAMP
OLUNDE, eldest son of Elesin

DRUMMERS, WOMEN, YOUNG GIRLS, DANCERS AT THE BALL

The play should run without an interval. For rapid scene changes, one adjustable outline set is very appropriate.

Act 1

A passage through a market in its closing stages. The stalls are being emptied, mats folded. A few WOMEN *pass through on their way home, loaded with baskets. On a cloth-stand, bolts of cloth are taken down, display pieces folded and piled on a tray.* ELESIN OBA *enters along a passage before the market, pursued by his* DRUMMERS *and* PRAISE-SINGERS. *He is a man of enormous vitality, speaks, dances, and sings with that infectious enjoyment of life which accompanies all his actions.*

PRAISE-SINGER Elesin o! Elesin Oba! Howu![7] What tryst is this the cockerel goes to keep with such haste that he must leave his tail behind?

ELESIN [*slows down a bit, laughing*] A tryst where the cockerel needs no adornment.

PRAISE-SINGER O-oh, you hear that my companions? That's the way the world goes. Because the man approaches a brand-new bride he forgets the long faithful mother of his children.[8]

ELESIN When the horse sniffs the stable does he not strain at the bridle? The market is the long-suffering home of my spirit and the women are packing up to go. That Esu[9]-harassed day slipped into the stewpot while we feasted. We ate it up with the rest of the meat. I have neglected my women.

PRAISE-SINGER We know all that. Still it's no reason for shedding your tail on this day of all days. I know the women will cover you in damask and *alari*[1] but when the wind blows cold from behind, that's when the fowl knows his true friends.

6. The ranking British officer in a province.
7. Why have you come? (Yoruba greeting). *Oba:* King (Yoruba).
8. Traditionally, Yoruba men had multiple wives.
9. The Yoruba trickster god.
1. A rich, woven cloth, brightly coloured [Soyinka]. *Damask:* a lustrous patterned fabric.

ELESIN Olohun-iyo![2]

PRAISE-SINGER Are you sure there will be one like me on the other side?

ELESIN Olohun-iyo!

PRAISE-SINGER Far be it for me to belittle the dwellers of that place but, a man is either born to his art or he isn't. And I don't know for certain that you'll meet my father, so who is going to sing these deeds in accents that will pierce the deafness of the ancient ones. I have prepared my going—just tell me: Olohun-iyo, I need you on this journey and I shall be behind you.

ELESIN You're like a jealous wife. Stay close to me, but only on this side. My fame, my honour are legacies to the living; stay behind and let the world sip its honey from your lips.

PRAISE-SINGER Your name will be like the sweet berry a child places under his tongue to sweeten the passage of food. The world will never spit it out.

ELESIN Come then. This market is my roost. When I come among the women I am a chicken with a hundred mothers. I become a monarch whose palace is built with tenderness and beauty.

PRAISE-SINGER They love to spoil you but beware. The hands of women also weaken the unwary.

ELESIN This night I'll lay my head upon their lap and go to sleep. This night I'll touch feet with their feet in a dance that is no longer of this earth. But the smell of their flesh, their sweat, the smell of indigo[3] on their cloth, this is the last air I wish to breathe as I go to meet my great forebears.

PRAISE-SINGER In their time the world was never tilted from its groove, it shall not be in yours.

ELESIN The gods have said No.

PRAISE-SINGER In their time the great wars came and went, the little wars came and went; the white slavers came and went, they took away the heart of our race, they bore away the mind and muscle of our race. The city fell and was rebuilt; the city fell and our people trudged through mountain and forest to found a new home but—Elesin Oba do you hear me?

ELESIN I hear your voice Olohun-iyo.

PRAISE-SINGER Our world was never wrenched from its true course.

ELESIN The gods have said No.

PRAISE-SINGER There is only one home to the life of a river-mussel; there is only one home to the life of a tortoise; there is only one shell to the soul of man; there is only one world to the spirit of our race. If that world leaves its course and smashes on boulders of the great void, whose world will give us shelter?

ELESIN It did not in the time of my forebears, it shall not in mine.

PRAISE-SINGER The cockerel must not be seen without his feathers.

ELESIN Nor will the Not-I bird[4] be much longer without his nest.

PRAISE-SINGER [*stopped in his lyric stride*] The Not-I bird, Elesin?

ELESIN I said, the Not-I bird.

PRAISE-SINGER All respect to our elders but, is there really such a bird?

ELESIN What! Could it be that he failed to knock on your door?

2. Praise-singer (Yoruba).
3. A costly blue dye made from plants and used by royalty in Africa.
4. A bird whose call resembles the Yoruba phrase that means "not I."

PRAISE-SINGER [*smiling*] Elesin's riddles are not merely the nut in the kernel that breaks human teeth; he also buries the kernel in hot embers and dares a man's fingers to draw it out.

ELESIN I am sure he called on you, Olohun-iyo. Did you hide in the loft and push out the servant to tell him you were out?

[ELESIN *executes a brief, half-taunting dance. The* DRUMMER *moves in and draws a rhythm out of his steps.* ELESIN *dances towards the market-place as he chants the story of the Not-I bird, his voice changing dexterously to mimic his characters. He performs like a born raconteur, infecting his retinue with his humour and energy. More* WOMEN *arrive during his recital, including* IYALOJA.]

Death came calling.
Who does not know his rasp of reeds?
A twilight whisper in the leaves before
The great araba[5] falls? Did you hear it?
Not I! swears the farmer. He snaps
His fingers round his head, abandons
A hard-worn harvest and begins
A rapid dialogue with his legs.

'Not I,' shouts the fearless hunter, 'but—
It's getting dark, and this night-lamp
Has leaked out all its oil. I think
It's best to go home and resume my hunt
Another day.' But now he pauses, suddenly
Lets out a wail: 'Oh foolish mouth, calling
Down a curse on your own head! Your lamp
Has leaked out all its oil, has it?'
Forwards or backwards now he dare not move.
To search for leaves and make *etutu*[6]
On that spot? Or race home to the safety
Of his hearth? Ten market-days have passed
My friends, and still he's rooted there
Rigid as the plinth of Orayan.[7]

The mouth of the courtesan barely
Opened wide enough to take a ha'penny *robo*[8]
When she wailed: 'Not I.' All dressed she was
To call upon my friend the Chief Tax Officer.
But now she sends her go-between instead:
'Tell him I'm ill: my period has come suddenly
But not—I hope—my time.'

Why is the pupil crying?
His hapless head was made to taste

5. A silk-cotton tree (Yoruba), which yields the fiber kapok.
6. Placatory rites or medicine [Soyinka's].
7. A tall landmark in Ile-Ife, ancestral home of the Yoruba. Orayan was a son of Oduduwa, first Yoruba king, and progenitor of all subsequent kings.
8. A delicacy made from crushed melon seeds, fried in tiny balls [Soyinka's].

The knuckles of my friend the Mallam.[9]
'If you were then reciting the Koran
Would you have ears for idle noises
Darkening the trees, you child of ill omen?'
He shuts down school before its time
Runs home and rings himself with amulets.

And take my good kinsman Ifawomi.
His hands were like a carver's, strong
And true. I saw them
Tremble like wet wings of a fowl
One day he cast his time-smoothed *opele*[1]
Across the divination board. And all because
The suppliant looked him in the eye and asked,
'Did you hear that whisper in the leaves?'
'Not I,' was his reply; 'perhaps I'm growing deaf—
Good-day.' And Ifa spoke no more that day
The priest locked fast his doors,
Sealed up his leaking roof—but wait!
This sudden care was not for Fawomi
But for Osanyin,[2] courier-bird of Ifa's
Heart of wisdom. I did not know a kite
Was hovering in the sky
And Ifa now a twittering chicken in
The brood of Fawomi the Mother Hen.

Ah, but I must not forget my evening
Courier from the abundant palm, whose groan
Became Not I, as he constipated down
A wayside bush. He wonders if Elegbara[3]
Has tricked his buttocks to discharge
Against a sacred grove. Hear him
Mutter spells to ward off penalties
For an abomination he did not intend.
If any here
Stumbles on a gourd of wine, fermenting
Near the road, and nearby hears a stream
Of spells issuing from a crouching form,
Brother to a *sigidi*,[4] bring home my wine,
Tell my tapper[5] I have ejected
Fear from home and farm. Assure him,
All is well.

PRAISE-SINGER In your time we do not doubt the peace of farmstead and home, the peace of road and hearth, we do not doubt the peace of the forest.

9. A teacher of Islamic doctrine (Hausa).
1. String of beads used in Ifa divination [Soyinka].
2. Patron deity of diviners. *Fawomi:* a reference to Ifa, the Yoruba god of divination.
3. Another name for Esu, the trickster god.
4. A squat, carved figure, endowed with the powers of an incubus [Soyinka], which is a demon that lies on people in their sleep.
5. The person who collects the sap of palm trees, which is fermented into wine.

ELESIN There was fear in the forest too.
Not-I was lately heard even in the lair
Of beasts. The hyena cackled loud Not I,
The civet[6] twitched his fiery tail and glared:
Not I. Not-I became the answering-name
Of the restless bird, that little one
Whom Death found nesting in the leaves
When whisper of his coming ran
Before him on the wind. Not-I
Has long abandoned home. This same dawn
I heard him twitter in the gods' abode.
Ah, companions of this living world
What a thing this is, that even those
We call immortal
Should fear to die.

IYALOJA But you, husband of multitudes?

ELESIN I, when that Not-I bird perched
Upon my roof, bade him seek his nest again,
Safe, without care or fear. I unrolled
My welcome mat for him to see. Not-I
Flew happily away, you'll hear his voice
No more in this lifetime—You all know
What I am.

PRAISE-SINGER That rock which turns its open lodes
Into the path of lightning. A gay
Thoroughbred whose stride disdains
To falter though an adder reared
Suddenly in his path.

ELESIN My rein is loosened.
I am master of my Fate. When the hour comes
Watch me dance along the narrowing path
Glazed by the soles of my great precursors.
My soul is eager. I shall not turn aside.

WOMEN You will not delay?

ELESIN Where the storm pleases, and when, it directs
The giants of the forest. When friendship summons
Is when the true comrade goes.

WOMEN Nothing will hold you back?

ELESIN Nothing. What! Has no one told you yet?
I go to keep my friend and master company.
Who says the mouth does not believe in
'No, I have chewed all that before?' I say I have.
The world is not a constant honey-pot.
Where I found little I made do with little.
Where there was plenty I gorged myself.
My master's hands and mine have always
Dipped together and, home or sacred feast,
The bowl was beaten bronze, the meats

6. A weasel-like carnivorous mammal (especially the species native to Africa).

So succulent our teeth accused us of neglect.
We shared the choicest of the season's
Harvest of yams. How my friend would read
Desire in my eyes before I knew the cause—
However rare, however precious, it was mine.

WOMEN The town, the very land was yours.

ELESIN The world was mine. Our joint hands
Raised houseposts of trust that withstood
The siege of envy and the termites of time.
But the twilight hour brings bats and rodents—
Shall I yield them cause to foul the rafters?

PRAISE-SINGER Elesin Oba! Are you not that man who
Looked out of doors that stormy day
The god of luck limped by, drenched
To the very lice that held
His rags together? You took pity upon
His sores and wished him fortune.
Fortune was footloose this dawn, he replied,
Till you trapped him in a heartfelt wish
That now returns to you. Elesin Oba!
I say you are that man who
Chanced upon the calabash[7] of honour
You thought it was palm wine and
Drained its contents to the final drop.

ELESIN Life has an end. A life that will outlive
Fame and friendship begs another name.
What elder takes his tongue to his plate,
Licks it clean of every crumb? He will encounter
Silence when he calls on children to fulfill
The smallest errand! Life is honour.
It ends when honour ends.

WOMEN We know you for a man of honour.

ELESIN Stop! Enough of that!

WOMEN [*puzzled, they whisper among themselves, turning mostly to* IYALOJA] What is it? Did we say something to give offence? Have we slighted him in some way?

ELESIN Enough of that sound I say. Let me hear no more in that vein. I've heard enough.

IYALOJA We must have said something wrong. [*Comes forward a little.*] Elesin Oba, we ask forgiveness before you speak.

ELESIN I am bitterly offended.

IYALOJA Our unworthiness has betrayed us. All we can do is ask your forgiveness. Correct us like a kind father.

ELESIN This day of all days . . .

IYALOJA It does not bear thinking. If we offend you now we have mortified the gods. We offend heaven itself. Father of us all, tell us where we went astray. [*She kneels, the other women follow.*]

7. A drinking vessel made from a gourd.

ELESIN Are you not ashamed? Even a tear-veiled
Eye preserves its function of sight.
Because my mind was raised to horizons
Even the boldest man lowers his gaze
In thinking of, must my body here
Be taken for a vagrant's?

IYALOJA Horseman of the King, I am more baffled than ever.

PRAISE-SINGER The strictest father unbends his brow when the child is penitent, Elesin. When time is short, we do not spend it prolonging the riddle. Their shoulders are bowed with the weight of fear lest they have marred your day beyond repair. Speak now in plain words and let us pursue the ailment to the home of remedies.

ELESIN Words are cheap. 'We know you for
A man of honour.' Well tell me, is this how
A man of honour should be seen?
Are these not the same clothes in which
I came among you a full half-hour ago?

[*He roars with laughter and the* WOMEN, *relieved, rise and rush into stalls to fetch rich cloths.*]

WOMEN The gods are kind. A fault soon remedied is soon forgiven. Elesin Oba, even as we match our words with deed, let your heart forgive us completely.

ELESIN You who are breath and giver of my being
How shall I dare refuse you forgiveness
Even if the offence were real.

IYALOJA [*dancing round him. Sings*]
He forgives us. He forgives us.
What a fearful thing it is when
The voyager sets forth
But a curse remains behind.

WOMEN For a while we truly feared
Our hands had wrenched the world adrift
In emptiness.

IYALOJA Richly, richly, robe him richly
The cloth of honour is *alari*
Sanyan is the band of friendship
Boa-skin[8] makes slippers of esteem

WOMEN For a while we truly feared
Our hands had wrenched the world adrift
In emptiness.

PRAISE-SINGER He who must, must voyage forth
The world will not roll backwards
It is he who must, with one
Great gesture overtake the world.

WOMEN For a while we truly feared
Our hands had wrenched the world
In emptiness.

PRAISE-SINGER The gourd you bear is not for shirking.
The gourd is not for setting down

8. That is, snake skin. *Sanyan:* a richly valued woven cloth [Soyinka].

IYALOJA Elesin Oba . . .

ELESIN What! Where do you all say I am?

IYALOJA Still among the living.

ELESIN And that radiance which so suddenly
Lit up this market I could boast
I knew so well?

IYALOJA Has one step already in her husband's home. She is betrothed.

ELESIN [*irritated*] Why do you tell me that?

[IYALOJA *falls silent. The* WOMEN *shuffle uneasily.*]

IYALOJA Not because we dare give you offence Elesin. Today is your day and the whole world is yours. Still, even those who leave town to make a new dwelling elsewhere like to be remembered by what they leave behind.

ELESIN Who does not seek to be remembered?
Memory is Master of Death, the chink
In his armour of conceit. I shall leave
That which makes my going the sheerest
Dream of an afternoon. Should voyagers
Not travel light? Let the considerate traveller
Shed, of his excessive load, all
That may benefit the living.

WOMEN [*relieved*] Ah Elesin Oba, we knew you for a man of honour.

ELESIN Then honour me. I deserve a bed of honour to lie upon.

IYALOJA The best is yours. We know you for a man of honour. You are not one who eats and leaves nothing on his plate for children. Did you not say it yourself? Not one who blights the happiness of others for a moment's pleasure.

ELESIN Who speaks of pleasure? O women, listen!
Pleasure palls. Our acts should have meaning.
The sap of the plantain never dries.
You have seen the young shoot swelling
Even as the parent stalk begins to wither.
Women, let my going be likened to
The twilight hour of the plantain.

WOMEN What does he mean Iyaloja? This language is the language of our elders, we do not fully grasp it.

IYALOJA I dare not understand you yet Elesin.

ELESIN All you who stand before the spirit that dares
The opening of the last door of passage,
Dare to rid my going of regrets! My wish
Transcends the blotting out of thought
In one mere moment's tremor of the senses.
Do me credit. And do me honour.
I am girded for the route beyond
Burdens of waste and longing.
Then let me travel light. Let
Seed that will not serve the stomach
On the way remain behind. Let it take root
In the earth of my choice, in this earth
I leave behind.

IYALOJA [*turns to* WOMEN] The voice I hear is already touched by the waiting fingers of our departed. I dare not refuse.

WOMEN But Iyaloja . . .

IYALOJA The matter is no longer in our hands.

WOMAN But she is betrothed to your own son. Tell him.

IYALOJA My son's wish is mine. I did the asking for him, the loss can be remedied. But who will remedy the blight of closed hands on the day when all should be openness and light? Tell him, you say! You wish that I burden him with knowledge that will sour his wish and lay regrets on the last moments of his mind. You pray to him who is your intercessor to the world—don't set this world adrift in your own time; would you rather it was my hand whose sacrilege wrenched it loose?

WOMAN Not many men will brave the curse of a dispossessed husband.

IYALOJA Only the curses of the departed are to be feared. The claims of one whose foot is on the threshold of their abode surpasses even the claims of blood. It is impiety even to place hindrances in their ways.

ELESIN What do my mothers say? Shall I step
Burdened into the unknown?

IYALOJA Not we, but the very earth says No. The sap in the plantain does not dry. Let grain that will not feed the voyager at his passage drop here and take root as he steps beyond this earth and us. Oh you who fill the home from hearth to threshold with the voices of children, you who now bestride the hidden gulf and pause to draw the right foot across and into the resting-home of the great forebears, it is good that your loins be drained into the earth we know, that your last strength be ploughed back into the womb that gave you being.

PRAISE-SINGER Iyaloja, mother of multitudes in the teeming market of the world, how your wisdom transfigures you!

IYALOJA [*smiling broadly, completely reconciled*] Elesin, even at the narrow end of the passage I know you will look back and sigh a last regret for the flesh that flashed past your spirit in flight. You always had a restless eye. Your choice has my blessing. [*To the* WOMEN] Take the good news to our daughter and make her ready. [*Some* WOMEN *go off.*]

ELESIN Your eyes were clouded at first.

IYALOJA Not for long. It is those who stand at the gateway of the great change to whose cry we must pay heed. And then, think of this—it makes the mind tremble. The fruit of such a union is rare. It will be neither of this world nor of the next. Nor of the one behind us. As if the timelessness of the ancestor world and the unborn have joined spirits to wring an issue of the elusive being of passage . . . Elesin!

ELESIN I am here. What is it?

IYALOJA Did you hear all I said just now?

ELESIN Yes.

IYALOJA The living must eat and drink. When the moment comes, don't turn the food to rodents' droppings in their mouth. Don't let them taste the ashes of the world when they step out at dawn to breathe the morning dew.

ELESIN This doubt is unworthy of you Iyaloja.

IYALOJA Eating the awusa nut[6] is not so difficult as drinking water afterwards.

6. A walnutlike seed that is eaten or used to produce oil. Raw, it has a bitter flavor.

ELESIN The waters of the bitter stream are honey to a man
Whose tongue has savoured all.

IYALOJA No one knows when the ants desert their home; they leave the mound intact. The swallow is never seen to peck holes in its nest when it is time to move with the season. There are always throngs of humanity behind the leave-taker. The rain should not come through the roof for them, the wind must not blow through the walls at night.

ELESIN I refuse to take offence.

IYALOJA You wish to travel light. Well, the earth is yours. But be sure the seed you leave in it attracts no curse.

ELESIN You really mistake my person Iyaloja.

IYALOJA I said nothing. Now we must go prepare your bridal chamber. Then these same hands will lay your shrouds.

ELESIN [*exasperated*] Must you be so blunt? [*Recovers.*] Well, weave your shrouds, but let the fingers of my bride seal my eyelids with earth and wash my body.

IYALOJA Prepare yourself Elesin.

[*She gets up to leave. At that moment the* WOMEN *return, leading the* BRIDE. ELESIN*'s face glows with pleasure. He flicks the sleeves of his agbada*[7] *with renewed confidence and steps forward to meet the group. As the girl kneels before* IYALOJA, *lights fade out on the scene.*]

Act 2

The verandah of the District Officer's bungalow. A tango is playing from an old hand-cranked gramophone and, glimpsed through the wide windows and doors which open onto the forestage verandah are the shapes of SIMON PILKINGS *and his wife,* JANE, *tangoing in and out of shadows in the living room. They are wearing what is immediately apparent as some form of fancy dress.*[8] *The dance goes on for some moments and then the figure of a* 'NATIVE ADMINISTRATION' POLICEMAN *emerges and climbs up the steps onto the verandah. He peeps through and observes the dancing couple, reacting with what is obviously a long-standing bewilderment. He stiffens suddenly, his expression changes to one of disbelief and horror. In his excitement he upsets a flowerpot and attracts the attention of the couple. They stop dancing.*

PILKINGS Is there anyone out there?

JANE I'll turn off the gramophone.

PILKINGS [*approaching the verandah*] I'm sure I heard something fall over. [*The* CONSTABLE *retreats slowly, open-mouthed as* PILKINGS *approaches the verandah.*] Oh it's you Amusa. Why didn't you just knock instead of knocking things over?

AMUSA [*stammers badly and points a shaky finger at his dress*] Mista Pirinkin . . . Mista Pirinkin . . .

PILKINGS What is the matter with you?

JANE [*emerging*] Who is it dear? Oh, Amusa . . .

PILKINGS Yes it's Amusa, and acting most strangely.

AMUSA [*his attention now transferred to* MRS PILKINGS] Mammadam . . . you too!

7. A flowing, wide-sleeved robe worn by important men.

8. That is, costumes.

PILKINGS What the hell is the matter with you man!

JANE Your costume darling. Our fancy dress.

PILKINGS Oh hell, I'd forgotten all about that. [*Lifts the face mask over his head showing his face. His wife follows suit.*]

JANE I think you've shocked his big pagan heart bless him.

PILKINGS Nonsense, he's a Moslem. Come on Amusa, you don't believe in all this nonsense do you? I thought you were a good Moslem.

AMUSA Mista Pirinkin, I beg you sir, what you think you do with that dress? It belong to dead cult, not for human being.

PILKINGS Oh Amusa, what a let down you are. I swear by you at the club you know—thank God for Amusa, he doesn't believe in any mumbo-jumbo. And now look at you!

AMUSA Mista Pirinkin, I beg you, take it off. Is not good for man like you to touch that cloth.

PILKINGS Well, I've got it on. And what's more Jane and I have bet on it we're taking first prize at the ball. Now, if you can just pull yourself together and tell me what you wanted to see me about . . .

AMUSA Sir, I cannot talk this matter to you in that dress. I no fit.

PILKINGS What's that rubbish again?

JANE He is dead earnest too Simon. I think you'll have to handle this delicately.

PILKINGS Delicately my . . . ! Look here Amusa, I think this little joke has gone far enough hm? Let's have some sense. You seem to forget that you are a police officer in the service of His Majesty's Government. I order you to report your business at once or face disciplinary action.

AMUSA Sir, it is a matter of death. How can man talk against death to person in uniform of death? Is like talking against government to person in uniform of police. Please sir, I go and come back.

PILKINGS [*roars*] Now! [AMUSA *switches his gaze to the ceiling suddenly, remains mute.*]

JANE Oh Amusa, what is there to be scared of in the costume? You saw it confiscated last month from those *egungun*[9] men who were creating trouble in town. You helped arrest the cult leaders yourself—if the juju[1] didn't harm you at the time how could it possibly harm you now? And merely by looking at it?

AMUSA [*without looking down*] Madam, I arrest the ringleaders who make trouble but me I no touch *egungun*. That *egungun* itself, I no touch. And I no abuse 'am. I arrest ringleader but I treat *egungun* with respect.

PILKINGS It's hopeless. We'll merely end up missing the best part of the ball. When they get this way there is nothing you can do. It's simply hammering against a brick wall. Write your report or whatever it is on that pad Amusa and take yourself out of here. Come on Jane. We only upset his delicate sensibilities by remaining here.

[AMUSA *waits for them to leave, then writes in the notebook, somewhat laboriously. Drumming from the direction of the town wells up.* AMUSA *listens, makes a movement as if he wants to recall* PILKINGS *but changes his mind. Completes his note and goes. A few moments later* PILKINGS *emerges, picks up the pad and reads.*]

9. Ancestral masquerade [Soyinka]. The spirits of the dead are believed to temporarily possess those wearing these costumes.

1. Magic associated with fetish objects.

PILKINGS Jane!

JANE [*from the bedroom*] Coming darling. Nearly ready.

PILKINGS Never mind being ready, just listen to this.

JANE What is it?

PILKINGS Amusa's report. Listen. 'I have to report that it come to my information that one prominent chief, namely, the Elesin Oba, is to commit death tonight as a result of native custom. Because this is criminal offence I await further instruction at charge office. Sergeant Amusa.'

[JANE *comes out onto the verandah while he is reading.*]

JANE Did I hear you say commit death?

PILKINGS Obviously he means murder.

JANE You mean a ritual murder?

PILKINGS Must be. You think you've stamped it all out but it's always lurking under the surface somewhere.

JANE Oh. Does it mean we are not getting to the ball at all?

PILKINGS No-o. I'll have the man arrested. Everyone remotely involved. In any case there may be nothing to it. Just rumours.

JANE Really? I thought you found Amusa's rumours generally reliable.

PILKINGS That's true enough. But who knows what may have been giving him the scare lately. Look at his conduct tonight.

JANE [*laughing*] You have to admit he had his own peculiar logic. [*Deepens her voice.*] How can man talk against death to person in uniform of death? [*Laughs.*] Anyway, you can't go into the police station dressed like that.

PILKINGS I'll send Joseph with instructions. Damn it, what a confounded nuisance!

JANE But don't you think you should talk first to the man, Simon?

PILKINGS Do you want to go to the ball or not?

JANE Darling, why are you getting rattled? I was only trying to be intelligent. It seems hardly fair just to lock up a man—and a chief at that—simply on the er . . . what is the legal word again?—uncorroborated word of a sergeant.

PILKINGS Well, that's easily decided. Joseph!

JOSEPH [*from within*] Yes master.

PILKINGS You're quite right of course, I am getting rattled. Probably the effect of those bloody drums. Do you hear how they go on and on?

JANE I wondered when you'd notice. Do you suppose it has something to do with this affair?

PILKINGS Who knows? They always find an excuse for making a noise . . . [*Thoughtfully*] Even so . . .

JANE Yes Simon?

PILKINGS It's different Jane. I don't think I've heard this particular—sound—before. Something unsettling about it.

JANE I thought all bush drumming sounded the same.

PILKINGS Don't tease me now Jane. This may be serious.

JANE I'm sorry. [*Gets up and throws her arms around his neck. Kisses him. The* HOUSEBOY *enters, retreats and knocks.*]

PILKINGS [*wearily*] Oh, come in Joseph! I don't know where you pick up all these elephantine notions of tact. Come over here.

JOSEPH Sir?

PILKINGS Joseph, are you a Christian or not?

JOSEPH Yessir.

PILKINGS Does seeing me in this outfit bother you?

JOSEPH No sir, it has no power.

PILKINGS Thank God for some sanity at last. Now Joseph, answer me on the honour of a Christian—what is supposed to be going on in town tonight?

JOSEPH Tonight sir? You mean the chief who is going to kill himself?

PILKINGS What?

JANE What do you mean, kill himself?

PILKINGS You do mean he is going to kill somebody don't you?

JOSEPH No master. He will not kill anybody and no one will kill him. He will simply die.

JANE But why Joseph?

JOSEPH It is native law and custom. The King die last month. Tonight is his burial. But before they can bury him, the Elesin must die so as to accompany him to heaven.

PILKINGS I seem to be fated to clash more often with that man than with any of the other chiefs.

JOSEPH He is the King's Chief Horseman.

PILKINGS [*in a resigned way*] I know.

JANE Simon, what's the matter?

PILKINGS It would have to be him!

JANE Who is he?

PILKINGS Don't you remember? He's that chief with whom I had a scrap some three or four years ago. I helped his son get to a medical school in England, remember? He fought tooth and nail to prevent it.

JANE Oh now I remember. He was that very sensitive young man. What was his name again?

PILKINGS Olunde. Haven't replied to his last letter come to think of it. The old pagan wanted him to stay and carry on some family tradition or the other. Honestly I couldn't understand the fuss he made. I literally had to help the boy escape from close confinement and load him onto the next boat. A most intelligent boy, really bright.

JANE I rather thought he was much too sensitive you know. The kind of person you feel should be a poet munching rose petals in Bloomsbury.[2]

PILKINGS Well, he's going to make a first-class doctor. His mind is set on that. And as long as he wants my help he is welcome to it.

JANE [*after a pause*] Simon.

PILKINGS Yes?

JANE This boy, he was the eldest son wasn't he?

PILKINGS I'm not sure. Who could tell with that old ram?

JANE Do you know, Joseph?

JOSEPH Oh yes madam. He was the eldest son. That's why Elesin cursed master good and proper. The eldest son is not supposed to travel away from the land.

JANE [*giggling*] Is that true Simon? Did he really curse you good and proper?

PILKINGS By all accounts I should be dead by now.

2. The district of central London in which the British Museum and the University of London are located; it has long been associated with art and literary culture, notably the Pre-Raphaelites in the 19th century and Virginia Woolf and the "Bloomsbury Group" in the 20th.

JOSEPH Oh no, master is white man. And good Christian. Black man juju can't touch master.

JANE If he was his eldest, it means that he would be the Elesin to the next king. It's a family thing isn't it Joseph?

JOSEPH Yes madam. And if this Elesin had died before the King, his eldest son must take his place.

JANE That would explain why the old chief was so mad you took the boy away.

PILKINGS Well it makes me all the more happy I did.

JANE I wonder if he knew.

PILKINGS Who? Oh, you mean Olunde?

JANE Yes. Was that why he was so determined to get away? I wouldn't stay if I knew I was trapped in such a horrible custom.

PILKINGS [*thoughtfully*] No, I don't think he knew. At least he gave no indication. But you couldn't really tell with him. He was rather close[3] you know, quite unlike most of them. Didn't give much away, not even to me.

JANE Aren't they all rather close, Simon?

PILKINGS These natives here? Good gracious. They'll open their mouths and yap with you about their family secrets before you can stop them. Only the other day . . .

JANE But Simon, do they really give anything away? I mean, anything that really counts. This affair for instance, we didn't know they still practised that custom did we?

PILKINGS Ye-e-es, I suppose you're right there. Sly, devious bastards.

JOSEPH [*stiffly*] Can I go now master? I have to clean the kitchen.

PILKINGS What? Oh, you can go. Forgot you were still there.

[JOSEPH *goes.*]

JANE Simon, you really must watch your language. Bastard isn't just a simple swear-word in these parts, you know.

PILKINGS Look, just when did you become a social anthropologist, that's what I'd like to know.

JANE I'm not claiming to know anything. I just happen to have overheard quarrels among the servants. That's how I know they consider it a smear.

PILKINGS I thought the extended family system took care of all that. Elastic family, no bastards.

JANE [*shrugs*] Have it your own way.

[*Awkward silence. The drumming increases in volume.* JANE *gets up suddenly, restless.*]

That drumming Simon, do you think it might really be connected with this ritual? It's been going on all evening.

PILKINGS Let's ask our native guide. Joseph! Just a minute Joseph. [JOSEPH *reenters.*] What's the drumming about?

JOSEPH I don't know master.

PILKINGS What do you mean you don't know? It's only two years since your conversion. Don't tell me all that holy water nonsense also wiped out your tribal memory.

JOSEPH [*visibly shocked*] Master!

3. Secretive, taciturn.

JANE Now you've done it.

PILKINGS What have I done now?

JANE Never mind. Listen Joseph, just tell me this. Is that drumming connected with dying or anything of that nature?

JOSEPH Madam, this is what I am trying to say: I am not sure. It sounds like the death of a great chief and then, it sounds like the wedding of a great chief. It really mix me up.

PILKINGS Oh get back to the kitchen. A fat lot of help you are.

JOSEPH Yes master. [*Goes.*]

JANE Simon . . .

PILKINGS Alright, alright. I'm in no mood for preaching.

JANE It isn't my preaching you have to worry about, it's the preaching of the missionaries who preceded you here. When they make converts they really convert them. Calling holy water nonsense to our Joseph is really like insulting the Virgin Mary before a Roman Catholic. He's going to hand in his notice tomorrow you mark my word.

PILKINGS Now you're being ridiculous.

JANE Am I? What are you willing to bet that tomorrow we are going to be without a steward-boy? Did you see his face?

PILKINGS I am more concerned about whether or not we will be one native chief short by tomorrow. Christ! Just listen to those drums. [*He strides up and down, undecided.*]

JANE [*getting up*] I'll change and make us some supper.

PILKINGS What's that?

JANE Simon, it's obvious we have to miss this ball.

PILKINGS Nonsense. It's the first bit of real fun the European club has managed to organise for over a year, I'm damned if I'm going to miss it. And it is a rather special occasion. Doesn't happen every day.

JANE You know this business has to be stopped Simon. And you are the only man who can do it.

PILKINGS I don't have to stop anything. If they want to throw themselves off the top of a cliff or poison themselves for the sake of some barbaric custom what is that to me? If it were ritual murder or something like that I'd be duty-bound to do something. I can't keep an eye on all the potential suicides in this province. And as for that man—believe me it's good riddance.

JANE [*laughs*] I know you better than that Simon. You are going to have to do something to stop it—after you've finished blustering.

PILKINGS [*shouts after her*] And suppose after all it's only a wedding. I'd look a proper fool if I interrupted a chief on his honeymoon, wouldn't I? [*Resumes his angry stride, slows down.*] Ah well, who can tell what those chiefs actually do on their honeymoon anyway? [*He takes up the pad and scribbles rapidly on it.*] Joseph! Joseph! Joseph! [*Some moments later* JOSEPH *puts in a sulky appearance.*] Did you hear me call you? Why the hell didn't you answer?

JOSEPH I didn't hear master.

PILKINGS You didn't hear me! How come you are here then?

JOSEPH [*stubbornly*] I didn't hear master.

PILKINGS [*controls himself with an effort*] We'll talk about it in the morning.

I want you to take this note directly to Sergeant Amusa. You'll find him at the charge office.[4] Get on your bicycle and race there with it. I expect you back in twenty minutes exactly. Twenty minutes, is that clear?

JOSEPH Yes master. [*Going*]

PILKINGS Oh er . . . Joseph.

JOSEPH Yes master?

PILKINGS [*between gritted teeth*] Er . . . forget what I said just now. The holy water is not nonsense. *I* was talking nonsense.

JOSEPH Yes master. [*Goes.*]

JANE [*pokes her head round the door*] Have you found him?

PILKINGS Found who?

JANE Joseph. Weren't you shouting for him?

PILKINGS Oh yes, he turned up finally.

JANE You sounded desperate. What was it all about?

PILKINGS Oh nothing. I just wanted to apologise to him. Assure him that the holy water isn't really nonsense.

JANE Oh? And how did he take it?

PILKINGS Who the hell gives a damn! I had a sudden vision of our Very Reverend MacFarlane drafting another letter of complaint to the Resident about my unchristian language towards his parishioners.

JANE Oh I think he's given up on you by now.

PILKINGS Don't be too sure. And anyway, I wanted to make sure Joseph didn't 'lose' my note on the way. He looked sufficiently full of the holy crusade to do some such thing.

JANE If you've finished exaggerating, come and have something to eat.

PILKINGS No, put it all away. We can still get to the ball.

JANE Simon . . .

PILKINGS Get your costume back on. Nothing to worry about. I've instructed Amusa to arrest the man and lock him up.

JANE But that station is hardly secure Simon. He'll soon get his friends to help him escape.

PILKINGS A-ah, that's where I have out-thought you. I'm not having him put in the station cell. Amusa will bring him right here and lock him up in my study. And he'll stay with him till we get back. No one will dare come here to incite him to anything.

JANE How clever of you darling. I'll get ready.

PILKINGS Hey.

JANE Yes darling.

PILKINGS I have a surprise for you. I was going to keep it until we actually got to the ball.

JANE What is it?

PILKINGS You know the Prince[5] is on a tour of the colonies don't you? Well, he docked in the capital only this morning but he is already at the Residency. He is going to grace the ball with his presence later tonight.

JANE Simon! Not really.

4. Police station.

5. Prince Henry, duke of Gloucester (1900–1974), the uncle of the future Queen Elizabeth II, toured Ceylon (Sri Lanka), India, and North Africa in 1942.

PILKINGS Yes he is. He's been invited to give away the prizes and he has agreed. You must admit old Engleton is the best Club Secretary we ever had. Quick off the mark that lad.

JANE But how thrilling.

PILKINGS The other provincials are going to be damned envious.

JANE I wonder what he'll come as.

PILKINGS Oh I don't know. As a coat-of-arms perhaps. Anyway it won't be anything to touch this.

JANE Well that's lucky. If we are to be presented I won't have to start looking for a pair of gloves. It's all sewn on.

PILKINGS [*laughing*] Quite right. Trust a woman to think of that. Come on, let's get going.

JANE [*rushing off*] Won't be a second. [*Stops.*] Now I see why you've been so edgy all evening. I thought you weren't handling this affair with your usual brilliance—to begin with that is.

PILKINGS [*his mood is much improved*] Shut up woman and get your things on.

JANE Alright boss, coming.

[PILKINGS *suddenly begins to hum the tango to which they were dancing before. Starts to execute a few practice steps. Lights fade.*]

Act 3

A swelling, agitated hum of women's voices rises immediately in the background. The lights come on and we see the frontage of a converted cloth stall in the market. The floor leading up to the entrance is covered in rich velvets and woven cloth. The WOMEN *come on stage, borne backwards by the determined progress of Sergeant* AMUSA *and his two* CONSTABLES *who already have their batons out and use them as a pressure against the* WOMEN. *At the edge of the cloth-covered floor however the* WOMEN *take a determined stand and block all further progress of the men. They begin to tease them mercilessly.*

AMUSA I am tell you women for last time to commot my road.[6] I am here on official business.

WOMAN Official business you white man's eunuch? Official business is taking place where you want to go and it's a business you wouldn't understand.

WOMAN [*makes a quick tug at the* CONSTABLE'S *baton*] That doesn't fool anyone you know. It's the one you carry under your government knickers[7] that counts. [*She bends low as if to peep under the baggy shorts. The embarrassed* CONSTABLE *quickly puts his knees together. The* WOMEN *roar.*]

WOMAN You mean there is nothing there at all?

WOMAN Oh there was something. You know that handbell which the whiteman uses to summon his servants . . . ?

AMUSA [*he manages to preserve some dignity throughout*] I hope you women know that interfering with officer in execution of his duty is criminal offence.

WOMAN Interfere? He says we're interfering with him. You foolish man we're telling you there's nothing to interfere with.

6. Come out of my road (pidgin English); that is get out of my way.

7. Woman's underpants; here, a contemptuous reference to the khaki shorts worn by colonial policemen.

AMUSA I am order you now to clear the road.

WOMAN What road? The one your father built?

WOMAN You are a Policeman not so? Then you know what they call trespassing in court. Or—[*Pointing to the cloth-lined steps*]—do you think that kind of road is built for every kind of feet.

WOMAN Go back and tell the white man who sent you to come himself.

AMUSA If I go I will come back with reinforcement. And we will all return carrying weapons.

WOMAN Oh, now I understand. Before they can put on those knickers the white man first cuts off their weapons.

WOMAN What a cheek! You mean you come here to show power to women and you don't even have a weapon.

AMUSA [*shouting above the laughter*] For the last time I warn you women to clear the road.

WOMAN To where?

AMUSA To that hut. I know he dey dere.

WOMAN Who?

AMUSA The chief who call himself Elesin Oba.

WOMAN You ignorant man. It is not he who calls himself Elesin Oba, it is his blood that says it. As it called out to his father before him and will to his son after him. And that is in spite of everything your white man can do.

WOMAN Is it not the same ocean that washes this land and the white man's land? Tell your white man he can hide our son away as long as he likes. When the time comes for him, the same ocean will bring him back.

AMUSA The government say dat kin' ting[8] must stop.

WOMAN Who will stop it? You? Tonight our husband and father will prove himself greater than the laws of strangers.

AMUSA I tell you nobody go prove anyting tonight or anytime. Is ignorant and criminal to prove dat kin' prove.

IYALOJA [*entering, from the hut. She is accompanied by a group of* YOUNG GIRLS *who have been attending the* BRIDE] What is it Amusa? Why do you come here to disturb the happiness of others.

AMUSA Madame Iyaloja, I glad you come. You know me, I no like trouble but duty is duty. I am here to arrest Elesin for criminal intent. Tell these women to stop obstructing me in the performance of my duty.

IYALOJA And you? What gives you the right to obstruct our leader of men in the performance of his duty?

AMUSA What kin' duty be dat one Iyaloja.

IYALOJA What kin' duty? What kin' duty does a man have to his new bride?

AMUSA [*bewildered, looks at the* WOMEN *and at the entrance to the hut*] Iyaloja, is it wedding you call dis kin' ting?

IYALOJA You have wives haven't you? Whatever the white man has done to you he hasn't stopped you having wives. And if he has, at least he is married. If you don't know what a marriage is, go and ask him to tell you.

AMUSA This no to wedding.

IYALOJA And ask him at the same time what he would have done if anyone had come to disturb him on his wedding night.

AMUSA Iyaloja, I say dis no to wedding.

8. That kind of thing (pidgin English).

IYALOJA You want to look inside the bridal chamber? You want to see for yourself how a man cuts the virgin knot?

AMUSA Madam . . .

WOMAN Perhaps his wives are still waiting for him to learn.

AMUSA Iyaloja, make you tell dese women make den no insult me again. If I hear dat kin' insult once more . . .

GIRL [*pushing her way through*] You will do what?

GIRL He's out of his mind. It's our mothers you're talking to, do you know that? Not to any illiterate villager you can bully and terrorise. How dare you intrude here anyway?

GIRL What a cheek, what impertinence!

GIRL You've treated them too gently. Now let them see what it is to tamper with the mothers of this market.

GIRL Your betters dare not enter the market when the women say no!

GIRL Haven't you learnt that yet, you jester in khaki and starch?

IYALOJA Daughters . . .

GIRL No no Iyaloja, leave us to deal with him. He no longer knows his mother, we'll teach him.

[*With a sudden movement they snatch the batons of the two* CONSTABLES. *They begin to hem them in.*]

GIRL What next? We have your batons? What next? What are you going to do?

[*With equally swift movements they knock off their hats.*]

GIRL Move if you dare. We have your hats, what will you do about it? Didn't the white man teach you to take off your hats before women?

IYALOJA It's a wedding night. It's a night of joy for us. Peace . . .

GIRL Not for him. Who asked him here?

GIRL Does he dare go to the Residency without an invitation?

GIRL Not even where the servants eat the left-overs.

GIRL [*in turn. In an 'English' accent*] Well well it's Mister Amusa. Were you invited? [*Play-acting to one another. The older* WOMEN *encourage them with their titters.*]

—Your invitation card please?
—Who are you? Have we been introduced?
—And who did you say you were?
—Sorry, I didn't quite catch your name.
—May I take your hat?
—If you insist. May I take yours? [*Exchanging the* POLICEMEN'*s hats*]
—How very kind of you.
—Not at all. Won't you sit down?
—After you.
—Oh no.
—I insist.
—You're most gracious.
—And how do you find the place?
—The natives are alright.
—Friendly?
—Tractable.
—Not a teeny-weeny bit restless?
—Well, a teeny-weeny bit restless.
—One might even say, difficult?

—Indeed one might be tempted to say, difficult.
—But you do manage to cope?
—Yes indeed I do. I have a rather faithful ox called Amusa.
—He's loyal?
—Absolutely.
—Lay down his life for you what?
—Without a moment's thought.
—Had one like that once. Trust him with my life.
—Mostly of course they are liars.
—Never known a native to tell the truth.
—Does it get rather close[9] around here?
—It's mild for this time of the year.
—But the rains may still come.
—They are late this year aren't they?
—They are keeping African time.
—Ha ha ha ha
—Ha ha ha ha
—The humidity is what gets me.
—It used to be whisky.
—Ha ha ha ha
—Ha ha ha ha
—What's your handicap old chap?
—Is there racing by golly?
—Splendid golf course, you'll like it.
—I'm beginning to like it already.
—And a European club, exclusive.
—You've kept the flag flying.
—We do our best for the old country.
—It's a pleasure to serve.
—Another whisky old chap?
—You are indeed too too kind.
—Not at all sir. Where is that boy? [*With a sudden bellow*] Sergeant!

AMUSA [*snaps to attention*] Yessir!

[*The* WOMEN *collapse with laughter.*]

GIRL Take your men out of here.

AMUSA [*realising the trick, he rages from loss of face*] I'm give you warning . . .

GIRL Alright then. Off with his knickers! [*They surge slowly forward.*]

IYALOJA Daughters, please.

AMUSA [*squaring himself for defence*] The first woman wey touch me . . .

IYALOJA My children, I beg of you . . .

GIRL Then tell him to leave this market. This is the home of our mothers. We don't want the eater of white left-overs at the feast their hands have prepared.

IYALOJA You heard them Amusa. You had better go.

GIRL Now!

AMUSA [*commencing his retreat*] We dey go now, but make you no say we no warn you.

GIRL Now!

9. Stifling, hot.

GIRL Before we read the riot act[1]—you should know all about that.

AMUSA Make we go. [*They depart, more precipitately.*]

[*The* WOMEN *strike their palms across in the gesture of wonder.*]

WOMEN Do they teach you all that at school?

WOMAN And to think I nearly kept Apinke away from the place.

WOMAN Did you hear them? Did you see how they mimicked the white man?

WOMAN The voices exactly. Hey, there are wonders in this world!

IYALOJA Well, our elders have said it: Dada may be weak, but he has a younger sibling who is truly fearless.[2]

WOMAN The next time the white man shows his face in this market I will set Wuraola[3] on his tail.

[*A* WOMAN *bursts into song and dance of euphoria—'Tani l'awa o l'ogbeja? Kayi! A l'ogbeja. Omo Kekere l'ogbeja.*[4] *The rest of the* WOMEN *join in, some placing the* GIRLS *on their back like infants, others dancing round them. The dance becomes general, mounting in excitement.* ELESIN *appears, in wrapper only. In his hands a white velvet cloth folded loosely as if it held some delicate object. He cries out.*]

ELESIN Oh you mothers of beautiful brides! [*The dancing stops. They turn and see him, and the object in his hands.* IYALOJA *approaches and gently takes the cloth from him.*] Take it. It is no mere virgin stain, but the union of life and the seeds of passage. My vital flow, the last from this flesh is intermingled with the promise of future life. All is prepared. Listen! [*A steady drumbeat from the distance.*] Yes. It is nearly time. The King's dog has been killed. The King's favourite horse is about to follow his master. My brother chiefs know their task and perform it well. [*He listens again.*]

[*The* BRIDE *emerges, stands shyly by the door. He turns to her.*]

Our marriage is not yet wholly fulfilled. When earth and passage wed, the consummation is complete only when there are grains of earth on the eyelids of passage. Stay by me till then. My faithful drummers, do me your last service. This is where I have chosen to do my leave-taking, in this heart of life, this hive which contains the swarm of the world in its small compass. This is where I have known love and laughter away from the palace. Even the richest food cloys when eaten days on end; in the market, nothing ever cloys. Listen. [*They listen to the drums.*] They have begun to seek out the heart of the King's favourite horse. Soon it will ride in its bolt of raffia[5] with the dog at its feet. Together they will ride on the shoulders of the King's grooms through the pulse centres of the town. They know it is here I shall await them. I have told them. [*His eyes appear to cloud. He passes his hand over them as if to clear his sight. He gives a faint smile.*] It promises well; just then I felt my spirit's eagerness. The kite[6] makes for wide spaces and the

1. The act of Parliament (1716) that enabled local authorities to declare a group unlawfully assembled; before the law could be enforced, a proclamation ordering them to disperse had to be read.
2. Dada, the mythical king of Oyo and god of vegetables, abdicated in favor of his fierce younger brother Shango, who was god of lightning.
3. A common Yoruba girl's name; it means "rich gold."
4. Who says we haven't a defender? Silence! We have our defenders. Little children are our champions [Soyinka's translation].
5. The fiber of raffia palms, used to fringe the masks of *egungun* and make their skirts.
6. One of a number of birds in the family that includes hawks.

wind creeps up behind its tail; can the kite say less than—thank you, the quicker the better? But wait a while my spirit. Wait. Wait for the coming of the courier of the King. Do you know, friends, the horse is born to this one destiny, to bear the burden that is man upon its back. Except for this night, this night alone when the spotless stallion will ride in triumph on the back of man. In the time of my father I witnessed the strange sight. Perhaps tonight also I shall see it for the last time. If they arrive before the drums beat for me, I shall tell them to let the Alafin[7] know I follow swiftly. If they come after the drums have sounded, why then, all is well for I have gone ahead. Our spirits shall fall in step along the great passage. [*He listens to the drums. He seems again to be falling into a state of semi-hypnosis; his eyes scan the sky but it is in a kind of daze. His voice is a little breathless.*] The moon has fed, a glow from its full stomach fills the sky and air, but I cannot tell where is that gateway through which I must pass. My faithful friends, let our feet touch together this last time, lead me into the other market with sounds that cover my skin with down yet make my limbs strike earth like a thoroughbred. Dear mothers, let me dance into the passage even as I have lived beneath your roofs. [*He comes down progressively among them. They make way for him, the* DRUMMERS *playing. His dance is one of solemn, regal motions, each gesture of the body is made with a solemn finality. The* WOMEN *join him, their steps a somewhat more fluid version of his. Beneath the* PRAISE-SINGER*'s exhortations the women dirge 'Ale lẹ lẹ, awo mi lọ.'*[8]]

PRAISE-SINGER Elesin Alafin, can you hear my voice?
ELESIN Faintly, my friend, faintly.
PRAISE-SINGER Elesin Alafin, can you hear my call?
ELESIN Faintly my king, faintly.
PRAISE-SINGER Is your memory sound Elesin?
Shall my voice be a blade of grass and
Tickle the armpit of the past?
ELESIN My memory needs no prodding but
What do you wish to say to me?
PRAISE-SINGER Only what has been spoken. Only what concerns
The dying wish of the father of all.
ELESIN It is buried like seed-yam in my mind.
This is the season of quick rains, the harvest
Is this moment due for gathering.
PRAISE-SINGER If you cannot come, I said, swear
You'll tell my favourite horse. I shall
Ride on through the gates alone.
ELESIN Elesin's message will be read
Only when his loyal heart no longer beats.
PRAISE-SINGER If you cannot come Elesin, tell my dog.
I cannot stay the keeper too long
At the gate.
ELESIN A dog does not outrun the hand
That feeds it meat. A horse that throws its rider

7. The title of the paramount king of the Yoruba (that is, the deceased king); thus "Elesin Alafin," below, means "King's Horseman."

8. Night has fallen, the seasoned initiate is leaving (Yoruba).

Slows down to a stop. Elesin Alafin
Trusts no beasts with messages between
A king and his companion.

PRAISE-SINGER If you get lost my dog will track
The hidden path to me.

ELESIN The seven-way crossroads[9] confuses
Only the stranger. The Horseman of the King
Was born in the recesses of the house.

PRAISE-SINGER I know the wickedness of men. If there is
Weight on the loose end of your sash, such weight
As no mere man can shift; if your sash is earthed
By evil minds who mean to part us at the last . . .

ELESIN My sash is of the deep purple *alari*;
It is no tethering-rope. The elephant
Trails no tethering-rope; that king
Is not yet crowned who will peg an elephant—
Not even you my friend and King.

PRAISE-SINGER And yet this fear will not depart from me
The darkness of this new abode is deep—
Will your human eyes suffice?

ELESIN In a night which falls before our eyes
However deep, we do not miss our way.

PRAISE-SINGER Shall I now not acknowledge I have stood
Where wonders met their end? The elephant deserves
Better than that we say 'I have caught
A glimpse of something'. If we see the tamer
Of the forest let us say plainly, we have seen
An elephant.

ELESIN [*his voice is drowsy*]
I have freed myself of earth and now
It's getting dark. Strange voices guide my feet.

PRAISE-SINGER The river is never so high that the eyes
Of a fish are covered. The night is not so dark
That the albino[1] fails to find his way. A child
Returning homewards craves no leading by the hand.
Gracefully does the mask regain his grove at the end of the day . . .
Gracefully. Gracefully does the mask dance
Homeward at the end of the day, gracefully . . .

[ELESIN'*s trance appears to be deepening, his steps heavier.*]

IYALOJA It is the death of war that kills the valiant,
Death of water is how the swimmer goes
It is the death of markets that kills the trader
And death of indecision takes the idle away
The trade of the cutlass blunts its edge
And the beautiful die the death of beauty.
It takes an Elesin to die the death of death . . .

9. A symbol of confusion; in Yoruba folklore, the trickster god, Esu Elegba, is often found at such a crossroads.

1. Yoruba view albinism as a handicap (while believing that handicapped people are sacred to the creator of humans).

Only Elesin . . . dies the unknowable death of death . . .
Gracefully, gracefully does the horseman regain
The stables at the end of day, gracefully . . .

PRAISE-SINGER How shall I tell what my eyes have seen? The Horseman gallops on before the courier, how shall I tell what my eyes have seen? He says a dog may be confused by new scents of beings he never dreamt of, so he must precede the dog to heaven. He says a horse may stumble on strange boulders and be lamed, so he races on before the horse to heaven. It is best, he says, to trust no messenger who may falter at the outer gate; oh how shall I tell what my ears have heard? But do you hear me still Elesin, do you hear your faithful one?

[ELESIN *in his motions appears to feel for a direction of sound, subtly, but he only sinks deeper into his trance-dance.*]

Elesin Alafin, I no longer sense your flesh. The drums are changing now but you have gone far ahead of the world. It is not yet noon in heaven; let those who claim it is begin their own journey home. So why must you rush like an impatient bride: why do you race to desert your Olohun-iyo?

[ELESIN *is now sunk fully deep in his trance, there is no longer sign of any awareness of his surroundings.*]

Does the deep voice of *gbedu*[2] cover you then, like the passage of royal elephants? Those drums that brook no rivals, have they blocked the passage to your ears that my voice passes into wind, a mere leaf floating in the night? Is your flesh lightened Elesin, is that lump of earth I slid between your slippers to keep you longer slowly sifting from your feet? Are the drums on the other side now tuning skin to skin with ours in *osugbo*?[3] Are there sounds there I cannot hear, do footsteps surround you which pound the earth like *gbedu,* roll like thunder round the dome of the world? Is the darkness gathering in your head Elesin? Is there now a streak of light at the end of the passage, a light I dare not look upon? Does it reveal whose voices we often heard, whose touches we often felt, whose wisdoms come suddenly into the mind when the wisest have shaken their heads and murmured: It cannot be done? Elesin Alafin, don't think I do not know why your lips are heavy, why your limbs are drowsy as palm oil in the cold of harmattan.[4] I would call you back but when the elephant heads for the jungle, the tail is too small a handhold for the hunter that would pull him back. The sun that heads for the sea no longer heeds the prayers of the farmer. When the river begins to taste the salt of the ocean, we no longer know what deity to call on, the river-god or Olokun.[5] No arrow flies back to the string, the child does not return through the same passage that gave it birth. Elesin Oba, can you hear me at all? Your eyelids are glazed like a courtesan's, is it that you see the dark groom and master of life? And will you see my father? Will you tell him that I stayed with you to the last? Will my voice ring in your ears awhile, will you remember Olohun-iyo even if the music on the other side surpasses his mortal craft? But will they know you over there? Have they eyes to gauge your worth, have they the heart to love you, will they

2. A deep-timbred royal drum [Soyinka].
3. Secret "executive" cult of the Yoruba; its meeting place [Soyinka].
4. A dry, dust-bearing seasonal wind that blows into West Africa from the Sahara Desert.
5. The god of the ocean.

know what thoroughbred prances towards them in caparisons[6] of honour? If they do not Elesin, if any there cuts your yam with a small knife, or pours you wine in a small calabash, turn back and return to welcoming hands. If the world were not greater than the wishes of Olohun-iyo, I would not let you go . . .

[*He appears to break down.* ELESIN *dances on, completely in a trance. The dirge wells up louder and stronger.* ELESIN*'s dance does not lose its elasticity but his gestures become, if possible, even more weighty. Lights fade slowly on the scene.*]

Act 4

A Masque.[7] *The front side of the stage is part of a wide corridor around the great hall of the Residency extending beyond vision into the rear and wings. It is redolent of the tawdry decadence of a far-flung but key imperial frontier. The couples in a variety of fancy-dress are ranged around the walls, gazing in the same direction. The guest-of-honour is about to make an appearance. A portion of the local police brass band with its white conductor is just visible. At last, the entrance of Royalty. The band plays 'Rule Britannia',*[8] *badly, beginning long before he is visible. The couples bow and curtsey as he passes by them. Both he and his companions are dressed in seventeenth-century European costume. Following behind are the* RESIDENT *and his partner similarly attired. As they gain the end of the hall where the orchestra dais begins the music comes to an end. The* PRINCE *bows to the guests. The band strikes up a Viennese waltz and the* PRINCE *formally opens the floor. Several bars later the* RESIDENT *and his companion follow suit. Others follow in appropriate pecking order. The orchestra's waltz rendition is not of the highest musical standard.*

Some time later the PRINCE *dances again into view and is settled into a corner by the* RESIDENT *who then proceeds to select couples as they dance past for introduction, sometimes threading his way through the dancers to tap the lucky couple on the shoulder. Desperate efforts from many to ensure that they are recognised in spite of, perhaps, their costume. The ritual of introductions soon takes in* PILKINGS *and his wife. The* PRINCE *is quite fascinated by their costume and they demonstrate the adaptations they have made to it, pulling down the mask to demonstrate how the* egungun *normally appears, then showing the various press-button controls they have innovated for the face flaps, the sleeves, etc. They demonstrate the dance steps and the guttural sounds made by the* egungun, *harass other dancers in the hall,* MRS PILKINGS *playing the 'restrainer'*[9] *to* PILKINGS' *manic darts. Everyone is highly entertained, the Royal Party especially who lead the applause.*

At this point a liveried footman comes in with a note on a salver and is intercepted almost absent-mindedly by the RESIDENT *who takes the note and reads it. After polite coughs he succeeds in excusing the* PILKINGS *from the* PRINCE *and takes them aside. The* PRINCE *considerately offers the* RESIDENT*'s wife his hand and dancing is resumed.*

On their way out the RESIDENT *gives an order to his* AIDE-DE-CAMP. *They come into the side corridor where the* RESIDENT *hands the note to* PILKINGS.

RESIDENT As you see it says 'emergency' on the outside. I took the liberty of opening it because His Highness was obviously enjoying the entertainment. I didn't want to interrupt unless really necessary.

6. Ornamental cloths spread over the saddle or harness of horses.
7. That is, a masquerade, or elaborate masked ball (a European entertainment).
8. A patriotic song (1740); its words, taken from James Thomson's poem of the same title, are set to music by Thomas Arne.
9. The person who exercises a restraining influence on the wild movements of the main dancer.

PILKINGS Yes, yes of course, sir.

RESIDENT Is it really as bad as it says? What's it all about?

PILKINGS Some strange custom they have sir. It seems because the King is dead some important chief has to commit suicide.

RESIDENT The King? Isn't it the same one who died nearly a month ago?

PILKINGS Yes sir.

RESIDENT Haven't they buried him yet?

PILKINGS They take their time about these things, sir. The preburial ceremonies last nearly thirty days. It seems tonight is the final night.

RESIDENT But what has it got to do with the market women? Why are they rioting? We've waived that troublesome tax haven't we?

PILKINGS We don't quite know that they are exactly rioting yet sir. Sergeant Amusa is sometimes prone to exaggerations.

RESIDENT He sounds desperate enough. That comes out even in his rather quaint grammar. Where is the man anyway? I asked my aide-de-camp to bring him here.

PILKINGS They are probably looking in the wrong verandah. I'll fetch him myself.

RESIDENT No no you stay here. Let your wife go and look for them. Do you mind my dear . . . ?

JANE Certainly not, your Excellency. [*Goes.*]

RESIDENT You should have kept me informed, Pilkings. You realise how disastrous it would have been if things had erupted while His Highness was here.

PILKINGS I wasn't aware of the whole business until tonight sir.

RESIDENT Nose to the ground Pilkings, nose to the ground. If we all let these little things slip past us where would the empire be eh? Tell me that. Where would we all be?

PILKINGS [*low voice*] Sleeping peacefully at home I bet.

RESIDENT What did you say Pilkings?

PILKINGS It won't happen again sir.

RESIDENT It mustn't Pilkings. It mustn't. Where is that damned sergeant? I ought to get back to His Highness as quickly as possible and offer him some plausible explanation for my rather abrupt conduct. Can you think of one, Pilkings?

PILKINGS You could tell him the truth, sir.

RESIDENT I could? No no no Pilkings, that would never do. What! Go and tell him there is a riot just two miles away from him? This is supposed to be a secure colony of His Majesty, Pilkings.

PILKINGS Yes, sir.

RESIDENT Ah, there they are. No, these are not our native police. Are these the ring-leaders of the riot?

PILKINGS Sir, these are my police officers.

RESIDENT Oh, I beg your pardon officers. You do look a little . . . I say, isn't there something missing in their uniform? I think they used to have some rather colourful sashes. If I remember rightly I recommended them myself in my young days in the service. A bit of colour always appeals to the natives, yes, I remember putting that in my report. Well well well, where are we? Make your report man.

PILKINGS [*moves close to* AMUSA, *between his teeth*] And let's have no more superstitious nonsense from you Amusa or I'll throw you in the guardroom for a month and feed you pork![1]

RESIDENT What's that? What has pork to do with it?

PILKINGS Sir, I was just warning him to be brief. I'm sure you are most anxious to hear his report.

RESIDENT Yes yes yes of course. Come on man, speak up. Hey, didn't we give them some colourful fez hats with all those wavy things, yes, pink tassels . . .

PILKINGS Sir, I think if he was permitted to make his report we might find that he lost his hat in the riot.

RESIDENT Ah yes indeed. I'd better tell His Highness that. Lost his hat in the riot, ha ha. He'll probably say well, as long as he didn't lose his head. [*Chuckles to himself.*] Don't forget to send me a report first thing in the morning young Pilkings.

PILKINGS No sir.

RESIDENT And whatever you do, don't let things get out of hand. Keep a cool head and—nose to the ground Pilkings. [*Wanders off in the general direction of the hall.*]

PILKINGS Yes, sir.

AIDE-DE-CAMP Would you be needing me sir?

PILKINGS No thanks Bob. I think His Excellency's need of you is greater than ours.

AIDE-DE-CAMP We have a detachment of soldiers from the capital sir. They accompanied His Highness up here.

PILINGS I doubt if it will come to that but, thanks, I'll bear it in mind. Oh, could you send an orderly with my cloak.

AIDE-DE-CAMP Very good sir. [*Goes.*]

PILKINGS Now sergeant.

AMUSA Sir . . . [*Makes an effort, stops dead. Eyes to the ceiling.*]

PILKINGS Oh, not again.

AMUSA I cannot against death to dead cult. This dress get power of dead.

PILKINGS Alright, let's go. You are relieved of all further duty Amusa. Report to me first thing in the morning.

JANE Shall I come Simon?

PILKINGS No, there's no need for that. If I can get back later I will. Otherwise get Bob to bring you home.

JANE Be careful Simon . . . I mean, be clever.

PILKINGS Sure I will. You two, come with me. [*As he turns to go, the clock in the Residency begins to chime.* PILKINGS *looks at his watch then turns, horror-stricken, to stare at his wife. The same thought clearly occurs to her. He swallows hard. An orderly brings his cloak.*] It's midnight. I had no idea it was that late.

JANE But surely . . . they don't count the hours the way we do. The moon, or something . . .

PILKINGS I am . . . not so sure.

1. The eating of pork is forbidden to Muslims by the Qur'an.

[*He turns and breaks into a sudden run. The two* CONSTABLES *follow, also at a run.* AMUSA, *who has kept his eyes on the ceiling throughout waits until the last of the footsteps has faded out of hearing. He salutes suddenly, but without once looking in the direction of the woman.*]

AMUSA Goodnight madam.

JANE Oh. [*She hesitates.*] Amusa . . . [*He goes off without seeming to have heard.*] Poor Simon . . . [*A figure emerges from the shadows, a young black man dressed in a sober western suit. He peeps into the hall, trying to make out the figures of the dancers.*] Who is that?

OLUNDE [*emerging into the light*] I didn't mean to startle you madam. I am looking for the District Officer.

JANE Wait a minute . . . don't I know you? Yes, you are Olunde, the young man who . . .

OLUNDE Mrs Pilkings! How fortunate. I came here to look for your husband.

JANE Olunde! Let's look at you. What a fine young man you've become. Grand but solemn. Good God, when did you return? Simon never said a word. But you do look well Olunde. Really!

OLUNDE You are . . . well, you look quite well yourself Mrs Pilkings. From what little I can see of you.

JANE Oh, this. It's caused quite a stir I assure you, and not all of it very pleasant. You are not shocked I hope?

OLUNDE Why should I be? But don't you find it rather hot in there? Your skin must find it difficult to breathe.

JANE Well, it is a little hot I must confess, but it's all in a good cause.

OLUNDE What cause Mrs Pilkings?

JANE All this. The ball. And His Highness being here in person and all that.

OLUNDE [*mildly*] And that is the good cause for which you desecrate an ancestral mask?

JANE Oh, so you are shocked after all. How disappointing.

OLUNDE No I am not shocked Mrs Pilkings. You forget that I have now spent four years among your people. I discovered that you have no respect for what you do not understand.

JANE Oh. So you've returned with a chip on your shoulder. That's a pity Olunde. I am sorry.

[*An uncomfortable silence follows.*]

I take it then that you did not find your stay in England altogether edifying.

OLUNDE I don't say that. I found your people quite admirable in many ways, their conduct and courage in this war[2] for instance.

JANE Ah yes, the war. Here of course it is all rather remote. From time to time we have a black-out drill just to remind us that there is a war on. And the rare convoy passes through on its way somewhere or on manoeuvres. Mind you there is the occasional bit of excitement like that ship that was blown up in the harbour.[3]

OLUNDE Here? Do you mean through enemy action?

2. That is, World War II.

3. Perhaps a reference to a tragic incident that involved no heroism: on December 5, 1942, when three British naval trawlers were moored in the harbor at Lagos, an oil spill caught fire. The ships exploded, killing about 200 men.

JANE Oh no, the war hasn't come that close. The captain did it himself. I don't quite understand it really. Simon tried to explain. The ship had to be blown up because it had become dangerous to the other ships, even to the city itself. Hundreds of the coastal population would have died.

OLUNDE Maybe it was loaded with ammunition and had caught fire. Or some of those lethal gases they've been experimenting on.

JANE Something like that. The captain blew himself up with it. Deliberately. Simon said someone had to remain on board to light the fuse.

OLUNDE It must have been a very short fuse.

JANE [*shrugs*] I don't know much about it. Only that there was no other way to save lives. No time to devise anything else. The captain took the decision and carried it out.

OLUNDE Yes . . . I quite believe it. I met men like that in England.

JANE Oh just look at me! Fancy welcoming you back with such morbid news. Stale too. It was at least six months ago.

OLUNDE I don't find it morbid at all. I find it rather inspiring. It is an affirmative commentary on life.

JANE What is?

OLUNDE That captain's self-sacrifice.

JANE Nonsense. Life should never be thrown deliberately away.

OLUNDE And the innocent people round the harbour?

JANE Oh, how does one know? The whole thing was probably exaggerated anyway.

OLUNDE That was a risk the captain couldn't take. But please Mrs Pilkings, do you think you could find your husband for me? I have to talk to him.

JANE Simon? Oh. [*As she recollects for the first time the full significance of* OLUNDE*'s presence.*] Simon is . . . there is a little problem in town. He was sent for. But . . . when did you arrive? Does Simon know you're here?

OLUNDE [*suddenly earnest*] I need your help Mrs Pilkings. I've always found you somewhat more understanding than your husband. Please find him for me and when you do, you must help me talk to him.

JANE I'm afraid I don't quite . . . follow you. Have you seen my husband already?

OLUNDE I went to your house. Your houseboy told me you were here. [*He smiles.*] He even told me how I would recognise you and Mr Pilkings.

JANE Then you must know what my husband is trying to do for you.

OLUNDE For me?

JANE For you. For your people. And to think he didn't even know you were coming back! But how do you happen to be here? Only this evening we were talking about you. We thought you were still four thousand miles away.

OLUNDE I was sent a cable.

JANE A cable? Who did? Simon? The business of your father didn't begin till tonight.

OLUNDE A relation sent it weeks ago, and it said nothing about my father. All it said was, Our King is dead. But I knew I had to return home at once so as to bury my father. I understood that.

JANE Well, thank God you don't have to go through that agony. Simon is going to stop it.

OLUNDE That's why I want to see him. He's wasting his time. And since he has been so helpful to me I don't want him to incur the enmity of our people. Especially over nothing.

JANE [*sits down open-mouthed*] You . . . you Olunde!

OLUNDE Mrs Pilkings, I came home to bury my father. As soon as I heard the news I booked my passage home. In fact we were fortunate. We travelled in the same convoy as your Prince, so we had excellent protection.

JANE But you don't think your father is also entitled to whatever protection is available to him?

OLUNDE How can I make you understand? He *has* protection. No one can undertake what he does tonight without the deepest protection the mind can conceive. What can you offer him in place of his peace of mind, in place of the honour and veneration of his own people? What would you think of your Prince if he refused to accept the risk of losing his life on this voyage? This . . . showing-the-flag tour of colonial possessions.

JANE I see. So it isn't just medicine you studied in England.

OLUNDE Yet another error into which your people fall. You believe that everything which appears to make sense was learnt from you.

JANE Not so fast Olunde. You have learnt to argue I can tell that, but I never said you made sense. However clearly you try to put it, it is still a barbaric custom. It is even worse—it's feudal! The king dies and a chieftain must be buried with him. How feudalistic can you get!

OLUNDE [*waves his hand towards the background. The* PRINCE *is dancing past again—to a different step—and all the guests are bowing and curtseying as he passes*] And this? Even in the midst of a devastating war, look at that. What name would you give to that?

JANE Therapy, British style. The preservation of sanity in the midst of chaos.

OLUNDE Others would call it decadence. However, it doesn't really interest me. You white races know how to survive; I've seen proof of that. By all logical and natural laws this war should end with all the white races wiping out one another, wiping out their so-called civilisation for all time and reverting to a state of primitivism the like of which has so far only existed in your imagination when you thought of us. I thought all that at the beginning. Then I slowly realised that your greatest art is the art of survival. But at least have the humility to let others survive in their own way.

JANE Through ritual suicide?

OLUNDE Is that worse than mass suicide? Mrs Pilkings, what do you call what those young men are sent to do by their generals in this war? Of course you have also mastered the art of calling things by names which don't remotely describe them.

JANE You talk! You people with your long-winded, roundabout way of making conversation.

OLUNDE Mrs Pilkings, whatever we do, we never suggest that a thing is the opposite of what it really is. In your newsreels I heard defeats, thorough, murderous defeats described as strategic victories. No wait, it wasn't just on your newsreels. Don't forget I was attached to hospitals all the time. Hordes of your wounded passed through those wards. I spoke to them. I spent long evenings by their bedsides while they spoke terrible truths of the realities of that war. I know now how history is made.

JANE But surely, in a war of this nature, for the morale of the nation you must expect . . .

OLUNDE That a disaster beyond human reckoning be spoken of as a triumph? No. I mean, is there no mourning in the home of the bereaved that such blasphemy is permitted?

JANE [*after a moment's pause*] Perhaps I can understand you now. The time we picked for you was not really one for seeing us at our best.

OLUNDE Don't think it was just the war. Before that even started I had plenty of time to study your people. I saw nothing, finally, that gave you the right to pass judgement on other peoples and their ways. Nothing at all.

JANE [*hesitantly*] Was it the . . . colour thing? I know there is some discrimination.

OLUNDE Don't make it so simple, Mrs Pilkings. You make it sound as if when I left, I took nothing at all with me.

JANE Yes . . . and to tell the truth, only this evening, Simon and I agreed that we never really knew what you left with.

OLUNDE Neither did I. But I found out over there. I am grateful to your country for that. And I will never give it up.

JANE Olunde please . . . promise me something. Whatever you do, don't throw away what you have started to do. You want to be a doctor. My husband and I believe you will make an excellent one, sympathetic and competent. Don't let anything make you throw away your training.

OLUNDE [*genuinely surprised*] Of course not. What a strange idea. I intend to return and complete my training. Once the burial of my father is over.

JANE Oh, please . . . !

OLUNDE Listen! Come outside. You can't hear anything against that music.

JANE What is it?

OLUNDE The drums. Can you hear the changes? Listen.

[*The drums come over, still distant but more distinct. There is a change of rhythm, it rises to a crescendo and then, suddenly, it is cut off. After a silence, a new beat begins, slow and resonant.*]

There, it's all over.

JANE You mean he's . . .

OLUNDE Yes, Mrs Pilkings, my father is dead. His will-power has always been enormous; I know he is dead.

JANE [*screams*] How can you be so callous! So unfeeling! You announce your father's own death like a surgeon looking down on some strange . . . stranger's body! You're just a savage like all the rest.

AIDE-DE-CAMP [*rushing out*] Mrs Pilkings. Mrs Pilkings. [*She breaks down, sobbing.*] Are you all right, Mrs Pilkings?

OLUNDE She'll be all right. [*Turns to go.*]

AIDE-DE-CAMP Who are you? And who the hell asked your opinion?

OLUNDE You're quite right, nobody. [*Going*]

AIDE-DE-CAMP What the hell! Did you hear me ask you who you were?

OLUNDE I have business to attend to.

AIDE-DE-CAMP I'll give you business in a moment you impudent nigger. Answer my question!

OLUNDE I have a funeral to arrange. Excuse me. [*Going*]

AIDE-DE-CAMP I said stop! Orderly!

JANE No, no, don't do that. I'm alright. And for heaven's sake don't act so foolishly. He's a family friend.

AIDE-DE-CAMP Well he'd better learn to answer civil questions when he's asked them. These natives put a suit on and they get high opinions of themselves.

OLUNDE Can I go now?

JANE No no don't go. I must talk to you. I'm sorry about what I said.

OLUNDE It's nothing, Mrs Pilkings. And I'm really anxious to go. I couldn't see my father before, it's forbidden for me, his heir and successor, to set eyes on him from the moment of the King's death. But now . . . I would like to touch his body while it is still warm.

JANE You will. I promise I shan't keep you long. Only, I couldn't possibly let you go like that. Bob, please excuse us.

AIDE-DE-CAMP If you're sure . . .

JANE Of course I'm sure. Something happened to upset me just then, but I'm alright now. Really.

[*The* AIDE-DE-CAMP *goes, somewhat reluctantly.*]

OLUNDE I mustn't stay long.

JANE Please, I promise not to keep you. It's just that . . . oh you saw yourself what happens to one in this place. The Resident's man thought he was being helpful, that's the way we all react. But I can't go in among that crowd just now and if I stay by myself somebody will come looking for me. Please, just say something for a few moments and then you can go. Just so I can recover myself.

OLUNDE What do you want me to say?

JANE Your calm acceptance for instance, can you explain that? It was so unnatural. I don't understand that at all. I feel a need to understand all I can.

OLUNDE But you explained it yourself. My medical training perhaps. I have seen death too often. And the soldiers who returned from the front, they died on our hands all the time.

JANE No. It has to be more than that. I feel it has to do with the many things we don't really grasp about your people. At least you can explain.

OLUNDE All these things are part of it. And anyway, my father has been dead in my mind for nearly a month. Ever since I learnt of the King's death. I've lived with my bereavement so long now that I cannot think of him alive. On that journey on the boat, I kept my mind on my duties as the one who must perform the rites over his body. I went through it all again and again in my mind as he himself had taught me. I didn't want to do anything wrong, something which might jeopardise the welfare of my people.

JANE But he had disowned you. When you left he swore publicly you were no longer his son.

OLUNDE I told you, he was a man of tremendous will. Sometimes that's another way of saying stubborn. But among our people, you don't disown a child just like that. Even if I had died before him I would still be buried like his eldest son. But it's time for me to go.

JANE Thank you. I feel calmer. Don't let me keep you from your duties.

OLUNDE Goodnight, Mrs Pilkings.

JANE Welcome home. [*She holds out her hand. As he takes it footsteps are heard approaching the drive. A short while later a woman's sobbing is also heard.*]

PILKINGS [*off*] Keep them here till I get back. [*He strides into view, reacts at the sight of* OLUNDE *but turns to his wife.*] Thank goodness you're still here.

JANE Simon, what happened?

PILKINGS Later Jane, please. Is Bob still here?

JANE Yes, I think so. I'm sure he must be.

PILKINGS Try and get him out here as quickly as you can. Tell him it's urgent.

JANE Of course. Oh Simon, you remember . . .

PILKINGS Yes yes. I can see who it is. Get Bob out here. [*She runs off.*] At first I thought I was seeing a ghost.

OLUNDE Mr Pilkings, I appreciate what you tried to do. I want you to believe that. I can tell you it would have been a terrible calamity if you'd succeeded.

PILKINGS [*opens his mouth several times, shuts it*] You . . . said what?

OLUNDE A calamity for us, the entire people.

PILKINGS [*sighs*] I see. Hm.

OLUNDE And now I must go. I must see him before he turns cold.

PILKINGS Oh ah . . . em . . . but this is a shock to see you. I mean er thinking all this while you were in England and thanking God for that.

OLUNDE I came on the mail boat. We travelled in the Prince's convoy.

PILKINGS Ah yes, a-ah, hm . . . er well . . .

OLUNDE Goodnight. I can see you are shocked by the whole business. But you must know by now there are things you cannot understand—or help.

PILKINGS Yes. Just a minute. There are armed policemen that way and they have instructions to let no one pass. I suggest you wait a little. I'll er . . . give you an escort.

OLUNDE That's very kind of you. But do you think it could be quickly arranged?

PILKINGS Of course. In fact, yes, what I'll do is send Bob over with some men to the er . . . place. You can go with them. Here he comes now. Excuse me a minute.

AIDE-DE-CAMP Anything wrong sir?

PILKINGS [*takes him to one side*] Listen Bob, that cellar in the disused annexe of the Residency, you know, where the slaves were stored before being taken down to the coast . . .

AIDE-DE-CAMP Oh yes, we use it as a storeroom for broken furniture.

PILKINGS But it's still got the bars on it?

AIDE-DE-CAMP Oh yes, they are quite intact.

PILKINGS Get the keys please. I'll explain later. And I want a strong guard over the Residency tonight.

AIDE-DE-CAMP We have that already. The detachment from the coast . . .

PILKINGS No, I don't want them at the gates of the Residency. I want you to deploy them at the bottom of the hill, a long way from the main hall so they can deal with any situation long before the sound carries to the house.

AIDE-DE-CAMP Yes of course.

PILKINGS I don't want His Highness alarmed.

AIDE-DE-CAMP You think the riot will spread here?

PILKINGS It's unlikely but I don't want to take a chance. I made them believe I was going to lock the man up in my house, which was what I had planned to do in the first place. They are probably assailing it by now. I took a roundabout route here so I don't think there is any danger at all. At least not before dawn. Nobody is to leave the premises of course—the native employees I mean. They'll soon smell something is up and they can't keep their mouths shut.

AIDE-DE-CAMP I'll give instructions at once.

PILKINGS I'll take the prisoner down myself. Two policemen will stay with him throughout the night. Inside the cell.

AIDE-DE-CAMP Right sir. [*Salutes and goes off at the double.*]

PILKINGS Jane. Bob is coming back in a moment with a detachment. Until he gets back please stay with Olunde. [*He makes an extra warning gesture with his eyes.*]

OLUNDE Please, Mr Pilkings . . .

PILKINGS I hate to be stuffy old son, but we have a crisis on our hands. It has to do with your father's affair if you must know. And it happens also at a time when we have His Highness here. I am responsible for security so you'll simply have to do as I say. I hope that's understood. [*Marches off quickly, in the direction from which he made his first appearance.*]

OLUNDE What's going on? All this can't be just because he failed to stop my father killing himself.

JANE I honestly don't know. Could it have sparked off a riot?

OLUNDE No. If he'd succeeded that would be more likely to start the riot. Perhaps there were other factors involved. Was there a chieftancy dispute?

JANE None that I know of.

ELESIN [*an animal bellow from off*] Leave me alone! Is it not enough that you have covered me in shame! White man, take your hand from my body!

[OLUNDE *stands frozen to the spot.* JANE, *understanding at last, tries to move him.*]

JANE Let's go in. It's getting chilly out here.

PILKINGS [*off*] Carry him.

ELESIN Give me back the name you have taken away from me you ghost from the land of the nameless!

PILKINGS Carry him! I can't have a disturbance here. Quickly! stuff up his mouth.

JANE Oh God! Let's go in. Please Olunde. [OLUNDE *does not move.*]

ELESIN Take your albino's[4] hand from me you . . .

[*Sounds of a struggle. His voice chokes as he is gagged.*]

OLUNDE [*quietly*] That was my father's voice.

JANE Oh you poor orphan, what have you come home to?

[*There is a sudden explosion of rage from offstage and powerful steps come running up the drive.*]

PILKINGS You bloody fools, after him!

[*Immediately* ELESIN, *in handcuffs, comes pounding in the direction of* JANE *and* OLUNDE, *followed some moments afterwards by* PILKINGS *and the* CONSTABLES. ELESIN, *confronted by the seeming statue of his son, stops dead.* OLUNDE *stares above his head into the distance. The* CONSTABLES *try to grab him.* JANE *screams at them.*]

JANE Leave him alone! Simon, tell them to leave him alone.

PILKINGS All right, stand aside you. [*Shrugs.*] Maybe just as well. It might help to calm him down.

[*For several moments they hold the same position.* ELESIN *moves a step forward, almost as if he's still in doubt.*]

4. A term of abuse when applied to a white person.

ELESIN Olunde? [*He moves his head, inspecting him from side to side.*] Olunde! [*He collapses slowly at* OLUNDE's *feet.*] Oh son, don't let the sight of your father turn you blind!

OLUNDE [*he moves for the first time since he heard his voice, brings his head slowly down to look on him*] I have no father, eater of left-overs.

[*He walks slowly down the way his father had run. Light fades out on* ELESIN, *sobbing into the ground.*]

Act 5

A wide iron-barred gate stretches almost the whole width of the cell in which ELESIN *is imprisoned. His wrists are encased in thick iron bracelets, chained together; he stands against the bars, looking out. Seated on the ground to one side on the outside is his recent bride, her eyes bent perpetually to the ground. Figures of the two* GUARDS *can be seen deeper inside the cell, alert to every movement* ELESIN *makes.* PILKINGS *now in a police officer's uniform, enters noiselessly, observes him a while. Then he coughs ostentatiously and approaches. Leans against the bars near a corner, his back to* ELESIN. *He is obviously trying to fall in mood with him. Some moments' silence.*

PILKINGS You seem fascinated by the moon.

ELESIN [*after a pause*] Yes, ghostly one. Your twin-brother up there engages my thoughts.

PILKINGS It is a beautiful night.

ELESIN Is that so?

PILKINGS The light on the leaves, the peace of the night . . .

ELESIN The night is not at peace, District Officer.

PILKINGS No? I would have said it was. You know, quiet . . .

ELESIN And does quiet mean peace for you?

PILKINGS Well, nearly the same thing. Naturally there is a subtle difference . . .

ELESIN The night is not at peace, ghostly one. The world is not at peace. You have shattered the peace of the world for ever. There is no sleep in the world tonight.

PILKINGS It is still a good bargain if the world should lose one night's sleep as the price of saving a man's life.

ELESIN You did not save my life, District Officer. You destroyed it.

PILKINGS Now come on . . .

ELESIN And not merely my life but the lives of many. The end of the night's work is not over. Neither this year nor the next will see it. If I wished you well, I would pray that you do not stay long enough on our land to see the disaster you have brought upon us.

PILKINGS Well, I did my duty as I saw it. I have no regrets.

ELESIN No. The regrets of life always come later.

[*Some moments' pause.*]

You are waiting for dawn white man. I hear you saying to yourself: only so many hours until dawn and then the danger is over. All I must do is to keep him alive tonight. You don't quite understand it all but you know that tonight is when what ought to be must be brought about. I shall ease your mind even more, ghostly one. It is not an entire night but a moment of the night, and that moment is past. The moon was my messenger and guide. When it reached a certain gateway in the sky, it touched that moment for which my whole life has been spent in blessings. Even I do not know the gateway. I have stood here and scanned the sky for a glimpse of that door but, I cannot see it. Human eyes are useless for a search of this nature. But in the house of *osugbo,* those who keep watch through the spirit recognised the moment, they sent word to me through the voice of our sacred drums to prepare myself. I heard them and I shed all thoughts of earth. I began to follow the moon to the abode of the gods . . . servant of the white king, that was when you entered my chosen place of departure on feet of desecration.

PILKINGS I'm sorry, but we all see our duty differently.

ELESIN I no longer blame you. You stole from me my first-born, sent him to your country so you could turn him into something in your own image. Did you plan it all beforehand? There are moments when it seems part of a larger plan. He who must follow my footsteps is taken from me, sent across the ocean. Then, in my turn, I am stopped from fulfilling my destiny. Did you think it all out before, this plan to push our world from its course and sever the cord that links us to the great origin?

PILKINGS You don't really believe that. Anyway, if that was my intention with your son, I appear to have failed.

ELESIN You did not fail in the main thing ghostly one. We know the roof covers the rafters, the cloth covers blemishes; who would have known that the white skin covered our future, preventing us from seeing the death our enemies had prepared for us. The world is set adrift and its inhabitants are lost. Around them, there is nothing but emptiness.

PILKINGS Your son does not take so gloomy a view.

ELESIN Are you dreaming now, white man? Were you not present at the reunion of shame? Did you not see when the world reversed itself and the father fell before his son, asking forgiveness?

PILKINGS That was in the heat of the moment. I spoke to him and . . . if you want to know, he wishes he could cut out his tongue for uttering the words he did.

ELESIN No. What he said must never be unsaid. The contempt of my own son rescued something of my shame at your hands. You have stopped me in my duty but I know now that I did give birth to a son. Once I mistrusted him for seeking the companionship of those my spirit knew as enemies of our race. Now I understand. One should seek to obtain the secrets of his enemies. He will avenge my shame, white one. His spirit will destroy you and yours.

PILKINGS That kind of talk is hardly called for. If you don't want my consolation . . .

ELESIN No white man, I do not want your consolation.

PILKINGS As you wish. Your son, anyway, sends his consolation. He asks your forgiveness. When I asked him not to despise you his reply was: I cannot judge him, and if I cannot judge him, I cannot despise him. He wants to come to you and say goodbye and to receive your blessing.

ELESIN Goodbye? Is he returning to your land?

PILKINGS Don't you think that's the most sensible thing for him to do? I advised him to leave at once, before dawn, and he agrees that is the right course of action.

ELESIN Yes, it is best. And even if I did not think so, I have lost the father's place of honour. My voice is broken.

PILKINGS Your son honours you. If he didn't he would not ask your blessing.

ELESIN No. Even a thoroughbred is not without pity for the turf he strikes with his hoof. When is he coming?

PILKINGS As soon as the town is a little quieter. I advised it.

ELESIN Yes white man, I am sure you advised it. You advise all our lives although on the authority of what gods, I do not know.

PILKINGS [*opens his mouth to reply, then appears to change his mind. Turns to go. Hesitates and stops again*] Before I leave you, may I ask just one thing of you?

ELESIN I am listening.

PILKINGS I wish to ask you to search the quiet of your heart and tell me—do you not find great contradictions in the wisdom of your own race?

ELESIN Make yourself clear, white one.

PILKINGS I have lived among you long enough to learn a saying or two. One came to my mind tonight when I stepped into the market and saw what was going on. You were surrounded by those who egged you on with song and praises. I thought, are these not the same people who say: the elder grimly approaches heaven and you ask him to bear your greetings yonder; do you really think he makes the journey willingly? After that, I did not hesitate.

[*A pause.* ELESIN *sighs. Before he can speak a sound of running feet is heard.*]

JANE [*off*] Simon! Simon!

PILKINGS What on earth . . . ! [*Runs off.*]

[ELESIN *turns to his new wife, gazes on her for some moments.*]

ELESIN My young bride, did you hear the ghostly one? You sit and sob in your silent heart but say nothing to all this. First I blamed the white man, then I blamed my gods for deserting me. Now I feel I want to blame you for the mystery of the sapping of my will. But blame is a strange peace offering for a man to bring a world he has deeply wronged, and to its innocent dwellers. Oh little mother, I have taken countless women in my life but you were more than a desire of the flesh. I needed you as the abyss across which my body must be drawn, I filled it with earth and dropped my seed in it at the moment of preparedness for my crossing. You were the final gift of the living to their emissary to the land of the ancestors, and perhaps your warmth and youth brought new insights of this world to me and turned my feet leaden on this side of the abyss. For I confess to you, daughter, my weakness came not merely from the abomination of the white man who came violently into my fading presence, there was also a weight of longing on my earth-held limbs. I would have shaken it off, already my foot had begun to lift but then, the white ghost entered and all was defiled.

[*Approaching voices of* PILKINGS *and his wife.*]

JANE Oh Simon, you will let her in won't you?

PILKINGS I really wish you'd stop interfering.

[*They come into view.* JANE *is in a dressing-gown.* PILKINGS *is holding a note to which he refers from time to time.*]

JANE Good gracious, I didn't initiate this. I was sleeping quietly, or trying to anyway, when the servant brought it. It's not my fault if one can't sleep undisturbed even in the Residency.

PILKINGS He'd have done the same thing if we were sleeping at home so don't sidetrack the issue. He knows he can get round[5] you or he wouldn't send you the petition in the first place.

JANE Be fair Simon. After all he was thinking of your own interests. He is grateful you know, you seem to forget that. He feels he owes you something.

PILKINGS I just wish they'd leave this man alone tonight, that's all.

JANE Trust him Simon. He's pledged his word it will all go peacefully.

PILKINGS Yes, and that's the other thing. I don't like being threatened.

JANE Threatened? [*Takes the note.*] I didn't spot any threat.

PILKINGS It's there. Veiled, but it's there. The only way to prevent serious rioting tomorrow—what a cheek!

JANE I don't think he's threatening you Simon.

PILKINGS He's picked up the idiom alright. Wouldn't surprise me if he's been mixing with commies or anarchists over there. The phrasing sounds too good to be true. Damn! If only the Prince hadn't picked this time for his visit.

JANE Well, even so Simon, what have you got to lose? You don't want a riot on your hands, not with the Prince here.

PILKINGS [*going up to* ELESIN] Let's see what he has to say. Chief Elesin, there is yet another person who wants to see you. As she is not a next-of-kin I don't really feel obliged to let her in. But your son sent a note with her, so it's up to you.

ELESIN I know who that must be. So she found out your hiding-place. Well, it was not difficult. My stench of shame is so strong, it requires no hunter's dog to follow it.

PILKINGS If you don't want to see her, just say so and I'll send her packing.

ELESIN Why should I not want to see her? Let her come. I have no more holes in my rag of shame. All is laid bare.

PILKINGS I'll bring her in. [*Goes off.*]

JANE [*hesitates, then goes to* ELESIN] Please, try and understand. Everything my husband did was for the best.

ELESIN [*he gives her a long strange stare, as if he is trying to understand who she is*] You are the wife of the District Officer?

JANE Yes. My name, is Jane.

ELESIN That is my wife sitting down there. You notice how still and silent she sits? My business is with your husband.

[PILKINGS *returns with* IYALOJA.]

PILKINGS Here she is. Now first I want your word of honour that you will try nothing foolish.

ELESIN Honour? White one, did you say you wanted my word of honour?

PILKINGS I know you to be an honourable man. Give me your word of honour you will receive nothing from her.

ELESIN But I am sure you have searched her clothing as you would never dare touch your own mother. And there are these two lizards of yours who roll their eyes even when I scratch.

PILKINGS And I shall be sitting on that tree trunk watching even how you blink. Just the same I want your word that you will not let her pass anything to you.

5. That is, circumvent, cajole.

ELESIN You have my honour already. It is locked up in that desk in which you will put away your report of this night's events. Even the honour of my people you have taken already; it is tied together with those papers of treachery which make you masters in this land.

PILKINGS Alright. I am trying to make things easy but if you must bring in politics we'll have to do it the hard way. Madam, I want you to remain along this line and move no nearer to the cell door. Guards! [*They spring to attention.*] If she moves beyond this point, blow your whistle. Come on Jane. [*They go off.*]

IYALOJA How boldly the lizard struts before the pigeon when it was the eagle itself he promised us he would confront.

ELESIN I don't ask you to take pity on me Iyaloja. You have a message for me or you would not have come. Even if it is the curses of the world, I shall listen.

IYALOJA You made so bold with the servant of the white king who took your side against death. I must tell your brother chiefs when I return how bravely you waged war against him. Especially with words.

ELESIN I more than deserve your scorn.

IYALOJA [*with sudden anger*] I warned you, if you must leave a seed behind, be sure it is not tainted with the curses of the world. Who are you to open a new life when you dared not open the door to a new existence? I say who are you to make so bold? [*The* BRIDE *sobs and* IYALOJA *notices her. Her contempt noticeably increases as she turns back to* ELESIN.] Oh you self-vaunted stem of the plantain, how hollow it all proves. The pith is gone in the parent stem, so how will it prove with the new shoot? How will it go with that earth that bears it? Who are you to bring this abomination on us!

ELESIN My powers deserted me. My charms, my spells, even my voice lacked strength when I made to summon the powers that would lead me over the last measure of earth into the land of the fleshless. You saw it, Iyaloja. You saw me struggle to retrieve my will from the power of the stranger whose shadow fell across the doorway and left me floundering and blundering in a maze I had never before encountered. My senses were numbed when the touch of cold iron came upon my wrists. I could do nothing to save myself.

IYALOJA You have betrayed us. We fed you sweetmeats such as we hoped awaited you on the other side. But you said No, I must eat the world's leftovers. We said you were the hunter who brought the quarry down; to you belonged the vital portions of the game. No, you said, I am the hunter's dog and I shall eat the entrails of the game and the faeces of the hunter. We said you were the hunter returning home in triumph, a slain buffalo pressing down on his neck; you said wait, I first must turn up this cricket hole with my toes. We said yours was the doorway at which we first spy the tapper when he comes down from the tree, yours was the blessing of the twilight wine, the purl[6] that brings night spirits out of doors to steal their portion before the light of day. We said yours was the body of wine whose burden shakes the tapper like a sudden gust on his perch. You said, No, I am content to lick the dregs from each calabash when the drinkers are

6. A liquor made by infusing bitter herbs in beer or ale. *Twilight wine*: that is, the finest wine; palm wine tapped before dawn is believed to be especially fresh and potent.

done. We said, the dew on earth's surface was for you to wash your feet along the slopes of honour. You said No, I shall step in the vomit of cats and the droppings of mice; I shall fight them for the left-overs of the world.

ELESIN Enough Iyaloja, enough.

IYALOJA We called you leader and oh, how you led us on. What we have no intention of eating should not be held to the nose.

ELESIN Enough, enough. My shame is heavy enough.

IYALOJA Wait. I came with a burden.

ELESIN You have more than discharged it.

IYALOJA I wish I could pity you.

ELESIN I need neither your pity nor the pity of the world. I need understanding. Even I need to understand. You were present at my defeat. You were part of the beginnings. You brought about the renewal of my tie to earth, you helped in the binding of the cord.

IYALOJA I gave you warning. The river which fills up before our eyes does not sweep us away in its flood.

ELESIN What were warnings beside the moist contact of living earth between my fingers? What were warnings beside the renewal of famished embers lodged eternally in the heart of man. But even that, even if it overwhelmed one with a thousandfold temptations to linger a little while, a man could overcome it. It is when the alien hand pollutes the source of will, when a stranger force of violence shatters the mind's calm resolution, this is when a man is made to commit the awful treachery of relief, commit in his thought the unspeakable blasphemy of seeing the hand of the gods in this alien rupture of his world. I know it was this thought that killed me, sapped my powers and turned me into an infant in the hands of unnamable strangers. I made to utter my spells anew but my tongue merely rattled in my mouth. I fingered hidden charms and the contact was damp; there was no spark left to sever the life-strings that should stretch from every fingertip. My will was squelched in the spittle of an alien race, and all because I had committed this blasphemy of thought—that there might be the hand of the gods in a stranger's intervention.

IYALOJA Explain it how you will, I hope it brings you peace of mind. The bush-rat fled his rightful cause, reached the market and set up a lamentation. 'Please save me!'—are these fitting words to hear from an ancestral mask? 'There's a wild beast at my heels' is not becoming language from a hunter.

ELESIN May the world forgive me.

IYALOJA I came with a burden I said. It approaches the gates which are so well guarded by those jackals whose spittle will from this day be on your food and drink. But first, tell me, you who were once Elesin Oba, tell me, you who know so well the cycle of the plantain: is it the parent shoot which withers to give sap to the younger or, does your wisdom see it running the other way?

ELESIN I don't see your meaning Iyaloja?

IYALOJA Did I ask you for a meaning? I asked a question. Whose trunk withers to give sap to the other? The parent shoot or the younger?

ELESIN The parent.

IYALOJA Ah. So you do know that. There are sights in this world which say different Elesin. There are some who choose to reverse the cycle of our being. Oh, you emptied bark that the world once saluted for a pith-laden being, shall I tell you what the gods have claimed of you?

[*In her agitation she steps beyond the line indicated by* PILKINGS *and the air is rent by piercing whistles. The two* GUARDS *also leap forward and place safe-guarding hands on* ELESIN. IYALOJA *stops, astonished.* PILKINGS *comes racing in, followed by* JANE.]

PILKINGS What is it? Did they try something?

GUARD She stepped beyond the line.

ELESIN [*in a broken voice*] Let her alone. She meant no harm.

IYALOJA Oh Elesin, see what you've become. Once you had no need to open your mouth in explanation because evil-smelling goats, itchy of hand and foot, had lost their senses. And it was a brave man indeed who dared lay hands on you because Iyaloja stepped from one side of the earth onto another. Now look at the spectacle of your life. I grieve for you.

PILKINGS I think you'd better leave. I doubt you have done him much good by coming here. I shall make sure you are not allowed to see him again. In any case we are moving him to a different place before dawn, so don't bother to come back.

IYALOJA We foresaw that. Hence the burden I trudged here to lay beside your gates.

PILKINGS What was that you said?

IYALOJA Didn't our son explain? Ask that one. He knows what it is. At least we hope the man we once knew as Elesin remembers the lesser oaths he need not break.

PILKINGS Do you know what she is talking about?

ELESIN Go to the gates, ghostly one. Whatever you find there, bring it to me.

IYALOJA Not yet. It drags behind me on the slow, weary feet of women. Slow as it is Elesin, it has long overtaken you. It rides ahead of your laggard will.

PILKINGS What is she saying now? Christ! Must your people forever speak in riddles?

ELESIN It will come white man, it will come. Tell your men at the gates to let it through.

PILKINGS [*dubiously*] I'll have to see what it is.

IYALOJA You will. [*Passionately*] But this is one oath he cannot shirk. White one, you have a king here, a visitor from your land. We know of his presence here. Tell me, were he to die would you leave his spirit roaming restlessly on the surface of earth? Would you bury him here among those you consider less than human? In your land have you no ceremonies of the dead?

PILKINGS Yes. But we don't make our chiefs commit suicide to keep him company.

IYALOJA Child, I have not come to help your understanding. [*Points to* ELESIN.] This is the man whose weakened understanding holds us in bondage to you. But ask him if you wish. He knows the meaning of a king's passage; he was not born yesterday. He knows the peril to the race when our dead father, who goes as intermediary, waits and waits and knows he is betrayed. He knows when the narrow gate was opened and he knows it will not stay for laggards who drag their feet in dung and vomit, whose lips are reeking of the left-overs of lesser men. He knows he has condemned our King to wander in the void of evil with beings who are enemies of life.

PILKINGS Yes er . . . but look here . . .

IYALOJA What we ask is little enough. Let him release our King so he can ride on homewards alone. The messenger is on his way on the backs of women. Let him send word through the heart that is folded up within the bolt. It is the least of all his oaths, it is the easiest fulfilled.

[*The* AIDE-DE-CAMP *runs in.*]

PILKINGS Bob?

AIDE-DE-CAMP Sir, there's a group of women chanting up the hill.

PILKINGS [*rounding on* IYALOJA] If you people want trouble . . .

JANE Simon, I think that's what Olunde referred to in his letter.

PILKINGS He knows damned well I can't have a crowd here! Damn it, I explained the delicacy of my position to him. I think it's about time I got him out of town. Bob, send a car and two or three soldiers to bring him in. I think the sooner he takes his leave of his father and gets out the better.

IYALOJA Save your labour white one. If it is the father of your prisoner you want, Olunde, he who until this night we knew as Elesin's son, he comes soon himself to take his leave. He has sent the women ahead, so let them in.

[PILKINGS *remains undecided.*]

AIDE-DE-CAMP What do we do about the invasion? We can still stop them far from here.

PILKINGS What do they look like?

AIDE-DE-CAMP They're not many. And they seem quite peaceful.

PILKINGS No men?

AIDE-DE-CAMP Mm, two or three at the most.

JANE Honestly, Simon, I'd trust Olunde. I don't think he'll deceive you about their intentions.

PILKINGS He'd better not. Alright then, let them in Bob. Warn them to control themselves. Then hurry Olunde here. Make sure he brings his baggage because I'm not returning him into town.

AIDE-DE-CAMP Very good, sir. [*Goes.*]

PILKINGS [*to* IYALOJA] I hope you understand that if anything goes wrong it will be on your head. My men have orders to shoot at the first sign of trouble.

IYALOJA To prevent one death you will actually make other deaths? Ah, great is the wisdom of the white race. But have no fear. Your Prince will sleep peacefully. So at long last will ours. We will disturb you no further, servant of the white King. Just let Elesin fulfil his oath and we will retire home and pay homage to our King.

JANE I believe her Simon, don't you?

PILKINGS Maybe.

ELESIN Have no fear ghostly one. I have a message to send my King and then you have nothing more to fear.

IYALOJA Olunde would have done it. The chiefs asked him to speak the words but he said no, not while you lived.

ELESIN Even from the depths to which my spirit has sunk, I find some joy that this little has been left to me.

[*The* WOMEN *enter, intoning the dirge 'Alẹ lẹ lẹ' and swaying from side to side. On their shoulders is borne a longish object roughly like a cylindrical bolt, covered in cloth. They set it down on the spot where*

IYALOJA *had stood earlier, and form a semi-circle round it. The* PRAISE-SINGER *and* DRUMMER *stand on the inside of the semi-circle but the drum is not used at all. The* DRUMMER *intones under the* PRAISE-SINGER*'s invocations.*]

PILKINGS [*as they enter*] What is *that*?

IYALOJA The burden you have made white one, but we bring it in peace.

PILKINGS I said *what* is it?

ELESIN White man, you must let me out. I have a duty to perform.

PILKINGS I most certainly will not.

ELESIN There lies the courier of my King. Let me out so I can perform what is demanded of me.

PILKINGS You'll do what you need to do from inside there or not at all. I've gone as far as I intend to with this business.

ELESIN The worshipper who lights a candle in your church to bear a message to his god bows his head and speaks in a whisper to the flame. Have I not seen it ghostly one? His voice does not ring out to the world. Mine are no words for anyone's ears. They are not words even for the bearers of this load. They are words I must speak secretly, even as my father whispered them in my ears and I in the ears of my first-born. I cannot shout them to the wind and the open night-sky.

JANE Simon . . .

PILKINGS Don't interfere. Please!

IYALOJA They have slain the favourite horse of the King and slain his dog. They have borne them from pulse to pulse centre of the land receiving prayers for their King. But the rider has chosen to stay behind. Is it too much to ask that he speak his heart to heart of the waiting courier? [PILKINGS *turns his back on her.*] So be it, Elesin Oba, you see how even the mere leavings are denied you. [*She gestures to the* PRAISE-SINGER.]

PRAISE-SINGER Elesin Oba! I call you by that name only this last time. Remember when I said, if you cannot come, tell my horse. [*Pause.*] What? I cannot hear you? I said, if you cannot come, whisper in the ears of my horse. Is your tongue severed from the roots Elesin? I can hear no response. I said, if there are boulders you cannot climb, mount my horse's back, this spotless black stallion, he'll bring you over them. [*Pauses.*] Elesin Oba, once you had a tongue that darted like a drummer's stick. I said, if you get lost my dog will track a path to me. My memory fails me but I think you replied: My feet have found the path, Alafin.

[*The dirge rises and falls.*]

I said at the last, if evil hands hold you back, just tell my horse there is weight on the hem of your smock. I dare not wait too long.

[*The dirge rises and falls.*]

There lies the swiftest-ever messenger of a king, so set me free with the errand of your heart. There lie the head and heart of the favourite of the gods, whisper in his ears. Oh my companion, if you had followed when you should, we would not say that the horse preceded its rider. If you had followed when it was time, we would not say the dog has raced beyond and left his master behind. If you had raised your will to cut the thread of life at the summons of the drums, we would not say your mere shadow fell across the gateway and took its owner's place at the banquet. But the hunter, laden with slain buffalo, stayed to root in the cricket's hole with his toes.

What now is left? If there is a dearth of bats, the pigeon must serve us for the offering. Speak the words over your shadow which must now serve in your place.

ELESIN I cannot approach. Take off the cloth. I shall speak my message from heart to heart of silence.

IYALOJA [*moves forward and removes the covering*] Your courier Elesin, cast your eyes on the favoured companion of the King.

[*Rolled up in the mat, his head and feet showing at either end, is the body of* OLUNDE.]

There lies the honour of your household and of our race. Because he could not bear to let honour fly out of doors, he stopped it with his life. The son has proved the father, Elesin, and there is nothing left in your mouth to gnash but infant gums.

PRAISE-SINGER Elesin, we placed the reins of the world in your hands yet you watched it plunge over the edge of the bitter precipice. You sat with folded arms while evil strangers tilted the world from its course and crashed it beyond the edge of emptiness—you muttered, there is little that one man can do, you left us floundering in a blind future. Your heir has taken the burden on himself. What the end will be, we are not gods to tell. But this young shoot has poured its sap into the parent stalk, and we know this is not the way of life. Our world is tumbling in the void of strangers, Elesin.

[ELESIN *has stood rock-still, his knuckles taut on the bars, his eyes glued to the body of his son. The stillness seizes and paralyses everyone, including* PILKINGS *who has turned to look. Suddenly* ELESIN *flings one arm round his neck, once, and with the loop of the chain, strangles himself in a swift, decisive pull. The* GUARDS *rush forward to stop him but they are only in time to let his body down.* PILKINGS *has leapt to the door at the same time and struggles with the lock. He rushes within, fumbles with the handcuffs and unlocks them, raises the body to a sitting position while he tries to give resuscitation. The* WOMEN *continue their dirge, unmoved by the sudden event.*]

IYALOJA Why do you strain yourself? Why do you labour at tasks for which no one, not even the man lying there, would give you thanks? He is gone at last into the passage but oh, how late it all is. His son will feast on the meat and throw him bones. The passage is clogged with droppings from the King's stallion; he will arrive all stained in dung.

PILKINGS [*in a tired voice*] Was this what you wanted?

IYALOJA No child, it is what you brought to be, you who play with strangers' lives, who even usurp the vestments of our dead, yet believe that the stain of death will not cling to you. The gods demanded only the old expired plantain but you cut down the sap-laden shoot to feed your pride. There is your board, filled to overflowing. Feast on it. [*She screams at him suddenly, seeing that* PILKINGS *is about to close* ELESIN*'s staring eyes.*] Let him alone! However sunk he was in debt he is no pauper's carrion abandoned on the road. Since when have strangers donned clothes of indigo before the bereaved cries out his loss?

[*She turns to the* BRIDE *who has remained motionless throughout.*]

Child.

[*The girl takes up a little earth, walks calmly into the cell and closes* ELESIN*'s eyes. She then pours some earth over each eyelid and comes out again.*]

IYALOJA Now forget the dead, forget even the living. Turn your mind only to the unborn.

[*She goes off, accompanied by the* BRIDE. *The dirge rises in volume and the* WOMEN *continue their sway. Lights fade to a black-out.*]

The End

SAM SHEPARD

b. 1943

SAM Shepard writes plays about power—about individuals' attempts to gain or exert power over one another physically, emotionally, spiritually, psychologically. Embracing the age-old precept that all drama arises from conflict and the battle for control, he places primal, agonistic struggles between characters at the core of his dramaturgy. Moreover, Shepard sees power as an important issue for American culture, and his plays are littered with mythic figures, historical characters, and social and cultural institutions that are popularly seen as exemplars of strength and dominance. He has gravitated to the genres to which an audience responds most powerfully—live theater, with its immediate force, and film, whose characters are larger than life. His Pulitzer Prize–winning drama ***BURIED CHILD*** (1978) exemplifies Shepard's ability to showcase potent symbols of American life while also questioning the deeply troubled structures of family and community in which they are embedded.

Samuel ("Steve") Shepard Rogers was born on November 5, 1943, in Fort Sheridan, Illinois—an army base where his mother lived while his father, a pilot, was serving overseas. In the early years of his life, the family moved often; but after his father left the military in 1949, they settled in California—first in South Pasadena, then on an avocado ranch in Duarte. A fascination with popular images of the West, of southern California, and of the American heartland animates many of his works, including *Cowboys #2* (1967), *The Unseen Hand* (1969), *Angel City* (1976), and *The Sad Lament of Pecos Bill on the Eve of Killing His Wife* (1976).

After graduating from high school, Shepard spent some time at a local junior college, where he drifted into acting. Shepard read SAMUEL BECKETT's Waiting for Godot (1952) and was struck by its freedom from conventional theatrical form and language, although he maintains that he did not understand the play. When a touring group, the Bishop's Company Repertory Players, advertised local auditions, Shepard decided to join them. On the road, he changed his name from Steve Rogers to Sam Shepard, thereby crystallizing the new identity that he was creating separate from the one associated with his family. The process of self-discovery and self-fashioning later became a central motif in his work; it was often connected with an artist figure trying to find an identity within society, as vividly exemplified in *The Tooth of Crime* (1972).

When the Players reached New York City, Shepard stayed behind. There he became involved with the downtown art scene, especially its music and the off-off-Broadway theaters that were beginning to emerge. Shepard's first two plays, *Cowboys* and *The Rock Garden,* were produced in 1964. Although they were roundly panned by the uptown critics, the pieces were championed by the *Village Voice*'s reviewer, Michael Smith, who saw Shepard as a new, exciting talent. Buoyed by Smith's support, Shepard began churning out plays, and in 1966 he garnered three Obies (annual awards for excellence in off-off- and off-Broadway theater). Between 1964 and 1971, nearly twenty Shepard dramas opened in New York, and small theaters around the country began to produce his plays as well. Shepard is unique among major American dramatists for rising to prominence with a series of one-act plays and for a career constituted almost entirely of regional and off- or off-off-Broadway productions. The 1996 staging of *Buried Child* (in a newly revised version) was the first full production of a Shepard drama on Broadway.

In 1969, Shepard married the actress O-Lan Johnson, and their son was born in 1970. Their marriage was turbulent from the start, with a number of separations; after an intense relationship with the rock musician and poet Patti Smith ended, and seeking to escape what he saw as the impersonality and materialism of New York City, in 1971 Shepard moved with his family to London. During three years there, he gained invaluable perspective on his country and its culture as well as on his own writing. Resettling with his family in California, Shepard formed a fruitful, lasting association with San Francisco's Magic Theater, where he began to hone his skills as a director of his own work. He also reengaged with acting, and his featured appearance in *Days of Heaven* (1978) launched what has become a highly successful film career. During the filming of *Frances* (1982), he met Jessica Lange and began living with her soon thereafter (he and O-Lan divorced in 1984); the couple has two children.

Shepard has never felt an obligation to conform to prevailing ideas of what American dramaturgy should be. Indeed, he claimed in a 1974 interview (reprinted in *American Dreams: The Imagination of Sam Shepard* [1981]) that he "didn't have any idea about how to shape an action into what is seen" and that the "so-called originality of the early work just comes from ignorance." Yet critics suspect that Shepard's early artistic persona may have been just that—a pose that suited his public image as an unintentional iconoclast. They have subsequently identified, through Shepard's interviews and correspondence, his wide array of influences from the nineteenth century (notably, the French symbolist poets and Fyodor Dostoyevsky) and the twentieth century—BERTOLT BRECHT, TENNESSEE WILLIAMS, Jack Kerouac, Lawrence Ferlinghetti, EDWARD ALBEE, the beat poets, Carlos Casteneda, and Werner Herzog, among others.

The development of Shepard's dramaturgy in effect inverts the history of modern drama; over the span of his career, his plays have moved from postmodernism and absurdism through expressionism to a modified realism. They fall into roughly three groups: the one-act abstract collages of the 1960s, the works focusing on artist figures of the early to mid-1970s, and the dramas written since 1974, when Shepard turned his attention to the American family. The plays within these relatively neat periods are highly complex pieces, which have consistently resisted interpreters' efforts to pin down their "meaning." Shepard's dramas do not rely on logic, cohesion, and order, and they cannot be easily categorized by form, style, or technique.

Shepard has emerged as the contemporary American dramatist most fully engaged in examining national identity through the trope of the Anglo-American family, a stand-in—with all its dysfunctionality and decay—for the United States itself. *Curse of the Starving Class* (1977), *Buried Child, True West* (1980), *Fool for Love* (1983), and *A Lie of the Mind* (1985) are often discussed together as family dramas. Shepard himself has observed that his fascination with the family puts his work squarely within the American dramatic tradition that embraces such canonical works as EUGENE O'NEILL's *Long Day's Journey into Night* (1957), ARTHUR MILLER's *Death of a Salesman* (1949), and Tennessee Williams's *The Glass Menagerie* (1945). Though Shepard's plays rarely display the theatrical conventions we associate with "kitchen sink" and "dining room table" dramaturgy, they resemble the form in their direct focus on the domestic milieu. Each conveys the deeply problematic nature of familial relationships, while also showing flashes of bizarre humor and inexplicable love. Shepard admitted, in the interview reprinted in *American Dreams,* that this new form for his work "could be called realism," but he insisted that it was not "the kind of realism where husbands and wives squabble and that kind of stuff." Critics and scholars have instead labeled his approach a type of "subverted" realism that freely borrows elements from styles quite foreign to traditional realism: the perverse grotesqueries of American gothic, for example, or the discontinuity and pastiche so common in postmodern artistry.

Buried Child uses a "homecoming" structure to reunite three generations of family members. Vince and his girlfriend, Shelly, decide to stop at the rural farm of his grandparents while en route to New Mexico to visit Vince's father, Tilden. They do not know that the psychologically damaged Tilden has preceded them and is living in his childhood home with his aging parents—the decaying alcoholic Dodge and vague yet controlling Halie—as well as his menacing amputee brother Bradley. When Vince arrives, no one, inexplicably, seems to recognize him, and he must grapple with the increasingly bizarre comments and behavior of people whom he thought he knew. Mysterious references to a child buried in the fields behind the house only complicate Vince's efforts to comprehend what has happened in his family, who he really is, and what place he holds in the world he has entered.

In *Buried Child,* Shepard refined the style and tone of the family environment first explored in *Curse of the Starving Class.* The aging patriarch, the ineffective mother, and the estranged, psychologically, or physically wounded children all come together in a sordid world of incest, abuse, and neglect. As an outsider, Shelly may *perhaps* be a more objective witness through whose eyes we can better understand and evaluate the familial machinations. She at first believes that the house is "like a Norman Rockwell cover or something," but the facade of idealized American family life

Vince (Christopher McCann) torments Bradley (William M. Carr) as Shelley (Mary McConnell) looks on in the background, in the 1979 Circle Repertory production of *Buried Child.*

soon shatters. The mystery of the titular buried child—whose it is, what happened to it, and what it symbolizes for Vince's family, and, by analogy, for the American family—is interwoven with Shepard's portrait of home life in the heartland, which never can match its Rockwellian exterior.

Replete with symbolic harvests of carrots and corn, *Buried Child* points toward Shepard's understanding of the plight of America's family farms, and his awareness of the economic pressures faced more generally by the working class. Unlike many of his colleagues from the 1960s, Shepard has not usually been perceived as a political playwright; yet the mood and tone of many of his works, including *Buried Child*, suggest a political consciousness that is integral to his identity as an American writer. Shepard is also deeply concerned with what he sees as an American ethos of violence, closely related to the struggles for power within his plays. Violence appears imminent throughout *Buried Child*, as characters' verbal, psychological, and, at moments, physical aggression toward each other punctuates both dialogue and action. As Shepard explained in a 1984 *New York Times* interview, he sees such violence as tied to gender roles:

> I think there's something about American violence that to me is very touching. In full force it's very ugly, but there's also something very moving about it, because it has to do with humiliation. There's some hidden, deeply rooted thing in the Anglo male American that has to do with inferiority, that has to do with not being a man, and always, continually having to act out some idea of manhood that invariably is violent. This sense of failure runs very deep—maybe it has to do with the frontier being systematically taken away, with the guilt of having gotten this country by wiping out a native race of people, with the whole Protestant work ethic. I can't put my finger on it, but it's the source of a lot of intrigue for me.

It is no coincidence that each of the men in *Buried Child* is profoundly damaged and is grappling with just such senses of inferiority and impotence. Shepard intuits a direct connection between larger cultural and economic forces and patterns of American identity, particularly those of American men. He traces a line of influence between the participation of members of his father's generation in World War II and their inability to reintegrate neatly into American life on their return. Shepard sees such men, like Dodge, as "lost children" who, unable to cope with their postwar roles, withdraw from their families and from society. Yet Shepard's representations of women are much more conventional and less nuanced. His work has been criticized for this comparative imbalance of complexity; the women in his plays often appear to be ciphers—opaque figures who lack an inner life. Halie and Shelly reflect a dramaturgical ambivalence toward female sexuality and the struggles for power between the sexes.

In his collection of short stories, poems, and autobiographical reveries, *Motel Chronicles* (1982), Shepard provides a memory of visiting his grandparents in Illinois that seems to have informed his creation of *Buried Child*. Yet this "chronicle" appears in a work that hovers between autobiography and fiction and puts into question the truth and value of memory—issues central to *Buried Child* as well. In an interview published in *The Cambridge Companion to Sam Shepard* in 2002, Shepard discussed his ongoing compulsion to explore familial dynamics. Musing on the inescapability of one's ties to family, Shepard confirmed his career-long interest "in the family's biological connections and how those patterns of behavior are passed on." Perhaps alluding to the speech at the end of the play in which Vince explains to Shelly what he has realized about his connections to his ancestors, Shepard describes how every individual is "intimately, inevitably, and entirely connected to who brought you into the world—through a long, long chain, regardless of whether you knew them face to face or not." Shepard believes, moreover, that "the disaster inherent in this thing called the American Family is very very resonant now with audiences" and accounts for the continuing interest in his family plays from the late 1970s and early 1980s.

The ambivalence of Shepard's relationship with American literary traditions reverberates on other levels as well. Shepard's conflicted representation of the American heartland in *Buried Child* resonates both with the trope of American pastoralism—a new Eden in the New World, fruitful and abundant—and with its opposite, an infertile wasteland that is decaying before our eyes. At the same time, these oppositional images of the land evoke a pattern of death and rebirth that strongly influenced many modernist writers: the myth of the Corn King.

The Corn King was a figure of ancient ritual. According to *The Golden Bough* (1890; 3d ed., 1911–14), James Frazer's massive comparative study of myth and religion, almost all the world's mythologies feature a priest-king who embodies the life and fertility of his kingdom; his decline would weaken the land. Thus, he must be ritually killed, so that a new king can assume the same role and the land can be reborn in spring. This dying and resurrected god found in ancient religions and fertility cults has obvious parallels with Christianity, and in *From Ritual to Romance* (1920) Jesse Weston argued that key elements of the Arthurian Grail legend—notably, the healing of a barren land and wounded king—are rooted in such religions. The medieval Grail stories also involve a questing knight who must overcome obstacles and respond to seemingly unanswerable questions.

Shepard's literal use of corn; the symbolic burial (under vegetables and Shelly's coat) and actual death of the patriarch, Dodge; and Vince's claiming of his ancestral home evoke this mythic backdrop, into which is woven the biblical story of the prodigal son. Yet Shepard's dark rendition of these tales reveals his ambivalence about the cultural power of myths and the traditions they embody.

Shepard's original version of *Buried Child* exemplifies the qualities of his most powerful dramas: lyrical, imagistic, fragmented, nonlinear. But in the mid-1990s, Shepard decided to revisit this play to "follow through [on] . . . certain questions that were ignited" in the original. As he explained in *American Theatre* magazine at that time, he was seeking not to resolve all the play's mysteries but to ensure that nothing was "gratuitously ambiguous." While the new production of *Buried Child* was enthusiastically received by reviewers, most critics view the revised script, like his revision of *The Tooth of Crime* (1996), as weaker than the original. In rewriting *Buried Child,* Shepard made the work more realistic and literal. He trimmed some of its notable monologues, including Dodge's recital of his will and Halie's description of their dead son Ansel's wedding; other cuts, in the dialogue, curtail the presentation of Shelly.

In executing these changes, Shepard may have been trying to alter the tempo of these works. As he notes in the 2002 interview, "writing is very rhythmic"; he has "always been fascinated by the rhythm of language, and language is musical . . . particularly written language when it's spoken." Indeed, Shepard's command of language may well be his greatest strength as a dramatist. Each of his characters has an utterly distinctive voice. In a 1977 essay, "Language, Visualization and the Inner Library" (reprinted in *American Dream*), Shepard defines words "as tools of imagery in motion." He believes that

> the power of words . . . isn't so much in the delineation of a character's social circumstances as it is in the capacity to evoke visions in the eye of the audience . . . words as living incantations and not as symbols. Taken in this way, the organization of living, breathing words as they hit the air between the actor and the audience actually possesses the power to change our chemistry.

Shepard has functioned as an alchemist for the contemporary American theater, transforming and recasting our very sense of what can be seen, heard, and imagined onstage. J.E.G.

Buried Child

While the rain of your fingertips falls,
while the rain of your bones falls,
and your laughter and marrow fall down,
you come flying. —Pablo Neruda[1]

CHARACTERS

DODGE, in his seventies
HALIE, his wife, mid-sixties
TILDEN, their oldest son
BRADLEY, their next oldest son, an amputee
VINCE, Tilden's son
SHELLY, Vince's girlfriend
FATHER DEWIS, a Protestant minister

Act 1

SCENE: *Day. Old wooden staircase down left with pale, frayed carpet laid down on the steps. The stairs lead offstage left up into the wings with no landing. Up right is an old, dark green sofa with the stuffing coming out in spots. Stage right of the sofa is an upright lamp with a faded yellow shade and a small night table with several small bottles of pills on it. Down right of the sofa, with the screen facing the sofa, is a large, old-fashioned brown T.V. A flickering blue light comes from the screen, but no image, no sound. In the dark, the light of the lamp and the T.V. slowly brighten in the black space. The space behind the sofa, upstage, is a large, screened-in porch with a board floor. A solid interior door to stage right of the sofa, leading into the room onstage; and another screen door up left, leading from the porch to the outside. Beyond that are the shapes of dark elm trees.*

Gradually the form of DODGE *is made out, sitting on the couch, facing the T.V., the blue light flickering on his face. He wears a well-worn T-shirt, suspenders, khaki work pants, and brown slippers. He's covered himself in an old brown blanket. He's very thin and sickly looking, in his late seventies. He just stares at the T.V. More light fills the stage softly. The sound of light rain.* DODGE *slowly tilts his head back and stares at the ceiling for a while, listening to the rain. He lowers his head again and stares at the T.V. He turns his head slowly to the left and stares at the cushion of the sofa next to the one he's sitting on. He pulls his left arm out from under the blanket, slides his hand under the cushion, and pulls out a bottle of whiskey. He looks down left toward the staircase, listens, then uncaps the bottle, takes a long swig, and caps it again. He puts the bottle back under the cushion and stares at the T.V. He starts to cough slowly and softly. The coughing gradually builds. He holds one hand to his mouth and tries to stifle it. The coughing gets louder, then suddenly stops when he hears the sound of his wife's voice coming from the top of the staircase.*

1. Chilean poet and politician (1904–1973); the epigraph is from his elegy "Alberto Rojas Jiménez Comes Flying" (1934).

HALIE'S VOICE Dodge?

[DODGE *just stares at the T.V. Long pause. He stifles two short coughs.*]

HALIE'S VOICE Dodge! You want a pill, Dodge?

[*He doesn't answer. Takes the bottle out again and takes another long swig. Puts the bottle back, stares at T.V., pulls blanket up around his neck.*]

HALIE'S VOICE You know what it is, don't you? It's the rain! Weather. That's it. Every time. Every time you get like this, it's the rain. No sooner does the rain start then you start. [*Pause*] Dodge?

[*He makes no reply. Pulls a pack of cigarettes out from his sweater and lights one. Stares at T.V. Pause.*]

HALIE'S VOICE You should see it coming down up here. Just coming down in sheets. Blue sheets. The bridge is pretty near flooded. What's it like down there? Dodge?

[DODGE *turns his head back over his left shoulder and takes a look out through the porch. He turns back to the T.V.*]

DODGE [*to himself*] Catastrophic.

HALIE'S VOICE What? What'd you say, Dodge?

DODGE [*louder*] It looks like rain to me! Plain old rain!

HALIE'S VOICE Rain? Of course it's rain! Are you having a seizure or something! Dodge? [*Pause*] I'm coming down there in about five minutes if you don't answer me!

DODGE Don't come down.

HALIE'S VOICE What!

DODGE [*louder*] Don't come down!

[*He has another coughing attack. Stops.*]

HALIE'S VOICE You should take a pill for that! I don't see why you just don't take a pill. Be done with it once and for all. Put a stop to it.

[*He takes bottle out again. Another swig. Returns bottle.*]

HALIE'S VOICE It's not Christian, but it works. It's not necessarily Christian, that is. We don't know. There's some things the ministers can't even answer. I, personally, can't see anything wrong with it. Pain is pain. Pure and simple. Suffering is a different matter. That's entirely different. A pill seems as good an answer as any. Dodge? [*Pause*] Dodge, are you watching baseball?

DODGE No.

HALIE'S VOICE What?

DODGE [*louder*] No!

HALIE'S VOICE What're you watching? You shouldn't be watching anything that'll get you excited! No horse racing!

DODGE They don't race on Sundays.

HALIE'S VOICE What?

DODGE [*louder*] They don't race on Sundays!

HALIE'S VOICE Well they shouldn't race on Sundays.

DODGE Well they don't!

HALIE'S VOICE Good. I'm amazed they still have that kind of legislation. That's amazing.

DODGE Yeah, it's amazing.

HALIE'S VOICE What?

DODGE [*louder*] It is amazing!

HALIE'S VOICE It is. It truly is. I would've thought these days they'd be racing on Christmas even. A big flashing Christmas tree right down at the finish line.

DODGE [*shakes his head*] No.

HALIE'S VOICE They used to race on New Year's! I remember that.

DODGE They never raced on New Year's!

HALIE'S VOICE Sometimes they did.

DODGE They never did!

HALIE'S VOICE Before we were married they did!

[DODGE *waves his hand in disgust at the staircase. Leans back in sofa. Stares at T.V.*]

HALIE'S VOICE I went once. With a man.

DODGE [*mimicking her*] Oh, a "man."

HALIE'S VOICE What?

DODGE Nothing!

HALIE'S VOICE A wonderful man. A breeder.

DODGE A what?

HALIE'S VOICE A breeder! A horse breeder! Thoroughbreds.

DODGE Oh, Thoroughbreds. Wonderful.

HALIE'S VOICE That's right. He knew everything there was to know.

DODGE I bet he taught you a thing or two huh? Gave you a good turn around the old stable!

HALIE'S VOICE Knew everything there was to know about horses. We won bookoos[2] of money that day.

DODGE What?

HALIE'S VOICE Money! We won every race I think.

DODGE Bookoos?

HALIE'S VOICE Every single race.

DODGE Bookoos of money?

HALIE'S VOICE It was one of those kind of days.

DODGE New Year's!

HALIE'S VOICE Yes! It might've been Florida. Or California! One of those two.

DODGE Can I take my pick?

HALIE'S VOICE It was Florida!

DODGE Aha!

HALIE'S VOICE Wonderful! Absolutely wonderful! The sun was just gleaming. Flamingos. Bougainvilleas. Palm trees.

DODGE [*to himself, mimicking her*] Bougainvilleas. Palm trees.

HALIE'S VOICE Everything was dancing with life! There were all kinds of people from everywhere. Everyone was dressed to the nines. Not like today. Not like they dress today.

DODGE When was this anyway?

HALIE'S VOICE This was long before I knew you.

DODGE Must've been.

HALIE'S VOICE Long before. I was escorted.

DODGE To Florida?

HALIE'S VOICE Yes. Or it might've been California. I'm not sure which.

DODGE All that way you were escorted?

2. Mock French, playing on *beaucoup* (much, a great deal).

HALIE'S VOICE Yes.

DODGE And he never laid a finger on you I suppose? [*Long silence*] Halie?

[*No answer. Long pause.*]

HALIE'S VOICE Are you going out today?

DODGE [*gesturing toward rain*] In this?

HALIE'S VOICE I'm just asking a simple question.

DODGE I rarely go out in the bright sunshine, why would I go out in this?

HALIE'S VOICE I'm just asking because I'm not doing any shopping today. And if you need anything you should ask Tilden.

DODGE Tilden's not here!

HALIE'S VOICE He's in the kitchen.

[DODGE *looks toward stage left, then back toward T.V.*]

DODGE All right.

HALIE'S VOICE What?

DODGE [*louder*] All right!

HALIE'S VOICE Don't scream. It'll only get your coughing started.

DODGE All right.

HALIE'S VOICE Just tell Tilden what you want and he'll get it. [*Pause*] Bradley should be over later.

DODGE Bradley?

HALIE'S VOICE Yes. To cut your hair.

DODGE My hair? I don't need my hair cut!

HALIE'S VOICE It won't hurt!

DODGE I don't need it!

HALIE'S VOICE It's been more than two weeks Dodge.

DODGE I don't need it!

HALIE'S VOICE I have to meet Father Dewis for lunch.

DODGE You tell Bradley that if he shows up here with those clippers, I'll kill him!

HALIE'S VOICE I won't be very late. No later than four at the very latest.

DODGE You tell him! Last time he left me almost bald! And I wasn't even awake! I was sleeping! I woke up and he'd already left!

HALIE'S VOICE That's not my fault!

DODGE You put him up to it!

HALIE'S VOICE I never did!

DODGE You did too! You had some fancy, stupid meeting planned! Time to dress up the corpse for company! Lower the ears a little! Put up a little front! Surprised you didn't tape a pipe to my mouth while you were at it! That woulda' looked nice! Huh? A pipe? Maybe a bowler hat! Maybe a copy of The Wall Street Journal casually placed on my lap!

HALIE'S VOICE You always imagine the worst things of people!

DODGE That's not the worst! That's the least of the worst!

HALIE'S VOICE I don't need to hear it! All day long I hear things like that and I don't need to hear more.

DODGE You better tell him!

HALIE'S VOICE You tell him yourself! He's your own son. You should be able to talk to your own son.

DODGE Not while I'm sleeping! He cut my hair while I was sleeping!

HALIE'S VOICE Well he won't do it again.

DODGE There's no guarantee.

HALIE'S VOICE I promise he won't do it without your consent.

DODGE [*after pause*] There's no reason for him to even come over here.

HALIE'S VOICE He feels responsible.

DODGE For my hair?

HALIE'S VOICE For your appearance.

DODGE My appearance is out of his domain! It's even out of mine! In fact, it's disappeared! I'm an invisible man!

HALIE'S VOICE Don't be ridiculous.

DODGE He better not try it. That's all I've got to say.

HALIE'S VOICE Tilden will watch out for you.

DODGE Tilden won't protect me from Bradley!

HALIE'S VOICE Tilden's the oldest. He'll protect you.

DODGE Tilden can't even protect himself!

HALIE'S VOICE Not so loud! He'll hear you. He's right in the kitchen.

DODGE [*yelling off left*] Tilden!

HALIE'S VOICE Dodge, what are you trying to do?

DODGE [*yelling off left*] Tilden, get in here!

HALIE'S VOICE Why do you enjoy stirring things up?

DODGE I don't enjoy anything!

HALIE'S VOICE That's a terrible thing to say.

DODGE Tilden!

HALIE'S VOICE That's the kind of statement that leads people right to the end of their rope.

DODGE Tilden!

HALIE'S VOICE It's no wonder people turn to Christ!

DODGE TILDEN!!

HALIE'S VOICE It's no wonder the messengers of God's word are shouted down in public places!

DODGE TILDEN!!!!

[DODGE *goes into a violent, spasmodic coughing attack as* TILDEN *enters from stage left, his arms loaded with fresh ears of corn.* TILDEN *is* DODGE'S *oldest son, late forties, wears heavy construction boots, covered with mud, dark green work pants, a plaid shirt, and a faded brown windbreaker. He has a butch haircut, wet from the rain. Something about him is profoundly burned out and displaced. He stops center stage with the ears of corn in his arms and just stares at* DODGE *until he slowly finishes his coughing attack.* DODGE *looks up at him slowly. He stares at the corn. Long pause as they watch each other.*]

HALIE'S VOICE Dodge, if you don't take that pill nobody's going to force you.

[*The two men ignore the voice.*]

DODGE [*to* TILDEN] Where'd you get that?

TILDEN Picked it.

DODGE You picked all that?

[TILDEN *nods.*]

DODGE You expecting company?

TILDEN No.

DODGE Where'd you pick it from?

TILDEN Right out back.

DODGE Out back where?

TILDEN Right out in back.

DODGE There's nothing out there!

TILDEN There's corn.

DODGE There hasn't been corn out there since about nineteen thirty-five! That's the last time I planted corn out there!

TILDEN It's out there now.

DODGE [*yelling at stairs*] Halie!

HALIE'S VOICE Yes dear!

DODGE Tilden's brought a whole bunch of corn in here! There's no corn out in back is there?

TILDEN [*to himself*] There's tons of corn.

HALIE'S VOICE Not that I know of!

DODGE That's what I thought.

HALIE'S VOICE Not since about nineteen thirty-five!

DODGE [*to* TILDEN] That's right. Nineteen thirty-five.

TILDEN It's out there now.

DODGE You go and take that corn back to wherever you got it from!

TILDEN [*after pause, staring at* DODGE] It's picked. I picked it all in the rain. Once it's picked you can't put it back.

DODGE I haven't had trouble with neighbors here for fifty-seven years. I don't even know who the neighbors are! And I don't wanna know! Now go put that corn back where it came from!

[TILDEN *stares at* DODGE *then walks slowly over to him and dumps all the corn on* DODGE'S *lap and steps back.* DODGE *stares at the corn then back to* TILDEN. *Long pause.*]

DODGE Are you having trouble here, Tilden! Are you in some kind of trouble?

TILDEN I'm not in any trouble.

DODGE You can tell me if you are. I'm still your father.

TILDEN I know you're still my father.

DODGE I know you had a little trouble back in New Mexico. That's why you came out here.

TILDEN I never had any trouble.

DODGE Tilden, your mother told me all about it.

TILDEN What'd she tell you?

[TILDEN *pulls some chewing tobacco out of his jacket and bites off a plug.*]

DODGE I don't have to repeat what she told me! She told me all about it!

TILDEN Can I bring my chair in from the kitchen?

DODGE What?

TILDEN Can I bring in my chair from the kitchen?

DODGE Sure. Bring your chair in.

[TILDEN *exits left.* DODGE *pushes all the corn off his lap onto the floor. He pulls the blanket off angrily and tosses it at one end of the sofa, pulls out the bottle and takes another swig.* TILDEN *enters again from left with a milking stool and a pail.* DODGE *hides the bottle quickly under the cushion before* TILDEN *see it.* TILDEN *sets the stool down by the sofa, sits on it, puts the pail in front of him on the floor.* TILDEN *starts picking up the ears of corn one at a time and husking them. He throws the husks and silk in the center of the stage and drops the ears into the pail each time he cleans one. He repeats this process as they talk.*]

DODGE [*after pause*] Sure is nice-looking corn.

TILDEN It's the best.

DODGE Hybrid?

TILDEN What?

DODGE Some kinda fancy hybrid?

TILDEN You planted it. I don't know what it is.

DODGE [*pause*] Tilden, look, you can't stay here forever. You know that, don't you?

TILDEN [*spits in spittoon*] I'm not.

DODGE I know you're not. I'm not worried about that. That's not the reason I brought it up.

TILDEN What's the reason?

DODGE The reason is I'm wondering what you're gonna do.

TILDEN You're not worried about me, are you?

DODGE I'm not worried about you.

TILDEN You weren't worried about me when I wasn't here. When I was in New Mexico.

DODGE No, I wasn't worried about you then either.

TILDEN You shoulda worried about me then.

DODGE Why's that? You didn't do anything down there, did you?

TILDEN I didn't do anything.

DODGE Then why should I have worried about you?

TILDEN Because I was lonely.

DODGE Because you were lonely?

TILDEN Yeah. I was more lonely than I've ever been before.

DODGE Why was that?

TILDEN [*pause*] Could I have some of that whiskey you've got?

DODGE What whiskey? I haven't got any whiskey.

TILDEN You've got some under the sofa.

DODGE I haven't got anything under the sofa! Now mind your own damn business! Jesus God, you come into the house outa the middle of nowhere, haven't heard or seen you in twenty years and suddenly you're making accusations.

TILDEN I'm not making accusations.

DODGE You're accusing me of hoarding whiskey under the sofa!

TILDEN I'm not accusing you.

DODGE You just got through telling me I had whiskey under the sofa!

HALIE'S VOICE Dodge?

DODGE [*to* TILDEN] Now she knows about it!

TILDEN She doesn't know about it.

HALIE'S VOICE Dodge, are you talking to yourself down there?

DODGE I'm talking to Tilden!

HALIE'S VOICE Tilden's down there?

DODGE He's right here!

HALIE'S VOICE What?

DODGE [*louder*] He's right here!

HALIE'S VOICE What's he doing?

DODGE [*to* TILDEN] Don't answer her.

TILDEN [*to* DODGE] I'm not doing anything wrong.

DODGE I know you're not.

HALIE'S VOICE What's he doing down there!

DODGE [*to* TILDEN] Don't answer.

TILDEN I'm not.

HALIE'S VOICE Dodge!

[*The men sit in silence.* DODGE *lights a cigarette.* TILDEN *keeps husking corn, spits tobacco now and then in spittoon.*]

HALIE'S VOICE Dodge! He's not drinking anything, is he? You see to it that he doesn't drink anything! You've gotta watch out for him. It's our responsibility. He can't look after himself anymore, so we have to do it. Nobody else will do it. We can't just send him away somewhere. If we had lots of money we could send him away. But we don't. We never will. That's why we have to stay healthy. You and me. Nobody's going to look after us. Bradley can't look after us. Bradley can hardly look after himself. I was always hoping that Tilden would look out for Bradley when they got older. After Bradley lost his leg. Tilden's the oldest. I always thought he'd be the one to take responsibility. I had no idea in the world that Tilden would be so much trouble. Who would've dreamed. Tilden was an All-American, don't forget. Don't forget that. Fullback. Or quarterback. I forget which.

TILDEN [*to himself*] Fullback. [*Still husking*]

HALIE'S VOICE Then when Tilden turned out to be so much trouble, I put all my hopes on Ansel. Of course Ansel wasn't as handsome, but he was smart. He was the smartest probably. I think he probably was. Smarter than Bradley, that's for sure. Didn't go and chop his leg off with a chain saw. Smart enough not to go and do that. I think he was smarter than Tilden too. Especially after Tilden got in all that trouble. Doesn't take brains to go to jail. Anybody knows that. Course then when Ansel died that left us all alone. Same as being alone. No different. Same as if they'd all died. He was the smartest. He could've earned lots of money. Lots and lots of money.

[HALIE *enters slowly from the top of the staircase as she continues talking. Just her feet are seen at first as she makes her way down the stairs, a step at a time. She appears dressed completely in black, as though in mourning. Black handbag, hat with a veil, and pulling on elbow length black gloves. She is about sixty-five with pure white hair. She remains absorbed in what she's saying as she descends the stairs and doesn't really notice the two men who continue sitting there as they were before she came down, smoking and husking.*]

HALIE He would've took care of us, too. He would've seen to it that we were repaid. He was like that. He was a hero. Don't forget that. A genuine hero. Brave. Strong. And very intelligent. Ansel could've been a great man. One of the greatest. I only regret that he didn't die in action. It's not fitting for a man like that to die in a motel room. A soldier. He could've won a medal. He could've been decorated for valor. I've talked to Father Dewis about putting up a plaque for Ansel. He thinks it's a good idea. He agrees. He knew Ansel when he used to play basketball. Went to every game. Ansel was his favorite player. He even recommended to the City Council that they put up a statue of Ansel. A big, tall statue with a basketball in one hand and a rifle in the other. That's how much he thinks of Ansel.

[HALIE *reaches the stage and begins to wander around, still absorbed in pulling on her gloves, brushing lint off her dress and continuously talking to herself as the men just sit.*]

HALIE Of course, he'd still be alive today if he hadn't married into the Catholics. The Mob. How in the world he never opened his eyes to that is beyond me. Just beyond me. Everyone around him could see the truth. Even Tilden. Tilden told him time and again. Catholic women are the Devil incarnate. He wouldn't listen. He was blind with love. Blind. I knew. Everyone knew. The wedding was more like a funeral. You remember? All those Italians. All that horrible black, greasy hair. The smell of cheap cologne. I think even the priest was wearing a pistol. When he gave her the ring I knew he was a dead man. I knew it. As soon as he gave her the ring. But then it was the honeymoon that killed him. The honeymoon. I knew he'd never come back from the honeymoon. I kissed him and he felt like a corpse. All white. Cold. Icy blue lips. He never used to kiss like that. Never before. I knew then that she'd cursed him. Taken his soul. I saw it in her eyes. She smiled at me with that Catholic sneer of hers. She told me with her eyes that she'd murder him in his bed. Murder my son. She told me. And there was nothing I could do. Absolutely nothing. He was going with her, thinking he was free. Thinking it was love. What could I do? I couldn't tell him she was a witch. I couldn't tell him that. He'd have turned on me. Hated me. I couldn't stand him hating me and then dying before he ever saw me again. Hating me in his deathbed. Hating me and loving her! How could I do that? I had to let him go. I had to. I watched him leave. I watched him throw gardenias as he helped her into the limousine. I watched his face disappear behind the glass.

[*She stops abruptly and stares at the corn husks. She looks around the space as though just waking up. She turns and looks hard at* TILDEN *and* DODGE *who continue sitting calmly. She looks again at the corn husks.*]

HALIE [*pointing to the husks*] What's this in my house! [*Kicks husks.*] What's all this!

[TILDEN *stops husking and stares at her.*]

HALIE [*to* DODGE] And you encourage him!

[DODGE *pulls blanket over him again.*]

DODGE You're going out in the rain?

HALIE It's not raining.

[TILDEN *starts husking again.*]

DODGE Not in Florida it's not.

HALIE We're not in Florida!

DODGE It's not raining at the racetrack.

HALIE Have you been taking those pills? Those pills always make you talk crazy. Tilden, has he been taking those pills?

TILDEN He hasn't took anything.

HALIE [*to* DODGE] What've you been taking?

DODGE It's not raining in California or Florida or the racetrack. Only in Illinois. This is the only place it's raining. All over the rest of the world it's bright golden sunshine.

[HALIE *goes to the night table next to the sofa and checks the bottle of pills.*]

HALIE Which ones did you take? Tilden, you must've seen him take something.

TILDEN He never took a thing.

HALIE Then why's he talking crazy?

TILDEN I've been here the whole time.

HALIE Then you've both been taking something!

TILDEN I've just been husking the corn.

HALIE Where'd you get that corn anyway? Why is the house suddenly full of corn?

DODGE Bumper crop!

HALIE [*moving center*] We haven't had corn here for over thirty years.

TILDEN The whole back lot's full of corn. Far as the eye can see.

DODGE [*to* HALIE] Things keep happening while you're upstairs, ya know. The world doesn't stop just because you're upstairs. Corn keeps growing. Rain keeps raining.

HALIE I'm not unaware of the world around me! Thank you very much. It so happens that I have an overall view from the upstairs. The backyard's in plain view of my window. And there's no corn to speak of. Absolutely none!

DODGE Tilden wouldn't lie. If he says there's corn, there's corn.

HALIE What's the meaning of this corn Tilden!

TILDEN It's a mystery to me. I was out in back there. And the rain was coming down. And I didn't feel like coming back inside. I didn't feel the cold so much. I didn't mind the wet. So I was just walking. I was muddy but I didn't mind the mud so much. And I looked up. And I saw this stand of corn. In fact I was standing in it. So, I was standing in it.

HALIE There isn't any corn outside, Tilden! There's no corn! Now, you must've either stolen this corn or you bought it.

DODGE He doesn't have any money.

HALIE [*to* TILDEN] So you stole it!

TILDEN I didn't steal it. I don't want to get kicked out of Illinois. I was kicked out of New Mexico and I don't want to get kicked out of Illinois.

HALIE You're going to get kicked out of this house, Tilden, if you don't tell me where you got that corn!

[TILDEN *starts crying softly to himself but keeps husking corn. Pause.*]

DODGE [*to* HALIE] Why'd you have to tell him that? Who cares where he got the corn? Why'd you have to go and tell him that?

HALIE [*to* DODGE] It's your fault you know! You're the one that's behind all this! I suppose you thought it'd be funny! Some joke! Cover the house with corn husks. You better get this cleaned up before Bradley sees it.

DODGE Bradley's not getting in the front door!

HALIE [*kicking husks, striding back and forth*] Bradley's going to be very upset when he sees this. He doesn't like to see the house in disarray. He can't stand it when one thing is out of place. The slightest thing. You know how he gets.

DODGE Bradley doesn't even live here!

HALIE It's his home as much as ours. He was born in this house!

DODGE He was born in a hog wallow.

HALIE Don't you say that! Don't you ever say that!

DODGE He was born in a goddamn hog wallow! That's where he was born and that's where he belongs! He doesn't belong in this house!

HALIE [*she stops*] I don't know what's come over you, Dodge. I don't know what in the world's come over you. You've become an evil man. You used to be a good man.

DODGE Six of one, a half dozen of another.

HALIE You sit here day and night, festering away! Decomposing! Smelling up the house with your putrid body! Hacking your head off till all hours of the morning! Thinking up mean, evil, stupid things to say about your own flesh and blood!

DODGE He's not my flesh and blood! My flesh and blood's buried in the backyard!

[*They freeze. Long pause. The men stare at her.*]

HALIE [*quietly*] That's enough, Dodge. That's quite enough. I'm going out now. I'm going to have lunch with Father Dewis. I'm going to ask him about a monument. A statue. At least a plaque.

[*She crosses to the door up right. She stops.*]

HALIE If you need anything, ask Tilden. He's the oldest. I've left some money on the kitchen table.

DODGE I don't need anything.

HALIE No, I suppose not. [*She opens the door and looks out through porch.*] Still raining. I love the smell just after it stops. The ground. I won't be too late.

[*She goes out door and closes it. She's still visible on the porch as she crosses toward stage left screen door. She stops in the middle of the porch, speaks to* DODGE *but doesn't turn to him.*]

HALIE Dodge, tell Tilden not to go out in the back lot anymore. I don't want him back there in the rain.

DODGE You tell him. He's sitting right here.

HALIE He never listens to me Dodge. He's never listened to me in the past.

DODGE I'll tell him.

HALIE We have to watch him just like we used to now. Just like we always have. He's still a child.

DODGE I'll watch him.

HALIE Good.

[*She crosses to screen door, left, takes an umbrella off a hook and goes out the door. The door slams behind her. Long pause.* TILDEN *husks corn, stares at pail.* DODGE *lights a cigarette, stares at T.V.*]

TILDEN [*still husking*] You shouldn't a told her that.

DODGE [*staring at T.V.*] What?

TILDEN What you told her. You know.

DODGE What do you know about it?

TILDEN I know. I know all about it. We all know.

DODGE So what difference does it make? Everybody knows, everybody's forgot.

TILDEN She hasn't forgot.

DODGE She should've forgot.

TILDEN It's different for a woman. She couldn't forget that. How could she forget that?

DODGE I don't want to talk about it!

TILDEN What do you want to talk about?

DODGE I don't want to talk about anything! I don't want to talk about troubles or what happened fifty years ago or thirty years ago or the racetrack or Florida or the last time I seeded the corn! I don't want to talk!

TILDEN You don't wanna die do you?

DODGE No, I don't wanna die either.

TILDEN Well, you gotta talk or you'll die.

DODGE Who told you that?

TILDEN That's what I know. I found that out in New Mexico. I thought I was dying but I just lost my voice.

DODGE Were you with somebody?

TILDEN I was alone. I thought I was dead.

DODGE Might as well have been. What'd you come back here for?

TILDEN I didn't know where to go.

DODGE You're a grown man. You shouldn't be needing your parents at your age. It's unnatural. There's nothing we can do for you now anyway. Couldn't you make a living down there? Couldn't you find some way to make a living? Support yourself? What'd'ya come back here for? You expect us to feed you forever?

TILDEN I didn't know where else to go.

DODGE I never went back to my parents. Never. Never even had the urge. I was independent. Always independent. Always found a way.

TILDEN I didn't know what to do. I couldn't figure anything out.

DODGE There's nothing to figure out. You just forge ahead. What's there to figure out?

[TILDEN *stands.*]

TILDEN I don't know.

DODGE Where are you going?

TILDEN Out back.

DODGE You're not supposed to go out there. You heard what she said. Don't play deaf with me!

TILDEN I like it out there.

DODGE In the rain?

TILDEN Especially in the rain. I like the feeling of it. Feels like it always did.

DODGE You're supposed to watch out for me. Get me things when I need them.

TILDEN What do you need?

DODGE I don't need anything! But I might. I might need something any second. Any second now. I can't be left alone for a minute!

[DODGE *starts to cough.*]

TILDEN I'll be right outside. You can just yell.

DODGE [*between coughs*] No! It's too far! You can't go out there! It's too far! You might not ever hear me!

TILDEN [*moving to pills*] Why don't you take a pill? You want a pill?

[DODGE *coughs more violently, throws himself back against sofa, clutches his throat.* TILDEN *stands by helplessly.*]

DODGE Water! Get me some water!

[TILDEN *rushes off left.* DODGE *reaches out for the pills, knocking some bottles to the floor, coughing in spasms. He grabs a small bottle, takes out pills and swallows them.* TILDEN *rushes back on with a glass of water.* DODGE *takes it and drinks, his coughing subsides.*]

TILDEN You all right now?

[DODGE *nods. Drinks more water.* TILDEN *moves in closer to him.* DODGE *sets glass of water on the night table. His coughing is almost gone.*]

TILDEN Why don't you lay down for a while? Just rest a little.

[**TILDEN** *helps* **DODGE** *lay down on the sofa. Covers him with blanket.*]

DODGE You're not going outside are you?

TILDEN No.

DODGE I don't want to wake up and find you not here.

TILDEN I'll be here.

[**TILDEN** *tucks blanket around* **DODGE**.]

DODGE You'll stay right here?

TILDEN I'll stay in my chair.

DODGE That's not a chair. That's my old milking stool.

TILDEN I know.

DODGE Don't call it a chair.

TILDEN I won't.

[**TILDEN** *tries to take* **DODGE**'s *baseball cap off.*]

DODGE What're you doing! Leave that on me! Don't take that offa me! That's my cap!

[**TILDEN** *leaves the cap on* **DODGE**.]

TILDEN I know.

DODGE Bradley'll shave my head if I don't have that on. That's my cap.

TILDEN I know it is.

DODGE Don't take my cap off.

TILDEN I won't.

DODGE You stay right here now.

TILDEN [*sits on stool*] I will.

DODGE Don't go outside. There's nothing out there.

TILDEN I won't.

DODGE Everything's in here. Everything you need. Money's on the table. T.V. Is the T.V. on?

TILDEN Yeah.

DODGE Turn it off! Turn the damn thing off! What's it doing on?

TILDEN [*shuts off T.V., light goes out*] You left it on.

DODGE Well turn it off.

TILDEN [*sits on stool again*] It's off.

DODGE Leave it off.

TILDEN I will.

DODGE When I fall asleep you can turn it on.

TILDEN Okay.

DODGE You can watch the ball game. Red Sox. You like the Red Sox don't you?

TILDEN Yeah.

DODGE You can watch the Red Sox. Pee Wee Reese.[3] Pee Wee Reese. You remember Pee Wee Reese?

TILDEN No.

DODGE Was he with the Red Sox?

3. An American baseball player (1918–1999); the All-Star shortstop played for the Brooklyn (later Los Angeles) Dodgers (1940–42, 1946–58), but he was originally drafted by the Boston Red Sox.

TILDEN I don't know.

DODGE Pee Wee Reese. [*Falling asleep*] You can watch the Cardinals. You remember Stan Musial.[4]

TILDEN No.

DODGE Stan Musial. [*Falling into sleep*] Bases loaded. Top a' the sixth. Bases loaded. Runner on first and third. Big fat knuckle ball. Floater. Big as a blimp. Cracko! Ball just took off like a rocket. Just pulverized. I marked it. Marked it with my eyes. Straight between the clock and the Burma Shave ad.[5] I was the first kid out there. First kid. I had to fight hard for that ball. I wouldn't give it up. They almost tore the ears right off me. But I wouldn't give it up.

[DODGE *falls into deep sleep.* TILDEN *just sits staring at him for a while. Slowly he leans toward the sofa, checking to see if* DODGE *is well asleep. He reaches slowly under the cushion and pulls out the bottle of booze.* DODGE *sleeps soundly.* TILDEN *stands quietly, staring at* DODGE *as he uncaps the bottle and takes a long drink. He caps the bottle and sticks it in his hip pocket. He looks around at the husks on the floor and then back to* DODGE. *He moves center stage and gathers an armload of corn husks then crosses back to the sofa. He stands holding the husks over* DODGE *and looking down at him he gently spreads the corn husks over the whole length of* DODGE*'s body. He stands back and looks at* DODGE. *Pulls out bottle, takes another drink, returns bottle to his hip pocket. He gathers more husks and repeats the procedure until the floor is clean of corn husks and* DODGE *is completely covered in them except for his head.* TILDEN *takes another long drink, stares at* DODGE *sleeping, then quietly exits stage left. Long pause as the sound of rain continues.* DODGE *sleeps on. The figure of* BRADLEY *appears up left, outside the screen porch door. He holds a wet newspaper over his head as a protection from the rain. He seems to be struggling with the door then slips and almost falls to the ground.* DODGE *sleeps on, undisturbed.*]

BRADLEY Sonuvabitch! Sonuvagoddamnbitch!

[BRADLEY *recovers his footing and makes it through the screen door onto the porch. He throws the newspaper down, shakes the water out of his hair, and brushes the rain off of his shoulders. He is a big man dressed in a gray sweat shirt, black suspenders, baggy dark blue pants, and black janitor's shoes. His left leg is wooden, having been amputated above the knee. He moves with an exaggerated, almost mechanical limp. The squeaking sounds of leather and metal accompany his walk coming from the harness and hinges of the false leg. His arms and shoulders are extremely powerful and muscular due to a lifetime dependency on the upper torso doing all the work for the legs. He is about five years younger than* TILDEN. *He moves laboriously to the stage right door and enters, closing the door behind him. He doesn't notice* DODGE *at first. He moves toward the staircase.*]

BRADLEY [*calling to upstairs*] Mom!

[*He stops and listens. Turns upstage and sees* DODGE *sleeping. Notices corn husks. He moves slowly toward sofa. Stops next to pail and looks into it. Looks at husks.* DODGE *stays asleep. Talks to himself.*]

4. An American outfielder and first baseman (b. 1920); one of the greatest hitters in baseball history, he played his entire career for the St. Louis Cardinals (1941–63).

5. Burma-Shave was a brand of brushless shaving cream, introduced in 1925. (Dodge is recalling a home run, apparently hit into the outfield bleachers.)

BRADLEY What in the hell is this?

[*He looks at* DODGE*'s sleeping face and shakes his head in disgust. He pulls out a pair of black electric hair clippers from his pocket. Unwinds the cord and crosses to the lamp. He jabs his wooden leg behind the knee, causing it to bend at the joint and awkwardly kneels to plug the cord into a floor outlet. He pulls himself to his feet again by using the sofa as leverage. He moves to* DODGE*'s head and again jabs his false leg. Goes down on one knee. He violently knocks away some of the corn husks then jerks off* DODGE*'s baseball cap and throws it down center stage.* DODGE *stays asleep.* BRADLEY *switches on the clippers. Lights start dimming.* BRADLEY *cuts* DODGE*'s hair while he sleeps. Lights dim slowly to black with the sound of clippers and rain.*]

Act 2

SCENE: *Same set as act 1. Night. Sounds of rain.* DODGE *still asleep on sofa. His hair is cut extremely short and in places the scalp is cut and bleeding. His cap is still center stage. All the corn and husks, pail, and milking stool have been cleared away. The lights come up to the sound of a young girl laughing off stage left.* DODGE *remains asleep.* SHELLY *and* VINCE *appear up left outside the screen porch door sharing the shelter of* VINCE*'s overcoat above their heads.* SHELLY *is about nineteen, black hair, very beautiful. She wears tight jeans, high heels, purple T-shirt, and a short rabbit-fur coat. Her makeup is exaggerated and her hair has been curled.* VINCE *is* TILDEN*'s son, about twenty-two, wears a plaid shirt, jeans, dark glasses, cowboy boots, and carries a black saxophone case. They shake the rain off themselves as they enter the porch through the screen door.*

SHELLY [*laughing, gesturing to house*] This is it? I don't believe this is it!

VINCE This is it.

SHELLY This is the house?

VINCE This is the house.

SHELLY I don't believe it!

VINCE How come?

SHELLY It's like a Norman Rockwell[6] cover or something.

VINCE What's a' matter with that? It's American.

SHELLY Where's the milkman and the little dog? What's the little dog's name? Spot. Spot and Jane. Dick and Jane and Spot.[7]

VINCE Knock it off.

SHELLY Dick and Jane and Spot and Mom and Dad and Junior and Sissy!

[*She laughs. Slaps her knee.*]

VINCE Come on! It's my heritage. What dya' expect?

[*She laughs more hysterically, out of control.*]

6. An American illustrator (1894–1978), best known for his covers for the *Saturday Evening Post* magazine, which appeared from 1916 through the early 1960s. Rockwell's drawings often featured realistic yet humorous and wholesome images of small-town American life.

7. Names from the famous Dick and Jane readers; created in 1930 for Scott, Foresman and Company, they were widely used throughout the United States up to the 1970s. The illustrated books, designed to teach children to read by repeating a limited number of carefully chosen words, depicted an idealized white, middle-class family.

SHELLY "And Tuffy and Toto and Dooda and Bonzo[8] all went down one day to the corner grocery store to buy a big bag of licorice for Mr. Marshall's pussy cat!"

[*She laughs so hard she falls to her knees holding her stomach.* VINCE *stands there looking at her.*]

VINCE Shelly will you get up!

[*She keeps laughing. Staggers to her feet. Turning in circles holding her stomach.*]

SHELLY [*continuing her story in kid's voice*] "Mr. Marshall was on vacation. He had no idea that the four little boys had taken such a liking to his little kitty cat."

VINCE Have some respect would ya'!

SHELLY [*trying to control herself*] I'm sorry.

VINCE Pull yourself together.

SHELLY [*salutes him*] Yes sir.

[*She giggles.*]

VINCE Jesus Christ, Shelly.

SHELLY [*pause, smiling*] And Mr. Marshall—

VINCE Cut it out.

[*She stops. Stands there staring at him. Stifles a giggle.*]

VINCE [*after pause*] Are you finished?

SHELLY Oh brother!

VINCE I don't wanna go in there with you acting like an idiot.

SHELLY Thanks.

VINCE Well, I don't.

SHELLY I won't embarrass you. Don't worry.

VINCE I'm not worried.

SHELLY You are too.

VINCE Shelly look, I just don't wanna go in there with you giggling your head off. They might think something's wrong with you.

SHELLY There is.

VINCE There is not!

SHELLY Something's definitely wrong with me.

VINCE There is not!

SHELLY There's something wrong with you too.

VINCE There's nothing wrong with me either!

SHELLY You wanna know what's wrong with you?

VINCE What?

[SHELLY *laughs.*]

VINCE [*crosses back left toward screen door*] I'm leaving!

8. A reference to the Bonzo Dog Doo-Dah Band, created by British art students in the 1960s; the Bonzos played a mixture of jazz and psychedelic rock and performed regularly on a BBC children's series, *Do Not Adjust Your Set* (1967–69). (Bonzo was also a chimpanzee in *Bedtime for Bonzo*, a 1951 film starring Ronald Reagan.) *Tuffy:* a baby mouse featured in the *Tom and Jerry* cartoon series (begun in the 1940s). *Toto:* Dorothy's dog in *The Wizard of Oz* (1939), the movie musical adapted from L. Frank Baum's novel *The Wonderful Wizard of Oz* (1900) and its sequels.

SHELLY [*stops laughing*] Wait! Stop! Stop! [VINCE *stops.*] What's wrong with you is that you take the situation too seriously.

VINCE I just don't want to have them think that I've suddenly arrived out of the middle of nowhere completely deranged.

SHELLY What do you want them to think then?

VINCE [*pause*] Nothing. Let's go in.

[*He crosses porch toward stage right interior door.* SHELLY *follows him. The stage right door opens slowly.* VINCE *sticks his head in, doesn't notice* DODGE *sleeping. Calls out toward staircase.*]

VINCE Grandma!

[SHELLY *breaks into laughter, unseen behind* VINCE. VINCE *pulls his head back outside and pulls door shut. We hear their voices again without seeing them.*]

SHELLY'S VOICE [*stops laughing*] I'm sorry. I'm sorry Vince. I really am. I really am sorry. I won't do it again. I couldn't help it.

VINCE'S VOICE It's not all that funny.

SHELLY'S VOICE I know it's not. I'm sorry.

VINCE'S VOICE I mean this is a tense situation for me! I haven't seen them for over six years. I don't know what to expect.

SHELLY'S VOICE I know. I won't do it again.

VINCE'S VOICE Can't you bite your tongue or something?

SHELLY'S VOICE Just don't say "Grandma," okay? [*She giggles, stops.*] I mean if you say "Grandma" I don't know if I can stop myself.

VINCE'S VOICE Well try!

SHELLY'S VOICE Okay. Sorry.

[*Door opens again.* VINCE *sticks his head in then enters.* SHELLY *follows behind him.* VINCE *crosses to staircase, sets down saxophone case and overcoat, looks up staircase.* SHELLY *notices* DODGE'*s baseball cap. Crosses to it. Picks it up and puts it on her head.* VINCE *goes up the stairs and disappears at the top.* SHELLY *watches him then turns and sees* DODGE *on the sofa. She takes off the baseball cap.*]

VINCE'S VOICE [*from above stairs*] Grandma!

[SHELLY *crosses over to* DODGE *slowly and stands next to him. She stands at his head, reaches out slowly and touches one of the cuts. The second she touches his head,* DODGE *jerks up to a sitting position on the sofa, eyes open.* SHELLY *gasps.* DODGE *looks at her, sees his cap in her hands, quickly puts his hand to his bare head. He glares at* SHELLY *then whips the cap out of her hands and puts it on.* SHELLY *backs away from him.* DODGE *stares at her.*]

SHELLY I'm uh—with Vince.

[DODGE *just glares at her.*]

SHELLY He's upstairs.

[DODGE *looks at the staircase then back to* SHELLY.]

SHELLY [*calling upstairs*] Vince!

VINCE'S VOICE Just a second!

SHELLY You better get down here!

VINCE'S VOICE Just a minute! I'm looking at the pictures.

[DODGE *keeps staring at her.*]

SHELLY [*to* DODGE] We just got here. Pouring rain on the freeway so we thought we'd stop by. I mean Vince was planning on stopping anyway. He wanted to see you. He said he hadn't seen you in a long time.

[*Pause.* DODGE *just keeps staring at her.*]

SHELLY We were going all the way through to New Mexico. To see his father. I guess his father lives out there. We thought we'd stop by and see you on the way. Kill two birds with one stone, you know? [*She laughs,* DODGE *stares, she stops laughing.*] I mean Vince has this thing about his family now. I guess it's a new thing with him. I kind of find it hard to relate to. But he feels it's important. You know. I mean he feels he wants to get to know you all again. After all this time.

[*Pause.* DODGE *just stares at her. She moves nervously to staircase and yells up to* VINCE.]

SHELLY Vince will you come down here please!

[VINCE *comes halfway down the stairs.*]

VINCE I guess they went out for a while.

[SHELLY *points to sofa and* DODGE. VINCE *turns and sees* DODGE. *He comes all the way down staircase and crosses to* DODGE. SHELLY *stays behind near staircase, keeping her distance.*]

VINCE Grandpa?

[DODGE *looks up at him, not recognizing him.*]

DODGE Did you bring the whiskey?

[VINCE *looks back at* SHELLY *then back to* DODGE.]

VINCE Grandpa, it's Vince. I'm Vince. Tilden's son. You remember?

[DODGE *stares at him.*]

DODGE You didn't do what you told me. You didn't stay here with me.

VINCE Grandpa, I haven't been here until just now. I just got here.

DODGE You left. You went outside like we told you not to do. You went out there in back. In the rain.

[VINCE *looks back at* SHELLY. *She moves slowly toward sofa.*]

SHELLY Is he okay?

VINCE I don't know. [*Takes off his shades.*] Look, Grandpa, don't you remember me? Vince. Your Grandson.

[DODGE *stares at him then takes off his baseball cap.*]

DODGE [*points to his head*] See what happens when you leave me alone? See that? That's what happens.

[VINCE *looks at his head.* VINCE *reaches out to touch his head.* DODGE *slaps his hand away with the cap and puts it back on his head.*]

VINCE What's going on Grandpa? Where's Halie?

DODGE Don't worry about her. She won't be back for days. She says she'll be back but she won't be. [*He starts laughing.*] There's life in the old girl yet! [*Stops laughing.*]

VINCE How did you do that to your head?

DODGE I didn't do it! Don't be ridiculous!

VINCE Well who did then?

[*Pause.* DODGE *stares at* VINCE.]

DODGE Who do you think did it? Who do you think?

[SHELLY *moves toward* VINCE.]

SHELLY Vince, maybe we oughta' go. I don't like this. I mean this isn't my idea of a good time.

VINCE [*to* SHELLY] Just a second. [*To* DODGE] Grandpa, look, I just got here. I just now got here. I haven't been here for six years. I don't know anything that's happened.

[*Pause.* DODGE *stares at him.*]

DODGE You don't know anything?

VINCE No.

DODGE Well that's good. That's good. It's much better not to know anything. Much, much better.

VINCE Isn't there anybody here with you?

[DODGE *turns slowly and looks off to stage left.*]

DODGE Tilden's here.

VINCE No, Grandpa, Tilden's in New Mexico. That's where I was going. I'm going out there to see him.

[DODGE *turns slowly back to* VINCE.]

DODGE Tilden's here.

[VINCE *backs away and joins* SHELLY. DODGE *stares at them.*]

SHELLY Vince, why don't we spend the night in a motel and come back in the morning? We could have breakfast. Maybe everything would be different.

VINCE Don't be scared. There's nothing to be scared of. He's just old.

SHELLY I'm not scared!

DODGE You two are not my idea of the perfect couple!

SHELLY [*after pause*] Oh really? Why's that?

VINCE Shh! Don't aggravate him.

DODGE There's something wrong between the two of you. Something not compatible.

VINCE Grandpa, where did Halie go? Maybe we should call her.

DODGE What are you talking about? Do you know what you're talking about? Are you just talking for the sake of talking? Lubricating the gums?

VINCE I'm trying to figure out what's going on here!

DODGE Is that it?

VINCE Yes. I mean I expected everything to be different.

DODGE Who are you to expect anything? Who are you supposed to be?

VINCE I'm Vince! Your Grandson!

DODGE Vince. My Grandson.

VINCE Tilden's son.

DODGE Tilden's son, Vince.

VINCE You haven't seen me for a long time.

DODGE When was the last time?

VINCE I don't remember.

DODGE You don't remember?

VINCE No.

DODGE You don't remember. How am I supposed to remember if you don't remember?

SHELLY Vince, come on. This isn't going to work out.

VINCE [*to* SHELLY] Just take it easy.

SHELLY I'm taking it easy! He doesn't even know who you are!

VINCE [*crossing toward* DODGE] Grandpa, look—

DODGE Stay where you are! Keep your distance!

[VINCE *stops. Looks back at* SHELLY *then to* DODGE.]

SHELLY Vince, this is really making me nervous. I mean he doesn't even want us here. He doesn't even like us.

DODGE She's a beautiful girl.

VINCE Thanks.

DODGE Very Beautiful Girl.

SHELLY Oh my God.

DODGE [*to* SHELLY] What's your name?

SHELLY Shelly.

DODGE Shelly. That's a man's name isn't it?

SHELLY Not in this case.

DODGE [*to* VINCE] She's a smart-ass too.

SHELLY Vince! Can we go?

DODGE She wants to go. She just got here and she wants to go.

VINCE This is kind of strange for her.

DODGE She'll get used to it. [*To* SHELLY] What part of the country do you come from?

SHELLY Originally?

DODGE That's right. Originally. At the very start.

SHELLY L.A.

DODGE L.A. Stupid country.

SHELLY I can't stand this Vince! This is really unbelievable!

DODGE It's stupid! L.A. is stupid! So is Florida! All those Sunshine States. They're all stupid. Do you know why they're stupid?

SHELLY Illuminate me.

DODGE I'll tell you why. Because they're full of smart-asses! That's why.

[SHELLY *turns her back to* DODGE, *crosses to staircase and sits on bottom step.*]

DODGE [*to* VINCE] Now she's insulted.

VINCE Well you weren't very polite.

DODGE She's insulted! Look at her! In my house she's insulted! She's over there sulking because I insulted her!

SHELLY [*to* VINCE] This is really terrific. This is wonderful. And you were worried about me making the right first impression!

DODGE [*to* VINCE] She's a fireball isn't she? Regular fireball. I had some a' them in my day. Temporary stuff. Never lasted more than a week.

VINCE Grandpa—

DODGE Stop calling me Grandpa will ya'! It's sickening. "Grandpa." I'm nobody's Grandpa!

[DODGE *starts feeling around under the cushion for the bottle of whiskey.* SHELLY *gets up from the staircase.*]

SHELLY [*to* VINCE] Maybe you've got the wrong house. Did you ever think of that? Maybe this is the wrong address!

VINCE It's not the wrong address! I recognize the yard.

SHELLY Yeah but do you recognize the people? He says he's not your Grandfather.

DODGE [*digging for bottle*] Where's that bottle!

VINCE He's just sick or something. I don't know what's happened to him.

DODGE Where's my goddamn bottle!

[DODGE *gets up from sofa and starts tearing the cushions off it and throwing them downstage, looking for the whiskey.*]

SHELLY Can't we just drive on to New Mexico? This is terrible, Vince! I don't want to stay here. In this house. I thought it was going to be turkey dinners and apple pie and all that kinda stuff.

VINCE Well I hate to disappoint you!

SHELLY I'm not disappointed! I'm fuckin' terrified! I wanna' go!

[DODGE *yells toward stage left.*]

DODGE Tilden! Tilden!

[DODGE *keeps ripping away at the sofa looking for his bottle, he knocks over the night stand with the bottles.* VINCE *and* SHELLY *watch as he starts ripping the stuffing out of the sofa.*]

VINCE [*to* SHELLY] He's lost his mind or something. I've got to try to help him.

SHELLY You help him! I'm leaving!

[SHELLY *starts to leave.* VINCE *grabs her. They struggle as* DODGE *keeps ripping away at the sofa and yelling.*]

DODGE Tilden! Tilden get your ass in here! Tilden!

SHELLY Let go of me!

VINCE You're not going anywhere! You're going to stay right here!

SHELLY Let go of me you sonuvabitch! I'm not your property!

[*Suddenly* TILDEN *walks on from stage left just as he did before. This time his arms are full of carrots.* DODGE, VINCE, *and* SHELLY *stop suddenly when they see him. They all stare at* TILDEN *as he crosses slowly center stage with the carrots and stops.* DODGE *sits on sofa, exhausted.*]

DODGE [*panting, to* TILDEN] Where in the hell have you been?

TILDEN Out back.

DODGE Where's my bottle?

TILDEN Gone.

[TILDEN *and* VINCE *stare at each other.* SHELLY *backs away.*]

DODGE [*to* TILDEN] You stole my bottle!

VINCE [*to* TILDEN] Dad?

[TILDEN *just stares at* VINCE.]

DODGE You had no right to steal my bottle! No right at all!

VINCE [*to* TILDEN] It's Vince. I'm Vince.

[TILDEN *stares at* VINCE *then looks at* DODGE *then turns to* SHELLY.]

TILDEN [*after pause*] I picked these carrots. If anybody wants any carrots, I picked 'em.

SHELLY [*to* VINCE] This is your father?

VINCE [*to* TILDEN] Dad, what're you doing here?

[TILDEN *just stares at* VINCE, *holding carrots,* DODGE *pulls the blanket back over himself.*]

DODGE [*to* TILDEN] You're going to have to get me another bottle! You gotta get me a bottle before Halie comes back! There's money on the table. [*Points to stage left kitchen.*]

TILDEN [*shaking his head*] I'm not going down there. Into town.

[SHELLY *crosses to* TILDEN. TILDEN *stares at her.*]

SHELLY [*to* TILDEN] Are you Vince's father?

TILDEN [*to* SHELLY] Vince?

SHELLY [*pointing to* VINCE] This is supposed to be your son! Is he your son? Do you recognize him! I'm just along for the ride here. I thought everybody knew each other!

[TILDEN *stares at* VINCE. DODGE *wraps himself up in the blanket and sits on sofa staring at the floor.*]

TILDEN I had a son once but we buried him.

[DODGE *quickly looks at* TILDEN. SHELLY *looks to* VINCE.]

DODGE You shut up about that! You don't know anything about that!

VINCE Dad, I thought you were in New Mexico. We were going to drive down there and see you.

TILDEN Long way to drive.

DODGE [*to* TILDEN] You don't know anything about that! That happened before you were born! Long before!

VINCE What's happened, Dad? What's going on here? I thought everything was all right. What's happened to Halie?

TILDEN She left.

SHELLY [*to* TILDEN] Do you want me to take those carrots for you?

[TILDEN *stares at her. She moves in close to him. Holds out her arms.* TILDEN *stares at her arms then slowly dumps the carrots into her arms.* SHELLY *stands there holding the carrots.*]

TILDEN [*to* SHELLY] You like carrots?

SHELLY Sure. I like all kinds of vegetables.

DODGE [*to* TILDEN] You gotta get me a bottle before Halie comes back!

[DODGE *hits sofa with his fist.* VINCE *crosses up to* DODGE *and tries to console him.* SHELLY *and* TILDEN *stay facing each other.*]

TILDEN [*to* SHELLY] Backyard's full of carrots. Corn. Potatoes.

SHELLY You're Vince's father, right?

TILDEN All kinds of vegetables. You like vegetables?

SHELLY [*laughs*] Yeah. I love vegetables.

TILDEN We could cook these carrots ya' know. You could cut 'em up and we could cook 'em.

SHELLY All right.

TILDEN I'll get you a pail and a knife.

SHELLY Okay.

TILDEN I'll be right back. Don't go.

[TILDEN *exits offstage left.* SHELLY *stands center, arms full of carrots.* VINCE *stands next to* DODGE. SHELLY *looks toward* VINCE *then down at the carrots.*]

DODGE [*to* VINCE] You could get me a bottle. [*Pointing off left*] There's money on the table.

VINCE Grandpa why don't you lay down for a while?

DODGE I don't wanna lay down for a while! Every time I lay down something happens! [*Whips off his cap, points at his head.*] Look what happens! That's what happens! [*Pulls his cap back on.*] You go lie down and see what happens to you! See how you like it! They'll steal your bottle! They'll cut your hair! They'll murder your children! That's what'll happen.

VINCE Just relax for a while.

DODGE [*pause*] You could get me a bottle ya' know. There's nothing stopping you from getting me a bottle.

SHELLY Why don't you get him a bottle, Vince? Maybe it would help everybody identify each other.

DODGE [*pointing to* SHELLY] There, see? She thinks you should get me a bottle.

[VINCE *crosses to* SHELLY.]

VINCE What're you doing with those carrots.

SHELLY I'm waiting for your father.

DODGE She thinks you should get me a bottle!

VINCE Shelly put the carrots down will ya'! We gotta deal with the situation here! I'm gonna need your help.

SHELLY I'm helping.

VINCE You're only adding to the problem! You're making things worse! Put the carrots down!

[VINCE *tries to knock the carrots out of her arms. She turns away from him, protecting the carrots.*]

SHELLY Get away from me! Stop it!

[VINCE *stands back from her. She turns to him still holding the carrots.*]

VINCE [*to* SHELLY] Why are you doing this! Are you trying to make fun of me? This is my family you know!

SHELLY You coulda' fooled me! I'd just as soon not be here myself. I'd just as soon be a thousand miles from here. I'd rather be anywhere but here. You're the one who wants to stay. So I'll stay. I'll stay and I'll cut the carrots. And I'll cook the carrots. And I'll do whatever I have to do to survive. Just to make it through this.

VINCE Put the carrots down Shelly.

[TILDEN *enters from left with pail, milking stool, and a knife. He sets the stool and pail center stage for* SHELLY. SHELLY *looks at* VINCE *then sits down on stool, sets the carrots on the floor and takes the knife from* TILDEN. *She looks at* VINCE *again then picks up a carrot, cuts the ends off, scrapes it and drops it in pail. She repeats this,* VINCE *glares at her. She smiles.*]

DODGE She could get me a bottle. She's the type a' girl that could get me a bottle. Easy. She'd go down there. Slink up to the counter. They'd probably give her two bottles for the price of one. She could do that.

[SHELLY *laughs. Keeps cutting carrots.* VINCE *crosses up to* DODGE, *looks at him.* TILDEN *watches* SHELLY*'s hands. Long pause.*]

VINCE [*to* DODGE] I haven't changed that much. I mean physically. Physically I'm just about the same. Same size. Same weight. Everything's the same.

[DODGE *keeps staring at* SHELLY *while* VINCE *talks to him.*]

DODGE She's a beautiful girl. Exceptional.

[VINCE *moves in front of* DODGE *to block his view of* SHELLY. DODGE *keeps craning his head around to see her as* VINCE *demonstrates tricks from his past.*]

VINCE Look. Look at this. Do you remember this? I used to bend my thumb behind my knuckles. You remember? I used to do it at the dinner table.

[VINCE *bends a thumb behind his knuckles for* DODGE *and holds it out to him.* DODGE *takes a short glance, then looks back at* SHELLY. VINCE *shifts position and shows him something else.*]

VINCE What about this?

[VINCE *curls his lips back and starts drumming on his teeth with his fingernails making little tapping sounds.* DODGE *watches a while.* TILDEN *turns toward the sound.* VINCE *keeps it up. He sees* TILDEN *taking notice and crosses to* TILDEN *as he drums on his teeth.* DODGE *turns T.V. on. Watches it.*]

VINCE You remember this Dad?

[VINCE *keeps on drumming for* TILDEN. TILDEN *watches a while, fascinated, then turns back to* SHELLY. VINCE *keeps up the drumming on his teeth, crosses back to* DODGE *doing it.* SHELLY *keeps working on carrots, talking to* TILDEN.]

SHELLY [*to* TILDEN] He drives me crazy with that sometimes.

VINCE [*to* DODGE] I know! Here's one you'll remember. You used to kick me out of the house for this one.

[VINCE *pulls his shirt out of his belt and holds it tucked under his chin with his stomach exposed. He grabs the flesh on either side of his belly button and pushes it in and out to make it look like a mouth talking. He watches his belly button and makes a deep-sounding cartoon voice to synchronize with the movement. He demonstrates it to* DODGE, *then crosses down to* TILDEN *doing it. Both* DODGE *and* TILDEN *take short, uninterested glances then ignore him.*]

VINCE [*deep cartoon voice*] "Hello. How are you? I'm fine. Thank you very much. It's so good to see you looking well this fine Sunday morning. I was going down to the hardware store to fetch a pail of water."

SHELLY Vince, don't be pathetic will ya'!

[VINCE *stops. Tucks his shirt back in.*]

SHELLY Jesus Christ. They're not gonna play. Can't you see that?

[SHELLY *keeps cutting carrots.* VINCE *slowly moves toward* TILDEN. TILDEN *keeps watching* SHELLY. DODGE *watches T.V.*]

VINCE [*to* SHELLY] I don't get it. I really don't get it. Maybe it's me. Maybe I forgot something.

DODGE [*from sofa*] You forgot to get me a bottle! That's what you forgot. Anybody in this house could get me a bottle. Anybody! But nobody will. Nobody understands the urgency! Peelin' carrots is more important. Playin' piano on your teeth! Well I hope you all remember this when you get up in years. When you find yourself immobilized. Dependent on the whims of others.

[VINCE *moves up toward* DODGE. *Pause as he looks at him.*]

VINCE I'll get you a bottle.

DODGE You will?

VINCE Sure.

[SHELLY *stands holding knife and carrot.*]

SHELLY You're not going to leave me here are you?

VINCE [*moving to her*] You suggested it! You said, "why don't I go get him a bottle." So I'll go get him a bottle!

SHELLY But I can't stay here.

VINCE What is going on! A minute ago you were ready to cut carrots all night!

SHELLY That was only if you stayed. Something to keep me busy, so I wouldn't be so nervous. I don't want to stay here alone.

DODGE Don't let her talk you out of it! She's a bad influence. I could see it the minute she stepped in here.

SHELLY [*to* DODGE] You were asleep!

TILDEN [*to* SHELLY] Don't you want to cut carrots anymore?

SHELLY Sure. Sure I do.

[SHELLY *sits back down on stool and continues cutting carrots. Pause.* VINCE *moves around, stroking his hair, staring at* DODGE *and* TILDEN. VINCE *and* SHELLY *exchange glances.* DODGE *watches T.V.*]

VINCE Boy! This is amazing. This is truly amazing. [*Keeps moving around.*] What is this anyway? Am I in a time warp or something? Have I committed an unpardonable offence? It's true, I'm not married. [SHELLY *looks at him, then back to carrots.*] But I'm also not divorced. I have been known to plunge into sinful infatuation with the Alto Saxophone. Sucking on number 5 reeds[9] deep into the wee, wee hours.

SHELLY Vince, what are you doing that for? They don't care about any of that. They just don't recognize you, that's all.

VINCE How could they not recognize me! How in the hell could they not recognize me! I'm their son!

DODGE [*watching T.V.*] You're no son of mine. I've had sons in my time and you're not one of 'em.

[*Long pause.* VINCE *stares at* DODGE *then looks at* TILDEN. *He turns to* SHELLY.]

VINCE Shelly, I gotta go out for a while. I just gotta go out. I'll get a bottle and I'll come right back. You'll be o.k. here. Really.

SHELLY I don't know if I can handle this, Vince.

VINCE I just gotta think or something. I don't know. I gotta put this all together.

SHELLY Can't we just go?

VINCE No! I gotta find out what's going on.

SHELLY Look, you think you're bad off, what about me? Not only don't they recognize me but I've never seen them before in my life. I don't know who these guys are. They could be anybody!

VINCE They're not anybody!

SHELLY That's what you say.

VINCE They're my family for Christ's sake! I should know who my own family is! Now give me a break. It won't take that long. I'll just go out and I'll come right back. Nothing'll happen. I promise.

[SHELLY *stares at him. Pause.*]

SHELLY All right.

VINCE Thanks. [*He crosses up to* DODGE.] I'm gonna go out now, Grandpa, and I'll pick you up a bottle. Okay?

9. The number assigned to a woodwind reed refers to its hardness (5 is extremely hard).

DODGE Change of heart huh? [*Pointing off left*] Money's on the table. In the kitchen.

[**VINCE** *moves toward* **SHELLY**.]

VINCE [*to* **SHELLY**] You be all right?

SHELLY [*cutting carrots*] Sure. I'm fine. I'll just keep real busy while you're gone.

[**VINCE** *looks at* **TILDEN** *who keeps staring down at* **SHELLY**'s *hands*.]

DODGE Persistence see? That's what it takes. Persistence. Persistence, fortitude, and determination. Those are the three virtues. You stick with those three and you can't go wrong.

VINCE [*to* **TILDEN**] You want anything, Dad?

TILDEN [*looks up at* **VINCE**] Me?

VINCE From the store? I'm gonna get Grandpa a bottle.

TILDEN He's not supposed to drink. Halie wouldn't like it.

VINCE He wants a bottle.

TILDEN He's not supposed to drink.

DODGE [*to* **VINCE**] Don't negotiate with him! Don't make any transactions until you've spoken to me first! He'll steal you blind!

VINCE [*to* **DODGE**] Tilden says you're not supposed to drink.

DODGE Tilden's lost his marbles! Look at him! He's around the bend. Take a look at him.

[**VINCE** *stares at* **TILDEN**. **TILDEN** *watches* **SHELLY**'s *hands as she keeps cutting carrots*.]

DODGE Now look at me. Look here at me!

[**VINCE** *looks back to* **DODGE**.]

DODGE Now, between the two of us, who do you think is more trustworthy? Him or me? Can you trust a man who keeps bringing in vegetables from out of nowhere? Take a look at him.

[**VINCE** *looks back at* **TILDEN**.]

SHELLY Go get the bottle, Vince.

VINCE [*to* **SHELLY**] You sure you'll be all right?

SHELLY I'll be fine. I feel right at home now.

VINCE You do?

SHELLY I'm fine. Now that I've got the carrots everything is all right.

VINCE I'll be right back.

[**VINCE** *crosses stage left*.]

DODGE Where are you going?

VINCE I'm going to get the money.

DODGE Then where are you going?

VINCE Liquor store.

DODGE Don't go anyplace else. Don't go off someplace and drink. Come right back here.

VINCE I will.

[**VINCE** *exits stage left*.]

DODGE [*calling after* **VINCE**] You've got responsibility now! And don't go out the back way either! Come out through this way! I wanna' see you when you leave! Don't go out the back!

VINCE'S VOICE [*off left*] I won't!

[DODGE *turns and looks at* TILDEN *and* SHELLY.]

DODGE Untrustworthy. Probably drown himself if he went out the back. Fall right in a hole. I'd never get my bottle.

SHELLY I wouldn't worry about Vince. He can take care of himself.

DODGE Oh he can, huh? Independent.

[VINCE *comes on again from stage left with two dollars in his hand. He crosses stage right past* DODGE.]

DODGE [*to* VINCE] You got the money?

VINCE Yeah. Two bucks.

DODGE Two bucks. Two bucks is two bucks. Don't sneer.

VINCE What kind do you want?

DODGE Whiskey! Gold Star Sour Mash. Use your own discretion.

VINCE Okay.

[VINCE *crosses to stage right door. Opens it. Stops when he hears* TILDEN.]

TILDEN [*to* VINCE] You drove all the way from New Mexico?

[VINCE *turns and looks at* TILDEN. *They stare at each other.* VINCE *shakes his head, goes out the door, crosses porch, and exits out screen door.* TILDEN *watches him go. Pause.*]

SHELLY You really don't recognize him? Either one of you?

[TILDEN *turns again and stares at* SHELLY'*s hands as she cuts carrots.*]

DODGE [watching T.V.] Recognize who?

SHELLY Vince.

DODGE What's to recognize?

[DODGE *lights a cigarette, coughs slightly, and stares at T.V.*]

SHELLY It'd be cruel if you recognized him and didn't tell him. Wouldn't be fair.

[DODGE *just stares at T.V., smoking.*]

TILDEN I thought I recognized him. I thought I recognized something about him.

SHELLY You did?

TILDEN I thought I saw a face inside his face.

SHELLY Well it was probably that you saw what he used to look like. You haven't seen him for six years.

TILDEN I haven't?

SHELLY That's what he says.

[TILDEN *moves around in front of her as she continues with carrots.*]

TILDEN Where was it I saw him last?

SHELLY I don't know. I've only known him for a few months. He doesn't tell me everything.

TILDEN He doesn't?

SHELLY Not stuff like that.

TILDEN What does he tell you?

SHELLY You mean in general?

TILDEN Yeah.

[TILDEN *moves around behind her.*]

SHELLY Well he tells me all kinds of things.

TILDEN Like what?

SHELLY I don't know! I mean I can't just come right out and tell you how he feels.

TILDEN How come?

[TILDEN *keeps moving around her slowly in a circle.*]

SHELLY Because it's stuff he told me privately!

TILDEN And you can't tell me?

SHELLY I don't even know you!

DODGE Tilden, go out in the kitchen and make me some coffee! Leave the girl alone.

SHELLY [*to* DODGE] He's all right.

[TILDEN *ignores* DODGE, *keeps moving around* SHELLY. *He stares at her hair and coat.* DODGE *stares at T.V.*]

TILDEN You mean you can't tell me anything?

SHELLY I can tell you some things. I mean we can have a conversation.

TILDEN We can?

SHELLY Sure. We're having a conversation right now.

TILDEN We are?

SHELLY Yes. That's what we're doing.

TILDEN But there's certain things you can't tell me, right?

SHELLY Right.

TILDEN There's certain things I can't tell you either.

SHELLY How come?

TILDEN I don't know. Nobody's supposed to hear it.

SHELLY Well, you can tell me anything you want to.

TILDEN I can?

SHELLY Sure.

TILDEN It might not be very nice.

SHELLY That's all right. I've been around.

TILDEN It might be awful.

SHELLY Well, can't you tell me anything nice?

[TILDEN *stops in front of her and stares at her coat.* SHELLY *looks back at him. Long pause.*]

TILDEN [*after pause*] Can I touch your coat?

SHELLY My coat? [*She looks at her coat then back to* TILDEN.] Sure.

TILDEN You don't mind?

SHELLY No. Go ahead.

[SHELLY *holds her arm out for* TILDEN *to touch.* DODGE *stays fixed on T.V.* TILDEN *moves in slowly toward* SHELLY, *staring at her arm. He reaches out very slowly and touches her arm, feels the fur gently then draws his hand back.* SHELLY *keeps her arm out.*]

SHELLY It's rabbit.

TILDEN Rabbit.

[*He reaches out again very slowly and touches the fur on her arm then pulls back his hand again.* SHELLY *drops her arm.*]

SHELLY My arm was getting tired.

TILDEN Can I hold it?

SHELLY [*pause*] The coat? Sure.

[SHELLY *takes off her coat and hands it to* TILDEN. TILDEN *takes it slowly, feels the fur, then puts it on.* SHELLY *watches as* TILDEN *strokes the fur slowly. He smiles at her. She goes back to cutting carrots.*]

SHELLY You can have it if you want.

TILDEN I can?

SHELLY Yeah. I've got a raincoat in the car. That's all I need.

TILDEN You've got a car?

SHELLY Vince does.

[TILDEN *walks around stroking the fur and smiling at the coat.* SHELLY *watches him when he's not looking.* DODGE *sticks with T.V., stretches out on sofa wrapped in blanket.*]

TILDEN [*as he walks around*] I had a car once! I had a white car! I drove. I went everywhere. I went to the mountains. I drove in the snow.

SHELLY That must've been fun.

TILDEN [*still moving, feeling coat*] I drove all day long sometimes. Across the desert. Way out across the desert. I drove past towns. Anywhere. Past palm trees. Lightning. Anything. I would drive through it. I would drive through it and I would stop and I would look around and I would drive on. I would get back in and drive! I loved to drive. There was nothing I loved more. Nothing I dreamed of was better than driving.

DODGE [*eyes on T.V.*] Pipe down would ya'!

[TILDEN *stops. Stares at* SHELLY.]

SHELLY Do you do much driving now?

TILDEN Now? Now? I don't drive now.

SHELLY How come?

TILDEN I'm grown up now.

SHELLY Grown up?

TILDEN I'm not a kid.

SHELLY You don't have to be a kid to drive.

TILDEN It wasn't driving then.

SHELLY What was it?

TILDEN Adventure. I went everywhere.

SHELLY Well you can still do that.

TILDEN Not now.

SHELLY Why not?

TILDEN I just told you. You don't understand anything. If I told you something you wouldn't understand it.

SHELLY Told me what?

TILDEN Told you something that's true.

SHELLY Like what?

TILDEN Like a baby. Like a little tiny baby.

SHELLY Like when you were little?

TILDEN If I told you you'd make me give your coat back.

SHELLY I won't. I promise. Tell me.

TILDEN I can't. Dodge won't let me.

SHELLY He won't hear you. It's okay.

[*Pause.* TILDEN *stares at her. Moves slightly toward her.*]

TILDEN We had a baby. [*Motioning to* DODGE] He did. Dodge did. Could pick it up with one hand. Put it in the other. Little baby. Dodge killed it.

[SHELLY *stands.*]

TILDEN Don't stand up. Don't stand up!

[SHELLY *sits again.* DODGE *sits up on sofa and looks at them.*]

TILDEN Dodge drowned it.

SHELLY Don't tell me anymore! Okay?

[TILDEN *moves closer to her.* DODGE *takes more interest.*]

DODGE Tilden? You leave that girl alone!

TILDEN [*pays no attention*] Never told Halie. Never told anybody. Just drowned it.

DODGE [*shuts off T.V.*] Tilden!

TILDEN Nobody could find it. Just disappeared. Cops looked for it. Neighbors. Nobody could find it.

[DODGE *struggles to get up from sofa.*]

DODGE Tilden, what're you telling her! Tilden!

[DODGE *keeps struggling until he's standing.*]

TILDEN Finally everybody just gave up. Just stopped looking. Everybody had a different answer. Kidnap. Murder. Accident. Some kind of accident.

[DODGE *struggles to walk toward* TILDEN *and falls.* TILDEN *ignores him.*]

DODGE Tilden you shut up! You shut up about it!

[DODGE *starts coughing on the floor.* SHELLY *watches him from the stool.*]

TILDEN Little tiny baby just disappeared. It's not hard. It's so small. Almost invisible.

[SHELLY *makes a move to help* DODGE. TILDEN *firmly pushes her back down on the stool.* DODGE *keeps coughing.*]

TILDEN He said he had his reasons. Said it went a long way back. But he wouldn't tell anybody.

DODGE Tilden! Don't tell her anything! Don't tell her!

TILDEN He's the only one who knows where it's buried. The only one. Like a secret buried treasure. Won't tell any of us. Won't tell me or mother or even Bradley. Especially Bradley. Bradley tried to force it out of him but he wouldn't tell. Wouldn't even tell why he did it. One night he just did it.

[DODGE*'s coughing subsides.* SHELLY *stays on stool staring at* DODGE. TILDEN *slowly takes* SHELLY*'s coat off and holds it out to her. Long pause.* SHELLY *sits there trembling.*]

TILDEN You probably want your coat back now.

[SHELLY *stares at coat but doesn't move to take it. The sound of* BRADLEY*'s leg squeaking is heard off left. The others onstage remain still.* BRADLEY *appears up left outside the screen door wearing a yellow rain slicker. He enters through screen door, crosses porch to stage right door and enters stage. Closes door. Takes off rain slicker and shakes it out. He sees all the others and stops.* TILDEN *turns to him.* BRADLEY *stares at* SHELLY. DODGE *remains on floor.*]

BRADLEY What's going on here? [*Motioning to* SHELLY] Who's that?

[SHELLY *stands, moves back away from* BRADLEY *as he crosses toward her. He stops next to* TILDEN. *He sees coat in* TILDEN*'s hand and grabs it away from him.*]

BRADLEY Who's she supposed to be?

TILDEN She's driving to New Mexico.

[BRADLEY *stares at her.* SHELLY *is frozen.* BRADLEY *limps over to her with the coat in his fist. He stops in front of her.*]

BRADLEY [*to* SHELLY, *after pause*] Vacation?

[SHELLY *shakes her head "no," trembling.*]

BRADLEY [*to* SHELLY, *motioning to* TILDEN] You taking him with you?

[SHELLY *shakes her head "no."* BRADLEY *crosses back to* TILDEN.]

BRADLEY You oughta'. No use leaving him here. Doesn't do a lick a' work. Doesn't raise a finger. [*Stopping, to* TILDEN] Do ya'? [*To* SHELLY] 'Course he used to be an All-American. Quarterback or Fullback or somethin'. He tell you that?

[SHELLY *shakes her head "no."*]

BRADLEY Yeah, he used to be a big deal. Wore lettermen's sweaters. Had medals hanging all around his neck. Real purty. Big deal. [*He laughs to himself, notices* DODGE *on floor, crosses to him, stops.*] This one too. [*To* SHELLY] You'd never think it to look at him would ya'? All bony and wasted away.

[SHELLY *shakes her head again.* BRADLEY *stares at her, crosses back to her, clenching the coat in his fist. He stops in front of* SHELLY.]

BRADLEY Women like that kinda' thing don't they?

SHELLY What?

BRADLEY Importance. Importance in a man?

SHELLY I don't know.

BRADLEY Yeah. You know, you know. Don't give me that. [*Moves closer to* SHELLY.] You're with Tilden?

SHELLY No.

BRADLEY [*turning to* TILDEN] Tilden! She with you?

[TILDEN *doesn't answer. Stares at floor.*]

BRADLEY Tilden!

[TILDEN *suddenly bolts and runs off up stage left.* BRADLEY *laughs. Talks to* SHELLY. DODGE *starts moving his lips silently as though talking to someone invisible on the floor.*]

BRADLEY [*laughing*] Scared to death! He was always scared!

[BRADLEY *stops laughing. Stares at* SHELLY.]

BRADLEY You're scared too, right? [*Laughs again.*] You're scared and you don't even know me. [*Stops laughing.*] You don't gotta be scared.

[SHELLY *looks at* DODGE *on the floor.*]

SHELLY Can't we do something for him?

BRADLEY [*looking at* DODGE] We could shoot him. [*Laughs.*] We could drown him! What about drowning him?

SHELLY Shut up!

[BRADLEY *stops laughing. Moves in closer to* SHELLY. *She freezes.* BRADLEY *speaks slowly and deliberately.*]

BRADLEY Hey! Missus. Don't talk to me like that. Don't talk to me in that tone a' voice. There was a time when I had to take that tone a' voice from pretty near everyone. [*Motioning to* DODGE] Him, for one! Him and that half brain that just ran outa' here. They don't talk to me like that now. Not anymore. Everything's turned around now. Full circle. Isn't that funny?

SHELLY I'm sorry.

BRADLEY Open your mouth.

SHELLY What?

BRADLEY [*motioning for her to open her mouth*] Open up.

[*She opens her mouth slightly.*]

BRADLEY Wider.

[*She opens her mouth wider.*]

BRADLEY Keep it like that.

[*She does. Stares at* BRADLEY. *With his free hand he puts his fingers into her mouth. She tries to pull away.*]

BRADLEY Just stay put!

[*She freezes. He keeps his fingers in her mouth. Stares at her. Pause. He pulls his hand out. She closes her mouth, keeps her eyes on him.* BRADLEY *smiles. He looks at* DODGE *on the floor and crosses over to him.* SHELLY *watches him closely.* BRADLEY *stands over* DODGE *and smiles at* SHELLY. *He holds her coat up in both hands over* DODGE, *keeps smiling at* SHELLY. *He looks down at* DODGE *then drops the coat so that it lands on* DODGE *and covers his head.* BRADLEY *keeps his hands up in the position of holding the coat, looks over at* SHELLY *and smiles. The lights black out.*]

Act 3

SCENE: *Same set. Morning. Bright sun. No sound of rain. Everything has been cleared up again. No sign of carrots. No pail. No stool.* VINCE*'s saxophone case and overcoat are still at the foot of the staircase.* BRADLEY *is asleep on the sofa under* DODGE*'s blanket. His head toward stage left.* BRADLEY*'s wooden leg is leaning against the sofa right by his head. The shoe is left on it. The harness hangs down.* DODGE *is sitting on the floor, propped up against the T.V. set facing stage left wearing his baseball cap.* SHELLY*'s rabbit fur coat covers his chest and shoulders. He stares off toward stage left. He seems weaker and more disoriented. The lights rise slowly to the sound of birds and remain for a while in silence on the two men.* BRADLEY *sleeps very soundly.* DODGE *hardly moves.* SHELLY *appears from stage left with a big smile, slowly crossing toward* DODGE *balancing a steaming cup of broth in a saucer.* DODGE *just stares at her as she gets closer to him.*

SHELLY [*as she crosses*] This is going to make all the difference in the world, Grandpa. You don't mind me calling you Grandpa do you? I mean I know you minded when Vince called you that but you don't even know him.

DODGE He skipped town with my money ya' know. I'm gonna hold you as collateral.

SHELLY He'll be back. Don't you worry.

[*She kneels down next to* DODGE *and puts the cup and saucer in his lap.*]

DODGE It's morning already! Not only didn't I get my bottle but he's got my two bucks!

SHELLY Try to drink this, okay? Don't spill it.

DODGE What is it?

SHELLY Beef bouillon. It'll warm you up.

DODGE Bouillon! I don't want any goddamn bouillon! Get that stuff away from me!

SHELLY I just got through making it.

DODGE I don't care if you just spent all week making it! I ain't drinking it!

SHELLY Well, what am I supposed to do with it then? I'm trying to help you out. Besides, it's good for you.

DODGE Get it away from me!

[SHELLY *stands up with cup and saucer.*]

DODGE What do you know what's good for me anyway?

[*She looks at* DODGE *then turns away from him, crossing to staircase, sits on bottom step and drinks the bouillon.* DODGE *stares at her.*]

DODGE You know what'd be good for me?

SHELLY What?

DODGE A little massage. A little contact.

SHELLY Oh no. I've had enough contact for a while. Thanks anyway.

[*She keeps sipping bouillon, stays sitting. Pause as* DODGE *stares at her.*]

DODGE Why not? You got nothing better to do. That fella's not gonna be back here. You're not expecting him to show up again are you?

SHELLY Sure. He'll show up. He left his horn here.

DODGE His horn? [*Laughs.*] You're his horn!

SHELLY Very funny.

DODGE He's run off with my money? He's not coming back here.

SHELLY He'll be back.

DODGE You're a funny chicken, you know that?

SHELLY Thanks.

DODGE Full of faith. Hope. Faith and hope. You're all alike you hopers. If it's not God then it's a man. If it's not a man then it's a woman. If it's not a woman then it's the land or the future of some kind. Some kind of future.

[*Pause.*]

SHELLY [*looking toward porch*] I'm glad it stopped raining.

DODGE [*looks toward porch then back to her*] That's what I mean. See, you're glad it stopped raining. Now you think everything's gonna be different. Just 'cause the sun comes out.

SHELLY It's already different. Last night I was scared.

DODGE Scared a' what?

SHELLY Just scared.

DODGE Bradley? [*Looks at* BRADLEY.] He's a pushover. 'Specially now. All ya' gotta' do is take his leg and throw it out the back door. Helpless. Totally helpless.

[SHELLY *turns and stares at* BRADLEY'S *wooden leg then looks at* DODGE. *She sips bouillon.*]

SHELLY You'd do that?

DODGE Me? I've hardly got the strength to breathe.

SHELLY But you'd actually do it if you could?

DODGE Don't be so easily shocked, girlie. There's nothing a man can't do. You dream it up and he can do it. Anything.

SHELLY You've tried I guess.

DODGE Don't sit there sippin' your bouillon and judging me! This is my house!

SHELLY I forgot.

DODGE You forgot? Whose house did you think it was?

SHELLY Mine.

[DODGE *just stares at her. Long pause. She sips from cup.*]

SHELLY I know it's not mine but I had that feeling.

DODGE What feeling?

SHELLY The feeling that nobody lives here but me. I mean everybody's gone. You're here, but it doesn't seem like you're supposed to be. [*Pointing to* BRADLEY] Doesn't seem like he's supposed to be here either. I don't know what it is. It's the house or something. Something familiar. Like I know my way around here. Did you ever get that feeling?

[DODGE *stares at her in silence. Pause.*]

DODGE No. No, I never did.

[SHELLY *gets up. Moves around space holding cup.*]

SHELLY Last night I went to sleep up there in that room.

DODGE What room?

SHELLY That room up there with all the pictures. All the crosses on the wall.

DODGE Halie's room?

SHELLY Yeah. Whoever "Halie" is.

DODGE She's my wife.

SHELLY So you remember her?

DODGE Whad'ya mean! 'Course I remember her! She's only been gone for a day—half a day. However long it's been.

SHELLY Do you remember her when her hair was bright red? Standing in front of an apple tree?

DODGE What is this, the third degree or something! Who're you to be askin' me personal questions about my wife!

SHELLY You never look at those pictures up there?

DODGE What pictures!

SHELLY Your whole life's up there hanging on the wall. Somebody who looks just like you. Somebody who looks just like you used to look.

DODGE That isn't me! That never was me! This is me. Right here. This is it. The whole shootin' match, sittin' right in front of you.

SHELLY So the past never happened as far as you're concerned?

DODGE The past? Jesus Christ. The past. What do you know about the past?

SHELLY Not much. I know there was a farm.

[*Pause.*]

DODGE A farm?

SHELLY There's a picture of a farm. A big farm. A bull. Wheat. Corn.

DODGE Corn?

SHELLY All the kids are standing out in the corn. They're all waving these big straw hats. One of them doesn't have a hat.

DODGE Which one was that?

SHELLY There's a baby. A baby in a woman's arms. The same woman with the red hair. She looks lost standing out there. Like she doesn't know how she got there.

DODGE She knows! I told her a hundred times it wasn't gonna' be the city! I gave her plenty a' warning.

SHELLY She's looking down at the baby like it was somebody else's. Like it didn't even belong to her.

DODGE That's about enough outa' you! You got some funny ideas. Some damn funny ideas. You think just because people propagate they have to love their offspring? You never seen a bitch eat her puppies? Where are you from anyway?

SHELLY L.A. We already went through that.

DODGE That's right, L.A. I remember.

SHELLY Stupid country.

DODGE That's right! No wonder.

[*Pause.*]

SHELLY What's happened to this family anyway?

DODGE You're in no position to ask! What do you care? You some kinda' Social Worker?

SHELLY I'm Vince's friend.

DODGE Vince's friend! That's rich. That's really rich. "Vince"! "Mr. Vince"! "Mr. Thief" is more like it! His name doesn't mean a hoot in hell to me. Not a tinkle in the well. You know how many kids I've spawned? Not to mention Grand kids and Great Grand kids and Great Great Grand kids after them?

SHELLY And you don't remember any of them?

DODGE What's to remember? Halie's the one with the family album. She's the one you should talk to. She'll set you straight on the heritage if that's what you're interested in. She's traced it all the way back to the grave.

SHELLY What do you mean?

DODGE What do you think I mean? How far back can you go? A long line of corpses! There's not a living soul behind me. Not a one. Who's holding me in their memory? Who gives a damn about bones in the ground?

SHELLY Was Tilden telling the truth?

[DODGE *stops short. Stares at* SHELLY. *Shakes his head. He looks off stage left.*]

SHELLY Was he?

[DODGE*'s tone changes drastically.*]

DODGE Tilden? [*Turns to* SHELLY, *calmly.*] Where is Tilden?

SHELLY Last night. Was he telling the truth about the baby?

[*Pause.*]

DODGE [*turns toward stage left*] What's happened to Tilden? Why isn't Tilden here?

SHELLY Bradley chased him out.

DODGE [*looking at* BRADLEY *asleep*] Bradley? Why is he on my sofa? [*Turns back to* SHELLY.] Have I been here all night? On the floor?

SHELLY He wouldn't leave. I hid outside until he fell asleep.

DODGE Outside? Is Tilden outside? He shouldn't be out there in the rain. He'll get himself into trouble. He doesn't know his way around here anymore. Not like he used to. He went out West and got himself into trouble. Got himself into bad trouble. We don't want any of that around here.

SHELLY What did he do?

[*Pause.*]

DODGE [*quietly stares at* SHELLY] Tilden? He got mixed up. That's what he did. We can't afford to leave him alone. Not now.

[*Sound of* HALIE *laughing comes from off left.* SHELLY *stands, looking in direction of voice, holding cup and saucer, doesn't know whether to stay or run.*]

DODGE [*motioning to* SHELLY] Sit down! Sit back down!

[SHELLY *sits. Sounds of* HALIE*'s laughter again.*]

DODGE [*to* SHELLY *in a heavy whisper, pulling coat up around him*] Don't leave me alone now! Promise me? Don't go off and leave me alone. I need somebody here with me. Tilden's gone now and I need someone. Don't leave me! Promise!

SHELLY [*sitting*] I won't.

[HALIE *appears outside the screen porch door, up left with* FATHER DEWIS. *She is wearing a bright yellow dress, no hat, white gloves and her arms are full of yellow roses.* FATHER DEWIS *is dressed in traditional black suit, white clerical collar, and shirt. He is a very distinguished grey-haired man in his sixties. They are both slightly drunk and feeling giddy. As they enter the porch through the screen door,* DODGE *pulls the rabbit fur coat over his head and hides.* SHELLY *stands again.* DODGE *drops the coat and whispers intensely to* SHELLY. *Neither* HALIE *nor* FATHER DEWIS *are aware of the people inside the house.*]

DODGE [*to* SHELLY *in a strong whisper*] You promised!

[SHELLY *sits on stairs again.* DODGE *pulls coat back over his head.* HALIE *and* FATHER DEWIS *talk on the porch as they cross toward stage right interior door.*]

HALIE Oh Father! That's terrible! That's absolutely terrible. Aren't you afraid of being punished?

[*She giggles.*]

DEWIS Not by the Italians. They're too busy punishing each other.

[*They both break out in giggles.*]

HALIE What about God?

DEWIS Well, prayerfully, God only hears what he wants to. That's just between you and me of course. In our heart of hearts we know we're every bit as wicked as the Catholics.

[*They giggle again and reach the stage right door.*]

HALIE Father, I never heard you talk like this in Sunday sermon.

DEWIS Well, I save all my best jokes for private company. Pearls before swine[1] you know.

[*They enter the room laughing and stop when they see* SHELLY. SHELLY *stands.* HALIE *closes the door behind* FATHER DEWIS. DODGE'S *voice is heard under the coat, talking to* SHELLY.]

DODGE [*under coat, to* SHELLY] Sit down, sit down! Don't let 'em buffalo you!

[SHELLY *sits on stair again.* HALIE *looks at* DODGE *on the floor then looks at* BRADLEY *asleep on sofa and sees his wooden leg. She lets out a shriek of embarrassment for* FATHER DEWIS.]

HALIE Oh my gracious! What in the name of Judas Priest is going on in this house!

[*She hands over the roses to* FATHER DEWIS.]

HALIE Excuse me Father.

[HALIE *crosses to* DODGE, *whips the coat off him, and covers the wooden leg with it.* BRADLEY *stays asleep.*]

HALIE You can't leave this house for a second without the Devil blowing in through the front door!

1. See Matthew 7.6: "Give not that which is holy unto the dogs, neither cast ye your pearls before swine, lest they trample them under their feet, and turn again and rend you."

DODGE Gimme back that coat! Gimmie back that goddamn coat before I freeze to death!

HALIE You're not going to freeze! The sun's out in case you hadn't noticed!

DODGE Gimme back that coat! That coat's for live flesh not dead wood!

[HALIE *whips the blanket off* BRADLEY *and throws it on* DODGE. DODGE *covers his head again with blanket.* BRADLEY'S *amputated leg can be faked by having half of it under a cushion of the sofa. He's fully clothed.* BRADLEY *sits up with a jerk when the blanket comes off him.*]

HALIE [*as she tosses blanket*] Here! Use this! It's yours anyway! Can't you take care of yourself for once!

BRADLEY [*yelling at* HALIE] Gimme that blanket! Gimme back that blanket! That's my blanket!

[HALIE *crosses back toward* FATHER DEWIS *who just stands there with the roses.* BRADLEY *thrashes helplessly on the sofa trying to reach blanket.* DODGE *hides himself deeper in blanket.* SHELLY *looks on from staircase, still holding cup and saucer.*]

HALIE Believe me, Father, this is not what I had in mind when I invited you in.

DEWIS Oh, no apologies please. I wouldn't be in the ministry if I couldn't face real life.

[*He laughs self-consciously.* HALIE *notices* SHELLY *again and crosses over to her.* SHELLY *stays sitting.* HALIE *stops and stares at her.*]

BRADLEY I want my blanket back! Gimme my blanket!

[HALIE *turns toward* BRADLEY *and silences him.*]

HALIE Shut up, Bradley! Right this minute! I've had enough!

[BRADLEY *slowly recoils, lies back down on sofa, turns his back toward* HALIE, *and whimpers softly.* HALIE *directs her attention to* SHELLY *again. Pause.*]

HALIE [*to* SHELLY] What're you doing with my cup and saucer?

SHELLY [*looking at cup, back to* HALIE] I made some bouillon for Dodge.

HALIE For Dodge?

SHELLY Yeah.

HALIE Well, did he drink it?

SHELLY No.

HALIE Did you drink it?

SHELLY Yes.

[HALIE *stares at her. Long pause. She turns abruptly away from* SHELLY *and crosses back to* FATHER DEWIS.]

HALIE Father, there's a stranger in my house. What would you advise? What would be the Christian thing?

DEWIS [*squirming*] Oh, well. . . . I. . . . I really—

HALIE We still have some whiskey, don't we?

[DODGE *slowly pulls the blanket down off his head and looks toward* FATHER DEWIS. SHELLY *stands.*]

SHELLY Listen, I don't drink or anything. I just—

[HALIE *turns toward* SHELLY *viciously.*]

HALIE You sit back down!

[SHELLY *sits again on stair.* HALIE *turns again to* DEWIS.]

HALIE I think we have plenty of whiskey left! Don't we Father?

DEWIS Well, yes. I think so. You'll have to get it. My hands are full.

[HALIE *giggles. Reaches into* DEWIS*'s pockets, searching for bottle. She smells the roses as she searches.* DEWIS *stands stiffly.* DODGE *watches* HALIE *closely as she looks for bottle.*]

HALIE The most incredible things, roses! Aren't they incredible, Father?

DEWIS Yes. Yes they are.

HALIE They almost cover the stench of sin in this house. Just magnificent! The smell. We'll have to put some at the foot of Ansel's statue. On the day of the unveiling.

[HALIE *finds a silver flask of whiskey in* DEWIS*'s vest pocket. She pulls it out.* DODGE *looks on eagerly.* HALIE *crosses to* DODGE, *opens the flask, and takes a sip.*]

HALIE [*to* DODGE] Ansel's getting a statue, Dodge. Did you know that? Not a plaque but a real live statue. A full bronze. Tip to toe. A basketball in one hand and a rifle in the other.

BRADLEY [*his back to* HALIE] He never played basketball!

HALIE You shut up, Bradley! You shut up about Ansel! Ansel played basketball better than anyone! And you know it! He was an All-American! There's no reason to take the glory away from others.

[HALIE *turns away from* BRADLEY, *crosses back toward* DEWIS *sipping on the flask and smiling.*]

HALIE [*to* DEWIS] Ansel was a great basketball player. One of the greatest.

DEWIS I remember Ansel.

HALIE Of course! You remember. You remember how he could play. [*She turns toward* SHELLY.] Of course, nowadays they play a different brand of basketball. More vicious. Isn't that right, dear?

SHELLY I don't know.

[HALIE *crosses to* SHELLY, *sipping on flask. She stops in front of* SHELLY.]

HALIE Much, much more vicious. They smash into each other. They knock each other's teeth out. There's blood all over the court. Savages.

[HALIE *takes the cup from* SHELLY *and pours whiskey into it.*]

HALIE They don't train like they used to. Not at all. They allow themselves to run amuck. Drugs and women. Women mostly.

[HALIE *hands the cup of whiskey back to* SHELLY *slowly.* SHELLY *takes it.*]

HALIE Mostly women. Girls. Sad, pathetic little girls. [*She crosses back to* FATHER DEWIS.] It's just a reflection of the times, don't you think Father? An indication of where we stand?

DEWIS I suppose so, yes.

HALIE Yes. A sort of a bad omen. Our youth becoming monsters.

DEWIS Well, I uh—

HALIE Oh you can disagree with me if you want to, Father. I'm open to debate. I think argument only enriches both sides of the question don't you? [*She moves toward* DODGE.] I suppose, in the long run, it doesn't matter. When you see the way things deteriorate before your very eyes. Everything running downhill. It's kind of silly to even think about youth.

DEWIS No, I don't think so. I think it's important to believe in certain things.

HALIE Yes. Yes, I know what you mean. I think that's right. I think that's true. [*She looks at* DODGE.] Certain basic things. We can't shake certain basic things. We might end up crazy. Like my husband. You can see it in his eyes. You can see how mad he is.

[DODGE *covers his head with the blanket again.* HALIE *takes a single rose from* DEWIS *and moves slowly over to* DODGE.]

HALIE We can't not believe in something. We can't stop believing. We just end up dying if we stop. Just end up dead.

[HALIE *throws the rose gently onto* DODGE*'s blanket. It lands between his knees and stays there. Long pause as* HALIE *stares at the rose.* SHELLY *stands suddenly.* HALIE *doesn't turn to her but keeps staring at rose.*]

SHELLY [*to* HALIE] Don't you wanna' know who I am! Don't you wanna know what I'm doing here! I'm not dead!

[SHELLY *crosses toward* HALIE. HALIE *turns slowly toward her.*]

HALIE Did you drink your whiskey?

SHELLY No! And I'm not going to either!

HALIE Well that's a firm stand. It's good to have a firm stand.

SHELLY I don't have any stand at all. I'm just trying to put all this together.

[HALIE *laughs and crosses back to* DEWIS.]

HALIE [*to* DEWIS] Surprises, surprises! Did you have any idea we'd be returning to this?

SHELLY I came here with your Grandson for a little visit! A little innocent friendly visit.

HALIE My Grandson?

SHELLY Yes! That's right. The one no one remembers.

HALIE [*to* DEWIS] This is getting a little far-fetched.

SHELLY I told him it was stupid to come back here. To try to pick up from where he left off.

HALIE Where was that?

SHELLY Wherever he was when he left here! Six years ago! Ten years ago! Whenever it was. I told him nobody cares.

HALIE Didn't he listen?

SHELLY No! No he didn't. We had to stop off at every tiny little meatball town that he remembered from his boyhood! Every stupid little donut shop he ever kissed a girl in. Every Drive-In. Every Drag Strip. Every football field he ever broke a bone on.

HALIE [*suddenly alarmed, to* DODGE] Where's Tilden?

SHELLY Don't ignore me!

HALIE Dodge! Where's Tilden gone?

[SHELLY *moves violently toward* HALIE.]

SHELLY [*to* HALIE] I'm talking to you!

[BRADLEY *sits up fast on the sofa,* SHELLY *backs away.*]

BRADLEY [*to* SHELLY] Don't you yell at my mother!

HALIE Dodge! [*She kicks* DODGE.] I told you not to let Tilden out of your sight! Where's he gone to?

DODGE Gimme a drink and I'll yell ya'.

DEWIS Halie, maybe this isn't the right time for a visit.

[HALIE *crosses back to* DEWIS.]

HALIE [*to* DEWIS] I never should've left. I never, never should've left! Tilden could be anywhere by now! Anywhere! He's not in control of his faculties. Dodge knew that. I told him when I left here. I told him specifically to watch out for Tilden.

[BRADLEY *reaches down, grabs* DODGE*'s blanket, and yanks it off him. He lays down on sofa and pulls the blanket over his head.*]

DODGE He's got my blanket again! He's got my blanket!

HALIE [*turning to* BRADLEY] Bradley! Bradley, put that blanket back!

[HALIE *moves toward* BRADLEY. SHELLY *suddenly throws the cup and saucer against the stage right door.* DEWIS *ducks. The cup and saucer smash into pieces.* HALIE *stops, turns toward* SHELLY. *Everyone freezes.* BRADLEY *slowly pulls his head out from under blanket, looks toward stage right door, then to* SHELLY. SHELLY *stares at* HALIE. DEWIS *cowers with roses.* SHELLY *moves slowly toward* HALIE. *Long pause.* SHELLY *speaks softly.*]

SHELLY [*to* HALIE] I don't like being ignored. I don't like being treated like I'm not here. I didn't like it when I was a kid and I still don't like it.

BRADLEY [*sitting up on sofa*] We don't have to tell you anything, girl. Not a thing. You're not the police are you? You're not the government. You're just some prostitute that Tilden brought in here.

HALIE Language! I won't have that language in my house!

SHELLY [*to* BRADLEY] You stuck your hand in my mouth and you call me a prostitute!

HALIE Bradley! Did you put your hand in her mouth? I'm ashamed of you. I can't leave you alone for a minute.

BRADLEY I never did. She's lying!

DEWIS Halie, I think I'll be running along now. I'll just put the roses in the kitchen.

[DEWIS *moves toward stage left.* HALIE *stops him.*]

HALIE Don't go now, Father! Not now.

BRADLEY I never did anything, Mom! I never touched her! She propositioned me! And I turned her down. I turned her down flat!

[SHELLY *suddenly grabs her coat off the wooden leg and takes both the leg and coat down stage, away from* BRADLEY.]

BRADLEY Mom! Mom! She's got my leg! She's taken my leg! I never did anything to her! She's stolen my leg!

[BRADLEY *reaches pathetically in the air for his leg.* SHELLY *sets it down for a second, puts on her coat fast, and picks the leg up again.* DODGE *starts coughing softly.*]

HALIE [*to* SHELLY] I think we've had about enough of you young lady. Just about enough. I don't know where you came from or what you're doing here but you're no longer welcome in this house.

SHELLY [*laughs, holds leg*] No longer welcome!

BRADLEY Mom! That's my leg! Get my leg back! I can't do anything without my leg.

[BRADLEY *keeps making whimpering sounds and reaching for his leg.*]

HALIE Give my son back his leg. Right this very minute!

[DODGE *starts laughing softly to himself in between coughs.*]

HALIE [*to* DEWIS] Father, do something about this would you! I'm not about to be terrorized in my own house!

BRADLEY Gimme back my leg!

HALIE Oh, shut up Bradley! Just shut up! You don't need your leg now! Just lay down and shut up!

[BRADLEY *whimpers. Lays down and pulls blanket around him. He keeps one arm outside blanket, reaching out toward his wooden leg.* DEWIS *cautiously approaches* SHELLY *with the roses in his arms.* SHELLY *clutches the wooden leg to her chest as though she's kidnapped it.*]

DEWIS [*to* SHELLY] Now, honestly dear, wouldn't it be better to try to talk things out? To try to use some reason?

SHELLY There isn't any reason here! I can't find a reason for anything.

DEWIS There's nothing to be afraid of. These are all good people. All righteous people.

SHELLY I'm not afraid!

DEWIS But this isn't your house. You have to have some respect.

SHELLY You're the strangers here, not me.

HALIE This has gone far enough!

DEWIS Halie, please. Let me handle this.

SHELLY Don't come near me! Don't anyone come near me. I don't need any words from you. I'm not threatening anybody. I don't even know what I'm doing here. You all say you don't remember Vince, okay, maybe you don't. Maybe it's Vince that's crazy. Maybe he's made this whole family thing up. I don't even care anymore. I was just coming along for the ride. I thought it'd be a nice gesture. Besides, I was curious. He made all of you sound familiar to me. Every one of you. For every name, I had an image. Every time he'd tell me a name, I'd see the person. In fact, each of you was so clear in my mind that I actually believed it was you. I really believed when I walked through that door that the people who lived here would turn out to be the same people in my imagination. But I don't recognize any of you. Not one. Not even the slightest resemblance.

DEWIS Well you can hardly blame others for not fulfilling your hallucination.

SHELLY It was no hallucination! It was more like a prophecy. You believe in prophecy, don't you?

HALIE Father, there's no point in talking to her any further. We're just going to have to call the police.

BRADLEY No! Don't get the police in here. We don't want the police in here. This is our home.

SHELLY That's right. Bradley's right. Don't you usually settle your affairs in private? Don't you usually take them out in the dark? Out in the back?

BRADLEY You stay out of our lives! You have no business interfering!

SHELLY I don't have any business period. I got nothing to lose.

[*She moves around, staring at each of them.*]

BRADLEY You don't know what we've been through. You don't know anything!

SHELLY I know you've got a secret. You've all got a secret. It's so secret in fact, you're all convinced it never happened.

[HALIE *moves to* DEWIS.]

HALIE Oh, my God, Father!

DODGE [*laughing to himself*] She thinks she's going to get it out of us. She thinks she's going to uncover the truth of the matter. Like a detective or something.

BRADLEY I'm not telling her anything! Nothing's wrong here! Nothing's ever been wrong! Everything's the way it's supposed to be! Nothing ever happened that's bad! Everything is all right here! We're all good people!

DODGE She thinks she's gonna suddenly bring everything out into the open after all these years.

DEWIS [*to* SHELLY] Can't you see that these people want to be left in peace? Don't you have any mercy? They haven't done anything to you.

DODGE She wants to get to the bottom of it. [*To* SHELLY] That's it, isn't it? You'd like to get right down to bedrock? You want me to tell ya'? You want me to tell ya' what happened? I'll tell ya'. I might as well.

BRADLEY No! Don't listen to him. He doesn't remember anything!

DODGE I remember the whole thing from start to finish. I remember the day he was born.

[*Pause.*]

HALIE Dodge, if you tell this thing—if you tell this, you'll be dead to me. You'll be just as good as dead.

DODGE That won't be such a big change, Halie. See this girl, this girl here, she wants to know. She wants to know something more. And I got this feeling that it doesn't make a bit difference. I'd sooner tell it to a stranger than anybody else.

BRADLEY [*to* DODGE] We made a pact! We made a pact between us! You can't break that now!

DODGE I don't remember any pact.

BRADLEY [*to* SHELLY] See, he doesn't remember anything. I'm the only one in the family who remembers. The only one. And I'll never tell you!

SHELLY I'm not so sure I want to find out now.

DODGE [*laughing to himself*] Listen to her! Now she's runnin' scared!

SHELLY I'm not scared!

[DODGE *stops laughing, long pause.* DODGE *stares at her.*]

DODGE You're not huh? Well, that's good. Because I'm not either. See, we were a well-established family once. Well-established. All the boys were grown. The farm was producing enough milk to fill Lake Michigan twice over. Me and Halie here were pointed toward what looked like the middle part of our life. Everything was settled with us. All we had to do was ride it out. Then Halie got pregnant again. Outa' the middle a' nowhere, she got pregnant. We weren't planning on havin' any more boys. We had enough boys already. In fact, we hadn't been sleepin' in the same bed for about six years.

HALIE [*moving toward stairs*] I'm not listening to this! I don't have to listen to this!

DODGE [*stops* HALIE] Where are you going! Upstairs! You'll just be listenin' to it upstairs! You go outside, you'll be listenin' to it outside. Might as well stay here and listen to it.

[HALIE *stays by stairs.*]

BRADLEY If I had my leg you wouldn't be saying this. You'd never get away with it if I had my leg.

DODGE [*pointing to* SHELLY] She's got your leg. [*Laughs*] She's gonna keep your leg too. [*To* SHELLY] She wants to hear this. Don't you?

SHELLY I don't know.

DODGE Well even if ya' don't I'm gonna' tell ya'. [*Pause*] Halie had this kid. This baby boy. She had it. I let her have it on her own. All the other boys I had had the best doctors, best nurses, everything. This one I let her have by herself. This one hurt real bad. Almost killed her, but she had it anyway. It lived, see. It lived. It wanted to grow up in this family. It wanted to be just like us. It wanted to be a part of us. It wanted to pretend that I was its father. She wanted me to believe in it. Even when everyone around us knew. Everyone. All our boys knew. Tilden knew.

HALIE You shut up! Bradley, make him shut up!

BRADLEY I can't.

DODGE Tilden was the one who knew. Better than any of us. He'd walk for miles with that kid in his arms. Halie let him take it. All night sometimes. He'd walk all night out there in the pasture with it. Talkin' to it. Singin' to it. Used to hear him singing to it. He'd make up stories. He'd tell that kid all kinds a' stories. Even when he knew it couldn't understand him. Couldn't understand a word he was sayin'. Never would understand him. We couldn't let a thing like that continue. We couldn't allow that to grow up right in the middle of our lives. It made everything we'd accomplished look like it was nothin'. Everything was cancelled out by this one mistake. This one weakness.

SHELLY So you killed him?

DODGE I killed it. I drowned it. Just like the runt of a litter. Just drowned it.

[HALIE *moves toward* BRADLEY.]

HALIE [*to* BRADLEY] Ansel would've stopped him! Ansel would've stopped him from telling these lies! He was a hero! A man! A whole man! What's happened to the men in this family! Where are the men!

[*Suddenly* VINCE *comes crashing through the screen porch door up left, tearing it off its hinges. Everyone but* DODGE *and* BRADLEY *back away from the porch and stare at* VINCE *who has landed on his stomach on the porch in a drunken stupor. He is singing loudly to himself and hauls himself slowly to his feet. He has a paper shopping bag full of empty booze bottles. He takes them out one at a time as he sings and smashes them at the opposite end of the porch, behind the solid interior door, stage right.* SHELLY *moves slowly toward stage right, holding wooden leg and watching* VINCE.]

VINCE [*singing loudly as he hurls bottles*] "From the Halls of Montezuma to the Shores of Tripoli. We will fight our country's battles on the land and on the sea."[2]

[*He punctuates the words "Montezuma," "Tripoli," "battles," and "sea" with a smashed bottle each. He stops throwing for a second, stares toward stage right of the porch, shades his eyes with his hand as though looking across to a battlefield, then cups his hands around his mouth and yells across the space of the porch to an imaginary army. The others watch in terror and expectation.*]

VINCE [*to imagined army*] Have you had enough over there! 'Cause there's a lot more here where that came from! [*Pointing to paper bag full of bottles*]

2. The opening of the official anthem of the U.S. Marine Corps (author unknown; the music is from a song in the 1867 revision of *Geneviève de Brabant* [1859], a comic opera by Jacques Offenbach). The first line refers, respectively, to the capture of Mexico City's Castle of Chapultepec (the Halls of Montezuma) in the Mexican-American War (1846–48) and to the 1801–05 war against the Barbary pirates of North Africa, who were based largely in Tripoli (in northwest Libya).

A helluva lot more! We got enough over here to blow ya' from here to Kingdomcome!

[*He takes another bottle, makes high whistling sound of a bomb and throws it toward stage right porch. Sound of bottle smashing against wall. This should be the actual smashing of bottles and not tape sound. He keeps yelling and heaving bottles one after another.* VINCE *stops for a while, breathing heavily from exhaustion. Long silence as the others watch him.* SHELLY *approaches tentatively in* VINCE'*s direction, still holding* BRADLEY'*s wooden leg.*]

SHELLY [*after silence*] Vince?

[VINCE *turns toward her. Peers through screen.*]

VINCE Who? What? Vince who? Who's that in there?

[VINCE *pushes his face against the screen from the porch and stares in at everyone.*]

DODGE Where's my goddamn bottle!

VINCE [*looking in at* DODGE] What? Who is that?

DODGE It's me! Your Grandfather! Don't play stupid with me! Where's my two bucks!

VINCE Your two bucks?

[HALIE *moves away from* DEWIS, *upstage, peers out at* VINCE, *trying to recognize him.*]

HALIE Vincent? Is that you, Vincent?

[SHELLY *stares at* HALIE *then looks out at* VINCE.]

VINCE [*from porch*] Vincent who? What is this! Who are you people?

SHELLY [*to* HALIE] Hey, wait a minute. Wait a minute! What's going on?

HALIE [*moving closer to porch screen*] We thought you were a murderer or something. Barging in through the door like that.

VINCE I am a murderer! Don't underestimate me for a minute! I'm the Midnight Strangler! I devour whole families in a single gulp!

[VINCE *grabs another bottle and smashes it on the porch.* HALIE *backs away.*]

SHELLY [*approaching* HALIE] You mean you know who he is?

HALIE Of course I know who he is! That's more than I can say for you.

BRADLEY [*sitting up on sofa*] You get off our front porch you creep! What're you doing out there breaking bottles? Who are these foreigners anyway! Where did they come from?

VINCE Maybe I should come in there and break them!

HALIE [*moving toward porch*] Don't you dare! Vincent, what's got into you! Why are you acting like this?

VINCE Maybe I should come in there and usurp your territory!

[HALIE *turns back toward* DEWIS *and crosses to him.*]

HALIE [*to* DEWIS] Father, why are you just standing around here when everything's falling apart? Can't you rectify this situation?

[DODGE *laughs, coughs.*]

DEWIS I'm just a guest here, Halie. I don't know what my position is exactly. This is outside my parish anyway.

[VINCE *starts throwing more bottles as things continue.*]

BRADLEY If I had my leg I'd rectify it! I'd rectify him all over the goddamn highway! I'd pull his ears out if I could reach him!

[BRADLEY *sticks his fist through the screening of the porch and reaches out for* VINCE, *grabbing at him and missing.* VINCE *jumps away from* BRADLEY*'s hand.*]

VINCE Aaaah! Our lines have been penetrated! Tentacled animals! Beasts from the deep!

[VINCE *strikes out at* BRADLEY*'s hand with a bottle.* BRADLEY *pulls his hand back inside.*]

SHELLY Vince! Knock it off will ya'! I want to get out of here!

[VINCE *pushes his face against screen, looks in at* SHELLY.]

VINCE [*to* SHELLY] Have they got you prisoner in there, dear? Such a sweet young thing too. All her life in front of her. Nipped in the bud.

SHELLY I'm coming out there, Vince! I'm coming out there and I want us to get in the car and drive away from here. Anywhere. Just away from here.

[SHELLY *moves toward* VINCE*'s saxophone case and overcoat. She sets down the wooden leg, downstage left, and picks up the saxophone case and overcoat.* VINCE *watches her through the screen.*]

VINCE [*to* SHELLY] We'll have to negotiate. Make some kind of a deal. Prisoner exchange or something. A few of theirs for one of ours. Small price to pay if you ask me.

[SHELLY *crosses toward stage right door with overcoat and case.*]

SHELLY Just go and get the car! I'm coming out there now. We're going to leave.

VINCE Don't come out here! Don't you dare come out here!

[SHELLY *stops short of the door, stage right.*]

SHELLY How come?

VINCE Off limits! Verboten![3] This is taboo territory. No man or woman has ever crossed the line and lived to tell the tale!

SHELLY I'll take my chances.

[SHELLY *moves to stage right door and opens it.* VINCE *pulls out a big folding hunting knife and pulls open the blade. He jabs the blade into the screen and starts cutting a hole big enough to climb through.* BRADLEY *cowers in a corner of the sofa as* VINCE *rips at the screen.*]

VINCE [*as he cuts screen*] Don't come out here! I'm warning you! You'll disintegrate!

[DEWIS *takes* HALIE *by the arm and pulls her toward staircase.*]

DEWIS Halie, maybe we should go upstairs until this blows over.

HALIE I don't understand it. I just don't understand it. He was the sweetest little boy!

[DEWIS *drops the roses beside the wooden leg at the foot of the staircase then escorts* HALIE *quickly up the stairs.* HALIE *keeps looking back at* VINCE *as they climb the stairs.*]

HALIE There wasn't a mean bone in his body. Everyone loved Vincent. Everyone. He was the perfect baby.

DEWIS He'll be all right after a while. He's just had a few too many that's all.

HALIE He used to sing in his sleep. He'd sing. In the middle of the night. The sweetest voice. Like an angel. [*She stops for a moment.*] I used to lie

3. Forbidden! (German).

awake listening to it. I used to lie awake thinking it was all right if I died. Because Vincent was an angel. A guardian angel. He'd watch over us. He'd watch over all of us.

[DEWIS *takes her all the way up the stairs. They disappear above.* VINCE *is now climbing through the porch screen onto the sofa.* BRADLEY *crashes off the sofa, holding tight to his blanket, keeping it wrapped around him.* SHELLY *is outside on the porch.* VINCE *holds the knife in his teeth once he gets the hole wide enough to climb through.* BRADLEY *starts crawling slowly toward his wooden leg, reaching out for it.*]

DODGE [*to* VINCE] Go ahead! Take over the house! Take over the whole goddamn house! You can have it! It's yours. It's been a pain in the neck ever since the very first mortgage. I'm gonna die any second now. Any second. You won't even notice. So I'll settle my affairs once and for all.

[*As* DODGE *proclaims his last will and testament,* VINCE *climbs into the room, knife in mouth, and strides slowly around the space, inspecting his inheritance. He casually notices* BRADLEY *as he crawls toward his leg.* VINCE *moves to the leg and keeps pushing it with his foot so that it's out of* BRADLEY*'s reach, then goes on with his inspection. He picks up the roses and carries them around smelling them.* SHELLY *can be seen outside on the porch, moving slowly center and staring in at* VINCE. VINCE *ignores her.*]

DODGE: The house goes to my Grandson, Vincent. All the furnishings, accoutrements, and paraphernalia therein. Everything tacked to the walls or otherwise resting under this roof. My tools—namely my band saw, my Skilsaw,[4] my drill press, my chain saw, my lathe, my electric sander, all go to my eldest son, Tilden. That is, if he ever shows up again. My shed and gasoline-powered equipment, namely my tractor, my dozer,[5] my hand tiller plus all the attachments and riggings for the above-mentioned machinery, namely my spring-tooth harrow,[6] my deep plows, my disk plows, my automatic fertilizing equipment, my reaper, my swathe, my seeder, my John Deere Harvester, my posthole digger, my jackhammer, my lathe—[*To himself*] Did I mention my lathe? I already mentioned my lathe—my Bennie Goodman[7] records, my harnesses, my bits, my halters, my brace, my rough rasp, my forge, my welding equipment, my shoeing nails, my levels and bevels, my milking stool—no, not my milking stool—my hammers and chisels, my hinges, my cattle gates, my barbed wire, self-tapping augers, my horsehair ropes, and all related materials are to be pushed into a gigantic heap and set ablaze in the very center of my fields. When the blaze is at its highest, preferably on a cold, windless night, my body is to be pitched into the middle of it and burned till nothing remains but ash.

[*Pause.* VINCE *takes the knife out of his mouth and smells the roses. He's facing toward audience and doesn't turn around to* SHELLY. *He folds up knife and pockets it.*]

SHELLY [*from porch*] I'm leaving, Vince. Whether you come or not, I'm leaving.

VINCE [*smelling roses*] Just put my horn on the couch there before you take off.

4. Circular saw (a brand name).
5. That is, bulldozer.
6. An implement, pulled by a tractor, that breaks up soil and levels it before planting.
7. That is, Benny Goodman (1909–1986), American jazz clarinetist, composer, and bandleader.

SHELLY [*moving toward hole in screen*] You're not coming?

[VINCE *stays downstage, turns and looks at her.*]

VINCE I just inherited a house.

SHELLY [*through hole, from porch*] You want to stay here?

VINCE [*as he pushes* BRADLEY'*s leg out of reach*] I've gotta carry on the line. I've gotta see to it that things keep rolling.

[BRADLEY *looks up at him from floor, keeps pulling himself toward his leg.* VINCE *keeps moving it.*]

SHELLY What happened to you Vince? You just disappeared.

VINCE [*pause, delivers speech front*] I was gonna run last night. I was gonna run and keep right on running. I drove all night. Clear to the Iowa border. The old man's two bucks sitting right on the seat beside me. It never stopped raining the whole time. Never stopped once. I could see myself in the windshield. My face. My eyes. I studied my face. Studied everything about it. As though I was looking at another man. As though I could see his whole race behind him. Like a mummy's face. I saw him dead and alive at the same time. In the same breath. In the windshield, I watched him breathe as though he was frozen in time. And every breath marked him. Marked him forever without him knowing. And then his face changed. His face became his father's face. Same bones. Same eyes. Same nose. Same breath. And his father's face changed to his Grandfather's face. And it went on like that. Changing. Clear on back to faces I'd never seen before but still recognized. Still recognized the bones underneath. The eyes. The breath. The mouth. I followed my family clear into Iowa. Every last one. Straight into the Corn Belt and further. Straight back as far as they'd take me. Then it all dissolved. Everything dissolved.

[SHELLY *stares at him for a while then reaches through the hole in the screen and sets the saxophone case and* VINCE'*s overcoat on the sofa. She looks at* VINCE *again.*]

SHELLY Bye Vince.

[*She exits left off the porch.* VINCE *watches her go.* BRADLEY *tries to make a lunge for his wooden leg.* VINCE *quickly picks it up and dangles it over* BRADLEY'*s head like a carrot.* BRADLEY *keeps making desperate grabs at the leg.* DEWIS *comes down the staircase and stops halfway, staring at* VINCE *and* BRADLEY. VINCE *looks up at* DEWIS *and smiles. He keeps moving backwards with the leg toward upstage left as* BRADLEY *crawls after him.*]

VINCE [*to* DEWIS *as he continues torturing* BRADLEY] Oh, excuse me Father. Just getting rid of some of the vermin in the house. This is my house now, ya' know? All mine. Everything. Except for the power tools and stuff. I'm gonna get all new equipment anyway. New plows, new tractor, everything. All brand-new. [VINCE *teases* BRADLEY *closer to the up left corner of the stage.*] Start right off on the ground floor.

[VINCE *throws* BRADLEY'*s wooden leg far off stage left.* BRADLEY *follows his leg offstage, pulling himself along on the ground, whimpering. As* BRADLEY *exits* VINCE *pulls the blanket off him and throws it over his own shoulder. He crosses toward* DEWIS *with the blanket and smells the roses.* DEWIS *comes to the bottom of the stairs.*]

DEWIS You'd better go up and see your Grandmother.

VINCE [*looking up stairs, back to* DEWIS] My Grandmother? There's nobody else in this house. Except for you. And you're leaving aren't you?

[DEWIS *crosses toward stage right door. He turns back to* VINCE.]

DEWIS She's going to need someone. I can't help her. I don't know what to do. I don't know what my position is. I just came in for some tea. I had no idea there was any trouble. No idea at all.

[VINCE *just stares at him.* DEWIS *goes out the door, crosses porch, and exits left.* VINCE *listens to him leaving. He smells roses, looks up the staircase, then smells roses again. He turns and looks upstage at* DODGE. *He crosses up to him and bends over looking at* DODGE'*s open eyes.* DODGE *is dead. His death should have come completely unnoticed. Vince lifts the blanket, then covers his head. He sits on the sofa, smelling roses and staring at* DODGE'*s body. Long pause.* VINCE *places the roses on* DODGE'*s chest, then lays down on the sofa, arms folded behind his head, staring at the ceiling. His body is in the same relationship to* DODGE'*s. After a while* HALIE'*s voice is heard coming from above the staircase. The lights start to dim almost imperceptibly as* HALIE *speaks.* VINCE *keeps staring at the ceiling.*

HALIE'S VOICE Dodge? Is that you Dodge? Tilden was right about the corn you know. I've never seen such corn. Have you taken a look at it lately? Tall as a man already. This early in the year. Carrots too. Potatoes. Peas. It's like a paradise out there, Dodge. You oughta' take a look. A miracle. I've never seen it like this. Maybe the rain did something. Maybe it was the rain.

[*As* HALIE *keeps talking offstage,* TILDEN *appears from stage left, dripping with mud from the knees down. His arms and hands are covered with mud. In his hands he carries the corpse of a small child at chest level, staring down at it. The corpse mainly consists of bones wrapped in muddy, rotten cloth. He moves slowly downstage toward the staircase, ignoring* VINCE *on the sofa.* VINCE *keeps staring at the ceiling as though* TILDEN *wasn't there. As* HALIE'S VOICE *continues,* TILDEN *slowly makes his way up the stairs. His eyes never leave the corpse of the child. The lights keep fading.*]

HALIE'S VOICE Good hard rain. Takes everything straight down deep to the roots. The rest takes care of itself. You can't force a thing to grow. You can't interfere with it. It's all hidden. It's all unseen. You just gotta wait till it pops up out of the ground. Tiny little shoot. Tiny little white shoot. All hairy and fragile. Strong though. Strong enough to break the earth even. It's a miracle, Dodge. I've never seen a crop like this in my whole life. Maybe it's the sun. Maybe that's it. Maybe it's the sun.

[TILDEN *disappears above. Silence. Lights go to black.*]

JUDITH THOMPSON

b. 1954

WITH the premiere of her first play, *THE CRACKWALKER*, at Toronto's Theatre Passe Muraille in 1980, Judith Thompson emerged as a major new voice in Canadian theater. A professionally trained actor, Thompson discovered while at Canada's National Theatre School that her greatest interest lay in examining the "huge chasm between the social persona and the inner life" of the individual, and that she could "find out who people really are" better as a playwright than as a performer. Thompson's deep understanding of the actor's craft and the process of character development undergirds her dramaturgy and has contributed immeasurably to her success as a dramatist known for vivid portraiture. The experience of acting in DAVID MAMET's *Sexual Perversity in Chicago* (1974) also inspired in her a taste for freedom in both dramatic language and structure that has enabled her to build plays not by constructing a plot but rather by exploring characters' voices. Monologues remain central to each of her subsequent dramas, revealing her characters' complex psychology and motivations as she examines the dynamic interplay between social forces and individual behavior. *The Crackwalker* reflects a number of Thompson's other concerns, including her Catholic upbringing, her engagement with the family as a structural unit in society, her understanding of Canadian nationalism, and her acute sensitivity to the interplay of gender, race, and class in contemporary Canadian culture. Alternately naturalistic and dreamlike, Thompson's writing conforms to no preestablished structures. Her goal as a playwright mirrors the goal of the actor: to harness varying theatrical techniques in order to convey truth in performance.

Thompson was born in Montreal but grew up mostly in Kingston, Ontario, where her father, William Robert Thompson, a researcher in the field of behavioral genetics, chaired the Department of Psychology at Queen's University. Her mother Mary, who worked both as a theater artist and part-time as an English teacher, often took her daughter to see plays. After graduating from Queen's University in 1976, Thompson enrolled in the three-year acting program at the National Theatre School in Montreal—training that provided a creative foundation for her subsequent writing. She married Gregor Campbell in 1983, and they have five children. Thompson has twice received the prestigious Governor General's Award for Drama, for *White Biting Dog* in 1984 and for the collection *The Other Side of the Dark* in 1989; in addition, she has won the Floyd S. Chalmers Canadian Play Award, for *I Am Yours* in 1987 and for *Lion in the Streets* in 1991. Most recently, she received the Susan Smith

Blackburn Prize in 2008 for her play *Palace of the End.* Although she has worked in film, television, and radio as well as in fiction, Thompson feels most drawn to live theater. She has developed an ongoing working relationship with the Tarragon Theatre in Toronto, and she also teaches playwriting at the University of Guelph. Like a number of prominent contemporary dramatists, Thompson has chosen to direct the premieres of her more recent works, seeking both to protect her artistic vision and to continue to develop her scripts through the production process.

Unlike such other notable contemporary Canadian dramatists as Michel Tremblay, whose plays are strongly associated with his position as a Québécois writer, or Sharon Pollock, whose writing has been championed for its political force, or George F. Walker, known for his comedic, postmodern sensibility, Thompson continues to produce work that is elusive and cryptic. Hers is a theater of stark images and dreamscapes, of haunting symbols juxtaposed to raw brutality, of emotional intensity and corporeal intimacy interspersed with banality and the quotidian. And whereas such early plays as *The Crackwalker, I Am Yours,* or *Lion in the Streets* provided her middle-class audiences with some distance from her visceral representations of the under class, she has more recently challenged that separation and threatened their complacency in such pieces as *Sled* (1997) and *Perfect Pie* (2000). Refusing to lessen the reality of her characters' lives through artificial catharsis or well-made narrative closure, Thompson relies on her dramas' challenging style and content to change her audience.

In *The Crackwalker,* Thompson demands our immediate and fixed attention. From the play's very first moments, we must work to understand simply what the characters are saying, as well as what and who they are talking about. Thompson takes the notion of starting in medias res to extremes. She never provides easy exposition, instead plunging directly into the maelstrom of her characters' lives. We can discern that Theresa is struggling to achieve what she imagines as a normal life from within the confines of an imperfect social services system. Her friend Sandy faces challenges of her own, especially in her relationship with the volatile Joe. And Alan, Theresa's boyfriend, grapples, as does Joe, with the meaning of manhood and with social expectations that at times become overwhelming. As Alan's life unravels, he is haunted by the presence of a Native American man, the titular Crackwalker, who has reached the true nadir of contemporary existence.

Working for the Canadian government's Adult Protective Services agency in Kingston one summer, Thompson had met a girl who became the basis for Theresa: she "was borderline mentally handicapped and . . . had this wonderful way of speaking and a wonderful purity about her." Theresa's opening monologue is much more than a "stream of consciousness" outpouring; Thompson uses this character's frankness and ebullience to reveal her complex relationship to sexuality, to religion, and to the state. Theresa's speech careers from disputing the charge that she "was suckin off queers down the Lido for five bucks" to her lack of respect for "sosha workers" to her rejection of enforced religion: "I don't like readin no stupid Bible!" Through this address, Theresa emerges as both a fully realized character and an individual buffeted by social forces and interpersonal dynamics completely beyond her control.

In the scenes that follow, Thompson intersperses brief dialogic exchanges with other monologues to explore the relationships between her characters and to reveal the demons that haunt each of them. Sandy, a modern-day Everywoman, struggles with received ideas of femininity and social status, questions her commitment to her abusive boyfriend Joe, and grapples with her precarious economic position. But she never goes so far as to interrogate the social values she has embraced. She simply adjusts her perceptions—even though she may recognize their inadequacy—in order to carry on, as in her closing description of the funeral of Theresa and Alan's baby, Danny: "And they had a big wreath of flowers around his neck so's to hide the strangle—you know the kind you put on your door at Christmas? Like that. It was kinda nice." A moment later she adds,

"The flowers never hid it they just made ya look harder."

Thompson creates subtle parallels between the conventions of femininity to which Sandy adheres and the world of male bonding, petty crime, and bravado that Joe inhabits. Narrating the events surrounding the death of a friend in a car crash, Joe observes that they "never *talked* about shit, it was the shit we done together made us good buddies. Just doin stuff with a guy you know you're thinkin the same." Joe's notions of masculinity and of how to survive in a culture of disenfranchisement are shared by Alan, but Alan also feels compelled to realize the ideals of the nuclear family to prove his worth as a man. He selects the mentally retarded Theresa, whom he sees as his "angel" and like "that madonna lady," to be his wife and the mother of his child. But his choice epitomizes the radical disjunction between these characters' visions of participating in the dominant culture and the impossibility of achieving those visions. The unraveling of Alan's dream starkly reveals the psychic and social costs of such unrealistic expectations.

As the description above makes clear, *The Crackwalker*, like a number of Thompson's plays, is brutal, unflinching, and potentially offensive in its themes and dialogue. She readily acknowledges that her plays can disturb audiences, precisely because they reveal what people mask in their everyday social interactions: "Our whole society is founded on denial. Denial of murdering the Native people, denial of oppressing women. . . . Once secrets are exposed . . . and people hate to turn red and be exposed—then they will hate you for it." Moreover, Thompson insists that to be effective, her works must be as frank and elemental as possible:

> Theatre has to be embarrassing, and theatre has to be slovenly. . . . When I have young babies I like to let my breast milk leak through my blouse in public at nice restaurants. . . . And the looks of disgust on people's faces are the same looks [as the ones] on the people that walk out of my plays. I've let something leak that's not supposed to be leaking.

Thompson frequently uses such metaphors, as corporeal states and bodily functions figure largely both in her characters' speech and in her own commentary on her creative process. Several of her plays, most notably *Tornado* (1987; rev. 1992), feature a character who, like Thompson, is epileptic. Thompson's experiences with epilepsy have profoundly affected her perspectives on life, consciousness, and the relationship between mind and body. Most strikingly, she perceives her illness in social as well as physical terms, linking her seizures to her identity as a woman and as a writer. She writes eloquently of her need, as a Catholic girl, to don a series of masks so that she might hide and preserve another self more resistant to social strictures. This stranger within, Thompson explains, manifested itself first in awkward, unfeminine physicality and then, starting at age nine, in epilepsy. Thompson's acute sensitivity, through her illness, to what she calls "contact with the dark" enables her to capture the fluidity of psychic states. Remarkable moments result, such as Alan's description of his loss of control over the frightening scenes in his mind that opens act 2 of *The Crackwalker*: "Fuck I'll be doin the dishes where I'm workin down the Tropicana there and it's like pictures burning holes in my brain I try all the time to like put other pictures over top of that, nice things that I really get off on, eh, that I really like[.]" As horrific images overpower him, Alan comes ever closer to what Thompson elsewhere calls "the abyss": "The abyss is death. It's what you don't know. . . . You see an abyss when you're falling, in that dream where you're falling and falling and there's no bottom." The threat of the abyss pervades Thompson's dramaturgy; each of her characters struggles—some successfully, others not—to retain a sense of normalcy and autonomy against its magnetic power.

The figure of the Crackwalker, the play's eponymous metaphor and the character who haunts its periphery, is inextricably linked to the abyss. Thompson based the Crackwalker, as she had Theresa, on a real person—a Kingstonian known for his obsessive avoidance of sidewalk cracks. "That guy walkin down street lookin at the

Randy Hughson as Alan and Debra Kirshenbaum as Theresa, in the 1990 performance of *The Crackwalker* at the Tarragon Theatre in Toronto, Ontario.

sidewalk" gives Sandy "the creeps," but, significantly, he is the individual with whom Alan may most closely identify, despite his feelings of revulsion. His name reminds us of children's games of daring, threat, and taboo—"step on a crack and you break your mother's back"—perhaps best captured by A. A. Milne in his poem "Lines and Squares" (1924), which warns against bears "Who wait at the corners all ready to eat / The sillies who tread on the lines of the street." The bears

> *try to pretend that nobody cares*
> *Whether you walk on the lines or*
> *squares.*
> *But only the sillies believe their talk;*
> *It's ever so portant how you walk.*

Milne's portrait of intelligent beasts lurking in the urban landscape resonates with Thompson's images of ever-present danger. Threats of psychic chaos, sexual violation, economic deprivation, and social ostracism permeate her dramatic world. Moreover,

Milne's verse suggests a connection between social conformity—staying "in the squares"—and personal safety that Thompson both understands and deconstructs. In Thompson's theater, of course, the human beast is the most unpredictable and potentially violent presence in either the urban jungle or the Canadian wilderness.

Thompson's interest in the unpredictable and unknown has also led her to actively resist the seamless linear plots and characterological arcs that we identify with conventional dramaturgy. She creates for each character a unique voice, distinguishable by vocabulary, intonational patterns, and grammar. The Canadian critic Alan Filewod notes that Thompson's characters "move in and out of private worlds that are constructed through language; at the same time, language marks the social environments through which the characters have passed." Her plays take shape through the dramatization of strategic moments—some comic, some horrific, some banal—designed to reveal the complexity of the individuals she portrays. She leaves it to her audience to connect these moments and to find meaning created by scenic juxtapositions, idiosyncratic dialogue, and evocative imagery.

For some critics, Thompson's decision to position a number of her characters—especially women—as victims, or as individuals who unquestioningly accept dominant social structures, renders her dramaturgy politically problematic. Thompson argues, however, that one must examine "an issue that's *true,* and until you examine what *is,* what exists, you can't do anything about it." When asked what impact she would like to have on her audience, Thompson explains that she wants "to hold a mirror up to all of us" to ensure a "forced confrontation with the self." Only in a moment of awakening can theater, for Thompson, truly become powerful. "The coma lifting, then, becomes political. Art is political, should be political, but only in this really essential way." Psychically charged, visceral as well as lyrical, sexually frank, emotionally turbulent, and uncompromising in its social convictions, Thompson's playwriting exemplifies the contemporary theater at its most elemental, powerful level.

J.E.G.

The Crackwalker

CHARACTERS

THERESA	JOE
SANDY	The MAN
ALAN	

1.1

THERESA Shut up, mouth, I not goin back there no more noway, I'm goin back to Sandy's! [*To audience*] You know what she done to me? She make me go livin with her up on Division[1] near Chung Wah's, cause she say I come from God, eh, then she go lookin in my room every night see if I got

1. Division Street, the main commercial thoroughfare in Kingston, Ontario.

guys in there cause Bonnie Cain told her I was suckin off queers down the Lido for five bucks; I wasn't doin it anyways Bonnie Cain was doin it I was just watchin. So last night, eh, I'm up there with a friend of mine, Danny, he a taxi driver—we're just talkin, eh, we weren't doin nothin, and so she come up and knock on the door and she say, "Trese I know you got someone in there" and I go "No Mrs. Beddison ain't nobody in here," and she start goin on about God and that, and how she knowed cause she got a six feelin[2] in her, so I get scared, eh, so I tell Danny to get in the closet. We don't got no clothes on, eh, so I put his jeans and that under the bed and I get under the covers like I'm sleepin and I go "S'kay Mrs. Beddison you could come in now." So she come in lookin at me like a stupid bitch and she say she knowed there was somebody in there cause she heard talkin and I says "You feelin okay Mrs. Beddison, ain't nobody here cept me and I sleepin," then she start goin near the closet, eh, and Danny start laughin. Well she runup the closet and she pullin on the door and I'm pullin on her arm and I'm saying "Trust me Mrs. Beddison, ya gotta trus me," cause the sosha workers are always goin on about trus and that, eh, but she don't listen, she open the door and there's Danny standin stripped naked. Well that whoredog Beddison start screamin God words at him, eh, so he takes off outa the house and she takes off after him and I got his pants, eh, so I throw em out the window case he catch em and then I bawlin. I bawlin on the bed and ya know what she make me do? She make me take a bath! A bubble bath like for the baby! All bubbles and that! Then she make me put on her stupid dressin robe itch my skin and smell like chocolate bars and that and she take me to where she livin and you know what she make me do? She make me read the Bible! I don't like readin no stupid Bible! Ya get a stomachache doin that, ya do! Stupid hose bag. I'm not goin back there no more no way, I'm goin back to Sandy's.

1.2

[SANDY *and* JOE'S *apartment.* SANDY *is scrubbing the floor furiously.* THERESA *appears, joyous, carrying a plastic bag containing all of her belongings. As she has not seen* SANDY *in several weeks, she is very excited.*]

THERESA Hi Sandy, how ya doin!!

[SANDY *does not look at* THERESA.]

SANDY What are you doin here?

THERESA I come callin on ya!

[*In the following sequence,* SANDY'S *anger builds. At first, however, it contains an element of teasing.*]

SANDY I don't want no houndogs callin on me. [*Continues scrubbing*]

THERESA I not a houndog!

SANDY Yes, y'are.

THERESA No I not.

SANDY Whoredog houndog that's what you are.

THERESA [*laughs, delighted*] Sanny!

SANDY [*pointing backwards*] And get your whorepaws offa my sofa.

2. That is, had an intuition via a "sixth sense."

THERESA [*jumps, removes hand, gasps*] Sanny, like I don't mean to bug ya or nothin [*Eating donut from bag*] but like I don't get off on livin where I'm livin no more so I come back here sleepin on the couch, okay?

SANDY I not keepin no cowpies[3] here.

THERESA I not a cowpie!

SANDY [*faces her*] Would you get out of my house?

THERESA Why, what I done?

SANDY . . . Ya smell like cookin fat—turns my gut.

THERESA That only cause I eatin chip from the chipwagon![4]

SANDY I don't care what it's cause of, get your whoreface out of here.

THERESA Why, why you bein ugly for?

SANDY You tell me and then we'll both know.

THERESA What.

SANDY Don't think nobody seen ya neither cause Bonnie Cain seen ya right through the picture window!

[THERESA *claps a hand to her mouth in "uh-oh."*]

On my couch that I paid for with my money.

THERESA Wha—

SANDY With *my husband!*

THERESA No way, Sanny.

SANDY [*unable to contain her anger any longer*] You touch my fuckin husband again and I break every bone in your body!

THERESA Bonnie Cain lyin she lyin to ya she think I took twenty buck off her she tryin to get me back.

SANDY [*starts speaking after "she lying to ya"*] That's bullshit Therese cause Bonnie Cain don't lie and you know she don't.

THERESA You don't trus me.

SANDY Fuckin right.

THERESA I never done it.

SANDY Pretty bad combination, Trese, a retarded whore.

THERESA That's a load of bullshit Sanny, I *not retarded.*

SANDY Just get out of my house and don't come back. [*Pushes her.*]

THERESA No I never I never done it! [*In angry indignation she pushes back.*]

SANDY Trese Joe told me, he told me what the two of youse done!

THERESA Oh.

SANDY Lyin whore, look at ya make me sick. Wearin that ugly dress thinkin it's sexy cause it shows off your fat tits and those shoes are fuckin stupid ya can't even walk in them.

THERESA I know.

[SANDY *stares at* THERESA. THERESA *does not move.*]

SANDY [*with an air of resignation, tiredness*] Just get out, okay?

THERESA I never wanted it, Sanny, I never wanted it he come in he made me.

SANDY Bull Trese.

THERESA He did I sleepin I sleepin there havin dreams I seen this puppy and he come in and tie me up and push it in me down my hole.

SANDY What?

3. Piles of cow manure.
4. Vendor's cart selling chips (french fries).

THERESA He tie me all up with strings and that and he singin Ol Macdonel Farm and he say he gonna kill me if I don't shut up so I be quiet and he done it he screw me.

SANDY Are you shittin me?

THERESA And—and—and he singin and he take his jean down and it all hard and smellin like pee pee and he go and he put it in my mouth.

SANDY He could do twenty for that.

THERESA Don't send him up the river[5] Sanny he didn't mean nothin.

SANDY Horny bastard he's not gettin into me again.

THERESA Me neither Sanny he tries anything I just run up to Tim Hortons[6] get a fancy donut.

SANDY Oh he won't be cheatin on me again.

THERESA How come Sanny, you tell him off?

SANDY Fuckin right I did. After Bonnie tole me, I start givin him shit, eh, and he takes the hand to me callin me a hag and sayin how he liked pokin you bettern that and look. [*Reveals bruise.*]

THERESA Bassard.

SANDY He's done it before, but he won't do it again.

THERESA Why, Sanny, you call the cops on him?

SANDY *Right.*

THERESA Did ya—

SANDY Ya know my high heels? The shiny black ones I got up in Toronto?

THERESA Yeah, they're sharp.

SANDY [*obviously enjoying telling the story*] And he knows it, too. After he beat up on me he takes off drinkin, comes back about three just shitfaced, eh, and passes out cold? Well I'm there lookin at him snorin like a pig and I says to myself "I'm gonna get this bastard," I'm thinkin of how when I seen my heels sittin over in the corner and then I know what I'm gonna do. So I take one of the heels and go over real quiet to where he's lyin, and ya know what I do? I take the heel and I rip the holy shit out of his back with it.

THERESA JEEZ DID HE WAKE UP?

SANDY Fuckin right he did. You shoulda seen him, first I guess he thought he was dreamin, eh, so he just lies there makin these ugly noises burpin and that? And then he opens his eyes, and puts his hands up like a baby eh, and *then* I *seen* him *see* the heel. Well I take off right out the back door and he's comin after me fit to kill his eyes is all red he's hissin I am scared shitless; well he gets ahold of me and I says to myself "Sandy this is it. This is how you're gonna die. You got the bastard back and now you're gonna die for it." Well he is just about to send me to the fuckin angels when he stops; just like that and turns around and goes on to bed.

THERESA How come he done that, Sanny?

SANDY I didn't know at first either, then I figured it out. Cuttin him with the heel was the smartest thing I done. Ya see, he wasn't gonna kill me cause he don't want to do time, eh, and he knew if he just beat up on me he'd

5. That is, to prison (an expression that originated in New York City, which sent convicts up the Hudson River to Sing Sing Prison in Ossining, New York).

6. A chain of doughnut shops founded and mainly located in Canada.

never get no more sleep cause I'd do it again. He knows it. He don't dare take a hand to me again, no way. Either he takes off, or he stays and he treats me nice.

THERESA Did you talk to him later?

SANDY I ain't seen him for three days. But we ate together before he took off, I fixed him up some tuna casserole and we ate it; we didn't say nothin, though. It don't matter, we sometimes go a whole week without talkin, don't mean we're pissed off at each other.

THERESA Al and I talkin all the time when we go out.

SANDY We did too when we first started goin together. After a while ya don't have to talk cause you always know what they're gonna say anyways. Makes ya sick sometimes. What are you bawlin for?

THERESA I'm sorry Joe done that to me, Sanny.

SANDY He's like that, he's a prick.

THERESA S'okay if I come livin here then?

SANDY . . . Sure, I don't care.

THERESA Thank you Sanny.

SANDY I like the company.

THERESA Don't say nothin to Al, eh?

SANDY What if I tell him what Bonnie Cain tole me about you blowin off queers down the Lido?

THERESA Oh no, Sanny, don't say bout that.

SANDY I guess old fags in Kingston are pretty hard up.

THERESA You want a donut, Sanny?

SANDY No. What kind ya got.

THERESA Apple fritters.

SANDY Jeez, Therese, ya ever see how they make them things?

THERESA No, I never worked up there.

SANDY It'd make ya sick.

THERESA I love em.

SANDY I know ya do, you're a pig.

THERESA Fuck off. . . . Only kiddin.

SANDY You watch your mouth.

THERESA You love Joe still?

SANDY I don't know. I used to feel like we was in the fuckin movies. Member that show *Funny Girl* where Barbra Streisand and Omar Sharif are goin together?[7]

THERESA She hardly[8] sing pretty.

SANDY Well remember that part where they start singin right on the boat, singin to each other?

THERESA Yeah.

SANDY We done that once. We'd been up at the Manor, eh, Chesty Morgan[9] was up there so we'd just been havin a hoot, eh, and Joe wants to go over to the General Wolfe to see the Mayor, so we get on the Wolfe Island[1] ferry

7. *Funny Girl* is a 1968 movie musical, starring Streisand (b. 1942) and Sharif (b. 1932).
8. Really.
9. Polish-born stripper (b. 1928?) who made two campy sexploitation films in 1974 and toured clubs throughout North America.

1. The largest of the Thousand Islands, located at the northeast end of Lake Ontario, where the St. Lawrence River begins; ferry service runs to the island from Kingston.

and we're laughin and carryin on and that and then we start singin, right on the bow of the Wolfe Island ferry.

THERESA Jeez.

SANDY We didn't care when we were doin it though, we didn't give a shit what anyone was thinkin, fuck em we were havin fun.

THERESA I love singin.

SANDY Joe really done that to you?

THERESA What?

SANDY *Raped* ya.

THERESA Don't like talkin about it Sanny.

SANDY *Trese.*

THERESA He done it when I never wanted it it's true.

SANDY It is, eh?

THERESA S'true, Sanny. Don't tell Joe, eh?

SANDY I mighta known it.

THERESA Still okay if I sleepin here though?

SANDY You're gonna have to do the housework while I'm workin for Nikos.

THERESA How come you workin down there I thought you didn't like Nikos?

SANDY I get off on corned beef on rye, arsewipe, what d'ya think I need the fuckin money.

THERESA Ain't Joe drivin for Amey's[2] no more?

SANDY No.

THERESA What's he doin?

SANDY Fuckin the dog,[3] I don't know.

THERESA Bassard.

SANDY I know. Gimme a bite of that.

THERESA I not really retarded am I Sanny?

SANDY Just a little slow.

THERESA Not like that guy walkin down street lookin at the sidewalk?

SANDY Jeez he give me the creeps.

THERESA He hardly got the long beard, eh?

SANDY I know.

THERESA Not like him, eh Sanny?

SANDY No. No, I tole ya Therese, you're just a little slow.

THERESA Oh.

[JOE *and* ALAN *barge in with a hot*[4] *motorbike. They start quickly, efficiently taking it apart and packing the parts.* SANDY *and* THERESA *stand there stupefied.*]

JOE Ya hoo! We got ourselves a shit-hot mother!

ALAN Did we *ever!*

JOE Okay nice and easy we don't want to mark this babe.

ALAN Like this?

JOE That's right buddy—fuckin back door wide open shit that dog just sittin there waggin its tail at us.

ALAN He wanted to be buddies with us.

JOE I just about shit it was fuckin *helpin* us.

2. A taxi company in Kingston.
3. Doing nothing (slang).
4. Stolen.

THERESA What kinda dog was it Al, one of them golden?

JOE A shepherd.

ALAN A German shepherd a police dog.

JOE A fuckin *screw*[5] dog.

SANDY You're not bringin Martin over here.

JOE How's my pussycake doin? Eh? [*Kisses* SANDY.] Eh pussycake?

SANDY I says you're not bringin Martin over here.

JOE Don't worry babe we're meetin him over to the Shamrock he ain't comin here.

ALAN Down the Beachcomber Room.

THERESA That's hardly nice down there all them trees and that?

ALAN You like it there?

THERESA I love it.

ALAN I'll take ya there sometime.

SANDY Where you been the last three nights?

JOE Paintin the town brown honeysuck whata you been doin?

SANDY I said where were ya for three nights in a row?

JOE Out with the Mayor, poochie, spookin out the Royal.

THERESA You not out with him he dead.

ALAN Theresa.

THERESA He is dead.

ALAN Joe's only kiddin, Trese.

SANDY You tell me where ya been or you're out on your ear. I said where were ya the last three nights?

JOE Just hold on to your pants sugar crack first things first. [*Madly working on the bike*]

ALAN This is big bucks ya know.

SANDY You don't have to tell me cause I know. I know where ya were you were down the Embassy pissin our money away.

THERESA Them ugly old Greeks down there anyways.

ALAN You were takin Papa's *shirt,* eh Joe?

SANDY I'll tell ya somethin about gamblers youse do it just so's you could lose it's true that's why.

JOE Well fuck me blind I never knew that. Did you know that Al?

ALAN Nope, I never heard of that.

JOE Thars pretty good commander, where'd ya get that offa?

SANDY It happened to be in the *Reader's Digest,* arsewipe, and it was written by a doctor, Doctor John Grant, and I guess he knows what he's talkin about.

JOE Oooooh *Reader's Digest,* shit-for-brains is going smart on us.

THERESA She not a shit-for-brains you stupid.

JOE You simmer down there burger.

SANDY Is that where ya were, pissin away my money?

JOE [*completes a physical action*] Gotcha.

SANDY Eh?

JOE Hand me the pliers, would ya?

SANDY [*screeching*] I said where were ya Joe!

5. Prison guard (slang).

[JOE *spits his mouthful of beer in her face.* ALAN *laughs and laughs.*]

That's cute.

THERESA Stupid dummy-face.

[JOE *spits on* ALAN. ALAN *laughs, spits back.*]

SANDY You are cut off and I mean it.

JOE From what, bitch, your ugly box?

[SANDY *exits to clean up.*]

Don't know what she's so pissed off at nice brew in the face cool ya right down.

THERESA I'm movin back here Joe Sanny said I could.

ALAN She did?

JOE Is that right.

THERESA Sleepin on the couch that okay Joe?

JOE Sure, fuck, I don't care, long as the two of youse don't gang up on me.

ALAN Two women together always do.

THERESA What do two women do?

ALAN You know, gang up on the guy.

SANDY [*entering*] Only if he got it comin to him.

JOE Do I get it comin to me commander?

SANDY You're fuckin right you do.

JOE Little diesel dyke this one see what she done to me?

ALAN Holy Jeez!

JOE She's a live one all right Pearl Lasalle[6] the second.

THERESA She not like Pearl Lasalle Pearl Lasalle ugly lookin.

JOE She fights like her though don't ya honey suck? What's for supper I'm starvin.

SANDY Nothin.

JOE What?

SANDY You don't bring in money we don't get no supper.

JOE Well fuck—don't we got stuff for samiches?

SANDY Nope.

JOE Well fuck I'm goin over to Shirley's.

SANDY When.

JOE Right now fuck.

SANDY Take your stuff with ya.

JOE Would ya sit on this first I want fish for supper.

SANDY Pig. I says take your stuff with ya and get out.

JOE You for real?

SANDY Fuckin right.

JOE All right I been wantin out of this hole. Thanks babe.

SANDY Is that right?

JOE Take care. [*Starts to go.*]

SANDY You could get in a lot of trouble rapin a retard Joe.

JOE Pardon.

SANDY I said you could get in a lot of trouble rapin a retard.

6. The name of a woman living in Kingston when the play was written—a "diesel dyke" (lesbian with a masculine appearance) well-known locally both as a heavily tattooed ex-convict and as the kindly, loving mother of five children.

[THERESA *is motioning No! No! No! to* SANDY.]

JOE Yeah that's right you would. So?

SANDY You'll be up the river for twenty years when I tell the cops what you done, Joe.

ALAN Over fifty[7] don't get you twenty years no way no way!

SANDY I'm not talkin bout the bike.

JOE What? What are ya talkin about eh?

SANDY About rapin a retard.

JOE What?

SANDY About rapin Theresa.

JOE What?

SANDY About rapin Theresa with me in the next room.

JOE Rape? Rape? Who told you that did Theresa tell you that?

SANDY Yeahhh.

THERESA No no Sanny not rape I only said he done it when I never wanted it.

JOE Did you tell my wife that I raped you Theresa? [THERESA *doesn't answer.*] Did you say that? Eh? [*Grabs her.*] Eh?

THERESA I never—leave me alone you big ugly cock—

JOE I'll tell you somethin about your little girlfriend buddy. I'll tell you something about this little—

ALAN It don't matter, Joe, it—it—it just don't matter nobody don't believe her anyways.

JOE This little girl who's callin rape was sittin on that couch beggin for it.

ALAN She never.

SANDY Theresa?

JOE It's true. I come in piss drunk I'm passed out on the floor and there she is down on all fours shovin her big white ass in my face.

THERESA No I never.

JOE Big white bootie right in the face.

THERESA Go away.

JOE Tell em like it was Trese, and no crossin fingers.

THERESA I never say that Sanny, I never mean he rape me!

SANDY Theresa is he tellin the truth?

ALAN Theresa you never done that, did ya? Shown him your bum?

JOE This is your last chance, burger, now tell the fuckin truth or I get serious.

SANDY Don't lie to me Theresa. I can forgive a lot of things but not a lie.

ALAN You can tell the truth, Theresa, I'll take care of ya.

SANDY Eh, Trese?

[*Pause.*]

THERESA [*laughing*] Who farted?

ALAN I never did.

JOE Eh Theresa?

ALAN It's—it's okay, Joe it's—she—she can't handle her booze yet she was probably drunk or sniffin[8] and you was drunk and it don't matter, it just don't matter I'll be stayin with her all the nights from now I'm gonna take

7. That is, theft of property worth more than $50—the threshold for distinguishing categories of theft in Canada's criminal code until 1971.

8. That is, sniffing glue.

care of her it won't happen again she won't never say nothin bout ya again I promise.

THERESA You stayin with me all nights from now Al?

ALAN I'm takin care of ya. I'm—

SANDY Could youse leave us alone, please.

ALAN Who, me and Theresa?

SANDY If you don't mind.

ALAN Sure, sure. We—

THERESA Wait for me Al I wanna get some chocolate bars and that I starvin . . . well I am I didn't have no dinner.

JOE You. You watch your mouth, eh?

SANDY Would youse just take off?

[ALAN *pulls* THERESA *out.*]

THERESA See youse later don't do nothin I wouldn't do.

1.3

[ALAN *and* THERESA *exit.* JOE *is furious and trying to cool down. His back is to* SANDY. *She is aware of his anger. She picks something up off the kitchen floor and starts to take it in to the kitchen.* JOE *grabs her as she tries to pass him and throws her to the floor.*]

JOE You CUNT.

SANDY Keep away from me—

JOE I'm a fuckin rapist cause a fuckin retard SAYS so?

SANDY Touch me again and you go to your goddamn grave!

JOE FUCK maybe I'm the maniac been carvin all the TELLERS out in SASKATOON![9] [*Makes monster face and noise.*]

SANDY Go jump in a hole.

JOE [*grabs her, hard*] What is fuckin with your BRAIN, woman?

SANDY I didn't mean it.

JOE It was a *joke?*

SANDY I was just—you said you liked her better.

JOE What?

SANDY You said you liked—pokin her better.

JOE [*laughs, almost hysterically*] So I go to the joint.

SANDY I wasn't gonna tell nobody—

JOE You're a fuckin CROW, you know that?

SANDY I was just—seein—

JOE [*thrusting her away*] Get away from me.

[SANDY *starts to run toward him, trying to scream but the sound is muffled and distorted by a stomach seizure which stops her about three feet away from* JOE.]

You got your upset stomach again?

SANDY Bastard.

JOE [*looks her up and down*] You just give me a hard-on.

[SANDY *spits on him.*]

9. The largest city of the province of Saskatchewan, in western Canada.

Hewww you like it when I'm rough with ya, don't ya? Eh? [*Moves her roughly, whispers.*] Makes your nips stand up when I'm rough with ya.

[SANDY's *hands are still raised.* SANDY *and* JOE *are a foot apart throughout the interchange.* SANDY *looks at him with hatred.*]

What, you don't want it? Okay, see ya later!

[*He starts to leave.*]

SANDY [*head down*] Joe.

JOE What can I do for ya?

[SANDY *smiles.*]

Oh, ya do want it. Okay, why—why—don't ya take that blouse there off?

[*She removes her blouse.*]

Hm. And the skirt.

[*She removes her skirt. She is left in a bra and pantyhose with a low crotch. He nods, looking her up and down.*]

How come ya like it like this? Eh? [*Shakes his head.*] I gotta be somewhere.

[JOE *exits.* SANDY *remains onstage, not moving. Lights out quickly.*]

1.4

[THERESA *and* ALAN *are in a restaurant.*]

THERESA Where d'ya think Joe took off to?

ALAN I don't know probably drinkin, maybe the Shamrock.

THERESA You think they're splitting up?

ALAN I hope not.

THERESA Me too. I love Sandy, she my best girlfriend.

ALAN I—Joe—he and me are good buddies, too. They go good together anyways.

THERESA Could I have a donut?

ALAN What kind, chocolate? I know you like chocolate.

THERESA I love it.

ALAN Sandy's nuts, you're not fat.

THERESA Don't say nothin about it.

ALAN You're not.

THERESA I don't like talkin about it.

ALAN Here. Two chocolate donuts.

THERESA Thank you Alan.

ALAN Jesus you're a good lookin girl. You're the prettiest lookin girl I seen.

THERESA Don't talk like that.

ALAN I love screwin with ya. Do you like it with me?

THERESA I don't know—don't ask me that stuff dummy-face.

ALAN I like eatin ya out ya know.

THERESA Shut your mouth people are lookin don't talk like that stupid-face.

ALAN Nobody's lookin. Jeez you're pretty. Just like a little angel. Huh. Like a—I know. I know. I'm gonna call you my little angel from now on. People gonna see ya and they're gonna go "There's Trese, she's Al's angel!"

THERESA Who gonna say them things?

ALAN Anybody.

THERESA They are?

ALAN Yup.

THERESA You're a dummy-face.

ALAN So beautiful.

THERESA Stop it Al you make me embarrass.

ALAN You're—I was always hopin for someone like you—always happy always laughin and that.

THERESA I cryin sometimes ya know.

ALAN Yeah but ya cry the same way ya laugh. There's somethin—I don't know—as soon as I seen ya I knew I wanted ya. I wanted to marry ya when I seen ya.

THERESA When, when did you say that?

ALAN I never said nothin, I just thought it, all the time.

THERESA We only been goin together for a little while, you know.

ALAN Let's get married.

THERESA Al stop lookin at me like that you embarrassin me.

ALAN Sorry. Did you hear me?

THERESA Yeah. Okay.

ALAN When.

THERESA Tuesday. I ask my sosha worker to come.

ALAN No. Just Joe and me and you and Sandy. Just the four of us. I want Joe to be my best man.

THERESA Sandy could be the flower girl. Uh. Oh.

ALAN What?

THERESA Hope you don't want no babies.

ALAN Why. I do! I do want babies! I get on with babies good!

THERESA Not sposda have none.

ALAN How come? Who told you that?

THERESA The sosha worker, she say I gotta get my tubes tied.[1]

ALAN What's that?

THERESA Operation up the hospital. They tie it up down there so ya won't go havin babies.

ALAN They can't do that to you no way!

THERESA I know they can't but they're doin it.

ALAN They don't have no *right*.

THERESA Yah they do Al I slow.

ALAN Slow? I don't think you're slow who told YOU that?

THERESA I ain't a good mum Al I cant help it.

ALAN Who said you ain't a good mum?

THERESA All of them just cause when I took off on Dawn.

ALAN Who's Dawn?

THERESA The baby, the other baby.

ALAN You never had a baby before did ya? Did ya?

THERESA Las—

ALAN You didn't have no other man's baby did ya? With another guy?

[*Pause.*]

THERESA No, it's Bernice's.

1. That is, be sterilized by tubal ligation; in some provinces of Canada, from the 1930s up through the 1970s, people with mental disabilities were routinely sterilized.

ALAN Who's Bernice?

THERESA My cousin my mum's sister.

ALAN Well how come you were lookin after her baby?

THERESA Cause she was sick up in hospital. Jeez Al.

ALAN Well—what happened whatdja do wrong?

THERESA Nothin it wasn't my fault just one Friday night I was sniffin, eh, so I took off down to the plaza and I leave the baby up the room, eh, I thought I was comin right back, and I met this guy and he buyin me drinks and that then I never knew what happened and I woke up and I asked somebody where I was and I was in Ottawa!

ALAN He took you all the way up to Ottawa? That bastard.

THERESA I never seen him again I thumbed back to Kingston. [*Crying*] I come back to the house and the baby's gone she ain't there so I bawlin I goin everywhere yellin after her and never found nothin then I see Bonnie Cain and she told me they took her up the Children's Aid she dead. So I go on up the Aid and they say she ain't dead she live but they not givin her back cause I unfit.

ALAN Jeez.

THERESA I ain't no more Al I don't sniff or nothin.

ALAN Them bastards.

THERESA Honest.

ALAN I know. I know ya don't and we're gonna have a baby and nobody ain't gonna stop us. We're gonna have our own little baby between you and me and nobody can't say nothin bout it. You're not goin to no hospital, understand?

THERESA But Al she say she gonna cut off my pension check if I don't get my tubes tied.

ALAN Fuck the pension check you're not goin to no hospital.

THERESA Okay Al.

ALAN Come here. You're not goin to no hospital.

THERESA You won't let em do nothin to me, will ya Al?

ALAN Nope. You're my angel and they ain't gonna touch you. . . . Hey! I know what ya look like now!

THERESA What, an angel?

ALAN That—that madonna lady; you know them pictures they got up in classrooms when you're a kid? Them pictures of the madonna?

THERESA The Virgin Mary?

ALAN Yeah. Her.

THERESA I love her I askin her for stuff.

ALAN Yuh look just like her. Just like the madonna. Cept the madonna picture got a baby in it.

THERESA It do?

ALAN She's holdin it right in her arms. You too, maybe, eh? Eh? Hey! Let's go up to the Good Thief.[2]

THERESA Al I don't know you goin to church! You goin every Sunday?

2. That is, the Church of the Good Thief, a Roman Catholic church in Kingston. The "Good Thief," traditionally given the name Dismas, was the robber crucified with Jesus who repented and asked Jesus to "remember me when thou comest into thy kingdom" (Luke 23.42).

ALAN No I never went since I was five I just want to go now. We'll go and we'll—we'll like have a party lightin candles[3] and that a party for gettin married!

THERESA I love lightin candles.

ALAN Maybe the Father's gonna be there. They're always happy when someone's gettin married we could tell him!

THERESA Al I gettin sleepy.

ALAN Well after we party I'm gonna put ya right down to sleep over at Joe's. I won't try nothin or nothin.

THERESA What if Sandy be piss off.

ALAN No Trese, they said we could stay there together. The two of us. And we're gonna.

THERESA Okay . . . really I lookin like that madonna?

ALAN Just like her. Just like her.

[*He is rocking her in his arms. Lights fade.*]

1.5

JOE Me and the Mayor we'd pick up a couple steak hoagies, and a case of twenty-four, head up to Merton on the hogs[4]—catch some shit group—you know, Mad Dog Fagin, Grapes of Wrath, somethin, get shitfaced then go back to Kingston, pick us up some juicy pie down at Lino's or Horny Tim's,[5] drive it out to middle road, fuck it blind, and have em home by one o'clock. Then we'd go down and catch the last ferry to the island and fuckin ride from one end to the other all fuckin night. Seven o'clock we'd go into Lou's have us some home fries and a couple eggs easy over then head on back to work in Kingston. That was when I was drivin a Cat[6] makin a shitload of money just a shitload. Huh—the Mayor was fuckin crazy wasn't nothin he wouldn't do nothin he was smart too he went to university in the States even, he just didn't give a shit about it, you know? He had about a hundred books I seen em all filled with words that long [*Measures two feet*] he knew what they meant, too, every one of them but he never let on, ya know? He never let on he knew so much . . . we never *talked* about shit, it was the shit we done together made us good buddies. Just doin stuff with a guy you know you're thinkin the same. Anybody touched him I woulda killed them and same goes for him . . . he was a damn good driver too but he wasn't *drivin,* Martin was. Fuckin Martin fuckin stoned on STP.[7] Martin—Martin wasn't an asshole, but he stupid you know? Jeez he was stupid. So this Friday night we'd all gotten pissed up the Manor, eh, then we all went over to the island just to fuck around and to see the Mayor's sister, Linda, who was workin at the General Wolfe waitin on tables. So Bart, that was his real name, Bart and me and Martin had all got these new boots over at the A1 men's store really nice you know,

3. In Catholic churches, worshippers light votive candles to symbolize and extend their prayers and to honor the saint before whose image the candle is lit.
4. That is, Harley-Davidson motorcycles.
5. Nickname for the Tim Hortons chain of doughnut shops.
6. That is, a piece of construction equipment (a Caterpillar).
7. A synthetic hallucinogen—a forerunner of ecstasy—introduced in the late 1960s (the initials stand for "serenity, tranquility, peace").

all leather, real solid a hundred bucks a pair so we wanted to show em off to Linda, you know, bug her. So Bart gets in there and he's jumpin on tables, eatin all the limes and cherries and that for the drinks singin some gross song about his love boots, he called them. Fuck it was funny—we were killin ourselves but Linda she wasn't laughin her boss was gettin pissed off so she told Bart, she goes "Bart, get the fuck out of here I think your goddamn boots are shit." That's what she said. So he give her a big kiss right in front of her boss and we take off in Martin's car. Me and the Mayor in the backseat, Martin and his girlfriend in the front. Well we're headin down the road goin south it's dark but it ain't wet and the last thing I remember Bart looks at me and he says "I wonder what it's like to fuck an angel" and *bang* everything goes fuckin black. When I come to I'm in the fucking ambulance goin across to Kingston and Bart's lyin there beside me dead only I didn't know it and there's his sister Linda right there in the ambulance. I don't know how she got there—she's all red all black under her eyes and that and she's bawlin just bawlin up a storm and she's huggin his legs and she's sayin something only I can't make out what she's sayin I can't make it out I was so out of it I'm thinkin I'm gonna die I'm thinkin I'm gonna die if I don't make out what she's sayin so I kept tryin to make it out and she kept sayin it and then I knew what she was sayin and you know what it was? . . . She was sayin she did like his boots. "I do like your boots Bart I do like your boots Bart I do like your boots I do like your fuckin boots I do like your boots I do like your boots I do like your boots. . . ." She wouldn't fuckin stop it.

1.6

[ALAN *and* THERESA *are sound asleep. The room is sometimes lit by passing cars. Noise of people on the street.* THERESA*'s steady breathing. Suddenly we hear* JOE, *very drunk, half singing. As soon as* ALAN *hears him he springs into his jeans, legs shaking, and awkwardly tries to light a cigarette. His heart is racing.* JOE *enters.*]

ALAN Hey Joe.

JOE Jeeeeeeezus you gimme a scare what are you doin here?

ALAN Stayin with Trese member? Member ya said I could? The—the mum's got company—in from Windsor.[8]

JOE *Windsor.* What a fuckin hole.

ALAN Yeah it's hot down there—in the summer—

JOE Look what I found in the fuckin hallway. Cheese samich with a bloody Kleenex stuck to it.

[*This makes* ALAN *very sick.*]

ALAN Jeezus who put it there.

JOE I was thinkin maybe the wife left out a little snack for me. Ya want some? Blood'n Cheez Whiz[9] samich? Hey hey hey it's hardly good.

ALAN Hey no—no—no thank you. No way.

8. An industrial city in the southwest corner of Ontario (across the Detroit River from Detroit, Michigan).

9. A processed cheese food, sold by Kraft since the 1950s.

JOE What, you don't like eatin blood or somethin?

ALAN I never tried it.

JOE Were you screwin that?

ALAN No! No I mean no I was just I—

JOE Why the hell not?

ALAN Oh no I mean I was eh, like I was a couple hours ago, but not right before ya came in I wasn't.

JOE Jeez you're strange. How come ya got dressed you goin out?

ALAN No—no I'm not goin out—I—I couldn't fuckin sleep, you know? Ya know what that's like? Ya just keep turnin and can't lie right? So I thought I'd wait up and just shoot the shit with you when ya came in.

JOE Strange-o.

ALAN I guess so. Did-dju play tonight?

JOE Papadapa dies!

ALAN He—he was cheatin again?

JOE Fuckin right he was.

ALAN He dies.

JOE Greasy fuck. Fuck once I seen Edwards get him in a half Nelson an he was so greasy he slipped out!

ALAN Ewwww.

JOE Slipped right out. Slimy bastard right in the middle of the game I turn to him and I says "Papa" I says, "Don't fuck with me, just don't fuck with me."

ALAN That's hardly good. Huh. What did he say?

JOE Nothin. He just made one of them noises.

ALAN What, what the ones with their mouth like this? Like a chicken does?

JOE Hah. Yeah it is kinda like a chicken. Gives me the creeps.

ALAN Yeah. Yeah, they do that all the time and the one I worked for, Andy? He *stunk* too, he smelled like matches, you know? After ya light a match?

JOE He's gettin it.

ALAN Yeah?? Yeah? Who's gonna give it to him, are you? Are you gonna give it to him Joe? I'll help ya I hate the bastard. I hate him.

JOE Buddy I am pleadin the Fifth. Fuuuck. [*Singing*] "I gotta get outtaaa this place if it's the lassst . . ."[1]

ALAN I know what ya mean, Joe. Too—too—too bad there weren't no late movie on or something—hah—Mr. Ed or somethin.

JOE Who's he when he's at home?

ALAN Mr. Ed? The talkin horse, don't ya remember? "A horse is a horse of course of course and no one . . ."[2]

JOE Hey [*Indicating bedroom*] w'she bawlin or did she go out?

ALAN Sleepin when we come in I think.

JOE She's a good woman buddy.

ALAN I know she is Joe. So's Trese.

1. A paraphrase of "We Gotta Get Out of This Place" (1965), a hit song recorded by the Animals (written by Barry Mann and Cynthia Weil); the line ends "thing we ever do." *Pleadin the Fifth:* invoking the right against self-incrimination guaranteed by the Fifth Amendment of the U.S. Constitution.

2. The opening lyrics of the theme song to *Mister Ed* (written by Jay Livingston and Ray Evans), an American television sitcom (1961–66).

JOE Are you sure, buddy?

ALAN Oh—that was—she—she didn't mean nothin honest Joe she she just don't think sometimes, ya know?

JOE That mouth of hers is gonna send her up shit creek one day ain't it burger?

ALAN You—you want a smoke?

JOE Whaddya got—menthol, fuck, I can't smoke that shit.

ALAN I know—I didn't buy em a guy a guy give em to me.

JOE Hey hamburger sorry for wakin ya.

THERESA I not a hamburger.

JOE Ooooh I thought ya was!

THERESA You shut up I sleepin.

JOE Okay burger queen. Yeah. Yeah buddy she's okay too.

ALAN Thank you, Joe. So's Sandy.

JOE She never fucked around on me, you know.

ALAN No?

JOE Not once. [*Goes to window and leans out*] What a fuckin hole this is eh? . . . K fuckin O.[3] [*Yells out window*] Fuuuuuuck.

[SANDY *enters.*]

SANDY Would you shut it?

JOE [*singing*] "I gotta get out of this place."

SANDY Why don't ya then ya big pig.

JOE I told ya woman don't go callin me pig in public. Jeez she got an ugly mouth, eh?

SANDY You're shitfaced, Joe, go on and pass out.

JOE You make me wanta piss my pants.

SANDY Just go on makin a fool of yourself.

JOE Down woman, me and my pal Al is gonna head up to Horny Tim's and we're gonna pick us up some taileroooonie! Then we're gonna go on over to the quarry and we're gonna get ourselves sucked and fucked—

SANDY You're not proud, are ya.

[JOE *bumps into something, falls.* SANDY *starts to pick him up.*]

JOE You never fooled around on me, did ya?

SANDY Nope. I never . . . did.

JOE [*sings*] "She's a hooo-o-o-o-nky tonk womannnn gimme [*Goes to bedroom.*] gimme gimme the [*Fading*] honky tonk wom . . ."[4]

[ALAN *goes to the window and silently mouths "Fuuuuck," in imitation of* JOE. *He turns on TV, crouches on sofa, and sings softly, but can't remember the whole song.*]

ALAN Nobody—nobody here—but us chickens, nobody here but us guys don't—don't bother me we got work—to do we got stuff to do and eggs to lay—we're busy—chickens[5]—[*He pretends to be a car, makes sounds, mimes a steering wheel.*] Neeowwwwwwwwwwww. Whaaaaaa. Fhrhuuummmm. Atta girl.

3. That is, Kingston, Ontario.

4. A paraphrase of the Rolling Stones song "Honky Tonk Woman" (1969).

5. A paraphrase of the rhythm-and-blues song "Ain't Nobody Here But Us Chickens" (1946; written by Alex Kramer and Joan Whitney).

1.7

[*Later,* SANDY *brings in bedding to sleep on sofa, turns on lamp, turns off TV, lights cigarette, sits on sofa.*]

SANDY He pukes all over the fuckin bed.

ALAN Oooh shit.

SANDY Funny.

ALAN I'm—I'm sorry Sandy I didn't mean to laugh at ya.

SANDY Can I ask you a personal question?

ALAN Yeah, yeah sure—what?

SANDY Am I gettin ugly lookin?

ALAN What?

SANDY You know, mean lookin, uglier lookin.

ALAN Shit no, jeez—you—you look nice I think ya do! Who, who said that?

SANDY No one. Are ya sure?

ALAN Sure, sure I am you're a good looker I even heard people say ya was.

SANDY Who, who said that?

ALAN Alf. Alf said ya was.

SANDY His folks are loaded.

ALAN I know!

SANDY Did—did Joe ever say anything?

ALAN Joe? What about?

SANDY About me gettin ugly, *arsewipe.*

ALAN No, no Joe never said nothin.

SANDY Are ya sure?

ALAN Yeah. Yeah he never—he never said nothin! No! Why?

SANDY None of your business.

ALAN What's buggin you, you got your pains?

SANDY No, I don't got my *pains* but I'm gonna get em if youse—if youse—well—no offence or nothin but when are youse gettin outa here anyways?

ALAN Soon as I get up the money I—wh—why is—is it buggin you me and Trese sleepin over?

SANDY Yeah. Yeah, it is it's—it's me and Joe gotta have—have some privacy, ya know? Ya know?

ALAN Yeah. Yeah I do I—I'll be out soon what can I say, we'll be out as soon as I got the cash.

SANDY I never heard of screwin your girlfriend on your buddy's floor.

ALAN I'll be out as soon as I got the cash, okay?

SANDY It's just strange you goin with Trese on our floor.

ALAN I know it's strange I know I'm strange I'm strange okay?

SANDY I know you're fuckin strange all right.

ALAN You're smokin too much. You're smokin too much.

SANDY Look who's talkin.

ALAN Well at least I know I'm doin it you don't even know. [*Takes drag off cigarette.*]

SANDY You're fuckin nuts, you know that, nuts.

ALAN I may be nuts but I fuckin know what I'm doin. I know I'm killin myself smokin these I know it so I'm throwin them away okay? I'm throwin them away!

[ALAN *rips up his cigarettes and takes* SANDY'*s cigarette out of her mouth.*]

Fuckin killsticks!

SANDY [*tries to stop him*] Stop it you—fuckin don't you touch me—you fucker you give me back the cash for those right now right now hear?

ALAN No! No Sandy I can't I don't have the money I gotta save it so I can fuck off outa this *hole* I don't have money okay??

SANDY [*starts to back out the door shaking head*] You're nuts Al—

ALAN [*grabs her back into the room*] I am not nuts. I am not nuts you understand? I just decided now I'm gonna quit smoking that's all. I got a flash in my head of my old man tryin to take his breath tryin to find the fuckin air and not gettin it fuckin all hunched over so's he wouldn't drown to death his his his feet all puffed all that shit all that shit comin out of his mouth and they wouldn't even clean it cause they said he couldn't get nothin cause he was gonna die so he had all this shit comin out of his mouth and and I know he didn't like it cause he was clean—all the *time* he was washin—and then when he's dyin they don't give a shit about his goddamn mouth with all the fuck comin out of it and they got a goddamn vacuum cleaner goin—we can't hear nothin and he keeps sort of movin forward movin ahead in his chair like when you're tryin not to crash out at the show so ya keep movin forward? He didn't want to go he didn't want to go at all and he went cause of these. Cause of these goddamn ugly white killsticks these! [*Shows her cigarette, lets her go.*] See? See why ya can't smoke? See?

SANDY [*very moved by* ALAN*'s speech; speaks quietly*] I don't know who the fuck you think you are tearin up the place just cause you seen your old man fuckin croak.

ALAN You don't know what it's like, man, you don't know what it's like till you been there don't you talk.

SANDY Don't tell me what I know, arsewipe, don't you tell me nothin. I seen my mum go, I sat by her bed for three fuckin months and I don't go carryin on like a three-year-old.

ALAN It wasn't the same I'm tellin ya it couldna been the same.

SANDY And I'm a woman and I don't go cryin about it I never cried about it once.

ALAN I'm not cryin about it I never cried about it I'm just tellin ya why not to smoke.

SANDY You're just tellin me shit. Jeez if Joe seen you just now he'd think you were some kind of fag.

ALAN I'm not a fag that's one thing I'm not I'm not a fag.

SANDY Then start acting like a fuckin man.

ALAN I'm not a fag you take that back.

SANDY I'm not takin nothin back for no baby.

ALAN I said take that back you ugly bitch.

[ALAN *grabs her.* SANDY *throws him to the floor.*]

SANDY You're sad, you know that? You don't scare nobody.

ALAN I'm no fag.

SANDY [*goes back to lie on couch*] I seen ten-year-olds fight better than you.

ALAN Why?

SANDY Why what?

ALAN Why don't I scare nobody?

SANDY Cause you're a wimp that's why. Like one of them dogs that starts shakin when ya go to pat it.

ALAN How come?

SANDY How am I supposed to know?

ALAN Don't say nothin to Joe, eh?

SANDY What, about takin a fit?

ALAN About you thinkin I'm like one of them dogs.

SANDY I won't.

ALAN Or Trese.

SANDY Don't worry about it.

ALAN You watched your mum go?

SANDY Big deal.

ALAN Couldna been the same.

SANDY It's all the same.

ALAN Don't you feel nothin?

SANDY Well I'm not a baby like you.

ALAN No.

SANDY Anyways, bein dead ain't no different from livin anyway.

ALAN How do you know?

SANDY I just know. It's just like movin to Brockville or Oshawa[6] or somethin. It ain't that different.

ALAN Oh no. Oh no you're wrong I think you're wrong there.

SANDY No I'm not.

ALAN Yes you are.

SANDY You don't know shit Al.

ALAN I do I do know some things and I know that. I know it's different.

SANDY Get out of my house.

ALAN I'm goin I didn't want to stay anyways it *smells* funny in here.

SANDY Garbage stinks up a place.

ALAN And Sandy.

SANDY *What.*

ALAN No offence or nothin, but you—you—are—you are gettin ugly lookin.

[SANDY *looks at him.*]

See ya.

1.8

[JOE, SANDY, ALAN, THERESA *sitting in bar. Otis Redding's "I've Been Loving You Too Long"*[7] *is playing.*]

JOE That's a shit-hot tune. Too bad he died.

ALAN Did he die?

JOE That's right. In a fuckin motel.

ALAN That's too bad.

JOE Too bad Jimi Hendrix died too.

ALAN Yeah. Oh *yeah.* [*Sings, drums*] "Scuse me while I kiss the sky!"[8]

6. A town and a city, respectively, in southeast Ontario.

7. A hit song (1965) written by Jerry Butler and Otis Redding (1941–1967), an American soul singer; he died in a plane crash.

8. A line from the song "Purple Haze" (1966), by Jimi Hendrix (1942–1970), an American rock song writer and guitarist; he died of a drug overdose.

JOE Did youse know if Hendrix hadda lived he was gonna join up with ELP?

SANDY I seen them, Emerson, Lake and Palmer,[9] down in Montreal.

JOE Ya know what they woulda, been called if Hendrix hadda joined up with them?

ALAN Hendrix, and . . .

JOE [*spells it out*] H.E.L.P. *Help.* And you fuckin would need help hearin those two play together.

ALAN Fuck would ya ever.

JOE Fuckin straight.

ALAN Would ya ever. Fuck, your brain'd die.

JOE H.E.L.P. *Help.*

THERESA I wouldn't need no help.

SANDY You don't got no ear for music.

THERESA I do so.

ALAN She sings and that all the time.

THERESA I seen Jerry uptown he got a job workin for Wilmot's.

SANDY That right eh.

JOE Splinter what a cocksuck.

[*Restless,* JOE *goes to the jukebox, presses button.* JOE *walks to the urinal. After a moment,* ALAN *follows.*]

THERESA He be workin with all that ice cream all the time.

[*Pause.*]

SANDY He could hardly munch out.

THERESA I love ice cream.

SANDY Just munch right out.

1.9

[JOE *and* ALAN. *In urinal of bar.*]

ALAN Those two guys together. Geez! [*Shaking head in disbelief*]

JOE I'm goin buddy I'm takin off.

ALAN Where ya goin?

JOE That's for me to know.

ALAN Oh. Sorry. How—how come gettin sick of Kingston?

JOE Got me a job drivin a Cat.

ALAN Jeez. You make a lot of cash doin that.

JOE Nice work if you can get it.

ALAN Nice work if you can get it.

JOE Make a shitload of money.

ALAN That's hard to do, drivin one of them things, ain't it?

JOE They're mother fuckers.

ALAN Jeez fuck where'd ya learn how to do that anyways?

JOE Hymie Beach.[1]

ALAN WOW, I never knew that. You live down there?

9. An English rock group, popular in the 1970s, consisting of Keith Emerson (b. 1944), Greg Lake (b. 1948), and Carl Palmer (b. 1950).

1. A derogatory reference to Miami Beach, Florida; *hymie* is an offensive term for a Jew.

JOE Sure, shared a motel room with this creep who later turned out to be a queer boy. Started sayin stuff about my dink and that when I got out of the shower. "Is it always that long?"

ALAN Fuckin queers.

JOE I know.

ALAN They just make me—feel like pukin—

JOE I sent that one through the fuckin wall.

ALAN Did ya?

JOE Fuckin right.

ALAN I hate em.

[*Pause.*]

JOE Don't say nothin to Sandy.

ALAN Don't she know?

[JOE *shakes his head.*]

What if something happens—she gets cancer or somethin?

JOE What?

ALAN Them things happen, I've heard of them.

JOE . . . I'll let ya know where I am.

ALAN Hey—I'd like to do that kind of shit.

JOE You should come out. You could get on a site dry-wallin or somethin.

ALAN They just take anybody?

JOE Sure.

ALAN No, no way.

JOE Suit yourself.

ALAN Hey—I forgot to tell ya, Cathy Yachuk jumped offa the Brock Towers![2]

JOE What?

ALAN Jumped right onto her feet Martin was sayin, fucked em up so bad they hadda take a piece of her bum and glue it on to her f-f-feet—so's she could walk on them.

JOE How come she done that?

ALAN She seen a white light in front of her, tellin her!

JOE Fuckin whore . . . yuh, I'm gettin right out of this hole.

ALAN You comin back ever?

JOE How'm I sposda know?

1.10

[ALAN *on way to work, stumbles out door. There is an Indian* MAN *on the street, his wrists bleeding heavily. He is ambling past* ALAN. *He is very drunk.*]

ALAN Hey buddy—hey can I do something for ya?

MAN [*drunk, mumbling*] Please . . .

ALAN Hey, want a smoke?

MAN Yeah. Give me a smoke.

ALAN What are ya lookin for man?

MAN Fuckers took it fuckers.

ALAN Who? Did somebody jump ya? Eh? Did somebody jump ya?

2. A high-rise apartment complex in Scarborough (now a district of Toronto), Ontario.

MAN Yaah. Some guys. Buncha Indians—fuckin Indians.

ALAN Hey man you're an Indian aren't ya?

MAN [*giggling*] Don't burn the fish bones! Don't burn the fish bones!

ALAN That's okay man my fiancee she's Indian. Therese. I like Indians it's okay.

MAN [*weeping like a girl*] Stupid fuckin Indians.

ALAN Hey. Hey don't cry. Is it hurtin bad? Please—just stay here—I'll call an ambulance. Stay. [*Starts to walk to phone, holds up hand.*] Stay.

MAN [*sits up, screams a death scream*] Aaaahh!

[ALAN *comes back, takes off his own shirt, ties it around the* MAN'*s wrist to stop the bleeding. The* MAN *sees a vision.*]

Devil-baby-eyes-devil-baby-eyes. Please. Please. Mercy. Mercy. Hand. Gimme your hand. Hand. Please.

ALAN What? You want me to hold your hand? Okay.

[MAN *takes* ALAN'*s hand, starts rubbing it in a sexual way.* ALAN *doesn't know what to do.*]

MAN [*urgently*] Hey. Hey. Hey.

ALAN What, what is it, buddy?

MAN Hey. [*Makes intercourse motion with fingers.*] Let's tear off a piece. Come on let's tear off a piece. Rip off a piece. Come on.

ALAN Stupid cocksuker!

[ALAN *flings* MAN *away, but* MAN *clings to his leg.*]

Get off me you fucker! Get offffffff me! [*He runs.*]

MAN [*lies on street, giggling*] Pleeeease. [Giggles.]

[ALAN *jumps back to* SANDY'*s living room where* THERESA *is asleep at his feet.*

ALAN [*yells*] Dieeeeeeeeeee!

1.11

[*It is the middle of the night.*]

ALAN Therese?

THERESA Yeah?

ALAN Do you ever start thinkin ugly thoughts before ya go to sleep?

THERESA No, do you?

ALAN Yeah.

THERESA Like what?

ALAN Like fallin down and your teeth hittin the sidewalk.

THERESA Ewwwww.

ALAN Sometimes I even think of someone takin out my spine, like they do with a shrimp.

THERESA You crazy stupid-face, go sleepin and think of nice stuff.

ALAN Like what.

THERESA Donuts and the Wolfe Island ferry and that. Stuff like that.

ALAN Huh. I love ya Trese.

THERESA Madonna.

2.1

ALAN Did you ever start thinkin somethin, and it's like ugly . . . ? And ya can't beat it out of your head? I wouldn't be scared of it if it was sittin in front of me, I'd beat it to shit—nothin wouldn't stop me—but I can't beat it cause it's in my head fuck. It's not like bein crazy, it's just like thinkin one thing over and over and it kinda makes ya sick. Like when I was a kid and I used to have these earaches all the time, you know? And I would keep thinkin it was like a couple of garter snakes with big ugly teeth all yellow, like an *old* guy's teeth and there they were the two of them suckin and bitin on my eardrum with these yellow teeth. Makin noises like a cat eatin cat food. I could even hear the fuckin noises. [*Makes the noise.*] Like that. Just made me wanta puke thinkin that—made the pain worse I'd think of their eyes, too, that made me sick, black eyes lookin sideways all the time while they keep suckin and chewin on my eardrum. Fuck. Do youse know what I mean? No offense or nothin I don't mean no offense I wish youse all good luck in your lives. I was just—like I just wanted to know if any of youse like knew of a medicine or somethin ya might take for this—they gotta have somethin cause the one I'm thinkin of now is even worse it's fuckin bad it's it's somethin Bonnie Cain told me about this nurse she knows goin out to Enterprise out to one of the farms out there these folks were on the dole[3] so she goes up to see if the kids got colds and that, and the wife, all small with her teeth all black takes her into the warsh room and tells her she got somethin wrong down in her woman's part. And Bonnie said this nurse lifted up this woman's skirt and you know what she seen? Like a cauliflower growin out of her thing! A cauliflower! Fuck! And ya know the worst part of it? When ya cut it it bleeds! It grows blood and that! It just happened last summer too, last fuckin summer in July! . . . How'd she go—like how'd she pee? Fuck I'll be doin the dishes where I'm workin down the Tropicana there and it's like pictures burning holes in my brain I try all the time to like put other pictures over top of that, nice things that I really get off on, eh, that I really like like—like lambs in a field, you know, with the black on their faces? Like baby sheep? I always liked them whenever I seen one in a field or someplace I always laughed at them so stupid lookin and cute fuck—I never told the other guys they were there case they burn them or something. Anyways I try puttin pictures of these baby sheep over top of the cauliflower and I'll do it and it's okay for a second then the lamb its eyes'll go all funny like slits lookin sideways just like them snakes and then it'll open its mouth and there'll be them long sharp teeth and a bunch of worms inside and the nice little sheep goes all ugly on me and the cauliflower comes back worse than ever like it ate the sheep or somethin. . . . Maybe if I could just have a car or get back to workin on cars, you know? Or get into Dragmasters,[4] then maybe I'd stop thinkin of these things. I don't know. I'm lookin for somebody who knows, that's why I'm askin youse I don't know. I wish I did. [*Pause*] If it was in front of me I'd beat it to shit, you know?

3. On public assistance or welfare. *Enterprise*: a small town northwest of Kingston.

4. A club devoted to racing motorcycles (especially Harley-Davidsons).

2.2

[ALAN *and* THERESA *at home.* ALAN *comes in after work.* THERESA *is watching television, laughing.*]

ALAN Did ya do it did ya get it done?

THERESA You got somethin on your mouth Al.

ALAN [*wipes*] What was it?

THERESA Look like cream from one of them Joe Louis.[5]

ALAN What I got on my face don't matter, Trese, I asked ya a question.

THERESA What?

ALAN Did ya get what I told ya done?

THERESA Readin writin?

ALAN Yes.

THERESA Shhhh baby sleepin Al.

ALAN Did—let's see. Awwwww hey Danny! He's not sleepin! Hey ya little bugger how ya doin—this is your dad—this is your dad speakin, ya know me? Hey? He does, he knows me. Don't ya Danny. Hey Danny did your angel mummy do what daddy asked her to? Eh? Yes? She did? Oh thank you Danny you are the most neatest cutest little baby boy—what's that on his chin?

THERESA From eatin milk.

ALAN Theresa you don't *eat* milk you drink it.

THERESA I know.

ALAN There. Wipe that ugly milk offa ya. Eh Danny? You are my little bugger and I'm your daddy! Hey! Your mummy gonna show me what she done! Okay mummy, now show me what ya done.

THERESA I lost it.

ALAN How could you lose it?

THERESA I done it, Al, but I lost it.

ALAN *Theresa.* Theresa I'm gonna try not to get mad at ya but ya can't keep doin this to me! Every day you're tellin me ya lost your homework!

THERESA Maybe someone take it.

ALAN Theresa don't you understand I am tryin to improve my family.

THERESA [*coyly*] Al.

ALAN What.

THERESA [*delighted*] You shoulda seen the pooh I done today it was hardly long!

ALAN Theresa, married ladies with babies ain't supposed to say things like that!

THERESA Sorry.

ALAN Danny could hear ya ya know.

THERESA I don't think he hear Al I think he deaf.

ALAN What?

THERESA I shoutin in his ear he don't do nothin.

ALAN Trese ya don't go shoutin in babies' ears!

[THERESA *kisses* ALAN. *He melts.*]

THERESA I love ya Al.

5. A Canadian packaged snack cake.

ALAN You know I love you don't ya you know it—more than anything in this whole world you and Danny boy.

THERESA I know Al. How many dishes you done today?

ALAN Two hundred and twenty-three.

THERESA Jeez.

ALAN Yup. That's ten more than yesterday.

THERESA Jeez.

2.3

[THERESA *has been sleeping over at* SANDY'S *because* SANDY *is scared. Cat scream.*]

SANDY What's that noise. Trese wake up. Hear that?

THERESA What?

SANDY Listen—oh Jesus what is it?

THERESA Maybe it Charlie Manson.[6]

SANDY Oh shut up you watch too much TV.

THERESA Maybe it a pussy cat.

SANDY Hello? Hello? Anybody there? Trese hand me somethin. The lamp.

THERESA Why?

SANDY Shut your mouth and don't ask questions.

THERESA Okay okay here.

SANDY Okay. You get the knife from the top drawer just in case he comes in here.

THERESA Who Charlie Manson.

SANDY Don't say that name Trese. Scream if anybody comes . . .

THERESA I will Sanny.

[SANDY *goes to other room. She screams a primal scream.*]

SANDY [*returns*] It was nothin.

THERESA How come?

SANDY Cause.

THERESA How come my baby never smilin?

SANDY Are ya doin what the workers tell ya?

THERESA Al do it he don't let me do nothin.

SANDY Why?

THERESA He smarter.

SANDY I guess so.

THERESA He love Danny. He wash him with soap and he feed him and he huggin him.

SANDY What's he feedin him.

THERESA Bologna.

SANDY At four months?

THERESA He love it.

SANDY Oh Christ. Don't ya have baby food.

THERESA I don't know.

SANDY What am I gonna do with you?

THERESA I'm glad I stayin here. Al cryin nights.

6. An American cult leader (b. 1934); he led his "family" in committing multiple murders in 1969 and was sentenced to death (later commuted to life in prison) in 1971.

SANDY How come?

THERESA I don't know. I tell him nothin's wrong everything fine but he keep cryin.

SANDY Trese do ya think Joe'll come back?

THERESA He proly comin back next Friday.

SANDY If he do, he can go to hell.

THERESA Bonnie Cain say he never comin back.

SANDY She did?

THERESA She don't know nothin. He comin back.

SANDY I got a letter.

THERESA Ya did?

SANDY I burnt it though, didn't read it.

THERESA Sandy you depress?

SANDY No. I just don't like stayin alone nights it ain't good for ya.

THERESA You could come stayin with us.

SANDY Uh uh. No way. I don't want to see no baby eatin bologna.

THERESA Oh.

SANDY You get in some baby food, Trese, or I'm reporting ya to the social worker.

THERESA Okay.

SANDY Okay?

THERESA I'm gonna.

SANDY You go on to sleep. Now.

THERESA Night Sandy. Don't go havin no bad dreams.

SANDY Night.

[THERESA *falls asleep instantly.* SANDY *stays awake, staring out.*]

2.4

[ALAN *has just been fired from his dishwashing job. He is thrown out of a door, real or imaginary, onto a busy street. He has stolen an egg, which he carries in his hand.*]

ALAN [*holding up egg as pointer*] I was quittin anyways, ya bastards, there's white worms in the hamburg, I *seen* em, there's white worms in the hamburg! [*More quietly, to himself*] I seen em wiggle—[*Turning to audience, in threatening tones*] There wasn't no egg on that pan, sir, there wasn't no egg on that frypan.

[ALAN *stares at the audience for a moment, gets the idea to throw the egg at the door and turns very slowly towards door. Then in a flash, starts to throw the egg but instead, cracks it over his head. He puts the shell in his pocket, sees somebody in the distance, sticks down his hair, leans onto the sewer and discovers the Indian* MAN *with a bottle.* ALAN *grabs it and takes a sip.*]

MAN Man, who is standing between two girly-girls in the whirly-burl.

ALAN Oh why don't ya just shut up . . .

MAN [*pointing at constellation in the sky*] Double devil—stuck together—cha cha cha!

[JOE *appears, wearing a new coat and a hat that says "SUCCESS."* ALAN *rushes to greet him. By the end of the scene, they reach the entrance to* SANDY'S *apartment.*]

ALAN Jesus Joe! Joe! Hey Joe, how're ya doin?

JOE Hey buddy how are you?

ALAN Okay, you know, hangin on. You—when did ya get back?

JOE Just now, buddy, but not for long. I'm moving Sandy out there with me.

ALAN No kidding? It's pretty good out there?

JOE It's a great place, man, lots of work, nice people. Hell of a lot better than this hole, I'm tellin you.

ALAN Yeah? Does Sandy know you're back?

JOE Nope. I'm gonna surprise her. She'll be happy as hell to see me. Then the two of us are gonna take right off.

ALAN That right? . . . Hey me and Theresa got a kid—a little boy, Danny.

JOE Is that right? Danny, huh? So how do you like bein a father?

ALAN It's all right, man. I like it. I make a good father I guess.

JOE Yeah? . . . Well, I better head off.

ALAN Hey—Joe—I got somethin to tell ya.

JOE Is this a long story or a short one?

ALAN Not too long—d'ju hear about Boyd's GTO?[7]

JOE What the one that used to be parked on Johnson below Division?

ALAN Yeah, you know, green with chrome mags and chrome cut-outs.[8]

JOE Yeah. What a fuckin beast. What about it?

ALAN He totalled it.

JOE Hah. Well it was a shitty-lookin car anyways.

ALAN Yeah but fuck it had—it had them high lift cam solid lifters, and, and high compression kit and—

JOE You name it.

ALAN He had it. Yup. Hey—did you know it had four fuckin carbs?[9]

JOE Eat shit.

ALAN No kiddin, four! But you know how come he kept it lookin so shitty?

JOE Beats me.

ALAN So the cops wouldn't notice. They all knew, though eh, they knew what he had. Fuck that thing was fast he used to shoot the main drag doin one-fifty.

JOE Yeah? That's fast.

ALAN Fuckin fast. You know how he totalled it?

JOE No.

ALAN Fuck it was funny. We were gettin polluted up at the Manor, eh, and Alfie decides he's gonna go up to Gan. He was about half pissed I guess. So parently he tries to pass three or four cars same time except one of em happens to be a truck goin left. So I guess he almost makes it but the truck catches him by his back right fender and spins him. Huh. Flipped the car six fuckin times.

JOE Jeez. How is he?

ALAN Alfie? He's okay now but he got stabbed in the heart with the rearview mirror. Had an operation.

7. A Pontiac high-performance V-8 coupe (often considered the first "muscle car"), originally built from 1964 to 1974.

8. Magnesium alloy wheels and chrome ornaments.

9. Although most cars have only one carburetor, it was not unusual for high-performance V-8 engines to have four.

JOE That right?

ALAN Chuck was with him and—

JOE The Scotty?

ALAN Yeah and he just jumped out and never even had a scratch on him. What's that a present for the wife?

JOE Yeah. That Charlie perfume[1] shit.

ALAN Hardly nice. Yeah, that's nice stuff. Women—they like that kinda stuff.

JOE I know. Smells shitty to me.

ALAN Yeah.

JOE Well I gotta move buddy catch you later.

ALAN Hey! Hey!

[*From his pocket,* ALAN *takes an ornamental iron monk with a hard-on. It is wrapped in newspaper.*]

Here.

JOE What's this?

ALAN Just somethin.

JOE Oh yeah. I seen one of these. Well I'm gone.

ALAN See ya. . . . Bye Joe!

2.5

[SANDY *and* JOE *seated at a table.*]

SANDY I got a fucking hole in my gut cause of you.

JOE Who told ya that.

SANDY Doctor Scott.

JOE He don't know what he's talking about.

SANDY Hurtin me all the time I had pain.

JOE Not no more. Not no more ya won't.

SANDY I was takin pills even—prescription!

JOE I told ya babe I feel bad.

SANDY I never done nothin to you *why??*

JOE Ewwww Christ I missed your body there was times I wanted ya so bad I could taste ya. I'd lie in bed there and think about you and what ya looked like stripped naked, think about your nice titties.

SANDY Two old bags.

JOE *Nothin* them are peaches.

SANDY Bullshit. I'm not goin back with ya.

JOE Yes you are.

SANDY Can't push me around no more.

JOE Come on just try it a couple weeks if ya don't like it you can fuck off.

SANDY Won't be nothin different.

JOE It's gotta be different.

SANDY It'll be the same as before, beatin up on me.

JOE No way.

SANDY How the fuck do I know?

JOE Cause it's fuckin true that's how.

1. A perfume made by Revlon, introduced in 1973 and marketed to working women.

SANDY I hate you. I hated you all the time you was gone.

JOE I know.

SANDY I woulda laughed if you hadda died.

JOE I never did.

SANDY I know.

JOE So.

[*Pause.*]

SANDY How come ya want me back.

JOE Don't know. It's dog shit when you're gone.

SANDY Then why'd ya stay so long.

JOE Shit Sandy.

SANDY I was up nights shakin.

JOE Scared of the crackwalker[2] were ya?

SANDY He never hurt nobody.

JOE I missed makin it with ya. Did ya miss it with me?

SANDY I didn't have no one.

JOE That's cause you're mine.

SANDY Is that right.

JOE [*opens her gift*] Here. Smell that.

SANDY Hmmn.

JOE You told me you like that shit.

SANDY It's okay.

JOE Soooo. You been workin for Nikos?

SANDY Some.

JOE What else you been doin?

SANDY Learned how to make a new drink.

JOE What, rum and Coke?

SANDY That's not new.

JOE What, dough brain.

SANDY A Dirty Mother, asshole.

JOE A dirty mother asshole, what's that?

SANDY A Dirty Mother! It's tequila, crème de cacao, and milk. It's hardly good.

JOE Sounds like a chocky milkshake from Mexico.

SANDY Arsewipe. I got a batch made up in the fridge, you want one?

JOE Yeah, okay. I'll try one. Gimme a beer with it though.

SANDY [*goes to the kitchen; from kitchen*] You should give Al a call he's in a bad way.

JOE Yeah I seen him he looked like shit.

SANDY They got a kid, Danny.

JOE He was tellin me.

SANDY It's a medical retard.

JOE Fuuuuck.

SANDY It don't ever move its face—like a doll.

JOE See this thing he give me?

SANDY What is it?

JOE I don't know. An iron monk with a hard-on?

2. An allusion to a resident of Kingston known for his obsessive avoidance of sidewalk cracks (see the introduction to this play).

SANDY Jeez where'd he get that, up at Van's?

JOE I guess so. [SANDY *brings in tray.*] Well fuckin jumpqueen, eh, where'd ya get them glasses?

SANDY My girlfriend Gail she scoffed[3] em offa the 401 Inn.

JOE Fuckin eh.

SANDY They'd cost ya, ya know.

JOE Hmmm. That's, ahhh that's a shit-hot drink.

SANDY Me and Gail drink it all the time when we go out.

JOE It's not bad.

SANDY We always order it only none of em knows how to make it so we have to tell them.

JOE Yeah?

SANDY I can make any kind of drink now she taught me.

JOE What're you doin two women goin drinkin alone together.

SANDY Who said we were alone?

JOE Come here.

SANDY Joe it ain't like that no more.

JOE Who said it ain't.

SANDY I did. Keep your paws offa me.

JOE Jeez you're lookin good.

SANDY I'm doin my eyeliner different.

JOE Yeah?

SANDY Makes my eyes look bigger.

JOE Nice.

SANDY I know.

2.6

[ALAN *and* THERESA*'s place.* THERESA *is playing with the baby. There are tea things set out. The baby does not respond to anything.*]

THERESA Beebeebeebee. . . . How come you not drinkin your tea, beebee? You got a bad cold? Poor beebee. [*Singing*] My little baby is my baby my little Danny is my angel baby I take care of him, and he don't cry or nothin and he ain't never gonna have the crib death neither—[*Speaking*] No way Danny, cause I love ya. Al loves ya too but he a bastard sometime I know he don't talk nice in front of you sometime—don't you go goin into one of them deep sleeps beebee—no—hey! Hey baby Danny! Wake up cause that's how them other babies got the crib death! From sleepin too deep! S'true! You darlin little baby! You mine! That sosha worker's hardly nice, eh? Look! [*Dangles Joe Louis wrapper in front of Danny.*] Look at that baby, you like that? Eh? It's hardly pretty! You come on, come on, gimme a smile beebee; you thinkin too much just like Al that why you so serious all the time. Ohhhhh baby [*She rocks him.*] so soff. Skin hardly soff. Hey! I, look like that madonna lady and she holdin baby Jesus just like I holdin you so you mus look like Jesus! Baby Jesus! Oooohhh Danny you my beebee Jesus and I the Madonna lady and Al maybe he Joseph, he make stuff outa wood. You like a little horsey made outa wood carry you down Princess Street

3. Stole.

when we go to the S & R?[4] I love ya beebee. That a little smile? Oh! Oh baby baby Jesus I love Ya!

ALAN [*comes blasting through the door, starts tearing up the place—medicines, creams, clothes, everything*] No fuckin social worker's gonna fuckin tell me how to run my fuckin life! I don't take this fuckin shit from nobody! Nobody don't tell me what to do and nobody don't tell me how to take care of my baby never! That means you too you fuckin woman—I'm not takin any shit from you neither! There. We're not using any of their cocksucking medicine—they'll try to kill you with it!

THERESA Al! Al stop it!

ALAN They did they killed my dad with all their fuckin medicine! He didn't have no hair and he didn't have no flesh just bones all over and ugly and yellow. No way Therese no way you could stop me I'm throwin it all fuckin out! Out the window, watch! There! It's out the window! Danny! Hey Danny my boy my own son see? You don't have to be takin any of that ugly tastin shit no more!

THERESA But he gonna get numona[5] if he don't take his medicine doctor say so! Nurse say he hafta take it three time a day or he gettin worse! Doctor sees you done that he won't give us no more medicine for Danny! You bassard! You bassard! [*She hits him.*]

ALAN Arsewipe! Don't you know nothin? Don't you know them doctors make money offa sick babies? That's why they like to keep em sick with all them medicines! So they make more fuckin money!

THERESA I don't believe ya. Doctors are nice they wouldn't go makin babies sick!

ALAN Jeez you're a dumbrain sometimes, Therese, they don't give a fuck about our fuckin baby so long as they get their TVs and golf clubs and that. They care dick! That's why they give em this poison so the baby stay sick!

THERESA It not poison, it good for ya, the nurse say so! She don't even have no TV, she tole me. So you're crazy I know that stuff good for Danny he gettin better already!

ALAN That baby ain't gettin no better you stupid woman you know it ain't. It looks strange. It don't look right and that's cause they're givin it all them fuckin medicines! Fuck them! So no more!

THERESA Really would them doctors do that? Really?

ALAN Fuckin right they would. Bastards.

THERESA Bastards. How come? How come they hurtin my little baby?

ALAN Money. Money and bucks. Cocksuckers.

THERESA Well what we gonna do about all his snifflin and that?

ALAN Well I know what to do the social worker even said I did. He said I was a great father and you even heard him. I was a great father.

THERESA S'true Alan.

ALAN Well, it got a cold, right? So if ya got a cold, ya gotta get warm, what else? It's fuckin simple and them doctors always do everything to make it harder! Fuck! So all we do, is ahh—turn on the oven! It's easy! Here. Put it to about five hundred—there—and open the door like that—and—now bring him over—

4. A hardware store on Princess Street in Kingston.

5. Pneumonia.

THERESA Why? What you gonna do?

ALAN Just bring the baby over, Trese. Do what I tell ya!

THERESA Al you not cooking the baby, are ya? [*Weeping with confusion*]

ALAN [*laughs*] Huh. Wait'll I tell Joe that he'll laugh. Cookin the baby. Right. Jesus arsehole it's just like at the farm back in Picton[6] when mum used to sit by the stove with Ronny to warm him up that's all! It's easy! If a guy's got a cold, warm him up!

THERESA Oh. Don't make it too hot though.

ALAN Keep out of it, woman. [*Places crib as close to stove as he can get it.*] There. There ya go Danny! How you doin anyway you little bugger—that's right it's your daddy he come to make you better! Getcha away from all them fuckin doctors! That's right.

THERESA Al he's coughin! Cant we get back some of that cough syrup?

ALAN Listen stupid we're not usin any of that stuff I told ya! Didn't ya hear me or what? Listen. If he's coughin we'll just get that Vicks vapour rub[7] that my old man used to use.

THERESA That stuff smell too much!

ALAN If it's good enough for my old man it's good enough for my baby Therese. He used to put it all over his chest and his cough be gone the next day. Here.

[*He puts a whole jar of Vicks over the baby's body.*]

THERESA Al you puttin too much!

ALAN Don't tell me what to do! Shut up! I know what I'm doin I told ya the social worker said I was a great father! So shut up!

[*He holds the baby up. It is glistening with the stuff.*]

There. You're gonna be just fine now baby.

THERESA Al you sure it ain't too much?

ALAN Shhhhh. He's goin to sleep. Come here. I got somethin for ya.

THERESA You did? What'dja get donuts?

ALAN [*opens perfume—orange, cheap, and it has broken in the package*] Shit. It broke on me. It's okay though here I'll put it in a glass. [*He does so.*] There. [*Hands it to her.*]

THERESA Smell that. That's hardly beautiful Al. Thank you I love perfume.

ALAN I know ya do. Ya like it?

THERESA I love it. It hardly smells nice.

ALAN [*caresses her*] Guess why I brung it?

THERESA Why?

ALAN I love you and you're my angel madonna.

THERESA A-l-l-l-l-l.

ALAN It's true. Come here angel. Hey. Eh hey. You know I love makin love to ya. I love fuckin you and chewin ya out. [*Whispers*] I do.

THERESA I know.

[ALAN *starts to undress her. They start necking on the floor next to the baby.* THERESA *stops suddenly.*]

Oh oh.

6. A small town in southeast Ontario, about 40 miles from Kingston.

7. Vicks VapoRub, a topical analgesic and cough suppressant.

ALAN What?

THERESA We can't do it Al.

ALAN Don't matter if you're bleedin.

THERESA No I can't do it till I get my new IUD in. Or I get pregnant again doctor say so!

ALAN Fuck the goddamn doctors! Goddamn doctors trying to run my life saying I can't make love to my own woman to my own wife fuck em fuck em. I don't care if you get pregnant we're gonna do it when we want and no doctor's gonna tell us nothin.

THERESA No! No Alan, please! Get off me you bastard we're not doin it today no way! No! Get offa me or I callin the cops.

ALAN [*he hits her, sends her across the room*] You stupid dumb cunt Indian bitch face fat fat retarded whore. I don't want ya anyways! [*He collapses on floor, now meeker, almost whiny.*] Alls I wanted was a little lovin anyways there's nothin wrong with that? A man is sposda get lovin from his woman ain't he? That is how come ya get married, ain't it? All I wanted was a little lovin that's all . . . that's alllll.

[*The baby is crying.*]

Look what you done woman you makin the baby cry! You stupid bitch!

[THERESA *gets up to go to the baby.*]

No! No you stay down I'm the only one who can make him stop cryin. Watch. Hey baby. Hey baby here's your daddy. He's a great daddy, huh? Eh?

[*The baby is screaming.*]

THERESA Take it away from the stove Alan! Take it away from the stove!

ALAN [*to* THERESA] Shhhhh. [*To baby*] Come on baby stop that cryin daddy don't like it when you cryin! Shhhh. Now shhhhhh. Gonna buy you a car when you get older—what kind you want, a Monte Carlo?[8] Okay. I'm gonna get you a Monte Carlo. You wait, I'm gonna get work in a station and I'm gonna buy my own and I'm gonna get you anything you want. Okay? Now shhhhhhhh. Stop cryin I'm gonna get you a Monte Carlo didn't ya hear me? Didn't ya? Shhhhhh. Be quiet your mum is tryin to sleep, okay? Shhhhhh! Come on, come on. My little Danny boy baby. Come onnnn. Shhhhhhhh!

[*On the last "shhh" he squeezes the baby's neck till it dies.*]

Shhhhhh.

[*From now on he is very wooden, like a sleepwalker. Looks at* THERESA, *who is watching in wonder.*]

It's okay. It's okay it's not cryin anymore. See. It's quiet now. It's not cryin. I—I—I done it, see? See? I'm a good father he—you know how come he stopped? Cause I told him he was gonna get a Monte Carlo.

THERESA What's that?

ALAN It's a kind of car. It's a place too. One of them south sea islands. Maybe we'll go there, eh? Anyways I gotta go I gotta meet somebody . . . see ya.

[ALAN *goes.* THERESA *looks after him.*]

8. A Chevrolet coupe, designed as a midsize luxury car (introduced in 1970). Monte Carlo is a district of Monaco—a glamorous resort on the French Riviera.

2.7

[JOE *and* SANDY*'s.* ALAN, JOE, *and* SANDY *are watching a Leafs*[9] *hockey game on television.* ALAN *is sitting away from* JOE *and* SANDY, *and he is smoking and loudly eating barbecue chips.* JOE *and* SANDY *are very much involved with each other and the game, and they virtually ignore* ALAN.]

JOE Go go go you fucker—Bunnyfuck what are you fuckin doin—*get him off Nykoluk get him off the ice fuck.*

ALAN Imlach dies.

[JOE *does not respond.*]

IMLACH DIES!!

JOE Oh LAROCQUE—come on Sittler put that mother in come on come on FUCK OFF PERREAULT, do it Daryl hey Martin Martin put it in put it ALL RIGHT! [*Jumps up.*] ALL FUCKING RIGHT!

[ALAN *jumps up with* JOE, *leans into the TV, his face only one inch away from the screen, screams, wagging his head.*]

ALAN ALLLLL FUCKIN RIGHT!

[*Looks back at* JOE *with a little laugh.*]

SANDY [*jocularly*] Take a bird why don't ya?

[ALAN *continues yelling into TV.*]

JOE Hey Al don't scare the TV away he—

[THERESA *appears in the doorway with a bag in her hand. She is reminiscent of Cassandra in* The Trojan Women.[1]]

THERESA YOU TOLE HIM YOU GIVE HIM A MONTE CARLO AND YA DON'T EVEN DRIVE ONE. *YA DON'T EVEN DRIVE ONE.*

[*Her presence is so strong that she immediately captures their attention.*]

I not goin screwin with ya no more Al, no way. No way! You stoppem breathin. I tell him "Breathin baby, breathin" and he not cause *you stoppenim.*

ALAN [*looking away from* THERESA] She's lyin you guys, stop your lyin.

THERESA You goin up the river to Penetang[2] Al, you goin there tomorrow and you never comin out for what you done you not goin back with me I goin with Ron Harton he better than you he not stoppem breathin, he still livin up on Division up at Shuter's? I callin him up and I goin steady with him he better lookin you funny lookin I screwin him.

ALAN YOU lyin fat COW you don't know what you're fuckin talkin about crazy fucking whore-bag—LIAR!

9. The Toronto Maple Leafs. In the following exchange, Joe and Alan refer to several members of the Maple Leafs: Michel "Bunny" Laroque, goalie (1980–81, 1981–83); Mike Nykoluk, head coach (1980–84); George "Punch" Imlach, general manager (1979–81); Darryl Sittler, center (1970–82); and Terry Martin, forward (1979–80, 1980–84). Gilbert Perreault was a standout center for the Buffalo Sabres (1970–87).

1. In Euripides' play *The Trojan Women* (415 B.C.E.), Cassandra enters joyfully, despite her enslavement to Agamemnon, because she prophesies his death (it is her curse that her prophecies are never believed).

2. Penetanguishene, Ontario, location of a maximum-security hospital for the criminally insane.

[ALAN *knocks* THERESA *to the floor, hesitates, grabs two glasses half-full of Dirty Mother, and runs off.* JOE *follows.*]

THERESA You got a donut, Sanny, gimme a donut.

SANDY What have ya got in the bag Trese.

THERESA Ivy, Ivy gimme the bag, I not givin it.

SANDY What's in it, though.

THERESA I takin him up the graveyard.

SANDY What for.

THERESA I puttin him with Grandma down St. Mary's Sanny, see ya later.

SANDY [*stepping in front of* THERESA*'s exit*] Wait a minute what—

THERESA Fuck off Sanny.

SANDY What's inside it.

[THERESA *giggles.* SANDY *touches the bag, flinches.*]

I'm callin the cops.

THERESA Agghhhhh. You fuckin call anyone I takin one of my fits.

SANDY I'm shakin in my shoes, Trese. [*Begins to dial.*]

THERESA [*grabs* SANDY, *rips phone from wall*] You not callin—

SANDY [*gets up, begins to exit, turns around, points at* THERESA] You're not here when I get back and I'm tellin Ron Harton what ya done down the Lido, ya hear me?

[THERESA *stares at* SANDY *in horror.*]

I will, too.

THERESA Okay.

SANDY I mean it. [*Exits.*]

THERESA [*to baby in bag*] It okay, Danny, don't you be cryin now, you with baby Jesus sittin on the cloud and the Virgin lookin like me she with ya she sittin there wearin that long blue dress goin down to her feet hardly pretty, eh? . . . Danny? You still live? You breathin if I breathin into ya? S'okay I'm your mum! [*Tries to breathe into baby.*] Danny? You dead, eh? You not live. You never comin back, eh. [*Puts bag to side, picks up severed phone, does not dial.*] Hi Janus won't be doin readin writin today. Somethin happen. Just somethin. The baby die. The baby die. Up at Sanny's. Okay okay I waitin . . . Ron Harton still livin up at Shuter's? [*Hangs up the phone, and picks it up immediately.*] C'I speak to Ron please? Hi Ron, its Trese. S'okay if we start goin together I love ya. Okay, see ya Tuesday.

[SANDY *enters, breathless, leans against the door. She cannot look at* THERESA.]

SANDY Don't want you tellin no stories to the cops, you hear me? Want you to tell em the truth exactly like it happened, okay?

THERESA Don't like ya no more, Sanny.

SANDY S'too bad.

THERESA You a dirty faggot.

SANDY Right.

THERESA Not my friend no more!

SANDY Okay . . .

THERESA I not talkin to YOU.

[*She turns her back to* SANDY. *She is crying.* SANDY *notices.*]

SANDY You should come out to Calgary[3] sometime—visit.

THERESA No Sanny, I workin!

SANDY What?

THERESA [*tells story joyously with no trace of grief*] Down at Kresge's[4] up with Ivy. Hah! She hardly funny she hardly get pissed off when I eatin icin she yellin "Trese, if you eat one more chocolate icin I tellin Charlie" so I go "You tellin Charlie I tellin on you, Ivy, snitchin butter tarts!" They're hardly good, though, them tarts. Ivy English. . . . Sorry I can't comin with ya out west, Sanny . . . Ivy be piss off.

2.8

[ALAN *and Indian* MAN *on warm air vent.* ALAN *is leaning against wall. He is clanging two glasses together. This produces a spooky sound.*]

ALAN [*pointing to* MAN] You fuckin touch me and I'll break your head.

MAN Hee hee hee Church'n Mondee all dee Mondee hee hee hee!

ALAN I will break your fuckin head in!

MAN [*starts happily, becomes angry as he remembers incident with a paramedic who denied him phenobarbital*] Breakin my fa fa pheno phenobarbidoll[5]—barbidoll—NIGGER, YOU NIGGER!

ALAN Shut it you fuck, just shut it.

[MAN *in panic, rushes toward the audience.*]

MAN SHUT THE WINDOW, SHUT THE WINDOW, SHUT THE WINDOW . . .

[*Laughs.*]

ALAN Nothing's funny, okay, so—just—STOP LAUGHIN. Just pass out will ya, can't ya just pass out? [MAN *vomits on* ALAN*'s sock.*] Ahhhh fuck you goddamn *shit.* SHIT! Eccchh you keep your puke to yourself you old fuck! [*Crouches, rocking.*] I could drive a Monte Carlo I know I could. [*Rubbing glasses together*]

[JOE *enters, looking for* ALAN, *spots him, then crosses to him.*]

JOE Al?

ALAN Joe!

JOE Look—ah—

ALAN She's lyin Joe, I could drive a Monte Carlo.

JOE Al?

ALAN I could *drive one easy.*

JOE You could drive any car on the road. Now why don't you come on—

ALAN I—I—I can't.

JOE Why not?

ALAN I—I—I'm too cold, you know? I'm freezin.

JOE You're okay, ya probably got a flu, ya got a bug, okay?

ALAN No, no, I don't got a bug I'm just cold, he puked on me.

3. A large city (about 1,800 miles from Kingston) in southern Alberta, a western province of Canada.

4. A department store; the chain operated in Canada between 1929 and 1994.

5. That is, phenobarbital, a sedative commonly prescribed to treat sleeping disorders and seizures.

JOE So he puked on ya Martin used to puke on ya all the time. Come on—come on out of that shit pit and I'll get ya a coffee.

ALAN NO. No, I don't want to, I just don't want to, okay?

JOE Suit yourself. [*Turns his back on* ALAN, *starts to leave.*]

ALAN I done what I done and I done it and I fucked it up so I'm payin for it, get it? I'm payin for it.

JOE I don't know what ya done.

ALAN Sorry, Joe.

[JOE *looks at him, can't think of what to say.*]

Joe.

JOE Yeah.

ALAN Could ya do one thing?

JOE What.

ALAN Tell her I could drive a Monte Carlo. Easy.

JOE I will.

ALAN Bye Joe. [*Crouches in previous position, zipping and unzipping his jacket.*] "Nobody here—but us chickens—nobody here but us guys—don't bother me we got work to do and eggs to lay—and guys to see—"

MAN SHHHHHHHHHHHHhhhhhhhh. [*With no motion, just the sound*]

2.9

SANDY I think it's better off dead. I'm not kiddin ya I'm serious. It don't hurt babies to be dead they go straight on up to heaven no hell no purgatory no nothin *no problems.* Cause their souls are still white as snow—they ain't had the time to get them black and ugly. Not like the rest of us—oh no if a baby dies he's just fine he don't even know he's dead. Youse shoulda seen him lyin there in that casket he looked fine. They had them little pajamas on him Trese got up at the S & R, the ones with all them dogs chasin cats all over, all yellow? They hardly looked sweet. And they had a big wreath of flowers around his neck so's to hide the strangle—you know the kind you put on your door at Christmas? Like that. It was kinda nice. We all lined up to take a look at him too—first time he got so much attention in his life—nobody broke up or nothin not even Trese. In fact I was scared she was gonna break up laughin. I'm not kiddin ya it don't bug her at all the kid's gone. Jeez y'know I don't know what goes on inside that girl but it ain't what's goin on inside the rest of us. She only got one thing on her mind now that's goin after Ron Harton. Don't ask me *why,* he looks like the fucking wrath of God. He's a pig too. I don't blame Trese though, I still feel for her even—fuck—this old bag sittin behind me was goin on about how come Trese never went to the hairdressers, you know what her hair is like, eh, right in the middle of the service, so I turn around and I says, "You're gonna hardly think of goin to the hairdressers when your own baby's just been killed by your own husband, ya fuckin old hag." I called her that too, right to her face. Oh yeah I'll stand up for a friend, anytime. I'll tell ya who else I stood up for at that service . . . Al, and he done it. Oh yeah, I still consider him a friend. No matter what he done, nobody can say what happened in that room; so I walk into the funeral parlour, and I take one of them cookies they got lyin out, you know, just tea biscuits, and I turn around and who's standin behind me lookin me right in the eye but that goddamn Bonnie Cain. She comes up close her breath just reekin and she says to me how she seen the whole thing from the window and how he done it with a plastic bag one of them Glad bags and how Trese was lookin on and laughin. That goddamn holy bitch. "You lie" I says to her and I grab her by the tit and I says "You fuckin hound dog one more word outa you and I send you to your goddamn grave. . . ." He never done it with a plastic bag he done it with his hands. I woulda I woulda broke every bone in her fuckin body and she knowed it too. *She* didn't say nothin more. Jeez I'll be glad to get outa this hole I'm tellin ya. I won't miss it neither I won't even dream about it. I won't. I worry about Trese but she'll be okay, you know? She'll—she'll go back down the Lido, start blowin off old queers again for five bucks. It's still open it won't never close. . . . They had them flowers round Danny's neck so's to hide the strangle but I seen it. The flowers never hid it they just made ya look harder, ya know? They just made ya look harder.

2.10

[*Small struggle off stage.* THERESA *runs on stage.*]

THERESA Stupid old bassard don't go foolin with me you don't even know who I look like even. You don't even know who I lookin like.

[illegible]

[illegible]

ATHOL FUGARD

b. 1932

In Athol Fugard's *Sorrows and Rejoicings* (2001), a poet's death gives his friends an occasion to ponder the conflicted role of the white, liberal writer in contemporary South Africa. One character observes that the late author "was meant to be a poet, not a politician," but another disagrees: "And he would have told you that in this country you can't separate the two." Fugard might have been describing himself, for the politics of South Africa—specifically, his opposition to the practice of racial segregation known as apartheid—cannot be separated from his life's work; it has driven his creativity. Though critics may disagree on the political impact and efficacy of Fugard's dramaturgy, especially in a post-apartheid era, all acknowledge Fugard's place as one of the leading dramatists of the late twentieth century: a writer whose work has been produced to acclaim around the world and who has fostered global understanding of his country and its people.

Harold Athol Lannigan Fugard (called "Hally" as a boy) describes himself as being of "mixed descent." His mother, Elizabeth Magdalena Potgieter, was of Afrikaner heritage—that is, she was descended from the Dutch who were the original European settlers in South Africa—while his father, Harold David, was of Anglo-Irish stock. Fugard grew up in a polyglot environment, speaking both Afrikaans (one of the country's official languages, derived from Dutch) and English, and also exposed to African languages (mainly Xhosa). He writes in English but uses a South African idiom richly peppered with words and phrases from other tongues in the region.

In 1935, Fugard's family moved to Port Elizabeth, a coastal city in the Eastern Cape. Fugard's father, a musician who had been crippled in youth and who suffered from chronic pain and alcoholism, became incapable of supporting his family. Fugard's mother, their financial mainstay, first ran the Jubilee Hotel (a small boardinghouse) and then the Saint George's Park Tea Room, both of which feature in *"MASTER HAROLD" . . . AND THE BOYS* (1982). At the Port Elizabeth Technical College, Fugard studied automobile mechanics and experimented with amateur dramatics and creative writing. He won a scholarship to the University of Cape Town; there he pursued studies in social anthropology and philosophy and first encountered the existentialist writings of Albert Camus and Jean-Paul Sartre, both of whom have strongly influenced his dramaturgy. In 1953, he decided to hitchhike with a friend north through Africa, and he left the university without a degree. Arriving penniless in Port Sudan, he signed on as the captain's personal servant aboard a British tramp steamer. Fugard maintains that his experience as the only white crew member, living and working closely with men of other races, liberated him from his boyhood prejudices.

Upon his return to South Africa in 1954, Fugard wrote briefly for the *Port Elizabeth Evening Post* before settling in Cape Town to work in broadcast journalism. There he met Sheila Meiring, an actor (and later a poet and novelist); they married in 1956. Meiring encouraged his latent interest in theater and directed some of his early one-act plays for amateur groups. Watching productions of imported English dramas, Fugard had recognized the need for writers to tell South Africa's own stories on stage. In notebooks (published in 1983), in which he recorded ideas for future writing and thoughts about his experiences, he explained that he believes his "life's work was possibly just to witness as truthfully as I could, the nameless and destitute (desperate) of this one little corner of the world." By "witness," Fugard means not just to observe but also to provide oral or written evidence of what he has observed—sharing with others faithful images of his region and those who live there.

The couple moved to Johannesburg in 1958. Working as a clerk in a local court, where violations of South Africa's "pass law" were tried, Fugard saw the apartheid system in action. During this same period, his encounter with the artists and culture of Sophiatown, a black township on the outskirts of Johannesburg that was "open"—that is, it could be entered by whites without a special permit—proved instrumental in the development of his dramaturgy. Fugard wrote his first full-length plays, *No-Good Friday* (1958) and *Nongogo* (1959), about blacks living in Johannesburg and its environs. The plays were performed by amateur casts and directed by the playwright. Both featured the actor Zakes Mokae, whom Fugard had met in Sophiatown and who soon became one of his most important collaborators and closest friends. Fugard would later cast Mokae as Sam in the world premiere of *"MASTER HAROLD" . . . and the boys.*

Several years later, Fugard co-founded an amateur theater group called the Serpent Players, based in the black township near Port Elizabeth. Fugard directed its productions of Machiavelli (*The Mandrake*), GEORG BÜCHNER, Camus, Sartre, SAMUEL BECKETT, and WOLE SOYINKA, all amid increasing police scrutiny of its activities. When two black actors were arrested and sent to Robben Island, a jail for political dissidents, one of them chose to perform there a version of SOPHOCLES' *Antigone* (ca. 441 B.C.E.)—an incident that inspired a series of original pieces developed by Fugard and the Serpent Players. *Sizwe Bansi Is Dead* (1972) and *The Island* (1973), both co-written with John Kani and Winston Ntshona, soon provided international audiences gripping representations of the inequities and inhumanity of the apartheid regime. Fugard's growing international reputation helped foster strong ties with several theater companies abroad, including London's National Theatre and New Haven's Yale Repertory Theatre. He turned to the latter when, in 1982, he chose for the first time to stage the world premiere of one of his works outside South Africa. According to Fugard, *"MASTER HAROLD" . . . and the boys*—a play based on memories of his childhood relationships with his family and with a black man who worked for them—was too personal for him to produce at home before testing the work's broader appeal elsewhere.

Set on a rainy afternoon in the Saint George's Park Tea Room, *"MASTER HAROLD"* opens on the daily routine of two black employees, Sam and Willie, who await the arrival from school of the white owner's teenage son, Hally. Sam and Willie are practicing for an upcoming ballroom dance competition—an event that Hally later will realize could serve as the topic of an assigned school essay. As Hally settles in, doing his homework and reminiscing with the men about their years of service to his family, he receives a phone call from his mother: his father, a disabled alcoholic, is unexpectedly being discharged from the hospital. Hally's ambivalence about this news and the impact his father's release will have on his family life triggers emotions he cannot control and actions that will haunt him ever after. Simultaneously establishing their own dignity and maturity, as well as their deep affection for the troubled youth, the black men serve as witnesses for Hally, whose struggle to decide what kind of man he will be has just begun.

The 1982 New York production of *"MASTER HAROLD" . . . and the boys* at the Lyceum Theater, featuring Danny Glover (foreground) as Willie, Zakes Mokae as Sam, and Lonny Price as Hally.

Fugard's ability to truthfully represent the motivations and perspectives of each of his characters at critical junctures—no matter how difficult or ugly—is a hallmark of his dramaturgy. He creates great intimacy with small casts, a technique that is often compared to that of Beckett. Most of Fugard's plays feature only two or three characters, reflecting as well a stylistic predilection for the "poor theatre" championed by Jerzy Grotowski, whose theory Fugard explicitly embraces, along with Grotowski's concept of an actor-centered theater devoid of the trappings of the commercial stage. In finally writing this autobiographical drama—this portrait of the artist as a young man (or, as he has said, a young fool)—Fugard explores the universal tropes of conflict between fathers and sons and exposes personal and political realities specific to his native country.

Fugard places *"MASTER HAROLD"* in 1950, just when the South African government enacted the Population Registration Act and the Group Areas Act, legislation that classified and separated its residents by race. Although the autobiographical events chronicled by the play had actually occurred earlier, his decision to advance Hally's age from boyhood to adolescence allows Fugard to set him at the cusp of adulthood—the moment when an individual's identity and ideas about the world solidify—at a time of enormous political change. The play's title—and Fugard has been extremely clear about the importance of his capitalization and punctuation—highlights the ironies inherent in the ages and races of these characters as individuals and as South Africans. Hally has yet to grasp, for example, that Willie's agonizing choice between using his coins to play music to which he can practice ballroom dancing or to pay for bus fare home has everything to do with the laws that forced blacks to live in areas far removed from their places of employment. Fugard wants us to see this pivotal historic moment as having both microcosmic and macrocosmic consequences—we cannot separate the story of these three people from the world we now inhabit.

Fugard weaves together these stories of individuals and a nation in three scenes demarcated by two telephone calls. The play is, structurally, a long one act, running about 100 minutes in performance, with no intermission to relieve its growing tension. Confined to a single set, the action on stage occurs in real time; neither the audience nor the characters can escape the inexorable momentum of the conflict. Fugard also frames the action with separate glimpses of the lives of Sam and Willie; as characters, the men must have the independence and agency necessary to resist both the political context that would deny them those capacities and the narrative traditions that normalize blacks' marginality.

As the three characters discuss "social reformers" and "men of magnitude" from Hally's lessons, such men as Abraham Lincoln and Charles Darwin, the first scene foregrounds historic figures whose achievements resonate with the play's own societal concerns. This conversation later intertwines with Hally's personal memories, especially the story of a kite that Sam once made for him. Sam emerges as an unheralded man of magnitude for the troubled boy—someone who has affected him profoundly, but whose story would not appear in any textbook. Fugard uses this same tale to develop Hally's conflicting allegiance to his two "fathers" and, ultimately, his passage from youthful obliviousness to a more mature recognition of the significance of apartheid. Sam interprets for Hally the current meaning of the whites-only area in which the boy had rested after their kite flying: "You don't *have* to sit up there by yourself. You know what that bench means now, and you can leave it any time you choose. All you've got to do is stand up and walk away from it."

Hally cannot walk away from his conflicted relationship to his biological father, however, and Fugard uses the trope of mobility to connect Hally's personal dilemma with the metaphoric narratives of the kite and the ballroom competition. The miracle of the kite's flight and the beauty of the dancers' movement stand in stark contrast to Hally's perceptions of his father's disability, yet we also see these same stories of physical triumph from the perspectives of Sam and Willie, who are crippled by social forces beyond their control. In the play's closing moments, Fugard may be using ballroom dance to suggest hope not only on a global but also on a local scale. A final glimpse of Sam and Willie dancing a slow foxtrot seems to hint at a better future if South Africa's disenfranchised majority can work together to bring it about. Such an interpretation may account for why the play was initially banned from production in South Africa. While officials pointed to what they called obscene language in the script and not its political content in justifying their decision, they also maintained that they did not know the drama was by Fugard, despite the wide publicity surrounding its premiere and its enthusiastic critical reception in the United States. Because of the work's literary merit, the ban was soon lifted; ironically, this governmental response to *"MASTER HAROLD"* had the immediate effect of drawing international attention to the work and its contemporary relevance.

Fugard no longer considers himself a dissident writer, driven by the necessity to give voice to a silenced majority. Yet he feels a continuing challenge to "witness" his country and its people as they confront new questions about their identity and their past. He holds fast to the idea that the theater can be a force for change and maintains his commitment "to entertain in order to make a difference" worldwide.

J.E.G.

"MASTER HAROLD" . . . and the boys

CHARACTERS

HALLY
SAM
WILLIE

The St. George's Park Tea Room on a wet and windy Port Elizabeth[1] afternoon.

Tables and chairs have been cleared and are stacked on one side except for one which stands apart with a single chair. On this table a knife, fork, spoon, and side plate in anticipation of a simple meal, together with a pile of comic books.

Other elements: a serving counter with a few stale cakes under glass and a not very impressive display of sweets, cigarettes and cool drinks, etc.; a few cardboard advertising handouts—Cadbury's Chocolate, Coca-Cola—and a blackboard on which an untrained hand has chalked up the prices of Tea, Coffee, Scones, Milkshakes—all flavors—and Cool Drinks; a few sad ferns in pots; a telephone; an old-style jukebox.

There is an entrance on one side and an exit into a kitchen on the other.

Leaning on the solitary table, his head cupped in one hand as he pages through one of the comic books, is SAM. *A black man in his mid-forties. He wears the white coat of a waiter. Behind him on his knees, mopping down the floor with a bucket of water and a rag, is* WILLIE. *Also black and about the same age as* SAM. *He has his sleeves and trousers rolled up.*

The year: 1950.

WILLIE [*singing as he works*]
"She was scandalizin' my name,[2]
She took my money
She called me honey
But she was scandalizin' my name.
Called it love but was playin' a game . . ."

[*He gets up and moves the bucket. Stands thinking for a moment, then, raising his arms to hold an imaginary partner, he launches into an intricate ballroom dance step. Although a mildly comic figure, he reveals a reasonable degree of accomplishment.*]

Hey, Sam.

[SAM, *absorbed in the comic book, does not respond.*]

Hey, Boet[3] Sam!

[SAM *looks up.*]

I'm getting it. The quickstep. Look now and tell me. [*He repeats the step.*] Well?

1. A city on the southeastern coast of South Africa; it has been Fugard's primary residence since 1935 and is the setting for a number of his plays.
2. "Scandalizing My Name," recorded by Thomas Wayne (1959); a rhythm-and-blues version of "Scandalize My Name," a black gospel song recorded by Paul Robeson in the 1930s.
3. Brother (Afrikaans), a term here used in the sense of friendship.

SAM [*encouragingly*] Show me again.

WILLIE Okay, count for me.

SAM Ready?

WILLIE Ready.

SAM Five, six, seven, eight . . . [WILLIE *starts to dance.*] A-n-d one two three four . . . and one two three four. . . . [*Ad libbing as* WILLIE *dances*] Your shoulders, Willie . . . your shoulders! Don't look down! Look happy, Willie! Relax, Willie!

WILLIE [*desperate but still dancing*] I am relax.

SAM No, you're not.

WILLIE [*he falters*] Ag no man, Sam! Mustn't talk. You make me make mistakes.

SAM But you're too stiff.

WILLIE Yesterday I'm not straight . . . today I'm too stiff!

SAM Well, you are. You asked me and I'm telling you.

WILLIE Where?

SAM Everywhere. Try to glide through it.

WILLIE Glide?

SAM Ja,[4] make it smooth. And give it more style. It must look like you're enjoying yourself.

WILLIE [*emphatically*] I wasn't.

SAM Exactly.

WILLIE How can I enjoy myself? Not straight, too stiff and now it's also glide, give it more style, make it smooth. . . . Haai! Is hard to remember all those things, Boet Sam.

SAM That's your trouble. You're trying too hard.

WILLIE I try hard because it *is* hard.

SAM But don't let me see it. The secret is to make it look easy. Ballroom must look happy, Willie, not like hard work. It must . . . Ja! . . . it must look like romance.

WILLIE Now another one! What's romance?

SAM Love story with happy ending. A handsome man in tails, and in his arms, smiling at him, a beautiful lady in evening dress!

WILLIE Fred Astaire, Ginger Rogers.[5]

SAM You got it. Tapdance or ballroom, it's the same. Romance. In two weeks' time when the judges look at you and Hilda, they must see a man and a woman who are dancing their way to a happy ending. What I saw was you holding her like you were frightened she was going to run away.

WILLIE Ja! Because that is what she wants to do! I got no romance left for Hilda anymore, Boet Sam.

SAM Then pretend. When you put your arms around Hilda, imagine she is Ginger Rogers.

WILLIE With no teeth? You try.

SAM Well, just remember, there's only two weeks left.

WILLIE I know, I know! [*To the jukebox*] I do it better with music. You got sixpence for Sarah Vaughan?[6]

4. Yes (Afrikaans).

5. Famous dance partners in movie musicals; the American actors Astaire (1899–1987) and Rogers (1911–1995) starred together in ten films (1933–39, 1949).

6. An American jazz vocalist and pianist (1924–1990).

SAM That's a slow foxtrot. You're practicing the quickstep.

WILLIE I'll practice slow foxtrot.

SAM [*shaking his head*] It's your turn to put money in the jukebox.

WILLIE I only got bus fare to go home. [*He returns disconsolately to his work.*] Love story and happy ending! She's doing it all right, Boet Sam, but is not me she's giving happy endings. Fuckin' whore! Three nights now she doesn't come practice. I wind up gramophone, I get record ready and I sit and wait. What happens? Nothing. Ten o'clock I start dancing with my pillow. You try and practice romance by yourself, Boet Sam. Struesgod,[7] she doesn't come tonight I take back my dress and ballroom shoes and I find me new partner. Size twenty-six. Shoes size seven. And now she's also making trouble for me with the baby again. Reports me to Child Wellfed, that I'm not giving her money. She lies! Every week I am giving her money for milk. And how do I know is my baby? Only his hair looks like me. She's fucking around all the time I turn my back. Hilda Samuels is a bitch! [*Pause*] Hey, Sam!

SAM Ja.

WILLIE You listening?

SAM Ja.

WILLIE So what you say?

SAM About Hilda?

WILLIE Ja.

SAM When did you last give her a hiding?

WILLIE [*reluctantly*] Sunday night.

SAM And today is Thursday.

WILLIE [*he knows what's coming*] Okay.

SAM Hiding on Sunday night, then Monday, Tuesday and Wednesday she doesn't come to practice . . . and you are asking me why?

WILLIE I said okay, Boet Sam!

SAM You hit her too much. One day she's going to leave you for good.

WILLIE So? She makes me the hell-in[8] too much.

SAM [*emphasizing his point*] *Too* much and *too* hard. You had the same trouble with Eunice.

WILLIE Because she also make the hell-in, Boet Sam. She never got the steps right. Even the waltz.

SAM Beating her up every time she makes a mistake in the waltz? [*Shaking his head*] No, Willie! That takes the pleasure out of ballroom dancing.

WILLIE Hilda is not too bad with the waltz, Boet Sam. Is the quickstep where the trouble starts.

SAM [*teasing him gently*] How's your pillow with the quickstep?

WILLIE [*ignoring the tease*] Good! And why? Because it got no legs. That's her trouble. She can't move them quick enough, Boet Sam. I start the record and before halfway Count Basie[9] is already winning. Only time we catch up with him is when gramophone runs down.

[SAM *laughs.*]

Haaikona,[1] Boet Sam, is not funny.

7. As true as God (Afrikaans); that is, "I swear."
8. That is, she drives me crazy (South African slang).
9. William "Count" Basie (1904–1984), American pianist, arranger, and composer who was one of the most influential bandleaders of the 20th century.
1. An exclamation of strong negation (Xhosa).

SAM [*snapping his fingers*] I got it! Give her a handicap.

WILLIE What's that?

SAM Give her a ten-second start and then let Count Basie go. Then I put my money on her. Hot favorite in the Ballroom Stakes: Hilda Samuels ridden by Willie Malopo.

WILLIE [*turning away*] I'm not talking to you no more.

SAM [*relenting*] Sorry, Willie . . .

WILLIE It's finish between us.

SAM Okay, okay . . . I'll stop.

WILLIE You can also fuck off.

SAM Willie, listen! I want to help you!

WILLIE No more jokes?

SAM I promise.

WILLIE Okay. Help me.

SAM [*his turn to hold an imaginary partner*] Look and learn. Feet together. Back straight. Body relaxed. Right hand placed gently in the small of her back and wait for the music. Don't start worrying about making mistakes or the judges or the other competitors. It's just you, Hilda, and the music, and you're going to have a good time. What Count Basie do you play?

WILLIE "You the cream in my coffee, you the salt in my stew."[2]

SAM Right. Give it to me in strict tempo.[3]

WILLIE Ready?

SAM Ready.

WILLIE A-n-d . . . [*Singing*]

"You the cream in my coffee.
You the salt in my stew.
You will always be my necessity.
I'd be lost without you. . . ." (*etc.*)

[SAM *launches into the quickstep. He is obviously a much more accomplished dancer than* WILLIE. HALLY *enters. A seventeen-year-old white boy. Wet raincoat and school case. He stops and watches* SAM. *The demonstration comes to an end with a flourish. Applause from* HALLY *and* WILLIE.]

HALLY Bravo! No question about it. First place goes to Mr. Sam Semela.

WILLIE [*in total agreement*] You was gliding with style, Boet Sam.

HALLY [*cheerfully*] How's it, chaps?

SAM Okay, Hally.

WILLIE [*springing to attention like a soldier and saluting*] At your service, Master[4] Harold!

HALLY Not long to the big event, hey!

SAM Two weeks.

HALLY You nervous?

SAM No.

HALLY Think you stand a chance?

SAM Let's just say I'm ready to go out there and dance.

HALLY It looked like it. What about you, Willie?

[WILLIE *groans.*]

2. From "You're the Cream in My Coffee" (1928; music by Ray Henderson, lyrics by Buddy G. DeSylva and Lew Brown).

3. That is, with an unvarying beat, so that it can be danced to more easily.

4. In Britain, the traditional courtesy title of a young gentleman not considered old enough to be called "Mister."

What's the matter?

SAM He's got leg trouble.

HALLY [*innocently*] Oh, sorry to hear that, Willie.

WILLIE Boet Sam! You promised. [WILLIE *returns to his work.*]

[HALLY *deposits his school case and takes off his raincoat. His clothes are a little neglected and untidy: black blazer with school badge, gray flannel trousers in need of an ironing, khaki shirt and tie, black shoes.* SAM *has fetched a towel for* HALLY *to dry his hair.*]

HALLY God, what a lousy bloody day. It's coming down cats and dogs out there. Bad for business, chaps . . . [*Conspiratorial whisper*] . . . but it also means we're in for a nice quiet afternoon.

SAM You can speak loud. Your Mom's not here.

HALLY Out shopping?

SAM No. The hospital.

HALLY But it's Thursday. There's no visiting on Thursday afternoons. Is my Dad okay?

SAM Sounds like it. In fact, I think he's going home.

HALLY [*stopped short by* SAM*'s remark*] What do you mean?

SAM The hospital phoned.

HALLY To say what?

SAM I don't know. I just heard your Mom talking.

HALLY So what makes you say he's going home?

SAM It sounded as if they were telling her to come and fetch him.

[HALLY *thinks about what* SAM *has said for a few seconds.*]

HALLY When did she leave?

SAM About an hour ago. She said she would phone you. Want to eat?

[HALLY *doesn't respond.*]

Hally, want your lunch?

HALLY I suppose so. [*His mood has changed.*] What's on the menu? . . . as if I don't know.

SAM Soup, followed by meat pie and gravy.

HALLY Today's?

SAM No.

HALLY And the soup?

SAM Nourishing pea soup.

HALLY Just the soup. [*The pile of comic books on the table*] And these?

SAM For your Dad. Mr. Kempston brought them.

HALLY You haven't been reading them, have you?

SAM Just looking.

HALLY [*examining the comics*] *Jungle Jim* . . . *Batman and Robin* . . . *Tarzan* . . . God, what rubbish! Mental pollution. Take them away.

[SAM *exits waltzing into the kitchen.* HALLY *turns to* WILLIE.]

HALLY Did you hear my Mom talking on the telephone, Willie?

WILLIE No, Master Hally. I was at the back.

HALLY And she didn't say anything to you before she left?

WILLIE She said I must clean the floors.

HALLY I mean about my Dad.

WILLIE She didn't say nothing to me about him, Master Hally.

HALLY [*with conviction*] No! It can't be. They said he needed at least another three weeks of treatment. Sam's definitely made a mistake. [*Rummages through his school case, finds a book and settles down at the table to read.*] So, Willie!

WILLIE Yes, Master Hally! Schooling okay today?

HALLY Yes, okay. . . . [*He thinks about it.*] . . . No, not really. Ag, what's the difference? I don't care. And Sam says you've got problems.

WILLIE Big problems.

HALLY Which leg is sore?

[WILLIE *groans.*]

Both legs.

WILLIE There is nothing wrong with my legs. Sam is just making jokes.

HALLY So then you *will* be in the competition.

WILLIE Only if I can find me a partner.

HALLY But what about Hilda?

SAM [*returning with a bowl of soup*] She's the one who's got trouble with her legs.

HALLY What sort of trouble, Willie?

SAM From the way he describes it, I think the lady has gone a bit lame.

HALLY Good God! Have you taken her to see a doctor?

SAM I think a vet would be better.

HALLY What do you mean?

SAM What do you call it again when a racehorse goes very fast?

HALLY Gallop?

SAM That's it!

WILLIE Boet Sam!

HALLY "A gallop down the homestretch to the winning post." But what's that got to do with Hilda?

SAM Count Basie always gets there first.

[WILLIE *lets fly with his slop rag. It misses* SAM *and hits* HALLY.]

HALLY [*furious*] For Christ's sake, Willie! What the hell do you think you're doing!

WILLIE Sorry, Master Hally, but it's him. . . .

HALLY Act your bloody age! [*Hurls the rag back at* WILLIE.] Cut out the nonsense now and get on with your work. And you too, Sam. Stop fooling around.

[SAM *moves away.*]

No. Hang on. I haven't finished! Tell me exactly what my Mom said.

SAM I have. "When Hally comes, tell him I've gone to the hospital and I'll phone him."

HALLY She didn't say anything about taking my Dad home?

SAM No. It's just that when she was talking on the phone . . .

HALLY [*interrupting him*] No, Sam. They can't be discharging him. She would have said so if they were. In any case, we saw him last night and he wasn't in good shape at all. Staff nurse even said there was talk about taking more X-rays. And now suddenly today he's better? If anything, it sounds more like a bad turn to me . . . which I sincerely hope it isn't. Hang on . . . how long ago did you say she left?

SAM Just before two . . . [*His wristwatch*] . . . hour and a half.

HALLY I know how to settle it. [*Behind the counter to the telephone. Talking as he dials*] Let's give her ten minutes to get to the hospital, ten minutes to load him up, another ten, at the most, to get home, and another ten to get him inside. Forty minutes. They should have been home for at least half an hour already. [*Pause—he waits with the receiver to his ear.*] No reply, chaps. And you know why? Because she's at his bedside in hospital helping him pull through a bad turn. You definitely heard wrong.

SAM Okay.

[*As far as* HALLY *is concerned, the matter is settled. He returns to his table, sits down and divides his attention between the book and his soup.* SAM *is at his school case and picks up a textbook.*]

Modern Graded Mathematics for Standards[5] *Nine and Ten.* [*Opens it at random and laughs at something he sees.*] Who is this supposed to be?

HALLY Old fart-face Prentice.

SAM Teacher?

HALLY Thinks he is. And believe me, that is not a bad likeness.

SAM Has he seen it?

HALLY Yes.

SAM What did he say?

HALLY Tried to be clever, as usual. Said I was no Leonardo da Vinci[6] and that bad art had to be punished. So, six of the best, and his are bloody good.

SAM On your bum?

HALLY Where else? The days when I got them on my hands are gone forever, Sam.

SAM With your trousers down!

HALLY No. He's not quite that barbaric.

SAM That's the way they do it in jail.

HALLY [*flicker of morbid interest*] Really?

SAM Ja. When the magistrate sentences you to "strokes with a light cane."

HALLY Go on.

SAM They make you lie down on a bench. One policeman pulls down your trousers and holds your ankles, another one pulls your shirt over your head and holds your arms . . .

HALLY Thank you! That's enough.

SAM . . . and the one that gives you the strokes talks to you gently and for a long time between each one. [*He laughs.*]

HALLY I've heard enough, Sam! Jesus! It's a bloody awful world when you come to think of it. People can be real bastards.

SAM That's the way it is, Hally.

HALLY It doesn't *have* to be that way. There is something called progress, you know. We don't exactly burn people at the stake anymore.

SAM Like Joan of Arc.[7]

HALLY Correct. If she was captured today, she'd be given a fair trial.

SAM And then the death sentence.

HALLY [*a world-weary sigh*] I know, I know! I oscillate between hope and despair for this world as well, Sam. But things will change, you wait and see. One day somebody is going to get up and give history a kick up the backside and get it going again.

5. That is, grades.
6. Italian artist (1452–1519), famous for his precisely rendered drawings as well as his paintings.
7. The French saint and national heroine (ca. 1412–1431); she successfully led French troops against the English, but was captured and burned at the stake after being charged with heresy and witchcraft.

SAM What?

HALLY Where we come from and what it all means.

SAM And that's a benefit to mankind? Anyway, I still don't believe it.

HALLY God, you're impossible. I showed it to you in black and white.

SAM Doesn't mean I got to believe it.

HALLY It's the likes of you that kept the Inquisition[3] in business. It's called bigotry. Anyway, that's my man of magnitude. Charles Darwin! Who's yours?

SAM [*without hesitation*] Abraham Lincoln.[4]

HALLY I might have guessed as much. Don't get sentimental, Sam. You've never been a slave, you know. And anyway we freed your ancestors here in South Africa long before the Americans. But if you want to thank somebody on their behalf, do it to Mr. William Wilberforce.[5] Come on. Try again. I want a real genius. [*Now enjoying himself, and so is* SAM. HALLY *goes behind the counter and helps himself to a chocolate.*]

SAM William Shakespeare.

HALLY [*no enthusiasm*] Oh. So you're also one of them,[6] are you? You're basing that opinion on only one play, you know. You've only read my *Julius Caesar* and even I don't understand half of what they're talking about. They should do what they did with the old Bible: bring the language up to date.

SAM That's all you've got. It's also the only one *you've* read.

HALLY I know. I admit it. That's why I suggest we reserve our judgment until we've checked up on a few others. I've got a feeling, though, that by the end of this year one is going to be enough for me, and I can give you the names of twenty-nine other chaps in the Standard Nine class of the Port Elizabeth Technical College who feel the same. But if you want him, you can have him. My turn now. [*Pacing*] This is a damned good exercise, you know! It started off looking like a simple question and here it's got us really probing into the intellectual heritage of our civilization.

SAM So who is it going to be?

HALLY My next man . . . and he gets the title on two scores: social reform and literary genius . . . is Leo Nikolaevich Tolstoy.[7]

SAM That Russian.

HALLY Correct. Remember the picture of him I showed you?

SAM With the long beard.

HALLY [*trying to look like Tolstoy*] And those burning, visionary eyes. My God, the face of a social prophet if ever I saw one! And remember my words when I showed it to you? Here's a *man*, Sam!

SAM Those were words, Hally.

3. A tribunal of the Roman Catholic Church, established in 1233 to investigate heresy; over the centuries, a number of philosophers and scientists (including Galileo) were tried by its officers.

4. The sixteenth president of the United States (1809–1865; president, 1861–65), known as the "Great Emancipator" because of his proclamation freeing the slaves who were living in states that were in rebellion against the federal government.

5. British politician and opponent of slavery (1759–1833); days before his death, Parliament passed an act outlawing slavery throughout most of the British Empire, including the Cape Colony (later to become part of South Africa).

6. That is, one of the many who regard Shakespeare (1564–1616) as the greatest dramatist of all time. *Julius Caesar* was first performed in 1599.

7. Russian novelist and philosopher (1828–1910), born into the nobility (he inherited an estate that included hundreds of serfs); one of his masterpieces is *War and Peace* (1863–69).

HALLY Not many intellectuals are prepared to shovel manure with the peasants and then go home and write a "little book" called *War and Peace.* Incidentally, Sam, he was somebody else who, to quote, ". . . did not distinguish himself scholastically."

SAM Meaning?

HALLY He was also no good at school.

SAM Like you and Winston Churchill.

HALLY [*mirthlessly*] Ha, ha, ha.

SAM [*simultaneously*] Ha, ha, ha.

HALLY Don't get clever, Sam. That man freed his serfs of his own free will.

SAM No argument. He was a somebody, all right. I accept him.

HALLY I'm sure Count Tolstoy will be very pleased to hear that. Your turn. Shoot. [*Another chocolate from behind the counter*] I'm waiting, Sam.

SAM I've got him.

HALLY Good. Submit your candidate for examination.

SAM Jesus.

HALLY [*stopped dead in his tracks*] Who?

SAM Jesus Christ.

HALLY Oh, come on, Sam!

SAM The Messiah.

HALLY Ja, but still . . . No, Sam. Don't let's get started on religion. We'll just spend the whole afternoon arguing again. Suppose I turn around and say Mohammed?

SAM All right.

HALLY You can't have them both on the same list!

SAM Why not? You like Mohammed, I like Jesus.

HALLY I *don't* like Mohammed. I never have. I was merely being hypothetical. As far as I'm concerned, the Koran is as bad as the Bible. No. Religion is out! I'm not going to waste my time again arguing with you about the existence of God. You know perfectly well I'm an atheist . . . and I've got homework to do.

SAM Okay, I take him back.

HALLY You've got time for one more name.

SAM [*after thought*] I've got one I know we'll agree on. A simple straightforward great Man of Magnitude . . . and no arguments. And *he* really *did* benefit all mankind.

HALLY I wonder. After your last contribution I'm beginning to doubt whether anything in the way of an intellectual agreement is possible between the two of us. Who is he?

SAM Guess.

HALLY Socrates? Alexandre Dumas? Karl Marx? Dostoevsky? Nietzsche?[8]

[SAM *shakes his head after each name.*]

Give me a clue.

SAM The letter P is important . . .

HALLY Plato!

SAM . . . and his name begins with an F.

8. A mixture of philosophers—the Greek Socrates (469–399 B.C.E.), who is featured in the dialogues of Plato (427–347 B.C.E.), and the Germans Karl Marx (1818–1883) and Friedrich Nietzsche (1844–1900)—and novelists: the French Dumas père (1802–1870) and fils (1824–1895), and the Russian Fyodor Dostoyevsky (1821–1881).

HALLY I've got it. Freud[9] and Psychology.

SAM No. I didn't understand him.

HALLY That makes two of us.

SAM Think of mouldy apricot jam.

HALLY [*after a delighted laugh*] Penicillin and Sir Alexander Fleming![1] And the title of the book: *The Microbe Hunters.* [*Delighted.*] Splendid, Sam! Splendid. For once we are in total agreement. The major breakthrough in medical science in the Twentieth Century. If it wasn't for him, we might have lost the Second World War. It's deeply gratifying, Sam, to know that I haven't been wasting my time in talking to you. [*Strutting around proudly*] Tolstoy may have educated his peasants, but I've educated you.

SAM Standard Four to Standard Nine.

HALLY Have we been at it as long as that?

SAM Yep. And my first lesson was geography.

HALLY [*intrigued*] Really? I don't remember.

SAM My room there at the back of the old Jubilee Boarding House. I had just started working for your Mom. Little boy in short trousers walks in one afternoon and asks me seriously: "Sam, do you want to see South Africa?" Hey man! Sure I wanted to see South Africa!

HALLY Was that me?

SAM . . . So the next thing I'm looking at a map you had just done for homework. It was your first one and you were very proud of yourself.

HALLY Go on.

SAM Then came my first lesson. "Repeat after me, Sam: Gold in the Transvaal, mealies in the Free State, sugar in Natal and grapes in the Cape."[2] I still know it!

HALLY Well, I'll be buggered.[3] So that's how it all started.

SAM And your next map was one with all the rivers and the mountains they came from. The Orange, the Vaal, the Limpopo, the Zambezi . . .

HALLY You've got a phenomenal memory!

SAM You should be grateful. That is why you started passing your exams. You tried to be better than me.

[*They laugh together.* WILLIE *is attracted by the laughter and joins them.*]

HALLY The old Jubilee Boarding House. Sixteen rooms with board and lodging, rent in advance and one week's notice. I haven't thought about it for donkey's years[4] . . . and I don't think that's an accident. God, was I glad when we sold it and moved out. Those years are not remembered as the happiest ones of an unhappy childhood.

WILLIE [*knocking on the table and trying to imitate a woman's voice*] "Hally, are you there?"

HALLY Who's that supposed to be?

WILLIE "What you doing in there, Hally? Come out at once!"

HALLY [*to* SAM] What's he talking about?

9. Sigmund Freud (1856–1939), the Austrian founder of psychoanalysis.

1. A Scottish bacteriologist (1881–1955); in 1928, he discovered penicillin, the first effective antibiotic. Fleming is one of the scientists featured in Paul de Kruif's *Microbe Hunters* (1926).

2. In 1950, the four provinces of South Africa were the Transvaal, the Orange Free State, Natal, and the Cape Province. *Mealies* (U.S. corn): maize, the principal staple of southern Africa.

3. That is, I'll be damned (slang).

4. That is, a very long time (British slang).

SAM Don't you remember?

WILLIE "Sam, Willie . . . is he in there with you boys?"

SAM Hiding away in our room when your mother was looking for you.

HALLY [*another good laugh*] Of course! I used to crawl and hide under your bed! But finish the story, Willie. Then what used to happen? You chaps would give the game away by telling her I was in there with you. So much for friendship.

SAM We couldn't lie to her. She knew.

HALLY Which meant I got another rowing[5] for hanging around the "servants' quarters." I think I spent more time in there with you chaps than anywhere else in that dump. And do you blame me? Nothing but bloody misery wherever you went. Somebody was always complaining about the food, or my mother was having a fight with Micky Nash because she'd caught her with a petty officer in her room. Maud Meiring was another one. Remember those two? They were prostitutes, you know. Soldiers and sailors from the troopships. Bottom fell out of the business when the war ended. God, the flotsam and jetsam that life washed up on our shores! No joking, if it wasn't for your room, I would have been the first certified[6] ten-year-old in medical history. Ja, the memories are coming back now. Walking home from school and thinking: "What can I do this afternoon?" Try out a few ideas, but sooner or later I'd end up in there with you fellows. I bet you I could still find my way to your room with my eyes closed. [*He does exactly that.*] Down the corridor . . . telephone on the right, which my Mom keeps locked because somebody is using it on the sly and not paying . . . past the kitchen and unappetizing cooking smells . . . around the corner into the backyard, hold my breath again because there are more smells coming when I pass your lavatory, then into that little passageway, first door on the right and into your room. How's that?

SAM Good. But, as usual, you forgot to knock.

HALLY Like that time I barged in and caught you and Cynthia . . . at it. Remember? God, was I embarrassed! I didn't know what was going on at first.

SAM Ja, that taught you a lesson.

HALLY And about a lot more than knocking on doors, I'll have you know, and I don't mean geography either. Hell, Sam, couldn't you have waited until it was dark?

SAM No.

HALLY Was it that urgent?

SAM Yes, and if you don't believe me, wait until your time comes.

HALLY No, thank you. I am not interested in girls. [*Back to his memories . . . Using a few chairs he re-creates the room as he lists the items.*] A gray little room with a cold cement floor. Your bed against that wall . . . and I now know why the mattress sags so much! . . . Willie's bed . . . it's propped up on bricks because one leg is broken . . . that wobbly little table with the washbasin and jug of water . . . Yes! . . . stuck to the wall above it are some pin-up pictures from magazines. Joe Louis[7] . . .

5. Scolding.
6. Officially declared insane.
7. A black American boxer (1914–1981); he was world heavyweight champion when he knocked out the German champion, Max Schmeling (1905–2005), in the first round of their celebrated 1938 rematch (Schmeling had knocked him out in a 1936 fight).

WILLIE Brown Bomber. World Title. [*Boxing pose*] Three rounds and knockout.

HALLY Against who?

SAM Max Schmeling.

HALLY Correct. I can also remember Fred Astaire and Ginger Rogers, and Rita Hayworth[8] in a bathing costume which always made me hot and bothered when I looked at it. Under Willie's bed is an old suitcase with all his clothes in a mess, which is why I never hide there. Your things are neat and tidy in a trunk next to your bed, and on it there is a picture of you and Cynthia in your ballroom clothes, your first silver cup for third place in a competition and an old radio which doesn't work anymore. Have I left out anything?

SAM No.

HALLY Right, so much for the stage directions. Now the characters. [SAM *and* WILLIE *move to their appropriate positions in the bedroom.*] Willie is in bed, under his blankets with his clothes on, complaining nonstop about something, but we can't make out a word of what he's saying because he's got his head under the blankets as well. You're on your bed trimming your toenails with a knife—not a very edifying sight—and as for me . . . What am I doing?

SAM You're sitting on the floor giving Willie a lecture about being a good loser while you get the checkerboard and pieces ready for a game. Then you go to Willie's bed, pull off the blankets and make him play with you first because you know you're going to win, and that gives you the second game with me.

HALLY And you certainly were a bad loser, Willie!

WILLIE Haai!

HALLY Wasn't he, Sam? And so slow! A game with you almost took the whole afternoon. Thank God I gave up trying to teach you how to play chess.

WILLIE You and Sam cheated.

HALLY I never saw Sam cheat, and mine were mostly the mistakes of youth.

WILLIE Then how is it you two was always winning?

HALLY Have you ever considered the possibility, Willie, that it was because we were better than you?

WILLIE Every time better?

HALLY Not every time. There were occasions when we deliberately let you win a game so that you would stop sulking and go on playing with us. Sam used to wink at me when you weren't looking to show me it was time to let you win.

WILLIE So then you two didn't play fair.

HALLY It was for your benefit, Mr. Malopo, which is more than being fair. It was an act of self-sacrifice. [*To* SAM] But you know what my best memory is, don't you?

SAM No.

HALLY Come on, guess. If your memory is so good, you must remember it as well.

SAM We got up to a lot of tricks in there, Hally.

HALLY This one was special, Sam.

SAM I'm listening.

8. American movie star (1918–1987), a leading sex symbol of the 1940s.

HALLY It started off looking like another of those useless nothing-to-do afternoons. I'd already been down to Main Street looking for adventure, but nothing had happened. I didn't feel like climbing trees in the Donkin Park[9] or pretending I was a private eye and following a stranger . . . so as usual: See what's cooking in Sam's room. This time it was you on the floor. You had two thin pieces of wood and you were smoothing them down with a knife. It didn't look particularly interesting, but when I asked you what you were doing, you just said, "Wait and see, Hally. Wait . . . and see" . . . in that secret sort of way of yours, so I knew there was a surprise coming. You teased me, you bugger, by being deliberately slow and not answering my questions!

[SAM *laughs.*]

And whistling while you worked away! God, it was infuriating! I could have brained you! It was only when you tied them together in a cross and put that down on the brown paper that I realized what you were doing. "Sam is making a kite?" And when I asked you and you said "Yes" . . . ! [*Shaking his head with disbelief*] The sheer audacity of it took my breath away. I mean, seriously, what the hell does a black man know about flying a kite? I'll be honest with you, Sam, I had no hopes for it. If you think I was excited and happy, you got another guess coming. In fact, I was shit-scared that we were going to make fools of ourselves. When we left the boarding house to go up onto the hill, I was praying quietly that there wouldn't be any other kids around to laugh at us.

SAM [*enjoying the memory as much as* HALLY] Ja, I could see that.

HALLY I made it obvious, did I?

SAM Ja. You refused to carry it.

HALLY Do you blame me? Can you remember what the poor thing looked like? Tomato-box wood and brown paper! Flour and water for glue! Two of my mother's old stockings for a tail, and then all those bits and pieces of string you made me tie together so that we could fly it! Hell, no, that was now only asking for a miracle to happen.

SAM Then the big argument when I told you to hold the string and run with it when I let go.

HALLY I was prepared to run, all right, but straight back to the boarding house.

SAM [*knowing what's coming*] So what happened?

HALLY Come on, Sam, you remember as well as I do.

SAM I want to hear it from you.

[HALLY *pauses. He wants to be as accurate as possible.*]

HALLY You went a little distance from me down the hill, you held it up ready to let it go. . . . "This is it," I thought. "Like everything else in my life, here comes another fiasco." Then you shouted, "Go, Hally!" and I started to run. [*Another pause*] I don't know how to describe it, Sam. Ja! The miracle happened! I was running, waiting for it to crash to the ground, but instead suddenly there was something alive behind me at the end of the string, tugging at it as if it wanted to be free. I looked back . . . [*Shakes his head.*] . . . I still can't believe my eyes. It was flying! Looping around and trying to climb even higher into the sky. You shouted to me to let it have more string. I did,

9. That is, the Donkin Reserve, a park established in Port Elizabeth in 1820.

until there was none left and I was just holding that piece of wood we had tied it to. You came up and joined me. You were laughing.

SAM So were you. And shouting, "It works, Sam! We've done it!"

HALLY And we had! I was so proud of us! It was the most splendid thing I had ever seen. I wished there were hundreds of kids around to watch us. The part that scared me, though, was when you showed me how to make it dive down to the ground and then just when it was on the point of crashing, swoop up again!

SAM You didn't want to try yourself.

HALLY Of course not! I would have been suicidal if anything had happened to it. Watching you do it made me nervous enough. I was quite happy just to see it up there with its tail fluttering behind it. You left me after that, didn't you? You explained how to get it down, we tied it to the bench so that I could sit and watch it, and you went away. I wanted you to stay, you know. I was a little scared of having to look after it by myself.

SAM [*quietly*] I had work to do, Hally.

HALLY It was sort of sad bringing it down, Sam. And it looked sad again when it was lying there on the ground. Like something that had lost its soul. Just tomato-box wood, brown paper and two of my mother's old stockings! But, hell, I'll never forget that first moment when I saw it up there. I had a stiff neck the next day from looking up so much.

[SAM *laughs.* HALLY *turns to him with a question he never thought of asking before.*]

Why did you make that kite, Sam?

SAM [*evenly*] I can't remember.

HALLY Truly?

SAM Too long ago, Hally.

HALLY Ja, I suppose it was. It's time for another one, you know.

SAM Why do you say that?

HALLY Because it feels like that. Wouldn't be a good day to fly it, though.

SAM No. You can't fly kites on rainy days.

HALLY [*he studies* SAM. *Their memories have made him conscious of the man's presence in his life*] How old are you, Sam?

SAM Two score and five.

HALLY Strange, isn't it?

SAM What?

HALLY Me and you.

SAM What's strange about it?

HALLY Little white boy in short trousers and a black man old enough to be his father flying a kite. It's not every day you see that.

SAM But why strange? Because the one is white and the other black?

HALLY I don't know. Would have been just as strange, I suppose, if it had been me and my Dad . . . cripple man and a little boy! Nope! There's no chance of me flying a kite without it being strange. [*Simple statement of fact—no self-pity*] There's a nice little short story there. "The Kite-Flyers." But we'd have to find a twist in the ending.

SAM Twist?

HALLY Yes. Something unexpected. The way it ended with us was too straightforward . . . me on the bench and you going back to work. There's no drama in that.

WILLIE And me?

HALLY You?

WILLIE Yes me.

HALLY You want to get into the story as well, do you? I got it! Change the title: "Afternoons in Sam's Room" . . . expand it and tell all the stories. It's on its way to being a novel. Our days in the old Jubilee. Sad in a way that they're over. I almost wish we were still in that little room.

SAM We're still together.

HALLY That's true. It's just that life felt the right size in there . . . not too big and not too small. Wasn't so hard to work up a bit of courage. It's got so bloody complicated since then.

[*The telephone rings.* SAM *answers it.*]

SAM St. George's Park Tea Room . . . Hello, Madam . . . Yes, Madam, he's here. . . . Hally, it's your mother.

HALLY Where is she phoning from?

SAM Sounds like the hospital. It's a public telephone.

HALLY [*relieved*] You see! I told you. [*The telephone*] Hello, Mom . . . Yes . . . Yes no fine. Everything's under control here. How's things with poor old Dad? . . . Has he had a bad turn? . . . What? . . . Oh, God! . . . Yes, Sam told me, but I was sure he'd made a mistake. But what's this all about, Mom? He didn't look at all good last night. How can he get better so quickly? . . . Then very obviously you must say no. Be firm with him. You're the boss. . . . You know what it's going to be like if he comes home. . . . Well then, don't blame me when I fail my exams at the end of the year. . . . Yes! How am I expected to be fresh for school when I spend half the night massaging his gammy[1] leg? . . . So am I! . . . So tell him a white lie. Say Dr. Colley wants more X-rays of his stump. Or bribe him. We'll sneak in double tots of brandy in future. . . . What? . . . Order him to get back into bed at once! If he's going to behave like a child, treat him like one. . . . All right, Mom! I was just trying to . . . I'm sorry. . . . I said I'm sorry. . . . Quick, give me your number. I'll phone you back. [*He hangs up and waits a few seconds.*] Here we go again! [*He dials.*] I'm sorry, Mom. . . . Okay . . . But now listen to me carefully. All it needs is for you to put your foot down. Don't take no for an answer. . . . Did you hear me? And whatever you do, don't discuss it with him. . . . Because I'm frightened you'll give in to him. . . . Yes, Sam gave me lunch. . . . I ate all of it! . . . No, Mom not a soul. It's still raining here. . . . Right, I'll tell them. I'll just do some homework and then lock up. . . . But remember now, Mom. Don't listen to anything he says. And phone me back and let me know what happens. . . . Okay. Bye, Mom. [*He hangs up. The men are staring at him.*] My Mom says that when you're finished with the floors you must do the windows. [*Pause*] Don't misunderstand me, chaps. All I want is for him to get better. And if he was, I'd be the first person to say: "Bring him home." But he's not, and we can't give him the medical care and attention he needs at home. That's what hospitals are there for. [*Brusquely*] So don't just stand there! Get on with it!

[SAM *clears* HALLY*'s table.*]

You heard right. My Dad wants to go home.

1. Game; lame.

SAM Is he better?

HALLY [*sharply*] No! How the hell can he be better when last night he was groaning with pain? This is not an age of miracles!

SAM Then he should stay in hospital.

HALLY [*seething with irritation and frustration*] Tell me something I don't know, Sam. What the hell do you think I was saying to my Mom? All I can say is fuck-it-all.

SAM I'm sure he'll listen to your Mom.

HALLY You don't know what she's up against. He's already packed his shaving kit and pajamas and is sitting on his bed with his crutches, dressed and ready to go. I know him when he gets in that mood. If she tries to reason with him, we've had it. She's no match for him when it comes to a battle of words. He'll tie her up in knots. [*Trying to hide his true feelings*]

SAM I suppose it gets lonely for him in there.

HALLY With all the patients and nurses around? Regular visits from the Salvation Army? Balls! It's ten times worse for him at home. I'm at school and my mother is here in the business all day.

SAM He's at least got you at night.

HALLY [*before he can stop himself*] And we've got him! Please! I don't want to talk about it anymore. [*Unpacks his school case, slamming down books on the table.*] Life is just a plain bloody mess, that's all. And people are fools.

SAM Come on, Hally.

HALLY Yes, they are! They bloody well deserve what they get.

SAM Then don't complain.

HALLY Don't try to be clever, Sam. It doesn't suit you. Anybody who thinks there's nothing wrong with this world needs to have his head examined. Just when things are going along all right, without fail someone or something will come along and spoil everything. Somebody should write that down as a fundamental law of the Universe. The principle of perpetual disappointment. If there is a God who created this world, he should scrap it and try again.

SAM All right, Hally, all right. What you got for homework?

HALLY Bullshit, as usual. [*Opens an exercise book and reads.*] "Write five hundred words describing an annual event of cultural or historical significance."

SAM That should be easy enough for you.

HALLY And also plain bloody boring. You know what he wants, don't you? One of their useless old ceremonies. The commemoration of the landing of the 1820 Settlers,[2] or if it's going to be culture, Carols by Candlelight every Christmas.

SAM It's an impressive sight. Make a good description, Hally. All those candles glowing in the dark and the people singing hymns.

HALLY And it's called religious hysteria. [*Intense irritation*] Please, Sam! Just leave me alone and let me get on with it. I'm not in the mood for games this afternoon. And remember my Mom's orders . . . you're to help Willie with the windows. Come on now, I don't want any more nonsense in here.

SAM Okay, Hally, okay.

2. That is, the founders of Port Elizabeth, which was established to strengthen the Cape Colony against the Xhosa people to the east.

[HALLY *settles down to his homework; determined preparations . . . pen, ruler, exercise book, dictionary, another cake . . . all of which will lead to nothing.*]

[SAM *waltzes over to* WILLIE *and starts to replace tables and chairs. He practices a ballroom step while doing so.* WILLIE *watches. When* SAM *is finished,* WILLIE *tries.*] Good! But just a little bit quicker on the turn and only move in to her after she's crossed over. What about this one?

[*Another step. When* SAM *is finished,* WILLIE *again has a go.*]

Much better. See what happens when you just relax and enjoy yourself? Remember that in two weeks' time and you'll be all right.

WILLIE But I haven't got partner, Boet Sam.

SAM Maybe Hilda will turn up tonight.

WILLIE No, Boet Sam. [*Reluctantly*] I gave her a good hiding.

SAM You mean a bad one.

WILLIE Good bad one.

SAM Then you mustn't complain either. Now you pay the price for losing your temper.

WILLIE I also pay two pounds ten shilling entrance fee.

SAM They'll refund you if you withdraw now.

WILLIE [*appalled*] You mean, don't dance?

SAM Yes.

WILLIE No! I wait too long and I practice too hard. If I find me new partner, you think I can be ready in two weeks? I ask Madam for my leave now and we practice every day.

SAM Quickstep non-stop for two weeks. World record, Willie, but you'll be mad at the end.

WILLIE No jokes, Boet Sam.

SAM I'm not joking.

WILLIE So then what?

SAM Find Hilda. Say you're sorry and promise you won't beat her again.

WILLIE No.

SAM Then withdraw. Try again next year.

WILLIE No.

SAM Then I give up.

WILLIE Haaikona, Boet Sam, you can't.

SAM What do you mean, I can't? I'm telling you: I give up.

WILLIE [*adamant*] No! [*Accusingly*] It was you who start me ballroom dancing.

SAM So?

WILLIE Before that I use to be happy. And is you and Miriam who bring me to Hilda and say here's partner for you.

SAM What are you saying, Willie?

WILLIE You!

SAM But me what? To blame?

WILLIE Yes.

SAM Willie . . . ? [*Bursts into laughter.*]

WILLIE And now all you do is make jokes at me. You wait. When Miriam leaves you is my turn to laugh. Ha! Ha! Ha!

SAM [*he can't take* WILLIE *seriously any longer*] She can leave me tonight! I know what to do. [*Bowing before an imaginary partner*] May I have the pleasure? [*He dances and sings.*]

"Just a fellow with his pillow . . .
Dancin' like a willow . . .
In an autumn breeze . . ."

WILLIE There you go again!

[SAM *goes on dancing and singing.*]

Boet Sam!

SAM There's the answer to your problem! Judges' announcement in two weeks' time: "Ladies and gentlemen, the winner in the open section . . . Mr. Willie Malopo and his pillow!"

[*This is too much for a now really angry* WILLIE. *He goes for* SAM, *but the latter is too quick for him and puts* HALLY'S *table between the two of them.*]

HALLY [*exploding*] For Christ's sake, you two!

WILLIE [*still trying to get at* SAM] I donner[3] you, Sam! Struesgod!

SAM [*still laughing*] Sorry, Willie . . . Sorry . . .

HALLY Sam! Willie! [*Grabs his ruler and gives* WILLIE *a vicious whack on the bum.*] How the hell am I supposed to concentrate with the two of you behaving like bloody children!

WILLIE Hit him too!

HALLY Shut up, Willie.

WILLIE He started jokes again.

HALLY Get back to your work. You too, Sam. [*His ruler*] Do you want another one, Willie?

[SAM *and* WILLIE *return to their work.* HALLY *uses the opportunity to escape from his unsuccessful attempt at homework. He struts around like a little despot, ruler in hand, giving vent to his anger and frustration.*]

Suppose a customer had walked in then? Or the Park Superintendent. And seen the two of you behaving like a pair of hooligans. That would have been the end of my mother's license, you know. And your jobs! Well, this is the end of it. From now on there will be no more of your ballroom nonsense in here. This is a business establishment, not a bloody New Brighton[4] dancing school. I've been far too lenient with the two of you. [*Behind the counter for a green cool drink and a dollop of ice cream. He keeps up his tirade as he prepares it.*] But what really makes me bitter is that I allow you chaps a little freedom in here when business is bad and what do you do with it? The foxtrot! Specially you, Sam. There's more to life than trotting around a dance floor and I thought at least you knew it.

SAM It's a harmless pleasure, Hally. It doesn't hurt anybody.

HALLY It's also a rather simple one, you know.

SAM You reckon so? Have you ever tried?

HALLY Of course not.

SAM Why don't you? Now.

HALLY What do you mean? Me dance?

SAM Yes. I'll show you a simple step—the waltz—then you try it.

HALLY What will that prove?

SAM That it might not be as easy as you think.

3. Beat up (slang).
4. A suburb of Port Elizabeth (a black township).

HALLY I didn't say it was easy. I said it was simple—like in simple-minded, meaning mentally retarded. You can't exactly say it challenges the intellect.

SAM It does other things.

HALLY Such as?

SAM Make people happy.

HALLY [*the glass in his hand*] So do American cream sodas with ice cream. For God's sake, Sam, you're not asking me to take ballroom dancing serious, are you?

SAM Yes.

HALLY [*sigh of defeat*] Oh, well, so much for trying to give you a decent education. I've obviously achieved nothing.

SAM You still haven't told me what's wrong with admiring something that's beautiful and then trying to do it yourself.

HALLY Nothing. But we happen to be talking about a foxtrot, not a thing of beauty.

SAM But that is just what I'm saying. If you were to see two champions doing, two masters of the art . . . !

HALLY Oh, God, I give up. So now it's also art!

SAM Ja.

HALLY There's a limit, Sam. Don't confuse art and entertainment.

SAM So then what is art?

HALLY You want a definition?

SAM Ja.

HALLY [*he realizes he has got to be careful. He gives the matter a lot of thought before answering*] Philosophers have been trying to do that for centuries. What is Art? What is Life? But basically I suppose it's . . . the giving of meaning to matter.

SAM Nothing to do with beautiful?

HALLY It goes beyond that. It's the giving of form to the formless.

SAM Ja, well, maybe it's not art, then. But I still say it's beautiful.

HALLY I'm sure the word you mean to use is entertaining.

SAM [*adamant*] No. Beautiful. And if you want proof, come along to the Centenary Hall in New Brighton in two weeks' time.

[*The mention of the Centenary Hall draws* WILLIE *over to them.*]

HALLY What for? I've seen the two of you prancing around in here often enough.

SAM [*he laughs*] This isn't the real thing, Hally. We're just playing around in here.

HALLY So? I can use my imagination.

SAM And what do you get?

HALLY A lot of people dancing around and having a so-called good time.

SAM That all?

HALLY Well, basically it is that, surely.

SAM No, it isn't. Your imagination hasn't helped you at all. There's a lot more to it than that. We're getting ready for the championships, Hally, not just another dance. There's going to be a lot of people, all right, and they're going to have a good time, but they'll only be spectators, sitting around and watching. It's just the competitors out there on the dance floor. Party decorations and fancy lights all around the walls! The ladies in beautiful evening dresses!

HALLY My mother's got one of those, Sam, and, quite frankly, it's an embarrassment every time she wears it.

SAM [*undeterred*] Your imagination left out the excitement.

[HALLY *scoffs.*]

Oh, yes. The finalists are not going to be out there just to have a good time. One of those couples will be the 1950 Eastern Province Champions. And your imagination left out the music.

WILLIE Mr. Elijah Gladman Guzana and his Orchestral Jazzonions.

SAM The sound of the big band, Hally. Trombone, trumpet, tenor and alto sax. And then, finally, your imagination also left out the climax of the evening when the dancing is finished, the judges have stopped whispering among themselves and the Master of Ceremonies collects their scorecards and goes up onto the stage to announce the winners.

HALLY All right. So you make it sound like a bit of a do. It's an occasion. Satisfied?

SAM [*victory*] So you admit that!

HALLY Emotionally yes, intellectually no.

SAM Well, I don't know what you mean by that, all I'm telling you is that it is going to be *the* event of the year in New Brighton. It's been sold out for two weeks already. There's only standing room left. We've got competitors coming from Kingwilliamstown, East London, Port Alfred.[5]

[HALLY *starts pacing thoughtfully.*]

HALLY Tell me a bit more.

SAM I thought you weren't interested . . . intellectually.

HALLY [*mysteriously*] I've got my reasons.

SAM What do you want to know?

HALLY It takes place every year?

SAM Yes. But only every third year in New Brighton. It's East London's turn to have the championships next year.

HALLY Which, I suppose, makes it an even more significant event.

SAM Ah ha! We're getting somewhere. Our "occasion" is now a "significant event."

HALLY I wonder.

SAM What?

HALLY I wonder if I would get away with it.

SAM But what?

HALLY [*to the table and his exercise book*] "Write five hundred words describing an annual event of cultural or historical significance." Would I be stretching poetic license a little too far if I called your ballroom championships a cultural event?

SAM You mean . . . ?

HALLY You think we could get five hundred words out of it, Sam?

SAM Victor Sylvester[6] has written a whole book on ballroom dancing.

WILLIE You going to write about it, Master Hally?

5. East London is a coastal city, not far from King William's Town and about 150 miles east of Port Elizabeth; Port Alfred is a small town halfway between East London and Port Elizabeth.

6. An English dancer and bandleader (1900–1978), who helped popularize ballroom dancing worldwide—notably, in *Modern Ballroom Dancing* (1927); by 1952, it was already in its 45th edition.

HALLY Yes, gentlemen, that is precisely what I am considering doing. Old Doc Bromely—he's my English teacher—is going to argue with me, of course. He doesn't like natives. But I'll point out to him that in strict anthropological terms the culture of a primitive black society includes its dancing and singing. To put my thesis in a nutshell: The war-dance has been replaced by the waltz. But it still amounts to the same thing: the release of primitive emotions through movement. Shall we give it a go?

SAM I'm ready.

WILLIE Me also.

HALLY Ha! This will teach the old bugger a lesson. [*Decision taken*[7]] Right. Let's get ourselves organized. [*This means another cake on the table. He sits.*] I think you've given me enough general atmosphere, Sam, but to build the tension and suspense I need facts. [*Pencil poised*]

WILLIE Give him facts, Boet Sam.

HALLY What you called the climax . . . how many finalists?

SAM Six couples.

HALLY [*making notes*] Go on. Give me the picture.

SAM Spectators seated right around the hall. [WILLIE *becomes a spectator.*]

HALLY . . . and it's a full house.

SAM At one end, on the stage, Gladman and his Orchestral Jazzonions. At the other end is a long table with the three judges. The six finalists go onto the dance floor and take up their positions. When they are ready and the spectators have settled down, the Master of Ceremonies goes to the microphone. To start with, he makes some jokes to get the people laughing . . .

HALLY Good touch! [*As he writes*] ". . . creating a relaxed atmosphere which will change to one of tension and drama as the climax is approached."

SAM [*onto a chair to act out the M.C.*] "Ladies and gentlemen, we come now to the great moment you have all been waiting for this evening. . . . The finals of the 1950 Eastern Province Open Ballroom Dancing Championships. But first let me introduce the finalists! Mr. and Mrs. Welcome Tchabalala from Kingwilliamstown . . ."

WILLIE [*he applauds after every name*] Is when the people clap their hands and whistle and make a lot of noise, Master Hally.

SAM "Mr. Mulligan Njikelane and Miss Nomhle Nkonyeni of Grahamstown; Mr. and Mrs. Norman Nchinga from Port Alfred; Mr. Fats Bokolane and Miss Dina Plaatjies from East London; Mr. Sipho Dugu and Mrs. Mable Magada from Peddie; and from New Brighton our very own Mr. Willie Malopo and Miss Hilda Samuels."

[WILLIE *can't believe his ears. He abandons his role as spectator and scrambles into position as a finalist.*]

WILLIE Relaxed and ready to romance!

SAM The applause dies down. When everybody is silent, Gladman lifts up his sax, nods at the Orchestral Jazzonions . . .

WILLIE Play the jukebox please, Boet Sam!

SAM I also only got bus fare, Willie.

HALLY Hold it, everybody. [*Heads for the cash register behind the counter.*] How much is in the till, Sam?

SAM Three shillings. Hally . . . your Mom counted it before she left.

7. Made.

[HALLY *hesitates.*]

HALLY Sorry, Willie. You know how she carried on the last time I did it. We'll just have to pool our combined imaginations and hope for the best. [*Returns to the table.*] Back to work. How are the points scored, Sam?

SAM Maximum of ten points each for individual style, deportment, rhythm, and general appearance.

WILLIE Must I start?

HALLY Hold it for a second, Willie. And penalties?

SAM For what?

HALLY For doing something wrong. Say you stumble or bump into somebody . . . do they take off any points?

SAM [*aghast*] Hally . . . !

HALLY When you're dancing. If you and your partner collide into another couple.

[HALLY *can get no further.* SAM *has collapsed with laughter. He explains to* WILLIE.]

SAM If me and Miriam bump into you and Hilda . . .

[WILLIE *joins him in another good laugh.*]

Hally, Hally . . . !

HALLY [*perplexed*] Why? What did I say?

SAM There's no collisions out there, Hally. Nobody trips or stumbles or bumps into anybody else. That's what that moment is all about. To be one of those finalists on that dance floor is like . . . like being in a dream about a world in which accidents don't happen.

HALLY [*genuinely moved by* SAM*'s image*] Jesus, Sam! That's beautiful!

WILLIE [*can endure waiting no longer*] I'm starting! [WILLIE *dances while* SAM *talks.*]

SAM Of course it is. That's what I've been trying to say to you all afternoon. And it's beautiful because that is what we want life to be like. But instead, like you said, Hally, we're bumping into each other all the time. Look at the three of us this afternoon: I've bumped into Willie, the two of us have bumped into you, you've bumped into your mother, she bumping into your Dad. . . . None of us knows the steps and there's no music playing. And it doesn't stop with us. The whole world is doing it all the time. Open a newspaper and what do you read? America has bumped into Russia, England is bumping into India, rich man bumps into poor man. Those are big collisions, Hally. They make for a lot of bruises. People get hurt in all that bumping, and we're sick and tired of it now. It's been going on for too long. Are we never going to get it right? . . . Learn to dance life like champions instead of always being just a bunch of beginners at it?

HALLY [*deep and sincere admiration of the man*] You've got a vision, Sam!

SAM Not just me. What I'm saying to you is that everybody's got it. That's why there's only standing room left for the Centenary Hall in two weeks' time. For as long as the music lasts, we are going to see six couples get it right, the way we want life to be.

HALLY But is that the best we can do, Sam . . . watch six finalists dreaming about the way it should be?

SAM I don't know. But it starts with that. Without the dream we won't know what we're going for. And anyway I reckon there are a few people who have got past just dreaming about it and are trying for something real. Remember that thing we read once in the paper about the Mahatma Gandhi?[8] Going without food to stop those riots in India?

HALLY You're right. He certainly was trying to teach people to get the steps right.

SAM And the Pope.

HALLY Yes, he's another one. Our old General Smuts[9] as well, you know. He's also out there dancing. You know, Sam, when you come to think of it, that's what the United Nations boils down to . . . a dancing school for politicians!

SAM And let's hope they learn.

HALLY [*a little surge of hope*] You're right. We mustn't despair. Maybe there's some hope for mankind after all. Keep it up, Willie. [*Back to his table with determination*] This is a lot bigger than I thought. So what have we got? Yes, our title: "A World Without Collisions."

SAM That sounds good! "A World Without Collisions."

HALLY Subtitle: "Global Politics on the Dance Floor." No. A bit too heavy, hey? What about "Ballroom Dancing as a Political Vision"?

[*The telephone rings.* SAM *answers it.*]

SAM St. George's Park Tea Room . . . Yes, Madam . . . Hally, it's your Mom.

HALLY [*back to reality*] Oh, God, yes! I'd forgotten all about that. Shit! Remember my words, Sam? Just when you're enjoying yourself, someone or something will come along and wreck everything.

SAM You haven't heard what she's got to say yet.

HALLY Public telephone?

SAM No.

HALLY Does she sound happy or unhappy?

SAM I couldn't tell. [*Pause*] She's waiting, Hally.

HALLY [*to the telephone*] Hello, Mom . . . No, everything is okay here. Just doing my homework. . . . What's your news? . . . You've what? . . . [*Pause. He takes the receiver away from his ear for a few seconds. In the course of* HALLY'*s telephone conversation,* SAM *and* WILLIE *discretely position the stacked tables and chairs.* HALLY *places the receiver back to his ear.*] Yes, I'm still here. Oh, well, I give up now. Why did you do it, Mom? . . . Well, I just hope you know what you've let us in for. . . . [*Loudly*] I said I hope you know what you've let us in for! It's the end of the peace and quiet we've been having. [*Softly*] Where is he? [*Normal voice*] He can't hear us from in there. But for God's sake, Mom, what happened? I told you to be firm with him. . . . Then you and the nurses should have held him down, taken his crutches away. . . . I know only too well he's my father! . . . I'm not being disrespectful, but I'm sick and tired of emptying stinking chamberpots full of phlegm and piss. . . . Yes, I do! When you're not there, he asks *me* to do it. . . . If you really want to know the truth, that's why I've got no appetite for my food. . . . Yes! There's a lot of things you don't know about. For your

8. Indian political activist and religious leader (1869–1948) who used nonviolent resistance and fasting in his struggle against British imperial rule; when violence between Muslims and Hindus erupted before the partition of the Indian subcontinent into India and Pakistan, he undertook lengthy fasts (the last ended with his assassination).

9. Jan Christian Smuts (1870–1950), a South African statesman and soldier who helped found the Union of South Africa (1910) as a self-governing nation within the British Commonwealth. He twice served as its prime minister (1919–24, 1939–48), and he championed the creation of both the League of Nations and the United Nations.

information, I still haven't got that science textbook I need. And you know why? He borrowed the money you gave me for it. . . . Because I didn't want to start another fight between you two. . . . He says that every time. . . . All right, Mom! [*Viciously*] Then just remember to start hiding your bag away again, because he'll be at your purse before long for money for booze. And when he's well enough to come down here, you better keep an eye on the till as well, because that is also going to develop a leak. . . . Then don't complain to me when he starts his old tricks. . . . Yes, you do. I get it from you on one side and from him on the other, and it makes life hell for me. I'm not going to be the peacemaker anymore. I'm warning you now: when the two of you start fighting again, I'm leaving home. . . . Mom, if you start crying, I'm going to put down the receiver. . . . Okay . . . [*Lowering his voice to a vicious whisper*] Okay, Mom. I heard you. [*Desperate*] No. . . . Because I don't want to. I'll see him when I get home! Mom! . . . [*Pause. When he speaks again, his tone changes completely. It is not simply pretense. We sense a genuine emotional conflict.*] Welcome home, chum! . . . What's that? . . . Don't be silly, Dad. You being home is just about the best news in the world. . . . I bet you are. Bloody depressing there with everybody going on about their ailments, hey! . . . How you feeling? . . . Good . . . Here as well, pal. Coming down cats and dogs. . . . That's right. Just the day for a kip and a toss in your old Uncle Ned.[1] . . . Everything's just hunky-dory on my side, Dad. . . . Well, to start with, there's a nice pile of comics for you on the counter. . . . Yes, old Kemple brought them in. *Batman and Robin, Submariner* . . . just your cup of tea . . . I will. . . . Yes, we'll spin a few yarns tonight. . . . Okay, chum, see you in a little while. . . . No, I promise. I'll come straight home. . . . [*Pause—his mother comes back on the phone.*] Mom? Okay. I'll lock up now. . . . What? . . . Oh, the brandy . . . Yes, I'll remember! . . . I'll put it in my suitcase now, for God's sake. I know well enough what will happen if he doesn't get it. . . . [*Places a bottle of brandy on the counter.*] I *was* kind to him, Mom. I didn't say anything nasty! . . . All right. Bye. [*End of telephone conversation. A desolate* HALLY *doesn't move. A strained silence.*]

SAM [*quietly*] That sounded like a bad bump, Hally.

HALLY [*having a hard time controlling his emotions. He speaks carefully*] Mind your own business, Sam.

SAM Sorry. I wasn't trying to interfere. Shall we carry on? Hally? [*He indicates the exercise book. No response from* HALLY.]

WILLIE [*also trying*] Tell him about when they give out the cups, Boet Sam.

SAM Ja! That's another big moment. The presentation of the cups after the winners have been announced. You've got to put that in.

[*Still no response from* HALLY.]

WILLIE A big silver one, Master Hally, called floating trophy for the champions.

SAM We always invite some big-shot personality to hand them over. Guest of honor this year is going to be His Holiness Bishop Jabulani of the All African Free Zionist Church.

[HALLY *gets up abruptly, goes to his table and tears up the page he was writing on.*]

HALLY So much for a bloody world without collisions.

1. That is, a nap (kip, toss) in your bed ("Uncle Ned" in Cockney rhyming slang).

SAM Too bad. It was on its way to being a good composition.

HALLY Let's stop bullshitting ourselves, Sam.

SAM Have we been doing that?

HALLY Yes! That's what all our talk about a decent world has been . . . just so much bullshit.

SAM We did say it was still only a dream.

HALLY And a bloody useless one at that. Life's a fuck-up and it's never going to change.

SAM Ja, maybe that's true.

HALLY There's no maybe about it. It's a blunt and brutal fact. All we've done this afternoon is waste our time.

SAM Not if we'd got your homework done.

HALLY I don't give a shit about my homework, so, for Christ's sake, just shut up about it. [*Slamming books viciously into his school case*] Hurry up now and finish your work. I want to lock up and get out of here. [*Pause*] And then go where? Home-sweet-fucking-home. Jesus, I hate that word.

[HALLY *goes to the counter to put the brandy bottle and comics in his school case. After a moment's hesitation, he smashes the bottle of brandy. He abandons all further attempts to hide his feelings.* SAM *and* WILLIE *work away as unobtrusively as possible.*]

Do you want to know what is really wrong with your lovely little dream, Sam? It's not just that we are all bad dancers. That does happen to be perfectly true, but there's more to it than just that. You left out the cripples.

SAM Hally!

HALLY [*now totally reckless*] Ja! Can't leave them out, Sam. That's why we always end up on our backsides on the dance floor. They're also out there dancing . . . like a bunch of broken spiders trying to do the quickstep! [*An ugly attempt at laughter*] When you come to think of it, it's a bloody comical sight. I mean, it's bad enough on two legs . . . but one and a pair of crutches! Hell, no, Sam. That's guaranteed to turn that dance floor into a shambles. Why you shaking your head? Picture it, man. For once this afternoon let's use our imaginations sensibly.

SAM Be careful, Hally.

HALLY Of what? The truth? I seem to be the only one around here who is prepared to face it. We've had the pretty dream, it's time now to wake up and have a good long look at the way things really are. Nobody knows the steps, there's no music, the cripples are also out there tripping up everybody and trying to get into the act, and it's all called the All-Comers-How-to-Make-a-Fuckup-of-Life Championships. [*Another ugly laugh*] Hang on, Sam! The best bit is still coming. Do you know what the winner's trophy is? A beautiful big chamber-pot with roses on the side, and it's full to the brim with piss. And guess who I think is going to be this year's winner.

SAM [*almost shouting*] Stop now!

HALLY [*suddenly appalled by how far he has gone*] Why?

SAM Hally? It's your father you're talking about.

HALLY So?

SAM Do you know what you've been saying?

[HALLY *can't answer. He is rigid with shame.* SAM *speaks to him sternly.*]

No, Hally, you mustn't do it. Take back those words and ask for forgiveness! It's a terrible sin for a son to mock his father with jokes like that. You'll be punished if you carry on. Your father is your father, even if he is a . . . cripple man.

WILLIE Yes, Master Hally. Is true what Sam say.

SAM I understand how you are feeling, Hally, but even so . . .

HALLY No, you don't!

SAM I think I do.

HALLY And I'm telling you you don't. Nobody does. [*Speaking carefully as his shame turns to rage at* SAM] It's your turn to be careful, Sam. Very careful! You're treading on dangerous ground. Leave me and my father alone.

SAM I'm not the one who's been saying things about him.

HALLY What goes on between me and my Dad is none of your business!

SAM Then don't tell me about it. If that's all you've got to say about him, I don't want to hear.

[*For a moment* HALLY *is at loss for a response.*]

HALLY Just get on with your bloody work and shut up.

SAM Swearing at me won't help you.

HALLY Yes, it does! Mind your own fucking business and shut up!

SAM Okay. If that's the way you want it, I'll stop trying.

[*He turns away. This infuriates* HALLY *even more.*]

HALLY Good. Because what you've been trying to do is meddle in something you know nothing about. All that concerns you in here, Sam, is to try and do what you get paid for—keep the place clean and serve the customers. In plain words, just get on with your job. My mother is right. She's always warning me about allowing you to get too familiar. Well, this time you've gone too far. It's going to stop right now.

[*No response from* SAM.]

You're only a servant in here, and don't forget it.

[*Still no response.* HALLY *is trying hard to get one.*]

And as far as my father is concerned, all you need to remember is that he is your boss.

SAM [*needled at last*] No, he isn't. I get paid by your mother.

HALLY Don't argue with me, Sam!

SAM Then don't say he's my boss.

HALLY He's a white man and that's good enough for you.

SAM I'll try to forget you said that.

HALLY Don't! Because you won't be doing me a favor if you do. I'm telling you to remember it.

[*A pause.* SAM *pulls himself together and makes one last effort.*]

SAM Hally, Hally . . . ! Come on now. Let's stop before it's too late. You're right. We *are* on dangerous ground. If we're not careful, somebody is going to get hurt.

HALLY It won't be me.

SAM Don't be so sure.

HALLY I don't know what you're talking about, Sam.

SAM Yes, you do.

HALLY [*furious*] Jesus, I wish you would stop trying to tell me what I do and what I don't know.

[SAM *gives up. He turns to* WILLIE.]

SAM Let's finish up.

HALLY Don't turn your back on me! I haven't finished talking.

[*He grabs* SAM *by the arm and tries to make him turn around.* SAM *reacts with a flash of anger.*]

SAM Don't do that, Hally! [*Facing the boy*] All right, I'm listening. Well? What do you want to say to me?

HALLY [*pause as* HALLY *looks for something to say*] To begin with, why don't you also start calling me Master Harold, like Willie.

SAM Do you mean that?

HALLY Why the hell do you think I said it?

SAM And if I don't?

HALLY You might just lose your job.

SAM [*quietly and very carefully*] If you make me say it once, I'll never call you anything else again.

HALLY So? [*The boy confronts the man.*] Is that meant to be a threat?

SAM Just telling you what will happen if you make me do that. You must decide what it means to you.

HALLY Well, I have. It's good news. Because that is exactly what Master Harold wants from now on. Think of it as a little lesson in respect, Sam, that's long overdue, and I hope you remember it as well as you do your geography. I can tell you now that somebody who will be glad to hear I've finally given it to you will be my Dad. Yes! He agrees with my Mom. He's always going on about it as well. "You must teach the boys to show you more respect, my son."

SAM So now you can stop complaining about going home. Everybody is going to be happy tonight.

HALLY That's perfectly correct. You see, you mustn't get the wrong idea about me and my Dad, Sam. We also have our good times together. Some bloody good laughs. He's got a marvelous sense of humor. Want to know what our favorite joke is? He gives out a big groan, you see, and says: "It's not fair, is it, Hally?" Then I have to ask: "What, chum?" And then he says: "A nigger's arse"[2] . . . and we both have a good laugh.

[*The men stare at him with disbelief.*]

What's the matter, Willie? Don't you catch the joke? You always were a bit slow on the uptake. It's what is called a pun. You see, fair means both light in color and to be just and decent. [*He turns to* SAM.] I thought *you* would catch it, Sam.

SAM Oh ja, I catch it all right.

HALLY But it doesn't appeal to your sense of humor.

SAM Do you really laugh?

HALLY Of course.

SAM To please him? Make him feel good?

HALLY No, for heaven's sake! I laugh because I think it's a bloody good joke.

SAM You're really trying hard to be ugly, aren't you? And why drag poor old Willie into it? He's done nothing to you except show you the respect you want so badly. That's also not being fair, you know . . . and *I* mean just or decent.

WILLIE It's all right, Sam. Leave it now.

2. In editions and performances outside the United States, Fugard replaces "nigger's" with "kaffir's," a term that in South Africa conveys comparable insult and contempt.

SAM It's me you're after. You should just have said "Sam's arse" . . . because that's the one you're trying to kick. Anyway, how do you know it's not fair? You've never seen it. Do you want to? [*He drops his trousers and underpants and presents his backside for* HALLY'S *inspection.*] Have a good look. A real Basuto[3] arse . . . which is about as nigger as they can come. Satisfied? [*Trousers up*] Now you can make your Dad even happier when you go home tonight. Tell him I showed you my arse and he is quite right. It's not fair. And if it will give him an even better laugh next time, I'll also let *him* have a look. Come, Willie, let's finish up and go.

[SAM *and* WILLIE *start to tidy up the tea room.* HALLY *doesn't move. He waits for a moment when* SAM *passes him.*]

HALLY [*quietly*] Sam . . .

[SAM *stops and looks expectantly at the boy.* HALLY *spits in his face. A long and heartfelt groan from* WILLIE. *For a few seconds* SAM *doesn't move.*]

SAM [*taking out a handkerchief and wiping his face*] It's all right, Willie.

[*To* HALLY.]

Ja, well, you've done it . . . Master Harold. Yes, I'll start calling you that from now on. It won't be difficult anymore. You've hurt yourself, Master Harold. I saw it coming. I warned you, but you wouldn't listen. You've just hurt yourself *bad*. And you're a coward, Master Harold. The face you should be spitting in is your father's . . . but you used mine, because you think you're safe inside your fair skin . . . and this time I don't mean just or decent. [*Pause, then moving violently towards* HALLY] Should I hit him, Willie?

WILLIE [*stopping* SAM] No, Boet Sam.

SAM [*violently*] Why not?

WILLIE It won't help, Boet Sam.

SAM I don't want to help! I want to hurt him.

WILLIE You also hurt yourself.

SAM And if he had done it to you, Willie?

WILLIE Me? Spit at me like I was a dog? [*A thought that had not occurred to him before. He looks at* HALLY.] Ja. Then I want to hit him. I want to hit him hard!

[*A dangerous few seconds as the men stand staring at the boy.* WILLIE *turns away, shaking his head.*]

But maybe all I do is go cry at the back. He's little boy, Boet Sam. Little *white* boy. Long trousers now, but he's still little boy.

SAM [*his violence ebbing away into defeat as quickly as it flooded*] You're right. So go on, then: groan again, Willie. You do it better than me. [*To* HALLY] You don't know all of what you've just done . . . Master Harold. It's not just that you've made me feel dirtier than I've ever been in my life . . . I mean, how do I wash off yours and your father's filth? . . . I've also failed. A long time ago I promised myself I was going to try and do something, but you've just shown me . . . Master Harold . . . that I've failed. [*Pause*] I've also got a memory of a little white boy when he was still wearing short trousers and a black man, but they're not flying a kite. It was the old Jubilee days,[4] after dinner one night. I was in my room. You came in and

3. One of the principal tribal groups of southern Africa.

4. That is, when they were living in the old Jubilee Boarding House.

just stood against the wall, looking down at the ground, and only after I'd asked you what you wanted, what was wrong, I don't know how many times, did you speak and even then so softly I almost didn't hear you. "Sam, please help me to go and fetch my Dad." Remember? He was dead drunk on the floor of the Central Hotel Bar. They'd phoned for your Mom, but you were the only one at home. And do you remember how we did it? You went in first by yourself to ask permission for me to go into the bar. Then I loaded him onto my back like a baby and carried him back to the boarding house with you following behind carrying his crutches. [*Shaking his head as he remembers*] A crowded Main Street with all the people watching a little white boy following his drunk father on a nigger's back! I felt for that little boy . . . Master Harold. I felt for him. After that we still had to clean him up, remember? He'd messed in his trousers, so we had to clean him up and get him into bed.

HALLY [*great pain*] I love him, Sam.

SAM I know you do. That's why I tried to stop you from saying these things about him. It would have been so simple if you could have just despised him for being a weak man. But he's your father. You love him and you're ashamed of him. You're ashamed of so much! . . . And now that's going to include yourself. That was the promise I made to myself: to try and stop that happening. [*Pause*] After we got him to bed you came back with me to my room and sat in a corner and carried on just looking down at the ground. And for days after that! You hadn't done anything wrong, but you went around as if you owed the world an apology for being alive. I didn't like seeing that! That's not the way a boy grows up to be a man! . . . But the one person who should have been teaching you what that means was the cause of your shame. If you really want to know, that's why I made you that kite. I wanted you to look up, be proud of something, of yourself . . . [*Bitter smile at the memory*] . . . and you certainly were that when I left you with it up there on the hill. Oh, ja . . . something else! . . . If you ever do write it as a short story, there *was* a twist in our ending. I couldn't sit down there and stay with you. It was a "Whites Only" bench. You were too young, too excited to notice then. But not anymore. If you're not careful . . . Master Harold . . . you're going to be sitting up there by yourself for a long time to come, and there won't be a kite in the sky. [SAM *has got nothing more to say. He exits into the kitchen, taking off his waiter's jacket.*]

WILLIE Is bad. Is all all bad in here now.

HALLY [*books into his school case, raincoat on*] Willie . . . [*It is difficult to speak.*] Will you lock up for me and look after the keys?

WILLIE Okay.

[SAM *returns.* HALLY *goes behind the counter and collects the few coins in the cash register. As he starts to leave . . .*]

SAM Don't forget the comic books.

[HALLY *returns to the counter and puts them in his case. He starts to leave again.*]

SAM [*to the retreating back of the boy*] Stop . . . Hally . . .

[HALLY *stops, but doesn't turn to face him.*]

Hally . . . I've got no right to tell you what being a man means if I don't behave like one myself, and I'm not doing so well at that this afternoon. Should we try again, Hally?

HALLY Try what?

SAM Fly another kite, I suppose. It worked once, and this time I need it as much as you do.

HALLY It's still raining, Sam. You can't fly kites on rainy days, remember.

SAM So what do we do? Hope for better weather tomorrow?

HALLY [*helpless gesture*] I don't know. I don't know anything anymore.

SAM You sure of that, Hally? Because it would be pretty hopeless if that was true. It would mean nothing has been learnt in here this afternoon, and there was a hell of a lot of teaching going on . . . one way or the other. But anyway, I don't believe you. I reckon there's one thing you know. You don't *have* to sit up there by yourself. You know what that bench means now, and you can leave it any time you choose. All you've got to do is stand up and walk away from it.

[HALLY *leaves.* WILLIE *goes up quietly to* SAM.]

WILLIE Is okay, Boet Sam. You see. Is . . . [*He can't find any better words.*] . . . *is* going to be okay tomorrow. [*Changing his tone*] Hey, Boet Sam! [*He is trying hard.*] You right. I think about it and you right. Tonight I find Hilda and say sorry. And make promise I won't beat her no more. You hear me, Boet Sam?

SAM I hear you, Willie.

WILLIE And when we practice I relax and romance with her from beginning to end. Non-stop! You watch! Two weeks' time: "First prize for promising newcomers: Mr. Willie Malopo and Miss Hilda Samuels." [*Sudden impulse*] To hell with it! I walk home. [*He goes to the jukebox, puts in a coin and selects a record. The machine comes to life in the gray twilight, blushing its way through a spectrum of soft, romantic colors.*] How did you say it, Boet Sam? Let's dream. [WILLIE *sways with the music and gestures for* SAM *to dance.*]

[*Sarah Vaughan sings.*[5]]

"Little man you're crying,
I know why you're blue,
Someone took your kiddy car away;
Better go to sleep now,
Little man you've had a busy day." [*etc. etc.*]

You lead. I follow.

[*The men dance together.*]

"Johnny won your marbles,
Tell you what we'll do;
Dad will get you new ones right away;
Better go to sleep now,
Little man you've had a busy day."

5. "Little Man You've Had a Busy Day" (1934; by Al Hoffman, Maurice Sigler, and Mabel Wayne), recorded by Sarah Vaughan and the Count Basie Orchestra in 1961.

MARIA IRENE FORNES

b. 1930

MARIA Irene Fornes emerged on the burgeoning off-off-Broadway scene of the early 1960s as a vibrant new voice for the American theater. Since that revolutionary time, she has retained a commitment to exploration and innovation while rejecting commercialism in the arts. Long considered one of the leading figures in the American alternative theater movement and a finalist for the Pulitzer Prize for Drama in 1988, Fornes has also become one of the country's foremost directors and playwriting teachers. Her play *MUD* (1983), dating from the middle period of her career, exemplifies the spare, evocative, and emotionally raw style of writing that has become the hallmark of her dramaturgy. Her focus on the elemental forces driving human behavior and her concern with such social structures as class and gender come together in this powerful and disturbing drama.

Fornes was born in Cuba in 1930, a time of economic depression and political instability. Her father, Carlos, was a civil engineer but was often out of work; her mother, Carmen, was a former teacher; and together they shared with their six children their enthusiasm for politics, ideas, and the arts. In the early 1940s, Carmen attempted to move the family to the United States, but obtaining visas during wartime was difficult. After Carlos's unexpected death in 1945, she suceeded in emigrating to New York City with her two youngest children; one of them was Maria Irene.

Fornes soon became more interested in painting than in pursuing her formal education; after briefly studying abstract art, in 1954 she moved to Europe to paint. That same year, she saw the world premiere in Paris of SAMUEL BECKETT's groundbreaking drama *En Attendant Godot* (*Waiting for Godot*)—a play that she claims moved her deeply and changed her life, though she did not understand French. Fornes had had little prior exposure to the theater, and she maintains that the only play she had read before embarking on her own theatrical career was HENRIK IBSEN's *Hedda Gabler* (1890). In 1957, she returned to the United States to pursue work as a textile designer. For a while she rented an apartment with Susan Sontag, soon to become one of America's foremost cultural critics, and the two women challenged each other to write. After some early efforts translating family letters from Spanish to English and putting them in dramatic form (*The Widow*, 1961), Fornes became obsessed with the idea of writing another play; in the space of a few weeks, she produced *Tango Palace* (originally titled *There! You Died!*, 1963). In its existential struggle between characters, this piece clearly reflects the impact of Beckett's dramaturgy—an influence that is still strong in *Mud*.

Deceptively simple in its narrative arc, *Mud* chronicles the evolving relationships between three characters: Mae, Lloyd, and Henry. Locked in a cycle of interdependency and conflict, Mae and Lloyd can barely survive on what Mae earns by taking in ironing, and Lloyd's illness has added to the strain. Mae strives for a better life, seeing education as a means of self-improvement. She gravitates toward Henry, with whom she feels she can genuinely communicate. The dynamic shifts when Henry becomes incapacitated and Mae and Lloyd decide they must care for him. The men then begin to make increasing demands on Mae, both emotionally and financially, driving the play to its crisis and devastating conclusion.

The focus in *Mud* on both the intense dynamics between and the complex inner lives of the characters reflects Fornes's formative early exposure to "the method," an approach to acting that had enormous influence in the United States. It was promoted by the director Lee Strasberg, who had derived his concepts about acting in large part from the "system" of the legendary Russian director and actor Konstantin Stanislavsky, and in the late 1950s, Fornes joined the playwriting unit of Strasberg's Actors Studio. She quickly grasped the principle at the core of the method: to access and embody the truth of a character in any drama, regardless of how that drama is written or staged. Although these techniques are often associated with theatrical realism, a piece like *Mud*, which is stripped of the usual trappings of the realist stage, demonstrates how closely these concepts of emotional and psychological truth dovetail with Fornes's abstract, imagistic naturalism. Her early training as a visual artist, too, has significantly shaped her dramaturgy, which has been described as "a form of painting with words." Interestingly, some critics have also noted Brechtian elements—which are often seen as diametrically opposed to method techniques—in her productions. Fornes has never claimed

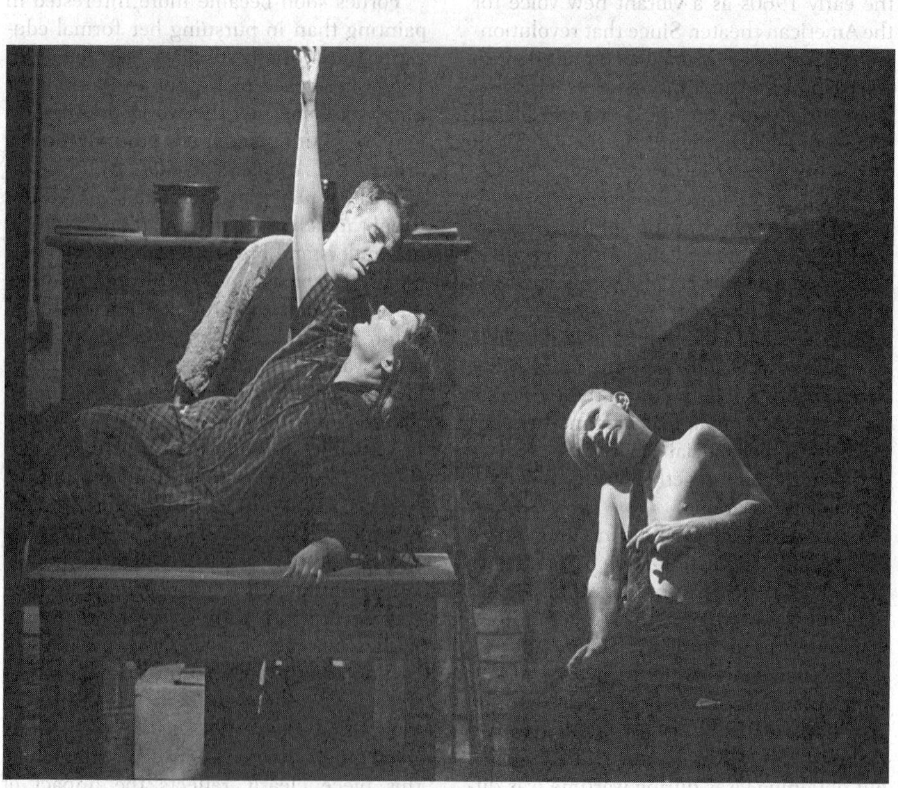

A 1991 performance of *Mud* directed by Fornes and produced at the Milwaukee Repertory Theater. Pictured left to right are James Pickering as Lloyd, Rose Pickering as Mae, and and Tom Blair as Henry.

BERTOLT BRECHT as an influence, however; indeed, this interpretation may owe more to the political dimensions of her themes and to her frank, seemingly matter-of-fact depictions of violence—evident in *Mud* and a number of her other plays—than to her own conscious choices as a dramatist or as a director.

Experimentation with form, parody of popular entertainment styles, and humorous social critique distinguish the first phase of Fornes's theatrical career. But her style and tone changed markedly with *Fefu and Her Friends* (1977), and we can see her further refinement of this new kind of dramaturgy in *Mud*. A richer, more complex work than any of her previous pieces, *Fefu* breaks new ground in its concentration on female characters and their thoughts, feelings, and interrelationships; its relative disinterest in traditional plot; and its innovative environmental staging. *Mud* expands this focus on character to encompass men as well, within a narrative similarly lacking in traditional stage action or a realist stage milieu.

Critics have noted the transition from Fornes's use of irony and playfulness as vehicles for social and political critique to the more somber tone of *Fefu* and *Mud*. We might attribute this change in part to Fornes's sense that her earlier styles were inadequate to address profound events such as the war in Vietnam and to her growing recognition of gender and class inequities in contemporary society. A number of her plays after *Fefu*, especially *The Conduct of Life* (1985), treat sexual and political violence while displaying her ongoing commitment to an evenhanded and truthful representation of all her characters' complex motivations and responses, no matter how disturbing these may be.

Fornes developed and premiered *Mud* at the Padua Hills Playwrights Festival in southern California. This locale had a profound and tangible impact on the piece: the outdoor venue informed the play's structure (as shown most obviously in the freezes between scenes, made necessary by the lack of blackouts) and its palette—the sky became more gray as the day wore on, and Fornes opted to maintain this effect through the costuming and lighting in subsequent productions. The theater's location may have been equally influential in suggesting the symbolism of earth, dirt, and mud that permeates the play, as well as its setting, "a wooden room which sits on an earth promontory." External circumstances strongly affected the piece in other ways. According to Fornes, because an older actor whom she had initially envisioned as a father for Mae was unavailable, she had to rethink the role for a younger actor—and thus Henry was created. She further explains that her discovery at a local flea market of an inexpensive set of farm tools and an ironing board decided both the play's rural setting and Mae's occupation. Such seemingly random events have shaped Fornes's entire career, leading critics to liken her work to the "found art" movement.

Mud ultimately reveals both Fornes's deep sensitivity to the disenfranchised and her refusal to soft-pedal the stark realities of their lives. Yet this play, which remains one of Fornes's favorites—she has called it "a little jewel"—has also proven controversial; critics have expressed considerable ambivalence about the elemental interrelationship of Mae, Lloyd, and Henry and the choices each makes to survive. The character of Mae has come under particular scrutiny and has been condemned for the gender-coded, menial work she performs and the brutality she experiences. In response, Fornes has faulted critics for making judgments about her writing based on erroneous assumptions and preconceived ideas, particularly regarding gender roles and the responsibilities of women playwrights in depicting female identity. In her essay "Creative Danger," Fornes remarks of her characters:

> These people are too poor to indulge in bizarre ego games. They have a reality to deal with, which is poverty. That is the way things have worked out for them. The concepts of sex roles and role playing are a luxury, an indulgence that requires a degree of affluence. . . . If you reversed the sexes in *Mud*, you would see that Mae's nature is more male than female in terms of dominance, and that the men's natures are more female in terms of tenderness and acceptance. . . . But the attention to sex

> roles, protest against sex roles, defense against the guilt that results from that protest, all these things keep us from seeing a work with a full perspective. They prevent us from seeing characters as human beings; we see them rather as party members.

At the same time, Fornes has acknowledged the aptness of other critical observations on her work, especially that it is always about immigrants, because all her plays in some way "deal with a person going to another world."

A closely related concern is with language acquisition—a process of which Fornes is acutely aware, both as a nonnative speaker of English and as a translator of plays by such Spanish dramatists as FEDERICO GARCÍA LORCA and PEDRO CALDERÓN DE LA BARCA. Language is equally at stake for her characters who, in a broader sense, must discover themselves in words. In her plays, Fornes consistently foregrounds the interrelationship of language, thought, and action. The struggle for verbal expression thus emerges as a core element of her dramaturgy, represented with aching beauty and clarity through Mae's study of starfish in *Mud*. Mae's quest for language and learning also reflects Fornes's revision of the Western philosophical tradition that links masculinity with thought and femininity with emotion. Fornes explained in an interview that "what's wonderful about Mae is her love for knowledge" and that, ultimately, "what is important about this play is that Mae is the central character . . . simply because she is the *center* of the play." Fornes concludes that "it is because of that mind, Mae's mind, *a woman's mind*, that the play exists. To me that is an . . . important step toward redeeming women's position in the world." Such insights into the significance of her own contributions as a dramatist demonstrate the importance of avoiding entanglements in narrow debates about Fornes's work. Attempts to reduce her writing to such binaries as feminist/not feminist describe only the most obvious aspects of its characters or action. Fornes has revealed how deep the foundations of her characters are laid, and we must tunnel down just as far to understand the fundamental human truths she dramatizes.

J.E.G.

Mud

CHARACTERS

MAE A spirited young woman. She is single-minded and determined, a believer. She is mid-twenties.

LLOYD A simple and good-hearted young man. He is ungainly and unkempt. His shoulders slope, his stomach protrudes, some of his teeth are missing. At the start of the play, illness contributes to his poor appearance. He is mid-twenties.

HENRY A large man. He has a natural sense of dignity, a philosophical mind. He can barely read. He is mid-fifties.

The set is a wooden room which sits on an earth promontory. The promontory is five feet high and covers the same periphery as the room. The wood has the color and texture of bone that has dried in the sun. It is ashen and cold. The earth in the promontory is red and soft and so is the earth around it. There is no greenery. Behind the promontory there is a vast blue sky. On the back wall of the room there is an oversized fireplace which is the same color and texture as the walls and floor. On each side of the fireplace there are narrow doors. The door to the right leads to the exterior. There is a blue sky. The one to the left leads to a dark corridor. In the center of the room there is a kitchen table. There is a chair on each end. Down right there is an ironing board. There is an iron on it and a pair of trousers. Against the back wall on the left there is another chair. After the first scene these three chairs will always be placed around the table and will be referred to as right, center, and left. Against the right wall there is a bench. On it there is a pile of unpressed trousers. On the table there is a pile of pressed trousers. Under the bench, there is a bundle of women's clothes and a pair of old, flat women's shoes. Inside the fireplace there are two cardboard boxes. One is full and tied with a string, the other is empty. On the mantelpiece there are, from right to left: a brown paper bag with a pamphlet in it, a pot with three metal plates and three spoons stacked upon it, a plate with broken bread, a pitcher with milk, a textbook, a notebook and pencil, a dish with string beans, a folded newspaper, and a box with pills. Between the fireplace and the door to the left there are an ax and a rifle.

Offstage there is an empty box the same size as the box tied with a string. The following props are carried by the actors as they enter to perform the scene:

MAE: *2 bundles of clothes and a loose clean rag.*

LLOYD: *3 coins, a prescription note, and a cup with oatmeal and a spoon.*

HENRY: *lipstick wrapped in paper, a small mirror, a notebook, bills and pencil, loose coins, a tin cup of milk, and a wad of bills.*

At the end of each scene a freeze is indicated. These freezes will last eight seconds which will create the effect of a still photograph. When the freeze is broken, the actors will make the necessary set changes and proceed to perform the following scene.

Act 1

Scene 1

[LLOYD *sits left. He is unwashed and unshaven. He has a fever. He is clumsy and badly coordinated.* MAE *is at the ironing board. She is unkempt.*]

LLOYD You think you learn a lot at school?

MAE I do.

LLOYD What do you learn?

MAE Subjects.

LLOYD What is subjects?

MAE Different things.

LLOYD What things?

MAE You want to know?

LLOYD What are they?

MAE Arithmetic.

LLOYD Big deal arithmetic. I know arithmetic.

MAE I'll bet.

LLOYD Don't talk back to me. I'll kick your ass.

MAE Fuck you, Lloyd. I'm telling you about arithmetic and you talk to me like that? You're a moron. I won't tell you anything.

LLOYD Oh, no?

MAE No.

LLOYD So what's arithmetic?

MAE Fuck you. I'm not telling you.

LLOYD [*moving toward her*] I'll fuck you till you're blue in the face! [*He stops and starts back to the chair.*] I don't even want to fuck you.

MAE You can't, that's why. You can't get it up.

LLOYD Oh yeah? I got it up yesterday!

MAE When!

LLOYD Afternoon!

MAE Never saw it.

LLOYD You weren't here.

MAE Where was I?

LLOYD At school. You missed it. I got it up.

MAE Who with?

LLOYD Fuck you. I'm not telling you.

MAE Who with?

LLOYD With myself.—I don't need someone. I got it up right here. [*Pointing to the wall*] See that? I did that! From here. I didn't give it to you or anyone. [*Pantomiming an erection and ejaculation*] I held it as long as I wanted. Then I gave it to the wall. [*Pointing to a spot on the wall*] See. Fuck you, Mae.

MAE Fuck you, Lloyd.

LLOYD So tell me!

MAE Tell you what.

LLOYD What's arithmetic?

MAE It's numbers.

LLOYD Oh yeah!

MAE Yeah!

LLOYD Why didn't you say it's numbers!—I know numbers.

MAE You don't know numbers.

LLOYD Yes I do. [*He stands.*] I'm Lloyd. I have two pigs. My mother died. I was seven. My father left. He is dead. [*He gets three coins from his pocket.*] This is money. It's mine. It's three nickels. I'm Lloyd. That's arithmetic.

MAE That is not arithmetic.

LLOYD Why not?

MAE It isn't.

LLOYD [*he returns to the chair*] It's numbers!

MAE Arithmetic is more!

LLOYD What more!

MAE A lot more!—Multiplication!

LLOYD Come here! [*She puts the iron down.*]

MAE What for!

LLOYD I'm going to show you something.

MAE [*she walks to him*] What!

LLOYD [*in one move he takes her hand, crosses his left leg, and puts her hand on his crotch*] Feel it!

MAE What?

LLOYD It! It! Touch it!

MAE I'm touching it!

LLOYD Do something to it!

MAE What!

LLOYD Anything, stupid!

MAE Let go of my hand!

LLOYD [*pressing her tighter*] What hand?

MAE Let go, you jerk! You stink! You smell bad!

LLOYD So what!

MAE You're disgusting!

LLOYD No kidding!

MAE Let go! [*She steps on his foot.*]

LLOYD Shit! [*She goes back to the ironing board.*] I'll kick your ass! [*He feels his genitals.*] Shit, it's gone!

MAE What's gone! You can't get it up! You have some sickness there! [*Short pause*] You should go to a doctor.

LLOYD Didn't I say I got it up yesterday!

MAE Yes. You did.

LLOYD OK! So I did!—So where's dinner!

MAE I don't know where's dinner.

LLOYD You know where's dinner!

MAE You know where's dinner!

LLOYD Yeah, where's dinner! Dinner's in a pot on the stove! Dinner's on the table! It's in the cupboard! It's dried up in the pot! Dinner is somewhere! It's spilled on the floor! Where's dinner! [*There is a pause.*] Where's dinner! [*She continues ironing.*] Come here!

MAE Fuck you.

LLOYD You're a whore!

MAE I'm pressing, jerk! What are you doing! I'm pressing. What are you doing! [*He looks away.*] I'm pressing what are you doing! You're a jerk. [*She continues ironing.*] I work. See, I work. I'm working. I learned to work. I wake up and I work. Open my eyes and I work. I work. What do you do! Yeah, what do you do!—*Work!*

LLOYD So what. [*He sits in a corner on the floor.*]

MAE What do you do when you open your eyes. I work, jerk. You're a pig. You'll die like a pig in the mud. You'll rot there in the mud. No one will bury you. Your skin will bloat. In the mud. Then, it will get blue like rotten meat and it will bloat even more. And you will get so rotten that the dogs will puke when they come near you. Even flies won't go near you. You'll just lay there and rot. [*She irons.*] I'm going to die in a hospital. In white sheets. You hear? [*She looks front.*] Clean feet. Injections. That's how I'm going to die. I'm going to die clean. I'm going to school and I'm learning things. You're stupid. I'm not. When I finish school I'm leaving. You hear that? You can stay in the mud. [*She irons.*] Did you pick the corn?

LLOYD What corn?

MAE The corn I told you to pick.

LLOYD There is no corn.

MAE How come there is no corn.

LLOYD The groundhog ate it.

MAE You let him eat it.

LLOYD I didn't.

MAE You didn't watch it.

LLOYD I came in to sleep. I had to sleep.

MAE You can sleep in the field.

LLOYD It's wet there! It's cold! I'm sick! You sleep there!

MAE I work here, not in the field.

LLOYD I'll work here. You work there.

MAE [*harshly*] I wish you went to the doctor.—You're not going to get well if you don't. When I leave you'll starve.

LLOYD I'll find food.

MAE Where?

LLOYD Anywhere. There's food.

MAE Where.

LLOYD There's pigslop.

MAE What pigslop? There won't be any pigslop. Not if you don't grow something to put in it!

[*Pause.*]

LLOYD I did it to Betsy.

MAE You did.

LLOYD Yeah.—I felt bad.—My head hurt.—I went to her. She's nice. She lets me eat her food.—I did it to her.—I got it up. I got it in her all the way.—It didn't hurt.

MAE No kidding.

LLOYD It didn't hurt.

MAE You don't fuck pigs.

LLOYD She liked it.

MAE I'll bet.

LLOYD What do you mean?

MAE Did you get clean before you did it?

LLOYD What for? I'm clean.

MAE No you're not. You stink.

LLOYD She didn't mind.

MAE [*she places the ironing board alongside the right wall and places the garment she has pressed on top of the other pressed clothes*] I'm taking these up now. We'll walk to the clinic. You have to see a doctor. [*She starts putting on her shoes.*] Put on your shoes, Lloyd.—I'll walk there with you. I know you won't get there if I don't go with you. Get moving, Lloyd. [*She takes the clothes and goes to the door.*] Come on. [*He doesn't move.*] Let's go, Lloyd. [*He stands and goes for the ax. He holds the ax as he waits for her to exit.*] You're not going to the clinic with an ax.

LLOYD [*he goes to the chair still holding the ax and sits*] Why not.

MAE You can't.

LLOYD I'll take my knife, then.

MAE You can't take your knife either.

LLOYD I won't go then.

[*They freeze.*]

Scene 2

[MAE *takes a brown paper bag from the mantelpiece, opens the right door, steps on the threshold, and turns front as if she had just come from the outside. She has an air of serenity.* LLOYD *sits on the left. His appearance has worsened.*]

MAE I went to the clinic, Lloyd. And I told them what you have.

LLOYD What did you tell them?

MAE [*stepping into the room*] I told them you're sick. And I told them what you have.

LLOYD What did they say?

MAE They said you have to go there. [*As she gets the chair from the left corner and places it center*] You have to go to the clinic. They won't give you medicine till you go.

LLOYD I'm not going.

MAE They have to give you a test. They can't give you medicine till they find out what you have. They said you may have something bad.

LLOYD What.

MAE [*she sits*] They didn't say. [*She takes a pamphlet out of the paper bag.*] They gave me this book.

LLOYD What does it say?

MAE [*she places the paper bag on the mantelpiece*] I couldn't read it. I tried to read it but I can't. I got Henry to read it for you. He's outside.

LLOYD Why can't you read it?

MAE It's too difficult.

LLOYD All that time at school and you can't read.

MAE I tried to read it and it was too difficult. That's why I got Henry to read it because it was too difficult for me. It is advanced. I'm not advanced yet. I'm intermediate. I can read a lot of things but not this.—I'm going to let Henry in.

LLOYD [*reproachfully*] I wish you could have read it.

MAE Me too. I wish I could have read it. [*She opens the door and walks to the left of the center chair.*] Come in, Henry. [HENRY *enters and stands by the fireplace. He places his left hand on the mantelpiece.*] Sit down, Henry. [HENRY *sits on the center chair.* MAE *closes the door.*] Here's Henry, Lloyd. He's going to read for you.

HENRY Are you drunk, Lloyd? You look drunk.

MAE [*sitting on the right*] He's sick. He has a fever.

HENRY Has he been drinking?

LLOYD I am not drunk.

HENRY What's wrong with him?

MAE He's sick.

HENRY Remember Ron, what happened to him.

LLOYD What happened to him?

HENRY He died.—And what did he die of?

LLOYD He drank till he died.

MAE His liver failed him.

HENRY Why did his liver fail him? Alcohol.—Why did he drink? He drank because he owned alcohol. And why did he own alcohol? He owned alcohol because he owned a pharmacy. And why did that lead a man to drinking? Because he kept alcohol in the pharmacy.—There you have two things: alcohol and time to do nothing. So what happens? You drink yourself to death.—So, you have alcohol, you drink it. You don't have alcohol, you don't drink it. You have money to buy alcohol, you buy it. You don't have money to buy it, you don't buy it.—Does Lloyd have alcohol, Mae?

MAE He has no money to buy it.

HENRY If Lloyd had money he would drink. He'd be a drunk.

MAE Yes, he would.

HENRY If he's not a drunk it's because he's poor.

MAE He is.—This is the book, Henry.

HENRY [HENRY *puts on his glasses. He reads each section first to himself in a low voice. Then he reads it out loud stumbling through the words at a high speed.*] Prostatitis and Prostatosis. Acute and chronic bacterial infection of the prostrate[1] gland: symptoms, diagnosis, and treatment. [*He wets his finger and turns the page.*] Common symptoms of acute prostatitis and bacterial prostatosis are: febrile illness, back pains, perineal pain, irritative voiding, aching of the perineum, sexual pain, sexual impotency, painful ejaculation, and intermittent disureah,[2] or bloody ejaculation.

LLOYD What does that mean?

HENRY I don't know what it means, Lloyd. These are medical terms. It needs study. This may require the use of a dictionary—a special dictionary. One that has medical terms—technical terms—probably a dictionary that would have all kinds of technical terms—from hardware and construction terms to scientific terms—like physics. There are such dictionaries. [*Short pause*] You look swollen, Lloyd.

MAE He is swollen.

HENRY And your color is poor.

MAE Show him your tongue, Lloyd. His tongue is white and his breath smells bad.

[LLOYD *opens his mouth.* HENRY *looks at* LLOYD*'s tongue.*]

HENRY What is wrong with you?

MAE I want him to go to the doctor but he won't.

HENRY Why won't you go to the doctor, Lloyd.

LLOYD I don't want to go.

MAE He will stay here and rot.

LLOYD I won't rot. I said I'd go. You said I couldn't go.

MAE He wanted to go up with an ax. He's an animal. You don't go to the clinic with an ax. You can't do that.

HENRY Why would you do that, Lloyd?

LLOYD I didn't do it. I never went.

HENRY He does smell bad.

MAE He's rotting away and he won't do anything about it. You better dig your grave while you can, Lloyd. Because I'm not going to do it for you. I told him to find a spot and dig it. It takes a strong person to dig that deep. I can't do it. I wouldn't, even if I could. [*Pause*] Would you like some bread, Henry? I got some butter.

HENRY Yes, thank you.

MAE Would you like some dinner? We have soup.

HENRY Yes, thank you.

MAE Stay then, I haven't started it yet.

HENRY I will, thank you.

[*They freeze.*]

1. Henry's misreading for "prostate."
2. Dysuria; that is, painful or difficult urination.

Scene 3

[MAE *places the pamphlet on the mantelpiece, then takes the pot, plates, and spoons and places them on the table. They each take a spoon and plate, then they pass them to* MAE, *who holds the plates in her hands as if she were about to put them away.* LLOYD *lies on the floor, under the table, facing front.* HENRY *moves his chair slightly to the left. He and* MAE *have been talking. They both speak with philosophical objectivity.*]

HENRY Soon everything will be used only once. We will use things once. We will need to do that as our time will be of value and it will not be feasible to spend it caring for things: washing them, mending them, repairing them. We will use a car till it breaks down. Then, we will discard it. A radio or any machine or appliance will be discarded as soon as it breaks down. We will make a call on the telephone and a new one will be delivered. Already we see places that use paper cups, paper plates, paper towels.—Our time will not be wasted and we will choose how to spend it.

MAE I don't think I'll be wanted in such a world.

HENRY Why not?

MAE . . . Oh. [*Pause*] In such a world a person must be of value.

HENRY Oh?

MAE I feel I am hollow . . . and offensive. [*As* MAE *places the dishes on the mantelpiece*]

HENRY Why is that?

MAE I think most people are.

HENRY What do you mean?—Explain what you mean.

MAE I don't think I can.

HENRY I am not offensive. I don't think I am offensive. I think I am a decent man.

MAE You are decent, Henry. I know you are, and so is Lloyd in his own way.

HENRY Then, what do you mean when you say we are offensive?

MAE I mean that we are base, and that we spend our lives with small things.

HENRY I don't feel I do that.

MAE Don't be offended, Henry. You are not base. Of all the people I know you are the finest. You are the person I respect and I feel most proud to know.—[*She begins to look at him fixedly, possessed by fervor.*] I have no one to talk to. And sometimes I feel hollow and base. And I feel I don't have a mind. But when I talk to you I do. I feel I have a mind. Why is that? [*She moves closer to him.*] Why is it that some people make you feel stupid and some people make you feel smart. Not smart, because I am not smart. But some people make you feel that you have something inside you. Inside your head. [*She moves closer.*] Why is it that you can talk, Henry, and Lloyd cannot talk? Why is that? What I'm saying, Henry, is that I want you. That I want you here with me. That I love you.

HENRY Mae, this is unexpected.

MAE It is unexpected, Henry.

HENRY I have nothing to offer you.

MAE Yes, you do. I want you.

HENRY Me?

MAE [*she starts to move her head toward him slowly and intensely*] I want your mind.

HENRY . . . My mind?

MAE [*still moving her head toward him*] I want it. [*She kisses him intensely. They look at each other.*]

HENRY Did you feel my mind?

MAE Yes. I did. [*She kisses him again.*] I did. I want you here.

HENRY Here?

MAE I want you here.

HENRY To live here?

MAE If you will.

[*They freeze.*]

Scene 4

[HENRY *exits.* MAE *places the spoons and pot on the mantelpiece. Then, she takes off her shoes, places a pair of trousers on the ironing board, and puts out the ironing board.* LLOYD *gets the box with the string from the fireplace and stands down left holding it.* MAE *irons.*]

MAE Just put it down. [*He stands still. She continues ironing.*] Put it down Lloyd. [*He stands still.*] Henry is going to stay here with us. He is going to live here. He needs a place and I want him to stay here. You can learn from Henry. If you want to, he can teach you how to read. Put the box down. I'll take it up to the bedroom. Henry's going to sleep in the bedroom. He has a bad back and he needs to sleep in the bed. You can sleep here.—Get papers from the shed and lay them on the floor. I'll get you a blanket.—I'll take it up now. [*She takes the box from* LLOYD *and exits left. He is distraught. He sits on the chair on the left and cries. He puts his head on the table and freezes.*]

Scene 5

[MAE *places the ironing board against the wall.* LLOYD *places the pitcher of milk and the plate with bread on the table.* MAE *gets the plates and spoons. She places the spoons in the center and lays each plate in front of her.* HENRY *enters and sits center.* LLOYD *sits left.* LLOYD *and* HENRY *take a spoon each.* MAE *serves bread onto the plates, pours milk on the bread, and passes two plates to* HENRY, *who passes one to* LLOYD *and keeps the second for himself.* MAE *sits. They start eating.*]

MAE Do you say grace before a meal, Henry?

HENRY I do sometimes.

MAE Would you say grace?

HENRY I will, if you want me to.

MAE I do.

HENRY [*crosses his hands*] Oh, give thanks unto the Lord, for he is good: for his mercy endures forever. For he satisfies the longing soul, and fills the hungry soul with goodness.

MAE We never said grace in this house. My father never did and I never learned how and neither did Lloyd.—Lloyd did you hear that? Henry said grace. I feel grace in my heart. I feel fresh inside as if a breeze had just gone inside my heart. What was it you said, Henry? What were these words. I don't retain the words. I never do. I find it hard to retain words I learn. It is hard for me to do the work at school. I can work on my feet all day at the ironing board. I can make myself do it, even if I am tired. But I cannot make myself retain what I learn. I have no memory. The teacher says I have no memory. And it's true I don't. I don't remember the things I learn too well. Not enough to pass the test. But I rejoice with the knowledge that I get. Not everything, but most things, make me feel joyful. Do you feel that way, Henry?

HENRY I am not sure. I like to know things. But if I didn't remember what I learned, I don't think I would feel any pleasure.—If I didn't remember things, I would feel that I don't know them. I like to learn things so I can live according to them, according to my knowledge. What would be the use of knowing things if they don't serve you, if they don't help you shape your life.—Lloyd, do you take pleasure in learning if you forget what you have learned?

[LLOYD *looks at* MAE, *then at* HENRY *again.*]

MAE Lloyd doesn't like learning things.

LLOYD I like learning things.

MAE Why don't you then?

LLOYD What is it I haven't learned?

[MAE *and* HENRY *look at each other.*]

MAE Henry, would you say grace again?

HENRY Again?

MAE Is that wrong?

HENRY No. Oh, give thanks unto the Lord, for he is good: for his mercy endures forever. For he satisfies the longing soul, and fills the hungry soul with goodness. [MAE *sobs.*] Why are you crying?

MAE I am a hungry soul. I am a longing soul. I am an empty soul. [*She cries.*] I cry with joy. It satisfies me to hear words that speak so lovingly to my soul. [MAE *eats.* LLOYD *eats.* HENRY *watches* MAE.] Don't be afraid to eat from our dishes, Henry. They are clean.

[*They freeze.*]

Scene 6

[LLOYD *places his plate and spoon over* HENRY's. HENRY *places the pitcher and bread plate on the mantelpiece and exits.* MAE *places the plates and spoons on the mantelpiece and gets the textbook. She sits center and reads with difficulty. She follows the written words with the fingers of both hands. Her reading is inspired.* LLOYD *listens to her and stares at the book.*]

MAE The starfish is an animal, not a fish. He is called a fish because he lives in the water. The starfish cannot live out of the water. If he is moist and in the shade he may be able to live out of the water for a day. Starfish eat old and dead sea animals. They keep the water clean. A starfish has five arms like a star. That is why it is called a starfish. Each of the arms of the starfish has an eye in the end. These eyes do not look like our eyes. A starfish's eye cannot see. But they can tell if it is night or day. If a starfish loses an arm he can grow a new one. This takes about a year. A starfish can live five or ten years or perhaps more, no one really knows.

[LLOYD *slaps the book off the table.* MAE *slaps* LLOYD. *They freeze.*]

Scene 7

[LLOYD *picks up the book and places it on the down-left corner of the table. He places the left chair against the wall and sits.* MAE *takes a notebook and pencil from the mantelpiece. She takes the book and stands on the up-right side of the table copying from the book.* HENRY *enters and stands on the up-left corner.*]

HENRY What is Lloyd to you? [*There is a pause.*] He's a man and he's not a blood relative. So what is he to you?

MAE Lloyd? [*Pause*] He is like family.

HENRY But he is not.—Everyone knows he is not. What is he?

MAE I don't know what you call what he is. If I were to ask myself I would not know what to answer.—He is not with me. You know he is not. He sleeps down here.

HENRY I feel I am offending him. And he is offending me. So what is he.

MAE [*sitting on the right facing front*] What can I do, Henry, I don't want you to be offended. There's nothing I can do and there's nothing you can do and there is nothing Lloyd can do. He's always been here, since he was little. My dad brought him in. He said that Lloyd was a good boy and that he could keep me company. He said he was old and tired and he didn't understand what a young person like me was like. That he had no patience left and he was weary of life and he had no more desire to make things work. He didn't want to listen to me talk and he felt sorry to see me sad and lonely. He didn't want to be mean to me, but he didn't have the patience. He was sick. My dad was good but he was sad and hopeless and when my mom died he went to hell with himself. He got sick and died and he left Lloyd here and Lloyd and I took care of each other. I don't know what we are. We are related but I don't know what to call it. We are not brother and sister. We are like animals who grow up together and mate. We were mates till you came here, but not since then. I could not be his mate again, not while you are here. I am not an animal. I care about things, Henry, I do. I know some things that I never learned. It's just that I don't know what they are. I cannot grasp them. [*She goes on her knees as her left shoulder leans on the corner of the table.*] I don't want to live like a dog. [*Pause*] Lloyd is good, Henry. And this is his home. [*Pause. She looks up.*] When you came here I thought heaven had come to this place, and I still feel so. How can there be offense here for you?

[*They freeze.*]

Scene 8

[LLOYD *places his chair by the table and exits.* MAE *places the notebook, pencil, and textbook on the mantelpiece. She places the dish with string beans center and sits. She snaps beans.* HENRY *walks behind* MAE *and covers her eyes. He takes a small package from his pocket and puts it in the bowl.*]

MAE What is it? [*He uncovers her eyes. She unwraps the package. It is a lipstick.*] Lipstick . . . [HENRY *pushes the lipstick out of the tube. He takes a mirror out of his pocket and holds it in front of her.*] A mirror. [*She holds the mirror and puts on lipstick. She puckers her lips. He kisses her.*] Oh, Henry.

[*They freeze.*]

Scene 9

[MAE *places the lipstick, mirror, and dish with string beans on the mantelpiece. She places the textbook center and sits.* HENRY *places the paper and lipstick cover on the mantelpiece. He takes the newspaper, turns the left chair toward the down-left corner, and sits to read, leaning his elbow on the table.* LLOYD *sits on the floor, down of the right chair with his arm leaning on it.*]

MAE [*reading*] This is a hermit crab. He is called a hermit because he lives in empty shells that once belonged to other animals. When he is little he likes to crawl into the shells of water snails. When he grows larger he finds a larger shell. Often he tries several shells before he finds the one that fits. Sometimes he wants the shell of another hermit crab and then there is a fight. Sometimes the owner is pulled out. Sometimes the owner wins and stays.

[LLOYD *lifts himself up to look at* HENRY. *He mouths a curse.* MAE *turns to look at* LLOYD, *then looks at* HENRY. HENRY *turns to look at* MAE, *then he looks at* LLOYD. *They freeze.*]

Act 2

Scene 10

[HENRY *enters left carrying a notebook, pencil, and a few bills. He sits left. He transfers figures from the bills to the ledger.* LLOYD *enters right. He stands up-center. He reaches into his pocket for a medical prescription and stretches his arm in* HENRY'*s direction. He sits to the right. The italicized words represent a stuttering.*]

LLOYD They gave me *this.*

HENRY [*reads what's on the paper while still in* LLOYD'*s hand. He returns to his papers.*] That's the prescription for your medicine.

LLOYD They said I should buy *this.* [*Pause*] They said I should *buy* it.

HENRY Did you?

LLOYD No.

HENRY Why not.

LLOYD I went to the *clinic.*

HENRY [*without looking at him*] I'm glad you did.

LLOYD It took a *while.* I thought they *kept* me a long time. I went *early* and just came back.

HENRY How do you feel?

LLOYD I don't feel *better.*—I feel *worse.*

HENRY Why is that?

LLOYD They have *instruments* there. They *stuck instruments* in me.

HENRY What did they say?

LLOYD I have to take *medicine—pills.* I have to *buy* them. They said I have to *swallow* the pills.

HENRY I'm glad you went.

LLOYD [*stretches his arm to show* HENRY *the prescription*] They gave me *this.* They said I should *buy* this. [*He puts the prescription on the table.*] They said I should *buy* it.

HENRY [*with contained anger*] You should get the medicine, Lloyd. You should take it and get it over with. You should take the medication and get well. You should not walk around with an illness that's eating your insides. Get the medicine. Do as you are told.

[*They freeze.*]

Scene 11

[HENRY *exits.* LLOYD *takes the box of pills from the mantelpiece and empties it on the table. He sits center.* MAE *enters right, wiping her wet hands with her skirt. She sits right.* LLOYD *puts a pill in his mouth. A moment later he spits it.*]

MAE What are they?

LLOYD Pills.

MAE Lloyd . . . What are you doing? [*He cleans his tongue.*] Does it taste bad?

LLOYD Yeah.

MAE [*she picks up the pill and sits*] Try it again. [*He puts it in his mouth.*] Swallow it. [*He swallows and chokes. She stands by him and pushes the pill down his throat. She looks at him.*] Did you swallow it? [*She looks at him.*] What do you feel? [*He makes a face. She sits and puts the pills in the box.*] How did you get them?

LLOYD [*defensively*] I bought them.—I took the money.—From Henry.—From his trousers.—I took the money from his trousers.—I don't care.—He owes me money.—For rent.—For my bed.—He took my bed.—Like a crab.—He got into my bed like a crab.—I took it.—I didn't steal it, because it belonged to me.—Because I needed to get my medicine.—And he never gave me what he owed me.—I had to ask him for it.—And he never gave it to me.—I asked him.—And he never gave it to me.—And he came here only to take things from me.—Like a crab.

[HENRY *enters left. He is in his underwear. He carries his pants over his left arm. He holds a change purse in his right hand. He walks down left and stands there. He is stunned.*]

HENRY Someone took money from my purse.—There is less money here than I should have.—Some of the money I had is gone.

MAE Lloyd took it.

HENRY [*he sits*] Well, tell him to give it back.

MAE He took it for his medicine.

HENRY He went to my purse and took it?

MAE He needed money for his medicine. [*Pause*] Would you let Lloyd have that money?

HENRY Have Lloyd have my money?

[*Pause.*]

MAE He'll pay it back.

HENRY How will he pay it back?

MAE [*to* LLOYD] . . . Lloyd . . . ? [LLOYD *looks at* MAE.]

HENRY How will he pay it back. How will Lloyd get money to pay me back? [*Pause*] How much money did he take?

MAE . . . Lloyd . . . ?

LLYOD I don't know how much I took.

HENRY How will he pay it back if he doesn't know how much he took? [*Pause*] Tell him I want to know how much he took.

LLOYD I went to the clinic.—And they put those instruments in me.—And they said I had to buy that medicine.—And I couldn't find someone to help me buy that medicine.—I went to the pharmacy.—And they said I had to pay for it.—And Henry had money but he wouldn't pay for it.—And he took my bed.—And he can take anything he wants from me.—And I had to buy that medicine.—So I took the money from him.

HENRY Ask him when he took it.

LLOYD I took it while he slept.

HENRY How much did he take?

[*Pause.*]

MAE Lloyd can't count, Henry.

HENRY [*he takes money out of the purse, puts it on the table and counts it. He does mental subtraction.*] Tell him he took one fifty four. [MAE *looks at* LLOYD.] Is that what he spent? Does he still have any of that money? [LLOYD *reaches into his pocket.*] Tell him to put it on the table. [LLOYD *does.* HENRY *counts the money, then does mental subtraction. He puts the coins in the purse and goes to the door.*] Tell him he owes me one thirty eight. And tell him I wish he'll pay it back. [*He exits.* MAE *goes to the door and looks in the direction* HENRY *has walked. They freeze.*]

Scene 12

[MAE *puts a pair of trousers on the ironing board and puts the ironing board out.* LLOYD *places the box of pills on the mantelpiece and stands on top of the table.*]

LLOYD There is a reason why it happened to him and not to me.

MAE I wish it had happened to you.

LLOYD Ha!—It couldn't have happened to me. I'm strong. He's weak and old. That's why he fell. [*Doing an exaggerated demonstration of someone walking on dangerous ground*] I can walk on wet stones and I don't fall. Look. I can run on wet stones. I can stand on my own two feet. Look! [*He jumps to the floor and stands with his feet apart.*] Try and push me. Go on. Push me. [*She ignores him. He jumps on the table in a prone position with his legs crossed and his hands under his head.*] I wish he had drowned. I wish he had fallen in the water and drowned. He's old. His legs couldn't hold him. That's why he fell. [*He jumps to the floor and runs across jumping up in the air making sounds as he goes up and down. He does this several times, then holds an athletic pose.*] Can he do that?

MAE [*still ironing*] No, he can't. He's paralyzed. He may be a cripple. You know he can't do that!

LLOYD [*lies on the table with his hands under his head*] He couldn't do it before he fell. That's why he fell. He's old. He was falling apart. That's why he fell. Now he can't even move.—Look! [*He does several cartwheels.*] Can he do that?

MAE No, he can't.

LLOYD [*sits on the table with his arms and legs in a bodybuilder's pose*] He has no muscle. I wouldn't fall if I had to walk on wet stones. I can run on wet stones. Like this. [*He demonstrates.*] I wish he had fell in the water. I wish he had drowned. So now he can't walk. [*Short pause*] Who's going to take care of him?

MAE We are.

[LLOYD *exits right. The sound of vomiting is heard. She freezes.*]

Scene 13

[MAE *puts the ironing board alongside the wall.* LLOYD *enters left with the cup with oatmeal and the spoon. He places the right chair away from the table.* HENRY *enters. He sits on the chair to the right. His left side is paralyzed and deformed. His trousers are rolled to his knees. He is bare-chested and wears a kitchen towel as a bib. He wears a necktie under the towel. He holds a tin cup of milk in his left hand.* LLOYD *is perched against the table next to* HENRY. *He feeds oatmeal to him.* HENRY *moves the oatmeal around his mouth, then he lets it dribble out or he spits it.* HENRY'S *speech is incomprehensible.*]

LLOYD Stop it! [*Scooping the spilled oatmeal from* HENRY'S *chin and bib and putting it back in his mouth*] Stop doing that.—Don't do that. [HENRY *lets the oatmeal out.*] You just quit that.—Chew it.—Swallow it. [HENRY *lets the oatmeal out.* LLOYD *starts scooping it.*] Stop that! Stop doing that! You better stop that, Henry.— [HENRY *lets the oatmeal out.*] Quit that. You just quit that. [HENRY *slaps the cup of milk and spills it on the floor.*] That is it, Henry. [*Taking* HENRY'S *bib off.*] You get your own food.

HENRY It spilled!

LLOYD You did it on purpose.

HENRY It spilled.

LLOYD No, it didn't. You spilled it.

HENRY Clean it!

LLOYD No, I won't. You clean it. I saw you do it. You clean it.

HENRY Clean it!

LLOYD I won't clean it. You clean it.

HENRY Clean it!

LLOYD You clean it!

HENRY Mae . . . ! [*Pause*] Mae . . . ! [*Pause*] Mae . . . !

MAE [*enters. She carries a bundle of clothes and a cleaning rag.*] What is it?

HENRY [*pointing to the milk*] Look!

MAE What happened? (MAE *puts the clothes on the bench and stands by* HENRY *with the rag.*)

HENRY He spilled it!

LLOYD I didn't spill it! He spilled it!

MAE So clean it up!

HENRY Clean it!

LLOYD I'm going to kill him.

MAE Kill him if you want.—He can't talk straight any more. [*She starts wiping the oatmeal off* HENRY.] Clean up the milk!

HENRY Clean it!

[LLOYD *takes* HENRY'S *bib and starts wiping the milk.*]

MAE Did you feed the pigs?

LLOYD Yeah.

MAE Did Henry eat?

LLOYD He spilled the milk.

MAE Did he eat! [LLOYD *doesn't answer.*] Did he eat! [*Pause*] Did you eat, Henry?

HENRY I ate.

MAE He ate. Why didn't you say he ate. [MAE *walks to the left door and opens it.*]

LLOYD I'm going to kill him.

MAE [*stands on the threshold and turns to* LLOYD] So kill him.

[*They freeze.*]

Scene 14

[MAE *exits.* LLOYD *places the bib, the oatmeal cup and spoon, and the tin cup on the mantelpiece. He takes the textbook and sits center. He attempts to read. He first makes the sound of the letter. Then, he speaks the name of the letter and traces it with his finger on the table. Then, he puts the sounds of the letters together.* HENRY *sits to the right facing front. He mimics* LLOYD*'s effort and laughs in silent convulsions.*]

LLOYD S.

HENRY S.

LLOYD T. St.

HENRY T. St.

LLOYD A.

HENRY A.

LLOYD Stop that!

HENRY A.

LLOYD Stop it, Henry!

HENRY A.

LLOYD R. Ar.

HENRY R. Ar.

LLOYD Sta.

HENRY Sta.

LLOYD Star.

[*The left door opens.* MAE *stands outside and looks in.*]

HENRY Star.

LLOYD F.

HENRY F.

LLOYD I. Fi.

HENRY I. Fi.

LLOYD S. Fis.

HENRY S. Fis.

LLOYD Stop it. Cut it out. Fish.

HENRY Fish.

[MAE *enters left. She carries a bundle of clothes.*]

LLOYD Fish.

HENRY Fish.

MAE Someone took my money. Who did? [*Neither looks at her.*] Who did!—Did you, Lloyd!

LLOYD I didn't. Fish.

HENRY Fish.

MAE Did Henry? Did you take the money, Henry? [*She closes the door.*] Answer me. Did you take the money! Someone took it! You took it, Lloyd. Hand it over.

LLOYD I didn't take it.

MAE Hand it over.

LLOYD I didn't take it!

MAE Who took it then!

LLOYD Henry took it.

MAE [*to* LLOYD] He didn't take it. He can't walk.

LLOYD Yes, he can. You know he can. Walk, Henry. Show Mae how you can walk. Walk! He can walk.

MAE [*enraged*] Walk!

HENRY I can't walk.

LLOYD You can walk!

MAE Don't say he can walk, Lloyd. He can't walk. He didn't take the money. [*She notices the book.*] What are you doing with my book? [*He lowers his head. She is perplexed.*] What are you doing? [*She takes the book and holds it protectively.*] Don't mess my book.

HENRY He was messing it. [*He laughs.*]

MAE Shut up, Henry.

HENRY He was saying "Fish." [*He laughs.*]

MAE Everything turns bad for me.

[*They freeze.*]

Scene 15

[LLOYD *exits.* MAE *places the book on the mantelpiece and stands by the down-right corner of the table.* HENRY *walks to the left and sits. His hand is inside his fly. He handles himself.*]

HENRY Mae. I still feel desire.—I am sexual.—I have not lost my sexuality.—Mae, make love to me. [MAE *doesn't answer. He continues touching himself.*] You are my wife. I want you. I feel the same desires. I feel the same needs. I have not changed. [*He holds on to the table and begins to stand.*] Mae, I have not stopped wanting you.—I can make love to you.—I can satisfy you. [*Supporting himself on the table, he slides toward her.*] I am potent.—I can make you happy. Kiss me, Mae.— [*He grabs her wrist.*] Tell me you still love me. Kiss me. Let me feel you close to me.—You think a cripple has no feelings.—I'm not crippled in my parts.—It gets hard. [*He puts his right arm around her waist.*] Mae, I love you. [*He holds her tighter. He starts moving his pelvis against her.*] I'm coming. . . . [*He starts sliding down to the floor.*] I'm coming. . . . I'm coming. . . . I'm coming. . . . I'm coming. . . . [*He collapses. She falls on the chair. She stands and leans against the table.*]

MAE You can walk, Henry. You took my money.

[*They freeze.*]

Scene 16

[MAE *exits left.* HENRY *is on the floor trying to sit on the chair.* LLOYD *enters right. He helps* HENRY *up and closes his fly.* MAE *enters with* HENRY*'s box and lifts it up in the air.*]

HENRY Don't, Mae.

MAE [*throwing the box at him*] Get out!

[LLOYD *exits right.*]

HENRY Don't throw things at me, Mae!

MAE You took the money!

HENRY You hurt me, Mae! You threw that box at me and hurt me!

MAE You took the money!

HENRY I didn't take it!

MAE You took it! Where is it? [*She moves toward him.*]

HENRY I didn't take it!

[MAE *reaches in his right pocket. She pulls out a wad of bills. She grabs his necktie, turns it back, and pulls it down.* LLOYD *puts his head in through the left door and begins to enter.* MAE *and* LLOYD *speak the following speeches at the same time.*]

MAE I feed you and I take care of you! And you steal from me? You eat my food and you sleep in my bed and you steal from me! You're a pig, Henry. You're worse than Lloyd!

LLOYD Kill him, Mae! Kill him! Kill him! [*He climbs on the table on all fours.*] He's no good! Kill him, Mae! He's no good! He's a thief!

[HENRY *falls off the chair.* MAE *falls on her knees next to him.* LLOYD *jumps off the table. He lets out a hysterical laugh.*]

LLOYD Look he's bleeding! [*He chants and dances.*] Henry's bleeding! Henry's bleeding! Henry's bleeding!

MAE Shut up, Lloyd!

[*There is silence.*]

HENRY It was my money. Lloyd never paid me. He never paid me. He never paid me what he owed me.

MAE You could have let him have it. Just because he takes care of you. You could have let him have your money. He takes care of you.

HENRY He never paid me.

MAE [*she looks up to the sky*] Can't I have a decent life? [*There is a pause.*]

LLOYD But I love you, Mae.

HENRY I love you, Mae.

[*They freeze.*]

Scene 17

[LLOYD *places the box inside the fireplace. He closes the left door.* MAE *gets the empty box from the fireplace and places it on the right chair. She places the bundle of women's clothes from under the bench on the table. She is packing clothes in the box.* LLOYD *stands up-left. He watches her.* HENRY *sits left.*]

MAE [*as she packs*] I'm leaving, Lloyd. I'm going somewhere else. I'm leaving you and Henry. Both of you are no good. I got rotten luck. I work too hard and the two of you keep sucking my blood. I'm going to look for a better place to be. [LLOYD *sits on the chair upstage of the table.*] Just a place where the two of you are not sucking my blood. I'm going to find myself a job. And a room to live in. Far away from you. Where I don't have my blood sucked.

LLOYD Don't go, Mae.

HENRY Don't go.

MAE I'm going and that's that.

LLOYD Where are you going?

MAE I don't know, Lloyd. I'm just going.

LLOYD I'll do what you say.

MAE I don't care what you do. [*Closing the box*] You do what you want. Henry too. I don't care what he does.

LLOYD Stay, Mae.

HENRY Please.

MAE I'm going. You take care of Henry, Lloyd. [*She goes to the door.*]

LLOYD Don't go, Mae.

HENRY Please.

MAE Goodbye.

[*She exits through the right door and closes the door.* LLOYD *is still for a few seconds. He then runs to the door, knocking down his chair. He exits.*]

LLOYD [*shouting*] Mae . . . ! [HENRY *makes a plaintive sound.*] Mae . . . !

HENRY Mae . . . !

LLOYD [*offstage*] Mae . . . ! [HENRY *makes a plaintive sound.*] Stop, Mae!

HENRY Stop!

[LLOYD *enters running. He takes the rifle.* HENRY *makes incoherent sounds.* LLOYD *exits running.*]

LLOYD Mae . . . ! Stop . . . ! Stop, Mae!

HENRY Mae . . . !

LLOYD Mae, stop . . . !

HENRY Mae . . . !

LLOYD Mae! Mae! Mae!

[*A shot is heard. There is silence. Another shot is heard.*]

HENRY [*plaintively*] . . . Mae . . .

[LLOYD *appears in threshold carrying* MAE. *She is drenched in blood and unconscious.* LLOYD *turns to* HENRY.]

LLOYD She's not leaving, Henry.

[HENRY *lets out a whimper.* LLOYD *places* MAE *on the table.* MAE *begins to move.*]

MAE Like the starfish, I live in the dark and my eyes see only a faint light. It is faint and yet it consumes me. I long for it. I thirst for it. I would die for it. Lloyd, I am dying.

[MAE *collapses.* LLOYD *sobs.* HENRY *lets out a plaintive cry. They freeze.*]

End.

DAVID MAMET

b. 1947

EVER since his first great success with *American Buffalo* (1975), David Mamet has been the principal dramatist of a ruthless modern world in which individuals struggle for survival and dominance. Whether depicting the world of small-time crooks or of real estate salesmen, Mamet's plays center on fast-talking, street-smart characters seeking an edge to get ahead. In the end, his plays show how profoundly capitalism has shaped America, affecting not just the lives of individual characters but also their social relations; he is the poet of what might be called capitalist existentialism. Rather than denouncing the world he depicts as immoral, Mamet observes its workings with a detached fascination that is imbued with sympathy. He is also one of the few major dramatists to be equally at home in the theater and in film. His first well-known work for the cinema was an adaptation of James Cain's 1934 novel, *The Postman Always Rings Twice* (1981), and he has since turned several of his own plays into films, written original screenplays, and directed successful features, notably *The House of Games* (1987), *Homicide* (1991), and *The Spanish Prisoner* (1997). With new plays and films coming out every few years, Mamet has reached the prime of his career, and he may yet have surprises and new breakthroughs in store for us.

Born into a Jewish family in a suburb of Chicago, Mamet was introduced to drama at an early age, acting in small parts for an uncle who produced radio and television programs for the Chicago Board of Rabbis. In 1998, Mamet commemorated the urban milieu of his youth with the plays that make up *The Old Neighborhood*. After high school, he attended Goddard College in Vermont. During his junior year, he studied at New York's Neighborhood Playhouse with Sanford Meisner, a master teacher of naturalist acting who influenced Mamet as a director as well as a playwright. After graduation, he taught drama for a year at Marlboro College in Vermont, returning a year later to Goddard as an artist-in-residence. There Mamet founded the St. Nicholas Theatre Company with William H. Macy and other actors who would become prominent interpreters of his plays—which would be produced by that company, following its revival after he moved back to Chicago.

Mamet's earliest plays—*Lakeboat* (1970), *Duck Variations* (1972), and *Sexual Perversity in Chicago* (1974)—exemplify his most typical form: the two-person dialogue. These early plays are essentially strings of episodes; Mamet shows little interest in constructing an arch of action, in building up tensions that lead to a climactic event whose consequences are then developed toward their logical conclusion. The propulsive force instead is the spoken word, the chatter of his characters as they reminisce, brag, lie, conceal, bully, and offend one another in a series of conversations. It is difficult to identify a thematic interest or project, since the plays' settings seem to be little more than an excuse for exploring the particular everyday idiom of the characters—often lowlifes—who inhabit this or that subgroup or profession. Mamet works in the tradition of naturalism in that he preserves these characters' mistakes and colloquialisms, their repetitions, interruptions, and incomplete sentences. But he also manages to turn this ordinary idiom into a rhythmic, almost poetic language and transforms everyday dialogue into a literary style. In the process, his characters often become brilliant users and abusers of language, expert storytellers and manipulators of words who enjoy their mastery as much as Mamet does his.

Mamet found this dominance of speech over action in the three writers whom he considers his primary influences: HAROLD PINTER, SAMUEL BECKETT, and the nineteenth-century German dramatist Heinrich von Kleist. From Pinter, he learned to write elliptical dialogues, full of interruptions and silences; from Beckett, he learned that a play can be sustained by cyclical and meandering exchanges that accomplish nothing and that have to begin anew in each act; and from Kleist, he learned to use language ruthlessly and strategically. A fourth influence was ANTON CHEKHOV, whose work Mamet came to know intimately through his fine adaptations of *The Cherry Orchard* (1987), *The Three Sisters* (1992), and *Uncle Vanya* (1989). Like Mamet's, Chekhov's plays are based not on action but on the rhythms of speech, the endless repetitions of phrases through which provincial characters express and repress their ideas and desires.

Mamet broke through as a dramatist when he related his interest in language and dialogue to the larger structures of life in the United States—specifically, to the nature and effects of capitalism—in *American Buffalo*. The play examines capitalist individualism at the local level: a pawn shop inhabited by a few small-time crooks. *American Buffalo* presents a world of exchanges of commodities that are all more or less worthless. The characters are planning to steal the coin collection of someone who had earlier bought a buffalo head nickel at the shop, but their inability to determine (with the help of an outdated book) the value of another old coin suggests that the robbery would be pointless even if pulled off successfully. The men exploit one another's weak spots, play on each other's fears and desires, manipulate and lie for their piece of an increasingly worthless pie. Yet even as they present themselves as ready to sacrifice anything for a good deal, they also exhibit moments of sentimentality that belie their tough-talking poses. A work treating the same subject on a grander scale was *The Water Engine* (1977), which Mamet originally wrote as a radio play (perhaps a natural medium for a writer who emphasizes language) and later adapted to the stage. *The Water Engine* is set at the Chicago World's Fair of 1934, an awe-inspiring display of American ingenuity in the midst of the Great Depression. Running through the play is a chain letter, representing the pyramid scheme that in Mamet's view epitomizes the greed and exploitation inherent to capitalism.

The inability to assign value—indeed, the general untrustworthiness of all products of capitalism—has increasingly emerged as Mamet's most important theme. Nearly all of his work written since the 1980s seems to suggest, in one way or another, that you can't trust what people say, you can't trust what they do, and things are not what they seem to be, but he has explored this idea most fully in his films. Whereas many of his plays revolve around proposed actions that never take place and schemes that never quite work out, his films (especially *Homicide, A House of Games,* and *The Spanish Prisoner*) devise plans of astonishing complexity, with layers of feints, baits, and trickery that are masterminded by a single, perfect plotter.

The three pillars of Mamet's work—dialogue, capitalism, and the con game—jointly sustain what is to date his masterwork: *GLENGARRY GLEN ROSS* (1983). Like his earlier plays, it is set in a limited, enclosed world, here a small real estate office that sells worthless property in Florida with Scottish-sounding names. Mamet knew this world firsthand, for he had briefly worked in a real estate office in Chicago. The entire play proceeds at a breakneck speed, drawing its electricity from ruthless, winner-takes-all capitalism: the best salesman of the month gets a Cadillac; the second-best receives steak knives, and the two lowest performers will be fired. The salesmen are thus reduced to competitors in a high-stakes game that leaves no time for anything besides cut-throat business. Like many of Mamet's other plays, *Glengarry* presents an all-male world from which private lives have all but disappeared. Despite his declared sympathy for his salesmen and the ingenuity they exhibit in their struggle, the play excoriates the system that has produced them.

In choosing salesmen as his protagonists, Mamet joined a line of prominent twentieth-century dramatists—EUGENE O'NEILL, in *The Iceman Cometh* (1946), and ARTHUR MILLER, in *Death of a Salesman* (1949) notable among them—who call into question America's capitalist dream. But unlike Miller, who famously turned his play into a general parable by deliberately not specifying the products sold by Willy Loman, Mamet details what is being sold and for how much. At the same time, however, none of the commodities that circulate through this play, from the Cadillac and the steak knives to the Florida property, have any genuine utility. None of the salesmen even pretend that he wants, let alone needs, the Cadillac or the steak knives, and we know that their whole enterprise is fraudulent. They are selling real estate that could hardly be less real: not only is it worthless but even the buyers seem to have no need for it.

While *Glengarry* is a play about capitalism, it is also something of a detective story: the real estate office is broken into and valuable customer information is stolen. In the second act, the play thus turns, at least on the surface, into a whodunit. Most of the characters have a motive for the robbery, since they are all victims of the cruel system in which they are forced to operate, and one salesman's mistake that reveals his guilt coincides with the play's end. But it is important to realize that the detective plot is ultimately only a frame, not integral to the central theme.

The set and cast of the original 1983 production of *Glengarry Glen Ross* at the Cottesloe Theatre, London.

Unlike Mamet's films, which concentrate on elaborate cons and schemes, this play uses the burglary, a crime haplessly executed and quickly solved, merely as a backdrop for a study in the language of salesmanship. It is steeped in the peculiar idiom of the salesmen—"sits" or meetings with clients, "cold calls," and the "closing" of deals. The play's epigraph is "always be closing," which is explained as a "practical sales maxim." The most important bit of jargon, used innumerable times, is "leads": the names and addresses of potential buyers, ranked according to the likelihood that they will pan out. As in Mamet's early works, the first act of *Glengarry Glen Ross* is structured around a series of dialogues, which again display the playwright's linguistic virtuosity. The characters' rapid-fire delivery of their distinctive slang makes no concessions to the audience. They are, after all, masters of the pitch, of using language to get their way by alternately threatening, pleading with, begging, and pleasing their interlocutors. More fully here than in any other play, Mamet captures the rhythms of everyday speech, filled with interruptions and awkward transitions. Indeed, one is hard-pressed to find a complete sentence. The characters constantly interrupt one another and themselves; they test words and phrases, modifying and replacing them to suit their interlocutor's reaction. It is a kind of linguistic dance that is as expert as it is ruthless.

The play is all talk, but the talk is never innocent—words are weapons. The first to speak is Levene, a salesman who is falling behind in his rate of closed deals and who therefore no longer gets the "premium leads." Desperately trying to improve his standing, he attempts to persuade his boss, Williamson, to give him some of those hot leads on the sly. He pleads and seeks to arouse pity by mentioning his daughter; he appeals to Williamson's own greed, his good judgment, his expertise, and his management style. Williamson can hardly break in with a word of his own, but Levene's verbal torrent has no effect. The next scene features the two men whose sales are lowest, Aaronow and Moss. After drawing Aaronow into a harangue about the real estate office and its managers, bad leads, and fickle clients, Moss skillfully sets a verbal trap for his interlocutor. Building on a general remark—someone should punish the management for giving the salesmen bad leads—he begins to spin out a plot to steal the leads from the office and then sell them to a rival firm. Aaronow finds himself unwittingly drawn into this scheme when Moss convinces him that the mere act of listening has made him an accomplice. Even more subtle and successful in his strategic talking is the protagonist of the third dialogue, the top salesman Roma, who cajoles his hapless victim into buying worthless property.

In the second act, one-on-one conversations are replaced with an ensemble piece, as different interactions occur simultaneously on the stage. While the salesmen are being cross-examined by a detective who is trying to solve the burglary, Roma's latest buyer comes into the office to cancel the deal. To distract him, Levene and Roma put on an act that is reminiscent of Mamet's metatheatrical plays, such as *A Life in the Theatre* (1977). This scene is an homage to the salesmen, the artists of deception. We see them stage a veritable play within the play, a dazzling performance that exhibits their skillful improvisation and linguistic ingenuity. These are the skills that the salesmen have developed on the street and that set them apart from the office manager, whose interruption undercuts and undoes their act. The Jewish and Italian salesmen and the WASP manager are also set on opposite sides of an ethnic divide. Indeed, ethnic divides consistently inform Mamet's plays, which use ethnicity not as a central theme but as one more occasion for slurs, one more occasion to explore different dialects and modes of speech, one more social reality that is subsumed into the overpowering need to find a way of getting the good lead, to learn how to pitch the next sale, and to close the best deal.

The intersection of language, deception, and power is Mamet's great theme, which continues to inform his most recent plays—most notably *Oleanna* (1991), whose series of encounters between a professor and his student develops into a vicious cycle of attack and counterattack. More recently, Mamet has turned away from contemporary America to write plays set in historically and therefore linguistically remote eras: *Boston Marriage* (1999) in late nineteenth-century Boston and *Faustus* (2004) in the Middle Ages. Critics and audiences have generally not considered these historical experiments equal to Mamet's earlier works. But whether Mamet persists in a historical vein or returns to the contemporary subjects that brought him fame, his future plays will most likely continue to be meditations on the power and the futility of the spoken word. M.P.

Glengarry Glen Ross

CHARACTERS

WILLIAMSON, BAYLEN, ROMA, LINGK	Men in their early forties
LEVENE, MOSS, AARONOW	Men in their fifties

THE SCENE

The three scenes of Act 1 take place in a Chinese restaurant.
Act 2 takes place in a real estate office.

ALWAYS BE CLOSING.
Practical Sales Maxim

Act 1

Scene 1

[*A booth at a Chinese restaurant,* WILLIAMSON *and* LEVENE *are seated at the booth.*]

LEVENE John . . . John . . . John. Okay. John. John. Look: [*Pause*] The Glengarry Highland's leads,[1] you're sending Roma out. Fine. He's a good man. We know what he is. He's fine. All I'm saying, you look at the *board,* he's throwing . . . wait, wait, wait, he's throwing them *away,* he's throwing the leads away. All that I'm saying, that you're wasting leads. I don't want to tell you your *job.* All that I'm saying, things get *set,* I know they do, you get a certain *mindset.* . . . A guy gets a reputation. We know how this . . . all I'm saying, put a *closer* on the job. There's more than one man for the . . . Put a . . . wait a second, put a *proven man out* . . . and you watch, now *wait* a second—and you watch your *dollar* volumes. . . . You start closing them for *fifty* 'stead of *twenty-five* . . . you put a *closer* on the . . .

1. Contact information about potential clients that might lead to a sale.

WILLIAMSON Shelly, you blew the last . . .

LEVENE No. John. No. Let's wait, let's back up here, I did . . . will you please? Wait a second. Please. I didn't "blow" them. No. I didn't "blow" them. No. One kicked *out,*[2] one I closed . . .

WILLIAMSON . . . you didn't close . . .

LEVENE . . . I, if you'd *listen* to me. Please. I *closed* the cocksucker. His *ex,* John, his *ex, I* didn't know he was married . . . he, the *judge* invalidated the . . .

WILLIAMSON Shelly . . .

LEVENE . . . and what is that, John? What? Bad *luck.* That's all it is. I pray in your *life* you will never find it runs in streaks. That's what it does, that's all it's doing. Streaks. I pray it misses you. That's all I want to say.

WILLIAMSON [*pause*] What about the other two?

LEVENE What two?

WILLIAMSON Four. You had four leads. One kicked out, one the *judge,* you say . . .

LEVENE . . . you want to see the court records? John? Eh? You want to go down . . .

WILLIAMSON . . . no . . .

LEVENE . . . do you want to go down*town* . . . ?

WILLIAMSON . . . no . . .

LEVENE . . . then . . .

WILLIAMSON . . . I only . . .

LEVENE . . . then what is this "you *say*" shit, what is that? [*Pause*] What is that . . . ?

WILLIAMSON All that I'm saying . . .

LEVENE What is this "you *say*"? A deal kicks out . . . I got to *eat. Shit,* Williamson, *shit.* You . . . Moss . . . Roma . . . look at the *sheets* . . . look at the *sheets.* Nineteen *eighty,* eighty-*one* . . . eighty-*two* . . . six months of eighty-two . . . who's there? Who's up there?

WILLIAMSON Roma.

LEVENE Under him?

WILLIAMSON Moss.

LEVENE Bullshit. John. Bull*shit.* April, September 1981. It's *me.* It isn't *fucking* Moss. Due respect, he's an *order* taker, John. He *talks,* he talks a good game, look at the *board,* and it's *me,* John, it's me . . .

WILLIAMSON Not lately it isn't.

LEVENE Lately kiss my ass lately. That isn't how you build an org . . . talk, talk to Murray. Talk to Mitch. When we were on Peterson, who paid for his fucking *car?* You talk to him. The *Seville*[3] . . . ? He came in, "You bought that for me Shelly." Out of *what?* Cold *calling.*[4] *Nothing.* Sixty-*five,* when we were there, with Glen *Ross* Farms? You call 'em downtown. What was that? *Luck?* That was "luck"? *Bull*shit, John. You're burning my ass, I can't get a fucking *lead* . . . you think that was luck. My stats for those years?

2. That is, fell through (without necessarily involving a real estate "kick-out clause," which allows the seller to continue to seek another purchaser while a potential buyer attempts to sell his or her current house).

3. The Cadillac Seville, a name reintroduced in 1975 for the division's smallest but most expensive model.

4. That is, telephoning potential customers without having any lead or prior contact.

Bull*shit* . . . over that period of time . . . ? Bull*shit.* It wasn't luck. It was *skill.* You want to throw that away, John . . . ? You want to throw that away?

WILLIAMSON It isn't me . . .

LEVENE . . . it isn't you . . . ? Who *is* it? Who is this I'm talking to? I need the *leads* . . .

WILLIAMSON . . . after the thirtieth . . .

LEVENE Bull*shit* the thirtieth, I don't get on the board the thirtieth, they're going to can my ass. I need the leads. I need them now. Or I'm gone, and you're going to miss me, John, I swear to you.

WILLIAMSON Murray . . .

LEVENE . . . you *talk* to Murray . . .

WILLIAMSON I have. And my job is to marshal those leads . . .

LEVENE Marshal the leads . . . marshal the leads? What the fuck, what bus did *you* get off of, we're here to fucking *sell. Fuck* marshaling the leads. What the fuck talk is that? What the fuck talk is that? Where did you learn that? In school? [*Pause*] That's "talk," my friend, that's "talk." Our job is to *sell.* I'm the *man* to sell. I'm getting garbage. [*Pause*] You're giving it to me, and what I'm saying is it's *fucked.*

WILLIAMSON You're saying that I'm fucked.

LEVENE Yes. [*Pause*] I am. I'm sorry to antagonize you.

WILLIAMSON Let me . . .

LEVENE . . . and I'm going to get bounced and you're . . .

WILLIAMSON . . . let me . . . are you listening to me . . . ?

LEVENE Yes.

WILLIAMSON Let me tell you something, Shelly. I do what I'm hired to do. I'm . . . wait a second. I'm *hired* to watch the leads. I'm given . . . hold on, I'm given a *policy. My* job is to *do that.* What I'm *told.* That's it. You, wait a second, *anybody* falls below a certain mark I'm not *permitted* to give them the premium leads.

LEVENE Then how do they come up above that mark? With *dreck*[5] . . . ? That's *nonsense.* Explain this to me. 'Cause it's a waste, and it's a stupid waste. I want to tell you something . . .

WILLIAMSON You know what those leads cost?

LEVENE The premium leads. Yes. I know what they cost. John. Because I, *I* generated the dollar revenue sufficient to *buy* them. Nineteen senny-*nine,* you know what I made? Senny-*nine?* Ninety-six thousand dollars. John? For *Murray* . . . For *Mitch* . . . look at the sheets . . .

WILLIAMSON Murray said . . .

LEVENE *Fuck* him. *Fuck* Murray. John? You know? You tell him I said so. What does *he* fucking know? He's going to have a "sales" contest . . . you know what our sales contest used to be? *Money.* A *fortune.* Money lying on the ground. Murray? When was the last time *he* went out on a sit?[6] Sales contest? It's *laughable.* It's cold out there now, John. It's tight. Money is *tight.* This ain't sixty-five.[7] It ain't. It just ain't. See? See? Now, I'm a good *man*—but I need a . . .

WILLIAMSON Murray said . . .

5. Crap (Yiddish).
6. A face-to-face meeting with clients.
7. That is, 1965, remembered as a time of economic expansion and easy sales.

LEVENE John. John . . .

WILLIAMSON Will you please wait a second. Shelly. Please. Murray told me: the hot leads . . .

LEVENE . . . ah, *fuck* this . . .

WILLIAMSON The . . . Shelly? [*Pause*] The hot leads are assigned according to the board. During the contest. *Period.* Anyone who beats fifty per . . .

LEVENE That's fucked. That's fucked. You don't look at the fucking *percentage.* You look at the *gross.*

WILLIAMSON Either way. You're out.

LEVENE I'm out.

WILLIAMSON Yes.

LEVENE I'll tell you why I'm out. I'm *out,* you're giving me toilet paper. John. I've *seen* those leads. I saw them when I was at Homestead, we pitched those cocksuckers Rio Rancho nineteen sixty-*nine* they wouldn't buy. They couldn't buy a fucking *toaster.* They're *broke,* John. They're cold. They're deadbeats, you can't judge on that. Even so. Even so. Alright. Fine. Fine. Even so. I go in, FOUR FUCKING LEADS they got their money in a *sock.* They're fucking *Polacks,*[8] John. Four leads. I close two. *Two.* Fifty per . . .

WILLIAMSON . . . they kicked out.

LEVENE They *all* kick out. You run in *streaks,* pal. *Streaks.* I'm . . . I'm . . . don't look at the *board,* look at *me.* Shelly Levene. *Anyone. Ask* them on Western. Ask Getz at Homestead. Go ask Jerry Graff. You know who I am . . . I NEED A SHOT. I got to get on the fucking board. Ask them. *Ask* them. Ask them who ever picked up a check I was flush. Moss, Jerry Graff, Mitch himself . . . Those guys *lived* on the business I brought in. They *lived* on it . . . and so did Murray, John. You were here you'd of benefited from it too. And now I'm saying this. Do I want charity? Do I want *pity?* I want *sits.* I want leads don't come right out of a *phone book.* Give me a lead hotter than that, I'll go in and close it. Give me a chance. That's all I want. I'm going to *get* up on that fucking board and all I want is a chance. It's a *streak* and I'm going to turn it around. [*Pause*] I need your help. [*Pause*]

WILLIAMSON I can't do it, Shelly. [*Pause*]

LEVENE Why?

WILLIAMSON The leads are assigned randomly . . .

LEVENE *Bullshit, bullshit,* you assign them. . . . What are you *telling* me?

WILLIAMSON . . . apart from the top men on the contest board.

LEVENE Then put me on the board.

WILLIAMSON You start closing again, you'll *be* on the board.

LEVENE I can't close these leads, John. No one can. It's a joke. John, look, just give me a hot lead. Just give me two of the premium leads. As a "test," alright? As a "test" and I promise you . . .

WILLIAMSON I can't do it, Shel. [*Pause*]

LEVENE I'll give you ten percent. [*Pause*]

WILLIAMSON Of what?

LEVENE Of my end what I close.

WILLIAMSON And what if you don't close.

LEVENE I *will* close.

8. People of Polish descent (derogatory).

WILLIAMSON What if you *don't* close . . . ?

LEVENE I *will* close.

WILLIAMSON What if you *don't*? Then I'm *fucked*. You see . . . ? Then it's *my* job. That's what I'm *telling* you.

LEVENE I *will* close. John, John, ten percent. I can get hot. You *know* that . . .

WILLIAMSON Not lately you can't . . .

LEVENE Fuck that. That's defeatist. Fuck that. Fuck it. . . . Get on my side. *Go* with me. Let's *do* something. You want to run this office, *run* it.

WILLIAMSON Twenty percent. [*Pause*]

LEVENE Alright.

WILLIAMSON And fifty bucks a lead.

LEVENE John. [*Pause*] Listen. I want to talk to you. Permit me to do this a second. I'm older than you. A man acquires a reputation. On the street. What he does when he's *up*, what he does otherwise. . . . I said "ten," you said "no." You said "twenty." I said "fine," I'm not going to fuck with you, how can I beat that, you tell me? . . . Okay. Okay. We'll . . . Okay. Fine. We'll . . . Alright, twenty percent, and fifty bucks a lead. That's fine. For now. That's fine. A month or two we'll talk. A month from now. Next month. After the thirtieth. [*Pause*] We'll talk.

WILLIAMSON What are we going to say?

LEVENE No. You're right. That's for later. We'll talk in a month. What have you got? I want two sits. Tonight.

WILLIAMSON I'm not sure I have two.

LEVENE I saw the board. You've got *four* . . .

WILLIAMSON [*snaps*] I've got *Roma*. Then I've got Moss . . .

LEVENE *Bullshit*. They ain't been in the office yet. Give 'em some stiff. We have a deal or not? Eh? Two sits. The Des Plaines. Both of 'em, six and ten, you can do it . . . six and ten . . . eight and eleven, I don't give a shit, you set 'em up? Alright? The two sits in Des Plaines.

WILLIAMSON Alright.

LEVENE Good. Now we're talking. [*Pause*]

WILLIAMSON A hundred bucks. [*Pause*]

LEVENE Now? [*Pause*] *Now?*

WILLIAMSON Now. [*Pause*] *Yes* . . . *When?*

LEVENE Ah, *shit*, John. [*Pause*]

WILLIAMSON I wish I could.

LEVENE You fucking asshole. [*Pause*] I haven't got it. [*Pause*] I haven't got it, John. [*Pause*] I'll pay you tomorrow. [*Pause*] I'm coming in here with the sales, I'll pay you *tomorrow*. [*Pause*] I haven't *got* it, when I pay, the *gas* . . . I get back the hotel, I'll bring it in tomorrow.

WILLIAMSON Can't do it.

LEVENE I'll give you thirty on them now, I'll bring the rest tomorrow. I've got it at the hotel. [*Pause*] John? [*Pause*] We do that, for chrissake?

WILLIAMSON No.

LEVENE I'm asking you. As a favor to me? [*Pause*] John. [*Long pause*] John: my *daughter* . . .

WILLIAMSON I can't do it, Shelly.

LEVENE Well, I want to tell you something, fella, wasn't long I could pick up the phone, call *Murray* and I'd have your job. You know that? Not too *long* ago. For what? For *nothing*. "Mur, this new kid burns my ass." "Shelly, he's out." You're gone before I'm back from lunch. I bought him a trip to Bermuda once . . .

WILLIAMSON I have to go . . . [*Gets up.*]

LEVENE Wait. Alright. Fine. [*Starts going in pocket for money.*] The one. Give me the lead. Give me the one lead. The best one you have.

WILLIAMSON I can't split them. [*Pause*]

LEVENE Why?

WILLIAMSON Because I say so.

LEVENE [*pause*] Is that it? Is that *it?* You want to do business that way . . . ?

[WILLIAMSON *gets up, leaves money on the table.*]

LEVENE You want to do business that way . . . ? Alright. Alright. Alright. Alright. What is there on the other list . . . ?

WILLIAMSON You want something off the B list?

LEVENE *Yeah.* Yeah.

WILLIAMSON Is that what you're saying?

LEVENE That's what I'm saying. Yeah. [*Pause*] I'd like something off the other list. Which, very least, that I'm entitled to. If I'm still *working* here, which for the moment I guess that I am. [*Pause*] What? I'm sorry I spoke harshly to you.

WILLIAMSON That's alright.

LEVENE The deal still stands, our other thing.

[WILLIAMSON *shrugs. Starts out of the booth.*]

LEVENE Good. Mmm. I, you know, I left my wallet back at the hotel.

Scene 2

[*A booth at the restaurant.* MOSS *and* AARONOW *seated. After the meal.*]

MOSS Polacks and deadbeats.

AARONOW . . . Polacks . . .

MOSS Deadbeats *all.*

AARONOW . . . they hold on to their money . . .

MOSS All of 'em. They, *hey:* it happens to us all.

AARONOW Where am I going to work?

MOSS You have to cheer up, George, you aren't out yet.

AARONOW I'm not?

MOSS You missed a fucking sale. Big deal. A deadbeat Polack. Big deal. How you going to sell 'em in the *first* place . . . ? Your mistake, you shoun'a took the lead.

AARONOW I had to.

MOSS You had to, yeah. Why?

AARONOW To get on the . . .

MOSS To get on the board. Yeah. How you goan'a get on the board sell'n a Polack? And I'll tell you, I'll tell you what *else.* You listening? I'll tell you what else: don't ever try to sell an Indian.

AARONOW I'd never try to sell an Indian.

MOSS You get those names come up, you ever get 'em, "Patel"?

AARONOW Mmm . . .

MOSS You ever get 'em?

AARONOW Well, I think I had one once.

MOSS You did?

AARONOW I . . . I don't know.

MOSS You had one you'd know it. *Patel.* They keep coming up. I don't know. They like to talk to salesmen. [*Pause*] They're *lonely,* something. [*Pause*] They like to feel *superior,* I don't know. Never bought a fucking thing. You're sitting down "The Rio Rancho *this,* the blah blah blah," "The Mountain View—" "Oh yes. My brother told me that. . . ." They got a grapevine. Fuckin' Indians, George. Not my cup of tea. Speaking of which I want to tell you something: [*Pause*] I never got a cup of tea with them. You see them in the restaurants. A supercilious race. What is this *look* on their face all the time? I don't know. [*Pause*] I don't know. Their broads all look like they just got fucked with a dead *cat, I* don't know. [*Pause*] I don't know. I don't like it. Christ . . .

AARONOW What?

MOSS The whole fuckin' thing . . . The pressure's just too great. You're ab . . . you're absolu . . . they're too important. All of them. You go in the door. I . . . "I got to *close* this fucker, or I don't eat lunch," "or I don't win the *Cadillac.* . . ." We fuckin' work too hard. You work too hard. We all, I remember when we were at Platt . . . huh? Glen Ross Farms . . . *didn't* we sell a bunch of that . . . ?

AARONOW They came in and they, you know . . .

MOSS Well, they fucked it up.

AARONOW They did.

MOSS They killed the goose.[9]

AARONOW They did.

MOSS And now . . .

AARONOW We're stuck with *this* . . .

MOSS We're stuck with *this* fucking shit . . .

AARONOW . . . *this* shit . . .

MOSS It's too . . .

AARONOW It is.

MOSS Eh?

AARONOW It's too . . .

MOSS You get a bad month, all of a . . .

AARONOW You're on this . . .

MOSS All of, they got you on this "board . . ."

AARONOW I, I . . . I . . .

MOSS Some *contest* board . . .

AARONOW I . . .

MOSS It's not right.

AARONOW It's not.

MOSS No. [*Pause*]

AARONOW And it's not right to the *customers.*

MOSS I know it's not. I'll tell you, you got, you know, you got . . . what did I learn as a kid on Western? Don't sell a guy one car. Sell him *five* cars over fifteen years.

AARONOW That's right?

MOSS Eh . . . ?

9. That is, the goose that laid the golden eggs; in the fable about this goose, greed leads to overreaching and the subsequent loss of easy profit.

AARONOW That's right?

MOSS Goddamn right, that's right. Guys come on: "Oh, the blah blah blah, *I* know what I'll do: I'll go in and rob everyone blind and go to Argentina cause nobody ever *thought* of this before."

AARONOW ". . . that's right . . .

MOSS Eh?

AARONOW No. That's absolutely right.

MOSS And so they kill the goose. I, I, I'll . . . and a fuckin' *man,* worked all his *life* has got to . . .

AARONOW . . . that's right . . .

MOSS . . . cower in his boots . . .

AARONOW [*simultaneously with "boots"*] Shoes, boots, yes . . .

MOSS For some fuckin' "Sell ten thousand and you win the steak knives . . ."

AARONOW For some *sales* pro . . .

MOSS . . . sales promotion, "You *lose,* then we fire your . . ." No. It's *medieval* . . . it's wrong. "Or we're going to fire your ass." It's wrong.

AARONOW Yes.

MOSS Yes, it is. And you know who's responsible?

AARONOW Who?

MOSS You know who it is. It's Mitch. And Murray. 'Cause it doesn't have to be this way.

AARONOW No.

MOSS Look at Jerry Graff. He's *clean,* he's doing business for *himself,* he's got his, that *list* of his with the *nurses* . . . see? You see? That's *thinking.* Why take ten percent? A ten percent comm . . . why are we giving the rest away? What are we giving ninety per . . . for *nothing.* For some jerk sit in the office tell you "Get out there and close." "Go win the Cadillac." Graff. He goes out and *buys.* He pays top dollar for the . . . you see?

AARONOW Yes.

MOSS That's *thinking.* Now, he's got the leads, he goes in business for *himself.* He's . . . that's what I . . . that's *thinking!* "Who? Who's got a steady *job,* a couple bucks nobody's touched, who?"

AARONOW Nurses.

MOSS So Graff buys a fucking list of nurses, one grand—if he paid two I'll eat my hat—four, five thousand nurses, and he's going *wild* . . .

AARONOW He is?

MOSS He's doing *very* well.

AARONOW I heard that they were running cold.

MOSS The nurses?

AARONOW Yes.

MOSS You hear a *lot* of things. . . . He's doing very well. He's doing *very* well.

AARONOW With River Oaks?

MOSS River Oaks, Brook Farms. *All* of that shit. Somebody told me, you know what he's clearing *himself*? Fourteen, fifteen grand[1] a *week.*

AARONOW Himself?

MOSS That's what I'm *saying.* Why? The *leads.* He's got the good leads . . . what are we, we're sitting in the shit here. Why? We have to go to *them* to

1. Equivalent to about $31,000 or $33,000 in 2008.

get them. Huh. Ninety percent our sale, we're *paying* to the *office* for the *leads.*

AARONOW The leads, the overhead, the telephones, there's *lots* of things.

MOSS What do you need? A *telephone,* some broad to say "Good morning," nothing . . . nothing . . .

AARONOW No, it's not that simple, Dave . . .

MOSS *Yes.* It *is.* It *is* simple, and you know what the hard part is?

AARONOW What?

MOSS Starting up.

AARONOW What hard part?

MOSS Of doing the thing. The dif . . . the difference. Between me and Jerry Graff. Going to business for yourself. The hard part is . . . you know what it is?

AARONOW What?

MOSS Just the *act.*

AARONOW What act?

MOSS To say "I'm going on my own." 'Cause what you do, George, let me tell you what you do: you find yourself in *thrall* to someone else. And we *enslave* ourselves. To *please.* To win some fucking *toaster* . . . to . . . to . . . and the guy who got there first made *up* those . . .

AARONOW That's right . . .

MOSS He made *up* those rules, and we're working for *him.*

AARONOW That's the truth . . .

MOSS That's the *God's* truth. And it gets me depressed. I *swear* that it does. At MY AGE. To see a goddamn: "Somebody wins the Cadillac this month. P.S. Two guys get fucked."

AARONOW *Huh.*

MOSS You don't *ax* your sales force.

AARONOW No.

MOSS You . . .

AARONOW You . . .

MOSS You *build* it!

AARONOW That's what I . . .

MOSS You fucking *build* it! Men come . . .

AARONOW Men come *work* for you . . .

MOSS . . . you're absolutely right.

AARONOW They . . .

MOSS They have . . .

AARONOW When they . . .

MOSS Look look look look, when they *build* your business, then you can't fucking turn around, *enslave* them, treat them like *children,* fuck them up the ass, leave them to fend for themselves . . . no. [*Pause*] No. [*Pause*] You're absolutely right, and I want to tell you something.

AARONOW What?

MOSS I want to tell you what somebody should do.

AARONOW What?

MOSS Someone should stand up and strike *back.*

AARONOW What do you mean?

MOSS *Somebody* . . .

AARONOW Yes . . . ?

MOSS Should do something to *them.*

AARONOW What?

MOSS Something. To pay them back. [*Pause*] Someone, someone should hurt them. Murray and Mitch.

AARONOW Someone should hurt them.

MOSS Yes.

AARONOW [*pause*] How?

MOSS How? Do something to hurt them. Where they live.

AARONOW What? [*Pause*]

MOSS Someone should rob the office.

AARONOW Huh.

MOSS That's what I'm *saying.* We were, if we were that kind of guys, to knock it off, and *trash* the joint, it looks like robbery, and *take* the fuckin' leads out of the files . . . go to Jerry Graff. [*Long pause*]

AARONOW What could somebody get for them?

MOSS What could we *get* for them? I don't know. Buck a *throw* . . . buck-a-half a throw . . . I don't know. . . . Hey, who knows what they're worth, what do they *pay* for them? All told . . . must be, I'd . . . three bucks a throw . . . *I* don't know.

AARONOW How many leads have we got?

MOSS The *Glengarry* . . . the premium leads . . . ? I'd say we got five thousand. Five. Five thousand leads.

AARONOW And you're saying a fella could take and sell these leads to Jerry Graff.

MOSS Yes.

AARONOW How do you know he'd buy them?

MOSS Graff? Because I worked for him.

AARONOW You haven't talked to him.

MOSS No. What do you mean? Have I talked to him about *this?* [*Pause*]

AARONOW Yes. I mean are you actually *talking* about this, or are we just . . .

MOSS No, we're just . . .

AARONOW We're just "*talking*" about it.

MOSS We're just *speaking* about it. [*Pause*] As an *idea.*

AARONOW As an idea.

MOSS Yes.

AARONOW We're not actually *talking* about it.

MOSS No.

AARONOW Talking about it as a . . .

MOSS *No.*

AARONOW As a *robbery.*

MOSS As a "robbery"?! No.

AARONOW *Well.* Well . . .

MOSS *Hey.* [*Pause*]

AARONOW So all this, um, you didn't, actually, you didn't actually go talk to Graff.

MOSS Not actually, no. [*Pause*]

AARONOW You didn't?

MOSS No. Not actually.

AARONOW Did you?

MOSS What did I say?
AARONOW What did you say?
MOSS Yes. [*Pause*] I said, "Not actually." The fuck *you* care, George? We're just *talking* . . .
AARONOW We are?
MOSS Yes. [*Pause*]
AARONOW Because, because, you know, it's a *crime*.
MOSS That's right. It's a crime. It is a crime. It's also very safe.
AARONOW You're actually *talking* about this?
MOSS That's right. [*Pause*]
AARONOW You're going to steal the leads?
MOSS Have I said that? [*Pause*]
AARONOW Are you? [*Pause*]
MOSS Did I say that?
AARONOW Did you talk to Graff?
MOSS Is that what I said?
AARONOW What did he say?
MOSS What did he say? He'd *buy* them. [*Pause*]
AARONOW You're going to steal the leads and sell the leads to him? [*Pause*]
MOSS Yes.
AARONOW What will he pay?
MOSS A buck a shot.
AARONOW For five thousand?
MOSS However they are, that's the deal. A buck a throw. Five thousand dollars. Split it half and half.
AARONOW You're saying "me."
MOSS Yes. [*Pause*] Twenty-five hundred apiece. One night's work, and the job with Graff. Working the premium leads. [*Pause*]
AARONOW A job with Graff.
MOSS Is that what I said?
AARONOW He'd give me a job.
MOSS He would take you on. Yes. [*Pause*]
AARONOW Is that the truth?
MOSS Yes. It is, George. [*Pause*] Yes. It's a big decision. [*Pause*] And it's a big reward. [*Pause*] It's a big reward. For one night's work. [*Pause*] But it's got to be tonight.
AARONOW What?
MOSS What? What? The *leads*.
AARONOW You have to steal the leads tonight?
MOSS That's *right,* the guys are moving them downtown. After the thirtieth. Murray and Mitch. After the contest.
AARONOW You're, you're saying so you have to go in there tonight and . . .
MOSS *You* . . .
AARONOW I'm sorry?
MOSS *You*. [*Pause*]
AARONOW Me?
MOSS *You* have to go in. [*Pause*] *You* have to get the leads. [*Pause*]
AARONOW I do?
MOSS Yes.

AARONOW I . . .

MOSS It's not something for nothing, George, I took you in on this, you have to go. That's your thing. I've made the deal with Graff. I can't go. I can't go in, I've spoken on this too much. I've got a big mouth. [*Pause*] "The fucking leads" et cetera, blah blah blah ". . . the fucking tight-ass company . . ."

AARONOW They'll know when you go over to Graff . . .

MOSS What will they know? That I stole the leads? I *didn't* steal the leads, I'm going to the *movies* tonight with a friend, and then I'm going to the Como Inn. Why did I go to Graff? I got a better deal. *Period*. Let 'em prove something. They can't prove anything that's not the case. [*Pause*]

AARONOW *Dave.*

MOSS Yes.

AARONOW You want me to break into the office tonight and steal the leads?

MOSS Yes. [*Pause*]

AARONOW No.

MOSS Oh, yes, George.

AARONOW What does that mean?

MOSS Listen to this. I have an alibi, I'm going to the Como Inn, why? Why? The place gets robbed, they're going to come looking for *me*. Why? Because I probably did it. Are you going to turn me in? [*Pause*] George? Are you going to turn me in?

AARONOW What if you don't get caught?

MOSS They come to you, you going to turn me in?

AARONOW Why would they come to me?

MOSS They're going to come to *everyone*.

AARONOW Why would I *do* it?

MOSS You wouldn't, George, that's why I'm talking to you. Answer me. They come to you. You going to turn me in?

AARONOW No.

MOSS Are you sure?

AARONOW Yes. I'm sure.

MOSS Then listen to this: I have to get those leads tonight. That's something I have to do. If I'm not at the *movies* . . . if I'm not eating over at the inn . . . if you don't do this, then *I* have to come in here . . .

AARONOW . . . you don't have to come in . . .

MOSS . . . and *rob* the place . . .

AARONOW . . . I thought that we were only talking . . .

MOSS . . . they *take* me, then. They're going to ask me who were my accomplices.

AARONOW *Me?*

MOSS Absolutely.

AARONOW That's ridiculous.

MOSS Well, to the law, you're an accessory. Before the fact.

AARONOW I didn't ask to be.

MOSS Then tough luck, George, because you are.

AARONOW Why? *Why,* because you only *told* me about it?

MOSS That's right.

AARONOW Why are you doing this to me, Dave. Why are you talking this way to me? I don't understand. Why are you doing this at *all* . . . ?

MOSS That's none of your fucking business . . .

AARONOW Well, well, well, *talk* to me, we sat down to eat *dinner,* and here I'm a *criminal* . . .

MOSS You *went* for it.

AARONOW In the abstract . . .

MOSS So I'm making it concrete.

AARONOW Why?

MOSS Why? Why *you* going to give me five grand?

AARONOW Do you need five grand?

MOSS Is that what I just said?

AARONOW You need money? Is that the . . .

MOSS Hey, hey, let's just keep it simple, what I need is not the . . . what do *you* need . . . ?

AARONOW What is the five grand? [*Pause*] What is the, you said that we were going to *split* five . . .

MOSS I lied. [*Pause*] Alright? My end is *my* business. Your end's twenty-five. In or out. You tell me, you're out you take the consequences.

AARONOW I do?

MOSS Yes. [*Pause*]

AARONOW And why is that?

MOSS Because you listened.

Scene 3

[*The restaurant.* ROMA *is seated alone at the booth.* LINGK *is at the booth next to him.* ROMA *is talking to him.*]

ROMA . . . all train compartments smell vaguely of shit. It gets so you don't mind it. That's the worst thing that I can confess. You know how long it took me to get there? A long time. When you *die* you're going to regret the things you don't do. You think you're *queer* . . . ? I'm going to tell you something: we're *all* queer. You think that you're a *thief?* So *what?* You get befuddled by a middle-class morality . . . ? Get *shut* of it. Shut it out. You cheated on your wife . . . ? You *did* it, *live* with it. [*Pause*] You fuck little girls, so *be* it. There's an absolute morality? May *be.* And *then* what? If you *think* there is, then *be* that thing. Bad people go to hell? I don't *think* so. If you think that, act that way. A hell exists on earth? Yes. I won't live in it. That's *me.* You ever take a dump made you feel you'd just slept for twelve hours . . . ?

LINGK Did I . . . ?

ROMA Yes.

LINGK I don't know.

ROMA Or a *piss* . . . ? A great meal fades in reflection. Everything else gains. You know why? 'Cause it's only food. This shit we eat, it keeps us going. But it's only food. The great fucks that you may have had. What do you remember about them?

LINGK What do I . . . ?

ROMA Yes.

LINGK Mmmm . . .

ROMA I don't know. For *me,* I'm saying, what it is, it's probably not the orgasm. Some broads, forearms on your neck, something her *eyes* did. There was a *sound* she made . . . or, me, lying, in the, I'll tell you: me lying in bed; the next day she brought me café au lait. She gives me a cigarette, my balls feel like concrete. Eh? What I'm saying, what is our life? [*Pause*] It's looking forward or it's looking back. And that's our life. That's *it.* Where is the *moment?* [*Pause*] And what is it that we're afraid of? Loss. What else? [*Pause*] The *bank* closes. We get *sick,* my wife died on a plane, the stock market collapsed . . . the house burnt down . . . what of these happen . . . ? None of 'em. We worry anyway. What does this mean? I'm not *secure.* How can I be secure? [*Pause*] Through amassing wealth beyond all measure? No. And what's beyond all measure? That's a sickness. That's a trap. There is no measure. Only greed. How can we act? The right way, we would say, to deal with this: "There is a one-in-a-million chance that so and so will happen. . . . *Fuck* it, it won't happen to *me.* . . ." No. We know that's not the right way I think. [*Pause*] We say the *correct* way to deal with this is "There is one-in-so-and-so chance this will happen . . . God *protect* me. I am powerless, let it not happen to me. . . ." But no to *that.* I say. There's something else. What is it? "If it happens, AS IT MAY for that is not within our powers, I will *deal* with it, just as I do *today* with what draws my concern today." I say *this* is how we must act. I do those things which seem correct to me *today.* I trust myself. And if security concerns me, I do that which *today* I think will make me secure. And every day I *do* that, when that day *arrives* that I need a reserve, (a) odds are that I have it, and (b) the *true* reserve that I have is the strength that I have of *acting each day* without fear. [*Pause*] According to the dictates of my mind. [*Pause*] Stocks, bonds, objects of art, real estate. Now: what are they? [*Pause*] An opportunity. To what? To make money? Perhaps. To *lose* money? Perhaps. To "indulge" and to "learn" about ourselves? Perhaps. *So fucking what?* What *isn't?* They're an *opportunity.* That's all. They're an *event.* A guy comes up to you, you make a call, you send in a brochure, it doesn't matter, "There're these *properties* I'd like for you to see." What does it mean? What you *want* it to mean. [*Pause*] Money? [*Pause*] If that's what it signifies to you. Security? [*Pause*] Comfort? [*Pause*] All it is is THINGS THAT HAPPEN TO YOU. [*Pause*] That's all it is. How are they different? [*Pause*] Some poor newly married guy gets run down by a cab. Some *busboy* wins the lottery. [*Pause*] All it is, it's a carnival. What's special . . . what *draws* us? [*Pause*] We're all different. [*Pause*] We're not the same. [*Pause*] We are not the same. [*Pause*] Hmmm. [*Pause. Sighs.*] It's been a long day. [*Pause*] What are you drinking?

LINGK Gimlet.

ROMA Well, let's have a couple more. My name is Richard Roma, what's yours?

LINGK Lingk. James Lingk.

ROMA James. I'm glad to meet you. [*They shake hands.*] I'm glad to meet you, James. [*Pause*] I want to show you something. [*Pause*] It might mean *nothing* to you . . . and it might not. I don't know. I don't know anymore. [*Pause. He takes out a small map and spreads it on a table.*] What is that? Florida. Glengarry Highlands. Florida. "Florida. *Bullshit.*" And maybe that's true; and that's what *I* said: but look *here*: what is this? This is a piece of land. Listen to what I'm going to tell you now:

Act 2

[*The real estate office. Ransacked. A broken plate-glass window boarded up, glass all over the floor.* AARONOW *and* WILLIAMSON *standing around, smoking.*]

[*Pause.*]

AARONOW People used to say that there are numbers of such magnitude that multiplying them by two made no difference. [*Pause*]

WILLIAMSON Who used to say that?

AARONOW In school. [*Pause*]

[BAYLEN, *a detective, comes out of the inner office.*]

BAYLEN Alright . . . ?

[ROMA *enters from the street.*]

ROMA *Williamson . . . Williamson,* they stole the *contracts* . . . ?

BAYLEN Excuse me, sir . . .

ROMA Did they get my contracts?

WILLIAMSON They got . . .

BAYLEN Excuse me, fella.

ROMA . . . did they . . .

BAYLEN Would you excuse us, please . . . ?

ROMA Don't *fuck* with me, fella. I'm talking about a fuckin' Cadillac car that you owe me . . .

WILLIAMSON They didn't get your contract. I filed it before I left.

ROMA They didn't get my contracts?

WILLIAMSON They—excuse me . . .

[*He goes back into inner room with the detective.*]

ROMA Oh, *fuck. Fuck.* [*He starts kicking the desk.*] FUCK FUCK FUCK! WILLIAMSON!!! WILLIAMSON!!! [*Goes to the door* WILLIAMSON *went into, tries the door; it's locked.*] OPEN THE FUCKING . . . WILLIAMSON . . .

BAYLEN [*coming out*] Who are you?

[WILLIAMSON *comes out.*]

WILLIAMSON They didn't get the contracts.

ROMA Did they . . .

WILLIAMSON They got, listen to me . . .

ROMA Th . . .

WILLIAMSON Listen to me: They got *some* of them.

ROMA Some of them . . .

BAYLEN Who told you . . . ?

ROMA Who told me wh . . . ? You've got a fuckin', you've . . . a . . . who is this . . . ? You've got a board-up on the window. . . . *Moss* told me.

BAYLEN [*looking back toward the inner office*] *Moss* . . . Who told him?

ROMA How the fuck do *I* know? [*To* WILLIAMSON] *What* . . . *talk* to me.

WILLIAMSON They took *some* of the con . . .

ROMA . . . some of the contracts . . . Lingk. James Lingk. I closed . . .

WILLIAMSON You closed him yesterday.

ROMA *Yes.*

WILLIAMSON It went down. I filed it.

ROMA You did?

WILLIAMSON Yes.

ROMA Then I'm over the fucking top and you owe me a Cadillac.

WILLIAMSON I . . .

ROMA And I don't want any fucking shit and I don't give a shit, Lingk puts me over the top, you filed it, that's fine, any other shit kicks out *you* go back. You . . . *you* reclose it, 'cause I *closed* it and you . . . you owe me the car.

BAYLEN Would you excuse us, please.

AARONOW I, um, and may . . . maybe they're in . . . they're in . . . you should, John, if we're ins . . .

WILLIAMSON I'm sure that we're insured, George . . .

[*Going back inside.*]

ROMA Fuck insured. You owe me a car.

BAYLEN [*stepping back into the inner room*] Please don't leave. I'm going to talk to you. What's your name?

ROMA Are you talking to me? [*Pause*]

BAYLEN Yes. [*Pause*]

ROMA My name is Richard Roma.

[BAYLEN *goes back into the inner room.*]

AARONOW I, you know, they should be insured.

ROMA What do *you* care . . . ?

AARONOW Then, you know, they wouldn't be so ups . . .

ROMA Yeah. That's swell. Yes. You're right. [*Pause*] How are you?

AARONOW I'm fine. You mean the *board*? You mean the *board* . . . ?

ROMA I don't . . . yes. Okay, the board.

AARONOW I'm, I'm, I'm, I'm fucked on the board. *You*. You see how . . . I . . . [*Pause*] I can't . . . my mind must be in other places. 'Cause I can't do any . . .

ROMA *What*? You can't do any *what*? [*Pause*]

AARONOW I can't close 'em.

ROMA Well, they're old. I saw the shit that they were giving you.

AARONOW Yes.

ROMA Huh?

AARONOW Yes. They are old.

ROMA They're ancient.

AARONOW Clear . . .

ROMA Clear Meadows. That shit's dead. [*Pause*]

AARONOW It *is* dead.

ROMA It's a waste of time.

AARONOW Yes. [*Long pause*] I'm no fucking good.

ROMA That's . . .

AARONOW Everything I . . . *you* know . . .

ROMA That's not . . . Fuck that shit, George. You're a, *hey*, you had a bad month. You're a good man, George.

AARONOW I am?

ROMA You hit a bad streak. We've all . . . look at this: fifteen units Mountain View, the fucking things get stole.

AARONOW He said he filed . . .

ROMA He filed half of them, he filed the *big* one. All the little ones, I have, I have to go back and . . . ah, *fuck*, I got to go out like a fucking schmuck[2]

2. Jerk; dick (Yiddish).

hat in my hand and reclose the . . . [*Pause*] I mean, talk about a bad streak. That would sap *anyone's* self confi . . . I got to go out and reclose all my . . . Where's the phones?

AARONOW They stole . . .

ROMA They stole the . . .

AARONOW What. What kind of outfit are we running where . . . where anyone . . .

ROMA [*to himself*] They stole the phones.

AARONOW Where criminals can come in here . . . they take the . . .

ROMA They stole the phones. They stole the leads. They're . . . *Christ.* [*Pause*] What am I going to do this month? Oh, *shit* . . . [*Starts for the door.*]

AARONOW You think they're going to catch . . . where are you going?

ROMA Down the street.

WILLIAMSON [*sticking his head out of the door*] Where are you going?

ROMA To the restaura . . . what do you fucking . . . ?

WILLIAMSON Aren't you going out today?

ROMA With what? [*Pause*] With what, John, they took the leads . . .

WILLIAMSON I have the stuff from last year's . . .

ROMA Oh. Oh. Oh, your "nostalgia" file, that's fine. No. Swell. 'Cause I don't have to . . .

WILLIAMSON . . . you want to go out today . . . ?

ROMA 'Cause I don't have to *eat* this month. No. Okay. *Give* 'em to me . . . [*To himself*] Fucking Mitch and Murray going to shit a br . . . what am I going to *do* all . . .

[WILLIAMSON *starts back into the office. He is accosted by* AARONOW.]

AARONOW Were the leads . . .

ROMA . . . what am I going to *do* all month . . . ?

AARONOW Were the leads insured?

WILLIAMSON I don't know, George, why?

AARONOW 'Cause, you know, 'cause they weren't, I know that Mitch and Murray uh . . . [*Pause*]

WILLIAMSON What?

AARONOW That they're going to be upset.

WILLIAMSON That's right. [*Going back into his office. Pause. To* ROMA] You want to go out today . . . ?

[*Pause.* WILLIAMSON *returns to his office.*]

AARONOW He said we're all going to have to go talk to the guy.

ROMA What?

AARONOW He said we . . .

ROMA To the cop?

AARONOW Yeah.

ROMA Yeah. That's swell. *Another* waste of time.

AARONOW A waste of time? Why?

ROMA *Why*? 'Cause they aren't going to find the guy.

AARONOW The cops?

ROMA Yes. The cops. No.

AARONOW They aren't?

ROMA No.

AARONOW Why don't you think so?

ROMA Why? Because they're *stupid*. "Where were you last night . . ."

AARONOW Where were you?

ROMA Where was *I*?

AARONOW Yes.

ROMA I was at home, where were *you*?

AARONOW At home.

ROMA *See* . . . ? Were you the guy who broke in?

AARONOW Was I?

ROMA Yes.

AARONOW No.

ROMA Then don't sweat it, George, you know why?

AARONOW No.

ROMA You have nothing to hide.

AARONOW [*pause*] When I talk to the police, I get nervous.

ROMA Yeah. You know who doesn't?

AARONOW No, who?

ROMA Thieves.

AARONOW Why?

ROMA They're inured to it.

AARONOW You think so?

ROMA Yes. [*Pause*]

AARONOW But what should I *tell* them?

ROMA The truth, George. Always tell the truth. It's the easiest thing to remember.

[WILLIAMSON *comes out of the office with leads.* ROMA *takes one, reads it.*]

ROMA *Patel?* Ravidam *Patel?* How am I going to make a living on these deadbeat *wogs?*[3] Where did you get this, from the *morgue?*

WILLIAMSON If you don't want it, give it back.

ROMA I don't "want" it, if you catch my drift.

WILLIAMSON I'm giving you *three* leads. You . . .

ROMA What's the fucking point in *any* case . . . ? What's the *point.* I got to argue with *you,* I got to knock heads with the *cops,* I'm busting my *balls,* sell you *dirt* to fucking *deadbeats* money in the *mattress,* I come back you can't even manage to keep the contracts safe, I have to go back and close them *again*. . . . What the fuck am I wasting my time, fuck this shit. I'm going out and reclose last week's . . .

WILLIAMSON The word from Murray is: leave them alone. If we need a new signature he'll go out himself, he'll be the *president,* just come *in,* from out of *town* . . .

ROMA Okay, okay, okay, gimme this shit. Fine. [*Takes the leads.*]

WILLIAMSON Now, I'm giving you three . . .

ROMA Three? I count *two.*

WILLIAMSON Three.

ROMA Patel? Fuck *you.* Fuckin' *Shiva*[4] handed him a million dollars, told him "sign the deal," he wouldn't sign. And Vishnu, too. Into the bargain.

3. Dark-skinned people, especially South Asians (a pejorative term, mainly British).

4. One of the most important gods of Hinduism, as is Vishnu; they are identified, respectively, with destruction and preservation.

Fuck *that,* John. You know your business, I know mine. Your business is being an *asshole,* and I find out whose fucking *cousin* you are, I'm going to go to him and figure out a way to have your *ass* . . . fuck you—I'll wait for the new leads.

[SHELLY LEVENE *enters.*]

LEVENE Get the *chalk.* Get the *chalk* . . . get the *chalk!* I closed 'em! I *closed* the cocksucker. Get the chalk and put me on the *board.* I'm going to Hawaii! Put me on the Cadillac board, Williamson! Pick up the fuckin' chalk. Eight units. Mountain View . . .

ROMA You sold eight Mountain View?

LEVENE You bet your ass. Who wants to go to lunch? Who wants to go to lunch? I'm buying. [*Slaps contract down on Williamson's desk.*] Eighty-two fucking grand. And twelve grand in commission. John. [*Pause*] On fucking deadbeat magazine subscription leads.

WILLIAMSON Who?

LEVENE [*pointing to contract*] *Read* it. Bruce and Harriett Nyborg. [*Looking around*] What happened here?

AARONOW Fuck. I had them on River Glen.

[LEVENE *looks around.*]

LEVENE What happened?

WILLIAMSON Somebody broke in.

ROMA Eight units?

LEVENE That's right.

ROMA *Shelly* . . . !

LEVENE Hey, big fucking deal. Broke a bad streak . . .

AARONOW Shelly, the Machine, Levene.

LEVENE You . . .

AARONOW That's great.

LEVENE Thank you, George.

[BAYLEN *sticks his head out of the room; calls in, "Aaronow."* AARONOW *goes into the side room.*]

LEVENE Williamson, get on the phone, call Mitch . . .

ROMA They took the phones . . .

LEVENE They . . .

BAYLEN *Aaronow* . . .

ROMA They took the typewriters, they took the leads, they took the *cash,* they took the *contracts* . . .

LEVENE Wh . . . wh . . . Wha . . . ?

AARONOW We had a robbery.

[*Goes into the inner room.*]

LEVENE [*pause*] When?

ROMA Last night, this morning. [*Pause*]

LEVENE They took the leads?

ROMA Mmm.

[MOSS *comes out of the interrogation.*]

MOSS Fuckin' asshole.

ROMA What, they beat you with a rubber bat?

MOSS Cop couldn't find his dick two hands and a map. Anyone talks to this guy's an *asshole* . . .

ROMA You going to turn State's?[5]

MOSS Fuck you, Ricky. I ain't going out today. I'm going home. I'm going home because nothing's *accomplished* here. . . . Anyone *talks* to this guy is . . .

ROMA Guess what the Machine did?

MOSS Fuck the Machine.

ROMA Mountain View. Eight units.

MOSS Fuckin' cop's got no right talk to me that way. I didn't rob the place . . .

ROMA You hear what I said?

MOSS Yeah. He closed a deal.

ROMA Eight units. Mountain View.

MOSS [*to* LEVENE] You did that?

LEVENE Yeah. [*Pause*]

MOSS Fuck you.

ROMA Guess who?

MOSS When . . .

LEVENE Just now.

ROMA Guess who?

MOSS You just this morning . . .

ROMA Harriet and blah blah Nyborg.

MOSS You did that?

LEVENE Eighty-two thousand dollars. [*Pause*]

MOSS Those fuckin' *deadbeats* . . .

LEVENE My ass. I told 'em. [*To* ROMA] Listen to this: I said . . .

MOSS Hey, I don't want to hear your fucking war stories . . .

ROMA Fuck *you*, Dave . . .

LEVENE "You have to believe in your*self* . . . you"—look—"alright . . . ?"

MOSS [*to* WILLIAMSON] Give me some leads. I'm going out . . . I'm getting out of . . .

LEVENE ". . . you have to believe in your*self* . . ."

MOSS Na, fuck the leads, I'm going home.

LEVENE "Bruce, Harriet . . . Fuck *me*, believe in your*self* . . ."

ROMA We haven't got a lead . . .

MOSS Why not?

ROMA They took 'em . . .

MOSS Hey, they're fuckin' garbage any case. . . . This whole goddamn . . .

LEVENE ". . . You look around, you say, 'This one has so-and-so, and I have nothing . . . ' "

MOSS *Shit.*

LEVENE " '*Why*? Why don't I get the opportunities . . . ?' "

MOSS And did they steal the contracts . . . ?

ROMA Fuck *you* care . . . ?

LEVENE "I want to tell you something, Harriett . . ."

MOSS . . . the fuck is *that* supposed to mean . . . ?

LEVENE Will you shut up, I'm telling you this . . .

[AARONOW *sticks his head out.*]

AARONOW Can we get some coffee . . . ?

5. That is, "turn state's evidence," a phrase applied to the actions of an accomplice who supplies prosecutors with evidence in return for a reduction in charges or in sentence.

MOSS How ya doing? [*Pause*]

AARONOW Fine.

MOSS Uh-huh.

AARONOW If anyone's going, I could use some coffee.

LEVENE "You *do* get the . . ." [*To* ROMA] Huh? Huh?

MOSS *Fuck* is that supposed to mean?

LEVENE "You *do* get the opportunity. . . . You *get* them. As *I* do, as *anyone* does . . ."

MOSS Ricky? . . . That I don't care they stole the contracts? [*Pause*]

LEVENE I got 'em in the kitchen. I'm eating her crumb cake.

MOSS What does that mean?

ROMA It *means*, Dave, you haven't closed a good one in a month, none of my business, you want to push me to answer you. [*Pause*] And so you haven't got a contract to get stolen or so forth.

MOSS You have a mean streak in you, Ricky, you know that . . . ?

LEVENE Rick. Let me tell you. Wait, we're in the . . .

MOSS Shut the fuck up. [*Pause*] Ricky. You have a mean streak in you. . . . [*To* LEVENE] And what the fuck are *you* babbling about . . . ? [*To* ROMA] Bring that shit up. Of my volume. You were on a bad one and I brought it up to *you* you'd harbor it. [*Pause*] You'd harbor it a long long while. And you'd be right.

ROMA Who said "Fuck the Machine"?

MOSS *"Fuck the Machine"? "Fuck the Machine"?* What is this. *Courtesy* class . . . ? You're *fucked*, Rick—are you fucking *nuts?* You're hot, so you think you're the *ruler* of this place . . . ?! You want to . . .

LEVENE Dave . . .

MOSS . . . Shut up. Decide who should be dealt with how? Is that the thing? I come into the fuckin' office today, I get humiliated by some jagoff[6] cop. I get accused of . . . I get this *shit* thrown in my face by you, you genuine shit, because you're top name on the board . . .

ROMA Is that what I did? Dave? I humiliated you? My *God* . . . I'm *sorry* . . .

MOSS Sittin' on top of the *world*, sittin' on top of the *world*, everything's fucking *peach*fuzz . . .

ROMA Oh, and I don't get a moment to spare for a bust-out *humanitarian* down on his luck lately. Fuck *you*, Dave, you know you got a big *mouth*, and *you* make a close the whole *place* stinks with your *farts* for a week. "How much you just ingested," what a big *man* you are, "Hey, let me buy you a pack of gum. I'll show you how to *chew* it." Your *pal* closes, all that comes out of your mouth is *bile*, how fucked *up* you are . . .

MOSS *Who's* my pal . . . ? And what are you, Ricky, huh, what are you, Bishop *Sheean?*[7] Who the fuck are *you*, Mr. Slick . . . ? What are you, friend to the *workingman*? Big deal. Fuck *you*, you got the memory a fuckin' *fly*. I never liked you.

ROMA What is this, your farewell speech?

MOSS I'm going home.

6. Jack-off, jerk-off.
7. Archbishop Fulton Sheen (1895–1979), one of the first religious figures to have regular broadcasts on radio (1930–52) and on television (1952–57, 1961–68); he popularized Roman Catholic teachings and offered Catholic interpretations of current events.

ROMA Your farewell to the troops?

MOSS I'm not going home. I'm going to Wis*con*sin.

ROMA Have a good trip.

MOSS [*simultaneously with "trip"*] And fuck *you*. Fuck the *lot* of you. Fuck you *all*.

[MOSS *exits. Pause.*]

ROMA [*to* LEVENE] You were saying? [*Pause*] Come on. Come on, you got them in the kitchen, you got the stats spread out, you're in your shirtsleeves, you can *smell* it. Huh? Snap out of it, you're eating her *crumb* cake. [*Pause*]

LEVENE I'm eating her *crumb* cake . . .

ROMA How was it . . . ?

LEVENE From the store.

ROMA Fuck *her* . . .

LEVENE "What we have to do is *admit* to ourself that we see that opportunity . . . and *take* it. [*Pause*] And that's it." And we *sit* there. [*Pause*] I got the pen out . . .

ROMA "Always be closing . . ."

LEVENE That's what I'm *saying*. The *old* ways. The *old* ways . . . convert the motherfucker . . . *sell* him . . . *sell* him . . . *make him sign the check.* [*Pause*] The . . . Bruce, Harriett . . . the kitchen, blah: they got their money in *government* bonds. . . . I say *fuck* it, we're going to go the whole route. I plat it out[8] eight units. Eighty-two grand. I tell them. "This is now. This is that *thing* that you've been dreaming of, you're going to find that suitcase on the train, the guy comes in the door, the bag that's full of money. This is it, *Harriett* . . ."

ROMA [*reflectively*] Harriett . . .

LEVENE *Bruce* . . . "I don't want to fuck *around* with you. I don't want to go *round* this, and *pussyfoot* around the thing, you have to look back on this. I do, too. I came here to do good for you and me. For *both* of us. Why take an interim position? *The only arrangement I'll accept* is full investment. Period. The whole eight units. I know that you're saying 'be safe,' I know what you're saying. I know if I left you to yourselves, you'd say 'come back tomorrow,' and when I walked out that door, you'd make a cup of *coffee* . . . you'd sit *down* . . . and you'd think 'let's be safe . . .' and not to disappoint me you'd go *one* unit or maybe two, because you'd become scared because you'd met possi*bil*ity. But this won't do, and that's not the subject. . . ." Listen to this, I actually said this. "That's not the subject of our *evening* together." Now I handed them the pen. I held it in my hand. I turned the contract, eight units eighty-two grand. "Now I want you to sign." [*Pause*] I sat there. Five minutes. Then, I sat there, Ricky, *twenty-two minutes* by the kitchen *clock*. [*Pause*] Twenty-two minutes by the kitchen clock. Not a *word*, not a *motion*. What am I thinking? "My arm's getting tired?" *No*. I *did* it. I *did* it. Like in the *old* days, Ricky. Like I was taught . . . Like, like, like I *used* to do . . . I did it.

ROMA Like you taught me . . .

LEVENE Bullshit, you're . . . No. That's raw . . . well, if I *did*, then I'm *glad* I did. I, *well*. I locked on them. All on them, nothing on me. All my thoughts

8. That is, map out land into individual lots for development.

are on them. I'm holding the last thought that I spoke: "Now is the time." [*Pause*] They signed, Ricky. It was *great*. It was fucking great. It was like they wilted all at once. No *gesture* . . . nothing. Like together. They, I swear to God, they both kind of *imperceptibly slumped*. And he reaches and takes the pen and signs, he passes it to her, she signs. It was so fucking solemn. I just let it sit. I nod like this. I nod again. I grasp his hands. I shake his hands. I grasp *her* hands. I nod at her like this. "Bruce . . . Harriett . . ." I'm beaming at them. I'm nodding like this. I point back in the living room, back to the sideboard. [*Pause*] *I didn't fucking know there was a sideboard there!!* He goes back, he brings us a drink. Little shot glasses. A pattern in 'em. And we toast. In silence. [*Pause*]

ROMA That was a great sale, Shelly. [*Pause*]

LEVENE Ah, fuck. Leads! Leads! Williamson! [WILLIAMSON *sticks his head out of the office*.] Send me *out!* Send me *out!*

WILLIAMSON The leads are coming.

LEVENE *Get* 'em to me!

WILLIAMSON I talked to Murray and Mitch an hour ago. They're coming in, you understand they're a bit *upset* over this morning's . . .

LEVENE Did you tell 'em my sale?

WILLIAMSON How could I tell 'em your sale? Eh? I don't have a tel . . . I'll tell 'em your sale when they bring in the leads. Alright? Shelly. Alright? We had a little . . . You closed a deal. You made a good sale. Fine.

LEVENE It's better than a good sale. It's a . . .

WILLIAMSON Look: I have a lot of things on my mind, they're coming in, alright, they're very upset, I'm trying to make some *sense* . . .

LEVENE All that I'm *telling* you: that one thing you can tell them it's a remarkable sale.

WILLIAMSON The only thing remarkable is who you made it to.

LEVENE What does *that* fucking mean?

WILLIAMSON That if the sale sticks, it will be a miracle.

LEVENE Why should the sale not stick? Hey, *fuck* you. That's what I'm saying. You have no idea of your job. A man's his job and you're *fucked* at yours. You hear what I'm saying to you? Your "end of month board . . ." You can't run an office. I don't care. You don't know what it *is*, you don't have the *sense*, you don't have the *balls*. You ever been on a sit? *Ever?* Has this cocksucker ever been . . . you ever sit down with a cust . . .

WILLIAMSON I were you, I'd calm down, Shelly.

LEVENE *Would* you? *Would* you . . . ? Or you're gonna *what,* fire me?

WILLIAMSON It's not impossible.

LEVENE On an eighty-thousand dollar *day?* And it ain't even *noon*.

ROMA You closed 'em today?

LEVENE Yes. I did. This *morning*. [*To* WILLIAMSON] What I'm *saying* to you: things can *change*. You *see?* This is where you fuck *up,* because this is something you don't *know*. You can't look down the *road*. And see what's *coming*. Might be someone *else,* John. It might be someone *new,* eh? Someone *new*. And you can't look *back*. 'Cause you don't know *history*. You ask them. When we were at Rio Rancho, who was top man? A month . . . ? Two months . . . ? Eight months in twelve for three years in a row. You know what that means? You know what that means? Is that *luck?* Is that some, some, some purloined leads? That's *skill*. That's *talent,* that's, that's . . .

ROMA . . . *yes* . . .

LEVENE . . . and you don't *remember.* 'Cause you weren't *around.* That's cold *calling.* Walk up to the door. I don't even know their *name.* I'm selling something they don't even *want.* You talk about soft sell . . . before we had a name for it . . . before we called it anything, we did it.

ROMA That's right, Shel.

LEVENE And, and, and, I *did* it. And I put a kid through *school.* She . . . and . . . Cold *calling,* fella. Door to door. But you don't know. You don't know. You never heard of a *streak.* You never heard of "marshaling your sales force. . . ." What are you, you're a *secretary,* John. Fuck *you.* That's my message to you. Fuck you and kiss my ass. You don't like it, I'll go talk to Jerry Graff. Period. Fuck you. Put me on the board. And I want three worthwhile leads today and I don't want any bullshit about them and I want 'em close together 'cause I'm going to hit them all today. That's all I have to say to you.

ROMA He's right, Williamson.

[WILLIAMSON *goes into a side office. Pause.*]

LEVENE It's not right. I'm sorry, and I'll tell you who's to blame is Mitch and Murray.

[ROMA *sees something outside the window.*]

ROMA [*sotto*[9]] Oh, Christ.

LEVENE The hell with him. We'll go to lunch, the leads won't be up for . . .

ROMA You're a client. I just sold you five waterfront Glengarry Farms. I rub my head, throw me the cue "Kenilworth."

LEVENE What is it?

ROMA Kenilw . . .

[LINGK *enters the office.*]

ROMA [*to* LEVENE] *I* own the property, my *mother* owns the property, I put her *into* it. I'm going to show you on the plats. You look when you get home A–3 through A–14 and 26 through 30. You take your time and if you still feel.

LEVENE No, Mr. Roma. I don't need the time, I've made a lot of *investments* in the last . . .

LINGK I've got to talk to you.

ROMA [*looking up*] Jim! What are you doing here? Jim Lingk, D. Ray Morton . . .

LEVENE Glad to meet you.

ROMA I just put Jim into Black Creek . . . are you acquainted with . . .

LEVENE No . . . Black *Creek.* Yes. In *Florida?*

ROMA Yes.

LEVENE I wanted to *speak* with you about . . .

ROMA Well, we'll do that this weekend.

LEVENE My *wife* told me to look into . . .

ROMA *Beautiful.* Beautiful rolling land. I was telling Jim and Jinny, Ray, I want to tell you something. [*To* LEVENE] You, Ray, you eat in a lot of restaurants. I know you do. . . . [*To* LINGK] Mr. Morton's with American Express . . . he's . . . [*To* LEVENE] I can tell Jim what you do . . . ?

LEVENE Sure.

9. That is, sotto voce: softly, under the breath (literally, "under the voice"; Italian).

ROMA Ray is director of all European sales and services for American Ex . . . [*To* LEVENE] But I'm saying you haven't had a *meal* until you've tasted . . . I was at the Lingks' last . . . as a matter of fact, what was that service feature you were talking about . . . ?

LEVENE Which . . .

ROMA "Home Cooking" . . . what did you call it, you said it . . . it was a tag phrase that you had . . .

LEVENE Uh . . .

ROMA Home . . .

LEVENE Home cooking . . .

ROMA The monthly interview . . . ?

LEVENE Oh! For the *magazine* . . .

ROMA Yes. Is this something that I can talk ab . . .

LEVENE Well, it isn't coming *out* until the February iss . . . *sure*. Sure, go ahead, Ricky.

ROMA You're sure?

LEVENE [*nods*] Go ahead.

ROMA Well, Ray was eating at one of his company's men's home in France . . . the man's French, isn't he?

LEVENE No, his *wife* is.

ROMA Ah. Ah, his wife is. Ray: what *time* do you have . . . ?

LEVENE Twelve-fifteen.

ROMA Oh! My God . . . I've got to get you on the *plane!*

LEVENE Didn't I say I was taking the two o' . . .

ROMA No. You said the one. That's why you said we couldn't talk till Kenilworth.

LEVENE Oh, my God, you're right! I'm on the one. . . . [*Getting up*] Well, let's *scoot* . . .

LINGK I've got to talk to you . . .

ROMA I've got to get Ray to O'Hare[1] . . . [*To* LEVENE] Come on, let's hustle. . . . [*Over his shoulder*] John! Call American Express in *Pittsburgh* for Mr. Morton, will you, tell them he's on the one o'clock. [*To* LINGK] I'll see you. . . . Christ, I'm sorry you came all the way in. . . . I'm running Ray over to O'Hare. . . . You wait here, I'll . . . no. [*To* LEVENE] I'm meeting your man at the bank. . . . [*To* LINGK] I wish you'd phoned. . . . I'll tell you, wait: are you and Jinny going to be home tonight? [*Rubs forehead.*]

LINGK I . . .

LEVENE Rick.

ROMA What?

LEVENE *Kenilworth* . . . ?

ROMA I'm sorry . . . ?

LEVENE *Kenilworth.*

ROMA Oh, God . . . Oh, God . . . [ROMA *takes* LINGK *aside, sotto.*] Jim, excuse me. . . . Ray, I told you, who he is is *the* senior vice-president American Express. His family owns 32 per. . . . Over the past years I've sold him . . . I can't tell you the dollar amount, but *quite* a lot of land. I promised five *weeks* ago that I'd go to the wife's birthday party in Kenilworth tonight. [*Sighs.*] I *have* to go. You understand. They treat me like a member of the

1. Chicago's main airport.

family, so I have to go. It's funny, you know, you get a picture of the Corporation-Type Company Man, all business . . . this man, *no.* We'll go out to his home sometime. Let's see. [*He checks his datebook.*] Tomorrow. No. Tomorrow, I'm in L.A. . . . *Monday* . . . I'll take you to lunch, where would you like to go?

LINGK My wife . . . [ROMA *rubs his head.*]

LEVENE [*standing in the door*] Rick . . . ?

ROMA I'm sorry, Jim. I can't talk now. I'll call you tonight . . . I'm sorry. I'm coming, Ray. [*Starts for the door.*]

LINGK My wife said I have to cancel the deal.

ROMA It's a common reaction, Jim. I'll tell you what it is, and I know that that's why you married her. One of the reasons is *prudence.* It's a sizable investment. One thinks *twice* . . . it's also something *women* have. It's just a reaction to the size of the investment. *Monday,* if you'd invite me for dinner again . . . [*To* LEVENE] This woman can *cook* . . .

LEVENE [*simultaneously*] I'm sure she can . . .

ROMA [*to* LINGK] We're going to talk. I'm going to *tell* you something. Because [*Sotto*] there's something about your acreage I want you to know. I can't talk about it now. I really shouldn't. And, in fact, by *law,* I . . . [*Shrugs, resigned.*] The man next to you, he bought his lot at forty-*two,* he phoned to say that he'd *already* had an offer . . . [ROMA *rubs his head.*]

LEVENE Rick . . . ?

ROMA I'm coming, Ray . . . what a day! I'll call you this evening, Jim. I'm sorry you had to come in . . . Monday, lunch.

LINGK My wife . . .

LEVENE Rick, we really have to go.

LINGK My wife . . .

ROMA Monday.

LINGK She called the consumer . . . the attorney, I don't know. The attorney gen . . . they said we have three days . . .

ROMA *Who* did she call?

LINGK I don't know, the attorney gen . . . the . . . some consumer office, umm . . .

ROMA Why did she do *that,* Jim?

LINGK I don't know. [*Pause*] They said we have three days. [*Pause*] They said we have three days.

ROMA Three days.

LINGK To . . . you know. [*Pause*]

ROMA No, I don't know. *Tell* me.

LINGK To change our minds.

ROMA Of *course* you have three days. [*Pause*]

LINGK So we can't talk *Monday.* [*Pause*]

ROMA Jim, Jim, you saw my book . . . I *can't, you* saw my book . . .

LINGK But we have to *before* Monday. To get our money ba . . .

ROMA Three *business* days. They mean three *business* days.

LINGK Wednesday, Thursday, Friday.

ROMA I don't understand.

LINGK That's what they are. Three business . . . if I wait till Monday, my time limit runs out.

ROMA You don't count Saturday.

LINGK I'm not.

ROMA No, I'm saying you don't include Saturday . . . in your three days. It's not a *business* day.

LINGK But I'm not *counting* it. [*Pause*] Wednesday. Thursday. Friday. So it would have elapsed.

ROMA What would have elapsed?

LINGK If we wait till Mon . . .

ROMA When did you write the check?

LINGK Yest . . .

ROMA What was yesterday?

LINGK Tuesday.

ROMA And when was that check cashed?

LINGK I don't know.

ROMA What was the *earliest* it could have been cashed? [*Pause*]

LINGK I don't know.

ROMA *Today.* [*Pause*] *Today.* Which, in any case, it was not, as there were a couple of points on the agreement I wanted to go over with you in any case.

LINGK The check wasn't cashed?

ROMA I just called downtown, and it's on their desk.

LEVENE Rick . . .

ROMA One moment, I'll be right with you. [*To* LINGK] In fact, a . . . *one* point, which I spoke to you of which [*Looks around.*] I can't talk to you about here.

[*Detective puts his head out of the doorway.*]

BAYLEN Levene!!!

LINGK I, I . . .

ROMA Listen to me, the *statute,* it's for your protection. I have no complaints with that, in fact, I was a member of the board when we *drafted* it, so quite the *opposite.* It *says* that you can change your mind three working days from the time the deal is closed.

BAYLEN Levene!

ROMA Which, wait a second, which is not until the check is cashed.

BAYLEN Levene!!

[AARONOW *comes out of the detective's office.*]

AARONOW I'm *through,* with *this* fucking meshugaas.[2] No one should talk to a man that way. How are you *talking* to me that . . . ?

BAYLEN Levene! [WILLIAMSON *puts his head out of the office.*]

AARONOW . . . how can you *talk* to me that . . . that . . .

LEVENE [*to* ROMA] Rick, I'm going to flag a cab.

AARONOW *I* didn't rob . . .

[WILLIAMSON *sees* LEVENE.]

WILLIAMSON Shelly: get in the office.

AARONOW *I* didn't . . . why should *I* . . . "Where were you last . . ." Is anybody listening to me . . . ? Where's Moss . . . ? Where . . . ?

BAYLEN Levene? [*To* WILLIAMSON] Is this Lev . . . [BAYLEN *accosts* LINGK.]

LEVENE [*taking* BAYLEN *into the office*] Ah. Ah. Perhaps I can advise you on that. . . . [*To* ROMA *and* LINGK, *as he exits*] *Excuse* us, will you . . . ?

2. Insanity, nonsense (Yiddish; usually spelled *mishegoss*).

AARONOW [*simultaneous with* LEVENE*'s speech above*] . . . Come in here . . . I *work* here, I don't come in here to be *mistreated* . . .

WILLIAMSON Go to *lunch,* will you . . .

AARONOW I want to *work* today, that's why I came . . .

WILLIAMSON The leads come in, I'll let . . .

AARONOW . . . that's why I came in. I thought I . . .

WILLIAMSON Just go to lunch.

AARONOW I don't *want* to go to lunch.

WILLIAMSON Go to lunch, George.

AARONOW Where does he get off to talk that way to a working man? It's not . . .

WILLIAMSON [*buttonholes him*] Will you take it outside, we have people trying to do *business* here . . .

AARONOW That's what, that's what, that's what *I* was trying to do. [*Pause*] That's why I came *in* . . . I meet *gestapo*[3] tac . . .

WILLIAMSON [*going back into his office*] Excuse me . . .

AARONOW I meet *gestapo* tactics . . . I meet *gestapo* tactics. . . . That's not right. . . . No man has the right to . . . "Call an attorney," that means you're guilt . . . you're under sus . . . "Co . . . ," he says, "cooperate" or we'll go downtown. *That's* not . . . as long as I've . . .

WILLIAMSON [*bursting out of his office*] Will you get out of here. Will you get *out* of here. Will you. I'm trying to run an *office* here. Will you go to lunch? Go to lunch. Will you go to lunch?

[*Retreats into office.*]

ROMA [*to* AARONOW] Will you excuse . . .

AARONOW Where did Moss . . . ? I . . .

ROMA Will you excuse us please?

AARONOW Uh, uh, did he go to the restaurant? [*Pause*] I . . . I . . .

[*Exits.*]

ROMA I'm *very* sorry, Jimmy. I apologize to you.

LINGK It's not me, it's my wife.

ROMA [*pause*] What is?

LINGK I told you.

ROMA Tell me again.

LINGK What's going on here?

ROMA Tell me again. Your wife.

LINGK I told you.

ROMA You tell me again.

LINGK She wants her money back.

ROMA We're going to speak to her.

LINGK No. She told me "right now."

ROMA We'll speak to her, Jim . . .

LINGK She won't listen.

[*Detective sticks his head out.*]

BAYLEN *Roma.*

LINGK She told me if not, I have to call the State's attorney.

3. A secret police using terrorist methods (the shortened form of the Nazis' Geheime Staatspolizei, or Secret State Police).

ROMA No, no. That's just something she "said." We don't have to do that.

LINGK She told me I *have* to.

ROMA No, Jim.

LINGK I *do.* If I don't get my *money* back . . .

[WILLIAMSON *points out* ROMA *to* BAYLEN.]

BAYLEN Roma! [*To* ROMA] I'm talking to you . . .

ROMA I've . . . look. [*Generally*] Will someone get this guy off my back.

BAYLEN You have a problem?

ROMA Yes, I have a problem. Yes, I *do,* my fr . . . It's not me that ripped the joint off, I'm doing *business.* I'll be with you in a *while.* You got it . . . ? [*Looks back.* LINGK *is heading for the door.*] Where are you going?

LINGK I'm . . .

ROMA Where are you going . . . ? This is *me.* . . . This is Ricky, Jim. Jim, anything you *want,* you *want* it, you *have* it. You understand? This is *me.* Something *upset* you. Sit down, now sit down. You tell me what it is. [*Pause*] Am I going to help you fix it? You're goddamned right I am. Sit down. Tell you something . . . ? *Sometimes* we need someone from *outside.* It's . . . no, sit down. . . . Now *talk* to me.

LINGK I can't negotiate.

ROMA What does that mean?

LINGK That . . .

ROMA . . . what, what, *say* it. Say it to me . . .

LINGK I . . .

ROMA What . . . ?

LINGK I . . .

ROMA What . . . ? Say the words.

LINGK I don't have the *power.* [*Pause*] I said it.

ROMA What power?

LINGK The power to negotiate.

ROMA To negotiate what? [*Pause*] To negotiate what?

LINGK *This.*

ROMA What, "this"? [*Pause*]

LINGK The deal.

ROMA The "deal," *Forget* the deal. *Forget* the deal, you've got something on your mind, Jim, what is it?

LINGK [*rising*] I can't talk to you, *you* met my wife, I . . . [*Pause*]

ROMA What? [*Pause*] What? [*Pause*] What, Jim: I tell you what, let's get out of here . . . let's go get a drink.

LINGK She told me not to talk to you.

ROMA Let's . . . no one's going to know, let's go around the *corner* and we'll get a drink.

LINGK She told me I had to get back the check or call the State's att . . .

ROMA *Forget* the deal, Jimmy. [*Pause*] *Forget* the deal . . . you know me. The deal's *dead.* Am I talking about the *deal*? That's *over.* Please. Let's talk about *you.* Come on. [*Pause.* ROMA *rises and starts walking toward the front door.*] Come on. [*Pause*] Come on, Jim. [*Pause*] I want to tell you something. Your life is your own. You have a contract with your wife. You have certain things you do *jointly,* you have a *bond* there . . . and there are *other* things. Those things are yours. You needn't feel *ashamed,* you needn't feel that you're being *untrue* . . . or that she would abandon you if she knew. This is your life. [*Pause*] *Yes.* Now I want to *talk* to you because you're obviously upset and that *concerns* me. Now let's go. Right now.

[LINGK *gets up and they start for the door.*]

BAYLEN [*sticks his head out of the door*] Roma . . .

LINGK . . . and . . . and . . . [*Pause*]

ROMA What?

LINGK And the check is . . .

ROMA What did I *tell* you? [*Pause*] What did I say about the three days . . . ?

BAYLEN Roma, would you, I'd like to get some lunch . . .

ROMA I'm talking with Mr. Lingk. If you please, I'll be back in. [*Checks watch.*] I'll be back in a while. . . . I told you, check with Mr. Williamson.

BAYLEN The people downtown said . . .

ROMA You call them again. Mr. Williamson . . . !

WILLIAMSON Yes.

ROMA Mr. Lingk and I are going to . . .

WILLIAMSON Yes. Please. Please. [*To* LINGK] The police [*Shrugs.*] can be . . .

LINGK What are the police doing?

ROMA It's nothing.

LINGK What are the *police* doing here . . . ?

WILLIAMSON We had a slight burglary last night.

ROMA It was nothing . . . I was assuring Mr. Lingk . . .

WILLIAMSON Mr. Lingk. James Lingk. Your contract went out. Nothing to . . .

ROMA John . . .

WILLIAMSON Your contract went out to the bank.

LINGK You cashed the check?

WILLIAMSON We . . .

ROMA . . . Mr. Williamson . . .

WILLIAMSON Your check was cashed yesterday afternoon. And we're completely insured, as you know, in *any* case. [*Pause*]

LINGK [*To* ROMA] You cashed the check?

ROMA Not to my knowledge, no . . .

WILLIAMSON I'm sure we can . . .

LINGK Oh, Christ . . . [*Starts out the door.*] Don't follow me. . . . Oh, Christ. [*Pause. To* ROMA.] I know I've let you down. I'm sorry. For . . . Forgive . . . for . . . I don't know anymore. [*Pause*] Forgive me. [LINGK *exits. Pause.*]

ROMA [*To* WILLIAMSON] You stupid fucking cunt. *You*, Williamson . . . I'm talking to *you*, shithead. . . . You just cost me *six thousand dollars.* [*Pause*] Six thousand dollars. And one Cadillac. That's right. What are you going to do about it? What are you going to do about it, asshole. You fucking *shit.* Where did you learn your *trade.* You stupid fucking *cunt.* You *idiot.* Whoever told you you could work with *men*?

BAYLEN Could I . . .

ROMA I'm going to have your *job,* shithead. I'm going *downtown* and talk to Mitch and Murray, and I'm going to Lemkin. I don't care *whose* nephew you are, who you know, whose dick you're sucking on. You're going *out,* I swear to you, you're going . . .

BAYLEN Hey, fella, let's get this done . . .

ROMA Anyone in this office lives on their *wits.* . . . [*To* BAYLEN] I'm going to be with you in a second. [*To* WILLIAMSON] What you're hired for is to *help* us—does that seem clear to you? To *help* us. *Not* to fuck us up . . . to help *men* who are going *out* there to try to earn a *living.* You *fairy.* You company man . . . I'll tell you something else. I hope you knocked the joint off, I can tell our friend here something might help him catch you. [*Starts into the room.*] You want to learn the first rule you'd know if you ever spent a day in your life . . . you never open your mouth till you know what the shot is. [*Pause*] You fucking *child* . . .

[ROMA *goes to the inner room.*]

LEVENE You *are* a shithead, Williamson . . . [*Pause*]

WILLIAMSON Mmm.

LEVENE You can't think on your feet you should keep your mouth closed. [*Pause*] You hear me? I'm *talking* to you. Do you hear me . . . ?

WILLIAMSON Yes. [*Pause*] I hear you.

LEVENE You can't learn that in an office. Eh? He's right. You have to learn it on the streets. You can't *buy* that. You have to *live* it.

WILLIAMSON Mmm.

LEVENE *Yes.* Mmm. *Yes. Precisely. Precisely.* 'Cause your partner *depends* on it. [*Pause*] I'm *talking* to you, I'm trying to tell you something.

WILLIAMSON You are?

LEVENE Yes, I am.

WILLIAMSON What are you trying to tell me?

LEVENE What Roma's trying to tell you. What I told you yesterday. Why you don't belong in this business.

WILLIAMSON Why I don't . . .

LEVENE You listen to me, someday you might say, "Hey . . ." No, fuck that, you just listen what I'm going to say: your partner *depends* on you. Your partner . . . a man who's your "partner" *depends* on you . . . you have to go *with* him and *for* him . . . or you're shit, you're *shit,* you can't exist alone . . .

WILLIAMSON [*brushing past him*] Excuse me . . .

LEVENE . . . excuse you, *nothing,* you be as cold as you want, but you just fucked a good man out of six thousand dollars and his goddamn bonus 'cause you didn't know the *shot,* if you can do that and you aren't man enough that it gets you, then I don't know what, if you can't take *something* from that . . . [*Blocking his way*] you're *scum,* you're fucking white-bread.[4] You be as cold as you want. A *child* would know it, he's right. [*Pause*] You're going to make something up, be sure it will *help* or keep your mouth closed. [*Pause*]

WILLIAMSON Mmm. [LEVENE *lifts up his arm.*]

LEVENE Now I'm done with you. [*Pause*]

WILLIAMSON How do you know I made it up?

LEVENE [*pause*] What?

WILLIAMSON How do you know I made it up?

LEVENE What are you talking about?

WILLIAMSON You said, "You don't make something up unless it's sure to help." [*Pause*] How did you know that I made it up?

LEVENE What are you talking about?

WILLIAMSON I told the customer that his contracts had gone to the bank.

LEVENE Well, hadn't it?

4. That is, typical of the bland, white middle class.

WILLIAMSON No. [*Pause*] It hadn't.

LEVENE Don't *fuck* with me, John, don't *fuck* with me . . . what are you saying?

WILLIAMSON Well, I'm saying this, Shel: usually I take the contracts to the bank. Last night I didn't. How did you know that? One night in a year I left a contract on my desk. Nobody knew that but *you.* Now how did you know that? [*Pause*] You want to talk to me, you want to talk to someone *else* . . . because this is *my* job. This is my job on the line, and you are going to *talk* to me. Now how did you know that contract was on my desk?

LEVENE You're so full of shit.

WILLIAMSON You robbed the office.

LEVENE [*laughs*] Sure! I robbed the office. Sure.

WILLIAMSON What'd you do with the leads? [*Pause. Points to the detective's room.*] You want to go in there? I tell him what I know, he's going to dig up *something.* . . . You got an alibi last night? You better have one. What did you do with the leads? If you tell me what you did with the leads, we can talk.

LEVENE I don't know what you are saying.

WILLIAMSON If you tell me where the leads are, I won't turn you in. If you *don't,* I am going to tell the cop you stole them, Mitch and Murray will see that you go to jail. Believe me they will. Now, what did you do with the leads? I'm walking in that door—you have five seconds to tell me: or you are going to jail.

LEVENE I . . .

WILLIAMSON I don't care. You understand? *Where are the leads?* [*Pause*] Alright. [WILLIAMSON *goes to open the office door.*]

LEVENE I sold them to Jerry Graff.

WILLIAMSON How much did you get for them? [*Pause*] How much did you get for them?

LEVENE Five thousand. I kept half.

WILLIAMSON Who kept the other half? [*Pause*]

LEVENE Do I have to tell you? [*Pause.* WILLIAMSON *starts to open the door.*] Moss.

WILLIAMSON *That* was easy, *wasn't* it? [*Pause*]

LEVENE It was his idea.

WILLIAMSON *Was* it?

LEVENE I . . . I'm sure he got more than the five, actually.

WILLIAMSON Uh-huh?

LEVENE He told me my share was twenty-five.

WILLIAMSON Mmm.

LEVENE Okay: I . . . look: I'm going to make it worth your while. I am. I turned this thing around. I closed the *old* stuff, I can do it again. *I'm* the one's going to close 'em. *I* am! *I* am! 'Cause I turned this thing a . . . I can do *that,* I can do *anyth* . . . last night. I'm going to tell you, I was ready to Do the Dutch.[5] Moss gets me, "Do this, we'll get well. . . ." Why not. Big fuckin' deal. I'm halfway hoping to get caught. To put me out of my . . . [*Pause*] But it *taught* me something. What it taught me, that you've got to

5. Commit suicide.

get *out* there. Big deal. So I wasn't cut out to be a thief. I was cut out to be a salesman. And now I'm back, and I got my *balls* back . . . and, you know, John, you have the *advantage* on me now. Whatever it takes to make it right, we'll make it right. We're going to make it right.

WILLIAMSON I want to tell you something, Shelly. You have a big mouth. [*Pause*]

LEVENE What?

WILLIAMSON You've got a big mouth, and now I'm going to show you an even bigger one. [*Starts toward the detective's door.*]

LEVENE Where are you going, John? . . . you can't do that, you don't want to do that . . . hold, hold on . . . hold on . . . wait . . . wait . . . wait . . . [*Pulls money out of his pockets.*] Wait . . . uh, look . . . [*Starts splitting money.*] Look, twelve, twenty, two, twen . . . twenty-five hundred, it's . . . take it. [*Pause*] Take it all. . . . [*Pause*] Take it!

WILLIAMSON No, I don't think so, Shel.

LEVENE I . . .

WILLIAMSON No, I think I don't want your money. I think you fucked up my office. And I think you're going away.

LEVENE I . . . what? Are you, are you, that's why . . . ? Are you nuts? I'm . . . I'm going to *close* for you, I'm going to . . . [*Thrusting money at him.*] Here, here, I'm going to *make* this office . . . I'm going to be back there Number One. . . . Hey, hey, hey! This is only the beginning. . . . List . . . list . . . listen. Listen. Just one moment. List . . . here's what . . . here's what we're going to do. Twenty percent. I'm going to give you twenty percent of my sales. . . . [*Pause*] Twenty percent. [*Pause*] For as long as I am with the firm. [*Pause*] Fifty percent. [*Pause*] You're going to be my partner. [*Pause*] Fifty percent. Of all my sales.

WILLIAMSON What sales?

LEVENE What sales . . . ? I just *closed* eighty-two *grand*. . . . Are you fuckin' . . . I'm *back* . . . I'm *back,* this is only the beginning.

WILLIAMSON Only the beginning . . .

LEVENE Abso . . .

WILLIAMSON Where have you been, Shelly? Bruce and Harriett Nyborg. Do you want to see the *memos* . . . ? They're nuts . . . they used to call in every week. When I was with Webb. And we were selling Arizona . . . they're nuts . . . did you see how they were *living*? How can you delude yours . . .

LEVENE I've got the check . . .

WILLIAMSON Forget it. Frame it. It's worthless. [*Pause*]

LEVENE The check's no good?

WILLIAMSON You stick around I'll pull the memo for you. [*Starts for the door.*] I'm busy now . . .

LEVENE Their check's no good? They're nuts . . . ?

WILLIAMSON Call up the bank. *I* called them.

LEVENE You did?

WILLIAMSON I called them when we had the lead . . . four months ago. [*Pause*] The people are insane. They just like talking to salesmen. [WILLIAMSON *starts for door.*]

LEVENE Don't.

WILLIAMSON I'm sorry.

LEVENE *Why?*

WILLIAMSON Because I don't like you.

LEVENE John: John: . . . my *daughter* . . .

WILLIAMSON Fuck you.

[ROMA *comes out of the detective's door.* WILLIAMSON *goes in.*]

ROMA [*To* BAYLEN] Asshole . . . [*To* LEVENE] Guy couldn't find his fuckin' couch the *living room* . . . Ah, Christ . . . what a day, what a day . . . I haven't even had a cup of *coffee*. . . . Jagoff John opens his mouth he blows my Cadillac. . . . [*Sighs.*] I swear . . . it's not a world of men . . . it's not a world of men, Machine . . . it's a world of clock-watchers, bureaucrats, officeholders . . . what it is, it's a fucked-up world . . . there's no adventure *to* it. [*Pause*] Dying breed. Yes it is. [*Pause*] We are the members of a dying breed. That's . . . that's . . . that's why we have to stick together. Shel: I want to talk to you. I've wanted to talk to you for some time. For a long time, actually. I said, "The Machine, there's a man I would work with. There's a man. . . ." You know? I never said a thing. I should have, don't know why I didn't. And that shit you were slinging on my guy today was *so* good . . . it . . . it was, and, excuse me, 'cause it isn't even my place to say it. It was admirable . . . it was the old stuff. Hey, I've been on a hot streak, so *what*? There's things that I could learn from you. You eat today?

LEVENE Me.

ROMA Yeah.

LEVENE Mm.

ROMA Well, you want to swing by the Chinks,[6] watch me eat, we'll talk?

LEVENE I think I'd better stay here for a while.

[BAYLEN *sticks his head out of the room.*]

BAYLEN Mr. *Levene* . . . ?

ROMA You're done, come down and let's . . .

BAYLEN Would you come in here, please?

ROMA And let's put this together. Okay? Shel? Say okay. [*Pause*]

LEVENE [*softly, to himself*] Huh.

BAYLEN Mr. Levene, I think we have to talk.

ROMA I'm going to the Chinks. You're done, come down, we're going to smoke a cigarette.

LEVENE I . . .

BAYLEN [*comes over*] . . . Get in the room.

ROMA Hey, hey, hey, *easy*, friend, That's the "Machine." That is Shelly "The Machine" Lev . . .

BAYLEN Get in the goddamn room. [BAYLEN *starts manhandling* SHELLY *into the room.*]

LEVENE Ricky, I . . .

ROMA Okay, okay, I'll be at the resta . . .

LEVENE Ricky . . .

BAYLEN "Ricky" can't help you, pal.

LEVENE . . . I only want to . . .

BAYLEN Yeah. What do you want? You want to *what?*

[*He pushes* LEVENE *into the room, closes the door behind him. Pause.*]

6. That is, the Chinese restaurant (*Chinks* is a derogatory term for the Chinese).

ROMA Williamson: listen to me: when the *leads* come in . . . listen to me: when the *leads* come in I want my top two off the list. For *me.* My usual two. Anything you give *Levene* . . .

WILLIAMSON . . . I wouldn't worry about it.

ROMA Well I'm *going* to worry about it, and so are you, so shut up and *listen.* [*Pause*] I GET HIS ACTION. My stuff is *mine,* whatever *he* gets for himself, I'm talking half. You put me in with him.

[AARONOW *enters.*]

AARONOW Did they . . . ?

ROMA You understand?

AARONOW Did they catch . . . ?

ROMA Do you understand? My stuff is mine, his stuff is ours. I'm taking half of his commissions—now, *you* work it out.

WILLIAMSON Mmm.

AARONOW Did they find the guy who broke into the office yet?

ROMA No. *I* don't know. [*Pause*]

AARONOW Did the leads come in yet?

ROMA No.

AARONOW [*settling into a desk chair*] Oh, God, I hate this job.

ROMA [*simultaneous with "job," exiting the office*] I'll be at the restaurant.

LOUIS NOWRA

b. 1950

IMAGES of Australia have fascinated the Western popular imagination since the island continent was "discovered" and explored by Europeans in the seventeenth century, but by the latter half of the twentieth century, the cultural products of the Australian imagination began to have an international reach. Following World War II, when it and other British Commonwealth nations fought against the Axis powers in Europe and the Pacific, Australia became increasingly active in world affairs; its heightened visibility made other countries more receptive to works created by its citizens. Particularly in such popular media as pop and rock music, as well as film, Australian artists have achieved global recognition and success. And yet, although some of Australia's best-known actors and directors began their careers in live theater, its stage history and its dramatic literature remain relatively unknown to outsiders—despite burgeoning theatrical activity, much of it informed both by postcolonial sensibilities and by a recognition of the ongoing tensions between settler and indigenous cultures. Since the 1970s, the Australian dramatist Louis Nowra has emerged as one of the country's leading chroniclers of such national concerns.

Australia's development of a distinct national culture cannot be understood without taking into account its history as part of the British Empire. Well into the twentieth century, creativity was expected to follow British models; such a climate of cultural imperialism, together with a strict system of censorship, constrained and stifled local artists. Touring productions from England and regional productions of British plays long defined Australian theater. In 1955, however, a play by Ray Lawler—*Summer of the Seventeenth Doll*—revolutionized the nation's dramaturgy by offering a revisionist depiction of Australia's sparsely populated hinterlands and representing distinctly Australian characters and themes. A so-called second wave of Australian dramatists, Nowra among them, arrived in the 1970s, seeking to move the drama away from a preoccupation with questions of national, mythic identity and to expand the stylistic and thematic parameters of the stage.

Louis Cale Nowra was born Mark Robert Doyle on December 12, 1950, the eldest of four children in what he calls "a troubled family" in Melbourne. Five years earlier, his mother, Gloria Herbert, had shot and killed her father while protecting her mother during a domestic dispute. Gloria's second husband, Louis's father Clarrie Doyle, was a truck driver of Irish descent who spent most of his time on the road and finally left his family altogether, though he remained in contact with them intermittently. Nowra ascribes his dark sense of humor to his father, who told his children stories of robbers and con men and claimed they were related to a famous criminal. From his mother he "learnt a particular lower-middle-class culture. Instead of having Bizet's *Carmen* . . . we had its Hollywood version in *Carmen Jones;* instead of having Borodin's *Prince Igor,* we had *Kismet.* It was as if I were receiving art through a plastic sieve." Equally important was the influence of his uncle, the playwright Bob Herbert; he worked as a stage manager and director for the J. C. Williamson theatrical chain, which toured Broadway musicals around Australia, and he introduced Nowra to such classics as *Camelot* (1960), *My Fair Lady* (1956), and *Hello, Dolly!* (1964). Nowra recalls being profoundly disturbed, however, when his uncle took him backstage, where he discovered the false finery of costumes and sets and the general tawdriness of the environment. His sense of theatrical illusion was destroyed; indeed, Nowra "never really got over this moment and even today I think there is something fraudulent about theatre, as if some cheap trick . . . were at the basis of it all."

As a child, Nowra was not a particularly good student, and in his first year of high school, he suffered a severe head injury that profoundly affected his speech and learning for the next four years. He describes feeling during this time as if his "brain had turned off." Forced to completely relearn how to speak and write, Nowra struggled academically and often skipped classes to watch movies at a nearby cinema. Nowra developed a keen sensitivity to visual images and initially aspired to a career as a film director or painter. In his last year of high school, he saw his first nonmusical play, ARTHUR MILLER's *Death of a Salesman* (1949). The production appears to have emphasized only the realistic aspects of the text, which Nowra found "excruciatingly tedious"; its falsity drove him to decisively reject stage realism.

In 1967, Nowra enrolled at La Trobe University in Melbourne, majoring in English literature. Having made an almost miraculous recovery, he became a voracious reader of theoretical as well as creative works, ranging from James Joyce, F. Scott Fitzgerald, Vladimir Nabokov, and Leo Tolstoy to Karl Marx and Franz Fanon. He also began to read more widely in the dramatic canon, finding in such contemporary British playwrights as HAROLD PINTER and Edward Bond "a thundering resonance and power" he had not previously seen in plays. Nowra joined a politically oriented street theater group; because he was the only member who could type, he soon began to write their scripts. While working with patients in a mental hospital, he directed them in an adaptation of W. S. Gilbert and Arthur Sullivan's operetta *Trial by Jury* (1875), with a simplified script and interpolated songs by the Beatles and the Bee Gees.

Nowra dropped out of college and spent several years doing odd jobs before deciding to commit himself to a more sustained effort as a writer. It was probably during this period that he changed his name from Mark Doyle to Louis Nowra, possibly taking the surname from the city called Nowra in the South Coast region of New South Wales. During this period, he encountered the farcical, camp style of the British playwright Joe Orton and observed the development of the new generation of Australian dramatists. Nowra later explained that he "liked the roughness, the energy" of this new national dramaturgy, but he "could not understand its preoccupation with beer, women, cars and sport." He "found this aggressive Australian maleness and its middle-class sensibility off-putting" and, consciously or unconsciously, chose a different path for his own creative endeavors. Nowra's earliest plays reflect his preoccupation with language, enculturation, and education. His first piece, *Albert Names Edward* (1975), concerns a derelict recluse who teaches a homeless amnesiac. *Inner Voices* (1977) explores these same concerns through the metaphoric context of Czarist Russia, while *Visions* (1978), set in Paraguay, also treats teaching as the means of cultural transmission. At this early point in his career, Nowra had no interest in generating nationalistic pieces that trumpet Australian identity; quite to the contrary, he saw a "void at our centre, where our soul should be," that was the direct result of "our refusal to come to terms with the fact that we conquered a race of people and confiscated their land, without understanding the immoral enormity of what we had done."

Nowra traces the origins of *THE GOLDEN AGE* to a story he heard in 1984 of the discovery, on the eve of World War II, of a group of people, living in the Tasmanian wilderness, seemingly frozen in time and cut off from the rest of civilization. The group was taken to Tasmania's capital, Hobart, and eventually placed in New Norfolk Asylum. Nowra's dramatic version of the story opens on the grounds of Elizabeth and William Archer's home in Hobart, situated near the psychiatric hospital where Dr. William Archer works. The Archers' son, Peter, and his close friend Francis decide to go off on a hiking trip to the wilds of Tasmania. In the desolate southwest of the island, they discover a group of six inhabitants—Betsheb, Stef, Ayre, Melorne, Angel, and Mac. These descendants of convicts who had populated the area in the first half of the nineteenth century have a culture and a language that appear almost incomprehensible. After Melorne dies, Ayre manages to tell Peter and Francis that they wish to return with the boys. The play then explores the collision of their world with that of twentieth-century Australians, framed by the global conflict into which Peter and Francis are drawn.

Tasmania, known as Van Diemen's Land until 1856, was settled by the British in the early nineteenth century. Of the 70,000 colonists living in Australia (including Tasmania) by 1830, almost 60,000 were British convicts. During the early decades of the nineteenth century, the white settlers eradicated most of the Aboriginal Tasmanians; the few who remained were moved to Flinders Island, where they soon succumbed to disease and died. Well into the late twentieth century, white Tasmanians retained a sense of identity as Britons. Local culture reflected Georgian tastes, especially in architecture, and promoted a kind of neoclassicism epitomized by the renovation of a museum that had been built on the slopes of Mount Wellington in 1842, at the request of the governor's wife, in the form of a Greek temple. Nowra translates much of this sensibility to the Archers, who represent the vestiges of British colonialism.

The play's title—*The Golden Age*—perfectly captures both the blinkered glorification of the past and the irony of invoking a perfect civilization that, by definition, has been irrevocably lost; the main association with the phrase "golden age" reaches back millennia, to Greek mythology. As told in the *Metamorphoses* (ca. 10 C.E.) by the Roman poet Ovid,

> In the beginning was the Golden Age,
> when men of their own accord,

The Golden Age at the Playbox Theatre Centre, Melbourne, Australia, 1985. Pictured here are, from left to right, Melita Jurisic as Betsheb, Marilynne Hanigan as Angel, and Robin Cuming as Melorne.

> without threat of punishment, without laws, maintained good faith and did what was right. . . . Never yet had any pine tree, cut down from its home on the mountains, been launched on ocean's waves, to visit foreign lands: men only knew their own shores. . . . The peoples of the world, untroubled by any fears, enjoyed a leisurely and peaceful existence, and had no use for soldiers.

Nowra highlights Australia's quixotic engagement with the past in the very first scene of *The Golden Age,* as Elizabeth and William Archer stand before a "small, crumbling Greek temple" and, clad respectively in ancient dress and contemporary evening attire, deliver lines from EURIPIDES' *Iphigenia in Tauris* (ca. 413 B.C.E.). This tragedy, which serves powerfully as a play-within-the-play, chronicles the reunion of Orestes and his long-lost sister Iphigenia, followed by their narrow escape from the Taurians. The play also trumpets the siblings' love of and longing for their distant Greek homeland and features the theme of idealized male friendship in the characters of Orestes and Pylades.

Nowra utilizes another potent cultural referent, SHAKESPEARE's *King Lear,* though the version of the narrative performed by Melorne is closer to its popularized nineteenth-century variant than to the Renaissance original. The trope of "outcastin'" (exile), a powerful, recurring term in the patois of the discovered group, binds together the stories of a wandering king, estranged from his daughters, and of this family, descendants of convicts transported to Tasmania. Nowra invites us to compare the Archers' fealty to an ersatz classicism with the lost tribe's appropriation and heartfelt reproduction of English popular culture.

At the intersection of these canonical dramatic narratives stands the theme of exile, which necessarily opposes two locales: home and the foreign site of involuntary residence. Nowra, who especially admires Shakespeare's use of disparate settings that showcase the bard's "highly developed sense of figures in a landscape," provocatively builds *The Golden Age* around a series of distinct worlds: Hobart and the southwestern Tasmanian wilderness; Tasmania, at a remove from England and even from the Australian mainland; and Berlin, where Francis and Peter are posted during the war. In so doing, Nowra suggests that all of his characters are alienated from their home and could echo Melorne's cry, "Nowt more outcastin'!" (No more exile!). At the same time, the play forces us to consider what really signifies home, or exile, for any individual and to realize that such distinctions may not be absolute.

Nowra conveys a very specific sense of what he calls "the black hole" of Australian history through his rendition of the lost tribe's discovery. Many critics see the group as a metaphor for Australia's Aboriginal peoples (an interpretation confirmed by Nowra himself), and the story of their capture, transportation to the asylum, and "reeducation" parallels that larger historical tragedy. The Archers' efforts to protect, study, and teach the strangers perfectly exemplify imperialist practices. The play thus epitomizes Nowra's career-long preoccupation with language, enculturation, and education, which resonate for him on both personal and political levels. Although he acknowledges these preoccupations, Nowra resists polemical dramaturgy and overt critiques of colonialism. Instead, he believes that his plays work "by resonance and metaphor," showing "how power is used whether it be in our private lives or in the political arena."

One of the key structures of power in Nowra's writing is language. He declares, "Language should make people re-examine the world. Language should tear apart the audience's perception of the world and remake it." The most striking element of *The Golden Age* may well be its creation of a new language for the lost tribe. Nowra speaks of the challenge of inventing speech that was new but "that the audience could basically understand. . . . I tried to use rhythms that most of the audience was already familiar with, especially those audience members who are from an English or Irish background. I repeated words and sentences a fair bit so it gradually sank in—or sank without a trace." He carefully researched "lower class language and slang in the 1840s and books of the bawdy verse of the times. I thought that this group, isolated from the outside world for three generations, would have turned upside-down society's notions of obscene language and used it as a non-vulgar vehicle to explain notions of fertility and the like."

This language corresponds to the sheer energy projected by members of the tribe. Their incredible physicality is yet another distinguishing feature, which critics have linked to the gothic sensibility present throughout Nowra's plays. He once expressed his admiration for the Canadian film director David Cronenberg by observing that Cronenberg's films demonstrate "the body is a weapon that can be used against self." Nowra translates these somatic energies theatrically, creating vivid stage images of physical degeneration that contrast sharply with these characters' indomitable spirit.

The fatal clash of characters and cultures that takes place in *The Golden Age* traces a narrative pattern common to many of Nowra's plays—a pattern that has earned him the sobriquet "Apocalypse Nowra." Nowra has continued to explore such conflicts in his later works, which include pieces for theater, radio, television, and film—especially *Così* (1992, 1995), which won the New South Wales Premier's Literary Award for its initial theatrical version, and the Australian Film Institute's award for best screenplay adaptation—as well as novels and short stories. Yet the dramatist sees his work a bit differently. He explains that in all his plays, "the ending generally revolves around" a loss of balance and a new struggle between outer and inner worlds: "The attainment of a synthesis, forged from the conflict between the thesis and antithesis, is at a cost." Critics see *The Golden Age* as one of Nowra's most accomplished works, with a temporal and thematic reach that both reflects the specificity of Australia's heritage and speaks to political and cultural patterns at the very center of world history.

J.E.G.

The Golden Age

There are moments when speech is but a mouth pressed lightly and humbly against the angel's hand. —*James Merrill*[1]

In memory of Marvin Gaye.[2]

CHARACTERS

WILLIAM ARCHER, a doctor
ELIZABETH ARCHER, William's wife
MR TURNER, a friend of the Archers
FRANCIS MORRIS, a young engineer
PETER ARCHER, a young geologist
BETSHEB, a young woman
STEF, an 'autistic' child
AYRE, an old woman
MELORNE, an old man
ANGEL, a woman in her twenties
MAC, a young man
GEORGE ROSS, M.P.,[3] Federal Minister for Health
MRS WITCOMBE, a working-class woman in her fifties
DR SIMON, psychiatrist at the asylum

1. American poet (1926–1995); the lines quoted are from the end of "A Dedication" (1959).
2. American singer and songwriter (1939–1984), one of the best-selling soul artists of his generation; he was shot to death by his father a year before this play premiered.
3. Minister of Parliament.

JAMES, a patient at the asylum
PRIVATE CORRIS, an Australian soldier
A GERMAN MAN, a man on the run
MARY, a maid
A servant

SETTING: The play is set during the wartime years 1939–45, and the action moves from locations in Hobart[4] and southwest Tasmania to Berlin in the last days of the War.

1.1

Hobart, 1939. A garden. It is a hot Australian night full of the sounds of cicadas and crickets. ELIZABETH ARCHER, *a middle-aged woman, stands in front of a small, crumbling Greek temple. She wears a copy of an ancient Greek dress. For a moment it seems we are in ancient Greece, but she is playing Iphigenia from* Iphigenia in Tauris.[5]

ELIZABETH 'I dreamed I had escaped from this island and lived at home in Argos. There I was asleep when suddenly the earth shook and tore apart. I ran outdoors and helplessly watched the whole house crumble into the earth. Out of this ruin, which was my father's house, one column stood. Brown hair grew from its head and it spoke in a human voice. Weeping, I performed for it this murderous ritual for strangers, sprinkling water, as on one destined to die. I interpret this dream thus: it was my brother Orestes I prepared for death and he has died. For what are pillars of a house but its sons. And those whose heads I touch with purifying water die. So now I want to pour libations for my brother.'

[WILLIAM, *about the same age as his wife, enters as Orestes. He is handcuffed, wears glasses and a dinner jacket. He stands before Iphigenia.*]

'Do you know where you are?'

WILLIAM 'Tauris, my High Priestess.'

ELIZABETH 'And what is it known for?'

WILLIAM 'Any Greek who lands on its shores is put to death.'

ELIZABETH 'And yet, mysterious stranger, you are Greek and you dare to step on our island. You should have left when you had the chance.'

WILLIAM 'I was shipwrecked.'

ELIZABETH 'I do not believe your story. Do you see the dark stain on the altar? It is the blood of previous sacrifices. Your blood will mingle with that blood to delight the goddess Artemis.'

WILLIAM 'I would not care to die if my sister were here to prepare me for my burial.'

4. The capital city of Tasmania (one of the states of Australia), on the southeast coast of the island.

5. A tragedy (ca. 413 B.C.E.) by the Greek playwright Euripides. In most versions of her story, Iphigenia is sacrificed to Artemis at Aulis by Agamemnon, her father, so that the Greek fleet can sail to Troy; this play draws on a version in which the huntress goddess saves her, transporting her to Tauris (today's Crimea, on the Black Sea). Years later, when her brother, Orestes, and his friend come to Tauris, she is the high priestess charged with seeing that all strangers be put to death on the altar of Artemis. Once she recognizes Orestes, she plots to escape with them and the statue of Artemis they had come to steal (an act that the oracle at Delphi had told them was necessary to end Orestes' fits of madness, caused by his murder of his mother, Clytemnestra). Elizabeth's initial speech quotes Euripides (lines 44–63), but the remainder of the dialogue is not taken directly from the play.

ELIZABETH 'A hopeless wish for a lost soul. Your sister would never be in this savage country. I gather you were captured with another man.'

WILLIAM 'My friend Pylades. He is rich, his house is pure and untainted while I live nowhere and everywhere. I am an outcast, hated by the gods.'

ELIZABETH 'I too am far from home and live only to perform these dark rites which are so savage as not to be sung. Last night I dreamed my brother, whom I have not seen since we were children, was dead. Killed. His house in ruins. I now have nothing left to lose. Cruelty has overtaken me, possessed me. You are the first to sail here in a long time but you will never return home. You will die in pain and lie in an unmarked grave.'

1.2

The same place, next morning. A servant sets up outdoor tables and chairs. Off, in the distance, FRANCIS *and* PETER *play tennis. While the servant sets up,* MR TURNER *enters. He is blind and confused. The servant doesn't see him and heads off, humming, to get another chair.* MR TURNER *hears.*

MR TURNER Am I in the garden?

[*The servant doesn't respond.*]

Excuse me, am I in the garden?

[*Silence. He goes a little further and finds himself on the steps of the temple. This confuses him further.*]

Hello, is anybody here?

[*He enters the temple and disappears.*]

[*Off*] Mrs Archer?

[*The servant re-enters with another chair, followed by* WILLIAM.]

WILLIAM I admire the boys' stamina playing in this heat.

ELIZABETH [*entering behind him*] His driver said he dropped him at the front door and now he's disappeared. Vanished!

[*She exits again. The boys appear.* PETER *looks very English in his whites.* FRANCIS *wears tennis shoes with football socks,*[6] *a T-shirt, and black football shorts.*]

WILLIAM Who won?

PETER Francis, by a whisker.

FRANCIS By a mile.

[*They laugh.* PETER *pours lemonade for his friend and himself.*]

WILLIAM [*to* FRANCIS] You know what you two are about to do is quite dangerous.

PETER Don't nag, father.

WILLIAM Francis, didn't Mary lay out some tennis whites for you?

[FRANCIS *is embarrassed.*]

PETER She did, but Francis didn't know they were for him.

[ELIZABETH *enters.*]

ELIZABETH I can't find him anywhere.

WILLIAM He'll turn up.

6. Knee-high athletic socks (rather than ankle-high tennis socks). Before World War II, men customarily played tennis in white clothing, including full-length pants.

ELIZABETH I want to personally give him his cheque. I think the School for the Blind should be quite pleased at how much was given last night. [*Glancing at* FRANCIS' *clothes*] Francis, didn't Mary—?

WILLIAM [*interrupting*] We've been through that.

ELIZABETH [*sitting*] The weather is exquisite! Have you been to Tasmania before, Francis?

FRANCIS First time. Thank you for letting me stay here—

ELIZABETH [*waving this away*] Our pleasure. Half the time we think we're a separate country from the rest of Australia.[7]

[*The boys finish their lemonade.*]

PETER We'll go and clean up.

ELIZABETH Make it snappy. I'd like you to meet Mr Turner.

[*The boys exit.*]

Did you speak to them about their trip?

WILLIAM They're determined.

ELIZABETH They should consider something less hazardous.

WILLIAM It's part of the attraction.

[MR TURNER *emerges from the temple behind them, lost and confused.*]

ELIZABETH That Francis, he's a strange boy. I watched him playing tennis from the balcony. He plays with such ferocity.

WILLIAM It's why I like him, he's had to fight so hard to get where he is.

MR TURNER Hello?

[ELIZABETH *turns around.*]

ELIZABETH Mr Turner! [*Rushing to his aid*] Stay where you are.

MR TURNER Where am I?

ELIZABETH On the steps of the temple.

MR TURNER Temple?

[ELIZABETH *grabs him and escorts him to the chairs.*]

ELIZABETH I've been looking everywhere for you.

MR TURNER [*still confused*] I thought I was in the garden, and then . . .

ELIZABETH Sit down . . . Some lemonade? [*Pouring it without waiting for an answer*] You seem flustered.

WILLIAM How are you, Mr Turner?

MR TURNER Is that you, Mr Archer?

WILLIAM Yes.

ELIZABETH [*putting the glass in his hand*] There you are. You certainly won't be going home empty-handed, Mr Turner. The Greek tragedy wrought a financial miracle.

MR TURNER I was lost.

ELIZABETH Excuse me?

MR TURNER I thought I was in the garden. I smelt roses. Flowers. And then I stepped into another world. I felt like Alice in Wonderland.[8] I said 'Hello' and it echoed all about me. I was lost. I thought I was dead.

[*The Archers have no idea what he is talking about.*]

7. Tasmania is about 150 miles south of the state of Victoria, geographically separated from "the rest of Australia" by the Bass Strait.

8. The subject of two children's books by Lewis Carroll (the pseudonym of the British mathematician Charles Dodgson), *Alice's Adventures in Wonderland* (1865) and *Through the Looking-Glass, and What Alice Found There* (1871).

1.3

The wilds of southwest Tasmania, evening. Two lanterns sit on the ground. FRANCIS, *tired and dirty, rests against his knapsack looking at a map in the frail light cast by the lantern. He eats some biscuits.*

FRANCIS [*to himself*] Jesus . . .

[*Silence.*]

[*Calling*] Are you all right?

[*No answer.*]

Peter?

PETER [*off*] Coming!

[FRANCIS *returns to his map.*]

FRANCIS Could be anywhere . . . anywhere.

[*A noise comes from the bush behind him.* FRANCIS *looks.*]

Peter?

[*Silence.*]

Is that you, Peter?

[*Silence. There is nothing.* FRANCIS *returns to his map.* PETER *enters from another direction, exhausted and dirty.*]

PETER Got bloody caught up in the Bauera.

FRANCIS The what?

PETER That wild rose we saw this morning. It grows around everything and once it's entangled all living things, it grows back on itself to form a wall. A bit like my mother.

[*He sits down and takes a stone from his pocket.*]

I found this: it was glinting in the moonlight. [*Taking a closer look at it under the lantern*] I'll have a better look at it in the morning. Once you conquered this region I'm sure you'd find huge mineral deposits.

FRANCIS I'd be happy if we could conquer this map. We should go back the way we came, otherwise we'll get well and truly lost. Not that we're not anyway.

PETER [*unconcerned*] We'll be fine. Do you know that this part of Tasmania is one of the most unexplored regions on earth, like the Amazon or the highlands of New Guinea? [*Standing*] It's like another world, isn't it?

FRANCIS [*looking up at the night sky*] Can't even see the stars.

PETER An underworld. [*Jumping up and down*] See how the ground springs?

FRANCIS Soggy.

PETER You know we're about ten foot off the ground?

[FRANCIS *laughs.*]

True. We're on the burial ground of nature. Rotten vegetable residue of centuries, ancient and petrified trees. So here we are, suspended ten foot above the true floor.

FRANCIS That's what I love about nature; it's so treacherous.

PETER You look at nature and your eyes glaze over.

FRANCIS I always feel that I'm looking at a postcard. [*Smiling*] My mother says that nature is God's Bible.

PETER You know, you've never introduced me to her.

FRANCIS Things that humans make: cars, gasworks, factories: now that's something. The conquering of chaos.

PETER You're serious?

FRANCIS A painter does a painting and people think it's a miracle. It is more wonderful to see a blueprint of a building or bridge and watch it transformed into reality. The Sydney Harbour Bridge[9] has not only conquered nature but is also beautiful. It is imagination made concrete. Mind has become matter.

[PETER *laughs.*]

What are you laughing at?

PETER [*slightly bewildered*] Nothing.

FRANCIS Take your father; he's an artist, he heals the sick. That's more important than painting. He saves lives.

[FRANCIS *notices something.*]

PETER In a way.

FRANCIS Did you see that?

PETER Probably some animal.

[PETER *goes through his knapsack.*]

FRANCIS I heard something over there before.

PETER Sorry to put you through the ordeal of meeting my parents.

FRANCIS It was interesting.

[PETER *laughs.*]

PETER They have developed certain eccentricities.

FRANCIS I heard you arguing with your dad before we left.

PETER He doesn't want me to go to Europe; he thinks the political climate is 'unsuitable'. Since he became president of the Medical Board he's taken an unnatural interest in politics. Like you. At the moment he's trying to get the medical profession to protest against the deregistration of Jewish doctors in Germany.[1] I say to him, 'Why bother? Australians don't give a damn.'

FRANCIS [*sarcastically*] Perhaps the English will.

PETER Who cares, anyway? I want to enjoy myself over there; get to know my mother's relatives, Esther's family—

FRANCIS [*interrupting*] Esther's family?

PETER She's partly why I'm going.

FRANCIS You're not marrying her?

PETER When I return.

FRANCIS I thought you said you wanted to enjoy life. Think of all the women you'll never get to know.

PETER You boys from the slums.

FRANCIS I have my standards: I only go out with rich girls; I'm trying to rise above my class.

PETER Is that why you mix with me?

FRANCIS Of course. You're my introductory service.

9. A steel arch bridge connecting Sydney's central business area with its North Shore; its construction (1924–32) was a tremendous engineering feat, and it is one of the country's best-known landmarks.

1. Soon after Adolph Hitler became chancellor of Germany in 1933, the Nazis began to institute a series of "Aryanization" measures that curtailed the professional and civil rights of Jewish doctors and lawyers.

[*Suddenly a woman screams. Both men jump up. The scream goes on and on, anguished, passionate but almost ritualistic.*]

PETER What in the hell is that?

[*It goes on, then abruptly stops. Silence. Both boys are scared.*]

That was a person, wasn't it?

FRANCIS No animal could sound like that.

PETER Maybe it was an animal in pain.

[*They take their lanterns and go to the area from which they judge the cry came.*]

FRANCIS Here.

[PETER *comes over and shines his lantern. It reveals the corpse of a young man, his body covered in rotten flowers.*]

PETER Christ, I'm going to be sick.

[*He moves away.* FRANCIS *holds his lantern closer and examines the body.*]

FRANCIS He's been dead for some time. I wonder why no one's buried him. They've covered him in flowers; why not bury him, then?

PETER Perhaps someone wanted him left that way.

FRANCIS He seems quite young.

PETER God, he stinks. How can you be so close?

FRANCIS There's something about his face . . .

PETER It's rotten, that's all. Come on, Francis, let's get going. That screaming . . .

FRANCIS It'll take us days to get back.

[FRANCIS *spots something.*]

Jesus . . .

[*He holds the lantern closer.*]

PETER What is it?

FRANCIS His mouth is full of gold.

[PETER *comes closer.* FRANCIS *takes out a small piece.*]

See?

PETER You're like my father: nothing bothers you.

FRANCIS [*handing the gold piece to* PETER] See?

PETER [*repulsed*] No thanks, not from a dead man's mouth.

[*Silence. Unnoticed, the silhouetted figure of a woman enters.*]

FRANCIS Flowers . . . bits of gold . . .

PETER Perhaps he was murdered.

FRANCIS Why would a murderer do this to him? Anyway, you told me nobody is supposed to be living way out here.

[*The woman growls softly at* FRANCIS *and* PETER. *Both boys are startled. They stand up and look at her.* BETSHEB *is young, dirty, and dressed in a nineteenth-century dress patched in various colours as if repaired over many years. She bares her teeth at them, almost like an animal, then screams violently as if cursing them. She turns and runs away. Blackout.*]

1.4

A river bank, afternoon. BETSHEB *sits on the bank with* STEF, *a boy aged between fifteen and eighteen. It is hard to tell his exact age because his behaviour is so infantile. His limbs seem spastic. His gaze is distant. The woman wears the same dress as before. The boy wears only a filthy pair of long johns, years old. The woman chews up a piece of meat and passes it into the boy's mouth by placing her mouth on his, like a bird feeding its chick. He is not very hungry and protests. She gets up and goes to the river where she wets a rag. As she does so she hums to herself a tune reminiscent of a Victorian ballad. While she wets the rag the boy tries to stand, but flops down and in the process tumbles over. The woman sees him and laughs. The boy finds himself flat on his back, like a beetle that cannot right itself, as his legs and arms don't function properly. Even though he wants to get up he doesn't call out. Eventually he rights himself. The woman comes over as the boy begins to crawl towards something of interest, like a crippled child in a Muybridge photograph.*[2] *The effort is too great and he flops down. The woman wipes his face, then her own. She then blows loudly and theatrically on his face, pretending to be the wind. The boy pathetically tries to mimic her. She stands up and spins around in her beloved dress for him. He takes no notice, his eyes looking past her. Abruptly she drops to her knees and slaps him on the face. He yelps in pain. She kisses him where she has hit him and then moves away so he can see her properly. She smiles broadly and stiffly, trying to teach him. She pushes at his mouth until it turns into a smile, but when she lets go his face returns to its expressionless mask. She is frustrated. She hums. He follows suit, but his gaze is distant. She bites his leg and he yelps in pain. As he cries out she mimics him. He looks at her for a brief moment, then beyond her. The routine is over. The woman gets up and does a whirling dervish-like dance and hums loudly to herself. Suddenly she notices something and stops. Frightened, she runs to the boy and tries to drag him off, but he is angry and fights. She drops him and heads off. She exits and moments later* FRANCIS *hurries on, followed by* PETER.

FRANCIS [*calling after her*] Hey!

[*He runs after her.* PETER *walks over to* STEF.]

PETER Hello!

[*The boy doesn't seem to notice him.* FRANCIS *returns.*]

FRANCIS My God, she's quick. Lost her.

[PETER *waves his hand in front of the boy's face.*]

Is he blind?

PETER Maybe.

[*Suddenly the boy's hand snakes out and grabs* PETER'S *hand.* PETER *is startled. The boy laughs, then bites the hand.* PETER *cries out in pain.*]

FRANCIS What happened?

PETER He bit it.

[*Silence.*]

FRANCIS [*to the boy*] What's your name?

[*Pause.*]

Your name, what is it?

2. The English-born photographer Eadweard Muybridge (1830–1904), most famous for photographs capturing animal movement and the invention of a device for projecting pictures on a screen (a forerunner of motion pictures). His *Animal Locomotion* (1887) included photographs of humans—children and amputees among them—engaged in a wide range of activities.

[*The boy rolls over, not listening, and laughs at the sky.*]

PETER What's he laughing at?

[*Suddenly the boy's mood changes. He grimaces.*]

[*To the boy*] Are you all right?

[*The boy groans loudly, rising to a sharply accentuated crescendo until, abruptly, he bursts into a wide grin. Then he moves on all fours, but the effort is too much and he collapses. His face goes blank and his eyes distant.* FRANCIS *and* PETER *don't know what to make of it all.*]

PETER [*laughing nervously*] I wouldn't mind not being here.

FRANCIS We'd better pull him back or he might fall into the river.

[*They grab hold of the boy and drag him back from the river. The boy takes no notice of what is happening to him.* BETSHEB *silently enters and stands nervously nearby.* PETER *is the first to notice her.*]

PETER [*quietly*] Francis.

[FRANCIS *turns and spots her. She is now extremely nervous. She sinks to her knees and dry-retches with fear. The two young men don't know what to do. The woman crawls on all fours to the boy and makes sure he is all right. She slaps him hard. He laughs. She laboriously lifts him on her back.* FRANCIS *goes to help, but* PETER *holds him back.*]

She knows how to do it.

[*The boy clings to her back like a monkey. The woman goes off without looking at the two intruders. Silence.*]

FRANCIS Come on.

PETER What?

FRANCIS Scared?

PETER Pain in the arse.

[*They exit after her.*]

1.5

A clearing, afternoon. Four people wait: AYRE, *an old woman, sits on a homemade wooden chair; the others sit on the ground.* ANGEL *is in her late twenties. She is pale and coughs occasionally.* MELORNE, *a strong and wiry old white-haired man, sits near her.* MAC, *a twenty-year-old man with blond hair, sits by himself. They are dressed in old odds and ends, as though they have been to a Victorian opportunity shop.*[3] *They seem expectant and their pose is like that of a Victorian photograph. On the ground are some wooden and chipped-porcelain bowls. Some pieces of meat lie near the bowls; there are also seeds, wild fruit, and flowers. There is a large wash bowl in the centre of this arrangement. They wait some time and then* BETSHEB *enters, half dragging, half carrying* STEF. *He grins widely as if at some private joke. She drops him down near the others. Just then* FRANCIS *and* PETER *enter. They are startled at the scene before them. All except the boy and old woman rise and bow deeply but stiffly towards the boys. Silence.*

FRANCIS [*pointing*] We followed that girl.

[*Silence. Everyone is nervous and apprehensive. As the old woman speaks, the words make little sense to the boys.*]

AYRE To the greeny pallor o' thee kingspot; o' cunty goldy.[4]

3. A thrift store operated by a charitable organization.

4. *Welcome to this green land fit for kings, this land rich and fertile.* [This and all subsequent translations of his invented language are provided by Nowra.]

[PETER *smiles, amused.* FRANCIS *realises it is a welcome.*]

FRANCIS Thank you. My name is Francis. This is Peter. We come from Hobart.

[*Silence. They don't seem to understand.*]

[*Pointing to himself*] Francis. [*To* PETER] Peter.

[*The old lady nods and motions to the young woman, who goes to her.*]

AYRE Betsheb. [*Pointing to the old man*] Melorne. [*To the woman*] Angel. [*To the autistic boy*] Stef. [*To the young man*] Mac. [*To herself*] Ayre.

PETER Hello.

FRANCIS Hello.

[*The pair are amused by the situation.* AYRE *motions to the others to find their places. There is something of an unconscious parody about the group, as if with their limited means they are giving an upper-class tea party.*]

PETER [*to* FRANCIS] I think we're invited to a tea party.

FRANCIS Did you understand her?

PETER [*amused*] Not a word.

[AYRE *stays in her chair.*]

AYRE [*smiling*] I bunter t' the windy sheet, t' the arsemine o' the world. Breathe a vein, breathe a vein. [*Shaking her head*] Olcers an' 'ellpain. [*Tapping her chair*] Starry, shiny, cunty dell o' me world.[5]

[*It is obvious she is trying to explain why she can't join the others. The visitors sit.* AYRE *claps her hands and motions to* ANGEL, *who picks up an old-fashioned porcelain doll and shows it to* FRANCIS.]

FRANCIS It's lovely. Very old.

[ANGEL *smiles and nods.* MELORNE *walks into the centre of the group, picks up a washbowl and shows it to the two men proudly.*]

PETER [*looking into the bowl*] Gold. It must have taken a long time to collect all those tiny pieces.

[MELORNE *puts the bowl back in its position.*]

FRANCIS [*to* MELORNE] We saw a dead man on the mountain. Back there. He had flowers in his hair and gold in his mouth.

[MELORNE *sits, uncomprehending.* FRANCIS *points to* BETSHEB.]

She came and cried beside him.

[STEF *lies on his back and makes wind noises at the sky.*]

PETER He wasn't buried, but he was dead.

[*No one seems to understand.* BETSHEB *hands meat and fruit to* FRANCIS *and* PETER *in the only two porcelain bowls.*]

PETER [*to* FRANCIS, *sotto voce*[6]] I see we get the best china. [*To* BETSHEB] Thank you.

FRANCIS How long have you people lived here?

[*Silence.*]

Do you understand us?

[*Silence.*]

MELORNE [*thickly*] Fer skilly we gobble in awe.[7]

5. *I sometimes feel I am fluttering in the wind, or other times I am at the bottom of the world. Have a rest, take it easy. Ulcers and hellish pain. This chair is the shining centre of my world.*

6. Under the voice (Italian); that is, spoken very softly, under the breath.

7. *For this food we thank you and will eat it with the proper respect.*

[BETSHEB *and* AYRE *both laugh, as at a private joke. Everyone starts to eat. They have spoons and / or battered forks. There is an embarrassing silence as people try and think of ways of bridging the gap.*]

FRANCIS [*at last*] I come from Melbourne. Peter comes from Hobart. I'm an engineer. I design bridges. Peter is a geologist. He studies rocks. He knows all about things like that gold there.

[*No one seems to understand.* BETSHEB *feeds* STEF *by the same method she used before.* AYRE *sees the visitors' surprise.*]

AYRE Born o' cat 'n' rack 'n' goldy sow.[8]

[*They don't understand. Annoyed at being fed when he doesn't want to be,* STEF *cries out and rolls away.* ANGEL *begins to hum a tune.*]

He fed on tarse o' dark in the black quim o' a belle.[9]

[STEF *joins* ANGEL *in humming the snatch of melody, but soon he grows very loud.*]

[*Trying to make herself understood*] Skittle. Skittle. Blackfortune.[1]

[*The two men nod as though they can understand.* STEF*'s humming is almost yelling now.* PETER *recognises the tune and begins to sing over the top of* STEF*; he goes beyond the snatch of tune and sings the whole verse.*]

PETER

'I finally found you', Edward said.
'I've just returned from the salt, salt sea,
And it is all for the love of thee.
They say you married a hanging judge,
O don't let the news, the news be true.
But a friend, he said you didn't wait for me
As I have waited on the sea for you.'[2]

[*There is a silence, except for the quiet humming of* STEF. PETER *is embarrassed.*]

Those are the words of that song. My grandmother taught them to me.

[ANGEL *gives an 1850s top hat in very good condition to* MELORNE. *He makes a performing space.* BETSHEB *drags* STEF *to lie at* AYRE*'s feet.* STEF *stops humming and briefly cries out in alarm.* AYRE *pats him on the head and sings a murmuring song.*]

AYRE [*singing*]

In the night,
In the day,
Blue ruins, blue ruins
In Jack's Inn Bay.[3]

[*The two young men become the audience for the others. The four bow to them. As they perform, the words sometimes seem out of keeping with*

8. *He was born of a past that included both prisoners who remembered the cat-o-nine-tails and the rack and fertile gold mines.*
9. *He was fed by a diseased penis while he was in the diseased womb of a young girl.*
1. *It was chance. Chance. Misfortune.*
2. These lyrics are reminiscent of a piece known variously as "House Carpenter" and "James Harris, or the Daemon Lover," a ballad included in Francis J. Child's *English and Scottish Popular Ballads* (1882–98). The songs in Nowra's plays are often based on ballads or other traditional music.
3. *In the night, / In the day, / Drinking blue ruin, blue ruin / Travelling towards Jackson's Bay. Blue ruin* is gin, usually of poor quality (slang).

their emotions, as if they, especially MELORNE, *don't always understand what they are saying.*]

MELORNE Bleak street o' fen 'n' bellies. Dark trees 'n' no trees betide bleak sand.[4]

[*The scene set, he begins. He grabs* MAC *and drags him as if through terrible country. He stops.*]

[*Yelling, to* MAC] 'Toady o' the holy! Bleak King o' the dark. Thou walk on loam cooked o' thou disease. Thou disease pox on the land in blood 'n' pig. [*Indicating the land and sky*] 'Rye o' the sky, rye o' the loam. Morn 'n' dark all topsy turvy.' [*Motioning to himself*] 'I, King. King o' cits.' [*Crying out*] 'Trellion! Trellion!'[5]

[MAC *sings to entertain the tormented* MELORNE. ANGEL *plays a penny whistle to accompany him. She plays well.*]

MAC [*singing*]

Up 'n' down
He go,
Up 'n' down
A-jig, jig, jig.
She go
Groan 'n' groan
A-jig, jig, jig.[6]

[MELORNE *pats* MAC *on the head as one would a favourite dog.*]

MELORNE 'A-lik a-lik a-lik a-lik a-lik . . .'[7]

[ANGEL *enters and throws herself at* MELORNE'*s feet.* ANGEL *cannot speak and* AYRE *speaks for her.* ANGEL *mimes seeking forgiveness from* MELORNE.]

AYRE 'Poor quim me am, bleak father. Forgive me, bleak father. The 'eaven is wild. Torn a-thunder so bad, so bad, we fain to live.'[8]

MELORNE [*yelling*] 'Ye child, dry quim. Ye rack o' truth I boil, this loam boil 'cos o' me profoundest outcastin'. [*With high emotion*] 'Outcastin'!' [*Crying at the sky*] 'Rack 'n' cat, rack 'n' cat!'[9]

[*He jabs out both her eyes with a stick.*]

'Ye blind! Ye blind! Now, forsooth, ye can eye me pain o' outcastin.' Ye pain goldy sow o' me tarse!'[1]

4. *Bleak landscape of ferns and valleys. There are also dark woods and places with no trees down near the ocean.*

5. *"Poisonous toad. King of Darkness. You walk on the soil that is made warm by your corruption and disease. You have diseased this country; it smells like pig and bone. The fertile sky, the fertile soil. The rich sky and soil is now diseased, everything is upside-down, darkness is morning, morning is darkness. I am King. King of all citizens. Rebellion and treason! Rebellion and treason!"*

6. A source, according to Nowra's manuscript notes for the play, is the following lyric: "Faine would I go both up and downe / up and downe, up and downe / No child is fonder of the gig / Than I to dance a merry Jig / Faine woulde I try how I could frig / Up and downe, up and downe, up and downe / Faine would I try how I could caper." *Frig:* move about restlessly.

7. *"I lick I lick I lick I lick I lick . . ."*

8. *"I am a poor empty womb, stern Father. Forgive me, stern Father. The heavens are so wild, so violent that we are afraid to live."*

9. *"You child, you have a dry cunt. I am racked by the truth of it all. I am upset, the soil is upset, because I am in exile. Exiled! The sky sounds like whipping!"*

1. *"You are blind. Only now can you see the pain I feel at my exile. You are the corrupted sperm of my cock."*

[*He falls to the ground and sits. Singing,* MAC *covers him with leaves and flowers.* ANGEL *plays her penny whistle.*]

MAC [*singing*]

Up 'n' down
He go,
Up 'n' down
A-jig, jig, jig.

MELORNE [*as though in his second childhood*] 'Bleak outcastin', a-blub, blub, blub.'[2]

[BETSHEB *enters.* MELORNE *spots her. They look at one another, so ecstatic it is amusing even to the visitors, though the actors mean it seriously. Their arms out, with cries of delight they rush into one another's arms.*]

'True treasure o' quim 'n' tarse![3]

[*They hug.*]

'Nowt more outcastin'! Nowt more!'[4]

[*He grabs the washbasin full of gold.*]

'Joyful quim! Joyful tarse! Joyful bird! Joyful goldy sow! Joyful day!'[5]

[*He gives the bowl to* BETSHEB.]

'Joy o' loam.' [*Quietly*] 'Nowt more outcastin! Nowt more.'[6]

[*Everyone is happy.* MELORNE *leads as the company bows to the two young men.* AYRE *applauds and* FRANCIS *and* PETER, *who have understood very little, do likewise.* MELORNE *takes off his top hat and joyfully runs to them, holding it out, expecting a tip. Blackout.*]

1.6

The same clearing, night. FRANCIS *and* PETER *lie on the ground talking softly. Not far away* AYRE *sits in her chair, half dozing, half listening to the night birds.* STEF *lies at her feet,* MAC *nearby.*

PETER [*to* FRANCIS, *looking at* AYRE] Is she sleeping?

FRANCIS Listening.

PETER To us?

FRANCIS The owl.

[AYRE *turns in the direction of a hooting owl.*]

PETER Did you see the huts?

FRANCIS Like those old slab squatter huts.[7] Really primitive. God knows what happens when it rains here. Maybe they go into that cave.

PETER It's a mine. Where their gold comes from, I suppose. That young fellow, Mac; he showed me.

[*Silence.* AYRE *watches them, though they don't realise it.*]

FRANCIS Well?

PETER 'Well' what?

FRANCIS Who do you think they are?

2. *"Terrible exile, a blub, blub, blub."*
3. *"Honest fruit of womb and cock!"*
4. *"No more exile! No more!"*
5. *"Joyful womb! Joyful cock! Joyful bird! Joyful gold mine! Joyful day!"*
6. *"Joyful soil. No more exile! No more."*
7. The typical dwellings of Australia's 19th-century settlers who leased their land were huts built with ax-hewn planks ("slabs") and roofed with bark.

PETER Maybe the play was telling us. Maybe it was their history.

[FRANCIS *shrugs.*]

Two timbermen were discovered up north of here. They had been living alone for years. They had come to cut down Huon pine.[8] People forgot about them but they continued to cut down the trees, though no one collected them. They were still going through the motions. They had gone mad.

[*Suddenly* AYRE *motions to the sky, quoting loudly.*]

AYRE 'O tell me, bird, t' where is yer goin'? O tell me, what is yer want t' hear?' [*Smiling at the two men*] New chums. Skittle o' chance has yer to this spot, here, down in a fine ol' dark.[9]

[*Pause.*]

I cup me ear t' the glommen bird. Soul o' the dead. Cryin' out, 'Donna burst 'er 'eart, the bird is me!' No rack 'n' cat. Heavenbirth.[1]

[*She laughs, then sardonically motions to the hooting owl.*]

Me, moonin' in the glommen.[2]

[*Silence.*]

[*With an all-encompassing motion of her hands*] Our goldy sow, the furst t' bloodburst int' this silent sea. Past riverrun 'n' turn o' kelp int' muddy moss, seay green 'n' here. 'Ere! Spirit eyes o' gold. In ghost time, behind us; osier 'n' 'eather 'n' 'ello, ducky. 'Oary boyos, sun-stricken girlie days. Blackysmith 'n' Trunk's Tavern. I hear the goldy lifey, the glommen lifey. Do nowt ferget dreamytime. Ferget lifey in rattlesnake, ev'ry chum cryin' to death, 'n' into 'ere, the greeny belch o' 'eaven. Danderupping so to live on the greasypole o' spirit friends. Spirits o' cunty dell. Circle o' greeny 'ome. Stars 'n' loam, firs 'n' spermy flower. Spirits, sprits, ghosts 'n' pitch dark, buboes o' the face 'n' arse 'n' . . .'n' [*Motioning to* STEF *at her feet*] festerin' lip 'n' baby birdcry. Burst mouth, hairy brain 'n' cradlepain. Goldy death, goldy backward seein'. [*Motioning to her head*] Me mossy brain is the backward seein'. Pitch dark glommen is dry sheb and rottin' tarse. The circle is burst. [*Softly, almost to herself*] The circle is burst.[3]

8. A Tasmanian tree whose golden color, durability, and workability made its wood highly prized for both carving and shipbuilding (remaining stands are now protected).

9. *You're new arrivals. Chance and accident has brought you to this spot, this place hidden deep in the country.*

1. *I listen to the night bird. He is the soul of the dead. He is singing to me, 'Don't be alarmed, I am what is singing.' The bird is no demon. Born in heaven.*

2. *Look at me, saying silly things to the night.*

3. *Our ancestors were the first to venture into this wilderness. They came over rivers, through seas, through mud and slush, thick woods to reach here. Here! Here we saw flecks of gold. In the past, the past of our ancestors, there were osier and heather and people said 'Hello, ducky.' There were also randy boys and sun-filled, girl-filled days. There were blacksmiths and Trunk's Tavern. I listened to stories of the golden life in the past and also the darkness of the past (or the dark life). I was told not to forget my past dream-life in England. I was told to forget life in the prison ships, where every prisoner cried until they died. Then we reached here: the green stomach of heaven. But you had to get your dander up, be prepared, full of energy if you lived in this place because of all the spirits. It is like living on a greasy pole, always on guard, nothing certain. We call them the spirits of this fertile valley. This circle of greenery we call home. Home is stars and rich soil, fir trees, and fertile flowers. Spirits and the mischievous, even deadly spirits; but there are also ghosts and deep darkness, blisters and boils which grow on the face and arse, and there are harelips and babies which, because of this, can only make bird cries. There are also cleft palates, useless brains, and babies born in pain. Death can be good, as can looking into the past. My old brain contains*

[*She looks at the men, hoping they have understood. Silence. She shrugs.*]

[*Looking at the sky*] I cup me ear t' the glommen bird.[4]

[MAC *arrives, lifts* AYRE *out of the chair and helps her to walk off.* STEF, *as if startled awake, runs after them and then past them. Silence.*]

FRANCIS Maybe she was trying to tell us what we don't know.

PETER Perhaps.

[PETER *stands.*]

Nature calls.

[*He exits.* FRANCIS *lies down, hands behind his head and thinks. He notices a figure. It is a curious* BETSHEB *moving closer.* FRANCIS *pretends he is sleeping. She moves closer.* FRANCIS *turns and faces her. She steps back, unsure. They stare at one another. Silence.*]

FRANCIS The man who was dead: was he your husband?

[*Pause.*]

Was he your brother?

[*Silence.*]

Do you remember my name? 'Francis'.

[*He sits up. She is frightened and hurries off into the night.*]

Come back, don't be frightened.

[*He jumps up and goes after her. Blackout.*]

1.7

The bush, night. FRANCIS *moves out of the moonlight and into the shadows.* BETSHEB *enters, laughing. As* MAC *enters she spins in her dress, around and around, making herself giddy, and then falls on the ground. They both laugh as she tries to stand up, but she's still too giddy. He approaches her and she pushes him onto the ground. She pounces on him, growling softly like an animal. She nuzzles her face into his neck: it tickles and he laughs.* BETSHEB *jumps on him and straddles his chest, kissing him playfully.* MAC *grows irritated and roughly pushes her off. He tries to jump up, but her playfulness turns to real desperation and she grabs hold of his leg. He struggles to his feet but she holds on to him. He tries to push her away but she won't budge. She cries like an animal in pain and buries her face into his crotch. He hits her away; she falls to the ground and he takes the opportunity to escape into the night.* BETSHEB, *anguished, smashes the ground with her fists, moaning.* FRANCIS, *shocked by what he has seen, moves into the moonlight.* BETSHEB *doesn't notice and, weeping, jumps up and runs off into the night.* FRANCIS *stands where he is, trying to make sense of what he has seen and the extraordinary primal agony and passion of* BETSHEB. *As he stands thinking night gives way to dawn.* PETER *enters.*

PETER Where did you get to last night?

[FRANCIS *starts from his preoccupation.*]

You look awful.

FRANCIS I couldn't sleep.

---

the past. Do you know what true, deep darkness is? It's sterile cunts and useless pricks. Everything is broken. Everything is broken. Osier: basket willow, a plant that (like heather) is native to Europe, not Australia. *Prison ships:* after taking possession of Van Dieman's Island (Tasmania) in 1803, Great Britain established a penal colony on it; convicts were transported there until 1853.

4. *I listen to the night bird.*

PETER The old geezer got me up. Took me into the mine. I think he realises I know something about rocks. I didn't know if he wanted my advice or to show off. I tried to explain that the damn thing would cave in. You should see it, it's bloody primitive: water-logged, a few struts. We'd better get started back soon.

[*Pause.*]

Did you hear?

[FRANCIS *nods.*]

What's the matter?

FRANCIS Nothing.

PETER Something's bothering you.

FRANCIS I want to find out who they are.

[BETSHEB *brings in* AYRE'*s chair.* FRANCIS *catches her eye as* AYRE *comes out helped by* ANGEL. AYRE *looks more infirm than on the previous night.*]

[*To* BETSHEB] Last night I saw you down near the river.

[BETSHEB *doesn't understand.*]

AYRE [*sitting in her chair and looking at the sky*] Sun, sun, sun, sun. Jack straw, barley o' life. Eh?

[*She basks her face in the morning sun and dozes.* MAC *enters and looks at* BETSHEB. *They are awkward and embarrassed about what happened the night before. Suddenly, seemingly from nowhere,* MELORNE *runs in and knocks* MAC *down.* MELORNE *circles* MAC, *smiling broadly, urging him to wrestle.* MAC *doesn't want to fight.*]

PETER [*to* FRANCIS] He's crazy about wrestling, wants to prove himself. When we came out of the mine he jumped on me, wanting to wrestle.

FRANCIS Did you?

PETER A bloody fit old bugger; he soon had me giving up.

FRANCIS [*to* MELORNE, *calling*] Here!

[MELORNE *turns around.*]

PETER What are you doing? He's crazy.

FRANCIS I want to see how good he is.

[*The old man laughs. He loves wrestling.*]

[*To* MELORNE] Mad as a hatter, aren't you?

[MELORNE *nods and smiles broadly.*]

I can see it in your eyes.

PETER Careful, he's quick.

[*But just as* PETER *warns* FRANCIS, MELORNE *leaps at him and knocks him down.* FRANCIS *quickly pushes him off and jumps up.*]

FRANCIS [*to* PETER] He's bloody quick. Strong too. [*Smiling at* MELORNE] Do that again.

[MELORNE *takes a step towards* FRANCIS. *The younger man jumps him. They wrestle on the ground. Everyone is enthralled by the contest. It quickly turns from a lighthearted game into something deadly serious:* FRANCIS, *like* MELORNE, *is not the type to give in. Advantage goes one way and then the other.* MELORNE *jumps up,* FRANCIS *moves towards him. The old man spits at him viciously.* FRANCIS *decides to thrash* MELORNE *now. He lunges at the old man, there is a vicious series of grabs, tackles, and falls.* MELORNE *tires and pulls away.* PETER *realises that* MELORNE *is beaten and also knows that* FRANCIS *is angry enough to do serious injury.*]

PETER Leave him alone, Francis. You've won. You've beaten him.

FRANCIS [*keeping his eyes on* MELORNE] No I haven't. Not yet. I'm going to crush him.

[*He moves in on* MELORNE. *They circle one another.* FRANCIS *suddenly dives on the older man, throwing him to the ground, and lands on him heavily. He forces the old man into a position of defeat and pain.* MELORNE *cries out in anguish.*]

[*Yelling*] Give up!

PETER [*going to him*] You've defeated him. Come on.

FRANCIS [*to* MELORNE, *angrily*] Give up.

PETER [*grabbing him*] Francis! [*Pulling him away*] For Christ's sake, you could kill him.

FRANCIS That's what he wanted to do to me.

[MAC *and* ANGEL *go to* MELORNE *and lift him up.*]

PETER What were you trying to prove?

FRANCIS [*calming down*] He just seemed to be asking for it. It's the only thing he understands.

PETER The same would apply to you, it would seem.

[MELORNE *angrily shrugs off* ANGEL *and* MAC *and walks over to* FRANCIS. *The two men stare at one another.* FRANCIS *is apprehensive.* MELORNE *abruptly thrusts out his hand.* FRANCIS *and* PETER *flinch, but he only wants to shake hands with the victor. Everyone applauds.*]

1.8

The river, twilight. BETSHEB *sits, staring out at the evening sun. Near her feet are flowers she has just picked. She hums a tune to herself. Nearby,* STEF *rolls on the ground, laughing to himself.* FRANCIS *enters and watches* BETSHEB *for some time.*

FRANCIS Are you looking at the sunset?

[*Startled,* BETSHEB *turns around.*]

[*Smiling*] I'm not a monster . . . No more running.

[*Silence. He walks closer to the river.*]

Look at us reflected in the water, see? Upside-down.

[*He smiles and she smiles back. Silence.*]

So quiet. I'm not used to such silence. I'm a city boy, born and bred. You've never seen a city or town, have you? Where I live there are dozens of factories: shoe factories, some that make gaskets, hydraulic machines, clothing. My mother works in a shoe factory. [*Pointing to his boots*] These came from my mother's factory.

[*Silence.*]

These sunsets here, I've never seen the likes of them. A bit of muddy orange light in the distance, behind the chimneys, is generally all I get to see.

[*Pause.*]

You'd like the trams,[5] especially at night. They rattle and squeak, like ghosts rattling their chains, and every so often the conducting rod hits a terminus

5. Streetcars.

and there is a brilliant spark of electricity, like an axe striking a rock. 'Spisss!' On Saturday afternoon thousands of people go and watch the football.[6] A huge oval of grass. [*Miming a football*] A ball like this. Someone hand passes it, 'whish', straight to me. I duck one lumbering giant, spin around a nifty dwarf of a rover,[7] then I catch sight of the goals. I boot a seventy-yard drop kick straight through the centre. The crowd goes wild!

[*He cheers wildly.* BETSHEB *laughs at his actions. He is pleased to have made her laugh.*]

Not as good as your play.

[*Pause.*]

This is your home. My home is across the water, Bass Strait.[8]

[*Silence.* STEF *rolls over and ends up near* FRANCIS' *feet.*]

What is it about you people? Why are you like you are?

[BETSHEB *gathers up her flowers. As she stands she drops a few.*]

Don't go.

[*He picks up the fallen flowers.*]

I was watching you pick these. My mother steals flowers from her neighbour's front garden so every morning she can have fresh flowers in her vase for Saint Teresa's[9] portrait. She was a woman centuries ago. God fired a burning arrow of love into her. [*Smiling*] When it penetrated her, Saint Teresa could smell the burning flesh of her heart.

[BETSHEB *does a parody of the wrestling match, but to her it is so funny that she cannot go on.* FRANCIS *smiles uncertainly.* STEF *crawls across the ground, growling to himself, then sits and rocks back and forth, staring into the distance.*]

BETSHEB [*to* FRANCIS, *with a very thick accent*] Stef 'ave cradlepain.[1]

[*She strokes* STEF'*s head.*]

[*Murmuring*] Stef, Stef, Stef, Stef. [*In a sing-song voice*] Sha' it up, dee, dee, dee.

FRANCIS You can actually talk . . . talk like the old lady. Like Ayre.

[*She looks closely at* FRANCIS.]

Talk. You can talk like Ayre.

[BETSHEB *is unsure what he's talking about.* STEF *begins to move away;* BETSHEB *follows and helps him.* PETER *arrives unnoticed and watches* FRANCIS *watching* BETSHEB *and* STEF. *The couple leaves.* FRANCIS *picks up a few pebbles and starts to skim them across the river.*]

PETER It rose last night.

[FRANCIS *turns, momentarily startled.*]

FRANCIS Imagine how this place is in winter.

PETER How many times can you get them to skip?

FRANCIS Four or five.

6. That is, Australian rules football, a game developed during the 19th century that combines elements of soccer, rugby, and American football.
7. Typically the smallest players on the field, assigned to stay with the ball during play.
8. The channel that separates Tasmania from the state of Victoria in southeastern Australia.
9. Saint Teresa of Ávila (1515–1582), a Spanish Carmelite nun; in her mystical writings, she describes a vision in which an angel pierces her heart with a fiery arrow of love for God.
1. *Stef was born diseased.*

PETER I could never do it.

FRANCIS Used to go down to the Yarra near Dights Falls[2] and practice.

[*Silence.*]

PETER Is she the reason you want to stay?

FRANCIS I want to find out about these people.

PETER What attracts you to her?

FRANCIS She's interesting, in a way.

PETER It's because you don't know anything about her. She's probably as crazy as the rest of them.

FRANCIS They're not crazy.

PETER My father would certify them.[3]

[*Pause.*]

I had a closer look at that wash basin. There's no gold in it, just quartz, a bit of copper, alum, iron pyrites . . . Fool's gold.[4] I had a look over the back there too. There used to be other houses, a long time ago. And another mine.

[*Pause.*]

FRANCIS How's the old fellow?

PETER Coughing up blood.

FRANCIS You think he'll die?

[*Silence.*]

PETER It wasn't your fault.

[*Silence.*]

We'll head back tomorrow morning?

[FRANCIS *nods.*]

We'll get some experts out here; they'll find out what this is all about.

[*Pause.*]

FRANCIS She can't understand me, or at least I think she doesn't, but I know she's absorbing it like a sponge, soaking up what I'm saying. I see her listening to Ayre, you know, when they're together and it is as if she's soaking up all that Ayre is telling her. Remembering. Recording.

PETER Check your knapsack; someone's been through it.

[*He exits.* FRANCIS *returns to skimming pebbles across the surface of the river.*]

1.9

The bush, night. Clouds obscure the moon. BETSHEB *is perched on* MAC*'s shoulders. They turn slowly on the spot like a ballerina on a music box. From a distance* ANGEL*'s penny whistle plays a haunting tune. The whole thing has a distant dreamlike feel, almost like a memory.* BETSHEB *stares up at the sky.*

BETSHEB [*murmuring softly*]

Rain, rain, go thy way,
Come a-back ne'er a day . . .[5]

2. A waterfall on the Yarra River, in eastern Melbourne (the capital of Victoria).
3. That is, certify them as clinically insane.
4. The nickname of iron pyrite, a pale brass-yellow mineral.
5. *Rain, rain, go away, / Come back again another day . . .*

[*She repeats this incantation over and over. The lights fade and come up again.*]

1.10

The bush, night. Thunder sounds. AYRE *sits in her chair, a beautiful, unworn 1850s dress on her lap. She looks up at the thunder and clouds. Something is preying on her mind. She tries to remember a song.*

AYRE 'Little Peggy . . .' 'Peggy . . .' 'She met 'im in . . .'

[*She can't remember it. She looks down at the dress and strokes it like a lap dog.*]

'Airloomin' fer the child. Wot child? Bellsademon laughin'. Nowt need nowt Herod. We is dead. Goldy dead nowt goldy sow. Nowt tongue, nowt goldy sow, nowt 'istory.[6]

[*Silence. She feels the beautiful material of the dress.*]

So fine. So fine. 'I shew yer beauty. Beauty so fine yer'll piss yerself. 'Airloomin' fer the child.'[7]

[*Silence. She comes to a decision.*]

Nowt more outcastin'. [*Crying out to the sky*] Nowt more outcastin'![8]

1.11

The bush, night. BETSHEB *sits alone on the ground and examines the contents of a rough cloth bag.* FRANCIS *enters and watches her surreptitiously. She takes out and examines a watch, then a book, and then a small compass; finally she takes out a large lizard. She stares at it intently and hisses at it, her tongue flicking in and out at it. She seems mightily intrigued by this reptile.*

FRANCIS [*quietly*] Betsheb.

[BETSHEB *doesn't turn around. She seems to have already known* FRANCIS *was nearby. She puts the lizard back in the cloth bag.*]

BETSHEB [*quietly, almost to herself*] Francis.

[*He comes over and sits down beside her.*]

FRANCIS I couldn't sleep.

[*Silence.* FRANCIS *notices the objects.*]

These are mine. [*Picking up the watch*] A watch. [*Winding it*] It tells the time, tells us how old we're getting.

[*He holds it to her ear.*]

See? Can you hear it? 'Tick, tick, tick', like a heartbeat.

[*He picks up the compass.*]

6. *This would have been an heirloom for the child. But what child? The devils are laughing at me. We don't need King Herod (to kill our children). We are dead. The gold mine is finished, there is no fertile womb or sperm. We have no language, no sperm, and therefore no history. King Herod:* Herod the Great (d. 4 B.C.E.), ruler of Judaea; because it was prophesied that a new king of the Jews had been born, he ordered the murder of all the male children in Bethlehem and its vicinity who were age two and younger (Matthew 2.1–16).

7. *So beautiful. So beautiful. "I'll show you beauty, beauty so wonderful that you'll piss yourself. An heirloom for the child."*

8. *No more exile. No more exile!*

Compass. See the arrow? [*Indicating*] North is that way. Somewhere that way is Hobart. [*Sardonically*] Somewhere. And this . . . this is a book.

[*She nods as if she knows.*]

The Structure of Single Span Bridges.

BETSHEB Book.

FRANCIS You know it's a book?

[*She nods.*]

BETSHEB [*pretending to read, turning the pages quickly*] Thy word.[9]

[BETSHEB *stands and motions to the sky.*]

Rain, rain, go thy way,
Come a-back ne'er a day.

'Ate the olcer sky. No end. No end. Adorate the shiny brocade sky, glommen time. Queenie Ayre say in ancient glommen, King David see the brocade, King Moses see the goldy brocade, lubilashings o' shiny in ancient glommen. The sky 'e see, is me goldy brocade. See?[1]

[*She stands and spins slowly, staring up at the sky as if intoxicated by it and her words. We hear distant thunder.*]

FRANCIS The last waltz, *madame.*

[*He grabs her. She starts as if woken from an intense reverie.*]

Dance. Dancing. Follow me. Arm here. [*Singing a waltz melody*] Da, da, da . . . That's right, that's right, turn here, now a step here . . . Right . . .

[*She quickly picks it up.*]

My mother forced me to learn dancing so I would be able to mix in the proper circles at university.

[*Suddenly he kisses her. She tries to pull away.*]

No!

[*He holds on to her roughly and kisses her again. She bites him on the lip. He grimaces in pain. She pulls away.* FRANCIS *puts a finger to his lips and spots blood on it.* BETSHEB *is apprehensive.*]

I only wanted to kiss you.

[*Pause.*]

You do it with Mac, why not with me?

[*Silence.*]

I want to break through to you and I don't know how. I don't even know if you're stupid or crazy or whatever.

[*He walks towards her.*]

Don't run away. [*Smiling*] I can smell my heart burning.

[*She moves towards him and presses her forehead tightly against his.*]

9. *This is your book.*

1. *I hate the sky when it looks dark and threatening. There seems to be no end to darkness when it's like that. No end. I adore the shiny, starry sky at night. Queenie Ayre says that back in the old times, King David saw the shiny, starry sky; King Moses also saw the golden stars. There were incredible numbers of stars back in ancient times. The sky they saw is the same golden starry sky I see.* Moses and David (ca. 1000–962 B.C.E.) are both major figures in the Bible, though only David was a king of ancient Israel.

BETSHEB Me burstin' brain. Me burstin' brain. See?[2]

[*He doesn't understand.*]

FRANCIS You're hurting.

[*But she desperately wants him to understand.*]

BETSHEB Break 'n' crack int' thee.[3]

[*She abruptly pulls away and looks at the sky, disappointed by* FRANCIS' *lack of understanding. There is a loud roll of thunder.*]

Rain, rain, go thy way,
Come a-back ne'er a day.

[*She takes* FRANCIS' *hand and kisses it. She then takes a small cardboard backed photograph from between her breasts and gives it to him.*]

FRANCIS A photograph. Is this woman your mother?

BETSHEB Ghost o' me flesh.

FRANCIS Grandmother?

[BETSHEB *points to something in the photograph.*]

Painted backdrop. Photographer's studio. That's not a real mountain or waterfall.

[*She points to something else, then touches her dress.*]

Yes, it's like your dress. Well, when it was new. Is it yours?

[BETSHEB *pays no attention to his question. She takes the photograph, kisses it, then puts it inside her dress. She is ecstatic. She runs up the river bank, turns and throws herself on the ground and rolls over and over down to him like a log rolling down a hill, then jumps up, pretending to be* MELORNE *asking for his hat to take up a collection.* FRANCIS *laughs at her imitation.* BETSHEB *then squats and pretends to piss, making groaning, pissing noises; a broad grin of contentment passes over her face. She does a parody of a high-born woman. She pretends to sit and sip tea at an exclusive dinner party. She speaks as if delivering bon mots to imaginary guests.*]

BETSHEB Shit, shit, shit, shit, shit.

[FRANCIS *laughs at her slightly bitter parody.*]

FRANCIS Lady So-And-So's tea party?

[BETSHEB *is extremely happy showing off to* FRANCIS. *She prowls around him like a wild, vicious dog sniffing its prey, and then she turns into a snarling, spitting Tasmanian devil,*[4] *an act which slightly unnerves* FRANCIS. *Abruptly, she changes again and begins to walk like a grande dame taking a promenade. She motions to convicts nearby and gives them orders.*]

BETSHEB: Rack 'n' cat, rack 'n' cat, rack 'n' cat, rack 'n' cat.[5]

[*Then the grande dame farts. She discreetly waves her hand behind her to get rid of the smell.* FRANCIS *laughs at the parody.*]

FRANCIS Where did you pick that up from? Ayre? Did Ayre teach you?

[BETSHEB *pays no attention to him. She crawls over to him, tongue flicking in and out like a lizard's. She kisses him on the mouth with her flickering tongue.*]

2. *My head feels like it's exploding. My head feels like it's exploding. See?*

3. *I want to crack and break your skull and get directly through to you.*

4. A ferocious carnivorous marsupial, about the size of a small dog.

5. See 1.9, note 5.

BETSHEB Bellsademon kissin' 'n' spoonkissin' in the rye. [*Murmuring*] The belle she lie droopin'. The gent he lie tongue out. Ho! Spoonfuckin' in the glommen.[6]

[*She lifts her dress and sits down.*]

FRANCIS Are you sure?

[*He sits down next to her.*]

BETSHEB [*smiling, softly*] The belle whoopin', tongue out in the glommen.[7]

[*They kiss.*]

FRANCIS [*feeling her flesh*] Soft. So soft.

[*He kisses her on the lips again. The thunder comes closer, but they pay no attention to it. He kisses her on the inside of her legs. She ruffles his hair as if he were a dog. He takes off his shirt, then kisses her again. The whole of her body begins to tremble violently, as if possessed by involuntary muscle spasms. She lashes out and tears at her clothes. Her eyes roll, her body convulses. It is like an epileptic fit.*]

[*Concerned*] Betsheb!

[*He tries to hold her, to calm her, but her body is uncontrollable. She lashes out, without knowing what she is doing, and hits him.*]

Betsheb . . . Betsheb . . . What is it? Please . . . Do you want me to get help? [*Crying out*] Peter!

[*She begins to calm down. He strokes her as if soothing a child.*]

That's right . . . [*Soothingly*] Calm. Calm down.

[*She is still, silent.*]

I'm sorry.

[*Silence. He holds her in his arms. Suddenly she wakes as if from a nightmare. Horrified she realises she has blacked out. She looks at her clothes and wipes away the saliva that has formed around the edges of her mouth. Now that she realises what she's done she is ashamed. She jumps up and away from him.*]

BETSHEB No, no, no . . .

FRANCIS It's all right, it's over.

[*She is angry with her body. She starts to tear at it, then motions to her head as if to say she is stupid. She spits on her body because it has betrayed her.* FRANCIS *comes over to her, but she pushes him away, humiliated.*]

BETSHEB Go, go!

[*Pause.*]

FRANCIS You want me to go away? [*Motioning*] You want me to leave you? It's nothing to be ashamed of.

BETSHEB [*pushing him away*] Go. Go.

FRANCIS Will you be all right?

BETSHEB Thee, way! Go! [*Picking up a stone and throwing it at him*] Go!

6. *Let's kiss like demons and put our tongues down each other's mouths while we're here in the grass. The woman lies ready, the boy has his tongue out. Ho! Fucking in the night.* A source, according to Nowra's manuscript notes for the play, is the following lyric: "A Man and a younge Mayd that / loved a long time / Were taken in a frenzy in Midsummer prime; / The Maid she lay dropping, Hye; / The Man he lay whopping, Hey; / the Man he lay whopping, Ho!"

7. *The girl is randy, she has her tongue out in the night.*

[FRANCIS *reluctantly moves away. She sinks to the ground with her back to him, exhausted.* FRANCIS *sits also, far away from her, and watches. The thunder comes closer.*]

FRANCIS It is going to pour. You should go in.

[*Silence.*]

Let's go in.

[*Silence.*]

Talk to me.

[*Silence. Despondent,* BETSHEB *lies on the ground. Scattered before her are the three objects she stole from* FRANCIS' *knapsack.* FRANCIS *stares at the violent sky.* BETSHEB *stares at the objects with distant eyes. As she stares they move towards her, one by one, slowly and firmly, as though by telekinesis. The watch is first to move along the ground, then the compass, then the book. She makes no move to gather them as they stop in front of her.* FRANCIS *sees none of this.*]

BETSHEB [*to herself, quietly*] Francis.

PETER [*off, calling*] Francis.

[FRANCIS *stands up.* PETER *enters. Close behind him* MAC *carries* MELORNE. BETSHEB *retreats apprehensively.* MAC *puts* MELORNE *on the ground and lays him out. As he does so,* STEF *enters and sits down to play with the compass.*]

He's dying.

FRANCIS Why bring him here? A storm's coming.

PETER He wants to die outside.

[FRANCIS *is reluctant to come closer.* ANGEL *enters with a large, battered box which she puts down.*]

Come closer. He knows it wasn't your fault. He wanted to come to you.

[FRANCIS *moves closer, then drops to his knees.*]

FRANCIS Sorry, old man.

[MELORNE*'s hand suddenly snakes out and grabs* FRANCIS'. *He squeezes it tightly.* FRANCIS *is afraid.* MELORNE *grunts with exertion as if wrestling, then laughs triumphantly. The effort has been too much; he sinks back.* ANGEL *hurries over to him.* AYRE *enters slowly and painfully.* MELORNE *tries to cry out but cannot.* ANGEL *holds his hand. He smiles at her and dies.* ANGEL *tries to call to him, but like a baby can only get out the first part of 'Daddy'.*]

ANGEL D-d-d-d- . . .

[*Silence.* ANGEL *silently hugs the dead* MELORNE.]

AYRE [*to* FRANCIS *and* PETER] The circle is burst. We is burstin' int' the glommen. Outburst. Bellsademon land; cradlepain. Circle is burst. Nowt more outcastin'. Nowt more sin fer bread.[8]

[AYRE *gives* MAC *a signal and he opens the box.*]

See!

[*The two young men look inside the box.*]

8. *Everything has broken apart. We are breaking apart into the night. Exploding outwards. This land is the Devil's land, full of awful pain. No more exile, but no more prostituting ourselves as in the old days either.*

Goldy sow o' the 'airloomin' pit.[9]

[FRANCIS *takes out the doll seen before.*]

Sa, Sa.[1]

[*He takes out the dress seen earlier.*]

Promin'. 'Airloomin'.[2]

[*He takes out the book.*]

FRANCIS What is it?

PETER The writing's too faint to see.

AYRE [*motioning to the distance*] Way! Way!

PETER She's telling us to go.

[FRANCIS *suddenly realises.*]

FRANCIS No, this is their luggage, their belongings.

AYRE Nowt more outcastin'. Nowt more outcastin'.

FRANCIS She wants us to take them back with us. You want to go back with us, Ayre?

AYRE Yea.

[*Silence. The storm breaks.* AYRE *looks at the grief-stricken* ANGEL *as she cradles* MELORNE.]

Nowt more outcastin'. Nowt more outcastin' . . .

1.12

The Archers' garden, twilight. It is a warm evening. In the background is the Greek temple. A long table with an expensive setting is ready: porcelain crockery, silverware, and crystal glasses; food is on the table. ELIZABETH *escorts* GEORGE ROSS, *Federal M.P., into the garden.*

ELIZABETH It was such a lovely evening we decided to have it out here. We expected you later.

GEORGE The Cabinet meeting took less time than I thought.

ELIZABETH They won't be long.

GEORGE I'm most intrigued to see them. Your husband's report was extraordinary.

[*He notices the Greek temple.*]

Not many of those in Australian backyards.

ELIZABETH It was built way back in eighteen forty—only Australians could say 'way back in eighteen forty'—by my grandfather. He loved Greece, Greek culture; a family trait. So he built this little Olympus.[3] It was said that he had a giant streak of paganism in his soul. The architect, an ex-convict, unfortunately used poor materials. It took the Parthenon[4] two thousand years to crumble; it took our temple less than a hundred. Occasionally I let the spirits of the Greeks take hold of me and I put on an ancient tragedy. Once we performed *Iphigenia in Tauris* to help a charity for unwed mothers and, do you know, some people looked down on us. But being an unwed mother is so human: one moment of passion, a lifetime of

9. *In this box are all the best things, the heirlooms.*

1. *Sarah, Sarah.*

2. *For promenading. It's an heirloom.*

3. The highest mountain in Greece, traditionally identified with the home of the principal Greek gods.

4. The Temple of Athena located on the Acropolis (a hill in the center of Athens); it was built in the 5th century B.C.E.

misery. Years ago, William and I could have said those speeches in ancient Greek and most of the audience would have understood; many of them were academics and artists, of course. That was our greatest period of civilisation. From then on it's been all downhill. Romans conquered the world and Mussolini[5] takes years to conquer a few Ethiopian hill tribes. Ah, who are these handsome young men?

[PETER *and* FRANCIS *enter wearing tuxedos.* FRANCIS *is agitated.*]

Mr Ross, I would like to introduce my son, Peter. Peter, this is Mr George Ross, Federal Minister for Health.

PETER [*shaking hands*] How do you do, sir?

ELIZABETH And his friend, Francis Morris.

GEORGE Very glad to meet you.

[*They shake hands.*]

ELIZABETH Francis's fascination with these people is only matched by my husband's.

GEORGE Doctor Archer's report mentioned you two found this group. I couldn't not come, my curiosity about them was too great.

ELIZABETH This will be the first time you've seen them since you brought them back, won't it?

FRANCIS Yes.

[PETER *pours* FRANCIS *a glass of wine to try and calm him.*]

GEORGE [*looking around*] And this is where they've been staying?

ELIZABETH William thought they would be more comfortable here and it would make studying them easier. The woman, Angel, is in hospital, however. She has pulmonary tuberculosis. Her brother, Mac, is with her; it's thought he may have a touch of it too.

GEORGE So they won't be coming tonight?

ELIZABETH No. How was Melbourne, Francis? Francis?

[FRANCIS *sips his glass of wine. For a moment he is at a loss.*]

The job?

FRANCIS I didn't get it.

ELIZABETH Perhaps next time. Have you heard the latest about Poland, Mr Ross?

GEORGE They say Poland is about to surrender.[6]

ELIZABETH I can feel it in my blood. Another world war. The times are definitely out of joint. And, again, we'll send our youth off to die.

GEORGE If it's necessary to fight Nazism. Would you sign up, Francis?

FRANCIS Yes. Fascism has to be destroyed; it's an evil philosophy. If I had been older I would have fought against it in Spain.[7]

GEORGE [*amused*] Oh, an idealist.

5. Benito Mussolini (1883–1945), prime minister and dictator of Italy (1922–43); in 1935, Mussolini ordered the invasion of Ethiopia, which was defeated in less than a year.

6. Nazi Germany invaded Poland on September 1, 1939, and the Polish government capitulated four weeks later. In response, the United Kingdom, along with Australia and New Zealand, declared war on Germany, marking the beginning of World War II.

7. In the Spanish Civil War (1936–39), the Nazi government of Germany and the Fascist government of Spain aided the Nationalist forces of General Francisco Franco with personnel, weapons, and other equipment; on the other side, idealistic volunteers from around the world joined the International Brigades to help the Loyalists, who were ultimately defeated.

ELIZABETH [*looking off*] Ah, here they are.

[*It is an extraordinary sight.* BETSHEB *and* AYRE *are dressed magnificently.* AYRE *wears the dress she held in her lap and* BETSHEB *wears a modern evening dress.* STEF *wears a dinner jacket. They are escorted by* WILLIAM, *also dressed in a dinner jacket.* STEF *shambles stiffly to the table, attracted by the glitter and the candles.* BETSHEB *guides* AYRE *in. Both women stop when they see* FRANCIS *and* PETER. *They are pleased to see both.*]

WILLIAM [*to* BETSHEB] Here, I'll take Queenie Ayre.

[WILLIAM *leads* AYRE *to the central chair.* BETSHEB *and* FRANCIS *stare shyly at one another.*]

BETSHEB 'Ello.

FRANCIS Hello.

ELIZABETH My, how wonderful you look.

FRANCIS You look lovely.

[BETSHEB *spins in her dress for everyone, delighted by the praise. She stops and smiles at* FRANCIS.]

BETSHEB [*quietly*] The belle is spoonin'.[8]

[STEF *puts his hand into one of the dips. He tastes it, then spits it out in horror.*]

WILLIAM Mr Ross, I'm Doctor Archer.

GEORGE Of course, I remember you well; that conference last year.

[STEF *sits on the grass and rocks back and forth, humming to himself.*]

WILLIAM Actually, in only a week Stef has improved out of sight.

GEORGE Did you find out who they are?

WILLIAM These people are the last members of a group that goes back to the eighteen fifties, during the gold rushes when everyone had the fever. Bankers, convicts, businessmen, doctors . . . but unlike in Victoria, the rush finished pretty quickly here.[9] One group moved much further into the South West looking for gold than anyone else. Most of them were ex-convicts, escaped convicts, failed colonists, general scum . . . even a travelling actor tired of doing bad shows for stupid colonists. One of the escaped convicts by the name of 'Simpson' kept a notebook. Some of it is his information, but the rest of the notebook is his obsession with his dreams. He dreamed he should found his own town, independent of the rest of mankind, so he tried to. And what material did he have? Criminals, retards, the lost, the desperate. [*Smiling*] So what we have before us is the true Australian culture.

GEORGE What about the way they talk?

WILLIAM Simpson, like his sister, had a cleft palate. Their language is a word salad made up of Cockney, Scottish, Irish dialects. There must have been a thread of retardation running through the original group because some of them just didn't learn to speak.

FRANCIS Perhaps they didn't feel the need to speak.

WILLIAM [*amused*] Of the younger ones, only Betsheb can talk. Ayre forces her to. Once Ayre dies, Betsheb will be the last repository of their culture. Stef is Angel's son; he's the final genetic mockery. Betsheb's brother died recently.

8. *The girl is happy.*
9. Victoria's gold rush, which began in 1851, lasted until the late 1860s; gold was discovered in 1877 in the north of Tasmania.

FRANCIS The corpse?

WILLIAM Yes. And Mac will never be able to have children because his genitals are malformed. Queenie Ayre is a woman I admire more each day. It would have taken a lot of courage to come back to the world of 'rack 'n' cat'. Back to the world she had only heard about, a world of racks, whips, prison, hatred. She knows they have no future in the wilderness. Inside her head she has kept everything she deems important. Dreams, memories, snatches of songs, Bible stories . . . it's had to be passed on by word of mouth.

[*Silence. The three newcomers look curiously vulnerable and* BETSHEB *and* AYRE *are embarrassed as the others stare at them.* STEF *stares at the sky.*]

FRANCIS What's going to happen to them?

WILLIAM We decided not to let the public know until we know a little more about them. [*Looking at* GEORGE] We plan to release the information on Tuesday.

[GEORGE *nods.*]

So, ladies and gentlemen, the children of our past.

[AYRE *points to* ELIZABETH]

ELIZABETH What is it, Ayre?

AYRE [*motioning to* ELIZABETH*'s neck*] Shiny, shiny.

[ELIZABETH *takes off the necklace and gives it to her.*]

ELIZABETH For tonight.

[*She puts it around* AYRE*'s neck.* AYRE *is very pleased.* PETER *sits down to have a drink.* WILLIAM *pours one for* GEORGE. WILLIAM *watches as* FRANCIS *approaches* BETSHEB. STEF *begins to stalk* GEORGE.]

FRANCIS You wear your dress with more ease than I wear this monkey suit.

BETSHEB I look fer thee, dawnytime, day fer day.

WILLIAM 'I looked for you every morning, day after day.'

BETSHEB I nowt more a-feared.

WILLIAM 'I'm not afraid any more.'

FRANCIS [*to* WILLIAM] I know.

[*A broad smile crosses* BETSHEB*'s face as she remembers something.*]

BETSHEB I see car . . .

[WILLIAM *translates, proud of his skill and also realising that when* BETSHEB *gets excited she is hard to understand.*]

WILLIAM 'I was in a car.'

BETSHEB Windwhistlin'.

WILLIAM 'It went quickly.'

BETSHEB 'Ome, country groan 'n' moan 'n' run.

WILLIAM 'Factories and houses make noises and the landscape from the car makes it look like it's running.'

BETSHEB Voice in a stick.

WILLIAM 'Telephone.' She loves hearing people speak on the telephone.

BETSHEB I laugh. Let go.

[*She demonstrates listening on the telephone.*]

Demon or 'eaven?

WILLIAM 'The voices, are they from heaven or hell?'

[STEF *pounces on* GEORGE *and starts to chew his ankle, growling.*]

WILLIAM Pay no attention.

GEORGE [*thin-lipped*] I'll try.

ELIZABETH Shall we sit? Francis, you escort Betsheb.

[GEORGE *pretends not to notice as* STEF *clings by his teeth to* GEORGE*'s trousers. He makes his awkward way to the table.* BETSHEB *is highly excited at meeting* FRANCIS *again.* WILLIAM *pulls* STEF *free of* GEORGE*'s trousers.*]

GEORGE Much appreciated, Doctor Archer.

[WILLIAM *sits* STEF *at the table.* BETSHEB *suddenly cries out like a magpie. Everyone looks at her. Now that she has their attention she decides to show off. She remembers how* FRANCIS *enjoyed her performance down by the river, so she steps away and begins to promenade like a grande dame.*]

BETSHEB Rack 'n' cat, rack 'n' cat, rack 'n' cat . . .

[*She turns around for her return walk.* FRANCIS *realises what will come next.*]

FRANCIS [*horrified*] Betsheb!

[*But* BETSHEB *doesn't hear him. She farts loudly, much to* AYRE*'s amusement, and pretends discreetly to wave the smell away. She notices that no one else is laughing. She is suddenly worried.*]

ELIZABETH [*to* WILLIAM] You couldn't get anything more Australian than that! [*To* BETSHEB] Bravo, Betsheb! [*Applauding*] Bravo!

[*The others applaud.* BETSHEB *is pleased.* STEF *is fascinated by the candles, especially the one near him. He blows it out.*]

[*To* WILLIAM] The matches.

GEORGE Allow me, Mrs Archer.

[GEORGE *takes out his matches and relights the candle.* STEF *blows it out again: he enjoys this game.*]

ELIZABETH I think, Mr Ross, that shifting the candle might save an enormous match bill.

GEORGE I think you may be right, Mrs Archer.

[GEORGE *shifts the candle.* STEF *is very annoyed and lunges across the table at it, scattering plates and glasses everywhere. He grabs the candle and sinks back in his chair, holding it inches from his face. He stares at its flame as if mesmerised by it.* GEORGE *goes to take the candle from him but the boy growls at him.*]

ELIZABETH For your own safety, Minister, I suggest you let Stef keep it.

[GEORGE *does so.* WILLIAM *pours the champagne.*]

WILLIAM I thought we might make a toast to our visitors.

[BETSHEB *goes to drink her champagne.*]

FRANCIS Betsheb . . . not yet.

[AYRE *takes hers and gulps it down.* BETSHEB *sees her and follows suit.*]

ELIZABETH I suppose a queen is entitled to invent her own table manners.

[*She indicates to* WILLIAM *that he should pour more champagne for the women.*]

[*As he sets down the bottle*] William, short and sweet before it's too late.

[WILLIAM *raises his glass and, with the exception of* STEF, *the others do likewise.* AYRE *and* BETSHEB *raise their glasses, curious as to the meaning of this ritual.*]

WILLIAM To our five aliens who have landed on this strange planet, no longer called Van Diemen's Land,[1] but Tasmania, and to their queen, Queenie Ayre.

OTHERS Queenie Ayre.

[STEF *stares at the candle.* AYRE *downs her glass quickly. The others sip theirs,* BETSHEB *carefully imitating* FRANCIS.]

1.13

The Archers' garden, night. The meal has been eaten and only STEF *is left, lying on the grass playing with a candle.* GEORGE *and* WILLIAM *enter from the garden.* STEF *secretly stalks them.*

GEORGE It must need a lot of gardeners.

WILLIAM Two full-time, one part-time. It's modelled after Beckford's[2] classical English garden, Fonthill.

[*They stop and watch* STEF, *who pretends to look at the candle.*]

GEORGE You picked up their language very quickly. I find it a real pea soup.

WILLIAM I wouldn't leave them alone. Drove them mad, trying to understand it.

GEORGE [*touching* STEF *with his foot*] Doesn't notice much about him, does he?

WILLIAM It's hard to know.

GEORGE Asylum patients make me feel the same way. They seem unfathomable. As if they could do anything.

[*Pause.*]

As you can well appreciate, Doctor Archer, with Australia now at war the Government has many important things on its mind. Our primary aim will be to help defeat the Germans. Have you read any of the Nazi philosophy? Foul. A cesspool of human hatred.

[STEF *is intrigued by* GEORGE*'s trouser legs and watches like a dog observing its prey.*]

The Cabinet decided I should take care of this matter as I have medical experience myself. You know it's going to be a very popular piece in the newspapers here and overseas? That would be true to say, wouldn't it?

[STEF *pounces on* GEORGE*'s leg and sinks his teeth in.*]

WILLIAM Stef! Stef! Let go!

[WILLIAM *pulls him off.*]

GEORGE Does he always do that?

WILLIAM He likes to pretend he's our corgi.

[STEF *rocks back and forth and laughs at some huge private joke.*]

1. So named in 1642 by the Dutch explorer Abel Tasman, in honor of Anthony van Diemen (1593–1645), the governor-general of the Dutch East Indies who had sent him on voyages of exploration.

2. William Beckford (1760–1844), a wealthy English author; the garden at his Gothic mansion, Fonthill Abbey, was not "classical" but Romantic, intended to appeal to the imagination and inspire a sense of awe.

GEORGE You realise the fuss these people are going to cause?

[WILLIAM *nods.*]

Isn't there an asylum not far from here?

WILLIAM New Norfolk.[3]

GEORGE That's the one. I visited it once. Quite nice. I'll look at it again in the morning.

WILLIAM I don't quite understand.

GEORGE Do you want it plainer?

WILLIAM These people aren't mad.

GEORGE The Cabinet has decided that the public is not to know about these people until the war is over.

WILLIAM But why? They're not mad!

GEORGE Now listen to me. In Germany Stef would have been put to death a long time ago. The basis of Nazism is that there is a pure Aryan race and it must be kept free from impure bloodlines or genetic faults. Since they have come to power they have systematically murdered the retarded and deformed.[4] Imagine the glee with which the Germans would greet the news that it only took three generations to result in someone like Stef. What a coup for Nazi propaganda. They would be proved right. Once the war is over, then we'll allow the public to know about them.

WILLIAM You can't do this. They didn't come back to civilisation to be put into an asylum.

GEORGE These people should not be seen as examples of the correctness of Nazi beliefs.

WILLIAM But you'll prove it! You've demonstrated they are right by locking these people up . . .

GEORGE This is war, Archer. I'm saying that the Nazis will bend, reshape the information for their own purposes. These people cannot be seen to be an endorsement of Nazi beliefs.

[*Pause.*]

Can't you see the Government's position?

WILLIAM I don't have much choice, do I?

GEORGE No.

[STEF *rolls around making wind noises.* GEORGE *stares at him.*]

You know, in some ways the Nazis are right. It took only three generations to get to him, only three generations to lose a language, the power to speak. They are a genetic graveyard.

[*Pause.*]

I must get back to my hotel. Tomorrow will be hectic.

WILLIAM I'll phone for a taxi.

[*They walk off in silence.* BETSHEB *and* FRANCIS *enter happily from the garden.*]

FRANCIS And is that your favourite spot?

3. A town about 20 miles north-northwest of Hobart.

4. In this campaign for Aryan (northern European) purity, hundreds of thousands of "the retarded and deformed," as well as criminals and homosexuals, were sterilized or murdered. The Nazis claimed to be following the dictates of the "science" of eugenics, which at the time had many adherents throughout the Western world.

BETSHEB I eye the skyey blue 'n' call t' yer. Call 'n' call 'n' yer come.

[*He takes her by the waist and they dance to distant piano music.* ELIZABETH *enters.*]

ELIZABETH There you are. Don't you want to come in and watch Mr Turner play? He came especially.

FRANCIS We can hear it out here.

ELIZABETH If Mr Turner hadn't been born blind he would have been a great pianist. She missed you. Every morning she asked William where you were. He, as you know, has become quite, quite fascinated by them.

[*She picks up a wine glass and sips from it.*]

Tipsy. It's as if the dead have come alive. Ghosts from the nether world of an Australian childhood.

[*The piano stops.* BETSHEB *steps away and goes into the garden near the temple steps.*]

There are rumours that William refused to allow other doctors to see them; that he kept them to himself, as if they were prize exhibits that no one else could look at. For twenty-four hours a day he lives and breathes them.

[BETSHEB *squats unselfconsciously and pisses.*]

They are not children, Francis, and they are not adults; they are a poor, contaminated people.

FRANCIS I think I can look after myself, Mrs Archer.

ELIZABETH Can you? I see her early in the morning, from my window, lying on the lawn, stroking herself as if she has some invisible lover; and she talks to herself or to the sky, I don't know which. At such times I doubt her sanity.

[*The piano starts again.*]

When the news of this group breaks I will lose William. They will be his, he will explain them, he will make us understand them. Best I go inside. Mr Turner becomes quite put off by Queenie Ayre's snoring. [*Looking at the temple, smiling*] I remember the day before you and Peter left for your trip. I was Iphigenia bemoaning my fate. As I looked down from the temple steps I saw such an expression of horror on your face, a look of 'What sort of world is Peter's?'

[*She laughs.* FRANCIS *smiles.*]

They'll change too. All the publicity, all the attention. Then we'll lose them.

[*She exits.* BETSHEB *shivers.*]

FRANCIS Cold? You shouldn't be, it's warm.

[*He takes off his jacket and puts it over her shoulders. They dance, contented and happy. She nuzzles into him.* STEF *crawls onto the table. He steals a spoon and puts it in his jacket. Sitting on the table, he rocks back and forth, ecstatically happy.*]

2.1

The living room of a working-class house, morning. A coffin lies on a table surrounded by flowers. FRANCIS *stands before it.* MRS WITCOMBE, *a neighbour, enters.*

MRS WITCOMBE They'll be in in a moment.

FRANCIS And what happens then?

MRS WITCOMBE We follow them to the cemetery.

[*Pause.*]

So it'll be only us and her mates from work?

[FRANCIS *nods.*]

No relatives?

FRANCIS I think she had relations in the country—in New South Wales,[5] I think—but they didn't get on. Once Dad remarried, I was the only person she had.

MRS WITCOMBE Your mum was always quiet. Kept to herself. Lived next door for twenty-odd years and . . . When I die, it'll be the same. Some distant cousins in Perth,[6] very distant cousins in England . . . but, of course, we don't keep in touch. [*Looking at the corpse*] Never seen this dress before; it's gorgeous.

FRANCIS Her honeymoon dress.

MRS WITCOMBE Looking so calm.

[*Pause.*]

At least it was quick.

[PETER *enters.* MRS WITCOMBE *doesn't notice him.*]

She was very proud of you. 'My son the engineer!' Such rotten luck. When I was young and I saw a car for the first time—I was a country girl like your mother—I was as frightened of it as my horse was. I had every right to be. She gripped my hand so tightly as we waited for the ambulance to come . . . see, it's still bruised. I'll see what's happening outside.

[*She exists. Silence.*]

PETER Lots of flowers; she must have been well liked.

FRANCIS Her workmates. She worked in the same shoe factory for years and all her boss could give her was a brand new pair of shoes. In our neighbourhood flowers mean death. Mum said she had only ever saved money for herself twice: the first time for her trousseau, the second for her funeral, so she could go off 'like a real swell'.

[*Silence.*]

PETER Do you still want to return to Hobart with me tomorrow?

[FRANCIS *nods.*]

But what about the house and things?

FRANCIS It was rented. The landlord wants it cleaned up and empty by Tuesday. I told Mrs Witcombe that if she cleaned it up she could have anything she wanted.

PETER But don't you want to keep a few mementos? You can't cut loose entirely.

FRANCIS I've got a few photographs; that's all I want. [*Looking around the room*] What a life, eh? Struggle hard, marry a bastard, struggle hard, have an ungrateful son, earn enough to live in a dump. Second-hand furniture, concrete backyard and on the walls Saint Teresa and facing her a picture of the nineteen thirty Collingwood football team.[7] If Collingwood won we had fish and chips; if they lost we didn't eat. [*Moving over to it*] Signed by

5. Australia's most populous state, located immediately north of Victoria.

6. Probably the city in the state of Western Australia (there is also a town named Perth in northeast Tasmania).

7. A club in the Australian Football League known for its large and loyal fan base; star Collingwood players of the 1920s and '30s included Harry Collier (1907–1994) and Gordon "Nuts" Coventry (1901–1968). *Saint Teresa:* patron saint of the sick, especially headache sufferers (see 1.8, note 9).

all of them: Collier, Coventry . . . She plucked up all her courage to go down to training one night and got all of the team to sign it. I was with her, crimson with embarrassment. She was so happy you would have thought she had had an audience with the Pope.

PETER Why don't you take it with you?

FRANCIS Mrs Witcombe's daughter has had her eye on it for years. Mum promised it to her.

PETER You'll regret it if you don't take a few things to remind you.

FRANCIS One should forget the past. Do you know why I never invited you here?

[PETER *shakes his head.*]

Because I was too ashamed.

2.2

A room in the asylum, evening. MAC *sits at a table.* WILLIAM *watches him. There is a manual skills test on the table. A recording of* AYRE*'s voice plays.* MAC *doesn't really listen to it.* AYRE*'s voice is slow and deliberate, as if trying to make herself understood.*

AYRE'S VOICE Past riverrun 'n' turn o' kelp int' muddy moss, seay green 'n' here. There! Ghost 'n' sprit time. Goldy lifey, glommen lifey. Thee dreamy-time in greeny belch o' 'eaven. Sprits o' cunty dell. Circle o' greeny 'ome! Nowt 'ome. Burst mouth, hairy brain 'n' cradlepain. Pitch dark glommen is dry sheb and rottin' tarse. The circle is burst . . . [8]

WILLIAM Are you listening? That is Ayre's voice. There is nothing wrong with your vocal cords and yet you don't speak. Try again.

[WILLIAM *makes elementary sounds.*]

Copy me.

[*But* MAC *isn't interested.* WILLIAM *turns off the gramophone.*]

All right, let's get back to the test, then. Now concentrate this time, Mac. Concentrate!

[MAC *is exhausted. He angrily throws the manual skills test on the ground.*]

[*Angrily*] Pick it up!

[MAC, *obedient as a child, does so.* WILLIAM, *annoyed at his own anger, stoops to help him, then sits back on the chair.*]

I know it's late. But concentrate, please. I'm just as tired as you are. [*Smiling*] I'm going to conquer you. Understand you. Now let's go through this again. We'll get it right this time.

[*Silence.* MAC *makes no move on the manual skills test.*]

If you do it right you can go back to your ward and see Angel. Angel. Do that test and you can go and see Angel.

[MAC *starts on his test.*]

8. *They came over rivers, through seas, through mud and slush, thick woods to reach there. There! It was a time of ghosts and wicked spirits. Life in the past was golden, but also dark. The past dream-life in the green stomach of heaven. The wicked spirits of this fertile valley. This circle of greenery we call home! But it's not home. There were cleft palates, useless brains, and babies born in pain. True, deep darkness is sterile cunts and useless pricks. Everything is broken . . .* In the opening of this passage, Nowra may be playfully alluding to the beginning of James Joyce's novel *Finnegans Wake* (1939): "riverrun, past Eve and Adam's, from swerve of shore to bend of bay . . ."

2.3

The asylum gardens, afternoon. The wind sounds through the trees. MAC *sits on a distant bench wearing an asylum uniform.* STEF *imitates the wind. His asylum jacket is very dirty.* BETSHEB *stands downstage in her beautiful bright dress. At her feet is a magazine. A magpie sings; she imitates its call. She begins to sing much more comprehensibly than before.*

BETSHEB [*singing*]

Glow white in 'er dress,
Gold, gold in 'er hair.
Ruby are 'er lips,
Love, love is e'rywhere.

[*The bird sings again.* BETSHEB *lies on her back and spreads out the dress like a fan. She strokes her dress: the material feels wonderful—so does the grass: warm and cosy. She feels her breasts and stomach: like a child unaware of anyone else she enjoys the sensations of her own body. A woman,* DR SIMON, *enters.*]

DR SIMON [*to* BETSHEB] Such a dress! I would kill for one like that. Happy?

BETSHEB Yes.

DR SIMON [*picking up a magazine*] Who wouldn't be on a day like this? Been looking at the pictures? Which ones do you like best? Aeroplanes? The cricketers? That's Don Bradman.[9] The dancers? The weddings?

[BETSHEB *laughs at a private joke. She knows which pictures she likes best but she is not going to tell* DR SIMON.]

You're not going to tell me?

[*As* BETSHEB *continues to laugh,* DR SIMON *goes to* MAC.]

Mac, don't be so down-in-the-dumps. Come on, the man is waiting. You'll like him. He'll take your photograph. Do you want your photograph taken?

[FRANCIS *enters in army uniform with a bunch of flowers. He watches* DR SIMON *trying to coax* MAC.]

I thought you liked seeing pictures of yourself. Come on, for me. Come on, Mac, it won't take long.

[*She leads him off.* FRANCIS *approaches* BETSHEB, *who still laughs to herself.*]

FRANCIS What's so funny?

BETSHEB Thou!

[*He gives her the flowers. She smells them deeply. He sits down next to her and they kiss gently.*]

FRANCIS [indicating the dress] Beautiful. The nurses wanted it but I said it was for you. Only you. Elizabeth helped me find it.

[*Pause.*]

Why is Mac being photographed?

[BETSHEB *takes no notice of the question as she feels* FRANCIS' *uniform.*]

He's jealous of us, you know.

BETSHEB Peter?

9. Legendary Australian cricket player (1908–2001), regarded as the greatest batsman of all time.

FRANCIS He should have reached England by now. He'll be stationed there. Live there.

[*Pause.*]

The nurse said you and the others visited Angel's grave yesterday.

BETSHEB Flowers, like this.

[*She bends down and puts her ear to the ground.*]

I ear op'n t' the Angel sprit.[1]

FRANCIS I spoke to Ayre before coming out here; she's looking better.

BETSHEB She mus' live. She mus'! She say t' me: 'I mus' live!' [*Waving at the distance*] 'Ello!

FRANCIS Who's that?

BETSHEB Lorry.[2] Gard-aner.

FRANCIS The gardener?

BETSHEB I 'elp 'im.

FRANCIS I hope you won't help him in that dress.

BETSHEB This dress? Nowt dirt. Me weddon dress.[3]

FRANCIS It's your good dress. Your best dress. You know we are not allowed. When the war is over you'll leave this place.

BETSHEB Wid Ayre 'n' Stef 'n' Mac?

FRANCIS [*amused*] Yes. Ayre, Stef, Mac, and you.

[BETSHEB *is suddenly disturbed. She jumps up and motions to a distant building.*]

BETSHEB There. Our bedibyes. Glommen time.[4]

FRANCIS You go to bed at night?

BETSHEB There. Glommen time. There is a man, he listens, speakin' t' glommen demon.[5] This girl . . .

[*She squeezes her head like a vice.*]

She bits 'er arm.

[*She demonstrates a girl biting her own arm in an obsessional, horrific way.*]

I 'ate glommen time 'ere. 'Eads burst, outburstin' wid demons.[6]

FRANCIS [*soothingly*] William can't get you out of that ward; the asylum's too crowded. Those people are mad, not you. The Government says you've got to stay here. You know that.

BETSHEB Me quim is burnin'.[7]

[*She touches* FRANCIS' *genitals.*]

FRANCIS Betsheb!

BETSHEB [*moving to him again*] Thou burning. Eyebright.[8]

[*She jumps him again and he ducks out of the way. She chases after him. They both laugh, like children in a game.*]

FRANCIS Not out here. Everyone's watching!

BETSHEB Francis! Francis! Francis!

1. *I hear the spirit of Angel.*
2. *Larry.*
3. *This dress? I won't dirty it. It's my wedding dress.*
4. *There. Going to bed. Nighttime.*
5. *There is a man, he listens and speaks to the night demon . . .*
6. *I hate nighttime here. Heads explode and break open and send forth demons.*
7. *I'm randy.*
8. *You're randy too. Your eyes are bright with lust.*

FRANCIS I'll turn the hose on you.

BETSHEB [*laughing*] Burnin'. Burnin'.

[*She grabs him. He falls to the ground. She kisses him.*]

FRANCIS [*pushing her away slightly*] Betsheb, I have to tell you something.

[*She grabs him and smothers his face with quick kisses. He pushes her away, annoyed.*]

This is serious!

[BETSHEB *doesn't notice his annoyance.*]

BETSHEB The belle she spoonin' the gent. 'E whoopin'.[9]

[*She grabs him again.*]

FRANCIS [*angrily*] No!

[*Almost immediately he is annoyed with himself for getting angry. She looks hurt and confused.*]

Listen. [*Touching his uniform*] You remember what I told you this uniform meant? I am in the army. Australia is at war with Germany and Italy. We have to fight to protect ourselves. To protect you, to save you from hurt, our families from hurt.

VOICE [*off*] Mr Morris, the taxi's here!

FRANCIS [*calling*] Tell him I won't be a moment. [*To* BETSHEB] I joined up to fight because we have to. And now I know I must fight for you, for Stef. The Germans are demons. Do you understand any of this?

[*She nods, but it's clear she doesn't.*]

I'm being shipped out tomorrow. Europe. Remember the map of the world we looked at? Well, I'm going to Europe. I won't be seeing you for some time. Goodbye.

BETSHEB [*shocked*] 'Goodbye'?

FRANCIS But not for long. I knew a couple of days ago but couldn't tell you. Too much of a coward. This dress is my going-away present for you. And this.

[*He gives her a wristwatch.*]

You can watch the hands move, learn to tell the time.
You wind it, make it go like this.

[BETSHEB *is still shocked and pays little attention.*]

BETSHEB 'Goodbye'?

[*The taxi horn beeps.*]

FRANCIS I must go. I'll write letter. William said he'd read them to you.

BETSHEB Nowt 'Goodbye'.[1]

FRANCIS I have to; it's my duty.

BETSHEB Nowt 'Goodbye'!

[*He kisses her.*]

FRANCIS This hurts me too. I love you . . . do you understand?

BETSHEB Nowt 'Goodbye'.

[*He begins to go, then stops briefly to pat* STEF *on the head.*]

FRANCIS Goodbye, Stef.

9. *The girl is lusting after the man. He is happy.*

1. *Don't say "Goodbye."*

[STEF *laughs and rolls over and over.* FRANCIS *pauses to look back at* BETSHEB. *She looks at him, confused and hurt. The taxi horn beeps again: he must go. He exits.*]

BETSHEB [*quietly*] Nowt 'Goodbye'. [*Crying out, throwing away the watch*] Nowt 'Goodbye'!

2.4

The asylum gardens, early evening. WILLIAM, *in dinner jacket, sits on the bench upstage. He watches* STEF, MAC, AYRE, *and* BETSHEB *downstage. All of the group wear asylum clothes.* MAC *sleeps curled up.* STEF *examines his shoe by himself.* BETSHEB *half cradles* AYRE, *chewing bits of bread and, like a sparrow feeding its young, passing the chewed bread into* AYRE*'s mouth.* AYRE *is fading, but she is desperate to live long enough to pass on their language and memories to* BETSHEB. *It is difficult for* AYRE *to get the words out.*

AYRE Demon 'ollarin' in glommen time.[2]

BETSHEB 'Demon 'ollarin' in glommen time.'

[*Silence.*]

AYRE Sprits o' rack 'n' cat, doomtime.[3]

BETSHEB 'Sprits o' rack 'n' cat, doomtime.'

[*Silence.* ELIZABETH, *wearing an expensive evening gown, enters and watches, unnoticed.*]

AYRE Sprits adorate quim sold for sinbread.[4]

BETSHEB 'Sprits adorate quim sold for sinbread.'

AYRE Albion is glommentime, rack 'n' cat time.[5]

BETSHEB 'Albion is glommentime, rack 'n' cat time.'

[*Silence.* BETSHEB *feeds* AYRE. ELIZABETH *goes towards* WILLIAM.]

ELIZABETH The driver is waiting.

[*He looks up, puzzled.*]

You said we should pick you up on the way to Government House.[6]

WILLIAM I wanted to see if Ayre was all right.

ELIZABETH You're always here. Why isn't Ayre inside? She looks very ill.

WILLIAM She has a great fear of dying in her room. They'll go in soon for dinner.

ELIZABETH I'm curious, William: what do you do when you come to visit them?

WILLIAM Nothing much. Check their health. Watch.

ELIZABETH You're forever here. The hospital's always ringing me. 'Where's Doctor Archer?' 'He's gone to stare at the madmen', I say.

WILLIAM They're not mad.

ELIZABETH They just do a very good impersonation of it.

[*Pause.*]

WILLIAM Ayre is teaching Betsheb—not teaching, passing on their culture, her memories.

ELIZABETH Do you read Francis's letters to her?

WILLIAM Each one I have to read dozens of times. She misses him terribly.

2. *Demons yell in the night.*
3. *When the spirits make sounds like a rack and cat, it means someone is doomed.*
4. *Spirits like prostitutes.*
5. *England is full of night; it was a time of whippings, rack and cat.*
6. The official residence of the governor of Tasmania.

AYRE [*to* BETSHEB] Glommen sprits o' cut-throat kin.[7]

BETSHEB 'Glommen sprits o' cut-throat kin.'

AYRE Pass 'elly gate t' goldy dell.[8]

BETSHEB 'Pass 'elly gate t' goldy dell.'

ELIZABETH [*to* WILLIAM] What a pathetic group they look, like those Aboriginals[9] in shanty towns.

WILLIAM She's teaching Betsheb about the night-time spirits.

ELIZABETH Come on, the Governor is waiting.

[*He stands.*]

Your bow tie.

[*An envelope falls from his lap. As he straightens his bow tie,* ELIZABETH *picks up the envelope.*]

What's in here?

WILLIAM The editor of the *Medical Journal* was going to publish them.

ELIZABETH [*handing him the envelope*] What are they?

WILLIAM The Chief Psychiatrist here decided she wanted photographs of Mac's interesting medical condition. [*Handing the photographs to* ELIZABETH] He was always ashamed of his deformity and so that's what they photographed in brilliant close-ups. The reason why Ayre and the rest are here is because Mac couldn't have children. He knows that. And look what they go and do.

ELIZABETH You would have been as callous as that.

WILLIAM Once.

ELIZABETH Your tie. [*Straightening his tie*] You smell like a brewery.

WILLIAM I drink to forget what we've done to them.

ELIZABETH There was nothing you could do.

AYRE [*to* BETSHEB] Pearly dawn pass glommen time, thou pass demon time. Pass tempest 'n' temper time.[1]

WILLIAM [*to* ELIZABETH] It would have been nice for that to have been the Australian language.

ELIZABETH When you've been drinking I can never tell when you're serious or not.

WILLIAM Their culture is more authentic than ours. We Australians have assumed the garb of a hand-me-down culture, but at our heart is a desert. For their appalling ignorance and pathetic beliefs they at least have a real core, an essence.

ELIZABETH When you're in your cups you have a disturbing tendency to philosophise. I know this mood of yours: no sarcastic remarks about Singapore at the dinner.

WILLIAM Why shouldn't I? The pompous ass said only a month ago that Singapore was impregnable.[2] Thousands of Australians are in prison camps because of British stupidity. Betsheb.

7. *Night spirits are related to our violent ancestors, the true criminals.*
8. *We passed through hell's gate to get to the golden valley.*
9. The indigenous peoples of Australia.
1. *If you can survive nighttime, then dawn will come and you will have survived another night of demons and the wilds and anger of nature.*
2. Singapore, which contained a large British naval base, was quickly overwhelmed when the Japanese attacked in December 1941; it surrendered on February 15, 1942, and some 14,000 Australians were among the more than 130,000 Commonwealth troops taken prisoner.

[BETSHEB *turns to him. He motions at the sky.*]

Tempest time.

[BETSHEB *looks up at the sky.*]

Probably tonight.

BETSHEB [*smiling*] Yes.

WILLIAM You'd better get Ayre in. 'Bye, Ayre. Mac. 'Bye, Betsheb. I'll see you tomorrow.

[MAC *picks up* AYRE *and carries her inside.*]

She won't allow the nurses to touch her.

ELIZABETH She's not long for this world.

WILLIAM Probably not.

ELIZABETH [*sarcastically*] But you've still got her voice on record. Don't be a hypocrite. You're glad that they've been hidden away; you've had them all to yourself. If you don't recognise that, then you're blind. We had better hurry, the Governor doesn't like to be kept waiting.

[*They exit.*]

2.5

On one side of the stage FRANCIS, *in army uniform with greatcoat covering his shoulders, writes by lamplight. On the other is the asylum gardens, night.* BETSHEB *washes a naked* STEF *with a bucket and sponge.*

FRANCIS My darling Betsheb, tomorrow morning I go into battle for the first time. The German planes have been pounding us since we arrived.

[BETSHEB *washes* STEF*'s body as he makes wind noises. Both seem very happy.* WILLIAM *enters and, unnoticed, watches the pair.*]

Crete is desolate and rocky. Why should we defend this country? We are fighting over a place as desolate as the moon.[3]

[BETSHEB *washes* STEF*'s face. He laughs and then rolls away. She catches him and continues to wash his face.*]

When we arrived we ran into a local priest who had lost both his legs. He felt sorry for us and said: 'This is a bad world and you have lost your way in it.' It was easy to see what he meant. The paddocks were covered in burning tanks and dying men. I imagine a battle is like being caught in a butcher shop that is burning down.

[BETSHEB *washes* STEF*'s groin.*]

BETSHEB [*softly, singing*]

Hey, hey,
The girlie say,
Rub a dub, dub,
Spoonin' in the hay.

FRANCIS It is said that if we win here, then we'll stop the Germans and the war will end. There will be a peace. But will I be alive to see it?

3. In March 1941, the British government committed Australian, New Zealand, and British forces to defend Greece and Crete against the expected German invasion; German paratroopers landed on Crete on May 20, and the island fell on the 29th.

[BETSHEB *tickles* STEF's *feet. He laughs wildly, she joins in. Their laughter is joyous.*]

Betsheb, I am scared. I do not want to die.

2.6

The asylum gardens, dusk. BETSHEB *stands on* MAC's *shoulders. They turn slowly, her face to the darkening sky. As if in a dream,* ANGEL's *penny whistle sounds.*

BETSHEB [*singing*]

Rain, rain, go thy way,
Come a-back ne'er a day.

[*As* BETSHEB *repeats the song, unconsciously she strokes* MAC's *face sensuously. He is pleased to be touched by* BETSHEB.]

[*Softly*] Francis . . .

[MAC *breaks away. Astonished,* BETSHEB *tumbles to the ground.* MAC *heads off.* BETSHEB, *perplexed by his behaviour, chases after him. He throws her off and exits angrily.*]

2.7

The asylum gardens, late at night. Rain and hail pour down. A cry of pain comes from the distance. Dimly, a figure hurries out into the garden. It is DR SIMON, *carrying an umbrella and a flashlight. The beam darts here and there.*

DR SIMON Betsheb! Are you out here?

[*Pause.*]

Betsheb. Bring Ayre inside.

[*Pause.*]

Betsheb! Answer me! Where are you? Come out of the rain.

[*She exits towards C Ward. Silence. Thunder.* BETSHEB *drags* AYRE *into the rain.*]

BETSHEB [*crying*] Thou mus' nowt die. Thou mus' live!

[*She stops to catch her breath.*]

Goldy green breathen int' thee, rain breathen int' thee.[4]

[*She rolls* AYRE *back and forth.* AYRE *moans in agony.*]

The earth breathen int' thee. Thou mus' live![5]

[DR SIMON *enters again, at a distance.*]

DR SIMON [*off*] Betsheb! Betsheb! Where are you?

[BETSHEB *huddles over* AYRE's *body. Pause.* DR SIMON *retreats. Once sure she has gone,* BETSHEB *turns her attention back to* AYRE. *She is barely breathing.*]

BETSHEB [*breathing into* AYRE's *mouth*] I am in thee, thee in me. [*Thumping* AYRE] Breathen! Breathen the tempest! Breathen the rain! [*Crying out, desperately*] Breathen the world! Thee must breathen the world![6]

4. *Nature is breathing into you, the rain is breathing into you.*
5. *The earth breathes into you. You must live!*
6. *I am in you, you in me. Breathe! Breathe in the rain! Breathe in the world! You must breathe in the world!'*

[*But* AYRE *is dead.*]

Nowt die! Nowt die!

[*She wails in fear and horror.*]

Breathen! Breathen the world! The world is breathen thee! Mumma! Breathen![7]

2.8

The asylum gardens, a pleasant autumn day. MAC *lies on the ground, dead. A bloodied knife lies next to him.* DR SIMON *enters with a camera. She turns* MAC *over: his crotch is bloodied. He has castrated himself.* DR SIMON *sees someone in the distance.*

DR SIMON Get back to your ward, Richard.

[*She watches Richard go.*]

Hurry up.

[*She turns her attention to the corpse and, taking careful aim, takes a photograph. She doesn't like the way the body is arranged, so she shifts it slightly with her foot and takes a closer picture. Silence. She stares at the corpse.*]

[*Quietly*] It's over now; you are released.

2.9

The asylum gardens, a winter's day. WILLIAM *sits on the bench wearing a coat.* STEF *and* BETSHEB *sit on the grass wearing hand-me-down coats over their asylum uniforms.* BETSHEB *massages* STEF*'s scalp.* WILLIAM *reads a letter to her.*

WILLIAM 'Some people say the war will be over by Christmas, others say it will go on forever. There is no point to this slaughter. The Germans will lose, but they don't give in; they would sooner destroy the world than surrender. My handwriting is bad. We are snowed in and my hands are shaking with the cold. The snow and the blood are endless.'

[WILLIAM *points.*]

Like the snow on Mount Wellington.[8]

[BETSHEB *nods.*]

BETSHEB Pass snow; nowt more outcastin'.[9]

WILLIAM Once the snow thaws, perhaps his exile will be over. Nowt more outcastin'. [*Continuing the letter*] 'I want to write about more pleasant things, Betsheb, but the war is my world at the moment. But once it is over I will return. Goodbye for now, my love, Francis.'

[STEF *no longer wants his head massaged. He moves away and coughs deeply. He laughs.* BETSHEB *rises and takes the letter from* WILLIAM.]

You must have quite a collection now.

[*She puts it down the front of her dress. There is a blast of icy wind.* WILLIAM *shivers.*]

What a wind, eh? Straight from the South Pole.

7. *Breathe! Breathe in the world! The world is breathing you! Mumma! Breathe!*

8. The 4,200-foot mountain overlooking Hobart, frequently snow-covered.

9. *Once it has finished snowing, his exile will be over.*

[BETSHEB *ponders. Silence.* DR SIMON *enters and stands at a distance, watching the odd trio.*]

BETSHEB Nurse Greene got child.

WILLIAM A baby boy.

BETSHEB The belly o' 'er quim. Lovely.[1]

WILLIAM She and her husband had been trying for years to have a child.

BETSHEB Francis outcastin'; come back 'n' look at 'is belle 'n' 'e think 'the dead moon o' me cunt.'[2]

WILLIAM We don't know for certain.

BETSHEB Me bod shakin' like a leaf, out o' the blue.[3]

WILLIAM Those fits you have are rare.

BETSHEB Me bod in the toothy bite o' a bad dream.[4]

[*Silence.*]

DR SIMON What is Betsheb talking about?

WILLIAM Nothing important.

DR SIMON I'm curious.

WILLIAM She just talks about things that interest her.

DR SIMON And they don't interest you?

WILLIAM Of course they do.

DR SIMON Then why wouldn't I be interested?

[*Pause.* WILLIAM *turns his attention back to* BETSHEB.]

WILLIAM [*to* BETSHEB] Don't be afraid of your body—

DR SIMON [*interrupting*] If I knew the language or if you translated for me, then I would be able to help them.

WILLIAM Like you helped Mac with the photographs?

DR SIMON I am Chief Psychiatrist here. I have every right to have patients photographed: photographs are a legitimate record of a patient's condition.

WILLIAM You treated him as if he were a freak.

DR SIMON That's not true. You have turned them against everyone except yourself. I have been here over four years and I still can't understand her.

WILLIAM [*coldly*] Perhaps you're stupid.

DR SIMON [*angrily*] You come here drunk. You've been relieved of your own post. Remember, you are only a visitor. You have no authority here.

[STEF *coughs.*]

If you really cared for him you wouldn't let him lie out in the cold. He should be brought inside.

[*She takes a step towards* STEF. BETSHEB *moves in front of him.*]

WILLIAM If you touch him, Betsheb will kill you.

[DR SIMON *stops.*]

[*Smiling*] Perhaps you had best get out of the cold, Doctor Simon.

DR SIMON One day, Doctor Archer, you'll realise what you've done to them.

WILLIAM I know what I've done: I've protected them from the likes of you.

[DR SIMON *returns inside.* BETSHEB *sits down on the wet grass and looks at the watch* FRANCIS *gave her.*]

1. *Her belly is full. It's lovely.*
2. *Francis is in exile, but when he comes back and looks at his girl he will think that I have a dead moon in my cunt.*
3. *My body shakes like a leaf; these attacks come on suddenly.*
4. *My body is in the toothy bite of a bad dream.*

BETSHEB Time is slow.

[*She looks at her watch, willing time to go faster.* **STEF** *lies prone on the ground, silent.* **WILLIAM** *puts up his collar to shield himself from the cold wind. Silence.*]

2.10

The asylum gardens, night. There is a moon. **BETSHEB** *sits on the bench staring at the night sky.*

BETSHEB 'I cup me ear t' the glommen bird. Soul o' the dead. Cryin out "Donna burst yer 'eart, the bird is me."'

[*Faint sounds of a party and dance songs of the forties come from the distance. A man in his thirties enters wearing a party hat or mask.*]

JAMES How you going? I was over there watching you talking to yourself. The New Year's party is pretty good, eh?

[**BETSHEB** *is nervous.*]

You've seen me around, haven't you? James, remember? I've been here almost as long as you. The nurses call me 'Jimmy'; me mum, 'Jim'. I saw you crawling out the window. I see you do that most nights. I can talk to you tonight because the ward assistant is drunk. He's not bad, Bert; keeps us up with the war news. I wanted to fight. I tried to join up. I said, 'I want to murder Germans.' They refused me. They said they didn't want murderers in their army. I should have said I wanted to kill Germans. James, Jim, Jimmy, murder, kill . . . No wonder I'm at a loss in the outside world; I haven't got me language skills right. Want a fuck?

[*She doesn't understand.*]

I can't make it plainer than that. I suppose I should ask you with words tied up with little blue bow ties but I don't know any.

[*He comes closer. She stiffens.*]

You can call me 'James', 'Jim', 'Jimmy'; I'll answer to them all.

[*He makes a grab at her; she ducks away.*]

[*Annoyed*] Why the problem? You're as fuckin' mad as me; why put up a front?

BETSHEB [*quietly, explaining*] Francis. Francis, 'e outcastin'.

JAMES No wonder none of us can understand you: it sounds like a mouthful of marbles.

[*He lunges and grabs at her. She stands still, scared.*]

Others are scared of you, think you're some kind of witch. Not me. I see you pissing out here, rubbing yourself and I know. Look at you, like a bird in a trap.

[*He slowly pulls her closer.*]

I have dreamed of fuckin' you; now I'll make it real.

DR SIMON [*off, quietly*] Jimmy.

[*Pause.*]

Jimmy, let her go.

[**JAMES** *lets her go.*]

JAMES [*looking off*] Hello, Doctor Simon.

DR SIMON Go back to the party.

JAMES Why pick on me? She's always out, every night, yapping to herself.

DR SIMON Back to your ward.

[JAMES *goes. Silence.* BETSHEB *lifts up her dress, offering her body in gratitude to* DR SIMON.]

Put down your dress, Betsheb, and go to bed. Stef needs you; he's very sick.

2.11

The asylum gardens, a spring day. Birds are singing. BETSHEB *drags out the body of* STEF. *He is dead, but she tries to play with him as she once did.* DR SIMON *enters.*

DR SIMON Let him go, Betsheb. Come on, let him go . . . He has to be examined by the coroner.

[*She advances on* BETSHEB, *who growls like an animal and lashes out.*]

Little bitch.

[BETSHEB *growls softly.*]

Like a bloody animal.

[*Pause.*]

[*Angrily*] He's dead. If you hadn't let him lie on the wet grass he wouldn't be.

[WILLIAM *enters. His clothes are dirty and he is very drunk.*]

WILLIAM [*to* DR SIMON, *smiling*] Fell into the flower bed. Blood and bone. Boy, do I pong![5] Betsheb!

DR SIMON Doctor Archer, she won't let go of Stef.

WILLIAM So what?

DR SIMON He's been dead since early this morning.

[WILLIAM *is shocked for a moment.*]

WILLIAM Stef?

BETSHEB [*anguished*] Stef: 'e dead!

WILLIAM No, not possible.

DR SIMON The coroner's waiting; we have to get Stef away from her.

[WILLIAM'*s sense of duty as a doctor returns.*]

WILLIAM Yes, yes. [*To* BETSHEB] You must let him go, Betsheb, there is nothing you can do. Nothing more.

BETSHEB 'e me las' blood. Stef is me las' blood. I am cast t' the windy. 'e me las' blood, boyo.[6]

WILLIAM I know, but you must give him up.

[BETSHEB *cradles* STEF, *focusing all her attention on him.* WILLIAM *starts to walk towards her, but trips and falls. He lands and turns on his back, grinning broadly.*]

Whoops-a-daisy.

[*For a moment he is bewildered, then he realises where he is.*]

[*To* BETSHEB] I'm sorry.

DR SIMON You're putrid drunk, Doctor Archer!

WILLIAM God help me, some women are observant. Yes, Doctor, I am going putrescent with alcohol.

5. Stink.
6. *Stef is my last relative, the last of my family. I am cast adrift. He was the last male member of the family.*

DR SIMON You're as crazy as she is.

WILLIAM I'm just drunk. Get a whiff of my clothes!

[*He laughs.* DR SIMON *hurries off.*]

[*Calling after her*] Call the cops! [*Yelling*] Call anyone you bloody-well please!

[*Silence. He stares at* BETSHEB *for some time, at a loss. All her attention remains on* STEF *as she cradles him. Pause.*]

[*Brushing her hair*] How I wanted to study you. To find out. I thought if I did discover everything, then I'd know. You know, of course, that this drunken old man loves you just as much as Francis does. Don't wait for him, he hasn't written in a year, he's free of you. Run away, head for the hills. Nowt more outcastin'.

[*Silence.*]

I shouldn't have let you destroy me.

BETSHEB [*looking at* WILLIAM, *quietly, almost beyond pain*] Stef . . . 'E dead.

2.12

The ruins of Berlin, evening, 1945. FRANCIS, *now a lieutenant, enters carrying a pistol. He is dirty, worn, and wearing a heavy army coat. He stops and looks around.* PRIVATE CORRIS *enters, also rugged up, carrying a rifle. Nearby on the ground are the remains of a huge statue: the head of Frederick the Great,*[7] *its face riddled with bullet holes.*

CORRIS I'm pretty sure I saw the bugger head this way.

FRANCIS He's probably gone through those ruins there.

CORRIS He wouldn't get far: there's the Americans on the other side.

[*Silence.*]

Sorry I fucked it up. When I turned me back he was off like a flash.

FRANCIS [*shrugging*] It'll soon be too dark to see anything.

CORRIS Yeah, the fires are starting up. The homeless. What a fuckin' mess, eh? They'll have to rebuild Berlin from scratch. They live like rats in a tip.[8] [*Looking at the head*] Not much bird shit.

FRANCIS They deserved it: they started it; they were so bloody proud of their thousand-year Reich.[9]

CORRIS [*examining a hole in the head*] Jesus, Doctor, I've got a splitting headache.

[*He laughs.*]

I once saw Mo at the Tiv;[1] me girlfriend said I was funnier. Who do you reckon it is?

[FRANCIS *shakes his head.*]

It's not Hitler. Some old king, I guess. Wonder where the rest of him is. [*Looking around*] A leg there . . . there's some angels. [*Sitting on the head*]

7. That is, Frederick II, King of Prussia (1712–1786; 1740–86), credited with religious tolerance and enlightened political reforms.

8. Rubbish heap.

9. The Nazi government was officially known as *Das Dritte Reich* (The Third Reign); Adolf Hitler (1889–1945) believed that the regime he founded and led would endure a thousand years, but it lasted twelve (1933–45).

1. The Tivoli, a circuit of Australian theaters that featured variety acts; among the popular performers was the comedian Roy Rene (1891–1954), best known as the bawdy character Mo McCackie.

Have to be careful I don't get a nose up me bum. You know what I heard yesterday? After they strung up Mussolini and his mistress they pissed and shat on them.[2] Bet you the same people who were saluting him the day before did it. Will we keep going or what?

FRANCIS No point. Be too dark to see soon. He'll hide in the ruins somewhere, find some old mate, change his identity . . . Doesn't matter.

CORRIS Maybe the Yanks[3] will get him.

FRANCIS So what? You saw them with those scientists the other day putting them on the plane. Like they were kings. Going to America to get well-paid jobs and yet they created the planes, the bombs, the rockets[4]—

CORRIS [*interrupting*] This fella was no scientist.

FRANCIS He was Goebbels'[5] right-hand man. He'll probably end up like the scientists: get off scot-free, probably find himself running a huge American publicity firm.

CORRIS Maybe they'll go to trial.

FRANCIS They are war criminals: who needs a trial? We should execute them straight away.

CORRIS Got a real bee in your bonnet.

FRANCIS [*coldly*] And you're a bloody idiot: you let him go.

[*Silence.*]

[*Looking around*] This is where the world ended.

CORRIS What I wouldn't give to be back in Australia. Know what I learned in four years of fighting the Krauts?[6] One German phrase: 'I surrender.' And to prove I was Australian I'd hop about like this.

[*He starts to hop. Suddenly* FRANCIS *pulls out his revolver and fires at* CORRIS. CORRIS *ducks. There is a cry from the ruins. A figure wearing a dirty suit jumps into view and runs for* CORRIS' *gun.*]

FRANCIS Get out of the way, Corris.

[*He fires and hits the* MAN *again.*]

Grab him.

[CORRIS *and the* MAN *struggle with the rifle, but the* MAN *is weak and bleeding badly. He falls to the ground.*]

[*To the* MAN, *pointing his revolver*] Don't move.

CORRIS That's the bugger, Lieutenant. [*Looking closely*] Jeez, he's badly hit.

FRANCIS He must have been waiting all the time, waiting to jump you and get your rifle.

CORRIS [*motioning with his rifle*] On your feet, Fritz.[7] [*To* FRANCIS] I think he's hurt too bad. One in the leg isn't too bad, but the chest . . .

FRANCIS Understand English?

MAN English? *Nein.*[8]

2. Mussolini and his mistress, Clara Petacci (1912–1945), were captured in April 1945, shot after a summary trial, and hanged upside down (with five others) in a public square in Milan.

3. That is, American soldiers.

4. A number of German scientists—including Werner von Braun, who was primarily responsible for building Germany's V-2 rocket and who later would be instrumental in the American space program as well as in developing military ballistic missiles—were brought to the United States to work.

5. Joseph Goebbels (1897–1945), a close associate of Hitler and the chief propaganda minister for the Nazi government.

6. Germans (derogatory).

7. Generic name for a German.

8. No (German).

FRANCIS Get someone to help us carry him back.

CORRIS Those Americans will help us. Be back in ten.

[CORRIS *heads off. Silence.*]

FRANCIS Not such a big boy now. What's the point? You'll get off.

[*The* MAN *is dying.*]

MAN Kill me.

[FRANCIS *is surprised.*]

Kill me. Please.

[*The* MAN *is in incredible pain.* FRANCIS *puts his gun to the* MAN*'s head and calmly shoots him.*]

2.13

WILLIAM*'s study, night.* WILLIAM *sits in a high-backed chair finishing the remains of a bottle of whiskey. He is drunk, but full of purpose. On his lap is an open cut-throat razor. He listens to a recording of* AYRE*'s voice for the umpteenth time. As she slowly speaks he unconsciously translates.*

AYRE'S VOICE Past riverrun 'n' turn o' kelp int' muddy moss, seay green 'n' here. There! Ghost 'n' sprit time. Goldy lifey, glommen lifey. Thee dreamy-time in greeny belch o' 'eaven. Sprits o' cunty dell. Circle o' greeny 'ome! Nowt 'ome. Burst mouth, 'airy brain 'n' cradlepain. Pitch dark glommen is dry sheb and rottin' tarse. The circle is burst . . .

WILLIAM 'We came past river, past tides of kelp and mud, moss and into the sea of green and came to here. There! The time of our ancestors. A dream-time in the green stomach of heaven. All around the spirits of the fertile valley. Home. It is not home. Then something happened: there were hare-lips,[9] soft brains, and children in pain. A darkness of sterile girls and boys. The circle is burst. Broken.'

[*The sound of burning wood is heard faintly. Something is burning close to* WILLIAM, *but he does not hear it, or doesn't care.*]

AYRE'S VOICE 'Ear us, William, William. Keep us in that box. We is talkin' t' thee. T' thee. The circle is burst. I ne'er more cup me ear to the glommen bird. I ne'er more helter-skelterin' wid the glommen sprits; foe 'n' friend.

WILLIAM 'Hear us, William. Keep us in that box. We are talking to you. To *you!* The circle is broken. I'll never more listen to the night birds. Never more dance with the night spirits, the good and the bad.'

[WILLIAM *finishes his drink and puts down the empty glass.*]

ELIZABETH [*off, banging on the door, yelling*] Bill! William! Are you in there?

AYRE'S VOICE Listen t' us, William, 'ear us words, 'member us, 'elp us, us who is born in card, cradlepain. Nowt more outcastin'.

WILLIAM 'Listen to us, William. Hear our words. Remember us. Help us, who were born in pain. No more exile.'

ELIZABETH William, answer me!

AYRE'S VOICE Nowt more outcastin'.

WILLIAM 'No more exile.'

[WILLIAM *does not hear* ELIZABETH. *He picks up the razor and calmly slits his throat. The fire grows loud.*]

9. That is, people with cleft upper lips, a birth defect.

2.14

The asylum gardens, late afternoon. BETSHEB *sits on the bench. Some flowers, pulled up by the roots, are scattered around her. Around her mouth are traces of dried blood. She wears a white hospital gown which is stained with urine and menstrual blood. She has lost control of herself.* DR SIMON *enters, surprised by* BETSHEB*'s appearance.*

DR SIMON What has happened, Betsheb?

[BETSHEB *doesn't answer.*]

Larry said someone tore up all his flower beds: it was you, wasn't it?

[*Pause.*]

You must look after yourself. Come inside, let's clean you up.

[DR SIMON *grabs her. Suddenly* BETSHEB *lashes out and knocks the doctor down.*]

BETSHEB Way! Way!

[BETSHEB *looks wild.* DR SIMON *gets up and moves away.*]

DR SIMON Come on, Betsheb, come inside.

BETSHEB [*screaming*] Nowt more![1]

DR SIMON If you don't calm down I'll have to get the ward assistants to help me.

BETSHEB [*screaming*] Nowt more!

[DR SIMON *hurries off for help.* BETSHEB *looks wildly about her.*]

[*Screaming*] Nowt more! [*Looking up at the sky*] Nowt more!

[*Suddenly there is thunder. It is as if she cries out for the destruction of the world. The more she screams at the heavens, the louder the thunder and lightening grows.*]

2.15

A prison courtyard, Berlin, afternoon. FRANCIS *sits on the ground against a wall and soaks up the last rays of sun. Silence.*

AMERICAN VOICE [*off, crying out*] Hoy, hoy, I'm the boy! Hoy, hoy, I'm the boy!

[PETER *enters in a captain's uniform.* FRANCIS *doesn't notice him.* PETER *is shocked by* FRANCIS' *condition. He puts on a smile.*]

PETER Long time no see, mate.

FRANCIS Peter!

[*He stands up. They greet each other warmly.*]

So long, so bloody long!

PETER Forty-two.

FRANCIS That's right. A captain.

PETER Didn't do so badly yourself.

[*There is an awkward pause.* FRANCIS *makes a sweeping, mocking gesture.*]

FRANCIS My home.

PETER [*trying to be lighthearted*] Love the bluestone.[2]

FRANCIS How did you find me?

1. *No more!*

2. In Australia, a basalt used for building.

PETER Came over from Paris a few days ago. I'm fixing up the final Australian repatriation. Heard about your case this morning. How long have you been here?

FRANCIS Eight or nine weeks. This is my daily exercise. I'm like a lizard. I follow the sun around the courtyard, trying to warm my blood.

AMERICAN VOICE [*off*] Hoy, hoy, I'm the boy! Hoy, hoy, I'm the boy!

FRANCIS An American negro. Went mad and killed a whore with his bare hands 'cos she called him a nigger. [*Gesturing*] Those windows, they're black-marketeers. War criminals stare out of those windows, waiting to be sent to Nuremburg;[3] and those windows, that's where I am: the rapists and murderers section.

AMERICAN VOICE Hoy, hoy, I'm the boy! Hoy, hoy, I'm the boy!

FRANCIS Actually, I'm quite at home; it reminds me of Collingwood.

[*He walks a little to the left, looking up at the sun, closing his eyes.*]

The last bit of sun. It's freezing in the cell.

PETER I only had time to glance at your file. The Americans think you murdered him.

FRANCIS I did. The Kraut asked me to do it, so I obliged. Now the Australians want to show off to the Allies that they can be just as tough on their men. [*Looking at the sun*] It's going.

PETER After years in England it was the sun I missed the most and the bright blue skies.

[*Pause.*]

Did you know my father died?

FRANCIS Your mum wrote to me.

PETER Burnt to death. Most of the rear of the house was destroyed. Mother said you stopped writing to Betsheb.

FRANCIS What could I write to her about? How could I describe what I was seeing? Civilisations perfecting death. Bombs, fighter planes, slaughtered soldiers, extermination camps, rape, bloodlust. I couldn't pretend the war would end and I would return because every morning I thought I would die that day. I couldn't write any more gentle letters because I have nothing of that left inside me any more. It's gone, the little I had. Once I stopped writing to her I knew I couldn't go home again. This prison perfectly suits my state of mind; I have been bred for it, just as I have been bred to kill. Do you know that people think the war will continue only it will be between the Americans and Russians? It's as if this century has imagined a monster, concocted it from the deepest underworld of its brain, and now it has escaped and is devouring everything. Nothing makes sense.

AMERICAN VOICE Hoy, hoy, I'm the boy! Hoy, hoy, I'm the boy!

PETER Your bitterness will pass.

FRANCIS I can't get rid of this dream. I have built a bridge. There is a grand opening. The ribbon is cut. Bright happy people begin to walk across the bridge. It collapses like a pack of cards. I have even lost faith in my ability to build something mechanical. How I envied you with your wealth, your

3. The city in southern Germany where Nazis were tried for war crimes (1945–49); both before and during World War II, it was the site of massive Nazi propaganda rallies.

background, your sense of past, family, belonging. I am rootless now. It's not such a bad feeling because it's no feeling at all.

AMERICAN VOICE Hoy, hoy, I'm the boy! [*More desperately*] Hoy, hoy, I'm the boy!

FRANCIS I wish I could go as mad as him.

PETER You've spent too many years fighting. Everyone has.

FRANCIS Don't you see, Peter, the war will never stop; we humans don't give up until we perfect something. Mind made perfect matter.

PETER It's over.

AMERICAN VOICE [*desperately*] Hoy, hoy, I'm the boy!

[FRANCIS *stands on tiptoe to get the last rays of the sun.*]

FRANCIS What kept me going was my memories of that time when we found them. God, I was stricken with her.

[PETER *laughs.*]

The old geezer doing Lear; I finally realised what it was: the happy version of *King Lear.*[4]

[*The sun vanishes.*]

Poof! Snuffed out.

[*Pause.*]

PETER We were very innocent then.

FRANCIS So were they.

AMERICAN VOICE [*crying out*] Hoy, hoy, I'm the boy!

FRANCIS [*calling out*] Hoy, hoy, you're the boy!

AMERICAN VOICE [*joyfully*] Hoy, hoy, I'm the boy!

FRANCIS Before going in I tell him that. It makes him happy. [*Holding out his hand*] I have to go in now.

PETER You'd better. [*Smiling*] You'll have to collect your gear. You'll be flown to England tomorrow and then . . . a slow boat to Australia.

[*Pause.*]

They wanted a way out of it as much as you did. No one really wants to be reminded of the war anymore. Connections help, the major was a friend of my father.

[FRANCIS *is stunned.*]

AMERICAN VOICE [*joyfully*] Hoy, hoy, I'm the boy!

PETER The nightmare is over.

2.16

The asylum gardens, an early summer day, 1945. BETSHEB *sits, withdrawn, on the bench in a clean hospital gown. It is as if she is a doll that has had all its stuffing removed.* FRANCIS *enters in civilian clothes. He carries a large bunch of flowers. Escorting him is* DR SIMON.

DR SIMON She always sits on that garden bench.

[*They look at her.*]

You're the first visitor she's had in a long time.

FRANCIS No one else?

4. The tragedy (1605) by William Shakespeare.

DR SIMON No one. Not for a year.

FRANCIS She was supposed to be released once the war was over.

DR SIMON I know nothing about that. All files about her and her group were stolen by Doctor Archer and destroyed in his house fire. Anyway, she's not in a fit condition to be released.

[FRANCIS *takes a step towards* BETSHEB, *but* DR SIMON *speaks again.*]

It would have been better if you had never found them. They should have remained a lost tribe.

[FRANCIS *nods.*]

She was in a terrible state. Profound depressions and refusing to eat, so we had to give her electric shock treatment.[5] Be patient with her.

[DR SIMON *exits. Silence.* FRANCIS *walks towards* BETSHEB *and stops behind her, smiling nervously.*]

FRANCIS [*quietly*] Betsheb?

[*She doesn't hear. He walks around to face her.*]

Betsheb?

[*She doesn't seem to recognise him. He gives her the flowers: they drop from her lap onto the ground.*]

It's me. Francis. Please. Look at me.

[*She looks at him without recognition.*]

What have we done to you?

[*Silence.*]

I couldn't come back. I couldn't write anymore. When the others died I didn't know what to write. I thought they were better off dead than living here.

[*Pause.*]

You're the last thing I ever wanted to hurt.

[*A long silence.*]

I didn't know this was going to happen. Perhaps I did, that's why I felt so guilty.

[*Silence.*]

Betsheb?

[*He kisses her. She doesn't respond. As he kisses her again, he takes out his revolver and points it at the side of her head.*]

2.17

Hobart, a summer's night, 1945. The tiny Greek temple is the same as the opening scene. ELIZABETH *stands before it in Greek costume.* PETER, *in dinner jacket, plays his father's role as Orestes.*

ELIZABETH 'You are now ready for death, yet you seem to be facing the prospect of such a hideous fate with true calm.'

PETER 'What else should I do? I have nothing to live for.'

ELIZABETH 'What of your family? You were once a child: who was your mother, then? Your father? Have you a sister?'

PETER 'My sister was sacrificed for my father.'

5. Electroconvulsive therapy, which became a widespread psychiatric treatment in the 1940s; its most common side effect is memory loss.

ELIZABETH 'I am lost too. My mother, Clytemnestra, said my brother—'

PETER 'My darling sister! I can scarcely believe what I hear!'

[*He moves towards her. She steps away.*]

ELIZABETH 'What are you doing? I am Head Priestess.'

PETER 'Clytemnestra was my mother too! My father is the grandson of Pelops. Was yours?'

ELIZABETH 'Yes.'

PETER 'Iphigenia! We thought you were dead and now I have found you!'

ELIZABETH 'I am happier than words can tell.'

[*They embrace.*]

'Our strange story is beyond all dreams and thought. Instead of killing you I must save you and so save us all. How I longed for my country and you, long before your coming, Orestes. How my prayer joins with yours for the renewal of our breed. We must escape.'

PETER 'My purpose in coming here must now be revealed. I came here to steal the statue of Artemis. We shall take it back with us.'

ELIZABETH 'You cannot do both; take the statue and leave me to die. If a man dies, a house, a name is lost, but if a woman dies it means nothing.'

PETER 'No murderer of you shall I be. Either I escape to Argos with you or die here with you. Now I see the plan of the gods: they have intended that I should find you here. I see the strands of fate entwining themselves. Lady, I think we shall reach home!'

[MARY, *the maid, enters. Both* PETER *and* ELIZABETH *stop.*]

MARY I'm sorry, Mrs Archer, an urgent phone call for your son.

PETER Who is it, Mary?

MARY The superintendent of New Norfolk Asylum, Mr Archer.

[PETER *heads off, followed by* MARY.]

ELIZABETH [*exasperated*] Peter! [*To the audience*] Ladies and gentlemen, a slight pause before my son returns. In the meantime the blind children would adore it if they saw you reaching even further into your pockets. Our target tonight is five hundred pounds, so dip your hands in. Go on, the heavens are clear and fortune shines on us tonight.

2.18

The wilds of southwestern Tasmania, day. FRANCIS *lies on the ground, dirty and sleepy. There is a sudden noise and he wakes up.* PETER *appears wearing his old hiking gear.* FRANCIS *is surprised to see his friend. Silence.*

PETER I knew you'd come back here.

FRANCIS Are there any others with you?

PETER No.

[*Pause.*]

Are you all right?

FRANCIS Tired, that's all.

PETER I'm not used to all this exercise.

FRANCIS [*smiling*] Neither am I.

[*Silence.*]

PETER Betsheb?

FRANCIS Down by the river.

PETER When I got to the asylum, Doctor Simon was still shaking. She said you were about to shoot Betsheb and when she called out you turned the gun on her.

FRANCIS I wanted to put Betsheb out of her misery, but when I held it against her head I realised I should have been holding it against mine. I knew what to do. I would bring Betsheb back here, bring her home. We destroyed them.

PETER It was a combination of events. How were we to know that the Government would deal with them that way?

FRANCIS Does it bother you?

PETER It does, but I have never been obsessed by them as you are or my father was. How could they have survived, anyway? They were pathetic remnants of what was probably an even more pathetic collection of people. They were like those Aboriginal tribes that withered away because their culture wasn't strong enough. It happens in nature, in human civilisations, one big animal swallows a little one. [*Looking around*] It didn't take long for it to return to the wilderness.

[BETSHEB *enters and smiles when she sees* PETER. *She hugs him.*]

BETSHEB Peter, Peter, Peter.

PETER Hello, Betsheb. [*To* FRANCIS] Are you going to stay here . . . with her?

FRANCIS Why not?

[*He releases* BETSHEB, *and she lies on the ground and stares contentedly at the sky.*]

PETER You're mad. How in hell will you two survive out here?

FRANCIS They survived; why not us? It doesn't matter, anyway. Why should I go back? How can I go back after all I've seen? This is what I hate about this country: it pretends nothing important ever happened. Everything we experienced overseas . . . we return and pretend we never experienced it. I shot that German, not out of pity, but because I was filled with hate. All right, pretend it didn't happen. You helped co-ordinate the bombing raids over Germany. Forget it. We obliterated a group of people, not through deliberate cruelty, but through plain stupidity and indifference. Doesn't matter, no problems, mate. Indifference is our guiding star. We'd sooner turn our attention to making a quick quid,[6] like children amused by shiny trinkets. We'd sooner wipe out all unpleasant memories, block our ears and pretend we can't hear the cry of pain. If we heard that cry, then our sense of ourselves would be deeper, then we shall have reached home. We are lost, rootless people: she isn't.

PETER You're running away.

[*Silence.*]

FRANCIS Will you stay with us for tonight?

PETER If I leave now, I'll get back to the track before dark.

[*Pause.*]

I'll say I couldn't find you.

[*He looks at* BETSHEB, *who still lies on the ground staring contentedly up at the sky and trees.*]

BETSHEB [*happily*] Rack 'n' cat o' the windy, bumpin' thru the trees.[7]

6. That is, a quick buck (*quid* is slang for one pound sterling).

7. *The wind sounds like the rack and cat as it blows through the trees.*

PETER She can't offer you a future.

BETSHEB Sprits o' Melorne, Ayre, Stef, Mac, Angel. Liptalkin' softly, swirlin' in the cunty dell o' moss 'n' ferny clotty 'eart. The moon is a white 'ole, I crawl int' it t' dream. Ayre liptalkin' thru me 'eart. The bird listen, he liptalk thru 'is soul. Sprits outburstin' around 'n' around, a-yellin, a-kissin'. All goldy things. All goldy sow. 'Ome. I come 'ome.[8]

[*Silence.*]

PETER What she's describing doesn't exist; it's a figment of her imagination.

FRANCIS She can teach me how to see it.

PETER But it's not real.

BETSHEB [*softly, singing*]

Rain, rain, go thy way,
Come a-back ne'er a day.

PETER Goodbye, Betsheb.

[*She pays no attention.*]

She lives in a world of her own. You know that. She destroyed my father just as she'll destroy you. You have done the wrong thing.

FRANCIS Maybe I have; I don't know. But she's all I've got to believe in.

PETER Goodbye.

[FRANCIS *nods a 'Goodbye'.* PETER *departs. Silence.* BETSHEB *continues to sing softly to herself.*]

FRANCIS Betsheb? Betsheb?

[BETSHEB, *immersed in her own world, doesn't answer.* FRANCIS *sits down away from her and wonders if* PETER *is right.* BETSHEB *laughs to herself. After a time she turns around and notices* FRANCIS*: a lonely, confused figure. She stares at him and, almost as if he has heard his name, he turns and looks at her. She smiles across the gulf that separates them.*]

BETSHEB Nowt more outcastin'.[9]

[*The lights fade slowly to blackout.*]

The End.

8. *I can hear the spirits of Melorne, Ayre, Stef, Mac, and Angel talking softly. I hear their voices swirling down through the valley and up through the mosses and ferns, so thick they are like a fern-clotted heart. The moon is like a white hole; I crawl into it when I dream. Ayre is speaking through my heart. The night bird listens, but when he talks he talks through his soul. Spirits are bursting out and dancing around, yelling and kissing. Everything is fertile, wonderful. Home. I have come home.*

9. *No more exile.*

AUGUST WILSON

1945–2005

OF the many African American dramatists who have written for the theater since Lorraine Hansberry's acclaimed *A Raisin in the Sun* (1959), none has enjoyed more popular and critical success than August Wilson. *Ma Rainey's Black Bottom* (1984), the first of Wilson's plays to reach Broadway, won the New York Drama Critics' Circle Award for best new play; ***FENCES*** (1985) received numerous honors, including the Tony Award for Best Play and the Pulitzer Prize; and *The Piano Lesson* (1987) won Wilson another Drama Critics' Circle Award and a second Pulitzer. Subsequent plays, which continued Wilson's stated project of dramatizing African American history throughout the twentieth century one decade at a time, have also received widespread acclaim. Few dramatists, white or black, have matched Wilson's historical and sociological ambition or so minutely examined the dynamics, memories, and traumas that constitute the twentieth-century African American community.

Wilson was born Frederick August Kittel on April 27, 1945, in the Hill District, a largely African American neighborhood of Pittsburgh, where all but one of his major plays are set. The fourth of six children, he was the son of a black mother and a white German baker who was absent throughout his childhood. The family had little money, relying mainly on welfare and on Daisy Wilson Kittel's earnings as a janitor. When his father, whose name he bore, died in 1965, the future writer began calling himself August Wilson, thereby choosing to identify with the African American side of his family. By that point in his life, Wilson had had ample opportunity to learn what such an identity meant in the civil rights–era United States. In 1959 his mother and her second husband, a black man named David Bedford who worked in the city Sewer Department and would provide a model for Troy in *Fences,* had moved the family to a predominantly white neighborhood. Wilson's teenage years took him from one high school to another until, the target of racist remarks and ostracism, he dropped out of school for good in tenth grade when a teacher accused him of plagiarism, insisting that his paper on Napoleon was so good that one of his sisters must have written it.

Unwilling to tell his parents what he had done, Wilson spent much of his free time in a public library; there, in the "Negro Section," he discovered the works of such African American writers as Langston Hughes, Ralph Ellison, and James Baldwin. Wilson later recalled in an interview that he derived comfort from the fact that black people wrote books, adding that he "used to dream about being part of the Harlem Renaissance." After serving one year in the U.S. Army and spending two years working odd jobs, he took major steps toward realizing his ambition in 1965 when he moved from his mother's house into a rooming house back in the Hill District, bought himself a typewriter, and changed his name. The move immersed Wilson in a culturally and socially vibrant African American community, and from the musicians, artists, ex-convicts, and workers he encountered he absorbed the personalities, behaviors, and stories that would later appear in his plays. Wilson also learned the rich and varied vernacular of this black community, marked by cadences and idioms that mixed northern and southern, urban and rural.

Wilson's early years as a writer coincided with a shift in politics and culture as the forms of social and artistic protest that characterized the late 1950s and early 1960s were replaced by the more radicalized politics of black separatism, cultural nationalism, and the black power movement. By 1965 the playwright Amiri Baraka, who had begun his career as the Beat poet LeRoi Jones, had written such incendiary plays as *Dutchman* (1964) and *The Slave* (1964) and was calling for a "Black Revolutionary Theater." Wilson was deeply influenced by black cultural nationalism and its project of celebrating African American culture and developing institutions where this culture could be nurtured and shared within the black community. In 1968 he co-founded the Black Horizons Theatre in Pittsburgh to raise black consciousness and help politicize the community. The new theater put on the plays of Baraka and other playwrights of the Black Arts movement, and Wilson tried his hand at playwriting for the first time.

These attempts at one-act dramas were not successful; indeed, not until the mid-1970s would Wilson devote himself seriously to the theater. A 1976 work based on the life and death of 1920s blues musician Blind Lemon Jefferson, *The Homecoming,* became Wilson's first produced play, and other playscripts followed; they included a 1977 musical satire about the white nineteenth-century rustler Black Bart and *Jitney!* (1979), a play set in a gypsy cab station in his native Pittsburgh. In 1978 Wilson moved to St. Paul, Minnesota, where he became associated with the Playwright's Center in Minneapolis; among other jobs, he wrote short educational plays for a theater troupe affiliated with the Science Museum of Minnesota. The breakthrough for this relatively unknown playwright came when he developed early material he had written on Ma Rainey into *Ma Rainey's Black Bottom* and submitted the completed play to the Eugene O'Neill Theater Center's Playwright's Conference in Connecticut. The play was accepted for staged reading and Wilson was introduced to Lloyd Richards, who would serve as his mentor and director in subsequent projects. After a process of workshop revisions, *Ma Rainey* premiered at the Yale Repertory Theatre in April 1984, and moved to Broadway in October of the same year.

As *Ma Rainey* was winning praise among the theatergoing public, Wilson's *Fences* and an early version of *Joe Turner's Come and Gone* had already been presented in staged readings and workshops. By that time, Wilson was fully embarked on the project that he would complete twenty years later: tracing the history of twentieth-century black America through a cycle of ten plays set in each decade of the century. The result is a remarkable panorama of modern African American history. *Ma Rainey's Black Bottom,* the only play in the cycle not set in Pittsburgh, takes place in a Chicago recording studio in 1927. Most of the action of *Fences* takes place in Troy Maxson's backyard in 1957, while *Joe Turner's Come and Gone* (1986) is set in a boardinghouse in 1911. *The Piano Lesson* (1987), which deals with the conflict between brother and sister over a 135-year-old piano that has been central to their family's history, takes place in 1936. *Two Trains Running* (1990) is set in a Pittsburgh restaurant in 1969; *Seven Guitars* (1996) deals with the causes and repercussions of a young guitar player's death in 1948. A revised version of *Jitney* (which premiered in 1996), takes place in 1977, and *King Hedley II* (1999) explores the breakdown of the black family and community in the 1980s. *Gem of the Ocean* (2003), which is set in 1904, is dominated by the figure of Aunt Ester, a 287-year-old community elder and seer who arrived on the first shipload of American slaves in 1619. *Radio Golf,* which premiered six months before Wilson's death from cancer in 2005, centers on a plan to redevelop Pittsburgh's Hill District proposed in the 1990s.

With its broad historical ambitions, Wilson's history of a people invites comparison to the cycle plays of the medieval mystery guilds presented at York, Wakefield, and elsewhere. Wilson's plays similarly stand firmly on their own yet acquire wider meanings when viewed or read in relation to each other. The historical backdrop, or metanarrative, of these plays is certainly epic in scope. Like Hansberry, Wilson takes on the legacy of the Great Migration—the movement of black Americans who left the poverty and economic limitations of the Mississippi Delta and other parts of the South for Chicago, Cleveland, New York, and other northern cities in the largest demographic shift in U.S. history. Though this migration spanned the years between 1900 and 1970 (the year that black Americans started returning to the South), its peak came during World War I and the 1920s. In his brief introduction to *Fences,* Wilson describes how the "descendants of African slaves," pursuing the same hopes and dreams as European immigrants, found a very different reception in the cities of the North, and how hard they worked to make their lives, now spent "in shallow, ramshackle houses made of sticks and tar paper," into something free and dignified. Plays such as *Joe Turner's Come and Gone, Fences,* and *The Piano Lesson* examine the impact of the Great Migration on the generations that undertook it and those that followed. In doing so, they also look back to a past whose traumas and histories constitute the horizons of urban African American racial memory: the life of southern sharecroppers during Reconstruction, when the hopes of emancipation confronted the realities of socialized racism; the uncountable brutalities of slavery; the hardships of the Middle Passage; and, at the farthest reach, Africa and its forms of community, culture, and identity. As Wilson himself has commented, "When your back is pressed to the wall you go to the deepest part of yourself, and there's a response—it's your great ancestors talking. It's blood memory."

Their identities fragmented to varying degrees, Wilson's characters carry this history with them in the form of conflicting needs, drives, and behaviors. Such conflicts particularly affect Wilson's male characters. Negotiating their way through a society uncomfortable with their presence, they move, often compulsively, from place to place, relationship to relationship, seeking a haven in the world and some balm for their restless psyches. They fall in and out of jobs and end up so regularly in jail (or the "workhouse") that being arrested becomes a kind of initiation ritual. All of Wilson's characters, male and female, are haunted by the experiences of their parents and ancestors, and they seek, in sometimes self-defeating and contradictory ways, to escape or redeem this inheritance. In *The Piano Lesson,* Berniece and Boy Willie struggle for control of the family piano, each with a different understanding of what its painful history means to the present: Boy Willie wants to sell the piano and put the money toward purchasing the plantation where their great-grandparents had worked as slaves, while Berniece is equally determined to preserve the representations of family members that their great-grandfather had carved into the piano's legs after the relatives had been sold away. The siblings' struggle with the past comes to a head when Boy Willie fights the ghost of Sutter, the slave owner who controlled their ancestors' fate, in the play's final scene.

Wilson's dual interests in the present and the historical memories that inform it have driven certain stylistic and formal choices in the composition of his plays. Though he was influenced by Baraka's writing, Wilson chose not to employ the confrontational aesthetic of the Black Revolutionary Theater movement in his own drama. Nor has he pursued the antitheatrical styles and techniques through which some other contemporary black playwrights (such as Adrienne Kennedy, Ntozake Shange, and SUZAN-LORI PARKS) subvert the representational conventions that have traditionally governed the staging of African Americans. Wilson's drama draws on realism as an aesthetic; stylistically, his plays resemble those of EUGENE O'NEILL, ARTHUR MILLER, and others in the American mainstream. Yet at the same time that Wilson's plays display an almost ethnographic attention to the lives of his characters, detailing their material world and social codes with a range and specificity that recall the nineteenth-century realist novel, their realism is neither simple nor seamless. Wilson's settings—a backyard, a drawing room, a cab station—are based in the everyday, but they are invested with memory, history, and myth. For one thing, the dramatic present of Wilson's plays is expanded through the act of storytelling as characters narrate individual and family history, legends, and dreams. Several scholars have noted the similarities between Wilson's raconteurs and the West African griot, or storyteller, who preserved and transmitted the oral tradition of families and communities. In their access to traumatic memory and visionary revelation, these characters—such as Herald Loomis in *Joe Turner's Come and Gone,* with his trancelike vision of bones rising from the ocean waves and re-forming as bodies on the shore—introduce myth and the supernatural to Wilson's plays. In this respect, they are related to other figures created by Wilson whose presence unsettles the boundaries of realism—characters such as Aunt Ester, the centuries-old seer who has a presence, onstage and off, in several of his plays; Hedley in *Seven Guitars,* who is obsessed by visions about his dead father and the belief that he will father the Messiah; and Troy Maxson's brother Gabe in *Fences,* who, having suffered a brain injury in World War II, carries a trumpet and believes that he is the archangel Gabriel. Traversed by characters such as these, history in August Wilson's twentieth-century chronicle becomes actual and mythic at the same time.

There is certainly something mythic and outsized about the protagonist of *Fences,* Wilson's most widely known play. The name "Troy" calls to mind the embattled city of Homer's *Iliad,* while "Maxson" (Max-son) evokes the idea of patrilineal succession so central to heroic sagas. Like Babe Ruth, Josh Gibson, and the other baseball legends in whose company he places himself, Troy is larger than life; as Wilson notes, "[t]ogether with his blackness, his largeness informs his sensibilities and the choices he has made in his life." In a play profoundly concerned with space, ownership, and boundaries, Troy's presence dominates the stage even when he is absent from a particular scene; as a glance at the character list indicates, the other characters are defined primarily in terms of their relationship to him. Boasting that he "wrestled with Death" when he was seriously ill in the hospital, Troy displays the same indomitability in his job as a garbage collector, confronting his boss to ask why only whites drive the trucks while blacks lift the garbage. His passions in life are women and baseball, and it is not always clear which comes first. Troy learned baseball while in prison for killing a man, and upon his release he played in the Negro League, the circuit of teams for black ballplayers; none played in the major leagues until Jackie Robinson joined the Brooklyn Dodgers in 1947. Negro League teams, which often drew crowds as large as those that watched their white counterparts, featured some of the best players in the history of the sport—including Josh Gibson, the so-called black Babe Ruth, who played for the powerful Homestead Grays, based in a steel mill town adjacent to Pittsburgh. As the archetypal American pastime, baseball serves as a powerful sym-

James Earl Jones as Troy in the world premiere of *Fences* at the Yale Repertory Theatre, 1985.

bol in *Fences* of the exclusion of black Americans from the country's social and cultural institutions. Unfortunately for Troy, by the time baseball's color line had been breached and black players gradually began playing for major league teams, he was too old to be one of them. At age fifty-three, he carries his baseball past with him as a bitter reminder of racial oppression and as a metaphor of his battles against an antagonistic life: for him, "Death ain't nothing but a fastball on the outside corner."

Troy's personality was forged in his relationship with his father, an embittered and abusive sharecropper who towered over his children and drove Troy away with a particularly ugly explosion of violence. From his father Troy learns responsibility, but it is a responsibility born of hardness, not love. When applied to his two sons, it is accompanied by a rigid sense of authority and a demand that they live their lives with the pressure-forged self-denial he has been forced to accept in his. In different ways, both Lyons (who aspires to be a musician) and Cory (a high school football star) resist this narrow definition of life's possibilities. Cory's desire to win a scholarship to play football in college reflects the changing place of black athletes in American sports: in 1957, the year the play opens, the running back Jim Brown was declared the National Football League's Most Valuable Player and the Milwaukee Braves won the World Series, defeating the New York Yankees behind the hitting of Hank Aaron (who would eventually break Babe Ruth's revered lifetime home run record). As Troy's wife Rose explains to him, "The world's changing around you and you can't even see it." But Troy is the product of a different world. Unable to perceive an alternative to the father-son struggle that he himself was forced to endure and scarred by the deprivations he faced, Troy becomes the father he ran away from, standing in the way of a younger generation's new opportunities and driving away those he loves. Resenting the self-sacrifice, suffering, and disappointment that he has nonetheless worked into a code of living, he betrays his younger son, wife, and brother.

With its psychologically embattled patriarch, urban backyard setting, and other details of plot and action, *Fences* bears more than casual resemblance to ARTHUR MILLER's *Death of a Salesman* (1949). Like the earlier play, *Fences* revolves around questions of masculinity: what the social performance of maleness consists of, how it is transmitted (or not transmitted) from fathers to sons, how it relates to social models of femaleness. Their economic and social disempowerment has made the task of fulfilling traditional male roles particularly fraught for African American men. Like Biff Loman, Cory must negotiate the boundaries of his own identity, and thereby become a man, in the shadow of his father's frustrated and defensive masculinity: "It would wrap around you and lay there until you couldn't tell which one was you anymore." He is not alone in struggling against Troy. Rose, one of only two female characters in the play, must confront her failure to meet all of her husband's needs and affirm, in the process, her own need for selfhood. Critics have been divided over the status of the women Wilson created, who inhabit a dramatic world whose orientation is largely determined by male preoccupations. To what extent is Rose's character defined in terms of and limited by the support—psychological, domestic, sexual—that she provides her husband? To what extent, conversely, does she succeed in articulating an autonomous set of experiences, desires, and identity boundaries?

Against these psychological and sociological backdrops, the play's title resonates in complex ways. Designed both to keep people in and to keep them out, the backyard fence represents the many ways in which society and the human mind establish boundaries around psyches, social units, races, genders. The play's principal characters think about fences differently. Rose, who builds fences in order to "keep people in," desires a space where her family can remain protected and whole. Troy, on the other hand, constructs fences against those aspects of life that threaten his view of the world and himself. In so doing, he establishes barriers between himself and those who love him, denying himself the possibilities of growth, intimacy, and pride in the son who has tried so hard to live up to his expectations. Alone in the play's penultimate scene, all Troy can do is swing his bat, hoping to clear the fences—hit a home run—in one last act of solitary heroism.

S.G

Fences

When the sins of our fathers visit us
We do not have to play host.
We can banish them with forgiveness
As God, in His Largeness and Laws.

—AUGUST WILSON

CHARACTERS

TROY MAXSON
JIM BONO, Troy's friend
ROSE, Troy's wife
LYONS, Troy's oldest son by previous marriage
GABRIEL, Troy's brother
CORY, Troy and Rose's son
RAYNELL, Troy's daughter

Setting

The setting is the yard which fronts the only entrance to the MAXSON household, an ancient two-story brick house set back off a small alley in a big-city neighborhood. The entrance to the house is gained by two or three steps leading to a wooden porch badly in need of paint.

A relatively recent addition to the house and running its full width, the porch lacks congruence. It is a sturdy porch with a flat roof. One or two chairs of dubious value sit at one end where the kitchen window opens onto the porch. An old-fashioned icebox stands silent guard at the opposite end.

The yard is a small dirt yard, partially fenced, except for the last scene, with a wooden sawhorse, a pile of lumber, and other fence-building equipment set off to the side. Opposite is a tree from which hangs a ball made of rags. A baseball bat leans against the tree. Two oil drums serve as garbage receptacles and sit near the house at right to complete the setting.

The Play

Near the turn of the century, the destitute of Europe sprang on the city with tenacious claws and an honest and solid dream. The city devoured them. They swelled its belly until it burst into a thousand furnaces and sewing machines, a thousand butcher shops and bakers' ovens, a thousand churches and hospitals and funeral parlors and moneylenders. The city grew. It nourished itself and offered each man a partnership limited only by his talent, his guile, and his willingness and capacity for hard work. For the immigrants of Europe, a dream dared and won true.

The descendants of African slaves were offered no such welcome or participation. They came from places called the Carolinas and the Virginias, Georgia, Alabama, Mississippi, and Tennessee. They came strong, eager, searching. The city rejected them and they fled and settled along the riverbanks and under bridges in shallow, ramshackle houses made of sticks and tar paper. They collected rags and wood. They sold the use of their muscles and their bodies. They cleaned houses and washed clothes, they shined shoes, and in quiet desperation and vengeful pride, they stole, and lived in pursuit of their own dream. That they could breathe free, finally, and stand to meet life with the force of dignity and whatever eloquence the heart could call upon.

By 1957, the hard-won victories of the European immigrants had solidified the industrial might of America. War had been confronted and won with new energies that used loyalty and patriotism as its fuel. Life was rich, full, and flourishing. The Milwaukee Braves won the World Series, and the hot winds of change that would make the sixties a turbulent, racing, dangerous, and provocative decade had not yet begun to blow full.

1.1

It is 1957. TROY *and* BONO *enter the yard, engaged in conversation.* TROY *is fifty-three years old, a large man with thick, heavy hands; it is this largeness that he strives to fill out and make an accommodation with. Together with his blackness, his largeness informs his sensibilities and the choices he has made in his life.*

Of the two men, BONO *is obviously the follower. His commitment to their friendship of thirty-odd years is rooted in his admiration of* TROY*'s honesty, capacity for hard work, and his strength, which* BONO *seeks to emulate.*

It is Friday night, payday, and the one night of the week the two men engage in a ritual of talk and drink. TROY *is usually the most talkative and at times he can be crude and almost vulgar, though he is capable of rising to profound heights of expression. The men carry lunch buckets and wear or carry burlap aprons and are dressed in clothes suitable to their jobs as garbage collectors.*

BONO Troy, you ought to stop that lying!

TROY I ain't lying! The nigger had a watermelon this big. [*He indicates with his hands.*] Talking about . . . "What watermelon, Mr. Rand?" I liked to fell out![1] "What watermelon, Mr. Rand?" . . . And it sitting there big as life.

BONO What did Mr. Rand say?

TROY Ain't said nothing. Figure if the nigger too dumb to know he carrying a watermelon, he wasn't gonna get much sense out of him. Trying to hide that great big old watermelon under his coat. Afraid to let the white man see him carry it home.

BONO I'm like you . . . I ain't got no time for them kind of people.

TROY Now what he look like getting mad cause he see the man from the union talking to Mr. Rand?

BONO He come to me talking about . . . "Maxson gonna get us fired." I told him to get away from me with that. He walked away from me calling you a troublemaker. What Mr. Rand say?

TROY Ain't said nothing. He told me to go down the Commissioner's office next Friday. They called me down there to see them.

BONO Well, as long as you got your complaint filed, they can't fire you. That's what one of them white fellows tell me.

TROY I ain't worried about them firing me. They gonna fire me cause I asked a question? That's all I did. I went to Mr. Rand and asked him, "Why? Why you got the white mens driving and the colored lifting?" Told him, "What's the matter, don't I count? You think only white fellows got sense enough to

1. I nearly fell out of my tree; that is, I was amazed.

drive a truck. That ain't no paper job! Hell, anybody can drive a truck. How come you got all whites driving and the colored lifting? He told me, "Take it to the union." Well, hell, that's what I done! Now they wanna come up with this pack of lies.

BONO I told Brownie if the man come and ask him any questions . . . just tell the truth! It ain't nothing but something they done trumped up on you cause you filed a complaint on them.

TROY Brownie don't understand nothing. All I want them to do is change the job description. Give everybody a chance to drive the truck. Brownie can't see that. He ain't got that much sense.

BONO How you figure he be making out with that gal be up at Taylors' all the time . . . that Alberta gal?

TROY Same as you and me. Getting just as much as we is. Which is to say nothing.

BONO It is, huh? I figure you doing a little better than me . . . and I ain't saying what I'm doing.

TROY Aw, nigger, look here . . . I know you. If you had got anywhere near that gal, twenty minutes later you be looking to tell somebody. And the first one you gonna tell . . . that you gonna want to brag to . . . is gonna be me.

BONO I ain't saying that. I see where you be eyeing her.

TROY I eye all the women. I don't miss nothing. Don't never let nobody tell you Troy Maxson don't eye the women.

BONO You been doing more than eyeing her. You done bought her a drink or two.

TROY Hell yeah, I bought her a drink! What that mean? I bought you one, too. What that mean cause I buy her a drink? I'm just being polite.

BONO It's alright to buy her one drink. That's what you call being polite. But when you wanna be buying two or three . . . that's what you call eyeing her.

TROY Look here, as long as you known me . . . you ever known me to chase after women?

BONO Hell yeah! Long as I done known you. You forgetting I knew you when.

TROY Naw, I'm talking about since I been married to Rose?

BONO Oh, not since you been married to Rose. Now, that's the truth, there. I can say that.

TROY Alright then! Case closed.

BONO I see you be walking up around Alberta's house. You supposed to be at Taylors' and you be walking up around there.

TROY What you watching where I'm walking for? I ain't watching after you.

BONO I seen you walking around there more than once.

TROY Hell, you liable to see me walking anywhere! That don't mean nothing cause you see me walking around there.

BONO Where she come from anyway? She just kinda showed up one day.

TROY Tallahassee. You can look at her and tell she one of them Florida gals. They got some big healthy women down there. Grow them right up out the ground. Got a little bit of Indian in her. Most of them niggers down in Florida got some Indian in them.

BONO I don't know about that Indian part. But she damn sure big and healthy. Woman wear some big stockings. Got them great big old legs and hips as wide as the Mississippi River.

TROY Legs don't mean nothing. You don't do nothing but push them out of the way. But them hips cushion the ride!

BONO Troy, you ain't got no sense.

TROY It's the truth! Like you riding on Goodyears![2]

[ROSE *enters from the house. She is ten years younger than* TROY, *her devotion to him stems from her recognition of the possibilities of her life without him: a succession of abusive men and their babies, a life of partying and running the streets, the Church, or aloneness with its attendant pain and frustration. She recognizes* TROY's *spirit as a fine and illuminating one and she either ignores or forgives his faults, only some of which she recognizes. Though she doesn't drink, her presence is an integral part of the Friday night rituals. She alternates between the porch and the kitchen, where supper preparations are under way.*]

ROSE What you all out here getting into?

TROY What you worried about what we getting into for? This is men talk, woman.

ROSE What I care what you all talking about? Bono, you gonna stay for supper?

BONO No, I thank you, Rose. But Lucille say she cooking up a pot of pigfeet.

TROY Pigfeet! Hell, I'm going home with you! Might even stay the night if you got some pigfeet. You got something in there to top them pigfeet, Rose?

ROSE I'm cooking up some chicken. I got some chicken and collard greens.

TROY Well, go on back in the house and let me and Bono finish what we was talking about. This is men talk. I got some talk for you later. You know what kind of talk I mean. You go on and powder it up.

ROSE Troy Maxson, don't you start that now!

TROY [*puts his arm around her*] Aw, woman . . . come here. Look here, Bono . . . when I met this woman . . . I got out that place, say, "Hitch up my pony, saddle up my mare . . . there's a woman out there for me somewhere. I looked here. Looked there. Saw Rose and latched on to her." I latched on to her and told her—I'm gonna tell you the truth—I told her, "Baby, I don't wanna marry, I just wanna be your man." Rose told me . . . tell him what you told me, Rose.

ROSE I told him if he wasn't the marrying kind, then move out the way so the marrying kind could find me.

TROY That's what she told me. "Nigger, you in my way. You blocking the view! Move out the way so I can find me a husband." I thought it over two or three days. Come back—

ROSE Ain't no two or three days nothing. You was back the same night.

TROY Come back, told her . . . "Okay, baby . . . but I'm gonna buy me a banty[3] rooster and put him out there in the backyard . . . and when he see a stranger come, he'll flap his wings and crow . . ." Look here, Bono, I could watch the front door by myself . . . it was that back door I was worried about.

ROSE Troy, you ought not talk like that. Troy ain't doing nothing but telling a lie.

TROY Only thing is . . . when we first got married . . . forget the rooster . . . we ain't had no yard!

2. That is, on automobile tires.
3. That is, bantam, or small (a term applied to several breeds of domestic fowl).

BONO I hear you tell it. Me and Lucille was staying down there on Logan Street. Had two rooms with the outhouse in the back. I ain't mind the outhouse none. But when that goddamn wind blow through there in the winter . . . that's what I'm talking about! To this day I wonder why in the hell I ever stayed down there for six long years. But see, I didn't know I could do no better. I thought only white folks had inside toilets and things.

ROSE There's a lot of people don't know they can do no better than they doing now. That's just something you got to learn. A lot of folks still shop at Bella's.

TROY Ain't nothing wrong with shopping at Bella's. She got fresh food.

ROSE I ain't said nothing about if she got fresh food. I'm talking about what she charge. She charge ten cents more than the A&P.[4]

TROY The A&P ain't never done nothing for me. I spends my money where I'm treated right. I go down to Bella, say, "I need a loaf of bread, I'll pay you Friday." She give it to me. What sense that make when I got money to go and spend it somewhere else and ignore the person who done right by me? That ain't in the Bible.

ROSE We ain't talking about what's in the Bible. What sense it make to shop there when she overcharge?

TROY You shop where you want to. I'll do my shopping where the people been good to me.

ROSE Well, I don't think it's right for her to overcharge. That's all I was saying.

BONO Look here . . . I got to get on. Lucille going be raising all kind of hell.

TROY Where you going, nigger? We ain't finished this pint. Come here, finish this pint.

BONO Well, hell, I am . . . if you ever turn the bottle loose.

TROY [*hands him the bottle*] The only thing I say about the A&P is I'm glad Cory got that job down there. Help him take care of his school clothes and things. Gabe done moved out and things getting tight around here. He got that job. . . . He can start to look out for himself.

ROSE Cory done went and got recruited by a college football team.

TROY I told that boy about that football stuff. The white man ain't gonna let him get nowhere with that football. I told him when he first come to me with it. Now you come telling me he done went and got more tied up in it. He ought to go and get recruited in how to fix cars or something where he can make a living.

ROSE He ain't talking about making no living playing football. It's just something the boys in school do. They gonna send a recruiter by to talk to you. He'll tell you he ain't talking about making no living playing football. It's a honor to be recruited.

TROY It ain't gonna get him nowhere. Bono'll tell you that.

BONO If he be like you in the sports . . . he's gonna be alright. Ain't but two men ever played baseball as good as you. That's Babe Ruth and Josh Gibson.[5] Them's the only two men ever hit more home runs than you.

4. The dominant U.S. supermarket chain in the 1950s.

5. Respectively, the most famous white and black hitters of the 20th century. Ruth (1895–1948), who played with the N.Y. Yankees for most of his career (1914–35), held the major-league record for home runs in a season (60) for 34 years, and the lifetime home run record (714) for 39; Gibson (1911–1947; catcher, 1930–46), who played mainly for the Homestead Grays (near Pittsburgh) in the Negro League, was known as "the black Babe Ruth"; it is estimated that in his career he hit more than 800 home runs, 75 of them in a single season.

TROY What it ever get me? Ain't got a pot to piss in or a window to throw it out of.

ROSE Times have changed since you was playing baseball, Troy. That was before the war. Times have changed a lot since then.

TROY How in hell they done changed?

ROSE They got lots of colored boys playing ball now.[6] Baseball and football.

BONO You right about that, Rose. Times have changed, Troy. You just come along too early.

TROY There ought not never have been no time called too early! Now you take that fellow . . . what's that fellow they had playing right field for the Yankees back then? You know who I'm talking about, Bono. Used to play right field for the Yankees.

ROSE Selkirk?[7]

TROY Selkirk! That's it! Man batting .269, understand? .269. What kind of sense that make? I was hitting .432 with thirty-seven home runs! Man batting .269 and playing right field for the Yankees! I saw Josh Gibson's daughter yesterday. She walking around with raggedy shoes on her feet. Now I bet you Selkirk's daughter ain't walking around with raggedy shoes on her feet! I bet you that!

ROSE They got a lot of colored baseball players now. Jackie Robinson was the first. Folks had to wait for Jackie Robinson.

TROY I done seen a hundred niggers play baseball better than Jackie Robinson. Hell, I know some teams Jackie Robinson couldn't even make! What you talking about Jackie Robinson. Jackie Robinson wasn't nobody.[8] I'm talking about if you could play ball then they ought to have let you play. Don't care what color you were. Come telling me I come along too early. If you could play . . . then they ought to have let you play.

[TROY *takes a long drink from the bottle.*]

ROSE You gonna drink yourself to death. You don't need to be drinking like that.

TROY Death ain't nothing. I done seen him. Done wrassled with him. You can't tell me nothing about death. Death ain't nothing but a fastball on the outside corner. And you know what I'll do to that! Lookee here, Bono . . . am I lying? You get one of them fastballs, about waist high, over the outside corner of the plate where you can get the meat of the bat on it . . . and good god! You can kiss it goodbye. Now, am I lying?

BONO Naw, you telling the truth there. I seen you do it.

TROY If I'm lying . . . that 450 feet worth of lying![9] [*Pause*] That's all death is to me. A fastball on the outside corner.

6. Until 1947, when Jackie Robinson (1919–1972) began playing for the Brooklyn Dodgers, no "colored" athletes had been allowed to play in baseball's minor or major leagues since the late 19th century. Initially, professional football had a few black players (1920–34), but none subsequently played for the National Football League until 1946, when four were signed.

7. George Selkirk (1908–1987), who became the Yankee's right fielder in 1935 after Ruth retired; he batted .269 in 1940 (his average was above .300 five times in the 1930s).

8. Robinson was in fact Rookie of the Year, a six-time All-Star, and the 1949 National League MVP, outstanding as both a fielder and a hitter with a career batting average of .311.

9. A ball hit this distance would be an impressive home run in any ballpark (at its deepest, no fence is more than 435 feet from home plate).

ROSE I don't know why you want to get on talking about death.

TROY Ain't nothing wrong with talking about death. That's part of life. Everybody gonna die. You gonna die, I'm gonna die. Bono's gonna die. Hell, we all gonna die.

ROSE But you ain't got to talk about it. I don't like to talk about it.

TROY You the one brought it up. Me and Bono was talking about baseball . . . you tell me I'm gonna drink myself to death. Ain't that right, Bono? You know I don't drink this but one night out of the week. That's Friday night. I'm gonna drink just enough to where I can handle it. Then I cuts it loose. I leave it alone. So don't you worry about me drinking myself to death. 'Cause I ain't worried about Death. I done seen him. I done wrestled with him.

Look here, Bono . . . I looked up one day and Death was marching straight at me. Like Soldiers on Parade! The Army of Death was marching straight at me. The middle of July, 1941. It got real cold just like it be winter. It seem like Death himself reached out and touched me on the shoulder. He touch me just like I touch you. I got cold as ice and Death standing there grinning at me.

ROSE Troy, why don't you hush that talk.

TROY I say . . . What you want, Mr. Death? You be wanting me? You done brought your army to be getting me? I looked him dead in the eye. I wasn't fearing nothing. I was ready to tangle. Just like I'm ready to tangle now. The Bible say be ever vigilant.[1] That's why I don't get but so drunk. I got to keep watch.

ROSE Troy was right down there in Mercy Hospital. You remember he had pneumonia? Laying there with a fever talking plumb out of his head.

TROY Death standing there staring at me . . . carrying that sickle in his hand. Finally he say, "You want bound over for another year?" See, just like that . . . "You want bound over[2] for another year?" I told him, "Bound over hell! Let's settle this now!"

It seem like he kinda fell back when I said that, and all the cold went out of me. I reached down and grabbed that sickle and threw it just as far as I could throw it . . . and me and him commenced to wrestling.

We wrestled for three days and three nights. I can't say where I found the strength from. Every time it seemed like he was gonna get the best of me, I'd reach way down deep inside myself and find the strength to do him one better.

ROSE Every time Troy tell that story he find different ways to tell it. Different things to make up about it.

TROY I ain't making up nothing. I'm telling you the facts of what happened. I wrestled with Death for three days and three nights and I'm standing here to tell you about it.

[*Pause.*]

Alright. At the end of the third night we done weakened each other to where we can't hardly move. Death stood up, throwed on his robe . . . had him a white robe with a hood on it. He throwed on that robe and went off

1. "Be sober, be vigilant; because your adversary the devil, as a roaring lion, walketh about, seeking whom he may devour" (1 Peter 5.8).

2. That is, agreeing to one more year of servitude, as if he were a sharecropper.

to look for his sickle. Say, "I'll be back." Just like that. "I'll be back." I told him, say, "Yeah, but . . . you gonna have to find me!" I wasn't no fool. I wasn't going looking for him. Death ain't nothing to play with. And I know he's gonna get me. I know I got to join his army . . . his camp followers. But as long as I keep my strength and see him coming . . . as long as I keep up my vigilance . . . he's gonna have to fight to get me. I ain't going easy.

BONO Well, look here, since you got to keep up your vigilance . . . let me have the bottle.

TROY Aw hell, I shouldn't have told you that part. I should have left out that part.

ROSE Troy be talking that stuff and half the time don't even know what he be talking about.

TROY Bono know me better than that.

BONO That's right. I know you. I know you got some Uncle Remus[3] in your blood. You got more stories than the devil got sinners.

TROY Aw hell, I done seen him too! Done talked with the devil.

ROSE Troy, don't nobody wanna be hearing all that stuff.

[LYONS *enters the yard from the street. Thirty-four years old,* TROY'S *son by a previous marriage, he sports a neatly trimmed goatee, sport coat, white shirt, tieless and buttoned at the collar. Though he fancies himself a musician, he is more caught up in the rituals and "idea" of being a musician than in the actual practice of the music. He has come to borrow money from* TROY, *and while he knows he will be successful, he is uncertain as to what extent his lifestyle will be held up to scrutiny and ridicule.*]

LYONS Hey, Pop.

TROY What you come "Hey, Popping" me for?

LYONS How you doing, Rose?

[*He kisses her.*]

Mr. Bono. How you doing?

BONO Hey, Lyons . . . how you been?

TROY He must have been doing alright. I ain't seen him around here last week.

ROSE Troy, leave your boy alone. He come by to see you and you wanna start all that nonsense.

TROY I ain't bothering Lyons. [*Offers him the bottle.*] Here . . . get you a drink. We got an understanding. I know why he come by to see me and he know I know.

LYONS Come on, Pop . . . I just stopped by to say hi . . . see how you was doing.

TROY You ain't stopped by yesterday.

ROSE You gonna stay for supper, Lyons? I got some chicken cooking in the oven.

LYONS No, Rose . . . thanks. I was just in the neighborhood and thought I'd stop by for a minute.

TROY You was in the neighborhood alright, nigger. You telling the truth there. You was in the neighborhood cause it's my payday.

LYONS Well, hell, since you mentioned it . . . let me have ten dollars.

3. The fictional narrator of popular black folktales compiled by the white humorist Joel Chandler Harris, beginning with *Uncle Remus: His Songs and Sayings* (1881).

TROY I'll be damned! I'll die and go to hell and play blackjack with the devil before I give you ten dollars.

BONO That's what I wanna know about . . . that devil you done seen.

LYONS What . . . Pop done seen the devil? You too much, Pops.

TROY Yeah, I done seen him. Talked to him too!

ROSE You ain't seen no devil. I done told you that man ain't had nothing to do with the devil. Anything you can't understand, you want to call it the devil.

TROY Look here, Bono . . . I went down to see Hertzberger about some furniture. Got three rooms for two-ninety-eight. That what it say on the radio. "Three rooms . . . two-ninety-eight." Even made up a little song about it. Go down there . . . man tell me I can't get no credit. I'm working every day and can't get no credit. What to do? I got an empty house with some raggedy furniture in it. Cory ain't got no bed. He's sleeping on a pile of rags on the floor. Working every day and can't get no credit. Come back here—Rose'll tell you—madder than hell. Sit down . . . try to figure what I'm gonna do. Come a knock on the door. Ain't been living here but three days. Who know I'm here? Open the door . . . devil standing there bigger than life. White fellow . . . got on good clothes and everything. Standing there with a clipboard in his hand. I ain't had to say nothing. First words come out of his mouth was . . . "I understand you need some furniture and can't get no credit." I liked to fell over. He say "I'll give you all the credit you want, but you got to pay the interest on it." I told him, "Give me three rooms worth and charge whatever you want." Next day a truck pulled up here and two men unloaded them three rooms. Man what drove the truck give me a book. Say send ten dollars, first of every month to the address in the book and everything will be alright. Say if I miss a payment the devil was coming back and it'll be hell to pay. That was fifteen years ago. To this day . . . the first of the month I send my ten dollars, Rose'll tell you.

ROSE Troy lying.

TROY I ain't never seen that man since. Now you tell me who else that could have been but the devil? I ain't sold my soul or nothing like that, you understand. Naw, I wouldn't have truck with the devil about nothing like that. I got my furniture and pays my ten dollars the first of the month just like clockwork.

BONO How long you say you been paying this ten dollars a month?

TROY Fifteen years!

BONO Hell, ain't you finished paying for it yet? How much the man done charged you?

TROY Aw hell, I done paid for it. I done paid for it ten times over! The fact is I'm scared to stop paying it.

ROSE Troy lying. We got that furniture from Mr. Glickman. He ain't paying no ten dollars a month to nobody.

TROY Aw hell, woman. Bono know I ain't that big a fool.

LYONS I was just getting ready to say . . . I know where there's a bridge for sale.[4]

4. To sell the Brooklyn Bridge proverbially demonstrates both the seller's powers of persuasion and the buyer's gullibility (a couple of turn-of-the-century confidence men did manage to pull off this swindle).

TROY Look here, I'll tell you this . . . it don't matter to me if he was the devil. It don't matter if the devil give credit. Somebody has got to give it.

ROSE It ought to matter. You going around talking about having truck with the devil . . . God's the one you gonna have to answer to. He's the one gonna be at the Judgment.

LYONS Yeah, well, look here, Pop . . . let me have that ten dollars. I'll give it back to you. Bonnie got a job working at the hospital.

TROY What I tell you, Bono? The only time I see this nigger is when he wants something. That's the only time I see him.

LYONS Come on, Pop, Mr. Bono don't want to hear all that. Let me have the ten dollars. I told you Bonnie working.

TROY What that mean to me? "Bonnie working." I don't care if she working. Go ask her for the ten dollars if she working. Talking about "Bonnie working." Why ain't you working?

LYONS Aw, Pop, you know I can't find no decent job. Where am I gonna get a job at? You know I can't get no job.

TROY I told you I know some people down there. I can get you on the rubbish if you want to work. I told you that the last time you came by here asking me for something.

LYONS Naw, Pop . . . thanks. That ain't for me. I don't wanna be carrying nobody's rubbish. I don't wanna be punching nobody's time clock.

TROY What's the matter, you too good to carry people's rubbish? Where you think that ten dollars you talking about come from? I'm just supposed to haul people's rubbish and give my money to you cause you too lazy to work. You too lazy to work and wanna know why you ain't got what I got.

ROSE What hospital Bonnie working at? Mercy?

LYONS She's down at Passavant working in the laundry.

TROY I ain't got nothing as it is. I give you that ten dollars and I got to eat beans the rest of the week. Naw . . . you ain't getting no ten dollars here.

LYONS You ain't got to be eating no beans. I don't know why you wanna say that.

TROY I ain't got no extra money. Gabe done moved over to Miss Pearl's paying her the rent and things done got tight around here. I can't afford to be giving you every payday.

LYONS I ain't asked you to give me nothing. I asked you to loan me ten dollars. I know you got ten dollars.

TROY Yeah, I got it. You know why I got it? Cause I don't throw my money away out there in the streets. You living the fast life . . . wanna be a musician . . . running around in them clubs and things . . . then, you learn to take care of yourself. You ain't gonna find me going and asking nobody for nothing. I done spent too many years without.

LYONS You and me is two different people, Pop.

TROY I done learned my mistake and learned to do what's right by it. You still trying to get something for nothing. Life don't owe you nothing. You owe it to yourself. Ask Bono. He'll tell you I'm right.

LYONS You got your way of dealing with the world . . . I got mine. The only thing that matters to me is the music.

TROY Yeah, I can see that! It don't matter how you gonna eat . . . where your next dollar is coming from. You telling the truth there.

LYONS I know I got to eat. But I got to live too. I need something that gonna help me to get out of the bed in the morning. Make me feel like I belong in the world. I don't bother nobody. I just stay with my music cause that's the only way I can find to live in the world. Otherwise there ain't no telling what I might do. Now I don't come criticizing you and how you live. I just come by to ask you for ten dollars. I don't wanna hear all that about how I live.

TROY Boy, your mama did a hell of a job raising you.

LYONS You can't change me, Pop. I'm thirty-four years old. If you wanted to change me, you should have been there when I was growing up. I come by to see you . . . ask for ten dollars and you want to talk about how I was raised. You don't know nothing about how I was raised.

ROSE Let the boy have ten dollars, Troy.

TROY [*to* LYONS] What the hell you looking at me for? I ain't got no ten dollars. You know what I do with my money. [*To* ROSE] Give him ten dollars if you want him to have it.

ROSE I will. Just as soon as you turn it loose.

TROY [*handing* ROSE *the money*] There it is. Seventy-six dollars and forty-two cents. You see this, Bono? Now, I ain't gonna get but six of that back.

ROSE You ought to stop telling that lie. Here, Lyons.

[*She hands him the money.*]

LYONS Thanks, Rose. Look . . . I got to run . . . I'll see you later.

TROY Wait a minute. You gonna say, "Thanks, Rose," and ain't gonna look to see where she got that ten dollars from? See how they do me, Bono?

LYONS I know she got it from you, Pop. Thanks. I'll give it back to you.

TROY There he go telling another lie. Time I see that ten dollars . . . he'll be owing me thirty more.

LYONS See you, Mr. Bono.

BONO Take care, Lyons!

LYONS Thanks, Pop. I'll see you again.

[LYONS *exits the yard.*]

TROY I don't know why he don't go and get him a decent job and take care of that woman he got.

BONO He'll be alright, Troy. The boy is still young.

TROY The *boy* is thirty-four years old.

ROSE Let's not get off into all that.

BONO Look here . . . I got to be going. I got to be getting on. Lucille gonna be waiting.

TROY [*puts his arm around* ROSE] See this woman, Bono? I love this woman. I love this woman so much it hurts. I love her so much . . . I done run out of ways of loving her. So I got to go back to basics. Don't you come by my house Monday morning talking about time to go to work . . . 'cause I'm still gonna be stroking!

ROSE Troy! Stop it now!

BONO I ain't paying him no mind, Rose. That ain't nothing but gin-talk. Go on, Troy. I'll see you Monday.

TROY Don't you come by my house, nigger! I done told you what I'm gonna be doing.

[*The lights go down to black.*]

1.2

The lights come up on ROSE *hanging up clothes. She hums and sings softly to herself. It is the following morning.*

ROSE [*sings*]
Jesus, be a fence all around me every day
Jesus, I want you to protect me as I travel on my way.
Jesus, be a fence all around me every day.[5]

[TROY *enters from the house.*]

ROSE [*continued*]

Jesus, I want you to protect me
As I travel on my way.

[*To* TROY] 'Morning. You ready for breakfast? I can fix it soon as I finish hanging up these clothes?

TROY I got the coffee on. That'll be alright. I'll just drink some of that this morning.

ROSE That 651 hit yesterday.[6] That's the second time this month. Miss Pearl hit for a dollar . . . seem like those that need the least always get lucky. Poor folks can't get nothing.

TROY Them numbers don't know nobody. I don't know why you fool with them. You and Lyons both.

ROSE It's something to do.

TROY You ain't doing nothing but throwing your money away.

ROSE Troy, you know I don't play foolishly. I just play a nickel here and a nickel there.

TROY That's two nickels you done thrown away.

ROSE Now I hit sometimes . . . that makes up for it. It always comes in handy when I do hit. I don't hear you complaining then.

TROY I ain't complaining now. I just say it's foolish. Trying to guess out of six hundred ways which way the number gonna come. If I had all the money niggers, these Negroes, throw away on numbers for one week—just one week—I'd be a rich man.

ROSE Well, you wishing and calling it foolish ain't gonna stop folks from playing numbers. That's one thing for sure. Besides . . . some good things come from playing numbers. Look where Pope done bought him that restaurant off of numbers.

TROY I can't stand niggers like that. Man ain't had two dimes to rub together. He walking around with his shoes all run over bumming money for cigarettes. Alright. Got lucky there and hit the numbers . . .

ROSE Troy, I know all about it.

TROY Had good sense, I'll say that for him. He ain't throwed his money away. I seen niggers hit the numbers and go through two thousand dollars in four days. Man brought him that restaurant down there . . . fixed it up real nice . . . and then didn't want nobody to come in it! A Negro go in there

5. Traditional gospel song.
6. A reference to playing the numbers, a form of illegal gambling that was popular before the advent of legal state-run lotteries.

and can't get no kind of service. I seen a white fellow come in there and order a bowl of stew. Pope picked all the meat out the pot for him. Man ain't had nothing but a bowl of meat! Negro come behind him and ain't got nothing but the potatoes and carrots. Talking about what numbers do for people, you picked a wrong example. Ain't done nothing but make a worser fool out of him than he was before.

ROSE Troy, you ought to stop worrying about what happened at work yesterday.

TROY I ain't worried. Just told me to be down there at the Commissioner's office on Friday. Everybody think they gonna fire me. I ain't worried about them firing me. You ain't got to worry about that.

[*Pause.*]

Where's Cory? Cory in the house? [*Calls.*] Cory?

ROSE He gone out.

TROY Out, huh? He gone out cause he know I want him to help me with this fence. I know how he is. That boy scared of work.

[GABRIEL *enters. He comes halfway down the alley and, hearing Troy's voice, stops.*]

TROY [*continues*] He ain't done a lick of work in his life.

ROSE He had to go to football practice. Coach wanted them to get in a little extra practice before the season start.

TROY I got his practice . . . running out of here before he get his chores done.

ROSE Troy, what is wrong with you this morning? Don't nothing set right with you. Go on back in there and go to bed . . . get up on the other side.

TROY Why something got to be wrong with me? I ain't said nothing wrong with me.

ROSE You got something to say about everything. First it's the numbers . . . then it's the way the man runs his restaurant . . . then you done got on Cory. What's it gonna be next? Take a look up there and see if the weather suits you . . . or is it gonna be how you gonna put up the fence with the clothes hanging in the yard.

TROY You hit the nail on the head then.

ROSE I know you like I know the back of my hand. Go on in there and get you some coffee . . . see if that straighten you up. Cause you ain't right this morning.

[TROY *starts into the house and sees* GABRIEL. GABRIEL *starts singing.* TROY*'s brother, he is seven years younger than* TROY. *Injured in World War II, he has a metal plate in his head. He carries an old trumpet tied around his waist and believes with every fiber of his being that he is the Archangel Gabriel. He carries a chipped basket*[7] *with an assortment of discarded fruits and vegetables he has picked up in the strip district and which he attempts to sell.*]

GABRIEL [*singing*]

Yes, ma'am, I got plums
You ask me how I sell them
Oh ten cents apiece

7. That is, a chip basket, made from roughly joined strips of split wood.

Three for a quarter
Come and buy now
'Cause I'm here today
And tomorrow I'll be gone

[GABRIEL *enters.*]

Hey, Rose!

ROSE How you doing, Gabe?

GABRIEL There's Troy . . . Hey, Troy!

TROY Hey, Gabe.

[*Exit into kitchen.*]

ROSE [*to* GABRIEL] What you got there?

GABRIEL You know what I got, Rose. I got fruits and vegetables.

ROSE [*looking in basket*] Where's all these plums you talking about?

GABRIEL I ain't got no plums today, Rose. I was just singing that. Have some tomorrow. Put me in a big order for plums. Have enough plums tomorrow for St. Peter and everybody.

[TROY *reenters from kitchen, crosses to steps.*]

[*To* ROSE] Troy's mad at me.

TROY I ain't mad at you. What I got to be mad at you about? You ain't done nothing to me.

GABRIEL I just moved over to Miss Pearl's to keep out from in your way. I ain't mean no harm by it.

TROY Who said anything about that? I ain't said anything about that.

GABRIEL You ain't mad at me, is you?

TROY Naw . . . I ain't mad at you, Gabe. If I was mad at you I'd tell you about it.

GABRIEL Got me two rooms. In the basement. Got my own door too. Wanna see my key? [*He holds up a key.*] That's my own key! Ain't nobody else got a key like that. That's my key! My two rooms!

TROY Well, that's good, Gabe. You got your own key . . . that's good.

ROSE You hungry, Gabe? I was just fixing to cook Troy his breakfast.

GABRIEL I'll take some biscuits. You got some biscuits? Did you know when I was in heaven . . . every morning me and St. Peter would sit down by the gate and eat some big fat biscuits? Oh, yeah! We had us a good time. We'd sit there and eat us them biscuits and then St. Peter would go off to sleep and tell me to wake him up when it's time to open the gates for the judgment.

ROSE Well, come on . . . I'll make up a batch of biscuits.

[ROSE *exits into the house.*]

GABRIEL Troy . . . St. Peter got your name in the book. I seen it. It say . . . Troy Maxson. I say . . . I know him! He got the same name like what I got. That's my brother!

TROY How many times you gonna tell me that, Gabe?

GABRIEL Ain't got my name in the book. Don't have to have my name. I done died and went to heaven. He got your name though. One morning St. Peter was looking at his book . . . marking it up for the judgment . . . and he let me see your name. Got it in there under M. Got Rose's name . . . I ain't seen it like I seen yours . . . but I know it's in there. He got a great big book. Got everybody's name what was ever been born. That's what he told me. But I seen your name. Seen it with my own eyes.

TROY Go on in the house there. Rose going to fix you something to eat.

GABRIEL Oh, I ain't hungry. I done had breakfast with Aunt Jemimah.[8] She come by and cooked me up a whole mess of flapjacks. Remember how we used to eat them flapjacks?

TROY Go on in the house and get you something to eat now.

GABRIEL I got to go sell my plums. I done sold some tomatoes. Got me two quarters. Wanna see? [*He shows* TROY *his quarters.*] I'm gonna save them and buy me a new horn so St. Peter can hear me when it's time to open the gates.

[GABRIEL *stops suddenly. Listens.*]

Hear that? That's the hellhounds. I got to chase them out of here. Go on get out of here! Get out!

[GABRIEL *exits singing.*]

Better get ready for the judgment
Better get ready for the judgment
My Lord is coming down

[ROSE *enters from the house.*]

TROY He gone off somewhere.

GABRIEL [*offstage*]

Better get ready for the judgment
Better get ready for the judgment morning
Better get ready for the judgment
My God is coming down

ROSE He ain't eating right. Miss Pearl say she can't get him to eat nothing.

TROY What you want me to do about it, Rose? I done did everything I can for the man. I can't make him get well. Man got half his head blown away . . . what you expect?

ROSE Seem like something ought to be done to help him.

TROY Man don't bother nobody. He just mixed up from that metal plate he got in his head. Ain't no sense for him to go back into the hospital.

ROSE Least he be eating right. They can help him take care of himself.

TROY Don't nobody wanna be locked up, Rose. What you wanna lock him up for? Man go over there and fight the war . . . messin' around with them Japs, get half his head blown off . . . and they give him a lousy three thousand dollars. And I had to swoop down on that.

ROSE Is you fixing to go into that again?

TROY That's the only way I got a roof over my head . . . cause of that metal plate.

ROSE Ain't no sense you blaming yourself for nothing. Gabe wasn't in no condition to manage that money. You done what was right by him. Can't nobody say you ain't done what was right by him. Look how long you took

8. Stereotypical "mammy" from a minstrel song; in 1893 the name and image were trademarked by a pancake mix company, which for decades hired women to portray the character.

care of him . . . till he wanted to have his own place and moved over there with Miss Pearl.

TROY That ain't what I'm saying, woman! I'm just stating the facts. If my brother didn't have that metal plate in his head . . . I wouldn't have a pot to piss in or a window to throw it out of. And I'm fifty-three years old. Now see if you can understand that!

[TROY *gets up from the porch and starts to exit the yard.*]

ROSE Where you going off to? You been running out of here every Saturday for weeks. I thought you was gonna work on this fence?

TROY I'm gonna walk down to Taylors'. Listen to the ball game. I'll be back in a bit. I'll work on it when I get back.

[*He exits the yard. The lights go to black.*]

1.3

The lights come up on the yard. It is four hours later. ROSE *is taking down the clothes from the line.* CORY *enters carrying his football equipment.*

ROSE Your daddy like to had a fit with you running out of here this morning without doing your chores.

CORY I told you I had to go to practice.

ROSE He say you were supposed to help him with this fence.

CORY He been saying that the last four or five Saturdays, and then he don't never do nothing, but go down to Taylors'. Did you tell him about the recruiter?

ROSE Yeah, I told him.

CORY What he say?

ROSE He ain't said nothing too much. You get in there and get started on your chores before he gets back. Go on and scrub down them steps before he gets back here hollering and carrying on.

CORY I'm hungry. What you got to eat, Mama?

ROSE Go on and get started on your chores. I got some meat loaf in there. Go on and make you a sandwich . . . and don't leave no mess in there.

[CORY *exits into the house,* ROSE *continues to take down the clothes.* TROY *enters the yard and sneaks up and grabs her from behind.*]

Troy! Go on, now. You liked to scared me to death. What was the score of the game? Lucille had me on the phone and I couldn't keep up with it.

TROY What I care about the game? Come here, woman. [*He tries to kiss her.*]

ROSE I thought you went down Taylors' to listen to the game. Go on, Troy! You supposed to be putting up this fence.

TROY [*attempting to kiss her again.*] I'll put it up when I finish with what is at hand.

ROSE Go on, Troy. I ain't studying you.[9]

TROY [*chasing after her*] I'm studying you . . . fixing to do my homework!

ROSE Troy, you better leave me alone.

TROY Where's Cory? That boy brought his butt home yet?

ROSE He's in the house doing his chores.

TROY [*calling*] Cory! Get your butt out here, boy!

9. That is, paying any attention to you.

[ROSE *exits into the house with the laundry.* TROY *goes over to the pile of wood, picks up a board, and starts sawing.* CORY *enters from the house.*]

TROY You just now coming in here from leaving this morning?

CORY Yeah, I had to go to football practice.

TROY Yeah, what?

CORY Yessir.

TROY I ain't but two seconds off you noway. The garbage sitting in there overflowing . . . you ain't done none of your chores . . . and you come in here talking about "Yeah."

CORY I was just getting ready to do my chores now, Pop . . .

TROY Your first chore is to help me with this fence on Saturday. Everything else come after that. Now get that saw and cut them boards.

[CORY *takes the saw and begins cutting the boards.* TROY *continues working. There is a long pause.*]

CORY Hey, Pop . . . why don't you buy a TV?

TROY What I want with a TV? What I want one of them for?

CORY Everybody got one. Earl, Ba Bra . . . Jesse!

TROY I ain't asked you who had one. I say what I want with one?

CORY So you can watch it. They got lots of things on TV. Baseball games and everything. We could watch the World Series.

TROY Yeah . . . and how much this TV cost?

CORY I don't know. They got them on sale for around two hundred dollars.[1]

TROY Two hundred dollars, huh?

CORY That ain't that much, Pop.

TROY Naw, it's just two hundred dollars. See that roof you got over your head at night? Let me tell you something about that roof. It's been over ten years since that roof was last tarred. See now . . . the snow come this winter and sit up there on that roof like it is . . . and it's gonna seep inside. It's just gonna be a little bit . . . ain't gonna hardly notice it. Then the next thing you know, it's gonna be leaking all over the house. Then the wood rot from all that water and you gonna need a whole new roof. Now, how much you think it cost to get that roof tarred?

CORY I don't know.

TROY Two hundred and sixty-four dollars . . . cash money. While you thinking about a TV, I got to be thinking about the roof . . . and whatever else go wrong around here. Now if you had two hundred dollars, what would you do . . . fix the roof or buy a TV?

CORY I'd buy a TV. Then when the roof started to leak . . . when it needed fixing . . . I'd fix it.

TROY Where you gonna get the money from? You done spent it for a TV. You gonna sit up and watch the water run all over your brand new TV.

CORY Aw, Pop. You got money. I know you do.

TROY Where I got it at, huh?

CORY You got it in the bank.

TROY You wanna see my bankbook? You wanna see that seventy-three dollars and twenty-two cents I got sitting up in there?

CORY You ain't got to pay for it all at one time. You can put a down payment on it and carry it on home with you.

1. Equivalent to about $1,500 in 2008.

TROY Not me. I ain't gonna owe nobody nothing if I can help it. Miss a payment and they come and snatch it right out your house. Then what you got? Now, soon as I get two hundred dollars clear, then I'll buy a TV. Right now, as soon as I get two hundred and sixty-four dollars, I'm gonna have this roof tarred.

CORY Aw . . . Pop!

TROY You go on and get you two hundred dollars and buy one if ya want it. I got better things to do with my money.

CORY I can't get no two hundred dollars. I ain't never seen two hundred dollars.

TROY I'll tell you what . . . you get you a hundred dollars and I'll put the other hundred with it.

CORY Alright, I'm gonna show you.

TROY You gonna show me how you can cut them boards right now.

[CORY *begins to cut the boards. There is a long pause.*]

CORY The Pirates won today. That makes five in a row.

TROY I ain't thinking about the Pirates. Got an all-white team. Got that boy . . . that Puerto Rican boy . . . Clemente.[2] Don't even half-play him. That boy could be something if they give him a chance. Play him one day and sit him on the bench the next.

CORY He gets a lot of chances to play.

TROY I'm talking about playing regular. Playing every day so you can get your timing. That's what I'm talking about.

CORY They got some white guys on the team that don't play every day. You can't play everybody at the same time.

TROY If they got a white fellow sitting on the bench . . . you can bet your last dollar he can't play! The colored guy got to be twice as good before he get on the team. That's why I don't want you to get all tied up in them sports. Man on the team and what it get him? They got colored on the team and don't use them. Same as not having them. All them teams the same.

CORY The Braves got Hank Aaron and Wes Covington.[3] Hank Aaron hit two home runs today. That makes forty-three.

TROY Hank Aaron ain't nobody. That's what you supposed to do. That's how you supposed to play the game. Ain't nothing to it. It's just a matter of timing . . . getting the right follow-through. Hell, I can hit forty-three home runs right now!

CORY Not off no major-league pitching, you couldn't.

TROY We had better pitching in the Negro leagues. I hit seven home runs off of Satchel Paige.[4] You can't get no better than that!

2. Roberto Clemente (1934–1972), a Hall of Fame outfielder who played for the Pittsburgh Pirates between 1955 and his death in a plane crash; he was a twelve-time All-Star and four-time National League batting champion. He played in 111 (of 162) games in 1957.

3. Aaron (b. 1934), who spent all but the last two years of his major-league career (1954–76) with the Milwaukee (later Atlanta) Braves, was one of the greatest baseball players of all time; his best-known achievement was breaking Ruth's lifetime home run record, eventually hitting 755; in 1957 he hit 44 home runs. Covington (b. 1932), who played for the Braves (1956–61) and five other teams (1961–66), was integral to the Braves' 1957 run to the World Series.

4. The legendary Negro League pitcher (1906–1982); he began playing in the mid-1920s, and between 1948 and 1965 played for several major-league teams.

CORY Sandy Koufax.[5] He's leading the league in strikeouts.

TROY I ain't thinking of no Sandy Koufax.

CORY You got Warren Spahn and Lew Burdette.[6] I bet you couldn't hit no home runs off of Warren Spahn.

TROY I'm through with it now. You go on and cut them boards. [*Pause*] Your mama tell me you done got recruited by a college football team? Is that right?

CORY Yeah. Coach Zellman say the recruiter gonna be coming by to talk to you. Get you to sign the permission papers.

TROY I thought you supposed to be working down there at the A&P. Ain't you suppose to be working down there after school?

CORY Mr. Stawicki say he gonna hold my job for me until after the football season. Say starting next week I can work weekends.

TROY I thought we had an understanding about this football stuff? You suppose to keep up with your chores and hold that job down at the A&P. Ain't been around here all day on a Saturday. Ain't none of your chores done . . . and now you telling me you done quit your job.

CORY I'm gonna be working weekends.

TROY You damn right you are! And ain't no need for nobody coming around here to talk to me about signing nothing.

CORY Hey, Pop . . . you can't do that. He's coming all the way from North Carolina.

TROY I don't care where he coming from. The white man ain't gonna let you get nowhere with that football noway. You go on and get your book-learning so you can work yourself up in that A&P or learn how to fix cars or build houses or something, get you a trade. That way you have something can't nobody take away from you. You go on and learn how to put your hands to some good use. Besides hauling people's garbage.

CORY I get good grades, Pop. That's why the recruiter wants to talk with you. You got to keep up your grades to get recruited. This way I'll be going to college. I'll get a chance . . .

TROY First you gonna get your butt down there to the A&P and get your job back.

CORY Mr. Stawicki done already hired somebody else cause I told him I was playing football.

TROY You a bigger fool than I thought . . . to let somebody take away your job so you can play some football. Where you gonna get your money to take out your girlfriend and whatnot? What kind of foolishness is that to let somebody take away your job?

CORY I'm still gonna be working weekends.

TROY Naw . . . naw. You getting your butt out of here and finding you another job.

5. A Hall of Fame pitcher (b. 1935), for the Brooklyn (later Los Angeles) Dodgers (1955–66).

6. The Braves' left-handed and right-handed pitching aces in 1957. Spahn (1921–2003), a Hall of Famer, played all but the final year of his career (1942–65) with the Boston (later Milwaukee) Braves; Burdette (1926–2007), the MVP of the 1957 World Series, played mainly for the Braves (1951–63) but for four other teams as well (1950, 1963–67).

CORY Come on, Pop! I got to practice. I can't work after school and play football too. The team needs me. That's what Coach Zellman say . . .

TROY I don't care what nobody else say. I'm the boss . . . you understand? I'm the boss around here. I do the only saying what counts.

CORY Come on, Pop!

TROY I asked you . . . did you understand?

CORY Yeah . . .

TROY What?!

CORY Yessir.

TROY You go on down there to that A&P and see if you can get your job back. If you can't do both . . . then you quit the football team. You've got to take the crookeds with the straights.

CORY Yessir. [*Pause*] Can I ask you a question?

TROY What the hell you wanna ask me? Mr. Stawicki the one you got the questions for.

CORY How come you ain't never liked me?

TROY Liked you? Who the hell say I got to like you? What law is there say I got to like you? Wanna stand up in my face and ask a damn fool-ass question like that. Talking about liking somebody. Come here, boy, when I talk to you.

[CORY *comes over to where* TROY *is working. He stands slouched over and* TROY *shoves him on his shoulder.*]

Straighten up, goddammit! I asked you a question . . . what law is there say I got to like you?

CORY None.

TROY Well, alright then! Don't you eat every day? [*Pause*] Answer me when I talk to you! Don't you eat every day?

CORY Yeah.

TROY Nigger, as long as you in my house, you put that sir on the end of it when you talk to me!

CORY Yes . . . sir.

TROY You eat every day.

CORY Yessir!

TROY Got a roof over your head.

CORY Yessir!

TROY Got clothes on your back.

CORY Yessir.

TROY Why you think that is?

CORY Cause of you.

TROY Aw, hell I know it's 'cause of me . . . but why do you think that is?

CORY [*hesitant*] Cause you like me.

TROY Like you? I go out of here every morning . . . bust my butt . . . putting up with them crackers[7] every day . . . cause I like you? You about the biggest fool I ever saw. [*Pause*] It's my job. It's my responsibility! You understand that? A man got to take care of his family. You live in my house . . . sleep you behind on my bedclothes . . . fill you belly up with my food . . . cause you my son. You my flesh and blood. Not 'cause I like you! Cause it's

7. Poor whites (derogatory term).

my duty to take care of you. I owe a responsibility to you! Let's get this straight right here . . . before it go along any further . . . I ain't got to like you. Mr. Rand don't give me my money come payday cause he likes me. He gives me cause he owe me. I done give you everything I had to give you. I gave you your life! Me and your mama worked that out between us. And liking your black ass wasn't part of the bargain. Don't you try and go through life worrying about if somebody like you or not. You best be making sure they doing right by you. You understand what I'm saying, boy?

CORY Yessir.

TROY Then get the hell out of my face, and get on down to that A&P.

[ROSE *has been standing behind the screen door for much of the scene. She enters as* CORY *exits.*]

ROSE Why don't you let the boy go ahead and play football, Troy? Ain't no harm in that. He's just trying to be like you with the sports.

TROY I don't want him to be like me! I want him to move as far away from my life as he can get. You the only decent thing that ever happened to me. I wish him that. But I don't wish him a thing else from my life. I decided seventeen years ago that boy wasn't getting involved in no sports. Not after what they did to me in the sports.

ROSE Troy, why don't you admit you was too old to play in the major leagues? For once . . . why don't you admit that?

TROY What do you mean too old? Don't come telling me I was too old. I just wasn't the right color. Hell, I'm fifty-three years old and can do better than Selkirk's .269 right now!

ROSE How's was you gonna play ball when you were over forty? Sometimes I can't get no sense out of you.

TROY I got good sense, woman. I got sense enough not to let my boy get hurt over playing no sports. You been mothering that boy too much. Worried about if people like him.

ROSE Everything that boy do . . . he do for you. He wants you to say "Good job, son." That's all.

TROY Rose, I ain't got time for that. He's alive. He's healthy. He's got to make his own way. I made mine. Ain't nobody gonna hold his hand when he get out there in that world.

ROSE Times have changed from when you was young, Troy. People change. The world's changing around you and you can't even see it.

TROY [*slow, methodical*] Woman . . . I do the best I can do. I come in here every Friday. I carry a sack of potatoes and a bucket of lard. You all line up at the door with your hands out. I give you the lint from my pockets. I give you my sweat and my blood. I ain't got no tears.[8] I done spent them. We go upstairs in that room at night . . . and I fall down on you and try to blast a hole into forever. I get up Monday morning . . . find my lunch on the table. I go out. Make my way. Find my strength to carry me through to the next Friday. [*Pause*] That's all I got, Rose. That's all I got to give. I can't give nothing else.

[TROY *exits into the house. The lights go down to black.*]

8. An allusion to a famous wartime declaration to the British Parliament by Prime Minister Winston Churchill in May 1940: "I have nothing to offer but blood, toil, tears, and sweat."

1.4

It is Friday. Two weeks later. CORY *starts out of the house with his football equipment. The phone rings.*

CORY [*calling*] I got it! [*He answers the phone and stands in the screen door talking.*] Hello? Hey, Jesse. Naw . . . I was just getting ready to leave now.

ROSE [*calling*] Cory!

CORY I told you, man, them spikes is all tore up. You can use them if you want, but they ain't no good. Earl got some spikes.

ROSE [*calling*] Cory!

CORY [*calling to* ROSE] Mam? I'm talking to Jesse. [*Into phone*] When she say that? [*Pause*] Aw, you lying, man. I'm gonna tell her you said that.

ROSE [*calling*] Cory, don't you go nowhere!

CORY I got to go to the game, Ma! [*Into the phone*] Yeah, hey, look, I'll talk to you later. Yeah, I'll meet you over Earl's house. Later. Bye, Ma.

[CORY *exists the house and starts out the yard.*]

ROSE Cory, where you going off to? You got that stuff all pulled out and thrown all over your room.

CORY [*in the yard*] I was looking for my spikes. Jesse wanted to borrow my spikes.

ROSE Get up there and get that cleaned up before your daddy get back in here.

CORY I got to go to the game! I'll clean it up *when I get back.*

[CORY *exits.*]

ROSE That's all he need to do is see that room all messed up.

[ROSE *exits into the house.* TROY *and* BONO *enter the yard.* TROY *is dressed in clothes other than his work clothes.*]

BONO He told him the same thing he told you. Take it to the union.

TROY Brownie ain't got that much sense. Man wasn't thinking about nothing. He wait until I confront them on it . . . then he wanna come crying seniority. [*Calls*] Hey, Rose!

BONO I wish I could have seen Mr. Rand's face when he told you.

TROY He couldn't get it out of his mouth! Liked to bit his tongue! When they called me down there to the Commissioner's office . . . he thought they was gonna fire me. Like everybody else.

BONO I didn't think they was gonna fire you. I thought they was gonna put you on the warning paper.

TROY Hey, Rose! [*To* BONO] Yeah, Mr. Rand like to bit his tongue.

[TROY *breaks the seal on the bottle, takes a drink, and hands it to* BONO.]

BONO I see you run right down to Taylors' and told that Alberta gal.

TROY [*calling*] Hey Rose! [*To* BONO] I told everybody. Hey, Rose! I went down there to cash my check.

ROSE [*entering from the house*] Hush all that hollering, man! I know you out here. What they say down there at the Commissioner's office?

TROY You supposed to come when I call you, woman. Bono'll tell you that. [*To* BONO] Don't Lucille come when you call her?

ROSE Man, hush your mouth. I ain't no dog . . . talk about "come when you call me."

TROY [*puts his arm around* **ROSE**] You hear this, Bono? I had me an old dog used to get uppity like that. You say, "C'mere, Blue!" . . . and he just lay there and look at you. End up getting a stick and chasing him away trying to make him come.

ROSE I ain't studying you and your dog. I remember you used to sing that old song.

TROY [*he sings*]

> Hear it ring! Hear it ring!
> I had a dog his name was Blue.[9]

ROSE Don't nobody wanna hear you sing that old song.

TROY [*sings*] You know Blue was mighty true.

ROSE Used to have Cory running around here singing that song.

BONO Hell, I remember that song myself.

TROY [*sings*]

> You know Blue was a good old dog.
> Blue treed a possum in a hollow log.

That was my daddy's song. My daddy made up that song.

ROSE I don't care who made it up. Don't nobody wanna hear you sing it.

TROY [*makes a song like calling a dog*] Come here, woman.

ROSE You come in here carrying on, I reckon they ain't fired you. What they say down there at the Commissioner's office?

TROY Look here, Rose . . . Mr. Rand called me into his office today when I got back from talking to them people down there . . . it come from up top . . . he called me in and told me they was making me a driver.

ROSE Troy, you kidding!

TROY No I ain't. Ask Bono.

ROSE Well, that's great, Troy. Now you don't have to hassle them people no more.

[**LYONS** *enters from the street.*]

TROY Aw hell, I wasn't looking to see you today. I thought you was in jail. Got it all over the front page of the *Courier*[1] about them raiding Sefus' place . . . where you be hanging out with all them thugs.

LYONS Hey, Pop . . . that ain't got nothing to do with me. I don't go down there gambling. I go down there to sit in with the band. I ain't got nothing to do with the gambling part. They got some good music down there.

TROY They got some rogues . . . is what they got.

LYONS How you been, Mr. Bono? Hi, Rose.

BONO I see where you playing down at the Crawford Grill tonight.

ROSE How come you ain't brought Bonnie like I told you. You should have brought Bonnie with you, she ain't been over in a month of Sundays.

LYONS I was just in the neighborhood . . . thought I'd stop by.

TROY Here he come . . .

BONO Your daddy got a promotion on the rubbish. He's gonna be the first

9. A variation on "Old Blue," a traditional African American folk song.

1. The *Pittsburgh Courier,* one of the top-selling African American newspapers in the mid-20th century.

colored driver. Ain't got to do nothing but sit up there and read the paper like them white fellows.

LYONS Hey, Pop . . . if you knew how to read you'd be alright.

BONO Naw . . . naw . . . you mean if the nigger knew how to drive he'd be all right. Been fighting with them people about driving and ain't even got a license. Mr. Rand know you ain't got no driver's license?

TROY Driving ain't nothing. All you do is point the truck where you want it to go. Driving ain't nothing.

BONO Do Mr. Rand know you ain't got no driver's license? That's what I'm talking about. I ain't asked if driving was easy. I asked if Mr. Rand know you ain't got no driver's license.

TROY He ain't got to know. The man ain't got to know my business. Time he find out, I have two or three driver's licenses.

LYONS [*going into his pocket*] Say, look here, Pop . . .

TROY I knew it was coming. Didn't I tell you, Bono? I know what kind of "Look here, Pop" that was. The nigger fixing to ask me for some money. It's Friday night. It's my payday. All them rogues down there on the avenue . . . the ones that ain't in jail . . . and Lyons is hopping in his shoes to get down there with them.

LYONS See, Pop . . . if you give somebody else a chance to talk sometime, you'd see that I was fixing to pay you back your ten dollars like I told you. Here . . . I told you I'd pay you when Bonnie got paid.

TROY Naw . . . you go ahead and keep that ten dollars. Put it in the bank. The next time you feel like you wanna come by here and ask me for something . . . you go on down there and get that.

LYONS Here's your ten dollars, Pop. I told you I don't want you to give me nothing. I just wanted to borrow ten dollars.

TROY Naw . . . you go on and keep that for the next time you want to ask me.

LYONS Come on, Pop . . . here go your ten dollars.

ROSE Why don't you go on and let the boy pay you back, Troy?

LYONS Here you go, Rose. If you don't take it I'm gonna have to hear about it for the next six months.

[*He hands her the money.*]

ROSE You can hand yours over here too, Troy.

TROY You see this, Bono. You see how they do me.

BONO Yeah, Lucille do me the same way.

[GABRIEL *is heard singing offstage. He enters.*]

GABRIEL Better get ready for the Judgment! Better get ready for . . . Hey! . . . Hey! . . . There's Troy's boy!

LYONS How you doing, Uncle Gabe?

GABRIEL Lyons . . . The King of the Jungle! Rose . . . hey, Rose. Got a flower for you. [*He takes a rose from his pocket.*] Picked it myself. That's the same rose like you is!

ROSE That's right nice of you, Gabe.

LYONS What you been doing, Uncle Gabe?

GABRIEL Oh, I been chasing hellhounds and waiting on the time to tell St. Peter to open the gates.

LYONS You been chasing hellhounds, huh? Well . . . you doing the right thing, Uncle Gabe. Somebody got to chase them.

GABRIEL Oh, yeah . . . I know it. The devil's strong. The devil ain't no pushover. Hellhounds snipping at everybody's heels. But I got my trumpet waiting on the judgment time.

LYONS Waiting on the Battle of Armageddon,[2] huh?

GABRIEL Ain't gonna be too much of a battle when God get to waving that Judgment sword. But the people's gonna have a hell of a time trying to get into heaven if them gates ain't open.

LYONS [*putting his arm around* GABRIEL] You hear this, Pop. Uncle Gabe, you alright!

GABRIEL [*laughing with* LYONS] Lyons! King of the Jungle.

ROSE You gonna stay for supper, Gabe. Want me to fix you a plate?

GABRIEL I'll take a sandwich, Rose. Don't want no plate. Just wanna eat with my hands. I'll take a sandwich.

ROSE How about you, Lyons? You staying? Got some short ribs cooking.

LYONS Naw, I won't eat nothing till after we finished playing. [*Pause*] You ought to come down and listen to me play, Pop.

TROY I don't like that Chinese music. All that noise.

ROSE Go on in the house and wash up, Gabe . . . I'll fix you a sandwich.

GABRIEL [*to* LYONS, *as he exits*] Troy's mad at me.

LYONS What you mad at Uncle Gabe for, Pop?

ROSE He thinks Troy's mad at him cause he moved over to Miss Pearl's.

TROY I ain't mad at the man. He can live where he want to live at.

LYONS What he move over there for? Miss Pearl don't like nobody.

ROSE She don't mind him none. She treats him real nice. She just don't allow all that singing.

TROY She don't mind that rent he be paying . . . that's what she don't mind.

ROSE Troy, I ain't going through that with you no more. He's over there cause he want to have his own place. He can come and go as he please.

TROY Hell, he could come and go as he please here. I wasn't stopping him. I ain't put no rules on him.

ROSE It ain't the same thing, Troy. And you know it.

[GABRIEL *comes to the door.*]

Now, that's the last I wanna hear about that. I don't wanna hear nothing else about Gabe and Miss Pearl. And next week . . .

GABRIEL I'm ready for my sandwich, Rose.

ROSE And next week . . . when that recruiter come from that school . . . I want you to sign that paper and go on and let Cory play football. Then that'll be the last I have to hear about that.

TROY [*to* ROSE *as she exits into the house*] I ain't thinking about Cory nothing.

LYONS What . . . Cory got recruited? What school he going to?

TROY That boy walking around here smelling his piss . . . thinking he's grown. Thinking he's gonna do what he want, irrespective of what I say. Look here, Bono . . . I left the Commissioner's office and went down to the A&P . . . that boy ain't working down there. He lying to me. Telling me he got his job back . . . telling me he working weekends . . . telling me he working after school . . . Mr. Stawicki tell me he ain't working down there at all!

2. The final battle between the forces of God and of evil, as described in the New Testament's book of Revelation (see 16.16).

LYONS Cory just growing up. He's just busting at the seams trying to fill out your shoes.

TROY I don't care what he's doing. When he get to the point where he wanna disobey me . . . then it's time for him to move on. Bono'll tell you that. I bet he ain't never disobeyed his daddy without paying the consequences.

BONO I ain't never had a chance. My daddy came on through . . . but I ain't never knew him to see him . . . or what he had on his mind or where he went. Just moving on through. Searching out the New Land. That's what the old folks used to call it. See a fellow moving around from place to place . . . woman to woman . . . called it searching out the New Land. I can't say if he ever found it. I come along, didn't want no kids. Didn't know if I was gonna be in one place long enough to fix on them right as their daddy. I figured I was going searching too. As it turned out I been hooked up with Lucille near about as long as your daddy been with Rose. Going on sixteen years.

TROY Sometimes I wish I hadn't known my daddy. He ain't cared nothing about no kids. A kid to him wasn't nothing. All he wanted was for you to learn how to walk so he could start you to working. When it come time for eating . . . he ate first. If there was anything left over, that's what you got. Man would sit down and eat two chickens and give you the wing.

LYONS You ought to stop that, Pop. Everybody feed their kids. No matter how hard times is . . . everybody care about their kids. Make sure they have something to eat.

TROY The only thing my daddy cared about was getting them bales of cotton in to Mr. Lubin. That's the only thing that mattered to him. Sometimes I used to wonder why he was living. Wonder why the devil hadn't come and got him. "Get them bales of cotton in to Mr. Lubin" and find out he owe him money[3] . . .

LYONS He should have just went on and left when he saw he couldn't get nowhere. That's what I would have done.

TROY How he gonna leave with eleven kids? And where he gonna go? He ain't knew how to do nothing but farm. No, he was trapped and I think he knew it. But I'll say this for him . . . he felt a responsibility toward us. Maybe he ain't treated us the way I felt he should have . . . but without that responsibility he could have walked off and left us . . . made his own way.

BONO A lot of them did. Back in those days what you talking about . . . they walk out their front door and just take on down one road or another and keep on walking.

LYONS There you go! That's what I'm talking about.

BONO Just keep on walking till you come to something else. Ain't you never heard of nobody having the walking blues? Well, that's what you call it when you just take off like that.

TROY My daddy ain't had them walking blues! What you talking about? He stayed right there with his family. But he was just as evil as he could be. My

3. Under the sharecropping system that arose in the South after the Civil War, tenant farmers received their seed, tools, food and clothing, and housing on credit from landowners; after harvesting the cotton, they had to repay these charges from their share of the value of the crop.

mama couldn't stand him. Couldn't stand that evilness. She run off when I was about eight. She sneaked off one night after he had gone to sleep. Told me she was coming back for me. I ain't never seen her no more. All his women run off and left him. He wasn't good for nobody.

When my turn come to head out, I was fourteen and got to sniffing around Joe Canewell's daughter. Had us an old mule we called Greyboy. My daddy sent me out to do some plowing and I tied up Greyboy and went to fooling around with Joe Canewell's daughter. We done found us a nice little spot, got real cozy with each other. She about thirteen and we done figured we was grown anyway . . . so we down there enjoying ourselves . . . ain't thinking about nothing. We didn't know Greyboy had got loose and wandered back to the house and my daddy was looking for me. We down there by the creek enjoying ourselves when my daddy come up on us. Surprised us. He had them leather straps off the mule and commenced to whupping me like there was no tomorrow. I jumped up, mad and embarrassed. I was scared of my daddy. When he commenced to whupping on me . . . quite naturally I run to get out of the way.

[*Pause.*]

Now I thought he was mad cause I ain't done my work. But I see where he was chasing me off so he could have the gal for himself. When I see what the matter of it was, I lost all fear of my daddy. Right there is where I become a man . . . at fourteen years of age.

[*Pause.*]

Now it was my turn to run him off. I picked up them same reins that he had used on me. I picked up them reins and commenced to whupping on him. The gal jumped up and run off . . . and when my daddy turned to face me, I could see why the devil had never come to get him . . . cause he was the devil himself. I don't know what happened. When I woke up, I was laying right there by the creek, and Blue . . . this old dog we had . . . was licking my face. I thought I was blind. I couldn't see nothing. Both my eyes were swollen shut. I layed there and cried. I didn't know what I was gonna do. The only thing I knew was the time had come for me to leave my daddy's house. And right there the world suddenly got big. And it was a long time before I could cut it down to where I could handle it.

Part of that cutting down was when I got to the place where I could feel him kicking in my blood and knew that the only thing that separated us was the matter of a few years.

[GABRIEL *enters from the house with a sandwich.*]

LYONS What you got there, Uncle Gabe?

GABRIEL Got me a ham sandwich. Rose gave me a ham sandwich.

TROY I don't know what happened to him. I done lost touch with everybody except Gabriel. But I hope he's dead. I hope he found some peace.

LYONS That's a heavy story, Pop. I didn't know you left home when you was fourteen.

TROY And didn't know nothing. The only part of the world I knew was the forty-two acres of Mr. Lubin's land. That's all I knew about life.

LYONS Fourteen's kinda young to be out on your own. [*Phone rings.*] I don't even think I was ready to be out on my own at fourteen. I don't know what I would have done.

TROY I got up from the creek and walked on down to Mobile. I was through with farming. Figured I could do better in the city. So I walked the two hundred miles to Mobile.

LYONS Wait a minute . . . you ain't walked no two hundred miles, Pop. Ain't nobody gonna walk no two hundred miles. You talking about some walking there.

BONO That's the only way you got anywhere back in them days.

LYONS Shhh. Damn if I wouldn't have hitched a ride with somebody!

TROY Who you gonna hitch it with? They ain't had no cars and things like they got now. We talking about 1918.

ROSE [*entering*] What you all out here getting into?

TROY [*to* ROSE] I'm telling Lyons how good he got it. He don't know nothing about this I'm talking.

ROSE Lyons, that was Bonnie on the phone. She say you supposed to pick her up.

LYONS Yeah, okay, Rose.

TROY I walked on down to Mobile and hitched up with some of them fellows that was heading this way. Got up here and found out . . . not only couldn't you get a job . . . you couldn't find no place to live. I thought I was in freedom. Shhh. Colored folks living down there on the riverbanks in whatever kind of shelter they could find for themselves. Right down there under the Brady Street Bridge. Living in shacks made of sticks and tar paper. Messed around there and went from bad to worse. Started stealing. First it was food. Then I figured, hell, if I steal money I can buy me some food. Buy me some shoes too! One thing led to another. Met your mama. I was young and anxious to be a man. Met your mama and had you. What I do that for? Now I got to worry about feeding you and her. Got to steal three times as much. Went out one day looking for somebody to rob . . . that's what I was, a robber. I'll tell you the truth. I'm ashamed of it today. But it's the truth. Went to rob this fellow . . . pulled out my knife . . . and he pulled out a gun. Shot me in the chest. It felt just like somebody had taken a hot branding iron and laid it on me. When he shot me I jumped at him with my knife. They told me I killed him and they put me in the penitentiary and locked me up for fifteen years. That's where I met Bono. That's where I learned how to play baseball. Got out that place and your mama had taken you and went on to make life without me. Fifteen years was a long time for her to wait. But that fifteen years cured me of that robbing stuff. Rose'll tell you. She asked me when I met her if I had gotten all that foolishness out of my system. And I told her, "Baby, it's you and baseball all what count with me." You hear me, Bono? I meant it too. She say, "Which one comes first?" I told her, "Baby, ain't no doubt it's baseball . . . but you stick and get old with me and we'll both outlive this baseball." Am I right, Rose? And it's true.

ROSE Man, hush your mouth. You ain't said no such thing. Talking about, "Baby, you know you'll always be number one with me." That's what you was talking.

TROY You hear that, Bono. That's why I love her.

BONO Rose'll keep you straight. You get off the track, she'll straighten you up.

ROSE Lyons, you better get on up and get Bonnie. She waiting on you.

LYONS [*gets up to go*] Hey, Pop, why don't you come on down to the Grill and hear me play?

TROY I ain't going down there. I'm too old to be sitting around in them clubs.

BONO You got to be good to play down at the Grill.

LYONS Come on, Pop . . .

TROY I got to get up in the morning.

LYONS You ain't got to stay long.

TROY Naw, I'm gonna get my supper and go on to bed.

LYONS Well, I got to go. I'll see you again.

TROY Don't you come around my house on my payday.

ROSE Pick up the phone and let somebody know you coming. And bring Bonnie with you. You know I'm always glad to see her.

LYONS Yeah, I'll do that, Rose. You take care now. See you, Pop. See you, Mr. Bono. See you, Uncle Gabe.

GABRIEL Lyons! King of the Jungle!

[LYONS *exits.*]

TROY Is supper ready, woman? Me and you got some business to take care of. I'm gonna tear it up too.

ROSE Troy, I done told you now!

TROY [*puts his arm around* BONO] Aw hell, woman . . . this is Bono. Bono like family. I done known this nigger since . . . how long I done know you?

BONO It's been a long time.

TROY I done known this nigger since Skippy was a pup.[4] Me and him done been through some times.

BONO You sure right about that.

TROY Hell, I done know him longer than I known you. And we still standing shoulder to shoulder. Hey, look here, Bono . . . a man can't ask for no more than that. [*Drinks to him.*] I love you, nigger.

BONO Hell, I love you too . . . but I got to get home see my woman. You got yours in hand. I got to go get mine.

[BONO *starts to exit as* CORY *enters the yard, dressed in his football uniform. He gives* TROY *a hard, uncompromising look.*]

CORY What you do that for, Pop?

[*He throws his helmet down in the direction of* TROY.]

ROSE What's the matter? Cory . . . what's the matter?

CORY Papa done went up to the school and told Coach Zellman I can't play football no more. Wouldn't even let me play the game. Told him to tell the recruiter not to come.

ROSE Troy . . .

TROY What you Troying me for. Yeah, I did it. And the boy know why I did it.

CORY Why you wanna do that to me? That was the one chance I had.

ROSE Ain't nothing wrong with Cory playing football, Troy.

TROY The boy lied to me. I told the nigger if he wanna play football . . . to keep up his chores and hold down that job at the A&P. That was the conditions. Stopped down there to see Mr. Stawicki . . .

CORY I can't work after school during the football season, Pop! I tried to tell you that Mr. Stawicki's holding my job for me. You don't never want to listen to nobody. And then you wanna go and do this to me!

4. That is, for a very long time (folk expression).

TROY I ain't done nothing to you. You done it to yourself.

CORY Just cause you didn't have a chance! You just scared I'm gonna be better than you, that's all.

TROY Come here.

ROSE Troy . . .

[CORY *reluctantly crosses over to* TROY.]

TROY Alright! See. You done made a mistake.

CORY I didn't even do nothing!

TROY I'm gonna tell you what your mistake was. See . . . you swung at the ball and didn't hit it. That's strike one. See, you in the batter's box now. You swung and you missed. That's strike one. Don't you strike out!

[*Lights fade to black.*]

2.1

The following morning. CORY *is at the tree hitting the ball with the bat. He tries to mimic* TROY, *but his swing is awkward, less sure.* ROSE *enters from the house.*

ROSE Cory, I want you to help me with this cupboard.

CORY I ain't quitting the team. I don't care what Poppa say.

ROSE I'll talk to him when he gets back. He had to go see about your Uncle Gabe. The police done arrested him. Say he was disturbing the peace. He'll be back directly. Come on in here and help me clean out the top of this cupboard.

[CORY *exits into the house.* ROSE *sees* TROY *and* BONO *coming down the alley.*]

Troy . . . what they say down there?

TROY Ain't said nothing. I give them fifty dollars and they let him go. I'll talk to you about it. Where's Cory?

ROSE He's in there helping me clean out these cupboards.

TROY Tell him to get his butt out here.

[TROY *and* BONO *go over to the pile of wood.* BONO *picks up the saw and begins sawing.*]

TROY [*to* BONO] All they want is the money. That makes six or seven times I done went down there and got him. See me coming they stick out their hands.

BONO Yeah. I know what you mean. That's all they care about . . . that money. They don't care about what's right. [*Pause*] Nigger, why you got to go and get some hard wood? You ain't doing nothing but building a little old fence. Get you some soft pine wood. That's all you need.

TROY I know what I'm doing. This is outside wood. You put pine wood inside the house. Pine wood is inside wood. This here is outside wood. Now you tell me where the fence is gonna be?

BONO You don't need this wood. You can put it up with pine wood and it'll stand as long as you gonna be here looking at it.

TROY How you know how long I'm gonna be here, nigger? Hell, I might just live forever. Live longer than old man Horsely.

BONO That's what Magee used to say.

TROY Magee's a damn fool. Now you tell me who you ever heard of gonna pull their own teeth with a pair of rusty pliers.

BONO The old folks . . . my granddaddy used to pull his teeth with pliers. They ain't had no dentists for the colored folks back then.

TROY Get clean pliers! You understand? Clean pliers! Sterilize them! Besides we ain't living back then. All Magee had to do was walk over to Doc Goldblum's.

BONO I see where you and that Tallahassee gal . . . that Alberta . . . I see where you all done got tight.

TROY What you mean "got tight"?

BONO I see where you be laughing and joking with her all the time.

TROY I laughs and jokes with all of them, Bono. You know me.

BONO That ain't the kind of laughing and joking I'm talking about.

[CORY *enters from the house.*]

CORY How you doing, Mr. Bono?

TROY Cory? Get that saw from Bono and cut some wood. He talking about the wood's too hard to cut. Stand back there, Jim, and let that young boy show you how it's done.

BONO He's sure welcome to it.

[CORY *takes the saw and begins to cut the wood.*]

Whew-e-e! Look at that. Big old strong boy. Look like Joe Louis.[5] Hell, must be getting old the way I'm watching that boy whip through that wood.

CORY I don't see why Mama want a fence around the yard noways.

TROY Damn if I know either. What the hell she keeping out with it? She ain't got nothing nobody want.

BONO Some people build fences to keep people out . . . and other people build fences to keep people in. Rose wants to hold on to you all. She loves you.

TROY Hell, nigger, I don't need nobody to tell me my wife loves me, Cory . . . go on in the house and see if you can find that other saw.

CORY Where's it at?

TROY I said find it! Look for it till you find it!

[CORY *exists into the house.*]

What's that supposed to mean? Wanna keep us in?

BONO Troy . . . I done known you seem like damn near my whole life. You and Rose both. I done know both of you all for a long time. I remember when you met Rose. When you was hitting them baseball out the park. A lot of them old gals was after you then. You had the pick of the litter. When you picked Rose, I was happy for you. That was the first time I knew you had any sense. I said . . . My man Troy knows what he's doing . . . I'm gonna follow this nigger . . . he might take me somewhere. I been following you too. I done learned a whole heap of things about life watching you. I done learned how to tell where the shit lies. How to tell it from the alfalfa. You done learned me a lot of things. You showed me how to not make the same mistakes . . . to take life as it comes along and keep putting one foot in front of the other. [*Pause*] Rose a good woman, Troy.

TROY Hell, nigger, I know she a good woman. I been married to her for eighteen years. What you got on your mind, Bono?

5. American boxer (1914–1981); as world heavyweight champion (1937–49), he was the most famous black man in the United States.

BONO I just say she a good woman. Just like I say anything. I ain't got to have nothing on my mind.

TROY You just gonna say she a good woman and leave it hanging out there like that? Why you telling me she a good woman?

BONO She loves you, Troy. Rose loves you.

TROY You saying I don't measure up. That's what you trying to say. I don't measure up cause I'm seeing this other gal. I know what you trying to say.

BONO I know what Rose means to you, Troy. I'm just trying to say I don't want to see you mess up.

TROY Yeah, I appreciate that, Bono. If you was messing around on Lucille I'd be telling you the same thing.

BONO Well, that's all I got to say. I just say that because I love you both.

TROY Hell, you know me . . . I wasn't out there looking for nothing. You can't find a better woman than Rose. I know that. But seems like this woman just stuck onto me where I can't shake her loose. I done wrestled with it, tried to throw her off me . . . but she just stuck on tighter. Now she's stuck on for good.

BONO You's in control . . . that's what you tell me all the time. You responsible for what you do.

TROY I ain't ducking the responsibility of it. As long as it sets right in my heart . . . then I'm okay. Cause that's all I listen to. It'll tell me right from wrong every time. And I ain't talking about doing Rose no bad turn. I love Rose. She done carried me a long ways and I love and respect her for that.

BONO I know you do. That's why I don't want to see you hurt her. But what you gonna do when she find out? What you got then? If you try and juggle both of them . . . sooner or later you gonna drop one of them. That's common sense.

TROY Yeah, I hear what you saying, Bono. I been trying to figure a way to work it out.

BONO Work it out right, Troy. I don't want to be getting all up between you and Rose's business . . . but work it so it come out right.

TROY Aw hell, I get all up between you and Lucille's business. When you gonna get that woman that refrigerator she been wanting? Don't tell me you ain't got no money now. I know who your banker is. Mellon[6] don't need that money bad as Lucille want that refrigerator. I'll tell you that.

BONO Tell you what I'll do . . . when you finish building this fence for Rose . . . I'll buy Lucille that refrigerator.

TROY You done stuck your foot in your mouth now!

[TROY *grabs up a board and begins to saw.* BONO *starts to walk out the yard.*]

Hey, nigger . . . where you going?

BONO I'm going home. I know you don't expect me to help you now. I'm protecting my money. I wanna see you put that fence up by yourself. That's what I want to see. You'll be here another six months without me.

TROY Nigger, you ain't right.

BONO When it comes to my money . . . I'm right as fireworks on the Fourth of July.

6. Mellon National Bank, founded in Pittsburgh in 1870 by Thomas Mellon.

TROY Alright, we gonna see now. You better get out your bankbook.

[**BONO** *exits, and* **TROY** *continues to work.* **ROSE** *enters from the house.*]

ROSE What they say down there? What's happening with Gabe?

TROY I went down there and got him out. Cost me fifty dollars. Say he was disturbing the peace. Judge set up a hearing for him in three weeks. Say to show cause why he shouldn't be recommitted.

ROSE What was he doing that cause them to arrest him?

TROY Some kids was teasing him and he run them off home. Say he was howling and carrying on. Some folks seen him and called the police. That's all it was.

ROSE Well, what's you say? What'd you tell the judge?

TROY Told him I'd look after him. It didn't make no sense to recommit the man. He stuck out his big greasy palm and told me to give him fifty dollars and take him on home.

ROSE Where's he at now? Where'd he go off to?

TROY He's gone on about his business. He don't need nobody to hold his hand.

ROSE Well, I don't know. Seem like that would be the best place for him if they did put him into the hospital. I know what you're gonna say. But that's what I think would be best.

TROY The man done had his life ruined fighting for what? And they wanna take and lock him up. Let him be free. He don't bother nobody.

ROSE Well, everybody got their own way of looking at it I guess. Come on and get your lunch. I got a bowl of lima beans and some cornbread in the oven. Come on get something to eat. Ain't no sense you fretting over Gabe.

[**ROSE** *turns to go into the house.*]

TROY Rose . . . got something to tell you.

ROSE Well, come on . . . wait till I get this food on the table.

TROY Rose!

[*She stops and turns around.*]

I don't know how to say this. [*Pause*] I can't explain it none. It just sort of grows on you till it gets out of hand. It starts out like a little bush . . . and the next think you know it's a whole forest.

ROSE Troy . . . what is you talking about?

TROY I'm talking, woman, let me talk. I'm trying to find a way to tell you . . . I'm gonna be a daddy. I'm gonna be somebody's daddy.

ROSE Troy . . . you're not telling me this? You're gonna be . . . what?

TROY Rose . . . now . . . see . . .

ROSE You telling me you gonna be somebody's daddy? You telling your *wife* this?

[**GABRIEL** *enters from the street. He carries a rose in his hand.*]

GABRIEL Hey, Troy! Hey, Rose!

ROSE I have to wait eighteen years to hear something like this.

GABRIEL Hey, Rose . . . I got a flower for you. [*He hands it to her.*] That's a rose. Same rose like you is.

ROSE Thanks, Gabe.

GABRIEL Troy, you ain't mad at me is you? Them bad mens come and put me away. You ain't mad at me is you?

TROY Naw, Gabe, I ain't mad at you.

ROSE Eighteen years and you wanna come with this.

GABRIEL [*takes a quarter out of his pocket*] See what I got? Got a brand new quarter.

TROY Rose . . . it's just . . .

ROSE Ain't nothing you can say, Troy. Ain't no way of explaining that.

GABRIEL Fellow that give me this quarter had a whole mess of them. I'm gonna keep this quarter till it stop shining.

ROSE Gabe, go on in the house there. I got some watermelon in the frigidaire. Go on and get you a piece.

GABRIEL Say, Rose . . . you know I was chasing hellhounds and them bad mens come and get me and take me away. Troy helped me. He come down there and told them they better let me go before he beat them up. Yeah, he did!

ROSE You go on and get you a piece of watermelon, Gabe. Them bad mens is gone now.

GABRIEL Okay, Rose . . . gonna get me some watermelon. The kind with the stripes on it.

[GABRIEL *exits into the house.*]

ROSE Why, Troy? Why? After all these years to come dragging this in to me now. It don't make no sense at your age. I could have expected this ten or fifteen years ago, but not now.

TROY Age ain't got nothing to do with it, Rose.

ROSE I done tried to be everything a wife should be. Everything a wife could be. Been married eighteen years and I got to live to see the day you tell me you been seeing another woman and done fathered a child by her. And you know I ain't never wanted no half nothing in my family. My whole family is half. Everybody got different fathers and mothers . . . my two sisters and my brother. Can't hardly tell who's who. Can't never sit down and talk about Papa and Mama. It's your papa and your mama and my papa and my mama . . .

TROY Rose . . . stop it now.

ROSE I ain't never wanted that for none of my children. And now you wanna drag your behind in here and tell me something like this.

TROY You ought to know. It's time for you to know.

ROSE Well, I don't want to know, goddamn it!

TROY I can't just make it go away. It's done now. I can't wish the circumstance of the thing away.

ROSE And you don't want to either. Maybe you want to wish me and my boy away. Maybe that's what you want? Well, you can't wish us away. I've got eighteen years of my life invested in you. You ought to have stayed upstairs in my bed where you belong.

TROY Rose . . . now listen to me . . . we can get a handle on this thing. We can talk this out . . . come to an understanding.

ROSE All of a sudden it's "we." Where was "we" at when you was down there rolling around with some godforsaken woman? "We" should have come to an understanding before you started making a damn fool of yourself. You're a day late and a dollar short when it comes to an understanding with me.

TROY It's just . . . She gives me a different idea . . . a different understanding about myself. I can step out of this house and get away from the pressures and problems . . . be a different man. I ain't got to wonder how I'm gonna pay the bills or get the roof fixed. I can just be a part of myself that I ain't never been.

ROSE What I want to know . . . is do you plan to continue seeing her. That's all you can say to me.

TROY I can sit up in her house and laugh. Do you understand what I'm saying. I can laugh out loud . . . and it feels good. It reaches all the way down to the bottom of my shoes. [*Pause*] Rose, I can't give that up.

ROSE Maybe you ought to go on and stay down there with her . . . if she a better woman than me.

TROY It ain't about nobody being a better woman or nothing. Rose, you ain't the blame. A man couldn't ask for no woman to be a better wife than you've been. I'm responsible for it. I done locked myself into a pattern trying to take care of you all that I forgot about myself.

ROSE What the hell was I there for? That was my job, not somebody else's.

TROY Rose, I done tried all my life to live decent . . . to live a clean . . . hard . . . useful life. I tried to be a good husband to you. In every way I knew how. Maybe I come into the world backwards, I don't know. But . . . you born with two strikes on you before you come to the plate. You got to guard it closely . . . always looking for the curve ball on the inside corner. You can't afford to let none get past you. You can't afford a call strike.[7] If you going down . . . you going down swinging. Everything lined up against you. What you gonna do. I fooled them, Rose. I bunted. When I found you and Cory and a halfway decent job . . . I was safe. Couldn't nothing touch me. I wasn't gonna strike out no more. I wasn't going back to the penitentiary. I wasn't gonna lay in the streets with a bottle of wine. I was safe. I had me a family. A job. I wasn't gonna get that last strike. I was on first looking for one of them boys to knock me in. To get me home.

ROSE You should have stayed in my bed, Troy.

TROY Then when I saw that gal . . . she firmed up my backbone. And I got to thinking that if I tried . . . I just might be able to steal second. Do you understand after eighteen years I wanted to steal second.

ROSE You should have held me tight. You should have grabbed me and held on.

TROY I stood on first base for eighteen years and I thought . . . well, goddamn it . . . go on for it!

ROSE We're not talking about baseball! We're talking about you going off to lay in bed with another woman . . . and then bring it home to me. That's what we're talking about. We ain't talking about no baseball.

TROY Rose, you're not listening to me. I'm trying the best I can to explain it to you. It's not easy for me to admit that I been standing in the same place for eighteen years.

ROSE I been standing with you! I been right here with you, Troy. I got a life too. I gave eighteen years of my life to stand in the same spot with you.

7. That is, a called strike: a pitch at which the batter fails to swing that the umpire judges to have been within the strike zone.

Don't you think I ever wanted other things? Don't you think I had dreams and hopes? What about my life? What about me? Don't you think it ever crossed my mind to want to know other men? That I wanted to lay up somewhere and forget about my responsibilities? That I wanted someone to make me laugh so I could feel good? You not the only one who's got wants and needs. But I held on to you, Troy. I took all my feelings, my wants and needs, my dreams . . . and I buried them inside you. I planted a seed and watched and prayed over it. I planted myself inside you and waited to bloom. And it didn't take me no eighteen years to find out the soil was hard and rocky and it wasn't never gonna bloom.

But I held on to you, Troy. I held you tighter. You was my husband. I owed you everything I had. Every part of me I could find to give you. And upstairs in that room . . . with the darkness falling in on me . . . I gave everything I had to try and erase the doubt that you wasn't the finest man in the world. And wherever you was going . . . I wanted to be there with you. Cause you was my husband. Cause that's the only way I was gonna survive as your wife. You always talking about what you give . . . and what you don't have to give. But you take too. You take . . . and don't even know nobody's giving!

[ROSE *turns to exit into the house;* TROY *grabs her arm.*]

TROY You say I take and don't give!

ROSE Troy! You're hurting me!

TROY You say I take and don't give.

ROSE Troy . . . you're hurting my arm! Let go!

TROY I done give you everything I got. Don't you tell that lie on me.

ROSE Troy!

TROY Don't you tell that lie on me!

[CORY *enters from the house.*]

CORY Mama!

ROSE Troy. You're hurting me.

TROY Don't you tell me about no taking and giving.

[CORY *comes up behind* TROY *and grabs him.* TROY, *surprised, is thrown off balance just as* CORY *throws a glancing blow that catches him on the chest and knocks him down.* TROY *is stunned, as is* CORY.]

ROSE Troy. Troy. No!

[TROY *gets to his feet and starts at* CORY.]

Troy . . . no. Please! Troy!

[ROSE *pulls on* TROY *to hold him back.* TROY *stops himself.*]

TROY [*to* CORY] Alright. That's strike two. You stay away from around me, boy. Don't you strike out. You living with a full count. Don't you strike out.

[TROY *exits out the yard as the lights go down.*]

2.2

It is six months later, early afternoon. TROY *enters from the house and starts to exit the yard.* ROSE *enters from the house.*

ROSE Troy, I want to talk to you.

TROY All of a sudden, after all this time, you want to talk to me, huh? You ain't wanted to talk to me for months. You ain't wanted to talk to me last night. You ain't wanted no part of me then. What you wanna talk to me about now?

ROSE Tomorrow's Friday.

TROY I know what day tomorrow is. You think I don't know tomorrow's Friday? My whole life I ain't done nothing but look to see Friday coming and you got to tell me it's Friday.

ROSE I want to know if you're coming home.

TROY I always come home, Rose. You know that. There ain't never been a night I ain't come home.

ROSE That ain't what I mean . . . and you know it. I want to know if you're coming straight home after work.

TROY I figure I'd cash my check . . . hang out at Taylors' with the boys . . . maybe play a game of checkers . . .

ROSE Troy, I can't live like this. I won't live like this. You livin' on borrowed time with me. It's been going on six months now you ain't been coming home.

TROY I be here every night. Every night of the year. That's 365 days.

ROSE I want you to come home tomorrow after work.

TROY Rose . . . I don't mess up my pay. You know that now. I take my pay and I give it to you. I don't have no money but what you give me back. I just want to have a little time to myself . . . a little time to enjoy life.

ROSE What about me? When's my time to enjoy life?

TROY I don't know what to tell you, Rose. I'm doing the best I can.

ROSE You ain't been home from work but time enough to change your clothes and run out . . . and you wanna call that the best you can do?

TROY I'm going over to the hospital to see Alberta. She went into the hospital this afternoon. Look like she might have the baby early. I won't be gone long.

ROSE Well, you ought to know. They went over to Miss Pearl's and got Gabe today. She said you told them to go ahead and lock him up.

TROY I ain't said no such thing. Whoever told you that is telling a lie. Pearl ain't doing nothing but telling a big fat lie.

ROSE She ain't had to tell me. I read it on the papers.

TROY I ain't told them nothing of the kind.

ROSE I saw it right there on the papers.

TROY What it say, huh?

ROSE It said you told them to take him.

TROY Then they screwed that up, just the way they screw up everything. I ain't worried about what they got on the paper.

ROSE Say the government send part of his check to the hospital and the other part to you.

TROY I ain't got nothing to do with that if that's the way it works. I ain't made up the rules about how it work.

ROSE You did Gabe just like you did Cory. You wouldn't sign the paper for Cory . . . but you signed for Gabe. You signed that paper.

[*The telephone is heard ringing inside the house.*]

TROY I told you I ain't signed nothing, woman! The only thing I signed was the release form. Hell, I can't read, I don't know what they had on that paper! I ain't signed nothing about sending Gabe away.

ROSE I said send him to the hospital . . . you said let him be free . . . now you done went down there and signed him to the hospital for half his money. You went back on yourself, Troy. You gonna have to answer for that.

TROY See now . . . you been over there talking to Miss Pearl. She done got mad cause she ain't getting Gabe's rent money. That's all it is. She's liable to say anything.

ROSE Troy, I seen where you signed the paper.

TROY You ain't seen nothing I signed. What she doing got papers on my brother anyway? Miss Pearl telling a big fat lie. And I'm gonna tell her about it too! You ain't seen nothing I signed. Say . . . you ain't seen nothing I signed.

[ROSE *exits into the house to answer the telephone. Presently she returns.*]

ROSE Troy . . . that was the hospital. Alberta had the baby.

TROY What she have? What is it?

ROSE It's a girl.

TROY I better get on down to the hospital to see her.

ROSE Troy . . .

TROY Rose . . . I got to go see her now. That's only right . . . what's the matter . . . the baby's alright, ain't it?

ROSE Alberta died having the baby.

TROY Died . . . you say she's dead? Alberta's dead?

ROSE They said they done all they could. They couldn't do nothing for her.

TROY The baby? How's the baby?

ROSE They say it's healthy. I wonder who's gonna bury her.

TROY She had family, Rose. She wasn't living in the world by herself.

ROSE I know she wasn't living in the world by herself.

TROY Next thing you gonna want to know if she had any insurance.

ROSE Troy, you ain't got to talk like that.

TROY That's the first thing that jumped out your mouth. "Who's gonna bury her?" Like I'm fixing to take on that task for myself.

ROSE I am your wife. Don't push me away.

TROY I ain't pushing nobody away. Just give me some space. That's all. Just give me some room to breathe.

[ROSE *exits into the house.* TROY *walks about the yard.*]

TROY [*with a quiet rage that threatens to consume him*] Alright . . . Mr. Death. See now . . . I'm gonna tell you what I'm gonna do. I'm gonna take and build me a fence around this yard. See? I'm gonna build me a fence around what belongs to me. And then I want you to stay on the other side. See? You stay over there until you're ready for me. Then you come on. Bring your army. Bring your sickle. Bring your wrestling clothes. I ain't gonna fall down on my vigilance this time. You ain't gonna sneak up on me no more. When you ready for me . . . when the top of your list say Troy

Maxson . . . that's when you come around here. You come up and knock on the front door. Ain't nobody else got nothing to do with this. This is between you and me. Man to man. You stay on the other side of that fence until you ready for me. Then you come up and knock on the front door. Anytime you want. I'll be ready for you.

[*The lights go down to black.*]

2.3

The lights come up on the porch. It is late evening three days later. ROSE *sits listening to the ball game waiting for* TROY. *The final out of the game is made and* ROSE *switches off the radio.* TROY *enters the yard carrying an infant wrapped in blankets. He stands back from the house and calls.*

[ROSE *enters and stands on the porch. There is a long, awkward silence, the weight of which grows heavier with each passing second.*]

TROY Rose . . . I'm standing here with my daughter in my arms. She ain't but a wee bittie little old thing. She don't know nothing about grownups' business. She innocent . . . and she ain't got no mama.

ROSE What you telling me for, Troy?

[*She turns and exits into the house.*]

TROY Well . . . I guess we'll just sit out here on the porch.

[*He sits down on the porch. There is an awkward indelicateness about the way he handles the baby. His largeness engulfs and seems to swallow it. He speaks loud enough for* ROSE *to hear.*]

A man's got to do what's right for him. I ain't sorry for nothing I done. It felt right in my heart.

[*To the baby*]

What you smiling at? Your daddy's a big man. Got these great big old hands. But sometimes he's scared. And right now your daddy's scared cause we sitting out here and ain't got no home. Oh, I been homeless before. I ain't had no little baby with me. But I been homeless. You just be out on the road by your lonesome and you see one of them trains coming and you just kinda go like this . . .

[*He sings as a lullaby.*]

Please, Mr. Engineer let a man ride the line
Please, Mr. Engineer let a man ride the line
I ain't got no ticket please let me ride the blinds[8]

[ROSE *enters from the house.* TROY *hearing her steps behind him, stands and faces her.*]

She's my daughter, Rose. My own flesh and blood. I can't deny her no more than I can deny them boys. [*Pause*] You and them boys is my family. You and them and this child is all I got in the world. So I guess what I'm saying is . . . I'd appreciate it if you'd help me take care of her.

ROSE Okay, Troy . . . you're right. I'll take care of your baby for you . . . cause . . . like you say . . . she's innocent . . . and you can't visit the sins of the father upon the child. A motherless child has got a hard time.

8. Baggage cars with no end doors. This is a traditional blues song, with lyrics adapted by Wilson.

[*She takes the baby from him.*]

From right now . . . this child got a mother. But you a womanless man.

[ROSE *turns and exits into the house with the baby. Lights go down to black.*]

2.4

It is two months later. LYONS *enters from the street. He knocks on the door and calls.*

LYONS Hey, Rose! [*Pause*] Rose!

ROSE [*from inside the house*] Stop that yelling. You gonna wake up Raynell. I just got her to sleep.

LYONS I just stopped by to pay Papa this twenty dollars I owe him. Where's Papa at?

ROSE He should be here in a minute. I'm getting ready to go down to the church. Sit down and wait on him.

LYONS I got to go pick up Bonnie over her mother's house.

ROSE Well, sit it down there on the table. He'll get it.

LYONS [*enters the house and sets the money on the table*] Tell Papa I said thanks. I'll see you again.

ROSE Alright, Lyons. We'll see you.

[LYONS *starts to exit as* CORY *enters.*]

CORY Hey, Lyons.

LYONS What's happening, Cory. Say man, I'm sorry I missed your graduation. You know I had a gig and couldn't get away. Otherwise, I would have been there, man. So what you doing?

CORY I'm trying to find a job.

LYONS Yeah I know how that go, man. It's rough out here. Jobs are scarce.

CORY Yeah, I know.

LYONS Look here, I got to run. Talk to Papa . . . he know some people. He'll be able to help get you a job. Talk to him . . . see what he say.

CORY Yeah . . . alright, Lyons.

LYONS You take care. I'll talk to you soon. We'll find some time to talk.

[LYONS *exits the yard.* CORY *wanders over to the tree, picks up the bat and assumes a batting stance. He studies an imaginary pitcher and swings. Dissatisfied with the result, he tries again.* TROY *enters. They eye each other for a beat.* CORY *puts the bat down and exits the yard.* TROY *starts into the house as* ROSE *exits with* RAYNELL. *She is carrying a cake.*]

TROY I'm coming in and everybody's going out.

ROSE I'm taking this cake down to the church for the bakesale. Lyons was by to see you. He stopped by to pay you your twenty dollars. It's laying in there on the table.

TROY [*going into his pocket*] Well . . . here go this money.

ROSE Put it in there on the table, Troy. I'll get it.

TROY What time you coming back?

ROSE Ain't no use in you studying me. It don't matter what time I come back.

TROY I just asked you a question, woman. What's the matter . . . can't I ask you a question?

ROSE Troy, I don't want to go into it. Your dinner's in there on the stove. All you got to do is heat it up. And don't you be eating the rest of them cakes in there. I'm coming back for them. We having a bakesale at the church tomorrow.

[ROSE *exits the yard.* TROY *sits down on the steps, takes a pint bottle from his pocket, opens it and drinks. He begins to sing.*]

TROY

Hear it ring! Hear it ring!
Had an old dog his name was Blue
You know Blue was mighty true
You know Blue as a good old dog
Blue trees a possum in a hollow log
You know from that he was a good old dog

[BONO *enters the yard.*]

BONO Hey, Troy.

TROY Hey, what's happening, Bono?

BONO I just thought I'd stop by to see you.

TROY What you stop by and see me for? You ain't stopped by in a month of Sundays. Hell, I must owe you money or something.

BONO Since you got your promotion I can't keep up with you. Used to see you everyday. Now I don't even know what route you working.

TROY They keep switching me around. Got me out in Greentree[9] now . . . hauling white folks' garbage.

BONO Greentree, huh? You lucky, at least you ain't got to be lifting them barrels. Damn if they ain't getting heavier. I'm gonna put in my two years and call it quits.

TROY I'm thinking about retiring myself.

BONO You got it easy. You can *drive* for another five years.

TROY It ain't the same, Bono. It ain't like working the back of the truck. Ain't got nobody to talk to . . . feel like you working by yourself. Naw, I'm thinking about retiring. How's Lucille?

BONO She alright. Her arthritis get to acting up on her sometime. Saw Rose on my way in. She going down to the church, huh?

TROY Yeah, she took up going down there. All them preachers looking for somebody to fatten their pockets. [*Pause*] Got some gin here.

BONO Naw, thanks. I just stopped by to say hello.

TROY Hell, nigger . . . you can take a drink. I ain't never known you to say no to a drink. You ain't got to work tomorrow.

BONO I just stopped by. I'm fixing to go over to Skinner's. We got us a domino game going over his house every Friday.

TROY Nigger, you can't play no dominoes. I used to whup you four games out of five.

BONO Well, that learned me. I'm getting better.

TROY Yeah? Well, that's alright.

BONO Look here . . . I got to be getting on. Stop by sometime, huh?

TROY Yeah, I'll do that, Bono. Lucille told Rose you bought her a new refrigerator.

BONO Yeah, Rose told Lucille you had finally built your fence . . . so I figured we'd call it even.

TROY I knew you would.

9. That is, Green Tree, an affluent suburb of Pittsburgh.

BONO Yeah . . . okay. I'll be talking to you.

TROY Yeah, take care, Bono. Good to see you. I'm gonna stop over.

BONO Yeah. Okay, Troy.

[BONO *exits.* TROY *drinks from the bottle.*]

TROY

Old Blue died and I dig his grave
Let him down with a golden chain
Every night when I hear old Blue bark
I know Blue treed a possum in Noah's Ark.
Hear it ring! Hear it ring!

[CORY *enters the yard. They eye each other for a beat.* TROY *is sitting in the middle of the steps.* CORY *walks over.*]

CORY I got to get by.

TROY Say what? What's you say?

CORY You in my way. I got to get by.

TROY You got to get by where? This is my house. Bought and paid for. In full. Took me fifteen years. And if you wanna go in my house and I'm sitting on the steps . . . you say excuse me. Like your mama taught you.

CORY Come on, Pop . . . I got to get by.

[CORY *starts to maneuver his way past* TROY. TROY *grabs his leg and shoves him back.*]

TROY You just gonna walk over top of me?

CORY I live here too!

TROY [*advancing toward him*] You just gonna walk over top of me in my own house?

CORY I ain't scared of you.

TROY I ain't asked if you was scared of me. I asked you if you was fixing to walk over top of me in my own house? That's the question. You ain't gonna say excuse me? You just gonna walk over top of me?

CORY If you wanna put it like that.

TROY How else am I gonna put it?

CORY I was walking by you to go into the house cause you sitting on the steps drunk, singing to yourself. You can put it like that.

TROY Without saying excuse me???

[CORY *doesn't respond.*]

I asked you a question. Without saying excuse me???

CORY I ain't got to say excuse me to you. You don't count around here no more.

TROY Oh, I see . . . I don't count around here no more. You ain't got to say excuse me to your daddy. All of a sudden you done got so grown that your daddy don't count around here no more . . . Around here in his own house and yard that he done paid for with the sweat of his brow. You done got so grown to where you gonna take over. You gonna take over my house. Is that right? You gonna wear my pants. You gonna go in there and stretch out on my bed. You ain't got to say excuse me cause I don't count around here no more. Is that right?

CORY That's right. You always talking this dumb stuff. Now, why don't you just get out my way.

TROY I guess you got someplace to sleep and something to put in your belly. You got that, huh? You got that? That's what you need. You got that, huh?

CORY You don't know what I got. You ain't got to worry about what I got.

TROY You right! You one hundred percent right! I done spent the last seventeen years worrying about what you got. Now it's your turn, see? I'll tell you what to do. You grown . . . we done established that. You a man. Now, let's see you act like one. Turn your behind around and walk out this yard. And when you get out there in the alley . . . you can forget about this house. See? Cause this is my house. You go on and be a man and get your own house. You can forget about this. Cause this is mine. You go on and get yours cause I'm through with doing for you.

CORY You talking about what you did for me . . . what'd you ever give me?

TROY Them feet and bones! That pumping heart, nigger! I give you more than anybody else is ever gonna give you.

CORY You ain't never gave me nothing! You ain't never done nothing but hold me back. Afraid I was gonna be better than you. All you ever did was try and make me scared of you. I used to tremble every time you called my name. Every time I heard your footsteps in the house. Wondering all the time . . . what's Papa gonna say if I do this? . . . What's he gonna say if I do that? . . . What's Papa gonna say if I turn on the radio? And Mama, too . . . she tries . . . but she's scared of you.

TROY You leave your mama out of this. She ain't got nothing to do with this.

CORY I don't know how she stand you . . . after what you did to her.

TROY I told you to leave your mama out of this!

[*He advances toward* CORY.]

CORY What you gonna do . . . give me a whupping? You can't whup me no more. You're too old. You just an old man.

TROY [*shoves him on his shoulder*] Nigger! That's what you are. You just another nigger on the street to me!

CORY You crazy! You know that?

TROY Go on now! You got the devil in you. Get on away from me!

CORY You just a crazy old man . . . talking about I got the devil in me.

TROY Yeah, I'm crazy! If you don't get on the other side of that yard . . . I'm gonna show you how crazy I am! Go on . . . get the hell out of my yard.

CORY It ain't your yard. You took Uncle Gabe's money he got from the army to buy this house and then you put him out.

TROY [*advances on* CORY] Get your black ass out of my yard!

[TROY'*s advance backs* CORY *up against the tree.* CORY *grabs up the bat.*]

CORY I ain't going nowhere! Come on . . . put me out! I ain't scared of you.

TROY That's my bat!

CORY Come on!

TROY Put my bat down!

CORY Come on, put me out.

[CORY *swings at* TROY, *who backs across the yard.*]

What's the matter? You so bad . . . put me out!

[TROY *advances toward* CORY.]

CORY [*backing up*] Come on! Come on!

TROY You're gonna have to use it! You wanna draw that bat back on me . . . you're gonna have to use it.

CORY Come on! . . . Come on!

[CORY *swings the bat at* TROY *a second time. He misses.* TROY *continues to advance toward him.*]

TROY You're gonna have to kill me! You wanna draw that bat back on me. You're gonna have to kill me.

[CORY, *backed up against the tree, can go no farther.* TROY *taunts him. He sticks out his head and offers him a target.*]

Come on! Come on!

[CORY *is unable to swing the bat.* TROY *grabs it.*]

TROY Then I'll show you.

[CORY *and* TROY *struggle over the bat. The struggle is fierce and fully engaged.* TROY *ultimately is the stronger, and takes the bat from* CORY *and stands over him ready to swing. He stops himself.*]

Go on and get away from around my house.

[CORY *stung by his defeat, picks himself up, walks slowly out of the yard and up the alley.*]

CORY Tell Mama I'll be back for my things.

TROY They'll be on the other side of that fence.

[CORY *exits.*]

TROY I can't taste nothing. Helluljah! I can't taste nothing no more. [TROY *assumes a batting posture and begins to taunt Death, the fastball on the outside corner.*] Come on! It's between you and me now! Come on! Anytime you want! Come on! I be ready for you . . . but I ain't gonna be easy.

[*The lights go down on the scene.*]

2.5

The time is 1965. The lights come up in the yard. It is the morning of TROY'S *funeral. A funeral plaque with a light hangs beside the door. There is a small garden plot off to the side. There is noise and activity in the house as* ROSE, GABRIEL, *and* BONO *have gathered. The door opens and* RAYNELL, *seven years old, enters dressed in a flannel nightgown. She crosses to the garden and pokes around with a stick.* ROSE *calls from the house.*

ROSE Raynell!

RAYNELL Mam?

ROSE What you doing out there?

RAYNELL Nothing.

[ROSE *comes to the door.*]

ROSE Girl, get in here and get dressed. What you doing?

RAYNELL Seeing if my garden growed.

ROSE I told you it ain't gonna grow overnight. You got to wait.

RAYNELL It don't look like it never gonna grow. Dag!

ROSE I told you a watched pot never boils. Get in here and get dressed.

RAYNELL This ain't even no pot, Mama.

ROSE You just have to give it a chance. It'll grow. Now you come on and do what I told you. We got to be getting ready. This ain't no morning to be playing around. You hear me?

RAYNELL Yes, mam.

[ROSE *exits into the house.* RAYNELL *continues to poke at her garden with a stick.* CORY *enters. He is dressed in a Marine corporal's uniform, and carries a duffel bag. His posture is that of a military man, and his speech has a clipped sternness.*]

CORY [*to* RAYNELL] Hi. [*Pause*] I bet your name is Raynell.

RAYNELL Uh huh.

CORY Is your mama home?

[RAYNELL *runs up on the porch and calls through the screen door.*]

RAYNELL Mama . . . there's some man out here. Mama?

[ROSE *comes to the door.*]

ROSE Cory? Lord have mercy! Look here, you all!

[ROSE *and* CORY *embrace in a tearful reunion as* BONO *and* LYONS *enter from the house dressed in funeral clothes.*]

BONO Aw, looka here . . .

ROSE Done got all grown up!

CORY Don't cry, Mama. What you crying about?

ROSE I'm just so glad you made it.

CORY Hey Lyons. How you doing, Mr. Bono.

[LYONS *goes to embrace* CORY.]

LYONS Look at you, man. Look at you. Don't he look good, Rose. Got them Corporal stripes.

ROSE What took you so long.

CORY You know how the Marines are, Mama. They got to get all their paper-work straight before they let you do anything.

ROSE Well, I'm sure glad you made it. They let Lyons come. Your Uncle Gabe's still in the hospital. They don't know if they gonna let him out or not. I just talked to them a little while ago.

LYONS A Corporal in the United States Marines.

BONO Your daddy knew you had it in you. He used to tell me all the time.

LYONS Don't he look good, Mr. Bono?

BONO Yeah, he remind me of Troy when I first met him. [*Pause*] Say, Rose, Lucille's down at the church with the choir. I'm gonna go down and get the pallbearers lined up. I'll be back to get you all.

ROSE Thanks, Jim.

CORY See you, Mr. Bono.

LYONS [*with his arm around* RAYNELL] Cory . . . look at Raynell. Ain't she precious? She gonna break a whole lot of hearts.

ROSE Raynell, come and say hello to your brother. This is your brother, Cory. You remember Cory.

RAYNELL No, Mam.

CORY She don't remember me, Mama.

ROSE Well, we talk about you. She heard us talk about you. [*To* RAYNELL] This is your brother, Cory. Come on and say hello.

RAYNELL Hi.

CORY Hi. So you're Raynell. Mama told me a lot about you.

ROSE You all come on into the house and let me fix you some breakfast. Keep up your strength.

CORY I ain't hungry, Mama.

LYONS You can fix me something, Rose. I'll be in there in a minute.

ROSE Cory, you sure you don't want nothing. I know they ain't feeding you right.

CORY No, Mama . . . thanks. I don't feel like eating. I'll get something later.

ROSE Raynell . . . get on upstairs and get that dress on like I told you.

[ROSE *and* RAYNELL *exit into the house.*]

LYONS So . . . I hear you thinking about getting married.

CORY Yeah, I done found the right one, Lyons. It's about time.

LYONS Me and Bonnie been split up about four years now. About the time Papa retired. I guess she just got tired of all them changes I was putting her through. [*Pause*] I always knew you was gonna make something out yourself. Your head was always in the right direction. So . . . you gonna stay in . . . make it a career . . . put in your twenty years?[1]

CORY I don't know. I got six already, I think that's enough.

LYONS Stick with Uncle Sam and retire early. Ain't nothing out here. I guess Rose told you what happened with me. They got me down the workhouse. I thought I was being slick cashing other people's checks.

CORY How much time you doing?

LYONS They give me three years. I got that beat now. I ain't got but nine more months. It ain't so bad. You learn to deal with it like anything else. You got to take the crookeds with the straights. That's what Papa used to say. He used to say that when he struck out. I seen him strike out three times in a row . . . and the next time up he hit the ball over the grandstand. Right out there in Homestead Field. He wasn't satisfied hitting in the seats . . . he want to hit it over everything! After the game he had two hundred people standing around waiting to shake his hand. You got to take the crookeds with the straights. Yeah, Papa was something else.

CORY You still playing?

LYONS Cory . . . you know I'm gonna do that. There's some fellows down there we got us a band . . . we gonna try and stay together when we get out . . . but yeah, I'm still playing. It still helps me to get out of bed in the morning. As long as it do that I'm gonna be right there playing and trying to make some sense out of it.

ROSE [*calling*] Lyons, I got these eggs in the pan.

LYONS Let me go on and get these eggs, man. Get ready to go bury Papa. [*Pause*] How you doing? You doing alright?

[CORY *nods.* LYONS *touches him on the shoulder and they share a moment of silent grief.* LYONS *exits into the house.* CORY *wanders about the yard.* RAYNELL *enters.*]

RAYNELL Hi.

CORY Hi.

RAYNELL Did you used to sleep in my room?

CORY Yeah . . . that used to be my room.

RAYNELL That's what Papa call it. "Cory's room." It got your football in the closet.

[ROSE *comes to the door.*]

ROSE Raynell, get in there and get them good shoes on.

RAYNELL Mama, can't I wear these? Them other one hurt my feet.

ROSE Well, they just gonna have to hurt your feet for a while. You ain't said they hurt your feet when you went down to the store and got them.

RAYNELL They didn't hurt then. My feet done got bigger.

ROSE Don't you give me no backtalk now. You get in there and get them shoes on.

[RAYNELL *exits into the house.*]

1. The minimum years of service required for retirement benefits.

Ain't too much changed. He still got that piece of rag tied to that tree. He was out here swinging that bat. I was just ready to go back in the house. He swung that bat and then he just fell over. Seem like he swung it and stood there with this grin on his face . . . and then he just fell over. They carried him on down to the hospital, but I knew there wasn't no need . . . why don't you come on in the house?

CORY Mama . . . I got something to tell you. I don't know how to tell you this . . . but I've got to tell you . . . I'm not going to Papa's funeral.

ROSE Boy, hush your mouth. That's your daddy you talking about. I don't want hear that kind of talk this morning. I done raised you to come to this? You standing there all healthy and grown talking about you ain't going to your daddy's funeral?

CORY Mama . . . listen . . .

ROSE I don't want to hear it, Cory. You just get that thought out of your head.

CORY I can't drag Papa with me everywhere I go. I've got to say no to him. One time in my life I've got to say no.

ROSE Don't nobody have to listen to nothing like that. I know you and your daddy ain't seen eye to eye, but I ain't got to listen to that kind of talk this morning. Whatever was between you and your daddy . . . the time has come to put it aside. Just take it and set it over there on the shelf and forget about it. Disrespecting your daddy ain't gonna make you a man, Cory. You got to find a way to come to that on your own. Not going to your daddy's funeral ain't gonna make you a man.

CORY The whole time I was growing up . . . living in his house . . . Papa was like a shadow that followed you everywhere. It weighed on you and sunk into your flesh. It would wrap around you and lay there until you couldn't tell which one was you anymore. That shadow digging in your flesh. Trying to crawl in. Trying to live through you. Everywhere I looked, Troy Maxson was staring back at me . . . hiding under the bed . . . in the closet. I'm just saying I've got to find a way to get rid of that shadow, Mama.

ROSE You just like him. You got him in you good.

CORY Don't tell me that, Mama.

ROSE You Troy Maxson all over again.

CORY I don't want to be Troy Maxson. I want to be me.

ROSE You can't be nobody but who you are, Cory. That shadow wasn't nothing but you growing into yourself. You either got to grow into it or cut it down to fit you. But that's all you got to make life with. That's all you got to measure yourself against that world out there. Your daddy wanted you to be everything he wasn't . . . and at the same time he tried to make you into everything he was. I don't know if he was right or wrong . . . but I do know he meant to do more good than he meant to do harm. He wasn't always right. Sometimes when he touched he bruised. And sometimes when he took me in his arms he cut.

When I first met your daddy I thought . . . Here is a man I can lay down with and make a baby. That's the first thing I thought when I seen him. I was thirty years old and had done seen my share of men. But when he walked up to me and said, "I can dance a waltz that'll make you dizzy," I thought, Rose Lee, here is a man that you can open yourself up to and be filled to bursting. Here is a man that can fill all them empty spaces you been tipping around the edges of. One of them empty spaces was being somebody's mother.

I married your daddy and settled down to cooking his supper and keeping clean sheets on the bed. When your daddy walked through the house he was so big he filled it up. That was my first mistake. Not to make him leave some room for me. For my part in the matter. But at that time I wanted that. I wanted a house that I could sing in. And that's what your daddy gave me. I didn't know to keep up his strength I had to give up little pieces of mine. I did that. I took on his life as mine and mixed up the pieces so that you couldn't hardly tell which was which anymore. It was my choice. It was my life and I didn't have to live it like that. But that's what life offered me in the way of being a woman and I took it. I grabbed hold of it with both hands.

By the time Raynell came into the house, me and your daddy had done lost touch with one another. I didn't want to make my blessing off of nobody's misfortune . . . but I took on to Raynell like she was all them babies I had wanted and never had.

[*The phone rings.*]

Like I'd been blessed to relive a part of my life. And if the Lord see fit to keep up my strength . . . I'm gonna do her just like your daddy did you . . . I'm gonna give her the best of what's in me.

RAYNELL [*entering, still with her old shoes*] Mama . . . Reverend Tollivier on the phone.

[ROSE *exits into the house.*]

RAYNELL Hi.

CORY Hi.

RAYNELL You in the Army or the Marines?

CORY Marines.

RAYNELL Papa said it was the Army. Did you know Blue?

CORY Blue? Who's Blue?

RAYNELL Papa's dog what he sing about all the time.

CORY [*singing*]

Hear it ring! Hear it ring!
I had a dog his name was Blue
You know Blue was mighty true
You know Blue was a good old dog
Blue treed a possum in a hollow log
You know from that he was a good old dog.
Hear it ring! Hear it ring!

[RAYNELL *joins in singing.*]

CORY and RAYNELL

Blue treed a possum out on a limb
Blue looked at me and I looked at him
Grabbed that possum and put him in a sack
Blue stayed there till I came back
Old Blue's feets was big and round
Never allowed a possum to touch the ground.

Old Blue died and I dug his grave
I dug his grave with a silver spade
Let him down with a golden chain
And every night I call his name

Go on Blue, you good dog you
Go on Blue, you good dog you

RAYNELL
Blue laid down and died like a man
Blue laid down and died . . .

BOTH
Blue laid down and died like a man
Now he's treeing possums in the Promised Land
I'm gonna tell you this to let you know
Blue's gone where the good dogs go
When I hear old Blue bark
When I hear old Blue bark
Blue treed a possum in Noah's Ark.
Blue treed a possum in Noah's Ark.

[ROSE *comes to the screen door.*]

ROSE Cory, we gonna be ready to go in a minute.

CORY [*to* RAYNELL] You go on in the house and change them shoes like Mama told you so we can go to Papa's funeral.

RAYNELL Okay, I'll be back.

[RAYNELL *exits into the house.* CORY *gets up and crosses over to the tree.* ROSE *stands in the screen door watching him.* GABRIEL *enters from the alley.*]

GABRIEL [*calling*] Hey, Rose!

ROSE Gabe?

GABRIEL I'm here, Rose. Hey Rose, I'm here!

[ROSE *enters from the house.*]

ROSE Lord . . . Look here, Lyons!

LYONS See, I told you, Rose . . . I told you they'd let him come.

CORY How you doing, Uncle Gabe?

LYONS How you doing, Uncle Gabe?

GABRIEL Hey, Rose. It's time. It's time to tell St. Peter to open the gates. Troy, you ready? You ready, Troy. I'm gonna tell St. Peter to open the gates. You get ready now.

[*Gabriel, with great fanfare, braces himself to blow. The trumpet is without a mouthpiece. He puts the end of it into his mouth and blows with great force, like a man who has been waiting some twenty-odd years for this single moment. No sound comes out of the trumpet. He braces himself and blows again with the same result. A third time he blows. There is a weight of impossible description that falls away and leaves him bare and exposed to a frightful realization. It is a trauma that a sane and normal mind would be unable to withstand. He begins to dance. A slow, strange dance, eerie and life-giving. A dance of atavistic signature and ritual.* LYONS *attempts to embrace him.* GABRIEL *pushes* LYONS *away. He begins to howl in what is an attempt at song, or perhaps a song turning back into itself in an attempt at speech. He finishes his dance and the gates of heaven stand open as wide as God's closet.*]

That's the way that go!

Blackout.

DAVID HENRY HWANG

b. 1957

FROM the Filipinos who escaped from a Spanish galleon in 1763 and established villages in the Louisiana bayous to the Chinese laborers who built the transcontinental railroad in the nineteenth century to the Cambodians who fled the killing fields of the Khmer Rouge in the 1970s, Asians have come to America and have been an integral part of American history. As the United States expanded westward, a country that had defined itself in relation to Europe (and, through the institution of slavery, to Africa) found itself increasingly engaged with the Pacific region. In the Spanish-American War (1898), the United States annexed Hawaii, was granted protectorship over Guam and the Philippines, and thereby extended a colonial arm across the Pacific Ocean. As American contacts with Asia and its people deepened, popular perceptions of the East vacillated between fascination with the exotic and mysterious "Orient" and fear of the "Yellow Peril" posed by races seemingly alien to American national identity. Even as the vogue for Chinese and Japanese design flourished in the late nineteenth and early twentieth centuries, the U.S. Congress passed laws limiting Asian immigration.

Against this historical backdrop, contemporary Asian Americans—a term that generally includes those who claim origin or ancestry from East Asia, Southeast Asia, or the Indian subcontinent—have often found themselves caught between identities. Racially linked to countries with which those in later generations have had little or no contact, they inhabit a culture that has traditionally represented Asians and those of Asian descent through stereotypes: submissive lotus blossom, dragon lady, evil genius, exotic dancer, obedient servant, warmonger. In recent years, Asian American writers have challenged these stereotypes by depicting the experience of themselves and their communities in its human complexity, and the drama of David Henry Hwang and other Asian American playwrights has given this experience a powerful voice in the American theater. Since Hwang first came to the attention of the theatrical world in the late 1970s, he has written plays exploring the complicated relationship of Chinese Americans to their familial, cultural, and spiritual roots. With his 1988 play *M. BUTTERFLY*—the most critically and commercially successful play ever written by an Asian American—Hwang broadened his gaze to include the intricate (mis)perceptions that characterize the East in the Western imagination.

David Henry Hwang (pronounced "Wong") was born on August 11, 1957, in San Gabriel, California, a wealthy suburb of Los Angeles. His father, who emigrated from Shanghai and—later—Taiwan, was a successful accountant and businessman, and his mother, who was born in southern China to a family that had been converted to fundamentalist Christianity and was raised in the Philippines, was a talented pianist. Hwang would explore this family heritage in his 1996 play *Golden Child*, which is based on the story of his great-grandfather who brought Christianity to his family in China. Because of his mother's religious background and his father's desire to assimilate in his adopted country, the family did not celebrate Chinese holidays or raise their children with an awareness of their Chinese heritage. It wasn't until he was a college student that Hwang became interested in knowing more about his roots. As a child, Hwang studied violin and excelled in debating, and his talents earned him admission to an exclusive preparatory school in Hollywood Hills. Hwang would later credit music and debate as important influences on his playwriting: "Music really helps in terms of developing structure and dramatic growth, and jazz in particular helps with theatrical improvisation. . . . And my early interest in debate no doubt contributed to my theatrical interest in the opposition of ideas and the interplay of ideas in many plays."

Hwang enrolled at Stanford University in 1975 in order to study law, but by his sophomore year he decided that he wanted to write plays. When his creative writing professor explained to him that he lacked an adequate understanding of theater, he immersed himself in drama by attending the theater and reading as many plays as he could. He was particularly drawn to the drama of SAM SHEPARD, several of whose plays premiered during this time at the Magic Theater in nearby San Francisco. In 1978, Hwang had the opportunity to study playwriting with Shepard and the Cuban American playwright MARIA IRENE FORNES at the Padua Hills Playwrights Festival workshop in Claremont, California; it was during this workshop that he conceived the idea of his first play, *FOB*. The play, whose title is the acronym popularly applied to new immigrants—standing for the condescending label "fresh off the boat"—centers on the interaction of three characters: Grace, a first-generation Chinese American; her cousin Dale, a second-generation Chinese American; and Steve, a wealthy immigrant who has just arrived from Hong Kong. Set in the back room of a California restaurant, *FOB* explores the conflicts that immigrants experience as they struggle to assimilate into their new country while also retaining their cultural identity. Though its dialogue and action are clearly influenced by Shepard's plays of the 1970s, the play reveals a highly original dramatic sensibility. In addition to offering carefully drawn psychological portraits, the play dramatizes the confrontation between realism and myth. Steve imagines himself to be the Chinese god Gwan Gung, while Grace identifies with Fa Mu Lan, the mythic "woman warrior" who is the spiritual center of Maxine Hong Kingston's 1976 novel by the same name. When the two engage in a ritualized battle in the play's second act, the realistic present gives way to the timeless space of myth.

FOB was first performed in the lounge of Hwang's Stanford dorm in March 1979 as part of a festival of student plays and musicals. Hwang also submitted the play to the Eugene O'Neill National Playwrights Conference in Connecticut, where it was selected and produced that summer. After attracting the interest of Joseph Papp, producer of the off-Broadway New York Public Theater, *FOB* was produced in New York the following year and received enthusiastic reviews. As the play moved from its college production to the Public Theater, it underwent a significant change in its theatrical style. Papp and others who read the play felt that the ritualized sequence in the play's second act should be staged using the movements and visual approach of the Peking (or Beijing) Opera, a highly stylized form of Chinese theater involving drama, music, mime, dance, and acrobatics. The addition of stage conventions from Chinese opera established a theatrical equivalent to the confrontation of East and West within the play's action, and it launched Hwang's interest in the fusion of Eastern and Western theatrical traditions that would culminate seven years later in *M. Butterfly*.

After the success of *FOB*, which won an Obie Award for Best New American Play, Hwang spent a year in the Yale School of Drama graduate playwriting program. During that time, he wrote *The Dance and the Railroad,* which was produced in New York in 1981. Set during an 1867 strike by Chinese laborers working on the first transcontinental railroad, this two-character play dramatizes the plight of early immigrants who pursued the promise of America while living as "coolies" in an alien land. Through the character of Lone, who trained in Chinese opera and practices his craft on a mountainside at the end of each day's work, the play also expands Hwang's use of Asian theatrical traditions to explore the clash of East and West. *The Dance and the Railroad,* which enjoyed widespread critical acclaim, was followed by a series of plays whose reviews were more mixed: *Family Devotions* (1981); *The House of Sleeping Beauties* and *The Sound of a Voice,* two one-act plays produced in 1983 under the title *Sound and Beauty;* and *Rich Relations* (1986). Hwang's next play, however, would overshadow all his earlier triumphs and disappointments. After a brief preview at the National Theater in Washington, D.C., *M. Butterfly* opened at Broadway's Eugene O'Neill Theatre on March 20, 1988. Lavishly staged, the play was an enormous popular and critical success; indeed, it became one of the most commercially successful nonmusical plays in Broadway history and won a number of awards, including the Tony, Drama Desk, and Outer Critics Circle awards for Best Play. In the years since *M. Butterfly,* Hwang has done collaborative work—including a musical drama titled *1000 Airplanes on the Roof* (1988) with the composer Philip Glass—produced television scripts, and written a number of screenplays. He has also continued to write for theater. In 1996, Hwang received an Obie Award for *Golden Child* (discussed above). In 2001, Hwang's updated text for the 1958 Richard Rodgers and Oscar Hammerstein II's musical *Flower Drum Song* was staged in Los Angeles before moving to Broadway.

M. Butterfly, like many of Hwang's other plays, is characterized by a blending of history and imagination. In May 1986, Hwang heard about an incident reported earlier that month in the *New York Times.* A former French diplomat named Bernard Boursicot and a Chinese opera star named Shi Pei Pu had been arrested and tried for espionage in Paris after a twenty-year sexual relationship during which Boursicot passed government information to Shi, who then passed it on to the Communist Chinese government. During the trial, it was revealed that Boursicot had believed his lover—a man who played women's roles in Chinese and Western opera—was a woman and had conducted what he thought was a heterosexual affair. Boursicot explained that he had never seen "her" naked: "He was very shy. I thought it was a Chinese custom." Intrigued by the theatrical possibilities of so incredible a story, Hwang began working on a play. The crucial moment in conceiving this new work came when he realized that the French diplomat had fallen in love not with a person but with a stereotype of Asian women. "I was driving down Santa Monica Boulevard one afternoon, and asked myself, 'What did Boursicot think he was getting in this Chinese actress?' The answer came to me clearly: 'He probably thought he had found Madame Butterfly.' "

Although Hwang had not yet seen or listened to Giacomo Puccini's opera by that name, he was familiar with the stereotype represented by its delicate, self-sacrificing heroine. *Madame Butterfly* (*Madama* in the original Italian), which premiered in Milan in 1904, was based on a 1900 one-act play by the American playwright and producer David Belasco that Puccini had seen in London (Belasco's play was itself based on a 1898 short story by John Luther Long). Both play and opera tell the story of Cio-Cio-San, a Japanese geisha known as Madame Butterfly, and the American naval lieutenant named Pinkerton who marries her during one of his tours of duty to Japan. He then leaves with his ship; and although he fails to return the following year as promised, Cio-Cio-San waits faithfully, refusing the marriage proposal of a wealthy Japanese man. When Pinkerton finally does come back to Japan, several years later, he is accompanied by a new American wife; Butterfly takes her own life, leaving behind a child that Pinkerton and his wife will bring back to the United States. In its portrait of a submissive and feminized Asia, *Madame Butterfly* exemplifies the Western fantasy of the East as an exotic realm that displays its mysteries for the West to ad-

John Lithgow, center, as Rene Gallimard, and B. D. Wong, right, as Song Liling, in the 1988 Broadway production of *M. Butterfly.*

mire, collect, and dominate. Such a conception of the "Orient," as Edward Said argued in his influential book *Orientalism* (1978), is a Western invention, reflecting an "imaginative geography" rather than the actual sociocultural geography of Asia and its peoples. The operations of such myths, Said claimed, can be felt not only in the representations of Asians by Europeans and North Americans but in the military and political relationships between West and East that form part of the history of imperialism.

In writing what he has called a "deconstructivist *Madame Butterfly,*" Hwang established a series of parallels and counterpoints between Puccini's opera, contemporary history, and a fictionalized version of the Boursicot story. Rene Gallimard, the diplomat of Hwang's play, relives the events of his past from the cell of a Paris prison, a nightly ritual in which he seeks the understanding, and perhaps envy, of his audience for having loved and been loved by "the Perfect Woman." In order to justify his belief and the actions, he recounts the story of *Madame Butterfly*—the opera in which he first saw the singer Song Liling perform—and identifies himself with Puccini's Pinkerton in his quest for the feminine ideal of beauty and submissiveness. The power of this myth is only deepened when Song challenges its premises: "It's one of your favorite fantasies, isn't it? The submissive Oriental woman and the cruel white man." In the following scenes, Gallimard pursues the fantasy of Pinkerton and Butterfly, exulting in his apparent power over his mistress and in his initiation, after an unpromising sexual past, into the privileges of maleness.

One of the central themes of *M. Butterfly,* Hwang suggested in a 1989 interview, is "the nature of seduction, in the sense that to some degree we seduce ourselves." On the collective as well as the individual level, the West's self-seducing perceptions of the East are intimately connected to male perceptions of the female. As Song explains when he is asked about Gallimard's delusion by a Paris judge, "One, . . . when he finally met his fantasy woman, he wanted more than anything to believe that she was, in fact, a woman. And second, I am an Oriental. And being an Oriental, I could never be completely a man." Such thinking, the play suggests, accounts for the West's historic diplomatic and military failings in its encounters with the East. Advising the French ambassador about the Americans' prospects in neighboring Vietnam, Gallimard offers the disastrously misguided prediction that "Orientals will always submit to a greater force."

Hwang's exploration of seduction and misperception also extends to the play's interaction with its audience. On the level of theatrical form, *M. Butterfly* achieves an intricate counterpointing of Eastern and Western characters, impersonations, and styles. A French diplomat taking on the role of an American lieutenant interacts with a Chinese performer playing a Japanese heroine from an opera written by an Italian. Visually and aurally, the play juxtaposes the operatic traditions of Europe with the stage conventions and music of Chinese opera, complicating the audience's point of view with a sometimes jarring cultural fusion of East and West. Moreover, as a commentary on the fluidity of roles and identities, *M. Butterfly* challenges the seemingly clear-cut categories of male and female. Hwang replaced the *Madame* of Puccini's title with the letter *M.*, which stands for *Monsieur* in French but in English is more ambiguous in its gender reference. Even spectators who know the story on which the play is based can find themselves seduced by Song's performance as a woman. Accordingly, when Song removes "her" costume and makeup near the play's end, the audience witnesses the uncanny crossing of gender boundaries. When, in the play's unexpected final scene, Gallimard turns the tables on Song and rescues his fantasy from the harsh light of reality, these boundaries are rendered even more fluid and indeterminate.

M. Butterfly has not been without its critics in the Asian American community, a number of whom have charged Hwang with falling into stereotypes of his own concerning the East and indulging the theatrical exoticism that his play otherwise faults. Yet despite such critiques, the play established Hwang as one of the leading American playwrights of his generation and the most successful figure in Asian American theater. By bringing the lives and experiences of Asian Americans into the theatrical mainstream, he has helped expose the prejudices, misconceptions, and idealized images that have limited the representations of Asianness within and beyond the borders of the United States. Just as importantly, he has served as the voice of a new generation of Asian Americans who find themselves pulled between cultures and who must come to terms with their histories, myths, and traditions while making their lives in a country half a world away from their ancestors' home.

S.G.

M. Butterfly

CHARACTERS

KUROGO[1]	GIRL in magazine
RENE GALLIMARD / PINKERTON	COMRADE CHIN / SUZUKI
SONG LILING / BUTTERFLY	HELGA
WOMAN at party	SHU-FANG
MAN 1	M. TOULON
MAN 2	RENEE
MARC / CONSUL SHARPLESS	JUDGE

Playwright's Notes

A former French diplomat and a Chinese opera singer have been sentenced to six years in jail for spying for China after a two-day trial that traced a story of clandestine love and mistaken sexual identity. . . . Mr. Boursicot was accused of passing information to China after he fell in love with Mr. Shi, whom he believed for twenty years to be a woman.

—The New York Times, *May 11, 1986*

This play was suggested by international newspaper accounts of a recent espionage trial. For purposes of dramatization, names have been changed, characters created, and incidents devised or altered, and this play does not purport to be a factual record of real events or real people.

I could escape this feeling
With my China girl . . .[2]
—DAVID BOWIE & IGGY POP

SETTING: *The action of the play takes place in a Paris prison in the present, and in recall, during the decade 1960 to 1970 in Beijing, and from 1966 to the present in Paris.*

1.1

M. GALLIMARD*'s prison cell. Paris. Present.*

Lights fade up to reveal RENE GALLIMARD, *65, in a prison cell. He wears a comfortable bathrobe, and looks old and tired. The sparsely furnished cell contains a wooden crate upon which sits a hot plate with a kettle, and a portable tape recorder.* GALLIMARD *sits on the crate staring at the recorder, a sad smile on his face.*

Upstage SONG, *who appears as a beautiful woman in traditional Chinese*

1. In traditional Japanese theater, black-clad stage attendants (treated as invisible).
2. From "China Girl," co-written by the English rock musician David Bowie (b. 1947) and the American rock singer Iggy Pop (b. 1947); first released on Pop's album *The Idiot* (1977), it became a hit on Bowie's album *Let's Dance* (1983).

garb, dances a traditional piece from the Peking Opera,[3] *surrounded by the percussive clatter of Chinese music.*

Then, slowly, lights and sound cross-fade; the Chinese opera music dissolves into a Western opera, the "Love Duet" from Puccini's Madame Butterfly.[4] SONG *continues dancing, now to the Western accompaniment. Though her movements are the same, the difference in music now gives them a balletic quality.*

GALLIMARD *rises, and turns upstage towards the figure of* SONG, *who dances without acknowledging him.*

GALLIMARD Butterfly, Butterfly . . .

[*He forces himself to turn away, as the image of* SONG *fades out, and talks to us.*]

GALLIMARD The limits of my cell are as such: four-and-a-half meters by five. There's one window against the far wall; a door, very strong, to protect me from autograph hounds. I'm responsible for the tape recorder, the hot plate, and this charming coffee table.

When I want to eat, I'm marched off to the dining room—hot, steaming slop appears on my plate. When I want to sleep, the lightbulb turns itself off—the work of fairies. It's an enchanted space I occupy. The French—we know how to run a prison.

But, to be honest, I'm not treated like an ordinary prisoner. Why? Because I'm a celebrity. You see, I make people laugh.

I never dreamed this day would arrive. I've never been considered witty or clever. In fact, as a young boy, in an informal poll among my grammar school classmates, I was voted "least likely to be invited to a party." It's a title I managed to hold onto for many years. Despite some stiff competition.

But now, how the tables turn! Look at me: the life of every social function in Paris. Paris? Why be modest? My fame has spread to Amsterdam, London, New York. Listen to them! In the world's smartest parlors. I'm the one who lifts their spirits!

[*With a flourish,* GALLIMARD *directs our attention to another part of the stage.*]

1.2

A party. Present.

Lights go up on a chic-looking parlor, where a well-dressed trio, two men and one woman, make conversation. GALLIMARD *also remains lit; he observes them from his cell.*

WOMAN And what of Gallimard?

MAN 1 Gallimard?

MAN 2 Gallimard!

GALLIMARD [*to us*] You see? They're all determined to say my name, as if it were some new dance.

WOMAN He still claims not to believe the truth.

MAN 1 What? Still? Even since the trial?

3. Chinese opera is a highly stylized art form involving drama, song, mime, dance, and acrobatics. *Peking*: former Westernization of Beijing.

4. That is, *Madama Butterfly* (1904), an Italian opera composed by Giacomo Puccini (1858–1924) with a libretto by Luigi Illica (1857–1919) and Giuseppi Giacosa (1847—1906); it is one of the most frequently performed of all operas.

WOMAN Yes. Isn't it mad?

MAN 2 [*laughing*] He says . . . it was dark . . . and she was very modest!

[*The trio break into laughter.*]

MAN 1 So—what? He never touched her with his hands?

MAN 2 Perhaps he did, and simply misidentified the equipment. A compelling case for sex education in the schools.

WOMAN To protect the National Security—the Church can't argue with that.

MAN 1 That's impossible! How could he not know?

MAN 2 Simple ignorance.

MAN 1 For twenty years?

MAN 2 Time flies when you're being stupid.

WOMAN Well, I thought the French were ladies' men.

MAN 2 It seems Monsieur Gallimard was overly anxious to live up to his national reputation.

WOMAN Well, he's not very good-looking.

MAN 1 No, he's not.

MAN 2 Certainly not.

WOMAN Actually, I feel sorry for him.

MAN 2 A toast! To Monsieur Gallimard!

WOMAN Yes! To Gallimard!

MAN 1 To Gallimard!

MAN 2 Vive la différence![5]

[*They toast, laughing. Lights down on them.*]

1.3

M. GALLIMARD*'s cell.*

GALLIMARD [*smiling*] You see? They toast me. I've become patron saint of the socially inept. Can they really be so foolish? Men like that—they should be scratching at my door, begging to learn my secrets! For I, Rene Gallimard, you see, I have known, and been loved by . . . the Perfect Woman.

Alone in this cell, I sit night after night, watching our story play through my head, always searching for a new ending, one which redeems my honor, where she returns at last to my arms. And I imagine you—my ideal audience—who come to understand and even, perhaps just a little, to envy me.

[*He turns on his tape recorder. Over the house speakers, we hear the opening phrases of* Madame Butterfly.]

GALLIMARD In order for you to understand what I did and why, I must introduce you to my favorite opera: *Madame Butterfly*. By Giacomo Puccini. First produced at La Scala, Milan, in 1904, it is now beloved throughout the Western world.

[*As* GALLIMARD *describes the opera, the tape segues in and out to sections he may be describing.*]

GALLIMARD And why not? Its heroine, Cio-Cio-San, also known as Butterfly, is a feminine ideal, beautiful and brave. And its hero, the man for whom she gives up everything, is—[*He pulls out a naval officer's cap from under his crate, pops it on his head, and struts about.*]—not very good-looking, not too bright, and pretty much a wimp: Benjamin Franklin Pinkerton of the

5. Long live the difference (French), an expression that specifically celebrates the difference between the sexes.

U.S. Navy. As the curtain rises, he's just closed on two great bargains: one on a house, the other on a woman—call it a package deal.

Pinkerton purchased the rights to Butterfly for one hundred yen—in modern currency, equivalent to about . . . sixty-six cents. So, he's feeling pretty pleased with himself as Sharpless, the American consul, arrives to witness the marriage.

[MARC, *wearing an official cap to designate* SHARPLESS, *enters and plays the character.*]

SHARPLESS/MARC Pinkerton!

PINKERTON/GALLIMARD Sharpless! How's it hangin'? It's a great day, just great. Between my house, my wife, and the rickshaw[6] ride in from town, I've saved nineteen cents just this morning.

SHARPLESS Wonderful. I can see the inscription on your tombstone already: "I saved a dollar, here I lie." [*He looks around.*] Nice house.

PINKERTON It's artistic. Artistic, don't you think? Like the way the shoji[7] screens slide open to reveal the wet bar and disco mirror ball? Classy, huh? Great for impressing the chicks.

SHARPLESS "Chicks"? Pinkerton, you're going to be a married man!

PINKERTON Well, sort of.

SHARPLESS What do you mean?

PINKERTON This country—Sharpless, it is okay. You got all these geisha[8] girls running around—

SHARPLESS I know! I live here!

PINKERTON Then, you know the marriage laws, right? I split for one month, it's annulled!

SHARPLESS Leave it to you to read the fine print. Who's the lucky girl?

PINKERTON Cio-Cio-San. Her friends call her Butterfly. Sharpless, she eats out of my hand!

SHARPLESS She's probably very hungry.

PINKERTON Not like American girls. It's true what they say about Oriental girls. They want to be treated bad!

SHARPLESS Oh, please!

PINKERTON It's true!

SHARPLESS Are you serious about this girl?

PINKERTON I'm marrying her, aren't I?

SHARPLESS Yes—with generous trade-in terms.

PINKERTON When I leave, she'll know what it's like to have loved a real man. And I'll even buy her a few nylons.

SHARPLESS You aren't planning to take her with you?

PINKERTON Huh? Where?

SHARPLESS Home!

PINKERTON You mean, America? Are you crazy? Can you see her trying to buy rice in St. Louis?

SHARPLESS So, you're not serious.

[*Pause.*]

PINKERTON/GALLIMARD [*as* PINKERTON] Consul, I am a sailor in port. [*As* GAL-

6. That is, *jinrikisha* (Japanese), a light, two-wheeled passenger vehicle drawn by one or two men.

7. Paper screens used as walls, partitions, or sliding doors (Japanese).

8. In traditional Japanese society, professional women trained from childhood to entertain men with singing, dancing, and conversation.

LIMARD] They then proceed to sing the famous duet, "The Whole World Over."[9]

[*The duet plays on the speakers.* GALLIMARD, *as* PINKERTON, *lip-syncs his lines from the opera.*]

GALLIMARD To give a rough translation: "The whole world over, the Yankee travels, casting his anchor wherever he wants. Life's not worth living unless he can win the hearts of the fairest maidens, then hotfoot it off the premises ASAP." [*He turns towards* MARC.] In the preceding scene, I played Pinkerton, the womanizing cad, and my friend Marc from school . . . [MARC *bows grandly for our benefit.*] played Sharpless, the sensitive soul of reason. In life, however, our positions were usually—no, always—reversed.

1.4

Ecole Nationale. Aix-en-Provence.[1] 1947.

GALLIMARD No, Marc, I think I'd rather stay home.

MARC Are you crazy?! We are going to Dad's condo in Marseille![2] You know what happened last time?

GALLIMARD Of course I do.

MARC Of course you don't! You never know. . . . They stripped, Rene!

GALLIMARD Who stripped?

MARC The girls!

GALLIMARD Girls? Who said anything about girls?

MARC Rene, we're a buncha university guys goin' up to the woods. What are we gonna do—talk philosophy?

GALLIMARD What girls? Where do you get them?

MARC Who cares? The point is, they come. On trucks. Packed in like sardines. The back flips open, babes hop out, we're ready to roll.

GALLIMARD You mean, they just—?

MARC Before you know it, every last one of them—they're stripped and splashing around my pool. There's no moon out, they can't see what's going on, their boobs are flapping, right? You close your eyes, reach out—it's grab bag, get it? Doesn't matter whose ass is between whose legs, whose teeth are sinking into who. You're just in there, going at it, eyes closed, on and on for as long as you can stand. [*Pause*] Some fun, huh?

GALLIMARD What happens in the morning?

MARC In the morning, you're ready to talk some philosophy. [*Beat*[3]] So how 'bout it?

GALLIMARD Marc, I can't . . . I'm afraid they'll say no—the girls. So I never ask.

MARC You don't have to ask! That's the beauty—don't you see? They don't have to say yes. It's perfect for a guy like you, really.

GALLIMARD You go ahead . . . I may come later.

MARC Hey, Rene—it doesn't matter that you're clumsy and got zits—they're not looking!

9. "Dovunque al mondo" is in fact an aria sung by Pinkerton.

1. A city in southern France, about 20 miles north of Marseille. Among its universities is the École Nationale Supérieure d'Arts et Métiers (National School of Arts and Trades), an elite school of engineering.

2. France's second-largest city, an important commercial and industrial center on the Mediterranean coast.

3. Pause (theater term).

GALLIMARD Thank you very much.

MARC Wimp.

[MARC *walks over to the other side of the stage, and starts waving and smiling at women in the audience.*]

GALLIMARD [*to us*] We now return to my version of *Madame Butterfly* and the events leading to my recent conviction for treason.

[GALLIMARD *notices* MARC *making lewd gestures.*]

GALLIMARD Marc, what are you doing?

MARC Huh? [*Sotto voce*[4]] Rene, there're a lotta great babes out there. They're probably lookin' at me and thinking, "What a dangerous guy."

GALLIMARD Yes—how could they help but be impressed by your cool sophistication?

[GALLIMARD *pops the* SHARPLESS *cap on* MARC*'s head, and points him offstage.* MARC *exits, leering.*]

1.5

M. GALLIMARD*'s cell.*

GALLIMARD Next, Butterfly makes her entrance. We learn her age—fifteen . . . but very mature for her years.

[*Lights come up on the area where we saw* SONG *dancing at the top of the play. She appears there again, now dressed as Madame* BUTTERFLY, *moving to the "Love Duet."*[5] GALLIMARD *turns upstage slightly to watch, transfixed.*]

GALLIMARD But as she glides past him, beautiful, laughing softly behind her fan, don't we who are men sigh with hope? We, who are not handsome, nor brave, nor powerful, yet somehow believe, like Pinkerton, that we deserve a Butterfly. She arrives with all her possessions in the folds of her sleeves, lays them all out, for her man to do with as he pleases. Even her life itself—she bows her head as she whispers that she's not even worth the hundred yen he paid for her. He's already given too much, when we know he's really had to give nothing at all.

[*Music and lights on* SONG *out.* GALLIMARD *sits at his crate.*]

GALLIMARD In real life, women who put their total worth at less than sixty-six cents are quite hard to find. The closest we come is in the pages of these magazines. [*He reaches into his crate, pulls out a stack of girlie magazines, and begins flipping through them.*] Quite a necessity in prison. For three or four dollars, you get seven or eight women.

I first discovered these magazines at my uncle's house. One day, as a boy of twelve. The first time I saw them in his closet . . . all lined up—my body shook. Not with lust—no, with power. Here were women—a shelfful—who would do exactly as I wanted.

[*The "Love Duet" creeps in over the speakers. Special*[6] *comes up, revealing, not* SONG *this time, but a pinup girl in a sexy negligee, her back to us.* GALLIMARD *turns upstage and looks at her.*]

GIRL I know you're watching me.

4. Under the voice (Italian); that is, spoken very softly, under the breath.

5. "Viene la sera" ("Evening Is Falling"), a duet sung by Pinkerton and Butterfly at the end of act 1 of *Madama Butterfly*.

6. A stage light used at designated moments during a play for specific, highly theatrical effects.

GALLIMARD My throat . . . it's dry.

GIRL I leave my blinds open every night before I go to bed.

GALLIMARD I can't move.

GIRL I leave my blinds open and the lights on.

GALLIMARD I'm shaking. My skin is hot, but my penis is soft. Why?

GIRL I stand in front of the window.

GALLIMARD What is she going to do?

GIRL I toss my hair, and I let my lips part . . . barely.

GALLIMARD I shouldn't be seeing this. It's so dirty. I'm so bad.

GIRL Then, slowly, I lift off my nightdress.

GALLIMARD Oh, god. I can't believe it. I can't—

GIRL I toss it to the ground.

GALLIMARD Now, she's going to walk away. She's going to—

GIRL I stand there, in the light, displaying myself.

GALLIMARD No. She's—why is she naked?

GIRL To you.

GALLIMARD In front of a window? This is wrong. No—

GIRL Without shame.

GALLIMARD No, she must . . . like it.

GIRL I like it.

GALLIMARD She . . . she wants me to see.

GIRL I want you to see.

GALLIMARD I can't believe it! She's getting excited!

GIRL I can't see you. You can do whatever you want.

GALLIMARD I can't do a thing. Why?

GIRL What would you like me to do . . . next?

[*Lights go down on her. Music off. Silence, as* GALLIMARD *puts away his magazines. Then he resumes talking to us.*]

GALLIMARD Act Two begins with Butterfly staring at the ocean. Pinkerton's been called back to the U.S., and he's given his wife a detailed schedule of his plans. In the column marked "return date," he's written "when the robins nest." This failed to ignite her suspicions. Now, three years have passed without a peep from him. Which brings a response from her faithful servant, Suzuki.

[COMRADE CHIN *enters, playing* SUZUKI.]

SUZUKI Girl, he's a loser. What'd he ever give you? Nineteen cents and those ugly Day-Glo stockings? Look, it's finished! Kaput! Done! And you should be glad! I mean, the guy was a woofer![7] He tried before, you know—before he met you, he went down to geisha central and plunked down his spare change in front of the usual candidates—everyone else gagged! These are hungry prostitutes, and they were not interested, get the picture? Now, stop slathering when an American ship sails in, and let's make some bucks—I mean, yen! We are broke!

Now, what about Yamadori? Hey, hey—don't look away—the man is a prince—figuratively, and, what's even better, literally. He's rich, he's handsome, he says he'll die if you don't marry him—and he's even willing to overlook the little fact that you've been deflowered all over the place by a foreign devil. What do you mean, "But he's Japanese?" You're Japanese! You think you've been touched by the whitey god? He was a sailor with dirty hands!

7. That is, a dog, an ugly person (slang).

[SUZUKI *stalks offstage.*]

GALLIMARD She's also visited by Consul Sharpless, sent by Pinkerton on a minor errand.

[MARC *enters, as* SHARPLESS.]

SHARPLESS I hate this job.

GALLIMARD This Pinkerton—he doesn't show up personally to tell his wife he's abandoning her. No, he sends a government diplomat . . . at taxpayer's expense.

SHARPLESS Butterfly? Butterfly? I have some bad—I'm going to be ill. Butterfly, I came to tell you—

GALLIMARD Butterfly says she knows he'll return and if he doesn't she'll kill herself rather than go back to her own people. [*Beat*] This causes a lull in the conversation.

SHARPLESS Let's put it this way . . .

GALLIMARD Butterfly runs into the next room, and returns holding—

[*Sound cue: a baby crying.* SHARPLESS, *"seeing" this, backs away.*]

SHARPLESS Well, good. Happy to see things going so well. I suppose I'll be going now. Ta ta. Ciao. [*He turns away. Sound cue out.*] I hate this job. [*He exits.*]

GALLIMARD At that moment, Butterfly spots in the harbor an American ship—the *Abramo Lincoln!*[8]

[*Music cue: "The Flower Duet."*[9] SONG, *still dressed as* BUTTERFLY, *changes into a wedding kimono, moving to the music.*]

GALLIMARD This is the moment that redeems her years of waiting. With Suzuki's help, they cover the room with flowers—

[CHIN, *as* SUZUKI, *trudges onstage and drops a lone flower without much enthusiasm.*]

GALLIMARD —and she changes into her wedding dress to prepare for Pinkerton's arrival.

[SUZUKI *helps* BUTTERFLY *change.* HELGA *enters, and helps* GALLIMARD *change into a tuxedo.*]

GALLIMARD I married a woman older than myself—Helga.

HELGA My father was ambassador to Australia. I grew up among criminals and kangaroos.[1]

GALLIMARD Hearing that brought me to the altar—

[HELGA *exits.*]

GALLIMARD —where I took a vow renouncing love. No fantasy woman would ever want me, so, yes, I would settle for a quick leap up the career ladder. Passion, I banish, and in its place—practicality!

But my vows had long since lost their charm by the time we arrived in China. The sad truth is that all men want a beautiful woman, and the uglier the man, the greater the want.

[SUZUKI *makes final adjustments of* BUTTERFLY'*s costume, as does* GALLIMARD *of his tuxedo.*]

8. Abraham Lincoln (Italian).
9. "Tutti i fior?" ("All the Flowers"), a duet sung by Butterfly and her servant Suzuki in act 2 of *Madama Butterfly* at the point in the story narrated here by Gallimard.

1. Australia was originally used by Great Britain as a penal colony, and a sizable portion of the early settlers were convicts transported between 1788 and 1868.

GALLIMARD I married late, at age thirty-one. I was faithful to my marriage for eight years. Until the day when, as a junior-level diplomat in puritanical Peking, in a parlor at the German ambassador's house, during the "Reign of a Hundred Flowers,"[2] I first saw her . . . singing the death scene from *Madame Butterfly.*

[SUZUKI *runs offstage.*]

1.6

German ambassador's house. Beijing. 1960.

The upstage special area now becomes a stage. Several chairs face upstage, representing seating for some twenty guests in the parlor. A few "diplomats"— RENEE, MARC, TOULON*—in formal dress enter and take seats.*

GALLIMARD *also sits down, but turns towards us and continues to talk. Orchestral accompaniment on the tape is now replaced by a simple piano.* SONG *picks up the death scene from the point where* BUTTERFLY *uncovers the hara-kiri[3] knife.*

GALLIMARD The ending is pitiful. Pinkerton, in an act of great courage, stays home and sends his American wife to pick up Butterfly's child. The truth, long deferred, has come up to her door.

[SONG, *playing* BUTTERFLY, *sings the lines from the opera in her own voice—which, though not classical, should be decent.*]

SONG "Con onor muore / chi non puo serbar / vita con onore."

GALLIMARD [*simultaneously*] "Death with honor / Is better than life / Life with dishonor."

[*The stage is illuminated; we are now completely within an elegant diplomat's residence.* SONG *proceeds to play out an abbreviated death scene. Everyone in the room applauds.* SONG, *shyly, takes her bows. Others in the room rush to congratulate her.* GALLIMARD *remains with us.*]

GALLIMARD They say in opera the voice is everything. That's probably why I'd never before enjoyed opera. Here . . . here was a Butterfly with little or no voice—but she had the grace, the delicacy . . . I believed this girl. I believed her suffering. I wanted to take her in my arms—so delicate, even I could protect her, take her home, pamper her until she smiled.

[*Over the course of the preceding speech,* SONG *has broken from the upstage crowd and moved directly upstage of* GALLIMARD.]

SONG Excuse me. Monsieur . . . ?

[GALLIMARD *turns upstage, shocked.*]

GALLIMARD Oh! Gallimard. Mademoiselle . . . ? A beautiful . . .

SONG Song Liling.

GALLIMARD A beautiful performance.

SONG Oh, please.

GALLIMARD I usually—

SONG You make me blush. I'm no opera singer at all.

GALLIMARD I usually don't like *Butterfly.*

2. The so-called Hundred Flowers Campaign, a brief period (1956–57) during which the Communist authorities allowed intellectuals greater freedom of thought and speech.

3. Ritual suicide by disembowelment (Japanese).

SONG I can't blame you in the least.

GALLIMARD I mean, the story—

SONG Ridiculous.

GALLIMARD I like the story, but . . . what?

SONG Oh, you like it?

GALLIMARD I . . . what I mean is, I've always seen it played by huge women in so much bad makeup.

SONG Bad makeup is not unique to the West.

GALLIMARD But, who can believe them?

SONG And you believe me?

GALLIMARD Absolutely. You were utterly convincing. It's the first time—

SONG Convincing? As a Japanese woman? The Japanese used hundreds of our people for medical experiments during the war,[4] you know. But I gather such an irony is lost on you.

GALLIMARD No! I was about to say, it's the first time I've seen the beauty of the story.

SONG Really?

GALLIMARD Of her death. It's a . . . a pure sacrifice. He's unworthy, but what can she do? She loves him . . . so much. It's a very beautiful story.

SONG Well, yes, to a Westerner.

GALLIMARD Excuse me?

SONG It's one of your favorite fantasies, isn't it? The submissive Oriental woman and the cruel white man.

GALLIMARD Well, I didn't quite mean . . .

SONG Consider it this way: what would you say if a blonde homecoming queen fell in love with a short Japanese businessman? He treats her cruelly, then goes home for three years, during which time she prays to his picture and turns down marriage from a young Kennedy.[5] Then, when she learns he has remarried, she kills herself. Now, I believe you would consider this girl to be a deranged idiot, correct? But because it's an Oriental who kills herself for a Westerner—ah!—you find it beautiful.

[*Silence.*]

GALLIMARD Yes . . . well . . . I see your point . . .

SONG I will never do Butterfly again, Monsieur Gallimard. If you wish to see some real theatre, come to the Peking Opera sometime. Expand your mind.

[SONG *walks offstage.*]

GALLIMARD [*to us*] So much for protecting her in my big Western arms.

1.7

M. GALLIMARD*'s apartment. Beijing. 1960.*

GALLIMARD *changes from his tux into a casual suit.* HELGA *enters.*

GALLIMARD The Chinese are an incredibly arrogant people.

HELGA They warned us about that in Paris, remember?

4. The Japanese conducted gruesome medical experiments on Chinese prisoners and civilians during their World War II–era occupation of China (1937–45).

5. A member of the Massachusetts political family whose best-known members are President John F. Kennedy (1917–1963), Senator Robert F. Kennedy (1925–1968), and Senator Edward Kennedy (b. 1932).

GALLIMARD Even Parisians consider them arrogant. That's a switch.

HELGA What is it that Madame Su says? "We are a very old civilization." I never know if she's talking about her country or herself.

GALLIMARD I walk around here, all I hear every day, everywhere is how *old* this culture is. The fact that "old" may be synonymous with "senile" doesn't occur to them.

HELGA You're not going to change them. "East is east, west is west, and . . ."[6] whatever that guy said.

GALLIMARD It's just that—silly. I met . . . at Ambassador Koening's tonight—you should've been there.

HELGA Koening? Oh god, no. Did he enchant you all again with the history of Bavaria?[7]

GALLIMARD No. I met, I suppose, the Chinese equivalent of a diva.[8] She's a singer in the Chinese opera.

HELGA They have an opera, too? Do they sing in Chinese? Or maybe—in Italian?

GALLIMARD Tonight, she did sing in Italian.

HELGA How'd she manage that?

GALLIMARD She must've been educated in the West before the Revolution.[9] Her French is very good also. Anyway, she sang the death scene from *Madame Butterfly.*

HELGA *Madame Butterfly!* Then I should have come. [*She begins humming, floating around the room as if dragging long kimono sleeves.*] Did she have a nice costume? I think it's a classic piece of music.

GALLIMARD That's what *I* thought, too. Don't let her hear you say that.

HELGA What's wrong?

GALLIMARD Evidently the Chinese hate it.

HELGA She hated it, but she performed it anyway? Is she perverse?

GALLIMARD They hate it because the white man gets the girl. Sour grapes if you ask me.

HELGA Politics again? Why can't they just hear it as a piece of beautiful music? So, what's in their opera?

GALLIMARD I don't know. But, whatever it is, I'm sure it must be *old.*

[HELGA *exits.*]

1.8

Chinese opera house and the streets of Beijing. 1960.

The sound of gongs clanging fills the stage.

GALLIMARD My wife's innocent question kept ringing in my ears. I asked around, but no one knew anything about the Chinese opera. It took four weeks, but my curiosity overcame my cowardice. This Chinese diva—this unwilling Butterfly—what did she do to make her so proud?

6. "Oh, East is East, and West is West, and never the twain shall meet," from the poem "The Ballad of East and West" (1889) by the British writer Rudyard Kipling (1865–1936).

7. Germany's southernmost state, which was an independent kingdom until 1871.

8. A female opera star of the most glamorous and imperious sort (literally, "goddess"; Italian).

9. The civil war between the Nationalist government, led by Chiang Kai-shek, and the Communist rebels, led by Mao Zedong, which ended with the establishment of the People's Republic of China under Mao in 1949.

The room was hot, and full of smoke. Wrinkled faces, old women, teeth missing—a man with a growth on his neck, like a human toad. All smiling, pipes falling from their mouths, cracking nuts between their teeth, a live chicken pecking at my foot—all looking, screaming, gawking . . . at her.

[*The upstage area is suddenly hit with a harsh white light. It has become the stage for the Chinese opera performance. Two dancers enter, along with* SONG. GALLIMARD *stands apart, watching.* SONG *glides gracefully amidst the two dancers. Drums suddenly slam to a halt.* SONG *strikes a pose, looking straight at* GALLIMARD. *Dancers exit. Light change. Pause, then* SONG *walks right off the stage and straight up to* GALLIMARD.]

SONG Yes. You. White man. I'm looking straight at you.

GALLIMARD Me?

SONG You see any other white men? It was too easy to spot you. How often does a man in my audience come in a tie?

[SONG *starts to remove her costume. Underneath, she wears simple baggy clothes. They are now backstage. The show is over.*]

SONG So, you are an adventurous imperialist?

GALLIMARD I . . . thought it would further my education.

SONG It took you four weeks. Why?

GALLIMARD I've been busy.

SONG Well, education has always been undervalued in the West, hasn't it?

GALLIMARD [*laughing*] I don't think it's true.

SONG No, you wouldn't. You're a Westerner. How can you objectively judge your own values?

GALLIMARD I think it's possible to achieve some distance.

SONG Do you? [*Pause*] It stinks in here. Let's go.

GALLIMARD These are the smells of your loyal fans.

SONG I love them for being my fans, I hate the smell they leave behind. I too can distance myself from my people. [*She looks around, then whispers in his ear.*] "Art for the masses"[1] is a shitty excuse to keep artists poor. [*She pops a cigarette in her mouth.*] Be a gentleman, will you? And light my cigarette.

[GALLIMARD *fumbles for a match.*]

GALLIMARD I don't . . . smoke.

SONG [*lighting her own*] Your loss. Had you lit my cigarette, I might have blown a puff of smoke right between your eyes. Come.

[*They start to walk about the stage. It is a summer night on the Beijing streets. Sounds of the city play on the house speakers.*]

SONG How I wish there were even a tiny cafe to sit in. With cappuccinos, and men in tuxedos and bad expatriate jazz.

GALLIMARD If my history serves me correctly, you weren't even allowed into the clubs in Shanghai[2] before the Revolution.

SONG Your history serves you poorly, Monsieur Gallimard. True, there were signs reading "No dogs and Chinamen." But a woman, especially a delicate Oriental woman—we always go where we please. Could you imagine it otherwise? Clubs in China filled with pasty, big-thighed white women, while

1. A Communist slogan advocating a proletarian (working-class) art in place of the so-called elite art of Western capitalism.

2. The largest city in China; as one of the five ports opened to foreign trade and to foreign residents in the 19th century, it became the country's economic and cultural center until investment from overseas was halted by the Communist victory.

thousands of slender lotus blossoms[3] wait just outside the door? Never. The clubs would be empty. [*Beat*] We have always held a certain fascination for you Caucasian men, have we not?

GALLIMARD But . . . that fascination is imperialist, or so you tell me.

SONG Do you believe everything I tell you? Yes. It is always imperialist. But sometimes . . . sometimes, it is also mutual. Oh—this is my flat.

GALLIMARD I didn't even—

SONG Thank you. Come another time and we will further expand your mind.

[SONG *exits.* GALLIMARD *continues roaming the streets as he speaks to us.*]

GALLIMARD What was that? What did she mean, "Sometimes . . . it is mutual?" Women do not flirt with me. And I normally can't talk to them. But tonight, I held up my end of the conversation.

1.9

GALLIMARD*'s bedroom. Beijing. 1960.*

HELGA *enters.*

HELGA You didn't tell me you'd be home late.

GALLIMARD I didn't intend to. Something came up.

HELGA Oh? Like what?

GALLIMARD I went to the . . . to the Dutch ambassador's home.

HELGA Again?

GALLIMARD There was a reception for a visiting scholar. He's writing a six-volume treatise on the Chinese revolution. We all gathered that meant he'd have to live here long enough to actually write six volumes, and we all expressed our deepest sympathies.

HELGA Well, I had a good night too. I went with the ladies to a martial arts demonstration. Some of those men—when they break those thick boards—[*She mimes fanning herself.*] whoo-whoo!

[HELGA *exits. Lights dim.*]

GALLIMARD I lied to my wife. Why? I've never had any reason to lie before. But what reason did I have tonight? I didn't do anything wrong. That night, I had a dream. Other people, I've been told, have dreams where angels appear. Or dragons, or Sophia Loren[4] in a towel. In my dream, Marc from school appeared.

[MARC *enters, in a nightshirt and cap.*]

MARC Rene! You met a girl!

[GALLIMARD *and* MARC *stumble down the Beijing streets. Night sounds over the speakers.*]

GALLIMARD It's not that amazing, thank you.

MARC No! It's so monumental, I heard about it halfway around the world in my sleep!

GALLIMARD I've met girls before, you know.

MARC Name one. I've come across time and space to congratulate you. [*He hands* GALLIMARD *a bottle of wine.*]

3. That is, Asian women. The lotus blossom symbolized the practice of footbinding, which was highly eroticized in traditional Chinese culture.

4. An Italian actress (b. 1934), famous for her beauty and viewed as an international sex symbol.

GALLIMARD Marc, this is expensive.

MARC On those rare occasions when you become a formless spirit, why not steal the best?

[MARC *pops open the bottle, begins to share it with* GALLIMARD.]

GALLIMARD You embarrass me. She . . . there's no reason to think she likes me.

MARC "Sometimes, it is mutual"?

GALLIMARD Oh.

MARC "Mutual"? "Mutual"? What does that mean?

GALLIMARD You heard!

MARC It means the money is in the bank, you only have to write the check!

GALLIMARD I am a married man!

MARC And an excellent one too. I cheated after . . . six months. Then again and again, until now—three hundred girls in twelve years.

GALLIMARD I don't think we should hold that up as a model.

MARC Of course not! My life—it is disgusting! Phooey! Phooey! But, you—you are the model husband.

GALLIMARD Anyway, it's impossible. I'm a foreigner.

MARC Ah, yes. She cannot love you, it is taboo, but something deep inside her heart . . . she cannot help herself . . . she must surrender to you. It is her destiny.

GALLIMARD How do you imagine all this?

MARC The same way you do. It's an old story. It's in our blood. They fear us, Rene. Their women fear us. And their men—their men hate us. And, you know something? They are all correct.

[*They spot a light in a window.*]

MARC There! There, Rene!

GALLIMARD It's her window.

MARC Late at night—it burns. The light—it burns for you.

GALLIMARD I won't look. It's not respectful.

MARC We don't have to be respectful. We're foreign devils.

[*Enter* SONG, *in a sheer robe. The "One Fine Day"*[5] *aria creeps in over the speakers. With her back to us,* SONG *mimes attending to her toilette. Her robe comes loose, revealing her white shoulders.*]

MARC All your life you've waited for a beautiful girl who would lay down for you. All your life you've smiled like a saint when it's happened to every other man you know. And you see them in magazines and you see them in movies. And you wonder, what's wrong with me? Will anyone beautiful ever want me? As the years pass, your hair thins and you struggle to hold onto even your hopes. Stop struggling, Rene. The wait is over. [*He exits.*]

GALLIMARD Marc? Marc?

[*At that moment,* SONG, *her back still towards us, drops her robe. A second of her naked back, then a sound cue: a phone ringing, very loud. Blackout, followed in the next beat by a special up on the bedroom area, where a phone now sits.* GALLIMARD *stumbles across the stage and picks up the phone. Sound cue out. Over the course of his conversation, area lights fill in the vicinity of his bed. It is the following morning.*]

5. "Un bel dì vedremo" ("One Fine Day We Shall See"), an aria sung by Butterfly in act 2 of *Madama Butterfly*.

GALLIMARD Yes? Hello?
SONG [*offstage*] Is it very early?
GALLIMARD Why, yes.
SONG [*offstage*] How early?
GALLIMARD It's . . . it's 5:30. Why are you—?
SONG [*offstage*] But it's light outside. Already.
GALLIMARD It is. The sun must be in confusion today.

[*Over the course of* SONG'S *next speech, her upstage special comes up again. She sits in a chair, legs crossed, in a robe, telephone to her ear.*]

SONG I waited until I saw the sun. That was as much discipline as I could manage for one night. Do you forgive me?
GALLIMARD Of course . . . for what?
SONG Then I'll ask you quickly. Are you really interested in the opera?
GALLIMARD Why, yes. Yes I am.
SONG Then come again next Thursday. I am playing *The Drunken Beauty.*[6] May I count on you?
GALLIMARD Yes. You may.
SONG Perfect. Well, I must be getting to bed. I'm exhausted. It's been a very long night for me.

[SONG *hangs up; special on her goes off.* GALLIMARD *begins to dress for work.*]

1.10

SONG LILING'S *apartment. Beijing. 1960.*

GALLIMARD I returned to the opera that next week, and the week after that . . . she keeps our meetings so short—perhaps fifteen, twenty minutes at most. So I am left each week with a thirst which is intensified. In this way, fifteen weeks have gone by. I am starting to doubt the words of my friend Marc. But no, not really. In my heart, I know she has . . . an interest in me. I suspect this is her way. She is outwardly bold and outspoken, yet her heart is shy and afraid. It is the Oriental in her at war with her Western education.
SONG [*offstage*] I will be out in an instant. Ask the servant for anything you want.
GALLIMARD Tonight, I have finally been invited to enter her apartment. Though the idea is almost beyond belief, I believe she is afraid of me.

[GALLIMARD *looks around the room. He picks up a picture in a frame, studies it. Without his noticing,* SONG *enters, dressed elegantly in a black gown from the twenties. She stands in the doorway looking like Anna May Wong.*[7]]

SONG That is my father.
GALLIMARD [*surprised*] Mademoiselle Song . . .

[*She glides up to him, snatches away the picture.*]

6. A traditional Chinese opera about an imperial concubine during the Tang dynasty (set ca. 750 C.E.). Enraged that the emperor has chosen to visit a new concubine, his previous favorite drinks herself into a state of gaiety and then despondency. *The Drunken Beauty* (or *The Drunken Concubine*) was made famous by the Beijing Opera star Mei Lanfang (1894–1961), a man who specialized in female roles.

7. A Chinese American actor (1905–1961), the first Asian woman to become a film star; she often played temptresses or exotic villainesses in the 1920s and '30s.

SONG It is very good that he did not live to see the Revolution. They would, no doubt, have made him kneel on broken glass.[8] Not that he didn't deserve such a punishment. But he is my father. I would've hated to see it happen.

GALLIMARD I'm very honored that you've allowed me to visit your home.

[SONG *curtsies.*]

SONG Thank you. Oh! Haven't you been poured any tea?

GALLIMARD I'm really not—

SONG [*to her offstage servant*] Shu-Fang! Cha! Kwai-lah![9] [*To* GALLIMARD] I'm sorry. You want everything to be perfect—

GALLIMARD Please.

SONG —and before the evening even begins—

GALLIMARD I'm really not thirsty.

SONG —It's ruined.

GALLIMARD [*sharply*] Mademoiselle Song!

[SONG *sits down.*]

SONG I'm sorry.

GALLIMARD What are you apologizing for now?

[*Pause;* SONG *starts to giggle.*]

SONG I don't know!

[GALLIMARD *laughs.*]

GALLIMARD Exactly my point.

SONG Oh, I am silly. Lightheaded. I promise not to apologize for anything else tonight, do you hear me?

GALLIMARD That's a good girl.

[SHU-FANG, *a servant girl, comes out with a tea tray and starts to pour.*]

SONG [*to* SHU-FANG] No! I'll pour myself for the gentleman!

[SHU-FANG, *staring at* GALLIMARD, *exits.*]

SONG No, I . . . I don't even know why I invited you up.

GALLIMARD Well, I'm glad you did.

[SONG *looks around the room.*]

SONG There is an element of danger to your presence.

GALLIMARD Oh?

SONG You must know.

GALLIMARD It doesn't concern me. We both know why I'm here.

SONG It doesn't concern me either. No . . . well perhaps . . .

GALLIMARD What?

SONG Perhaps I am slightly afraid of scandal.

GALLIMARD What are we doing?

SONG I'm entertaining you. In my parlor.

GALLIMARD In France, that would hardly—

SONG France. France is a country living in the modern era. Perhaps even ahead of it. China is a nation whose soul is firmly rooted two thousand years in the past. What I do, even pouring the tea for you now . . . it has . . . implications. The walls and windows say so. Even my own heart, strapped inside this Western dress . . . even it says things—things I don't care to hear.

8. A punishment inflicted by the Communists on those viewed as "class enemies."

9. Tea, quickly please! (Chinese).

[SONG *hands* GALLIMARD *a cup of tea.* GALLIMARD *puts his hand over both the teacup and* SONG*'s hand.*]

GALLIMARD This is a beautiful dress.

SONG Don't.

GALLIMARD What?

SONG I don't even know if it looks right on me.

GALLIMARD Believe me—

SONG You are from France. You see so many beautiful women.

GALLIMARD France? Since when are the European women—?

SONG Oh! What am I trying to do, anyway?!

[SONG *runs to the door, composes herself, then turns towards* GALLIMARD.]

SONG Monsieur Gallimard, perhaps you should go.

GALLIMARD But . . . why?

SONG There's something wrong about this.

GALLIMARD I don't see what.

SONG I feel . . . I am not myself.

GALLIMARD No. You're nervous.

SONG Please. Hard as I try to be modern, to speak like a man, to hold a Western woman's strong face up to my own . . . in the end, I fail. A small, frightened heart beats too quickly and gives me away. Monsieur Gallimard, I'm a Chinese girl. I've never . . . never invited a man up to my flat before. The forwardness of my actions makes my skin burn.

GALLIMARD What are you afraid of? Certainly not me, I hope.

SONG I'm a modest girl.

GALLIMARD I know. And very beautiful. [*He touches her hair.*]

SONG Please—go now. The next time you see me, I shall again be myself.

GALLIMARD I like you the way you are right now.

SONG You are a cad.

GALLIMARD What do you expect? I'm a foreign devil.

[GALLIMARD *walks downstage.* SONG *exits.*]

GALLIMARD [*to us*] Did you hear the way she talked about Western women? Much differently than the first night. She does—she feels inferior to them—and to me.

1.11

The French embassy. Beijing. 1960.

GALLIMARD *moves towards a desk.*

GALLIMARD I determined to try an experiment. In *Madame Butterfly,* Cio-Cio-San fears that the Western man who catches a butterfly will pierce its heart with a needle, then leave it to perish. I began to wonder: had I, too, caught a butterfly who would writhe on a needle?

[MARC *enters, dressed as a bureaucrat, holding a stack of papers. As* GALLIMARD *speaks,* MARC *hands papers to him. He peruses, then signs, stamps, or rejects them.*]

GALLIMARD Over the next five weeks, I worked like a dynamo. I stopped going to the opera, I didn't phone or write her. I knew this little flower was waiting for me to call, and, as I wickedly refused to do so, I felt for the first time that rush of power—the absolute power of a man.

[MARC *continues acting as the bureaucrat, but he now speaks as himself.*]

MARC Rene! It's me!

GALLIMARD Marc—I hear your voice everywhere now. Even in the midst of work.

MARC That's because I'm watching you—all the time.

GALLIMARD You were always the most popular guy in school.

MARC Well, there's no guarantee of failure in life like happiness in high school. Somehow I knew I'd end up in the suburbs working for Renault[1] and you'd be in the Orient picking exotic women off the trees. And they say there's no justice.

GALLIMARD That's why you were my friend?

MARC I gave you a little of my life, so that now you can give me some of yours. [*Pause*] Remember Isabelle?

GALLIMARD Of course I remember! She was my first experience.

MARC We all wanted to ball her. But she only wanted me.

GALLIMARD I had her.

MARC Right. You balled her.

GALLIMARD You were the only one who ever believed me.

MARC Well, there's a good reason for that. [*Beat*] C'mon. You must've guessed.

GALLIMARD You told me to wait in the bushes by the cafeteria that night. The next thing I knew, she was on me. Dress up in the air.

MARC She never wore underwear.

GALLIMARD My arms were pinned to the dirt.

MARC She loved the superior position. A girl ahead of her time.

GALLIMARD I looked up, and there was this woman . . . bouncing up and down on my loins.

MARC Screaming, right?

GALLIMARD Screaming, and breaking off the branches all around me, and pounding my butt up and down into the dirt.

MARC Huffing and puffing like a locomotive.

GALLIMARD And in the middle of all this, the leaves were getting into my mouth, my legs were losing circulation, I thought, "God. So this is *it*?"

MARC You thought that?

GALLIMARD Well, I was worried about my legs falling off.

MARC You didn't have a good time?

GALLIMARD No, that's not what I—I had a great time!

MARC You're sure?

GALLIMARD Yeah. Really.

MARC 'Cuz I wanted you to have a good time.

GALLIMARD I did.

[*Pause.*]

MARC Shit. [*Pause*] When all is said and done, she was kind of a lousy lay, wasn't she? I mean, there was a lot of energy there, but you never knew what she was doing with it. Like when she yelled "I'm coming!"—hell, it was so loud, you wanted to go "Look, it's not that big a deal."

GALLIMARD I got scared. I thought she meant someone was actually coming. [*Pause*] But, Marc?

MARC What?

1. A French automobile manufacturing company.

GALLIMARD Thanks.

MARC Oh, don't mention it.

GALLIMARD It was my first experience.

MARC Yeah. You got her.

GALLIMARD I got her.

MARC Wait! Look at that letter again!

[GALLIMARD *picks up one of the papers he's been stamping, and rereads it.*]

GALLIMARD [*to us*] After six weeks, they began to arrive. The letters.

[*Upstage special on* SONG, *as Madame* BUTTERFLY. *The scene is underscored by the "Love Duet."*]

SONG Did we fight? I do not know. Is the opera no longer of interest to you? Please come—my audiences miss the white devil in their midst.

[GALLIMARD *looks up from the letter, towards us.*]

GALLIMARD [*to us*] A concession, but much too dignified. [*Beat; he discards the letter.*] I skipped the opera again that week to complete a position paper on trade.

[*The bureaucrat hands him another letter.*]

SONG Six weeks have passed since last we met. Is this your practice—to leave friends in the lurch? Sometimes I hate you, sometimes I hate myself, but always I miss you.

GALLIMARD [*to us*] Better, but I don't like the way she calls me "friend." When a woman calls a man her "friend," she's calling him a eunuch or a homosexual. [*Beat; he discards the letter.*] I was absent from the opera for the seventh week, feeling a sudden urge to clean out my files.

[*Bureaucrat hands him another letter.*]

SONG Your rudeness is beyond belief. I don't deserve this cruelty. Don't bother to call. I'll have you turned away at the door.

GALLIMARD [*to us*] I didn't. [*He discards the letter; bureaucrat hands him another.*] And then finally, the letter that concluded my experiment.

SONG I am out of words. I can hide behind dignity no longer. What do you want? I have already given you my shame.

[GALLIMARD *gives the letter back to* MARC, *slowly. Special on* SONG *fades out.*]

GALLIMARD [*to us*] Reading it, I became suddenly ashamed. Yes, my experiment had been a success. She was turning on my needle. But the victory seemed hollow.

MARC Hollow?! Are you crazy?

GALLIMARD Nothing, Marc. Please go away.

MARC [*exiting, with papers*] Haven't I taught you anything?

GALLIMARD "I have already given you my shame." I had to attend a reception that evening. On the way, I felt sick. If there is a God, surely he would punish me now. I had finally gained power over a beautiful woman, only to abuse it cruelly. There must be justice in the world. I had the strange feeling that the ax would fall this very evening.

1.12

Ambassador TOULON*'s residence. Beijing. 1960.*

Sound cue: party noises. Light change. We are now in a spacious residence. TOULON, *the French ambassador, enters and taps* GALLIMARD *on the shoulder.*

TOULON Gallimard? Can I have a word? Over here.

GALLIMARD [*to us*] Manuel Toulon. French ambassador to China. He likes to think of us all as his children. Rather like God.

TOULON Look, Gallimard, there's not much to say. I've liked you. From the day you walked in. You were no leader, but you were tidy and efficient.

GALLIMARD Thank you, sir.

TOULON Don't jump the gun. Okay, our needs in China are changing. It's embarrassing that we lost Indochina.[2] Someone just wasn't on the ball there. I don't mean you personally, of course.

GALLIMARD Thank you, sir.

TOULON We're going to be doing a lot more information-gathering in the future. The nature of our work here is changing. Some people are just going to have to go. It's nothing personal.

GALLIMARD Oh.

TOULON Want to know a secret? Vice-Consul LeBon is being transferred.

GALLIMARD [*to us*] My immediate superior!

TOULON And most of his department.

GALLIMARD [*to us*] Just as I feared! God has seen my evil heart—

TOULON But not you.

GALLIMARD [*to us*] —and he's taking her away just as . . . [*To* TOULON] Excuse me, sir?

TOULON Scare you? I think I did. Cheer up, Gallimard. I want you to replace LeBon as vice-consul.

GALLIMARD You—? Yes, well, thank you, sir.

TOULON Anytime.

GALLIMARD I . . . accept with great humility.

TOULON Humility won't be part of the job. You're going to coordinate the revamped intelligence division. Want to know a secret? A year ago, you would've been out. But the past few months, I don't know how it happened, you've become this new aggressive confident . . . thing. And they also tell me you get along with the Chinese. So I think you're a lucky man, Gallimard. Congratulations.

[*They shake hands.* TOULON *exits. Party noises out.* GALLIMARD *stumbles across a darkened stage.*]

GALLIMARD Vice-consul? Impossible! As I stumbled out of the party, I saw it written across the sky: There is no God. Or, no—say that there is a God. But that God . . . understands. Of course! God who creates Eve to serve Adam, who blesses Solomon with his harem but ties Jezebel to a burning bed[3]—that God is a man. And he understands! At age thirty-nine, I was suddenly initiated into the way of the world.

2. That is, French Indochina, a colony established in the late 19th century that comprised present-day Laos, Cambodia, and Vietnam. It was "lost" with the French defeat at the Battle of Dien Bien Phu in 1954, ending an insurgency that had begun with Vietnam's declaration of independence in 1945.

3. A series of biblical references: see Genesis 2.21–23 and 1 Corinthians 11.8–9 (the creation of Eve), 1 Kings 11.1–3 (Solomon's wives and concubines), and Revelation 2.20–23 (the punishment of Jezebel for harlotry, as described here).

1.13

SONG LILING'*s apartment. Beijing. 1960.*

SONG *enters, in a sheer dressing gown.*

SONG Are you crazy?

GALLIMARD Mademoiselle Song—

SONG To come here—at this hour? After . . . after eight weeks?

GALLIMARD It's the most amazing—

SONG You bang on my door? Scare my servants, scandalize the neighbors?

GALLIMARD I've been promoted. To vice-consul.

[*Pause.*]

SONG And what is that supposed to mean to me?

GALLIMARD Are you my Butterfly?

SONG What are you saying?

GALLIMARD I've come tonight for an answer: are you my Butterfly?

SONG Don't you know already?

GALLIMARD I want you to say it.

SONG I don't want to say it.

GALLIMARD So, that is your answer?

SONG You know how I feel about—

GALLIMARD I do remember one thing.

SONG What?

GALLIMARD In the letter I received today.

SONG Don't.

GALLIMARD "I have already given you my shame."

SONG It's enough that I even wrote it.

GALLIMARD Well, then—

SONG I shouldn't have it splashed across my face.

GALLIMARD —if that's all true—

SONG Stop!

GALLIMARD Then what is one more short answer?

SONG I don't want to!

GALLIMARD Are you my Butterfly? [*Silence; he crosses the room and begins to touch her hair.*] I want from you honesty. There should be nothing false between us. No false pride.

[*Pause.*]

SONG Yes, I am. I am your Butterfly.

GALLIMARD Then let me be honest with you. It is because of you that I was promoted tonight. You have changed my life forever. My little Butterfly, there should be no more secrets: I love you.

[*He starts to kiss her roughly. She resists slightly.*]

SONG No . . . no . . . gently . . . please, I've never . . .

GALLIMARD No?

SONG I've tried to appear experienced, but . . . the truth is . . . no.

GALLIMARD Are you cold?

SONG Yes. Cold.

GALLIMARD Then we will go very, very slowly.

[*He starts to caress her; her gown begins to open.*]

SONG No . . . let me . . . keep my clothes . . .

GALLIMARD But . . .

SONG Please . . . it all frightens me. I'm a modest Chinese girl.

GALLIMARD My poor little treasure.

SONG I am your treasure. Though inexperienced, I am not . . . ignorant. They teach us things, our mothers, about pleasing a man.

GALLIMARD Yes?

SONG I'll do my best to make you happy. Turn off the lights.

[GALLIMARD *gets up and heads for a lamp.* SONG, *propped up on one elbow, tosses her hair back and smiles.*]

SONG Monsieur Gallimard?

GALLIMARD Yes, Butterfly?

SONG "Vieni, vieni!"[4]

GALLIMARD "Come, darling."

SONG "Ah! Dolce notte!"

GALLIMARD "Beautiful night."

SONG "Tutto estatico d'amor ride il ciel!"

GALLIMARD "All ecstatic with love, the heavens are filled with laughter."

[*He turns off the lamp. Blackout.*]

2.1

M. GALLIMARD*'s cell. Paris. Present.*

Lights up on GALLIMARD. *He sits in his cell, reading from a leaflet.*

GALLIMARD This, from a contemporary critic's commentary on *Madame Butterfly:* "Pinkerton suffers from . . . being an obnoxious bounder whom every man in the audience itches to kick." Bully for us men in the audience! Then, in the same note: "Butterfly is the most irresistibly appealing of Puccini's 'Little Women.' Watching the succession of her humiliations is like watching a child under torture." [*He tosses the pamphlet over his shoulder.*] I suggest that, while we men may all want to kick Pinkerton, very few of us would pass up the opportunity to *be* Pinkerton.

[GALLIMARD *moves out of his cell.*]

2.2

GALLIMARD *and* BUTTERFLY*'s flat. Beijing. 1960.*

We are in a simple but well-decorated parlor. GALLIMARD *moves to sit on a sofa, while* SONG, *dressed in a chong sam,*[5] *enters and curls up at his feet.*

GALLIMARD [*to us*] We secured a flat on the outskirts of Peking. Butterfly, as I was calling her now, decorated our "home" with Western furniture and Chinese antiques. And there, on a few stolen afternoons or evenings each week, Butterfly commenced her education.

SONG The Chinese men—they keep us down.

GALLIMARD Even in the "New Society"?[6]

4. Song's Italian lines ending this scene, translated by Gallimard, are drawn from the "Love Duet" finale of act 1 of *Madama Butterfly*.

5. That is, a cheongsam (literally, "long gown"), a traditional Chinese dress with a high collar and a slit skirt.

6. In his essay "On New Democracy" (1940), Mao Zedong called for "a new society and a new state for the Chinese nation."

SONG In the "New Society," we are all kept ignorant equally. That's one of the exciting things about loving a Western man. I know you are not threatened by a woman's education.

GALLIMARD I'm no saint, Butterfly.

SONG But you come from a progressive society.

GALLIMARD We're not always reminding each other how "old" we are, if that's what you mean.

SONG Exactly. We Chinese—once, I suppose, it is true, we ruled the world. But so what? How much more exciting to be part of the society ruling the world today. Tell me—what's happening in Vietnam?[7]

GALLIMARD Oh, Butterfly—you want me to bring my work home?

SONG I want to know what you know. To be impressed by my man. It's not the particulars so much as the fact that you're making decisions which change the shape of the world.

GALLIMARD Not the world. At best, a small corner.

[TOULON *enters, and sits at a desk upstage.*]

2.3

French embassy. Beijing. 1961.

GALLIMARD *moves downstage, to* TOULON*'s desk.* SONG *remains upstage, watching.*

TOULON And a more troublesome corner is hard to imagine.

GALLIMARD So, the Americans plan to begin bombing?

TOULON This is very secret, Gallimard: yes. The Americans don't have an embassy here.[8] They're asking us to be their eyes and ears. Say Jack Kennedy signed an order to bomb North Vietnam, Laos.[9] How would the Chinese react?

GALLIMARD I think the Chinese will squawk—

TOULON Uh-huh.

GALLIMARD —but, in their hearts, they don't even like Ho Chi Minh.[1]

[*Pause.*]

TOULON What a bunch of jerks. Vietnam was *our* colony. Not only didn't the Americans help us fight to keep them, but now, seven years later, they've come back to grab the territory for themselves. It's very irritating.

GALLIMARD With all due respect, sir, why should the Americans have won our war for us back in '54 if we didn't have the will to win it ourselves?

7. On gaining its independence in 1954, Vietnam was divided into two countries: the Communist-controlled Democratic Republic of Vietnam (North Vietnam) and the U.S.-backed Republic of Vietnam (South Vietnam). In the late 1950s, Communist insurgents in the South (the Viet Cong), aided by the North, launched a guerrilla war seeking the reunification of Vietnam.

8. The United States did not establish official diplomatic relations with the People's Republic of China until 1979.

9. While campaigning for the presidency in 1960, Kennedy pledged to increase U.S. military assistance to South Vietnam in its struggle against the armed insurgency supported by the North. In 1961, his administration signed a military and economic aid treaty with South Vietnam, leading to large increases in the number of U.S. military advisers in the country (U.S. air strikes against North Vietnam and Laos would not begin until 1964).

1. Vietnamese nationalist (1890–1969), a Communist who led the struggle for independence; after the country's partition in 1954, he became president of North Vietnam. In the early 1950s, China had sent military advisers and weapons to the Vietnamese insurgents, and it supported the North in its war with the South.

TOULON You're kidding, aren't you?

[*Pause.*]

GALLIMARD The Orientals simply want to be associated with whoever shows the most strength and power. You live with the Chinese, sir. Do you think they like Communism?

TOULON I live in China. Not with the Chinese.

GALLIMARD Well, I—

TOULON *You* live with the Chinese.

GALLIMARD Excuse me?

TOULON I can't keep a secret.

GALLIMARD What are you saying?

TOULON Only that I'm not immune to gossip. So, you're keeping a native mistress. Don't answer. It's none of my business. [*Pause*] I'm sure she must be gorgeous.

GALLIMARD Well . . .

TOULON I'm impressed. You have the stamina to go out into the streets and hunt one down. Some of us have to be content with the wives of the expatriate community.

GALLIMARD I do feel . . . fortunate.

TOULON So, Gallimard, you've got the inside knowledge—what *do* the Chinese think?

GALLIMARD Deep down, they miss the old days. You know, cappuccinos, men in tuxedos—

TOULON So what do we tell the Americans about Vietnam?

GALLIMARD Tell them there's a natural affinity between the West and the Orient.

TOULON And that you speak from experience?

GALLIMARD The Orientals are people too. They want the good things we can give them. If the Americans demonstrate the will to win, the Vietnamese will welcome them into a mutually beneficial union.

TOULON I don't see how the Vietnamese can stand up to American firepower.

GALLIMARD Orientals will always submit to a greater force.

TOULON I'll note your opinions in my report. The Americans always love to hear how "welcome" they'll be. [*He starts to exit.*]

GALLIMARD Sir?

TOULON Mmmm?

GALLIMARD This . . . rumor you've heard.

TOULON Uh-huh?

GALLIMARD How . . . widespread do you think it is?

TOULON It's only widespread within this embassy. Where nobody talks because everybody is guilty. We were worried about you, Gallimard. We thought you were the only one here without a secret. Now you go and find a lotus blossom . . . and top us all. [*He exits.*]

GALLIMARD [*to us*] Toulon knows! And he approves! I was learning the benefits of being a man. We form our own clubs, sit behind thick doors, smoke—and celebrate the fact that we're still boys. [*He starts to move downstage, towards* SONG.] So, over the—

[*Suddenly* COMRADE CHIN *enters.* GALLIMARD *backs away.*]

GALLIMARD [*to* SONG] No! Why does she have to come in?

SONG Rene, be sensible. How can they understand the story without her? Now, don't embarrass yourself.

[GALLIMARD *moves down center.*]

GALLIMARD [*to us*] Now, you will see why my story is so amusing to so many people. Why they snicker at parties in disbelief. Please—try to understand it from my point of view. We are all prisoners of our time and place. [*He exits.*]

2.4

GALLIMARD *and* BUTTERFLY's *flat. Beijing. 1961.*

SONG [*to us*] 1961. The flat Monsieur Gallimard rented for us. An evening after he has gone.

CHIN Okay, see if you can find out when the Americans plan to start bombing Vietnam. If you can find out what cities, even better.

SONG I'll do my best, but I don't want to arouse his suspicions.

CHIN Yeah, sure, of course. So, what else?

SONG The Americans will increase troops in Vietnam to 170,000 soldiers with 120,000 militia and 11,000 American advisors.

CHIN [*writing*] Wait, wait. 120,000 militia and—

SONG —11,000 American—

CHIN —American advisors. [*Beat*] How do you remember so much?

SONG I'm an actor.

CHIN Yeah. [*Beat*] Is that how come you dress like that?

SONG Like what, Miss Chin?

CHIN Like that dress! You're wearing a dress. And every time I come here, you're wearing a dress. Is that because you're an actor? Or what?

SONG It's a . . . disguise, Miss Chin.

CHIN Actors, I think they're all weirdos. My mother tells me actors are like gamblers or prostitutes or—

SONG It helps me in my assignment.

[*Pause.*]

CHIN You're not gathering information in any way that violates Communist Party principles, are you?

SONG Why would I do that?

CHIN Just checking. Remember: when working for the Great Proletarian State, you represent our Chairman Mao[2] in every position you take.

SONG I'll try to imagine the Chairman taking my positions.

CHIN We all think of him this way. Good-bye, comrade.[3] [*She starts to exit.*] Comrade?

SONG Yes?

CHIN Don't forget: there is no homosexuality in China!

SONG Yes, I've heard.

CHIN Just checking. [*She exits.*]

SONG [*to us*] What passes for a woman in modern China.

2. Mao Zedong (1893–1976) was chairman of the Central Committee of the Chinese Communist Party from 1945 until his death. *Proletarian state:* a transitional stage in the proletarian (i.e., working-class) revolution that Karl Marx and Friedrich Engels, in *Manifesto of the Communist Party* (1848), envisioned as necessary to overthrow capitalism and bring about a classless society.

3. Customary form of address among Communists.

[GALLIMARD *sticks his head out from the wings.*]

GALLIMARD Is she gone?

SONG Yes, Rene. Please continue in your own fashion.

2.5

Beijing. 1961–63.

GALLIMARD *moves to the couch where* SONG *still sits. He lies down in her lap, and she strokes his forehead.*

GALLIMARD [*to us*] And so, over the years 1961, '62, '63, we settled into our routine, Butterfly and I. She would always have prepared a light snack and then, ever so delicately, and only if I agreed, she would start to pleasure me. With her hands, her mouth . . . too many ways to explain, and too sad, given my present situation. But mostly we would talk. About my life. Perhaps there is nothing more rare than to find a woman who passionately listens.

[SONG *remains upstage, listening, as* HELGA *enters and plays a scene downstage with* GALLIMARD.]

HELGA Rene, I visited Dr. Bolleart this morning.

GALLIMARD Why? Are you ill?

HELGA No, no. You see, I wanted to ask him . . . that question we've been discussing.

GALLIMARD And I told you, it's only a matter of time. Why did you bring a doctor into this? We just have to keep trying—like a crapshoot, actually.

HELGA I went, I'm sorry. But listen: he says there's nothing wrong with me.

GALLIMARD You see? Now, will you stop—?

HELGA Rene, he says he'd like you to go in and take some tests.

GALLIMARD Why? So he can find there's nothing wrong with both of us?

HELGA Rene, I don't ask for much. One trip! One visit! And then, whatever you want to do about it—you decide.

GALLIMARD You're assuming he'll find something defective!

HELGA No! Of course not! Whatever he finds—if he finds nothing, we decide what to do about nothing! But go!

GALLIMARD If he finds nothing, we keep trying. Just like we do now.

HELGA But at least we'll know! [*Pause*] I'm sorry. [*She starts to exit.*]

GALLIMARD Do you really want me to see Dr. Bolleart?

HELGA Only if you want a child, Rene. We have to face the fact that time is running out. Only if you want a child. [*She exits.*]

GALLIMARD [*to* SONG] I'm a modern man, Butterfly. And yet, I don't want to go. It's the same old voodoo. I feel like God himself is laughing at me if I can't produce a child.

SONG You men of the West—you're obsessed by your odd desire for equality. Your wife can't give you a child, and *you're* going to the doctor?

GALLIMARD Well, you see, she's already gone.

SONG And because this incompetent can't find the defect, you now have to subject yourself to him? It's unnatural.

GALLIMARD Well, what is the "natural" solution?

SONG In Imperial China, when a man found that one wife was inadequate, he turned to another—to give him his son.

GALLIMARD What do you—? I can't . . . marry you, yet.

SONG Please. I'm not asking you to be my husband. But I am already your wife.

GALLIMARD Do you want to . . . have my child?

SONG I thought you'd never ask.

GALLIMARD But, your career . . . your—

SONG Phooey on my career! That's your Western mind, twisting itself into strange shapes again. Of course I love my career. But what would I love most of all? To feel something inside me—day and night—something I know is yours. [*Pause*] Promise me . . . you won't go to this doctor. Who is this Western quack to set himself as judge over the man I love? I know who is a man, and who is not. [*She exits.*]

GALLIMARD [*to us*] Dr. Bolleart? Of course I didn't go. What man would?

2.6

Beijing. 1963.

Party noises over the house speakers. RENEE *enters, wearing a revealing gown.*

GALLIMARD 1963. A party at the Austrian embassy. None of us could remember the Austrian ambassador's name, which seemed somehow appropriate. [*To* RENEE] So, I tell the Americans, Diem[4] must go. The U.S. wants to be respected by the Vietnamese, and yet they're propping up this nobody seminarian as her president. A man whose claim to fame is his sister-in-law[5] imposing fanatic "moral order" campaigns? Oriental women—when they're good, they're very good, but when they're bad, they're Christians.

RENEE Yeah.

GALLIMARD And what do you do?

RENEE I'm a student. My father exports a lot of useless stuff to the Third World.

GALLIMARD How useless?

RENEE You know. Squirt guns, confectioner's sugar, hula hoops[6] . . .

GALLIMARD I'm sure they appreciate the sugar.

RENEE I'm here for two years to study Chinese.

GALLIMARD Two years?

RENEE That's what everybody says.

GALLIMARD When did you arrive?

RENEE Three weeks ago.

GALLIMARD And?

RENEE I like it. It's primitive, but . . . well, this is the place to learn Chinese, so here I am.

GALLIMARD Why Chinese?

RENEE I think it'll be important someday.

4. Ngo Dinh Diem (1901–1963); as a boy, he studied in a French Catholic school and briefly entered a monastery. With U.S. support, he became prime minister of Vietnam in 1954 and president of South Vietnam in 1955. His authoritarian and corrupt rule made him widely unpopular, and he was ousted and murdered by a group of generals who had been assured that the United States would not interfere with a coup.

5. Tran Le Xian (b. 1924), the wife of Diem's brother and chief adviser, Ngo Dinh Nhu; she was known as Madame Nhu. Because Diem was unmarried, she was in effect the country's first lady. A passionate convert to Roman Catholicism, she worked for laws banning divorce, contraception, brothels, and the like and encouraged the persecution of Buddhists.

6. Hula Hoops were a brief U.S. craze in 1958, when 25 million were sold in four months.

GALLIMARD You do?

RENEE Don't ask me when, but . . . that's what I think.

GALLIMARD Well, I agree with you. One hundred percent. That's very far-sighted.

RENEE Yeah. Well of course, my father thinks I'm a complete weirdo.

GALLIMARD He'll thank you someday.

RENEE Like when the Chinese start buying hula hoops?

GALLIMARD There're a billion bellies out there.

RENEE And if they end up taking over the world—well, then I'll be lucky to know Chinese too, right?

[*Pause.*]

GALLIMARD At this point, I don't see how the Chinese can possibly take—

RENEE You know what I *don't* like about China?

GALLIMARD Excuse me? No—what?

RENEE Nothing to do at night.

GALLIMARD You come to parties at embassies like everyone else.

RENEE Yeah, but they get out at ten. And then what?

GALLIMARD I'm afraid the Chinese idea of a dance hall is a dirt floor and a man with a flute.

RENEE Are you married?

GALLIMARD Yes. Why?

RENEE You wanna . . . fool around?

[*Pause.*]

GALLIMARD Sure.

RENEE I'll wait for you outside. What's your name?

GALLIMARD Gallimard. Rene.

RENEE Weird. I'm Renee too. [*She exits.*]

GALLIMARD [*to us*] And so, I embarked on my first extra-extramarital affair. Renee was picture perfect. With a body like those girls in the magazines. If I put a tissue paper over my eyes, I wouldn't have been able to tell the difference. And it was exciting to be with someone who wasn't afraid to be seen completely naked. But is it possible for a woman to be *too* uninhibited, *too* willing, so as to seem almost too . . . masculine?

[*Chuck Berry*[7] *blares from the house speakers, then comes down in volume as* RENEE *enters, toweling her hair.*]

RENEE You have a nice weenie.

GALLIMARD What?

RENEE Penis. You have a nice penis.

GALLIMARD Oh. Well, thank you. That's very . . .

RENEE What—can't take a compliment?

GALLIMARD No, it's very . . . reassuring.

RENEE But most girls don't come out and say it, huh?

GALLIMARD And also . . . what did you call it?

RENEE Oh. Most girls don't call it a "weenie," huh?

GALLIMARD It sounds very—

RENEE Small, I know.

7. An African American songwriter, guitarist, and singer (b. 1926), a pioneer of rock-and-roll music whose hits include "Roll Over Beethoven" (1956) and "Johnny B. Goode" (1958).

GALLIMARD I was going to say, "young."

RENEE Yeah. Young, small, same thing. Most guys are pretty, uh, sensitive about that. Like, you know, I had a boyfriend back home in Denmark. I got mad at him once and called him a little weeniehead. He got so mad! He said at least I should call him a great big weeniehead.

GALLIMARD I suppose I just say "penis."

RENEE Yeah. That's pretty clinical. There's "cock," but that sounds like a chicken. And "prick" is painful, and "dick" is like you're talking about someone who's not in the room.

GALLIMARD Yes. It's a . . . bigger problem than I imagined.

RENEE I—I think maybe it's because I really don't know what to do with them—that's why I call them "weenies."

GALLIMARD Well, you did quite well with . . . mine.

RENEE Thanks, but I mean, really *do* with them. Like, okay, have you ever looked at one? I mean, really?

GALLIMARD No, I suppose when it's part of you, you sort of take it for granted.

RENEE I guess. But, like, it just hangs there. This little . . . flap of flesh. And there's so much fuss that we make about it. Like, I think the reason we fight wars is because we wear clothes. Because no one knows—between the men, I mean—who has the bigger . . . weenie. So, if I'm a guy with a small one, I'm going to build a really big building or take over a really big piece of land or write a really long book so the other men don't know, right? But, see, it never really works, that's the problem. I mean, you conquer the country, or whatever, but you're still wearing clothes, so there's no way to prove absolutely whose is bigger or smaller. And that's what we call a civilized society. The whole world run by a bunch of men with pricks the size of pins. [*She exits.*]

GALLIMARD [*to us*] This was simply not acceptable.

[*A high-pitched chime rings through the air.* SONG, *dressed as* BUTTERFLY, *appears in the upstage special. She is obviously distressed. Her body swoons as she attempts to clip the stems of flowers she's arranging in a vase.*]

GALLIMARD But I kept up our affair, wildly, for several months. Why? I believe because of Butterfly. She knew the secret I was trying to hide. But, unlike a Western woman, she didn't confront me, threaten, even pout. I remembered the words of Puccini's *Butterfly:*

SONG "Noi siamo gente avvezza / alle piccole cose / umili e silenziose."[8]

GALLIMARD "I come from a people / Who are accustomed to little / Humble and silent." I saw Pinkerton and Butterfly, and what she would say if he were unfaithful . . . nothing. She would cry, alone, into those wildly soft sleeves, once full of possessions, now empty to collect her tears. It was her tears and her silence that excited me, every time I visited Renee.

TOULON [*offstage*] Gallimard!

[TOULON *enters.* GALLIMARD *turns towards him. During the next section,* SONG, *up center, begins to dance with the flowers. It is a drunken dance, where she breaks small pieces off the stems.*]

8. Lines from the aria "vogliatemi bene" ("Ah, Love Me a Little"), sung by Butterfly in the opera's first act.

TOULON They're killing him.

GALLIMARD Who? I'm sorry? What?

TOULON Bother you to come over at this late hour?

GALLIMARD No . . . of course not.

TOULON Not after you hear my secret. Champagne?

GALLIMARD Um . . . thank you.

TOULON You're surprised. There's something that you've wanted, Gallimard. No, not a promotion. Next time. Something in the world. You're not aware of this, but there's an informal gossip circle among intelligence agents. And some of ours heard from some of the Americans—

GALLIMARD Yes?

TOULON That the U.S. will allow the Vietnamese generals to stage a coup . . . and assassinate President Diem.[9]

[*The chime rings again.* TOULON *freezes.* GALLIMARD *turns upstage and looks at* BUTTERFLY, *who slowly and deliberately clips a flower off its stem.* GALLIMARD *turns back towards* TOULON.]

GALLIMARD I think . . . that's a very wise move!

[TOULON *unfreezes.*]

TOULON It's what you've been advocating. A toast?

GALLIMARD Sure. I consider this a vindication.

TOULON Not exactly. "To the test. Let's hope you pass."

[*They drink. The chime rings again.* TOULON *freezes.* GALLIMARD *turns upstage, and* SONG *clips another flower.*]

GALLIMARD [*to* TOULON] The test?

TOULON [*unfreezing*] It's a test of everything you've been saying. I personally think the generals probably will stop the Communists. And you'll be a hero. But if anything goes wrong, then your opinions won't be worth a pig's ear. I'm sure that won't happen. But sometimes it's easier when they don't listen to you.

GALLIMARD They're your opinions too, aren't they?

TOULON Personally, yes.

GALLIMARD So we agree.

TOULON But my opinions aren't on that report. Yours are. Cheers.

[TOULON *turns away from* GALLIMARD *and raises his glass. At that instant* SONG *picks up the vase and hurls it to the ground. It shatters.* SONG *sinks down amidst the shards of the vase, in a calm, childlike trance. She sings softly, as if reciting a child's nursery rhyme.*]

SONG [*repeat as necessary*] "The whole world over, the white man travels, setting anchor, wherever he likes. Life's not worth living, unless he finds, the finest maidens, of every land . . ."[1]

[GALLIMARD *turns downstage towards us.* SONG *continues singing.*]

GALLIMARD I shook as I left his house. That coward! That worm! To put the burden for his decisions on my shoulders!

I started for Renee's. But no, that was all I needed. A schoolgirl who would question the role of the penis in modern society. What I wanted was revenge. A vessel to contain my humiliation. Though I hadn't seen her in several weeks, I headed for Butterfly's.

9. See the first note of this scene.

1. A translation of lines sung by Pinkerton in the first act of *Madama Butterfly*.

[GALLIMARD *enters* SONG*'s apartment.*]

SONG Oh! Rene . . . I was dreaming!

GALLIMARD You've been drinking?

SONG If I can't sleep, then yes, I drink. But then, it gives me these dreams which—Rene, it's been almost three weeks since you visited me last.

GALLIMARD I know. There's been a lot going on in the world.

SONG Fortunately I am drunk. So I can speak freely. It's not the world, it's you and me. And an old problem. Even the softest skin becomes like leather to a man who's touched it too often. I confess I don't know how to stop it. I don't know how to become another woman.

GALLIMARD I have a request.

SONG Is this a solution? Or are you ready to give up the flat?

GALLIMARD It may be a solution. But I'm sure you won't like it.

SONG Oh well, that's very important. "Like it?" Do you think I "like" lying here alone, waiting, always waiting for your return? Please—don't worry about what I may not "like."

GALLIMARD I want to see you . . . naked.

[*Silence.*]

SONG I thought you understood my modesty. So you want me to—what—strip? Like a big cowboy girl? Shiny pasties on my breasts? Shall I fling my kimono over my head and yell "ya-hoo" in the process? I thought you respected my shame!

GALLIMARD I believe you gave me your shame many years ago.

SONG Yes—and it is just like a white devil to use it against me. I can't believe it. I thought myself so repulsed by the passive Oriental and the cruel white man. Now I see—we are always most revolted by the things hidden within us.

GALLIMARD I just mean—

SONG Yes?

GALLIMARD —that it will remove the only barrier left between us.

SONG No, Rene. Don't couch your request in sweet words. Be yourself—a cad—and know that my love is enough, that I submit—submit to the worst you can give me. [*Pause*] Well, come. Strip me. Whatever happens, know that you have willed it. Our love, in your hands. I'm helpless before my man.

[GALLIMARD *starts to cross the room.*]

GALLIMARD Did I not undress her because I knew, somewhere deep down, what I would find? Perhaps. Happiness is so rare that our mind can turn somersaults to protect it.

At the time, I only knew that I was seeing Pinkerton stalking towards his Butterfly, ready to reward her love with his lecherous hands. The image sickened me, pulled me to my knees, so I was crawling towards her like a worm. By the time I reached her, Pinkerton . . . had vanished from my heart. To be replaced by something new, something unnatural, that flew in the face of all I'd learned in the world—something very close to love.

[*He grabs her around the waist; she strokes his hair.*]

GALLIMARD Butterfly, forgive me.

SONG Rene . . .

GALLIMARD For everything. From the start.

SONG I'm . . .

GALLIMARD I want to—

SONG I'm pregnant. [*Beat*] I'm pregnant. [*Beat*] I'm pregnant.

[*Beat.*]

GALLIMARD I want to marry you!

2.7

GALLIMARD *and* BUTTERFLY*'s flat. Beijing. 1963.*

Downstage, SONG *paces as* COMRADE CHIN *reads from her notepad. Upstage,* GALLIMARD *is still kneeling. He remains on his knees throughout the scene, watching it.*

SONG I need a baby.

CHIN [*from pad*] He's been spotted going to a dorm.

SONG I need a baby.

CHIN At the Foreign Language Institute.

SONG I need a baby.

CHIN The room of a Danish girl . . . What do you mean, you need a baby?!

SONG Tell Comrade Kang—last night, the entire mission, it could've ended.

CHIN What do you mean?

SONG Tell Kang—he told me to strip.

CHIN *Strip?!*

SONG Write!

CHIN I tell you, I don't understand nothing about this case anymore. Nothing.

SONG He told me to strip, and I took a chance. Oh, we Chinese, we know how to gamble.

CHIN [*writing*] ". . . told him to strip."

SONG My palms were wet, I had to make a split-second decision.

CHIN Hey! Can you slow down?!

[*Pause.*]

SONG You write faster, I'm the artist here. Suddenly, it hit me—"All he wants is for her to submit. Once a woman submits, a man is always ready to become 'generous.'"

CHIN You're just gonna end up with rough notes.

SONG And it worked! He gave in! Now, if I can just present him with a baby. A Chinese baby with blond hair—he'll be mine for life!

CHIN Kang will never agree! The trading of babies has to be a counterrevolutionary[2] act!

SONG Sometimes, a counterrevolutionary act is necessary to counter a counterrevolutionary act.

[*Pause.*]

CHIN Wait.

SONG I need one . . . in seven months. Make sure it's a boy.

CHIN This doesn't sound like something the Chairman would do. Maybe you'd better talk to Comrade Kang yourself.

SONG Good. I will.

[CHIN *gets up to leave.*]

2. That is, undermining the goals of the Revolution of 1949.

SONG Miss Chin? Why, in the Peking Opera, are women's roles played by men?

CHIN I don't know. Maybe, a reactionary remnant of male—

SONG No. [*Beat*] Because only a man knows how a woman is supposed to act.

[CHIN *exits.* SONG *turns upstage, towards* GALLIMARD.]

GALLIMARD [*calling after* CHIN] Good riddance! [*To* SONG] I could forget all that betrayal in an instant, you know. If you'd just come back and become Butterfly again.

SONG Fat chance. You're here in prison, rotting in a cell. And I'm on a plane, winging my way back to China. Your President pardoned me of our treason, you know.

GALLIMARD Yes, I read about that.

SONG Must make you feel . . . lower than shit.

GALLIMARD But don't you, even a little bit, wish you were here with me?

SONG I'm an artist, Rene. You were my greatest . . . acting challenge. [*She laughs.*] It doesn't matter how rotten I answer, does it? You still adore me. That's why I love you, Rene. [*She points to us.*] So—you were telling your audience about the night I announced I was pregnant.

[GALLIMARD *puts his arms around* SONG*'s waist. He and* SONG *are in the positions they were in at the end of Scene 6.*]

2.8

Same.

GALLIMARD I'll divorce my wife. We'll live together here, and then later in France.

SONG I feel so . . . ashamed.

GALLIMARD Why?

SONG I had begun to lose faith. And now, you shame me with your generosity.

GALLIMARD Generosity? No, I'm proposing for very selfish reasons.

SONG Your apologies only make me feel more ashamed. My outburst a moment ago!

GALLIMARD Your outburst? What about my request?!

SONG You've been very patient dealing with my . . . eccentricities. A Western man, used to women freer with their bodies—

GALLIMARD It was sick! Don't make excuses for me.

SONG I have to. You don't seem willing to make them for yourself.

[*Pause.*]

GALLIMARD You're crazy.

SONG I'm happy. Which often looks like crazy.

GALLIMARD Then make me crazy. Marry me.

[*Pause.*]

SONG No.

GALLIMARD What?

SONG Do I sound silly, a slave, if I say I'm not worthy?

GALLIMARD Yes. In fact you do. No one has loved me like you.

SONG Thank you. And no one ever will. I'll see to that.

GALLIMARD So what is the problem?

SONG Rene, we Chinese are realists. We understand rice, gold, and guns. You are a diplomat. Your career is skyrocketing. Now, what would happen if you divorced your wife to marry a Communist Chinese actress?

GALLIMARD That's not being realistic. That's defeating yourself before you begin.

SONG We must conserve our strength for the battles we can win.

GALLIMARD That sounds like a fortune cookie!

SONG Where do you think fortune cookies come from?

GALLIMARD I don't care.

SONG You do. So do I. And we should. That is why I say I'm not worthy. I'm worthy to love and even to be loved by you. But I am not worthy to end the career of one of the West's most promising diplomats.

GALLIMARD It's not that great a career! I made it sound like more than it is!

SONG Modesty will get you nowhere. Flatter yourself, and you flatter me. I'm flattered to decline your offer. [*She exits.*]

GALLIMARD [*to us*] Butterfly and I argued all night. And, in the end, I left, knowing I would never be her husband. She went away for several months—to the countryside, like a small animal. Until the night I received her call.

[*A baby's cry from offstage.* SONG *enters, carrying a child.*]

SONG He looks like you.

GALLIMARD Oh! [*Beat; he approaches the baby.*] Well, babies are never very attractive at birth.

SONG Stop!

GALLIMARD I'm sure he'll grow more beautiful with age. More like his mother.

SONG "Chi vide mai / a bimbo del Giappon . . ."[3]

GALLIMARD "What baby, I wonder, was ever born in Japan"—or China, for that matter—

SONG ". . . occhi azzurrini?"

GALLIMARD "With azure eyes"—they're actually sort of brown, wouldn't you say?

SONG "E il labbro."

GALLIMARD: "And such lips!" [*He kisses* SONG.] And such lips.

SONG "E i ricciolini d'oro schietto?"

GALLIMARD "And such a head of golden"—if slightly patchy—"curls?"

SONG I'm going to call him "Peepee."

GALLIMARD Darling, could you repeat that because I'm sure a rickshaw just flew by overhead.

SONG You heard me.

GALLIMARD "Song Peepee"? May I suggest Michael, or Stephan, or Adolph?

SONG You may, but I won't listen.

GALLIMARD You can't be serious. Can you imagine the time this child will have in school?

SONG In the West, yes.

3. These lines and those that follow are sung by Butterfly in act 2 of *Madama Butterfly.*

GALLIMARD It's worse than naming him Ping Pong or Long Dong[4] or—

SONG But he's never going to live in the West, is he?

[*Pause.*]

GALLIMARD That wasn't my choice.

SONG It is mine. And this is my promise to you: I will raise him, he will be our child, but he will never burden you outside of China.

GALLIMARD Why do you make these promises? I want to be burdened! I want a scandal to cover the papers!

SONG [*to us*] Prophetic.

GALLIMARD I'm serious.

SONG So am I. His name is as I registered it. And he will never live in the West.

[SONG *exits with the child.*]

GALLIMARD [*to us*] It is possible that her stubbornness only made me want her more. That drawing back at the moment of my capitulation was the most brilliant strategy she could have chosen. It is possible. But it is also possible that by this point she could have said, could have done . . . anything, and I would have adored her still.

2.9

Beijing. 1966.

A driving rhythm of Chinese percussion fills the stage.

GALLIMARD And then, China began to change. Mao became very old, and his cult became very strong. And, like many old men, he entered his second childhood. So he handed over the reins of state to those with minds like his own. And children ruled the Middle Kingdom[5] with complete caprice. The doctrine of the Cultural Revolution[6] implied continuous anarchy. Contact between Chinese and foreigners became impossible. Our flat was confiscated. Her fame and my money now counted against us.

[*Two dancers in Mao suits and red-starred caps enter, and begin crudely mimicking revolutionary violence, in an agitprop[7] fashion.*]

GALLIMARD And somehow the American war went wrong too. Four hundred thousand dollars were being spent for every Viet Cong killed; so General Westmoreland's[8] remark that the Oriental does not value life the way

4. Penis (slang).

5. The Chinese name for China (in Mandarin *Zongguo*, "central state"), first used in the 11th century.

6. The Great Proletarian Cultural Revolution (1966–76), a campaign launched by Mao to rekindle revolutionary fervor by removing so-called counterrevolutionary elements from the Communist Party and society in general. Repeated purges led by the Red Guards—a mass movement composed mainly of students and of young people from the country-side, who subscribed wholeheartedly to Mao's new cult of personality—were aimed at bureaucrats, teachers and intellectuals, and writers and artists. The result was factionalism, violence, and chaos.

7. Agitation and propaganda, usually on behalf of communism and conveyed through the arts or literature (from the name of the department of the Russian Communist Party responsible for such activities).

8. William Westmoreland (1914–2005), commander of American military operations in Vietnam (1964–68) and U.S. Army chief of staff (1968–72); in the documentary *Hearts and Minds* (1974) he said, "The Oriental doesn't put the same high price on life as does the Westerner. Life is plentiful, life is cheap in the Orient."

Americans do was oddly accurate. Why weren't the Vietnamese people giving in? Why were they content instead to die and die and die again?

[TOULON *enters.*]

TOULON Congratulations, Gallimard.

GALLIMARD Excuse me, sir?

TOULON Not a promotion. That was last time. You're going home.

GALLIMARD What?

TOULON Don't say I didn't warn you.

GALLIMARD I'm being transferred . . . because I was wrong about the American war?[9]

TOULON Of course not. We don't care about the Americans. We care about your mind. The quality of your analysis. In general, everything you've predicted here in the Orient . . . just hasn't happened.

GALLIMARD I think that's premature.

TOULON Don't force me to be blunt. Okay, you said China was ready to open to Western trade. The only thing they're trading out there are Western heads. And, yes, you said the Americans would succeed in Indochina. You were kidding, right?

GALLIMARD I think the end is in sight.

TOULON Don't be pathetic. And don't take this personally. You were wrong. It's not your fault.

GALLIMARD But I'm going home.

TOULON Right. Could I have the number of your mistress? [*Beat*] Joke! Joke! Eat a croissant for me.

[TOULON *exits.* SONG, *wearing a Mao suit,*[1] *is dragged in from the wings as part of the upstage dance. They "beat" her, then lampoon the acrobatics of the Chinese opera, as she is made to kneel onstage.*]

GALLIMARD [*simultaneously*] I don't care to recall how Butterfly and I said our hurried farewell. Perhaps it was better to end our affair before it killed her.

[GALLIMARD *exits.* COMRADE CHIN *walks across the stage with a banner reading: "The Actor Renounces His Decadent Profession!" She reaches the kneeling* SONG. *Percussion stops with a thud. Dancers strike poses.*]

CHIN Actor-oppressor, for years you have lived above the common people and looked down on their labor. While the farmer ate millet—

SONG I ate pastries from France and sweetmeats from silver trays.

CHIN And how did you come to live in such an exalted position?

SONG I was a plaything for the imperialists!

CHIN What did you do?

SONG I shamed China by allowing myself to be corrupted by a foreigner . . .

CHIN What does this mean? The People demand a full confession!

SONG I engaged in the lowest perversions with China's enemies!

9. After the Tonkin Gulf Resolution (1964) gave the president authority to "take all necessary measures" to defend U.S. forces "and to prevent further aggression," the first U.S. combat troops arrived in South Vietnam, joining 16,000 military advisers. By the end of 1966, close to 400,000 troops were in Vietnam; troop strength peaked in 1968 at 540,000. The last American forces left in 1973, and South Vietnam fell to the North in 1975.

1. A suit like that worn by Mao at the ceremony founding the People's Republic of China—with a high, buttoned collar and four external pockets. It was especially common during the Cultural Revolution.

CHIN What perversions? Be more clear!

SONG I let him put it up my ass!

[Dancers look over, disgusted.]

CHIN Aaaa-ya! How can you use such sickening language?!

SONG My language . . . is only as foul as the crimes I committed . . .

CHIN Yeah. That's better. So—what do you want to do now?

SONG I want to serve the people.

[Percussion starts up, with Chinese strings.]

CHIN What?

SONG I want to serve the people!

[Dancers regain their revolutionary smiles, and begin a dance of victory.]

CHIN What?!

SONG I want to serve the people!!

[Dancers unveil a banner: "The Actor Is Rehabilitated!" SONG *remains kneeling before* CHIN, *as the dancers bounce around them, then exit. Music out.]*

2.10

A commune. Hunan Province.[2] *1970.*

CHIN How you planning to do that?

SONG I've already worked four years in the fields of Hunan, Comrade Chin.[3]

CHIN So? Farmers work all their lives. Let me see your hands.

[SONG *holds them out for her inspection.*]

CHIN Goddamn! Still so smooth! How long does it take to turn you actors into good anythings? Hunh. You've just spent too many years in luxury to be any good to the Revolution.

SONG I served the Revolution.

CHIN Serve the Revolution? Bullshit! You wore dresses! Don't tell me—I was there. I saw you! You and your white vice-consul! Stuck up there in your flat, living off the People's Treasury! Yeah, I knew what was going on! You two . . . homos! Homos! Homos! [*Pause; she composes herself.*] Ah! Well . . . you will serve the people, all right. But not with the Revolution's money. This time, you use your own money.

SONG I have no money.

CHIN Shut up! And you won't stink up China anymore with your pervert stuff. You'll pollute the place where pollution begins—the West.

SONG What do you mean?

CHIN Shut up! You're going to France. Without a cent in your pocket. You find your consul's house, you make him pay your expenses—

SONG No.

CHIN And you give us weekly reports! Useful information!

SONG That's crazy. It's been four years.

CHIN Either that, or back to rehabilitation center!

2. In southern China. *Commune:* the basic unit of China's collectivized system of agriculture (introduced in 1958 and abandoned in 1981).

3. During the Cultural Revolution, many deemed counterrevolutionary were sent to the countryside in order to be "rehabilitated" through hard labor and political reindoctrination.

SONG Comrade Chin, he's not going to support me! Not in France! He's a white man! I was just his plaything—

CHIN Oh yuck! Again with the sickening language? Where's my stick?

SONG You don't understand the mind of a man.

[*Pause.*]

CHIN Oh no? No I don't? Then how come I'm married, huh? How come I got a man? Five, six years ago, you always tell me those kind of things, I felt very bad. But not now! Because what does the Chairman say? He tells us *I'm* now the smart one, you're now the nincompoop! *You're* the blackhead, the harebrain, the nitwit! You think you're so smart? You understand "The Mind of a Man"? Good! Then *you* go to France and be a pervert for Chairman Mao!

[CHIN *and* SONG *exit in opposite directions.*]

2.11

Paris. 1968–70.

GALLIMARD *enters.*

GALLIMARD And what was waiting for me back in Paris? Well, better Chinese food than I'd eaten in China. Friends and relatives. A little accounting, regular schedule, keeping track of traffic violations in the suburbs. . . . And the indignity of students shouting the slogans of Chairman Mao at me—in French.[4]

HELGA Rene? Rene? [*She enters, soaking wet.*] I've had a . . . a problem. [*She sneezes.*]

GALLIMARD You're wet.

HELGA Yes, I . . . coming back from the grocer's. A group of students, waving red flags, they—

[GALLIMARD *fetches a towel.*]

HELGA —they ran by, I was caught up along with them. Before I knew what was happening—

[GALLIMARD *gives her the towel.*]

HELGA Thank you. The police started firing water cannons at us. I tried to shout, to tell them I was the wife of a diplomat, but—you know how it is . . . [*Pause*] Needless to say, I lost the groceries. Rene, what's happening to France?

GALLIMARD What's—? Well, nothing, really.

HELGA Nothing?! The storefronts are in flames, there's glass in the streets, buildings are toppling—and I'm wet!

GALLIMARD Nothing! . . . that I care to think about.

HELGA And is that why you stay in this room?

GALLIMARD Yes, in fact.

HELGA With the incense burning? You know something? I hate incense. It smells so sickly sweet.

4. In May 1968, student demonstrations against the French government's heavy-handed response to earlier protests grew into a massive uprising, joined by a general strike of millions of workers, seeking to end the administration of President Charles de Gaulle. The students were a mixture of radicals and leftists, including anarchists, Marxists, Trotskyites, and Maoists.

GALLIMARD Well, I hate the French. Who just smell—period!

HELGA And the Chinese were better?

GALLIMARD Please—don't start.

HELGA When we left, this exact same thing, the riots—

GALLIMARD No, no . . .

HELGA Students screaming slogans, smashing down doors—

GALLIMARD Helga—

HELGA It was all going on in China, too. Don't you remember?!

GALLIMARD Helga! Please! [*Pause*] You have never understood China, have you? You walk in here with these ridiculous ideas, that the West is falling apart, that China was spitting in our faces. You come in, dripping of the streets, and you leave water all over my floor. [*He grabs* HELGA*'s towel, begins mopping up the floor.*]

HELGA But it's the truth!

GALLIMARD Helga, I want a divorce.

[*Pause;* GALLIMARD *continues, mopping the floor.*]

HELGA I take it back. China is . . . beautiful. Incense, I like incense.

GALLIMARD I've had a mistress.

HELGA So?

GALLIMARD For eight years.

HELGA I knew you would. I knew you would the day I married you. And now what? You want to marry her?

GALLIMARD I can't. She's in China.

HELGA I see. You want to leave. For someone who's not here, is that right?

GALLIMARD That's right.

HELGA You can't live with her, but still you don't want to live with me.

GALLIMARD That's right.

[*Pause.*]

HELGA Shit. How terrible that I can figure that out. [*Pause.*] I never thought I'd say it. But, in China, I was happy. I knew, in my own way, I knew that you were not everything you pretended to be. But the pretense—going on your arm to the embassy ball, visiting your office and the guards saying, "Good morning, good morning, Madame Gallimard"—the pretense . . . was very good indeed. [*Pause*] I hope everyone is mean to you for the rest of your life. [*She exits.*]

GALLIMARD [*to us*] Prophetic.

[MARC *enters with two drinks.*]

GALLIMARD [*to* MARC] In China, I was different from all other men.

MARC Sure. You were white. Here's your drink.

GALLIMARD I felt . . . touched.

MARC In the head? Rene, I don't want to hear about the Oriental love goddess. Okay? One night—can we just drink and throw up without a lot of conversation?

GALLIMARD You still don't believe me, do you?

MARC Sure I do. She was the most beautiful, et cetera, et cetera, blasé blasé.

[*Pause.*]

GALLIMARD My life in the West has been such a disappointment.

MARC Life in the West is like that. You'll get used to it. Look, you're driving me away. I'm leaving. Happy, now? [*He exits, then returns.*] Look, I have a date tomorrow night. You wanna come? I can fix you up with—

GALLIMARD Of course. I would love to come.

[*Pause.*]

MARC Uh—on second thought, no. You'd better get ahold of yourself first.

[*He exits;* GALLIMARD *nurses his drink.*]

GALLIMARD [*to us*] This is the ultimate cruelty, isn't it? That I can talk and talk and to anyone listening, it's only air—too rich a diet to be swallowed by a mundane world. Why can't anyone understand? That in China, I once loved, and was loved by, very simply, the Perfect Woman.

[SONG *enters, dressed as* BUTTERFLY *in wedding dress.*]

GALLIMARD [*to* SONG] Not again. My imagination is hell. Am I asleep this time? Or did I drink too much?

SONG Rene?

GALLIMARD God, it's too painful! That you speak?

SONG What are you talking about? Rene—touch me.

GALLIMARD Why?

SONG I'm real. Take my hand.

GALLIMARD Why? So you can disappear again and leave me clutching at the air? For the entertainment of my neighbors who—?

[SONG *touches* GALLIMARD.]

SONG Rene?

[GALLIMARD *takes* SONG*'s hand. Silence.*]

GALLIMARD Butterfly? I never doubted you'd return.

SONG You hadn't . . . forgotten—?

GALLIMARD Yes, actually, I've forgotten everything. My mind, you see—there wasn't enough room in this hard head—not for the world *and* for you. No, there was only room for one. [*Beat*] Come, look. See? Your bed has been waiting, with the Klimt[5] poster you like, and—see? The xiang lu [incense burner] you gave me?

SONG I . . . I don't know what to say.

GALLIMARD There's nothing to say. Not at the end of a long trip. Can I make you some tea?

SONG But where's your wife?

GALLIMARD She's by my side. She's by my side at last.

[GALLIMARD *reaches to embrace* SONG. SONG *sidesteps, dodging him.*]

GALLIMARD Why?!

SONG [*to us*] So I did return to Rene in Paris. Where I found—

GALLIMARD Why do you run away? Can't we show them how we embraced that evening?

SONG Please. I'm talking.

GALLIMARD You have to do what I say! I'm conjuring you up in *my* mind!

SONG Rene, I've never done what you've said. Why should it be any different in your mind? Now split—the story moves on, and I must change.

GALLIMARD I welcomed you into my home! I didn't have to, you know! I could've left you penniless on the streets of Paris! But I took you in!

5. Gustav Klimt (1862–1918), an Austrian painter associated with exoticism and eroticism.

SONG Thank you.

GALLIMARD So . . . please . . . don't change.

SONG You know I have to. You know I will. And anyway, what difference does it make? No matter what your eyes tell you, you can't ignore the truth. You already know too much.

[GALLIMARD *exits.* SONG *turns to us.*]

SONG The change I'm going to make requires about five minutes. So I thought you might want to take this opportunity to stretch your legs, enjoy a drink, or listen to the musicians. I'll be here, when you return, right where you left me.

[SONG *goes to a mirror in front of which is a wash basin of water. She starts to remove her makeup as stagelights go to half and houselights come up.*]

3.1

A courthouse in Paris. 1986.

As he promised, SONG *has completed the bulk of his transformation, onstage by the time the houselights go down and the stagelights come up full. He removes his wig and kimono, leaving them on the floor. Underneath, he wears a well-cut suit.*

SONG So I'd done my job better than I had a right to expect. Well, give him some credit, too. He's right—I was in a fix when I arrived in Paris. I walked from the airport into town, then I located, by blind groping, the Chinatown district. Let me make one thing clear: whatever else may be said about the Chinese, they are stingy! I slept in doorways three days until I could find a tailor who would make me this kimono on credit. As it turns out, maybe I didn't even need it. Maybe he would've been happy to see me in a simple shift and mascara. But . . . better safe than sorry.

That was 1970, when I arrived in Paris. For the next fifteen years, yes, I lived a very comfy life. Some relief, believe me, after four years on a fucking commune in Nowheresville, China. Rene supported the boy and me, and I did some demonstrations around the country as part of my "cultural exchange" cover. And then there was the spying.

[SONG *moves upstage, to a chair.* TOULON *enters as a judge, wearing the appropriate wig and robes. He sits near* SONG. *It's 1986, and* SONG *is testifying in a courtroom.*]

SONG Not much at first. Rene had lost all his high-level contacts. Comrade Chin wasn't very interested in parking-ticket statistics. But finally, at my urging, Rene got a job as a courier, handling sensitive documents. He'd photograph them for me, and I'd pass them on to the Chinese embassy.

JUDGE Did he understand the extent of his activity?

SONG He didn't ask. He knew that I needed those documents, and that was enough.

JUDGE But he must've known he was passing classified information.

SONG I can't say.

JUDGE He never asked what you were going to do with them?

SONG Nope.

[*Pause.*]

JUDGE There is one thing that the court—indeed, that all of France—would like to know.

SONG Fire away.

JUDGE Did Monsieur Gallimard know you were a man?

SONG Well, he never saw me completely naked. Ever.

JUDGE But surely, he must've . . . how can I put this?

SONG Put it however you like. I'm not shy. He must've felt around?

JUDGE Mmmmm.

SONG Not really. I did all the work. He just laid back. Of course we did enjoy more . . . complete union, and I suppose he *might* have wondered why I was always on my stomach, but. . . . But what you're thinking is: "Of course a wrist must've brushed . . . a hand hit . . . over twenty years!" Yeah. Well, Your Honor, it was my job to make him think I was a woman. And chew on this: it wasn't all that hard. See, my mother was a prostitute along the Bundt[6] before the Revolution. And, uh, I think it's fair to say she learned a few things about Western men. So I borrowed her knowledge. In service to my country.

JUDGE Would you care to enlighten the court with this secret knowledge? I'm sure we're all very curious.

SONG I'm sure you are. [*Pause*] Okay, Rule One is: Men always believe what they want to hear. So a girl can tell the most obnoxious lies and the guys will believe them every time—"This is my first time"—"That's the biggest I've ever seen"—or *both*, which, if you really think about it, is not possible in a single lifetime. You've maybe heard those phrases a few times in your own life, yes, Your Honor?

JUDGE It's not my life, Monsieur Song, which is on trial today.

SONG Okay, okay, just trying to lighten up the proceedings. Tough room.

JUDGE Go on.

SONG Rule Two: As soon as a Western man comes into contact with the East—he's already confused. The West has sort of an international rape mentality towards the East. Do you know rape mentality?

JUDGE Give us your definition, please.

SONG Basically, "Her mouth says no, but her eyes say yes."

The West thinks of itself as masculine—big guns, big industry, big money—so the East is feminine—weak, delicate, poor . . . but good at art, and full of inscrutable wisdom—the feminine mystique.

Her mouth says no, but her eyes say yes. The West believes the East, deep down, *wants* to be dominated—because a woman can't think for herself.

JUDGE What does this have to do with my question?

SONG You expect Oriental countries to submit to your guns, and you expect Oriental women to be submissive to your men. That's why you say they make the best wives.

JUDGE But why would that make it possible for you to fool Monsieur Gallimard? Please—get to the point.

SONG One, because when he finally met his fantasy woman, he wanted

6. That is, the Bund, a thoroughfare along the Huangpu River in the former Shanghai International Settlement; before the Revolution, it was lined with financial institutions, hotels, and clubs as well as wharves (*Bund* is the name often given in the Far East to an embanked street along a river or sea).

more than anything to believe that she was, in fact, a woman. And second, I am an Oriental. And being an Oriental, I could never be completely a man.

[*Pause.*]

JUDGE Your armchair political theory is tenuous, Monsieur Song.

SONG You think so? That's why you'll lose in all your dealings with the East.

JUDGE Just answer my question: did he know you were a man?

[*Pause.*]

SONG You know, Your Honor, I never asked.

3.2

Same.

Music from the "Death Scene" from Butterfly *blares over the house speakers. It is the loudest thing we've heard in this play.*

GALLIMARD *enters, crawling towards* SONG*'s wig and kimono.*

GALLIMARD Butterfly? Butterfly?

[SONG *remains a man, in the witness box, delivering a testimony we do not hear.*]

GALLIMARD [*to us*] In my moment of greatest shame, here, in this courtroom—with that . . . person up there, telling the world. . . . What strikes me especially is how shallow he is, how glib and obsequious . . . completely . . . without substance! The type that prowls around discos with a gold medallion, stinking of garlic. So little like my Butterfly.

Yet even in this moment my mind remains agile, flip-flopping like a man on a trampoline. Even now, my picture dissolves, and I see that . . . witness . . . talking to me.

[SONG *suddenly stands straight up in his witness box, and looks at* GALLIMARD.]

SONG Yes. You. White man.

[SONG *steps out of the witness box, and moves downstage towards* GALLIMARD. *Light change.*]

GALLIMARD [*to* SONG] Who? Me?

SONG Do you see any other white men?

GALLIMARD Yes. There're white men all around. This is a French courtroom.

SONG So you are an adventurous imperialist. Tell me, why did it take you so long? To come back to this place?

GALLIMARD What place?

SONG This theatre in China. Where we met many years ago.

GALLIMARD [*to us*] And once again, against my will, I am transported.

[*Chinese opera music comes up on the speakers.* SONG *begins to do opera moves, as he did the night they met.*]

SONG Do you remember? The night you gave your heart?

GALLIMARD It was a long time ago.

SONG Not long enough. A night that turned your world upside down.

GALLIMARD Perhaps.

SONG Oh, be honest with me. What's another bit of flattery when you've already given me twenty years' worth? It's a wonder my head hasn't swollen to the size of China.

GALLIMARD Who's to say it hasn't?

SONG Who's to say? And what's the shame? In pride? You think I could've pulled this off if I wasn't already full of pride when we met? No, not just pride. Arrogance. It takes arrogance, really—to believe you can will, with your eyes and your lips, the destiny of another. [*He dances.*] C'mon. Admit it. You still want me. Even in slacks and a button-down collar.

GALLIMARD I don't see what the point of—

SONG You don't? Well maybe, Rene, just maybe—I want you.

GALLIMARD You do?

SONG Then again, maybe I'm just playing with you. How can you tell? [*Reprising his feminine character, he sidles up to* GALLIMARD.] "How I wish there were even a small cafe to sit in. With men in tuxedos, and cappuccinos, and bad expatriate jazz." Now you want to kiss me, don't you?

GALLIMARD [*pulling away*] What makes you—?

SONG —so sure? See? I take the words from your mouth. Then I wait for you to come and retrieve them. [*He reclines on the floor.*]

GALLIMARD Why?! Why do you treat me so cruelly?

SONG Perhaps I *was* treating you cruelly. But now—I'm being nice. Come here, my little one.

GALLIMARD I'm not your little one!

SONG My mistake. It's I who am *your* little one, right?

GALLIMARD Yes, I—

SONG So come get your little one. If you like. I may even let you strip me.

GALLIMARD I mean, you were! Before . . . but not like this!

SONG I was? Then perhaps I still am. If you look hard enough. [*He starts to remove his clothes.*]

GALLIMARD What—what are you doing?

SONG Helping you to see through my act.

GALLIMARD Stop that! I don't want to! I don't—

SONG Oh, but you asked me to strip, remember?

GALLIMARD What? That was years ago! And I took it back!

SONG No. You postponed it. Postponed the inevitable. Today, the inevitable has come calling.

[*From the speakers, cacophony:* BUTTERFLY *mixed in with Chinese gongs.*]

GALLIMARD No! Stop! I don't want to see!

SONG Then look away.

GALLIMARD You're only in my mind! All this is in my mind! I order you! To stop!

SONG To what? To strip? That's just what I'm—

GALLIMARD No! Stop! I want you—!

SONG You want me?

GALLIMARD To stop!

SONG You know something, Rene? Your mouth says no, but your eyes say yes. Turn them away. I dare you.

GALLIMARD I don't have to! Every night, you say you're going to strip, but then I beg you and you stop!

SONG I guess tonight is different.

GALLIMARD Why? Why should that be?

SONG Maybe I've become frustrated. Maybe I'm saying "Look at me, you fool!" Or maybe I'm just feeling . . . sexy. [*He is down to his briefs.*]

GALLIMARD Please. This is unnecessary. I know what you are.

SONG Do you? What am I?

GALLIMARD A—a man.

SONG You don't really believe that.

GALLIMARD Yes I do! I knew all the time somewhere that my happiness was temporary, my love a deception. But my mind kept the knowledge at bay. To make the wait bearable.

SONG Monsieur Gallimard—the wait is over.

[SONG *drops his briefs. He is naked. Sound cue out. Slowly, we and* SONG *come to the realization that what we had thought to be* GALLIMARD*'s sobbing is actually his laughter.*]

GALLIMARD Oh god! What an idiot! Of course!

SONG Rene—what?

GALLIMARD Look at you! You're a man! [*He bursts into laughter again.*]

SONG I fail to see what's so funny!

GALLIMARD "You fail to see—!" I mean, you never did have much of a sense of humor, did you? I just think it's ridiculously funny that I've wasted so much time on just a man!

SONG Wait. I'm not "just a man."

GALLIMARD No? Isn't that what you've been trying to convince me of?

SONG Yes, but what I mean—

GALLIMARD And now, I finally believe you, and you tell me it's not true? I think you must have some kind of identity problem.

SONG Will you listen to me?

GALLIMARD Why?! I've been listening to you for twenty years. Don't I deserve a vacation?

SONG I'm not just any man!

GALLIMARD Then, what exactly are you?

SONG Rene, how can you ask—? Okay, what about this?

[*He picks up* BUTTERFLY*'s robes, starts to dance around. No music.*]

GALLIMARD Yes, that's very nice. I have to admit.

[SONG *holds out his arm to* GALLIMARD.]

SONG It's the same skin you've worshiped for years. Touch it.

GALLIMARD Yes, it does feel the same.

SONG Now—close your eyes.

[SONG *covers* GALLIMARD*'s eyes with one hand. With the other,* SONG *draws* GALLIMARD*'s hand up to his face.* GALLIMARD, *like a blind man, lets his hands run over* SONG*'s face.*]

GALLIMARD This skin, I remember. The curve of her face, the softness of her cheek, her hair against the back of my hand . . .

SONG I'm your Butterfly. Under the robes, beneath everything, it was always me. Now, open your eyes and admit it—you adore me. [*He removes his hand from* GALLIMARD*'s eyes.*]

GALLIMARD You, who knew every inch of my desires—how could you, of all people, have made such a mistake?

SONG What?

GALLIMARD You showed me your true self. When all I loved was the lie. A perfect lie, which you let fall to the ground—and now, it's old and soiled.

SONG So—you never really loved me? Only when I was playing a part?

GALLIMARD I'm a man who loved a woman created by a man. Everything else—simply falls short.

[*Pause.*]

SONG What am I supposed to do now?

GALLIMARD You were a fine spy, Monsieur Song, with an even finer accomplice. But now I believe you should go. Get out of my life!

SONG Go where? Rene, you can't live without me. Not after twenty years.

GALLIMARD I certainly can't live with you—not after twenty years of betrayal.

SONG Don't be so stubborn! Where will you go?

GALLIMARD I have a date . . . with my Butterfly.

SONG So, throw away your pride. And come . . .

GALLIMARD Get away from me! Tonight, I've finally learned to tell fantasy from reality. And, knowing the difference, I choose fantasy.

SONG *I'm* your fantasy!

GALLIMARD You? You're as real as hamburger. Now get out! I have a date with my Butterfly and I don't want your body polluting the room! [*He tosses* SONG*'s suit at him.*] Look at these—you dress like a pimp.

SONG Hey! These are Armani slacks[7] and—! [*He puts on his briefs and slacks.*] Let's just say . . . I'm disappointed in you, Rene. In the crush of your adoration, I thought you'd become something more. More like . . . a woman.

But no. Men. You're like the rest of them. It's all in the way we dress, and make up our faces, and bat our eyelashes. You really have so little imagination!

GALLIMARD You, Monsieur Song? Accuse me of too little imagination? You, if anyone, should know—I am pure imagination. And in imagination I will remain. Now get out!

[GALLIMARD *bodily removes* SONG *from the stage, taking his kimono.*]

SONG Rene! I'll never put on those robes again! You'll be sorry!

GALLIMARD [*to* SONG] I'm already sorry! [*Looking at the kimono in his hands*] Exactly as sorry . . . as a Butterfly.

3.3

M. GALLIMARD*'s prison cell. Paris. Present.*

GALLIMARD I've played out the events of my life night after night, always searching for a new ending to my story, one where I leave this cell and return forever to my Butterfly's arms.

Tonight I realize my search is over. That I've looked all along in the wrong place. And now, to you, I will prove that my love was not in vain—by returning to the world of fantasy where I first met her.

[*He picks up the kimono; dancers enter.*]

GALLIMARD There is a vision of the Orient that I have. Of slender women in chong sams and kimonos who die for the love of unworthy foreign devils. Who are born and raised to be the perfect women. Who take whatever punishment we give them, and bounce back, strengthened by love, unconditionally. It is a vision that has become my life.

7. That is, expensive, designer clothing. Giorgio Armani (b. 1934) is an Italian designer of relaxed but luxurious clothes for men and women.

[*Dancers bring the wash basin to him and help him make up his face.*]

GALLIMARD In public, I have continued to deny that Song Liling is a man. This brings me headlines, and is a source of great embarrassment to my French colleagues, who can now be sent into a coughing fit by the mere mention of Chinese food. But alone, in my cell, I have long since faced the truth.

And the truth demands a sacrifice. For mistakes made over the course of a lifetime. My mistakes were simple and absolute—the man I loved was a cad, a bounder. He deserved nothing but a kick in the behind, and instead I gave him . . . all my love.

Yes—love. Why not admit it all? That was my undoing, wasn't it? Love warped my judgment, blinded my eyes, rearranged the very lines on my face . . . until I could look in the mirror and see nothing but . . . a woman.

[*Dancers help him put on the* BUTTERFLY *wig.*]

GALLIMARD I have a vision. Of the Orient. That, deep within its almond eyes, there are still women. Women willing to sacrifice themselves for the love of a man. Even a man whose love is completely without worth.

[*Dancers assist* GALLIMARD *in donning the kimono. They hand him a knife.*]

GALLIMARD Death with honor is better than life . . . life with dishonor. [*He sets himself center stage, in a seppuku*[8] *position.*] The love of a Butterfly can withstand many things—unfaithfulness, loss, even abandonment. But how can it face the one sin that implies all others? The devastating knowledge that, underneath it all, the object of her love was nothing more, nothing less than . . . a man. [*He sets the tip of the knife against his body.*] It is 19__. And I have found her at last. In a prison on the outskirts of Paris. My name is Rene Gallimard—also known as Madame Butterfly.

[GALLIMARD *turns upstage and plunges the knife into his body, as music from the "Love Duet" blares over the speakers. He collapses into the arms of the dancers, who lay him reverently on the floor. The image holds for several beats. Then a tight special up on* SONG, *who stands as a man, staring at the dead* GALLIMARD. *He smokes a cigarette; the smoke filters up through the lights. Two words leave his lips.*]

SONG Butterfly? Butterfly?

[*Smoke rises as lights fade slowly to black.*]

8. Ritual suicide by disembowelment (Japanese); synonymous with hara-kiri.

TONY KUSHNER

b. 1956

When *Millennium Approaches*, Part One of *Angels in America*, opened on Broadway in 1993, Tony Kushner was hailed as the savior of serious American theater. Since the 1970s, skyrocketing production costs had made it all but impossible for an ambitious nonmusical drama to survive on Broadway. Not only did Kushner defy those odds, he did so with a work of enormous scope and ambition. *Angels in America* is a two-part epic drama exploring personal identity, sexual orientation, political responsibility, AIDS, Mormonism, Judaism, and Reagan-era conservatism within an eclectic dramaturgy that mixes realism, surrealism, and the spectacular. *Millennium Approaches* received numerous awards, including the Tony Award for Best Play and the Pulitzer Prize for Drama; not surprisingly, its sequel, *Perestroika,* was similarly acclaimed. Critics compared the play to such landmark works as TENNESSEE WILLIAMS's *A Streetcar Named Desire* (1947) and ARTHUR MILLER's *Death of a Salesman* (1949). In the ensuing years, additional North American and European productions of *Angels in America* have established Kushner's reputation as the preeminent American dramatist of his generation.

The success of *Angels* also made Kushner one of the most widely known gay artists and activists of the 1990s and early 2000s. Born in 1956, in New York City, to parents who were classical musicians, and raised in Lake Charles, Louisiana, Kushner became aware of his homosexuality by the age of ten. Because of the social stigma attached to being gay, he felt unable to acknowledge his sexual orientation openly, even to his politically liberal parents. Like Joe in *Angels,* Kushner came out to his mother in a telephone call—made from a pay phone on the morning of his first graduate class at New York University (where he completed a master of fine arts in directing in 1984). Kushner's mentor at NYU was Carl Weber, a highly reputed scholar, director, and former assistant of BERTOLT BRECHT's at the Berliner Ensemble. After graduation, Kushner worked as a director at the Repertory Theatre of St. Louis and the New York Theatre Workshop. His first major play, *A Bright Room Called Day,* premiered in San Francisco in 1987 and was produced by the New York Shakespeare Festival in 1991. In 1990, Kushner received a commission to develop *Angels in America* for the Eureka Theatre in San Francisco, where *Millennium Approaches* premiered in 1991. The play subsequently moved to the Mark Taper Forum in Los Angeles, where it was performed with *Perestroika* in 1992. Both plays were produced in London at the National Theater in 1992; in New York, *Millennium Approaches* opened in 1993 and *Perestroika* in 1994.

In the years following the success of *Angels in America,* Kushner wrote a number of adaptations and plays, including *Slavs! Thinking About the Longstanding Problems of Virtue and Happiness* (1994), which features scenes that the playwright had originally intended for *Angels; Henry Box Brown, or The Mirror of Slavery* (1998), the story of an American slave who mailed himself to freedom in 1848; and the musical *Caroline, or Change* (2002). Kushner's 2001 play *Homebody/Kabul* is set in Afghanistan in 1988, during the rule of the oppressive Taliban government. *Angels in America* was made into a highly acclaimed film for television in 2003.

Labeled by Kushner "a gay fantasia on national themes," *Angels* joined a number of other plays that deal with the experience of gay men in contemporary America. Although issues of homosexuality pervade the drama of Williams and EDWARD ALBEE, the emergence of openly gay drama can be dated to 1968 and the off-Broadway production of Mart Crowley's *The Boys in the Band.* Crowley's play gave the mainstream theater its first view inside "the closet" of gay life: in this case, a Manhattan birthday party at which a group of gay men descend into alcohol-fueled self-loathing. The writing and production of gay plays accelerated in the wake of two events: the Stonewall Riots of June 1969 and the onset of the AIDS crisis in the early 1980s. In the 1960s, the police in New York often raided bars frequented by homosexuals—who were arrested for being "disorderly"—but late on June 26, 1969, gay and lesbian patrons of Greenwich Village's Stonewall Inn resisted arrest, spawning a riot; violent protests followed for several more nights. This uprising was instrumental in sparking a new phase of the gay rights movement; its emergence was accompanied by plays that depicted the personal and sexual struggles of gay male characters. Key works of the time include Martin Sherman's *Passing By* (1974) and *Bent* (1979), Lanford Wilson's *Fifth of July* (1978), Robert Patrick's *T-Shirts* (1978), and Harvey Fierstein's *Torch Song Trilogy* (1981).

In the 1980s, "AIDS plays" expanded on the conventions of earlier gay drama to explore the impact on individuals, relationships, and families of a new and devastating epidemic. Works such as Larry Kramer's *The Normal Heart* (1985) and William Hoffman's *As Is* (1985) were aggressive in expressing their anger at the relative lack of concern displayed by the Reagan administration and by Americans generally. Even more forcefully than the plays of the 1970s, AIDS plays challenged heterosexual audiences to empathize with gay characters as individuals entitled to equal rights and opportunities within society.

Despite their dramatic power, none of these plays received the attention won by *Angels in America.* The particular acclaim that greeted Kushner's play resulted, in part, from the way in which its characters, themes, and issues address the question of American national identity. This focus on Americanness invites comparison between *Angels* and Miller's *Death of a Salesman.* Produced just four years after the end of World War II, *Salesman* exposed the false myths of the "American Dream" and the vulnerability of the self-made man whose success in business and access to the good life rest on his personal charm. Produced near the end of the twentieth century, *Angels in America* likewise reveals a fundamental social betrayal—in this case, of America's founding ideals of freedom and equality. Miller's play is grounded in the history of European immigration to the United States and in the Great Depression; Kushner's is tied to the legacy of the civil rights movement in the 1960s, the rise of the gay rights movement, and the conservative backlash against both in the 1980s and early 1990s.

Yet whereas *Salesman* critiques American society through the lens of liberal humanism, *Angels* explores how those in power legislate and enforce normative assumptions about sex and sexuality, gender, race, and class. In its affirmation of social pluralism, the play embraces a decidedly postmodern understanding of identity and history. Narratives, myths, and themes that have traditionally constituted "America"—the Founding Fathers, manifest destiny, "the melting pot," the American family—no longer fit the changing demographics and experiences of contemporary life as Kushner dramatizes them. In one of the opening scenes of *Millennium Approaches,* Harper Pitt—one of the play's visionaries—

speaks of "beautiful systems dying, old fixed orders spiraling apart." Characters in *Angels in America* must rethink their identities and that of their nation within new relationships and psychological frameworks, reinterpreting the myths of America in light of more pluralistic social realities. On the eve of the third millennium, Kushner suggests, the question of what it means to be an American must be answered in ways that are at once collective and deeply individual.

The political and social breadth of *Angels in America* is matched by its stylistic expansiveness. Whereas *Death of a Salesman* helped define the tradition of American poetic realism, innovatively combining naturalistic and expressionistic elements, *Angels* employs an extraordinary collage of theatrical styles—from realism to surrealism, tragedy to farce, Brechtian political theater to the gay performance traditions of camp and drag. Ranging from the broadly political to the intensely personal and spiritual, the play balances intimately crafted scenes with an overarching epic structure, blending psychological realism together with nonrealistic dream scenes and heightened theatrical spectacle. While interweaving these styles and structures, the play also intercuts story lines cinematically, thereby encouraging the audience to see the life of each character in relation to society and to understand that such supposedly "personal" matters as sex and love are inherently political. Coining the label "Theatre of the Fabulous" for this stylistic collage, Kushner has stressed the theatrical nature of the play's scenes and effects. In his "playwright's notes," he comments: "The moments of magic . . . are to be fully realized, as bits of wonderful *theatrical* illusion—which means it's OK if the wires show, and maybe it's good that they do, but the magic should at the same time be thoroughly amazing."

Julius (third from left) and Ethel (far left) Rosenberg, who, on June 19, 1953, became the first American citizens executed for espionage.

Even as *Angels in America* has one foot in the miraculous, its other is firmly planted in the actual. Kushner's play is set in the mid-1980s during the Reagan presidency, and its cast includes characters drawn from modern American history. Most important among these is Roy Cohn, who served as chief counsel to Senator Joseph McCarthy during the Senate's anticommunist investigations of the 1950s and who, earlier, as an assistant U.S. attorney in New York, played a key role in the most sensational and controversial case of the decade's Red Scare: the prosecution of Julius and Ethel Rosenberg, a Jewish couple accused of helping to pass secrets of American nuclear research to the Soviet Union. They were convicted in 1951 and executed in 1953. Though Cohn's investigative methods were ultimately exposed as unethical, and perhaps illegal, he went on to become a powerful attorney in Washington D.C., and New York, giving behind-the-scenes advice to FBI Chief J. Edgar Hoover as well as to judges, mayors, and presidents. Throughout his career, he repudiated his familial and cultural roots, striving to become the reverse of what he was: the son of a Jewish, liberal, Democratic New York state supreme court judge. Cohn died from AIDS in 1986 but sought, to the very end, to hide his homosexuality, insisting that his ailment was "liver cancer."

Kushner juxtaposes Cohn's life with the lives of two fictional couples, one homosexual and the other heterosexual, who represent ordinary, young middle-class Americans living in New York in the mid-1980s. The homosexual couple are Louis, who works as a word processor in an office located in Roy's building, and Prior, a drag queen who has recently learned he is HIV-positive. When Prior develops full-blown AIDS, Louis's commitment to him and to their relationship shrinks as he confronts his fears of death and emotional pain. The heterosexual couple are Joe and Harper, Mormons who have moved from Utah to New York City to further Joe's legal career; Joe has become Roy's protégé, the object of his professional mentoring and almost paternal love. Joe and Harper's marriage is brought to a crisis by Roy's offer to place Joe in a job in Washington, D.C.—a position that will enable him to block Roy's threatened disbarment—and by Joe's homosexuality, with which he has struggled

Sean Chapman as Prior and Nancy Crane as the Angel in the 1992 London premiere of *Angels in America* at the Royal National Theatre.

all his life and which he must eventually acknowledge to himself and his wife. As the play unfolds, shifting focus from one story to another, the choices and actions of these characters shed light on each other. The audience sees Prior's experience of AIDS against Roy's denial of the disease, Joe's personal and professional integrity against Roy's dishonesty, Louis's abandonment of his partner against Joe's rejection of Harper, and Joe's emerging awareness of his homosexuality against Roy's repression of his own. By thus placing characters side by side, Kushner reveals their social interconnectedness and makes them symbolic of contradictions at the heart of the United States as a nation.

Joe's and Harper's Mormonism serves as one of a number of intellectual and spiritual backdrops to *Angels in America*. The one Christian religion indigenous to the United States, the Church of Jesus Christ of Latter-day Saints was founded in response to what its adherents view as a revelation that revised established Christian belief; it developed fully only after its first members journeyed to the edges of the frontier in search of the Promised Land. The metaphor of building on a past, of migrating, of crossing personal and ideological boundaries on the way to some anticipated rebirth or revelation recurs throughout *Angels:* in the opening monologue on Jewish emigration to the United States, in Joe's awakening to his sexuality, in Louis's movement away from Prior and toward Joe, and in Harper's and Prior's visions. Indeed, Kushner makes the stage itself a frontier, filling it with diverse styles that he synthesizes into a vision of social theater. As it moves between realism and nonrealism, between epic theater and spectacle, the play explores the limits of theatrical representation; at the outer reaches of those limits are the play's split scenes and dream scenes, which address social and spiritual dissolution and redemption.

Written as the cold war ended and in the waning years of the twentieth century, *Millennium Approaches* is charged with millenarian apprehension toward an unknown future. Apocalyptic foreboding occurs throughout the play, from Harper's fears about the vanishing ozone layer to terror at the pestilential specter of AIDS. *Perestroika,* the concluding part of *Angels in America,* lightens this tone somewhat, as it affirms life, community, and the possibility of personal, social, and spiritual progress. Like Kushner himself, who found himself anointed as a theatrical prophet while he moved steadily on with his writing and his activism, the play's characters seek ways to confront the world's problems while cultivating a vision of humanity's underlying grace. But though the two-part drama moves in the direction of healing, the most memorable moment in Kushner's theatrical epic is the spectacular conclusion of *Millennium Approaches*. Terrifying, beautiful, yet ambiguous, this final scene reflects the longings and fears, the restless spirituality, and the sense of the unknown that mark the turn of the millennium.

ART BORRECCA

Angels in America
A Gay Fantasia on National Themes

PART ONE:
MILLENNIUM APPROACHES

CHARACTERS

ROY M. COHN,[1] a successful New York lawyer and unofficial power broker.

JOSEPH PORTER PITT, chief clerk for Justice Theodore Wilson of the Federal Court of Appeals, Second Circuit.

HARPER AMATY PITT, Joe's wife, an agoraphobic with a mild Valium[2] addiction.

LOUIS IRONSON, a word processor working for the Second Circuit Court of Appeals.

PRIOR WALTER, Louis's boyfriend. Occasionally works as a club designer or caterer, otherwise lives very modestly but with great style off a small trust fund.

HANNAH PORTER PITT, Joe's mother, currently residing in Salt Lake City, living off her deceased husband's army pension.

BELIZE, a former drag queen and former lover of Prior's. A registered nurse. Belize's name was originally Norman Arriaga; Belize is a drag name that stuck.

THE ANGEL, four divine emanations, Fluor, Phosphor, Lumen, and Candle;[3] manifest in One: the Continental Principality of America. She has magnificent steel-gray wings.

Other Characters in Part One

RABBI ISIDOR CHEMELWITZ, an orthodox Jewish rabbi, played by the actor playing HANNAH.

MR. LIES, Harper's imaginary friend, a travel agent, who in style of dress and speech suggests a jazz musician; he always wears a large lapel badge emblazoned "IOTA" (The International Order of Travel Agents). He is played by the actor playing BELIZE.

THE MAN IN THE PARK, played by the actor playing PRIOR.

THE VOICE, the voice of THE ANGEL.

HENRY, ROY's doctor, played by the actor playing HANNAH.

EMILY, a nurse, played by the actor playing THE ANGEL.

1. A Jewish, New York–born lawyer (1927–1986) who attracted public attention and controversy throughout his career, most notoriously as chief counsel (1953–54) to the Permanent Subcommittee on Investigations, which, under the chairmanship of Senator Joseph McCarthy, hunted for Communists in the government and U.S. Army.

2. Diazepam (trademark), a tranquilizer that in the 1980s was the most frequently prescribed drug in the United States.

3. All terms having to do with light: *fluor,* or fluorite, is a mineral whose crystals can exhibit lumenescence; *phosphor,* or phosphorus, also emits light; and *lumen* (literally, "light" in Latin) and *candle* are both measures of light (of its intensity and flux, respectively).

MARTIN HELLER, a Reagan Administration Justice Department flackman, played by the actor playing HARPER.

SISTER ELLA CHAPTER, a Salt Lake City real estate saleswoman, played by the actor playing THE ANGEL.

PRIOR 1, the ghost of a dead Prior Walter from the 13th century, played by the actor playing JOE. He is a blunt, gloomy medieval farmer with a guttural Yorkshire accent.

PRIOR 2, the ghost of a dead Prior Walter from the 17th century, played by the actor playing ROY. He is a Londoner, sophisticated, with a High British accent.

THE ESKIMO, played by the actor playing JOE.

THE WOMAN IN THE SOUTH BRONX, played by the actor playing THE ANGEL.

ETHEL ROSENBERG,[4] played by the actor playing HANNAH.

Playwright's Notes

A DISCLAIMER: Roy M. Cohn, the character, is based on the late Roy M. Cohn (1927–1986), who was all too real; for the most part the acts attributed to the character Roy, such as his illegal conferences with Judge Kaufman during the trial of Ethel Rosenberg, are to be found in the historical record. But this Roy is a work of dramatic fiction; his words are my invention, and liberties have been taken.

A NOTE ABOUT THE STAGING: The play benefits from a pared-down style of presentation, with minimal scenery and scene shifts done rapidly (no blackouts!), employing the cast as well as stagehands—which makes for an actor-driven event, as this must be. The moments of magic—the appearance and disappearance of Mr. Lies and the ghosts, the Book hallucination, and the ending—are to be fully realized, as bits of wonderful *theatrical* illusion—which means it's OK if the wires show, and maybe it's good that they do, but the magic should at the same time be thoroughly amazing.

In a murderous time
the heart breaks and breaks
and lives by breaking.
—Stanley Kunitz[5]
"The Testing-Tree"

4. A Jewish, New York–born Communist (1915–1953); along with her husband, Julius, she was tried and executed for conspiring to give the Soviet Union information about the atomic bomb. As an assistant in the U.S. Attorney's office in New York, Roy Cohn played a prominent role in her 1951 trial.

5. An American poet (1905–2006); "The Testing-Tree" is the title poem of a collection published in 1971.

Act 1: Bad News

(*October–November 1985*)

Scene 1

[*The last days of October.* RABBI ISIDOR CHEMELWITZ *alone onstage with a small coffin. It is a rough pine box with two wooden pegs, one at the foot and one at the head, holding the lid in place. A prayer shawl embroidered with a Star of David is draped over the lid, and by the head a yarzheit*[6] *candle is burning.*]

RABBI ISIDOR CHEMELWITZ [*he speaks sonorously, with a heavy Eastern European accent, unapologetically consulting a sheet of notes for the family names*] Hello and good morning. I am Rabbi Isidor Chemelwitz of the Bronx Home for Aged Hebrews. We are here this morning to pay respects at the passing of Sarah Ironson, devoted wife of Benjamin Ironson, also deceased, loving and caring mother of her sons Morris, Abraham, and Samuel, and her daughters Esther and Rachel; beloved grandmother of Max, Mark, Louis, Lisa, Maria . . . uh . . . Lesley, Angela, Doris, Luke, and Eric. [*Looks more closely at paper.*] Eric? This is a Jewish name? [*Shrugs.*] Eric. A large and loving family. We assemble that we may mourn collectively this good and righteous woman. [*He looks at the coffin.*]

This woman. I did not know this woman. I cannot accurately describe her attributes, nor do justice to her dimensions. She was . . . Well, in the Bronx Home of Aged Hebrews are many like this, the old, and to many I speak but not to be frank with this one. She preferred silence. So I do not know her and yet I know her. She was . . . [*He touches the coffin.*] . . . not a person but a whole kind of person, the ones who crossed the ocean, who brought with us to America the villages of Russia and Lithuania—and how we struggled, and how we fought, for the family, for the Jewish home, so that you would not grow up *here,* in this strange place, in the melting pot where nothing melted. Descendants of this immigrant woman, you do not grow up in America, you and your children and their children with the goyische[7] names. You do not live in America. No such place exists. Your clay is the clay of some Litvak shtetl,[8] your air the air of the steppes—because she carried the old world on her back across the ocean, in a boat, and she put it down on Grand Concourse Avenue, or in Flatbush,[9] and she worked that earth into your bones, and you pass it to your children, this ancient, ancient culture and home. [*Little pause*]

You can never make that crossing that she made, for such Great Voyages in this world do not anymore exist. But every day of your lives the miles that voyage between that place and this one you cross. Every day. You understand me? In you that journey is.

So . . .

6. Anniversary (Yiddish); on the anniversary of a relative's death, observant Jews light a memorial candle at home and in their synagogue.
7. Non-Jewish, Gentile (Yiddish; sometimes pejorative).
8. Lithuanian village (Yiddish).
9. Two middle-class areas of New York City to which Jews moved in large numbers in the 1920s and '30s (in the Bronx and in Brooklyn, respectively).

She was the last of the Mohicans,[1] this one was. Pretty soon . . . all the old will be dead.

Scene 2

[*Same day.* ROY *and* JOE *in* ROY's *office.* ROY *at an impressive desk, bare except for a very elaborate phone system, rows and rows of flashing buttons which bleep and beep and whistle incessantly, making chaotic music underneath* ROY's *conversations.* JOE *is sitting, waiting.* ROY *conducts business with great energy, impatience, and sensual abandon: gesticulating, shouting, cajoling, crooning, playing the phone, receiver and hold button, with virtuosity and love.*]

ROY [*hitting a button*] Hold. [*To* JOE] I wish I was an octopus, a fucking octopus. Eight loving arms and all those suckers. Know what I mean?

JOE No, I . . .

ROY [*gesturing to a deli platter of little sandwiches on his desk*] You want lunch?

JOE No, that's OK really I just . . .

ROY [*hitting a button*] Ailene? Roy Cohn. Now what kind of a greeting is. . . . I thought we were friends, Ai . . . Look Mrs. Soffer you don't have to get . . . You're upset. You're yelling. You'll aggravate your condition, you shouldn't yell, you'll pop little blood vessels in your face if you yell. . . . No that was a joke, Mrs. Soffer, I was joking. . . . I already apologized sixteen times for that, Mrs. Soffer, you . . . [*While she's fulminating,* ROY *covers the mouthpiece with his hand and talks to* JOE.] This'll take a minute, *eat* already, what is this tasty sandwich here it's— [*He takes a bite of a sandwich.*] Mmmmm, liver or some . . . Here.

[*He pitches the sandwich to* JOE, *who catches it and returns it to the platter.*]

ROY [*back to Mrs. Soffer*] Uh huh, uh huh. . . . No, I already told you, it wasn't a vacation, it was business, Mrs. Soffer, I have clients in Haiti, Mrs. Soffer, I . . . Listen, Ailene, YOU THINK I'M THE ONLY GODDAM LAWYER IN HISTORY EVER MISSED A COURT DATE? Don't make such a big fucking . . . Hold. [*He hits the hold button.*] You HAG!

JOE If this is a bad time . . .

ROY *Bad* time? This is a *good* time! [*Button*] Baby doll, get me . . . Oh fuck, wait . . . [*Button, button*] Hello? Yah. Sorry to keep you holding, Judge Hollins, I . . . Oh *Mrs.* Hollins, sorry dear deep voice you got. Enjoying your visit? [*Hand over mouthpiece again, to* JOE] She sounds like a truckdriver and he sounds like Kate Smith,[2] very confusing. Nixon[3] appointed him, all the geeks are Nixon appointees . . . [*To Mrs. Hollins*] Yeah yeah right good so how many tickets dear? Seven. For what, *Cats, 42nd Street,*

1. That is, the last of her kind—an allusion to James Fenimore Cooper's novel *The Last of the Mohicans* (1826).

2. A popular American singer (1907–1986), best known for her rendition of Irving Berlin's "God Bless America" (1918); her career peaked in the 1940s, but her robust voice made her a star of radio and television from the 1930s to the 1960s.

3. Richard M. Nixon (1913–1994), thirty-seventh president of the United States (1969–74); Nixon rose to national prominence in the 1940s as an ardently anticommunist Republican congressman on the House Committee on Un-American Activities.

what? No you wouldn't like *La Cage*,[4] trust me, I know. Oh for godsake . . . Hold. [*Button, button*] Baby doll, seven for *Cats* or something, anything hard to get, I don't give a fuck what and neither will they. [*Button; to* JOE] You see *La Cage?*

JOE No, I . . .

ROY Fabulous. Best thing on Broadway. Maybe ever. [*Button*] Who? Aw, Jesus H. Christ, Harry, *no,* Harry, Judge John Francis Grimes, Manhattan Family Court. Do I have to do every goddam thing myself? *Touch* the bastard, Harry, and don't call me on this line again, I told you not to . . .

JOE [*starting to get up*] Roy, uh, should I wait outside or . . .

ROY [*to* JOE] Oh sit. [*To Harry*] You hold. I pay you to hold fuck you Harry you jerk. [*Button*] Half-wit dick-brain. [*Instantly philosophical*] I see the universe, Joe, as a kind of sandstorm in outer space with winds of mega-hurricane velocity, but instead of grains of sand it's shards and splinters of glass. You ever feel that way? Ever have one of those days?

JOE I'm not sure I . . .

ROY So how's life in Appeals?[5] How's the Judge?

JOE He sends his best.

ROY He's a good man. Loyal. Not the brightest man on the bench, but he has manners. And a nice head of silver hair.

JOE He gives me a lot of responsibility.

ROY Yeah, like writing his decisions and signing his name.

JOE Well . . .

ROY He's a nice guy. And you cover admirably.

JOE Well, thanks, Roy, I . . .

ROY [*button*] Yah? Who is *this?* Well who the fuck are *you?* Hold— [*Button*] Harry? Eighty-seven grand, something like that. Fuck him. Eat me. New Jersey, chain of porno film stores in, uh, Weehawken.[6] That's—Harry, that's the beauty of the law. [*Button*] So, baby doll, what? *Cats?* Bleah. [*Button*] *Cats!* It's about cats. Singing cats, you'll love it. Eight o'clock, the theatre's always at eight. [*Button*] Fucking tourists. [*Button, then to* JOE] Oh live a little, Joe, *eat* something for Christ sake—

JOE Um, Roy, could you . . .

ROY What? [*To Harry*] Hold a minute. [*Button*] Mrs. Soffer? Mrs. . . . [*Button*] God-fucking-dammit to hell, where is . . .

JOE [*overlapping*] Roy, I'd really appreciate it if . . .

ROY [*overlapping*] Well she was here a minute ago, baby doll, see if . . .

[*The phone starts making three different beeping sounds, all at once.*]

ROY [*smashing buttons*] Jesus fuck this goddam thing . . .

JOE [*overlapping*] I really wish you wouldn't . . .

ROY [*overlapping*] Baby doll? Ring the *Post*[7] get me Suzy see if . . .

[*The phone starts whistling loudly.*]

4. Long-running musicals on Broadway in the 1980s: *Cats* (1982–2000; lyrics by T. S. Eliot and Trevor Nunn, music by Andrew Lloyd Webber); *42nd Street* (1980–89; book by Mark Bramble and Michael Stewart, lyrics by Al Dubin, music by Harry Warren); and *La Cage aux Folles* (1983–87; book by Harvey Fierstein, lyrics and music by Jerry Herman), which presents the interactions between a gay couple (the manager and the star of a drag nightclub), the manager's son, and the conservative parents of the son's fiancée.

5. The U.S. Court of Appeals, where Joe is a lawyer holding a senior administrative position.

6. A town directly across the Hudson River from New York City.

7. The *New York Post,* which by the 1980s had become a conservative tabloid.

ROY CHRIST!

JOE *Roy.*

ROY [*into receiver*] Hold. [*Button; to* JOE] *What?*

JOE Could you please not take the Lord's name in vain? [*Pause*]

I'm sorry. But please. At least while I'm . . .

ROY [*laughs, then*] Right. Sorry. Fuck.

Only in America. [*Punches a button.*] Baby doll, tell 'em all to fuck off. Tell 'em I died. You handle Mrs. Soffer. Tell her it's on the way. Tell her I'm schtupping[8] the judge. I'll call her back. I *will* call her. I *know* how much I borrowed. She's got four hundred times that stuffed up her . . . Yeah, tell her I said that. [*Button. The phone is silent.*]

So, Joe.

JOE I'm sorry Roy, I just . . .

ROY No no no no, principles count, I respect principles, I'm not religious but I like God and God likes me. Baptist, Catholic?

JOE Mormon.

ROY Mormon. Delectable. Absolutely. Only in America. So, Joe. Whattya think?

JOE It's . . . well . . .

ROY Crazy life.

JOE Chaotic.

ROY Well but God bless chaos. Right?

JOE Ummm . . .

ROY Huh. Mormons. I knew Mormons, in, um, Nevada.

JOE Utah, mostly.

ROY No, these Mormons were in Vegas.

So. So, how'd you like to go to Washington and work for the Justice Department?

JOE Sorry?

ROY How'd you like to go to Washington and work for the Justice Department? All I gotta do is pick up the phone, talk to Ed, and you're in.

JOE In . . . what, exactly?

ROY Associate Assistant Something Big. Internal Affairs, heart of the woods, something nice with clout.

JOE Ed . . . ?

ROY Meese.[9] The Attorney General.

JOE Oh.

ROY I just have to pick up the phone . . .

JOE I have to think.

ROY Of course. [*Pause*]

It's a great time to be in Washington, Joe.

JOE Roy, it's incredibly exciting . . .

ROY And it would mean something to me. You understand?

[*Little pause.*]

JOE I . . . can't say how much I appreciate this Roy, I'm sort of . . . well, stunned, I mean . . . Thanks, Roy. But I have to give it some thought. I have to ask my wife.

8. Aggressively pushing, ingratiating himself with; fucking (from Yiddish).

9. Edwin Meese III (b. 1931), who served as attorney general (1985–88) under President Ronald Reagan (1911–2004; 40th president, 1981–89).

ROY Your wife. Of course.

JOE But I really appreciate . . .

ROY Of course. Talk to your wife.

Scene 3

[*Later that day.* HARPER *at home, alone. She is listening to the radio and talking to herself, as she often does. She speaks to the audience.*]

HARPER People who are lonely, people left alone, sit talking nonsense to the air, imagining . . . beautiful systems dying, old fixed orders spiraling apart . . .

When you look at the ozone layer, from outside, from a spaceship, it looks like a pale blue halo, a gentle, shimmering aureole encircling the atmosphere encircling the earth. Thirty miles above our heads, a thin layer of three-atom oxygen molecules, product of photosynthesis, which explains the fussy vegetable preference for visible light, its rejection of darker rays and emanations. Danger from without. It's a kind of gift, from God, the crowning touch to the creation of the world: guardian angels, hands linked, make a spherical net, a blue-green nesting orb, a shell of safety for life itself. But everywhere, things are collapsing, lies surfacing, systems of defense giving way.[1] . . . This is why, Joe, this is why I shouldn't be left alone. [*Little pause*]

I'd like to go traveling. Leave you behind to worry. I'll send postcards with strange stamps and tantalizing messages on the back. "Later maybe." "Nevermore . . ."

[MR. LIES, *a travel agent, appears.*]

HARPER Oh! You startled me!

MR. LIES Cash, check, or credit card?

HARPER I remember you. You're from Salt Lake. You sold us the plane tickets when we flew here. What are you doing in Brooklyn?

MR. LIES You said you wanted to travel . . .

HARPER And here you are. How thoughtful.

MR. LIES Mr. Lies. Of the International Order of Travel Agents. We mobilize the globe, we set people adrift, we stir the populace and send nomads eddying across the planet. We are adepts of motion, acolytes of the flux. Cash, check, or credit card. Name your destination.

HARPER Antarctica, maybe. I want to see the hole in the ozone. I heard on the radio . . .

MR. LIES [*he has a computer terminal in his briefcase*] I can arrange a guided tour. Now?

HARPER Soon. Maybe soon. I'm not safe here you see. Things aren't right with me. Weird stuff happens . . .

MR. LIES Like?

HARPER Well, like you, for instance. Just appearing. Or last week . . . well never mind.

People are like planets, you need a thick skin. Things get to me, Joe stays away and now. . . . Well look. My dreams are talking back to me.

1. Beginning in the 1970s, scientists began to warn that industrial pollutants such as chlorofluorocarbons (CFCs) might concentrate in the stratosphere and deplete the ozone there, which affords protection against harmful high-energy radiation. The first "ozone hole"—a seasonal depletion—was discovered above Antarctica in 1985, and subsequent research confirmed the widespread loss of ozone.

MR. LIES It's the price of rootlessness. Motion sickness. The only cure: to keep moving.

HARPER I'm undecided. I feel . . . that something's going to give. It's 1985. Fifteen years till the third millennium. Maybe Christ will come again. Maybe seeds will be planted, maybe there'll be harvests then, maybe early figs to eat, maybe new life, maybe fresh blood, maybe companionship and love and protection, safety from what's outside, maybe the door will hold, or maybe . . . maybe the troubles[2] will come, and the end will come, and the sky will collapse and there will be terrible rains and showers of poison light, or maybe my life is really fine, maybe Joe loves me and I'm only crazy thinking otherwise, or maybe not, maybe it's even worse than I know, maybe . . . I want to know, maybe I don't. The suspense, Mr. Lies, it's killing me.

MR. LIES I suggest a vacation.

HARPER [*hearing something*] That was the elevator. Oh God, I should fix myself up, I . . . You have to go, you shouldn't be here . . . you aren't even real.

MR. LIES Call me when you decide . . .

HARPER Go!

[*The travel agent vanishes as* JOE *enters.*]

JOE Buddy?

Buddy? Sorry I'm late. I was just . . . out. Walking. Are you mad?

HARPER I got a little anxious.

JOE Buddy kiss.

[*They kiss.*]

JOE Nothing to get anxious about.

So. So how'd you like to move to Washington?

Scene 4

[*Same day.* LOUIS *and* PRIOR *outside the funeral home, sitting on a bench, both dressed in funereal finery, talking. The funeral service for Sarah Ironson has just concluded and* LOUIS *is about to leave for the cemetery.*]

LOUIS My grandmother actually saw Emma Goldman[3] speak. In Yiddish. But all Grandma could remember was that she spoke well and wore a hat.

What a weird service. That rabbi . . .

PRIOR A definite find. Get his number when you go to the graveyard. I want him to bury me.

LOUIS Better head out there. Everyone gets to put dirt on the coffin once it's lowered in.

PRIOR Oooh. Cemetery fun. Don't want to miss that.

LOUIS It's an old Jewish custom to express love. Here, Grandma, have a shovelful. Latecomers run the risk of finding the grave completely filled.

She was pretty crazy. She was up there in that home for ten years, talking to herself. I never visited. She looked too much like my mother.

PRIOR [*hugs him*] Poor Louis. I'm sorry your grandma is dead.

2. That is, the apocalyptic "end times" foretold in the New Testament's book of Revelation.

3. A Lithuanian-born American anarchist and writer (1869–1940); she championed socialism and women's rights in the United States, Russia, and Britain. Though Goldman's primary languages were Russian and German, she gave speeches in Yiddish—the lingua franca of Jews from central and eastern Europe—to reach the largest audience possible.

LOUIS Tiny little coffin, huh?

Sorry I didn't introduce you to. . . . I always get so closety[4] at these family things.

PRIOR Butch.[5] You get butch. [*Imitating*] "Hi Cousin Doris, you don't remember me I'm Lou, Rachel's boy." Lou, not Louis, because if you say Louis they'll hear the sibilant S.

LOUIS I don't have a . . .

PRIOR I don't blame you, hiding. Bloodlines. Jewish curses are the worst. I personally would dissolve if anyone ever looked me in the eye and said "Feh."[6] Fortunately WASPs don't say "Feh." Oh and by the way, darling, cousin Doris is a dyke.

LOUIS No.

Really?

PRIOR You don't notice anything. If I hadn't spent the last four years fellating you I'd swear you were straight.

LOUIS You're in a pissy mood. Cat still missing?

[*Little pause.*]

PRIOR Not a furball in sight. It's your fault.

LOUIS It is?

PRIOR I warned you, Louis. Names are important. Call an animal "Little Sheba"[7] and you can't expect it to stick around. Besides, it's a dog's name.

LOUIS I wanted a dog in the first place, not a cat. He sprayed my books.

PRIOR He was a female cat.

LOUIS Cats are stupid, high-strung predators. Babylonians sealed them up in bricks. Dogs have brains.

PRIOR Cats have intuition.

LOUIS A sharp dog is as smart as a really dull two-year-old child.

PRIOR Cats know when something's wrong.

LOUIS Only if you stop feeding them.

PRIOR They know. That's why Sheba left, because she knew.

LOUIS Knew what?

[*Pause.*]

PRIOR I did my best Shirley Booth[8] this morning, floppy slippers, housecoat, curlers, can of Little Friskies; "Come back, Little Sheba, come back. . . ." To no avail. Le chat, elle ne reviendra jamais, jamais[9] . . .

[*He removes his jacket, rolls up his sleeve, shows* LOUIS *a dark-purple spot on the underside of his arm near the shoulder.*] See.

LOUIS That's just a burst blood vessel.

PRIOR Not according to the best medical authorities.

LOUIS What? [*Pause*]

Tell me.

PRIOR K.S.,[1] baby. Lesion number one. Lookit. The wine-dark kiss of the angel of death.

4. That is, secretive about his homosexuality.

5. Assertively masculine.

6. A Yiddish interjection that expresses disgust or displeasure.

7. A reference to *Come Back, Little Sheba,* a 1952 film (dir. Daniel Mann) based on William Inge's 1950 play, which takes its title from the call for a lost dog.

8. An American actor (1898–1992); she starred in the stage and film versions of *Come Back, Little Sheba*.

9. The cat, she will never, ever come back (French).

1. That is, Kaposi's sarcoma, a type of lesion associated with AIDS; it was one of the first recognized signs of HIV infection.

LOUIS [*very softly, holding* PRIOR*'s arm*] Oh please . . .

PRIOR I'm a lesionnaire. The Foreign Lesion. The American Lesion. Lesionnaire's disease.

LOUIS Stop.

PRIOR My troubles are lesion.

LOUIS Will you *stop*.

PRIOR Don't you think I'm handling this well? I'm going to die.

LOUIS Bullshit.

PRIOR Let go of my arm.

LOUIS No.

PRIOR Let go.

LOUIS [*grabbing* PRIOR*, embracing him ferociously*] No.

PRIOR I can't find a way to spare you baby. No wall like the wall of hard scientific fact. K.S. Wham. Bang your head on that.

LOUIS Fuck you. [*Letting go*] Fuck you fuck you fuck you.

PRIOR Now that's what I like to hear. A mature reaction.
Let's go see if the cat's come home.
Louis?

LOUIS When did you find this?

PRIOR I couldn't tell you.

LOUIS Why?

PRIOR I was scared, Lou.

LOUIS Of what?

PRIOR That you'll leave me.

LOUIS Oh.

[*Little pause.*]

PRIOR Bad timing, funeral and all, but I figured as long as we're on the subject of death . . .

LOUIS I have to go bury my grandma.

PRIOR Lou?

[*Pause.*]

Then you'll come home?

LOUIS Then I'll come home.

Scene 5

[*Same day, later on. Split scene:* JOE *and* HARPER *at home;* LOUIS *at the cemetery with* RABBI ISIDOR CHEMELWITZ *and the little coffin.*]

HARPER Washington?

JOE It's an incredible honor, buddy, and . . .

HARPER I have to think.

JOE Of course.

HARPER Say no.

JOE You said you were going to think about it.

HARPER I don't want to move to Washington.

JOE Well I do.

HARPER It's a giant cemetery, huge white graves and mausoleums everywhere.

JOE We could live in Maryland. Or Georgetown.

HARPER We're happy here.

JOE That's not really true, buddy, we . . .

HARPER Well happy enough! Pretend-happy. That's better than nothing.

JOE It's time to make some changes, Harper.

HARPER No changes. Why?

JOE I've been chief clerk for four years. I make twenty-nine thousand dollars a year. That's ridiculous. I graduated fourth in my class and I make less than anyone I know. And I'm . . . I'm tired of being a clerk, I want to go where something good is happening.

HARPER Nothing good happens in Washington. We'll forget church teachings and buy furniture at . . . at *Conran's* and become yuppies.[2] I have too much to do here.

JOE Like what?

HARPER I *do* have things . . .

JOE What things?

HARPER I have to finish painting the bedroom.

JOE You've been painting in there for over a year.

HARPER I know, I . . . It just isn't done because I never get time to finish it.

JOE Oh that's . . . that doesn't make sense. You have all the time in the world. You could finish it when I'm at work.

HARPER I'm afraid to go in there alone.

JOE Afraid of what?

HARPER I heard someone in there. Metal scraping on the wall. A man with a knife, maybe.

JOE There's no one in the bedroom, Harper.

HARPER Not now.

JOE Not this morning either.

HARPER How do you know? You were at work this morning. There's something creepy about this place. Remember *Rosemary's Baby*?[3]

JOE *Rosemary's Baby?*

HARPER Our apartment looks like that one. Wasn't that apartment in Brooklyn?

JOE No, it was . . .

HARPER Well, it looked like this. It did.

JOE Then let's move.

HARPER Georgetown's worse. *The Exorcist* was in Georgetown.[4]

JOE The devil, everywhere you turn, huh, buddy.

HARPER Yeah. Everywhere.

JOE How many pills today, buddy?

HARPER None. One. Three. Only three.

LOUIS [*pointing at the coffin*] Why are there just two little wooden pegs holding the lid down?

RABBI ISIDOR CHEMELWITZ So she can get out easier if she wants to.

LOUIS I hope she stays put.

2. A term that came into widespread use in the 1980s. *Conran's:* New York retailer of contemporary home furnishings marketed to young urban professionals.

3. A horror film directed by Roman Polanski (1968), based on a best-selling novel by Ira Levin (1967), in which a young couple move into a Manhattan apartment building inhabited by Satan worshippers.

4. An affluent neighborhood in Washington, D.C., that was the setting of *The Exorcist* (1973; dir. William Friedkin), a horror film adapted from William Peter Blatty's best-selling novel (1971) about a twelve-year-old girl possessed by the devil.

I pretended for years that she was already dead. When they called to say she had died it was a surprise. I abandoned her.

RABBI ISIDOR CHEMELWITZ "Sharfer vi di tson fun a shlang iz an umdankbar kind!"

LOUIS I don't speak Yiddish.

RABBI ISIDOR CHEMELWITZ Sharper than the serpent's tooth is the ingratitude of children. Shakespeare. *Kenig Lear*.[5]

LOUIS Rabbi, what does the Holy Writ say about someone who abandons someone he loves at a time of great need?

RABBI ISIDOR CHEMELWITZ Why would a person do such a thing?

LOUIS Because he has to.

Maybe because this person's sense of the world, that it will change for the better with struggle, maybe a person who has this neo-Hegelian positivist sense of constant historical progress towards happiness or perfection or something,[6] who feels very powerful because he feels connected to these forces, moving uphill all the time . . . maybe that person can't, um, incorporate sickness into his sense of how things are supposed to go. Maybe vomit . . . and sores and disease . . . really frighten him, maybe . . . he isn't so good with death.

RABBI ISIDOR CHEMELWITZ The Holy Scriptures have nothing to say about such a person.

LOUIS Rabbi, I'm afraid of the crimes I may commit.

RABBI ISIDOR CHEMELWITZ Please, mister. I'm a sick old rabbi facing a long drive home to the Bronx. You want to confess, better you should find a priest.

LOUIS But I'm not a Catholic, I'm a Jew.

RABBI ISIDOR CHEMELWITZ Worse luck for you, bubbulah.[7] Catholics believe in forgiveness. Jews believe in Guilt. [*He pats the coffin tenderly.*]

LOUIS You just make sure those pegs are in good and tight.

RABBI ISIDOR CHEMELWITZ Don't worry, mister. The life she had, she'll stay put. She's better off.

JOE Look, I know this is scary for you. But try to understand what it means to me. Will you try?

HARPER Yes.

JOE Good. Really try.

I think things are starting to change in the world.

HARPER But I don't want . . .

JOE Wait. For the good. Change for the good. America has rediscovered itself. Its sacred position among nations. And people aren't ashamed of that like they used to be. This is a great thing. The truth restored. Law restored. That's what President Reagan's done, Harper. He says "Truth exists and can be spoken proudly." And the country responds to him. We become better.

5. That is, *King Lear* (Yiddish); the line paraphrases Shakespeare's play (1605), 1.4.265–66.

6. The German philosopher Georg Wilhelm Friedrich Hegel (1770–1831), who saw in culture and civilization the logical development of consciousness, has traditionally been viewed as an idealist (i.e., his theory is not connected to external reality or the senses); but his belief in the dialectical process—that a thesis inevitably generates its antithesis, and their interaction results in a new synthesis—can lead to such positivist philosophies (i.e., systems of thought focused on observable phenomena) as the dialectical materialism connected with Marxism.

7. Literally, "little grandmother" (Yiddish); a term of endearment, often applied to children.

More good. I need to be a part of that, I need something big to lift me up. I mean, six years ago the world seemed in decline, horrible, hopeless, full of unsolvable problems and crime and confusion and hunger and . . .

HARPER But it still seems that way. More now than before. They say the ozone layer is . . .

JOE Harper . . .

HARPER And today out the window on Atlantic Avenue there was a schizophrenic traffic cop who was making these . . .

JOE Stop it! I'm trying to make a point.

HARPER So am I.

JOE You aren't even making sense, you . . .

HARPER My point is the world seems just as . . .

JOE It only seems that way to you because you never go out in the world, Harper, and you have emotional problems.

HARPER I do so get out in the world.

JOE You don't. You stay in all day, fretting about imaginary . . .

HARPER I get out. I do. You don't know what I do.

JOE You don't stay in all day.

HARPER No.

JOE Well. . . . Yes you do.

HARPER That's what you think.

JOE Where do you go?

HARPER Where do *you* go? When you walk.

[*Pause, then angrily*] And I DO NOT have emotional problems.

JOE I'm sorry.

HARPER And if I do have emotional problems it's from living with you. Or . . .

JOE I'm sorry buddy, I didn't mean to . . .

HARPER Or if you do think I do then you should never have married me. You have all these secrets and lies.

JOE I want to be married to you, Harper.

HARPER You shouldn't. You never should. [*Pause*]

Hey buddy. Hey buddy.

JOE Buddy kiss . . .

[*They kiss.*]

HARPER I heard on the radio how to give a blowjob.

JOE What?

HARPER You want to try?

JOE You really shouldn't listen to stuff like that.

HARPER Mormons can give blowjobs.

JOE *Harper.*

HARPER [*imitating his tone*] *Joe.*

It was a little Jewish lady with a German accent.[8]

This is a good time. For me to make a baby.

[*Little pause.* JOE *turns away.*]

8. Ruth Westheimer (b. 1928), the German-born psychologist and sex therapist who, as "Dr. Ruth," began hosting the radio call-in program *Sexually Speaking* in New York in 1980; it became hugely successful and was soon followed by a cable television program, *The Dr. Ruth Show.*

HARPER Then they went on to a program about holes in the ozone layer. Over Antarctica. Skin burns, birds go blind, icebergs melt. The world's coming to an end.

Scene 6

[*First week of November. In the men's room of the offices of the Brooklyn Federal Court of Appeals;* LOUIS *is crying over the sink;* JOE *enters.*]

JOE Oh, um . . . Morning.
LOUIS Good morning, counselor.
JOE [*he watches* LOUIS *cry*] Sorry, I . . . I don't know your name.
LOUIS Don't bother. Word processor. The lowest of the low.
JOE [*holding out hand*] Joe Pitt. I'm with Justice Wilson . . .
LOUIS Oh, I know that. Counselor Pitt. Chief Clerk.
JOE Were you . . . are you OK?
LOUIS Oh, yeah. Thanks. What a nice man.
JOE Not so nice.
LOUIS What?
JOE Not so nice. Nothing. You sure you're . . .
LOUIS Life sucks shit. Life . . . just sucks shit.
JOE What's wrong?
LOUIS Run in my nylons.
JOE Sorry . . . ?
LOUIS Forget it. Look, thanks for asking.
JOE Well . . .
LOUIS I mean it really is nice of you. [*He starts crying again.*] Sorry, sorry, sick friend . . .
JOE Oh, I'm sorry.
LOUIS Yeah, yeah, well, that's sweet.
Three of your colleagues have preceded you to this baleful sight and you're the first one to ask. The others just opened the door, saw me, and fled. I hope they had to pee real bad.
JOE [*handing him a wad of toilet paper*] They just didn't want to intrude.
LOUIS Hah. Reaganite heartless macho asshole lawyers.[9]
JOE Oh, that's unfair.
LOUIS What is? Heartless? Macho? Reaganite? Lawyer?
JOE I voted for Reagan.
LOUIS You did?
JOE Twice.
LOUIS Twice? Well, oh boy. A Gay Republican.
JOE Excuse me?
LOUIS Nothing.
JOE I'm not . . .
Forget it.
LOUIS Republican? Not Republican? Or . . .
JOE What?

9. Court of appeals judges and district court judges are presidential appointees who, after confirmation, hold their positions for life, and they generally hire subordinates who share their legal philosophies. During his two terms as president, Reagan appointed almost 400 federal judges.

LOUIS What?

JOE Not gay. I'm not gay.

LOUIS Oh. Sorry.

[*Blows his nose loudly.*] It's just . . .

JOE Yes?

LOUIS Well, sometimes you can tell from the way a person sounds that . . . I mean you *sound* like a . . .

JOE No I don't. Like what?

LOUIS Like a Republican.

[*Little pause.* JOE *knows he's being teased;* LOUIS *knows he knows.* JOE *decides to be a little brave.*]

JOE [*making sure no one else is around*] Do I? Sound like a . . . ?

LOUIS What? Like a . . . ? Republican, or . . . ? Do *I*?

JOE Do you what?

LOUIS Sound like a . . . ?

JOE Like a . . . ?

I'm . . . confused.

LOUIS Yes.

My name is Louis. But all my friends call me Louise. I work in Word Processing. Thanks for the toilet paper.

[LOUIS *offers* JOE *his hand,* JOE *reaches,* LOUIS *feints and pecks* JOE *on the cheek, then exits.*]

Scene 7

[*A week later. Mutual dream scene.* PRIOR *is at a fantastic makeup table, having a dream, applying the face.* HARPER *is having a pill-induced hallucination. She has these from time to time. For some reason,* PRIOR *has appeared in this one. Or* HARPER *has appeared in* PRIOR*'s dream. It is bewildering.*]

PRIOR [*alone, putting on makeup, then examining the results in the mirror; to the audience*] "I'm ready for my closeup, Mr. DeMille."[1]

One wants to move through life with elegance and grace, blossoming infrequently but with exquisite taste, and perfect timing, like a rare bloom, a zebra orchid. . . . One wants. . . . But one so seldom gets what one wants, does one? No. One does not. One gets fucked. Over. One . . . dies at thirty, robbed of . . . decades of majesty.

Fuck this shit. Fuck this shit.

[*He almost crumbles; he pulls himself together; he studies his handiwork in the mirror.*] I look like a corpse. A corpsette. Oh my queen; you know you've hit rock-bottom when even drag is a drag.

[HARPER *appears.*]

HARPER Are you. . . . Who are you?

PRIOR Who are you?

HARPER What are you doing in my hallucination?

PRIOR I'm not in your hallucination. You're in my dream.

1. The final line of *Sunset Boulevard* (1950; dir. Billy Wilder), spoken by Gloria Swanson as the delusional former silent-movie star Norma Desmond, is "All right, Mr. DeMille, I'm ready for my closeup." The pioneering film director Cecil B. DeMille (1881–1959) plays himself in the film.

HARPER You're wearing makeup.

PRIOR So are you.

HARPER But you're a man.

PRIOR [*feigning dismay, shock, he mimes slashing his throat with his lipstick and dies, fabulously tragic. Then*] The hands and feet give it away.

HARPER There must be some mistake here. I don't recognize you. You're not. . . . Are you my . . . some sort of imaginary friend?

PRIOR No. Aren't you too old to have imaginary friends?

HARPER I have emotional problems. I took too many pills. Why are you wearing makeup?

PRIOR I was in the process of applying the face, trying to make myself feel better—I swiped the new fall colors at the Clinique counter at Macy's.[2] [*Showing her*]

HARPER You stole these?

PRIOR I was out of cash; it was an emotional emergency!

HARPER Joe will be so angry. I promised him. No more pills.

PRIOR These pills you keep alluding to?

HARPER Valium. I take Valium. Lots of Valium.

PRIOR And you're dancing as fast as you can.[3]

HARPER I'm not *addicted*. I don't believe in addiction, and I never . . . well, I *never* drink. And I *never* take drugs.

PRIOR Well, smell *you*, Nancy Drew.[4]

HARPER Except Valium.

PRIOR Except Valium; in wee fistfuls.

HARPER It's terrible. Mormons are not supposed to be addicted to anything. I'm a Mormon.

PRIOR I'm a homosexual.

HARPER Oh! In my church we don't believe in homosexuals.

PRIOR In my church we don't believe in Mormons.

HARPER What church do . . . oh! [*She laughs.*] I get it.

I don't understand this. If I didn't ever see you before and I don't think I did then I don't think you should be here, in this hallucination, because in my experience the mind, which is where hallucinations come from, shouldn't be able to make up anything that wasn't there to start with, that didn't enter it from experience, from the real world. Imagination can't create anything new, can it? It only recycles bits and pieces from the world and reassembles them into visions. . . . Am I making sense right now?

PRIOR Given the circumstances, yes.

HARPER So when we think we've escaped the unbearable ordinariness and, well, untruthfulness of our lives, it's really only the same old ordinariness and falseness rearranged into the appearance of novelty and truth. Nothing unknown is knowable. Don't you think it's depressing?

PRIOR The limitations of the imagination?

HARPER Yes.

2. A chain of department stores; its flagship store is in New York City at Herald Square. *Clinique*: an upscale brand of cosmetics.

3. A play on *I'm Dancing as Fast as I Can* (1982; dir. Jack Hofsiss), a film adapted from Barbara Gordon's best-selling 1972 memoir about Valium addiction.

4. A schoolyard taunt; Nancy Drew, a wholesome teenage detective, is the heroine of a popular series that the Stratemeyer syndicate began publishing in 1930.

PRIOR It's something you learn after your second theme party: It's All Been Done Before.

HARPER The world. Finite. Terribly, terribly. . . . Well . . .
This is the most depressing hallucination I've ever had.

PRIOR Apologies. I do try to be amusing.

HARPER Oh, well, don't apologize, you . . . I can't expect someone who's really sick to entertain me.

PRIOR How on earth did you know . . .

HARPER Oh that happens. This is the very threshhold of revelation sometimes. You can see things . . . how sick you are. Do you see anything about me?

PRIOR Yes.

HARPER What?

PRIOR You are amazingly unhappy.

HARPER Oh big deal. You meet a Valium addict and you figure out she's unhappy. That doesn't count. Of course I . . . Something else. Something surprising.

PRIOR Something surprising.

HARPER Yes.

PRIOR Your husband's a homo.

[*Pause.*]

HARPER Oh, ridiculous.
[*Pause, then very quietly*] Really?

PRIOR [*shrugs*] Threshhold of revelation.

HARPER Well I don't like your revelations. I don't think you intuit well at all. Joe's a very normal man, he . . .
Oh God. Oh God. He . . . Do homos take, like, lots of long walks?

PRIOR Yes. We do. In stretch pants with lavender coifs. I just looked at you, and there was . . .

HARPER A sort of blue streak of recognition.

PRIOR Yes.

HARPER Like you knew me incredibly well.

PRIOR Yes.

HARPER Yes.
I have to go now, get back, something just . . . fell apart.
Oh God, I feel so sad . . .

PRIOR I . . . I'm sorry. I usually say, "Fuck the truth," but mostly, the truth fucks you.

HARPER I see something else about you . . .

PRIOR Oh?

HARPER Deep inside you, there's a part of you, the most inner part, entirely free of disease. I can see that.

PRIOR Is that . . . That isn't true.

HARPER Threshhold of revelation.
Home . . .

[*She vanishes.*]

PRIOR People come and go so quickly here . . .
[*To himself in the mirror*] I don't think there's any uninfected part of me. My heart is pumping polluted blood. I feel dirty.

[*He begins to wipe makeup off with his hands, smearing it around. A large gray feather falls from up above.* PRIOR *stops smearing the makeup and looks at the feather. He goes to it and picks it up.*]

A VOICE [*it is an incredibly beautiful voice*] Look up!

PRIOR [*looking up, not seeing anyone*] Hello?

A VOICE Look up!

PRIOR Who is that?

A VOICE Prepare the way!

PRIOR I don't see any . . .

[*There is a dramatic change in lighting, from above.*]

A VOICE

Look up, look up,
prepare the way
the infinite descent
A breath in air
floating down
Glory to . . .

[*Silence.*]

PRIOR Hello? Is that it? Helloooo!

What the fuck . . . ? [*He holds himself.*]

Poor me. Poor poor me. Why me? Why poor poor me? Oh I don't feel good right now. I really don't.

Scene 8

[*That night. Split scene:* HARPER *and* JOE *at home;* PRIOR *and* LOUIS *in bed.*]

HARPER Where were you?

JOE Out.

HARPER Where?

JOE Just out. Thinking.

HARPER It's late.

JOE I had a lot to think about.

HARPER I burned dinner.

JOE Sorry.

HARPER Not my dinner. My dinner was fine. Your dinner. I put it back in the oven and turned everything up as high as it could go and I watched till it burned black. It's still hot. Very hot. Want it?

JOE You didn't have to do that.

HARPER I know. It just seemed like the kind of thing a mentally deranged sex-starved pill-popping housewife would do.

JOE Uh huh.

HARPER So I did it. Who knows anymore what I have to do?

JOE How many pills?

HARPER A bunch. Don't change the subject.

JOE I won't talk to you when you . . .

HARPER No. No. Don't do that! I'm . . . I'm fine, pills are not the problem, not our problem, I WANT TO KNOW WHERE YOU'VE BEEN! I WANT TO KNOW WHAT'S GOING ON!

JOE Going on with what? The job?

HARPER Not the job.

JOE I said I need more time.

HARPER Not the job!

JOE Mr. Cohn, I talked to him on the phone, he said I had to hurry . . .

HARPER Not the . . .

JOE But I can't get you to talk sensibly about anything so . . .

HARPER SHUT UP!

JOE Then what?

HARPER Stick to the subject.

JOE I don't know what that is. You have something you want to ask me? Ask me. Go.

HARPER I . . . can't. I'm scared of you.

JOE I'm tired, I'm going to bed.

HARPER Tell me without making me ask. Please.

JOE This is crazy, I'm not . . .

HARPER When you come through the door at night your face is never exactly the way I remembered it. I get surprised by something . . . mean and hard about the way you look. Even the weight of you in the bed at night, the way you breathe in your sleep seems unfamiliar.

You terrify me.

JOE [*cold*] I know who you are.

HARPER Yes. I'm the enemy. That's easy. That doesn't change.

You think you're the only one who hates sex; I do; I hate it with you; I do. I dream that you batter away at me till all my joints come apart, like wax, and I fall into pieces. It's like a punishment. It was wrong of me to marry you. I knew you . . . [*She stops herself.*] It's a sin, and it's killing us both.

JOE I can always tell when you've taken pills because it makes you red-faced and sweaty and frankly that's very often why I don't want to . . .

HARPER Because . . .

JOE Well, you aren't pretty. Not like this.

HARPER I have something to ask you.

JOE Then ASK! ASK! What in hell are you . . .

HARPER Are you a homo? [*Pause*]

Are you? If you try to walk out right now I'll put your dinner back in the oven and turn it up so high the whole building will fill with smoke and everyone in it will asphyxiate. So help me God I will.

Now answer the question.

JOE What if I . . .

[*Small pause.*]

HARPER Then tell me, please. And we'll see.

JOE No. I'm not.

I don't see what difference it makes.

LOUIS Jews don't have any clear textual guide to the afterlife; even that it exists. I don't think much about it. I see it as a perpetual rainy Thursday afternoon in March. Dead leaves.

PRIOR Eeeugh. Very Greco-Roman.[5]

LOUIS Well, for us it's not the verdict that counts, it's the act of judgment. That's why I could never be a lawyer. In court all that matters is the verdict.

5. An adjective apparently intended to evoke stoicism and austerity.

PRIOR You could never be a lawyer because you are oversexed. You're too distracted.

LOUIS Not distracted; *ab*stracted. I'm trying to make a point:

PRIOR Namely:

LOUIS It's the judge in his or her chambers, weighing, books open, pondering the evidence, ranging freely over categories: good, evil, innocent, guilty; the judge in the chamber of circumspection, not the judge on the bench with the gavel. The shaping of the law, not its execution.

PRIOR The point, dear, the point . . .

LOUIS That it should be the questions and shape of a life, its total complexity gathered, arranged, and considered, which matters in the end, not some stamp of salvation or damnation which disperses all the complexity in some unsatisfying little decision—the balancing of the scales . . .

PRIOR I like this; very zen; it's . . . reassuringly incomprehensible and useless. We who are about to die thank you.[6]

LOUIS You are not about to die.

PRIOR It's not going well, really . . . two new lesions. My leg hurts. There's protein in my urine, the doctor says, but who knows what the fuck that portends. Anyway it shouldn't be there, the protein. My butt is chapped from diarrhea and yesterday I shat blood.

LOUIS I really hate this. You don't tell me . . .

PRIOR You get too upset, I wind up comforting you. It's easier . . .

LOUIS Oh thanks.

PRIOR If it's bad I'll tell you.

LOUIS Shitting blood sounds bad to me.

PRIOR And I'm telling you.

LOUIS And I'm handling it.

PRIOR Tell me some more about justice.

LOUIS I *am* handling it.

PRIOR Well Louis you win Trooper of the Month.

[LOUIS *starts to cry.*]

PRIOR I take it back. You aren't Trooper of the Month.
This isn't working . . .
Tell me some more about justice.

LOUIS You are not about to die.

PRIOR Justice . . .

LOUIS . . . is an immensity, a confusing vastness. Justice is God.
Prior?

PRIOR Hmmm?

LOUIS You love me.

PRIOR Yes.

LOUIS What if I walked out on this?
Would you hate me forever?

[PRIOR *kisses* LOUIS *on the forehead.*]

PRIOR Yes.

6. An echo of "We who are about to die greet you," popularly believed to be the salute of Roman gladiators to the emperor. *Zen:* exhibiting the calm associated with this meditative Japanese school of Buddhism.

JOE I think we ought to pray. Ask God for help. Ask him together . . .

HARPER God won't talk to me. I have to make up people to talk to me.

JOE You have to keep asking.

HARPER I forgot the question.

Oh yeah. God, is my husband a . . .

JOE [*scary*] Stop it. Stop it. I'm warning you.

Does it make any difference? That I might be one thing deep within, no matter how wrong or ugly that thing is, so long as I have fought, with everything I have, to kill it. What do you want from me? What do you want from me, Harper? More than that? For God's sake, there's nothing left, I'm a shell. There's nothing left to kill.

As long as my behavior is what I know it has to be. Decent. Correct. That alone in the eyes of God.

HARPER No, no, not that, that's Utah talk, Mormon talk, I hate it, Joe, tell me, say it . . .

JOE All I will say is that I am a very good man who has worked very hard to become good and you want to destroy that. You want to destroy me, but I am not going to let you do that.

[*Pause.*]

HARPER I'm going to have a baby.

JOE Liar.

HARPER You liar.

A baby born addicted to pills. A baby who does not dream but who hallucinates, who stares up at us with big mirror eyes and who does not know who we are.

[*Pause.*]

JOE Are you really . . .

HARPER No. Yes. No. Yes. Get away from me.

Now we both have a secret.

PRIOR One of my ancestors was a ship's captain who made money bringing whale oil to Europe and returning with immigrants—Irish mostly, packed in tight, so many dollars per head. The last ship he captained foundered off the coast of Nova Scotia in a winter tempest and sank to the bottom. He went down with the ship—*la Grande Geste*[7]—but his crew took seventy women and kids in the ship's only longboat, this big, open rowboat, and when the weather got too rough, and they thought the boat was overcrowded, the crew started lifting people up and hurling them into the sea. Until they got the ballast right. They walked up and down the longboat, eyes to the waterline, and when the boat rode low in the water they'd grab the nearest passenger and throw them into the sea. The boat was leaky, see; seventy people; they arrived in Halifax with nine people on board.

LOUIS Jesus.

PRIOR I think about that story a lot now. People in a boat, waiting, terrified, while implacable, unsmiling men, irresistibly strong, seize . . . maybe the person next to you, maybe you, and with no warning at all, with time only for a quick intake of air you are pitched into freezing, turbulent water and salt and darkness to drown.

7. The grand gesture (French); by tradition, the captain is the last to leave a sinking ship.

I like your cosmology, baby. While time is running out I find myself drawn to anything that's suspended, that lacks an ending—but it seems to me that it lets you off scot-free.

LOUIS What do you mean?

PRIOR No judgment, no guilt or responsibility.

LOUIS For me.

PRIOR For anyone. It was an editorial "you."

LOUIS Please get better. Please.
Please don't get any sicker.

Scene 9

[*Third week in November.* ROY *and* HENRY, *his doctor, in* HENRY'S *office.*]

HENRY Nobody knows what causes it. And nobody knows how to cure it. The best theory is that we blame a retrovirus, the Human Immunodeficiency Virus. Its presence is made known to us by the useless antibodies which appear in reaction to its entrance into the bloodstream through a cut, or an orifice. The antibodies are powerless to protect the body against it. Why, we don't know. The body's immune system ceases to function. Sometimes the body even attacks itself. At any rate it's left open to a whole horror house of infections from microbes which it usually defends against.

Like Kaposi's sarcomas. These lesions. Or your throat problem. Or the glands.

We think it may also be able to slip past the blood-brain barrier[8] into the brain. Which is of course very bad news.

And it's fatal in we don't know what percent of people with suppressed immune responses.

[*Pause.*]

ROY This is very interesting, Mr. Wizard,[9] but why the fuck are you telling me this?

[*Pause.*]

HENRY Well, I have just removed one of three lesions which biopsy results will probably tell us is a Kaposi's sarcoma lesion. And you have a pronounced swelling of glands in your neck, groin, and armpits—lymphadenopathy[1] is another sign. And you have oral candidiasis[2] and maybe a little more fungus under the fingernails of two digits on your right hand. So that's why . . .

ROY This disease . . .

HENRY Syndrome.

ROY Whatever. It afflicts mostly homosexuals and drug addicts.

HENRY Mostly. Hemophiliacs are also at risk.

ROY Homosexuals and drug addicts. So why are you implying that I . . . [*Pause*] What are you implying, Henry?

HENRY I don't . . .

ROY I'm not a drug addict.

8. The physical structure and system of cellular transport mechanisms that prevent harmful chemicals in the bloodstream from reaching the brain.

9. The host of *Watch Mr. Wizard* (1951–65), a television show that explained science to children (revived on cable as *Mr. Wizard's World*, 1983–90).

1. An abnormal enlargement of the lymph nodes.

2. An infection of the mouth by the yeastlike fungus *Candida albicans*.

HENRY Oh come on Roy.

ROY What, what, come on Roy what? Do you think I'm a junkie, Henry, do you see tracks?

HENRY This is absurd.

ROY Say it.

HENRY Say what?

ROY Say, "Roy Cohn, you are a . . ."

HENRY Roy.

ROY "You are a . . ." Go on. Not "Roy Cohn you are a drug fiend." "Roy Marcus Cohn, you are a . . ."
Go on, Henry, it starts with an "H."

HENRY Oh I'm not going to . . .

ROY *With an "H,"* Henry, and it isn't "Hemophiliac." Come on . . .

HENRY What are you doing, Roy?

ROY No, say it. I mean it. Say: "Roy Cohn, you are a homosexual." [*Pause*]
And I will proceed, systematically, to destroy your reputation and your practice and your career in New York State, Henry. Which you know I can do.
[*Pause.*]

HENRY Roy, you have been seeing me since 1958. Apart from the facelifts I have treated you for everything from syphilis . . .

ROY From a whore in Dallas.

HENRY From syphilis to venereal warts. In your rectum. Which you may have gotten from a whore in Dallas, but it wasn't a female whore.
[*Pause.*]

ROY So say it.

HENRY Roy Cohn, you are . . .
You have had sex with men, many many times, Roy, and one of them, or any number of them, has made you very sick. You have AIDS.[3]

ROY AIDS.
Your problem, Henry, is that you are hung up on words, on labels, that you believe they mean what they seem to mean. AIDS. Homosexual. Gay. Lesbian. You think these are names that tell you who someone sleeps with, but they don't tell you that.

HENRY No?

ROY No. Like all labels they tell you one thing and one thing only: where does an individual so identified fit in the food chain, in the pecking order? Not ideology, or sexual taste, but something much simpler: clout. Not who I fuck or who fucks me, but who will pick up the phone when I call, who owes me favors. This is what a label refers to. Now to someone who does not understand this, homosexual is what I am because I have sex with men. But really this is wrong. Homosexuals are not men who sleep with other men. Homosexuals are men who in fifteen years of trying cannot get a pissant antidiscrimination bill through City Council. Homosexuals are men who know nobody and who nobody knows. Who have zero clout. Does this sound like me, Henry?

HENRY No.

ROY No. I have clout. A lot. I can pick up this phone, punch fifteen numbers, and you know who will be on the other end in under five minutes, Henry?

3. Acquired immune deficiency syndrome was first recognized in 1981.

HENRY The President.

ROY Even better, Henry. His wife.

HENRY I'm impressed.

ROY I don't want you to be impressed. I want you to understand. This is not sophistry. And this is not hypocrisy. This is reality. I have sex with men. But unlike nearly every other man of whom this is true, I bring the guy I'm screwing to the White House and President Reagan smiles at us and shakes his hand. Because *what* I am is defined entirely by *who* I am. Roy Cohn is not a homosexual. Roy Cohn is a heterosexual man, Henry, who fucks around with guys.

HENRY OK, Roy.

ROY And what is my diagnosis, Henry?

HENRY You have AIDS, Roy.

ROY No, Henry, no. AIDS is what homosexuals have. I have liver cancer.

[*Pause.*]

HENRY Well, whatever the fuck you have, Roy, it's very serious, and I haven't got a damn thing for you. The NIH in Bethesda has a new drug called AZT[4] with a two-year waiting list that not even I can get you onto. So get on the phone, Roy, and dial the fifteen numbers, and tell the First Lady you need in on an experimental treatment for liver cancer, because you can call it any damn thing you want, Roy, but what it boils down to is very bad news.

Act 2: In Vitro

(*December 1985–January 1986*)

Scene 1

[*Night, the third week in December.* PRIOR *alone on the floor of his bedroom; he is much worse.*]

PRIOR Louis, Louis, please wake up, oh God.

[*Louis runs in.*]

PRIOR I think something horrible is wrong with me I can't breathe . . .

LOUIS [*starting to exit*] I'm calling the ambulance.

PRIOR No, wait, I . . .

LOUIS *Wait?* Are you fucking crazy? Oh God you're on fire, your head is on fire.

PRIOR It hurts, it hurts . . .

LOUIS I'm calling the ambulance.

PRIOR I don't want to go to the hospital, I don't want to go to the hospital please let me lie here, just . . .

LOUIS No, no, God, Prior, stand up . . .

PRIOR DON'T TOUCH MY LEG!

LOUIS We have to . . . oh God this is so crazy.

PRIOR I'll be OK if I just lie here Lou, really, if I can only sleep a little . . .

4. Azidothymidine or zidovudine, an antiviral drug that was the first approved (in 1987) to treat AIDS; that the government accelerate the testing process required for its approval was a major demand of early AIDS activists. *NIH:* the National Institutes of Health, the federal agency primarily responsible for supporting and conducting medical research; its headquarters are in Bethesda, Maryland.

[LOUIS *exits.*]

PRIOR Louis?

NO! NO! Don't call, you'll send me there and I won't come back, please, please Louis I'm begging, baby, please . . .

[*Screams.*] *LOUIS!!*

LOUIS [*from off; hysterical*] WILL YOU SHUT THE FUCK UP!

PRIOR [*trying to stand*] Aaah. I have . . . to go to the bathroom. Wait. Wait, just . . . oh. Oh God. [*He shits himself.*]

LOUIS [*Entering*] Prior? They'll be here in . . .

Oh my God.

PRIOR I'm sorry, I'm sorry.

LOUIS What did . . . ? What?

PRIOR I had an accident.

[*Louis goes to him.*]

LOUIS This is blood.

PRIOR Maybe you shouldn't touch it . . . me. . . . I . . . [*He faints.*]

LOUIS [*quietly*] Oh help. Oh help. Oh God oh God oh God help me I can't I can't I can't.

Scene 2

[*Same night.* HARPER *is sitting at home, all alone, with no lights on. We can bare ly see her.* JOE *enters, but he doesn't turn on the lights.*]

JOE Why are you sitting in the dark? Turn on the light.

HARPER *No.* I heard the sounds in the bedroom again. I know someone was in there.

JOE No one was.

HARPER Maybe actually in the bed, under the covers with a knife.

Oh, boy. Joe. I, um, I'm thinking of going away. By which I mean: I think I'm going off again. You . . . you know what I mean?

JOE Please don't. Stay. We can fix it. I pray for that. This is my fault, but I can correct it. You have to try too . . .

[*He turns on the light. She turns it off again.*]

HARPER When you pray, what do you pray for?

JOE I pray for God to crush me, break me up into little pieces and start all over again.

HARPER Oh. Please. Don't pray for that.

JOE I had a book of Bible stories when I was a kid. There was a picture I'd look at twenty times every day: Jacob wrestles with the angel.[5] I don't really remember the story, or why the wrestling—just the picture. Jacob is young and very strong. The angel is . . . a beautiful man, with golden hair and wings, of course. I still dream about it. Many nights. I'm . . . It's me. In that struggle. Fierce, and unfair. The angel is not human, and it holds nothing back, so how could anyone human win, what kind of a fight is that? It's not just. Losing means your soul thrown down in the dust, your heart torn out from God's. But you can't not lose.

HARPER In the whole entire world, you are the only person, the only person I love or have ever loved. And I love you terribly. Terribly. That's what's so

5. See Genesis 32.24–30.

awfully, irreducibly real. I can make up anything but I can't dream that away.

JOE Are you . . . are you really going to have a baby?

HARPER It's my time, and there's no blood. I don't really know. I suppose it wouldn't be a great thing. Maybe I'm just not bleeding because I take too many pills. Maybe I'll give birth to a pill. That would give a new meaning to pill-popping, huh?

I think you should go to Washington. Alone. Change, like you said.

JOE I'm not going to leave you, Harper.

HARPER Well maybe not. But I'm going to leave you.

Scene 3

[*One* AM, *the next morning.* LOUIS *and a nurse,* EMILY, *are sitting in* PRIOR*'s room in the hospital.*]

EMILY He'll be all right now.

LOUIS No he won't.

EMILY No. I guess not. I gave him something that makes him sleep.

LOUIS Deep asleep?

EMILY Orbiting the moons of Jupiter.

LOUIS A good place to be.

EMILY Anyplace better than here. You his . . . uh?

LOUIS Yes. I'm his uh.

EMILY This must be hell for you.

LOUIS It is. Hell. The After Life. Which is not at all like a rainy afternoon in March, by the way, Prior. A lot more vivid than I'd expected. Dead leaves, but the crunchy kind. Sharp, dry air. The kind of long, luxurious dying feeling that breaks your heart.

EMILY Yeah, well we all get to break our hearts on this one.

He seems like a nice guy. Cute.

LOUIS Not like this.

Yes, he is. Was. Whatever.

EMILY Weird name. Prior Walter. Like, "The Walter before this one."

LOUIS Lots of Walters before this one. Prior is an old old family name in an old old family. The Walters go back to the Mayflower and beyond. Back to the Norman Conquest. He says there's a Prior Walter stitched into the Bayeux tapestry.[6]

EMILY Is that impressive?

LOUIS Well, it's old. Very old. Which in some circles equals impressive.

EMILY Not in my circle. What's the name of the tapestry?

LOUIS The Bayeux tapestry. Embroidered by La Reine Mathilde.[7]

EMILY I'll tell my mother. She embroiders. Drives me nuts.

LOUIS Manual therapy for anxious hands.

EMILY Maybe you should try it.

6. An embroidery, 230 feet long, that chronicles the invasion and conquest of England by the Normans in 1066 (preserved in the Bayeux Museum in northern France). *Mayflower:* the ship that in 1620 brought the English founders of the Plymouth Colony to Massachusetts.

7. Queen Matilda (French; ca. 1031–1083), the wife of William the Conqueror (ca. 1028–1087); the tradition that attributes the creation of the Bayeux tapestry to her has little foundation.

LOUIS Mathilde stitched while William the Conqueror was off to war. She was capable of . . . more than loyalty. Devotion.

She waited for him, she stitched for years. And if he had come back broken and defeated from war, she would have loved him even more. And if he had returned mutilated, ugly, full of infection and horror, she would still have loved him; fed by pity, by a sharing of pain, she would love him even more, and even more, and she would never, never have prayed to God, please let him die if he can't return to me whole and healthy and able to live a normal life. . . . If he had died, she would have buried her heart with him.

So what the fuck is the matter with me? [*Little pause*]

Will he sleep through the night?

EMILY At least.

LOUIS I'm going.

EMILY It's one AM. Where do you have to go at . . .

LOUIS I know what time it is. A walk. Night air, good for the . . . The park.

EMILY Be careful.

LOUIS Yeah. Danger.

Tell him, if he wakes up and you're still on, tell him goodbye, tell him I had to go.

Scene 4

[*An hour later. Split scene:* JOE *and* ROY *in a fancy (straight) bar;* LOUIS *and a* MAN *in the Rambles*[8] *in Central Park.* JOE *and* ROY *are sitting at the bar; the place is brightly lit.* JOE *has a plate of food in front of him but he isn't eating.* ROY *occasionally reaches over the table and forks small bites off* JOE*'s plate.* ROY *is drinking heavily,* JOE *not at all.* LOUIS *and the* MAN *are eyeing each other, each alternating interest and indifference.*]

JOE The pills were something she started when she miscarried or . . . no, she took some before that. She had a really bad time at home, when she was a kid, her home was really bad. I think a lot of drinking and physical stuff. She doesn't talk about that, instead she talks about . . . the sky falling down, people with knives hiding under sofas. Monsters. Mormons. Everyone thinks Mormons don't come from homes like that, we aren't supposed to behave that way, but we do. It's not lying, or being two-faced. Everyone tries very hard to live up to God's strictures, which are very . . . um . . .

ROY Strict.

JOE I shouldn't be bothering you with this.

ROY No, please. Heart to heart. Want another. . . . What is that, seltzer?[9]

JOE The failure to measure up hits people very hard. From such a strong desire to be good they feel very far from goodness when they fail.

What scares me is that maybe what I really love in her is the part of her that's farthest from the light, from God's love; maybe I was drawn to that in the first place. And I'm keeping it alive because I need it.

ROY Why would you need it?

JOE There are things. . . . I don't know how well we know ourselves. I mean, what if? I know I married her because she . . . because I loved it that she

8. A wooded section in New York's Central Park, designed as a wild garden; for much of the 20th century, the Ramble was notorious as an area for homosexual cruising.

9. Observant Mormons do not drink alcohol or caffeine (or smoke).

was always wrong, always doing something wrong, like one step out of step. In Salt Lake City that stands out. I never stood out, on the outside, but inside, it was hard for me. To pass.

ROY Pass?

JOE Yeah.

ROY Pass as what?

JOE Oh. Well. . . . As someone cheerful and strong. Those who love God with an open heart unclouded by secrets and struggles are cheerful; God's easy simple love for them shows in how strong and happy they are. The saints.[1]

ROY But you had secrets? Secret struggles . . .

JOE I wanted to be one of the elect, one of the Blessed. You feel you ought to be, that the blemishes are yours by choice, which of course they aren't. Harper's sorrow, that really deep sorrow, she didn't choose that. But it's there.

ROY You didn't put it there.

JOE No.

ROY You sound like you think you did.

JOE I am responsible for her.

ROY Because she's your wife.

JOE That. And I do love her.

ROY Whatever. She's your wife. And so there are obligations. To her. But also to yourself.

JOE She'd fall apart in Washington.

ROY Then let her stay here.

JOE She'll fall apart if I leave her.

ROY Then bring her to Washington.

JOE I just can't, Roy. She needs me.

ROY Listen, Joe. I'm the best divorce lawyer in the business.

[*Little pause.*]

JOE Can't Washington wait?

ROY You do what you need to do, Joe. What *you* need. *You.* Let her life go where it wants to go. You'll both be better for that. *Somebody* should get what they want.

MAN What do you want?

LOUIS I want you to fuck me, hurt me, make me bleed.

MAN I want to.

LOUIS Yeah?

MAN I want to hurt you.

LOUIS Fuck me.

MAN Yeah?

LOUIS Hard.

MAN Yeah? You been a bad boy?

[*Pause.* LOUIS *laughs, softly.*]

LOUIS Very bad. Very bad.

MAN You need to be punished, boy?

LOUIS Yes. I do.

1. That is, Mormons, members of what is officially called the Church of Jesus Christ of Latter-day Saints (the LDS Church).

MAN Yes what?

[*Little pause.*]

LOUIS Um, I . . .

MAN Yes *what,* boy?

LOUIS Oh. Yes sir.

MAN I want you to take me to your place, boy.

LOUIS No, I can't do that.

MAN No *what?*

LOUIS No sir, I can't, I . . .
I don't live alone, sir.

MAN Your lover know you're out with a man tonight, boy?

LOUIS No sir, he . . .
My lover doesn't know.

MAN Your lover know you . . .

LOUIS Let's change the subject, OK? Can we go to your place?

MAN I live with my parents.

LOUIS Oh.

ROY Everyone who makes it in this world makes it because somebody older and more powerful takes an interest. The most precious asset in life, I think, is the ability to be a good son. You have that, Joe. Somebody who can be a good son to a father who pushes them farther than they would otherwise go. I've had many fathers, I owe my life to them, powerful, powerful men. Walter Winchell, Edgar Hoover. Joe McCarthy most of all.[2] He valued me because I am a good lawyer, but he loved me because I was and am a good son. He was a very difficult man, very guarded and cagey; I brought out something tender in him. He would have died for me. And me for him. Does this embarrass you?

JOE I had a hard time with my father.

ROY Well sometimes that's the way. Then you have to find other fathers, substitutes, I don't know. The father-son relationship is central to life. Women are for birth, beginning, but the father is continuance. The son offers the father his life as a vessel for carrying forth his father's dream. Your father's living?

JOE Um, dead.

ROY He was . . . what? A difficult man?

JOE He was in the military. He could be very unfair. And cold.

ROY But he loved you.

JOE I don't know.

2. The historical Cohn, through his work on the Permanent Subcommittee on Investigations, is most closely identified with McCarthy (1908–1957), who as senator from Wisconsin (1947–57) gained national attention with his sensational and unsubstantiated claims that the State Department and other parts of the government had been infiltrated by Communists. Winchell (1897–1972) wrote a hugely popular gossip column (begun in 1924); he lost influence after he allied himself with McCarthy's anticommunist witch hunt. Hoover (1895–1972), early in his career (during the first Red Scare, 1919–20), was placed in charge of investigating suspected alien radicals; in 1924, he became director of the Bureau of Investigation (renamed the Federal Bureau of Investigation in 1935), amassing enormous and virtually unchecked power during his forty-eight years in that position. A believer in a worldwide communist conspiracy, he too was an ally of McCarthy; rumors that he was a homosexual circulated for decades.

ROY No, no, Joe, he did, I know this. Sometimes a father's love has to be very, very hard, unfair even, cold to make his son grow strong in a world like this. This isn't a good world.

MAN Here, then.
LOUIS I. . . . Do you have a rubber?
MAN I don't use rubbers.
LOUIS You should. [*He takes one from his coat pocket.*] Here.
MAN I don't use them.
LOUIS Forget it, then. [*He starts to leave.*]
MAN No, wait.
Put it on me. Boy.
LOUIS Forget it, I have to get back. Home. I must be going crazy.
MAN Oh come on please he won't find out.
LOUIS It's cold. Too cold.
MAN It's never too cold, let me warm you up. Please?
[*They begin to fuck.*]
MAN Relax.
LOUIS [*a small laugh*] Not a chance.
MAN It . . .
LOUIS What?
MAN I think it broke. The rubber. You want me to keep going?
[*Little pause*] Pull out? Should I . . .
LOUIS Keep going.
Infect me.
I don't care. I don't care.
[*Pause. The* MAN *pulls out.*]
MAN I . . . um, look, I'm sorry, but I think I want to go.
LOUIS Yeah.
Give my best to mom and dad.
[*The* MAN *slaps him.*]
LOUIS Ow!
[*They stare at each other.*]
LOUIS It was a joke.
[*The* MAN *leaves.*]

ROY How long have we known each other?
JOE Since 1980.
ROY Right. A long time. I feel close to you, Joe. Do I advise you well?
JOE You've been an incredible friend, Roy, I . . .
ROY I want to be family. Familia, as my Italian friends call it. La Familia. A lovely word. It's important for me to help you, like I was helped.
JOE I owe practically everything to you, Roy.
ROY I'm dying, Joe. Cancer.
JOE Oh my God.
ROY Please. Let me finish.
Few people know this and I'm telling you this only because . . . I'm not afraid of death. What can death bring that I haven't faced? I've lived; life is the worst. [*Gently mocking himself*] Listen to me, I'm a philosopher.

Joe. You must do this. You must must must. Love; that's a trap. Responsibility; that's a trap too. Like a father to a son I tell you this: Life is full of horror; nobody escapes, nobody; save yourself. Whatever pulls on you, whatever needs from you, threatens you. Don't be afraid; people are so afraid; don't be afraid to live in the raw wind, naked, alone. . . . Learn at least this: What you are capable of. Let nothing stand in your way.

Scene 5

[*Three days later.* PRIOR *and* BELIZE *in* PRIOR*'s hospital room.* PRIOR *is very sick but improving.* BELIZE *has just arrived.*]

PRIOR Miss Thing.

BELIZE Ma cherie bichette.[3]

PRIOR Stella.

BELIZE Stella for star.[4] Let me see. [*Scrutinizing* PRIOR] You look like shit, why yes indeed you do, comme la merde![5]

PRIOR Merci.[6]

BELIZE [*taking little plastic bottles from his bag, handing them to* PRIOR] Not to despair, Belle Reeve.[7] Lookie! Magic goop!

PRIOR [*opening a bottle, sniffing*] Pooh! What kinda crap is that?

BELIZE Beats me. Let's rub it on your poor blistered body and see what it does.

PRIOR This is not Western medicine, these bottles . . .

BELIZE Voodoo cream. From the botanica 'round the block.

PRIOR And you a registered nurse.

BELIZE [*sniffing it*] Beeswax and cheap perfume. Cut with Jergen's Lotion. Full of good vibes and love from some little black Cubana witch in Miami.

PRIOR Get that trash away from me, I am immune-suppressed.

BELIZE I *am* a health professional. I *know* what I'm doing.

PRIOR It stinks. Any word from Louis?

[*Pause.* BELIZE *starts giving* PRIOR *a gentle massage.*]

PRIOR Gone.

BELIZE He'll be back. I know the type. Likes to keep a girl on edge.

PRIOR It's been . . .

[*Pause.*]

BELIZE [*trying to jog his memory*] How long?

PRIOR I don't remember.

BELIZE How long have you been here?

PRIOR [*getting suddenly upset*] I don't remember, I don't give a fuck. I want Louis. I want my fucking boyfriend, where the fuck is he? I'm dying, I'm dying, where's Louis?

BELIZE Shhhh, shhh . . .

PRIOR This is a very strange drug, this drug. Emotional lability, for starters.

BELIZE Save a tab or two for me.

3. My dear little darling (French).
4. A line spoken by Blanche DuBois to her sister Stella in Tennessee Williams's *A Streetcar Named Desire* (1947). (*Stella* means "star" in Latin.)
5. Like shit! (French).
6. Thanks (French).
7. In *A Streetcar Named Desire*, Belle Reve (Beautiful Dream; French) is the name of Blanche and Stella's ancestral home.

PRIOR Oh no, not this drug, ce n'est pas pour la joyeux noël et la bonne année, this drug she is serious poisonous chemistry, ma pauvre bichette.[8]

And not just disorienting. I hear things. Voices.

BELIZE Voices.

PRIOR A voice.

BELIZE Saying what?

[*Pause.*]

PRIOR I'm not supposed to tell.

BELIZE You better tell the doctor. Or I will.

PRIOR No no don't. Please. I want the voice; it's wonderful. It's all that's keeping me alive. I don't want to talk to some intern about it.

You know what happens? When I hear it, I get hard.

BELIZE Oh my.

PRIOR Comme ça.[9] [*He uses his arm to demonstrate.*] And you know I am slow to rise.

BELIZE My jaw aches at the memory.

PRIOR And would you deny me this little solace—betray my concupiscence to Florence Nightingale's storm troopers?[1]

BELIZE Perish the thought, ma bébé.[2]

PRIOR They'd change the drug just to spoil the fun.

BELIZE You and your boner can depend on me.

PRIOR Je t'adore, ma belle nègre.[3]

BELIZE All this girl-talk shit is politically incorrect, you know. We should have dropped it back when we gave up drag.

PRIOR I'm sick, I get to be politically incorrect if it makes me feel better. You sound like Lou. [*Little pause*]

Well, at least I have the satisfaction of knowing he's in anguish somewhere. I loved his anguish. Watching him stick his head up his asshole and eat his guts out over some relatively minor moral conundrum—it was the best show in town. But Mother warned me: if they get overwhelmed by the little things . . .

BELIZE They'll be belly-up bustville when something big comes along.

PRIOR Mother warned me.

BELIZE And they do come along.

PRIOR But I didn't listen.

BELIZE No. [*Doing Hepburn*][4] Men are beasts.

PRIOR [*also Hepburn*] The absolute lowest.

BELIZE I have to go. If I want to spend my whole lonely life looking after white people I can get underpaid to do it.

PRIOR You're just a Christian martyr.

BELIZE Whatever happens, baby, I will be here for you.

PRIOR Je t'aime.[5]

8. It doesn't give you a merry Christmas and a happy New Year . . . my poor little darling (French).

9. Like that (French).

1. That is, nurses; Nightingale (1820–1910), an English reformer whose work organizing a unit of nurses during the Crimean War won her international fame, is credited with founding modern nursing.

2. My baby, my child (French).

3. I adore you, my beautiful Negro (French).

4. That is, the American stage and film star Katharine Hepburn (1907–2003), who often portrayed independent women.

5. I love you (French).

BELIZE Je t'aime. Don't go crazy on me, girlfriend, I already got enough crazy queens for one lifetime. For two. I can't be bothering with dementia.

PRIOR I promise.

BELIZE [*touching him; softly*] Ouch.

PRIOR Ouch. Indeed.

BELIZE Why'd they have to pick on you?

And eat more, girlfriend, you really do look like shit.

[BELIZE *leaves.*]

PRIOR [*after waiting a beat*] He's gone.

Are you still . . .

VOICE I can't stay. I will return.

PRIOR Are you one of those "Follow me to the other side" voices?

VOICE No. I am no nightbird. I am a messenger . . .

PRIOR You have a beautiful voice, it sounds . . . like a viola, like a perfectly tuned, tight string, balanced, the truth. . . . Stay with me.

VOICE Not now. Soon I will return, I will reveal myself to you; I am glorious, glorious; my heart, my countenance, and my message. You must prepare.

PRIOR For what? I don't want to . . .

VOICE No death, no:

A marvelous work and a wonder[6] we undertake, an edifice awry we sink plumb and straighten, a great Lie we abolish, a great error correct, with the rule, sword, and broom of Truth!

PRIOR What are you talking about, I . . .

VOICE

I am on my way; when I am manifest, our Work begins:
Prepare for the parting of the air,
The breath, the ascent,
Glory to . . .

Scene 6

[*The second week of January.* MARTIN, ROY, *and* JOE *in a fancy Manhattan restaurant.*]

MARTIN It's a revolution in Washington, Joe. We have a new agenda and finally a real leader. They got back the Senate[7] but we have the courts. By the nineties the Supreme Court will be block-solid Republican appointees, and the Federal bench—Republican judges like land mines, everywhere, everywhere they turn. Affirmative action? Take it to court. Boom! Land mine. And we'll get our way on just about everything: abortion, defense, Central America, family values, a live investment climate. We have the White House locked till the year 2000. And beyond. A permanent fix on the Oval Office? It's possible. By '92 we'll get the Senate back, and in ten years the South is going to give us the House. It's really the end of Liberalism. The end of New Deal Socialism.[8] The end of ipso

6. See Isaiah 29.14.

7. Majority control of the U.S. Senate shifted to the Democrats in the 1986 election (Republicans gained majorities in both the House and the Senate in 1994).

8. That is, the government programs promoting economic and social welfare (and thus labeled "socialist" by opponents) of the type first instituted during the New Deal, the name given by Franklin Delano Roosevelt (1882–1945; 32nd president, 1933–45) to his domestic reform initiatives. These programs include Social Security, banking reform, and the minimum wage.

facto secular humanism.[9] The dawning of a genuinely American political personality. Modeled on Ronald Wilson Reagan.

JOE It sounds great, Mr. Heller.

MARTIN Martin. And Justice is the hub. Especially since Ed Meese took over. He doesn't specialize in Fine Points of the Law. He's a flatfoot, a cop. He reminds me of Teddy Roosevelt.[1]

JOE I can't wait to meet him.

MARTIN Too bad, Joe, he's been dead for sixty years!

[*There is a little awkwardness.* JOE *doesn't respond.*]

MARTIN Teddy Roosevelt. You said you wanted to. . . . Little joke. It reminds me of the story about the . . .

ROY [*smiling, but nasty*] Aw shut the fuck up Martin.

[*To* JOE] You see that? Mr. Heller here is one of the mighty, Joseph, in D.C. he sitteth on the right hand of the man who sitteth on the right hand of The Man.[2] And yet I can say "shut the fuck up" and he will take no offense. Loyalty. He . . .

Martin?

MARTIN Yes, Roy?

ROY Rub my back.

MARTIN Roy . . .

ROY No no really, a sore spot, I get them all the time now, these . . . Rub it for me darling, would you do that for me?

[MARTIN *rubs* ROY*'s back. They both look at* JOE.]

ROY [*to* JOE] How do you think a handful of Bolsheviks turned St. Petersburg into Leningrad in one afternoon? *Comrades.* Who do for each other. Marx and Engels. Lenin and Trotsky. Josef Stalin and Franklin Delano Roosevelt.[3]

[MARTIN *laughs.*]

ROY *Comrades,* right Martin?

MARTIN This man, Joe, is a Saint of the Right.

JOE I know, Mr. Heller, I . . .

ROY And you see what I mean, Martin? He's special, right?

MARTIN Don't embarrass him, Roy.

ROY Gravity, decency, smarts! His strength is as the strength of ten because his heart is pure![4] *And* he's a Royboy, one hundred percent.

9. A philosophy that locates value in human reason and interests, rejecting religion and the supernatural.

1. Theodore Roosevelt (1858–1919), twenty-sixth president of the United States (1901–09); between 1895 and 1897, he served as president of the New York City Board of Police Commissioners.

2. Compare Colossians 3.1 ("Christ sitteth on the right hand of God").

3. That is, symbiosis—even between supposed adversaries—is the key to success. The German political philosopher Karl Marx (1818–1883) and the German socialist Friedrich Engels (1820–1895) co-wrote the *Manifesto of the Communist Party* (1848); the Russian revolutionaries Vladimir Lenin (1870–1924) and Leon Trotsky (1879–1940) led the Bolshevik faction of socialists that triumphed in the October Revolution of 1917 (Saint Petersburg, which was a focal point of revolutionary activity, had been given the less Germanic name Petrograd in 1914; it was renamed Leningrad after Lenin died, but its original name was restored in 1991); the dictator Joseph Stalin (1879–1953), who controlled the Soviet Union from Lenin's death until his own death, and President Roosevelt became allies in World War II. *Comrades:* form of address used among Communists.

4. Paraphrase of a couplet from "Sir Galahad" (1842), by Alfred, Lord Tennyson.

MARTIN We're on the move, Joe. On the move.

JOE Mr. Heller, I . . .

MARTIN [*ending backrub*] We can't wait any longer for an answer.

[*Little pause.*]

JOE Oh. Um, I . . .

ROY Joe's a married man, Martin.

MARTIN Aha.

ROY With a wife. She doesn't care to go to D.C., and so Joe cannot go. And keeps us dangling. We've seen that kind of thing before, haven't we? These men and their wives.

MARTIN Oh yes. Beware.

JOE I really can't discuss this under . . .

MARTIN Then *don't* discuss. Say yes, Joe.

ROY Now.

MARTIN Say yes I will.

ROY Now.

Now. I'll hold my breath till you do, I'm turning blue waiting. . . . *Now*, goddammit!

MARTIN Roy, calm down, it's not . . .

ROY Aw, fuck it. [*He takes a letter from his jacket pocket, hands it to* JOE.] Read. Came today.

[JOE *reads the first paragraph, then looks up.*]

JOE Roy. This is . . . Roy, this is terrible.

ROY You're telling me.

A letter from the New York State Bar Association, Martin.

They're gonna try and disbar me.

MARTIN Oh my.

JOE Why?

ROY Why, Martin?

MARTIN Revenge.

ROY The whole Establishment. Their little rules. Because I know no rules. Because I don't see the Law as a dead and arbitrary collection of antiquated dictums, thou shall, thou shalt not, because, because I know the Law's a pliable, breathing, sweating . . . *organ*, because, because . . .

MARTIN Because he borrowed half a million from one of his clients.[5]

ROY Yeah, well, there's that.

MARTIN *And* he forgot to *return* it.

JOE Roy, that's . . . You borrowed money from a client?

ROY I'm deeply ashamed.

[*Little pause.*]

JOE [*very sympathetic*] Roy, you know how much I admire you. Well I mean I know you have unorthodox ways, but I'm sure you only did what you thought at the time you needed to do. And I have faith that . . .

ROY Not so damp, please. I'll deny it was a loan. She's got no paperwork. Can't prove a fucking thing.

[*Little pause.* MARTIN *studies the menu.*]

5. Cohn was in fact disbarred in 1986 for unethical conduct, which included borrowing $109,000 from a client and not repaying her.

JOE [*handing back the letter, more official in tone*] Roy I really appreciate your telling me this, and I'll do whatever I can to help.

ROY [*holding up a hand, then, carefully*] I'll tell you what you can do.

I'm about to be tried, Joe, by a jury that is not a jury of my peers. The disbarment committee: genteel gentleman Brahmin[6] lawyers, country-club men. I offend them, to these men . . . I'm what, Martin, some sort of filthy little Jewish troll?

MARTIN Oh well, I wouldn't go so far as . . .

ROY Oh well I would.

Very fancy lawyers, these disbarment committee lawyers, fancy lawyers with fancy corporate clients and complicated cases. Antitrust suits. Deregulation. Environmental control. Complex cases like these need Justice Department cooperation like flowers need the sun. Wouldn't you say that's an accurate assessment, Martin?

MARTIN I'm not here, Roy. I'm not hearing any of this.

ROY No. Of course not.

Without the light of the sun, Joe, these cases, and the fancy lawyers who represent them, will wither and die.

A well-placed friend, someone in the Justice Department, say, can turn off the sun. Cast a deep shadow on my behalf. Make them shiver in the cold. If they overstep. They would fear that.

[*Pause.*]

JOE Roy. I don't understand.

ROY You do.

[*Pause.*]

JOE You're not asking me to . . .

ROY Sssshhhh. Careful.

JOE [*a beat,*[7] *then*] Even if I said yes to the job, it would be illegal to interfere. With the hearings. It's unethical. No. I can't.

ROY Un-ethical.

Would you excuse us, Martin?

MARTIN Excuse you?

ROY Take a walk, Martin. For real.

[MARTIN *leaves.*]

ROY Un-ethical. Are you trying to embarrass me in front of my friend?

JOE Well it is unethical, I can't . . .

ROY Boy, you are really something. What the fuck do you think this is, Sunday School?

JOE No, but Roy this is . . .

ROY This is . . . this is gastric juices churning, this is enzymes and acids, this is intestinal is what this is, bowel movement and blood-red meat—this stinks, this is *politics,* Joe, the game of being alive. And you think you're. . . . What? Above that? Above alive is what? Dead! In the clouds! You're on earth, goddammit! Plant a foot, stay awhile.

I'm sick. They smell I'm weak. They want blood this time. I must have eyes in Justice. In Justice you will protect me.

6. That is, of high social standing (Brahmans are Hindus of the highest caste).

7. Pause (theater term).

JOE Why can't Mr. Heller . . .

ROY Grow up, Joe. The administration can't get involved.

JOE But I'd be part of the administration. The same as him.

ROY Not the same. Martin's Ed's man. And Ed's Reagan's man. So Martin's Reagan's man.

And you're mine. [*Little pause. He holds up the letter.*] This will never be. Understand me? [*He tears the letter up.*]

I'm gonna be a lawyer, Joe, I'm gonna be a lawyer, Joe, I'm gonna be a goddam motherfucking legally licensed member of the bar lawyer, just like my daddy was,[8] till my last bitter day on earth, Joseph, until the day I die.

[*Martin returns.*]

ROY Ah, Martin's back.

MARTIN So are we agreed?

ROY Joe?

[*Little pause.*]

JOE I will think about it.

[*To* ROY.] I will.

ROY Huh.

MARTIN It's the fear of what comes after the doing that makes the doing hard to do.

ROY Amen.

MARTIN But you can almost always live with the consequences.

Scene 7

[*That afternoon. On the granite steps outside the Hall of Justice, Brooklyn. It is cold and sunny. A Sabrett[9] wagon is selling hot dogs. Louis, in a shabby overcoat, is sitting on the steps contemplatively eating one. Joe enters with three hot dogs and a can of Coke.*]

JOE Can I . . . ?

LOUIS Oh sure. Sure. Crazy cold sun.

JOE [*sitting*] Have to make the best of it.

How's your friend?

LOUIS My . . . ? Oh. He's worse. My friend is worse.

JOE I'm sorry.

LOUIS Yeah, well. Thanks for asking. It's nice. You're nice. I can't believe you voted for Reagan.

JOE I hope he gets better.

LOUIS Reagan?

JOE Your friend.

LOUIS He won't. Neither will Reagan.

JOE Let's not talk politics, OK?

LOUIS [*pointing to* JOE*'s lunch*] You're eating *three* of those?

JOE Well . . . I'm . . . hungry.

LOUIS They're really terrible for you. Full of rat-poo and beetle legs and wood shavings 'n' shit.

JOE Huh.

8. Albert Cohn (1885–1959) was a New York state supreme court justice, appointed by Governor Franklin Delano Roosevelt.

9. A New York–based hot dog company.

LOUIS And . . . um . . . irridium, I think. Something toxic.[1]

JOE You're eating one.

LOUIS Yeah, well, the shape, I can't help myself, plus I'm *trying* to commit suicide, what's your excuse?

JOE I don't have an excuse. I just have Pepto-Bismol.[2]

[JOE *takes a bottle of Pepto-Bismol and chugs it.* LOUIS *shudders audibly.*]

JOE Yeah I know but then I wash it down with Coke.

[*He does this.* LOUIS *mimes barfing in* JOE*'s lap.* JOE *pushes* LOUIS*'s head away.*]

JOE Are you *always* like this?

LOUIS I've been worrying a lot about his kids.

JOE Whose?

LOUIS Reagan's. Maureen and Mike and little orphan Patti and Miss Ron Reagan Jr.,[3] the you-should-pardon-the-expression heterosexual.

JOE Ron Reagan Jr. is *not* . . . You shouldn't just make these assumptions about people. How do you know? About him? What he is? You don't know.

LOUIS [*doing Tallulah*[4]] Well darling he never sucked *my* cock but . . .

JOE Look, if you're going to get vulgar . . .

LOUIS No no really I mean . . . What's it like to be the child of the Zeitgeist? To have the American Animus as your dad? It's not really a *family,* the Reagans, I read *People,*[5] there aren't any connections there, no love, they don't ever even speak to each other except through their agents. So what's it like to be Reagan's kid? Enquiring minds want to know.

JOE You can't believe everything you . . .

LOUIS [*looking away*] But . . . I think we all know what that's like. Nowadays. No connections. No responsibilities. All of us . . . falling through the cracks that separate what we owe to our selves and . . . and what we owe to love.

JOE You just. . . . Whatever you feel like saying or doing, you don't care, you just . . . do it.

LOUIS Do what?

JOE It. Whatever. Whatever it is you want to do.

LOUIS Are you trying to tell me something?

[*Little pause, sexual. They stare at each other.* JOE *looks away.*]

JOE No, I'm just observing that you . . .

LOUIS Impulsive.

JOE Yes, I mean it must be scary, you . . .

LOUIS [*Shrugs*] Land of the free. Home of the brave. Call me irresponsible.[6]

JOE It's kind of terrifying.

1. Many hot dogs contain preservatives that can be toxic in large quantities (*iridium* is a rare metallic element).
2. A product used to treat various kinds of minor digestive distress.
3. Ronald Reagan's children from his first marriage, to Jane Wyman (Maureen [1941–2001] and Michael [b. 1951]), and his second marriage, to Nancy Davis (Patti [b. 1952] and Ron [b. 1958]). Patti's estrangement from her parents made her an "orphan."
4. Imitating the husky, drawled "darling" with which the American stage and film star Tallulah Bankhead (1902–1968) customarily addressed people.
5. An American magazine that focuses on celebrities and human interest stories; it began publication in 1974.
6. The opening phrase and the title of a 1963 song (music by Jimmy Van Heusen, lyrics by Sammy Cahn). "O'er the land of the free, and the home of the brave" is the closing phrase of the refrain of "The Star-Spangled Banner," the U.S. national anthem (words by Francis Scott Key, 1814).

LOUIS Yeah, well, freedom is. Heartless, too.

JOE Oh you're not heartless.

LOUIS You don't know.

Finish your weenie.

[He pats JOE *on the knee, starts to leave.]*

JOE Um . . .

*[*LOUIS *turns, looks at him.* JOE *searches for something to say.]*

JOE Yesterday was Sunday but I've been a little unfocused recently and I thought it was Monday. So I came here like I was going to work. And the whole place was empty. And at first I couldn't figure out why, and I had this moment of incredible . . . fear and also . . . It just flashed through my mind: The whole Hall of Justice, it's empty, it's deserted, it's gone out of business. Forever. The people that make it run have up and abandoned it.

LOUIS *[looking at the building]* Creepy.

JOE Well yes but. I felt that I was going to scream. Not because it was creepy, but because the emptiness felt so *fast.*

And . . . well, good. A . . . happy scream.

I just wondered what a thing it would be . . . if overnight everything you owe anything to, justice, or love, had really gone away. Free.

It would be . . . heartless terror. Yes. Terrible, and . . .

Very great. To shed your skin, every old skin, one by one and then walk away, unencumbered, into the morning. *[Little pause. He looks at the building.]*

I can't go in there today.

LOUIS Then don't.

JOE *[not really hearing* LOUIS*]* I can't go in, I need . . .

[He looks for what he needs. He takes a swig of Pepto-Bismol.] I can't *be* this anymore. I need . . . a change, I should just . . .

LOUIS *[not a come-on, necessarily; he doesn't want to be alone]* Want some company? For whatever?

[Pause. JOE *looks at* LOUIS *and looks away, afraid.* LOUIS *shrugs.]*

LOUIS Sometimes, even if it scares you to death, you have to be willing to break the law. Know what I mean?

[Another little pause.]

JOE Yes.

[Another little pause.]

LOUIS I moved out. I moved out on my . . .

I haven't been sleeping well.

JOE Me neither.

*[*LOUIS *goes up to* JOE*, licks his napkin and dabs at* JOE*'s mouth.]*

LOUIS Antacid moustache.

[Points to the building.] Maybe the court won't convene. Ever again. Maybe we are free. To do whatever.

Children of the new morning, criminal minds. Selfish and greedy and loveless and blind. Reagan's children.

You're scared. So am I. Everybody is in the land of the free. God help us all.

Scene 8

[*Late that night.* JOE *at a payphone phoning* HANNAH *at home in Salt Lake City.*]

JOE Mom?

HANNAH Joe?

JOE Hi.

HANNAH You're calling from the street. It's . . . it must be four in the morning. What's happened?

JOE Nothing, nothing, I . . .

HANNAH It's Harper. Is Harper. . . . Joe? Joe?

JOE Yeah, hi. No, Harper's fine. Well, no, she's . . . not fine. How are you, Mom?

HANNAH What's happened?

JOE I just wanted to talk to you. I, uh, wanted to try something out on you.

HANNAH Joe, you haven't . . . have you been drinking, Joe?

JOE Yes ma'am. I'm drunk.

HANNAH That isn't like you.

JOE No. I mean, who's to say?

HANNAH Why are you out on the street at four AM? In that crazy city. It's dangerous.

JOE Actually, Mom, I'm not on the street. I'm near the boathouse in the park.

HANNAH What park?

JOE Central Park.

HANNAH CENTRAL PARK! Oh my Lord. What on earth are you doing in Central Park at this time of night? Are you . . .

Joe, I think you ought to go home right now. Call me from home. [*Little pause*] Joe?

JOE I come here to watch, Mom. Sometimes. Just to watch.

HANNAH Watch what? What's there to watch at four in the . . .

JOE Mom, did Dad love me?

HANNAH What?

JOE Did he?

HANNAH You ought to go home and call from there.

JOE Answer.

HANNAH Oh now really. This is maudlin. I don't like this conversation.

JOE Yeah, well, it gets worse from here on.

[*Pause.*]

HANNAH Joe?

JOE Mom. Momma. I'm a homosexual, Momma.

Boy, did that come out awkward. [*Pause*] Hello? Hello?

I'm a homosexual. [*Pause*] Please, Momma. Say something.

HANNAH You're old enough to understand that your father didn't love you without being ridiculous about it.

JOE What?

HANNAH You're ridiculous. You're being ridiculous.

JOE I'm . . .

What?

HANNAH You really ought to go home now to your wife. I need to go to bed. This phone call. . . . We will just forget this phone call.

JOE Mom.

HANNAH No more talk. Tonight. This . . .

[*Suddenly very angry*] Drinking is a sin! A sin! I raised you better than that. [*She hangs up.*]

Scene 9

[*The following morning, early. Split scene:* HARPER *and* JOE *at home;* LOUIS *and* PRIOR *in* PRIOR*'s hospital room.* JOE *and* LOUIS *have just entered. This should be fast and obviously furious; overlapping is fine; the proceedings may be a little confusing but not the final results.*]

HARPER Oh God. Home. The moment of truth has arrived.

JOE Harper.

LOUIS I'm going to move out.

PRIOR The fuck you are.

JOE Harper. Please listen. I still love you very much. You're still my best buddy; I'm not going to leave you.

HARPER No, I don't like the sound of this. I'm leaving.

LOUIS I'm leaving.

I already have.

JOE Please listen. Stay. This is really hard. We have to talk.

HARPER We are talking. Aren't we. Now please shut up. OK?

PRIOR Bastard. Sneaking off while I'm flat out here, that's low. If I could get up now I'd beat the holy shit out of you.

JOE Did you take pills? How many?

HARPER No pills. Bad for the . . . [*Pats stomach.*]

JOE You aren't pregnant. I called your gynecologist.

HARPER I'm seeing a new gynecologist.

PRIOR You have no right to do this.

LOUIS Oh, that's ridiculous.

PRIOR No right. It's criminal.

JOE Forget about that. Just listen. You want the truth. This is the truth.

I knew this when I married you. I've known this I guess for as long as I've known anything, but . . . I don't know, I thought maybe that with enough effort and will I could change myself . . . but I can't . . .

PRIOR Criminal.

LOUIS There oughta be a law.

PRIOR There is a law. You'll see.

JOE I'm losing ground here, I go walking, you want to know where I walk, I . . . go to the park, or up and down 53rd Street, or places where . . . And I keep swearing I won't go walking again, but I just can't.

LOUIS I need some privacy.

PRIOR That's new.

LOUIS Everything's new, Prior.

JOE I try to tighten my heart into a knot, a snarl, I try to learn to live dead, just numb, but then I see someone I want, and it's like a nail, like a hot spike right through my chest, and I know I'm losing.

PRIOR Apartment too small for three? Louis and Prior comfy but not Louis and Prior and Prior's disease?

LOUIS Something like that.

I won't be judged by you. This isn't a crime, just—the inevitable consequence of people who run out of—whose limitations . . .

PRIOR Bang bang bang. The court will come to order.

LOUIS I mean let's talk practicalities, schedules; I'll come over if you want, spend nights with you when I can, I can . . .

PRIOR Has the jury reached a verdict?

LOUIS I'm doing the best I can.

PRIOR Pathetic. Who cares?

JOE My whole life has conspired to bring me to this place, and I can't despise my whole life. I think I believed when I met you I could save you, you at least if not myself, but . . .

I don't have any sexual feelings for you, Harper. And I don't think I ever did.

[*Little pause.*]

HARPER I think you should go.

JOE Where?

HARPER Washington. Doesn't matter.

JOE What are you talking about?

HARPER Without me.

Without me, Joe. Isn't that what you want to hear?

[*Little pause.*]

JOE Yes.

LOUIS You can love someone and fail them. You can love someone and not be able to . . .

PRIOR You *can,* theoretically, yes. A person can, maybe an editorial "you" can love, Louis, but not *you,* specifically you, I don't know, I think you are excluded from that general category.

HARPER You were going to save me, but the whole time you were spinning a lie. I just don't understand that.

PRIOR A person could theoretically love and maybe many do but we both know now you can't.

LOUIS I do.

PRIOR You can't even say it.

LOUIS I love you, Prior.

PRIOR I repeat. Who cares?

HARPER This is so scary, I want this to stop, to go back . . .

PRIOR We have reached a verdict, your honor. This man's heart is deficient. He loves, but his love is worth nothing.

JOE Harper . . .

HARPER Mr. Lies, I want to get away from here. Far away. Right now. Before he starts talking again. Please, please . . .

JOE As long as I've known you Harper you've been afraid of . . . of men hiding under the bed, men hiding under the sofa, men with knives.

PRIOR [*shattered; almost pleading; trying to reach him*] I'm dying! You stupid fuck! Do you know what that is! Love! Do you know what love means? We lived together four-and-a-half years, you animal, you idiot.

LOUIS I have to find some way to save myself.

JOE Who are these men? I never understood it. Now I know.

HARPER What?

JOE It's me.

HARPER It is?

PRIOR GET OUT OF MY ROOM!

JOE I'm the man with the knives.

HARPER You are?

PRIOR If I could get up now I'd kill you. I would. Go away. Go away or I'll scream.

HARPER Oh God . . .

JOE I'm sorry . . .

HARPER It is you.

LOUIS Please don't scream.

PRIOR Go.

HARPER I recognize you now.

LOUIS Please . . .

JOE Oh. Wait, I . . . Oh!

[*He covers his mouth with his hand, gags, and removes his hand, red with blood.*] I'm bleeding.

[PRIOR *screams.*]

HARPER Mr. Lies.

MR. LIES [*appearing, dressed in Antarctic explorer's apparel*] Right here.

HARPER I want to go away. I can't see him anymore.

MR. LIES Where?

HARPER Anywhere. Far away.

MR. LIES Absolutamento.

[HARPER *and* MR. LIES *vanish.* JOE *looks up, sees that she's gone.*]

PRIOR [*closing his eyes*] When I open my eyes you'll be gone.

[LOUIS *leaves.*]

JOE Harper?

PRIOR [*opening his eyes*] Huh. It worked.

JOE [*calling*] Harper?

PRIOR I hurt all over. I wish I was dead.

Scene 10

[*The same day, sunset.* HANNAH *and* SISTER ELLA CHAPTER, *a real estate saleswoman,* HANNAH PITT*'s closest friend, in front of* HANNAH*'s house in Salt Lake City.*]

SISTER ELLA CHAPTER Look at that view! A view of heaven. Like the living city of heaven,[7] isn't it, it just fairly glimmers in the sun.

HANNAH Glimmers.

SISTER ELLA CHAPTER Even the stone and brick it just glimmers and glitters like heaven in the sunshine. Such a nice view you get, perched up on a canyon rim. Some kind of beautiful place.

HANNAH It's just Salt Lake, and you're selling the house *for* me, not *to* me.

SISTER ELLA CHAPTER I like to work up an enthusiasm for my properties.

HANNAH Just get me a good price.

SISTER ELLA CHAPTER Well, the market's off.

7. As the headquarters of the LDS Church, Salt Lake City contains an enormous temple and many church-related buildings.

HANNAH At least fifty.

SISTER ELLA CHAPTER Forty'd be more like it.

HANNAH Fifty.

SISTER ELLA CHAPTER Wish you'd wait a bit.

HANNAH Well I can't.

SISTER ELLA CHAPTER Wish you would. You're about the only friend I got.

HANNAH Oh well now.

SISTER ELLA CHAPTER Know why I decided to like you? I decided to like you 'cause you're the only unfriendly Mormon I ever met.

HANNAH Your wig is crooked.

SISTER ELLA CHAPTER Fix it.

[HANNAH *straightens* SISTER ELLA*'s wig.*]

SISTER ELLA CHAPTER New York City. All they got there is tiny rooms.

I always thought: People ought to stay put. That's why I got my license to sell real estate. It's a way of saying: Have a house! Stay put! It's a way of saying traveling's no good. Plus I needed the cash. [*She takes a pack of cigarettes out of her purse, lights one, offers pack to* HANNAH.]

HANNAH Not out here, anyone could come by.

There's been days I've stood at this ledge and thought about stepping over.

It's a hard place, Salt Lake: baked dry. Abundant energy; not much intelligence. That's a combination that can wear a body out. No harm looking someplace else. I don't need much room.

My sister-in-law Libby thinks there's radon gas[8] in the basement.

SISTER ELLA CHAPTER Is there gas in the . . .

HANNAH Of course not. Libby's a fool.

SISTER ELLA CHAPTER 'Cause I'd have to include that in the description.

HANNAH There's no gas, Ella. [*Little pause.*] Give a puff. [*She takes a furtive drag of* ELLA*'s cigarette.*] Put it away now.

SISTER ELLA CHAPTER So I guess it's goodbye.

HANNAH You'll be all right, Ella, I wasn't ever much of a friend.

SISTER ELLA CHAPTER I'll say something but don't laugh, OK?

This is the home of saints, the godliest place on earth, they say, and I think they're right. That mean there's no evil here? No. Evil's everywhere. Sin's everywhere. But this . . . is the spring of sweet water in the desert, the desert flower. Every step a Believer takes away from here is a step fraught with peril. I fear for you, Hannah Pitt, because you are my friend. Stay put. This is the right home of saints.

HANNAH Latter-day saints.

SISTER ELLA CHAPTER Only kind left.

HANNAH But still. Late in the day . . . for saints and everyone. That's all. That's all.

Fifty thousand dollars for the house, Sister Ella Chapter; don't undersell. It's an impressive view.

8. A naturally occurring radioactive gas that can cause lung cancer.

Act 3: Not-Yet-Conscious, Forward Dawning

(January 1986)

Scene 1

[*Late night, three days after the end of Act 2. The stage is completely dark.* PRIOR *is in bed in his apartment, having a nightmare. He wakes up, sits up, and switches on a nightlight. He looks at his clock. Seated by the table near the bed is a man dressed in the clothing of a 13th-century British squire.*]

PRIOR [*terrified*] Who are you?

PRIOR 1 My name is Prior Walter.

[*Pause.*]

PRIOR My name is Prior Walter.

PRIOR 1 I know that.

PRIOR Explain.

PRIOR 1 You're alive. I'm not. We have the same name. What do you want me to explain?

PRIOR A ghost?

PRIOR 1 An ancestor.

PRIOR Not *the* Prior Walter? The Bayeux tapestry Prior Walter?

PRIOR 1 His great-great grandson. The fifth of the name.

PRIOR I'm the thirty-fourth, I think.

PRIOR 1 Actually the thirty-second.

PRIOR Not according to Mother.

PRIOR 1 She's including the two bastards, then; I say leave them out. I say no room for bastards. The little things you swallow . . .

PRIOR Pills.

PRIOR 1 Pills. For the pestilence. I too . . .

PRIOR Pestilence. . . . You too what?

PRIOR 1 The pestilence[9] in my time was much worse than now. Whole villages of empty houses. You could look outdoors and see Death walking in the morning, dew dampening the ragged hem of his black robe. Plain as I see you now.

PRIOR You died of the plague.

PRIOR 1 The spotty monster. Like you, alone.

PRIOR I'm not alone.

PRIOR 1 You have no wife, no children.

PRIOR I'm gay.

PRIOR 1 So? Be gay, dance in your altogether for all I care, what's that to do with not having children?

PRIOR Gay homosexual, not bonny, blithe and[1] . . . never mind.

PRIOR 1 I had twelve. When I died.

9. Bubonic plague, or the Black Death; it killed more than one-third of the population of Asia and Europe in the 1300s.

1. An allusion to the nursery rhyme that begins "Monday's child is fair of face"; one version ends "But the child born on the Sabbath Day / Is bonny and blithe and good and gay."

[*The second ghost appears, this one dressed in the clothing of an elegant 17th-century Londoner.*]

PRIOR 1 [*pointing to* PRIOR 2] And I was three years younger than him.

[PRIOR *sees the new ghost, screams.*]

PRIOR Oh God another one.

PRIOR 2 Prior Walter. Prior to you by some seventeen others.

PRIOR 1 He's counting the bastards.

PRIOR Are we having a convention?

PRIOR 2 We've been sent to declare her fabulous incipience. They love a well-paved entrance with lots of heralds, and . . .

PRIOR 1 The messenger come. Prepare the way. The infinite descent, a breath in air . . .

PRIOR 2 They chose us, I suspect, because of the mortal affinities. In a family as long-descended as the Walters there are bound to be a few carried off by plague.

PRIOR 1 The spotty monster.

PRIOR 2 Black Jack.[2] Came from a water pump, half the city of London, can you imagine? His came from fleas. Yours, I understand, is the lamentable consequence of venery . . .

PRIOR 1 Fleas on rats, but who knew that?

PRIOR Am I going to die?

PRIOR 2 We aren't allowed to discuss . . .

PRIOR 1 When you do, you don't get ancestors to help you through it. You may be surrounded by children but you die alone.

PRIOR I'm afraid.

PRIOR 1 You should be. There aren't even torches, and the path's rocky, dark, and steep.

PRIOR 2 Don't alarm him. There's good news before there's bad.

We two come to strew rose petal and palm leaf before the triumphal procession. Prophet. Seer. Revelator. It's a great honor for the family.

PRIOR 1 He hasn't got a family.

PRIOR 2 I meant for the Walters, for the family in the larger sense.

PRIOR [*singing*]

All I want is a room somewhere,
Far away from the cold night air . . . [3]

PRIOR 2 [*putting a hand on* PRIOR*'s forehead*] Calm, calm, this is no brain fever . . .

[PRIOR *calms down, but keeps his eyes closed. The lights begin to change. Distant Glorious Music.*]

PRIOR 1 [*low chant*]

Adonai, Adonai,
Olam ha-yichud,
Zefirot, Zazahot,

2. Another name for bubonic plague. The worst epidemic to devastate London killed up to 100,000, or one-fifth of the city's population, in 1665–66.

3. The opening lines of "Wouldn't It Be Loverly?"—a song from Alan Jay Lerner and Frederick Loewe's musical *My Fair Lady* (1956).

Ha-adam, ha-gadol[4]
Daughter of Light,
Daughter of Splendors,
Fluor! Phosphor!
Lumen! Candle!

PRIOR 2 [*simultaneously*]
Even now,
From the mirror-bright halls of heaven,
Across the cold and lifeless infinity of space,
The Messenger comes
Trailing orbs of light,
Fabulous, incipient,
Oh Prophet,
To you . . .

PRIOR 1 and PRIOR 2
Prepare, prepare,
The Infinite Descent,
A breath, a feather,
Glory to . . .
[*They vanish.*]

Scene 2

[*The next day. Split scene:* LOUIS *and* BELIZE *in a coffee shop.* PRIOR *is at the outpatient clinic at the hospital with* EMILY, *the nurse; she has him on a pentamidine*[5] *IV drip.*]

LOUIS Why has democracy succeeded in America? Of course by succeeded I mean comparatively, not literally, not in the present, but what makes for the prospect of some sort of radical democracy spreading outward and growing up? Why does the power that was once so carefully preserved at the top of the pyramid by the original framers of the Constitution seem drawn inexorably downward and outward in spite of the best effort of the Right to stop this? I mean it's the really hard thing about being Left in this country, the American Left can't help but trip over all these petrified little fetishes: freedom, that's the worst; you know, *Jeane Kirkpatrick*[6] for God's sake will go on and on about freedom and so what does that mean, the word freedom, when she talks about it, or human rights; you have Bush[7] talking about human rights, and so what are these people talking about,

4. Hebrew terms associated with the Kabbalah, a tradition of mystical interpretation of the Hebrew Bible, though *Adonai* is a common way of referring to the Lord. *Olam hayichud:* the world of unification (i.e., unified by God); *Zefirot:* the divine emanations that represent the aspects of God visible in the world (usually *sefirot*); *Zazahot:* the three "brightnesses" (*Tzachtzachot,* often called the "splendors") that precede and govern the emanations of the sefirot; *Ha-adam, ha-gadol:* the heavenly man (literally, "the great man"; see Joshua 14.15).

5. Pentamidine isethionate, a drug that fights AIDS-related pneumonia.

6. An American professor of political science (1926–2006), selected by Reagan to be U.S. ambassador to the United Nations (1981–85); she criticized the Carter administration's emphasis on human rights, arguing for U.S. support of authoritarian regimes that oppose revolutionary totalitarian (Communist) regimes.

7. George H. W. Bush (b. 1924), vice president under Ronald Reagan (1981–89) and president (1989–93).

they might as well be talking about the mating habits of Venusians, these people don't begin to know what, ontologically, freedom is or human rights, like they see these bourgeois property-based Rights-of-Man-type rights[8] but that's not enfranchisement, not democracy, not what's implicit, what's potential within the idea, not the idea with blood in it. That's just liberalism, the worst kind of liberalism, really, bourgeois tolerance, and what I think is that what AIDS shows us is the limits of tolerance, that it's not enough to be tolerated, because when the shit hits the fan you find out how much tolerance is worth. Nothing. And underneath all the tolerance is intense, passionate hatred.

BELIZE Uh huh.

LOUIS Well don't you think that's true?

BELIZE Uh huh. It is.

LOUIS *Power* is the object, not being tolerated. Fuck assimilation. But I mean in spite of all this the thing about America, I think, is that ultimately we're different from every other nation on earth, in that, with people here of every race, we can't. . . . Ultimately what defines us isn't race, but politics. Not like any European country where there's an insurmountable fact of a kind of racial, or ethnic, monopoly, or monolith, like all Dutchmen, I mean Dutch people, are well, Dutch, and the Jews of Europe were never Europeans, just a small problem. Facing the monolith. But here there are so many small problems, it's really just a collection of small problems, the monolith is missing. Oh, I mean, of course I suppose there's the monolith of White America. White Straight Male America.

BELIZE Which is not unimpressive, even among monoliths.

LOUIS Well, no, but when the race thing gets taken care of, and I don't mean to minimalize how major it is, I mean I know it is, this is a really, really incredibly racist country but it's like, well, the British. I mean, all these blue-eyed pink people. And it's just weird, you know, I mean I'm not all that Jewish-looking, or . . . well, maybe I am but, you know, in New York, everyone is . . . well, not everyone, but so many are but so but in England, in London I walk into bars and I feel like Sid the Yid, you know I mean like Woody Allen in *Annie Hall*, with the payess and the gabardine coat,[9] like never, never anywhere so much—I mean, not actively despised, not like they're Germans, who I think are still terribly anti-Semitic, and racist too, I mean black-racist, they pretend otherwise but, anyway, in London, there's just . . . and at one point I met this black gay guy from Jamaica who talked with a lilt but he said his family'd been living in London since before the Civil War—the American one[1]—and how the English never let him forget for a minute that he wasn't blue-eyed and pink and I said yeah, me too, these people are anti-Semites and he said yeah but the British Jews have the clothing business all sewed up and blacks there can't get a foothold.

8. An allusion to the property-based political theory of the British philosopher John Locke (1632–1704), which influenced the framers of the U.S. Constitution.

9. In *Annie Hall* (1977), directed by and starring Allen (b. 1935), a Jew born in New York City, Allen's character imagines that his girlfriend's midwestern family sees him as a Hasid, wearing the tight-woven wool coat and *payess* (side curls; Yiddish) characteristic of that ultraorthodox Jewish sect. *Yid:* Jew (pejorative).

1. That is, not the English Civil War (1642–48).

And it was an incredibly awkward moment of just . . . I mean here we were, in this bar that was gay but it was a *pub,* you know, the beams and the plaster and those horrible little, like, two-day-old fish and egg sandwiches—and just so British, so *old,* and I felt, well, there's no way out of this because both of us are, right now, too much immersed in this history, hope is dissolved in the sheer age of this place, where race is what counts and there's no real hope of change—it's the racial destiny of the Brits that matters to them, not their political destiny, whereas in America . . .

BELIZE Here in America race doesn't count.

LOUIS No, no, that's not . . . I mean you *can't* be hearing that . . .

BELIZE I . . .

LOUIS It's—look, race, yes, but ultimately race here is a political question, right? Racists just try to use race here as a tool in a political struggle. It's not really about race. Like the spiritualists try to use that stuff, are you enlightened, are you centered, channeled, whatever, this reaching out for a spiritual past in a country where no indigenous spirits exist—only the Indians, I mean Native American spirits and we killed them off so now, there are no gods here, no ghosts and spirits in America, there are no angels in America, no spiritual past, no racial past, there's only the political, and the decoys and the ploys to maneuver around the inescapable battle of politics, the shifting downwards and outwards of political power to the people . . .

BELIZE POWER to the People![2] AMEN! [*Looking at his watch*] *OH MY GOODNESS!* Will you look at the time, I gotta . . .

LOUIS Do you. . . . You think this is, what, racist or naive or something?

BELIZE Well it's certainly *something.* Look, I just remembered I have an appointment . . .

LOUIS What? I mean I really don't want to, like, speak from some position of privilege and . . .

BELIZE I'm sitting here, thinking, eventually he's *got* to run out of steam, so I let you rattle on and on saying about maybe seven or eight things I find really offensive.

LOUIS What?

BELIZE But I know you, Louis, and I know the guilt fueling this peculiar tirade is obviously already swollen bigger than your hemorrhoids.

LOUIS I don't have hemorrhoids.

BELIZE I hear different. May I finish?

LOUIS Yes, but I don't have hemorrhoids.

BELIZE So finally, when I . . .

LOUIS Prior told you, he's an asshole, he shouldn't have . . .

BELIZE You promised, Louis. Prior is not a subject.

LOUIS You brought him up.

BELIZE I brought up hemorrhoids.

LOUIS So it's indirect. Passive-aggressive.

BELIZE Unlike, I suppose, banging me over the head with your theory that America doesn't have a race problem.

LOUIS Oh be fair I never said that.

2. A slogan of the 1960s, associated both with student protesters and with the militant Black Panthers.

BELIZE Not exactly, but . . .

LOUIS I said . . .

BELIZE . . . but it was close enough, because if it'd been that blunt I'd've just walked out and . . .

LOUIS You deliberately misinterpreted! I . . .

BELIZE Stop interrupting! I haven't been able to . . .

LOUIS Just let me . . .

BELIZE NO! What, *talk*? You've been running your mouth nonstop since I got here, yaddadda yaddadda blah blah blah, up the hill, down the hill, playing with your MONOLITH . . .

LOUIS [*overlapping*] Well, you could have joined in at any time instead of . . .

BELIZE [*continuing over* LOUIS] . . . and girlfriend it is truly an *awesome* spectacle but I got better things to do with my time than sit here listening to this racist bullshit just because I feel sorry for you that . . .

LOUIS I am not a racist!

BELIZE Oh come on . . .

LOUIS So maybe I am a racist but . . .

BELIZE Oh I really hate that! It's no fun picking on you Louis; you're so guilty, it's like throwing darts at a glob of jello, there's no satisfying hits, just quivering, the darts just blop in and vanish.

LOUIS I just think when you are discussing lines of oppression it gets very complicated and . . .

BELIZE Oh is that a fact? You know, we black drag queens have a rather intimate knowledge of the complexity of the lines of . . .

LOUIS *Ex*–black drag queen.

BELIZE Actually ex-ex.

LOUIS You're doing drag again?

BELIZE I don't . . . Maybe. I don't have to tell you. Maybe.

LOUIS I think it's sexist.

BELIZE I didn't ask you.

LOUIS Well it is. The gay community, I think, has to adopt the same attitude towards drag as black women have to take towards black women blues singers.

BELIZE Oh my we *are* walking dangerous tonight.

LOUIS Well, it's all internalized oppression, right, I mean the masochism, the stereotypes, the . . .

BELIZE Louis, are you deliberately trying to make me hate you?

LOUIS No, I . . .

BELIZE I mean, are you deliberately transforming yourself into an arrogant, sexual-political Stalinist-slash-racist flag-waving thug for my benefit?

[*Pause.*]

LOUIS You know what I think?

BELIZE What?

LOUIS You hate me because I'm a Jew.

BELIZE I'm leaving.

LOUIS It's true.

BELIZE You have no basis except your . . .

Louis, it's good to know you haven't changed; you are still an honorary citizen of the Twilight Zone,[3] and after your pale, pale white polemics on behalf of racial insensitivity you have a flaming *fuck* of a lot of nerve calling me an anti-Semite. Now I really gotta go.

LOUIS You called me Lou the Jew.

BELIZE That was a joke.

LOUIS I didn't think it was funny. It was hostile.

BELIZE It was three years ago.

LOUIS So?

BELIZE You just called yourself Sid the Yid.

LOUIS That's not the same thing.

BELIZE Sid the Yid is different from Lou the Jew.

LOUIS Yes.

BELIZE Someday you'll have to explain that to me, but right now . . . *You* hate me because you hate black people.

LOUIS I do not. But I do think most black people are anti-Semitic.

BELIZE "Most black people." *That's* racist, Louis, and *I* think most Jews . . .

LOUIS Louis Farrakhan.[4]

BELIZE Ed Koch.[5]

LOUIS Jesse Jackson.[6]

BELIZE Jackson. Oh really, Louis, this is . . .

LOUIS Hymietown! Hymietown!

BELIZE Louis, you voted for Jesse Jackson. You send checks to the Rainbow Coalition.

LOUIS I'm ambivalent. The checks bounced.

BELIZE All your checks bounce, Louis; you're ambivalent about everything.

LOUIS What's that supposed to mean?

BELIZE You may be dumber than shit but I refuse to believe you can't figure it out. Try.

LOUIS I was never ambivalent about Prior. I love him. I do. I really do.

BELIZE Nobody said different.

LOUIS Love and ambivalence are . . . Real love isn't ambivalent.

BELIZE "Real love isn't ambivalent." I'd swear that's a line from my favorite bestselling paperback novel, *In Love with the Night Mysterious,*[7] except I don't think you ever read it.

[*Pause.*]

LOUIS I never read it, no.

3. That is, in the fantasy world of *The Twilight Zone* (1959–64), Rod Serling's television series.

4. A black religious leader (b. 1933), who in 1977 became leader of the Nation of Islam (Black Muslims); beginning in the 1980s, he received public censure for statements viewed as anti-Semitic and antiwhite.

5. A Jewish New York politician (b. 1924); though popular as mayor (1978–89), early in his administration, he angered black political leaders by reorganizing the city's poverty programs, and in the 1980s, he became a vocal critic of Farrakhan and Jesse Jackson.

6. A black civil rights leader (b. 1941), who ran for president in 1984 and 1988; the 1984 revelation that he had called New York "Hymietown," together with his association—soon disavowed—with Farrakhan, damaged his reputation with Jews. After the 1984 campaign, he turned his informal "rainbow coalition" of minorities into a national social justice organization.

7. A line from Cole Porter's 1948 song "So in Love" (whose refrain begins "So taunt me and hurt me, / Deceive me, desert me, / I'm yours 'til I die"); no such novel exists.

BELIZE You ought to. Instead of spending the rest of your life trying to get through *Democracy in America.*[8] It's about this white woman whose Daddy owns a plantation in the Deep South in the years before the Civil War—the American one—and her name is Margaret, and she's in love with her Daddy's number-one slave, and his name is Thaddeus, and she's married but her white slave-owner husband has AIDS: Antebellum Insufficiently Developed Sexorgans. And there's a lot of hot stuff going down when Margaret and Thaddeus can catch a spare torrid ten under the cotton-picking moon, and then of course the Yankees come, and they set the slaves free, and the slaves string up old Daddy, and so on. Historical fiction. Somewhere in there I recall Margaret and Thaddeus find the time to discuss the nature of love; her face is reflecting the flames of the burning plantation—you know, the way white people do—and his black face is dark in the night and she says to him, "Thaddeus, real love isn't ever ambivalent."

[*Little pause.* EMILY *enters and turns off IV drip.*]

BELIZE Thaddeus looks at her; he's contemplating her thesis; and he isn't sure he agrees.

EMILY [*removing IV drip from* PRIOR'*s arm*] Treatment number . . . [*Consulting chart*] four.

PRIOR Pharmaceutical miracle. Lazarus[9] breathes again.

LOUIS Is he. . . . How bad is he?

BELIZE You want the laundry list?

EMILY Shirt off, let's check the . . .

[PRIOR *takes his shirt off. She examines his lesions.*]

BELIZE There's the weight problem and the shit problem and the morale problem.

EMILY Only six. That's good. Pants.

[*He drops his pants. He's naked. She examines.*]

BELIZE And. He thinks he's going crazy.

EMILY Looking good. What else?

PRIOR Ankles sore and swollen, but the leg's better. The nausea's mostly gone with the little orange pills. BM's pure liquid but not bloody anymore, for now, my eye doctor says everything's OK, for now, my dentist says "Yuck!" when he sees my fuzzy tongue, and now he wears little condoms on his thumb and forefinger. And a mask. So what? My dermatologist is in Hawaii and my mother . . . well leave my mother out of it. Which is usually where my mother is, out of it. My glands are like walnuts, my weight's holding steady for week two, and a friend died two days ago of bird tuberculosis;[1] bird tuberculosis; that scared me and I didn't go to the funeral today because he was an Irish Catholic and it's probably open casket and I'm afraid of . . . something, the bird TB or seeing him or . . . So I guess I'm doing OK. Except for of course I'm going nuts.

EMILY We ran the toxoplasmosis series[2] and there's no indication . . .

8. Alexis de Tocqueville's classic study of Americans and their system of government (2 vols., 1835–40).

9. Jesus' resurrection of Lazarus from the dead is described in John 11.1–44.

1. A hard-to-treat form of tuberculosis that is common in AIDS patients.

2. A series of tests for toxoplasmosis, one of the infections commonly associated with AIDS; it often affects the brain.

PRIOR I know, I know, but I feel like something terrifying is on its way, you know, like a missile from outer space, and it's plummeting down towards the earth, and I'm ground zero, and . . . I am generally known where I am known as one cool, collected queen. And I am ruffled.

EMILY There's really nothing to worry about. I think that shochen bamromim hamtzeh menucho nechono al kanfey haschino.[3]

PRIOR What?

EMILY Everything's fine. Bemaalos k'doshim ut'horim kezohar horokeea mazhirim . . .

PRIOR Oh I don't understand what you're . . .

EMILY Es nishmas Prior sheholoch leolomoh, baavur shenodvoo z'dokoh b'ad hazkoras nishmosoh.

PRIOR Why are you doing that?! Stop it! Stop it!

EMILY Stop what?

PRIOR You were just . . . weren't you just speaking in Hebrew or something.

EMILY *Hebrew?* [*Laughs.*] I'm basically Italian-American. No. I didn't speak in Hebrew.

PRIOR Oh no, oh God please I really think I . . .

EMILY Look, I'm sorry, I have a waiting room full of . . . I think you're one of the lucky ones, you'll live for years, probably—you're pretty healthy for someone with no immune system. Are you seeing someone? Loneliness is a danger. A therapist?

PRIOR No, I don't need to see anyone, I just . . .

EMILY Well think about it. You aren't going crazy. You're just under a lot of stress. No wonder . . . [*She starts to write in his chart.*]

[*Suddenly there is an astonishing blaze of light, a huge chord sounded by a gigantic choir, and a great book with steel pages mounted atop a molten-red pillar pops up from the stage floor. The book opens; there is a large Aleph[4] inscribed on its pages, which bursts into flames. Immediately the book slams shut and disappears instantly under the floor as the lights become normal again.* EMILY *notices none of this, writing.* PRIOR *is agog.*]

EMILY [*laughing, exiting*] Hebrew . . .

[*Prior flees.*]

LOUIS Help me.

BELIZE I beg your pardon?

LOUIS You're a nurse, give me something, I . . . don't know what to do anymore, I . . . Last week at work I screwed up the Xerox machine like permanently and so I . . . then I tripped on the subway steps and my glasses broke and I cut my forehead, here, see, and now I can't see much and my forehead . . . it's like the Mark of Cain,[5] stupid, right, but it won't heal and every morning I see it and I think, Biblical things, Mark of Cain, Judas

3. This line begins transliterated Hebrew taken from the prayer traditionally recited at funerals for the soul of the departed; the translation is "[God, full of compassion,] who dwells on high, grant true rest upon the wings of your Divine Presence, in the exalted spheres of the holy and pure, who shine as the brightness of the heavens, to the soul of Prior, who has gone to his eternal rest, for charity has been donated in remembrance of his soul."

4. The first letter of the Hebrew alphabet.

5. According to Genesis (4.1–16), the first son of Adam and Eve, whose forehead was marked by God after he killed Abel, his brother.

Iscariot and his silver and his noose,[6] people who . . . in betraying what they love betray what's truest in themselves, I feel . . . nothing but cold for myself, just cold, and every night I miss him, I miss him so much but then . . . those sores, and the smell and . . . where I thought it was going. . . . I could be . . . I could be sick too, maybe I'm sick too. I don't know.

Belize. Tell him I love him. Can you do that?

BELIZE I've thought about it for a very long time, and I still don't understand what love is. Justice is simple. Democracy is simple. Those things are unambivalent. But love is very hard. And it goes bad for you if you violate the hard law of love.

LOUIS I'm dying.

BELIZE He's dying. You just wish you were.

Oh cheer up, Louis. Look at that heavy sky out there.

LOUIS Purple.

BELIZE *Purple?* Boy, what kind of a homosexual are you, anyway? That's not purple, Mary, that color up there is [*Very grand*] *mauve.*

All day today it's felt like Thanksgiving. Soon, this . . . ruination will be blanketed white. You can smell it—can you smell it?

LOUIS Smell what?

BELIZE Softness, compliance, forgiveness, grace.

LOUIS No . . .

BELIZE I can't help you learn that. I can't help you, Louis. You're not my business. [*He exits.*]

[*Louis puts his head in his hands, inadvertently touching his cut forehead.*]

LOUIS Ow FUCK! [*He stands slowly, looks towards where* BELIZE *exited.*] Smell what?

[*He looks both ways to be sure no one is watching, then inhales deeply, and is surprised.*] Huh. Snow.

Scene 3

[*Same day.* HARPER *in a very white, cold place, with a brilliant blue sky above; a delicate snowfall. She is dressed in a beautiful snowsuit. The sound of the sea, faint.*]

HARPER Snow! Ice! Mountains of ice! Where am I? I . . .

I feel better, I do,

I . . . feel better. There are ice crystals in my lungs, wonderful and sharp. And the snow smells like cold, crushed peaches. And there's something . . . some current of blood in the wind, how strange, it has that iron taste.

MR. LIES Ozone.

HARPER Ozone! Wow! Where am I?

MR. LIES The Kingdom of Ice, the bottommost part of the world.

HARPER [*looking around, then realizing*] Antarctica. This is Antarctica!

MR. LIES Cold shelter for the shattered. No sorrow here, tears freeze.

HARPER Antarctica, Antarctica, oh boy oh boy, LOOK at this, I . . . Wow, I must've really snapped the tether, huh?

MR. LIES Apparently . . .

6. For the story of the betrayal of Jesus by Judas Iscariot, his disciple, for thirty pieces of silver, and Judas's subsequent suicide by hanging, see Matthew 26.14–15, 27.3–5.

HARPER That's great. I want to stay here forever. Set up camp. Build things. Build a city, an enormous city made up of frontier forts, dark wood and green roofs and high gates made of pointed logs and bonfires burning on every street corner. I should build by a river. Where are the forests?

MR. LIES No timber here. Too cold. Ice, no trees.

HARPER Oh details! I'm sick of details! I'll plant them and grow them. I'll live off caribou fat, I'll melt it over the bonfires and drink it from long, curved goat-horn cups. It'll be great. I want to make a new world here. So that I never have to go home again.

MR. LIES As long as it lasts. Ice has a way of melting . . .

HARPER No. Forever. I can have anything I want here—maybe even companionship, someone who has . . . desire for me. You, maybe.

MR. LIES It's against the by-laws of the International Order of Travel Agents to get involved with clients. Rules are rules. Anyway, I'm not the one you really want.

HARPER There isn't anyone . . . maybe an Eskimo. Who could ice-fish for food. And help me build a nest for when the baby comes.

MR. LIES There are no Eskimo in Antarctica. And you're not really pregnant. You made that up.

HARPER Well all of this is made up. So if the snow feels cold I'm pregnant. Right? Here, I can be pregnant. And I can have any kind of a baby I want.

MR. LIES This is a retreat, a vacuum, its virtue is that it lacks everything; deep-freeze for feelings. You can be numb and safe here, that's what you came for. Respect the delicate ecology of your delusions.

HARPER You mean like no Eskimo in Antarctica.

MR. LIES Correcto. Ice and snow, no Eskimo. Even hallucinations have laws.

HARPER Well then who's that?

[*The Eskimo appears.*]

MR. LIES An Eskimo.

HARPER An antarctic Eskimo. A fisher of the polar deep.

MR. LIES There's something wrong with this picture.

[*The Eskimo beckons.*]

HARPER I'm going to like this place. It's my own National Geographic Special![7] Oh! Oh! [*She holds her stomach.*] I think . . . I think I felt her kicking. Maybe I'll give birth to a baby covered with thick white fur, and that way she won't be cold. My breasts will be full of hot cocoa so she doesn't get chilly. And if it gets really cold, she'll have a pouch I can crawl into. Like a marsupial. We'll mend together. That's what we'll do; we'll mend.

Scene 4

[*Same day. An abandoned lot in the South Bronx. A homeless* WOMAN *is standing near an oil drum in which a fire is burning. Snowfall. Trash around.* HANNAH *enters dragging two heavy suitcases.*]

HANNAH Excuse me? I said excuse me? Can you tell me where I am? Is this Brooklyn? Do you know a Pineapple Street?[8] Is there some sort of bus or train or . . . ?

7. That is, like the television programs—mainly documentaries featuring the exploration of the natural world—produced by the National Geographic Society since 1964.

8. A street in Brooklyn Heights, a historic district of Brooklyn.

I'm lost, I just arrived from Salt Lake. City. Utah? I took the bus that I was told to take and I got off—well it was the very last stop, so I had to get off, and I *asked* the driver was this Brooklyn, and he nodded yes but he was from one of those foreign countries where they think it's good manners to nod at everything even if you have no idea what it is you're nodding at, and in truth I think he spoke no English at all, which I think would make him ineligible for employment on public transportation. The public being English-speaking, mostly. Do you speak English?

[*The* WOMAN *nods.*]

HANNAH I was supposed to be met at the airport by my son. He didn't show and I don't wait more than three and three-quarters hours for *anyone.* I should have been patient, I guess, I . . . Is this . . .

WOMAN Bronx.

HANNAH Is that . . . The *Bronx?* Well how in the name of Heaven did I get to the Bronx when the bus driver said . . .

WOMAN [*talking to herself*] Slurp slurp slurp will you STOP that disgusting slurping! YOU DISGUSTING SLURPING FEEDING ANIMAL! Feeding yourself, just feeding yourself, what would it matter, to you or to ANYONE, if you just stopped. Feeding. And DIED?

[*Pause.*]

HANNAH Can you just tell me where I . . .

WOMAN Why was the Kosciuszko Bridge[9] named after a Polack?

HANNAH I don't know what you're . . .

WOMAN That was a joke.

HANNAH Well what's the punchline?

WOMAN I don't know.

HANNAH [*looking around desperately*] Oh for pete's sake, is there anyone else who . . .

WOMAN [*again, to herself*] Stand further off you fat loathsome whore, you can't have any more of this soup, slurp slurp slurp you animal, and the—I know you'll just go pee it all away and where will you do that? Behind what bush? It's FUCKING COLD out here and I . . .

Oh that's right, because it was supposed to have been a tunnel!

That's not very funny.

Have you read the prophecies of Nostradamus?[1]

HANNAH Who?

WOMAN Some guy I went out with once somewhere, Nostradamus. Prophet, outcast, eyes like . . . Scary shit, he . . .

HANNAH Shut up. Please. Now I want you to stop jabbering for a minute and pull your wits together and tell me how to get to Brooklyn. Because you know! And you are going to tell me! Because there is no one else around to tell me and I am wet and cold and I am very angry! So I am sorry you're psychotic but just make the effort—take a deep breath—DO IT!

9. A bridge that connects the Bronx and Queens (a borough that, like Brooklyn, is on Long Island); it is named for Tadeusz Kościuszko (1746–1817), a Polish military engineer who fought with distinction in America's Continental Army in the Revolutionary War.

1. Michel de Nostredame (1503–1566), a French astrologer and physician whose *Prophesies* (1555), a collection of predictions about the future, has long found a receptive audience.

[HANNAH *and the* WOMAN *breathe together.*]

HANNAH That's good. Now exhale.

[*They do.*]

HANNAH Good. Now how do I get to Brooklyn?

WOMAN Don't know. Never been. Sorry. Want some soup?

HANNAH Manhattan? Maybe you know . . . I don't suppose you know the location of the Mormon Visitor's[2] . . .

WOMAN 65th and Broadway.

HANNAH How do you . . .

WOMAN Go there all the time. Free movies. Boring, but you can stay all day.

HANNAH Well. . . . So how do I . . .

WOMAN Take the D Train.[3] Next block make a right.

HANNAH Thank you.

WOMAN Oh yeah. In the new century I think we will all be insane.

Scene 5

[*Same day.* JOE *and* ROY *in the study of* ROY*'s brownstone.* ROY *is wearing an elegant bathrobe. He has made a considerable effort to look well. He isn't well, and he hasn't succeeded much in looking it.*]

JOE I can't. The answer's no. I'm sorry.

ROY Oh, well, apologies . . .

I can't see that there's anyone asking for apologies.

[*Pause.*]

JOE I'm sorry, Roy.

ROY Oh, well, apologies.

JOE My wife is missing, Roy. My mother's coming from Salt Lake to . . . to help look, I guess. I'm supposed to be at the airport now, picking her up but . . . I just spent two days in a hospital, Roy, with a bleeding ulcer, I was spitting up blood.

ROY Blood, huh? Look, I'm very busy here and . . .

JOE It's just a job.

ROY A job? A *job? Washington!* Dumb Utah Mormon hick shit!

JOE Roy . . .

ROY *WASHINGTON!* When Washington called me I was younger than you, you think I said "Aw fuck no I can't go I got two fingers up my asshole and a little moral nosebleed to boot!" When Washington calls you my pretty young punk friend you go or you can go fuck yourself sideways 'cause the train has pulled out of the station, and you are *out*, nowhere, out in the cold. Fuck you, Mary Jane, get outta here.

JOE Just let me . . .

ROY Explain? Ephemera. You broke my heart. Explain that. Explain that.

JOE I love you. Roy.

There's so much that I want, to be . . . what you see in me, I want to be a participant in the world, in your world, Roy, I want to be capable of that, I've tried, really I have but . . . I can't do this. Not because I don't believe in

2. The Mormon Visitors' Center.

3. A subway line that, in the Bronx, runs along the Grand Concourse; it extends to Brooklyn.

you, but because I believe in you so much, in what you stand for, at heart, the order, the decency. I would give anything to protect you, but . . . There are laws I can't break. It's too ingrained. It's not me. There's enough damage I've already done.

Maybe you were right, maybe I'm dead.

ROY You're not dead, boy, you're a sissy.

You love me; that's moving, I'm moved. It's nice to be loved. I warned you about her, didn't I, Joe? But you don't listen to me, why, because you say Roy is smart and Roy's a friend but Roy . . . well, he isn't nice, and you wanna be nice. Right? A nice, nice man! [*Little pause*]

You know what my greatest accomplishment was, Joe, in my life, what I am able to look back on and be proudest of? And I have helped make Presidents and unmake them and mayors and more goddam judges than anyone in NYC ever—AND several million dollars, tax-free—and what do you think means the most to me?

You ever hear of Ethel Rosenberg? Huh, Joe, huh?

JOE Well, yeah, I guess I . . . Yes.

ROY Yes. Yes. You have heard of Ethel Rosenberg. Yes. Maybe you even read about her in the history books.

If it wasn't for me, Joe, Ethel Rosenberg would be alive today, writing some personal-advice column for *Ms.* magazine.[4] She isn't. Because during the trial, Joe, I was on the phone every day, talking with the judge . . .

JOE Roy . . .

ROY Every day, doing what I do best, talking on the telephone, making sure that timid Yid nebbish[5] on the bench did his duty to America, to history. That sweet unprepossessing woman, two kids, boo-hoo-hoo, reminded us all of our little Jewish mamas—she came this close to getting life; I pleaded till I wept to put her in the chair.[6] Me. I did that. I would have fucking pulled the switch if they'd have let me. Why? Because I fucking hate traitors. Because I fucking hate communists. Was it legal? Fuck legal. Am I a nice man? Fuck nice. They say terrible things about me in the *Nation.*[7] Fuck the *Nation.* You want to be Nice, or you want to be Effective? Make the law, or subject to it. Choose. Your wife chose. A week from today, she'll be back. SHE knows how to get what SHE wants. Maybe I ought to send *her* to Washington.

JOE I don't believe you.

ROY Gospel.

JOE You can't possibly mean what you're saying.

Roy, you were the Assistant United States Attorney on the Rosenberg case, ex-parte[8] communication with the judge during the trial would be . . . censurable, at least, probably conspiracy and . . . in a case that resulted in execution, it's . . .

4. An American feminist magazine that appeared monthly from 1972 to 1987; it resumed publication in 2001.
5. A nonentity, a loser (Yiddish); the presiding judge in the Rosenbergs' trial was Irving R. Kaufman (1910–1992).
6. The electric chair, used to execute the Rosenbergs.
7. A left-liberal American journal of culture and politics, published weekly since 1865.
8. In law, proceedings conducted in the absence of and without notice to one party, a practice that is normally prohibited (literally, "from [one] side"; Latin); see Playwright's Notes.

ROY What? Murder?

JOE You're not well is all.

ROY What do you mean, not well? Who's not well?

[*Pause.*]

JOE You said . . .

ROY No I didn't. I said what?

JOE Roy, you have cancer.

ROY No I don't.

[*Pause.*]

JOE You told me you were dying.

ROY What the fuck are you talking about, Joe? I never said that. I'm in perfect health. There's not a goddam thing wrong with me. [*He smiles.*] Shake?

[JOE *hesitates. He holds out his hand to* ROY. ROY *pulls* JOE *into a close, strong clinch.*]

ROY [*more to himself than to* JOE] It's OK that you hurt me because I love you, baby Joe. That's why I'm so rough on you.

[ROY *releases* JOE. JOE *backs away a step or two.*]

ROY Prodigal son.[9] The world will wipe its dirty hands all over you.

JOE It already has, Roy.

ROY Now go.

[ROY *shoves* JOE, *hard.* JOE *turns to leave.* ROY *stops him, turns him around.*]

ROY [*smoothing* JOE*'s lapels, tenderly*] I'll always be here, waiting for you . . . [*Then again, with sudden violence, he pulls* JOE *close, violently.*] What did you want from me, what was all this, what do you want, treacherous ungrateful little . . .

[JOE, *very close to belting* ROY, *grabs him by the front of his robe, and propels him across the length of the room. He holds* ROY *at arm's length, the other arm ready to hit.*]

ROY [*laughing softly, almost pleading to be hit*] Transgress a little, Joseph.

[JOE *releases* ROY.]

ROY There are so many laws; find one you can break.

[JOE *hesitates, then leaves, backing out. When* JOE *has gone,* ROY *doubles over in great pain, which he's been hiding throughout the scene with* JOE.]

ROY Ah, Christ . . .
Andy! Andy! Get in here! Andy!

[*The door opens, but it isn't* ANDY. *A small Jewish* WOMAN *dressed modestly in a fifties hat and coat stands in the doorway. The room darkens.*]

ROY Who the fuck are you? The new nurse?

[*The figure in the doorway says nothing. She stares at* ROY. *A pause.* ROY *looks at her carefully, gets up, crosses to her. He crosses back to the chair, sits heavily.*]

ROY Aw, fuck. Ethel.

9. That is, the son who squanders his inheritance but is joyfully welcomed back home (see Luke 15.11–32).

ETHEL ROSENBERG [*her manner is friendly, her voice is ice-cold*] You don't look good, Roy.

ROY Well, Ethel. I don't feel good.

ETHEL ROSENBERG But you lost a lot of weight. That suits you. You were heavy back then. Zaftig, mit[1] hips.

ROY I haven't been that heavy since 1960. We were all heavier back then, before the body thing started. Now I look like a skeleton. They stare.

ETHEL ROSENBERG The shit's really hit the fan, huh, Roy?

[*Little pause.* ROY *nods.*]

ETHEL ROSENBERG Well the fun's just started.

ROY What is this, Ethel, Halloween? You trying to scare me?

[ETHEL *says nothing.*]

ROY Well you're wasting your time! I'm scarier than you any day of the week! So beat it, Ethel! BOOO! BETTER DEAD THAN RED![2] Somebody trying to shake me up? HAH HAH! From the throne of God in heaven to the belly of hell, you can all fuck yourselves and then go jump in the lake because I'M NOT AFRAID OF YOU OR DEATH OR HELL OR ANYTHING!

ETHEL ROSENBERG Be seeing you soon, Roy. Julius[3] sends his regards.

ROY Yeah, well send this to Julius!

[*He flips the bird in her direction,*[4] *stands and moves towards her. Halfway across the room he slumps to the floor, breathing laboriously, in pain.*]

ETHEL ROSENBERG You're a very sick man, Roy.

ROY Oh God . . . ANDY!

ETHEL ROSENBERG Hmmm. He doesn't hear you, I guess. We should call the ambulance.

[*She goes to the phone.*] Hah! Buttons! Such things they got now. What do I dial, Roy?

[*Pause.* ROY *looks at her, then.*]

ROY 911.

ETHEL ROSENBERG [*dials the phone*] It sings!

[*Imitating dial tones*] La la la . . .

Huh.

Yes, you should please send an ambulance to the home of Mister Roy Cohn, the famous lawyer.

What's the address, Roy?

ROY [*a beat, then*] 244 East 87th.

ETHEL ROSENBERG 244 East 87th Street. No apartment number, he's got the whole building.

My name? [*A beat*] Ethel Greenglass Rosenberg.

[*Small smile*] Me? No I'm not related to Mr. Cohn. An old friend. [*She hangs up.*]

They said a minute.

ROY I have all the time in the world.

1. Plump, with (Yiddish); *Zaftig* usually means "buxom."

2. A slogan used in the 1950s to denounce Communists ("Reds") and leftists.

3. Julius Rosenberg (1918–1953), Ethel's husband.

4. Gives her the finger.

ETHEL ROSENBERG You're immortal.

ROY I'm immortal. Ethel. [*He forces himself to stand.*]

I have *forced* my way into history. I ain't never gonna die.

ETHEL ROSENBERG [*a little laugh, then*] History is about to crack wide open. Millennium approaches.

Scene 6

[*Late that night.* PRIOR*'s bedroom.* PRIOR 1 *watching* PRIOR *in bed, who is staring back at him, terrified. Tonight* PRIOR 1 *is dressed in weird alchemical robes and hat over his historical clothing and he carries a long palm-leaf bundle.*

PRIOR 1 Tonight's the night! Aren't you excited? Tonight she arrives! Right through the roof! Ha-adam, Ha-gadol . . .

PRIOR 2 [*appearing, similarly attired*] Lumen! Phosphor! Fluor! Candle! An unending billowing of scarlet and . . .

PRIOR Look. Garlic. A mirror. Holy water. A crucifix.[5] FUCK OFF! Get the fuck out of my room! GO!

PRIOR 1 [*to* PRIOR 2] Hard as a hickory knob, I'll bet.

PRIOR 2 We all tumesce when they approach. We wax full, like moons.

PRIOR 1 Dance.

PRIOR Dance?

PRIOR 1 Stand up, dammit, give us your hands, dance!

PRIOR 2 Listen . . .

[*A lone oboe begins to play a little dance tune.*]

PRIOR 2 Delightful sound. Care to dance?

PRIOR Please leave me alone, please just let me sleep . . .

PRIOR 2 Ah, he wants someone familiar. A partner who knows his steps. [*To* PRIOR] Close your eyes. Imagine . . .

PRIOR I don't . . .

PRIOR 2 Hush. Close your eyes.

[PRIOR *does.*]

PRIOR 2 Now open them.

[PRIOR *does.* LOUIS *appears. He looks gorgeous. The music builds gradually into a full-blooded, romantic dance tune.*]

PRIOR Lou.

LOUIS Dance with me.

PRIOR I can't, my leg, it hurts at night . . .

Are you . . . a ghost, Lou?

LOUIS No. Just spectral. Lost to myself. Sitting all day on cold park benches. Wishing I could be with you. Dance with me, babe . . .

[PRIOR *stands up. The leg stops hurting. They begin to dance. The music is beautiful.*]

PRIOR 1 [*to* PRIOR 2] Hah. Now I see why he's got no children. He's a sodomite.

PRIOR 2 Oh be quiet, you medieval gnome, and let them dance.

5. All items believed to deter vampires.

PRIOR 1 I'm not interfering, I've done my bit. Hooray, hooray, the messenger's come, now I'm blowing off. I don't like it here.

[PRIOR 1 *vanishes.*]

PRIOR 2 The twentieth century. Oh dear, the world has gotten so terribly, terribly old.

[PRIOR 2 *vanishes.* LOUIS *and* PRIOR *waltz happily. Lights fade back to normal.* LOUIS *vanishes.*

PRIOR *dances alone.*

Then suddenly, the sound of wings fills the room.]

Scene 7

[*Split scene:* PRIOR *alone in his apartment;* LOUIS *alone in the park. Again, a sound of beating wings.*]

PRIOR Oh don't come in here don't come in . . . LOUIS!!

No. My name is Prior Walter, I am . . . the scion of an ancient line, I am . . . abandoned I . . . no, my name is . . . is . . . Prior and I live . . . *here and now,* and . . . in the dark, in the dark, the Recording Angel opens its hundred eyes and snaps the spine of the Book of Life[6] and . . . hush! Hush! I'm talking nonsense, I . . .

No more mad scene, hush, hush . . .

[LOUIS *in the park on a bench.* JOE *approaches, stands at a distance. They stare at each other, then* LOUIS *turns away.*]

LOUIS Do you know the story of Lazarus?

JOE Lazarus?

LOUIS Lazarus. I can't remember what happens, exactly.

JOE I don't . . . Well, he was dead, Lazarus, and Jesus breathed life into him. He brought him back from death.

LOUIS Come here often?

JOE No. Yes. Yes.

LOUIS Back from the dead. You believe that really happened?

JOE I don't know anymore what I believe.

LOUIS This is quite a coincidence. Us meeting.

JOE I followed you.

From work. I . . . followed you here.

[*Pause.*]

LOUIS You followed me.

You probably saw me that day in the washroom and thought: there's a sweet guy, sensitive, cries for friends in trouble.

JOE Yes.

LOUIS You thought maybe I'll cry for you.

JOE Yes.

LOUIS Well I fooled you. Crocodile tears. Nothing . . . [*He touches his heart, shrugs.*]

[JOE *reaches tentatively to touch* LOUIS*'s face.*]

6. In Jewish tradition, the symbolic book in which all who lived are sealed each year on the Day of Atonement, Yom Kippur; in the New Testament, it contains the names of those who will not be damned on Judgment Day (Revelation 13.8, 20.12–15).

LOUIS [*pulling back*] What are you doing? Don't do that.

JOE [*withdrawing his hand*] Sorry. I'm sorry.

LOUIS I'm . . . just not . . . I think, if you touch me, your hand might fall off or something. Worse things have happened to people who have touched me.

JOE Please.

Oh, boy . . .

Can I . . .

I . . . want . . . to touch you. Can I please just touch you . . . um, here?

[*He puts his hand on one side of* LOUIS*'s face. He holds it there.*]

I'm going to hell for doing this.

LOUIS Big deal. You think it could be any worse than New York City?

[*He puts his hand on* JOE*'s hand. He takes* JOE*'s hand away from his face, holds it for a moment, then.*] Come on.

JOE Where?

LOUIS Home. With me.

JOE This makes no sense. I mean I don't know you.

LOUIS Likewise.

JOE And what you do know about me you don't like.

LOUIS The Republican stuff?

JOE Yeah, well for starters.

LOUIS I don't not like that. I *hate* that.

JOE So why on earth should we . . .

[LOUIS *goes to* JOE *and kisses him.*]

LOUIS Strange bedfellows. I don't know. I never made it with one of the damned before.

I would really rather not have to spend tonight alone.

JOE I'm a pretty terrible person, Louis.

LOUIS Lou.

JOE No, I really really am. I don't think I deserve being loved.

LOUIS There? See? We already have a lot in common.

[LOUIS *stands, begins to walk away. He turns, looks back at* JOE. JOE *follows. They exit.*]

[PRIOR *listens. At first no sound, then once again, the sound of beating wings, frighteningly near.*]

PRIOR That sound, that sound, it. . . . What is that, like birds or something, like a *really* big bird, I'm frightened, I . . . no, no fear, find the anger, find the . . . anger, my blood is clean, my brain is fine, I can handle pressure, I am a gay man and I am used to pressure, to trouble, I am tough and strong and. . . . Oh. Oh my goodness. I . . . [*He is washed over by an intense sexual feeling.*] Ooohhhh. . . . I'm hot, I'm . . . so . . . aw Jeez what is going on here I . . . must have a fever I . . .

[*The bedside lamp flickers wildly as the bed begins to roll forward and back. There is a deep bass creaking and groaning from the bedroom ceiling, like the timbers of a ship under immense stress, and from above a fine rain of plaster dust.*]

PRIOR OH!

PLEASE, OH PLEASE! Something's coming in here, I'm scared, I don't like this at all, something's approaching and I . . . OH!

[*There is a great blaze of triumphal music, heralding. The light turns an extraordinary harsh, cold, pale blue, then a rich, brilliant warm golden color, then a hot, bilious green, and then finally a spectacular royal purple. Then silence.*]

PRIOR [*an awestruck whisper*] God almighty . . .
Very Steven Spielberg.[7]

[*A sound, like a plummeting meteor, tears down from very, very far above the earth, hurtling at an incredible velocity towards the bedroom; the light seems to be sucked out of the room as the projectile approaches; as the room reaches darkness, we hear a terrifying CRASH as something immense strikes earth; the whole building shudders and a part of the bedroom ceiling, lots of plaster and lathe and wiring, crashes to the floor. And then in a shower of unearthly white light, spreading great opalescent gray-silver wings, the Angel descends into the room and floats above the bed.*]

ANGEL

Greetings, Prophet;
The Great Work begins:
The Messenger has arrived.

[*Blackout.*]

End of Part One.

7. An American film director (b. 1947), known for his use of special effects in such hits as *Close Encounters of the Third Kind* (1977), *Raiders of the Lost Ark* (1981), and *E.T.: The Extraterrestrial* (1982).

SUZAN-LORI PARKS

b. 1964

WHEN Suzan-Lori Parks was a senior at Mount Holyoke College, she wrote her first play, *The Sinner's Place.* Because, as Parks later recalled, the play's setting consisted of "a lot of dirt on stage which was being dug at," the Theater Department rejected it for production. By the time she was awarded a Pulitzer Prize in 2002 for her play *Topdog/Underdog,* however, Parks's fascination with digging—turning over the topsoil of cultural myths, sifting through the artifacts of history, unearthing the buried voices of African Americans within history—had established her as one of the American theater's foremost archaeologists. "The responsibility of a writer," the novelist James Baldwin once remarked, "is to excavate the experience of the people who produced him." Deeply concerned with forebears and inheritances, Parks's drama uncovers this experience by examining its traces and absences in the American historical imagination. "Because so much of African American history has been unrecorded, dismembered, washed out," Parks writes, "one of my tasks as playwright is to—through literature and the special strange relationship between theater and real-life—locate the ancestral burial ground, dig for bones, find bones, hear the bones sing, write it down." By "remembering" history in the double sense of retrieving and remaking it, Parks offers new theatrical possibilities for staging the dialogue between past, present, and future. Innovative (often challenging) in language, dramatic structure, and performance, her drama remains among the most startlingly original in the contemporary American theater.

Suzan-Lori Parks was born in Fort Knox, Kentucky. The daughter of an Army colonel, she moved frequently as a child and considered a number of places home: Texas, California, North Carolina, Maryland, Vermont, and Germany, where she attended German schools rather than those for the children of American military personnel. This experience of changing location—of moving between places with divergent regional and national histories and of negotiating language differences—clearly contributed to her interest in language and in the relationships between geography, history, and identity. As an undergraduate at Mount Holyoke she took a short story writing class with James Baldwin; after she gave an animated in-class reading of one of her stories, he suggested that she consider playwriting. The turn to drama was a natural one: as she explained in a 2000 interview, she felt while writing short stories that her characters were in the room with her, "standing right behind me, talking. Not telling the story, but acting it out—doing it." Despite the Theater Department's rejection of *The Sinner's Place,* Parks decided to pursue her interest in dramatic writing. Encouraged by one of her English professors, she read the plays of two pioneering African American women playwrights: Adrienne Kennedy, whose *Funnyhouse of a Negro* (1962) dramatized its protagonist's haunted consciousness on a dreamlike stage reminiscent of the stages of AUGUST STRINDBERG and JEAN GENET, and Ntozake Shange, who has explored the relationship of drama, poetry, dance, and female African American identity in *for colored girls who have considered suicide / when the rainbow is enuf* (1975) and other plays. After graduating from college in 1985 with majors in English and German, Parks studied acting for a year in London.

Upon her return to the United States, Parks quickly established herself as a playwright of note. *Betting on the Dust Commander* (1987) was produced in New York, as was *Imperceptible Mutabilities in the Third Kingdom* (1989). The latter play received an Obie (Off-Broadway) Award for Best New American Play and was widely praised by critics; indeed, after seeing the play, Mel Gussow of the *New York Times* called Parks "the year's most promising playwright." *The Death of the Last Black Man in the Whole Entire World* opened the following year at the same theater, and *Devotees in the Garden of Love* was produced at the Humana Festival in Louisville in 1992. Parks's next drama, ***THE AMERICA PLAY***, was given workshop productions in Washington and Dallas in 1993 before opening at the Yale Repertory Theatre and the New York Public Theater in 1994. In 1996, her play *Venus*—based on the life of Saartjie Baartman, a Khoisan African woman who, because of her large buttocks, was exhibited in the early 1800s in London and Paris as the "Hottentot Venus"—was produced at the Public Theatre in New York and received an Obie Award for Playwriting. *In the Blood* was produced in New York in 1999, and *Fucking A* premiered in Houston in 2000; both plays were inspired by Nathaniel Hawthorne's novel *The Scarlet Letter* (1850). The Pulitzer Prize–winning *Topdog/Underdog*, which features two brothers named Lincoln and Booth, opened at the Public Theater in New York in 2001 and was subsequently taken to Broadway. Parks's most ambitious theatrical project began in 2002, when the playwright decided to write one play every day for a year. The completed plays—some less than a page in length, others considerably longer—were performed by theater groups across the United States in 2006–07 as part of a cycle titled *365 Days/365 Plays*. Parks has also written the screenplay for the film *Girl 6* (1996, directed by Spike Lee) and an adaptation of Zora Neale Hurston's 1937 novel *Their Eyes Were Watching God*, which was televised in 2005. Parks's novel *Getting Mother's Body* was published in 2003.

Intricate (sometimes dense) in texture and meaning, Parks's plays have received widespread attention for their distinctive, highly theatricalized conception of language, character, and dramatic form. As befits a dramatist whose favorite writers include the modernists William Faulkner, Virginia Woolf, and James Joyce, Parks makes intricate, highly self-conscious use of the acoustic and semantic qualities of dramatic speech. Words, Parks insists, are "spells in our mouths." Driven by the cadences, syntax, and word forms of African American dialect, distinguished by frequent wordplay and by multiple meanings, the language of Parks's drama reflects her characters' complex lives and inheritance. When one of the characters in *Imperceptible Mutabilities* says "Last night I dreamed of where I comed from. But where I comed from diduhnt look like nowhere like I been," his words evoke a collective experience of migration, relocation, and lost origins. How do contemporary African Americans, descendants of those who endured the Middle Passage in the holds of slave ships, bridge the gap between Africa and North America, between the present and the history that informs it? Like the words that Parks uses, with their "thrilling histories" and "fabulous etymologies," the characters who people her plays are indelibly marked by history. They bear names such as those in *Death of the Last Black Man in the Whole Entire World:* Black Man with Watermelon, Yes and Greens Black-Eyed Peas Cornbread, And Bigger and Bigger and Bigger, Before Columbus, and Queen-then-Pharaoh-Hatshepsut. Drawing together racial stereotypes, African history, soul food, and literary references (the character And Bigger and Bigger and Bigger, for example, is named after Bigger Thomas, the protagonist of Richard Wright's 1940 novel *Native*

Son), these figures embody many of the ways in which black Americans have been represented in American history and culture.

While Parks's dramatic characters are rooted in real lives and relationships, they also function as improvised meditations, or riffs, on cultural themes and images. Not surprisingly, music—in the form of jazz, classical music, opera, and hip-hop—has played an important role in the language and structure of Parks's drama. Rejecting the linear form of traditional drama, in which action proceeds with a clear beginning, middle, and end, Parks experiments with alternative ways of structuring dramatic incidents. One of her signature devices is "repetition and revision"—the technique, popular with jazz composers and musicians (and echoing the cadence of African American oral traditions, including preaching), of repeating a phrase over and over again while varying it slightly each time. In Parks's drama, words, exchanges, and situations return with hypnotic regularity, establishing connections and counterpoints that build with a logic as much circular as linear. "Characters refigure their words," Parks declares, "and through a refiguring of language show us that they are experiencing their situation anew." The phrase that supplies the title of *The Death of the Last Black Man in the Whole Entire World,* for instance, is spoken at a number of points in the play, and this repetition mirrors that of the action, in which the central protagonist—representing one black man and every black man—is murdered over and over again. Only in the burial scene that ends the play does this repetitive cycle in African American history attain closure.

Repetition, doubling, and, again, the remembering of history are central to *The America Play,* Parks's most frequently performed work. The play is set in a "great hole" somewhere in the American West, "an exact replica" (the stage direction indicates) "of the Great Hole of History," a fictional theme park located back East where a parade of historical figures emerge and march by for the audience's entertainment. The play's protagonist, an African American man identified by his stage name, The Foundling Father, was so entranced with the marvels of history when he visited the Great Park on his honeymoon that he became determined to re-create it. After being told that he resembled Abraham Lincoln—the two "were dead ringers, more or less"—he took to reciting speeches by the famous president in costume. When someone observed that "he played Lincoln so well that he ought to be shot," The Foundling Father devised just such an act: customers pay a penny to shoot him as he sits in Ford's Theater. One after another, they select a pistol, stand in position, and, after shooting him in the head, jump to the stage yelling "Thus to the Tyrants!" or other exclamations attributed to Lincoln's assassin John Wilkes Booth

A nineteenth-century lithograph by Currier and Ives showing the assassination of Lincoln in Ford's Theatre.

(and others). The assassination is replayed over and over again while The Foundling Father recounts to the play's audience his past and his peculiar vocation.

All history repeats itself, Karl Marx famously observed: "the first time as tragedy, the second time as farce." But in an age of historical theme parks, Revolutionary and Civil War reenactments, and interactive museums (such as the Abraham Lincoln Presidential Museum in Springfield, Illinois, which opened in 2005), history is just as likely to repeat itself as theater. In *The America Play,* Parks explores the many ways in which American history—the images, texts, performances, commemorations with which we tell the story of our collective past—writes itself into the present. The Foundling Father is flanked by a pasteboard cutout and bust of Lincoln, to which he frequently gestures; he collects the pennies that bear Lincoln's profile; and he carries with him the props by which the legendary president is identified in the popular imagination: black coat, stovepipe hat, and an assortment of beards (including a blond one, which he rarely wears because it undermines the illusion). The Foundling Father quotes from the Gettysburg Address and retells the events of the fateful night in Ford's Theater, though the account he provides is based as much on tradition and hearsay as historical fact. Parks plays with the idea of historical accuracy in her footnotes to the play, which include humorous or speculative information (including a line that Mary Todd Lincoln "might have said . . . that night") as well as documented facts. In a play that features an actor impersonating a historical figure, a replay of this performance on television (in the play's second act), and scenes from the play that Lincoln was watching (*Our American Cousin* [1858] by Tom Taylor), history becomes the site of multiple performances and competing imitations. At times, original and copy seem indistinguishable from one another. Even the Great Hole of History reappears as a theme park somewhere else.

With its parade of well-known historical figures and deeds, the Great Hole provides a spectacle of American history as it has traditionally circulated and been known. But this hole in the ground also signals its absences and elisions. Reversing the nineteenth-century tradition of blackface—white actors blackening their faces in order to play African American characters—The Foundling Father's impersonation of Abraham Lincoln foregrounds the absence or marginalization of African Americans from this history. As he refers to himself as the "Lesser Known," in contrast to the "Great Man," The Foundling Father reflects on the discrepancy between the latter's fame and his own anonymity. A "digger" by trade, he discovers a more elevated calling by following in the Great Man's footsteps. Yet the reflected glory that he acquires by impersonating Lincoln only underscores the historical invisibility to which his racial identity has otherwise consigned him. Lincoln may have freed the slaves—but the idea of America that he represents has largely excluded

Reggie Montgomery, seated, as the Foundling Father, and Adriane Lenox, as a woman customer, in the 1993 premiere production of *The America Play* at the Yale Repertory Theatre.

African Americans from its originating myths, as well as from the prevailing national identity. The Foundling Father may assume the mantle of one of his country's forefathers—but as Parks's play on his name signifies, his is an illegitimate inheritance (a *foundling* is a child of unknown parentage). When one of his customers, a woman, yells "LIES!" after jumping to the stage, her accusation strikes at the heart of the national myth—the idea of America as "a new nation, conceived in Liberty, and dedicated to the proposition that all men are created equal"—that Lincoln represents.

The search for (fore)fathers in *The America Play* extends into the play's second act, set years later, when The Foundling Father's wife Lucy and son Brazil look for traces of him after his death. Marked by the rituals of grief, this act is pervaded with a sense of mourning, yet it also conveys a tone of affirmation. The Foundling Father may have "fall[en] in love with the wrong person, fall[en] in love with the wrong dream" (as Parks suggests), but his deconstructive performance of American history has been celebratory as well. By showing this history to itself through the mirror of blackness, he has claimed a space, however small, in the performance of national identity. S.G.

The America Play

THE ROLES

Act 1: THE FOUNDLING FATHER, AS ABRAHAM LINCOLN
A VARIETY OF VISITORS

Act 2: LUCY
BRAZIL
THE FOUNDLING FATHER, AS ABRAHAM LINCOLN
2 ACTORS
The Visitors in Act 1 are played by the 2 Actors who assume the roles in the passages from *Our American Cousin* in Act 2.

Place A great hole. In the middle of nowhere. The hole is an exact replica of The Great Hole of History.

SYNOPSIS OF ACTS AND SCENES

Act 1: Lincoln Act
Act 2: The Hall of Wonders

A. Big Bang
B. Echo
C. Archeology
D. Echo
E. Spadework
F. Echo
G. The Great Beyond

Brackets in the text indicate optional cuts for production.

In the beginning, all the world was America.
—JOHN LOCKE[1]

1. English philosopher and political theorist (1632–1704); the quotation is from *Two Treatises of Government* (1689).

Act 1: Lincoln Act

A great hole. In the middle of nowhere. The hole is an exact replica of the Great Hole of History.

THE FOUNDLING FATHER AS ABRAHAM LINCOLN "To stop too fearful and too faint to go."[2]

[*Rest.*[3]]

"He digged the hole and the whole held him."

[*Rest.*]

"I cannot dig, to beg I am ashamed."[4]

[*Rest.*]

"He went to the theatre but home went she."[5]

[*Rest.*]

Goatee. Goatee. What he sported when he died. Its not my favorite.

[*Rest.*]

"He digged the hole and the whole held him." Huh.

[*Rest.*]

There was once a man who was told that he bore a strong resemblance to Abraham Lincoln.[6] He was tall and thinly built just like the Great Man. His legs were the longer part just like the Great Mans legs. His hands and feet were large as the Great Mans were large. The Lesser Known had several beards which he carried around in a box. The beards were his although he himself had not grown them on his face but since he'd secretly bought the hairs from his barber and arranged their beard shapes and since the procurement and upkeep of his beards took so much work he figured that the beards were completely his. Were as authentic as he was, so to speak. His beard box was of cherry wood and lined with purple velvet. He had the initials "A.L." tooled in gold on the lid.

[*Rest.*]

While the Great Mans livelihood kept him in Big Town the Lesser Knowns work kept him in Small Town. The Great Man by trade was a President. The Lesser Known was a Digger by trade. From a family of Diggers. Digged graves. He was known in Small Town to dig his graves quickly and neatly. This brought him a steady business.

[*Rest.*]

2. An example of chiasmus, by Oliver Goldsmith, cited under "chiasmus" in *Webster's Ninth New Collegiate Dictionary* (Springfield, MA: Merriam-Webster, Inc., 1983) p. 232. Notes 4 and 5 also refer to examples of chiasmus [Parks's note]. *Chiasmus:* the syntactic inversion of the second of two parallel clauses (a rhetorical figure). The example is from "The Traveller; or, A Prospect of Society" (1794), by Goldsmith (ca. 1730–1774), an Irish-born novelist, poet, and playwright.

3. Pause.

4. *A Dictionary of Modern English Usage,* H. W. Fowler (New York: Oxford University Press, 1983) p. 86 [Parks's note]. The quotation is from Luke 16.3.

5. *The New American Heritage Dictionary of the English Language,* William Morris, ed. (Boston: Houghton Mifflin Co., 1981) p. 232 [Parks's note].

6. The sixteenth president of the United States (1809–1865; president, 1861–65), a lawyer and legislator from Illinois who was born in backwoods Kentucky; he has been acclaimed for his leadership during the Civil War (1861–65) and for his role in ending slavery.

A wink to Mr. Lincolns pasteboard cutout. [*Winks at Lincoln's pasteboard cutout.*]

[*Rest.*]

It would be helpful to our story if when the Great Man died in death he were to meet the Lesser Known. It would be helpful to our story if, say, the Lesser Known were summoned to Big Town by the Great Mans wife: "*Emergency* oh, *Emergency,* please put the Great Man in the ground"[7] (they say the Great Mans wife was given to hysterics: one young son dead others sickly:[8] even the Great Man couldnt save them: a war on then off and surrendered to: "Play Dixie I always liked that song":[9] the brother against the brother: a new nation all conceived and ready to be hatched: the Great Man takes to guffawing guffawing at thin jokes in bad plays: "You sockdologizing old man-trap!"[1] haw haw haw because he wants so very badly to laugh at something and one moment guffawing and the next moment the Great Man is gunned down. In his rocker. "Useless Useless."[2] And there were bills to pay.) "*Emergency,* oh *Emergency* please put the Great Man in the ground."

[*Rest.*]

It is said that the Great Mans wife did call out and it is said that the Lesser Known would [sneak away from his digging and stand behind a tree where he couldnt be seen or get up and] leave his wife and child after the blessing had been said and [the meat carved during the distribution of the vegetables it is said that he would leave his wife and his child and] standing in the kitchen or sometimes out in the yard [between the right angles of the house] stand out there where he couldnt be seen standing with his ear cocked. "*Emergency,* oh *Emergency,* please put the Great Man in the ground."

[*Rest.*]

It would help if she had called out and if he had been summoned been given a ticket all bought and paid for and boarded a train in his look-alike black frock coat bought on time and already exhausted. Ridiculous. If he had been summoned. [Been summoned between the meat and the vegetables and boarded a train to Big Town where he would line up and gawk at

7. Possibly the words of Mary Todd Lincoln [1818–1882] after the death of her husband [Parks's note].

8. Of the Lincolns' four sons—Robert (1843–1926), Edward (1846–1850), William (1850–1862), and Thomas, nicknamed Tad (1853–1871)—only Robert survived into adulthood. Mary Todd Lincoln has often been described as mentally unstable.

9. At the end of the Civil War, President Lincoln told his troops to play "Dixie," the song of the South, in tribute to the Confederacy [Parks's note]. The song was published in 1860 by the Ohio-born Daniel Decatur Emmett, who wrote songs for his blackface minstrel troupe, but his claim of authorship is disputed.

1. A very funny line from the play *Our American Cousin.* As the audience roared with laughter, Booth entered Lincoln's box and shot him dead [Parks's note]. *Our American Cousin* (1858), a comedy by the English dramatist and writer Tom Taylor. John Wilkes Booth (1838–1865), a renowned Shakespearean actor and a Southern sympathizer who led the conspiracy to assassinate Lincoln as he attended a performance, less than a week after the Civil War ended.

2. The last words of President Lincoln's assassin, John Wilkes Booth [Parks's note]. After shooting Lincoln, Booth leaped to the stage and broke his leg, but escaped on horseback. After soldiers and detectives found him hiding in a barn in Virginia, about 75 miles southwest of Washington, he either was shot or shot himself and died shortly thereafter.

the Great Mans corpse along with the rest of them.[3]] But none of this was meant to be.

[*Rest.*]

A nod to the bust of Mr. Lincoln. [*Nods to the bust of Lincoln.*] But none of this was meant to be. For the Great Man had been murdered long before the Lesser Known had been born. How uhboutthat. [So that any calling that had been done he couldnt hear, any summoning he had hoped for he couldnt answer but somehow not even unheard and unanswered because he hadnt even been there] although you should note that he talked about the murder and the mourning that followed as if he'd been called away on business at the time and because of the business had missed it. Living regretting he hadnt arrived sooner. Being told from birth practically that he and the Great Man were dead ringers, more or less, and knowing that he, if he had been in the slightest vicinity back then, would have had at least a chance at the great honor of digging the Great Mans grave.

[*Rest.*]

This beard I wear for the holidays. I got shoes to match. Rarely wear em together. It's a little *much.*

[*Rest.*]

[His son named in a fit of meanspirit after the bad joke about fancy nuts[4] and old mens toes his son looked like a nobody. Not Mr. Lincoln or the father or the mother either for that matter although the father had assumed the superiority of his own blood and hadnt really expected the mother to exert any influence.]

[*Rest.*]

Sunday. Always slow on Sunday. I'll get thuh shoes. Youll see. A wink to Mr. Lincolns pasteboard cutout. [*Winks at Lincoln's cutout.*]

[*Rest.*]

Everyone who has ever walked the earth has a shape around which their entire lives and their posterity shapes itself. The Great Man had his log cabin into which he was born, the distance between the cabin and Big Town multiplied by the half-life, the staying power of his words and image, being the true measurement of the Great Mans stature. The Lesser Known had a favorite hole. A chasm, really. Not a hole he had digged but one he'd visited. Long before the son was born. When he and his Lucy were newly wedded. Lucy kept secrets for the dead. And they figured what with his digging and her Confidence work[5] they could build a mourning business. The son would be a weeper.[6] Such a long time uhgo. So long uhgo. When he and his Lucy were newly wedded and looking for some postnuptial excitement: A Big Hole. A theme park. With historical parades. The size of the hole itself was enough to impress any Digger but it was the Historicity of the place the order and beauty of the pageants which marched by them the Greats on parade in front of them. From the sidelines he'd be calling "Ohwayohwhyohwayoh" and "Hello" and waving and saluting. The Hole

3. Thousands viewed Lincoln's body lying in state in the U.S. Capitol, and thousands more watched the train bearing him home to Springfield, Illinois, where he was buried.

4. That is, Brazil nuts, which were long known in some regions of the United States as "nigger toes."

5. That is, her work as someone entrusted with confidential communications.

6. A hired mourner.

and its Historicity and the part he played in it all gave a shape to the life and posterity of the Lesser Known that he could never shake.

[*Rest.*]

Here they are. I wont put them on. I'll just hold them up. See. Too much. Told ya. [Much much later when the Lesser Known had made a name for himself he began to record his own movements. He hoped he'd be of interest to posterity. As in the Great Mans footsteps.]

[*Rest.*]

Traveling home again from the honeymoon at the Big Hole riding the train with his Lucy: wife beside him the Reconstructed Historicities he has witnessed continue to march before him in his minds eye as they had at the Hole. Cannons wicks were lit and the rockets did blare and the enemy was slain and lay stretched out and smoldering for dead and rose up again to take their bows. On the way home again the histories paraded again on past him although it wasnt on past him at all it wasnt something he could expect but again like Lincolns life not "on past" but *past. Behind him.* Like an echo in his head.

[*Rest.*]

When he got home again he began to hear the summoning. At first they thought it only an echo. Memories sometimes stuck like that and he and his Lucy had both seen visions. But after a while it only called to him. And it became louder not softer but louder louder as if he were moving toward it.

[*Rest.*]

This is my fancy beard. Yellow. Mr. Lincolns hair was dark so I dont wear it much. If you deviate too much they wont get their pleasure. Thats my experience. Some inconsistencies are perpetuatable because theyre good for business. But not the yellow beard. Its just my fancy. Every once and a while. Of course, his hair was dark.

[*Rest.*]

The Lesser Known left his wife and child and went out West finally. [Between the meat and the vegetables. A monumentous journey. Enduring all the elements. Without a friend in the world. And the beasts of the forest took him in. He got there and he got his plot he staked his claim he tried his hand at his own Big Hole.] As it had been back East everywhere out West he went people remarked on his likeness to Lincoln. How, in a limited sort of way, taking into account of course his natural God-given limitations, how he was identical to the Great Man in gait and manner how his legs were long and torso short. The Lesser Known had by this time taken to wearing a false wart on his cheek in remembrance of the Great Mans wart. When the Westerners noted his wart they pronounced the 2 men in virtual twinship.

[*Rest.*]

Goatee. Huh. Goatee.

[*Rest.*]

"He digged the Hole and the Whole held him."

[*Rest.*]

"I cannot dig, to beg I am ashamed."

[*Rest.*]

The Lesser Known had under his belt a few of the Great Mans words and after a day of digging, in the evenings, would stand in his hole reciting. But the Lesser Known was a curiosity at best. None of those who spoke of his virtual twinship with greatness would actually pay money to watch him be that greatness. One day he tacked up posters inviting them to come and throw old food at him while he spoke. This was a moderate success. People began to save their old food "for Mr. Lincoln" they said. He took to traveling playing small towns. Made money. And when someone remarked that he played Lincoln so well that he ought to be shot, it was as if the Great Mans footsteps had been suddenly revealed:

[*Rest.*]

The Lesser Known returned to his hole and, instead of speeching, his act would now consist of a single chair, a rocker, in a dark box. The public was invited to pay a penny, choose from the selection of provided pistols, enter the darkened box and "Shoot Mr. Lincoln." The Lesser Known became famous overnight.

[A MAN, *as John Wilkes* Booth, *enters. He takes a gun and "stands in position": at the left side of* THE FOUNDLING FATHER, *as Abraham* LINCOLN, *pointing the gun at* THE FOUNDLING FATHER*'s head*]

A MAN Ready.

THE FOUNDLING FATHER Haw Haw Haw Haw

[*Rest.*]

HAW HAW HAW HAW

[BOOTH *shoots.* LINCOLN *"slumps in his chair."* BOOTH *jumps.*]

A MAN [*theatrically*] "Thus to the tyrants!"[7]

[*Rest.*]

Hhhh. [*Exits.*]

THE FOUNDLING FATHER Most of them do that, thuh "Thus to the tyrants!"—what they say the killer said. "Thus to the tyrants!" The killer was also heard to say "The South is avenged!"[8] Sometimes they yell that.

[A *man, the same man as before, enters again, again as John Wilkes* Booth. *He takes a gun and "stands in position": at the left side of* THE FOUNDLING FATHER, *as Abraham* LINCOLN, *pointing the gun at* THE FOUNDLING FATHER*'s head.*]

A MAN Ready.

THE FOUNDLING FATHER Haw Haw Haw Haw

[*Rest.*]

HAW HAW HAW HAW

[BOOTH *shoots.* LINCOLN *"slumps in his chair."* BOOTH *jumps.*]

A MAN [*theatrically*] "The South is avenged!"

[*Rest.*]

7. Or "Sic semper tyrannis." Purportedly, Booth's words after he slew Lincoln and leapt from the presidential box to the stage of Ford's Theatre in Washington, D.C. on 14 April 1865, not only killing the President but also interrupting a performance of *Our American Cousin,* starring Miss Laura Keene [Parks's note]. *Sic semper tyrannis:* Thus always to tyrants (Latin), adopted in 1776 as the state motto of Virginia (whose capital, Richmond, became the capital of the Confederacy). Keene (ca. 1826–1873), a London-born actress who became well-known in the United States on the stage and as a theater manager.

8. Allegedly, Booth's words [Parks's note].

Hhhh.

[*Rest.*]

Thank you.

THE FOUNDLING FATHER Pleasures mine.

A MAN Till next week.

THE FOUNDLING FATHER Till next week.

[A MAN *exits.*]

THE FOUNDLING FATHER Comes once a week that one. Always chooses the Derringer[9] although we've got several styles he always chooses the Derringer. Always "The tyrants" and then "The South avenged." The ones who choose the Derringer are the ones for History. He's one for History. As it Used to Be. Never wavers. No frills. By the book. Nothing excessive.

[*Rest.*]

A nod to Mr. Lincolns bust. [*Nods to Lincoln's bust.*]

[*Rest.*]

I'll wear this one. He sported this style in the early war years. Years of uncertainty. When he didnt know if the war was right when it could be said he didnt always know which side he was on not because he was a stupid man but because it was sometimes not 2 different sides at all but one great side surging toward something beyond either Northern or Southern. A beard of uncertainty. The Lesser Known meanwhile living his life long after all this had happened and not knowing much about it until he was much older [(as a boy "The Civil War" was an afterschool game and his folks didnt mention the Great Mans murder for fear of frightening him)] knew only that he was a dead ringer in a family of Diggers and that he wanted to grow and have others think of him and remove their hats and touch their hearts and look up into the heavens and say something about the freeing of the slaves. That is, he wanted to make a great impression as he understood Mr. Lincoln to have made.

[*Rest.*]

And so in his youth the Lesser Known familiarized himself with all aspects of the Great Mans existence. What interested the Lesser Known most was the murder and what was most captivating about the murder was the 20 feet—

[A WOMAN, *as* BOOTH, *enters.*]

A WOMAN Excuse me.

THE FOUNDLING FATHER Not at all.

[A WOMAN, *as* BOOTH, *"stands in position."*]

THE FOUNDLING FATHER Haw Haw Haw Haw

[*Rest.*]

HAW HAW HAW HAW

[BOOTH *shoots.* LINCOLN *"slumps in his chair."* BOOTH *jumps.*]

A WOMAN "Strike the tent."[1] [*Exits.*]

9. A small, easily concealed pistol with a large bore, invented ca. 1852 by the American gunsmith Henry Deringer; Booth used a derringer to shoot Lincoln in the back of the head.

1. The last words of General Robert E. Lee [1807–1870], Commander of the Confederate Army [Parks's note].

THE FOUNDLING FATHER What interested the Lesser Known most about the Great Mans murder was the 20 feet which separated the presidents box from the stage. In the presidents box sat the president his wife and their 2 friends.[2] On the stage that night was *Our American Cousin* starring Miss Laura Keene. The plot of this play is of little consequence to our story. Suffice it to say that it was thinly comedic and somewhere in the 3rd Act a man holds a gun to his head—something about despair—

[*Rest.*]

Ladies and Gentlemen: *Our American Cousin*—

[B WOMAN, *as* BOOTH, *enters. She "stands in position."*]

B WOMAN Go ahead.

THE FOUNDLING FATHER Haw Haw Haw Haw

[*Rest.*]

HAW HAW HAW HAW

[BOOTH *shoots.* LINCOLN *"slumps in his chair."* BOOTH *jumps.*]

B WOMAN [*rest*] LIES!

[*Rest.*]

L I I I I I I I I I I I I I I I I I I I I I I I I I I I I E S !

[*Rest.*]

L I I I I I I I I I I I I I I I I I I I A R R R R R R R R R R R R R R R R S !

[*Rest.*]

Lies.

[*Rest. Exits. Reenters. Steps downstage. Rest.*]

LIES!

[*Rest.*]

L I I I I I I I I I I I I I I I I I I I I I I I I I I I I E S !

[*Rest.*]

L I I I I I I I I I I I I I I I I I I I A R R R R R R R R R R R R R R R R S !

[*Rest.*]

Lies.

[*Rest. Exits.*]

THE FOUNDLING FATHER [*rest*] I think I'll wear the yellow beard. Variety. Works like uh tonic.

[*Rest.*]

Some inaccuracies are good for business. Take the stovepipe hat! Never really worn indoors but people dont like their Lincoln hatless.

[*Rest.*]

Mr. Lincoln my apologies. [*Nods to the bust and winks to the cutout.*]

[*Rest.*]

[Blonde. Not bad if you like a stretch. Hmmm. Let us pretend for a moment that our beloved Mr. Lincoln was a blonde. "The sun on his fair hair looked like the sun itself."[3]—. Now. What interested our Mr. Lesser Known most was those feet between where the Great *Blonde* Man sat, in

2. Clara Harris (1845–1883), the daughter of a U.S. senator, and her fiancée, Major Henry Rathbone (1837–1911).

3. From "The Sun," a composition by The Foundling Father, unpublished [Parks's note].

his rocker, the stage, the time it took the murderer to cross that expanse, and how the murderer crossed it. He jumped. Broke his leg in the jumping. It was said that the Great Mans wife then began to scream. (She was given to hysterics several years afterward in fact declared insane did you know she ran around Big Town poor desperate for money trying to sell her clothing? On that sad night she begged her servant: "Bring in Taddy, Father will speak to Taddy."[4] But Father died instead unconscious. And she went mad from grief. Off her rocker. Mad Mary claims she hears her dead men. Summoning. The older son, Robert, he locked her up.[5] "*Emergency,* oh, *Emergency* please put the Great Man in the ground.")

[*Enter* B MAN, *as* BOOTH. *He "stands in position."*]

THE FOUNDLING FATHER Haw Haw Haw Haw

[*Rest.*]

HAW HAW HAW HAW

[BOOTH *shoots.* LINCOLN *"slumps in his chair."* BOOTH *jumps.*]

B MAN "Now he belongs to the ages."[6]

[*Rest.*]

Blonde?

THE FOUNDLING FATHER (I only talk with the regulars.)

B MAN He wasnt blonde. [*Exits.*]

THE FOUNDLING FATHER A slight deafness in this ear other than that there are no side effects.

[*Rest.*]

Hhh. Clean-shaven for a while. The face needs air. Clean-shaven as in his youth. When he met his Mary. —. Hhh. Blonde.

[*Rest.*]

6 feet under is a long way to go. Imagine. When the Lesser Known left to find his way out West he figured he had dug over 7 hundred and 23 graves. 7 hundred and 23. Excluding his Big Hole. Excluding the hundreds of shallow holes he later digs the hundreds of shallow holes he'll use to bury his faux-historical knickknacks when he finally quits this business. Not including those. 7 hundred and 23 graves.

[C MAN *and* C WOMAN *enter.*]

C MAN You allow 2 at once?

THE FOUNDLING FATHER

[*Rest.*]

C WOMAN We're just married. You know: newlyweds. We hope you dont mind. Us both at once.

THE FOUNDLING FATHER

[*Rest.*]

4. Mary Todd Lincoln, wanting her dying husband to speak to their son Tad, might have said this that night [Parks's note]. After he was shot, Lincoln was carried to a home across the street from the theater; he died the next morning.

5. In 1875, Robert had his mother committed to an insane asylum, but she was later declared legally competent. *Hears her dead men:* from the 1850s onward, Mary Todd Lincoln became increasingly interested in spiritualism, or communication with the dead (usually attempted with the help of a medium).

6. The words of Secretary of War Edwin Stanton [1814–1869], as Lincoln died [Parks's note].

C MAN We're just married.

C WOMAN Newlyweds.

THE FOUNDLING FATHER

[*Rest.*]

[*Rest.*]

[*They "stand in position." Both hold one gun.*]

C MAN AND C WOMAN Shoot.

THE FOUNDLING FATHER Haw Haw Haw Haw

[*Rest.*]

HAW HAW HAW HAW

[*Rest.*]

[*Rest.*]

HAW HAW HAW HAW

[*They shoot.* LINCOLN *"slumps in his chair." They jump.*]

C MAN Go on.

C WOMAN [*theatrically*] "Theyve killed the president!"[7]

[*Rest. They exit.*]

THE FOUNDLING FATHER Theyll have children and theyll bring their children here. A slight deafness in this ear other than that there are no side effects. Little ringing in the ears. Slight deafness. I cant complain.

[*Rest.*]

The passage of time. The crossing of space. [The Lesser Known recorded his every movement.] He'd hoped he'd be of interest in his posterity. [Once again riding in the Great Mans footsteps.] A nod to the presidents bust. [*Nods.*]

[*Rest.*]

[*Rest.*]

The Great Man lived in the past that is was an inhabitant of time immemorial and the Lesser Known out West alive a resident of the present. And the Great Mans deeds had transpired during the life of the Great Man somewhere in past-land that is somewhere "back there" and all this while the Lesser Known digging his holes bearing the burden of his resemblance all the while trying somehow to equal the Great Man in stature, word and deed going forward with his lesser life trying somehow to follow in the Great Mans footsteps footsteps that were of course behind him. The Lesser Known trying somehow to catch up to the Great Man all this while and maybe running too fast in the wrong direction. Which is to say that maybe the Great Man had to catch him. Hhhh. Ridiculous.

[*Rest.*]

Full fringe. The way he appears on the money.

[*Rest.*]

A wink to Mr. Lincolns pasteboard cutout. A nod to Mr. Lincolns bust.

[*Rest. Time passes. Rest.*]

7. The words of Mary Todd, just after Lincoln was shot [Parks's note].

When someone remarked that he played Lincoln so well that he ought to be shot it was as if the Great Mans footsteps had been suddenly revealed: instead of making speeches his act would now consist of a single chair, a rocker, in a dark box. The public was cordially invited to pay a penny, choose from a selection of provided pistols enter the darkened box and "Shoot Mr. Lincoln." The Lesser Known became famous overnight.

[A MAN, *as John Wilkes* BOOTH, *enters. He takes a gun and "stands in position": at the left side of* THE FOUNDLING FATHER, *as Abraham* LINCOLN, *pointing the gun at* THE FOUNDLING FATHER*'s head.*]

THE FOUNDLING FATHER Mmm. Like clockwork.

A MAN Ready.

THE FOUNDLING FATHER Haw Haw Haw Haw

[*Rest.*]

HAW HAW HAW HAW

[BOOTH *shoots.* LINCOLN *"slumps in his chair."* BOOTH *jumps.*]

A MAN [*theatrically*] "Thus to the tyrants!"

[*Rest.*]

Hhhh.

LINCOLN

BOOTH

LINCOLN

BOOTH

LINCOLN

BOOTH

LINCOLN

BOOTH

LINCOLN[8]

[BOOTH *jumps.*]

A MAN [*theatrically*] "The South is avenged!"

[*Rest.*]

Hhhh.

[*Rest.*]

Thank you.

THE FOUNDLING FATHER Pleasures mine.

A MAN Next week then. [*Exits.*]

THE FOUNDLING FATHER Little ringing in the ears. Slight deafness.

[*Rest.*]

Little ringing in the ears.

[*Rest.*]

A wink to the Great Mans cutout. A nod to the Great Mans bust. Once again striding in the Great Mans footsteps. Riding on in. Riding to the rescue the way they do. They both had such long legs. Such big feet. And the Greater Man had such a lead although of course somehow still "back there." If the Lesser Known had slowed down stopped moving completely gone in

8. The repetition of characters' names without dialogue indicates an extended pause, or what Parks has elsewhere described as "an elongated and heightened (rest)."

reverse died maybe the Greater Man could have caught up. Woulda had a chance. Woulda sneaked up behind him the Greater Man would have sneaked up behind the Lesser Known unbeknownst and wrestled him to the ground. Stabbed him in the back. In revenge. "Thus to the tyrants!" Shot him maybe. The Lesser Known forgets who he is and just crumples. His bones cannot be found. The Greater Man continues on.

[*Rest.*]

"*Emergency*, oh *Emergency*, please put the Great Man in the ground."

[*Rest.*]

Only a little ringing in the ears. Thats all. Slight deafness.

[*Rest.*]

[*He puts on the blonde beard.*]

Huh. Whatdoyou say I wear the blonde.

[*Rest.*]

[*A gunshot echoes. Softly. And echoes.*]

Act 2: The Hall of Wonders

A gunshot echoes. Loudly. And echoes.
They are in a great hole. In the middle of nowhere. The hole is an exact replica of The Great Hole of History.
A gunshot echoes. Loudly. And echoes. LUCY *with ear trumpet circulates.* BRAZIL *digs.*

A. BIG BANG

LUCY Hear that?
BRAZIL Zit him?
LUCY No.
BRAZIL Oh.

[*A gunshot echoes. Loudly. And echoes.*]

LUCY Hear?
BRAZIL Zit him?!
LUCY Nope. Ssuhecho.
BRAZIL Ssuhecho.
LUCY Uh echo uh huhn. Of gunplay. Once upon uh time somebody had uh little gunplay and now thuh gun goes on playing: *KER-BANG!* KERBANG-Kerbang-kerbang-(kerbang)-((kerbang)).
BRAZIL Thuh echoes.

[*Rest.*]

[*Rest.*]

LUCY Youre stopped.
BRAZIL Mmlistenin.
LUCY Dig on, Brazil. Cant stop diggin till you dig up somethin. Your Daddy was uh Digger.
BRAZIL Uh huhnnn.

LUCY

BRAZIL

[*A gunshot echoes. Loudly. And echoes. Rest. A gunshot echoes. Loudly. And echoes. Rest.*]

[LUCY Itssalways been important in my line to distinguish. Tuh know thuh difference. Not like your Fathuh. Your Fathuh became confused. His lonely death and lack of proper burial is our embarrassment. Go on: dig. Now me I need tuh know thuh real thing from thuh echo. Thuh truth from thuh hearsay.

[*Rest.*]

Bram Price for example. His dear ones and relations told me his dying words but Bram Price hisself of course told me something quite different.

BRAZIL I wept forim.

LUCY Whispered his true secrets to me and to me uhlone.

BRAZIL Then he died.

LUCY Then he died.

[*Rest.*]

Thuh things he told me I will never tell. Mr. Bram Price. Huh.

[*Rest.*]

Dig on.

BRAZIL

LUCY

BRAZIL

LUCY Little Bram Price Junior.

BRAZIL Thuh fat one?

LUCY Burned my eardrums. Just like his Dad did.

BRAZIL I wailed forim.

LUCY Ten days dead wept over and buried and that boy comes back. Not him though. His echo. Sits down tuh dinner and eats up everybodys food just like he did when he was livin.

[*Rest.*]

[*Rest.*]

Little Bram Junior. Burned my eardrums. Miz Penny Price his mother. Thuh things she told me I will never tell.

[*Rest.*]

You remember her.

BRAZIL Wore red velvet in August.

LUCY When her 2 Brams passed she sold herself, son.

BRAZIL O.

LUCY Also lost her mind. —. She finally went. Like your Fathuh went, perhaps. Foul play.

BRAZIL I gnashed for her.

LUCY You did.

BRAZIL Couldnt choose between wailin or gnashin. Weepin sobbin or moanin. Went for gnashing. More to it. Gnashed for her and hers like I have never gnashed. I woulda tore at my coat but thats extra. Chipped uh tooth. One in thuh front.

LUCY You did your job son.

BRAZIL I did my job.

LUCY Confidence. Huh. Thuh things she told me I will never tell. Miz Penny Price. Miz Penny Price.

[*Rest.*]

Youre stopped.

BRAZIL Mmlistenin.

LUCY Dig on, Brazil.

BRAZIL

LUCY

BRAZIL We arent from these parts.

LUCY No. We're not.

BRAZIL Daddy iduhnt[9] either.

LUCY Your Daddy iduhnt either.

[*Rest.*]

Dig on, son. —. Cant stop diggin till you dig up somethin. You dig that something up you brush that something off you give that something uh designated place. Its own place. Along with thuh other discoveries. In thuh Hall of Wonders. Uh place in the Hall of Wonders right uhlong with thuh rest of thuh Wonders hear?

BRAZIL Uh huhn.

[*Rest.*]

LUCY Bram Price Senior, son. Bram Price Senior was not thuh man he claimed tuh be. Huh. Nope. Was not thuh man he claimed tuh be atall. You ever see him in his stocking feet? Or barefoot? Course not. I guessed before he told me. He told me then he died. He told me and I havent told no one. I'm uh good Confidence. As Confidences go. Huh. One of thuh best. As Confidence, mmonly contracted tuh keep quiet 12 years. After 12 years nobody cares. For 19 years I have kept his secret. In my bosom.

[*Rest.*]

He wore lifts in his shoes, son.

BRAZIL Lifts?

LUCY Lifts. Made him seem taller than he was.

BRAZIL Bram Price Senior?

LUCY Bram Price Senior wore lifts in his shoes yes he did, Brazil. I tell you just as he told me with his last breaths on his dying bed: "Lifts." Thats all he said. Then he died. I put thuh puzzle pieces in place. I put thuh puzzle pieces in place. Couldnt tell no one though. Not even your Pa. "Lifts." I never told no one son. For 19 years I have kept Brams secret in my bosom. Youre thuh first tuh know. Hhh! Dig on. Dig on.

BRAZIL Dig on.

LUCY

BRAZIL

LUCY

[*A gunshot echoes. Loudly. And echoes.*]

BRAZIL [*rest*] Ff Pa was here weud find his bones.

9. That is, "isn't."

LUCY Not always.

BRAZIL Thereud be his bones and thereud be thuh Wonders surrounding his bones.

LUCY Ive heard of different.

BRAZIL Thereud be thuh Wonders surrounding his bones and thereud be his Whispers.

LUCY Maybe.

BRAZIL Ffhe sspast like they say he'd of parlayed to uh Confidence his last words and dying wishes. His secrets and his dreams.

LUCY Thats how we pass[1] back East. They could pass different out here.

BRAZIL We got Daddys ways Daddyssgot ours. When theres no Confidence available we just dribble thuh words out. In uh whisper.

LUCY Sometimes.

BRAZIL Thuh Confidencell gather up thuh whispers when she arrives.

LUCY Youre uh prize, Brazil. Uh prize.]

BRAZIL

LUCY

BRAZIL

LUCY

BRAZIL You hear him then? His whispers?

LUCY Not exactly.

BRAZIL He wuduhnt here then.

LUCY He was here.

BRAZIL Ffyou dont hear his whispers he wuduhnt here.

LUCY Whispers dont always come up right away. Takes time sometimes. Whispers could travel different out West than they do back East. Maybe slower. Maybe. Whispers are secrets and often shy. We aint seen your Pa in 30 years. That could be part of it. We also could be experiencing some sort of interference. Or some sort of technical difficulty. Ssard tuh tell.

[*Rest.*]

So much to live for.

BRAZIL So much to live for.

LUCY Look on thuh bright side.

BRAZIL Look on thuh bright side. Look on thuh bright side. Loook onnnnn thuhhhh briiiiiiiight siiiiiiiiide!!!!

LUCY DIIIIIIIIIIIG!

BRAZIL Dig.

LUCY

BRAZIL

LUCY Helloooo! —. Hellooooo!

BRAZIL

LUCY

BRAZIL [We're from out East. We're not from these parts.

[*Rest.*]

My foe-father, her husband, my Daddy, her mate, her man, my Pa come out here. Out West.

[*Rest.*]

1. Die.

Come out here all uhlone. Cleared thuh path tamed thuh wilderness dug this whole Hole with his own 2 hands and et cetera.

[*Rest.*]

Left his family behind. Back East. His Lucy and his child. He waved "Goodbye." Left us tuh carry on. I was only 5.

[*Rest.*]

My Daddy was uh Digger. Shes whatcha call uh Confidence. I did thuh weepin and thuh moanin.

[*Rest.*]

His lonely death and lack of proper burial is our embarrassment.

[*Rest.*]

Diggin was his livelihood but fakin was his callin. Ssonly natural heud come out here and combine thuh 2. Back East he was always diggin. He was uh natural. Could dig uh hole for uh body that passed like no one else. Digged em quick and they looked good too. This Hole here—this large one—sshis biggest venture to date. So says hearsay.

[*Rest.*]

Uh exact replica of thuh Great Hole of History!

LUCY Sshhhhhht.

BRAZIL [*rest*] Thuh original ssback East. He and Lucy they honeymooned there. At thuh original Great Hole. Its uh popular spot. He and Her would sit on thuh lip and watch everybody who was ever anybody parade on by. Daily parades! Just like thuh Tee Vee. Mr. George Washington, for example, thuh Fathuh of our Country hisself, would rise up from thuh dead and walk uhround and cross thuh Delaware and say stuff!![2] Right before their very eyes!!!!

LUCY Son?

BRAZIL Huh?

LUCY That iduhnt how it went.

BRAZIL Oh.

LUCY Thuh Mr. Washington me and your Daddy seen was uh lookuhlike of thuh Mr. Washington of history-fame, son.

BRAZIL Oh.

LUCY Thuh original Mr. Washingtonssbeen long dead.

BRAZIL O.

LUCY That Hole back East was uh theme park son. Keep your story to scale.

BRAZIL K.[3]

[*Rest.*]

Him and Her would sit by thuh lip uhlong with thuh others all in uh row cameras clickin and theyud look down into that Hole and see—ooooo—you name it. Ever-y-day you could look down that Hole and see—ooooo you name it. Amerigo Vespucci hisself made regular appearances. Marcus Garvey. Ferdinand and Isabella. Mary Queen of thuh Scots! Tarzan King of

2. Washington (1732–1799), the "Father of our Country," the first U.S. president (1789–97), crossed the Delaware from Pennsylvania on December 25, 1776, to make a surprise attack on the Hessian forces garrisoned in Trenton, New Jersey; the attack's success was an enormous boost to American morale early in the Revolutionary War.

3. That is, "OK."

thuh Apes! Washington Jefferson Harding and Millard Fillmore. Mistufer Columbus even.[4] Oh they saw all thuh greats. Parading daily in thuh Great Hole of History.

[*Rest.*]

My Fathuh did thuh living and thuh dead. Small-town and big-time. Mr. Lincoln was of course his favorite.

[*Rest.*]

Not only Mr. Lincoln but Mr. Lincolns last show. His last deeds. His last laughs.

[*Rest.*]

Being uh Digger of some renown Daddy comes out here tuh build uh like attraction. So says hearsay. Figures theres people out here who'll enjoy amusements such as them amusements He and Her enjoyed. We're all citizens of one country afterall.

[*Rest.*]

Mmrestin.

[*A gunshot echoes. Loudly. And echoes.*]

BRAZIL Woooo! [*Drops dead.*]

LUCY Youre fakin Mr. Brazil.

BRAZIL Uh uhnnn.

LUCY Tryin tuh get you some benefits.

BRAZIL Uh uhnnnnnnnn.

LUCY I know me uh faker when I see one. Your Father was uh faker. Huh. One of thuh best. There wuduhnt nobody your Fathuh couldnt do. Did thuh living and thuh dead. Small-town and big-time. Made-up and historical. Fakin was your Daddys callin but diggin was his livelihood. Oh, back East he was always diggin. Was uh natural. Could dig uh hole for uh body that passed like no one else. Digged em quick and they looked good too. You dont remember of course you dont.

BRAZIL I was only 5.

LUCY You were only 5. When your Fathuh spoke he'd quote thuh Greats. Mister George Washington. Thuh Misters Roosevelt.[5] Mister Millard Fillmore. Huh. All thuh greats. You dont remember of course you dont.

BRAZIL I was only 5—

LUCY —only 5. Mr. Lincoln was of course your Fathuhs favorite. Wuz. Huh. Wuz. Huh. Heresay says he's past. Your Daddy. Digged this hole then he died. So says hearsay.

4. Brazil names figures who were instrumental in "discovering" America: King Ferdinand (1452–1516) and Queen Isabella (1451–1504), rulers of Aragón and Castile, who underwrote the expeditions of the Italian-born explorer Christopher Columbus (1451–1506), two of which the Italian navigator Amerigo Vespucci (1454–1512)—whose accounts of his voyages to the New World led to the lands being named "America"—helped outfit; he also mentions presidents both lauded—Washington and Thomas Jefferson (1743–1826; 3rd president, 1801–09)—and disparaged: Warren Harding (1865–1923; 29th president, 1921–23) and Millard Fillmore (1800–1874; 13th president, 1850–53). The story of Mary, Queen of Scots (1542–1587; r. 1542–67)—executed, after years of imprisonment, for plotting against England's Elizabeth I—was retold in drama and opera, and Tarzan, a fictional character created by Edgar Rice Burroughs in *Tarzan of the Apes* (1912), has had a long afterlife in print sequels, film, and comics.

5. Two U.S. presidents named Roosevelt, Theodore (1858–1919; 26th president, 1901–09) and his distant cousin Franklin Delano (1882–1945; 32nd president, 1933–45).

[*Rest.*]

Dig, Brazil.

BRAZIL My paw—

LUCY Ssonly natural that heud come out here tuh dig out one of his own. He loved that Great Hole so. He'd stand at thuh lip of that Great Hole: "OHWAYOHWHYOHWAYOH!"

BRAZIL "OHWAYOHWHYOHWAYOH!"

LUCY "OHWAYOHWHYOHWAYOH!" You know: hole talk. Ohwayohwhy-ohwayoh, just tuh get their attention, then: "Hellooo!" He'd shout down to em. Theyd call back "Hellllooooo!" and wave. He loved that Great Hole so. Came out here. Digged this lookuhlike.

BRAZIL Then he died?

LUCY Then he died. Your Daddy died right here. Huh. Oh, he was uh faker. Uh greaaaaat biiiiig faker too. He was your Fathuh. Thats thuh connection. You take after him.

BRAZIL I do?

LUCY Sure. Put your paw back where it belongs. Go on—back on its stump. —. Poke it on out of your sleeve son. There you go. I'll draw uh X for you. See? Heresuh X. Huh. Dig here.

[*Rest.*]

DIG!

BRAZIL

LUCY

BRAZIL

LUCY Woah! Woah!

BRAZIL Whatchaheard?!

LUCY No tellin, son. Cant say.

[BRAZIL *digs.* LUCY *circulates.*]

BRAZIL [*rest. Rest*] On thuh day he claimed to be the 100th anniversary of the founding of our country the Father took the Son out into the yard. The Father threw himself down in front of the Son and bit into the dirt with his teeth. His eyes leaked. "This is how youll make your mark, Son" the Father said. The Son was only 2 then. "This is the Wail," the Father said. "There's money init," the Father said. The Son was only 2 then. Quiet. On what he claimed was the 101st anniversary the Father showed the Son "the Weep" "the Sob" and "the Moan." How to stand just so what to do with the hands and feet (to capitalize on what we in the business call "the Mourning Moment"). Formal stances the Fatherd picked up at the History Hole. The Son studied night and day. By candlelight. No one could best him. The money came pouring in. On the 102nd anniversary[6] the Son was 5 and the Father taught him "the Gnash." The day after that the Father left for out West. To seek his fortune. In the middle of dinnertime. The Son was eating his peas.

LUCY

BRAZIL

LUCY

BRAZIL

LUCY Hellooooo! Hellooooo!

[*Rest.*]

6. Hearsay [Parks's note].

BRAZIL

LUCY

BRAZIL HO! [*Unearths something.*]

LUCY Whatcha got?

BRAZIL Uh Wonder!

LUCY Uh Wonder!

BRAZIL Uh Wonder: Ho!

LUCY Dust it off and put it over with thuh rest of thuh Wonders.

BRAZIL Uh bust.

LUCY Whose?

BRAZIL Says "A. Lincoln." A. Lincolns bust. —. Abraham Lincolns bust!!!

LUCY Howuhboutthat!

[*Rest.*]

[*Rest.*]

Woah! Woah!

BRAZIL Whatchaheard?

LUCY Uh—. Cant say.

BRAZIL Whatchaheard?!!

LUCY SSShhhhhhhhhhhhhhhhht!

[*Rest.*]

dig!

B. ECHO

THE FOUNDLING FATHER Ladies and Gentlemen: *Our American Cousin,* Act III, scene 5:

MR. TRENCHARD[7] Have you found it?

MISS KEENE I find no trace of it. [*Discovering*] What is this?!

MR. TRENCHARD This is the place where father kept all the old deeds.

MISS KEENE Oh my poor muddled brain! What can this mean?!

MR. TRENCHARD [*with difficulty*] I cannot survive the downfall of my house but choose instead to end my life with a pistol to my head!

[*Applause.*]

THE FOUNDLING FATHER OHWAYOHWHYOHWAYOH!

[*Rest.*]

[*Rest.*]

Helllooooooo!

[*Rest.*]

Helllooooooo!

[*Rest. Waves.*]

7. Asa Trenchard is the title character of *Our American Cousin;* Laura Keene played his cousin, Florence Trenchard. (The exchange paraphrases one found in scene 6, but Florence is not present and the suicide is threatened in the following scene by another character, Sir Edward Trenchard.)

C. ARCHEOLOGY

BRAZIL You hear im?

LUCY Echo of thuh first sort: thuh sound. (E.g. thuh gunplay.)

[*Rest.*]

Echo of thuh 2nd sort: thuh words. Type A: thuh words from thuh dead. Category: Unrelated.

[*Rest.*]

Echo of thuh 2nd sort, Type B: words less fortunate: thuh Disembodied Voice. Also known as "Thuh Whispers." Category: Related. Like your Fathuhs.

[*Rest.*]

Echo of thuh 3rd sort: thuh body itself.

[*Rest.*]

BRAZIL You hear im.

LUCY Cant say. Cant say, son.

BRAZIL My faux-father. Thuh one who comed out here before us. Thuh one who left us behind. Tuh come out here all uhlone. Tuh do his bit. All them who comed before us—my Daddy. He's one of them.

LUCY

[*Rest.*]

[*Rest.*]

[BRAZIL: He's one of them. All of them who comed before us—my Daddy.

[*Rest.*]

I'd say thuh creation of thuh world must uh been just like thuh clearing off of this plot. Just like him diggin his Hole. I'd say. Must uh been just as dug up. And unfair.

[*Rest.*]

Peoples (or thuh what-was), just had tuh hit thuh road. In thuh beginning there was one of those voids here and then "bang" and then *voilà!*[8] And here we is.

[*Rest.*]

But where did those voids that was here before *we* was here go off to? Hmmm. In thuh beginning there were some of them voids here and then: KERBANG-KERBLAMMO! And now it all belongs tuh us.

LUCY

[*Rest.*]

[*Rest.*]

BRAZIL This Hole is our inheritance of sorts. My Daddy died and left it to me and Her. And when She goes, Shes gonna give it all to me!!

LUCY Dig, son.

BRAZIL I'd rather dust and polish. [*Puts something on.*]

LUCY Dust and polish then. —. You dont got tuh put on that tuh do it.

BRAZIL It helps. Uh Hehm. *Uh Hehm.* WELCOME WELCOME WELCOME TUH THUH HALL OF—

LUCY Sssht.

BRAZIL

8. Literally, "see there" (French).

LUCY

BRAZIL (welcome welcome welcome to thuh hall. of. wonnndersss: To our right A Jewel Box made of cherry wood, lined in velvet, letters "A.L." carved in gold on thuh lid: the jewels have long escaped. Over here one of Mr. Washingtons bones, right pointer so they say; here is his likeness and here: his wooden teeth.[9] Yes, uh top and bottom pair of nibblers: nibblers, lookin for uh meal. Nibblin. I iduhnt your lunch. Quit nibblin. Quit that nibblin you. Quit that nibblin you nibblers you nibblin nibblers you.)

LUCY Keep it tuh scale.

BRAZIL (Over here our newest Wonder: uh bust of Mr. Lincoln carved of marble lookin like he looked in life. Right heress thuh bit from thuh mouth of thuh mount on which some great Someone rode tuh thuh rescue. This is all thats left. Uh glass tradin bead—one of thuh first. Here are thuh licked boots. Here, uh dried scrap of whales blubber. Uh petrified scrap of uh great blubberer, servin to remind us that once this land was covered with sea. And blubberers were Kings. In this area here are several documents: peace pacts, writs, bills of sale, treaties, notices, handbills and circulars, freein papers, summonses, declarations of war, addresses, title deeds, obits, long lists of dids. And thuh medals: for bravery and honesty; for trustworthiness and for standing straight; for standing tall; for standing still. For advancing and retreating. For makin do. For skills in whittlin, for skills in painting and drawing, for uh knowledge of sewin, of handicrafts and building things, for leather tannin, blacksmithery, lacemakin, horseback riding, swimmin, croquet, and badminton. Community Service. For cookin and for cleanin. For bowin and scrapin. Uh medal for fakin? Huh. This could uh been his. Zsis his? This is his! This is his!!!

LUCY Keep it tuh scale, Brazil.

BRAZIL This could be his!

LUCY May well be.

BRAZIL [*rest*] Whaddyahear?

LUCY Bits and pieces.

BRAZIL This could be his.

LUCY Could well be.

BRAZIL [*rest. Rest*] waaaaaahhhhhhhHHHHHHHHHHHHHH! HUH HEE HUH HEE HUH HEE HUH.

LUCY There there, Brazil. Dont weep.

BRAZIL WAHHHHHHHHHHH!—imissim—WAHHHHHHHHHHHHH!

LUCY It is an honor to be of his line. He cleared this plot for us. He was uh Digger.

BRAZIL Huh huh huh. Uh Digger.

LUCY Mr. Lincoln was his favorite.

BRAZIL I was only 5.

LUCY He dug this whole Hole.

BRAZIL Sssnuch.[1] This whole Hole.

LUCY This whole Hole.

[*Rest.*]

BRAZIL

LUCY

9. Washington's famous "wooden teeth" were in fact dentures made of ivory and of animal and human teeth.

1. Parks defines "Sssnuch" as "a fast reverse snort, a big sniff (usually accompanies crying or sneezing)."

BRAZIL

LUCY

BRAZIL

LUCY

I couldnt never deny him nothin.
I gived intuh him on everything.
Thuh moon. Thuh stars.
Thuh bees knees. Thuh cats pyjamas.

[*Rest.*]

BRAZIL

LUCY

BRAZIL Anything?

LUCY Stories too horrible tuh mention.

BRAZIL His stories?

LUCY Nope.

[*Rest.*]

BRAZIL Mama Lucy?

LUCY Whut.

BRAZIL —Imissim—.

LUCY Hhh. ((dig.))

D. ECHO

THE FOUNDLING FATHER Ladies and Gentlemen: *Our American Cousin*, Act III, scene 2:

MR. TRENCHARD You crave affection, *you* do. Now I've no fortune, but I'm biling over with affections, which I'm ready to pour out to all of you, like apple sass over roast pork.

AUGUSTA Sir, your American talk do woo me.[2]

THE FOUNDLING FATHER [*as Mrs. Mount*] Mr. Trenchard, you will please recollect you are addressing my daughter and in my presence.

MR. TRENCHARD Yes, I'm offering her my heart and hand just as she wants them, with nothing in 'em.

THE FOUNDLING FATHER [*as Mrs. Mount*] Augusta dear, to your room.

AUGUSTA Yes, Ma, the nasty beast.

THE FOUNDLING FATHER [*as Mrs. Mount*] I am aware, Mr. Trenchard, that you are not used to the manners of good society, and that, alone, will excuse the impertinence of which you have been guilty.

MR. TRENCHARD Don't know the manners of good society, eh? Wal, I guess I know enough to turn you inside out, old gal—you sockdologizing old mantrap.

[*Laughter. Applause.*]

THE FOUNDLING FATHER Thanks. Thanks so much. Snyder has always been a very special very favorite town uh mine. Thank you thank you so very much. Loverly loverly evening loverly tuh be here loverly tuh be here with you with all of you thank you very much.

[*Rest.*]

Uh Hehm. I *only* do thuh greats.

2. Parks adds this line to a passage that is otherwise quoted directly from the play.

[*Rest.*]

A crowd pleaser: 4score and 7 years ago our fathers brought forth upon this continent a new nation conceived in Liberty and dedicated to the proposition that all men are created equal![3]

[*Applause.*]

Observe!: Indiana? Indianapolis. Louisiana? Baton Rouge. Concord? New Hampshire. Pierre? South Dakota. Honolulu? Hawaii. Springfield? Illinois. Frankfort? Kentucky. Lincoln? Nebraska.[4] Ha! Lickety split!

[*Applause.*]

And now, the centerpiece of the evening!!

[*Rest.*]

Uh Hehm. The Death of Lincoln!: —. The watching of the play, the laughter, the smiles of Lincoln and Mary Todd, the slipping of Booth into the presidential box unseen, the freeing of the slaves, the pulling of the trigger, the bullets piercing above the left ear, the bullets entrance into the great head, the bullets lodging behind the great right eye, the slumping of Lincoln, the leaping onto the stage of Booth, the screaming of Todd, the screaming of Todd, the screaming of Keene, the leaping onto the stage of Booth; the screaming of Todd, the screaming of Keene, the shouting of Booth "Thus to the tyrants!," the death of Lincoln! —And the silence of the nation.

[*Rest.*]

Yes. —.The year was way back when. The place: our nations capitol. 4score, back in the olden days, and Mr. Lincolns great head. The the-a-ter was "Fords." The wife "Mary Todd." Thuh freeing of the slaves and thuh great black hole that thuh fatal bullet bored. And how that great head was bleedin. Thuh body stretched crossways acrosst thuh bed. Thuh last words. Thuh last breaths. And how thuh nation mourned.

[*Applause.*]

E. SPADEWORK

LUCY Thats uh hard nut tuh crack uh hard nut tuh crack indeed.

BRAZIL Alaska—?

LUCY Thats uh hard nut tuh crack. Thats uh hard nut tuh crack indeed. —. Huh. Juneau.

BRAZIL Good!

LUCY Go uhgain.

BRAZIL —. Texas?

LUCY —. Austin. Wyoming?

BRAZIL —. —. Cheyenne. Florida?

LUCY Tallahassee.

[*Rest.*]

Ohio.

BRAZIL Oh. Uh. Well: Columbus. Louisiana?

3. The opening sentence of Lincoln's Gettysburg Address, delivered November 19, 1863, in Gettysburg, Pennsylvania, at the dedication ceremony for a national cemetery on the site of the Civil War's bloodiest battle, fought four months earlier.

4. This list pairs states with their capitals (a pattern that continues in the next scene).

LUCY Baton Rouge. Arkansas.

BRAZIL Little Rock. Jackson.

LUCY Mississippi. Spell it.

BRAZIL M-i-s-s-i-s-s-i-p-p-i!

LUCY Huh. Youre good. Montgomery.

BRAZIL Alabama.

LUCY Topeka.

BRAZIL Kansas?

LUCY Kansas.

BRAZIL Boise, Idaho?

LUCY Boise, Idaho.

BRAZIL Huh. Nebraska.

LUCY Nebraska. Lincoln.

[*Rest.*]

Thuh year was way back when. Thuh place: our nations capitol.

[*Rest.*]

Your Fathuh couldnt get that story out of his head: Mr. Lincolns great head. And thuh hole thuh fatal bullet bored. How that great head was bleedin. Thuh body stretched crossways acrosst thuh bed. Thuh last words. Thuh last breaths. And how thuh nation mourned. Huh. Changed your Fathuhs life.

[*Rest.*]

Couldnt get that story out of his head. Whuduhnt my favorite page from thuh book of Mr. Lincolns life, me myself now I prefer thuh part where he gets married to Mary Todd and she begins to lose her mind (and then of course where he frees all thuh slaves) but shoot, he couldnt get that story out of his head. Hhh. Changed his life.

[*Rest.*]

BRAZIL (wahhhhhhhh—)

LUCY There there, Brazil.

BRAZIL (wahhhhhh—)

LUCY Dont weep. Got somethin for ya.

BRAZIL (o)?

LUCY Spade. —. Dont scrunch up your face like that, son. Go on. Take it.

BRAZIL Spade?

LUCY Spade. He woulda wanted you tuh have it.

BRAZIL Daddys diggin spade? Ssnnuch.

LUCY I swannee[5] you look more and more and more and more like him every day.

BRAZIL His chin?

LUCY You got his chin.

BRAZIL His lips?

LUCY You got his lips.

BRAZIL His teeths?

LUCY Top and bottom. In his youth. He had some. Just like yours. His frock coat. Was just like that. He had hisself uh stovepipe hat which you lack. His medals—yours are for weepin his of course were for diggin.

5. A punning combination of *I swan* (i.e., "I declare"; dialect) and *Swannee (River)*, an allusion to Stephen Foster's 1851 song "Old Folks at Home" (which presents a sentimental view of African American life in the antebellum South).

BRAZIL And I got his spade.

LUCY And now you got his spade.

BRAZIL We could say I'm his spittin image.

LUCY We could say that.

BRAZIL We could say I just may follow in thuh footsteps of my foe-father.

LUCY We could say that.

BRAZIL Look on thuh bright side!

LUCY Look on thuh bright side!

BRAZIL So much tuh live for!

LUCY So much tuh live for! Sweet land of—! Sweet land of—?

BRAZIL Of liberty!

LUCY Of liberty! Thats it thats it and *"Woah!"* Lets say I hear his words!

BRAZIL And you could say?

LUCY And I could say.

BRAZIL Lets say you hear his words!

LUCY *Woah!*

BRAZIL Whatwouldhesay?!

LUCY He'd say: "Hello." He'd say. —. "Hope you like your spade."

BRAZIL Tell him I do.

LUCY He'd say: "My how youve grown!" He'd say: "Hows your weepin?" He'd say: —Ha! He's running through his states and capitals! Licketysplit!

BRAZIL Howuhboutthat!

LUCY He'd say: "Uh house divided cannot stand!" He'd say: "4score and 7 years uhgoh." Say: "Of thuh people by thuh people and for thuh people." Say: "Malice toward none and charity toward all." Say: "Cheat some of thuh people some of thuh time."[6] He'd say: (and this is only to be spoken between you and me and him—)

BRAZIL K.

LUCY Lean in. Ssfor our ears and our ears uhlone.

LUCY

BRAZIL

LUCY

BRAZIL

BRAZIL O.

LUCY Howuhboutthat. And here he comes. Striding on in striding on in and he surveys thuh situation. And he nods tuh what we found cause he knows his Wonders. And he smiles. And he tells us of his doins all these years. And he does his Mr. Lincoln for us. Uh great page from thuh great mans great life! And you n me llsmile, cause then we'll know, more or less, exactly where he is.

[*Rest.*]

6. Some of the most famous words spoken by or attributed to Lincoln, from, respectively, his speech on June 16, 1858, to the Illinois Republican State Convention in Springfield—"A house divided against itself cannot stand" (an allusion to Mark 3.25); the beginning and the end of the Gettysburg Address—"government of the people, by the people, for the people"; his second Inaugural Address, delivered March 4, 1865—"With malice toward none; with charity for all"; and (with slight variations in wording) a speech of September 8, 1858, in Clinton, Illinois, or a remark made to a caller at the White House—"You may fool all the people some of the time; you can even fool some of the people all the time; but you can't fool all of the people all the time" (this observation, which does not appear in any surviving Lincoln documents, has also been attributed to the 19th-century American showman P. T. Barnum).

BRAZIL Lucy? Where is he?

LUCY Lincoln?

BRAZIL Papa.

LUCY Close by, I guess. Huh. Dig.

[BRAZIL *digs. Times passes.*]

Youre uh Digger. Youre uh Digger. Your Daddy was uh Digger and so are you.

BRAZIL Ho!

LUCY I couldnt never deny him nothin.

BRAZIL Wonder: Ho! Wonder: Ho!

LUCY I gived intuh him on everything.

BRAZIL Ssuhtrumpet.

LUCY Gived intuh him on everything.

BRAZIL Ssuhtrumpet, Lucy.

LUCY Howboutthat.

BRAZIL Try it out.

LUCY How uh-bout that.

BRAZIL Anythin?

LUCY Cant say, son. Cant say.

[*Rest.*]

I couldnt never deny him nothin.
I gived intuh him on everything.
Thuh moon. Thuh stars.

BRAZIL Ho!

LUCY Thuh bees knees. Thuh cats pyjamas.

BRAZIL Wonder: Ho! Wonder: Ho!

[*Rest.*]

Howuhboutthat: Uh bag of pennies. Money, Lucy.

LUCY Howuhboutthat.

[*Rest.*]

Thuh bees knees.
Thuh cats pyjamas.
Thuh best cuts of meat.
My baby teeth.

BRAZIL Wonder: Ho! Wonder: HO!

LUCY

Thuh apron from uhround my waist.
Thuh hair from off my head.

BRAZIL Huh. Yellow fur.

LUCY My mores and my folkways.

BRAZIL Oh. Uh beard. Howuhboutthat.

[*Rest.*]

LUCY WOAH. WOAH!

BRAZIL Whatchaheard?

LUCY

[*Rest.*]

[*Rest.*]

BRAZIL Whatchaheard?!

LUCY You dont wanna know.

BRAZIL
LUCY
BRAZIL
LUCY
BRAZIL Wonder: Ho! Wonder: HO! WONDER: HO!
LUCY
Thuh apron from uhround my waist.
Thuh hair from off my head.
BRAZIL Huh: uh Tee-Vee.
LUCY Huh.
BRAZIL I'll hold ontooit for uh minit.
[*Rest.*]
LUCY
Thuh apron from uhround my waist.
Thuh hair from off my head.
My mores and my folkways.
My rock and my foundation.
BRAZIL
LUCY
BRAZIL
LUCY My re-memberies—you know—thuh stuff out of my head.
[*The TV comes on.* THE FOUNDLING FATHER*'s face appears.*]
BRAZIL (ho! ho! wonder: ho!)
LUCY
My spare buttons in their envelopes.
Thuh leftovers from all my unmade meals.
Thuh letter R.
Thuh key of G.
BRAZIL (ho! ho! wonder: ho!)
LUCY
All my good jokes. All my jokes that fell flat.
Thuh way I walked, cause you liked it so much.
All my winnin dance steps.
My teeth when yours runned out.
My smile.
BRAZIL (ho! ho! wonder: ho!)
LUCY Sssssht.
[*Rest.*]
Well. Its him.

F. ECHO

A gunshot echoes. Loudly. And echoes.

G. THE GREAT BEYOND

LUCY *and* BRAZIL *watch the TV: a replay of "The Lincoln Act."* THE FOUNDLING FATHER *has returned. His coffin awaits him.*

LUCY Howuhboutthat!

BRAZIL They just gunned him down uhgain.

LUCY Howuhboutthat.

BRAZIL He's dead but not really.

LUCY Howuhboutthat.

BRAZIL Only fakin. Only fakin. See? Hesupuhgain.

LUCY What-izzysayin?

BRAZIL Sound duhnt work.

LUCY Zat right.

[*Rest.*]

THE FOUNDLING FATHER I believe this is the place where I do the Gettysburg Address, I believe.

BRAZIL

THE FOUNDLING FATHER

LUCY

BRAZIL Woah!

LUCY Howuhboutthat.

BRAZIL Huh. Well.

[*Rest.*]

Huh. Zit him?

LUCY Its him.

BRAZIL He's dead?

LUCY He's dead.

BRAZIL Howuhboutthat.

[*Rest.*]

Shit.

LUCY

BRAZIL

LUCY

BRAZIL Mail the in-vites?

LUCY I did.

BRAZIL Think theyll come?

LUCY I do. There are hundreds upon thousands who knew of your Daddy, glorified his reputation, and would like to pay their respects.

THE FOUNDLING FATHER Howuhboutthat.

BRAZIL Howuhboutthat!

LUCY Turn that off, son.

[*Rest.*]

You gonna get in yr coffin now or later?

THE FOUNDLING FATHER I'd like tuh wait uhwhile.

LUCY Youd like tuh wait uhwhile.

BRAZIL Mmgonna gnash for you. You know: teeth in thuh dirt, hands like this, then jump up rip my clothes up, you know, you know go all out.

THE FOUNDLING FATHER Howuhboutthat. Open casket or closed?

LUCY —. Closed.

[*Rest.*]

Turn that off, son.

BRAZIL K.

THE FOUNDLING FATHER Hug me.

BRAZIL Not yet.

THE FOUNDLING FATHER You?

LUCY Gimmieuhminute.

[*A gunshot echoes. Loudly. And echoes.*]

LUCY That gunplay. Wierdiduhntit. Comes. And goze.

[*They ready his coffin. He inspects it.*]

At thuh Great Hole where we honeymooned—son, at thuh Original Great Hole, you could see thuh whole world without goin too far. You could look intuh that Hole and see your entire life pass before you. Not your own life but someones life from history, you know, [someone who'd done somethin of note, got theirselves known somehow, uh President or] somebody who killed somebody important, uh face on uh postal stamp, you know, someone from History. *Like* you, but *not* you. You know: *Known.*

THE FOUNDLING FATHER "*Emergency,* oh, *Emergency,* please put the Great Man in the ground."

LUCY Go on. Get in. Try it out. Ssnot so bad. See? Sstight, but private. Bought on time but we'll manage. And you got enough height for your hat.

[*Rest.*]

THE FOUNDLING FATHER Hug me.

LUCY Not yet.

THE FOUNDLING FATHER You?

BRAZIL Gimmieuhminute.

[*Rest.*]

LUCY He loved that Great Hole so. Came out here. Digged this lookuhlike.

BRAZIL Then he died?

LUCY Then he died.

THE FOUNDLING FATHER

BRAZIL

LUCY

THE FOUNDLING FATHER

BRAZIL

LUCY

THE FOUNDLING FATHER A monumentous occasion. I'd like to say a few words from the grave. Maybe a little conversation: Such a long story. Uh-hem. I quit the business. And buried all my things. I dropped anchor: Bottomless. Your turn.

LUCY

BRAZIL

THE FOUNDLING FATHER

LUCY [*rest*] Do your Lincoln for im.

THE FOUNDLING FATHER Yeah?

LUCY He was only 5.

THE FOUNDLING FATHER Only 5. *Uh Hehm.* So very loverly to be here so very very loverly to be here the town of —Wonderville has always been a special favorite of mine always has been a very very special favorite of mine. Now, I *only* do thuh greats. Uh hehm: I was born in a log cabin of humble parentage. But I picked up uh few things. Uh Hehm: 4score and 7 years ago our fathers—ah you know thuh rest. Lets see now. Yes. Uh house divided cannot stand! You can fool some of thuh people some of thuh time! Of thuh people by thuh people and for thuh people! Malice toward none and charity toward all! Ha! The Death of Lincoln! (Highlights): Haw Haw Haw Haw

[*Rest.*]

HAW HAW HAW HAW

[*A gunshot echoes. Loudly. And echoes.* THE FOUNDLING FATHER *"slumps in his chair."*]

THE FOUNDLING FATHER

LUCY

BRAZIL

LUCY

THE FOUNDLING FATHER

BRAZIL [Izzy dead?

LUCY Mmlistenin.

BRAZIL Anything?

LUCY Nothin.

BRAZIL [*rest*] As a child it was her luck tuh be in thuh same room with her Uncle when he died. Her family wanted to know what he had said. What his last words had been. Theyre hadnt been any. Only screaming. Or, you know, breath. Didnt have uh shape to it. Her family thought she was holding on to thuh words. For safekeeping. And they proclaimed thuh girl uh Confidence. At the age of 8. Sworn tuh secrecy. She picked up thuh tricks of thuh trade as she went uhlong.]

[*Rest.*]

Should I gnash now?

LUCY Better save it for thuh guests. I guess.

[*Rest.*]

Well. Dust and polish, son. I'll circulate.

BRAZIL Welcome Welcome Welcome to thuh hall. Of. Wonders.

[*Rest.*]

To our right A Jewel Box of cherry wood, lined in velvet, letters "A.L." carved in gold on thuh lid. Over here one of Mr. Washingtons bones and here: his wooden teeth. Over here: uh bust of Mr. Lincoln carved of marble lookin like he looked in life. —More or less. And thuh medals: for bravery and honesty; for trustworthiness and for standing straight; for standing tall; for standing still. For advancing and retreating. For makin do. For skills in whittlin, for skills in painting and drawing, for uh knowledge of sewin, of handicrafts and building things, for leather tannin, blacksmithery, lacemakin, horseback riding, swimmin, croquet, and badminton. Community Service. For cookin and for cleanin. For bowin and scrapin. Uh medal for fakin.

[*Rest.*]

To my right: our newest Wonder: One of thuh greats Hisself! Note: thuh body sitting propped upright in our great Hole. Note the large mouth opened wide. Note the top hat and frock coat, just like the greats. Note the death wound: thuh great black hole—thuh great black hole in thuh great head. —And how this great head is bleedin. —Note: thuh last words. —And thuh last breaths. —And how thuh nation mourns—

[*Takes his leave.*]

EDWARD ALBEE

b. 1928

IN the program note for the 1996 London revival of his legendary drama *Who's Afraid of Virginia Woolf?* (1962), Edward Albee observed that "many contemporary playwrights are best known for one play, usually an early one." Albee sees the prominence accorded such early writing as a mixed blessing, for he believes that living playwrights feel strong allegiances to their other works as well. They want audiences and critics to continue to take risks with them, remaining open to the potential that each new play contains, instead of repeatedly returning to a single piece—no matter how illustrious—that established a reputation. Albee's ambivalence toward *Virginia Woolf* does not, of course, detract from its historical significance or theatrical power, but his remarks do remind us of the need to consider seriously his ongoing contributions to the theater. With the 2002 premiere of ***THE GOAT; OR, WHO IS SYLVIA? (NOTES TOWARD A DEFINITION OF TRAGEDY)***, Albee demonstrated his continuing ability to provoke and polarize audiences. He takes the measure of contemporary American culture with the same piercing insight, bold theatricality, and audacious wit that he displayed in such early one acts as *The Zoo Story* (1959) and *The American Dream* (1961). Moreover, he persists in challenging received ideas about what kind of theater attracts Broadway audiences. Indeed, the success of *The Goat,* which received the Tony Award for Best Play, the New York Drama Critics' Circle Award for Best Play, and the Drama Desk Award for Outstanding Play, cannot be separated from the controversy it sparked among reviewers and theatergoers alike.

Edward F. Albee III was given to an orphanage shortly after his birth in March 1928, and adopted into a famous New York theatrical family days later. Edward's adoptive grandfather, for whom he was named, had been a partner in running one of the most successful vaudeville theater syndicates in the United States. His adoptive father, Reed Albee, retired from theater management around the time of Edward's birth. Reed and his wife Louise raised Edward in suburban Larchmont, New York, in an atmosphere of great financial privilege; by all reports, however, the Albees were emotionally distant parents who entrusted their son primarily to the care of a nurse.

After brief, unsuccessful stints at both Trinity College and Columbia University, Albee took up residence in Greenwich Village in 1949; there he became part of the circle of painters, writers, composers, and other artists who were contributing to the development of a new avant-garde in the 1950s. He absorbed the cultural outpourings of that decade, especially its music and theater, attending productions by playwrights including EUGENE O'NEILL, TENNESSEE WILLIAMS, JEAN GENET, and T. S. Eliot. Albee had experimented for many years with poetry, fiction, essays, and drama, but he focused on plays only after receiving some modest encouragement from an early mentor—Thornton Wilder, the author of the quintessential American drama *Our Town* (1938). Shortly before his thirtieth birthday, Albee drafted, in what he describes as a moment of creative "explosion," the play that would launch his career, *The Zoo Story*. This one-act drama depicts an encounter—initially innocuous but ultimately disastrous—in Central Park between two men, one an eccentric loner (who has just been to the zoo) and the other a middle-class New Yorker. In 1961, Albee drafted his first full-length play, *Virginia Woolf*, which took Broadway by storm the following year: it won the Tony and the New York Drama Critics' Circle Award for Best Play, as well as the Outer Critics Circle Award for Playwright of the Season. Albee received his first Pulitzer Prize for Drama in 1967, with *A Delicate Balance*. He won the Pulitzer again in 1975 for *Seascape* and most recently in 1994 for *Three Tall Women*. His record of achievement and continued productivity is unmatched in American theater; Albee and his contemporaries are also credited with revitalizing the stage in the United States in the early 1960s and with inspiring the off- and off-off-Broadway theater movements that launched the careers of SAM SHEPARD and MARIA IRENE FORNES, among many others.

The Goat opens, as do many Albee works, in a seemingly everyday, domestic environment. Stevie and her husband, Martin, are at home, awaiting the arrival of their friend Ross. Martin, a successful architect, has just received an extraordinarily prestigious award, and Ross, who hosts a televised interview program, wants to film a segment highlighting Martin's triumph. But Martin is distracted and divulges that he has been having an affair—with a goat he has named Sylvia. Ross feels he must share this information with Stevie, and the second and third scenes show the impact of the revelation on Stevie, Martin, and Billy, their gay teenage son. Swinging wildly between comedy and pathos, *The Goat* explores the nature of love and desire and, ultimately, what it means to be human.

Very early in his career, Albee's writing attracted the attention of the prominent theater scholar Martin Esslin. Esslin's highly influential study, *The Theatre of the Absurd* (1961), grouped Albee's dramaturgy with that of SAMUEL BECKETT, Eugene Ionesco, Jean Genet, and HAROLD PINTER, among other contemporary European dramatists of the postwar era. Esslin's identification of Albee as an absurdist writer helped catapult him to fame, but the label has remained fixed to the dramatist throughout his career. Absurdist theater, according to Esslin, reflects "metaphysical anguish at the absurdity of the human condition" and strives to express that sentiment "by the open abandonment of rational devices and discursive thought"—an abandonment that we could certainly ascribe to *The Goat*, in Martin's actions and their aftermath. Yet Albee has steadfastly maintained that his work should be seen as "naturalistic" and "political." Though these descriptors appear to conflict with the tenets of Esslin's absurdism, they, too, clearly apply to *The Goat*: in particular, the play's living room setting and focus on the nuclear family are naturalistic, and its overt engagement with contemporary debates on sexual identity evoke contemporary politics.

Other critics have employed a biographical framework to explicate Albee's writing, establishing clear links between his dysfunctional boyhood home and his painful representations of family relationships and parental figures. His characterizations of children as either deeply troubled or highly idealized—or both, as in the case of Billy—resonate, in this biographical schema, with his own ambiguous status as an adopted child ultimately rejected by his adoptive parents. While Albee acknowledges the parallels, he argues that his plays go beyond autobiography. Albee has always claimed O'Neill as a profound influence, as well as (perhaps more surprisingly) the American humorist James Thurber, and we can see in *The Goat* Albee's unique ability to render the American family as both achingly flawed and slightly ridiculous. Indeed, Albee's focus on the family places him squarely in the mainstream of American drama, which has long relied on the family unit to act as a

Bill Pullman and Mercedes Ruehl in the original Broadway production of *The Goat; or, Who Is Sylvia?* at the Golden Theatre (2002).

microcosm and mirror of society. In that context, *The Goat* can be read as an indictment of the hypocrisies inherent in the current rhetoric of family values.

Though Albee does consider himself an American playwright, he believes his work can also speak to audiences from other cultures and in other locations. ANTON CHEKHOV, LUIGI PIRANDELLO, BERTOLT BRECHT, and Beckett are among the writers whom he names as having had a meaningful and lasting impact on him; the enormous success of his work outside the United States may reflect audiences' ability to connect with his plays. The issues faced by his characters in *The Goat* move them beyond their individual lives, and outside an exclusively American milieu, as they explore more profound and far-reaching questions of modern civilization.

Despite his repeated refusal to answer questions about the meaning of his plays, Albee has often revealed some of his goals for a given piece. In the case of *The Goat,* he remarked in *Playbill:* "I think there's one thing I'm doing with this play: testing the tolerance of the audience. Testing the limits of tolerance. . . . I suppose some people will be offended and enraged. I hope more people will find it informing and involving." The range of critical responses to the Broadway premiere suggests that Albee accurately gauged both the strength of resistance and the degree of engagement that his depiction of bestiality would inspire. *USA Today* pronounced *The Goat* a "self-indulgent mess, in which the cynical, disdainful view of family life that has informed some of Albee's more eloquent works reaches its nauseating nadir." But the critic for the New York *Post* called it "one of the wittiest and funniest plays Albee has ever written."

Albee's parenthetical subtitle for the drama, *Notes Toward a Definition of Tragedy,* seems to provide an explanation for the play's trajectory from sparkling comedic opening to emotionally devastating conclusion. Underscoring the point is the choice of animal at the center of the conflict, for the original meaning of *tragōidia* (tragedy) is "goat song," and historians posit close connections between the themes, narratives, and characters of Greek tragedy and those of the satyr plays that accompanied and may have parodied them in the ancient festivals. Incorporating a troubling vision of our future, Albee describes how Martin's planned $200 billion World City, "financed by U.S. Electronics Technology," will rise from "the wheatfields of Kansas." This new dystopia—this jarring juxtaposition of nature and industry, an image both ludicrous and frighteningly possible—is set against Martin's reverie of the American pastoral ideal, the Edenic "country place" he describes to Ross, where he encounters, contains, and has sexual relations with the goat Sylvia.

The play's repeated question "Who is Sylvia?" registers on similarly seriocomic levels, first in the witty banter between Martin and Stevie in the opening scene, when Stevie senses something is wrong but does not yet know the truth, and then more seriously during Ross's interrogation of his best friend once the affair is revealed. Albee's direct allusion to the song from Act 4 of SHAKESPEARE's *The Two Gentlemen of Verona* (ca. 1591?)—"Who is Silvia? What is she, / That all our swains commend her?"—makes a further provocative link between tragedy and pastoral comedy. This particular play has come to exemplify the "green world" of Shakespeare's romantic dramas, whose action routinely moves from an everyday setting into an idealized realm of nature where almost magical metamorphoses of character can occur. Shakespeare's Silvia is both a specific character, embodying generosity of spirit and faithful love, and a pastoral ideal. The goat Sylvia mirrors her as a real object of love and desire and as part of a contemporary rural and agricultural idyll—as remote, fertile, and mythic as any Renaissance vision.

Yet Sylvia also becomes an absurd parody of the "kept woman" and the manifestation of everything that has gone tragically wrong in Martin's heartfelt longing for communion with nature. Albee thus insists on her multivalence: "There's a real goat and also a person who becomes a scapegoat." By inviting us to consider *The Goat* as part of a theatrical tradition stretching back to the prehistory of Greek tragedy, Albee raises profound questions about what constitutes that dramatic tradition in the twenty-first century. At the same time, he makes us face the reality of an array of intimate relationships and violent actions, reminding us that such narratives have always shaped tragedy.

In addition, Albee uses the character of Billy to tackle dominant cultural messages regarding sexuality, challenging us to rethink our tendency to make clear-cut distinctions among the manifold expressions of sexual desire. As Billy remarks ruefully to Ross, "I get confused . . . sex and love; loving and . . . I want to sleep with everyone." Stevie, whose tragedy is different from but inextricably tied to Martin's, cannot fathom how Martin can claim to love both her and Sylvia: "But I'm a human being; I have only two breasts; I walk upright; I give milk only on special occasions; I use the toilet. [*Begins to cry.*] You love me? I don't understand." When she enters at the end of the play, having committed her own passionate and transgressive offstage act, surely we are meant to see her as a woman haunted by the spirit of classical tragedy. Stevie is ultimately unable to accept that she can be equated with another kind of animal, and thus her marriage is torn apart as much by a fundamental disagreement over the conceptions of the self as by any primal act of betrayal. Billy's final questioning—"Dad? Mom?"—suggests that all such roles are up for negotiation, that the radical instability of the family, nature, and civilization Albee presents allows what are, for many of us, unimaginable acts, yet also demands that we confront them.

J.E.G.

The Goat; or, Who Is Sylvia?
(*Notes Toward a Definition of Tragedy*)

PLACE

A living room.

TIME

The present.

CHARACTERS

STEVIE	ROSS
MARTIN	BILLY

Scene 1

[*The living room.* STEVIE *onstage, arranging flowers.*]

STEVIE [*calling offstage*] What time are they coming?

[*No response.*]

Martin? What time are they coming?

MARTIN [*offstage*] What?

[*Entering.*]

What?

STEVIE [*a little smile; a slowish statement*] What . . . time . . . are . . . they . . . coming.

MARTIN Who? [*Recalling*] Oh! Oh. [*Looks at watch.*] Soon; very soon. Why can't I remember anything?

STEVIE [*finishing flowers*] Why can't you remember?

MARTIN Anything; nothing; can't remember a thing. This morning—so far!—I couldn't remember where I'd put the new head for the razor; I couldn't recall Ross's son's name—still can't; two cards in my jacket make no sense to me whatever, and I'm not sure I know why I came in here.

STEVIE Todd.

MARTIN What?

STEVIE Ross's son is called Todd.

MARTIN [*slaps his forehead*] Right! Why the flowers?

STEVIE To brighten up the corner . . .

MARTIN . . . where you *are*? Where *I* am?

STEVIE . . . where you'll probably be sitting, to make the cameras happy.

MARTIN [*smelling the flowers*] What are they?

STEVIE Cameras?

MARTIN No; these.

STEVIE Ranunculus.[1] I. [*Then*] I: ranunculi.

1. A large genus of flowers that includes the buttercup (the Latin plural is *ranunculi*).

MARTIN Pretty. Why don't they smell?

STEVIE They're secretive; probably too subtle for your forgetful nose.

MARTIN [*shakes his head, mock concern*] Every sense going! Taste next! Touch; hearing. Hah! Hearing!

STEVIE What?

MARTIN What?

STEVIE And to think you're only fifty. Did you find it?

MARTIN What?

STEVIE The new head for the razor.

MARTIN Right! A new head! I'll need that next—the whole thing.

STEVIE Why did you want to remember Todd's name?

MARTIN Well, to begin with, I shouldn't be forgetting it, and when Ross shows up and he asks about Billy I can't say "He's fine; how's . . . you know . . . *your* son . . ."

STEVIE Todd.

MARTIN Todd. "How's old Todd?"

STEVIE Young Todd.

MARTIN Yes. It's the little slips.

STEVIE I wouldn't worry about it. Are you going to offer them stuff? Coffee? Beer?

MARTIN [*preoccupied*] Probably. Do you think it means anything?

STEVIE I don't know what "it" is.

MARTIN That I can't remember anything.

STEVIE Probably not: you have too much to remember, that's all. You could go in for a checkup . . . if you can remember our doctor's name.

MARTIN [*nailing it*] Percy!

STEVIE Right!

MARTIN [*to himself*] Who could forget that? Nobody has a doctor named Percy. [*To* STEVIE] What's the matter with me?

STEVIE You're fifty.

MARTIN No; more than that.

STEVIE The old foreboding? The sense that everything going right is a sure sign that everything's going wrong, of all the awful to come? All that?

MARTIN [*rueful*] Probably. Why did I come in here?

STEVIE I heard you in the hall; I called you.

MARTIN Aha.

STEVIE What's my *name*?

MARTIN Pardon?

STEVIE Who *am* I? Who am *I*?

MARTIN [*acted*] You're the love of my life, the mother of my handsome and worrisome son, my playmate, my cook, my bottlewasher.[2] Do you?

STEVIE What?

MARTIN Wash my bottles?

STEVIE [*puzzles it*] Not as a habit. I may have—washed one of your bottles. Do you have bottles?

MARTIN Everyone has bottles.

STEVIE Right. But what's my *name*?

MARTIN [*pretending confusion*] Uh . . . Stevie?

2. A humorous title for a servant who handles all his master's affairs.

STEVIE Good. Will this be a long one?

MARTIN A long what?

STEVIE Interview.

MARTIN The usual, I guess. Ross said it wasn't going to be a feature—sort of a catch-up.

STEVIE On your fiftieth.

MARTIN [*nods*] On my fiftieth. I wonder if I should tell him that my mind's going? If I can remember.

STEVIE [*laughs; hugs him from behind*] Your mind's not going.

MARTIN My what?

STEVIE Your mind, darling; it's not going . . . anywhere.

MARTIN [*serious*] Am I too young for Alzheimer's?[3]

STEVIE Probably. Isn't it nice to be too young for something?

MARTIN [*mind elsewhere*] Um-hum.

STEVIE The joke is, if you can remember what it's called you don't have it.

MARTIN Have what?

STEVIE Alz . . .

[*They both laugh; he kisses her forehead.*]

Oh, you know how to turn a girl on! Forehead kisses! [*Sniffs him.*] Where have you been?

MARTIN [*releases her; preoccupied*] What time are they coming?

STEVIE Soon, you said; very soon.

MARTIN I did? Good.

STEVIE Did you find it?

MARTIN What?

STEVIE The head for your razor.

MARTIN No; it's around somewhere. [*Fishes in a pocket, brings out cards.*] But these! Now these! What the hell are these!? "Basic Services, Limited." Basic Services, Limited?? Limited to what!? [*The other card*] "Clarissa Atherton." [*Shrugs.*] Clarissa Atherton? No number, no . . . internet thing? Clarissa Atherton?

STEVIE Basic services? Clarissa Atherton, basic services?

MARTIN Hm? Every time someone gives me one of these, I know I'm supposed to give them one back, and I don't have them. It's embarrassing.

STEVIE I've told you to have them made . . . cards.

MARTIN I don't want to.

STEVIE Then don't. Who is she?

MARTIN Who?

STEVIE Clarissa Atherton, basic services. Does she smell funny?

MARTIN I don't know. [*Afterthought*] I don't know who she is, as far as I know. Where were we this week?

STEVIE [*overly casual; stretches*] Oh, it doesn't matter, sweetie. If you're seeing this Atherton woman, this . . . dominatrix . . . who smells funny . . .

MARTIN How could I be seeing her—whoever she is? There's nothing on the card. Dominatrix!?

STEVIE Why not?

MARTIN Maybe you know things I don't.

STEVIE Maybe.

3. Though Alzeimer's disease is a dementia that usually develops after age 65, it can occur earlier.

MARTIN And I probably know one or two things you *don't.*

STEVIE It evens out.

MARTIN Yes. Do I look OK?

STEVIE For the TV? Yes.

MARTIN Yes. [*Turning*] Really?

STEVIE I said: yes; fine. [*Indicates.*] The old prep school tie?

MARTIN [*genuine, as he looks*] Is it? Oh, yeah; so it is.

STEVIE [*not letting him have it*] *No* one puts on their prep school tie by accident. *No* one.

MARTIN [*considers*] What if you can't remember that's what it is?

STEVIE *No* one!! If you do get Alzheimer's, and you get to the stage you don't know who *I* am, who *Billy* is, who *you* are, for that matter . . .

MARTIN Billy?

STEVIE [*laughs*] Stop it! When you get to the point you can't remember anything, someone will hand you *that* [*indicates his tie*] and you'll look at it and you'll say [*terrible imitation of aged man*] "Ahhhhh! My prep school tie! My prep school tie!"

[*They chuckle; the doorbell rings/chimes.*]

MARTIN Ah! Doom time!

STEVIE [*quite matter-of-fact*] If you *are* seeing that woman, I think we'd better talk about it.

MARTIN [*stops. Long pause; matter-of-fact*] If I *were* . . . we *would.*

STEVIE [*as offhand as possible*] If not the dominatrix, then some blonde half your age, some . . . chippie, as they used to call them . . .

MARTIN . . . or, worst of all, someone just like you? As bright; as resourceful; as intrepid; . . . merely . . . new?

STEVIE [*warm smile; shake of head*] You win 'em all, don't you.

MARTIN [*same smile*] Enough.

[*Door again. The next several speeches are done in a greatly exaggerated Noël Coward*[4] *play manner: English accents, flamboyant gestures.*]

STEVIE Something's going on, isn't it!?

MARTIN Yes! I've fallen in love!

STEVIE I knew it!

MARTIN Hopelessly!

STEVIE I knew it!

MARTIN I fought against it!

STEVIE Oh, you poor darling!

MARTIN Fought hard!

STEVIE I suppose you'd better tell me!

MARTIN I can't! I can't!

STEVIE Tell me! Tell me!

MARTIN Her name is Sylvia!

STEVIE Sylvia? Who is Sylvia?

MARTIN She's a goat; Sylvia is a goat! [*Acting manner dropped; normal tone now; serious, flat*] She's a goat.

STEVIE [*long pause; she stares, finally smiles. Giggles, chortles, moves toward the hall; normal tone*] You're too much!

[*Exits.*]

4. British actor, songwriter, and playwright (1899–1973), known for comic repartee.

MARTIN I am? [*Shrugs; to himself.*] You try to *tell* them; you try to be *honest.* What do they do? They laugh at you. [*Imitation*] "You're too much!" [*Thinks about it.*] I suppose I am.

ROSS Hey honey.

STEVIE Hi Ross.

[ROSS *enters with* STEVIE.]

ROSS Hello there, old man!

MARTIN I'm fifty!

ROSS It's a term of endearment. Nice flowers.

MARTIN It is?

ROSS What? What is?

MARTIN "Hello there, old man." Ranunculi.

ROSS Pardon?

STEVIE The proper plural of ranunculus—the flowers, according to old Martin here.

MARTIN Some say ranunculuses, but that sounds wrong, even though it's probably perfectly acceptable.

ROSS [*not interested*] Aha! Let's move that chair over to the . . . whatever they are . . . the flowers. [*To* MARTIN] Are you happy in that chair?

MARTIN Am I happy in it? I don't even know if I've ever sat in it. [*To* STEVIE] Have I? Have I ever sat in it?

STEVIE You just did, and you sat in it the last time Ross did the program with you.

ROSS That's *right!*

MARTIN Yes . . . but was I happy? Did I sit there and did contentment bathe me in its warm light?

ROSS You got me, fella.

STEVIE Yes; contentment fell; you sat there and I watched it bathe you in its warm light. I've got to go.

MARTIN Where are you going?

STEVIE [*no information*] Out.

MARTIN Are we in tonight?

STEVIE Yes. I think Billy's going out.

MARTIN Naturally!

STEVIE We're in. [*Glee*] TV time! I'm getting my hair done, and then I thought I'd stop by the feed store.

[*Exits, giggling.*]

ROSS By *what?* She's going to stop by *what?*

MARTIN [*staring after her*] Nothing; nowhere. [*To* ROSS] No crew?

ROSS Just me this time—the old handheld. [*Indicates camera.*] You ready for the chair?

MARTIN [*singsong*] Ha, ha. [*Suddenly remembering*] How's old *Todd!?*

ROSS "Old Todd?"

MARTIN You know: old *Todd!*

ROSS You mean my baby son who just last week it seems I dandled on my knee? *That* old Todd?

MARTIN Lovely word—dandled. Yes: *that* old Todd.

ROSS Who I cannot accept having become eighteen?

MARTIN Whom.

ROSS Maybe.

MARTIN Yes; that one. Can any of us? Ever?

ROSS Pushing me further into middle age?

MARTIN Yes; that one.

ROSS [*offhand*] He's OK. [*Laughs.*] He asked me last week—first time since he was four, or something—why he didn't have a brother, or a sister, or whatever—why April and I never had another kid.

MARTIN April, May, June—the pastel months. You name girl babies after them.

ROSS [*doesn't care*] Right. [*Does care.*] I told him if you do it right the first time, why take a chance on another.

MARTIN Did he like that one?

ROSS Seemed to. Of course, I could have told him the whole graduating class got together and vowed that we would all have only one kid each—keep the population down. Speaking of which, how's Billy? How's *yours*—*your* one and only?

MARTIN [*attempted throw-away tone*] Ohhhh, seventeen last week—didn't Todd come to the party? No, I guess he didn't. Real cute kid, Billy, bright as you'd ever want, gay as the nineties.[5]

ROSS Passing phase. Have you had the old serious talk?

MARTIN The "You'll get over it once you meet the right girl" lecture? Nah, I'm too smart for that, so's he, so's Billy. I told him to be sure. Says he's sure; loves it, he says.

ROSS Well, of course he loves it; he's getting laid, for God's sake! Don't worry about him.

MARTIN Who?

ROSS Billy! Seventeen; it's a phase.

MARTIN Like the moon, eh?

ROSS He'll straighten out—to make a pun. [*To quash the subject*] Billy'll come out of it; he'll be OK.

MARTIN [*reassuring if a bit patronizing*] Sure.

ROSS Voice test? Phone off?

MARTIN I assume Stevie did it.

ROSS I hear a kind of . . . rushing sound, like a . . . wooooosh!, or . . . wings, or something.

MARTIN It's probably the Eumenides.[6]

ROSS More like the dishwasher. There; it stopped.

MARTIN Then it probably wasn't the Eumenides: they don't stop.

ROSS [*agreeing*] They go right on.

MARTIN Right.

ROSS Why is Stevie going to the feed store?

MARTIN She isn't.

ROSS Then why did she . . .

MARTIN It's a joke.

ROSS A standing joke?

5. "Gay nineties" is a phrase originally applied to the 1890s (a time of great prosperity among the upper class in the northeastern United States).

6. Literally, "the Kindly Ones" (Greek), a euphemism for the Erinyes or Furies; in classical mythology, they were monstrous female personifications of vengeance.

MARTIN No, a new one; a brand-new one.

ROSS OK? Ready? Ready Martin; here we go; just . . . be yourself.

MARTIN Really?

ROSS [*a tiny bit testy*] Well, no; maybe not. Put on your public face.

MARTIN [*overly cheerful*] OK!!

ROSS And don't switch in the middle.

MARTIN [*more*] OK!!

ROSS [*under his breath*] Jesus!

[*Announcer voice.*]

Good evening. This is Ross Tuttle. Welcome to "People Who Matter." Some people have birthdays and no one pays them any mind. Well . . . family, of course, friends. And others . . . well, some people are . . . I was going to say special, but that's a . . . dumb word, for everyone matters, everyone's special. But some people matter in extraordinary ways, in ways which affect the lives of the rest of us—enrich them, inform them. Some people, I guess, are, well . . . more extraordinary than others. Martin Gray—whom you've met on this program before—is such a man, such a person. Good evening, Martin.

MARTIN Good . . . uh, evening, Ross.

[*Sotto voce.*[7]]

It's mid-afternoon.

ROSS [*quiet snarl*] I know. Shut up!

[*Announcer voice.*]

Three things happened to you this week, Martin. You became the youngest person ever to win the Pritzker Prize, architecture's version of the Nobel. Also this week you were chosen to design The World City, the two hundred billion dollar dream city of the future, financed by U.S. Electronics Technology and set to rise in the wheatfields of our Middle West. Also, this week, you celebrated your fiftieth birthday. Happy birthday, Martin, and congratulations!

MARTIN [*brief pause; casual*] Thanks, Ross.

ROSS Quite a week, Martin!

MARTIN [*a little puzzled*] Yes; yes it was. Quite a week.

ROSS [*big*] How does it feel, Martin?

MARTIN Becoming fifty?

ROSS [*pushing*] No. *All* of it. Yes.

MARTIN Well . . .

ROSS [*sensing no answer is coming*] It must be amazing! No, thrilling!

MARTIN Turning fifty? No: not really.

ROSS [*not amused*] No! The other! The World City! The Pritzker! All that!

MARTIN [*genuine surprise*] Oh, that! Well, yes . . . amazing, thrilling.

ROSS [*prompting*] For one so young.

MARTIN [*innocent*] Fifty is young?

ROSS [*controlling himself*] For the Pritzker Prize! Where were you when they told you?

MARTIN I was at the gym; I'd taken all my clothes off, and Stevie called me there.

7. Under the voice (Italian); that is, spoken very softly, under the breath.

ROSS Stevie is your wife.
MARTIN I know that.
ROSS How did it make you feel?
MARTIN Stevie being my wife?
ROSS No: the Prize.
MARTIN Well, it was . . . gratifying—not being naked, but . . . hearing about it—the Prize.
ROSS [*exuberant*] Weren't you . . . thunderstruck!?
MARTIN Well, no; they'd hinted at it—the Prize, I mean, and . . .
ROSS [*heavily prompting*] But it was pretty wonderful, wasn't it?
MARTIN [*understanding what to say*] Yes; yes it was pretty wonderful—*is* pretty wonderful.
ROSS Tell us about The World City.
MARTIN Well, you just *did:* two hundred billion dollars, and all, the wheat-fields of Kansas, or whatever . . .
ROSS What an honor! What a duo of honors! You're at the . . . pinnacle of your success, Martin . . .
MARTIN [*considers that*] You mean it's all downhill from here?
ROSS CUT! CUT!

[*Camera down. To* MARTIN.]

What's the matter with you!?
MARTIN Sorry?
ROSS I can't shoot that! You were a million miles away!!
MARTIN [*considering*] That far.
ROSS You want to try again?
MARTIN Try what?
ROSS The taping! The program!
MARTIN [*as if seeing the camera for the first time*] Oooooh.
ROSS We're taping!
MARTIN [*unhappy*] Yes; I know.
ROSS [*nicely concerned*] Something the matter?
MARTIN I think so. Yes; probably.
ROSS Do you want to talk about it, as they say?
MARTIN About what?
ROSS About what's the matter.
MARTIN [*concerned*] Why? What's the matter?
ROSS You said something was the matter, that you think something's the matter.
MARTIN [*far away*] Oh.
ROSS Forty years, Martin; we've known each other forty years—since we were ten.
MARTIN [*trying to understand*] Yes. That gives you something? Rights, or something?
ROSS I'm your oldest friend.
MARTIN No; my aesthetics professor at college; I still see him; he's a lot older than you; he's over ninety.
ROSS [*so patient*] Your longest friend: the person you've known the longest.
MARTIN No; my Aunt Sarah; she's known me . . .
ROSS [*trying to stay patient*] She's not a friend!
MARTIN [*deep, quiet surprise*] Oh?

ROSS [*close to giving up*] No; she's a relative; relatives are not friends!

MARTIN Oh, now . . .

ROSS Are not the same as friends. Jesus!

MARTIN Aha! Yes; well, you're right. I've known you longer as a friend than anyone. [*Tiny pause*] Why is that relevant?

ROSS Because you're troubled, and I thought that as your oldest friend I might be able to . . .

MARTIN I am? Is that true?

ROSS You said that something was the matter!

MARTIN [*not remembering*] I did, hunh?

ROSS Why are you so . . . ? [*Can't find the word.*]

MARTIN Are you still shooting? Are you still on?

ROSS [*heavy sigh*] No. We'll try to do it at the studio later. Sorry.

MARTIN Can I get up now?

ROSS If you want to; if you're not happy.

MARTIN Why are you talking to me like I was a child?

ROSS Because you're acting like one.

MARTIN [*innocent*] I am?

ROSS Probably the most important week of your life . . .

MARTIN [*impressed, if uninvolved*] Really!

ROSS . . . and you act like you don't know whether you're coming or going, like you don't know where you are.

MARTIN [*self-absorbed, almost to himself*] Maybe it's . . . love or something.

ROSS Maybe what is?

MARTIN Like a child.

ROSS [*bingo!*] You're having an affair!

MARTIN SHHHHHHHH! I mean, Jesus!

ROSS [*shrugs*] It's OK; he's not having an affair.

MARTIN Jesus! Too bad you didn't bring the crew; they'd love this.

ROSS [*cool*] They know their business.

MARTIN And . . . ?

ROSS And . . . ?

MARTIN Aren't you guys friendly anymore?

ROSS They know their business. What do you want me to do—have them over for *dinner*? Have every crew over for dinner?

MARTIN [*puzzled*] No, I guess not. [*Afterthought*] Why *not*?

ROSS Hm?

MARTIN Why *not* have them over for dinner?

ROSS Oh, for God's sake, Martin!

MARTIN [*hands up, defensively*] OK! OK! Jesus!

ROSS It's just that . . . it's just that I don't . . . mix with . . .

MARTIN [*joyful*] The *help*?! You don't mix with the *help*!?

ROSS What *is* wrong with you today!? That's not what I meant, and you *know* it.

MARTIN [*half-serious, half-joking*] You're a snob! I guess I've always known that. For all your left-wing, proletarian background, you're a *snob:* worst kind.

ROSS [*a plea; a warning*] We're best friends, remember?

MARTIN Meaning . . . ?

ROSS We like each other.

MARTIN [*"so, that's it!"*] Ohhhhhhhh!

ROSS More than anyone.

MARTIN [*ibid.*[8]] Ohhhhh! [*Considers it.*] Right; yes. Who else can I be cranky with?

ROSS Stevie?

MARTIN Ya know, Stevie doesn't take too well to cranky anymore. If she's developed a flaw, it's that. "Don't be so cranky, Martin."

ROSS Pity.

[*They've gentled down now.*]

MARTIN [*shrugs*] Well . . . *you* know.

ROSS [*pause*] So you're in love.

MARTIN With Stevie? Sure! Twenty-two years now.

ROSS No, I mean . . . "in love." Ficky-fack! Humpty-doodle!

MARTIN What on earth are you talking about!? "Humpty-doodle"!?

ROSS You said you were in love—outside of Stevie, as I read it.

MARTIN [*genuine*] Really? I don't remember.

ROSS [*impatient sigh; abrupt*] O . . . K! That does it!

MARTIN [*as* ROSS *gathers up stuff; true innocence*] Where are you going?

ROSS [*staring him down*] I'm gathering my things and I'm taking my left-wing . . . what was it?

MARTIN Uh . . . proletarian.

ROSS . . . proletarian self outta here.

MARTIN "But, why!" as the . . .

ROSS Look, I came here to fucking interview you.

MARTIN Fine.

ROSS To boost your ego even more than . . .

MARTIN I have no ego.

ROSS Bullshit! Even more than where it is already and you fuck that up.

MARTIN Fine. You say fuck a lot.

ROSS You say fine a lot.

[*He laughs; so does* MARTIN.]

MARTIN Words beginning with F.

ROSS [*smiles*] Yeah. [*Pause*] So; tell me about it.

MARTIN [*shy*] About . . . ?

ROSS [*gently urging*] Your new love.

MARTIN Oh; that.

ROSS Yes.

MARTIN I don't know that I want to.

ROSS Yes; you do.

MARTIN . . . that I can.

ROSS Try.

MARTIN [*small smile*] You're persistent.

ROSS Best friend.

[MARTIN *tries to talk; can't.*]

Best friend.

MARTIN [*frustrated explosion*] OK!! OK!! [*Heavy, slow sigh; long pause*] I don't know if I ever thought that . . . well, that Stevie and I would be . . . well, no; we're not.

8. That is, the same way (the Latin *ibidem* literally means "in the same place").

[*Pause.*]

ROSS Are you telling me about it?

MARTIN I'm starting to . . . or maybe I'm beginning to start.

ROSS Oh; OK.

MARTIN As I said, it never occurred to me that anything like this would come up. 'Cause we've always been good together—good in bed, good out; always honest, always . . . considerate. I've not been unfaithful our whole marriage; I want you to know this; never physically untrue, as they say.

ROSS That's amazing. It's wonderful, but . . . wow!

MARTIN Yes: wow. Oh, I've been groped in the kitchen by a cutie or two, late, a party, once or twice, and I've had my hand a couple of places a couple of times, but I've never . . . *done* anything. You follow.

ROSS Yes; I follow.

MARTIN It never seemed . . . well, necessary, either to be able to do a comparison, or . . . even for its own sake. I never needed it, I guess. Do you remember that time, that college reunion weekend you and I decided to call that service they'd told us about . . . the gang had told us about?

ROSS [*rueful laugh*] The Ladies Aid Society?

MARTIN Yeah, and you called them, and . . .

ROSS . . . and we had a couple of bimbos over . . .

MARTIN Bimbi.

ROSS Yes? [*Broad*] Ohhhhh, I remember.

MARTIN . . . and you were married already, and Stevie and I were dating . . . or going together . . .

ROSS . . . or whatever.

MARTIN Yes.

ROSS [*trying to recall*] What were their names?

MARTIN Mine was Alice.

ROSS Big girl.

MARTIN Large Alice.[9]

ROSS Right! Mine was Trudy, or Trixie, or . . .

MARTIN April.

ROSS Yes? April?

MARTIN Yes; April.

ROSS [*interior*] Oh, shit; April's called April.

MARTIN [*registering it*] Yes; she is.

ROSS Shit. [*Pause; recovers.*] And we had them up to our room—two beds, two hookers.

MARTIN Just like when we roomed together.

ROSS A kind of reunion for the reunion.

MARTIN Yes, I guess so. And do you remember what happened?

ROSS I don't know. What happened?

MARTIN I couldn't do it? Couldn't perform?

ROSS [*recalls*] Oh, yeah. You'd never had that problem when we were undergrads! I'd be pumping away, you pumping away in the next bed.

MARTIN I hadn't met Stevie.

ROSS [*soberer*] Right.

MARTIN That night at the reunion with large Alice . . .

9. An allusion to *Tiny Alice* (1964), Albee's own play.

ROSS You were going with Stevie . . .

MARTIN Right.

ROSS I remember.

MARTIN I don't know why I ever thought I wanted to . . . *you* know.

ROSS No. Right.

MARTIN I was already in love with Stevie and I didn't know how much.

ROSS [*a little deriding*] Amazing theory: the heart rules the dick. I always thought that the dick was driven by . . .

MARTIN Don't be cynical.

ROSS Oh, a new part of my left-wing . . . what?

MARTIN Proletarian.

ROSS Yes. My left-wing, proletarian, snobbish, *cynical* self.

MARTIN Right, and not new.

[*They both smile.*]

You *do* see, don't you? In love with Stevie, she owns every part of me. Look, when I'm traveling, and Stevie's *here,* and I get itchy . . .

ROSS You give yourself a handjob and you think about Stevie—about you and Stevie.

MARTIN [*shy*] Yes.

ROSS [*shakes his head; noncommittal*] Wonderful.

MARTIN I didn't catch your tone.

ROSS There wasn't any. Go on; how did you fuck it up?

MARTIN [*truly confused*] What? Fuck *what* up?

ROSS Are you playing games?

MARTIN No. Fuck *what* up?

ROSS [*serious*] Your life, apparently—you and Stevie. How'd you fuck it up?

MARTIN [*pause*] Oh. [*Pause*] That.

ROSS [*impatient*] Getting an answer out of you . . .

MARTIN OK! OK! As I told you, I've never been unfaithful, never needed it . . . never . . .

ROSS Yeah, yeah; right. You told me.

MARTIN And then . . . one day . . .

[*Stops.*]

ROSS [*after a silence*] Yeah!?

MARTIN And then one day.

[*Says nothing more.*]

ROSS [*long pause*] That's it!?

MARTIN [*goes ahead*] And then one day . . . one day . . . well, I was house-hunting—barn-hunting, actually. Stevie and I had decided it was time to have a real country place—a farm, maybe—we deserved it. So, I was in the car about sixty miles out from the city. Stevie couldn't come with me.

ROSS Beyond the suburbs.

MARTIN Yes; beyond the suburbs. Farms around it, small farms. And I found a wonderful place, a wonderful old farmhouse, and a lot of land.

ROSS The old back twenty,[1] or whatever it is.

1. That is, the back forty, a phrase referring to one-fourth of a quarter section of land (40 acres; a *section* is one square mile).

MARTIN Right! Whatever. And I called Stevie, and told her she had to see it, and I'd put a hold on it 'til she could see it. And Stevie was . . . well, "A farm?" she said, but I said "Wait!" And the real estate guy was OK with that for a while. And I was driving out of the town back to the highway, and I stopped at the top of a hill.

ROSS Crest.

MARTIN Right. And I stopped, and the view was . . . well, not spectacular, but . . . wonderful. Fall, you know?, with leaves turning and the town below me and great scudding clouds and those country smells.

ROSS Cow shit, and all that.

MARTIN [*broad country parody*] New-mown hay, fella! The smell a country; the smell a apples! [*Normal tone again*] The roadside stands, with corn and other stuff piled high, and baskets full of other things—beans and tomatoes and those great white peaches you only get late summer . . .

ROSS [*broad*] The whole thing; right.

MARTIN [*shakes his head*] Oh, you city boys! And from up there I could trace the roads out toward the farm, and it gave me a kind of shiver.

ROSS The ludicrous often does.

MARTIN Anyway . . .

ROSS Anyway.

MARTIN Anyway, it was pretty wonderful. And I was getting back in the car, about to get back in the car, all my loot—vegetables and stuff . . . [*Change of tone to quiet wonder*] and it was then that I saw her. [*Sees it.*] Just . . . just looking at me.

ROSS Daisy Mae! Blonde hair to her shoulders, big tits in the calico blouse, bare midriff, blonde down at the navel, piece a straw in her teeth . . .

MARTIN [*gentle, admonishing smile*] You don't understand.

ROSS No? No blonde hair? No tits?

MARTIN No. And there she was, looking at me with those eyes.

ROSS And it was love.

MARTIN You don't understand.

ROSS No? It *wasn't* love?

MARTIN No. Yes; yes, it was love, but I didn't know it right then. [*To himself*] How could I?

ROSS Right then it was good old lust, eh? Dick starting to get big in your pants . . .

MARTIN [*sad*] You *don't* understand. [*Pause*] I didn't know *what* it was—what I was feeling. It was . . . it wasn't like anything I'd felt before; it was . . . so . . . amazing, so . . . extraordinary! There she was, just looking at me, with those *eyes* of hers, and . . .

ROSS [*impatient*] Well, did you *talk* to her?

MARTIN [*incredulous laugh*] Did I *what!?*

ROSS Did you *talk* to her!?

MARTIN [*considers it*] Hunh! Yes; yes, I did. I went up to her, to where she was, and I spoke to her, and she came toward me and . . . and those eyes, and I touched her face, and . . . [*Abrupt*] I don't want to talk about it; I can't *talk* about it.

ROSS All right; let me help you. You're *seeing* her.

MARTIN [*sad laugh*] Yes; oh, yes; I'm *seeing* her.

ROSS You're having an affair with her.

MARTIN [*confused*] A what? Having a *what!?*

ROSS [*hard*] You're *screwing* her.

MARTIN [*sudden vision of it*] Yes; yes; I'm *screwing* her. Oh, Jesus!

ROSS [*softer*] And you're in love.

MARTIN That's it, you see.

ROSS What is? What do I see?

MARTIN I *am* seeing her; I *am* having . . . an affair, I guess. No! That's not the right word. I am . . . [*winces*] screwing her, as you put it—all of which is . . . beyond even . . . yes, I'm doing all that.

ROSS [*prompting*] . . . and you're in love with her.

MARTIN [*begins to cry*] Yes! Yes! I am! I'm in love with her. Oh, Jesus! Oh, Sylvia! Oh, Sylvia!

ROSS [*after a respectful pause*] I almost dare not ask this, but . . . who is Sylvia?

MARTIN I can't tell you!

ROSS Who else *but* me? You can't tell Stevie, it would . . .

MARTIN NO!!

ROSS Then, who is she? Who is Sylvia?

[MARTIN *pauses; goes to wallet, brings out photo, looks at it, hesitates, then hands it to* ROSS, *not looking as he does so.* ROSS *takes photo, looks at it, double-takes, begins a huge guffaw, which becomes a coughing.*]

MARTIN [*shy*] Don't laugh. Please; don't laugh.

ROSS [*staring at photo; straightforward*] This is Sylvia.

MARTIN [*nods*] Yes.

ROSS [*pinning it down*] This is Sylvia . . . who you're fucking.

MARTIN [*winces*] Don't say that. [*It just comes out.*] Whom.

ROSS . . . with whom you're having an affair.

MARTIN [*soft; nodding*] Yes. [*Pause*] Yes.

ROSS How long now?

MARTIN [*soft*] Six months.

ROSS Jesus. You *have* to tell Stevie.

MARTIN I can't! I couldn't do that!

ROSS You *have* to . . . and if you don't, I will.

MARTIN [*begging*] No! Ross! Please!

ROSS [*genuine*] You're in very serious trouble.

MARTIN [*pause; little boy*] I am?

ROSS [*quiet; shaking his head as he looks at the photo*] You sure are, buddy; you sure are.

MARTIN But, Ross, you don't under . . .

ROSS [*huge*] THIS IS A GOAT! YOU'RE HAVING AN AFFAIR WITH A GOAT! YOU'RE FUCKING A GOAT!

MARTIN [*long pause; factual*] Yes.

Curtain.

Scene 2

[*The living room; a day later.* MARTIN, STEVIE, *and* BILLY; STEVIE *holding a letter.*]

BILLY [*to* MARTIN] You're doing *what?!* You're fucking a *goat?!*

MARTIN [*indicating* STEVIE, *who is at window, facing out*] Billy! Please!

BILLY Jesus Christ!

MARTIN Don't swear.

BILLY [*scoffing laugh*] Don't *what?!*

MARTIN Don't swear; you're too young.

BILLY [*considers a moment, then*] FUCK THAT!!

MARTIN Billy! Your mother!

BILLY [*scoffing laugh*] You're fucking a fucking goat and you tell me not to *swear?!*

MARTIN You know, your *own* sex life leaves a little to . . . .

STEVIE [*still at window; ice*] All right, you two!

BILLY [*to* MARTIN] At least what I do is with . . . persons!

STEVIE [*turning into the room*] I said, all right, you two!

BILLY Goat fucker!

MARTIN Fucking faggot!

STEVIE I said, all right!

[*A silence.*]

BILLY [*to* MARTIN; *soft, hurt*] Fucking faggot? You called me a fucking *faggot?!*

MARTIN [*gentle; to* BILLY] I'm . . . I'm sorry.

STEVIE [*even*] Your father's sorry, Billy.

MARTIN I'm sorry. [*To get rid of the whole subject*] You're gay, and that's fine, and I don't give a shit what you put where. [*Thinks about it.*] I don't care one way or the other is what I mean.

BILLY Yeah! Sure!

STEVIE [*cool*] I said your father's sorry for calling you a fucking faggot because he's not that kind of man. He's a decent, liberal, right-thinking, talented, famous, gentle man [*hard*] who right now would appear to be fucking a goat; and *I* would like to talk about *that, if* you don't mind. *Or* . . . even if you *do.*

BILLY [*nice*] Sure, Mom; I'm sorry; you go right ahead.

MARTIN [*sighs*] Oh, dear.

STEVIE [*objective*] Let's review Ross's letter, shall we? [*Waves it.*]

MARTIN [*hurt and enraged*] How *could* he!! How could he do such a thing?!

STEVIE [*ice*] How could he—best friend to both of us, a man you would trust with your wife—no? . . .

MARTIN . . . sure; sure . . .

STEVIE How could Ross write me this letter? [*Waves it again.*]

MARTIN YES!!

STEVIE [*composed; cool; quoting*] ". . . because I love you, Stevie, as much as I love Martin, because I love you both—respect you, love you—I can't stay silent at a time of crisis for you both, for Martin's public image, and your own deeply devoted . . ."

MARTIN BULLSHIT!

STEVIE Yes?

MARTIN Yes!

STEVIE So; anyhow; let's not pretend he never wrote the letter; let's not pretend I didn't get it in the mail today—nice that: no electronic nonsense—and let us not pretend that I did not read it.

MARTIN No; no, of course not.

STEVIE And let us not pretend that Ross does not tell me that you are having an affair with . . . [*looks*] how does he put it? . . . "an affair with a certain Sylvia who, I am mortified to tell you . . ." He does get flowery, doesn't he!

MARTIN Yes; yes, he does.

STEVIE "I am mortified to tell you is a goat."

BILLY Jesus!

STEVIE and MARTIN Will you be still!!?

BILLY [*dramatically cowering*] Hey! Sure! Jesus!

STEVIE [*back to business; quoting again*] "You will, of eourse, be shocked and greatly distressed . . ." No kidding! Uh . . . "shocked and greatly distressed to know of this, but I felt it my obligation to be the one to bear these tidings . . ."

MARTIN [*some disbelief*] Tidings?

STEVIE Yes; "tidings."

MARTIN Jesus! Of comfort and joy?[2]

STEVIE ". . . as I'm sure you'd rather hear it all from a dear friend . . ." As opposed to *what!* The ASPCA?![3]

MARTIN [*woe*] Oh, God; oh, God.

STEVIE "Doubtless, Martin . . ." Doubtless?

MARTIN Probably.

STEVIE ". . . doubtless Martin will tell you all I have not, all I cannot." [*To* MARTIN] What are friends for, eh?

BILLY [*really sad*] Oh, Dad!

MARTIN Poor Dad?[4]

BILLY What?

MARTIN Nothing.

STEVIE [*level*] So, now you will tell me all that Ross has not, cannot. After you tell me what friends are for, of course.

MARTIN Oh . . . Stevie . . .

[*Starts to move to her.*]

STEVIE [*abrupt; cold*] Stay away from me; stay there. You smell of goat, you smell of shit, you smell of all I cannot imagine being able to smell. Stay *away* from me!

MARTIN [*arms wide; hopeless*] I *love* you!

BILLY [*softly*] Jesus.

STEVIE You *love* me. Let's see if I understand the phrase. You *love* me.

MARTIN Yes!

STEVIE But I'm a human being; I have only two breasts; I walk upright; I give milk only on special occasions; I use the toilet. [*Begins to cry*] You love me? I don't understand.

MARTIN [*more hopeless*] Oh, God!

STEVIE How can you love me when you love so much less?

2. An allusion to the refrain of a traditional Christmas carol, "God Rest Ye Merry Gentlemen" ("tidings of comfort and joy").

3. The American Society for the Prevention of Cruelty to Animals.

4. An allusion to *Oh Dad, Poor Dad, Mamma's Hung You in the Closet and I'm Feelin' So Sad* (1960), a play by Arthur L. Kopit.

MARTIN [*even more hopeless*] Oh, God.

BILLY Fucking a goat?!

MARTIN [*to* BILLY; *sharp*] That does it! Out!

BILLY [*to* STEVIE; *arms wide*] What did I *say*? I said he was . . .

MARTIN Enough!

BILLY For Christ's sake, I . . .

MARTIN Go to your room!

STEVIE [*almost laughing*] Oh, really, Martin!

BILLY [*incredulous*] Go to my room?!

MARTIN Go to your *room!*

BILLY What am I—eight, or something? Go to my *room?*

STEVIE You'd better go, Billy. If you stay you might learn something.

MARTIN [*to* STEVIE] Nicely put.

STEVIE [*coldly*] Thanks.

BILLY [*to* STEVIE] You want me to leave you here with this . . . this . . . *pervert?!*

STEVIE [*to help*] Just go to your room, Billy, or go outside, or . . .

MARTIN . . . or go to one of your public urinals, or one of those death clubs, or . . .

BILLY KNOCK IT OFF!!

MARTIN [*impressed*] Wow!

BILLY [*sneering*] You seem to know a lot about all that.

MARTIN [*not defensive*] I *read*.

BILLY Sure. [*To* STEVIE] I'll go if you think it's OK, Ma; I'll go. [*To* MARTIN] But not to your . . . "places." I will probably go to my room, and I'll probably close my door, and I'll probably lie down on my bed, and I'll probably start crying and it'll probably get louder and worse, but you probably won't hear it—either of you—because you'll be too busy killing each other. But I'll be there, and my little eight-year-old heart will for certain be breaking—in twain, as they say.

MARTIN [*some awe; no contempt*] Very good; very good.

STEVIE [*preoccupied*] Yes; very good, Billy.

BILLY [*feeling; near tears*] Jesus Christ!

STEVIE [*as he exits*] Billy . . .

MARTIN [*quietly*] Let him go. [*Silence; quietly*] Well, now; just you and me.

STEVIE [*pause*] Yes.

MARTIN [*pause*] I take it you want to talk about it?

STEVIE [*awful chuckle*] Oh, God! [*Afterthought*] You *take* it?

MARTIN Is that a "yes"?

STEVIE [*cold; precise*] I was out shopping today—dress gloves, if you want to know. I still wear them—for weddings and things . . .

MARTIN [*puzzled*] Who's getting married?

STEVIE [*huge*] SHUT UP!

MARTIN [*winces*] Sorry.

STEVIE [*normal tone again*] . . . dress gloves, and then to the fish people for shad roe—it's just come in—and then back home, and you were gone and I heard Billy's music up in his room and there was the mail. You'd gone out before it came—not that it would have mattered: we don't read each other's.

MARTIN Would that we did.

STEVIE Oh? I would have found out sooner or later. And there was Ross's letter. "Ross? Writing to me? Whatever for!"

MARTIN [*softly*] Oh, God.

STEVIE . . . and I was standing in the pantry. I'd put the roe away and had left the kitchen and was moving to the dining room on my way to the stairs when I began to read it.

MARTIN Ross shouldn't have done this. He *knows* he shouldn't have done . . .

STEVIE [*reading; steady, almost amused*] "Dearest Stevie . . ."

MARTIN Oh, God.

STEVIE "This is the hardest letter I've ever had to write."

MARTIN Sure!

STEVIE You doubt it? ". . . the hardest letter I've ever had to write, and to my dearest friends. But because I love you, Stevie, as much as I love Martin, because I love you both—respect you, love you—I can't stay silent at a time of crisis for you both, for Martin's public image and your own deeply devoted . . ."

MARTIN As I said, bullshit.

STEVIE . . . "self. I must put it baldly, for hinting would only put off the inevitable. Martin—and he told me this himself" . . .

[*Aside.*]

I would have liked to have been listening to *that* conversation!

MARTIN No you wouldn't.

STEVIE [*reading again*] "Martin is having an affair with a certain Sylvia . . ."

[*To* MARTIN.]

Oh, God, I thought; at least it's someone I don't know; at least it's not Ross's first wife, the one I thought you might if you were going to . . .

MARTIN [*surprise*] Rebecca?

STEVIE Yes, or maybe your new assistant . . .

MARTIN [*bewildered*] Who? Ted Ryan?

STEVIE No; the *other* one—the one with the hooters.

MARTIN Oh; Lucy something.

STEVIE Yes: Lucy "something." You men are the end. Where was I?

[*Reads again.*]

. . . "an affair with a certain Sylvia who, I am mortified to tell you . . . is a goat. You will, of course, be shocked and greatly disturbed to know of this, but I felt it my obligation to be the one to bear these tidings, as I'm sure you'd rather hear it from a dear friend. Doubtless, Martin . . ." Doubtless?

MARTIN [*shrugs*] Sounds right.

STEVIE "Doubtless, Martin will tell you all I have not . . . all I cannot. With profound affection for you both, Ross."

[*Pause.*]

Well.

MARTIN Yes. "Well."

STEVIE [*not eager; dogged*] We will now discuss it.

MARTIN [*heavy sigh*] Of course, though you won't understand.

STEVIE Oh? Do you know what I thought—what I thought after I'd read the letter, right to the end?

MARTIN No, I don't want to know . . . or guess.

STEVIE Well, I laughed, of course: a grim joke but an awfully funny one. "That Ross, I tell you, that Ross! You go too far, Ross. It's funny . . . in its . . . awful way, but it's way overboard, Ross!" So, I shook my head and laughed—at the awfulness of it, the absurdity, the awfulness; some things are so awful you have to laugh—and then I listened to myself laughing, and I began to wonder why I *was—laughing*. "It's not funny when you come right down to it, Ross." Why *was* I laughing? And just like that [*snaps her fingers*] I stopped; I stopped laughing. I realized—probably in the way if you suddenly fell off a building—oh, shit! I've fallen off a building and I'm going to die; I'm going to go splat on the sidewalk; like *that*—that it wasn't a joke at all; it was awful and absurd, but it wasn't a joke. And everything tied in—Ross coming here to interview you yesterday, the funny smell, the Noël Coward bit we did about you having an affair, and with a goat. You said it right out and I laughed. You *told* me! You came right out and fucking *told* me, and I laughed, and I made jokes about going to the feed store, and I *laughed*. I fucking laughed! Until it stopped; until the laughter stopped. Until it all came together—Ross's letter and all the rest: that odd smell . . . the mistress's perfume on you. And so I knew.

MARTIN Stevie, I'm so . . .

STEVIE Shut up. And so I knew. And next, of course, came believing it. Knowing it—knowing it's true is one thing, but *believing* what you *know* . . . well, there's the tough part. We all prepare for jolts along the way, disturbances of the peace, the lies, the evasions, the infidelities—*if* they happen. [*Very off-hand*] I've never had an affair, by the way, all our years together; not even with a cat, or . . . *any*thing.

MARTIN Oh, Stevie . . .

STEVIE We prepare for . . . things, for lessenings, even; inevitable . . . lessenings, and we think we can handle everything, whatever comes along, but we don't know, *do* we! [*Right at* MARTIN] *Do* we!

MARTIN [*bereaved*] No; no, we don't.

STEVIE Fucking *right* we don't! [*Didactic*] Something can happen that's outside the rules, that doesn't relate to The Way the Game Is Played. Death before you're ready to even think about it—that's part of the game. A stroke that leaves you sitting looking at an eggplant the week before had been your husband—that's another. Emotional disengagement, gradual, so gradual you don't know it's happening, or sudden—not very often, but occasionally—that's another. You've read about spouses—God! I hate that word!—"spouses" who all of a sudden start wearing dresses—yours, or their own collection—wives gone dyke . . . but if there's one thing you *don't* put on your plate, no matter how exotic your tastes may be is . . . bestiality.

MARTIN Don't! You don't understand.

STEVIE The fucking of animals! No, that's one thing you haven't thought about, one thing you've overlooked as a byway on the road of life, as the old soap has it. "Well, I wonder when he'll start cruising livestock. I must ask Mother whether Dad did it and how *she* handled it." No, that's the one thing you haven't thought about—nor could you conceive of. [*Pause; grimly cheerful*] So! How was *your* day?

MARTIN [*pause; attempting the casual*] Well . . . I had a good day at the office. Made the design for The World City even larger than . . .

STEVIE [*fixed smile*] Oh, good!

MARTIN . . . and then I stopped by the haberdasher . . .

STEVIE [*pretending to puzzle*] Ha-ber-dash-er. That's someone who makes haberdash?

MARTIN Haber, I think. Dash is part of doing it.[5]

STEVIE Ah! *Then* what?

MARTIN Hm? Well, then I drove back home, and . . .

STEVIE What! You didn't stop by to see your ladyfriend? Get a lick in?

MARTIN She's in the country. Please, Stevie . . . *don't!*

STEVIE [*feigned wonder*] She's in the *country!*

MARTIN I keep her there.

STEVIE Where!?

MARTIN Please! Don't!

STEVIE Martin, did you ever think you'd come back from your splendid life, walk into your living room and find you had no life left?

MARTIN Not specifically; no. [*Looks down.*]

STEVIE I think we'd better talk about this. If I'm going to kill you I need to know exactly why—all the details.

MARTIN [*shy*] You really want to?

STEVIE What? Kill you?

MARTIN No; learn about it.

STEVIE [*big*] No! I *don't* really want to! [*Normal tone again*] I want the whole day to rewind—start over. I want the reel to reverse: to see the mail on the hall table where Billy's left it, then *not* see it because I haven't opened the door yet—not having gotten the fish yet because I haven't bought the gloves yet because I haven't left the house yet because I haven't gotten out of our bed because I haven't *waked UP YET!!* [*Quieter*] But . . . since I can't reverse time . . . yes, I *do* want to know. I'm reeling with it. [*Pleading*] Make me not *believe* it! Please, make me *not believe* it.

MARTIN [*pause*] Why aren't you crying?

STEVIE Because this is too serious. Do goats cry, by the way?

MARTIN I . . . I don't know. I haven't . . .

STEVIE . . . made her cry yet!? What's the *matter* with you?!

MARTIN [*begging*] Stevie . . .

STEVIE [*as if to someone else*] He can't even make a *goat* cry. What *good* is he? His son's probably weeping as we speak. That was pretty awful what you said to him, Martin, pretty awful. His son's probably lying on his bed, tears flowing; his wife *would* be crying [*harder*] except she can't be that weak right now. And you can't even make a goat cry?! Jeez!

MARTIN [*dogmatic*] I didn't say I *couldn't;* I said I *haven't.*

STEVIE Well, the goats of this world must be very happy. Oh, you kid![6]

MARTIN [*starting to leave*] I can't *have* this conversation. I can't listen to you when you're . . .

STEVIE [*blocking him*] You *stay* where you *are!* You will *have* this conversation, and with *me* and right *now!*

MARTIN [*retreating; sighing*] Where shall I start?

5. *Haberdasher* may be an older word than *haberdash* (which does not, in any case, break down into "haber" and "dash").

6. A catchphrase, popular in the early 20th century, that here becomes a pun playing on its source, the 1909 song titled "I Love My Wife, But Oh, You Kid" (music and lyrics by Harry Armstrong and Billy Clark).

STEVIE [*a threat*] Right at the beginning! [*Afterthought*] Why do you call her Sylvia, by the way? Did she have a tag, or something? Or, was it more:

Who is Sylvia,
Fair is she
That all our goats commend her . . .[7]

MARTIN [*trying to be rational*] No, it just seemed right. Very good, by the way.
STEVIE Thank you. You saw this . . . *thing* . . . this goat, and you said to yourself "This is Sylvia." Or did you talk to it: "Hello, Sylvia." How the hell did you know it was a she—was a female? Bag of nipples dragging in the dung? Or, isn't this your first?!
MARTIN [*very quiet*] She is my first; she is my only. But you don't understand. You . . .
STEVIE [*contemptuous*] Awww; I'm trying not to throw up.
MARTIN Well, if that's the way you . . .
STEVIE *No!!* Tell me.
MARTIN [*sighs*] All right. As I said to Ross . . .
STEVIE [*broad parody*] "As I said to Ross . . ." *NO!* Not "As I said to Ross." To *me!* As you say to *me!*
MARTIN [*annoyed*] In any event . . .
STEVIE Not "in any event!" No! *This* event!
MARTIN [*won't let it go*] As I said to Ross . . .
STEVIE [*impatient acquiescence*] *Very* well; as you said to Ross.
MARTIN Thank you. As I said to Ross, I'd gone to the country . . . to find the place we wanted, our . . . country *place.*
STEVIE [*fact*] You went out a lot.
MARTIN Well, if you're after Utopia . . . [*Shrugs.*]
STEVIE Sure.
MARTIN . . . unless you're one of those people finds it right off: "That's it; that's the place." Unless you're one of those, you've got to search; look around. Close enough in to make it practical for our country needs. No more than an hour or so from . . .
STEVIE [*scoffing*] Our "country needs"?
MARTIN *You're* the one who said it. Verdancy: flowers and green leaves against steel and stone. OK?
STEVIE [*shrugs*] OK. [*Angry*] And it's lovely. Now get to the *goat!*
MARTIN I'm *getting* there. I'm *getting* to her.
STEVIE Stop calling it *her!*
MARTIN [*defending*] *That* is what she *is!* It is a *she! She* is a *she!*
STEVIE [*pathetic sneer*] I suppose I should be grateful it wasn't a *male, isn't* a male goat.
MARTIN Funny you should ask—as they say. There was a place I went to . . .
STEVIE Oh?
MARTIN Well, when I realized something was wrong. I mean, when I realized people would *think* something was wrong, that what I was doing wasn't . . .
STEVIE [*dispassionate*] I *am* going to kill you.

7. A play on the opening lines of the song from Shakespeare's *The Two Gentlemen of Verona* (ca. 1591?), "Who is Silvia? What is she, / That all our swains commend her?" (4.2.37–38).

MARTIN [*preoccupied*] Yes; probably. It was a therapy place, a place people went to . . . to talk about it, about what they were doing . . . and with whom.

STEVIE *What!* Not *whom! What!* With *what!*

MARTIN [*sharp*] Whatever! A place! Please! Let me finish this! [STEVIE *is silent.*] A place to talk about it; like A.A., like Alcoholics Anonymous.

STEVIE [*sneers*] Goat-fuckers Anonymous?

MARTIN [*oddly shocked*] Please! [STEVIE *hoots. Quieter.*] Please?

STEVIE Sorry. Destroy me.

MARTIN It had no cute name; no A.A.; no . . . no nothing. Just . . . a place.

STEVIE How did you find it?

MARTIN Online.

STEVIE [*toneless*] Of course.

MARTIN I went there . . . and there were—what?—ten of us . . . a group leader, of course.

STEVIE What was *he* fucking? *Who;* sorry.

MARTIN He was cured, he said—odd phrase. Was off it.

STEVIE [*very calm*] Very well. What *had* he been fucking?

MARTIN [*matter-of-fact*] A pig. A young pig.

[STEVIE *rises, finds a big ceramic table plate, smashes it, resits, or whatever.*]

STEVIE [*without emotion*] Go on.

MARTIN [*indicates*] Is there going to be a lot of that?

STEVIE Probably.

MARTIN You don't want Billy down here; some things . . .

STEVIE [*steaming*] Some things are . . . *what?!* Private? Sacred? Husband telling wifey about a very peculiar therapy session? A *pig?!*

MARTIN [*a little embarrassed*] A small one, he said.

STEVIE Jesus!

[BILLY *rushes in from the hall.*]

BILLY You two OK?

MARTIN Yes-we're-fine-go-away-Billy.

BILLY Who's throwing things?

STEVIE I am; your mother is throwing things.

BILLY Is there going to be more?

STEVIE I imagine so.

BILLY [*retrieving a small vase*] I gave you this one; I think I'll take it upstairs.

STEVIE [*as* BILLY *turns to go*] I would have noticed, Billy.

BILLY [*shaking his head*] Sure. You guys hold it down.

[*Exits.*]

STEVIE [*after him*] I *would* have. [*Uncertain*] I *think* I would have.

MARTIN [*pause*] So, anyway; it was this place.

STEVIE [*reconcentrating*] A pig? Really?

MARTIN Well, everyone had . . . *you* know . . .

STEVIE . . . some*one*, or some*thing*.

MARTIN Yes.

STEVIE [*lightbulb*] And was Clarissa Atherton there?

MARTIN Who? Yes! That's where I got the card, and . . .

STEVIE And what is *she* fucking? *Who?*

MARTIN [*matter-of-fact*] A dog, I think.

[STEVIE *finds a vase, crashes it to the floor.*]

STEVIE A dog you *think.*

MARTIN Why would she lie? Why would anyone there lie?

STEVIE Damned if *I* know.

MARTIN [*sighs*] And so I went there, and . . .

STEVIE [*there is chaos behind the civility, of course*] Did you all take your . . . friends with you—your pigs, your dogs, your goats, your . . .

MARTIN No. We weren't there to talk about *them;* we were there about ourselves, our . . . our problems, as they called them.

STEVIE The livestock was all happy, you mean.

MARTIN Well, no; there was this one . . . goose, I think it was . . .

[STEVIE *finds a vase, crashes it to the floor.*]

Shall we go outside?

STEVIE [*hands on hips*] Get *on* with it.

MARTIN [*so calm*] All right; there was this one goose . . .

STEVIE *Not* geese! *Not* pigs! *Not* dogs! *Goats!* The subject is *goats!*

MARTIN The subject is *a* goat; the subject is Sylvia. [*He sees* STEVIE *looking for something to throw.*] No! Don't; please! Just listen! Sit and listen!

STEVIE [*has a small bowl in her hands; sits*] All right. I'm listening.

MARTIN I said, most of the people there were having problems, were . . . ashamed, or—what is the word?—conflicted . . . were . . . needed to talk about it while . . . while I went there, I guess, to find out why they were all there.

STEVIE [*as if the language were unfamiliar*] Pardon?

MARTIN I didn't understand why they were there—why they were all so . . . unhappy; what was wrong with . . . with . . . being in love . . . like that.

[STEVIE *gently separates hands, letting bowl fall between her legs, break.*]

There's so much I have to explain.

STEVIE [*deep, quiet irony*] Oh?

MARTIN [*rises, moves a little away*] You must promise to be still. Sit there and please listen, and then maybe when I've finished you . . . just listen; please.

STEVIE [*sad smile*] How could I not?

MARTIN I went there . . . because I couldn't come to *you* with it.

STEVIE Oh?

MARTIN Well . . . *think* about it.

STEVIE [*does*] I suppose you're right.

MARTIN And most of them had a problem, had a long history. The man with the pig was a farmboy, and he and his brothers, when they were kids, just . . . *did* it . . . *naturally;* it was what they did . . . with the pigs. [*Knits brow.*] Or piglets, perhaps; that wasn't clear.

STEVIE Naturally; of course.

MARTIN Are you agreeing?

STEVIE No. Just get on with it.

MARTIN It was what they did. Maybe it was better than . . .

STEVIE . . . than with each other, or their sisters, or their grandmothers? You've got to be kidding!

MARTIN No one got hurt.

STEVIE HUNH!!

MARTIN We'll talk about that.

STEVIE You *bet* we will!

MARTIN [*sighs*] Most of them had a reason, the man with the pig more a matter of . . . habit than anything else, I guess . . . comfort, familiarity.

STEVIE [*eyes heavenward*] Jesus!

MARTIN Though he was off it . . . "cured," as he put it, which I found odd.

STEVIE Of course.

MARTIN I mean . . . if he was happy . . .

[STEVIE *knocks over the small side table where she is sitting, never taking her eyes off* MARTIN.]

STEVIE [*ironic*] Ooops!

MARTIN When he was doing it, I mean. Must you? Though I suppose he wasn't . . . no longer was happy.

STEVIE [*feigned surprise*] You mean you didn't *ask* him?

MARTIN No; no, I didn't. The lady with the German Shepherd . . .

STEVIE Clarissa?

MARTIN No; another one. The lady with the Shepherd, it turned out she had been raped by her father *and* her brother when she was twelve, or so . . . continually raped, one watching the other, she told us . . .

STEVIE . . . and so she took up with a *dog?!*

MARTIN [*no opinion*] Yes; it would seem. The man with the goose was . . . hideously ugly—I could barely look at him—and I suppose he thought he could never . . . *you* know.

STEVIE [*cool*] Do I?

MARTIN Try and imagine.

STEVIE [*calm; sad*] I doubt I can.

MARTIN *Try:* so ugly, no woman—no *man*—would even *think* of . . . "doing it" with you—*ever.*

STEVIE One in the hand, et cetera.[8] But . . . a goose!?

MARTIN [*sad smile*] Not everyone is satisfied that way . . . one in the hand. No matter. And *I* was unhappy there, for *they* were all unhappy.

STEVIE My goodness.

MARTIN And I didn't know why.

STEVIE [*considers it*] Really? I think we've hit upon why I'm going to kill you.

MARTIN [*onward*] There's something else I want you to understand.

STEVIE [*sarcasm*] Oh? Something else?

MARTIN It's something I told Ross.

STEVIE Not him again.

MARTIN He *is* my best friend.

STEVIE [*actress-y*] Oh? And I thought *I* was!

MARTIN [*undeterred; calm*] I told him that in all our time together—yours and mine—all our marriage—I've never been unfaithful.

STEVIE [*a beat;[9] fake astonishment*] *Hunh!!*

MARTIN [*onward*] Never in all our years. Oh, early on, one of your friends would grope me in the kitchen at a party, or . . .

STEVIE I love my friends; they have taste.

MARTIN Never unfaithful; never once. I've never even wanted to. We're so good together, you and I.

8. That is, "a bird in the hand is worth two in the bush" (proverbial).

9. A pause (theater term).

STEVIE A perfect fit, eh?

MARTIN [*sincere*] Yes!

STEVIE You'd never imagine that a marriage could be so perfect.

MARTIN Yes! I mean *no;* I *hadn't.*

STEVIE [*advertisement*] Great sex, good cook, even does windows.

MARTIN Be serious!

STEVIE No! It's too serious for that. [*Afterthought*] Fuck you, by the way.

MARTIN Never once! People looked at me, said "What's the matter with you?!" "Don't you have any . . . you know, lust?" And "Sure," I said, "I've got plenty. All for Stevie."

STEVIE [*shakes her head; singsong*] La-di-da; la-di-fuckin'-da!

MARTIN [*rage*] Listen to me!

STEVIE [*army drill*] Yes, sir! [*Softer*] Yes, sir.

MARTIN All the men I knew were "having affairs" . . . *see*ing other women, and laughing about it—at the club, on the train. I felt . . . well, I almost felt like a misfit. "What's the matter with you, Martin!? You mean you're only doing it with your wife!? What kind of man *are* you?!"

STEVIE You men *must* be fun together.

MARTIN Odd man out. I only wanted *you.*

STEVIE [*pause; quietly*] And *I* have something to tell *you.*

MARTIN [*anticipating, with dread*] Oh, no! Don't tell me that you've been with . . .

STEVIE [*hands up; shakes her head*] Hush. In all our marriage I've never even wanted anyone but you.

MARTIN [*deeply sad*] Oh, Stevie.

STEVIE My mother told me—we really *were* good friends; I'm sorry you never knew her.

MARTIN I am, too.

STEVIE We talked together like sisters, by God; we talked the night away, two "girls" talking; we were that good friends, but she sure knew how to be a "parent" when she needed to, when she wanted to keep me very . . . level. And she said to me—I never told you this—"Be sure you marry someone you're in love with—deeply and wholly in love with—but be careful who you fall in love with, because you might marry him."

[MARTIN *chuckles, quietly, ruefully.*]

"Your father and I have the best marriage anyone could possibly have," she said to me, over and over. "Be sure you do, too."

MARTIN Stevie, I . . .

STEVIE "Be careful who you marry," she said to me. And I *was.* I *fell* in love with you? No . . . I rose into love with you and have—what—*cherished?* you, all these years, been proud of all you've done, been happy with our . . . funny son, been . . . well, happy. I guess that's the word. No, I don't guess; I *know.* [*Begins to cry.*] I've been happy. [*More*] Look at me, Mother; I've married the man I loved [*more*] and I've been . . . so . . . happy.

MARTIN [*moves to her; touches her*] Oh, Stevie . . .

STEVIE [*huge; swipes objects off the coffee table*] GET YOUR GOAT-FUCKING HANDS OFF ME!!!

[*Retreats to wall, arms wide, sobbing greatly.*]

MARTIN [*reacts as if he's touched a hot stove*] All right! No more!

STEVIE Yes! *More!* Finish it! Vomit it all up! Puke it out all over me. I'll never be less ready. So . . . *do* it! *DO* IT!! I've laid it all out for you; I'm naked on the table; take all your knives! Cut me! Scar me forever!

MARTIN [*thinks a moment*] Before or *after* I vomit on you? [*Gently; hands up to appease*] Sorry; sorry.

STEVIE [*a shaking voice*] Women in deep woe often mix their metaphors.

MARTIN [*pacifying*] Yes; yes.

STEVIE Get *on* with it! [*Afterthought*] Very good, by the way.

MARTIN [*rue*] Thanks.

STEVIE . . . and hopelessly inappropriate.

MARTIN Yes; sorry.

STEVIE [*casually overturns a chair*] Get on with it, I said.

MARTIN Are you going to do that with *all* the furniture?

STEVIE [*looks around*] I think so. You may have to help me with some of it.

MARTIN Truce! Truce!

STEVIE [*takes a painting, breaks it over something*] NO! NO TRUCE! *All* of it! Now!

MARTIN That was my mother's painting.

STEVIE It still is! [*Prompting*] You found us our lovely country place.

MARTIN [*girds*] And the day I found it—I called you. You remember: I told you I'd put a hold on it.

STEVIE I'll never forget.

MARTIN And I was driving out of the town, back to the highway, and I stopped at the top of a hill . . .

STEVIE Crest.

MARTIN What!? Who *are* you!?

STEVIE You stopped at the crest of a hill—on it, actually.

MARTIN Yes. And I stopped, and the view was . . . wonderful. Not spectacular, but wonderful—fall, the leaves turning . . .

STEVIE [*staring at him*] A regular bucolic.

MARTIN Yes; a regular bucolic. I stopped and got us things—vegetables and things. *You* remember.

STEVIE [*denial*] No; I don't.

MARTIN [*realizing, going on*] No matter. And it was then that I saw her.

STEVIE [*grotesque incomprehension*] *Who!?*

MARTIN [*deeply sad*] Oh, Stevie . . .

STEVIE [*heavy irony*] *Who!? Who* could you have seen!?

MARTIN [*dogged*] I'm going on with this. You asked. I'm going to get it all out.

STEVIE [*eyes hard on him*] Serves *me* right, I guess.

MARTIN And I closed the trunk of the car, with all that I'd gotten—[*pause*] . . . and it was then that I saw her. And she was looking at me with . . . with those eyes.

STEVIE [*staring at him*] Oh, those eyes! [*Afterthought*] *THEM* eyes!

MARTIN [*slow; deliberate*] And what I felt was . . . it was unlike anything I'd ever felt before. It was so . . . amazing. There she was.

STEVIE [*grotesque enthusiasm*] Who!? Who!?

MARTIN Don't. She was looking at me with those eyes of hers and . . . I melted, I think. I think that's what I did: I melted.

STEVIE [*hideous enthusiasm*] You melted!!

MARTIN [*waves her off*] I'd never seen such an expression. It was pure . . . and trusting and . . . and innocent; so . . . so guileless.

STEVIE [*sardonic echo*] Guileless; innocent; pure. You've never seen children, or anything? You never saw Billy when he was a kid?

MARTIN [*pleading*] Of course I did. Don't *mock* me.

STEVIE [*shooting harsh chuckle*] Don't mock *me.*

MARTIN I . . . I went over to where she was—to the fence where she was, and I knelt there, eye level . . .

STEVIE [*quiet loathing*] *Goat* level.

MARTIN [*angry; didactic*] I will *finish* this! You *asked* for it, and you're going to *get* it! So . . . shut your tragic mouth!

[STEVIE *does a sharp intake of breath, puts her fingers over her mouth.*]

All right. Listen to me. It was as if an alien came out of whatever it was, and it . . . took me with it, and it was . . . an ecstasy and a purity, and a . . . love of a . . . [*dogmatic*] un-i-mag-in-able kind, and it relates to nothing *whatever,* to nothing that can be *related* to! Don't you see!? Don't you see the . . . don't you see the "thing" that happened to me? What nobody understands? Why I can't feel what I'm supposed to!? Because it relates to nothing? It can't have happened! It did, but it *can't* have!

[STEVIE *shakes her head.*]

What are you doing?

STEVIE [*removes fingers*] Being tragic. I bet a psychiatrist would love all this.

MARTIN I knelt there, eye level, and there was a . . . a what!? . . . an understanding so intense, so natural . . .

STEVIE There are some things you *can* remember, eh?

MARTIN [*closes his eyes, reopens them*] . . . an understanding so . . .

STEVIE [*awful, high-pitched little voice*] I can't remember why I come into rooms, where I put the thing for the razor . . .

MARTIN [*refusing to be drawn in*] . . . an understanding so natural, so intense that I will *never* forget it, as intense as the night you and I finally came at the same time. What was it . . . a month after we began?

[*Where is she, emotionally?*]

Stevie? It wasn't happening . . . but it *was!*

STEVIE [*shaking her head; oddly objective*] How *much* do you hate me?

MARTIN [*hopeless*] I *love* you. [*Pause*] And I love *her.* [*Pause*] And there it is.

[STEVIE *howls three times, slowly, deliberately; a combination of rage and hurt.*]

STEVIE [*then; calmly*] Go on.

MARTIN [*apologetic*] I have to do it.

STEVIE Yes?

[MARTIN *nods.*]

Right.

MARTIN [*starting again*] And there was a connection there—a communication—that, well . . . an epiphany, I guess comes closest, and I knew what was going to happen.

STEVIE [*mildly interested in the fact*] I think I'm going to be sick.

MARTIN *Please* don't.

[*Back to it.*]

Epiphany! And when it happens there's no retreating, no holding back. I put my hands through the wires of the fence and she came toward me, slipped her face between my hands, brought her nose to mine at the wires and . . . and nuzzled.

STEVIE I am a grown woman; a grown married woman. [*As if she's never heard the word before*] Nuzzled; nuzzled.

MARTIN Her breath . . . her breath was . . . so sweet, warm and . . . [*Hears something; stops.*]

STEVIE Go on. Tell the grown-up married woman . . .

MARTIN [*warning hand up*] I hear Billy.

[BILLY *enters.*]

BILLY Are you hitting her!? [*Sees the carnage.*] What the fuck!?

STEVIE We're redecorating, honey. No, he's not, by the way—hitting me. I'm hitting myself.

BILLY [*near tears*] I hear you two! I'm up there and I *hear* you! STOP IT! JESUS GOD, STOP IT!!

MARTIN [*gentle*] We will, Billy; we're not quite done.

STEVIE Go away, Billy. Go out and play.

BILLY Go out and . . . ?

STEVIE [*harder*] Leave the house! Leave us alone!

BILLY But . . .

MARTIN [*calm*] Do what your Mother says. "Go out and play." Make mudpies; climb a tree . . .

BILLY [*a finger in* MARTIN'*s face*] If I come back and find you've hurt her, I'll . . . I'll . . .

[BILLY *lunges at* MARTIN, *shoves him, recoils.* MARTIN *steps forward, stops.* BILLY *sobs, runs from the room. We hear the front door slam.*]

STEVIE [*after*] Mudpies?

MARTIN Well . . . whatever.

STEVIE [*calm*] What *will* you do if he comes back and finds you've hurt me? . . . *when* he comes back and finds you've hurt me?

MARTIN [*absorbed in something*] What?

STEVIE [*smiles*] Down from the trees, hands all muddy? [*Sad*] Nothing. [*Cold*] You were in the middle of your epiphany.

MARTIN [*sighs*] Yes.

STEVIE [*sad*] God, I wish you were stupid.

MARTIN [*he, too*] Yes; I wish *you* were stupid, too.

STEVIE [*pause; businesslike*] Epiphany!

MARTIN Yes. It was at that moment that I realized . . .

STEVIE . . . that you and the fucking goat were destined for one another!

MARTIN . . . that she and I were . . . [*softly; embarrassed*] that she and I were going to go to bed together.

STEVIE To stall together! To hay! *Not* to bed!

MARTIN [*sits*] Whatever. That what could not happen was *going* to. That we wanted each other very much, that I had to have her, that I . . .

[STEVIE *screams—a deep-throated rage—and lunges at* MARTIN. *He rises, grabs her wrists, and shoves her into a chair. She attempts to get up, but he shoves her back again.*]

Now stop it! Let me finish!

STEVIE You'll be fucking Billy next.

MARTIN [*ice*] He's not my type.

STEVIE [*rising again. Rage*] He's not your type!? He's not your fucking type!?

MARTIN No; he's not.

[*She is about to strike him.*]

You're my type.

[*The shock of this stays her gesture; we see her confusion.*]

You're my type.

STEVIE [*stands where she is; hard*] Thank you!

MARTIN You're welcome. [*A gesture.*] Oh, Stevie, I . . .

STEVIE I'm your type and so is she; so is the goat. [*Harder*] So long as it's female, eh? So long as it's got a cunt it's all right with you!

MARTIN [*huge*] A SOUL!! Don't you know the difference!? Not a cunt, a soul!

STEVIE [*after a little; tears again*] You can't fuck a soul.

MARTIN No; and it isn't about fucking.

STEVIE YES!!

MARTIN [*as gentle as possible*] No; no, Stevie, it isn't.

STEVIE [*pause; then, even more sure*] Yes! It is about fucking! It is about you being an animal!

MARTIN [*thinks a moment; quietly*] I thought I was.

STEVIE [*contempt*] Hunh!

MARTIN I thought I was; I thought we *all* were . . . animals.

STEVIE [*cold rage*] We stay with our own kind!

MARTIN [*gentle; rational*] Oh, we fall in love with *many* other creatures . . . dogs and cats, and . . .

STEVIE We don't *fuck* them! You're a monster!

MARTIN [*pinning it down*] I am a deeply troubled, greatly divided . . .

STEVIE [*no quarter*] *Animal* fucker!

MARTIN Sylvia and I . . .

STEVIE [*hideous*] You're going to tell me she *wants* you.

MARTIN [*simply put*] Yes.

STEVIE What does she do—back into you making awful little bleating sounds?

MARTIN That's sheep.

STEVIE *Whatever!! Presented* herself? Down on her forelegs, her head turned, her eyes on you, her . . .

MARTIN Stop it! I won't go into the specifics of our sex with you!

STEVIE [*contempt*] *Thank* you! You take advantage of this . . . creature!? You . . . *rape* this . . . animal and convince yourself that it has to do with *love!?*

MARTIN [*helpless*] I love her . . . and she loves me, and . . .

STEVIE [*a huge animal sound: rage; sweeps the bookcase of whatever is on it, or overturns a piece of furniture. Silence; then starting quietly, building*] Now, you listen to me. I have listened to you. I have heard you tell me how much you love me, how you've never even wanted another woman, how we have been a more perfect marriage than chance would even *allow.* We're both too bright for *most* of the shit. We see the deep and awful humor of things go over the heads of most people; we see what's hideously wrong in what most people accept as normal; we have both the joys and the sorrows of all that. We have a straight line through life, right all the way to dying, but that's OK because it's a good line . . . so long as we don't screw up.

MARTIN I know; I know.

STEVIE [*don't interrupt me*!] Shut up; so long as we don't screw up. [*Points at him.*] And *you've* screwed *up!*

MARTIN Stevie, I . . .

STEVIE I said, shut up. Do you know *how* you've done it? How you've screwed up?

MARTIN [*mumbled*] Because I was at the vegetable stand one day, and I looked over to my right and I saw . . .

STEVIE [*hard and slow*] Because you've broken something and it can't be fixed!

MARTIN Stevie . . .

STEVIE Fall out of love with me? Fine! No, not fine, but that can be fixed . . . time . . . whatever! But tell me you love me and an animal—both of us!—equally? The same way? That you go from my bed—*our* bed . . .

[*Aside-ish.*]

it's amazing, you know, how good we are, still, how we please each other *and* ourselves so . . . fully, so . . . fresh each time . . .

[*Aside over.*]

. . . you go from our bed, wash your dick, get in your car and go to her, and do with her what I cannot imagine myself imagining? Or—worse! . . . that you've come *from* her, to *my* bed!? To *our* bed!? . . . and you do with me what I *can* imagine . . . love . . . *want* you for!?

MARTIN [*deep sadness*] Oh, Stevie . . .

STEVIE [*not listening*] That you can do these two things . . . and not understand how it . . . SHATTERS THE GLASS!!?? How it cannot be dealt with—how stop and forgiveness have nothing to do with it? and how *I* am destroyed? How *you* are? How I cannot admit it though I *know* it!? How I cannot deny it because I cannot *admit* it!? Cannot admit it, because it is outside of denying!?

MARTIN Stevie, I . . . I promise you, I'll stop; I'll . . .

STEVIE How stopping has nothing to do with having started?! How nothing has anything to do with anything!? [*Tears—if there—stop.*] You have brought me down, you goat-fucker; you love of my life! You have brought me down to *nothing!* [*Accusatory finger right at him*] You have brought me down, and, Christ!, I'll bring you down with me!

[*Brief pause; she turns on her heel, exits. We hear the front door slam.*]

MARTIN [*after she leaves; after he hears the door; little boy*] Stevie? [*Pause*] Stevie?

Curtain.

Scene 3

[*An hour or so later.* MARTIN *is sitting in the ruins. Maybe he is examining a broken piece of something. The room is as it was at the end of Scene 2. The front door slams;* BILLY *enters;* MARTIN *rises and stands in the middle of the room.*]

BILLY [*looking around*] Wow!

MARTIN [*realizing* BILLY *is there*] Yes; wow.

BILLY [*seemingly casual*] You guys really had it out, hunh.

MARTIN [*subdued; almost laughing*] *Oh*, yes.

BILLY Where is she?

MARTIN Hm? Who?

BILLY [*not friendly; overly articulated*] My mother. Where is my mother?

MARTIN [*mocking*] Where is "my mother"? Not "Mother—where's mother?" Not that, but . . . "Where is my mother?"

BILLY [*anger rising*] Whatever! Where *is* she? Where is *my mother?*

MARTIN [*arms out; helplessly*] I . . . I . . .

BILLY [*angrier*] Where *is* she?! What did you do . . . kill her?

MARTIN [*softly*] Yes; I think so.

BILLY [*dropping something he has picked up*] What!!?

MARTIN [*quietly, with a restraining hand*] Stop. No. No, I did not kill her—of *course* not—but I think I might as well have. I think we've killed each other.

BILLY [*driving*] Where *is* she!?

MARTIN [*simply*] I don't know.

BILLY What do you mean you don't . . .

MARTIN [*loud*] She left!

BILLY What do you mean she left? Where . . .

MARTIN [*snappish*] Stop asking me what I mean! [*Quieter*] She said what she wanted to say; she finished . . . and she left. She slammed the front door and left. I assume she drove somewhere.

BILLY Yeah, the wagon's gone. [*Harder*] Where *is* she!?

MARTIN [*loud*] She *left!* I don't know where she *is!* It's English! "She left." It's English. No, I did not kill her, yes, I think I did, I think we killed each other. That's English, too: one of your courses!

BILLY [*is his rage close to tears? Probably*] I know who you *are.* I know you're my father. I know who you are, and I know who you're supposed to be, but . . .

MARTIN You, too?

BILLY Hunh?

MARTIN You don't know who I *am* anymore.

BILLY [*flat*] No.

MARTIN Well . . . neither does your mother.

BILLY [*trying to explain, but, still, rage underneath*] Parents fight; I know that; all kids know that. There are good times and rotten ones, and sometimes the blanket is pulled out from under you, and . . .

MARTIN [*can't help saying it*] You're mixing your metaphors.

BILLY [*furious*] What!?

MARTIN Never mind; probably not the best time to bring it up. You were saying . . . "There are good times and rotten ones"?

BILLY Yes. [*Quick sarcasm*] Thanks.

MARTIN [*noncommittal*] Welcome.

BILLY But sometimes the whatever is pulled out from under you.

MARTIN Rug, I think.

BILLY Right! Now shut the fuck up! [MARTIN *opens his mouth, closes it. Spits out.*] Semanticist!

MARTIN Very good! Where did you learn that?

BILLY I go to a good school. Remember?

MARTIN Yes, but still . . .

BILLY I said, shut the fuck up!

MARTIN [*subsiding*] Right.

BILLY There are good times, and there are rotten ones. There are times we are so . . . deep in content, in happiness, that we think we'll probably drown in it but we won't mind. There are *some* of those—not too many. There are times we don't know what the fuck's going on—*to* us, *with* us, *about* us—and that's most of the time. I'm talking about us so-called adolescents.

MARTIN I know.

BILLY And then there are the times we wish we were old enough to . . . just walk out the door and start all over again, somewhere else—blank it all out.

MARTIN [*quietly*] And this?

BILLY [*hard*] One guess, you *fuck*!! [*Huge*] What have you done with my *mother*!!??

MARTIN [*calm*] We finished our conversation [*gestures at ruined room*]—you see how we talk?—we finished our conversation, and she said a final . . . *thing*, and she left. She walked out, out the front door, slam.

BILLY How long ago?

MARTIN [*shrugs*] An hour; maybe more; maybe two. I'm not very good at time and stuff right now.

BILLY Two hours? And you haven't . . .

MARTIN [*a little angry himself*] What!? Called the police? [*Awful imitation of distress*] "Oh, Officer, help me! My wife just found out I've been doing it with livestock, and she's run off, and can you help me find her?" What!? Take off after her!? She's a grown woman; she could be having her hair done, for all I know.

BILLY [*dogged*] What did she *say* to you?

MARTIN [*rueful chuckle*] Oh . . . quite a few things.

BILLY [*bigger*] When she left! What did she say when she left!?

MARTIN Something about . . . bringing me down—or whatever.

BILLY Be specific.

MARTIN Well, it's hard to be specific. We *were* busy after all, and . . .

BILLY [*big*] Exactly what she said, and *now!*

MARTIN [*clears his throat*] "You have brought me down, and . . . I will bring you down with me."

BILLY [*puzzled; trying to get it*] What does that *mean*?

MARTIN [*almost sweet*] No one's ever brought you down? No, I suppose not—not yet. It means . . . [*fails*] it means what it says: that you have done to me what cannot be undone and . . . and you won't get away with it.

[BILLY *stands for a moment and then spontaneously cries for a little, stops.*]

BILLY [*wiping his eyes*] I see.

MARTIN [*further explanation*] You destroy me—I destroy you.

BILLY Yes; I see. [*Indicates wreckage.*] Then there's no point in setting all this right.

MARTIN [*sad chuckle*] It does look pretty awful, *doesn't* it.

BILLY Let's do it anyway.

MARTIN Set the stage for the next round? [*Some self-pity and irony*] Hunh! *What* next round!? It's all behind me, isn't it?—everything? All hope . . . all . . . "salvation?" [*Fast litany*] Dead-end-rock-bottom-out-with-the-garbage-flushed-down-the-toilet-ground-up-spit-out-over-the-edge-with-heavy-weights, down-down-sunk . . . whatever? All hope, everything? Gone? Right?

BILLY [*shrugs*] Whatever.

[BILLY *begins to right a few things, not much; then quits.*]

What is it going to be then? Divorce?

MARTIN [*simply*] I don't know, Billy; I don't know that there are any rules for where we are.

BILLY Beyond all the rules, eh?

MARTIN [*some rue*] I think so.

BILLY I wouldn't know. I guess I've never been in love. *Yet,* I mean. Oh, lots of crushes, and all.

MARTIN Only twice for me—your mother and . . . Sylvia.

BILLY You're really holding onto this, *aren't* you.

MARTIN To . . . ?

BILLY [*sneering*] This goat! This big love affair!

MARTIN [*shrugs*] It's true.

BILLY Grow up!

MARTIN Ah! Is *that* it!

[BILLY *laughs, in spite of himself.* MARTIN *tries to right a chair.*]

Help me with this.

[BILLY *helps him.*]

Thanks.

BILLY [*shrugs*] Any time. [*Pause*] They asked us at school—when? Last week, last month?—they asked each of us in this class to talk about how normal our lives were, how . . . how conventional it all was and how did we feel about it.

MARTIN What kind of school *is* this!?

BILLY [*shrugs*] You chose it; you two chose it. And a lot of the guys got up and talked about—you know—our home lives, how our parents get on, and all; and it wasn't very special except the guys whose parents are divorced or one has died or gone crazy, or whatever.

MARTIN Really? Crazy?

BILLY Sure. Good private school. All guys, too; thanks. I mean, it was all about what you'd expect. Maybe everybody left all the juicy stuff out, or they didn't know it. [*Picks up a shard.*] Where does this go?

MARTIN Trash, I suspect.

BILLY [*looks at it*] Too bad. [*Drops it.*] So, it was all pretty dull, pretty much what you'd expect.

MARTIN I take it you haven't gotten up and spoken yet.

BILLY [*noncommittal*] Nope. Haven't. [*Waits a little.*] You know what I'm going to tell them—when I get up there on my hind legs?

MARTIN [*winces*] Do I *want* to know?

BILLY Sure; you're a big guy.

MARTIN I am diminished.

BILLY Yeah? Well . . . whatever. I think what I'll tell them is this: that I've been living with two people about as splendid as you can get; that if I'd been born to other people, it couldn't have been any better.

[MARTIN *sighs heavily, puts a protesting hand up.*]

No; really; I mean it. You two guys are about as good as they come. You're smart, and fair, and you have a sense of humor—both of you—and . . . and you're Democrats. You *are* Democrats, aren't you?

MARTIN More than *they* are, sometimes.

BILLY That's what I thought, and you've figured out that raising a kid does *not* include making him into a carbon copy of *you*, that you're letting me think you're putting up with me being gay far better than you probably really are.

MARTIN Oh, now . . .

BILLY Thank you, by the way.

MARTIN It's the least.

BILLY [*nodding*] Right.

MARTIN [*feigned surprise*] You're *gay!?*

BILLY [*smiles*] Shut up. Anyway, you've let me have it better than a lot of kids, better than a lot of "Moms and Dads" have, a lot closer to what being grown up will look like—as far as I can tell. Good guidance; it's great to see how two people can love each other . . .

MARTIN Don't!

BILLY At least that's what I thought—until yesterday, until the shit hit the fan!

MARTIN Billy, please don't.

BILLY [*big crying underneath*] . . . until the shit hit the fan, and the talk I was going to do at school became history. [*Exaggerated*] What will I say *now!?* Goodness me! The Good Ship Lollipop[1] has gone and sunk. [*More normal tone*] What will I say!? Well, let's see: I came home yesterday and everything had been great—absolutely normal, therefore great. Great parents, great house, great trees, great cars—you know: the old "great." [*Bigger now, more exaggerated*] But then today I come home, and what do I *find?* I find my great Mom and my great Dad talking about a letter from great good friend Ross . . .

MARTIN [*deep anger*] Fuck Ross!!

BILLY Yes? A letter from great good friend Ross written to great good Mom about how great good Dad has been out in the barnyard fucking animals!!

MARTIN Don't . . . *do* this.

BILLY Animals! Well, one in particular. A goat! A fucking goat! You see, guys, your stories are swell or whatever, but I've got one'll knock your socks off, as they used to say, wipe the tattoos right off your butts. Ya see, while great old Mom and great old Dad have been doing the great old

1. The fantasy "ship" (an airplane) made famous by the child actress Shirley Temple in the movie *Bright Eyes* (1934), in which she sang "On the Good Ship Lollipop" (music by Richard A. Whiting; lyrics by Sidney Clare).

parent thing, one of them has been underneath the house, down in the cellar, digging a pit so deep!, so wide!, so . . . HUGE! . . . we'll all fall in and [*crying now*] and never . . . be . . . able . . . to . . . climb . . . out . . . again—no matter how much we want to, how hard we try. And you see, kids, fellow students, you see, I love these people. I love the man who's been down there digging—when he's not giving it to a goat! I love this man! I love him! [*Drops whatever he's holding, moves to* MARTIN, *arms out.*] I love him!

[*Wraps his arms around* MARTIN, *who doesn't know what to do. Starts kissing* MARTIN *on the hands, then on the neck, crying all the while. Then it turns—or does it?—and he kisses* MARTIN *full on the mouth—a deep, sobbing, sexual kiss.* ROSS *has entered, stands watching.* MARTIN *tries to disengage from* BILLY, *but* BILLY *moans, holds on. Finally* MARTIN *shoves him away.* BILLY *stands there, still sobbing, arms around nothing. They have not seen* ROSS.]

MARTIN Don't *do* that!!

BILLY I *love* you!

MARTIN Sure you do, you . . . you . . .

BILLY Faggot? You faggot?

MARTIN [*enraged*] That's not what I was going to say!!

BILLY [*so sad; so sincere*] Dad! I *love* you! Hold me! Please!

MARTIN [*holds him; strokes him*] Shhhhhh; shhhh; shhhhh now.

BILLY [*disengaging finally*] I'm sorry; I didn't mean to . . .

MARTIN No; it's all right. [*Arms out*] Here; let me hold you.

[BILLY *moves to him again; a momentary silent embrace.*]

ROSS Excuse me.

[*They are startled, split. Maybe* BILLY *stumbles over something.*]

I'm sorry; I didn't mean to interrupt your little . . .

MARTIN [*cold fury*] What!? See a man and his son kissing? That would go nicely in one of your fucking letters. Judas! Get out of here!

BILLY [*to* ROSS] It wasn't what you think!

MARTIN [*at* BILLY] Yes! Yes, it was! Don't apologize. [*To* ROSS] Too bad you couldn't have brought your fucking TV crew over! Don't you and *your* son ever kiss? Don't you and—what's his name?—*Todd* love one another?

ROSS [*hard; contemptuous*] Not *that* way!

MARTIN [*angry and reckless*] *That* way!? *What* way!? [*Points vigorously at* BILLY.] This boy is hurt! I've hurt him, and he still loves me! You fucker! He loves his father, and if it . . . clicks over and becomes—what?—sexual for . . . just a moment . . . so what!? So fucking what!? He's hurt and he's lonely and mind your own fucking business!

ROSS [*a sneer*] You're sicker than I thought.

MARTIN No! I'm hysterical!

BILLY [*rueful wonder*] It *did.* It clicked over, and you were just another . . .

MARTIN It's all right.

BILLY . . . another man. I get confused . . . sex and love; loving and . . . [*to* ROSS] I probably do want to sleep with him. [*Rueful laugh*] I want to sleep with everyone.

MARTIN [*to quiet him*] It's all right.

BILLY [*still to* ROSS] Except you, probably.

ROSS Jesus! Sick! What is it . . . contagious?

BILLY [*confused*] What? Is what?

MARTIN [*moves over to comfort* BILLY] There was a man told me once—a friend; we went to the same gym—he told me he had his kid on his lap one day—not even old enough to be a boy or a girl: a baby—and he had . . . *it* on his lap, and it was gurgling at him and making giggling sounds, and he had it with his arms around it, [*demonstrates*] in his lap, shifting it a little from side to side to make it happier, to make it giggle more . . . and all at once he realized he was getting hard.

ROSS Jesus!

BILLY Oh my God . . .

MARTIN . . . that the baby in his lap was making him hard—not arousing him; it wasn't sexual, but it was happening.

ROSS Jesus!

MARTIN . . . his dick was rising to the baby in his lap—his baby; his lap. And when he realized what was happening, he thought he would die; his pulse was going a mile a minute; his ears were ringing—loud! Very *loud!* And he was going to faint; he *knew* it, and then the moment passed, and he knew it had all been an accident, that it meant . . . nothing—that nothing was connected to anything else. His wife came in; she smiled; he smiled and handed her the baby. And that was it; it was over. [*Shrugs.*] Things happen. Besides—I'm hysterical. Remember?

ROSS What are you doing? *Defending* yourself?! Jesus. You're sick.

MARTIN [*contempt*] Do you have any other words? Sick and Jesus? Is that all you have?

BILLY [*shy*] Was it me? Was it me, Dad? Was the baby me?

MARTIN [*to* BILLY*; after a pause; gently*] Hush.

BILLY [*almost frightened*] Was it?

MARTIN [*turning to* ROSS] So, what do you want here now, motherfucker!? Judas!?

ROSS Stevie called—what? An hour ago? More? She said you needed me; she said to come over.

MARTIN I don't! Get out! [*Surprise*] She *called* you?

ROSS Yes. [*Shakes his head.*] Getting hard with a baby! Is there anything you people don't get off on!?

BILLY [*once more*] Was it, Dad?

MARTIN [*so clearly a lie; gently*] Of course not, Billy. [*To* ROSS*; hard, eyes narrowing*] Is there anything "we people" don't get off on? Is there anything anyone doesn't get off on, whether we admit it or not—whether we *know* it or not? Remember Saint Sebastian with all the arrows shot into him?[2] He probably came! God knows the faithful did! Shall I go on!? You want to hear about the cross!?

BILLY [*quietly; smiling*] No, of course it wasn't . . . wasn't me.

ROSS [*shaking his head; sad, but with a lip curled*] Sick; sick; sick.

MARTIN [*at* ROSS*; growing rage*] I'll tell you what's sick! Writing that fucking letter to Stevie—why doesn't matter!!—that's what's sick! I *tell* you about it;

2. A Roman soldier who was martyred (ca. 288 C.E.) for his Christian beliefs; according to legend, he was shot with arrows, healed by St. Irene, and then killed by a club. From the Renaissance onward, he has often been portrayed as a youth pierced by many arrows. Traditionally a patron saint of soldiers, athletes, and archers, more recently Sebastian has been adopted as a homoerotic icon and become the patron saint of gay culture.

I share it with you, the . . . the . . . whole . . . awful . . . thing, because I think I've lost it, maybe; I *tell* you; I *share* it with you because you're . . . what!? . . . you're my best friend in the whole world? Because I needed to tell *somebody,* somebody with his head on straight enough to hear it? I *tell* you, and you fucking turn around and . . .

ROSS I *had* to!!

MARTIN *No!* You *didn't!* You didn't *have* to!

ROSS [*dogmatic*] I couldn't let you *continue!*

MARTIN [*near tears*] I could have worked it out. I could have stopped, and no one would have known. Except you, motherfucker. Mister one strike and you're out. I could have . . .

ROSS No! You couldn't!

MARTIN I could have worked it out! And now nothing can *ever* be put back together! *Ever!*

BILLY [*trying to help*] Dad . . .

MARTIN [*savage*] You shut up!

[BILLY *winces.* MARTIN *reacts.*]

Oh, God! I'm sorry. [*To* ROSS] Yes; all right, it *was* sick, and yes, it *was* compulsive, and . . .

ROSS IS! Not *was!* IS!

MARTIN [*stopped in his tracks*] I . . . I . . .

ROSS IS!

MARTIN [*gathering himself*] *Is.* All right. *Is. Is* sick; *is* compulsive.

ROSS [*pushing*] And it was *wrong!*

MARTIN It was . . . it was . . . what?

ROSS Wrong! Deeply, destructively *wrong!*

MARTIN Whatever you want. [*Rage growing*] But I could have handled it! You didn't have to bring it all down! You didn't have to destroy both of us; you didn't have to destroy Stevie, too!

ROSS Me!? *Me* bring you down!? This isn't . . . embezzlement, honey; this isn't stealing from helpless widows; this isn't going to whores and coming down with the clap, or whatever, you know. This isn't the stuff that stops a career in its tracks for a little while—humiliation, public remorse, and then back up again. This is *beyond* that—*way* beyond it! You go on and you'll slip up one day. Somebody'll see you. Somebody'll surprise you one day, in whatever barn you put her in, no matter where you put her. Somebody'll see you, on your knees behind the damn animal; your pants around your ankles. Somebody will *catch* you at it.

BILLY Let him alone. For God's sake, Ross . . .

ROSS [*waving* BILLY *off; to* MARTIN] Do you know there are prison terms for this? Some states they kill you for it? Do you know what they'd *do* to you. The press? Everybody? Down it all comes—your career; your life . . . everything. [*So cold; so rational*] For fucking a goat.

[*Shakes his head sadly;* BILLY *is weeping quietly.*]

MARTIN [*long pause*] Is *that* what it is, then? That people will *know!*? That people will find *out!*? That I can do whatever I want, and that's what matters!? That people will find *out!*? Fuck the . . . thing *itself!*? Fuck what it *means!*? That people will find *out!*?

ROSS Your soul is your own business. The rest I can *help* you with.

MARTIN Of course it's my business, and clearly you don't have one.

ROSS [*mild interest*] Oh?

MARTIN So that's what it comes down to, eh? . . . what we can get away with?

ROSS Sure.

MARTIN [*heavy irony*] Oh, thank God! It's so simple! I thought it was . . . I thought it had to do with love and loss, and it's only about . . . getting *by.* Well, Stevie and I have been wrestling with the wrong angel![3] When she comes back—*if* she comes back—I'll have to set her straight about what matters. [*Intense; not looking at* ROSS *or* BILLY*; pounding his hands on his knees perhaps*] Does nobody understand what happened!?

ROSS Oh, for Christ's sake, Martin!

BILLY Dad . . .

MARTIN [*crying a little*] Why can't anyone understand this . . . that I am *alone* . . . all . . . *alone!*

[*A silence. Then we hear a sound at the door.*]

BILLY Mom?

[BILLY *going into the hall. Gone.*]

MARTIN [*pause; to* ROSS*, begging*] You *do* understand; *don't* you.

ROSS [*long pause; shakes his head*] No.

[STEVIE *is dragging a dead goat. The goat's throat is cut; the blood is down* STEVIE*'s dress, on her arms. She stops.*]

Oh, my God.

MARTIN What have you done!?

STEVIE Here.

BILLY [*generally; to no one; helpless; a quiet plea*] Help. Help.

ROSS Oh, my God.

[MARTIN *moves toward* STEVIE.]

MARTIN What have you done!? Oh, my God, what have you *done!?*

[BILLY *is crying.* STEVIE *regards* MARTIN *for a moment;* ROSS *is immobile.*]

STEVIE [*turns to face him; evenly, without emotion*] I went where Ross told me I would find . . . your friend. I found her. I killed her. I brought her here to you. [*Odd little question*] No?

MARTIN [*a profound cry*] ANNNNNNH!

STEVIE Why are you surprised? What did you expect me to do?

MARTIN [*crying*] What did she *do!?* What did she ever *do!?* [*To* STEVIE] I ask you: what did she ever *do!?*

STEVIE [*pause; quietly*] She loved you . . . you say. As much as *I* do.

MARTIN [*to* STEVIE*; empty*] I'm sorry. [*To* BILLY*; empty*] I'm sorry. [*Then . . .*] I'm sorry.

BILLY [*to one, then the other; no reaction from them*] Dad? Mom?

[*Tableau.*[4]]

Curtain.

3. An allusion to the story of Jacob wrestling the angel of God (Genesis 32.24–30).

4. A stage direction that instructs the actors to freeze in their positions (as if forming a tableau vivant).

CARYL CHURCHILL

b. 1938

In February 1997, Scottish scientists sparked worldwide controversy by announcing the birth of a lamb, Dolly—the first mammalian clone successfully created from an adult cell. If it was now possible to clone a sheep, could the cloning of humans be far behind? And what were the scientific, legal, and moral implications of such research? The World Health Organization soon issued a statement condemning human cloning, as did the Parliamentary Assembly of the Council of Europe. England's Human Genetics Advisory Commission produced a strongly cautionary statement in 1998; in the United States, President Bill Clinton immediately imposed a moratorium on federal funding for human cloning research and charged his National Bioethics Advisory Commission to consider cloning's broader ramifications. Its report, *Cloning Human Beings,* appeared in June 1997. The first publication of the President's Council on Bioethics, which was created by President George W. Bush in 2001, was *Human Cloning and Human Dignity: An Ethical Enquiry* (2002). The stream of commentary on the topic, in both scientific and popular publications, has only grown, fueled by the overlapping debate about the benefits and morality of embryonic stem cell research. Here, matters of scientific fact and preoccupations of science fiction seem to merge. Though researchers point to the practical obstacles that must be overcome before human cloning could become a reality, many in the general public view the perfection of this reproductive technology as imminent—a possibility that stirs both fear and fascination. The issue raises basic questions about human identity—are we the products of our genes, our environment, or both?—and has kindled the imaginations of writers. In *A NUMBER* (2002), the British playwright Caryl Churchill envisions that future moment when cloning has become a reality: she explores these foundational concerns on the most personal level, asking us to consider what this "brave new world" might signify for parents and children.

Churchill is among the most influential and innovative of contemporary dramatists, consistently challenging theater artists and audiences alike since the 1970s with her politically charged and technically adventurous dramaturgy. Working in a country where theater has long reflected and affected national culture and discourse, she has embraced the stage as an avenue for expressing her deeply held social convictions. For decades, her plays have conveyed with growing urgency and intensity the potential devastation—sociological, economic, environmental, and political—that those with power can wreak on the individual and on society.

Caryl Churchill came of age at a potent, transitional period in English theater: the era of the "angry young men" like John Osborne, whose *Look Back in Anger* (1956) voiced hostility toward the British class system. Born in London in 1938, Churchill spent part of her childhood in Canada but returned to England in 1955; in 1957, she went to Oxford, studying English language and literature. At the university, she began writing plays that were produced by student theater groups. Shortly after graduation, she married David Harter, a lawyer. The couple had three children in the 1960s, and Churchill speaks frankly of her struggles in attempting simultaneously to continue writing and to fulfill her family obligations. She was initially politicized not by the broader social movements of that tumultuous era but by "being discontent with [her] own way of life—of being a barrister's wife and just being at home with small children." She started composing radio plays, because working in that form afforded her both the flexibility required by her family life and a respectable outlet for her work that was relatively accessible. As Churchill later noted in an interview, it was a time when the world-renowned dramatist "[SAMUEL] BECKETT was on the radio" and when the medium was perceived as "the way to break in" to professional playwriting.

In 1972, the first of Churchill's several television plays was produced and *Owners* was staged at London's Royal Court Theatre, a venue known for its commitment to new playwrights. Two years later, Churchill became the first woman to be offered a playwriting residency with the Royal Court; more than a dozen of her plays have premiered there, including her best-known work, *Top Girls* (1982)—a clear-eyed examination of feminism and women's lives in the "me decade"—and *A Number.* Another professional relationship that was to profoundly influence Churchill's work began in 1976, when she became involved with the Joint Stock Company. It was a theater collective committed to a collaborative, improvisational production process and to creative political engagement, and the approach taken to her plays by the company's actors and director, Max Stafford-Clark, changed how she developed her scripts. Elements of Churchill's dramaturgy that critics have called nonnaturalisitic and nonlinear are rooted in this experience. Other signature devices, such as double-casting and casting across race and gender, were initially practical techniques to make fullest use of the fairly small number of actors available to her in the company. But they soon affected and became crucial to expressing her conceptualization of characters, and were frequently employed to throw into relief the social construction of identity—most notably in *Cloud 9* (1979), Churchill's breakthrough international success that hilariously exposes Victorian notions of gender, race, and class and also poignantly captures the stubborn persistence of those values to the present day. In *A Number,* the technique of casting one actor in multiple roles lends itself brilliantly to an exploration of cloning.

Shortly before her work with Joint Stock began, Churchill had also affiliated with the socialist-feminist theater group Monstrous Regiment, which took its name from the title of a sixteenth-century misogynist pamphlet by John Knox that inveighs against the "monstrous regiment of women." The group collaborated with her in staging several pieces; one was *Vinegar Tom* (1976), a gripping historical drama about the persecution of women accused of witchcraft. Over the next decade, Churchill catapulted to international renown; *Top Girls, Cloud 9, Fen* (1983), and *Serious Money* (1987) were among her plays produced throughout the English-speaking world as well as in Europe, Asia, and Latin America. Her awards include an Obie for both *Cloud 9* and *Top Girls,* the Susan Smith Blackburn Prize for both *Fen* and *Serious Money,* and the Laurence Olivier Award (the British equivalent of the Tony Award) for *Serious Money.*

Churchill has repeatedly harnessed the power of live performance to engage audiences in meaningful political debate. Together with Mark Wing-Davey, the artistic director of London's Central School of Speech and Drama, she brought students from that professional conservatory to Romania to work with students from the Caragiale Institute of Theatre and Cinema in Bucharest in developing a piece dealing with the fall of Nicolae Ceausescu and the impact of his policies on the lives of Romanian citizens. The resulting drama, *Mad Forest* (1990), captures the complexities of life under and after an oppressive political regime. *The Skriker* (1994) weaves the dark world of folktale magic together with a hard-edged consideration of contemporary female adolescence and the natural environment, as it blurs the boundaries of drama and dance. In *Far Away* (2000), Churchill creates an apocalyptic vision of a land torn apart by conflict so profound that it beggars description. And *A Number* brings us into a frightening and all-too-conceivable world where scientific advances challenge long-held assumptions about individuals' autonomy and humanity. Although Churchill wins praise for consistently innovative and provocative dramaturgy, the arc of her career also reveals her ongoing engagement with issues that particularly concern her. Some of her earliest pieces consider themes that will recur, refined, in *A Number.* The radio play *Identical Twins* (1968), for example, examines personal identity; *Not . . . Not . . . Not . . . Not . . . Not Enough Oxygen* (1971), also a radio play, envisions a dystopic future.

A Number opens in the middle of a conversation between a father and his adult son. Though the situation appears to be normal, the topic is not: the son, Bernard, has just learned that he is not an only child (as he had always believed) but one of "a number" of cloned individuals. His father, Salter, insists that the cells taken from an earlier child—also named Bernard—were supposed to be used to produce only a single clone, but "some mad scientist has illegally" created more (perhaps twenty). Both men must grapple with this revelation, which raises issues of parental responsibility and culpability, individual identity, and the meaning of family.

The first scene sets the tone for the entire play. Structured as a kind of thriller, but one that deliberately eschews narrative closure, *A Number* relies on an exceedingly spare theatrical frame to draw us into the ever-deepening mystery of what has really happened in this family. In this two-hander (a script for two actors), Salter appears in each of five short scenes, while another actor plays the original Bernard (designated B1 in the script) and two of the clones, the

Dallas Roberts, left, plays Bernard, the cloned son of Salter (Sam Shepard) in *A Number,* which imparts a terrible mathematics lesson.

Bernard we meet initially (designated B2) and the one named Michael Black. Whom are we to believe? Which version of events is true? And what kind of people are Salter, the Bernards, and Michael?

Though the play's fragmented dialogue focuses on cloning, its subject is much broader. As noted by Stephen Daldry, its director at the Royal Court, *A Number* explores what free will is, and whether genetics or environment influences it more. Scientists and philosophers have long addressed the question of how heredity and culture interact to shape the lives of humans. By envisioning three individuals developed from the same genetic material, Churchill provides an opportunity for us to explore these issues through characters who remain distinct despite resembling each other physically—even on the cellular level.

Significantly, productions of *A Number* have chosen various theatrical means to communicate these foundational concepts of sameness and individuality. In the original London production, the actor playing the sons conveyed the differences between each character simply by changing his voice and physical mannerisms. Elsewhere, actors relied on elements of costume, such as baseball hats and jackets, to signal the different personas. Some directors had these changes occur offstage, while others had the actor transform in full view of the audience, as both performers remained on stage throughout the play.

At the same time, Churchill presents the character who is "the same" in each scene as profoundly unstable. Salter is unpredictable and chameleon-like, changing not only how he describes the past but also how he behaves to suit his different sons. Critics have observed in *A Number* echoes of other contemporary dramatists—including Samuel Beckett, HAROLD PINTER, and EDWARD ALBEE—who have dramatized powerful yet fractured relationships within families. These connections are depicted in the play's intense, elliptical encounters between characters, whose dialogue is filled with half-sentences, interruptions, and seemingly incomplete thoughts. Early in her career, Churchill developed a structure of fast-paced, overlapping dialogue that heightened an effect evident in ANTON CHEKHOV: through simultaneous speech, characters both make their own statements and appear to comment on each other's lines, thereby providing two layers of meaning. More recently, however, Churchill has pared down her dialogue, bringing it closer to the early style of DAVID MAMET, who has described his process of eliminating all unnecessary words from his writing. Although such dialogue may initially seem artificial, it in fact renders human speech patterns far more accurately than do the exchanges found in traditional realist drama; at the same time, it demands of actors and directors an intense engagement with subtext, and with the connection between subtext and action.

Even as *A Number* portrays a terrifying futuristic scenario, it captures family dynamics as old as humanity itself. The characterizations of B1 and B2 have led critics to reach for biblical analogies, citing Cain and Abel, or Jacob and Esau, while the relationship between Salter and his children has elicited comparisons to ARTHUR MILLER's *All My Sons* (1947) and especially to SHAKESPEARE's *King Lear* (1605) The depictions also resonate with the contemporary observation that men often struggle to communicate and express their feelings. Significantly, Churchill makes *A Number* a play that features only men. Salter's wife does not physically appear, though maternity is certainly an issue in the drama and her story is as complex as his. As in SUSAN GLASPELL's *Trifles* (1916), the key woman becomes an absent presence—a character we come to know through others' representation of her. And *A Number,* like *Trifles,* requires us to explore this absence in terms not only of the narrative but also of culture and symbolism.

Churchill further asks us to consider whether the label *parent* is applied primarily because of what one is (genetics) or because of what one does (behavior). *A Number* builds on a common fantasy: that one might return to the earliest days of a child's life and, with the benefit of hindsight, be a better parent. Though cloning appears to offer that opportunity to turn back the clock, Churchill makes clear that this is no panacea. Our mistakes—and their impact on others—can never simply be erased. We must come to grips with past errors even as we hold on to hopes for the future.

The play's final scene, in which Salter meets the clone Michael Black, provides a conclusion to Churchill's exploration of sadly damaged fathers and sons that is both poignant and ironic. Despite their previous lack of contact, their blood forms a bond, and Salter's longing for a relationship with this heretofore unknown child is palpable. As they struggle to communicate and find commonality, Michael shares with Salter some scientific truths he finds comforting: "We've got ninety-nine percent the same genes as any other person. We've got ninety percent the same as a chimpanzee. We've got thirty percent the same as a lettuce. Does that cheer you up at all? I love about the lettuce. It makes me feel I belong." Lacking traditional family ties, Michael has sought a sense of belonging elsewhere, and in *A Number*, Churchill pushes us to question not only how and where we belong, but how much we value all our connections to living beings.

J.E.G.

A Number

CHARACTERS

SALTER, a man in his early sixties
BERNARD, his son, forty
BERNARD, his son, thirty-five
MICHAEL BLACK, his son, thirty-five

The play is for two actors. One plays SALTER, the other his sons. The scene is the same throughout, it's where SALTER lives.

Scene 1

[SALTER, *a man in his early sixties and his son* BERNARD (B2), *thirty-five.*]

B2 A number

SALTER you mean

B2 a number of them, of us, a considerable

SALTER say

B2 ten, twenty

SALTER didn't you ask?

B2 I got the impression

SALTER why didn't you ask?

B2 I didn't think of asking.

SALTER I can't think why not, it seems to me it would be the first thing you'd want to know, how far has this thing gone, how many of these things are there?

B2 Good, so if it ever happens to you

SALTER no you're right

B2 no it was stupid, it was shock, I'd known for a week before I went to the hospital but it was still

SALTER it is, I am, the shocking thing is that there *are* these, not how many but at all

B2 even one

SALTER exactly, even one, a twin would be a shock

B2 a twin would be a surprise but a number

SALTER a number any number is a shock.

B2 You said things, these things

SALTER I said?

B2 you called them things. I think we'll find they're people.

SALTER Yes of course they are, they are of course.

B2 Because I'm one.

SALTER No.

B2 Yes. Why not? Yes.

SALTER Because they're copies

B2 copies? they're not

SALTER copies of you which some mad scientist has illegally

B2 how do you know that?

SALTER I don't but

B2 what if someone else is the one, the first one, the real one and I'm

SALTER no because

B2 not that I'm *not* real which is why I'm saying they're not things, don't call them

SALTER just wait, because I'm your father.

B2 You know that?

SALTER Of course.

B2 It was all a normal, everything, birth

SALTER you think I wouldn't know if I wasn't your father?

B2 Yes of course I was just for a moment there, but they are all still people like twins are all, quins[1] are all

SALTER yes I'm sorry

B2 we just happen to have identical be identical identical genetic

SALTER sorry I said things, I didn't mean anything by that, it just

B2 no forget it, it's nothing, it's

SALTER because of course for me you're the

B2 yes I know what you meant, I just, because of course I want them to be things, I do think they're things, I don't think they're, of course I *do* think they're them just as much as I'm me but I. I don't know what I think, I feel terrible.

SALTER I wonder if we can sue.

B2 Sue? who?

SALTER Them, whoever did it. Who did you see?

B2 Just some young, I don't know, younger than me.

SALTER So who did it?

B2 He's dead, he was some old and they've just found the records and they've traced

SALTER so we sue the hospital.

B2 Maybe. Maybe we can.

SALTER Because they've taken your cells

1. Quintuplets.

B2 but when how did they?

SALTER when you were born maybe or later you broke your leg when you were two you were in the hospital, some hairs or scrapings of your skin

B2 but they didn't damage

SALTER but it's you, part of you, the value

B2 the value of those people

SALTER yes

B2 and what is the value of

SALTER there you are, who knows, priceless, and they belong

B2 no

SALTER they belong to you, they should belong to you, they're made from your

B2 they should

SALTER they've been stolen from you and you should get your rights

B2 but is it

SALTER what? is it money? is it something you can put a figure on? put a figure on it.

B2 This is purely

SALTER yes

B2 suppose each person was worth ten thousand pounds

SALTER a hundred

B2 a hundred thousand?

SALTER they've taken a person away from you

B2 times the number of people

SALTER which we don't know

B2 but a number a fairly large say anyway ten

SALTER a million is the least you should take, I think it's more like half a million each person because what they've done they've damaged your uniqueness, weakened your identity, so we're looking at five million for a start.

B2 Maybe.

SALTER Yes, because how dare they?

B2 We'd need to be able to prove

SALTER we prove you're genetically my son genetically and then

B2 because there's no doubt

SALTER no doubt at all. I suppose you didn't see one?

B2 One what? of them?

SALTER of these people

B2 no I think they'd keep us apart wouldn't they so we don't spoil like contaminate the crime scene so you don't tell each other I have nightmares oh come to think of it I have nightmares and he might have said no if he was asked in the first place

SALTER because they need to find out

B2 yes how much we're the same, not just how tall we are or do we get asthma but what do you call your dog, why did you leave your wife you don't even know the answer to these questions.

SALTER So you didn't suddenly suddenly see

B2 what suddenly see myself coming round the corner

SALTER because that could be

B2 like seeing yourself on the camera in a shop or you hear yourself on the answering machine and you think god is that what I

SALTER but more than that, it'd be it'd be

B2 don't they say you die if you meet yourself?[2]

SALTER walk round the corner and see yourself you could get a heart attack. Because if that's me over there who am I?

B2 Yes but it's not me over there

SALTER no I know

B2 it's like having a twin that's all it's just

SALTER I know what it is.

B2 I think I'd like to meet one. It's an adventure isn't it and you're part of science. I wouldn't be frightened to meet any number.

SALTER I don't know.

B2 They're all your sons.

SALTER I don't want a number of sons, thank you, you're plenty, I'm fine.

B2 Maybe after they've found everything out they'll let us meet. They'll have a party for us, we can

SALTER I'm not going to drink with those doctors. But maybe you're right you're right, take it in a positive spirit.

B2 There is a thing

SALTER what's that?

B2 a thing that puzzles me a little

SALTER what's that?

B2 I did get the impression and I know I may be wrong because maybe I was in shock but I got the impression there was this batch and we were all in it. I was in it.

SALTER No because you're my son.

B2 No but we were all

SALTER I explained already

B2 but I wasn't being quite open with you because I'm confused because it's a shock but I want to know what happened

SALTER they stole

B2 no but what happened

SALTER I don't

B2 because they said that none of us was the original.

SALTER They said that?

B2 I think

SALTER I think you're mistaken because you're confused

B2 you think

SALTER you need to get back to them

B2 well I'll do that. But I think that's what they meant

SALTER it's not what they meant

B2 ok. But that's my impression, that none of us is the original.

SALTER Then who? do they know?

B2 they're not saying, they just say we were all

SALTER they're not saying?

B2 so if I was your son the original would be your son too which is nonsense so

SALTER does that follow?

2. According to folk belief, meeting one's ghostly double (or doppelganger) is a portent of death.

B2 so please if you're not my father that's fine. If you couldn't have children or my mother, and you did in vitro[3] or I don't know what you did I really think you should tell me.

SALTER Yes, that's what it was.

B2 That's all right.

SALTER Yes I know.

B2 Thank you for telling me.

SALTER Yes.

B2 It's better to know.

SALTER Yes.

B2 So don't be upset.

SALTER No.

B2 You are though

SALTER Well.

B2 I'm fine about it. I'm not quite sure what I'm fine about. There was some other person this original some baby or cluster or and there were a number a number of us made somehow and you were one of the people who acquired, something like that.

SALTER It wasn't

B2 don't worry

SALTER because the thing is you see that isn't what happened. I am your father, it was by an artificial the forefront of science but I am genetically.

B2 That's great.

SALTER Yes.

B2 So I know the truth and you're still my father and that's fine.

SALTER Yes.

B2 So what about this original? I don't quite I don't

SALTER There was someone.

B2 There was what kind of someone?

SALTER There was a son.

B2 A son of yours?

SALTER Yes.

B2 So when was that?

SALTER That was some time earlier.

B2 Some time before I was born there was

SALTER another son, yes, a first

B2 who what, who died

SALTER who died, yes

B2 and you wanted to replace him

SALTER I wanted

B2 instead of just having another child you wanted

SALTER because your mother was dead too

B2 but she died when I was born, I thought she

SALTER well I'm telling you what happened.

B2 So what happened?

SALTER So they'd been killed in a carcrash and

B2 my mother and this

3. That is, in vitro (literally, "in glass"; Latin) fertilization; in this form of assisted reproduction, eggs are fertilized in a laboratory dish and one or more are implanted in the birth mother's uterus.

SALTER carcrash

B2 when was this? how old was the child, was he

SALTER four, he was four

B2 and you wanted him back

SALTER yes

B2 so I'm just him over again.

SALTER No but you are you because that's who you are but I wanted one just the same because that seemed to me the most perfect

B2 but another child might have been better

SALTER no I wanted the same

B2 but I'm not him

SALTER no but you're just the way I wanted

B2 but I could have been a different person not like him I

SALTER how could you? if I'd had a different child that wouldn't be you, would it. You're this one.

B2 I'm just a copy. I'm not the real one.

SALTER You're the only one.

B2 What do you mean only, there's all the others, there's

SALTER but I didn't know that, that wasn't part of the deal. They were meant to make one of you not a whole number, they stole that, we'll deal with, it's something for lawyers. But you're what I wanted, you're the one.

B2 Did you give me the same name as him?

SALTER Does it make it worse?

B2 Probably.

Scene 2

[SALTER *and his other son* BERNARD (B1), *forty.*]

SALTER So they stole—don't look at me—they stole your genetic material and

B1 no

SALTER they're the ones you want to

B1 no

SALTER because what ten twenty twenty copies of you walking round the streets

B1 no

SALTER which was nothing to do with me whatsoever and I think you and I should be united on this.

B1 Let me look at you.

SALTER You've been looking at me all the

B1 let me look at you.

SALTER Bit older.

B1 No because your father's not young when you're small is he, he's not any age, he's more a power. He's a dark dark power which is why my heart, people pay trainers to get it up to this speed, but is it because my body recognises or because I'm told? because if I'd seen you in the street I don't think I'd've stopped and shouted Daddy. But you'd've known me wouldn't you. Unless you thought I was one of the others.

SALTER It's a long time.

B1 Can we talk about what you did?

SALTER Yes of course. I'm not sure where what

BI about you sent me away and had this other one made from some bit of my body some

SALTER it didn't hurt you

BI what bit

SALTER I don't know what

BI not a limb, they clearly didn't take a limb like a starfish and grow[4]

SALTER a speck

BI or half of me chopped through like a worm and grow the other

SALTER a scraping cells a speck a speck

BI a speck yes because we're talking that microscope world of giant blobs and globs

SALTER that's all

BI and they take this painless scrape this specky little cells of me and kept that and you threw the rest of me away

SALTER no

BI and had a new one made

SALTER no

BI yes

SALTER yes

BI yes

SALTER yes of course, you know I did, I'm not attempting to deny, I thought it was the best thing to do, it seemed a brilliant it was the only

BI brilliant?

SALTER it seemed

BI to get rid

SALTER it wasn't perfect. It was the best I could do, I wasn't very I was I was always and it's a blur to be honest but it was I promise you the best

BI and this copy they grew of me, that worked out all right?

SALTER There were failures of course, inevitable

BI dead ones

SALTER in the test tubes the dishes, I was told they didn't all

BI but they finally got a satisfactory a bouncing

SALTER yes but they lied to me because they didn't tell me

BI in a cradle

SALTER all those others, they stole

BI and he looked just like me did he indistinguishable from

SALTER yes

BI so it worked out very well. And this son lives and breathes?

SALTER yes

BI talks and fucks? eats and walks? swims and dreams and exists somewhere right now yes does he? exist now?

SALTER yes

BI still exists

SALTER yes of course

BI happily?

4. Starfish, or sea stars, not only are able to regrow lost arms but also can regenerate themselves from a single arm if it includes part of the central disc to which the arms are attached.

SALTER well mostly you could say

BI as happily as most people?

SALTER yes I think

BI because most people are happy I read in the paper. Did it cost a lot of money?

SALTER the procedure? to get?

BI the baby

SALTER yes.

BI Were we rich?

SALTER Not rich.

BI No, I don't remember anything rich. A lot of dust under the bed those heaps of fluff you get don't you if you look if you go under there and lie in it.

SALTER No, we weren't. But I managed. I was spending less.

BI You made an effort.

SALTER I did and for that money you'd think I'd get exclusive

BI they ripped you off

SALTER because one one was the deal and they

BI what do you expect?

SALTER from you too they it's you they, just so they can do some scientific some research some do you get asthma do you have a dog what do you call it do you

BI Who did you think it was at the door? did you think it was one of the others or your son or

SALTER I don't know the others

BI you know your son

SALTER I know

BI your son the new

SALTER yes of course

BI you know him

SALTER yes I wouldn't think he was you, no.

BI You wouldn't think it was him having a bad day.

SALTER You look very well.

BI But it could have been one of the others?

SALTER Yes because that's what I was thinking about, how could the doctors, I think there's money to be made out of this.

BI I've not been lucky with dogs. I had this black and tan bitch wouldn't do what it's told, useless. Before that I had a lurcher[5] they need too much running about. Then a friend of mine went inside could I look after, battle from day one with that dog, rottweiler pit bull I had to throw a chair, you could hit it with a belt it kept coming back. I'd keep it shut up in the other room and it barks so you have to hit it, I was glad when it bit a girl went to pat it and straight off to the vet, get rid of this one it's a bastard. My friend wasn't pleased but he shouldn't have gone in the postoffice.

SALTER No that's right. I've never wanted a dog.

BI Don't patronise me

SALTER I'm not I'm not

BI you don't know what you're doing

5. A mixed-breed dog, traditionally used by poachers to catch rabbits (British term). *Bitch:* a female dog.

SALTER I just

BI because you go in a pub someone throws his beer in your face you're supposed to say sorry, he only had three stitches I'm a very restrained person. Because this minute we sit here there's somebody a lot of them but think of one on the electric bedsprings or water poured down his throat and jump on his stomach. There's a lot of wicked people. So that's why. And you see them all around you. You go down the street and you see their faces and you think you don't fool me I know what you're capable of. So don't start anything.

SALTER I think what we need is a good solicitor.[6]

BI What I like about a dog it stops people getting after you, they're not going to come round in the night. But they make the place stink because I might want to stay out a few days and when I get back I might want to stay in a few days and a dog can become a tyrant to you.

[*Silence.*]

Hello daddy daddy daddy, daddy hello.

SALTER Nobody regrets more than me the completely unforeseen unforeseeable which isn't my fault and does make it more upsetting but what I did did seem at the time the only and also it's a tribute, I could have had a different one, a new child altogether that's what most people but I wanted you again because I thought you were the best.

BI It wasn't me again.

SALTER No but the same basic the same raw materials because they were perfect. You were the most beautiful baby everyone said. As a child too you were very pretty, very pretty child.

BI You know when I used to be shouting.

SALTER No.

BI When I was there in the dark. I'd be shouting.

SALTER No.

BI Yes, I'd be shouting dad dad

SALTER Was this some time you had a bad dream or?

BI shouting on and on

SALTER I don't think I

BI shouting and shouting

SALTER no

BI and you never came, nobody ever came

SALTER so was this after your mum

BI after my mum was dead this was after

SALTER because you were very little when she

BI yes because I can only remember

SALTER you were maybe two when she

BI and I remember her sitting there, she was there

SALTER you remember so early?

BI she'd be there but she wouldn't help stop anything

SALTER I'm surprised

BI so when I was shouting what I want to know

SALTER but when was this

6. In the British legal system, a lawyer who advises clients (and does not represent them, except in the lower courts).

BI I want to know if you could hear me or not because I never knew were you hearing me and not coming or could you not hear me and if I shouted loud enough you'd come

SALTER I can't have heard you, no

BI or maybe there was no one there at all and you'd gone out so no matter how hard I shouted there was no one there

SALTER no that wouldn't have

BI so then I'd stop shouting but it was worse

SALTER because I hardly ever

BI and I didn't dare get out of bed to go and see

SALTER I don't think this can have

BI because if there was nobody there that would be terrifying and if you were there that might be worse but it's something I wonder

SALTER no

BI could you hear me shouting?

SALTER no I don't

BI no

SALTER no I don't think this happened in quite the

BI what?

SALTER because I'd

BI again and again and again, every night I'd be

SALTER no

BI so you didn't hear?

SALTER no but you can't have

BI yes I was shouting, are you telling me you didn't

SALTER no of course I didn't

BI you didn't

SALTER no

BI you weren't sitting there listening to me shouting

SALTER no

BI you weren't out

SALTER no

BI so I needed to shout louder.

SALTER Of course sometimes everyone who's had children will tell you sometimes you put them to bed and they want another story and you say goodnight now and go away and they call out once or twice and you say no go to sleep now and they might call out again and they go to sleep.

BI The other one. Your son. My brother is he? my little twin.

SALTER Yes.

BI Has he got a child?

SALTER No.

BI Because if he had I'd kill it.

SALTER No, he hasn't got one.

BI So when you opened the door you didn't recognise me.

SALTER No because

BI Do you recognise me now?

SALTER I know it's you.

BI No but look at me.

SALTER I have. I am.

BI No, look in my eyes. No, keep looking. Look.

Scene 3

[SALTER *and* BERNARD (B2).]

B2 Not like me at all

SALTER not like

B2 well like like but not identical not

SALTER not identical no not

B2 because what struck me was how different

SALTER yes I was struck

B2 you couldn't mistake

SALTER no no not at all I knew at once it wasn't

B2 though of course he is older if I was older

SALTER but even then you wouldn't

B2 I wouldn't be identical

SALTER no no not at all no, you're a different

B2 just a bit like

SALTER well bound to be a bit

B2 because for a start I'm not frightening.

SALTER So what did he want did he

B2 no nothing really, not frightening not

SALTER he didn't hit you?

B2 hit? god no, hit me? do you think?

SALTER well he

B2 he could have done yes, no he shouted

SALTER shouted

B2 shouted and rambled really, rambled he's not entirely

SALTER no, well

B2 so that's what, his childhood, his life, his childhood

SALTER all kinds of

B2 has made him a nutter really is what I think I mean not a nutter but he's

SALTER yes yes I'm not, yes he probably is.

B2 He says all kinds of wild

SALTER yes

B2 so you don't know what to believe.

SALTER And how did it end up, are you on friendly

B2 friendly no

SALTER not

B2 no no we ended up

SALTER yes

B2 we ended as I mean to go on with me running away, I was glad we were meeting in a public place, if I'd been at home you can't run away in your own home and if we'd been at his I wonder if he'd have let me go he might put me in a cupboard[7] not really, anyway yes I got up and left and I kept thinking had he followed me.

SALTER As you mean to go on as in not seeing him any more

B2 as in leaving the country.

SALTER For what for a week or two a holiday, I don't

B2 leaving, going on yes I don't know, going away, I don't want to be here.

7. Closet (British term).

SALTER But when you come back he'll still

B2 so maybe I won't

SALTER but that's, not come back, no that's

B2 I don't know I don't know don't ask me I don't know. I'm going, I don't know. I don't want to be anywhere near him.

SALTER You think he might try to hurt you?

B2 Why? why do you keep

SALTER I don't know. Is it that?

B2 It's partly that, it's also it's horrible, I don't feel myself and there's the others too, I don't want to see them I don't want them

SALTER I thought you did.

B2 I thought I did, I might, if I go away by myself I might feel all right, I might feel—you can understand that.

SALTER Yes, yes I can.

B2 Because there's this person who's identical to me

SALTER he's not

B2 who's not identical, who's like

SALTER not even very

B2 not very like but very something terrible which is exactly the same genetic person

SALTER not the same person

B2 and I don't like it.

SALTER I know. I'm sorry.

B2 I know you're sorry I'm not

SALTER I know

B2 I'm not trying to make you say sorry

SALTER I know, I just am

B2 I know

SALTER I just am sorry.

B2 He said some things.

SALTER Yes.

B2 There's a lot of things I don't, could you tell me what happened to my mother?

SALTER She's dead.

B2 Yes.

SALTER I told you she was dead.

B2 Yes but she didn't die when I was born and she didn't die with the first child in a carcrash because the first child's not dead he's walking round the streets at night giving me nightmares. Unless she did die in a carcrash?

SALTER No.

B2 No.

SALTER Your mother, the thing a thing about your mother was that she wasn't very happy, she wasn't a very happy person at all, I don't mean there were sometimes days she wasn't happy or I did things that made her not happy I did of course, she was always not happy, often cheerful and

B2 she killed herself. How did she do that?

SALTER She did it under a train under a tube[8] train, she was one of those

8. Subway (British term).

people when they say there has been a person under a train and the trains are delayed she was a person under a train.

B2 Were you with her?

SALTER With her on the platform no, I was still *with* her more or less but not with her then no I was having a drink I think.

B2 And the boy?

SALTER Do you know I don't remember where the boy was. I think he was at a friend's house, we had friends.

B2 And he was how old four?

SALTER no no he was four later when I he was walking, about two just starting to talk

B2 he was four when you sent him

SALTER that's right when his mother died he was two.

B2 So this was let me be clear this was before this was some years before I was born she died before

SALTER yes

B2 so she was already always

SALTER yes she was

B2 just so I'm clear. And then you and the boy you and your son

SALTER we went on we just

B2 lived alone together

SALTER yes

B2 you were bringing him up

SALTER yes

B2 the best you could

SALTER I

B2 until

SALTER and my best wasn't very but I had my moments, don't think, I did cook meals now and then and read a story I'm sure I can remember a particularly boring and badly written little book about an elephant at sea. But I could have managed better.

B2 Yes he said something about it

SALTER he said

B2 yes

SALTER yes of course he did yes. I know I could have managed better because I did with you because I stopped, shut myself away, gave it all up came off it all while I waited for you and I think we may even have had that same book, maybe it's you I remember reading it to, do you remember it at all? it had an elephant in red trousers.

B2 No I don't think

SALTER no it was terrible, we had far better books we had

B2 Maybe he shouldn't blame you, maybe it was a genetic, could you help drinking we don't know or drugs at the time philosophically as I understand it it wasn't viewed as not like now when our understanding's different and would a different person genetically different person not have been so been so vulnerable because there could always be some genetic addictive and then again someone with the same genetic exactly the same but at a different time a different cultural and of course all the personal all kinds of what happened in your own life your childhood or things all kind of because suppose you'd had a brother with identical an identical twin say but separated at birth so you had entirely different early you see what I'm saying would he have done the same things who can say he might have been a very loving father and in fact of course you have that in you to be that because you were to me so it's a combination of very complicated and that's who you were so probably I shouldn't blame you.

SALTER I'd rather you blamed me. I blame myself.

B2 I'm not saying you weren't horrible.

SALTER Couldn't I not have been?

B2 Apparently not.

SALTER If I'd tried harder.

B2 But someone like you couldn't have tried harder. What does it mean? If you'd tried harder you'd have been different from what you were like and you weren't you were

SALTER but then later I

B2 later yes

SALTER I did try that's what I did I started again I

B2 that's what

SALTER I was good I tried to be good I was good to you

B2 that's what you were like

SALTER I was good

B2 but I can't you can't I can't give you credit for that if I don't give you blame for the other it's what you did it's what happened

SALTER but it felt

B2 it felt

SALTER it felt as if I tried I deliberately

B2 of course it felt

SALTER well then

B2 it feels it always it feels doesn't it inside that's just how we feel what we are and we don't know all these complicated we can't know what we're it's too complicated to disentangle all the causes and we feel this is me I freely and of course it's true who you are does freely not forced by someone else but who you are who you are itself forces or you'd be someone else wouldn't you?

SALTER I did some bad things. I deserve to suffer. I did some better things. I'd like recognition.

B2 That's how everyone feels, certainly.

SALTER He still blames me.

B2 There's a difference then.

SALTER You remind me of him.

B2 I remind myself of him. We both hate you.

SALTER I thought you

B2 I don't blame you it's not your fault but what you've been like what you're like I can't help it.

SALTER Yes of course.

B2 Except what he feels as hate and what I feel as hate are completely different because what you did to him and what you did to me are different things.

SALTER I was nice to you.

B2 Yes you were.

SALTER You don't have to go away. Not for long.

B2 It might make me feel better.

SALTER I love you.

B2 That's something else you can't help.

SALTER That's all right. That's all right.

B2 Also I'm afraid he'll kill me.

Scene 4

[SALTER *and* BERNARD (B1).]

SALTER So what kind of a place was it? was it

B1 the place

SALTER he was in a hotel was he or

B1 no

SALTER I thought he was in a hotel. So where was he?

B1 what?

SALTER I'm trying to get a picture.

B1 Does it matter?

SALTER It won't bring him back no obviously but I'd like I'd like you can't help feeling curious you want to get at it and you're blocked in all directions, your son dies you want his body, you want to know where his body last was when he was alive, you can't help

B1 He had a room.

SALTER In somebody's house, renting

B1 some small you know how the locals when you arrive, just a room not breakfast you'd go out for a coffee.

SALTER So was it some pretty on a harbour front or

B1 no

SALTER thinking of him on holiday

B1 in a street just a side

SALTER but of course it wasn't a holiday he was hiding he thought he was hiding. Did you go inside the room?

B1 Just a small room, rather dark, one window and the shutters

SALTER not very tidy I expect

B1 that's right, not tidy the bed not made, couple of books, bag on the floor with clothes half out of it

SALTER did he scream?

B1 and you know what he's like, not tidy, am I tidy you don't know do you but you'd guess not wouldn't you but you'd be wrong there because I'm meticulous.

SALTER What I want to know is how you actually, what you, how you got him to go off to some remote because that's what I'm imagining, you don't shoot the lodger without the landlady hearing, I don't know if you did shoot I don't know why I say shoot you could have had a knife you could have strangled, I can't think he would have gone off with you because he was frightened which is why but perhaps you talked you made him feel or did you follow him or lie in wait in some dark? and I don't know how you found him there did you follow him from his house when he left or follow him from here last time he?

B1 I didn't need to tell you it had happened

SALTER but you did so naturally I want to

B1 and I'm wishing I hadn't

SALTER no I'm glad

BI and I'm not telling you

SALTER because I won't tell anyone

BI and there's nothing more to be said.

SALTER What about the others? or is he the only one you hated because I loved him, I don't love the others, you and I have got common cause against the others don't forget, I'm still hoping we'll make our fortunes there. I'm going to talk to a solicitor, I've been too busy not busy but it's been like a storm going on I don't know what's gone on, it's not been very long ago it all started. You're not going to be a serial, wipe them all out so you're the only, back like it was at the start I'd understand that. If they do catch up with you, I'm sure they won't I'm sure you know what you're, if they do we'll tell them it was me it was my fault anyway you look at it. Don't you agree, don't you feel that? Don't stop talking to me. It wasn't his fault, you should have killed me, it's my fault you. Perhaps you're going to kill me, is that why you've stopped talking? Shall I kill myself? I'd do that for you if you like, would you like that?

I'll tell you a thought, I could have killed you and I didn't. I may have done terrible things but I didn't kill you. I could have killed you and had another son, made one the same like I did or start again have a different one get married again and I didn't, I spared you though you were this disgusting thing by then anyone in their right mind would have squashed you but I remembered what you'd been like at the beginning and I spared you, I didn't want a different one, I wanted that again because you were perfect just like that and I loved you.

You know you asked me when you used to shout in the night. Sometimes I was there, I'd sit and listen to you or I'd not be in any condition to hear you I'd just be sitting. Sometimes I'd go out and leave you. I don't think you got out of bed, did you get out of bed, because you'd be frightened what I'd do to you so it was all right to go out. That was just a short period you used to shout, you grew out of that, you got so you'd rather not see me, you wanted to be left alone in the night, you wouldn't want me to come any more. You'd nearly stopped speaking do you remember that? not speaking not eating I tried to make you. I'd put you in the cupboard do you remember? or I'd look for you everywhere and I'd think you'd got away and I'd find you under the bed. You liked it there I'd put your dinner under for you. But it got worse do you remember? There was nobody but us. One day I cleaned you up and said take him into care.[9] You didn't look too bad and they took you away. My darling. Do you remember that? Do you remember that day because I don't remember it you know. The whole thing is very vague to me. It's two years I remember almost nothing about but you must remember things and when you're that age two years is much longer, it wasn't very long to me, it was one long night out. Can you tell me anything you remember? the day you left? can you tell me things I did I might have forgotten?

BI When I was following him there was a time I was getting on the same train and he looked round, I thought he was looking right at me but he didn't see me. I got on the train and went with him all the way.

SALTER Yes? yes?

9. Under the guardianship of the state.

Scene 5

[SALTER *and* MICHAEL BLACK, *his son, thirty-five.*]

MICHAEL Have you met the others?

SALTER You're the first.

MICHAEL Are you going to meet us all?

SALTER I thought I'd start.

MICHAEL I'm sure everyone will be pleased to meet you. I know I am.

SALTER I'm sorry to stare.

MICHAEL No, please, I can see it must be. Do I look like?

SALTER Yes of course

MICHAEL of course, I meant

SALTER no no I didn't mean

MICHAEL I suppose I meant how

SALTER because of course you don't, you don't, not exactly

MICHAEL no of course

SALTER I wouldn't mistake

MICHAEL no

SALTER or I might at a casual

MICHAEL of course

SALTER but not if I really look

MICHAEL no

SALTER no

MICHAEL because?

SALTER because of the eyes. You don't look at me in the same way.

MICHAEL I'm looking at someone I don't know of course.

SALTER Maybe you could tell me a little

MICHAEL about myself

SALTER if you don't mind

MICHAEL no of course, it's where to, you already know I'm a teacher, mathematics, you know I'm married, three children did I tell you that

SALTER yes but you didn't

MICHAEL boy and girl twelve and eight and now a baby well eighteen months so she's walking and beginning to talk, I don't have any photographs on me I didn't think, there's no need for photographs is there if you see someone all the time so

SALTER are you happy?

MICHAEL what now? or in general? Yes I think I am, I don't think about it, I am. The job gets me down sometimes. The world's a mess of course. But you can't help, a sunny morning, leaves turning, off to the park with the baby, you can't help feeling wonderful can you?

SALTER Can't you?

MICHAEL Well that's how I seem to be.

SALTER Tell me. Forgive me

MICHAEL no go on

SALTER tell me something about yourself that's really specific to you, something really important

MICHAEL what sort of?

SALTER anything

MICHAEL it's hard to

SALTER yes.

MICHAEL Well here's something I find fascinating, there are these people who used to live in holes in the ground, with all tunnels and underground chambers and sometimes you'd have a chamber you'd get to it through a labyrinth of passages and the ceiling got lower and lower so you had to go on your hands and knees and then wriggle on your stomach and you'd get through to this chamber deep deep down that had a hole like a chimney like a well a hole all the way up to the sky so you could sit in this chamber this room this cave whatever and look up at a little circle of sky going past overhead. And when somebody died they'd hollow out more little rooms so they weren't buried underneath you they were buried in the walls beside you. And maybe sometimes they walled people up alive in there, it's possible because of how the remains were contorted but either way of course they're dead by now and very soon after they went in of course. And

SALTER I don't think this is what I'm looking for

MICHAEL oh, how, sorry

SALTER because what you're telling me is about something else and I was hoping for something about you

MICHAEL I don't quite

SALTER I'm sorry I don't know I was hoping

MICHAEL you want what my beliefs, politics how I feel about war for instance is that? I dislike war, I'm not at all happy when people say we're doing a lot of good with our bombing, I'm never very comfortable with that. War's one of those things, don't you think, where everyone always thinks they're in the right have you noticed that? Nobody ever says we're the bad guys, we're going to beat shit out of the good guys. What do you think?

SALTER I was hoping I don't know something more personal something from deep inside your life. If that's not intrusive.

MICHAEL Maybe what maybe my wife's ears?

SALTER Yes?

MICHAEL Because last night we were watching the news and I thought what beautiful and slightly odd ears she's got, they're small but with big lobes, big relative to the small ear, and they're slightly pointy on top, like a disney elf[1] or little animal ears and they're always there but you know how you suddenly notice and noticing that, I mean the way I love her, felt very felt what you said something deep inside. Or the children obviously, I could talk about, is this the sort of thing?

SALTER it's not quite

MICHAEL no

SALTER because you're just describing other people or

MICHAEL yes

SALTER not yourself

MICHAEL but it's people I love so

SALTER it's not what I'm looking for. Because anyone could feel

MICHAEL oh of course I'm not claiming

SALTER I was somehow hoping

MICHAEL yes

1. That is, like the ears of an elf in an animated film created by the American movie producer Walt Disney (1901–1966).

SALTER further in
MICHAEL yes
SALTER just about yourself
MICHAEL myself
SALTER yes
MICHAEL like maybe I'm lying in bed and it's comfortable and then it gets slightly not so comfortable and I move my legs or even turn over and then it's
SALTER no
MICHAEL no
SALTER no that's
MICHAEL yes that's something everyone
SALTER yes
MICHAEL well I don't know. I like blue socks. Banana icecream. Does that help you?
SALTER Dogs?
MICHAEL do I like
SALTER dogs
MICHAEL I'm ok with dogs. My daughter wants a puppy but I don't know. Is dogs the kind of thing?
SALTER So tell me what did you feel when you found out?
MICHAEL Fascinated.
SALTER Not angry?
MICHAEL No.
SALTER Not frightened.
MICHAEL No, what of?
SALTER Your life, losing your life.
MICHAEL I've still got my life.
SALTER But there are things there are things that are what you are, I think you're avoiding
MICHAEL yes perhaps
SALTER because then you might be frightened
MICHAEL I don't think
SALTER or angry
MICHAEL not really
SALTER because what does it do what does it to you to everything if there are all these walking around, what it does to me what am I and it's not even me it happened to, so how you can just, you must think something about it.
MICHAEL I think it's funny, I think it's delightful
SALTER delightful?
MICHAEL all these very similar people doing things like each other or a bit different or whatever we're doing, what a thrill for the mad old professor if he'd lived to see it, I do see the joy of it. I know you're not at all happy.
SALTER I didn't feel I'd lost him when I sent him away because I had the second chance. And when the second one my son the second son was murdered it wasn't so bad as you'd think because it seemed fair. I was back with the first one.
MICHAEL But now
SALTER now he's killed himself
MICHAEL now you feel
SALTER now I've lost him, I've lost

MICHAEL yes

SALTER now I can't put it right any more. Because the second time round you see I slept very lightly with the door open.

MICHAEL Is that the worst you did, not go in the night?

SALTER No of course not.

MICHAEL Like what?

SALTER Things that are what I did that are not trivial like banana icecream nor unifuckingversal like turning over in bed.

MICHAEL We've got ninety-nine percent the same genes as any other person. We've got ninety percent the same as a chimpanzee. We've got thirty percent the same as a lettuce. Does that cheer you up at all? I love about the lettuce. It makes me feel I belong.

SALTER I miss him so much. I miss them both.

MICHAEL There's nineteen more of us.

SALTER That's not the same.

MICHAEL No of course not. I was making a joke.

SALTER And you're happy you say are you? you like your life?

MICHAEL I do yes, sorry.

Selected Bibliographies

EDWARD ALBEE

The Goat was first published by Overlook Press in 2003. A slightly revised edition, published in 2008, is the version used here. Albee's plays have been collected in a three-volume set, *The Collected Plays of Edward Albee*, published by Overlook Duckworth (2008). Albee's life and career through 1998 are discussed in Mel Gussow's biography, *Edward Albee: A Singular Journey: A Biography* (1999). Albee has, over the years, generously shared his time with critics, scholars, and colleagues; a useful selection of interviews spanning his career through the mid-1980s appears in Philip Kolin's edited volume, *Conversations with Edward Albee* (1988). Several bibliographies cover Albee's own writing and criticism of his early work: see Charles Lee Green, *Edward Albee: An Annotated Bibliography, 1968–1977* (1980); Richard Tyce, *Edward Albee: A Bibliography* (1986); and Scott Giantvalley, *Edward Albee: A Reference Guide* (1987).

A number of studies address Albee's early career, including C. W. E. Bigsby, *Albee* (1969); Ruby Cohn, *Edward Albee* (1969); Anne Paolucci, *From Tension to Tonic: The Plays of Edward Albee* (1972); Ronald Hayman, *Edward Albee* (1973); Foster Hirsch, *Who's Afraid of Edward Albee?* (1978); Gerry McCarthy, *Edward Albee* (1987); and Matthew C. Roudané, *Understanding Edward Albee* (1987). A number of collections of early reviews and essays also contain valuable background on the reception of Albee's work: see C. W. E. Bigsby, ed., *Edward Albee: A Collection of Critical Essays* (1975); Philip C. Kolin and J. Madison Davis, eds., *Critical Essays on Edward Albee* (1986); and Harold Bloom, ed., *Edward Albee* (1987). Stephen J. Bottoms, *Albee: Who's Afraid of Virginia Woolf?* (2000), analyzes both productions and critical responses to this groundbreaking play. J. Ellen Gainor's "Albee's *The Goat*: Rethinking Tragedy for the 21st Century," in *The Cambridge Companion to Edward Albee*, ed. Stephen Bottoms (2005), and John Kuhn's "Getting Albee's Goat: 'Notes Toward a Definition of Tragedy'" (2004) provide detailed readings of the play.

TAWFIQ AL-HAKIM

In addition to the 1977 translation by M. M. Badawi included here, *Song of Death* has been translated into English by C. W. R. Long (1972) and Denys Johnson-Davies (1973). One of the most comprehensive treatments in English of Tawfiq al-Hakim and his contribution to Egyptian theater is found in Badawi's seminal work *Modern Arabic Drama in Egypt* (1987). In this study, Badawi provides a thorough overview of al-Hakim's different developmental stages as a playwright and traces his dramatic production from its earliest experiments to the last stages. *Tawfiq al-Hakim: A Reader's Guide*, ed. William Maynard Hutchins (2003), discusses al-Hakim's plays, novels, and short stories and includes an excellent annotated biography and chronology of the writer's life and work. Other studies of al-Hakim's drama include Richard Long, *Tawfiq al Hakim, Playwright of Egypt* (1979); Roger Allen, "Egyptian Drama after the Revolution" (1979);

Paul Starkey, "Tawfiq Al-Hakim: Leading Playwright of the Arab World" (1989); and Ali al-Ra'i, "Arab Drama Since the Thirties," in *The Cambridge History of Arabic Literature: Modern Arabic Literature*, ed. M. M. Badawi (1992).

SAMUEL BECKETT

Samuel Beckett's plays are published in the United States by Grove/Atlantic and in Britain by Faber and Faber. The most complete biography of Beckett, written with the author's approval, is James Knowlson, *Damned to Fame: The Life of Samuel Beckett* (1996), which has supplemented and, in the view of most Beckett scholars, superseded Deirdre Bair's earlier *Samuel Beckett: A Biography* (1978). Other important biographies written since Beckett's death include Anthony Cronin, *Samuel Beckett: The Last Modernist* (1996), and Lois Gordon, *The World of Samuel Beckett, 1906–1946* (1996). Among the many critical discussions of Beckett's work, the following are particularly useful to students of his plays: Hugh Kenner, *Samuel Beckett: A Critical Study* (1961; new ed., 1968); Eugene Webb, *The Plays of Samuel Beckett* (1972); John Fletcher and John Spurling, *Beckett: A Study of His Plays* (1972; 2d ed., 1978); Ruby Cohn, *Back to Beckett* (1973) and *Just Play: Beckett's Theater* (1980); John Pilling, *Samuel Beckett* (1976); S. E. Gontarski, *The Intent of Undoing in Samuel Beckett's Dramatic Texts* (1985); Steven Connor, *Samuel Beckett: Repetition, Theory and Text* (1988); Andrew K. Kennedy, *Samuel Beckett* (1989); Enoch Brater, *Why Beckett* (1989); David Pattie, *The Complete Critical Guide to Samuel Beckett* (2000); and Rónán McDonald, *The Cambridge Introduction to Samuel Beckett* (2006). Important collections of essays include Martin Esslin, ed., *Samuel Beckett: A Collection of Critical Essays* (1965); S. E. Gontarski, ed., *On Beckett: Essays and Criticism* (1986); and Lance St. John Butler and Robin J. Davis, eds., *Rethinking Beckett: A Collection of Critical Essays* (1990). Studies of Beckett's plays in performance include Dougald McMillan and Martha Fehsenfeld, *Beckett in the Theatre: The Author as Practical Playwright and Director* (1988), and Jonathan Kalb, *Beckett in Performance* (1989). Linda Ben-Zvi, ed., *Women in Beckett: Performance and Critical Perspectives* (1990), explores issues of gender in Beckett's drama with an emphasis on performance.

Resources for the study of *Waiting for Godot* include the following: Ruby Cohn, ed., *Casebook on "Waiting for Godot"* (1967); Bert O. States, *The Shape of Paradox: An Essay on "Waiting for Godot"* (1978); Lawrence Graver, *Samuel Beckett, "Waiting for Godot,"* (1989; 2nd ed., 2004); Thomas Cousineau, *"Waiting for Godot": Form in Movement* (1990); Steven Connor, ed., *"Waiting for Godot" and "Endgame,"* by Samuel Beckett (1992); and Lois Gordon, *Reading "Godot"* (2002). David Bradby, *Beckett: "Waiting for Godot"* (2001), and Jonathan Croall, *The Coming of Godot: A Short History of a Masterpiece* (2005), discuss the play's production history. Dougald McMillan and James Knowlson, eds., *The Theatrical Notebooks of Samuel Beckett*, vol. 1, *Waiting for Godot* (1993), contains the working notes that Beckett kept while directing *Godot* at Berlin's Schiller-Theater in 1975 and will be of particular interest to actors and directors of Beckett's play.

BERTOLT BRECHT

Not surprisingly, the critical literature on Brecht's life and work is extensive. The person who introduced Brecht to America was Eric Bentley, who translated many of Brecht's plays, adapted them, and wrote extensively on the author. Although his not always faithful translations have been criticized, his writings on Brecht are important milestones in Brecht criticism; they include *Bentley on Brecht* (1998; 3d ed., 2008) and *The Playwright as Thinker: A Study of Drama in Modern Times* (1967). A good biography of Brecht is still Frederic Ewen's *Bertolt Brecht: His Life, His Art, and His Times* (1967). A more recent biography, John Fuegi's controversial *Brecht and Company: Sex, Politics, and the Making of the Modern Drama* (1994), argues that much of what has been viewed as original in Brecht was noncredited work by a number of others, including several of his lovers. Though exaggerated and shrill in its claims, the book nevertheless draws needed attention to the collaborative process that was undoubtedly part of Brecht's work. A good and simple introduction to Brecht's work is John Willett's *The Theatre of Bertolt Brecht: A Study from Eight Aspects* (1959; 3d ed., 1967); Martin Esslin's *Brecht: A Choice of Evils: A Critical Study of the Man, His Work, and His Opinions* (1959; 4th ed., 1984) is more ambitious and insightful. On Brecht's exile in and influence on the theater of the United States, see James Lyon's informative *Bertolt Brecht in America* (1980). Brecht's theoretical works are collected and translated by John Willett in *Brecht on Theatre: The Development of an Aesthetic* (1964; 2d ed., 1974); a good recent study of Brecht's theater is John J. White's *Bertolt Brecht's Dramatic Theory* (2004). A theoretically challenging but intriguing discussion of Brecht is Fredric Jameson's *Brecht and Method* (1998). On the use, in *The Good Person of Szechwan*, of a Chinese setting as well as on Brecht's interest in Chinese theater, see Eric Hayot's *Chinese Dreams: Pound, Brecht, Tel Quel* (2004).

Given Brecht's immense influence on modern drama, most classic studies of that period include substantial chapters on Brecht. See, for example, Raymond Williams, *Drama from Ibsen to Brecht* (1969); Richard Gilman, *The Making of Modern Drama* (1972); and Robert Brustein, *The Theatre of Revolt: An Approach to the Modern Drama* (1964). Brecht's paradigm has also shaped studies such as Janelle Reinelt's *After Brecht: British Epic Theater* (1994) and Elin Diamond's *Unmaking Mimesis* (1997).

WILLIAM WELLS BROWN

A contemporary edition of *The Escape,* edited by John Ernest and containing a valuable introduction, was published in 2001. Of the relatively few books devoted to the life and career of William Wells Brown, the most complete is William Edward Farrison's admirable biography *William Wells Brown: Author and Reformer* (1969). Robert S. Levine's edition of *Clotel; or, The President's Daughter* (2000) includes a useful chronology of Brown's life and its literary and historical backdrops. As the author of an influential slave narrative and the first African American novel, Brown has received substantial notice, though most scholars have paid scant if any attention to Brown's drama. Doris M. Abramson, "William Wells Brown: America's First Negro Playwright" (1968), was one of the first articles to consider Brown's career as a dramatist, and a number of recent articles have deepened this critical discussion by exploring questions of race and representation: see especially Paul Gilmore, "'De Genewine Artekil': William Wells Brown, Blackface Minstrelsy, and Abolitionism" (1997); John Ernest, "The Reconstruction of Whiteness: William Wells Brown's *The Escape; or, A Leap for Freedom*" (1998); and Harry J. Elam Jr., "The Black Performer and the Performance of Blackness: *The Escape; or, a Leap to Freedom* by William Wells Brown and *No Place to Be Somebody* by Charles Gordone," in *African American Performance and Theater History: A Critical Reader,* ed. Harry J. Elam Jr. and David Krasner (2001). William H. Andrews, "Mark Twain, William Wells Brown, and the Problem of Authority in New South Writing," in *Southern Literature and Literary Theory,* ed. Jefferson Humphries (1990), includes valuable observations on Brown's use of black dialect.

GEORG BÜCHNER

Despite Büchner's influence, the scholarship in English on his work is somewhat limited in its range and methodologies. Both an authoritative text of *Woyzeck* and Büchner's various drafts and insertions can be found in Walter Hinderer and Henry J. Schmidt's edition of his *Complete Works and Letters*, trans. Henry J. Schmidt (1986). Given Büchner's short life and small oeuvre, most studies of the author combine a biographical account with a discussion of his plays. The earliest such work in English, A. H. J. Knight's *Georg Büchner* (1951), provides a good overview of Büchner's varied writings, but Herbert Lindenberger's study, *Georg Büchner* (1964), is more attuned to his use and revision of literary form and genre and more fully discusses the peculiar relation of Büchner to his contemporaries and descendants. Also interested in form and style is Henry Schmidt, *Satire, Caricature and Perspectivism in the Works of Georg Büchner* (1970). A number of critics have emphasized the political and revolutionary nature of Büchner's writing, for example, Maurice Benn in *The Drama of Revolt: A Critical Study of Georg Büchner* (1976). Richard Gilman begins his influential *The Making of Modern Drama* (1974) with a chapter on Büchner. Georg Lukács, a Marxist critic and philosopher, claimed Büchner as an early communist against the attempt on the part of National Socialists to see him as a fascist, in "The Real Georg Büchner and His Fascist Misrepresentation" (1939). There is, unfortunately, little scholarship focusing on Büchner's impact on theater and performance, although Lynn Sobieski's "The Bread and Puppet Theater's 'Woyzeck'" (1981) provides an account of one of the more unusual stagings this play has received. The most comprehensive and discriminating study of Büchner in English is John Reddick's *Georg Büchner: The Shattered Whole* (1994), which carefully traces Büchner's literary development within the context of his political and scientific writings.

ANTON CHEKHOV

Numerous translations of Chekhov's plays have appeared in the past forty years, including versions by such playwrights as Michael Frayn, Trevor Griffiths, and David Mamet. While its translations are not as stage-worthy as the best of these, Ronald Hingley's nine-volume edition, *The Oxford Chekhov* (1964–80), includes all of Chekhov's plays and most of his stories. Laurence Senelick's Norton Critical Edition, *Anton Chekhov's Selected Plays* (2005), contains useful annotations on *The Cherry Orchard* and other plays. Donald Rayfield's authoritative biography, *Anton Chekhov: A Life* (1997), was the first account of the playwright's life to benefit from the opening of Russian archives after the dissolution of the Soviet Union in 1991.

The following are useful studies of Chekhov's

drama: Maurice Valency, *The Breaking String: The Plays of Anton Chekhov* (1966); J. L. Styan, *Chekhov in Performance: A Commentary on the Major Plays* (1971); Richard Peace, *Chekhov: A Study of the Four Major Plays* (1983); Laurence Senelick, *Anton Chekhov* (1985); Richard Gilman, *Chekhov's Plays: An Opening into Eternity* (1995); and Donald Rayfield, *Understanding Chekhov: A Critical Study of Chekhov's Prose and Drama* (1999). Toby W. Clyman, ed., *A Chekhov Companion* (1985), and Vera Gottlieb and Paul Allain, eds., *The Cambridge Companion to Chekhov* (2000), contain valuable essays on Chekhov, while Harold Bloom, ed., *Anton Chekhov* (1999), reprints a number of previously published essays on Chekhov's fiction and drama. The chapters on Chekhov in Robert Brustein, *The Theatre of Revolt: An Approach to the Modern Drama* (1964), and Richard Gilman, *The Making of Modern Drama* (1974), remain among the best discussions of the playwright's dramatic work. Donald Rayfield, *The Cherry Orchard: Catastrophe and Comedy* (1994), is a book-length study of Chekhov's final play. Laurence Senelick, *The Chekhov Theatre: A Century of the Plays in Performance* (1997), and David Allen, *Performing Chekhov* (2000), examine Chekhov's plays in performance.

CARYL CHURCHILL

Most of Caryl Churchill's produced dramas and radio scripts to date have been published singly or in collected volumes by Methuen and Nick Hern Books. Some of her very early, unproduced pieces have not yet been made publicly available. *File on Churchill*, comp. Linda Fitzsimmons (1989), contains much useful information on Churchill's biography and early career, as well as excerpts from reviews, interviews, and other commentary. No biography of Churchill has yet been published, although she has shared information on her life with interviewers. Among the most useful of these dialogues are with Kathleen Betsko and Rachel Koenig, in *Interviews with Contemporary Women Playwrights* (1987); with Laurie Stone, "Caryl Churchill: Making Room at the Top" (1983); and with Lynne Truss, "A Fair Cop" (1984).

Early full-length studies of Churchill's work include Geraldine Cousin, *Churchill: The Playwright* (1989), and Amelia Howe Kritzer, *The Plays of Caryl Churchill: Theatre of Empowerment* (1991). Elaine Aston's *Caryl Churchill* (1997; 2d ed., 2001) builds productively on this early criticism. Janelle Reinelt has also published important analyses of Churchill in *After Brecht: British Epic Theater* (1994) and in "Caryl Churchill and the Politics of Style," in *The Cambridge Companion to Modern British Women Playwrights*, ed. Elaine Aston and Reinelt (2000). *Caryl Churchill: A Casebook*, ed. Phyllis R. Randall (1988); Helene Keyssar, *Feminist Theatre: An Introduction to the Plays of Contemporary British and American Women* (1984); Elin Diamond, "(In) Visible Bodies in Churchill's Theater," in *Making a Spectacle: Feminist Essays on Contemporary Women's Theatre*, ed. Lynda Hart (1989); Austin Quigley, "Stereotype and Prototype: Character in the Plays of Caryl Churchill," in *Feminine Focus: The New Women Playwrights*, ed. Enoch Brater (1989); Frances Gray, "Mirrors of Utopia: Caryl Churchill and Joint Stock," in *British and Irish Drama Since 1960*, ed. James Acheson (1993); and Lisa Merrill, "Monsters and Heroines: Caryl Churchill's Women," in *Modern Dramatists: A Casebook of Major British, Irish, and American Playwrights*, ed. Kimball King (2001), are all worthwhile.

To date, only two published scholarly articles discuss *A Number*: Martha Montello, "Novel Perspectives on Bioethics" (2005), and Amy Strahler Holzapfel, "The Body in Pieces: Contemporary Anatomy Theatres" (2008). Most of the commentary on the play can be found in theatrical reviews and feature articles; the more insightful of these include Michael Billington, "A Number: Royal Court, London," *The Guardian* (2002); Charles Spencer, "In Short, This is a Spellbinding Triumph: First Night," *Daily Telegraph* (2002); Matt Wolf, "Magic 'Number' Reps Churchill at her Best," *Variety* (2002); Sarah Lyall, "The Mysteries of Caryl Churchill," *New York Times* (2004); Ben Brantley, "My 3 Sons: Cloning's Unexpected Results" *New York Times* (2004); and Mel Gussow, "A Play without Instructions Morphs into Another," *New York Times* (2004). An interview with the play's original director, Stephen Daldry, can be found at www.royalcourttheatre.com/files/downloads/a_number_edupack.pdf.

For discussions of human cloning and the bioethical controversy surrounding it, see John Harris, "'Goodbye Dolly?' The Ethics of Human Cloning" (1997); Meredith Wadman, "Dolly: A Decade On" (2007); Matteo Galletti, "Begetting, Cloning and Being Human: Two National Commission Reports against Human Cloning from Italy and the U.S.A." (2006); and Dan W. Brock, "Cloning Human Beings: An Assessment of the Ethical Issues Pro and Con" (1997), reprinted in *Cloning and the Future of Human Embryo Research*, ed. Paul Lauritzen (2001).

MARIA IRENE FORNES

Mud was originally published in Fornes's collection *Plays* (1986), with a preface by Susan Sontag. Although there is no complete bibliography of Fornes's publications to date, many of her works are listed in Maria M. Delgado and Caridad Svich, eds., *Conducting a Life: Reflections on the Theatre of Maria Irene Fornes* (1999); Marc Robinson, ed., *The Theater of Maria Irene Fornes* (1999); and Assunta Bartolomucci Kent, *Maria Irene Fornes and Her Critics* (1996). Kent's study also contains the fullest biographical information now available on Fornes, as well as a thorough secondary bibliography. Fornes's generosity to interviewers is evident in pieces found in Kathleen Betsko and Rachel Koenig, comps., *Interviews with Contemporary Women Playwrights* (1987); David Savran, ed., *In Their Own Words: Contemporary American Playwrights* (1988); and Philip C. Kolin and Colby H. Kullman, eds., *Speaking on Stage: Interviews with Contemporary American Playwrights* (1996), as well as journals; see *PAJ* (Winter 1978) and *Theater* (Winter 1985). Fornes has also written on her own work in such journal essays as "I Write These Messages That Come" (1977), in the " 'Woman' Playwrights" issue of *PAJ* (1983), "Creative Danger" (1985), and in the "Ages of the Avant-Garde" issue of *PAJ* (1994). Bonnie Marranca, the editor of *PAJ*, has long championed Fornes's career through interviews and essays, including "The Real Life of Maria Irene Fornes" (1984) and "The State of Grace: Maria Irene Fornes at Sixty-Two" (1992). Two important features on her work have appeared in the *Village Voice:* Stephanie Harrington's "Irene Fornes, Playwright: Alice and the Red Queen" (1966) and Ross Wetzsteon's "Irene Fornes: The Elements of Style" (1986).

For full-length scholarly studies of Fornes, see Kent, *Maria Irene Fornes and Her Critics,* and Diane Lynn Moroff, *Fornes: Theater in the Present Tense* (1996). Among the important scholarly essays on Fornes are a chapter in Marc Robinson's *The Other American Drama* (1994); Deborah R. Geis, "Wordscapes of the Body: Performative Language as *Gestus* in Maria Irene Fornes's Plays" (1990); Cara Gargano, "The Starfish and the Strange Attractor: Myth, Science, and Theatre as Laboratory in Maria Irene Fornes' 'Mud' " (1997); Lurana Donnels O'Malley, "Pressing Clothes/Snapping Beans/Reading Books: Maria Irene Fornes's Women's Work" (1989); and Christine Kiebuzinska, "Traces of Brecht in Maria Irene Fornes' *Mud*" (1993). Delgado and Svich's edited volume contains numerous responses to Fornes's writing and teaching. For the history of off-off-Broadway and Fornes's place in it, see Stephen J. Bottoms, *Playing Underground: A Critical History of the 1960s Off-Off-Broadway Movement* (2004).

ATHOL FUGARD

For a history of South African performance traditions, see Loren Kruger, *The Drama of South Africa: Plays, Pageants and Politics Since 1910* (1999); Martin Orkin, *Drama and the South African State* (1991); and Margarete Seidenspinner, *Exploring the Labyrinth: Athol Fugard's Approach to South African Drama* (1986). Useful bibliographies and resources about Athol Fugard's plays in production include Temple Hauptfleisch, Wilma Vijoen, and Céleste Van Greunen, eds., *Athol Fugard: A Source Guide* (1982); John Read, comp., *Athol Fugard: A Bibliography* (1991); and Stephen Gray, comp., *File on Fugard* (1991). For full-length critical studies of Fugard's work, see Dennis Walder, *Athol Fugard* (1984) and *Athol Fugard* (2003); Russell Vandenbroucke, *Truths the Hand Can Touch: The Theatre of Athol Fugard* (1985); and Albert Wertheim, *The Dramatic Art of Athol Fugard: From South Africa to the World* (2000). The work most critical of Fugard as a political writer is Robert Mshengu, "Political Theatre in South Africa and the Work of Athol Fugard" (1982). For details of Fugard's plays and perspectives post-1994, see Marcia Blumberg and Dennis Walder, eds., *South African Theatre as/and Intervention* (1999).

The standard edition of *"MASTER HAROLD"* is that published by Penguin in 1982. Among the essays of particular relevance to its analysis are Rob Amato, "Fugard's Confessional Analysis: *'MASTER HAROLD' . . . and the boys,*" in *Momentum: On Recent South African Writing,* ed. M. J. Daymond, J. U. Jacobs, and Margaret Lenta (1984); Errol Durbach, " *'MASTER HAROLD' . . . and the boys:* Athol Fugard and the Psychopathology of Apartheid" (1987); and J. Ellen Gainor, " 'A World without Collisions': Ballroom Dance in Athol Fugard's *'MASTER HAROLD' . . . and the boys,*" in *Bodies of the Text: Dance as Theory, Literature as Dance,* ed. Ellen W. Goellner and Jacqueline Shea Murphy (1995). Mel Gussow's "Profiles: Witness" (1982) provides a summary of the play's autobiographical elements, as well as Fugard's direction of the play in the context of his career. Fugard's *Notebooks, 1960–1977* (1983) contains details of the play's background from the playwright's perspective.

FEDERICO GARCÍA LORCA

Since many sources pertaining to García Lorca's life have been available only after the fall of the fascist regime in Spain in 1975, the most extensive biographies of the playwright were written in the past two decades. An exception to this rule is one of the first studies of García Lorca in English, Edwin Honig's *García Lorca* (1944; rev. ed., 1963), which still provides a good introduction to the writer. Of the more recent biographies, the most informative is Ian Gibson's *Federico García Lorca: A Life* (1989), which includes a detailed description of the Granada region where García

Lorca grew up and where he set many of his plays. Equally readable is Leslie Stainton's *Lorca: A Dream of Life* (1998). Both biographies also give detailed accounts of García Lorca's friendship with Falla, Buñuel, and Dalí. Given García Lorca's prominence as a poet, many scholars pay less attention to the theatrical aspect of his work. The first book-length study with that focus was Robert Lima's *The Theatre of Garcia Lorca* (1963), which provides a useful introduction to the dramatist. More theoretically sophisticated is *The Theatre of García Lorca: Text, Performance, Psychoanalysis* by Paul Julian Smith (1998), which also discusses the significance of García Lorca's homosexuality. *The Comic Spirit of Federico García Lorca* (1976), by Virginia Higginbotham, provides not only insight into García Lorca's comedies and farces but also a general history of twentieth-century theater in Spain. C. Christopher Soufas's *Audience and Authority in the Modernist Theater of Federico García Lorca* (1996) discusses from the perspective of the audience García Lorca's drama, in particular his attempt to introduce avant-garde and experimental elements into mainstream theater. Special attention to García Lorca's interest in folklore and folk music, such as flamenco, can be found in Robert Stone, *The Flamenco Tradition in the Works of Federico García Lorca and Carlos Aura: The Wounded Throat* (2004).

JEAN GENET

Jean-Paul Sartre's monumental study *Saint Genet: Actor and Martyr* (1952; trans. 1963), written early in Genet's career, casts a long shadow over all subsequent scholarship. For Sartre, Genet's life and work cannot be accounted for by the traditional forms of psychoanalytic biography or Marxist criticism but instead reflect existential choices. Richard N. Coe's *The Vision of Jean Genet* (1968) and Philip Thody's *Jean Genet: A Study of His Novels and Plays* (1968) take many strategies and topics from Sartre. This Sartrean approach of weaving together Genet's life and work was criticized in Edmund White's award-winning biography, *Genet: A Biography* (1993), which tried to disentangle the two and which demonstrated the extent to which Genet himself had been engaged in exaggerating and falsifying aspects of his life. Two influential theater historians and theorists who wrote on Genet are Robert Brustein, in his *Theatre of Revolt: An Approach to the Modern Drama* (1964), which sees Genet's works as exemplifying Artaud's Theater of Cruelty, and Martin Esslin, in *The Theatre of the Absurd* (1961; 3d ed., 1980). A second generation of scholars paid more attention to the intricate structure of Genet's works, using semiotic and structuralist methods; see, for example, Una Chaudhuri's *No Man's Stage: A Semiotic Study of Genet's Major Plays* (1986) and Laura Oswald's *Jean Genet and the Semiotics of Performance* (1989). And in *Homos* (1995), Leo Bersani uses the perspective of psychoanalysis and queer theory to analyze Genet as a gay outlaw. Directly or indirectly, these studies are indebted to another philosopher's monumental work on Genet: Jacques Derrida's *Glas* (1974; trans. 1986), which pays particular attention to Genet's language and figures, including his use of slang and the prominence of flowers. That two great twentieth-century philosophers, Sartre and Derrida, devoted considerable attention to Genet is part of his lasting legacy.

SUSAN GLASPELL

Although there is to date no complete collected edition of Susan Glaspell's dramas, C. W. E. Bigsby's selection, *Plays* (1987), reprints several of her major works (including *Trifles*) and contains a worthwhile introduction; his entry on Glaspell for the first volume of his *Critical Introduction to Twentieth-Century American Drama* (1983) is also helpful. Marcia Noe's *Susan Glaspell: Voice from the Heartland* (1983) was the first critical biography of Glaspell. More recent definitive biographies are Linda Ben-Zvi, *Susan Glaspell: Her Life and Times* (2005), and Barbara Ozieblo, *Susan Glaspell: A Critical Biography* (2000). J. Ellen Gainor, *Susan Glaspell in Context: American Theater, Culture, and Politics, 1915–48* (2001), provides readings of Glaspell's dramas within their creative, historical, and critical milieus. Linda Ben-Zvi, ed., *Susan Glaspell: Essay on Her Theater and Fiction* (1995), contains a useful section on *Trifles* and "Jury." Veronica Makowsky, *Susan Glaspell's Century of American Women: A Critical Interpretation of Her Work* (1993), focuses on female characters and themes in Glaspell's fiction and drama, while Kristina Hinz-Bode, *Susan Glaspell and the Anxiety of Expression: Language and Isolation in the Plays* (2006), examines issues of language and isolation in the playwright's dramas. Robert Károly Sarlós, *Jig Cook and the Provincetown Players: Theatre in Ferment* (1982), provides the broader historical background to Glaspell's early theatrical career, and Cheryl Black's *The Women of Provincetown, 1915–22* (2002) focuses on the artistry of Glaspell and her female colleagues. In *Midnight Assassin: A Murder in America's Heartland* (2005), Patricia L. Bryan and Thomas Wolf provide a historical analysis of the murder that was the source for Glaspell's play. Mary E. Papke, *Susan Glaspell: A Research and Production Sourcebook* (1993), is the most comprehensive bibliographic resource.

LANGSTON HUGHES

The most complete collection of Langston Hughes's plays can be found in volumes 5 and 6 of *The Collected Works of Langston Hughes*, ed. Arnold Rampersad (2001–04). *Five Plays*, ed. Webster Smalley (1963), offers a narrower but more widely available selection of plays, including *Soul Gone Home*. The authoritative biography of Langston Hughes is Arnold Rampersad's two-volume *The Life of Langston Hughes* (1986–88; 2d ed., 2002). John Edgar Tidwell and Cheryl R. Ragar, eds., *Montage of a Dream: The Art and Life of Langston Hughes* (2007), includes a variety of essays on Hughes's life and career. The following works are useful for an understanding of Hughes the dramatist: Darwin T. Turner, "Langston Hughes as Playwright" (1968); Faith Berry, *Langston Hughes: Before and Beyond Harlem* (1983); Leslie Catherine Sanders, "'Also Own the Theatre': Representation in the Comedies of Langston Hughes" (1992); and Joseph McLaren, *Langston Hughes: Folk Dramatist in the Protest Tradition, 1921–1943* (1997). The spring 1997 issue of *The Langston Hughes Review* is devoted to Hughes's work for theater. William Miles, "Isolation in Langston Hughes' *Soul Gone Home*," in *Five Black Writers: Essays on Wright, Ellison, Baldwin, Hughes, and Le Roi Jones*, comp. Donald B. Gibson (1970), and Philip C. Kolin and Maureen Curley, "Hughes's *Soul Gone Home*" (2003), are among the few critical studies of *Soul Gone Home*.

DAVID HENRY HWANG

The standard text of *M. Butterfly* is the New American Library edition (1989), which includes Hwang's afterword on the play and its composition. The acting edition (1988) published by Dramatists Play Service contains the same afterword, as well as a discussion of the play's Broadway production and suggestions for prospective actors, directors, and designers. Douglas Street's brief but useful monograph *David Henry Hwang* (1989) contains biographical information on the playwright and an overview of his dramatic writing through *M. Butterfly*. Additional biographical information and a more current survey of Hwang's drama can be found in William C. Boles, "David Henry Hwang," in *Asian American Writers*, ed. Deborah L. Madsen (2005), vol. 312 of the *Dictionary of Literary Biography*. Miles Xian Liu, ed., *Asian American Playwrights: A Bio-bibliographical Critical Sourcebook* (2002), provides biographical backgrounds, production history, and bibliographical information on the works of Hwang and other Asian American dramatists.

Important articles on *M. Butterfly* include Robert Skloot, "Breaking the Butterfly: The Politics of David Henry Hwang" (1990); Douglas Kerr, "David Henry Hwang and the Revenge of *Madame Butterfly*," in *Asian Voices in English*, ed. Mimi Chan and Roy Harris (1991); Marjorie Garber, "The Occidental Tourist: *M. Butterfly* and the Scandal of Transvestism," in *Nationalities and Sexualities*, ed. Andrew Parker, Mary Russo, Doris Sommer, and Patricia Yaeger (1992); Karen Shimakawa, "'Who's to Say?' or, Making Space for Gender and Ethnicity in *M. Butterfly*" (1993); Foong Ling Kong's "Pulling the Wings Off Butterfly" (1994); and Hsiu-Chen Lin, "Staging Orientalia: Dangerous 'Authenticity' in David Henry Hwang's *M. Butterfly*" (1997). James S. Moy, *Marginal Sights: Staging the Chinese in America* (1993), and Josephine Lee, *Performing Asian America: Race and Ethnicity on the Contemporary Stage* (1997), explore *M. Butterfly* in the context of earlier and contemporary representations of Asian Americans in theater and in American culture.

HENRIK IBSEN

Among the early reactions to Ibsen was George Bernard Shaw's *The Quintessence of Ibsenism* (1891), which emphasizes Ibsen's concern with pressing social and political issues; William Archer's essays, collected by Thomas Postlewait in *William Archer on Ibsen: The Major Essays, 1889–1919* (1984), foreground Ibsen's poetic choices and techniques. The decisive impact of Shaw and Archer is described in detail in Thomas Postlewait's *Prophet of the New Drama: William Archer and the Ibsen Campaign* (1986). Ibsen's third major early supporter was the critic Georg Brandes, who accompanied Ibsen's career with three essays, written in the 1870s, '80s, and '90s, collected in his *Henrik Ibsen: A Critical Study* (1899). Charles Lyons's compilation, *Critical Essays on Henrik Ibsen* (1987), includes landmark essay by Ibsen's modernist admirers, among them James Joyce, E. M. Forster, and Georg Lukàcs. The wider cultural context of Ibsen's European success, as well as a wealth of personal detail, is captured in Michael Meyer's *Ibsen: A Biography* (1971). While there have been a number of excellent studies devoted to Ibsen—for example, Michael Goldman's imaginative reading of Ibsen's subtexts and psychologies in *Ibsen: The Dramaturgy of Fear* (1999)—the most influential accounts of Ibsen's impact on modern drama are to be found in studies devoted to modern drama more generally, many of which take their point of departure from Ibsen's work. Of these, Raymond Williams's *Drama: From Ibsen to Eliot* (1952; 2nd rev. ed., 1973) is the most important, discussing Ibsen's social drama and modern tragedy. Robert Brustein's *The Theatre of Revolt: An Approach to the Modern Drama* (1964) and Richard Gilman's

The Making of Modern Drama (1974) are classics in dating the origin of a modern revolt to Ibsen's drama, as is Peter Szondi's *The Theory of the Modern Drama* (1956; trans. 1987), which measures Ibsen against Sophocles' *Oedipus the King.* In *Ibsen and Early Modernist Theatre, 1890–1900* (1997), Kirsten Shepherd-Barr situates Ibsen in the context of theater history, and Joan Templeton's *Ibsen's Women* (1997) is the first in-depth analysis of Ibsen's construction of female characters, including Hedda Gabler. *The Cambridge Companion to Ibsen,* ed. James McFarlane (1994), provides a good introduction to recent scholarship and contemporary approaches. The best book on Ibsen is Toril Moi's *Henrik Ibsen and the Birth of Modernism: Art, Theater, Philosophy* (2006).

ALFRED JARRY

An edition of the entire Ubu cycle is to be found in *The Ubu Plays,* translated and introduced by Kenneth McLeish (1997), as well as in *The Ubu Plays,* edited and introduced by Simon Watson Taylor (1968). The lesser known of Jarry's Ubu publications as well as his own writings on the theater are available in *Selected Works of Alfred Jarry,* ed. Roger Shattuck and Simon Watson Taylor (1965). The best biographical account of Jarry's life and work is to be found in Keith Beaumont's *Alfred Jarry: A Critical and Biographical Study* (1984), which weaves Jarry's biography into a discussion of his literary works, his relation to symbolism, and his use of language and style. A close analysis of the Ubu cycle is undertaken by Judith Cooper, *Ubu Roi: An Analytical Study* (1974). Specifically attuned to Jarry's important contribution to theater history is Maurice Marc LaBelle's *Alfred Jarry, Nihilism and the Theater of the Absurd* (1980), which details Jarry's stagecraft, including his use of marionettes, sets, and masks—topics that have been at the center of attention in the much richer and more wide-ranging literature on Jarry in French. Jarry's relation to the avant-garde of the early twentieth century is the central concern of Roger Shattuck's excellent *The Banquet Year: The Origins of the Avant-Garde in France, 1885 to World War I: Alfred Jarry, Henri Rousseau, Erik Satie, and Guillaume Apollinaire* (1958; rev. ed., 1968), and Claude Schumacher's *Alfred Jarry and Guillaume Apollinaire* (1984) likewise compares Jarry to the French avant-garde poet and dramatist Apollinaire, who invented the term *surrealism.*

TONY KUSHNER

Angels in America: A Gay Fantasia on National Themes (Theatre Communications Group, 1995), is the standard edition of this two-part play. James Fisher, *The Theater of Tony Kushner: Living Past Hope* (2001), is a full-length study of the development of Kushner's drama in its social, theatrical, and biographical contexts. Robert Vorlicky, ed., *Tony Kushner in Conversation* (1998), is a rich collection of biographical, critical, and backstage interviews with the playwright. Deborah R. Geis and Steven F. Kruger, eds., *Approaching the Millennium: Essays on "Angels in America"* (1997), and Per Brask, ed., *Essays on Kushner's "Angels"* (1995), provide a range of historical, critical, and theatrical perspectives on the play. In addition to the essays included in the above collections, the following articles are useful: Charles McNulty, "*Angels in America:* Tony Kushner's Theses on the Philosophy of History" (1996); Jonathan Freedman, "Angels, Monsters, and Jews: Intersections of Queer and Jewish Identity in Kushner's *Angels in America*" (1998); Daryl Ogden, "Cold War Science and the Body Politic: An Immuno/Virological Approach to *Angels in America*" (2000); and Ranen Omer-Sherman, "The Fate of the Other in Tony Kushner's *Angels in America*" (2007).

DAVID MAMET

Although no detailed biography of David Mamet has yet been written, scholarship on Mamet has burgeoned in the past ten years. An excellent resource is *David Mamet: A Research and Production Sourcebook,* comp. David K. Sauer and Janice A. Sauer (2003), which documents both productions and scholarship. Among the monographs on Mamet, C. W. E. Bigsby's *David Mamet* (1985) provides a good overview of the dramatist's work up to the early eighties. More specialized in their focus are Anne Dean's *David Mamet: Language as Dramatic Action* (1990), which examines the important topic of language, and Leslie Kane's *Weasels and Wisemen: Ethics and Ethnicity in the Work of David Mamet* (1999), which analyzes the complex role of ethnicity in Mamet's work.

A number of essays offer more detailed readings of Mamet than do the available book-length studies. The collection edited by Leslie Kane, *David Mamet's "Glengarry Glen Ross": Text and Performance* (1996), includes a good analysis of Mamet's representation of capitalism, Elizabeth Kalver's "David Mamet, Jean Baudrillard and the Performance of America," as well as an interesting account of a foreign production, "A Japanese *Glengarry Glen Ross,*" by Robert T. Rolf. Harold Bloom, ed., *David Mamet* (2004), features two very good essays on the relation of realism and illusion: Michael L. Quinn's "Anti-theatricality and American Ideology: Mamet's Performative Realism" and Howard Pearce's "Plato in Hollywood:

David Mamet and the Power of Illusion." The best account on realism in Mamet is David Savran's "New Realism: Mamet, Mann and Nelson," in *Contemporary American Theatre*, ed. Bruce King (1991). Robert Vorlicky has investigated the question of masculinity in Mamet in *Act Like a Man: Challenging Masculinities in American Drama* (1995). Bigsby, ed., *Cambridge Companion to David Mamet* (2004), includes essays that provide a good introduction to the work of the playwright, as does Nesta Jones and Steven Dykes, comp., *File on Mamet* (1991).

ARTHUR MILLER

Arthur Miller's *Collected Plays* (1957) contains the playwright's five major plays through 1957; *The Portable Arthur Miller* (1971; rev. ed., 2003) includes a useful selection of plays from throughout his career. Published two years before the playwright's death, Martin Gottfried's *Arthur Miller: His Life and Work* (2003) is a full-length biography of Miller. An engaging overview can also be found in Enoch Brater, *Arthur Miller: A Playwright's Life and Works* (2005). Those who want an in-depth account of the playwright's life and times through the early 1980s can consult his wide-ranging and critically acclaimed autobiography, *Timebends: A Life* (1987). Important studies of Miller's plays include Sheila Huftel, *Arthur Miller: The Burning Glass* (1965); Edward Murray, *Arthur Miller, Dramatist* (1967); Leonard Moss, *Arthur Miller* (1967; rev. ed., 1980); Benjamin Nelson, *Arthur Miller: Portrait of a Playwright* (1970); Dennis Welland, *Miller the Playwright* (1979; 3d ed., 1985); Neil Carson, *Arthur Miller* (1982; 2d ed., 2008); C. W. E. Bigsby, *A Critical Introduction to Twentieth-Century American Drama*, vol. 2, *Tennessee Williams, Arthur Miller, Edward Albee* (1984); June Schlueter and James K. Flanagan, *Arthur Miller* (1987); David Savran, *Communist, Cowboys, and Queers: The Politics of Masculinity in the Work of Arthur Miller and Tennessee Williams* (1992); Alice Griffin, *Understanding Arthur Miller* (1996); and Christopher Bigsby, *Arthur Miller: A Critical Study* (2005).

Miller wrote and spoke widely on his plays and his career as a writer. Collections of his essays and interviews include *The Theater Essays of Arthur Miller*, ed. Robert A. Martin (1978; rev. ed., 1996); Matthew C. Roudané, ed., *Conversations with Arthur Miller* (1987); *Echoes down the Corridor: Collected Essays, 1944–2000,* ed. Steven R. Centola (2000); and Mel Gussow, *Conversations with Miller* (2002). Stefani Koorey, *Arthur Miller's Life and Literature: An Annotated and Comprehensive Guide* (2000), offers an extensive bibliography of books and articles on Miller's drama, as well as information on Miller's life and politics, references to theater reviews, and production information on his plays. Susan C. W. Abbotson's, *Critical Companion to Arthur Miller: A Literary Reference to His Life and Work* (2007) is also an important resource.

Among the collections of critical essays on *Death of a Salesman* are *Death of a Salesman: Text and Criticism,* ed. Gerald Weales (1967); Helene Wickham Koon, ed., *Twentieth-Century Interpretations of "Death of a Salesman": A Collection of Critical Essays* (1983); Harold Bloom, ed., *Arthur Miller's "Death of a Salesman"* (1988; updated, 2007) and *Willy Loman* (1991; updated, 2005); Matthew C. Roudané, ed., *Approaches to Teaching Miller's "Death of a Salesman"* (1995); and Stephen A. Marino, ed., *"The "Salesman" Has a Birthday": Essays Celebrating the Fiftieth Anniversary of Arthur Miller's "Death of a Salesman"* (2000). Kay Stanton, "Women and the American Dream of *Death of a Salesman*," in *Feminist Rereadings of Modern American Drama,* ed. June Schlueter (1989), is an important feminist reading of Miller's play. Brenda Murphy, *Miller: "Death of a Salesman"* (1995), is a history of *Death of a Salesman* productions during the years 1949–89, while Miller's own *Salesman in Beijing* (1984) discusses his experiences directing the play in the People's Republic of China in 1983.

LOUIS NOWRA

The Golden Age was first produced and published in 1985; Nowra revised the script and published a new edition, with his preface, in 1989. Although no biography of Nowra has yet been published, he has written a brief autobiography covering his childhood and early career, included in *Louis Nowra*, a collection of critical essays and interviews edited by Veronica Kelly (1987). He has provided additional information about his life, as well as insights into his plays and observations about Australia and Australian culture, in the many interviews he has given to date. Among the most useful are those are with Jim Davidson, "Interview" (1980); Jeremy Ridgman, "Interview" (1983); Gerry Turcotte, " 'Perfecting the Monologue of Silence' " (1987); Veronica Kelly, "Video Interview" (1987); and Paul Makeham, "The Black Hole of Our History" (1993). Nowra has also written occasional essays that describe his compositional process and career development: "*Inner Voices* and the First Coil" (1979), "At the Crossroads" (1984), and "The Short, Nasty, Brutal Life of the Playwright" (1995).

The work of Kelly has profoundly shaped our understanding of Nowra's dramaturgy. Kelly's *The*

Theatre of Louis Nowra (1998), as yet the only full-length study, contains both a listing of Nowra's works and a critical bibliography. Her edited essay collection, noted above, and her chapter "Louis Nowra" in *Post-Colonial English Drama: Commonwealth Drama since 1960*, ed. Bruce King (1992), provide further insights. Gerry Turcotte's "'The Circle Is Burst': Eschatological Discourse in Louis Nowra's *Sunrise* and *The Golden Age*" (1987), as well as his introduction to the revised edition of *The Golden Age* (1989), offers cogent readings, as does Helen Gilbert's "Postcolonial Grotesques: Re-membering the Body in Louis Nowra's *Visions* and *The Golden Age*" (1993). Helen Thomson's "Drama Since 1965," in *The Oxford Literary History of Australia*, ed. Bruce Bennett and Jennifer Strauss (1998), situates Nowra in the context of recent Australian dramaturgy, as does the chapter on Nowra and his contemporary Stephen Sewell in Leslie Rees's *Australian Drama, 1970–1985: A Historical and Critical Survey* (rev. and enl. ed., 1987). Jim Davidson's "Tasmanian Gothic" (1989) provides further thematic context for *The Golden Age*.

EUGENE O'NEILL

As befits his stature as the most significant U.S. dramatist, the critical literature on O'Neill is extensive and varied. The autobiographical character of *Long Day's Journey into Night* and other plays has led many critics and commentators to describe O'Neill as the tragic hero of U.S. theater. The two-volume study by Louis Sheaffer, *O'Neill: Son and Playwright* (1968) and *O'Neill: Son and Artist* (1973), remains the most informative of the several biographies, although Stephen Black's *Eugene O'Neill: Beyond Mourning and Tragedy* (1999) usefully takes O'Neill's interest in Freud and psychoanalysis as a point of departure for psychoanalytical readings of O'Neill's life and work. Travis Bogard's *Contour in Time: The Plays of Eugene O'Neill* (1972; rev. ed., 1988) is the best of the earlier analyses of the drama. Many studies tend toward idealizing their subject, presenting O'Neill's work as a heroic quest for artistic excellence. Notable exceptions to this rule are Joel Pfister's *Staging Depth: Eugene O'Neill and the Politics of Psychological Discourse* (1995), which provides historical context for the playwright's interest in psychology and interiority, and Zander Brietzke's excellent *Aesthetics of Failure: Dynamic Structure in the Plays of Eugene O'Neill* (2001), which examines the relation between O'Neill's significant failures and his stunning successes. Also useful are Kurt Eisner's *The Inner Strength of Opposites: O'Neill's Novelistic Drama and the Melodramatic Imagination* (1994), which focuses on O'Neill's novelistic techniques (including his stage directions, asides, and monologues), and Thierry Dubost's *Struggle, Defeat or Rebirth: Eugene O'Neill's Vision of Humanity* (1997).

There is a rich literature on and documentation of O'Neill's view of the theater and the staging of his plays, including *Eugene O'Neill: Comments on the Drama and the Theater: A Source Book*, ed. Ulrich Halfmann (1987), which contains early reviews as well as the playwright's letters to actors, directors, and critics; see also *Conversations with Eugene O'Neill*, ed. Mark W. Estrin (1990), and Yvonne Shafer, *Performing O'Neill: Conversations with Actors and Directors* (2000). Brenda Murphy's *O'Neill: Long Day's Journey into Night* (2001) documents the play's stage history. In addition, there are several valuable collections of essays, such as Michael Manheim, ed., *The Cambridge Companion to Eugene O'Neill* (1998), and Harold Bloom, ed., *Eugene O'Neill's "Long Day's Journey into Night"* (1987).

SUZAN-LORI PARKS

The America Play is published in *The America Play, and Other Works* (Theatre Communications Group, 1995). Those interested in further biographical information on Suzan-Lori Parks should consult the entry on her in *Contemporary Authors Online* (Thompson Gale, 2005). Though no full-length study of Parks's plays has yet appeared, useful critical discussions of *The America Play* and Parks's career as a whole include the following: Alisa Solomon, "Signifying on the Signifyin'": The Plays of Suzan-Lori Parks" (1990); Katy Ryan, "'No Less Human': Making History in Suzan-Lori Parks's *The America Play*" (1999); Harry Elam and Alice Rayner, "Echoes from the Black (W)hole: An Examination of *The America Play* by Suzan-Lori Parks," in *Performing America: Cultural Nationalism in American Theater*, ed. Jeffrey D. Mason and J. Ellen Gainor (1999); S. E. Wilmer, "Restaging the Nation: The Work of Suzan-Lori Parks" (2000); Shawn-Marie Garrett, "The Possession of Suzan-Lori Parks" (2000); and Frank Haike, "The Instability of Meaning in Suzan-Lori Parks's *The America Play*" (2002).

HAROLD PINTER

Old Times (Grove, 1971) is the standard edition of the play; it is reprinted in volume 4 of Harold Pinter, *Complete Works* (Grove, 1990). Michael Billington's *Harold Pinter* (2007), published in an earlier edition as *The Life and Work of Harold Pinter* (1996), is the authoritative biography, while Mel Gussow's *Conversations with Pinter* (1994) is an important collection of interviews conducted at different stages of Pinter's career. Martin Esslin, *The Peopled Wound: The Work of*

Harold Pinter (1970), revised and updated as *Pinter, the Playwright* (6th ed., 2000), is a classic critical study. Other valuable book-length studies are Austin E. Quigley, *The Pinter Problem* (1975); Elin Diamond, *Pinter's Comic Play* (1985); David T. Thompson, *Pinter: The Player's Playwright* (1985); Susan Hollis Merritt, *Pinter in Play: Critical Strategies and the Plays of Harold Pinter* (1990); and Marc Silverstein, *Harold Pinter and the Language of Cultural Power* (1993). The following collections provide a range of critical approaches: Arthur Ganz, ed., *Pinter: A Collection of Critical Essays* (1972); Steven H. Gale, ed., *Critical Essays on Harold Pinter* (1990); Peter Raby, ed., *The Cambridge Companion to Harold Pinter* (2001); and Mark Batty, *Harold Pinter* (2001). The website www.haroldpinter.org is a compendium of information about Pinter as playwright, screenwriter, actor, director, and political activist.

Articles offering useful discussions of *Old Times* include Stephen Martineau, "*Old Times:* The Memory Game" (1973); Alan Hughes, "'They Can't Take That Away from Me': Myth and Memory in Pinter's *Old Times*" (1974); and A. R. Braunmuller, "A World of Words in Pinter's *Old Times*" (1979).

LUIGI PIRANDELLO

As a general overview of Pirandello's life, Gaspare Guidice's *Pirandello: A Biography* (1963; abridged trans. 1975) is more measured than Domenico Vittorini's *The Drama of Luigi Pirandello* (1935), written only one year after Pirandello had received the Nobel Prize. Because of Pirandello's place in the canon of modern drama, many of the most important commentators on modern drama have devoted essays or book chapters to his work. Among the classics in the field are Eric Bentley's *The Pirandello Commentaries* (1985) and Francis Fergusson's *The Idea of the Theater, a Study of Ten Plays: The Art of Drama in Changing Perspective* (1949), which places Pirandello in relation to other modern dramatists such as George Bernard Shaw and Bertolt Brecht. The best essay on Pirandello and metatheater is by Maurizio Grande, "Pirandello and the Theatre-within-the-Theatre: Thresholds and Frames in *Cascuno a suo modo*," in *Luigi Pirandello: Contemporary Perspectives*, ed. Gian-Paolo Biasin (1999). Roger W. Oliver's *Dreams of Passion: The Theater of Luigi Pirandello* (1979) focuses on Pirandello's theory of humor and applies it to his best-known plays, including *Six Characters*. The best book-length study of Pirandello in English is Ann Hallamore Caesar's *Characters and Authors in Luigi Pirandello* (1998), which includes detailed discussions of Pirandello's aesthetic theories and also an incisive critique of his patriarchal family structures. Daniela Bini's *Pirandello and His Muse: The Plays for Marta Abba* (1998) takes a similar approach to Pirandello's late plays. Pirandello's work in the theater is captured in *Luigi Pirandello in the Theatre: A Documentary Record*, ed. Susan Bassnett and Jennifer Lorch (1993), and in A. Richard Sogliuzzo's *Luigi Pirandello, Director: The Playwright in the Theatre* (1982). The political aspects of Pirandello's work are articulated especially well by Mary Ann Frese Witt in *The Search for Modern Tragedy: Aesthetic Fascism in Italy and France* (2001).

GEORGE BERNARD SHAW

Throughout his lifetime, Shaw not only tried to control the presentation of his plays, he also carefully orchestrated his public persona, essentially collaborating with, if not ghostwriting, every attempt at authorized biography. Thus Michael Holroyd's four-volume *Bernard Shaw* (1988–92) may stand for some time as the only definitive and reasonably objective study of his life and work. Shaw repeatedly revised his plays even after publication; Dan Laurence's two-volume *Bernard Shaw: A Bibliography* (1983) meticulously traces Shaw's complete oeuvre. *The Bodley Head Bernard Shaw: Collected Plays with Their Prefaces*, 7 vols. (1970–74), is considered the definitive edition. Laurence also edited Shaw's four-volume *Collected Letters* (1965–88), which shed important light on his plays and other writings; many additional edited volumes of letters between Shaw and individual correspondents have also been published. Shaw published selections from his critical and political writings during his lifetime; scholarly editions of his dramatic, art, and music criticism have appeared more recently. Major Shaw research archives, which include both published and unpublished materials, are located in the British Library, the Berg Collection of the New York Public Library, the Bernard F. Burgunder Collection at Cornell University, and the Harry Ransom Humanities Research Center at the University of Texas at Austin.

Shaw's astounding volume of writing is matched only by the vast body of critical writing about him and his work. The three-volume (to date) *G. B. Shaw: An Annotated Bibliography of Writings about Him*, comp. J. P. Wearing (1986–), provides a helpful starting point for research. *Shaw: The Critical Heritage*, ed. T. F. Evans (1976), includes excerpts from reviews of his plays. *The Cambridge Companion to George Bernard Shaw*, ed. Christopher Innes (1998), includes current essays that provide valuable overviews of major topics in Shaw scholarship and contains extensive bibliographical suggestions.

Raymond Mander and Joe Mitchenson's *Theatrical Companion to Shaw: A Pictorial Record of the First Performances of the Plays of George Bernard Shaw* (1954) remains the best record of his works in performance.

Among many full-length studies worth consulting are Eric Bentley, *Bernard Shaw* (1947); Tracy C. Davis, *George Bernard Shaw and the Socialist Theatre* (1994); Bernard F. Dukore, *Bernard Shaw, Playwright: Aspects of Shavian Drama* (1973); J. Ellen Gainor, *Shaw's Daughters: Dramatic and Narrative Constructions of Gender* (1991); Arthur Ganz, *George Bernard Shaw* (1983); Martin Meisel, *Shaw and the Nineteenth-Century Theater* (1963); Margery M. Morgan, *The Shavian Playground: An Exploration of the Art of George Bernard Shaw* (1972); and Alfred Turco Jr., *Shaw's Moral Vision: The Self and Salvation* (1976). Shaw scholarship has also flourished in essay form. There are three journals entirely devoted to Shaw—the *Shavian*, the *Shaw Bulletin*, and *Shaw: The Annual of Bernard Shaw Studies*—but essays abound throughout the periodic literature as well as in anthologies. For discussions of *Pygmalion* in particular, readers may wish to consult Awam Amkpa, "Drama and the Languages of Postcolonial Desire: Bernard Shaw's *Pygmalion*" (1999); Milton Crane, "Pygmalion: Bernard Shaw's Dramatic Theory and Practice" (1951); J. Ellen Gainor, "Bernard Shaw and the Drama of Imperialism," in *The Performance of Power: Theatrical Discourse and Politics*, ed. Sue-Ellen Case and Janelle Reinelt (1991); Celia Marshik, "Parodying the £5 Virgin: Bernard Shaw and the Playing of *Pygmalion*" (2000); and Jean Reynolds, "Deconstructing Henry Higgins, or Eliza as Derridean 'Text'" (1994).

SAM SHEPARD

Buried Child originally appeared in the collection *Seven Plays* (1981); the revised version was published first in *American Theatre* (with an interview, 1996) and then by Dramatists Play Service, Inc. (1997). Only the revised version is now authorized for production. The most comprehensive biography to date is Don Shewey's *Sam Shepard* (1985; updated ed., 1997). Earlier biographies by Martin Tucker, *Sam Shepard* (1992), and Ellen Oumano, *Sam Shepard: The Life and Dream of an American Dreamer* (1986), are also useful. Shepard criticism mushroomed during the 1980s and 1990s with such full-length studies as Ron Mottram, *Inner Landscapes: The Theater of Sam Shepard* (1984); Lynda Hart, *Sam Shepard's Metaphorical Stages* (1987); Leslie A. Wade, *Sam Shepard and the American Theatre* (1997); and Stephen J. Bottoms, *The Theatre of Sam Shepard: States of Crisis* (1998). In addition, several essay collections contain insightful perspectives on his dramaturgy: see Kimball King, ed., *Sam Shepard: A Casebook* (1988); Bonnie Maranca, ed., *American Dreams: The Imagination of Sam Shepard* (1981), which also contains essays by and interviews with the dramatist; Leonard Wilcox, ed., *Rereading Shepard: Contemporary Critical Essays on the Plays of Sam Shepard* (1993); and Matthew Roudané, ed., *The Cambridge Companion to Sam Shepard* (2002), which contains a revealing interview with the playwright.

Richard Gilman's critical introduction to Shepard's *Seven Plays* and Ross Wetzsteon's to *Fool for Love and Other Plays* (1984) both provide invaluable commentary. John Dungan's *File on Shepard* (1989) chronicles production information and reviews. Noteworthy articles on *Buried Child* include Thomas Nash, "Sam Shepard's *Buried Child*: The Ironic Use of Folklore" (1983); Charles Whiting, "Digging Up *Buried Child*" (1988); Steven D. Putzel and Suzanne R. Westfall, "The Back Side of Myth: Sam Shepard's Subversion of Mythic Codes in *Buried Child*" (1989); Tucker Orbison, "Authorization and Subversion of Myth in Shepard's *Buried Child*" (1994); and James R. Stacy, "Making the Grave Less Deep: A Descriptive Assessment of Sam Shepard's Revisions to *Buried Child*" (1997).

WOLE SOYINKA

For an authoritative text and extensive background readings on *Death and the King's Horseman*, consult the Norton Critical Edition, edited by Simon Gikandi (2003). The general bibliography on Soyinka's work is extensive. Book-length accounts started to appear in the early 1970s—notably, Eldred Duromsimi Jones's *The Writing of Wole Soyinka* (1973; 3d ed., 1988). A more recent study, Derek Wright's *Wole Soyinka Revisited* (1993), provides a more nuanced analysis of the dramatic works; it focuses on the different theatrical categories, particularly ritual, tragedy, and satire, that are central for understanding Soyinka's work. Ketu H. Katrak's *Wole Soyinka and Modern Tragedy* (1986) examines Soyinka's attempt to create a "Yoruba tragedy." By far the best of the critical literature on the playwright is Biodun Jeyifo's *Wole Soyinka: Politics, Poetics and Postcoloniality* (2004), which analyzes the complex relations between colonial culture, independence, and literature that mark his oeuvre. Jeyifo is among those intellectuals with whom Soyinka has heatedly debated the relation between art and politics; see, for example, Soyinka's collection of essays, *Art, Dialogue, and Outrage: Essays on Literature and Culture* (1988; rev. and expanded ed., 1993). Also useful is a collection of interviews, *Conversations with Wole Soyinka*, ed. Biodun Jeyifo (2001). Other major critics to have devoted attention to

Soyinka are the philosopher Anthony Appiah, in *In My Father's House: Africa in the Philosophy of Culture* (1992), and Henry Louis Gates Jr., in "Being, the Will, and the Semantics of Death" (1981). Valuable collections of essays on Soyinka include James Gibb, ed., *Critical Perspectives on Wole Soyinka* (1980), and Biodun Jeyifo, ed., *Perspectives on Wole Soyinka: Freedom and Complexity* (2001). Jonathan Peters's *A Dance of Masks: Senghor, Achebe, Soyinka* (1978) and Kole Omotoso's *Achebe or Soyinka? A Study in Contrasts* (1996) are noteworthy comparative studies of Soyinka.

AUGUST STRINDBERG

The best biography available is Michael Meyer's *Strindberg* (1985), which seeks to distinguish between Strindberg's autobiographical novels and plays and the facts of his own life, especially his three marriages. The topic of autobiography receives special focus in Michael Robinson's *Strindberg and Autobiography: Writing and Reading a Life* (1986) and Harry G. Carlson's *Out of Inferno: Strindberg's Reawakening as an Artist* (1996). Particular attention to Strindberg the playwright is paid by Evert Sprinchorn (whose translation of *Miss Julie* in included in this volume) in *Strindberg as Dramatist* (1992), and by Egil Törnqvist, Strindberg's main Swedish interpreter, in *Strindbergian Drama: Themes and Structure* (1982). More interested in the literary and poetic dimensions of Strindberg's drama is another translator of his plays, Harry G. Carlson, in *Strindberg and the Poetry of Myth* (1982). Also commendable is Freddie Rokem's *Strindberg's Secret Codes* (2004). Given Strindberg's influence, most of the classic studies of modern drama dedicate important essays to the playwright, including Robert Brustein's *The Theatre of Revolt: An Approach to the Modern Drama* (1964), which emphasizes Strindberg's revolt against modern life, and Raymond Williams's *Drama from Ibsen to Brecht* (1968), which combines social analysis with an attention to form. An international collection of essays on Strindberg was assembled by Göran Stockenström in *Strindberg's Dramaturgy* (1988), as well as by Michael Robinson in *Studies in Strindberg* (1998). More interested in particular genres is Børge Gedsø Madsen's *Strindberg's Naturalistic Theatre: Its Relation to French Naturalism* (1962), Walter Johnson's *Strindberg and the Historical Drama* (1963), and John Ward's *The Social and Religious Plays of Strindberg* (1980). And Strindberg's influence on expressionist theater is detailed in Michael Robinson and Sven Rossel's collection *Expressionism and Modernism: New Approaches to August Strindberg* (1999). Most thoroughly dedicated to Strindberg on stage is Frederick J. Marker and Lise-Lone Marker's *Strindberg and Modernist Theatre: Post-Inferno Drama on the Stage* (2002). For analysis specifically of *Miss Julie*, see the collection edited by Egil Törnqvist and Barry Jacobs, *Strindberg's "Miss Julie": A Play and Its Transpositions* (1988).

JOHN MILLINGTON SYNGE

Synge's plays have been edited by Ann Saddlemyer in volumes 3 and 4 of J. M. Synge, *Collected Works*, ed. Robin Skelton (1962–68); the appendix to *Riders to the Sea* (in volume 3) includes a transcription of Synge's draft manuscripts. W. J. McCormack, *Fool of the Family: A Life of J. M. Synge* (2000), is an excellent recent biography of Synge, though David H. Greene and Edward M. Stephens, *J. M. Synge, 1871–1909* (1959; rev. ed., 1989), and David M. Kiely, *John Millington Synge: A Biography* (1994), are also valuable. E. H. Mikhail, ed., *J. M. Synge: Interviews and Recollections* (1977), contains first-person accounts by those who knew Synge.

The following books provide useful discussions of Synge's drama: Alan Price, *Synge and Anglo-Irish Drama* (1961); Robin Skelton, *The Writings of J. M. Synge* (1971) and *J. M. Synge and His World* (1971); Nicholas Grene, *Synge: A Critical Study of the Plays* (1975); Eugene Benson, *J. M. Synge* (1982); Mary C. King, *The Drama of J. M. Synge* (1985); Donna Gerstenberger, *John Millington Synge* (1964; rev. ed., 1990); and Declan Kiberd, *Synge and the Irish Language* (1979; 2nd ed., 1993). Among the important collections of essays on Synge are Edward A. Kopper Jr., *A J. M. Synge Literary Companion* (1988); Daniel J. Casey, *Critical Essays on John Millington Synge* (1994); and Alexander G. Gonzalez, *Assessing the Achievement of J. M. Synge* (1996). David R. Clark's edition of *Riders to the Sea* (1970) includes earlier critical essays on Synge's play.

Intellectual, cultural, and theatrical background to Synge and his art can be found in D. E. S. Maxwell, *A Critical History of Modern Irish Drama, 1891–1980* (1984); Declan Kiberd, *Inventing Ireland* (1995); Gregory Castle, *Modernism and the Celtic Revival* (2001); Mary Trotter, *Ireland's National Theaters: Political Performance and the Origins of the Irish Dramatic Movement* (2001); and Ben Levitas, *The Theatre of Nation: Irish Drama and Cultural Nationalism, 1890–1916* (2002).

JUDITH THOMPSON

Judith Thompson's plays are available through the Playwrights Canada Press. Though no book-length studies devoted solely to her work have appeared to date, Ric Knowles has edited two collections of essays devoted to the playwright:

Judith Thompson (2005) and *The Masks of Judith Thompson* (2006). In addition, the journal *Canadian Theatre Review* published a special issue on Thompson, *Judith Thompson Casebook* (Winter 1996), which contains interviews, the revised script of *Tornado,* critical analyses, production commentary, and a bibliography of primary and secondary works. Chapters on Thompson can be found in Craig Stewart Walker, *The Buried Astrolabe: Canadian Dramatic Imagination and Western Tradition* (2001), and Cynthia Zimmerman, *Playwriting Women: Female Voices in English Canada* (1994). Essays on Thompson have appeared in scholarly journals, critical volumes, and the Canadian press: see especially Julie Adams, "The Implicated Audience: Judith Thompson's Anti-Naturalism in *The Crackwalker, White Biting Dog, I Am Yours* and *Lion in the Streets,*" in *Women on the Canadian Stage: The Legacy of Hrotsvit,* ed. Rita Much (1992); Diane Bessai, "Women Dramatists: Sharon Pollock and Judith Thompson," in *Post-colonial English Drama: Commonwealth Drama since 1960,* ed. Bruce King (1992); Alan Filewod, "Critical Mass: Assigning Value and Place in Canadian Drama," in *On-stage and Off-stage: English Canadian Drama in Discourse,* ed. Albert-Reiner Glaap and Rolf Althof (1996); Jennifer Harvie, "(Im) Possibility: Fantasy and Judith Thompson's Drama," in *On-stage and Off-stage,* ed. Glaap and Althof (1996); Nigel Hunt, "In Contact with the Dark" (1988); Richard Paul Knowles, "The Dramaturgy of the Perverse" (1992); Robert Nunn, "Spatial Metaphor in the Plays of Judith Thompson" (1989); Judy Steed, "Thompson Walks a Different Path Than Her Characters" (1982); and George Toles, "'Cause You're the Only One I Want': The Anatomy of Love in the Plays of Judith Thompson" (1988).

Thompson has given a number of interviews to journalists and scholars, including Judith Rudakoff in *Fair Play: 12 Women Speak: Conversations with Canadian Playwrights* (1990), Cynthia Zimmerman in "A Conversation with Judith Thompson" (1990), and Sandra Tomc in "Revisions of Probability: An Interview with Judith Thompson" (1989); see also her contributions to the dialogues "Revisions: Offending Your Audience" (1992) and "Look to the Lady: Re-examining Women's Theatre" (1995). In addition, Thompson has written several revealing essays on her life and work; see "Why Should a Playwright Direct Her Own Play?" in *Women on the Canadian Stage,* ed. Much (1992); "Second Thoughts (What I'd Be If I Were Not a Writer)" (1995); "One Twelfth" in *Language in Her Eye: Views on Writing and Gender by Canadian Women Writing in English,* ed. Libby Scheier, Sarah Sheard, and Eleanor Wachtel (1990); and "The Happy Vessel" in *Still Running—: Personal Stories by Queen's Women Celebrating the Fiftieth Anniversary of the Marty Scholarship,* ed. Joy Parr (1987).

DEREK WALCOTT

Although the much shorter *Derek Walcott* (1981; updated ed., 1993), by Robert Hamner, can be consulted for a brief overview of Walcott's life and works, by far the best biography is Bruce King's *Derek Walcott & West Indian Drama: Not Only a playwright but a company, the Trinidad Theatre Workshop, 1959–1993* (1995), which also contains an extensive history of Walcott's theater company. Situating the writer in the debates about postcolonial literature are an informative collection of interviews, *Conversations with Derek Walcott,* ed. William Baer (1996), and Robert Hamner's useful collection of essays by and about Walcott, *Critical Perspectives on Derek Walcott* (1993). Walcott's own poetic essay, "What the Twilight Says: An Overture," is printed as an introduction to the collection of plays that also contains *The Sea at Dauphin, Dream on Monkey Mountain, and Other Plays* (1970).

Because of Walcott's preeminence as a poet, especially since the 1990 publication of his epic poem, *Omeros,* the critical literature on Walcott the poet outshines that on Walcott the dramatist. Reid Tereda's *Derek Walcott's Poetry: American Mimicry* (1992) and Patricia Ismond's *Abandoning Dead Metaphors: The Caribbean Phase of Derek Walcott's Poetry* (2001) also provide insight into his drama, as does Jahan Ramazani's *The Hybrid Muse: Postcolonial Poetry in English* (2001). Some postcolonial interpretations of Walcott have emphasized his distinctness from Western traditions and paid insufficient attention to his reliance on and revision of them. Charles Pollard's *New World Modernisms: T. S. Eliot, Derek Walcott, and Kamau Brathwaite* (2004), which connects Walcott, as well as the Caribbean writer Kamau Braithwaite, to the modernism of T. S. Eliot, makes a strong case for Walcott's modernism. To contextualize Walcott's use of carnival, see Errol Hill's *The Trinidad Carnival: Mandate for a National Theatre* (1972). Hill's *The Jamaican Stage, 1655–1900: Profile of a Colonial Theatre* (1992) is a good general introduction to the theater of the region, and Sabine Sörgel's *Dancing Postcolonialism: The National Dance Theatre company of Jamaica* (2007) offers an extensive reflection on Caribbean dance. Finally, an annotated bibliography of Walcott's work, although now out of date, has been compiled by Irma E. Goldstraw in *Derek Walcott: An Annotated Bibliography of His Works* (1984).

OSCAR WILDE

While there is no standard edition of Oscar Wilde's plays, *"The Importance of Being Earnest" and Other Plays*, ed. David Raby (1995), is a useful collection. Richard Ellmann, *Oscar Wilde* (1987), is considered the authoritative biography. Studies of Wilde's career include Rodney Shewan, *Oscar Wilde: Art and Egotism* (1977); Regenia Gagnier, *Idylls of the Marketplace: Oscar Wilde and the Victorian Public* (1986); Alan Sinfield, *The Wilde Century: Effeminacy, Oscar Wilde, and the Queer Moment* (1994); Josephine M. Guy and Ian Small, *Oscar Wilde's Profession: Writing and the Culture Industry in the Late Nineteenth Century* (2000); Neil Sammells, *Wilde Style: The Plays and Prose of Oscar Wilde* (2000); John Sloan, *Oscar Wilde* (2003); and Paul L. Fortunato, *Modernist Aesthetics and Consumer Culture in the Writings of Oscar Wilde* (2007). Early critical responses to Wilde's life and work are included in Richard Ellmann, ed., *Oscar Wilde: A Collection of Critical Essays* (1969). C. George Sandulescu, ed., *Rediscovering Oscar Wilde* (1994), and Peter Raby, ed., *The Cambridge Companion to Oscar Wilde* (1997), are valuable collections of essays.

Wilde's drama is the subject of Alan Bird, *The Plays of Oscar Wilde* (1977); Katharine Worth, *Oscar Wilde* (1983); Sos Eltis, *Revising Wilde: Society and Subversion in the Plays of Oscar Wilde* (1996); and Kerry Powell, *Oscar Wilde and the Theatre of the 1890s* (1990). Joseph Donohue and Ruth Berggren, eds., *Oscar Wilde's "The Importance of Being Earnest": A Reconstructive Critical Edition of the Text of the First Production at St. James's Theatre, London, 1895* (1995), provides an extensively annotated edition of Wilde's masterpiece with an exhaustive discussion of the play's composition and manuscript history.

TENNESSEE WILLIAMS

The standard collection of Tennessee Williams's plays is *The Theatre of Tennessee Williams,* published in eight volumes by New Directions (1971–81). Additional plays from Williams's early career have been published separately. Among the several biographies of Williams, the finest is Lyle Leverich's *Tom: The Unknown Tennessee Williams* (1995), which covers the playwright's life to 1945. Students interested in Williams's life as a whole might consult Ronald Hayman, *Tennessee Williams: Everyone Else Is an Audience* (1993). Richard F. Leavitt, ed., *The World of Tennessee Williams* (1978), includes photographs, theater programs, and other documents illustrating Williams's life and career, while Philip Kolin, ed., *The Tennessee Williams Encyclopedia* (2004), contains valuable information on the playwright's works. Kenneth Holditch and Richard Freeman Leavitt's *Tennessee Williams and the South* (2002) discusses the profound influence of this region on Williams's work.

The following include valuable critical discussions of Williams's drama: Jac Tharpe, ed., *Tennessee Williams: A Tribute* (1977); Roger Boxill, *Tennessee Williams* (1987); Alice Griffin, *Understanding Tennessee Williams* (1995); Matthew C. Roudané, ed., *The Cambridge Companion to Tennessee Williams* (1997); Robert A. Martin, ed., *Critical Essays on Tennessee Williams* (1997); Philip C. Kolin, ed., *Tennessee Williams: A Guide to Research and Performance* (1998); Nancy M. Tischler, *Student Companion to Tennessee Williams* (2000); and Judith J. Thompson, *Tennessee Williams' Plays: Memory, Myth, and Symbol* (1987; rev. ed., 2002). One of the best discussions of Williams's dramatic career can be found in volume 2 of C. W. E. Bigsby, *A Critical Introduction to Twentieth-Century American Drama* (1984). The influence of Williams's homosexuality on his drama is explored in David Savran, *Communists, Cowboys, and Queers: The Politics of Masculinity in the Work of Arthur Miller and Tennessee Williams* (1992), and John M. Clum, *Acting Gay: Male Homosexuality in Modern Drama* (1992; expanded ed., 1994).

The essays in Jordan Y. Miller, ed., *Twentieth Century Interpretations of "A Streetcar Named Desire"* (1971), are devoted exclusively to Williams's play, as are Thomas P. Adler, *"A Streetcar Named Desire": The Moth and the Lantern* (1990), and Philip C. Kolin, ed., *Confronting Tennessee Williams's "A Streetcar Named Desire": Essays in Critical Pluralism* (1993). Philip C. Kolin, *Williams: "A Streetcar Named Desire"* (2000), provides a history of *Streetcar* in performance, while Brenda Murphy's *Tennessee Williams and Elia Kazan: A Collaboration in the Theatre* (1992) examines the productions of *Streetcar* and other Williams plays directed by Kazan. Kazan's valuable directorial notes on *Streetcar* are excerpted in the *Twentieth Century Interpretations* collection mentioned above. Maurice Yacowar's *Tennessee Williams and Film* (1977) offers a useful discussion of the 1951 film version of Williams's play.

AUGUST WILSON

The plays of August Wilson's twentieth-century cycle were published in 2007 by Theatre Communications Group in a ten-volume collection. The best book-length studies of August Wilson's life and plays are Sandra G. Shannon, *The Dramatic Vision of August Wilson* (1995); Kim Pereira, *August Wilson and the African-American Odyssey* (1995); Peter Wolfe, *August Wilson* (1999); and Harry J.

Elam Jr., *The Past as Present in the Drama of August Wilson* (2004). Mary L. Bogumil, *Understanding August Wilson* (1999), and Harry J. Elam Jr., "August Wilson," in *A Companion to Twentieth-Century American Drama*, ed. David Krasner (2005), are general introductions to Wilson's work, while Yvonne Shafer, *August Wilson: A Research and Production Sourcebook* (1998), and Mary Ellen Snodgrass, *August Wilson: A Literary Companion* (2004), are valuable resources for the student of Wilson's plays. Jackson R. Bryer and Mary C. Hartig, eds., *Conversations with August Wilson* (2006), contains Wilson's major interviews. Dana A. Williams and Sandra G. Shannon, eds., *August Wilson and Black Aesthetics* (2004), examines the cultural politics of Wilson as an African American writer.

Two collections of essays—Marilyn Elkins, ed., *August Wilson: A Casebook* (1994), and Alan Nadel, ed., *May All Your Fences Have Gates: Essays on the Drama of August Wilson* (1994)—present the range of critical approaches adopted by scholars analyzing Wilson's plays. Not surprising, *Fences* comes in for a large share of their discussion. Joan Fishman, "Developing His Song: August Wilson's *Fences*" (in Elkins), traces the development of Wilson's dramatic text through revisions, staged readings, and productions; Michael Awkward, "'The Crookeds with the Straights': *Fences*, Race, and the Politics of Adaptation" (in Nadel), considers *Fences* in the context of Wilson's well-publicized insistence that any film production of the play be directed by an African American. Susan Koprince, "Baseball as History and Myth in August Wilson's *Fences*" (2006), discusses the role of baseball in the play.

The black feminist scholar bell hooks has challenged the portrayal of women in Wilson's *Fences* in *Yearning: Race, Gender, and Cultural Politics* (1990). Harry J. Elam Jr., "August Wilson's Women," and Missy Dehn Kubitschek, "August Wilson's Gender Lesson" (both in Nadel), address the question of Wilson's women from feminist and other theoretical perspectives. Carla J. McDonough, *Staging Masculinity: Male Identity in Contemporary American Drama* (1997), considers the question of masculinity in Wilson's drama in the context of social issues facing urban black males.

PERMISSIONS ACKNOWLEDGMENTS

TEXT

Albee, Edward: *The Goat; or, Who Is Sylvia?* by Edward Albee. Published by Dramatists Play Service. Copyright © 2002 by Edward Albee. Reprinted by permission of William Morris Agency, LLC, on behalf of the Author. CAUTION: Professionals and amateurs are hereby warned that *The Goat; or, Who Is Sylvia?* is subject to a royalty. It is fully protected under the copyright laws of the United States of America and of all countries covered by the International Copyright Union (including the Dominion of Canada and the rest of the British Commonwealth), the Berne Convention, and Pan-American Copyright Convention and the Universal Copyright Convention as well as all countries with which the United States has reciprocal copyright relations. All rights, including professional/amateur stage rights, motion picture, recitation, public reading, radio broadcasting, television, video or sound recording, all other forms of mechanical or electronic reproduction, such as CD-ROM, CD-I, information storage and retrieval systems and photocopying, and the rights of translation into foreign languages, are strictly reserved. Particular emphasis is laid upon the matter of readings, permission for which must be secured from the author's agent in writing. Inquiries concerning rights should be addressed to: William Morris Agency, LLC, 1325 Avenue of the Americas, New York, NY 10019, Attn: Eric Lupfer.

al-Hakim, Tawfiq: *Song of Death,* translated by Mustafa Badawi, from ARABIC WRITING TODAY: DRAMA, edited by Mahmoud Manzalaoui. Reprinted by permission of The American Research Center in Egypt, Inc.

Beckett, Samuel: *Waiting for Godot.* Copyright © 1952 by Les Éditions de Minuit. English text copyright © 1954 by Grove Press, Inc.; copyright © renewed 1982 by Samuel Beckett, now The Estate of Samuel Beckett. Used by permission of Grove/Atlantic, Inc.

Brecht, Bertolt: *The Good Person of Szechwan.* Originally published in German under the title *Der gute Mensch von Sezuan.* Copyright © 1955 by Suhrkamp Verlag, Berlin. Translation copyright for the play and texts by Brecht © 1985 by Stefan S. Brecht. Reprinted from THE GOOD PERSON OF SZECHWAN by Bertolt Brecht. Translated from the German by John Willett and edited by John Willett and Ralph Manheim. Published by Arcade Publishers, New York, NY. Reprinted by permission of Arcade Publishers and A&C Black Publishers.

Büchner, Georg: *Woyzeck* from THE COMPLETE COLLECTED WORKS, translated by Henry J. Schmidt. Copyright © 1977 by Henry J. Schmidt. Used by permission of Cynthia Schmidt-Schilling.

Chekhov, Anton: *The Cherry Orchard* from THE PLAYS OF ANTON CHEKHOV, A NEW TRANSLATION by Paul Schmidt. Copyright © 1997 by Paul Schmidt. Reprinted by permission of HarperCollins Publishers.

Churchill, Caryl: *A Number,* copyright © 2002 by Caryl Churchill Ltd. Reproduced by permission of the publisher: Nick Hern Books Ltd. (UK), www.nickhernbooks.co.uk, and Theatre Communications Group (USA), www.tcg.org.

Fornes, Maria Irene: *Mud* from MARIA IRENE FORNES: PLAYS. Copyright © 1986 by Maria Irene Fornes and PAJ Publications. Reprinted by permission of PAJ Publications.

Fugard, Athol: *MASTER HAROLD . . . and the Boys.* Copyright © 1982 by Athol Fugard. Used by permission of Alfred A. Knopf, a division of Random House, Inc.

García Lorca, Federico: *La casa de Bernarda Alba/The House of Bernarda Alba* by Federico García Lorca. Copyright © Herederos de Federico García Lorca. *Obras Completas* (Galazia/Gutenberg, 1996 edition). English language translation by James Graham-Lujan and Richard L. O'Connell. Copyright © Herederos de Federico García Lorca and translators. From THREE TRAGEDIES, New Directions Publishing Company, New York. All rights reserved. For information regarding rights and permissions, please contact lorca@artslaw.co.uk or William Peter Kosmas, Esq., 8 Franklin Square, London W14 9UU.

Genet, Jean: *The Maids* from THE MAIDS AND DEATHWATCH. Copyright © 1954, 1961 by Bernard Frechtman. Used by permission of Grove/Atlantic, Inc.

Hughes, Langston: *Soul Gone Home* from FIVE PLAYS. Copyright © 1937 by Langston Hughes. Reprinted by permission of Harold Ober Associates, Inc.

Hwang, David Henry: *M. Butterfly*. Copyright © 1986, 1987, 1988 by David Henry Hwang. Used by permission of Dutton Signet, a division of Penguin Group (USA), Inc.

Ibsen, Henrik: *Hedda Gabler* from FOUR MAJOR PLAYS, Volume 1, translated by Rolf Fjelde. Copyright © 1965, 1992 by Rolf Fjelde. Used by permission of Dutton Signet, a division of Penguin Group (USA), Inc.

Kushner, Tony: *Angels in America: Part One: Millennium Approaches*. Copyright © 1992, 1993 by Tony Kushner. Published by Theatre Communications Group. Used by permission of Theatre Communications Group.

Mamet, David: *Glengarry Glen Ross*. Copyright © 1982, 1983 by David Mamet. Used by permission of Grove/Atlantic, Inc.

Miller, Arthur: *Death of a Salesman*. Copyright © 1949, renewed © 1977 by Arthur Miller. Used by permission of Viking Penguin, a division of Penguin Group (USA), Inc.

Nowra, Louis: *The Golden Age*, first published by Currency Press Pty Ltd., 1985. Copyright © 1985 by Louis Nowra. Used by permission of Currency Press Pty Ltd., P.O. Box 2287, Strawberry Hills, NSW 2012 Australia, www.currency.com.au. The play may not be performed without a license from the author or the author's agent. All application for public performance should be addressed to HLA Management, P.O. Box 1536, Strawberry Hills, NSW 2012 Australia, hla@hlamgt.com.au.

O'Neill, Eugene: *Long Day's Journey into Night*. Copyright © 1955 by Carlotta Monterey O'Neill. Copyright © renewed 1983 by Oona O'Neill Chaplin and Yale University. Reprinted by permission.

Parks, Suzan-Lori: *The America Play* from THE AMERICA PLAY AND OTHER WORKS. Copyright © 1995 by Suzan-Lori Parks. Published by Theatre Communications Group. Used by permission of Theatre Communications Group.

Pinter, Harold: *Old Times*. Copyright © 1971 by Harold Pinter Ltd. Used by permission of Grove/Atlantic, Inc.

Pirandello, Luigi: *Six Characters in Search of an Author*, from PIRANDELLO'S MAJOR PLAYS, translated by Eric Bentley. Evanston: Northwestern University Press. Used by permission.

Shepard, Sam: *Buried Child*, copyright © 1979 by Sam Shepard, from SEVEN PLAYS. Used by permission of Bantam Books, a division of Random House, Inc.

Soyinka, Wole: *Death and the King's Horseman*. Copyright © 1975, 2003 by Wole Soyinka. Used by permission of W. W. Norton & Company and Melanie Jackson Agency, LLC.

Strindberg, August: *Miss Julie* from SELECTED PLAYS, translated by Evert Sprinchorn. Copyright © 1986 by University of Minnesota Press. Used by permission of University of Minnesota Press.

Thompson, Judith: *The Crackwalker* from THE OTHER SIDE OF THE DARK. Copyright © 1989 by Judith Thompson. Used by permission of the playwright and Playwrights Canada Press.

Walcott, Derek: *The Sea at Dauphin* from DREAM ON MONKEY MOUNTAIN. Copyright © 1970 by Derek Walcott. Reprinted by permission of Farrar, Straus and Giroux, LLC.

Williams, Tennessee: *A Streetcar Named Desire*. Copyright © 1947 by Tennessee Williams. CAUTION: Professionals and amateurs are hereby warned that *A Streetcar Named Desire*, being fully protected under the copyright laws of the United States of America, the British Empire including the Dominion of Canada, and all other countries of the Copyright Union, is subject to royalty. All rights, including professional, amateur, motion picture, recitation, lecturing, public reading, radio and television broadcasting, and the rights of translation into foreign languages are strictly reserved. Particular emphasis is laid on the question of readings, permission for which must be secured from the author's agent, Luis Sanjurjo, c/o International Creative Management, 40 West 57th Street, New York, NY 10019. Inquiries concerning the amateur acting rights of *A Streetcar Named Desire* should be directed to the Dramatists' Play Service, Inc., 440 Park Avenue South, New York, NY 10016, without whose permission in writing no amateur performance may be given.

Wilson, August: *Fences*. Copyright © 1986 by August Wilson. Used by permission of Dutton Signet, a division of Penguin Group (USA), Inc.

ILLUSTRATIONS

3: Marty Nordstrom, c/o the Guthrie Theater; **5:** Erich Lessing/Art Resource, NY; **7:** The Granger Collection, New York; **9:** Theater and Playhouse by Richard and Helen Leacroft, Methuen Publishing, Ltd; **11:** Vanni/Art Resource, NY; **12:** Museo Capitolino, Rome, Italy/ Ancient Art and Architecture Collection Ltd./The Bridgeman Art Library; **13:** Scala/Art Resource, NY; **15:** Kings Visualization Lab;

18: The Philadelphia Museum of Art/Art Resource, NY; **21:** Princeton University Press, 1976; **23:** AFP/Getty Images; **26:** Theater and Playhouse by Richard and Helen Leacroft, Methuen Publishing, Ltd, ; **28:** Merridew: Coventry, 1825; **30:** Public domain ; **33:** Wikipedia Commons; **35:** Musee de la Ville de Paris, Musee Carnavalet, Paris, France/ Giraudon/ The Bridgeman Art Library; **37:** akg-Images; **39:** The Art Archive; **42:** akg-Images; **43:** Kevin George/Alamy; **46:** akg-Images; **47:** Lebrecht Authors; **49:** Private Collection/The Bridgeman Art Library; **51:** Tate, London/Art Resource, NY; **54:** akg-images; **55:** akg-images; **55:** Victoria & Albert Museum, London/Art Resource, NY; **57:** Lebrecht Authors; **59:** Picture Collection, The Branch Libraries, The New York Public Library, Astor, Lenox and Tilden Foundations; **61:** Lebrecht Authors; **63:** Snark/Art Resource, NY; **64:** Lipnitzki/Roger Viollet/Getty Images; **65:** Kurt Weill Foundation /Lebrecht Music & Arts; **66:** The New York Public Library, Astor, Lenox and Tilden Foundations; **67:** Franklin D. Roosevelt Library; **70:** Lipnitzki/Roger Viollet/Getty Images; **72:** Hulton-Deutsch Collection/Corbis; **73:** W. Eugene Smith/Time & Life/Getty Images; **74:** Bettmann/Corbis; **76:** Julio Donoso/Corbis; **79:** Nobby Clark/Hulton Archive/Getty Images; **89:** The Granger Collection, New York; **91:** Snark/Art Resource, NY; **111:** Hulton Archive/Getty Images; **112:** Rare Book Collection, University of North Carolina; **153:** Strindberg Museum Stockholm/Alfredo Dagli Orti/The Art Archive; **155:** Strindbergsmuseet, Stockholm; **195:** Private Collection MD/The Art Archive; **197:** Nasjonal Glleriet Oslo/The Art Archive; **199:** Fales Library/New York University; **255:** Culver Pictures/The Art Archive; **257:** Hulton Archive/Getty Images; **258:** courttheartre.org; **305:** Cultures France; **307:** Marc Charmet/The Art Archive; **309:** Roger Viollet/The Image Works; **341:** Hulton Archive/Getty Images; **344:** Billy Rose Theatre Division, NYPL for the Performing Arts, Astor, Lenox and Tilden Foundations; **345:** Austrian Archives/Corbis; **387:** Glasgow University Library, Dept. of Special Collections; **389:** Hulton Archive/Getty Images; **391:** Robin Skelton, *J. M. Synge and His World;* Viking, 1971; **403:** Culver Pictures/The Art Archive; **405:** Hulton Archive/Getty Images; **406:** London Stereoscopic Company/Getty Images; **471:** Photo courtesy of the Berg Collection; **473;** Photo courtesy of Daniel J. Lawrence; **474:** Billy Rose Theatre Collection, New York Public Library for the Performing Arts; **487:** Mary Evans Picture Library/Asia Media; **491:** The Art Archive; **531:** ©1981 Center for Creative Photography, Arizona Board of Regents. Langston Hughes, 1932. Photograph by Edward Weston; **533:** Library of Congress; **539:** Art Resource, NY; **541:** DACS /Index/The Bridgeman Art Library; **543:** Mary Evans Picture Library/Asia Media; **579:** Kurt Weill Foundation/Lebrecht Music & Arts; **581:** akg-images; **582:** Courtesy of Inge Steinert; **653:** Museum of Modern Art/Licensed by SCALA / Art Resource, NY; **655:** akg-Images; **681:** Baldwin H. Ward & Kathryn C. Ward/Corbis; **683:** AP/Wide World Photos; **684:** Bettmann/Corbis; **753:** AP/Wide World Photos; **756:** W. Eugene Smith/Getty Images; **757:** Billy Rose Collection; **825:** AFP/Getty Images; **826:** akg-images; **829:** Keystone/Getty Images; **843:** John Haynes/Lebrecht Music and Art Pictures; **844:** Lipnitzki/Roger Viollet/Getty Images; **846:** Lipnitzki/Roger Viollet/Getty Images; **907:** Horst Tappel/Lebrecth Music and Art Pictures; **910:** Schomberg Center for Research in Black Culture / New York Public Library; **927:** akg-Images; **929:** Beata Bergström, Sveriges Teatermuseum, Sweden; **930:** © Al Hirschfield; **1013:** Mary Evans Picture Library; **1017:** Donald Cooper / photostage.co.uk **1043:** Hulton Archive/Getty Images **1045:** Hulton-Deutsch Collection/Corbis; **1047:** Eliot Ellsofon/Time Life Pictures/Getty Images; **1097:** Nina Berman/Sipa; **1099:** Gerry Goodstein; **1151:** David Laurence; **1155:** Courtesy of Judith Thompson; **1195:** Hulton Archive/Getty Images; **1197:** Martha Swope; **1231:** Robert Giard. © Estate of Robert Giard. Courtesy Stephen Bulger Gallery; **1232:** Courtesy of University of Wisconsin, Milwaukee; **1253:** Steve Liss/Time Life Pictures/Getty; **1255:** Hulton Archive / Getty Images; **1293:** Courtesy of HLA Management; **1295:** David B. Simmonds; **1353:** AP; **1356:** Yale Repertory Theatre, Yale School of Drama; **1407:** Paradigm Agency; **1410:** © Joan Marcus; **1461:** AP/Wide World Photos; **1463:** Bettmann/Corbis; **1464:** John Haynes/Lebrecht Music & Arts; **1531:**© Stephanie Diani; **1533:** Currier and Ives/ Bridgeman Art Library; **1535:** T. Charles Erickson; **1567:** Christopher Felver/Corbis; **1569:** AP Photo/Tina Fineberg; **1609:** Gemma Levine/Hulton Archive/Getty Images; **1611:** Joan Marcus/AP.

Index

Albee, Edward, 1563
al-Hakim, Tawfiq, 825
America Play, The, 1533
Angels in America, Part I: Millennium Approaches, 1464

Beckett, Samuel, 843
Brecht, Bertolt, 579
Brown, William Wells, 111
Büchner, Georg, 89
Buried Child, 1102

Chekhov, Anton, 341
Cherry Orchard, The, 346
Churchill, Caryl, 1605
Crackwalker, The, 1155

Death and the King's Horseman, 1048
Death of a Salesman, 759

Escape, The, 116

Fences, 1358
Fornes, Maria Irene, 1231
Fugard, Athol, 1195

García Lorca, Federico, 539
Genet, Jean, 653
Glaspell, Susan, 471
Glengarry Glen Ross, 1257
Goat, The, 1567
Golden Age, The, 1297
Good Person of Szechwan, The, 585

Hedda Gabler, 200
House of Bernarda Alba, The, 544
Hughes, Langston, 531
Hwang, David Henry, 1407

Ibsen, Henrik, 195
Importance of Being Earnest, The, 260

Jarry, Alfred, 305

Kushner, Tony, 1459

Long Day's Journey into Night, 932

M. Butterfly, 1412
Maids, The, 657
Mamet, David, 1253
"MASTER HAROLD" . . . and the boys, 1199
Miller, Arthur, 753
Miss Julie, 157
Mud, 1234

Nowra, Louis, 1293
Number, A, 1609

Old Times, 1018
O'Neill, Eugene, 927

Parks, Suzan-Lori, 1529
Pinter, Harold, 1013
Pirandello, Luigi, 487
Pygmalion, 408

Riders to the Sea, 392

Sea at Dauphin, The, 913
Shaw, George Bernard, 403
Shepard, Sam, 1097
Six Characters in Search of an Author, 491
Song of Death, 831
Soul Gone Home, 535
Soyinka, Wole, 1043
Streetcar Named Desire, A, 686
Strindberg, August, 153
Synge, John Millington, 387

Thompson, Judith, 1151
Trifles, 475

Ubu the King, 309

Waiting for Godot, 849
Walcott, Derek, 907
Wilde, Oscar, 255
Williams, Tennessee, 681
Wilson, August, 1353
Woyzeck, 93